FOURTH EDITION

Making America

A HISTORY OF THE UNITED STATES

Carol Berkin
Baruch College, City University of New York

Christopher L. Miller
The University of Texas—Pan American

Robert W. Cherny
San Francisco State University

James L. Gormly
Washington and Jefferson College

Houghton Mifflin Company

Boston   New York

Publisher: Charles Hartford
Senior Sponsoring Editor: Sally Constable
Development Editor: Lisa Kalner Williams
Editorial Assistant: Arianne Vanni
Senior Project Editor: Bob Greiner
Editorial Assistant: Robert Woo
Senior Art and Design Coordinator: Jill Haber
Senior Photo Editor: Jennifer Meyer Dare
Senior Composition Buyer: Sarah Ambrose
Senior Manufacturing Coordinator: Marie Barnes
Senior Marketing Manager: Sandra McGuire

Cover image: *Broadway, New York City, 1885.* Lithograph by J. J. Fogarty. The Granger Collection, N.Y.

Printed in the U.S.A.

Library of Congress Catalog Number: 2004113041

ISBN: 0-618-61514-8

1 2 3 4 5 6 7 8 9-DOW-08 07 06 05

BRIEF CONTENTS

CONTENTS

MAPS

FEATURES

Chronologies

Figures

Tables

Authors of textbooks may dream of cheering audiences and mountains of fan mail, but this is rarely their reality. Yet there are occasional moments of glory. A colleague drops by our office to tell us she has been using our text and the students seem more prepared and more interested in class. A former student, now teaching, sends an e-mail, saying he has used our book as a basis for his first set of class lectures and discussions. Or a freshman in a survey class adds a note at the end of her exam, saying, "thanks for writing a text that isn't boring." Maybe none of this adds up to an Academy Award or a photo on the cover of *People* magazine, but comments like these do assure us that the book we envisioned a decade ago is, if not perfect, at least on the right track. And the improvements we have made in this fourth edition of *Making America* make us even more confident.

From the beginning, our goal has been to create a different kind of textbook, one that meets the real needs of the modern college student. Every history classroom reflects the rich cultural diversity of today's student body, with its mixture of native-born Americans and recent immigrants, and its significant number of serious-minded men and women whose formal skills lag behind their interest and enthusiasm for learning. As professors in large public universities located on three of the nation's borders—the Pacific Ocean, the Atlantic, and the Rio Grande—we know the basic elements both the professor and the students need in the survey text for that classroom. These elements include a historical narrative that does not demand a lot of prior knowledge about the American past; information organized sequentially, or chronologically, so that students are not confused by too many topical digressions; and a full array of integrated and supportive learning aids to help students at every level of preparedness comprehend and retain what they read.

Making America has always provided an account of the American past firmly anchored by a political chronology. In it, people and places are brought to life not only through words but also with maps, paintings, and photos. Students can see a genuine effort to communicate with them rather than impress them. And *Making America* presents history as a dynamic process shaped by human expectations, difficult choices, and often surprising consequences. With this focus on history as a process, *Making America* encourages students to think historically and to develop into citizens who value the past.

Yet, as veteran teachers, we the authors of *Making America* know that any history project, no matter how good, can be improved. Having scrawled "Revise" across the top of student papers for several decades, we impose the same demands on ourselves. For every edition, we subjected our text to the same critical reappraisal. We eliminated features that professors and students told us did not work as well as we had hoped; we added features that we believed would be more effective; and we tested our skills as storytellers and biographers more rigorously this time around. This fourth edition reflects the same willingness to revise and improve the textbook we offer to you.

The Approach

Professors and students who have used the previous editions of *Making America* will recognize immediately that we have preserved many of its central features. We have again set the nation's complex story within an explicitly political chronology, relying on a basic and familiar structure that is nevertheless broad enough to accommodate generous attention to social, economic, and diplomatic aspects of our national history. We remain confident that this political framework allows us to integrate the experiences of all Americans into a meaningful and effective narrative of our nation's development. Because our own scholarly research often focuses on the experiences of women, African Americans, and Native Americans, we would not have been content with a framework that excluded or marginalized their history. *Making America* continues to be built on the premise that all Americans are historically active figures, playing significant roles in creating the history that we and other authors narrate. We have also continued what is now a tradition in *Making America*, that is, providing pedagogical tools for students that allow them to master complex material and enable them to develop analytical skills.

Themes

This edition continues to thread the five central themes through the narrative of *Making America* that professors and students who used earlier editions will recognize. The first of these themes, the political development of the nation, is evident in the text's coverage of the creation and revision of the federal and local governments, the contests waged over domestic and diplomatic policies, the internal and external crises faced by the United States and its political institutions, and the history of political parties.

The second theme is the diversity of a national citizenry created by immigrants. To do justice to this theme, *Making America* explores not only English and European immigration but immigrant communities from Paleolithic times to the present. The text attends to the tensions and conflicts that arise in a diverse population, but it also examines the shared values and aspirations that define middle-class American lives.

Making America's third theme is the significance of regional economies and cultures. This regional theme is developed for society before European colonization and for the colonial settlements of the seventeenth and eighteenth centuries. It is evident in our attention to the striking social and cultural divergences that existed between the American Southwest and the Atlantic coastal regions as well as between the antebellum South and North.

A fourth theme is the rise and impact of large social movements, from the Great Awakening in the 1740s to the rise of youth cultures in the post–World War II generations, movements prompted by changing material conditions or by new ideas challenging the status quo.

The fifth theme is the relationship of the United States to other nations. In *Making America* we explore in depth the causes and consequences of this nation's role in world conflict and diplomacy, whether in the era of colonization of the Americas, the eighteenth-century independence movement, the removal of Indian nations from their traditional lands, the impact of the rhetoric of manifest destiny, American policies of isolationism and interventionism, or in the modern role of the United States as a dominant player in world affairs.

In this edition, however, we have added a sixth theme: American history in a global context. This new focus allows us to set our national development within the broadest context, to point out the parallels and the contrasts between our society and those of other nations. It also allows us to integrate the exciting new scholarship in this emerging field of world or global history.

Learning Features

The chapters in *Making America* follow a format that provides students essential study aids for mastering the historical material. Each chapter begins with a map and timeline that set the scene for the most sig-

nificant events and developments in the narrative that follows. While the opening timeline sets significant events in a broader time frame, a chronological chart in the interior of the chapter outlines more fully the events of the given time period. On the chapter-opening page, there is a topical outline of the material students will encounter in the chapter. Then, to help students focus on the broad questions and themes, we provide critical thinking, or focus, questions at the beginning of each major chapter section. Each chapter narrative begins with "Individual Choices" that offers a brief biography of a woman or man whose life reflects or illustrates the central themes of the chapter. At the end of the chapter narrative, "Individual Voices" provides a primary source and a series of thought-provoking questions about that source. These primary sources allow historical figures to speak for themselves and encourage students to engage directly in historical analysis. Finally, each chapter concludes with a summary that reinforces the most important themes and information the student has read.

To ensure that students have full access to the material in each chapter, we provide an on-page glossary, defining terms and explaining their historically specific usage the first time they appear in the narrative. The glossary also provides brief identifications of the major historical events, people, or documents discussed on the page. This on-page glossary will help students build their vocabularies and review for tests. The glossary reflects our concern about communicating fully with student readers without sacrificing the complexity of the history we are relating.

The illustrations in each chapter provide a visual connection to the past, and their captions analyze the subject of the painting, photograph, or artifact and comment on its significance. For this edition we have selected many new illustrations to reinforce or illustrate the themes of the narrative.

New to the Fourth Edition

In this new edition we have preserved what our colleagues and their students considered the best and most useful aspects of *Making America*. We also have replaced what was less successful, revised what could be improved, and added new elements to strengthen the book—and, miraculously, we have achieved these goals without increasing the length of the text.

You will find many features that you told us worked well in the past: biographical sketches, primary sources, timelines and maps that set the scene for each chapter. You will also find new features that you told us you would like to see. For example, we have added global events to every chapter opening timeline, in recognition of the fact that citizens of the twenty-first century live in a global rather than a local setting. We have also added global focus questions to the set of questions that introduce each major section of a chapter. We believe that this attention to global developments will help students place American events in their larger context and encourage them to compare and contrast their national history with the history of other nations. The fourth edition also introduces "It Matters," a feature in each chapter that points out connections between current events and past ones. Each "It Matters" will challenge students to see the links between past and present.

Each chapter opening map is now accompanied by a focus question. This question invites students to think critically about the map and familiarizes them with the content that is to come in the chapter.

Naming in *Making America*

We have thought carefully about the names by which we have identified ethnic groups. As a general rule, we have tried to use terms that were in use among members of that group at the time under consideration. At times, however, this would have distracted readers from the topic to the terminology, and we wanted to avoid that. In such instances, we have tried to use the terms in general use today among members of that group.

Thus, we have used *African American* and *black* relatively interchangeably. The same applies to the terms *American Indian* and *Native American*. If we are writing about a particular Indian group, we have tried to use the most familiar names by which those groups prefer to be identified, for example, *Lakota* rather than *Sioux*.

Sometimes the names by which groups are identified are controversial within the group itself. Thus, in identifying people from Latin America, some prefer *Latino* and others *Hispanic*. Our usage in this regard often reflects our own regional perspective—Bob Cherny has tended to use *Latino* as that term is more widely used in California, and Chris Miller has often used *Hispanic* because that term is more widely used in Texas. In other places, we have used more specific terms; for example, we have used *Mexican* or *Mexican American* to identify groups that migrated to the United States from Mexico and because that is the usage most common among scholars who have studied those migrants in recent years.

Finally, in a few instances when we have discussed nondominant groups, we have indicated the names that such groups used for dominant groups. In some discussions of the Southwest, for example, you will encounter the term *Anglo* to indicate those people who spoke English rather than Spanish, although we are well aware that many who were (and are) called *Anglo* are not of English (or Anglo-Saxon) descent. *Anglo* has to do with language usage, from the perspective of those who spoke Spanish, rather than having to do with those English-speakers' own sense of ethnicity. Similarly, we sometimes use the term *haole* in our discussions of Hawai`i, to indicate those people whom the indigenous Hawaiians considered to be outsiders.

We the authors of *Making America* believe that this new edition will be effective in the history classroom. Please let us know what you think by sending us your views through Houghton Mifflin's web site, located at **http://college.hmco.com.**

Learning and Teaching Ancillaries

The program for this edition of *Making America* includes a number of useful learning and teaching aids. These ancillaries are designed to help students get the most from the course and to provide instructors with useful course management and presentation tools.

The **history companion**

The **Houghton Mifflin History Companion** is a collection of resources designed to complement the use of *Making America*. It is organized according to the chapters in the text and has four parts—the **Instructor Companion web site**, the **Instructor Companion CD-ROM**, the **Student Study Companion**, and the **Student Research Companion**.

The **Instructor Companion web site** and **Instructor Companion CD-ROM** features the **Instructor's Resource Manual** written by Kelly Woestman of Pittsburg State University, primary sources with instructor notes in addition to hundreds of maps, images, audio and video clips, and PowerPoint slides for classroom presentation. The Instructor Companion CD-ROM offers additional audio and video clips for classroom use, the **Test Items** written by Matthew McCoy of University of Arkansas at Fort Smith, and **HM Testing™**, a computerized version of the Test Items with flexible test-editing capabilities.

The **Student Study Companion** is a free, online study guide to accompany *Making America*. The Study Companion contains a variety of tutorial resources including the **Study Guide** written by Kelly Woestman, ACE quizzes with feedback, annotated links to history sites, chronology exercises, flashcards, and other interactivities.

The **Student Research Companion** is a free, online tool with a wealth of interactive maps and primary sources. Students can use the maps for research, classroom assignments, or review of their geography skills. Primary sources provide a real-world introduction to historical evidence. The sources include headnotes that provide pertinent background information and questions that students can answer and e-mail to their instructors.

Please contact your local Houghton Mifflin sales representative for more information about these learning and teaching tools in addition to the **Rand McNally Atlas of American History,** WebCT and Blackboard cartridges, and transparencies for United States History.

Acknowledgments

The authors of *Making America* have benefited greatly from the critical reading of this edition of the book by instructors from across the country. We would like to thank these scholars and teachers: Linda J. Cross, Tyler Junior College; John Hosmer, University High School; Dennis Judd, Cuesta College; Barbara A. Klemm, Broward Community College; Lorraine M. Lees, Old Dominion University; Matthew G. McCoy, University of Arkansas—Fort Smith; Victoria McKain, Butler County Community College; Pamela Riney-Kehrberg, Iowa State University; Kristen L. Streater, Collin County Community College; Theman R. Taylor, Sr., The University of Central Arkansas; and Steven D. Woodsum, Brunswick High School.

Carol Berkin, who is responsible for Chapters 3 through 7, would like to thank Greg Toft, her undergraduate research assistant on this fourth edition. She also thanks the librarians at Baruch College and The Graduate Center of CUNY and the Gilder Lehrman Institute of American History for providing help in locating interesting primary sources, and colleagues and students in the Baruch history department for their ongoing, stimulating discussion of history and historical methods. She thanks her children, Hannah and Matthew, for their patience and support while she revised this book.

Christopher L. Miller, who is responsible for Chapters 1 and 2 and 8 through 15, is indebted to his students at the University of Texas—Pan American for providing the constant inspiration to innovate. Thanks, too, are due to the many students throughout the state of Texas who have participated in his fully online courses taught through the University of Texas TeleCampus. The variety of these students and the novelty of the delivery system have encouraged constant rethinking of both historical content and delivery. Online students at Lansing Community College have provided similar motivation and worthwhile feedback. Several colleagues at University of Texas—Pan American, including Charles Prather, Kenneth Buckman, Steve Rice, and the late Paul Henggeler have been particularly helpful. Colleagues on various H-NET discussion lists as always were generous with advice, guidance, and often abstruse points of information. His coauthors also proved again to be the ideal partners in an often frustrating and difficult task. Personal thanks are due to Ryan Leigh Zimmerman and Madelyn Trinity Weaver for providing a rich life away from the academy, which has made life in the academy much more bearable.

Robert W. Cherny, who is responsible for Chapters 16 through 23, wishes to thank his students who, over the years, have provided the testing ground for much that is included in these chapters, and especially to thank his research assistants who have helped with the first, second, or third edition, Randolf Arguelles, Marie Bolton, Katherine Davis, Beth Haigin, Michelle Kleehammer, Cynthia Taylor, David Winn, and Peter Gray, who helped with this fourth edition. The staff of the Leonard Library at San Francisco State has always been most helpful; the staff of the Kansas State Historical Society was also very helpful with locating the material on Annie Diggs in Chapter 20. Among his colleagues at San Francisco State, Jerry Combs, Tony D'Agostino, Bill Issel, Paul Longmore, Barbara Loomis, Abdiel Oñate, and Jules Tygiel have provided valuable advice on particular sections. Rebecca Marshall Cherny, Sarah Cherny, and Lena Hobbs Kracht Cherny have been unfailing in their encouragement, inspiration, and support.

James L. Gormly, who is responsible for Chapters 24 through 31, would like to acknowledge the support and encouragement he received from Washington and Jefferson College. He wants to gives a special thanks to Sharon Gormly, whose support, ideas, advice, and critical eye have helped to shape and refine his chapters.

As always, this book is a collaborative effort between authors and the editorial staff of Houghton Mifflin. We would like to thank Sally Constable, senior sponsoring editor; Lisa Kalner Williams, development editor; Sandra McGuire, senior marketing manager; Bob Greiner, senior project editor; Robert Woo, editorial assistant; and Pembroke Herbert, who helped us fill this edition with remarkable illustrations, portraits, and photographs. These talented, committed members of the publishing world encouraged us and generously assisted us every step of the way.

Dear Student:

History is about people—brilliant and insane, brave and treacherous, loveable and hateful, murderers and princesses, daredevils and visionaries, rule breakers and rule makers. It has exciting events, major crises, turning points, battles, and scientific breakthroughs. We, the authors of *Making America*, believe that knowing about the past is critical for anyone who hopes to understand the present and chart the future. In this book, we want to tell you the story of America from its earliest settlement to the present and to tell it in a language and format that helps you enjoy learning that history.

This book is organized and designed to help you master your American History course. The narrative is chronological, telling the story as it happened, decade by decade or era by era. We have developed special tools to help you learn. In the next few pages, we'll introduce you to the unique features of this book that will help you to understand the complex and fascinating story of American history.

At the back of the book, you will find some additional resources. In the Appendix, you will find an annotated, chapter-by-chapter list of suggested readings. You will also find reprinted several of the most important documents in American history: the Declaration of Independence, the Articles of Confederation, and the Constitution. Here, too, are tables that give you quick access to important data on the presidents and their cabinets. In addition, you will find a complete list of glossary terms used in the book. Finally, you will see the index, which will help you locate a subject quickly if you want to read about it.

In addition, the Houghton Mifflin History Companion, available online, provides you with free exercises, quizzes, maps, and primary sources to help you study, do research, and take tests effectively. You will also be able to access the *Making America* study guide on the History Companion.

We hope that our textbook conveys to you our own fascination with the American past and sparks your curiosity about the nation's history. We invite you to share your feedback on the book: you can reach us through Houghton Mifflin's American history web site, which is located at http://college.hmco.com.

Carol Berkin, Chris Miller, Bob Cherny, and Jim Gormly

EUROPEANS AND INDIANS IN NORTH AMERICA Although Europeans were at first unsure about the implications of stumbling over a portion of the world that was new to them, they quickly came to understand the economic, political, and military potential involved in American colonization. As this map shows, exploration continued into the seventeenth century as Europeans scrambled to claim individual pieces of New World real estate.

ARCTIC OCEAN

SWEDEN

THE NETHERLANDS

EUROPE

ENGLAND

FRANCE

Greenland

SPAIN

PORTUGAL

AFRICA

HUDSON 1610

HUDSON 1609

ATLANTIC OCEAN

INUIT

ALEUT

INUIT

INUIT

DOGRIB

INUIT

TLINGIT

CHIPEWYAN

Hudson Bay

INUIT

KWAKIUTL

CREE

CREE

BLACKFOOT

MONTAGNAIS

GRAND BANKS

CHINOOK

NEZ PERCE

CROW

MANDAN

CAYUSE

SIOUX

ALGONQUIN

OTTAWA

•Quebec

CHAMPLAIN 1615

CHIPPEWA

HURON

Montréal

MODOC

SHOSHONE

MARQUETTE AND JOLIET 1673

SAUK

FOX

IROQUOIS

Fort Orange (Albany)

Boston

PACIFIC OCEAN

CHEYENNE

ARAPAHO

MIAMI

ILLINOIS

Plymouth

WAMPANOAG

POMO

ONATE 1604–05

ONATE 1601

Taos

DELAWARE

New Amsterdam (New York)

Fort Christina (Wilmington)

POWHATAN

Acoma

ONATE 1598

Quivira

LA SALLE 1679–1682

SHAWNEE

Jamestown

El Paso

Santa Fe

CHEROKEE

TUSCARORA

Roanoke Island

CABEZA DE VACA 1528–36

COMANCHE

WICHITA

CHICKASAW

CREEK

DE SOTO 1539–42

CORONADO 1540–42

New Orleans

CHOCTAW

San Antonio

NARVAEZ 1528

San Agostín (St. Augustine)

SEMINOLE

Gulf of Mexico

Havana

Mexico City

TAINO

Caribbean Sea

ARAWAK

SOUTH AMERICA

Demarcation Line, Treaty of Tordesillas, 1494

→ Spanish exploration
→ French exploration
→ English exploration
→ Dutch exploration

Extent of settlements
■ Spanish
■ French
■ English
■ Swedish
■ Dutch
■ Portuguese

CROW Indian nation
▪ Indian settlement
⚲ Mission
■ Fort
• European settlement

0 400 800 Km.
0 400 800 Mi.

Each chapter opens with a **Map** and **Timeline**. The map geographically reinforces trends that you will read about in the chapter. The caption, boxed in the upper left-hand corner, provides the author's interpretation of what you see in the map.

1494	Treaty of Tordesillas
1521	Cortés conquers Mexico
1588	Defeat of the Spanish Armada
1608	French/Huron alliance
1623	Dutch/Iroquois alliance
1680	Pueblo Revolt
ca.1700	French/ Choctaw alliance

1500 1520 1540 1560 1580 1600 1620 1640 1660 1680 1700 1720

1500 Portugese discover Brazil

1550 Scientific revolution begins in Europe

ca.1640 Dutch take over African slave trade

1700 West Indies become the world's main source for sugar

1618 Thirty Years War begins in Europe

1691 British open trading post at Calcutta

1591 Morocco conquers Songhai Empire

ca.1680 Asante kingdom in Africa

The timeline presents the chapter's sequence of historical happenings in a chronological fashion so that you can see what happened when. This edition of *Making America* now places events in United States history in an international context.

The **Map Focus Question,** seen on the page facing the map, asks you to analyze specific information in the map. This will prepare you for the material you will soon read in the chapter.

Individual Choices

Bartolomé de Las Casas

In 1550 Spanish church officials ordered a council of learned theologians to assemble in the city of Valladolid to hear a debate over an issue so important that it challenged the entire underpinning of Spain's New World empire. At issue was the question of whether Native American Indians were human beings. Arguing that they were not was the well-respected scholar Juan Ginés de Sepúlveda. Arguing on the Indians' behalf was a former conquistador and *encomandero* named Bartolomé de Las Casas.

Born in 1474, Las Casas was the son of a small merchant in Seville. His family was privileged enough that young Bartolomé had both access and the leisure time to study at Seville's cathedral school. Like many of his contemporaries, Las Casas decided to pursue a military career, going to Granada as a soldier in 1497. Then in 1502 he embarked to the West Indies to seek his fortune in the conquest of the Americas.

Apparently Las Casas was successful as a **conquistador:** within a few years he had earned an imperial land grant with a full complement of Indian laborers. Meeting the demands of both church and king, he taught the Indians Catholicism while he exploited their labor. Eventually, however, the former came to outweigh the latter, and Las Casas's religious devotion grew in proportion. After a decade as a soldier and land baron, he became perhaps the first person to be ordained as a priest in America. His new status, however, did not prevent him from pursuing his

BARTOLOMÉ DE LAS CASAS

Himself a former conquistador, Bartolomé de Las Casas was ordained as a Catholic priest in 1512 and later became one of the most vocal opponents of Spain's brutal exploitation of Native American people. He petitioned the King in 1540 and won major reforms in the way Spaniards were supposed to treat Indians, but these reforms were never well enforced

Individual Choices provides a portrait of an individual whose life illustrates a central theme in the chapter. Some of the individuals are famous historical figures, while others are ordinary people who played a role in shaping the events of their era. Individual Choices shows how historical events are the result of real people making real choices.

Individual Voices

Examining a Primary Source

Bartolomé de Las Casas Argues for the American Indians

In his debate with Juan Ginés de Sepúlveda before the Council of Valladolid in 1550 and 1551, Bartolomé de Las Casas repeatedly stressed the many remarkable accomplishments made by Indians, both in creating advanced civilizations of their own and in adapting to Spanish civilization. Many witnesses (most of whom had never been to America) disputed these claims, but more damaging was the argument that such accomplishments were irrelevant. Though perhaps clever, Sepúlveda argued, Indians lacked souls and therefore could never become truly civilized Christians. Like animals, then, they could be exploited but never embraced. Las Casas thought otherwise, and drew on Church doctrine to refute this claim. In the end, Las Casas's argument won the day and became the official position for the Catholic Church and the Spanish Crown.

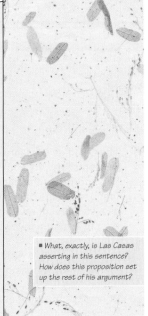

■ *What, exactly, is Las Casas asserting in this sentence? How does this proposition set up the rest of his argument?*

Who, therefore, except one who is irreverent toward God and contemptuous of nature, has dared to write that countless numbers of natives across the ocean are barbarous, savage, uncivilized, and slow witted when, if they are evaluated by an accurate judgment, they completely outnumber all other men? ■ *This is consistent with what Saint Thomas writes: "The good which is proportionate to the common state of nature is to be found in most men and is lacking only in a few. . . . Thus it is clear that the majority of men have sufficient knowledge to guide their lives, and the few who do not have this knowledge are said to be half-witted or fools." Therefore, since barbarians of that kind, as Saint Thomas says, lack that good of the intellect which is knowledge of the truth, a good proportionate to the com-*

Individual Voices allows you to explore a primary source as a historian would. Each document is written by or is closely connected to the person featured in Individual Choices. These primary source documents include personal letters, poems, speeches, political statements, and newspaper articles. Brief introductions set the scene for each primary source, and color-coded **Exploration Points** in the margin pose provocative questions and provide interesting facts about what the document reveals.

Chronology

Partisan Tension and Jeffersonian Optimism

1796 George Washington's Farewell Address
First contested presidential election: John Adams elected president, Thomas Jefferson vice president

1797 XYZ affair

1798 Quasi-War with France begins
Alien and Sedition Acts
Kentucky and Virginia Resolutions
George Logan's mission to France

1799 Fries's Rebellion
Napoleon seizes control in France

1800 Convention of Mortefontaine ends Quasi-War
Jefferson and Aaron Burr tie in Electoral College
Spain gives Louisiana back to France

1801 Jefferson elected president in House of Representatives; Burr vice president
Judiciary Act of 1801
John Marshall becomes chief justice

War begins between American navy ships and Barbary pirates
Outdoor revival meeting at Cane Ridge, Kentucky

1802 Congress repeals all internal taxes
Congress repeals Judiciary Act of 1801
French invade Santo Domingo

1803 *Marbury v. Madison*
Impeachment of Justices John Pickering and Samuel Chase
Louisiana Purchase

1804 Twelfth Amendment ratified
Jefferson reelected

1804–1806 Lewis and Clark expedition

1806–1807 Zebulon Pike's expedition

1816 African Methodist Episcopal Church formed in Philadelphia

The **Chronology** lists the important events that we discuss in the chapter. This list reinforces the sequencing seen earlier in the chapter timeline. You can refer to this chart while reading the chapter. Afterward, you can use it to review the major events of the period.

The Politics of War

■ What problems did Abraham Lincoln and Jefferson Davis face as they led their respective nations into war?

■ How did each chief executive deal with those problems?

■ What role did European nations play during the opening years of the war?

Running the war posed complex problems for both Abraham Lincoln and Jefferson Davis. At the out-

Focus Questions begin major sections of the chapter and guide you to the most important themes in the section. These critical thinking questions help you prioritize and understand events and developments in their context. These questions also have you examine the connection of relevant moments in United States and global history.

The **On-Page Glossary** defines key terms, concepts, and vocabulary in the lower right-hand corner of the page where the term is first used in the narrative. The glossary serves as a convenient review tool, and is of special benefit to non-native speakers of English and students who need help with vocabulary. This edition of *Making America* provides a complete listing of these glossary terms in an appendix. Glossary terms are also bolded in the index, making it easier for you to relate them to their place in history.

amnesty A general pardon granted by a government, especially for political offenses.

suffrage The right to vote.

Thirteenth Amendment Constitutional amendment, ratified in 1865, that abolished slavery in the United States and its territories.

It Matters

The Nation Transformed

The Senate's decision not to remove Clinton from office reaffirmed the principle that the process of impeachment and removal of a president, or any government official, should not rest on political passions. In writing the Constitution, the drafters in Article II, Section 4, stated: "The President . . . and all civil Officials of the United States, shall be removed from Office on Impeachment for, and Conviction of, Treason, Bribery, or other high Crimes and Misdemeanors." While the Constitution does not provide a definition of "high Crimes and Misdemeanors," Congress historically has required a high standard of guilt, preventing the process from being used as a political weapon by a Congressional majority.

It Matters, a feature new to this edition, shows how a particular person, event, or theme in each chapter is relevant today. Through this feature, you will see how the past impacts the present.

HOUGHTON MIFFLIN *The history companion*

Houghton Mifflin History Companion
Your primary source for Teaching and Learning

The **History Companion,** available online for **students** and on CD and online for **instructors,** provides a single source for tutorial materials and presentation materials that make teaching and learning even more dynamic. The History Companion has four components:

FOR STUDENTS:

The Student Study Companion
• ACE quizzes
• Flashcards
• Chronology exercises
• History connection exercises
• Web links and Internet resources
• Study Guide

The Student Research Companion
• Interactive maps and map exercises
• Primary sources with pedagogy and exercises

FOR INSTRUCTORS:

The Instructor Companion CD
• Test Items and HM Testing™
• Instructors Resource Manual
• Historical images in PowerPoint with notes
• Maps in PowerPoint
• Video and audio clips for classroom presentation

The Instructor Companion web site
The content from the Instructor Companion CD can also be accessed on the web site with the following exceptions:
• For security reasons, HM Testing is only available on the Instructor Companion CD.
• Many of the video clips are only available on the CD due to bandwidth concerns.

More resources will become available on the History Companion components. Please check with your local Houghton Mifflin sales representative.

Carol Berkin

Born in Mobile, Alabama, Carol Berkin received her undergraduate degree from Barnard College and her Ph.D. from Columbia University. Her dissertation won the Bancroft Award. She is now professor of history at Baruch College and the Graduate Center of City University of New York. She has written *Jonathan Sewall: Odyssey of an American Loyalist* (1974); *First Generations: Women in Colonial America* (1996); *A Brilliant Solution: Inventing the American Constitution* (2002); and *Revolutionary Mothers: Women in the Struggle for America's Independence* (2005). She has edited *Women of America: A History* (with Mary Beth Norton, 1979); *Women, War and Revolution* (with Clara M. Lovett, 1980); and *Women's Voices, Women's Lives: Documents in Early American History* (with Leslie Horowitz, 1998). She was contributing editor on southern women for *The Encyclopedia of Southern Culture* and has appeared in the PBS series *Liberty! The American Revolution* and The Learning Channel series *The American Revolution*. Professor Berkin chaired the Dunning Beveridge Prize Committee for the American Historical Association, the Columbia University Seminar in Early American History, and the Taylor Prize Committee of the Southern Association of Women Historians, and she served on the program committees for both the Society for the History of the Early American Republic and the Organization of American Historians. She has served on the Planning Committee for the U.S. Department of Education's National Assessment of Educational Progress, and chaired the CLEP Committee for Educational Testing Service.

Christopher L. Miller

Born and raised in Portland, Oregon, Christopher L. Miller received a Bachelor of Science from Lewis and Clark College and his Ph.D. from the University of California, Santa Barbara. He is currently associate professor of history at the University of Texas—Pan American. He is the author of *Prophetic Worlds: Indians and Whites on the Columbia Plateau* (1985), and his articles and reviews have appeared in numerous scholarly journals. Dr. Miller is also active in contemporary Indian affairs, having served, for exam-ple, as a participant in the American Indian Civics Project through Humboldt State University and as a member of the National Advisory Council for the Brothertown Indian Nation of New York. Professor Miller has also been active in projects designed to improve history teaching, including programs funded by the Meadows Foundation, the U.S. Department of Education, and other agencies.

Robert W. Cherny

Born in Marysville, Kansas, and raised in Beatrice, Nebraska, Robert W. Cherny received his B.A. from the University of Nebraska and his M.A. and Ph.D. from Columbia University. He is professor of history at San Francisco State University. His books include *Competing Visions: A History of California* (2005); *American Politics in the Gilded Age, 1868–1900* (1997); *San Francisco, 1865–1932: Politics, Power, and Urban Development* (with William Issel, 1986); *A Righteous Cause: The Life of William Jennings Bryan* (1985, 1994); and *Populism, Progressivism, and the Transformation of Nebraska Politics, 1885–1915* (1981). His articles on politics and labor in the late nineteenth and early twentieth centuries have appeared in journals, anthologies, and historical dictionaries and encyclopedias. In 2000, he and Ellen Du Bois co-edited a special issue of the *Pacific Historical Review* that surveyed woman suffrage movements in nine locations around the Pacific Rim. He has been an NEH Fellow, Distinguished Fulbright Lecturer at Moscow State University (Russia), and Visiting Research Scholar at the University of Melbourne (Australia). He has served as president of the Society for Historians of the Gilded Age and Progressive Era and of the Southwest Labor Studies Association and a member of the council of the American Historical Association, Pacific Coast Branch. He helped to found and continues to edit e-mail discussion lists for historians on the Gilded Age and Progressive Era (H-SHGAPE) and the history of California (H-California), both parts of H-Net, and he has served as a member of the council of H-Net (an association of more than one hundred electronic networks for scholars in the humanities and social sciences). He has also served several terms on the Academic Senate of the California State University system and has been a member of that body's executive committee.

James L. Gormly

Born in Riverside, California, James L. Gormly received a B.A. from the University of Arizona and his M.A. and Ph.D. from the University of Connecticut. He is now professor of history and chair of the history department at Washington and Jefferson College. He has written *The Collapse of the Grand Alliance* (1970) and *From Potsdam to the Cold War* (1979). His articles and reviews have appeared in *Diplomatic History, The Journal of American History, The American Historical Review, The Historian, The History Teacher,* and *The Journal of Interdisciplinary History.*

Making America

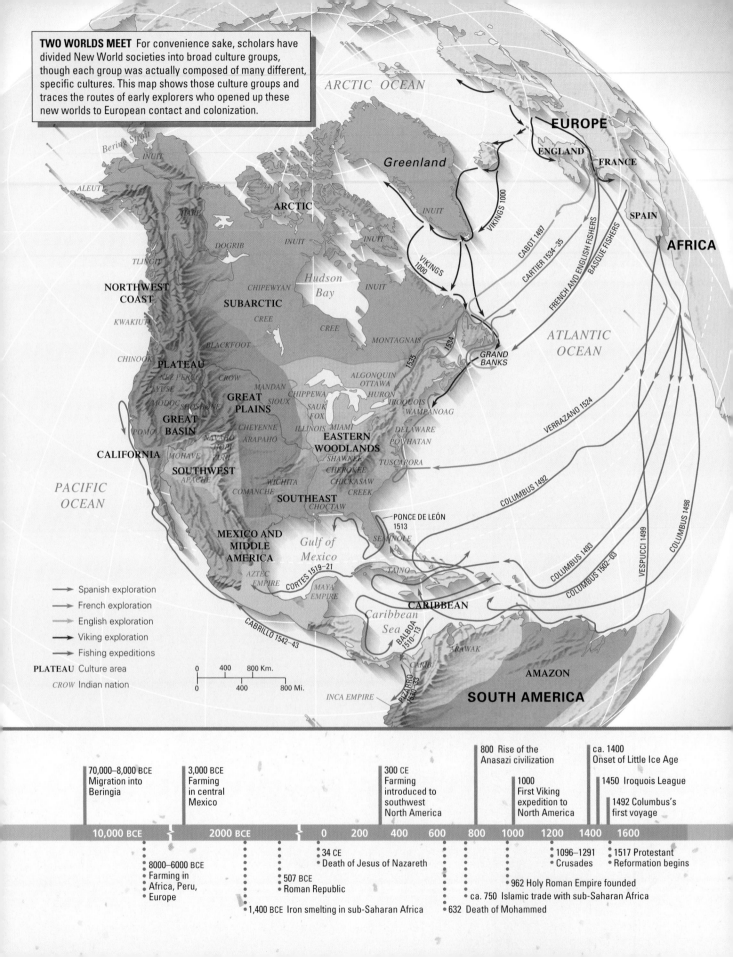

TWO WORLDS MEET For convenience sake, scholars have divided New World societies into broad culture groups, though each group was actually composed of many different, specific cultures. This map shows those culture groups and traces the routes of early explorers who opened up these new worlds to European contact and colonization.

ARCTIC OCEAN

EUROPE

Greenland

ENGLAND

FRANCE

ARCTIC

SPAIN

AFRICA

BERING STRAIT

INUIT

ALEUT

HARE

INUIT

INUIT

DOGRIB

TLINGIT

NORTHWEST COAST

KWAKIUTL

CHINOOK

PLATEAU

NEZ PERCE

CAYUSE

MODOC SHOSHONE

POMO

CALIFORNIA

GREAT BASIN

MOHAVE

SOUTHWEST

APACHE

Hudson Bay

CHIPEWYAN

SUBARCTIC

CREE

CREE

BLACKFOOT

CROW

MANDAN

SIOUX

GREAT PLAINS

CHEYENNE

ARAPAHO

NAVAHO

HOPI

ZUNI

COMANCHE

WICHITA

MEXICO AND MIDDLE AMERICA

AZTEC EMPIRE

Gulf of Mexico

MAYA EMPIRE

PACIFIC OCEAN

CHIPPEWA

SAUK FOX

ILLINOIS

MIAMI

ALGONQUIN

OTTAWA

HURON

IROQUOIS

WAMPANOAG

DELAWARE

POWHATAN

EASTERN WOODLANDS

SHAWNEE

CHEROKEE

CHICKASAW

CREEK

SOUTHEAST

CHOCTAW

TUSCARORA

MONTAGNAIS

GRAND BANKS

ATLANTIC OCEAN

VIKINGS 1000

VIKINGS 1000

CABOT 1497

CARTIER 1534-35

FRENCH AND ENGLISH FISHERS

BASQUE FISHERS

1534

1535

VERRAZANO 1524

COLUMBUS 1492

COLUMBUS 1493

COLUMBUS 1502-03

VESPUCCI 1499

COLUMBUS 1498

PONCE DE LEÓN 1513

SEMINOLE

CORTES 1519-21

TAINO

CARIBBEAN

Caribbean Sea

BALBOA 1510-13

ARAWAK

CARIB

CABRILLO 1542-43

PIZARRO 1530-33

INCA EMPIRE

AMAZON

SOUTH AMERICA

→ Spanish exploration
→ French exploration
→ English exploration
→ Viking exploration
→ Fishing expeditions

PLATEAU Culture area
CROW Indian nation

0 400 800 Km.
0 400 800 Mi.

70,000–8,000 BCE Migration into Beringia

3,000 BCE Farming in central Mexico

300 CE Farming introduced to southwest North America

800 Rise of the Anasazi civilization

ca. 1400 Onset of Little Ice Age

1000 First Viking expedition to North America

1450 Iroquois League

1492 Columbus's first voyage

10,000 BCE   2000 BCE   0   200   400   600   800   1000   1200   1400   1600

8000–6000 BCE Farming in Africa, Peru, Europe

34 CE Death of Jesus of Nazareth

507 BCE Roman Republic

1,400 BCE Iron smelting in sub-Saharan Africa

632 Death of Mohammed

962 Holy Roman Empire founded

ca. 750 Islamic trade with sub-Saharan Africa

1096–1291 Crusades

1517 Protestant Reformation begins

Making a "New" World, to 1588

1

Two Worlds Meet

Using the map on the facing page, examine the patterns of
European exploration and expansion into the Western Hemisphere. How would you say that New World geography
interacted with European economic, political, and diplomatic
interests to influence different colonizing powers to concentrate in certain areas? What sorts of consequences would
these patterns lead to?

Individual Choices

HIENWATHA

New conditions in North America led to increasing conflicts among the five northeastern Iroquois tribes during the fifteenth and sixteenth centuries. Hienwatha overcame resistance—even the murder of his family— to convince Iroquois leaders to form the Iroquois League, a political, military, and religious alliance that helped them survive massive changes and made them a major force in world diplomacy. *Newberry Library.*

Hienwatha

Things were bad, and getting worse, for the people who lived in North America's northeastern woodlands (see the chapter-opening map). For generations they had lived peacefully in their largely self-sufficient villages on the corn that the women grew and the game that the men hunted. Warfare was infrequent, and famine all but unknown. But around the time that Europeans would call 1400, a long-lasting change in the weather made corn production less dependable, and the people were forced to hunt and gather more wild foods to supplement their diets. As hunters from individual villages roamed deeper and deeper into the forests looking for food, they encountered others who, like themselves, were desperate to harvest the diminishing resources. Conflicts became common. "Everywhere there was peril and everywhere mourning," says one version of the story. "Feuds with outer nations and feuds with brother nations, feuds of sister towns and feuds of families and clans made every warrior a stealthy man who liked to kill."

In the midst of the crisis, a child who would be called Hienwatha (or Hiawatha, Maker of Rivers) was born among the woodland people. Oral accounts among the various Indian groups disagree about Hienwatha's early life. According to some sources, he was born among the Onondaga Nation sometime shortly after 1400 but came to live with the neighboring Mohawks. If so, he may well have been a war captive, taken to replace a Mohawk killed in the ever-accelerating violence that raged through the woodlands.

Having grown to adulthood among the Mohawks, the still young and unmarried outsider left his village to seek survival on his own in the woods. Food was scarce, and Hienwatha became a cannibal, killing lone travelers to eat their flesh. One day, as Hienwatha was butchering a victim, he discovered that he had a visitor. The man, a Huron Indian called Dekanahwideh (Two River Currents Flowing Together), shamed Hienwatha for his sad and dishonorable state. The stranger then told him of a spirit being called Peacemaker, who had given Dekanahwideh a vision and a mission: he was to unify all the Iroquois into a great and peaceful nation. Inspired by the stranger's words, Hienwatha vowed never to eat human flesh again and to spend his life making Dekanahwideh's vision a reality.

Hienwatha moved back among the Mohawks, married, and began telling the people about Dekanahwideh's vision and Peacemaker's message. Although many found his words inspiring, some, including Onondaga leader Tadadaho, opposed him. Tadadaho and his supporters finally attacked Hienwatha, killing his family and forcing him to flee once again into the woods.

Undaunted, Hienwatha tried to think of some way to convince his enemies among the Iroquois to accept the idea of cooperation. His solution was to weave a belt of wampum-shell strings that showed a great chain connecting the five northern Iroquois nations—Mohawk, Oneida, Onondaga, Cayuga, and Seneca. Carrying his belt, Hienwatha traveled among the five nations, telling them that they could

survive only if they ceased fighting among themselves and began cooperating. He finally won over even Tadadaho, whose Onondaga Nation became the keeper of the council fires. Together Hienwatha, Dekanahwideh, Tadadaho, and the other leaders of the Five Nations created a confederation government that Europeans later would call the League of the Iroquois. Under its provisions each member nation maintained complete sovereignty in its own affairs, but all agreed fully to defend the others, share resources, and promote the confederation's overall welfare. They also vowed to carry forward Peacemaker's design by offering peace to all who would agree to live with them under the Great Tree of Peace that symbolized the new covenant. Many agreed, but many also resisted what they saw as Iroquois aggression. That included Dekanahwideh's own Huron people, who formed their own alliance system to oppose the Iroquois League.

As remarkable as Hienwatha's story is, his experience was not entirely unique. Faced with changing conditions, natural ones at first and then those brought by invading Europeans, Indians throughout the Americas struggled valiantly and creatively to restructure their societies and their lives. Sometimes the effort brought success, as it did for the Iroquois, but the new political, diplomatic, and spiritual alignments just as often triggered more struggle and war, as it did between the Iroquois and the Hurons. But whatever else might be said for the achievements of Hienwatha and his contemporary visionaries, they succeeded in reshaping America, crafting what Europeans naively—but in this one sense quite correctly—called the New World. And in the process, they helped shape the entire Atlantic world, where the making of America would soon take center stage.

INTRODUCTION

The emergency that led the Iroquois to form their confederacy was but one in a long series of unsettling events that would entirely transform their world and that of their neighbors. Nor was this the first time that America's original population had experienced upheaval in response to changing historical conditions. Having come to a highly varied and ever-changing continent **millennia** earlier, Native Americans had continually modified their environments and been modified by them, giving shape to both the physical and the human world in which America would be made.

For nearly a thousand years before the Iroquois formed their league, a combination of natural and human forces truly global in scope was having a profound impact throughout the Atlantic basin. For example, during the several centuries following the death of Mohammed in 632, the vibrant new religion that he founded, Islam, swept out of the Arabian Peninsula to conquer virtually the entire Mediterranean world. In response, native Europeans, who had themselves adopted a new and dynamic religion, Christianity, only a few centuries earlier, struck back in a series of Crusades designed to break Islamic power. At the same time, climatic changes encouraged expansion by Viking warlords out of Scandinavia southward into the European mainland and westward all the way into North America. Together these expansive societies introduced new technologies and knowledge of distant and mysterious worlds that would engender an air of restlessness throughout Europe.

One of those mysterious worlds lay to the south of the forbidding Sahara Desert in Africa. There, as in both America and Europe, people had been dealing with changing conditions by crafting societies and economies that made the most of varying environments. When Islamic trading caravans began penetrating this region in the eighth century, they found highly developed cities that could draw on massive populations and natural resources to produce goods that were in great demand throughout the evolving Atlantic world. Like Native Americans, Africans too

millennia The plural of *millennium,* a period of one thousand years.

would be drawn into the restlessness that characterized this dynamic age.

Within decades after Hienwatha convinced the Five Nations to unite, Christopher Columbus, a Genoese navigator in Spain's employ, rediscovered the **Western Hemisphere** while trying to find the hidden and distant worlds known to Islamic traders. Columbus's accident brought two historical streams together, and from that point onward, the history of each helped to form the future of both. On a global scale, this event launched a new era in human history. On a more local scale, it began a process we call *Making America.*

A World of Change

■ How did environmental changes influence the development of various societies in North America during the millennia before the emergence of the Atlantic world?

■ What forces came into play in the centuries before 1500 that would launch Europeans on a program of outward exploration?

■ What factors in sub-Saharan African history helped lead to the development of the slave trade?

Christopher Columbus's accidental encounter with the Western Hemisphere came after nearly a thousand years of increasing restlessness and dramatic change that affected all of the areas surrounding the Atlantic Ocean. After millennia of relative isolation, the natural and human environments in America were opened to the flow of people, animals, and goods from the rest of the Atlantic world. During the centuries before 1492, Christian monarchs and church leaders conducted a series of **Crusades** to wrest control of the **Holy Land** from the **Muslims.** As armies of Crusaders pushed their way into the region, they came into contact with many desirable commodities—fine silks, exotic spices, and precious stones and metals. As word spread of the finery Muslims obtained through trade with Africa and Asia, enterprising individuals began looking for ways to profit by supplying such luxuries to European consumers. At the same time, northern European **Vikings** were extending their holdings throughout many parts of Europe and westward all the way to North America. Both Crusaders and Vikings came into contact with equally restless and vibrant societies in Africa and the Western Hemisphere, lending greater impetus to continuing exploration.

American Origins

American history, both before and after Columbus's intrusion, was shaped by the peculiar landscape that had developed over millennia in the Western Hemisphere. Floating plates of the earth's crust meet along the continent's western flank, rubbing and sometimes crashing together. Like a car fender after a collision, the earth has crumpled from the impact, forming rugged mountain ranges all the way from the Arctic to the extreme tip of South America. These collisions also left gaps and weak points in the earth's crust that gave rise to volcanoes and other geological activity. The resulting upheavals constantly changed the region's face: whole mountains were created and then destroyed, rich veins of minerals formed and then were buried, and varied local habitats emerged that would house an incredible array of plant and animal species.

While upheaval was shaping the western portion of the hemisphere, erosion was the sculptor in the east. Old granite rock formations were carved by winter frosts and running water. Thousands of rivers and streams crisscrossed the flattening land, carrying the minerals eroding from higher ground to form rich and deep soil downstream. Upstream, often all that remained was bedrock with only a shallow cover of topsoil. Throughout these regions, too, different habitats supported varied life forms.

Western Hemisphere   When discussing the world longitudinally (lengthwise), geographers often divide the globe into two halves (hemispheres). The **Western Hemisphere** includes North America, Mexico, Central America, and South America; the **Eastern Hemisphere** includes Europe, Asia, and Africa.

Crusades   Military expeditions undertaken by European Christians in the eleventh through the thirteenth centuries to recover the Holy Land from the Muslims.

Holy Land   Palestine, which now is divided between Israel, Jordan, and Syria; called the Holy Land because it is the region in which the events described in the Old and New Testaments of the Bible took place; it is sacred to Christians, Jews, and Muslims.

Muslims   People who practice the religion of Islam, a monotheistic faith that accepts Mohammed as the chief and last prophet of God.

Vikings   Late-medieval Danish, Swedish, and Norwegian groups who responded to land shortages and climatic conditions in Scandinavia by taking to the sea and establishing communities in various parts of western Europe, Iceland, Greenland, and North America.

Chronology

The New World

ca. 70,000–8,000 BCE	Human migration from Asia into Beringia
ca. 7000 BCE	Plant cultivation begins in North America
ca. 1400 BCE	Sub-Saharan Africans perfect iron smelting
ca. 34 CE	Death of Jesus of Nazareth and beginning of Christianity
632	Death of Mohammed and beginning of Islamic expansion
ca. 750	Islamic caravans travel to West Africa; African slave trade begins
ca. 500–1000	Rise of Hopewell culture
ca. 800–1700	Rise of Mississippian culture
ca. 1000–1400	Vikings in North America
1096–1291	The Crusades
ca. 1200	Aztecs arrive in the Valley of Mexico
ca. 1400	Beginning of Little Ice Age
ca. 1450	Hienwatha and Dekanahwideh found Iroquois League
1492	Reconquista completed; Columbus's first voyage
1500	Portuguese begin to transport and trade African slaves
1517	Martin Luther presents Ninety-five Theses
1527–1535	Henry VIII initiates English Reformation
1558	Elizabeth I becomes queen of England

Note: BCE means "before the common era."

About 2.5 million years ago, a new force came to dominate the landscape with the onset of the Great Ice Age. During the height of the Ice Age, great sheets of ice advanced and withdrew across the world's continents, and temperatures were between fifteen and twenty degrees colder than they are today. Glaciers moved southward, grinding away at the central part of North America, carving a flat corridor all the way from the Arctic Circle to the Gulf of Mexico. During the last ice advance, the Wisconsin glaciation, a sheet of ice more than 8,000 feet thick covered the northern half of both Europe and North America.

Not only did this massive ice sheet affect the underlying geology, but so much water was frozen into the glaciers that sea levels dropped as much as 450 feet. Migratory animals found vast regions closed to them by the imposing ice fields and ventured into areas exposed by the receding sea. One such region, Beringia, lay between present-day Siberia on the Asian continent and Alaska in North America (see Map 1.1). Now covered by the waters of the Bering Sea and Arctic Ocean, Beringia during the Ice Age was a dry, frigid grassland—a perfect grazing ground for animals such as giant bison and huge-tusked woolly mammoths. Hosts of predators, including large wolves and saber-toothed cats, followed them. Human populations, which until this time had been confined to the **Eastern Hemisphere,** appear to have followed as well (see page 6).

Sea levels were low enough to expose Beringia about 70,000 years ago, and the area remained above sea level more or less continually until about 10,000 years ago. Although movement southward into North America would have been difficult because of the rugged terrain and mountainous glaciers, determined people may have begun populating the continent at any time between these dates. In fact, recent archaeological finds and isolated discoveries such as that of the **Kenniwick Man** suggest that many different groups of migrating people may have arrived and

Kenniwick Man   The name given to a human skeleton discovered next to the Columbia River near Kenniwick, Washington, in 1996. The skeleton is believed to be over 9,000 years old and appears to have facial features unlike those of other ancient Indian relics.

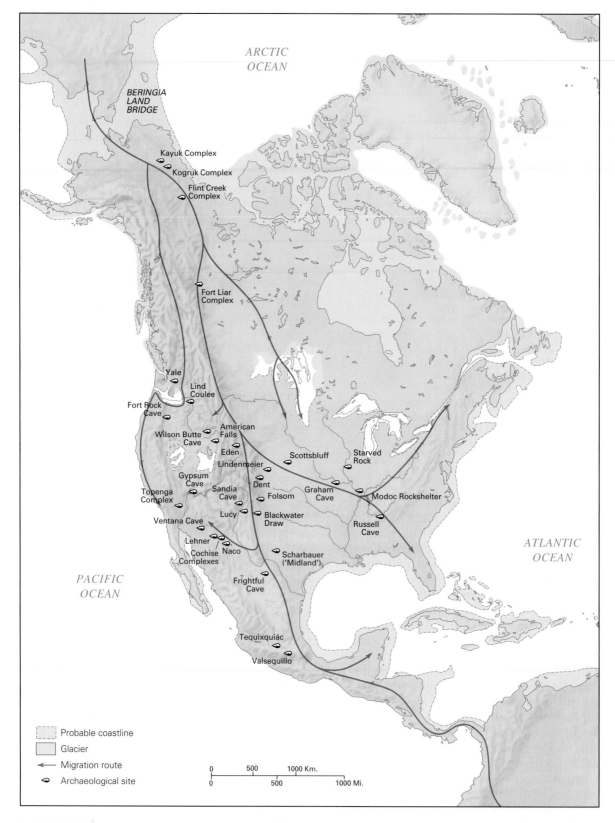

MAP 1.1 First Americans Enter the New World   Although DNA evidence indicates that all early migrants to the Western Hemisphere were genetically related, at least two cultural groups moved into North America between 70,000 and 40,000 years ago. The Old Cordilleran group, to the west of the Rocky Mountains, and the Clovis group, to the east, left records of their passing at numerous sites, the most prominent of which are labeled here.

Although some archaeologists and many Native Americans dispute the accuracy of this forensic reconstruction, many experts consider this bust of the Kenniwick Man based on a skull discovered on the banks of the Columbia River in 1996 to be the best indication of both the deep antiquity and diversity of Old World migrations to North America during the Ice Age. *James Chatters and Thomas McClelland.*

either coexisted or succeeded each other over this 60,000-year period.

Biological evidence collected from modern Indians suggests that the majority of Native Americans are descended from three distinct migrating groups, each of which arrived at a different time. The first of these groups, called the Paleo-Indians, probably entered the continent between 30,000 and 40,000 years ago, and their descendants eventually occupied the entire area of the Western Hemisphere. The second group, collectively called the Na-Dene people, appears to have arrived very near the end of the Wisconsin era, between 10,000 and 11,000 years ago, and their descendants are concentrated in the subarctic regions of Canada and the southwestern United States. The final group, the Arctic-dwelling Inuits, or Eskimos, arrived sometime later, perhaps after Beringia had flooded again (see Map 1.1).

Even after the Ice Age came to an end, it took between 4,000 and 5,000 years for the massive glaciers to melt. During that time the melting ice kept the climate cold and damp everywhere on the continent. But by about 9,000 years ago temperatures began warming. The Ice Age creatures whose presence supplied early hunters with their primary source of meat and whose movements set the tempo for Paleo-Indian life began to die out. The hunters faced the unpleasant prospect of following the large animals into extinction if they kept trying to survive by hunting big game.

It Matters

Native Americans Shape a New World

It may be hard to imagine why understanding the original peopling of North America and how Native cultures evolved during the millennia before Columbus could possibly matter to the history of the United States or, more specifically, to how we live our lives today. Without this chapter in our history, there would likely have been no United States history at all. First and foremost, as the eminent historian Francis Jennings pointed out, if the American continent had truly been a wilderness at the time of European discovery, it would probably still be a wilderness today. Europeans in the fifteenth century lacked the tools, the organization, the discipline, and the economic resources to conquer a wilderness—such a feat would have been the equivalent of our establishing a successful colony on the moon today. But the environmental and genetic engineering conducted through the millennia of North American history created a hospitable environment into which European crops, animals, and people could easily insinuate themselves. And while the descendants of those Europeans may fool themselves into thinking that they constructed an entirely new world in North America, the fact is that they simply grafted new growth onto ancient rootstock, creating the unique hybrid that is today's America.

People everywhere in North America abandoned big-game hunting and began to explore the newly emerging local environments for new sources of food, clothing, shelter, and tools. In the forests that grew up to cover the eastern half of the continent, they developed finely polished stone tools, which they used to make functional and beautiful implements out of wood, bone, shell, and other materials. There and along the Pacific shore, people used large, heavy stone tools to hollow out massive tree trunks, making boats from which they could harvest food from inland waterways and from the sea. During this time domesticated dogs were introduced into North America, probably by newly arriving migrants from Asia. With dogs to help carry loads on land and boats

Maize (corn), which was genetically engineered by Native Americans in what is now Mexico some 7,000 years ago, became one of the staple food sources for many Indian groups in North America. This sixteenth-century illustration depicts traditional Native American agricultural practices and typical foods, including corn, squashes, and gourds. *The Pierpont Morgan Library/Art Resource, NY.*

comes from north-central Mexico, where, beginning perhaps 7,000 years ago, human intervention helped a wild strain of grass develop bigger seedpods with more nutritious seeds. Such intervention eventually transformed a fairly unproductive plant into an enormously nourishing and prolific food crop: **maize.**

Maize (corn), along with other engineered plants like beans, squash, and chilies, formed the basis for an agricultural revolution in North America, allowing many people to settle in larger villages for longer periods. Successful adaptation—including plant cultivation and eventually agriculture—along with population growth and the constructive use of spare time allowed some Indians in North America to build large, ornate cities. The map of ancient America is dotted with such centers. Along the Ohio River, a complex of sites that archaeologists call the **Adena culture** was constructed about 3,000 years ago. Large quantities of both practical and purely decorative artifacts from all over North America have been found at Adena sites. In Illinois and elsewhere in eastern North America, **Hopewell culture** took the place of Adena culture and in time was itself eclipsed by a larger **Mississippian tradition.**

Then, about 800 years ago, midwestern **mound builder** sites fell into decline, and the people who once had congregated there withdrew to separated

for river transportation, Native American people were able to make the best use of their local environments by moving around to different spots during different seasons of the year. Thus they did not establish permanent towns or villages. Rather, they followed an annual round of movement from camp to camp—perhaps collecting shellfish for several weeks at the mouth of a river, then moving on to where wild strawberries were ripening, and later in the summer relocating to fields in which maturing wild onions or sunflower seeds could be harvested.

Although these ancestors of modern Indians believed in and celebrated the animating spirits of the plants and animals that they depended on for survival, they nonetheless engaged in large-scale environmental engineering. They used fire to clear forests of unwanted scrub and to encourage the growth of berries and other plants they found valuable. In this way they produced vegetables for themselves and also provided food for browsing animals such as deer, which increased in number while other species, less useful to people, declined. They also engaged in genetic engineering. A highly significant example

maize Corn; the word *maize* comes from an Indian word for this plant.

Adena culture An early nonagricultural American Indian society centered in the Ohio River valley and spreading as far as West Virginia; it is known for having built large trading centers, where artifacts from all over North America have been found.

Hopewell culture A successor to the Adena culture also centered in the Ohio River valley and spreading as far as New York; Hopewell Indians introduced maize agriculture in about 200 BCE and built larger and more elaborate mound cities in which large-scale trading activities continued.

Mississippian tradition A culture shared by a number of American Indian societies centered in the southern Mississippi River valley; influenced by Mexican culture, it is known for its pyramid building and urban centers.

mound builder Name applied to a number of Native American societies, including the Adena, Hopewell, and Mississippian cultures, that constructed massive earthen mounds as monuments and building foundations.

villages or bands. No single satisfactory explanation accounts for why this happened, but it is interesting to note that other changes were taking place at around this time elsewhere in the Atlantic world that would have profound effects on the American story.

Change and Restlessness in the Atlantic World

During the few centuries following the death of the prophet **Mohammed** in 632, Muslim Arabs, Turks, and **Moors** made major inroads into western Asia and northern Africa, eventually encroaching on Europe's southern and eastern frontiers (see Map 1.2). During these same years, Scandinavian Vikings, who controlled the northern frontiers of Europe, began expanding southward and westward. Accomplished and fearless seamen, the Vikings swept down Europe's western shore and through Russia by river to the Mediterranean. They also began colonizing Iceland and Greenland. Then, according to Viking sagas, a captain named Bjarni Herjólfsson sighted North America in 986. Fourteen years later, Viking chieftain Leif Eriksson led an expedition to the new land, and over the decades that followed, Vikings established several American colonies.

By about the year 1000, then, the heartland of Europe was surrounded by dynamic societies that served as conduits to a much broader world. Although Europeans resented and resisted both Viking and Islamic invasion, the newcomers brought with them tempting new technologies, food items, and expansive knowledge. These contributions not only enriched European culture but also improved the quality of life. For example, new farming methods increased food production so much that Europe began to experience a population explosion. Soon Europeans would begin turning this new knowledge and these new tools against the people who brought them.

Iberians launched a **Reconquista,** an effort to break Islamic rule on the peninsula, and in 1096, European Christians launched the first in a series of Crusades to sweep the Muslims from the Holy Land. With the aid of English Crusaders, Portugal attained independence in 1147. Meanwhile in the Holy Land, hordes of Crusaders captured key points only to be expelled by Muslim counterattacks. The effort to dislodge Islamic forces from Jerusalem and other sacred sites came largely to an end in 1291, but the struggle continued in the Iberian Peninsula. By 1380 Portugal's King John I had united that country's various

principalities under his rule. In Spain, unification took much longer, but in 1469 **Ferdinand and Isabella,** heirs to the rival thrones of Aragon and Castile, married and created a united state in Spain. Twenty-three years later, in 1492, the Spanish subdued the last Moorish stronghold on the peninsula, completing the Reconquista.

Dealings with the Vikings in the north took a somewhat different turn. Although they maintained trading contacts with North America for several hundred years, the Vikings began to retreat in the middle of the 1300s. By 1450 or so, they had withdrawn entirely from their transatlantic colonies. The most likely cause of their departure was a shift in climate. Although experts disagree about the exact timing, it appears that at some time between 1350 and 1450 a significant climatic shift called the Little Ice Age began to affect the entire world. In the Arctic and subarctic, temperatures fell, snowfall increased, and sea ice became a major hazard to navigation. This shift made it impossible for the Vikings to practice the herding, farming, and trading that supported their economy in Greenland and elsewhere. Finding themselves cut off from a vibrant North Atlantic empire, Viking settlements in the British Isles, Russia, France, and elsewhere merged with local populations.

These Viking refugees often joined with their neighbors in recognizing the value of large-scale political organization. Consolidation began in France in around 1480, when Louis XI took control of five rival provinces to create a unified kingdom. Five years later in

---

Mohammed   Born ca. 570 into an influential family in Mecca, on the Arabian Peninsula, around 610 Mohammed began having religious visions in which he was revealed as "the Messenger of God." The content of his various visions was recorded as the Qur'an, the sacred text that is the foundation for the Islamic religion.

Moors   Natives of northern Africa who converted to Islam in the eighth century, becoming the major carriers of the Islamic religion and culture both to southern Africa and to the Iberian Peninsula (Spain and Portugal), which they conquered and occupied from the eighth century until their ouster in the late fifteenth century.

Reconquista   The campaign undertaken by European Christians to recapture the Iberian Peninsula from the Moors.

Ferdinand and Isabella   Joint rulers of Spain (r. 1469–1504); their marriage in 1469 created a united Spain from the rival kingdoms of Aragon and Castile.

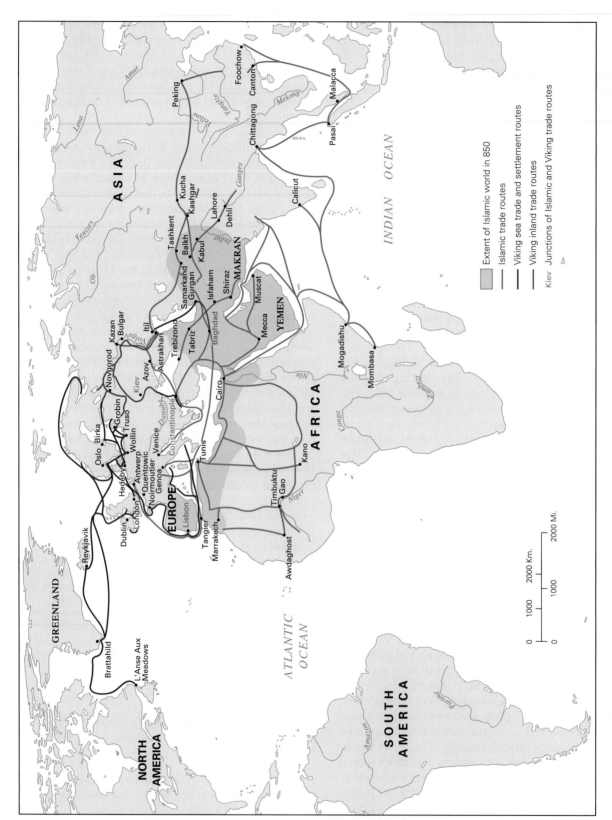

MAP 1.2 Europe and Its Neighbors, ca. 1000 Europe was not isolated during medieval times. As shown here, Viking and Islamic empires surrounded western Europe, and their trade routes crisscrossed the region, bringing far-away goods and ideas from many lands, including North America, long before Columbus "discovered" the New World.

Beginning in about the year 1000, two dynamic seafaring societies controlled the European continent's perimeters: various allied Islamic societies to the south and Vikings on all other sides. Both groups used innovative technologies and advanced geographical knowledge to continually expand their holdings, including holdings in North America. Their ships carried many new commodities as well as new knowledge into Europe, helping to create a restless, exploring spirit among Europeans. *Left: The Pierpont Morgan Library/Art Resource, NY; right: Bibliothèque Nationale, France.*

England, Henry Tudor and the House of Lancaster defeated the rival House of York in the Wars of the Roses, ending nearly a hundred years of civil war. Tudor, now styling himself King Henry VII, cemented this victory by marrying into the rival house, wedding Elizabeth of York to finally unify the English throne. As in Spain and Portugal, the formation of unified states in France and England opened the way to new expansive activity that would accelerate the creation of an Atlantic world.

The Complex World of Indian America

The world into which Vikings first sailed at the beginning of the second millennium and into which other Europeans would intrude half a millennium later was not some static realm stuck in the Stone Age. Native American societies were every bit as progressive, adaptable, and historically dynamic as those that would invade their homes. In fact, adaptive flexibility characterized Indian life throughout North America, and so the vast variety in environmental conditions that characterize the continent led to the emergence of enormous differences between various Indian groups. **Anthropologists** have tried to make

the extremely complicated cultural map of North America understandable by dividing the continent into a series of culture areas—regions where the similarities among native societies were greater than the differences. The chapter-opening map shows eleven such areas.

In the southeastern region of North America, peoples speaking Siouan, Caddoan, and Muskogean languages formed vibrant agricultural and urban societies that had ties with exchange centers farther north as well as with adventurous traders from Mexico. At places like Natchez, fortified cities housed gigantic pyramids, and farmland radiating outward provided food for large residential populations. These were true cities and, like their counterparts in Europe and Asia, were magnets attracting ideas, technologies, and religious notions from all parts of the Western Hemisphere.

Farther north, in the region called the Eastern Woodlands, people lived in smaller villages and combined agriculture with hunting and gathering. The

> **anthropologist**   A scholar who studies human behavior and culture in the past or the present.

Iroquois towns consisted of rows of longhouses, often surrounded by defensive walls. This partial reconstruction of a sixteenth-century Iroquois town that stood near what is now London, Ontario, illustrates how such sites looked. The staked areas to the right of the rebuilt longhouses show where neighboring longhouses used to stand. *Richard Alexander Cooke III.*

Iroquois, for example, lived in towns numbering three thousand or more people, changing locations only as soil fertility, firewood, and game became exhausted. Before Hienwatha and the formation of the Iroquois League, each village was largely self-governed by clan mothers and their chosen male civil servants. Each town was made up of a group of **longhouses,** structures often 60 feet or more in length.

A tradition that may go back to the time when the Iroquois lived as nomadic hunters and gatherers dictated that men and women occupy different spheres of existence. The women's world was the world of plants, healing, nurturing, and order. The men's was the world of animals, hunting, war, and disorder. By late **pre-Columbian** times, the Iroquois became strongly agricultural, and because plants were in the women's sphere, women occupied places of high social and economic status in Iroquois society. Families were

matrilineal, meaning that they traced their descent through the mother's line, and matrilocal, meaning that a man left his home to move in with his wife's family upon marriage. Women distributed the rights to cultivate specific fields and controlled the harvest.

Variations on this pattern were typical throughout the Eastern Woodlands and in the neighboring Great Plains and Southwest. Agricultural village life was the dominant lifestyle in each region before Europeans came. In fact, migrants into the plains probably came from the east carrying seed corn from settlements in the Southeast and Woodlands. Groups such as the Mandans began settling on bluffs overlooking the many streams that eventually drain into the Missouri River. Living in substantial houses insulated against the cold winters, these people divided their time among hunting, crop raising, and trade. Over a five-hundred-year period, populations increased, and agricultural settlements expanded. By 1300, such villages could be found along every stream ranging southward from North Dakota into present-day Kansas.

Just as agriculturalists in the Great Plains had strong connections to the Eastern Woodlands, Indians in the Southwest were closely tied to Mexico. As early as 3,200 years ago, corn appears to have been brought into the area. But the southwestern Indians, unlike their contemporaries farther south, continued to depend extensively on hunting and food gathering for a long time after experiencing the agricultural revolution. Not until about the year 400 did Indians in this region begin building larger and more substantial houses and limiting their migrations. The greatest change, however, came during the eighth century, when a shift in climate made the region drier and a pattern of late-summer thunderstorms triggered dangerous and erosive flash floods.

There seem to have been two quite different responses to this change in climate. A group called the Anasazi expanded their agricultural ways, cooperating to build flood-control dams and irrigation canals. The need for cooperative labor meant forming larger communities, and between about 900 and 1300 the Anasazi built whole cities of multistory apartment houses along the high cliffs, safe from flooding but near their irri-

longhouse   A communal dwelling, usually built of poles and bark and having a central hallway with family apartments on either side (see illustration).
pre-Columbian   Existing in the Americas before the arrival of Columbus.

gated fields. In these densely populated towns Anasazi craft specialists such as potters, weavers, basket makers, and tool smiths manufactured goods for the community while farmers tended fields and priests attended to the spiritual needs of the society.

Another contingent of southwestern Indians abandoned the region, moving southward into Mexico. Here they came upon the remnants of classical city-states like Teotihuacán. One of several highly developed societies of central Mexico, Teotihuacán was the largest city-state in the Western Hemisphere, with a population of nearly 200,000. However, by around the year 600, Teotihuacán and other such societies were in decline. Over the next several hundred years, migrants from southwestern North America—so-called Chichimecs or "wild tribes"—borrowed architectural and agricultural skills from the fallen societies and built new monumental cities. The first of these, Tula, entered its heyday in about the year 1000, but a civil war two centuries later brought that civilization to an end. Shortly thereafter, another Chichimec tribe rose to prominence in central Mexico. The **Aztecs** arrived in the Valley of Mexico soon after 1200, settling on a small island in the middle of a brackish lake. From this unappealing center, a series of strong leaders used a combination of diplomacy and brutal warfare to establish a **tributary empire** that eventually ruled as many as 6 million people.

Other major changes occurred in the Southwest after 1300. During the last quarter of the thirteenth century, a long string of summer droughts and bitterly cold winters forced the Anasazi to abandon their cities. They disappeared as a people, splitting into smaller communities that eventually became the various Pueblo groups. At the same time, an entirely new population entered the region. These hunter-gatherers brought new technologies, including the bow and arrow, into the Southwest. About half of them continued to be hunter-gatherers, while the rest borrowed cultivating and home-building techniques from the Pueblos. Europeans who later entered the area called the hunter-gatherers Apaches and the settled agriculturalists Navajos.

In the balance of North America, agriculture was practiced only marginally, if at all. In areas like the Great Basin, desert conditions made agriculture too risky, and in California, the Northwest Coast, and the intermountain Plateau (see the chapter-opening map), the bounty of available wild foods made it unnecessary. In these regions, hunting and gathering remained the chief occupations.

The Nez Perces and their neighbors living in the Plateau region, for example, occupied permanent vil-

lage sites in the winter but did not stay together in a single group all year. Rather, they formed task groups—temporary villages that came together to share the labor required to harvest a particular resource—and then went their separate ways when the task was done. These task groups brought together not only people who lived in different winter villages but often people from different tribes and even different language groups. In such groups, political authority passed among those who were best qualified to supervise particular activities. If the task group was hunting, the best and most senior hunters—almost always men—exercised political authority. If the task group was gathering roots, then the best and most senior diggers—almost always women—ruled. Thus among such hunting-gathering people, political organization changed from season to season, and social status depended on what activities were most important to the group at a particular time.

As these examples illustrate, variations in daily life and social arrangements in pre-Columbian North America reflected variations in climate, soil conditions, food supplies, and cultural heritages from place to place across the vast continent. But despite the enormous size of the continent and amazing variety of cultures spread across it, economic and social connections within and between ecological regions tied the people together in complex ways. For example, varieties of shell found only along the Northwest Pacific Coast passed in trade to settlements as far away as Florida, having been passed from hand to hand over thousands of miles of social and physical space.

A World of Change in Africa

Like North America, Africa was home to an array of societies that developed in response to varying natural and historical conditions. But unlike contemporary Indian groups, Africans maintained continual if perhaps only sporadic contacts with societies in

---

Aztecs   An Indian group living in central Mexico; the Aztecs used military force to dominate nearby tribes; their civilization was at its peak at the time of the Spanish conquest.

tributary empire   An empire in which subjects rule themselves but make payments, called tribute, to an imperial government in return for protection and services.

After being separated from the rest of Africa by the formation of the Sahara Desert, the Bantu people—aided perhaps by their mastery of iron-smelting technology—expanded throughout the sub-Saharan portion of the continent. This painting rendered by non-Bantu Bushmen, records a battle between themselves and Bantus. Note the relatively huge size and menacing quality of the Bantus compared with the retreating Bushmen, an indication of how the newly dominant group was perceived by its neighbors. *Private Collection.*

Europe and Asia, societies to which they had at one time been intimately linked.

Tendrils of trade between the Mediterranean and **sub-Saharan Africa** can be traced back to ancient Egypt and before, but the creation of the Sahara Desert, the product of a 1,500-year-long drought that began about 4,500 years ago, cut most of Africa off from the fertile areas of the Mediterranean coast. The people living south of the new desert were forced largely to reinvent civilization in response to changing conditions. They abandoned the wheat and other grain crops that had predominated in earlier economies, domesticating new staples such as **millet** and native strains of rice. They also abandoned the cattle and horses that had been common in earlier times, adopting sheep and goats, which were better suited to arid environments. Depending on immediate conditions, groups could establish large villages and live on a balance of vegetables, meat, and milk or, if necessary, shift over to a purely nomadic lifestyle following their herds.

Social organization tended to follow a similar adaptive strategy. The entire region was dominated by a single group of people, speakers of closely related dialects of the common Bantu language (see Map 1.3). Among these Bantu descendants and their neighbors, the social structure was based on the belief that large subgroups were descended from a common **fictive ancestor.** These larger organizations were then subdivided into smaller and smaller groups, each independent—as a modern nuclear family might be—but tied through an elaborate family tree to hundreds or even thousands of other similar groups.

The status of each group was determined by seniority in the line of descent—those descended from the oldest offspring of the common ancestor were socially and politically superior to those descended from younger branches. This fundamental hierarchy created an organizational structure that permitted large-group cooperation and management when appropriate but also permitted each small band to function independently when conditions required. Within each group, seniority also determined political and social status: the eldest descendant of the common ancestor within each group held superior power, whereas those on the lowest branch of the family tree were treated more or less as slaves.

sub-Saharan Africa   The region of Africa south of the Sahara Desert.

millet   A large family of grain grasses that produce nutritious, carbohydrate-rich seeds used for both human and animal feed.

fictive ancestor   A mythical figure believed by a social group to be its founder and from whom all members are believed to be biologically descended.

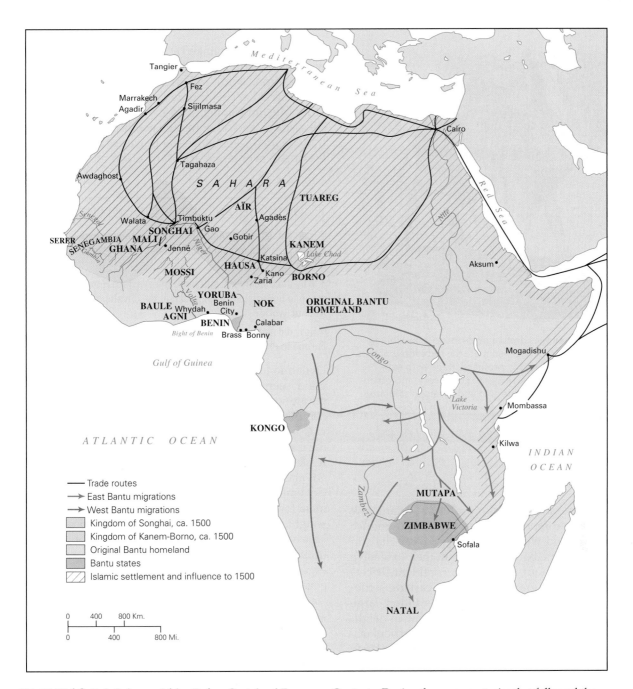

MAP 1.3 Sub-Saharan Africa Before Sustained European Contact   During the many centuries that followed the formation of the Sahara Desert, Bantu people expanded throughout the southern half of Africa. They and other groups established a number of powerful kingdoms, the capitals of which served as major trading centers among these kingdoms and for Islamic traders, who finally penetrated the desert after the year 750.

Much of the technology in place in sub-Saharan Africa can be traced to common roots that preceded the formation of the desert. Evidence suggests that pottery and simple metallurgy were part of an ancient pan-African technological tradition. However, sometime between two and three thousand years ago, sub-Saharan groups appear to have discovered iron smelting. Inventing a shaft furnace—a furnace shaped like a long tube that permitted both the high heat and air draft necessary for melting iron ore—

Introducing camels as draft animals made it possible for Arab and other traders to penetrate the forbidding Sahara Desert to open up a highly profitable trade with sub-Saharan states that were rich with gold, ivory, and other valuable commodities. This gold and diamond miniature (the sculpture is only about two-and-a-half inches tall) celebrates the riches that these animals carried out of Africa. *The Metropolitan Museum of Art, Gift of The Shaw Foundation, Inc., 1959.*

caravan routes that linked sub-Saharan trading centers with the outside world. Increasingly after 1100, metal goods—iron, gold, and precious gems—and slaves were carried across the desert by Arab, Berber, and other Muslim traders, who gave African middlemen silks, spices, and other foreign goods in exchange. This trade tended to enhance the power of African elites, leading to ever larger and more elaborate states.

Exploiting Atlantic Opportunities

■ How did various groups of Europeans seek to exploit opportunities that arose from new discoveries leading up to and following 1492?

■ Why did Columbus's entry into the Western Hemisphere prove to be a major turning point in the development of the Atlantic world?

■ How did Native Americans and Africans respond initially to European expansion?

Dynamic forces in America, Europe, Africa, and beyond seemed unavoidably to be drawing the disparate societies that occupied the Atlantic shore into a complex world of mutual experience. But this process was not automatic. Enterprising people throughout the globe seized opportunities created by the spirit of restlessness and the merging of historical streams, advancing the process and giving it peculiar shape. Generally seeking profits for themselves and advancement for their own nations, tribes, or classes, those who sought to exploit the emerging new world nonetheless had enormous impact on the lives of all who occupied it. The process of outreach and historical evolution that helped to launch the American experience grew directly from these efforts at exploitation.

The Portuguese, Africa, and Plantation Slavery

The first of the European states to pull itself together was also the first to challenge Islamic dominance in both the Asian and African trade. Portugal's John I encouraged exploration by establishing a school of navigation on his kingdom's southwestern shore. Under the directorship of John's son **Henry the Navigator,**

craftsmen were able to make use of abundant raw iron deposits common in southern Africa to produce tools, vessels, and weapons. This discovery may, in fact, have aided the Bantu-speakers in their extensive expansion throughout most of the continent. It certainly gave African groups an edge in carving settlements out of the jungles and grasslands. Often, large cities with elaborate social hierarchies grew in neighborhoods where iron and other ores were particularly abundant. These would then become centers for trade as well as political hubs, the seeds from which later kingdoms and empires would sprout.

These trading centers became particularly important when Islamic expansion brought new, outside sources for trade into the sub-Saharan world. The first mention of trade between Islamic adventurers and African communities stems from the eighth century, and it seems to have developed slowly over the next several hundred years. One catalyst to the trade growth was the introduction of the camel as a draft animal. Native to Asia and the Arabian Peninsula, camels were ideally suited for crossing the inhospitable desert, making it possible to establish regular

> **Henry the Navigator** Prince who founded an observatory and school of navigation and directed voyages that helped build Portugal's colonial empire.

During the years before European penetration into the region, western Africa became a center for Islamic culture. Islamic scholars congregated at holy sites like the Sankoré Mosque in Timbuktu (left). Here they discussed Islamic law and wrote scholarly treatises like Sayyid al-Mukhtur ibn Ahmed ibn Abi Bakr al-Kunti al-Kabir's "An Argument for Peace," which emphasized the Qur'an's message of peace and harmony (right). Writings like these not only helped win more Africans over to Islam but also influenced Qur'anic scholarship throughout the expanding Muslim world. *Left: Photo © www.danheller.com; right: Mamma Haidara Commemorative Library, Timbuktu, Mali.*

the school sent numerous expeditions in search of new sources of wealth. By the 1430s, the Portuguese had discovered and taken control of islands off the western shore of Africa, and within thirty years Prince Henry's protégés had pushed their way to Africa itself, opening relations with the Songhai Empire.

The **Songhai Empire** was typical of the sub-Saharan trading states that emerged through Muslim contacts (see Map 1.3). As was common in the region, the Songhai state consisted of numerous smaller societies, all related through a common ancestor and organized along hierarchical lines. Society remained largely village based, with slaves at the bottom, skilled craftsmen in the middle, and a small noble class at the top. These nobles assembled in Timbuktu, a trading hub and the Songhai capital, which became a cosmopolitan center where African and Islamic influences met. Its art, architecture, and the accomplishments of its scholars impressed all who ventured there. From Timbuktu, Songhai traders shipped valuable trade goods across the Sahara by means of caravans. The Portuguese, however, offered speedier shipment and higher profits by carrying trade goods directly to Europe by sea.

By the end of the fifteenth century, Portuguese navigators had gained control over the flow of prized items

such as gold, ivory, and spices out of West Africa, and Portuguese colonizers were growing sugar and other crops on the newly conquered Azores and Canary Islands. From the beginning of the sixteenth century onward, the Portuguese also became increasingly involved in slave trafficking, at first to their own plantations and then to Europe itself. By 1550, Portuguese ships were carrying African slaves throughout the world.

The Continued Quest for Asian Trade

Meanwhile, the Portuguese continued to venture outward. In 1487 Bartolomeu Dias became the first European to reach the **Cape of Good Hope** at the southern

Songhai Empire   A large empire in West Africa whose capital was Timbuktu; its rulers accepted Islam around the year 1000.

Cape of Good Hope   A point of land projecting into the Atlantic Ocean at the southern tip of Africa; to trade with Asia, European mariners had to sail around the cape to pass from the South Atlantic into the Indian Ocean.

tip of Africa. Ten years later Vasco da Gama sailed around the cape and launched the Portuguese exploration of eastern Africa and the Indian Ocean.

By the end of the fifteenth century, England, Spain, and France were vying with Portugal to find the shortest, cheapest, and safest sea route between Europe and Asia. Because of its early head start, Portugal remained fairly cautious in its explorations, hugging the coast around Africa before crossing the ocean to India. As latecomers, Spain and England could not afford to take such a conservative approach to exploration. Voyagers from those countries took advantage of technologies borrowed from China and the Arab world to expand their horizons. From China, Europeans acquired the magnetic compass, which allowed mariners to know roughly in what direction they were sailing, even when out of sight of land. An Arab invention, the **astrolabe,** which allowed seafarers to calculate the positions of heavenly bodies, also reduced the uncertainty of navigation. These inventions—together with improvements in steering mechanisms and hull design that improved a captain's control over his ship's direction, speed, and stability—made voyages much less risky.

Eager to capitalize on the new technology and knowledge, an ambitious sailor from the Italian port city of Genoa, **Christopher Columbus,** approached John II of Portugal in 1484 and asked him to support a voyage westward from Portugal, across the Atlantic, to the East Indies. The king refused when his geographers warned that Columbus had underestimated the distance. Undeterred, Columbus peddled his idea to various European governments over the next several years but found no one willing to take the risk. Finally, in 1492, Ferdinand and Isabella's defeat of the Moors provided Columbus with an opportunity.

The Spanish monarchs had just thrown off Islamic rule and added the coastal province of Granada to their holdings. They were eager to break into overseas trading, which was dominated in the east by the Arabs and in the south and west by the Portuguese. Ferdinand and Isabella agreed to equip three ships in exchange for a short, safe route to the Orient. On August 3, 1492, Columbus and some ninety sailors departed on the *Niña, Pinta,* and *Santa Maria* for the uncharted waters of the Atlantic. More than three months later, they finally made landfall. Columbus thought he had arrived at the East Indies, but in fact he had reached the islands we now call the **Bahamas.**

Over the next ten weeks, Columbus explored the mysteries of the Caribbean, making landfalls on the islands now known as Cuba and Hispaniola. He collected spices, coconuts, bits of gold, and some native captives. He described the natives as "a loving people" who, he thought, would make excellent servants. Columbus then returned to Spain, where he was welcomed with great celebration and rewarded with backing for three more voyages. Over the next several years, the Spanish gained a permanent foothold in the region that Columbus had discovered and became aware that the area was a world entirely new to them.

England, like Spain, was jealous of Portugal's trade monopoly, and in 1497 Henry VII commissioned another Italian mariner, Giovanni Caboto, to search for a sea route to India. **John Cabot,** as the English called him, succeeded in crossing the North Atlantic, arriving in the area that Leif Eriksson had colonized nearly five hundred years earlier. Shortly thereafter, another Italian, **Amerigo Vespucci,** sailing under the Spanish flag, sighted the northeastern shore of South America and sailed northward into the Caribbean in search of a passage to the East. Finally, in 1524, Giovanni da Verrazano, sailing for France, explored the Atlantic coast of North America, charting the coastline of what later became the thirteen English mainland colonies.

A New Transatlantic World

At first, European monarchs greeted the discovery of a new world as bad news: they wanted access to the riches of Asia, not contact with some undiscovered place. As knowledge of the **New World** spread, the

astrolabe   An instrument for measuring the position of the sun and stars; using these readings, navigators could calculate their latitude—their distance north or south of the equator.

Christopher Columbus   (Cristoforo Colombo) Italian explorer in the service of Spain who attempted to reach Asia by sailing west from Europe, thereby arriving in America in 1492.

Bahamas   A group of islands in the Atlantic Ocean east of Florida and Cuba.

John Cabot   (Giovanni Caboto) Italian explorer who led the English expedition that sailed along the North American mainland in 1497.

Amerigo Vespucci   Italian explorer of the South American coast; Europeans named America after him.

New World   A term that Europeans used during the period of early contact and colonization to refer to the Americas, especially in the context of their discovery and colonization.

primary goal of exploration became finding a route around or through it—the fabled **Northwest Passage.** But gradually Europeans learned that the new land had attractions of its own.

Ambitious adventurers from Britain, France, and Iberia began exploring the fertile fishing grounds off the northern shores of North America. By 1506, such voyages became so commonplace and so profitable that the king of Portugal placed a 10 percent tax on fish imported from North America in an effort to harness this new source of wealth. But these voyages did more than feed the European imagination and the continent's appetite for seafood. It appears that these fishermen established temporary camps along the shores of North America to provide land support for their enterprises. Gradually, as the Native Americans and the fishermen came to know each other, they began to exchange goods. Europeans, even relatively poor fishermen, had many things that the Indians lacked: copper pots, knives, jewelry, woolen blankets, and hundreds of other novelties. For their part, the Indians provided firewood, food, ivory, and furs. Apparently the trade grew quickly. By 1534, when **Jacques Cartier** made the first official exploration of the Canadian coast for the French government, he was approached by party after party of Indians offering to trade furs for the goods he carried. He could only conclude that many other Europeans had come before him.

The presence of explorers such as Verrazano and Cartier and of unknown numbers of anonymous fishermen and part-time traders had several effects on the native population. The Micmacs, Hurons, and other northeastern Indian groups approached the invading Europeans in friendship, eager to trade and to learn more about the strangers. In part this response was a sign of natural curiosity, but it also reflected some serious changes taking place in the native world of North America.

As we have noted, the onset of the Little Ice Age had far-reaching effects. As the climate got colder, hunter-gatherers in the subarctic responded by withdrawing farther south, where they began to encroach on Algonquin and Iroquoian Indians. Meanwhile, the deteriorating climate made it more difficult for groups like the Iroquois to depend on their corn crops for food. Forced to rely more on hunting and gathering, the Iroquois had to expand their territory, and in doing so they came into conflict with their neighbors. As warfare became more common, groups increasingly formed alliances for mutual defense—systems like the Iroquois League. And Indians found it beneficial to welcome European newcomers into their midst—as trading partners bearing new tools, as al-

lies in the evolving conflicts with neighboring Indian groups, and as powerful magicians whose **shamans** might provide explanations and remedies for the hard times that had befallen them.

The Challenges of Mutual Discovery

▪ How did Native Americans respond to increasing contact with European explorers and settlers?

▪ In what ways did Europeans seek to incorporate Africans and Native Americans into their world of understanding?

▪ In what ways was the world made different through the process called the Columbian Exchange?

Europeans approached the New World with certain ideas in mind and defined what they found there in terms that reflected what they already believed. American Indians approached Europeans in the same way. Both of these groups—as well as Africans—were thrown into a new world of understanding that challenged many of their fundamental assumptions. They also exchanged material goods that affected their physical well-being profoundly.

A Meeting of Minds in America

Most Europeans had a firm sense of how the world was arranged, who occupied it, and how they had come to be where they were. The existence of America—and even more the presence there of American Indians—challenged that secure knowledge. In the first stages of mutual discovery in America, most Europeans were content mentally to reshape what they found in the New World to fit with what they expected to find. Columbus expected to find India and Indians, and he believed that was precisely what he had found. Other

> **Northwest Passage**   The rumored and much-hoped-for water route from Europe to Asia by way of North America was sought by early explorers.
>
> **Jacques Cartier**   French explorer who, by navigating the St. Lawrence River in 1534, gave France its primary claim to territories in the New World.
>
> **shaman**   A person who acts as a link between the visible material world and an invisible spirit world; a shaman's duties include healing, conducting religious ceremonies, and foretelling the future.

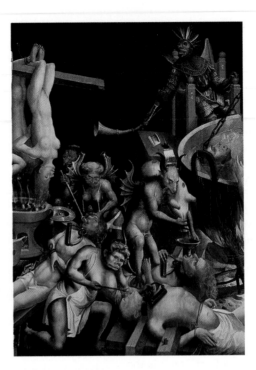

Europeans had trouble fitting American Indians into their preconceived ideas about the world. Native Americans were sometimes cast as noble savages and other times as devils. The Brazilian Indian shown in these two works illustrates the conflicting views. In one, the feather-clad Indian is shown as a wise magus paying homage to the Christ-child; in the other, an Indian devil wears the same costume while presiding over the tortures of Hell. *Left: "Adoration of the Magi" by Master of Viseu. Museu de Grao Vasco; right: "Inferno" anonymous, Portuguese. Giraudon/Art Resource, NY.*

Europeans understood that America was a new land and that the Indians were a new people, but they attempted to fit both into the cosmic map outlined in the Bible. Some Europeans assumed that the inhabitants of the new land were more pure and less corrupted than Europeans, people of God. Others viewed them as poor, ignorant savages.

Columbus's initial comments about the American Indians set the tone for many future encounters. "Of anything that they possess, if it be asked of them, they never say no," Columbus wrote; "on the contrary, they invite you to share it and show as much love as if their hearts went with it." Such writings were widely circulated in Europe and led to a perception of the Indians as noble savages, men and women free from the temptations and vanities of modern civilization.

Not all Europeans held this view of American Indians. Amerigo Vespucci, for one, found them less than noble. "They marry as many wives as they please," he explained. "The son cohabits with mother, brother with sister, male cousin with female, and any man with the first woman he meets. . . . Beyond the fact that they have no church, no religion and are not **idolaters,** what more can I say?" Much more, actually. Vespucci reported that the Indians practiced cannibalism and prostitution and decorated themselves in gaudy and "monstrous" ways.

In some ways, the arrival of Europeans may have been easier for American Indians to understand and explain than the existence of American Indians was for the Europeans. To Indians, the world was alive, animated by a spiritual force that was both universal and intelligent. This force took on many forms. Some of these forms were visible in the everyday world of ex-

idolater   A person who practices *idolatry,* idol worship, a practice forbidden in the Judeo-Christian and Muslim traditions.

perience, some were visible only at special times, and some were never visible. Social ties based on fictive kinship and **reciprocal trade** linked all creatures—human and nonhuman—together into a common cosmos. These connections were chronicled in myth and were maintained through ritual, which often involved the exchange of ceremonial items believed to have spiritual value. Such objects included quartz and volcanic-glass crystals, copper, mica, shells, and other rare and light-reflecting objects. In the pre-Columbian trading world, such prized goods passed from society to society, establishing a spiritual bond between the initial givers and the eventual receivers, even though the two groups might never meet.

Europeans and European goods slipped easily into this ceremonial trading system. The trade items that the Europeans generally offered to American Indians on first contact—glass beads, mirrors, brass bells—resembled closely the items that the Indians traditionally used to establish friendly spiritual and economic relations with strangers. The perceived similarity of the trade goods offered by the Europeans led Indians to accept the newcomers as simply another new group in the complex social cosmos uniting the spiritual and material worlds.

On the other hand, Europeans perceived such items as worthless trinkets, valuing instead Indian furs and Indian land. This difference in perception became a major source of misunderstanding and conflict. To the Indians, neither the furs nor the land was of much value because by their understanding they did not "own" either. According to their beliefs, all things had innate spirits and belonged to themselves. Thus passing animal pelts along to Europeans was simply extending the social connection that had brought the furs into Indian hands in the first place. Similarly, according to Indian belief, people could not own land: the land was seen as a living being—a mother—who feeds, clothes, and houses people as long as she receives proper respect. The idea of buying or selling land was unthinkable to Indians. When Europeans offered spiritually significant objects in exchange for land on which to build, farm, or hunt, Indians perceived the offer as an effort to join an already existing relationship, and not as a contract transferring ownership.

The Columbian Exchange

Even though Europeans and American Indians saw some similarities in each other, their worlds differed greatly, sometimes in ways hidden to both groups. The natural environments of these worlds were dif-

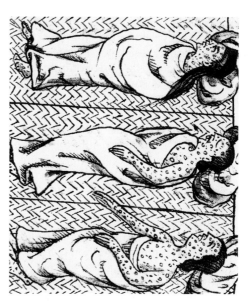

European diseases killed many millions of Indians during the initial stages of contact because they had no immunity to such epidemic illnesses as influenza, measles, and plague. Smallpox was one of the deadliest of these imported diseases. This Aztec drawing illustrates smallpox's impact, from the initial appearance of skin lesions through death. Not only were traditional Indian medical practices unable to cure such diseases, but physical contact between shamans and patients actually helped to spread them. *Biblioteca Medicea Laurenziana.*

ferent, and the passage of people, plants, and animals among Europe, Africa, and North America wrought profound changes in all three continents. Historians call this process the **Columbian Exchange.**

Perhaps the most tragic trade among the three continents came about as the direct and unavoidable consequence of human contact. During the period leading up to the age of exploration, many Europeans lost their lives to epidemic diseases. The Black Death of the fourteenth century, for example, wiped out over a third of Europe's population. Exposure to

reciprocal trade   A system of trading in which the objective is equal exchange of commodities rather than profit.

Columbian Exchange   The exchange of people, plants, and animals between Europe, Africa, and North America that occurred after Columbus's arrival in the New World.

smallpox, measles, typhus, and other serious diseases had often had devastating results, but Europeans gradually developed resistance to infection. In contrast, the Indian peoples whom Columbus and other European explorers encountered lived in an environment in which contagious diseases were never a serious threat until the Europeans arrived. They had no **acquired immunity** to the various bacteria and viruses that Europeans carried. As a result, the new diseases spread very rapidly and were much more deadly among the native peoples than they were among Europeans.

Controversy rages over the number of Indians killed by imported European diseases. Estimates of how many people lived in America north of Mexico in 1492 run from a high of 25 million to a low of 1 million. At the moment, most scholars accept a range of from 3 to 10 million. Even if the most conservative estimate is correct, the raw numbers of people who died of smallpox, typhus, measles, and other imported diseases were enormous. In areas of early and continuing association between Europeans and Indians, between 90 and 95 percent of the native population appear to have died of disease during the first century of contact. Although the percentage was probably lower in areas where contact was infrequent and where native populations were sparse, disease took a terrible toll as it followed the lines of kinship and trade that held native North America together.

Disease, however, did not flow in only one direction. Some diseases that originated in Africa found their way to both North America and Europe and at least one, **syphilis,** may have originated in the Western Hemisphere and migrated eastward. American Indians appear to have been less debilitated physically by syphilis, to which they may have possessed partial immunity. Africans were largely unaffected by various **malarial** fevers that ravaged both European and native populations. Europeans found measles to be a mildly unpleasant childhood disease, but for both Africans and Indians it was a mass killer. The march of exchanged diseases across the North American landscape and their effects on various populations provided a constant backdrop for the continent's history.

Less immediate but perhaps equally extreme ecological effects arose from the passage of plants among Europe, North America, and Africa. The introduction of plants into the New World extended a process that had been taking place for centuries in the Old World. Trade with Asia had carried exotic plants such as bananas, sugar cane, and rice into Africa as early as 2,300 years ago. From Africa, these plants were imported to Iberian-claimed islands such as the Ca-

naries and eventually to America, where, along with cotton, indigo, coffee, and other imports, they would become **cash crops** on European-controlled plantations. Grains such as wheat, barley, and millet were readily transplanted to some areas in North America, as were grazing grasses and various vegetables, including turnips, spinach, and cabbage.

North American plants also traveled from west to east in the Columbian Exchange. Leading the way in economic importance was tobacco, a stimulant used widely in North America for ceremonial purposes and broadly adopted by Europeans and Africans as a recreational drug. Another stimulant, cocoa, also enjoyed significant popularity among Old World consumers. In addition, New World vegetables helped to revolutionize world food supplies. Remarkably easy to grow, maize thrived virtually everywhere. In addition, the white potato, tomato, **manioc,** squash, and beans native to the Western Hemisphere were soon cultivated throughout the world. Animals also moved in the Columbian Exchange. Europeans brought horses, pigs, cattle, oxen, sheep, goats, and domesticated fowl to America, where their numbers soared.

The transplanting of European grain crops and domesticated animals reshaped the American landscape. Changing the contours of the land by clearing trees and undergrowth and by plowing and fencing altered the flow of water, the distribution of seeds, the nesting of birds, and the movement of native animals. Gradually, imported livestock pushed aside native species, and imported plants choked out indigenous ones.

Probably the most important and far-reaching environmental impact of the Columbian Exchange was its overall influence on human populations. Although exchanged diseases killed many millions of Indians

---

acquired immunity   Resistance or partial resistance to a disease; acquired immunity develops in a population over time as a result of exposure to harmful bacteria and viruses.

syphilis   An infectious disease usually transmitted through sexual contact; if untreated, it can lead to paralysis and death.

malarial   Related to malaria, an infectious disease characterized by chills, fever, and sweating; malaria is often transmitted through mosquito bites.

cash crop   A crop raised in large quantities for sale rather than for local or home consumption.

manioc   Also called cassava, a root vegetable native to South America that became a staple food source throughout the tropical world after 1500.

and lesser numbers of Africans and Europeans, the transplantation of North American plants significantly expanded food production in what had been marginal areas of Europe and Africa. At the same time, the environmental changes that Europeans wrought along the Atlantic shore of North America permitted the region to support many more people than it had sustained under Indian cultivation. The overall result in Europe and Africa was a population explosion that eventually spilled over to repopulate a devastated North America.

New Worlds in Africa and America

As the Columbian Exchange redistributed plants, animals, and populations among Europe, Africa, and North America, it permanently altered the history of both hemispheres. In North America, for example, the combination of disease, environmental transformation, and immigrant population pressure changed American Indian life and culture in profound ways.

Clearly, imported disease had the most ruinous influence on the lives of Indians. Cooperative labor was required for hunting and gathering, and native groups that continued to depend on those activities faced extinction if disease caused a shortage of labor. Also, most societies in North America were **nonliterate:** elders and storytellers passed on their collective knowledge from one generation to another. Wholesale death by disease wiped out these bearers of practical, religious, and cultural knowledge. The result of this loss was confusion and disorientation among survivors. In an effort to avert extinction, remnant groups banded together to share labor and lore. Members of formerly self-sustaining kinship groups joined together in composite villages or, in some cases, intertribal leagues or confederacies. And the devastation that European diseases wrought eased the way for the deeper penetration of Europeans into North America as Indians sought alliances with the newcomers in order to gain new tools, new sources of information, and new military partners, pushing Indians into increasingly tangled relationships with Europeans.

The Columbian Exchange also severely disrupted life in Africa. Africa had long been a key supplier of labor in the Old World. The ancient Egyptians had imported slaves from Ethiopia and other regions south of the Sahara Desert, a practice that continued through Roman times. But it was Islamic traders who turned the enslavement of Africans into a thriving enterprise. When North African Muslims established

Parties of captured villagers from Africa's interior were bound together and marched to trading centers on the coast, where they were sold to European or Arab traders. The slave drivers were heavily influenced by outside contact. One of those shown here is wearing an Arab-influenced turban, while the clothing of the other is more European. Note, too, that the latter carries both a gun and a traditional African spear. *The Granger Collection.*

regular caravan routes across the desert into sub-Saharan Africa, slaves quickly became a dominant trade item, second only to gold in overall value. Perhaps as many as 4 million slaves were carried across the desert between 800 and the time the Portuguese redirected the trade in the sixteenth century.

Portuguese entry, however, revolutionized this economy. European technology, wealth, and ideas fostered the development of aggressive centralized states along the **Slave Coast** on the western shore of

---

nonliterate   Lacking a system of reading and writing, relying instead on storytelling and mnemonic (memory-assisting) devices such as pictures.

Slave Coast   A region of coastal West Africa adjacent to the Gold Coast; it was the principal source of the slaves taken out of West Africa from the sixteenth to the early nineteenth century.

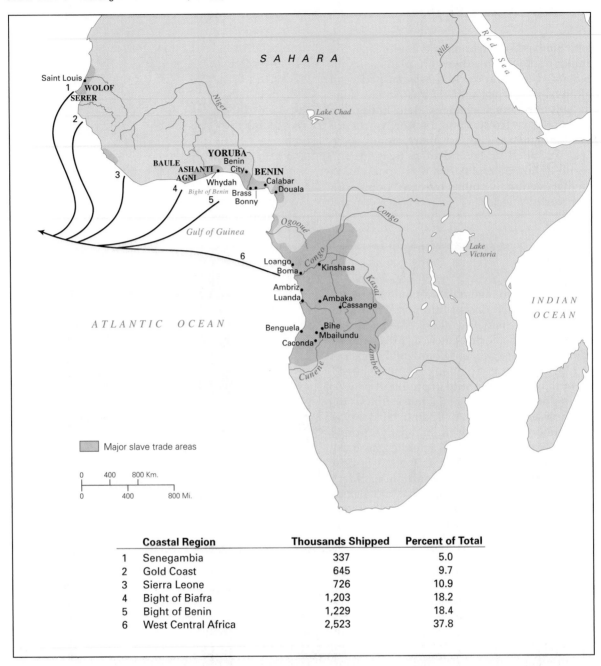

	Coastal Region	Thousands Shipped	Percent of Total
1	Senegambia	337	5.0
2	Gold Coast	645	9.7
3	Sierra Leone	726	10.9
4	Bight of Biafra	1,203	18.2
5	Bight of Benin	1,229	18.4
6	West Central Africa	2,523	37.8

MAP 1.4 Western Africa and the Atlantic Slave Trade   Africa's western shore was the major source for slaves that were transported to European colonies on the Atlantic islands, the Caribbean islands, and mainland North and South America. Powerful coastal kingdoms mounted organized raids into many inland areas to capture people who were then marched to the coast for shipment to the New World. This map shows the several regions from which slaves were extracted, and the accompanying table gives approximate numbers of people who were exported from each.

Africa's Gulf of Guinea (see Map 1.4). Armed with European firearms, aggressive tribes such as the Ashanti engaged in large-scale raiding deep into the Niger and Congo river regions. These raiders captured millions of prisoners, whom they herded back to the coast and sold to Portuguese, Spanish, Dutch, and other European traders to supply labor for mines and plantations in the New World.

It is difficult to determine the number of people sold in the West African slave trade between 1500 and

1800. The most recent estimates suggest that more than 9.5 million enslaved Africans arrived in the New World during this three-hundred-year period. And they were only a small portion of the total number of Africans victimized by the system. On average, between 10 and 20 percent of the slaves shipped to the Americas died in transit. Adding in the numbers who were shipped to other locations in the Eastern Hemisphere, who were kept in slavery within Africa, and who died during the raids and on the marches to the coast yields a staggering total.

A New World in Europe

The discovery of America and the Columbian Exchange also had staggering repercussions on life in Europe. New economic opportunities and new ideas demanded new kinds of political and economic organization. The discovery of the New World clearly forced a new and more modern society onto Europeans.

Europe's population was already rising when potatoes, maize, and other New World crops began to revolutionize food production. Populations then began to soar despite nearly continuous wars and a flood of migration to the New World. With populations on the rise and overseas empires to run, European rulers and their advisers saw that centralized states appeared to offer the most promising device for harnessing the riches of the New World while controlling ever-increasing numbers of people at home. The sons and daughters of Europe's first generation of **absolute monarchs** chose to continue the consolidation of authority begun by their parents.

As Europeans responded to social, political, and economic changes, traditional patterns of authority broke down, especially in the realm of religion. A particularly devastating blow to religious authority came from the pen of Martin Luther, a German monk. Luther preached that salvation was God's gift to the faithful. In 1517 he presented a set of arguments, the **Ninety-five Theses,** maintaining that only individual repentance and the grace of God could save sinners. The implications of this simple formula were profound: if Luther was right, then Christians could achieve salvation without the intercession of the Roman Catholic or any other church, undermining the keystone of both religious and political authority upon which order in Europe was based.

Luther's ideas took root among a generation of theologians who were dissatisfied with the corruption and superstition they found in the medieval Catholic Church, launching the period known as the

Reformation. A Frenchman, John Calvin, further undermined the church's authority by suggesting that God had preselected only some people for salvation. Calvin called these individuals **the Elect.** For all others, no earthly effort—no good works, no prayers, no church intervention—could save them. Thus neither popes nor kings had any claim to authority, and no one held the keys to salvation except God, but happiness on earth might be attained by wresting worldly authority from the hands of kings and putting it into the hands of the Elect.

Known as **Protestantism,** the doctrines of Luther, Calvin, and others who wanted to reform the Catholic Church formed an ideology that appealed to a broad audience in the rapidly changing European world of the sixteenth century. Ever critical of entrenched authority, the new doctrines attracted lawyers, bureaucrats, merchants, and manufacturers, whose economic and political status was on the rise thanks to increased prosperity generated by the Columbian Exchange. But many in the ruling classes also found aspects of the new theology attractive. In Germany, Luther's challenge to the priesthood, and by extension to the Catholic Church itself, led many local princes to question the **divine right** to authority

absolute monarch The ruler of a kingdom in which every aspect of national life—including politics, religion, the economy, and social affairs—comes under royal authority.

Ninety-five Theses A document prepared by Martin Luther in 1517 protesting certain Roman Catholic practices that he believed were contrary to the will of God as revealed in Scripture.

Reformation The sixteenth-century rise of Protestantism, with the establishment of state-sponsored Protestant churches in England, the Netherlands, parts of Germany and Switzerland, and elsewhere.

the Elect According to Calvinism, the people chosen by God for salvation.

Protestantism From the root word *protest*, the beliefs and practices of Christians who broke with the Roman Catholic Church; rejecting church authority, the doctrine of "good works," and the necessity of the priesthood, Protestants accepted the Bible as the only source of revelation, salvation as God's gift to the faithful, and a direct, personal relationship with God as available to every believer.

divine right The idea that monarchs derive their authority to rule directly from God and are accountable only to God.

claimed by the ruler of the **Holy Roman Empire.** Similarly, **Henry VIII** of England, at one time a critic of Luther's ideas, found Protestantism convenient when he wanted to resist the authority of the pope and expand English national power.

Henry VIII, the son of Henry VII and Elizabeth of York, was the first undisputed heir to the English throne in several generations, and he was consumed with the desire to avoid renewed civil war by having a son who could inherit the Crown. When his wife Catherine of Aragon, daughter of Spain's Ferdinand and Isabella, failed to bear a boy, Henry demanded in 1527 that Pope Clement VII grant him a divorce and permission to marry someone else. Fearful of Spanish reprisals on Catherine's behalf, Clement refused. In desperation, Henry launched an English Reformation by seizing the Catholic Church in England, gaining complete control of it by 1535.

Henry was not a staunch believer in the views aired by Luther and others, but the idea of unifying religious and civil authority under his personal control did appeal to him. In addition, the Catholic Church owned extensive and valuable lands in England, estates that Henry could use to enhance his wealth and power. He needed Protestant support in his war against the pope's authority, so he reluctantly opened the door to Protestant practices in his newly created Church of England.

After Henry's death, his very young son—finally born to his third wife, Jane Seymour—ascended the throne as Edward VI. In the absence of a strong king, Protestants had virtual free rein, and the pace of reform quickened. Young King Edward, however, was a frail child and died after ruling for only six years. Mary, his oldest sister, succeeded him. The daughter of Henry's first wife, Mary had married Philip II of Spain and was a devout Roman Catholic. She attempted to reverse the reforming trend, cruelly suppressing Protestantism by executing several hundred leading reformers. But her brutality only drove the movement underground and made it more militant. By the time her half-sister Elizabeth, who was born and raised a Protestant, inherited the crown in 1558, the Protestant underground had become powerful and highly motivated. In fact, **Elizabeth I** spent her entire half-century reign trying to reach a workable settlement with Protestant **dissenters** that would permit them free worship without endangering her control over church and state.

Holy Roman Empire   A political entity, authorized by the Catholic Church in 1356, unifying central Europe under an emperor elected by four princes and three Catholic archbishops.

Henry VIII   King of England (r. 1509–1547); his desire to divorce his first wife led him to break with Catholicism and establish the Church of England.

Elizabeth I   Queen of England (r. 1558–1603); she succeeded the Catholic Mary I and reestablished Protestantism in England; her reign was a time of domestic prosperity and cultural achievement.

dissenter   A person who does not accept the doctrines of an established or national church.

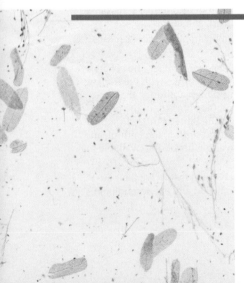

Individual Voices

Examining a Primary Source

The Five Nations Adopt the Great Law

Pressed on all sides by radically changing conditions, five Indian nations among the Iroquoian-speaking people in the Eastern Woodlands listened to Hienwatha (Hiawatha) and joined him in embracing the message of Dekanahwideh. The Peacegiver presented a plan for government, often referred to as "The Great Law," which would become the constitution for the Iroquois League. But Dekanahwideh's vision

■ Clearly Dekanahwideh chose the image of the "great tree" for a reason. What do you see as the meaning behind this image? What do you think the four "great, long, white roots" symbolize?

■ What is Dekanahwideh advocating in this passage? How do you suppose this advice steered Five Nations policy during the three centuries after the adoption of the Great Law?

■ What does the Great Law suggest about the responsibility of each of the Five Nations to the confederacy as a whole? How would the scheme advocated here help the Iroquois deal with changing historical conditions?

included much more than just peace among the Five Nations. Like similar strategies for cooperation that were being crafted by Indian groups throughout North America during this critical time, in the mid-1400s, the Great Law was a creative device that would carry the Iroquois into a new era of history.

Then Dekanahwideh said: "We have now completed arranging the system of our local councils and we shall hold our annual Confederate Council at the settlement of Thadodahho, the capitol or seat of government of the Five Nations Confederacy."

Dekanahwideh said: "Now I and you lords of the Confederate Nations shall plant a tree Ska-renj-heh-se-go-wah (meaning a tall and mighty tree) and we shall call it Jo-ne-rak-deh-ke-wah (the tree of the great long leaves)."

"Now this tree which we have planted shall shoot forth Jo-doh-ra-ken-rah-ko-wah (four great, long, white roots). These great, long, white roots shall shoot forth one to the north and one to the south and one to the east and one to the west, and we shall place on the top of it Oh-don-yonh (an eagle) which has great power of long vision, and we shall transact all our business beneath the shade of this great tree. ■ The meaning of planting this great tree, Skareh-hehsegowah, is to symbolize Ka-yah-ne-renh-ko-wa, which means Great Peace, and Jo-deh-ra-ken-rah-ke-wah, meaning Good Tidings of Peace and Power. The nations of the earth shall see it and shall accept and follow the roots and shall follow them to the tree and when they arrive here you shall receive them and shall seat them in the midst of your confederacy. ■ The object of placing an eagle on the top of the great, tall tree is that it may watch the roots which extend to the north and to the south and to the east and to the west, and whose duty shall be to discover if any evil is approaching your confederacy, and he shall scream loudly and give the alarm and all the nations of the confederacy at once shall heed the alarm and come to the rescue." ■

Summary

Making America began perhaps as long as 70,000 years ago, when the continent's first human occupants began the long process of fitting themselves to a land they would call their own. Hoping to find better conditions than they were leaving behind in Asia, they migrated across Beringia and then overcame or adapted to the ever-changing new environment in which they found themselves. Over thousands of years, they continually crafted economic strategies, social arrangements, and political systems to preserve and enhance their lives. The result was a rich and flourishing world of different cultures, linked by common religious and economic bonds.

At first, the arrival of Europeans only added another society to an already cosmopolitan sphere. The Vikings came and went, as perhaps did other non-Indians. But ultimately, the dynamic European society that arose after the Crusades and plagues of the Middle Ages became more intrusive. As a result, Native Americans faced challenges that they had never imagined: economic crises, disease, war, and the unfolding environmental changes wrought by the Europeans who followed Columbus.

In addition, influences from the New World reached out to accelerate processes that were already affecting the Old World. The flow of wealth and food out of the West was increasing populations, and this growth, with the accompanying rise of powerful kings and unified nations, led to continuing conflict over newfound resources. In Africa, strong coastal states raided weaker neighboring groups, more than doubling the flow of slaves out of Africa. This, in turn, influenced further developments in America. As disease destroyed millions of Indians, newcomers from the entire Atlantic rim poured in to replace them. These newcomers came from very different physical environments and had distinctly foreign ideas about nature. Their novel practices and ideas helped to create a new America on top of the old, rendering drastic changes to the landscape. Continuing interactions among these various newcomers, and between them and the survivors of America's original people, would launch the process of Making America.

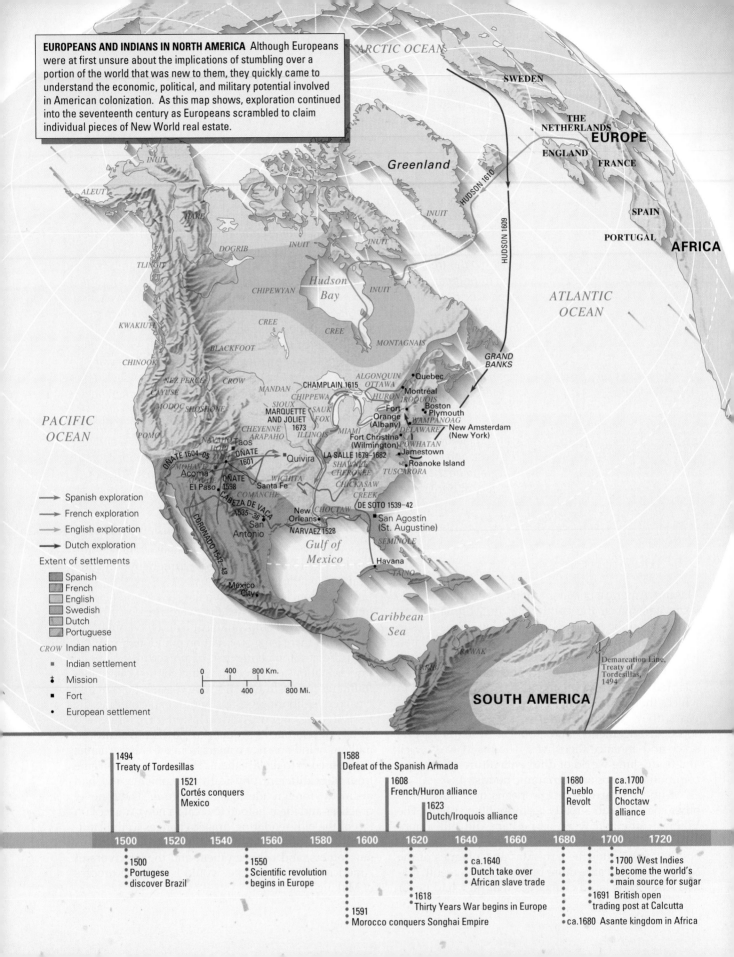

EUROPEANS AND INDIANS IN NORTH AMERICA Although Europeans were at first unsure about the implications of stumbling over a portion of the world that was new to them, they quickly came to understand the economic, political, and military potential involved in American colonization. As this map shows, exploration continued into the seventeenth century as Europeans scrambled to claim individual pieces of New World real estate.

ARCTIC OCEAN

SWEDEN

THE NETHERLANDS
ENGLAND

EUROPE

FRANCE

SPAIN

PORTUGAL

AFRICA

Greenland

HUDSON 1610

HUDSON 1609

INUIT

ALEUT

HARE

DOGRIB

TLINGIT

CHIPEWYAN

INUIT

INUIT

Hudson Bay

INUIT

ATLANTIC OCEAN

KWAKIUTL

CREE

CREE

CHINOOK

BLACKFOOT

MONTAGNAIS

NEZ PERCE

CROW

MANDAN

ALGONQUIN

Quebec

GRAND BANKS

CAYUSE

SIOUX

CHIPPEWA

OTTAWA

Montréal

MODOC

SHOSHONE

CHAMPLAIN 1615

HURON

IROQUOIS

Boston

PACIFIC OCEAN

POMO

MARQUETTE AND JOLIET 1673

SAUK FOX

Fort Orange (Albany)

Plymouth

WAMPANOAG

CHEYENNE
ARAPAHO

ILLINOIS

MIAMI

DELAWARE

New Amsterdam (New York)

NAVAHO
HOPI

Taos

Fort Christina (Wilmington)

POWHATAN

OÑATE 1604–05

OÑATE 1601

Quivira

LA SALLE 1679–1682

Jamestown

Acoma

Roanoke Island

MOHAVE

OÑATE 1598

SHAWNEE

El Paso

APACHE

Santa Fe

WICHITA

CHEROKEE

TUSCARORA

CABEZA DE VACA 1535–36

COMANCHE

CHICKASAW

CREEK

DE SOTO 1539–42

CORONADO 1542–43

San Antonio

New Orleans

CHOCTAW

San Agostín (St. Augustine)

NARVAEZ 1528

Gulf of Mexico

SEMINOLE

Havana

TAINO

Mexico City

Caribbean Sea

ARAWAK

CARIB

Demarcation Line, Treaty of Tordesillas, 1494

SOUTH AMERICA

→ Spanish exploration
→ French exploration
→ English exploration
→ Dutch exploration

Extent of settlements
- Spanish
- French
- English
- Swedish
- Dutch
- Portuguese

CROW Indian nation
■ Indian settlement
⚲ Mission
■ Fort
• European settlement

| 0 | 400 | 800 Km. |
| 0 | 400 | 800 Mi. |

1494
Treaty of Tordesillas

1521
Cortés conquers Mexico

1588
Defeat of the Spanish Armada

1608
French/Huron alliance

1623
Dutch/Iroquois alliance

1680
Pueblo Revolt

ca.1700
French/Choctaw alliance

| 1500 | 1520 | 1540 | 1560 | 1580 | 1600 | 1620 | 1640 | 1660 | 1680 | 1700 | 1720 |

1500
Portugese discover Brazil

1550
Scientific revolution begins in Europe

ca.1640
Dutch take over African slave trade

1700 West Indies become the world's main source for sugar

1618
Thirty Years War begins in Europe

1691 British open trading post at Calcutta

1591
Morocco conquers Songhai Empire

ca.1680 Asante kingdom in Africa

A Continent on the Move, 1400–1725

Europeans and Indians in North America

Using the map on the facing page, examine the continued expansion of Europeans into the North American continent during the early colonial period and the Native Americans with whom they came into contact. In what ways did the specific groups of people that each European colonizing power encountered influence patterns of settlement and the eventual shape of the colonial world in America?

Individual Choices

BARTOLOMÉ DE LAS CASAS

Himself a former conquistador, Bartolomé de Las Casas was ordained as a Catholic priest in 1512 and later became one of the most vocal opponents of Spain's brutal exploitation of Native American people. He petitioned the King in 1540 and won major reforms in the way Spaniards were supposed to treat Indians, but these reforms were never well enforced and soon were challenged in the Spanish court. In 1550, Las Casas debated Juan Ginés de Sepúlveda, a well-respected court scholar, who insisted that Native Americans were not human and deserved no protections under law. Las Casas brought his biblical learning and his New World experience to bear, winning the debate and Catholic support for continued reforms in Spanish colonial policy. *Archivo de Indias, Seville, Spain/Bridgeman Art Library Ltd.*

Bartolomé de Las Casas

In 1550 Spanish church officials ordered a council of learned theologians to assemble in the city of Valladolid to hear a debate over an issue so important that it challenged the entire underpinning of Spain's New World empire. At issue was the question of whether Native American Indians were human beings. Arguing that they were not was the well-respected scholar Juan Ginés de Sepúlveda. Arguing on the Indians' behalf was a former conquistador and **encomandero** named Bartolomé de Las Casas.

Born in 1474, Las Casas was the son of a small merchant in Seville. His family was privileged enough that young Bartolomé had both access and the leisure time to study at Seville's cathedral school. Like many of his contemporaries, Las Casas decided to pursue a military career, going to Granada as a soldier in 1497. Then in 1502 he embarked to the West Indies to seek his fortune in the conquest of the Americas.

Apparently Las Casas was successful as a **conquistador**: within a few years he had earned an imperial land grant with a full complement of Indian laborers. Meeting the demands of both church and king, he taught the Indians Catholicism while he exploited their labor. Eventually, however, the former came to outweigh the latter, and Las Casas's religious devotion grew in proportion. After a decade as a soldier and land baron, he became perhaps the first person to be ordained as a priest in America. His new status, however, did not prevent him from pursuing his career as a conquistador; in 1513 he embarked with the Spanish force that would ravage Cuba.

Perhaps the bloodiness of the Cuba campaign or maybe just a growing Catholic conscience influenced Las Casas's next choice: he began advocating Christian rights for conquered Indians. He devised a plan that would organize Indians into farming communities under church protection, allowing them to become self-sufficient contributors to the Spanish Empire. His plan won support from the archbishop of Toledo and the Spanish Parliament. In 1519 he was given permission to start an experimental community in what is now Venezuela. But Indians in the region understandably were suspicious, and Spanish landlords were hostile; the experiment failed. Despite this setback, Las Casas remained convinced that Indians deserved full Christian recognition. He joined the Dominican order in 1523 and began writing a history of the Spanish Empire in America. As an outgrowth, he sent a series of long letters to the Council of the Indies in Madrid exposing the harsh exploitation of the natives throughout Spanish America. Las Casas then took his case personally to Spain. In 1540 he petitioned for an audience with King Charles V. As he waited for Charles to respond, he wrote a report, *Brevísima relación de la destrucción de las Indias* ("A Brief Report on the Destruction of the Indians") summarizing his experiences and views.

By the time he finally met with Charles V, Las Casas was well prepared to argue for wholesale reform of Spanish Indian policy in America. And Charles was con-

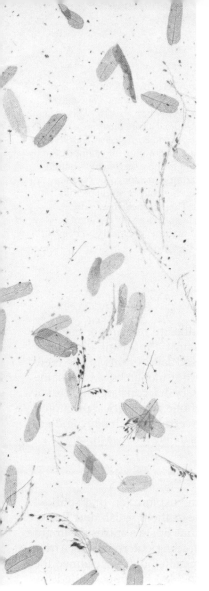

vinced. He signed a series of new laws in 1542—the *Leyes Nuevas*—reforming the *encomienda* system and placing Indian relations under church authority.

To ensure that these reforms would be carried out, Las Casas was appointed bishop of Chiapas and sent back to the New World with forty fellow Dominicans to oversee the enforcement of the laws.

Las Casas served as bishop until 1547, when hostility from landowners in America and growing opposition to humane colonization at home prompted him to return to Spain. The chief spokesman for that growing opposition was Juan Ginés de Sepúlveda, a well-respected scholar whose star was rising in court circles. Las Casas's return prompted demands for a face-off between the two, leading to the Council of Valladolid.

The debate went on for a year, extending through 1550 into 1551. Speaking for Spanish investors and court-based politicians who, like himself, had never been to the Western Hemisphere, Sepúlveda based his argument solely on logic and Scripture. According to his view, it was impossible for Indians in the Americas to be descendants of Adam and Eve; hence they were, in his words, "as apes are to men." As such, Indians did not deserve protection from the church. Las Casas countered with firsthand evidence, drawing on his varied experiences as priest, historian, conquistador, and *encomendero* in an attempt to prove that Indians truly were human beings.

Despite Sepúlveda's great learning and his influence at court, he lost the debate: his writings were denied official recognition by the church, whereas Las Casas's were accepted. But this official victory for Las Casas was actually a failure. Though Sepúlveda's views were rejected by the church, they were embraced by conquistadors as justification for the continuing conquest and enslavement of the native population. In arguing effectively for the recognition of Indians as human beings, however, Las Casas established an undercurrent of official disapproval that served as a braking mechanism against the extreme abuse of the Native population. The resulting three-way tension— between those who would exploit the Indians, those who sought to protect them, and the Indians themselves—would shape the colonial process and would punctuate life in the Americas for generations to come.

INTRODUCTION

The debate in the Council of Valladolid in 1550 focused early attention on a situation that all European colonizers would have to face. Despite Sepúlveda's claims, the population native to the Americas *was* human. Of course, changing natural conditions and the influx of new forces such as epidemic disease had weakened them, but for centuries successful European settlement continued to require Indian cooperation. Court-based scholars like Sepúlveda might fool themselves into thinking that the Indians did not matter, but experienced veterans like Las Casas knew better. Conflicts with the Indians could spell disaster for vulnerable overseas colonies.

Conflicts with other imperial powers could lead to disaster as well. It was virtually inevitable that other nations would join Spain in seeking a share of the wealth promised by the New World. Forced into a

encomandero a land owner/proprietor in the *encomienda* system, Spain's system of bonded labor in which Indians were assigned to Spanish plantation and mine owners in exchange for a tax payment and an agreement to "civilize" and convert them to Catholicism.

conquistadors Spanish soldiers who conquered Indian civilizations in the New World.

The differences between European and Native American styles and conceptions of warfare were often striking. This scene, from the Codex Durán, illustrates a Spanish force besieged by Aztec warriors. Note the contrast in clothing, for example. For most Indian groups, warfare was a highly spiritual affair surrounded by ceremony, often involving colorful and fanciful costumes. The European battle dress, however, bespeaks a very different conception of warfare: practical and deadly. *Archivo fotografico.*

defensive posture and unable to fend off the ambitions of numerous European rivals, Spain had to watch as the Dutch and the French carved out substantial inroads into North America.

The presence of so many, and such varied, Europeans presented both challenges and exceptional opportunities for Indians. In areas where a single European power was asserting dominance, often Indians could do little but bear up under relentless economic and religious pressures. Sometimes the encounter facilitated friendship, intermarriage, and the formation of complex composite societies; sometimes it led to open hostilities and even war. But in areas where two or more European powers were contesting for control, Indians could take advantage of their pivotal position and play one side off against the other in seeking their own ends.

The constant interplay among different European traditions, a novel physical environment, and a dynamic Indian presence forged a series of new societies across the North American continent. Throughout the colonial era and beyond, these hybrid societies continued to influence historical development and to color the life of the people and the nation.

The New Europe and the Atlantic World

▪ Why did European rulers promote exploration and colonization in North America?

▪ How did religious and political rivalries influence the ways in which each European power approached New World colonization?

Expansion into the New World and the subsequent economic and political pressures of colonization ag-

gravated the crisis of authority in Europe. Eager to enlist political allies against Protestant dissenters, popes during this era used land grants in the New World as rewards to faithful monarchs. At the same time, Henry VIII and Elizabeth I, constantly fearful of being outflanked by Catholic adversaries, promoted the development of a powerful English navy and geographical exploration as defensive measures.

Spanish Expansion in America

Spain's entry into Atlantic exploration first sparked a diplomatic crisis between the Spanish and Portuguese. Portugal feared that Spain's intrusion might endanger its hard-won trading enterprises in Africa and the Atlantic islands. Spain, however, claimed the right to explore freely. In 1493 the pope settled the dispute by drawing a line approximately 300 miles west of Portugal's westernmost holdings. Spanish exploration, he declared, was to be confined to areas west of the line (that is, to the New World) and Portuguese activity to areas east of it (to Africa and India). A year later, Spain and Portugal updated the agreement in the **Treaty of Tordesillas,** which moved the line an additional 1,000 miles westward. Most of the Western Hemisphere fell exclusively to Spain, at least in the eyes of Roman Catholics.

Over the next several decades the Spanish monarchs recruited hardened veterans of the Reconquista

> **Treaty of Tordesillas** The agreement, signed by Spain and Portugal in 1494, that moved the line separating Spanish and Portuguese claims to territory in the non-Christian world, giving Spain most of the Western Hemisphere.

Chronology

New World Colonies and Native Americans

1494	Treaty of Tordesillas
1512	Creation of the *encomienda* system
1519–1521	Hernando Cortés invades Mexico
1542	de Las Casas convinces Spain to implement the Leyes Nuevas
1551	Council of Valladolid rules that American Indians are human beings with souls
1558	Elizabeth I becomes queen of England
1565	Spanish found St. Augustine in present-day Florida
1588	English defeat Spanish Armada
1598	Don Juan de Oñate destroys Ácoma pueblo
1608	French-Huron alliance
1609	Henry Hudson sails up Hudson River Spanish found Santa Fe in present-day New Mexico
1623	Beginning of Dutch-Iroquois alliance
1627	Creation of Company of New France
1645	Dutch West India Company reorganized under Peter Stuyvesant
1680	Pueblo Revolt
1683	La Salle expedition down the Mississippi River to the Gulf of Mexico
ca. 1700	Beginning of French-Choctaw alliance

(see page 11) to lead its New World colonization efforts. **Hernando Cortés** was one such figure. In 1519 Cortés landed on the mainland of Mexico with an army of six hundred soldiers. Within three years he and his small force had conquered the mighty Aztec Empire. Although it is tempting to suppose that Cortés's victory was the product of technological superiority, his weapons made less difference in the outcome than did several other factors. More important than guns and swords were the warhorses and attack dogs that Cortés used to instill anxiety. More important than even these, however, was the Spanish philosophy of war, which emphasized hard strikes against both armed and civilian targets. This type of campaign stood in stark contrast to the Aztec art of war, which was much more ceremonial in nature and limited in scope. Cortés was also adept at cultivating diplomatic advantages. An Indian woman whom he called Doña Marina served as his translator and cultural adviser, and with her help the conquistadors gained military support from numerous tribes of Mexican Indians who resented the Aztecs' power and their continuous demands for tribute. And finally, crucially, smallpox and other European germs weakened the Aztecs during the two years in which Cortés maintained strained but peaceful relations with them.

The Spanish Crown supported many other exploratory ventures designed to bring new regions under Spain's control. In 1513 and again in 1521, Juan Ponce de León led expeditions to Florida. Following up on these voyages, Pánfilo de Narváez embarked on a colonizing mission to Florida in 1527. When his party became stranded, local Indians killed most of its members but took a few captives. One of these captives, Álvar Núñez Cabeza de Vaca, escaped with three others in 1534. The four men eventually walked all the way to Mexico, keeping detailed notes of what they saw. Cabeza de Vaca's accounts led the Spanish to send Hernando de Soto to claim the Mississippi River, and he penetrated into the heart of the mound builders' territory in present-day Louisiana and Mississippi. One year later, **Francisco Vásquez de Coronado** left

Hernando Cortés   Spanish soldier and explorer who conquered the Aztecs and claimed Mexico for Spain.

Francisco Vásquez de Coronado   Spanish soldier and explorer who led an expedition northward from Mexico in search of fabled cities of gold, passing through present-day New Mexico, Arizona, Colorado, Oklahoma, and Kansas, giving Spain a claim to most of the American Southwest.

Captured by Indians along the Gulf Coast of Spanish Florida, Álvar Núñez Cabeza de Vaca was made a slave. Most of his companions were afraid to resist or run away, but Cabeza de Vaca chose freedom over safety; in 1534 he led a small party of fellow captives all the way back to Mexico. His experiences and the many stories he collected from his various Indian hosts provided important intelligence for the expanding Spanish Empire. *Courtesy of Frederick Remington Art Museum, Ogdensburg, NY.*

Mexico to look for seven cities that Cabeza de Vaca had heard glittered with gold. Coronado eventually crossed what are now the states of New Mexico, Arizona, Colorado, Oklahoma, and Kansas. These explorations were but a few of the ambitious adventures undertaken by Spanish conquistadors.

Coronado never found Cabeza de Vaca's "cities of gold," but other Spaniards did locate enormous sources of wealth. In Bolivia, Colombia, and north-central Mexico, rich silver deposits rewarded the conquistadors. To the south, in present-day Peru, Francisco Pizarro in 1533 conquered the Inca Empire, an advanced civilization that glittered with gold. Enslaving local Indians for labor, Spanish officials everywhere in the New World quickly moved to rip precious metals out of the ground and from what they characterized as "heathen temples." Between 1545 and 1660, Indian and later African slaves extracted over 7 million pounds

of silver from Spanish-controlled areas, twice the volume of silver held by all of Europe before 1492. In the process, Spain became the richest nation in Europe, perhaps in the world.

Dreams of an English Eden

Given the stormy political and religious climate that prevailed during the sixteenth century, it is not surprising that Spain's early successes in the New World stirred up conflict with the other emerging states in Europe. To England, France, and other European countries, the massive flow of wealth made Spanish power a growing threat that had to be checked. The continuing religious controversies that accompanied the Reformation (see page 27) worsened the situation. Economic, religious, and political warfare was the rule throughout the century. One of the most celebrated of these early conflicts involved Spain and England.

Tension between Spain and England had been running high ever since Henry VIII had divorced his Spanish wife, Catherine of Aragon. That he quit the Catholic Church to do so and began permitting Protestant reforms in England added to the affront. Firmly wedded to the Catholic Church politically and religiously, Spain was aggressive in denouncing England. For his part, Henry was concerned primarily with domestic issues and steered away from direct confrontations with Spain or any of the other outraged Catholic countries.

The main exception to Henry's isolationism was an effort to bring Ireland and other outlying parts of his realm more firmly under his control. In 1541 Henry engineered a parliamentary change in title from "Lord of Ireland" to "King of Ireland" and used his new status to institute both religious and political reforms. He confiscated lands controlled by Irish Catholic monasteries and the estates of local lords who opposed him, channeling the money into building a stronger administrative structure. During the years to come, both Henry's heirs and the **Stuart kings** who would follow continued a systematic policy of colonization in Ireland. In the process, British authorities instituted a new set of colonial offices and encouraged generations of military adventurers, both of which would shape and advance later ventures in North America.

> **Stuart kings** The dynasty of English kings who claimed the throne after the death of Elizabeth I, who left no heirs.

Queen Elizabeth I used her charm and intelligence to turn England into a major world power and restored order to a kingdom shaken by religious and political turmoil following the death of her father, Henry VIII. This pendant from the 1570s not only captures the queen's elegance and austere grace, but was also a powerful political statement. Note the intertwining of white and red roses—emblems of the Houses of York and Lancaster, respectively—symbolizing the unified monarchy forged by her grandfather. On the reverse is an image of a phoenix rising from the flames of its nest, symbolizing the renewal of the true monarchy. Already in her 40s by the time the "Phoenix Jewel" was crafted, it may have been the last portrait to capture Elizabeth's true age; future images of the queen always depict her as being much younger than she really was. While this may have been the product of vanity, it seems more likely that the queen wanted to diminish concerns among her subjects that aging might undermine her resolve and bring back an era of disorder. © *The British Museum.*

During the reign of Henry's younger daughter, Elizabeth, the continuing flow of New World wealth into Spain and that nation's anti-Protestant aggression led to an upturn in hostile activity. When Philip II of Spain, Elizabeth's brother-in-law and most vehement critic, sent an army of twenty thousand soldiers to root out Protestantism in **the Netherlands,** only a few miles across the English Channel from Elizabeth's kingdom, the English queen began providing covert aid to the Protestants rebels. Elizabeth also struck at Philip's most valuable and vulnerable possession: his New World empire. In 1577 Elizabeth secretly authorized English **privateer** and explorer Francis Drake to attack Spanish ships in the area reserved for Spain under the Treaty of Tordesillas. Drake carried out his task with enthusiasm, raiding

Spanish ships and seizing tons of gold and silver during a three-year cruise around the world.

Elizabeth was open to virtually any venture that might vex her troublesome brother-in-law. New World colonizing efforts promised to do that and had the potential for enriching the kingdom as well. Like the rest of Europe, sixteenth-century England was experiencing a population boom that put great stress on traditional economic institutions. Although Elizabeth's father had confiscated and redistributed large tracts of church-owned land during his reign, farmland was becoming extremely scarce, and members of both the traditional nobility and the **gentry**—a class that was becoming increasingly important because of its investments in manufacturing and trading ventures—wanted more space for expansion. A relatively small island, England could acquire more territory only by conquest or by carving it out of the New World.

Thus in 1578 Elizabeth granted her friend and political supporter Sir Humphrey Gilbert permission to found a colony in America. Gilbert claimed that John Cabot's voyages gave England a legitimate right to settle America's eastern shore, and in 1583 he set out with two hundred colonists. When the entire party was lost at sea, Gilbert's half-brother, **Sir Walter Raleigh,** petitioned the queen to take over the colonizing effort. She gladly agreed, commanding Raleigh to locate on the northern frontier of Spanish Florida, where an English settlement was sure to irritate Philip. Raleigh chose an island off the coast of present-day North Carolina. He advertised **Roanoke Island** as an "American Eden," where "the earth bringeth forth all things in abundance, as in the first Creation, without toile or labour." To honor his benefactor, he decided to call this paradise Virginia, tribute to the unwed, and thus officially virgin, queen.

---

the Netherlands/Holland/Dutch Often used interchangeably, the first two terms refer to the low-lying area in western Europe north of France and Belgium and across the English Channel from Great Britain; the Dutch are the inhabitants of the Netherlands.

privateer A ship captain who owned his own boat, hired his own crew, and was authorized by his government to attack and capture enemy ships.

gentry The class of English landowners ranking just below the nobility.

Sir Walter Raleigh English courtier, soldier, and adventurer who attempted to establish the Virginia Colony.

Roanoke Island Island off North Carolina that Raleigh sought to colonize beginning in 1585.

In 1585 Elizabeth further angered the Spanish king by openly sending an army of six thousand troops across the Channel to aid Dutch rebels. In the meantime, Philip was supporting various Catholic plots within England to subvert Elizabeth's authority and bring down the Protestant state. As tensions increased, so did Drake's piracy. In 1586 Drake intensified his campaign, not only raiding Spanish ships at sea but attacking settlements in the Caribbean. Thus by 1586, British troops were fighting the Spanish alongside Dutch rebels in Holland; Spanish spies were encouraging rebellion in England, Scotland, and Ireland; and British ships were raiding Spanish settlements in the New World. War loomed on the horizon.

The Decline of Spanish Power

Despite dreams of a New World Eden, the realities of discovery and colonization were beginning to have a severe, and in many ways negative, impact on life in Europe. The enormous inflow of wealth from the New World brought Spain power that no European country since the Roman Empire had enjoyed, but such rapid enrichment was a mixed blessing. Starting in Spain and radiating outward, prices began to climb as the growth of the money supply outpaced the growth of European economies. Too much money was chasing too few goods. Between 1550 and 1600, prices doubled in much of Europe, and **inflation** continued to soar for another half-century.

In addition, the social impact of the new wealth was forcing European monarchs to expand geographically and crack down domestically. As prices rose, the traditional landholding classes earned enormous profits from the sale of food and other necessities. Other groups fared less well. Artisans, laborers, and landless peasants—by far the largest class of people in Europe—found the value of their labor constantly shrinking. Throughout Europe, social unrest increased as formerly productive and respected citizens were reduced to poverty and begging. Overseas expansion seemed an inviting solution to the problem of an impoverished population. It was a safety valve that relieved a potentially dangerous source of domestic pressure while opening opportunities for enhancing national wealth through the development of colonies.

Sitting at the center of the new economy, Philip's Spain had the most to lose from rapid inflation and popular unrest. It also had the most to lose from New World expansion by any other European nation. Each New World claim asserted by England, France, or some other country represented the loss of a piece of treasure that Spain claimed as its own. Philip finally chose to confront building tensions by taking a desperate gamble: he would destroy England. This ploy, he thought, would effectively remove the Protestant threat, rid him of Elizabeth's ongoing harassment, and demonstrate to the rest of Europe that Spain intended to exercise absolute authority over the Atlantic world. In the spring of 1585, when tensions were at their peak, Philip began massing what was to be the largest marine force Europe had ever witnessed.

Philip wanted to attack England in the spring or summer of 1587. But Francis Drake frustrated his plans by staging a surprise attack on the Spanish port of Cádiz, disabling part of Philip's navy. The Spanish king remained resolute, however, and by the spring of 1588 he succeeded in launching an **armada** of 132 warships carrying more than three thousand cannon and an invasion force of thirty thousand men. Arriving off the shores of England in July, the so-called Invincible Armada ran up against small, maneuverable British defense ships commanded by Elizabeth's skilled pirate captains. Drake and his fleet harassed the Spanish ships, preventing them from launching a successful attack. Then a storm blowing down from the North Sea scattered the Spanish fleet, ruining Philip's expected conquest of England. Though Spanish power remained great for some time to come, the Armada disaster effectively ended Spain's near monopoly over New World colonization.

European Empires in America

■ What similarities and differences characterized Spanish, French, and Dutch patterns of empire building in North America?

■ What role did natural environments play in shaping the colonial enterprises engineered by the Spanish, the French, and the Dutch?

■ How did the colonists' experiences challenge and help to reshape imperial policies?

In the seventeenth and eighteenth centuries, Spain, France, England, and a number of lesser European nations vied for control of the Americas and for domination of the transatlantic trade. For reasons that are explained in Chapter 3, England was somewhat de-

> **inflation**   Rising prices that occur when the supply of currency or credit grows faster than the available supply of goods and services.
> **armada**   A fleet of warships.

layed in its colonizing efforts, and by the time it became deeply involved in New World ventures, Spain, France, and Holland had already made major progress toward establishing empires in America. These European settlements not only affected England's colonization process profoundly, but through their interactions among themselves and with the Native Americans, they also created unique societies in North America whose presence influenced the entire course of the continent's history.

The Troubled Spanish Colonial Empire

Although the destruction of the Armada in 1588 struck a terrible blow at Spain's military power and its New World monopoly, the Spanish Empire continued to grow. By the end of the seventeenth century, it stretched from New Mexico southward through Central America and much of South America into the Caribbean islands and northward again into Florida. Governing such a vast empire was difficult, and periodic efforts to reform the system usually failed. Two agencies in Spain, the House of Trade and the Council of the Indies, set Spanish colonial policy. In the colonies, Crown-appointed viceroys wielded military and political power in each of the four divisions of the empire. The Spanish colonies set up local governments as well; each town had a *cabildo secular,* a municipal council, as well as judges and other minor officials. The colonial administrators were appointed rather than elected, and most were envoys from Spain rather than native-born individuals.

Over the centuries, as the layers of bureaucracy developed, corruption and inefficiency developed as well. The Spanish government made efforts to regulate colonial affairs, sending *visitadores* to inspect local government operations and creating new watchdog agencies. Despite these safeguards, colonial officials ignored their written instructions and failed to enforce laws.

One major source of corruption and unrest stemmed from a persistent New World problem: the shortage of labor. The Spanish had adapted traditional institutions to address the demand for workers in mines and on plantations. In Spain, work was directed by **feudal** landlords, *encomenderos,* whose military service to the king entitled them to harness the labor of Spanish peasants. In New Spain, Indians took the place of the peasants in what was called the *encomienda* system. Under a law passed in 1512, administrators gave Indian workers to *encomenderos* and

required them to labor for the landlords for nine months each year. The *encomendero* paid a tax to the Crown for each Indian he received and agreed to teach his workers the Catholic faith, the Spanish language and culture, and a "civilized" vocation.

Despite some commitment to uplifting local Indians, the system in reality was brutally exploitative. As Bartolomé de Las Casas reported both to the Council of the Indies and to the king himself, landlords frequently overworked their Indian **serfs** and failed in their "civilizing" responsibilities. As the result of Las Casas's appeal, the Leyes Nuevas turned Indian relations in New Spain over to the church, and priests were assigned to enforce the laws. Among the new regulations was a stipulation that a priest accompany all expeditions to serve as witnesses that Indians were treated lawfully. For their part, the conquistadors were required to explain to Indians that they were subject to the Spanish king and to the Catholic Church, offering to absorb them peacefully. As Las Casas discovered, however, colonists often ignored even these slim protections. Some simply forged a priest's signature, anticipating that by the time the document reached administrators in faraway Madrid, no one would know the difference. Others disregarded the law altogether.

As such behavior demonstrates, Spanish colonists were seldom entirely law-abiding citizens, and a degree of tension always existed between New Spain and Old. Bureaucratic and church interference in the labor system was one source of tension. Taxes were another. Spanish colonists were taxed to support the huge and largely corrupt, unrepresentative, and self-serving imperial bureaucracy. But for many decades the wealth produced within this empire overshadowed all governing problems. The gold, silver, and copper mined by Indian and later African slaves so dazzled Spanish officials that imperial authorities took few serious steps toward practical reform until the end of the seventeenth century.

---

cabildo secular   Secular municipal council that provided local government in Spain's New World empire.

feudal   Relating to a system in which landowners held broad powers over peasants or tenant farmers, providing protection in exchange for loyalty and labor.

serfs   Peasants who were bound to a particular estate but, unlike slaves, were not the personal property of the estate owner and received traditional feudal protections.

The French Presence in America

Although France made a number of efforts to compete with Spain's New World projects during the sixteenth century, Spanish power was sufficient to prevent any major successes. For example, when a force of French Protestants established a colony in Florida in 1564, Spanish authorities sent an army to root them out. This led to increased Spanish vigilance, prompting Pedro Menéndez de Aviles to build the city of **Saint Augustine** the following year.

Unable to penetrate Spain's defenses in the south, the French concentrated their efforts farther north. A powerful incentive came from a fashion trend that seized Europe late in the sixteenth century: the broad-brimmed beaver felt hat. The felt hat's immense popularity led to the virtual extinction of fur-bearing animals in the Eastern Hemisphere by the beginning of the seventeenth century. However, early French explorers and fishermen along America's North Atlantic shore indicated that a near endless supply was ripe for the trapping in the New World (see page 21). Early in the seventeenth century, **Samuel de Champlain,** the "father of **New France,**" established trading posts in Nova Scotia and elsewhere, founded the city of Quebec, and in 1608 formed an enduring alliance with the Huron Indians. But despite these efforts and the potential profitability of the fur trade, French colonial authorities at first took little interest in overseas enterprises.

In 1627 French minister Cardinal Richelieu chartered the **Company of New France,** awarding a group of the king's favorites a charter to establish plantations in New France, but the venture failed to attract much interest. French Protestants, who might have emigrated to avoid religious persecution, were forbidden to move to the colony, and few French Catholics wanted to migrate to America. Thus the colonizing effort did not attract enough rent-paying tenants to make the envisioned estates profitable. Equally important was the fact that the few French peasants and small farmers who did venture to the New World found life in the woods and the company of Indians preferable to life as a tenant farmer. So-called *coureurs de bois,* or "runners of the woods," married Indian women and lived among the tribes, returning to the French settlements only when they had enough furs to sell to make the trip worthwhile.

Frustrated by the lack of profits, Richelieu reorganized the Company of New France in 1633, dispatching Champlain, now bearing the title Lieutenant of New France, with three ships of supplies, workmen, and soldiers who, it was hoped, would breathe new

IT MATTERS

The Felt Hat Fad

Changes in fashion come and go and we seldom give much thought to them as being historically significant. But the sudden popularity of felt hats in the late sixteenth century had a profound impact on not just America's history, but the history of the entire world. The flood of new wealth flowing into Europe from America permitted people of means—not just the nobility, but the landed gentry and even urban craftsmen and small business owners—to keep up with the latest fashion trends. Being in style became increasingly important to status-conscious merchants, manufacturers, and other beneficiaries of the New World boom. Demand for the beaver fur to make the felt became so steep that virtually the entire population of Old World beavers was wiped out and entire industries arose in France, the Netherlands, Great Britain, and Russia to import this "brown gold" from the Americas. Fur drew Europeans up virtually every waterway in North America, leading to the founding of many of the most prominent cities in America today. It is safe to say that without this seemingly silly fashion trend that little in the United States would be as we know it today.

life into the colony. In its new form, the company ignored the government's demands that it establish agricultural settlements and focused instead on the

Saint Augustine   First colonial city in the present-day United States; located in Florida and founded by Pedro Menéndez de Aviles for Spain in 1565.

Samuel de Champlain   French explorer who traced the St. Lawrence River inland to the Great Lakes, founded the city of Quebec, and formed the French alliance with the Huron Indians.

New France   The colony established by France in what is now Canada and the Great Lakes region of the United States.

Company of New France   Company established by Cardinal Richelieu to bring order to the running of France's North American enterprises.

coureurs de bois   Literally, "runners of the woods"; independent French fur traders who lived among the Indians and sold furs to the French.

Although this scene in Quebec was not painted until 1820, back streets in the old part of the city still looked very much as they had during the heyday of the French *coureurs de bois*. So did the people. Shops, like the one on the left, sold provisions and tools—often on credit—to the outward-bound runners of the woods, binding them to bring their next load of furs back to satisfy their debt. Thus, while the French Crown did little to encourage the fur business, it formed the core for Canada's woodland and urban economies. *Royal Ontario Museum © COM.*

continued technically to own the land and retained the power to appoint the governor and court officials in the colony.

Local authorities managed most of the colony's affairs until 1663, when the Crown began to intervene seriously in Canada. Having taken the functions of state into his own hands, young Louis XIV gave his finance minister, Jean-Baptiste Colbert, considerable authority over all monetary matters, including colonial enterprises. Seeking to make New France more efficient and to increase its contribution to the empire at large, Colbert founded the **Company of the West,** modeled on the highly successful Dutch West India Company. He also revoked the land titles held by the Company of New France, putting them directly into the king's hands, and overturned the political power of the Community of Habitants, making New France a royal colony.

Although the king reaped enormous profits from the fur trade, his colonial interests ranged beyond this single source of income. In 1673 a French expedition led by Louis Joliet and Jacques Marquette set out on a systematic exploration of New France's many waterways in search of new resources. They discovered a promising water route, but failed to follow it up. It fell to **Robert Cavelier, Sieur de La Salle,** to prove the strategic and economic value in Joliet and Marquette's discovery. In 1683 he and a party of French *coureurs de bois* and Indians retraced the earlier expedition and then followed the Mississippi River all the way to the Gulf of Mexico. La Salle immediately claimed the new territory for Louis XIV of France, naming it **Louisiana** in his honor. In 1698 the king sent settlers to the lower Mississippi Valley under the leadership of Pierre LeMoyne d'Iberville,

fur trade. Setting up posts in Quebec, Montreal, and a few more remote locations, the company became the primary outfitter of and buyer from the *coureurs de bois* and amassed huge profits by reselling the furs in Europe. After Richelieu's death in 1642, queen mother and French regent Anne of Austria acted on complaints filed by both fur trade investors and Jesuit missionaries that the Company of New France was not governing effectively. She chose to empower a new company, the **Community of Habitants of New France,** with a monopoly on the fur trade and the privilege of granting land claims. Then, in 1647, Anne approved the formation of a council that consisted of the governor, the local director of the Jesuits, the colony's military commandant, and three elected officials. Meanwhile, the Company of New France

Community of Habitants of New France Company chartered by Anne of Austria to make operations in New France more efficient and profitable; it gave significant political power to local officials in Canada.

Company of the West Company chartered by Colbert after New France became a royal colony; modeled on the Dutch West India Company, it was designed to maximize profits to the Crown.

Robert Cavelier, Sieur de La Salle French explorer who followed the Mississippi River from its origin in present-day Illinois to the Gulf of Mexico in 1683, giving France a claim to the entire river way and adjoining territory.

Louisiana French colony south of New France; it included the entire area drained by the Mississippi River and all its tributary rivers.

who in 1699 raised Louisiana's first French fort, near present-day Biloxi, Mississippi. In 1718 French authorities built the city of New Orleans to serve as the capital of the new territory.

The acquisition of Louisiana was a major accomplishment for La Salle and for France. The newly discovered river way gave the French a rich, untapped source of furs as well as an alternative shipping route, allowing them to avoid the cold, stormy North Atlantic. Also, if an agricultural venture could be started in the new territory, it might serve as an inexpensive source of supplies to support both the fur trade in Canada and France's sugar plantations in the Caribbean. But perhaps of greatest importance was Louisiana's strategic location between Spain's claims in the Southwest and the Dutch and other colonies along the eastern seaboard. Controlling this piece of real estate gave Louis considerable leverage in international diplomacy.

The Dutch Enterprise

Another source of competition to Spain's New World monopoly came from one of its former colonies: the Netherlands. The Armada disaster in 1588 had tipped the scales in favor of Dutch Protestant rebels, and the newly independent nation quickly developed a thriving commercial economy. Holland's first serious claim to American territory came in 1609, when Dutch sea captain **Henry Hudson** explored the East Coast in search of the elusive Northwest Passage (see page 21). He sailed up a large river that he hoped would lead him west to the Pacific. After realizing that he had not found the hoped-for route to the Far East, he returned to Holland and reported to his sponsor, the Dutch East India Company, that the territory surrounding this river—which he named after himself—was "pleasant with Grasse & Flowers and Goodly Trees" and that the Indians were friendly. Surely, he added, profits could be made there. Hudson's employers did not share his enthusiasm. Although the Dutch created one trading post on the Hudson River at Albany and another on Manhattan Island in 1614, the Dutch were not yet in a position to take maximum advantage of this claim.

With significant government encouragement, investors formed the **Dutch West India Company** in 1621 in order to marshal resources to expand their growing enterprises in the New World. The new company financed Dutch privateers who successfully raided Spanish and Portuguese treasure ships and, in 1634, overcame weak Spanish and Portuguese resistance to conquer a number of islands in the Caribbean.

The Dutch also pushed the Portuguese aside to take control of the transatlantic slave trade. Holland's next goal was to establish an empire on the North American mainland.

Seeking to compete with France's early efforts in the fur trade, Dutch West India Company official Peter Minuit negotiated a lease for the entire island of Manhattan from the Manhates Indians in 1626. This acquisition gave the Dutch control over the mouth of the river that Hudson had discovered and the land of "Grasses & Flowers" that it drained. Minuit's main motive, however, was to safeguard Dutch claims against those of rival European traders. For three more years, the company did nothing to attract settlers, and by 1629 only three hundred colonists had spread themselves in a thin ribbon from the capital, New Amsterdam, on Manhattan Island, upriver to Albany.

In that year, the Dutch West India Company drew up a comprehensive business plan to maximize profits and minimize dependence on local Indians for food and other support. To encourage the agricultural development necessary to support the fur industry, the company offered huge estates called **patroonships** to any company stockholder willing and able to bring fifty colonists to **New Netherland** at his own expense. In exchange, the patroons would enjoy near-feudal powers over their tenants. But few prosperous Dutchmen were interested in becoming New World barons. Rensselaerswyck, the estate of Kilian van Rensselaer, was the only patroonship to develop in accordance with the company's plan. The colony's development came to rely instead on many poorer migrants who were drawn by unofficial promises of land ownership and economic betterment.

Settlers from just about anywhere were welcome in New Netherland—the colony attracted an extremely

---

Henry Hudson Dutch ship captain and explorer who sailed up the Hudson River in 1609, giving the Netherlands a claim to the area now occupied by New York.

Dutch West India Company Dutch investment company formed in 1621 to develop colonies for the Netherlands in North America.

patroonship A huge grant of land given to any Dutch West India Company stockholder who, at his own expense, brought fifty colonists to New Netherland; the colonists became the tenants of the estate owner, or patroon.

New Netherland The colony founded by the Dutch West India Company in present-day New York; its capital was New Amsterdam on Manhattan Island.

Its location at the mouth of the Hudson River made the Dutch settlement of New Amsterdam a particularly important colonial trading center. Furs flowed down the river from Fort Orange (near modern Albany, New York), while guns, tools, and other trade goods traveled the other way. This etching (detail), based on a watercolor illustration painted in around 1553, captures the city's colorful vibrancy after Peter Stuyvesant and the Dutch burghers merged their power to bring order and prosperity. The weighing beam in the foreground illustrates both the prosperity and quest for order: it was used not only to weigh the loads of goods flowing through the town, but was also used as a whipping post and gallows when necessary. *Museum of the City of New York. Gift of Dr. N. Sulzberger.*

diverse population, including German and French Protestants, free and enslaved Africans, Catholics, Jews, and Muslims. In 1638 the Dutch even encouraged Swedish fur traders to create their own colony, New Sweden, within its boundaries. Local government in such a disparate community was a persistent problem. Although the Dutch West India Company was officially in charge, the actual conduct of day-to-day affairs was run by an elite group of **burghers,** men in New Amsterdam whose economic and political successes gave them significant influence. In an effort to reassert its power, the company reorganized its New World operations in 1645, appointing Peter Stuyvesant to manage all of its operations in the Western Hemisphere. Stuyvesant immediately came into conflict with the local burghers in New Amsterdam, and in 1647 he was forced to create a compromise government that gave the burghers an official

voice through a council of nine appointed representatives. Six years later, Stuyvesant and the council created a municipal government modeled on those back home in Holland. Despite this nod to democratic government, Stuyvesant ran company affairs with an iron hand, significantly tightening operations throughout the colony. In 1655 he even invaded and rooted out the Swedes, eliminating that source of dissension and competition.

burghers Town dwellers who were free from feudal obligations and were responsible for civic government during the medieval period in Europe; in New Amsterdam these were men who were not Dutch West India Company officials, but who governed civic affairs through their political influence.

MAP 2.1 Indian Economies in North America   Indian economic activities helped to shape patterns of European settlement and investment in the New World. Regions that were primarily agricultural, like the Atlantic shoreline, lent themselves to European farming activities. Farther north and west, however, where hunting played a more prominent role in native life, the fur trade was a more attractive investment for European settlers.

Indians and the European Challenge

- How did changes in the natural environment affect Indian societies during the early colonial period?

- How did the arrival of Europeans influence continuing adaptations by Native American groups?

Native Americans did not sit idly by while the European powers carved out empires in North America. Some joined the newcomers, serving as advisers and companions. Others sought to use the Europeans as allies to accomplish their own economic, diplomatic, or military goals (see Map 2.1). Still others, overwhelmed by the onset of European diseases and shifting population pressures, withdrew into the interior. The changes in native America created both obstacles and opportunities, giving shape to the patterns of expansion and conflict that characterized the colonial world.

The Indian Frontier in New Spain

Indian assistance had been critical in Spain's successful campaigns against the Aztecs and Incas. In Mexico, for example, groups who had been forced to pay tribute to the Aztec Empire gladly allied themselves with the Spanish in what the natives perceived as an opportunity to win their independence. Their hopes were soon dashed when the Spanish simply replaced the Aztecs as the new lords of a tributary empire.

Once their New World empire was firmly rooted, Spanish expansion met little native resistance until 1598, when a particularly brutal conquistador named **Don Juan de Oñate** led a large expedition to the Rio Grande region of New Mexico. When some Pueblos resisted Oñate's efforts to impose Spanish culture and religion, the conquistador chose to make an example of **Ácoma pueblo.** It took Oñate's troops three days to subdue the settlement, but Spanish steel finally overcame Ácoma clubs and stone knives. When the battle was over, Oñate ordered eight hundred Indians executed and made slaves of the nearly seven hundred survivors, mostly women and children. In addition, each male survivor over the age of 25 had one foot chopped off to prevent his escape from slavery. Two **Hopi Indians** who had been visiting Ácoma at the time of the battle had their right hands cut off and then were sent home as examples of the price of resistance.

This blatant cruelty disgusted even the most cynical authorities in New Spain, and both the church and state stepped in. Oñate was removed, and the surviving Indians were placed under joint military and religious protection. Some members of Oñate's company remained, however, founding the town of **Santa Fe** in 1609. Others scattered to set up ranches throughout the region.

Thanks in part to Las Casas's efforts, the church played a key role in developing the colonies, especially in the stark regions along Mexico's northern frontier where there were no gold mines or profitable plantations. The Franciscan order led church efforts in New Mexico and put a peculiar stamp on the pattern of Indian relations. A highly **ascetic** and disciplined order, the Franciscans were particularly offended by Pueblo religion and the Pueblo lifestyle. Indian ceremonies that involved various types of traditional religious objects smacked of idolatry to the Franciscans. Seeking to root out what they viewed as evil, the priests embarked on a wholesale effort to destroy every vestige of the Indians' religion. One priest, Fray

Thinking of themselves as agents of God and invincible, the Spanish arrogantly sought to impose their cultural and religious views on the peaceful Pueblo people of New Mexico during the seventeenth century. Much to their surprise, the Pueblos unified under a traditional leader named Popé and drove the Europeans entirely out of the region. No one knows what Popé looked like, but this sculpture by Jemez Pueblo artist Cliff Fragua is a realistic depiction of a common Pueblo man from the period. In the words of the artist, "Popé was not a trained fighter, but a man who tended gardens, hunted, and participated in the Kiva ceremonies." "My rendition of Popé depicts a simple man, one who is concerned for survival of his family, his culture, and the history and beliefs of the Pueblo People," Fragua continues. "His actions against the Spaniards were not acts of defiance, but rather, acts of survival." © *Cliff Fragua & the New Mexico Statuary Hall Commission. (This statue was selected for the National Statuary Hall in the U.S. Capitol to represent the state of New Mexico.)*

Don Juan de Oñate   Spaniard who conquered New Mexico and claimed it for Spain in the 1590s.

Ácoma pueblo   Pueblo Indian community that resisted Spanish authority in 1598 and was subdued by the Spanish.

Hopi Indians   Indians who were related to the Comanches and Shoshones and took up residence among the Pueblo Indians as agricultural town-dwellers; their name means "peaceful ones."

Santa Fe   Spanish colonial town established in 1609; eventually the capital of the province of New Mexico.

ascetic   Practicing severe abstinence or self-denial, generally in pursuit of spiritual awareness.

Before the arrival of European explorers like Hernando de Soto in the early 1540s, Indians in the American Southeast had lived in huge cities characterized by monumental architecture and a stratified class system with priest kings at the top, skilled craftsmen and traders in the middle, and common farmers and laborers at the bottom. This painting by archaeological reconstruction artist Tom Hall captures the bustling marketplace at Moundville, a large pre-Columbian city in present-day Alabama. Moundville appears to have begun to decline in around 1350—perhaps a consequence of climate change—and collapsed altogether following the introduction of European diseases. Scholars are unsure about what became of Moundville's survivors, but it is likely that they formed smaller villages that were easier to support in the new environment. All of the Southeastern Indian societies—the Cherokees, Choctaws, Creeks, Natchez, and many others—went through a similar transition during this period. *Tom Hall/National Geographic Society Image Collection.*

life, imposing foreign ideas about sexual relations and family structure, punishing most of the Pueblos' traditional practices as sinful.

After nearly a century of enduring these assaults on their most fundamental values, the Pueblos struck back. In 1680 a traditional leader named Popé led an uprising that united virtually all of the Indians in New Mexico against Spanish rule. The **Pueblo Revolt** left four hundred Spaniards dead as the rebels captured Santa Fe and drove the invaders from their land. It took almost a decade for the Spanish to regroup sufficiently to reinvade New Mexico. In 1689 troops moved back into the region and over the next several years waged a brutal war to recapture the territory. The fighting continued off and on until the end of the century, but Spanish settlers began returning to New Mexico after the recapture of Santa Fe in 1693.

Elsewhere along the northern frontier of New Spain, the unsettled nature of Indian life and the arid and uninviting character of the land made settlement unappealing to the Spaniards. Efforts at mining, raising livestock, and missionizing in Arizona and Texas were largely unsuccessful until after 1700.

The Indian World in the Southeast

Members of Spanish-exploring expeditions under would-be conquistadors such as Ponce de León and de Soto were the first Europeans to contact the mound builder societies and other Indian groups in the Southeast. Although their residential and ceremonial centers often impressed the Spaniards, these Mississippian agricultural groups had no gold and could not easily be enslaved. The conquistadors moved on without attempting to force Spanish rule or the Catholic religion on them.

Given sufficient incentive, however, the Spanish were quick to strike at Indian independence and culture. In Florida, for example, the need to protect Spanish ships from French settlers led Spain to establish garrisons such as Saint Augustine. With this and other similar military posts in place, Jesuit and Franciscan missionaries ranged outward to bring Catholicism to Indians in the region. By 1600 they had

Alonso de Benavides, bragged in the 1620s that in one day he confiscated "more than a thousand idols of wood," which he then burned. The priests also interfered in the most intimate social aspects of Pueblo

Pueblo Revolt Indian rebellion against Spanish authority in 1680 led by Popé; succeeded in driving the Spanish out of New Mexico for nearly a decade.

established missions from the gulf coast of Florida all the way to Georgia.

Although the Spanish presence in the region was small, its impact was enormous. The Spanish introduced European diseases into the densely populated towns in the Mississippi River region. Epidemics wiped out entire Native American civilizations and forced survivors to abandon their towns and entirely modify their ways of life. Certain groups, among them the Cherokees and Creeks, formed village-based economies that combined agriculture, hunting, and gathering. As had happened earlier in the Northeast among the Iroquois and others, this change in economy led to increasing intergroup warfare. And like the Iroquois, many southeastern groups created formal confederacies as a way of coping. One example is the **Creek Confederacy,** a union of many groups who had survived the Spanish epidemics. Internally, members created an economic and social system in which each population contributed to the welfare of all and differences were settled through athletic competition— a ballgame not unlike modern lacrosse—rather than warfare. And when new Europeans arrived in the seventeenth and eighteenth centuries, the Creeks and other confederacies found it beneficial to welcome them as trading partners and allies, balancing the competing demands of the Spanish and French, and later the English. To some degree, they took advantage of the European rivalries to advance their own interests against those of neighboring confederacies.

The Indian World in the Northeast

By the time Europeans had begun serious exploration and settlement of the Northeast, the economic and cultural changes among Eastern Woodlands Indians that had begun between 1350 and 1450 had resulted in the creation of two massive—and opposing—alliance systems. On one side were the Hurons, Algonquins, Abenakis, Micmacs, Ottawas, and several smaller tribes. On the other was the Iroquois League.

The costs and benefits of sustained European contact first fell to the Hurons and their allies. The Abenakis, Micmacs, and others who lived along the northern shore of the Atlantic were the first groups drawn into trade with the French, and it was among them that the *coureurs de bois* settled and intermarried. These family ties became firm economic bonds when formal French exploration brought these groups into more direct contact with the European trading world. Seeking advantage against the Iroquois, the

Hurons and their neighbors created a great wheel of alliance with the fur trade at its hub and France as its axle.

The strong partnership between these Indians and the French posed a serious threat to the Iroquois. Having moved south out of the territory now firmly held by the Hurons when the climate first turned colder, the Iroquois Confederacy now wished to wield its combined power to reclaim the area. The presence of the French and the fur trade only made this objective all the more desirable. If they could push the Hurons and their allies out and take control of the St. Lawrence River, the French would then have to trade exclusively with the Iroquois. But the French presence also complicated the situation in that the Hurons had a ready source for guns, iron arrowheads, and other tools that gave them a military edge.

The arrival of the Dutch in the Albany area, however, offered the Iroquois an attractive diplomatic alternative. In 1623 the Dutch West India Company invited representatives from the Iroquois League to a meeting at **Fort Orange,** offering them friendship and trade. The Iroquois responded enthusiastically, but in a way that the Dutch had not anticipated. Instead of entering peacefully into the trade, the Iroquois imposed their authority over all of the Indian groups already trading with the Dutch. They began a bloody war with the **Mohicans,** who had been the Dutch traders' main source for furs in the Hudson Valley. As they had planned to do to the Hurons in the St. Lawrence Valley, by 1627 the Iroquois had driven the Mohicans out of the Hudson Valley and had taken control over the flow of furs.

Trade was so vigorous that the Iroquois soon wiped out fur supplies in their own territory and began a serious push to acquire new sources. Beginning in the late 1630s, the Iroquois Confederacy entered into a long-term aggressive war against the Hurons and their allies in New France; against the Munsees, Delawares, and other groups in the Susquehanna and Delaware River valleys to the south; and even against

---

Creek Confederacy Alliance of Indians living in the Southeast; formed after the lethal spread of European diseases to permit a cooperative economic and military system among survivors.

Fort Orange Dutch trading post established near present-day Albany, New York, in 1614.

Mohicans Algonquin-speaking Indians who lived along the Hudson River, were dispossessed in a war with the Iroquois confederacy, and eventually were all but exterminated.

Alfred Jacob Miller based this 1837 painting of eighteenth-century mounted buffalo hunters on interviews with Shoshone Indians he met on a trip through the American West. It illustrates clearly the enormous impact the arrival of horses had on Plains Indian life. Note how few mounted men it took to drive vast numbers of animals over a cliff to their deaths. At the bottom of the cliff, women would butcher the dead animals and the meat, bones, and hides would provide food, clothing, tools, tents, and trade goods sufficient to support an entire band of Indians for some time. The arrival of the horse on the Great Plains in the late 1600s marked the beginning of 150 years of unprecedented wealth and power for the Indians in the region. *Alfred Jacob Miller, Walters Art Gallery, Baltimore.*

the Iroquois-speaking Eries to the west. Citing Hienwatha's legacy, the Iroquois justified their aggression by claiming that their conquests were simply bringing more people into the shelter of the Great Tree of Peace, expanding the confederacy to include all the northeastern Indians.

The New Indian World of the Plains

Though largely unexplored and untouched by Europeans, the vast area of the Great Plains also underwent profound transformation during the period of initial contacts. Climate change, the pressure of shifting populations, and the introduction of novel European goods through lines of kinship and trade created an altogether new culture and economy among the Indians in this region.

Before about 1400, Indians living on the plains rarely strayed far from the river ways that form the Missouri River drainage, where they lived in villages sustained by agriculture, hunting, and gathering (see page 14). The climate cooldown that affected their neighbors to the east had a similar effect on the Plains Indians: growing seasons became shorter, and the need to hunt became greater. But at the same time, this shift in climate produced an increase in one food source: **buffalo.**

A survivor of the great ice ages, the American bison is particularly well adapted to cold climates. Unlike European cattle, which often starve when snow buries the grasses on which they graze, buffalo use their hooves to dig out the grass they need, and their efficient metabolism extracts nutrients from even poor-

buffalo   The American bison, a large member of the ox family, native to North America and the staple of the Plains Indian economy between the fifteenth and mid-nineteenth centuries.

quality pasturage. Although buffalo had long been a presence on the plains, the cold weather during the Little Ice Age spurred a massive increase in their numbers. Between 1300 and 1800, herds numbering in the millions emerged in the new environment created by the climate change.

Some groups—such as the **Caddoan**-speaking Wichitas, Pawnees, and Arikaras—virtually abandoned their agricultural villages and became hunters. Others, such as the Hidatsas, split in two: a splinter group calling themselves Crows went off permanently to the grasslands to hunt while the remainder stayed in their villages growing corn and tobacco. These and others who chose to continue their agricultural ways, the Mandans, for example, established a thriving trade with the hunters, exchanging vegetables and tobacco for fresh meat and other buffalo products.

The increase in buffalo not only provided a welcome resource for the Indians already on the Great Plains but also drew new populations to the area. As the climate farther north became unbearably severe, the Blackfeet and other Indians swept down from the subarctic Northeast to hunt on the plains. Other Algonquin-speaking Indians, including the Gros Ventres, Cheyennes, and Arapahos, soon followed. These were then joined by other northeastern groups fleeing the violence and disease that were becoming endemic in the Eastern Woodlands. Some groups, even war-weary Hurons and Iroquois, came as small parties and sought adoption among Great Plains societies. Others came en masse. The **Lakotas,** for example, once the westernmost family of Siouan agriculturalists, were pushed onto the plains by continuing pressure from the east, but they maintained close relations with their **Dakota** neighbors in Minnesota, who continued to farm and harvest wild rice and other crops. This continued tie, like that between the Crows and Hidatsas, increased both the hunters' and the farmers' chances for survival in an ever more hostile world by expanding available resources. Intergroup trade became the key to the welfare of all.

The buffalo also began to play an important role on the southern plains. There, groups such as the Apaches, Comanches, and Kiowas specialized in hunting the ever-increasing herds and then exchanging part of their kill for village-based products from their neighbors and kinsmen, the Navajos, Hopis, and Pueblos. And it was in these intergroup trades that the Plains Indians would acquire a new advantage in their efforts to expand their hunting economy: the horse.

One unintentional outcome of the Pueblo Revolt was the liberation of thousands of Spanish horses. The Pueblos had little use for these animals, but their trading partners, the Kiowas and Comanches, quickly adopted them. Horses could carry much larger loads than dogs and could survive on a diet of grass rather than taking a share of the meat. In less than a generation, horses became a mainstay of the buffalo-hunting cultures on the southern plains. And from there, horses spread quickly to other hunting people.

Northern plains dwellers such as the Shoshones quickly began acquiring horses from their southwestern kinsmen. Following a northward path along the eastern flank of the Rocky Mountains, horses were passed from one group to another in the complex trading system that had come into existence in the plains region. Well adapted to grasslands, virtually free from natural predators or diseases, and highly prized and thus well protected by their new human owners, horses greatly increased in number. By 1730, virtually all of the plains hunting peoples had some horses and were clamoring for more.

The steady demand for horses and hunting grounds created a new dynamic on the Great Plains and set a new economy into motion (see Map 2.2). After the Spanish reconquest of New Mexico, Indians could obtain horses only through warfare and trade, and both increased significantly. Surprise raids to steal horses from neighboring Indian groups and European settlements brought both honor and wealth to those who were successful. Human captives also became valuable prizes, both as replacements for individuals lost in the fighting and as items of trade. In exchange for horses, human captives might be bartered as slaves to the Spanish. Thus horse trading and slave trading became linked.

Conquest and Accommodation in a Shared New World

■ What forces shaped the day-to-day lives of settlers in New Mexico, Louisiana, and New Netherland?

■ How did settlers and American Indians adapt to changing conditions in the different regions of colonial occupation?

Caddoan A family of languages spoken by the Wichitas, Pawnees, Arikaras, and other Plains Indians.

Lakotas/Dakotas Subgroups of the Sioux Nation of Indians; Lakotas make up the western branch, living mostly on the Great Plains; Dakotas, the eastern branch, live mostly in the prairie and lakes region of the Upper Midwest.

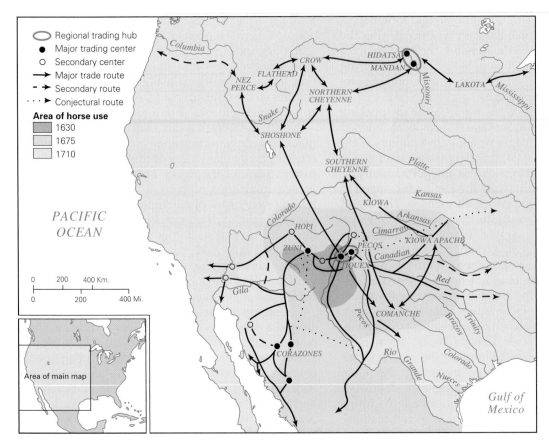

MAP 2.2 Intergroup Trading on the Plains   Although movies portray Plains Indians as unsophisticated hunters and warriors, Native American societies in America's midsection maintained extremely complex and cosmopolitan trading networks. As this map shows, trade routes that had existed before Europeans entered the region acquired added importance in distributing the novel technologies and ideas that the newcomers brought with them. The most important of these was horses, which were passed very quickly from group to group along these trade routes.

Old World cultures, Native American historical dynamics, and New World environmental conditions combined to create vibrant new societies in European pioneer settlements. Despite the regulatory efforts of Spanish bureaucrats, French royal officials, and Dutch company executives, life in the colonies developed in its own peculiar ways. Entire regions in what would become the United States assumed cultural contours that would shape all future developments in each.

New Spain's Northern Frontiers

Life along New Spain's northern fringe was punctuated by friction between the empire's highly organized official structure and the disorderliness common to frontier settings. For the Spanish, notions of civil order were rooted in the local community—city, town, or village—and its ruling elite. Responsibility for maintaining order belonged to the *cabildo secular,* the municipal town council composed of members of the elite or their appointees. Spain established towns in all of its New World colonies and immediately turned over local authority to a ruling *cabildo.* In Mexico, Peru, and elsewhere this practice was appropriate and usually successful, but in the high desert of New Mexico the *cabildo* system was at odds with environmental and cultural conditions.

After suppressing the Pueblo Revolt during the 1690s, Spaniards began drifting back into New Mexico. Unlike areas to the south, New Mexico offered no

San Esteban Rey, a Catholic church built at Pueblo de Ácoma in about 1642, stands as a monument to the mixing of cultures in colonial New Mexico. The building's adobe construction, rising towers, and curving corners reflect traditional Pueblo architecture, while the crosses on the top identify its European purpose. Churches like this provided an anchor for the multicultural society that emerged in the region. *Lee Marmon.*

rich deposits of gold or silver, and the climate was unsuitable for large-scale agriculture. With neither mines nor plantations to support the *encomienda* system, the basic underpinnings of the traditional ruling order never emerged. Even so, the Spanish colonial bureaucracy followed conventional imperial procedures and made Santa Fe the official municipal center for the region after its recapture from the Indians in 1693. But there were no *encomenderos* to provide wealth. The church, which was channeling money to missions, and the Spanish government, which allocated both military and civic support funds, were the only major employers in the region. Those in neither the church's nor the state's employ had to scramble for a living.

As in the days before the Pueblo Revolt, the most rewarding economic enterprise in the region was ranching. Under Pueblo control following the revolt, the small flocks of sheep abandoned by the fleeing Spanish grew dramatically. By the time the Spanish returned, sheep ranching had become a reliable way to make a living. Thus, rather than concentrating near the municipal center in Santa Fe, the population in New Mexico spread out across the land, forming two sorts of communities. South of Santa Fe, people settled on scattered ranches. Elsewhere, they gathered in small villages along streams and pooled their labor to make a living from irrigated **subsistence farming.**

Like colonists elsewhere in Spain's New World empire, the New Mexico colonists were almost entirely male. Isolated on sheep ranches or in small villages, these men sought Indian companionship and married into local populations. These marriages gave birth not only to a new hybrid population but also to lines of kinship, trade, and authority that were in sharp contrast to the imperial ideal. For example, when Navajo or Apache raiding parties struck, ranchers and villagers turned to their Indian relatives for protection rather than to Spanish officials in Santa Fe.

Far away from the imperial economy centered in Mexico City, New Mexicans looked northward for trading opportunities. Southern Plains Indians—Apaches, Comanches, Kiowas, and their kin—needed a continuous supply of horses. They could obtain them by raiding Spanish ranches, but doing so brought reprisals by ranchers and their Indian relatives. Trade was a safer option. Facing labor shortages and too poor to take advantage of traditional Spanish labor systems, New Mexicans accepted Indian slaves—especially children—in exchange for horses. Soon, these young captives became another important commodity in the already complex trading and raiding system that prevailed among the southwestern Indians and Spanish New Mexicans.

In this frontier world, unlike the rest of Spanish America, a man's social status came to depend less on his Spanish connections than on his ability to work effectively in the complicated world of kinship that prevailed in the Indian community. The people who eventually emerged as the elite class in New Mexico were those who best perfected these skills. Under their influence, Santa Fe was transformed from a traditional mission and imperial town into a cosmopolitan frontier trading center. During the next two centuries, this multiethnic elite absorbed first French and then Anglo-American newcomers while maintaining its own social, political, and economic style.

Life in French Louisiana

France's colony in Louisiana had many of the same qualities and faced many of the same problems as Spain's North American possessions. Like most European settlements, Louisiana suffered from a critical shortage of labor, leading first to dependence on the Indians and eventually to the wholesale adoption of African slavery. And like all Europeans who settled in North America, Louisianans found themselves

---

subsistence farming Farming that produces enough food for survival but no surplus that can be sold.

The French had difficulty persuading settlers to come to their New World province in Louisiana. As a result, the region's development depended on a mixture of various European refugees, native Indians, and imported Africans for labor. Alexander de Batz's 1735 painting gives us a good idea of what the population around New Orleans looked like at that time. As in neighboring New Mexico, a multiracial and multicultural society emerged in Louisiana that left a permanent legacy in the region. *Peabody Museum, Harvard University.*

embroiled in a complicated Native American world that usually defied European understanding.

Despite the territory's strategic location, fertile soils, and fur-bearing animals, few Frenchmen showed any interest in settling there. In the first years of the colony's existence, the population consisted primarily of three groups: military men, who were generally members of the lower nobility; *coureurs de bois* from Canada looking for new and better sources of furs; and French craftsmen seeking economic independence in the New World. The men in each group had little in common with those in the other groups, and, more important, none had knowledge of or interest in food production. In the absence of an agricultural establishment, the small number of settlers in Louisiana had to depend on imported food. At first, ships from France carried provisions to the colonies, but war in Europe frequently interrupted this source. In desperation, the colonists turned to the Indians.

The **Natchez, Chickasaws,** and **Choctaws** were all close by and well provisioned. The Chickasaws refused to deal with the French, and the Natchez, divided into quarreling factions, were sometimes helpful and sometimes hostile. But the Choctaws, locked into a war with the Chickasaws and a tense relationship with the Natchez, found the prospect of an alliance with the French quite attractive. In the realignment process, the Choctaws helped shape France's Indian policies and expansion plans. For example, af-

Natchez Indians An urban, mound-building Indian people who lived on the lower Mississippi River until they were destroyed in a war with the French in the 1720s; survivors joined the Creek Confederacy.

Chickasaw Indians An urban, mound-building Indian people who lived on the lower Mississippi River and became a society of hunters after the change in climate and introduction of disease after 1400; they were successful in resisting French aggression throughout the colonial era.

Choctaw Indians Like the Chickasaws, a mound-building people who became a society of hunters after 1400; they were steadfast allies of the French in wars against the Natchez and Chickasaws.

ter disastrous flooding along the Gulf Coast during the winter of 1719–1720, the French chose to relocate settlements onto Natchez land rather than in Choctaw territory. When the Natchez resisted French incursion, the Choctaws helped their European allies destroy the tribe—the entire Natchez Nation was either killed or exiled. The Choctaws also assisted the French in a thirty-year-long conflict with the Chickasaws, though with less success.

Despite the Choctaw alliance, which guaranteed ample food supplies and facilitated territorial acquisitions, Louisiana remained unappealing to French farmers. Recognizing the problem, the French government tried several tactics to lure settlers, occasionally resorting to some rather odd and extreme measures. For example, in the late 1690s, officials in Louisiana, aware that the absence of women was one serious deterrent to immigration, proposed that the government pay the passage of young women of good character to the colony. For several years, agents in France tried to recruit females but enlisted only twenty-four or so, who arrived in the colony in 1704. Like the noblemen and craftsmen who preceded them, these potential brides—refugees from orphanages and other public institutions—were ill suited for the primitive life offered by Louisiana and were entirely unprepared to work as farm laborers. By 1708, even officials who had been enthusiastic about the project were advising that it be discontinued. As a result, French men, like their Spanish neighbors, married Indians and, later, African slaves, creating a hybrid **creole** population.

Although Louisiana officials advised against it, the French government finally resorted to recruiting paupers, criminals, and religious or political refugees from central Europe and elsewhere to people the new land. But even with these newcomers, labor was inadequate to ensure survival, much less prosperity. Increasingly, settlers in Louisiana imported slaves to do necessary work. By 1732, slaves made up two-thirds of the population.

The Dutch Settlements

The existence of Rensselaerswyck and other great landed estates made it seem as though the New Netherland colony was prosperous and secure, but it actually was neither. Few of the wealthy stockholders in the Dutch West India Company wanted to trade their lives as successful gentleman investors for a pioneering existence on a barely tamed frontier. The economy in Holland was booming, and only the most desperate or adventurous wanted to leave. But having no one to pay their way, even the few who were willing were hard-pressed to migrate to the colony.

Desperate to draw settlers, the Dutch West India Company created an alternative to the patroonship, agreeing to grant a tract of land to any free man who would agree to farm it. This offer appealed to many groups in Europe who were experiencing hardship in their own countries but who, for one reason or another, were unwelcome in the colonies of their homelands. French Protestants, for example, were experiencing terrible persecution in France but were forbidden from going to Canada or Louisiana. Roman Catholics, Quakers, Jews, Muslims, and a wide variety of others also chose to migrate to New Netherland. Most of the colonists settled on small farms, called *bouweries* in Dutch, and engaged in the same agricultural pursuits they had practiced in Europe. Thus New Netherland was dotted with little settlements, each having its own language, culture, and internal economy.

Farming was the dominant activity among the emigrants, but some followed the example of the French *coureurs du bois* and went alone or in small groups into the woods to live and trade with the Indians. Called **bosch loopers,** these independent traders traveled through the forests, trading cheap brandy and rum for the Indians' furs, which they then sold for enormous profits. Although both tribal leaders and legitimate traders complained about the *bosch loopers'* illegal activities, company authorities could not control them.

In fact, the Dutch West India Company was unable to control much of anything in New Netherland. The incredible diversity of the settlers no doubt contributed to this administrative impotence. For example, Dutch law and company policy dictated that the Calvinistic **Dutch Reform Church** was to be the colony's official and only church. But instead of drawing everyone into one religion, the policy had the opposite effect. As late as 1642 not a single church of any

---

creole In colonial times, a term referring to anyone of European or African heritage who was born in the colonies; in Louisiana, refers to the ethnic group resulting from intermarriage by people of mixed languages, races, and cultures.

bosch loopers Dutch term meaning "woods runners"; independent Dutch fur traders.

Dutch Reform Church Calvinistic Protestant denomination; the established church in the Dutch Republic and the official church in New Netherland.

denomination had been planted. Poor leadership and unimaginative policies also contributed to the general air of disorder. Following Peter Minuit's dismissal by the company in 1631, a long line of incompetent governors ruled the colony. In the absence of any legislative assembly or other local body to help keep matters on track, for years one bad decision followed another. It took a major reorganization by the West India Company and its appointment of Peter Stuyvesant in 1645 to turn the colony around.

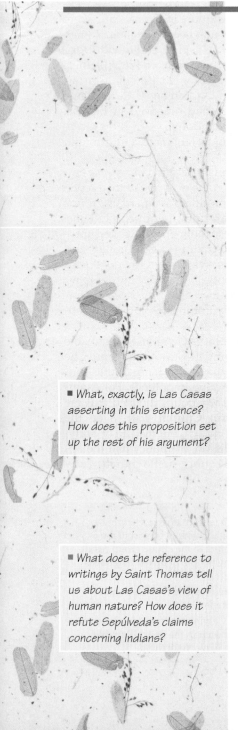

Individual Voices

Examining a Primary Source

Bartolomé de Las Casas Argues for the American Indians

In his debate with Juan Ginés de Sepúlveda before the Council of Valladolid in 1550 and 1551, Bartolomé de Las Casas repeatedly stressed the many remarkable accomplishments made by Indians, both in creating advanced civilizations of their own and in adapting to Spanish civilization. Many witnesses (most of whom had never been to America) disputed these claims, but more damaging was the argument that such accomplishments were irrelevant. Though perhaps clever, Sepúlveda argued, Indians lacked souls and therefore could never become truly civilized Christians. Like animals, then, they could be exploited but never embraced. Las Casas thought otherwise, and drew on Church doctrine to refute this claim. In the end, Las Casas's argument won the day and became the official position for the Catholic Church and the Spanish Crown.

■ What, exactly, is Las Casas asserting in this sentence? How does this proposition set up the rest of his argument?

■ What does the reference to writings by Saint Thomas tell us about Las Casas's view of human nature? How does it refute Sepúlveda's claims concerning Indians?

Who, therefore, except one who is irreverent toward God and contemptuous of nature, has dared to write that countless numbers of natives across the ocean are barbarous, savage, uncivilized, and slow witted when, if they are evaluated by an accurate judgment, they completely outnumber all other men? ■ *This is consistent with what Saint Thomas writes: "The good which is proportionate to the common state of nature is to be found in most men and is lacking only in a few. . . . Thus it is clear that the majority of men have sufficient knowledge to guide their lives, and the few who do not have this knowledge are said to be half-witted or fools." Therefore, since barbarians of that kind, as Saint Thomas says, lack that good of the intellect which is knowledge of the truth, a good proportionate to the common condition of rational nature, it is evident that in each part of the world, or anywhere among the nations, barbarians of this sort or freaks of rational nature can only be quite rare. For since God's love of mankind is so great and it is his will to save all men, it is in accord with his wisdom that in the whole universe, which is perfect in all its parts, his supreme wisdom should shine more and more in the most perfect thing: rational nature. Therefore, the barbarians of the kind we have placed in the third category are most rare, because with such natural endowments they cannot seek God, know him, call upon him, or love him. They do not have a capacity for doctrine or for performing the acts of faith or love.* ■

■ *Judging from this brief excerpt from Las Casas's argument, why do you suppose he won the debate? Why would the Catholic Church have chosen to endorse and publicize his views and not Sepúlveda's?*

Again, if we believe that such a huge part of mankind is barbaric, it would follow that God's design has for the most part been ineffective, with so many thousands of men deprived of the natural light that is common to all peoples. And so there would be a great reduction in the perfection of the entire universe—something that is unacceptable and unthinkable for any Christian. ■

Source: Bartolomé de las Casas, *In Defense of the Indians: The Defense of the Most Reverend Lord, Don Fray Bartolomé de las Casas, of the Order of Preachers, Late Bishop of Chiapa, Against the Persecutors and Slanderers of the Peoples of the New World Discovered Across the Seas.* Translated, edited and annotated by Stafford Poole (Dekalb, Northern Illinois University Press, © 1974). Used by permission of Northern Illinois University Press.

Summary

Spain's opening ventures in the Americas had been wildly successful, making the Iberian kingdom the envy of the world. Hoping to cash in on the bounty, other European nations challenged Spain's monopoly on American colonization, creating an outward explosion of exploring energy. Although slow to consolidate an imperial presence in North America, England was the first to confront the Spanish in force, wounding them severely. France and the Netherlands took advantage of the situation to begin building their own American empires.

For Native Americans, the entry of Europeans into their realms combined with other forces to create an air of crisis. Presented with a series of new challenges, Indians sought new ways to solve their problems and created altogether new societies. This often involved difficult choices: perhaps allying with the newcomers, resisting them, or fleeing. As different groups exercised different options, the outcome was a historically dynamic world of interaction involving all of the societies that were coming together in North America.

This dynamic interaction yielded interesting fruit. In New Spain, New France, Louisiana, New Netherland, and throughout the Great Plains, truly cosmopolitan societies emerged. Bearing cultural traits and material goods from throughout the world, these new transatlantic societies set the tone for future development in North America. As we will see in Chapter 3, societies on the Atlantic coast, too, were evolving as English colonists interacted with the land and its many occupants. The outcome of such interchange, over the centuries, was the emergence of a multicultural, multiethnic, and extraordinarily rich culture—an essential element in Making America.

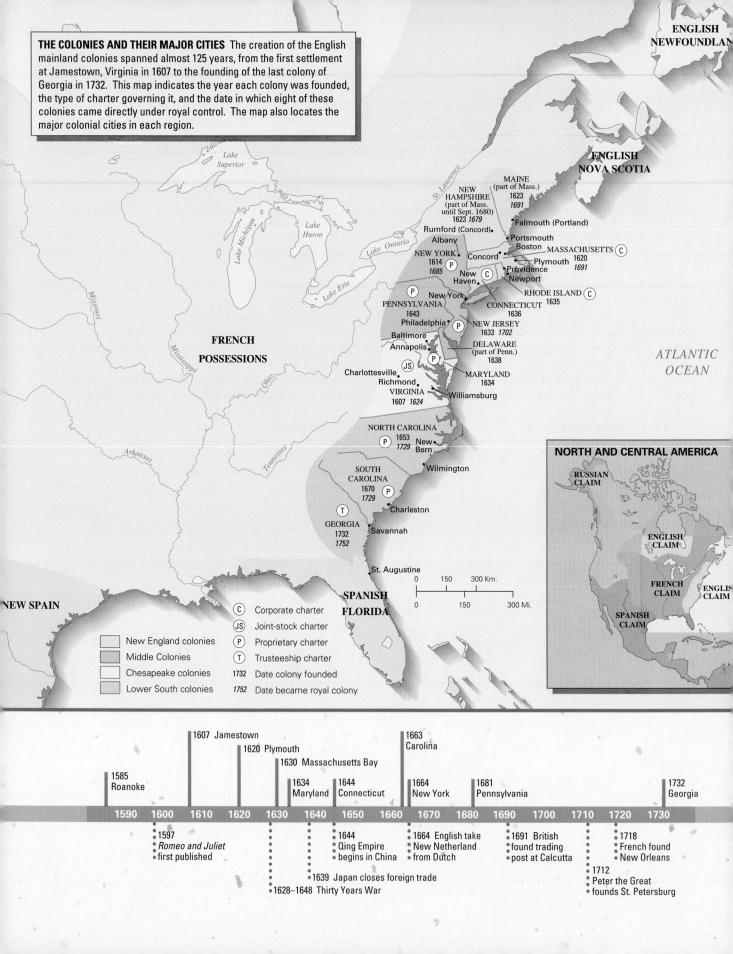

THE COLONIES AND THEIR MAJOR CITIES The creation of the English mainland colonies spanned almost 125 years, from the first settlement at Jamestown, Virginia in 1607 to the founding of the last colony of Georgia in 1732. This map indicates the year each colony was founded, the type of charter governing it, and the date in which eight of these colonies came directly under royal control. The map also locates the major colonial cities in each region.

ENGLISH NEWFOUNDLAN

Lake Superior

Lake Michigan

Lake Huron

Lake Ontario

Lake Erie

St. Lawrence

ENGLISH NOVA SCOTIA

MAINE (part of Mass.) 1623 *1691*

NEW HAMPSHIRE (part of Mass. until Sept. 1680) 1623 *1679*

Falmouth (Portland)

Rumford (Concord)

Albany

Portsmouth
Boston

MASSACHUSETTS Ⓒ

NEW YORK 1614 *1685* Ⓟ

Concord

Plymouth 1620 *1691*

New Haven Ⓒ

Providence
Newport

RHODE ISLAND Ⓒ 1635

Ⓟ

New York

CONNECTICUT 1636

PENNSYLVANIA 1643

Philadelphia

Ⓟ

NEW JERSEY 1633 *1702*

Baltimore

Annapolis

DELAWARE (part of Penn.) 1638

Ⓟ

FRENCH POSSESSIONS

Missouri

Mississippi

Ohio

JS

Charlottesville
Richmond

VIRGINIA 1607 *1624*

Williamsburg

MARYLAND 1634

ATLANTIC OCEAN

Arkansas

Tennessee

NORTH CAROLINA 1653 *1729* Ⓟ

New Bern

Wilmington

SOUTH CAROLINA 1670 *1729* Ⓟ

Charleston

Ⓣ

GEORGIA 1732 *1752*

Savannah

St. Augustine

NEW SPAIN

SPANISH FLORIDA

0 150 300 Km.
0 150 300 Mi.

NORTH AND CENTRAL AMERICA

RUSSIAN CLAIM

ENGLISH CLAIM

FRENCH CLAIM

ENGLIS CLAIM

SPANISH CLAIM

Ⓒ Corporate charter
ⒿⓈ Joint-stock charter
Ⓟ Proprietary charter
Ⓣ Trusteeship charter
1732 Date colony founded
1752 Date became royal colony

New England colonies
Middle Colonies
Chesapeake colonies
Lower South colonies

1607 Jamestown

1620 Plymouth

1630 Massachusetts Bay

1663 Carolina

1585 Roanoke

1634 Maryland

1644 Connecticut

1664 New York

1681 Pennsylvania

1732 Georgia

1590 1600 1610 1620 1630 1640 1650 1660 1670 1680 1690 1700 1710 1720 1730

1597 *Romeo and Juliet* first published

1644 Qing Empire begins in China

1664 English take New Netherland from Dutch

1691 British found trading post at Calcutta

1718 French found New Orleans

1639 Japan closes foreign trade

1712 Peter the Great founds St. Petersburg

1628–1648 Thirty Years War

Founding the English Mainland Colonies, 1585–1732

The Colonies and Their Major Cities
Using the map on the facing page, discuss the four types of colonies created on the mainland of British North America. What differences in political participation and political institutions do you think might develop between corporate colonies and proprietary ones?

Individual Choices

NATHANIEL BACON

Nathaniel Bacon came to Virginia as a gentleman in the 1670s, but his resentment of the economic and political domination of the colony by a small group of planters transformed him into a backwoods rebel. In 1676, Bacon led an army of discontented farmers, servants, and slaves against the powerful coastal planters—and almost won. In this stained glass window, discovered and restored in the twentieth century, Bacon's social class and his commanding presence are both evident. *The Association for the Preservation of Virginia Antiquities at Bacon's Castle, Library of Virginia.*

Nathaniel Bacon

One hundred years before the English colonies of North America declared their independence, Nathaniel Bacon led a group of Virginia colonists in a rebellion against the corrupt royal governor and the elite planters who supported him. Bacon's 1670s backcountry movement came at a time when the Virginia economy was in trouble. A recent drought and a drop in the price of tobacco had diminished the fortunes of many colonists. In the backcountry, raids by the neighboring Indian tribes had led to the deaths of many farm families and their servants. Small farms were being heavily taxed, while the larger plantations, owned by Governor William Berkeley's friends, remained tax-exempt and prosperous. New arrivals to the colony, eager for land, found the governor unwilling to open the western frontier for further settlement.

In 1674 a new face arrived in the colony of Virginia. Nathaniel Bacon, a charismatic 27-year-old, had been born to privilege in Suffolk County, England, and had studied law at Cambridge. After the young Nathaniel's involvement in a series of misadventures in England, his father decided to pack him off to the colonies to keep him out of trouble. Using his father's money, Bacon was able to purchase a large plantation 40 miles up the river from the capital city of Jamestown, as well as a tract of undeveloped land in the backcountry. Bacon's social status gained him a place among the colony's elite, and within six months he was appointed to Governor Berkeley's advisory council. But Bacon's relentless ambition and his impulsiveness soon made him an unpopular figure in the wealthy planter circles.

In the spring of 1676 the militant Susquehanna Indians raided Bacon's backcountry farm, killing the overseer and three servants. Bacon, speaking for himself and his neighbors, demanded that Governor Berkeley raise a militia and rid the area of its entire Indian population. Bold and ruthless action like this would not only end the attacks but also open up more land for settlement. But the governor, who was engaged in a lucrative fur-trading business with several of the local tribes, refused. He insisted that the existing plan of building forts along the frontier would protect Bacon and his fellow backcountry friends. The angry Bacon decided to take matters into his own hands. He returned to the backcountry and raised a militia of volunteers from the area. This vigilante army began a war against not just the Susquehanna but all the Indians on the Virginia frontier. Now the equally angry Governor Berkeley stripped Bacon of his seat on the council and branded him a traitor.

After leading successful campaigns against the Indians, Bacon returned to Jamestown with forty bodyguards. He demanded that his seat on the council be restored. The intimidated Governor Berkeley gave in to this demand, but only if Bacon confessed to his crimes and asked for forgiveness. Bacon agreed—and his supporters returned home, satisfied that all was well. They were wrong. As soon as Bacon's men left the city, the governor had Bacon arrested and condemned to

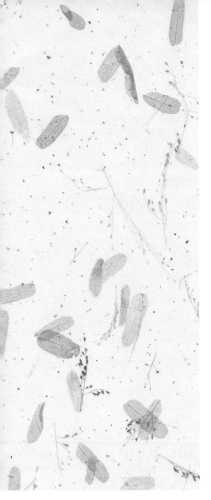

death for treason. Fortunately for Bacon, he had been warned of the governor's intentions and he escaped arrest.

Bacon realized that there could be no peaceful resolution to his clash with the governor and returned to the backcountry to reassemble his army. Within two weeks Bacon had recruited a force of over five hundred men. On June 23, 1676, this frontier army marched into Jamestown and demanded an audience with the governor. When Berkeley refused, Bacon ordered his troops to surround the state-house, making prisoners of all of the political leaders in the building. Bacon then demanded that the captive legislators pass several reforms, including an act barring the governor's friends from office. Bacon also demanded that all those who participated in the rebellion receive pardons. With little choice in the matter, the colonial government agreed, and Bacon ordered his men to let the governor and his planter friends return to their homes. Allowing the governor to go free would turn out to be a crucial mistake.

Over the next several months "General" Bacon (as his troops were now calling him) and Governor Berkeley continued to fight for control of the colony. After a series of failed attempts, the governor finally reclaimed Jamestown on September 7. Within two weeks Bacon recaptured the city, but realizing that he would never be able to hold it, he took drastic steps: he burned Jamestown to the ground.

By October 20 Bacon's supporters controlled over two-thirds of Virginia. New leaders had been installed at all levels of the government, and the power of the coastal planters seemed broken. Then tragedy struck. On October 26 Nathaniel Bacon died of dysentery. Without Bacon's strong leadership the revolution soon faltered. The following spring British troops arrived to put an end to the rebellion. For the next hundred years, the royal governors of the British Crown and the wealthy coastal planters would dominate Virginia political life.

INTRODUCTION

Bacon's Rebellion reflects many of the contradictory themes and patterns of the early colonial period: the determination to create new communities and the willingness to uproot Native American communities in the process; the sense of new opportunities for success and the continuing influence of wealth and social prestige in a frontier world; and the challenge of creating a unified society in the face of the conflicting economic interests of coastal planters and backcountry farmers.

The seventeenth century saw thousands of English men and women risk the dangers of the Atlantic crossing, the hardships of frontier life, the threat of violence from other settlers and local Indian groups, and the often overwhelming sense of isolation that were all part of the colonizing experience. What motivated them? Many left England to escape religious persecution or, at the least, discrimination and harassment because of their dissenting religious views.

Puritans, Catholics, and Quakers all felt compelled to resist demands for allegiance to the Church of England. Given a choice between silence and exile, many chose to journey to what Europeans called the "New World." These English religious radicals were not alone in seeking freedom of worship. Jews, French Protestants, and German pietists also came to America to escape persecution.

Still other colonists faced the difficult choice of poverty or flight. The economic transformation of England from a feudal society to a market society disrupted the lives of the country's rural population of tenant farmers. Thrown off their land as wealthy landlords turned to sheep raising, thousands of these victims of an emerging capitalism became nomads and vagabonds, traveling from country towns to seaport cities in search of work. Desperation drove them to sign away several years of their lives to a ship captain or plantation owner in Virginia or Maryland in exchange for passage to America.

But if desperation prompted them to leave England,

Grassroots Movements, Then and Now

Bacon's Rebellion is one of the first instances of a grassroots movement in American history. These movements often give voice to people who are not, or feel they are not, being heard by the government, or feel that their goals are not being considered by the government. Many things we take for granted today began as demands by grassroots movements, including the end to slavery, the direct election of senators, and women's suffrage. The antiwar movement of the 1960s, the environmental movements of the 1990s, and the antismoking movement of today are recent examples of grassroots movements. Often grassroots movements provide insights into changing values in American society, and, equally often, they arise as part of a cluster of reform movements.

dreams and expectations often motivated them too. These young men and woman agreed to years of servitude and backbreaking labor in the tobacco fields of the **Chesapeake,** without wages and with the most meager rations, because they hoped to acquire land when they were released from bondage. The promise of land was perhaps the most powerful appeal to more fortunate colonists as well. Families of modest means sold off their belongings and said their goodbyes to familiar faces and a familiar landscape, determined to build new and more independent lives for themselves in the colonies.

This expectation of opportunity was not the monopoly of English men and women. Dutch colonists, Swedes, Finns, and Germans also risked life and limb to reach America in order to improve their economic circumstances. Only one group of colonists, enslaved Africans, arrived on the mainland against their wills. Although their numbers were small in the seventeenth century, thousands of enslaved men, women, and children would become unwilling colonists in the decades that followed.

Colonists recorded their experiences in diaries, letters, journals, and reports to government, church, or trading company officials. These accounts dramatize the hardships and risks that settlers confronted and testify that many did not survive. Ships carrying colonists sank in ocean storms or fell victim to pirates or enemy vessels. Diseases unknown in England decimated settlements. Poor planning and simple ignorance of survival techniques destroyed others. Conflicts with local Indian populations produced violence, bloodshed, and atrocities on both sides. And though colonists lived far from the seats of power in Europe, the rivalries between English, French, Dutch, and Spanish governments spilled across the ocean, erupting in border raids and full-scale wars throughout the century.

Yet the records left by these colonists were not always tales of tragedy. New Englanders recorded the wonders of new vegetation and towering forests. New Yorkers described rolling farmlands, wide rivers, deep harbors. Virginians marveled at rich black soil, exotic flowers, and blooming plants. And throughout the colonies that emerged during the seventeenth and eighteenth centuries, settlers observed, with equal measures of amazement and contempt, the customs and appearances of a race of people entirely new to them: Native Americans.

England and Colonization

■ What was the impact of the failure of the Roanoke Colony on England's colonizing effort?

■ What circumstances or conditions in England prompted people to migrate to America?

By the end of the century, twelve distinct colonies hugged the Atlantic coastline of English America. The thirteenth, Georgia, was founded in 1732. Although each colony had its own unique history, climate and geography produced four distinct regions: New England, the Middle Colonies, the Chesapeake, and the Lower South. The colonies within each region shared a common economy and labor system, or a similar religious heritage, or a special character that defined the population, such as ethnic diversity. And by the end of the century, as frontier outposts developed into well-established communities, certain institutions emerged in every colony. Thus, whether its founders had been religious refugees or wealthy businessmen, each colony developed a representative assembly, established courts, built houses of worship—and constructed jails. Car-

Chesapeake   The Chesapeake was the common term for the two colonies of Maryland and Virginia, both of which border on Chesapeake Bay.

Chronology

Settling the Mainland Colonies

1585	English colonize Roanoke Island		**1655**	Civil war in Maryland
1603	James I becomes king of England		**1660**	Restoration of English monarchy
1607	Virginia Company founds Jamestown		**1663**	Carolina chartered
1619	Virginia House of Burgesses meets		**1664**	New Netherland becomes New York
1620	Pilgrims found Plymouth Plantations		**1675**	King Philip's War in New England
1625	Charles I becomes king of England		**1676**	Bacon's Rebellion in Virginia
1630	Puritans found Massachusetts Bay Colony		**1681**	Pennsylvania chartered
1634	Lord Baltimore establishes Maryland		**1685**	James II becomes king of England
1635	Roger Williams founds Providence		**1686**	Dominion of New England established
1636	Anne Hutchinson banished from Massachusetts Pequot War in New England Connecticut settled		**1688**	Glorious Revolution in England
1642–1648	English civil war		**1689**	Leisler's Rebellion in New York
1649	Charles I executed Cromwell and Puritans come to power in England		**1691**	Massachusetts becomes royal colony
			1692	Salem witch trials
			1732	Georgia chartered

olinians may have thought they shared little in common with the people of Connecticut, but both sets of colonists were subject to English law, English trade policies, and English conflicts with rival nations. Separate, yet linked to one another and to what they affectionately called the "Mother Country" in crucial ways, between 1607 and 1700 the colonies transformed themselves from struggling settlements to complex societies.

England's First Attempts at Colonization

In July 1584, two small ships entered the calm waters between the barrier islands and the mainland of North Carolina. On board were a group of Englishmen, sent by the wealthy nobleman Sir Walter Raleigh with orders to reconnoiter the area and locate a likely spot for settlement. The men were impressed by the peaceful, inviting scene before them: a forest of cypress,

sweet gums, pines, and flowering dogwood rising up from the sandy shores; the scent of flowers; and the gentle rustling of treetops filled with birds. The exhausted travelers could not fail to see the contrast between this exotic, lush environment, seemingly untamed by human efforts, and the carefully cultivated farmlands and pastures of their native land. But if they were awed, they were not naive. To protect themselves from unseen dangers, each man wore a suit of armor and carried weapons. Sometime that afternoon, the Englishmen got their first glimpse of the local population as three Indians approached in a canoe. It would be difficult to say which group was more amazed by what they saw. Despite all that they had read, and the many sketches they had seen, the Englishmen surely found these native people strange to behold, dressed as they were in loincloths, their bodies decorated with tattoos and adorned with necklaces and bracelets of shells. The Indians were perhaps equally astonished by the sight of strangers, encased in heavy metal on a humid summer's day.

The encounter passed without incident. Within a month, the Englishmen were gone, returning to make their report to the eagerly awaiting Raleigh. But the following year, a new group of Englishmen sank anchor off the North Carolina shore. These men, many of them soldiers recruited by Raleigh, settled on Roanoke Island. Among them was a 25-year-old historian, surveyor, and cartographer, Thomas Harriot, who published his remarkable account of his nation's first colonizing attempt, *A Briefe and True Report of the New Found Land of Virginia*, in 1588. In his *Briefe and True Report*, Harriot described the Indians the colonists encountered but failed to report the almost immediate clashes between natives and invaders. The Englishmen's unshakable sense of superiority, despite their dependence on the Indians for food, destroyed the possibility of cooperation. Before the year was over, Harriot and his shipmates returned to England.

Undaunted, Raleigh tried a second time in 1587, spending most of his remaining fortune to send over a hundred colonists to the area. Unfortunately, war with Spain made it impossible for Raleigh to send supplies to his colony for over three years. When a ship finally did reach the colony, the men on board could find no trace of the colonists. Instead they found abandoned ruins, and a single word carved into the bark of a nearby tree: "Croatan." Whether the Roanoke colonists had fled from attack by the Croatan Indians, or been rescued by them in the face of starvation, epidemic, or some other natural disaster, such as a severe drought, no one knows. News of the Roanoke mystery spread rapidly. So too did news that Sir Walter Raleigh had lost his entire fortune in his attempts at colonization. Thus, although Harriot's account stressed the possibilities for wealth and profit in America, the chilling outcome discouraged others from following Raleigh's lead.

Turmoil and Tensions in England

Although no one was willing to risk personal fortune on colonizing America, many English aristocrats believed the country needed to get rid of its numerous poor and, in their minds, dangerous men and women. Pamphlets suggested that the solution to crime and riots was to find a dumping ground for the thousands who had been displaced by the changing economy—desperate people without money or shelter, removed from their lands but having no new means of livelihood. As farmlands were turned into pastures for sheep that supplied the new woolens industries, the resentful evicted farmers carried signs reading "Sheep Eat Men."

The kings and their advisers also worried about the unrest stirred by growing demands for religious reform within the **Church of England.** The movement to "purify" the church had grown steadily, led by men and women who believed the church had kept too many Catholic rituals and customs despite its claim to be Protestant. For the seventeenth-century monarchs, the Stuart kings, this Puritan criticism smacked of treason since the king was not only head of the nation but also head of the Anglican Church. Mistrust between Puritan reformers and the Crown grew under King James I and his son Charles I, for both men were rumored to be secretly practicing Catholicism.

These economic and religious problems were not the only sources of tension in English society in the early decades of the century. A political struggle between the Crown and the legislative branch of the English government, the **Parliament,** was building to a crisis. In 1642 a civil war erupted, bringing together many of the threads of discontent and conflict. A Puritan army led by Oliver Cromwell overthrew the monarchy and in 1649 executed King Charles I. Cromwell's success established the supremacy of the Parliament. For almost a dozen years, the nation was a **Commonwealth,** a republic dominated by Puritans, merchants, and gentry rather than noblemen. Cromwell headed the government until his death in 1658, but to many English citizens his rule was as dictatorial as an absolute monarch's. In 1660 the Stuart family was invited to take the throne once again. For twenty-five years, a period called the **Restoration,** Charles II ruled the nation. But when the Crown passed to his brother James II, an avowed Catholic, a second revolution occurred. This time, no blood was

---

Church of England   The Protestant church established in the sixteenth century by King Henry VIII as England's official church; also known as the Anglican Church.

Parliament   The lawmaking branch of the English government, composed of the House of Lords, representing England's nobility, and the House of Commons, an elected body of untitled English citizens.

Commonwealth   The republic established after the victory of Oliver Cromwell in the English civil war; the Commonwealth lasted from 1649 until the monarchy was restored in 1660.

Restoration   The era following the return of monarchy to England, beginning in 1660 with King Charles II and ending in 1688 with the exile of King James II.

shed in England. James fled to the safety of France, and his Protestant daughter Mary and her Dutch husband, William, came to the throne of England. This **Glorious Revolution** of 1688 ended almost a century of political, ideological, and economic instability. By then, twelve American colonies were already perched on the mainland shores.

Settling the Chesapeake

▪ What were the goals of the Virginia Company and of the Calvert family in creating their Chesapeake colonies? Did the colonies achieve these goals?

▪ What events illustrate the racial, class, and religious tensions in the Chesapeake?

▪ How did the Chesapeake colonists resolve conflicts within their communities?

Fears of financial ruin had prevented any Englishman from following in Sir Walter Raleigh's footsteps. But a new method of financing high-risk ventures, the **joint-stock company,** sparked new colonization efforts. English **entrepreneurs** had devised a way to share the burdens of potentially profitable but risky shipping deals. In a joint-stock company, merchants joined together and purchased shares in a venture. Any profits had to be shared by all, but likewise any losses would be absorbed by all. Two groups of investors realized that the same principles that were being applied to overseas commerce could also be applied to planting colonies. In 1603 both the Plymouth Company and the London Company appealed to King James I for a charter to settle Virginia. The king agreed to both requests.

Although in theory these two joint-stock companies were rivals, neither worried much about its settlements intruding on the other's. Virginia was, after all, a huge and vaguely defined region, covering much of the Atlantic coast of North America and extending from one ocean to the other. The Plymouth Company chose a poor site for its colony, however. The rocky coast of Maine proved uninviting to the settlers, and sickness and Indian attacks soon sent the survivors hurrying home to England. With its sole rival out of the way, the London Company (now calling itself simply the Virginia Company) launched its enterprise. The first colonists did not set out until December 1606, heading far to the south of the ill-fated Maine colony. Here, near the Chesapeake Bay, they would create the first successful English colony in America.

Glorious Revolution   A term used to describe the removal of James II from the English throne and the crowning of the Protestant monarchs, William and Mary.

joint-stock company   A business financed through the sale of shares of stock to investors; the investors share in both the profits and losses from a risky venture.

entrepreneur   A person who organizes and manages a business enterprise that involves risk and requires initiative.

The Jamestown Colony

The 101 men and four boys sent by the Virginia Company aboard the *Susan Constant,* the *Godspeed,* and the *Discovery* had been tossed on the Atlantic waters for over five months when they at last entered the calm, broad waters of the Chesapeake Bay and made their way up a river they would name the James in honor of their king. Happy at last to feel dry land under their feet, the men disembarked on a small peninsula that jutted out into the river (see Map 3.1). They named their settlement **Jamestown.** If they had known what lay in store for them in the next decade, they might have sailed home at once.

The early years of this Jamestown colony were a seemingly endless series of survival challenges. The colonists discovered, too late, that they had encamped in an unhealthy spot. Summer brought intense heat, and the men were attacked by swarms of insects, bred in the wetlands that surrounded them. The water of the James was polluted by ocean salt water, making it dangerous to drink. One by one, the settlers fell ill, suffering typhus, malaria, or dysentery. Few of the men had any experience in wilderness survival. Indeed, most were gentlemen adventurers, hoping to discover gold and other precious metals just as the Spanish had in Central and South America. These adventurers, as one Englishman bluntly put it, "never knew what a day's labour meant." They assumed that they could enslave the local Indians and force them to do all the "labour."

Had they known more about the local Indians, they might not have relied on this solution. The Powhatan Confederacy, made up of some thirty Algonquin-speaking tribes on the coastal plains, was a powerful force in the Indian world of the east coast of North America. The chief of the Powhatans had forged this confederacy in the 1570s, in response to Spanish attempts at colonization. When the English arrived, the confederacy was led by Wahunsonacock, who effectively controlled tidewater Virginia and the eastern shore of Chesapeake Bay. Although Wahunsonacock's Powhatan tribe had only about forty warriors, he could count on the assistance of some three thousand others, drawn from member tribes such as the Pamunkeys, Mattoponis, and Arrohatecks. While the English adventurers expended their energies on a futile search for gold rather than on building shelters or stockpiling food for the winter, the Indians harvested their corn—and waited to see what this group of Europeans would do.

What the English did was not impressive. Lacking any farming skills, disorganized, and unaccustomed to following orders or working hard, the colonists soon

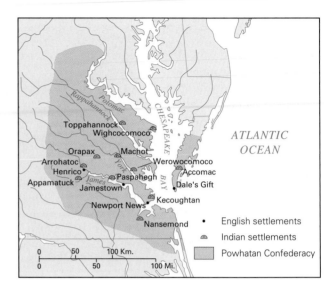

MAP 3.1 Early Chesapeake Settlement This map shows the location of both Indian and English colonial settlements in the early seventeenth century. As the English communities grew in number and size, conflicts between the Indians of the Powhatan Confederacy and the colonists also grew, eventually leading to warfare and considerable loss of life.

faced disease, starvation, and exposure to the elements. Temporary relief came when John Smith took command. Smith was hardly a well-liked man: he was overconfident and self-centered, full of exaggerated tales of his heroic deeds as a mercenary in exotic lands. He had narrowly escaped execution on the voyage from England for his role in organizing a mutiny. Smith did have some survival knowledge, however, and he did know how to discipline men. He established a "no work, no food" policy, and he negotiated with the Powhatans for corn and other supplies. When Smith left in 1609, the discipline and order he had established quickly collapsed. The original colonists and those who joined them the following spring remembered that winter as "the starving time." The desperate colonists burned their housing to keep warm and ate dogs, cats, mice, snakes, even shoe leather in their struggle to survive. Only sixty settlers were alive at winter's end.

The Powhatans had little sympathy for the desperate colonists. Even before Smith had departed, cooper-

Jamestown First permanent English settlement in mainland America, established in 1607 by the Virginia Company and named in honor of King James I.

ation between the two groups had begun to disintegrate, for despite all their problems, the English exhibited a sense of superiority and entitlement that alienated Wahunsonacock and his confederacy. By 1609 tension and resentment had turned to bloodshed, and raids and counterattacks defined Anglo-Indian relationships for over a decade. Wahunsonacock made several efforts to establish peace, but English encroachments on Indian lands made any lasting truce impossible. Wahunsonacock and his successor, Opechancanough, the chief of the Pamunkeys, recognized that dealing with the English colonists would require warfare, not words.

If the settlers were learning hard lessons in survival, the Virginia Company was learning hard lessons, too. The colony was hanging on by a thread, but the stockholders saw no profits. Their yearly expenses—passage for new colonists, supplies for old ones—gave them a new, more realistic understanding of the slow and costly nature of colonization. The Virginia Company seemed caught in an investor's nightmare, pumping good money after bad in hopes of delaying a total collapse. Prospects seemed bleak: the only gold the colonists had found was "fool's gold," and the investors could see nothing else of economic value in the Chesapeake.

Fortunately the investors were wrong. Tobacco, a weed native to the Americas, proved to be the colony's salvation. Pipe smoking had been a steady habit in England since the mid-sixteenth century, and Englishmen were a steady market for this "brown gold." The local strain of tobacco in Virginia was too harsh for English tastes, but one of the colonists, an enterprising young planter named John Rolfe, managed to transplant a milder strain of West Indian tobacco to the colony. This success changed Rolfe's life, earning him both wealth and the admiration of his neighbors. Rolfe made a second contribution to the colony soon afterward, easing the strained Indian-white relationships by his marriage to the same Indian princess, Pocahontas, who John Smith insisted had saved his life.

By 1612, the Virginia Colony was caught up in a tobacco craze as its settlers engaged in a mad race to plant and harvest as many acres of tobacco as possible. Yet the Virginia Company was unable to take full advantage of this unexpected windfall, for it had changed its policies in an effort to ease its financial burdens. In the beginning the company owned all the land but also bore all the costs of colonization. But by 1618, the company's new policy allowed individual colonists to own land if they paid their own immigration expenses. This **head right system** granted each

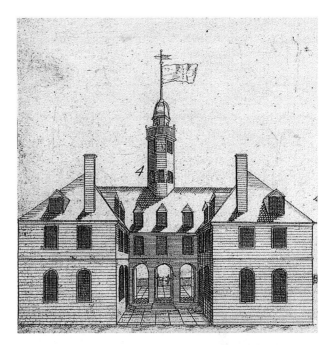

The Virginia House of Burgesses was the first representative assembly to be established in the British colonies. The legislators held their first session in a small Jamestown church, but by 1669, the tobacco planters who served in this assembly had moved into elegant quarters in the colonial capital of Williamsburg. The imposing building sent a clear message to all Virginians that government was the proper domain of gentlemen of wealth and social standing. *Library of Congress.*

male colonist a deed for 50 acres of land for himself and for every man, woman, or child whose voyage he financed. In this way the Virginia Company shifted the cost of populating and developing the colony to others. But the head rights also ended the company's monopoly on the suddenly valuable farmland.

Other important concessions to the colonists soon followed. The military-style discipline instituted by John Smith and continued by later leaders was abandoned. At the same time, a measure of self-government was allowed. In 1618 the company created an elected, representative lawmaking body called the **House of Burgesses,** which gave the landholders—tobacco

head right system The grant of 50 acres of land for each settler brought over to Virginia by a colonist.

House of Burgesses The elected lawmaking body of Virginia, established by the Virginia Company in 1618; the assembly first met in 1619.

planters—of Virginia a measure of control over local political matters. In effect, a business enterprise had finally become a colonial society.

The Virginia Company did retain one of the colony's earliest traditions: a bad relationship with the Powhatan Indians. By 1622, the English seemed to have the upper hand, for the population had grown and tobacco had brought a measure of prosperity. As Virginia planters pressed farther inland, seizing Indian land along local rivers, the new Powhatan chief, Opechancanough, decided to strike back. On what the Christian settlers called Good Friday, he mounted a deadly attack on Jamestown, killing a quarter of the colonists in a single day. The company responded as quickly as it could, sending weapons to the Virginians. For two years, war raged between Indians and the English. Although the bloodshed became less frequent by 1625, a final peace was not reached for a decade. By that time, disease and violence had taken its toll on the Powhatans. Once over forty thousand strong, they had dwindled to fewer than five hundred people.

The Good Friday Massacre, as the English called it, brought important changes for the colony. King James I had already begun an investigation of the Virginia Company's management record—and the colony's growing profit potential. When he learned of the renewed conflict between Indians and colonists, he decided to take action. The king took away the company's charter and declared Virginia to be a royal possession.

If the king's advisers had tallied the cost in human life for the planting of this first English colony in the same manner that the company tallied expenses in pence and pounds, they would have found the outcome sobering. By 1624, only 1,275 of the 8,500 settlers who had arrived since 1607 remained alive. Fortunately, no other English colony would pay such a price for its creation.

Maryland: A Catholic Refuge

As Virginians spread out along the riverways of their colony, searching for good tobacco land, plans for a second Chesapeake colony were brewing in England. The man behind this project was not a merchant or entrepreneur, and profit was not his motive. George Calvert, the wealthy Catholic who King Charles I had just made Lord Baltimore, was motivated by a strong concern for the fate of England's dwindling number of Catholics. He envisioned a religious refuge in America, a safe haven in the face of growing harassment and discrimination against members of his faith. Calvert acquired a charter from the king that granted him a generous tract of land east and north of Chesapeake Bay. Here, Calvert planned to establish a highly traditional society, dominated by powerful noblemen and populated by obedient tenant farmers. Thus, in the 1630s, George Calvert was a reactionary thinker with a radical vision.

Calvert never realized his dream. He died before a single colonist could be recruited for his Maryland.

Baltimore was founded in 1629 and served as a shipping center for Maryland tobacco growers. By 1752, when this view was drawn, it had begun to show signs of developing into a prosperous port city. After the American Revolution, Baltimore expanded and by the 1790s boasted a population of over twenty thousand. *"Baltimore 1752," from a sketch by John Moale, Esq. Maryland Historical Society, Baltimore.*

His oldest son, Cecilius Calvert, the second Lord Baltimore, took on the task of establishing the colony. To Calvert's surprise, few English Catholics showed any enthusiasm for the project. When the first boatload of colonists sailed up the Chesapeake Bay in 1634, most of these two hundred volunteers were young Protestants seeking a better life. Calvert wisely adopted the head right system developed by the Virginia Company to attract additional settlers. The lure of land ownership, he realized, was the key to populating Maryland.

Calvert's colony quickly developed along the same lines as neighboring Virginia. Marylanders immediately turned to planting the profitable **staple crop,** tobacco, and joined the scramble for good riverfront land. Like the Virginians, these colonists used trickery, threats, and violence to pry acres of potential farmland from resisting Indians. By midcentury, the Chesapeake colonies could claim a modest prosperity, even though their populations grew slowly. But they could not claim a peaceful existence. The political crises that shook England during the mid-seventeenth century sent shock waves across the Atlantic Ocean to the American shores. These crises intertwined with local tensions among colonists or between colonists and Indians to produce rebellions, raids, and civil wars.

Troubles on the Chesapeake

In Maryland, tensions ran high between the Catholic minority, who had political influence beyond their numbers because of Lord Baltimore's support, and the Protestant majority in the colony. But with the rise to power of the Puritan leader Oliver Cromwell and his Commonwealth government in England, Calvert realized that his power to protect Maryland's Catholics was in jeopardy. Hoping to avoid any open persecution of the Catholic colonists, Calvert offered religious toleration to both Protestant and Catholic Marylanders. In 1649 he issued the innovative Toleration Act, protecting all Christians from being "troubled [or] molested . . . in respect of his or her religion." Calvert's liberal policy offended the staunchly Puritan Cromwell, who promptly repealed the act. In 1654 the Puritan-dominated Parliament went further, seizing Maryland from the Calvert family and establishing a Protestant assembly in the colony. The outcome was exactly as Calvert had feared: a wave of anti-Catholic persecution swept over Maryland.

Within a year, a bloody civil war was raging in Maryland. Protestant forces won the fiercely fought Battle of the Severn, but their victory proved futile for, once again, events in England made their impact

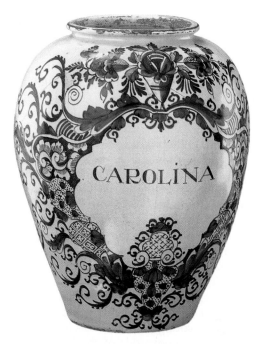

The ceramic jar shown above was used to store the tobacco that Europeans and Englishmen loved to smoke, sniff, or chew. Most of that tobacco was grown in Virginia and Maryland, in fields worked by slaves and servants on plantations owned by white colonists. The jar was valued both for its attractive appearance and its practical use, for it was elaborately decorated and it kept the tobacco fresh. It also served as a free advertisement for the "Carolina" brand of tobacco inside. *Colonial Williamsburg Foundation.*

felt on the colony. Oliver Cromwell died, and soon afterward the monarchy was restored. Charles II returned Maryland to the Calvert family, who had always been loyal supporters of the Stuart dynasty. Despite this reversal of fortunes, Protestants in Maryland continued their struggle, organizing unsuccessful rebellions in 1659, 1676, and again in 1681. Then, in 1689, William and Mary ascended to the throne of England in the Glorious Revolution, and Maryland's Protestants rallied once again. Led by an unlikely looking hero, the stooped and nearly crippled minister **John Coode,** colonists formed an army they called

---

staple crop   A basic or necessary agricultural item, produced for sale or export.

John Coode   Leader of a rebel army, the Protestant Association, that won control of Maryland in 1691.

the Protestant Association. By 1691, Coode had persuaded the Crown to make Maryland a royal colony. The story did not end here, however. In 1715 the fourth Lord Baltimore gave up the Catholic faith and joined the Church of England, leading the Crown to restore Maryland yet again to the Calverts.

Virginia was less affected by religious controversy than its neighbor. There, colonists were primarily Anglicans although small communities of Quakers, Puritans, and even members of the radical Dutch Labadist sect were scattered throughout Virginia. Religious differences, however, did not spark hostilities. Instead, the fault lines in Virginia society developed between the wealthy planters of the tidewater region and the ambitious newcomers seeking to make their fortunes in the backcountry.

The antagonism between the western, or backcountry, colonists and their more prosperous tidewater rivals was coming to a head as tobacco prices fell in the 1660s. It was in this highly volatile atmosphere that the brash young Nathaniel Bacon rose to challenge the established order of the Virginia Colony. While Bacon's rebellion ultimately failed after the death of its leader, many of the ideas behind the rebellion would resurface one hundred years later during the events leading up to the Revolutionary War.

Colonial Chesapeake Life

Every aspect of life in the Chesapeake colonies, observers noted, seemed to be shaped by tobacco. Its cultivation set rhythms of work and play in both Maryland and Virginia that were dramatically different from those in England. Planting, tending, harvesting, and drying tobacco leaves took almost ten months of the year, beginning in late winter and ending just before Christmas. In the short period between the holiday and the start of a new planting cycle, Chesapeake planters, their families, and their servants worked frantically to catch up on other, neglected farm chores. They did repairs, sewed and mended, built new cabins and sheds, cut timber and firewood. They also compressed what meager social life they had into these winter weeks, engaging—whenever possible—in hasty courtships followed by marriage.

Because tobacco quickly exhausted the soil in which it grew, planters moved frequently to new acres on their estates or to newly acquired lands farther west. Because they rarely stayed in one place very long, planters placed little value on permanent homes or on creating permanent social institutions such as schools. Throughout the century, Chesapeake colonists

sacrificed many of the familiar forms of community life to the demands of their profitable crop.

Planters engaged in an exhaustive search for a labor force large enough and cheap enough to ensure their profits. As long as poverty and social unrest plagued England, they found the workers they needed from their homeland. Over 175,000 young, single, and impoverished immigrants flooded the Chesapeake during the seventeenth century, their passages paid by the ship captain or the planter. In exchange for their transatlantic voyage, these **indentured servants** toiled for several years in the tobacco fields without pay. Planters preferred a male work force, for they shared the general European assumption that farming was a masculine activity. As a result, these colonies had an unusual population profile: men outnumbered women in most areas of Virginia and Maryland by 3 to 1. In some areas, the ratio was a remarkable 6 to 1 until the end of the century.

For these indentured servants, and often for their masters as well, life was short and brutal. They spent long, backbreaking days in the fields. Their food rations were meager, their clothing and bedding inadequate, and their shoulders frequently scarred by the master's whip. Servants wrote letters home describing their miserable existence. "People cry out day, and night," wrote one young man, who told his father that most servants would give up "any limb to be in England again."

Most servants also expressed doubts that they would survive to win their freedom. In many cases, they were correct. Disease and malnutrition took the lives of perhaps a quarter of these bound laborers. Free colonists fared little better than servants. Typhus, dysentery, and malaria killed thousands. Over one-quarter of the infants born in the Chesapeake did not live to see their first birthdays; another quarter of the population died before reaching the age of 20. Early death, the skewed ratio of men to women, and high infant mortality combined to create a **demographic disaster** that continued until the last decades of the century.

By the end of the 1600s, the labor force had become increasingly biracial. The steady supply of English

---

indentured servants Compulsory service for a fixed period of time, usually from four to seven years, most often agreed to in exchange for passage to the colonies; a labor contract called an indenture spelled out the terms of the agreement.

demographic disaster The outcome of a high death rate and an unbalanced ratio of men to women in the Chesapeake colonies.

workers dried up as economic conditions in England improved. At the same time, the cost of purchasing an African slave declined. During the next century, the shift from English servants to African slaves would be completed.

New England: Colonies of Dissenters

- Why did English religious dissenters settle in New England?
- What type of society did the Puritans create in Massachusetts?
- How did the Puritan authorities deal with dissent?

While Captain John Smith was barking orders at the settlers in Jamestown, some religious dissenters in a small English village were preparing to escape King James's wrath. These residents of Scrooby Village were people of modest means, without powerful political allies or a popular cause. But they had gone one step further than the majority of Puritans, who continued to be members of the Anglican Church despite their criticisms of it. The Scrooby villagers had left the church altogether, forming a separate sect of their own. James I despised these **separatists** and declared his intention to drive them out of England—or worse.

The Scrooby separatists took James's threats seriously. In 1611 they fled to the city of Leyden in the Netherlands. They saw themselves as **Pilgrims** on a spiritual journey to religious freedom. The Dutch welcomed them warmly, but several Pilgrims feared that the comfortable life they had found in Holland was diminishing their devotion to God. By 1620, **William Bradford** was leading a small group of these transplanted English men and women on a second pilgrimage—to America.

The Plymouth Colony

The Leyden Pilgrims were joined by other separatists in England. Together, they set sail on an old, creaky ship called the *Mayflower*. On board, too, were a band of "strangers," outsiders to the religious sect who simply wanted passage to America. Crammed together in close and uncomfortable quarters, Pilgrims and strangers weathered a nightmare of violent storms and choppy waters. After nine weeks at sea, the captain anchored the *Mayflower* at Cape Cod, almost 1,000 miles north of the original Virginia destination (see Map 3.2). The exhausted passengers did not complain; they fell to the ground to give thanks. Once

The Bible was the most cherished book, and often the only book, in a colonist's home. To safeguard this treasure, many Pilgrims stored their Bibles in hand-carved boxes like this one belonging to William Bradford. This box, once decorated with the lion and unicorn symbol of England, was politicized during the American Revolution, when the British lion was scraped off. *Pilgrim Society, Pilgrim Hall Museum.*

the thrill of standing on dry land had passed, however, many of them sank into depression. The early winter landscape of New England was dreary, alien, and disturbingly empty. William Bradford's own wife, Dorothy, may have committed suicide in the face of this bleak landscape.

Talk of setting sail for Virginia spread through the ranks of the ship's crew and the passengers. Mutiny was in the air. To calm the situation, Bradford negotiated an unusual contract with every man aboard the ship—Pilgrim, crew, servant, and stranger.

This document, known as the **Mayflower Compact,** granted political rights to any man willing to remain

---

separatists English Protestants who chose to leave the Church of England because they believed it was corrupt.

Pilgrims A small group of separatists who left England in search of religious freedom and sailed to America on the *Mayflower* in 1620.

William Bradford The separatist who led the Pilgrims to America; he became the first governor of Plymouth Plantations.

Mayflower Compact An agreement drafted in 1620 when the Pilgrims reached America that granted political rights to all male colonists who would abide by the colony's laws.

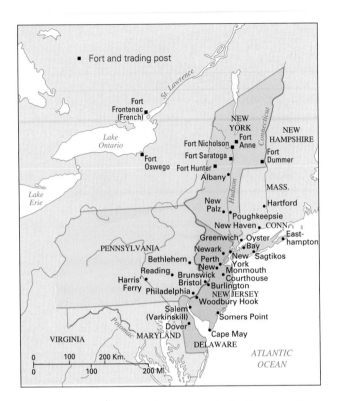

■ Fort and trading post

MAP 3.2 **New England Settlement in the Seventeenth and Early Eighteenth Centuries**   This map shows the major towns and cities of New England and their settlement dates. By the end of the seventeenth century, the region had four colonies. Colonists seeking land moved west and south toward the New York border and north toward French Canada. Those involved in trade, shipping, and crafts migrated to the seaport cities.

and to abide by whatever laws the new colony enacted. Here was an unheard-of opportunity for poor men to participate in governing themselves. All agreed, and the new colony of Plymouth Plantations began to prepare for the long winter ahead.

In Plymouth Plantations, as in Virginia, the first winter brought sickness, hunger, and death. Half of the colonists did not survive. When a Patuxet Indian, **Squanto,** came upon the remaining men and women in the spring of 1621, he found them huddled in flimsy shelters, trapped between a menacing forest and a dangerous ocean. Squanto sympathized with their confusion and their longings for home, for he had crossed the Atlantic in 1605 aboard an English trading ship and spent several years in an alien environment. He also understood what it meant to be a survivor, for the Pilgrims had settled where his own village had once stood. His entire family and tribe had been wiped out by disease carried by English traders and fishermen.

Squanto helped the colonists, teaching them how to plant corn, squash, and pumpkins. Perhaps his greatest service, however, was in helping William Bradford negotiate a peace treaty with Massasoit, leader of the local Wampanoag Indians. Agreeing that "if any did unjustly war against him, we would aid him," the Pilgrims got a similar pledge of assistance from Massasoit. The Wampanoags also agreed to spread the word to neighboring Indian communities that the Pilgrims were allies rather than enemies. The combined efforts of Squanto and Massasoit saved the Plymouth Colony, and in the fall of 1621, English settlers and Indian guests sat down together in a traditional harvest celebration of thanksgiving.

Plymouth grew slowly, its colonists earning their livings by farming, fishing, and lumbering. A few Pilgrims grew wealthy by developing a fur trade with the Indians. Unlike the Jamestown settlers, the Plymouth community worked hard for many years to preserve good relations with the local Indians. They purchased land rather than seizing it, and they proved to be strong allies when warfare broke out between Massasoit's people and their enemies. In fact, the colonists proved to be such ferocious fighters that they were known as Wotoroguenarge, or "Cutthroats."

Massachusetts Bay and Its Settlers

A second colony soon appeared beside Plymouth Plantations. In 1629 a group of prosperous Puritans, led by the 41-year-old lawyer and landowner **John Winthrop,** secured a charter for their Massachusetts Bay Company from King Charles I. These Puritans had grown increasingly worried about the government's attitude toward dissenters. The systematic harassment they suffered, coupled with a deepening economic depression in England, spurred them to set sail for New England. Advertising their colony as "a refuge for many who [God] means to save out of the general calamity," Winthrop and his colleagues had no trouble recruiting like-minded Puritans to migrate.

From the beginning, the Massachusetts Bay Colony had several advantages over Jamestown and Plymouth

Squanto   A Patuxet Indian who taught the Pilgrims survival techniques in America and acted as translator for the colonists.

John Winthrop   One of the founders of Massachusetts Bay Colony and the colony's first governor.

This statue of Anne Hutchinson conveys her as a courageous and determined woman. Massachusetts Bay's Puritan officials would not have approved. They considered her a dangerous heretic who overstepped her proper place as a woman by challenging the established religious and political authorities. Like Roger Williams, Anne Hutchinson was exiled from the colony for her unorthodox views. *Picture Research Consultant & Archives.*

Plantations. The colonists were well equipped and well prepared for their venture. The company had even sent an advance crew over to clear fields and build shelters for the newcomers. As religious tensions and economic distress increased in England, Massachusetts attracted thousands of settlers. This **Great Migration** continued until Oliver Cromwell's Puritan army took control of England.

While profit motivated the Virginia colonists and a desire to worship in peace prompted the Pilgrims to sail to America, the Puritans of Massachusetts were people with a mission. They hoped to create a model Christian community, a "city upon a hill" that would persuade all English men and women that Puritanism promoted godliness and prosperity. John Winthrop set out their mission in a speech to the passengers aboard the *Arabella*. "The eyes of all peoples are upon us," Winthrop warned, and, more importantly, God was watching them as well. If they abandoned or forgot their mission, the consequences would surely include divine punishment.

This sense of mission influenced the physical as well as spiritual shape of the colony. Massachusetts colonists created tight-knit farming villages and small seaport towns in which citizens could monitor one another's behavior as well as come together in prayer. This settlement pattern fit well with the realities of New England's climate and terrain, since the short growing season and the rocky soil made large, isolated plantations based on staple crops impossible. The colonists, homesick for English villages in regions such as East Anglia, did their best to reproduce familiar architecture and placement of public buildings. The result was often a hub-and-spoke design, with houses tightly clustered around a village green or common pasture, a church beside this green, and most of the fields and farms within walking distance of this village center. This design set natural limits on the size of any village because beyond a certain point— usually measured in a winter's walk to church—a farm family was considered outside the community circle. As a town's population grew and the available farmland was farther from the village green, settlers on the outer rim of the town usually chose to create a new community for themselves. The Puritans called this process of establishing a new village "hiving off."

Like Massachusetts, New Haven and the other New England settlements that followed were societies of families. Many, although not all, of the colonists arriving during the Great Migration came as members of a family. Of course, each ship carried unmarried male and female servants too, but unlike in the Chesapeake, the gender ratio in the northern colonies was never dramatically skewed. Imbalances between the sexes did occur in border towns decimated by war with the Indians or in older communities where land was scarce and the young men ventured farther west. On the whole, however, the number of men and women

Great Migration The movement of Puritans from England to America in the 1630s, caused by political and religious unrest in England.

was roughly equal. And, unlike their Chesapeake counterparts, New Englanders never endured a demographic disaster. The cool temperatures and clean drinking water made the region an extremely healthy place for Europeans, healthier than England itself. Infant mortality was low, and most children lived to reach marriageable age and produce families of their own. A couple could expect to live a long life together and raise a family of five to seven children. One outcome of this longevity was a rare phenomenon in the seventeenth-century English world: grandparents.

Both Puritans and neighboring Pilgrims spoke of the family as "a little commonwealth," the building block on which the larger society was constructed. They set a high priority on obedience in child rearing, in part because they believed that sinfulness and disobedience were the twin results of **original sin.** Breaking a child's will was thus a necessary step toward ensuring the child's salvation. The larger society actively supported a parent's right to demand respect and a child's duty to obey. In fact, Massachusetts law made criticizing a parent a crime punishable by death. The penalty was rarely administered, but the existence of such a harsh law shows the importance of obedience within the family.

A wife was also expected to obey her husband. Puritan ministers reinforced this ideal of a **hierarchy,** or well-defined chain of command, within a family. "Wives," they preached, "are part of the House and Family, and ought to be under a Husband's Government: they should Obey their own Husbands." A husband, however, was bound by sacred obligations to care for and be respectful toward his wife. He must rule his household, he was instructed, without "rigour, haughtiness, harshness, severity; but with the greatest love, gentleness, kindness, tenderness." Marriage involved many practical duties as well. Wives were expected to strive to be "notable housewives"—industrious, economical managers of resources and skilled at several crafts. They were to spin yarn, sew, cook, bake, pickle, butcher farm animals, cure meat, churn butter, and set cheeses. In close-knit New England communities, women were able to help one another by exchanging butter for eggs, assisting with a neighbor's childbirth, or nursing the sick back to health. Husbands were expected to labor in the fields, or in the shop, in order to provide for their families.

Although obligated to be tender and loving, the husband controlled the resources of the family. This was true in all English colonies, although in the Chesapeake, early death often left the wife in charge of the family farm or shop and its profits until sons came of age. Under English law, a married woman, or *femme couverte,* lost many of her legal rights because she came under the protection and governance of her husband. Married women could not acquire, sell, or bequeath property to another person. They could not sue or be sued or claim the use of any wages they earned. They could gain such basic legal rights only through special contracts made with their husbands. Puritan communities, however, frowned on any such arrangements. In the "little commonwealth" of the family, a man was the undisputed head of the household and thus had authority over all its economic resources and all its members. He also represented the family's interests in the realm of politics. No matter how wise or wealthy a woman might become, she was denied a political voice.

Government in Puritan Massachusetts

In order to create the "city upon a hill" the directors of the Massachusetts Bay Company needed, and expected, the full cooperation of all colonists. This did not mean that all colonists had an equal voice or an equal role in fulfilling this vision of a perfect community. During his speech aboard the *Arabella,* John Winthrop made it clear that the "wilderness Zion" was not intended to be an egalitarian society. Like most of his audience, Winthrop believed that it was natural and correct for some people to be rich and some to be poor—"some high and eminent in power and dignity, others mean and in subjugation." Women, children, servants, young men, and adult men without property owed obedience to others in most English communities. But in Massachusetts, there were further limitations on participation. Not even all free males with property were granted a voice in governing the colony. The first government, in fact, consisted solely of Winthrop and the eleven other stockholders of the company who had emigrated to New England. Later, the company relaxed its control and allowed a

---

original sin   In Christian doctrine, the condition of sinfulness that all humans share because of Adam and Eve's disobedience to God in the Garden of Eden.

hierarchy   A system in which people or things are ranked above one another.

femme couverte   From the French for "covered woman"; a legal term for a married woman; this legal status limited women's rights, denying them the right to sue or be sued, own or sell property, or earn wages.

representative assembly to be elected, but the qualifications for political participation in electing these representatives or serving in the assembly were dramatically different from those set by Maryland or Virginia. No man in Massachusetts had a full political voice unless he was an acknowledged church member, not just a churchgoer. Church membership, or **sainthood,** was granted only after a person testified to an experience of "saving grace," a moment of intense awareness of God's power and a reassuring conviction of personal salvation. Thus Massachusetts made religious qualifications as important as gender or economic status in the colony's political life.

Massachusetts differed from the Chesapeake colonies in other significant ways. The colony's government enforced biblical law as well as English civil and criminal law. This meant that the government regulated a colonist's religious beliefs and practices, style of dress, sexual conduct, and personal behavior. For example, every colonist was required to attend church and to observe the Sabbath as Puritan custom dictated. The church played a role in supervising business dealings, parent-child relationships, and marital life.

In the early decades of the colony, the Puritan sense of mission left little room for religious toleration. Colonial leaders saw no reason to welcome anyone who disagreed with their religious views. English America was large, they argued, and people of other faiths could settle elsewhere. Winthrop's government was particularly aggressive against members of a new sect called the **Quakers,** who came to Massachusetts on a mission of their own—to convert Puritans to their faith. Quakers entering the colony were beaten, imprisoned, or branded with hot irons. If they returned, they were hanged. Puritan leaders showed just as little tolerance toward members of their own communities who criticized or challenged the rules of the Bay Colony or the beliefs of its church. They drove out men and women who they perceived to be **heretics,** or religious traitors, including Roger Williams and Anne Hutchinson.

Almost anyone could be labeled a heretic—even a Puritan minister. Only a year after the colony was established, the church at Salem invited **Roger Williams** to serve as its assistant minister. His electrifying sermons and his impressive knowledge of Scripture attracted a devoted following. But he soon attracted the attention of local authorities as well, for his sermons were highly critical of the colonial government. From his pulpit, Williams condemned political leaders for seizing Indian land, calling their tactics of intimidation and violence a "National Sinne." He also denounced laws requiring church attendance.

True religious faith, he said, was a matter of personal commitment. It could not and should not be compelled. "Forced religion," he told his congregation, "stinks in God's nostrils."

In 1635 John Winthrop's government banished Roger Williams from the colony. With snow thick on the ground, Williams left Salem and sought refuge with the Narragansett Indians. When spring came, many of his Salem congregation joined him in exile. Together, in 1635, they created a community called Providence that welcomed dissenters of all kinds, including Quakers, Jews, and Baptists.

Providence also attracted other Massachusetts colonists tired of the tight controls imposed on their lives by Winthrop and his colleagues. In 1644 the English government granted Williams a charter for his colony, which he eventually called Rhode Island. Within their borders, Rhode Islanders firmly established the principle of separation of church and state.

Soon after the Massachusetts authorities rid the colony of Roger Williams, a new challenge to their religious precepts and theocratic government arose. In 1634 Puritan **Anne Hutchinson,** her husband, William, and their several children emigrated to Massachusetts. The Hutchinsons made an impressive addition to the colonial community. He was a successful merchant. She had received an exceptionally fine education from her father and was eloquent, witty, and well versed in Scripture. In addition, she was clearly knowledgeable about the religious debates of the day. Like Williams, Hutchinson put little stock in the power of a minister or in any rules of behavior to assist an individual in his or her search for salvation.

---

sainthood   Full membership in a Puritan church.

Quakers   Members of the Society of Friends, a radical Protestant sect that believed in the equality of men and women, pacifism, and the presence of a divine "inner light" in every individual.

heretic   A person who does not behave in accordance with an established attitude, doctrine, or principle, usually in religious matters.

Roger Williams   Puritan minister banished from Massachusetts for criticizing its religious rules and government policies; in 1635, he founded Providence, a community based on religious freedom and the separation of church and state.

Anne Hutchinson   A religious leader banished from Massachusetts in 1636 because of her criticism of the colonial government and what were judged to be heretical beliefs.

She believed that only God's grace could save a person's soul. And she declared that God made a "covenant of grace," or a promise of salvation, that did not depend on any church, minister, or worship service.

Hutchinson's opinions, aired in popular meetings at her home, disturbed the Puritan authorities. That she was a woman made her outspoken defiance even more shocking. Men like John Winthrop believed that women ought to be silent in the church and had no business criticizing male authorities, particularly ministers and **magistrates,** or government officials. A surprising number of Puritans, however, were untroubled by Hutchinson's sex. Male merchants and craftsmen who lacked political rights because they were not members of the saintly elect welcomed her attacks on these authorities. Hutchinson also attracted Puritan saints who resented the tight grip of the colonial government on their business, personal, and social lives.

In the end, none of Hutchinson's supporters could protect her against the determined opposition of the Puritan leadership. In 1637 she was arrested and brought to trial. Although she was in the last months of a troubled pregnancy, her judges forced her to stand throughout their long, exhausting, repetitive examination. Hutchinson seemed to be winning the battle of words despite her physical discomfort, but eventually she blundered. In one of her answers, she seemed to claim that she had direct communication with God. Such a claim went far beyond the acceptable bounds of Puritan belief. Triumphantly, John Winthrop and his colleagues declared her a heretic, "unfit to our society." They banished her from Massachusetts. Even after her departure, the government seemed to worry about her influence. They encouraged rumors that she was a witch and claimed that the miscarriage she suffered shortly after the trial indicated a demonic fetus.

Many Puritans who left Massachusetts did so by choice, not because they were banished. For example, in 1636 the Reverend Thomas Hooker and his entire Newton congregation abandoned Massachusetts and resettled in the Connecticut River valley. They sought freedom from Winthrop's domination, and the richer soils of the river valley attracted them. Other Puritan congregations followed these Newton families. By 1639 the Connecticut Valley towns of Hartford, Wethersfield, and Windsor had drafted their own governments, and in 1644 they united with the Saybrook settlement at the mouth of the Connecticut River to create the colony of Connecticut. In 1660 the independent New Haven community joined them.

Other Bay colonists, searching for new or better lands, made their way north to what later became Maine and New Hampshire. New Hampshire settlers won a charter for their own colony in 1679, but Maine remained part of Massachusetts until it became a state in 1820.

Indian Suppression

Although the Puritan colonists hoped to create a godly community, they were often motivated by greed and jealousy. Between 1636 and the 1670s, New Englanders came into conflict with one another over desirable land. They also waged particularly violent warfare against the Indians of the region.

When the Connecticut Valley towns sprang up, for example, Winthrop tried to assert Bay Colony authority over them. His motives were personal: he and his friends had expected to develop the valley area lands themselves someday. The Connecticut settlers ignored Winthrop's claims and successfully rebuffed his attempts to block their independence from Massachusetts. But they could not ignore the Indians of the area, who understood clearly the threat that English settlers posed to their territories and their way of life. Sassacus, leader of the Pequots, hoped that an armed struggle would break out between Winthrop and the new Connecticut towns, destroying them both. Instead, however, the two English rivals concentrated on destroying the Pequots.

By 1636, the **Pequot War** had begun, with the Indians under attack from both Massachusetts and Connecticut armies and their Indian allies, the Narragansetts and the Mohicans. Mounting a joint effort, the colonists targeted the Pequot town of Mystic Village. Although the village was defenseless and contained only civilians, Captain John Mason gave the orders for the attack. Captain John Underhill of the Massachusetts army recorded the slaughter with obvious satisfaction: "Many [Pequots] were burnt in the fort, both men, women, and children." When the survivors tried to surrender to the Narragansetts, Puritan soldiers killed them. The brutal war did not end

---

magistrate   A civil officer charged with administering the law.

Pequot War   Conflict in 1636 between the Pequot Indians inhabiting eastern Connecticut and the colonists of Massachusetts Bay and Connecticut: the Indians were destroyed and driven from the area.

No portrait of Metacomet, or King Philip, was painted during his lifetime. In this nineteenth-century painting, Metacomet wears traditional New England Indian clothing, yet he is armed with a European musket. This provides a stark reminder that even the bitterest enemies borrowed from one another's culture. *Library of Congress.*

settlements, the colonists retaliated by burning Indian crops and villages and selling Indian captives into slavery. By the end of the year, Metacomet had forged an alliance with the Narragansetts and several small regional tribes. Metacomet's early, devastating raids on white settlements terrified the colonists, but soon the casualties grew on both sides. Atrocities were committed by everyone involved in this struggle, which the English called King Philip's War. With the help of Iroquois troops sent by the governor of New York, the colonists finally defeated the Wampanoags. Metacomet was murdered, and his head was impaled on a stick.

Indian objections to colonial expansion in New England had been silenced. Indeed, few native peoples remained to offer resistance of any sort. Several tribes had been wiped out entirely in the war, or their few survivors sold into slavery in the Caribbean. Those who escaped enslavement or death scattered to the north and the west. The victory had cost the English dearly also. More than two thousand New England colonists lost their lives as the war spread from Plymouth to nearby settlements. And the war left a legacy of hate that prompted Indian tribes west of Massachusetts to block Puritan expansion whenever possible. The costs of New England's Indian policy prompted colonial leaders in other regions to try less aggressive tactics in dealing with local Indians. For the Wampanoags, the Narragansetts, and the Pequots, however, this decision came too late.

Change and Reaction in England and New England

Both Pilgrim and Puritan leaders had expected the broad expanse of the Atlantic Ocean to protect their colonies from the political turmoil and religious tensions that wracked seventeenth-century England. Like their Chesapeake counterparts, both were wrong. From the beginning, of course, Puritan migration to New England had been prompted by Charles I's

until all the Pequot men had been killed and the women and children sold into slavery. Connecticut claimed credit for this victory and, despite the massacre at Mystic, Massachusetts grudgingly conceded. If the Narragansett Indians believed their alliance with Winthrop provided some protection against English aggression, they were mistaken. Within five years the Puritans had assassinated the Narragansett chief, an act of insurance against problems with these Indian allies.

For almost three decades, an uneasy peace existed between New England colonists and Indians. But the struggle over the land continued. When war broke out again, it was two longtime allies—the Plymouth colonists and the Wampanoags—who took up arms against each other. By 1675, the friendship between these two groups had been eroded by Pilgrim demands for new Indian lands. Chief **Metacomet,** known to the English as King Philip, made the difficult decision to resist. When Metacomet used **guerrilla tactics** effectively, staging raids on white

> **Metacomet** A Wampanoag chief, known to the English as King Philip, who led the Indian resistance to colonial expansion in New England in 1675.
>
> **guerrilla tactics** A method of warfare in which small bands of fighters in occupied territory harass and attack their enemies, often in surprise raids; the Indians used these tactics during King Philip's War.

hostility to dissenters. When Oliver Cromwell and his Puritan armies challenged the Stuart king in 1642, Bay Colony settlers rejoiced. Many chose to return home to fight with Cromwell's armies. Throughout the decade, the Massachusetts population shrank.

Massachusetts faced a crisis in the post–civil war years. The sense of mission and the religious commitment that had accompanied its founding seemed to be declining. Few native-born colonists petitioned for full membership, or sainthood, in their local churches, perhaps because of their growing involvement with trade and commerce. And few new saints migrated to the Bay Colony after Cromwell's victory or during the Restoration era. In fact, most of the newcomers in the 1660s were not Puritans at all but Anglicans or members of other Protestant groups seeking economic opportunities. The Bay Colony leaders could not prevent them from settling, as John Winthrop had once done, for King Charles II would not allow it.

The decline in religious zeal troubled ministers and government officials alike, for it marked a sharp decline in eligible voters and officeholders. It troubled the saints, who feared their own children would never join the church and thus never become full citizens in the colony. The problem was made worse by the growing demands of prosperous non-Puritan men for an active role in the government. Some towns began to compromise, allowing men of property and good standing in the community to participate in local decision making. But the saints were not willing to set aside the church membership requirement. In 1662 they decided to introduce the **Half-Way Covenant,** an agreement that allowed the children of church members to join the church even if they did not make a convincing declaration of their own salvation. This compromise kept political power in the hands of Puritans—for the moment.

Pressures from England could not be dealt with so easily, however. Charles II cast a doubtful eye on a colony that sometimes ignored English civil law if it conflicted with biblical demands. In 1683 Charles insisted that the Bay Colony revise its charter to weaken the influence of biblical teachings and eliminate the stringent voting requirements. The Massachusetts government said no. With that, Charles revoked the charter. Massachusetts remained in political limbo until 1685, when James II came to the throne. Then conditions worsened.

In an effort to centralize administration of his growing American empire, King James II combined several of the northern colonies into one large unit under direct royal control. This megacolony, the Do-

minion of New England, included Massachusetts, Rhode Island, Connecticut, Plymouth Plantations, and the newly acquired colonies of New Jersey and New York. James expected the Dominion to increase the **patronage,** or political favors, he could provide to his loyal supporters—favors such as generous land grants or colonial administrative appointments. He also expected to increase revenues by imposing duties and taxes on colonial goods in the vast region he now controlled.

What King James did not expect was how strongly colonists resented his Dominion and the man he chose to govern it. That man was the arrogant and greedy Sir Edmund Andros. Andros immediately offended New England Puritans by establishing the Church of England as the official religion of the new colony. Then he added insult to injury by commandeering a Puritan church in Boston for Anglican worship. Andros also alienated many non-Puritans in Massachusetts by abolishing the representative assembly there. These men had been struggling to be included in the assembly, not to have the assembly dismantled. Andros's high-handed tactics united Massachusetts colonists who had been at odds with each other. One sign of this cooperation surfaced when the Dominion governor imposed new taxes: saints and nonsaints alike refused to pay them.

When Boston citizens received news of the Glorious Revolution, they imprisoned Edmund Andros and shipped him back to England to stand trial as a traitor to the nation's new Protestant government. Massachusetts Puritans hoped to be rewarded for their patriotism, but they were quickly disappointed. Although William and Mary abolished the Dominion, they chose not to restore the Bay Colony charter. In 1691 Massachusetts became a royal colony, its governor appointed by the Crown. **Suffrage,** or voting rights, was granted to all free males who met

---

Half-Way Covenant   An agreement (1662) that gave partial membership in Puritan churches to the children of church members even if they had not had a "saving faith" experience.

Dominion of New England   A megacolony created in 1686 by James II that brought Massachusetts, Plymouth Plantations, Connecticut, Rhode Island, New Jersey, and New York under the control of one royal governor; William and Mary dissolved the Dominion when they came to the throne in 1689.

patronage   Jobs or favors distributed on a political basis, usually as rewards for loyalty or service.

suffrage   The right to vote.

the standard English **property requirement.** Church membership would never again be a criterion for citizenship in the colony.

Over the course of its sixty-year history, Massachusetts had undergone many significant changes. The Puritan ideal of small, tightly knit farming communities whose members worshiped together and shared common values and goals had been replaced for many colonists by an emerging "Yankee" ideal of trade and commerce, bustling seaport cities, diverse beliefs, and a more secular, or nonreligious, orientation to daily life. This transition increased tensions in every community, especially during the difficult years of the 1680s. Those tensions were the context for one of the most dramatic events in the region's history: the Salem witch trials.

In 1692 a group of young women and girls in Salem Village began to show signs of what seventeenth-century society diagnosed as bewitchment. They fell into violent fits, contorting their bodies and showing great emotional distress. Under questioning, they named several local women, including a West Indian slave named Tituba, as their tormentors. The conviction that the devil had come to Massachusetts spread quickly, and the number of people accused of witchcraft mushroomed. By summer, more than a hundred women, men, and children were crowded into local jails, awaiting trial. Accusations, trials, and even executions—nineteen in all—continued until the new royal governor, Sir William Phips, arrived in the colony and forbade any further arrests. Phips dismissed the court that had passed judgment based on "spectral evidence"—that is, testimony by the alleged victims that they had seen the spirits of the accused tormenting them. In January 1693, Phips assembled a new court that acquitted the remaining prisoners.

The witch trials expressed the struggle between saintly Puritan farmers of Salem Village and the town's more worldly merchants: the accusers were invariably members of the farming community; the accused were often associated with commercial activities. Nevertheless, the witch-hunts reflected the belief among people—whether farmers or merchants—that the devil and his disciples could work great harm in a community.

The Pluralism of the Middle Colonies

■ Why did the Dutch and the English encourage a multicultural population in New York?

■ What cultural and economic tensions came to a head in Leisler's Rebellion?

■ What made William Penn's vision for Pennsylvania so distinctive?

Between the Chesapeake and New England lay the vast stretch of forest and farmland called New Netherland, a Dutch colony that was home to settlers from Holland, Sweden, Germany, and France. In the 1660s, Charles II seized the area and drove the Dutch from the Atlantic coast of North America. The English divided the conquered territory into three colonies: New York, New Jersey, and Pennsylvania. Although the region changed hands, it did not change its character: the Middle Colonies remained a multicultural, commercially oriented, and competitive society no matter whose flag flew over them.

From New Amsterdam to New York

Before 1650, Europe's two major Protestant powers had maintained a degree of cooperation, and their American colonies remained on friendly terms, assisting each other, for example, in conflicts with Indians. But a growing rivalry over the transatlantic trade and conflicting land claims in the Connecticut Valley soon eroded this neighborliness. Beginning in 1652, England and Holland fought three naval wars as both nations tried to control the transatlantic trade in raw materials and manufactured goods. After each, the Dutch lost ground, and their decline made it likely that the New Netherland settlement would be abandoned.

King Charles II of England wanted New Netherland very much, and James, Duke of York (later King James II), was eager to satisfy his brother's desires. In 1664 Charles agreed to give James control of the region lying between the Connecticut and Delaware Rivers—if James could wrest it from the Dutch (see Map 3.3). The promise and the prize amounted to a declaration of war on New Netherland.

When the duke's four armed ships arrived in New Amsterdam harbor and aimed their cannon at the town, Governor Peter Stuyvesant tried to rally the local residents to resist. They refused. Life under the English, they reasoned, would probably be no worse than life under the Dutch. Perhaps it might be better. The humiliated governor surrendered the colony, and

> **property requirement** The limitation of voting rights to citizens who own certain kinds or amounts of property.

This portrait of Peter Stuyvesant, the governor of the Dutch colony of New Netherland, was painted by Henrick Courturier when the feisty Stuyvesant was fifty years old. Stuyvesant governed with a heavy hand, flying into a rage if colonists challenged his decisions. He was not popular, but he did bring much-needed order to the colony. *New York Historical Society.*

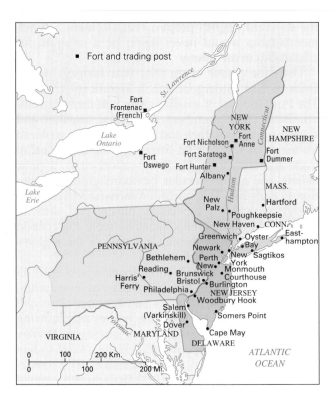

MAP 3.3 The Middle Colonies   This map shows the major towns, cities, and forts in the colonies of New York, Pennsylvania (including Delaware), and New Jersey. The prosperity of the region was based on the thriving commerce of its largest cities, Philadelphia and New York, and on the commercial production of wheat.

in 1664 New Netherland became New York without a shot being fired.

James proved to be a very liberal ruler, allowing the Dutch and other European colonists to keep their lands, practice their religions, and conduct their business in their native languages. But the duke's generosity and tolerance did not extend to taxation matters. James saw his colonists much as his brother the king saw every colonist: as a source of personal revenue. James taxed New Yorkers heavily and allowed no representative assembly that might interfere with his use of the treasury. All political offices in the new colony, high or low, went to the duke's friends, creating a patronage system that impressed even King Charles.

James's colony did not develop as he had hoped, however. Settlement did not expand to the north and east as he wished. He could not enlist the aid of influential New Yorkers in his expansion plans, even though he offered them the incentive of a representative assembly in 1682. By 1685, James—now king of England—had lost interest in the colony, abandoning his schemes for its growth and abolishing the representative assembly as well.

Leisler's Rebellion

Although James viewed New York as a failure, the colony actually grew rapidly during his rule. The population doubled between 1665 and 1685, reaching fifteen thousand the year the duke ascended to the English throne. These new settlers added to the cultural diversity that had always characterized the region. The colony became a religious refuge for French

Protestants, English Quakers, and Scottish **Presbyterians.** New York's diverse community, however, did not always live in harmony. English, Dutch, and German merchants competed fiercely for control of New York City's trade and for dominance in the city's cultural life. An equally intense rivalry existed between Manhattan's merchants and Albany's fur traders. Only one thing united these competitors: a burning resentment of James's political control and the men he chose to enforce his will. Their anger increased when James created the Dominion of New England, merging New York with the Puritan colonies.

In 1689 news of the Glorious Revolution prompted a revolt in New York City similar to the one that shook Boston. **Jacob Leisler,** a German merchant, emerged as its leader. Although Leisler lacked the charisma and commanding presence that had allowed Nathaniel Bacon to rise to power in 1667, he was able to take control of the entire colony. Acting in the name of the new English monarchs, William and Mary, he not only removed Dominion officials but imprisoned several of his local opponents, declaring them enemies of Protestantism. He then called for city elections to oust James's remaining appointees. Leisler expected an era of home rule to follow his rebellion, but England's new monarchs had no intention of leaving a local merchant in charge of a royal colony. When William and Mary sent a new governor to New York, Leisler refused to surrender the reins of government. This time, the abrasive, headstrong merchant found few supporters, and eventually he was forced to step down. To Leisler's surprise, he was then arrested and charged with treason. Both he and his son-in-law were tried, found guilty, and executed. As befit traitors in the seventeenth century, the two rebels were hanged, disemboweled while still alive, and then beheaded. Afterward, their mutilated bodies were quartered. In death, Leisler became a hero and a martyr. Popular anger was so great that to quiet the discontent, the new governor had to permit formation of a representative assembly. Several of the men elected to this new legislature were ardent Leislerians, and for many years New York politics remained a battleground between home rule advocates and supporters of the royal governor and the king.

William Penn's Holy Experiment

More than most dissenting sects, Quakers had paid a high price for their strongly held convictions. Members of the Society of Friends had been jailed in England and Scotland and harassed by their neighbors throughout the empire. Quaker leaders had strong

William Penn was about 50 years old when this chalk drawing was done. Although Pennsylvania was famous for its religious tolerance and welcoming of non-English immigrants, Penn held many views in common with New England's Puritan leaders. He believed that government should impose and enforce a moral code, because drunkenness, luxury, gambling, and cursing were not only "sins against Nature" but "sins against Government." *"William Penn" by Francis Place. The Historical Society of Pennsylvania.*

motives to create a refuge for members of their beleaguered church. In the 1670s, a group of wealthy Friends purchased New Jersey from its original proprietors and offered religious freedom and generous political rights to its current and future colonists, many of whom were Puritans. The best known of these Quaker proprietors was **William Penn,** who had given up a life of privilege, luxury, and self-indulgence in Restoration society and embraced the morally demanding life of the Friends.

Penn's father, Admiral Sir William Penn, was one of England's naval heroes and a political adviser to

Presbyterians Members of a Protestant sect that eventually became the established church of Scotland but which in the seventeenth century was sometimes persecuted by Scotland's rulers.

Jacob Leisler German merchant who led a revolt in New York in 1689 against royal officials representing the Dominion of New England; he was executed as a traitor when he refused to surrender control of the colony to a governor appointed by William and Mary.

William Penn English Quaker who founded the colony of Pennsylvania in 1681.

King Charles II. The senior Penn and his son had little in common except their loyalty to the king and their willingness to provide liberal loans to support their monarch's extravagant lifestyle. Eventually, Charles rewarded the Penns' devotion. In 1681, he granted the younger Penn a charter to a huge area west of the Delaware River. This gave Penn the opportunity to create for Quakers a refuge that fully embodied their religious principles.

Penn called his new colony Pennsylvania, meaning "Penn's Woods," in memory of his father. (The southernmost section of Penn's grant, added later by Charles II, developed independent of Penn's control and in 1776 became the state of Delaware.) Like most colonial proprietors, Penn expected to profit from his charter, and he set a quitrent, or small fee, on all land purchased within his colony. But his religious devoutness ensured that he would not govern by whim. Instead, Quaker values and principles were the basis for his "holy experiment." At the heart of the Quaker faith was the conviction that the divine spirit, or "inner light," resided in every human being. Quakers thus respected all individuals. By their plain dress and their refusal to remove their hats in the presence of their social "betters," Quakers demonstrated their belief that all men and women were equal. In keeping with their egalitarian principles, Quakers also recognized no distinctions of wealth or social status in their places of worship. At the strikingly simple Quaker meeting, or worship service, any member who felt moved to speak was welcome to participate, no matter how poor or uneducated and no matter what sex or age. Although they actively sought converts, Quakers were always tolerant of other religions.

Pennsylvania's political structure reflected this **egalitarianism.** All free male residents had the right to vote during Penn's lifetime, and the legislature they elected had full governing powers. Unlike his patron, Charles II, William Penn had no intention of interfering in his colony's lawmaking process. He honored the legislature's decisions even when they disturbed or amazed him. The political quarrels that developed in Pennsylvania's assembly actually shocked Penn, but his only action was to urge political leaders not to be "so noisy, and open, in your dissatisfactions."

Penn's land policy also reflected Quaker principles. Unlike many proprietors, he wanted no politically powerful landlords and no economically dependent tenant farmers. Instead, he actively promoted a society of independent, landowning farm families. Penn also insisted that all land be purchased fairly from the Indians, and he pursued a policy of peaceful coexistence between the two cultures. William Penn took an

This sketch of a Quaker meeting highlights one of the most radical of Quaker practices: allowing women to speak in church. Most Protestant denominations, because of their reading of Saint Paul, enforced the rule of silence on women. But Quakers struck a blow at seventeenth-century gender notions by granting women an active ministerial role, a voice in church policy, and decision-making responsibilities on issues relating to the church and the family. *"The Quaker Meeting" (detail) by Egbert Van Heemskerk. The Quaker Collection, Haverford College Library.*

active role in making Pennsylvania a multicultural society, recruiting non-English settlers through pamphlets that stressed the religious and political freedoms and economic opportunities his colony offered. More than eight thousand immigrants poured into the colony in the first four years. Many did come from England, but Irish, Scottish, Welsh, French, Scandinavian, and German settlers came as well. To their English neighbors who did not speak German, newcomers from Germany such as the Mennonites and Amish were known as the "Pennsylvania Dutch" (*Deutsch,* meaning "German," would have been correct).

When William Penn died in 1717, he left behind a successful, dynamic colony. Philadelphia was already emerging as a great shipping and commercial center, rivaling the older seaports of Boston and New York City. But this success came at some cost to Penn's original vision and to his Quaker principles. The commercial orientation here, as in Puritan Massachusetts, attracted colonists who were more secular in their interests and objectives than the colony's founders.

egalitarianism   A belief in human equality.

These colonists had no strong commitment to egalitarianism. For example, many newcomers saw Penn's Indian policy as a check on their ambitions and preferred to seize land from the Indians rather than purchase it. The demand for military protection from Indians by these land-hungry farmers in the western part of the colony became a major political issue and a matter of conscience for Quakers, whose religious principles included **pacifism.** Eventually many Quakers chose to resign from the colonial government rather than struggle to uphold a holy experiment that their neighbors did not support.

The Colonies of the Lower South

■ What type of society did the founders of Carolina hope to create? How did the colony differ from their expectations?

■ Why did philanthropists create Georgia? Why did the king support this project?

William Penn was not the only Englishman to benefit from the often extravagant generosity of King Charles II. In 1663 the king surprised eight of his favorite supporters by granting them several million acres lying south of Virginia and stretching from the Atlantic to the Pacific Ocean. This gesture by Charles was both grand and calculated. France, Spain, Holland, and the Indian tribes that inhabited this area all laid claim to it, and Charles thought it would be wise to secure England's control of the region by colonizing it. The eight new colonial proprietors named their colony Carolina to honor the king's late father, who had lost his head to the Puritan Commonwealth (and whose name in Latin was Carolus; see Map 3.4).

The Carolina Colony

The proprietors' plan for Carolina was similar to Lord Baltimore's medieval dream. The philosopher John Locke helped draw up the Fundamental Constitution of Carolina, an elaborate blueprint for a society of great landowners, **yeomen** (small, independent farmers), and serfs (agricultural laborers) bound to work for their landlords. Locke later became famous for his essays on freedom and human rights (see Chapter 4)—a far cry from the social hierarchy proposed in the Carolina constitution. Like the Calverts, however, the Carolina proprietors discovered that few English people were willing to travel 3,000 miles across the ocean to become serfs. Bowing to reality, the proprietors offered the incentive of the head right system used in Virginia and Maryland decades earlier.

MAP 3.4 The Settlements of the Lower South   This map shows the towns and fortifications of North Carolina, South Carolina, and Georgia, as well as the overlapping claims by the Spanish and the English to the territory south and west of Fort King George. The many Georgia forts reflect that colony's role as a buffer state between rice-rich South Carolina and the Spanish troops stationed in Florida.

The early settlers in Carolina, many of them relocating from the Caribbean island of Barbados, made their way to the southeastern portion of the colony, drawn there by the fine natural harbor of the port city, Charles Town (later Charleston), and its fertile surroundings. Despite the dangers of the Spanish to the south in Florida and the Yamasee Indians to the southwest, Charles Town grew rapidly, becoming the most important city in the southern colonies. These early Carolinians experimented with several money-making activities. Some established trade with the Indians of the region, exchanging English goods for deerskins and for captive victims of tribal warfare. The deerskins were shipped to England. The Indians were shipped as slaves to the Caribbean. Other colonists tapped the region's pine forests to produce

pacifism   Opposition to war or violence of any kind.
yeoman   Independent landowner entitled to suffrage.

The Lynch family, wealthy rice planters of South Carolina, built this elegant home on the banks of the North Santee River in the 1730s. Hopsewee Plantation is a striking example of the luxury enjoyed by the small number of elite white planters whose fortunes depended on the labor of enslaved African field workers. *Courtesy of the Hopsewee Plantation.*

naval stores—the timber, tar, resin, pitch, and turpentine that were used in building and maintaining wooden ships.

Carolinians experimented with several cash crops, including sugar cane, tobacco, silk, cotton, ginger, and olives. But none of these crops was particularly profitable. The first real success turned out to be cattle raising, a skill the settlers learned from African slaves brought into the colony by planters relocating from the West Indian sugar island of Barbados. By the 1680s, Carolina cattlemen had begun to use their profits to begin a new enterprise: rice cultivation. In 1719, when members of the Charleston planter elite wrested control of their part of Carolina from the original proprietors, the southern part of the colony, now called South Carolina, boasted the richest English colonists on the mainland.

The northern region of Carolina developed in the shadow of its southern neighbor. Bordered by the Great Dismal Swamp to the north and by smaller swamps to the south, this isolated area attracted few colonists. The land around Albemarle Sound was fertile enough, but the remaining coastline was cut off from the Atlantic by a chain of barrier islands that blocked access to oceangoing vessels. Despite all these constraints, some poor farm families and freed white indentured servants had drifted in from Virginia, searching for unclaimed land and a fresh start. They had modest success in Carolina growing tobacco and producing naval stores.

In 1729 the Albemarle colonists followed the lead of their elite neighbors around Charleston and rid themselves of proprietary rule. Then these North Carolinians went one step further: they officially separated from the rice-rich southern section of the colony. In this way, the colonists of Carolina restored to the Crown what King Charles II had once given away, for both South Carolina and North Carolina became royal colonies.

Georgia, the Last Colony

More than one hundred years after the first Jamestown colonists struggled against starvation and disease in Virginia, the last of the original thirteen colonies was established in the Lower South. In 1732 **James Oglethorpe,** a wealthy English social reformer, and several of his friends requested a charter for a colony on the Florida border. Oglethorpe's motives were philanthropic: he hoped to provide a new, moral life for many of the English men and women imprisoned for minor debts. He and his colleagues wanted no profits from the colony. King George II had other motives for granting the charter: he was anxious to create a protective buffer between the valuable rice-producing colony of South Carolina and the Spanish in Florida. The king inserted a clause in the Georgia charter requiring military service from every male settler. Thus

James Oglethorpe English philanthropist who established the colony of Georgia in 1732 as a refuge for debtors.

he guaranteed that the poor men of Georgia would protect the rich men of South Carolina.

Oglethorpe and his associates added their own special restrictions on the lives of the Georgia colonists. Although their concern about the welfare of English debtors was genuine, they believed that poverty was the outcome of a weak character or, worse, of an addiction to vice. Thus they forbade a representative assembly and denied the settlers a voice in selecting political leaders and military officers. Because they were eager to reform the character of their colonists, the trustees set other rules, including banning all alcoholic beverages to ensure that everyone worked hard and led a modest, moral life. All land grants were to be small, and no colonist could legally buy or sell property within Georgia. Slavery, the main source of labor in the southern colonies by this time, was banned, and free blacks were barred from the colony. The colonists

would have to work their own fields and harvest their own crops.

Oglethorpe interviewed many imprisoned debtors, searching for members of the "deserving poor" who would benefit from Georgia. But few of these men and women met his standards. Most of the colony's settlers turned out to be South Carolinians looking for new land, and English immigrants from their society's middling ranks. These colonists did not welcome the trustees' paternalistic attitudes, and they soon challenged all the restrictive rules and regulations in the charter. They won the right to accumulate and sell land. They introduced slave labor in defiance of the trustees, and by the 1740s, illegal slave auctions were a common sight in Georgia's largest town, Savannah. By 1752, Oglethorpe and his fellow trustees had lost enthusiasm for their reform project and, with relief, returned Georgia to the king.

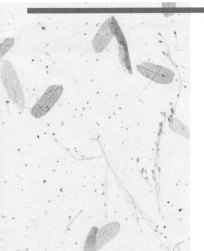

Individual Voices

Examining a Primary Source

Nathaniel Bacon: Manifesto Concerning the Troubles in Virginia, 1676

Nathaniel Bacon began his defiance of the colonial government with one specific objective: to remove the threat of Indian aggression in the backcountry of Virginia. Yet Bacon soon found himself the leader of a civil war between backcountry farmers, apprentices and servants on the one hand and the wealthy coastal planters and the royal governor on the other. Labeled a traitor by Governor Berkeley, Bacon defended himself and his actions in "The Declaration of the People." In it, he also listed his followers' many grievances against the governor.

■ *Here Bacon declares that a just God would condone his attacks on the Indian population since they had slaughtered innocent colonists. Yet Bacon attacked peaceful Indians as well as those who had threatened white settlements. Do Bacon's attacks on these peaceful Indian communities suggest a larger issue of racism in the colonies?*

If virtue be a sin, if piety be guilt, all the principles of morality, goodness and justice be perverted, we must confess that those who are now called rebels may be in danger of those high imputations. Those loud and several bulls would affright innocents and render the defense of our brethren and the inquiry into our sad and heavy oppressions, treason. ■ But if there be, as sure there is, a just God to appeal to; if religion and justice be a sanctuary here; if to plead the cause of the oppressed; if sincerely to aim at his Majesty's honour and die public good without any reservation or by interest; if to stand in the gap after so much blood of our dear brethren bought and sold; if after the loss of a great part of his Majesty's colony deserted and dispeopled, freely with our lives and estates to endeavour to save the remainders be treason; God Almighty judge and let guilty die. But since

■ In this section Bacon reminds his readers that the haughty tidewater planters came to Virginia as poor men, not as gentlemen, and are thus no better than his followers. Today, they would be accused of "putting on airs" or of being social climbers.

■ Bacon argues that the governor and his friends have done nothing to earn the public's trust or admiration, and have failed to provide basic protection for the citizens of the colony. One hundred years later, American revolutionaries will make the same claim against the king and Parliament of Great Britain. Do you think Bacon's claims are accurate?

we cannot in our hearts find one single spot of rebellion or treason, or that we have in any manner aimed at the subverting of the settled government or attempting of the person of any either magistrate or private man, notwithstanding the several reproaches and threats of some who for sinister ends were disaffected to us and censured our innocent and honest designs, and since all people in all places where we have yet been can attest our civil, quiet, peaceable behaviour far different from that of rebellion and tumultuous persons, let truth be bold and all the world know the real foundations of pretended guilt. We appeal to the country itself what and of what nature their oppressions have been, or by what cabal and mystery the designs of many of those whom we call great men have been transacted and carried on; but let us trace these men in authority and favour to whose hands the dispensation of the country's wealth has been committed. ■ *Let us observe the sudden rise of their estates composed with the quality in which they first entered this country, or the reputation, they have held here amongst wise and discerning men. And let us see whether their extractions and education have not been vile, and by what pretence of learning and virtue they could so soon [come] into employments of so great trust and consequence.* ■ *Let us consider their sudden advancement and let us also consider whether any public work for our safety and defence or for the advancement and propagation of trade, liberal arts, or sciences is here extant in any way adequate to our vast charge. Now let us compare these things together and see what sponges have sucked up the public treasure, and whether it has not been privately contrived away by unworthy favourites and juggling parasites whose tottering fortunes have been repaired and supported at the public charge. Now if it be so, judge what greater guilt can be than to offer to pry into these and to unriddle the mysterious wiles of a powerful cabal; let all people judge what can be of more dangerous import than to suspect the so long safe proceedings of some of our grandees, and whether people may with safety open their eyes in so nice a concern.*

Summary

After the failure of the Roanoke Colony in 1587, the English did not attempt to settle mainland America until the seventeenth century, when political conflict, economic instability, and religious persecution persuaded many English men and women that colonization might ease their national problems. Borrowing the idea of a joint-stock enterprise from English shippers, the Virginia Company financed the first successful colony at Jamestown in 1607. Between 1607 and 1732, thirteen colonies were founded on mainland America, with four distinct regions emerging: the Chesapeake, New England, the Middle Colonies, and the Lower South.

Although the Virginia Company expected to grow rich from the discovery of gold and silver, the real wealth of the first colony proved to be in agriculture.

Tobacco became known as the "brown gold" of Virginia. In 1634 the Calvert family established the second Chesapeake colony of Maryland as a refuge for English Catholics. Maryland settlers, most of whom turned out to be Protestants, chose to cultivate tobacco also. Chesapeake society was shaped by this decision. Both colonies filled with young, single males who came to America as indentured servants, working in the tobacco fields for several years in order to repay their masters for their Atlantic voyages. The demand for male field workers resulted in a skewed sex ratio. The unhealthy climate, hard labor, and poor diet produced a demographic disaster in the seventeenth-century Chesapeake. The relatively small number of women and high mortality rates prevented a traditional family structure from developing. Major conflicts among the settlers emerged in both colonies. In Maryland, Protestants and Catholics waged a long battle for control, and in Virginia, backcountry farmers rose up against the established coastal planters in 1676 in Bacon's Rebellion.

Religious dissenters seeking freedom of worship created the New England colonies. Pilgrims, or separatists, founded the first of these colonies at Plymouth in 1620. Pilgrim leader William Bradford assured the success of the colony by offering broad political rights to all the men on board the *Mayflower,* including the crew and servants, in an agreement known as the Mayflower Compact. Unlike the Chesapeake settlers, the Pilgrims established peaceful relations with the local Indians. The outcome was seventy-one years of stability in this small colony.

Puritans, who wished to "purify" the Anglican Church of all traces of Catholicism, founded Massachusetts in 1630. They expected to create a model Protestant community, a "city upon a hill," that would convince all English men and women to accept Puritan reforms. The colony's leaders required all settlers to obey biblical as well as English civil and criminal laws. Political rights were restricted to full church members, known as saints. Dissent arose, however. Roger Williams and Anne Hutchinson—both discovered that although the colony was founded for religious freedom, that freedom did not extend to everyone. Because they challenged Puritan practices or rituals or beliefs, they were exiled from Massachusetts. Roger Williams founded Rhode Island, a colony that established separation of church and state. Many colonists left Massachusetts voluntarily, exasperated by the regulation of their personal lives or seeking new land to settle. Connecticut was founded by such colonists. The Puritans ultimately lost control over Massachusetts in 1691 when the Crown revoked the charter and made it a royal colony. The tensions produced by this political change and by economic growth contributed to the Salem witch-hunts of 1691.

The region between the Chesapeake and New England, originally claimed and settled by both the Dutch and the Swedes, was "conquered" by the English in 1664. New Sweden and New Netherland became New Jersey and New York. In 1681 Quaker William Penn created the colony of Pennsylvania, known as the "holy experiment," west of New Jersey. The Middle Colonies, as they were called, were noted for their diverse populations—including Quakers, Germans, French Protestants, Dutch, Swedes, Finns, and a small community of Jews—and for their policies of religious toleration.

In the Lower South, the proprietors of Carolina expected to create a hierarchical society but discovered, as had the Calverts of Maryland, that they had to offer land under the head right system in order to attract colonists. Georgia, the last of the colonies, was founded by philanthropists who hoped to reform "worthy debtors" in English prisons. The king approved the colony because he wanted a buffer state between the Spanish-held Florida and the prosperous rice-growing colony of South Carolina.

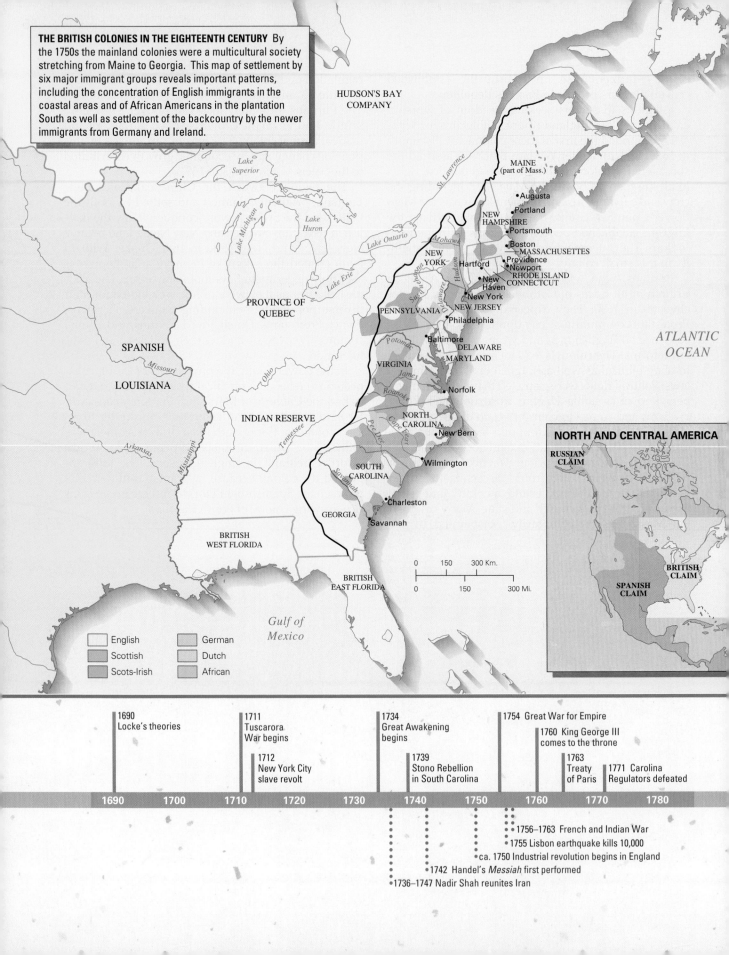

THE BRITISH COLONIES IN THE EIGHTEENTH CENTURY By the 1750s the mainland colonies were a multicultural society stretching from Maine to Georgia. This map of settlement by six major immigrant groups reveals important patterns, including the concentration of English immigrants in the coastal areas and of African Americans in the plantation South as well as settlement of the backcountry by the newer immigrants from Germany and Ireland.

HUDSON'S BAY COMPANY

Lake Superior

Lake Michigan

Lake Huron

Lake Ontario

Lake Erie

PROVINCE OF QUEBEC

SPANISH LOUISIANA

Missouri

Ohio

INDIAN RESERVE

Tennessee

Arkansas

Mississippi

St. Lawrence

MAINE (part of Mass.)

• Augusta

• Portland

NEW HAMPSHIRE

• Portsmouth

Mohawk

NEW YORK

Susquehanna

Delaware

Hudson

• Boston

MASSACHUSETTES

• Providence

• Newport

RHODE ISLAND

CONNECTCUT

Hartford •

• New Haven

• New York

NEW JERSEY

PENNSYLVANIA

• Philadelphia

Potomac

• Baltimore

DELAWARE

MARYLAND

VIRGINIA

James

Roanoke

• Norfolk

NORTH CAROLINA

Pee Dee

Cape Fear

• New Bern

SOUTH CAROLINA

Savannah

• Wilmington

• Charleston

GEORGIA

• Savannah

BRITISH WEST FLORIDA

BRITISH EAST FLORIDA

Gulf of Mexico

ATLANTIC OCEAN

| 0 | 150 | 300 Km. |
| 0 | 150 | 300 Mi. |

English
Scottish
Scots-Irish
German
Dutch
African

NORTH AND CENTRAL AMERICA

RUSSIAN CLAIM

SPANISH CLAIM

BRITISH CLAIM

1690 Locke's theories

1711 Tuscarora War begins

1712 New York City slave revolt

1734 Great Awakening begins

1739 Stono Rebellion in South Carolina

1754 Great War for Empire

1760 King George III comes to the throne

1763 Treaty of Paris

1771 Carolina Regulators defeated

| 1690 | 1700 | 1710 | 1720 | 1730 | 1740 | 1750 | 1760 | 1770 | 1780 |

1756–1763 French and Indian War

1755 Lisbon earthquake kills 10,000

ca. 1750 Industrial revolution begins in England

1742 Handel's *Messiah* first performed

1736–1747 Nadir Shah reunites Iran

The English Colonies in the Eighteenth Century, 1689–1763

The British Colonies in the Eighteenth Century
Using the map on the facing page, discuss immigrant settlement patterns in the mainland colonies. What role would regional economies play in determining where German, Scots-Irish, and African immigrants were concentrated?

Individual Choices

ELIZA LUCAS PINCKNEY'S GOWN

As the daughter of one prosperous South Carolina planter and the wife of another, Eliza Lucas Pinckney could afford luxury goods most colonists could not hope to enjoy. But the gown shown above was made of silk produced on her own plantation and sent to England to be woven and dyed. Eliza Lucas Pinckney, who became the manager of her father's three plantations when she was only a teenager, took great pride in experimenting with new crops, including silk from silkworms and the blue dye indigo. *National Museum of American History, Smithsonian Institution, Behring Center.*

Eliza Lucas Pinckney

Eliza Lucas was the daughter of a British military officer who moved his family to the colonies when she was a child. Here they settled in the new colony of South Carolina, where George Lucas acquired several thriving rice plantations. When Eliza was only sixteen, her father was recalled to active duty in the Caribbean, leaving behind a young family and an ailing wife. But George Lucas did not turn to outsiders or male relatives to take charge of his plantations while he was away; instead he turned over the daunting task to his bright, energetic daughter, Eliza. The choice may have surprised colonists who did not know Eliza, but friends and family shared her father's confidence in her. She had already shown her maturity and her organizing skills when she took over the management of the large family household from her invalid mother.

With the family's fortunes in her hands, Eliza proved her father had made the right choice. At a time when most wealthy young women in Carolina were preoccupied with thoughts of marriage and children, Eliza Lucas busied herself with planting and harvesting, paying bills, directing overseers, and selling crops. Despite her responsibilities, she did not ignore her duties as a member of her community's female social elite: she attended teas, visited the sick, and mastered the arts of dancing and music. To do all this, she set herself a grueling daily schedule. She began the day at 5:00 A.M. with two hours of reading, then toured the work in the fields, returned to the house to study music and French, and finally sat down to tutor her sister and two of the plantation's slave girls. All this was accomplished before noon. In the afternoon and evening she would do needlework, read the classics as well as the influential books of the day, and see to personal and business correspondence. One day a week, she set aside all her female duties and attended entirely to plantation business.

Under Eliza's management, the Lucas plantations prospered. From the beginning she took a bold approach, experimenting with new crops that might grow in South Carolina's climate and soil. Her father approved wholeheartedly of her unorthodox methods and assisted her in the search for potentially profitable crops. In the midst of his military duties, he found time to send her **indigo** seeds, from which blue dye could be made. He also sent her a talented indigo maker from the Caribbean island of Montserrat. It took Eliza five years of experimentation to turn a profit from indigo, but her persistence paid off. Indigo became a staple crop of South Carolina for several years.

Eliza's entrepreneurial spirit and business skills are well documented in her letters. But these letters also show the pride she took in her successes and the confidence she felt that she deserved to reap the rewards of her accomplishments. When Eliza described a "large plantation of Oaks" she had planted, she not only took credit for the project but also asserted her right to any profits in timber the grove generated. She even went so far as to insist that the oaks were "my own property, whether my father gives me the land or not." The men who worked for

her would not have been surprised by such a claim, for they knew her temperament and her business skills firsthand. Eliza hired and fired the overseers, who reported directly to her, and she wrote regularly to the family's agent in London on matters of property deeds, sales of land and livestock, and the purchase of goods through local Charles Town merchants. In matters of business and legal affairs, as in other areas, Eliza's father had laid the groundwork for her expertise. He had instructed her fully on her legal rights as a single woman, or *femme sole,* and encouraged her to make good use of the legal library left behind in her care. And she did just that. Many of her neighbors relied on her to make their wills or assist them in suing for debts. Male or female, these colonists knew less about protecting their property than this teenage girl who read law books, legal treatises, and philosophers of civil society such as John Locke.

Despite the many attempts by her father to find a suitable husband for Eliza, she stubbornly protected her independence. Believing herself too young to marry, she vowed to remain single until she was ready to live otherwise. When Eliza finally married it was to an old friend, a widower twice her age. Charles Pinckney was a leading lawyer and political figure in the colony and had acted as Eliza's mentor while her father was away. Eliza judged him to be a worthy companion for a woman of her intellect and abilities.

As Charles's wife, Eliza turned all her attention to domestic concerns, especially maternal ones, and within five years she gave birth to four children. Eliza undertook motherhood with the same energy and clarity of purpose she had shown in her years as a planter and businesswoman. She believed that the education of her children was the most important work she would ever undertake, and she prepared herself for the task well. She chose to follow John Locke's modern theories of childhood education, theories that stressed the power of nurture rather than older notions that children were burdened by original sin. Locke's advice served Eliza Lucas Pinckney well: both of her two surviving sons grew up to be political leaders during the revolutionary struggle, and her only daughter followed in Eliza's footsteps, eventually running her own plantation.

After fourteen years of marriage, Eliza was left a widow. Once again she rose to the challenge of managing a large plantation, just as she had done as a sixteen-year-old girl. She continued to manage the complex family business until her death from cancer in 1793. As a tribute to her place in colonial society, George Washington requested to be a pallbearer at her funeral.

INTRODUCTION

Despite the economic, political, intellectual, and religious ties that bound England and the colonies into a transatlantic community, many visitors to the colonies argued that Americans had a distinctive character of their own. The **unprecedented** degree of personal liberty for all except African and African American slaves struck many observers as uniquely American. The rich natural resources of the land impressed others as a key to an extraordinary American optimism. Liberty and economic opportunity drew thousands of new immigrants to the colonies every decade, not

only from England but from Germany, Ireland, and France as well. Quakers and other English dissenters flocked to colonies that offered religious toleration,

> **indigo**   Shrublike plant with clusters of red or purple flowers, grown on plantations in the South; it was a primary source of blue dye in the 18th century.
>
> *femme sole*   From the French for "woman alone"; a legal term for an unmarried, widowed, or divorced woman with the legal right to own or sell property, sue or be sued, or earn wages.
>
> **unprecedented**   Unheard of or novel.

The sugar-producing islands of the Caribbean were the jewels in the British empire of trade. Ship captains and ship owners made their fortunes out of the sugar or, as it was often called in the 18th century, molasses they carried from the West Indies to the mainland colonies, as well as to England and to Africa. The sugar planters lived in luxury in England, among the wealthiest men in the empire. Meanwhile, slaves labored in the cane fields in order to produce the profits these men enjoyed. *British Library; London, UK/ Bridgeman Art Library Ltd.*

such as Pennsylvania. Of course not everyone lived, as one observer insisted, "in his house like a king." The poor as well as the wealthy filled the crowded streets of Philadelphia, New York, and Boston. In western New England, land shortages in settled areas and urban unemployment were altering the social landscape. In the South, the steady flow of new immigrants to the backcountry of Virginia and the Carolinas produced subsistence-level farm families, struggling to survive. And throughout these regions of tobacco and rice production, slavery set the African and African American labor force outside the realm of economic advancement or basic personal liberties. Even so, many free white colonists would agree with Michel de Crèvecoeur, the French writer who called America "this smiling country."

Few members of the English or European elite bothered to chart these changes in American colonial life. Most continued to think of the colonies as a dumping ground for misfits and hayseeds who would struggle to survive, or not, on a violent frontier. Members of the English Parliament viewed the colonists as a constant source of problems and continued to expect the worst from them. They expected insubordinate colonial legislatures, defiant merchants who violated trade regulations, and a dangerously unstable political atmosphere in a society that gave common men such a great voice in government. To the king and his political advisers, this "smiling country" produced more gloom than sunshine. From the colonists' perspective, England and its rivals were responsible for most of the clouds on their horizon. A series of imperial wars between England and its competitors disrupted colonial life until

the 1760s, casting a long shadow over communities from Maine to Georgia. In the end, England would vanquish every rival for a North American empire, but neither the king nor the colonists could predict the surprising outcome of their nation's victory.

The English Transatlantic Communities of Trade

■ What were the main regional differences in colonial commerce?

■ In which region, and for what reasons, did new immigrants seem to have the best economic choices?

■ How were the Carolina plantation owners' profits affected by rising tensions between England and Spain and Portugal?

Although the English spoke of "the colonial trade," British America did not have a single, unified economy. Instead, four distinctive regional economies had developed on the mainland, concentrated along the Atlantic coastline and bordered on the west by the primarily **subsistence society** commonly found on the edge of white settlement. To the south, the sugar islands of the Caribbean made up a fifth unique regional economy. Each of these economies was shaped by environmental conditions, natural resources, Eng-

> **subsistence society** A society that produces the food and supplies necessary for its survival but which does not produce a surplus that can be marketed.

Chronology

From Settlements to Societies

1690–1691	John Locke's *Essay Concerning Human Understanding* and *Two Treatises of Government*	**1734**	Great Awakening spreads to New England
1701	Yale College founded	**1739**	Stono Rebellion in South Carolina
1702	Queen Anne's War begins	**1740**	King George's War begins George Whitefield begins his preaching tour
1704	Pro-French Indians attack Deerfield, Massachusetts	**1756**	Great War for Empire begins
1711	Tuscarora War begins in North Carolina	**1759**	British capture Quebec
1712	New York City slave revolt	**1763**	Treaty of Paris ends French and Indian or Seven Years, War Paxton Boys revolt in Pennsylvania
1715	Colonists defeat Creek and Yamasee Indians of Georgia	**1771**	North Carolina Regulator movement defeated

lish commercial policy, the available labor force, and the available technological know-how.

Regions of Commerce

The sugar-producing islands of the West Indies were the brightest jewels in the English imperial crown. Spain had first laid claim to most of these islands, but England had gobbled up many of them when the Spanish chose to concentrate instead on the gold- and silver-mining colonies of Peru and Mexico. By the eighteenth century, the English flag flew over St. Kitts, Barbados, Nevis, Montserrat, and Jamaica. On each island, English plantation owners built fabulous fortunes on the sugar that African slaves produced. While the **absentee planters** lived in luxury in England, black slaves lived—and died in staggering numbers—on the islands, working the cane fields and tending the fires that burned day and night under the sugar vats of the "great Boiling houses."

Few mainland colonists enjoyed the wealth of this "Sugar Interest." Still, in the Lower South, planters of South Carolina and Georgia, like Eliza Lucas Pinckney, amassed considerable fortunes by growing rice in the lowlands along the Atlantic coast. By the 1730s, this American rice was feeding the people of the Mediterranean, Portugal, and Spain. By midcentury, planters were making additional profits from indigo, which Eliza Lucas Pinckney had recently introduced to the re-

gion. Other Carolinians found cattle raising a profitable enterprise. Like the sugar planters, Carolina and Georgia rice growers based their production on slave labor, but unlike the island moguls, these plantation masters never became permanent absentee landowners.

Tobacco continued to dominate the economy of the Chesapeake, although by the eighteenth century, "brown gold" was no longer the only crop Virginians and Marylanders were willing to plant. In fact, at the turn of the century, when the price of tobacco was driven down by high taxes and competition from Mediterranean sources, many **tidewater** planters chose to diversify. They began producing wheat and other grains for export. As a result, tobacco production shifted west to the area along the Potomac, the James River valley, and the **piedmont** foothills. The second major shift came in the labor force used in tobacco cultivation. By the eighteenth century, African slaves had replaced indentured servants in the fields. Planters who could afford to purchase a number of slaves

absentee planters An estate owner who collects profits from farming or rent but does not live on the land or help cultivate it.

tidewater Low coastal land drained by tidal streams in Maryland and Virginia.

piedmont Land lying at the foot of a mountain range.

It Matters

Women's Roles, Then and Now

In her character and her life choices, Eliza Lucas Pinckney seems remarkably modern. Yet she lived in an era when women were assumed to be best suited for the domestic duties known as "house-wifery." Of course, Pinckney had advantages many other eighteenth-century women did not enjoy: wealth, social standing, and a father and a husband who had confidence in her abilities. Without these advantages, Pinckney might never have been able to venture outside the domestic realm. Today, Pinckney would find herself in the company of many women who are able to make careers in business, medicine, scientific research—and in an area completely closed out to Pinckney, politics. The contrast between a life that was extraordinary in the eighteenth century and ordinary in the twenty-first century prompts us to examine what changes have occurred in women's lives between the colonial era and today.

enjoyed a competitive advantage over their neighbors in both the old and the new tobacco areas because they had enough workers to plant and harvest bigger crops. This large-scale production kept tobacco the number one export of the mainland colonies.

Together, these two southern regions provided the bulk of the mainland's agricultural exports to Great Britain. By contrast, the New England regional economy depended far less on Britain as a market. Except in the Connecticut River valley, where tobacco was grown, the rocky soil of their region made large-scale farming unfeasible for New Englanders. Instead, they developed both a fishing and a lumbering industry, shipping the dried fish and timber to the West Indies. But it was shipbuilding and the ambitious **carrying trade** connected to it that dominated New England's economy. Colonists made great profits from an extensive shipping network that carried colonial exports across the Atlantic and distributed foreign goods and English manufactured products to the colonies. Some merchant-shippers—the slave traders of Newport, Rhode Island, for example—specialized in a certain commodity, but most were willing to carry any cargo that promised a profit. By the eighteenth century,

New England shipping made these colonists rivals of English merchants rather than useful sources of profit for the Mother Country.

Sandwiched between the South and New England, the colonies of New York, New Jersey, Pennsylvania, and later Delaware developed their own regional economy. The Middle Colonies combined the successes of their neighbors, creating profits from both staple-crop farming and trade. The forests of the Pocono Mountains and upper New York were a source of wood and wood products for the shipbuilding industry, and locally harvested flaxseed was exported to Ireland for its linen industry. The central crop, however, was wheat. Fortunately for the colonists of this area, the price of wheat rose steadily during the eighteenth century. The carrying trade was equally important in this region's mixed economy. Ships carrying cargoes of grain and flour milled in New York City across the Atlantic and into the Caribbean crossed paths with other colonial ships bringing manufactured goods and luxury items from Europe through the region's two major port cities, New York and Philadelphia. By 1775, Philadelphia had become the second-largest city in the British Empire.

Not everyone in Maryland grew tobacco for the market, of course, and not everyone in Massachusetts was a sailor, lumberjack, ship captain, or urban shopkeeper. The market-oriented activity was largely confined to the older coastal settlements of each region, where harbors and river ways provided the necessary transportation routes for the shipment of crops, goods, and supplies. Inland from these farms, towns, and cities, most colonies had a backcountry that was sparsely populated and farmed by European immigrants, ex-servants, or the families of younger sons from older communities. There, on what white settlers thought of as the frontier and Indians despised as the invasion line, colonists struggled to produce enough for survival. They lacked the labor force to clear the land or work sufficient acreage for a marketable crop, or they lacked the means to get that crop to market. And with no financial or political resources, they had little hope of solving either the manpower or the transport problem. As a result, this belt of subsistence economy extended like a border from Maine to western Pennsylvania, to inland Carolina, along every region of the mainland colonies. But even these backcountry

carrying trade   The business of transporting goods across the Atlantic or to and from the Caribbean.

farms had a fragile link to the world of international trade, for settlers brought with them the farm tools and the basic household supplies that had been manufactured in England or imported through colonial ports.

The Cords of Commercial Empire

England's mainland colonists traded, both directly and indirectly, with many European nations and their colonies. Salt, wine, and spices reached colonial tables from southern Europe, and sugar, rum, molasses, and cotton came to their households from the West Indies. But the deepest and broadest channels in the transatlantic trade were those that connected the Mother Country and the colonies. The British purchased over half of all the crops, furs, and mined resources that colonists produced for market and supplied 90 percent of all colonial imports. Strong cords of exchange thus bound America to England, even if many colonists were second-, third-, or even fourth-generation Americans and others traced their roots to different nations and even different continents. The English mainland colonies were also bound to one another, despite a deserved reputation for dispute, disagreement, and endless rivalries. New Englanders might exchange insults with Pennsylvanians, but in the shops and on the wharfs, Pennsylvania flour, Massachusetts mackerel, Carolina rice, and scores of domestic products and produce changed hands in a lively and cheerful commerce. Domestic trade was greater in volume, although lower in value, than all foreign trade in this eighteenth-century world.

Community and Work in Colonial Society

■ How did Yankee society differ from Puritan society in early eighteenth-century New England?

■ Why did non-English settlers migrate to the British North American colonies?

■ Why did colonists in the Chesapeake and Lower South shift from indentured servants to slaves as their primary labor force? What problems faced Africans in slavery?

■ What was distinctive about life in the Middle Colonies?

■ What motivated colonists to migrate to the backcountry?

Despite the belief of many observers that there was an "American character," visitors could not fail to note striking physical and social differences as they traveled from New England to the Lower South. Moving from the carefully laid-out towns of New England, through the crowded seaport cities of the Middle Colonies, and into the isolated rural worlds of the plantation South, they could see that the Yankee culture of Connecticut was strikingly different from the elegant lifestyle and social attitudes of Charles Town planter elite.

The Emergence of the "Yankee"

In the early eighteenth century, New England's seaport towns and cities grew steadily in size and economic importance. With the rise of a profitable international commerce, the Puritan culture of the village gave way to a more secular "Yankee" culture. In this milieu, a wealthy man could rise to political prominence without any need to demonstrate his piety. Economic competition and the pursuit of profit eclipsed older notions that the well-being of the community was more important than the gains of the individual. Not merely sentiments, these changes were substantive: seventeenth-century laws regulating prices and interest rates, for example, were repealed or simply ignored. Still, some sense of obligation to the community remained in New Englanders' willingness to create and maintain public institutions such as schools and colleges. In 1701, for example, Yale College opened its doors in New Haven, Connecticut, giving the sons of elite New Englanders an alternative to Massachusetts's Harvard College, founded in 1636. And New Englanders supported newspapers and printing presses that kept their communities informed about local, regional, and even international events.

Even in more traditional New England villages, changes were evident. By the eighteenth century, many fathers no longer had enough farmland to provide adequately for all their sons. Thus many younger sons left their families and friends behind and sought their fortunes elsewhere. Some chose to go west, pushing the frontier of settlement as they searched for fertile land. Others went north, to less developed areas such as Maine. In the process, they created new towns and villages, causing the number of backcountry New England towns to grow steadily until the end of the colonial period. Still other young men abandoned farming entirely and relocated to the commercial cities of the region. Whatever their expectations, urban life often disappointed them, for inequality of wealth and opportunity went hand in hand with the overall prosperity. In Boston a growing number of poor widows

John Smibert painted his "Vew of Boston," in 1738. There are two striking feature of the town: the number of church steeples that dot the urban landscape, testimony to the importance of religion in the founding of the colony of Massachusetts, and the presence of so many ships in the busy harbor, testimony to the importance of Boston as colonial entrepot. *Courtesy of the Childs Gallery.*

and landless young men scrambled for employment and often wound up dependent on public charity. As news spread about the scarcity of farmland in the countryside and the poverty and competition for work in the cities, European immigrants to America tended to bypass New England and settle in the Middle Colonies or along the southern frontier.

Planter Society and Slavery

Southern society was changing as dramatically as New England's. By the end of the seventeenth century, the steady supply of cheap labor from England had begun to disappear. The English economy was improving, and young men who might once have signed on as indentured servants in Virginia or Maryland now chose to remain at home. Those who did immigrate preferred to indenture themselves to farmers and merchants of the Middle Colonies, where work conditions were bearable and economic opportunities were brighter. While this supply of indentured servants was declining, however, a different labor supply was beginning to increase: enslaved Africans.

Although a small number of Africans had been brought to Virginia as early as 1619, the legal differences between black workers and white workers remained vague until the 1660s. By that time, the slowly increasing numbers of African Americans elicited the different, and harsher, treatment that defined slavery in the Caribbean and South America. By midcentury, it became the custom in the Chesapeake to hold black servants for life terms, although their children were still considered free. By the 1660s, colonists turned these customs of **discrimination** into law. In 1662 Virginia took a major step toward making slavery an inherited condition by declaring that "all children born in this country shall be held bond or free according to the condition of the mother."

Slaves did not become the dominant labor force in southern agriculture until the end of the century, although southern planters were probably well aware

discrimination   Treatment based on class, gender, or racial category rather than on merit; prejudice.

of the advantages of slave labor over indentured servitude. First, a slave, bound for life, would never compete with his former master the way freed white servants did. Second, most white colonists did not believe that the English customs regulating a master's treatment of servants had to be applied to African workers. For example, Christian holidays need not be honored for African laborers, and the workday itself could be lengthened without any outcry from white neighbors. Why, then, were the early Chesapeake planters reluctant to import slaves as colonists in the Caribbean and South America had done? Two factors made them hesitate. Dutch control of the African slave trade kept purchasing prices high, and the disease environment of the Chesapeake cut human life short. Until the end of the seventeenth century, therefore, planters considered the financial investment in African laborers both too costly and too risky.

In the 1680s, however, the drawbacks to African slavery began to vanish. Mortality rates fell in the Chesapeake, and the English broke the Dutch monopoly on the slave trade. Fierce competition among English slavers drove prices down and at the same time ensured a steady supply of slaves. Under these conditions, the demand for slaves grew in the Chesapeake. Although only 5 percent of the roughly 9.5 million Africans brought to the Americas came to the North American mainland colonies, their numbers in Virginia and Maryland rose dramatically in the eighteenth century. By 1700, 13 percent of the Chesapeake population was African or of African descent. In Virginia, where only 950 Africans lived in 1660, the black population grew to 120,000 by 1756. At the end of the colonial period, blacks made up 40 percent of Virginia's population.

Colonists who could not afford to purchase African slaves now found themselves at an economic disadvantage. These poorer white Virginians and Marylanders moved west, and new immigrants to the colonies avoided the coastal and piedmont plantation society altogether. Colonial merchants and skilled craftspeople also avoided the Chesapeake, for the planters purchased goods directly from England or used slave labor to manufacture barrels, bricks, and other products. As a result, this region saw the development of few towns or cities that could provide a dense community life. The Chesapeake remained a rural society, dominated by a slaveowning class made prosperous by the labor of African Americans who lived in bondage all their lives.

If tobacco provided a comfortable life for an eighteenth-century planter, rice provided a luxurious one. The Lower South, too, was a plantation society, headed by the wealthiest mainland colonists, the rice growers of the coastal regions of Carolina and Georgia. Members of this planter elite concentrated their social life in elegant Charles Town, where they moved each summer to avoid the heat, humidity, and unhealthy environment of their lowland plantations. With its beautiful townhouses, theaters, and parks, Charles Town was the single truly cosmopolitan city of the South and perhaps the most sophisticated of all mainland cities in North America.

The prosperity that these Lower South planters enjoyed, like the prosperity of the tidewater planters, was based on the forced labor of their slaves. Indeed, the families from Barbados who settled South Carolina had never relied on indentured servants because they arrived with slaves from their Caribbean plantations. By 1708, one-half of the colonial population in Carolina was black, and by 1720, Africans and African Americans outnumbered their white masters. Farther south, in Georgia, the colonists openly defied the trustees' ban on slavery until that ban was finally lifted.

Slave Experience and Slave Culture

Most slaves brought to the mainland colonies did not come directly from Africa. Instead, these men and women were reexported to the Chesapeake or the Lower South after a short period of **seasoning** in the tropical climate of the West Indies. But all imported slaves, whether seasoned or new to the Americas, began their bondage when African slavers, often armed with European weapons, captured men, women, and children and delivered them in chains to European ships anchored along the coast of West Africa (see Map 1.2). While many of those enslaved were considered war captives, others were simply kidnap victims. The slave trader John Barbot recounted the theft of "little Blacks" who had been sent by their parents to "scare away the devouring small birds" in the family cornfield. Even before these captives reached the coast and the European slave ships waiting there, they were introduced to the horrors of slavery. Their captors treated them "severely and barbarously," beating them and inflicting wounds on their bodies. The many who died on the long march from the interior to the coast were left unburied, their bodies to be

seasoning A period during which slaves from Africa were held in the West Indies so they could adjust to the climate and disease environment of the American tropics.

Both Africans and Europeans played critical roles in the African slave trade. In this illustration, African slave drivers march their captives, wearing chains and neck-clamps, from their village. Their likely destination: European ships waiting along the west coast of Africa. *Journey of the Discovery of the Source of the Nile, New York, 1869.*

"devoured by . . . beasts of prey." As the surviving captives were branded and then put into canoes to be rowed to the waiting ships, some committed suicide, leaping overboard into the ocean waters. Slave traders tried to prevent these suicides—every death meant a smaller profit—but were not surprised by them. The slaves, they commented, dreaded life in America more than their captors dreaded hell.

The transatlantic voyage, or **middle passage,** was a nightmare of death, disease, suicide, and sometimes mutiny. The casualties included the white officers and crews of the slave ships, who died of diseases in such great numbers that the waters near Benin in West Africa were known as the "white man's grave." But the loss of black lives was far greater. Slave ships were breeding grounds for scurvy, yellow fever, malaria, dysentery, smallpox, measles, and typhus—each bringing painful death. When smallpox struck his slave ship, one European recorded that "we hauled up eight or ten slaves dead of a morning. The flesh and skin peeled off their wrists when taken hold of." Perhaps 18 percent of all the Africans who began the middle passage died on the ocean.

Until the 1720s, most Chesapeake slaves worked alone on a tobacco farm with the owner and his family or in small groups of two or three, in a system known as "gang labor." This isolation made both marriage and the emergence of a slave community almost impossible. Even on larger plantations, community formation was discouraged by the use of "gangs" made up entirely of women and children or of men only. The steady influx of newly imported slaves, or "outlanders," during the first decades of the eighteenth century also made it difficult for African Americans to work together to create a culture in response to their disorienting circumstances. The new arrivals had to be taught to speak English and to adapt to the demands of slavery. Slowly, however, these involuntary immigrants from different African societies, speaking different languages, practicing different religions, and surviving under the oppressive conditions of slavery, did create a sense of community, weaving together African and European traditions. The result was an African American culture that gave meaning to, and a sense of identity within, the slave's oppressive world.

In the Lower South, where Eliza Lucas Pinckney ran her plantation, slaves were concentrated on large plantations where they had limited or no contact with white society. This isolation from the dominant society allowed them an earlier opportunity to develop a creole, or native, culture. In contrast to gang labor, here a "task labor" system prevailed, in which slaves were assigned certain chores to be completed within a certain time period. This alternative gave rice plan-

middle passage The transatlantic voyage of indentured servants or African slaves to the Americas.

tation slaves some control over their pace of work and some opportunities to manage their free time. Local languages evolved that mixed a basic English vocabulary with words from a variety of African tongues. One of these languages, Gullah, spoken on the Sea Islands off the coast of Georgia and South Carolina, remained the local dialect until the end of the nineteenth century.

For many slaves, the bonds of community that were fostered and forged within this culture became a form of resistance to the enslavement they were forced to endure. But African Americans also developed other ways to show their hatred of slavery. The diary of Virginia planter William Byrd is filled with accounts of daily resistance: slaves who challenged orders, field hands who broke tools and staged work slowdowns, men who pretended sickness and women who claimed pregnancies, household servants who stole supplies and damaged property, and slaves of all ages who ran away to the woods for a day or two or to the slave quarters of a neighboring plantation. African Americans with families, and those who understood the odds against escape, preferred to take disruptive actions like these rather than risk almost certain death in open rebellion.

The Urban Culture of the Middle Colonies

The small family farms of Pennsylvania, with their profitable wheat crops, earned the colony its reputation as the "best poor man's country." Tenant farmers, hired laborers, and even African slaves were not unknown in eastern Pennsylvania, but the colony boasted more comfortable or middling-class farm families than neighboring New York or New Jersey. In New York great estates along the Hudson River controlled much of the colony's good land, and in New Jersey wealthy owners dominated the choicest acreage, a situation that often resulted in tensions between the landlords and their tenants.

What made the Middle Colonies distinctive was not the expansive Hudson River estates or the comfortable farmhouses in seas of wheat. The region's distinguishing feature was the dynamic urban life of its two major cities, New York and Philadelphia. Although only 3 percent of the colonial population lived in the eighteenth-century cities, they were a magnet for young men and women, widows, free African Americans and slaves, and some of the immigrant population pouring into the colonies from Europe. By 1770, Philadelphia's 40,000 residents made it

Enslaved Africans living on the Sea Islands off the Georgia and South Carolina coasts had little contact with white colonists. Although they learned English, they were able to retain many language patterns from their homeland, developing a dialect known as Gullah, which their descendants still speak today. In 1995, the American Bible Society published the Gospel of Luke in this Sea Island dialect. *Courtesy of the Penn Center, History and Culture Department, St. Helena Island, SC.*

the second-largest city in the British Empire. In the same year, 25,000 people crowded onto the tip of New York's Manhattan Island.

New York residents shared their cramped living spaces with chickens and livestock and their streets with roving packs of dogs and pigs. On the narrow cobblestone or gravel streets, pedestrians jostled one another and struggled to avoid being run down by carts, carriages, men on horseback, or cattle being driven to slaughter. Although colonial cities were usually thought to be cleaner than European cities, with better sewerage and drainage systems, garbage and excrement left to rot on the streets provided a feast for flies and scavenging animals, including free-roaming pigs.

City residents faced more serious problems than runaway carts and snarling dogs. Sailors on the ships docked at Philadelphia or New York often carried venereal diseases. These and other communicable diseases spread rapidly in overcrowded areas. Fires also raced through these cities of wooden houses, wharfs, and shops. And crime—especially robbery and assault—was no stranger in the urban environment, where taverns, brothels, and gambling houses were common.

These eighteenth-century cities offered a wide range of occupations and experiences that attracted many a farmer's daughter or son but sometimes overwhelmed a new arrival from the countryside. One farm boy wrote to his father of the "Noise and confusion and Disturbance. I must confess, the jolts of Waggons, the Ratlings of Coaches, the crying of meat for the Market, the [hollering] of negroes and the ten thousand junggles and Noises, that continually Surround us in every Part almost of the Town, confuse my Thinking."

Young men who could endure the noise and confusion sought work as **apprentices** in scores of artisan trades ranging from the luxury crafts of silver- and goldsmithing or cabinet making to the profitable trades of shipbuilding, blacksmithing, or butchering, to the more modest occupations of ropemaking, baking, barbering, or shoemaking. The poorest might find work on the docks or as servants, or they might go to sea. Young women had fewer choices because few trades were open to them. Some might become dressmakers or **milliners,** but domestic service or prostitution were more likely choices. In the Middle Colony cities, as in Boston, widowed farm wives came seeking jobs as nurses, laundresses, teachers, or seamstresses. A widow or an unmarried woman who had a little money could open a shop or set up a tavern or a boarding house.

New York City had the highest concentration of African Americans in the northern colonies. The city attracted many free African American men and women. Only perhaps 5 percent of all mainland colony African Americans were free, and those **manumitted** by their plantation masters frequently chose to remain in the South, although they faced legal and social harassment, including special taxes and severe punishments—for example, striking a white person in self-defense could cost a black man his life. Others, though, made their way to the cities of New England and the Middle Colonies, making a living as laborers and servants or sailors. In addition, although slave labor was not common in New England or on the family farms of the Middle Colonies, slaves were used on New York's docks and wharfs as manual laborers.

Life in the Backcountry

Thomas Malthus, a well-known English economist and diligent student of **demographics,** believed the eighteenth-century population explosion in the English mainland colonies was "without parallel in history." The colonial white population climbed from 225,000 in 1688 to over 2 million in 1775, and the number of African Americans reached 500,000 in the same year. Natural increase accounted for much of this growth, and over half of the colonists were under age 16 in 1775. But hundreds of thousands of white immigrants arrived during the eighteenth century, risking hunger, thirst, discomfort, fear, and death on the transatlantic voyage to start life over in America. The majority of these immigrants ended up in the backcountry of the colonies.

The migration west, whether by native-born or immigrant white colonists, gradually shifted the population center of mainland society. Newcomers from Europe and Britain, as well as descendants of original New England settlers and the younger sons of the tidewater Chesapeake, all saw their best opportunities in the sparsely settled regions of western New York, northern New England, western Pennsylvania, Virginia's Shenandoah Valley, or the Carolina backcountry. Many of these settlers were squatters who cleared a few acres and laid claim by their presence to a promising piece of land.

The westward flow of settlers was part of the American landscape throughout the century, but it became a flood after 1760. A seemingly endless train of carts, sledges, and wagons moved along Indian paths to the west, and the rivers were crowded with rafts and canoes carrying families, farm tools, and livestock. Many of these new immigrants traveled south from Pennsylvania along a wagon road that ran 800 miles from Philadelphia to Virginia, North Carolina, and Augusta, Georgia. Others chose to remain in the Middle Colonies. New York's population rose 39 percent between 1760 and 1776, and in 1769, on the day the land office opened at Fort Pitt (Pittsburgh), over twenty-seven hundred applicants showed up to register for land.

By 1760, perhaps 700,000 new colonists had made their homes in the mainland colonies. In the early

apprentice   A person bound by legal agreement to work for an employer for a specific length of time in exchange for instruction in a trade, craft, or business.

milliner   A maker or designer of hats.

manumit   To free from slavery or bondage; to emancipate.

demographics   Statistical data on population.

Few women worked in the skilled trades or crafts, although widows and daughters might manage a shop after a husband or father died. The mantua maker shown here was considered an artisan and could command a good price for her skills, which were making fancy gowns and other elaborately sewn clothing. *Courtesy of the American Antiquarian Society.*

part of the century, the largest immigrant group was the **Scots-Irish.** Later, German settlers dominated. But an occasional traveler on the wagon roads might be Italian, Swiss, Irish, Welsh, or a European Jew. Most striking, the number of British immigrants swelled after 1760, causing anger and alarm within the British government. The steady stream of young English men and women out of the country prompted government officials to consider passing laws curbing emigration. What prompted this transatlantic population shift? It was not always desperation or oppression. Many arrived with enough resources to finance their new life in the colonies. Some became indentured servants or redemptioners only to preserve those savings. While unemployment, poverty, the oppression of landlords, and crop failures pushed men and women out of Europe or Britain, it is also true that the availability of cheap land, a greater likelihood of religious freedom, and the chance to pursue a craft successfully pulled others toward the colonies.

Conflicts Among the Colonists

■ What events illustrated the tensions between races in colonial society?

■ What conflicts arose between elites and poorer colonists?

The strains of economic inequality being felt in every region of mainland British America frequently erupted into violent confrontations. At the same time, tensions between Indians and colonists continued, and tensions between black and white colonists increased as both slave and free black populations grew during the eighteenth century. In almost every decade, blood was shed as colonist battled colonist over economic opportunity, personal freedom, western lands, or political representation.

Slave Revolts, North and South

White slave masters in both the Chesapeake and the Lower South knew that a slave revolt was always a possibility, for enslaved Africans and African Americans shared with other colonists what one observer called a "fondness for freedom." Planters thus took elaborate precautions to prevent rebellions, assembling armed patrols that policed the roads and woods near their plantations. These patrols were usually efficient, and the punishment they inflicted was deadly. Even if rebels escaped immediate capture, few safe havens were available to them. Individual runaways had a hard time sustaining their freedom, but dozens of rebels from one plantation were usually doomed once whites on neighboring plantations were alerted. Despite these odds, slaves continued to seek their liberty, often timing their revolts to coincide with epidemics or imperial wars that distracted the white community.

The most famous slave revolt of the eighteenth century, the **Stono Rebellion,** took place in the midst of a yellow fever epidemic in Charles Town just as news of war between England and Spain reached the colony of South Carolina. Early on a Sunday morning in September 1739, about twenty slaves gathered at the Stono River, south of Charles Town. Their leader, Jemmy, had been born in Africa, possibly in the Congo but more likely Angola, for twenty or more of those who

Scots-Irish   Protestant Scottish settlers in British-occupied northern Ireland, many of whom migrated to the colonies in the eighteenth century.

Stono Rebellion   Slave revolt in South Carolina in 1739; it prompted the colony to pass harsher laws governing the movement of slaves and the capture of runaways.

eventually joined the revolt were Angolan. The rebels seized guns and gunpowder, killed several planter families and storekeepers, and then headed south. Rather than traveling quietly through the woods, the rebels marched boldly in open view, beating drums to invite slaves on nearby plantations to join them in their flight to Spanish Florida. Other slaves answered the call, and the Stono rebels' ranks grew to almost one hundred. But in Charleston, planters were gathering to put an end to the uprising. By late Sunday afternoon white militias had overtaken and surrounded the escaping slaves. The Stono rebels stood and fought, but the militiamen killed almost thirty of them. Those who were captured were executed. Those who escaped into the countryside were hunted down.

The Stono Rebellion terrified white South Carolinians, who hurried to make the colony's already harsh slave codes even more brutal. The government increased the slave patrols in both size and frequency. It also raised the bounties, or rewards offered for the capture of runaways, to make sure that fleeing slaves taken alive and unharmed, or brought in dead and scalped, were worth hunting down.

Hostilities between black colonists and white colonists were not confined to the South. In the crowded environment of New York City, white residents showed the same fear of slave rebellions as Carolina or Virginia planters. Their fears became reality at midnight on April 6, 1712, when two dozen blacks, armed with guns, hatchets, and swords, set fire to a downtown building. Startled New Yorkers who rushed to keep the flames from spreading were attacked by the rebels, leaving nine people shot, stabbed, or beaten to death. Six more were wounded. Militia units from as far away as Westchester were called out to quell the riot and to cut off any hope of escape for the slaves. Realizing the hopelessness of their situation, six committed suicide. Those who were taken alive suffered horrible punishment. According to the colonial governor, Robert Hunter, "some were burnt, others were hanged, one broke on the wheel, and one hung alive in chains in the town." Twenty-nine years later, the mere rumor of a conspiracy by African Americans to commit arson was enough to move white residents to violent reprisals. Despite the lack of any evidence to support the charge, 101 of the city's black residents were arrested—18 of them were hanged and 18 burned alive.

Clashes Between the Rich and the Poor

Most often, class tensions erupted into violence as tenant farmers battled landlords or their agents and backcountry farmers took up arms against the elite planters who dominated their colonial governments. New York tenant farmers had long resented the legal and economic power that manor lords wielded over their lives, and protests, labeled "land riots" by the wealthy landlords, were common throughout the century. Likewise, New Jersey landlords who tried to squeeze higher rents out of their tenants provoked bitterness—and frequent bloodshed. In January 1745, for example, tenants in Essex County, New Jersey, rioted after three of their number were arrested by local authorities. When the sheriff tried to bring one of the alleged troublemakers to the county courthouse, he was "assaulted by a great number of persons, with clubbs and other weapons," who rescued the prisoner. Later, a "multitude" armed with axes stormed the jail and rescued the remaining prisoners. Such tenant uprisings in both colonies continued during the 1750s and 1760s, as landless men expressed their resentment and frustration at their inability to acquire land of their own.

In the backcountry, settlers were likely to face two enemies: Indians and the established political powers of their own colonies. Often the clashes with the colonial government were about Indian policy. Eighteenth-century colonial legislatures and governors preferred diplomacy to military action, but western settlers wanted a more aggressive program to push Indians out of the way. Even when frontier hostilities led to bloodshed, the colonists of the coastal communities were reluctant to spend tax money to provide protection along the settlement line. In the end, bitter western settlers frequently took matters into their own hands. Bacon's Rebellion was the best example of this kind of vigilante action in the seventeenth century.

The revolt by Pennsylvania's Paxton Boys was the most dramatic eighteenth-century episode. More than most colonies, Pennsylvania's Quaker-dominated government encouraged settlers to find peaceful ways to coexist with local tribes. But the eighteenth-century Scots-Irish settlers did not share the Quaker commitment to pacifism. They demanded protection against Indian raids on isolated homesteads and small frontier towns. In 1763 frustrated settlers from Paxton, Pennsylvania, attacked a village of peaceful Conestoga Indians. Although the murder of these Indians solved nothing and could not be justified, hundreds of western colonists supported this vigilante group known as the Paxton Boys. The group marched on Philadelphia, the capital city of Pennsylvania, to press their demands for an aggressive Indian policy. With Philadelphia residents fearing their city would be attacked

Tensions between backcountry farmers and the colonial officials of North and South Carolina came to a head in the 1760s and 1770s. Calling themselves "Regulators," frontier farmers voiced their complaints about corrupt government agencies or the absence of vital services, but their protests went unheeded. By 1768, the Regulators had taken up arms against the government. Their rebellions, however, were crushed by officials like Governor Tryon of North Carolina. *Courtesy of the North Carolina Department of Archives & History, Raleigh, North Carolina.*

and looted, the popular printer and political leader Benjamin Franklin met the **Paxton Boys** on the outskirts of the city and negotiated a truce. The outcome was a dramatic shift in Pennsylvania Indian policy, illustrated by an official bounty for Indian scalps.

Vigilante action, however, was not always connected to Indian conflicts. In South Carolina, trouble arose because coastal planters refused to provide basic government services to the backcountry. Settlers in western South Carolina paid their taxes, but because their counties had no courts, they had to travel long distances to register land transactions or file lawsuits. The government provided no sheriffs either, and outlaws preyed on these communities. With the coastal planters refusing to admit any backcountry representatives to the colonial legislature, settlers could do little but complain, petition, and demand relief. In the 1760s, the farmers took matters into their own hands, choosing to "regulate" backcountry affairs themselves through vigilante action. These **Regulators** pursued and punished backcountry outlaws, dispensing justice without the aid of courts or judges.

In North Carolina, a similar power struggle led to a brief civil war. Here, a Regulator movement was organized against legal outlaws, a collection of corrupt local officials in the backcountry appointed because of their political connections to the colony's slaveholding elite. These officials awarded contracts to friends for building roads and bridges. They charged exorbitant fees to register deeds, surveys, or even the sale of cattle. And they set high poll taxes on their backcountry neighbors. The North Carolina Regula-

tors wanted these men removed, and when their demands were ignored, they mounted a taxpayers' rebellion. When tax collection dried up, the governor acted, raising a militia of twelve hundred men to march on the rebels. The showdown took place in 1771 near the Alamance River, where the governor's army easily defeated the two thousand poorly armed Regulators. Six of the movement's leaders were then hanged. The brief east-west war ended in North Carolina, but the bitterness remained. During the Revolutionary War, when most of North Carolina's coastal elite cast their lot for independence, many of the farmers of the backcountry—disgusted with colonial government—sided with England.

Reason and Religion in Colonial Society

■ What political and personal expectations arose from Enlightenment philosophy?

■ What was the impact of the Great Awakening on colonial attitudes toward authority?

> **Paxton Boys** Settlers in Paxton, Pennsylvania, who massacred Conestoga Indians in 1763 and then marched on Philadelphia to demand that the colonial government provide better defense against the Indians.
>
> **Regulators** Frontier settlers in the Carolinas who protested the lack or abuse of government services in their area; the North Carolina Regulators were suppressed by government troops in 1771.

Trade routes tied the eighteenth-century colonial world to parent societies across the Atlantic. The bonds of language and custom tied the immigrant communities in America to their homelands too. In addition to these economic and cultural ties, the flow of ideas and religious beliefs helped sustain a transatlantic community.

The Impact of the Enlightenment

At the end of the seventeenth century, a new intellectual movement arose in Europe: the **Enlightenment.** Enlightenment thinkers argued that reason, or rational thinking, rather than divine revelation, tradition, intuition, or established authority, was the true path to reliable knowledge and to human progress. A group of brilliant French thinkers called **philosophes,** including Voltaire, Rousseau, Diderot, Buffon, and Montesquieu, were the central figures of the Enlightenment. These philosophers, political theorists, and scientists disagreed about many issues, but all embraced the belief that nature could provide for all human wants and that human nature was basically good rather than flawed by original sin. Humans, they insisted, were rational and capable of making progress toward a perfect society if they studied nature, unlocked its secrets, and carefully nurtured the best human qualities in themselves and their children. This belief in progress and perfectibility became a central Enlightenment theme.

The Enlightenment was the handiwork of a small, intensely intellectual elite in Europe, and only the colonial elite had access to the books and essays that these philosophers produced. Elite colonists were drawn to two aspects of Enlightenment thought: its new religious philosophy of **deism** and the political theory of the "social contract." Deism appealed to colonists such as the Philadelphia scientist, writer, and political leader Benjamin Franklin and Virginia planters George Washington and Thomas Jefferson, men who were intensely interested in science and the scientific method. Deists believed that the universe operated according to logical, natural laws, without divine intervention. They thus denied the existence of any miracles after the Creation and rejected the value of prayer in this rational universe.

The most widely accepted Enlightenment ideas in the colonies were those of the English political theorist John Locke, who published his *Essay Concerning Human Understanding* in 1690 and *Two Treatises of Government* in 1691. In his political essays Locke argued that

human beings have certain natural rights that they cannot give away—or alienate—and that no one can take from them. Those rights include the right to own themselves and their own labor and the right to own that part of nature on which they have labored productively—that is, their property. However, in exchange for the government's protection of their natural rights to life, liberty, and property, people make a social contract to give up absolute freedom and to live under a rule of law. According to Locke, the government created by the **social contract** receives its political power from the consent of those it governs, and it cannot claim a divine right to rule. In Locke's scheme, the people express their will, or their demands and interests, through a representative assembly, and the government is obligated to protect and respect the natural rights of its citizens and serve their interests. If the government fails to do this, Locke said, the people have a right, even a duty, to rebel. Locke's theory was especially convincing because it meshed with political developments in England from the civil war to the Glorious Revolution that were familiar to the colonists.

Religion and Religious Institutions

Deism attracted little attention among ordinary colonists, but many eighteenth-century Americans were impressed by the growing religious diversity of their society. The waves of immigration had greatly increased the number of Protestant sects in the colonies, and colonists began to see religious toleration as a practical matter. The commitment to religious toleration did not come at an even pace, of course, nor did it extend to everyone. No colony allowed Catholics to vote or hold elective office after Rhode Island disfranchised Catholics in 1729, and even Maryland

Enlightenment An eighteenth-century intellectual movement that stressed the pursuit of knowledge through reason and challenged the value of religious belief, emotion, and tradition.

philosophe Any of the popular French intellectuals or social philosophers of the Enlightenment, such as Voltaire, Diderot, or Rousseau.

deism The belief that God created the universe in such a way that it could operate without any further divine intervention such as miracles.

social contract A theoretical agreement between the governed and the government that defines and limits the rights and obligations of each.

did not permit Catholics to celebrate Mass openly until Catholics in the city of Baltimore broke the law and founded a church in 1763. Connecticut granted freedom of worship to "sober dissenters" such as Anglicans, Quakers, and Baptists as early as 1708, but in 1750 its legislature declared it a felony to deny the **Trinity.** When colonists spoke of religious toleration, they did not mean the separation of church and state. On the contrary, the tradition of an **established church,** supported by taxes from all members of a community regardless of where they worshiped, went unchallenged in the southern colonies, where Anglicanism was established, and in Massachusetts and Connecticut, where **Congregationalism** was established.

As the diversity in churches was growing, the number of colonists who did not regularly attend any church at all was growing too. Some colonists were more preoccupied with secular concerns, such as their place in the economic community, than with spiritual ones. Others were losing their devotion to churches where the sermons were more intellectual than impassioned and the worship service was more formal than inspiring.

Into this moment stepped that group of **charismatic** preachers who, like Jonathan Edwards, denounced the obsession with profit and wealth they saw around them, condemned the sinfulness and depravity of all people, warned of the terrible punishments of eternal hellfires, and praised the saving grace of Jesus Christ. In a society divided by regional disputes, racial conflicts, and economic competition, these preachers held out a promise of social harmony based on the surrender of individual pride and a renewed love and fear of God. In voices filled with "Thunder and Lightning," they called for a revival of basic Protestant belief.

The Great Awakening

The religious revival of the eighteenth century was based as much on a new approach to preaching as on the message itself. This new-style preaching first appeared in New Jersey and Pennsylvania in the 1720s, when two **itinerant** preachers—Theodore Frelinghuysen and William Tennent Jr.—began calling the local churches to task for lack of devotion to God and for "cold" preaching. Tennent established what he called a "log college" to train fiery preachers who could spread a Christian revival throughout the colonies. Soon afterward, Jonathan Edwards spread the revival to Massachusetts. Like Frelinghuysen and Tennent, Edwards berated the lukewarm preaching

of local ministers and then turned to the task of saving lost souls. The revival, or **Great Awakening,** sparked by men like Edwards and Tennent, spread rapidly throughout the colonies, carried from town to town by the wandering ministers called "Awakeners." These preachers stirred entire communities to renewed religious devotion.

The Great Awakening's success was ensured in 1740, when **George Whitefield** toured the colonies from Charles Town to Maine. Everywhere this young preacher went, crowds gathered to hear him. Often the audiences grew so large that church sanctuaries could not hold them and Whitefield would finish his service in a nearby field or village green. His impact was electric. "Hearing him preach gave me a heart wound," wrote one colonist, and even America's most committed deist, Benjamin Franklin, confessed that Whitefield's sermons moved him. Whitefield himself recorded his effect on a crowd: "A wonderful power was in the room and with one accord they began to cry out and weep most bitterly for the space of half an hour." As the sermon progressed, the audience response became more intense: "Some of the people were as pale as death; others were wringing their hands; others lying on the ground; others sinking into the arms of their friends; and most lifting their eyes to heaven, and crying to God for mercy."

The Great Awakening did not go unchallenged. Some ministers had gladly turned over their pulpits to Awakeners. But others, angered by the criticisms of

---

Trinity   In Christian doctrine, the belief that God has three divine aspects—Father, Son, and Holy Spirit.

established church   The official church of a nation or colony, usually supported by taxes collected from all citizens, no matter what their religious beliefs or place of worship.

Congregationalism   A form of Protestant church government in which the local congregation is independent and self-governing; in the colonies, the Puritans were Congregationalists.

charismatic   Having a spiritual power or personal quality that stirs enthusiasm and devotion in large numbers of people.

itinerant   Traveling from place to place.

Great Awakening   A series of religious revivals based on fiery preaching and emotionalism that swept across the colonies during the second quarter of the eighteenth century.

George Whitefield   English evangelical preacher of the Great Awakening whose charismatic style attracted huge crowds during his preaching tours of the colonies.

The English evangelical minister, George Whitefield, inspired awe and prompted renewed commitment to Christianity everywhere he preached. Crowds overflowed into the fields outside of colonial country churches, and men and women in his audiences often fainted or cried out in ecstasy. As the leading figure of the Great Awakening, Whitefield was loved by thousands and criticized by ministers who opposed the religious enthusiasm he represented. *Bridgeman Art Library Ltd.*

became Anglicans. These religious conflicts frequently became intertwined with secular disputes. Colonists who had long-standing disagreements over Indian policy or economic issues lined up on opposite sides of the Awakening. Class tensions influenced religious loyalties, as poor colonists pronounced judgment on their rich neighbors using religious vocabulary that equated luxury, dancing, and gambling with sin.

Thus, rather than fulfilling its promise of social harmony, the Great Awakening increased strife and tension among colonists. Yet it had positive effects as well. For example, the Awakening spurred the growth of higher education. During the complicated theological arguments between Old Lights and Awakeners, the revivalists came to see the value of theological training. They founded new colleges, including Rutgers, Brown, Princeton, and Dartmouth, to prepare their clergy just as the Old Lights relied on Harvard and Yale to train theirs. One of the most important effects of the Great Awakening was also one of the least expected. The resistance to authority, the activism involved in creating new institutions, the participation in debate and argument—these experiences reinforced a sense that protest and resistance were acceptable, not just in religious matters but in the realm of politics as well.

Government and Politics in the Mainland Colonies

■ What circumstances limited a colonial governor's exercise of royal power?

■ What was the result of the struggle for power between the colonial assemblies and the colonial governors?

The English mainland colonies were part of a large and complex empire, and the English government had created many agencies to set and enforce imperial policy. Parliament passed laws regulating colonial affairs, the royal navy and army determined colonial defense, and English diplomats decided which foreign nations were friends and which were foes. But from the beginning, most **proprietors,** joint-stock

their preaching and suggestions that they themselves were unsaved, launched a counterattack against the revivalists and their "beastly brayings." Members of the colonial elite were roused to political action against a movement that constantly condemned the worldly amusements they enjoyed, such as dancing, gambling, drinking, theater, and elegant clothing. In Connecticut, for example, the assembly passed a law banning itinerant ministers from preaching outside their own parishes.

Bitter fights within congregations and denominations also developed. "Old Light" Congregationalists upheld the established service but "New Lights" chose revivalism, and "Old Side" Presbyterians battled "New Sides" over preaching styles and the content of the worship service. Congregations split, and the minority groups hurriedly formed new churches. Many awakened believers left their own **denominations** entirely, joining the Baptists or the Methodists. Antirevivalists also left their strife-ridden churches and

> **denomination**   A group of religious congregations that accept the same doctrines and are united under a single name.
>
> **proprietor**   In colonial America, a proprietor was a wealthy Englishman who received a large grant of land in America from the king or queen in order to create a new colony.

companies, and kings had also found it convenient to create local governments within their colonies to handle day-to-day affairs. Virginia's House of Burgesses was the first locally elected legislative body in the colonies, but by 1700 every mainland colony boasted a representative assembly generally made up of its wealthiest men.

In the first half of the eighteenth century, the British government decided to restructure its colonial administration, hoping to make it more efficient. Despite this reorganization, the government was notably lax in enforcing colonial regulations. Even so, colonists often objected to the constraints of imperial law and challenged the role of the king or the proprietors in shaping local political decisions. This **insubordination** led to a long and steady struggle for power between colonial governors and colonial assemblies. Over the first half of the century, the colonists did wrest important powers from the governors. But the British government remained adamant that ultimate power, or **sovereignty,** rested in the hands of king and Parliament.

Imperial Institutions and Policies

By the eighteenth century, the British government had divided responsibility for colonial regulation and management among several departments, commissions, and agencies. Even though the Lords Commissioners of Trade and Plantations had been created in 1696 to coordinate colonial **policy,** authority remained fragmented. The treasury board, for example, continued to supervise all colonial financial affairs, and its customs office collected all trade revenues. The admiralty board, however, had the authority to enforce trade regulations. The potential for conflict among all these departments, commissions, and agencies was great. But British indifference to colonial affairs helped to preserve harmony.

Parliament set the tone for colonial administration in the eighteenth century with a policy that came to be known unofficially as **salutary neglect.** Salutary, or healthy, neglect meant the government was satisfied with relaxed enforcement of most regulations as long as the colonies remained dutifully loyal in military and economic matters. As long as specific, or **enumerated,** colonial raw materials continued to flow into British hands and the colonists continued to rely on British manufactured goods, salutary neglect suited the expectations of the king, Parliament, and most government officials.

Salutary neglect did not mean that the colonists were free to do exactly as they pleased. Even in purely domestic matters the colonial governments could not operate as freely as many of them desired. The most intense political conflicts before the 1760s centered on the colonial assemblies' power to govern local affairs as they chose.

Local Colonial Government

The eighteenth-century mainland colonies remained a mixture of royal, proprietary, and corporate colonies, although the majority were held directly by the king. Whatever the form of ownership, however, the colonies were strikingly similar in the structure and operation of their governments. Each colony had a governor appointed by the king or the proprietor or, in Connecticut and Rhode Island (the two **corporate colonies**), elected to executive office. Each had a council, usually appointed by the governor, though sometimes elected by the assembly, which served as an advisory body to the governor. And each had an elected representative assembly with lawmaking and taxing powers.

The governor was the linchpin of local government because he represented royal authority and imperial interests in the local setting. In theory, his powers were impressive. He alone could call the assembly into session, and he had the power to dismiss it. He also could veto any act passed by the assembly. He had the sole power to appoint and dismiss judges, justices of the peace, and all government officials. He could grant pardons and reprieves. The governor made all land grants, oversaw all aspects of colonial trade, and conducted all diplomatic negotiations with the Indians. Because he was commander in chief of the military and naval forces of the colony, he decided what action, if any, to take in conflicts between colonists and Indians. Armed with such extensive powers, the man who sat in the English colonial governor's seat ought to have been respected—or at least obeyed.

---

insubordination   Resistance to authority; disobedience.

sovereignty   The ultimate power in a nation or a state.

policy   A course of action taken by a government or a ruler.

salutary neglect   The British policy of relaxed enforcement of most colonial trade regulations as long as the mainland colonies remained loyal to the government and profitable within the British economy.

enumerated   Added to the list of regulated goods or crops.

corporate colony   A self-governing colony, not directly under the control of proprietors or the Crown.

Historians are sometimes simply wrong. For over a century, experts in New York history were certain that this was a portrait of Lord Cornbury, royal governor of New York from 1702 to 1708. Cornbury, it was said, bore a striking resemblance to his cousin Queen Anne and had dressed in women's clothing in order to emphasize his connection to her authority and power. A great story, isn't it? But recently a scholar has proven that this is not Lord Cornbury. Now the task is to discover who the person in the portrait really is. *New York Historical Society.*

A closer look, however, reveals that the governor was not so powerful after all. First, in many cases he was not free to exercise his own judgment because he was bound by a set of instructions written by the board of trade. Though highly detailed and specific, these instructions often bore little relation to the realities the governor encountered in his colony. Instead, by limiting his ability to improvise and compromise, they proved more burdensome than helpful to many a frustrated governor.

Second, the governor's own skills and experience were often limited. Few men in the prime of their careers sought posts 3,000 miles from England, in the provinces. Thus governorships went to **bureaucrats** nearing the end of sometimes unimpressive careers or to younger men who were new to the rough-and-tumble games of politics. Many colonial governors were honorable and competent, but enough of them were fools, scoundrels, or eccentrics to give the office a poor reputation.

Finally, most governors served brief terms, sometimes too brief for them to learn which local issues were critical or to discern friend from foe in the colonial government. For many, the goal was simply to survive the ordeal. They were willing to surrender much of their authority to the local assemblies in exchange for a calm, uneventful, and, they hoped, profitable term in office.

Even the most ignorant or incompetent governor might have managed to dominate colonial politics had he been able to apply the grease that oiled eighteenth-century political wheels: patronage. The kings of England had learned that political loyalty could be bought on the floor of Parliament with royal favors. By midcentury, over half of the members of Parliament held Crown offices or had received government contracts. Unfortunately for the colonial governor, he had few favors to hand out. The king could also bribe voters or intimidate them to ensure the election of his supporters to Parliament, but the governor lacked this option as well. The number of eligible voters in most colonies was far too great for a governor's resources.

The most significant restraint on the governor's authority was not his rigid instructions, his inexperience, or his lack of patronage, but the fact that the assembly paid his salary. England expected the colonists to foot the bill for local government, including compensation for the governor. Governors who challenged the assembly too strongly or too often usually found a sudden, unaccountable budget crisis delaying or diminishing their allowances. Those who bent to assembly wishes could expect bonuses in the form of cash or grants of land.

While the governors learned that their great powers were not so great after all, the assemblies in every colony were making an opposite discovery: they learned they could broaden their powers far beyond the king's intent. They fought for and won more freedom from the governor's supervision and influence, gaining the right to elect their own speaker of the assembly, make their own procedural rules, and settle contested elections. They also increased their power over taxation and the use of revenues, or, in eighteenth-century parlance, their **power of the purse.**

> **bureaucrat**   A government official, usually appointed, who is deeply devoted to the details of administrative procedures.
>
> **power of the purse**   The political power that is enjoyed by the branch of government that controls taxation and the use of tax monies.

In their pursuit of power, these local political leaders had several advantages besides the governor's weakness. They came from a small social and economic elite who were regularly elected to office for both practical and social reasons. First, they could satisfy the high property qualifications set for most officeholding. Second, they could afford to accept an office that cost more to win and to hold than its modest salary could cover. Third, a habit of **deference**—respect for the opinions and decisions of the more educated and wealthy families in a community—won them office. Although as many as 50 to 80 percent of adult free white males in a colony could vote, few were considered suitable to hold office. Generations of fathers and sons from elite families thus dominated political offices. These men knew one another well, and although they fought among themselves for positions and power, they could effectively unite against outsiders such as an arrogant governor. Finally, through long careers in the legislature they honed the political, administrative, and even **oratorical** skills that would enable them to contend successfully with the royal appointees.

Conflicting Views of the Assemblies

The king and Parliament gave local assemblies the authority to raise taxes, pay government salaries, direct the care of the poor, and maintain bridges and roads. To the colonists, this division of authority indicated an acceptance of a two-tiered system of government: (1) a central government that created and executed imperial policy and (2) a set of local governments that managed colonial domestic affairs. If these levels of government were not equal in their power and scope, at least—in the minds of the colonists—they were equally legitimate. On both points, however, the British disagreed. They did not acknowledge a multilevel system. They saw a single vast empire ruled by one government consisting of king and Parliament. The colonial governments may have acquired the power to establish temporary operating procedures and to pass minor laws, but British leaders did not believe they had acquired a share of the British government's sovereign power. As the governor of Pennsylvania put it in 1726, the assembly's actions and decisions should in "no ways interfere . . . with the Legal Prerogative of the Crown or the true Legislative Power of the Mother State." "True Legislative Power" belonged with Parliament, and most British political leaders considered the assemblies to

be little more than **ad hoc** bodies, specially created to meet immediate needs and serve as surrogates, or deputies, for those with real authority.

North America and the Struggle for Empire

- What were the diplomatic and military goals of Europeans and American Indians in North America?
- What were the major effects of the imperial wars on the American colonists?
- How did the English victory in 1763 affect people in North America?

During the seventeenth century, most of the violence and warfare in colonial America arose from struggles either between Indians and colonists over land or among colonists over political power and the use of revenues and resources. These struggles continued to be important during the eighteenth century. By 1690, however, the most persistent dangers to colonial peace and safety came from the fierce rivalries between the French, Spanish, and the English (see Map 4.1). Between 1688 and 1763, these European powers waged five bloody and costly wars. Most of these conflicts were motivated by politics at home, although colonial ambitions spurred the last and most decisive of them. No matter where these worldwide wars began, or what their immediate cause, colonists were usually drawn into them.

When imperial wars included fighting in America, English colonists were expected to fight without the assistance of British troops. Often the enemy the colonists faced was neither French nor Spanish but Indian, a result of the alliances Indians had formed with Europeans to advance their own interests. For example, until the mid-seventeenth century, the Huron-dominated confederacy to the north supported the French (see Map 4.2). These two allies had a strong economic bond: the French profited from the fur trade while the Hurons enjoyed the benefits of European manufactured goods. The English colonists were not without their Indian allies, however. Although

deference Yielding to the judgment or wishes of a social or intellectual superior.

oratorical Related to the art of persuasive and eloquent public speaking.

ad hoc Created for, or concerned with, one specific purpose; Latin for "to this [end]."

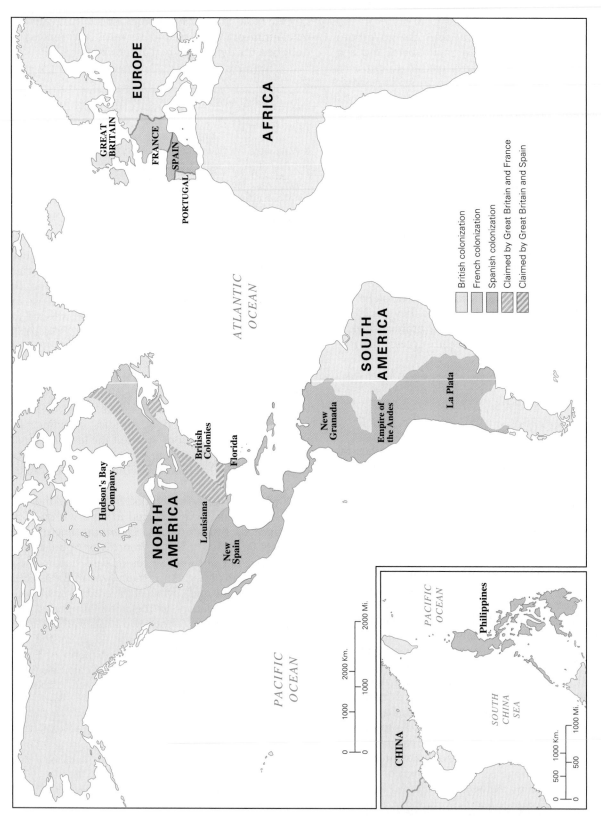

MAP 4.1 The European Empires in Eighteenth-Century America This map shows the colonization of the Americas and the Philippines by three rival powers. It is clear from the map why British colonists felt vulnerable to attack by England's archenemies, France and Spain, until English victory in the Great War for Empire in 1763.

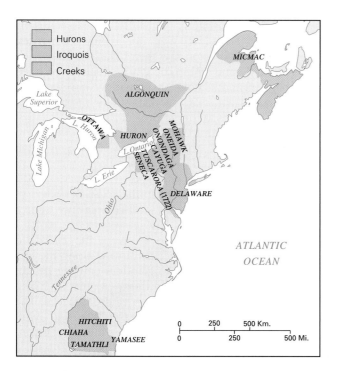

MAP 4.2 The Indian Confederacies This map shows the three major Indian military and political coalitions—the Huron, Iroquois, and Creek Confederacies. Unlike the squabbling English mainland colonies, these Indian tribes understood the value of military unity in the face of threats to their land and their safety and the importance of diplomatic unity in negotiating with their European allies.

the older, seventeenth-century alliances between the Wampanoags and the Plymouth settlers had ended in violence, other alliances held. Ties with the Iroquois League were carefully nurtured by the English, who appreciated the advantages of friendship with Indians living south of the Great Lakes, along crucial fur trading routes. For their part, the Iroquois were willing to cooperate with a European power who was the enemy of their perpetual rival, the Hurons. The southern English colonists turned to the **Creek Confederacy** when wars with Spain erupted. Yet the colonists' own land hunger always worked to undermine—if not unravel—these Indian alliances. Thus the southern tribes' support was unreliable, and the Iroquois, wary of the English westward expansion, often chose to pursue an independent strategy of neutrality.

The wars that raged from 1689 until 1763 were part of a grand effort by rival European nations to control the balance of power at home and abroad. The colonists often felt like pawns in the hands of the more powerful players, and resentment sometimes overshadowed their patriotic pride when England was victorious. Whatever their views on imperial diplomacy, few colonists escaped the impact of this nearly century-long struggle for power between England, France, and Spain, for periods of peace were short and the long shadow of war hung over them until Britain's major triumph in 1763.

An Age of Imperial Warfare

William and Mary's ascent to the throne in 1689 ushered in an era of political stability and religious tolerance in Britain. But it also ushered in an age of imperial warfare. Almost immediately, France took up arms against England, Holland, Sweden, and Spain in what the Europeans called the War of the League of Augsburg but which colonists called simply King William's War. With France as the enemy, New England and northern New York bore the brunt of the fighting. Because the English sent no troops to defend the border communities there, colonial armies, composed largely of untrained militia companies, and their Iroquois allies defended British interests—and their own families—in this long and vicious war. As reports of atrocities mounted, the governments of Massachusetts, Plymouth, Connecticut, and New York made a rare attempt at cooperation. They pledged to combine their resources in order to invade Canada. In the end, however, few made good on their promises of men or money, and colonial attacks on Montreal and Quebec both failed. When the war finally ended with the Treaty of Ryswick in 1697, 659 New Englanders had died in battle, in raids, or in captivity. The death toll for the Iroquois nations was higher—between 600 and 1,300. The lessons of the war were equally apparent. First, colonists paid a high price for their disunity and lack of cooperation. Second, no New Englander could ever feel secure until the French had been driven out of Canada. Third, the colonists needed the aid of the English army and navy to effectively drive the French away.

The colonists had little time to enjoy peace. Five years later, in 1702, the conflict colonists called Queen Anne's War began, once again pitting France and its now dependent ally, Spain, against England, Holland, and Austria. In this eleven-year struggle, colonists faced enemies on both their southern and northern borders. Once again, those enemies included Indians.

> **Creek Confederacy** Alliance of the Creeks and smaller Indian tribes living in the Southeast.

Imperial wars between England and her rivals often drew the colonists and neighboring Indian tribes into conflict. Between 1711 and 1713, land-hungry North Carolinians, joined by South Carolina and Virginia militias and by Creek and Yamasee troops, turned Queen Anne's War into a brutal and successful war on the nearby Tuscarora Indians. *South Carolina Historical Society.*

Between 1711 and 1713, southern colonists were caught up in fierce warfare with the Tuscaroras, who were angered by North Carolina land seizures. The casualties were staggering. Some 150 settlers were killed in the opening hours of the war, and in the following months both sides outdid one another in cruelty. Stakes were run through the bodies of women, children were murdered, and Indian captives were roasted alive. South Carolina and Virginia sent arms and supplies to aid the North Carolina colonists, and the Creek and Yamasee Indians fought beside the white settlers against the Tuscaroras. When this war-within-a-war ended in 1713, more than a thousand Tuscaroras were dead and nearly four hundred had been sold into slavery. The survivors took refuge in the land of the Iroquois.

The war in the north was just as deadly. Indian and French raids, such as the one on Deerfield, Massachusetts, cost the lives of many New Englanders. Despite repeated calls for help, the British did not send troops to defend their northern colonies. Disappointed New Englanders raised an army of nearly thirty-five hundred men and, in 1710, triumphantly took control of the military post at Port Royal and with it all of Acadia, or as the English called it, Nova Scotia.

The war, which ended in 1713, cost New Englanders dearly. The high death toll of King William's War and Queen Anne's War was staggering: nearly one of every four soldiers in uniform had died. The financial cost was equally devastating. Four-fifths of Massachusetts revenues in 1704–1705 went for military expenses. Homeowners in Boston saw their taxes rise 42 percent between 1700 and 1713. The city's streets were filled with beggars and its homes with widows. In Connecticut and Massachusetts, colonists spoke bitterly of the Mother Country's failure to protect them. Yet this time New Englanders could see tangible gains from the imperial struggle. The English flag now flew over Nova Scotia, Newfoundland, and Hudson Bay, which meant that Maine settlers no longer had to fear enemy raids. New England fleets could fish the cod-rich waters of Newfoundland more safely. And colonial fur traders could profit from Hudson Bay's resources.

For a generation, Europeans kept the peace. In America, however, violence continued along the line of settlement, with New Englanders battling Indian allies of the French and southern colonists making war on their own former allies, the Yamasees. The short but ferociously fought Yamasee War of 1715 left four hundred of South Carolina's five thousand colonists dead in the first twelve months of fighting, a higher death rate than white Massachusetts had sustained in King Philip's War.

At the end of the 1730s, the calm in Europe was fractured. By 1740, France, Spain, and Prussia were at war with England and its ally, Austria. This war, known in the colonies as King George's War, again meant enemy attacks on both the northern and southern colonies. New Englanders, swept up in the Great Awakening, viewed the war as a Protestant crusade against Catholicism, a holy war designed to rid the continent of religious enemies. Yet when the war ended in 1748, France still retained its Canadian territories.

The Great War for Empire

Despite three major wars and countless border conflicts, the map of North America had changed very little. Colonial efforts to capture Canada or to rid the southwest of Indian enemies had not succeeded. Yet veterans of the wars, and their civilian colonial supporters, spoke with pride of the colonial armies as excellent military forces. Without assistance from British regulars or the British navy, militiamen and volunteer armies had defended their communities, defeated Indian enemies, and captured important French forts.

Many colonists remained angry and bewildered, however, by the Mother Country's military neglect. From their perspective, they were being dragged into European wars that did not concern them. Then, in 1756, the tables seemed to turn: this time, Europe was dragged into a colonial war. Westward expansion

Louisbourg was an imposing fortress capital in Nova Scotia, almost 600 miles northeast of Boston. In May of 1745, during King George's War, Massachusetts merchant William Pepperrell led four thousand New England volunteers in a successful campaign to seize Louisbourg from the French. The New Englanders hailed their victory as a Protestant triumph over Catholicism and were stunned when Britain returned the city to the enemy at war's end. *Yale University Art Gallery, Mabel Brady Garven Collection.*

deeper into North America triggered a great war for empire, referred to in Europe as the Seven Years' War and in the colonies as the French and Indian War.

The problem began in the 1740s, as the neutral zone between the French colonial empire and the British mainland settlements began to shrink. As thousands of new immigrants poured into the English colonies, the colonists pressed farther westward, toward the Ohio Valley. Virginia land speculators began to woo the Indians of the region with trading agreements. The English colonial interest in the valley alarmed the French, who had plans to unite their mainland empire, connecting Canada and Louisiana with a chain of forts, trading posts, and missions across the Ohio Valley.

Virginia's governor, Robert Dinwiddie, was troubled by French military buildup in the Ohio Valley. He warned the British that a potential crisis was developing thousands of miles from London. In 1754 Britain responded; the government agreed to send an expedition to assess French strength and warn the French to abandon a new fort on French Creek. Dinwiddie chose an inexperienced Virginia planter and colonial militia officer, Major George Washington, to lead the expedition. When Washington conveyed the warning, the French commander responded with insulting sarcasm. Tensions escalated rapidly. Dinwiddie later sent Major Washington to challenge the French at Fort Duquesne, near present-day Pittsburgh, but the French forced him to surrender.

Fearing another war, colonial political leaders knew it was time to act decisively—and to attempt cooperation. In June 1754, seven colonies sent representatives to Albany, New York, to organize a united defense. Unfortunately this effort at cooperation failed. When the Albany Plan of Union was presented to the colonial assemblies, none was willing to approve it. Instead, American colonists looked to Britain to act. This time, Britain did. Parliament sent Major General Edward Braddock, a battle-hardened veteran, to drive the French out of Fort Duquesne. Braddock's humiliating failure was only the first of many for the English in America.

English and French forces engaged each other in battle four times before war was officially declared in 1756. Soon, every major European power was involved, and the fighting spread rapidly across Europe, the Philippines, Africa, India, the Caribbean, and North America. In America, France's Indian allies joined the war more readily than England's. Iroquois tribes opted for neutrality, waiting until 1759 to throw in their lot with the English. Although Mohawks fought as mercenaries in New York and Iroquois in western Pennsylvania suppressed Delaware attacks on English colonists there, Iroquois support was erratic. In fact, some members of the League, including the Senecas, fought with the French in 1757 and 1758. Given these circumstances, a British defeat seemed likely.

In the south, the Cherokees played the French and English against each other. About 250 Cherokee warriors did sign up to fight with the Virginia militia in 1757, but as mercenaries rather than allies. By 1760, a full-scale war between colonists and Cherokees had erupted in the southern colonies. Although this Cherokee Rebellion of 1759–1761 ended in Indian defeat, the war drained off many of the southern colonial resources that might have been used against the French.

In 1756 the worried British government turned over the direction of the war to the ardent imperialist William Pitt. More than willing to take drastic steps, Pitt committed the British treasury to the largest war expenditures the nation had ever known and then put together the largest military force that North America had ever seen, combining 25,000 colonial troops with 24,000 British regulars. The fortunes of war soon reversed. By the end of 1759, the upper Ohio Valley had been taken from the French. And in August of that year, General James Wolfe took the war to the heart of French Canada: the fortress city of Quebec.

With his piercing eyes and his long red hair, the 31-year-old Wolfe looked the part of the military hero he was. Despite his eighteen years of military service, even Wolfe admitted he was daunted by the difficult

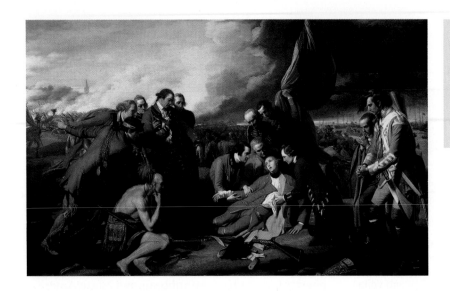

For most Americans, the English victory in the Battle of Quebec was the most dramatic event of the Seven Years' War. When Benjamin West painted "The Death of General Wolfe," he acknowledged the role Indian allies had played on both sides of this imperial struggle by adding an Indian observer to the scene. *National Gallery of Canada, Ottawa.*

task ahead of him. Quebec, heavily manned and well armed, sat on top of steep cliffs rising high above the St. Lawrence River. Inside, the formidable French general Louis-Joseph Montcalm was in command. The only possible approach was from the west of the city, across the Plains of Abraham. The problem was how to get to that battlefield.

Wolfe was uncharacteristically hesitant until he discovered a blockaded roadway running to the top of the 175-foot cliff. On the evening of September 12, forty-five hundred British soldiers climbed this diagonal path to the top. When the thoroughly surprised Montcalm saw a double line of scarlet uniforms forming on the plain at dawn, he gathered a force of more than four thousand and marched out to meet the British. The French fired several rounds, but Wolfe ordered his men to hold their fire until the enemy was within 60 yards. Then the redcoats fired, and the French turned and ran. Among the British wounded was General James Wolfe, shot through the chest. Hearing that the French were in retreat, the dying general murmured, "Now, God be praised, I will die in peace." Among the French casualties was Louis-Joseph, Marquis de Montcalm, who died the following day from internal injuries caused by a musket ball to his midsection.

Five days after the Battle of the Plains of Abraham, Quebec formally surrendered. In 1760 the city of Montreal also fell to the British. With that, the French governor surrendered the whole of New France to his enemies, and the war in North America was over. The fighting in this most global of eighteenth-century wars continued elsewhere until 1763. Spain entered the struggle as a French ally in 1761, but English victories in India, the Caribbean, and the Pacific squelched any hopes the French had. The **Treaty of Paris** established the supremacy of the British Empire.

The Outcomes of the Great War for Empire

The war had redrawn the map of the world (see Table 4.1). The French Empire had shriveled, with nothing remaining of New France but two tiny islands between Nova Scotia and Newfoundland. Ten thousand Acadians—French colonists of Nova Scotia—were refugees of the war, deported from their homes by the English because their loyalty was suspect. These Acadians, who either relocated to France, settled in New England, or made the exhausting trek to French-speaking Louisiana, were living reminders of the French Empire's eclipse. The only other remnants of the French Empire in the Western Hemisphere were the sugar islands of Guadeloupe, Martinique, and St. Domingue, left to France because England's so-called Sugar Interest wanted no further competition in the British market. Across the ocean, France lost trading posts in Africa, and on the other side of the world, the French presence in India vanished.

The 1763 peace treaty dismantled the French Empire but did not destroy France itself. Although the nation's treasury was empty, its borders were intact.

Treaty of Paris The treaty ending the French and Indian War in 1763; it gave all of French Canada and Spanish Florida to Britain.

T A B L E   4 . 1   Imperial and Colonial Wars

Name	Date	Participants	Treaty
In colonies: King William's War *In Europe:* War of the League of Augsburg	1688–1697	*In Europe:* France vs. England, Holland, Sweden, and Spain *In North America*: Colonists and their Iroquois allies vs. French and their Indian allies *Area:* New England and northern New York	Treaty of Ryswick (1697) *Results* Port Royal in Acadia (Nova Scotia) is returned to France France is still a presence in North America
In colonies: Queen Anne's War *In Europe:* War of the Spanish Succession	1702–1713	*In Europe:* England, Holland, and Austria vs. France and Spain *In North America:* English colonists vs. French and Spanish powers in North and South and their Indian allies	Treaty of Utrecht (1713) *Results* France renounces plans to unite with Spain under one crown England gains Caribbean islands, St. Kitts, Gibraltar, and Minorca English flag flies over Nova Scotia, New Foundland, and Hudson Bay War takes a financial toll on the colonies
War of Jenkins's Ear	1739–1740	*In Europe:* England vs. Spain *In North America:* English colonists clash with Spanish in interior regions (Georgia, South Carolina, Virginia)	None—Conflict expands into King George's War
In colonies: King George's War *In Europe:* War of the Austrian Succession	1740–1748	*In Europe:* Austria and England vs. Prussia, France, and Spain *In North America:* English colonists in New England vs. French and their Indian allies	Treaty of Aix-la-Chapelle (1748) *Results* England returns Louisbourg to French in exchange for Madras (in India)
In colonies: French and Indian War *In Europe:* Seven Years' War	1756–1763	*In Europe:* England and Prussia vs. France and Austria *In North America:* English colonists vs. French and their Indian allies *Area:* Global war; in colonies, all regions	Treaty of Paris (1763) *Results* French Empire shrinks France's presence in North America is greatly reduced France loses trading posts in Africa and exits India Britain takes Florida from Spain and Canada from France France gives up Louisiana to Spain for compensation for Florida British government is deeply in debt The borders of Britain's North American colonies are secured

France's alliance with Spain held firm, cemented by the experience of defeat. Britain was victorious, but victory did not mean Britain had escaped unharmed. The British government was deeply in debt and faced new problems associated with managing and protecting its greatly enlarged empire.

In the mainland colonies, people lit bonfires and staged parades to celebrate Britain's victory and the safety of their own borders. But the tension of being both members of a colonial society and citizens of a great empire could not be easily dismissed. The war left scars, including memories of the British military's arrogance toward provincial soldiers and lingering resentment over the quartering of British soldiers at colonial expense. The colonists were aware that the British had grounds for resentment also, particularly the profitable trade some Americans had carried on with the enemy even in the midst of the war. Suspicion and resentment, a growing sense of difference, a tug of loyalties between the local community and the larger empire—these were the unexpected outcomes of a glorious victory.

Individual Voices

Examining a Primary Source

Eliza Lucas Challenges Traditional Plantation Life

The eighteenth-century plantation world of South Carolina was a patriarchal society dedicated to the production of a single staple crop, rice. When Eliza Lucas began experimenting with indigo, figs, and hemp at Wappoo, her family plantation, it was the beginning of a new era of prosperity and diversification in the South Carolina plantation economy. As one of the few women to manage a large plantation at the time, Lucas was unique in her desire to experiment with new crops and stretch old gender roles. In her letters, Miss Lucas provides insight into the experiences of a woman succeeding in a male-dominated society. In this letter to her young niece, Lucas describes the demanding schedule she maintained in order to balance her roles as a society woman and a plantation master.

■ In this section Eliza Lucas shows us some of the ways in which she juggles her feminine and masculine roles? Do you think the men of the period spent the same amount of time devoted to learning?

■ Eliza Lucas hoped that the two African American slave girls she was educating would educate other slaves on the plantation. What arguments could be raised against this program to educate slaves? What benefits might come from the education of slaves?

Dr. Miss B.

. . . Why, my dear Miss B, will you so often repeat your desire to know how I triffle away my time in our retirement in my fathers absence. Could it afford you advantage or pleasure I should not have hesitated, but as you can expect neither from it I would have been excused; however, to show you my readiness in obeying your commands, here it is.

■ *In general then I rise at five o'Clock in the morning, read till Seven, then take a walk in the garden or field, see that the Servants are at their respective business, then to breakfast. The first hour after breakfast is spent at my musick, the next is constantly employed in recolecting something I have learned least for want of practise it should be quite lost, such as French and short hand.* ■ *After that I devote the rest of the time till I dress for dinner to our little Polly and two black girls who I teach to read, and if I have my papa's approbation (my Mamas I have got) I intend [them] for school mistres's for the rest of the negro children—another scheme you see. But to proceed, the first hour after dinner as the first after breakfast at musick, the rest of the afternoon in Needle work till candle light, and from that time to bed time read or write. 'Tis the fashion here to carry our work abroad*

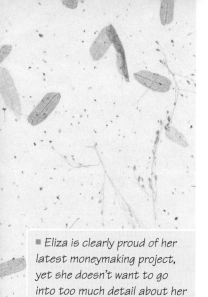

so that having company, without they are great strangers, is no interruption to that affair; but I have particular matters for particular days, which is an interruption of mine. Monday my musick Master is here. Tuesdays my friend Mrs. Chardon (about 3 mile distant) and I are constantly engaged to each other, she at our house one Tuesday—I at hers the next and this is one of the happiest days I spend at Woppoe. Thursday the whole day except what necessary affairs of the family take up is spent in writing, either on the business of the plantations, or letters to my friends. Every other Fryday, if no company, we go a vizeting so that I go abroad once a week and no oftener.

O! I had like to forgot the last thing I have done a great while. I have planted a large figg orchard with design to dry and export them. ■ I have reconed [reckoned] my experience and the propfets [profits] to arise from these figgs, but was I to tell you how great an Estate I am to make this way, and how 'tis to be laid out you would think me far gone in romance. Your good Uncle I know has long thought I have a fertile brain at schemeing. I only confirm him in his opinion; but I own I love the vegitable world extremly. I think it an innocent and useful amusement. Pray tell him, if he laughs much at my project, I never intend to have my hand in a silver mine and he will understand as well as you what I mean. . . .

■ Eliza is clearly proud of her latest moneymaking project, yet she doesn't want to go into too much detail about her plans to her friend. What reason does she give for this hesitancy?

Summary

Each of the colonial regions developed a unique culture and society. Each region was directly connected to Britain by a well-established pattern of trade, but trade also connected them to one another. The colonists were often at odds among themselves, yet they could and did unite when common enemies threatened.

The social and cultural diversity among the colonies developed within a common imperial structure. In many regions, society changed significantly in the eighteenth century. In New England, the outcome of increased commercial activity and a royal government was a shift from a "Puritan" culture to a more secular "Yankee" culture, despite the religious revival that Jonathan Edwards helped spark. In the South, the planter elite continued to focus on the production of staple crops but shifted from a labor force of indentured servants to one of African slaves. By midcentury, these enslaved Africans had begun to develop their own community life and their own African American culture. The Middle Colonies developed a lively urban culture, but most people who immigrated to British North America after 1700 chose to settle in the backcountry. Here opportunities were greater, although the conflict with Native Americans was a constant fact of life.

Intellectual life in the eighteenth century changed dramatically as Enlightenment ideas encouraged the expectation of progress through reliance on reason. Colonial elites affirmed John Locke's theory of natural rights as well as a skepticism about religious dogmas. The Great Awakening unleashed a second, and opposing, intellectual current. Revivalists such as Jonathan Edwards and George Whitefield spread a renewed commitment to religious salvation throughout the colonies. At the same time, "Awakeners" challenged all authority except the individual spirit, and many ordinary colonists embraced the same notion.

A similar challenge to authority emerged in politics and imperial relations. Despite England's policy of salutary neglect in governing the colonies, colonial assemblies resented royal officials and asserted their own claims to power against appointed governors and other British officials. Strains in the relationship between colonial assemblies and imperial officers ran deep.

Intense rivalry between England, France, and Spain led to five major wars between 1688 and 1763. Colonists were expected to defend their own borders in most of the wars. In the French and Indian War, however, the British played an active role in driving the French out of mainland America. The British victory in 1763 altered the colonial map of North America and changed power relations throughout the European world.

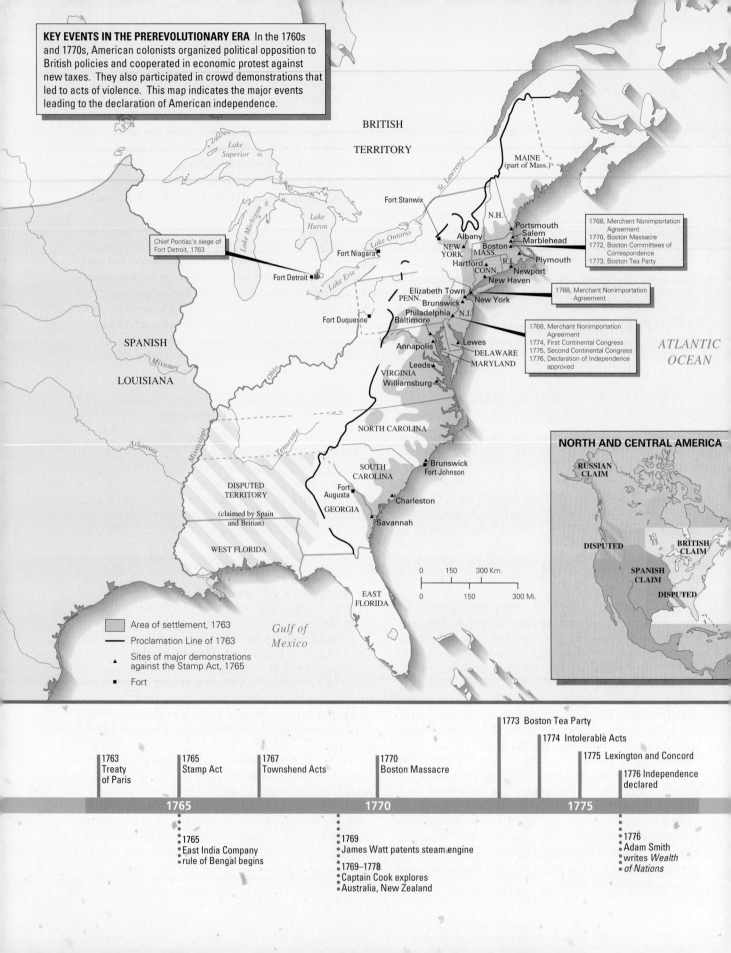

KEY EVENTS IN THE PREREVOLUTIONARY ERA In the 1760s and 1770s, American colonists organized political opposition to British policies and cooperated in economic protest against new taxes. They also participated in crowd demonstrations that led to acts of violence. This map indicates the major events leading to the declaration of American independence.

BRITISH

TERRITORY

MAINE
(part of Mass.)

Fort Stanwix

Chief Pontiac's siege of
Fort Detroit, 1763

Fort Niagara

Fort Detroit

Lake Superior
Lake Michigan
Lake Huron
Lake Ontario
Lake Erie
St. Lawrence

N.H.

Albany
NEW
YORK
Hartford
CONN.

Portsmouth
Salem
Marblehead
Boston
MASS.
R.I.
Newport
Plymouth
New Haven

1768, Merchant Nonimportation
Agreement
1770, Boston Massacre
1772, Boston Committees of
Correspondence
1773, Boston Tea Party

Elizabeth Town
PENN.
Brunswick
Philadelphia
Baltimore
N.J.
New York

1768, Merchant Nonimportation
Agreement

Fort Duquesne

Annapolis
Lewes
DELAWARE
MARYLAND
Leeds
VIRGINIA
Williamsburg

1768, Merchant Nonimportation
Agreement
1774, First Continental Congress
1775, Second Continental Congress
1776, Declaration of Independence
approved

SPANISH

LOUISIANA

Missouri

Ohio

Arkansas

Mississippi

Tennessee

NORTH CAROLINA

ATLANTIC
OCEAN

SOUTH
CAROLINA

Brunswick
Fort Johnson

Fort
Augusta
GEORGIA

Charleston

DISPUTED
TERRITORY

(claimed by Spain
and Britian)

WEST FLORIDA

Savannah

EAST
FLORIDA

Gulf of
Mexico

0   150   300 Km.

0   150   300 Mi.

NORTH AND CENTRAL AMERICA

RUSSIAN
CLAIM

DISPUTED

BRITISH
CLAIM

SPANISH
CLAIM

DISPUTED

Area of settlement, 1763

Proclamation Line of 1763

Sites of major demonstrations
against the Stamp Act, 1765

Fort

1773 Boston Tea Party

1774 Intolerable Acts

1775 Lexington and Concord

1776 Independence
declared

1763
Treaty
of Paris

1765
Stamp Act

1767
Townshend Acts

1770
Boston Massacre

1765

1770

1775

1765
East India Company
rule of Bengal begins

1769
James Watt patents steam engine

1769–1778
Captain Cook explores
Australia, New Zealand

1776
Adam Smith
writes *Wealth
of Nations*

Deciding Where Loyalties Lie, 1763–1776

The Events in the Prerevolutionary Era
Using the map on the facing page, suggest the reasons for
the concentration of prerevolutionary events in New England
and the Middle Colonies. What British policies during the
1760s and early 1770s might have affected these regions more
than others?

Individual Choices

CHARLES INGLIS

This portrait of the Anglican minister and later bishop Charles Inglis reveals a proud, intelligent, self-confident gentleman. Yet Inglis, like many loyalists, was spurned by his fellow colonists after he wrote a pamphlet urging all Americans to remain loyal to the king. He risked his neighbors' ridicule, he said, because he was a true patriot and a friend to America's best interests. *National Portrait Gallery, London.*

Charles Inglis

Charles Inglis was born in Donegal, Ireland, in 1734. Like many bright young men with only modest resources, he chose a career in the ministry. He was ordained in the Anglican Church in 1758 and, perhaps to his dismay, was immediately sent across the Atlantic Ocean to begin missionary work among the Mohawk Indians of Delaware. Inglis remained among the Mohawks for almost six years. At last, in 1765, he was called to New York City to serve as assistant to the rector of the prestigious Trinity Church. Unfortunately for Inglis, New Yorkers did not esteem the Anglican Church as highly as the young cleric might have expected. Presbyterians and other dissenting sects, members of the Dutch Reformed Church, French Protestants, and even Jews populated the bustling seaport city. And in the wake of the Stamp Act and England's determination to tighten controls over colonial life, open hostility to the Church of England increased. Many of New York's leading political figures linked the church with the king's plan to oppress and tyrannize the colonists. Inglis chose to speak out in defense of both his church and his king. He antagonized local radicals by campaigning actively for the appointment of an American bishop. From Virginia to Connecticut, many American leaders saw the effort to establish a bishop in the colonies as a blow to religious freedom similar to the Crown's assaults on economic and political freedom.

By the 1770s, Inglis found himself increasingly at odds with his neighbors. Yet he chose not to be silent. He had taken an oath of loyalty to both the Anglican Church and the English Crown, and so, under the pseudonym "Papinian," he wrote pamphlets and published letters in the local newspapers in support of Parliament's right to tax the colonies and the colonists' duty to submit. When Thomas Paine published his radical *Common Sense* in 1776, Charles Inglis was one of the few conservatives who dared to repudiate this open call for revolution. In *The True Interest of America Impartially Stated in Certain Strictures on a Pamphlet Intitled Common Sense,* Inglis condemned Paine and warned of the "evils which inevitably must attend our separating" from the Mother Country. He carefully listed the advantages of a reconciliation with Great Britain and then listed the horrors that would befall the colonies if they continued on the reckless path to rebellion. He painted a portrait of "the greatest confusion, and most violent convulsions" that would be the inevitable outcome of American protest and resistance to the king's sovereignty. Pointing out the hopelessness of waging a war against the most powerful navy and army in the world, he reminded Americans that they were still "properly Britons . . . [with] . . . the manners, habits, and ideas of Britons. . . ." Those ideas, he added emphatically, did not include a republican form of government.

In 1777 Charles Inglis was named rector of Trinity Church. From his pulpit, he continued boldly to pray for the king's well-being, despite the Declaration of Independence. He would not allow the revolutionaries to constrain him; he would not let their threats silence him. He remained an outspoken loyalist even when his

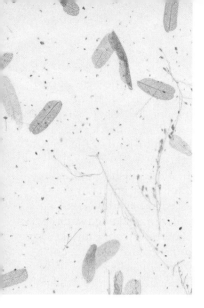

church was burned and his personal property was confiscated by the new state government.

Inglis was safe from personal harm throughout most of the war, for the British occupied New York City from 1776 until 1783. That year, Inglis joined thousands of other loyalists who sought refuge aboard British transport ships headed for Nova Scotia. Despite the criticism leveled against him, despite the loss of property he suffered, despite the enforced exile from what had been his home for almost two decades, Inglis refused to speak bitterly of his American enemies. "I do not leave behind me an individual," he wrote, "against whom I have the smallest degree of resentment or ill-will." Perhaps his generosity of spirit was the result of his good fortune in Canada, for in 1787 he was made the first Anglican bishop of Nova Scotia, Newfoundland, Quebec, Prince Edward Island, and Bermuda. Ironically, when he died in 1816, the United States and Britain had just ended their second war.

INTRODUCTION

During the very years that Charles Inglis was a missionary among the Mohawks, Britain and France were engaged in their final struggle for control of eastern North America. Britain's victory in 1763, would, many colonists believed, usher in a new era of economic growth, westward settlement, and cooperation between Mother Country and colonies that would continue "for Ages to come." But, like Inglis's expectations that his new post in New York City would bring him social status and respect, the colonists' hopes for harmony and good will were quickly dashed. Less than two years after the Treaty of Paris ended the war, colonists were protesting against British Indian policy and trade regulations. In the thirteen strife-filled years that followed, the colonists and the British government discovered that fundamental political differences existed between them. They found that they did not agree over the meaning of representative government or the proper division of power between Parliament and the local elected assemblies. And they found themselves in conflict over major imperial policies. English officials, for example, thought it was wise to curtail westward settlement in order to prevent costly Indian wars. American colonists, however, were certain that westward settlement would provide economic opportunity for loyal citizens. The British government and the colonists also disagreed on what obligations the colonists shared with men and women in England. The British insisted that the Americans ought to help pay the costs of maintaining the empire, but the colonists believed that this was the duty of those who remained in the Mother Country. By the 1770s, Americans who had once toasted the king and the empire drank instead to liberty and resistance to tyrants. By 1775, a new choice faced the colonists: loyalty or rebellion. And men such as Charles Inglis seemed caught in the midst of a struggle they had never anticipated and could not avoid.

The colonists who chose to protest taxation by the British government in 1765 and 1767, or to oppose the creation of courts without jury trials, or to complain of the presence of troops in their towns in peacetime did not know they were laying the groundwork for a revolution. Indeed, most of them would have been shocked at the suggestion that they were no longer British patriots. Yet events between 1763 and 1776 forced these colonists to choose between two versions of patriotism—loyalty to the king or loyalty to colonial independence—and between two visions of the future—as members of a great and powerful empire or as citizens of a struggling new nation. These events also forced Indians and African American slaves to choose an alliance with England or with the rebels, just as it forced churchmen such as Inglis and royal officials who had taken a solemn oath of allegiance to the king to decide if that oath was binding under all circumstances. The war that resulted set neighbor against neighbor, father against son, wife against husband, and slave against master. For thousands, the outcome of this crisis of loyalty was exile from home and family. For others, it meant death or injury on the battlefield, widowhood, or life as an orphan. In 1776, however, the outcome was unclear.

It Matters

The Right to Dissent

Charles Inglis was a man of integrity who considered himself as much an American patriot as his opponent in the pamphlet wars, Alexander Hamilton. But unlike Hamilton, Inglis believed that the protests against Parliament and the king were dangerous and unjustified and would lead to an unjust and tragic war. Throughout American history, men and women have opposed political and social choices made by the nation, including the entrance of the United States into World War I, woman suffrage, Prohibition, and the war in Vietnam. The right to dissent, guaranteed by the Constitution, has been a critical part of the American political tradition since the nation began. Examining how dissent has been offered and how it has been received is part of the historical narrative of major controversial events.

Victory's New Problems

■ Why did Prime Minister Grenville expect the colonists to accept part of the burden of financing the British Empire in 1764?

■ How did mercantile theory affect the colonies' trade with other nations?

■ Why were the colonists alarmed by Grenville's 1765 stamp tax?

■ How did the colonists protest Parliament's taxation policies?

In the midst of the French and Indian War, King George II died in his bed. Loyal subjects mourned the old king and in 1760 crowned his young grandson **George III**. At 22, the new monarch was hardworking but highly self-critical, and he was already showing the symptoms of an illness that produced **delusions** and severe depression. Although he was inexperienced in matters of state, George III meant to rule—even if he had to deal with politicians, whom he distrusted, and engage in politics, which he disliked. He chose **George Grenville**, a no-nonsense, practical man to assist him. It fell to Grenville to handle the two most pressing postwar tasks: negotiating England's victory treaty with France and its allies and designing Britain's peacetime policies.

Grenville's diplomats met with little resistance at the negotiating table. France was defeated, and it was up to the British government to decide what the spoils of war would be. England could take possession of a French Caribbean sugar island or the French mainland territory of Canada, a vast region stretching north and northwest of the English colonies. English sugar planters raised loud objections to the first option, for another sugar island would mean new competitors in the profitable English sugar markets. There was strong support, however, for adding Canada (see Map 5.1). Doing so would ensure the safety of the mainland colonies, whose people were increasingly important as consumers of English-made goods. With Canada, too, would come the rich fishing grounds off the Newfoundland coast and the fertile lands of the Ohio Valley. Such arguments in favor of Canada carried the day. By the end of 1763, George III could look with pride on an empire that had grown in physical size, on a nation that dominated the markets of Europe, and on a navy that ruled the seas.

Unfortunately, victory also brought new problems. First, the new English glory did not come cheaply. To win the war, William Pitt had spent vast sums of money, leaving the new king with an enormous war debt. English taxpayers, who had groaned under the wartime burden, now demanded tax relief, not tax increases. Second, the new Canadian territory posed serious governance problems because the Indians were unwilling to pledge their allegiance to the English king and, despite the change in flag, the French Canadians were unwilling to abandon their traditions, laws, or the Catholic Church.

Dealing with Indian and French Canadian Resistance

Both the Canadian tribes and Spain's former Indian allies along the southeastern borders of the English colonies felt threatened by Britain's victory. For decades, Indian diplomats had protected their lands by play-

George III King of England (r. 1760–1820); his government's policies produced colonial discontent that led to the American Revolution in 1776.

delusion A false belief strongly held in spite of evidence to the contrary.

George Grenville British prime minister who sought to tighten controls over the colonies and to impose taxes to raise revenues.

Chronology

Loyalty or Rebellion?

1763	Treaty of Paris ends French and Indian War
	Pontiac's Rebellion
	Proclamation Line
1764	Sugar Act
1765	Stamp Act
	Sons of Liberty organized
	Stamp Act Congress
	Nonimportation of British goods
1766	Stamp Act repealed
	Declaratory Act
1767	Townshend Acts
	John Dickinson's *Letters from a Farmer in Pennsylvania*
1768	Nonimportation of British goods
	Massachusetts Circular Letter
1770	Boston Massacre
	Townshend Acts repealed
1772	Burning of the *Gaspée*
1773	Tea Act
	Boston Tea Party
1774	Intolerable Acts
	First Continental Congress
	Continental Association
	Declaration of Rights and Grievances
	Suffolk Resolves
1775	Battles of Lexington and Concord
	Second Continental Congress
	Olive Branch Petition
	Declaration of the Causes and Necessity of Taking Up Arms
1776	Tom Paine's *Common Sense*
	Declaration of Independence

ing European rivals against one another, but with the elimination of France and the weakening of Spain in mainland America, this strategy was impossible. The Creeks and Cherokees of the Southeast expected the worst—and it soon came. English settlers from the southern colonies poured into their lands, and although the Cherokees mounted full-scale resistance along the Virginia and Carolina western settlement line, the British crushed their resistance. Cherokee leaders were forced to sign treaties that opened their lands to both English settlement and military bases.

A similar invasion of Delaware and Mingo territory began in the Ohio Valley and the Great Lakes region in 1763. The British added insult to injury by raising the price of the weapons, tools, clothing, and liquor that, by now, the tribes depended on. The crisis united the Indians, who acted quickly to create an intertribal alliance known as the **Covenant Chain.** The Covenant Chain brought together Senecas, Ojibwas, Potowatomis, Hurons, Ottawas, Delawares, Shawnees, and Mingoes, all of whom stood ready to resist colonial settlers, British trading policy, and the terms of military occupation of frontier forts. Led by the Ot-

tawa chief **Pontiac,** the Indians mounted their attack on British forts and colonial settlements in the spring of 1763. By fall, their resistance had evaporated, and the Covenant Chain tribes were forced to acknowledge British control of the Ohio Valley.

The British realized that such costly victories would not ensure permanent peace in the West. As long as the "middle ground" between Indian and colonial populations continued to shrink, Indians would mount resistance. And as long as Indians resisted what Creeks bluntly called "people greedily grasping after the lands of red people," settlers would demand expensive military protection as they pushed westward. If the army did not respond, settlers were ready to take action on

Covenant Chain   An alliance of Indian tribes established to resist colonial settlement in the Ohio Valley and Great Lakes region and to oppose British trading policies.

Pontiac   Ottawa chief who led the unsuccessful resistance against British policy in 1763.

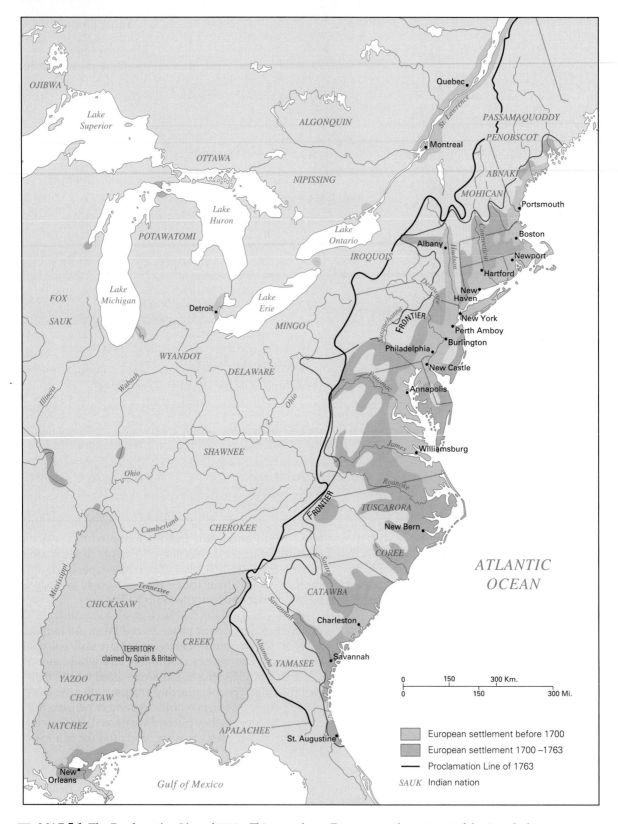

MAP 5.1 The Proclamation Line of 1763 This map shows European settlement east of the Appalachian Mountains and the numerous Indian tribes with territorial claims to the lands between the Appalachians and the Mississippi River. The Proclamation Line, which roughly follows the mountain range, was the British government's effort to temporarily halt colonial westward expansion and thus to prevent bloodshed between settlers and Indians. This British policy was deeply resented by land-hungry colonists.

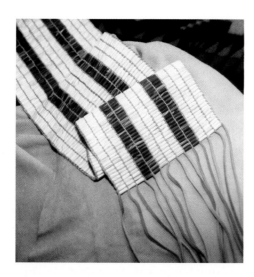

Among the Iroquis nations, wampum belts were the equivalent of the written documents familiar to English and European officials. The belt above was a treaty, stating the terms and conditions under which white people were welcomed to Indian lands. The two strands of yellow signified the equality of colonist and Iroquis, or as the Oneida explained, "We will not be like Father and Son, but like Brothers." *Oneida Indian Nation.*

their own. When the Paxton Boys of western Pennsylvania avenged an Indian raid by murdering a village of innocent Conestogas (see page 100), the dangers of this type of vigilante action became painfully clear. Violence would lead to violence—unless Grenville could keep Indians and settlers at arm's length. Grenville's solution was a proclamation, issued in 1763, temporarily banning all colonial settlement west of the Appalachian Mountains.

Grenville's **Proclamation Line of 1763** outraged colonists hoping to move west and wealthy land speculators hoping to reap a profit from their western investments. With the Indian enemy reeling from defeat, settlers insisted that this was the perfect moment to cross the mountains and stake claims to the land. Most colonists simply ignored Grenville's Proclamation Line. Over the next decade, areas such as Kentucky began to fill with eager homesteaders, creating a wedge that divided northern from southern Indian tribes and increasing Indian anxiety about their own futures.

Because of their long tradition of anti-Catholic sentiment, American colonists also objected to Grenville's policy toward French-speaking Catholic Canadians. George III's advisers preferred to win over these new subjects rather than strong-arm them. Thus, to balance the French Canadians' loss of their fishing and

fur-trading industries, Grenville promised them the right to preserve their religious and cultural way of life. Britain's colonists were scandalized by this concession to the losers in the war.

Demanding More from the Colonists

Colonists were not the only ones growing discontent. In London, the king, his ministers, and many members of Parliament were impatient with colonial behavior and attitudes. Hadn't the colonists benefited more than anyone from the French defeat? asked George Grenville. And hadn't they contributed less than anyone to securing that victory? Such questions revealed the subtle but important rewriting of the motives and goals of the French and Indian War. Although Britain had waged the war to win dominance in European affairs, not to benefit the colonies, Grenville now declared that the war had been fought to protect the colonists and to expand their opportunities for settlement.

This new interpretation fit well with the government's increasing doubts about colonial commitments to the empire's trade interests. It seemed clear to Grenville that something had gone wrong in the economic relationship between England and the colonies. Colonial cities such as Boston, Philadelphia, and New York had grown considerably, yet their growth did not make England as rich as **mercantile theory** said it should. One reason was that in every colony locally produced goods competed with English-made goods. A more important reason, however, was illegal trade. Colonists seized economic opportunity wherever they found it—even in trade with England's rivals. In fact, to English amazement, colonials had continued to trade with the French Caribbean islands throughout the French and Indian War. In peacetime, colonists avoided paying **import duties** on foreign goods by

Proclamation Line of 1763 Boundary that Britain established in the Appalachian Mountains, west of which white settlement was banned; it was intended to reduce conflict between Indians and colonists.

mercantile theory The economic notion that a nation should amass wealth by exporting more than it imports; colonies are valuable in a mercantile system as a source of raw materials and as a market for manufactured goods.

import duties Taxes on imported goods.

bribing customs officials or landing cargoes where no customs officers were stationed.

George Grenville was often mocked for having a bookkeeper's mentality, but few laughed at what the prime minister discovered when he examined the imperial trade books. By the 1760s, the Crown had collected less than £2,000 in revenue from colonial trade with other nations while the cost of collecting these duties was over £7,000 a year. Such discoveries fueled British suspicions that the colonies were underregulated and undergoverned, as well as ungrateful and uncooperative. When the strong doubts about colonial loyalty met the reality of the British government debts and soaring expenses, something drastic could be expected to follow. And it did. In 1764 Parliament approved the reforms of colonial policy proposed by Grenville. Colonists greeted those reforms with shock and alarm.

Separately, each of Grenville's measures addressed a loophole in the proper relationship between Mother Country and colonies. For example, a **Currency Act** outlawed the use of paper money as legal tender in the colonies. In part, this was done to ensure the colonial market for English manufacturers. Although the colonists had to pay for imported English products with hard currency (gold and silver), they could use paper money to pay for locally produced goods. With paper money now banned, local manufacturers would be driven out of business.

Grenville believed the major problem was smuggling. Lawbreakers were so common, and customs officers so easily bribed, that smuggling had become an acceptable, even respectable, form of commerce. To halt this illicit traffic, Grenville set about to reform the **customs service.** In his 1764 American Revenue Act, he increased the powers of the customs officers, allowing them to use blanket warrants, called writs of assistance, to search ships and warehouses for smuggled goods. He also changed the regulations regarding key foreign imports, including sugar, wine, and coffee. This startling shift in policy, known popularly as the **Sugar Act,** revealed Grenville's practical bent. He knew that any attempt to stop the flow of French sugar into the colonies was a waste of time and resources. So he decided to make a profit for the Crown from this trade. He would lower the tax on imported sugar—but he would make sure it was collected. Until 1764, a colonist accused of smuggling was tried before a jury of his neighbors in a **civil court.** He expected, and usually got, a favorable verdict from his peers. Grenville now declared that anyone caught smuggling would be tried in a juryless **vice-admiralty court,** where a conviction was likely.

Once smuggling became too costly and too risky, Grenville reasoned, American shippers would declare their cargoes of French sugar and pay the Crown for the privilege of importing them.

The Colonial Response

Grenville's reforms were spectacularly ill timed as far as Americans were concerned. The colonial economy was suffering from a postwar **depression,** brought on in part by the loss of the British army as a steady market for American supplies and of British soldiers as steady customers who paid in hard currency rather than paper money. In 1764 unemployment was high among urban artisans, dockworkers, and sailors. Colonial merchants were caught in a credit squeeze—unable to pay their debts to British merchants because their colonial customers had no cash to pay for their purchases. These colonists were not likely to cheer a currency act that shut off a source of money or a Sugar Act that established a new get-tough policy on foreign trade. In the eyes of many colonists, the English government was turning into a greater menace than the French army had ever been.

Some colonists, however, saw these hard times and the need to tighten their belts as a welcome brake on their society's **materialism.** These Americans believed that a love of luxuries weakened people's spirit, sapped their independence, and would soon lead to the same moral decay they saw in England, where they believed extravagance and corruption infected society and tainted the nation's political leaders. After 1763, these colonists appealed to their neighbors to embrace simplicity and sacrifice. They urged prosper-

---

Currency Act British law of 1764 banning the printing of paper money in the American colonies.

customs service A government agency authorized to collect taxes on foreign goods entering a country.

Sugar Act British law of 1764 that taxed sugar and other colonial imports to pay for some of Britain's expenses in protecting the colonies.

civil court Any court that hears cases regarding the rights of private citizens.

vice-admiralty court Nonjury British court in which a judge heard cases involving shipping.

depression A period of drastic economic decline, marked by decreased business activity, falling prices, and high unemployment.

materialism Excessive interest in worldly matters, especially in acquiring goods.

ous women, for example, to abandon fashion, with its "gaudy, butterfly, vain, fantastick and expensive Dresses bought from Europe," and put on the "decent plain Dresses made in their own Country." Convinced that the eighteenth-century **consumer revolution** in the colonies had eroded virtue, these colonists called for a **boycott** of all goods manufactured in England.

Other views and other proposals for action soon filled the pages of colonial newspapers. This concern suggested that Grenville's reforms had raised profound issues of liberty and the rights of citizens and of the relationship between Parliament and the colonial governments—issues that needed to be resolved. The degree to which Parliament had, or ought to have, power over colonial economic and political life required serious, public pondering. Years later, with the benefit of hindsight, Massachusetts lawyer and revolutionary John Adams stressed the importance of the Sugar Act in starting America down the road to independence. "I know not why we should blush to confess," wrote Adams, "that molasses [liquid sugar] was an essential ingredient in American independence. Many great events have proceeded from much smaller causes." But in 1764 colonists were far from agreement over the issue of parliamentary and local political powers. They were not even certain how to respond to the Sugar Act.

The Stamp Act

Did Grenville stop to consider the possibility of "great events" arising from his postwar policies? Probably not. He was hardly a stranger to protest and anger, for he had often heard British citizens grumble about taxes and assert their rights against the government. As he saw it, his duty was to fill the treasury, reduce the nation's staggering debt, arm its troops, and keep the royal navy afloat. The duty of loyal British citizens, he believed, was to obey the laws of their sovereign government. Grenville had no doubt that the measures he and Parliament were taking to regulate the colonies and their revenue-producing trade were constitutional. Some colonists, however, had doubts. Thus the next piece of colonial legislation Grenville proposed was designed not only to raise revenue but to settle the principle of parliamentary sovereignty.

The **Stamp Act** of 1765 was to be the first **direct tax** ever laid on the colonies by Parliament, and its purpose was to raise revenue by taxing certain goods and services. There was nothing startling or novel about the revenue-collecting method Grenville proposed to use. A stamp tax raised money by requiring the use of government "stamped paper" on certain goods or as

part of the cost for certain services. It was simple and efficient, and several colonial legislatures had adopted this method themselves. What was startling, however, was that Parliament would consider imposing a tax on the colonists that was not aimed at regulation of foreign trade. Up until 1765, Parliament had passed many acts regulating colonial trade. Sometimes these regulations on imports generated revenue for the Crown, and the colonists accepted them as a form of **external taxation.** But colonists expected direct taxation only from their local assemblies. If Grenville's Stamp Act became law, it would mark a radical change in the distribution of political power between assemblies and Parliament. It would be the powerful assertion of Parliament's sovereignty that Grenville intended.

Most members of Parliament saw the Stamp Act as an efficient and modest redistribution of the burdens of the empire—and a constitutional one. Colonists were certainly not being asked to shoulder the entire burden, since the estimated £160,000 in revenue from the stamped paper would cover only one-fifth of the cost of maintaining a British army in North America. Under these circumstances, Parliament saw no reason to deny Grenville's proposed tax. Thus the Stamp Act passed in February 1765 and was set to go into effect in November. The nine-month delay gave Grenville time to print the stamped paper, arrange for its shipment across the Atlantic, and appoint agents to receive and distribute the stamps in each colony. News of the tax, however, crossed the ocean rapidly and was greeted with outrage and anger. Opposition was widespread among the colonists because virtually every free man and woman was affected by a tax that required stamps on all legal documents, on newspapers and pamphlets, and even on playing cards and dice. Grenville was reaching into the pockets of

---

consumer revolution The rising market for manufactured goods, particularly luxury items, that occurred in the early eighteenth century in the colonies.

boycott An organized political protest in which people refuse to buy goods from a nation or group of people whose actions they oppose.

Stamp Act British law of 1765 that directly taxed a variety of items, including newspapers, playing cards, and legal documents.

direct tax A tax imposed to raise revenue rather than to regulate trade.

external taxation Revenue raised in the course of regulating trade with other nations.

the rich, who would need stamped paper to draw up wills and property deeds and to bring suit in court. And he was emptying the pockets of the poor, who would feel the pinch when dealing a hand of cards in a tavern or buying a printed **broadside** filled with advertising. Other segments of the colonial society would also feel the sting of the new tax. Unless colonial merchants and ship captains used stamped clearances for all shipments, the royal navy could seize their cargoes. Lawyers feared the loss of clients if they had to add the cost of the stamps to their fees. With the stamp tax Grenville united northern merchants and southern planters, rural women and urban workingmen, and he riled the most articulate and argumentative of all Americans: lawyers and newspaper publishers.

The Popular Response

Many colonists were ready to resist the new legislation. Massachusetts, whose smugglers were already choking on the new customs regulations, and whose assembly had a long history of struggle with local Crown officers, led the way. During the summer of 1765, a group of Bostonians formed a secret resistance organization called the **Sons of Liberty.** Spearheading the Sons was the irrepressible **Samuel Adams,** a Harvard-educated member of a prominent Massachusetts family who preferred the company of local working men and women to the conversation of the elite. More at home in the dockside taverns than in the comfortable parlors of his relatives, Adams was a quick-witted, dynamic champion of working-class causes. He had a genius for writing propaganda and for mobilizing popular sentiment on political and community issues. Most members of the Sons of Liberty were artisans and shopkeepers, and the group's main support came from men of the city's laboring classes who had been hard hit by the postwar depression and would suffer from the stamp tax. These colonists had little influence in the legislature or with Crown officials, but they compensated by staging public demonstrations and protests to make their opinions known.

The Sons of Liberty had been created to oppose British policies, but with class divisions widening in Boston, they sometimes added protests against local issues and local elites. Prosperous Bostonians saw a potential danger in the mobilization of lower-class crowds. For these elites, crowd protest was a double-edged sword, a useful weapon that could be deadly in the wrong hands. By January 1765, New York City also had a Sons of Liberty organization, and by Au-

gust, the Sons could be found in other cities and towns across the colonies.

Demonstrations and protests escalated, and once again Boston led the way. On August 14, shoemaker **Ebenezer McIntosh** led a crowd to protest the appointment of the colony's stamp agent, wealthy merchant Andrew Oliver. Until recently, McIntosh had headed one of two major workers' organizations in town, a **fraternal** group of artisans, apprentices, and day laborers known to the city's disapproving elite as the South End "gang." But on this August day, city gentlemen disguised themselves as workingmen and joined McIntosh's gang members as they paraded through the city streets, carrying an effigy of Oliver. The crowd destroyed the stamp agent's dockside warehouse and later broke all the windows in his home. The message was clear—and Oliver understood it well. The following day Andrew Oliver resigned as stamp agent. Boston Sons of Liberty celebrated by declaring the tree on which they hanged Oliver's effigy the "liberty tree."

Oliver's resignation did not end the protest. Customs officers and other Crown officials living in Boston were threatened with words and worse. The chief target of abuse, however, was the haughty merchant **Thomas Hutchinson,** hated by many of the ambitious younger political leaders because he monopolized appointive offices in the colony's government and by the workingmen because of his obvious disdain for ordinary people. Late one August evening, a large crowd surrounded Hutchinson's elegant brick mansion. Warned of the impending attack, Hutchinson and his family had wisely fled, escaping just before rocks began to shatter the parlor windows. By

broadside   An advertisement, public notice, or other publication printed on one side of a large sheet of paper.

Sons of Liberty   A secret organization first formed in Boston to oppose the Stamp Act.

Samuel Adams   Massachusetts revolutionary leader and propagandist who organized opposition to British policies after 1764.

Ebenezer McIntosh   Boston shoemaker whose workingman's organization, the South End "gang," became the core of the city's Sons of Liberty in 1765.

fraternal   Describes a group of people with common purposes or interests.

Thomas Hutchinson   Boston merchant and judge who served as lieutenant governor and later governor of Massachusetts; Stamp Act protesters destroyed his home in 1765.

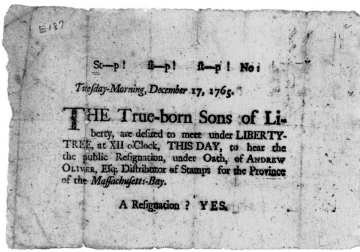

The Sons of Liberty first appeared in Boston, but this organization that united elite and working-class protesters spread quickly to other American cities. In the 1765 broadside above, the Boston Sons call a meeting to demand the resignation of local stamp agent, Andrew Oliver. Ten years later, New York's pro-British editor, James Rivington, used the illustration above while reporting that a New Brunswick mob had hanged him in effigy. The New York Sons promptly made good on the threat to Rivington, attacking his office, destroying his press, and forcing his paper to close. *Mr. Rivington: Library of Congress; Sons of Liberty Broadside: Massachusetts Historical Society.*

dawn, the house was in ruins, and Hutchinson's furniture, clothing, and personal library had been trashed.

Thomas Hutchinson was a political target of those who opposed the Stamp Act. But because he represented the privilege and power of the few and the well placed, he was also a social target of the working people in the crowd. The savage destruction of his home led many of Boston's elite to withdraw their support from popular protests of any kind. Perhaps, they reasoned, the tensions between rich and poor were more dangerous than any parliamentary reform. Like the challenge to authority of the Great Awakening, these political protests carried the seeds of social revolution.

The campaign against the stamp agents spread like a brushfire across the colonies. Agents in Connecticut, Rhode Island, Maryland, and New York were mercilessly harassed. Most stamp agents resigned. When the stamps reached colonial ports in November, only the young and conservative colony of Georgia could produce anyone willing to distribute them. Colonial governors retaliated by refusing to allow any colonial ships to leave port. They hoped this disruption of trade would persuade local merchants to help end the resistance. Their strategy backfired. Violence increased as hundreds of unemployed sailors took to the streets, terrorizing customs officers and any colonists suspected of supporting the king's taxation policy.

Political Debate

While the Sons of Liberty and their supporters demonstrated in the streets, most colonial political leaders were proceeding with caution. Virginia lawyer and planter **Patrick Henry** briefly stirred the passions of his colleagues in the House of Burgesses when he suggested that the Stamp Act was evidence of the king's tyranny. Not everyone agreed with him that the measure was so serious. Many did agree, however, that the heart of the matter was not stamped paper but parliamentary sovereignty versus the rights of colonial citizens. "No taxation without representation"—the principle that citizens cannot be taxed by a government unless they are represented in it—was a fundamental

Patrick Henry   Member of the Virginia House of Burgesses and American revolutionary leader noted for his oratorical skills.

Virginia planter and lawyer Patrick Henry may have acquired his oratorical brilliance from his father, a fiery Virginia preacher. Henry chose politics rather than the pulpit, and throughout the 1760s and 1770s, he stirred the House of Burgesses to resist British policy and the British king. *Colonial Williamsburg Foundation.*

assumption of free white Englishmen on both sides of the Atlantic. The crucial question was, Did the House of Commons represent the colonists even though no colonist sat in the House and none voted for its members? If the answer was no, then the Stamp Act violated the colonists' most basic "rights of Englishmen."

Stating the issue in this way led to other concerns. Could colonial political leaders oppose a single law such as the Stamp Act without completely denying the authority of the government that was responsible for its passage? Massachusetts lawyer James Otis pondered this question when he sat down to write his *Rights of the British Colonists Asserted and Proved.* Any opposition to the Stamp Act, he decided, was ultimately a challenge to parliamentary authority over the colonies, and it would surely lead to colonial rebellion and a declaration of colonial independence. He, for one, was not prepared to become a rebel.

The logic of his own argument disturbed Otis and prompted him to propose a compromise: the colonists should be given representation in the House of Commons. Few political leaders took this suggestion seriously. Even if Parliament agreed, a small contingent of colonists could be easily ignored in its decision making. Most colonial leaders thought it best to declare that American rights and liberties were under attack and to issue warnings that the assemblies

would oppose any further threats to colonial rights. They carefully avoided, however, any treasonous statements or threats of rebellion. In the most popular pamphlet of 1765, Pennsylvania lawyer Daniel Dulaney captured this combination of criticism and caution. His *Considerations on the Propriety of Imposing Taxes on the British Colonies* reaffirmed the dependence of the colonies on Great Britain. But it also reminded Parliament that Americans knew the difference between dependence and slavery.

Colonial assemblymen knew that a final question hung in the air. If Parliament asserted its right to govern the colonies directly, what powers would remain to them as members of the colonial legislatures? These men had much to lose—status, prestige, and the many benefits that came from deciding how tax monies would be allocated. In the end, the majority agreed that a firm stand had to be taken. After much debate, most assemblies followed the lead of the Virginia House of Burgesses and issued statements condemning the Stamp Act and demanding its repeal. Massachusetts reinforced this unusual show of unity among the colonies when its assembly put out a call for an intercolonial meeting of delegates to discuss the Stamp Act crisis. The call to meet was greeted with enthusiasm.

Grenville's policies appeared to be bringing about what had once seemed impossible: united political action by the colonies. Until the Stamp Act, competition among the colonial governments was far more common than cooperation. Yet in the fall of 1765 delegates from nine colonies met in New York "to consider a general and unified, dutiful, loyal and humble Representation [petition]" to the king and Parliament. The petitions this historic Stamp Act Congress ultimately produced were far bolder than the delegates first intended. They were powerful, tightly argued statements that conceded parliamentary authority over the colonies but denied Parliament's right to impose any direct taxes on them. "No taxes," the Congress said, "ever have been, or can be Constitutionally imposed" on the colonies "but by their respective Legislatures." Clearly Americans expected this tradition to be honored.

Repeal of the Stamp Act

Neither the protest in the streets nor the arguments of the Stamp Act Congress moved the king or Parliament to repeal the stamp tax. But economic pressure did. English manufacturers relied heavily on their colonial markets and were certain to be hurt by any interruption in the flow and sale of goods to America.

Thus the most powerful weapon in the colonial arsenal was a refusal to purchase English goods. On Halloween night, just one day before the stamp tax officially went into effect, two hundred New York merchants announced that they would not import any new British goods. Local artisans and laborers rallied to support this boycott. A mixture of patriotism and self-interest motivated both these groups. The merchants saw the possibility of emptying warehouses bulging with unsold goods because of the postwar depression. Unemployed and underemployed artisans and laborers saw the chance to sell their own products if the supply of cheaper English-made goods dried up. The same combination of interests existed in other colonial cities, and thus the nonimportation movement spread quickly. By the end of November, several colonial assemblies had publicly endorsed the nonimportation agreements signed by local merchants. Popular support widened as well. In many cities and towns, women publicly announced their commitment to nonimportation and vowed to spend long hours spinning and weaving their own cloth rather than purchase it ready-made from England. Their participation was crucial to the success of the boycott.

English exporters complained bitterly of the damage done to their businesses and pressured Parliament to take colonial protest seriously. Talk of repeal grew bolder and louder in the halls of Parliament. The Grenville government reluctantly conceded that enforcement of the Stamp Act had failed miserably. Even in colonies where royal officials dared to distribute the stamped paper, Americans refused to purchase it. Colonists simply ignored the hated law and continued to sue their neighbors, sell their land, publish their newspapers, and buy their playing cards as if the stamped paper and the Stamp Act did not exist.

By winter's end, Grenville was no longer prime minister. For the king's new head of state, Lord Rockingham, the critical issue was not whether to repeal the Stamp Act but how to do so without appearing to cave in to colonial pressure. After much debate and political maneuvering, the government came up with a satisfactory solution. In 1766, Great Britain repealed the Stamp Act but at the same time passed a Declaratory Act, which asserted that the colonies "have been, are, and of right ought to be subordinate unto, and dependent upon the imperial Crown and parliament of Great Britain," and thus Parliament's right to pass legislation for and raise taxes from the North American colonies was reaffirmed as absolute.

Colonists celebrated the repeal with public outpourings of loyalty to England that were as impressive as their public protests had been. There were cannon salutes, bonfires, parades, speeches, and public toasts to the king and Rockingham. In Boston, Sons of Liberty built a pyramid and covered its three sides with patriotic poetry. In Anne Arundel County, Maryland, colonists erected a "liberty pillar" and buried "Discord" beneath it. And in a spectacular but poorly executed gesture, the Liberty Boys of Plymouth, Massachusetts, tried to move Plymouth Rock to the center of town. When the famous rock on which the Pilgrims were said to have landed split in two, half of it was carried to Liberty Pole Square, where it remained until 1834.

Asserting American Rights

■ Why did Charles Townshend expect his revenue-raising measures to be successful?

■ What forms of resistance did the colonists use to force the repeal of Townshend's measures?

■ How did the Townshend Acts affect the northern colonies' trade with the West Indies?

■ What were the results of colonial resistance?

The Declaratory Act firmly asserted that Parliament had "the sole and exclusive right" to tax the colonists. This was a clear rejection of the colonial assemblies' claim to power, yet the colonists responded with indifference. Those who commented on it at all dismissed it as a face-saving device. To a degree, they were correct. But the Declaratory Act expressed the views of powerful men in Parliament, and within a year they put it to the test.

By the summer of 1766, William Pitt had returned to power within George III's government. But Pitt was old and preoccupied with his failing health. He lacked the energy to exercise the control over the government he had demonstrated during the French and Indian War. A young playboy named Charles Townshend, serving as chancellor of the exchequer, rushed in to fill the leadership void. This brash young politician wasted little time foisting a new package of taxes on the colonies.

The Townshend Acts and Colonial Protest

During the Stamp Act crisis, Benjamin Franklin had assured Parliament that American colonists accepted indirect taxation even if they violently protested a direct tax such as the Stamp Act. In other words,

Americans conceded the British government's right to any revenue arising from the regulation of colonial trade. In 1767 Townshend decided to test this distinction by proposing new regulations on a variety of imported necessities and luxuries. But the Townshend Acts were import taxes unlike any other the colonies had ever seen: they were tariffs on products made in Britain.

The Townshend Acts taxed glass, paper, paint, and lead products made in England, all part of the luxury trade. The acts also placed a three-penny tax on tea, the most popular drink among colonists everywhere and considered a necessity by virtually everyone. Townshend wanted to be certain these taxes were collected, so he ordered new customs boards established in the colonies and created new vice-admiralty courts in the major port cities of Boston, Charleston, and Philadelphia to try any cases of smuggling or tax evasion that might occur. In case Americans tried to harass customs officials, as they had so effectively done during the stamp tax protests, Townshend ordered British troops transferred from the western regions to the major colonial port cities. He knew this troop relocation would anger the colonists, but he was relying on the presence of uniformed soldiers—known as "redcoats" because of their scarlet jackets—to keep the peace. To help finance this military occupation of key cities, Townshend invoked the 1766 Quartering Act, a law requiring colonists to provide room and board, "candles, firing, bedding, cooking utensils, salt and vinegar" and a ration of beer, cider, or rum to troops stationed in their midst.

Clearly, Townshend was taking every precaution to avoid the embarrassment Grenville had suffered in the Stamp Act disaster. But he made a serious error in believing that colonists would meekly agree to pay import duties on British-made goods. When news of the new regulations reached the colonies, the response was immediate, determined, and well-organized resistance.

If the newspapers reflected popular sentiment accurately, the colonists were united in their opposition to the Townshend Acts and to the Mother Country's repressive enforcement policies. Some were incensed that the government was once again trampling on the principle of "no taxation without representation." In Boston, Samuel Adams voiced his outrage: "Is it possible to form an idea of Slavery, more compleat, more miserable, more disgraceful than that of a people, where justice is administer'd, government exercis'd, and a standing army maintain'd at the expense of the people, and yet without the least dependence upon them?" Others worried more about the economic burden of the new taxes and the quartering of the troops than about political rights. Boston lawyer Josiah Quincy Jr. asked readers of the *Boston Gazette*: "Is not the bread taken out of the children's mouths and given unto the Dogs?"

John Dickinson, a well-respected Pennsylvania landowner and lawyer, laid out the basic American position on imperial relations in his pamphlet *Letters from a Farmer in Pennsylvania* (1767). Direct taxation without representation violated the colonists' rights as English citizens, Dickinson declared. But by imposing any tax that did not regulate foreign trade, Parliament also violated those rights. Dickinson also considered, and rejected, the British claim that Americans were represented in the House of Commons. According to the British argument, colonists enjoyed "virtual representation" because the House of Commons represented the interests of all citizens in the empire who were not members of the nobility, whether those citizens participated directly in elections to the House or not. Like most Americans, Dickinson discounted virtual representation. What Englishmen were entitled to, he wrote, was *actual* representation by men they had elected to government to protect their interests. For qualified voters in the colonies, who enjoyed actual representation in their local assemblies, virtual representation was nothing more than a weak excuse for exclusion and exploitation. As one American quipped: "Our privileges are all virtual, our sufferings are real."

While political theorists set out the American position in newspaper essays and pamphlets, protest leaders organized popular resistance against acts that were clearly designed to raise revenue as well as make daily life more expensive in the colonies. Samuel Adams set in motion a massive boycott of British goods to begin on January 1, 1768. Just as before, some welcomed the chance a boycott provided to "mow down luxury and high living." But simple economics also contributed forcefully to support for the boycott. Boston artisans remained enthusiastic about any action that stopped the flow of inexpensive English-made goods to America. Small-scale merchants were also eager to see nonimportation enforced. They had little access to British credit or goods under normal circumstances, and the boycott would eliminate the advantages enjoyed by the merchant elite who did. Merchants and shippers who made their living smuggling goods from the West Indies supported the boycott because it cut out the competing English-made products. The large-scale merchants who had led the 1765 boycott were not enthusiastic, however. By 1767, their warehouses were no longer overflowing with

Massachusetts playwright, poet, and historian Mercy Otis Warren penned some of the most popular and effective propaganda for the American cause. In her plays, she portrayed pro-British officeholders as greedy, power-hungry traitors, while she praised Boston radicals as noble heroes. *"Mercy Otis Warren" by John Singleton Copley. Courtesy of the Museum of Fine Arts, Boston, bequest of Winslow Warren.*

unsold English stock, and the boycott might cut off their livelihoods. Many of these elite merchants delayed signing the agreements. Others did not sign at all.

The strongest voices raised against the boycott, and against resistance to the Townshend Acts in general, were the voices of colonists holding Crown-appointed government offices. These fortunate few—including judges and customs men—shared their neighbors' sensitivity to abuse or exploitation by the Crown. But they had sworn to uphold and carry out the programs and policies of the British government. And many of their salaries came from England. Because their careers and their identities were closely tied to the power and authority of the Crown, they were inclined to see British policymakers as well intentioned and acceptance of British policy as a patriotic duty. Jonathan Sewall, the king's attorney general in Massachusetts, was perhaps typical of these royal officeholders. Sewall had deep roots in his colonial community, for his family went back many generations and included

lawyers, judges, merchants, and assemblymen. His closest friend was John Adams, cousin of Samuel Adams, and the wealthy Boston merchant and smuggler John Hancock would soon become his brother-in-law. Yet Sewall became a staunch public defender of Crown policy. In his newspaper articles he urged his neighbors to ignore the call to resistance, and he questioned the motives of the leading activists, suggesting that greed, thwarted ambition, and envy rather than high-minded principles motivated the rabble-rousers. But despite their prestige and their positions of authority, Crown officers like Sewall were no more able to prevent the boycott or slow the spread of resistance than Anglican ministers like Charles Inglis.

Just as the Sons of Liberty and the Stamp Act demonstrations brought common men into the political arena, the 1768 boycott brought politics into the lives of women. When in 1765 the inexpensive, factory-made cloth produced in England had been placed high on the list of boycotted goods, an old, neglected, and tedious domestic skill became both a real and a symbolic element in the American protest strategy. In 1768 many women responded to the challenge. Taking a bold political stance, women, including wealthy mothers and daughters, formed groups called the Daughters of Liberty and staged large public spinning bees to show support for the boycott. Wearing clothing made of "homespun" became a mark of honor and a political statement. As one male observer noted, "The ladies . . . while they vie with each other in skill and industry in their profitable employment, may vie with the men in contributing to the preservation and prosperity of their country and equally share in the honor of it." Through the boycott, politics had entered the domestic circle.

The British Humiliated

Townshend and his new taxation policy faced sustained defiance in almost every colony, but Massachusetts provided the greatest embarrassment for Parliament and the king. Massachusetts governor Francis Bernard had lost his control over local politics ever since he tried to punish the assembly for issuing a call in 1768 for collective protest, called a Circular Letter, against the Townshend Acts to other colonies. Although Bernard forced the assembly to rescind, or call back, the letter, the men chosen for the legislature in the next election simply reissued it. The helpless governor could do nothing to save face except dismiss the assembly, leaving the colony without any representative government. Bernard's ability to ensure law and order eroded rapidly after this. Throughout 1768, enforcers of the boycott roamed the streets of Boston, intimidating pro-British merchants and harassing anyone wearing British-made clothing. Boston mobs of men and women openly threatened customs officials, and the Sons of Liberty protected smuggling operations. Despite the increased number of customs officers policing the docks and wharves, the colony was doing a thriving business in smuggling foreign goods and the items listed in the hated Townshend Acts. One of the town's most notorious smugglers, the flamboyant John Hancock, grew more popular with his neighbors each time he broke the customs laws and unloaded his illegal cargoes of French and Spanish wines or West Indian sugar. When customs officers seized Hancock's vessel, aptly named the *Liberty*, in June 1768, protesters beat up senior customs men and mobs visited the homes of other royal officials. The now-desperate Governor Bernard sent an urgent plea for help to the British government.

In October 1768, four thousand troops arrived in Boston. The Crown clearly believed that the presence of one soldier for every four citizens would be enough to restore order quickly. John Adams marveled at what he considered British thickheadedness. The presence of so many young soldiers, far from home and surrounded by a hostile community, was certain to worsen the situation. Military occupation of Boston, Adams warned, made more violence inevitable. Adams was right. With time on their hands, the soldiers passed the hours courting any local women who would speak to them and pestering those who would not. They angered local dockworkers by moonlighting in the shipyards when off duty and taking jobs away from colonists by accepting lower pay. For their part, civilians taunted the sentries, insulted the soldiers, and refused the military any sign of hospitality. News of street-corner fights and tavern brawls inflamed feelings on both sides. Samuel Adams and his friends did their best to fan the flames of hatred, publishing daily accounts of both real and imaginary confrontations in which soldiers threatened the honor or endangered the safety of innocent townspeople.

The military occupation dragged on through 1769 and early 1770. On March 5, the major confrontation most people expected occurred. An angry crowd began throwing snowballs—undoubtedly laced with bricks and rocks—at British sentries guarding the customs house. The redcoats, under strict orders not to fire on civilians, issued a frantic call for help in withdrawing to safety. When Captain Thomas Preston and his men arrived to rescue the sentries, the growing crowd immediately enveloped them. How, and under whose orders, Preston's soldiers began to fire is un-

Paul Revere's engraving of the Boston Massacre appeared in newspapers the day after the confrontation between redcoats and Boston citizens. Despite the fact that Captain Preston and most of his soldiers were acquitted of wrongdoing, Revere's striking image of innocent civilians and murderous soldiers remained fixed in the popular mind. It reinforced suspicion that the British were plotting to deprive Americans of their rights and liberties. *"Boston Massacre" by Paul Revere. Library of Congress.*

known, but they killed five men and wounded eight other colonists. Four of the five victims were white laborers. The fifth, Crispus Attucks, was a free black sailor.

Massachusetts protest leaders' account of what they called the Boston Massacre appeared in colonial newspapers everywhere and included a dramatic anti-British illustration engraved by silversmith Paul Revere. A jury of colonists later cleared Preston and all but two of his men of the charges against them. But nothing that was said at their trial—no sworn testimony, no lawyer's arguments—could erase the image of British brutality against British subjects.

Even before the bloodshed of March 5, Edmund Burke, a member of Parliament known for his sympathy to the colonial cause, had warned the House of Commons that the relationship between Mother Country and colonies was both desperate and tragic. "The Americans," Burke said, "have made a discovery, or think they have made one, that we mean to oppress them; we have made a discovery, or think we have made one, that they intend to rise in rebellion. We do not know how to advance; they do not know how to retreat." Burke captured well the growing American conviction of a conspiracy or plot by Parliament to deprive the colonists of their rights and liberties. He also captured the British government's growing sense that a rebellion was being hatched. But Parliament was ready to act to ease the crisis and make a truce possible. A new minister, Frederick Lord North, was given the reins of government, and on the very day Captain Preston's men fired on the crowd at Boston, Lord North repealed the Townshend Acts and allowed the hated Quartering Act to expire. Yet Lord North wanted to give no ground on the question of parliamentary control of the colonies. For this reason, North kept the tax on tea—to preserve a principle rather than fill the king's treasury.

Success Weakens Colonial Unity

Repeal of the Townshend Acts allowed the colonists to return to the ordinary routine of their lives. But it was not true that all tensions had vanished. Troubling ones remained—and they were largely among the colonists themselves.

The economic boycott begun in 1768 exposed and deepened the growing divisions between the merchant elite and the coalition of smaller merchants, artisans, and laborers in the urban centers of the North. During the years of nonimportation, many of the wealthy merchants had secretly imported and sold British goods whenever possible. When repeal came in 1770, the demand for locally manufactured goods was still low, and artisans and laborers still faced poor economic prospects. These groups were reluctant to abandon the boycott even after repeal. But few merchants, large or small, would agree to continue it.

Many elite colonists gladly abandoned the radical activism they had shown in the 1760s in favor of social conservatism. Their fear of British tyranny dimmed, but their fear of the lower classes' clamor for political power grew. Artisans and laborers did indeed continue to press for broader participation in local politics and for more representative political machinery. The tyranny that some of them opposed was close to home. "Many of the poorer People," observed one supporter of expanded political participation, "deeply felt the Aristocratic Power, or rather the intolerable Tyranny of the great and opulent." The new political language in which these common men justified their demands made their social superiors uneasy. Their own impassioned appeals for rights and liberties were returning to haunt some of the colonial elite.

The Crisis Renewed

■ What British policies led Americans to imagine a plot against their rights and liberties?

■ How did the king hope to crush resistance in Massachusetts?

■ How did the Continental Congress respond to the Intolerable Acts?

Lord North's government took care not to disturb the calm created by the repeal of the Townshend Acts. Between 1770 and 1773, North proposed no new taxes on the colonists and made no major changes in colonial policy. American political leaders took equal care not to make any open challenges to British authority. Both sides recognized that their political truce had its limits. It did not extend to smugglers and customs men, who continued to lock horns; it did not end the bitterness of southern colonists who wished to settle beyond the Proclamation Line; nor did it erase the distrust colonial political leaders and the British government felt for each other.

Disturbing the Peace of the Early 1770s

Despite the repeal of the Townshend duties, the British effort to crack down on American smuggling continued. New England merchants whose fortunes were built on trade with the Caribbean resented the sight of customs officers at the docks and customs ships patrolling the coastline (see Map 5.2). Rhode Island merchants were especially angry and frustrated by the determined—and highly effective—customs operation in their colony. They took their revenge one June day in 1772 when the customs patrol boat, the *Gaspée,* ran aground as it chased an American vessel. That evening a band of colonists boarded the *Gaspée,* taunted the stranded customs men, and then set fire to their boat.

Rhode Islanders called the burning of the *Gaspée* an act of political resistance. The English called it an act of vandalism and appointed a royal commission to investigate. To their amazement, no witnesses came forward, and no evidence could be gathered to support any arrests. The British found the conspiracy of silence among the Rhode Islanders appalling.

Many American political leaders found the royal commission equally appalling. They were convinced that the British government had intended to bring its suspects to England for trial and thus deprive them of a jury of their peers. They read this as further evidence of the plot to destroy American liberty, and

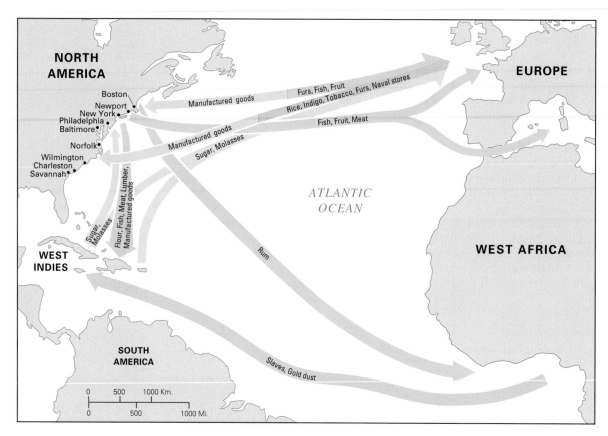

MAP 5.2 Colonial Transatlantic Trade in the 1770s This map shows the major trade routes between the British mainland colonies, West Africa, the Caribbean, and Europe and the most important export and import cargoes carried along these routes. The central role northern seaport cities played in carrying colonial agricultural products across the Atlantic and bringing British manufactured goods into the colonies is clear. Note also the role the northern colonies played in the slave trade.

they decided to keep in close contact in order to monitor British moves. Following the Virginia assembly's lead, five colonies organized a communications network called the committees of correspondence, instructing each committee to circulate detailed accounts of any questionable royal activities in its colony. These committees of correspondence were also a good mechanism for coordinating protest or resistance should the need arise. Thus the colonists put in place their first permanent machinery of protest.

The Tea Act and the Tea Party

During the early 1770s, colonial activists worked to keep the political consciousness of the 1760s alive. They commemorated American victories over British policy and observed the anniversary of the Boston Massacre with solemn speeches and sermons. The New York Sons of Liberty celebrated their founding day with dinners, endless toasts, and rituals that linked the Sons with a tradition of English radicalism. Without major British provocation, however, a revival of mass action was unlikely.

In 1773 Parliament provided that provocation. This time the government was not setting new colonial policy. It was trying to save a major commercial enterprise, the East India Tea Company. Mismanagement, coupled with the American boycott and the tendency of colonists to buy smuggled Dutch tea, had left the company in serious financial trouble. With its warehouses bursting with unsold tea, the company appealed to Parliament to rescue them.

The company directors had a plan: if Parliament allowed them to ship their tea directly to the colonial

The famous "Boston Tea Party" of December 1773 was neither secretive nor quiet. As this illustration shows, a noisy crowd gathered on the docks to cheer the men who boarded British ships to toss thousands of pounds' worth of tea into the harbor. Although the radicals donned Indian disguises, most of them were no doubt easily recognized by their supporters. Although this artist painted an all-male crowd, written accounts tell us that women were present at the Tea Party too. *Library of Congress.*

market, eliminating the English merchants who served as middlemen, they could lower their prices and compete effectively against the smuggled Dutch tea. Even with the three-penny tax on tea that remained from the Townshend era, smart consumers would see this as a bargain. Lord North liked the plan and saw in it the opportunity for vindication: Americans who purchased the cheaper English tea would be confirming Parliament's right to tax the colonies. With little debate, Parliament made the company's arrangement legal through passage of the Tea Act. No one expected the colonists to object.

Once again, British politicians had seriously misjudged the impact of their decisions. Colonists read the Tea Act as an insult, a challenge, another chilling sign of a conspiracy against their well-being and their liberty. They distrusted the arrangement, believing that the East India Tea Company would raise its prices dramatically once all foreign teas were driven off the market. And they were concerned that if other British companies marketing products in the colonies followed the East India Tea Company's example, prices for scores of products would soar. These objections, however, paled beside the colonists' immediate grasp of Lord North's strategy: purchasing cheaper English

tea would confirm Parliament's right to tax the colonies. The tea that Americans drank might be cheap, but the price of conceding the legitimacy of the tea tax was too high.

Colonists mobilized their resistance in 1773 with the skill acquired from a decade of experience. In several cities, crowds met the ships carrying the East India tea and prevented the unloading of their cargoes. They used the threat of violence to persuade ship captains to return to England with the tea still on board. As long as both the captains and the local royal officials gave in to these pressures, no serious confrontation occurred. But in Massachusetts, the most famous victim of mob violence, now Governor Thomas Hutchinson, was not willing to give in. A stalemate resulted: colonists refused to allow crews to unload the tea, but Hutchinson refused to allow the tea ships to depart without unloading. Boston activists broke the stalemate on December 16, 1773, when some sixty men, thinly disguised as Mohawk Indians, boarded the tea ships. Working calmly and methodically, they dumped 342 chests of tea, worth almost £10,000, into the waters of Boston Harbor.

The Intolerable Acts

The Boston Tea Party delighted colonists everywhere. The Crown, however, failed to see the humor in this deliberate destruction of valuable private property. The tea chests had barely settled into the harbor mud before Parliament retaliated. The king and his minister meant to make an example of everyone in Boston, the source of so much trouble and embarrassment over the past decade. Americans on the scene in England warned friends and family back home of the growing rage against the colonies. Arthur Lee, serving in London as Massachusetts's colonial agent, drew a gloomy picture of the dangers ahead in a letter to his brother. "The storm, you see, runs high," he wrote, "and it will require great prudence, wisdom and resolution, to save our liberties from shipwreck."

The four acts that Parliament passed in 1774 to discipline Massachusetts were as harsh and uncompromising as Arthur Lee predicted. The colonists called them the Intolerable Acts. The Port Act declared the port of Boston closed to all trade until the citizens compensated the East India Tea Company fully for its losses. This was a devastating blow to the colony's economy. The Massachusetts Government Act transferred much of the power of the colony's assembly to the royal governor, including the right to appoint judges, sheriffs, and members of the colonial legislature's upper house. The colony's town meetings,

An Act of Parliament

Passed in the Fourteenth Year of the Reign of His Majesty King GEORGE the Third. 1774.

An Act for the better regulating the Government of the Province of the Massachuset's Bay, in New-England.

WHEREAS by Letters Patent under the Great Seal of England, made in the Third Year of the Reign of Their late Majesties King William and Queen Mary, for uniting, erecting, and Incorporating, the several Colonies, Territories, and Tracts of Land therein mentioned, into one real Province, by the Name of Their Majesties Province of the Massachuset's Bay, in New-England; whereby it was, amongst other Things, ordained and established, That the Governor of the said Province should, from thenceforth, be appointed and commissioned by Their Majesties, Their Heirs and Successors: It was, however, granted and ordained, That, from the Expiration of the Term for and during which the Eight and twenty Persons named in the said Letters Patent were appointed to be the first Counsellors or Assistants to the Governor of the said Province for the Time being, the aforesaid Number of Eight and twenty Counsellors or Assistants should yearly, Once in every Year, for ever thereafter, be, by the General Court or Assembly, newly chosen: And whereas the said Method of electing such Counsellors or Assistants, to be vested with the several Powers, Authorities, and Privileges, therein mentioned, although conformable to the Practice theretofore used in such of the Colonies thereby united, in which the Appointment of the respective Governors had been vested in the General Courts or Assemblies of the said Colonies, hath, by repeated Experience, been found to be extremely ill adapted to the Plan of Government established in the Province of the Massachuset's Bay, by the said Letters Patent herein-before mentioned, and hath been so far from contributing to the Attainment of A the

The destruction of tea in Boston Harbor provoked harsh reprisals from the king and Parliament. In 1774, the British government issued a series of measures that colonists called the "Intolerable Acts." The most shocking of these was the reorganization of the Massachusetts government and the closing of the port of Boston to all trade. But instead of crushing the rebellion brewing in the colonies, the Intolerable Acts radicalized many colonists. *National Archives Image Library.*

which had served as forums for anti-British sentiment and protests, also came under the governor's direct control. A third measure, the Justice Act, allowed royal officials charged with capital crimes to stand trial in London rather than before local juries. And a new Quartering Act gave military commanders the authority to house troops in private homes. To see that these laws were enforced, the king named General Thomas Gage, commander of the British troops in North America, as the acting governor of Massachusetts.

At the same time that Parliament passed these punitive measures, the British government issued a comprehensive plan for the government of Canada. The timing of the Quebec Act may have been a coincidence, but its provisions infuriated Americans. The Quebec Act granted the French in Canada the right to worship as Catholics, retain their language, and keep many of their legal practices—all marks of a tolerance that the Crown had refused to show its English colonists. The Quebec Act also expanded the borders of Canada into the Ohio Valley at the expense of the English-speaking colonies' claim to western land. This dealt a harsh blow to Virginia planters who hoped to profit from land speculation in the region. The endorsement of Catholicism and the stifling of western expansion seemed to connect the Quebec Act to the attack on American liberty that Parliament had launched with the Intolerable Acts.

The king expected the severe punishment of Massachusetts to isolate that colony from its neighbors. But the Americans resisted this divide-and-conquer strategy. In every colony, newspaper essays and editorials urged readers to see Boston's plight as their own. "This horrid attack upon the town of Boston," said the *South Carolina Gazette,* "we consider not as an attempt upon that town singly, but upon the whole Continent." George Washington, by now an influential Virginia planter and militia officer—and a major land speculator—declared that "the cause of Boston now is and ever will be the cause of America." Indeed, the Intolerable Acts produced a wave of sympathy for the beleaguered Bostonians, and relief efforts sprang up across the colonies. The residents of Surry County, Virginia, declared they had gathered "upwards of 150 barrels of Indian corn and wheat . . . for the benefit of those firm and intrepid sons of Liberty." Throughout the year, much-needed supplies found their way to Boston despite British efforts to isolate the city.

Colonists did not stop at sympathy for the victims of the Intolerable Acts. In pamphlets and political essays, they placed these acts into the larger context of systematic oppression by the Mother Country. Political writers referred to the British government as the "enemy," conspiring to deprive Americans of their liberty, and urged colonists to defend themselves against the "power and cunning of our adversaries." This unity of sentiments, however, was more fragile than it appeared. In the cities, bitter divisions quickly developed, and artisans struggled with merchants to control the mass meetings that would make strategy choices. Samuel Adams and the radical artisans and workers of Boston suggested what might be at stake in this struggle between elites and ordinary citizens when they formed a "solemn league and covenant" to lead a third intercolonial boycott of British goods. As most Bostonians knew, the words *solemn league* referred to a pact between the Scottish Presbyterians and English Puritans who had overthrown royal government in the 1640s and beheaded a king. Adams and his allies had made their choice: armed rebellion. Yet even in crisis-torn Boston, not everyone wanted matters to go that far. And in the southern colonies, planters fearful of the social instability that resistance might bring worried that slave revolts and class antagonisms between the elite and the poorer farmers might be the ultimate outcome of escalating protest.

Creating a National Forum: The First Continental Congress

On September 5, 1774, delegates from every colony but Georgia gathered in Philadelphia for a continental congress. Few of the delegates or the people they represented thought of themselves as revolutionaries. "We want no revolution," a North Carolina delegate bluntly stated. Yet in the eyes of their British rulers, he and other colonists were treading dangerously close to treason. After all, neither the king nor Parliament had authorized the congress to which colonial assemblies and self-appointed committees had sent representatives. And that congress was intent on resisting acts of Parliament and defying the king. English men and women had been hanged as traitors for far less serious betrayals of the English government.

Some of the most articulate political leaders in the colonies attended this First Continental Congress. Conservative delegates such as Joseph Galloway of Pennsylvania hoped to slow the pace of colonial resistance by substituting petitions to Parliament for the total boycott proposed by Samuel Adams. Their radical opponents—including Samuel Adams and his cousin John, Patrick Henry, and delegates from the artisan community of Philadelphia—demanded the boycott and more. Most of the delegates were desperately searching for a third choice: a way to express their grievances and demand that injustices be corrected without further eroding their relationship with England.

The mounting crisis in Massachusetts diminished the chances of a moderate solution. Rumors spread that the royal navy was planning to bombard Boston and that General Gage was preparing to invade the countryside. Thousands of Massachusetts militiamen had begun mustering in Cambridge. The growing conflict drove many delegates into the radical camp. In this atmosphere of dread and anxiety, the Continental Congress approved the Continental Association, a boycott of all English goods to begin on December 1, 1774. The Congress also passed strong resolutions demanding the repeal of the Intolerable Acts.

The First Continental Congress had chosen radical tactics, but many delegates were torn between loyalties to two governments and their conflicting claims to power. Parliament insisted on an unconditional right to make laws for and regulate the colonies. The colonial assemblies claimed that they alone had the right to tax the colonists. Thomas Jefferson, a young Virginia planter and intellectual, tried to find a way out of this dilemma by separating loyalty to the king from resistance to Parliament. He argued that the colonists owed allegiance to the nation's king, not to Parliament, and that each colony did indeed have the right to legislate for itself. Not everyone agreed.

If no compromise could be reached, the delegates—and Americans everywhere—would have to choose where their strongest loyalties lay. Joseph Galloway believed that he had worked out the necessary compromise. In his Plan of Union, Galloway proposed a drastic restructuring of imperial relations. The plan called for a Grand Council, elected by each colonial legislature, that would share with Parliament the right to originate laws for the colonies. The Grand Council and Parliament would have the power to veto or disallow each other's decisions if necessary. A governor-general, appointed by the Crown, would oversee council operations and preserve imperial interests.

After much discussion and debate, Congress rejected Galloway's compromise by the narrowest of margins. Then it was John Adams's turn to propose a solution. Under his skillful urging and direction, the Congress adopted the Declaration of Rights and Grievances. The declaration politely but firmly established the colonial standard for acceptable legislation by Parliament. Colonists, said the declaration, would consent to acts meant to regulate "our external commerce." But they absolutely denied the legitimacy, or lawfulness, of an "idea of taxation, internal or external, for raising a revenue on the subjects of America, without their consent."

The delegates knew that the force behind the declaration came neither from the logic of its argument nor from the genius of its political reasoning. Whatever force it carried came from the unspoken but nevertheless real threat of rebellion that would occur if the colonists' demands were not met. To make this threat clearer, Congress endorsed a set of resolutions rushed to Philadelphia from Suffolk County, Massachusetts. These Suffolk Resolves called on the residents of that county to arm themselves and prepare to resist British military action. Congressional support for these resolves sent an unmistakable message that American leaders were willing to choose rebellion if politics failed.

The delegates adjourned and headed home, bringing news of the Congress's decisions with them to their families and their communities. There was nothing to do now but wait for the Crown's response. When it came, it was electric. "Blows must decide," declared King George III, "whether they are to be subject to this country or independent."

The Decision for Independence

- Could the Revolutionary War have been avoided?
- What alternatives might have kept compromise alive?
- What motivated some colonists to become loyalists and others to become patriots?

Americans were anxious while they waited for the king and Parliament to respond to the Declaration of Rights and Grievances, but they were not idle. In most colonies, a transfer of political power was occurring as the majority of Americans withdrew their support for and obedience to royal governments and recognized the authority of anti-British, patriot governments. The king might expect blows to decide the issue of colonial autonomy, but independent local governments were becoming a reality before any shots were fired.

Taking Charge and Enforcing Policies

Imperial control broke down as communities in each colony refused to obey royal laws or acknowledge the authority of royal officers. For example, when General Thomas Gage, the acting governor of Massachusetts, refused to convene the Massachusetts assembly, its members met anyway. Their first order of business was to prepare for military resistance to Gage and his army. While the redcoats occupied Boston, the rebellious assembly openly ordered the colonists to stockpile military supplies near the town of Concord (see Map 5.3).

The transition from royal to patriot political control was peaceful in communities where anti-British sentiment was strong. Where it was weak, or where the community was divided, radicals used persuasion, pressure, and open intimidation to advance the patriot cause. These radicals became increasingly impatient with dissent, disagreement, or even indecision among their neighbors. They insisted that people choose sides and declare loyalties.

In most colonial cities and towns, patriot committees arose to enforce compliance with the boycott of British goods. These committees publicly exposed those who did not obey the Continental Association, publishing violators' names in local newspapers and calling on the community to shun them. These tactics were effective against merchants who wanted to break the boycott and consumers willing to purchase English goods if they could find them. When public shaming did not work, most committees were ready to use threats of physical violence and to make good on them.

Colonists suspected of sympathizing with the British were brought before committees and made to swear oaths of support for the patriot cause. Such political pressure often gave way to violence. In Connecticut a group of patriots hauled a 70-year-old Anglican man from his bed, dragged him naked into the winter night, and beat him brutally because his loyalty to the Church of England made him suspect. In New England, many pro-British citizens, or **loyalists,** came to fear for their lives. In the wake of the Intolerable Acts, hundreds of them fled to the city of Boston, hoping General Gage could protect them from their neighbors.

The Shot Heard 'Round the World

The American situation was frustrating, but King George continued to believe that resistance in most colonies would fade if the Massachusetts radicals were crushed. In January 1775, he ordered General Gage to arrest the most notorious leaders of rebellion in that colony, Samuel Adams and John Hancock. Although storms on the Atlantic prevented the king's orders from reaching Gage until April, the general had independently decided it was time to take action. Gage planned to dispatch a force of redcoats to Concord with orders to seize the rapidly growing stockpile of weapons and arrest the two radical leaders along the way.

The patriots, of course, had their spies in Boston. Reports of the arrest orders and of suspicious troop preparations reached the militias gathered outside the occupied city. The only question was when and where Gage would attack. The Americans devised a warning system: as soon as Gage's troops began to move out of Boston, spies would signal the route with lanterns hung in the bell tower of the North Church. On April 18, 1775, riders waiting outside

---

loyalist An American colonist who remained loyal to the king during the Revolution.

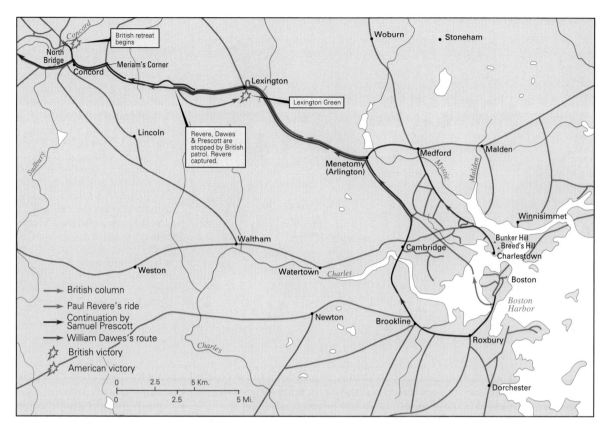

MAP 5.3 The First Battles in the War for Independence, 1775   This map shows the British march to Concord and the routes taken by the three Americans who alerted the countryside of the enemy's approach. Although Paul Revere was captured by the British and did not complete his ride, he is the best remembered and most celebrated of the nightriders who spread the alarm.

Boston saw one lantern, then another, flash from the bell tower. Within moments, silversmith Paul Revere and his fellow messengers rode off to give news of the British army's approach to the militia and the people living in the countryside.

Around sunrise on April 19, an advance guard of a few hundred redcoats reached the town of Lexington, where they expected to apprehend Adams and Hancock. In the pale light, they saw about seventy colonial militiamen waiting on the village green. As the badly outnumbered colonists began to disperse, eager and nervous redcoats broke ranks and rushed forward, sending up a triumphant cheer. No order came to fire, but in the confusion shots rang out. Eight Americans were killed, most of them shot in the back as they ran for safety. Nine more were wounded. Later Americans who told the story of the skirmish at Lexington would insist that the first musket fired there sounded a "shot heard 'round the world."

The British troops marched from Lexington to Concord. Surprised to find the town nearly deserted, they began a methodical search for weapons. All they uncovered were five hundred musket balls, which they dumped into a nearby pond. They then burned the town's liberty tree. Ignoring this act of provocation, the Concord **Minutemen,** in hiding nearby, waited patiently. When the moment seemed right, they swooped down on the unsuspecting British troops guarding the town's North Bridge.

The sudden attack by the Americans shocked the redcoats, who fled in a panic back toward Boston. The Minutemen followed, gathering more men along

Minutemen   Nickname first given to the Concord militia because of their speed in assembling and later applied generally to colonial militia during the Revolution.

The Pennsylvania State House in Philadelphia is best known to modern-day Americans as Independence Hall. It was here that the Declaration of Independence was debated and approved, and it was here that delegates gathered to draft a new constitution for the United States in the hot and humid summer of 1787. Although the State House boasted large windows in the East Room where the delegates met, the shutters were tightly closed—to preserve the secrecy of the debates and to prevent the huge bottlenecked flies swarming throughout the city from entering the room. *Independence National Historic Park.*

the path of pursuit. Together, these American farmers, artisans, servants, and shopkeepers terrorized the young British soldiers, firing on them at will from behind barns, stone walls, and trees. When the shaken troops reached the British encampment across the Charles River from Boston, 73 of their comrades were dead, 174 were wounded, and 26 were missing. The day after the **Battles of Lexington and Concord,** thousands of New England militiamen poured in from the surrounding countryside, dug trenches, and laid siege to Boston. As far as they and thousands of other Americans were concerned—including the loyalist refugees crowded into the city—war had begun.

The Second Continental Congress

When the Continental Congress reconvened in May 1775, it began at once to ready the colonies for war. This Second Continental Congress authorized the printing of American paper money for the purchase of supplies and appointed a committee to oversee foreign relations. It approved the creation of a Continental Army and chose George Washington, the Virginia veteran of the French and Indian War, to serve as its commander.

The Congress was clearly ready to defend Americans' rights and protect their liberties. But was it ready to declare a complete break with England? Some delegates still hoped to find a peaceful solution to the crisis, despite the bloodshed at Lexington and Concord. This sentiment led the Congress to draft the **Olive Branch Petition,** which offered the king a choice: the colonists would end their armed resistance if the king would withdraw the British military and revoke the Intolerable Acts. Many delegates must have doubted the king's willingness to make such concessions, for the very next day the Congress issued a public statement in defense of the war preparations. This "Declaration of the Causes and Necessity of Taking Up Arms" boldly accused the British government of tyranny. It stopped short, however, of declaring colonial independence.

Across the Atlantic, British leaders struggled to find some negotiating points despite the king's refusal to bend. Almost two months before the battles at Lexington and Concord, Lord North had drafted a set of Conciliatory Propositions for Parliament and

Battles of Lexington and Concord   Two confrontations in April 1775 between British soldiers and patriot Minutemen; the first recognized battles of the Revolution.

Olive Branch Petition   Resolution, adopted by the Second Continental Congress in 1775 after the Battles of Lexington and Concord, that offered to end armed resistance if the king would withdraw his troops and repeal the Intolerable Acts.

the American Continental Congress to consider. North's proposals gave no ground on Parliament's right to tax the colonies, but they did offer to suspend taxation if Americans would raise funds for their own military defense. Members of Parliament who were sympathetic toward the Americans also pressed for compromise. They insisted that it made better sense to keep the colonies as a market for English goods than to lose them in a battle over raising revenue.

Cooler heads, however, did not prevail. Americans rejected Lord North's proposals in July 1775. The king, loathe to compromise, rejected the Olive Branch Petition. George III then persuaded Parliament to pass an **American Prohibitory Act** instructing the royal navy to seize American ships engaged in any form of trade, "as if the same were the ships . . . of open enemies." For all intents and purposes, King George III declared war on his colonies before the colonies declared war on their king.

The Impact of *Common Sense*

War was a fact, yet few American voices were calling for a complete political and emotional break with Britain. Even the most ardent patriots continued to justify their actions as upholding the British constitution. They were rebelling, they said, to preserve the rights guaranteed English citizens, not to establish an independent nation. Their drastic actions were necessary because a corrupt Parliament and corrupt ministers were trampling on those rights.

Although in 1764 Patrick Henry had dramatically warned the king to remember that tyrants were often deposed, few colonists had yet traced the source of their oppression to George III himself. If any American political leaders believed the king was as corrupt as his advisers and his Parliament, they did not make this view public. Then, in January 1776, Thomas Paine, an Englishman who had emigrated to America a few years earlier, published a pamphlet he called *Common Sense.* Paine's pamphlet broke the silence about King George III.

Tom Paine was a corsetmaker by trade but a political radical by temperament. As soon as he settled in Philadelphia, he became a wholehearted and vocal supporter of the colonial protest to defend colonial rights, but he preferred American political independence. In *Common Sense,* Paine spoke directly to ordinary citizens, not to their political leaders. Like the preachers of the Great Awakening, he rejected the formal language of the elite, adopting instead a plain, urgent, and emotional vocabulary and writing style designed to reach a mass audience.

Common Sense was unique in its content as well as its style. Paine made no excuses for his revolutionary zeal. He expressed no admiration for the British constitution or reverence for the British political system. Instead, he attacked the **sanctity** of the monarchy head-on. He challenged the idea of a hereditary ruler, questioned the value of monarchy as an institution, and criticized the personal character of the men who ruled as kings. The common man, Paine insisted, had the ability to be his own king and was surely more deserving of that position than most of the men who had worn crowns. Paine put it bluntly and sarcastically: "Of more worth is one honest man to society, and in the sight of God, than all the crowned ruffians that ever lived." He dismissed George III as nothing more than a "Royal Brute," and he urged Americans to establish their own republic. No wonder Charles Inglis felt compelled to respond to such radical and treasonous arguments!

Common Sense sold 120,000 copies in its first three months in print. Paine's defiance of traditional authority and open criticism of the men who wielded it helped many of his readers, both male and female, discard the last shreds of loyalty to the king and to the empire. The impact of Paine's words resounded in the taverns and coffeehouses, where ordinary farmers, artisans, shopkeepers, and laborers took up his call for independence and the creation of a republic. Political leaders acknowledged Paine's importance, although some begrudged the popular admiration lavished on this poorly educated artisan. The Harvard-trained John Adams reluctantly admitted that *Common Sense* was a "tolerable summary of the arguments I have been repeating again and again in Congress for nine months." But Adams's social snobbery led him to criticize Paine's language and his flamboyant writing style, suitable, Adams insisted, only "for an emigrant from new Gate [an English prison] or one chiefly associated with such company." Unshaken by such criticism, Tom Paine was content to see his message move so many into the revolutionary camp.

American Prohibitory Act   British law of 1775 that authorized the royal navy to seize all American ships engaged in trade; it amounted to a declaration of war.

Common Sense   Revolutionary pamphlet written by Thomas Paine in 1776; it attacked George III, argued against monarchy, and advanced the patriot cause.

sanctity   Saintliness or holiness; the quality of being sacred or beyond criticism.

Declaring Independence

The Second Continental Congress, lagging far behind popular sentiment, inched its way toward a formal declaration of independence. But even John Adams, who had fumed at its snail's pace, took heart when the Congress opened American trade to all nations except Great Britain in early April 1776 and instructed the colonies to create official state governments. Then, on June 7, Adams's close ally in the struggle to announce independence, Virginia lawyer Richard Henry Lee, rose on the floor of the Congress and offered this straightforward motion: "That these United Colonies are, and of right ought to be, free and independent States, that they are absolved from all allegiance to the British Crown, and that all political connection between them and the State of Great Britain is, and ought to be, totally dissolved."

Lee's resolution was no more than a statement of reality, yet the Congress chose to postpone its final vote until July. The delay would give members time to win over the few fainthearted delegates from the Middle Colonies. It also would allow the committee appointed to draft a formal declaration of independence time to complete its work.

Congress had chosen an all-star group to draft the declaration, including John Adams, Connecticut's Roger Sherman, Benjamin Franklin, and New York landowner Robert Livingston. But these men delegated the task of writing the document to the fifth and youngest member of the committee, Thomas Jefferson. They chose well. The 33-year-old Virginian was not a social radical like Samuel Adams and Tom Paine. He was not an experienced politician like John Adams and Benjamin Franklin. And he lacked the reputation of fellow Virginians George Washington and Richard Henry Lee. But he had his strengths, and the committee members recognized them. Jefferson could draw on a deep and broad knowledge of political theory and philosophy. He had read the works of Enlightenment philosophers, classical theorists, and seventeenth-century English revolutionaries. And though shy and somewhat halting in his speech, Thomas Jefferson was a master of written prose. Jefferson began the **Declaration of Independence** with a defense of revolution based on "self-evident" truths about humanity's "inalienable rights"—rights that included life, liberty, and the pursuit of property. (In a later draft, the rights became "unalienable" and "property" became "happiness.") Jefferson argued that these rights were natural rather than historical. In other words, they came from the "Creator" rather than developing out of human law, government, or tradi-

In 1776, patriots everywhere celebrated independence by destroying local symbols of royal authority. New Yorkers, however, combined the practical with the symbolic, tearing down an imposing statue of King George III that had stood near the tip of Manhattan since 1770 and recycling its lead to make ammunition for the Revolutionary army. *"Pulling Down the Statue of George III" by William Walcott. Private Collection.*

tion. Thus they were broader and more sacred than the specific "rights of Englishmen." With this philosophical groundwork in place, Jefferson moved on to list the grievances that demanded that America end its relationship with Britain. He focused on the king's abuse of power rather than on the oppressive legislation passed by Parliament. All government rested on the consent of the governed, Jefferson asserted, and the people had the right to overthrow any government that tyrannized rather than protected them, that threatened rather than respected their unalienable rights.

The genius of Jefferson's Declaration was not that it contained novel ideas but that it contained ideas that were commonly accepted by America's political leaders and by most ordinary citizens as well. Jefferson gave voice to these beliefs, clearly and firmly. He also gave voice to the sense of abuse and injustice that had been growing in colonial society for several decades.

Declaration of Independence A formal statement, adopted by the Second Continental Congress in 1776, that listed justifications for rebellion and declared the American mainland colonies to be independent of Britain.

Declaring Loyalties

Delegates to the Second Continental Congress approved the Declaration of Independence on July 2, 1776, and made their approval public on July 4 (the text of the Declaration is reprinted in the Documents section at the end of this book). As John Adams was fond of saying, "The die had been cast," and Americans had to weigh loyalty to king against loyalty to a new nation. For Americans of every region, religion, social class, and race, this decision weighed heavily. In the face of such a critical choice, many wavered. Throughout the war that followed the Declaration, a surprising number of colonists clung to neutrality, hoping that the breach could be resolved without their having to participate or choose sides.

Those who did commit themselves based their decisions on deeply held beliefs and personal considerations, as well as fears. Many loyalists believed that tradition, commitment, and common sense argued for acknowledging parliamentary supremacy and the king's right to rule. These colonists had an abiding respect for the structure of the British government, with its balance between royalty, aristocracy, and the common people and its ability to preserve the rights of each group. In their judgment, the advantages of remaining within the protective circle of the most powerful nation in Europe seemed too obvious to debate. And the likelihood of swift and bloody defeat at the hands of the British army and navy seemed too obvious to risk. Many of the men who articulated the loyalist position were members of the colonial elite. They frankly admitted their fears that a revolution would unleash the "madness of the multitude." The tyranny of the mob, they argued, was far more damaging than the tyranny of which the king stood accused.

Not all colonists who chose loyalism feared the mob or revered the principles on which the British political system was based. For many, the deciding issues were economic. Holders of royal offices and merchants who depended on trade with British manufacturers found loyalty the compelling option. The loyalist ranks were also filled with colonists from the "multitude." Many small farmers and tenant farmers gave their support to the Crown when their political and economic foes—the great planters of the South or the New York manor lords—became patriots. The choice of which side to back often hinged, therefore, on local struggles and economic conflicts rather than on imperial issues.

For some of the perhaps 150,000 active loyalists, loyalism was a matter of personal character as much as conscious self-interest. Reluctance to break a solemn

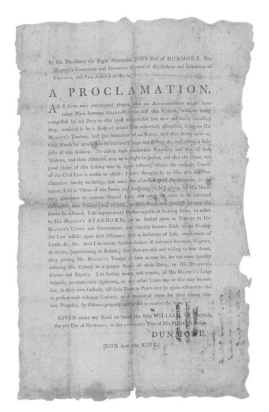

In November 1775, Virginia's royal governor, Lord Dunmore, enraged and frightened patriots by issuing this proclamation, which offered freedom to "all indentured Servants, Negroes, or others" who would help Britain squelch the impending rebellion. Thousands of enslaved men, women, and children eventually made their way to freedom behind British lines, choosing loyalism as their route to liberty. *Special Collections, University of Virginia Alderman Library.*

oath of allegiance to the king, anxiety over cutting ties with the past, fear of the chaos and violence that were a real part of revolution—any and all of these feelings could motivate a colonist to remain loyal rather than rebel.

For African Americans, the rallying call of liberty was familiar long before the Revolution began. Decades of slave resistance and rebellion demonstrated that black colonists did not need the impassioned language of a Patrick Henry or a Samuel Adams to remind them of the value of freedom. Instead, many slaves viewed the Revolution as they viewed epidemics and imperial warfare: as a potential opportunity to gain their own liberty. In the same way, free blacks saw the Revolution as a possible opportunity to win civil rights they had been denied before 1776.

African Americans had pointed out the inconsistencies of the radical position even before the Declaration of Independence. In 1773, a group of enslaved blacks in Boston petitioned the governor and the assembly for their freedom, "in behalf of all those, who . . . are held in a state of SLAVERY, within the bowels of a FREE country." There were white colonists who appreciated the injustice of a white slaveholding community in crisis over threats to its liberty. In 1774, while John Adams debated the threat of political slavery for colonial Englishmen in the First Continental Congress, his wife Abigail observed: "It always appeared a most iniquitous [sinful] scheme to me—to fight ourselves for what we are daily robbing and plundering from those who have as good a right to freedom as we have." Tom Paine agreed. Writing as "Humanus" in a Philadelphia newspaper, Paine urged white patriots to abolish slavery and give freed blacks western land grants.

Other patriots worried that slaves would seek their freedom by supporting the British in the war. The royal governor of Virginia was ready to make an offer of freedom to the colony's slaves. In 1775 Governor Dunmore expressed his intention to "arm all my own Negroes and receive all others that will come to me whom I shall declare free." Rumors of this plan horrified neighboring Maryland planters, who demanded that their governor issue arms and ammunition to protect against slave **insurrection.** Throughout the South, white communities braced themselves for a black struggle for freedom that would emerge in the midst of the colonial struggle for independence.

When Dunmore did offer freedom to "all indentured Servants, negroes or others . . . able and willing to bear Arms who escaped their masters," he was more interested in disrupting the slave-based plantation economy of his American enemies than in African American rights. Yet slaves responded, crossing into British lines in great enough numbers to create an "Ethiopian Regiment" of soldiers. These black loyalists wore a banner across their uniforms that read "Liberty to Slaves." Only six hundred to two thousand slaves managed to escape their masters in 1775–1776, but in the southern campaigns of the long war that followed, thousands of black men, women, and children made their way to the British lines. Once in uniform, black soldiers were usually assigned to work in road construction and other manual labor tasks rather than participate in combat. Perhaps as many as fifty thousand slaves gained their freedom during the war, as a result of either British policy or the disruptions that made escape possible.

Indians' responses to news of the war were far from uniform. At first, many considered the Revolution a family quarrel that should be avoided. The revolutionaries would have been satisfied to see Indians adopt this policy of neutrality. They knew they were unlikely to win Indian support given the legacy of border warfare and the actions of land-hungry settlers. As early as 1775, the Second Continental Congress issued a proclamation warning Indians to remain neutral. But the British, recognizing their advantage, made strong efforts to win Indian support. Indian leaders proceeded cautiously, however. When a British negotiator boasted to Flying Crow that British victory was inevitable, the Seneca chief was unimpressed. "If you are so strong, Brother, and they but as a weak Boy, why ask our assistance?" The chief was unwilling to commit his tribe based on issues that divided Crown and colonists but meant little to the welfare of his own people. "You say they are all mad, foolish, wicked, and deceitful—I say you are so and they are wise for you want us to destroy ourselves in your War and they advise us to live in Peace."

The British continued to press for Indian participation in the war, and many Indian tribes and confederations eventually decided that the Crown would better serve their interests and respect their rights than would the colonists. First, the British were much more likely than the colonists to be able to provide a steady supply of the manufactured goods and weapons the Indians relied on in the eighteenth century. Second, colonial territorial ambitions threatened the Indians along the southern and northwestern frontiers. Third, an alliance with the British offered some possibility of recouping land and trading benefits lost in the past. No uniformity emerged, however. Among the Iroquois, for example, conflicting choices of loyalties led pro-British Senecas to burn the crops and houses of Oneidas who had joined forces with the patriots. Among the Potowatomis, similar divisions occurred. Intertribal rivalries and Indians' concerns about the safety of their own villages often determined alignments. In the southern backcountry, fierce fighting between Indians and revolutionaries seemed a continuation of the century's many border wars. But even there, alignments could shift. Although the Cherokees began the war as British allies, a split developed, producing an internal civil war similar to the one among the Iroquois tribes.

Fewer than half of the colonists threw in their lot with the revolutionaries. Among those who did were

---

insurrection An uprising against a legitimate authority or government.

people whose economic interests made independence seem worth the risk, including artisans and urban laborers, merchants who traded outside the British Empire, large and small farmers, and many members of the southern planter elite. For these Americans, it was not simply a matter of escaping unfair taxation. A release from Britain's mercantile policies, which restricted colonial trade with other nations, held out the promise of expanded trade and an end to the risks of smuggling. Sometimes the pressure for independence came from below rather than from a colony's political leadership. For example, although Virginia's elite produced many radical spokesmen for independence such as Patrick Henry, many southern planters only reluctantly endorsed independence in order to retain their authority over the more radical ordinary farmers. Colonists affected by the Great Awakening and by its message of egalitarianism often chose the patriot side. Americans with a conscious, articulated radical vision of society—

the Tom Paines and Samuel Adamses—supported the Revolution and its promise of a republic. Many who became revolutionaries shared the hope for a better life under a government that encouraged its citizens to be virtuous and to live in simplicity.

As Americans—English, European, Indian, and African American—armed themselves or fled from the violence and bloodshed they saw coming, they realized that the conflict wore two faces: this was a war for independence, but it was also a civil war. In the South, it pitted slave against master, Cherokee against Cherokee, and frontier farmer against tidewater planter. In New England, it set neighbor against neighbor, forcing scores of loyalist families to flee. In some instances, children were set against parents, and wives refused to support the cause their husbands had chosen. Whatever the outcome of the struggle ahead, Americans knew that it would come at great cost.

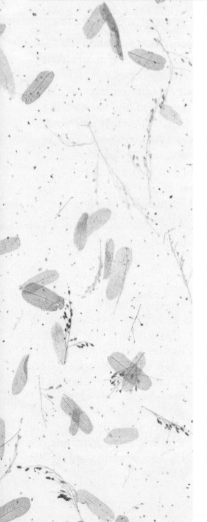

Individual Voices

Examining a Primary Source

Charles Inglis Calls for Reconcilation

Charles Inglis, Anglican minister and rector of New York City's Trinity Church, was one of the few loyalists who dared take issue with Thomas Paine's dramatic and powerful call to revolution, *Common Sense.* His response came in the form of a 1776 pamphlet called *The True Interest of America Impartially Stated.* In the portion of his pamphlet reprinted below, Inglis expresses horror at the prospect of breaking a sacred oath of allegiance to the Church of England and the Crown. Most loyalists who held appointed office and most Anglican ministers shared his feelings on this issue. In *The True Interest,* Inglis also predicts that the British army and navy would crush the rebellion at the cost of many American lives. His vision of the chaos, devastation, and humiliation the rebellious colonists would suffer was echoed in the private letters of loyalists everywhere. Finally, he points to the loss of property and the resulting poverty that would befall the colonies if they rose up against the Crown. Although fighting had already begun at Lexington and Concord, and the Continental Congress had started to muster an army, Inglis pleaded for the colonists to seek a reconciliation with Britain. But as John Adams was so fond of saying, "The die had been cast"; the Declaration of Independence was issued on July 4, 1776.

In many ways, Inglis proved correct. Much American blood was spilled during the Revolution and the long home-front war saw much devastation. Many of the ministers and officeholders who remained loyal saw the new state governments confiscate and sell their land and their homes. Once-wealthy loyalists such as Jonathan Sewall of Massachusetts and Joseph Galloway of Pennsylvania ended their lives in

■ *Inglis is referring to the battles in Massachusetts at Lexington, Concord, and Bunker Hill, in April and June 1775.*

■ *Although revolutionaries suffered the loss of crops, homes, and livestock, it was the loyalists who, in the end, saw their estates seized by the state governments and sold to patriotic neighbors. Do you think that confiscating their lands and possessions was justified?*

■ *Modern nations have also established colonies and fought wars to keep them. What economic advantages do colonies provide? Can you think of noneconomic reasons why colonies might be valuable?*

■ *If you were writing a response to Inglis's dire scenario, how would you refute his predictions of American defeat? What American advantages would you cite? What British disadvantages? What do you think were the most important factors in the American victory?*

exile and in poverty. Inglis was wrong, however, about the outcome of the war: in one of the greatest military upsets of Western history, the Americans brought the English to their knees.

The blood of the slain, the weeping voice of nature cries—it is time to be reconciled, it is time to lay aside those animosities which have pushed on Britons to shed the blood of Britons; ■ *it is high time that those who are connected by the endearing ties of religion, kindred and country, should resume their former friendship, and be united in the bond of mutual affection, as their interests are inseparably united. . . . By a Reconciliation with Great-Britain, Peace—that fairest offspring and gift of Heaven—will be restored. . . . What uneasiness and anxiety, what evils, has this short interruption of peace with the parent-state, brought on the whole British empire!*

Suppose we were to revolt from Great-Britain, declare ourselves Independent, and set up a Republic of our own—what would be the consequence? I stand aghast at the prospect—my blood runs chill when I think of the calamities, the complicated evils that must ensue. . . . All our property throughout the continent would be unhinged; the greatest confusion, and most violent convulsions would take place. . . . What a horrid situation would thousands be reduced to who have taken the oath of allegiance to the King; yet contrary to their oath, as well as inclination, must be compelled to renounce that allegiance, or abandon all their property in America! ■ *How many thousands more would be reduced to a similar situation; who, although they took not that oath, yet would think it inconsistent with their duty and a good conscience to renounce their Sovereign. . . .*

By a Declaration of Independency, every avenue to an accommodation with Great-Britain would be closed; the sword only could then decide the quarrel; and the sword would not be sheathed till one had conquered the other.

The importance of these colonies to Britain need not be enlarged on, it is a thing so universally known. ■ *The greater their importance is to her, so much the more obstinate will her struggle be not to lose them. . . . Great-Britain therefore must, for her own preservation, risk everything, and exert her whole strength, to prevent such an event from taking place. This being the case—Devastation and ruin must mark the progress of this war along the sea coast of America. Hitherto, Britain has not exerted her power. . . . But as soon as we declare for independency . . . ruthless war, with all its aggravated horrors, will ravage our once happy land. . . . Torrents of blood will be spilt, and thousands reduced to beggary and wretchedness. . . .* ■

Summary

The British victory over France and Spain in the Great War for Empire made Britain the most powerful European nation. Yet this victory produced new problems. The British had to govern the French population in Canada and maintain security against Indians on a greatly expanded colonial frontier. They had to pay an enormous war debt while maintaining a strong and well-equipped army and navy to keep the empire they

had won. To deal with these new circumstances, the English government chose to impose revenue-raising measures on the colonies. The outcome was growing tension between Mother Country and colonies.

The Sugar Act of 1764 tightened customs collections, the Stamp Act of 1765 placed a direct tax on legal documents, and the Townshend Acts of 1767 set import taxes on English products such as paint and tea. In response to this sharp shift in policy, the colonists chose protest, including crowd actions directed by the Sons of Liberty and boycotts of English goods. Crowds attacked royal officials, and in Boston five civilians died in the Boston Massacre, a clash with British troops. American colonists saw Parliament's revenue-raising acts as an abuse of power, and political debate began to focus on colonial rights and the possibility that the British government was threatening to curtail American liberties.

Protest led to the repeal of the acts, but political activists prepared for a quick and united response to any new crises by creating organizations such as the committees of correspondence. In 1773 the British passed the Tea Act, expecting little American opposition. The outcome was immediate protest, and in Boston a group of activists dumped thousands of pounds' worth of tea into the harbor.

Moving to punish the colonists, the English closed the port of Boston to all trade. This and other Intolerable Acts infuriated colonists, who took united action in support of Massachusetts. A new colonial forum, the First Continental Congress, met in 1774 to debate the colonies' relationship to England and to issue united protests. A Declaration of Rights and Griev-

ances was sent to the king, who rejected the colonists' appeal for compromise. Instead he declared that "blows must decide."

After British troops and militiamen fought at Lexington and Concord, a Second Continental Congress began to prepare for war. Tom Paine's pamphlet *Common Sense* pushed many reluctant colonists into the revolutionary camp. Not even a reasoned rebuttal of this call to revolution, such as the one written by Charles Inglis, could halt the progress toward independence after this. In July 1776, Congress issued the Declaration of Independence, drafted by Thomas Jefferson, defending the colonists' right to resist the destruction of their liberty by a tyrannical king. In 1776 Americans faced the difficult task of choosing sides: loyalty to the Crown or revolution. Not only white colonists but African Americans and Indians had to decide whether to offer support to one side or the other or try to remain neutral in the midst of revolution. The outcome was both a war for colonial independence and a civil war that divided families and communities across America.

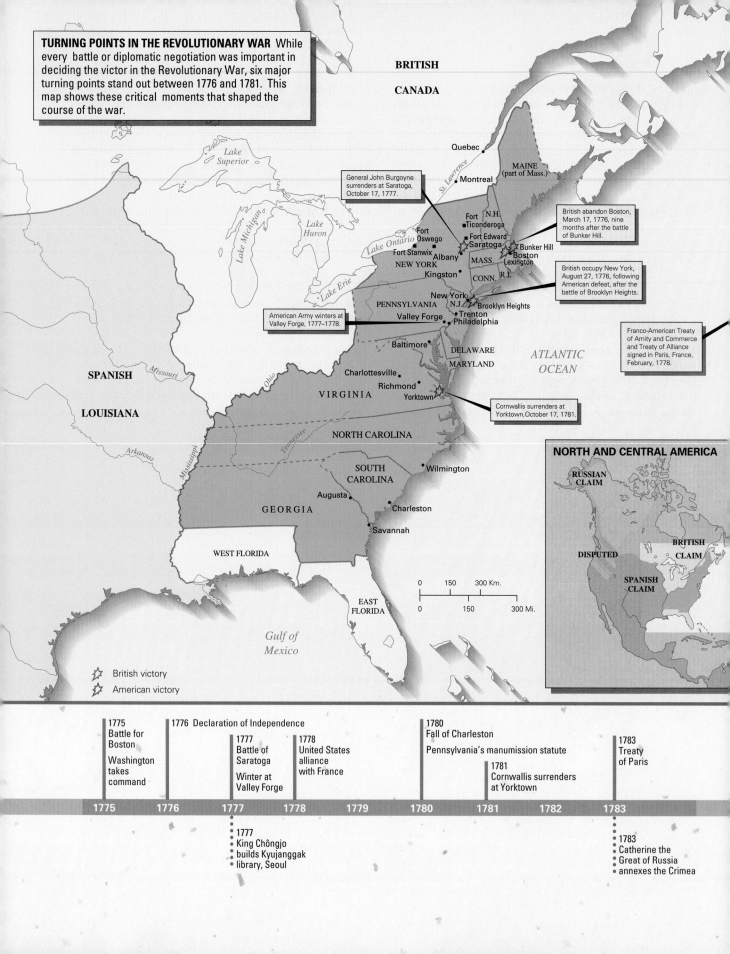

TURNING POINTS IN THE REVOLUTIONARY WAR While every battle or diplomatic negotiation was important in deciding the victor in the Revolutionary War, six major turning points stand out between 1776 and 1781. This map shows these critical moments that shaped the course of the war.

BRITISH

CANADA

Lake Superior

Lake Michigan

Lake Huron

Lake Erie

Lake Ontario

St. Lawrence

Quebec

Montreal

MAINE (part of Mass.)

General John Burgoyne surrenders at Saratoga, October 17, 1777.

Fort Ticonderoga

N.H.

Fort Edward

Fort Oswego

Fort Stanwix

Saratoga

Albany

NEW YORK

Kingston

British abandon Boston, March 17, 1776, nine months after the battle of Bunker Hill.

Bunker Hill

Boston

Lexington

MASS.

CONN.

R.I.

British occupy New York, August 27, 1776, following American defeat, after the battle of Brooklyn Heights.

New York

N.J.

Brooklyn Heights

PENNSYLVANIA

American Army winters at Valley Forge, 1777–1778.

Valley Forge

Trenton

Philadelphia

Baltimore

DELAWARE

MARYLAND

ATLANTIC OCEAN

Franco-American Treaty of Amity and Commerce and Treaty of Alliance signed in Paris, France, February, 1778.

SPANISH

LOUISIANA

Missouri

Ohio

Charlottesville

Richmond

Yorktown

VIRGINIA

Cornwallis surrenders at Yorktown, October 17, 1781.

Arkansas

Mississippi

Tennessee

NORTH CAROLINA

NORTH AND CENTRAL AMERICA

SOUTH CAROLINA

Wilmington

RUSSIAN CLAIM

Augusta

GEORGIA

Charleston

Savannah

DISPUTED

BRITISH CLAIM

SPANISH CLAIM

WEST FLORIDA

EAST FLORIDA

Gulf of Mexico

0   150   300 Km.

0   150   300 Mi.

✩ British victory

✩ American victory

1775
Battle for Boston

Washington takes command

1776 Declaration of Independence

1777
Battle of Saratoga

Winter at Valley Forge

1778
United States alliance with France

1780
Fall of Charleston

Pennsylvania's manumission statute

1781
Cornwallis surrenders at Yorktown

1783
Treaty of Paris

1775   **1776**   **1777**   **1778**   **1779**   **1780**   **1781**   **1782**   **1783**

1777
King Chôngjo builds Kyujanggak library, Seoul

1783
Catherine the Great of Russia annexes the Crimea

Recreating America: Independence and a New Nation, 1775–1783

6

Turning Points in the Revolutionary War
Using the map on the facing page, discuss the major military campaigns of the Revolutionary War. Can you explain why Burgoyne's campaign was located in New York and why Cornwallis's army was in Virginia? What role can you conclude the French played in the American victory?

Individual Choices

DEBORAH SAMPSON

Whether attracted by adventure, the promise of a pension, or the bounty soldiers received upon enlistment, Deborah Sampson decided to disguise herself as a man and enlist in the Continental Army in 1781. She served for over two years before officers discovered she was a woman and discharged her. This portrait, drawn by Joseph Stone Framingham in 1797, depicts Sampson in female dress but surrounds her with the military emblems befitting a veteran of the Revolutionary War. *Rhode Island Historical Society.*

Deborah Sampson

The Great War for Empire was still raging when Deborah Sampson was born in a small village outside Plymouth, Massachusetts, in 1760. Sampson's family tree had deep roots in New England, for her father was a descendant of two of the original Pilgrim settlers and her mother could trace her heritage back to the colony's first governor, William Bradford. Yet Deborah's parents had neither wealth nor status: the Sampsons were only a poor, struggling farm family. When Deborah was a small child, her father abandoned his wife and six children. Deborah's mother was forced to hire out some of her children, including Deborah, as servants in her neighbors' homes.

By the time the Revolutionary War began, Deborah Sampson was a tall, healthy young woman, made physically strong by years of farm work. When her term of service ended in 1779, Sampson had few choices for a next step in life. Without a dowry or an inheritance, she was unlikely to marry; without any special training, she was destined to spend her life as a servant in rural Massachusetts. But Deborah discovered another option—and chose to take it. Disguising herself as a man, she enlisted as a soldier in the Continental Army. Just as the colonies changed themselves into an independent nation, Deborah Sampson changed herself into Private Robert Shurtleff.

As a woman, Sampson might have played a role in the war by serving as a **courier** or a spy. Or she might have joined thousands of other women in the army camps, performing valuable services such as cooking, laundering, or nursing. She might have remained safely at home, knitting socks or making uniforms for the poorly clad soldiers serving under General Washington. But none of these alternatives would have given her what military service offered: the chance to see new places and have new experiences, an enlistment bonus, a pension if she survived, and a promise of land when the war ended. Thousands of poor young men risked the dangers of the battlefield for these rewards. Why not Deborah Sampson?

Perhaps patriotism also prompted her to abandon her petticoats for a uniform. Years later, when her story was published, she insisted that she had joined the army because she believed in liberty and wanted to play a meaningful part in the birth of her nation. But whatever her motives, Deborah Sampson proved herself a fine soldier and a brave one. She also managed to hide her identity for several years, even when she was wounded by a musket ball that lodged in her leg. The truth of her sex was not discovered until she was hospitalized for a fever while stationed in Philadelphia.

When the authorities realized that Private Shurtleff was actually a young woman, they dismissed her from military service at once. On October 25, 1783, eight months after the Treaty of Paris ending the war was signed, Deborah Sampson was granted an honorable discharge—and Robert Shurtleff disappeared forever.

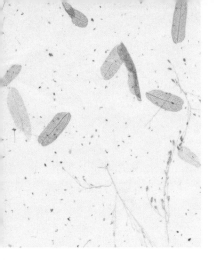

Deborah Sampson returned to Massachusetts in November of 1783. In the spring of the following year, she married a local farmer named Benjamin Gannett and began a family. As a wife and mother, Deborah Sampson Gannett was expected to give up any role in the public sphere. Once again, however, she proved herself a rebel: in 1802 she began to travel throughout New England giving public lectures on her military career. The tales she told the crowds who flocked to hear and see her were undoubtedly full of exaggerated claims of daring battlefield exploits. Yet dressed in her uniform once again, performing a precision drill on stage that would have made Washington's drillmaster Baron von Steuben proud, Deborah Sampson demonstrated the unexpected impact of the Revolution on an ordinary American's life.

INTRODUCTION

The war that so changed Deborah Sampson's life, and the lives of most colonists, began in April 1775 as a skirmish at Concord's North Bridge. In the first months of the war, Great Britain expected an easy victory over the colonial rebels. On paper, at least, the odds against an American victory were staggering. To crush the colonial rebellion, Great Britain was ready and able to commit vast human and material resources. The well-trained and harshly disciplined British ground troops were assisted and supplied by the most powerful navy in the world, and they carried the flag of the richest imperial power of Europe. Many Indian tribes, including most of the Iroquois, allied with the British, and the Crown could expect thousands of white and black loyalists to fight beside them as well.

The American war effort was far less impressive. The Continental Congress had a nearly empty treasury, and the country's resources did not include the foundries or factories needed to produce arms, ammunition, or other military supplies. The army administration was inefficient, the population was wary of professional soldiers, and the new state governments were unwilling to raise tax monies to contribute to the Congress's war chest. Through most of the war, therefore, American officers and enlisted men could expect to be underpaid or not paid at all. They were likely to go into battle poorly equipped, often half-starved, and frequently dressed in rags. Unlike the British redcoats, these Americans had little military skill or formal military training. Most were as new to military life as Deborah Sampson.

Britain's advantage thus seemed great, but it was not absolute. To fight the war, the British had to transport arms, provisions, and men across thousands of miles of ocean. They risked delays, disasters, and destruction of supplies on the open seas. The Americans, on the other hand, were fighting on familiar terrain, and geography gave them an additional advantage: their vast, rural society could not be easily conquered even if major colonial cities were taken or an entire region were occupied. Long-standing European rivalries also worked to the advantage of the Americans and gave them valuable allies. Holland, France, and Spain all stood to gain from England's distress and were therefore willing to lend money and provide much-needed supplies to the rebellion. And in 1778, when France and Spain decided to recognize American independence formally, the war suddenly expanded into a global struggle. The support of the French navy transformed General Washington's military strategy and led eventually to the defeat of the British army at Yorktown. Even the most patriotic American had to concede that international politics, as much as military heroism or popular commitment to the Revolution, had won the colonies their independence.

No matter what eighteenth-century Americans felt about the war, no matter which side they supported or what role they played, they shared the experience of extraordinary events and the need to make extraordinary choices when the war disrupted the flow of their ordinary lives. In this most personal and immediate sense, the war was as revolutionary for them as it was for a young woman who became, for a brief but critical moment, a soldier in the name of liberty.

courier A messenger carrying official information, sometimes secretly.

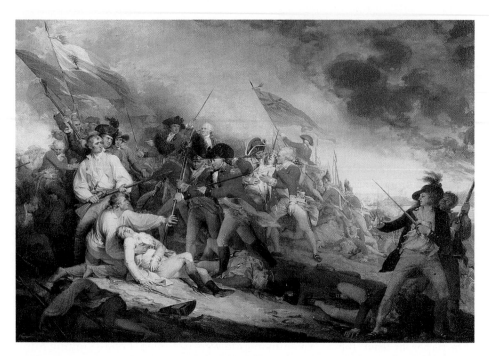

American artist John Trumbull painted *The Battle of Bunker Hill* in 1786, over a decade after the bloody encounter between redcoats and American militiamen. Trumbull was a student of the famous American painter Benjamin West, who had won his reputation celebrating the English victories of the French and Indian War. Trumbull and other American students of West built their reputations by celebrating American victories in the artistic style that West taught them. *"The Death of General Warren at Bunker Hill" by John Trumbull, Yale University Art Gallery. Trumbull Collection.*

The First Two Years of War

■ What were the British and American strategies in the early years of the war?

■ What decisions and constraints kept the British from achieving the quick victory many expected?

In 1775 **Thomas Gage,** the British general serving as military governor of Massachusetts and commander of the British army of occupation there, surely wished he were anywhere but Boston. The town was unsophisticated by British standards, many of its inhabitants were unfriendly, and its taverns and lodging houses bulged at the seams with complaining loyalist refugees from the countryside. Gage's army was restless, and his officers were bored. The American encampments outside the city were growing daily, filling with local farmers and artisans after the bloodshed of Lexington and Concord. These thousands of colonial **militiamen** gathering on the hills surrounding Boston were clearly the military enemy. Yet in 1775 they were still citizens of the British Empire, not foreign invaders

or foes. Gage, like his American opponents, was caught up in the dilemmas of an undeclared war.

The Battle for Boston

With proper artillery, well placed on the hills surrounding the city, the Americans could have done serious damage to Gage's army of occupation. The problem was that the rebels had no cannon. A New Haven druggist named **Benedict Arnold** joined forces

> **Thomas Gage**   British general who was military governor of Massachusetts and commander of the army occupying Boston in 1775.
>
> **militiamen**   Soldiers who were not members of a regular army but ordinary citizens called out in case of an emergency.
>
> **Benedict Arnold**   Pharmacist-turned-military-leader whose bravery and daring made him an American hero and a favorite of George Washington until he committed treason in 1780.

Chronology

Rebellion and Independence

1775	Battle for Boston George Washington assumes command of Continental Army
1776	Declaration of Independence British campaigns in South and mid-Atlantic region George Mason's Declaration of Rights
1777	Burgoyne's New York campaign Battle of Saratoga Winter at Valley Forge
1778	American-French alliance
1778	British begin second southern campaign
1780	Fall of Charleston Treason of Benedict Arnold Pennsylvania enacts manumission statute
1781	Cornwallis surrenders at Yorktown Loyalists evacuate United States Articles of Confederation government established
1782	British Parliament votes to end war
1783	Treaty of Paris signed

with a Vermont farmer named Ethan Allen to solve the problem. In May 1775 their troops captured Fort Ticonderoga in New York and began the difficult task of transporting the fort's cannon across hundreds of miles of mountains and forests to Boston. By the time the artillery reached the city, however, a bloody battle between Gage and the American militia had already taken place.

In early June, Gage had issued a proclamation declaring all armed colonists traitors, but he offered **amnesty** to any rebel who surrendered to British authorities. When the militiamen ignored the general's offer, Gage decided a show of force was necessary. On June 17, 1775, under cover of cannon fire from a British warship in Boston harbor, Gage's fellow officer **William Howe** led a force of twenty-four hundred soldiers against rebel-held Breed's Hill. Despite the oppressive heat and humidity of the day, General Howe ordered his men to advance in full dress uniform, weighed down with wool jackets and heavy knapsacks. Howe also insisted on making a "proper" frontal attack on the Americans. From the top of the hill, Captain William Prescott's militiamen immediately opened fire on the unprotected redcoats. The result was a near massacre. The tables turned, however, when the Americans ran out of ammunition. Most of Prescott's men fled in confusion, and the British soldiers bayoneted the few who remained to defend their position.

Even battle-worn veterans were shocked at the carnage of the day. The British suffered more casualties that June afternoon than they would in any other battle of the war. The Americans, who retreated to the safety of Cambridge, learned a costly lesson on the importance of an effective supply line of arms and ammunition to their fighting men. Little was gained by either side. That the battle was misnamed the **Battle of Bunker Hill** captured perfectly the confusion and the absurdity of the encounter.

Congress Creates an Army

While militiamen and redcoats turned the Boston area into a war zone, the Continental Congress took its first steps toward recruiting and supplying an army. The "regular" army that took shape was not really a national force. It was a collection of small state armies whose recruits preserved their local or regional identities. While this army was expected to follow the war wherever it led, the Continental Congress still relied on each state's militia to join in any battles that took place within its borders.

amnesty A general pardon granted by a government, especially for political offenses.

William Howe British general in command at the Battle of Bunker Hill; three years later he became commander in chief of British forces in America.

Battle of Bunker Hill British assault on American troops on Breed's Hill near Boston in June 1775; the British won the battle but suffered heavy losses.

Congress chose French and Indian War veteran **George Washington** to command the Continental forces. Washington wrote gloomily of the enormity of the task before him. Nothing he saw when he reached Massachusetts on July 3, 1775, made him more optimistic. A carnival atmosphere seemed to prevail inside the militiamen's camps. Farm-boys-turned-soldiers fired their muskets at random, often using their weapons to start fires or to shoot at geese flying overhead. In the confusion, they sometimes accidentally wounded or killed themselves and others. "Seldom a day passes but some persons are shot by their friends," Washington noted in amazement.

The camps resembled pigsties. The stench from open latrines was terrible, and rotting animal carcasses, strewn everywhere, added to the aroma. The men were dirty and infected with lice, and most soldiers were constantly scratching, trying to relieve an itch that left them covered with scabs and raw, peeling skin. General Washington was disturbed but not surprised by what he saw. He knew that the men in these camps were country boys, away from home for the first time in their lives. The chaos they created resulted from a combination of fear, excitement, boredom, inexperience, and plain homesickness, all brewing freely under poor leadership. Despite his sympathy for these young men, Washington acted quickly to reorganize the militia units, replace incompetent officers, and tighten discipline within the camps.

The British meanwhile laid plans for the evacuation of Boston, spurred in part by the knowledge that Arnold's wagon train of cannon was nearing Massachusetts. In March 1776 a fleet arrived to carry Thomas Gage, his officers, the British army, and almost a thousand loyalist refugees north to the safety of Halifax, Nova Scotia. By this time, command of His Majesty's war was in the hands of the Howe brothers—General William Howe, commander of the Breed's Hill attack, and **Richard Howe,** an admiral in the royal navy. With the help of military strategists and the vast resources of the Crown, the Howes were expected to bring the rebellion to a speedy end and restore order to the colonies.

The British Strategy in 1776

General Howe was less concerned with suppressing the radicalism of New England than the king had been. He thought the most effective strategy would be to locate areas with high concentrations of loyalists and mobilize them to secure the allegiance of their undecided and even rebellious neighbors. Howe and his advisers targeted two reputed centers of loyalist strength. The first—New York, New Jersey, Pennsylvania—had a legacy of social and economic conflicts, such as the revolt of the Paxton Boys, that had caused many of the region's elite families to fear that independence threatened their prosperity. But loyalism was not confined to the conservative and wealthy. Its second stronghold was among the poor settlers of the Carolina backcountry. There, decades of bitter struggle between the coastal planters and the backcountry farmers had led to the Regulator movement (see page 101) and to intense loyalist sentiment among many of the embattled westerners.

General Howe's strategy had its flaws, however. First, although many people in these two regions were loyal, their numbers were never as great as the British assumed. Second, everywhere they went, British and **Hessian troops** left behind a trail of destruction and memories of abuse that alienated many Americans who might have considered remaining loyal. Howe was not likely to win over families who saw their "cattle killed and lying about the fields and pastures . . . household furniture hacked and broken into pieces . . . wells filled up and . . . tools destroyed."

Nevertheless, in 1776 Howe launched his first major military assaults in the South and the mid-Atlantic region. The campaign in the South, directed by General Henry Clinton, went badly. In North Carolina, loyalists did turn out to fight for the Crown, but the British failed to provide them the military support they needed. Poorly armed and badly outnumbered, Carolina loyalists were decisively defeated by the rebel militia on February 27 in the Battle of Moore's Creek. Rather than rush to their defense, the British abandoned their loyalist allies in favor of taking revenge on South Carolina. Clinton and an impressive fleet of fifty ships and three thousand men sailed into Charleston harbor. But the British had unexpected bad luck. As the troops started to wade ashore, they found themselves stranded on small islands surrounded by a sudden rush of tidal waters. The Americans, on the

George Washington   Commander in chief of the Continental Army; he led Americans to victory in the Revolution and later became the first president of the United States.

Richard Howe   British admiral who commanded British naval forces in America; he was General William Howe's brother.

Hessian troops   German soldiers from the state of Hesse who were hired by Britain to fight in the American Revolution.

other hand, had unexpected good luck. Working frantically to defend the harbor, they constructed a flimsy fort out of local palmetto wood. To the surprise of both sides, the cannon balls fired by British ships sank harmlessly into the absorbent, pulpy palmetto stockade. The fort—and the city of Charleston—remained standing.

Embarrassed and frustrated, the British command abruptly ended its southern campaign. General Clinton, a gloomy man under the best of circumstances, sailed north, eager to escape the scene of his humiliation. The South Carolina loyalists, however, could not escape British failures. They had been denounced, mobbed, imprisoned, and sometimes tortured since 1775. Their situation grew even worse after the British withdrew.

Escape from New York

While Clinton was failing in the Carolinas, the Howe brothers were preparing a massive invasion of the mid-Atlantic region. In July 1776, Admiral Howe and General Howe sailed into New York harbor with the largest expeditionary force of the eighteenth century. With thirty thousand men, one-third of them Hessian mercenaries, this British army was larger than the peacetime population of New York City.

The Howes were not eager to demolish New York, however. Unlike most British officers, the brothers were genuinely fond of Americans, and they preferred to be agents of compromise and negotiation rather than of destruction. They hoped that a spectacular show of force and a thorough humiliation of rebel commander George Washington would be enough to bring the Americans to their senses and end the rebellion.

General Washington rushed his army south from Massachusetts to defend the city, but he had few illusions that his twenty-three thousand men, many of them sick and most of them inexperienced at war, could repel the invading British forces. In the middle of his defense preparations, Washington received a copy of the newly approved Declaration of Independence. He immediately ordered his brigades to line up on the parade grounds so that he could read Thomas Jefferson's stirring words aloud to them. He was gratified to hear the men cheer the Declaration. But privately, Washington wondered if these men would fight when they faced the enemy in battle.

For a month, the Howes made no move on the city. Finally, in the early morning of August 22, 1776, the British began their advance, landing unopposed, and moving toward the Brooklyn neck of Long Island (see Map 6.1). Just as Washington had feared, his raw and inexperienced troops quickly broke when fighting be-

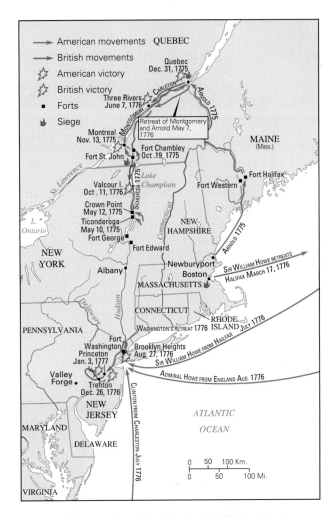

MAP 6.1 The War of the North, 1775–1777   The American attempt to capture Canada and General George Washington's effort to save New York from British occupation were failures, but Washington did manage to stage successful raids in New Jersey before retreating to safety in the winter of 1777. This map details the movements of both British and American troops during the Northern Campaign, and it indicates the victories and defeats for both armies.

gan five days later. Cut off from one another, confused by the sound and sight of the attack, almost all the American troops surrendered or ran. A single Maryland regiment made a heroic stand against the landing forces but was destroyed by the oncoming British. Washington, at the scene himself, might have been captured had the Howes pressed their advantage. But they withdrew, content that they had made the American commander look foolish.

Washington took advantage of the Howes' delay to bring his troops to the safety of Manhattan Island. The safety proved temporary, for on September 15, a British attack again sent his farm-boys-turned-soldiers into flight. Angry and frustrated, Washington threw his hat to the ground and shouted, "Are these the men with whom I am to defend America!"

Washington's army fled north, with the British in hot pursuit. In a skirmish at Harlem Heights, the American commander was relieved to see his men stand their ground and win their first combat victory. He was even more relieved by the strange failure of the British to press their advantage. The British had only to follow his army into Westchester County and deliver a crushing blow, but they did not. When the redcoats finally engaged the Continentals again at White Plains, the Americans managed to retreat safely. Soon afterward, Washington took his army across the Hudson River to New Jersey and marched them farther west, across the Delaware River into Pennsylvania.

Winter Quarters and Winter Victories

Following European customs, General Howe established winter quarters for his troops before the cold set in. Redcoats and Hessians made their camps in the New York area and in Rhode Island that December, expecting Washington to make camp somewhere as well. But Washington, safe for the moment in

Most American school children are familiar with paintings of General George Washington and his Continental Army crossing the ice-covered Delaware River on December 25, 1776, in order to mount a daring surprise attack on enemy troops at Trenton, New Jersey. This painting, done in 1851 by Emanuel Leutze, recreates an event that took place 75 years earlier—and forty years before the artist was born. What role does art play in creating national myths? *The Metropolitan Museum of Art, Gift of John S. Kennedy, 1987. Photograph © The Metropolitan Museum of Art.*

Pennsylvania, was too restless to settle in just yet. Enlistment terms in his army would soon be up, and without some encouraging military success he feared few of his soldiers would reenlist. Thus Washington looked eagerly for a good target to attack—and found one. Across the Delaware, on the Jersey side, two or three thousand Hessian troops held a garrison near the town of Trenton.

On Christmas night, amid a howling storm, General Washington led twenty-four hundred of his men back across the river. Marching 9 miles through a raging blizzard, the Americans arrived to find the Hessians asleep. The surprised enemy surrendered immediately. Without losing a single man, Washington had captured nine hundred prisoners and many badly needed military supplies. Taking full advantage of the moment, Washington made a rousing appeal to his men to reenlist. About half of the soldiers agreed to remain.

The **Battle of Trenton** was a crucial victory, but Washington enjoyed his next success even more. In early January he again crossed into New Jersey from the safety of Pennsylvania and made his way toward the British garrison at Princeton. On the way, his advance guard ran into two British regiments. As both sides lined up for battle, Washington rode back and forth in front of his men, shouting encouragement and urging them to stand firm. His behavior was reckless, for it put him squarely in the line of fire, but it was also effective. When the British turned in retreat, Washington rashly rode after them, clearly delighted to be in pursuit for once in the war.

The Trenton and Princeton victories raised the morale of the Continental Army as it settled at last into its winter quarters near Morristown, New Jersey. They stirred popular support also. Americans everywhere referred to the two winter raids as a "nine-day wonder." Of course, Howe's army was still poised to march on Philadelphia when warm weather revived the war again. And Congress still had few resources to spare for Washington and his men. When Washington pleaded for supplies, Congress urged him to commandeer what he needed from civilians nearby. The general wisely refused. English high-handedness and cruelty had turned many people of the area into staunch supporters of the Revolution, and Washington had no intention of alienating them by seizing their livestock, food, or weapons.

Burgoyne's New York Campaign

In July 1777 General William Howe sailed with fifteen thousand men up the Chesapeake Bay toward Philadelphia. The Continental Congress had already fled the city, knowing that Washington could not prevent the enemy occupation. Although the Americans made two efforts to block Howe, first at Brandywine Creek and then at Germantown, the British had little problem capturing Philadelphia. The problems they did face in 1777 came not from Washington but from the poor judgment of one of their own, a flamboyant young general named **John Burgoyne.**

Burgoyne had won approval for an elaborate plan to sever New England from the rest of the American colonies. He would move his army south from Montreal, while a second army of redcoats and Iroquois, commanded by Colonel Barry St. Leger, would veer east across the Mohawk Valley from Fort Oswego. At the same time, William Howe would send a third force north from New York City. The three armies would rendezvous at Albany, effectively isolating New England and, it was assumed, giving the British a perfect opportunity to crush the rebellion.

The plan was daring and—on paper—seemed to have every chance of success. In reality, however, it had serious flaws. First, neither Burgoyne nor the British officials in England had any knowledge of the American terrain that had to be covered. Second, they badly misjudged the Indian support St. Leger would receive. Third, General Howe, no longer in New York City, knew absolutely nothing of his own critical role in the plan. Blissfully unaware of these problems, Burgoyne led his army from Montreal in high spirits in June 1777 (see Map 6.2). The troops floated down Lake Champlain in canoes and flatbottom boats and easily retook Fort Ticonderoga. From Ticonderoga, the invading army continued to march toward Albany. From this point on, however, things began to go badly for Burgoyne.

In true eighteenth-century British style, "Gentleman Johnny" Burgoyne chose to travel well rather than lightly. The thirty wagons moving slowly behind the general contained over fifty pieces of artillery for the campaign. They also contained Burgoyne's mistress, her personal wardrobe and his, and a generous supply of champagne. When the caravan encountered New York's swamps and gullies, movement

Battle of Trenton Battle on December 26, 1776, when Washington led his troops by night across the Delaware River and captured a Hessian garrison wintering in New Jersey.

John Burgoyne British general forced to surrender his entire army at Saratoga, New York, in October 1777.

In July 1777 Jane McCrea was on her way to join her loyalist fiancé, marching with General Burgoyne's army, when she was brutally murdered. The American general, Horatio Gates, accused Iroquois Indian allies of the British army of the murder. The news of McCrea's violent death added to the American army's determination to stop Burgoyne's invasion into upstate New York. This early nineteenth-century painting depicts McCrea sympathetically as a helpless, innocent victim of savagery. The fact that she was not a patriot but a supporter of King George did not seem to diminish the artist's vision of her as a martyr. Does this suggest that McCrea's politics were less important than her race and gender? *Wadsworth Atheneum.*

slowed to a snail's pace. The Americans took full advantage of Burgoyne's folly. Ethan Allen and his Green Mountain Boys harassed the British as they entered Allen's home region of Vermont. A bloody, head-on battle near Bennington further slowed Burgoyne's progress. When the general's army finally reached Albany in mid-September, neither St. Leger nor Howe were in sight.

The full support St. Leger had counted on from the Iroquois had not materialized, and he met fierce resistance as he made his way to the rendezvous point. When news reached him that Benedict Arnold and an army of a thousand Americans were approaching, St. Leger simply turned around and took his exhausted men to safety at Fort Niagara. Howe, of course, had no idea that he was expected in Albany. This left John Burgoyne stranded in the heart of New York. By mid-September 1777, his supplies dwindling, he realized his only option was to break northward through the American lines and take refuge in Canada—or surrender. On September 19, Burgoyne attacked, hoping to clear a path of retreat for his army. The elderly American general, **Horatio "Granny" Gates,** was nei-

ther bold nor particularly clever, but it took little daring or genius to defeat Burgoyne's weary, dispirited British soldiers. When Burgoyne tried once again to break through on October 7, Gates and his men held their ground. On October 17, 1777, General John Burgoyne surrendered.

News that a major British army had been defeated spread quickly on both sides of the Atlantic. It was a powerful boost to American confidence and an equally powerful blow to British self-esteem. The report also reversed the fortunes of American diplomatic efforts. Until Saratoga, American appeals to the governments of Spain, France, and Holland for supplies, loans, and military support had met with only moderate success. Now, hopes ran high that France would recognize independence and join the war effort.

Horatio "Granny" Gates   Elderly Virginia general who led the American troops to victory in the Battle of Saratoga.

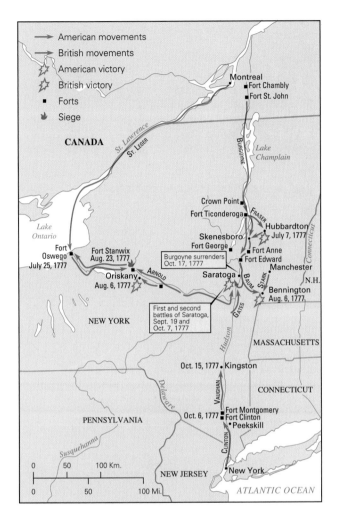

MAP 6.2 The Burgoyne Campaign, 1777 The defeat of General John Burgoyne and his army at Saratoga was a major turning point in the war. It led to the recognition of American independence by France and later by Spain and to a military alliance with both these European powers. This map shows American and British troop movement and the locations and dates of the Saratoga battles leading to the British surrender.

Winter Quarters in 1777

John Adams, who never wore a uniform, had once toasted a "short and Violent war." After Burgoyne's defeat, many Americans believed that Adams's wish was coming true. General Washington, however, did not share their optimism. French help might be coming, he pointed out, but who knew when? In the meantime, he reminded Congress the Continental Army

still needed funds and supplies. Congress ignored all his urgent requests. The result was the long and dreadful winter at Valley Forge. **Valley Forge** was 20 miles from Philadelphia, where General Howe and his army were comfortably housed for the winter. Throughout December 1777, Washington's men labored to build the huts and cabins they needed. While two officers were assigned to share quarters, a dozen enlisted men were expected to crowd into a 14-by-16-foot hut. Rations were a problem from the start. Technically, each man was entitled to raw or cured meat, yet most soldiers at Valley Forge lived entirely on a diet of fire cakes, made of flour and water baked in the coals or over the fire on a stick. Blankets were scarce, coats were rare, and firewood was precious. An army doctor summed up conditions when he wrote: "Poor food—hard lodgings—cold weather—fatigue—nasty clothes—nasty cookery—vomit half my time—smoked out of my senses—the devil's in it—I can't endure it."

The doctor, however, did endure it. So did the soldiers he tended to daily, men such as the barefoot, half-naked, dirty young man who cried out in despair, "I am sick, my feet lame, my legs are sore, my body covered with this tormenting itch." While civilians mastered the steps of the latest dance craze, "the Burgoyne surrender," soldiers at Valley Forge traded the remains of their uniforms and sometimes their muskets for the momentary warmth and sense of well-being provided by liquor.

The enlisted men who survived the winter at Valley Forge were strangers to luxury even in peacetime. Like Deborah Sampson, most were from the humblest social classes: farm laborers, servants, apprentices, even former slaves. They were exactly the sort of person most Americans believed ought to fight the war. But if poverty had driven them into the army, a commitment to see the war through kept them there. The contrast between their own patriotism and the apparent indifference of the civilian population made many of these soldiers bitter. Private Joseph Plumb Martin expressed the feelings of most when he said "a kind and holy Providence" had done more to help the army while it was at Valley Forge "than did the

> **Valley Forge** Winter encampment of Washington's army in Pennsylvania in 1777–1778; because the soldiers suffered greatly from cold and hunger, the term *Valley Forge* has become synonymous with "dire conditions."

Throughout the war, both the British and the American armies settled into winter quarters until they resumed military operations in the spring. While the British usually enjoyed the comforts of urban life, in Philadelphia, Charleston, or New York, the American army made its camps in the countryside. Here, soldiers endured the snow and freezing winds in makeshift shacks or in tents, although officers often commandeered the homes of local civilians. The winter at Valley Forge was among the most brutal endured by the Continental troops, and it has come to signify the determination of the common soldiers and their commitment to the cause of independence. *Stock Montage.*

country in whose service we were wearing away our lives by piecemeal."

What these soldiers desperately needed, in addition to new clothes, good food, and hot baths, was professional military training. And that is the one thing they did get, beginning in the spring of 1778, when an unlikely Prussian volunteer arrived at Valley Forge. **Baron Friedrich von Steuben** was almost 50 years old, dignified, elegantly dressed, with a dazzling gold and diamond medal always displayed on his chest. Like most foreign volunteers, many of whom plagued Washington more than they helped him, the baron claimed to be an aristocrat, to have vast military experience, and to have held high rank in a European army. In truth, he had purchased his title only a short time before fleeing his homeland in bankruptcy and he had only been a captain in the Prussian army. A penniless refugee, von Steuben hoped to receive a military pension for his service in the American army. He had not, however, exaggerated his talent as a military drillmaster. All spring, the baron could be seen drilling Washington's troops, alternately shouting in rage and applauding with delight. Washington had little patience with most of the foreign volunteers who joined the American cause, but he considered von Steuben a most unexpected and invaluable surprise.

In the spring of 1778, Washington received the heartening news that France had formally recognized the independence of the United States. He immediately declared a day of thanks, ordering cannon to be fired in honor of the new alliance. That day, the officers feasted with their commander, and Washington issued brandy to each enlisted man at Valley Forge. American diplomacy had triumphed; Washington hoped the combined forces of France and America would soon bring victory as well.

Baron Friedrich von Steuben   Prussian military officer who served as Washington's drillmaster at Valley Forge.

Diplomacy Abroad and Profiteering at Home

- Why did the French assist the Americans secretly in the early years of the war?
- Why did France enter the war after Saratoga?
- Besides the French, what other European power supported the American colonists' struggle against the British?
- How did the French alliance affect the war effort and wartime spending?

Like most wars, the Revolutionary War was not confined to the battlefields. Diplomacy was essential, and popular morale and support had to be sustained for any war to be won. American diplomats hoped to secure supplies, safe harbors for American ships, and if at all possible, formal recognition of independence and the open military assistance that would allow. British diplomats, on the other hand, worked to prevent any formal alliances between European powers and the American rebels. Both sides issued propaganda to ensure continued popular support for the war. General Burgoyne's defeat, and the widening of the war into an international struggle, affected popular morale in both America and Britain.

The Long Road to Formal Recognition

In 1776 England had many enemies and rivals in Europe who were only too happy to see George III expend his resources and military personnel in an effort to quell a colonial rebellion. Although these nations expected the American Revolution to fail, they were more than eager to keep the conflict going as long as possible. Before Saratoga, they preferred to keep their support for the Revolution unofficial. Thus, with the help of King Louis XVI's chief minister, the comte de Vergennes, an American entrepreneur named Arthur Lee set up a private commercial firm, supposedly for trading with France. In reality, the firm siphoned weapons and funds from France to the revolutionaries. France also agreed to open ports to American privateers and to provide French ships and seamen for raids on British commercial shipping.

The Americans hoped for more, however. In December 1776, Congress sent the printer-politician-scientist **Benjamin Franklin** to Paris in hopes of winning formal recognition of American independence. The charming and witty Franklin was the toast of Paris, adored by aristocrats and common people

alike, but even he could not persuade the king to support the Revolution openly. Burgoyne's surrender changed everything. After Saratoga, the British government began scrambling to end a war that had turned embarrassing, and the French government began scrambling to reassess its diplomatic position. Vergennes suspected that the English would quickly send a peace commission to America after Burgoyne's defeat. If the American Congress agreed to a compromise ending the rebellion, France could gain nothing more. But if the French kept the war alive by giving Americans reason to hope for total victory, perhaps they could recoup some of the territory and prestige lost to England in the Seven Years' War. This meant, of course, recognizing the United States and entering a war with Britain. Vergennes knew a choice had to be made—but he was not yet certain what to do.

Meanwhile, the English government was indeed preparing a new peace offer for Congress. At the heart of the British offer were two promises that George III considered to be great concessions. First, Parliament would renounce all intentions of ever taxing the colonies again. Second, the Intolerable Acts, the Tea Act, and any other objectionable legislation passed since 1763 would be repealed. Many members of Parliament thought these overtures were long overdue. They had been vocal critics of their government's policies in the 1760s and 1770s and had refused to support the war. After Burgoyne's defeat, popular support for compromise also increased in England. The Americans, however, were unimpressed by the offers. For Congress, a return to colonial status was now unthinkable.

Benjamin Franklin knew that Congress would reject the king's offer. But he was too shrewd to relieve the comte de Vergennes's fear that a compromise was in the works. Franklin warned that France must act quickly and decisively or accept the consequences. His gamble worked, and in 1778 France and the United States signed a treaty. The pact linked French and American fates tightly together, for under its provisions neither country could make a separate peace with Great Britain. By 1779, Spain had also formally acknowledged the United States, and in 1780 the Netherlands did so too. George III had little choice but to declare war against these European nations.

> **Benjamin Franklin** American writer, inventor, scientist, and diplomat instrumental in bringing about a French alliance with the United States in 1778 and who later helped negotiate the treaty ending the war.

The Revolution had grown into an international struggle that taxed British resources further and made it impossible for Britain to concentrate all its military might and naval power in America. With ships diverted to the Caribbean and to the European coast, Britain could no longer blockade American ports as effectively as before or transport troops to the American mainland as quickly. Above all, the entry of the French into the war opened new strategic possibilities for General Washington and his army. If the Americans could count on the cooperation of the French fleet, a British army could be trapped on American soil, cut off by French ships from supplies, reinforcements, and any chance of escape.

War and the American Public

News of the alliance with France helped release an orgy of spending and purchasing by American civilians. The conditions were ripe for such a spree in 1778. With the value of government-issued paper money dropping steadily, spending made more sense than saving. And with profits soaring from the sale of supplies to the army, many Americans had more money to spend than ever before. Also, not all of the credit that diplomats had negotiated with European allies went toward military supplies. Some of it was available for the purchase of manufactured goods. This combination of optimism, **cheap money,** and plentiful foreign goods led to a wartime spending bonanza.

Many of the goods that were imported into America in the next few years were actually British-made. American consumers apparently saw no contradiction between their strong patriotism and the purchase of enemy products. A **black market**—a network for the sale of illegally imported English goods—grew rapidly, and profits from it skyrocketed. Abandoning the commitment to "virtuous simplicity" that had led them to dress in homespun, Americans stampeded to purchase tea and other imported luxuries.

Both the government and the military succumbed to this spirit of self-indulgence. Corruption and **graft** grew common, as both high- and low-ranking officials sold government supplies for their own profit or charged the army excessive rates for goods and services. Cheating the government and the army was a game civilians could play, too. Wagoners carting pickled meat to military encampments drained the brine from the barrels to lighten their load so they could carry more. The results were spoiled meat, soldiers suffering from food poisoning—and a greater profit for the cartmen. Soldiers became accustomed to defective

The state governments, like the Continental Congress, resorted to printing paper money in order to finance the war effort. These certificates were used to pay soldiers and civilians who supplied the army with food, horses, or lodgings. Unfortunately, there was little in many of the state treasuries to back these paper certificates, and this, combined with inflation, soon made some paper money worthless. The Continental Congress's paper money declined in value faster than most. "Not worth a continental" became popular slang for anything that was worthless. *Picture Research Consultants & Archives.*

weapons, defective shoes, and defective ammunition, but many of them joined the profit game by selling off their army-issued supplies to any available buyers. Recruiters pocketed the bounties given to them to attract enlistees. Officers accepted bribes from enlisted men seeking discharges.

Popular optimism and the spending frenzy unleashed by the French treaty contrasted sharply with the financial realities facing Congress. Bluntly put, the government was broke. By 1778, both Congress and the states had exhausted their meager sources

cheap money Paper money that is readily available but has declined in value.

black market The illegal business of buying and selling goods that are banned or restricted.

graft Misuse of one's position for profit or advantage.

of hard currency. The government met the crisis by printing more paper money. The result was rampant inflation. The value of the "continental," as the congressional paper money was called, dropped steadily with each passing day. The government's inability to pay soldiers became widely known—and enlistments plummeted. Both the state militias and the Continental Army resorted to impressment, or forced military service, to fill their ranks. Men forced to serve, however, were men more likely to mutiny or to desert. Officers did not know whether to sympathize with their unpaid and involuntary soldiers or to enforce stricter discipline upon them. Some officers executed deserters or mutineers; some ordered the men whipped. And some pardoned their men, despite the severity of their crimes. Congress acknowledged the justice of the soldiers' complaints by giving them pay raises in the form of certificates that they could redeem—after the war.

From Stalemate to Victory

■ What did France hope to achieve by coming to the aid of the struggling American army?

■ What led to General Cornwallis's surrender at Yorktown?

■ What were the most important results of the peace treaty negotiations?

The French presence in the war did not immediately alter the strategies of British or American military leaders. English generals in the North displayed caution after Burgoyne's surrender, and Washington waited impatiently for signs that the French fleet would come to his aid. The result was a stalemate. The active war shifted to the South once again in late 1778 as the British mounted a second major campaign in the Carolinas.

The War Stalls in the North

Sir Henry Clinton, now the commander of the British army in North America, knew that the French fleet could easily blockade the Delaware River and thus cut off supplies to occupied Philadelphia. So, by the time warm weather had set in, his army was on the march, heading east through New Jersey en route to New York. Clinton's slow-moving caravan, burdened by a long train of bulky supply wagons, made an irresistible target—and Washington decided to strike.

Unfortunately, Washington entrusted the unreliable **General Charles Lee** with the initial attack. Lee marched his men to Monmouth, New Jersey, and as

the British approached, the Americans opened fire. Yet as soon as the British army began to return fire, Lee ordered his men to retreat. When Washington arrived on the scene, the Americans were fleeing and the British troops were closing in.

Washington rallied the retreating Americans, calling on them to re-form their lines and stand their ground. Trained by von Steuben, the men responded well. They moved forward with precision and speed, driving the redcoats back. The **Battle of Monmouth** was not the decisive victory Washington had dreamed of, but it was a fine recovery from what first appeared to be certain defeat. As for Lee, Washington saw to it that he was discharged from the army.

Monmouth was only the first of several missed opportunities that summer of 1778. In August the French and Americans launched their first joint effort, sending a combined land and naval attack against the British base at Newport, Rhode Island. At the last minute, however, French admiral D'Estaing decided that the casualty rate would be too high. He abruptly gathered up his own men and sailed to safety on the open seas. The American troops were left to retreat as best they could.

Throughout the fall and winter of 1778 Washington waited in vain for French naval support for a major campaign. Early news coming from the western front did little to improve Washington's bleak mood. In Kentucky and western Virginia, deadly Indian attacks had decimated many American settlements. The driving force behind these attacks was a remarkable British official named Harry Hamilton, who had won the nickname "Hair Buyer" because of the bounties he paid for American scalps. In October Hamilton led Indian troops from the Great Lakes tribes into the Illinois-Indiana region and captured the fort at Vincennes. The American counterattack was organized by a stocky young frontiersman, **George Rogers Clark,** whose own enthusiasm for scalping earned him the

Sir Henry Clinton General who replaced William Howe as commander of the British forces in America in 1778 after the British surrender at Saratoga.

Charles Lee Revolutionary general who tried to undermine Washington's authority on several occasions; he was eventually dismissed from the military.

Battle of Monmouth New Jersey battle in June 1778 in which Charles Lee wasted a decisive American advantage.

George Rogers Clark Virginian who led his troops to successes against the British and Indians in the Ohio Territory in 1778.

Mohawk chief Thayendanegea (Joseph Brant) believed that Iroquois lands would be lost if the Americans were victorious. He urged an Iroquois alliance with the British, fought for the British, and directed a series of deadly raids against settlements in New York. After the war—as Brant had feared—his people were forced to relocate to Canada. *"Joseph Brant" by Wilhelm von Moll Berczy, ca. 1800. National Gallery of Canada, Ottawa.*

nickname "Long-Knife." To Washington's relief, Clark and his volunteer forces managed to drive the British from Vincennes.

Border conflict with Britain's Indian allies remained a major problem, and when loyalist troops joined these Indians, the danger increased. So did the atrocities. When patriot General John Sullivan's regular army was badly defeated by Mohawk chief **Thayendanegea,** known to the Americans as Joseph Brant, and local loyalists, Sullivan took revenge by burning forty Indian villages. It was an act of violence and cruelty that deeply shocked and shamed General Washington.

Spring and summer of 1779 passed and still Washington waited for the French navy's cooperation. Fall brought the general the worst possible news: Admiral D'Estaing and his fleet had sailed for the West Indies under orders to protect valuable French possessions in the Caribbean and, if possible, to seize English possessions there. News of D'Estaing's departure spurred a new wave of discipline problems among Washington's idle troops. Mutinies and desertions increased. From his winter headquarters in Morristown Heights,

New Jersey, Washington wrote to von Steuben: "The prospect, my dear Baron, is gloomy, and the storm thickens." The real storm, however, was raging not in New Jersey but in the Carolinas.

The Second Carolinas Campaign

Since the fall of 1778, the British had been siphoning off New York–based troops for a new invasion of the South. The campaign began in earnest with the capture of Savannah, Georgia (see Map 6.3). Then, in the winter of 1779, General Henry Clinton sailed for Charleston, South Carolina, eager to avenge his embarrassing retreat in the 1776 campaign. Five thousand Continental soldiers hurried to join the South Carolina militia in defense of the city. From the Citadel, a fortification spanning the northern neck of the city's peninsula, these American forces bombarded the British with all they could find, firing projectiles made of glass, broken shovels, hatchets, and pickaxes. From aboard their ships, the British answered with a steady stream of mortar shells. On May 12, 1780, after months of deadly bombardment and high casualties on both sides, the Citadel fell. The American commander, General Benjamin Lincoln, surrendered his entire army to the British, and a satisfied General Clinton returned to New York.

Clinton left the southern campaign in the hands of **Charles Cornwallis,** an ambitious and able general who set out with more than eight thousand men to conquer the rest of South Carolina. Cornwallis and his regular army were joined by loyalist troops who were as eager to take their revenge on their enemies as Clinton had been. Since the British had abandoned the South in 1776, small, roving bands of loyalist guerrillas had kept resistance to the Revolution alive. After the British victory at Charleston, the guerrillas increased their attacks, and a bloody civil war of ambush, arson, and brutality on both sides resulted. By the summer of 1780, fortunes had reversed: the revolutionaries were now the resistance, and the loyalists were in control.

Thayendanegea Mohawk chief known to the Americans as Joseph Brant; his combined forces of loyalists and Indians defeated John Sullivan's expedition to upstate New York in 1779.

Charles Cornwallis British general who was second in command to Henry Clinton; his surrender at Yorktown in 1781 brought the Revolution to a close.

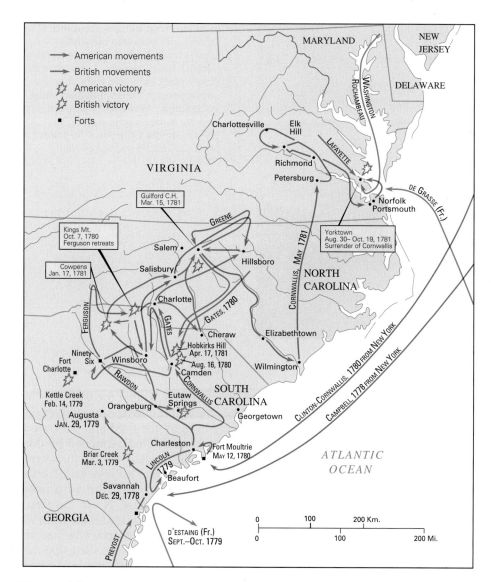

MAP 6.3 The Second Southern Campaign, 1778–1781 This map of the second attempt by Britain to crush the rebellion in the South shows the many battles waged in the Lower South before Cornwallis's encampment at Yorktown and his surrender there. This decisive southern campaign involved all the military resources of the combatants, including British, loyalist, French, and American ground forces and British and French naval fleets.

The revolutionary resistance produced legendary guerrilla leaders, including **Francis Marion,** known as the "Swamp Fox." Marion organized black and white recruits into raiding bands that steadily harassed Cornwallis's army and effectively cut British lines of communication between Charleston and the interior. While Marion did his best to trouble the British, Thomas Sumter's guerrillas and other resistance forces focused their energies on the loyalists. When these

guerrillas and loyalists met head-on in battle, they honored few of the rules of war. In October 1780, for

Francis Marion South Carolina leader of guerrilla forces during the war; known as the "Swamp Fox," he harassed British forces during the second southern campaign.

In this painting, patriots stand their ground against cavalrymen led by Lieutenant Banastre Tarleton in a 1781 skirmish near Cowpens. As the painting shows, black as well as white Americans supported the revolutionary cause in the South. *"Tarleton's Cavalrymen After the Battle of Cowpens, 1781" by William Ranney. Collection of the State of South Carolina. Photograph by Hunter Clarkson, Alt Lee, Inc.*

example, in the **Battle of King's Mountain,** revolutionaries surrounded loyalist troops and picked them off one by one. As this bitter civil war continued, marauding bands terrorized civilians and plundered their farms. Often the worst damage was done by outlaws posing as soldiers.

The regular American army, under the command of the Saratoga hero, "Granny" Gates, had little success against Cornwallis. In August 1780, Gates and his men suffered a crushing defeat at Camden, South Carolina. That fall, Washington wisely replaced Gates with a younger, more energetic officer from Rhode Island, **Nathanael Greene.** The fourteen hundred Continental soldiers Greene found when he arrived in South Carolina were tired, hungry, and clothed in rags. They were also, Greene discovered, "without discipline and so addicted to plundering that the utmost exertions of the officers cannot restrain them." Greene's first steps were to ease the strains caused by civil war, raids, and plundering by offering pardons to loyalists and proposing alliances with local Indian tribes. In the end, Greene managed to win all but the Creeks away from the British.

Greene's military strategy was attrition: wear the British out by making them chase his small army across the South. He sent Virginian Daniel Morgan and six hundred riflemen to western South Carolina to tempt troops under the command of Banastre Tarleton into pursuit. Tarleton finally caught up with

Morgan on an open meadow called the Cowpens in January 1781. When the outnumbered Americans stood their ground, ready to fight, the tired and frustrated British soldiers panicked and fled. Annoyed by this turn of events, Cornwallis decided to take the offensive. Now it was Greene's turn to lead the British on a long, exhausting chase. In March 1781, the two armies finally met at Guilford Courthouse, North Carolina. Although the Americans lost the battle and withdrew, British losses were so great that Cornwallis had to rethink the southern campaign. He decided that the price of conquering the Lower South was more than he was willing to pay. Disgusted, Cornwallis ordered his army northward to Virginia. Perhaps, he mused, he would have better luck there.

Treason and Triumph

In the fall of 1780, the popular general Benedict Arnold, one of Washington's protégés, defected to the British. Although Arnold's bold plot to turn over control of

Battle of King's Mountain Battle fought in October 1780 on the border between the Carolinas in which revolutionary troops defeated loyalists.

Nathanael Greene American general who took command of the Carolinas campaign in 1780.

John Trumbull celebrates the surrender of Cornwallis at Yorktown in this painting. However, neither Cornwallis nor Washington actually participated in the surrender ceremonies. The British commander claimed illness and sent his general of the guards as his deputy. Washington, always sensitive to status as well as to protocol, promptly appointed an officer of equal rank, General Benjamin Lincoln, to serve as his deputy. *"Surrender of Lord Cornwallis" by John Trumbull. Yale University Art Gallery. Trumbull Collection.*

the Hudson River by surrendering the fort at **West Point,** New York, to the British was foiled, Arnold's treason saddened Washington and damaged American morale. Washington's unhappiness over Arnold's betrayal was eased the following spring, however, when news came that French help was at last on its way. The general sat down at a strategy session with his French counterpart, General Rochambeau, in May 1781. The results were not exactly what Washington had hoped for: he had pressed for an attack on British-occupied New York, whereas Rochambeau insisted on a move against Cornwallis in Virginia. Since the French general had already ordered Admiral de Grasse and his fleet to the Chesapeake, Washington had little choice but to concur.

Thus, on July 6, 1781, a French army joined Washington's Continental forces just north of Manhattan for the long march to Virginia. The French soldiers, elegant in their sparkling uniforms, were openly amazed and impressed by their bedraggled allies. "It is incredible," wrote one French officer, "that soldiers composed of whites and blacks, almost naked, unpaid,

and rather poorly fed, can march so well and stand fire so steadfastly."

Within a few months, General Cornwallis too would be forced to admire the American army's stamina. In July, however, the British commander was unaware that a combined army was marching toward him. His first clue that trouble lay ahead came when a force of regular soldiers, led by Baron von Steuben and the marquis de Lafayette, appeared in Virginia. Soon afterward, Cornwallis moved his army to the peninsula port of Yorktown to prepare for more serious battles ahead. The choice of **Yorktown** was one he would heartily regret.

West Point   Site of a fort overlooking the Hudson River, north of New York City.

Yorktown   Site of the last major battle of the Revolution; American and French troops trapped Cornwallis's army here, on a peninsula on the York River near the Chesapeake Bay, and forced him to surrender.

By September 1781, the French and American troops coming from New York had joined forces with von Steuben and Lafayette's men. Admiral de Grasse's fleet of twenty-seven ships, seventy-four cannon, and an additional three thousand French soldiers were in place in Chesapeake Bay. General Clinton, still in New York, had been devastatingly slow to realize what the enemy intended. In desperation, he now sent a naval squadron from New York to rescue the trapped Cornwallis. He could do little more, since most of the British fleet was in the Caribbean.

Admiral de Grasse had no trouble fending off Clinton's rescue squadron. Then he turned his naval guns on the redcoats at Yorktown. From his siege positions on land, Washington also directed a steady barrage of artillery fire against the British, producing a deafening roar both day and night. The noise dazed the redcoats and prevented them from sleeping. On October 19, 1781, Lord Cornwallis admitted the hopelessness of his situation and surrendered. Despite the stunning turn of events at Yorktown, fighting continued in some areas. Loyalists and patriots continued to make war on each other in the South for another year. Bloody warfare against the Indians also meant more deaths along the frontier. The British occupation of Charleston, Savannah, and New York continued. But after Yorktown the British gave up all hope of military victory against their former colonies. On March 4, 1782, Parliament voted to cease "the further prosecution of offensive war on the Continent of North America, for the purpose of reducing the Colonies to obedience by force." The war for independence had been won.

Winning Diplomatic Independence

What Washington and his French and Spanish allies had won, American diplomats had to preserve. Three men represented the United States at the peace talks in Paris: Benjamin Franklin, John Adams, and John Jay. At first glance, this was an odd trio. The elderly Franklin, witty and sophisticated, had spent most of the war years in Paris, where he earned a deserved reputation as an admirer of French women and French wines. Adams, competitive, self-absorbed, and socially inept, did not hide his distaste for Franklin's flamboyance. Neither man found much comfort in the presence of the prudish, aristocratic John Jay of New York. Yet they proved to be a highly effective combination. Franklin brought a crafty skill and a love of strategy to the team as well as a useful knowledge of French politics. Adams provided the backbone, for in the face of

any odds he was stubborn, determined, fiercely patriotic, and a watchdog of American interests. Jay was calm, deliberate, and though not as aggressive as his New England colleague, he matched Adams in patriotism and integrity.

European political leaders expected the Americans to fare badly against the more experienced British and French diplomats. But Franklin, Jay, and Adams were far from naive. They were all veterans of wartime negotiations with European governments, having pursued loans, supplies, and military support. And they understood what was at stake at the peace table. They knew that their chief ally, France, had its own agenda and that England still wavered on the degree of independence America had actually won at Yorktown. Thus, despite firm orders from Congress to rely on France at every phase of the negotiations, the American diplomats quickly put their own agenda on the table. They issued a direct challenge to Britain: you must formally recognize American independence as a precondition to any negotiations at all. The British commissioner reluctantly agreed. Negotiations continued for more than a year, with all sides debating, arguing, and compromising until the terms of a treaty were finally set.

In the **Treaty of Paris of 1783** the Americans emerged with two clear victories. First, although the British did not give up Canada as the Americans had hoped, the boundaries of the new nation were extensive. Second, the treaty granted the United States unlimited access to the fisheries off Newfoundland, a particular concern of New Englander John Adams. It was difficult to measure the degree of success on other issues, however, since the terms for carrying out the agreements were so vague. For example, Britain ceded the Northwest to the United States. But the treaty said nothing about approval of this transfer of power by the Indians of the region, and it failed to set a timetable for British evacuation of the forts in the territory. This lack of clarity would cause problems for the Americans. In other cases, however, the treaty's vague language worked to American advantage. The treaty contained only the most general promise that the American government would not interfere with collection of the large prewar debts southern planters owed to British merchants. The promise to urge the states to return confiscated property to loyalists was equally inexact.

Treaty of Paris Treaty that ended the Revolutionary War in 1783 and secured American independence.

The peacemakers were aware of the treaty's shortcomings and its lack of clarity on key issues. But this was the price for avoiding stalemate and dangerous confrontation on controversial issues. Franklin, Adams, and Jay knew the consequences might be serious, but for the moment they preferred to celebrate rather than to worry.

Republican Expectations in a New Nation

- How did the Revolution affect Americans' expectations regarding individual rights, social equality, and the role of women in American society?
- What opportunities were open to African Americans during and after the Revolution?
- What was the fate of the loyalists?

As an old man, John Adams reminisced about the American Revolution with his family and friends. Although he spoke of the war as a remarkable military event, Adams insisted that the Revolution was more than battlefield victories and defeats. The Revolution took place, Adams said, "in the hearts and the minds of the people." What he meant was that changes in American social values and political ideas were as critical as artillery, swords, and battlefield strategies in creating the new nation. "The people" were, of course, far more diverse than Adams was ever willing to admit. And they often differed in their "hearts and minds." Race, region, social class, gender, religion, even the national origin of immigrants—all played a part in creating diverse interests and diverse interpretations of the Revolution. Adams was correct, however, that significant changes took place in American thought and behavior during the war and the years immediately after. Many of these changes reflected a growing identification of the new American nation as a **republic** that ensured not only representative government but also the protection of individual rights, an educated citizenry, and an expanded suffrage.

The Protection of Fundamental Rights

The Declaration of Independence expressed the commonly held American view that government must protect the fundamental rights of life, liberty, property, and, as Jefferson put it, "the pursuit of happiness." The belief that Britain was usurping these rights was a major justification for the Revolution. Thus, whatever form Americans chose for their new, independent government, they were certain to demand the protection of these fundamental rights. This emphasis had many social consequences.

The protection of many individual rights—freedom of speech, assembly, and the press, and the right to a trial by jury—were written into the new constitutions of several states. But some rights were more difficult to define than others. While many Americans supported "freedom of conscience," not all of them supported separation of church and state. In the seventeenth century, individual dissenters such as Roger Williams and Anne Hutchinson had fought for the separation of church and state. After the Great Awakening, the same demands were made by organized dissenter communities such as the Baptists, who protested the privileges that established churches enjoyed in most colonies. When Virginia took up the question in 1776, political leaders were not in agreement. The House of Burgesses approved George Mason's Declaration of Rights, which guaranteed its citizens "the free exercise of religion," yet Virginia continued to use tax monies to support the Anglican Church. Even with the strong support of Thomas Jefferson, dissenters' demands were not fully met until 1786, when the Statute of Religious Freedom ended tax-supported churches and guaranteed complete freedom of conscience, even for atheists. Other southern states followed Virginia's lead, ending tax support for their Anglican churches.

The battle was more heated in New England. Many descendants of the Puritans wished to continue government support of the Congregational Church. Others simply wished to keep the principle of an established church alive. As a compromise, communities were sometimes allowed to decide which local church received their tax money, although each town was required to make one church the established church. New England did not separate church and state entirely until the nineteenth century.

Protection of Property Rights

Members of the revolutionary generation who had a political voice were especially vocal about the importance of private property and protection of a citizen's

---

republic   A nation in which supreme power resides in the citizens, who elect representatives to govern them.

right to own property. In the decade before the Revolution, much of the protest against British policy had focused on this issue. For free, white, property-holding men—and for those white male servants, tenant farmers, or apprentices who hoped to join their ranks someday—life, liberty, and happiness were interwoven with the right of landownership.

The property rights of some infringed on the freedoms of others, however. Claims made on western lands by white Americans often meant the denial of Indian rights to that land. Masters' rights included a claim to the time and labor of their servants or apprentices. In the white community, a man's property rights usually included the restriction of his wife's right to own or sell land, slaves, and even her own personal possessions. Even the independent-minded Deborah Sampson lost her right to own property when she became Mrs. Gannett. And the institution of slavery transformed human beings into the private property of others.

The right to property was a principle, not a guarantee. Many white men were unable to acquire land during the revolutionary era or in the decades that followed. When the Revolution began, one-fifth of free American people lived in poverty or depended on public charity. The uneven distribution of wealth among white colonists was obvious on the streets of colonial Boston, in the rise in **almshouses** in Philadelphia, and in the growth of voluntary relief organizations that aided the homeless and the hungry in other cities and towns. For some, taking advantage of opportunities to acquire property was difficult even when those opportunities arose. Washington's Continental soldiers, for example, were promised western lands as delayed payment for their military service. But when they left the army in 1783, most were penniless, jobless, and sometimes homeless. They had little choice but to sell their precious land warrant certificates, trading their future as property owners for bread today.

Legal Reforms

Although economic inequality actually grew in the decades after the Revolution, several legal reforms were spurred by a commitment to the republican belief in social equality. Chief targets of this legal reform included the laws of **primogeniture** and **entail.** In Britain, these inheritance laws had led to the creation of a landed aristocracy. The actual threat they posed in America was small, for few planters ever adopted them. But the principle they represented remained important to republican spokesmen such as Thomas

In this portrait of Mary Harvey Champneys and her stepdaughter, Sarah Champneys, the two women pose in the respectable attire of a matron and an unmarried girl. The artist, Edward Savage, began his career making copies of paintings by more notable artists such as John Singleton Copley, but later managed to earn his living as a portraitist. In an era without photography, family portraits served as memorials as well as a display of wealth. *The Gibbes Museum of Art/Carolina Art Association.*

Jefferson, who pressed successfully for their abolition in Virginia and North Carolina.

The passion for social equality—in appearance if not in fact—affected customs as well as laws. To downplay their elite status as landowners, revolution-

almshouse A public shelter for the poor.
primogeniture The legal right of the eldest son to inherit the entire estate of his father.
entail A legal limitation that prevents property from being divided, sold, or given away.

Sheet music such as "The Ladies Patriotic Song" found its way into the parlors of many revolutionary and early republic homes. This song, which celebrates the heroes of independence, George Washington and John Adams, also celebrates what postwar society considered to be feminine virtues: beauty, innocence, and patriotic devotion. *Chicago Historical Society.*

aries stopped the practice of adding "**Esquire** (abbreviated "Esq.") after their names. (George Washington, Esq., became plain George Washington.)

Even unintentional elitist behavior could have embarrassing consequences. When General George Washington and the officers who served with him in the Revolutionary War organized the Society of the Cincinnati in 1783, they were motivated by the desire to sustain wartime friendships. The society's rules, however, brought protest from many Americans, for membership was hereditary, passing from officer fathers to their eldest sons. Grumblings that the club would spawn a military aristocracy—incompatible with republican government—drove Washington and his comrades to revise the offending society bylaws.

In some states, the principle of social equality had concrete political consequences. Pennsylvania and Georgia eliminated all property qualifications for voting among free white males. Other states lowered their property requirements for voters but refused to go as far as universal white manhood suffrage. They feared that the outcome of such a sweeping reform was unpredictable. Even women might demand a political voice.

Women in the New Republic

The war did not erase differences of class, race, region, or age for either men or women. Thus its impact was not uniform for all American women. Yet some

experiences, and the memories of them, were probably shared by the majority of white and even many black women. They would remember the war years as a time of constant shortages, anxiety, harassment, and unfamiliar and difficult responsibilities. Men going off to war left women to manage farms or shops in addition to caring for large families and household duties. Women had to cope with the critical shortages of food and supplies and to survive on meager budgets in inflationary times. Many, like the woman who pleaded with her soldier husband to "pray come home," may have feared they would fail in these new circumstances. After the war, however, many remembered with satisfaction how well they had adapted to new roles. They expressed their sense of accomplishment in letters to husbands that no longer spoke of "your farm" and "your crop" but of "our farm" and even "my crop."

Many women found they enjoyed the sudden independence from men and from the domestic hierarchy that men ruled in peacetime. Even women in difficult circumstances experienced this new sense of freedom. Grace Galloway, wife of loyalist exile Joseph Galloway of Pennsylvania, remained in America during the war in an effort to preserve her husband's

Esquire A term used to indicate that a man was a gentleman.

It Matters

Tracking Changes in Gender Roles

Eighteenth-century women like Deborah Sampson and Esther DeBerdt Reed tested the limits of traditional gender roles, demonstrating bravery on the battlefield and political organizing skills during the American Revolution. But it would be over 140 years before their descendants could vote in a national election and decades more before they could serve in the military. The impact of this social change can be seen today in the accomplishments of women such as Lt. General Claudia J. Kennedy, the United States Army's first female three-star general; Sandra Day O'Connor, the first woman to become a Supreme Court justice; and Geraldine Ferraro, the first woman to be the vice-presidential nominee of a national party. Tracking major changes in gender roles and examining why those changes occurred is a critical part of the historian's task.

property. Shunned by her patriot neighbors, reduced from wealth to painful poverty, Grace Galloway nevertheless confided to her diary that "Ye liberty of doing as I please Makes even Poverty more agreable than any time I ever spent since I married." If Galloway experienced new self-confidence and liberty during wartime, not all women were so fortunate. For the victims of rape and physical attack by soldiers on either side, the war meant more traditional experiences of vulnerability. American soldiers sang songs of flirtation and of their hopes for kisses from admiring young women, but occupying armies, guerrilla bands, and outlaws posing as soldiers left trails of abuse, particularly in New Jersey, along the frontier, and in the Carolinas.

For women, just as for men, the war meant adapting traditional behavior and skills to new circumstances. Women who followed the eighteenth-century custom of joining husbands or fathers in army camps took up the familiar domestic chores of cooking, cleaning, laundering, and providing nursing care. Outside the army camps, loyalist and patriot women served as spies or saboteurs and risked their lives by sheltering soldiers or hiding weapons in their cellars. Sometimes they opted to burn their crops or destroy their homes to prevent the enemy from using them. These were conscious acts of patriotism rather than wifely duties. On some occasions, women crossed gender boundaries dramatically. Although few behaved like Deborah Sampson and disguised themselves as men, women such as **Mary Ludwig** and Margaret Corbin did engage in military combat. These "Molly Pitchers" carried water to cool down the cannon in American forts across the country; but if men fell wounded, nearby women frequently took their place in line. After the war, female veterans of combat, including Corbin, applied to the government for pensions, citing as evidence the wounds they had received in battle.

In the postwar years, members of America's political and social elite engaged in a public discussion of women's role in the family and in a republican society. Spurred by Enlightenment assertions that all humans were capable of rational thought and action and by the empirical evidence of women's patriotic commitments and behavior, these Americans set aside older colonial notions that women lacked the ability to reason and to make moral choices. They urged a new role for women within the family: the moral training of their children. This training would include the inculcating of patriotism and republican principles. Thus the republic would rely on wives and mothers to sustain its values and to raise a new generation of concerned citizens.

This new ideal, **"republican womanhood,"** reflected Enlightenment ideals, but it also had roots in economic and social changes that began before the Revolution, including the growth of a prosperous urban class able to purchase many household necessities. No longer needing to make cloth or candles or butter, prosperous urban wives and mothers had time to devote to raising children. Republican womanhood probably had little immediate impact in the lives of free ordinary women, who remained unable to purchase essential goods or to pay others to do household chores, or in the lives of African American or Indian women.

Although women's active role in the education of the next generation was often applauded as a public,

Mary Ludwig Wife of a soldier at Fort Monmouth; one of many women known popularly as "Molly Pitchers" because they carried water to cool down the cannon their husbands fired in battle.

"republican womanhood" A role for mothers that became popularized following the Revolution; it stressed women's importance in instructing children in republican virtues such as patriotism and honor.

political contribution, not simply a private, family duty, it did not lead to direct political participation for female Americans. The Constitution left suffrage qualifications to the state governments, and no state chose to extend voting rights to women. Only one state, New Jersey, failed to stipulate "male" as a condition for suffrage in its first constitution, and this oversight was soon revised.

Although American republicanism expected mothers to instill patriotism in their children, it also expected communities to provide formal education for future citizens. Arguing that a citizen could not be both "ignorant and free," several states allotted tax money for public elementary schools. Some went even further. By 1789, for example, Massachusetts required every town to provide free public education to its children. After the Revolution, *children* meant girls as well as boys.

This new emphasis on female education was a radical departure for women. Before the Revolution, the education of daughters was haphazard at best. Colleges and the preparatory schools that trained young men for college were closed to female students. A woman got what formal knowledge she could by reading her father's or her brother's books. Some women, most notably Anne Hutchinson and the Massachusetts revolutionary propagandist Mercy Otis Warren, were lucky enough to receive fine educations from the men in their family. But most women had to be content to learn domestic skills rather than geography, philosophy, or history. After the Revolution, however, educational reformers reasoned that mothers must be well versed in history and even political theory if they were to teach their children the essential principles of citizenship. By the 1780s, private academies had opened to educate the daughters of wealthy American families. These privileged young women enjoyed the rare opportunity to study mathematics, history, and geography. Although their curriculum was often as rigorous as that in a boys' preparatory school, the addition of courses in fancy needlework reminded the girls that their futures lay in marriage and motherhood.

The War's Impact on Slaves and Slavery

The protection of liberty and the fear of enslavement were major themes of the Revolution. Yet the denial of liberty was a central reality in the lives of most African Americans. As the movement for independence developed, slaves' political and military loyalties reflected their best guess as to which side offered them the greatest chance of freedom. Ironically, the desire for freedom set many of them against the Revolution. Of the fifty thousand or so slaves who won their freedom in the war, half did so by escaping to the British army. Only about five thousand African American men joined the Continental Army once Congress opened enlistment to them in 1776. Black soldiers were generally better treated by the British than by the revolutionaries. In both armies, however, African American troops received lower

The blessings of liberty and equality at the heart of the Revolution did not extend to all Americans. In New England, slavery was abolished after the war, but free blacks were not welcomed into white society. The illustration above of a celebration sponsored in 1793 by Massachusetts governor John Hancock for free African Americans was accompanied by a satiric poem that mocked blacks and what the poet saw as their crude attempts to mimic polite society. *Library Company of Philadelphia.*

As a child, Phillis Wheatley was brought from Africa and sold to a Boston couple who came to recognize and encourage her literary talent. Wheatley's patriotic poetry won approval from George Washington and praise from many revolutionary leaders. She died free but in poverty in the 1780s. *Library of Congress.*

pay than white soldiers and were often assigned to the most dangerous or menial duties.

With American victory in 1781, African American loyalist soldiers faced a difficult decision: to remain in America and risk reenslavement or to evacuate along with the British army. Many stayed, prompting a group of angry owners to complain that there was "reason to believe that a great number of slaves which were taken by the British army are now passing in this country as free men." The British transported those who chose to leave to Canada, to England, to British Florida, to the Caribbean, or to Africa. Three thousand former slaves settled initially in Nova Scotia, but the racism of their white loyalist neighbors led more than a thousand of these veterans to emigrate a second time. Led by an African-born former slave named Thomas Peters, they sailed to Sierra Leone, in West Africa, where they established a free black colony. Slaves found other routes to freedom besides military service during the war. Some escaped from farms and plantations to the cities, where they passed as free people. Others fled to the frontier, where they joined sympathetic Indian tribes. Women and children, in particular, took advantage of wartime disruptions to flee their masters' control.

The long war affected the lives of those who remained in slavery. Control and discipline broke down when the southern campaigns dragged on, distracting slaveowners and disrupting work routines. Slave masters complained loudly and bitterly that their slaves "all do now what they please every where" and "pay no attention to the orders of the overseer." These exaggerated complaints point to real but temporary opportunities for slaves to alter the conditions under which they worked and lived.

In the northern states, the revolutionaries' demand for liberty undermined black slavery. Loyalists taunted patriots, asking, "How is it that we hear the loudest yelps for liberty among the drivers of negroes?" The question made the contradiction between revolutionary ideals and American reality painfully clear. Not all slaveowners, however, needed to be shamed by others into grappling with the hypocrisy of their position. In the 1760s and 1770s, influential political leaders such as James Otis, Thomas Paine, and Benjamin Rush campaigned against the continuation of slavery. In Boston, Phillis Wheatley, a young African-born slave whose master recognized and encouraged her literary talents, called on the revolutionaries to acknowledge the universality of the wish for freedom. "In every human breast," Wheatley wrote, "God had implanted a Principle, which we call love of freedom; it is impatient of Oppression, and pants for Deliverance. . . . I will assert, that the same Principles live in us." George Washington was among those who admired Wheatley's talents and respected her demands for black freedom, and he publicly acknowledged her as an American poet.

Free black Americans joined with white reformers to mobilize antislavery campaigns in Pennsylvania, Massachusetts, Rhode Island, and Connecticut. In Boston and Philadelphia, slaves petitioned on their own behalf to be "liberated from a state of Bondage, and made Freemen of this Community." Of course, these states were home to few slaves, and the regional economy did not depend on unfree labor. Thus it was easier there to acknowledge the truth in the slave's cry: "We have no property! . . . we have no children! . . . we have no city! . . . we have no country!"

Manumission increased during the 1770s, especially in the North. In 1780, Pennsylvania became the first state to pass an emancipation statute, making

manumit To free from slavery or bondage; to emancipate.

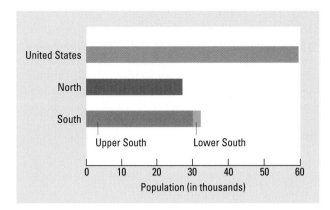

FIGURE 6.1 Free Black Population, 1790 This graph shows the number of free African Americans in the United States in 1790, as well as their regional distribution. These almost 60,000 free people were less than 10 percent of the African American population of the nation. Although 40 percent of northern blacks were members of this free community, only about 5.5 percent of the Upper South African Americans and less than 2 percent of those in the Lower South lived outside the bounds of slavery.

manumission a public policy rather than a private matter of conscience. Pennsylvania lawmakers, however, compromised on a gradual rather than an immediate end to slavery. Only slaves born after the law was enacted were eligible, and they could not expect to receive their freedom until they had served a twenty-eight-year term of indenture. By 1804, all northern states except Delaware had committed themselves to a slow end to slavery.

Slavery was far more deeply embedded in the South, as a labor system and as a system that regulated race relations. In the Lower South, white Americans ignored the debate over slavery and took immediate steps to replace missing slaves and to restore tight control over work and life on their plantations. Manumission did occur in the Upper South. Free black communities grew in both Maryland and Virginia after the Revolutionary War, and planters openly debated the morality of slavery in a republic and the practical benefits of slave labor. They did not all reach the same conclusions. George Washington freed all his slaves on the death of his wife, but Patrick Henry, who had often stirred his fellow Virginia legislators with his spirited defense of American liberty, justified his decision to continue slavery with blunt honesty. Freeing his slaves, he said, would be inconvenient (see Figure 6.1).

The Fate of the Loyalists

Before independence was declared, white Americans loyal to the Crown experienced the isolation and disapproval of their communities. Some faced the physical danger of tarring and feathering, imprisonment, or beatings. Still others saw their property destroyed. After 1775, loyalists flocked to the safety of British-occupied cities, crowding first into Boston and later into New York City and Philadelphia. When the British left an area, the loyalists evacuated with them. More than a thousand Massachusetts loyalists boarded British ships when Boston was abandoned in 1776, and fifteen thousand more sailed out of New York harbor when the war ended in 1781. Altogether, as many as a hundred thousand men, women, and children left their American homes to take up new lives in England, Canada, and the West Indies.

Wealth often determined a loyalist's destination. Rich and influential men such as Thomas Hutchinson of Massachusetts took refuge in England during the war. But life in England was so expensive that it quickly ate up their resources and drove them into debt. Accustomed to comfort, many of these exiles passed their days in seedy boarding houses in the small cities outside London. They lost more than servants and fine clothes, however. In a society dominated by aristocrats and royalty, loyalist men who had enjoyed status and prestige in America suddenly found themselves socially insignificant, with no work and little money. Loyalists in England grew more desperately homesick each day.

When the war ended, most of the loyalists in England departed for Nova Scotia, New Brunswick, or the Caribbean. Many of these exiles were specifically forbidden to return to the United States by the new state governments. Others refused to go back to America because they equated the new republican society with mob rule. Those who were willing to adjust to the new American nation returned slowly.

Less prosperous loyalists, especially those who served in the loyalist battalions during the war, went to Canada after 1781. The separation from family and friends, as much as the bleak climate of Canada, at first caused depression and despair in some exiles. One woman who had bravely endured the war and its deprivations broke down and cried when she landed at Nova Scotia. Like the revolutionaries, these men and women had chosen their political loyalty based on a mixture of principle and self-interest. Unlike the revolutionaries, they had chosen the losing side. They lived with the consequences for the rest of their lives.

Canada became the refuge of another group of loyalists: members of the Indian tribes that had supported the Crown. The British ceded much of the Iroquois land to the United States in the Treaty of Paris, and American hostility toward "enemy savages" made peaceful postwar coexistence unlikely. Thus, in the 1780s, Mohawks, Onondagas, Tuscaroras, Senecas, Oneidas, and Cayugas along with Delawares, Tutelos, and Nanticokes created new, often multiethnic settlements on the banks of the Grand River in Ontario. These communities marked an end to the dislocation and suffering many of these refugees had experienced during the Revolution, when steady warfare depleted Indian resources and made thousands dependent on the British for food, clothing, and military supplies. A majority of the Indians who settled in Canada had already spent years in makeshift encampments near Fort Niagara after American armies destroyed their farms, homes, and villages.

Individual Voices

Examining a Primary Source

Esther DeBerdt Reed Glories in the Usefulness of Women

Deborah Sampson took the most daring path to participation in the Revolution. But other women also pushed the boundaries of women's traditional sphere by organizing to play a public role in the war effort. Wealthy Philadelphia matron Esther DeBerdt Reed, for example, helped organize women's voluntary associations to raise funds and supplies for the American army. Openly political activities by women were not always greeted favorably by the community, however. Women who expressed their patriotism through public actions were accused of overstepping the boundaries of their gender—that is, of unfeminine behavior. Reed defended her activism in "The Sentiments of an American Woman," printed in 1780. In this unusual document, she connects the patriotic women of the Revolution with heroic women of history, and she discusses female patriotism in terms that Deborah Sampson would surely have applauded.

■ Here, Constitution does not mean a written plan of government but the natural characteristics and appropriate behaviors of women—and of men. Do you think Reed is challenging the notion that women are constitutionally, or naturally, weak and incapable of making decisions and acting on them? Or is she saying that women are decisive and competent only in times of great crisis?

On the commencement of actual war, the Women of America manifested a firm resolution to contribute as much as could depend on them, to the deliverance of this country. Animated by the purest patriotism they are sensible of sorrow at this day, in not offering more than barren wishes for the success of so glorious a Revolution. They aspire to render themselves more really useful; and this sentiment is universal from the north to the south of the Thirteen United States. ■ *Our ambition is kindled by the fame of those heroines of antiquity, who have rendered their sex illustrious, and have proved to the universe, that, if the weakness of our Constitution, if opinion and manners did not forbid us to march to glory by the same paths as the Men, we should at least equal and sometimes surpass them in our love for the public good. I glory in all that which my sex has done great and*

■ Male revolutionary leaders often drew analogies between their choices and actions and those of biblical heroes and leaders of the Roman republic. Why do you think Reed referred to the women of the Bible and Ancient Rome?

■ If you were opposed to the activities Reed was engaged in, what arguments would you make against this type of female activism?

commendable. ■ I call to mind with enthusiasm and with admiration, all those acts of courage, of constancy and patriotism, which history has transmitted to us: The people favoured by Heaven, preserved from destruction by the virtues, the zeal and the resolution of Deborah, of Judith, of Esther! . . . Rome saved from the fury of a victorious enemy by the efforts of Volunia, and other Roman ladies: So many famous sieges where the Women have been seen forgetting the weakness of their sex, building new walls, digging trenches with their feeble hands; furnishing arms to their defenders, they themselves darting the missile weapons on the enemy, resigning the adornments of their apparel, and their fortunes to fill the public treasury, and to hasten the deliverance of their country. . . . [We are] Born for liberty, disdaining to bear the irons of a tyrannic Government. ■ . . . Who knows if persons disposed to censure, and sometimes too severely with regard to us, may not disapprove our appearing acquainted even with the actions of which our sex boasts? We are at least certain, that he cannot be a good citizen who will not applaud our efforts for the relief of the armies which defend our lives, our possessions, our liberty.

Summary

When the colonies declared their independence, many people on both sides doubted that the Americans could win the war. The British outnumbered and outgunned the Americans, and their troops were better trained and better equipped. The Americans' major advantage was logistic: they were fighting a war on familiar terrain.

The early British strategy was to invade New York and the southern colonies, where they expected to rally strong loyalist support. But this strategy proved unsuccessful, not only because they were waging war on unfamiliar territory but because they had overestimated loyalist strength and persisted in alienating would-be sympathizers. Also, Washington's hit-and-run tactics made it impossible for the British to deliver a crushing blow.

The most dramatic turning point in the war came in 1777 when British general John Burgoyne's plan to isolate New England from the rest of the rebelling colonies failed. Burgoyne was forced to surrender at Saratoga, New York. The surprising American victory led to an alliance between France and the United States and the expansion of the war into an international conflict. The British again chose to invade the South in 1778, but despite early victories, their campaign ended in disaster. American victory was assured when French and American forces defeated General Cornwallis at Yorktown, Virginia, in October 1781. Fighting continued for a time, but in March 1782, the British Parliament ended the conflict. The war for American independence had been won. The Treaty of Paris was negotiated in 1783, and to the surprise of many European diplomats, the Americans gained important concessions.

Independence from British rule was not the only outcome of the war. Victory led to transformations in American society. Individual rights were strengthened for free white men. A republican spirit changed the outlook, if not the condition, of many Americans, as customs that signaled a hierarchical society gave way to more egalitarian behavior. The wartime experiences of women such as Deborah Sampson led American intellectuals to reconsider women's "nature" and their abilities. Although full citizenship was confined to free white males, white women's capacity for rational thought was acknowledged, and their new role as the educators of their children led to expanded formal education for women. Black Americans also made some gains. Fifty thousand slaves won their freedom during the war, thousands by serving in the Continental Army. Some northerners moved to outlaw slavery, but southern slaveholders chose to preserve the institution despite intense debate. Loyalists, having made their political choices, had to live with the consequences of defeat. For most, the outcome was permanent exile from their homeland.

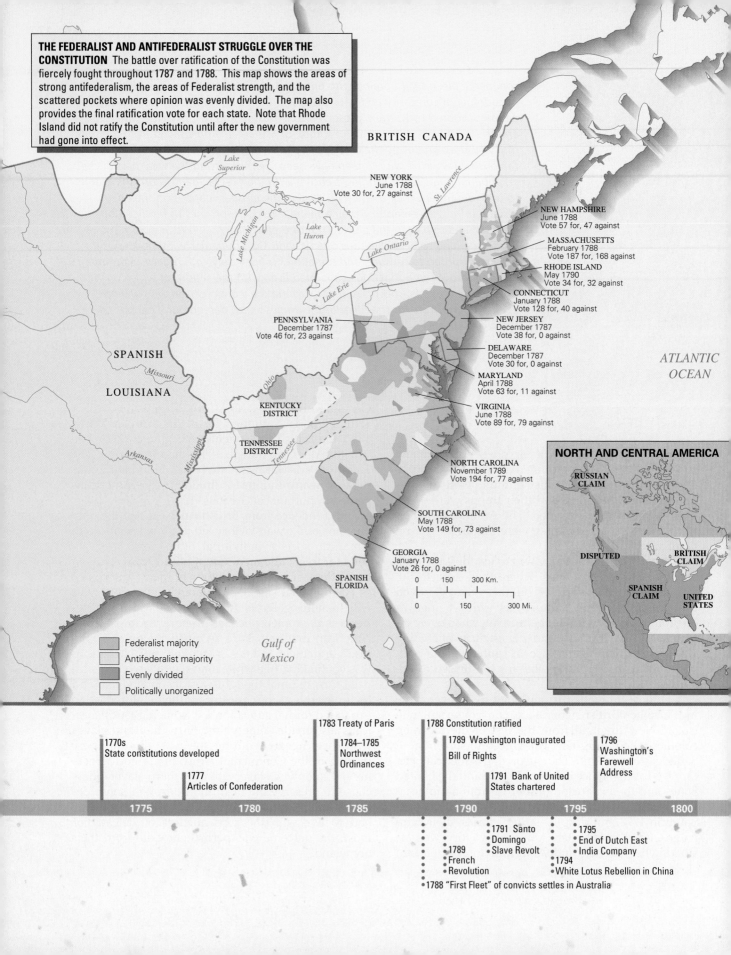

THE FEDERALIST AND ANTIFEDERALIST STRUGGLE OVER THE CONSTITUTION The battle over ratification of the Constitution was fiercely fought throughout 1787 and 1788. This map shows the areas of strong antifederalism, the areas of Federalist strength, and the scattered pockets where opinion was evenly divided. The map also provides the final ratification vote for each state. Note that Rhode Island did not ratify the Constitution until after the new government had gone into effect.

BRITISH CANADA

Lake Superior

Lake Michigan

Lake Huron

Lake Ontario

Lake Erie

St. Lawrence

NEW YORK
June 1788
Vote 30 for, 27 against

NEW HAMPSHIRE
June 1788
Vote 57 for, 47 against

MASSACHUSETTS
February 1788
Vote 187 for, 168 against

RHODE ISLAND
May 1790
Vote 34 for, 32 against

CONNECTICUT
January 1788
Vote 128 for, 40 against

NEW JERSEY
December 1787
Vote 38 for, 0 against

PENNSYLVANIA
December 1787
Vote 46 for, 23 against

DELAWARE
December 1787
Vote 30 for, 0 against

MARYLAND
April 1788
Vote 63 for, 11 against

VIRGINIA
June 1788
Vote 89 for, 79 against

SPANISH

LOUISIANA

Missouri

Ohio

KENTUCKY
DISTRICT

TENNESSEE
DISTRICT

Tennessee

Arkansas

Mississippi

NORTH CAROLINA
November 1789
Vote 194 for, 77 against

SOUTH CAROLINA
May 1788
Vote 149 for, 73 against

GEORGIA
January 1788
Vote 26 for, 0 against

ATLANTIC
OCEAN

0   150   300 Km.

0   150   300 Mi.

SPANISH
FLORIDA

Gulf of
Mexico

NORTH AND CENTRAL AMERICA

RUSSIAN
CLAIM

DISPUTED

BRITISH
CLAIM

SPANISH
CLAIM

UNITED
STATES

Federalist majority

Antifederalist majority

Evenly divided

Politically unorganized

1783 Treaty of Paris

1788 Constitution ratified

1770s
State constitutions developed

1784–1785
Northwest
Ordinances

1789 Washington inaugurated

Bill of Rights

1796
Washington's
Farewell
Address

1777
Articles of Confederation

1791 Bank of United
States chartered

| 1775 | 1780 | 1785 | 1790 | 1795 | 1800 |

1791 Santo
Domingo
Slave Revolt

1795
End of Dutch East
India Company

1789
French
Revolution

1794
White Lotus Rebellion in China

1788 "First Fleet" of convicts settles in Australia

Competing Visions of the Virtuous Republic, 1770–1796

7

The Federalist and Antifederalist Struggle over the Constitution
Using the map on the facing page, support or challenge the idea that small states and large states had different attitudes toward ratification of the Constitution.

Individual Choices

ALEXANDER HAMILTON

Author of many of *The Feder-alist Papers* essays and first secretary of the treasury, Alexander Hamilton was admired for his intellectual brilliance and his political vision, even by bitter political opponents. Hamilton was a true American success story: an illegitimate son of a Scot-tish merchant, he immigrated to the mainland during his teenage years, where he en-joyed a meteoric career. Hamilton served as Washing-ton's aide-de-camp, became a leader of the New York bar, and entered New York's social elite by his marriage into the Schuyler family. In 1804, a political enemy, Aaron Burr, killed Hamilton in a duel. *"Alexander Hamilton" by Charles Wilson Peale. Courtesy of the Independence National Historical Park Collection.*

Alexander Hamilton

Alexander Hamilton came into the world in 1757 without any of the at-tributes needed for success in the eighteenth century. He was poor, iso-lated on a tiny island in the Caribbean, and as John Adams once crudely put it, "the bastard brat of a Scots peddlar." But if Hamilton had few social or material resources, he had many intellectual ones. His genius and ambition catapulted him into the elite social circles of New York and into the very center of political power and influence in the new American nation. Hamilton's life was, in every respect, a tale of rags to riches.

By the time he was 13, Hamilton's brilliance had attracted the atten-tion of influential men. His employer on the island of St. Croix paid his passage to New York, where other gentlemen saw to his education. He arrived at King's College (now Columbia University) in 1774, just as the bonds of affection and loyalty between Great Britain and the colonies were about to come permanently undone. He quickly set aside his studies to join the protests and demonstrations. His charisma was immediately evident: at 17 he could hold a crowd spellbound, delivering an extemporaneous speech against taxation and government corruption. He wrote pamphlets attacking Parliament's colonial policy that made him an overnight leader of the radical movement in New York City. When the war began, the 19-year-old Hamilton immediately took command of an artillery company. By 1777, he had found the most important mentor in his life: General George Washington. Hamilton became Washington's secretary and aide-de-camp, a protégé to the most admired man in America.

By 1780, Hamilton was married to the daughter of one of the richest, most politically prominent men in New York, General Philip Schuyler. He could have spent the rest of his life enjoying the rounds of parties and balls, fishing at his father-in-law's Hudson Valley estate, and practicing law for elite clients. But Hamilton chose to be a statesman, not simply a gentleman. He had a bold vision for his adopted country. He was convinced that it could quickly rise to be the most productive, prosperous nation in the world, rivaling its former Mother Country, England. And he had an equally bold plan to ensure that this vision became a reality.

Hamilton was a driving force behind the move to discard the Articles of Confed-eration and create a strong central government, empowered to set a national economic agenda, regulate trade and commerce, encourage entrepreneurial en-terprises, maintain law and order, and win the respect of foreign powers through military strength and diplomacy. When the Constitution was drafted, Hamilton campaigned brilliantly for its ratification, writing many of the most effective *Fed-eralist* essays and outmaneuvering the Antifederalists in New York's ratifying con-vention. In 1789 Hamilton took his place in the cabinet of the first president, his longtime mentor George Washington. As secretary of the Treasury, a post Hamil-ton interpreted as the prime ministership, he initiated programs to realize his vision: establishing the Bank of the United States, funding the national debt, im-

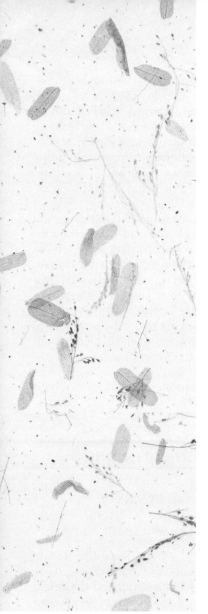

posing tariffs, and proposing an ambitious plan to encourage the rapid development of manufacturing in America. Although Thomas Jefferson and James Madison were soon organizing opposition to his policies and his vision, Hamilton left his mark on the nation's future.

In 1795, at the age of 37, Alexander Hamilton chose to resign from office. Despite Washington's continued confidence in him, Hamilton knew that any new programs he proposed would be blocked by his Jeffersonian opponents in the Congress. By the following year, he was back in New York City, practicing law, helping to organize the Bank of New York, and working for the abolition of slavery with fellow Federalist John Jay. Although Hamilton was an elitist, he believed in a hierarchy built on ability, not birthright. Slavery was unacceptable to him because it denied thousands of people the right to rise to power and wealth by their talent, ambition, and intelligence.

Hamilton's fiercely nationalistic politics, his commitment to a nation built on commerce and manufacturing rather than agriculture, his open admiration for England, and his vocal opposition to the French Revolution made him a controversial figure until his death in 1804. In that year, Aaron Burr, furious with Hamilton for blocking his political career, challenged Hamilton to a duel. Burr knew the emotional impact of such a challenge, for Hamilton's oldest son had been killed in a duel only three years earlier. The two men met at dawn on the cliffs of Weehawken, New Jersey—a site chosen because, after his son's death, Hamilton had helped pass a law making dueling illegal in New York. No one is certain what happened that July morning. Friends say that Burr aimed directly at his opponent and fired a fatal shot while Hamilton discharged his gun into the air. Alexander Hamilton died that afternoon.

All New York City seemed to turn out for the funeral. In a slow march to Trinity Church, Revolutionary War artillery, infantry, and militia companies, fellow military officers, clergymen, friends, and family were followed by long lines of foreign diplomats, city officers, trustees, faculty and students from Columbia College, and directors of the city's major financial institutions. Both British and French ships in the harbor fired their guns in salute. The champion of an active, strong central government, the architect of American industrialization, was dead. But, as Jefferson himself conceded, the economic direction Alexander Hamilton had chosen for the United States would not be altered.

INTRODUCTION

Between 1776 and 1783, Americans fought to create an independent nation. But what kind of nation would that be? Most free white Americans rejected the notion of an American monarchy and embraced the idea of a republic. Yet a republic could take many forms, and Americans who enjoyed a political voice disagreed on what form was best for the new nation. As a consequence, the transition from independence to nationhood generated heated debate.

How should power be divided between local and national governments? How should laws be made, and by whom? Who should be empowered to administer those laws? What programs and policies should the national government endorse? And, finally, how could the government be designed to protect the unalienable individual rights that free white Americans believed they possessed? Men such as Alexander Hamilton and James Madison knew as well as Tom Paine these questions had to be answered, and soon.

The Articles of Confederation was the nation's first effort at republican government. The Confederation, which joined the states together in friendship, guided Americans through the last years of the war and the

The men who drafted the New Jersey constitution took care to include a property qualification for voting but forgot to specify the sex of an eligible voter. Thus women who owned property had the right to vote from 1776 to 1807, when the "error" was corrected. New Jersey did not choose to grant women the vote again for over a century. *Corbis/Bettmann.*

peace negotiations. It also organized the northwest territories for settlement and established the political steps toward statehood within each territory. These were major achievements. But the Confederation government did not survive the decade of postwar adjustment, for many political leaders believed it was too weak to solve the nation's economic and social problems or set America's course for the future.

In 1787 delegates to a Constitutional Convention produced a new plan of government, the Constitution. It was fashioned from compromises between the interests of small states and large ones, between southern and northern regional interests, and between those who sought to preserve the sovereignty of the states and those who wished to increase the power of the national government. The Constitution created a strong central government with the right to regulate interstate and foreign trade and the power to tax.

Not everyone supported the adoption of this new government. Its opponents, known as Antifederalists, charged that it rejected many of the basic ideals of the Revolution, especially the commitment to local representative government and the guarantee of protection from the dangers of centralized authority. Many continued to believe that state governments were the best

guarantee that republican values would be maintained. Others feared the new government would be dominated by the wealthiest citizens. The Federalists, or pro-Constitution group, responded by arguing that the new government would save America from economic disaster, international scorn, and domestic unrest. Leading patriots of the 1760s and 1770s could be found on both sides of this debate, but the Federalists carried the day.

The adoption of the Constitution did not magically solve all America's problems. Tensions between northern and southern states were becoming as serious as those between the West and the more settled regions of the Atlantic coast. The nation was deeply divided over foreign policy and the lineup of allies and enemies in Europe. And even after the Constitution was ratified, many Americans continued to believe that strong local governments rather than an active central government best protected their liberties. Nevertheless, when President George Washington said his farewells to public life in 1796, most Americans were confident that their young nation would survive.

America's First Constitutions

- What types of legislatures did the states create?
- What were the major elements of the Articles of Confederation?
- What problems arose in ratifying the Articles?

The writers of state constitutions were the first to grapple with troubling but fundamental issues—in particular, the definition of citizenship and the extent of political participation. Should women be allowed to vote? Could landless men, servants, free blacks, or apprentices enjoy a political voice? These were exactly the kinds of questions John Adams feared might arise in any discussion of voting rights, or suffrage. They raised the specter of democracy, which he considered a dangerous system. Once the question was posed, he predicted, "There will be no end of it . . . women will demand a vote, lads from twelve to twenty-one will think their rights are not enough attended to, and every man who has not a **farthing** will demand an equal voice with any other in all acts of state."

---

farthing A British coin worth one-fourth of a penny and thus a term used to indicate something of very little value.

Chronology

From Revolution to Nationhood

1770s	State constitutions developed
1776	Oversight in New Jersey constitution gives property-holding women right to vote
1777	Congress adopts Articles of Confederation
1781	States ratify Articles of Confederation Cornwallis surrenders at Yorktown
1784–1785	First two Northwest Ordinances
1786	Annapolis Convention Shays's Rebellion
1787	Constitutional Convention Third Northwest Ordinance
1787–1788	States ratify U.S. Constitution
1789	First congressional elections George Washington inaugurated as first president Judiciary Act of 1789 French Revolution
1791	First Bank of the United States chartered Bill of Rights added to Constitution Alexander Hamilton's *Report on Manufactures*
1792	Washington reelected
1793	Genêt affair Jefferson resigns as secretary of state
1794	Whiskey Rebellion in Pennsylvania Battle of Fallen Timbers
1795	Congress approves Jay's Treaty Treaty of San Lorenzo
1796	Washington's Farewell Address

English political tradition supported Adams's view that political rights were not universal. Under English law, "rights" were, in fact, particular *privileges* that a group enjoyed because of special social circumstances—including age, sex, wealth, or family ties. In their first constitutions, several states extended these privileges to all free white men, a democratic reform but one that still sets special conditions of race and sex.

The state constitutions reflected the variety of opinion on this matter of democracy within a republic. At one end of the spectrum was Pennsylvania, whose constitution abolished all property qualifications and granted the vote to all white males in the state. At the other end were states such as Maryland, whose constitution continued to link the ownership of property to voting. To hold office, a Marylander had to meet even higher standards of wealth than the voters.

While constitution writers in every state believed that the legislature was the primary branch of government, they were divided over other issues. Should there be a separate executive branch? Should the legislature have one house or two? What qualifications should be set for officeholders? Again, Pennsylvania produced the most democratic answer to this question. Pennsylvania's constitution concentrated all power to make and to administer law in a one-house, or **unicameral,** elected assembly. The farmers and artisans who helped draft this state constitution eliminated both the executive office and the upper house of the legislature, remembering that these had been strongholds for the wealthy in colonial times. Pennsylvania also required annual elections of all legislators to ensure that the assembly remained responsive to the people's will. In contrast, Maryland and the other states divided powers among a governor, or executive branch, and a **bicameral** legislature, although the legislature enjoyed the broader powers. Members of the upper house in Maryland's legislature had to meet higher property qualifications than those in the lower house, or assembly. In this manner, political leaders in this state ensured their elite citizens a secure voice in lawmaking.

Pennsylvania and Maryland represented the two ends of the democratic spectrum. The remaining states fell between these poles. The constitutions of New

---

unicameral Having a single legislative house.
bicameral Having a legislature with two houses.

I t M a t t e r s

Having a Vision for the Future

In 1791, Alexander Hamilton outlined his vision for the economic future of the United States. When Hamilton predicted that manufacturing would overtake agriculture as the basis for the American economy, he knew he would be setting himself against some of the most important people in the nation. Hamilton's *Report on Manufactures* was not adopted by Congress, but the ideas set forth in it would eventually become central to the economy of the United States. Hamilton's belief that a strong central government with broad economic powers could encourage the fledgling manufacturing industries of the new country set the stage for the United States to become the economic superpower it is today.

Hampshire, North Carolina, and Georgia followed the democratic tendencies of Pennsylvania. New York, South Carolina, and Virginia chose Maryland's more conservative or traditional approach. New Jersey and Delaware took the middle ground, with at least one surprising result. New Jersey's first constitution, written in 1776, gave the vote to "all free inhabitants" who met certain property qualifications. This requirement denied the ballot to propertyless men but granted voting rights to property-holding women. A writer in the *New York Spectator* in 1797 snidely remarked that New Jersey women "intermeddl[ing] in political affairs" made that state's politics as strange as those of the "emperor of Java [who] never employs any but women in his embassies." Nevertheless, for thirty-one years, at least a few New Jersey women regularly exercised their right to elect the men who governed them. Then, in 1807, state lawmakers took away that right, arguing that "the weaker sex" was too easily manipulated by political candidates to be allowed to vote.

A state's particular history often determined the type of constitution it produced. For example, coastal elites and lowland gentry had dominated the colonial governments of New Hampshire, South Carolina, Virginia, and North Carolina. These states sought to correct this injustice by ensuring representation to small farming districts in interior and frontier regions. The memory of high-handed colonial governors and elitist

upper houses in the legislature led Massachusetts lawmakers to severely limit the powers of their first state government. The constitutions in all of these states reflected the strong political voice that ordinary citizens had acquired during the Revolution.

Beginning in the 1780s, however, many states revised their constitutions, increasing the power of the government. At the same time, they added safeguards they believed would prevent abuse. The 1780 Massachusetts constitution was the model for many of these revisions. Massachusetts political leaders built in a system of so-called checks and balances among the legislative, judicial, and executive branches to ensure that no branch of the government could grow too powerful or overstep its assigned duties. Over the opposition of many farmers and townspeople, these newer state constitutions also curbed the democratic extension of voting and officeholding privileges. Thus wealth returned as a qualification to govern, although the revised constitutions did not allow the wealthy to tamper with the basic individual rights of citizens. In seven states, these individual rights were safeguarded by a **bill of rights** guaranteeing freedom of speech, religion, and the press as well as the right to assemble and to petition the government.

The Articles of Confederation

There was little popular support for a powerful central government in the early years of the Revolution. Instead, as John Adams later recalled, Americans wanted "a Confederacy of States, each of which must have a separate government." When Pennsylvania's **John Dickinson** submitted a blueprint for a strong national government to the Continental Congress in July of 1776, he watched in wonder and dismay as his colleagues transformed his plan, called **Articles of Confederation,** into a government that preserved the rights and privileges of the states.

Members of the one-house Continental Congress agreed that the new government should also be a uni-

---

bill of rights   A formal statement of essential rights and liberties under law.

John Dickinson   Philadelphia lawyer and revolutionary pamphleteer who drafted the Articles of Confederation.

Articles of Confederation   The first constitution of the United States; it created a central government with limited powers, and it was replaced by the Constitution in 1788.

The Articles of Confederation were debated for almost as many years as they were in effect. Proposed in 1775, they were not ratified by the states until 1781. Eight years later, the Constitution replaced them. Eighteenth-century citizens hotly debated the virtues and shortcomings of the Articles, and historians have continued to disagree over the merits of this blueprint for a first American government. *The National Archives of the United States, published by Harry N. Abrams, Inc. Photograph by Jonathan Wallen.*

cameral legislature, without an executive branch or a separate judiciary. Democrats like Tom Paine and Samuel Adams praised the Articles' concentration of lawmaking, administrative, and judicial powers in the hands of an elected assembly, whereas conservatives like John Adams condemned the new government as "too democratical," lacking "any equilibrium" among the social classes.

Both Paine and Adams were eager to see a government that could protect the nation from tyranny. Paine, however, feared tyranny from above, from a power-grasping executive or an aristocratic upper house. Adams feared tyranny from below, from a majority of ordinary citizens who might exercise their will recklessly. Tyranny of any sort seemed unlikely from the proposed Confederation government since its powers were so limited. It had no authority to tax or to regulate trade or commerce. These powers remained with the state governments, reflecting the view of many Americans that the behavior of their local governments could be closely monitored. Because it had no taxing power, the Confederation had to depend on the states to finance its operations.

Dickinson's colleagues agreed that the state legislatures, not the voters themselves, should choose the members of the Confederation Congress. But they did not agree on how many members each state should be allotted. The question boiled down to this: should the states have equal representation or **proportional representation** based on population? Dickinson argued for a one-state, one-vote rule, but fellow Pennsylvanian Benjamin Franklin insisted that large states such as his own deserved more influence in the new government. This time, Dickinson's argument carried the day, and the Articles established that each state, large or small, was entitled to a single vote when the Confederation roll was called. The same jealous protection of state power also shaped the Confederation's amendment process. Any amendment required the unanimous consent of the states.

Arguments over financial issues were as fierce as those over representation and sovereignty. How was each state's share of the federal operating budget to be determined? Dickinson reasoned that a state's contribution should be based on its population, including inhabitants of every age, sex, and legal condition (free or unfree). This proposal brought southern political leaders to their feet in protest. Because their states had large, dependent slave populations, the burden of tax assessment would fall heavily on slave masters and other free white men. In the end, state assessments for the support of the new federal government were based on the value of land, buildings, and improvements rather than on population. The Continental Congress thus shrewdly avoided any final decision on the larger question of whether slaves were property or people.

When Congress finally submitted the Articles to the states for their approval in November of 1777, the fate of the western territories proved to be the major stumbling block to **ratification.** In his draft of the Articles, Dickinson had designated the Northwest Territory as a national domain. The states with colonial charters granting them land from the Atlantic to the Pacific Oceans protested, each claiming the exclusive right to portions of this vast region bounded by the Ohio River, the Great Lakes, and the Mississippi River (see Map 7.1). New Jersey, Maryland, and other states whose colonial charters gave them no claim to western territory disagreed. While New Jersey and others eventually gave in, Maryland delegates dug in their heels, insisting that citizens of any state ought

proportional representation   Representation in the legislature based on the population of each state.

ratification   The act of approving or confirming a proposal.

MAP 7.1 Western Land Claims After American Independence This map indicates the claims made by several of the thirteen original states to land west of the Appalachian Mountains and in the New England region. The states based their claims on the colonial charters that governed them before independence. Until this land was ceded to the federal government, new states could not be created here as they were in the Northwest Territory.

to have the right to pioneer the northwestern territories. Maryland's ultimatum—no national domain, no ratification—produced a stalemate. To resolve the problem, Virginia, which claimed the lion's share of the Northwest, agreed to cede all claims to Congress. The other states with claims followed suit and the crisis was over. In 1781 Maryland became the thirteenth and final state to ratify the Confederation government. Establishing this first national government had taken three and a half years. (The text of the Articles of Confederation is reprinted in the Documents appendix at the back of this book.)

Challenges to the Confederation

■ What problems undermined the Confederation, and what changes did they produce?

■ What was the impact of Shays's Rebellion on national politics?

■ What gains did nationalists expect from a stronger central government?

■ How did the Confederation establish relations with other nations of the world?

The members of the first Confederation Congress had barely taken their seats in 1781 when Cornwallis surrendered at Yorktown and peace negotiations began in Paris. Even the most optimistic of the Confederation leaders could see that the postwar problems of the new nation were more daunting than negotiations with French or British diplomats. The physical, psychological, and economic damage caused by the long and brutal home-front war was extensive. In New Jersey and Pennsylvania, communities bore the scars of rape and looting by the British occupying armies. In the South, where civil war had raged, a steady stream of refugees filled the cities. In Charleston, "women and children . . . in the open air round a fire without blanket or any Cloathing but what they had on" were a common sight. In many communities, livestock had vanished, and crops had been seized or ruined. In New England, a natural disaster magnified problems created by the war: insects wiped out wheat crops, worsening food shortages and the local economic depression.

After the war, economic depression spread rapidly throughout the states. Four years after the American victory, Thomas Jefferson wrote enthusiastically from France that a visit to Europe would make Americans "adore [their] country, its climate, its equality, liberty, laws, people and manners." America's unemployed sailors, debt-ridden farmers, and destitute widows and orphans would have found it difficult to share his enthusiasm.

Depression and Financial Crisis

Financial problems plagued wealthy Americans as well as poor farmers and unpaid Revolutionary War veterans. Many merchants had overextended their credit importing foreign goods after the war. Land **speculators** had also borrowed too heavily in order to grab up confiscated loyalist lands or portions of the Northwest Territory. Merchants whose fortunes depended on English markets paid a high price for an American victory that cut ties with England. Planters were hard hit when the demand for staple crops such as rice dropped dramatically after the war, and by 1786 the New England fisheries were operating at only about 80 percent of their prewar level. Not surprisingly, the English did nothing to ease the plight of their former colonists. In fact, Britain banned the sale of American farm products in the West Indies and limited the rights of American vessels to carry goods to and from Caribbean ports. These restrictions hit New England shipbuilding so hard that whole communities were impoverished.

The Confederation government did not create these economic problems, but it had little success in deal-

ing with them. In fact, it was helpless to solve its own most pressing problem—debt. To finance the war, the Continental Congress had printed more than $240 million in paper money backed by "good faith" rather than by the hard currency of gold and silver. As doubts grew that the government could ever **redeem** these continentals for hard currency, their value fell rapidly. The scornful phrase "not worth a continental" indicated popular attitudes about the government as well as its finances. Congress was also embarrassed by the substantial debts to foreign nations it was unable to repay.

In 1781 the government turned to Philadelphia shipper and merchant **Robert Morris** for advice on how to raise funds. Morris, known as a financial wizard, came up with a solution: ask the states to approve federal **tariffs,** or import taxes, on certain foreign goods. The tariffs would provide desperately needed income for the Confederation and relieve the states from having to contribute funding many could scarcely afford. For three years, beginning in 1782, Congress sought the necessary unanimous approval for a duty of 5 percent on imported goods, payable in hard currency rather than paper money. But the plan failed because both Virginia and Rhode Island said no. To add insult to injury, some states promptly passed their own tariffs on imported goods. The failure of the tariff strategy prompted one critic of the Confederation government to comment: "Thirteen wheels require a steady and powerful regulation to keep them in good order." Until Congress could act without the unanimous consent of all states, nothing could "prevent the machine from becoming useless."

The Northwest Ordinances

Still in financial crisis, the Confederation pinned its hopes for solvency on the sale of western lands in the Northwest Territory. Here at least Congress had the

---

speculator A person who buys and sells land or some other commodity in the hope of making a profit.

redeem To pay a specified sum in return for something; in this case, to make good on paper money issued by the government by exchanging it for hard currency, silver or gold.

Robert Morris Pennsylvania merchant and financial expert who advised the Continental Congress during the Revolution and served as a fundraiser for the Confederation government.

tariff A tax on imported or exported goods.

During his years of diplomatic service in Paris, Thomas Jefferson is believed to have fallen in love with the British artist Maria Cosway. In 1788, he presented her with a miniature portrait, a replica of the model John Trumbull intended to use for his painting *The Declaration of Independence.* Cosway took this likeness of Jefferson with her to Italy where it remained until 1976, when it was given to the United States as a gift of the Italian government in honor of the 200th anniversary of American independence. ©*The White House Historical Association.*

authority to act, for it could set policy for the settlement and governance of all national territories. In 1784, 1785, and 1787, a national land policy took shape in three **Northwest Ordinances.** These regulations had political significance beyond their role in raising money for the government: they guaranteed that the men and women who moved west would not be colonial dependents of the original states.

The 1784 ordinance established that five new states would be carved out of the region, each to stand on an equal footing with the older, original states. In the earliest stages of settlement, each territory would have an appointed governor. As soon as the number of eligible voters in the territory increased sufficiently, however, they could elect a representative assembly, and the territory could begin to govern itself. Once a state constitution was drafted and approved by the territory's voters, the new state could send elected representatives to the Confederation Congress. Ohio, Indiana, Illinois, Michigan, and Wisconsin each followed this path to full statehood (see Map 7.2 and the table "Ad-

mission of States into the Union" in the Tables appendix at the back of the book).

The ordinance of 1785 spelled out the terms for sale of the land. Mapmakers divided the region into five districts and subdivided each district into townships. Each township, covering 36 square miles, was broken down in a gridlike pattern of thirty-six 640-acre plots. Congress intended to auction these plots off to individual settlers rather than to land speculators, but when the original selling price of $1 per acre in hard currency proved too high for the average farm family, Congress lowered the price and lifted the ban on sales to speculators.

The ordinance of 1787 established that sixty thousand white males were needed for a territory to apply for admission as a state. Thomas Jefferson, who drafted this ordinance, took care to protect the liberties of the settlers with a bill of rights and to ban slavery north of the Ohio River. Jefferson's provisions trampled on the rights of American Indians, however, for their claims to the land were ignored in favor of white settlement.

Diplomatic Problems

The Confederation's diplomatic record was as discouraging as its financial plight. Problems with the British and the Indians arose in the West as settlers began to pour into the Northwest Territory. Although the British had agreed in the Treaty of Paris (1783) to evacuate their western forts, they refused to take any steps until the Americans honored their treaty obligations to repay their war debts and return loyalists' confiscated property. From their strongholds in the territories, the British encouraged Indian resistance by selling arms and supplies to the Shawnees, Miamis, and Delawares. These tribes, and others, denied the legitimacy of the two treaties that turned over the northwest territories to the Americans.

American claims to western lands rested on the 1784 **Treaty of Fort Stanwix** and the 1785 **Hopewell Treaties.** The former, negotiated with the remnants

Northwest Ordinances   Three laws (1784, 1785, 1787) that dealt with the sale of public lands in the Northwest Territory and established a plan for the admission of new states to the Union.

Treaty of Fort Stanwix   Treaty signed in 1784 that opened all Iroquois lands to white settlement.

Hopewell Treaties   Treaties signed by 1785 in which the Choctaws, Chickasaws, and Cherokees granted American settlement rights in the Southwest.

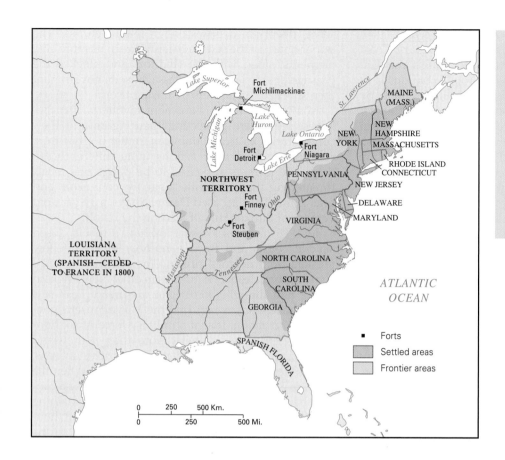

MAP 7.2 The United States in 1787 This map shows the extent of American westward settlement in 1787 and the limits placed on that settlement by French and Spanish claims west of the Mississippi and in Florida. Plans for the creation of five states in the Northwest Territory were approved by Congress in 1787, ensuring that the settlers in this region would enjoy the same political rights as the citizens of the original thirteen states.

of the Iroquois confederacy, opened all Iroquois lands to white settlement; the second, signed by Choctaw, Chickasaw, and Cherokee chiefs, granted Americans settlement rights in the Southwest. The Shawnees and their allies challenged both treaties. By what right, they asked, did those tribes speak for them? Throughout the 1780s, the Confederation and the Indians resorted to warfare rather than negotiation.

The Confederation preferred diplomacy to armed conflict when dealing with European powers. Congress sent John Adams to Great Britain, but not even this persistent and dedicated New Englander could wring any concessions from the British. The American bargaining position was weak. Commercial ties with France and Holland had not developed as rapidly after independence as some patriots had predicted, and thus American merchants remained economically dependent on England as a source of manufactured goods, and on British possessions in the Caribbean for trade. Britain had no desire to end America's economic dependency.

The Confederation had problems with allies as well as with enemies. Spain, for example, was alarmed by

American settlers pouring into the land east of the Mississippi. Almost fifty thousand Americans had already moved into what would become Kentucky and Tennessee, and thousands more were eager to farm the rich, river-fed lands of the region. The Spanish government, which controlled access to the Mississippi River and the port of New Orleans, responded by banning all American traffic on the river. The Confederation appointed **John Jay,** fresh from his success as a Paris peace commissioner, to negotiate with Spain on this and other issues, but Jay could make no headway.

The Confederation had no better luck in dealing with the **Barbary pirates.** For many years, the rulers

John Jay New York lawyer and diplomat who negotiated with Great Britain and Spain on behalf of the Confederation; he later became the first chief justice of the Supreme Court and negotiated the Jay Treaty with England.

Barbary pirates Pirates along the Barbary Coast of North Africa who attacked European and American vessels engaged in Mediterranean trade.

of Algiers, Tunisia, Tripoli, and Morocco had taken advantage of their location along the Barbary Coast of North Africa to attack European vessels engaged in Mediterranean trade. Most European nations kept this piracy under control by paying blackmail or by providing armed escorts for their merchant ships. The Barbary pirates showed no mercy to American ships, which were no longer protected by the British bribes or the royal navy. In 1785 a New England ship was captured, its cargo seized, and the crew stripped and sold into slavery. Though appalled and outraged, the Confederation Congress, with no navy and no authority to create one, could do little to ensure safe passage for American ships on the Mediterranean.

A Farmers' Revolt

From the "Wild Yankees" of Pennsylvania's Susquehanna Valley to the "Liberty-Men" of Maine, eighteenth-century backcountry settlers organized to resist speculators' claims on the land and to demand that political power remain with local communities rather than state governments. After the Revolution, these rebels used the language of republicanism to defend their protests and to justify the occasional violence that erupted in their areas. "We fought for land & liberty, & it is hard if we can't enjoy either," wrote one **squatter** in response to a land speculator's claim to his farm. "Who can have a better right to the land than we who have fought for it, subdued it & made it valuable." Farmers suffering from the postwar economic depression had a long list of complaints, including high rents, and land prices, heavy taxes, debts, burdensome legal fees, and the failure of central governments to provide protection from Indian attacks and frontier bandits. These backcountry settlers often made members of the political and economic elite uneasy just as their colonial counterparts—the Regulators and the Paxton Boys—had done. When farmers in western Massachusetts began an organized protest in 1786, this uneasiness reached crisis proportions.

The farmers of western Massachusetts were among the hardest hit by the postwar depression and the rising inflation that accompanied it. Many were deeply in debt to creditors who held mortgages on their farms and lands. In the 1780s, these farmers looked to the state government for temporary relief, hoping that it would pass **stay laws** that would temporarily suspend creditors' rights to foreclose on, or seize, lands and farm equipment. The Massachusetts assembly responded sympathetically and thus aroused the anger of merchants and other creditors who were them-

selves deeply in debt to foreign manufacturers. The upper house of the state legislature, with its more elite members, sided with the creditors and blocked the passage of stay laws. The Massachusetts government then shocked the farmers by raising taxes.

In 1786 hundreds of farmers revolted. They believed they were protecting their rights and their communities as true republicans must do, but their creditors viewed their actions quite differently. To them, the farmers appeared to be dangerous rebels threatening the state with "anarchy, confusion, and total ruin." They accused **Daniel Shays,** a 39-year-old veteran of Bunker Hill, of leading the revolt.

In 1786, farmers known as Shays's rebels closed several courts and freed a number of their fellow farmers from debtors' prison. Their actions struck a chord among desperate farmers in other New England states, and the rebellion began to spread. Fear of a widespread uprising spurred the Massachusetts government to action. It sent a military force of six hundred to Springfield, where more than a thousand farmers, most armed with pitchforks rather than guns, had gathered to close the local courthouse. When the farmers were within range, the troops let loose a cannon barrage that killed four and set the remaining men to flight. Then, on February 4, 1787, four thousand troops surprised the remaining "rebels" in the village of Petersham. Although Daniel Shays managed to escape, the farmers' revolt was over.

Shays's Rebellion revealed the temper of the times. When the government did not respond to their needs, the farmers acted as they had been encouraged to act in the prerevolutionary years. They organized and they protested—and when government still did not respond, they took up arms against what they considered to be injustice. Across the country, many Americans sympathized with these farmers. But just as many did not. Abigail Adams, whose husband, John, had been labeled an irresponsible troublemaker by loyalist opponents only a decade earlier, turned this language against the leaders of the farmers' revolt. She condemned them as "ignorant, restless, des-

---

squatter   A person who settles on unoccupied land to which he or she has no legal claim.

stay laws   Laws suspending the right of creditors to foreclose on debtors; they were designed to protect indebted farmers from losing their land.

Daniel Shays   Revolutionary War veteran considered the leader of the farmers' uprising in western Massachusetts called Shays's Rebellion.

In 1786, western Massachusetts farmers began an agrarian revolt against high taxes and mortgage foreclosures that soon spread to other New England states. Most of the leaders of the uprising, known as Shays's Rebellion, were veteran officers of the American Revolution; many had participated in the protest and resistance that preceded the war itself. The government of Massachusetts crushed the rebellion, jailing some leaders and driving Daniel Shays to seek asylum in Vermont. News of the uprising prompted elite political leaders like George Washington and Alexander Hamilton to press for a more powerful central government, able to ensure "law and order" throughout the nation. *National Portrait Gallery, Washington, D.C.; Art Resource, N.Y.*

peradoes, without conscience or principles," who were persuading a "deluded multitude to follow their standards."

The revolt stirred up fears of slave rebellions and pitched battles between debtors and creditors, haves and have-nots. Above all, it raised doubts among influential political figures about the ability of either state governments or the Confederation to preserve the rule of law. To men such as George Washington, now a planter and private citizen, Shays's Rebellion was a national tragedy, not for its participants but for the reputation of the United States. When the farmers' protest began, Washington wrote to authorities in Massachusetts urging them to act fairly but decisively. "If they have real grievances," he said, the government should acknowledge them. But if not, authorities should "employ the force of government against them at once. . . . To be more exposed to the eyes of the world, and more contemptible than we already are, is hardly possible."

The Revolt of the "Better Sort"

In important ways, the Articles of Confederation embodied the desires of the revolutionary generation for a limited central government that directed diplomacy and coordinated military defense but left the major tasks of governing to local representative governments. Yet such a government was proving to have troubling costs and trying consequences. By 1786, members of the nation's elite, or the "better sort," believed the survival of the nation was in question. Washington predicted "the worst consequences from

a half-starved, limping government, always moving upon crutches and tottering at every step." For him, for Hamilton, and for others like them who thought of themselves as **nationalists,** the solution was clear. "I do not conceive we can long exist as a nation," Washington remarked, "without having lodged somewhere a power which will pervade the whole Union in as energetic a manner as the authority of the State government extends over the several states." Here was a different form of republican government to consider.

Support for a stronger national government grew in the key states of Virginia, Massachusetts, and New York. Men of wealth and political experience urged a reform agenda that included giving the central government taxing powers, devising an easier amendment process, and providing some legal means to enforce national government policies that a state might oppose. They wanted a government that could establish stable diplomatic and trade relations with foreign countries. They also wanted a national government able to preserve their property and their peace of mind. One of the driving forces behind this appeal for reform was Alexander Hamilton.

In 1786 a group of influential Virginians called for a meeting on interstate trade restrictions that placed import taxes on goods carried from state to state. The

nationalists Americans who preferred a strong central government rather than the limited government prescribed in the Articles of Confederation.

In 1876, Thomas Pritchard Rossiter painted his *Signing of the Constitution of the United States* honoring a group of statesmen that included James Madison, Alexander Hamilton, and George Washington, who presided over the Constitutional Convention. Thomas Jefferson, absent because of his duties as ambassador to France, referred to the fifty-five delegates who crafted the Constitution as a gathering of "demigods." *Signing of the Constitution of the United States by Thomas Pritchard Rossiter, 1867. Fraunces Tavern Museum.*

Confederation Congress approved a meeting of state delegates at Annapolis, Maryland, to discuss this issue. But the meeting organizers had a second agenda: to test the waters on revising the nation's constitution. Although only a third of the states participated in the Annapolis conference, nationalists were convinced that their position had substantial support. They asked Congress to call a convention in Philadelphia so that political leaders could continue to discuss interstate commerce problems—and other aspects of government reform. Some members of Congress were reluctant, but news of Shays's Rebellion tipped the balance in favor of the convention.

Creating a New Constitution

■ What major compromises did the framers make in writing the new constitution?

■ What safeguards did James Madison see in his "checks and balances" system?

Late in May 1787, George Washington called the convention to order in Philadelphia. Before him sat delegates from eleven of the thirteen states (New Hampshire's delegates did not arrive until late July), closeted behind curtained windows and locked doors in the heat and humidity of a Philadelphia summer. These secrecy precautions stemmed, they said, from

their wish to speak frankly about the nation's political and economic problems without fear that foreign governments would use that information to their advantage. They were also looking out for thier own reputations in their home states for they quickly realized they might have to make comprises that would be unpopular with their state governments. Only Rhode Island refused to participate, accusing the convention of masquerading as a discussion of interstate trade in order to drastically revise the national government. The accusation by "Rogue's Island," as critics called the smallest state, was correct. The fifty-five prominent and prosperous men did expect to make significant changes in the structure of the government. Here was another reason to keep the deliberations secret.

Most of the men gathered in that room were lawyers, merchants, or planters—Americans of social standing though not necessarily intellectual achievement. When the absent Thomas Jefferson later referred to the convention members as "demigods," he was probably thinking of the likes of 81-year-old Benjamin Franklin, whose sparkling wit and crafty political style set him apart from his colleagues despite his advanced age; or of the articulate, brilliant Alexander Hamilton of New York, whose reputation as a financial mastermind equal to the Confederation's adviser Robert Morris was well established; or of Pennsylvania's Gouverneur Morris, who was widely admired for his intelligence as well as for his literary skills, and his fellow delegate, the logical and learned James Wilson; and finally of **James Madison,** the prim Virginia planter who turned out to be the chief architect of a new constitution. Several notable men were absent. Jefferson, author of the Declaration of Independence, was abroad serving as ambassador to France. John Adams, driving force behind the influential Massachusetts constitution of 1780, was representing the United States in the same capacity in London. And the two great propagandists of the Revolution, Samuel Adams and Thomas Paine, were also absent, for both opposed any revision of the Articles of Confederation.

Revise or Replace?

Most of the delegates were nationalists, but they did not necessarily agree on how best to proceed. Should they revise the Articles or abandon them? Eventually, Edmund Randolph of Virginia, Charles Pinckney of South Carolina, William Paterson of New Jersey, and Alexander Hamilton himself would present blueprints for the new government. But it was the Virginia planter and lawyer Edmund Randolph who first captured the convention's attention with his delegation's proposal, which effectively amended the Articles of Confederation out of existence.

Although Randolph introduced the **Virginia Plan** on the convention floor, James Madison was its guiding spirit. The 36-year-old Madison was no dashing figure. He was small, frail, charmless, and a hypochondriac. But he was highly respected as a scholar of philosophy and history and as an astute political theorist, and his long service as a member of the Virginia legislature and in the Confederation Congress gave him a practical understanding of politics and government. At the convention, Madison brought all his knowledge to bear on this question: what was the best form of government for a strong republic? He concluded, as John Adams had done early in the 1780s, that the fear of tyranny should not rule out a powerful national government. Any dangerous abuse of power could be avoided if internal checks and balances were built into the republican structure.

Madison's Virginia Plan embodied this conviction. It called for a government with three distinct branches—legislative, executive, and judicial—to replace the Confederation's Congress, which was performing all three functions. By dividing power in this way, Madison intended to ensure that no individual or group of men could wield too much authority, especially for self-interested reasons. Madison's plan also gave Congress the power to **veto** laws passed by

James Madison described himself as "feeble" and "sickly" and suffered all his life from dizzy spells and stomach disorders. But this small, shy Virginia planter won the respect of his colleagues as a brilliant political theorist during the drafting of the Constitution, and later as a genius for organizing the machinery of party politics. *Library of Congress.*

the state legislatures and the right to intervene directly if a state acted to interrupt "the harmony of the United States."

The notion of a strong government able, as Madison put it, "to control the governed" but also "obliged to control itself" was endorsed by the delegates. But they were in sharp disagreement over many specific issues in the Virginia Plan. The greatest controversy swirled around representation in the legislative branch—Congress—a controversy familiar to those who had helped draft the Articles of Confederation. Madison proposed a bicameral legislature with

James Madison Virginia planter and political theorist known as the "father of the Constitution"; he became the fourth president of the United States.

Virginia Plan Fourteen proposals by the Virginia delegation to the Constitutional Convention for creating a more powerful central government and giving states proportional representation in a bicameral legislature.

veto The power or right of one branch of government to reject the decisions of another branch.

membership in each house based on proportional representation. Large states supported the plan, for representation based on population worked to their advantage. Small states objected heatedly, calling for equal representation for each state. Small states argued that proportional representation would leave them helpless against a federal government dominated by the large ones. Small-state delegates threw their support behind a second proposal, the **New Jersey Plan,** which also called for three branches of government and gave Congress the power to tax and to control national commerce. This plan, however, preserved an equal voice and vote for every state within a unicameral legislature.

Debate over the two plans dragged on through the steamy days of a June heat wave. Tempers flared, and at times the deadlock seemed hopeless. Threats to walk out of the convention came from both sides. A compromise was needed to prevent distrust and hostility from destroying the convention. That compromise, hammered out by a special committee, was presented by Roger Sherman of Connecticut. Their **Great Compromise** used the idea of a two-house legislature in order to satisfy both sides. It proposed proportional representation in the lower house (the House of Representatives) and equal representation in the upper house (the Senate).

The Great Compromise resolved the first major controversy at the convention but opened the door to the next one. The delegates had to decide how the representatives to each house were to be elected. A compromise also settled this issue. State legislatures would select senators, and the eligible voters of each state would directly elect their state's representatives to the lower house. This formula allowed the delegates to acknowledge the sovereignty of the state governments but also to accommodate the republican commitment to popular elections in a representative government.

The delegates faced one last stumbling block over representation: which Americans were to be counted to determine a state's population? This issue remained as divisive as it had been when the Articles of Confederation were drafted. Southern delegates took care to argue that slaves, who composed as much as one-third and sometimes more of each plantation state's residents, should not be included in the population count on which a state's tax assessments were based. On the other hand, they insisted that these slaves should be included in the population count that determined a state's seats in the House of Representatives. Northern delegates protested, declaring that slaves should be considered property in both in-

stances. These delegates were motivated by self-interest rather than a desire for consistency, for if slaves were considered property, not people, the North would dominate the lower house.

A compromise that defied reason but made brilliant political sense settled this question. The **Three-Fifths Compromise** established that three-fifths of the slave population would be included in a state's critical headcount. A clause was then added guaranteeing that the slave trade would continue for a twenty-year period. Some southern leaders, especially in South Carolina, wanted this extension badly because they had lost many slaves during the Revolution. But not all slaveowners concurred. Virginia's George Mason, a slave owner himself, spoke passionately of the harm slavery did to his region. It not only prevented white immigration to the South, Mason said, but infected the moral character of the slave master. "Every master of slaves," Mason argued, "is born a petty tyrant." Slaveowners "bring the judgment of heaven upon a country," particularly one intended as a republic.

Drafting an Acceptable Document

The Three-Fifths Compromise ended weeks of debate over representation. No other issue arose to provoke such controversy, and the delegates proceeded calmly to implement the principle of checks and balances. For example, the president, or executive, was named commander in chief of the armed forces and given primary responsibility for foreign affairs. To balance these **executive powers,** Congress was given the right to declare war and to raise an army. Congress received the critical "power of the purse," but this power to tax and to spend the revenues raised by

---

New Jersey Plan   A proposal submitted by the New Jersey delegation at the Constitutional Convention for creating a government in which the states would have equal representation in a unicameral legislature.

Great Compromise   A proposal calling for a bicameral legislature with equal representation for the states in one house and proportional representation in the other.

Three-Fifths Compromise   An agreement to count three-fifths of a state's slave population for purposes of determining a state's representation in the House of Representatives.

executive powers   Powers given to the president by the Constitution.

taxation was checked in part by the president's power to veto congressional legislation. As yet another balance, Congress could override a presidential veto by the vote of a two-thirds majority. Following the same logic of distributing power, the delegates gave authority to the president to name federal court judges, but the Senate had to approve all such appointments.

Occasionally, as in the system for electing the president, the convention chose awkward or cumbersome procedures. For example, many delegates opposed direct popular election of the president. Some agreed with the elitist sentiments of George Mason, who said this "would be as unnatural . . . as it would [be] to refer a trial of colours to a blind man." Others simply doubted that the citizens of one state would be familiar enough with a candidate from a distant state to make a valid judgment. In an age of slow communication, few men besides George Washington had a truly national reputation. Should the president be chosen by state legislators who had perhaps worked in government with political leaders from outside their states? Delegates rose to object that this solution threatened too great a concentration of power in the legislators' hands. As a somewhat clumsy compromise, the delegates created the **Electoral College,** a group of special electors to be chosen by the states to vote for presidential candidates. Each state would be entitled to a number of electors equal to the number of its senators and representatives sitting in Congress, but no one serving in Congress at the time of a presidential election would be eligible to be an elector. If two presidential candidates received the same number of Electoral College votes, or if no candidate received a majority of the Electoral College votes, then the House of Representatives would choose the new president. This complex procedure honored the **discretion** of the state governments in appointing the electors but limited the power of individuals already holding office.

The long summer of conflict and compromise ended with a new plan for a national government. Would the delegates be willing to put their names to the document they had created in secrecy and by overreaching their authority? Benjamin Franklin fervently hoped so. Though sick and bedridden, Franklin was carried by friends to the convention floor, where he pleaded for unanimous support for the new government. When a weary George Washington at last declared the meetings adjourned on September 17, 1787, only a handful of delegates left without signing what the convention hoped would be the new American constitution.

Resolving the Conflict of Vision

- What were the Antifederalists' arguments against the Constitution? What were the Federalists' arguments in its favor?
- What was the outcome of the ratification process?

The framers of the Constitution called for special state **ratifying conventions** to discuss and then vote on the proposed change of government. They believed that these conventions would give citizens a more direct role in this important political decision. But the ratifying procedure also gave the framers two advantages. First, it allowed them to bypass the state legislatures, which stood to lose power under the new government and were thus likely to oppose it. Second, it allowed them to nominate their supporters and campaign for their election to the ratifying conventions. The framers added to their advantage by declaring that the approval of only nine states was necessary to establish the Constitution. Reluctantly, the Confederation Congress agreed to all these terms and procedures. By the end of September 1787, Congress had passed the proposed Constitution on to the states, triggering the next round of debates over America's political future.

The Ratification Controversy

As Alexander Hamilton boasted, "The new Constitution has in favor of its success . . . [the] very great weight of influence of the persons who framed it." Hamilton was correct. Men of wealth, political experience, and frequently great persuasive powers put their skills to the task of achieving ratification. But what Hamilton did not mention was that many revolutionary heroes and political leaders opposed the Constitution with equal intensity—most notably Patrick Henry, Samuel Adams, and George Clinton, the popular governor of New York. Boston's most effective revolutionary propagandist, **Mercy Otis Warren,** immediately

Electoral College A body of electors chosen by the states to elect the president and vice president; each state may select a number of electors equal to the number of its senators and representatives in Congress.

discretion The power or right to act according to one's own judgment.

ratifying conventions A meeting of delegates in each state to determine whether that state would ratify the Constitution.

Mercy Otis Warren Writer and historian known for her influential anti-British plays and essays during the prerevolutionary era; an active opponent of the Constitution.

took up her pen to attack the Constitution and even **canvassed** her neighbors to stand firm against what she called an assault on republican values. Thus the leadership on both sides of the issue was drawn from the political elite of the revolutionary generation.

The pro-Constitution forces won an early and important victory by clouding the language of the debate. They abandoned the label "nationalists," which drew attention to their belief in a strong central government, and chose to call themselves **Federalists,** a name originally associated with a system of strong state governments and limited national government. This shrewd tactic cheated opponents of the Constitution out of their rightful name. The pro-Constitution forces then dubbed their opponents **Antifederalists.** This label implied that their adversaries were negative thinkers, pessimists, and a group lacking a program of its own.

Although the philosophical debate over the best form of government for a republic was an important one, voters considered other, practical factors in choosing a Federalist or Antifederalist position. Voters in states with a stable or recovering economy were likely to oppose the Constitution because the Confederation system gave their states greater independent powers. Those in small, geographically or economically disadvantaged states were likely to favor a strong central government that could protect them from their competitive neighbors. Thus the small states of Delaware and Connecticut ratified the Constitution quickly, but in New York and Virginia ratification was hotly contested.

To some degree, Federalist and Antifederalist camps matched the divisions between the relatively urban, market-oriented communities of the Atlantic coast and the frontier or rural communities of the inland areas. For example, the backcountry of North and South Carolina and the less economically developed areas of Virginia saw little benefit in a stronger central government, especially one that might tax them. But coastal centers of trade and overseas commerce such as Boston, New York City, and Charleston were eager to see an aggressive and effective national policy regarding foreign and interstate trade. In these urban centers, artisans, shopkeepers, and even laborers joined forces with wealthy merchants and shippers to support the Constitution as they had once joined them to make the Revolution. No generalization can explain every political choice, of course. No economic or social group was unified under the Federalist or the Antifederalist banner. On the whole, however, it can be said that the Federalists were better organized, had more resources at their dis-

posal, and campaigned more effectively than the Antifederalists.

In the public debates, the political differences between the Federalists and Antifederalists were sharply defined. Antifederalists rejected the claim that the nation was in a "critical period," facing economic and political collapse. As one New Yorker put it: "I deny that we are in immediate danger of anarchy and commotions. Nothing but the passions of wicked and ambitious men will put us in the least danger. . . . The country is in profound peace . . . and the lives, the liberty and property of individuals is protected." Nevertheless, the Federalists were successful in portraying the moment as a crisis or turning point for the young republic—and in insisting that their plan for recovery was better than no plan at all.

The Antifederalists struck hard against the dangerous elitism they believed they saw in the Constitution. They portrayed the Federalists as a privileged, sophisticated minority, ready and able to tyrannize the people if their powerful national government were ratified. Be careful, one Massachusetts man warned, because "these lawyers, and men of learning, and moneyed men, that talk so finely and gloss over matters so smoothly, to make us poor illiterate people swallow down the pill, expect to get into Congress themselves." And New York Antifederalist Melancton Smith predicted that the proposed new government would lead inevitably to rule by a wealthy, unrepresentative minority. Smith argued with simple eloquence that members of a House of Representatives who had so much power ought to "resemble those they represent . . . and be disposed to seek their true interests." But this was impossible, Smith reasoned, when the representative body was so small and the political ambitions and financial resources of the elite were so great. The Virginia revolutionary leader Richard Henry Lee was flabbergasted that his generation would even consider ratification of the Constitution. "'Tis really astonishing," he wrote to a New York opponent in the summer of 1788, "that the same people, who have just emerged from a long and cruel

canvass A survey that is taken.

Federalists Supporters of the Constitution; they desired a strong central government.

Antifederalists Opponents of the Constitution; they believed a strong central government was a threat to American liberties and rights.

despotism Rule by a tyrant.

war in defense of liberty, should agree to fix an elective **despotism** upon themselves and posterity."

The Antifederalists' most convincing evidence of elitism and its potential for tyranny was that the Constitution lacked a bill of rights. The proposed new national Constitution contained no written guarantees of the people's right to assemble or to worship as they saw fit, and it gave no assurances of a trial by jury in civil cases or the right to bear arms. The framers believed these rights were secure because most state constitutions contained strong guarantees of these rights. But antifederalists put the question to both voters and delegates: what did this glaring omission tell Americans about the framers' respect for republican ideals? The only conclusion, Antifederalists argued, was that the Constitution was a threat to republican principles of representative government, a vehicle for elite rule, and a document unconcerned with the protection of the people's individual liberties. Its supporters, Antifederalists warned, were "crying 'wolf'" over economic and social problems in order to seize power.

The Federalist strategy was indeed to portray America in crisis. They pointed to the stagnation of the American economy, to the potential for revolt and social anarchy, and to the contempt that other nations showed toward the young republic. They also argued that the Constitution fulfilled and could preserve the republican ideals of the Revolution far better than the Articles of Confederation. Their cause was put forward most convincingly by Alexander Hamilton, James Madison, and John Jay, who entered the newspaper wars over ratification in the key state of New York. Together, they produced a series of essays known today as the *Federalist Papers.* Although these 85 essays were all signed "Publius," Hamilton wrote 51 of them, Madison 29, and Jay 5. Their common theme was the link between American prosperity and a strong central government.

The Federalist Victory

Practical politics rather than political theory seemed to influence the outcome of many of the ratifying conventions. Delaware, New Jersey, Georgia, and Connecticut—all small states—quickly approved the Constitution. In Pennsylvania, Antifederalists in the rural western regions lost control of the convention to the Federalists and thus that state also endorsed the Constitution. In the remaining states, including Massachusetts, Virginia, and New York, the two sides were more evenly matched.

Antifederalists were in the majority in the Massachusetts convention, where most of the delegates were

The unknown artist of *The Federal Procession in New York, 1788* captured the jubilant mood of Americans as they celebrated their new Constitution with parades, bonfires, and banquets. As the "Ship of State" float indicates, New Yorkers were particularly eager to acknowledge the role of their own Alexander Hamilton in launching the new government. *Library of Congress.*

small farmers from the western counties and more than twenty of them had participated in Shays's Rebellion. The Federalists' strategy was to make political deals with key delegates, winning over Antifederalists such as Samuel Adams and John Hancock, for example, with promises to demand the addition of a bill of rights to the Constitution. Class divisions, however, turned out to be critical during the convention balloting. Men of high social and economic status voted 107 to 34 for ratification. The less wealthy delegates were more divided, voting against the Constitution by a ratio of 2 to 1. At the final count, a 19-vote margin gave the Federalists a narrow victory in Massachusetts.

After Massachusetts ratified, the fight shifted to New Hampshire. Here, too, Federalists won by a small majority. Rhode Island, true to its history of opposition to strong central authority, rejected the Constitution decisively. But Maryland and South Carolina ratified it, and the tide in favor of the new government influenced the next critical vote: that of Virginia. There, Antifederalist leaders Lee, Henry, and James Monroe focused on the absence of a bill of rights in the proposed Constitution. James Madison, and George Washington

Federalist Papers   Essays written by Alexander Hamilton, John Jay, and James Madison in support of the Constitution.

directed the Federalist counterattack. In the end, the presence of Washington proved irresistible because Virginians knew that this war hero and admired colleague was certain to be the first president of the United States if the Constitution went into effect. When the vote was taken on June 25, 1788, Virginia became the tenth state to ratify the new government.

New York's battle was equally intense. Acknowledging that the absence of a bill of rights was a major political error, Federalist leaders Jay and Hamilton made a public pledge to support its inclusion. By then, however, ten states had already ratified the Constitution, and so the new government was a **fait accompli.** Realizing this, on July 26, 1788, a majority of New York delegates voted yes on ratification.

President George Washington

The election of senators and Congress members was almost complete by February 4, 1789, when presidential electors met in each state to choose the nation's first president. Although George Washington did not seek the position, he knew the nation expected him to serve. The general was among the very few in the revolutionary generation to have a national reputation. He was hailed as the hero of the Revolution, and he looked and acted the part of the dignified, virtuous patriot. Washington became president by a unanimous vote of the Electoral College. For regional balance, New Englander John Adams was chosen vice president.

In April 1789, as Washington made his way from Virginia to his inauguration in New York City, the temporary national capital, Americans thronged to greet him with parades, sharply dressed military escorts, and choruses of church bells and cannon fire. Near Trenton, New Jersey, the scene of his first victory in the Revolutionary War, he passed through a triumphal arch 20 feet high, supported by thirteen pillars, and inscribed in gold with the date of the Battle of Trenton. As his barge took him across the Hudson River, private boats sailed alongside, their passengers singing songs composed in his honor. Thousands of supporters gathered to see him take the oath of office. Yet amid the celebration, Washington and his closest advisers knew the future was uncharted and uncertain. "We are in a wilderness," Madison observed, "without a single footstep to guide us."

Washington agreed. The new president understood that he symbolized a national experiment in government and that friends and critics of the United States would be closely watching his behavior in office. Since he was the first to hold the presidency, his every action had the potential to become a ritual and to set

George Washington was a favorite subject of portrait artists in both the 18th and 19th centuries. In 1789, soon after Washington's first inauguration, the artist John Ramage painted this miniature for Mrs. Washington. Despite the fact that Ramage had been a loyalist during the Revolutionary War, by the 1780s his miniatures were in great demand during the early national period. The portrait of Washington is only 2⅛ inches high, but the case that holds it also holds strands of the president's hair. *Christies Images, Inc.*

a precedent for those who followed. "Few . . . can realize," he wrote, "the difficult and delicate part which a man in my situation has to act. . . . I walk on untrodden ground."

Washington proceeded with caution and deliberation. He labored carefully over each of his selections to the almost one thousand federal offices waiting to be filled. He took particular care in choosing the men to head four executive departments created with approval from Congress. Naming his **protégé** Alexander Hamilton to the Treasury Department was probably Washington's easiest decision. He asked the Massachusetts military strategist Henry Knox to head the War Department and fellow Virginian Edmund Randolph to serve as attorney general. Washington chose

fait accompli An accomplished deed or fact that cannot be reversed or undone.

protégé An individual whose welfare or career is promoted by an influential person.

another Virginian, Thomas Jefferson, to be secretary of state. Over time, the president established a pattern of meeting with this **cabinet** of advisers on a regular basis to discuss policy matters. Together, they made major decisions and, as Washington expected, expressed serious disagreements that exposed him to differing viewpoints on policy.

Competing Visions Re-emerge

■ How did Alexander Hamilton's expectations for the new nation differ from those of Thomas Jefferson? What were the consequences of this conflict of vision?

■ How did the French Revolution affect Washington's diplomatic policy?

A remarkable but, as it turned out, short-lived spirit of unity marked the early days of Washington's administration. Federalists had won the overwhelming majority of seats in the new Congress, and this success enabled them to work quickly and efficiently on matters they felt had priority. But the unity was fragile. By 1792, sectional divisions were deepening, and as the government debated foreign policy and domestic affairs, two distinct groups, voicing serious differences of opinion, began to form. Alexander Hamilton's vision for America guided one group. At the heart of the other was the vision of Thomas Jefferson.

Unity's Achievements

In addition to creating the four executive departments that became the cabinet, the First Congress passed the **Judiciary Act of 1789.** This act established a Supreme Court, thirteen district courts, and three circuit courts. It also empowered the Supreme Court to review the decisions of state courts and to nullify any state laws that violated either the Constitution or any treaty made by the federal government. President Washington chose John Jay to serve as first chief justice of the Supreme Court.

The First Congress also managed to break the stalemate on the tariff issue. Southern leaders had opposed a tariff because a tax on imports added to the cost of the consumer goods that southern agriculturalists had to purchase. Northeastern leaders had favored tariff legislation because such a tax, by making foreign goods more expensive, would benefit their region's merchants and manufacturers. During Washington's first term, southerner James Madison took the lead in conducting the delicate negotiations over tariffs. The result was an import tax on certain items such as rum, cocoa, and coffee.

For several years, New York City served as the capital of the new United States. But plans were soon laid for a new capital city to be created on the banks of the Potomac River, on land donated by Virginia and Maryland. This new city was to be named Washington, in honor of the hero of the Revolution and the first president of the new nation. Although elaborate plans for elegant, tree-lined streets such as this one were drawn up, for many years visitors and residents alike described Washington, D.C., as a dismal town of muddy streets and dreadful climate. *Library of Congress.*

Madison also prodded Congress to draft the promised **Bill of Rights.** Although more than two hundred suggestions were submitted to Congress, Madison honed them down to twelve. On December 15, 1791, ten of these were added to the Constitution as the Bill of Rights, and soon after, both Rhode Island and North Carolina ratified the Constitution and joined the union. Eight of these original constitutional amendments spelled out the government's commitment to

cabinet   A body of officials appointed by the president to run the executive departments of the government and to act as the president's advisers.

Judiciary Act of 1789   Law establishing the Supreme Court and the lower federal courts; it gave the Supreme Court the right to review state laws and state court decisions to determine their constitutionality.

Bill of Rights   The first ten amendments to the U.S. Constitution, added in 1791 to protect certain basic rights of American citizens.

protect individual **civil liberties.** They guaranteed that the new national government could not limit free speech, interfere with religious worship, deny U.S. citizens the right to keep or bear arms, force the quartering of troops in private homes, or allow homes to be searched without proper search warrants. The amendments prohibited the government from requiring persons accused of crimes to testify against themselves, nor could it deny citizens the right to a trial by jury. The government also could not deprive a citizen of life, liberty, or property without "due process of law," or impose excessive bail, or administer "cruel and unusual punishments." The Ninth Amendment made clear that the inclusion of these protections and rights did not mean that others were excluded. The Tenth Amendment stated that any powers not given to the federal government or denied to the states belonged solely to the states or the people.

Condensed into these ten amendments was a rich history of struggle for individual rights in the face of abusive power. It was a history that recalled the experiences of colonists protesting the illegal search and seizure of cargoes in Boston harbor, the British government's insistence on quartering troops in New York homes, and the religious persecution of men and women who dissented from established churches both in England and in the colonies.

Hamilton and Jefferson's Differences

Alexander Hamilton was consumed by a bold dream: to transform agricultural America into a manufacturing society that rivaled Great Britain. His blueprint for achieving this goal called for tariffs designed to protect developing American industry rather than simply raise revenue. It also called for **subsidies,** or government financial support, for new enterprises and incentives to support new industries. And it relied on strong economic and diplomatic ties with the mercantile interests of England. Hamilton's vision had great appeal in the Northeast but few advocates in the southern states. Indeed, his ambitious development program seemed to confirm Patrick Henry's worst fears: that the new government would produce "a system which I have ever dreaded—subserviency of Southern to Northern Interests."

Virginia planters Thomas Jefferson and James Madison offered a different vision of the new nation: a prosperous, agrarian society. Instead of government tariffs designed to encourage American manufacturing, they advocated a national policy of **free trade** to keep consumer prices low. The agrarian view did not entirely rule out commerce and industry in the United States. As long as commercial society remained "a handmaiden to agriculture," Jefferson saw no danger that citizens would be exploited or lured into the love of luxury that destroyed republics. In the same fashion, Hamilton was content to see agriculture thrive as long as it did not drain away the scarce resources of the national government or stand in the way of commercial or industrial growth. Hamilton and men of similar vision around him spoke of themselves as true **Federalists.** Those who agreed with Jefferson and Madison identified themselves as **Republicans.**

The emergence of two political camps was certain to trouble even the men who played a role in creating them. The revolutionary generation believed that **factions,** or special-interest parties, were responsible for the corruption of English politics. John Adams seemed to speak for all these political leaders when he declared: "A division of the republic into two great parties . . . is to be dreaded as the greatest political evil." Yet as President Washington was quick to see, **sectionalism** fueled the growth of just such a division.

Hamilton's Economic Plan

As secretary of the Treasury, Alexander Hamilton was expected to seek solutions to the nation's **fiscal** prob-

civil liberties Fundamental individual rights such as freedom of speech and religion, protected by law against interference from the government.

subsidy Financial assistance that a government grants to an enterprise considered to be in the public interest.

free trade Trade between nations without any protective tariffs.

Federalists Political group formed during Washington's first administration; led by Alexander Hamilton, they favored an active role for government in encouraging commercial and manufacturing growth.

Republicans Political group formed during Washington's first administration; led by Thomas Jefferson and James Madison, they favored limited government involvement in encouraging manufacturing and the continued dominance of agriculture in the national economy.

faction A political group with shared opinions or interests.

sectionalism Excessive concern for local or regional interests.

fiscal Relating to finances.

lems, particularly the foreign and domestic debts hanging over America's head. His proposals were the source of much of the conflict that divided Congress in the early 1790s.

In January 1790 Hamilton submitted a *Report on Public Credit* to the Congress. In it, he argued that the public debt fell into three categories, each requiring attention: (1) foreign debt, owed primarily to France; (2) state debts, incurred by the individual states to finance their war efforts; and (3) a national debt in the form of government securities (the notorious paper continentals) that had been issued to help finance the war. To establish credit, and thus to be able to borrow money and attract investors in American enterprises, Hamilton declared that the nation had to make good on all it owed.

Hamilton proposed that the federal government assume responsibility for the repayment of all three categories of debt. He insisted the continentals be redeemed for the amount shown on the certificate, regardless of what their current value might be. And he proposed that *current* holders of continentals should receive that payment regardless of how or when they had acquired them. These recommendations, and the political agenda for economic growth they revealed, raised furious debate within Congress.

Before Hamilton's *Report on Public Credit*, James Madison had been the voice of unity in Congress. Now, Madison leapt to his feet to protest the treasury secretary's plan. The government's debt, both financial and moral, Madison argued, was not to the current creditors holding the continentals but to the *original* holders. Many of the original holders were ordinary citizens and Continental soldiers who had sold these certificates to speculators at a tremendous loss during the postwar depression. The state treasuries of New York, Pennsylvania, and Maryland were three of the largest speculators, buying up great quantities of these bonds when they were disgracefully cheap. If Hamilton's plan were adopted, Madison protested, these speculators, rather than the nation's true patriots, would reap enormous unfair profits.

Madison's emotional opposition to Hamilton's debt program came from a deep distrust of certain ways of attaining wealth. Although enslaved men and women performed the work done on Madison's plantation, the Virginia planter believed that wealth acquired by productive labor was moral whereas wealth gained by the manipulation of money was corrupt. Hamilton simply sidestepped the moral issue by explaining the difficulty of identifying and locating the original holders of the continentals. Whatever the ethical merits of Madison's argument, Hamilton

said, his solution was impractical. Congress supported Hamilton, but the vote reflected the growing rift between regions.

Madison was far from silenced, however. Next, he led the opposition to Hamilton's proposal that the federal government assume, or take over, the states' debts. Here, Hamilton's motives were quite transparent: as a fierce nationalist, he wished to concentrate both political and economic power in the federal government at the expense of the states. He knew that creditors, who included America's wealthiest citizens, would take a particular interest in the welfare and success of any government that owed them money. By concentrating the debt in the federal government, Hamilton intended to give America's elite a clear stake in America's success. Hamilton also knew that a sizable debt provided a compelling reason for raising revenue. By assuming the state debts, the federal government could undercut state governments' need for new taxes—and justify its own.

Congress saw the obvious **inequities** of the plan. Members from states such as Maryland and Virginia quickly reminded Congress that their governments had paid all their war debts during the 1780s. If the national government assumed state debts and raised taxes to repay them, responsible citizens of Maryland and Virginia would be taxed for the failure of Massachusetts or New York to honor their obligations. Although the Senate approved the assumption of state debts, members of the House strongly objected and deferred a decision. Hamilton, realizing he faced defeat, moved to break the deadlock by a behind-the-scenes compromise with Madison and his ally Jefferson. Hamilton was confident he held a valuable bargaining chip: the location of the national capital.

In 1789 the new government had made New York its temporary home until Congress could settle on a permanent site. The choice turned out to be politically delicate because of regional jealousy and competition. Hamilton was willing to put the capital right in Jefferson's backyard in exchange for the Virginian's support on assumption of state debts. The deal clearly appealed to southern regional pride, but Madison and Jefferson had deeper motives for agreeing to it. Like many good Republicans, they believed it was important to monitor the deliberations of a powerful government. But in an age of slow land travel and slower communication, it was difficult to keep watch from a distance. New Englanders also knew that "watching"

---

inequities   Unfair circumstances or proceedings.

meant the chance to influence the government. "The climate of the Potomac," one New Englander quipped, would prove unhealthy, if not deadly, to "northern constitutions." Nevertheless, by trading away the capital location, Hamilton ensured the success of his assumption plan.

The year 1791 began with another controversial proposal from the secretary of the Treasury. This time, Hamilton outlined a plan for chartering a national bank. The bank, modeled on the Bank of England, would serve as fiscal agent for the federal government, although it would not be an exclusively public institution. Instead, the bank would be funded by both the government and private sources in a partnership that fit nicely with Hamilton's plan to tie national prosperity to the interests of private wealth.

Once again, James Madison led the opposition. He argued that the government had neither the express right nor the **implied power** to create a national institution such as the bank. The majority of Congress did not agree, but Madison's argument that the bank was unconstitutional did cause President Washington to hesitate over signing the congressional bill into law. As usual, Washington decided to consult advisers on the matter. He asked both Secretary of State Jefferson and the Treasury head Hamilton to set down their views.

Like Madison, Jefferson was at that time a **strict constructionist** in his interpretation of the Constitution. On February 15, 1791, he wrote of the dangers of interpreting the government's powers broadly. "To take a single step beyond the boundaries . . . specifically drawn around the powers of Congress," he warned, "is to take possession of a boundless field of power." A **broad constructionist,** Hamilton saw no such danger in the bank. He based his argument on Article 1, Section 8, of the Constitution, which granted Congress the right to "make all Laws which shall be necessary and proper" to exercise its legitimate powers. As he put it on February 23: "The powers contained in a constitution . . . ought to be construed liberally in advancement of the public good." And because it seemed obvious that "a bank has a natural relation to the power of collecting taxes," Hamilton believed there could be no reasonable constitutional argument against it. Hamilton's argument persuaded the president, and the bank was chartered on February 25, 1791. By July 4, 1791, stock in the newly established Bank of the United States was offered for sale.

Hamilton's assumption strategy and the creation of a bank were just preliminaries to the ambitious economic development program that he put forward in 1792 in his *Report on Manufactures.* But this time his package of policies for aggressively industrializing the nation—including protective tariffs and government incentives and subsidies—was too extreme to win support in Congress. Still, the Bank of the United States, which provided much-needed working **capital** for new commercial and manufacturing enterprises, and the establishment of sound national credit, which attracted foreign capital to the new nation, had gone far toward moving the economy in the direction of Hamilton's vision.

Foreign Affairs and Deepening Divisions

In 1789, just as George Washington became the first president of the United States, the **French Revolution** began. And in the years in which Hamilton was advancing his economic programs, that revolution stirred new controversy within American politics.

The first signs of serious resistance to the French monarchy came when **Louis XVI,** king of France, asked for new taxes. Reformers within the French parliament, or Estates General, refused, choosing instead to reduce the king's power and create a constitutional monarchy. Outside the halls of government, crowds took to the streets in the name of broad social reform. On July 14, 1789, Parisian radicals stormed the Bastille prison, a symbol of royal oppression, tear-

implied power Power that is not specifically granted to the government by the Constitution but can be viewed as necessary to carry out the governing duties listed in the Constitution.

strict constructionist A person who believes the government has only the powers specifically named in the Constitution.

broad constructionist A person who believes the government can exercise any implied powers that are in keeping with the spirit of the Constitution.

capital Money needed to start or sustain a commercial enterprise.

French Revolution Political rebellion against the French monarchy and aristocratic privileges; it began in 1789 and ended in 1799.

Louis XVI The king of France (r. 1774–1792) when the French Revolution began; he and his wife, Marie Antoinette, were executed in 1793 by the revolutionary government.

Edmund Genêt came to the United States in 1793 on a mission to recruit Americans to fight for France in that nation's war against Great Britain. Traveling from Charleston to New York, the charming, persuasive Genêt roused considerable popular support—and the wrath of President George Washington. The president viewed Genêt's unauthorized activities as an insult to American sovereignty and a threat to American foreign policy. At Washington's insistence, the French government issued a recall of "Citizen Genêt," but when news came that a warrant for Genêt's arrest had also been issued, Washington granted Genêt political asylum in America. The lively Frenchman settled in New York and married a daughter of Governor George Clinton. *Collection of the Albany Institute of History and Art. Bequest of George Genêt.*

ing down its walls and liberating its political prisoners. The crowds filling the Paris streets owed some of their political rhetoric and ideals to the American Revolution. The marquis de Lafayette acknowledged this debt when he sent his old friend President Washington the key to the Bastille. Like most Americans in these early days of the French Revolution, Washington was pleased to be identified with this new struggle for the "rights of man." Briefly, enthusiasm for the French Revolution united Hamilton's Federalists and Jefferson's Republicans.

By 1793, however, American public opinion began to divide sharply on the French Revolution. Popular support faded when the revolution's most radical party, the Jacobins, imprisoned and then executed the king and his wife. Many shocked Americans de-

nounced the revolution completely when the Jacobins, in their **Reign of Terror** against any who opposed their policies, began marching moderate French reformers as well as members of the nobility to the guillotine to be beheaded.

Soon after eliminating their revolutionary opponents, the Jacobin government vowed to bring "liberty, equality, and brotherhood" to the peoples of Europe, by force if necessary. This campaign to spread the revolution led France into war with England, Spain, Austria, and **Prussia.** At the very least, France expected the Americans to honor the terms of the treaty of 1778, which bound the United States to protect French possessions in the West Indies from enemy attack. The enemy most likely to strike was England, a fact that suddenly made a second war between England and the United States a possibility.

American opinion on a second war with England was contradictory and complex. George Blake, a Boston lawyer and political figure, reminded his fellow citizens, "The [French] cause is half our own, and does not our policy and our honor urge us to most forcibly cherish it?" But others who continued to support the French Revolution, including Thomas Jefferson, did not want the United States to become embroiled in a European war. Many who condemned the French Revolution nevertheless were eager to use any excuse to attack the British, who still were occupying forts in the Northwest and restricting American trade in the Caribbean. Political leaders such as Hamilton who were working toward better relations with England were appalled not only by the French assault on other nations but also by the prospect of American involvement in it. While Americans struggled with these contradictory views, the French plotted to mobilize American support directly.

In 1793 the new French republic sent a diplomatic minister to the United States. When Citizen **Edmund Genêt** arrived in Charleston, he wasted no time on formal matters such as presenting his credentials as

Reign of Terror   The period from 1793 to 1794 in the French Revolution when thousands of people were executed as enemies of the state.

Prussia   A northern European state that became the basis for the German Empire in the late nineteenth century.

Edmund Genêt   Diplomat sent by the French government to bring the United States into France's war with Britain and Spain.

an official representative from France to either the president or the secretary of state. Instead, he immediately launched a campaign to recruit Americans to the war effort. By all accounts, Genêt was charming, affable, and in the words of one observer, so humorous that he could "laugh us into the war." President Washington, however, was not amused. Genêt's total disregard for formal procedures infuriated Washington, who was undecided about whether to officially recognize the French minister. Genêt's bold attempts to provoke incidents between the United States and Spain stunned Hamilton. Even Thomas Jefferson grew uncomfortable when the Frenchman used the port of Philadelphia to transform a captured British ship into a French privateer!

On April 22, 1793, Washington decided to act. Publicly, the president issued a proclamation that declared American **neutrality** without actually using the term. While allowing Washington to avoid a formal **repudiation** of America's treaty with France, the proclamation made clear that the United States would give no military support to the French. Privately, Washington asked the French government to recall Genêt.

The Genêt affair had domestic as well as diplomatic repercussions. For the first time, George Washington came under public attack. A Republican newspaper whose editor was employed by Jefferson in the State Department questioned the president's integrity in refusing to honor the Franco-American treaty. Washington was furious with this assault on his character. Federalist newspapers struck back, insisting that Jefferson and his followers had actively encouraged the outrageous behavior of Genêt, and Federalists issued resolutions condemning Genêt. By the end of 1793, Jefferson had resigned from Washington's government, more convinced than ever that Hamilton and his supporters posed a serious threat to the survival of the American republic.

More Domestic Disturbances

Hamilton's Federalists agreed that the republic was in danger—from Jefferson's Republicans. By Washington's second term (he was reelected in 1792), both political groups were trying to rouse popular sentiment for their programs and policies and against those of their opponents. Just as in the prerevolutionary years, these appeals to popular opinion broadened participation in the debate over the future of the nation. Ordinary citizens did not always wait until their political leaders solicited their views, however. In the wake of the French Revolution and British in-terference in the West and on the seas, organizations rose up to make demands on the government. The most troubling of these to President Washington were the **Democratic-Republican societies.**

Between 1793 and 1794, thirty-five Democratic-Republican societies were created. Made up primarily of craftsmen and men of the "lower orders," these pro-French political groups also had their share of professional men, merchants, and planters. In Philadelphia, for example, noted scientist and inventor David Rittenhouse and Alexander Dallas, secretary to the governor of Pennsylvania, were society members. In Kentucky, which had split from Virginia in 1792, local elites organized their own society, separate from the one made up of western farmers. No matter what the background of the membership, these societies shared a common agenda: to serve as a platform for expressing the public's will. They insisted that political officeholders were "the agents of the people," not their leaders, and thus should act as the people wished.

In 1794 many western farmers were dismayed over what they considered the government's indifference toward the people. Kentucky settlers fretted about the navigation of the Mississippi, while Pennsylvania and Carolina farmers resented a new federal **excise** tax on whiskey. Although the Democratic-Republican societies denied an active role in spurring a new farmers' revolt against the government, a belief that the government ought to respond to its citizens' demands did seem to motivate Pennsylvania, Carolina, and Kentucky farmers to tar and feather **excise men,** burn the barns of tax supporters, and intimidate county officials. The most determined and organized resistance came from Pennsylvania, where, in July 1794, a crowd ransacked and burned the home of the federal excise inspector and then threatened to march on Pittsburgh if the tax on whiskey were not repealed.

---

neutrality   The policy of treating both sides in a conflict the same way and thus favoring neither.

repudiation   The act of rejecting the validity or the authority of something.

Democratic-Republican societies   Political organizations formed in 1793 and 1794 to demand greater responsiveness by the state and federal governments to the needs of the citizens.

excise   A tax on the production, sale, or consumption of a commodity or on the use of a service within a country.

excise men   Men who collected taxes on an article of trade or sale.

President Washington, haunted by the memory of Shays's Rebellion and worried that the radical spirit of the French Revolution was spreading throughout America, determined to crush this **Whiskey Rebellion** firmly. Calling up fifteen thousand militiamen, the president marched into the countryside to do battle with a few hundred citizens armed with rifles and pitchforks. In the face of such an overwhelming military force, the whiskey rebels abruptly dispersed.

Washington publicly laid the blame for the western insurrection on the Democratic-Republican societies. Federalists in Congress rushed to propose a resolution condemning those groups. Fisher Ames, an ardent Massachusetts Federalist, delivered an impassioned condemnation of the societies, accusing them of spreading "jealousies, suspicions, and accusations" against the government. They had, Ames declared, "arrogantly pretended sometimes to be the people and sometimes the [people's] guardians, the champions of the people." Instead, he said, they represented no one but themselves.

The Jeffersonians, generally believed to be sympathetic to the societies, knew it would be politically damaging to defend them in the aftermath of the Whiskey Rebellion. Instead, they worked to see a more moderate expression of disapproval emerge from Congress.

By 1796, the Democratic-Republican organizations had vanished from the American political scene. The president's public condemnation and Congress's censure undoubtedly damaged them. But improvements on the western borders also diminished the farmers' interest in protest organizations. In October 1795, Carolina planter Thomas Pinckney won the concession from Spain that Jay had been unable to obtain in earlier negotiations: free navigation of the Mississippi River. Pinckney's **Treaty of San Lorenzo** not only gave western farmers an outlet to ocean trade through the port of New Orleans but also ensured that Indian attacks would not be launched from Spanish-held territories.

Jay's Treaty

During Washington's second administration, the diplomatic crisis continued to worsen. England resented America's claim to neutrality, believing it helped France. The British, therefore, ignored American claims that "free ships made free goods" and began to seize American vessels trading with the French Caribbean islands. These seizures prompted new calls for war with Great Britain.

Anti-British emotion ran even higher when the governor of Canada actively encouraged Indian resistance to American settlement in the Northwest. Washington and the general public considered Indian relations dismal enough without such meddling, especially since efforts to crush the Miamis of Ohio had recently ended in two embarrassing American defeats. In February 1794, as General Anthony Wayne headed west for a third attempt against the Miamis, the Canadian governor's fiery remarks were particularly disturbing.

Jefferson's departure left little anti-British sentiment in the cabinet. But it remained strong in the Congress, where the House of Representatives considered restricting trade with England. Outside the government, war hysteria showed itself as mobs attacked English seamen and tarred and feathered Americans expressing pro-British views. What would Washington do?

Early in 1794, the president sent Chief Justice John Jay to England as his special **envoy.** Jay's mission was to produce a compromise that would prevent war between the two nations. Jay, however, was pessimistic. Britain wanted to avoid war with the United States, but what would British diplomats concede to his weak nation?

Jay's negotiations did resolve some old nagging issues. In the treaty that emerged, Britain agreed to evacuate the western forts although it did not promise to end support for Indian resistance to American western settlement. Britain also granted some small trade favors to America in the West Indies. For its part, the United States agreed to see that all prewar debts owed to British merchants were at last paid. Jay, a committed abolitionist, did not press for any provision compensating slaveholders for slaves lost during the Revolution. In the end, Jay knew he had given up more than he gained: he had abandoned America's demand for freedom of the seas and acknowledged

Whiskey Rebellion   A protest by grain farmers against the 1794 federal tax on whiskey; militia forces led by President Washington put down this Pennsylvania uprising.

Treaty of San Lorenzo   Treaty between the United States and Spain, negotiated in 1795 by Thomas Pinckney; Spain granted the United States the right to navigate the Mississippi River and use the port of New Orleans as an outlet to the sea.

envoy   A government representative charged with a special diplomatic mission.

In 1794, the new federal government passed an excise tax on whiskey made from surplus American grains. Farmers in western Pennsylvania rose up in protest against what they considered an unfair assault on their livelihood. Using tactics straight out of the pre–Revolutionary War era, including tarring and feathering the "revenooer" assigned to collect the taxes, the "Whiskey Rebels" challenged the federal government's authority. President Washington met this challenge by assembling an army of almost thirteen thousand men to put down the Whiskey Rebellion. Critics declared the president's response excessive. Do you agree? *Library of Congress.*

the British navy's right to remove French property from any neutral ship.

Jay's Treaty did little to enhance John Jay's reputation or popularity. After reading it, fellow New Yorker Robert R. Livingston said bluntly: "Mr. Jay has sacrificed the essential interests of this country." In Congress, judgments on the treaty were openly **partisan.** Federalists credited Jay's Treaty with preserving the peace, but Republicans condemned it as an embarrassment and a betrayal of France. Worried that the angry debate over ratification would fan popular outrage, the president banned public discussion of the treaty. Republican congressmen, however, leaked accounts to the press. Once again, the president came under attack, and Kentucky settlers threatened rebellion, warning Washington that if he signed Jay's Treaty, "western America is gone forever—lost to the Union." The treaty finally squeaked through the Senate in the spring of 1795 with only two southern senators supporting ratification. The House debate on appropriations for the treaty was equally bitter and prolonged. In the end, however, Congress endorsed Jay's handiwork. Despite the criticism, Jay knew he had accomplished his mission, for American neutrality in the European war continued.

Jay's negotiations with England damaged the prestige and authority of Washington's administration. The president did far better, however, in military and diplomatic affairs in the West. In August 1794, Anthony Wayne's army defeated the northwestern Indians at the **Battle of Fallen Timbers.** Wayne then lived up to his reputation as "Mad Anthony" by rampaging through enemy villages, destroying all that he could. These terror tactics helped produce the **Treaty of Greenville** in August 1795. By this treaty, the Indi-

Jay's Treaty Controversial 1794 treaty negotiated between the United States and Great Britain by John Jay to ensure American neutrality in the French and English war.

partisan Taking a strong position on an issue out of loyalty to a political group or leader.

Battle of Fallen Timbers 1794 battle in which Kentucky riflemen defeated Indians of several tribes, helping to end Indian resistance in the Northwest.

Treaty of Greenville 1795 treaty in which the United States agreed to pay northwestern Indians about $10,000 for the land that later became the state of Ohio.

ans ceded most of the land that later became the state of Ohio. These victories, combined with the auspicious terms of Pinckney's Treaty of San Lorenzo, won praise for the troubled president.

Washington's Farewell

The bitter political fight over Jay's Treaty, combined with the steady and nagging criticism of his policies in the press and the hardening of party lines between Federalists and Republicans, helped George Washington make an important decision: he would not seek a third term as president. Instead, in 1796 he would return to his beloved Virginia home, Mount Vernon, and resume the life of a gentleman planter.

When Washington retired, he left behind a nation very different from the one whose independence he had helped win and whose survival he had helped secure. The postwar economic depression was over, and the war raging in Europe had produced a steadily rising demand for American foodstuffs. More fundamentally, in the fifteen years since the Revolution, the U.S. economy had moved decisively in the direction that Alexander Hamilton had envisioned. The values and expectations of a **market economy**—with its stress on maximizing profit and the pursuit of individual economic interests—had captured the imagination and shaped the actions of many white Americans. Hamilton's policies as secretary of the treasury had both reflected and advanced a growing interest in the expansion of trade, the growth of markets, and the development of American manufacturing and industry. In its political life, the republic had been reorganized and the relationships between the states and the central government redefined. The new Constitution granted greater diplomatic and commercial powers to the federal government but protected individual citizens through the Bill of Rights. America's political leaders, though convinced that factions were dangerous to the survival of the republic, had nevertheless created and begun to work within an evolving party system.

In his Farewell Address to the public, Washington expressed his thoughts on many of these changes. Although Jefferson had believed the president was a Federalist partisan, Washington spoke with feeling against parties in a republic, urging the nation to return to nonpartisan cooperation. Washington also warned

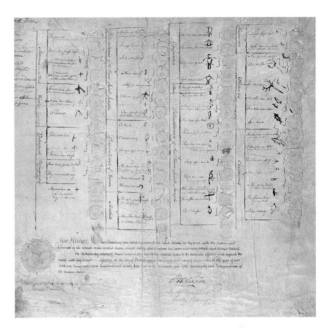

Independence sparked renewed westward migration by land-hungry Americans. The federal government took steps to legitimate these incursions into Indian homelands by persuading selected chiefs and warriors of the Northwest to cede all rights to vast tracts of this Ohio Valley land. The document above provides a sample of the eleven hundred signatures obtained in the Greenville Treaty of 1795, a treaty that ceded almost two-thirds of present-day Ohio and portions of Indiana. Many tribes protested such treaties on the grounds that the signers were not legitimate spokesmen for their people. *Library of Congress.*

America and its new leaders not to "interweave our destiny with any part of Europe" or "entangle our peace and prosperity in the toils of European ambition." An honorable country must "observe good faith and justice toward all nations," said the aging Virginian, but Americans must not let any alliance develop that draws the nation into a foreign war. The final ingredient in Washington's formula for America's success and its "permanent felicity" was the continuing virtue of its people.

market economy   An economy in which production of goods is geared to sale or profit.

Individual Voices

Examining a Primary Source

Alexander Hamilton Envisions a Prospering America

Alexander Hamilton made no effort to hide his grand vision for the new nation, even though many American leaders strongly opposed him. He had been an early and persistent advocate of a strong central government, and once it was created, he immediately proposed that it play an active role in developing the nation's economy. Hamilton's success in establishing a national bank and in funding the national debt led him to suggest an ambitious plan for government encouragement of manufacturing and industry. In his *Report on Manufactures,* which he submitted to Congress in 1791, Hamilton made a persuasive argument for the benefits of rapid economic growth in the manufacturing sector. Opposition to the report was immediate and effective, and this time, political leaders who shared Jefferson's agrarian vision for America managed to deal a crushing defeat to Hamilton. In fact, Congress refused to act on the Treasury secretary's suggestions.

■ Hamilton was well aware that the need for the national government to support manufacturing was still disputed. Why do you think he begins with the claim that most people now support this type of government involvement in the economy?

■ What arguments do you think Jefferson or Madison would use to defend the superiority of agriculture over manufacturing or commerce?

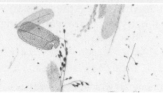

■ What were some of the "embarrassments" suffered by Americans during the war?

. . . The expediency of encouraging manufactures in the United States, which was not long since deemed very questionable, appears at this time to be pretty generally admitted. . . . ■ *It ought readily to be conceded that the cultivation of the earth—as the primary and most certain source of national supply—as the immediate and chief source of subsistence to man . . . as including a state most favourable to the freedom and independence of the human mind . . . has intrinsically a strong claim to pre-eminence over every other kind of industry.*

But, that it has a title to any thing like an exclusive predilection, in any country, ought to be admitted with great caution. That it is more productive than every other branch of Industry requires more evidence than has yet been given in support of that position. . . . ■ *To affirm, that the labour of the Manufacturer is unproductive, because he consumes as much of the produce of the land, as he adds value to the raw materials which he manufactures, is not better founded, than it would be to affirm, that the labour of the farmer, which furnishes materials to the manufacturer is unproductive, because he consumes an equal value of manufactured articles. Each furnishes a certain portion of the produce of his labor to the other. . . .*

Not only the wealth, but the independence and security of a Country, appear to be materially connected with the prosperity of manufactures. Every nation, with a view to those great objects, ought to endeavor to possess within itself all the essentials of national supply. These comprise the means of Subsistence, habitation, clothing, and defense.

The possession of these is necessary to the perfection of the body politic; to the safety as well as to the welfare of the society . . . the extreme embarrassments of the United States during the late War, from an incapacity of supplying themselves, are still matters of keen recollection. . . . ■

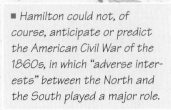

■ Hamilton could not, of course, anticipate or predict the American Civil War of the 1860s, in which "adverse interests" between the North and the South played a major role.

. . . It is not uncommon to meet with an opinion that though the promoting of manufactures may be the interest of a part of the Union, it is contrary to that of another part. The Northern & Southern regions are sometimes represented as having adverse interests in this respect. Those are called Manufacturing, these Agricultural states; and a species of opposition is imagined to exist between the Manufacturing and Agricultural interests. This idea . . . is the common error of the early periods of every country; but experience gradually dissipates it. . . . ■

Summary

After independence was declared, Americans faced the challenge of creating a new nation out of thirteen distinct states. Faced with enormous debt and still surrounded by real and potential enemies, the new nation's ability to survive seemed doubtful to many Americans and foreigners. As colonies became states, they drafted their own constitutions. Some put in place democratic forms of government whereas others built in more restrictive features such as high property qualifications for officeholding. The first national government, operating under the Articles of Confederation, reflected the states' strong desire to preserve their individual sovereignty. It also embodied the revolutionary generation's opposition to a strong centralized government with extensive powers. This Confederation government lacked basic powers: it could not raise taxes or regulate commerce, and its legislation required the unanimous approval of the states.

The Confederation could point to several achievements, however: it negotiated the peace treaty of 1783, and it established, through three Northwest Ordinances, the process by which territories achieved statehood on an equal footing with the original states. But with limited powers, the Confederation could not resolve the nation's financial problems, deal effectively with foreign nations, or ensure social order within its borders. Efforts to raise needed funds through the sale of western land resulted in renewed conflict with both the British and the Indians. Settlement on the southern frontier provoked retaliation by the Spanish. Barbary pirates seized American trading ships in the Mediterranean. Domestic violence erupted when Massachusetts farmers, hard hit by the postwar depression, rose up in revolt in Shays's Rebellion in 1786. By that time, many of the nation's elite political figures insisted that the system of national government had to be revised if the country wished to survive.

In the summer of 1787, Alexander Hamilton and other nationalists met in Philadelphia to consider a new constitution. The Constitution they produced, after long months of debate and compromise, steered a middle ground between a central government that was too powerful and one that was too weak. It established executive, legislative, and judicial branches, which could "check and balance" one another and thus safeguard the nation from tyranny. The new government was empowered both to raise taxes and regulate commerce. The new Constitution was ratified by the states in 1788 after intense battles between pro-Constitution forces, known as Federalists, and their Antifederalist adversaries. Federalist leaders such as Hamilton, Madison, and Jay campaigned tirelessly for ratification, convinced that the nation was in crisis and could not endure without the new government, and in time they prevailed. Soon after George Washington took office as the first president, serious differences in political opinion emerged. Alexander Hamilton's vision of a vigorous commercial and industrial nation came into conflict with Thomas Jefferson's hopes for an agrarian nation. These two factions disagreed over economic and foreign policy. The French Revolution intensified the divisions: while Hamilton argued against American support for the French in their war against England, Jefferson pressed the administration to align with America's fellow revolutionaries. Washington managed to steer a neutral course in this European conflict.

By the end of Washington's second term, the United States had expanded its borders, negotiated with Spain for access to the Mississippi River, and under Hamilton's guidance, established a national bank at the center of an economic system that promoted market-oriented growth. The country had survived domestic unrest and the development of political parties, which formed along largely sectional or regional lines. The departing Washington urged Americans to continue to cooperate and cautioned them not to allow competing visions of America's future to harm the new nation.

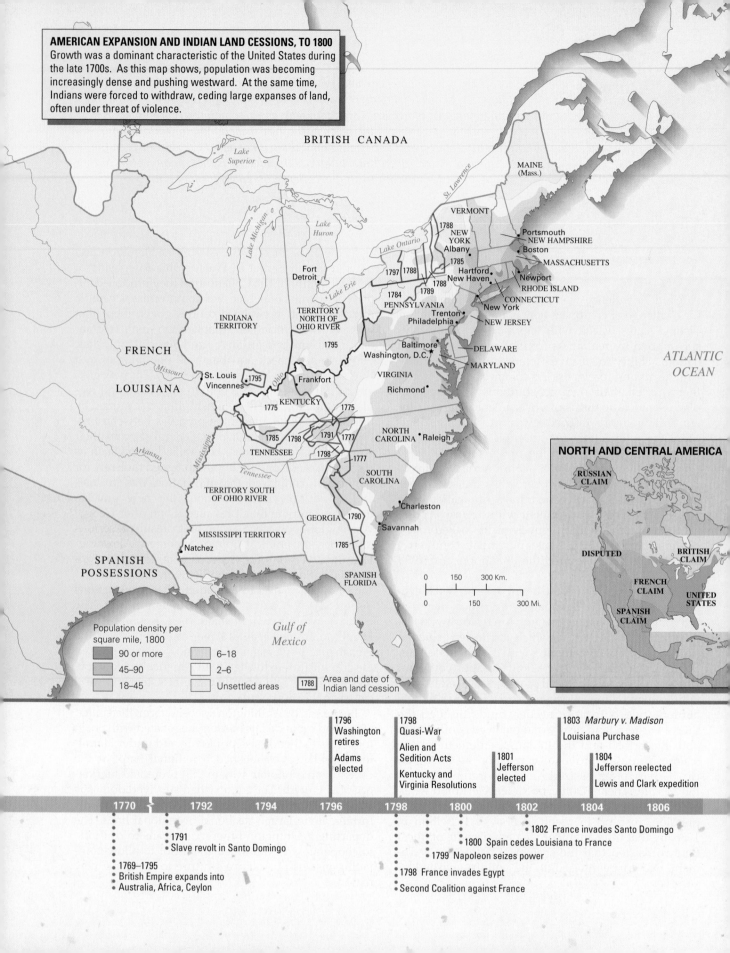

AMERICAN EXPANSION AND INDIAN LAND CESSIONS, TO 1800
Growth was a dominant characteristic of the United States during the late 1700s. As this map shows, population was becoming increasingly dense and pushing westward. At the same time, Indians were forced to withdraw, ceding large expanses of land, often under threat of violence.

BRITISH CANADA

Lake Superior

Lake Michigan

Lake Huron

Lake Ontario

Lake Erie

St. Lawrence

MAINE (Mass.)

VERMONT

1788
NEW YORK
Albany

1785
Hartford
New Haven

1797 1788

Fort Detroit

1784

1789

Portsmouth
NEW HAMPSHIRE
Boston
MASSACHUSETTS
Newport
RHODE ISLAND
CONNECTICUT
New York

INDIANA TERRITORY

TERRITORY NORTH OF OHIO RIVER

PENNSYLVANIA
Trenton
Philadelphia
NEW JERSEY

1795

Baltimore
Washington, D.C.
DELAWARE
MARYLAND

FRENCH

LOUISIANA

Missouri

St. Louis
Vincennes

1795

Ohio

Frankfort

VIRGINIA
Richmond

1775

KENTUCKY

1775

Arkansas

Mississippi

1785 1798

1791

1777

NORTH CAROLINA Raleigh

TENNESSEE

1798

1777

Tennessee

SOUTH CAROLINA

TERRITORY SOUTH OF OHIO RIVER

Charleston

GEORGIA 1790

Savannah

MISSISSIPPI TERRITORY

Natchez

1785

SPANISH POSSESSIONS

SPANISH FLORIDA

Gulf of Mexico

ATLANTIC OCEAN

0   150   300 Km.
0   150   300 Mi.

NORTH AND CENTRAL AMERICA

RUSSIAN CLAIM

DISPUTED

FRENCH CLAIM

SPANISH CLAIM

BRITISH CLAIM

UNITED STATES

Population density per square mile, 1800

- 90 or more
- 45–90
- 18–45
- 6–18
- 2–6
- Unsettled areas

1788 Area and date of Indian land cession

1770   1792   1794   1796   1798   1800   1802   1804   1806

1796
Washington retires

Adams elected

1798
Quasi-War

Alien and Sedition Acts

Kentucky and Virginia Resolutions

1801
Jefferson elected

1803 *Marbury v. Madison*

Louisiana Purchase

1804
Jefferson reelected

Lewis and Clark expedition

1791
• Slave revolt in Santo Domingo

1769–1795
• British Empire expands into
• Australia, Africa, Ceylon

1798 France invades Egypt

Second Coalition against France

1799 Napoleon seizes power

1800 Spain cedes Louisiana to France

1802 France invades Santo Domingo

The Early Republic, 1796–1804

American Expansion and Indian Land Cessions, to 1800
Using the map on the facing page, note the huge expanses of land that had come into the United States' possession and the enormous potential offered by French Louisiana, which would soon become part of the nation's public domain. What opportunities did the control of so much real estate offer to the young nation? What problems would the nation face, internally, from foreign sources, and from Native Americans as it sought to exploit this wealth?

Individual Choices

GEORGE LOGAN

The United States was caught up in a wave of patriotism when the French slighted President Adams's ambassadors in the XYZ affair. Federalists promoted a war against France, but George Logan chose to resist emotionalism and Federalist pressure by going to France to iron out the two nations' difficulties, thus ending the threat of war. *"George Logan" by Gilbert Stuart. Courtesy of the Historical Society of Pennsylvania Collection, Atwater Kent Museum of Philadelphia.*

George Logan

The very idea of the United States fighting a war presented a serious personal dilemma for George Logan. He was a loyal American with deep roots in the nation's history—his grandfather James Logan had been one of the first generation of pioneers in Pennsylvania. Like many descendants of Pennsylvania's first families, George was a Quaker and was morally opposed to war. His father, a conscientious objector during the Revolutionary War, had sent him to study medicine in Scotland and Paris while the war continued. Returning to the United States in 1780, George learned that his family was dead and that much of the considerable Logan estate had been destroyed.

Some of the family's landholdings had survived, but, Logan noted, his primary inheritance consisted of "piles of utterly depreciated paper currency." He turned to farming to support himself and then, in 1785, to politics, winning a seat in the Pennsylvania assembly. Ever a critic of Federalist economic and diplomatic strategies, he followed his friend Thomas Jefferson when the Republican faction became an opposition party.

By 1798, Logan seemed well on his way to recovering the fortune and prominence that the war had taken. But then the Federalists engineered a diplomatic crisis with France, and war again seemed inevitable. Recalling his father's frustration as the colonies were drawn into war in 1776, Logan made a fateful choice: he would risk his property, his reputation, even his life, to prevent another war.

Quietly Logan began selling off some of his land, accumulating cash to support a private peace effort. He then went to his friend Jefferson, who gave him letters of introduction to important people in France. Federalist agents learned of Logan's aims and put him under surveillance, but he slipped their noose and sailed for Germany during the summer of 1798. There he met with the marquis de Lafayette (see pages 167 and 203), who used his influence to get Logan into France and arrange an audience with French foreign minister Talleyrand.

Facing a newly formed coalition of antirevolutionary European powers including Russia, Britain, Austria, the Ottoman Empire, Portugal, Naples, and the Vatican, the last thing Talleyrand wanted was to further alienate the only other revolutionary and democratic nation in the world. Meeting with Talleyrand and other French officials in early August, Logan capitalized on this fact. He told them that most Americans supported democracy in France but warned that French seizure of American ships and other hostile actions were undermining that support. He assured them that if the French released the American sailors they were holding and ended the embargo placed on American ships, American popular support would turn back to France and force the Federalist government to end the Quasi-War. Talleyrand was convinced, assuring Logan that if Adams would send a new, official peace delegation, France would be happy to meet with it.

Logan's news was warmly received by his fellow Republicans and, surprisingly, by President Adams, who ignored his party's advice and immediately sought peace

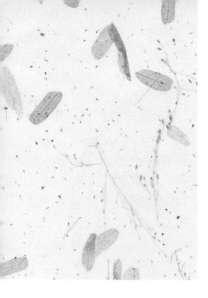

with France. Within a year, American ambassador William Vans Murray and Napoleon finalized the peace Logan had initiated. Logan had succeeded. Choosing to risk all for peace, he overcame official constraints and averted a war.

Outraged Federalists in Congress responded by passing the "Logan Act," which imposed a fine of $5,000 and a three-year prison term on any American citizen who conducted a private diplomatic mission to a foreign government. Passed after Logan's meetings with Talleyrand, the Logan Act could not be used to punish the courageous Quaker from Pennsylvania for his interference in 1798. But Logan might have been prosecuted under its provisions when, in 1810, he sailed to England in an effort to avert a war with that nation. This time Logan failed: war between the United States and England finally broke out in 1812. He then retired to his farm in Philadelphia, his name immortalized only in the federal law designed to punish the moral integrity he personified so well.

INTRODUCTION

That George Logan would undertake such a novel and highly risky venture as trying to negotiate a peace between the United States and France is a measure both of his personal Quaker faith and the nation's political state. George Washington had lent stability to a new and uncertain government, but his retirement reopened many of the divisions that had arisen during its formation. And Washington's replacement, John Adams, seemed incapable of calming these anxieties. Under his watch, the United States became involved in an undeclared war with France and saw its international reputation consistently decline.

Adams also seemed incapable of resolving deep divisions at home. Led by Alexander Hamilton, radical Federalists had tried to undermine the electoral process in 1796 and then used the war crisis to wage an internal war against their political enemies. Far from succeeding in the destruction of their critics, these Federalist efforts actually helped to crystallize opposition, giving Hamilton's key rival, Thomas Jefferson, a forum from which to assault the party in power. In 1800 these efforts backfired on the Federalists: despite trying to rig the election again, Federalists were soundly defeated in the national election and turned out of office.

Assuming the presidency in 1801, Jefferson ushered in a new era in American politics. Though there were strong undercurrents of opposition, even within his own party, Jefferson instituted a series of reforms that would launch the country on a heady, freewheeling adventure of continental expansion and global trade. His secretary of the Treasury, Albert Gallatin, implemented radical tax cuts and equally radical cuts in government spending. At the same time, Jefferson waged an aggressive foreign policy designed to restore American international trading and win new territory from the European powers that still owned large tracts along the nation's borders. His successes could be measured by a mounting federal Treasury surplus, increased national income, and expanding borders.

Under Jefferson's leadership most Americans saw significant improvement in their everyday lives, and the nation became increasingly optimistic. But for many, the promise in Jefferson's America was not as universal as it appeared. For women, Native Americans, and African Americans, life undoubtedly improved and opportunities certainly expanded, but underlying prejudices and rigid codes of public behavior prevented their full realization. Contradictions shot through the whole of Jeffersonian America, counterbalancing the enthusiastic optimism and giving peculiar shape to national life.

Conflict in the Adams Administration

■ How did diplomatic affairs in Europe affect Americans in the closing years of the eighteenth century?

■ How did Federalists manipulate the crisis with France in 1798 for their own political advantage?

■ What steps did Republicans take to counter Federalist manipulations?

Retiring president George Washington spoke for many in 1796 when he warned of "the baneful effects of the spirit of party" in his Farewell Address. Men like Washington believed in the ideal of republican citizenship, of sacrificing personal interest for the good of the republic. To such men, all political ideas that did not correspond with their vision of the republic's welfare were dangerous, even traitorous. Strong Federalists like Hamilton were sure that the Republican faction growing up around Jefferson constituted such a danger and wanted desperately to destroy it. For their part, Republicans were equally sure that Federalists were motivated by no higher motives than personal interest. And having spent several years organizing for a confrontation, Republicans were eager to unseat the politicians responsible for suppressing the Whiskey Rebellion and for tying the United States diplomatically to England. As the two groups prepared to face off, however, new factional lines opened.

The Split Election of 1796

As the broadly accepted leader of the opposition to Hamilton and his policies, Thomas Jefferson was the Republicans' logical choice to represent them in the presidential election in 1796. Most people at the time were not surprised that Republicans chose **Aaron Burr,** a brilliant young New York attorney and member of the Senate, to balance the ticket. Though many years apart in age and from vastly different backgrounds, both Jefferson and Burr were veterans of the revolutionary struggles in 1776 and outspoken champions of democracy.

Although he styled himself a spokesman for the common man, Burr definitely was not one—his father and uncle were presidents of Princeton and Yale Colleges, respectively, and his grandfather was the famous evangelical minister Jonathan Edwards (see page 103). During the Revolutionary War, Burr accepted a commission in the Continental Army, where he found common cause with the radical democrats who had formed the Sons of Liberty (see page 126). By 1784, he had used his political connections and backing from the Sons of Liberty to win a place in the New York state assembly. In 1791 the New York Sons of Liberty, now calling themselves the Society of St. Tammany, maneuvered Burr's election to the U.S. Senate.

Meanwhile, Jefferson had returned from Paris in 1789 to join Washington's cabinet as secretary of state. He was deeply disturbed to find that the once-unified revolutionary forces he knew from 1776 had divided into what he called a "republican side" and a "kingly one," and he complained that "a preference of kingly over republican government was evidently the favorite sentiment." His own preferences put him in

This miniature portrait of John Adams painted by John Trumbull in 1792 shows the stable (some said stodgy) statesman that Americans turned to after George Washington chose to step down as president. *"John Adams" by John Trumbull, 1792. Yale University Art Gallery, Trumbull Collection.*

league with, and eventually on the same ticket as, Burr and his associates in the Society of St. Tammany, who were equally dismayed.

The apparent unity among Republicans contrasted sharply with divisions in the Federalist faction. Most Federalists assumed that Vice President Adams would succeed Washington as president, but Hamilton and some other hardcore party members doubted the New Englander's loyalty to the party. They favored **Thomas Pinckney** of South Carolina. The younger son of a prestigious South Carolina planter, Pinckney had been a prominent military figure during the Revolution and became governor of South Carolina during the late 1780s. He emerged as a major political force when he successfully negotiated the treaty with Spain that opened the Mississippi River to American commerce. This coup won Pinckney the unreserved

Aaron Burr   New York lawyer and vice-presidential candidate in 1796; he became Thomas Jefferson's vice president in 1801 after the House of Representatives broke a deadlock in the Electoral College.

Thomas Pinckney   South Carolina politician and diplomat who was an unsuccessful Federalist candidate for president in 1796.

Chronology

Partisan Tension and Jeffersonian Optimism

1796	George Washington's Farewell Address First contested presidential election: John Adams elected president, Thomas Jefferson vice president
1797	XYZ affair
1798	Quasi-War with France begins Alien and Sedition Acts Kentucky and Virginia Resolutions George Logan's mission to France
1799	Fries's Rebellion Napoleon seizes control in France
1800	Convention of Mortefontaine ends Quasi-War Jefferson and Aaron Burr tie in Electoral College Spain gives Louisiana back to France
1801	Jefferson elected president in House of Representatives; Burr vice president Judiciary Act of 1801 John Marshall becomes chief justice

	War begins between American navy ships and Barbary pirates Outdoor revival meeting at Cane Ridge, Kentucky
1802	Congress repeals all internal taxes Congress repeals Judiciary Act of 1801 French invade Santo Domingo
1803	*Marbury v. Madison* Impeachment of Justices John Pickering and Samuel Chase Louisiana Purchase
1804	Twelfth Amendment ratified Jefferson reelected
1804–1806	Lewis and Clark expedition
1806–1807	Zebulon Pike's expedition
1816	African Methodist Episcopal Church formed in Philadelphia

admiration of both southerners and westerners (see page 205). Hamilton supported him, though, both because Pinckney was less associated with radical causes than was Adams and because Hamilton felt he could exercise more influence over the mild-mannered South Carolinian than he could over the stiff-necked Yankee.

Most Federalists, however, aligned behind the old warhorse from Massachusetts. A descendant of New England Calvinists (see page 27), Adams was a man of strong principles, fighting for what he believed was right despite anyone's contrary opinion. Though a thorough Federalist, he remained Thomas Jefferson's close friend: both he and his wife, Abigail, maintained a spirited correspondence with the red-haired Virginian during his stay in Paris. Like Washington, Adams was seen by many old revolutionaries as above politics, as a **statesman** whose conscience and integrity would help the new nation avoid the pitfalls of **factionalism.**

It was precisely Adams's statesmanship that led Hamilton to oppose him; the head of the radical Federalists sought to rig the election against Adams. According to the Constitution, each member of the Electoral College could cast votes for any two candidates; the highest vote getter became president, and the runner-up became vice president. Hamilton urged Pinckney supporters to cast only one vote—for Pinckney—so that Adams could not get enough votes to win the presidency. But Hamilton underestimated Pinckney's unpopularity in the North, Adams's unacceptability to southerners, and Jefferson's growing popularity among northern dissidents. Nor did the Treasury secretary expect Adams supporters to learn of the plot; when they did, they withheld votes from Pinckney to make up for the votes being withheld from Adams.

Because of the squabbling within the Federalist faction, Jefferson received the votes of disgruntled Federalist electors as well as electors within Republican ranks. He thus ended up with more votes than

statesman   A political leader who acts out of concern for the public good and not out of self-interest.

factionalism   In politics, the emergence of various self-interested parties (factions) that compete to impose their own views onto either a larger political party or the nation at large.

Pinckney—and only three fewer than Adams. So the nation emerged from the first truly contested presidential election with a split administration: the president and vice president belonged to different factions and held opposing political philosophies.

Never known for charm, subtlety, or willingness to compromise, Adams was ill suited to lead a deeply divided nation. Although he disavowed any monarchist sentiments in his inaugural address, the new president's aloofness did little to put Republicans' fears to rest, and he made few **conciliatory** gestures. In fact, from Washington's cabinet Adams retained Oliver Wolcott, James McHenry, and Timothy Pickering, all of whom were Hamilton men through and through. This move thoroughly angered Republicans, who had hoped Hamilton's influence would wane now that he had retired from government service to practice law. And then Adams further stung his foes by withholding an expected diplomatic appointment from James Madison. Clearly the factions were still alive and well and locked in conflict. This disunity enticed interested parties both at home and abroad to try to undermine Adams's authority and influence.

XYZ: The Power of Patriotism

One group seeking to take advantage of the divisions in the United States was the revolutionary government in France. America's minister to France, James Monroe, sympathized with the French cause, but the pro-British impact of Jay's Treaty (see pages 205–206) and the antirevolutionary rhetoric adopted by Federalists led the French to suspect American sincerity. During the election of 1796, France sought to influence American voting by actively favoring the Republican candidates, threatening to terminate diplomatic relations if the vocally pro-British Federalists won. True to its word, the revolutionary government of France broke off relations with the United States as soon as Adams was elected.

Angry at the French, Adams retaliated in 1796 by calling home the sympathetic Monroe and replacing him with devout Federalist **Charles Cotesworth Pinckney,** the older brother of Hamilton's favored candidate for the presidency. The French refused to acknowledge the hyper-Federalist Pinckney as ambassador and began seizing American ships. Faced with what was fast becoming a diplomatic crisis, and possibly a military one as well, Adams wisely chose to pursue two courses simultaneously. Asserting that the United States would not be "humiliated under a colonial spirit of fear and a sense of inferiority," he

Americans saw the XYZ affair as proof of European corruption standing in sharp contrast to American virtue. In this 1798 engraving by Charles Williams, a maidenly America is flattered to distraction by courtly Europeans while members of the French Directory prepare to plunder her wealth. *Lilly Library.*

pressed Congress in 1797 to build up America's military defenses. At the same time, he dispatched John Marshall and Elbridge Gerry to join Pinckney in Paris, where they were to arrange a peaceful settlement of the two nations' differences.

Playing a complicated diplomatic game, French foreign minister **Charles Maurice de Talleyrand-Périgord** declined to receive Pinckney and the peace delegation. As weeks passed, three businessmen residing in Paris, whose international trading profits stood at risk, offered themselves as go-betweens in solving the stalemate. According to Pinckney's report, these men suggested that if the Americans were willing to pay a bribe to key French officials and guarantee an American loan of several million dollars to

conciliatory   Striving to overcome distrust or to regain good will.

Charles Cotesworth Pinckney   Federalist politician and brother of Thomas Pinckney; he was sent on a diplomatic mission to Paris in 1796 during a period of unfriendly relations between France and the United States.

Charles Maurice de Talleyrand-Périgord   French foreign minister appointed by the revolutionary government in 1797; he later aided Napoleon Bonaparte's overthrow of that government and served as his foreign minister.

France, the three businessmen would be able to get them a hearing. Offended at such treatment, Pinckney broke off diplomatic relations. Reporting the affair to President Adams, Pinckney refused to name the would-be go-betweens, calling them only "X," "Y," and "Z."

Americans' response to the **XYZ affair** was overwhelming. France's diplomatic slight seemed a slap in the face to a new nation seeking international respect. In Philadelphia, people paraded in the streets to protest French arrogance. The crowds chanted Pinckney's reported response: "No, no, not a sixpence!" This wave of patriotism overcame the spirit of division that had plagued the Adams administration, giving the president a virtually unified Congress and country. In the heat of the moment, Adams pressed for increased military forces, and in short order Congress created the Department of the Navy and appropriated money to start building a fleet of warships. Then, on July 7, 1798, Congress rescinded all treaties with France and authorized privateering against French ships. Congress also created a standing army of twenty thousand troops and ordered that the militia be expanded to thirty thousand men. Washington added his prestige to the effort by coming out of retirement to lead the new army, with Hamilton as his second-in-command. Although running sea battles between French and American ships resulted in the sinking or capture of many vessels on both sides, Congress shied away from actually declaring war, which led to the conflict being labeled the **Quasi-War.**

The Home Front in the Quasi-War

Still disappointed over their failure to steal the presidential election, radical Federalists immediately seized upon the war as a means to crush their political enemies. In Congress, they began referring to Jefferson and his supporters as the "French Party" and accused the vice president and his faction of treason whenever they advised a moderate course. Arguing that the presence of this "French Party" constituted a danger to national security, congressional Federalists proposed a series of new laws to destroy all opposition to their political agenda.

One source of opposition was **naturalized** American citizens. The revolutionary promises of "life, liberty, and the pursuit of happiness" had drawn many immigrants to the United States. Disappointed by Hamilton's approach to government and economics,

they were drawn to Jefferson's political rhetoric—especially his stress on equal opportunity and his attacks on entrenched elites. In 1798 Federalists in Congress passed three acts designed to counter political activities by immigrants. The Naturalization Act extended the residency requirement for citizenship from five to fourteen years. The Alien Act authorized the president to deport any foreigner he judged "dangerous to the peace and safety of the United States." The Alien Enemies Act permitted the president to imprison or banish any foreigner he considered dangerous during a national emergency. The Naturalization Act was designed to prevent recent immigrants from supporting the Republican cause by barring them from the political process. The other two acts served as a constant reminder that the president or his agents could arbitrarily imprison or deport any resident alien who stepped out of line.

The other source of support for Jefferson was a partisan Republican press, which attempted to balance the biased news and criticism spewing forth from Federalist news sources. To counter this, congressional Federalists passed the Sedition Act. In addition to outlawing conspiracies to block the enforcement of federal laws, the Sedition Act prohibited the publication or utterance of any criticism of the government or its officials that would bring either "into contempt or disrepute." In the words of one Federalist newspaper, "It is patriotism to write in favour of our government, it is **sedition** to write against it." Federalists brandished the law against all kinds of criticism directed toward either the government or the president, including perfectly innocent political editorials. Not surprisingly, most of the defendants in the fifteen cases brought by federal authorities under the Sedition Act were prominent Republican newspaper editors.

XYZ affair   A diplomatic incident in which American envoys to France were told that the United States would have to loan France money and bribe government officials as a precondition for negotiation.

Quasi-War   Diplomatic crisis triggered by the XYZ affair; fighting occurred between the United States and France between the early summer of 1798 and the official end of the conflict in September 1800, but neither side issued a formal declaration of war.

naturalized   Granted full citizenship (after having been born in a foreign country).

sedition   Conduct or language inciting rebellion against the authority of a state.

Republicans complained that the **Alien and Sedition Acts** violated the Bill of Rights, but Congress and the federal judiciary, controlled as they were by Hamilton loyalists, paid no attention. Dissidents had little choice but to take their political case to the state governments, which they did in the fall of 1798. One statement, drafted by Madison, came before the Virginia legislature, and another, by Jefferson, was considered in Kentucky.

Madison and Jefferson based their **Virginia and Kentucky Resolutions** on the Tenth Amendment, contending that powers not specifically granted to the federal government under the Constitution or reserved to the people in the Bill of Rights fell to the states. By passing laws such as the Alien and Sedition Acts that were not explicitly permitted in the text of the Constitution, Congress had violated the states' rights. The two authors differed, however, in the responses they prescribed for states to take. For his part, Madison asserted that when the majority of states agreed that a federal law had violated their Tenth Amendment rights, they could collectively overrule federal authority. But Jefferson went further, arguing that each individual state had the "natural right" to **interpose** its own authority to protect its own rights and the rights of its citizens.

The Virginia and Kentucky Resolutions passed in their respective state legislatures, but no other states followed suit. Even within Kentucky and Virginia, great disagreement arose over how far state authority should extend. Nevertheless, this response to the Federalists' use of federal power brought the disputed relationship between federal law and **states' rights** into national prominence.

Another bone of contention was the methods used to finance the Quasi-War with France and the impact these methods had on various groups of Americans. Consistent with Hamilton's views on finance, tariffs and excises were to be the primary source of revenue, and they had the greatest impact on people who needed manufactured or imported items but had little hard cash. In addition, Federalists imposed a tax on land, hitting cash-poor farmers especially hard. In 1799 farmers in Northampton County, Pennsylvania, refused to pay the tax and began harassing tax collectors. Several tax resisters were arrested, but an auctioneer named John Fries, himself a Federalist, raised an armed force to break them out of jail. Later, federal troops sent by Adams to suppress what Federalists characterized as **Fries's Rebellion** arrested Fries and two of his associates. Charged with treason, the three were tried in federal court, found guilty, and condemned to death.

Settlement with France

The Federalists' seeming overreaction to French provocation and domestic protest alienated increasing numbers of Americans. Adams himself was eager to end the conflict, and when a private American citizen, George Logan, sent news from France that Foreign Minister Talleyrand was asking that a new American delegation be sent, Adams, who had grown impatient with the radical Federalist's lack of statesmanship, seized this opportunity to end the Quasi-War and regain control of his party. Telling the Federalist-dominated Congress that he would give them the details later, Adams instructed the American minister to the Netherlands, William Vans Murray, to go immediately to Paris. As rumors of negotiations began to circulate, Hamilton and his supporters became furious, all but accusing Adams of treason. This gave the president the ammunition he needed: he fired Pickering, Wolcott, and McHenry, Hamilton's primary supporters in his cabinet, and then embarrassed the Federalist judiciary by granting a presidential pardon to John Fries and his fellow Pennsylvania rebels.

Adams's diplomatic appeal to France was well timed. When Murray and his delegation arrived in Paris in November 1799, they found that whatever belligerence might have existed toward the United States had been swept away. On November 9, 1799,

Alien and Sedition Acts   Collectively, the four acts—Alien Act, Alien Enemies Act, Naturalization Act, and Sedition Act—passed by Congress in 1798 designed to prevent immigrants from participating in politics and to silence the anti-Federalist press.

Virginia and Kentucky Resolutions   Statements that the Virginia and Kentucky legislatures issued in 1798 in response to the Alien and Sedition Acts; they asserted the right of states to overrule the federal government.

interpose   To place a barrier between two objects or forces; to Jefferson, the principle of interposition meant that states had the right to use their sovereign power as a barrier between the federal government and the states' citizens when the natural rights of those citizens were at risk.

states' rights   The political position in favor of limiting federal power to allow the greatest possible self-government by the individual states.

Fries's Rebellion   A tax revolt by Pennsylvania citizens in 1799 that was suppressed by federal forces; leader John Fries was condemned to death for treason but received a presidential pardon from John Adams.

Napoleon Bonaparte had overthrown the government that was responsible for the XYZ affair. Napoleon was more interested in establishing an empire in Europe than in continuing an indecisive conflict with the United States. After some negotiation, Murray and Napoleon drew up and signed the Convention of Mortefontaine, ending the Quasi-War on September 30, 1800.

The "Revolution of 1800"

■ What did Thomas Jefferson mean by the statement "Every difference of opinion is not a difference of principles"?

■ How did Federalists respond to losing the election of 1800? What does this response reveal about their political attitudes?

■ How did Jefferson's vision for America differ from that of Hamilton, Adams, and other Federalists?

According to the partisan press, the political situation in 1800 was as simple as the contrast between the personalities of the major presidential candidates. The Republican press characterized Adams as a monarchist and a **spendthrift,** charging that Adams's efforts to expand the powers of the federal government were really attempts to rob citizens of freedom and turn the United States back into a colony of England. In contrast, the Republican press characterized Jefferson as a man of the people, sensitive to the appeals of southern and western agricultural groups who felt perpetually ignored or abused by northeastern Federalists and their constituents. According to Federalist newspapers, however, Vice President Jefferson was a dangerous radical and an atheist, a man who shared French tastes for radical politics, **dandyism,** and immorality. In the eyes of the Federalists, Adams was a man whose policies and steady-handed administration would bring stability and prosperity, qualities that appealed to manufacturers and merchants in New England, as well as to Calvinists and other supporters of a conservative social and political order. The rhetoric became so hateful that even Adams and Jefferson got caught up in it—the old friends stopped speaking to each other. Nearly twenty years would pass before they renewed their friendship.

The Lesser of Republican Evils

As the election of 1800 approached, the split between the Adams and Hamilton wings of the Federalist faction widened. Both agreed on the necessity of dumping Jefferson as vice president, putting forward Charles Cotesworth Pinckney, hero of the XYZ affair, to replace him. But Adams's behavior in the wake of George Logan's mission to France had angered the radicals; they now wanted Adams to be gone as well. Having gotten Pinckney into the Electoral College balloting, Hamilton again tried to steal the 1800 election. As before, he advised delegates to withhold votes, but this time he engaged in direct lobbying, even writing a pamphlet in which he questioned Adams's suitability for the presidency.

Hamilton's methods backfired again: Federalists cast one more vote for Adams than for Pinckney. But more important, Hamilton's scheming and his faction's consistent promanufacturing stance had so alienated southern Federalists that many chose to support Jefferson. With Jefferson pulling in the southern vote and his running mate—Burr again—pulling in the craftsmen and small-farm vote in New York, the Republicans outscored the Federalists by 16 votes in the Electoral College. But that still did not settle the election. Burr and Jefferson won the same number of electoral votes (see Map 8.1). The tie threw the election into the House of Representatives, which was still stocked with hard-line Federalists elected during the Quasi-War hysteria in 1798.

Undoubtedly many Federalists in the House wished they could overturn the election of 1800 altogether, but the Constitution specifically barred them from doing so. Instead, they faced the task of choosing between two men whom most of them viewed as being dangerous radicals bent on destroying the Federalists' hard work. Indecision was plain: in ballot after ballot over six grueling days early in 1801, neither Jefferson nor Burr could win the necessary majority.

In addition to exhaustion and frustration, two things finally combined to break the deadlock. First, Hamilton convinced several Federalists that even though Jefferson's rhetoric was dangerous, the Virginian was a gentleman of property and integrity, whereas Burr was "the most dangerous man of the community." Second, Virginia and Pennsylvania mobilized their militias, intent on preventing a "legislative usurpation"

Napoleon Bonaparte General who took control of the French government in November 1799, at the end of France's revolutionary period; he eventually proclaimed himself emperor of France and conquered much of the continent of Europe.

spendthrift A person who spends money recklessly or wastefully.

dandyism Dressing and behaving in an overly ornate and flamboyant fashion.

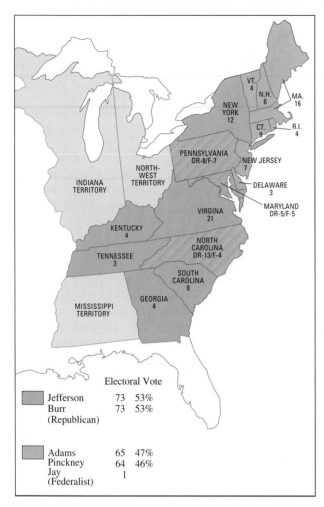

Electoral Vote

Jefferson	73	53%
Burr	73	53%
(Republican)		
Adams	65	47%
Pinckney	64	46%
Jay	1	
(Federalist)		

MAP 8.1 Election of 1800 The political partnership between Thomas Jefferson and Aaron Burr allowed the Republicans to unseat Federalist John Adams in the election of 1800. As this map shows, only New England voted as a bloc for the Federalist, while Burr's political home, New York, went entirely to Jefferson.

of the popular will. As Delaware senator James Bayard described the situation, Federalists had to admit "that we must risk the Constitution and a Civil War or take Mr. Jefferson." Finally, on the thirty-sixth ballot, on February 17, 1801, Jefferson emerged a winner.

Federalists and Republicans agreed about very little, but the threat of civil war frightened both factions equally. Not long after Jefferson's election, both parties aligned briefly to pass the **Twelfth Amendment** to the Constitution, which requires separate balloting in the Electoral College for president and vice president, thereby preventing deadlocks like the one that nearly wrecked the nation in 1800. The new electoral proce-

dure led to new sorts of political intrigues, but the manipulation that Hamilton attempted was no longer possible after the Twelfth Amendment was ratified in 1804.

Federalist Defenses and a Loyal Opposition

The Federalists had outmaneuvered themselves in the election of 1800, but they were not about to leave office without erecting some defenses for the political and economic machinery they had constructed. The Federalist-controlled judiciary, which had proved its clout during the controversy over the Alien and Sedition Acts, appeared to offer the strongest bulwark to prevent Republicans from tampering with the Constitution. Thus, during their last days in office, the Federalist **lame ducks** in Congress passed the **Judiciary Act of 1801,** which created sixteen new federal judgeships, six additional **circuit courts,** and a massive structure of **federal marshals** and clerks. President Adams then rushed to fill all these positions with loyal Federalists, signing appointments right up to midnight on his last day in office. The appointments came in such large numbers and so late in the day that **John Marshall,** Adams's secretary of state, was unable to deliver all the appointment letters before his own term ran out. But Marshall did deliver one letter promptly: the one addressed to himself, making him chief justice of the Supreme Court.

Twelfth Amendment Constitutional amendment, ratified in 1804, that provides for separate balloting in the Electoral College for president and vice president.

lame duck An officeholder who has failed to win, or is ineligible for, reelection but whose term in office has not yet ended.

Judiciary Act of 1801 Law that the Federalist Congress passed to increase the number of federal courts and judicial positions; President Adams rushed to fill these positions with Federalists before his term ended.

circuit court A court of appeals that has the power to review and either uphold or overturn decisions made by lower courts; in terms of authority, these stand between federal district courts and the Supreme Court.

federal marshal A law enforcement officer who works directly for the federal district court; each district court has one marshal, who in turn employs a staff of deputies to carry out orders from the court.

John Marshall Virginia lawyer and politician whom President Adams made chief justice of the Supreme Court; his legal decisions helped shape the role of the Supreme Court in American government.

Painted while he was at the height of his power and influence, this portrait of Chief Justice John Marshall captures the jurist's imposing presence—he would dominate the Supreme Court and American constitutional law for over thirty years after his appointment in 1801, setting many precedents that remain in force today. *Boston Athenaeum.*

Considering the ill will evident in the Alien and Sedition Acts and the presidential electioneering, Jefferson's inaugural address was oddly conciliatory. "We are all Republicans; we are all Federalists," Jefferson said, seeming to abandon partisan politics and align himself with those who had recently labeled him a "brandy-soaked defamer of churches" and a "contemptible hypocrite." In his mind, all Americans shared the same fundamental principles—the principles of 1776. But even Jefferson considered the election of 1800 a revolution—"as real a revolution in the principles of our government as that of 1776 was in its form."

Jefferson was right in many respects about the revolutionary nature of the election of 1800. Although his inaugural address preached kinship between Federalists and Republicans, the new president repeatedly criticized his opponents for their lack of faith in democracy and the American people. Unlike the Federalists, Jefferson was unalterably opposed to using the power of government against those who opposed his political position. "If there be any among us who would wish to dissolve this Union or to change its republican form," he said, "let them stand undisturbed as monuments of the safety with which error of opinion may be tolerated, where reason is left free to combat it."

As a result of Jefferson's reassuring address, the nation began to share the president's view that "every difference of opinion is not a difference of principles." Even extreme Federalists such as Fisher Ames came to understand that a "party is an association of honest men for honest purposes, and when the State falls into bad hands, is the only efficient defense; a champion who never flinches, a watchman who never sleeps." Ames went on to describe how a loyal **opposition party** should behave. "We are not to revile or abuse magistrates, or lie even for good cause," he said. "We must act as good citizens, using only truth, and argument, and zeal to impress them." With parties such as these, a system of loyal opposition could become a permanent part of a republican government without risk to security or freedom. And in keeping with the two-party spirit and Jefferson's philosophical commitment to free speech, Congress let the Sedition Act and the Alien Acts expire in 1801 and 1802 and did not seek to replace them. It also repealed the Naturalization Act, replacing its fourteen-year probationary interval with a five-year naturalization period.

Confident in Americans' ability to reason, Jefferson outlined a plan for a "wise and frugal government" that would seek "equal and exact justice to all men of whatever state or persuasion, religious or political." He would, he said, support state governments "in all their rights" but would not tear down the federal structure or fail to pay its debts.

Jefferson's Vision for America

Jefferson had a strong, positive vision for the nation, and the party made every effort to put his policies

opposition party   A political party opposed to the party or government in power.

The "Revolution of 1800"

Beginning with debates over the ratification of the Constitution and continuing with ever-increasing stridency through the Quasi-War, fears over the disloyalty of opposition party members set the tone for all political discourse in the infant United States. For example, in 1798, Representative John Rutledge shouted from the House floor that all who were critical of the Federalist administration "believe it to be their duty to do all in their power to overturn the whole system, to effect which, they may think a French army and a French invasion necessary." To which Republican John Nicholas replied: "More evil is to be apprehended in this country from the votaries of despotism, than from the votaries of France," accusing Federalists of seeking to "subvert all the liberties of our country." Yet despite this violent—and heartfelt—rhetoric, Federalist leaders like Alexander Hamilton came to agree with Jefferson that "every difference of opinion is not a difference of principles," and peacefully turned the reins of government over to the Republicans in 1800. This was the real "Revolution of 1800": the creation of the two-party political tradition that continues to allow the peaceful transit of power through elections rather than fostering foreign invasion or subverting liberties to put forward a political agenda.

into effect. He embraced a specific notion of proper political, economic, and social behavior. The greatest dangers to a republic, he believed, were (1) high population density and the social evils it generated and (2) the concentration of money and power in the hands of a few. Accordingly, Jefferson wanted to steer America away from the large-scale, publicly supported industry so dear to Hamilton and toward an economy founded on yeoman farmers—men who owned their own land, produced their own food, and were beholden to no one. Such men, Jefferson believed, could make political decisions based solely on pure reason and good sense.

But Jefferson was not naive. He knew Americans would continue to demand the comforts and luxuries found in industrial societies. His solution was simple. In America's vast lands, he said, a nation of farmers could produce so much food that "its surplus [could] go to nourish the now perishing births of Europe, who in return would manufacture and send us in exchange our clothes and other comforts." Overpopulation and **urbanization**—the twin causes of corruption in Europe—would not occur in America, for here, Jefferson said, "the immense extent of uncultivated and fertile lands enables every one who will labor, to marry young, and to raise a family of any size."

Making such a system work, however, would require a radical change in economic policy. The government would have to let businesses make their own decisions and succeed or fail in a marketplace free of government interference. In an economy with absolutely free trade and an open marketplace, the iron law of **supply and demand** would determine the cost of goods and services. This view of the economy was a direct assault on mercantilist notions of governments controlling prices and restricting trade to benefit the nation-state.

Jefferson believed that, given the shortage of raw materials and foodstuffs in war-torn and overcrowded Europe and its oversupply of manufactured items, free trade in a truly open international economy would benefit the United States. If the European nations could be convinced to drop trade restrictions and let the marketplace decide the value of goods, the principles of supply and demand would ensure profits for American producers and shippers.

Republicanism in Action

■ How did Republicans deal with the defenses that Federalists put in place in 1801? What successes did they have?

■ What policies did Jefferson pursue to carry out his vision for the country? What obstacles did he encounter?

When Jefferson assumed office, he ushered a new spirit into national politics and the presidency. A combination of circumstances moved him to lead a

urbanization   The growth of cities in a nation or region and the shifting of the population from rural to urban areas.

supply and demand   The two factors that determine price in an economy based on private property: (1) how much of a commodity is available (supply) and (2) how many people want it (demand).

Suffering a lifelong sensitivity to cold as well as a dislike for formality, Thomas Jefferson usually chose to dress practically, in fairly plain clothes that kept him warm. This 1822 portrait by Thomas Sully captures the former president in his customary greatcoat, unadorned suit, and well-worn boots. *"Thomas Jefferson" by Thomas Sully. West Point Museum, United States Military Academy, West Point, N.Y.*

much simpler life than his predecessors in office had led. For one thing, he was the first president to be inaugurated in the new national capital, the still largely uncompleted Washington City, which afforded quite different and much more limited **amenities.** Washington lacked the taverns, **salons,** and entertaining social circles that both previous capitals, New York and Philadelphia, had offered. Personal preferences also moved him in a simpler direction. He refused, for example, to ride in a carriage, choosing to go by horseback through Washington's muddy and rutted streets. He continued to give parties as he had done in Paris, but he sat his guests at a round table so that no one might be seen as more important than the others. He abandoned the fashion of wearing a wig, letting his red hair stand out, and he sometimes entertained with startling informality, wearing frayed slippers and work clothes.

But this show of simplicity and his conciliatory inaugural address were somewhat misleading. Jeffer-

son was a hardworking politician and administrator whose main objective was to turn the nation around with all possible speed. He quickly launched a program to revamp the American economy and give the United States a place in the international community. Along the way, he captured many Americans' affection and their political loyalty but also alienated those who did not share his vision or who lacked his zeal.

Assault on Federalist Defenses

Aware of the purpose behind the Judiciary Act of 1801 and Adams's midnight appointments, Republicans chose to wage an aggressive partisan war to reverse Federalist control of the justice system. In January 1802, Republicans in Congress proposed the repeal of the 1801 Judiciary Act, arguing that the new circuit courts were outrageously expensive and unnecessary. Federalists countered that if Congress repealed the act, it would in effect be terminating judges for reasons other than the "high crimes and misdemeanors" mentioned in the Constitution, thereby violating the separation of powers. Congress proceeded anyway, replacing the Judiciary Act of 1801 with the Judiciary Act of 1802, and awaited the response of the Federalist courts.

The **constitutionality** of the new Judiciary Act was never tested, but the power of the judicial branch to interpret and enforce federal law did become a major issue the following year. On taking office, Jefferson's secretary of state, James Madison, held back the appointment letters that John Marshall had been unable to deliver before the expiration of his term. One jilted appointee was William Marbury, who was to have been **justice of the peace** for the newly created District of Columbia (see page 199). Marbury, with the support of his party, filed suit in the Supreme Court.

amenities Conveniences, comforts, and services.

salon A gathering place, generally in a private home, where people came together to discuss their common interests; in the eighteenth and early nineteenth centuries, these were often the places where politicians gathered to discuss philosophy and policy issues.

constitutionality Accordance with the principles or provisions of the Constitution.

justice of the peace The lowest level of judge in some state court systems, usually responsible for hearing small claims and minor criminal cases; because Washington, D.C., is a federal territory rather than a state, the justice of the peace for that district is a federal appointee.

Marbury v. Madison was Chief Justice Marshall's first major case, and in it he proved his political as well as his judicial ingenuity. Marshall was certain that the Judiciary Act of 1789 required Madison to deliver the appointment letter, but the chief justice was keenly aware that if he ordered Madison to deliver it and Madison refused, the Court did not have the power to enforce the order. In such a direct confrontation between the executive and judicial branches, Marshall was sure to lose. Rather than risking a serious blow to the dignity of the Supreme Court, Marshall ruled in 1803 that the Constitution contained no provision for the Supreme Court to issue such orders as the Judiciary Act of 1789 required and that therefore the law was unconstitutional.

This decision put Jefferson and Madison in a difficult political position. On one hand, the authors of the Virginia and Kentucky Resolutions were on record for arguing that the states and not the courts should determine the constitutionality of federal laws. But political realities forced them to accept Marshall's decision in this case if they wanted to block Adams's handpicked men from assuming lifetime appointments in powerful judicial positions. Although this **precedent** for **judicial review** did not immediately invalidate the principles set forth in Jefferson's and Madison's earlier **manifestos,** it established the standard that federal courts, rather than states, could decide the constitutionality of acts of Congress.

Marshall's decision in *Marbury v. Madison* gave the Republicans the power to withhold undelivered letters of appointment from the Adams administration, but it gave them no power to control the behavior of judges whose appointments were already official. Thus, in the aftermath of the Marbury decision, Republican radicals in Congress decided to take aim at particularly partisan Federalist judges.

John Pickering of New Hampshire was an easy first target. An alcoholic who suffered from mental illness, he was known to rave incoherently both on and off the bench, usually about the evils of Jefferson and republicanism. No one, not even staunch Federalists, doubted that the besotted man was incompetent, but it was far from certain that he had committed the "high crimes and misdemeanors" for which he was **impeached** in 1803. Whether he had or not, the Senate found him guilty and removed him from office.

Emboldened by that easy victory and armed with a powerful precedent, radical Republicans took on Supreme Court justice Samuel Chase. Chase was notorious for making partisan decisions—such as condemning John Fries to death—and for using the federal bench as an anti-Republican soapbox. Unlike Pickering, Chase defended himself very competently, making the political motivations behind the impeachment effort obvious to all observers. In the end, both Federalists and many Republicans voted to dismiss the charges, returning Chase to his position on the Supreme Court. The Republican radicals' failure to impeach Chase reinforced Jefferson's authority in calling for conciliation. The radicals now had little choice but to accept Jefferson's more moderate position or bolt the party.

Implementing a New Economy

One area of general agreement among Republicans was the determination to tear down Hamilton's economic structure and replace it with a new one more consistent with Jefferson's vision. Responsibility for planning and implementing this economic policy fell to Treasury Secretary **Albert Gallatin.** Gallatin's first effort as secretary of the Treasury was to try to settle the nation's debts. His ambitious goal was to make the United States entirely debt free by 1817. With Jefferson's approval, Gallatin implemented a radical course of budget cutting, going so far as to close several American embassies overseas to save money. At home, Gallatin and Jefferson pared administrative costs by reducing staff and putting an end to the fancy receptions and other social events that President Adams had so enjoyed. The administration cut the military by half, reducing the army from four thousand to twenty-five hundred men and the navy from twenty-five ships to a mere seven.

But Gallatin's cost cutting did much more than just reduce the national budget. First, Gallatin was able to

---

Marbury v. Madison   Supreme Court decision (1803) declaring part of the Judiciary Act of 1789 unconstitutional, thereby establishing an important precedent in favor of judicial review.

precedent   An event or decision that may be used as an example in similar cases later on.

judicial review   The power of the Supreme Court to review the constitutionality of laws passed by Congress and by the states.

manifesto   A written statement publicly declaring the views of its author.

impeach   To formally charge a public official with criminal conduct in office; once the House of Representatives has impeached a federal official, the official is then tried in the Senate on the stated charges.

Albert Gallatin   Treasury secretary in Jefferson's administration; he favored limited government and reduced the federal debt by cutting spending.

Although Jefferson's efforts to stop Barbary pirate depredations against American shipping in the Mediterranean were largely a failure, the struggle provided a wonderful training ground for future military leaders. Young naval commander Stephen Decatur was one such figure. In the course of the fighting, Decatur boarded a pirate ship and engaged in hand-to-hand fighting against the crew, eventually winning the fight even though he had already been wounded by a bullet through his arm. *Naval Historical Foundation.*

mask the firing of loyal Federalists still employed in civil service in a seemingly nonpartisan appeal to fiscal responsibility. He accomplished another ideological goal by reducing the overall federal presence, putting more responsibilities onto the states, where his and Jefferson's philosophy said they belonged. In addition, Gallatin's plan called for a significant change in how the government raised money. In 1802 the Republican Congress repealed all **internal taxes,** leaving customs duties and the sale of western lands as the sole sources of federal revenue. With this one sweeping gesture, Gallatin struck a major blow for Jefferson's economic vision by tying the nation's financial future to westward expansion and foreign trade. But this vision would soon face serious challenges.

Threats to Jefferson's Vision

One threat to Jefferson's commitment to foreign trade came from pirates who patrolled the northern coast of Africa from Tangier to Tripoli, controlling access to the Mediterranean Sea. Ever since gaining independence, the United States had in effect been bribing the Barbary pirates not to attack American ships (see page 189). By 1800, fully a fifth of the federal budget was earmarked for this purpose, a cost Gallatin wished to see eliminated as he tried to balance the nation's books. To Jefferson, principle was as important as financial considerations. Jefferson decided on war.

Asserting presidential privilege as commander in chief, he dispatched navy ships to the Mediterranean in 1801.

The war that followed was a fiasco from anyone's point of view. After some indecisive engagements between the American fleet and the pirates, Jefferson's navy suffered a major defeat with the capture of a prize warship, the *Philadelphia,* and its entire crew. A bold but unsuccessful attempt to invade Tripoli by land across the Libyan Desert led only to a threat to kill the crew of the *Philadelphia* and other hostages. The war dragged along until 1805, when the United States finally negotiated peace terms, agreeing to pay $60,000 for the release of the hostages and accepting the pirates' promise to stop raiding American shipping.

In the meantime, France and Spain posed a serious threat to Jefferson's dream of rapid westward expansion. As settlers continued to pour into the region between the Appalachian Mountains and the Mississippi River, the commercial importance of that inland waterway increased. Whoever controlled the mouth of the Mississippi—the place where it flows past New Orleans and into the Gulf of Mexico and the open

> **internal taxes**   Taxes collected directly from citizens, like Alexander Hamilton's various excise taxes (see page 204), as opposed to tariffs or other taxes collected in connection with foreign trade.

With backing from the French, François Dominique Toussaint L'Ouverture (center) led his fellow slaves in a revolt against their French and Spanish masters, driving the Europeans from the West Indian island of Santo Domingo in 1791. Emperor Napoleon Bonaparte double-crossed Toussaint in 1802, sending a French army to seize the island. Although Toussaint was captured, his army defeated the French, creating the republic of Haiti in 1804. *"Toussaint L'Ouverture" by William Edouard Scott. Amistad Research Center, Tulane University, New Orleans, AFAC Collection.*

seas—would have the power to make or break the interior economy.

In accordance with the Treaty of San Lorenzo (1795) (see page 205), Spain had granted American farmers the right to ship cargoes down the Mississippi without paying tolls, and had given American merchants permission to **transship** goods from New Orleans to Atlantic ports without paying export duties. In 1800, however, Napoleon had traded some of France's holdings in southern Europe to Spain in exchange for Spain's land in North America. The United States had no agreement with France concerning navigation on the Mississippi, so the deal between Spain and France threatened to scuttle American commerce on the river. Anxiety over this issue turned to outright panic when, preparatory to the transfer of

the land to France, Spanish officials suspended free trade in New Orleans.

Jefferson responded on two fronts. Backing away from his usual anti-British position, he announced, "The day France takes possession of New Orleans we must marry ourselves to the British fleet and nation," and he dispatched James Monroe to talk with the British about a military alliance. He also had Monroe instruct the American minister to France, Robert Livingston, that he could spend as much as $2 million to try to purchase New Orleans and as much adjacent real estate as possible.

Napoleon may have been considering the creation of a Caribbean empire when he acquired Louisiana from Spain. Rich with sugar, the island of **Santo Domingo** was strategically well placed to serve as a hub for French exploitation of the North American interior. France and Spain had shared ownership of the island until an army under the leadership of a former slave named **François Dominique Toussaint L'Ouverture** liberated the French half in 1791 and the Spanish half ten years later. With backing from the French, Toussaint made himself president of the unified nation, but in 1802 Napoleon betrayed him by sending an invasion force to reclaim Santo Domingo. Americans feared that the French army's next destination would be New Orleans.

The French army was able to defeat and capture Toussaint, but no more. The rebels' military skills and yellow fever, malaria, and other tropical diseases destroyed the French force. Stymied in the Caribbean, Napoleon turned his full attention back to extending his holdings in Europe and was seeking funds to finance a continental war. Thus, by the time Monroe and Livingston entered into negotiations with the French in 1803, Napoleon had instructed Foreign Minister Talleyrand to offer the whole of Louisiana to the Americans for $15 million.

transship The practice of shipping cargo to a secondary port and then transferring it to other ships for transport to a final destination; cargos from up the Mississippi River were shipped by barge to New Orleans and then loaded onto ocean-going vessels to be carried to American ports along the Atlantic coast.

Santo Domingo Caribbean island (originally named Hispaniola by Christopher Columbus and also known as Saint Domingue) shared by the modern nations of Haiti and the Dominican Republic.

François Dominique Toussaint L'Ouverture Black revolutionary who liberated the island of Santo Domingo, only to see it reinvaded by the French in 1802.

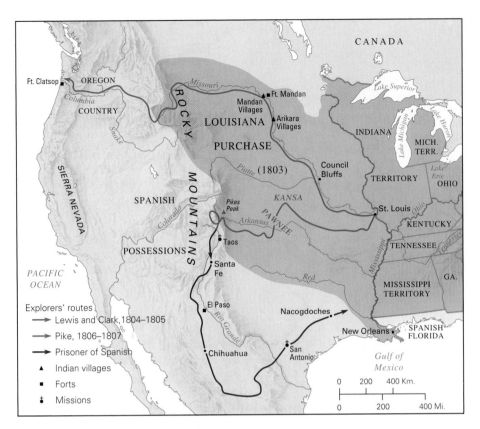

MAP 8.2 Louisiana Purchase and American Exploration   As this map shows, President Jefferson added an enormous tract of land to the United States when he purchased Louisiana from France in 1803. The president was eager to learn as much as possible about the new territory and sent two exploration teams into the West. In addition to collecting information, Lewis and Clark's and Pike's expeditions sought to commit Indian groups along their paths to alliances with the United States and to undermine French, Spanish, and British relations with the Indians, even in those areas that were not officially part of the United States. In Pike's case, this covert intelligence assignment led to his arrest by Spanish authorities and eventual expulsion from their territory.

Pushing Westward

Although Livingston and Monroe had been authorized to spend only $2 million for the purchase of Louisiana, they jumped at the deal offered by Talleyrand, hoping that President Jefferson would approve. The president not only approved but was overjoyed. The deal contained three important benefits for Jefferson and the nation. It removed one European power—France—from the continent and saved Jefferson from having to ally the United States with Britain. It secured the Mississippi River for shipments of American agricultural products to industrial Europe. And it doubled the size of the United States, opening uncharted new expanses for settlement by yeoman farmers.

The **Louisiana Purchase** was immensely popular among most Americans, but it raised significant constitutional questions that helped to keep party divisions alive. The framers of the Constitution had made

> **Louisiana Purchase**   The U.S. purchase of Louisiana from France for $15 million in 1803; the Louisiana Territory extended from the Mississippi River to the Rocky Mountains.

The winter that the Lewis and Clark expedition spent among the Mandan Indians proved to be a learning experience for both the explorers and the Native Americans. This painting by nineteenth-century artist C. M. Russell captures one of those experiences as leaders among the Hidatsa Indians encounter their first African American—William Clark's servant York. Puzzled by his color, the quizzical Indians rubbed at York's skin to see if the color would come off. *Montana Historical Society.*

no provision for the acquisition of new territories by the United States. Opponents of the Louisiana Purchase—mostly northeastern Federalists who feared the dilution of their political and economic power—asserted that the nation was prohibited from extending westward beyond its then-current boundaries without specific constitutional authorization. Ignoring the constitutional issue, Jefferson submitted the purchase to Congress for ratification in November 1803, winning an overwhelming majority. He later defended this action: "Strict observance to the written laws is doubtless one of the high duties of a good citizen, but it is not the highest. The laws of necessity, of self-preservation, of saving our country when in danger, are of a higher obligation."

Even before the Louisiana Purchase, "laws of necessity" had led Jefferson to exert presidential power in an unusual way. Although Spanish, French, and American fur traders, outlaws, and soldiers of fortune had crisscrossed Louisiana over the years, little systematic exploration had been done. When rumors of the land transfer between France and Spain began circulating, Jefferson started preparations to send his private secretary, **Meriwether Lewis,** and a small party into the territory to take a look at the land (see Map 8.2). In a series of confidential letters, Jefferson informed Lewis that the party was to pretend to be on a scientific mission, and the president issued false papers to that effect. Their primary mission, however, was to note the numbers of French, Spanish, and other agents in the area, along with the numbers and condition of the Indians, and to chart major water-

ways and other important strategic sites. They were also to open the way for direct dealings between the Indians and the United States, undermining the Indians' relations with the Spanish and French whenever possible. Early in 1803, months before Congress authorized the Louisiana Purchase, the president sought and received a secret congressional **appropriation** granting the funds necessary to finance the mission.

Lewis, his co-commander **William Clark,** and the rest of the Corps of Discovery set out by boat in the spring of 1804. Pushing its way up the Missouri River, the party arrived among the Mandan Indians (see pages 14; 49) in present-day North Dakota in the late fall. They chose to winter among the Mandans, a decision that may have ensured the expedition's success. The Mandans were a settled agricultural group who had been farming along the upper Missouri for over a thousand years. Unlike many of their neighbors, they had resisted the temptation to abandon their villages for mounted buffalo hunting

Meriwether Lewis   Jefferson aide who was sent to explore the Louisiana Territory in 1803; he later served as its governor.

appropriation   Public funds authorized for a specific purpose.

William Clark   Soldier and explorer who joined Meriwether Lewis as co-leader on the expedition to explore the Louisiana Territory; he was responsible for mapmaking.

when horses had arrived on the northern plains after 1700. Their villages, which offered food and shelter for the wandering hunting tribes, soon became hubs in the evolving Plains trading and raiding system (see pages 49; 50). By wintering with the Mandans, the expedition came into contact with many of the Indian and European groups that participated in the complex economy of the West. Lewis and Clark acted on Jefferson's secret instructions by learning all they could from the Mandans and their visitors about the fur trade, the nature of military alliances, and the tribes that lived farther west.

One particularly important contact Lewis and Clark made during the Mandan winter was with a French trapper named Charbonneau and his Shoshone wife, **Sacajawea.** Between the two of them, Sacajawea and Charbonneau spoke several of the languages understood by the Indians in the Far West and possessed knowledge about the geography and the various peoples in the area. With their help, Lewis and Clark were able to make contact with the Shoshones, who aided them in crossing the Rocky Mountains. From there, the expedition passed from Indian group to Indian group along a chain of friendship. The Nez Perce Indians, for example, were allied to the Shoshones and accepted the party hospitably. The Nez Perces then sent word down the Columbia River that these men were allies, ensuring their safe and speedy passage. Following this chain of Indian hospitality, the expedition finally reached the Pacific Ocean in November 1805.

While many Native American groups genuinely welcomed Lewis and Clark, others remained dubious about the newcomers. On the return trip, part of the expedition ventured off its original outward course to explore new territory and encountered a party of **Piegan Indians.** Allied closely with trading interests in Canada and involved in sporadic war with the Shoshones, the Piegans afforded the party no special diplomatic status, attempting to steal a gun from them while they slept. The Americans thwarted the theft and, in the melee that followed, were able to fight the Piegans off long enough to make a strategic retreat. Years later, Piegan Indians and their allies in the northern Rockies cited this encounter as justification for continuing hostilities toward Americans and their Indian trading partners.

Europeans in the interior were also skeptical of American "scientific" parties. In 1806 Lieutenant Zebulon M. Pike set out on a venture to explore the territory between the Missouri and Red Rivers south of Lewis and Clark's route. The Pawnee and Kansa Indians in the region received Pike with great reserve,

pointing out that the Spanish had recently sent an army through their territory demanding Indian allegiance. Undaunted, Pike continued his journey by following the trail left by the Spanish force, eventually arriving in what is now Colorado (see Map 8.2). From there, he pushed southward, venturing into New Mexico. Though he claimed that this trespass was an innocent navigational error, his party nonetheless was captured by a Spanish army detachment and held for three months. Pike and his men were finally escorted back to the United States and set free with a warning to stay out of Spanish lands and Spanish affairs.

Challenge and Uncertainty in Jefferson's America

■ How did the life of the average American change during Jefferson's presidency?

■ What place did Native Americans and African Americans have in the America Jefferson envisioned? How did each of these groups respond to these roles?

Jefferson's policies not only put the nation on a new road politically and economically but also brought a new spirit into the land. The Virginian's commitment to opportunity and progress, to openness and frugality, offered a stark contrast in approach and style to the policies of his predecessors. The congressional elections of 1802 and the presidential election in 1804 proved Jefferson's popularity and the Republican Party's strong appeal. Nevertheless, some disturbing social and intellectual undercurrents began to surface during his second term. National expansion strained conventional social institutions as white farmers, entrepreneurs, and adventurers seized the opportunities that Republican economic and expansion policies offered. Adding to the strain was the fact that the Jeffersonian spirit was more of a promise than a commitment and that Jefferson's vision for the republic excluded many.

The Heritage of Partisan Politics

The popularity of Jefferson's party was abundantly clear in 1804. Jefferson had won an extremely narrow

Sacajawea Shoshone woman who served as guide and interpreter on the Lewis and Clark expedition.

Piegan Indians The branch of the Blackfoot Indians who resided in areas of what is now Montana during the late eighteenth and early nineteenth centuries.

victory in 1800, and his Republican Party had won significant but hardly overwhelming majorities in Congress. The congressional elections of 1802, however, had virtually eclipsed Federalist power, and Federalists faced the presidential election of 1804 with dread. Former president John Adams commented, "The power of the Administration rests upon the support of a much stronger majority of the people throughout the Union than the former administrations ever possessed since the first establishment of the Constitution."

Despite an abiding faith in the emerging two-party system, staunch Federalist congressman Fisher Ames withdrew from public life, followed by John Jay and other prominent leaders. Some traditional Federalists, however, continued to fight. The party tapped former vice-presidential candidate Charles Cotesworth Pinckney to head the 1804 presidential ticket. For the vice presidency, the Federalists chose Rufus King, a defender of the notion of loyal opposition and the two-party system.

Federalists had trouble identifying issues on which to build a viable platform. Hoping to capitalize on **anti-expansionist** fears in New England and sentiments favoring states' rights in the South, the Federalists focused their campaign on Jefferson's acquisition of Louisiana. In a direct appeal to Yankee **frugality,** Federalists charged that Jefferson had paid too much for the new territory and was attempting to use the region to build a unified agrarian political faction. Pinckney accused Jefferson of violating his own political principles by exerting a federal power not explicitly granted in the Constitution. Some Republicans shared this view, but no one could question Jefferson's overall success in accomplishing the party's goals. During his first administration, Jefferson had eliminated internal taxes, stimulated westward migration, eliminated the hated Alien and Sedition Acts, and rekindled hope in the hearts of many disaffected Americans.

At the same time, he had proved that he was no threat to national commerce or to individual affluence. Despite Federalist fears, the economy continued to grow at the same rate during Jefferson's tenure in office as it had under the Federalists. In the process, those who engaged in international trade amassed enormous fortunes. Such economic growth permitted Jefferson to maintain a favorable **balance of payments** throughout his first administration, a feat the Federalists had never achieved. And with Gallatin's help, Jefferson had proved his fiscal responsibility by building up a multimillion-dollar Treasury surplus.

The enormous scope of Jefferson's successes and the limited scope of his opponent's platform helped swing the election of 1804 firmly over to the Republicans. Jefferson won 162 electoral votes to Pinckney's 14, carrying every state except Connecticut and Delaware.

Westward Expansion and Social Stress

Eastern Federalists and other critics of Jefferson's vision had some justification for their concerns about the rapid growth of the West. A baby boom had followed the Revolution, and as new territories opened in the West, young people streamed into the region at a rate that alarmed many. This had an unsettling effect on communities in the East. During the eighteenth century, older people maintained authority by controlling the distribution of land to their children. With only so much worthwhile land to go around, sons and daughters lived with and worked for their parents until their elders saw fit to deed property over to them. As a result, children living in the East generally did not become independent—that is, they did not become church members, marry, or operate their own farms or businesses—until they were in their thirties. Economic opportunities available on the frontier, however, lessened young people's need to rely on their parents for support and lowered the age at which they began to break away. During the early part of the nineteenth century, the age at which children attained independence fell steadily. By the 1820s, children were joining churches in their teens and marrying in their early to mid-twenties. Breathing the new air of independence, intrepid young people not only migrated west but also challenged their parents' authority at home. Obviously social and political traditionalists were upset. Business interests in the East were also upset as they witnessed westward expansion drawing off population, which in time would drive up the price of labor and reduce profits.

Conditions out west were even less stable as rapid growth put enormous stress on conventional institutions. The population of Ohio, for example, grew from 45,000 in 1800 to 231,000 in 1810, and similar

---

anti-expansionist One opposed to the policy of expanding a country by acquiring new territory.

frugality An unwillingness to spend money for unnecessary things; by stereotype, New Englanders (Yankees) supposedly have an ingrained tendency to frugality.

balance of payments The difference between a nation's total payments to foreign countries and its total receipts from abroad.

The Mississippi River drainage system was the only reliable transportation route for Americans moving into the West during the early 1800s. Farmers moved produce to market on keelboats like the one depicted here. Above decks, cargo and livestock endured weather and exposure to mosquitoes and other river menaces. Below decks, however, there was a cabin-like environment where people could eat, drink, and sleep in comfort during the often long trip downriver. One problem with this mode of transport was that the current on the giant river made upstream travel impossible during much of the year, so boats like this one were often sold for lumber after they reached New Orleans. *Miriam and Ira D. Wallach Division of Art, Prints and Photographs, The New York Public Library. Astor, Lenox and Tilden Foundations; Musee d'Histoire Naturelle, Le Havre, France.*

rates of growth occurred in the new states of Tennessee and Kentucky and in territories from Louisiana north to Michigan and west to Missouri. Authorities in the West found these increases challenging as they tried to deal with the practical matters of maintaining governments, economies, and peaceful relations among the new settlers and between the settlers and neighboring Indians.

Most of the people who moved west looked forward to achieving the agrarian self-sufficiency that Jefferson advocated, but life in the West was far from what Jefferson had hoped it would be. Inexpensive, reliable transportation was impossible in the vast, rugged interior, and Jefferson's notion of breadbasket America trading with industrial Europe was doomed without it. No navigable streams ran eastward from America's interior across the Appalachians to the Atlantic, and the ridges of those mountains made road building extremely difficult.

Only two reliable routes existed for transporting produce from the interior to shipping centers in the East. The Ohio-Mississippi-Missouri drainage system provided a reliable watercourse, and huge cargoes flowed along its stream. Shipping goods on the Mississippi, however, was a dangerous and expensive operation. Because of the river's strong current, loads could be shipped only one way—downstream. Rafts were built for the purpose and then were broken up and sold for lumber in New Orleans. Shippers had to return home by foot on the **Natchez Trace.** On both legs of the journey, travelers risked attack by river

Natchez Trace A road connecting Natchez, Mississippi, with Nashville, Tennessee; it was commercially and strategically important in the late eighteenth and early nineteenth centuries.

Evangelical denominations gained ever wider followings during the early nineteenth century as the uncertainties accompanying rapid expansion took their toll on national self-confidence. Mass baptisms like this one painted by Russian tourist Pavel Svinin celebrated the emotional moment of conversion and the individual's rebirth as a Christian. *"A Philadelphia Anabaptist Immersion During a Storm" by Pavel Svinin. The Metropolitan Museum of Art, Rogers Fund, 1942. (42.95.20. Photograph © 1979 The Metropolitan Museum of Art.)*

pirates, Indians, and sickness. Moreover, it was virtually impossible for shippers to take manufactured goods back with them because of the condition of the roads and the distances involved. The other river route—the St. Lawrence River, flowing east from the Great Lakes to the northern Atlantic—presented similar problems. In addition, that river passed through British Canada and therefore was closed to American commercial traffic.

As a result of geographical isolation and the rapid pace of settlement, the economy in the West became highly localized. Settlers arriving with neither food nor seed bought surplus crops produced by established farmers. The little capital that was generated in this way supported the development of local industries in hundreds of farming villages. Enterprising craftsmen ranging from **coopers** to **wheelwrights** produced hand-manufactured items on demand. As long as people kept moving into an area, local economies boomed. But when new arrivals slowed and then stopped, the market for surplus crops and local manufactures collapsed, and the economy went bust. Swinging from boom to bust and back again became a way of life in newly settled areas.

Along with economic instability, social instability was also common. The odd mixture of ethnic, religious, and national groups found in western villages did little to bring cohesiveness to community life.

The Religious Response to Social Change

The changes taking place in the young republic stirred conflicting religious currents. One was liberalism in religious thought. The other was a new **evangelicalism.**

Born of the Enlightenment (see page 102) in France, Scotland, and England, liberal religious thought emphasized the connection between **rationalism** and faith. To rationalists like both Jefferson and Adams, the possibility that a being as perfect as God might behave irrationally was unthinkable. In fact, for such

cooper   A person who makes or repairs wooden barrels.

wheelwright   A person who makes or repairs wheels for carts, wagons, or other vehicles.

evangelicalism   A Protestant religious persuasion that emphasizes the literal truth of the Gospels and salvation through faith alone; in the early nineteenth century, it became infused with increasing amounts of romantic emotionalism and an emphasis on converting others.

rationalism   The theory that the exercise of reason, rather than the acceptance of authority or spiritual revelation, is the only valid basis for belief and the best source of spiritual truth.

men, the more plain, reasonable, and verifiable religious claims were, the more likely it was that they emanated from God. Less perfect than God, it was man who had cluttered the plain revealed truth with irrational claims and insolvable mysteries. For his part, Jefferson was so convinced of this logic that he edited his own version of the Bible, keeping only the moral principles and the solid historical facts and discarding anything supernatural.

This liberal creed led many, including Jefferson, to abandon organized religion altogether. Not all liberals were so quick to bolt organized worship however. John Adams, for example, continued to adhere to New England Congregationalism, but he and others used their influence to promote a young and more liberal clergy who sought to insert a heavy dose of rationalism into the old Puritan structure. Rejecting such traditional mysteries as the **Trinity** and the literal divinity of Christ, a so-called **Unitarian** movement emerged and expanded inside Congregational churches during the years just before and following the American Revolution. Liberal influence within Congregationalism became so prominent in New England that Unitarians were able to engineer the election of their own **Henry Ware** as the senior professor of theology at Harvard College, formerly the educational heart of orthodox Calvinist America. Though outraged, more traditional Congregationalists did little immediately to oust liberals from their churches. In the decades to come, however, doctrinal disagreements between the parties would lead to outright religious war.

While deism and Unitarianism were gaining strong footholds in eastern cities, disorder, insecurity, and missionizing activities were helping to foster a very different kind of religious response in the West. Although Methodists, Baptists, Presbyterians, and evangelical Congregationalists disagreed on many specific principles, they all emphasized the spirited preaching that could bring about the emotional moment of conversion—the moment of realization that without the saving grace of God, every soul is lost. Each of these denominations concentrated on training a new, young ministry and sending it to preach in every corner of the nation. In this way, another religious awakening swept across America, beginning in Cane Ridge, Kentucky, in 1801 and spreading throughout the South and West.

The new evangelicalism stressed the individual nature of salvation but at the same time emphasized the importance of Christian community. Looking back to the first generation of Puritans in America, the new evangelicals breathed new life into the old Puritan notion of God's plan for the universe and the leading role that Americans were to play in its unfolding. As early nineteenth-century Presbyterian divine Lyman Beecher put it, "It was the opinion of [Jonathan] Edwards that the millennium would commence in America . . . all providential signs of the times lend corroboration to it."

Early nineteenth-century evangelicals formed official **synods,** councils, and conventions as well as hundreds of voluntary associations designed to carry out what they characterized as God's plan for America. These organizations helped counterbalance the forces of extreme individualism and social disorder by providing ideological underpinnings for the expansive behavior of westerners and a sense of mission to ease the insecurities produced by venturing into the unknown. They also provided an institutional framework that brought some stability to communities in which traditional controls were lacking. These attractive features helped evangelicalism to sweep across the West. During the early nineteenth century, it became the dominant religious persuasion in that region.

The Problem of Race in Jefferson's Republic

Jefferson's policies enabled many Americans to benefit from the nation's development, but they certainly did not help everyone. Neither Native Americans nor African Americans had much of a role in Jefferson's republic, and each group was subject to different forms of unequal treatment during the Jeffersonian era.

A slaveholder himself, Jefferson expressed strong views about African Americans. In his *Notes on the*

Trinity   The Christian belief that God consists of three divine persons: Father, Son, and Holy Spirit.

Unitarianism   A religion that denies the Trinity, teaching that God exists only in one person; it also stresses individual freedom of belief and the free use of reason in religion.

Henry Ware   Liberal Congregationalist who was elected senior theologian at Harvard College in 1805, making Unitarianism the dominant religious view at the previously Calvinist stronghold.

synod   An official governing council of a religious denomination that makes decisions on theological matters and matters of church law.

Born a free man in Maryland, Benjamin Banneker took full advantage of the educational opportunities that were offered to him and quickly displayed that he was a mathematical prodigy. Under the tutelage of businessman and gentleman scientist Joseph Ellicott, Banneker eventually became so proficient at trigonometry and calculus that he was invited to join the engineering team that helped to lay out the nation's capital at Washington, D.C., and published his own almanac of astronomical predictions. In doing so, he challenged prevailing stereotypes concerning the intellectual abilities possess by African Americans. He even engaged in a spirited correspondence with Thomas Jefferson himself, asserting that the president needed to revise his attitudes about race. *Courtesy of the American Antiquarian Society.*

State of Virginia (1781), Jefferson asserted that blacks were "inferior to whites in the endowments both of body and mind." Even when presented with direct evidence of superior black intellectual accomplishments, Jefferson remained unmoved. When the well-respected African American mathematician, astronomer, and engineer Benjamin Banneker sent a copy of an almanac he had prepared to Jefferson, the then secretary of state replied, "No body wishes more than I do to see such proofs as you exhibit, that nature has given to our black brethren, talents equal to those of the other colors of men." However, he refused to acknowledge that Banneker's work provided such proofs. "I have a long letter from Banneker," Jefferson later told his friend Joel Barlow, "which shows him to have had a

mind of very common stature indeed." He went on to suggest that the almanac had actually been written by a white engineer who was intent on "puffing" Banneker's reputation.

Jefferson was convinced, and stated publicly on many occasions, that the white and black races could not live together without inevitably polluting both. This was the key reason for what little opposition he voiced to slavery and for his continued involvement in various projects to remove African Americans by colonizing them in Africa. And yet despite this attitude, many of his contemporaries believed that he kept a slave mistress, Sally Hemings, by whom he fathered several children, a contention that modern DNA evidence has demonstrated as credible. Even so, almost no documentary evidence about the relationship exists despite the fact that hundreds of the nation's most prolific writers (and gossips) passed through Jefferson's home regularly. Circumstantial evidence, however, suggests that their relationship was an exclusive one and lasted for a long period of time. And traditions passed down through generations of Sally Hemings's descendants claim that theirs was a romantic, even sentimental, bond.

Given his belief in racial inequality, it would seem contradictory that Jefferson could have had a long-term affectionate relationship with an African American woman. If so, it reflects equally deep-seated contradictions that shot through American society at the time. Truly a man of his century and his social class, Jefferson was convinced that women, like slaves, existed to serve and entertain men. Thus his entanglement with Hemings, who probably was the half-sister of Martha Wayles Skelton, Jefferson's deceased wife, would have seemed no more unequal or unnatural than his marriage to Martha. But while the relationship may have seemed perfectly natural behind closed doors, the race code to which Jefferson gave voice in his various publications and official utterances defined it as entirely unacceptable in public. This rigid separation between public and private behavior led Jefferson to keep the relationship secret, and his friends and family—even most of his political enemies—joined him in a conspiracy of silence. This, too, was reflective of broader social ambiguities, contradictions that defined the sex lives of masters and slaves in Jefferson's South.

Throughout the Jeffersonian era, the great majority of African Americans lived in that South, and most of them were slaves. But from the 1790s onward, the number of free blacks increased steadily. Emancipation did not bring equality, however, even in northern states. Many states did not permit free blacks to testify in court, vote, or exercise other fundamental freedoms accorded to whites. Public schools often refused admission to black children. Even churches were often closed to blacks who wished to worship.

Some African Americans began to respond to systematic exclusion and to express their cultural and social identity by forming their own institutions. In Philadelphia, tension between white and free black Methodists led former slave Richard Allen to form the Bethel Church for Negro Methodists in 1793. Two years later, Allen became the first black deacon ordained in America. Ongoing tension with the white Methodist hierarchy, however, eventually led Allen to secede from the church and form his own **African Methodist Episcopal Church** (Bethel) in 1816. Similar controversies in New York led black divine James Varick to found an African Methodist Episcopal Church (Zion) in that city in 1821.

African American leadership was not confined to religious and intellectual realms. **James Forten,** for example, a free-born African American, followed up on his experience as a sailor in the Revolutionary navy with a career as a sailmaker in Philadelphia. Despite both overt and subtle racial discrimination, he acquired his own company in 1798, eventually becoming a major employer of both African American and white workers. Though himself a Quaker, Forten often cooperated with Richard Allen but did not subscribe to projects designed to separate the races, working consistently—even to the point of petitioning Congress and the Pennsylvania assembly—to pass laws ensuring desegregation and equal treatment. In cooperation with other African American entrepreneurs, such as Boston's Paul Cuffe, Forten invested expertise, capital, and personal influence in an effort to create jobs for black city-dwellers and opportunities for budding black businessmen. Despite these efforts, the overall racial atmosphere in Jefferson's America significantly limited the number of African American leaders who would attain positions of wealth or influence.

Jefferson thought differently of Native Americans than he did of African Americans. He considered Indians to be "savages" but was not convinced that they were biologically inferior to Europeans: "They are formed in mind as well as in body, on the same module with the 'Homo Sapiens Europaeus,'" he said. Jefferson attributed the differences between Indians and Europeans to what he termed the Indians' cultural retardation. He was confident that if whites lifted Indians out of their uncivilized state and put them on an equal footing with Europeans, Indian populations

would grow, their physical condition would improve, and they would be able to participate in the yeoman republic on an equal footing with whites.

Jefferson's Indian policy reflected this attitude. Jefferson created a series of government-owned trading posts at which Indians were offered goods at cheap prices. He believed that Indians who were exposed to white manufactures would come to agree that white culture was superior and would make the rational decision to adopt that culture wholesale. At the same time, both the government and right-minded philanthropists should engage in instructing Native Americans in European methods of farming, ensuring that these former "savages" would emerge as good, Republican-voting frontier farmers. Until this process of **acculturation** was complete, however, Jefferson believed the Indians, like children, should be protected from those who would take advantage of them or lead them astray. Also like children, the Indians were not to be trusted to exercise the rights and responsibilities of citizenship. Thus Indian rights were not protected by the Constitution but were subject to the whims of the Senate—which drafted and ratified Indian treaties—and of the army—which enforced those treaties.

The chief problem for Jeffersonian Indian policy was not the Indians' supposed cultural retardation but their rapid modernization. Among groups such as the Cherokees and Creeks, members of a rising new elite—often the offspring of European fathers and Indian mothers—led their people toward greater prosperity and diplomatic independence. Alexander McGillivray of the Creeks, for example, deftly manipulated American, French, and Spanish interests to Creek advantage while building a strong economic base founded on both communally and privately owned plantations. In similar fashion, the rising Cherokee elite in 1794 established a centralized government that

---

African Methodist Episcopal Church African American branch of Methodism established in Philadelphia in 1816 and in New York in 1821.

James Forten African American entrepreneur with a successful sailmaking business in Philadelphia who provided leadership for black business enterprises and advocated both racial integration and equal rights during the Jeffersonian era.

acculturation Changes in the culture of a group or an individual as a result of contact with a different culture.

began pushing the Cherokees into a new era of wealth and power.

Although Jefferson might have greeted such acculturation with enthusiasm, the Indians' white neighbors generally did not. Envisioning all-out war between the states and the Indians—war that his reduced government and shrunken military was helpless to prevent—Jefferson advanced an alternative. Having acquired Louisiana, Jefferson suggested the creation of large reserves to which Indians currently residing within states could relocate, taking themselves out of state jurisdictions and removing themselves from the corrupting influence of the "baser elements" of white society. Although he did not advocate the use of force to move Indians west of the Mississippi, he made every effort to convince them to migrate. This idea of segregating Native Americans from other Americans formed the basis for Indian policy for the rest of the century.

Individual Voices

Examining a Primary Source

Congress Debates George Logan's Mission to France

Even before any official news had reached Washington, rumors were flying about George Logan's trip to France to negotiate an end to the diplomatic crisis that was plaguing the nation. Less than a month after Logan had set off for Europe, Federalists in Congress proposed a new law that would make any such efforts at unofficial peacemaking a federal crime. Republican representative Albert Gallatin urged patience: wait for the president to present the facts to Congress as he had promised to do. But the Federalists persisted, leading Gallatin to ask why they were so eager to criminalize Logan's actions. In a moment of heated candor, Massachusetts Federalist Harrison G. Otis blurted out the answer, revealing what was really at work inside the radical circle.

■ *What is Otis saying here? What does he perceive as the motive behind the Republican criticism of a bill to outlaw acts like Logan's?*

■ *This speech is quoted from The Debates and Proceedings in the Congress of the United States, the official record of Congress from 1789 through 1824. In this source, speeches were generally reported in the third person; hence Otis is referred to as "he."*

■ *What is Otis saying was the actual motivation for proposing this bill? What conclusions can you draw from this statement about the nature of partisan politics in 1798? To what extent is such political practice in play today?*

Again: it is insisted that the secret of the resolution on the table, was to perpetuate the division of party, and that, although but few real causes of dissension remain, yet we are determined to throw down the gauntlet and excite the greatest possible irritation. ■ *This accusation he denied.* ■ *He did not believe that the resolution was introduced with any such design; but if such had been the object of the mover, the blame would not attach to him or to his friends. They might even then have justified themselves upon principles of self-defence. He appealed to the whole House that, within a few days after the commencement of this session, they were threatened with a notice that motions might be expected in favor of repealing the Alien and Sedition acts; which could owe their origin to no other intention but that of inflaming the public mind, and of persevering in the endeavor to expose the Administration and its friends to odious imputations. Therefore we should stand acquitted, if, instead of giving time to our adversaries to furnish their weapons, and carry war into our borders, we had seized this occasion to strike the first blow.* ■

Summary

Americans faced a difficult choice in 1796: to continue in a Federalist direction with John Adams or to move into new and uncharted regions of democracy with Thomas Jefferson. Factionalism and voter indecision led to Adams's election as president and Jefferson's as vice president. The split outcome frightened Federalists, and they used every excuse to make war on their political opponents. Diplomatically, they let relations with France sour to the point that the two nations were at war in all but name. At home, they used repressive measures such as the Alien and Sedition Acts to try to silence opponents, and they imposed tariffs and taxes that were hateful to many. Reminded of what they had rebelled against in the Revolution, in 1800 the American people decided to give Jefferson and the Republican faction a chance.

Although Jefferson would call the election "the revolution of 1800," even hard-line Federalists such as Hamilton were sure that the general direction in government would not change. Just to be safe, however, Federalists stacked the court system so that Republicans would face insurmountable constraints if they tried to change government too much. At the same time, they organized themselves into a true political party, an ever-present watchdog on the activities of their rivals.

Jefferson's inaugural address in 1801 seemed to announce an end to partisan warfare, but both Madison and hard-line Republicans in Congress attempted to restrict Federalist power in the court system. The Republican program, however, was not entirely negative. Jefferson looked toward a future in which most Americans could own enough land to produce life's necessities for themselves and would be beholden to no one and thus free to vote as their consciences and rationality dictated. To attain this end, Jefferson ordered massive reductions in the size of government, the elimination of internal federal taxes, and rapid westward expansion, including the purchase of the vast territory called Louisiana. For some the outcome was a spirit of excitement and optimism, but not everyone was so hopeful. Many were unsure and fearful of the new order's novelty and of the stresses that rapid expansion engendered; social change disrupted lives and communities.

Jefferson clearly wanted most Americans to share in the bounty of an expanded nation, but not all were free to share equally. For American Indians, the very success of Jefferson's expansion policy meant a contraction in their freedom of action. African Americans also found that the equality Jefferson promised to others was not intended for them, though many like Benjamin Banneker and Paul Cuffe grasped for it anyway. As to women, Jefferson himself observed, "The appointment of a woman to office is an innovation for which the public is not prepared, nor am I"; they were encouraged to play an active role in the new nation but were expected to do so only through their roles as wives and mothers.

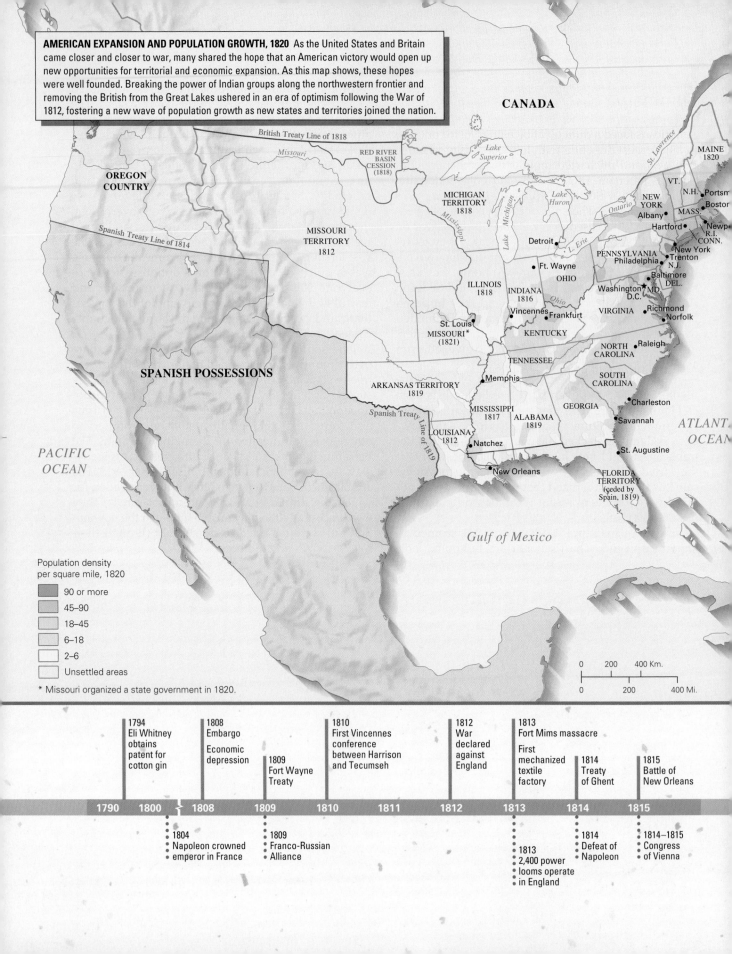

AMERICAN EXPANSION AND POPULATION GROWTH, 1820 As the United States and Britain came closer and closer to war, many shared the hope that an American victory would open up new opportunities for territorial and economic expansion. As this map shows, these hopes were well founded. Breaking the power of Indian groups along the northwestern frontier and removing the British from the Great Lakes ushered in an era of optimism following the War of 1812, fostering a new wave of population growth as new states and territories joined the nation.

CANADA

British Treaty Line of 1818

OREGON COUNTRY

Missouri

RED RIVER BASIN CESSION (1818)

Lake Superior

MAINE 1820

Spanish Treaty Line of 1814

MICHIGAN TERRITORY 1818

Lake Huron

VT.

N.H. Portsm

MISSOURI TERRITORY 1812

Lake Michigan

Mississippi

L. Ontario

St. Lawrence

NEW YORK
Albany

Detroit

L. Erie

Ft. Wayne

OHIO

NEW
YORK

MASS.
Boston

Newp

R.I.
CONN.

Hartford

New York

ILLINOIS 1818

INDIANA 1816

Ohio

PENNSYLVANIA

Trenton

Philadelphia

N.J.

Vincennes Frankfort

Washington
D.C.

Baltimore
MD.

DEL.

St. Louis
MISSOURI*
(1821)

KENTUCKY

VIRGINIA

Richmond
Norfolk

SPANISH POSSESSIONS

TENNESSEE

NORTH
CAROLINA

Raleigh

ARKANSAS TERRITORY 1819

Memphis

SOUTH
CAROLINA

Spanish Treaty Line of 1819

MISSISSIPPI 1817

ALABAMA 1819

GEORGIA

Charleston

LOUISIANA 1812

Savannah

ATLANT.
OCEAN

Natchez

St. Augustine

PACIFIC
OCEAN

New Orleans

FLORIDA
TERRITORY
(ceded by
Spain, 1819)

Gulf of Mexico

Population density
per square mile, 1820

	90 or more
	45–90
	18–45
	6–18
	2–6
	Unsettled areas

* Missouri organized a state government in 1820.

0   200   400 Km.

0   200   400 Mi.

1790   1800   1808   1809   1810   1811   1812   1813   1814   1815

1794
Eli Whitney
obtains
patent for
cotton gin

1808
Embargo

Economic
depression

1809
Fort Wayne
Treaty

1810
First Vincennes
conference
between Harrison
and Tecumseh

1812
War
declared
against
England

1813
Fort Mims massacre

First
mechanized
textile
factory

1814
Treaty
of Ghent

1815
Battle of
New Orleans

1804
Napoleon crowned
emperor in France

1809
Franco-Russian
Alliance

1813
2,400 power
looms operate
in England

1814
Defeat of
Napoleon

1814–1815
Congress
of Vienna

Increasing Conflict and War, 1805–1815

American Expansion and Population Growth, 1820

Using the map on the facing page, and comparing it to the opening map for Chapter 8 (see page 210), examine the twin dynamics of population growth and westward expansion that characterized this era. How did these twin dynamics influence American political and diplomatic decision making and social life for all Americans between Jefferson's second presidential administration and the years immediately following the War of 1812?

Individual Choices

TECUMSEH

Coming of age in the years when his people were facing their greatest challenge from invading Europeans, Tecumseh followed in his father's footsteps by becoming an influential war leader among the Shawnee people. And following his mother's influence, a Creek Indian who had married across tribal lines, he persistently emphasized the unity between all Native American people. Both influences would lead him to undertake heroic efforts to preserve what remained of the Indians' territory in the years following the American Revolution. But neither his war skills nor his diplomatic skills would win the day. Killed fighting American aggression in the War of 1812, Tecumseh's dismembered body foreshadowed the dismemberment of the Indian nations. According to many experts, this particular portrait, a composite of several sketches, comes closest to capturing what this inspiring Indian leader actually looked like at the peak of his career. *Benson J. Lossing,* The Pictorial Field Book of the War of 1812.

Tecumseh

In the opening days of the nineteenth century, most Americans believed the native people in the continent's interior were an odd survival from the Stone Age who lived in isolated tribes constantly warring among themselves and were doomed to extinction. It was only fair, then, that more progressive people like themselves deserved the Indians' land and inevitable that they would acquire it. Tecumseh knew better, and few did as much to try to stop the loss of Indian land that whites deemed inevitable.

Tecumseh's entire life stood in stark contrast to dominant white theories about Indian life. Although he was born among the Shawnee Indians in Ohio in around 1768, Tecumseh's mother was actually a Creek Indian from Alabama. His parents had met when his father had visited the Creeks in the 1750s. In the sophisticated Indian world of the American interior, such visitations were common, as were intergroup marriages. Because of their cosmopolitan connections, the children of such marriages often attained positions of high authority.

A combination of his family connections and a distinguished military career led to Tecumseh's emergence as war chief in the late 1780s. It was in this capacity that he helped defeat American general Arthur St. Clair in 1791. American vengeance came in 1794 when General "Mad" Anthony Wayne crushed an intertribal Indian army that included Tecumseh and his Shawnee warriors at the Battle of Fallen Timbers. Wayne then forced the Indians to sign the Treaty of Greenville, ceding a huge tract of land to the United States. In exchange, the American government promised to protect the Indians from further incursions.

This promise was not kept. In the years that followed, American agents used a combination of bribery, coercion, and outright violence to convince **civil chiefs** to cede more land. Seeking to stop these new invasions, Tecumseh approached war chiefs with a bold plan to stop American expansion once and for all. What he had in mind was a vast alliance system in which the warriors from all tribes along the American frontier would agree to stop civil chiefs from selling land and commit their military might to turn back any American armies that sought to push the Indians out. Joining Tecumseh was his younger brother, Tenskwatawa, the Shawnee Prophet. According to the Prophet, if the Indians gave up white ways and white goods, stopped selling their land, and resumed their traditional lives, the whites would vanish from their world. Taken together, the messages from the two brothers reinforced each other and proved quite compelling. Tecumseh began traveling throughout the frontier, inviting warriors from all tribes to join his expanding alliance.

Bent on continuing expansion, white leaders like Indiana territorial governor William Henry Harrison found the formation of a solid line of Indian resistance frightening. Harrison continually attacked both Tecumseh and the Prophet, trying to discredit them in the eyes of potential followers. For their part, the Prophet and

Tecumseh became increasingly strident in their insistence that Indian people should live out their own lives on their own land.

Abandoning argument and character assassination, Harrison resorted to violence, leading an army to invade the brothers' headquarters at Prophetstown on Tippecanoe Creek in November 1811. With Tecumseh absent seeking new allies, the Prophet attempted to save his village and the promise of his vision, but Harrison's forces overcame a spirited defense and burned the town, destroying its winter food supply. By the time Tecumseh reached Tippecanoe in January, few of his followers remained, and his carefully crafted alliance system was in the process of unraveling. Thinking first of the survivors' welfare, Tecumseh traveled extensively into British territory and among the various tribes in the West, seeking emergency relief supplies to replace what Harrison's forces had destroyed.

It was while he was in the process of raising that relief that war again broke out, this time between the United States and Great Britain. In Canada at the time, Tecumseh quickly learned that American troops were marching through Indian country, harassing villages and confiscating necessary food supplies. With his hopes for a unified Indian barrier to American expansion crushed, he decided that the only hope for the Shawnees' future lay in a British victory. He immediately delivered what was left of his alliance to the British. Tecumseh soon joined Colonel Henry Proctor in commanding an army of twelve hundred Indians from various tribes and nine hundred British regular troops. This joint force enjoyed great success against the Americans, but at the Battle of the Thames, on October 5, 1813, Tecumseh's forces were overrun and Tecumseh was shot. After the battle, triumphant American troops mutilated his body and left it lying on the field.

When Tecumseh died, hopes for a unified Indian resistance died with him, and his mutilated body foreshadowed the future for the Indian land base. Stinging from military defeats and with no more strong voices urging common cause, the once-cosmopolitan world of the Indian interior became what whites imagined it to be: isolated tribes constantly warring among themselves, each scrambling to salvage some small portion of land and dignity. Expansionists like Harrison used this desperation to play one group off against another, carving piece after piece out of the Indian domain until, by 1850, virtually no Indians remained in the territory Tecumseh had tried to preserve.

INTRODUCTION

Tecumseh's situation in Indiana reflected many of the more troubling problems that beset the nation during the opening decades of the nineteenth century. Sitting at the juncture of three worlds—the dynamic republican world of Jeffersonian America, the European imperial world in Canada, and his own Native American world—Tecumseh perceived that unless something happened soon, all three worlds were heading for a crisis.

Jefferson had set an ambitious agenda for the country that was extremely popular with many Americans, but it created serious stresses within the nation and across the world. Along the Atlantic frontier, imperial powers such as Great Britain and France challenged Jefferson's commitment to open trade and freedom of the seas. A war of words, blustering threats, and some open confrontations pushed the United States increasingly toward crisis and triggered economic disaster. Along the western frontier, a variety of Indian

civil chiefs   In many Native American societies, leadership was shared among different classes of chiefs, each of which was responsible for specific political tasks; civil chiefs generally were responsible for overseeing domestic affairs, while war chiefs were responsible for diplomacy.

groups opposed Jefferson's vision of rapid westward expansion. Here too, verbal and some armed conflicts engendered an air of crisis. And to many, including Harrison, these seemed not to be isolated phenomena. Convinced that a conspiracy was afoot between Indian dissidents like Tecumseh and imperial agents from Great Britain and France, an increasing number of Jeffersonians demanded aggressive action.

Try as they might to ease the growing tensions, neither Jefferson and his successor, James Madison, nor Federalist and Republican dissidents could stem the tide of crisis. Harrison finally took matters over the edge: his attack on Prophetstown precipitated a general call for a war that would set the nation on a new course altogether.

Troubling Currents in Jefferson's America

■ How did varying interests between regions of the country complicate Jefferson's political situation during his second term as president?

■ What impact did European politics have on the American economy between 1804 and 1808?

Jefferson's successes, culminating in his victory in the 1804 election, seemed to prove that Republicans had absolute control over the nation's political reins. But factions that would challenge Jefferson's control were forming. A small but vocal coalition of disgruntled Federalists threatened to **secede** from the Union. Even within his own party, Jefferson's supremacy eroded and dissidents emerged. Diplomatic problems also joined domestic ones to trouble Jefferson's second administration.

Emerging Factions in American Politics

The Federalists' failure in the election of 1804 nearly spelled the troubled party's demise. With the West and the South firmly in Jefferson's camp, disgruntled New England Federalists found their once-dominant voice being drowned out by those who shared Jefferson's rather than Hamilton's view of America's future (see page 230). Proclaiming that "the people of the East cannot reconcile their habits, views, and interests with those of the South and West," Federalist leader Timothy Pickering advocated radical changes in the Constitution that he thought might restore balance. Among other things, northeasterners demanded

much stricter standards for admitting new states in the West and the elimination of the Three-Fifths Compromise. Pickering brought together a tight political coalition called the **Essex Junto** to press for these changes.

Regional fissures began to open inside Jefferson's party as well. Throughout Jefferson's first administration, some within his party, especially those from the South, criticized the president for turning his back on republican principles by expanding federal power and interfering with states' rights. One of Jefferson's most vocal critics was his cousin **John Randolph.**

The two Virginia Republicans clashed on the eve of the 1804 election over the **Yazoo affair.** This complicated legal tangle had begun back in 1794 when a group of politically well-connected land speculators succeeded in using bribes and other questionable methods to secure over 40 million acres of land from the State of Georgia for a mere five hundred thousand dollars. Georgia voters were outraged and in the next election threw the corrupt state congressmen who were responsible for the deal out of office. When the new state legislature convened in 1796, it overturned the previous sale, but in the meantime, much of the land had already been sold to individual farmers, who had already taken possession. Georgia ordered these individuals to move off the disputed land, offering them financial compensation, but many refused, taking the matter to court. The political and legal infighting continued until 1802, when Georgia finally joined the other original states in ceding its western

---

secede   To withdraw formally from membership in a political union; threats of secession were used frequently during the early nineteenth century to bring attention to political issues.

Essex Junto   Junto—A group of political conspirators who seek power outside of the regular political process—composed of radical Federalists in Essex County, Massachusetts, who at first advocated constitutional changes that would favor New England politically and later called for New England and New York to secede from the United States.

John Randolph   Virginia Republican politician who was a cousin of Thomas Jefferson; he believed in limited government and objected to several of Jefferson's policies.

Yazoo affair   Corrupt deal in which the Georgia legislature sold a huge tract of public land to speculators for a low price but later overturned the sale; the basis for the Supreme Court case of *Fletcher v. Peck*, discussed in more detail in Chapter 10, which in 1810 established the sanctity of civil contracts over state legislation.

Chronology

Domestic Expansion and International Crisis

1794	Eli Whitney patents cotton gin
1803	Britain steps up impressment Renewal of war between France and Britain
1804	Duel between Alexander Hamilton and Aaron Burr Jefferson reelected
1805	Beginning of Shawnee religious revival
1806	Napoleon issues Berlin Decree
1807	Burr conspiracy trial Founding of Prophetstown *Chesapeake* affair
1808	Embargo of 1808 goes into effect Economic depression begins James Madison elected president
1809	Non-Intercourse Act Fort Wayne Treaty Chouteau brothers form Missouri Fur Company
1810	Macon's Bill No. 2 Vincennes Conference between Harrison and Tecumseh Formation of War Hawk faction
1811	United States breaks trade relations with Britain Second Vincennes Conference between Harrison and Tecumseh Battle of Tippecanoe and destruction of Prophetstown
1812	United States declares war against England United States invades Canada James Madison reelected
1813	Fort Mims massacre Battle of Put-in-Bay Embargo of 1813 First mechanized textile factory, Waltham, Massachusetts Battle of the Thames
1814	Battle of Horseshoe Bend Napoleon defeated British capture and burn Washington, D.C. Battle of Plattsburgh Treaty of Ghent 1815 Battle of New Orleans Treaty of Fort Jackson Portage des Sioux treaties
1819	Treaty of Edwardsville
1825	Prairie du Chien treaties

lands to the United States as part of the compromise necessary to gain ratification for the Constitution (see pages 185–186). With Jefferson's approval, Georgia included the disputed Yazoo lands with other claims, turning the state conflict into a federal one and involving the national government in a matter that Randolph and others believed should have been worked out by the state.

In 1806 Jefferson again irritated Randolph by approaching Congress for a $2 million appropriation to be used to win French influence in convincing Spain to sell Florida to the United States. Citing these and other perceived violations of Republican principles, Randolph announced, "I found I might co-operate or be an honest man." Randolph chose honesty, splitting with Jefferson to form a third party, the **Tertium Quid,** fracturing the Republican united political front.

A second fissure in the party opened over controversial vice president Aaron Burr's political scheming. Upset that Burr had not conceded the presidency immediately after the tied Electoral College vote in 1800, Jefferson snubbed him throughout his first four years in office and then dropped him as his vice-presidential nominee in 1804. But Burr's political failures constituted an opportunity for the Essex Junto: Pickering offered to help Burr become governor of

Tertium Quid   Republican faction formed by John Randolph in protest against Jefferson's plan for acquiring Florida from Spain; the name is Latin and means a "third thing," indicating Randolph's rejection of both the Federalist and Republican Parties.

New York if Burr would deliver the state to the northern confederacy and support secession. Burr agreed, but mainstream New York Federalists were furious, especially Alexander Hamilton. During the New York state election in the spring of 1804, Hamilton was quoted by the press as saying that Burr was "a dangerous man, and one who ought not to be trusted with the reins of government." Burr lost the election in a landslide, wrecking the junto's scheme and pushing himself into an even greater personal and political crisis. Never willing to accept defeat gracefully, Burr demanded that Hamilton retract his statements. When Hamilton refused, Burr challenged him to a duel. An excellent shot, the vice president put a bullet directly through Hamilton's liver, wounding him gravely. Hamilton soon died.

Killing Hamilton did not solve Burr's problem: he was indicted for murder and fled. While in hiding, he made contact with James Wilkinson, with whom he struck up some sort of business deal. A former Revolutionary War commander who had become a freelance adventurer, Wilkinson was employed simultaneously by Spain and the United States, each of which thought he represented their interests. Wilkinson's real loyalties and intentions remain mysterious. At one point, he told Spanish officials that he and Burr intended to establish an independent republic in the Mississippi Valley, but Burr informed the British that they intended to carve a republic out of Spanish territory. Once Congress reconvened in the fall of 1804, Burr became immune, as president of the Senate, from prosecution for killing Hamilton and emerged from hiding. He then used his political connections to gain an appointment for Wilkinson to be governor of the Louisiana Territory, providing an institutional foundation for whatever plot they had hatched.

When Burr's vice-presidential term expired in 1805, he ventured west, sailing down the Mississippi to recruit associates. Rumors of intrigue soon surfaced, and federal authorities became interested late in 1806 when they received a letter from Wilkinson implicating Burr in a "deep, dark, wicked, and wide-spread conspiracy" against the United States. Learning that Wilkinson had turned him in, Burr tried to reach Spanish Florida but was captured early in 1807 and put on trial for treason.

Burr's trial was a circus, an open arena for Jefferson and his critics to air their views on such touchy subjects as presidential power, westward expansion, and national loyalty. Presiding over the case, Chief Justice John Marshall, no friend to Jefferson, made it clear that he believed Burr was a victim, not the perpetrator, of a conspiracy. Jefferson, however, asserted his belief that Burr was guilty, and the president was determined to have him prosecuted to the full extent of the law. Using the powers of his office, Jefferson offered pardons to conspirators who would testify against Burr, and he leaked information that would make his former vice president look guilty. He also refused to honor a **subpoena** issued by Marshall requiring the president to appear in court and to produce official presidential documents that might have a bearing on the case. In this instance, Jefferson embarrassed the chief justice by recalling that Marshall had supported George Washington's assertion of presidential privilege when the first president refused to present key papers to Congress relating to Jay's Treaty (see pages 205–206). Marshall backed down, and neither Jefferson nor his executive papers appeared in court.

But Marshall struck back in his own way. The chief justice instructed the jury that the Constitution defined *treason* as "levying war against the United States or adhering to their enemies" and that a guilty verdict required direct evidence from two witnesses. Because Burr had not waged war, and because neither Spain nor Britain was at the moment an enemy of the United States, the jury acquitted the former vice president, to the glee of Jefferson's critics.

The Problem of American Neutrality

Internal tensions in American politics were matched by growing stress in the nation's diplomatic and economic relations. Jefferson's economic successes had been the product of continuing warfare in Europe. With their fleets engaged in naval battles, their people locked in combat, and their lands crisscrossed by opposing armies, Europeans needed American ships and the fruits of American labor, especially food. American neutrality assured continued prosperity as long as the contending parties in Europe agreed to the diplomatic principle of neutrality.

Americans immediately grasped at this opportunity. An upsurge in European campaigning in 1803 helped raise the total value of American exports by over 65 percent. A significant proportion of the in-

---

subpoena A writ, or order, requiring an individual to appear in court to give testimony.

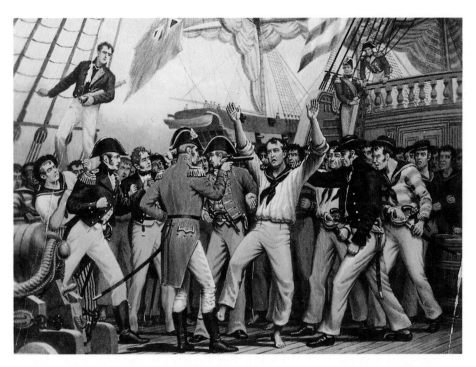

The impressment of sailors into the British navy from American ships was one of the more prominent causes of the War of 1812. This 1790 engraving shows an American sailor being seized at gunpoint while those who might try to assist him are elbowed aside. *Library of Congress.*

crease came from the shipment of foreign goods to foreign markets by way of neutral American ports: sugar from the Caribbean, for example, frequently passed through the United States on its way to Europe. These so-called **reexports** rose in value from $14 million in 1803 to $60 million in 1807, prompting a rapid growth in earnings for American shipping. In 1790, net income from shipping amounted to a mere $5.9 million; by 1807 the volume had surged to $42.1 million.

Prospects seemed bright for America's economic and diplomatic future and for Jefferson's dream of agricultural America feeding overcrowded, war-torn Europe. But politicians in both England and France cared about their own military victories, not about American prosperity. Their decisions, especially those relating to neutral shipping, disrupted American trade and created an atmosphere of hostility.

Another source of tension was a British law that empowered the king's warships to engage in **impressment.** For decades, British sailors had protested the exceedingly cruel conditions and low pay in His Majesty's navy by jumping ship in American ports and enlisting as merchant sailors on American vessels. Strapped for mariners by renewed warfare, England pursued a vigorous policy of reclaiming British sailors after 1803, even if they were on neutral American ships and, more provocatively, even if they were citizens of the United States. It is estimated that the British abducted as many as eight thousand sailors from American ships between 1803 and 1812. The loss of so many seamen hurt American shippers economically, but it wounded American pride even more. Like the XYZ affair, impressment seemed to be a direct denial of the United States' status as a legitimate nation.

reexports   Products shipped from one nation to another by way of a third; during wartime, neutral nations can be used as third parties to carry goods to combatants.

impressment   Procedure permitted under British maritime law that authorized commanders of warships to force English civilian sailors into military service.

Economic Warfare

Pressure on American neutrality increased after 1805, when a military deadlock emerged in the European war: Britain was supreme at sea, and France was in control on the continent of Europe. Stuck in a stalemate, both sides used whatever nonmilitary advantages were available in an effort to tip the balance in their favor. Thus the war changed from one of military campaigning to one of diplomatic and economic maneuvering. Seeking to close off foreign supplies to England, in November 1806 Napoleon issued the **Berlin Decree,** barring ships that had anchored at British harbors from entering ports controlled by France. The British Parliament responded by issuing a series of directives that permitted neutral ships to sail to European ports only if they first called at a British port to pay a transit tax. It was thus impossible for a neutral ship to follow the laws of either nation without violating the laws of the other. All this European blustering, however, had little immediate effect on the American economy. From the issuance of the Berlin Decree to the end of 1807, American exports and shipping rose more than they had risen during any similar period.

But such good fortune was not to last. Seeking to break France's dependence on America as a source for food and other supplies, Napoleon sought an alliance with Russia, and in the spring of 1807 his diplomatic mission succeeded. Having acquired an alternative source for grain and other foodstuffs, Napoleon immediately began enforcing the Berlin Decree, hoping to starve England into submission. The British countered by stepping up enforcement of their European blockade and aggressively pursuing impressment to strengthen the royal navy.

The escalation in both France's and Britain's economic war efforts quickly led to confrontation with Americans and a diplomatic crisis. A pivotal event occurred in June 1807. The British **frigate** *Leopard,* patrolling the American shoreline, confronted the American warship *Chesapeake.* Even though both ships were inside American territorial waters, the *Leopard* ordered the American ship to halt and hand over any British sailors on board. When the *Chesapeake*'s captain refused, the *Leopard* fired several **broadsides,** crippling the American vessel, killing three sailors, and injuring eighteen. The British then boarded the *Chesapeake* and dragged off four men, three of whom were naturalized citizens of the United States. Americans were outraged.

Americans were not the only ones galvanized by British aggression. Shortly after the *Chesapeake* affair, word arrived in the United States that Napoleon had responded to Britain's belligerence by declaring a virtual economic war against neutrals. In the **Milan Decree,** he vowed to seize any neutral ship that so much as carried licenses to trade with England. What was worse, the Milan Decree stated that ships that had been boarded by British authorities—even against their crew's will—would be subject to immediate French capture.

Many Americans viewed the escalating French and English sanctions as insulting treachery that cried out for an American response. The *Washington Federalist* newspaper observed, "We have never, on any occasion, witnessed . . . such a thirst for revenge." If Congress had been in session, the legislature surely would have called for war, but Jefferson stayed calm. War with England or France or, worse still, with both would bring Jefferson's whole political program to a crashing halt. He had insisted on inexpensive government, lobbied for American neutrality, and hoped for renewed prosperity through continuing trade with Europe. War would destroy his entire agenda. But clearly Jefferson had to do something.

Believing that Europeans were far more dependent on American goods and ships than Americans were on European money and manufactures, Jefferson chose to violate one of his cardinal principles: the U.S. government would interfere in the economy to force Europeans to recognize American neutral rights. In December 1807, the president announced the **Embargo Act,** which would, in effect, close all American foreign trade as of January 1 unless the Europeans agreed to recognize America's neutral rights to trade with anyone it pleased.

Berlin Decree Napoleon's order declaring the British Isles under blockade and authorizing the confiscation of British goods from any ship found carrying them.

frigate A very fast warship, rigged with square sails and carrying from thirty to fifty cannon on two gun decks.

broadside The simultaneous discharge of all the guns on one side of a warship.

Milan Decree Napoleon's order authorizing the capture of any neutral vessels sailing from British ports or submitting to British searches.

Embargo Act Embargo (a government-ordered trade ban) announced by Jefferson in 1807 in order to pressure Britain and France to accept neutral trading rights; it went into effect in 1808 and closed down all U.S. foreign trade.

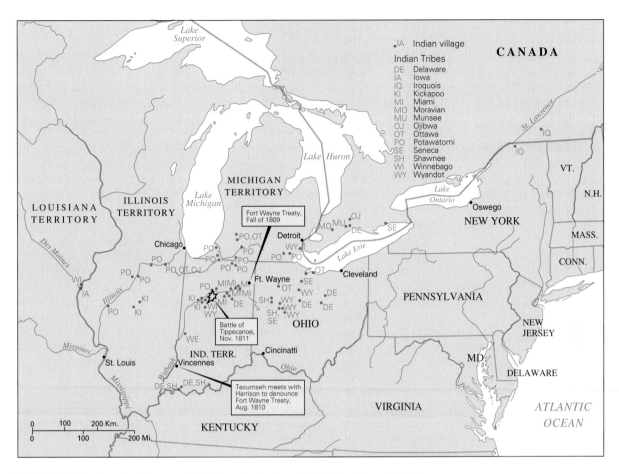

MAP 9.1 Indian Territory, ca. 1812 Frontier leaders like William Henry Harrison were very worried about unified Indian resistance in the years leading up to the War of 1812, and this map shows why. Strong Indian groups, some of which were allied with Tecumseh, formed a nearly solid frontier line on the nation's western borders. Harrison's efforts and the War of 1812 virtually destroyed this constraint on American expansion.

Crises in the Nation

■ How did Jefferson's economic and Indian policies influence national developments after 1808?

■ How did problems in Europe contribute to changing conditions in the American West?

■ What did the actions of frontier politicians such as William Henry Harrison do to bring the nation into war in 1812?

Jefferson's reaction to European aggression immediately began strangling American trade and with it America's domestic economic development. In addition, European countries still had legitimate claims on much of North America, and the Indians who continued to occupy most of the continent had enough military power to pose a serious threat to the United

States if properly motivated (see Map 9.1). While impressment, blockade, and embargo paralyzed America's Atlantic frontier, a combination of European and Indian hostility along the western frontier added to the air of national emergency. The resulting series of domestic crises played havoc with Jefferson's vision of a peaceful, prosperous nation.

Economic Depression

Although Jefferson felt justified in suspending free trade to protect neutral rights, the result was the worst economic depression since the founding of the British colonies in North America. Critics such as John Randolph pronounced Jefferson's solution worse than the problem—like trying "to cure corns by cutting off the toes." And while Jefferson's "damn-bargo," as critics called it, was only halfheartedly enforced, the economy slumped disastrously. Taken together, all American exports fell from $109 million to $22 million, and net earnings from shipping fell by almost 50 percent. During 1808, earnings from legitimate business enterprise in America declined to less than a quarter of their value in 1807.

The depression shattered economic and social life in many eastern towns. It has been estimated that thirty thousand sailors were thrown out of work and that as many as a hundred thousand people employed in support industries were laid off. During 1808 in New York City alone, 120 businesses went bankrupt, and the combination of unemployment and business failure led to the imprisonment of twelve hundred New Yorkers for debt. New England, where the economy had become almost entirely dependent on foreign trade, was hit harder still. In light of Jefferson's policies and the collapsing economy, the extremism expressed by the Essex Junto three years earlier began to sound reasonable.

New Englanders screamed loudest about the impact of the embargo, but southerners and westerners were just as seriously affected by it. The economy of the South had depended on the export of staple crops like tobacco since colonial times and was rapidly turning to cotton. There, embargo meant near-death to all legitimate trade. In response to the loss of foreign markets, tobacco prices fell from $6.75 per hundredweight to $3.25, and cotton from 21 to 13 cents per pound. In the West, wholesale prices for agricultural products spiraled downward also. Overall, the prices of farm products were 16 percent lower between 1807 and 1811 than they had been between 1791 and 1801. At the same time, the price of virtually every consumer item went up. For example, the price of building materials—hardware, glass, and milled lumber—rose 11 percent during the same period, and the price of textiles climbed 20 percent. In fact, the only consumer item that did not go up in price was the one item farmers did not need to buy: food. Faced with dropping incomes and soaring costs, farmers probably felt the trade restrictions more profoundly than others.

Rather than blaming their problems on the Republican administration, however, disaffected farmers directed their anger at the British. Frontiersmen believed, rightly or wrongly, that eliminating British interference with American trade would restore the boom economy that had drawn so many of them to the edge of American settlement. Thus westerners banded together to raise their voices in favor of American patriotism and war against Britain.

Political Upheaval

Despite the escalating crisis in the country, Jefferson remained popular and powerful, but like Washington, he chose to step down from the presidency after serving two terms, making it clear to party officials that he favored James Madison to replace him in the upcoming presidential election of 1808. Although Madison and Jefferson had much in common and were longtime friends, they seemed very different from each other. Few could say they knew Madison well, but those who did found him captivating: a man of few words but of piercing intellect and unflinching conviction. Those less well acquainted with him thought the quiet Virginian indecisive: where Jefferson tended to act on impulse, Madison approached matters of state as he approached matters of political philosophy—with caution, patience, and reason.

Riding his reputation as a brilliant political thinker and his status as Jefferson's chosen successor, Madison easily defeated his Federalist opponent, Charles Cotesworth Pinckney. But the one-sided results disguised deep political divisions in the nation at large. Federalist criticism of Jefferson's policies, especially of the embargo, was finding a growing audience as the depression deepened, and in the congressional election in 1808 the Republicans lost twenty-four seats to Federalists.

Internal dissent also weakened the Republican Party. Dissatisfied with Jefferson's policies, both southern and northeastern party members contested Madison's succession. The Tertium Quid challenged Jefferson's authority in the **party caucus** and tried to secure the nomination for the stately and conservative **James Monroe.** Jefferson managed to hold the party's southern wing in line, but northeasterners, stinging under the pressure of the embargo, bucked the decision of the party caucus and nominated their own presidential candidate: New Yorker George Clinton. Although Clinton polled only six electoral votes for the presidency, his nomination was a sign of growing divisions over the problems that the United States faced in 1808.

party caucus A meeting of members of a political party to decide on questions of policy or leadership or to register preferences for candidates running for office.

James Monroe Republican politician from Virginia who served in diplomatic posts under George Washington, John Adams, and Thomas Jefferson; he later became the fifth president of the United States.

During Madison's first two years in office, lack of any progress toward resolving the nation's woes seemed to confirm critics' perception of his indecisiveness. Despite that, Republicans actually made gains in the congressional elections in 1810: they regained fourteen of the seats they had lost in the House in 1808 and picked up two additional Senate seats. But this was no vote of confidence in Madison. Though the new congressmen were Republicans, sixty-three of them did not support Madison or his commitment to a conciliatory policy toward the British. These new members of Congress were mostly very young, extremely patriotic, and represented frontier constituents who were being ravaged by the agricultural depression. In the months to come, their increasingly strident demands for aggressive action against England earned them the nickname **War Hawks.**

The Rise of the Shawnee Prophet

A key reason for War Hawk militancy was the unsettled conditions along the western frontier. Relations with Indians in the West had been peaceful since the Battle of Fallen Timbers in 1794. The Shawnees and other groups had been thrown off their traditional homelands in Ohio by the Treaty of Greenville (see page 206) and forced to move to new lands in Indiana. There, food shortages, disease, and continuing encroachment by settlers caused many young Indians to lose faith in their traditional beliefs and in themselves as human beings.

In the midst of the crisis, one disheartened, diseased alcoholic rose above his afflictions to lead the Indians into a brief new era of hope. Tecumseh's younger brother Lalawethika had bragged that he would play an influential role in his people's affairs (his name meant "Noisemaker"). But his prospects had declined along with those of his people. Lacking his brother's training as a warrior, Lalawethika felt increasingly hopeless, turned to alcohol, and finally in 1805 became critically ill. He claimed that he remembered dying and meeting the Master of Life, who showed him the way to lead his people out of degradation and commanded him to return to the world of the living so he could tell the Indians what they must do to recover their dignity. He then awoke, cured of his illness. Launching a full-fledged religious and cultural revival designed to teach the ways revealed to him by the Master of Life, he adopted the name Tenskwatawa ("the Way"). Whites called him **"The Prophet."**

Blaming the decline of his people on their adoption of white ways, the Prophet taught them to go back to their traditional lifestyle—to discard whites' clothing, religion, and especially alcohol—and live as their ancestors had lived. He also urged his followers to unify against the temptations and threats of white exploiters and hold on to what remained of their lands. If they followed his teachings, the Prophet insisted, the Indians would regain control of their lives and their lands, and the whites would vanish from their world. In 1807 the Prophet established a religious settlement, Prophetstown, on the banks of Tippecanoe Creek in Indiana Territory. This community was to serve as a center for the Prophet's activities and as a living model for revitalized Indian life. The residents of Prophetstown worked together using traditional forms of agriculture, hunting, and gathering.

Although the Prophet preached a message of ethnic pride, nonviolence, and passive resistance, as white settlers continued to pressure his people, he began to advocate more forceful solutions to the Indians' problems. In a speech to an intertribal council in April 1807, he suggested for the first time that warriors unite to resist white expansion. Although he did not urge his followers to attack the whites, he made it clear that the Master of Life would defend him and his followers if war were pressed on them.

Prophecy and Politics in the West

While Tenskwatawa continued to stress spiritual means for stopping white aggression, his brother **Tecumseh** pushed for a more political course of action. Seven years older than the Prophet, Tecumseh had always inclined more toward politics and warfare. Known as a brave fighter and a persuasive political orator, Tecumseh traveled throughout the western frontier, working out political and military alliances designed to put a stop to white expansion once and for all. Although

---

War Hawks   Members of Congress elected in 1810 from the West and South who campaigned for war with Britain in the hopes of stimulating the economy and annexing new territory.

The Prophet   Shawnee religious visionary who called for a return to Indian traditions and founded the community of Prophetstown on Tippecanoe Creek in Indiana.

Tecumseh   Shawnee leader and brother of the Prophet; he established an Indian confederacy along the frontier that he hoped would be a barrier to white expansion.

Although they had enormous respect for each other, Indiana territorial governor William Henry Harrison and Tecumseh were both ferocious when it came to defending their political and diplomatic positions. This painting of their confrontation at the 1810 peace conference held at Vincennes makes this point clearly. The two never actually came to blows at this meeting or at another held one year later, but they never were able to find common ground. Tecumseh's refusal to compromise his people's rights to their land would eventually lead to renewed warfare and his own death. *Cincinnati Museum Center.*

he did not want to start a war against white settlers, Tecumseh exhorted Indians to defend every inch of land that remained to them. In 1807 he warned Ohio governor Thomas Kirker that they would do so with their lives.

Tecumseh's plan might have brought about his brother's goals. Faced by a unified defensive line of Indians stretching along the American frontier from Canada to the Gulf of Mexico, the United States probably would have found it virtually impossible to expand any farther, and the Indian confederacy would have become a significant force in America's future. The very brilliance of Tecumseh's reasoning and his success at organizing Indian groups caused a great deal of confusion among whites. Various white officials were convinced that the Shawnee leader was a spy either for the French or for the British and that his activities were an extension of some hidden plot by one European power or another. Though wrong, such theories helped to escalate the air of crisis in the West and in the nation at large.

Indiana governor William Henry Harrison had good reason to advance the impression of a conspiracy between Tecumseh and the British. Harrison and men like him believed the United States had the right to control all of North America and, accordingly, to brush aside anything standing in the way by any means available (see Map 9.1). Britain and the Indians were thus linked in their thinking. Both were seen as obstacles to national destiny—and many War Hawks prayed for the outbreak of war between the United States and

the British with the Indians in between. Such a war would provide an excuse for attacking the Indians along the frontier to break up their emerging confederation and dispossess them of their land. In addition, a war would justify invading and seizing Canada, fulfilling what many considered a logical but frustrated objective of the American Revolution. At the same time, taking Canada from the British would open rich timber, fur, and agricultural lands for American settlement. More important, it would secure American control of the Great Lakes and St. Lawrence River—potentially a very valuable shipping route for agricultural produce from upper New York, northern Ohio, and the newly opening areas of the **Old Northwest.**

Choosing War

With the nation reeling from the economic squeeze of the embargo, Congress replaced it with the **Non-Intercourse Act** early in 1809. The new law forbade

Old Northwest The area of the United States referred to at the time as the Northwest Territory, it would eventually be broken into the states of Indiana, Illinois, Michigan, and Wisconsin.

Non-Intercourse Act Law passed by Congress in 1809 reopening trade with all nations except France and Britain and authorizing the president to reopen trade with them if they lifted restrictions on American shipping.

trade only with England and France and gave the president the power to reopen trade if either of the combatants lifted its restrictions against American shipping. Even though this act was much less restrictive than the embargo, American merchants were relieved when it expired in the spring of 1810. At that point, Congress passed an even more permissive boycott, **Macon's Bill No. 2.** According to this new law, merchants could trade with the combatants if they wanted to take the risk, but if either France or England lifted its blockade, the United States would stop trading with the other.

Hoping to cut England off from needed outside supplies, Napoleon responded to Macon's Bill in August by sending a letter to the American government promising to suspend French restrictions on American shipping. In secret, however, the French emperor issued an order to continue seizing American ships. Despite Napoleon's devious intentions, Madison sought to use the French peace overture as a lever: he instructed the American mission in London to tell the British that he would close down trade with them unless they joined France in dropping trade restrictions. Sure that Napoleon was lying, the British refused, backing the president into a diplomatic corner. In February 1811, the provisions of Macon's Bill forced Madison to close trading with Britain for its failure to remove economic sanctions, stepping up tensions all around.

Later in the year, events in the West finally triggered a crisis. The underlying origin of the problem was an agreement, the Fort Wayne Treaty, signed in the fall of 1809 between the United States and representatives of the Miami, Potawatomi, and Delaware Indians. In return for an outright bribe of $5,200 and individual **annuities** ranging from $250 to $500, civil chiefs among these three tribes sold over 3 million acres of Indian land in Indiana and Illinois—land already occupied by many other Indian groups.

In August 1810, Tecumseh met with Governor Harrison in Vincennes, Indiana, to denounce the Fort Wayne Treaty. Harrison insisted that the agreement was legitimate. Speaking for those whose lands had been sold out from under them, Tecumseh said, "They want to save that piece of land, we do not wish you to take it. . . . I want the present boundary line to continue. Should you cross it, I assure you it will be productive of bad consequences." But Harrison refused to budge.

The Vincennes meeting convinced the Indians that they must prepare for a white attack. The Prophet increasingly preached the Master of Life's commitment to support the faithful in a battle against the whites.

It Matters

The Battle of Tippecanoe

Americans today largely accept unthinkingly that although Indians are an extremely interesting part of American history, they never really mattered. This modern dismissal of Indian significance is entirely incorrect. Throughout the years leading up to the Battle of Tippecanoe, Harrison warned officials in Washington that if Tecumseh's activities were allowed to continue unchecked, the combined military force he might assemble would be sufficient to stop American westward expansion altogether. This was not baseless exaggeration. As Harrison himself said of Tecumseh, "He is one of those uncommon geniuses, which spring up occasionally to produce revolutions and overturn the established order of things." We will never know how close Tecumseh came to overturning the established order. We do know, however, that he spent a considerable amount of time during 1810 and 1811 traveling throughout the frontier drumming up support. We know, too, that he experienced considerable success. Historians disagree about whether he could have succeeded in stopping American expansion, but there is no question that such a unified force along the American frontier would have compelled politicians like Jefferson to reconsider their policies. In either case, America today would be a profoundly different place had Harrison not destroyed Prophetstown and undermined the growing Indian confederacy.

Tecumseh traveled up and down the American frontier, enlisting additional allies into his growing Indian confederacy. Meanwhile, Harrison grew more and more eager to attack the Indians before they could unite fully. He got his chance when a second peace conference, also held at Vincennes in the summer of

Macon's Bill No. 2   Law passed by Congress in 1810 that offered exclusive trading rights to France or Britain, whichever recognized American neutral rights first.

annuity   An allowance or income paid annually.

1811, also failed. Citing the failed peace effort and sporadic skirmishes between frontier settlers and renegade bands of Indians, none of whom were directly connected to Tecumseh, Harrison ordered an attack. On November 7, in the so-called **Battle of Tippecanoe,** an army of enraged frontiersmen burned Prophetstown. Then, having succeeded in setting the Indian frontier ablaze, Harrison called for a declaration of war against the Indians and the British.

Headlining Harrison's call for war, a Kentucky newspaper proclaimed, "The war on the Wabash is purely BRITISH, the SCALPING KNIFE and TOMAHAWK of British savages, is now, again devastating our frontiers." Coming as it did while Congress was already embroiled in debate over economic sanctions and British impressment, the outbreak of violence on the frontier was finally enough to push Madison into action. Still hoping for some sort of peaceful resolution, the president chose his words carefully when he told Congress, "We behold . . . on the side of Great Britain, a state of war against the United States; and on the side of the United States, a state of peace toward Britain." As chairman of the House Foreign Relations Committee, however, **John C. Calhoun** was less circumspect: "The mad ambition, the lust of power, and the commercial avarice of Great Britain have left to neutral nations an alternative only between the base surrender of their rights, and a manly vindication of them." He then introduced a war bill in Congress.

When the vote was finally cast in 1812, the war bill passed by a vote of 79 to 49 in the House and 19 to 13 in the Senate. Although they seemed to have the most to lose from continued indecisive policies, representatives from the heavily Federalist regions that depended the most on overseas trade—Massachusetts, Connecticut, and New York, for example—voted against war, whereas strongly Republican western and southern representatives voted in favor.

awesome military power in the world. Not surprisingly, defeat and humiliation were the main fruits of American efforts as the two nations faced off.

The Fighting Begins

Despite years of agitation, the war's actual arrival in 1812 caught the United States terribly unprepared. Republican cost cutting had virtually disbanded the military during Jefferson's first term in office. Renewed fighting with pirates in the Mediterranean and building tensions in the Atlantic had forced Republicans to increase military spending, but the navy still had fewer than twenty vessels, and the army could field fewer than seven thousand men. And for all its war fever, Congress balked at appropriating new funds even after war had been declared. Thus the first ventures in the war went forward with only grudging financial support.

In line with what the War Hawks wanted, the first military campaign was a three-pronged drive toward Canada and against the Indians (see Map 9.2). One force, commanded by Harrison, was successful in raiding undefended Indian villages but was unable to make any gains against British troops. Farther east, a force led by Major General Stephen Van Rensselaer was defeated by a small British and Indian army. Meanwhile, the third force, commanded by Henry Dearborn, lunged at Montreal but nervously withdrew back into U.S. territory after an inconclusive battle against the British.

American sailors fared much better during the war's opening days. Leading the war effort at sea were three frigates: the *Constitution* (popularly known as **Old Ironsides**), the *President,* and the *United States.* In mid-August, the *Constitution* outmaneuvered and eventually sank what the British described as "one of our stoutest frigates," the H.M.S. *Guerrière.* The *United States,* under the command of Stephen Decatur, enjoyed a victory against the British frigate the H.M.S.

The Nation At War

■ What geographic and economic factors impeded American war efforts against Great Britain and Britain's Indian allies?

■ How did events in Europe influence the war in America?

■ To what extent were Americans' objectives in going to war accomplished?

The nation was dreadfully unprepared when the breach with England finally came. With virtually no army or navy, the United States was taking a terrible risk in engaging what was fast becoming the most

Battle of Tippecanoe   Battle near Prophetstown in 1811, where American forces led by William Henry Harrison defeated the followers of the Shawnee Prophet and destroyed the town.

John C. Calhoun   Congressman from South Carolina who was a leader of the War Hawks and the author of the official declaration of war in 1812.

Old Ironsides   Nickname of the U.S.S. *Constitution,* the forty-four-gun American frigate whose victory over the *Guerrière* bolstered sagging national morale during the War of 1812.

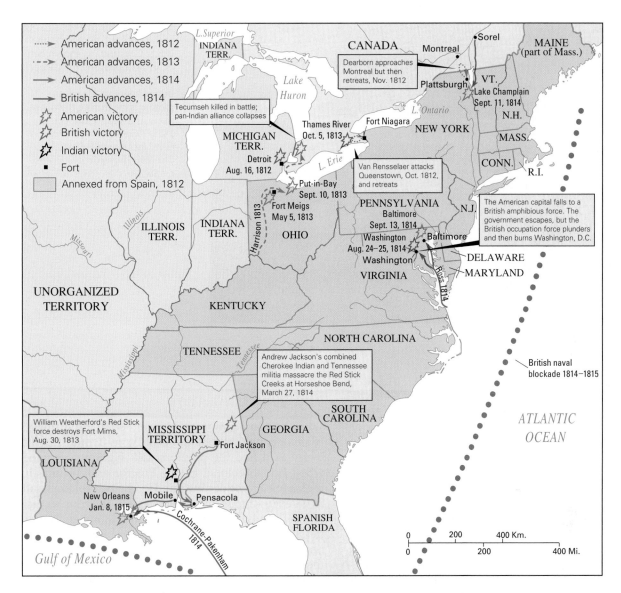

MAP 9.2 The War of 1812   The heaviest action during the first two years of the War of 1812 lay along the U.S./Canadian border. In 1814 the British sought to knock the United States out of the war by staging three offensives: one along the northern frontier at Plattsburgh, New York; one into the Chesapeake; and a third directed at the Mississippi River at New Orleans. All three offensives failed.

Macedonian. Enduring thirty broadsides fired by the *Macedonian,* Decatur's gunners splintered the British ship with seventy broadsides of their own. Though no stranger to the horrors of war, Decatur was shocked by what he found when he boarded the crippled vessel: "fragments of the dead scattered in every direction, the decks slippery with blood, and one continuous agonizing yell of the unhappy wounded." American privateers also enjoyed success, capturing

450 British merchant ships valued in the millions during the first six months of the war.

American naval victories were all that kept the nation's morale alive in 1812. Former Treasury secretary Albert Gallatin summarized the nation's humiliating military efforts: "The series of misfortunes," he wrote to Jefferson, "exceeds all anticipations made even by those who had least confidence in our inexperienced officers and undisciplined men." The land war had

Naval victories like the sinking of the H.M.S. *Guerrière* by the U.S.S. *Constitution,* shown here in an 1812 painting by Michael Felice Corne, were the only things keeping American morale alive during the disastrous first year of the War of 1812. *"Constitution & Guerrière" by Michael Felice Corne. The New Haven Colony Historical Society, gift of Mrs. S. Galpin.*

been, as another politician would recall, a "miscarriage, without even the heroism of disaster." Vowing to reverse the situation, Congress increased the size of the army to fifty-seven thousand men and offered a $16 bonus to encourage enlistments.

Thus in 1812 Madison stood for reelection at a time when the nation's military fate appeared uncertain and his own leadership seemed shaky. Although the majority of his party's congressional caucus supported him for reelection, nearly a third of the Republican congressmen—mostly those from New York and New England—rallied around New Yorker De-Witt Clinton, nephew and political ally of Madison's former challenger George Clinton. Like his uncle, De-Witt Clinton was a Republican who favored Federalist economic policies and agreed with New England Federalists that the war was unnecessary. Most Federalists supported Clinton, and the party did not field a candidate of its own.

When the campaign was over, the outcome was nearly the same as the congressional vote on the war bill earlier in the year. New York and New England rallied behind Clinton. The South and West continued to support Madison, the Republicans, and war. Madison won but was in no position to gloat. His share of electoral votes had fallen from 72 percent in 1808 to 58.9 percent. At the same time, Republican Party strength in the House dropped by over 13 percent, in the Senate by about 8 percent.

The War Continues

When military campaigning resumed in the spring of 1813, it appeared that the U.S. Army would fare as badly as it had the previous fall. Fighting resumed when British colonel Henry Proctor and Tecumseh, with a joint force of nine hundred British soldiers and twelve hundred Indians, laid siege to Harrison's command camped at Fort Meigs on the Maumee Rapids in Ohio. An army of twelve hundred Kentucky militiamen finally arrived and drove the enemy off, but they were so disorganized that they lost nearly half their number in pursuing the British and Indian force. Harrison was shocked, proclaiming the Kentuckians' "excessive ardour scarcely less fatal than cowardice." Having escaped virtually unscathed, Proctor and Tecumseh continued to harass American forces through the summer. Then, with winter approaching, the British and Indians withdrew to Canada. Harrison, who had been busy raising additional troops, decided to pursue.

No doubt Harrison's new effort would have proved as fruitless as his earlier ones, but an unexpected event turned the odds in his favor. One key problem plaguing Harrison and other commanders in the field was that the British controlled the Great Lakes and so could depend on an uninterrupted supply line. In contrast, American forces and their supplies moved along undeveloped roads and were easy targets for

Choosing to side with the British against the United States in the War of 1812, Tecumseh joined British commander Henry Proctor in leading a joint force of Indians and British regulars. On October 5, 1813, their force was attacked by an army led by Tecumseh's old rival William Henry Harrison. As shown in this painting of the battle, a penetrating cavalry charge (upper left) broke the British line while the Indian forces continued fighting. In the melee, Tecumseh was shot and died on the field. In this romanticized view, we see him, gun down and tomahawk raised as a bullet from a mounted officer's pistol moves unerringly toward him. *Library of Congress.*

Indian and British attackers. **Oliver Hazard Perry,** a young naval tactician, had been given command of a small fleet assigned to clear the lakes of British ships. After months of playing hide-and-seek among the shore islands, British and American ships met in battle at Put-in-Bay in September 1813. Two hours of cannon fire left Perry's **flagship,** the *Lawrence,* nearly destroyed, and 80 percent of the crew lay dead or wounded. Perry refused to surrender. He slipped off his damaged vessel and took command of another ship standing nearby. What remained of his command then sailed back into the heart of the British force and after three hours of close combat subdued and captured six British ships. Perry immediately sent a note to Harrison stating, "We have met the enemy and they are ours."

Buoyed by this news, Harrison's army closed in on Proctor and Tecumseh at the Thames River, about 50 miles northeast of Detroit, on October 5. The British force faced a piercing cavalry charge and lacking naval support was soon forced to surrender. The Indians held out longer, but when word spread that Tecumseh had been killed, they melted into the woods,

leaving the body of their fallen leader to be torn apart by the victorious Americans.

Another war front had also opened farther south during 1813. Although the Creek Confederacy as a whole wished to remain neutral, one faction calling themselves the Red Sticks had allied with Tecumseh in 1812. In the summer of 1813, Red Stick leader William Weatherford led a force against Fort Mims, killing all but about thirty of the more than three hundred occupants. The so-called Fort Mims massacre enraged whites in the Southeast. In Tennessee, twenty-five hundred militiamen rallied around **Andrew Jackson,**

Oliver Hazard Perry   American naval officer who led the fleet that defeated the British in the Battle of Put-in-Bay during the War of 1812.

flagship   The ship that carries the fleet commander and bears the commander's flag.

Andrew Jackson   General who defeated the Creeks at Horseshoe Bend in 1814 and the British at New Orleans in 1815; he later became the seventh president of the United States.

a young brawler and Indian fighter. Already called "Old Hickory" because of his toughness, Jackson made a bold promise: "The blood of our women & children shall not call for vengeance in vain." In the course of that summer and fall, Jackson's frontier ruffians fought multiple engagements against the Red Stick Creeks, driving them into hiding.

While these battles raged on land, the British shut down American forces at sea. Embarrassed by the success of Old Ironsides and the other American frigates, the British admiralty ordered that "the naval force of the enemy should be quickly and completely disposed of" and sent sufficient ships to do the job. The American naval fleet and **merchant marine** found themselves bottled up in port by the world's strongest navy.

The Politics of War

The war had wound down for the winter by the time Congress reconvened in December 1813, but the outlook was not good. Disappointed that American forces had not knocked the British out of the war, Republican representative William Murfree spoke for many when he said, "The result of the last campaign disappointed the expectations of every one." President Madison tried to be optimistic. Recalling the victories during the year, he said, "The war, with its **vicissitudes,** is illustrating the capacity and destiny of the United States to be a great, a flourishing, and a powerful nation."

Madison's optimism seemed justified later in December when the British offered to open direct peace negotiations with the Americans. The president quickly formed a peace commission, but until its work was done, Madison and Congress still had to worry about the practical issues of troops and money, both of which were in critically short supply.

Despite increases in army pay and bonuses for new recruits, enlistments were falling off in 1813. Congressional Republicans responded by adding further enticements for new recruits, including grants of 160 acres of land in the western territories. Congress also authorized the president to extend the term of enlistment for men already in service. By 1814, Congress had increased the size of the army to more than sixty-two thousand men but had not figured out how to pay for all the changes.

Presenting the federal budget for 1814, Treasury Secretary William Jones announced that the government's income would be approximately $16 million, but its expenses would amount to over $45 million. Traditional enemies of internal taxes, the Republicans faced a dilemma. Shortly after convening, members of Congress had passed a set of new taxes and could not imagine explaining another increase to their constituents. So congressional Republicans decided to borrow instead, authorizing a $35 million deficit.

Adding to the money problem was the fact that, to this point in the war, the United States had permitted neutral nations to trade freely in American ports, carrying American exports to England and Canada and English goods into eastern ports. As a result of this flourishing trade, American currency was flooding out of the United States at an alarming rate, weakening the nation's economy. At the same time, American food was rolling directly into British military commissaries, strengthening the enemy's ability and will to fight.

In a secret message to Congress, the president proposed an absolute embargo on all American ships and goods—neither was to leave port—and a complete ban on imports that were customarily produced in Great Britain. Federalists, especially those from New England, screamed in protest. They called the proposal "an engine of tyranny, an engine of oppression," no different, they said, from the Intolerable Acts imposed on American colonies by Britain in 1774 (see pages 135–137). But congressional Republicans passed the embargo a mere eight days after Madison submitted it.

The **Embargo of 1813** was the most far-reaching trade restriction bill ever passed by Congress. It confined all trading ships to port, and even fishing vessels could put to sea only if their masters posted sizable **bonds.** Government officials charged with enforcing the new law had unprecedented **discretionary powers.** The impact was devastating: the embargo virtually shut down the New England and New York economies, and it severely crippled the economy of nearly every other state.

New British Offensives

While Congress debated matters of finance and trade restrictions, events in Europe were changing the en-

---

merchant marine   A nation's commercial ships.

vicissitudes   Sudden or unexpected changes encountered during the course of life.

Embargo of 1813   An absolute embargo on all American trade and British imports.

bond   A sum of money paid as bail or security.

discretionary powers   Powers to be used at one's own judgment; in government, powers given to an administrative official to be used without outside consultation or oversight.

Although the British were successful in capturing the United States capital, defenders stalled the invasion long enough for the government to escape. In frustration, the British pillaged the deserted city and then burned the public buildings. The Capitol Building was badly damaged and all of the books in the Library of Congress, which was housed in the building, were destroyed. *"The Capitol," watercolor 1814, by George Munger. Photo by Israel Sack.*

tire character of the war. On March 31, 1814, the British and their allies took Paris, forcing Napoleon to abdicate his throne. Few in America mourned the French emperor's fall. Jefferson wrote, "I rejoice . . . in the downfall of Bonaparte. This scourge of the world has occasioned the deaths of at least ten millions of human beings." Napoleon's defeat, however, left the United States as Great Britain's sole military target. Republican Joseph Nicholson expressed a common lament when he observed, "We should have to fight hereafter not for 'free Trade and sailors rights,' not for the Conquest of the Canadas, but for our national Existence."

As Nicholson feared, a flood of combat-hardened British veterans began arriving in North America, and the survival of the United States as an independent nation was indeed at issue. By the late summer of 1814, British troop strength in Canada had risen to thirty thousand men. From this position of power, the British prepared a chain of three offensives to bring the war to a quick end.

In August 1814, twenty British warships and several troop transports sailed up Chesapeake Bay toward Washington, D.C. The British arrived outside Washington at midday on August 24. The troops defending the city could not withstand the force of hardened British veterans, but they delayed the invasion long enough for the government to escape. Angered at being foiled, the British sacked the city, torching most of the buildings. They then moved on toward the key port city of Baltimore.

At Baltimore, the British navy had to knock out Fort McHenry and take the harbor before the army could take the city. On September 13, British ships armed with heavy **mortars** and rockets attacked the

mortar   A portable, muzzle-loading cannon that fires large projectiles at high trajectories over a short range; traditionally used by mobile troops against fixed fortifications.

fort. Despite the pounding, when the sun rose on September 14, the American flag continued to wave over Fort McHenry. The sight moved a young Georgetown volunteer named **Francis Scott Key,** who had watched the shelling as a prisoner aboard one of the British ships, to record the event in a poem that was later set to music and became the national anthem of the United States. Having failed to reduce the fort, the British were forced to withdraw, leaving Baltimore undisturbed.

While this strike at the nation's midsection was raging, Sir George Prevost, governor-general of Canada, massed ten thousand troops for an invasion in the north. The British force arrived just north of Plattsburgh, New York, on September 6, where it was to join the British naval fleet that controlled Lake Champlain. However, a small American flotilla under the command of Lieutenant Thomas Macdonough outmaneuvered the imposing British armada and forced a surrender on September 11. Prevost had already begun his attack against the defenders at Plattsburgh, but when he learned that the British lake fleet was defeated and in flames, he lost his nerve and ordered his men to retreat.

On yet another front, the British pressed an offensive against the Gulf Coast designed to take pressure off Canada and close transportation on the Mississippi River. The defense of the Gulf Coast fell to Andrew Jackson and his Tennesseans. Having spent the winter raising troops and collecting supplies, in March 1814 Jackson and his army of four thousand militiamen and Cherokee volunteers resumed their mission to punish the Red Stick Creeks. Learning that the Red Sticks had established a camp on the peninsula formed by a bend in the Tallapoosa River, Jackson led his men on a forced march to attack. On March 27 in what was misleadingly called the **Battle of Horseshoe Bend,** Jackson's force trapped the Creeks and slaughtered nearly eight hundred people, destroying Red Stick opposition and severely crippling Indian resistance in the South.

After the massacre at Horseshoe Bend, Jackson moved his army toward the Gulf of Mexico, where a British offensive was in the making. Arriving in New Orleans on December 1, he found the city ill prepared to defend itself. The local militia, consisting mostly of French and Spanish residents, would not obey American officers. "Those who are not for us are against us, and will be dealt with accordingly," Jackson proclaimed. He turned increasingly to unconventional sources of support. Free blacks in the city formed a regular army corps, and Jackson created a special unit of black refugees from Santo Domingo under the

command of Colonel Jean Baptiste Savary. White citizens protested Jackson's arming of runaway slaves, but he ignored their objections. "Legitimate citizens" protested too when Jackson accepted a company of river pirates under the command of **Jean Lafitte,** awarding them a blanket pardon for all past crimes. "Hellish Banditti," Jackson himself called them, but the pirate commander and the general hit it off so well that Lafitte became Jackson's constant companion during the campaign.

Having pulled his ragtag force together, Jackson settled in to wait for the British attack. On the morning of January 8, 1815, it came. The British force, commanded by General Edward Pakenham, emerged from the fog at dawn, directly in front of Jackson's defenses. Waiting patiently behind hastily constructed barricades, Jackson's men began firing cannon, rifles, and muskets as the British moved within range. According to one British veteran, it was "the most murderous fire I have ever beheld before or since." Pakenham tried to keep his men from running but was cut in half by a cannonball.

When it was all over, more than two thousand British troops had been killed or wounded in the **Battle of New Orleans,** while a mere seventy-one Americans fell. This was by far the most successful battle fought by American forces during the War of 1812. But ironically, it was fought after the war was over.

The War's Strange Conclusion

While the British were closing in on Washington in the summer of 1814, treaty negotiations designed to end the war were beginning in Ghent, Belgium. Confident that their three-pronged attack against the United States would soon knock the Americans out of

---

Francis Scott Key Author of "The Star-Spangled Banner," which chronicles the British bombardment of Fort McHenry in 1814; Key's poem, set to music, became the official U.S. national anthem in 1931.

Battle of Horseshoe Bend Battle in 1814 in which Tennessee militia massacred Creek Indians in Alabama, ending Red Stick resistance to white westward expansion.

Jean Lafitte Leader of a band of pirates in southeast Louisiana; he offered to fight for the Americans at New Orleans in return for the pardon of his men.

Battle of New Orleans Battle in the War of 1812 in which American troops commanded by Andrew Jackson destroyed the British force attempting to seize New Orleans.

The nearly miraculous American victory in the Battle of New Orleans—fought two weeks after the Americans and British had signed a peace treaty—helped launch a new era in American nationalism. And, as this illustration from a popular magazine shows, it made Andrew Jackson, shown waving his hat to encourage his troops, a national hero of greater-than-human proportions. *Library of Congress.*

the war, the British delegates were in no hurry to end it by diplomacy. They refused to discuss substantive issues, insisting that all of the matters raised by Madison's peace commission were nonnegotiable.

At that point, however, domestic politics in England began to play a deciding role. After nearly a generation of armed conflict, the English people were war-weary, especially the taxpayers. As one British official put it, "Economy & relief from taxation are not merely the War Cry of Opposition, but they are the real objects to which public attention is turned." The failures at Plattsburgh and Baltimore made it appear that at best the war would drag on at least another year, at an estimated cost to Britain of an additional $44 million. Moreover, continuation of the American war was interfering with Britain's European diplomacy. Trying to arrive at a peace settlement for Europe at the **Congress of Vienna,** a British official commented, "We do not think the Continental Powers will continue in good humour with our Blockade of the whole Coast of America." Speaking for the military, the **Duke of Wellington** reviewed British military successes and failures in the American war and advised his countrymen, "You have no right . . . to demand any **concession** . . . from America."

In the end, the **Treaty of Ghent,** completed on December 24, 1814, simply restored diplomatic relations between England and the United States to what they had been prior to the outbreak of war. The treaty said nothing about impressment, blockades, or neutral trading rights. Neither military action nor diplomatic

finagling netted Canada for the War Hawks. And the treaty did nothing about the alleged conspiracies between Indians and British agents. Although Americans called the War of 1812 a victory, they actually won none of the prizes that Madison's war statement had declared the nation was fighting for.

Peace and the Rise of New Expectations

■ How did events during the War of 1812 help to move the American economy in new directions after peace was restored?

■ What impact did changes in the economy have on the institution of slavery and on the lives of slaves?

Congress of Vienna Conference between ambassadors from the major powers in Europe to redraw the continent's political map after the defeat of Napoleon; it also sought to uproot revolutionary movements and restore traditional monarchies.

Duke of Wellington The most respected military leader in Great Britain at this time, Wellington was responsible for the defeat of Napoleon.

concession In diplomacy, something given up during negotiations.

Treaty of Ghent Treaty ending the War of 1812, signed in Belgium in 1814; it restored peace but was silent on the issues over which the United States and Britain had gone to war.

Despite repeated military disasters, loss of life, and diplomatic failure, the war had a number of positive effects on the United States. Just to have survived a war against the British was enough to build national confidence, but to have scored major victories such as those at Plattsburgh, Baltimore, and especially New Orleans was truly worth boasting about. Americans emerged from the conflict with a new sense of national pride and purpose. And many side effects from the fighting itself gave Americans new hopes and plans.

New Expectations in the Northeastern Economy

Although trading interests in the Northeast suffered following Jefferson's embargo and were nearly ruined by the war and Madison's embargo, a new avenue of economic expansion opened in New England. Cut off from European manufactured goods, Americans started to make more textiles and other items for themselves.

Samuel Slater, an English immigrant who had been trained in manufacturing in Britain, introduced the use of machines for spinning cotton yarn to the United States in 1790. His mill was financially successful, but few others tried to copy his enterprise. Even with shipping expenses, tariffs, and other added costs, buying machine-made British cloth was still more practical than investing large sums at high risk to build competing factories in the United States. And after 1800, Jefferson's economic policies discouraged such investment. But his embargo changed all that. After it went into effect in 1808, British fabrics became increasingly unavailable and prices soared. Slater and his partners moved quickly to expand their spinning operations to fill the void. And now his inventiveness was widely copied.

Another entrepreneur, Francis Cabot Lowell, went even further than Slater. Left in the lurch economically by the embargo, Lowell ventured to England in 1810. While there, he engaged in wholesale industrial espionage, observing British textile-manufacturing practices and machinery and making detailed notes and sketches of what he saw. Returning to the United States just before war broke out in 1812, Lowell formed the Boston Manufacturing Company. In 1813 the company used the plans Lowell had smuggled back to the United States to build a factory in Waltham, Massachusetts. The new facility included spinning machines, power looms, and all the equipment necessary to **mechanize** every stage in the production of finished cloth, bringing the entire process under

one roof. Like Slater's innovations, Lowell's too were soon duplicated by economically desperate New Englanders.

The spread of textile manufacturing was astonishing. Prior to 1808, only fifteen cotton mills of the sort Slater had introduced had been built in the entire country. But between the passage of the embargo and the end of 1809, eighty-seven additional mills had sprung up, mostly in New England. And when war came, the pace increased, especially when Lowell's idea of a mechanized textile factory proved to be highly efficient and profitable. The number of people employed in manufacturing increased from four thousand in 1809 to perhaps as many as a hundred thousand in 1816. In the years to come, factories in New England and elsewhere supplied more and more of the country's consumer goods.

New Opportunities in the West

But business growth was not confined to the Northeast. Following the war, pioneers poured into the West in astounding numbers. The population of Ohio had already soared from 45,000 in 1800 to 231,000 in 1810, but it more than doubled again by 1820, reaching 581,000. Indiana, Illinois, Missouri, and Michigan experienced similar growth. Most of those who flooded into the newly opened West were small farmers, but subsistence agriculture was not the only economic opportunity that drew expectant Americans into the region. Big business, too, had great expectations for finding new wealth in the West.

One of the designs behind the Lewis and Clark and the Zebulon Pike expeditions had been to gain entry for the United States into the burgeoning economy in North America's interior (see pages 227–228). That economy was complex, with many commodities being traded, and few entirely understood all of its intricacies. There was one facet, though, that was well known and very desirable to entrepreneurs: the brown gold of beaver, mink, and other animal furs.

Even before the War of 1812, individual fur traders had tried to break the monopoly wielded by the English and Canadians over the trade along the northern frontier and by the Spanish and French farther south. One particularly visionary businessman had already put a plan in motion before the war to create a continent-wide trading network. John Jacob Astor, a German immigrant who had arrived in the United

---

mechanize   To substitute machinery for human labor.

Generally, when we think of the Far West in the early nineteenth century, especially the fur trade, we think of wild adventures experienced by colorful men who had little thought for responsibilities or wealth. Attractive though that image may be, the fact is that the early American fur trade was big business and the entrepreneurs who succeeded at it became true captains of industry. Here we see the home that fur profits built for the Chouteau family in St. Louis, a considerable mansion by any standards. *"St. Louis the Fourth City, 1764–1909" by Walter B. Stevens. S. J. Clarke Publishing Co. , 1909.*

States in 1783, announced that he intended to establish "a range of Posts or Trading houses" along the route that Lewis and Clark had followed from St. Louis to the Pacific (see Map 8.2).

Another visionary entrepreneur sought a similar fortune in the Southwest. Auguste Chouteau was French by birth, but like many frontiersmen, he changed nationalities as frequently as the borderlands changed owners. Chouteau had helped to found the town of St. Louis and had been instrumental in establishing that city as the capital for a fur-trading empire. He, his brother Pierre, and an extended family of business partners used intermarriage to create a massive kinship network that included important French, Spanish, and Indian connections. With kinship ensuring cooperative trading partners, the Chouteau brothers were able to extend their reach deep into the Missouri region and establish trade between St. Louis and the Spanish far western trading capital at Santa Fe (see page 51). As Americans began to penetrate the area, the Chouteau brothers took the change in stride, inviting William Clark of the Corps of Discov-

ery and fur entrepreneur Andrew Henry to join forces with them in founding the Missouri Fur Company in 1809.

The war disrupted both Astor's and the Missouri Fur Company's operations, but when the war was over, the fur business resumed with increasing vigor. Pierre Chouteau and his various American partners pushed continually farther into the West, using their strategy of forming traditional Indian trading partnerships, often rooted in intermarriage, to expand business. Chouteau also used his kin partnerships and capital from the fur trade to branch into other businesses. He was a cofounder of the Bank of Missouri and served as its president for a number of years. He also operated flour mills and distilleries and speculated in real estate. Members of his extended family later helped to found Kansas City, pioneered mining in Colorado, and financed railroad building in the Dakotas.

The joint efforts of individual farmers and business tycoons such as Astor and the Chouteaus opened the West and proved to the satisfaction of many that

Following the War of 1812 and the death of Tecumseh, aggressive American expansionists put great pressure on Indians living on the eastern side of the Mississippi River to move farther west. In location after location, American Indian agents and their military escorts set up treaty negotiations designed to acquire ever-increasing amounts of land that would accommodate ambitious would-be farmers. This painting captures one of the largest of these, the Prairie du Chien conference of 1825, at which the Sauk, Fox, Chippewa, and other Indians in Illinois, Wisconsin, and Michigan ceded huge portions of land in hopes of winning peace. *Wisconsin Historical Society.*

great fortunes and good lives could be had on the frontier. Though the promise was nearly always greater than the reality, the allure of the West was unmistakable. And after the War of 1812, the nation's aspirations became more and more firmly tied to that region's growth and development.

But American westward expansion posed a terrible threat to Native Americans. When Harrison's soldiers burned Prophetstown and later killed Tecumseh, they wiped out all hopes for a pan-Indian confederacy. In addition, the civil war among the Creeks, followed by Jackson's victories against the Red Stick faction, removed all meaningful resistance to westward expansion in the South. Many Indian groups continued to wield great power, but accommodationist leaders such as those who formed the Cherokee government suggested that cooperation with federal authorities was the best course.

Collaboration between the United States and Native Americans helped to prevent renewed warfare, but at enormous cost to the Indians. Within a year of the Battle of Horseshoe Bend, Jackson forced the Creeks to sign the Treaty of Fort Jackson, which confiscated over 20 million acres of land from the Creek Confederacy. A similar but more gradual assault on Indian landholding began in the Northwest in 1815. In a council meeting at Portage des Sioux in Illinois Territory, the United States signed peace accords with the various tribes that had joined the British during the war. Both sides pledged that their earlier hostilities would be "forgiven and forgotten" and that all the agreeing parties would live in "perpetual peace and friendship." The northwestern Indians, however, possessed some 2 million acres of prime real estate between the Illinois and Mississippi Rivers—land that the United States government had already given away as enlistment bonuses to white war volunteers. Moving the Indians off that land as quickly as possible thus became a matter of national priority.

Over the next several years, **federal Indian agents** used every tactic they could think of to coerce groups like the Kickapoo Indians into ceding their lands. Finally, in 1819, the Kickapoo Nation signed the Treaty of Edwardsville, turning over most of the land the United States had demanded. Having secured this massive tract, government agents then turned their attention to the vast holdings of more distant tribes—the Sauk, Fox, Chippewa, and Dakota Indians in western Illinois, Wisconsin, and Michigan. As they had done with the Kickapoos, American negotiators used bribery, threat, and manipulation of local tensions to pursue their goal, eventually winning an enormous cession of land in the Prairie du Chien treaties of 1825.

A Revolution in the Southern Economy

Indian dispossession and westward expansion also promised great economic growth for the South. In the years before the War of 1812, the southern economy had been sluggish, and the future of the region's single-crop agricultural system was doubtful. Tobacco, the mainstay of the South's economy, was no longer the glorious profit maker it had been during the colonial period. Sea Island cotton, rice, sugar, and other products continued to find markets, but they grew only in limited areas. However, the technological and economic changes that came in the war's wake pumped new energy into the South. In only a few decades, an entirely new South would emerge.

The mechanization of the British textile industry in the late eighteenth century created an enormous new demand for cotton. Southern planters had been growing the fibrous plant since colonial times, but soil and climatic conditions limited the growing area for the sort of **long-staple cotton** that could be harvested and sold economically. Large areas of the South and Southwest had proved suitable for growing **short-staple cotton,** but the time and labor required to pick the sticky seeds from the compact **cotton bolls** made the crop unprofitable. In 1793 a young Yale College graduate, **Eli Whitney,** was a guest at a plantation in Georgia, where he learned about the difficulty of removing the seeds from short-staple cotton. In a matter of weeks, Whitney helped to perfect a machine that allowed a small and unskilled work force to quickly comb out the seeds without damaging the fibers. He obtained a **patent** for the cotton gin (short for "cotton engine") in 1794 and set up a factory in New Haven, Connecticut, to manufacture the machine. Whitney's engine, though revolutionary in its impact, was a relatively simple mechanism, and despite his patent, other manufacturers and individual planters stole the design and built their own cotton gins.

The outcome of Whitney's inventiveness was the rapid spread of short-staple cotton throughout inland South Carolina and Georgia. Then, just as it seemed that the southern economy was about to bloom, embargo and war closed down exports to England. Although some cotton growers were able to shift sales from England to the rising new factories in New England, a true explosion of growth in cotton cultivation had to await war's end.

With the arrival of peace and the departure of the British naval blockade, cotton growing began to spread at an astounding rate. The massacre of the Red Stick Creeks removed the final major threat of Indian resistance in the South, and southerners rushed into frontier areas, spreading cotton agriculture into Alabama and Mississippi and then into Arkansas, northern Louisiana, and eastern Texas. From 1815 onward, the South's annual cotton crop grew by leaps and bounds. By 1840, annual exports reached nearly a million and a half bales, and increasing volumes were consumed within the United States by the mushrooming textile factories in the Northeast.

---

federal Indian agents   Government officials who were responsible for negotiating treaties with Native American groups; at this time they were employed by the War Department.

long-staple cotton   A variety of cotton with long and loosely packed pods of fiber that is easy to comb out and process.

short-staple cotton   A variety of cotton with short and tightly packed pods of fiber in which the plant's seeds are tangled.

cotton boll   The pod of the cotton plant; it contains the plant's seeds surrounded by the fluffy fiber that is spun into yarn.

Eli Whitney   American inventor and manufacturer; his perfecting of the cotton gin revolutionized the cotton industry.

patent   A government grant that gives the creator of an invention the sole right to produce, use, or sell that invention for a set period of time.

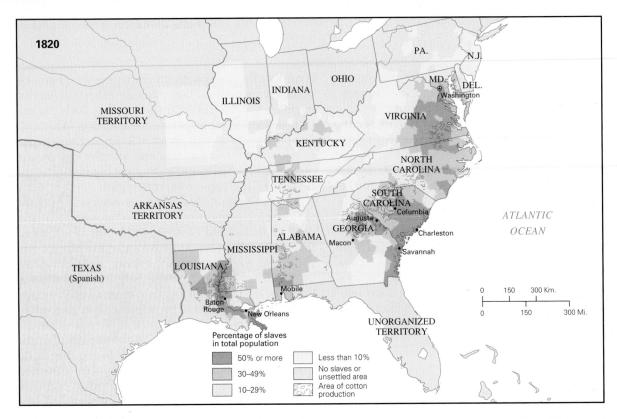

1820

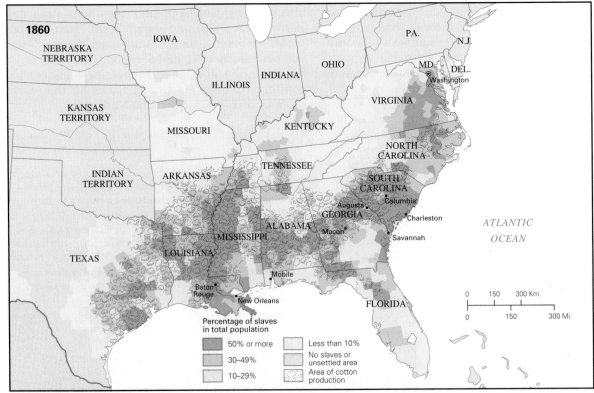

1860

MAP 9.3 Cotton Agriculture and Slave Population   Between 1820 and 1860, the expansion of cotton agriculture and the extension of slavery went hand in hand. As these maps show, cotton production was an isolated activity in 1820, and slavery remained isolated as well. By 1860, both had extended westward.

Reviving and Reinventing Slavery

Before the emergence of cotton, when the South's agricultural system was foundering, many southerners began to question the use of slaves. In 1782 Virginia made it legal for individual masters to free their slaves, and many did so. In 1784 Thomas Jefferson proposed (but saw defeated) a land ordinance that would have prohibited slavery in all of the nation's territories after 1800. Some southern leaders advocated abolishing slavery and transporting freed blacks to Africa. But the booming southern economy after the War of 1812 required more labor than ever. As a result, African American slavery expanded as never before.

Viewed side by side, a map showing cotton agriculture and one showing slave population would appear nearly identical (see Map 9.3). In the 1820s, when cotton production was most heavily concentrated in South Carolina and Georgia, the greatest density of slaves occurred in the same area. During the 1840s, as cotton growing spread to the West, slavery followed. By 1860, both cotton growing and slavery would appear on the map as a continuous belt stretching from the Carolinas through Georgia and Alabama and on to the Mississippi River.

The virtually universal shift to cotton growing throughout the South brought about not only the expansion and extension of slavery but also substantial modifications to the institution itself. The wide variety of economic pursuits in which slave labor had been employed from the colonial period onward led to varied patterns in slave employment. In many parts of the South, slaves traditionally exercised a great deal of control over their work schedules as they completed assigned tasks (see page 96). But the cotton business called for large gangs of predominantly unskilled workers, and increasingly slaves found themselves regimented like machines in tempo with the demands of cotton production.

At the same time, as northeastern factories were able to provide clothing, shoes, and other manufactured goods at ever more attractive prices and western farmers shipped cheap pork and grain into southern markets, plantation managers found it more practical to purchase such goods rather than to pro-

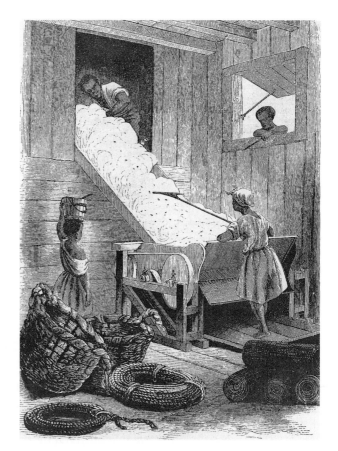

The invention of the cotton gin and the spread of cotton agriculture throughout the American South created an enormous new demand for slave workers and changed the nature of their work. A handful of slaves could process large amounts of fiber using the revolutionary new machine, but it took armies of field workers to produce the raw cotton. *Library of Congress.*

duce them. Thus slaves who formerly had performed various skilled tasks such as milling and weaving found themselves pressed into much less rewarding service as brute labor in the cotton fields. To a large extent, then, specialized manufacturing in the North and large-scale commercial food production in the West permitted an intensified cotton industry in the South and helped foster the increasing dehumanization of the peculiar labor system that drove it.

Individual Voices

Examining a Primary Source

Tecumseh Describes American Indian Policy Under William Henry Harrison

Between 1808 and 1811, Shawnee political spokesman Tecumseh and Indiana Territory governor William Henry Harrison engaged in a running war of words. In the course of these discussions, Tecumseh became increasingly frustrated at Harrison's apparent ignorance of political and social organization among the various groups of Indians in the American interior. He repeatedly explained that though relations among the various Indians were complex, they nevertheless constituted a single people and not a patchwork of separate nations. Finally, at a conference in Vincennes on August 20, 1810, Tecumseh lost his temper and accused Harrison of intentionally misunderstanding the nature of Native American intergroup relations as part of a larger effort to defraud the Indians of their land. The original handwritten transcript of this speech contains many abbreviations as well as some unusual spelling and punctuation. The excerpt that follows has been modernized for easier reading.

■ *What exactly is Tecumseh charging Harrison and his agents of doing? What does this suggest about Tecumseh's understanding of the nature of Indian organization and Harrison's misunderstandings about it?*

■ *Why would Tecumseh insist that warriors rather than village chiefs decide policy toward the United States?*

■ *The Wea Indians, a small Miami Indian group, did not sign the Fort Wayne Treaty but later were pressured by Harrison and his accomplice, Winamac, to give their approval. A political headman among the Potawatomi Indians, Winamac worked closely with Harrison, using threats and bribes to convince many of his peers to sign away their lands.*

■ *What did Tecumseh propose to do if Harrison persisted in conducting Indian policy and land acquisition as he had done at Fort Wayne? Why do you think Tecumseh chose this particular approach?*

You try to force the red people to do some injury. It is you that is pushing them on to do mischief. You endeavor to make distinctions. You wish to prevent the Indians to do as we wish them to: unite and let them consider their land as the common property of the whole. You take tribes aside and advise them not to come into this measure. . . .

The reason I tell you this is [that] you want by your distinctions of Indian tribes in allotting to each a particular tract of land to make them to war with each other. You never see an Indian come and endeavor to make the white people do so. You are continually driving the red people when at last you will drive them into the great Lake where they can't either stand or work. ■

You ought to know what you are doing with the Indians. Perhaps it is by direction of the President to make those distinctions. It is a very bad thing and we do not like it. Since my residence at Tippecanoe, we have endeavored to level all distinctions to destroy village chiefs by whom all mischief is done; it is they who sell our land to the Americans [so] our object is to let all our affairs be transacted by Warriors. ■

This land that was sold and the goods that were given for it was only done by a few. The treaty was afterwards brought here and the Weas were induced to give their consent because of their small numbers. The treaty at Fort Wayne was made through the threats [by] Winamac, ■ *but in future we are prepared to punish those chiefs who may come forward to propose to sell their land. If you continue to purchase [land from] them, it will produce war among the different tribes, and at last I do not know what will be the consequences to the white people. . . .*

I now wish you to listen to me. If you do not it will appear as if you wished me to kill all the chiefs that sold you the land. I tell you so because I am authorized by all the tribes to do so. I am at the head of them all. I am a Warrior and all the Warriors will meet together in two or three moons from this. Then I will call for those chiefs that sold you the land and shall know what to do with them. If you do not restore the land, you will have a hand in killing them. ■

Summary

After Jefferson's triumphal first four years in office, factional disputes at home and diplomatic deadlocks with European powers began to plague the Republicans. Although the Federalists were in full retreat, many within Jefferson's own party rebelled against some of his policies. When Jefferson stepped down in 1808, tapping James Madison as his successor, Republicans in both the Northeast and the South bucked the president, supporting George Clinton and James Monroe, respectively.

To a large extent, the Republicans' problems were the outcome of external stresses. On the Atlantic frontier, the United States tried to remain neutral in the wars that engulfed Europe. On the western frontier, the Prophet and Tecumseh were successfully unifying dispossessed Indians into an alliance devoted to stopping U.S. expansion. Things went from bad to worse when Jefferson's use of economic sanctions gave rise to the worst economic depression since the beginnings of English colonization. The embargo strangled the economy in port cities, and the downward spiral in agricultural prices threatened to bankrupt many in the West and South.

The combination of economic and diplomatic constraints brought aggressive politicians to power in 1808 and 1810. Men such as William Henry Harrison expected that war with England would permit the United States finally to realize independence—forcing freedom of the seas, eliminating Indian resistance, and justifying the conquest of the rest of North America. Despite Madison's continuing peace efforts, southern and western interests finally pushed the nation into war with England in 1812.

Although some glimmering moments of glory heartened the Americans, the war was mostly disastrous. But after generations of fighting one enemy or another, the English people demanded peace. When their final offensive in America failed to bring immediate victory in 1814, the British chose to negotiate. Finally, on Christmas Eve, the two nations signed the Treaty of Ghent, ending the war. From a diplomatic point of view, it was as though the war had never happened: everything was simply restored to pre-1812 status.

Nevertheless, in the United States the war created strong feelings of national pride and confidence, and Americans looked forward to even better things to come. In the Northeast, the constraints of war provoked entrepreneurs to explore new industries, creating the first stage of an industrial revolution in the country. In the West, the defeat of Indian resistance combined with bright economic opportunities to trigger a wave of westward migration. In the South, the economy was revolutionized by the cotton gin and the growing demand for fiber among English and then American manufacturers. Throughout the country, economic progress promised to improve life for most Americans, but as before, both African Americans and Native Americans would bear much of the cost.

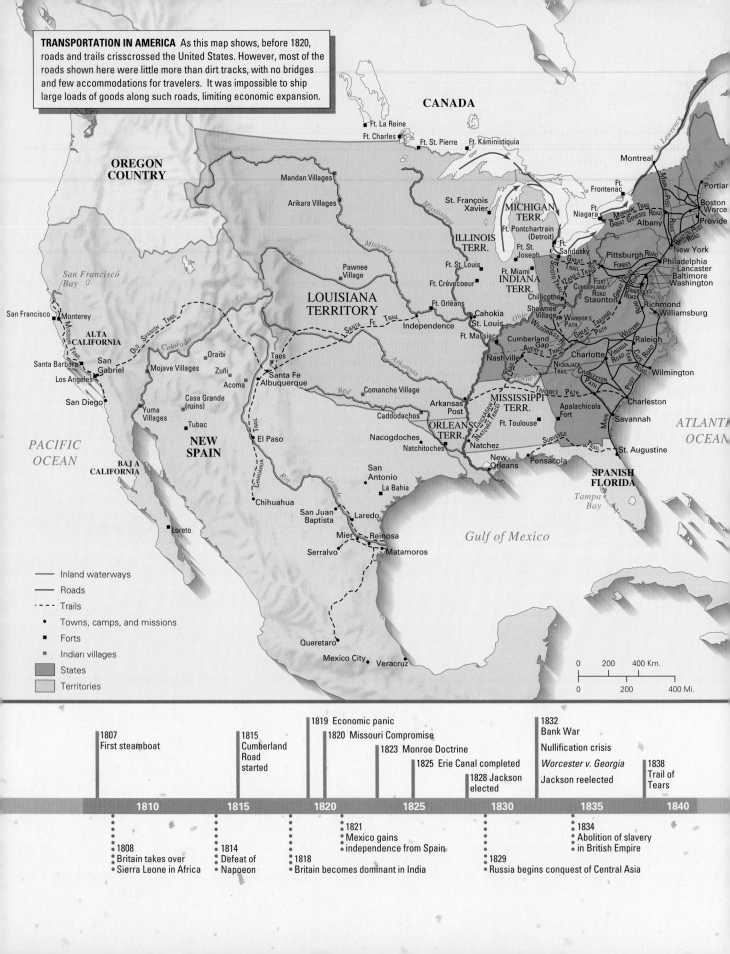

TRANSPORTATION IN AMERICA As this map shows, before 1820, roads and trails crisscrossed the United States. However, most of the roads shown here were little more than dirt tracks, with no bridges and few accommodations for travelers. It was impossible to ship large loads of goods along such roads, limiting economic expansion.

CANADA

OREGON COUNTRY

Ft. La Reine
Ft. Charles
Ft. St. Pierre
Ft. Kaministiquia

Mandan Villages

Arikara Villages

St. François Xavier

MICHIGAN TERR.
Ft. Pontchartrain (Detroit)

Montreal

Ft. Frontenac

Portlar

Boston
Worce
Provide

ILLINOIS TERR.

Ft. Niagara

Albany

San Francisco Bay

Pawnee Village

Ft. St. Louis
Ft. St. Joseph

Ft. Sandusky

Pittsburgh Road

New York

INDIANA TERR.
Ft. Miami

Ft. Crèvecoeur

Chillicothe

Philadelphia
Lancaster
Baltimore
Washington

LOUISIANA TERRITORY

Ft. Orleans

Shawnee Village

Staunton

Richmond
Williamsburg

San Francisco
Monterey

ALTA CALIFORNIA

Cahokia
St. Louis

Warrior's Path

Raleigh

Independence

Ft. Massiac

Santa Barbara
San Gabriel

Old Spanish Trail

Colorado

Oraibi
Zuñi
Acoma

Taos
Santa Fe
Albuquerque

Cumberland Gap

Nashville

Charlotte

Wilmington

Los Angeles

Mojave Villages

Comanche Village

Nickajack Trail

Charleston Path

San Diego

Casa Grande (ruins)

Red

Caddodachos

MISSISSIPPI TERR.

Charleston

Yuma Villages

Arkansas

Arkansas Post

Savannah

Tubac

NEW SPAIN

El Paso

Nacogdoches

Ft. Toulouse

Natchez

ORLEANS TERR.

Apalachicola Fort

ATLANTIC OCEAN

PACIFIC OCEAN

BAJA CALIFORNIA

Rio Grande

Natchitoches

New Orleans

Pensacola

St. Augustine

SPANISH FLORIDA

Loreto

San Antonio
La Bahia

Tampa Bay

Gulf of Mexico

Chihuahua

San Juan Baptista

Laredo

Mier
Reinosa

Serralvo
Matamoros

Querétaro

Mexico City
Veracruz

Inland waterways
Roads
Trails
● Towns, camps, and missions
■ Forts
■ Indian villages
States
Territories

0   200   400 Km.
0   200   400 Mi.

1807 First steamboat

1815 Cumberland Road started

1819 Economic panic
1820 Missouri Compromise
1823 Monroe Doctrine
1825 Erie Canal completed
1828 Jackson elected

1832 Bank War
Nullification crisis
Worcester v. Georgia
Jackson reelected

1838 Trail of Tears

1810   1815   1820   1825   1830   1835   1840

1808 Britain takes over Sierra Leone in Africa

1814 Defeat of Napoeon

1818 Britain becomes dominant in India

1821 Mexico gains independence from Spain

1829 Russia begins conquest of Central Asia

1834 Abolition of slavery in British Empire

The Rise of a New Nation, 1815–1836

Transportation in America

Using the map on the facing page, note the severe constraints that geography and the lack of an organized transportation system placed on American economic and physical
expansion. What efforts would individuals, states, and the
federal government have to make in order to make Americans' expectations for continuing growth a reality? What
expected and unexpected outcomes would flow from
these efforts?

Individual Choices

JOHN C. CALHOUN

As a young congressman in the years bracketing the War of 1812, John C. Calhoun was celebrated as a leading American nationalist. But in the years following the economic panic of 1819 and the sectional crisis in Missouri, Calhoun chose to abandon nationalism in favor of states' rights and southern sectionalism. As vehement in his new sentiments as he had been in his earlier ones, Calhoun became a virtual patron saint among states' rights advocates for generations to come. *National Portrait Gallery/Art Resource, NY.*

John C. Calhoun

The prosperity that followed the War of 1812 seemed to justify the nationalistic optimism that had guided the young War Hawks during the years before the war. Now dominant in Congress, these same young men joined Presidents Madison and Monroe in pushing for a carefully balanced economic system that supposedly would lead to increasing prosperity for the whole nation. Instead, unfounded economic optimism led to overspeculation, and in 1819 the bubble burst, setting off a six-year depression. Viewing the economic wreckage and shocked by solutions proposed by his political allies, former War Hawk John C. Calhoun made a fateful choice that would nearly tear the nation apart.

Little in Calhoun's background would have suggested that he would emerge as a controversial and divisive figure. A political prodigy, at age 29 he had been elected to the U.S. House of Representatives, where he joined forces with other up-and-coming legislators as part of the hyperpatriotic War Hawk faction. After the War of 1812 he continued to act as a dedicated nationalist, working closely with Henry Clay to build the American System—Clay's plan for a national **market economy.** Calhoun drafted specific bills necessary to the program; won House support for chartering a new national bank, spending federal funds for transportation development, and creating the nation's first protective tariff package; and convinced President Madison of the program's constitutionality. Calhoun quickly established a reputation as a solid nationalist; his admiring colleague John Quincy Adams found him to be "above all sectional and factious prejudices more than any other statesman of this Union with whom I have ever acted."

But in the wake of the economic Panic of 1819, Calhoun began entertaining serious "sectional and factious prejudices." To a large extent this was because of proposals on the part of his northeastern colleagues to use tight credit and higher tariffs as a way of fighting off the effects of the depression. While these solutions made sense to manufacturers and some other beneficiaries of the postwar boom, they threatened to strangle the growing cotton industry that was fast becoming the centerpiece in the economy of the South. But population growth in the Northeast and increasing economic specialization in parts of the West gave protariff forces all the votes they needed to promote their political agenda in Congress. Soon, Calhoun came to believe, the Northeast would emerge as a tyrannical mother country, and the rest of the nation would become its oppressed and dependent colonies.

Seeing incoming president Andrew Jackson as being perhaps even more nationalistic than his predecessors, and fearing extension of northeastern domination, in 1828 Calhoun drafted a pamphlet called *The South Carolina Exposition and Protest.* Drawing on ideas enunciated years before by James Madison and Thomas Jefferson in their Virginia and Kentucky Resolutions, Calhoun argued that the federal union was nothing more than a convenient mechanism for carrying out the collective will of the states. As such, its sovereignty was not superior to that of the states. More importantly, if a state determined that a federal law violated the

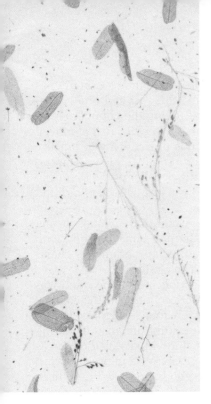

basic rights of its citizens, a popular assembly could declare that law null—having no legal force—within its borders. This doctrine became known as nullification.

The crisis itself centered on a hodgepodge of tariff legislation passed by Congress in 1828. By 1832, the so-called Tariff of Abominations had so alienated South Carolinians that they chose to act on Calhoun's nullification principle: a popular assembly declared the tariff null. Jackson responded by building up federal forces in South Carolina and demanding that Congress pass a "force bill" that would allow him to use federal troops to establish martial law in the state. South Carolina in turn mobilized its militia to defend its sovereignty. And Calhoun, the once-proud nationalist, resigned as Jackson's vice president to stand with his state for the principle of nullification.

Though civil war was avoided in 1832—cooler heads in Congress were able to craft a temporary solution to the tariff conflict—Calhoun's decision to apply his considerable political talent to the cause of sectionalism helped bring the nation to the very brink of war. In the years to come, Calhoun would continue to fan the flames of sectionalism. By the time of his death in 1850, Calhoun had become a virtual patron saint for the southern cause, and most people had forgotten that this paragon of sectionalism had at one time been an equally rabid nationalist. The transformations that unsettled the nation turned Calhoun completely around. And his new legacy would affect the nation every bit as profoundly as had his earlier one.

INTRODUCTION

Though certainly more talented than many Americans and more powerful than most, John C. Calhoun nonetheless was typical of his generation in many ways. Like most of his contemporaries he was angered by British invasions of American sovereignty and lobbied for war in 1812. Following the war he embraced the spirit of national unity and good feelings to promote economic consolidation, leading Congress to revolutionize public finance laws in order to encourage expansive growth. And these policies succeeded: the United States experienced an exciting growth spurt after 1815. But when the speculative bubble burst in 1819, the optimism and unity that had characterized the country faltered.

Calhoun was also typical of a growing number of Americans in his views on politics. Like his fellow prodigies Henry Clay and William Henry Harrison, Calhoun had made politics a career from very early in life. Of course, Calhoun, Clay, and Harrison were property owners, and their families had always exercised political rights, but during the 1820s more and more Americans gained those same rights and took politics every bit as seriously as Calhoun and his privileged colleagues. In this highly charged atmosphere, matters of state became for the first time in the nation's history a topic for debate among people from all regions and from a broad cross-section of occupations and communities. As for Calhoun, politics for these newly enfranchised voters was not some gentleman's game but a form of personal combat designed to make their own lives better and to test their wills and their loyalties. To such highly motivated men, even the risk of civil war was an acceptable price for claiming their personal and sectional rights.

An "Era of Good Feelings"

■ What were the sources for Americans' optimism as they emerged from the War of 1812?

■ What steps did the American government take to capitalize on this optimism?

■ How did new developments in the nation influence foreign affairs?

■ How did events in North Africa and Europe influence developments in the United States?

> **market economy** An economic system based on the buying and selling of goods and services, in which prices are determined by the forces of supply and demand.

James Madison had been the butt of jokes and the cause of dissension within his own party during the War of 1812, but he emerged from the war a national hero with considerable political clout. Although his fellow Republicans may have considered his wartime policies indecisive, after the war Madison immediately seized the political initiative to inaugurate vigorous new diplomatic and domestic programs. His successor, James Monroe, then picked up the beat, pressing on with a new nationalistic Republican agenda. The nationalism that arose after the war seemed to bring political dissension to a close. Commenting on the decline of partisan politics, a Federalist newspaper in Boston proclaimed the dawn of an **"Era of Good Feelings."**

The "American System" and New Economic Direction

The nation was much more unified politically in 1815 than it had been for years. The war's outcome and the growth that began to take place immediately following the peace settlement had largely silenced Madison's critics within the Republican Party. And during the waning days of the war, extreme Federalists had so embarrassed their party that they were at a severe political disadvantage.

The Essex Junto was primarily responsible for the Federalists' embarrassment. The junto had capitalized on the many military blunders and growing national debt to cast Republicans in a bad light and was drawing increasing support in the Northeast. In mid-December 1814 the Essex Junto staged the Hartford Convention, voting to secede from the union unless Congress repealed the Embargo of 1813 and passed the slate of constitutional reforms the junto had been pushing since its formation (see page 242). However, news of the Treaty of Ghent, which ended the War of 1812, and of the American victory in the Battle of New Orleans caused many to view the Federalists' efforts as either foolish or treasonous, and party popularity underwent a steep decline.

Facing no meaningful opposition, Madison chose in December 1815 to launch an aggressive new domestic policy. He challenged Congress to correct the economic ills that had caused the depression and helped to propel the nation into war. He also encouraged the states to invest in the nation's future by financing transportation systems and other internal improvements. Former critics such as DeWitt Clinton, Henry Clay, and John C. Calhoun quickly rallied behind the president and his nationalistic economic and political agenda.

Clay took the lead. He had come to Congress as one of the War Hawks in 1810 and had quickly become the dominant voice among the younger representatives. Born in Virginia in 1777, Clay had moved at the age of 20 to the wilds of Kentucky to practice law and carve out a career in politics. He was fantastically successful, becoming Speaker of the Kentucky state assembly when he was only 30 years old and winning a seat in the House of Representatives four years later. He became Speaker of the House during the prewar crisis. Now aligning himself firmly with the new economic agenda, Clay became its champion, calling it the **American System.**

What congressional Republicans had in mind was to create a national market economy. In the colonial period and increasingly thereafter, local market economies grew up around the trading and manufacturing centers of the Northeast. Individuals in these areas produced single items for cash sale and used the cash they earned to purchase goods produced by others. Specialization was the natural outcome. Farmers, for example, chose to grow only one or two crops and to sell the whole harvest for cash, which they used to buy various items they had once raised or made for themselves. Calhoun and others wanted to see such interdependence on a much larger scale. They envisioned a time when whole regions would specialize in producing commodities for which geography, climate, and the temperament of the people made each locale most suitable. Agricultural regions in the West, for example, would produce food for the industrializing Northeast and the fiber-producing South. The North would depend on the South for efficiently produced cotton, and both South and West would depend on the Northeast for manufactured goods. Improved transportation systems would make this flow of goods possible, and a strong national currency would ensure orderly trade between states. Advocates of the American System were confident that the balance eventually established among regions would free the nation as a whole from economic dependence on manufacturing centers in Europe.

Era of Good Feelings   The period from 1816 to 1823, when the decline of the Federalist Party and the end of the War of 1812 gave rise to a time of political cooperation.

American System   An economic plan sponsored by nationalists in Congress; it was intended to capitalize on regional differences to spur U.S. economic growth and the domestic production of goods previously bought from foreign manufacturers.

Chronology

New Optimism and a New Democracy

1807	Robert Fulton tests steam-powered *Clermont*
1810	*Fletcher v. Peck*
1814	Treaty of Ghent ends War of 1812
1814–1815	Hartford Convention
1815	Government funds Cumberland Road Stephen Decatur defeats Barbary pirates
1816	Tariff of 1816 First successful steamboat run, Pittsburgh to New Orleans James Monroe elected president
1817	Second Bank of the United States opens for business Rush-Bagot Agreement Construction of Erie Canal begins Congress suspends installment payments on public land purchases
1818	Convention of 1818 Andrew Jackson invades Spanish Florida
1819	*Dartmouth College v. Woodward* *McCulloch v. Maryland* Adams-Onís Treaty Missouri Territory applies for statehood Panic of 1819
1820	Monroe reelected Missouri Compromise Northeastern congressmen propose protective tariffs and reduction of public land prices
1823	Monroe Doctrine

1824–1828	Suffrage reform triples voter population
1824	*Gibbons v. Ogden* Western congressmen join northeastern congressmen to pass increased protective tariffs Jackson wins electoral plurality and popular majority in presidential election
1825	House of Representatives elects John Quincy Adams president Prairie du Chien treaties Completion of Erie Canal
1826	Disappearance of William Morgan and beginning of Antimasons
1827	Ratification of Cherokee constitution Federal removal of Winnebagos
1828	Tariff of Abominations Jackson elected president Publication of *The South Carolina Exposition and Protest* First issue of the *Cherokee Phoenix*
1830	Webster-Hayne debate Indian Removal Act
1831	Federal removal of Sauks and Choctaws *Cherokee Nation v. Georgia*
1832	*Worcester v. Georgia* Bank War Nullification crisis Black Hawk War Seminole War begins
1836–1838	Federal removal of Creeks, Chickasaws, and Cherokees

Clay and his cohorts recognized that one of the first steps in bringing all this about would have to be a national banking authority. True, Republicans had persistently opposed Alexander Hamilton's Bank of the United States (see page 202) and had killed it in 1811 by not renewing its initial twenty-year charter. During the war, however, bankers, merchants, and foreign shippers had chosen not to accept the paper currency issued by local and state banks. The postwar call for a unified national economy prompted Republicans to press again for a national currency and for a national bank to regulate its circulation. In 1816 Calhoun introduced legislation chartering a Second Bank of the United States, which Congress approved overwhelmingly. The Second Bank had many of the same powers and responsibilities as Hamilton's bank. Congress provided $7 million of its $35 million in opening capital and appointed one-fifth of its board of directors. The Second Bank opened for business in Philadelphia on January 1, 1817.

Proponents also saw improvements in transportation and communications as essential. Access to reliable transportation by means of the Great Lakes and the Ohio and Mississippi Rivers had been one of the principal planks in the War Hawk platform in 1812, and poor lines of supply and communication had spelled disaster for American military efforts during the war itself. Announcing that they would "bind the republic together with a perfect system of roads and canals," Republicans in Congress put forward a series of proposals designed to improve transportation and communications.

Finally, Calhoun took the lead in advocating **protective tariffs** to help the fledgling industries that had hatched during the war. Helped by the embargoes, American cotton-spinning plants had increased rapidly between 1808 and 1815. But with the return of open trade at war's end, British merchants dumped accumulated inventories of cotton and woolen cloth onto the U.S. market below cost in an effort to hamper further American development. Although some New England voices protested tariffs as unfair government interference, most northeasterners supported protection. Most southerners and westerners, however, remained leery of its impact on consumer prices. Still, shouting with nationalistic fervor about American economic independence, westerners such as Clay and southerners such as Calhoun were able to raise enough support to pass Madison's proposed **Tariff of 1816,** opening the way for continued tariff legislation in the years to come.

The popularity of these measures was apparent in the outcome of the 1816 elections. Madison's handpicked successor, fellow Virginian James Monroe, won by a decisive electoral majority: 184 votes to Federalist Rufus King's 34. Congressional Republicans enjoyed a similar sweep, winning more than three-fourths of the seats in the House of Representatives and the Senate. Presented with such a powerful mandate and the political clout necessary to carry it out, Republicans immediately set about expanding on the new nationalistic agenda.

The Transportation Problem

In the years before the War of 1812, travel on the nation's roads was a wearying experience. People who could afford transportation by stagecoach were crammed into an open wagon bouncing behind four horses on muddy, rutted, winding roads. Stagecoaches crept along at 4 miles per hour—when weather, equip-

ment, and local **blue laws** permitted them to move at all. And the enjoyment of such dubious luxury did not come cheaply: tolls for each mile of travel equaled the cost of a pint of good whiskey.

Recognizing the need for more and better roads, entrepreneurs sought to profit by building private **turnpikes** between heavily traveled points. In 1791, for example, a private company opened a 66-mile-long road between Philadelphia and Lancaster, Pennsylvania, hoping to make money on tolls. Between that time and the outbreak of war in 1812, private companies invested millions of dollars to construct several thousand miles of turnpikes.

Despite such private efforts, it was clear to many after the war that only the large-scale resources available to state and federal governments could make a practical difference in the transportation picture. Immediately after the war, Calhoun introduced legislation in Congress to finance a national transportation program. Congress approved, but Madison vetoed the bill, stating that the Constitution did not authorize federal spending on projects designed to benefit the states. But Calhoun finally won Madison's support by convincing the president that a government-funded national road between Cumberland, Maryland, and Wheeling, Virginia, was a military and postal necessity and therefore the initial federal expenditure of $30,000 for the **Cumberland Road** was permissible under the Constitution. That constitutional hurdle cleared, actual construction began in 1815.

Although people and light cargoes might move efficiently along the proposed national road, water transportation remained the most economical way to

---

protective tariff Tax on imported goods intended to make them more expensive than similar domestic goods, thus protecting the market for goods produced at home.

Tariff of 1816 First protective tariff in U.S. history; its purpose was to protect America's fledgling textile industry.

blue laws Local legislation designed to enforce Christian morality by forbidding certain activities, including traveling, on Sunday.

turnpike A road on which tolls are collected at gates set up along the way; private companies hoping to make a profit from the tolls built the first turnpikes.

Cumberland Road The initial section of what would be called the "National Road," a highway built with federal funds; this section stretched from Cumberland, Maryland, to Wheeling, Virginia. Later the road would be extended to Vandalia, Illinois, and beyond.

Before the transportation revolution, traveling was highly risky and uncomfortable. This painting shows a rather stylish stagecoach, but its well-dressed passengers are clearly being jostled. Note how the man in the front seat is bracing himself, while the man behind him loses his hat under the wheels. *"Travel by Stagecoach Near Trenton, New Jersey" by John Lewis Krimmel. The Metropolitan Museum of Art, Rogers Fund, 1942 (42.95.11). Photograph © 1984 The Metropolitan Museum of Art.*

ship bulky freight. Unfortunately, with few exceptions, navigable rivers and lakes did not link up conveniently to form usable transportation networks. Holland and other European countries had solved this problem by digging canals to expand the areas served by waterways. Before the War of 1812, some Americans had considered this solution, but enormous costs and engineering problems had limited canal construction to less than 100 miles. After the war, however, the entry of the state and federal governments into transportation development opened the way to an era of canal building.

New York State was most successful at canal development. In 1817 the state started work on a canal that would run more than 350 miles from Lake Erie at Buffalo to the Hudson River at Albany. Aided by Governor DeWitt Clinton's unswerving support and the gentle terrain in western New York, engineers planned the **Erie Canal.** Three thousand workers dug the huge ditch and built the **locks,** dams, and **aqueducts** that would transport barges carrying freight and passengers across the state. This vision became reality when the last section of the canal was completed and the first barge made its way from Buffalo to Albany and then on to New York City in 1825.

Canals were really little more than extensions of natural river courses, and fighting the currents of the great rivers that they connected remained a problem.

Pushed along by current and manpower, a barge could make the trip south from Pittsburgh to New Orleans in about a month. Returning north, against the current, took more than four months, if a boat could make the trip at all. As a result, most shippers barged their freight downriver, sold the barges for lumber in New Orleans, and walked back home along the **Natchez Trace,** a well-used path that eventually became another national road.

In 1807 Robert Fulton wedded steam technology borrowed from England with his own boat design to prove that steam-powered shipping was possible. Steam-driven water wheels pushed his 160-ton ship, the *Clermont,* upstream from New York City to Albany in an incredibly quick thirty-two hours. Unfortunately,

Erie Canal   A 350-mile canal stretching from Buffalo to Albany; it revolutionized shipping in New York State.

lock   A section of canal with gates at each end, used to raise or lower boats from one level to another by admitting or releasing water; locks allow canals to compensate for changes in terrain.

aqueduct   An elevated structure raising a canal to bridge rivers, canyons, or other obstructions.

Natchez Trace   A road connecting Natchez, Mississippi, with Nashville, Tennessee; it evolved from a series of Indian trails.

the design of the *Clermont* required deep water and large amounts of fuel to carry a limited **payload,** demands that rendered what many called "Fulton's Folly" impractical for most of America's rivers. After the war, however, Henry M. Shreve, a career boat pilot and captain, began experimenting with new designs and technologies. Borrowing the hull design of the shallow-draft, broad-beamed keelboats that had been sailing up and down inland streams for generations, Shreve added two lightweight high-compression steam engines, each one driving an independent side wheel. He also added an upper deck for passengers, creating the now-familiar multistoried steamboats of southern lore. Funded by merchants in Wheeling, Virginia—soon to be the western terminus for the Cumberland Road—Shreve successfully piloted one of his newly designed boats upriver, from Wheeling to Pittsburgh. Then, in 1816, he made the first successful run south, all the way to New Orleans.

Legal Anchors for New Business Enterprise

President Madison had raised serious constitutional concerns when Henry Clay and his congressional clique proposed spending federal money on road development. Though Calhoun was able to ease the president's mind on this specific matter, many constitutional issues needed clarification if the government was going to play the economic role that nationalists envisioned.

In 1819 the Supreme Court took an important step in clarifying the federal government's role in national economic life. The case arose over an effort by the state of Maryland to raise money by placing **revenue stamps** on federal currency. When a clerk at the Bank of the United States' Baltimore branch, James McCulloch, refused to apply the stamps, he was indicted by the state. In the resulting Supreme Court case, *McCulloch v. Maryland* (1819), the majority ruled that the states could not impose taxes on federal institutions and that McCulloch was right in refusing to comply with Maryland's revenue law. But more important, in rejecting Maryland's argument that the federal government was simply a creation of the several states and was therefore subject to state taxation, Chief Justice John Marshall wrote, "The Constitution and the laws made in pursuance thereof are supreme: that they control the constitution and laws of the respective states, and cannot be controlled by them." With this, Marshall declared his binding opinion that federal law was superior to state law in all matters.

Marshall demonstrated this principle again and reinforced it five years later in the landmark case of *Gibbons v. Ogden* (1824). In 1808 the state of New York had recognized Robert Fulton's accomplishments in steamboating by granting him an exclusive contract to run steamboats on rivers in that state. Fulton then used this monopoly power to sell licenses to various operators, including Aaron Ogden, who ran a ferry service between New York and New Jersey. Another individual, Thomas Gibbons, was also running a steamboat service in the same area, but he was operating under license from the federal government. When Ogden accused Gibbons of violating his contractual monopoly in a New York court, Gibbons took refuge in federal court. It finally fell to Marshall's Supreme Court to resolve the conflict. Consistent with its earlier decision, the Court ruled in favor of Gibbons, arguing that the New York monopoly conflicted with federal authority and was therefore invalid. In cases of interstate commerce, it ruled, Congress's authority "is complete in itself" and the states could not challenge it.

But it was going to take more than federal authority and investment to revolutionize the economy. Private money would be needed as well, and that too required some constitutional clarification. At issue were contracts, the basis for all business transactions, and their security from interference by either private or public challengers.

One case from before the war was important in clarifying how federal authorities would deal with matters of contract. The issue was the Yazoo affair, in which the Georgia state legislature had contracted to sell vast tracts of land to private investors (see page 242). The decision by the legislature to overturn that contract led to a great deal of political fuss, but it created a legal problem also: could a state legis-

---

payload The part of a cargo that generates revenue, as opposed to the part needed to fire the boiler or supply the crew.

revenue stamps Stickers affixed to taxed items by government officials indicating that the tax has been paid.

McCulloch v. Maryland Supreme Court case (1819) in which the majority ruled that federal authority is superior to that of individual states and that states cannot control or tax federal operations within their borders.

Gibbons v. Ogden Supreme Court case (1824) in which the majority ruled that the authority of Congress is absolute in matters of interstate commerce.

lature dissolve an executed contract? This came before Marshall's Court in 1810 with the case of *Fletcher v. Peck* (1810). In this case, the Court ruled that even if the original contract was fraudulently obtained, it still was binding and that the state legislature had no right to overturn it. Nor, it ruled in a later case, could a state modify a standing contract. That case, *Dartmouth College v. Woodward* (1819), involved Dartmouth College's founding charter, which specified that new members of the board of trustees were to be appointed by the current board. In 1816 the New Hampshire state legislature tried to take over the college by passing a bill that would allow the state's governor to appoint board members. The college brought suit, claiming that its charter was a legal contract and that the legislature had no right to abridge it. Announcing the Court's decision, Marshall noted that the Constitution protected the sanctity of contracts and that state legislatures could not interfere with them.

These and other cases helped ease the way for the development of new business ventures. With private contracts and federal financial bureaus safe from state and local meddling and the superiority of Congress in interstate commerce established, businesses had the security they needed to expand into new areas and attempt to turn Clay's dream of a national market economy into a reality. And private investors knew that their involvement in often risky ventures was protected, at least from the whims of politicians.

James Monroe and the Nationalist Agenda

While Congress and the courts were firmly in the hands of forward-looking leaders, the presidency passed in 1816 to the seemingly stolid James Monroe. Personally conservative, Monroe nonetheless was a strong nationalist as well as a graceful statesman. He had served primarily as a diplomat during the contentious period that preceded the War of 1812, and as president he turned his diplomatic skills to the task of calming political disputes. He was the first president since Washington to take a national goodwill tour, during which he persistently urged various political factions to merge their interests for the benefit of the nation at large.

Monroe's cabinet was well chosen to carry out the task of smoothing political rivalries while flexing nationalistic muscles. He selected John Quincy Adams, son and heir of Yankee Federalist John Adams, as secretary of state because of his diplomatic skill and to

This portrait of James Monroe, painted as he entered the White House in 1816, captures the president's conservative bearing. His clothing, for example, is much more typical of the revolutionary years than of the nineteenth century. His conservatism endeared him to many who were tired of political strife. *"James Monroe" by John Vanderlyn. National Portrait Gallery, Smithsonian Institution/Art Resource, NY.*

win political support in New England. Monroe tapped southern nationalist John C. Calhoun for secretary of war and balanced his appointment with that of southern states' rights advocate William C. Crawford as secretary of the Treasury. With his team assembled, Monroe launched the nation on a course designed to increase its control over the North American continent and improve its position in world affairs.

Fletcher v. Peck   Supreme Court case (1810) growing out of the Yazoo affair in which the majority ruled that the original land sale contract rescinded by the Georgia legislature was binding, establishing the superiority of contracts over legislation.

Dartmouth College v. Woodward   Supreme Court case (1819) in which the majority ruled that private contracts are sacred and cannot be modified by state legislatures.

Madison had already taken steps toward initiating a more aggressive diplomatic policy, setting the tone for the years to come. Taking advantage of U.S. involvement in the War of 1812, Barbary pirates (see page 189) had resumed their raiding activity against American shipping. In June 1815, Madison ordered a military force back to the Mediterranean to put an end to those raids. Naval hero Stephen Decatur returned to the region with a fleet of ten warships. Training his guns on the port of Algiers itself, Decatur threatened to level the city if the pirates did not stop raiding American shipping. The Algerians and the rest of the Barbary pirates signed treaties ending the practice of exacting **tribute.** They also released all American hostages and agreed to pay compensation for past seizures of American ships. Celebrating the victory, Decatur gave voice to a militant new American nationalism, proclaiming, "Our Country! In her intercourse with foreign nations may she always be in the right; but our country, right or wrong."

As though in direct response to Decatur's pronouncement, Monroe maintained Madison's firm stand as he attempted to resolve important issues not settled by earlier administrations. Secretary of State Adams began negotiating for strict and straightforward treaties outlining America's economic and territorial rights.

The first matter Adams addressed was the Treaty of Ghent (1814)—specifically, the loose ends it had left dangling. One problem had been the **demilitarization** of the Great Lakes boundary between the United States and British Canada. In the 1817 Rush-Bagot Agreement, both nations agreed to cut back their Great Lakes fleets to only a few vessels. A year later, the two nations drew up the Convention of 1818: the British agreed to honor American fishing rights in the Atlantic, to recognize a boundary between the Louisiana Territory and Canada at the 49th parallel, and to occupy the Oregon Territory jointly with the United States.

With these northern border issues settled, Adams set his sights on defining the nation's southern and southwestern frontiers. Conditions in Spanish Florida were extremely unsettled. Pirates and other renegades used Florida as a base for launching raids against American settlements and shipping, and runaway slaves found it a safe haven in their flight from southern plantations. By December 1817, matters in the Florida border region seemed critical. Reflecting on the situation there, General Andrew Jackson wrote the president advocating the invasion of Spanish Florida. "Let it be signified to me through any channel . . . that the possession of the Floridas would be desirable to the United States, and in sixty days it will be accomplished."

A short time later, Secretary of War Calhoun ordered Jackson to lead a military expedition into southern Georgia. Jackson's orders read that he was to patrol the border to keep raiders from crossing into the United States and runaway slaves from going out, but he later claimed that Monroe secretly authorized him to invade Florida. Jackson crossed the border, forcing the Spanish government to flee to Cuba. Spain vigorously protested, and Secretary of War Calhoun and others recommended that the general be severely disciplined. Adams, however, saw an opportunity to settle the Florida border issue. He announced that Jackson's raid was an act of self-defense that would be repeated unless Spain could police the area adequately. Fully aware that Spain could not guarantee American security, Adams knew that the Spanish would either have to give up Florida or stand by and watch the United States take it by force. Understanding his country's precarious position, Spanish minister Don Luis de Onís chose to cede Florida in the **Adams-Onís Treaty** of 1819. The United States got all of Florida in exchange for releasing Spain from $5 million in damage claims resulting from border raids. Spain also relinquished all previous claims to the Oregon Country in exchange for acknowledgment of its claims in the American Southwest.

Spain's inability to police its New World territories also led to a more general diplomatic problem. As the result of Spain's weakness, many of its colonies in Latin America had rebelled and established themselves as independent republics. Fearful of the anticolonial example being set in the Western Hemisphere, most members of the Congress of Vienna (see page 259) seemed poised to help Spain reclaim its overseas empire. Neither England, which had developed a thriving trade with the new Latin American republics, nor the United States felt that Europe should be allowed to intervene in the affairs of the Western Hemisphere. In 1823 British foreign minister George Canning proposed that the United States and England form an alliance to end European meddling in Latin America.

tribute A payment of money or other valuables that one group makes to another as the price of security.

demilitarization The removal of military forces from a region and the restoration of civilian control.

Adams-Onís Treaty Treaty between the United States and Spain in 1819 that ceded Florida to the United States, ended any Spanish claims in Oregon, and recognized Spanish rights in the American Southwest.

Most members of Monroe's cabinet supported allied action, but Adams protested that America would be reduced to a "cock-boat in the wake of the British man-of-war." Instead, he suggested a **unilateral** statement to the effect that "the American continents by the free and independent condition which they have assumed, and maintain, are henceforth not to be considered as subject for future colonization by any European power."

Monroe remained undecided. He trusted Adams's judgment but did not share the secretary of state's confidence in the nation's ability to fight off European colonization without British help. Monroe nevertheless conceded the nationalistic necessity for the United States to "take a bolder attitude . . . in favor of liberty." The president's indecision finally vanished in November 1823 when he learned that the alliance designed to restore Spain's colonies was faltering. With the immediate threat removed, Monroe rejected Canning's offer and in his annual message in December announced that the United States would regard any effort by European countries "to extend their system to any portion of this hemisphere as dangerous to our peace and safety." He went on to define any attempt at European intervention in the affairs of the Western Hemisphere as a virtual act of war against the United States and at the same time promised that the United States would steer clear of affairs in Europe.

The **Monroe Doctrine**, as this statement was later called, was exactly the proud assertion of principle "in favor of liberty" that Monroe had hoped for. It immediately won the support of the American people. The Monroe Doctrine, like Decatur's "Our country, right or wrong" speech, seemed to announce the arrival of the United States on the international scene. Both Europeans and Latin Americans, however, thought it was a meaningless statement. Rhetoric aside, the policy depended on the British navy and on Britain's informal commitment to New World autonomy.

tied up ships, making European nations dependent on America. After those wars ended in 1815, Europeans continued to need American food and manufactures as they rebuilt a peacetime economy. Encouraged by a ready European market and expanding credit offered by the Second Bank of the United States and by various state banks, budding southern planters, northern manufacturers, and western and southwestern farmers embarked on a frenzy of speculation. They rushed to borrow against what they were sure was a golden future to buy equipment, land, and slaves.

Although all shared the same sense of optimism, entrepreneurs in the North, West, and South had different ideas about the best course for the American economy. As the American System drew the regions together into increasing mutual dependency, the tensions among them increased as well. As long as economic conditions remained good, there was little reason for conflict, but when the speculative boom collapsed, sectional tensions increased dramatically.

The Panic of 1819

Earlier changes in federal land policy had contributed to the rise of speculation. In 1800 and again in 1804, Congress had passed bills lowering the minimum number of acres of federal land an individual could purchase and the minimum price per acre. After 1804 the minimum purchase became 160 acres and the minimum price, $1.64 per acre. The bill also permitted farmers to pay the government in **installments.** For most Americans, the minimum investment of $262.40 was still out of reach, but the installment option encouraged many to take the risk and buy farms they could barely afford.

Land speculators complicated matters considerably. Taking advantage of the new land prices, they too jumped into the game, buying land on credit. Unlike farmers, however, speculators never intended to put the land into production. They hoped to subdivide

Dynamic Growth and Political Consequences

■ How did the global economic situation contribute to American economics between 1815 and 1820?

■ How did postwar economic optimism help lead to economic panic in 1819?

■ How did economic growth and panic contribute to sectional conflict and political contention?

During the **Napoleonic wars,** massive armies had drained Europe's manpower, laid waste to crops, and

unilateral   Undertaken or issued by only one side and thus not involving an agreement made with others.

Monroe Doctrine   President Monroe's 1823 statement declaring the Americas closed to further European colonization and discouraging European interference in the affairs of the Western Hemisphere.

Napoleonic wars   Wars in Europe waged by or against Napoleon Bonaparte between 1803 and 1815.

installment   Partial payments of a debt to be made at regular intervals until the entire debt is repaid.

THE REMEMBRANCER,
OR
DEBTORS PRISON RECORDER.

"HE WHO'S ENTOMB'D WITHIN A PRISON'S WALLS
ENDURES THE ANGUISH OF A LIVING DEATH"

VOL. I.   NEW-YORK, SATURDAY, APRIL 8, 1820.   No. 1.

THE
DEBTORS PRISON RECORDER
IS ISSUED FROM THE PRESS OF
CHARLES N. BALDWIN,
AND PUBLISHED BY
JOHN B. JANSEN,
No. 15 Chatham-street,
NEW-YORK,
At two dollars per annum, payable quarterly in advance.

Persons at a distance may have the paper regularly forwarded to them by mail, provided they forward the requisite advance, *post paid.*

TO THE PUBLIC.

THE chief object of this publication will be to spread before an enlightened public the deplorable effects resulting from the barbarous practice of imprisonment for debt—to exhibit the misery of its wretched victims, and the unfeeling conduct of unpitying creditors. By these means, " with truth as its guide, and justice for its object," it will, it is hoped, gradually prepare the minds of the community for the entire abolition of a law which exists a dishonor to the precepts of Christianity, and as a blot on the statute book.

It will be published weekly, in an octavo form, each number to consist of eight pages, comprising a succinct and correct history of the interesting incidents which daily occur in the debtors prison—a correct Journal of prisoners received and discharged from

time to time, with such remarks as may grow out of peculiar persecution or other causes; nor will it neglect to announce the number of those who are supplied with food from that inestimable body, the Humane Society, to whom the profits of this publication will be faithfully applied, as a small testimonial of the gratitude felt by the unfortunate inmates of the prison, for their distinguished beneficence. It will contain interesting extracts from the latest European and American publications. In its columns will be found a variety of communications on various interesting subjects, from gentlemen without the prison walls, who have kindly volunteered their services to furnish us with essays on the ARTS and SCIENCES, criticisms on the DRAMA, POETRY, &c.

This work will be edited, and its matter carefully revised by several prisoners, who, if they cannot themselves enjoy the benefits of their labor, may at least feel a pleasure in the reflection that after ages will bestow a pitying tear on their sufferings, and bless them for the exertions made to rescue their country from the only vestage of feudal tyranny remaining in a land that boasts of freedom.

The small pittance paid for its perusal, will, it is beleived, procure for it the patronage of a generous public, who will be amply remunerated in performing a duty subserving the great and benign ends of Charity, while in return they are furnished with a species of reading not to be met with in any other publication.

Before the adoption of modern bankruptcy laws, it was not uncommon for people to be put in prison when they could not pay their debts. One impact of the Panic of 1819 was a huge upturn in such imprisonments. Responses varied: creditors stinging from gross losses insisted on vigorous enforcement of debtor laws, but many who were thrown out of work by forces beyond their control protested. Newspapers like *The Remembrancer, or Debtors Prison Recorder,* which began publication with this issue on April 8, 1820, called for reform in debtor laws and also reported gruesome stories about the sufferings of previously respectable people who found themselves in debtors' prison through no fault of their own. Debtors Prison Recorder, *Vol. 1., No. 1, New York, Saturday, April 8, 1820.*

and sell it to people who could not afford to buy 160-acre lots directly from the government. Speculators also offered installment loans, pyramiding the already huge tower of debt.

Banks—both relatively unsupervised state banks and the Second Bank of the United States—then added to the problem. Farmers who bought land on credit seldom had enough cash to purchase farm equipment, seed, materials for housing, and the other supplies necessary to put the land to productive use.

So the banks extended liberal credit on top of the credit already extended by the government and by land developers. Farmers thus had acreage and tools, but they also had an enormous debt.

Two developments in the international economy combined to undermine the nation's tower of debt. The economic optimism that fed the speculative frenzy rested on profitable markets. But as the 1810s drew to a close and recovery began in Europe, the profit bandwagon began to slow, and optimism to slip. Not only was Europe able to supply more of its own needs, but Europeans were also importing from other regions of the globe. Led by Great Britain, European nations were establishing colonies in Asia, Africa, and the Pacific. In addition, the recent independence of many of Europe's Latin American colonies deprived the Europeans of the gold and silver that had driven international economics since the discovery of America. Europe became less and less dependent on American goods and, at the same time, less and less able to afford them. Thus the bottom began to fall out of the international market that had fueled speculation within the United States.

Congress noted the beginning of the collapse late in 1817 and tried to head off disaster by tightening credit. The government stopped installment payments on new land purchases and demanded that they be transacted in hard currency. The Second Bank of the United States followed suit in 1818, demanding immediate repayment of loans in either gold or silver. State banks then followed and were joined by land speculators. Instead of curing the problem, however, tightening credit and recalling loans drove the economy over the edge. The speculative balloon burst, leaving nothing but a mass of debt behind. This economic catastrophe became known as the **Panic of 1819.**

Six years of economic depression followed the panic. As prices declined, individual farmers and manufacturers, unable to repay loans for land and equipment, faced **repossession** and imprisonment for debt. In Cincinnati and other agricultural cities, bankruptcy sales were a daily occurrence. In New England and the West, factories closed, throwing both employees and owners out of work. In New York and other manufacturing and trading cities, the ranks of the unem-

Panic of 1819 A financial panic that began when the Second Bank of the United States tightened credit and recalled government loans.

repossession The reclaiming of land or goods by the seller or lender after the purchaser fails to pay installments due.

ployed grew steadily. The number of **paupers** in New York City nearly doubled between 1819 and 1820, and in Boston thirty-five hundred people were imprisoned for debt. Shaken by the enormity of the problem, John C. Calhoun observed in 1820: "There has been within these two years an immense revolution of fortunes in every part of the Union; enormous numbers of persons utterly ruined; multitudes in deep distress."

Economic Woes and Political Sectionalism

Despite Monroe's efforts to merge southern, northern, and nationalist interests during the Era of Good Feelings, the Panic of 1819 drove a wedge between the nation's geographical sections. The depression touched each of the major regions differently, calling for conflicting solutions. For the next several years, the halls of Congress rang with debates rooted in each section's particular economic needs.

Tariffs were one proven method for handling economic emergencies, and as the Panic of 1819 spread economic devastation throughout the country, legislators from Pennsylvania and the Middle Atlantic states, southern New England, and then Ohio and Kentucky began clamoring for protection. Others disagreed, turning tariffs into the issue that would pit region against region more violently than any other during these years.

Farmers were split on the tariff issue. Irrespective of where they lived, so-called yeoman farmers favored a free market that would keep the price of the manufactures they had to buy as low as possible. In contrast, the increasing number of commercial farmers—those who had chosen to follow Henry Clay's ideas and were specializing to produce cash crops of raw wool, hemp, and wheat—joined mill owners, factory managers, and industrial workers in supporting protection against the foreign dumping of such products. So did those westerners who were producing raw minerals such as iron and tin that were in high demand in the industrializing economy.

Southern commercial farmers, however, did not join with their western counterparts in favoring protection. After supporting the protective Tariff of 1816, Calhoun and other southerners became firm opponents of tariffs. Their dislike of protection reflected a complex economic reality. Britain, not the United States, was the South's primary market for raw cotton and its main supplier of manufactured goods. Protective tariffs raised the price of the latter as well as the possibility that Britain might enact a **retaliatory tariff** on cotton imports from the South. If that happened,

southerners would pay more for manufactures but receive less profit from cotton.

When, in 1820, northern congressmen proposed a major increase in tariff rates, small farmers in the West and cotton growers in the South combined to defeat the measure. Northerners then wooed congressmen from the West, where small farmers were begging for relief from high land prices and debt. The northerners supported one bill that lowered the minimum price of public land to $1.25 per acre and another that allowed farmers who had bought land before 1820 to pay off their debts at the reduced price. The bill also extended the time over which those who were on the installment plan could make payments. Then, in 1822, northerners backed a bill authorizing increased federal spending on the Cumberland Road, an interest vital to westerners. Such **blandishments** finally had the desired outcome. In 1824 western congressmen joined with northern manufacturing interests to pass a greatly increased tariff.

This victory demonstrated an important new political reality. Of the six western states admitted to the Union after 1800, three—Ohio, Indiana, and Illinois—were predominantly farming states, split between commercial and nonspecialized farming. The other three—Louisiana, Mississippi, and Alabama—were increasingly dominated by cotton growing. As long as northern commercial interests could pull support from Ohio, Indiana, and Illinois, the balance of power in Congress remained relatively even. But new expansion in either the North or South had the potential to tip the political scale. As all three regions fought to implement specific solutions to the nation's economic woes, the regional balance of power in Congress became a matter of crucial importance.

The Missouri Compromise

The delicate balance in Congress began to wobble immediately in 1819 when Missouri Territory applied for statehood. New York congressman James Tallmadge Jr.

paupers A term popular in the eighteenth and nineteenth centuries to describe poor people; cities like New York and Boston often registered paupers so as to provide local relief.

retaliatory tariff A tariff on imported goods imposed neither to raise revenue nor control commerce but to retaliate against tariffs charged by another nation.

blandishment The use of flattery or manipulation to convince others to support a particular project or point of view.

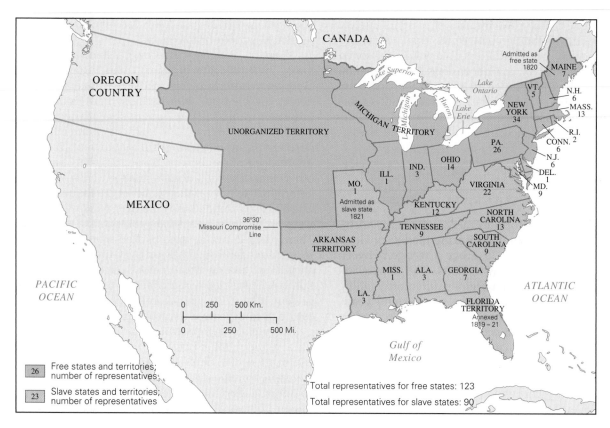

MAP 10.1 Missouri Compromise and Representative Strength The Missouri Compromise fixed the boundary between free and slave territories at 36°30′ north latitude. This map shows the result both in geographical and political terms. While each section emerged from the compromise with the same number of senators (24), the balance in the House of Representatives and Electoral College tilted toward the North.

realized that if Missouri was admitted as a free state, its economy would resemble the economies of states in the Old Northwest, and its congressmen would be susceptible to northern political deal making. This realization led Talmadge to propose that no new slaves be taken into Missouri and that those already in the territory be emancipated gradually. Southerners likewise understood that if Missouri was admitted as a slave state, its economy would resemble the economies of the southern states and its congressional **bloc** would undoubtedly support the southern position on tariffs and other key issues. They unified to oppose the **Tallmadge Amendment.**

Both sides in the debate were deeply entrenched, but in 1820 Henry Clay suggested a compromise. Late in 1819, Maine had separated from Massachusetts and applied for admission to the United States

as a separate state. The compromise proposed by Clay was to admit Missouri as a slave state and Maine as a free state. Clay also proposed that after the admission of Missouri, slavery be banned forever in the rest of the Louisiana Territory above 36°30′ north latitude, the line that formed Missouri's southern border (see Map 10.1). With this provision, Congress approved

---

bloc A group of people united for common action.

Tallmadge Amendment An amendment to a statehood bill for Missouri proposed by New York congressman James Tallmadge Jr. that would have banned slavery from the new state; it created a deadlock in Congress that necessitated the Missouri Compromise.

the **Missouri Compromise,** and the issue of slavery in the territories faded for a while.

The Missouri crisis was more than a simple debate over economic interests and congressional balances. Although economic issues had caused the conflict, slavery—its expansion and, for a few, its very existence—had become part of a struggle between sections over national power. For former Federalists such as Rufus King, the crisis offered an opportunity to use the slavery issue to woo northerners and westerners away from the traditionally southern-centered Republican coalition. Thus DeWitt Clinton and other northeastern dissidents joined with former Federalists to criticize their party's southern leadership and challenge Monroe's dominance. Wise to this political "party trick," Jefferson observed that "King is ready to risk the union for any chance of restoring his party to power and wriggling himself to the head of it." Still, the "trick" was an effective one: from 1820 onward, opportunistic politicians would attempt to use slavery to their own advantage.

New Politics and the End of Good Feelings

Conducted in the midst of the Missouri crisis, the presidential election of 1820 went as smoothly as could be: Monroe was reelected with the greatest majority ever enjoyed by any president except George Washington. Despite economic depression and sectional strife, the people's faith in Jefferson's party and his handpicked successors remained firm. As the election of 1824 approached, however, it became clear that the nation's continuing problems had broken Republican unity and destroyed the public's confidence in the party's ability to solve domestic problems.

Approaching the end of his second term, Monroe could identify no more gentleman Republicans from Virginia to carry the presidential torch. Although he probably favored John Quincy Adams as his successor, the president carefully avoided naming him as the party's **standard-bearer,** leaving that task to the Republican congressional caucus. If Monroe was hoping that the party would nominate Adams, he was disappointed when the southern-dominated party caucus tapped Georgia states' rights advocate William Crawford as its candidate. Certainly Clay and Adams were disappointed: each immediately defied party discipline by deciding to run against Crawford without the approval of the caucus. Encouraged by the apparent death of the caucus system for nominating presidential candidates, the Tennessee state legislature chose to put forward its own candidate, Andrew Jackson.

The election that followed was a painful demonstration of how deeply divided the nation had become. Northern regional political leaders rallied behind Adams, southern sectionalists supported Crawford, and northwestern commercial farmers and other backers of the American System lined up behind Clay. But a good portion of the American people—many of them independent yeoman farmers, traditional craftsmen, and immigrants—defied their political leaders by supporting the hero of New Orleans: Jackson.

The source of Jackson's political popularity is something of a mystery because the Tennessean remained almost entirely silent during the campaign. But his posture as a man of action—a doer rather than a talker—and the fact that he was a political outsider certainly played key roles. For whatever combination of reasons, once the ballots were cast, it became apparent that this groundswell of popular enthusiasm was a potent political force. Though a political **dark horse,** Jackson won the popular election, but the Electoral College vote was another matter (see Map 10.2). Jackson had 99 electoral votes to Adams's 84, Crawford's 41, and Clay's 37, but that was not enough to win the election. Jackson's opponents had a combined total of 162 of the 261 electoral votes cast. Thus Jackson won a **plurality** of electors but did not have the "majority of the whole number of electors" required by the Constitution. The Constitution specifies that in such cases, a list of the top three vote getters be passed to the House of Representatives for a final decision.

By the time the House had convened to settle the election, Crawford, the third-highest vote getter, had suffered a disabling stroke, so the list of candidates had only two names: John Quincy Adams and Andrew Jackson. Because Clay had finished fourth, he was not

Missouri Compromise   Law proposed by Henry Clay in 1820 admitting Missouri to the Union as a slave state and Maine as a free state and banning slavery in the Louisiana Territory north of latitude 36°30'.

standard-bearer   The recognized leader of a movement, organization, or political party.

dark horse   A political candidate who has little organized support and is not expected to win.

plurality   In an election with three or more candidates, the number of votes received by the winner when the winner receives less than half of the total number of votes cast.

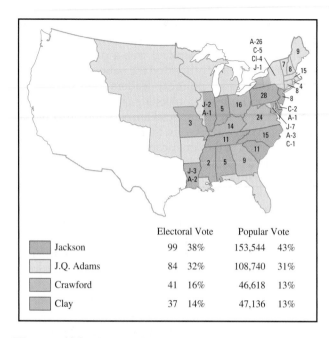

	Electoral Vote		Popular Vote	
Jackson	99	38%	153,544	43%
J.Q. Adams	84	32%	108,740	31%
Crawford	41	16%	46,618	13%
Clay	37	14%	47,136	13%

MAP 10.2 Election of 1824 This map showing the 1824 presidential election illustrates how divided the nation had become politically. William Crawford, the official Republican Party nominee, placed third in the Electoral College. The two most successful candidates, Andrew Jackson and John Quincy Adams, represented no political party. Speaker of the House Henry Clay, who finished fourth, played a key role in the outcome. Under his leadership, the House elected Adams.

The "New Man" in Politics

■ What factors helped change Americans' political options during the mid-1820s?

■ How did the election of Andrew Jackson in 1828 reflect those new options?

Since Washington's day the presidency had been considered an office for gentlemen and statesmen. The first several presidents had tried to maintain an air of polite dignity while in office, and voters were generally pleased with that orderly approach. But with the massive social changes taking place after the War of 1812, the conduct of national politics changed drastically. New voters from new professions with radically varying political and economic views began making demands. Many felt isolated from a political system that permitted the presidency to pass from one propertied gentleman to another. Clearly, changing times called for political change, and the American people began to press for it in no uncertain terms.

Adams's Troubled Administration

John Quincy Adams may have been the best-prepared man ever to assume the office of president. The son of revolutionary giant and former president John Adams, John Quincy had been born and raised in the midst of America's most powerful political circles. By the time of his controversial election in 1825, Adams had been a foreign diplomat, a U.S. senator, a Harvard professor, and an exceptionally effective secretary of state. Adams conducted himself in office as his father had, holding himself above partisan politics and refusing to use political favors to curry support. As a result, Adams had no effective means of rallying those who might have supported him or of pressuring his opponents. Thus, despite his impressive résumé, Adams's administration was a deeply troubled one.

Adams's policy commitments did nothing to boost his popularity. The new president promised to increase tariffs to protect American manufacturing and

in contention in the **runoff election.** As Speaker of the House, however, he was in a particularly strategic position to influence the outcome, and friends of both hopefuls sought his support. Adams's and Clay's views on tariffs, manufacturing, foreign affairs, and other key issues were quite compatible. Clay therefore endorsed Adams, who won the House election and in 1825 became the nation's sixth president.

Jackson and his supporters were outraged. They considered Clay a betrayer of western and southern interests, calling him the "Judas of the West." Then when Adams named Clay as his secretary of state—the position that had been the springboard to the presidency for every past Republican who held it—Jacksonians exploded. Proclaiming Adams's election a "corrupt bargain," Jackson supporters withdrew from the party of Jefferson, bringing an end to the one-party system that had emerged under the so-called **Virginia Dynasty** and dealing the knockout blow to the Era of Good Feelings.

runoff election A final election held to determine a winner after an earlier election has eliminated the weakest candidates.

Virginia Dynasty Term applied to the U.S. presidents from Virginia in the period between 1801 and 1825: Jefferson, Madison, and Monroe.

to raise funds necessary to pay for "the improvement of agriculture, commerce, and manufactures." He also wanted the Second Bank of the United States to stabilize the economy while providing ample loans to finance new manufacturing ventures. And he advocated federal spending to improve "the elegant arts" and advance "literature and the progress of the sciences, ornamental and profound." High sounding though Adams's objectives were, Thomas Jefferson spoke for many when he observed that such policies would establish "a single and splendid government of an aristocracy . . . riding and ruling over the plundered ploughman and beggared yeomanry." Jefferson's criticism seemed particularly apt in the economic turmoil that followed the Panic of 1819. Moreover, the increase in federal power implied by Adams's policies frightened southerners, and this fear, combined with their traditional distaste for tariffs, virtually unified opposition to Adams in the South.

Led by John C. Calhoun, Adams's opponents tried to manipulate tariff legislation to undercut the president's support. Calhoun proposed that Congress should propose an unprecedented increase in tariff rates. Northeastern Jacksonians should then voice support for the increase while Jackson supporters in the West and South opposed them. Calhoun and his colleagues envisioned a win-win situation: northeastern Jacksonians would win increasing support from manufacturing interests in their region by appearing to support tariffs; southern and western Jackson supporters could take credit for sinking tariff increases, cementing support in their districts; and Adams, who had promised increases as part of his political agenda, would appear ineffectual and his support undermined. But Calhoun and his fellow conspirators had miscalculated: when the tariff package came to the floor in May 1828, key northeastern congressmen engineered its passage. The resulting **Tariff of Abominations** was not what Calhoun had expected, but it served his ends by establishing tariff rates that were unpopular with almost every segment of the population, and the unpopular president would bear the blame.

Democratic Styles and Political Structure

Adams's demeanor and outlook compounded his problems. He seemed more a man of his father's generation than of his own. The enormous economic and demographic changes that occurred during the first decades of the nineteenth century created a new political climate, one in which Adams's archrival Andrew Jackson felt much more at ease than did the stiff Yankee who occupied the White House.

One of the most profound changes in the American political scene was an explosion in the number of voters. Throughout the early years of the republic's history, voting rights were limited to white men who held real estate. In a nation primarily of farmers, most men owned land, so the fact of limited suffrage raised little controversy. But as economic conditions changed, a smaller proportion of the population owned farms, and while bankers, lawyers, manufacturers, and other such men often were highly educated, economically stable, and politically concerned, their lack of real estate barred them from political participation. Not surprisingly, such elite and middle-class men urged suffrage reform. In 1800 only three of the sixteen states—Kentucky, Vermont, and New Hampshire—had no property qualifications for voting, and Georgia, North Carolina, and Pennsylvania permitted taxpayers to vote even if they did not own real property. By 1830, only five of the twenty-four states retained property qualifications, nine required tax payment only, and ten made no property demands at all. Of course, all of the states continued to bar women from voting, no matter how much property they may have owned, and most refused the ballot to African Americans, whether free or slave. Still, the raw number of voters grew enormously and rapidly. In the 1824 election, 356,038 men cast ballots for the presidency. Four years later, more than three times that number of men voted.

Complementing the impact of the expanding **electorate** were significant changes in the structure of politics itself. Key among them was the method for selecting members of the Electoral College (see page 195). Gradually, state after state adopted the popular election of electors until, by 1828, state legislatures in only two states continued to appoint them. At the same time, more and more government jobs that had traditionally been appointive became elective. Thus more voters would vote to fill more offices and could

---

Tariff of Abominations Tariff package designed to win support for anti-Adams forces in Congress; its passage in 1828 discredited Adams but set off sectional tension over tariff issues.

electorate The portion of the population that possesses the right to vote.

As suffrage requirements loosened, politicians began canvassing for votes among common people. This painting by George Caleb Bingham captures the spirit of the new politics, showing an office seeker drumming up support from people on the street. *"Canvassing for a Vote,"* 1852, by George Caleb Bingham. The Nelson Gallery–Atkins Museum of Art, Kansas City, MO (purchase: Nelson Trust), 54-9.

affect the political process in new, profound ways. In addition, states increasingly dropped property qualifications for officeholding as well as voting, opening new opportunities for breaking the gentlemanly monopoly on political power.

Political opportunists were not slow to take advantage of the new situation. Men such as New Yorker **Martin Van Buren** quickly came to the fore, organizing political factions into tightly disciplined local and statewide units. A longtime opponent of Governor DeWitt Clinton's faction in New York, Van Buren molded disaffected Republicans into the so-called Bucktail faction. In 1820 the Bucktails used a combination of political patronage—the ability of the party in power to distribute government jobs—**influence peddling,** and fiery speeches to draw newly qualified voters into the political process and swept Clinton out of office.

Many new voters were gratified at finally being allowed to participate in politics but sensed that their participation was not having the impact it should. They resented the "corrupt bargain" that had denied the presidency to the people's choice—Andrew Jackson—in the election of 1824. Voters in upstate New York and elsewhere pointed at organizations such as the **Masons,** claiming that they used secret signs and rituals to ensure the election of their own members,

thus maintaining the supremacy of political parties and thwarting the popular will. In the fall of 1826, William Morgan, a bricklayer and Mason from Canandaigua, New York, decided to publish some of the organization's lesser secrets. Morgan was promptly arrested—charged with owing a debt of $2.69—and jailed. What happened after that remains a mystery. Some unknown person paid Morgan's debt, and he was released. But as he emerged from jail, he was seized, bound and gagged, and dragged into a carriage that whisked him out of town. He was never seen again.

Morgan's disappearance caused a popular outcry, and political outsiders demanded a complete investigation. When no clues turned up, many assumed that

Martin Van Buren   New York politician known for his skillful handling of party politics; he helped found the Democratic Party and later became the eighth president of the United States.

influence peddling   Using one's influence with people in authority to obtain favors or preferential treatment for someone else, usually in return for payment.

Masons   An international fraternal organization with many socially and politically prominent members, including a number of U.S. presidents.

a Masonic conspiracy was afoot. Within a year, opportunistic young politicians, including New Yorkers Thurlow Weed and William Seward and Pennsylvanian **Thaddeus Stevens,** had harnessed this political anxiety by forming a new party: the **Antimasonic Party.** Based exclusively on the alienation felt by small craftsmen, farmers, and other marginalized groups, the Antimasons had no platform beyond their shared faith in conspiracies and opposition to them. The Antimasonic Party was, in effect, a political party whose sole cause was to oppose political parties.

What was happening in New York was typical of party and antiparty developments throughout the country. As the party of Jefferson dissolved, a tangle of political factions broke out across the nation. This was precisely the sort of petty politics that Adams disdained, but the chaos suited a man like Jackson perfectly. So, while the Antimasons were busy pursuing often highly fanciful conspiracy theories, Van Buren was busy forging with the hero of New Orleans an alliance that would fundamentally alter American politics.

The Rise of "King Andrew"

Within two years of Adams's election, Van Buren had brought together northern outsiders like himself, dissident southern Republicans like John C. Calhoun, and western spokesmen like **Thomas Hart Benton** of Missouri and John H. Eaton of Tennessee into a new political party. Calling themselves Democratic-Republicans—**Democrats** for short—this party railed against the neofederalism of Clay and Adams's National Republican platform. The Democrats called for a return to Jeffersonian simplicity, states' rights, and democratic principles. Behind the scenes, however, they employed the tight organizational discipline and manipulative techniques that Van Buren had used to such good effect against the Clintonians in New York. Lining up behind the recently defeated popular hero Andrew Jackson, the new party appealed to both opportunistic political outsiders and democratically inclined new voters. In the congressional elections of 1826, Van Buren's coalition drew the unqualified support of both groups, unseating enough National Republicans to gain a twenty-five-seat majority in the House of Representatives and an eight-seat advantage in the Senate.

Having Andrew Jackson as a candidate was probably as important to the Democrats' success as their ideological appeal and tight political organization. In many ways, Jackson was a perfect reflection of the new voters. Like many of them, he was born in a log cabin under rustic circumstances. His family had faced

more than its share of hardships: his father had died two weeks before Andrew's birth, and he had lost his two brothers and his mother during the Revolutionary War. In the waning days of the Revolution, at the age of 13, Jackson joined a mounted militia company and was captured by the British. His captors beat their young prisoner and then let him go, a humiliation he would never forgive.

At the end of the war, Jackson set out to make his own way in the world. Like many of his contemporaries, he chose the legal profession as the route to rapid social and economic advancement. In 1788 he was appointed **public prosecutor** for the North Carolina district that later split off to become Tennessee. Driven by an indomitable will and a wealth of native talent, Jackson became the first U.S. congressman from the state of Tennessee and eventually was elected to the Senate. He also was a judge on the Tennessee Supreme Court. Along the way, Jackson's exploits established his solid reputation as a heroic and natural leader. Even before the War of 1812, his toughness had earned him the nickname "Old Hickory" (see pages 255–256). Also, in the popular view, it was Jackson's brashness, not Adams's diplomacy, that had finally won Spanish Florida for the United States.

Jackson's popular image as a rough-hewn man of the people was somehow untarnished by his political alliance with business interests, his activities as a land speculator, and his large and growing personal fortune and stock of slaves. In the eyes of frontiersmen,

Thaddeus Stevens Opportunistic politician who was one of the founders of the Antimasonic Party; he later became a leader of the "Conscience Whigs" and later still became one of the key organizers of the Republican Party. During and after the Civil War, he was the leader of the Radical Republican faction in Congress.

Antimasonic Party Political party formed in 1827 to capitalize on popular anxiety about the influence of the Masons; it opposed politics-as-usual without offering any particular substitute.

Thomas Hart Benton U.S. senator from Missouri and legislative leader of the Democrats; he was a champion of President Jackson and a supporter of westward expansion.

Democrats Political party that brought Andrew Jackson into office; it recalled Jeffersonian principles of limited government and drew its support from farmers, craftsmen, and small businessmen.

public prosecutor A lawyer appointed by the government to prosecute criminal actions on behalf of the state.

During the nineteenth century many practical and purely decorative items were used to advertise political candidates. This campaign pendant for Andrew Jackson and the thread box depicting John Quincy Adams are good examples. The pictures themselves give insight into the public images of the two candidates: Jackson appears to be flamboyant and romantic, whereas Adams seems stern and conservative. *Collection of Janice L. and David J. Frent.*

small farmers, and to some extent urban working-men, he remained a common man like them. Having started with nothing, Jackson seemed to have drawn from a combination of will, natural ability, and divine favor to become a man of substance without becoming a snob.

Caricature and image making rather than substantive issues dominated the election campaign of 1828. Jackson supporters accused Adams of being cold, aristocratic, and corrupt in bowing to speculators and **special interests** when defining his tariff and land policies. Adams supporters charged Jackson with being a dueler, an insubordinate military adventurer, and an uncouth backwoodsman whose disregard for propriety had led him to live with a woman before she divorced her first husband.

The characterization of Adams as cold was accurate, but charges of corruption were entirely untrue, though Adams's refusal to respond led many to believe them. The charges against Jackson were all too true, but voters saw them as irrelevant. Rather than

damaging Jackson's image, such talk made him appear romantic and daring. When all was said and done, the Tennessean polled over a hundred thousand more popular votes than did the New Englander and won the vast majority of states, taking every one in the South and West (see Map 10.3).

As if in response to his supporters' desires and his opponents' fears, Jackson swept into the White House on a groundswell of unruly popular enthusiasm. Ten thousand visitors crammed into the capital to witness Jackson's inauguration on March 4, 1829. Showing his usual disdain for tradition, Jackson took the oath of office and then pushed through the crowd and

caricature An exaggerated image of a person, usually enhancing their most uncomplimentary features.

special interest A person or organization that seeks to benefit by influencing legislators to support particular policies.

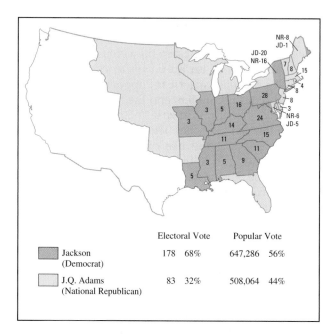

	Electoral Vote		Popular Vote	
Jackson (Democrat)	178	68%	647,286	56%
J.Q. Adams (National Republican)	83	32%	508,064	44%

MAP 10.3 Election of 1828 This map shows how the political coalition between Andrew Jackson and Martin Van Buren turned the tables in the election of 1828. Jackson's Democratic Party won every region except Adams's native New England.

mounted his horse, galloping off toward the White House followed by a throng of excited onlookers. When they arrived, the mob flowed behind him into the presidential mansion, where they climbed over furniture, broke glassware, and generally frolicked. The new president was finally forced to flee the near-riot by climbing out a back window. Clearly a boisterous new spirit was alive in the nation's politics.

Launching Jacksonian Politics

That he was a political outsider was a major factor in Jackson's popularity. Antimasons and others were convinced that politics consisted primarily of conspiracies among political insiders, and Jackson curried their support by promising **retrenchment** and reform in the federal system. In the process he initiated a personal style in government unlike that of any of his predecessors in office and alienated many both inside and outside Washington.

Retrenchment was first on the new president's agenda. Jackson challenged the notion that government work could be carried out best by an elite core of professional civil servants. Such duties, Jackson declared, were "so plain and simple that men of intel-

ligence may readily qualify themselves for their performance." And in order to keep such men from becoming entrenched, Jackson promised to institute regular rotation in office for federal bureaucrats: appointments in his administration would last only four years, after which civil servants would have to return to "making a living as other people do."

Like many of Jackson's policies, this rotation system was designed to accomplish more than a single goal. Because no new party had come to power since Jefferson's election in 1800, Jackson inherited some ten thousand civil servants who owed their jobs to Republican patronage. Rotation in office gave the president the excuse to fire people whom he associated with the "corrupt bargain" and felt he could not fully trust. It also opened up an unprecedented opportunity for Jackson to reward his loyal supporters by placing them in the newly vacated civil service jobs. The Jacksonian adage became "To the victor belong the **spoils**," and the Democrats made every effort to advance their party's hold on power by distributing government jobs to loyal party members.

Patronage appointments extended to the highest levels in government. Jackson selected cabinet members not for their experience or ability but for their political loyalty and value in satisfying the various factions that formed his coalition. The potential negative impact of these appointments was minimized by Jackson's decision to abandon his predecessors' practice of regularly seeking his cabinet members' advice on major issues: the president called virtually no cabinet meetings and seldom asked for his cabinet's opinion. Instead, he surrounded himself with an informal network of friends and advisers. This so-called **Kitchen Cabinet** worked closely with the president on matters of both national policy and party management.

Jackson's relationship with everyone in government was equally unconventional. He was known to rage, pout, and storm at suspected disloyalty. Earlier presidents had at least pretended to believe in the equal distribution of power among the three branches of government, but Jackson avowed that the executive

retrenchment In government, the elimination of unnecessary jobs or functions for reform or cost-cutting purposes.

spoils Jobs and other rewards for political support.

Kitchen Cabinet President Jackson's informal advisers, who helped him shape both national and Democrat Party policy.

should be supreme because the president was the only member of the government elected by all the people. He made it clear that he would stand in opposition to both private and congressional opponents and was not above threatening military action to get his way. Reflecting his generally testy relationship with the legislative branch, he vetoed twelve bills in the course of his administration, three more than all his predecessors combined. Nor did he feel any qualms about standing up to the judiciary. Such arrogant assertions of executive power led Jackson's opponents to call the new president "King Andrew."

The Reign of "King Andrew"

■ What was President's Jackson role in shaping U.S. Indian policy? How does his background account for his policy choices?

■ How did conditions in each region of the country influence the national divisions reflected in the nullification crisis and the Bank War?

Jackson had promised the voters "retrenchment and reform." He delivered retrenchment, but reform was more difficult to arrange. Jackson tried to implement reform in four broad areas: (1) the nation's banking and financial system, (2) internal improvements and public land policy, (3) Indian affairs, and (4) the collection of revenue and enforcement of federal law. The steps that Jackson took appealed to some of his supporters but strongly alienated others. Thus, as Jackson tried to follow through on his promise to reform the nation, he nearly tore the nation apart.

Jackson and the Bank

The Second Bank of the United States, chartered in 1816, was an essential part of Clay and Calhoun's American System. In addition to serving as the depository for federal funds, the Second Bank issued national currency, which could be exchanged directly for gold, and it served as a national clearing-house for notes issued by state and local banks. In that capacity, the Second Bank could regulate currency values and credit rates and help to control the activities of state banks by refusing to honor their notes if the banks lacked sufficient gold to back them. The Second Bank could also police state and local banks by calling in loans and refusing credit—actions that had helped bring on the Panic of 1819 and had made the Second Bank very unpopular.

In 1823 **Nicholas Biddle** became president of the Second Bank. An able administrator and talented econ-

omist, Biddle enforced firm and consistent policies that restored some confidence in the bank and its functions. But many Americans still were not ready to accept the notion of an all-powerful central banking authority. The vast majority of opponents were Americans who did not understand the function of the Second Bank, viewing it as just another instrument for helping the rich get richer. These critics tended instinctively to support the use of hard currency, called **specie.** Other critics, including many state bankers, opposed the Second Bank because they felt that Biddle's controls were too strict and that they were not receiving their fair share of federal revenues. Speculators and debtors also opposed the bank: when they gambled correctly, they could benefit from the sort of economic instability the bank was designed to prevent.

Hoping to fan political turmoil in the upcoming presidential election, Jackson's opponents in Congress proposed to renew the bank's twenty-year charter four years early, in 1832. They hoped that Biddle's leadership had established the bank as a necessary part of the nation's economy, even in critics' minds, and that Democratic Party discipline would break down if the president tried to prevent the early renewal of the charter. They were partially right—Congress passed the renewal bill, and Jackson vetoed it—but the anticipated rift between Jackson and congressional Democrats did not open. The president stole the day by delivering a powerful veto message geared to appeal to the mass of Americans on whose support his party's congressmen depended. Jackson denounced the Second Bank as an example of vested privilege and monopoly power that served the interests of "the few at the expense of the many" and injured "humbler members of society—the farmers, the mechanics, and laborers—who have neither the time nor the means of securing like favors to themselves." And Jackson went even further, asserting that foreign interests, many of which were seen as enemies to American rights, had used the bank to accumulate large blocks of American securities.

Although the charter was not renewed, the Second Bank could operate for four more years on the basis of its unexpired charter. Jackson, however, wanted to kill the Second Bank immediately, to "deprive the conspirators of the aid which they expect from it money

> **Nicholas Biddle** President of the Second Bank of the United States; he struggled to keep the bank functioning when President Jackson tried to destroy it.
>
> **specie** Coins minted from precious metals.

Published in 1833, this political cartoon entitled "The Diplomatic Hercules [Andrew Jackson] Attacking the Political Hydra [The Second Bank of the United States]" illustrates why the Bank War enhanced rather than hurt Jackson at the polls. Many voters saw the bank as a monster that used its tentacles of complicated financial policy to choke common people while enriching the speculators and merchants who supported it. *New York Historical Society.*

and power." The strategy Jackson chose was to withdraw federal funds and redeposit the money in state banks. Although this move was illegal, Jackson nonetheless ordered Treasury Secretary Louis McLane to withdraw the federal funds. When he refused, the president fired and replaced him with William J. Duane, who also refused to carry out Jackson's order. Jackson quickly fired him too and appointed Kitchen Cabinet member Roger B. Taney to head the Treasury Department. Stepping around the law rather than breaking it, Taney chose not to transfer federal funds directly from the Second Bank to state banks, but instead simply kept paying the government's bills from existing accounts in the Second Bank while placing all new deposits in so-called **pet banks.**

Bank president Biddle was not going to give up without a fight. Powerless to stop Taney's diversion of federal funds, Biddle sought to replace dwindling assets by raising interest rates and by calling in loans owed by state banks. In this way, the banker believed, he would not only head off the Second Bank's collapse but also trigger a business panic that might force the government to reverse its course. "Nothing but the evidence of suffering . . . will produce any effect," Biddle said as he pushed the nation toward economic instability. Biddle was correct that there would be "evidence of suffering," but the full effect of the **Bank War** would not be felt until after the reign of "King Andrew" had ended.

Jackson and the West

Although Jackson was a westerner, his views on federal spending for roads, canals, and other internal im-

provements seemed based more on politics than on ideology or regional interest. For example, when Congress passed a bill calling for federal money to build a road in Kentucky—from Maysville, on the Ohio border, to Lexington—Jackson vetoed it, claiming that it would benefit only one state and was therefore unconstitutional. But three practical political issues influenced his decision. First, party loyalists in places such as Pennsylvania and New York, where Jackson hoped to gain support, opposed federal aid to western states. Second, Lexington was the hub of Henry Clay's political district, and by denying aid that would benefit that city, Jackson was putting his western competitor in political hot water. Finally, Jackson's former congressional district centered on Nashville—already the terminus of a national road and therefore a legitimate recipient of federal funds. Thus Jackson could lavish money on his hometown while seeming to stand by strict constitutional limitations on federal power.

Disposing of the **public domain** was the other persistent problem Jackson faced. By the time he came to

---

pet banks State banks into which Andrew Jackson ordered federal deposits to be placed to help deplete the funds of the Second Bank of the United States.

Bank War The political conflict that occurred when Andrew Jackson tried to destroy the Second Bank of the United States, which he thought represented special interests at the expense of the common man.

public domain Land owned and controlled by the federal government.

Throughout the West, people without money simply camped on publicly owned land. This painting by George Caleb Bingham captures one such family as they pause outside their log cabin. Western politicians like Thomas Hart Benton argued that such "squatters" had a legitimate right to claim the land they settled and fought for legislation protecting squatters' rights. *"The Squatters" by George Caleb Bingham, 1850. Courtesy of Museum of Fine Arts, Boston.*

power, land policy had become a major factor in sectional politics. Although the price of $1.25 per acre for public land established in the wake of the Panic of 1819 was a significant improvement over the previous price, it was still too high for many hopeful farmers. Abandoning his predecessors' notion that public land sales should profit the government, Jackson took the position that small farmers should be able to buy federal land for no more than it cost the government to **survey** the plot and process the sale.

Jackson thus directed Congress that "public lands shall cease as soon as practicable to be a source of revenue," and western Jacksonians responded immediately. One of them, Senator Thomas Hart Benton of Missouri, proposed in 1830 that the price of government land be dropped gradually from $1.25 to just 25 cents an acre and that any lands not sold at that price simply be given away. He also suggested that squatters—anyone who was currently settled illegally on public land—be given the first chance to buy the tract where they were squatting when the government offered it for sale.

Such measures pleased Jackson's western supporters but frightened easterners and southerners. His supporters in the East and South feared that migration would give the West an even bigger say in the nation's economic and political future. In addition, southerners were concerned that Congress would replace revenues lost from the sale of public land by raising tariffs, threatening the South's economic relationship with Europe. Northerners were afraid that as people moved west, the drain on population would drive up the price of labor, increasing the cost of production and lowering profits. The result was nearly three years of debate in Congress. A frustrated Henry Clay, desperate to save any scrap of his economic plans for the nation, suggested that the distribution of public land be turned over to the states. Congress, relieved to have the matter taken out of its hands, passed Clay's bill in 1833, but Jackson vetoed it, taking another slap at Clay and affirming that the distribution of the public domain was a federal matter.

Jackson and the Indians

At the end of the War of 1812, the powerful Cherokees, Choctaws, Seminoles, Creeks, and Chickasaws—the so-called **Five Civilized Tribes**—numbered nearly seventy-five thousand people and occupied large holdings within the states of Georgia, North and South Carolina, Alabama, Mississippi, and Tennessee. These Indians had embraced Jefferson's vision of acculturation but were seen as an obstruction to westward migration, especially by grasping planters on the make who coveted Indian land for cotton fields. A similar situation prevailed in the Northwest. Though neither as numerous nor as Europeanized as the Civilized Tribes, groups such as the Peorias, Kaskaskias, Kickapoos, Sauks, Foxes, and Winnebagos were living settled and stable lives along the northern frontier.

Throughout the 1820s, the federal government tried to convince tribes along the frontier to move farther west. Promised money, new land, and relief from white harassment, many Indian leaders agreed. Others, however, resisted, insisting that they stay where they were. The outcome was terrible factionalism within Indian societies as some lobbied to sell out and move west while others fought to keep their lands.

survey   To determine the area and boundaries of land through measurement and mathematical calculation.

Five Civilized Tribes   Term used by whites to describe the Cherokee, Choctaw, Seminole, Creek, and Chickasaw Indians, many of whom were planters and merchants.

Playing on this factionalism, federal Indian agents were able to extract land cessions that consolidated the eastern tribes onto smaller and smaller holdings. One such transaction, the 1825 Treaty of Indian Springs, involved fraud and manipulation so obnoxious that President Adams overturned the ratified treaty and insisted on a new one.

Adams's protective attitude did not extend to all Indians, however. The Prairie du Chien treaties (see page 263) called for the gradual removal of the northwestern tribes to the west side of the Mississippi. Drawn by the presence of gold and rich soil, impatient white miners and farmers moved onto the treaty lands even before the Indians left. In 1827 the Winnebagos, under Red Bird, resisted this invasion by raiding mining settlements in what was still legally Indian territory. White miners called for federal troops to assist their militia companies in suppressing Winnebago resistance. Despite the illegality of the miners' actions, the Adams administration complied, driving Red Bird and his people out of the disputed region.

Adams at least paid lip service to honest dealings with the Indians and the sanctity of treaties. Jackson scoffed at both. In 1817 he had told President Monroe, "I have long viewed treaties with the Indians an absurdity not to be reconciled to the principles of our government." As president, Jackson advocated removing all the eastern Indians to the west side of the Mississippi, by force if necessary (see Map 10.4). Following Jackson's direction, Congress passed the **Indian Removal Act** in 1830, appropriating the funds necessary to purchase all of the lands held by Indian tribes east of the Mississippi River and to pay for their resettlement in the West.

It did not take Jackson long to begin implementing his new authority. Like the Winnebagos, the Sauk and Fox Indians also resisted violations of the Prairie du Chien treaties. When white farmers penetrated Sauk Indian territory during the summer of 1831, the Jackson administration authorized federal troops to forcibly move the entire band of more than a thousand Indian men, women, and children across the Mississippi. During the following spring, however, one Sauk leader, **Black Hawk,** led a party back "home." Harassed by Illinois militia units, Black Hawk's resistance force clung to their territory until federal troops marched in from Illinois and Missouri, killing more than three hundred Indians and capturing Black Hawk.

At the same time, whites were exerting similar pressure on the southern tribes. The case of the Cherokees provides an excellent illustration of the new, more aggressive attitude toward Indian policy. Having allied with Jackson against the Creeks in 1813, the Cherokees emerged from the War of 1812 with their lands pretty well intact, and a rising generation of progressive leaders pushed strongly for the tribe to embrace white culture. In the early 1820s the Cherokees created a formal government with a bicameral legislature, a court system, and a professional, salaried civil service. In 1827 the tribe drafted and ratified a written constitution modeled on the Constitution of the United States. In the following year the tribe began publication of its own newspaper, the *Cherokee Phoenix*, printed in both English and Cherokee, using the alphabet devised earlier in the decade by tribal member **George Guess (Sequoyah).**

Rather than winning the acceptance of their white neighbors, however, those innovations led to even greater friction. From the frontiersmen's point of view, Indians were supposed to be dying out, disappearing into history, not founding new governments and competing successfully for economic power. Thus in 1828 the Georgia legislature **annulled** the Cherokee constitution. In the following year, gold was found on Cherokee land. As more than three thousand greedy prospectors violated tribal territory, the state of Georgia extended its authority over the Cherokees and ordered all communal tribal lands seized.

That was the first in a series of laws that the Georgia legislature passed to make life as difficult as possible for the Cherokees in hopes of driving them out of the state. When Christian missionaries living with the tribe protested the state's actions and encouraged the Cherokees to seek federal assistance, Georgia passed a law that required teachers among the Indians to obtain licenses from the state—a law expressly designed to eliminate the missionaries' influence. When two missionaries, Samuel Austin Worcester and Elizur Butler, refused to comply, a company of

---

Indian Removal Act   Law passed by Congress in 1830 providing for the removal of all Indian tribes east of the Mississippi and the purchase of western lands for their resettlement.

Black Hawk   Sauk leader who brought his people back to their homeland in Illinois; he was captured in 1832 when U.S. troops massacred his followers.

George Guess (Sequoyah)   Cherokee silversmith and trader who created an alphabet that made it possible to transcribe the Cherokee language according to the sounds of its syllables.

annul   To declare a law or contract invalid.

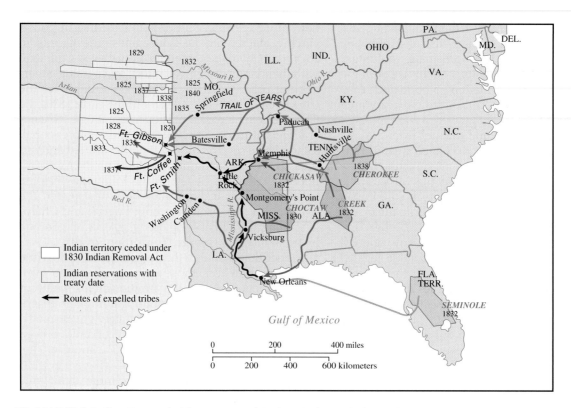

MAP 10.4 Indian Removal The outcome of Andrew Jackson's Indian policy appears clearly on this map. Between 1830 and 1835, all of the Civilized Tribes except Osceola's faction of Seminoles were forced to relocate west of the Mississippi River. Thousands died in the process. © Martin Gilbert, *The Routledge Atlas of American History*, Fourth Edition, ISBN: 0415281512 HB & 0415281520 PB.

Georgia militia invaded their mission in the heart of Cherokee country, arrested the teachers, and marched them off to jail.

Two notable lawsuits came out of the combined efforts of the missionaries and Cherokees to get justice. In the first case, *Cherokee Nation v. Georgia* (1831), the Cherokees claimed that Georgia's action in extending authority over them and enforcing state law within Cherokee territory was illegal because they were a sovereign nation in a treaty relationship with the United States. The U.S. Supreme Court refused to hear this case. Speaking for the Court, Chief Justice John Marshall stated that the Cherokee Nation was neither a foreign nor a domestic state but was a "domestic dependent nation" and as such had no standing in federal court.

As American citizens, however, Worcester and Butler did have legitimate standing under federal law, and in 1832 Marshall was able to render a decision in the case of *Worcester v. Georgia.* In this case,

the Court ruled that the Cherokee Nation was a distinct political community recognized by federal authority and that Georgia did not have legitimate power to pass laws regulating Indian behavior or to invade Indian land. He thus declared all the laws Georgia had passed to harass the Cherokees null and void and ordered the state to release Worcester and Butler from jail.

Cherokee Nation v. Georgia Supreme Court case (1831) concerning Georgia's annulment of all Cherokee laws; the Supreme Court ruled that Indian tribes did not have the right to appeal to the federal court system.

Worcester v. Georgia Supreme Court case (1832) concerning the arrest of two missionaries to the Cherokees in Georgia; the Court found that Georgia had no right to rule in Cherokee territory.

When white farmers began moving into territory that legally belonged to the Sauk and Fox Indians during the summer of 1831, Andrew Jackson's Department of War chose to remove the Indians by force rather than the renegade frontiersmen. Black Hawk chose to resist by moving his band back to their homeland to plant crops in the spring of 1832. Harassed by Illinois militia, the Sauk band attempted to flee back across the Mississippi River but were headed off by federal troops and massacred at the Battle of Bad Axe: the official report noted that 150 Indians were killed—though it acknowledged that number was too low "as a large proportion were slain in endeavoring to swim to the islands" and their bodies lost—while 40, including Black Hawk, were captured. *Chicago Historical Society.*

Although the Cherokees had grounds for celebration, their joy was short-lived. Jackson refused to use any federal authority to carry out the Court's order. When the Cherokees and their sympathizers pressed Jackson on the matter, he claimed that he was powerless to help and that the only way the Indians could get protection from the Georgians was to relocate west of the Mississippi.

It Matters

Worcester v. Georgia

It would be easy to conclude that Andrew Jackson's refusal to enforce the Supreme Court's decision in *Worcester v. Georgia* was an important first step in the decline of Indian power and sovereignty. In the long run, however, this landmark case became the foundation for American Indian survival. Emphasizing that Indians had once lived as truly sovereign nations, the Court declared that their relationship with the United States was as government to government and that the Constitution defined this relationship as exclusive: "The Cherokee nation, then, is a distinct community occupying its own territory, with boundaries accurately described." Within that territory local and state laws had no power and no one could enter without Indian permission. "The whole intercourse between the United States and this nation, is, by our constitution and laws, vested in the government of the United States." In the twentieth and twenty-first centuries Native Americans have used this recognition of national sovereignty successfully in the courts to revitalize their communities and have become a powerful economic and political force in today's America.

Under this sort of pressure, tribal unity broke down. The majority of Cherokees stood fast with their stalwart leader John Ross, fighting Georgia through the court system. But another faction emerged advocating relocation. Preying on the division, federal Indian agents named the dissenters as the true representatives of the tribe and convinced them to sign the **Treaty of New Echota** (1835), in which the minority faction sold the last 8 million acres of Cherokee land in the East to the U.S. government for $5 million.

Treaty of New Echota Treaty in 1835 by which a minority faction gave all Cherokee lands east of the Mississippi to the U.S. government in return for $5 million and land in Indian Territory.

It is easy to gloss over the brutality and dehumanization that were an essential part of removing the Cherokees and other Indians from the Southeast during the 1830s, but this last remaining landmark provides gruesome testimony to the actualities of the "Trail of Tears." This blockhouse at the former site of Fort Marr in Tennessee was one of four corner guard towers that were connected by high walls that contained Indians waiting to be transported to Indian Territory. Such confinement often lasted for months, during which time food, fresh water, adequate shelter, and sanitary facilities were either minimal or not supplied at all. Armed sentinels in the blockhouses could shoot through specially drilled gun ports if the Indian detainees ever protested their inhumane treatment. © Copyright 1994–2003 by Golden Ink. All Rights Reserved. Used with permission.

A similar combination of pressure, manipulation, and outright fraud led to the dispossession of all the other Civilized Tribes. During the winter of 1831–1832, the Choctaws in Mississippi and Alabama became the first tribe to be forcibly removed from their lands to a designated Indian Territory between the Red and Arkansas Rivers in what is now Oklahoma. They were joined by the Creeks in 1836 and by the Chickasaws in 1837. John Ross and the other anti-treaty Cherokee leaders continued to fight in court and to lobby in Congress, but in 1838 federal troops rounded up the entire Cherokee tribe and force-marched them to Indian Territory. Like all of the Indian groups who were forcibly removed from their native lands, the Cherokees suffered terribly. In the course of the long trek, which is known as the **Trail of Tears** (see Map 10.4), nearly a fourth of the twenty thousand Cherokees who started the march died of disease, exhaustion, or heartbreak.

The only one of the Civilized Tribes to abandon legal defenses and adopt a policy of military resistance was the Seminoles. Like the other tribes, the Semi-

> **Trail of Tears** Forced march of the Cherokee people from Georgia to Indian Territory in the winter of 1838, during which thousands of Cherokees died.

noles were deeply divided. Some chose peaceful relocation; others advocated rebellion. After the conciliatory faction signed the Treaty of Payne's Landing in 1832, a group led by **Osceola** broke with the tribe, declaring war on the protreaty group and on the United States. After years of guerrilla swamp fighting, Osceola was finally captured in 1837, but the antitreaty warriors fought on. The struggle continued until 1842, when the United States withdrew its troops, having lost fifteen hundred men during the ten-year conflict. Eventually, even the majority of Osceola's followers agreed to move west, though a small faction of the Seminoles remained in Florida's swamps, justly proud that they were neither conquered nor dispossessed by the United States.

The Nullification Crisis

Southern concerns about rising tariffs during the debate over western lands reflected the South's abiding political and economic posture during the Jackson administration. For years, southerners had complained that tariffs discriminated against them. From their point of view, they were paying at least as much in tariffs as the North and West but were not getting nearly the same economic benefits.

This matter had come to a head in 1829 when the impact of the ill-considered Tariff of Abominations (1828) began to be felt throughout the nation. The new tariffs roused loud protest from states such as South Carolina, where soil exhaustion and declining prices for agricultural produce were putting strong economic pressure on men who were deeply invested in land and slaves. Calhoun, who took office as Jackson's vice president in 1829, spearheaded the protest.

Though it guarded the author's identity, the South Carolina legislature published Calhoun's *South Carolina Exposition and Protest* in 1828, fanning the flames of sectionalism. Calhoun's **nullification** sentiments reflected notions being expressed throughout the nation. And as Calhoun's pamphlet circulated to wider and wider audiences, nationalists such as Clay and Jackson grew more and more anxious about the potential threat to federal power. The test came in 1830, when Senator Robert Y. Hayne of South Carolina and Senator **Daniel Webster** of Massachusetts entered into a debate over Calhoun's ideas. Hayne zealously supported Calhoun; Webster appealed to nationalism. Many have maintained that Hayne's speech was better argued than Webster's, but what mattered was how the president and the nation viewed the debate. Jackson soon made his position clear. At a political banquet, he offered the toast, "Our Federal Union—It must be preserved," indicating that he would brook no nullification arguments. Calhoun, who was sitting near the president, then rose and countered Jackson's toast with one of his own: "The Union—next to our liberty most dear." For Jackson, who valued loyalty above all else, his vice president's insubordination was inexcusable. Still, two years passed before the crisis finally came.

In 1832 nullification advocates in South Carolina called for a special session of the state legislature to consider the matter of state versus federal power. The convention met in November and voted overwhelmingly to nullify the despised tariff. The legislature also elected Hayne, nullification's most prominent spokesman, as governor and named Calhoun as his replacement in the Senate. The vice president, who realized that he would not be Jackson's running mate in the coming election, finally admitted writing the *Exposition and Protest* and resigned from the vice presidency to lead the pro-nullification forces from the Senate floor.

Jackson quickly proved true to his toast of two years before. Bristling that nullification violated the Constitution and was "destructive of the great object for which it was formed," Jackson immediately reinforced federal forts in South Carolina and sent warships to guarantee the tariff's collection. He also asked Congress to pass a "force bill" giving him the power to invade the rebellious state if doing so proved necessary to carry out federal law. In hopes of placating southerners and winning popular support in the upcoming election, Congress passed a lowered tariff, but it also voted to give Jackson the power he requested.

South Carolina nullifiers immediately called a new convention, which withdrew its nullification of the previous tariff but passed a resolution nullifying the force bill. Because Jackson no longer needed the force bill to apply federal law and collect the new tariff, he chose to ignore this action. Thus there was no real resolution to the problem, and the gash over federal versus states' rights remained unhealed. The wound continued to fester until it was finally cauterized thirty years later by civil war.

Osceola   Seminole leader in Florida who opposed removal of his people to the West and led resistance to U.S. troops; he was captured by treachery while bearing a flag of truce.

nullification   Refusal by a state to recognize or enforce a federal law within its boundaries.

Daniel Webster   Massachusetts senator and lawyer who was known for his forceful speeches and considered nullification a threat to the Union.

Individual Voices

Examining a Primary Source

John C. Calhoun Justifies the Principle and Practice of Nullification

■ *What is the significance of Calhoun's assertion that the federal union is a "union of States" and "not of individuals"?*

■ *How does Calhoun's description of the process by which the Constitution was ratified justify his claims concerning the rights of a statewide convention to declare federal laws null and void?*

■ *The expression "meum and tuum" is Latin for "mine and thine." Here Calhoun is saying that a citizen's claim that the government has wrongly taken his or her property—a conflict between "mine and thine"—would be an appropriate matter to take to court. In cases, however, where all citizens believe themselves deprived by the government, it falls to the state and not to the courts to act on their behalf.*

■ *On what basis does Calhoun justify the expulsion of federal authorities from a state? What assumptions is he making about federal rights versus states' rights?*

After resigning from the vice presidency in 1832 over the nullification crisis, John C. Calhoun was appointed by the South Carolina legislature to fill a vacancy in its U.S. Senate delegation. One year later, in February 1833, Calhoun stood before the Senate defending South Carolina's actions and the principle of nullification. In a brief statement, Calhoun summarized his views and attempted to justify his home state's act of disobedience in refusing to comply with federal tariff laws.

The people of Carolina believe that the Union is a union of States, and not of individuals; that it was formed by the States, and that the citizens of the several States were bound to it through the acts of their several States; that each State ratified the Constitution for itself, and that it was only by such ratification of a State that any obligation was imposed upon its citizens. ■ *Thus believing, it is the opinion of the people of Carolina that it belongs to the State which has imposed the obligation to declare, in the last resort, the extent of this obligation, as far as her citizens are concerned; and this upon the plain principles which exist in all analogous cases of compact between sovereign bodies. On this principle the people of the State, acting in their sovereign capacity in convention, precisely as they did in the adoption of their own and the Federal Constitution, have declared, by the ordinance, that the acts of Congress which imposed duties under the authority to lay imposts, were acts not for revenue, as intended by the Constitution, but for protection, and therefore null and void.* ■ *. . . It ought to be borne in mind that, according to the opinion which prevails in Carolina, the right of resistance to the unconstitutional acts of Congress belongs to the State, and not to her individual citizens; and that, though the latter may, in a mere question of* meum and tuum, ■ *resist through the courts an unconstitutional encroachment upon their rights, yet the final stand against usurpation rests not with them, but with the State of which they are members; and such act of resistance by a State binds the conscience and allegiance of the citizen. . . .*

The Constitution has admitted the jurisdiction of the United States within the limits of the several States only so far as the delegated powers authorize; beyond that they are intruders, and may rightfully be expelled; and that they have been efficiently expelled by the legislation of the State through her civil process, as has been acknowledged on all sides in the debate, is only a confirmation of the truth of the doctrine for which the majority in Carolina have contended. ■

Summary

With the end of the War of 1812, President Madison and the Republicans promoted a strong agenda for the nation. Joining with former critics such as Henry Clay and John C. Calhoun, Madison pushed for a national market economy by sponsoring federal legislation for a national bank, controlled currency, and tariff protection for American industry. In addition, Madison gave free rein to nationalists such as Stephen Decatur, John Quincy Adams, and Andrew Jackson, who succeeded in enhancing the nation's military reputation and expanding its sphere of influence.

While the nation moved forward in accomplishing its diplomatic goals, the Republicans' economic agenda suffered from a lack of viable transportation and communication systems. Expecting quick and enormous profits, New York built the Erie Canal, the first successful link between the increasingly urban and manufacturing East and the rural, agricultural West. Convinced finally that transportation improvements were necessary for national defense and for carrying out the work of the government, Madison and his successors joined with state officials to begin the process of building a truly national system of roads and canals.

But what had begun as an age of optimism closed in a tangle of conflict and ill will. A much-hoped-for prosperity dissolved in the face of shrinking markets, resulting in economic panic in 1819 and a collapse in the speculative economy. Economic hard times, in turn, triggered increased competition between the nation's geographical sections, as leaders wrestled for control over federal power in an effort to rid particular areas of economic despair. Supporters of the American System tried to craft a solution, but their compromise did not entirely satisfy anyone. And in the sea of contention that swelled around the Missouri Compromise, the Era of Good Feelings collapsed.

Meanwhile, distressed by what seemed an elite conspiracy to run American affairs, newly politicized voters swept the gentlemanly John Quincy Adams out of office and replaced him with the more exciting and presumably more democratic Andrew Jackson. Backed by a political machine composed of northern, western, and southern interests, Jackson had to juggle each region's financial, tariff, and Indian policy demands while trying to hold his political alliance and the nation together. The outcome was a series of regional crises—the Bank War, nullification, and Indian removal—that alienated each region and together constituted a crisis of national proportions.

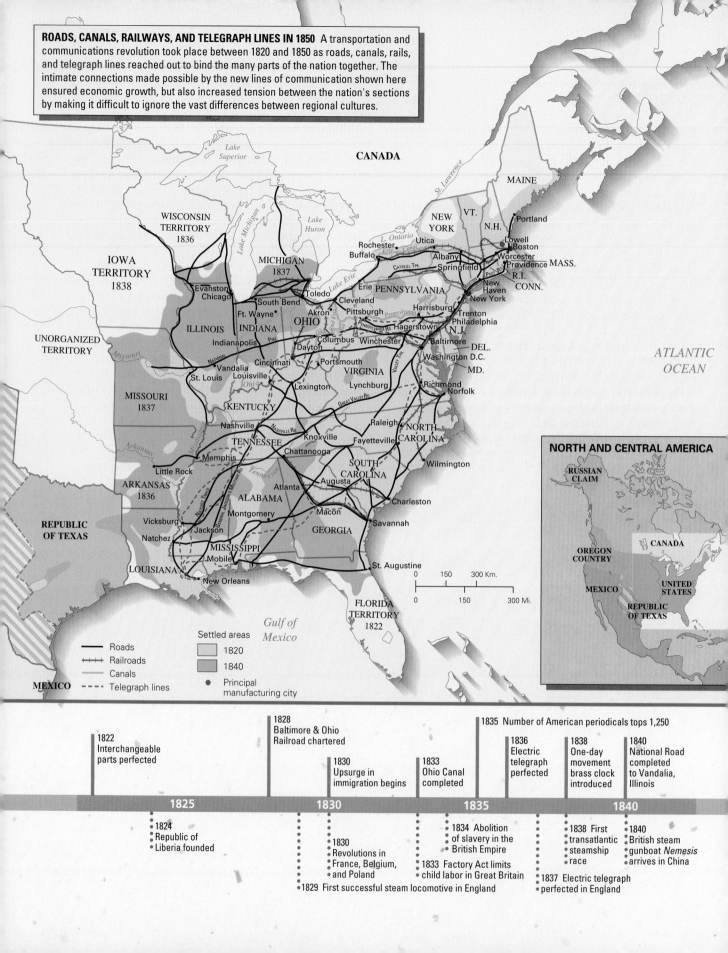

ROADS, CANALS, RAILWAYS, AND TELEGRAPH LINES IN 1850 A transportation and communications revolution took place between 1820 and 1850 as roads, canals, rails, and telegraph lines reached out to bind the many parts of the nation together. The intimate connections made possible by the new lines of communication shown here ensured economic growth, but also increased tension between the nation's sections by making it difficult to ignore the vast differences between regional cultures.

CANADA

NORTH AND CENTRAL AMERICA

RUSSIAN CLAIM

OREGON COUNTRY

MEXICO

CANADA

UNITED STATES

REPUBLIC OF TEXAS

ATLANTIC OCEAN

WISCONSIN TERRITORY 1836

IOWA TERRITORY 1838

UNORGANIZED TERRITORY

MICHIGAN 1837

MAINE

NEW YORK

VT.

N.H.

Portland

MASS.

R.I.

CONN.

Lowell

Boston

Worcester

Providence

Rochester

Buffalo

Utica

Albany

Springfield

New Haven

New York

Evanston

Chicago

South Bend

Ft. Wayne

Toledo

Cleveland

Erie

PENNSYLVANIA

Harrisburg

Trenton

Philadelphia

N.J.

Akron

Pittsburgh

Hagerstown

ILLINOIS

INDIANA

OHIO

Columbus

Winchester

Baltimore

DEL.

MD.

Indianapolis

Dayton

Washington D.C.

Vandalia

Cincinnati

Portsmouth

VIRGINIA

St. Louis

Louisville

Lexington

Lynchburg

Richmond

Norfolk

MISSOURI 1837

KENTUCKY

Nashville

Raleigh

NORTH CAROLINA

Knoxville

Fayetteville

TENNESSEE

Chattanooga

SOUTH CAROLINA

Memphis

Little Rock

Atlanta

Augusta

Wilmington

ARKANSAS 1836

ALABAMA

Montgomery

Macon

Charleston

REPUBLIC OF TEXAS

Vicksburg

Jackson

GEORGIA

Savannah

Natchez

MISSISSIPPI

Mobile

St. Augustine

LOUISIANA

New Orleans

FLORIDA TERRITORY 1822

Gulf of Mexico

MEXICO

0   150   300 Km.

0   150   300 Mi.

Roads
┼┼┼┼ **Railroads**
Canals
----- **Telegraph lines**

Settled areas
1820
1840

● **Principal manufacturing city**

1822 Interchangeable parts perfected

1828 Baltimore & Ohio Railroad chartered

1830 Upsurge in immigration begins

1833 Ohio Canal completed

1835 Number of American periodicals tops 1,250

1836 Electric telegraph perfected

1838 One-day movement brass clock introduced

1840 National Road completed to Vandalia, Illinois

1825   **1830**   **1835**   **1840**

1824 Republic of Liberia founded

1830 Revolutions in France, Belgium, and Poland

1834 Abolition of slavery in the British Empire

1838 First transatlantic steamship race

1840 British steam gunboat *Nemesis* arrives in China

1833 Factory Act limits child labor in Great Britain

1837 Electric telegraph perfected in England

1829 First successful steam locomotive in England

The Great Transformation, 1828–1840

11

Roads, Canals, Railways, and Telegraph Lines in 1850

Compare the map on the facing page with the opening map for Chapter 10, noting the changes that took place in transportation and communications systems. In what ways did these changes in transportation and communications change traditional patterns of economics, politics, and culture within the United States? How might they have facilitated greater tension as well as cooperation between different regions in the country?

Individual Choices

HELEN JEWETT

Blessed with natural beauty and a quick mind, Helen Jewett became a very successful prostitute in New York City. Although she had been born in poverty and had no valid claim to genteel status, she passed herself off as the dishonored daughter of an elite family. Called "confidence men" and "painted women" by contemporaries, such pretenders used the anonymity possible in newly emerging American cities in the 1830s to insinuate themselves into polite social circles. The press coverage of Helen Jewett's grisly murder brought attention to these unsavory types, and her death was used as a moral lesson illustrating the costs that might accompany sneaking through social barriers. *Courtesy of the American Antiquarian Society.*

Helen Jewett

Anonymity was something virtually unknown to most people in early America. In the villages where most people lived, everyone knew everyone, and strangers were viewed with suspicion. But increasingly during the 1830s the rise of new cities brought hordes of strangers together, making anonymity a very real factor in many people's lives. And in a city full of strangers, it was not only easier to hide an identity but also easier to invent one. In urban centers such as Boston, Philadelphia, and, most notoriously, New York, enterprising people could break social conventions, class restrictions, and other limitations on their ambitions by concocting new identities. Many undoubtedly got away with it, disappearing among the thousands of other faceless strangers. Others, however, came to public attention, and a few became objects of lurid fascination. Helen Jewett was one of those few.

Jewett's story begins with that of a little girl named Dorcas Doyen, the daughter of a poor and drunken Maine shoemaker. Dorcas's mother died when she was 10 years old, and her father decided to put her out as a domestic servant. After working for three years in a modest household, Dorcas was hired as a house servant by Maine's chief justice. While living in the judge's home, young Dorcas was exposed to a genteel lifestyle that she could never have known in her father's rustic cabin, and she worked very hard at trying to blend into her new environment. Her employers encouraged her desire to "better herself," giving her fashionable clothes to wear and access to books and the leisure time for reading. She was so successful in her efforts that visitors often mistook her for one of the judge's own daughters.

But Dorcas Doyen was not one of the judge's daughters and, given her background, could never aspire to the lifestyle to which she was so eagerly becoming accustomed. As a teenager rapidly approaching womanhood, Dorcas faced the unpleasant reality that as long as she remained in the relatively closed, face-to-face village world of rural Maine, she could never be anything more than a daughter of poverty, the serving girl that everyone knew her to be. Hemmed in by an apparent lack of choices, at age 17 she disappeared from the judge's house, taking with her some of her books and stylish clothes and all of the gracious manners she had acquired over the years. Dorcas Doyen was never seen again.

Almost immediately after Dorcas disappeared, a woman named Maria B. Benson established herself in the city of Portland, Maine. Her beauty, charm, and wit soon allowed Miss Benson to become a much-sought-after companion by the upwardly mobile young men in the city, who lavished her with gifts and showered her with cash. Though no one in polite society at the time would have used such an expression, Maria Benson was a high-class call girl, and a successful one, but three years later she disappeared from Portland, never to be seen again.

Not long after Maria vanished, a woman named Helen Jewett turned up in New York City. Beautiful and cultured, she quickly took up residence in one of the most

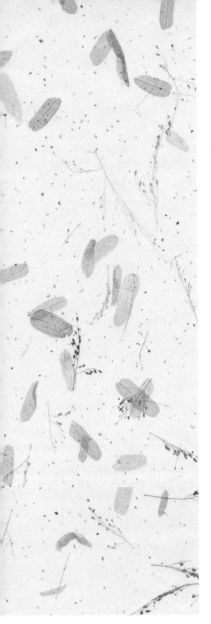

fashionable brothels in America's most fashionable city. There she entertained a following of educated, economically comfortable young clerks and junior managers who were putting off marriage while launching their careers. Whenever asked about her background, Jewett told her clients that she was a victim of circumstances. She claimed that she had been born into a respectable New England family. Orphaned at an early age, she had been adopted by a kindly local judge who raised her in genteel elegance. He had even sent her to an elite boarding school. There, however, she fell in with the reckless son of a wealthy merchant, who took advantage of her innocence by seducing and then abandoning her. Homeless and friendless, deserted on the cruel streets of New York, she turned to the only profession open to a dishonored woman.

This story line, so similar to plots in the best-selling sentimental novels of the time, explained the anomaly of a cultured and intelligent woman who made her living by disreputable means. "Soiled" and yet still genteel, she slipped through the cracks of social convention, living out a polite existence despite her fallen condition. And she probably would have continued this successful life if horror had not intervened. Late on the night of April 10, 1836, the fallen but fashionable Helen Jewett was murdered, literally hacked to death with an ax and then set on fire. The sparkling quality of Jewett's life and the gruesome nature of her death made her murder an overnight media sensation—newspapers scrambled for the latest tidbits about the death, and life, of this conventionally contradictory young woman. In the end, none of the investigations yielded definitive evidence about who killed her, but it was not long before they unearthed the truth about her identity: Helen Jewett, once also known as Maria Benson, was actually Dorcas Doyen.

In the terminology of the time, Dorcas Doyen had chosen to become a "painted woman," a pretender to social status that she could not otherwise legitimately claim. Becoming a prostitute apparently was an acceptable price to pay in order to escape the stifling constraints to which her birth and early life would have condemned her in the village world of rural Maine. And it all came about because the new economy that was emerging in America was creating peculiar urban spaces in which such masquerades were possible. Moralistic journalists were quick to point out that her deception caused her grisly death. Nevertheless, her story revealed not only the risks but also the expanding range of choices that were coming into being in a new, modern, and urbanizing America.

INTRODUCTION

Helen Jewett might be considered an exceptional woman in any era, but all the more so in the early nineteenth century. At a time when expectations for women increasingly constrained their public roles—confining them, at least ideally, to positions as mothers, teachers, and churchgoers at the high end of the social spectrum or factory workers or domestic servants at the lower end—her decision to become a prostitute certainly stands out. But in a way, her experience typifies much broader patterns in American life during this period. Like many in her generation, she followed the economic opportunities that were fleeing the countryside and concentrating in the newly arising cities. She also made a conscious choice to forego marriage and childbearing in exchange for a career. And like so many of her contemporaries, her success in that career was itself a product of changing times: the anonymity that came with the rise of cities permitted prostitution to thrive, just as the deferral of marriage for the sake of personal development may have encouraged upwardly mobile young men to seek out women like her. At the same time, the worsening of conditions for working people certainly provided an incentive for young Dorcas Doyen to create a false identity for herself that would allow her to transcend her lowly origins. She came to the city to make something

Networks of improved roads made travel much easier in the 1820s and 1830s than it had been earlier in the century but led to a new complication: traffic jams. This picture of the Fairview Inn in 1829 illustrates the problem, as riders, wagons, and herds of animals all crowd for space on the road outside Baltimore. *"The Fairview Inn, 1829" by Thomas Coke Ruckle. Maryland Historical Society.*

new and better of herself—transforming herself in line with the great transformation happening around her.

But the urbanization that was taking place in the northeastern section of the country was only one manifestation of the upheaval that was affecting the nation at large. As cotton production continued to offer staggering profits for efficient and lucky southern planters, that industry and its various features—especially slavery—underwent significant growth and change. That in turn affected the everyday lives of everyone of every race in the ever-expanding Cotton Belt.

These drastic changes in the Northeast and South reinforced each other. Factory development led to increased demand for cotton, while increased efficiency in cotton growing added to manufacturing profitability. The expanding transportation networks that allowed goods and people to move around the country fed this upsurge. Despite resistance by many, the United States was rapidly being knit into a single nation, a process that would reward many but which created a whole new catalog of problems.

The Transportation Revolution

■ What technological innovations contributed to the development of new transportation systems during the era between 1828 and 1840?

■ How did the exchange of scientific knowledge between Europe and the United States contribute to America's changing transportation systems?

■ How did newly emerging networks of transportation and communication change the lives of Americans in the North, West, and South?

To pull together the sort of integrated national market economy that leaders such as Henry Clay envisioned, Americans had to find ways to overcome the vast distances and difficult terrain that separated the various regions of the country. Directly after the War of 1812, politicians and inventive entrepreneurs established new transportation routes and technologies, but much more was needed. A truly integrated economy required intersecting networks of transportation and communications that could channel the produce of the West and South into the industrializing North, and the manufactures of the North into the markets of the South and West.

Extending the Nation's Roads

Both government and private enterprise embarked on road-building projects after the War of 1812. Between 1815 and 1820, the so-called National Road snaked its way across the Cumberland Gap in the Appalachian Mountains and wound from the Atlantic shore to the Ohio River at Wheeling, Virginia. Then, in 1822, a political deal between northeastern congressmen and their western colleagues extended funding and further extended the road (see page 281). By 1838 this state-of-the-art highway—with its evenly graded surface, gravel pavement, and stone bridges—had been pushed all the way to Vandalia, Illinois. Within a few more years, it reached St. Louis, the great jumping-off point for the Far West.

At the same time, a series of other roads were beginning to merge into a transportation network. The Natchez Trace (see page 275) also enjoyed federal patronage, as did the so-called Military Road con-

The Dawn of Modernization

1822	John H. Hall perfects interchangeable parts for gun manufacturing
1828	Baltimore and Ohio Railroad
1830	Steam locomotive *Tom Thumb* beaten in race by stagecoach horse
1830–1840	Ten-year immigration figure for United States exceeds 500,000
1833	Ohio Canal completed
1834	Main Line Canal from Philadelphia to Pittsburgh completed
1835	Number of U.S. periodicals exceeds 1,250, with combined circulation of 90 million
1836	Samuel F. B. Morse invents electric telegraph Bronson Alcott's *Conversations with Children on the Gospels* Murder of Helen Jewett
1838	National Road completed to Vandalia, Illinois First mass-produced brass clock

necting Nashville even more directly to New Orleans. The Nashville Road, in turn, connected Nashville to Knoxville, where a traveler could pick up the Great Valley Road to Lynchburg, Virginia, and from there the Valley Turnpike, which connected with the Cumberland Road. Eventually towns from Portland, Maine, to Saint Augustine, Florida, and from Natchez, Mississippi, to New Haven, Connecticut, were linked by intersecting highways (see the chapter-opening map). Increasing numbers of people used these new roads to head west looking for new opportunities. Farmers, craftsmen, fur hunters, and others already settled in the West used them too, moving small loads of goods to the nearby towns and small cities that always sprang up along the unfolding transportation routes. But the new roads did little to advance large-scale commerce. Heavy and bulky products were too expensive to move: at a minimum, hauling a ton of freight along the nation's roads cost 15 cents a mile. At that rate, the cost of shipping a ton of oats from Buffalo to New York City amounted to twelve times the value of the cargo.

A Network of Canals

But the new roads also linked rural America to an ever-expanding network of waterways that made relatively inexpensive long-distance hauling possible. Completed in 1825, the Erie Canal revolutionized shipping (see page 275): transporting a ton of oats

from Buffalo to Albany fell from $100 to $15, and the transit time dropped from twenty days to just eight. All of New York State celebrated. Businessmen in New York City were particularly happy. During the early nineteenth century, the flood of goods from America's interior made New York City the most important commercial center in the nation.

The spectacular success of the Erie Canal prompted businessmen, farmers, and politicians throughout the country to promote canal building. State governments offered exclusive charters to canal-building companies, giving them direct financial grants, guaranteeing their credit, and easing their way in every possible manner. The result was an explosion in canal building that lasted through the 1830s (see the chapter-opening map).

Pennsylvania's experiences were typical. Jealous of New York's success, Pennsylvania projected a massive system of canals, roads, and natural waterways designed to make Philadelphia the commercial center of the Western Hemisphere. Central to Pennsylvania's plan was the **Main Line Canal,** connecting the Delaware and Schuylkill Rivers at Philadelphia with the Ohio River at Pittsburgh. The problem was that a mountain range more than 2,000 feet high separated

Main Line Canal Ambitious canal-building enterprise by the state of Pennsylvania to connect the Delaware River at Philadelphia with the Ohio River at Pittsburgh.

The Allegheny Portage Railroad was an engineering marvel for its time, carrying canal boats over the Allegheny Mountains as part of the Main Line Canal system. This painting by Karl Bodmer illustrates how the portage system worked. Canal barges were floated onto submerged railcars. The railcars were attached to a cable, and steam winches pulled them up an incline. Four inclines later the canal boats were hauled across the mountain's peak and then lowered down another five inclines and into the water on the opposite side. *"View of Mauch Chunk, Pennsylvania with Railroad" by Karl Bodmer, 1832. Maximilian-Bodmer Collection, Joslyn Art Museum.*

the two cities. The Main Line Canal would have needed locks five times the size of those used on the Erie Canal—an engineering feat beyond the abilities of even the most skilled designers in the country. Engineering veterans of the New York effort finally resorted to a **portage** railroad over the Allegheny Mountains.

Completed in 1834, the **Allegheny Portage Railroad** permitted canal boats to make the trip across the mountains. On each side of the mountains, canal boats were floated onto submerged railcars. The railcars were attached to a cable, and steam winches pulled them up a series of inclined planes. At the top of one incline, horses (later locomotives) towed the railcars over level ground to the next incline. After being pulled up five steep inclines, the railcars—still carrying the canal boats with their passengers and cargo—were carefully lowered down the inclines, and the boats were placed in the canal to continue their trips by water.

The portage railroad was an engineering marvel, but it was expensive to build and was only one of several massive projects necessary to complete Pennsylvania's "Golden Link to the West." Engineers designed and built tunnels, aqueducts, and enormous locks, all at outrageous cost. By the time the Main Line system was completed, anyone intent on migrating to the West could travel at a good speed and in relative comfort all the way from Philadelphia to Pittsburgh, but the tolls alone cost as much as 6 acres of prime farmland. In the long run, the Main Line Canal was a dismal financial failure, never earning investors one cent of profit.

Despite Pennsylvania's bad experience, nearly every state in the North and West undertook some canal building between 1820 and 1840. States and private individuals invested more than $100 million on nearly 3,500 miles of canals during the heyday of canal building. One of the most important examples was Ohio's canal system. Seeking to complete a circuit of inland waterways, Ohio began building a canal connecting Cleveland on Lake Erie with Portsmouth on the Ohio River. After the **Ohio Canal** was completed in 1833, it became possible for a merchant in New York to ship manufactured goods up the Hudson River to Albany, along the Erie Canal to Buffalo, along the shore of Lake Erie to Cleveland, on the Ohio Canal to Portsmouth, then down the Ohio and Mississippi Rivers all the way to New Orleans without the cargo ever leaving the water. And with Henry Shreve's successful experiments with steamboats (see

portage   The carrying of boats or supplies overland between two waterways.

Allegheny Portage Railroad   A rail line that carried canal boats over the Allegheny Mountains as part of the Main Line Canal system.

Ohio Canal   A canal connecting Cleveland to Portsmouth, completing a network of waterways linking the Hudson River, the Great Lakes, and the Mississippi River system.

page 276), meat, grain, ore, and other western products could move just as easily in the other direction.

But this new mobility did not come cheaply. Canals like those in Ohio and neighboring Indiana cost as much as $20,000 to $30,000 a mile to build, and financing was always a problem. Hoping for large profits, entrepreneurs such as John Jacob Astor invested heavily in canal building. Before 1836, careful investors could make a 15 to 20 percent **return on capital** in canal building, but after that, most canal companies faced bankruptcy, as did the states that had helped finance them.

Steam Power

Steam power took canal building's impact on inland transportation a revolutionary step further. After Shreve's pioneer voyage in 1816, the cost of shipping a ton of goods down American rivers fell annually. By 1840, the price had declined from an average of 1¼ cents a mile to less than half a cent, and the cost of upstream transport from over 10 cents a mile to less than a cent. In addition, steamboats could carry bulky and heavy objects that could not be hauled upstream for any price by any other means. The impact of steam technology on the economies of the South and West was staggering. The presence of dependable transportation on the Mississippi drew cotton cultivation farther into the nation's interior, western farmers flooded into the Ohio Valley, and fur trappers and traders pressed up the Missouri River.

Steam technology also had applications in areas without navigable rivers. Towns lacking water routes to the interior began losing revenue from inland trade to canal towns such as Albany and Philadelphia. Predictably, entrepreneurs in places like Baltimore looked for other ways to move cargo. In fact, demands from Baltimore merchants spurred Maryland to take the lead in developing a new transportation technology: the steam railroad. In 1828 the state chartered the **Baltimore and Ohio Railroad** (B&O). The B&O soon demonstrated its potential when inventor Peter Cooper's steam locomotive *Tom Thumb* sped 13 miles along B&O track. Steam railroading, however, did not seem destined to succeed. In 1829, England's Liverpool and Manchester Railway drew attention and investment by pitting horse-drawn and steam-drawn trains against each other. The steam engines won easily. When Cooper tried the same stunt in the following year, however, the horse won. The B&O abandoned steam power, replacing it with coaches pulled along the rails by horses.

Despite the B&O's failure, South Carolina chose to invest in steam technology and chartered a 136-mile rail line from Charleston to Hamburg. Here, the first full-size American-built locomotive, the *Best Friend of Charleston*, successfully pulled cars until the engine exploded, taking much of the train and many of its

---

return on capital   The yield on money that has been invested in an enterprise or product.

Baltimore and Ohio Railroad   First steam railroad commissioned in the United States; it resorted to using horse-drawn cars after a stagecoach horse beat its pioneer locomotive in a race.

passengers with it. Rather than giving up on the idea of steam power, however, the Charleston and Hamburg Railroad had the engine rebuilt and began putting "buffer" cars filled with cotton bales between the engine and the other cars to protect passengers and cargoes from boiler explosions. Massachusetts followed this practice as well, as it tried to compete with New York by building a railroad from Boston to Albany.

Although rail transport enjoyed some success during this early period, it could not rival water-based transportation systems. By 1850 individual companies had laid approximately 9,000 miles of track, but not in any coherent network. Rails were laid with little or no standardization of track size, and the distance between tracks varied from company to company. As a result, railcars with their loads could not be transferred from one company's line to another's. Other problems also plagued the fledgling industry. Boiler explosions, fires, and derailments were common because pressure regulators, spark arresters, and brakes were inadequate. And in state capitals, investors who hoped to profit from canals, roads, and steam shipping lobbied to prevent legislatures from supporting rail expansion.

The Information Revolution

Distance impaired not only American commerce but also the conduct of the republic itself. Since the nation's founding, American leaders had expressed the fear that the continent's sheer size would make true federal democracy impractical. Voting returns, economic data, and other information crucial to running a republic seemed to take an impossibly long time to circulate, and the problem promised to get worse as the nation grew. During the 1790s, for example, it took a week for news to travel from Virginia to New York City and three weeks for a letter to get from Cincinnati to the Atlantic coast. This difficulty led Thomas Jefferson and others to speculate that the continent would become a series of allied republics, each small enough to operate efficiently given the slow speed of communication. The transportation revolution, however, made quite a difference in how quickly news got around. After the Erie Canal opened, letters posted in Buffalo could reach New York City within six days and might get to New Orleans within two weeks.

As the nation expanded, and as economics and social life became more complicated, Americans felt growing pressure to keep up with news at home and in the nation's new territories. The revolution in transportation helped them do so by making the transport of printed matter faster and cheaper. At the same time,

revolutions in printing technology and paper production significantly lowered the cost of printing and speeded up production. Organizations such as the American Bible Society and the American Tract Society joined newspaper and magazine publishers in producing a literal flood of printed material. In 1790 the 92 newspapers being published in America had a total **circulation** of around 4 million. By 1835 the number of periodicals had risen to 1,258, and circulation had surpassed 90 million.

The explosion in the volume and velocity of communications was enhanced by a true revolution in information technology that was in its starting phases. In the mid-1830s, both Samuel F. B. Morse in the United States and Charles Wheatstone and William Cooke in Great Britain began experimenting with the world's first form of electronic communication: the **electric telegraph.** Morse won the contest, perfecting his version in 1836. Simple in design, Morse's transmitter consisted of a key that closed an electrical circuit, thereby sending a pulse along a connected wire. Morse developed a code consisting of dots (short pulses) and dashes (longer pulses) that represented letters of the alphabet. With this device a skilled operator could quickly key out long messages and send them at nearly the speed of light. Over the next several years, Morse worked on improvements to extend the distance that the impulses would travel along the wires. Finally, in 1843, Congress agreed to finance an experimental telegraph line from Washington, D.C., to Baltimore. Morse sent his first message on the experimental line on May 24, 1844. His message, "What hath God wrought!" was a fitting opening line for the telecommunications revolution.

The New Cotton Empire in the South

■ Why did living conditions for southerners—black and white—change after 1820?

■ How did elite white southerners respond to the change? What were the impacts of their response on slaves, free blacks, and poor whites?

circulation   The number of copies of a publication sold or distributed.

electric telegraph   Device invented by Samuel F. B. Morse in 1836 that transmits coded messages along a wire over long distances; the first electronic communications device.

It was the South that was first to take advantage of expanding transportation systems, especially steam power. The South exploded outward, seeking new lands on which to grow the glamour crop of the century: cotton. In 1820 cotton was being grown heavily in parts of Virginia, South Carolina, and Georgia. With Shreve's shallow-draft steamboats in place, within a matter of decades, the cotton empire had expanded to include most of Alabama, Mississippi, and Louisiana and extensive portions of eastern Texas, Kentucky, Tennessee, Arkansas, and southern Missouri. The new dependence on a single crop changed the outlook and experiences not just of large planters but also of the slaves, free blacks, and poor whites whose labor made cotton king.

A New Birth for the Plantation System

Few images have persisted in American history longer than that of courtly southern planters in the years before the Civil War. Throughout the nineteenth and much of the twentieth centuries, songs and stories immortalized the myth of a wealthy and well-mannered southern aristocracy upholding a culture of romantic **chivalry.** Charming though this image is, it is not accurate.

Statistics from the **antebellum** South suggest that the great planters of popular myth were a tiny minority of the overall southern white population. By far the largest class of slaveholders—nearly three-quarters of the total—was the "farmer" class, people who owned between 80 and 160 acres of land and fewer than ten slaves. Next on the social ladder came a "gentry" class—about 15 percent of the slaveholding population—people who owned up to 800 acres and between ten and twenty slaves. The rest, about 12 percent of slaveholders, were true planters, possessing more than 800 acres and more than twenty slaves. Taken together, all three classes constituted less than one-third of white southerners. Though few in number, slaveholders in general, and the planter class in particular, controlled the biggest share of productive land and labor. As a result, their economic, political, and social importance was far out of proportion to the size of their population, and their legend equally inflated.

Even among the handful of true southern planters, the aristocratic manners and trappings of the idealized plantation were unusual. The rapidly rising cotton economy brought a new sort of man to the forefront. These new aristocrats were generally not related to the old colonial plantation gentry. Most had begun their careers as land speculators, financiers, and rough-and-tumble yeoman farmers who had capitalized on both ruthlessness and lucky speculations in the burgeoning cotton market to amass large landholdings and armies of slaves. Describing his master's cultural interests, one former slave recalled, "My master's habits were such as were common enough among the dissipated planters of the neighborhood; and one of their frequent practices was to assemble on Saturday or Sunday . . . and gamble, run horses, or fight game-cocks, discuss politics, and drink whisky and brandy and water all day long."

This is not to say that the image of grand plantations and lavish aristocratic living is entirely false. The owners of cotton plantations made an excellent living from the labor of their slaves. Although they often complained of debt and poor markets, it appears that large-scale planters could expect an annual return on capital of between 8 and 10 percent—the equivalent of what the most successful northern industrialists were making. Agricultural profits in non-cotton-producing areas were significantly lower, but even there slavery netted white landowners major profits. The enormous demand for workers in the heart of the **Cotton Belt** (see Map 9.3) created a profitable interstate trade in slaves, especially after Congress outlawed the importation of slaves from abroad in 1808. Although an unknown number of slaves continued to be smuggled in, mostly from the nearby Caribbean islands, most came to the Cotton Belt from the plantations of former tobacco, rice, and sugar growers who now went into the business of breeding and selling slaves. Thus even planters who did not grow cotton came to have a significant investment in its cultivation and in the labor system that was its cornerstone.

The increasing demand for slaves had a terribly unsettling effect on social stability in the plantation world. Whereas generations of slaves had coexisted with generations of slave owners on the traditional plantations in the colonial South, now the appeal of quick profits led planters in places like Virginia and Maryland to sell off their slaves, often breaking up

chivalry   The code of honor among medieval knights that was central to the romantic self-image among southern planters.

antebellum   The decades before the Civil War, the period from 1815 to 1860; Latin for "before the war."

Cotton Belt   The region in the southeastern United States in which cotton is grown.

Despite the popular image that antebellum planters lived lives of idle luxury in great mansions, most actually lived in modest homes and worked alongside their employees and slaves, as this 1838 painting by an anonymous artist shows. *"Ye Southern Planter"* 1838. Private collection.

families and deeply rooted social connections in the process. This fragmentation of slave society helped to further dehumanize an already dehumanizing institution and drove a deeper wedge between the races.

The enormous profits earned from cotton in the 1840s and 1850s permitted some planters—or, more often, the children of successful cotton capitalists—to build elegant mansions and to affect the lifestyle that they associated with a noble past. Voracious readers of romantic literature, planters assumed what they imagined were the ways of medieval knights, adopting courtly manners and the nobleman's **paternalistic** obligation to look out for the welfare of social inferiors, both black and white. Women decked out in the latest gowns flocked to formal balls and weekend parties. Young men were sent to academies where they could learn the twin aristocratic virtues of militarism and honor. Young women attended private "seminaries" where they were taught, in the words of one southern seminary mistress, "principles calculated to render them useful and rational companions." Courtship became highly ritualized, an imitation of imagined medieval court manners.

Practical concerns, however, always threatened to crack this romantic veneer. Although huge profits might be made in cotton planting, successful ventures required major capital investment. If land suitable for cotton could be purchased directly from the federal government, it might be had for as little as 25

cents an acre, but efficient planting called for huge blocks of land, and planters often had to pay a premium to get them. Contrary to popular perception, slave labor was not cheap. At the height of the slave trade, a healthy male field hand in his mid-twenties sold for an average of $1,800. Younger and older men or those in less than perfect health sold for less, but even a male child too young to work in the fields might cost anywhere from $250 to $500.

Often planters purchased slaves and fields on credit and genuinely feared that their carefully constructed empires and lifestyles might collapse in an instant. Aristocratic parents sought to use marriage as a means of adding to family and economic security. "As to my having any sweethearts that is not thought of," one young southern woman complained. "Money is too much preferred, for us poor Girls to be much caressed."

Even those girls whose fortunes earned caresses faced a strange and often difficult life. Planters' wives bore little resemblance to their counterparts in popular fiction. Far from being frail, helpless creatures, southern plantation mistresses carried a heavy burden of responsibility. A planter's wife was responsible for all domestic matters. She supervised large staffs of

paternalistic   Treating social dependents as a father treats his children, providing for their needs but denying them rights or responsibilities.

Slave life in the antebellum South presented an array of complex and often contradictory sides, as these two images illustrate. On the left, a parlor scene shows two young house slaves in absolute subjugation—one even serves as a footstool for his mistress. The nicely framed daguerreotype on the right, however, depicts slaves in a very different light; this couple either had the means to bear the cost of the expensive photograph or their owner thought highly enough of them to do so. These are but two striking images of a complex evolving world that emerged in the cotton South, the legacy of which we continue to live with today. *Ohio State University Libraries (left); Maryland Historical Society Library, Special Collections Department, Cased Photo #156 (right).*

slaves, organized and ran schools for the children on the plantation, looked out for the health of everyone, and managed all plantation operations in the absence of her husband. All those duties were complicated by a sex code that relegated southern women to a peculiar position in the plantation hierarchy—between white men and black slaves. On the one hand, southern white women were expected to exercise absolute authority over their slaves. On the other, they were to be absolutely obedient to white men. "He is master of the house," said plantation mistress Mary Boykin Chesnut about her husband. "To hear [him] is to obey." This contradiction put great pressure on southern women, adding severe anxiety to their other burdens. "All the comfort of my life depends upon his being in a good humor," Chesnut remarked. And while in some respects planters treated their slaves like machines, slaves were nonetheless human—and sexual—beings, a fact that produced even more stress for plantation mistresses. Like Thomas Jefferson before them (see page 234), antebellum planters found that their power over slave women afforded them sexual as well as financial benefits. One southerner rationalized this situation, saying, "The intercourse which takes place with enslaved females is less depraving in its effects [on white men] than when it is carried on with females of their own caste." As a result, a partic-

ularly beautiful young slave woman, who like Sally Hemings might herself have been the daughter of such a relationship, could bring as much as $5,000 at auction. Constrained as they were by the region's strict rules of conduct, the wives of these men generally were powerless to intercede. Though some may not have minded release from sexual pressures, they had to be mindful of slave concubines and their children, both of whom occupied an odd place in the domestic power structure. It is little wonder, then, that Chesnut concluded her observations about southern womanhood with the statement, "There is no slave . . . like a wife."

Life Among Common Southern Whites

Federal census figures for the early nineteenth century reveal that fully two-thirds of free southern families owned no slaves, and among the minority who did, half owned fewer than five. A small number of these families owned stores, craft shops, and other urban businesses in Charleston, New Orleans, Atlanta, and other southern cities. Some were attorneys, teachers, doctors, and other professionals. The great majority, however, were proud small farmers who owned, leased, or simply squatted on the land they farmed.

Often tarred with the label "poor white trash" by their planter neighbors, and described as shiftless, idle backcountry rabble, these people were often productive stock raisers and farmers. They concentrated on growing and manufacturing by hand what they needed to live, but all aspired to end up with small surpluses of grains, meat products, and other commodities that they could sell either to neighboring plantations or to merchants for export. Many of these small farmers tried to grow cotton in an effort to raise cash, though they generally could not do so on a large scale. Whatever cash they raised they usually spent on necessary manufactures, as well as on land and slaves.

These small farmers had a shaky relationship with white planters. On the one hand, many wanted to join the ranks of the great planters, hoping they could transform their small holdings into cotton empires. On the other hand, they resented the aristocracy and envied the planters' exalted status and power. They also feared the expansion of large plantations, which often forced small holders to abandon their hard-won farms and slaves.

Although they seldom rebelled openly against their social superiors, common white people often used the power of the ballot box to make their dissatisfactions known. For despite the enormous power of the plantation elite, they were greatly outnumbered by the lesser class of whites, who had the power to wreck the entire social and economic structure if they became sufficiently disgruntled. Thus the *noblesse oblige* practiced by aristocrats toward poorer whites was as much a practical necessity as it was a romantic affectation.

Large-scale planters also used racial tensions as a device for controlling their contentious neighbors. Although they were not above taking slave concubines or trusting African Americans with positions of authority on plantations, the white elite nonetheless emphasized white superiority and common cause when conversing with their poorer farmer neighbors. They pointed out that although poor farmers may have felt underprivileged when compared with their wealthier counterparts, they at least were spared the most demeaning of work: a still-lower class bore that burden. Thus what freedoms and privileges poor whites enjoyed were afforded by the existence of slavery. And should slavery ever end, planters avowed, whether because of poor white political maneuverings or outside pressures, it would be the farmers who would have the most to lose.

Free Blacks in the South

Caught in the middle between southern planters, slaves, and poor white farmers, African Americans in the South who were not slaves often faced extreme discrimination. Some communities of free blacks could trace their origins back to earliest colonial times, when Africans, like Europeans, served limited terms of indenture. The majority, however, had been freed recently because of diminishing plantation profits during the late 1700s. Most of these people lived not much differently from slaves, working for white employers as day laborers.

Mounting restrictions on free blacks during the first half of the nineteenth century limited their freedom of movement, economic options, and the protection they could expect to receive by law. In the town of Petersburg, Virginia, for example, when a free black woman named Esther Fells irritated her white neighbor, he took it upon himself to whip her for disturbing his peace. The sheriff did not arrest the assailant but instead took Mrs. Fells into custody, and the court ordered that she be given fifteen more lashes for "being insolent to a white person." Skin color left free African Americans open to abuses and forced them to be extremely careful in their dealings with their white neighbors.

Still, some opportunities were available for a handful of free blacks who had desirable skills. In the Upper South—Delaware, Maryland, and Virginia—master carpenters, coopers, painters, brick masons, blacksmiths, boatmen, bakers, and barbers hired young African American boys as apprentices. Those who could stick out their apprenticeship might make an independent living. The situation was different for African American girls. They had few opportunities as skilled laborers. Some became seamstresses and washers, others became cooks, and a few grew up to run small groceries, taverns, and restaurants. Folk healing, **midwifery,** and prostitution also led to economic independence for some black women.

It is worth noting that perhaps as many as 10 percent of free southern African American heads of household were slaveowners, but by itself this statistic may be somewhat misleading. Many free black men were

---

noblesse oblige The belief that members of the elite are duty-bound to treat others charitably, especially those of lower status than themselves.

midwifery The practice of assisting women in childbirth.

forced to buy their wives and children in order to re-unite families and often were prevented by restrictive slave codes from legally freeing them. Still, a good many people of African descent owned plantations and gangs of slave laborers, though these possessions seldom earned them entry into local elite circles.

Living Conditions for Southern Slaves

Slaveowners' enormous economic investment in their human property played a significant role in the treatment slaves received. Damaging or, worse, killing a healthy slave resulted in a significant financial loss. But to maintain profitability, slaveholders had to keep productivity levels high. This need led southern states to write increasingly harsh **slave codes** during the late eighteenth and early nineteenth centuries, giving slaveowners virtual life-and-death control over their human chattel. A delicate balance between power and profit shaped planters' policies toward slaves and set the tone for slave life. Like the vital machines in northern factories, slaves received the minimum maintenance required to keep them in proper working order.

As to the work itself, cotton planting led to increasing concentration in the tasks performed by slaves. A survey of large and medium-size plantations during the height of the cotton boom shows that the majority of slaves (58 percent of the men and 69 percent of the women) were employed primarily as **field hands.** Of the rest, only 2 percent of slave men and 17 percent of slave women were employed as **house slaves.** The remaining 14 percent of slave women were employed in nonfield occupations such as sewing, weaving, and food processing. Seventeen percent of slave men were employed in nonfield activities such as driving wagons, piloting riverboats, and herding cattle. Another 23 percent were managers and craftsmen.

The percentage of slave craftsmen was much higher in cities, where slave artisans were often allowed to hire themselves out on the open job market in return for handing part of their earnings over to their owners. In Charleston, Norfolk, Richmond, and Savannah, slave artisans formed guilds. Feeling threatened by their solidarity, white craftsmen appealed to state legislatures and city councils for restrictions on slave employment in skilled crafts. Such appeals, and the need for more and more field hands, led to a decline in the number of slave artisans during the 1840s and 1850s.

With the possible exception of sexual exploitation, no area of slave existence has captured the imagina-

Although slaves increasingly were being used in the burgeoning cotton industry during the antebellum years, some continued to practice skilled trades throughout the South. Horace King, for example, was a civil engineer who designed and built bridges and public buildings, including sections of the Alabama state capitol building. *Collection of the Columbus Museum, Columbus, Georgia; Museum purchase.*

tion as much as violence. The image of sadistic white men beating slaves permeates the dark side of the southern myth. Such behavior, however, though not unknown, was far from typical. Slaves were money, and injuring slaves was expensive behavior that most slaveowners could not afford. Still, given the need to keep up productivity, slaveowners were not shy about using measured force. "I always punish according to the crime," one plantation owner declared. "If it is a

---

slave codes   Laws that established the status of slaves, denying them basic rights and classifying them as the property of slaveowners.

field hands   People who do agricultural work such as planting, weeding, and harvesting.

house slaves   People who did domestic work such as cleaning and cooking.

This early photograph, taken on a South Carolina plantation before the Civil War, freezes slave life in time, giving us a view of what slave cabins looked like, how they were arranged, how the largest majority of slaves dressed, and how they spent what little leisure time they had. *Collection of William Gladstone.*

Large one I give him a genteel flogging with a strop, about 75 Lashes I think is a good whipping." Noting the practical limitations even to this "genteel" form of discipline, he continued, "When picking cotton I never put on more than 20 stripes and very frequently not more than 10 or 15." But not all plantation owners were gentle or even practical when it came to discipline. The historical record is filled with accounts of slaveowners who were willing to take a financial loss by beating slaves until they became useless or even died.

In keeping with demands for profitability, housing for slaves was seldom more than adequate. Generally, slaves lived in one-room log cabins with dirt floors and a fireplace or stove. Mindful of the need to maintain control and keep slaves productive, slaveowners tried to avoid crowding people into slave quarters. As one slaveowner explained, "The crowding [of] a number into one house is unhealthy. It breeds contention; is destructive of delicacy of feeling, and it promotes immorality between the sexes."

Though not all planters shared this view, census figures suggest that the average slave cabin housed five or six people.

Though not crammed fifty to a house, as were workers in some New York slums, slave quarters were not particularly comfortable. The cabins had windows, but generally only wooden shutters and no glass. The windows let in flies in summer and cold in winter, but closing the shutters shut out the light. When the shutters were closed against flies and cold, the most reliable source of light was an open fireplace or stove, which was also used for heat and cooking. Ever-present fires increased the danger of cabins burning down, especially because chimneys were generally made of sticks held together with dried mud. As one slave commented, "Many the time we have to get up at midnight and push the chimney away from the house to keep the house from burning up."

As in the cabin homes of common southern whites, furnishings in slave houses were usually fairly crude and often were crafted by the residents themselves.

Bedding generally consisted of straw pallets stacked on the floor or occasionally mounted on rough bedsteads. Other furnishings were equally simple—rough-hewn wooden chairs or benches and plank tables.

Clothing was very basic. One Georgia planter outlined the usual yearly clothing allowance for slaves: "The proper and usual quantity of clothes for plantation hands is two suits of cotton for spring and summer, and two suits of woolen for winter; four pair of shoes and three hats." On some plantations, slave women spun, wove, and sewed cotton fabric called osnaburg. This material was durable, but rough and uncomfortable to wear. As one slave complained, the material was "like needles when it was new." Women generally wore simple dresses or skirts and blouses made from the scratchy osnaburg. Children often went naked in the summer and were fitted with long, loose-hanging osnaburg shirts during the colder months.

It appears that the slave diet, like slave clothing and housing, was sufficient to maintain life but not particularly pleasing. One slave noted that there was "plenty to eat sich as it was," but in summer flies swarmed all over the food. Her master, she said, would laugh about that, saying the added protein provided by the flies "made us fat." Despite justified complaints, the fact is that the average slave diet was rich by comparison with the diet of many other Americans. Slaves in the American South ate significantly more meat than workers in the urban North. In addition to meat, slaves consumed milk and corn, potatoes, peas and beans, molasses, and fish. Generally the planter provided this variety of food, but owners also occasionally permitted slaves to hunt and fish and to collect wild roots, berries, and vegetables. Theft also added to the quantity and variety of foods available in the slave quarters.

Although the diet provided to slaves kept them alive and functioning, the southern diet in general lacked important nutrients, and diet-related diseases plagued southern communities. Slaves were also subject to hernia, pneumonia, and **lockjaw**, of which each, in its way, was the product of slaves' working and living conditions. Because of the lack of proper sanitation, slaves also suffered from dysentery and **cholera**.

One major public health risk that was **endemic** among slaves was in the realm of circulatory disease. Recent research reveals that slave children were generally undernourished because slaveowners would not allocate ample resources to feed people who did not work. Once children were old enough to work, however, they had access to a very high-calorie diet.

Such early malnutrition followed by an instant transition to a high-calorie and often high-fat diet may well have led to the high incidence of heart attacks, strokes, and similar ailments among slaves found in the historical record. And given the balance-sheet mentality among plantation owners, this phenomenon may not have been unwelcome. Old people who could not work hard were, like children, a liability; thus having slaves die from circulatory disease in middle age saved planters from unnecessary expenditures later on.

Most of what we know about living conditions for slaves comes from relatively large plantations in the Cotton Belt. Although most slaves lived under such circumstances, a very large minority lived on small farms in communities of between five and ten, or sometimes just one or two slaves. It appears that slaves on such farms were usually not much better off than slaves on large plantations. Economic life for southern farmers was always difficult; they lived a hand-to-mouth existence, often short of food, clothing, and housing. Small farmers saw slaves as vehicles for social and economic advancement; they were willing to starve, overwork, or sell their slaves if doing so meant economic betterment for their own families. When all was going well, slaves might be treated like members of the farmer's family—much as apprentices might be considered members of a northern craftsman's family. But when conditions were not good, slaves were the first casualties.

Whether on large plantations or small farms, the burden of slavery was a source of constant stress for both slaves and masters in the newly evolving South. The precarious nature of family life, the ever-present threat of violence, and the overwhelming sense of powerlessness weighed heavily on slaves. And among masters, the awareness that they often were outnumbered and thus vulnerable to organized slave rebellion was a source of anxiety. Locked into this fear-and hate-laden atmosphere, everyone in the cotton South was drawn into what would become a long-lasting legacy of racial tension and distrust.

---

lockjaw   A popular name for tetanus, an often fatal disease resulting primarily from deep wounds.

cholera   An infectious disease of the small intestines whose bacteria is often found in untreated water.

endemic   Present among a particular group or groups of people or geographical area.

The Manufacturing Boom

■ How did the process of manufacturing change in the United States after 1820? How did this change affect the nature of work?

■ In what ways did the American system of manufacturing change the traditional patterns of trade between the United States and the rest of the world?

■ How did the developing factory system affect the lives of artisans, factory owners, and middle-class Americans?

Although the South changed radically during the opening years of the nineteenth century, one thing persisted: the economy remained rooted in people's homes. Before the 1820s, households in the North also produced most of the things they used. For example, more than 60 percent of the clothing that Americans wore was spun from raw fibers and sewn by women in their own homes. Some householders even crafted sophisticated items—furniture, clocks, and tools—but skilled **artisans** usually made such products. These craftsmen, too, usually worked in their homes, assisted by family members and an extended family of artisan employees: **apprentices** and **journeymen.**

Beginning with the cotton-spinning plants that sprang up during the War of 1812, textile manufacturing led the way in pushing production in a radical new direction (see page 260). From 1820 onward, manufacturing increasingly moved out of the home and into factories, and cities began to grow up around the factories. The intimate ties between manufacturers and workers were severed, and both found themselves surrounded by strangers in the new urban environments. "In most large cities there may be said to be two nations, understanding as little of one another, having as little intercourse, as if they lived in different lands," said Unitarian minister William Ellery Channing in 1841. "This estrangement of men from men, of class from class, is one of the saddest features of a great city."

The "American System of Manufacturing"

The transition from home manufacturing to factory production did not take place overnight, and the two processes often overlapped. Pioneer manufacturers such as Samuel Slater relied on home workers to carry out major steps in the production of textiles. Using what was called the **putting-out system,** cotton spinners supplied machine-produced yarn to individual households, where families then wove fabric on their own looms during their spare time. Such activities pro-

vided much-needed cash to farm families, enabled less productive family members (like the elderly or children) to contribute, and gave entire families worthwhile pastimes during lulls in the farming calendar.

But innovations in manufacturing soon began displacing such home crafting. The factory designs pioneered by Francis Cabot Lowell and his various partners were widely copied during the 1820s and 1830s. Spinning and weaving on machines located in one building significantly cut both the time and the cost of manufacturing. Quality control became easier because the tools of the trade, owned by the manufacturer rather than by the worker, were standardized and employees were under constant supervision. As a result, the putting-out system for turning yarn into cloth went into serious decline, falling off by as much as 90 percent in some areas of New England. Even home production of clothes for family use slid into decline. Women discovered that spending their time producing cheese or eggs or other marketable items could bring in enough cash to purchase clothing and still have money left over. Throughout the 1830s and 1840s, ready-made clothing—often cut, machine-sewn, and finished by semiskilled workers in factory settings—became standard wearing apparel.

A major technological revolution helped to push factory production into other areas of manufacturing as well during these years. In traditional manufacturing, individual artisans crafted each item one at a time, from the smallest part to the final product. A clockmaker, for example, either cast or carved individually by hand all of the clock's internal parts. As a result, the mechanisms of a clock worked together only in the clock for which they had been made. If that clock ever needed repair, new parts had to be custom-made for it. The lack of **interchangeable parts**

---

artisan   A person whose primary employment is the specialized production of hand-manufactured items; a craftsperson.

apprentice   A person who is bound by contract to a craftsman, providing labor in exchange for learning the skills associated with the craft.

journeyman   A person who has finished an apprenticeship in a trade or craft and is a qualified worker in the employ of another.

putting-out system   Manufacturing system through which machine-made components were distributed to individual families who used them to craft finished goods.

interchangeable parts   Parts that are identical and which can be substituted for one another.

As American industry became increasingly mechanized in the decades after 1820, suitable mill sites—places with solid foundations for factory buildings and reliable water flow for powering machinery—became highly prized. Often long stretches of riverbanks would sprout factory after factory. This was the case in Brandywine Village near the present site of Wilmington, Delaware, which became the leading mechanized, flour-producing center in the United States during the early nineteenth century. *Historical Society of Delaware Collection.*

made manufacturing extremely slow and repairs difficult, and it limited employment in the manufacturing trades to highly skilled professionals.

While serving as ambassador to France, Thomas Jefferson had encountered the idea of standardizing parts, so that a wheel from any given clock could be used in any other similar clock. Eli Whitney, perfecter of the cotton gin (see page 265), was the first American to propose the large-scale use of interchangeable parts—for a gun-manufacturing scheme in 1798. Whitney's efforts failed because he lacked money and pre-

cision machine tools. But a quarter-century later, in 1822, one of Whitney's partners in this pioneering venture, John H. Hall, brought together the necessary skill, financing, and tools to prove that manufacturing guns from interchangeable parts was practical. Within twenty years this "American system of manufacturing," as it was called, was being used to produce a wide range of products—farm implements, padlocks, sewing machines, and clocks. Formerly, clocks had been a status symbol setting apart people of means from common folks; however, using standardized

Manufacturing and the Revolution in Time

Before the 1830s, complex manufactured items like guns and clocks were extremely expensive, generally beyond the means of most Americans. The manufacturing revolution changed all that. In 1838, Chauncey Jerome introduced the first mass-produced brass clock at a price that virtually any American could afford, and the clocks sold by the thousands. The distribution of clocks and the means by which they were produced reinforced each other. Factory production required a much greater degree of regimentation than had individual hand manufacturing: the efforts of armies of workers, clerks, managers, shippers, and others essential to industry had to be coordinated if factories were going to function effectively. No longer living at their place of work, all of these employees, from the highest to the lowest in status, needed to have a reliable way of telling time. Jerome's clocks provided that reliability, contributing to a revolution in the way Americans began thinking about time itself. Increasingly people looked to mechanical devices rather than to natural ones—the transit of the sun, the changing of seasons—to punctuate their lives, and industry profited accordingly. As American society has become increasingly complex, we have become even more dependent on time management and various devices for implementing it. As we look at our day planner or electronic personal information manager, we are participating in a world that was born in 1838 with the introduction of cheap brass clocks.

New Workplaces and New Workers

With machines now producing standardized parts for complex mechanisms such as clocks, the worker's job was reduced to simply assembling premade components. The centuries-old **guild** organization for artisans—preserved in the hierarchical system of apprentices, journeymen, and master craftsmen—rapidly fell away as extensive training in the manufacturing arts became irrelevant.

At first, owners found they had to use creative means to attract workers into the new factories. Some entrepreneurs developed **company towns.** In New England these towns resembled traditional New England villages. Families recruited from the economically depressed countryside were installed in neat row houses, each with its own small vegetable garden. The company employed each family member. Women worked on the production line. Men ran heavy machinery and worked as **millwrights,** carpenters, haulers, or as day laborers dredging out the **millraces.** Children did light work in the factories and tended gardens at home.

Lowell's company developed another system at its factories. Hard-pressed to find enough families to leave traditional employment and come to work in the factories, Lowell recruited unmarried farm girls. The company built dormitories to house these young working women, offering cash wages and reasonable prices for room and board, as well as cultural events and educational opportunities. Because most of the girls saw factory work as a transitional stage between girlhood and marriage, Lowell assured them and their families that the company would strictly control the moral atmosphere so that the girls' reputations would remain spotless.

Not everyone was convinced that factory work, even under strict supervision, was appropriate for

parts, pioneer manufacturers like Seth Thomas and Chauncey Jerome revolutionized clock making to the point where virtually all Americans could afford them. Not only that, Thomas's and Jerome's breakthroughs produced clocks so inexpensive and reliable that even the British and Europeans began importing them. This reversed the long-standing pattern of manufactures moving exclusively from Europe to America, a trend that would grow in the years to come.

guild   An association of craftspeople with the same skills who join together to protect their mutual interests.

company town   A town built and owned by a single company; its residents depend on the company not only for jobs but for stores, schools, and housing.

millwright   A person who designs, builds, or repairs mills or mill machinery.

millrace   The channel for the fast-moving stream of water that drives a mill wheel.

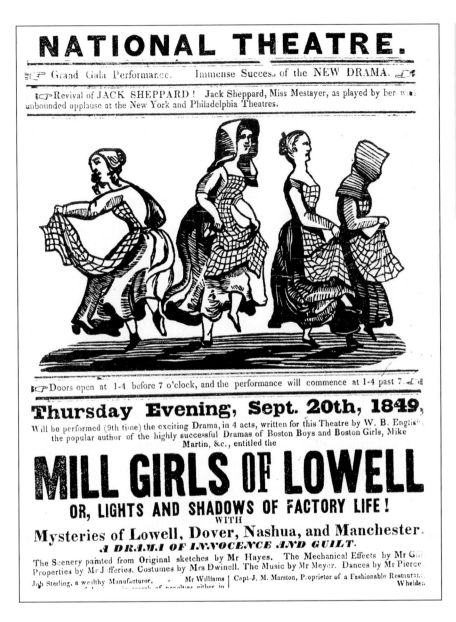

young women. "Few of them ever marry," Boston journalist Orestes A. Brownson incorrectly reported. "Fewer still ever return to their native places with reputations unimpaired." Others, however, even the young women themselves, defended the system. In a letter to the editor, one young woman attacked Brownson personally. "And now, if Mr. Brownson is a man . . . let him come among us: let him make himself as well acquainted with us as our pastors and superintendents are; . . . he would not see worthy and virtuous girls consigned to infamy, because they work in a factory."

In New York, Philadelphia, and other cities, immigrant slums offered opportunistic manufacturers an alternative source of labor. In the shoe industry, for example, one family would make soles, while a neighboring family made heels, and so forth. This type of operation was not as efficient as large shoe factories, but the money that urban manufacturers saved by not building factories and by paying rock-bottom wages to desperate slum-dwellers made it possible for the companies to compete successfully in the open market.

The combination of machine production and a growing pool of labor proved economically devastating to workers. No longer was the employer a master craftsman or a paternalistic entrepreneur who felt some responsibility to look out for his workers' domestic needs. Factory owners were obligated to investors and bankers and had to squeeze the greatest possible profit out of the manufacturing process. They kept wages low, regardless of the workers' cost of living. As the swelling supply of labor allowed employers to offer lower and lower wages, increasing numbers of working people faced poverty and squalor.

Immigration supplied much of this labor. Between 1820 and 1830 slightly more than 151,000 people immigrated to the United States. In the decade that followed, that number increased to nearly 600,000; between 1840 and 1850, well over a million and a half people moved to the United States from abroad (see Map 11.1). This enormous increase in immigration changed not only the **demographic** but also the cultural and economic face of the nation. The flood of immigrants collected in the port and manufacturing cities of the Northeast, where they joined Americans fleeing financial depression in the countryside after the economic panics of 1819 (see page 280) and 1837 (discussed in Chapter 12). Adding to the resulting brew were former master craftsmen, journeymen, and apprentices who no longer had a secure place in the changing economy. Together, though seldom cooperatively, these groups helped to form a new social class in America.

Nearly half of all the immigrants who flooded into the United States between 1820 and 1860 came from Ireland—a nation beset with poverty, political strife, and, after a devastating blight began killing the potato crop in 1841, starvation. For centuries Ireland had been a colony in the British Empire, and Irish immigrants had few marketable skills or more money than the voyage to America cost. They arrived penniless, many of them speaking not English but Gaelic, and most had little or no chance of finding employment.

Similar conditions beset many members of the second most numerous immigrant group: the Germans. Radical economic change and political upheaval in Germany were putting both peasants and skilled craftsmen to flight. Like Irish peasants, German farmers arrived in America destitute and devoid of opportunities. Trained German craftsmen had a better chance of finding employment, but the changeover from handicraft to industrial production—the very change that in many cases had driven them from Germany—was also taking place in America. And like the Irish, few spoke English well.

Not only were the new immigrants poor and often unskilled, but also most were culturally different from native-born Americans. Religion was their most notable cultural distinction: the majority were Roman Catholics. Their Catholicism separated them from most Americans, who claimed to be Protestant whether they worshiped actively or not. It also made them suspect in the minds of people steeped in anti-Catholic sentiments handed down from earlier generations of Lutheran, Presbyterian, Quaker, and other immigrants who had fled Catholic persecution. In religion, then, as well as in language, dress, and eating and drinking habits, the new immigrants were very different from the sorts of people whose culture had come to dominate American society.

Poverty, cultural distinctiveness, and a desire to live among people who understood their ways and spoke their language brought new immigrants to neighborhoods where their countrymen had already found places to live. In New York, Philadelphia, and other cities, people with the same culture and religion built churches, stores, pubs or beer halls, and other familiar institutions that helped them cope with the shock of transplantation from Europe and gave them a chance to adapt gradually to life in the United States. They also started fraternal organizations and clubs to overcome the loneliness, isolation, and powerlessness they were experiencing.

Because the new immigrants were poor, housing in their neighborhoods was often substandard, and living conditions were crowded, uncomfortable, and unsanitary. Desperate for work and eager to make their own way in their new country, these fresh immigrants were willing to do nearly anything to earn money. Lacking the resources to buy farms and lacking the skills to enter professional trades, they were the perfect work force for the newly evolving industrial economy. As the flow of immigrants increased, the traditional labor shortage in America was replaced by a **labor glut,** and the social and economic status of all workers declined accordingly.

Living Conditions in Blue-Collar America

Working conditions for **blue-collar workers** in factories reflected the labor supply, the amount of capital available to the manufacturing company, and the

---

demographic The statistical distribution of subpopulations (ethnic groups, for example) among the larger population of a community or nation.

labor glut Oversupply of labor in relation to the number of jobs available.

blue-collar workers Workers who wear work clothes, such as coveralls and jeans, on the job; their work is likely to involve manual labor.

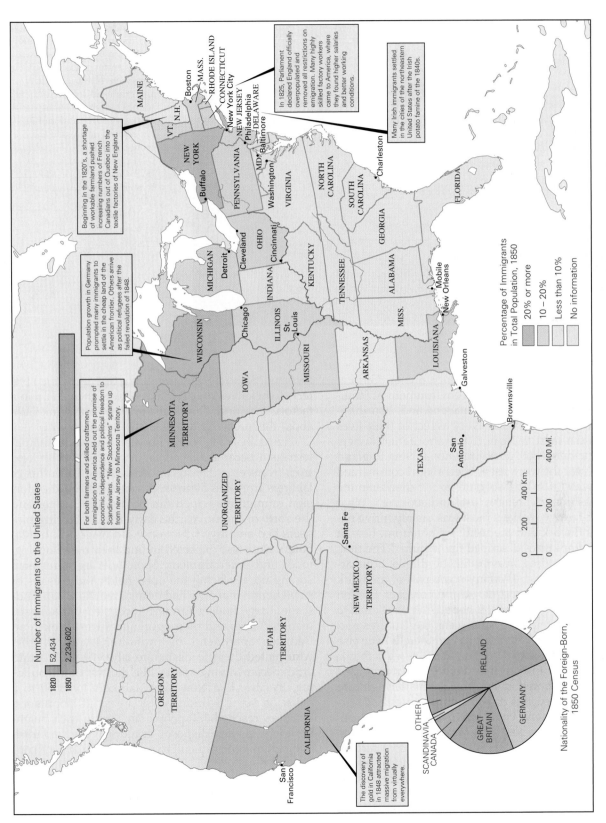

Number of Immigrants to the United States

1820 52,434
1850 2,234,602

In 1825, Parliament declared England officially overpopulated and removed all restrictions on emigration. Many highly skilled factory workers came to America, where they found higher salaries and better working conditions.

Many Irish immigrants settled in the cities of the northeastern United States after the Irish potato famine of the 1840s.

Beginning in the 1820's, a shortage of workable farmland pushed increasing numbers of French Canadians out of Quebec into the textile factories of New England.

Population growth in Germany prompted many immigrants to settle in the cheap land of the American frontier. Others arrive as political refugees after the failed revolution of 1848.

For both farmers and skilled craftsmen, immigration to America held out the promise of economic independence and political freedom to Scandinavians. "New Stockholms" sprang up from new Jersey to Minnesota Territory.

The discovery of gold in California in 1848 attracted massive migration from virtually everywhere.

Percentage of Immigrants in Total Population, 1850

20% or more
10–20%
Less than 10%
No information

Nationality of the Foreign-Born, 1850 Census

IRELAND
GERMANY
GREAT BRITAIN
CANADA
SCANDINAVIA
OTHER

MAP 11.1 Origin and Settlement of Immigrants, 1820–1850 Immigration was one of the most important economic, political, and social factors in American life during the antebellum period. As this map shows, with the exception of Louisiana, immigration was confined almost exclusively to areas where slavery was not permitted. This gave the North, Northwest, and California a different cultural flavor than the rest of the country and also affected the political balance between those areas and the South.

Working-class neighborhoods like the infamous Five Points District in New York, shown in this anonymous 1829 picture, were filthy, unhealthy, and crime-ridden. Reformers sought to help by changing workers' habits and morals but seldom addressed their economic plight. *"Five Points District," artist unknown, ca. 1829. Courtesy of Mr. and Mrs. Screven Lorillard. Photograph by Josh Nefsky.*

personal philosophy of the factory owner. Girls at Lowell's factories described an environment of familiar paternalism. Factory managers and boarding-house keepers supervised every aspect of their lives in much the same manner that authoritarian fathers saw to the details of life on traditional New England farms. As for the work itself, one mill girl commented that it was "not half so hard as . . . attending the dairy, washing, cleaning house, and cooking." What bothered factory workers most was the repetitive nature of the work and the resulting boredom. One of Lowell's employees described the tedium. "The time is often apt to drag heavily till the dinner hour arrives," she reported. "Perhaps some part of the work becomes deranged and stops; the constant friction causes a belt of leather to burst into a flame; a stranger visits the room, and scans the features and dress of its inmates inquiringly; and there is little else to break the monotony."

She went on to note that daydreaming provided relief from the boredom and the ear-shattering noise of the machinery. But daydreaming in front of fast-moving equipment could have disastrous consequences for what a New Jersey magazine called "the human portion of the machine." Inattentive factory workers were likely to lose fingers, hands, or whole arms to whirring, pounding, slashing mechanisms. Not a few lost their lives. Though managers may have wanted to make factories safer, investors vetoed any additional costs that safety devices might have

incurred. Samuel Slater, for example, complained bitterly to his investors after a child was chewed up in a factory machine. "You call for yarn but think little about the means by which it is to be made."

Gradually Slater's and Lowell's well-meaning paternalism became rare as factory owners withdrew from overseeing day-to-day operations. The influx of laborers from the depressed countryside and of foreign immigrants wiped out both decent wages and the sorts of incentives the early manufacturing pioneers had employed. Not only did wages fall but laborers were also expected to find their own housing, food, and entertainment. Soon hulking **tenements** sprang up, replacing the open fields and clusters of small homes that once had dominated the urban landscape. Large houses formerly occupied by domestic manufacturers and their apprentices were broken up into tiny apartments by profit-hungry speculators who rented them to desperate laborers. Cellars and attics became living spaces like the rest of the building. In cities like New York, laborers lived 50 to a house in some working-class areas. As population densities reached 150 people an acre in such neighborhoods, sewage disposal, drinking water, and trash removal became difficult to provide. Life in such con-

tenement   An urban apartment house, usually with minimal facilities for sanitation, safety, and comfort.

ditions was grossly unpleasant and extremely unhealthy: epidemics of typhus, cholera, and other crowd diseases swept through the slums periodically.

Investigating living and working conditions, a *New York Tribune* reporter found conditions deplorable. "The floor is made of rough plank laid loosely down, and the ceiling is not quite so high as a tall man," he reported. "The walls are dark and damp and the miserable room is lighted only by a shallow sash partly projecting above the surface of the ground and by the light that struggles from the steep and rotting stairs." In this dark and tiny space, he observed, "often lives the man and his work bench, the wife, and five or six children of all ages; and perhaps a palsied grandfather and grandmother and often both. Here they work, here they cook, they eat, they sleep, they pray."

Life and Culture Among a New Middle Class

Large-scale manufacturing not only changed industrial work but also introduced demands for a new class of skilled managerial and clerical employees. Under the old system of manufacturing, the master craftsman or his wife had managed the company's accounts, hired journeymen and apprentices, purchased raw materials, and seen to the delivery of finished products. The size of the new factories made such direct contact between owners, workers, and products impossible. To fill the void, a new class of professionals came into being. In these days before the invention of the typewriter, firms such as Lowell's Boston Manufacturing Company employed teams of young men as clerks. These clerks kept accounts, wrote orders, and drafted correspondence, all in longhand using **quill pens.** As elite owners such as Lowell and his partners became wrapped up in building new factories, pursuing investors, and entering new markets, both clerical and manufacturing employees were increasingly supervised by professional managers.

One distinguishing characteristic of the new **white-collar workers** was their relative youth. These young people, many of them the sons and daughters of rural farmers, had flocked to newly emerging cities in pursuit of formal education. They stayed to seek employment away from the economic instability and **provincialism** of the farm. The experience of Elizabeth Yale Hancock, a country girl from upstate New York, was fairly typical. After attending public school in Champlain, Elizabeth transferred to the Plattsburgh Academy. She studied there full-time for two terms before taking a job teaching at a public school while continuing classes at the academy part-time. She then went to the Female Seminary in Buffalo, where she enrolled in college-level classes. While pursuing her studies there, she worked as a nanny and resident tutor. Finally graduating from the seminary, Elizabeth took a job as a teacher at a select school.

Men too attended school when and where they could get financial assistance and then settled down where they could find employment and the company of others like themselves. And, as Elizabeth Hancock's experience indicates, women joined men in moving into new professions. While middle-class men found employment as clerks, bookkeepers, and managers, middle-class women parlayed their formal education and their gender's perceived gift for nurturing children into work as teachers. It became acceptable for women to work as teachers for several years before marriage, and many avoided marriage altogether to pursue their hard-won careers.

Middle-class men and women tended to put off marriage as long as possible while they established themselves socially and economically. They also tended to have fewer children than their parents had had. In the new urban middle-class setting, parents felt compelled to send their children to school so that they could take their place on the career ladder chosen by their parents. Adding nothing to family income, children thus became economic liabilities rather than assets, and middle-class adults used a combination of late marriage and various forms of birth control to keep families small.

A lack of traditional ties affected the lives of both married and unmarried middle-class people. Many unmarried men and women seeking their fortunes in town boarded in private homes or rooming houses. After marriage, middle-class men and women often moved into private town homes, isolating themselves and their children from perceived dangers in the faceless city but also cutting them off from the comforting sociability of traditional country life. Accordingly, these young people crafted new urban structures that might provide the missing companionship and guidance.

---

quill pen A pen made from the shaft of a feather; the end of the quill is sharpened with a knife and then dipped in ink.

white-collar workers Workers able to wear white shirts on the job because they do no grubby manual labor.

provincialism The limited and narrow perspective thought to be characteristic of people in rural areas.

Obviously some sought the company of women like Helen Jewett. Most, however, found companionship in **voluntary associations.** Students in colleges and universities formed a variety of discussion groups, preprofessional clubs, and benevolent societies. After graduation, groups such as the Odd Fellows and the Masons brought people together for companionship. Such organizations helped enforce traditional values through rigid membership standards stressing moral character, upright behavior, and, above all, order.

The *Odd Fellows' Manual* summarized the philosophy of these organizations well. "In the transaction of our business we pursue strict parliamentary rules, that our members may be qualified for any public stations to which they may be called by their fellow-citizens," the manual asserts. "And when business has been performed, we indulge in social intercourse, and even in cheerful and innocent hilarity and amusement. But all in strict order and decorum, good fellowship and prudence are constantly to be kept in view." In such clubs, people could discuss the latest books or world affairs with others of similar education and lifestyle in an affable setting. As the *Odd Fellows' Manual* went on to say, "Exercise yourself in the discussions of your Lodge not for the purpose of mere debate, contention, or 'love of opposition,' but to improve yourself in suitably expressing your sentiments." Young people also created and joined professional and trade groups. These associations served a social function, but they also became forums for training novices and for setting standards for professional methods and modes of conduct.

Members of the new middle class also used their organizing skills to press for reforms. While the elite class of factory owners and financiers generally formed the leadership for such organizations as the American Tract Society, the American Bible Society, and the American Board of Commissioners for Foreign Missions—each a multimillion-dollar reforming enterprise—young middle-class men and women provided the rank and file of charity workers.

In addition to their youth, another characteristic that prevailed among this newly forming class was deep anxiety. Although their education and skills earned them jobs with greater prestige than those of the average worker, these clerks and supervisors could be laid off or demoted to working-class status at any time. Also, because of the anonymity in the new cities, it was virtually impossible to know if a stranger was truly a member of one's own class or an imposter who might use the trappings of gentility to take advantage of the new urban scene. Such suspicions led to a very strict set of rules for making social connections, and the wary atmosphere also helps to explain the fascination with a woman like Helen Jewett, whose life, and especially whose death, illustrated the dangers posed by and to pretenders to middle-class gentility.

Social Life for a Genteel Class

The changes in lifestyle that affected working-class and middle-class Americans were in large part an outcome of changes in the daily lives of those who owned and operated manufacturing businesses. In earlier years, when journeymen and apprentices had lived with master craftsmen, they were in effect members of a craftsman's extended family. The master craftsman/owner exercised great authority over his workers but felt obligated to care for them almost as a parent would have done. Such working arrangements blurred the distinction between employee and employer. Crammed together in the same household, owner and workers shared the same general lifestyle, kept the same hours, ate the same food, and enjoyed the same leisure activities. The factory system ended this relationship. The movement of workers out of the owners' homes permitted members of the emerging elite class to develop a **genteel** lifestyle that set them off from the army of factory workers and lesser number of clerks. Genteel families aimed at the complete separation of their private and public lives. Men in the manufacturing elite class spent their leisure time in new activities. Instead of drinking, eating, and playing with their employees, business owners began to socialize with one another in private clubs and in church and civic organizations. Instead of attending the popular theater, elite patrons began endowing opera companies and other highbrow forms of entertainment.

The lives of the factory owners' wives also changed. The mistress of a traditional manufacturing household had been responsible for important tasks in the operation of the business. Genteel women, in contrast, were expected to leave business dealings to men. Ensconced in private houses set apart from the new centers of production and marketing, genteel women found themselves with time on their hands. To give themselves something to do, they sought areas of ac-

---

voluntary association An organization or club through which individuals engage in voluntary service, usually associated with charity or reform.

genteel The manner and style associated with elite classes, usually characterized by elegance, grace, and politeness.

The Oddfellow's March.

Voluntary associations and fraternal organizations sprang up by the hundreds in the new urban America that was emerging in the 1830s and 1840s. These organizations provided companionship and, more importantly, a sense of order for the newly emerging middle class. The Odd Fellows was one prominent example. This sheet music cover, from a piece entitled "The Oddfellows March," is but one piece of evidence of the enormous cultural contributions that these organizations made to emerging modern American life. *Maryland Historical Society.*

tivity that would provide focus and a sense of accomplishment without imperiling their elite status by involving them in what was now perceived as the crass, masculine world of commerce. Many found outlets for their creative energies in fancy needlework, reading, and art appreciation societies. But some wished for more challenging activities. Sarah Huntington Smith, for example, a member of Connecticut's elite, spoke for many when she complained in 1833, "To make and receive visits, exchange friendly salutations, attend to one's wardrobe, cultivate a garden, read good and entertaining books, and even attend religious meetings for one's own enjoyment; all this does not satisfy me."

One activity that consumed genteel women was motherhood. Magazines and advice manuals, which began appearing during the 1820s and 1830s, rejected the traditional adage of "spare the rod, spoil the child," replacing it with an insistence on gentle nurturing. One leader in this movement was author and teacher Bronson Alcott. Alcott denied the concept of **infant depravity** that had so affected Puritan parents during the colonial era and led them to break their children's will, often through harsh measures (see page 71). Instead, he stated emphatically that "the child must be treated as a free, self-guiding, self-controlling being."

Alcott was equally emphatic that child rearing was the mother's responsibility. As his wife, Abigail, wrote of family management in Alcott's household, "Mr. A aids me in general principles, though nobody can aid me in the detail." And, according to Alcott, women should feel especially blessed for having such an opportunity.

Books like Alcott's *Conversations with Children on the Gospels* (1836–1837) flooded forth during these years and appealed greatly to isolated and underemployed women. Many adopted the advertised **cult of domesticity** completely. Turning inward, these women centered their lives on their homes and children. In doing so, they believed they were performing an important duty for God and country and fulfilling their most important, perhaps their only, natural calling.

Other genteel women agreed with the general tone of the domestic message but widened the woman's supposedly natural sphere outward, beyond the nursery, to encompass the whole world. They banded together with like-minded women to get out into the world in order to reform it. "I want to be where every arrangement will have unreserved and constant reference to eternity," Sarah Huntington Smith explained. Smith herself chose to become a missionary. Others during the 1830s and 1840s involved themselves in a variety of reform movements, such as founding Sunday schools or opposing alcohol abuse. These causes let them use their nurturing and purifying talents to improve what appeared to be an increasingly chaotic and immoral society, the world represented by Helen Jewett.

infant depravity   The idea that children are naturally sinful because they share in the original sin of the human race but have not learned the discipline to control their evil instincts.

cult of domesticity   The belief that women's proper role lies in domestic pursuits.

Individual Voices

Examining a Primary Source

The Press "Remembers" Helen Jewett

The United States in 1836 was rapidly becoming more modern. One measure of its emerging modernity, a feature with which we are all too familiar today, was the rise of a sensationalist press. The murder of Helen Jewett (really Dorcas Doyen) presented an irresistible opportunity for this new medium. Although a few responsible newspapers printed factually based stories about the victim's early life, sensationalist newspapers seeking larger sales and plumped-up reputations for being investigative published ever more exaggerated accounts of Jewett's life and death. The *New York Herald,* for example, continued to print romanticized stories about Jewett even after it became generally known that her early life was rather unremarkable and that the charming Miss Jewett was a fictional creation by an intelligent and inventive woman who was intent on shaping her life on her own terms. The following is taken from a story printed in the *Herald* on April 12, 1836.

- *Although it was generally known that young Dorcas was actually hired as a serving girl in Judge Weston's household, this story suggests that she was a guest or companion in the justice's home. Why would a news writer choose to "revise" the facts?*

Her private history is most remarkable—her character equally so. . . . In Augusta, Maine, lived a highly respectable gentleman, Judge Western [sic], by name. Some of the female members of his family pitying the bereaved condition of young Dorcas invited her to live at the Judge's house. At that time Dorcas was young, beautiful, innocent, modest, and ingenuous. Her good qualities and sprightly temper won the good feelings of the Judge's family. She became a chere-amie of his daughters—a companion and a playmate. . . . ▪

- *How does the account of the seduction of the teenage Dorcas add to the story? Why might this version have had more appeal than the truth for popular audiences?*

   After having continued at the Academy for some time, Dorcas, during the summer of 1829, went to spend the vacation at a distant relative's at Norridgewock, a town on the Kennebeck river, about 28 miles above Augusta. Dorcas was then sixteen years of age—and one of the most lovely, interesting, black eyed girls, that ever appeared in that place.

   In this town, in the course of visiting, she became acquainted with a young man, by the name of H—— Sp——y, a fine youth, elegant and educated, since said to be a Cashier in one of the banks of Augusta. After a short acquaintance with him, all was gone that constitutes the honor and ornament of the female character. . . . ▪

   She returned after a short season to Augusta. Her situation soon became known in the Judge's family. A quarrel ensued. She left her protector, after having in a moment of passion lost all the rules of virtue and morality.

- *Aspasia was the mistress of Pericles, the foremost Athenian statesman of classical Greece. Despite a disreputable background, Aspasia used her intelligence and wit to charm the political elite of Athens in the fifth century BCE. Though charming, she frequently was the target of public attacks that painted her as a common harlot.*

- *Whom does the writer want the audience to blame for Dorcas Doyen's descent into prostitution? Why?*

   After having recovered from her first lapse from the path of virtue, she retreated to Portland, took the name of Maria B. Benson, and became a regular Aspasia ▪ among the young men, lawyers, and merchants. ▪

Summary

Although seemingly the most old-fashioned region of the country, the South that emerged during the years leading up to 1840 was a profoundly different place than it had been before the War of 1812. As an industrial revolution overturned the economies in Great Britain and the American Northeast, economic options for southerners changed radically. Although they clothed their new society in romanticized medieval garb, they were creating an altogether new kind of economy and society. The efficient production of cotton by the newly reorganized South was an essential aspect of the emerging national market economy and a powerful force in the Great Transformation.

Change in the North was more obvious. As factories replaced craft shops and cities replaced towns, the entire fabric of northern society seemed to come unraveled. The new economy and new technology created wonderful new opportunities but also imposed serious constraints. A revamped social structure replaced the traditional order as unskilled and semiskilled workers, a new class of clerks, and the genteel elite carved out new lives. The new cities also developed a dark underside where the tawdry glamour that characterized Helen Jewett's life often led to grotesque death. As in the South, the outcome was a remarkable transformation in the lives of everyone in the region.

Tying these two regions together was a new network of roads, waterways, and communications systems that accelerated the process of change. After 1840, it was possible to ship goods from any one section of the country to any other, and people in all sections were learning more about conditions in far distant parts of the growing country. Often this new information promised prosperity, but it also made more and more people aware of the enormity of the transformation taking place and the glaring differences between the nation's various regions. The twin outcomes would be greater integration in the national economy and increasing tension between mutually dependent participants in the new marketplace.

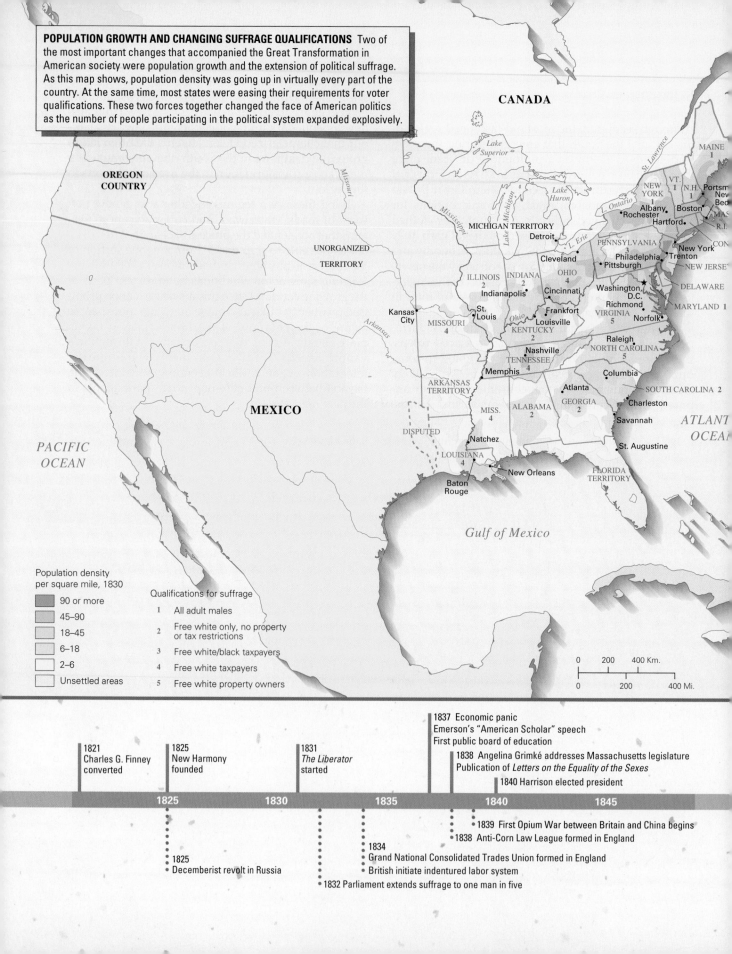

POPULATION GROWTH AND CHANGING SUFFRAGE QUALIFICATIONS Two of the most important changes that accompanied the Great Transformation in American society were population growth and the extension of political suffrage. As this map shows, population density was going up in virtually every part of the country. At the same time, most states were easing their requirements for voter qualifications. These two forces together changed the face of American politics as the number of people participating in the political system expanded explosively.

CANADA

OREGON COUNTRY

UNORGANIZED TERRITORY

MICHIGAN TERRITORY

MEXICO

DISPUTED

ARKANSAS TERRITORY

PACIFIC OCEAN

Lake Superior
Lake Michigan
Lake Huron
L. Ontario
L. Erie

St. Lawrence

Missouri

Mississippi

Arkansas

Ohio

Kansas City

St. Louis

MISSOURI 4

ILLINOIS 2
Indianapolis
INDIANA 2

OHIO 4
Cincinnati
Frankfort
Louisville
KENTUCKY 2

Detroit
Cleveland

PENNSYLVANIA 3
Pittsburgh
Philadelphia

Washington D.C.
Richmond
VIRGINIA 5
Norfolk

MAINE 1
NEW YORK
Albany
Rochester
VT. 1
N.H. 1
Portsm
New Bed
Boston
Hartford
CON
R.I.
MASS

New York
Trenton
NEW JERSE
DELAWARE
MARYLAND 1

Raleigh
NORTH CAROLINA 5

Nashville
TENNESSEE 4
Memphis

MISS. 4
ALABAMA 2
GEORGIA 2
Atlanta

Columbia
SOUTH CAROLINA 2
Charleston
Savannah
St. Augustine

LOUISIANA 4
Natchez
Baton Rouge
New Orleans

FLORIDA TERRITORY

ATLANT OCEA

Gulf of Mexico

Population density per square mile, 1830

- 90 or more
- 45–90
- 18–45
- 6–18
- 2–6
- Unsettled areas

Qualifications for suffrage

1 All adult males
2 Free white only, no property or tax restrictions
3 Free white/black taxpayers
4 Free white taxpayers
5 Free white property owners

| 0 | | 200 | | 400 Km. |
| 0 | | 200 | | 400 Mi. |

1821 Charles G. Finney converted

1825 New Harmony founded

1831 *The Liberator* started

1837 Economic panic
Emerson's "American Scholar" speech
First public board of education

1838 Angelina Grimké addresses Massachusetts legislature
Publication of *Letters on the Equality of the Sexes*

1840 Harrison elected president

| 1825 | 1830 | 1835 | 1840 | 1845 |

1839 First Opium War between Britain and China begins

1838 Anti-Corn Law League formed in England

1834 Grand National Consolidated Trades Union formed in England

British initiate indentured labor system

1832 Parliament extends suffrage to one man in five

1825 Decemberist revolt in Russia

Responses to the Great Transformation, 1828–1840

Population Growth and Changing Suffrage Qualifications

Using the map on the facing page, note the increasing concentration of population in certain areas and also the rules that controlled voting on a regional basis. How would these two factors manifest themselves in the presidential election of 1840? How was the face of American politics changed?

Individual Choices

ANGELINA GRIMKÉ

Born in the South to a prominent slaveholding family, Angelina Grimké moved to the North to distance herself from an institution she hated. When she discovered that northerners were no more sympathetic about the plight of slaves than southerners and would not give abolition a free hearing, she chose to do something about it. She toured the Northeast, speaking first to groups of women and then to large mixed audiences. She capped her tour by becoming the first woman to address the Massachusetts state legislature. Her courage won new respect both for abolitionists and for women. *Library of Congress.*

Angelina Grimké

On March 22, 1838, Boston newspapers reported an unprecedented historical event. On the day before, a young woman had become the first of her gender to address a committee of the Massachusetts state legislature. The young woman was Angelina Emily Grimké, and her speech was a ringing condemnation of slavery.

Many thought it odd that a woman barely out of her twenties would stand before the legislature to speak on any subject, but to speak so boldly on a topic so controversial was odder still. And more than just odd, to speak out against slavery, even in Boston, was dangerous. And that was precisely why Angelina Grimké had chosen to do it.

Born in 1808, Angelina was the thirteenth child of Judge John Faucheraud Grimké and his wife, Mary Smith Grimké. Both of Angelina's parents were descendants of old South Carolina aristocratic families and members in good standing of the state's social and political elite. But Angelina was never comfortable in this environment of carefree gentility. Raised mostly by her older sister Sarah, young Angelina was extremely serious-minded. When presented for confirmation in her parents' Episcopal faith, she refused, saying, "If, with my feelings and views as they now are, I should go through that form, it would be acting a lie. I cannot do it."

Sarah, too, was uncomfortable with plantation life and Episcopalian ritual. While on a trip to Philadelphia she became attracted to Quakerism and brought this new faith home. But being a Quaker in antebellum South Carolina was anything but easy—the Society of Friends in Charleston consisted of but two old men. Sarah finally chose to leave her family and move to Pennsylvania, where she could practice her faith. Angelina, too, eventually converted to the Quaker faith and, in 1829, followed her sister to Philadelphia.

One of the Quaker principles that attracted Sarah and Angelina was its rejection of slavery. Though raised in a slaveholding family, several of the Grimké children opposed the institution. Their brother Thomas, for example, was one of the key organizers of the American Colonization Society, which labored to free slaves and return them to Africa. Most of their Quaker friends, too, supported colonization and the Colonization Society's gradual approach, but this was not acceptable to Angelina. Just before leaving South Carolina, she had written about slavery in her diary: "May it not be laid down as an axiom, that the system must be radically wrong which can only be supported by transgressing the laws of God."

In fact, Angelina was at first disappointed and then angered by northern indifference to the slavery issue. Even in Quaker circles, conservative leaders sought to maintain peace in congregations by prohibiting the discussion of slavery. And non-Quakers treated those who vocally attacked the institution with outright hostility. In 1834 riots had broken out in New York and Philadelphia when abolitionist speakers had tried to give public addresses. Finally, in the late summer of 1835, after a year of repeated outbreaks, William Lloyd Garrison published an appeal in

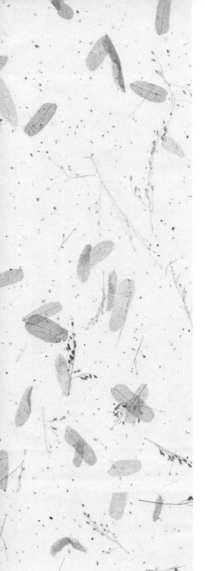

The Liberator calling for the citizens of Boston to stop mob violence and give abolitionist speakers a fair hearing. His courage in standing up to the mobs was like a personal call for Angelina. Although she tried to resist the temptation, she felt compelled to write a letter to Garrison praising his stand.

"The ground upon which you stand is holy ground," she wrote. "Never—never surrender it. If you surrender it, the hope of the slave is extinguished." Garrison was so moved by the letter that he immediately published it, casting a spotlight on its young female author. "I had some idea it might be published," Angelina wrote in her diary, "but did not feel at liberty to say it must not be. . . ." Friends, family members, even her sister Sarah begged Angelina to withdraw the letter, but she refused. "I cannot describe the anguish of my soul," she wrote. "Nevertheless I could not blame the publication of the letter, nor would I have recalled it if I could."

As to the danger, she had written to Garrison, "If persecution is the means which God has ordained for the accomplishment of this great end, EMANCIPATION; then . . . I feel as if I could say, LET IT COME; for it is my deep, solemn deliberate conviction, that this is a cause worth dying for. . . ."

From that point, there was no turning back. In 1836 she wrote an *Appeal to the Christian Women of the South,* calling for them to stand up and put an end to the institution of slavery. In the following year she addressed an *Appeal to the Women of the Nominally Free States.* Then she accepted an invitation from the American Anti-Slavery Society to begin a lecture tour, speaking at first only to groups of women, but eventually to large mixed audiences. The acclaim she won finally led to her appearance at the state house in Boston, where the committee not only listened to her arguments but invited her back for an additional session. "The chairman," she reported, "was in tears almost the whole time that I was speaking."

Angelina's choice and the wide acceptance she gained through her eloquence made it easier from then on for abolitionist speakers to win the hearing Garrison had begged for. And the precedent she set, first in speaking to large audiences of men and women together and then in addressing the Massachusetts legislature, proved to women that they could and should publicly proclaim their ideas, even on dangerous subjects.

INTRODUCTION

Standing before the Massachusetts state legislature in 1838, Angelina Grimké was violating nearly every standard for behavior that applied to her generation. The daughter of a southern plantation family, she nonetheless opposed slavery and was willing to declare her opinions publicly. As a woman, she was taking a step that no other of her sex had yet done by testifying about this controversial issue in the halls of government. A person of deep faith and unswerving commitment, she felt she had to speak out. And in that, she stood with many in her generation. Changing conditions wrought by the so-called Great Transformation in the nation's economy and society prompted unusual responses by many. In 1838 Grimké stood alone at the podium, but she was not alone in spirit.

In her many speeches and written works, Grimké gave voice to both a growing anxiety and a growing hopefulness that was sweeping over America. She and many of her fellow Christians shared with transcendentalists, socialists, and other communitarians a belief in human perfectibility that drove them all into a frenzy of work and experimentation. In northern cities, on southern plantations, and at western revival meetings, members of all social classes were crafting cultural expressions designed to give meaning to their lives and lend shape to a society that seemed to be losing all direction. At the same time, ambitious politicians were re-creating the art of politics in line with new economic and cultural imperatives. A new, modern, and much more complicated America clearly was in the making.

Toward an American Culture

■ To what extent were American cultural expressions influenced by international forces?

■ How did developments in American arts and letters reflect the spirit of change during the Jacksonian era?

■ What other cultural consequences emerged from this dynamic era?

As Angelina Grimké's life illustrates, profound changes were taking place during the first decades of the nineteenth century that were altering traditional relationships between individuals and society. Both frontiersmen and city-dwellers became increasingly self-reliant, giving rise to a widespread commitment to individualism. The changing economic, social, and political systems that came to maturity in the Jacksonian era, as well as the character of the popular president himself, helped to fix this individualistic creed as a dominant force in an evolving American culture.

Traditional community ties based on close-knit, longtime social and family relationships could not survive in towns and villages where migrating opportunity seekers came and went. Nor could such ties develop and thrive in the growing trading and manufacturing centers where throngs of strangers massed to seek a better living. Instead, as visiting French nobleman **Alexis de Tocqueville** observed, Americans seemed to be "animated by the most selfish **cupidity**." Indeed, a new world of opportunity seemed open to those with the talent, desire, and good luck to pursue it. As Tocqueville also observed, "The government of democracy brings the notion of political rights to the level of the humblest citizens, just as the dissemination of wealth brings the notion of property within the reach of all the members of society."

Romanticism and Genteel Culture

Underlying the new mood in American thought and culture was a philosophical attitude sweeping across the Atlantic. **Romanticism,** the European philosophers' rebellion against Enlightenment reason (see page 102), stressed the heart over the mind, the wild over the controlled, the mystical over the rational. The United States, with its millions of acres of wilder-

Giving voice to the Romantic sentimentalism that rapidly was setting the tone for middle-class culture in early nineteenth-century America, women writers like Lydia Sigourney became virtual overnight celebrities, selling thousands of books to newly emerging urban consumers. This early daguerreotype, by African American photographer Augustus Washington, captures Sigourney at the height of her popularity and influence. *Watkinson Library, Trinity College, Hartford, Connecticut.*

ness, teeming populations of wild animals, and colorful frontier myths, was the perfect setting for romanticism to flower. Uniting individualism and romanticism, many of the era's leading intellectuals emphasized the positive aspects of life in the United States, cele-

Alexis de Tocqueville   French traveler and historian who toured the United States in 1831 and wrote *Democracy in America*, a classic study of American institutions and the American character.

cupidity   The extreme desire for wealth; greed.

romanticism   Artistic and intellectual movement characterized by interest in nature, emphasis on emotion and imagination over rationality, and rebellion against social conventions.

Chronology

Modernization and Rising Stress

1806	Journeyman shoemakers' strike in New York City
1821	Charles G. Finney experiences a religious conversion
1823	James Fenimore Cooper's *The Pioneers*
1825	Thomas Cole begins Hudson River school of painting Robert Owen establishes community at New Harmony, Indiana
1826	Shakers have eighteen communities in the United States
1828	Weavers protest and riot in New York City Andrew Jackson elected president
1829	Grand jury in Rochester, New York, declares alcohol most prominent cause of crime
1830	Joseph Smith Jr. publishes Book of Mormon
1831	Nat Turner's Rebellion William Lloyd Garrison begins publishing *The Liberator*
1832	Jackson reelected
1833	Lydia Sigourney publishes bestsellers *Letters to Young Ladies* and *How to Be Happy*
1834	Riot in Charlestown, Massachusetts, leads to destruction of Catholic convent

	George Bancroft publishes volume 1 of his American history Formation of National Trades' Union Formation of Whig Party
1835	Five Points riot in New York City
1836	Congress passes the gag rule Martin Van Buren elected president
1837	Horace Mann heads first public board of education Panic of 1837 Ralph Waldo Emerson's "American Scholar" speech
1838	Emerson articulates transcendentalism Angelina Grimké addresses Massachusetts state legislature on evils of slavery Sarah Grimké publishes *Letters on the Equality of the Sexes and the Condition of Women*
1839	Mormons build Nauvoo, Illinois
1840	Log-cabin campaign William Henry Harrison elected president
1841	Brook Farm established
1842	*Commonwealth v. Hunt*
1843	Dorothea Dix advocates state-funded insane asylums

brating it in forms of religious, literary, and artistic expression. In the process, they launched new forms of thought and presentation that won broad recognition among the genteel and middle classes.

Romanticism and individualism had their earliest impact in the religious realm. Reeling under the shock of social change that was affecting every aspect of life, many young people sought a religious anchor to bring themselves some stability. Many, especially in the rising cities in the Northeast, found a voice in New Englander **Ralph Waldo Emerson.**

Emerson was pastor of the prestigious Second Unitarian Church in Boston when tragedy struck: his young wife, Ellen Louisa, died in 1831. Emerson ex-

perienced a religious crisis and, looking for new inspiration, traveled to Europe. There he met the famous Romantic poets William Wordsworth and Thomas Carlyle, who influenced him to seek truth in nature and spirit rather than in rationality and order. Emerson combined this Romantic influence with his already strong Unitarian leaning, creating a new

Ralph Waldo Emerson   Philosopher, writer, and poet whose essays and poems made him a central figure in the transcendentalist movement and an important figure in the development of literary expression in the United States.

philosophical creed called **transcendentalism.** Recovered from his grief, he returned to the United States to begin a new career as an essayist and lecturer, spreading the transcendentalist message.

"Historical Christianity has fallen into the error that corrupts all attempts to communicate religion," Emerson told the students at the Harvard Divinity School in 1838. "It has dwelt, it dwells, with noxious exaggeration about the person of Jesus. Men have come to speak of revelation as somewhat long ago given and done, as if God were dead." But Emerson believed that God was far from dead. "The world is not the product of manifold power," Emerson taught, "but of one will, of one mind; and that one mind is everywhere active, in each ray of the star, in each wavelet of the pool." This being the case, Emerson went on, "The prayers and even the dogmas of our church, are . . . wholly insulated from anything now extant in the life and business of the people." Only through direct contact with the **transcendent** power in the universe could men and women know the truth. "It cannot be received at second hand," Emerson insisted, but only through the independent working of the liberated mind.

Although Emerson emphasized **nonconformity** and dissent in his writings, his ideas were in tune with the cultural and economic currents of his day. In celebrating the individual, Emerson validated the surging individualism of Jacksonian America. In addition, because each person had to find his or her own path to knowledge, Emerson could extol many of the disturbing aspects of modernizing America as potentially liberating forces. Rather than condemning the "selfish cupidity" that Tocqueville said characterized Jacksonian America, Emerson stated that money represented the "prose of life" and was, "in its effects and laws, as beautiful as roses."

Emerson not only set the tone for American philosophical inquiry but also suggested a bold new direction for American literature. In 1837 he issued a declaration of literary independence from European models in an address at Harvard University entitled "The American Scholar." Young American writers responded enthusiastically. During the twenty years following this speech, Henry David Thoreau, Walt Whitman, Henry Wadsworth Longfellow, and other writers and poets refined the transcendentalist gospel, emphasizing the uniqueness of the individual and the role of literature as a vehicle for self-discovery. "I celebrate myself, and sing myself," Whitman wrote. They also carried the Romantic message, celebrating the primitive and the common. Longfellow wrote of the legendary Indian chief Hiawatha (Hienwatha; see page 4) and sang the praise of the village blacksmith.

In "I Hear America Singing," Whitman conveyed the poetry present in the everyday speech of mechanics, carpenters, and other common folk.

Perhaps the most radical of the transcendentalists was Emerson's good friend and frequent houseguest **Henry David Thoreau.** Emerson and his other followers made the case for self-reliance, but Thoreau embodied it, camping on the shore of Walden Pond near Concord, Massachusetts, where he did his best to live independent of the rapidly modernizing market economy. "I went to the woods because I wished to live deliberately," Thoreau wrote, "and not, when I came to die, discover that I had not lived."

Like Thoreau, a number of women were also seeking meaning through their writing. Sarah Moore Grimké, elder sister of abolitionist Angelina Grimké, published a well-received essay on women's rights called *Letters on the Equality of the Sexes and the Condition of Women* in 1838. Margaret Fuller picked up on the same theme in her *Woman in the Nineteenth Century* (1845), after demonstrating her own equality by editing the highly influential transcendentalist magazine *The Dial* as well as serving as chief literary critic for the *New York Tribune*.

But the most popular women writers of the day were those who were most successful at communicating the sentimentalized role for the new genteel woman. **Lydia Sigourney** was one of the first American women to carve out an independent living as a writer. Her first book, *Moral Pieces, in Prose and Verse,* was published in 1815. By 1830 she was a regular contributor to over thirty popular magazines. Like many critics, Edgar Allan Poe dismissed her work as shallow and **mawkish,** but he actively solicited her writing

transcendentalism   A philosophical and literary movement asserting the existence of God within human beings and in nature and the belief that intuition is the highest source of knowledge.

transcendent   Lying beyond the normal range of experience.

nonconformity   Refusal to accept or conform to the beliefs and practices of the majority.

Henry David Thoreau   Writer and naturalist and friend of Ralph Waldo Emerson; his best-known work is *Walden* (1854).

Lydia Sigourney   Nineteenth-century Romantic and sentimental author who was one of the first women in American history to make a living as a professional writer.

mawkish   Mushy, exaggerated, and insincere sentimentality.

This 1827 painting by Thomas Cole, capturing a scene from James Fenimore Cooper's *Last of the Mohicans*, illustrates the Romantic mood current during the early nineteenth century. In line with artistic romanticism, nature dwarfs all else. Even a large Indian camp seems insignificant in size, lost in an exaggerated image of the mountains in the Hudson River region of New York. *"Last of the Mohicans" by Thomas Cole. Fenimore House Museum, New York State Historical Association, Cooperstown, NY.*

for his own magazine, the *Southern Literary Messenger.* In 1833 she published two bestsellers, *How to Be Happy* and *Letters to Young Ladies,* both of which emphasized Christian activism and the domestic ideal. Catharine Beecher was another woman writer who enjoyed enormous success for her practical advice guides aimed at making women more effective homemakers. The novels of women writers E. D. E. N. Southworth and Susan Warner were among the most popular books published in the first half of the nineteenth century.

Other authors joined Sigourney, Southworth, and Warner in pushing American literature in Romantic directions. James Fenimore Cooper and Nathaniel Hawthorne each helped to popularize American themes and scenes in their writing. Even before Emerson's "American Scholar," Cooper had launched a new sort of American novel and American hero. In *The Pioneers* (1823), Cooper introduced Natty Bumppo, also called Hawkeye, a frontiersman whose honesty, independent-mindedness, and skill as a marksman represented the rough-hewn virtues so beloved by Romantics and popularly associated with the American frontier. Altogether, Cooper wrote five novels featuring the plucky Bumppo, and they all sold well.

Nathaniel Hawthorne explored a different but equally American literary theme: the tension between good and evil. In *Twice-Told Tales* (1837), Hawthorne presented readers with a collection of moral **allegories** stressing the evils of pride, selfishness, and secret guilt among puritanical New Englanders. He brought these themes to fruition in his novel *The Scarlet Letter* (1850), in which adulteress Hester Prynne overcomes shame to gain redemption while her secret lover, Puritan minister Arthur Dimmesdale, is destroyed by his hidden sins.

allegory   A story in which characters and events stand for abstract ideas and suggest a deep, symbolic meaning.

George Bancroft did for American history what novelists like Cooper did for American literature. A prominent Jacksonian, Bancroft set out to capture in writing the unique nature of the American experience. His history of the United States from the first settlement of the continent through the American Revolution eventually filled ten volumes, published between 1834 and 1874. From Bancroft's perspective, Jacksonian democracy was the perfect form for human government and was the product of the complex history of the American nation. Focusing on strong leaders who carried out God's design by bringing liberty into the world, Bancroft made clear that the middle-class qualities of individualism, self-sufficiency, and a passionate love of liberty were the essence of the American experience and the American genius. Bancroft's history became the definitive work of its kind, influencing generations of American students and scholars in their interpretations of the nation's past.

The drive to celebrate American scenes and the young nation's uniqueness also influenced the visual arts during this period. **Neoclassicism** had dominated the art scene during the late eighteenth century and first decades of the nineteenth. Influenced by Enlightenment rationalism, neoclassical artists brought to their painting and sculpture the simple, logical lines found in Greek and Roman art. They often used classical imagery in their portrayals of contemporary figures and events. Horatio Greenough's statue of George Washington, for example, presented the nation's first president wrapped in a toga, looking like a Greek god.

After 1825, however, classical scenes were gradually being replaced by American ones. Englishman Thomas Cole came to the United States in 1818 hoping to find a romantic paradise. Disappointed by the neoclassical art scene in Philadelphia, Cole began traveling into the American interior. In the Hudson River valley Cole found the paradise he was seeking, and he began painting romantically exaggerated renderings of these locales. The refreshing naturalness and Americanness of Cole's landscapes attracted a large following, and other artists took up the style. This group of landscapists is known as the **Hudson River school,** after the area where most of its members painted.

Another movement in American art that reflected the temper of the time is exemplified by the paintings of George Caleb Bingham. Bingham was born in Virginia and educated for a time in Pennsylvania before he went west to Missouri. There he painted realistic pictures of common people engaged in everyday activities. The flatboatmen, marketplace-dwellers, and electioneering politicians in Bingham's paintings were artistic testimony to the emerging democratic style of America in the Jacksonian period (see illustrations on pages 286 and 292).

Culture Among Workers and Slaves

Most genteel people in the antebellum era would have denied that working people, whether the wage-earning immigrants in northern cities or slaves in the South, had a "culture." But each of these groups crafted viable cultures that suited their living and working conditions and were distinct from the genteel culture of their owners or supervisors.

Wretched living conditions and dispiriting poverty encouraged working-class people in northern cities to choose social and cultural outlets that were very different from those of upper- and middle-class Americans. Offering temporary relief from unpleasant conditions, drinking was the social distraction of choice among working people. Whiskey and gin were cheap and available during the 1820s and 1830s as western farmers used the new roads and canals to ship distilled spirits to urban markets. In the 1830s, consumers could purchase a gallon of whiskey for 25 cents.

Even activities that did not center on drinking tended to involve it. While genteel and middle-class people remained in their private homes reading Sigourney or Hawthorne, working people attended popular theaters cheering entertainments designed to appeal to their less polished tastes. **Minstrel shows** featured fast-paced music and raucous comedy. Plays, such as Benjamin Baker's *A Glance at New York in 1848*, presented caricatures of working-class "Bowery B'hoys" and "G'hals" and of the well-off-Broadway "pumpkins" they poked fun at. To put the audience in the proper mood, theater owners sold cheap drinks in the lobby or in basement pubs. Alcohol was also usually sold at sporting events that drew large work-

---

neoclassicism   A revival in architecture and art in the eighteenth and nineteenth centuries inspired by Greek and Roman models and characterized by order, symmetry, and simplicity of style.

Hudson River school   The first native school of landscape painting in the United States (1825–1875); it attracted artists rebelling against the neoclassical tradition.

minstrel show   A variety show in which white actors made up as blacks presented jokes, songs, dances, and comic skits.

Slave artisans often fashioned beautiful and functional items that incorporated both European and African design motifs, creating a unique material culture in the American South. A potter, now known only as Dave, crafted enormous storage jars (some examples of his work hold 30 gallons or more) that he inscribed with original poetry. Slave women often used needlework as a means of self-expression, as exemplified by this Star of Bethlehem quilt, crafted by a slave in Texas known only as Aunt Peggy. *Storage jar: Collection of McKissick Museum, University of South Carolina; quilt: Cincinnati Art Museum. Gift of Mrs. Cletus T. Palmer.*

ing-class audiences—bare-knuckle boxing contests, for instance, where the fighting was seldom confined to the boxing ring.

Stinging from their low status in the urbanizing and industrializing society, angry about living in hovels, and freed from inhibitions by hours of drinking, otherwise rational workingmen often pummeled one another to let off steam. And in working-class neighborhoods, where police forces were small, fistfights often turned into brawls and then into riots pitting Protestants against Catholics, immigrants against the native-born, and whites against blacks.

Working-class women experienced the same dull but dangerous working conditions and dismal living circumstances as working-class men, but their lives were even harder. Single women were particularly bad off. They were paid significantly less than men but had to pay as much and sometimes more for living quarters, food, and clothing. Marriage could reduce a woman's personal expenses—but at a cost. While men

congregated in the barbershop or candy store drinking and socializing during their leisure hours, married women were stuck in tiny apartments caring for children and doing household chores.

Like their northern counterparts, slaves fashioned for themselves a culture that helped them to survive and to maintain their humanity under dehumanizing conditions. The degree to which African practices endured in America is remarkable, for slaves seldom came to southern plantations directly from Africa. What evolved was a truly unique African American culture.

Traces of African heritage were visible in slaves' clothing, entertainment, and folkways. Often the plain garments that masters provided were upgraded with colorful headscarves and other decorations similar to ornaments worn in Africa. Hairstyles often resembled those characteristic of African tribes. Music, dancing, and other forms of public entertainment and celebration also showed strong African roots. Musical instruments were copies of traditional ones, modified only by the use of New World materials. And stories that were told around the stoves at night were a New World adaptation of African **trickster tales.** Other links to Africa abounded. Healers among the slaves used African ceremonies, Christian rituals, and both imported and native herbs to effect cures. Taken together, these survivals and adaptations of African traditions provided a strong base underlying a solid African American culture.

Abiding family ties helped to make possible this cultural continuity. Slave families endured despite kinship ties made fragile by their highly precarious life. Children could be taken away from their parents, husbands separated from wives at the whim of masters. And anyone might be sold at any time. Families that remained intact, however, remained stable. When families did suffer separation, the **extended family** of grandparents and other relatives offered emotional support and helped maintain some sense of continuity. Another African legacy, the concept of fictive kinship (see page 16) also contributed to family stability by turning the whole community of slaves into a vast network of aunts and uncles.

Within families, the separation of work along age and gender lines followed traditional patterns. Slave women, when not laboring at the assigned tasks of plantation work, generally performed domestic duties and tended children, while the men hunted, fished, did carpentry, and performed other "manly" tasks. Children were likely to help out by tending family gardens and doing other light work until they were old enough to join their parents in the fields or learn skilled trades.

Slaves' religion, like family structure, was another means for preserving unique African American traits. White churches virtually ignored the religious needs of slaves before the mid-eighteenth century. During the Great Awakening (see page 103), however, many white evangelicals turned their attention to the spiritual life of slaves. "Your Negroes may be ignorant and stupid as to divine Things," evangelical Samuel Davies told slaveowners, "not for Want of Capacity, but for Want of Instruction; not through their Perverseness, but through your Negligence." In the face of slaveowners' negligence, evangelical Presbyterians, Baptists, and Methodists took it upon themselves to carry the Christian message to slaves.

Though the designation Baptist or Methodist would suggest that the Christianity practiced by slaves resembled the religion practiced by southern whites, it differed in significant ways. Slave preachers untrained in white theology often equated Christian and African

religious figures, creating unique African American religious symbols. Ceremonies too combined African practices such as group dancing with Christian prayer. The merging of African musical forms with Christian lyrics gave rise to a new form of Christian music: the **spiritual.** Masters often encouraged such worship, thinking that the Christian emphasis on obedience and meekness would make slaves more productive and more peaceful servants. Some, however, discouraged religion among their slaves, fearing that large congregations of slaves might be moved to rebellion. Thus some religious slaves had to meet in secret to practice their own particular form of Christianity.

Radical Attempts to Regain Community

To many of all classes, society seemed to be spinning out of control as modernization rearranged basic lifestyles during the antebellum period. Some religious groups and social thinkers tried to ward off the excesses of Jacksonian individualism by forming **utopian** communities that experimented with various living arrangements and ideological commitments. They hoped to strike a new balance between self-sufficiency and community support.

A wealthy Welsh industrialist, Robert Owen, began one of the earliest experiments along these lines. In 1825 he purchased a tract of land on the Wabash River in Indiana called **New Harmony.** Believing that the solution to poverty in modern society was to collect the unemployed into self-contained and self-supporting villages, Owen opened a textile factory in which own-

---

trickster tales Stories that feature as a central character a clever figure who uses his wits and instincts to adapt to changing times; a survivor, the trickster is used by traditional societies, including African cultures, to teach important cultural lessons.

extended family A family group consisting of various close relatives as well as the parents and children.

spiritual A religious folk song originated by African Americans, often expressing a longing for deliverance from the constraints and hardships of their lives.

utopian Idealistic reform sentiment based on the belief that a perfect society can be created on Earth and that a particular group or leader has the knowledge to actually create such a society.

New Harmony Utopian community that Robert Owen established in Indiana in 1825; economic problems and discord among members led to its failure two years later.

On one of his western tours, artist Karl Bodmer paused to paint this view of New Harmony, Welsh philanthropist Robert Owen's experimental utopian community in Indiana. Like many similar communities, this peaceful commune was destroyed by a combination of internal dissension and pressure from suspicious and often jealous outsiders. *"View of New Harmony" by Karl Bodmer, 1833. Maximilian-Bodmer Collection, Joslyn Art Museum.*

ership was held communally by the workers and decisions were made by group consensus. Even though the community instituted innovations like an eight-hour workday, cultural activities for workers, and the nation's first school offering equal education to boys and girls, New Harmony did not succeed. Owen and his son, Robert Dale Owen, were outspoken critics of organized religion and joined their close associate **Frances (Fanny) Wright** in advocating radical causes. These leanings made the Owenites unpopular with more traditional Americans, and when their mill experienced economic hardship in 1827, New Harmony collapsed.

A more famous experiment, **Brook Farm,** had its origin in the transcendentalist movement but later flirted with **socialistic** ideas like those practiced at New Harmony. The brainchild of George Ripley, Brook Farm was designed to "prepare a society of liberal, intelligent and cultivated persons, whose relations with each other would permit a more wholesome and simple life than can be led amidst the pressure of our competitive institutions." To carry out this enter-

prise Ripley set up a joint-stock company, selling the initial twenty-four shares of stock for $500 each. Most of the stockholders were transcendentalist celebrities such as Nathaniel Hawthorne and Ralph Waldo Emerson. Rather than living and working at the site as Ripley had hoped they would, most just dropped in from time to time. Disappointed, in 1844 Ripley adopted a

Frances (Fanny) Wright Infamous nineteenth-century woman who advocated what at the time were considered radical causes, including racial equality, equality for women, birth control, and open sexuality.

Brook Farm An experimental farm based on cooperative living; established in 1841, it first attracted transcendentalists and then serious farmers before fire destroyed it in 1845.

socialist Practicing socialism, the public ownership of manufacturing, farming, and other forms of production so that they benefit society rather than produce individual or corporate profits.

new constitution based on the socialist ideas of Frenchman Charles Fourier. **Fourierism** emphasized community self-sufficiency, the equal sharing of earnings among members of the community, and the periodic redistribution of tasks and status to prevent boredom and elitism. With this new disciplined ideology in place, Brook Farm began to appeal to serious artisans and farmers, but a disastrous fire in 1845 cut the experiment short. Other Fourierist communities were also founded during this period—nearly a hundred such organizations sprang up from Massachusetts to Michigan—and although none achieved Brook Farm's notoriety, all shared the same unsuccessful fate.

Some communal experiments were grounded in various religious beliefs. The **Oneida Community,** established in central New York in 1848, for example, reflected the notions of its founder, John Humphrey Noyes. Though educated in theology at Andover and Yale, Noyes could find no church willing to ordain him because of his strange belief that his followers could escape sin through faith in God, communal living, and group marriage. Unlike Brook Farm and New Harmony, the Oneida Community was very successful financially, establishing thriving logging, farming, and manufacturing businesses. It was finally dissolved as the result of local pressures directed at the "free love" practiced by its members.

Economically successful communes operated by the **Shakers,** an offshoot of the Quakers, tried to sidestep the Oneida Community's problems by banning sex altogether. Founded in Britain in 1770 and then transported to America in 1774, the sect grew slowly at first, but in the excitement of the early nineteenth century, it expanded at a more vigorous rate. By 1826 eighteen Shaker communities had been planted in eight states. Throughout the Jacksonian era and after, the Shakers established communal farms and grew to a population of nearly six thousand. The Shaker communities succeeded by pursuing farming activities and the manufacture and sale of furniture and handcrafts admired for their design and workmanship. But like the Oneida Community, the Shakers' ideas about marriage and family stirred up controversy. In a number of cases, converts deserted husbands or wives in order to join the organization, often bringing their children with them. This led to several highly publicized lawsuits. Controversy also raged over the practice in some areas of turning orphaned children or other public **wards** over to the Shakers. Like most such experiments, the Shaker movement went into decline after 1860, though vestiges of it remain operative today.

The group that was most successful at joining the religious fervor of the Second Great Awakening with the inclination to communalism was a peculiarly American movement founded by New York farmer **Joseph Smith Jr.** Smith's story is surrounded by a haze of religious zeal and myth, but he reported that in 1827 an angel named Moroni led him to a set of golden plates inscribed in a strange hieroglyphic language. Church tradition holds that Smith and a series of secretaries worked for nearly two years to translate the writing on the plates. The result of their effort was the Book of Mormon, first printed and available for purchase in 1830.

Although the Book of Mormon greatly resembled the books of the Old Testament and purported to be a truly ancient document, it captured many of the themes that most appealed to Americans during the restless Jacksonian era. In line with Romantic literature, the Book of Mormon evoked a mythic past. In adventure passages that rival Cooper's, Smith's testament traces the history of America back to the migrations of several Old World groups during biblical times. According to the Book of Mormon, one group, the Lamanites, sank into barbarity and became the forefathers of the American Indians. Another group, the Nephites, tried to return the Lamanites to the true religion but failed and was nearly destroyed by the Lamanites. Finally, only two Nephites remained: Mormon and his son Moroni. In the year 384, they buried the golden plates chronicling America's hidden past and its place in God's unfolding plan for the universe. Moroni, in the form of an angel, waited for a true spiritual descendant to whom he might reveal

Fourierism Social system advanced by Frenchman Charles Fourier, who argued that people were capable of living in perfect harmony under the right conditions, which included communal life and republican government.

Oneida Community A religious community established in central New York in 1848; its members shared property, practiced group marriage, and reared children under communal care.

Shakers A mid-eighteenth-century offshoot of the Quakers, founded in England by Mother Ann Lee; Shakers engaged in spirited worship, including dancing and rhythmic shaking, hence their name, and practiced communal living and strict celibacy.

ward A child who is legally put into the care of someone other than a parent.

Joseph Smith, Jr. Founder of the Church of Jesus Christ of Latter-day Saints, also known as the Mormon Church, who transcribed the Book of Mormon and led his congregation westward from New York to Illinois; he was later murdered by an anti-Mormon mob.

the plates and their truths. Smith proclaimed that he was that descendant.

In 1830 Smith founded the Church of Jesus Christ of Latter-day Saints—also called the Mormon Church, after the prophet Mormon. Announcing that he had experienced a revelation that called for him to establish a community "on the borders by the Lamanites," Smith led his congregation as a unit out of New York in 1831 to settle in the northeastern Ohio village of Kirtland. There the people known as Mormons thrived for a while, stressing notions of community, faith, and hard work. The Mormons tended to be clannish, however, keeping to themselves and excluding others, making outsiders suspicious. In addition, the tight discipline practiced by the Mormon community not only made them more prosperous than most surrounding farms and villages but also gave them considerable political clout as church members engaged in **block voting.**

There, too, economic pressure, internal dissension, and religious persecution convinced Smith to lead his followers farther west into Missouri. Again the Mormons faced serious resentment from frontiersmen. Smith then decided to relocate his congregation to the Illinois frontier, founding the city of Nauvoo in 1839. Continuing conversions to the new faith brought a flood of Mormons to Smith's Zion in Illinois. In 1844 Nauvoo, with a population of fifteen thousand Mormons, dwarfed every other Illinois city.

Reactions to Changing Conditions

■ How did Americans deal with the stresses created by rapid change during the Jacksonian era?

■ What were the cultural consequences of their actions?

In the grasping, competitive conditions that were emerging in the dynamic new America, an individual's status, reputation, and welfare seemed to depend exclusively on his or her economic position. The combination of rapid geographical expansion and unprecedented opportunities in business produced a highly precarious social world for all Americans. Desperate for some stability, many pushed for various reforms to bring the fast-spinning world under control.

A Second Great Awakening

Popular religion was a major counterbalance to the modernizing tendencies that shocked many Americans as the Great Transformation progressed. While some were drawn to transcendentalism and a hand-

ful chose to follow radical communitarian leaders, others sought solace within existing, mainstream denominations. Beginning in the 1790s both theologians and popular preachers sought to create a new Protestant creed that would maintain the notion of Christian community in an atmosphere of increasing individualism and competition.

Mirroring tendencies in the political and economic realms, Protestant thinking during the opening decades of the nineteenth century emphasized the role of the individual. Preachers such as Jonathan Edwards and George Whitefield had moved in this direction during the Great Awakening of the 1740s, but many Protestant theologians continued to share the conviction that salvation was a gift from God that individuals could do nothing to earn (see page 103). Timothy Dwight, Jonathan Edwards's grandson, took the first step toward liberalizing this position in the 1790s, but it fell to his students at Yale College, especially Nathaniel Taylor, to create a new theology that was entirely consistent with the prevailing secular creed of individualism. According to this new doctrine, God offers salvation to all, but it is the individual's responsibility to seek it. Thus the individual has "free will" to choose or not choose salvation. Taylor's ideas struck a responsive chord in a restless and expanding America. Hundreds of ordained ministers, licensed preachers, and **lay exhorters** carried the message of individual empowerment to an anxious populace.

Unlike Calvinist Puritanism, which characterized women as the weaker sex, the new evangelicalism stressed women's spiritual equality with—and even spiritual superiority to—men. Not surprisingly, young women generally were the first to respond to the new message: during the 1820s and 1830s, women often outnumbered men by two to one in new evangelical congregations. The most highly effective preachers of the day took advantage of this appeal, turning women into agents spreading the word to their husbands, brothers, and children.

Charles Grandison Finney was one of the most effective among the new generation of preachers. A former schoolteacher and lawyer, Finney experienced a soul-shattering religious conversion in 1821. Declaring that "the Lord Jesus Christ" had retained him "to

block voting The practice by organized groups of people to coordinate their voting so that all members vote the same way, thereby enhancing the group's political influence.

lay exhorter A church member who preaches but is not an ordained minister.

After becoming the president of Oberlin College, evangelist Charles G. Finney reenacted the traveling tent revivals that had brought him into national prominence as the leading spokesman for the new evangelicalism that arose during the Second Great Awakening. *Oberlin College Archives, Oberlin, Ohio.*

plead his cause," Finney performed on the pulpit as a spirited attorney might argue a case in court. A religious revival "is not a miracle, or dependent on a miracle in any sense," Finney announced, to the shock of conservative Calvinists. Arguing for souls was like moving a judge to make the right decision in a lawsuit—the result of effective persuasion. Seating those most likely to be converted on a special "anxious bench," Finney focused on them as a lawyer might a jury. The result was likely to be dramatic. Many of the targeted people fainted, experienced bodily spasms, or cried out in hysteria. Such dramatic presentations and results brought Finney enormous publicity, which he and an army of imitators used to gain access to communities all over the West and Northeast. The result was a nearly continuous season of religious revival. The **Second Great Awakening** spread from rural community to rural community like a wildfire until, in the late 1830s, Finney carried the fire into Boston and New York.

Revival meetings were remarkable affairs. Usually beginning on a Thursday and continuing until the following Tuesday, they drew together huge crowds who listened to spirited preaching in the evenings and engaged in religious study, conversation, and wrenching soul searching during the daylight hours.

Second Great Awakening An upsurge in religious fervor that began around 1800 and was characterized by revival meetings.

revival meeting A meeting for the purpose of reawakening religious faith, often characterized by impassioned preaching and emotional public testimony by converted sinners.

At one such meeting, as many as twenty-five thousand people listened to forty different preachers. As one witness proclaimed, there were "loud ejaculations of prayer . . . some struck with terror . . . others, trembling weeping and crying out . . . fainting and swooning away."

The new revivals led to the breakdown of traditional church organizations and the creation of various Christian denominations. **Evangelical sects** such as the Presbyterians, Baptists, and Methodists split into groups who supported the new theology and those who clung to more traditional notions. Church splits also occurred for reasons that now seem petty. One Baptist congregation, for example, split over the hypothetical question of whether it would be a sin to lie to marauding Indians in order to protect hidden family members. Those who said lying to protect one's family was no sin formed a separate congregation of so-called Lying Baptists. Those who said lying was sinful under any circumstances gathered as Truth-Telling Baptists.

In the face of such fragmentation, all denominations voiced concern that state support of any one church would give that denomination an artificial advantage in the continuing competition for souls. Oddly, those most fervent in their Christian beliefs joined deists and other Enlightenment-influenced thinkers in arguing steadfastly for the continued and even more stringent separation of church and state. This, in turn, added to the spirit of competition as individual congregations vied for voluntary contributions to keep their churches alive.

Even though religious conversion had become an individual matter and competition for tithes a genuine concern, revivalists did not ignore the notion of community. In fact, preachers like Finney put great emphasis on creating a single Christian community to stand in opposition to sin. One proclaimed deep impatience with "Old Church Hipocrites who think more of their particular denomination than Christ Church." Finney himself wrote that during his revivals, "Christians of every denomination generally seemed to make common cause, and went to work with a will, to pull sinners out of the fire." As one Finney convert wrote to his sister, "We are either marching toward heaven or towards hell. How is it with you?"

"I know this is all algebra to those who have never felt it," Finney said. "But to those who have experienced the agony of wrestling, prevailing prayer, for the conversion of a soul, you may depend on it, that soul . . . appears as dear as a child is to the mother who brought it forth with pain." This intimate connection forged bonds of mutual responsibility, giving a generation of isolated individuals something to rally around, a common starting point for joint action. According to the new theology, it was the convert's duty to carry the message of the free gift of salvation to the multitudes still in darkness. Another strong goad to Christian activism at this time was the rise of **postmillennialism** among Second Great Awakening theologians and other believers. Understanding it to be their divine commission to bring on the return of Christ by converting and perfecting the world, postmillennialists threw themselves into what they believed was God's design for them. Evangelicalism and postmillennialism together formed the core for an activist ideology by which new congregations, missionary societies, and a thousand other benevolent groups rose up to lead America and the world in the continuing battle against sin.

Free and Slave Labor Protests

While the new forms of religion appealed to many northern workers and southern slaves, others in both groups blamed their miseries not on sin but on their exploitation by others. In view of their grim working and living conditions, it is not surprising that some manufacturing workers and slave laborers protested their situations. In both cases, the most skilled and well educated took the lead in making their dissatisfaction with the new modes of production known to factory owners and plantation masters.

The first organized labor strike in America took place in 1806, when a group of journeyman shoemakers stopped work to protest the hiring of unskilled workers to perform some tasks that higher-paid journeymen and apprentices had been doing. The strike failed when a New York court declared the shoemakers' actions illegal, but in the years to come many other journeymen's groups would try the same tactic. In large part they were reacting to the mechanization that threatened their jobs and their social position. In addition, they bemoaned their loss of power to set hours, conditions, and wages for the work they

evangelical sects Protestant groups that emphasized the sole authority of the Bible and the necessity of actively striving to convert others.

postmillennialism The tenet in some Christian theology teaching that Christ will return to Earth after religious activists have succeeded in converting all people to Christianity and following a thousand years under their godly rule.

performed; industrialization robbed them of their status as independent contractors and forced many to become wage laborers.

Instead of attacking or even criticizing industrialization, however, journeymen simply asked for what they believed was their fair piece of the pie: decent wages and working conditions and some role in decision making—all of which they had traditionally possessed. Throughout the industrializing cities of the Northeast and the smaller manufacturing centers of the West, journeymen banded together in **trade unions:** assemblies of skilled workers grouped by specific occupation. During the 1830s, trade unions from neighboring towns merged with one another to form the beginnings of a national trade union movement. In this way, house carpenters, shoemakers, handloom weavers, printers, and comb makers established national unions through which they attempted to enforce uniform wage standards in their industries. In 1834 journeymen's organizations from a number of industries joined to form the **National Trades' Union,** the first labor organization in the nation's history to represent many different crafts.

The trade union movement, however, accomplished little during the antebellum period. Factory owners, bankers, and others who had a vested interest in keeping labor cheap and, in their view, making it more efficient used every device available to prevent unions from gaining the upper hand. Employers countered the national trade unions by forming associations to resist union activity. They also used the courts to keep organized labor from disrupting business.

Despite such efforts, a number of strikes affected American industries during the 1830s. In 1834 women working in the textile mills in Lowell, Massachusetts, closed down production in response to a 25 percent reduction in their wages. And they proved their organizational skills and economic clout again two years later when they struck over an increase in boarding house rates. Such demonstrations of power by workers frightened manufacturers, and gradually over the next two decades, employers replaced native-born women in the factories with immigrants, who were less liable to organize successfully and, more important, less likely to win approval from sympathetic judges or consumers.

Still, workers won some small victories in the battle to organize. A significant breakthrough finally came in 1842 when the Massachusetts Supreme Court decided in the case of *Commonwealth v. Hunt* that Boston's journeymen boot makers were within their rights to organize "in such manner as best to subserve their own interests" and to call strikes. By that time, however, economic changes had so undermined labor's ability to withstand the rigors of strikes and court cases that legal protection became somewhat meaningless.

Not all labor protests were as peaceful as the shoemakers' strike. In 1828, for example, immigrant weavers protested the pitiful wages paid by Alexander Knox, New York City's leading textile employer. Storming Knox's home to demand higher pay, the weavers invaded and vandalized the house and beat Knox's son and a cordon of police guards. The rioters then marched to the garret and basement homes of weavers who had refused to join the protest and destroyed their looms.

Not all the riots that occurred in American cities during these years were directly related to working conditions. Notable were ethnic riots that shook New York, Philadelphia, and Boston during the late 1820s and 1830s. In 1834, for example, rumors began circulating in Boston that innocent girls were being held captive and tortured in a Catholic convent in nearby Charlestown. A Protestant mob stormed the building, leaving it a heap of smoldering ashes. A year later, in New York's notoriously overcrowded and lawless Five Points District, roving gangs of native-born Protestant and immigrant Irish Catholic men battled in the streets. The ethnic tension evident in these and other riots was the direct result of declining economic power and terrible living conditions—and worker desperation. Native-born journeymen blamed immigrants for lowered wages and loss of status. Immigrants simmered with hatred at being treated like dirt by their native-born coworkers.

Unlike workers in the North, who at least had some legal protections and civil rights, slaves had nothing but their own wits to protect them against a society that classed them as disposable personal property. Slaves were skilled at the use of **passive resistance.** Clever strategies for getting extra food, clothing, and other supplies were passed on from generation to generation. Slaves often stole food, not because they were hungry but because its unexplainable disappearance flustered their masters. Farm ani-

---

trade union A labor organization whose members work in a specific trade or craft.

National Trades' Union The first national association of trade unions in the United States; it was formed in 1834.

passive resistance Resistance by nonviolent methods.

mals also disappeared mysteriously, tools broke in puzzling ways, people fell ill from unknown diseases, and workers got lost on the way to fields—all these events were subtle signs of slaves' discontent. Slaves also used flattery and trickery, convincing whites that slave-initiated improvements were really the master's idea.

The importance of passive resistance was evident in the folk tales and songs that circulated among slaves. Perhaps the best-known example is the stories of Br'er—that is, Brother—Rabbit, a classic trickster figure who uses deceit to get what he wants. In one particularly revealing tale, Br'er Rabbit is caught by Br'er Fox, who threatens Rabbit with all sorts of horrible tortures. Rabbit begs Br'er Fox to do anything but throw him into the nearby briar patch. Seizing on Rabbit's apparent fear, Fox unties Br'er Rabbit and pitches him deep into the middle of the briar patch, expecting to see the rabbit struggle and die amid the thorns. Br'er Rabbit, however, scampers away through the briars, calling back over his shoulder that he was born and bred in a briar patch and laughing at Br'er Fox's gullibility. Such stories taught slaves how to deal cleverly with powerful adversaries.

Not all slave resistance was passive. Perhaps the most common form of active resistance was running away (see Map 12.1). The number of slaves who escaped may never be known, though some estimate that an average of about a thousand made their way to freedom each year. Most of these lived in **border states,** where freedom lay perhaps only a few miles away from the slave quarters. Large numbers also escaped from Texas and other states where the nearby Mexican border or the Indian frontier promised protection and relative freedom.

Of all the slaves who made the run to freedom during the reign of King Cotton, fully a third were artisans, wagoners, boat pilots, and other specially skilled and privileged slaves, and more than 80 percent were men between the ages of 16 and 35. Young men were not likely to be burdened with family responsibilities and had the physical strength to resist capture, and artisans, almost all of whom were men, had viable economic options in the free world and the relative liberty to move around without constant supervision. But running away was always a dangerous gamble. One former slave recalled, "No man who has never been placed in such a situation can comprehend the thousand obstacles thrown in the way of the flying slave. Every white man's hand is raised against him—the patrollers are watching for him—the hounds are ready to follow on his track."

Anti-Catholic and anti-immigrant feelings often caused rioting in American cities during the 1830s and 1840s. In 1834, street violence escalated into a full-fledged riot in Massachusetts, leading to the burning of a Catholic convent in Charlestown, a Boston suburb. This engraving, which adorned the covers of a number of pamphlets that purported to tell the true lurid story of the events surrounding the fire, shows the convent ablaze as fire companies try in vain to smother the flames. Though the most notorious event of this kind that occurred during this era, this riot was anything but exceptional. *The Nun of St. Ursula: Burning of the Convent by Harry Hazel.*

Besides the undeniable appeal of freedom, some more immediate factors seem to have prompted slaves to risk running away. Frederick Douglass, who later became a famous abolitionist leader, was a skilled craftsman who ran away because he finally grew tired of turning his wages over to his master. Most contemporary observers thought that fear of punishment for some crime was the most common motivation for flight. Some slaves, however, reported that they ran not because they had done something that merited punishment but to keep themselves from doing so. "They didn't do something and run," one former slave reported. "They run before they did it, 'cause they knew that if they struck a white man there wasn't going to be a nigger. In them days they run to keep from doing something." Yet another strong motivation for running was to keep families together or to reunite, if only for a short time. Advertisements for runaway slaves often contained such comments as "He is no doubt trying to reach his wife."

border states   The slave states of Delaware, Maryland, Virginia, Kentucky, and Missouri, which shared a border with states in which slavery was illegal.

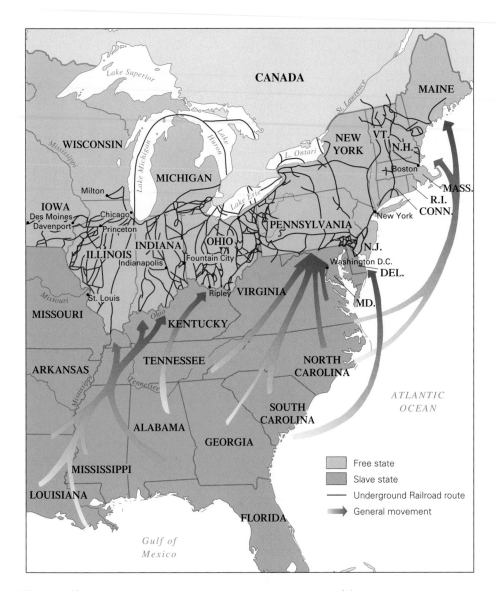

MAP 12.1 Escaping from Slavery Running away was one of the most prominent forms of slave resistance during the antebellum period. Success often depended on help from African Americans who had already gained their freedom and from sympathetic whites. Beginning in the 1820s an informal and secret network called the Underground Railroad provided escape routes for slaves who were daring enough to risk all for freedom. The routes shown here are based on documentary evidence, but the network's secrecy makes it impossible to know if they are drawn entirely accurately.

The most frightening form of slave resistance was open and armed revolt. Despite slaveholders' best efforts, slaves planned an unknown number of rebellions during the antebellum period, and many of them were actually carried out. The most serious and violent of these uprisings was the work of a black preacher, Nat Turner. After years of planning and organization, in 1831 Turner led a force of about seventy slaves in a predawn raid against the slaveholding households in Southampton County, Virginia. It took four days for white forces to stop the assault. During that time, the slaves slaughtered and mutilated fifty-

No pictures of famed slave revolt leader Nat Turner are known to exist, but this nineteenth-century painting illustrates how one artist imagined the appearance of Turner and his fellow conspirators. White southerners lived in terror of scenes such as this and passed severe laws designed to prevent African Americans from ever having such meetings. *Granger Collection.*

five white men, women, and children. Angry, terrified whites finally captured and executed Turner and sixteen of his followers.

In the wake of Nat Turner's Rebellion, fear of slave revolts reached paranoid levels in the South, especially in areas where slaves greatly outnumbered whites. After reading about and seeing a play depicting a slave insurrection, Mary Boykin Chesnut gave expression to the fear that plagued whites in the slave South: "What a thrill of terror ran through me as those yellow and black brutes came jumping over the parapets! Their faces were like so many of the same sort at home. . . . How long would they resist the seductive and irresistible call: 'Rise, kill, and be free!'"

Frightened and often outnumbered, whites felt justified in imposing stringent restrictions and using harsh methods to enforce them. Southern courts and legislatures clapped stricter controls on the freedoms granted to slaves and to free blacks. In most areas, free African Americans were denied the right to own guns, buy liquor, hold public assemblies, testify in court, and vote. Slaves were forbidden to own any private property, to attend unsupervised worship ser-

vices, and to learn reading and writing. Also, codes that prevented slaves from being unsupervised in towns virtually eliminated slaves as independent urban craftsmen after 1840. In many areas of the South, white citizens formed local **vigilance committees,** bands of armed men who rode through the countryside to overawe slaves and dissuade them from attempting to escape or rebel. Local authorities pressed court clerks, ship captains, and other officials to limit the freedom of blacks. White critics of slavery—who had been numerous, vocal, and well respected before the birth of King Cotton—were harassed, prosecuted, and sometimes beaten into silence.

The Middle Class and Moral Reform

Witnessing the squalor and violence in working-class districts and the deteriorating condition for slaves led many genteel and middle-class Americans to push for reforms. The missionary activism that accompanied the Second Great Awakening dovetailed with this reformist inclination. The **Christian benevolence** movement gave rise to hundreds of voluntary societies ranging from maternal associations designed to improve child rearing to political lobby groups aiming at outlawing alcohol, Sunday mail delivery, and other perceived evils. Such activism drew them together in common causes and led to deep friendships and a shared sense of commitment—antidotes to the alienation and loneliness common in the competitive world of the early nineteenth century.

As traditional family and village life broke down in the new America, voluntary societies pressed for public intervention to address social problems. The new theology reinforced the reforming impulse by emphasizing that even the most depraved might be saved if proper means were applied. This idea had immediate application in the realm of crime and punishment. Reformers characterized criminals not as evil but as lost and in need of divine guidance. In Auburn, New York, an experimental prison system

vigilance committees Groups of armed private citizens who use the threat of mob violence to enforce their own interpretation of the law.

Christian benevolence A tenet in some Christian theology teaching that the essence of God is self-sacrificing love and that the ultimate duty for Christians is to perform acts of kindness with no expectation of reward in return.

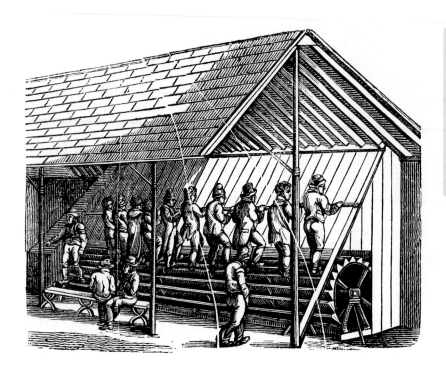

Prison reformers insisted that idleness was symptomatic of the criminal personality and insisted that only a combination of exhausting physical exercise, solitary confinement, and silence were necessary to affecting rehabilitation. At the experimental prison in Auburn, New York, officials erected a huge step-wheel, chaining prisoners and forcing them to climb for extended periods of time, seeking to instill discipline. © *Collection of the New York Historical Society.*

put prisoners to work during the day, condemned them to absolute silence during mealtimes, and locked them away in solitary confinement at night. Reformers believed that this combination of hard work, discipline, and solitude would put criminals on the path to productive lives and spiritual renewal.

Mental illness underwent a similar change in definition. Rather than viewing the mentally ill as hopeless cases doomed by an innate spiritual flaw, reformers now spoke of them as lost souls in need of help. **Dorothea Dix,** a young, compassionate, and reform-minded teacher, advocated publicly funded asylums for the insane. She told the Massachusetts state legislature in 1843: "I tell what I have seen. . . . Insane persons confined within the Commonwealth, in cages, closets, cellars, stalls, pens! Chained, naked, beaten with rods, and lashed into obedience!" For the balance of the century, Dix toured the country pleading the cause of the mentally ill, succeeding in winning both private and public support for mental health systems.

A hundred other targets for reform joined prisons and asylums on the agenda of middle-class Christian activists. Embracing their Puritan ancestors' strict observance of the Sabbath, newly awakened Christians insisted on stopping Sunday mail delivery and demanded that canals be closed on Sundays. Some joined Bible and tract societies that distributed Christian literature; others founded Sunday schools or operated domestic missions devoted to winning either the **irreligious** or the wrongly religious (as Roman Catholics were perceived to be) to the new covenant of the Second Great Awakening.

Many white-collar reformers acted in earnest and were genuinely interested in forging a new social welfare system. A number of their programs, however, seemed more like social control because they tried to force people to conform to a middle-class standard of behavior. For example, reformers believed that immigrants should willingly discard their traditional customs and beliefs and act like Americans. Immigrants who chose to cling to familiar ways were suspected of disloyalty. This aspect of benevolent reform was particularly prominent in two important movements: public education and **temperance.**

Before the War of 1812, most Americans believed that education was the family's or the church's re-

Dorothea Dix Philanthropist, reformer, and educator who was a pioneer in the movement for specialized treatment of the mentally ill.

irreligious Hostile or indifferent to religion.

temperance Moderation or abstinence in the consumption of alcoholic drinks.

sponsibility and did not require children to attend school. Many people depended on the apprenticeship system rather than on schools to provide the rudiments of reading, writing, and figuring. But as the complexity of economic, political, and cultural life increased during the opening decades of the nineteenth century, **Horace Mann** and other champions of education pushed states to introduce formal public schooling.

Like his contemporary Charles G. Finney, Mann was trained as a lawyer, but unlike Finney, he believed that ignorance, not sin, lay at the heart of the nation's problems. "If we do not prepare children to become good citizens," Mann proclaimed, "if we do not enrich their minds with knowledge, then our republic must go down to destruction, as others have gone before it." Democracy could continue only where there was equality, and, Mann believed, public education was "a great equalizer of the conditions of men—the balance wheel of the social machinery."

Mann and Massachusetts took the lead in formalizing schooling in 1837, when the state founded the country's first public board of education, with Mann at its head. Seizing control of Massachusetts's educational establishment, Mann immediately extended the school year to a minimum of six months, organized a state teachers' association, and increased teacher salaries. Gradually the state board changed the curriculum in Massachusetts schools to emphasize "practical" education, replacing classical learning and ministerial training with courses such as arithmetic, practical geography, and physical science.

Education reformers were interested in more than "knowledge." Mann and others were equally concerned that new immigrants and the children of the urban poor be trained in Protestant values and middle-class habits. Thus the books used in public schools emphasized virtues such as promptness, perseverance, discipline, and obedience to authority. In Philadelphia and other cities where Roman Catholic immigrants concentrated, Catholic parents resisted the cultural pressure applied on their children by Protestant-dominated public school boards. They supported the establishment of **parochial schools**—a development that aggravated the strain between native-born Protestants and immigrant Catholics.

Another source of such tension was a Protestant crusade against alcohol. Drinking alcohol had always been common in America and before the early nineteenth century was not broadly perceived as a significant social problem. Unhealthy drinking water, the absence of affordable alternatives like coffee and tea, and the desire for an escape from difficult and un-

comfortable surroundings had turned the United States into what one historian has termed "the alcoholic republic." But during the 1820s and 1830s, three factors contributed to a new, more ominous perception.

One was the increasing visibility of drinking and its consequence, drunkenness, as populations became more concentrated in manufacturing and trading cities, especially by immigrants and others in the working class. In Rochester, New York, for example, a town that went through the throes of modernization in the late 1820s, the number of drinking establishments multiplied rapidly as the population grew. Anyone with a few cents could get a glass of whiskey at grocery stores, either of two candy stores, barbershops, or even private homes—all within a few steps of wherever a person might be. By 1829 this proliferation of public drinking led the county grand jury sitting in Rochester to conclude that strong drink was "the cause of almost all of the crime and almost all of the misery that flesh is heir to."

The second factor was alcohol's economic impact in a new and more complex world of work. Factory owners and managers recognized that workers who drank often and heavily, on or off the job, threatened the quantity and quality of production. Owners and supervisors alike rallied around the temperance movement as a way of policing the undisciplined behavior of their employees, both in and out of the factory. By promoting temperance, these reformers believed they could clean up the worst aspects of city life and turn the raucous lower classes into clean-living, self-controlled, peaceful workers, increasing their productivity and business profits.

The third factor was a social and religious one. Like most of the reform movements, the temperance movement began in churches touched by the Second Great Awakening. Drunkenness earned special condemnation from reawakened Protestants, who believed that people were responsible not only for their sins but also for their own salvation. A person whose reason was besotted by alcohol simply could not rise to the demand. Christian reformers, therefore, believed that temperance was necessary not only to preserve the nation but also to win people's souls.

Horace Mann Educator who called for publicly funded education for all children and was head of the first public board of education in the United States.

parochial school A school supported by a church parish; in the United States, the term usually refers to a Catholic school.

Opposition to Slavery

Although some people had always had doubts about the morality of slavery, little organized opposition to it appeared before the American Revolution. During the Revolution, many Americans saw the contradiction between slavery and the "unalienable rights" of "life, liberty, and the pursuit of happiness." By the end of the Revolution, only Georgia and South Carolina continued to allow the importation of slaves, while Massachusetts specifically prohibited slavery altogether and Pennsylvania had begun to phase it out gradually. Even the plantation states showed increasing flexibility in dealing with slavery, as some elite southerners began to realize the unprofitability, though generally not the immorality, of the institution. After Virginia authorized owners to free their slaves in 1782, Delaware and Maryland soon did likewise. By the mid-1780s, most states, including those in the South, had active antislavery societies. In 1807, when Congress voted to outlaw permanently the importation of slaves in the following year, little was said in defense of slavery as an institution. But after 1815, the morality of slavery had begun to emerge as a national issue.

Public feeling about slavery during these years is reflected in the rise of the **American Colonization Society,** founded in 1817. This society was rooted in economic pragmatism, humanitarian concern for slaves' well-being, and a belief that blacks were not equal to whites and therefore the two races could not live together. Such ideas prompted the organization to propose that if slaveowners emancipated their slaves, or if funds could be raised to purchase their freedom, the freed slaves should immediately be shipped to Africa. Others noted that because many slaves had embraced Christianity, they might be agents in the extension of enthusiastic religious conversion. Theologian Samuel Hopkins, who believed slavery to be a sin, pointed out that God had allowed it "so that blacks could embrace the gospel in the New World and then bear the glad tidings back to Africa."

Although the American Colonization Society began in the South, its policies were particularly popular in the Northeast and West. In eastern cities, workers fearful for their jobs lived in dread of either enslaved or free blacks flooding in, lowering wages, and destroying job security. In western states such as Indiana and Illinois, farmers feared that competition could arise from a slaveholding aristocracy. In both regions, white supremacists argued that the extension of slavery beyond the Mississippi River and north

Not all African Americans supported the idea of transporting free-born and liberated slaves to Africa. Paul Cuffe believed that the opportunity should be encouraged. The son of a former slave and an American Indian woman, Cuffe became a sailor. He eventually purchased his own ship and then a fleet of ships, becoming a very successful Boston-area merchant and whaler. He supported many efforts to promote the welfare of American Americans, even supplying money and ships to transport freed slaves who wished to leave the United States to live in the former slave colony of Liberia in Africa. This portrait of a "Black Sailor" is thought to be the mature Paul Cuffe. *Christie's Images, Inc.*

of the **Mason-Dixon Line** would eventually lead to blacks mixing with the white population, a possibility they found extremely distasteful. Of course slaves had little to say about this strategy, but African Americans who were not slaves generally did not share their white neighbors' enthusiasm for the colonization movement. A few though, like Paul Cuffe (see

American Colonization Society Organization founded in 1817 to end slavery gradually by assisting individual slave owners to liberate their slaves and then transporting them to Africa.

Mason-Dixon Line The boundary between Pennsylvania and Maryland; it marked the northern division between free and slave states before the Civil War.

page 235), supported the idea of a black homeland in Africa for free African Americans who chose to go.

Most preachers active in the Second Great Awakening supported the idea of colonization, but a few individuals pressed for more radical reforms. The most vocal leader among the antislavery forces during the early nineteenth century was **William Lloyd Garrison.** A Christian reformer from Massachusetts, Garrison in the late 1820s concentrated all his energies in the antislavery cause. In 1831 he founded the nation's first prominent abolitionist newspaper, *The Liberator.* In it he advocated immediate emancipation for African Americans, with no compensation for slaveholders. In the following year, Garrison founded the New England Anti-Slavery Society and then, in 1833, branched out to found the national American Anti-Slavery Society.

At first, Garrison stood alone. Some Christian reformers joined his cause, but the majority held back. For the same reasons that they supported colonization, most northern whites detested the notion of immediate emancipation, and radical **abolitionists** at this early date were almost universally ignored or, worse, attacked when they denounced slavery. Throughout the 1830s, riots often accompanied abolitionist rallies, and angry mobs stormed stages and pulpits to silence abolitionist speakers. Still, support for the movement gradually grew. In 1836 petitions flooded into Congress demanding an end to the slave trade in Washington, D.C. Not ready to engage in an action quite so controversial, Congress passed a **gag rule** that automatically **tabled** any petition to Congress that addressed the abolition of slavery. The rule remained in effect for nearly a decade.

Despite this official denial by the national Congress, a neglect shared by many state assemblies, not all governments remained closed to the discussion of slavery. In Massachusetts, for example, the state legislature held hearings in 1838 to explore the slavery issue. Like many others who before had remained silent, Angelina Grimké spoke up in an effort to bring the problem of slavery to the attention of the nation at large.

The Whig Alternative to Jacksonian Democracy

■ What did Jackson's opponents hope to accomplish when they built their coalition to oppose the Democrats?

■ Did the coalition accomplish their purposes? Why or why not?

The same fundamental structural changes that led to such social and cultural transformations had an enormous impact on politics as well. Although Andrew Jackson was quite possibly the most popular president since George Washington, not all Americans agreed with his philosophy, policies, or political style. As the Bank War illustrates (see page 291), men like Henry Clay and Daniel Webster, who inherited the crumbling structure of Jefferson's Republican Party, continually opposed Jackson in and out of Congress but seemed unable to overcome sectional differences and culture wars enough to challenge Jackson's enormous national power. Gradually, however, anger over Jackson's policies and anxiety about change forged cooperation among the disenchanted, who coalesced into a new national party.

The End of the Old Party Structure

The end of Jackson's first term in office, 1832, was a landmark year in the nation's political history. In the course of that single year, the Seminoles declared war on the United States, Jackson declared war on the Second Bank, South Carolina declared war on the binding power of the Constitution, and the Cherokees waged a continuing war in the courts to hold on to their lands. The presidential election that year reflected the air of political crisis.

Henry Clay had started the Bank War for the purpose of creating a political cause to rally Jackson's opponents. The problem was that Jackson's enemies were deeply divided among themselves. Clay opposed Jackson because the president refused to support the American System (see pages 272–274) and used every tool at his disposal to attack Clay's economic policies. Southern politicians like Calhoun, however, feared and hated Clay's nationalistic policies as much as they did Jackson's assertions of federal power. And

William Lloyd Garrison   Abolitionist leader who founded and published *The Liberator,* an antislavery newspaper.

abolitionist   An individual who supported national legislation outlawing slavery, either gradually or immediately, with or without compensation to slave owners.

gag rule   A rule that limits or prevents debate on an issue.

table   Action taken by a legislative body (Congress, for example) to postpone debate on an issue until a positive vote to remove the topic from the table is taken.

political outsiders like the Antimasons distrusted all political organizations. These divisions were under-scored in the 1832 election.

The Antimasons (see page 287) kicked off the anti-Jackson campaign in September 1831 when they held the nation's first nominating convention in Baltimore. Thurlow Weed's skillful political manipulation had pulled in a wide range of people who were disgusted with what Jefferson had called "political party tricks," and the convention drew a broad con-stituency. Using all his charm and influence, Weed ca-joled the convention into nominating William Wirt, a respected lawyer from Maryland, as its presidential candidate.

Weed and Wirt fully expected that when the Re-publicans met in convention later in the year, they would rubber-stamp the Antimasonic nomination and present a united front against Jackson. But the Repub-licans, fearful of the Antimasons' odd combination of **machine politics** and antiparty paranoia, nominated Clay as their standard-bearer. The Republicans then issued the country's first formal **party platform,** a ringing document supporting Clay's economic ideas and attacking Jackson's use of the spoils system (see page 289).

Even having two anti-Jackson parties in the run-ning did not satisfy some. Distrustful of the Anti-masons and put off by Clay's nationalist philosophy, southerners in both parties refused to support any of the candidates. They finally backed nullification (see page 297) advocate John Floyd of Virginia.

Lack of unity spelled disaster for Jackson's oppo-nents. Wirt and Floyd received votes that might have gone to Clay. But even if Clay had gotten those votes, Jackson's popularity and the political machinery that he and Van Buren controlled would have given the victory to Jackson. The president was reelected with a total of 219 electoral votes to Clay's 49, Wirt's 7, and Floyd's 11. Jackson's party lost five seats in the Senate but gained six in the House of Representatives. De-spite unsettling changes in the land and continuing political chaos, the people still wanted the hero of New Orleans as their leader.

The New Political Coalition

If one lesson emerged clearly from the election of 1832, it was that Jackson's opponents needed to pull together if they expected to challenge the growing power of "King Andrew." Imitating political organiza-tions in Great Britain, Clay and his associates began calling Jackson supporters Tories—supporters of the king—and calling themselves Whigs. The antimonar-

BORN TO COMMAND.

OF VETO MEMORY.

HAD I BEEN CONSULTED.

KING ANDREW THE FIRST.

Calling themselves Whigs after the English political party that opposed royal authority, Henry Clay, John C. Cal-houn, and Daniel Webster joined forces to oppose what they characterized as Andrew Jackson's kingly use of power. This lithograph from 1834 depicting Jackson in royal dress stepping on the Constitution expresses their view quite vividly. *New York Historical Society.*

chial label stuck, and the new party formed in 1834 was called the **Whig Party.**

The Whigs eventually absorbed all the major fac-tions that opposed Jackson. At the heart of the party were Clay supporters: advocates of strong govern-ment and the American System in economics. The nullifiers in the South, however, quickly came around when Clay and Calhoun found themselves on the

machine politics   The aggressive use of influence, favors, and tradeoffs by a political organization, or "machine," to mobilize support among its followers.

party platform   A formal statement of the principles, policies, and promises on which a political party bases its appeal to the public.

Whig Party   Political party that came into being in 1834 as an anti-Jackson coalition and that charged "King Andrew" with executive tyranny.

same side in defeating Jackson's appointment of Van Buren as American minister to England. This successful campaign, combined with Calhoun's growing awareness that Jackson was perhaps more dangerous to his constituents' interests than was Clay, led the southerner and his associates back into Clay's camp. The Antimasons also joined the Whig coalition. Disgusted by Jackson's use of patronage and back-alley politics—not to mention the fact that the president was a Mason—they overcame their distrust of Clay's party philosophy. A final major group to rally to the Whigs was the collection of Christian reformers whose campaigns to eliminate alcohol, violations of the Sabbath, and dozens of other perceived evils had become increasingly political during the opening years of the 1830s. Evangelicals disapproved of Jackson's personal lifestyle, his views on slavery, his Indian policy, and his refusal to involve government in their moral causes. The orderly and sober society that Clay and the Whigs envisioned appealed to such people.

The congressional elections in 1834 provided the first test for the new coalition. In this first electoral contest, the Whigs won nearly 40 percent of the seats in the House of Representatives and more than 48 percent in the Senate. Clearly cooperation was paying off.

Van Buren in the White House

Jackson had seemed to be a tower of strength when he was first elected to the presidency in 1828, but by the end of his second term, he was aging and ill. Nearly 70 years old and plagued by various ailments, Old Hickory decided to follow Washington's example and not run for a third term. Instead, Jackson used all the power and patronage at his command to ensure that Martin Van Buren, his most consistent loyalist, would win the presidential nomination at the Democratic Party convention.

If Jackson personified the popular charisma behind Democratic Party success, Van Buren personified its political machinery. A skilled organizer, his ability at creating unlikely political alliances had earned him the nickname "the Little Magician." Throughout Jackson's first term, Van Buren had headed up the Kitchen Cabinet (see page 289) and increasingly became Jackson's chief political henchman. In 1832 Jackson had repaid his loyalty by making him vice president, with the intention of launching him into the presidency.

Meanwhile, Clay and his Whig associates were hatching a plot to deny the election to the Democrats. Instead of holding a convention and thrashing out a platform, the Whigs let each region's party organization nominate its own candidates. Whig leaders, especially experienced political manipulator Thurlow Weed, hoped a large number of candidates would confuse voters and throw the election into the House of Representatives, where skillful political management and Van Buren's unpopularity might unseat the Democrats. As a result, four **favorite sons** ran on the Whig ticket. Daniel Webster of Massachusetts represented the Northeast. Hugh Lawson White, a Tennessean and former Jackson supporter, ran for the Southwest. South Carolina nullifier W. P. Mangum represented the South. William Henry Harrison, former governor of Indiana Territory and victor at the Battle of Tippecanoe in 1811, was tapped to represent the Northwest.

Weed underestimated the Democrats' hold on the minds of the voters. Van Buren captured 765,483 popular votes—more than Jackson had won in the previous election—but his performance in the Electoral College was significantly weaker than Jackson's had been. Van Buren squeaked by with a winning margin of less than 1 percent, but it was a victory, and the presidential election did not go to the House of Representatives. House Democrats lost thirty-seven seats to Whigs. In the Senate, however, Democrats increased their majority to more than 62 percent. Even with that slight edge, Van Buren could expect trouble getting Democratic policies through Congress. This handicap was worsened by a total collapse in the economy just weeks after he took office.

The **Panic of 1837** was a direct outcome of the Bank War and Jackson's money policies, but it was Van Buren who would take the blame. The crisis had begun with Nicholas Biddle's manipulation of credit and interest rates in an effort to discredit Jackson and have the Second Bank rechartered in spite of the president's veto (see page 291). Jackson had added to the problem by removing paper money and credit from the economy in an effort to win support from hard-money advocates. Arguing that he wanted to end "the monopoly of the public lands in the hands of speculators and capitalists," Jackson had issued the **Specie Circular** on August 15, 1836. From that day

---

favorite son A candidate nominated for office by delegates from his or her own region or state.

Panic of 1837 An economic collapse that came as the result of Andrew Jackson's fiscal policies and led to an extended national economic depression.

Specie Circular Order issued by President Jackson in 1836 stating that the federal government would accept only specie—gold and silver—as payment for public land; one of the causes of the Panic of 1837.

forward payment for public land had to be made in specie.

The contraction in credit and currency had the same impact in 1836 as it had in 1819: the national economy collapsed. By May 1837, New York banks were no longer accepting any paper currency, and soon all banks had adopted the policy of accepting specie only. Unable to pay back or collect loans, buy raw materials, or conduct any other sort of commerce, hundreds of businesses, plantations, farms, factories, canals, and other enterprises spiraled into bankruptcy by the end of the year. More than a third of the population was thrown out of work, and people who were fortunate enough to keep their jobs found their pay reduced by as much as 50 percent. Fledgling industries and labor organizations were cast into disarray, and the nation sank into both an economic and an emotional depression.

As credit continued to collapse through 1838 and 1839, President Van Buren tried to address the problems. First, he extended Jackson's hard-money policy, which caused the economy to contract further. Next, in an effort to keep the government solvent, Van Buren cut federal spending to the bone, shrinking the money supply even more. Then, to replace the stabilizing influence lost when the Second Bank was destroyed, he created a national treasury system endowed with many of the powers formerly wielded by the bank. The new regional treasury offices accepted specie only in payment for federal lands and other obligations and used that specie to pay federal expenses and debts. As a result, specie was sucked out of local banks and local economies. While fiscally sound by the wisdom of the day, Van Buren's decisions only made matters worse for the average person and drove the last nail into his political coffin.

The Log-Cabin and Hard-Cider Campaign of 1840

The Whigs had learned their lesson in the election of 1836: only a unified party could possibly destroy the political machine built by Jackson and Van Buren. As the nation sank into depression, the Whigs lined up behind a single candidate for the 1840 election, determined to use whatever means were necessary to break the Democrats' grip on the voters.

Once again, Henry Clay hoped to be the party's nominee, but Thurlow Weed convinced the party that William Henry Harrison would have a better chance in the election. Weed chose Harrison because of his distinguished military record and because the gen-

Democrats tried to discredit Whig candidate William Henry Harrison by characterizing him as a backwoods hick. This strategy backfired when romantically inclined American voters rallied around the image Whigs painted of their candidate as a simple, honest, and hospitable frontiersman. In this cartoon, Harrison is shown dispensing hard cider to his supporters (which actually was done at campaign events), while Van Buren and Jackson wince at the taste of this simple, poor man's drink and plot to turn off the flow of Harrison's hospitality. *Boston Athenaeum.*

eral, who had been a political lion thirty years earlier, had been out of the public eye for a long time and had few enemies left. For Harrison's running mate, the party chose **John Tyler,** a Virginia senator who had

> **John Tyler** Virginia senator who left the Democratic Party after conflicts with Andrew Jackson; he was elected vice president in 1840 and became president when William Henry Harrison died in office.

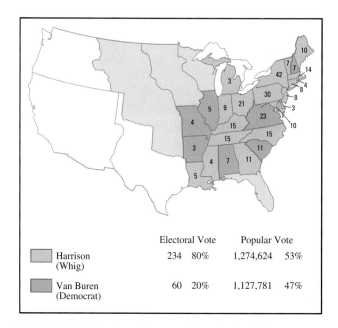

	Electoral Vote	Popular Vote
Harrison (Whig)	234 80%	1,274,624 53%
Van Buren (Democrat)	60 20%	1,127,781 47%

MAP 12.2 Election of 1840 Although the difference in popular votes between William Henry Harrison and Martin Van Buren was small in the election of 1840, Harrison won a landslide victory in the Electoral College. This map shows why. After floundering through several elections, the Whig Party was finally able to organize a national coalition, giving it solid victories in all of the most populous regions of the country. Only the Far West, which was still sparsely settled, voted as a block for Van Buren.

It Matters

The Log-Cabin and Hard-Cider Campaign

Political pundits revel in criticizing modern electioneering for its abundant use of spin, exaggeration, and mudslinging. But these qualities are certainly nothing new. As early as 1800, opposing Federalists and Republicans had resorted to name calling and political spin as they campaigned for John Adams or Thomas Jefferson, respectively. But something certainly changed with the election of 1840. By 1840, volunteer statesmen had been virtually replaced as candidates by professional politicians. And as political parties became more complex and coordinated, a corp of professional political managers also emerged. Now the outcome of an election meant more than a change in ideological tilt; it often meant that candidates and their ever-expanding staffs would be out of work. It is little wonder, then, that what is often called the first *modern* election in American history was so nasty. In fact, it set the style for presidential campaigning that continues today.

bolted from Jackson's Democratic Party during the Bank War. Weed clearly hoped that the Virginian would draw votes from the planter South while Harrison carried the West and North.

Although the economy was in bad shape, the Whig campaign avoided addressing any serious issues. Instead, the Whigs launched a smear campaign against Van Buren. Although he was the son of a lowly tavern keeper, the Whig press portrayed him as an aristocrat whose expensive tastes in clothes, food, and furniture were signs of dangerous excess during an economic depression. Harrison really was an aristocrat, but the Whigs played on the Romantic themes so popular among their genteel and middle-class constituents by characterizing him as a simple frontiersman—a Natty Bumppo—who had risen to greatness through his own efforts. Whig claims were so extravagant that the Democratic press soon satirized Harrison in political cartoons showing a rustic hick rocking on the porch of a log cabin swilling hard cider. The

satire backfired. Whig newspapers and speechmakers seized on the image and sold Harrison, the longtime political insider, as a simple man of the people who truly lived in a log cabin.

Van Buren had little with which to retaliate. Harrison had a fairly clean and certainly a distinguished political and military career behind him. Tyler, too, was well respected. And Van Buren had simply not done a good job of addressing the nation's pressing economic needs. Voters, from former Antimasons to Christian reformers, cried out for change, and Van Buren could not offer them one. The combination of political dissatisfaction and campaign hype brought the biggest voter turnout to that time in American history: nearly twice as many voters came to the polls in 1840 as had done so in 1836. And while Harrison won only 53 percent of the popular vote, Weed's successful political manipulations earned the Whigs nearly 80 percent of the electoral votes, sweeping the Democrats out of the White House (see Map 12.2).

Individual Voices

Examining a Primary Source

Angelina Grimké Corrects Catharine Beecher on Women's Activism

Her letter to William Lloyd Garrison and then her unprecedented testimony in the Massachusetts state legislature made Angelina Grimké a national celebrity. Many famous people began corresponding with her, including fellow abolitionist and frequent writer on women's issues Catharine Beecher. Despite Beecher's expectation that she and Grimké would agree on most matters, the two were often at odds. In fact, their correspondence reveals many of the strains that beset the nation (and the nation's women) during this difficult era. In the excerpt that follows, from an October 1827 letter, Grimké responds to a statement made by Beecher in an earlier letter.

Thou sayest, when a woman is asked to sign a petition, or join an Anti-Slavery Society, it is "for the purpose of contributing her measure of influence to keep up agitation in Congress, to promote the excitement of the North against the iniquities of the South, to coerce the South by fear, shame, anger, and a sense of odium, to do what she is determined not to do." Indeed! Are these the only motives presented to the daughters of America, for laboring in the glorious cause of Human Rights? . . . ■

*   But I had thought the principal motives urged by abolitionists were not these; but that they endeavored to excite men and women to active exertion—first, to* cleanse *their own* hands *of the sin of slavery, and secondly, to save the South, if possible, and the North, at any rate, from the impending judgments of heaven. The result of their mission in this country, cannot in the least affect the validity of that mission.* ■ *Like Noah, they may preach in vain; if so, the destruction of the South can no more be attributed to them, than the destruction of the antediluvian* ■ *world to him. "In vain," did I say? Oh no! The discussion of the rights of the slave has opened the way for the discussion of* other *rights, and the ultimate result will most certainly be, "the breaking of every yoke," the letting the oppressed of every grade and description go free, an emancipation far more glorious than any the world has ever yet seen, and introduction into that "liberty wherewith Christ hath made his people free."* ■

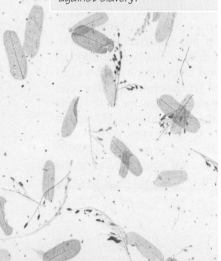

■ In the first paragraph of this passage, Grimké quotes from one of Catharine Beecher's earlier letters. What does Beecher seem to be saying about the extent to which women should be advocates for abolitionism? What limits to such activism do her words imply?

■ What sort of action does Grimké advocate in response to perceived evils such as slavery? How does her view differ from Beecher's?

■ Antediluvian is a term not heard much today. It refers to the time period before the Great Flood described in the Bible (ante means "before"; diluvian means "flood").

■ What does Grimké see as the appropriate goal for abolitionism? How might this explain her willingness to risk public ridicule and even physical danger by speaking out against slavery?

Summary

William Henry Harrison inherited an excitingly dynamic but deeply troubled country. An economic crisis triggered by Andrew Jackson's Specie Circular was worsened by Van Buren's treasury system, and both were compounded by Nicholas Biddle's manipulations. The emerging new party system promised great exhilaration and political sport but not much in the way of solutions. Still, Americans were caught up in the new politics as never before: nearly twice as many men voted in the 1840 election as had done so in any other presidential contest.

Political participation was only one of the many ways in which Americans responded to the many unsettling changes that had been taking place as part of the Great Transformation. Different economic classes responded by creating their own cultures and by adopting specific strategies for dealing with anxiety. Some chose violent protest, some passive resistance. Some looked to heaven for solutions and others to earthly utopias. And out of this complex swirl, something entirely new and unexpected emerged: a new America, on its way to being socially, politically, intellectually, and culturally modern.

In the election of 1840, a man who had become a national figure by fighting against Indian sovereignty and for westward expansion swept a new sentiment into national politics. Increasingly Americans came to believe that the West would provide the solutions to the problems ushered in during the Great Transformation. In the short term, this notion led to an exciting race by Americans toward the Pacific. But different visions about how the West would solve the nation's problems soon added to the ever-growing air of crisis.

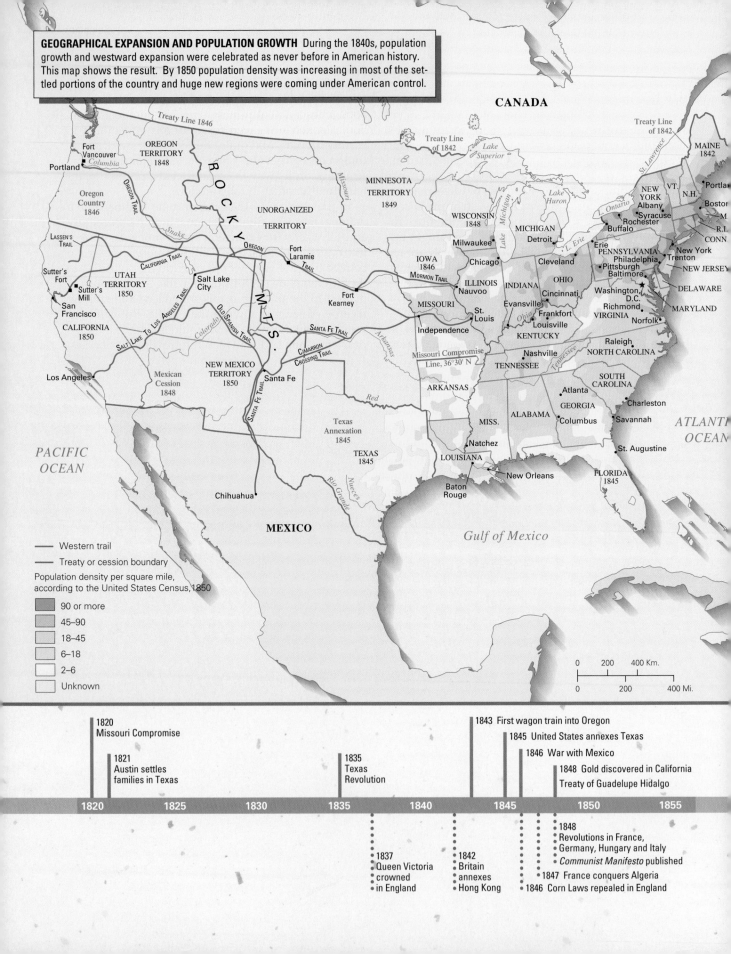

GEOGRAPHICAL EXPANSION AND POPULATION GROWTH During the 1840s, population growth and westward expansion were celebrated as never before in American history. This map shows the result. By 1850 population density was increasing in most of the settled portions of the country and huge new regions were coming under American control.

Westward Expansion and Manifest Destiny, 1841–1848

Geographical Expansion and Population Growth
Compare the map on the facing page with the opening maps for Chapter 8 and Chapter 12, noting the trends in population growth and concentration. How might these trends have contributed to the popularity of manifest destiny during the 1840s and the similarities and/or differences between how various regions in the country defined it?

Individual Choices

LORENZO DE ZAVALA

Lorenzo de Zavala fought against tyranny in his native Mexico. When the government he helped establish after a successful revolution against Spain refused to create a democracy, Zavala moved to Texas. In 1835 he joined the Texas Revolution against Mexico and was elected vice president of the Republic of Texas. *"Lorenzo de Zavala" by C. E. Proctor. Archives Division, Texas State Library. Photograph by Eric Beggs.*

Lorenzo de Zavala

Although Lorenzo de Zavala was a physician by training, his heart persistently pulled him into politics. An ardent federalist, he was elected to the Mérida city council in his native Yucatán, in southern Mexico, when he was only 23 years old. Then in 1814 he was elected as a delegate to the Spanish parliament. He never assumed his seat: the young liberal was imprisoned by Spain's King Ferdinand VII for expressing antimonarchical sentiments. Gaining his release in 1817, Zavala returned to Yucatán.

Zavala chafed at Spanish rule, and as revolutionary movements broke out in all parts of Mexico in 1820, he again entered politics, winning election as the secretary of the Yucatán assembly. From this position, he assisted the Mexican independence movement. Shortly after it succeeded in 1821, he was elected to the Mexican constituent congress, serving there and in the national senate until 1827, when he was appointed provincial governor.

By 1829, Zavala was having doubts about Mexico's future. The independent government had proved far from stable, and the ruling authorities seemed just as reactionary as the Spaniards. The liberals' pleas to allocate farmland to peasants, for example, were continually refused by the government. Seeking some way to help the peasants, Zavala resigned his governorship and secured an empresario grant to settle five hundred poor Mexican families in Texas.

For the next several years, Zavala traveled and wrote a history of the revolutionary movement in Mexico, which he published in 1831. Then, finding himself in Paris in 1833, Zavala returned to public service and politics by accepting a post as Mexico's ambassador to France. In the following year, Antonio López de Santa Anna pushed his way into power, suspending the constitution, dissolving the national congress, and assuming dictatorial control. Watching events unfold from his post in Paris, Zavala became increasingly disaffected by Santa Anna. In 1835 he resigned as ambassador and sailed for Texas, where he hoped to join with others in ousting Santa Anna and restoring the constitution. When Stephen F. Austin called for a "general consultation of the people" to consider appropriate responses to Santa Anna's aggression in the fall of 1835, Zavala sought and won a seat.

Like many settlers in Texas—whether they were originally from the United States, Europe, or Mexico—Zavala wanted reform but not necessarily independence. Thus he agreed with the Consultation's decision in November 1835 to form a provisional government using the Mexican constitution of 1824—a document he had helped write—as a legal foundation. But when Santa Anna declared all members of the Consultation traitors and ordered troops into Texas, Zavala gave up hope of a peaceful settlement. On March 2, 1836, he chose to join his colleagues in signing a declaration of independence, and then threw himself into the task of writing a constitution for Texas. The resulting document was an interesting hybrid: a mixture of Zavala's and James Madison's views concerning liberal federalism.

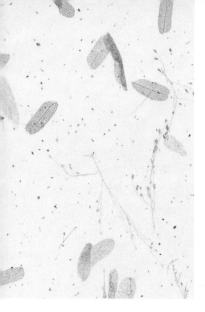

The Texas Consultation ratified the new constitution on March 16, 1836. Then, in recognition of Zavala's strong political voice and the significant role he had played in launching the revolution, the Consultation unanimously elected him vice president of the Republic of Texas.

The revolution and the establishment of the Texas Republic represented a victory for views that Zavala and many Mexican-born Texans had held for a lifetime. Throughout his political career, Zavala had fought for reform in Mexico, helping to win independence from Spain and pushing for liberal federalism. His expectations had been dashed by the tyranny of self-interested political factions, which had created such instability that Santa Anna had been able to bully his way to the top and suspend constitutional government. For Zavala and many others, the choice was clear: if Mexico could not be reformed, they would rally behind a new state where their ideals might become reality. The Republic of Texas became the seat for their dreams.

INTRODUCTION

Lorenzo de Zavala was but one of many westerners who found themselves in unexpected situations during the first half of the nineteenth century. In various regions of the American West, different ecological conditions, ideological commitments, Native American populations, and national claims created a series of complex settings. After William Henry Harrison's election to the presidency in 1840, the nation's political and cultural focus would tilt progressively westward. As transportation systems extended the American frontier, and as industrialization generated new capital, adventurous speculators would invest in the newly opened West. Expecting to find a wide-open land of opportunity, multitudes of Americans quickly followed. Many who hoped to move west, and more who saw in the West a fertile ground for expanding the political and ideological values they held dear, adopted a faith in the nation's **manifest destiny** to control the whole of the North American continent.

Had he lived to see it, Zavala would no doubt have been both surprised and disappointed when the United States fought a war with Mexico over westward expansion. But without doubt he would have celebrated the fact that the war once again forced the United States to confront the inconsistency between its promise of freedom and the reality of slavery. Even so, the divisive wedges that the slavery debate drove into the heart of the political nation would have disheartened this loyal Tejano. Instead of engaging in the sort of mature and rational discussion that Zavala would have advocated, Americans used slavery as a playing piece in an increasingly bitter game of sectional politics.

The Complicated Worlds of the West

■ How did most Americans imagine "the West"? To what extent were their imaginings accurate?

■ Who generally were the first pioneers to move into the West? How did they and those who followed actually move westward and establish communities there?

Americans entertained conflicting images about what they might find in the newly opening West. Many were convinced that most of the region was a vast wasteland, inhospitable to human civilization. Others were certain that it was a world full of promise. Enterprising capitalists often led the way in systematic exploration, looking for furs, gold, and other sources of quick profit. But it did not take long before a wide variety of others followed. Whether they expected a wasteland, a paradise, or something in between, what all of these newcomers to the West did find was a natural and cultural world that was much more complex than anything they had imagined.

Western Myths and Realities

Two views of the West, tied to Americans' earlier explorations there, dominated the popular imagination in the 1840s. One, traceable to Zebulon Pike's expedition in 1806–1807, envisioned the West as a "great American desert" unsuitable for habitation by any

> **manifest destiny** Term first used in the 1840s to describe the right and duty of the United States to expand westward.

but the hardiest and most primitive Indians. The other, traceable to the Lewis and Clark expedition, imagined a region rich in resources. Common to both was the notion that the West, whether desert or paradise, was largely unoccupied: a virgin land free for the taking.

Realities in the **Far West** were much more complex than the myths suggested. Indeed, vast areas of the region had extremely dry and fragile **ecologies** largely unfit for the sort of economic exploitation nineteenth-century Americans desired. At the other extreme, some regions were so wet that their rain forests were virtually impassable by horse or vehicle. And all over the West, in areas large and small, thousands of local ecologies stood between the two extremes. But none of it was virgin land.

For thousands of years, various Indian groups had extracted a rich living from the many different environments in the Far West. Through the twin strategies of geographic mobility and intergroup trading, Indians had taken advantage of the West's diversity, receiving what each ecological zone had to offer. Like Europeans, Indians managed and exploited resources, but this flexible approach to the complicated and often fragile ecology of the Far West provided an excellent living and did minimal damage (see page 13). If the land appeared to expansionists in the United States to be unoccupied, it was only because they would not, or could not, recognize a system of land use that was foreign to them.

With the arrival of Spanish, French, Russian, and other Europeans, the already complex world of interrelations in the West became even more complicated. Indians on the Great Plains used the mobility provided by European horses to expand not just their hunting range but also their trading range. Goods from the Plains made their way regularly to Spanish settlements in New Mexico, and replacement horses, guns, and other European goods flooded northward in return. This was the world into which early western entrepreneurs such as John Jacob Astor and Auguste Chouteau had entered earlier in the century (see pages 260–261). No unexploited land or great American desert could have supported their monumental visions of an inland empire providing rare furs to genteel consumers in the eastern states and Europe. What both men did was tap into an already sophisticated trading world, and both became extremely wealthy and influential as a result.

In the rough-and-tumble world of the Missouri fur trade, men earned respect through ability and toughness alone. Jim Beckwourth, a former slave from Virginia, had both, and was widely recognized as one of the era's leading mountain men. *Courtesy of the Colorado Historical Society.*

Western Enterprises

The image of the solitary trapper braving a hostile environment and even more hostile Indians is the stuff of American adventure novels and movies. Although characters such as Christopher "Kit" Carson and Jeremiah "Crow Killer" Johnson really did exist, these men were merely advance agents for an **extractive industry** geared to the efficient removal of animal pelts.

What drew men like Carson and Johnson into the Far West in the 1830s and 1840s was an innovation in the fur business instigated by a former Astor employee and one-time partner of Chouteau, William Henry Ashley. Taking advantage of the presence of large numbers of underemployed young men seeking fortune and adventure in the West, Ashley broke

Far West In North America, the lands west of the Mississippi River.

ecology Relating to the interactive relationships between organisms (animals, plants, microorganisms, etc.) and the physical environment in which they are found.

extractive industry An industry, such as fur trapping, logging, or mining, that removes natural resources from the environment.

Chronology

Expansion and Crisis

1820	Missouri Compromise
1821	Stephen F. Austin settles Americans in Texas William Becknell opens Santa Fe Trail
1831	Nez Perce and Flathead delegation ask whites to live among them
1834	Mexican government begins seizure of California mission lands
1835	Texas Revolution begins
1836	Rebellion in California against Mexican rule
1838	Senate rejects annexation of Texas Armed confrontation between Maine and New Brunswick
1839	John Sutter founds New Helvetia
1840	Split between moderates and radicals in American Anti-Slavery Society
1841	John Tyler becomes president Congress passes preemption bill
1842	Elijah White named federal Indian agent for Oregon
1843	First wagon train into Oregon Oregon adopts First Organic Laws
1844	James K. Polk elected president Murder of Joseph Smith
1845	United States annexes Texas Term "manifest destiny" coined
1846	War with Mexico begins Oregon boundary established; United States and Britain end joint occupancy California declares itself a republic
1847	Whitman massacre Mormons arrive in Utah
1848	Gold discovered in California Treaty of Guadalupe Hidalgo Zachary Taylor elected president

the long tradition of depending exclusively on Indian labor for collecting furs. In 1825 he set up the highly successful rendezvous system. Under this arrangement, individual trappers—white adventurers like Carson and Johnson, African Americans such as James Beckwourth, and a large number of Indians—combed the upper Missouri, trapping, curing, and packing furs. Each hunter carved out his own territory in the western Rocky Mountains and enforced his claim through a combination of mutual respect and violence. Once each year Ashley conducted a fur rendezvous in the mountains, where the trappers brought their furs and exchanged them for goods. Pioneer missionary Pierre Jean de Smet called these gatherings "one of the most picturesque features of early frontier life in the Far West."

Ashley's, Chouteau's, and Astor's strategies for extracting wealth from the Far West were successful and made these men very rich and important. But the success of their complex business inadvertently led to its decline. The expansion in international commerce flowing out of the fur trade helped open the way for importing vast amounts of silk from Asia. Soon silk hats became a fashion rage among luxury-loving consumers in both America and Europe, displacing the beaver hats that had consumed most American furs. In addition, the efficiency with which these gigantic organizations extracted fur from the western wilderness virtually wiped out beaver populations in the Rocky Mountains. Through the 1830s and 1840s, the beaver business slowed to a near standstill.

Many beaver hunters stayed in the West, however, becoming founding members of new communities. As early as 1840, fur trapper Robert "Doc" Newell reportedly told his companion Joe Meek, "Come, we are all done with this life in the mountains—done with wading in Beaver-dams, and freezing or starving alternately—done with Indian trading and Indian fighting. The fur trade is dead in the Rocky Mountains, and it is no place for us now, if ever it was." The two men then headed to the Willamette Valley in Oregon to become settlers. The great captains in the fur

This painting by Alfred Jacob Miller captures the color and spirit of the annual fur rendezvous and shows the wide variety of colorful people the event brought together—not only Indians and mountain men, but sightseeing English lords like William Drummond Steward (shown here on his white horse). *"Encampment on Green River" by Alfred Miller. Joslyn Art Museum, Omaha, Nebraska. Gift of the Enron Foundation.*

industry came to similar conclusions, pulling their capital out of trapping and diverting it to more attractive ventures: banks, mills, real estate, and the burgeoning canal and rail systems.

Often the first people to join the former fur trappers in settling the West were not rugged yeoman farmers but highly organized and well-financed land speculators and developers. From the earliest days of the republic, federal public land policy favored those who could afford large purchases and pay in cash. Liberalization of the land laws during the first half of the nineteenth century put smaller tracts—for less money and on credit terms—within reach of more citizens, but speculators continued to play a role in land distribution by offering often even smaller tracts and more liberal credit (see page 292). This was particularly true as states granted rights-of-way, first to canal companies and then, increasingly, to railroad developers as a way of financing internal improvements. Land along transportation routes was especially valuable, and developers could often turn an outright grant into enormous profits.

A third group of expectant fortune hunters was lured into the Far West by the same magnet that had drawn the Spanish to the American Southwest: gold.

Since colonial times, Americans had persistently hunted precious metals, usually without much success. The promise of gold continued to draw people westward, however, onto Winnebago lands in 1827 and into Cherokee territory in 1829 (see page 293). But the most impressive case of gold fever would not strike until 1848, when a group of laborers digging a millrace in northern California found flakes and then chunks of gold. Despite efforts to suppress the news, word leaked out, and by mid-May 1848 men were rushing from all over California and Oregon into the Sierra foothills northeast of Sacramento to prospect for gold. By September, news reached the East that the light work of panning for gold in California could yield $50 a day, two months' wages for an average northern workingman. In 1849 more than a hundred thousand **forty-niners** took up residence in California.

As in earlier gold rushes, most of these fortune hunters did not discover gold, but many of them stayed to establish trading businesses, banks, and

forty-niners Prospectors who streamed into California in 1849, after the discovery of gold northeast of New Helvetia in 1848.

farms. Others moved on, still seeking their fortunes. But eventually they too, for the most part, settled down to become shopkeepers, farmers, and entrepreneurs.

Moving Westward

Distinct waves of Americans pushed westward into the areas opened by gold seekers, fur trappers, and land speculators. All of these migrants were responding to promises of abundant land in America's interior. But different groups were reacting to very different conditions in the East, and those differences gave shape to their migrations and to the settlements they eventually created.

The underlying cause for most westward migration was the hope of economic opportunity. "To make money was their chief object," one young pioneer woman in Texas commented; "all things else were subsidiary to it." Like her family, many settlers went to the Southwest to improve their fortunes by taking advantage of rising cotton prices in hopes of becoming prosperous inland planters. Many, too, were pushed by economic forces to seek new lives in the West, especially after the panics of 1819 and 1837. New England Yankees, for example, were edged out of the Northeast by two forces. First, the long-established New England tradition of dividing family holdings equally among adult children had created a significant shortage of workable farms in the region. Second, innovations in spinning and weaving made large-scale wool processing economical, creating a new demand for this fiber. Starting after 1824, a sheep-raising craze swept New England, especially in the Connecticut River valley. Sheep required little labor but a lot of land, and people who had the capital to amass large herds soon began buying out their less fortunate neighbors. Between 1825 and 1840, sheep displaced people throughout much of the New England countryside. Thus young people in New England faced a choice between moving into cities or trying to establish New England–style farming in new areas. A significant number opted to migrate westward.

The image of the independent frontier farmer fleeing the restrictions of civilized life and hewing out a living with an ax, a hoe, and single-minded self-sufficiency is a persistent myth in American history, but the true picture is less romantic. Most people went west not solo but as part of a larger community and often as the result of organized land development efforts. In Texas, for example, most migrants in the 1820s and 1830s came in large groups under the direction of men such as **Stephen F. Austin** and Martín de León. The Spanish government in Mexico gave these *empresarios*

land grants and the right to assess fees in exchange for encouraging settlement in Spain's northern New World colonies. Austin's father, Moses Austin, was the first Anglo-American *empresario*. On January 17, 1821, Spanish authorities gave him permission to settle three hundred American families within a 200,000-acre tract between the Brazos and Colorado Rivers. Following his father's death, the younger Austin took over the enterprise and in the aftermath of the Panic of 1819 was able to offer families large plots of land for a filing fee of only 12½ cents an acre. "I am convinced," he exclaimed, "that I could take on fifteen hundred families as easily as three hundred if permitted to do so."

Beginning with Austin's first overland party in the winter of 1821, migrants to Texas generally traveled in small-to-medium-size groups. Some of them ventured overland, others by boat. One settler, Jared E. Groce, transported an entire plantation from Georgia to Texas—fifty wagons full of personal belongings and more than a hundred slaves—but that was unusual. More typical was the experience of a young woman named Rabb. She traveled in a family group of seven adults and eight children, who found and settled with other relatives when they arrived in Texas. Even those few who arrived alone seldom stayed that way. "Those of us who have no families of our own, reside with some of the families in the settlement," one young migrant observed. "We remain here notwithstanding the scarcity of provisions, to assist in protecting the settlement."

Migration to Oregon also involved group effort but followed a different pattern. The first permanent Anglo-American settlements in the Pacific Northwest were begun by missionaries carrying the Second Great Awakening's message of Christianity and Americanism to the Indians, who welcomed and in some cases had even invited them. These missionaries encouraged mass migration to the new territory. "Who will come & possess the land, who?" Henry H. Spalding wrote from his mission station in Oregon, urging farmers, mechanics, and additional missionaries to rush westward immediately. Missionaries all over the Northwest repeated his summons, which echoed in the religious and secular newspapers and magazines that enjoyed wide circulation during the 1830s and 1840s. Coming on the heels of the Panic of

Stephen F. Austin   American colonizer in Texas and leading voice in the Texas Revolution.

empresario   In the Spanish colonies, a person who organized and led a group of settlers in exchange for

Although modern movies and traditional folklore portray early Texas as a barely settled cowboy frontier, the region actually was attractive because vast areas in its eastern and central regions could support large-scale cotton, sugar, and other lucrative plantation businesses. This painting from 1845 captures the more genteel side of Texas life during the pioneer era. *Texas Memorial Museum, The University of Texas, Austin.*

1837, these calls appealed strongly to people eager for economic opportunity in familiar cultural surroundings. Thus, when the Methodist Church issued a call for a "great reinforcement" for its mission in Oregon, it received a flood of applications, and three separate reinforcements arrived in Oregon by ship in 1840. But large-scale immigration did not begin until 1843, when missionary Marcus Whitman led the first major emigration along what would later be called the **Oregon Trail.**

Every spring thereafter for decades, families from all over the East gathered in Missouri to start the overland trek. "Probably there were sixty-five or seventy, or possibly more than that, wagons in our train, and hundreds of loose cattle and horses," one young woman pioneer reported, and that was just one of the wagon trains on the trail that summer. "We were not allowed to travel across the plains in any haphazard manner," she continued. "No family or individual was permitted to go off alone from the company."

Although trail life was novel for most of the Oregon-bound emigrants, the division in domestic labor re-mained much as it had been at home. "Everybody was supposed to rise at daylight, and while the women were preparing breakfast, the men rounded up the cattle, took down the tents, yoked the oxen to the wagons and made everything ready for an immediate start after the morning meal was finished." Even social customs remained the same. "Life on the plains was a primitive edition of life in town or village," the same pioneer woman remarked. "We were expected to visit our neighbors when we paused for rest. If we did not, we were designated as 'high-toned' or 'stuck-up.' . . . Human nature is the same the world over. Bickerings and jealousies arose just as they would have done in a settlement of the same size."

And so life went on during the six months it took to cross the more than 2,000 miles separating the set-

Oregon Trail The overland route from St. Louis to the Pacific Northwest followed by thousands of settlers in the 1840s.

Though highly idealized, this painting of an emigrant wagon train settling down for the night on the Oregon Trail does capture many accurate details. Notice, for example, the division of labor: women are washing, cooking, and tending to small children while men are drawing water, herding animals, and preparing to hunt for food. Diaries kept by actual emigrants confirm this was the way life was on the trail. *The Corcoran Gallery of Art, Washington, D.C. Gift of Mr. & Mrs. Lansdell K. Christie.*

tled part of the nation and the **Oregon Country.** Once in Oregon, families arriving in the wagon trains tended to settle in rings around the already existing missions, which soon became the hubs for New England–style villages in the Pacific Northwest.

Another migration pattern led toward the **Great Basin.** Despite their growth in numbers and prosperity, Joseph Smith's community of Mormons in Nauvoo, Illinois, continued to be victims of religious and economic persecution. On June 27, 1844, Joseph Smith was murdered by a mob in neighboring Carthage, Illinois. The remaining church leaders concluded that the Mormons would never be safe until they moved far from mainstream American civilization. **Brigham Young,** Smith's successor, decided to search for a safe refuge beyond the Rocky Mountains and led sixteen hundred Mormons out of Nauvoo. After establishing

a base camp in Iowa, Young put together a contingent of 146 young men and women and set out for the Far West, laying out roads, building bridges, and planting crops so that the main body of the church could

Oregon Country   The region to the north of Spanish California extending from the crest of the Rocky Mountains to the Pacific Coast.

Great Basin   A desert region of the western United States including most of Nevada and parts of Utah, California, Idaho, Wyoming, and Oregon.

Brigham Young   Mormon leader who took over in 1844 after Joseph Smith's death and guided the Mormons from Illinois to Utah, where they established a permanent home for the church.

follow in comfort. On July 24, 1847, Young's party finally pushed into the valley of the **Great Salt Lake.** Young immediately assigned some followers to begin an irrigation project and sent others on to California to buy livestock. The rest of the congregation soon arrived, and within a matter of weeks the Mormon community had become a thriving settlement of nearly two thousand.

Despite their differences, pioneers shared one fundamental problem: hard cash was always in short supply. Frontier farmers in every region of the West lived on a shoestring, barely making ends meet when conditions were good and falling into debt when weather or other hazards interrupted farming. Still, those who were lucky and exercised careful management were able to carve out excellent livings. Strongly centralized authority and a deeply felt sense of community helped the Mormons, for example, to overcome even bad luck and deficient skills. Many in other communities, however, had to sell out to satisfy creditors or saw their land repossessed for debts. Pulling up stakes again, they often moved to new lands exhausted of furs and opened to settlement by merchant-adventurers and Indian agents.

Many pioneers had no legal claim to their lands. People bankrupted by unscrupulous speculators or by their own misfortune or mismanagement often settled wherever they could find a spread that seemed unoccupied. Thousands of squatters living on unsold federal lands were a problem for the national government when the time came to sell off the public domain. Always with an eye to winning votes, western politicians frequently advocated "squatter rights," as Thomas Hart Benton had done in 1830 (see page 294). Western congressmen finally maneuvered the passage of a **preemption bill** in 1841, allowing squatters to settle on unsurveyed federal land. Of course, this right did not guarantee that they would have the money to buy the land once it came on the market, or that they would make profitable use of it in the meantime. Thus shoestring farming, perpetual debt, and an uncertain future continued to challenge frontier farmers.

The Social Fabric in the West

■ What challenges did various communities in the West have to face?

■ What cultural arrangements helped settlers deal with these challenges?

■ Why did distinctly different western societies develop in the Far West?

Although migrants to places such as Texas, Oregon, and Utah headed for and found strange new lands, most had no intention of carving out a new social order in the West. Rather, they intended to re-create the society they were leaving behind. The physical and cultural environments into which they moved, however, forced change on them. The West, after all, was not an unpopulated place, and pioneers had to accommodate themselves to the geography and people they found there. Thus the different origins and eventual destinations of various migrants resulted in some significant differences in the cultures and societies of the Far West. The result was not one frontier but a patchwork of frontier areas.

The New Cotton Country

Migrants to cotton country in the Mississippi Valley and beyond brought a particular lifestyle with them. Often starting out as landless herders, migrating families carved out claims beyond the **frontier line** and survived on a mixture of raised and gathered food until they could put the land into agricultural production. The Indians who preceded them in the Mississippi Valley unintentionally simplified life for these families; the Indians had already cleared large expanses of land for agriculture. Removal of the Indians to the Far West and the continuing devastation of Indian populations by disease meant that southern frontiersmen could plant corn and cotton quickly and reap early profits with minimal labor.

Although some areas were cleared and extremely fertile, others were swampy, rocky, and unproductive. In these less desirable locales, settlers were allowed to survey their own claims. The result was odd-shaped farms, differences in the quality of land owned by neighboring farmers, and the re-creation of the southern class system in the new lands. Those fortunate enough to get profitable lands might become

Great Salt Lake   A shallow, salty lake in the Great Basin near which the Mormons established a permanent settlement in 1847.

preemption bill   A temporary law that gave squatters the right to buy land they had settled on before it was offered for sale at public auction.

frontier line   The outer limit of agricultural settlement bordering on areas still under Indian control or unoccupied.

great planters; those not so fortunate had to settle for lesser prosperity and lower status.

During the pioneer phase of southern frontier life, all the members of migrating families devoted most of their time to the various tasks necessary to keep the family alive. Even their social and recreational lives tended to center on practical tasks. House building, planting, and harvesting were often done in cooperation with neighbors. Such occasions saw plenty of food and homemade whiskey consumed, and at day's end, music and dancing often lasted long into the night. Women gathered together separately for large-scale projects such as group quilting. Another community event for southwestern settlers was the periodic religious revival, which brought people from miles around to revival meetings that might last for days (see pages 342–343). Here they could make new acquaintances, court sweethearts, and discuss the common failings in their souls and on their farms.

Westering Yankees

For migrants to areas such as Michigan and Oregon, the overall frontier experience differed in many respects from that in the Mississippi Valley. In the Old Northwest, Indians had also cleared the land for planting, easing the task for incoming farmers. As arriving whites pushed out the Winnebagos and others, pioneers snatched up the Indians' deserted farms. In this region, professional surveyors had already carved the land into neat rectangular lots before it was sold. These surveys generally included provision for a township, where settlers quickly established villages similar to those left behind in New England, in which they re-created the social institutions they already knew and respected—first and foremost, law courts, churches, and schools. These institutions helped to prevent the sort of social distinctions that developed so quickly along the southern frontier. That is not to say that all northern frontiersmen fared equally, but class differences among them were not so vast or so obvious as between members of the slaveholding elite and their poorer neighbors.

Conditions in the Oregon Country resembled those farther east in most respects, but some significant differences did exist. Most important, the Indians in the Oregon Country had never practiced agriculture—their environment was so rich in fish, meat, and wild vegetables that farming was unnecessary—and they still occupied their traditional homelands and outnumbered whites significantly. Although

both of these facts might have had a profound impact on life in Oregon, early pioneers were bothered by neither. Large open prairies flanking the Columbia, Willamette, and other rivers provided abundant fertile farmland. And the Indians helped rather than hindered the pioneers.

Much like the Indians in colonial New England, groups such as the Nez Perces, Cayuses, and Kalapuyas welcomed whites. In fact, in 1831 the Nez Perces, who had hosted Lewis and Clark in 1805 (see page 229), and the Flatheads issued an appeal for whites to come live among them, spurring the rush of missionaries who opened the Oregon Country for American settlement. Although occasional tensions arose between white settlers and Indians, no serious conflict took place until the winter of 1847, when a combination of disease, white population pressure, and factionalism within the tribe led a group of Cayuse Indians to kill missionaries Marcus and Narcissa Whitman. The Whitman massacre triggered the Cayuse War and led to a concerted effort by white Americans in the Oregon Country to remove Indians.

Like their southwestern counterparts, pioneers in both the Old and the Pacific Northwest cooperated in house building, annual planting and harvesting, and other big jobs, but a more sober air prevailed at these gatherings among the descendants of New England Puritans. Religious life was also more solemn. Religious revivals swept through Yankee settlements during the 1830s and 1840s, but the revival meetings tended to be held in churches at the center of communities rather than in outlying campgrounds. As a result, they were usually briefer and less emotional than their counterparts in the Southwest and strongly reinforced the Yankee notion of village solidarity.

The Hispanic Southwest

The physical and cultural environment in California differed greatly from the Pacific Northwest, and frontier life in California was in many ways unique. One major reason for the difference was that Spain had colonized California and the Spanish had left a lasting cultural imprint.

Although they could assert a claim extending back to the mid-1500s, systematic Spanish exploration into what is now the state of California did not begin until 1769. Prompted in part by Russian expansion into Spanish-claimed territory, Gaspar de Portolá, the governor of Baja California, led an expedition northward and established garrisons at San Diego and Monterey.

Using Indian labor, Franciscan missionaries transformed the dry California coastal hill country into a blooming garden and built a long string of missions in which to celebrate their religion. This painting of Mission San Gabriel conveys the beauty and the awesome size of these mission establishments. *Courtesy of the Santa Barbara Mission Archive-Library.*

Junípero Serra, a Franciscan monk, accompanied Portolá's expedition and established a mission, San Diego de Alcalá, near the present city of San Diego. Eventually Serra and his successors established twenty-one missions extending from San Diego to the town of Sonoma, north of San Francisco.

The mission system provided a framework for Spanish settlement in California. Established in terrain that resembled the hills of Spain, the missions were soon surrounded by groves, vineyards, and lush farms. California Indians were harnessed for the labor needed to create this new landscape, but not willingly: the missionaries often forced them into the missions, where they became virtual slaves. The death rate from disease and harsh treatment among the mission Indians

was terrible, but their labor turned California's coastal plain into a vast and productive garden.

The Franciscans continued to control the most fertile and valuable lands in California until after Mexico won independence from Spain. Between 1834 and 1840, however, the Mexican government seized the mission lands in California and sold them off to private citizens living in the region. An elite class of

> **Junípero Serra** Spanish missionary who went to California in 1769; he and his successors established near the California coast a chain of missions that depended on Indian labor.

Spanish-speaking Californians snatched up the rich lands. Taking advantage of continuing turmoil in the Mexican government and the distance between California's fertile coast and Mexico City, these landholding **Californios** amassed a great degree of political and economic power. Never numbering more than about a thousand people, this Hispanic elite class eventually owned some 15 million acres of California's richest land. In 1836 the Californios and non-Hispanic newcomers together rebelled against Mexico to make one of their own, Juan Bautista Alvarado, governor. The landholding elite never ended California's official relationship with Mexico but continued to run their own affairs.

At first, the Californios welcomed outsiders as neighbors and trading partners. Ships from the United States called at California ports regularly, picking up cargoes of beef **tallow,** cow hides, and other commodities to be shipped around the world, and settlers who promised to open new lands and business opportunities were given generous grants and assistance. **John Sutter,** for example, received an outright grant of land extending from the Sierra foothills southwest to the Sacramento Valley, where in 1839 he established a colony called New Helvetia.

People of many races and classes could be found strolling the lanes in New Helvetia and in other northern California settlements. Farther south, however, in the heartland of Spanish California, the Hispanic landholding elite resented intrusions by lower-class Mexicans and other newcomers. Thus, although new pioneers had been instrumental in elevating him to power, Governor Alvarado worried constantly about their designs and motivations. His henchmen arrested a number of American and British citizens on the suspicion that they were plotting to overthrow his government.

A similar but more harmonious pattern of interracial cooperation existed in other Spanish North American provinces. In 1821 trader William Becknell began selling and trading goods along the Santa Fe Trail from St. Louis to New Mexico. By 1824, the business had become so profitable that people from all over the frontier moved in to create a permanent Santa Fe trade. As had taken place in St. Louis, an elite class emerged in Santa Fe from the intermingled fortunes and intermarriages among Indian, European, and American populations, and a strong kinship system developed. Thus, based on kinship, the Hispanic leaders of New Mexico, unlike those of California, consistently worked across cultural lines, whether to fight off Texan aggression or eventually to lobby for **annexation** to the United States.

Intercultural cooperation also characterized the early history of Texas settlement. Spanish and then Mexican officials aided the empresarios, hoping that the aggressive Americans would form a frontier line between southern Plains Indians and prosperous silver-mining communities south of the **Rio Bravo.** Tensions rose, however, as population increased. Despite the best efforts of the Mexican government to encourage Hispanics to settle in Texas, fully four-fifths of the thirty-five hundred land titles perfected by the empresarios went to non-Hispanics, most of whom were impoverished but hopeful frontiersmen from the southern United States.

In Texas, economic desperation combined with cultural insensitivity and misunderstanding to create the sort of tensions that were rare in New Mexico. As a result of the relative lack of harmony and the enormous stretches of land that separated ethnic groups in Texas, both **Texians** and **Tejanos** tended to cling to their own ways.

The Mormon Community

Physical and cultural conditions in the Great Basin led to a completely different social and cultural order in that area. Utah is a high-desert plateau where water is scarce and survival depends on careful management. The tightly knit community of Mormons was perfectly suited to such an inhospitable place, and their social order responded well to the hostile environment.

Mormons followed a simple principle: "Land belongs to the Lord, and his Saints are to use so much as they can work profitably." The church measured off

---

Californios Spanish colonists in California in the eighteenth and nineteenth centuries.

tallow Hard fat obtained from the bodies of cattle and other animals and used to make candles and soap.

John Sutter Swiss immigrant who founded a colony in California; the discovery of gold on his property in the Coloma Valley, northeast of New Helvetia (Sacramento) in 1848 attracted hordes of miners who seized his land, leaving him financially ruined.

annexation The incorporation of a territory into an existing political unit such as a neighboring country.

Rio Bravo The Spanish and then Mexican name for the river that now forms the border between Texas and Mexico; the Rio Grande.

Texians Non-Hispanic settlers in Texas in the nineteenth century.

Tejanos Mexican settlers in Texas in the nineteenth century.

With two wives and several children to help share the burden of work, this Mormon settler was in a good position to do well, even in the harsh conditions that prevailed in the near-desert environment of Utah. Sensitive to disapproval from more traditional Christians, families like this tended to associate exclusively with other Mormons and pressured outsiders to leave as quickly as possible. *Denver Public Library, Western History Division.*

plots of various sizes, up to 40 acres, and assigned them to settlers on the basis of need. Thus a man with several wives, a large number of children, and enough wealth to hire help might receive a grant of 40 acres, but a man with one wife, few children, and little capital might receive only 10. The size of a land grant determined the extent to which the recipient was obligated to support community efforts. When the church ordered the construction of irrigation systems or other public works, a man who had been granted 40 acres had to provide four times the amount of labor as one who had been granted 10 acres. Like settlers elsewhere, the Mormons in Utah joined in community work parties, but cooperation among them was more rigidly controlled and formal. As on other frontiers, when the system worked it was because it was well suited to natural conditions.

Mormons had their own peculiar religious and social culture, and because of their bad experiences in Missouri and Illinois, they were unaccepting of strangers. The General Authorities of the church made every effort to keep Utah an exclusively Mormon so-ciety, welcoming all who would embrace the new religion and its practices but making it difficult for non-Mormons to stay in the region. The one exception was the American Indian population. Because Indians occupied a central place in Mormon sacred literature (see pages 340–341), the Mormons practiced an accepting and gentle Indian policy. Like other missionaries, Mormons insisted that Indians convert to their religion and lifestyle, but the Mormon hierarchy used its enormous power in Utah to prevent private violence against Indians whenever possible.

The Triumph of "Manifest Destiny"

■ What forces in American life contributed to the concept of manifest destiny?

■ To what extent did the actions taken by American settlers in Oregon and Texas reflect the ideal of manifest destiny?

■ What were the global implications of manifest destiny?

Economic opportunity was the primary reason for

westward movement before the Civil War erupted in 1861, but cultural and religious concerns also pushed people west, following migrants they knew personally or people whose religious views and cultural values resembled their own. Political ideology, too, promoted westward expansion. The idea that proved most influential in opening the West was not new, but it received a name only in 1845: manifest destiny.

The Rise of Manifest Destiny

To some extent, manifest destiny can be traced back to the sense of mission that had motivated colonial Puritans (see page 71). Like John Winthrop and his Massachusetts Bay associates, many early nineteenth-century Americans believed they had a duty to go into new lands. During the antebellum period, romantic nationalism, land hunger, and Second Great Awakening evangelicalism shaped this sense of divine mission into a new and powerful commitment to westward expansion. As the American Board of Commissioners for Foreign Missions noted in its annual report for 1827, "The tide of emigration is rolling westward so rapidly, that it must speedily surmount every barrier, till it reaches every habitable part of this continent." The power of this force led many to conclude that the westward movement was not just an economic process but was part of a divine plan for North America and the world.

Not surprisingly, the earliest and most aggressive proponents of expansion were Christian missionary organizations whose many magazines, newsletters, and reports were the first to give it formal voice. Politicians, however, were not far behind. Democratic warhorse and expansion advocate Thomas Hart Benton of Missouri borrowed both the tone and content of missionary rhetoric in his speeches promoting generous land policies, territorial acquisition, and even overseas expansion. In 1825, for example, Benton argued in favor of American colonization of the Pacific coast for two reasons: it would bring "great and wonderful benefits" not only to the Indians but also to the Chinese and Japanese; and it would allow "science, liberal principles in government, and true religion [to] cast their lights across the intervening sea."

Expansion to the North and West

One major complication standing in the way of the nation's perceived manifest destiny was the fact that Spain, Britain, Russia, and other countries already owned large parts of the continent. The continued presence of the British, for example, proved to be a constant source of irritation. During the War of 1812, the War Hawks had advocated conquering Canada and pushing the British from the continent altogether (see page 250). Although events thwarted this ambition, many continued to push for that objective by either legal or extralegal means.

One confrontation flared in 1838. The United States and Britain had been disputing Maine's boundaries since the Treaty of Paris in 1783. Growing impatient, Canadian loggers moved into the disputed region during the winter of 1838–1839 and began cutting trees. American lumberjacks resolved to drive them away, and fighting soon broke out. The Canadian province of New Brunswick and the state of Maine then mobilized their militias, the American Congress nervously called up fifty thousand men in case of war, and President Van Buren ordered in **Winfield Scott.** Once on the scene, General Scott was able to calm tempers and arrange a truce, but tension continued to run high.

Another source of dispute between the United States and Great Britain was the **Oregon Question.** The vast Oregon tract had been claimed at one time or another by Spain, Russia, France, England, and the United States (see Map 13.1). By the 1820s, only England and the United States continued to contest for its ownership. At the close of the War of 1812, the two countries had been unable to settle their claims, and in 1818 had agreed to joint occupation of Oregon for ten years (see page 278). They extended this arrangement indefinitely in 1827, with the **proviso** that either country could end it with one year's notice.

Oregon's status as neither British nor American was a problem even before wagon trains of Americans began pouring into the region. In 1841 wealthy American pioneer Ewing Young died without leaving a will. Because the Oregon Country had no laws, no guidelines existed on who was entitled to inherit his property. Finally, Methodist missionary officials

---

Winfield Scott   Virginia soldier and statesman who led troops in the War of 1812 and the War with Mexico; he was still serving as a general at the start of the Civil War.

Oregon Question   The question of the national ownership of the Pacific Northwest; the United States and England renegotiated the boundary in 1846, establishing it at 49° north latitude.

proviso   A clause making a qualification, condition, or restriction in a document.

MAP 13.1 Oregon Territory   This map shows the changing boundaries and shifting possession of the Oregon Country. As a result of Polk's aggressive stance and economic pressures, Britain ceded all land south of the 49th parallel to the United States in 1846.

created a **probate court** and instructed it to follow the statutes of the state of New York. At the same time, the missionaries appointed a committee to frame a constitution and draft a basic code of laws. Opposition from the British put an end to this early effort at self-rule, but the movement continued.

Two years later, Americans in Oregon began agitating again, this time supposedly because of wolves preying on their livestock. Settlers in the Willamette Valley held a series of "Wolf Meetings" in 1843 to discuss joint protection and resolved to create a civil government. They called a constitutional convention for May 2. Although the British tried to prevent the convention, the assembly passed the **First Organic Laws** of Oregon on July 5, 1843, making Oregon an independent republic in all but name. Independence, however, was not the settlers' long-term goal. The document's preamble announced that the code of laws would continue in force "until such time as the United States of America extend their jurisdiction over us."

Revolution in Texas

Questions about the nation's southwestern borders were quite different from boundary disputes in the Northeast and Pacific Northwest. Unlike the situation in northern Maine and the Oregon Country, the matter of ownership in the Southwest was fairly clear. The area including present-day Texas, New Mexico, Arizona, California, Nevada, and portions of Colorado, Oklahoma, Kansas, and Wyoming belonged to Spain prior to Mexico's successful revolution in 1821. After that revolution, common precedent dictated that it belonged to Mexico, despite Spain's continued protest to the contrary. But owning this vast region and controlling it were two different matters. The distance and rough terrain separating the capital in Mexico City from the northern provinces made governing the region problematic. Moreover, large areas of Texas and New Mexico were home to strong and independent Indian groups such as the Comanches, who made the extension of both settlement and law difficult.

Although the Spanish and then the Mexican government had invited Anglo-Americans to settle in the Southwest, these pioneers generally ignored Mexican customs, including their pledge to practice Roman Catholicism, and often disregarded Mexican law. This was particularly the case after 1829, when Mexico began attaching duties to trade items moving between the region and the neighboring United States. Mexico also abolished importing slaves. Bad feelings grew over the years, but the distant and politically unstable Mexican government could do little to enforce laws, customs, or faith. In addition, despite the friction between cultures in Texas, many Tejanos—men such as Lorenzo de Zavala—were disturbed by the corruption and political instability in Mexico City and were as eager as their Texian counterparts to participate in the United States' thriving cotton market.

Assuming responsibility for forging a peaceful settlement to the problems between settlers in Texas and the Mexican government, Stephen F. Austin went to

probate court   A court that establishes the validity of wills and administers the estates of people who have died.

First Organic Laws   A constitution adopted by American settlers in the Oregon Country on July 5, 1843, establishing a government independent from Great Britain and requesting annexation by the United States.

Mexico City in 1833. While Austin was there, **Antonio López de Santa Anna** seized power after a series of revolutions and disputed elections. A former supporter of federalism and a key figure in the adoption of a republican constitution in 1824, Santa Anna had come to the conclusion that Mexico was not ready for democracy. Upon assuming power, he suspended the constitution, dismissed congress, and set himself up as the self-declared "Napoleon of the West."

Throughout Mexico, former revolutionaries and common citizens who had anticipated democracy were outraged by Santa Anna's actions. To the south, in Yucatán and elsewhere, provinces openly rebelled. The same potential existed along the northern frontier as well. Trying to avoid an open break, Austin met with Santa Anna in 1834 and presented several petitions advocating reforms and greater self-government in Texas, but Santa Anna made it clear that he intended to exert his authority over the region. On his arrival back in Texas in 1835, Austin declared, "War is our only recourse." At a banquet given in his honor early in September, Austin announced to the mixed Tejano and Texian audience, "The constitutional rights and the security and peace of Texas—they ought to be maintained; and jeopardized as they now are, they demand a general consultation of the people." He was immediately made chairman of a committee to call for a convention of delegates from all over Texas. Members of the group that convened followed Austin's terminology, referring to themselves as the "Consultation."

Mexican officials, viewing the unrest in Texas as rebellion against their authority, issued arrest warrants for all the Texas troublemakers they could identify and **deployed** troops to San Antonio. Austin's committee immediately sent out word for Texans to arm themselves. The **Texas Revolution** started quickly thereafter when the little town of Gonzales refused to surrender a cannon to Mexican officials on September 29, 1835, and a battle ensued several days later (see Map 13.2).

After the battle in Gonzales and several other small encounters, the Texas Consultation formed itself into a provisional government in November 1835 and adopted the Mexican federalist constitution of 1824, recently suspended by Santa Anna, as its legal foundation. Angered by the rebellion, Santa Anna personally led the Mexican army into Texas, arriving in San Antonio on February 23, 1836. Knowing that Santa Anna was on his way, Texas commander William Travis had moved his troops into the **Alamo.** On March 6 Santa Anna ordered an all-out assault and despite sustaining staggering casualties was able

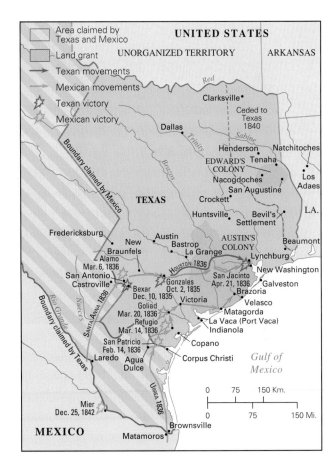

MAP 13.2 Texas Revolution This map shows troop movements and the major battles in the Texas Revolution, as well as the conflicting boundary claims made by Texans and the Mexican government. The Battle of San Jacinto and the Treaty of Velasco ended the war, but the conflicting land claims continued when Mexico repudiated the treaty.

to capture the former mission. Most of the post's defenders were killed in the assault, and Santa Anna executed those who survived the battle, including

Antonio López de Santa Anna Mexican general who was president of Mexico when he led an attack on the Alamo in 1836; he again led Mexico during its war with the United States in 1846–1848.

deploy To position military resources (troops, artillery, equipment) in preparation for action.

Texas Revolution A revolt by American colonists in Texas against Mexican rule; it began in 1835 and ended with the establishment of the Republic of Texas in 1836.

Alamo A fortified Franciscan mission at San Antonio; rebellious Texas colonists were besieged and annihilated there by Santa Anna's forces in 1836.

Following the Battle of San Jacinto, Mexican president Antonio López de Santa Anna was captured while trying to escape disguised as a private. Texas forces brought him to Sam Houston, who had been wounded in the battle, in order to convey his formal surrender. A month later, the captured president signed the Treaty of Valasco, granting Texas its independence in exchange for his own release and return to Mexico. *Texas State Library and Archives Commission.*

former American congressman and frontier celebrity Davy Crockett.

While Santa Anna was subduing San Antonio, Texas rebels elsewhere were occupied with consolidating the revolution. On March 2, a convention met at Washington-on-the-Brazos and issued a declaration of independence. The convention adopted a constitution written by former Mexican revolutionary and federalist Lorenzo de Zavala, ratifying it on March 16. On the following day, David G. Burnet was elected president of the new republic, and Zavala was elected vice president. **Sam Houston** had earlier been named commander of the army.

Despite the loss at the Alamo, Texans continued to underestimate Santa Anna's strength and his resolve to put down the rebellion. After a series of defeats, however, the Texans scored a stunning victory on April 21. Santa Anna had ordered his army to pause at the San Jacinto River. Arriving in the vicinity undetected, Houston's force of just over nine hundred formed up quietly and attacked. In just eighteen minutes, 630 Mexican soldiers lay dead. Disguised in a private's uniform, Santa Anna attempted to escape but was captured and brought to Houston. In exchange

for his release, in May 1836 the Mexican president signed the **Treaty of Velasco,** officially recognizing Texas's independence and acknowledging the Rio Grande as the border between Texas and Mexico. Santa Anna then returned to Mexico and was immediately deposed as president. The new government repudiated the treaty with Texas, but was in no immediate position to do anything about it.

As in Oregon, many leaders in Texas hoped their actions would lead to swift annexation by the United States. In 1838 Houston, by then president of the Republic of Texas, invited the United States to annex Texas. Because all of Texas lay below the Missouri Compromise line (see page 281–283), John Quincy Adams, elected to the House of Representatives after his loss

Sam Houston American general and politician who fought in the struggle for Texas's independence from Mexico and became president of the Republic of Texas.

Treaty of Velasco Treaty that Santa Anna signed in May 1836 after his capture at the San Jacinto River; it recognized the Republic of Texas but was later rejected by the Mexican congress.

in the presidential election of 1828, **filibustered** for three weeks against the acquisition of such a massive block of potential slave territory. Seeking to avoid national controversy, Congress refused to ratify the annexation treaty.

The Politics of Manifest Destiny

Although Adams was typical of one wing of the Whig coalition, he certainly did not speak for the majority of Whigs on the topic of national expansion. The party of manufacturing, revivalism, and social reform inclined naturally toward the blending of political, economic, and religious evangelicalism that was manifest destiny. William Henry Harrison himself, the united party's first national candidate, was a colorful figure in American westward expansion. He had been a prominent War Hawk and Indian fighter in the years leading up to the War of 1812 (see pages 250–252), and his political campaign in 1840 celebrated the simple pleasures and virtues of frontier life, appealing to a westering population. When Harrison died soon after taking office in 1841, his vice president, John Tyler, picked up the torch of American expansionism.

Tyler was a less typical Whig than even Adams. A Virginian and a states' rights advocate, he had been a staunch Democrat until the nullification crisis, when he bolted the party in protest against Jackson's strong assertion of federal power (see page 297). As president, Tyler seemed still to be more Democrat than Whig. Although he had objected to Jackson's use of presidential power, like Old Hickory, Tyler as president was unyielding where political principles were concerned. He vetoed high protective tariffs, internal improvement bills that he perceived as unnecessary, and attempts to revive the Second Bank of the United States. In fact, during Tyler's administration, Whigs accomplished only two moderate goals: they eliminated Van Buren's hated treasury system (see page 354), and they passed a slightly higher tariff. Tyler's refusal to promote Whig economic policies led to a general crisis in government in 1843, when his entire cabinet resigned over his veto of a bank bill.

Tyler did share his party's desire for expansion, however. He assigned his secretary of state, Daniel Webster, to negotiate a treaty with Britain to settle the Maine matter once and for all. The resulting **Webster-Ashburton Treaty** (1842) gave more than half of the disputed territory to the United States and finally established the nation's northeastern border with Canada. Tyler also adopted an aggressive stance on the Oregon Question by appointing a federal Indian agent

for the region in 1842—an act of doubtful legality in view of the mutual occupation agreement between the United States and Great Britain. His appointee, former missionary Elijah White, was one of the organizers of the Wolf Meetings and helped draft the First Organic Laws. Historians have speculated that Tyler also encouraged Marcus Whitman to help guide a large party of immigrants into Oregon in 1843 as a way of bolstering the U.S. claim to the region.

Tyler also pushed a forceful policy toward Texas and the Southwest. In 1842 Sam Houston repeated his invitation for the United States to annex Texas, only to be rebuffed by Secretary of State Webster, a New Englander who shared Adams's views. When Webster resigned with the other cabinet officers in 1843, however, Tyler replaced him with fellow Virginian Abel P. Upshur, who immediately reopened the matter of Texas annexation.

Negotiations between Houston's representatives and Tyler's secretary of state—Upshur at first, then, after Upshur's death, John C. Calhoun—led to a treaty of annexation on April 11, 1844. In line with the repudiated Treaty of Velasco, the annexation document named the Rio Grande as the southern boundary of Texas. Annexation remained a major arguing point between proslavery and antislavery forces, however, and the treaty failed ratification in the Senate. The issue of Texas annexation then joined the Oregon Question as a major campaign issue in the presidential election of 1844.

Expansion and the Election of 1844

As the Whigs and the Democrats geared up for a national election, it became clear that expansion would be the key issue. This put the two leading political figures of the day, Democrat Martin Van Buren and Whig Henry Clay, in an uncomfortable position. Van Buren was on record as opposing the extension of slavery and was therefore against the annexation of Texas. Clay, the architect of the American System (see page 272), was opposed to any form of uncontrolled

---

filibuster   To use obstructionist tactics, especially prolonged speechmaking, in order to delay legislative action.

Webster-Ashburton Treaty   Treaty that in 1842 established the present border between Canada and northeastern Maine.

This campaign banner celebrating the candidacy of James K. Polk and George M. Dallas on the Democratic ticket carries a subtle message conveying the party's platform. Surrounding Polk's picture are twenty-five stars, one for each state in the Union. Outside the corner box, a twenty-sixth star stands for Texas, which Polk promised to annex. *Collection of David J. and Janet L. Frent.*

expansion, especially if it meant fanning sectional tensions, and he too opposed immediate annexation of Texas. Approaching the election, both issued statements to the effect that they would back annexation only with Mexico's consent.

Clay's somewhat ambiguous stance on expansion contrasted sharply with Tyler's efforts to advance the cause of manifest destiny. However, President Tyler's constant refusal to support the larger Whig political agenda led the party to nominate Clay anyway. Van Buren was not so lucky. The strong southern wing of the Democratic Party was so put off by Van Buren's position on slavery that it blocked him, securing the nomination of Tennessee congressman **James K. Polk.**

The Democrats based their platform on the issues surrounding Oregon and Texas. They implied that the regions rightfully belonged to the United States, stating "that the re-occupation of Oregon and the re-annexation of Texas at the earliest practicable period are great American measures." Polk vowed to stand up to the British by claiming the entire Oregon Country up to 54°40′ north latitude and to defend the territorial claims of Texas. The Democrats played up both regions to appeal to the manifest destiny sentiments of both northerners and southerners. For his part,

Clay continued to waffle on expansionism, emphasizing economic policies instead.

The election demonstrated the people's commitment to manifest destiny. Clay was a national figure, well respected and regarded as one of the nation's leading statesmen, whereas Polk was barely known outside Tennessee. Still, Polk polled forty thousand more popular votes than Clay and garnered sixty-five more electoral votes. Seeing the election as a political barometer, outgoing president Tyler prepared a special message to Congress in December 1844 proposing a **joint resolution** annexing Texas. Many congressmen who had opposed annexation could not ignore the clear mandate given to manifest destiny in the presidential election, and the bill to annex Texas passed in February 1845, just as Tyler prepared to turn the White House over to his Democratic successor.

James K. Polk Tennessee congressman who was a leader of the Democratic Party and the dark-horse winner of the presidential campaign in 1844.

joint resolution A formal statement adopted by both houses of Congress and subject to approval by the president; if approved, it has the force of law.

Though Polk was not well known, he was a seasoned politician. Often called "Young Hickory" because of his political resemblance to Andrew Jackson, Polk had entered politics in Tennessee as a very young man, serving fourteen years in Congress and two years as governor of the state. Like Jackson, Polk was tenacious, seldom willing to surrender when locked into political struggles. He supported Jacksonian political notions, disavowing protective tariffs and national banks while embracing expansionism.

Holding to the position he had taken prior to the election, in his annual message for 1845 Polk asked Congress to end the joint occupation of Oregon. Referring to the largely forgotten Monroe Doctrine (see page 278–279), the president insisted that no nation other than the United States should be permitted to occupy any part of North America and urged Congress to assert exclusive control over the Oregon Country even if doing so meant war.

Neither the United States nor Britain intended to go to war over Oregon. The only issue—where the border would be—was a matter for the bargaining table, not the battlefield. Recalling the rhetoric that had gotten him elected, Polk insisted on 54°40'. The British lobbied for the Columbia River as the boundary, but their position softened quickly. The fur trade along the Columbia was in rapid decline and had become unprofitable by the early 1840s. As a result, in the spring of 1846, the British foreign secretary offered Polk a compromise boundary at the 49th parallel. The Senate recommended that Polk accept the offer, and a treaty settling the Oregon Question was ratified on June 15, 1846. Sectional politics, however, delayed the admission of Oregon as a territory for a few years.

Expansion and Sectional Crisis

■ On what bases did some Americans support and other Americans oppose the war with Mexico?

■ How did expansionism and economics help shape Americans' positions on slavery in the 1840s?

Slavery lay at the heart of the significant political controversy that accompanied expansion. Although only a few radicals totally opposed slavery, many people in the North and West strongly opposed its expansion. For them this was less a moral than an economic issue. The expansion of slavery meant open economic competition with slaves or slaveholders for jobs and profits. Southerners, in contrast, demanded that slavery be allowed to expand as far as economic opportunity permitted. And, not surprisingly, southerners

believed the nation's manifest destiny was to expand into areas where cotton would grow and slavery would be most profitable. Given these strong economic motives, the congressional gag rule passed in 1836 (see page 351) could not prevent the debate over expansion from turning into a debate over slavery.

The Texas Crisis and Sectional Conflict

Whatever President Polk chose to do about Texas would have promoted a political crisis, but action of some sort could not be avoided. In annexing Texas, Tyler and Calhoun had offended the Mexican government, which still considered Texas a province. When Congress adopted the joint resolution annexing Texas and establishing the Rio Grande as its southern border, Mexico's popular press linked the event with an uprising in New Mexico in 1837 and continued restlessness in California, raising fears of an American conspiracy against Mexican sovereignty. The press demanded that Mexico sever diplomatic relations with the United States. The government did so immediately, threatening war. Polk added to the tension, and seemed to confirm Mexican fears, by declaring that the entire Southwest should be annexed.

Polk sought his objectives peacefully but prepared to use force in case Mexico rejected his overtures. Late in 1845, the president dispatched John Slidell to Mexico City to negotiate the boundary dispute. He also authorized Slidell to purchase New Mexico and California if possible. At the same time, Polk dispatched American troops to Louisiana, ready to strike if Mexico resisted Slidell's offers. And he notified the American consul in California, Thomas O. Larkin, that the Pacific fleet had orders to seize California ports if war broke out with Mexico. If American citizens in the region then wished to rebel against Mexico, the president said, the United States would support them and invite them to join the Union.

Nervous but bristling over what seemed to be preparations for war, and rightfully upset that Polk had disregarded the break in diplomatic relations by sending an emissary, the Mexican government refused to receive Slidell. In January 1846, Slidell sent word to the president that his mission was a failure. Receiving that report, Polk ordered **Zachary Taylor** to

Zachary Taylor American general whose defeat of Santa Anna at Buena Vista in 1847 made him a national hero and the Whig choice for president in 1848.

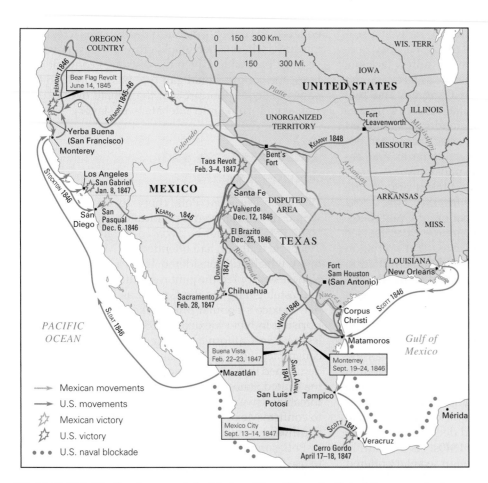

MAP 13.3 The Southwest and the Mexican War   When the United States acquired Texas, it inherited the Texans' boundary disputes with Mexico. This map shows the outcome: war with Mexico in 1846 and the acquisition of the disputed territories in Texas as well as most of Arizona, New Mexico, and California through the Treaty of Guadalupe Hidalgo.

lead troops from New Orleans toward the Rio Grande. Shortly thereafter, an American military party led by **John C. Frémont** entered California's Salinas Valley. By April, the Mexican government had had enough. On April 22, Mexico proclaimed that its territory had been violated by the United States and declared war. Two days later, Mexican troops engaged a detachment of Taylor's army at Matamoros on the Rio Grande, killing eleven and capturing the rest. When news reached Washington of Taylor's battle at Matamoros, Polk immediately called for war. Although the nation was far from united on the issue, Congress agreed on May 13, 1846 (see Map 13.3).

The outbreak of war disturbed many Americans. In New England, for example, protest ran high. Tran-scendentalist Henry David Thoreau was an outspo-ken critic and chose to be jailed rather than pay taxes that would support the war. It was not expansion as such that troubled Thoreau, but the connection be-tween Texas annexation and slavery. To southerners, the broad stretch of land lying south of 36°30′ (the Missouri Compromise line) represented both eco-nomic and political power. The adoption of proslav-ery constitutions in newly acquired territories would

John C. Frémont   Explorer, soldier, and politician who explored and mapped much of the American West and Northwest; he later ran unsuccessfully for president.

ensure the immigration of friendly voters and the installation of congenial governments, which would strengthen the South's economic and political interests in Congress. Northerners were perturbed by these implications but saw something even more alarming in the southern expansion movement. Since the Missouri Compromise (1820), some northerners had come to believe that a slaveholding **oligarchy** controlled life and politics in the South. Abolitionists warned that this "Slave Power" sought to expand its reach until it controlled every aspect of American life. Many viewed Congress's adoption of the gag rule in 1836 and the drive to annex Texas as evidence of the Slave Power's influence. Thus debates over Texas pitted two regions of the country against each other in what champions of both sides regarded as mortal combat.

Serious political combat began in August 1846 when David Wilmot, a Democratic representative from Pennsylvania, proposed an amendment to a military appropriations bill specifying that "neither slavery nor involuntary servitude shall ever exist" in any territory gained in the War with Mexico. The **Wilmot Proviso** passed in the House of Representatives but failed in the Senate, where equal state representation gave the South a stronger position. At Polk's request, Wilmot refused to propose his proviso when the House reconsidered the war appropriations bill, but Van Buren Democrats defied Polk by attaching the amendment again, and the House approved it once more. Again the Senate rejected the amended bill. In opposing the amendment, John C. Calhoun (reelected to the Senate after serving as Tyler's secretary of state) argued that any territory acquired in the war would belong to all the American people, and that for Congress to forbid any citizen from taking slaves into the area would violate the constitutional protection of life, liberty, and property. The House finally decided in April to appropriate money for the war without stipulating whether or not slavery would be permitted.

War with Mexico

While all this political infighting was going on in Washington, D.C., a real war was going on in the Southwest. In California, American settlers rallied in open rebellion in the Sacramento Valley. The rebels captured the town of Sonoma in June 1846 and declared themselves independent. They crafted a flag depicting a grizzly bear and announced the birth of the Bear Flag Republic. Rushing to Sonoma, Frémont's force joined the Bear Flag rebels and began to march south toward Monterey. The little army arrived on July 19, only to find that the Pacific fleet had

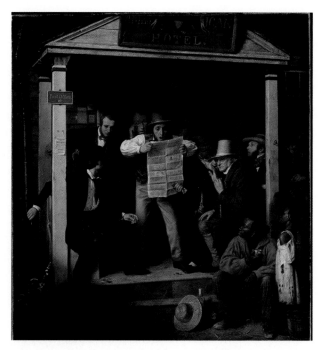

Slaves look on in obvious interest as men gathered at the post office devour the latest news from the front in the war with Mexico. One newspaperman in Baltimore reported, "The news from the army on the Rio Grande has caused more general excitement in this city than has before taken place, perhaps during the present generation." *"War News from Mexico" by Richard Caton Woodville, 1848. The Manogian Foundation © 1996. Board of Trustees, National Gallery of Art, Washington, D.C.*

already acted on Polk's orders and seized the city. The Mexican forces were in full flight southward.

To round out the greater southwestern strategy, Polk ordered Colonel Stephen Kearny to invade New Mexico on May 15. After leading his men across 800 miles of desert to Santa Fe, Kearny found a less-than-hostile enemy force facing him. Members of the interracial upper class of Santa Fe had already expressed interest in joining the United States. Given the opportunity, they surrendered without firing a shot.

---

oligarchy   A small group of people or families who hold power.

Wilmot Proviso   Amendment to an appropriations bill in 1846 proposing that any territory acquired from Mexico be closed to slavery; it was defeated in the Senate.

Within a short time, all of the New Mexico region and California were securely in the hands of U.S. forces. Zachary Taylor in Texas, however, faced more serious opposition. Marching across the Rio Grande, Taylor headed for the Mexican city of Monterrey, which he attacked in September 1846. He managed to capture the city, but only at the cost of agreeing to let the enemy garrison pass unmolested through his lines. From Monterrey, Taylor planned to turn southward toward Mexico City and lead the main attack against the Mexican capital, but politics intervened.

After Taylor's successful siege at Monterrey, Polk began to perceive the popular general as a political threat. In an attempt to undermine Taylor's political appeal, Polk turned the war effort over to Winfield Scott, ordering Scott to gather an army at the port of Tampico, on the Gulf of Mexico. Drawing men from Taylor's and other forces, Scott was then to sail down to Veracruz, from which the army was to move inland to take Mexico City (see Map 13.3).

Polk complicated the military situation by plotting with deposed Mexican president Santa Anna, who had been exiled to Cuba after his defeat at San Jacinto. In secret correspondence with the president, Santa Anna promised that he would end the war and settle the border dispute in Polk's favor if Polk would help him return to Mexico. The American president agreed to sneak Santa Anna back into Mexico, where he soon resumed the presidency. Going back on his agreement, however, Santa Anna also picked up his sword and vowed to resist American territorial expansion into the disputed territory. Thus, while Scott and Taylor were realigning the American forces, Mexico's most able general resumed command of the army and chose to strike.

Planning to crush Taylor's remaining force and then wheel around to attack Scott, Santa Anna and his numerically superior army encountered Taylor at Buena Vista in February 1847. Tired and dispirited from forced marching across the desert, the Mexican army was in no shape to fight, but Santa Anna ordered an attack anyway. Tactically speaking, the **Battle of Buena Vista** was a draw, but it was a strategic victory for the Americans: Taylor's fresher troops stalled Santa Anna's forces, permitting Scott's forces to capture Veracruz on March 9. His eyes firmly on a quick victory, Scott moved relentlessly toward Mexico City. By May 15, however, Scott had run into trouble. Many of his troops were serving under twelve-month enlistments, which had just expired. Feeling they had no obligation to stay, nearly a third of his army went home, leaving the general powerless to proceed. Finally, after three months of waiting, Scott received

supplies and reinforcements and resumed his march on Mexico City. After a crushing assault, Scott and his force routed the Mexican defenders and captured the city on September 13, 1847.

With Mexico City, all of Texas, New Mexico, and California in American hands, the direction of treaty talks should have been fairly predictable. Scott's enormous success, however, caused Santa Anna's government to collapse, leaving no one to negotiate with American peace commissioner Nicholas Trist. After a month had passed with no settlement, Polk concluded that Trist was not pressing hard enough and removed him as peace commissioner. But by the time Polk's orders arrived, the Mexican government had elected a new president and on November 11 told Trist that Mexico was ready to begin negotiations. When Trist received Polk's removal order, he ignored it and pressed on with negotiations. Finally, on February 2, 1848, Trist and the Mexican delegation signed the **Treaty of Guadalupe Hidalgo,** granting the United States all the territory between the Nueces River and the Rio Grande and between there and the Pacific. In exchange, Trist agreed that the United States would pay Mexico $15 million, and he committed the United States to honoring all claims made by Texans for damages resulting from the war.

Polk was very angry when he heard the terms of the treaty. Although the United States had obtained everything it had gone to war for, Polk felt that Scott's sweeping victory at Mexico City should have netted the United States more territory for less money. Political realities in Washington, however, prevented Polk from trying to get a more aggressive treaty ratified by the Senate. Although the president had strong support for his own position in favor of annexing all of Mexico, many antislavery voices loudly protested bringing so much land south of the Missouri Compromise line into the Union. Others opposed the annexation of Mexico because they feared that the largely Roman Catholic population might be a threat to Protestant institutions in the United States. Still others, many of whom had opposed the war to begin with, had moral objections to taking any territory by

Battle of Buena Vista   Battle in February 1847 during which U.S. troops led by Zachary Taylor forced Santa Anna's forces to withdraw into the interior of Mexico.

Treaty of Guadalupe Hidalgo   Treaty (1848) in which Mexico gave up Texas above the Rio Grande and ceded New Mexico and California to the United States in return for $15 million.

An American private, Samuel E. Chamberlain, made this drawing of the Battle of Buena Vista. Present at the battle, Chamberlain watched as Mexican forces overran an artillery emplacement. The Americans eventually turned the tide, and the battle came out a draw. Even so, troops under Santa Anna were forced to retreat into the Mexican interior, spoiling the general's hope for a quick and easy victory against the invading Americans. *"Battle of Buena Vista" by Samuel Chamberlain, 1847. San Jacinto Museum of History Association.*

force. Perhaps more convincing than these arguments, however, was the fact that the war had cost a lot of money, and congressmen were unwilling to allocate more if peace was within reach. Thus Polk submitted the treaty Trist had negotiated, and the Senate approved it by a vote of 38 to 14.

Politicizing Slavery

The American victory in the War with Mexico was an enormous shot in the arm for American nationalism and manifest destiny, but it also brought the divisive issue of slavery back into mainstream politics to a degree unknown since the Missouri Compromise. Opposed to slavery expansion for both political and ethical reasons, David Wilmot had broken a gentlemen's agreement among congressmen to skirt around slavery issues, firmly wedding American expansion and slavery in the minds of many. Even a largely unpolitical nonconformist like Henry David Thoreau found the connection obvious, and protested the war for that reason.

Of course, being opposed to the expansion of slavery was not the same thing as opposing the institution of slavery itself, and antislavery sentiments were still not widespread among the American people during the 1840s. However, as the debates over the Mexican War indicate, abolitionist voices were getting louder and more politically insistent. Despite strong and sometimes violent opposition, the abolition movement had continued to grow, especially among the privileged and educated classes in the Northeast. Throughout the 1830s, evangelicals increasingly stressed the sinful nature of slavery and broke away from the **gradualism** of the American Colonization Society (see page 350). Driven by their postmillennialism (see page 343), men and women steeped in evangelical zeal joined

> **gradualism** The belief that slavery in the United States should be abolished gradually, by methods such as placing territorial limits on slavery or settling free blacks in Africa.

Sojourner Truth was a remarkable woman for her time, or for any time. One anecdote claims that a white policeman in New York state demanded that she identify herself. Using her cane to thrust herself upright to her full six feet of height, she boomed out the same words that God used to identify himself to Moses: "I am that I am." The policeman was unnerved and scurried away. Showing such bravery and pride in both her race and sex, it is little wonder that she commanded great respect in both antislavery and women's rights circles throughout her lifetime. *Sophia Smith Collection, Smith College.*

with William Lloyd Garrison and Angelina Grimké in urging the immediate, uncompensated liberation of slaves.

Garrison, however, consistently alienated his followers. Calling the Constitution "a covenant with death and an agreement with hell," Garrison burned a copy of it, telling his followers, "so perish all compromises with tyranny," and he urged them to have no dealings with a government that permitted so great an evil as slavery. Citing the reluctance of most organized churches to condemn slavery outright, Garrison urged his followers to break with them as well. He also offended many of his white evangelical supporters by associating with and supporting free black advocates of abolition.

During the 1830s, even moderates within the abolition movement had celebrated **Frederick Douglass, Sojourner Truth,** and other African American abolitionists, welcoming them as members of the American Anti-Slavery Society. But more insistent black voices frightened white abolitionists. African American abolitionist David Walker cried, "The whites want slaves, and want us for their slaves, but some of them will curse the day they ever saw us." Walker advocated that African Americans should "kill or be killed." Another black spokesman, Henry Highland Garnet, proclaimed, "Strike for your lives and liberties. Now is the day and hour. Let every slave in the land do this and the days of slavery are numbered. Rather die freemen than live to be slaves."

Garrison's sentiments mobilized some, but most of his followers were more conservative. In 1840 this and other controversial issues caused many of those moderates to bolt from Garrison's American Anti-Slavery Society to form the more temperate American and Foreign Anti-Slavery Society. This new group forged strong ties with mainstream politicians and church leaders who, while opposed to any extension of slavery and sympathetic to moderate abolitionist proposals, had been relatively silent because of Garrison's reputation for radicalism.

Issues in the Election of 1848

Efforts by moderate antislavery supporters meshed with the political aspirations of both those who opposed slavery's expansion primarily for political and economic reasons and those who were motivated by purely ethical concerns to bring limited abolitionism into the political mainstream. Hoping to cash in on the popular attention created by debates over slavery during the War with Mexico, moderates in 1840 challenged both Whig and Democrat ambivalence by forming a third political party: the **Liberty Party.**

Specifically disavowing Garrison's radical aims, Liberty Party leaders argued that slavery would even-

Frederick Douglass Abolitionist and journalist who escaped from slavery in 1838 and became an influential lecturer in the North and abroad.

Sojourner Truth Abolitionist and feminist who was freed from slavery in 1827 and became a leading preacher against slavery and for the rights of women.

Liberty Party The first antislavery political party; it was formed in Albany, New York, in 1840.

The Moderate Split in the Abolition Movement

It is fitting to herald bold leaders like William Lloyd Garrison, celebrating their deep commitment to ethical causes and their willingness to engage in radical action to accomplish their goals. In doing so, we often ignore more moderate voices speaking to those same goals. In the case of abolitionism, however, one of the key events in moving the cause out of obscurity and bringing it into mainstream public attention was the split between radicals and moderates in 1840. By disavowing Garrison's growing radicalism, moderates were able to forge solid alliances with political, business, and religious leaders throughout the North and West as well as with British and other international slavery opponents, who would, together, make the elimination of slavery part of everyday conversation. According to Nobel Prize–winning author Robert William Fogel, it was this broad proliferation of abolitionist discourse, along with its unflinching refusal to go away, that eventually caused slavery's demise.

tually die on its own if it could be confined geographically. In addition, the Liberty Party called for the abolition of slavery in Washington, D.C., and in all the territories where it already existed. Though certainly more popular than Garrison's radical appeals, this moderate message drew little open political support: in 1840 Liberty Party presidential candidate James G. Birney had garnered only about 7,000 out of the nearly 2.5 million votes cast. But in 1844, when he again ran on the Liberty Party ticket, he won 62,000 popular votes. Clearly a moderate antislavery position was becoming more acceptable.

Even in the face of such evidence, both major parties continued to practice the politics of avoidance. Suffering ill health, Polk chose not to run for a second term in 1848, leaving the Democrats scrambling for a candidate. They chose Lewis Cass of Michigan—a longtime moderate on slavery issues—as their presidential candidate and balanced the ticket with General William Butler of Kentucky. The Whigs hoped to ride a wave of nationalism following the War with Mexico by running military hero Zachary Taylor, a Louisianan and a slaveholder, for president and moderate New Yorker Millard Fillmore for vice president.

During the election campaign, Cass tried to avoid offending anyone by suggesting that the federal government withdraw entirely from the slavery question. He advanced instead a policy of **popular sovereignty,** which would permit the territories to choose for themselves whether or not to admit slavery. Taylor refused to go even that far, echoing Calhoun's opinion that no one had the authority to control slavery in the territories.

As in 1840 and again in 1844, it took a third party to cut to the heart of the issues. A number of northern Democrats who had supported the Wilmot Proviso felt that Cass's and the Democratic Party's position on slavery was too weak-kneed. Casting about for alternatives, they joined with a number of northern Whigs who could not support the slaveholding Taylor and with former members of the Liberty Party, which had collapsed after its failure in 1844, to promote the candidacy of antislavery advocate Martin Van Buren. Adopting the slogan "Free soil, free speech, free labor, and free men," this northern antislavery coalition dubbed itself the **Free-Soil Party.** Even more than the Liberty Party before it, the Free-Soil Party avoided taking a radical stand on the issue of slavery itself but was firm about excluding slavery from the territories.

The two major parties split more than 2.5 million votes almost evenly—Taylor polled 1,360,000 to Cass's 1,220,000 and won the presidency with 163 electoral votes to Cass's 127. The Free-Soilers, however, made a stronger showing than their predecessors had made. When the votes were counted, Van Buren had won almost 300,000, nearly 10 percent of the total votes cast, but no electoral votes. Congress remained split between Whigs and Democrats, though many northern Whigs were leaning in a Free-Soil direction. Sectional issues had not yet fragmented the political system, but large cracks were now visible.

popular sovereignty   The doctrine that the people of a territory had the right to determine whether slavery would exist within their territory.

Free-Soil Party   A political party that opposed the extension of slavery into any of the territories newly acquired from Mexico.

Individual Voices

Examining a Primary Source

Lorenzo de Zavala Predicts the Spread of Liberal Democracy

Lorenzo de Zavala spent his entire adult life working for expanding freedoms in his native Mexico. Working at first within the Spanish Empire and then as both an elected and appointed administrative official in the independent Mexican republic, Zavala constantly chafed at what he characterized as the unnatural impositions that governments placed on a rational and freedom-loving citizenry. Having fled the military dictatorship that emerged in Mexico in the late 1820s, Zavala traveled extensively and recorded his views about government and his hopes for Mexico's future.

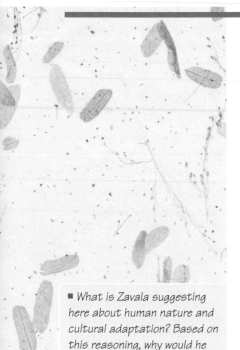

■ What is Zavala suggesting here about human nature and cultural adaptation? Based on this reasoning, why would he have opposed Mexican policies in Texas?

■ To whom and to what is Zavala referring in this passage? What does this say about his reasons for supporting revolution in Texas?

■ These seven Mexican states are the northernmost—that is, closest to the United States. The six states that follow all occupy the Mexican interior.

■ Zavala seems to be describing a process not unlike that which U.S. expansionists would call "manifest destiny." Is Zavala espousing manifest destiny? How do his views compare with those expressed by others at this time?

I have set forth my opinions concerning that beautiful and rich portion of land known formerly as the province of Texas. . . . Once the way was opened to colonization, as it should have been, under a system of free government, it was necessary that a new generation should appear within a few years and populate a part of the Mexican republic, and consequently that this new population should be entirely heterogeneous with respect to the other provinces or states of the country. Fifteen or twenty thousand foreigners distributed over the vast areas of Mexico, Oaxaca, Veracruz, etc., scattered among the former inhabitants cannot cause any sudden change in their ways, manners and customs. Rather they adopt the tendencies, manners, language, religion, politics and even the vices of the multitude that surrounds them. An Englishman will be a Mexican in Mexico City, and a Mexican an Englishman in London. ■

The same thing will not happen with colonies. Completely empty woods and lands, uninhabited a dozen years ago, converted into villages and towns suddenly by Germans, Irish, and North Americans, must of necessity form an entirely different nation, and it would be absurd to try to get them to renounce their religion, their customs and their deepest convictions. ■ *What will be the result?*

I have stated it many times. They will not be able to subject themselves to a military regime and ecclesiastical government such as unfortunately have continued in Mexican territory in spite of the republican-democratic constitutions. . . . When a military leader tries to intervene in civil transactions, they will resist, and they will triumph. They will organize popular assemblies to deal with political matters as is done in the United States and in England. They will build chapels for different faiths to worship the Creator according to their beliefs. . . . Within a few years this fortunate conquest of civilization will continue its course through other states toward the south, and those of Tamaulipas, Nuevo Leon, San Luis, Chihuahua, Durango, Jalisco, and Zacatecas ■ *will be the freest ones in the Mexican confederation. Meanwhile, those of Mexico, Puebla, Veracruz, Oaxaca, Michoacan and Chiapas will have to experience for some time the military and ecclesiastical influence.* ■

Summary

During the first half of the nineteenth century, the westward movement of Americans steadily gained momentum. Some successful entrepreneurs such as William Henry Ashley made enormous profits from their fur-trading empires. Land speculators and gold seekers, too, helped open areas to settlement. Such pioneers were usually followed by distinct waves of migrants who went west in search of land and opportunity. In Texas, Oregon, California, Utah, and elsewhere in the West, communities sprang up like weeds. Here they interacted—and often clashed—with one another, with those who had prior claims to the land, and with the land itself. As a result, a variety of cultures and economies developed in the expansive section of the country.

Outside the West, conflicting views about the country's manifest destiny promoted an air of crisis for the nation at large. Northerners wanted a West that would be free for diversified economic development. Southerners wanted to sow every suitable acre with cotton. And people from each region tried to use expansion to add to their power in Congress, hoping to further their economic and political demands—tariff, tax, and internal improvement measures that would favor their section of the country.

In the course of the debate, one issue—slavery—began to eclipse all others in symbolizing the differing demands made by the North and South. For northerners, the idea of going to war to win Oregon was acceptable because it was geographically unsuitable for slavery, but the idea of going to war to acquire Texas was quite another matter. The possibility of more southern senators and representatives filled northerners with dread. Nevertheless, the nation chose to fight a war with Mexico in 1846–1848, and won, gaining California and vast territories in the Southwest. Though the value of much of this territory was questionable, the discovery of gold in California in 1848 made it a prize well worth political contention.

Meanwhile, voices challenging slavery's moral implications gained a wider audience. Radical abolitionists, especially William Lloyd Garrison, still labored for acceptance, but by separating themselves from Garrison's radicalism and aligning with like-minded politicians, moderate abolitionists brought their cause into the political mainstream. The limited success enjoyed by the Liberty Party and then by the Free-Soil Party demonstrated that opposition to slavery's expansion was becoming more acceptable in the North, but it still was not popular enough to shatter the existing political party system. Though not broken, national unity certainly was experiencing severe stress as the nation continued to move westward.

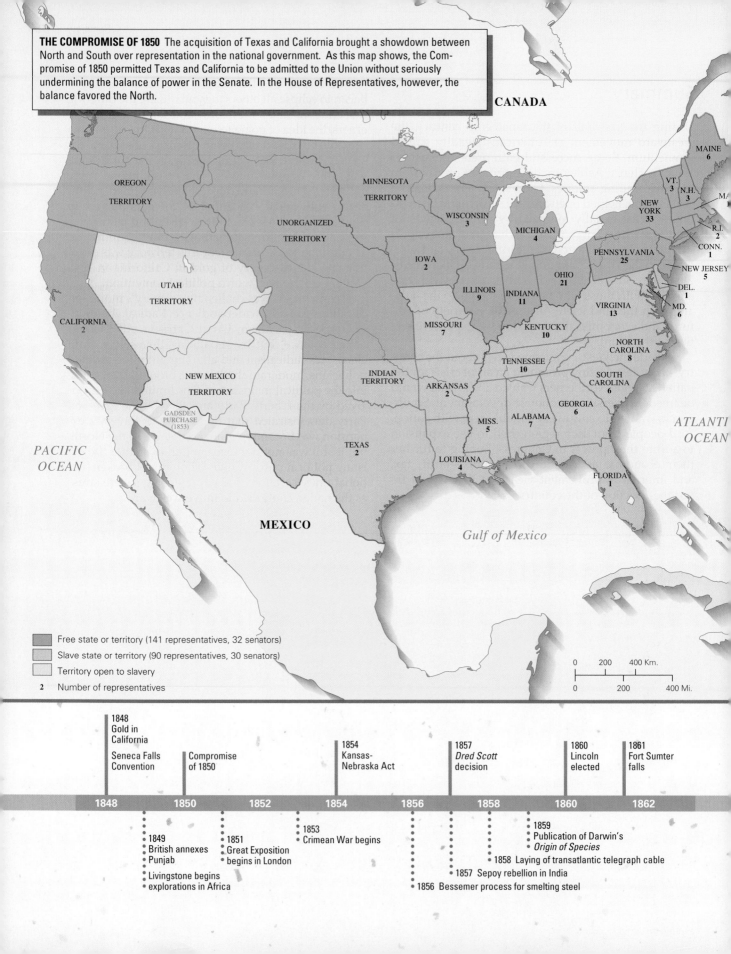

THE COMPROMISE OF 1850 The acquisition of Texas and California brought a showdown between North and South over representation in the national government. As this map shows, the Compromise of 1850 permitted Texas and California to be admitted to the Union without seriously undermining the balance of power in the Senate. In the House of Representatives, however, the balance favored the North.

CANADA

OREGON TERRITORY

MINNESOTA TERRITORY

MAINE
6

UNORGANIZED TERRITORY

WISCONSIN
3

MICHIGAN
4

VT.
3

N.H.
3

MA

NEW YORK
33

R.I.
2

CONN.
1

UTAH TERRITORY

IOWA
2

ILLINOIS
9

INDIANA
11

OHIO
21

PENNSYLVANIA
25

NEW JERSEY
5

DEL.
1

MD.
6

CALIFORNIA
2

MISSOURI
7

KENTUCKY
10

VIRGINIA
13

NORTH CAROLINA
8

NEW MEXICO TERRITORY

INDIAN TERRITORY

ARKANSAS
2

TENNESSEE
10

SOUTH CAROLINA
6

GADSDEN PURCHASE (1853)

MISS.
5

ALABAMA
7

GEORGIA
6

ATLANTIC OCEAN

PACIFIC OCEAN

TEXAS
2

LOUISIANA
4

FLORIDA
1

MEXICO

Gulf of Mexico

Free state or territory (141 representatives, 32 senators)

Slave state or territory (90 representatives, 30 senators)

Territory open to slavery

2   Number of representatives

0   200   400 Km.
0   200   400 Mi.

1848
Gold in California

Seneca Falls Convention

Compromise of 1850

1854
Kansas-Nebraska Act

1857
Dred Scott decision

1860
Lincoln elected

1861
Fort Sumter falls

1848   **1850**   **1852**   **1854**   **1856**   **1858**   **1860**   **1862**

1849
British annexes Punjab

Livingstone begins explorations in Africa

1851
Great Exposition begins in London

1853
Crimean War begins

1859
Publication of Darwin's *Origin of Species*

1858 Laying of transatlantic telegraph cable

1857 Sepoy rebellion in India

1856 Bessemer process for smelting steel

Sectional Conflict and Shattered Union, 1848–1860

The Compromise of 1850
Use the map on the facing page to analyze patterns of political representation between the three major sections of the country: the North, West, and South. Given the patterns of population growth and density noted on the opening map for Chapter 13, what expectations would reasonable people from each region of country have entertained as the result of the compromise?

Individual Choices

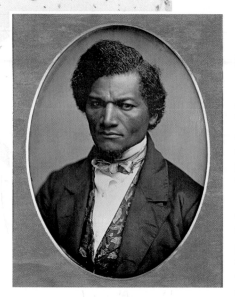

FREDERICK DOUGLASS
Working as a skilled craftsman in the shipyards of Baltimore, Frederick Douglass remained, nonetheless, a slave and was forced to turn his hard-earned wages over to his owner. Seeking economic self-sufficiency and personal freedom, he chose to escape from slavery in 1838 to seek employment as a free man in Massachusetts. Facing the constraint of severe racial discrimination, Douglass had difficulty making a living until abolitionist William Lloyd Garrison heard him speak at an antislavery rally. Garrison promoted Douglass as a lecturer and he soon became recognized as one of the most effective abolitionist activists in the country. Postcards like this one, which presents a daguerreotype of Douglass looking his most imposing and severe, were used to advertise his appearances and to promote the abolitionist cause. Douglass continued to be a leader in the African American rights movement until his death in 1895. *Art Institute of Chicago.*

Frederick Douglass

Although he was born a slave, Frederick Douglass gave a lot of thought to freedom while growing up in Baltimore, Maryland, during the 1820s. As a young boy he cultivated white friends, both for their companionship and because they were willing to teach him to read and write, but he was struck by the difference in their status. He would tell them, "You will be free as soon as you are twenty-one, *but I am a slave for life!*"

But escaping was not an easy thing to do, as he learned in 1834. He and two other slaves hit upon a plan to steal a canoe and paddle into Chesapeake Bay, drifting out of Maryland and into freedom. But their plan was betrayed; Douglass and his colleagues were arrested and dragged off to jail. Douglass was sure that he would be gravely punished for trying to escape—his master threatened to sell him to a cotton plantation in Alabama—but instead he was made an apprentice ship caulker.

Working as an apprentice, Douglass observed that he was "kept in such a perpetual whirl of excitement, I could think of nothing, scarcely, but my life; and in thinking of my life, I almost forgot my liberty." He soon became a master caulker, earning the highest wages in the yard. "I was now of some importance to my master," Douglass recalled. "I was bringing him from six to seven dollars per week." His productivity earned him a lot of freedom: he made his own contracts, set his own work schedule, and collected his own earnings. But he also remembered his liberty. "I have observed this in my experience of slavery," Douglass commented, "that whenever my condition was improved, instead of its increasing my contentment, it only increased my desire to be free."

In 1838 Douglass decided that he would again try to escape. He chose not to contact any of the white organizations that helped slaves to escape to the North because he believed that in seeking applause, such organizations undermined their purpose. "The *underground railroad* . . . by their open declarations, has been made most emphatically the *"upper-ground railroad*," Douglass observed, pointing out that such advertisement actually made it easier for masters to track runaway slaves. He chose instead to depend on personal friends for help. He had become engaged to a free black woman named Anna Murray, who sold a featherbed and other property to finance his escape. He also contacted a retired black sailor from whom he secured seaman's protection papers, legal documents entitling black sailors to pass unmolested through slave territory.

Bearing cash and the borrowed papers, Douglass disguised himself as a sailor and boarded a train heading north out of Baltimore on September 3, 1838. Switching from train to ferry boat, ferry boat to steamship, steamship back to train, and finally train back to ferry boat, Douglass made his way northward, arriving in New York City early on the morning of September 4. Although he had a couple of close calls—he ran into two men who knew he was not a sailor, one of whom apparently did not notice him and another who chose not to turn him in—Douglass's escape had succeeded.

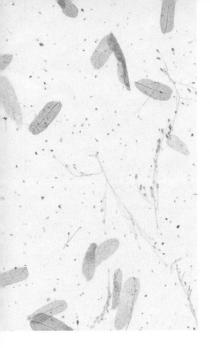

Douglass now had what the white boys he had known in his younger days also enjoyed: he was free. But the color of his skin still deprived him of equality. Moving to the town of New Bedford, Massachusetts, where he hoped to earn a living in the boatyards, Douglass found that "such was the strength of prejudice against color, among the white caulkers, that they refused to work with me, and of course I could get no employment." For three years he was forced to do odd jobs to keep himself and his wife alive. "There was no work too hard—none too dirty," he recalled.

But in 1841 Douglass found a new profession and a new life. Attending an antislavery conference in Nantucket, Douglass was cajoled by a white abolitionist to speak about his experiences. "It was a severe cross," Douglass recalled, "but I took it up reluctantly." Famed abolitionist William Lloyd Garrison heard Douglass's speech, declaring that "Patrick Henry, of revolutionary fame, never made a speech more eloquent in the cause of liberty." Garrison was so moved that he offered to support Douglass as a lecturer in the antislavery cause. Douglass accepted, lending a thundering voice to the cause of racial equality for the next fifty years.

INTRODUCTION

Though not a politician, Frederick Douglass certainly was not immune to the political wrangling going on around him. Like many Americans, Douglass's life was in a state of constant upheaval as politicians engaged in abstract power games that had all-too-real consequences.

Struggles over tariffs, coinage, internal improvements, public land policy, and dozens of other practical issues intersected in complicated ways with the overinflated egos of power-hungry politicians to create an air of political contention and national crisis. The discovery of gold in California followed by a massive rush of Americans into the new territory added greed to the equation. Then strong-willed men such as Jefferson Davis and Stephen A. Douglas threw more fuel on the fire as they fought over the best—that is, most profitable and politically advantageous—route for a transcontinental railroad that would tie California's wealth to the rest of the nation. The halls of Congress rang with debate, denunciation, and even physical violence.

Beneath it all lurked an institution that Frederick Douglass knew all too well: slavery. In a changing society rife with the problems of expansion, immigration, industrialization, and urbanization, political leaders tried either to seek compromise or to ignore the slavery question altogether. In reality, they could do neither. As the nation's leaders wrestled with a host of new issues, the confrontation between northern and southern societies peaked. Although many people wanted peace and favored reconciliation, ultimately both sides rejected compromise, leading to the end of the Union and the beginning of America's most destructive and deadly war.

New Political Options

■ How did the presidential election in 1848 help to foster political dissent?

■ How did events in Europe help to push the American economy forward during the 1850s? In what ways did this contribute to growing political tensions?

■ What new political options affected the political system during the 1850s? In what ways?

The presidential election in 1848 had celebrated American expansion and nationalism, but at the same time it revealed a strong undercurrent of dissent. The political system held together during the election, and the existing parties managed to maintain the politics of avoidance, but the successes enjoyed by Free-Soil challengers were evidence that significant problems churned under the surface. It was clear to many that the nation's political system was not meeting their economic and ideological needs, and they began looking for new options. Efforts at compromise might save the nation from the immediate consequences of growth, modernization, and sectional tension, but crisis clearly was in the air.

Disaffected Voices and Political Dissent

It did not take long after the election of 1848 for cracks in the system to become more prominent. In an effort to compete with Democrats in northeastern cities, the Whigs had tried to win Catholic and immigrant voters away from the rival party. The strategy backfired. Not only did the Whigs not attract large numbers of immigrants, but they alienated two core groups among their existing supporters. One such group was artisans, who saw immigrants as the main source of their economic and social woes. The other was Protestant evangelicals, to whom Roman Catholic Irish and German immigrants symbolized all that was wrong in the world and threatening to the American republic. Whig leaders could do little to address these voters' immediate concerns, and increasing numbers left the Whig Party to form state and local coalitions more in tune with their hopes and fears.

One of the most prominent of these locally oriented groups was the anti-Catholic, anti-immigrant **Know-Nothings.** This loosely knit political organization traced its origins back to secret **nativist** societies that had come into existence during the ethnic tension and rioting in Philadelphia, Boston, and New York in the 1830s. These secret fraternal groups at first dabbled in politics by endorsing candidates who shared their **xenophobic** views. Remaining underground, they told their members to say "I know nothing" if they were questioned about the organization or its political intrigues, hence the name Know-Nothings.

Increasingly after 1848, these secretive groups became more public and more vocal. To the artisans and others who formed the core of the Know-Nothing movement, the issues of slavery and sectionalism that seemed to dominate the national political debate were nothing but devices being used by political insiders and the established parties to divert ordinary Americans from real issues of concern. The Know-Nothings pointed instead at immigration, loss of job security, urban crowding and violence, and political corruption as the true threats to American liberties. They built a platform charging that immigrants were part of a Catholic plot to overthrow democracy in the United States. Seeking to counter this perceived threat, they contended that "Americans must rule America" and urged a twenty-one-year naturalization period, a ban against naturalized citizens holding public office, and the use of the Protestant Bible in public schools.

Know-Nothings from different regions disagreed about many things, but they all agreed that the Whig and Democratic Parties were corrupt and that the only hope for the nation lay in scrapping traditional politics and starting anew. Like the Antimasonic movement in the 1820s (see pages 287; 352), in which many Know-Nothing leaders got their start in politics, the Know-Nothing Party expressed antiparty sentiments, alleging wholesale voter fraud and government corruption by both major parties. As future president Rutherford B. Hayes noted, the people were expressing a "general disgust with the powers that be."

Many Know-Nothings had deep ties with the evangelical Protestant movement and indeed represented one dimension of Christian dissent, but not all Protestant dissenters shared their single-mindedness. Many evangelical reformers believed the nation was beset by a host of evils that imperiled its existence. Progress without Christian principles and individual morality, they thought, posed a great danger for the United States, and they viewed slavery, alcohol, Catholicism, religious heresy, and corrupt government as threats to the nation's moral fiber. In their efforts to create moral government and to direct national destiny, these reformers advocated social reform through both religious and political action. Temperance was one of the more prominent topics of their political concern (see page 349). The war on alcohol had made great gains since the 1830s: thirteen states had enacted laws prohibiting the manufacture and sale of liquor. Overall, however, progress seemed slow, and like Know-Nothings and others, temperance advocates became increasingly impatient with the traditional political parties.

Another group that was growing impatient with traditional politics brought an altogether new voice to the American scene. Having assumed the burden of eliminating sin from the world back in the 1830s (see page 325), many evangelical women had rallied around reform causes. Their growing prominence in the abolition movement, for example, had led William Lloyd Garrison to insist that they play a more equal role. In 1840 he proposed that a woman be elected to the executive committee of the American Anti-Slavery Society. And later that year women were members of Garrison's delegation to the first World Anti-Slavery Convention in London. British antislavery advocates,

---

Know-Nothings Members of anti-Catholic, anti-immigrant organizations who eventually formed themselves into a national political party.

nativist Favoring native-born inhabitants of a country over immigrants.

xenophobic Fearful of or hateful toward foreigners or those seen as being different.

Chronology

Toward a Shattered Union

1848	Seneca Falls Convention Zachary Taylor elected president Immigration to United States exceeds 100,000
1850	Compromise of 1850
1852	First railroad line completed to Chicago Harriet Beecher Stowe's *Uncle Tom's Cabin* Franklin Pierce elected president Whig Party collapses Know-Nothing Party emerges
1853	Gadsden Purchase
1854	Republican Party formed Kansas-Nebraska Act Ostend Manifesto
1855	Proslavery posse sacks Lawrence, Kansas Pottawatomie Massacre
1856	James Buchanan elected president Demise of Know-Nothing Party
1857	*Dred Scott* decision Proslavery Lecompton constitution adopted in Kansas
1858	Lincoln-Douglas debates Minnesota admitted to Union
1859	Oregon admitted to Union John Brown's raid on Harpers Ferry
1860	Abraham Lincoln elected president Crittenden compromise fails
1861	Confederate States of America formed Fort Sumter shelled Federal troops occupy Maryland and Missouri Confederate troops occupy east Tennessee

however, like most of their American counterparts, considered the presence of women inappropriate and refused to seat them.

Angelina Grimké was one of the first to announce the frustration women were feeling (see pages 330–331). In her speech before the Massachusetts state assembly in 1838, she had asked, "Are we aliens, because we are women? Are we bereft of citizenship because we are mothers, wives and daughters of a mighty people? Have women no country—no interests staked in public weal—no liabilities in the common peril—no partnership in a nation's guilt and shame?" In that same year, her sister Sarah went further, writing a powerful indictment against the treatment of women in America and a call for equality. In *Letters on the Equality of the Sexes and the Condition of Woman,* Sarah proclaimed, "The page of history teems with woman's wrongs . . . and it is wet with woman's tears." Women must, she said, "arise in all the majesty of moral power . . . and plant themselves, side by side, on the platform of human rights, with man, to whom they were designed to be companions, equals and helpers in every good word and work."

Like Sarah Grimké, many other women began backing away from male-dominated causes and began ad-

vancing their own cause. In 1848 two women who had been excluded from the World Anti-Slavery Convention, **Lucretia Mott** and **Elizabeth Cady Stanton,** called concerned women to a convention at Seneca Falls, New York, to discuss their common problems. At Seneca Falls, they presented a Declaration of Sentiments, based on the Declaration of Independence, citing "the history of repeated injuries and usurpations on the part of man toward woman, having in direct object the establishment of an absolute tyranny over her." The convention adopted eleven resolutions relating to equality under the law, rights to control property, and other prominent gender issues. A twelfth resolution, calling for the right to vote, failed to receive unanimous endorsement.

Lucretia Mott Quaker minister who founded the Philadelphia Female Anti-Slavery Society (1833) and co-organized the Seneca Falls Women's Rights Convention in 1848.

Elizabeth Cady Stanton Pioneering woman suffrage leader, co-organizer of the first Women's Rights Convention, held in Seneca Falls, New York, in 1848.

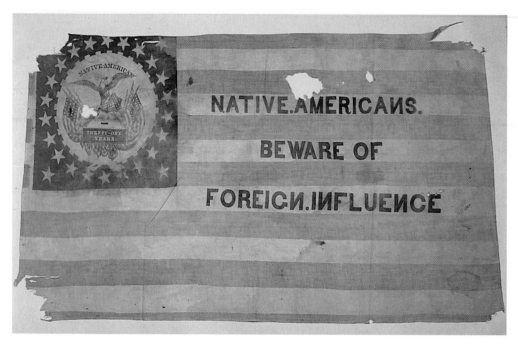

Convinced that slavery and other sectional issues were blinding Americans to the true dangers stemming from uncontrolled immigration and foreign influence, the Know-Nothing Party ran Millard Fillmore for president in 1856. Banners like this one warned Americans and solicited their votes. Fillmore succeeded in getting 21 percent of the popular vote. *Milwaukee County Historical Society.*

While none of these movements alone was capable of overturning the ruling political order, they were symptomatic of serious problems perceived by growing numbers of citizens. Though there were serious differences in the problems that each of these groups emphasized, they shared a number of perceptions in common. All that was missing was a catalyst that could bind them together into a unified dissenting force.

The Politics of Compromise

While Know-Nothings, evangelicals, and women attacked the political parties from outside, problems raised by national expansion were continuing to erode party unity from within. Immediately after Zachary Taylor's election in 1848, California's future became a new divisive issue.

California presented a peculiar political problem. Once word reached the rest of the nation that California was rich with gold, politicians immediately began grasping for control over the newly acquired territory. Although large parts of the area lay below the 36°30′ line that the Missouri Compromise had set for slavery expansion, that legislation had applied only

to territory acquired in the Louisiana Purchase. This left wide open the question of slavery in the new territories acquired from Great Britain and Mexico in the previous decade.

Having been primarily responsible for crafting the earlier compromise (see pages 281–283), Henry Clay took it upon himself to find a solution to the new situation. Clay was convinced that any successful agreement would have to address all sides of the issue. He thus proposed a complex **omnibus** bill to the Senate on January 20, 1850. California would enter the Union as a free state, but the slavery question would be left to popular sovereignty in all other territories acquired through the Treaty of Guadalupe Hidalgo (see page 382). The bill also directed Texas to drop a continuing border dispute with New Mexico in exchange for federal assumption of Texas's public debt. Then, to appease abolitionists, Clay called for an end to the slave trade in Washington, D.C., and balanced that with a

---

omnibus Including or covering many things; an omnibus bill is a piece of legislation with many parts.

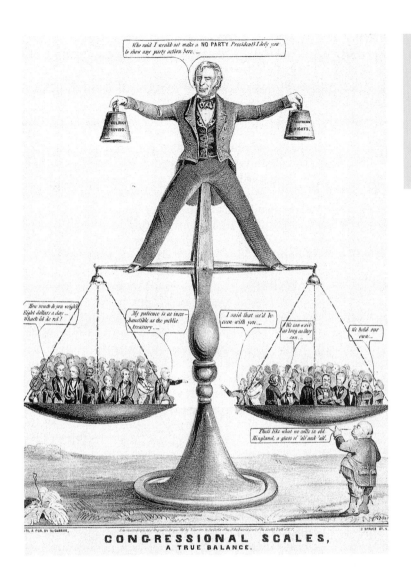

CONGRESSIONAL SCALES,
A TRUE BALANCE.

The question of how a war with Mexico might unbalance the nation politically weighed heavily on people's minds as the nation entered the 1850s. In this cartoon, lithographer Nathaniel Currier—who later would found the famous graphic art company Currier and Ives—illustrates the problem. Trying himself to balance the Wilmot Proviso against Southern Rights, the president seeks to keep congressional representatives from the North and the South in balance as well. *Library of Congress.*

clause popular with southerners: a new, more effective **fugitive slave law.**

Though Clay was trying to please all sectional interests, the omnibus bill satisfied no one; Congress debated it without resolution for seven months. Despite appeals to reason by Clay and Daniel Webster, Congress remained hopelessly deadlocked. Finally, in July 1850, Clay's proposals were defeated. The 73-year-old political veteran left the capital tired and dispirited, but **Stephen A. Douglas** of Illinois set himself to the task of reviving the compromise. Using practical economic arguments and backroom political arm twisting, Douglas proposed each component of Clay's omnibus package as a separate bill, steering each forward toward a comprehensive compromise. Finally, in September, Congress passed the **Compromise of 1850.**

Silenced by the political machinations of their mainstream colleagues, both antislavery and evangelical Whigs chafed at the provision that allowed slave catchers to follow runaway slaves into the North.

fugitive slave law   Law providing for the return of escaped slaves to their owners.

Stephen A. Douglas   Illinois senator who tried to reconcile northern and southern differences over slavery through the Compromise of 1850 and the Kansas-Nebraska Act.

Compromise of 1850   Plan intended to reconcile North and South on the issue of slavery; it recognized the principle of popular sovereignty and included a strong fugitive slave law.

Striking back, they increasingly joined forces with African Americans to seek solutions outside the political realm. Throughout the 1850s, both white and African American activists sought to help slaves escape from the South on the **Underground Railroad.** This covert network provided hiding places and aid for runaway slaves along routes designed to carry them from southern plantations through American territory made hostile by the fugitive slave law and on to safety in Canada. Individuals like **Harriet Tubman** made frequent excursions into the South. Along with Frederick Douglass and others, she also delivered lectures on their life in slavery to white audiences across the North, increasing northern awareness of the plight of slaves and stirring hostility toward the fugitive slave provisions of the Douglas package.

The Compromise of 1850 did little to relieve underlying regional differences and only aggravated political dissent. That slaveowners could pursue runaway slaves into northern states and return them into bondage brought slavery too close to home for many northerners. Nor did southerners find any reason to celebrate: admission of another nonslave state further drained their power in the Senate, and slavery had gained no positive protection, either in the territories or at home. Still, the compromise created a brief respite from the slavery-extension question at a time when the nation's attention increasingly needed to focus on other major changes in national life.

A Changing Political Economy

In the years following the Compromise of 1850, American economic and territorial growth continued to play a destabilizing role in both national and regional development. Most notably, during the 1850s industrial growth accelerated, further altering the nation's economic structure. By 1860 less than half of all northern workers made a living from agriculture as northern industry became more concentrated. Steam began to replace water as the primary power source, and factories were no longer limited to locations along rivers and streams. The use of interchangeable parts became more sophisticated and intricate. In 1851, for example, Isaac Singer devised an assembly line using this technology and began mass-producing sewing machines, fostering a boom in ready-made clothing. As industry expanded, the North became more reliant on the West and South for raw materials and for the food consumed by those working in northeastern factories.

Railroad development stimulated economic and industrial growth. Between 1850 and 1860, the number of miles of railroad track in the United States increased from 9,000 to more than 30,000. The vast majority of these lines linked the Northeast with the Midwest, carrying produce to eastern markets and eastern manufactures to western consumers. In 1852 the Michigan Southern Railroad completed the first line into Chicago from the East, and by 1855 that city had become a key transportation hub linking regions farther west with the eastern seaboard.

Developing this transportation system was difficult. A lack of bridges over major rivers, particularly over the Ohio, impeded rail traffic. Because there still was no standard **rail gauge**—at least twelve different measurements were used—cargo frequently had to be carted from one rail line to another. Despite these problems, railroads quickly became an integral part of the expanding American economy. Western farmers who had previously shipped their products downriver to New Orleans now sent them much more rapidly by rail to eastern industrial centers. The availability of reliable transportation induced farmers to cultivate more land, and enterprising individuals started up related businesses such as warehouses and **grain elevators,** simplifying storage and loading along railroad lines. Mining boomed, particularly the iron industry; the railroads not only transported ore but also became a prime consumer.

Building a railroad required huge sums of money. In populous areas, where passenger and freight traffic was heavy, the promise of a quick and profitable return on investment allowed railroads to raise sufficient capital by selling company stock. In sparsely settled regions, however, where investment returns were much slower, state and local governments loaned money directly to rail companies, financed them indirectly by purchasing stock, or extended state tax exemptions. The most crucial aid to railroads, however, was federal land grants.

The federal government, which owned vast amounts of unsettled territory, gave land to developers who

---

Underground Railroad   The secret network of northerners who helped fugitive slaves escape to Canada or to safe areas in free states.

Harriet Tubman   One of the most famous and most effective of the many African American "conductors" on the Underground Railroad; she is thought to have been personally responsible for leading at least three hundred slaves into freedom.

rail gauge   The distance between train tracks.

grain elevator   A building equipped with mechanical lifting devices and used for storing grain.

AN EXPRESS FREIGHT SHIPMENT OF 30 COACHES, APRIL 15, 1868
BY ABBOT, DOWNING & CO., CONCORD, N.H. TO WELLS, FARGO CO., OMAHA, NEB.

The expansion of railroads facilitated transportation in a number of ways. Not only could western farmers get their produce to market and buy bulky manufactured goods delivered by train, but other modes of transportation were made easier. This illustration shows thirty stagecoaches built by a New Hampshire firm being hauled in a single load to the Wells Fargo Company in Omaha, Nebraska, which, in turn, used them to haul passengers and small freight to places the trains did not go. *New Hampshire Historical Society, Concord.*

then leased or sold plots of ground along the proposed route to finance construction. In 1850 one such federal proposal made by Illinois senator Stephen A. Douglas resulted in a 2.6-million-acre land grant to Illinois, Mississippi, and Alabama for a railroad between Chicago and Mobile. Congress also invested heavily in plans for a transcontinental railroad and on March 4, 1853, appropriated $150,000 to survey potential routes across the continent.

While Americans were enjoying the rail boom, events in Europe were creating new markets for American produce. Several years of bad weather helped spur crop failures throughout the region. In the face of rising public protest over the high cost of food, in 1846 the British Parliament repealed the Corn Laws, which had outlawed the importation of grain since 1804. Two years later, revolutions spread throughout much of continental Europe, followed by the outbreak of several wars. During the 1850s, the price of grain rose sharply in world markets. Railroads allowed western farmers to ship directly to eastern seaports and on to Europe. Meanwhile, technological advances in farm-

ing equipment enabled American farmers to harvest enough grain to meet world demand.

Using the steel plow devised in 1837 by **John Deere,** farmers could cultivate more acres with greater ease. The mechanical reaper invented in 1831 by **Cyrus McCormick** allowed a single operator to harvest as much as fourteen field hands could by hand. Railroads distributed these new pieces of heavy equipment at a reasonable cost. The combination of greater production potential and speedy transportation prompted westerners to increase farm size and concentrate on cash crops. The outcome of these developments was a vast increase in the economic and political power of the West.

John Deere American industrialist who pioneered the manufacture of steel plows especially suited for working hard-packed prairie soil.

Cyrus McCormick Virginia inventor and manufacturer who developed and mass-produced the McCormick reaper, a machine that harvested grain.

M'Cormick's
REAPER.

PATENTED 1845.

Cyrus McCormick's mechanical reaper, shown here in an 1846 advertisement from *The Cultivator* magazine, was one of the technological wonders of its time, permitting a single farmer to harvest as much grain as fourteen field hands could using conventional tools. *State Historical Society of Wisconsin.*

Western grain markets provided the foodstuffs for American industrialization, and Europe provided much of the labor. Factories employed unskilled workers for the most part, and immigrants made up the majority of that labor pool as food shortages, poverty, and political upheaval drove millions from Europe, especially from Ireland and Germany (see page 320). Total immigration to the United States exceeded 100,000 for the first time in 1848, and in 1851, 221,000 people migrated to the United States from Ireland alone. In 1852 the number of German immigrants reached 145,000. Many of these newcomers, particularly the Irish, were not trained in skilled crafts and wound up settling in the industrial urban centers of the Northeast, where they could find work in the factories.

This combination of changes set the stage for political crisis. Liberalized suffrage rules transformed naturalized immigrants into voters, and both parties courted them, adding their interests to the political pot. Meanwhile, a mechanized textile industry hungry for southern fiber lent vitality to the continued growth of the cotton kingdom and the slave labor system that gave it life. Northern political leaders visualized an industrial nation based on free labor, but that view ran counter to the southern elites' ideals of **agrarian capitalism** based on slavery. In the West, most continued to believe in the Jeffersonian ideal of an agricultural nation of small and medium-size farms and could not accept either industrial or cotton capitalism as positive developments.

Political Instability and the Election of 1852

Dynamic economic progress improved material life throughout the nation, but it also raised serious questions about what course progress should take. As one clear-sighted northern minister pointed out in 1852, the debate was not about whether America should pursue progress but about "different kinds and methods of progress." Contradictory visions of national destiny were about to cause the breakdown of the existing party system.

Slavery seemed to loom behind every debate, but most Americans, even southerners, had no personal investment in the institution. Two-thirds of southerners owned no slaves, tolerating the institution but having only fleeting contact with the great plantations and the peculiar labor system operating on them. North-

agrarian capitalism A system of agriculture based on the efficient, specialized production of crops intended to generate profits rather than subsistence.

erners, too, were largely indifferent. Men like young Illinois state congressman **Abraham Lincoln** believed the institution was wrong but were not inclined to do anything about it. What mattered to these people was not slavery but autonomy—control over local affairs and over their own lives.

The slavery question challenged notions of autonomy in both the North and the South. In their widely disseminated rhetoric, abolitionists expanded the specter of the Slave Power conspiracy (see page 381), especially in the aftermath of the Compromise of 1850. Growing numbers perceived this conspiracy as intent on imposing southern ways onto all parts of the country and installing southern elites or their sympathizers in seats of power in every section of the nation. Whether they were farmers in western states like Illinois or artisans in Pennsylvania, common people were jealous of their own local institutions and would resist a southern takeover. Nor would common people in the South accept interference from outsiders, and the ever more vigorous antisouthern crusade by northern radicals alarmed them as well.

The Compromise of 1850 momentarily eased regional fears, but sectional tensions still smoldered beneath the surface. These embers flamed anew in 1852 with the publication of *Uncle Tom's Cabin* by **Harriet Beecher Stowe.** Stowe portrayed the darkest inhumanities of southern slavery in the first American novel to include African Americans as central characters. *Uncle Tom's Cabin* sold three hundred thousand copies in its first year. Adapted for the stage, it became one of the most popular plays of the period. The book stirred public opinion and breathed new life into antislavery sentiments, leading Free-Soilers and so-called **conscience Whigs** to renew their efforts to limit or end slavery. When these activists saw that the Whig Party was incapable of addressing the slavery question in any effective way, they began to look for other political options.

Superficially, the Whigs seemed well organized and surprisingly unified as a new presidential election approached. They passed over Millard Fillmore, who had advanced into the presidency when Zachary Taylor died in office in July 1850, in favor of General Winfield Scott, Taylor's military rival in the War with Mexico. The Democrats remained divided through forty-nine ballots, unable to decide between Lewis Cass of Michigan, Stephen A. Douglas of Illinois, and **James Buchanan** of Pennsylvania. They finally settled on the virtually unknown **Franklin Pierce** of New Hampshire, who pledged to live by and uphold the Compromise of 1850 and keep slavery out of politics. This promise was enough to bring Martin Van

Harriet Beecher Stowe's novel *Uncle Tom's Cabin* was historic for a number of reasons. Not only did it help to fire up northern antislavery sentiments, but it also was the first American novel that featured African American characters in prominent roles. It was issued in various editions with many different covers, but most of them featured the lead character, Uncle Tom—another first in American publishing. This particular cover, from an early "Young Folks' Edition" of the book, depicts the stooped old man with his young, sympathetic white mistress. *Collection of Picture Research Consultants & Archives.*

Buren back to the Democrats, and he brought many Free-Soilers back with him. Many others, though, abandoned Van Buren and joined forces with conscience Whigs.

Abraham Lincoln   Illinois lawyer and politician who argued against popular sovereignty in debates with Stephen Douglas in 1858; he lost the senatorial election to Douglas but was elected president in 1860.

Harriet Beecher Stowe   American novelist and abolitionist whose novel *Uncle Tom's Cabin* fanned antislavery sentiment in the North.

conscience Whigs   Members of the Whig Party who supported moderate abolitionism, as opposed to cotton Whigs, members who opposed abolitionism.

James Buchanan   Pennsylvania senator who was elected president in 1856 after gaining the Democratic nomination as a compromise candidate.

Franklin Pierce   New Hampshire lawyer and Democratic politician nominated as a compromise candidate and elected president in 1852.

Scott was a national figure and a distinguished military hero, but Pierce gathered 254 electoral votes to Scott's 42. This one-sided victory, however, revealed more about the disarray in the Whig Party than it did about Pierce's popularity or Democratic Party strength. Splits between "cotton" and "conscience" groups splintered Whig unity. Regional tension escalated as Free-Soil rhetoric clashed with calls for extending slavery. Confrontations between Catholics and Protestants and between native-born and immigrant laborers caused bitter animosity. In the North, where immigration, industrialization, and antislavery sentiment were most prevalent and economic friction was most pronounced, massive numbers of voters, believing the Whigs incapable of addressing current problems, deserted the party.

Increasing Tension Under Pierce

The Democratic Party and Franklin Pierce, its representative in the White House, were also not immune to the pressures of a changing electorate. Pierce was part of the **Young America Movement,** which, as a whole, tried to ignore the slavery issue, advocating romantic and aggressive nationalism, manifest destiny, and republican revolutions throughout the Americas. In line with the Young America agenda, Pierce emphasized expansion; choosing a route for a transcontinental railroad became the keystone in his agenda for the nation.

Southerners knew that a railroad based in the South would channel the flow of gold from California through their region and would also open new areas for settlement and allow cotton agriculture to spread beyond the waterways that had proved so necessary to its expansion so far. Eventually the new territories would become states, increasing the South's national political power.

That model of development was totally unacceptable to several groups: to northern evangelicals, who viewed slavery as a moral blight on the nation; to Free-Soil advocates, who believed the spread of slavery would degrade white workers; and to northern manufacturers, who wanted to maintain dominance in Congress to ensure continued economic protection. In May 1853, only two months after assuming office, Pierce inflamed all of these groups by sending James Gadsden, a southern railroad developer, to Mexico to purchase a strip of land lying below the southern border of the New Mexico Territory. Any rail line built westward from a southern city would have to cross that land as it proceeded from Texas to California, and Pierce and his southern supporters

wanted to make sure that it was part of the United States. The **Gadsden Purchase,** signed on December 30, 1853, added 29,640 square miles of land to the United States for a cost of $10 million. It also finalized the southwestern border of the United States.

Rather than enhancing Pierce's reputation as a nationalist, the Gadsden Purchase fed the perception that he was a southern sympathizer promoting the extension of slavery. It also led to a more serious sectional crisis. The Gadsden Purchase prompted proponents of a southern route for the transcontinental railroad, led by Secretary of War **Jefferson Davis,** to push for government sponsorship of the project. Rooted politically in Chicago and having invested his own money in rail development, Illinois senator Stephen A. Douglas rose to the challenge. He used his position as chairman of the Senate's Committee on Territories to block Davis's effort to build a transcontinental railroad through the South and pushed for a route westward from Chicago. This route passed through territory that had been set aside for a permanent Native American homeland and thus had not been organized into a federal territory. To rectify this problem, Douglas introduced a bill on January 4, 1854, incorporating the entire northern half of Indian Territory into a new federal entity called Nebraska.

Douglas knew that he would need both northern and southern support to get his bill through Congress, so he tried to structure the legislation so as to alienate neither section. Fearful that the bill would spark yet another debate over slavery, Douglas sought to silence possible opposition by proposing that the matter be left to popular sovereignty within the territory itself—let the voters of Nebraska decide. Noting that the proposed territory was above the Missouri Compromise line, southerners pointed out that Congress might prohibit popular sovereignty from functioning. Douglas responded that the Compromise of

---

Young America Movement A political movement popular among young voters during the 1840s and early 1850s that advocated free-market capitalism, national expansionism, and American patriotism; a strong force within the Democratic Party, Young America leaders tried to avoid antislavery debates and other divisive controversies.

Gadsden Purchase A strip of land in present-day Arizona and New Mexico that the United States bought from Mexico in 1853 to secure a southern route for a transcontinental railroad.

Jefferson Davis Secretary of war under Franklin Pierce; he later became president of the Confederacy.

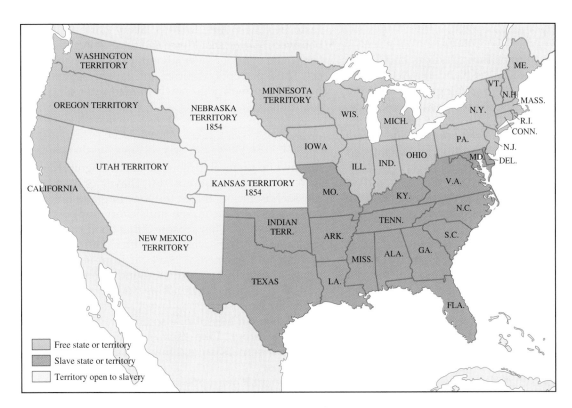

MAP 14.1 The Kansas-Nebraska Act This map shows Stephen Douglas's proposed compromise to resolve the dilemma of organizing the vast territory separating the settled part of the United States from California and Oregon. His solution, designed in part to win profitable rail connections for his home district in Illinois, stirred a political crisis by repealing the Missouri Compromise and replacing it with popular sovereignty.

1850 superseded the 1820 Missouri Compromise, but he finally supported an amendment to his original bill dividing the territory in half—Nebraska in the north and Kansas in the south (see Map 14.1). Assuming that popular sovereignty would lead to slavery in Kansas and a system of free labor in Nebraska, Douglas calculated that both northerners and southerners would be satisfied and support the bill.

Toward a House Divided

■ How did various political coalitions react to the Kansas-Nebraska Act?

■ What was the effect of these various reactions on the national political climate?

Once again slavery threatened national political stability. In the North, opponents of the bill formed local coalitions to defeat it. On January 24, 1854, a group of

Democrats including Salmon P. Chase, Gerrit Smith, Joshua Giddings, and **Charles Sumner** published "The Appeal of the Independent Democrats in Congress, to the People of the United States." They called the bill an "atrocious plot" to make Nebraska a "dreary region of despotism, inhabited by masters and slaves." On February 28, opponents of the Kansas-Nebraska bill met in Ripon, Wisconsin, and recommended the formation of a new political party. Similar meetings took place in several northern states as opposition to the bill grew. In the wake of these meetings, the existing party system would collapse and a new one would arise to replace it.

Charles Sumner Massachusetts senator who was brutally beaten by a southern congressman in 1856 after delivering a speech attacking the South.

A Shattered Compromise

Despite this strong opposition, Douglas and Pierce rallied support for the **Kansas-Nebraska Act** in Congress. On May 26, 1854, after gaining approval in the House of Representatives, the bill passed the Senate, and Pierce soon signed it into law. Passage of the Kansas-Nebraska Act crystallized northern antislavery sentiment. To protest, many northerners threatened **noncompliance** with the fugitive slave law of 1850. As Senator William Seward of New York vowed, "We will engage in competition for the virgin soil of Kansas, and God give the victory to the side which is stronger in numbers as it is in right."

Antislavery forces, however, remained divided into at least three major groups. The Free-Soil contingent opposed any extension of slavery but did not necessarily favor abolishing the institution. The other two groups—Garrisonians and evangelicals—wanted immediate abolition but disagreed on many particulars. William Lloyd Garrison and his followers believed that slavery was the primary evil facing the nation, and they embraced anyone who held that position. Evangelicals agreed that slavery was evil, but they believed it was one among many vices undermining the virtuous republic. All three groups constantly agitated against slavery and what they perceived as southern control of national politics. They weakened the Democratic Party's strength in the North but could not bring themselves to align behind a single opposition party.

Talk of expansion also threatened Democratic unity in the South. Many southerners believed that extending slavery was necessary to prevent northern domination. Increased northern wealth and continued conflict over the expansion of slavery convinced many southern Democrats that northern manufacturing and commercial power threatened to reduce the South to a "colony" controlled by northern bankers and industrialists.

Some southerners attempted to neutralize this perceived threat by acquiring colonies of their own in the Caribbean and Central America. Although all these efforts were the work of a few power-hungry individuals, many northerners believed them to be part of the Slave Power conspiracy. President Pierce unintentionally aggravated this sentiment by pushing to acquire Cuba, which he hoped to purchase from Spain. The Spanish, however, were unwilling to negotiate, and in October 1854 three of Pierce's European ministers met in Ostend, Belgium, and secretly drafted a statement outlining conditions that might justify taking Cuba by force. When the so-called **Ostend Mani-festo** became public in 1855, many northerners felt betrayed, fearing that Pierce and the Democratic Party approved of undercover adventurism to expand slavery. These perceptions stirred antislavery anxieties and fueled the growth of the newly formed anti-Democratic coalitions.

Bleeding Kansas

Meanwhile, political friction was about to ignite Kansas. In April 1854, abolitionist Eli Thayer of Worcester, Massachusetts, organized the New England Emigrant Aid Society to encourage antislavery supporters to move to Kansas. They reasoned that flooding a region subject to popular sovereignty with right-minded residents could effectively "save" it from slavery. This group eventually sent two thousand armed settlers to Kansas, founding Lawrence and other communities. With similar designs, proslavery southerners, particularly those in Missouri, also encouraged settlement in the territory. Like their northern counterparts, these southerners came armed and ready to fight for their cause.

President Pierce appointed governors in both Kansas and Nebraska and instructed them to organize elections for territorial legislatures. As proslavery and antislavery settlers vied for control of Kansas, the region became a testing ground for popular sovereignty. When the vote came on March 30, 1855, a large contingent of armed slavery supporters from Missouri—so-called border ruffians—crossed into Kansas and cast ballots for proslavery candidates. According to later Senate investigations, 60 percent of the votes cast were illegal. These unlawful ballots gave proslavery supporters a large majority in the Kansas legislature. They promptly expelled all abolitionist legislators and enacted the Kansas Code—a group of laws meant to drive all antislavery forces out of the territory. Antislavery advocates refused to acknowledge the validity of the election or the laws. They organized their own free-state government and drew up an alternative constitution, which they submitted to the voters.

Kansas-Nebraska Act Law passed by Congress in 1854 that allowed residents of Kansas and Nebraska territories to decide whether to allow slavery within their borders.

noncompliance Failure or refusal to obey a law or request.

Ostend Manifesto Declaration by American foreign ministers in 1854 that if Spain refused to sell Cuba, the United States might be justified in taking it by force.

Though no one would deny that their cause was noble, many of the men who flocked to Kansas to resist the expansion of slavery were no less violent than their proslavery adversaries. This photograph taken in 1859 shows a gang of armed antislavery men who had just broken an accomplice (John Doy, seated) out of jail in neighboring St. Joseph, Missouri. Like proslavery border ruffians, many of these men also served in guerrilla bands during the Civil War, and some went on to careers as famous outlaws after the war was over. *Kansas State Historical Society.*

Bloodshed soon followed. Attempting to bring the conflict to conclusion, proslavery territorial judge Samuel LeCompte called a grand jury of slavery supporters that indicted members of the free-state government for treason and sent a **posse** of about eight hundred men armed with rifles and five cannon to Lawrence. There they "arrested" the antislavery forces and sacked the town, burning buildings and plundering shops and homes. But the violence did not end there. Hearing news of the "Sack of Lawrence," **John Brown,** an antislavery zealot, vowed to "fight fire with fire." Reasoning that at least five antislavery supporters had been killed since the conflict erupted, he and seven others abducted five proslavery men living along the Pottawatomie River south of Lawrence and murdered them. The "Pottawatomie Massacre" triggered a series of episodes in which more than two hundred men were killed. Much of the violence was the work of border ruffians and zealots like Brown, but to many people in both the North and the South, the events symbolized the "righteousness" of their cause.

The Kansas issue also led to violence in Congress. During the debates over the admission of the territory, Charles Sumner, a senator from Massachusetts, delivered an abusive and threatening speech against proslavery advocates. In particular, he made insulting remarks about South Carolina and its 60-year-old senator Andrew Butler. Butler was out of town, but Butler's nephew, Representative Preston Brooks, accosted Sumner and nearly beat him to death with a cane. Though **censured** by the House of Representatives, Brooks was overwhelmingly reelected by his

posse   A group of people usually summoned by a sheriff to aid in law enforcement.

John Brown   Abolitionist who fought proslavery settlers in Kansas in 1855; he was hanged for treason after seizing the U.S. arsenal at Harpers Ferry in 1859 as part of an effort to liberate southern slaves.

censure   To issue an official rebuke, as by a legislature to one of its members.

home district and openly praised for his actions—he received canes as gifts from admirers all over the South.

Meanwhile the presidential election of 1856 was approaching. The Pierce administration's actions, southern expansionism, and the Kansas-Nebraska controversy swelled the ranks of dissenters like those who had convened in Ripon. Now formally calling themselves the **Republican Party,** these northern and western groups began actively seeking support. Immigration also remained a major issue, but the Know-Nothings, despite their success at the local and state levels, split over slavery at their initial national convention in 1855. Disagreement over a **plank** dealing with the Kansas-Nebraska Act caused most northerners to bolt from the convention. Some formed an anti-slavery group called the Know-Somethings, but many joined Republican coalitions. In 1856 the remaining Know-Nothings reconvened and nominated former president Millard Fillmore as the party's standard-bearer. John C. Frémont, a moderate abolitionist who had achieved fame as the liberator of California (see pages 380–381), got the Republican nomination. The few remaining Whigs endorsed Fillmore at their convention, while some former Know-Nothings met separately and endorsed Frémont. The Democrats rejected both Pierce and Douglas and nominated James Buchanan from Pennsylvania, selecting John C. Breckinridge of Kentucky as Buchanan's running mate to balance the ticket between the North and the South.

The election became a contest for party survival rather than a national referendum on slavery. Buchanan received 45 percent of the popular vote and 163 electoral votes. Frémont finished second with 33 percent of the popular vote and 114 electoral votes. Fillmore received 21 percent of the popular vote but only 8 electoral votes. Frémont's surprisingly narrow margin of defeat demonstrated the appeal of the newly formed Republican coalition to northern voters. The Know-Nothings, fragmented over slavery, disappeared and never again attempted a national organization.

Bringing Slavery Home to the North

On March 4, 1857, James Buchanan became president of the United States. The 65-year-old Pennsylvanian had begun his political career in Congress in 1821 and owed much of his success to southern support. His election came at a time when the nation needed strong leadership, but Buchanan seemed unable to provide it. During the campaign, he had emphasized national

In attempting to win his freedom, Dred Scott unintentionally set a legal process in motion that would deny Congress's right to control the extension of slavery. This 1858 painting captures Scott's resolution and strength of character. *"Dred Scott" by Louis Schultze, 1881. Missouri Historical Society.*

unity, but he proved incapable of achieving a unifying compromise. His attempt to preserve the politics of avoidance only strengthened radicalism in both the North and the South. **Regionalism** colored all political issues, and every debate became a contest between competing social, political, and economic ideologies.

Though Buchanan's shortcomings contributed to the rising crisis, an event occurred within days of his inauguration that sent shock waves through the al-

Republican Party Political party formed in 1854 that opposed the extension of slavery into the western territories.

plank One of the articles of a political platform.

regionalism Loyalty to the interests of a particular region of the country.

ready troubled nation. **Dred Scott,** a slave once owned by John Emerson, resided in Missouri, a slave state. But between 1831 and 1833, Emerson, an army surgeon, had taken Scott with him during various postings, including stints in Illinois and Wisconsin, where the Missouri Compromise banned slavery. Scott's attorney argued that living in Illinois and Wisconsin had made Scott a free man. When, after nearly six years in the Missouri courts, the state supreme court rejected this argument in 1852, Scott, with the help of abolitionist lawyers, appealed to the United States Supreme Court. In a 7-to-2 decision, the Court ruled against Scott. Chief Justice Roger B. Taney, formerly a member of Andrew Jackson's Kitchen Cabinet and a stalwart Democrat (see page 289), argued that in the eyes of the law slaves were not people but property; as such, they could not be citizens of the United States and had no right to petition the Court. Taney then ignited a political powder keg by ruling that Congress had no constitutional authority to limit slavery in a federal territory, thereby declaring the Missouri Compromise unconstitutional.

While southerners generally celebrated the decision, antislavery forces and northern evangelical leaders called the *Dred Scott* decision a mockery of justice and a crime against a "higher law." Some radical abolitionists argued that the North should separate from the Union. Others suggested impeaching the Supreme Court. Already incensed by events in Kansas, antislavery leaders predicted that the next move by the Slave Power conspiracy would be to get the Supreme Court to strike down antislavery laws in northern states.

Meanwhile, the Kansas issue still burned. The fact that very few slaveholders actually moved into the territory did nothing to deter proslavery leaders, who met in Lecompton, Kansas, in June 1857 to draft a state constitution favoring slavery. When the **Lecompton constitution** was submitted for voters' approval, antislavery forces protested by refusing to vote, so it was easily ratified. But when it was revealed that more than two thousand nonresidents had voted illegally, both Republicans and northern Democrats in Congress roundly denounced it. The Buchanan administration joined southerners in support of admitting Kansas to the Union as a slave state and managed to push the statehood bill through the Senate, but the House of Representatives rejected it. Congress then returned the Lecompton constitution to Kansas for another vote. This time Free-Soilers participated in the election and defeated the proposed constitution. Kansas remained a territory.

The Kansas controversy proved a hard pill for Douglas to swallow. He believed in popular sovereignty

It Matters

The *Dred Scott* Case

If one had to point to a single event that, perhaps more than any other, made civil war inevitable in the United States, it was the Taney Court's decision in *Dred Scott v. Sanford.* More than anything else, this decision revealed the shortsightedness of Federalists when they had cobbled together the Three-Fifths Compromise as a way of rushing a new Constitution out for state ratification. The mere mention of slavery in the Constitution would have given defenders of the institution an argument for its legitimacy, but to have made it integral to the basic representative structure of government gave them an iron defense. However, the Court's opinion went far beyond just legitimizing slavery. According to Justice Taney's argument, no state could "introduce any person, or description of persons, who were not intended to be embraced in this new political family, which the constitution brought into existence, but were intended to be excluded from it." Because no state at the time of ratification had included African Americans as citizens, then no one of African descent could become a citizen of the United States. Ever! It would take the Thirteenth and Fourteenth Amendments to the Constitution to reverse Taney's opinion and remove the errors that the Federalists' haste had inserted in that document in the first place.

but could not support the fraudulent election that brought the Lecompton constitution to Congress for approval. And the *Dred Scott* decision had virtually nullified his pet solution by ruling that even popular sovereignty could not exclude slavery from a state or territory. Still entertaining presidential ambitions,

---

Dred Scott Slave who sued for his liberty in the Missouri courts, arguing that four years on free soil had made him free; the Supreme Court's 1857 ruling against him negated the Missouri Compromise.

Lecompton constitution State constitution written for Kansas in 1857 at a convention dominated by proslavery forces; it would have allowed slavery, but Kansas voters rejected it.

Douglas sought a solution that might win him both northern and southern support in a run for the office in 1860. His immediate goal, however, was reelection to the Senate.

Illinois Republicans selected Abraham Lincoln to run against Douglas for the Senate in 1858. Born on the Kentucky frontier in 1809, Lincoln had accompanied his family from one failed farm to another, picking up schooling in Indiana and Illinois as opportunities arose. As a young man he worked odd jobs—farm worker, ferryman, flatboatman, surveyor, and store clerk—and was a member of the Illinois militia during the Black Hawk War in 1832 (see page 293). Two years after the war, Lincoln was elected to the Illinois legislature and began a serious study of law. He was admitted to the Illinois state bar in 1836. A strong Whig, Lincoln followed Henry Clay's economic philosophy and steered a middle course between the "cotton" and "conscience" wings of the Whig Party. Lincoln acknowledged that slavery was evil but contended that it was the unavoidable consequence of black racial inferiority. The only way to get rid of the evil, he believed, was to prevent the expansion of slavery into the territories, forcing it to die out naturally, and then make arrangements to separate the two races forever, either by transporting them to Africa or creating a segregated space for them in the Americas.

Lincoln was decidedly the underdog in the contest with Douglas and sought to improve his chances by challenging the senator to a series of debates about slavery and its expansion. Douglas agreed to seven debates in various parts of the state. During the debate at Freeport, Lincoln asked Douglas to explain how the people of a territory could exclude slavery in light of the *Dred Scott* ruling. Douglas's reply became known as the **Freeport Doctrine.** Slavery, he said, needed the protection of "local police regulations." In any territory, citizens opposed to slavery could elect representatives who would "by unfriendly legislation" prevent the introduction of slavery. Lincoln did not win Douglas's Senate seat, but the debate drew national attention to the Illinois race, and Lincoln won recognition as an up-and-coming Republican force.

Radical Responses to Abolitionism and Slavery

Southerners bristled at claims by Lincoln and others that slavery was immoral. Charles C. Jones and other southern evangelical leaders, for example, offered a religious defense of slavery. Such apologists argued that whites had a moral responsibility to care for blacks and instruct them in the Christian faith. Those who claimed that the Bible condoned slavery pointed out that the Israelites practiced slavery and that when Jesus walked among slaves he never mentioned freedom. The apostle Paul, they argued, even commanded slaves to obey their masters.

Many southerners, like some of their Republican opponents, were less interested in the slave than in how slavery affected white society and white labor. When the Republicans argued that slavery defiled labor, southern apologists countered that slavery was a "mudsill," or foundation, supporting democracy. Southerners contended that whites in the South enjoyed a greater degree of freedom than northern whites because slaves did all the demeaning work, freeing whites for more noble pursuits. Moreover, southern lawyer George Fitzhugh argued, both the North and the South relied equally on a subjugated work force: southerners on **chattel slavery** and northerners on **wage slavery.** Fitzhugh charged that poor northern whites were a "mudsill" as surely as slaves were in the South. The only meaningful difference between wage slaves and southern slaves, Fitzhugh concluded, was that northerners accepted no responsibility for housing and feeding their work force, condemning laborers to suffer at below-subsistence conditions.

These ideas infuriated northerners as much as antislavery arguments angered southerners because they challenged deeply held cultural and social values. Northern radicals increasingly called for the violent overthrow of slavery, and Kansas zealot John Brown moved to oblige them. In 1857 Brown came to the East, where he convinced several prominent antislavery leaders to finance a daring plan to raise an army of slaves in an all-out insurrection against their masters. Brown and a small party of followers attacked the federal arsenal at **Harpers Ferry,** Virginia, on October 16, 1859, attempting to seize weapons. The

Freeport Doctrine   Stephen Douglas's belief, stated at Freeport, Illinois, that a territory could exclude slavery by writing local laws or regulations that made slavery impossible to enforce.

chattel slavery   The bondage of people who are considered to be the movable personal property of their owners.

wage slavery   The bondage of workers who, though legally free, are underpaid, trapped in debt, and living in extreme poverty.

Harpers Ferry   Town in present-day West Virginia and site of the U.S. arsenal that John Brown briefly seized in 1859.

Seeing himself as an avenging angel, John Brown, shown here in an 1856 photograph, used the same terrorist tactics employed by border ruffians in Kansas. A year after this picture was taken, Brown began a two-year campaign to raise funds, volunteers, and political support for starting a massive armed slave uprising in Virginia, He finally struck at the federal armory at Harpers Ferry, Virginia, on October 16, 1859, where he and his force of volunteers were quickly overcome and arrested. He was hanged for treason on December 2, 1859. *Boston Athenaeum.*

arsenal proved an easy target, but no slaves joined the uprising. Local citizens surrounded the arsenal, firing on Brown and his followers until federal troops commanded by Colonel **Robert E. Lee** arrived. On October 18, Lee's forces battered down the barricaded entrance and arrested Brown. He was tried, convicted of treason, and hanged on December 2, 1859.

Brown's raid on Harpers Ferry captured the imagination of radical abolitionists. Republican leaders denounced it, but other northerners proclaimed Brown a martyr. Church bells tolled in many northern cities on the day of his execution. In New England, Ralph Waldo Emerson proclaimed Brown "that new saint." Such reactions caused many appalled southerners— even extreme moderates—to seriously consider **se-cession.** In Alabama, Mississippi, and Florida, state legislatures resolved that a Republican victory in the

upcoming presidential election would provide sufficient justification for such action.

The Divided Nation

■ How did the realignment of the political party system during the 1850s contribute to the conduct and results of the presidential election in 1860?

■ Why did the election results have the political effects that they did?

The Republicans were a new phenomenon on the American political scene: a purely regional political party. Rather than making any attempt to forge a national coalition, the party drew its strength and ideas almost entirely from the North. The Republican platform—"Free Soil, Free Labor, and Free Men"— stressed the defilement of white labor by slavery and contended that the Slave Power conspiracy was eroding the rights of free whites everywhere. By taking up a cry against "Rum, Romanism, and Slavery," the Republicans drew former Know-Nothings and temperance advocates into their ranks. The Democrats hoped to maintain a national coalition, but as the nation approached a new presidential election, their hopes began to fade.

The Dominance of Regionalism

During the Buchanan administration, Democrats found it increasingly difficult to achieve national party unity. Facing Republican pressure in their own states, northern Democrats realized that any concession to southern Democratic demands for extending or protecting slavery would cost them votes at home. In April 1860, as the party convened in Charleston, South Carolina, each side was ready to do battle for its political life.

The fight began when northern supporters of Stephen A. Douglas championed a popular sovereignty position. Southern radicals demanded a plank calling for the legal protection of slavery in the territories. After heated debates, neither side would compromise. When the delegates finally voted, the Douglas forces carried the day. Disgusted delegates from eight

Robert E. Lee A Virginian with a distinguished career in the U.S. Army who resigned to assume command of the Confederate army in Virginia when the Civil War began.

secession Withdrawal from the United States.

southern states walked out of the convention. Shocked, the remaining delegates adjourned the convention; they would reconvene in Baltimore in June. Most southern delegates boycotted the Baltimore proceedings, and Douglas easily won the Democratic presidential nomination. Moderate southerner Herschel V. Johnson of Georgia was his running mate. Hoping to attract moderate voters from both the North and the South, the party's final platform supported popular sovereignty and emphasized allegiance to the Union.

The southern Democratic contingent met one week later, also in Baltimore, and nominated Vice President John C. Breckinridge of Kentucky as its presidential candidate and Joseph Lane of Oregon as his running mate. The southern Democrats' platform vowed support for the Union but called for federal protection of the right to own slaves in the territories and for the preservation of slavery where it already existed.

In May 1860, a group of former Whigs and Know-Nothings along with some disaffected Democrats convened in Baltimore and formed the **Constitutional Union Party.** They nominated John Bell, a former southern Know-Nothing and wealthy slaveholder from Tennessee, for president and Edward Everett of Massachusetts, a former Whig leader, as his running mate. Hoping to resurrect the politics of compromise, the party resolved to take no stand on the sectional controversy and pledged to uphold the Constitution and the Union and to enforce the laws of the nation.

Having lost most of its moderates to the Constitutional Union coalition and having virtually no southerners in its ranks to start with, the Republican convention faced few ideological divisions, but personality conflicts were rife. The front-runner for the Republican nomination appeared to be William Seward of New York. A former Whig and longtime New York politician, Seward had actively opposed any extension of slavery during the early 1850s but had switched to the popular-sovereignty position during the Kansas controversy. Several other Republican favorites—Salmon P. Chase of Ohio, Simon Cameron of Pennsylvania, and Edward Bates of Missouri—agreed with Seward's position but sought their own nominations. Eventually, however, Illinois favorite son Abraham Lincoln emerged as Seward's major competition. Many delegates considered Seward too radical. Moreover, he and his campaign manager, Thurlow Weed (see page 287), had earned the distrust of many prominent Republicans for their political wheeling and dealing. Lincoln, in contrast, had a reputation for integrity and had not seriously alienated any of the Republican factions. He won the nomination on the third ballot.

The Election of 1860

The 1860 presidential campaign began as several separate contests. Lincoln and Douglas competed for northern votes; the Republicans were not even on the ballot in the **Deep South.** Douglas proclaimed himself the only national candidate but received most of his support from northerners who feared the consequences of a Republican victory. By the same token, Breckinridge and the southern Democrats expected no support in the North. Bell and the Constitutional Unionists attempted to campaign in both regions but attracted mostly southern voters anxious to stave off the crisis of disunion.

Slavery and sectionalism were the key issues. Even when a congressional investigation revealed evidence of graft, bribery, and shady dealings in the Buchanan administration, Republicans linked these charges to the supposed Slave Power conspiracy. The slaveholding elite, they contended, not only had attempted to subvert liberty but had used fraudulent means to keep the Democratic Party of Buchanan—and Douglas—in power. "Honest Abe Lincoln," the man of the people, would lead the fight against the forces of slavery and corruption. This argument drew in many northern voters, including a lot of former Know-Nothings.

Sensing that Lincoln would win the North, Douglas launched a last-ditch effort to win the election and hold the Union together by pushing his campaign into the South. Douglas and his forces tried unsuccessfully to form a coalition between moderate Democrats and Constitutional Unionists. Already in poor health, Douglas all but exhausted himself trying to prevent disunion.

As the election drew near, the likelihood of a Republican victory deeply alarmed southerners. Even moderate southerners started to believe that the Republicans intended to crush their way of life and to enslave southern whites economically while freeing southern blacks. Northern qualms were aroused as well when the pro-Democrat *New York Herald* contended that the election of Lincoln would bring "hundreds of thousands" of slaves north to compete with

Constitutional Union Party Political party that organized on the eve of the Civil War with no platform other than preservation of the Constitution, the Union, and the law.

Deep South The region of the South farthest from the North, usually said to comprise the states of Alabama, Florida, Georgia, Louisiana, Mississippi, and South Carolina.

Four candidates representing four different parties vied for the presidency in the election of 1860. As this political cartoon makes clear, the *Dred Scott* case set the agenda for the election. Here Scott provides the music as each of the four presidential candidates dances with a partner who symbolizes his perceived political orientation. John C. Breckinridge (upper left) dances with fellow southern Democrat James "Buck" Buchanan, illustrating his alignment with southern proslavery hard-liners. John H. Bell (lower right) dances with a Native American, symbolizing his nativist Know-Nothing affiliations, suggesting avoidance of the slavery issue. Meanwhile, Stephen A. Douglas (lower left) escorts a disheveled Irishman, suggesting his alignment with northeastern urban interests including immigrants and other "undesirables." Finally, Abraham Lincoln (upper right) is seen with an African American woman, an obvious reference to his party's perceived abolitionist leanings. *Lilly Library.*

whites for jobs, resulting in "African amalgamation with the fair daughters of the Anglo-Saxon, Celtic, and Teutonic races."

Seeking to counter such scare tactics, national Republican leaders forged a platform that advocated limits on slavery's expansion but contained no planks seeking an end to slavery in areas where it already existed. They also called for higher tariffs (to appeal to northern industrialists) and for internal improvements and public lands legislation (to appeal to westerners). Particularly in the Midwest, party leaders worked hard to portray themselves as "the white man's party." In line with the position Lincoln had taken in his 1858 debates with Douglas, Republicans argued that excluding slavery meant excluding blacks from competition with whites. These tactics alienated

a few abolitionists but persuaded many northerners and westerners to support the party.

On November 6, 1860, Abraham Lincoln was elected president of the United States with 180 electoral votes—a clear majority—but only 40 percent of the popular vote. Lincoln carried all the northern states, California, and Oregon (see Map 14.2). Douglas finished second with 29 percent of the popular vote but just 12 electoral votes. He won only Missouri. Bell won the 39 electoral votes of Virginia, Kentucky, and Tennessee. Breckinridge, as expected, carried the Deep South but tallied only 72 electoral votes and 18 percent of the popular vote nationwide. For the first time in American history, a purely regional party held the presidency. The Republicans, who had made no effort to win votes in the South,

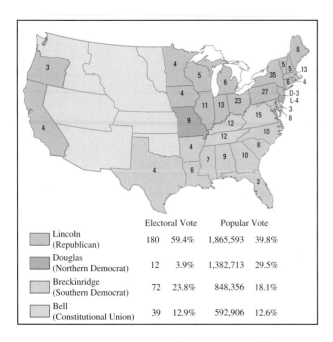

		Electoral Vote		Popular Vote	
■	Lincoln (Republican)	180	59.4%	1,865,593	39.8%
■	Douglas (Northern Democrat)	12	3.9%	1,382,713	29.5%
■	Breckinridge (Southern Democrat)	72	23.8%	848,356	18.1%
■	Bell (Constitutional Union)	39	12.9%	592,906	12.6%

MAP 14.2 Election of 1860 The election of 1860 confirmed the worst fears expressed by concerned Union supporters during the 1850s: changes in the nation's population made it possible for one section to dominate national politics. As this map shows, the Republican and southern Democratic Parties virtually split the nation, and the Republicans were able to seize the presidency.

also swept congressional races in the North and secured a large majority in the House of Representatives for the upcoming term.

The First Wave of Secession

After the Republican victory, southern sentiment for secession snowballed, especially in the Deep South. The Republicans were a "party founded on a single sentiment," stated the *Richmond Examiner*: "hatred of African slavery." The *New Orleans Delta* agreed, calling the Republicans "essentially a revolutionary party." But this party now controlled the national government. To a growing number of southerners, the Republican victory was proof that secession was the only alternative to political domination.

Calls for secession had been heard for decades, and most Republicans did not believe that the South would actually leave the Union. Seward had ridiculed threats of secession as an attempt "to terrify or alarm" the northern people. Lincoln himself believed that the "people of the South" had "too much sense" to launch an "attempt to ruin the government." During the campaign, he had promised "no interference by

the government, with slaves or slavery within the states," and he continued to urge moderation.

In a last-ditch attempt at compromise, **John J. Crittenden** proposed a block of permanent constitutional amendments—amendments that could never be repealed—to the Senate on December 18, 1860. He suggested extending the Missouri Compromise line westward across the continent, forbidding slavery north of the line, and protecting slavery to the south. Crittenden's plan also upheld the interstate trade in slaves and called for compensation to slaveowners who were unable to recover fugitive slaves from northern states. Although this plan seemed to favor the South, it had some appeal in the North, especially among businessmen who feared that secession would cause a major depression. Thurlow Weed, Seward's political adviser, seemed ready to listen to such a compromise, but Lincoln was "inflexible on the territorial question." The extension of the Missouri Compromise line, Lincoln warned, would "lose us everything we gained by the election." He let senators and congressmen know that he wanted no "compromise in regard to the extension of slavery." The Senate defeated Crittenden's proposals by a vote of 25 to 23. The Kentuckian then proposed putting the measure to a vote of the people, but Congress rejected that idea as well.

Meanwhile, on December 20, 1860, delegates in South Carolina met to consider seceding from the Union. South Carolina had long been a hotbed of resistance to federal authority, and state officials determined to take action to protect slavery before the newly elected Republican administration came to power. Amid general jubilation, South Carolina delegates voted unanimously to dissolve their ties with the United States. Just as the radicals hoped, other southern states followed. During January 1861, delegates convened in Mississippi, Florida, Alabama, Georgia, and Louisiana and voted to secede.

On February 4, 1861, delegates from the six seceding states met in Montgomery, Alabama, and formed the provisional government for the **Confederate States of America.** During the several weeks that followed,

John J. Crittenden Kentucky senator who made an unsuccessful attempt to prevent the Civil War by proposing a series of constitutional amendments protecting slavery south of the Missouri Compromise line.

Confederate States of America Political entity formed by the seceding states of South Carolina, Georgia, Florida, Alabama, Mississippi, and Louisiana in February 1861; Texas, Virginia, Arkansas, Tennessee, and North Carolina joined later.

the provisional congress drafted a constitution, and the six Confederate states ratified it on March 11, 1861.

The Confederate constitution emphasized the "sovereign and independent character" of the states and guaranteed the protection of slavery in any new territories acquired. It allowed tariffs solely for the purpose of raising government revenue and prohibited government funding of internal improvements. It also limited the president and vice president to a single six-year term. A cabinet composed of six executive department heads rounded out the executive branch. In all other respects, the Confederate government was identical to that in the United States. In fact, the U.S. Constitution was acknowledged as the supreme law in the Confederacy except in those particulars where it conflicted with provisions in the Confederate Constitution.

While this process was under way, the Confederate cause got a significant boost when Texas, which had been holding back, declared itself part of the new nation. Despite unionist pleas from Governor Sam Houston, the heavily populated cotton-growing region in the eastern part of the state opted to join neighboring Louisiana in rebellion, and the rest of the population followed suit. The Confederacy now numbered seven states.

Responses to Disunion

Even as late as March 1861, not all southerners favored secession. John Bell and Stephen Douglas together had received more than 50 percent of southern votes in 1860, winning support from southerners who desired compromise and had only limited stakes in upholding slavery. These "plain folk" joined together with some large planters, who stood to suffer economic loss from disunion, in calls for moderation and compromise. And the border states, which were less invested in cotton and had numerous ties with the North, were not strongly inclined toward secession. In February, Virginia had called for a peace conference to meet in Washington in an effort to forestall hostilities, but this attempt, like Crittenden's effort, also failed to hold the Union together.

The division in southern sentiments was a major stumbling block to the election of a Confederate president. Many moderate delegates to the constitutional convention refused to support radical secessionists, believing them to be equally responsible with the Republicans for initiating the crisis. The convention remained deadlocked until two prosecession Virginia legislators nominated Mississippi moderate Jefferson Davis as a compromise candidate.

Davis appeared to be the ideal choice. Austere and dignified, he had not sought the job but seemed extremely capable of handling it. A West Point graduate, he served during the War with Mexico, was elected to the Senate soon afterward, then left the Senate in 1851 to run unsuccessfully for governor in Mississippi. After serving as secretary of war under Franklin Pierce, he returned to the Senate in 1857. Although Davis had long championed southern interests and owned many slaves, he was no romantic, fire-eating secessionist. Before 1860 he had been a strong **Unionist,** arguing only that the South be allowed to maintain its own economy, culture, and institutions, including slavery. He had supported the Compromise of 1850. When he had fought for a southern route for a transcontinental railroad as secretary of war, he believed that it would benefit the South economically, but he also felt that it would tie the whole nation more firmly together. Like many of his contemporaries, however, Davis had become increasingly alarmed by the prospect of declining southern political power. Immediately after Mississippi's declaration of secession, Davis resigned his Senate seat and threw in with the Confederacy.

To moderates like Davis, the presidential election of 1860 was simply a forceful demonstration of a fact already in evidence: unless the South took a strong stand against outside interference, the region would no longer be able to control its own internal affairs. The initial northward tilt in the Senate created by California's admission in 1850 had been aggravated in 1858 by the admission of Minnesota and by Oregon's statehood in 1859. Southerners, Davis believed, needed to act in concert to convince northerners to either leave the South alone or face the region's withdrawal from the nation. "To rally the men of the North, who would preserve the government as our fathers found it," Davis proclaimed, "we . . . should offer no doubtful or divided front."

Elected provisional president of the Confederate States of America unanimously on February 9, 1861, Davis addressed the cheering crowds in Montgomery a week later and set forth the Confederate position: "The time for compromise has now passed," he said. "The South is determined to maintain her position, and make all who oppose her smell Southern powder and feel Southern steel." In his inaugural address several days later, he stressed a desire for peace but reiterated that the "courage and patriotism of the

Unionist Loyal to the United States of America.

A few months before being nominated by the Republican Party as its presidential candidate, Abraham Lincoln permitted Illinois artist Leonard Volk to cast the future president's face in plaster. Preserved for all these years, this casting and the many reproductions that have been struck from it remain the most accurate picture we have of Lincoln before the secession crisis tore the nation apart. Captured in time, we can see the noble and serious man whose unflinching determination saw the nation through its worst historical crisis. As the many hundreds of photographs and other images of Lincoln during his presidency attest, he would never look this young and confident again. *Picture History.*

Confederate States" would be "found equal to any measure of defense which honor and security may require."

Northern Democrats and Republicans alike watched developments in the South with dismay. President Buchanan argued that secession had no constitutional validity and that any state leaving the Union did so unlawfully. He confused the issue, however, by stating his belief that the federal government had no constitutional power to "coerce a State" to remain in the Union. He blamed the crisis on "incessant and violent agitation on the slavery question," chiding northern states for disregarding fugitive slave laws and calling for a constitutional amendment protecting slavery.

Waiting to assume the office he had just won, Lincoln wrestled with the twin problems of what he would do about secession and slavery. African American abolitionist Frederick Douglass summed up Lincoln's dilemma. "Much as I value the current apparent hostility to Slavery," Douglass stated, "I plainly see that it is less the outgrowth of high and moral conviction against Slavery, as such, than because of the trouble its friends have brought upon the country." The South had divided the nation by seceding, and as Douglass indicated, many northerners were much more concerned about the breakup of the nation and potential hostilities between the North and the South than they ever had been about slavery. Lincoln wrote, "My opinion is that no state can, in any way, lawfully get out of the Union, without the consent of the others." He attempted to clarify his position in a letter to Alexander H. Stephens, who would soon become vice president of the Confederacy. Trying to reassure him that "a republican administration" would not "directly or indirectly, interfere with their slaves, or with them, about their slaves," the president-elect still refused to consider any compromise on disunion or the extension of slavery.

Before he could do anything else, Lincoln first had to unite his party. In an attempt to appease all the Republican factions, he chose his cabinet with great care. His vice president, the moderate Hannibal Hamlin of Maine, had supported Lincoln but was also a friend of William Seward and had been chosen to balance the ticket factionally. Lincoln continued this balancing act by appointing to his cabinet his four main rivals for party control. Seward received the job of secretary of state. Moderate Edward Bates of Missouri became attorney general. Although many Republicans considered Simon Cameron of Pennsylvania to be "destitute of honor and integrity," in the interest of appeasing Cameron's supporters and maintaining party unity, Lincoln reluctantly named him secretary of war. Salmon P. Chase of Ohio, a longtime politician and sometime radical on the slavery question, became secretary of the Treasury. Despite Lincoln's evenhandedness, his political balancing act was not easy to maintain. Chase and Seward, for instance, had a long history of political infighting and hated each other. That Lincoln would appoint Chase to any position so angered Seward that he threatened to resign, and Lincoln had to persuade him to remain.

The Nation Dissolved

■ What problems confronted Abraham Lincoln and Jefferson Davis in March 1861?

■ How did their actions contribute to the escalating national crisis?

Abraham Lincoln was inaugurated on March 4, 1861. In his inaugural address he repeated themes that he had been stressing since the election: no interference with slavery in states where it existed, no extension of slavery into the territories, and no tolerance of secession. "The Union," he contended, was "perpetual." The Constitution, according to its **Preamble,** had been written to form a "more perfect union," and no state could withdraw. Lincoln believed that the nation remained unbroken, and he pledged to see "that the laws of the Union be faithfully executed in all the States." This policy, he continued, necessitated "no bloodshed or violence, and there shall be none, unless it is forced upon the national authority. The power confided in me will be used to hold, occupy, and possess the property and places belonging to the government, and to collect the duties and imposts." If war came, he argued, it would be over secession, not slavery, for the federal government had a duty to maintain the Union by any means, including force.

Lincoln, Sumter, and War

Lincoln's first presidential address drew mixed reactions. Most Republicans found it firm and reasonable, applauding its tone. Union advocates in both the North and the South thought the speech held promise for the future. Even former rival Stephen Douglas stated, "I am with him." Moderate southerners commended Lincoln's "temperance and conservatism" and believed the speech was all "any reasonable Southern man" could have expected. Confederates and their sympathizers, however, branded the speech a "Declaration of War." Lincoln had hoped the address would foster a climate of reconciliation, show his commitment to maintaining the Union, and demonstrate his determination to find a peaceful solution, for he desperately needed time to organize the new government and formulate a plan of action. But such luxuries were not forthcoming.

Even before Lincoln assumed office, South Carolina officials had ordered the state militia to seize two federal forts—Fort Moultrie and Castle Pinckney—and the federal arsenal at Charleston. In response, Major Robert Anderson had moved all federal troops from Charleston to **Fort Sumter,** an island stronghold in Charleston Harbor. The Confederate congress determined that "immediate steps be taken to obtain possession" of forts still under U.S. control and demanded that President Buchanan remove all federal troops from the sovereign territory of the Confederacy. Despite his sympathy for the southern cause, Buchanan had announced that Fort Sumter would be defended "against all hostile attacks, from whatever quarter." On January 9, 1861, a Charleston Harbor **battery** fired on a supply ship, the *Star of the West,* as it attempted to reach the fort. Buchanan denounced the action but did nothing.

Immediately after taking office in March, Lincoln received a report from Fort Sumter that supplies were running low. Under great pressure from northern public opinion to do something without starting a war, he responded cleverly. He informed South Carolina governor Francis Pickens of his peaceful intention to send unarmed boats carrying food and supplies to the besieged fort. Lincoln thus placed the Confederacy in a no-win position: if Pickens accepted the resupply of federal forts he would lose face, but firing on an unarmed ship would be sufficiently dishonorable to justify stronger federal action. After studying the situation, Confederate officials determined to beat Lincoln to the punch. President Davis ordered the Confederate commander at Charleston, General P. G. T. Beauregard, to demand the evacuation of Sumter and, if the federals refused, to "proceed, in such a manner as you may determine, to reduce it." On April 11, while the supply ships were still on their way, Beauregard called on Anderson to surrender. When Anderson rejected the ultimatum on the following day, shore batteries opened fire on the island fortress. After a thirty-four-hour artillery battle, Anderson surrendered. Neither side had inflicted casualties on the other, but civil war had officially begun.

Across the North, newspapers contrasted the president's resolute but restrained policy with the violent aggression of the Confederates, and the public rallied behind the Union cause. In New York City, where southern sympathizers had once vehemently criticized abolitionist actions, a million people attended a

---

Preamble   An introductory paragraph in a formal document setting out its underlying justification and purpose.

Fort Sumter   Fort at the mouth of the harbor of Charleston, South Carolina; it was the scene of the opening engagement of the Civil War in April 1861.

battery   An army artillery unit, usually supplied with heavy guns.

In this vivid engraving, South Carolina shore batteries under the command of P. G. T. Beauregard shell Fort Sumter, the last federal stronghold in Charleston Harbor, on the night of April 12, 1861. Curious and excited civilians look on from their rooftops, never suspecting the horrors that would be the outcome of this rash action. *Library of Congress.*

Union rally. Even northern Democrats rallied behind the Republican president, hearkening to Stephen Douglas's statement that "there can be no neutrals in this war, only patriots—or traitors." Spurred by the public outcry and confident of support, Lincoln called for seventy-five thousand militiamen to be mobilized "to maintain the honor, the integrity, and the existence of our National Union, and the perpetuity of popular government." Northern states responded immediately and enthusiastically. Across the Upper South and the border regions, however, the call to arms meant that a decision had to be made: whether to continue in the Union or join the Confederacy.

Choosing Sides in Virginia

The need for southern unity in the face of what he saw as northern aggression pushed Jefferson Davis to employ a combination of political finesse and force to create a solid southern alignment. He selected his cabinet with this in mind, choosing one cabinet member from each state except his own Mississippi and appointing men of varying degrees of radicalism. But unity among the seven seceding states was only one of Davis's worries. A perhaps more pressing concern was alignment

among the eight slave states that remained in the Union. These states were critical, for they contained more than half of the entire southern population (two-thirds of its white population), possessed most of the South's industrial capacity, produced most of its food, and raised more than half of its horses. In addition, many experienced and able military leaders lived in these states. If the Confederacy was to have any chance of survival, the human and physical resources of the whole South were essential.

It was not Davis's appeal for solidarity but Lincoln's call to mobilize the militia that won most of the other slave states for the Confederate cause. In Virginia, Governor John Letcher refused to honor Lincoln's demand for troops, and on April 17 a special convention declared for secession. Voters in Virginia overwhelmingly ratified this decision in a popular referendum on May 23. By then Letcher had offered **Richmond** as a site for the new nation's capital. The Confederate congress accepted the offer in order to strengthen ties with Virginia and because facilities in Montgomery were less than adequate.

Not all Virginians were flattered by becoming the seat for the Confederacy. Residents of the western portion of the state had strong Union ties and long-standing political differences with their neighbors east of the Allegheny Mountains. Forty-six counties called mass Unionist meetings to protest the state's secession, and in a June convention at Wheeling, they elected their own governor, Francis H. Pierpoint, and drew up a constitution. The document was ratified in an election open only to voters willing to take an oath of allegiance to the Union. Eastern Virginians considered the entire process illegal, but the West Virginia legislature finally convened in May 1862 and requested admission to the United States.

For many individuals in the Upper South, the decision to support the Confederacy was not an easy one. Virginian Robert E. Lee, for example, was deeply devoted to the Union. A West Point graduate and career officer in the U.S. Army, he had a distinguished record in the war with Mexico and as superintendent of West Point. General Winfield Scott, commander of the Union forces, called Lee "the best soldier I ever saw in the field." Recognizing his military skill, Lincoln offered Lee field command of the Union armies, but the Virginian refused, deciding that he should serve his

Richmond Port city on the James River in Virginia; already the state capital, it became the capital of the Confederacy.

native state instead. Lee agonized over the decision but told a friend, "I cannot raise my hand against my birthplace, my home, my children." He resigned his U.S. Army commission in April 1861. When he informed Scott, a personal friend and fellow Virginian, of his decision, Scott replied, "You have made the greatest mistake of your life, but I feared it would be so." Scott chose to remain loyal to the Union.

A Second Wave of Secession

Influenced by Virginia and by Lee's decision, three other states joined the Confederacy. Arkansas had voted against secession in March, hoping that bloodshed might be averted, but when Lincoln called for militia units, Governor Henry M. Rector answered, "None will be furnished. The demand is only adding insult to injury." The state then called a second convention and on May 6 seceded from the Union. North Carolinians had also hoped for compromise, but moderates turned secessionist when Secretary of War Simon Cameron **requisitioned** "two regiments of militia for immediate service" against the Confederacy. Governor John W. Ellis replied, "I regard the levy of troops made by this administration for the purpose of subjugating the states of the South [to be] in violation of the Constitution and a gross usurpation of power." North Carolina seceded on May 20.

Tennessee, the eleventh and final state to join the Confederacy, was the home of many moderates, including John Bell, the Constitutional Union candidate in 1860. Eastern residents favored the Union, and those in the west favored the Confederacy. The state's voters at first rejected disunion overwhelmingly, but after the fighting began, Governor Isham C. Harris and the state legislature initiated military ties with the Confederacy, forcing another vote on the issue. Western voters carried the election, approving the agreement and seceding from the Union on June 8. East Tennesseans, who remained loyal Unionists, tried to divide the state much as West Virginians had done, but Davis ordered Confederate troops to occupy the region, thwarting the effort.

Trouble in the Border States

Four slave states remained in the Union, and the start of hostilities brought political and military confrontation in three of the four. Delaware quietly stayed in the Union. Voters there had given Breckinridge a plurality in 1860, but the majority of voters disapproved of secession, and few of the state's citizens owned slaves. Maryland, Missouri, and Kentucky, however,

Like the citizens in western Virginia, people in eastern Tennessee remained faithful to the Union. Men like those shown here swore allegiance to the United States flag and tried to split the state in two—one rebel and the other loyal—but Confederate troops put a stop to their efforts. *Library of Congress.*

each contained large, vocal secessionist minorities and appeared poised to bolt to the Confederacy.

Maryland was particularly vital to the Union, for it enclosed Washington, D.C., on the three sides not bordered by Virginia. If Maryland were to secede, the Union would be forced to move its capital. Maryland voters had overwhelmingly supported Breckinridge in 1860, and southern sympathizers controlled the legislature. But Governor Thomas Hicks, a Unionist, refused to call a special legislative session to consider secession.

On April 6, a Massachusetts regiment responding to Lincoln's call for troops passed through Baltimore on the way to the capital. A mob confronted the soldiers, and rioters attacked the rear companies with bricks, bottles, and pistols. The soldiers returned fire. When the violence subsided, twelve Baltimore residents and four soldiers lay dead, and dozens more

requisition To demand for military use.

were wounded. Secessionists reacted violently, destroying railroad bridges to keep additional northern troops out of the state. In effect, Washington, D.C., was cut off from the North.

Lincoln and General Scott ordered the military occupation of Baltimore and declared **martial law.** The state legislature finally met and voted to remain neutral. Lincoln then instructed the army to arrest suspected southern sympathizers and hold them without formal hearings or charges. When the legislature met again and appeared to be planning secession, Lincoln ordered the army to surround Frederick, the legislative seat—just as Davis had dispatched Confederate troops to occupy eastern Tennessee. With southern sympathizers suppressed, new state elections were held. The new legislature, overwhelmingly Unionist, voted against secession.

Kentucky had important economic ties to the South but was strongly nationalistic. Like Kentuckians Henry Clay and John Crittenden, most in the state favored compromise. The governor refused to honor Lincoln's call for troops, but the state legislature voted to remain neutral. Both the North and the South honored that neutrality. Kentucky's own militia, however, split into two factions, and the state became a bloody battleground where even members of the same family fought against one another.

In Missouri, Governor Claiborne F. Jackson, a former proslavery border ruffian, pushed for secession arguing that Missourians were bound together "in one brotherhood with the States of the South." When Unionists frustrated the secession movement, Jackson's forces seized the federal arsenal at Liberty and wrote to Jefferson Davis requesting artillery to support an assault on the arsenal at St. Louis. Union sympathizers, however, fielded their own forces and fought Jackson at every turn. Rioting broke out in St. Louis as civilians clashed with soldiers, and mob violence marred the nights. Jackson's secessionist movement sent representatives to the Confederate congress in Richmond, but Union forces maintained nominal control of the state and drove prosouthern leaders into exile.

> **martial law** Temporary rule by military authorities, imposed on a civilian population in time of war or when civil authority has broken down.

Individual Voices

Examining a Primary Source

Frederick Douglass: What to the Slave Is the Fourth of July?

After escaping from slavery and then experiencing continuing denigration in the North, Frederick Douglass eventually became a very effective speaker for the abolition cause. Always very direct, Douglass often said things to white audiences that they *really* did not want to hear. In 1852 the Ladies' Anti-Slavery Society of Rochester invited Douglass to speak at their Fourth of July celebration. They were extremely shocked by what he said.

Fellow-citizens, pardon me, allow me to ask, why am I called upon to speak here today? What have I, or those I represent, to do with your national independence? ■ *Are the great principles of political freedom and of natural justice, embodied in that Declaration of Independence, extended to us? and am I, therefore, called upon to bring out humble offering to the national altar, and to confess the benefits and express devout gratitude for the blessings resulting from your independence to us?* . . .

But such is not the state of the case. I say it with a sad sense of the disparity between us. I am not included within the pale of this glorious anniversary! ■

■ To whom is Douglass referring here? Who did he consider his constituency to be?

■ Ironically, Douglass's statement predicted one of Roger Taney's points in the Dred Scott decision five years later. "In the opinion of the court, the legislation and histories of the times, and the language used in the declaration of independence, show, that neither the class of persons who had been imported as slaves, nor their descendants, whether they had become free or not, were then acknowledged as a part of the people, nor intended to be included in the general words used in that memorable instrument."

■ What is Douglass's point in denying connection to the holiday about which he had been invited to speak?

■ Douglass is quoting here from Psalm 137, which he had recited in full earlier in the speech. This Psalm, which relates to the fall of Israel and the Babylonian Captivity, is cited again when Douglass discusses the fate of nations that defy God. What point was Douglass making in citing this Psalm?

Your high independence only reveals the immeasurable distance between us. The blessings in which you, this day, rejoice, are not enjoyed in common. The rich inheritance of justice, liberty, prosperity and independence, bequeathed by your fathers, is shared by you, not by me. The sunlight that brought life and healing to you, has brought stripes and death to me. This Fourth [of] July is yours, not mine. ■ . . .

Fellow-citizens; above your national, tumultuous joy, I hear the mournful wail of millions! whose chains, heavy and grievous yesterday, are, to-day, rendered more intolerable by the jubilee shouts that reach them. If I do forget, if I do not faithfully remember those bleeding children of sorrow this day, "may my right hand forget her cunning, and may my tongue cleave to the roof of my mouth!" ■ *To forget them, to pass lightly over their wrongs, and to chime in with the popular theme, would be treason most scandalous and shocking, and would make me a reproach before God and the world.*

Summary

As the Compromise of 1850 failed to alleviate regional tension and debates over slavery dominated the political agenda, the Whig Party, strained by fragmentation among its factions, disintegrated. Two completely new groups—the Know-Nothings and the Republicans—competed to replace the Whigs. A series of events—including the Kansas-Nebraska Act and the *Dred Scott* decision—intensified regional polarization, and radicals on both sides fanned the flames of sectional rivalry.

The new regional political coalitions of the 1850s more accurately reflected the changed composition of the electorate, but their intense commitment to regional interests left them far less able than their more nationally oriented predecessors to achieve compromise. Even the Democratic Party could not hold together, splitting into northern and southern wings. By 1859, the young Republican Party, committed to restricting slavery's expansion, seemed poised to gain control of the federal government. Fearing that the loss of political power would doom their way of life, southerners recoiled in terror. Neither side felt it could afford to back down.

With the election of Abraham Lincoln in 1860, six southern states withdrew from the Union. Last-minute efforts at compromise, such as the Crittenden proposal, failed, and on April 12, 1861, five weeks after Lincoln's inauguration, Confederate forces fired on federal troops at Fort Sumter in Charleston Harbor. Certain that secession was illegal, Lincoln's constituency expected action, but the president's options were limited by the varied ideologies of his supporters. Similarly, Jefferson Davis and the newly created Confederacy faced problems resulting from disagreement about secession. But Lincoln believed that he had to call the nation to arms, and this move forced wavering states to choose sides. Internal divisions in Virginia, Tennessee, Maryland, Kentucky, and Missouri brought further violence and military action. Before summer, a second wave of secession finally solidified the lineup, and the boundary lines, between the two competing societies. The stakes were set, the division was complete: the nation was poised for the bloodiest war in its history.

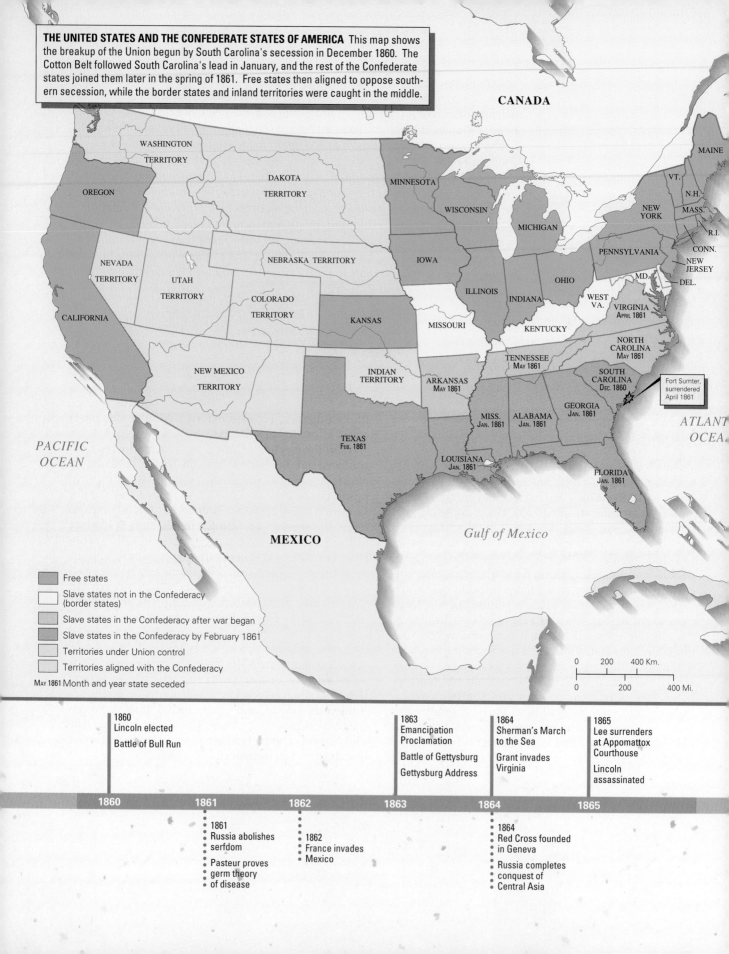

THE UNITED STATES AND THE CONFEDERATE STATES OF AMERICA This map shows the breakup of the Union begun by South Carolina's secession in December 1860. The Cotton Belt followed South Carolina's lead in January, and the rest of the Confederate states joined them later in the spring of 1861. Free states then aligned to oppose southern secession, while the border states and inland territories were caught in the middle.

CANADA

WASHINGTON TERRITORY

OREGON

DAKOTA TERRITORY

MINNESOTA

WISCONSIN

MICHIGAN

MAINE

VT.

N.H.

NEW YORK

MASS.

R.I.

NEVADA TERRITORY

UTAH TERRITORY

NEBRASKA TERRITORY

IOWA

PENNSYLVANIA

CONN.

NEW JERSEY

DEL.

CALIFORNIA

COLORADO TERRITORY

KANSAS

ILLINOIS

INDIANA

OHIO

MD.

WEST VA.

VIRGINIA
APRIL 1861

MISSOURI

KENTUCKY

NEW MEXICO TERRITORY

INDIAN TERRITORY

ARKANSAS
MAY 1861

TENNESSEE
MAY 1861

NORTH CAROLINA
MAY 1861

SOUTH CAROLINA
DEC. 1860

Fort Sumter, surrendered April 1861

GEORGIA
JAN. 1861

ATLANTIC OCEAN

TEXAS
FEB. 1861

MISS.
JAN. 1861

ALABAMA
JAN. 1861

LOUISIANA
JAN. 1861

FLORIDA
JAN. 1861

PACIFIC OCEAN

MEXICO

Gulf of Mexico

0   200   400 Km.

0   200   400 Mi.

Free states

Slave states not in the Confederacy (border states)

Slave states in the Confederacy after war began

Slave states in the Confederacy by February 1861

Territories under Union control

Territories aligned with the Confederacy

MAY 1861 Month and year state seceded

1860
Lincoln elected

Battle of Bull Run

1863
Emancipation Proclamation

Battle of Gettysburg

Gettysburg Address

1864
Sherman's March to the Sea

Grant invades Virginia

1865
Lee surrenders at Appomattox Courthouse

Lincoln assassinated

1860   **1861**   **1862**   **1863**   **1864**   **1865**

1861
Russia abolishes serfdom

Pasteur proves germ theory of disease

1862
France invades Mexico

1864
Red Cross founded in Geneva

Russia completes conquest of Central Asia

A Violent Choice: Civil War, 1861–1865

15

The United States and the Confederate States of America

Compare the map on the facing page to the opening maps for Chapters 10, 11, and 12 in terms of population, transportation systems, and industrial capacity. Given all of this information, why was the Confederacy at a distinct disadvantage at the beginning of the war? How was the conduct of the war influenced by these geographical factors, and what long-term consequences did this have on American history?

Individual Choices

MARY ASHTON RICE LIVERMORE

Having dedicated her life to women's education and national reform, Mary Ashton Rice Livermore and her husband, a crusading journalist, moved to Kansas in 1857 to lend their voices and votes to the antislavery effort in the new territory. Stalled in Chicago by their daughter's illness, they eventually founded an abolitionist newspaper in that city. When Civil War broke out in 1861, Mary immediately volunteered to create a local commission devoted to collecting medical supplies and other relief items to send to the battlefront. She also worked with other crusading women to raise public consciousness about sanitary conditions, eventually becoming a key official in Dorothea Dix's U.S. Sanitary Commission. Choices she made throughout her life convinced Livermore that women could and should assume expanding roles in American society and demand equality with men. *Chicago Historical Society.*

Mary Ashton Rice Livermore

Mary Ashton Rice was the daughter of strict Calvinists, but growing up in the heady intellectual atmosphere that permeated antebellum Boston, she soon joined many of her contemporaries in rejecting predestination and adopting a commitment to individual improvement and universal reform. With grudging support from her father, she attended several schools in Boston and finally took a job as a teacher to support herself while attending the Female Seminary in Charlestown, Massachusetts. After graduation, she took a position as a resident teacher on a Virginia plantation, where she learned firsthand about slavery and hated what she saw. After three years in the South, Rice made a choice to devote the balance of her life to two missions: personal involvement in reform movements such as temperance and abolition, and educating a new generation of young women to be reforming activists. She acted on the second of these by returning to Massachusetts to take charge of a female seminary in Duxbury. At the same time, she became active in the Boston-area temperance movement, where she met Universalist minister and reform editor Daniel P. Livermore, whom she married in 1845. Over the next ten years she and Daniel contributed regularly to local-area reform newspapers and magazines and became more and more active in increasingly radical organizations.

The Kansas-Nebraska Act and the subsequent outbreak of violence in Kansas proved to be a major turning point in the young couple's lives. Like many New Englanders and others who opposed the extension of slavery, the Livermores decided to move to Kansas in 1857 to lend their voices and votes to the struggle to make Kansas free. They got as far as Chicago; their daughter became ill, and the family decided to halt its journey. Still burning with reform fever, they decided to start a magazine, *The New Covenant,* to bring New England–style radical journalism to the Midwest.

When war broke out in 1861, Mary was no longer satisfied to apply herself exclusively in print. She immediately formed a female society devoted to "the relief of sick and wounded soldiers, and for the care of soldiers' families." Gathering a number of like-minded women into a tight organization, she and her lieutenants traveled to cities throughout the Midwest, even into hotly contested Missouri, gathering medical supplies and morale-raising cartons filled with homemade food, personal-care items, and often encouraging notes from sympathetic women addressed to anonymous soldiers in the field.

Over the next two years, women throughout the Midwest formed similar organizations and began to coordinate their efforts. In 1863 these various societies finally merged into the Northwestern Sanitary Commission, a major arm of reformer Dorothea Dix's national U.S. Sanitary Commission, with Livermore at its head. In that same year, she and her chief lieutenant, Jane C. Hoge, sponsored the first Sanitary Fair in Chicago, a four-month-long effort to raise money and educate the public about the deplorable health conditions in army camps. The crusade

brought in over $70,000, demonstrating the efficacy of fairs for raising funds as well as the public consciousness. This triumph also led communities around the country to begin giving formal recognition to female relief organizations and to their leaders as effective executives. In the years to come, Sanitary Fairs would become a regular part of the wartime environment, and women like Hoge and Livermore would gain the ear of both political leaders and military commanders.

Mary Livermore's choice to be an activist carried with it the realization that women were fully capable of performing the organizational work that many believed only men could do. Reflecting on popular writings about women, Livermore commented, "One would suppose in reading them that women possess but one class of physical organs, and that these are always diseased. Such teaching is pestiferous, and tends to cause and perpetuate the very evils it professes to remedy." Never shy about sharing her views with men—whether military camp commanders whose ignorance of public health endangered soldiers' lives or politicians who were slow to fund relief efforts—Livermore resolved after the war to work toward gaining for women the recognition that their efforts during the war had proved they deserved. As a feminist editor and activist, Livermore spent the rest of her life as it began, laboring for justice. As she advised her followers, "Courage, then, for the end draws near! A few more years of persistent, faithful work and the women of the United States will be recognized as the legal equals of men." She clearly had come a long way from her Boston Calvinist roots. A series of choices by this one woman not only changed her life but also contributed greatly to changing the country and the world.

INTRODUCTION

The outbreak of war between the states shocked many in the already deeply troubled nation. Many considered it a dire tragedy. Lying in a sickbed in Boston, Mary Livermore's father declared that he would rather die than see the nation divided. But for his daughter, this was a moment of triumph and opportunity. For years she and her husband had worked to bring about the end of slavery, and now it appeared that the time was at hand.

Many shared Livermore's enthusiasm. Over the previous decade, increasing numbers of people in the North had come to loathe the South and everything it stood for. Though many had no great love for slaves, they had grown to detest slavery, which they associated with a power-mad aristocracy bent on imposing their power, and their culture, on the entire nation. People in the South were also enthusiastic. Likening themselves to the American colonists of old standing up to a haughty empire, southerners were eager to reenact a war for independence.

It did not take long, however, for virtually everyone to become disillusioned. The South would find it more and more difficult to withstand the superior manpower and resources controlled by the Union. And the North would suffer frustrations of its own as President Lincoln's generals let opportunity after opportunity slip by. In desperation, Lincoln would finally redefine the war by issuing the Emancipation Proclamation, making it a struggle to end slavery as well as to prevent southern secession. From that point forward, hopes for a peaceful resolution evaporated: both sides would demand total victory or total destruction.

The war would affect many people in many different ways. For some, like Mary Livermore, it would afford great opportunities for advancement. For others, it would be a long, torturous ordeal. But one thing was true for everyone and for the nation at

"It is easy to understand how men catch the contagion of war," civilian relief worker Mary Ashton Rice Livermore asserted. Many on both sides certainly caught it during the opening days of the Civil War. These two Union cavalrymen (*left*) and Confederate infantrymen (*right*), father and son, volunteered for service and obviously were eager to fight. Such enthusiasm seldom lasted long as days and weeks of boredom, often accompanied by disease, punctuated by brief but heated battles caused enormous anxiety that eroded their fighting spirit. *Left: Richard Carlile; right: Bill Turner.*

large: nothing would be the same after the conflagration was over.

The Politics of War

- What problems did Abraham Lincoln and Jefferson Davis face as they led their respective nations into war?
- How did each chief executive deal with those problems?
- What role did European nations play during the opening years of the war?

Running the war posed complex problems for both Abraham Lincoln and Jefferson Davis. At the outset, neither side had the experience, soldiers, or supplies to wage an effective war, and foreign diplomacy and international trade were vital to both. But perhaps the biggest challenge confronting both Davis and Lincoln

was internal politics. Lincoln had to contend not only with northern Democrats and southern sympathizers but also with divisions in his own party. Not all Republicans agreed with the president's war aims. Davis also faced internal political problems. The Confederate constitution guaranteed a great deal of autonomy to the Confederate states, and each state had a different opinion about war strategy and national objectives.

Union Policies and Objectives

Abraham Lincoln took the oath of office in March 1861, but Congress did not convene until July. This delay placed Lincoln in an awkward position. The Constitution gives Congress, not the president, the power "to declare war" and "to provide for calling forth the militia to execute the laws of the Union, sup-

Chronology

War Between the States

1861   Lincoln takes office and runs Union by executive authority until July
Fort Sumter falls
Battle of Bull Run
McClellan organizes the Union army
Union naval blockade begins

1862   Grant's victories in Mississippi Valley
Battle of Shiloh
U.S. Navy captures New Orleans
Peninsular Campaign
Battle of Antietam
African Americans permitted in Union army

1863   Emancipation Proclamation takes effect
Union enacts conscription

Battle of Chancellorsville and death of Stonewall Jackson
Union victories at Gettysburg and Vicksburg
Draft riots in New York City

1864   Grant invades Virginia
Sherman captures Atlanta
Lincoln reelected
Sherman's March to the Sea
Congress passes the Thirteenth Amendment

1865   Sherman's march through the Carolinas
Lee abandons Petersburg and Richmond
Lee surrenders at Appomattox Courthouse
Lincoln proposes a gentle reconstruction policy
Lincoln is assassinated

---

press insurrection, and repel invasions." The secession of the southern states and the imminent threat to federal authority at Fort Sumter, however, required an immediate response.

In effect, Lincoln ruled by executive proclamation for three months, vastly expanding the wartime powers of the presidency. Lincoln called for seventy-five thousand militiamen from the states to put down the rebellion. And ignoring specific constitutional provisions, he suspended the civil rights of citizens in Maryland when it appeared likely that the border state would join the Confederacy (see page 416). At various times during the war, Lincoln would resort to similar invasions of civil liberties when he felt that dissent threatened either domestic security or the Union cause.

Having assumed nearly absolute authority, Lincoln faced the need to rebuild an army in disarray. When hostilities broke out, the Union had only sixteen thousand men in uniform, and nearly one-third of the officers resigned to support the Confederacy. What military leadership remained was aged: seven of the eight heads of army bureaus had been in the service since the War of 1812, including General in Chief Winfield Scott, who was 74 years old. Only two Union officers had ever commanded a brigade, and both were in their seventies. Weapons were old, and supplies were low. On May 3, Lincoln again exceeded his con-

stitutional authority by calling for regular army recruits to meet the crisis. "Whether strictly legal or not," he asserted, such actions were based on "a popular demand, and a public necessity," and he expected "that Congress would readily ratify them."

Lincoln had also ordered the U.S. Navy to stop all incoming supplies to the states in rebellion. The naval blockade became an integral part of Union strategy. Though the Union navy had as few resources as the army, leadership in the Navy Department quickly turned that situation around. Navy Secretary Gideon Welles, whom Lincoln called "Father Neptune," purchased ships and built an effective navy that could both blockade the South and support land forces. By the end of 1861, the Union navy had 260 warships on the seas and a hundred more under construction.

The aged Winfield Scott drafted the initial Union military strategy. He ordered that the blockade of southern ports be combined with a strong Union thrust down the Mississippi River, the primary artery in the South's transportation system. This strategy would break the southern economy and split the Confederacy into two isolated parts. Like many northerners, Scott believed that economic pressure would bring southern moderates forward to negotiate a settlement and perhaps return to the Union. However, this passive, diplomacy-oriented strategy did not appeal to

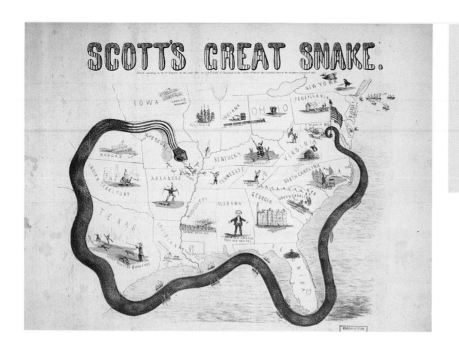

Though many northerners thought it was too passive, General Winfield Scott's "anaconda plan" was actually very well conceived. As this 1861 lithograph shows, Scott called for a naval blockade of the South and seizure of the Mississippi River, shutting down transportation routes to ruin the Confederate economy. Scott retired at the end of the war's first year, but his plan continued to shape the Union's overall strategy. *Library of Congress.*

war-fevered northerners who hungered for complete victory over those "arrogant southerners." The northern press ridiculed what it called the **anaconda plan.**

When Congress finally convened on July 4, 1861, Lincoln explained his actions and reminded congressmen that he had neither the constitutional authority to abolish slavery nor any intention of doing so. Rebellion, not slavery, had caused the crisis, he said, and the seceding states must be brought back into the Union, regardless of the cost. "Our popular government has been called an experiment," he argued, and the point to be settled now was "its successful maintenance against a formidable internal attempt to overthrow it." On July 22 and 25, 1861, both houses of Congress passed resolutions validating Lincoln's actions.

This seemingly unified front lasted only a short time. Viewing vengeance as the correct objective, **Radical Republicans** pressured Congress to create a special committee to oversee the conduct of the war. Radical leader Thaddeus Stevens (see page 287) of Pennsylvania growled, "If their whole country must be laid waste, and made a desert, in order to save this union, so let it be." Stevens and the Radicals pressed for and passed a series of confiscation acts that inflicted severe penalties against individuals in rebellion. Treason was punishable by death, and anyone aiding the Confederacy was to be punished with imprisonment, attachment of property, and confiscation

of slaves. All persons living in the eleven seceding states, whether loyal to the Union or not, were declared enemies of the Union and subject to the provisions of the law.

The Radicals splintered any consensus Lincoln might have achieved in his own party, and northern Democrats railed against his accumulation of power. To keep an unruly Congress from undermining his efforts, Lincoln shaped early Union strategy to appease all factions and used military appointments to smooth political feathers. His attitudes frequently enraged radical abolitionists, but Lincoln maintained his calm in the face of their criticism and merely reinforced his intentions. "What I do about slavery and the colored race," he stated in 1862, "I do because it helps to save the Union; and what I forbear, I forbear because I do not believe it would help to save the

anaconda plan   Winfield Scott's plan (named after a snake that smothers prey in its coils) to blockade southern ports and take control of the Mississippi River, thus splitting the Confederacy, cutting off southern trade, and causing an economic collapse.

Radical Republicans   Republican faction that tried to limit presidential power and enhance congressional authority during the Civil War; Radicals opposed moderation toward the South or any toleration of slavery.

TABLE 15.1   Comparison of Union and Confederate Resources

	Union (23 States)	Confederacy (11 States)
Total population	20,700,000	9,105,000[a]
Manufacturing establishments	110,000	18,000
Manufacturing workers	1,300,000	110,000
Miles of railroad	21,973	9,283
Troop strength (est.)	2,100,000	850,000

Source: Data from *Battles and Leaders of the Civil War* (1884–1888; reprinted ed., 1956).
[a]Includes 3,654,000 blacks, most of them slaves and not available for military duty.

Union." Such words, however, did not mend the ongoing divisiveness that hindered his efforts to run the war.

Nevertheless, Lincoln had far greater physical and human resources at his command than did the Confederates (see Table 15.1). The Union was home to more than twice as many people as the Confederacy, had vastly superior manufacturing and transportation systems, and enjoyed almost a monopoly in banking and foreign exchange. Lincoln also had a well-established government structure and formal diplomatic relations with other nations of the world. Still, these advantages could not help the war effort unless properly harnessed.

Confederate Policies and Objectives

At the start of the war, the Confederacy had no army, no navy, no war supplies, no government structure, no foreign alliances, and a political situation as ragged as the Union's. Each Confederate state had its own ideas about the best way to conduct the war. After the attack on Fort Sumter, amassing supplies, troops, ships, and war materials was the main task for Davis and his cabinet. Politics, however, influenced southern choices about where to field armies and who would direct them, how to run a war without offending state leaders, and how to pursue foreign diplomacy.

The Union naval blockade posed an immediate problem. The Confederacy had no navy and no capacity to build naval ships. But it did have the extremely resourceful Stephen Mallory as secretary of the navy. Under Mallory's direction, southern coastal defenders converted river steamboats, tugboats, and **revenue cutters** into harbor patrol gunboats, and they developed and placed explosive mines at the entrances to southern harbors.

Confederates pinned their main hope of winning the war on the army. Fighting for honor was praiseworthy behavior in the South, and southerners strongly believed they could "lick the Yankees" despite their disadvantage in manpower and resources. Southern boys rushed to enlist to fight the northern "popinjays," expecting a quick and glorious victory. Thousands volunteered before the Confederate war department was even organized. By the time Lincoln issued his call for seventy-five thousand militiamen, the Confederates already had sixty thousand men in uniform.

Despite this rush of fighting men, the South faced major handicaps. Even with the addition of the four Upper South states (Virginia, North Carolina, Tennessee, and Arkansas), the South built only 4 percent of all locomotives and only 3 percent of all firearms manufactured in the United States in 1860. The North produced almost all of the country's cloth, **pig iron,** boots, and shoes. Early in the war, the South could produce enough food but lacked the means to transport it where it was needed. Quartermaster General Abraham Myers drew the mammoth task of producing

revenue cutter   A small, lightly armed boat used by government customs agents to apprehend merchant ships violating customs laws.

pig iron   Crude iron, direct from a blast furnace, that is cast into rectangular molds called pigs in preparation for conversion into steel, cast iron, or wrought iron.

and delivering tents, shoes, uniforms, blankets, horses, and wagons. All were in short supply.

The miracle worker in charge of supplying southern troops with weapons and ammunition was Josiah Gorgas, who became chief of **ordnance** in April 1861. Gorgas purchased arms from Europe while his ordnance officers bought or stole copper pots and tubing to make **percussion caps,** bronze church bells to make cannon, and lead weights to make bullets. He built factories and foundries to manufacture small arms. But despite his extraordinary skill, he could not supply all of the Confederate troops. When the Confederate congress authorized the enlistment of four hundred thousand additional volunteers in 1861, the war department had to turn away more than half of the enlistees because it lacked equipment for them.

Internal politics also plagued the Davis administration. Despite the shortage of arms, state governors hoarded weapons seized from federal arsenals for their own state militias and then criticized Confederate strategies, particularly the actions of the war department. Although the South had many more qualified officers at the beginning of the war than did the North, powerful state politicians with little military experience—such as Henry A. Wise of Virginia and Robert A. Toombs of Georgia—received appointments as generals. That practice may have made good political sense, but it was military folly.

Going into the conflict, Davis favored waging a defensive war. He felt that by counterattacking and yielding territory when necessary to buy time, the Confederacy could prolong the war and make it so costly that the Union would finally give up. Although defensive strategies ran counter to southern notions of pride and honor, each state's leaders demanded that their state's borders be protected, ignoring that such a strategy would spread troops so thin that no state would be safe. In any case, most southerners preferred an aggressive policy. As one southern editor put it, the "idea of waiting for blows, instead of inflicting them is altogether unsuited to the genius of our people."

The Diplomatic Front

Perhaps the biggest challenge facing the Confederacy was gaining international recognition and foreign aid. The primary focus of Confederate foreign policy was Great Britain. For years, the South had been exporting huge amounts of cotton to Britain, and many southerners felt that formal recognition of the Confederate States of America as an independent nation would immediately follow secession. Political, diplo-

matic, and economic realities doomed them to disappointment. After all, the United States, divided as it was, was still an important player in international affairs, and the British were not going to risk offending the emerging industrial power without good cause. Also, many English voters were morally opposed to slavery and would have objected to an open alliance with the slaveholding Confederacy. Thus, while the British allowed southern agents to purchase ships and goods, they crafted a careful policy. On May 13, 1861, Queen Victoria proclaimed official neutrality but granted **belligerent status** to the South. This meant that Britain recognized the Confederates not as rebels but as responsible parties in a legitimate war for independence. But it also meant that they did not recognize the Confederate States of America as yet ready to enter the international community.

The British pronouncement set the tone for other European responses and was much less than southerners had hoped for. It was also a major blow to the North, however, for Britain rejected Lincoln's position that the conflict was rebellion against duly authorized government. Lincoln could do little but accept British neutrality, for to provoke Britain might lead to full recognition of the Confederacy or to calls for arbitration of the conflict. At the same time, he cautiously continued efforts to block all incoming aid to the Confederacy. In November 1861, however, an incident at sea nearly scuttled British-American relations. James Murray Mason, the newly appointed Confederate emissary to London, and John Slidell, the Confederate minister to France, were traveling to their posts aboard the *Trent,* a British merchant ship bound for London. After the *Trent* left Havana, the U.S. warship *San Jacinto,* under the command of Captain Charles Wilkes, stopped the British ship. Wilkes had Mason, Slidell, and their staffs removed from the *Trent* and taken to Boston for confinement at Fort Warren.

Northerners celebrated the action and praised Wilkes, but the British were not pleased. They viewed the *Trent* affair as aggression against a neutral government, a violation of international law, and an af-

---

ordnance   Weapons, ammunition, and other military equipment.

percussion cap   A thin metal cap containing an explosive compound, needed to fire the guns used in the Civil War.

belligerent status   Recognition that a participant in a conflict is a nation engaged in warfare rather than a rebel against a legally constituted government; full diplomatic recognition is one possible outcome.

front to their national honor. President Lincoln, Secretary of State William Seward, and U.S. Ambassador to England Charles Francis Adams (son of former president John Quincy Adams) calmed the British by arguing that Wilkes had acted without orders. They ordered the release of the prisoners and apologized to the British, handling the incident so adroitly that the public outcry was largely forgotten when Mason and Slidell arrived in London.

The Union's First Attack

Like most southerners, northerners were confident that military action would bring the war to a quick end. General Irvin McDowell made the first move when his troops crossed into Virginia to engage troops led by General P. G. T. Beauregard (see Map 15.1 and Table 15.2). McDowell's troops, though high-spirited, were poorly trained and undisciplined. They ambled along as if they were on a country outing, allowing Beauregard enough time to position his troops in defense of a vital rail center near Manassas Junction along a creek called **Bull Run.**

McDowell attacked on Sunday, July 21, and maintained the offensive most of the day. He seemed poised to overrun the Confederates until southern reinforcements under **Thomas J. Jackson** stalled the Union advance. Jackson's unflinching stand at Bull Run earned him the nickname "Stonewall," and under intense cannon fire, Union troops panicked and began fleeing into a throng of northern spectators who had brought picnic lunches and settled in to watch the battle. Thoroughly humiliated before a hometown crowd, Union soldiers retreated toward Washington. Jefferson Davis immediately ordered the invasion of the Union capital, but the Confederates were also in disarray and made no attempt to pursue the fleeing Union forces.

This battle profoundly affected both sides. In the South, the victory stirred confidence that the war would be short and victory complete. Northerners, disillusioned and embarrassed, pledged that no similar retreats would occur. Under fire for the loss and hoping to improve both the management of military affairs and the competence of the troops, Lincoln fired McDowell and appointed **George B. McClellan.** McClellan was assigned to create the **Army of the Potomac** to defend the capital from Confederate attack and spearhead any offensives into Virginia. Lincoln also replaced Secretary of War Simon Cameron with Edwin Stanton, a politician and lawyer from Pennsylvania. Scott remained in place as general in chief until his retirement at the end of the year.

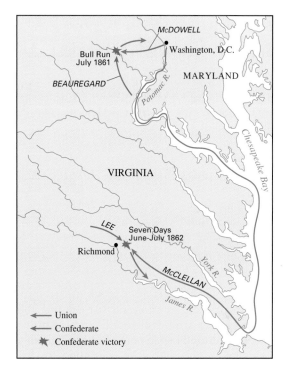

MAP 15.1 Union Offensives into Virginia, 1861–1862 This map shows two failed Union attempts to invade Virginia: the Battle of Bull Run (July 1861) and the Peninsular Campaign (August 1862). Confederate victories embarrassed the richer and more populous Union.

General McClellan's strengths were in organization and discipline. Both were sorely needed. Before Bull Run, Union officers had lounged around Washington while largely unsupervised raw recruits in army camps received no military instruction. Under

Bull Run A creek in Virginia not far from Washington, D.C., where Confederate soldiers forced federal troops to retreat in the first major battle of the Civil War, fought in July 1861.

Thomas J. Jackson Confederate general nicknamed "Stonewall"; he commanded troops at both battles of Bull Run and was mortally wounded by his own soldiers at Chancellorsville in 1863.

George B. McClellan U.S. general tapped by Lincoln to organize the Army of the Potomac; a skillful organizer but slow and indecisive as a field commander. He eventually replaced Winfield Scott as general in chief of Union forces.

Army of the Potomac Army created to guard the U.S. capital after the Battle of Bull Run in 1861; it became the main Union army in the East.

TABLE 15.2 Battle of Bull Run, July 22, 1861

	Union Army	Confederate Army
Commanders	Irvin McDowell	P. G. T. Beauregard
Troop strength	17,676	18,053
Losses		
Killed	460	387
Wounded	1,124	1,582
Captured	1,312	13
Total Losses	2,896	1,982

Source: Data from *Battles and Leaders of the Civil War* (1884–1888; reprinted ed., 1956).

McClellan, months of training turned the 185,000-man army into a well-drilled and efficient unit. Calls to attack Richmond began anew, but McClellan, seemingly in no hurry for battle, continued to drill the troops and remained in the capital. Finally on January 27, 1862, Lincoln called for a broad offensive, but his general in chief ignored the order and delayed for nearly two months. Completely frustrated, Lincoln removed McClellan as general in chief on March 11 but left him in command of the Army of the Potomac. Even so, Union forces in the East mounted no major offensives.

From Bull Run to Antietam

■ How did military action during the opening years of the war affect the people's perceptions of the war in the North and South?

■ In what ways did international diplomacy play into Lincoln's decision making as the war unfolded?

■ Why did Lincoln issue the Emancipation Proclamation when and in the way he did? What sorts of responses did it elicit?

Reorganizing the military and forming the Army of the Potomac did not accomplish Lincoln's and the nation's goal of toppling the Confederacy quickly and bringing the rebellious South back into the Union. In the second year of the war, frustration followed frustration as Confederate forces continued to outwit and outfight numerically superior and better-equipped federal troops. After Bull Run it was clear that the war would be neither short nor glorious. Military, political, and diplomatic strategies became increasingly entan-

gled as both North and South struggled for the major victories that would end the war.

The War in the West

While the war in the East slid into inactivity, events in the West seemed almost as futile for the Union forces. In the border state of Missouri, the conflict rapidly degenerated into guerrilla warfare. Confederate William Quantrill's Raiders matched atrocities committed by Unionist guerrilla units called Jayhawkers. Union officials seemed unable to stop the ambushes, arson, theft, and murder, and Missouri remained a lawless battleground throughout the war.

Both the United States and the Confederacy coveted the western territories nearly as much as they did the border states. In 1861 Confederate Henry Hopkins Sibley attempted to gain control of New Mexico and Arizona. Bearing authority directly from Jefferson Davis, Sibley recruited thirty-seven hundred Texans and marched into New Mexico. He defeated a Union force at Valverde, but his losses were high. Needing provisions to continue the operation, he sent units to raid abandoned Union storehouses at Albuquerque and Santa Fe, but withdrawing federal troops had burned whatever supplies they could not carry. The small Confederate force at Santa Fe encountered a much larger federal force and won a miraculous victory, but the effort left the Confederates destitute of supplies. Under constant attack, the starving Confederate detachment evaded Union troops and retreated back into Texas.

As the war intensified, leaders on both sides were forced to concentrate on regional defenses and focus

Angered by years of systematic mistreatment at the hands of federal authorities, many Native Americans in Indian Territory were eager to enlist for service with the Confederacy. Confederate president Jefferson Davis chose his Indian agents carefully in order to take advantage of this much-needed source of aid: his ambassador to Indian Territory, General Albert Pike, for example, had represented the Creeks in their battle against removal in the 1830s. As this daguerreotype illustrates, Davis's diplomacy was highly successful; many young Indians flocked to Confederate recruitment rallies to join the army. *Wisconsin Historical Society.*

on potential confrontations with enemy armies. Union officers pulled most of their troops back into the areas of concentrated fighting, leaving vast areas of the sparsely settled West with no military protection. In 1862 the Santee Sioux took advantage of the situation by attacking and killing more than eight hundred settlers in the Minnesota River valley. An army of fourteen hundred volunteers finally put down the uprising, but the lack of federal troops in frontier regions created severe anxiety in western communities.

Confederate leaders sought alliances with several Indian tribes at the onset of war, particularly tribes in the newly settled Indian Territory south of Kansas. Many of the residents there had endured the Trail of Tears (see page 296) and had no particular love for the Union. If these Indian tribes aligned with the Confederacy, they not only could supply troops but might also form a buffer between Union forces in Kansas and the thinly spread Confederate defenses west of the Mississippi River. Davis appointed General Albert Pike, an Arkansas lawyer who had represented the Creeks in court, as special commissioner for the Indian Territory in March 1861. Pike negotiated with several tribes and on October 7 signed a treaty with John Ross, chief of the Cherokee Nation (see pages 295–296). The treaty, which applied to some members of the Cherokee, Choctaw, Creek, Chickasaw, and Seminole tribes, granted the Indians more nearly equal status—at least on paper—than any previous federal treaty, and it guaranteed that Indians would be asked to fight only to defend their own territory. One Cherokee leader, Stand Watie, became a Confederate general and distinguished himself in battle, leading his Confederate troops in guerrilla warfare against Union forces.

Struggle for the Mississippi

While McClellan stalled in the East, one Union general finally had some success in the western theater of the war. Following the strategy outlined in General Scott's anaconda plan, **Ulysses S. Grant** moved against southern strongholds in the Mississippi Valley in 1862. On February 6, he took Fort Henry along the Tennessee River and ten days later captured Fort Donelson on the Cumberland River near Nashville, Tennessee (see Map 15.2). As Union forces approached Nashville, the Confederates retreated to Corinth, Mississippi. In this one swift stroke, Grant successfully penetrated Confederate western defenses and brought Kentucky and most of Tennessee under federal control.

At Corinth, Confederate general Albert Sidney Johnston finally reorganized the retreating southern troops while Grant was waiting for reinforcements. Early on April 6, to Grant's surprise, Johnston attacked at Pittsburg Landing, Tennessee, near a small country meetinghouse called Shiloh Church (see Table 15.3). Some

Ulysses S. Grant U.S. general who became general in chief of the Union army in 1864 after the Vicksburg campaign; he later became president of the United States.

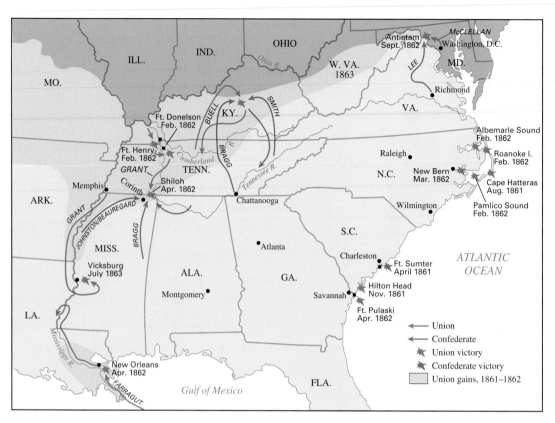

MAP 15.2 The Anaconda Plan and the Battle of Antietam This map illustrates the anaconda plan at work. The Union navy closed southern harbors while Grant's troops worked to seal the northern end of the Mississippi River. The map also shows the Battle of Antietam (September 1862), in which Confederate troops under Robert E. Lee were finally defeated by the Union army under General George McClellan.

Union forces under General **William Tecumseh Sherman** were driven back, but the Confederate attack soon lost momentum as Union defenses stiffened. The **Battle of Shiloh** raged until midafternoon. When Johnston was mortally wounded, General Beauregard took command and by day's end believed the enemy defeated. But Union reinforcements arrived during the night, and the next morning Grant counterattacked, pushing the Confederates back to Corinth.

The losses on both sides were staggering. The Battle of Shiloh made the reality of war apparent to everyone but made a particularly strong impression on the common soldier. After Shiloh, one Confederate wrote: "Death in every awful form, if it really be death, is a pleasant sight in comparison to the fearfully and mortally wounded." Few people foresaw that the horrible carnage at Shiloh was but a taste of what was to come.

Farther south, Admiral David G. Farragut led a fleet of U.S. Navy gunboats against New Orleans, the commercial and banking center of the South, and on April 25 forced the city's surrender. Farragut then sailed up the Mississippi, hoping to take the well-fortified city of **Vicksburg,** Mississippi. He scored several vic-

William Tecumseh Sherman U.S. general who captured Atlanta in 1864 and led a destructive march to the Atlantic coast.

Battle of Shiloh Battle in Tennessee in April 1862 that ended with an unpursued Confederate withdrawal; both sides suffered heavy casualties for the first time, but neither side gained ground.

Vicksburg Confederate-held city on the Mississippi River that surrendered on July 4, 1863, after a lengthy siege by Grant's forces.

TABLE 1 5 . 3   Battle of Shiloh, April 6–7, 1862

	Union Army	Confederate Army
Commanders	William Tecumseh Sherman Ulysses S. Grant	Albert Sidney Johnston (killed) P. G. T. Beauregard
Troop strength	75,000	44,000
Losses		
Killed	1,754	1,723
Wounded	8,408	8,012
Captured, missing	2,885	959
Total Losses	13,047	10,694

Source: Data from *Battles and Leaders of the Civil War* (1884–1888; reprinted ed., 1956).

tories until he reached Port Hudson, Louisiana, where the combination of Confederate defenses and shallow water forced him to halt. Meanwhile, on June 6, Union gunboats destroyed a Confederate fleet at Memphis, Tennessee, and brought the upper Mississippi under Union control. Vicksburg remained the only major obstacle to Union control over the entire river (see Map 15.2).

Realizing the seriousness of the situation in the West, the Confederates regrouped and invaded Kentucky. Union forces under General William S. Rosecrans stopped Confederate general Braxton Bragg's force on December 31 at Stone's River and did not pursue when the Confederates retreated. Back in Mississippi, Grant launched two unsuccessful attacks against Vicksburg in December, but then Union efforts stalled. Nevertheless, northern forces had wrenched control of the upper and lower ends of the river away from the Confederacy.

Lee's Aggressive Defense of Virginia

The anaconda plan was well on its way to cutting the Confederacy in two, but the general public in the North thought that the path to real victory led to Richmond, capital of the Confederacy. Thus, to maintain public support for the war, Lincoln needed victories over the Confederates in the East, and campaigns there were given higher priority than campaigns in the West. Confederate leaders, realizing that Richmond would be an important prize for the North, took dramatic steps to keep their capital city out of

enemy hands. In fact, defending Richmond was the South's primary goal: more supplies and men were assigned to campaigns in Virginia than to defending Confederate borders elsewhere.

Hoping to clear Virginia's coastline of Union blockaders and protect their capital from amphibious invasion, Confederate naval architects had redesigned a captured Union ship named the *Merrimac.* They encased the entire ship in iron plates and renamed it the *Virginia.* Learning of Confederate attempts to launch an armored ship, the Union navy began building the *Monitor,* a low-decked ironclad vessel with a revolving gun turret. In March the *Virginia* and the *Monitor* shelled each other for five hours. Both were badly damaged but still afloat when the *Virginia* withdrew, making its way back to Norfolk, never to leave harbor again.

With the *Virginia* out of service, McClellan devised precisely the amphibious assault that Virginians had been fearing. Expecting to surprise the Confederates by attacking Richmond from the south, he transported the entire Army of the Potomac by ship to Fort Monroe, Virginia. Initiating what would be called the **Peninsular Campaign,** the army marched up the peninsula between the York and James Rivers (see Map 15.1). In typical fashion, McClellan proceeded

Peninsular Campaign   McClellan's attempt in the spring and summer of 1862 to capture Richmond by advancing up the peninsula between the James and York Rivers; Confederate forces under Robert E. Lee drove his troops back.

Desperate to break the grip of the Union anaconda, the Confederate navy converted the captured Union ship U.S.S. *Merrimac* into the ironclad C.S.S. *Virginia*. Virtually immune to any weapon carried by Union frigates, the *Virginia* dominated the sea-lanes out of Norfolk Harbor. Though the *Virginia* carried cannon, its iron hull was its most effective weapon, as illustrated by this painting of the Confederate ironclad ramming the Union blockade vessel *Cumberland*. The Union navy eventually completed construction of its own ironclad, the U.S.S. *Monitor,* which defeated the *Virginia* in a dramatic sea battle, eliminating that weapon from the Confederate arsenal. *"Ramming of the U.S.S.* Cumberland *and the U.S.S.* Virginia*" by Alexander Charles Stuart. Courtesy of the Charleston Renaissance Gallery, Robert M. Hicklin Jr. Inc., Charleston, SC.*

cautiously. The outnumbered Confederate forces took advantage of his indecision and twice slipped away, retreating toward Richmond while McClellan followed. Hoping to overcome the odds by surprising his opponent, General Joseph E. Johnston, commander of the Confederate Army of Northern Virginia, wheeled about and attacked at Seven Pines on May 31. Though the battle was indecisive—both sides claimed victory—it halted McClellan's progress and disabled Johnston, who was seriously wounded.

With McClellan stalled, Confederate stalwart Stonewall Jackson staged a brilliant diversionary thrust down the Shenandoah Valley toward Washington. Jackson, who had grown up in the region, seemed to be everywhere at once. In thirty days, he and his men (who became known as the "foot cavalry") marched 350 miles, defeated three Union armies in five battles, captured and sent back to Richmond a fortune in provisions and equipment, inflicted twice as many casualties as they received, and confused and immobilized Union forces in the region.

Meanwhile, Union forces were marking time near Richmond while McClellan waited for reinforcements. Determined to remove this threat, Confederate forces launched a series of attacks to drive McClellan away from the Confederate capital. Though his army had already proved itself against the Confederates at Seven Pines, a new factor weighed in against McClelland. With Johnston wounded, Davis had been forced to re-

place him, choosing Robert E. Lee. Lee was probably the Confederacy's best general. Daring, bold, and tactically aggressive, he enjoyed combat, pushed his troops to the maximum, and was well liked by those serving under him. Lee had an uncanny ability to read the character of his opponents, predict their maneuvers, and exploit their mistakes. In a move that became typical of his generalship, Lee split his forces and attacked from all sides over a seven-day period in August, forcing McClellan into a defensive position. The Peninsular Campaign was over. The self-promoting Union general had been beaten in part by his own indecisiveness.

Fed up with McClellan, Lincoln transferred command of the Army of the Potomac to General John Pope, but Pope's command was brief. Union forces encountered Lee's army again at the Manassas rail line on August 30. The Confederates pretended to retreat, and when Pope followed, Lee soundly defeated Lincoln's new general in the **Second Battle of Bull Run.** Thoroughly disappointed with Pope's performance, but lacking any other viable replacement, Lincoln once again named McClellan commander of the Army of the Potomac.

Second Battle of Bull Run Union defeat near Bull Run in August 1862; Union troops led by John Pope were outmaneuvered by Lee.

Lee's Invasion of Maryland

Feeling confident after the second victory at Bull Run, Lee devised a bold offensive against Maryland. His plan had three objectives. First, he wanted to move the fighting out of war-torn Virginia so that farmers could harvest food. Second, he hoped that he might attract volunteers from among the many slaveowners and southern sympathizers in Maryland to beef up his undermanned army. Third, he believed that a strong thrust against Union forces might gain diplomatic recognition for the Confederacy from Europe. In the process, he hoped to win enough territory to force the Union to sue for peace. On September 4, Lee crossed the Potomac into Maryland, formulating an intricate offensive by dividing his army into three separate attack wings. But someone was careless— Union soldiers found a copy of Lee's detailed instructions wrapped around some cigars at an abandoned Confederate campsite.

If McClellan had acted swiftly on this intelligence, he could have crushed Lee's army piece by piece, but he waited sixteen hours before advancing. By then, Lee had learned of the missing orders and quickly withdrew. Lee reunited some of his forces at Sharpsburg, Maryland, around **Antietam Creek** (see Map 15.2). There, on September 17, the Army of the Potomac and the Army of Northern Virginia engaged in the bloodiest single-day battle of the Civil War.

The casualties in this one battle were more than double those suffered in the War of 1812 and the War with Mexico combined. "The air was full of the hiss of bullets and the hurtle of grapeshot," one Union soldier said, and "the whole landscape turned red." The bitter fighting exhausted both armies. After a day of rest, Lee retreated across the Potomac. Stonewall Jackson, covering Lee's retreat, soundly thrashed a force that McClellan sent in pursuit. But for the first time, General Lee experienced defeat.

Although Lee's offensive had been thwarted, Lincoln was in no way pleased with the performance of his army and its leadership. He felt that McClellan could have destroyed Lee's forces if he had attacked earlier or, failing that, had pursued the fleeing Confederate army with all haste. He fired McClellan again, this time for good, and placed Ambrose E. Burnside in command of the Army of the Potomac.

Burnside moved the Army of the Potomac to the east bank of the Rappahannock River overlooking **Fredericksburg,** Virginia (see Map 15.3), where he delayed for almost three weeks. Lee used the time to fortify the heights west of the city with men and artillery. On December 13, in one of the worst mistakes of the war, Burnside ordered a day-long frontal assault. The results were devastating. Federal troops, mowed down from the heights, suffered tremendous casualties, and once again the Army of the Potomac retreated to Washington.

Diplomacy and the Politics of Emancipation

The first full year of the war ended with mixed results for both sides. Union forces in the West had scored major victories, breaking down Confederate defenses and taking Memphis and New Orleans. But the failure of the Army of the Potomac under three different generals and against Lee and Jackson's brilliant maneuvers seemed to outweigh those successes. Lee's victories, however, carried heavy casualties, and the South's ability to supply and deploy troops was rapidly diminishing. A long, drawn-out conflict favored the Union unless Jefferson Davis could secure help for the Confederacy from abroad.

The Confederacy still expected British aid, but nothing seemed to shake Britain's commitment to neutrality. To a large extent, this obstinacy was due to the efforts of Charles Francis Adams, Lincoln's ambassador in London, who demonstrated his diplomatic skill repeatedly during the war. Also, Britain possessed a surplus of cotton and did not need southern supplies, neutralizing the South's only economic lever and frustrating Davis's diplomatic goals.

Radical Republicans were also frustrated. No aspect of the war was going as they had expected. They had hoped that the Union army would defeat the South in short order. Instead the war effort was dragging on. More important from the Radicals' point of view, nothing was being done about slavery. They pressed Lincoln to take a stand against slavery, and they pushed Congress for legislation to prohibit slavery in federal territories.

Politically astute as always, Lincoln acted to appease the Radical Republicans, foster popular support in the North for the war effort, and increase favorable sentiment for the Union cause abroad. During the

---

Antietam Creek   Site of a battle that occurred in September 1862 when Lee's forces invaded Maryland; both sides suffered heavy losses, and Lee retreated into Virginia.

Fredericksburg   Site in Virginia of a Union defeat in December 1862, which demonstrated the incompetence of the new Union commander, Ambrose E. Burnside.

Many soldiers entered the Civil War expecting excitement and colorful pageantry, but the realities of war were harsh and ugly. This photograph by Union cameraman Andrew J. Russell shows a line of southern soldiers who were killed while defending a position at Fredericksburg. Even after Union soldiers had breached the wall, the Confederates fought on, using their rifles as clubs until they were all mowed down. Scenes like this became so common that veterans reported that they became numb to the shock of death. *Library of Congress.*

summer of 1862, he drafted a proclamation freeing the slaves in the Confederacy and submitted it to his cabinet. Cabinet members advised that he postpone announcing the policy until after the Union had achieved a military victory. In August, **Horace Greeley,** founder of the *New York Tribune,* called for the immediate emancipation of all slaves, but Lincoln reiterated that his objective was "to save the Union," not "to save or destroy slavery." On September 22, however, five days after the Battle of Antietam, Lincoln unveiled the **Emancipation Proclamation,** which abolished slavery in the states "in rebellion" and would go into effect on January 1, 1863.

Although the Emancipation Proclamation was a major step toward ending slavery, it actually freed no slaves. The proclamation applied only to slavery in areas controlled by the Confederacy, not in any area controlled by the Union. Some found this exception troubling, labeling the proclamation an empty fraud, but the president's reasoning was sound. He could not afford to alienate the four slave states that had remained in the Union, nor could he commit any manpower to enforce emancipation in the areas that had been captured from the Confederacy. Lincoln made emancipation entirely conditional on a Union military victory, a gambit designed to force critics of the war, whether in the United States or Great Britain, to rally behind his cause.

Whether or not it was successful as a humanitarian action, issuing the Emancipation Proclamation at the time he did and in the form he did was a profoundly successful political step for Lincoln. Although a handful of northern Democrats and a few Union military leaders called it an "absurd proclamation of a political coward," more joined Frederick Douglass in proclaiming, "We shout for joy that we live to record this righteous decree." Meanwhile, some in Britain pointed to the paradox of the proclamation: it declared an end to slavery in areas where Lincoln could not enforce it, while having no effect on slavery in areas where he could. But even there, most applauded the document and rallied against recognition of the Confederacy.

Still, Lincoln's new general in chief, Henry Halleck, was chilled by the document. As he explained to Grant, the "character of the war has very much changed within the last year. There is now no possible hope of reconciliation." The war was now about slavery as well as secession, and the Emancipation Proclamation committed the Union to conquering the enemy. As Lincoln told one member of his cabinet, the war would now be "one of subjugation."

Horace Greeley Journalist and politician who helped found the Republican Party; his newspaper, the *New York Tribune,* was known for its antislavery stance.

Emancipation Proclamation Lincoln's order abolishing slavery as of January 1, 1863, in states "in rebellion" but not in border territories still loyal to the Union.

The Human Dimensions of the War

■ How did the burdens of war affect society in the North and the South during the course of the fighting?

■ How did individuals and governments in both regions respond to those burdens?

The Civil War imposed tremendous stress on American society. As the men marched off to battle, women faced the task of caring for families and property alone. As casualties increased, the number of voluntary enlistments decreased, and both sides searched for ways to find replacements for dead and wounded soldiers. The armies consumed vast amounts of manufactured and agricultural products—constantly demanding not only weapons and ammunition but also food, clothing, and hardware. Government spending was enormous, hard currency was scarce, and inflation soared as both governments printed paper money to pay their debts. Industrial capability, transportation facilities, and agricultural production often dictated when, where, and how well armies fought. Society in both North and South changed to meet an array of hardships as individuals facing unfamiliar conditions attempted to carry on their lives amid the war's devastation.

Instituting the Draft

By the end of 1862, heavy casualties, massive desertion, and declining enlistments had depleted both armies. Although the North had a much larger population pool than the South to draw from, its enlistments sagged with its military fortunes during 1862. More than a hundred thousand Union soldiers were absent without official leave. Most volunteers had enlisted in 1861 for limited terms, which would soon expire. Calling on state militias netted few replacements because the Democrats, who made tremendous political gains at the state level in 1862, openly criticized Republican policies and at times refused to cooperate. In March 1863, Congress passed the **Conscription Act,** trying to bypass state officials and ensure enough manpower to continue the war. The law in effect made all single men between the ages of 20 and 45 and married men between 20 and 35 eligible for service. Government agents collected names in a house-to-house survey, and draftees were selected by lottery.

The conscription law did offer "escape routes." Drafted men could avoid military service by providing—that is, hiring—an "acceptable substitute" or by paying a $300 fee to purchase exemption. The burden of service thus fell on farmers and urban workers—a large proportion of whom were immigrants—who were already suffering from the economic burden of high taxation and inflation caused by the war. Added to that was workers' fears that multitudes of former slaves freed by the Emancipation Proclamation would pour into the already crowded job market, further lowering the value of their labor. Together, conscription and emancipation created among the urban poor a sense of alienation, which exploded in the summer of 1863.

The trouble started on July 13 in New York City. Armed demonstrators protesting unfair draft laws engaged in a spree of violence, venting their frustration over the troubles plaguing working people. During three nights of rioting, white workingmen beat many African Americans and lynched six. The Colored Orphan Asylum and several homes owned by blacks were burned. Mobs ransacked businesses owned by African Americans and by people who employed them. Irish men and women and members of other groups that seemed to threaten job security also felt the fury as mobs attacked their churches, businesses, and homes. The rioters also expressed their frustration against Republican spokesmen and officials. Republican journalist Horace Greeley was **hanged in effigy,** and the homes of other prominent Republicans and abolitionists were vandalized. Protesting draft exemptions for the rich, rioters also set upon well-dressed strangers on the streets. After four days of chaos, federal troops put down the riot. Fearful of future violence, the city council of New York City voted to pay the $300 exemption fee for all poor draftees who chose not to serve in the army.

The Confederacy also instituted a draft after the first wave of enlistments dried up. Conscription in the South, as in the North, met with considerable resentment and resistance. Believing that plantations were necessary to the war effort and that slaves would not work unless directly overseen by masters, in 1862 Confederate officials passed the **Twenty Negro Law,**

Conscription Act   Law passed by Congress in 1863 that established a draft but allowed wealthy people to escape it by hiring a substitute or paying the government a $300 fee.

hang in effigy   To hang, as if on a gallows, a crude likeness or dummy—an effigy—representing a hated person.

Twenty Negro Law   Confederate law that exempted planters owning twenty or more slaves from the draft on the grounds that overseeing farm labor done by slaves was necessary to the war effort.

Angered by the fact that rich men were virtually exempt from the draft, frightened by the prospect of job competition from freed southern slaves, and frustrated by the lack of resolution on the battlefield, workingmen took to the streets in New York City during the summer of 1863 to protest against the war. Well-dressed men, African Americans, and leading war advocates were the main targets of mob violence during three nights of uncontrolled rioting. As this illustration shows, federal troops finally put down the rioting in a series of battles around the city. An unknown number of people were killed and injured. *Collection of Picture Research Consultants & Archives.*

which exempted planters owning twenty or more slaves from military service. Like the exemptions in the North, the southern policy fostered the feeling that the poor were going off to fight while the rich stayed safely at home. The law was modified in 1863, requiring exempted planters to pay $500, and in 1864, the number of slaves required to earn an exemption was lowered to fifteen. Nevertheless, resentment continued to smolder.

Confederate conscription laws also ran afoul of states' rights advocates, who feared that too much power was centered in Richmond. Southerners developed several forms of passive resistance to the draft laws. Thousands of draftees simply never showed up, and local officials, jealously guarding their political autonomy, made little effort to enforce the draft.

Wartime Economy in the North and South

Although riots, disorder, and social disruption plagued northern cities, the economy and industry of the Union actually grew stronger as the war progressed. In his 1864 message to Congress, Abraham Lincoln stated that the war had not depleted northern resources. Although the president exaggerated a bit, the statement con-

tained some truth. Northern industry and population did grow during the Civil War. Operating in cooperation with government, manufacturing experienced a boom. Manufacturers of war supplies benefited from government contracts. Textiles and shoemaking boomed as new labor-saving devices improved efficiency and increased production. Congress stimulated economic growth by means of subsidies and land grants to support a transcontinental railroad, higher tariffs to aid manufacturing, and land grants that states could use to finance higher education. In 1862 Congress passed the **Homestead Act** to make land available to more farmers. The law granted 160 acres of the public domain in the West to any citizen or would-be citizen who lived on, and improved, the land for five years.

Of course the economic picture was not entirely positive. The Union found itself resorting to financial

> **Homestead Act** Law passed by Congress in 1862 that promised ownership of 160 acres of public land to any citizen or would-be citizen who lived on and cultivated the land for five years.

tricks to keep the economy afloat. Facing a cash-flow emergency in 1862, Congress passed the Legal Tender Act, authorizing Treasury Secretary Salmon Chase to issue $431 million in paper money, known as **greenbacks,** that was backed not by specie but only by the government's commitment to redeem the bills. Financial support also came through selling bonds. In the fall of 1862, Philadelphia banker Jay Cooke started a bond drive. More than $2 billion worth of government bonds were sold, and most of them were paid for in greenbacks. These emergency measures helped the Union survive the financial pressures created by the war, but the combination of bond issues and paper money not backed by gold or silver set up a highly unstable situation that came back to haunt Republicans after the war.

The South, an agrarian society, began the war without an industrial base. In addition to lacking transportation, raw materials, and machines, the South lacked managers and skilled industrial workers. The Confederate government intervened more directly in the economy than did its Union counterpart, offering generous loans to new or existing companies that would produce war materials and agree to sell at least two-thirds of their production to the government. Josiah Gorgas started government-owned production plants in Alabama, Georgia, and South Carolina. These innovative programs, however, could not compensate for inadequate prewar industrialization.

The supply of money was also a severe problem in the South. Like the North, the South tried to ease cash-flow problems by printing paper money, eventually issuing more than $1 billion in unbacked currency. The outcome was runaway inflation. By the time the war ended, southerners were paying more than $400 for a barrel of flour and $10 a pound for bacon.

Southern industrial shortcomings severely handicapped the army. During Lee's Maryland campaign, many Confederate soldiers were barefoot because shoes were in such short supply. Ordnance was always in demand. Northern plants could produce more than five thousand muskets a day; Confederate production never exceeded three hundred. The most serious shortage, however, was food. Although the South was an agricultural region, most of its productive acreage was devoted to cotton, tobacco, and other crops that were essential to its overall economy but not suitable to eat. Corn and rice were the primary food products, but supplies were continually reduced by military campaigns and Union occupation of farmlands. Hog production suffered from the same disruptions as rice and corn growing, and while Southern cattle were abundant, most were range stock grown for hides and tallow rather than for food. Hunger became a miserable part of daily life for the Confederate armies.

Civilians in the South suffered from the same shortages as the army. Because of prewar shipping patterns, the few rail lines that crossed the Confederacy ran north and south. Distribution of goods became almost impossible as invading Union forces cut rail lines and disrupted production. The flow of cattle, horses, and food from the West diminished when Union forces gained control of the Mississippi. Imported goods had to evade the Union naval blockade. Southern society, cut off from the outside world, consumed its existing resources and found no way to obtain more.

Women in Two Nations at War

Because the South had fewer men than the North to send to war, a larger proportion of southern families were left in the care of women. Some women worked farms, herded livestock, and supported their families. Others found themselves homeless, living in complete poverty, as the ravages of war destroyed the countryside. One woman wrote to the Confederacy's secretary of war, pleading that he "discharge" her husband so that "he might do his children some good" rather than leaving them "to suffer." Some tried to persuade their husbands to desert, to come home to family and safety. One woman shouted to her husband, who was being drafted for the second time, "Desert again, Jake." The vast majority, however, fully supported the war effort despite the hardships at home and at the front.

Women became responsible for much of the South's agricultural and industrial production, overseeing the raising of crops, working in factories, managing estates, and running businesses. As one southern soldier wrote, women bore "the greatest burden of this horrid war." Indeed, the burden of a woman was great—working the fields, running the household, and waiting for news from loved ones at the front or for the dreaded message that she was now a widow or childless.

Women in the North served in much the same capacity as their southern counterparts. They maintained families and homes alone, working to provide income and raise children. Although they did not face the shortages and ravages of battle that made life so hard for southern women, they did work in factories, run family businesses, teach school, and supply soldiers. Many served in managerial capacities or as

greenbacks Paper money issued by the Union; it was not backed by gold.

As Mary Ashton Rice Livermore pointed out, many women served in many different capacities during the Civil War. An unknown number of them actually dressed as men to join the fighting. Frances Clayton was one of the few documented cases of such Civil War gender-bending. *Left and right: Trustees of the Boston Public Library.*

writers and civil servants. Even before the war ended, northern women were going south to educate former slaves and help them find a place in American society. Women thus assumed new roles that helped prepare them to become more involved in social and political life after the war.

Women from both South and North actively participated in the war itself. Many women on both sides served as scouts, couriers, and spies, and more than four hundred disguised themselves as men and served as active soldiers until they were discovered. General William S. Rosecrans expressed dismay when one of his sergeants was delivered of "a bouncing baby boy," which was, the general complained, "in violation of all military regulations." Army camps frequently included officers' wives, female employees, camp followers, and women who came to help in whatever way they could. One black woman served the 33rd U.S. Colored Troops for four years and three months without pay, teaching the men to read and write and binding up their wounds.

Free Blacks, Slaves, and War

The changes the Civil War brought for African Americans, both free and slave, were radical and not always for the better. At first, many free blacks attempted to enlist in the Union army but were turned away. In 1861 General Benjamin F. Butler began using runaway slaves, called contrabands, as laborers. Several other northern commanders quickly adopted the practice. As the number of contrabands increased, however, the Union grappled with problems of housing and feeding them.

In the summer of 1862, Congress authorized the acceptance of "persons of African descent" into the armed forces, but enlistment remained low. After the Emancipation Proclamation, Union officials actively recruited former slaves, raising troops from among the freedmen and forming them into regiments known as the U.S. Colored Troops. Some northern state governments sought free blacks to fill state draft quotas; agents offered generous bonuses to those who signed up. By the end of the war, about 180,000 African Americans had enlisted in northern armies.

Army officials discriminated against African American soldiers in a variety of ways. Units were segregated, and until 1864, blacks were paid less than whites. All black regiments had white commanders; the government refused to allow blacks to lead blacks. Only one hundred were commissioned as officers, and no African American soldier ever received a commission higher than major.

Eager to fill constantly depleting army ranks, Union officials appealed to African Americans to volunteer for military service. This recruiting poster, which bore the legend "Come Join Us, Brothers," presents a highly glorified vision of what conditions were like for black units. One accurate detail is that the only officer in the scene is white; in fact, no African Americans were permitted to command troops during the Civil War. *Chicago Historical Society.*

At first, African American regiments were used as laborers or kept in the rear rather than being allowed to fight. But several black regiments, when finally allowed into battle, performed so well that they won grudging respect. These men fought in 449 battles in every theater of the war and had a casualty rate 35 percent higher than white soldiers. Still, acceptance by white troops was slow, and discrimination was the rule, not the exception.

As the war progressed, the number of African Americans in the Union army increased dramatically. By 1865, almost two-thirds of Union troops in the Mississippi Valley were black. Some southerners violently resented the Union's use of these troops, and African American soldiers suffered atrocities because some Confederate leaders refused to take black prisoners. At Fort Pillow, Tennessee, for example, Confederate soldiers massacred more than a hundred African American soldiers who were trying to surrender.

About sixty-eight thousand black Union soldiers were killed or wounded in battle, and twenty-one were awarded the Congressional Medal of Honor. Probably no unit acquitted itself better in the field than the **54th Massachusetts.** On July 18, 1863, it led a frontal assault on Confederate defenses at Charleston Harbor. Despite sustaining grievous casualties, the African American troops captured the fort's front wall and held it for nearly an hour before being forced to retreat.

Their conduct in battle had a large impact on changing attitudes toward black soldiers and emancipation.

The war effort in the South relied heavily on the slave population, mostly as producers of food and as military laborers. Slaves constituted more than half of the work force in armament plants and military hospitals. Though crucial to the southern war effort, slaves suffered more than other southerners in the face of food shortages and other privations. And after Lincoln issued the Emancipation Proclamation, fears of slave revolts prompted whites to institute harsh security procedures. Hungry and even less free than usual, slaves became the greatest unsung casualties of the war.

Life and Death at the Front

Many volunteers on both sides in the Civil War had romantic notions about military service. Most were disappointed. Life as a common soldier was anything but glorious. Letters and diaries written by soldiers most frequently tell of long periods of boredom in

54th Massachusetts Regiment of African American troops from Massachusetts commanded by abolitionist Colonel Robert Gould Shaw; it led an assault on Fort Wagner at Charleston Harbor.

In this photograph, taken outside an army hospital in Fredericksburg, Virginia, one of the many women who served as nurses during the Civil War sits with some of her wounded charges. Despite the efforts of women like her, medical facilities and treatment for the wounded were woefully inadequate—most of those who were not killed outright by the primitive surgical practices of the day died from their wounds or from secondary infections. *Library of Congress.*

overcrowded camps punctuated by furious spells of dangerous action.

Though life in camp was tedious, it could be nearly as dangerous as time spent on the battlefield. Problems with supplying safe drinking water and disposing of waste constantly plagued military leaders faced with providing basic services for large numbers of people, often on short notice. Diseases such as dysentery and **typhoid fever** frequently swept through unsanitary camps. And in the overcrowded conditions that often prevailed, smallpox and other contagious diseases passed rapidly from person to person. At times, as many as a quarter of the uninjured people in camps were disabled by one or another of these ailments.

Lacking in resources, organization, and expertise, the South did little to upgrade camp conditions. In the North, however, women drew on the organizational skills they had gained as antebellum reformers and created voluntary organizations to address the problem. At the local level, women like Mary Livermore and Jane Hoge created small relief societies designed to aid soldiers and their families. Gradually these merged into regional organizations that would take the lead in raising money and implementing large-scale public health efforts, both in the army camps and at home. Mental health advocate and reformer Dorothea Dix (see page 348) was also one of these crusaders. In June 1861, President Lincoln responded to their concerns by creating the **United States Sanitary Commission,** a government agency responsible for advising the military on public health issues and investigating sanitary problems. Gradually enfolding many of the local and regional societies into its structure, "The Sanitary," as it was called, put hundreds of nurses into the field, providing much-needed relief for overburdened military doctors. Even with this official organization in place, many women continued to labor as volunteer nurses in the camps and in hospitals behind the lines.

Nurses on both sides showed bravery and devotion. Often working under fire at the front and with almost no medical supplies, these volunteers nursed sick and wounded soldiers, watched as they died not only from their wounds but also from infection and disease, and offered as much comfort and help as they could. **Clara Barton,** a famous northern nurse known as the "Angel of the Battlefield," recalled "speaking to and feeding with my own hands each soldier" as she attempted to nurse them back to health. Hospitals were unsanitary, overflowing, and underfunded.

The numbers of wounded who filled the hospital tents was unprecedented, largely because of technological innovations that had taken place during the antebellum period. New **rifled** muskets had many

typhoid fever An infectious disease transmitted through contact with contaminated water, milk, or food; causes severe intestinal distress and high fever.

United States Sanitary Commission Government commission established by Abraham Lincoln to improve public health conditions in military camps and hospitals.

Clara Barton Organizer of a volunteer service to aid sick and wounded Civil War soldiers; she later founded the American branch of the Red Cross.

rifled Having a series of spiral grooves inside the barrel of a gun that cause the bullet to spin, giving it greater range and accuracy.

times the range of the old smooth-bore weapons used during earlier wars—the effective range of the Springfield rifle used by many Union soldiers was 400 yards, and a stray bullet could still kill a man at 1,000 yards. Waterproof cartridges, perfected by gunsmith Samuel Colt, made these weapons much less prone to misfire and much easier to reload. And at closer range, the revolver, also perfected by Colt, could fire six shots without any reloading. Rifled artillery also added to the casualty count, as did exploding artillery shells, which sent deadly shrapnel ripping through lines of men.

Many surgeons at the front lines could do little more than amputate limbs to save lives. Hospitals, understaffed and lacking supplies and medicines, frequently became breeding grounds for disease. The war exacted a tremendous emotional toll on everyone, even on those who escaped physical injury. As one veteran put it, soldiers had seen "so many new forms of death" and "so many frightful and novel kinds of mutilation."

Conditions were even worse in prison camps. Throughout much of the war, an agreement provided for prisoner exchanges, but that did not prevent overcrowding and unsanitary conditions. And as the war dragged on, the exchange system stopped working effectively. In part the program collapsed because of the enormity of the task: moving and accounting for the large numbers of prisoners presented a serious organizational problem. Another contributing factor, though, was the refusal by Confederate officials to exchange African American prisoners of war—those who were not slaughtered like the men at Fort Pillow were enslaved. Also, late in the war, Union commanders suspended all prisoner exchanges in hopes of depriving the South of much-needed replacement soldiers.

The most notorious of the Civil War prison camps was **Andersonville,** in northern Georgia, where thousands of Union captives languished in an open stockade with only a small creek for water and virtually no sanitary facilities. Without enough food to feed its own armies and civilian population, the Confederacy could allocate little food for its overcrowded prison camps. Designed to house 10,000 men, Andersonville held more than 33,000 prisoners during the summer of 1864. As many as 100 men died of disease and malnutrition within its walls each day; estimates put the death toll at that one prison at nearly 14,000 over the course of the war.

Even death itself came to be redefined, as 8 percent of the white male population in the United States between the ages of 13 and 43 died in such a short time and in such grisly ways. People at the front reported being numbed by the horror. One army surgeon reported, "I pass over the putrefying bodies of the dead . . . and feel as . . . unconcerned as though they were two hundred pigs." Nor was distance any insulation from the horrors of death. The new art of photography brought graphic images of the gruesome carnage directly into the nation's parlors. "Death does not seem half so terrible as it did long ago," one Texas woman reported. "We have grown used to it."

Waging Total War

- What factors contributed to the Union's adoption of a total war strategy after 1863?

- Was total war a justifiable option in light of the human and property damage it inflicted and the overall consequences it achieved? Why or why not?

As northerners anticipated the presidential election of 1864, Lincoln faced severe challenges on several fronts. The losses to Lee and Jackson in Virginia and the failure to catch Lee at Antietam had eroded public support. Many northerners resented the war, conscription, and abolitionism. Others feared Lincoln's powerful central government.

Northern Democrats advocated a peace platform and turned to George B. McClellan, Lincoln's ousted general, as a potential presidential candidate. Lincoln also faced a challenge from within his own party. Radical Republicans, who felt he was too soft on the South and unfit to run the war, began planning a campaign to win power. They championed the candidacy of John C. Frémont (see page 404), who had become an ardent advocate of the complete abolition of slavery.

Lincoln's Generals and Southern Successes

The surest way for Lincoln to stop his opponents was through military success. Lincoln had replaced McClellan with Burnside, but the results had been disastrous. Lincoln tried again, demoting Burnside and elevating General Joseph Hooker. Despite Hooker's reputation for bravery in battle—his nickname was "Fighting Joe"—Lee soundly defeated his forces at **Chancellorsville** in May 1863 (see Map 15.3 and

> **Andersonville** Confederate prisoner-of-war camp in northern Georgia where some fourteen thousand Union prisoners died of disease and malnutrition.
>
> **Chancellorsville** Site in Virginia where in May 1863 Confederate troops led by Lee defeated a much larger Union force.

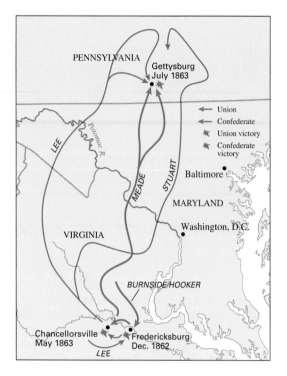

MAP 15.3 Fredericksburg, Chancellorsville, and Gettysburg   This map shows the campaigns that took place during the winter of 1862 and spring of 1863, culminating in the Battle of Gettysburg (July 1863). General Meade's victory at Gettysburg may have been the critical turning point of the war.

Table 15.4). After Hooker had maneuvered Lee into a corner, Stonewall Jackson unleashed a vicious attack, and Fighting Joe simply "lost his nerve," according to one of his subordinates. Hooker resigned, and Lincoln replaced him with General George E. Meade.

Chancellorsville was a devastating loss for the North, but it was perhaps more devastating for the Confederates. They lost Stonewall Jackson. After he led the charge that unnerved Hooker, Jackson's own men mistakenly shot him as he rode back toward his camp in the darkness. Doctors amputated Jackson's arm in an attempt to save his life. "He has lost his left arm," moaned Lee, "but I have lost my right." Eight days later, Jackson died of pneumonia.

In the West too, Union forces seemed mired during the first half of 1863. General Rosecrans was bogged down in a costly and unsuccessful campaign to take the vital rail center at Chattanooga, Tennessee. Grant had settled in for a long siege at Vicksburg (see Map 15.2). Nowhere did there seem to be a prospect for the dramatic victory Lincoln needed.

The summer of 1863, however, turned out to be a major turning point in the war. Facing superior northern resources and rising inflation, Confederate leaders met in Richmond to consider their options. Lee proposed another major invasion of the North, arguing that such a maneuver would allow the Confederates to gather supplies and might encourage the northern peace movement, revitalize the prospects of foreign recognition, and perhaps capture the Union capital. Confederate leaders agreed and approved Lee's plan.

Lee's advance met only weak opposition as the Army of Northern Virginia crossed the Potomac River and marched into Union territory (see Map 15.3). In Maryland and Pennsylvania the troops seized livestock, supplies, food, clothing, and shoes. Union forces had been converging on the area of **Gettysburg,** Pennsylvania, since early June, anticipating Lee's move but unsure of his exact intention. Learning that the Federals were waiting and believing them to be weaker than they were, on June 29 Lee moved to engage the Union forces. Meade, who had been trailing Lee's army as it marched north from Chancellorsville, immediately dispatched a detachment to reinforce Gettysburg. On the following day, the two armies began a furious three-day battle.

Arriving in force on July 1, Meade took up an almost impregnable defensive position on the hills along Cemetery Ridge. The Confederates hammered both ends of the Union line but could gain no ground. On the third day, Lee ordered a major assault on the middle of the Union position. Eleven brigades, more than thirteen thousand men, led by fresh troops under Major General George E. Pickett, tried to cross open ground and take the hills held by Meade while Major J. E. B. "Jeb" Stuart's cavalry attacked from the east. Lee made few strategic mistakes during the war, but Pickett's charge was foolhardy. Meade's forces drove off the attack. The whole field was "dotted with our soldiers," wrote one Confederate officer. Lee met his retreating troops with the words "It's all my fault, my fault." Losses on both sides were high (see Table 15.5), but Confederate casualties exceeded twenty-eight thousand men, more than half of Lee's army. Lee retreated, his invasion of the North a failure.

On the heels of this major victory for the North came news from Mississippi that Vicksburg had fallen to

Gettysburg   Site in Pennsylvania where in July 1863 Union forces under General George Meade defeated Lee's Confederate forces, turning back Lee's invasion of the North.

TABLE 15.4 Battle of Chancellorsville, May 1–4, 1863

	Union Army	Confederate Army
Commanders	Joseph Hooker	Robert E. Lee
Troop strength	75,000	50,000
Losses		
Killed	1,606	1,665
Wounded	9,762	9,081
Captured, missing	5,919	2,018
Total Losses	17,287	12,764

Source: Data from *Battles and Leaders of the Civil War* (1884–1888; reprinted ed., 1956).

TABLE 15.5 Battle of Gettysburg, July 1–3, 1863

	Union Army	Confederate Army
Commanders	George E. Meade	Robert E. Lee
Troop strength	75,000	50,000
Losses		
Killed	3,155	3,903
Wounded	14,529	18,735
Captured, missing	5,365	5,425
Total Losses	23,049	28,063

Source: Data from *Battles and Leaders of the Civil War* (1884–1888; reprinted ed., 1956).

Grant's siege on July 4. Sherman had been beating back Confederate forces in central Mississippi, and Union guns had been shelling the city continuously for nearly seven weeks, driving residents into caves and barricaded shelters. But it was starvation and disease that finally subdued the defenders. Then on July 9, after receiving news of Vicksburg's fate, **Port Hudson,** the last Confederate garrison on the Mississippi River, also surrendered. The Mississippi River was totally under Union control. The "Father of Waters," said Lincoln, "again goes unvexed to the sea."

Despite jubilation over the recent victories, Lincoln and the North remained frustrated. Northern newspapers proclaiming Gettysburg to be the last gasp of the South had anticipated an immediate southern surrender, but Meade, like McClellan, acted with extreme caution and failed to pursue Lee and his retreating troops. Back in Washington, Lincoln waited for word of Lee's capture, believing it would signal the end of the rebellion. When he learned of Lee's escape, the president said in disbelief, "Our Army held the war in the hollow of their hand and they would not close it."

Disappointment in Tennessee also soon marred the celebration over Gettysburg and Vicksburg. Rosecrans had taken Chattanooga, but on September 18, Bragg's forces attacked Rosecrans at Chickamauga Creek. Rosecrans scurried in retreat to take refuge

Port Hudson Confederate garrison in Louisiana that surrendered to Union forces in July 1863, thus giving the Union unrestricted control of the Mississippi River.

During the summer of 1863, Confederate General Robert E. Lee proposed a daring invasion into Pennsylvania in hopes that it might force the Union to end the war. It proved to be a turning point, but not the one Lee anticipated. At Gettysburg, a series of battles like the one shown here—this one on the first day of the fighting—cost Lee more than half of his entire army, and he was forced to retreat into Virginia. President Lincoln hoped that the Union army would pursue the fleeing Confederates and destroy the remnants of Lee's force, but he was disappointed when he learned that Lee had escaped. "Our Army held the war in the hollow of their hand," Lincoln complained, "and they would not close it." *West Point Museum, United States Military Academy, West Point, NY.*

back in Chattanooga, leaving part of his troops in place to cover his retreat. This force, under the command of George H. Thomas, delayed the Confederate offensive and, in the words of one veteran, "saved the army from defeat and rout." Bragg nonetheless was able to follow and laid siege to Chattanooga from the heights of Missionary Ridge and Lookout Mountain, overlooking the city.

With Lee and his army intact and Rosecrans pinned down in Tennessee, the war, which in July had appeared to be so nearly over, was, in Lincoln's words, "prolonged indefinitely." Lincoln needed a new kind of general.

Grant, Sherman, and the Invention of Total War

Among the available choices, Grant had shown the kind of persistence and boldness Lincoln thought

necessary. Lincoln placed him in charge of all Union forces in the West on October 16. Grant immediately replaced Rosecrans with the more intrepid and decisive Thomas. Sherman's troops joined Thomas under Grant's command on November 14. This united force rid the mountains above Chattanooga of Confederate strongholds and drove Bragg's forces out of southern Tennessee. Confederate forces also withdrew from Knoxville in December, leaving the state under Union control.

While fighting raged in Tennessee, Lincoln took a break from his duties in the White House to participate in the dedication of a national cemetery at the site where, just months before, the Battle of Gettysburg had taken the lives of thousands. In the speech he delivered on November 19, 1863, Lincoln dedicated not only the cemetery but the war effort itself to the fallen soldiers, and also to a principle. "Fourscore and seven years ago," Lincoln said, "our fathers brought forth on this continent a new nation, con-

It Matters

The Gettysburg Address

When the war began, Lincoln made it clear that his purpose in pursuing a military course was simply the defense of the Constitution. But when he spoke on the Gettysburg battlefield two years later, he gave voice to a broader vision that seems to have evolved as the bloodshed and horror escalated. Interestingly, Lincoln referenced the Declaration of Independence as the founding document for the republic, *not* the Constitution. Though the Declaration was an important document in American history, it was never a binding legal instrument; it had no power in law. Yet through this speech, Lincoln transformed Thomas Jefferson's stirring announcement of enlightenment principle into a central element in American legal thinking. When the war was over, and after Lincoln's death, Congress acted on this sentiment by framing the Fourteenth Amendment, which codified the central principle that "all men are created equal." Though enforced inconsistently through the years, this principle would become the foundation for all of the civil rights that Americans enjoy and continue to fight for.

ceived in liberty and dedicated to the proposition that all men are created equal." Though delivered in a low voice that most of the crowd could not hear, the **Gettysburg Address** was circulated in the media and galvanized many Americans who had come to doubt the war's purpose.

The president was delighted with Grant's successes in Tennessee. Lincoln promoted him again on March 10, 1864, this time to general in chief. Grant immediately left his command in the West to prepare an all-out attack on Lee and Virginia, authorizing Sherman to pursue a campaign into Georgia.

In Grant and Sherman, Lincoln had found what he needed. On the surface, neither seemed a likely candidate for a major role in the Union army. Both were West Point graduates but left the army after the War with Mexico to seek their fortunes. Neither had succeeded in civilian life: Grant was a binge drinker who had accomplished little, and Sherman had failed as a banker and a lawyer. Both were "political generals,"

owing their Civil War commissions to the influence of friends or relatives. Despite their checkered pasts, these two men invented a new type of warfare that eventually brought the South to its knees. Grant and Sherman were willing to wage **total war** in order to destroy the South's will to continue the struggle.

Preparing for the new sort of war he was about to inaugurate, Grant suspended prisoner-of-war exchanges. Realizing that the Confederates needed soldiers badly, he understood that one outcome of this policy would be slow death by starvation for Union prisoners. Cruel though his policy was, Grant reasoned that victory was his primary goal and that suffering and death were unavoidable in war. Throughout the remainder of the war, this single-mindedness pushed Grant to make decisions that cost tens of thousands of lives on both sides.

On May 4, Grant and Meade moved toward Richmond and Robert E. Lee. The next day, Union and Confederate armies collided in a tangle of woods called **The Wilderness,** near Chancellorsville (see Map 15.4). Two days of bloody fighting followed, broken by a night during which hundreds of the wounded burned to death in brushfires that raged between the two lines. Grant decided to skirt Lee's troops and head for Richmond, but Lee anticipated the maneuver and blocked Grant's route at Spotsylvania. Twelve days of fighting ensued. Grant again attempted to move around Lee, and again Lee anticipated him. On June 1, the two armies met at **Cold Harbor,** Virginia. After each side had consolidated its position, Grant ordered a series of frontal attacks against the entrenched Confederates on June 3. Lee's veteran troops waited patiently in perhaps the best position they had ever defended, while Union soldiers expecting to die marched toward them. The assault failed amid unspeakable slaughter.

Gettysburg Address A speech given by Abraham Lincoln on November 19, 1863, dedicating a national cemetery in Gettysburg, Pennsylvania; it enunciated Lincoln's maturing view of the war and its purpose.

total war War waged with little regard for the welfare of troops on either side or for enemy civilians; the objective is to destroy both the human and the economic resources of the enemy.

The Wilderness Densely wooded region of Virginia that was the site in May 1864 of a devastating but inconclusive battle between Union forces under Grant and Confederates under Lee.

Cold Harbor Area of Virginia, about 10 miles from Richmond, where Grant made an unsuccessful attempt to drive his forces through Lee's center.

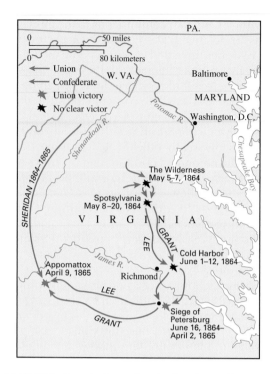

MAP 15.4 Grant's Campaign Against Lee This map shows the series of battles during the late spring of 1864 in which Grant's army suffered staggering casualties but finally drove Lee into retreat. After holding up for months behind heavy fortifications in Petersburg, Lee made a daring attempt to escape in April 1865 but was headed off by General Philip Sheridan's troops. Grant quickly closed in on the greatly weakened Confederate army, forcing Lee's surrender.

Disliked by most of his fellow officers because of his coarse behavior and binge drinking, Ulysses S. Grant had the right combination of daring, unconventionality, and ruthlessness to wear down Robert E. Lee's forces in Virginia and finally defeat the Confederate army. *National Archives.*

One southerner described Grant's assaults as "inexplicable and incredible butchery." The wounded were left to die between the lines while the living fell back exhausted into their trenches. Many of the young federal attackers at Cold Harbor had pinned their names on their shirts in the hope that their shattered bodies might be identified after the battle. Casualties on both sides at Spotsylvania and Cold Harbor were staggering, but Union losses were unimaginably horrible. As one Confederate officer put it, "We have met a man, this time, who either does not know when he is whipped, or who cares not if he loses his whole army." During the three encounters, Grant lost a total of sixty thousand troops, more than Lee's entire army. Said Lee, "This is not war, this is murder." But Grant's seeming wantonness was calculated, for the Confederates lost more than twenty-five thousand troops. And Grant knew, as did Lee, that the Union could afford the losses but the Confederacy could not.

After Cold Harbor, Grant guessed that Lee would expect him to try to assault nearby Richmond next. This time, though, he steered the Union army south of Richmond for Petersburg to try to take the vital rail center and cut off the southern capital. Once again, Lee reacted quickly: he rapidly shifted the **vanguard** of his troops, beat back Grant's advance, and occupied Petersburg. Grant bitterly regretted this failure, feeling that he could have ended the war. Instead, the campaign settled into a siege that neither side wanted. Lee and the Confederates could ill afford a siege that ate up supplies and munitions. And elections were rapidly approaching in the Union.

vanguard The foremost position in any army advancing into battle.

The Election of 1864 and Sherman's March to the Sea

Lincoln was under fire from two directions. On May 31, 1864, Radical Republicans met in Cleveland and officially nominated John C. Frémont as their presidential candidate. Lincoln's wing of the party, which began calling itself the Union Party, held its nominating convention in June and renominated Lincoln. To attract Democrats who still favored fighting for a clear victory, Union Party delegates dumped Vice President Hannibal Hamlin and chose **Andrew Johnson,** a southern Democrat, as Lincoln's running mate. Then, in August, the Democratic National Convention met at Chicago. The Democrats pulled together many **Copperheads** and other northerners who were so upset by the heavy casualties that they were determined to stop the war even at the cost of allowing slavery to continue. The Democrats selected McClellan as their presidential candidate and included a peace plank in their platform. Thus Lincoln sat squarely in the middle between one group that castigated him for pursuing the war and another group that rebuked him for failing to punish the South vigorously enough.

Confederate president Jefferson Davis did not face an election in 1864, but he too had plenty of political problems. As deprivation and military losses mounted, some factions began to resist the war effort. The Confederate congress called for a new draft, but several states refused to comply. Governors in Georgia, North Carolina, and South Carolina, who controlled their state's militia, kept troops at home and defied Davis to enforce conscription.

Eager to solve their problems, Lincoln and Confederate vice president Alexander H. Stephens had conversations about negotiating a settlement. Lincoln stated his terms: reunion, abolition, and amnesty for Confederates. Southern officials balked, pointing out that "amnesty" applied to criminals and that the South had "committed no crime." The only possible outcomes of the war for the South, they concluded, were independence or extermination, even if it meant enduring the sight of "every Southern plantation sacked and every Southern city in flames." The words proved prophetic.

Grant had instructed Sherman "to get into the interior of the enemy's country as far as you can, inflicting all the damage you can against their war resources." Sherman responded with a vengeance. Slowly and skillfully his army advanced southward from Tennessee toward Atlanta, one of the South's few remaining industrial centers, against Confederate armies under the command of General Joseph E. Johnston

(see Map 15.5). Only Johnston's skillful retreats kept Sherman from annihilating his army. President Davis then replaced Johnston with John Bell Hood, who vowed to take the offensive. Hood attacked, but Sherman inflicted such serious casualties that Hood had to retreat to Atlanta.

For days Sherman shelled Atlanta and wrought havoc in the surrounding countryside. When a last-ditch southern attack failed, Hood evacuated the city on September 1. The victorious Union troops moved in and occupied Atlanta on the following day. Sherman's victory caused tremendous despair among Confederates but gave great momentum to Lincoln's reelection campaign.

Also boosting Lincoln's reelection efforts was General Philip Sheridan's campaign in the Shenandoah Valley, an important source of food for Lee's army. Adopting the same sort of devastating tactics that Sherman used so successfully, Sheridan's men lived off the land and destroyed both military and civilian supplies whenever possible. Accepting high casualties, Sheridan drove Confederate forces from the region in October, laying waste to much of Lee's food supply in the process.

These victories proved the decisive factor in the election of 1864. Sherman's and Sheridan's successes defused McClellan's argument that Lincoln was not competent to direct the Union's military fortunes and quelled much antiwar sentiment in the North. Equally discredited, the Radical Republican platform and the Frémont candidacy disappeared before election day. As late as August, Lincoln had been expecting to lose the election in November, but the victory in Atlanta gave him some hope. When the votes were counted, Lincoln learned that he had defeated McClellan—by half a million popular votes and by a landslide margin of 212 to 21 in the Electoral College.

The southern peace movement had viewed a Democratic victory as the last chance to reach a settlement. Without it, all hope of negotiation appeared lost. Amid the bleak prospects, animosity toward Jefferson Davis increased in the South. But Lee's forces still remained in Petersburg, as did Hood's in Georgia. Southern hopes were dimmed but not extinguished.

Andrew Johnson   Tennessee senator who became Lincoln's running mate in 1864 and who succeeded to the presidency after Lincoln's assassination.

Copperheads   Derogatory term (the name of a poisonous snake) applied to northerners who supported the South during the Civil War.

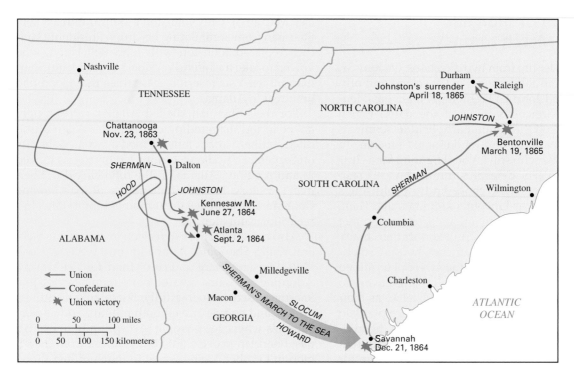

MAP 15.5 Sherman's Campaign in the South This map shows how William Tecumseh Sherman's troops slashed through the South, destroying both civilian and military targets and reducing the South's will to continue the war.

Sherman soon grew bored with the occupation of Atlanta and posed a bold plan to Grant. He wanted to ignore Hood, leave the battered Confederates loose at his rear, go on the offensive, and "cut a swath through to the sea." "I can make Georgia howl," he promised. Despite some misgivings, Grant agreed and convinced Lincoln.

A week after the election, Sherman began preparing for his 300-mile **March to the Sea** (see Map 15.5). His intentions were clear. "We are not only fighting hostile armies, but a hostile people," he stated. By devastating the countryside and destroying the South's ability to conduct war, he intended to break down southerners' will to resist. "We cannot change the hearts of those people of the South," he concluded, but we can "make them so sick of war that generations would pass away before they would again appeal to it." With that, he burned most of Atlanta and then set out on his march to Savannah, on the coast. His troops plundered and looted farms and towns on the way, foraging for food and supplies and destroying everything in their path.

While Sherman headed toward Savannah, Confederate general Hood turned north and attacked General George Thomas's Union forces at Franklin, Tennessee, on November 30. Hood lost convincingly in a bloody battle. The Confederate Army of Tennessee fragmented, and all opposition to Sherman's onslaught dissolved. Sherman entered Savannah unopposed on December 21.

The March to the Sea completed, Sherman turned north. In South Carolina, the first state to secede and fire shots, Sherman's troops took special delight in ravaging the countryside. When they reached Columbia, flames engulfed the city. Whether Sherman's men or retreating Confederates started the blaze was not clear, but African American regiments in Sher-

March to the Sea Sherman's march through Georgia from Atlanta to Savannah from November 15 to December 21, 1864, during which Union soldiers carried out orders to destroy everything in their path.

Determined to "make Georgia howl," William Tecumseh Sherman and his band of "bummers" slashed their way through the South during the winter of 1864, destroying military and civilian property along the way. This painting shows Sherman astride a white horse looking on while his men rip up a rail line and burn bridges and homes. *"Sherman's March to the Sea," engraving after F.O.C. Darley. Photo by Ben Lourie. Collection of David H. Sherman.*

man's command helped to put out the fires after Sherman occupied the South Carolina capital on February 17, 1865.

With the capital in flames, Confederate forces abandoned their posts in South Carolina, moving north to join with Joseph E. Johnston's army in an effort to stop Sherman from crossing North Carolina and joining Grant in Virginia. Union forces quickly moved into abandoned southern strongholds, including Charleston, where Major Robert Anderson, who had commanded Fort Sumter in April 1861, returned to raise the Union flag over the fort that he had surrendered four years earlier.

The Fall of Lee and Lincoln

Under increasing pressure from Sherman, the Confederacy's military situation was deteriorating rapidly. In a last-ditch effort to keep the Confederacy alive, Lee advised Davis to evacuate Richmond—the army intended to abandon the capital, moving west as rapidly as possible toward Lynchburg (see Map 15.4). From there Lee hoped to use surviving rail lines to move his troops south to join with Johnston's force in North Carolina. The unified armies might then halt Sherman's advance and wheel around to deal with Grant.

Suffering none of his predecessors' indecisiveness, Grant ordered an immediate assault as Lee's forces retreated from Petersburg. Lee had little ammunition, almost no food, and only thirty-five thousand men. As they retreated westward, under constant pressure from harassing attacks, hundreds of southern soldiers collapsed from hunger and exhaustion. By April 9, Union forces had surrounded Lee's broken army. Saying, "There is nothing left for me to do but go and see General Grant," Lee sent a note offering surrender.

The two generals met at a private home in the little village of Appomattox Courthouse, Virginia. Grant offered generous terms, allowing Confederate officers and men to go home "so long as they observe their paroles and the laws in force where they reside." This guaranteed them immunity from prosecution

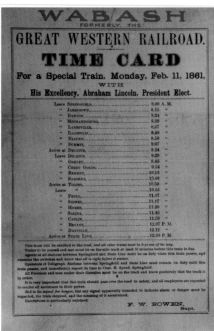

The nation's mood shifted from celebration to shock when it learned that President Lincoln had fallen to an assassin's bullet. His funeral provided an occasion for the entire country to mourn, not only his death but also the deaths of hundreds of thousands of Americans who had fallen in the Civil War. A specially constructed rail car pulled by an armored military locomotive carried the president's body on a route that retraced his 1860 campaign throughout the North. In large cities, Lincoln's body was paraded through the streets in mourning processionals. Throughout the countryside, however, people consulted published schedules of the train's route and lined the tracks at all hours of the day and night waiting for the train to pass so they could pay tribute to their fallen leader. *Left and right: Picture History.*

for treason and became the model for surrender. Grant sent the starving Confederates rations and let them keep their horses.

On the following day, Lincoln addressed a crowd outside the White House about his hopes and plans for rebuilding the nation. He talked about the need for flexibility in pulling the nation back together after the long and bitter conflict. He had already taken steps to bring southerners back into the Union. In December 1863, he had issued a Proclamation of Amnesty and Reconstruction offering pardons to any Confederates who would take a loyalty oath. After his re-election in 1864, Lincoln had begun to plan for the Confederacy's eventual surrender, and he pushed for a constitutional ban on slavery, which passed on January 31, 1865.

With victory at hand and a peace plan in place, on April 14 after an exhausting day in conference with his cabinet and with General Grant, Lincoln chose to relax by attending a play at Ford's Theater in Washington. At about ten o'clock, **John Wilkes Booth,** an actor and a southern sympathizer, entered the president's box and shot him behind the ear. Meanwhile, one of Booth's accomplices entered the home of Sec-

John Wilkes Booth Actor and southern sympathizer who on April 14, 1865, five days after Lee's surrender, fatally shot President Lincoln at Ford's Theater in Washington.

retary of State Seward, who was bedridden as a result of a carriage accident, and stabbed him several times before being driven out by Seward's son and a male nurse. Another accomplice was supposed to assassinate Vice President Johnson but apparently lost his nerve. Although the conspiracy had failed, one of its main objectives succeeded: the following morning, Lincoln died of his wound.

Even though Lincoln was dead and Lee had fallen, the war continued. Joseph E. Johnston, whose forces succeeded in preventing Sherman from joining Grant, did not surrender until April 18. And although most of his forces had been defeated, Jefferson Davis remained in hiding and called for guerrilla warfare and continued resistance. But one by one, the Confederate officers surrendered to their Union opponents. On May 10, Davis and the Confederate postmaster general were captured near Irwinville, Georgia, and placed in prison. Andrew Johnson, who had assumed the presidency upon Lincoln's death, issued a statement to the American people that armed rebellion against legitimate authority could be considered "virtually at an end." The last Confederate general to lay down his arms was Cherokee leader Stand Watie, who surrendered on June 23, 1865.

The price of victory was high for both the winner and the loser. More than 350,000 Union soldiers had been killed in action. No exact figures exist for the Confederacy, but southern casualties probably equaled or exceeded those of the Union. The war had wrecked the economy of the South, for most of the fighting had occurred there. Union military campaigns had wiped out most southern rail lines, destroyed the South's manufacturing capacity, and severely reduced agricultural productivity. Both sides had faced rising inflation during the war, but the Confederacy's actions to supply troops and keep the war effort going had bled the South of most of its resources and money. Secession had been defeated, but reunion remained a distant and difficult objective.

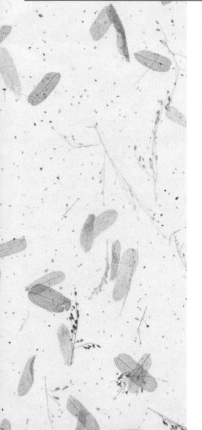

Individual Voices

Examining a Primary Source

Mary Ashton Rice Livermore Depicts Women's War Efforts

When Civil War broke out, women in both the North and South rallied in support of the war effort. An unknown number actually dressed up as men to enter the ranks as combat soldiers. Others carried on volunteer work, both at home and in the field, becoming fundraisers, nurses, and public health advocates. Mary Livermore served a short stint as a battlefield nurse but spent most of the war as a soldiers' relief worker. She urged other women to act on their patriotism by becoming involved in ways that would draw on the peculiar skills and affinities that nineteenth-century Americans believed belonged exclusively to women. After the war, she wrote a book recounting her experiences and presenting her perspectives. The following excerpt is taken from that 1888 publication.

It is easy to understand how men catch the contagion of war, especially when they feel their quarrel to be just. One can comprehend how, fired with enthusiasm, and

■ *How does Livermore characterize the differences between men and women in terms of their response to the appeals of war? What does this reflect about general attitudes toward gender in mid-nineteenth-century America?*

■ *What is Livermore suggesting here about the role of women during wartime? Does she portray this role as inferior, superior, or equal to that played by men?*

■ *In light of this eloquent description of women's efforts during the war, what would Livermore probably suggest about appropriate peacetime employment for women? Would you characterize this as a "feminist" or a "traditionalist" statement? What leads you to this conclusion?*

inspired by martial music, they march to the cannon's mouth, where the iron hail rains heaviest, and the ranks are mowed down like grain in harvest. But for women to send forth their husbands, sons, brothers and lovers to the fearful chances of the battle-field, knowing well the risks they run,—this involves exquisite suffering, and calls for another kind of heroism. . . . ■

The number of women who actually bore arms and served in the ranks during the war was greater than is supposed. . . . Such service was not the noblest that women rendered the country during its four years' struggle for life, and no one can regret that these soldier women were exceptional and rare. It is better to heal a wound than to make one. And it is to the honor of American women, not that they led hosts to the deadly charge, and battled amid contending armies, but that they confronted the horrid aspects of war with mighty life and earnestness. ■ They kept up their own courage and that of their households. They became ministering angels to their countrymen who periled health and life for the nation. They sent the love and impulses of home into the extended ranks of the army, through the unceasing correspondence they maintained with "the boys in blue." They planned largely, and toiled untiringly, and with steady persistence to the end, that the horrors of the battle-field might be mitigated, and the hospitals abound in needed comforts. ■

Summary

Both the Union and the Confederacy entered the war in 1861 with glowing hopes. Jefferson Davis pursued a defensive strategy, certain that northerners would soon tire of war and let the South withdraw from the Union. Abraham Lincoln countered by using the superior human, economic, and natural resources of the North to strangle the South into submission. But both leaders became increasingly frustrated during the first year of the war.

For Lincoln, the greatest frustration was military leadership. Beginning with the first Battle of Bull Run, Union forces seemed unable to win any major battles despite their numerical superiority. Although Union forces under Ulysses S. Grant's command scored victories in the Mississippi Valley, the Federals were stalemated. Robert E. Lee and Thomas "Stone-

wall" Jackson seemed able to defeat any Union general that Lincoln sent to oppose them.

The war's nature and direction changed after the fall of 1862, however. Lee invaded Maryland and was defeated at Antietam. Despite this crushing loss, Union generals still failed to capture Lee or to subdue Confederate forces in Virginia. Still vexed by military blundering, political attacks, and popular unrest, Lincoln issued the Emancipation Proclamation in an effort to undermine southern efforts and unify northern ones. After the proclamation, the only option for either side was total victory or total defeat.

After further reversals in the spring of 1863, Union forces turned the tide in the war by defeating Lee's army at Gettysburg and taking Vicksburg to gain full control of the Mississippi. With an election drawing near, Lincoln spurred his generals to deal the death blow to the Confederacy, and two in particular rose to the occasion. During the last half of 1864, William

Tecumseh Sherman wreaked havoc, making Georgia "howl." And Grant, in a wanton display of disregard for human life, drove Lee into a defensive corner. In November, buoyed by Sherman's victories in Georgia, Lincoln was reelected.

Suffering was not confined to those at the front. Governments in both the North and the South had to dig deep into depleting economic resources to keep the war effort going. Inflation plagued both nations, and common people faced hunger, disease, and insufficient police protection. Riots broke out in major cities, including New York. But throughout the country many people responded heroically to their own privations and to suffering at the front. Women such as Mary Livermore and others faced up to epidemics, enemy gunfire, and gender bias to institute public health standards and bring solace to suffering civilians and soldiers alike.

As hope dwindled for the South in the spring of 1865, Lee made a final desperate effort to keep the flagging Confederacy alive, racing to unify the last surviving remnants of the once-proud southern army. But Grant closed a net of steel around Lee's troops, forcing surrender. Lincoln immediately promoted a gentle policy for reunion, but his assassination ended this effort. The saintly American hero was gone, leaving a southern Democrat—Andrew Johnson—as president and a nation reeling in shock. The war was over, but the issues were still unresolved. Both the North and the South were beset with uncertainty about what would follow four years of suffering and sacrifice.

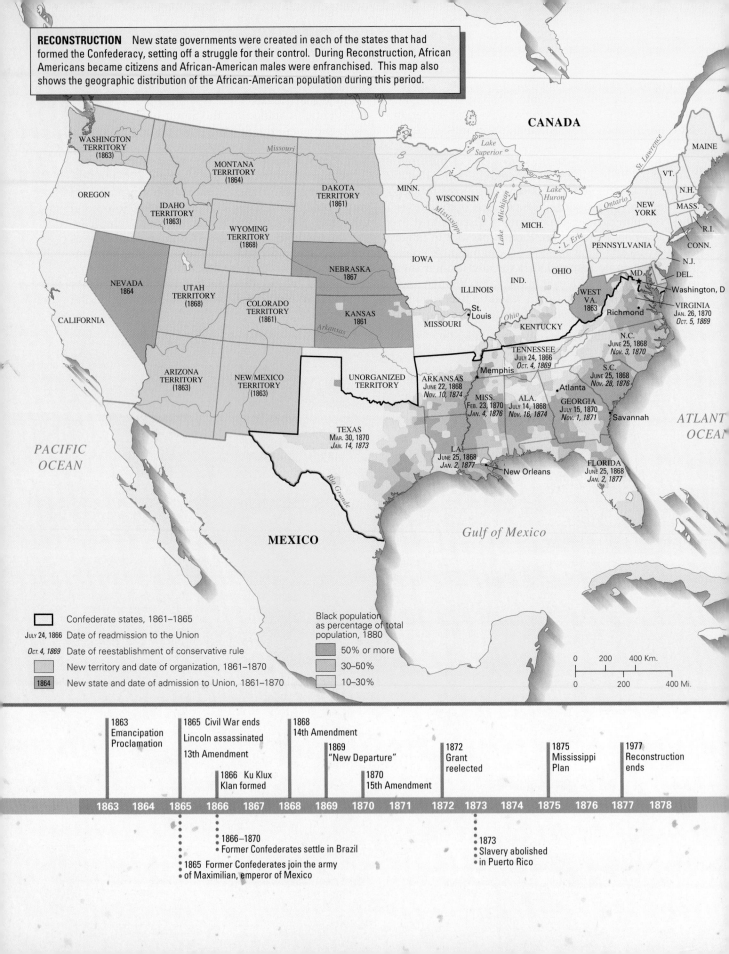

RECONSTRUCTION New state governments were created in each of the states that had formed the Confederacy, setting off a struggle for their control. During Reconstruction, African Americans became citizens and African-American males were enfranchised. This map also shows the geographic distribution of the African-American population during this period.

CANADA

MAINE

WASHINGTON TERRITORY (1863)

Missouri

MONTANA TERRITORY (1864)

OREGON

DAKOTA TERRITORY (1861)

IDAHO TERRITORY (1863)

MINN.

WISCONSIN

Lake Superior

Lake Huron

VT.

N.H.

WYOMING TERRITORY (1868)

MICH.

NEW YORK

MASS.

Mississippi

Lake Michigan

NEBRASKA 1867

IOWA

L. Ontario

L. Erie

PENNSYLVANIA

R.I.

CONN.

NEVADA 1864

UTAH TERRITORY (1868)

ILLINOIS

IND.

OHIO

N.J.

DEL.

MD.

Washington, D

CALIFORNIA

COLORADO TERRITORY (1861)

KANSAS 1861

Arkansas

MISSOURI

St. Louis

Ohio

KENTUCKY

WEST VA. 1863

Richmond

VIRGINIA
JAN. 26, 1870
OCT. 5, 1869

ARIZONA TERRITORY (1863)

NEW MEXICO TERRITORY (1863)

UNORGANIZED TERRITORY

ARKANSAS
JUNE 22, 1868
Nov. 10, 1874

TENNESSEE
JULY 24, 1866
OCT. 4, 1869

Memphis

N.C.
JUNE 25, 1868
Nov. 3, 1870

S.C.
JUNE 25, 1868
Nov. 28, 1876

MISS.
FEB. 23, 1870
JAN. 4, 1876

ALA.
JULY 14, 1868
Nov. 16, 1874

Atlanta

GEORGIA
JULY 15, 1870
Nov. 1, 1871

Savannah

ATLANT
OCEA

TEXAS
MAR. 30, 1870
JAN. 14, 1873

LA.
JUNE 25, 1868
JAN. 2, 1877

New Orleans

FLORIDA
JUNE 25, 1868
JAN. 2, 1877

PACIFIC OCEAN

Rio Grande

MEXICO

Gulf of Mexico

Confederate states, 1861–1865

JULY 24, 1866 Date of readmission to the Union

OCT. 4, 1869 Date of reestablishment of conservative rule

New territory and date of organization, 1861–1870

1864 New state and date of admission to Union, 1861–1870

Black population as percentage of total population, 1880

50% or more

30–50%

10–30%

0   200   400 Km.

0   200   400 Mi.

1863 Emancipation Proclamation

1865 Civil War ends
Lincoln assassinated
13th Amendment

1868 14th Amendment

1869 "New Departure"

1872 Grant reelected

1875 Mississippi Plan

1977 Reconstruction ends

1866 Ku Klux Klan formed

1870 15th Amendment

| 1863 | 1864 | 1865 | 1866 | 1867 | 1868 | 1869 | 1870 | 1871 | 1872 | 1873 | 1874 | 1875 | 1876 | 1877 | 1878 |

1866–1870 Former Confederates settle in Brazil

1873 Slavery abolished in Puerto Rico

1865 Former Confederates join the army of Maximilian, emperor of Mexico

Reconstruction: High Hopes and Shattered Dreams, 1865–1877

16

Reconstruction

What does the map on the facing page suggest regarding the connection between the proportion of the population that was African American and the length of time that each southern state experienced Black Reconstruction? Compare this map with Map 16.1 and consider which southern whites were most likely to vote Republican.

Individual Choices

ANDY ANDERSON

Andy Anderson was 94 years old when he was interviewed in 1937. Unfortunately, no photo of him has been found. This photo depicts an African American family from East Texas, the area where Anderson was born and grew up and where he began to farm. The photo shows what Anderson's home may have looked like in the 1880s or 1890s. *East Texas Research Center, Stephen F. Austin State University.*

Andy Anderson

Andy Anderson was born into slavery in East Texas in 1843. In 1937, when he was 94 years old, he told an interviewer about the day when he made the decision to be free. The interview was one of more than two thousand conversations with former slaves that the Federal Writers Project (a New Deal agency for unemployed professionals) collected between 1936 and 1938. Interviewers were instructed to record the interviews exactly, word for word.

Anderson explained that he had been born on the plantation of Jack Haley. Anderson remembered Haley as "kind to his cullud folks" and "kind to ever'body." Haley rarely whipped his slaves, Anderson recalled, and he had been "reasonable" when he did apply the lash. Anderson remembered that Haley treated his slaves so well that neighboring whites called them "petted niggers." With the coming of the Civil War, however, conditions changed. Haley sold Anderson to W. T. House, whom Anderson remembered as a man that "hell am too good fo'," and who whipped Anderson for a minor accident with a wagon.

> De overseer ties me to de stake an' ever' ha'f hour, fo' four hours, deys lay 10 lashes on my back. Aftah I's stood dat fo' a couple of hours, I's could not feel de pain so much an' w'en dey took me loose, I's jus' ha'f dead. I's could not feel de lash 'cause my body am numb, an' my mind am numb. De last thing I's 'membahs am dat I's wishin' fo' death. I's laid in the de bunk fo' two days gittin' over dat whuppin'. Dat is, gittin' over it in de body but not in de heart. No Sar! I's have dat in de heart 'til dis day.

Soon after the whipping, Anderson was sold again, to House's brother John, who, to Anderson's knowledge, had never struck a slave.

As the Civil War was winding down to its end, Anderson remembered the day when House called his slaves together and told them that they were free and that the official order would soon be given. He offered any who wished to stay the choice to work for wages or work the land as sharecroppers, and he urged the freed people to "stay with me." Anderson was standing near House and said to himself, not expecting anyone to hear, "Lak hell I's will." He meant only that he intended to take his freedom, but House heard him, took it as a challenge, and promised that he would "tend to yous later." Anderson recalled that he was sure to keep his lips closed when he thought, "I's won't be heah."

Toward sundown, Anderson left the House plantation for good. He traveled at night to avoid the patrollers, who were always on the lookout for African Americans on the road without passes, and hid in the brush during the day. Though he was 21 years old, he'd never been farther from home than a neighbor's house, and he was uncertain of his way. Nonetheless he managed to locate the Haley plantation and to find his father, who hid Anderson. Haley permitted Anderson to stay on his place until the final proclamation of freedom.

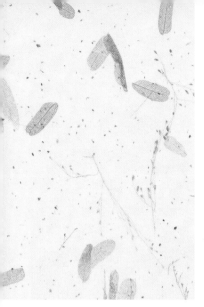

Sheldon Cauthier of the Federal Writers Project interviewed Andy Anderson on September 16, 1937, and Anderson gave him this account of his decision to take his freedom. By then, Anderson was living in Fort Worth, Texas. Anderson provided only limited information on his later life. He left Haley's farm soon after emancipation to work on another farm for $2 a month plus clothing and food, and he continued to do farm work until his old age. He married in 1883, when he was about 40, an indication, perhaps, that his labor did not provide enough income to support a family until then. He and his first wife had two children, but both children and his wife died. He married again in 1885, and he and second his wife had six children, of whom four were still living in 1937. His second wife died in 1934, and he married a third time in 1936. He joked with the interviewer that "dere am no chilluns yet f'om my third mai'age." Though we know little of what Anderson experienced during the years of Reconstruction, we do have his dramatic account of how he claimed his freedom.

INTRODUCTION

Andy Anderson was not the only African American who claimed freedom while the war was raging. Anderson's experience was repeated time and time again, with many variations, all across the South. Those decisions were made legal by the Emancipation Proclamation, the presence of Union armies, and later the Thirteenth Amendment to the Constitution. The **freed people** now faced a wide range of new decisions—where to live, where to work, how to create their own communities.

The war was a momentous event for nearly all Americans. By 1865, when the war ended, some 2.6 million men—and a few hundred women—had served in the Union or Confederate armies, equal to almost 40 percent of all the men ages 15 to 40 in the United States in 1860. More than a half-million had died—more deaths than in any other American war—and many others were permanently disabled. By 1865, the war had touched the lives of nearly every person living in the nation.

Nearly all the major battles occurred in the South or in the border states. Toward the end of the war, Union armies swept across the South, leaving havoc behind them: burned and shelled buildings, ravaged fields, twisted railroad tracks. This destruction, and the collapse of the region's financial system, devastated the southern economy.

More distressing for many white southerners than the ravaged countryside was the **emancipation** of 4 million slaves. In 1861 fears for the future of slavery under Republicans had caused the South to attempt to **secede** from the Union. With the end of the war, fears became reality. The end of slavery forced southerners of both races to develop new social, economic, and political patterns.

Historians identify the years between 1865 and 1877 as **Reconstruction.** Although the period was a time of physical rebuilding throughout the South, Reconstruction refers primarily to the rebuilding of the federal Union and to the political, economic, and social changes that came to the South as it was restored to the nation. Reconstruction involved some of the most momentous questions in American history. How was the defeated South to be treated? What was to be the future of the 4 million former slaves? Should key decisions be made by the federal government or in state capitols and county courthouses throughout the South? Which branch of the government was to establish policies?

---

freed people   Former slaves; *freed people* is the term used by historians to refer to former slaves, whether male or female.

emancipation   Release from slavery.

secede   To withdraw from membership in an organization; in this case, the attempted withdrawal of eleven southern states from the United States in 1860–1861, giving rise to the Civil War.

Reconstruction   Term applied by historians to the years 1865–1877, when the Union was restored from the Civil War; important changes were made to the federal Constitution; and social, economic, and political relations between the races were transformed in the South.

As the dominant Republicans turned their attention from waging war to reconstructing the Union, they wrote into law and the Constitution new definitions of the Union itself. They also defined the rights of the former slaves and the terms on which the South might rejoin the Union. And they permanently changed the definition of American citizenship.

Most white southerners disliked the new rules emerging from the federal government, and some resisted. Disagreement over the future of the South and the status of the former slaves led to conflict between the president and Congress. A temporary result of this conflict was a more powerful Congress and a less powerful executive. A lasting outcome of these events was a significant increase in the power of the federal government and new limits on local and state governments.

Reconstruction significantly changed many aspects of southern life. In the end, however, Reconstruction failed to fulfill many African Americans' hopes for their lives as free people.

Presidential Reconstruction

■ What did Presidents Lincoln and Johnson seek to accomplish through their Reconstruction policies? How did their purposes differ? In what ways were their policies similar?

■ How did white southerners respond to the Reconstruction efforts of Lincoln and Johnson? What does this suggest about the expectations of white southerners?

On New Year's Day 1863, the Emancipation Proclamation took effect. More than four years earlier, Abraham Lincoln had insisted that "this government cannot endure permanently half slave and half free. . . . It will become all one thing, or all the other." With the Emancipation Proclamation, President Lincoln began the legal process by which the nation became all free. At the time, however, the Proclamation did not affect any slave because it abolished slavery only in territory under Confederate control, where it was unenforceable. But every advance of a Union army after January 1, 1863, brought the law of the land—and emancipation—to the Confederacy.

Republican War Aims

For Lincoln and the Republican Party, freedom for the slaves became a central concern partly because **abolitionists** were an influential group within the party. The Republican Party had promised only to prohibit slavery in the territories during their 1860 electoral

This engraving celebrating the Emancipation Proclamation first appeared in 1863. While it places a white Union soldier in the center, it also portrays the important role of African American troops and emphasizes the importance of education and literacy. *The Library Company of Philadelphia.*

campaign, and Lincoln initially defined the war only as one to maintain the Union. Some leading Republicans, however, favored abolition of slavery everywhere in the Union. As Union troops moved into the South, some slaves took matters into their hands by walking away from their owners and seeking safety with the advancing army. Within a year, former slaves had become an important part of the Union army's work force. Abolitionists throughout the North—including Frederick Douglass, an escaped slave and an important leader of the abolition movement—began to argue that emancipation would be meaningless unless the government guaranteed the civil and political rights of the former slaves. Thus some Republicans expanded their definition of war objectives to include not just preserving the Union but also abolishing slavery, extending citizenship for the former slaves, and guaranteeing the equality of all citizens before the law. At the time, these were extreme views

Chronology

Reconstruction

1863	Emancipation Proclamation The Ten Percent Plan
1864	Abraham Lincoln reelected
1865	Freedmen's Bureau created Civil War ends Lincoln assassinated Andrew Johnson becomes president Thirteenth Amendment (abolishing slavery) ratified
1866	Ku Klux Klan formed Congress begins to assert control over Reconstruction Civil Rights Act of 1866 Riots by whites in Memphis and New Orleans
1867	Military Reconstruction Act Command of the Army Act Tenure of Office Act
1868	Impeachment of President Johnson Fourteenth Amendment (defining citizenship) ratified Ulysses S. Grant elected president
1869–1870	Victories of "New Departure" Democrats in some southern states
1870	Fifteenth Amendment (guaranteeing voting rights) ratified
1870–1871	Ku Klux Klan Acts
1872	Grant reelected
1875	Civil Rights Act of 1875 Mississippi Plan ends Reconstruction in Mississippi
1876	Disputed presidential election: Hayes versus Tilden
1877	Compromise of 1877 Rutherford B. Hayes becomes president End of Reconstruction

on abolition and equal rights, and the people who held them were called **Radical Republicans,** or simply Radicals.

Thaddeus Stevens, 73 years old in 1865 and perhaps the leading Radical in the House of Representatives, had made a successful career as a Pennsylvania iron manufacturer before he won election to Congress in 1858. Born with a clubfoot, he always seemed to identify with those outside the social mainstream. He became a compelling spokesman for abolition and an uncompromising advocate of equal rights for African Americans. A masterful parliamentarian, he was known for his honesty and his sarcastic wit. From the beginning of the war, Stevens urged that the slaves be not only freed but also armed, to fight the Confederacy. By the end of the war, some 180,000 African Americans, the great majority of them freedmen, had served in the Union army and a few thousand in the Union navy. Many more worked for the army as laborers.

Charles Sumner of Massachusetts, a prominent Radical in the Senate, had argued for **racial integration** of Massachusetts schools in 1849 and won election to the U.S. Senate in 1851. Immediately establishing himself as the Senate's foremost champion of abolition, he became a martyr to the cause after a severe beating he suffered in 1856 because of an antislavery speech. After emancipation, Sumner, like

abolitionist   An individual who condemns slavery as morally wrong and seeks to abolish (eliminate) slavery.

Radical Republicans   A group within the Republican Party during the Civil War and Reconstruction who advocated abolition of slavery, citizenship for the former slaves, and sweeping alteration of the South.

racial integration   Equal opportunities to participate in a society or organization by people of different racial groups; the absence of race-based barriers to full and equal participation.

President Andrew Johnson was initially seen by the Radical Republicans as a potential ally. Instead he proved to be unsympathetic to most Radical goals. His self-righteous and uncompromising personality led to conflict that eventually produced an unsuccessful effort to remove him from office in 1868. *Library of Congress.*

Stevens, fought for full political and civil rights for the freed people.

Stevens, Sumner, and other Radicals demanded a drastic restructuring not only of the South's political system but also of its economy. They opposed slavery not only on moral grounds but also because they believed free labor was more productive. Slaves worked to escape punishment, they argued, but free workers worked to benefit themselves. Eliminating slavery and instituting a free-labor system in its place, they claimed, would benefit everyone by increasing the productivity of the nation's work force. Free labor not only contributed centrally to the dynamism of the North's economy, they argued, but was crucial to democracy itself. "The middling classes who own the soil, and work it with their own hands," Stevens once proclaimed, "are the main support of every free government." For the South to be fully democratic, the Radicals concluded, it had to elevate free labor to a position of honor.

Not all Republicans agreed with the Radicals. All Republicans had objected to slavery, but not all Republicans were abolitionists. Similarly, not all Republicans wanted to extend full citizenship rights to the former slaves. Some favored rapid restoration of the South to the Union so that the federal government could concentrate on stimulating the nation's economy and developing the West. Republicans who did not immediately endorse severe punishment for the South or citizenship for the freed people are usually referred to as **moderates.**

Lincoln's Approach to Reconstruction: "With Malice Toward None"

After the Emancipation Proclamation, President Lincoln and the congressional Radicals agreed that the abolition of slavery had to be a condition for the return of the South to the Union. Major differences soon appeared, however, over other terms for reunion and the roles of the president and Congress in establishing those terms. In his second inaugural address, a month before his death, Lincoln defined the task facing the nation:

> With malice toward none; with charity for all; with firmness in the right, as God gives us to see the right, let us strive on to finish the work we are in: to bind up the nation's wounds; to care for him who shall have borne the battle, and for his widow and orphan, to do all which may achieve and cherish a just and lasting peace among ourselves, and with all nations.

Lincoln began to rebuild the Union on the basis of these principles. He hoped to hasten the end of the war by encouraging southerners to renounce the Confederacy and to accept emancipation. As soon as Union armies occupied portions of southern states, he appointed temporary military governors for those regions and tried to restore civil government as quickly as possible.

Drawing on the president's constitutional power to issue **pardons** (Article II, Section 2), Lincoln issued

moderates People whose views are midway between two more-extreme positions; in this case, Republicans who favored some reforms but not all the Radicals' proposals.

pardon A governmental directive canceling punishment for a person or people who have committed a crime.

a Proclamation of **Amnesty** and Reconstruction in December 1863. Often called the "Ten Percent Plan," it promised a full pardon and restoration of rights to those who swore their loyalty to the Union and accepted the abolition of slavery. Only high-ranking Confederate leaders were not eligible. Once those who had taken the oath in a state amounted to 10 percent of the number of votes cast by that state in the 1860 presidential election, the pardoned voters were to write a new state constitution that abolished slavery, elect state officials, and resume self-government. Some congressional Radicals disagreed with Lincoln's lenient approach. When they tried to set more stringent standards, however, Lincoln blocked them, fearing their plan would slow the restoration of civil government and perhaps even lengthen the war.

Under Lincoln's Ten Percent Plan, new state governments were established in Arkansas, Louisiana, and Tennessee during 1864 and early 1865. In Louisiana, the new government denied voting rights to men who were one-quarter or more black. Radicals complained, but Lincoln urged patience, suggesting the reconstructed government in Louisiana was "as the egg to the fowl, and we shall sooner have the fowl by hatching the egg than by smashing it." Events in Louisiana and elsewhere convinced Radicals that freed people were unlikely to receive equitable treatment from state governments formed under the Ten Percent Plan. Some moderates agreed and moved toward the Radicals' position that only **suffrage** could protect the freedmen's rights and that only federal action could secure black suffrage.

Abolishing Slavery Forever: The Thirteenth Amendment

Amid questions about the rights of freed people, congressional Republicans prepared the final destruction of slavery. The Emancipation Proclamation had been a wartime measure, justified partly by military necessity, and it never applied in Union states. State legislatures or conventions abolished slavery in West Virginia, Maryland, Missouri, and the reconstructed state of Tennessee. In early 1865, however, slavery remained legal in Delaware and Kentucky, and old, prewar state laws—which might or might not be valid—still permitted slavery in the states that had seceded. To destroy slavery forever, Congress in January 1865 approved the **Thirteenth Amendment,** which read simply, "Neither slavery nor involuntary servitude, except as a punishment for crime whereof the party shall have been duly convicted, shall exist

within the United States, or any place subject to their jurisdiction."

The Constitution requires any amendment to be ratified by three-fourths of the states—then 27 of 36. By December 1865, only 19 of the 25 Union states had ratified the amendment. The measure passed, however, when 8 of the reconstructed southern states approved it. In the end, therefore, the abolition of slavery hinged on action by reconstructed state governments in the South.

By abolishing slavery, the United States followed the lead of most of the nations of Europe and Latin America. Table 16.1 summarizes information on the abolition of slavery elsewhere in the world.

Andrew Johnson and Reconstruction

After the assassination of Lincoln in mid-April 1865, Vice President Andrew Johnson became president. Born in North Carolina, he never had the opportunity to attend school and spent his early life in a continual struggle against poverty. As a young man in Tennessee, he worked as a tailor and then turned to politics. After he married, his wife, Eliza McCardle Johnson, tutored him in reading, writing, and arithmetic. A Democrat, Johnson relied on his oratorical skills to win several terms in the Tennessee legislature. He was elected to Congress and afterward served as governor before winning election to the U.S. Senate in 1857. His political support came primarily from small-scale farmers and working people. The state's elite of plantation owners usually opposed him. Johnson, in turn, resented their wealth and power and blamed them for secession and the Civil War.

Johnson was the only southern senator who rejected the Confederacy. Early in the war, Union forces captured Nashville, the capital of Tennessee, and Lincoln appointed Johnson as military governor. Johnson dealt harshly with Tennessee secessionists, especially wealthy planters, and Radical Republicans thought that Johnson's severe treatment of former Confederates was exactly what the South needed. Johnson was

amnesty A general pardon granted by a government, especially for political offenses.
suffrage The right to vote.
Thirteenth Amendment Constitutional amendment, ratified in 1865, that abolished slavery in the United States and its territories.

TABLE 16.1   Abolition of Slavery Around the World

1772	Slavery abolished in England
1807	British navy begins operations to end the international slave trade
1808	United States prohibits the importation of slaves
1820s	Slavery abolished in most Spanish-speaking Latin American nations
1833	Slavery abolished within the British Empire
1848	Slavery abolished within the French Empire
1861	Abolition of serfdom in Russia
1863	Emancipation Proclamation (United States); abolition of slavery within the Dutch Empire
1865	Thirteenth Amendment abolishes slavery everywhere in the United States
1888	Slavery abolished in Brazil
1926	Thirty-five states sign a Convention to Suppress the Slave Trade and Slavery
1948	United Nations adopts the Universal Declaration of Human Rights, which includes a call for the abolition of slavery and the slave trade
1962	Abolition of slavery in Saudi Arabia
2004	International Year to Commemorate the Struggle against Slavery and its Abolition, proclaimed by the United Nations General Assembly

Though illegal throughout the world, chattel slavery still exists in some parts of Africa, notably Mauritania and Sudan, and in some parts of Asia, especially the Middle East. In other places throughout the world, people are still forced to work in conditions approaching that of slavery, through forced prostitution, debt bondage, and forced-labor camps.

elected vice president in 1864, receiving the nomination for vice president in part because Lincoln wanted to appeal to Democrats and to Unionists in border states.

When Johnson became president, Radicals hoped he would join their efforts to transform the South. Johnson, however, soon made clear that he was strongly committed to **states' rights** and opposed the Radicals' objective of a powerful federal government. "White men alone must manage the South," Johnson told one visitor, although he recommended limited political roles for the freedmen. Self-righteous and uncompromising, Johnson saw the major task of Reconstruction as **empowering** the region's white middle class and excluding the wealthy planters from power.

Johnson's approach to Reconstruction differed little from Lincoln's. Like Lincoln, he relied on the president's constitutional power to grant pardons. His desire for a quick restoration of the southern states to the Union apparently overcame his bitterness toward the southern elite, and he granted amnesty to most former Confederates who pledged loyalty to the Union and support for emancipation. In one of his last actions as president, he granted full pardon and amnesty to all southern rebels, although after 1868 the Fourteenth Amendment prevented him from restoring their right to hold office.

Johnson appointed **provisional** civilian governors for the southern states not already reconstructed. He instructed them to reconstitute functioning state administrations and to call constitutional conventions of delegates elected by pardoned voters. Some provisional governors, however, appointed former Confederates to state and local offices, outraging those who expected Reconstruction to bring to power loyal Unionists committed to a new southern society.

states' rights   A political position favoring limitation of the federal government's power and the greatest possible self-government by the individual states.

empower   To increase the power or authority of some person or group.

provisional   Temporary.

Before Emancipation, slaves typically made their own simple and rough clothing or they received the cast-off clothing of their owners and overseers. With Emancipation, those freed people who had an income could afford to dress more fashionably. The Harry Stephens family probably put on their best clothes for a visit to the photographer G. Gable in 1866. *Gilman Paper Company, NY.*

The Southern Response: Minimal Compliance

Johnson expected the state constitutional conventions to abolish slavery within each state, ratify the Thirteenth Amendment, renounce secession, and **repudiate** the states' war debts. The states were then to hold elections and resume their places in the Union. State conventions during the summer of 1865 usually complied with these requirements, though some did so grudgingly. Johnson had specified nothing about the rights of the freed people, and every state rejected black suffrage.

By April 1866, a year after the close of the war, all the southern states had fulfilled Johnson's requirements for rejoining the Union and had elected legislators, governors, and members of Congress. Their choices troubled Johnson. He had hoped for the emergence of new political leaders in the South and was dismayed at the number of rich planters and former Confederate officials who won state contests.

Most white southerners, however, viewed Johnson as their protector, standing between them and the Radicals. His support for states' rights and his opposition to federal determination of voting rights led white southerners to expect that they would shape the transition from slavery to freedom—that they, and not Congress, would define the status of the former slaves.

Freedom and the Legacy of Slavery

■ How did the freed people respond to freedom? What seem to have been the leading objectives among freed people as they explored their new opportunities?

■ How did southern whites respond to the end of slavery?

■ How do the differing responses of freed people and southern whites show different understandings of the significance of emancipation?

As state conventions wrote new constitutions and politicians argued in Washington, African Americans throughout the South set about creating new, free lives for themselves. In the antebellum South, all slaves and most free African Americans had led lives tightly constrained by law and custom. They were permitted few social organizations of their own. Eric Foner, in his comprehensive study *Reconstruction* (1988), described the central theme of the black response to emancipation as "a desire for independence from white control, for autonomy both as individuals and as members of a community." The prospect of **autonomy** touched every

---

repudiation   The act of rejecting the validity or authority of something; to refuse to pay.
autonomy   Control of one's own affairs.

aspect of life—family, churches, schools, newspapers, and a host of other social institutions. From this ferment of freedom came new black institutions that provided the basis for southern African American communities. At the same time, the economic life of the South had been shattered by the Civil War and was being transformed by emancipation. Thus white southerners also faced drastic economic and social change.

Defining the Meaning of Freedom

At the most basic level, freedom came every time an individual slave stopped working for a master and claimed the right to be free. Thus freedom did not come to all slaves at the same time or in the same way. For some, freedom came before the Emancipation Proclamation, when they walked away from their owners, crossed into Union-held territory, and asserted their liberty. Toward the end of the war, as civil authority broke down throughout much of the South, many slaves declared their freedom and left the lands they had worked when they were in bondage. Some left for good, but many remained nearby, though with a new understanding of their relationship to their former masters. For some, freedom did not come until ratification of the Thirteenth Amendment.

Across the South, the approach of Yankee troops set off a joyous celebration—called a Jubilee—among those who knew that their enslavement was ending. As one Virginia woman remembered, "Such rejoicing and shouting you never heard in your life." A man recalled that, with the appearance of the Union soldiers, "We was all walking on golden clouds. Hallelujah!" Once the celebrating was over, however, the freed people had to decide how best to use their freedom.

The freed people expressed their new status in many ways. Some chose new names to symbolize their new beginning. Andy Anderson (see page 456), for example, had been called Andy Haley, after the last name of his owner. On claiming his freedom, he changed his name to Anderson, the last name of his father. Many freed people changed their style of dress, discarding the cheap clothing provided to slaves. Some acquired guns. A significant benefit of freedom was the ability to travel without a pass and without being checked by the **patrollers** who had enforced the **pass system.**

Many freed people took advantage of this new opportunity to travel. Indeed, some felt they had to leave the site of their enslavement to experience full freedom. Andy Anderson refused to work for his last owner, not because he had anything against him but because he wanted "to take my freedom." One freed woman said, "If I stay here I'll never know I'm free." Most did not move, however. Those who did generally traveled only short distances, usually to find work or land to farm, to seek family members separated from them by slavery, or for other well-defined reasons.

The towns and cities of the South attracted some freed people. The presence of Union troops and officials promised protection from the random violence against freed people that occurred in many rural areas. A new federal program, the **Freedmen's Bureau,** offered assistance with finding work and necessities. Cities and towns also offered black churches, schools (which before the war had usually operated in secret), and other social institutions begun by free blacks before the war. Many African Americans also came to towns and cities looking for work. With little housing available, however, most crowded into hastily built shanties. Sanitation was poor and disease a common scourge. In September 1866, for example, more than a hundred people died of **cholera** in Vicksburg, Mississippi. Such conditions improved only very slowly.

Creating Communities

During Reconstruction, African Americans created their own communities with their own social institutions, beginning with family ties. Joyful families were reunited after years of separation caused by the sale of a spouse or children. Some people spent years searching for lost family members.

The new freedom to conduct religious services without white supervision was especially important. Churches quickly became the most prominent social organizations in African American communities.

---

patrollers   During the era of slavery, white guards who made the rounds of rural roads to make certain that slaves were not moving about the countryside without written permission from their masters.

pass system   Laws that forbade slaves from traveling without written authorization from their owners.

Freedmen's Bureau   Agency established in 1865 to aid former slaves in their transition to freedom, especially by administering relief and sponsoring education.

cholera   Infectious and often fatal disease associated with poor sanitation.

Churches were the first institutions in America to be completely controlled by African Americans, and ministers were highly influential figures in the African American communities that emerged during Reconstruction. This photograph shows the Reverend John Qualls at the pulpit of his church in New Orleans in the 1880s. *Historic New Orleans Collection.*

Churches were, in fact, among the very first social institutions that African Americans fully controlled. During Reconstruction, black denominations, including the African Methodist Episcopal, African Methodist Episcopal Zion, and several Baptist groups (all founded well before the Civil War), grew rapidly in the South. Black ministers helped to lead congregation members as they adjusted to the changes that freedom brought, and many ministers became key leaders within developing African American communities.

Throughout the cities and towns of the South, African Americans—especially ministers and church members—worked to create schools. Setting up a school, said one, was "the first proof" of independence. Many new schools were for both children and adults, whose literacy and learning had been restricted by state laws prohibiting education for slaves. The desire to learn was widespread and intense. One freedman in Georgia wrote to a friend: "The Lord has sent books and teachers. We must not hesitate a moment, but go on and learn all we can."

Before the war, free public education had been rudimentary in much of the South, and wholly absent in many places. When African Americans set up schools, they faced severe shortages of teachers, books, and schoolrooms—everything but students. As abolitionists and northern reformers tried to assist the transition from slavery to freedom, many of them focused first on education.

In March 1865, Congress created the Freedmen's Bureau to assist the freed people in their transition to freedom. It played an important role in organizing and equipping schools. Freedmen's Aid Societies also sprang up in most northern cities and, along with northern churches, collected funds and supplies for the freed people. Teachers—mostly white women, often from New England and often acting on religious impulses—came from the North. Northern aid societies and church organizations, together with the Freedmen's Bureau, established schools to train black teachers. Some of those schools evolved into black colleges. By 1870, the Freedmen's Bureau supervised more than 4,000 schools, with more than 9,000 teachers and 247,000 students. Still, in 1870, the schools had room for only one black child in ten of school age.

In addition to churches and schools, other African American social institutions emerged and grew, including **fraternal orders, benevolent societies,** and newspapers. By 1866, the South had ten black newspapers, led by the *New Orleans Tribune,* and black newspapers played important roles in shaping African American communities.

In politics, African Americans' first objective was recognition of their equal rights as citizens. Spokesman Frederick Douglass insisted, "Slavery is not abolished until the black man has the ballot." Political conventions of African Americans attracted hundreds of leaders of the emerging black communities. They called for equality and voting rights and pointed to black contributions in the American Revolution and the Civil War as evidence of patriotism

> **fraternal order** An organization of men, often with a ceremonial initiation, that typically provided rudimentary life insurance; many fraternal orders also had auxiliaries for the female relatives of members.
>
> **benevolent society** An organization of people dedicated to some charitable purpose.

During Reconstruction, the freed people gave a high priority to the establishment of schools, often with the assistance of the Freedmen's Bureau and northern missionary societies. This teacher and her barefoot pupils were photographed in the 1870s, in Petersburg, Virginia. In a school like this, one teacher typically taught grades 1–8. Note the daylight coming through the wall of the school behind the teacher's right shoulder, the gaps in the floorboards, and the benches for the students which seem to have been constructed from logs. *Clayton Lewis, William L. Clements Library, University of Michigan.*

and devotion. They also appealed to the nation's republican traditions, in particular the Declaration of Independence and its dictum that "all men are created equal."

Land and Labor

Former slaveowners reacted to emancipation in many ways. Some tried to keep their slaves from learning of their freedom. A very few white southerners welcomed the end of slavery—Mary Chesnut, for example, a plantation mistress from South Carolina, believed that the power of male slaveholders over female slaves led to sexual coercion and adultery, and she was glad to see the end of slavery. Few former slaveowners provided any compensation to assist their former slaves. One freedman later recalled, "I do know some of dem old slave owners to be nice enough to start der slaves off in freedom wid somethin' to live on . . . but dey wasn't in droves, I tell you."

Many freed people looked to Union troops for assistance. When General William T. Sherman led his victorious army through Georgia in the closing months of the war, thousands of African American men, women, and children claimed their freedom and followed in the Yankees' wake. Their leaders told Sherman that what they wanted most was to "reap the fruit of our own labor." In January 1865, Sherman issued Special Field Order No. 15, setting aside the Sea Islands and land along the South Carolina coast for

freed families. Each family, he specified, was to receive 40 acres and the loan of an army mule. By June, the area had filled with forty thousand freed people settled on 400,000 acres of "Sherman land."

Sherman's action encouraged many African Americans to expect that the federal government would redistribute land throughout the South. "Forty acres and a mule" became a rallying cry. Only land, Thaddeus Stevens proclaimed, would give the freed people control of their own labor. "If we do not furnish them with homesteads," Stevens said, "we had better left them in bondage."

By the end of the war, the Freedmen's Bureau controlled some 850,000 acres of land abandoned by former owners or confiscated from Confederate leaders. In July 1865, General Oliver O. Howard, head of the bureau, directed that this land be divided into 40-acre plots to be given to freed people. However, President Johnson ordered Howard to halt **land redistribution** and to reclaim land already handed over and return it to its former owners. Johnson's order displaced thousands of African Americans who had already taken their 40 acres. They and others who had hoped for land felt disappointed and betrayed. One later re-

> **land redistribution** The division of land held by large landowners into smaller plots that are turned over to people without property.

called that they had expected "a heap from freedom dey didn't git."

The congressional act that created the Freedmen's Bureau also authorized it to assist white refugees. In a few places, white recipients of aid outnumbered the freed blacks. The vast majority of southern whites had never owned slaves, and some opposed secession, but the outcome of the war meant that some lost their livelihood, and many feared that they would now have to compete with the freed people for farmland or wage labor. Like the freed people, many southern whites lacked the means to farm on their own. With the collapse of the Confederate government, Confederate money—badly devalued by rampant inflation—became worthless. This currency fiasco, together with the failure of southern banks and the devastation of the southern economy, meant that even many whites with large landholdings lacked the cash to hire farm workers.

Sharecropping slowly emerged across much of the South as an alternative both to land redistribution and to wage labor on the plantations. Sharecropping derived directly from the central realities of southern agriculture. Much of the land was in large holdings, but the landowners had no one to work it. Many families, black and white, wanted to raise their own crops with their own labor but had no land, no supplies, and no money. The entire region was short of **capital.** Under sharecropping, an individual—usually a family head—signed a contract with a landowner to rent land as home and farm. The tenant—the sharecropper—was to pay, as rent, a share of the harvest. The share might amount to half or more of the crop if the landlord provided mules, tools, seed, and fertilizer as well as land. Many landowners thought that sharecropping encouraged tenants to be productive, to get as much value as possible from their shares of the crop. The rental contract often allowed the landlord to specify what crop would be planted, and most landlords chose cotton so that their tenants would not hold back any of the harvest for personal consumption. Thus sharecropping helped to perpetuate the dependency of the South on cotton.

Southern farmers—black or white, sharecroppers or owners of small plots—often found themselves in debt to a local merchant who advanced supplies on credit. In return for credit, the merchant required a lien (a legal claim) on the growing crop. Many landlords ran stores that they required their tenants to patronize. Often the share paid as rent and the debt owed the store exceeded the value of the entire harvest. Furthermore, many rental contracts and **crop liens** were automatically renewed if all debts were not paid at the end of a year. Thus, in spite of their ef-

Sharecropping gave the African Americans more control over their labor than did labor contracts. But sharecropping also contributed to the South's dependence on one-crop agriculture and helped to perpetuate widespread rural poverty. This family of sharecroppers near Aiken, South Carolina, was photographed picking cotton around 1870. © *Collection of the New York Historical Society.*

forts to achieve greater control over their lives and labor, many southern farm families, black and white alike, found themselves trapped by sharecropping and debt. Still, sharecropping gave freed people more control over their daily lives than had slavery.

Landlords often exercised political as well as economic power over their tenants. Until the 1890s, the act of casting a ballot on election day was an open process, and any observer could see how an individual voted (see page 474). Thus, when a landlord or merchant advocated a particular candidate, the unspoken message was often an implicit threat to cut off credit at the store or to evict a sharecropper if he did

sharecropping   A system for renting farmland in which tenant farmers give landlords a share of their crops, rather than cash, as rent.

capital   Money, especially the money invested in a commercial enterprise.

crop lien   A legal claim to a farmer's crop, similar to a mortgage, based on the use of crops as collateral for extension of credit by a merchant.

not vote accordingly. Such forms of economic **coercion** had the potential to undercut voting rights.

The White South: Confronting Change

The Civil War and the end of slavery transformed the lives of white southerners as well as black southerners. For some, the changes were nearly as profound as for the freed people. Savings vanished. Some homes and other buildings were destroyed. Thousands left the South.

Before the war, few white southerners had owned slaves, and even fewer owned large numbers. Distrust or even hostility had always existed between the privileged planter families and the many whites who farmed small plots by themselves. Some regions populated by small-scale farmers had resisted secession, and some of them welcomed the Union victory and supported the Republicans during Reconstruction. Some southerners also welcomed the prospect of the economic transformation that northern capital might bring.

Most white southerners, however, shared what one North Carolinian described in 1866 as "the bitterest hatred toward the North." Even people with no attachment to slavery detested the Yankees who so profoundly changed their lives. For many white southerners, the "lost cause" of the Confederacy came to symbolize their defense of their prewar lives, not an attempt to break up the nation or protect slavery. During the early phases of Reconstruction, most white southerners apparently expected that, except for slavery, things would soon be put back much as they had been before the war.

As civil governments began to function in late 1865 and 1866, state legislatures passed **black codes** defining the new legal status of African Americans. These regulations varied from state to state, but every state placed significant restraints on black people. Various black codes required African Americans to have an annual employment contract, limited them to agricultural work, forbade them from moving about the countryside without permission, restricted their ownership of land, and provided for forced labor by those found guilty of **vagrancy**—which usually meant anyone without a job. Some codes originated in prewar restrictions on slaves and free blacks. Some reflected efforts to ensure that farm workers would be on hand for planting, cultivating, and harvesting. Taken together, however, the black codes represented an effort by white southerners to define a legally subordinate place for African Americans.

In this picture, the artist has portrayed a Republican leader, John Campbell, pleading for mercy from a group of bizarrely dressed Klansmen in Moore County, North Carolina, on August 10, 1871. Campbell was a white grocery store owner who was active in the local Republican Party; the Klansmen flogged him before releasing him. Those responsible were captured and photographed in their Klan costumes, providing the basis for this drawing. Curiously, the artist has depicted Campbell as an African American. *The Granger Collection, New York.*

Some white southerners also used violence to coerce freed people into accepting a subordinate status within the new southern society. Clara Barton, who had organized women as nurses for the Union army, visited the South from 1866 to 1870 and observed "a condition of lawlessness toward the blacks" and "a

coercion Use of threats or force to compel action.

black codes Laws passed by the southern states after the Civil War to define the status of freed people as subordinate to whites.

vagrancy The legal condition of having no fixed place of residence or means of support.

disposition . . . to injure or kill them on slight or no provocation."

Violence and terror became closely associated with the **Ku Klux Klan,** a secret organization formed in 1866 and led by a former Confederate general. Most Klan members were small-scale farmers and workers, but the leaders were often prominent within their own communities. As one Freedmen's Bureau agent observed about the Klan, "The most respectable citizens are engaged in it." Klan groups existed throughout the South, but operated with little central control. Their major goals were to restore **white supremacy** and to destroy the Republican Party. Other, similar organizations also formed and adopted terrorist tactics.

Klan members were called ghouls. Officers included cyclops, night-hawks, and grand dragons, and the national leader was called the grand wizard. Klan members covered their faces with hoods, wore white robes, and rode horses draped in white as they set out to intimidate black Republicans and their Radical white allies. Klan members also attacked less politically prominent people, whipping African Americans accused of not showing sufficient deference to whites. Nightriders also burned black churches and schools. By such tactics, the Klan devastated Republican organizations in many communities.

In 1866 two events dramatized the violence that some white southerners were inflicting on African Americans. In early May, in Memphis, Tennessee, black veterans of the Union army came to the assistance of a black man being arrested by white police, setting off a three-day riot in which whites, including police, indiscriminately attacked African Americans. Forty-five blacks and three whites died. In late July, in New Orleans, some forty people died, most of them African Americans, in an altercation between police and a largely black prosuffrage group. General Philip Sheridan, the military commander of the district, called it "an absolute massacre by the police." Memphis and New Orleans were unusual only in the numbers of casualties. Local authorities often seemed uninterested in stopping such violence, and federal troops were not always available when they were needed.

The black codes, violence against freed people, and the failure of southern authorities to stem the violence turned northern opinion against President Johnson's lenient approach to Reconstruction. Increasing numbers of moderate Republicans accepted the Radicals' arguments that the freed people required greater federal protection, and congressional Republicans moved to take control of Reconstruction. When Johnson's stubborn and uncompromising personality ran up against the equally stubborn and uncompromising Thaddeus Stevens, the nation faced a constitutional crisis.

Challenging Presidential Reconstruction

In December 1865, the Thirty-ninth Congress (elected in 1864) met for the first time. Republicans outnumbered Democrats by more than three to one. The president's annual message proclaimed Reconstruction complete and the Union restored. Few Republicans agreed. Events in the South had convinced most moderate Republicans of the need to protect free labor in the South and to establish basic rights for the freed people. Most also agreed that Congress could withhold representation from the South until reconstructed state governments met these conditions.

On the first day of the Thirty-ninth Congress, moderate Republicans joined Radicals to exclude newly elected congressmen from the South. Citing Article I, Section 5, of the Constitution (which makes each house of Congress the judge of the qualifications of its members), Republicans set up a Joint Committee on Reconstruction to evaluate the qualifications of the excluded southerners and to determine whether the southern states were entitled to representation. Some committee members wanted to launch an investigation of presidential Reconstruction. In the meantime, the former Confederate states had no representation in Congress.

Congressional Republicans also moved to provide more assistance to the freed people. Moderates and Radicals approved a bill extending the Freedmen's

---

Congressional Reconstruction

■ Why did congressional Republicans take control over Reconstruction policy? What did they seek to accomplish? How successful were they?

■ How did the Fourteenth and Fifteenth Amendments change the nature of the federal Union?

Ku Klux Klan   A secret society organized in the South after the Civil War to resurrect white supremacy by means of violence and intimidation.

white supremacy   The racist belief that whites are inherently superior to all other races and are therefore entitled to rule over them.

These white southerners are shown taking the oath of allegiance to the United States in 1865, as part of the process of restoring civil government in the South. The Union soldiers and officers are administering the oath. *Library of Congress.*

Bureau and giving it more authority against racial discrimination. When Johnson vetoed it, Congress drafted a slightly revised version. Similar Republican unity produced a **civil rights** bill, a far-reaching measure that extended citizenship to African Americans and defined some of the rights guaranteed to all citizens. Johnson vetoed both the civil rights bill and the revised Freedmen's Bureau bill, but Congress passed both over his veto. With creation of the Joint Committee on Reconstruction and passage of the Civil Rights and Freedmen's Bureau Acts, Congress took control of Reconstruction.

The Civil Rights Act of 1866

The Civil Rights Act of 1866 defined all persons born in the United States (except Indians not taxed) as citizens. It also listed certain rights of all citizens, including the right to testify in court, own property, make contracts, bring lawsuits, and enjoy "full and equal benefit of all laws and proceedings for the security of person and property." This was the first effort to define in law some of the rights of American citizenship. It placed significant restrictions on state actions on the grounds that the rights of national citizenship

took precedence over the powers of state governments. The law expanded the power of the federal government in unprecedented ways and challenged traditional concepts of states' rights. Though the law applied to all citizens, its most immediate consequence was to benefit African Americans.

Much of the debate in Congress over the measure focused on the situation of the freed people. Some supporters saw the Civil Rights Act as a way to secure the freed people's basic rights. Some northern Republicans hoped the law would encourage freed people to stay in the South. For other Republicans, the bill carried broader implications because it empowered the federal government to force states to abide by the principle of equality before the law. They applauded its redefinition of federal-state relations. Senator Lot Morrill of Maine described it as "absolutely revolutionary" but added, "Are we not in the midst of a revolution?"

> **civil rights** The rights, privileges, and protections that are a part of citizenship.

When President Johnson vetoed the bill, he argued that it violated states' rights. By defending states' rights and taking aim at the Radicals, Johnson may have hoped to generate enough political support to elect a conservative Congress in 1866 and to win the presidency in 1868. He probably expected the veto to appeal to voters and to turn them against the Radicals. Instead, the veto led most moderate Republicans to give up all hope of cooperation with him. In April 1866, when Congress passed the Civil Rights Act over Johnson's veto, it was the first time ever that Congress had overridden a presidential veto of major legislation.

Defining Citizenship: The Fourteenth Amendment

Leading Republicans, though pleased that the Civil Rights Act was now law, worried that it could be amended or repealed by a later Congress or declared unconstitutional by the Supreme Court. Only a constitutional amendment, they concluded, could permanently safeguard the freed people's rights as citizens.

The **Fourteenth Amendment** began as a proposal made by Radicals seeking a constitutional guarantee of equality before the law. But the final wording—the longest of any amendment—resulted from many compromises. Section 1 of the amendment defined American citizenship in much the same way as the Civil Rights Act of 1866, then specified that

> No State shall make or enforce any law which shall abridge the privileges or immunities of citizens of the United States; nor shall any State deprive any person of life, liberty, or property, without due process of law; nor deny to any person within its jurisdiction the equal protection of the laws.

The Constitution and Bill of Rights prohibit federal interference with basic civil rights. The Fourteenth Amendment extends this protection against action by state governments.

The amendment was vague on some points. For example, it penalized states that did not **enfranchise** African Americans by reducing their congressional and electoral representation, but it did not specifically guarantee to African Americans the right to vote.

Some provisions of the amendment stemmed from Republicans' fears that a restored South, allied with northern Democrats, might try to undo the outcome of the war. One section barred from public office anyone who had sworn to uphold the federal Constitution and then "engaged in insurrection or rebellion against the same." Only a two-thirds vote of Con-

It Matters

The Fourteenth Amendment

The Fourteenth Amendment is one of the most important amendments to the Constitution, next to the Bill of Rights (the first ten amendments). One key change was the definition of American citizenship. The Constitution had no provisions regarding citizenship until the Fourteenth Amendment. The Fourteenth Amendment cleared up any confusion about who was, and who was not, a citizen.

The amendment also specified that no state could abridge the liberties of a citizen "without due process of law." Until this time, the Constitution and the Bill of Rights restricted action by the *federal* government to restrict individual liberties. The Fourteenth Amendment extends many of these restrictions to *state* governments. For example, the Supreme Court has interpreted the Fourteenth Amendment to mean that the restrictions placed on Congress by the First Amendment also restrict state governments—that no state government could abridge the freedom of speech, press, assembly, and religion. The Supreme Court continues to interpret these provisions when it is presented with new cases. For example, the Supreme Court cited this provision to conclude that states may not prevent residents from buying contraceptives, and also cited the due process clause, among others, in *Roe v. Wade*, to conclude that state laws may not prevent women from having abortions.

gress could override this provision. (In 1872 Congress passed a blanket measure pardoning nearly all former Confederates.) The amendment also prohibited federal or state governments from assuming any of the Confederate debt or from paying any claim arising from emancipation.

Fourteenth Amendment Constitutional amendment, ratified in 1868, defining American citizenship and placing restrictions on former Confederates.

enfranchise To grant the right to vote to an individual or group.

Not everyone approved of the final wording. Charles Sumner condemned the provision that permitted a state to deny suffrage to male citizens if it accepted a penalty in congressional representation. Stevens wanted to bar former Confederates not just from holding office but also from voting. Woman suffrage advocates, led by **Susan B. Anthony** and **Elizabeth Cady Stanton,** complained that the amendment, for the first time, introduced the word *male* into the Constitution in connection with voting rights.

Despite such concerns, Congress approved the Fourteenth Amendment by a straight party vote in June 1866 and sent it to the states for ratification. Johnson protested that Congress should not propose constitutional amendments until all representatives of the southern states had taken their seats. Tennessee promptly ratified the amendment, became the first reconstructed state government to be recognized by Congress, and was exempted from most later Reconstruction legislation.

Although Congress adjourned in the summer of 1866, the nation's attention remained fixed on Reconstruction. In May and July, the bloody riots in Memphis and New Orleans turned more moderates against Johnson's Reconstruction policies. Some interpreted the congressional elections that fall as a referendum on Reconstruction and the Fourteenth Amendment, pitting Johnson against the Radicals. Johnson undertook a speaking tour to promote his views, but one of his own supporters calculated that Johnson's reckless tirades alienated a million voters. Republicans swept the 1866 elections, outnumbering Democrats 143 to 49 in the new House of Representatives, and 42 to 11 in the Senate. Lyman Trumbull, senator from Illinois and a leading moderate, voiced the consensus of congressional Republicans: Congress should now "hurl from power the disloyal element" in the South.

Radicals in Control

As congressional Radicals struggled with Johnson over control of Reconstruction, it became clear that the Fourteenth Amendment might fall short of ratification. Rejection by ten states could prevent its acceptance. By March 1867, the amendment had been rejected by twelve states—Delaware, Kentucky, and all the former Confederate states except Tennessee. Moderate Republicans who had expected the Fourteenth Amendment to be the final Reconstruction measure now became more receptive to other proposals that the Radicals put forth.

The Military Reconstruction Act of 1867, passed on March 2 over Johnson's veto, divided the Confeder-ate states (except Tennessee) into five military districts. Each district was to be governed by a military commander authorized by Congress to use military force to protect life and property. The ten states were to hold constitutional conventions, and all adult male citizens were to vote, except former Confederates barred from office under the proposed Fourteenth Amendment. The constitutional conventions were to create new state governments that permitted black suffrage, and the new governments were to ratify the Fourteenth Amendment. Congress would then evaluate whether those state governments were to regain representation in Congress.

Congress had wrested a major degree of control over Reconstruction from the president, but it was not finished with him. On the same day, March 2, Congress further limited Johnson's powers. The Command of the Army Act specified that the president could issue military orders only through the General of the Army, then Ulysses S. Grant, considered an ally of Congress. It also specified that the General of the Army could not be removed without Senate permission. Congress thereby blocked Johnson from direct communication with military commanders in the South. The Tenure of Office Act specified that officials appointed with the Senate's consent were to remain in office until the Senate approved a successor, thereby preventing Johnson from removing federal officials who opposed his policies. Johnson understood both measures as invasions of presidential authority.

Early in 1867, some Radicals began to consider impeaching President Johnson. The Constitution (Article I, Sections 2 and 3) gives the House of Representatives exclusive power to **impeach** the president—that is, to charge the chief executive with misconduct. The Constitution specifies that the Senate shall hold trial on those charges, with the chief justice of the Supreme Court presiding. If found guilty by a two-thirds vote of the Senate, the president is removed from office.

In January 1867, the House Judiciary Committee investigated charges against Johnson but found no convincing evidence of misconduct. Johnson, however, challenged Congress over the Tenure of Office Act by

Susan B. Anthony   Tireless campaigner for woman suffrage and close associate of Elizabeth Cady Stanton.

Elizabeth Cady Stanton   A founder and leader of the American woman suffrage movement from 1848, and the Seneca Falls Conference, until her death in 1902.

impeach   To charge a public official with improper, usually criminal, conduct.

Tickets such as these were in high demand, for they permitted the holder to watch the historic proceedings as the Radical leaders presented their evidence to justify removing Andrew Johnson from the presidency. *Collection of Janice L. and David J. Frent.*

removing Edwin Stanton as secretary of war. This provocation gave Johnson's opponents something resembling a violation of law by the president. Still, an effort to secure impeachment through the House Judiciary Committee failed. The Joint Committee on Reconstruction, led by Thaddeus Stevens, then took over and developed charges against Johnson. On February 24, 1868, the House adopted eleven articles, or charges, nearly all based on the Stanton affair. The actual reasons the Radicals wanted Johnson removed were clear to all: they disliked him and his actions.

To convict Johnson and remove him from the presidency required a two-thirds vote by the Senate. Johnson's defenders argued that he had done nothing to warrant impeachment. The Radicals' legal case was weak, but they urged senators to vote on whether they wished Johnson to remain as president. Republican unity unraveled when some moderates, fearing a precedent of removing a president for such flimsy reasons, joined with Democrats to defeat the Radicals. The vote, on May 16 and 26, 1868, was 35 in favor of conviction and 19 against, one vote short of the required two-thirds. By this tiny margin, the Congress maintained the principle that it should not remove the president from office simply because they disagreed with or disliked each other.

Political Terrorism and the Election of 1868

The Radicals' failure to unseat Johnson left him with less than a year remaining in office. As the election approached, the Republicans nominated Ulysses S. Grant for president. A war hero, popular throughout the North, Grant had fully supported Lincoln and Congress in implementing emancipation. By 1868, he had committed himself to the congressional view of Reconstruction. The Democrats nominated Horatio Seymour, a former governor of New York, and focused their energies on denouncing Reconstruction.

In the South, the campaign stirred up fierce activity by the Ku Klux Klan and similar groups. **Terrorists** assassinated an Arkansas congressman, three members of the South Carolina legislature, and several other Republican leaders. Throughout the South, mobs attacked Republican offices and meetings, and sometimes attacked any black person they could find. Such coercion had its intended effect at the ballot box. For example, as many as two hundred blacks were killed in St. Landry Parish, Louisiana, where the Republicans previously had a thousand-vote majority. On election day, not a single Republican vote was recorded from that parish.

Despite such violence, many Americans may have been anticipating a calmer political future. In June 1868 Congress had readmitted seven southern states that met the requirements of congressional Reconstruction. In July, the secretary of state declared the Fourteenth Amendment ratified. In November, Grant easily won the presidency, carrying twenty-six of the thirty-four states and 53 percent of the vote.

Voting Rights and Civil Rights

With Grant in the White House, Radical Republicans now considered pressing for voting rights for all African Americans. In 1867 Congress had removed racial barriers to voting in the District of Columbia and in the territories, but elsewhere the states still defined voting rights. Congress had required southern states to enfranchise black males as the price of readmission to the Union, but only seven northern states had taken that step by 1869. Further, any state that had enfranchised African Americans could change its law to reverse the policy. In addition to the principled arguments of Douglass and other Radicals, many Republicans concluded that they needed to guarantee black suffrage in the South if they were to continue to win presidential elections and enjoy majorities in Congress.

> **terrorists** Those who use threats and violence to achieve ideological or political goals.

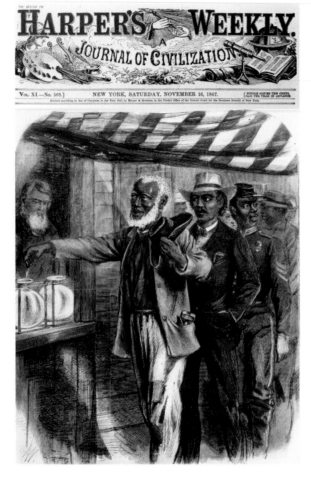

This engraving appeared on the cover of *Harper's Weekly* in November 1867. It shows black men lined up to cast their ballots in that fall's elections. Note that the artist has shown first an older black workingman, with his hammer in his pocket; and next a well-dressed young black man, probably a city-dweller and perhaps a leader in the emerging black community; and next a black Union soldier. Note, too, the open process of voting. Voters received a ballot (a "party ticket") from a party campaigner and deposited that ballot in a ballot box, in full sight of all. Voting was not secret until much later. *Harper's Weekly, Nov. 16, 1867. Granger Collection.*

moderates and Radicals. Some African American leaders argued for language guaranteeing voting rights to all male citizens, because prohibiting some grounds for **disfranchisement** might imply the legitimacy of other grounds. Some Radicals tried, unsuccessfully, to add "**nativity,** property, education, or religious beliefs" to the prohibited grounds. Democrats condemned the Fifteenth Amendment as a "revolutionary" change in the rights of states to define voting rights.

Elizabeth Cady Stanton, Susan B. Anthony, and other advocates of woman suffrage opposed the amendment because it ignored restrictions based on sex. For nearly twenty years, the cause of women's rights and the cause of black rights had marched together. Once black male suffrage came under discussion, however, this alliance began to fracture. When one veteran abolitionist declared it to be "the Negro's hour" and called for black male suffrage, Anthony responded that she "would sooner cut off my right hand than ask the ballot for the black man and not for woman." The break between the women's movement and the black movement was eventually papered over, but the wounds never completely healed.

Despite such opposition, within thirteen months the proposed amendment received the approval of enough states to take effect. Success came in part because Republicans, who might otherwise have been reluctant to impose black suffrage in the North, concluded that the future success of their party required black suffrage in the South.

The Fifteenth Amendment did nothing to reduce the violence—especially at election time—that had become almost routine in the South after 1865. When Klan activity escalated in the elections of 1870, southern Republicans looked to Washington for support. In 1870 and 1871, Congress adopted several Enforcement Acts—often called the Ku Klux Klan Acts—to enforce the Fourteenth and Fifteenth Amendments.

Despite a limited budget and many obstacles, the prosecution of Klansmen began in 1871. Across the South many hundreds were indicted, and many were convicted. In South Carolina, President Grant de-

To secure suffrage rights for all African Americans, Congress approved the **Fifteenth Amendment** in February 1869. Widely considered to be the final step in Reconstruction, the amendment prohibited both federal and state governments from restricting a person's right to vote because of "race, color, or previous condition of servitude." Like the Fourteenth Amendment, the Fifteenth marked a compromise between

Fifteenth Amendment Constitutional amendment, ratified in 1870, that prohibited states from denying the right to vote because of a person's race or because a person had been a slave.

disfranchisement The taking away of an individual's or group's right to vote.

nativity Place of birth.

clared martial law. By 1872, federal intervention had broken much of the strength of the Klan.

Congress eventually passed one final Reconstruction measure. Charles Sumner introduced a bill prohibiting **discrimination** in 1870 and in each subsequent session of Congress until his death in 1874. On his deathbed, Sumner urged his visitors to "take care of the civil-rights bill," begging them, "Don't let it fail." Passed after Sumner's death, the **Civil Rights Act of 1875** prohibited racial discrimination in the selection of juries and in public transportation and **public accommodations.**

This lithograph from 1883 depicts prominent African American men, several of whom had leading roles in Black Reconstruction. *Library of Congress.*

Black Reconstruction

■ What major groups made up the Republican Party in the South during Reconstruction? Compare their reasons for being Republicans, their relative size, and their objectives.

■ What were the most lasting results of the Republican state administrations?

Congressional Reconstruction set the stage for new developments at state and local levels throughout the South, as newly enfranchised black men organized for political action. African Americans never completely controlled any state government, but they did form a significant element in the governments of several states. The period when African Americans participated prominently in state and local politics is usually called **Black Reconstruction.** It began with efforts by African Americans to take part in politics as early as 1865 and lasted for more than a decade. A few African Americans continued to hold elective office in the South long after 1877, but they could do little to bring about significant political change.

The Republican Party in the South

Not surprisingly, nearly all African Americans who participated actively in politics did so as Republicans. African Americans formed the large majority of those who supported the Republican Party in the South. Nearly all black Republicans were new to politics, and they often braved considerable personal danger by participating in a party that many white southerners equated with the conquering Yankees. In the South, the Republican Party also included some southern whites along with a smaller number of transplanted northerners—both black and white.

Suffrage made politics a centrally important activity for African American communities. The state con-

stitutional conventions that met in 1868 included 265 black delegates. Only in Louisiana and South Carolina were half or more of the delegates black. With suffrage established, southern Republicans began to elect African Americans to public office. Between 1869 and 1877, fourteen black men served in the national House of Representatives, and Mississippi sent

discrimination   Denial of equal treatment based on prejudice or bias.

Civil Rights Act of 1875   Law passed by Congress in 1875 prohibiting racial discrimination in selection of juries and in transportation and other businesses open to the general public.

public accommodations   Hotels, bars and restaurants, theaters, and other places set up to do business with anyone who can pay the price of admission.

Black Reconstruction   The period of Reconstruction when African Americans took an active role in state and local government.

two African Americans to the U.S. Senate: Hiram R. Revels and Blanche K. Bruce.

Across the South, six African Americans served as lieutenant governors, and one of them, P. B. S. Pinchback, succeeded to the governorship of Louisiana for forty-three days. More than six hundred black men served in southern state legislatures during Reconstruction, but only in South Carolina did African Americans have a majority in the state legislature. Elsewhere they formed part of a Republican majority but rarely held key legislative positions. Only in South Carolina and Mississippi did legislatures elect black presiding officers.

Although politically inexperienced, most African Americans who held office during Reconstruction had some education. Of the eighteen who served in statewide offices, all but three are known to have been born free. P. B. S. Pinchback, for example, was educated in Ohio and served in the army as a captain before entering politics in Louisiana. Most black politicians first achieved prominence through service with the army, the Freedmen's Bureau, the new schools, or the religious and civic organizations of black communities.

Throughout the South, Republicans gained power only by securing some support from white voters. These white Republicans are usually remembered by the names fastened on them by their political opponents: "carpetbaggers" and "scalawags." Both groups included idealists who hoped to create a new southern society, but both also included opportunists expecting to exploit politics for personal gain.

Southern Democrats applied the term *carpetbagger* to northern Republicans who came to the South after the war, regarding them as second-rate schemers—outsiders with their belongings packed in a carpet bag. In fact, most northerners who came south were well-educated men and women from middle-class backgrounds. Most men had served in the Union army and moved south before blacks could vote. Some were lawyers, businessmen, or newspaper editors. Whether as investors in agricultural land, teachers in the new schools, or agents of the Freedmen's Bureau, most hoped to transform the South by creating new institutions based on northern models, especially free labor and free public schools. Few in number compared with southerners, transplanted northerners nonetheless took leading roles in state constitutional conventions and state legislatures. Some were also prominent advocates of economic modernization.

Southern Democrats reserved their greatest contempt for those they called *scalawags,* slang for

Bags made of carpeting, like this one, were inexpensive luggage for traveling. Southern opponents of Reconstruction fastened the label "carpetbaggers" on northerners who came south to participate in Reconstruction, suggesting that they were cheap opportunists. *Collection of Picture Research Consultants.*

someone completely unscrupulous and worthless. Scalawags were white southerners who became Republicans. They included many southern Unionists, who had opposed secession, and others who thought the Republicans offered the best hope for economic recovery. Scalawags included merchants, artisans, and professionals who favored a modernized South. Others were small-scale farmers who saw Reconstruction as a way to end political domination by the plantation owners.

The freedmen, carpetbaggers, and scalawags who made up the Republican Party in the South hoped to inject new ideas into that region. They tried to modernize state and local governments and make the postwar South more like the North. They repealed outdated laws and established or expanded schools, hospitals, orphanages, and penitentiaries.

carpetbagger Derogatory term for the northerners who came to the South after the Civil War to take part in Reconstruction.

scalawag Derogatory term for white southerners who aligned themselves with the Republican Party during Reconstruction.

The Hampton Normal and Agricultural Institute was founded in 1868 with financial assistance from the Freedmen's Bureau and the American Missionary Association. Its purpose was to provide education for African Americans to prepare males for jobs in agriculture or industry, and to prepare women as homemakers. As a normal school, it also trained teachers. One of Hampton's most prominent graduates was Booker T. Washington, who attended shortly after this picture was taken around 1870. *Archival and Museum Collection, Hampton University.*

Creating an Educational System and Fighting Discrimination

Free public education was perhaps the most permanent legacy of Black Reconstruction. Reconstruction constitutions throughout the South required tax-supported public schools. Implementation, however, was expensive and proceeded slowly. By the mid-1870s, only half of southern children attended public schools.

In creating public schools, Reconstruction state governments faced a central question: would white and black children attend the same schools? Many blacks favored racially integrated schools. On the other hand, southern white leaders, including many southern white Republicans, argued that integration would destroy the fledgling public school system by driving whites away. In consequence, no state required school integration. Similarly, southern states set up separate black normal schools (to train schoolteachers) and colleges.

On balance, most blacks probably agreed with Frederick Douglass that separate schools were "infinitely superior" to no public education at all. Some found other reasons to accept segregated schools: separate black schools gave a larger role to black parents, and they hired black teachers.

Funding for the new schools was rarely adequate. Creating and operating two educational systems, one white and one black, was costly. The division of limited funds posed an additional problem, and black schools almost always received less support per student than white schools. Despite their accomplishments, the segregated schools institutionalized discrimination.

Reconstruction state governments moved toward protection of equal rights in areas other than education.

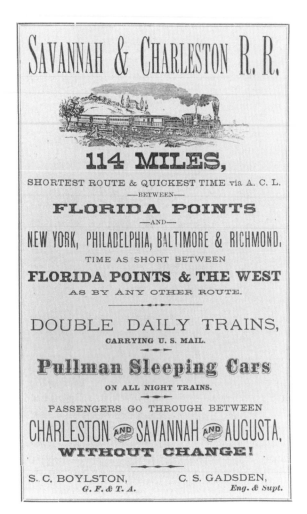

In the period after the Civil War, political leaders of all parties eagerly sought to encourage railroad construction because railroads were equated with economic development and prosperity. This advertisement for the Savannah and Charleston Railroad appeared in 1878. *Charleston City Directory for 1878, South Carolina Historical Society.*

As Republicans gained control in the South, they often wrote into the new state constitutions prohibitions against discrimination and protections for civil rights. Some Reconstruction state governments enacted laws guaranteeing **equal access** to public transportation and public accommodations. Elsewhere efforts to pass equal access laws foundered on the opposition of southern white Republicans, who often joined Democrats to favor **segregation.** Such conflicts pointed up the internal divisions within the southern Republican Party. Even when equal access laws were passed, they were often not enforced.

Railroad Development and Corruption

Across the nation, Republicans sought to use the power of government to encourage economic growth and development. Efforts to promote economic development—North, South, and West—often focused on encouraging railroad construction. In the South, as elsewhere in the nation, some state governments granted state lands to railroads, or lent them money, or committed the state's credit to **underwrite** bonds for construction. Sometimes they promoted railroads without adequate planning or determining whether companies were financially sound. Some efforts to promote railroad construction failed as companies squandered funds without building rail lines. During the 1870s, only 7,000 miles of new track were laid in the South, compared with 45,000 miles elsewhere in the nation. Even that was a considerable accomplishment for the South, given its dismal economic situation.

Railroad companies sometimes sought favorable treatment by bribing public officials. All too many officeholders—North, South, and West—accepted their offers. Given the excessive favoritism that most public officials showed to railroads, revelations and allegations of corruption became common from New York City to Mississippi to California.

Conditions in the South were ripe for political corruption as government responsibilities expanded rapidly and created new opportunities for scoundrels. Many Reconstruction officials—white and black—had only modest holdings of their own and wanted more. One South Carolina legislator bluntly described his attitude toward electing a U.S. senator: "I was pretty hard up, and I did not care who the candidate was if I got two hundred dollars." Corruption was usually nonpartisan, but it seemed more prominent among Republicans because they held the most important offices. One Louisiana Republican claimed, "Corruption is the fashion." Charges of corruption became

equal access The right of any person to use a public facility, such as streetcars, as freely as other people in the society.

segregation Separation on account of race or class from the rest of society, such as the separation of blacks from whites in most southern school systems.

underwrite To assume financial responsibility for; in this case, to guarantee the purchase of bonds so that a project can go forward.

common everywhere in the nation as politicians sought to discredit their opponents.

The End of Reconstruction

■ What major factors brought about the end of Reconstruction? Evaluate their relative significance.

■ Many historians began to reevaluate their interpretations of Reconstruction during the 1950s and 1960s. Why do you suppose that happened?

From the beginning, most white southerners resisted the new order that the conquering Yankees imposed on them. Initially, resistance took the form of black codes and the Klan. Later, some southern opponents of Reconstruction developed new strategies, but terror remained an important instrument of resistance.

The "New Departure"

By 1869, some leading southern Democrats had abandoned their last-ditch resistance to change, deciding instead to accept some Reconstruction measures and African American suffrage. At the same time, they also tried to secure restoration of political rights for former Confederates. Behind this **New Departure** for southern Democrats lay the belief that continued resistance would only cause more regional turmoil and prolong federal intervention.

Sometimes southern Democrats supported conservative Republicans for state and local offices instead of members of their own party, hoping to defuse concern in Washington and dilute Radical influence in state government. This strategy was tried first in Virginia, the last southern state to hold an election under its new constitution. There William Mahone, a former Confederate general, railroad promoter, and leading Democrat, forged a broad political **coalition** that accepted black suffrage. In 1869 Mahone's organization elected as governor a northern-born banker and moderate Republican. In this way, Mahone got state support for his railroad plans, and Virginia successfully avoided Radical Republican rule.

Coalitions of Democrats and moderate Republicans won in Tennessee in 1869 and in Missouri in 1870. Elsewhere leading Democrats endorsed the New Departure, accepted black suffrage, and attacked Republicans more for raising taxes and increasing state spending than for their racial policies. And Democrats almost always charged Republicans with corruption. Such campaigns brought a positive response

from many taxpayers because southern tax rates had risen drastically to support the new educational systems, railroad subsidies, and other modernizing programs. In 1870 Democrats won the governorship in Alabama and Georgia. For Georgia, it meant the end of Reconstruction.

The victories of so-called **Redeemers** and New Departure Democrats in the early 1870s coincided with renewed terrorist activity aimed at Republicans. The worst single incident occurred in 1873. A group of armed freedmen fortified the town of Colfax, Louisiana, to hold off Democrats who were planning to seize the county government. After a three-week siege, well-armed whites overcame the black defenders and killed 280 African Americans. Leading Democrats rarely endorsed such bloodshed, but they reaped political advantages from it.

The 1872 Presidential Election

The New Departure movement, at its peak in 1872, coincided with a division within the Republican Party in the North. The Liberal Republican movement grew out of several elements within the Republican Party. Some were moderates, concerned that the Radicals had gone too far, especially with the Enforcement Acts, and had endangered federalism. Others opposed Grant on issues unrelated to Reconstruction. All were appalled by growing evidence of corruption in Washington. Liberal Republicans found allies among Democrats by arguing against further Reconstruction measures.

Horace Greeley, editor of the *New York Daily Tribune,* won the Liberal nomination for president. An opponent of slavery before the Civil War, Greeley had given strong support to the Fourteenth and Fifteenth Amendments. But he had sometimes taken puzzling positions, including a willingness to let the South secede. His unkempt appearance and whining voice conveyed little of a presidential image. One political

---

New Departure   Strategy of cooperation with some Reconstruction measures adopted by some leading southern Democrats in the hope of winning compromises favorable to their party.

coalition   An alliance, especially a temporary one of different people or groups.

Redeemers   Southern Democrats who hoped to bring the Democratic Party back into power and to suppress Black Reconstruction.

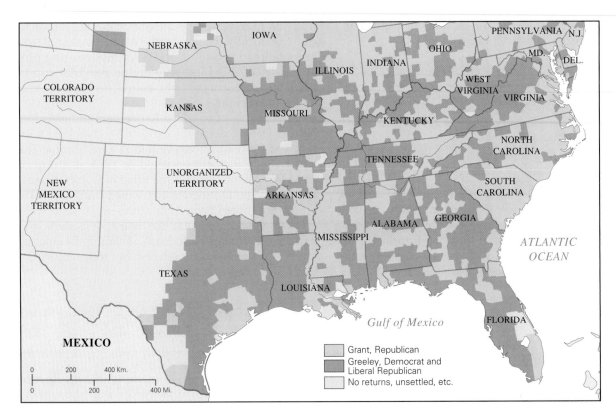

[[X-REF]]

MAP 16.1 Popular Vote for President in the South, 1872 This map shows which candidate carried each county in the southeastern United States in 1872. Looking at both this map and the chapter-opening map, you can see the relation between Republican voting and African American population in some areas, as well as where the southern Republican Party drew strong support from white voters.

observer described him as "honest, but . . . conceited, fussy, and foolish."

Greeley had long ripped the Democrats in his newspaper columns. Even so, the Democrats nominated him in an effort to defeat Grant. Many saw the Democrats' action as desperate opportunism, and Greeley alienated many northern Democrats by favoring restrictions on the sale of alcohol. Grant won convincingly, carrying 56 percent of the vote and winning every northern state and ten of the sixteen southern and border states (see Map 16.1).

The Politics of Terror: The "Mississippi Plan"

By the 1872 presidential race, nearly all southern whites had abandoned the Republicans, and Black Reconstruction had ended in several states. African Americans, however, maintained their Republican loyalties. As Democrats worked to unite all southern whites behind their banner of white supremacy, the South polarized politically along racial lines. Elections in 1874 proved disastrous for Republicans: Democrats won more than two-thirds of the South's seats in the House of Representatives and "redeemed" Alabama, Arkansas, and Texas.

Terrorism against black Republicans and their remaining white allies played a role in some victories by Democrats in 1874. Where the Klan had worn disguises and ridden at night, by 1874 in many places Democrats openly formed rifle companies, put on red-flannel shirts, and marched and drilled in public. In some areas, armed whites prevented African Americans from voting or terrorized prominent Republicans, especially African American Republicans.

Republican candidates in 1874 also lost support in the North because of scandals within the Grant administration and because a major economic **depression** that had begun in 1873 was producing high unemployment. Before the 1874 elections, the House of Representatives included 194 Republicans and 92 Democrats. After those elections, Democrats outnumbered Republicans by 169 to 109. Now southern Republicans could no longer look to Congress for assistance. Even though Republicans still controlled the Senate, the Democratic majority in the House of Representatives could block any new Reconstruction legislation.

During 1875 in Mississippi, political violence reached such levels that the use of terror to overthrow Reconstruction became known as the **Mississippi Plan.** Democratic rifle clubs broke up Republican meetings and attacked Republican leaders in broad daylight. One black Mississippian described the election of 1875 as "the most violent time we have ever seen." When Mississippi's carpetbagger governor, Adelbert Ames, requested federal help, President Grant declined, fearful that the southern Reconstruction governments had become so discredited that further federal military intervention might endanger the election prospects of Republican candidates in the North.

The Democrats swept the Mississippi elections, winning four-fifths of the state legislature. When the legislature convened, it impeached and removed from office Alexander Davis, the black Republican lieutenant governor, on grounds no more serious than those brought against Andrew Johnson. The legislature then brought similar impeachment charges against Governor Ames, who resigned and left the state. Ames had foreseen the result during the campaign when he wrote, "A revolution has taken place—by force of arms."

The Compromise of 1877

In 1876, on the centennial of American independence, the nation stumbled through a deeply troubled—and potentially dangerous—presidential election. As revelations of corruption multiplied, the issue of reform took center stage. The Democratic Party nominated Samuel J. Tilden, governor of New York, as its presidential candidate. A wealthy lawyer and businessman, Tilden had earned a reputation as a reformer by fighting political corruption in New York City. The Republicans selected **Rutherford B. Hayes,** a Civil War general and governor of Ohio, whose unblemished reputation proved to be his greatest asset. Not well known outside Ohio, he was a candidate nobody could object to. During the campaign in the South, intimidation of Republicans, both black and white, continued in many places.

First election reports indicated a victory for Tilden (see Map 16.2). In addition to the border states and South, he also carried New York, New Jersey, and Indiana. Tilden received 51 percent of the popular vote versus 48 percent for Hayes. Leading Republicans quickly realized that their party still controlled the counting and reporting of ballots in South Carolina, Florida, and Louisiana, and that those three states could change the Electoral College majority from Tilden to Hayes. Charging **voting fraud,** Republican election boards in those states rejected enough ballots so that the official count gave Hayes narrow majorities and thus a one-vote margin of victory in the Electoral College. Crying fraud in return, Democratic officials in all three states submitted their own versions of the vote count.

Angry Democrats vowed to see Tilden inaugurated, by force if necessary, and some Democratic newspapers ran headlines that read "Tilden or War." For the first time, Congress faced the problem of disputed electoral votes that could decide the outcome of an election. To resolve the challenges, Congress created a commission: five senators, chosen by the Senate, which had a Republican majority; five representatives, chosen by the House, which had a Democratic majority; and five Supreme Court justices, chosen by the justices. Initially, the balance was seven Republicans, seven Democrats, and one independent from the Supreme Court. The independent withdrew, however, and the remaining justices (all but one of whom had been appointed by Republican presidents) chose a Republican to replace him. The Republicans now had a one-vote majority on the commission.

This body needed to make its decision before the constitutionally mandated deadline of March 4. Some Democrats and Republicans worried over the potential for violence. However, as commission hearings droned on through January and into February 1877, informal discussions took place among leading

---

depression A period of economic contraction, characterized by decreasing business activity, falling prices, and high unemployment.

Mississippi Plan Use of threats, violence, and lynching by Mississippi Democrats in 1875 to intimidate Republicans and bring the Democratic Party to power.

Rutherford B. Hayes Ohio governor and former Union general who won the Republican nomination in 1876 and became president of the United States in 1877.

voting fraud Altering election results by illegal measures to bring about the victory of a particular candidate.

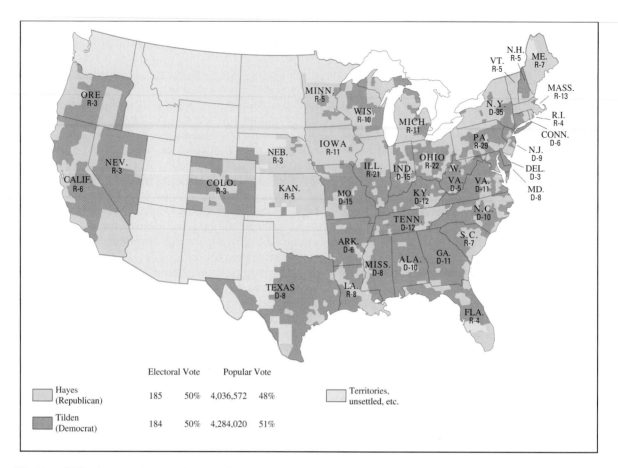

MAP 16.2 Election of 1876 The end of Black Reconstruction in most of the South combined with Democratic gains in the North to give a popular majority to Samuel Tilden, the Democratic candidate. The electoral vote was disputed, however, and was ultimately resolved in favor of Rutherford B. Hayes, the Republican.

Republicans and Democrats. The result was often called the **Compromise of 1877.**

Southern Democrats demanded an end to federal intervention in southern politics but insisted on federal subsidies for railroad construction and waterways in the South. And they wanted one of their own as postmaster general because that office held the key to most federal patronage. In return, southern Democrats seemed willing to abandon Tilden's claim to the White House.

Although the Compromise of 1877 was never set down in one place or agreed to by all parties, most of its conditions were met. By a straight party vote, the commission confirmed the election of Hayes. Soon after his peaceful inauguration, the new president ordered the last of the federal troops withdrawn from occupation duties in the South. The Radical era of a powerful federal government pledged to protect "equality before the law" for all citizens was over. The last three Republican state governments fell in 1877. The Democrats, the self-described party of white supremacy, now held sway in every southern state. One Radical journal bitterly concluded that African Americans had been forced "to relinquish the artificial right to vote for the natural right to live." In parts

Compromise of 1877 Name applied by historians to the resolution of the disputed presidential election of 1876; it gave the presidency to the Republicans and made concessions to southern Democrats.

of the South thereafter, election fraud and violence became routine. One Mississippi judge acknowledged in 1890 that "since 1875 . . . we have been preserving the ascendancy of the white people by . . . stuffing ballot boxes, committing perjury and here and there in the state carrying the elections by fraud and violence."

The Compromise of 1877 marked the end of Reconstruction. The Civil War was more than ten years in the past. Many moderate Republicans had hoped that the Fourteenth and Fifteenth Amendments and the Civil Rights Act would guarantee black rights without a continuing federal presence in the South. Southern Democrats tried hard to persuade northerners—on paltry evidence—that carpetbaggers and scalawags were all corrupt and self-serving, that they manipulated black voters to keep themselves in power, that African American officeholders were ignorant and illiterate and could not participate in politics without guidance by whites, and that southern Democrats wanted only to establish honest self-government. The truth of the situation made little difference.

Northern Democrats had always opposed Reconstruction and readily adopted the southern Democrats' version of reality. Such portrayals found growing acceptance among other northerners too, for many had shown their own racial bias when they resisted black suffrage and kept their public schools segregated. In 1875, when Grant refused to use federal troops to protect black rights, he declared that "the whole public are tired out with these . . . outbreaks in the South." He was quoted widely and with approval throughout the North.

In addition, a major depression in the mid-1870s, unemployment and labor disputes, the growth of industry, the emergence of big business, and the development of the West focused the attention of many Americans, including many members of Congress, on economic issues.

Some Republicans, to be certain, kept the faith of their abolitionist and Radical forebears and hoped the federal government might again protect black rights. After 1877, however, though Republicans routinely condemned violations of black rights, few Republicans showed much interest in using federal power to prevent such outrages.

After Reconstruction

Southern Democrats read the events of 1877 as permission to establish new systems of politics and race relations. Most Redeemers worked to reduce taxes, dismantle Reconstruction legislation and agencies, and grab political influence away from black citizens. They also began the process of turning the South into a one-party region, a situation that reached its fullest development around 1900 and persisted until the 1950s and in some areas later.

Voting and officeholding by African Americans did not cease in 1877, but the context changed profoundly. Without federal enforcement of black rights, the threat of violence and the potential for economic retaliation by landlords and merchants sharply reduced meaningful political involvement by African Americans. Black political leaders soon understood that efforts to mobilize black voters posed dangers to candidates and voters, and they concluded that their political survival depended on favors from influential white Republicans or even from Democratic leaders. The public schools survived, segregated and underfunded, but presenting an important opportunity. Many Reconstruction-era laws remained on the books. Through much of the 1880s, many theaters, bars, restaurants, hotels, streetcars, and railroads continued to serve African Americans without discrimination.

Not until the 1890s did black disfranchisement and thoroughgoing racial segregation become widely embedded in southern law. From the mid-1870s to the late 1890s, African Americans exercised some constitutional rights. White supremacy had been established by force of arms, however, and blacks exercised their rights at the sufferance of the dominant whites. Such a situation bore the seeds of future conflict.

After 1877, Reconstruction was held up as a failure. Although far from accurate, the southern version of Reconstruction—that conniving carpetbaggers and scalawags had manipulated ignorant freedmen—appealed to many white Americans throughout the nation, and it gained widespread acceptance among many novelists, journalists, and historians. William A. Dunning, for example, endorsed that interpretation in his history of Reconstruction, published in 1907. Thomas Dixon's popular novel *The Clansman* (1905) inspired the highly influential film *The Birth of a Nation* (1915). Historically inaccurate and luridly racist, the book and the movie portrayed Ku Klux Klan members as heroes who rescued the white South, and especially white southern women, from domination and debauchery at the hands of depraved freedmen and carpetbaggers.

Against this pattern stood some of the first black historians, notably George Washington Williams, a Union army veteran whose two-volume history of African

Americans appeared in 1882. *Black Reconstruction in America,* by W. E. B. Du Bois, appeared in 1935. Both presented fully the role of African Americans in Reconstruction and pointed to the accomplishments of the Reconstruction state governments and black leaders. Not until the 1950s and 1960s, however, did large numbers of American historians begin to reconsider their interpretations of Reconstruction. Historians today recognize that Reconstruction was not the failure that had earlier been claimed. The creation of public schools was the most important of the changes in southern life produced by the Reconstruction state governments. At a federal level, the Fourteenth and Fifteenth Amendments eventually provided the constitutional leverage to restore the principle of equality before the law that so concerned the Radicals. Historians also recognize that Reconstruction collapsed partly because of internal flaws, partly because of divisions within the Republican Party, and partly because of the political terrorism unleashed in the South and the refusal of the North to commit the force required to protect the constitutional rights of African Americans.

■ How does the author indicate that the lives of these freed people have changed by leaving Tennessee for Ohio?

Individual Voices

Examining a Primary Source

A Freedman Offers His Former Master a Proposition

This letter appeared in the *New York Daily Tribune* on August 22, 1865, with the notation that it was a "genuine document," reprinted from the *Cincinnati Commercial.* At that time, all newspapers had strong connections to political parties, and both of these papers were allied to the Republicans. By then, battle lines were being drawn between President Andrew Johnson and Republicans in Congress over the legal and political status of the freed people.

DAYTON, Ohio, August 7, 1865

To my Old Master, Col. P. H. Anderson, Big Spring, Tennessee

Sir: I got your letter and was glad to find that you had not forgotten Jordan, and that you wanted me to come back and live with you again, promising to do better for me than anybody else can. . . .

I want to know particularly what the good chance is you propose to give me. I am doing tolerably well here; I get $25 a month, with victuals and clothing; have a comfortable home for Mandy (the folks here call her Mrs. Anderson), and the children, Milly[,] Jane and Grundy, go to school and are learning well. . . . Now, if you will write and say what wages you will give me, I will be better able to decide whether it would be to my advantage to move back again. ■

As to my freedom, which you say I can have, there is nothing to be gained on that score, as I got my free-papers in 1864 from the Provost-Marshal-General of the Department at Nashville. Mandy says she would be afraid to go back without some proof that you are sincerely disposed to treat us justly and kindly—and we have concluded to test your sincerity by asking you to send us our wages for the time we served you. This will make us forget and forgive old sores, and rely on

■ Anderson's monthly wages of $25 in 1865 would be equivalent to about $2,280 today. The amount he asks for as compensation for his slave labor, $11,680, in 1865 would be equivalent to more than $130,000 today.

■ How does the author use this letter to raise a wide range of issues about the nature of slavery and about the uneasiness of freed people about life in the South in 1865?

■ Evaluate the likelihood that this letter was actually written by a former slave. What are the other possibilities? Why do you think this letter appeared in newspapers in August of 1865?

your justice and friendship in the future. I served you faithfully for thirty-two years, and Mandy twenty years, at $25 a month for me and $2 a week for Mandy. Our earnings would amount to $11,680. ■ *Add to this the interest for the time our wages has been kept back and deduct what you paid for our clothing and three doctor's visits to me, and pulling a tooth for Mandy, and the balance will show what we are in justice entitled to. . . . If you fail to pay us for faithful labors in the past we can have little faith in your promises in the future. We trust the good Maker has opened your eyes to the wrongs which you and your fathers have done to me and my fathers, in making us toil for you for generations without recompense. . . .*

In answering this letter please state if there would be any safety for my Milly and Jane, who are now grown up and both good looking girls. You know how it was with poor Matilda and Catherine. I would rather stay here and starve and die if it had to come to that than have my girls brought to shame by the violence and wickedness of their young masters. You will also please state if there has been any schools opened for the colored children in your neighborhood, the great desire of my life now is to give my children an education, and have them form virtuous habits. ■

From your old servant, ■ JOURDAN ANDERSON.

P.S.—Say howdy to George Carter, and thank him for taking the pistol from you when you were shooting at me.

Summary

At the end of the Civil War, the nation faced difficult choices regarding the restoration of the defeated South and the future of the freed people. Committed to ending slavery, President Lincoln nevertheless chose a lenient approach to restoring states to the Union, partly to persuade southerners to accept emancipation and abandon the Confederacy. When Johnson became president, he continued Lincoln's approach.

The end of slavery brought new opportunities for African Americans, whether or not they had been slaves. Taking advantage of the opportunities that freedom opened, they tried to create independent lives for themselves, and they developed social institutions that helped to define black communities. Because few were able to acquire land of their own, most became either sharecroppers or wage laborers. White southerners also experienced economic dislocation, and many also became sharecroppers. Most white southerners expected to keep African Americans in a subordinate role and initially used black codes and violence toward that end.

In reaction against the black codes and violence, Congress took control of Reconstruction away from President Johnson and passed the Civil Rights Act of 1866, the Fourteenth Amendment, and the Reconstruction Acts of 1867. An attempt to remove Johnson from the presidency was unsuccessful. Additional federal Reconstruction measures included the Fifteenth Amendment, laws directed against the Ku Klux Klan, and the Civil Rights Act of 1875. Several of these measures strengthened the federal government at the expense of the states.

Enfranchised freedmen, white and black northerners who moved to the South, and some southern whites created a southern Republican Party that governed most southern states for a time. The most lasting contribution of these state governments was the creation of public school systems. Like government officials elsewhere in the nation, however, some southern politicians fell prey to corruption.

In the late 1860s, many southern Democrats chose a "New Departure": they grudgingly accepted some features of Reconstruction and sought to recapture control of state governments. By the mid-1870s, however, southern politics turned almost solely on race. The 1876 presidential election was very close and hotly disputed. Key Republicans and Democrats developed a compromise: Hayes took office and ended the final stages of Reconstruction. Without federal protection for their civil rights, African Americans faced terrorism, violence, and even death if they challenged their subordinate role. With the end of Reconstruction, the South entered an era of white supremacy in politics and government, the economy, and social relations.

INDUSTRIALIZATION After the Civil War, manufacturing expanded significantly, especially in the Northeast. This map indicates the major types of manufacturing that had developed by the late nineteenth century, and also the locations of major natural resources. Some of these resources were not exploited until the twentieth century.

CANADA

WASHINGTON TERRITORY

OREGON

IDAHO TERRITORY

MONTANA TERRITORY

DAKOTA TERRITORY

WYOMING TERRITORY

NEVADA

UTAH TERRITORY

COLORADO

CALIFORNIA

San Francisco

ARIZONA TERRITORY

NEW MEXICO TERRITORY

NEBRASKA

KANSAS

UNORGANIZED TERRITORY

TEXAS

MINN.

WISCONSIN

Minneapolis

Milwaukee

Chicago

IOWA

ILLINOIS

MISSOURI

St. Louis

ARKANSAS

MEXICO

MICH.

Detroit

IND.

Cincinnati

KENTUCKY

Louisville

TENNESSEE

MISS.

ALABAMA

LOUISIANA

New York

Jersey City

Rochester

Buffalo

Cleveland

Pittsburgh

OHIO

WEST VA.

VIRGINIA

NORTH CAROLINA

SOUTH CAROLINA

GEORGIA

FLORIDA

MAINE

VT.

N.H.

MASS.

Bos

NEW YORK

CONN.

Provider R.I.

Brooklyn

Newark

PENNSYLVANIA

Philadelphia

N.J.

DEL.

MD.

Baltimore

Lake Superior

Lake Michigan

Lake Huron

L. Ontario

L. Erie

Missouri

Mississippi

Ohio

PACIFIC OCEAN

Gulf of Mexico

ATLANTIC OCEAN

Products manufactured in 20 largest cities
- Clothing
- Flour milling
- Food, beverage, and tobacco processing
- Foundry and machine shop products
- Iron and steel
- Printing and publishing
- Slaughtering and meatpacking
- Textiles
- Mixed or other

Natural resources
- Ag   Silver
- Au   Gold
- C   Coal
- Cu   Copper
- Fe   Iron ore
- O   Oil (petroleum)
- Pb   Lead
- Timber Timber

States with 25% or more of employees in manufacturing

0   200   400 Km.

0   200   400 Mi.

1865 Civil War ends

1866 First Grange

1867 Purchase of Alaska

1869 First transcontinental railroad

1873 Major depression begins U.S. adopts gold standard

1875 Carnegie opens largest steel plant in U.S.

1876 Disputed presidential election

1877 Reconstruction ends Great Railway Strike

| 1865 | 1866 | 1867 | 1868 | 1869 | 1870 | 1871 | 1872 | 1873 | 1874 | 1875 | 1876 | 1877 | 1878 |

1867 French troops withdraw from Mexico

Canada becomes self-governing dominion

1869 Suez Canal opens

1870–1871 Prussia defeats France in war

1871 Germany unifies and adopts gold standard

1875 Netherlands adopts gold standard

1876 Queen Victoria of England becomes Empress of India

1878 France adopts gold standard

An Industrial Order Emerges, 1865–1880

Industrialization
What relation does the map on the facing page suggest
among the location of raw materials, the location of the
twenty largest cities, and manufacturing?

Individual Choices

FRANK RONEY

This photograph of Frank Roney was probably taken in the 1880s when Roney was head of the San Francisco Trades Assembly, an umbrella organization for the city's trade unions. *Bancroft Library, University of California, Berkeley.*

Frank Roney

Frank Roney arrived in New York from Ireland in 1868. Born in 1841, he had served a seven-year apprenticeship to become an iron molder. (Iron molders make objects of cast iron by heating iron until it melts and pouring it into molds.) His father was a skilled carpenter and an officer in the carpenters' union. Some of the skilled iron molders from whom Roney learned his trade also taught him about the Friendly Society of Iron Molders, the Irish trade union for molders. Both his father and his mentors, then, had a role in introducing him to organized labor. Around the age of 21, Roney completed his apprenticeship and qualified as a journeyman (skilled) iron molder. Soon he became involved with the struggle for Irish independence from England and was imprisoned. A sympathetic judge gave Roney the chance to go free if he would leave Ireland and go to America.

Roney found that many American foundry workers lacked the self-respect he associated with his craft. In Ireland, molders "worked rationally, intelligently, and well, and had some of their work remaining for the next day." By contrast, "American molders seemed desirous of doing all the work required as if it were the last day of their lives." Roney learned that many American workers were paid by the piece rather than by the day, so that the more work they did, the more they were paid. Wages, he discovered, "were periodically reduced" and "the more this was done and the greater the reduction, the harder the men worked" to earn the same pay. Roney was appalled. For him, being a skilled iron molder was a mark of status, and he found the pace maintained by the American workers to be not only physically exhausting but personally degrading.

He worked for a time in Jersey City, New Jersey, and then sampled life in St. Louis and Chicago. Chicago foundries, he discovered, also "operated on the breakneck principle," and he lost his position there when he refused to work overtime without extra pay. Traveling to Omaha, he worked in the shops of the Union Pacific Railroad and quickly became an officer in Iron Molders Union No. 190. William Sylvis, the national president of the molders' union, was also head of the National Labor Union, and Roney eagerly joined up, hoping the new organization and its associated political party might accomplish its goal of abolishing poverty. After the collapse of that party, he went to Salt Lake City for a time, and then pushed on to San Francisco, arriving in 1875.

In San Francisco, Roney secured work in the Union Iron Works, the largest foundry on the Pacific Coast. He was again disgusted by the workers around him. "No foreman was needed to urge these men to work to the point of exhaustion. They labored hard of their volition and displayed an eagerness most discouraging to one who wished to see each of them [behave like] a man." Manliness, for Roney, involved dignity. He became active in the local molders' union and helped to form the Trades and Labor Assembly, a central body for trade unions. But a major concern remained—the work habits of his fellow molders. "Men who work

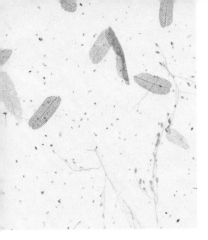

as hacks and drudges are not those from whom to expect high thoughts or ideas of social improvement," he wrote. "A slavish worker," he argued, "has a slavish mind." He set out, in the shop and in union meetings, to persuade his fellow workers by word and deed to recognize the evils of "rushing" and competing with one another. Gradually, he sensed some success, and with it came the growth of the union. Roney emerged as an officer and then became a leader of organized labor more generally in the city. Under his leadership, many San Francisco unions gained members and strength. Once again, however, union activism cost Roney his job, and eventually he stopped his union work to devote his full attention to supporting his family.

INTRODUCTION

Frank Roney's experiences in the iron works and the union hall came amidst an economy that was being dramatically and profoundly transformed. At the end of the Civil War, in 1865, more than half of all American workers toiled in agriculture. Anyone contemplating the prospects for manufacturing would have been struck by the obstacles: a poorly developed transportation system, limited amounts of capital, an unsophisticated system for mobilizing funds, and an uncertain labor force. Some, however, would have pointed to the great potential evident in America's vast natural resources and skilled workers

A generation later, by 1900, much of that potential had been realized, and the United States stood as a major industrial power. The changes in the nation's economy far exceeded the wildest expectations of Americans living in 1865. Many then probably anticipated economic growth, but few could have imagined that steel production could increase a thousand times by 1900, or that railroads could operate nearly six times as many miles of track, or that farms could triple their harvests. These economic changes and many others were the result of decisions by many individuals—where to seek work, where to invest, whether to expand production, how to react to a business competitor, whom to trust. Like Roney, many Americans also had to make choices about competition and cooperation.

As the industrial economy took off, many people found themselves in a love-hate relationship with competition. Andrew Carnegie, leader of the new steel industry, loved it, arguing that competition "insures the survival of the fittest" and "insures the future progress of the race" by producing the highest quality, largest quantity, and lowest prices. Other entrepreneurs saw competition as the single most unpredictable factor they faced and a serious constraint on economic progress. Carnegie's zeal for competition was, in fact, unusual. Although many entrepreneurs publicly applauded the idea of the "survival of the fittest," most loved competition only in the abstract and preferred to find alternatives to it in their own business affairs.

Other Americans also found themselves making choices regarding cooperation. Individualism was deeply entrenched in the American psyche, yet the increasing complexity of the economy presented repeated opportunities for cooperation. Railroad executives sometimes cooperated by dividing a market rather than competing in it. Like Frank Roney, wage earners sometimes joined with other workers in standing up to their employers and demanding better wages or working conditions. The result of these many decisions was the industrialization of the nation and the transformation of the economy. This chapter and the next explore various facets of the industrialization of America: the transformation of the economy, the spectacular growth of cities, a huge surge of immigration, and new social patterns.

Foundation for Industrialization

■ What were the most important factors that encouraged economic growth and industrial development after the Civil War?

■ What were the major changes in the U.S. economy from the Civil War to World War I?

By 1865, conditions in the United States were ripe for rapid industrialization. A wealth of natural resources, a capable work force, an agricultural base that produced enough food for a large urban population, and favorable government policies combined to lay the foundation.

Mineral resources were crucial to the development of an industrial economy, and petroleum was among the most essential. Oil was discovered in large quantities in northwestern Pennsylvania beginning in 1859. This photograph, from 1869, shows the oil well of Gordon Clifford, in the middle of Oil City, Pennsylvania. Clifford is the man wearing a top hat and posing proudly in front of his well. *William B. Becker Collection/American Museum of Photography.*

Resources, Skills, and Capital

At the end of the Civil War, **entrepreneurs** could draw on vast and virtually untapped natural resources. Americans had long since plowed the fertile farmland of the Midwest (where corn and wheat dominated) and the South (where cotton was king). They had just begun to farm the rich soils of Minnesota, Nebraska, Kansas, Iowa, and the Dakotas, as well as the productive valleys of California. Through the central part of the nation stretched vast grasslands that received too little rain for most farming but were well suited for grazing. The Pacific Northwest, the western Great Lakes region, and the South all held extensive forests untouched by the lumberman's saw.

The nation was also rich in mineral resources. Before the Civil War, the iron **industry** had become centered in Pennsylvania as a result of easy access to iron ore and coal. Pennsylvania was also the site of early efforts to tap underground pools of crude oil. The California gold rush, beginning in 1848, had drawn many people west, and some of them had found great riches. Reserves of other minerals lay unused and, in many cases, undiscovered at the end of the war, including iron ore in Michigan, Minnesota, and Alabama; coal throughout the Ohio Valley and in Wyoming and Colorado; oil in the Midwest, Oklahoma, Texas, Louisiana, southern California, and Alaska; gold or silver in Nevada, Colorado, and Alaska; and copper in Michigan, Montana, Utah, and Arizona. Many of these natural resources were far from population centers, and their use awaited adequate transportation facilities. Exploitation of some of these resources also required new technologies.

In addition to natural resources, a skilled and experienced work force was essential for economic growth. In the 1790s and early nineteenth century, New Englanders had developed manufacturing systems based on **interchangeable parts** (first used for manufacturing guns and clocks) and factories for producing cotton cloth. These accomplishments gave them a reputation for "Yankee ingenuity"—a talent for devising new tools and inventive methods. Such skills and problem-solving abilities, however, were not limited to New England—they were key ingredients in nearly all large-scale manufacturing because early factories usually relied on skilled **artisans** to direct less-skilled workers in assembling products. Some of the early artisans and factory owners came from Great Britain, where they had learned mechanical skills or honed entrepreneurial abilities in the world's first industrial nation.

Another crucial element for industrialization was capital, and institutions that could mobilize capital had developed before the Civil War. During the years before the war, capital became centered in the seaport

---

entrepreneur   A person who takes on the risks of creating, organizing, and managing a business enterprise.

industry   A basic unit of business activity in which the various participants do similar activities; for example, the railroad industry consists of railroad companies and the firms and factories that supply their equipment.

interchangeable parts   Mechanical parts that are identical and can be substituted for one another.

artisan   A skilled worker, whether self-employed or working for wages.

Chronology

The Growth of Industry

1823	Monroe Doctrine
1839-1842	First Opium War (Britain defeats China, China cedes Hong Kong to Britain)
1850s	Development of Bessemer and Kelly steel-making processes
1854	U.S. Navy opens trade with Japan
1856	Second Opium War (Britain and France defeat China, expanding opportunities for trade in China)
1859	Publication of Darwin's *On the Origin of Species*
1861	Protective tariff
1862	Homestead Act Land-Grant College Act Pacific Railway Act
1865	Civil War ends
1866	National Labor Union organized
1867	First Grange formed French troops leave Mexico Maximilian executed Senate rejects purchase of Danish West Indies United States purchases Alaska from Russia
1868	Ulysses S. Grant elected president
1869	First transcontinental railroad completed
1870	Senate rejects annexation of Santo Domingo
1871	William Marcy Tweed indicted

1872	Crédit Mobilier scandal Grant reelected Montgomery Ward opens first U.S. mail-order business Arbitration of *Alabama* claims
1872–1874	Granger laws
1873	"Salary Grab" Act Gold Standard adopted
1873–1879	Depression
mid-1870s	Grange membership peaks
1874	Republicans lose majority in House of Representatives
1875	Whiskey Ring scandal Andrew Carnegie opens nation's largest steel plant
1876	Secretary of War William Belknap resigns
1877	Disputed presidential election Rutherford B. Hayes becomes president Reconstruction ends Great Railway Strike *Munn v. Illinois*
1878	Bland-Allison Act Greenback Party peaks
1879	Publication of Henry George's *Progress and Poverty*
1881	Garfield becomes president
1882	U.S. Navy opens trade with Korea

cities of the Northeast—Boston, New York, and Philadelphia, especially—where prosperous merchants invested their profits in banks and factories. Banks were important instruments for mobilizing capital. Before the Civil War, some bankers had begun to specialize in arranging financing for large-scale enterprises, and some of these had opened permanent branch offices in Britain to tap sources of capital there. **Stock exchanges** had also developed long before the Civil War as important institutions for raising capital for new ventures.

stock exchange   A place where people buy and sell stocks (shares in the ownership of companies); stockholders may participate in election of the company's directors and share in the company's profits.

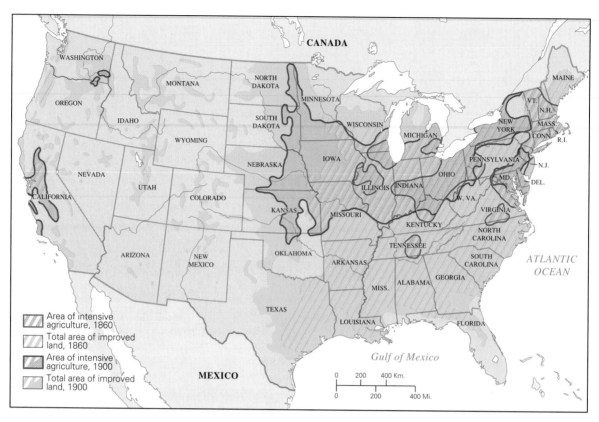

MAP 17.1 Expansion of Agriculture, 1860–1900 The amount of improved farmland more than doubled during these forty years. This map shows how agricultural expansion came in two ways—first, western lands were brought under cultivation; second, in other areas, especially the Midwest, land was cultivated much more intensely than before.

The Transformation of Agriculture

The expanding economy of the nineteenth century rested on a productive agricultural base. Improved transportation—canals early in the nineteenth century and railroads later—speeded the expansion of agriculture by making it possible to move large amounts of agricultural produce over long distances. Up to the Civil War, farmers had developed 407 million acres into productive farmland. During the next thirty-five years, this figure more than doubled, to 841 million acres. Map 17.1 indicates where this growth occurred.

The federal government contributed to the rapid settlement of Kansas, Nebraska, the Dakotas, and Minnesota through the **Homestead Act** of 1862, a leading example of the Republican Party's commitment to using federal landholdings to speed economic

development. Under this act, any person could receive free as much as 160 acres (a quarter of a square mile) of government land by building a house, living on the land for five years, and farming it. Between 1862 and 1890, 48 million acres passed from government ownership to private hands in this way. Other federally owned land could be purchased for as little as $1.25 per acre, and much more was obtained at this bargain price than was acquired free under the Homestead Act.

> **Homestead Act** Law passed by Congress in 1862 that offered ownership of 160 acres of designated public lands to any citizen who lived on and improved the land for five years.

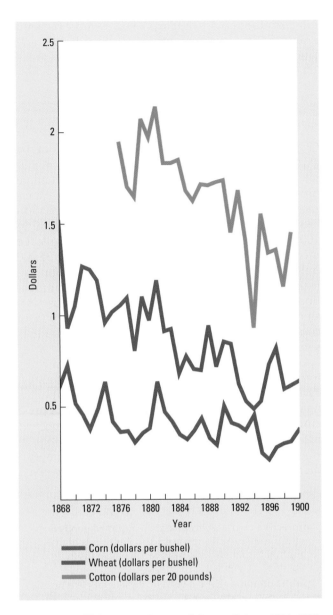

FIGURE 17.1 Corn, Wheat, and Cotton Prices, 1868–1900
From the late 1860s through the end of the century, prices for major crops fell. This graph shows the year-to-year fluctuations in prices and indicates the general downward trend in prices for all three crops. *Source:* U.S. Department of Commerce, Bureau of the Census, *Historical Statistics of the United States, Colonial Times to 1970,* Bicentennial edition, 2 vols. (Washington: Government Printing Office, 1975), I: 510–512, 517–518.

Production of leading commercial crops increased more rapidly than the overall expansion of farming. Though the total number of acres in farmland doubled between 1866 and 1900, the number of acres planted in corn, wheat, and cotton more than tripled. New farming methods increased harvests even more—corn by 264 percent, wheat by 252 percent, and cotton by 383 percent. Through these years, farm output grew more than twice as much as the population.

As production of major crops rose, prices for them fell. Fig. 17.1 shows the prices for wheat, corn, and cotton—the most significant commercial crops. Though several factors contributed to this decline in farm prices, the most obvious was that supply outpaced demand. Production increased more rapidly than both the population (which largely determined the demand within the nation) and the demand from other countries. According to economic theory, over-supply causes prices to fall, and falling prices lead producers to reduce their output. When American farmers received less for their crops, however, they usually raised *more* in an effort to maintain the same level of income. To increase their harvests, they bought fertilizers and elaborate machinery. Between 1870 and 1890, the amount of fertilizer consumed in the nation more than quadrupled. And the more the farmers raised, the lower prices fell—and with them, the economic well-being of many farmers.

New machinery especially affected the production of grain crops, greatly increasing the amount of land one person could farm. A single farmer with a hand-held scythe and cradle, for example, could harvest 2 acres of wheat in a day. Using the McCormick reaper (first produced in 1849), a single farmer and a team of horses could harvest 2 acres in an hour. For other crops too, a person with modern machinery could farm two or three times as much land as a farmer fifty years before.

During the thirty years following the Civil War, the growth of agriculture affected other segments of the economy. The expansion of farming stimulated the farm equipment industry and, in turn, the iron and steel industry. The large volume of agricultural exports—cotton, tobacco, wheat, meat—spurred oceanic shipping and shipbuilding, and increased shipbuilding meant a greater demand for iron and steel. Railroads played a crucial role in the expansion and commercialization of agriculture by carrying farm products to distant markets and transporting fertilizer and machinery from factories (usually in distant cities) to farming regions.

The Impact of War and New Government Policies

In 1865 nearly three times as many Americans worked in agriculture as in manufacturing. Most manufacturing was small in scale and local in nature—a shop with a few workers who made barrels or assembled farm wagons, mostly for people nearby. Nonetheless, many conditions were ripe for the emergence of large-scale manufacturing. The Civil War encouraged some entrepreneurs to deliver military supplies to distant parts of the nation, and some of them now sought to develop similar business patterns in peacetime. At the end of the war, too, some people found themselves looking for places to invest their wartime profits. By diverting labor and capital into war production, the Civil War may have slowed an expansion of manufacturing already under way. However, the war also brought important changes in the experience and expectations of some entrepreneurs. At the same time, new government policies encouraged a more rapid rate of economic growth.

When Republicans took command of the federal government in 1861, the South seceded in reaction to the new administration's opposition to slavery, and secession led to the Civil War. While the Republicans made war against the Confederacy, abolished slavery, and undertook Reconstruction, they also forged new policies intended to stimulate economic growth. First came a new **protective tariff,** passed in 1861. The tariff increased the price of imports to equal or exceed the price of American-made goods in order to protect domestic products from foreign competition and thereby encourage investment in manufacturing. Tariff rates changed from time to time, but the protective tariff remained central to federal economic policy for more than a half-century.

New federal land policies also stimulated economic growth. At the beginning of the Civil War, the federal government claimed a billion acres of land as federal property—the **public domain**—half of the land area of the nation. The Republicans used this land to encourage economic development in several ways, including free land for farmers, beginning with the Homestead Act (1862). Recognizing the importance of higher education, the **Land-Grant College Act** (1862)—often called the Morrill Act for its sponsor, Senator Justin Morrill of Vermont—gave federal land to each state (excluding those that had seceded) to sell or otherwise use to raise funds to establish a public university, which was required to provide education in engineering and agriculture and to train

military officers. Also in 1862, Congress approved land grants for the first transcontinental railroad, and more land grants to railroads followed.

Overview: The Economy from the Civil War to World War I

Given the solid foundation for industrialization, the expansion of agriculture, and favorable governmental policies, the nation grew dramatically in the late nineteenth and early twentieth centuries. For example, between 1865 and 1920, the nation's population increased by nearly 200 percent, from 36 million to 106 million. During the same years, railroad mileage increased by more than 1,000 percent, from 35,000 miles to 407,000 miles. The output of manufacturing increased by a similar margin. Agricultural production grew far faster than the population. Perhaps most significantly, the total domestic product, per capita, in constant dollars, nearly tripled. (Fig. 17.2 presents some of these patterns.)

Much of this growth was sporadic. Economic historians think of the economy as developing through a cycle in which periods of **expansion** (growth) alternate with times of **contraction** (**recession** or **depression,** characterized by high unemployment and low productivity). Though this alternation between expansion and contraction is predictable, there is no predictability or regularity to the duration of any given

---

protective tariff　A tax placed on imported goods for the purpose of raising the price of imports as high as or higher than the prices of the same item produced within the nation.

public domain　Land owned by the federal government.

Land-Grant College Act　Law passed by Congress in 1862 that gave states land to use to raise money to establish public universities that were to offer courses in engineering and agriculture and to train military officers.

expansion　In the economic cycle, a time when the economy is growing as indicated by increased production of goods and services and usually by low rates of unemployment.

contraction　In the economic cycle, a time when the economy has ceased to grow, characterized by decreased production of goods and services and often by high rates of unemployment.

recession/depression　A recession is an economic contraction of relatively short duration; a depression is an economic contraction of longer duration.

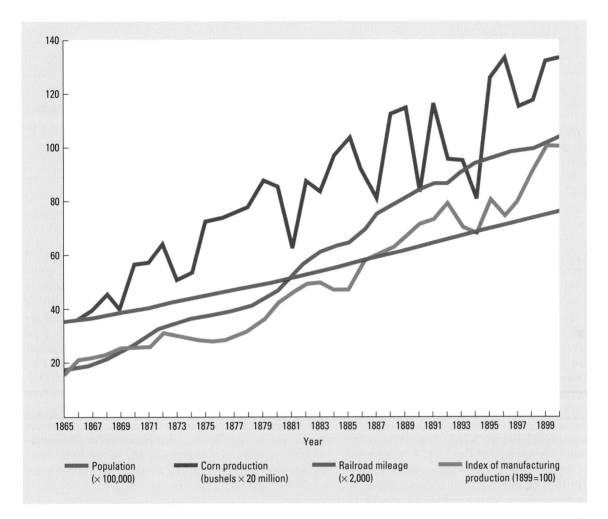

FIGURE 17.2 Measures of Growth, 1865–1900   Though many measures of economic productivity are related to population size, this graph shows how several measures of economic productivity grew at more rapid rates than did the population. *Source:* U.S. Department of Commerce, Bureau of the Census, *Historical Statistics of the United States, Colonial Times to 1970,* Bicentennial edition, 2 vols. (Washington: Government Printing Office, 1975), I: 8, 510–512; 2: 667, 727–731.

up or down period. During the late nineteenth century, contractions were sometimes severe, producing widespread unemployment and distress. After 1865, a postwar recession lasted until late 1867, reflecting sharp dislocations as the economy shifted from wartime production to other ventures. This was followed by several expansions and contractions of similar length. A major depression began in October 1873

and lasted until March 1879. The period from 1879 to 1893 was generally a period of expansion (105 months of growth), spurred in particular by railroad construction, but the growth was interrupted three times by contractions (totaling 61 months), two of them quite short. Another major depression began in January 1893 and lasted (despite a brief upswing) until June 1897 and was then followed by alternating periods of expansion and contraction of almost equal length, with the longest expansion in 1904–1907 (33 months) and the longest contraction in 1910–1912 (24 months).

During boom periods, companies advertised for labor and ran their operations at full capacity. When the demand for manufactured goods fell, companies reduced production, cutting hours of work or dismissing employees as they waited for business to pick up. Some businesses shut down temporarily; others closed permanently. Thus Americans living in the late nineteenth and early twentieth centuries came to expect that "hard times" were likely in the future, regardless of how prosperous life seemed at the moment. Until the early twentieth century, federal intervention in the economy was limited largely to stimulating growth through the protective tariff and land distribution programs. Unemployed workers had little to fall back on besides their savings or the earnings of other family members. Some churches and private charity organizations gave out food, but state and federal governments provided no unemployment benefits. Families who failed to find work might go hungry or even become homeless. In a depression, jobs of any sort were scarce, and competition for every opening was intense. Most adult Americans therefore understood the wisdom of saving up for hard times, whether or not they were able to do so.

The depression that began in 1873 was both severe and long-lasting. Between 1873 and 1879, 355 banks closed down, a number equivalent to one bank in nine that existed in 1873. Nearly 54,000 businesses failed—equivalent to one in nine operating in 1873. No reliable unemployment data exist, but evidence indicates that the contraction hit urban wage earners especially hard. Many lost their jobs or suffered a reduced workweek. Workers who kept their jobs saw their daily wages fall by 17 to 18 percent from 1873 to 1878 or 1879. For example, unskilled laborers' daily wages fell from an average of $1.52 in 1873 to a low of $1.26 in 1878, and blacksmiths' daily wages fell from $2.70 in 1873 to $2.21 in 1879. (One dollar in 1875 had the purchasing power of more than $16 today.) One Massachusetts worker described the consequences for his family in 1875:

> I have six children . . . Last year three of my children were promoted [to the next grade in school], and I was notified to furnish different books. [Schoolchildren then were responsible for providing their own textbooks.] I wrote a note to the school committee, stating that I was not able to do so. . . . I then received a note stating that, unless I furnished the books called for, I must keep my children at home. I then had to reduce the bread for my children and

> family, in order to get the required books to keep them at school. Every cent of my earnings is consumed in my family; and yet I have not been able to have a piece of meat on my table twice a month for the last eight months.

Thus, though long-term economic trends reflect dramatic growth, the short-run boom-and-bust nature of the economy repeatedly claimed its victims.

Railroads and Industry

■ What was the significance of the railroad and steel industries in the new industrial economy that emerged after the Civil War?

■ What might account for the changes in historians' views of the industrial entrepreneurs of the post–Civil War period?

To many Americans of the late nineteenth century, nothing symbolized economic growth so effectively as a locomotive—a huge, powerful, noisy, smoke-belching machine barreling forward. Railroads set much of the pace for economic expansion after the Civil War. Growth of the rail network stimulated industries that supplied materials for railroad construction and operation—especially steel and coal—and industries that relied on railroads to connect them to the emerging national economy. Railroad companies also came to symbolize "big business"—companies of great size, employing thousands of workers, operating over large geographic areas—and some Americans began to fear their power.

Railroad Expansion

At the end of the Civil War, the nation lacked a comprehensive national transportation network. Before the Civil War, much of the nation's commerce moved on water—on rivers, canals, and coastal waterways, and there was no national rail network until well after the war's end. Railroad companies operated on tracks of varying **gauges,** which made the transfer of railcars from one line to another impossible. Instead, freight had to be moved by hand or wagon from the cars of one line to those of another. Few railway bridges crossed major rivers. Until 1869, no railroad connected the eastern half of the country to the booming Pacific Coast region. Every route between the Atlantic and Pacific Coasts required more than a month

---

gauge In this usage, the distance between the two rails making up railroad tracks.

In his novel *The Octopus* (1901), Frank Norris described not just the physical power of the railroad but also its economic and political prowess: "The galloping terror of steam and steel, with its single eye, cyclopean, red, shooting from horizon to horizon, symbol of a vast power, huge and terrible; the leviathan with tentacles of steel, to oppose which meant to be ground to instant destruction beneath the clashing wheels." This Currier and Ives lithograph from 1863, entitled "The Lightning Express Trains: Leaving the Junction," captures some of that sense of power. *Museum of the City of New York.*

and posed serious discomfort if not outright danger. The choices were equally intimidating: a sea voyage around the storm-tossed tip of South America; or a boat trip to Central America, then transit over mountains and through malaria-infested jungles to the Pacific, and then another boat trip up the Pacific Coast; or a seemingly endless overland journey by riverboat and stagecoach.

By the mid-1880s, all the elements were finally in place for a national rail network. The first transcontinental rail line was completed in 1869, connecting California to Omaha, Nebraska (where Frank Roney briefly worked in the railroad's shops), and ultimately to eastern cities. (The construction of this railroad is described in Chapter 19.) Within the next fifteen years, three more rail lines linked the Pacific Coast to the eastern half of the nation, and a fourth was completed in 1893. Between 1865 and 1890, railroads grew from 35,000 miles of track to 167,000 miles (see Map 17.2). By the mid-1880s, most major rivers had been bridged. Companies had replaced many iron rails with steel ones, allowing them to haul heavier loads. New inventions increased the speed, carry-

ing capacity, and efficiency of trains. In 1886 the last major lines converted to a standard gauge, making it possible to transfer railcars from one line to another simply by throwing a switch. This rail network encouraged entrepreneurs to think in terms of a national economic system in which raw materials and finished products might move easily from one region to another.

Railroads, especially in the West, expanded with generous governmental assistance. The first transcontinental rail line was made possible by the **Pacific Railway Act** of 1862. Congress provided the Union Pacific and Central Pacific companies not only with sizable loans but also with 10 square miles of the public domain for every mile of track laid—an amount that was doubled in a subsequent act in 1864. By 1871, Congress had authorized some seventy railroad land

Pacific Railway Act   Law passed by Congress in 1862 that gave loans and land to the Central Pacific and Union Pacific Railroad companies to subsidize construction of a rail line between Omaha and the Pacific Coast.

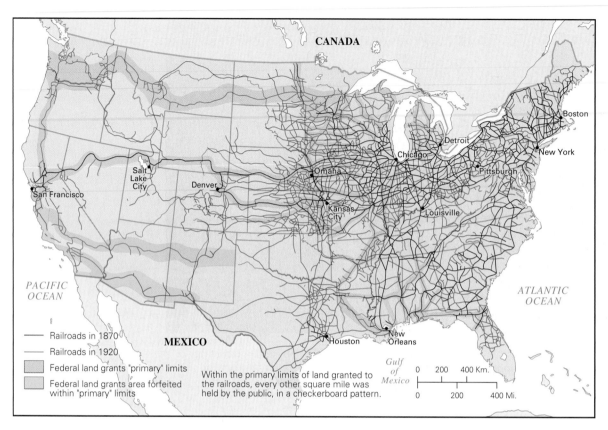

MAP 17.2 Railroad Expansion and Railroad Land Grants   Post–Civil War railroad expansion produced the transportation base for an industrial economy. In the West, federal land grants encouraged railroad construction. Within a grant, railroads received every other square mile. Land could be forfeited if construction did not meet the terms of the grant legislation.

grants, involving 128 million acres—more than one-tenth of the entire public domain, an area approximately equal to Colorado and Wyoming together—though not all companies proved able to claim their entire grants. Most railroads sold their land to raise capital for railroad operations. By encouraging farmers, businesses, or organizations to develop the land, railroad companies tried to build up the economies along their tracks and thereby to boost the demand for their freight trains to haul supplies to new settlers and carry their products (wheat, cattle, lumber, ore) to market.

Railroads: Model for Big Business

The expansion of railroads created the potential for a nationwide market, stimulated the economic devel-

opment of the West, and created a demand for iron, steel, locomotives, and similar products. Railroad companies also provided an organizational model for newly developing industrial enterprises.

Because they spanned such great distances and managed so many employees and so much equipment, railroads encountered problems of scale that few companies had faced before but that other industrial entrepreneurs soon had to address. Not surprisingly, businesses that came later often adopted solutions that railroads first developed.

Railroad companies required a much higher degree of coordination and long-range planning than most businesses up to that time. Earlier companies typically operated at a single location, but railroads functioned over long distances and in multiple sites of operation. They had to keep up numerous maintenance and repair facilities and maintain many stations to receive and discharge both freight and passengers.

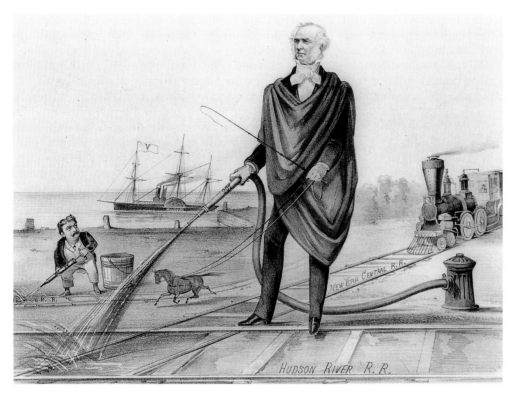

HUDSON RIVER R. R.

This cartoon appeared during the "Erie War," the struggle for control over the Erie Railroad. Vanderbilt is depicted "watering" the Hudson River Railroad, one of the connecting lines for his New York Central company, while Jim Fisk, in the distance, busily "waters" the Erie Railroad. Those people who saw this cartoon would have understand that "watering" meant watering the stock of the company, that is, issuing more stock than the total value of the assets of the company. *New York Historical Society.*

Financial transactions carried on over hundreds of miles by scores of employees required a centralized accounting office. One result was development of a company bureaucracy of clerks, accountants, managers, and agents. Railroads became training grounds for administrators, some of whom later entered other industries. Indeed, the experience of the railroads was central in defining the subject of business administration when it began to be taught in colleges at the turn of the century.

Railroads required far more capital than most manufacturing concerns. In 1875 the largest steel furnaces in the world cost $741,000; at the same time, the Pennsylvania Railroad was capitalized at $400 million. Even railroads that received government subsidies required large amounts of private capital—and Congress gave out the last federal land grant in 1871. Private capital and support from state and local governments underwrote the enormous railroad expansion of the 1880s. The railroads' huge appetite for capital made them the first American businesses to seek investors on a nationwide and international scale. Those who invested their money could choose to buy either stocks or **bonds.** Sales of railroad stocks provided the major activity for the New York Stock Exchange through the second half of the nineteenth century.

Railroads faced higher **fixed costs** than most previous companies. These costs included commitments to bondholders and the expense of maintaining and protecting far-flung equipment and property. To pay their fixed costs and keep profits high, railroad companies tried to operate at full capacity whenever

bond   A certificate of debt issued by a government or corporation guaranteeing payment of the original investment plus interest at a specified future date.

fixed costs   Costs that a company must pay even if it closes down all its operations—for example, interest on loans, dividends on bonds, and property taxes.

possible. Doing so, however, often proved difficult. Where two or more lines competed for the same traffic, one might choose to cut rates in an effort to lure business from the other. But if the other company responded with cuts in its rates, neither stood to gain significantly more business, and both took in less income. Competition between railroad companies sometimes became so intense that no line could show a profit.

Cornelius Vanderbilt, called "Commodore" because of his investments in steamships, controlled the New York Central Railroad (which ran along the Mohawk Valley in upstate New York) and connecting lines to New York City and into Ohio, and he hoped to extend his holdings all the way to Chicago. The Erie Railroad, controlled by Daniel Drew, ran parallel to Vanderbilt's lines in many places. Both Drew and Vanderbilt had reputations as hard-driving **moguls,** but no one could match Drew's reputation for deviousness. When Vanderbilt raised his freight rates, Drew undercut him by 20 percent. When Vanderbilt set out to buy enough stock to seize control of the Erie from Drew, Drew and his allies, James "Diamond Jim" Fisk and Jay Gould, issued more stock and even offered some of it for sale, keeping Vanderbilt from control and enriching themselves in the process. At one point, the battle shifted to the New York state legislature, where Gould tried to secure passage of a law to legalize their dubious Erie stock issues. Stories circulated through Albany about shameless bidding for legislators' votes, and a subsequent investigation indicated that Gould spent a million dollars in Albany. Both sides also sought friendly judges. Finally Vanderbilt sent a simple message to Drew: "I'm sick of the whole damned business. Come and see me."

Some railroad operators chose to defuse such intense competition by forming a **pool.** In a pool, the railroads agreed to divide the existing business among themselves and not to compete on rates. The most famous was the Iowa Pool, made up of the railroads running between Chicago and Omaha, across Iowa. Formed in 1870, the Iowa Pool operated until 1874, and some pooling continued until the mid-1880s. Few pools lasted very long. Often one or more pool members tired of a restricted market share and broke the pool arrangement in an effort to expand, thereby setting off a new price war. When a pooling arrangement became known, it brought loud complaints from customers, who concluded that they paid higher rates because of the pool.

To compete more effectively, railroads adjusted their rates to attract companies that did a great deal of shipping. Favored customers sometimes received a **rebate.** Large shipments sent over long distances cost the railroad companies less per mile than small shipments sent over short distances, so companies developed different rate structures for long hauls and short hauls. Thus the largest shippers, with the power to secure rebates and low rates, could ship more cheaply than small businesses and individual farmers. Railroad companies defended the differences on the basis of differences in costs, but small shippers who paid high prices saw themselves as victims of rate discrimination.

Railroads viewed state and federal governments as sources of valuable subsidies. At the same time, they constantly guarded against efforts by their customers to use government to restrict or regulate their enterprises—by outlawing rate discrimination, for example. Companies sometimes campaigned openly to secure the election of friendly representatives and senators and to defeat unfriendly candidates. They maintained well-organized operations to **lobby** public officials in Washington, D.C., and in state capitals. Most railroad companies issued free passes to public officials—a practice that reformers attacked as bribery. Some railroads won reputations as the most influential political power in entire states—the Southern Pacific in California, for example, or the Santa Fe in Kansas.

Stories of railroad officials bribing politicians became commonplace after the Civil War. The Crédit Mobilier scandal touched some of the most influential members of Congress in the 1870s (see the discussion later in this chapter). A decade later, Collis P. Huntington of the Southern Pacific Railroad candidly explained his expectations regarding public officials: "If you have to pay money to have the right thing done, it is only just and fair to do it." For Huntington, "the right thing" meant favorable treatment for his company.

Chicago: Railroad Metropolis

The financing of railroads was centered in New York, but Chicago experienced the most dramatic change as a consequence of railroad construction. Between 1850 and 1880, railroads transformed Chicago from a

mogul An important or powerful person, especially the head of a major company.

pool An agreement among businesses in the same industry to divide up the market and charge equal prices instead of competing.

rebate The refund of part of a payment.

lobby To try to influence the thinking of public officials for or against a specific cause.

Chicago was perhaps the most important single center for the nation's rail traffic in the late 19th century. Nearly all western railroads converged there, meeting several major lines from the East. This lithograph shows Chicago's Grand Passenger Station in 1880. The lithograph advertises some of the many rail connections possible through this station—to Kansas City, Denver, and San Francisco. The artist has also presented many different forms of street transportation in front of the station, including a coach, several varieties of carriages, and two high-wheel bicycles. *Chicago Historical Society.*

town of 30,000 residents to the nation's fourth-largest city, with a half-million people. By 1890, it was second only to New York in size, and in 1900 its population stood at 1.7 million people. Thanks in part to local promoters and in part to geography, Chicago emerged as the rail center not just of the Midwest but of much of the nation. By 1880, more than twenty railroad lines and 15,000 miles of tracks connected Chicago with nearly all of the United States and much of Canada. The boom in railroad construction during the 1880s only reinforced the city's prominence. Entrepreneurs in manufacturing and commerce soon developed new enterprises based on Chicago's unrivaled location at the hub of a great transportation network.

Chicago's rail connections made it the logical center for the new business of **mail-order sales,** and the two pioneers in that field—Montgomery Ward, in 1872, and Sears, Roebuck and Co., in 1895—began business there (see pages 534–535). Central location and rail connections also made Chicago a major manufacturing center. By the 1880s, Chicago's factories produced more farm equipment than those of any other city, and its iron and steel production rivaled that of Pittsburgh. Other leading Chicago industries produced railway cars and equipment, metal products, a wide variety of machinery, and clothing. At the same time, the city also claimed title as the world's largest grain market.

Location and rail lines made Chicago the nation's largest center for **meatpacking.** Livestock from across the Midwest and from as far as southern Texas was unloaded in Chicago's Union Stockyards—over 400 acres of railroad sidings, chutes, and pens filled with cattle, hogs, and sheep. Huge slaughterhouses flanking the stockyards received a steady stream of live animals and disgorged an equally steady stream of fresh, canned, and processed meat. The development in the 1870s of refrigeration for railroad cars and ships permitted fresh meat to be sent throughout the nation and even to Europe.

Chicago's rapid growth and rising economic significance gave it an aura of energy and vitality that impressed nearly all visitors. Louis Sullivan, later a leading architect, remembered his first impressions of the city in 1873: "An intoxicating rawness; a sense of big things to be done. 'Biggest in the world' was the braggart phrase on every tongue." A French visitor

mail-order sales   The business of selling goods using the mails; mail-order houses send out catalogs, customers submit orders, and the products are delivered all by mail.

meatpacking   The business of slaughtering animals and preparing their meat for sale as food.

called Chicago "the boldest" and "most American" of the cities of the United States. The poet Carl Sandburg celebrated this aspect of the city in his poem "Chicago" in 1914:

> Hog Butcher for the World,
> Tool Maker, Stacker of Wheat,
> Player with Railroads and the Nation's Freight
>   Handler;
> Stormy, husky, brawling,
> City of the Big Shoulders

Andrew Carnegie and the Age of Steel

The new, industrial economy rode on a network of steel rails, propelled by locomotives made of steel. Steel plows broke the tough sod of the western prairies. Skyscrapers, the first of which appeared in Chicago in 1885, relied on steel frames as they boldly shaped urban skylines (see page 546). Steel, a relative latecomer to the industrial revolution, defined the age. Made by combining carbon and molten iron and then burning out impurities, steel has greater strength, resilience, and durability than iron. This superior metal was difficult and expensive to make until the 1850s, when Henry Bessemer in England and William Kelly in Kentucky independently discovered ways to make steel in large quantities at a reasonable cost. Even so, the first Bessemer or Kelly process plants did not begin production in the United States until 1864. In that year, the entire nation produced only 10,000 tons of steel.

In 1875, just south of Pittsburgh, Pennsylvania, **Andrew Carnegie** opened the nation's largest steel plant, employing 1,500 workers. From then until 1901 (when the plant had grown to more than eight thousand workers), Carnegie held central place in the steel industry. Born in Scotland in 1835, Carnegie and his penniless parents came to the United States in 1848. Young Andrew worked first in a textile mill, then became a messenger in a telegraph office, and soon was promoted to telegraph operator. His impressive skill at the telegraph key won him a position as personal telegrapher for a high official of the Pennsylvania Railroad. Carnegie rose rapidly within that company and became a superintendent (a high management position) at the age of 25. At the end of the Civil War, he devoted his full attention to the iron and steel industry, in which he had previously invested money. He quickly applied to his own companies the management lessons he had learned with the railroad.

Andrew Carnegie, as depicted by an unknown painter around 1901, when he sold his steel holdings to J. P. Morgan and transformed himself from a fiercely competitive entrepreneur into a generous philanthropist. *National Portrait Gallery.*

Carnegie's basic rule was "Cut the prices; scoop the market; run the mills full." An aggressive competitor, he took every opportunity to cut costs so that he might show a profit while charging less than his rivals. He usually chose to undersell competitors rather than cooperate with them. In 1864, steel rails sold for $126 per ton; by 1875, Carnegie was selling them for $69 per ton. Driven by improved technology and Carnegie's competitiveness, steel prices continued to fall, reaching $29 a ton in 1885 and less than $20 a ton in the late 1890s. By then, the nation produced nearly 10 million tons of steel each year.

Andrew Carnegie   Scottish-born industrialist who made a fortune in steel and believed the rich had a duty to act for the public benefit.

Vertical Integration

From the time of Andrew Carnegie to our own time, vertical integration has been an important competitive strategy for American businesses. Today, students of business administration learn that companies often follow one or both varieties of vertical integration: *backward,* or upstream, vertical integration, in which the company acquires control over suppliers of raw materials or other components for the company's manufacturing process; and *forward,* or downstream, vertical integration, in which the company acquires control over distribution or marketing of the company's product.

Since the late nineteenth century, vertical integration has been a central feature of American corporate history. In the 1920s, motion picture studios controlled chains of motion picture theaters, an example of forward vertical integration; similarly, in 1995, Disney, a producer of films, bought ABC, which distributed films via its television broadcasting. In the 1950s, the Supreme Court blocked the acquisition of Kinney shoe stores, the largest chain of retail shoe stores, by Brown Shoe Company, one of the largest shoe manufacturers, on the grounds that vertical integration on that scale would inhibit competition. In the past few decades, much of food production and processing has become vertically integrated—Smithfield, for example, controls the process of pork production from the time a sow is inseminated until packaged pork chops are delivered to supermarkets. When McDonald's opened fast-food restaurants in Russia, the company also became the largest lettuce grower in that country, to provide an important ingredient of the Биг Мак (Big Mac).

tive factory. The size of such operations continued to grow. In 1900 the three largest steel plants each employed 8,000 to 10,000 workers, and seventy other factories employed more than 2,000, producing everything from watches to locomotives, and from cotton cloth to processed meat.

During the late nineteenth century, drawing in part on railroads' innovations in managing large-scale operations, Carnegie and other entrepreneurs transformed the organizational structure of manufacturing. They often joined a range of operations formerly conducted by separate businesses—acquisition of raw materials, processing, distribution of finished goods—into one company, achieving **vertical integration.** Companies usually developed vertical integration to ensure steady operations and to gain a competitive advantage. Control over the sources and transportation of raw materials, for example, guaranteed a reliable flow of crucial supplies at predictable prices. Such control may also have denied materials to a competitor.

Steel plants stood at one end of a long chain of operations that Carnegie owned or controlled: iron ore mines in Michigan and Wisconsin, a fleet of ships that transported iron ore across the Great Lakes, hundreds of miles of railway lines, tens of thousands of acres of coal lands, ovens to produce coke (coal treated to burn at high temperatures), and plants for turning iron ore into bars of crude iron. Carnegie Steel was vertically integrated from the point where the raw materials came out of the ground through the delivery of steel rails and beams.

Survival of the Fittest or Robber Barons?

Many Americans were uneasy with the new economic powerhouses bred by industrialization. In a book published in 1889, economist David A. Wells remarked on the "wholly unprecedented" size of the new businesses, the "rapidity" with which they emerged, and their tendency to be "far more complex than what has been familiar." Such giant enterprises, he noted, "are

Carnegie's company was larger and more complex than any manufacturing enterprise in pre–Civil War America. In its own day, however, it was by no means unique. Other companies operated plants that were as complex, and several challenged it in size. By 1880, five steel companies had more than 1,500 employees, as did an equal number of textile mills and a locomo-

> **vertical integration**   The process of bringing together into a single company several of the activities in the process of creating a manufactured product, such as the acquiring of raw materials, the manufacturing of products, and the marketing, selling, and distributing of finished goods.

regarded to some extent as evils." But, he added, "they are necessary, as there is apparently no other way in which the work of production and distribution . . . can be prosecuted."

The concentration of power and wealth during the late nineteenth century generated extensive comment and concern. One prominent view on the subject was known as **Social Darwinism,** reflecting its roots in Charles Darwin's work on evolution. In his book *On the Origin of Species* (published in 1859), Darwin had concluded that those creatures that survive in competition against other creatures and in the face of an often inhospitable environment are those that have best adapted to their surroundings. Such adaptation, he suggested, leads to the evolution of different species, each uniquely suited to a particular ecological niche.

Two philosophers, Herbert Spencer, writing in England in the 1870s and after, and William Graham Sumner, in the United States in the 1880s and after, put their own interpretations on Darwin's reasoning and applied it to the human situation, producing Social Darwinism (a philosophical perspective that bore little relation to Darwin's original work). Social Darwinists contended that competition among people produced "progress" through "survival of the fittest" and that competition provided the best possible route for improving humankind and advancing civilization. Further, they argued that efforts to ease the harsh impact of competition only protected the unfit and thereby worked to the long-term disadvantage of all. Some concluded that powerful entrepreneurs constituted "the fittest" and benefited all humankind by their accomplishments.

Andrew Carnegie enthusiastically embraced Spencer's arguments and endorsed individualism and self-reliance as the cornerstones of progress. "Civilization took its start from that day that the capable, industrious workman said to his incompetent and lazy fellow, 'If thou dost not sow, thou shalt not reap,'" Carnegie wrote. When applied to government, this notion became a form of **laissez faire.**

Carnegie, though, was inconsistent, also preaching what he called the **Gospel of Wealth:** the idea that the wealthy should return their riches to the community by creating parks, art museums, and educational institutions. He spent his final eighteen years giving away his fortune: he funded 3,000 public library buildings and 4,100 church organs all across the nation, gifts to universities, Carnegie Hall in New York City, and several foundations. (One humorist, though, poked fun at Carnegie's libraries by suggesting that they would serve the community better if they con-

tained a kitchen and beds so that the poor might eat and sleep in them.) Like Carnegie, other great entrepreneurs of the late nineteenth century gave away vast sums—even as some of them also built ostentatious mansions, threw extravagant parties, and otherwise flaunted their wealth. Duke University, Stanford University, Vanderbilt University, the Morgan Library in New York City, and the Huntington Library in southern California all carry the names of men who amassed fortunes in the new, industrial economy and donated part of their riches to promote learning and research.

Although many Americans subscribed to the vision of Social Darwinism propounded by Spencer and Sumner, many others did not. Entrepreneurs themselves often welcomed some forms of government intervention in the economy—from railroad land grants to the protective tariff to suppression of strikes—although most agreed with the Social Darwinists that government should not assist the poor and destitute.

Furthermore, many Americans disagreed with the Social Darwinists' equating of laissez faire with progress. Henry George, a San Francisco journalist, pointed out in *Progress and Poverty* (1879) that "amid the greatest accumulations of wealth, men die of starvation," and he concluded that "material progress does not merely fail to relieve poverty—it actually produces it." Lester Frank Ward, a sociologist, in 1886 posed a carefully reasoned refutation of Social Darwinism, suggesting that biological competition produced bare survival, not civilization. Civilization, he argued, represented "a triumph of mind" that derived not from "ceaseless and aimless competition" but from rationality and cooperation.

Americans also disagreed about whether the railroad magnates and powerful industrialists were heroes or villains. Some accepted them wholeheartedly as benefactors of the nation. Others sided with E. L. God-

---

Social Darwinism The philosophical argument, inspired by Charles Darwin's theory of evolution, that competition in human society produced "the survival of the fittest" and therefore benefited society as a whole; Social Darwinists opposed efforts to regulate competitive practices.

laissez faire The principle that the government should not interfere in the workings of the economy.

Gospel of Wealth Andrew Carnegie's idea that all possessors of great wealth have an obligation to spend or otherwise disburse their money to help people help themselves.

The McCormick plant in Chicago (*left*) produced farm equipment, and this Richmond, Virginia, factory (*right*) employed women to make cigars. In both factories, individual machines drew their power from a central source through a system of belts and shafts, and workers toiled under the watchful eye of the foreman, who could usually adjust the speed of the belts and shafts to speed up the machines of the individual workers. (*left*) *McCormick factory: State Historical Society of Wisconsin; (right) Valentine Museum.*

kin, a journalist who in 1869 compared Vanderbilt to a medieval robber baron—a feudal lord who stole from travelers passing through his domain. Those who have called the wealthy industrialists and bankers **robber barons** point out that they were unscrupulous, greedy, exploitative, and antisocial. Looking only at the deeds or misdeeds of individual entrepreneurs, however, hides more about the economy than it reveals. Understanding these men and the larger economic changes of the era requires more than an examination of individual behavior, whether despicable or praiseworthy.

Thomas C. Cochran, a historian, has looked at the broad cultural context that affected not just prominent entrepreneurs but also most Americans. He identified three broadly shared "cultural themes" as central for understanding the period: (1) a belief that the economy operated according to self-correcting principles, especially the law of supply and demand; (2) the ideas of Social Darwinism; and (3) an assumption that people were motivated primarily by a desire for material gain. These themes shed light not only on the actions of the entrepreneurs of the late nineteenth century but also on those of the political leaders of the day and on the reception those actions received from other Americans.

Workers in Industrial America

■ How did industrialization change the lives of those who came to work in the new industries?

■ What was the basis for craft unionism? How does the nature of its organization help to explain both its successes and its shortcomings?

The rapid expansion of railroads, mining, and manufacturing created a demand for labor to lay the rails, dig the ore, tend the furnaces, operate the refineries, and carry out a thousand other tasks. America's new workers—men, women, and children from many ethnic groups—came from across the nation and around the world. Despite hopes for a rags-to-riches triumph such as Andrew Carnegie's, very few rose from the shop floor to the manager's office.

> **robber baron** In medieval times, a feudal aristocrat who laid exorbitant charges on all who crossed his territory; in the late nineteenth century, an insulting term applied to powerful industrial and financial figures, especially those who disregarded the public interest in their haste to make profits.

The Transformation of Work

Most adult industrial workers had been born into a rural society, either in the United States or in another part of the world. They found industrial work quite different from work they had done in the past. Farm families might toil from sunrise to sunset, but they did so at their own speed. They could take a break when they felt the need and adjust the pace of their work to avoid exhaustion. Self-employed blacksmiths, carpenters, dressmakers, and other skilled workers also controlled the speed and intensity of their work, although, like the farmer, they might work very long hours. Frank Roney considered this autonomy to be part of the dignity of labor. In many early factories, the most skilled workers, such as Roney, often set the pace of work around them. They also earned more than other workers and were difficult to replace.

By the late nineteenth century, the workday in most industries averaged ten or twelve hours, six days a week. People from rural settings expected to work long hours, but they found that industrial work controlled them, rather than the other way around. The speed of the machines set the pace of the work, and machine speeds were often centrally controlled. If managers ordered a **speed-up,** workers worked faster but rarely received an increase in pay. Foremen, too, pushed workers to work faster and faster. Ten- or twelve-hour days at a constant, rapid pace drained the workers. A woman textile worker in 1882 said, "I get so exhausted that I can scarcely drag myself home when night comes." The pace of the work and the resulting exhaustion, together with inadequate safety precautions, contributed to a high rate of industrial accidents, injuries, and deaths, but careful records were not kept until much later.

Workers for Industry

The labor force grew rapidly after the Civil War, almost doubling by 1890. The largest increases occurred in industries undergoing the greatest changes (see Fig,17.3). Agriculture continued to employ the largest share of the labor force, ranging downward from more than half in 1870 to two-fifths in 1900, but the proportional growth of the agricultural work force was the smallest of all major categories of workers.

Some workers for the rapidly expanding economy came from within the nation, especially from rural areas. Throughout rural parts of New England and the Middle Atlantic states, many people found it difficult to make a living from agriculture and moved to urban or industrial areas. In New England, some farms—

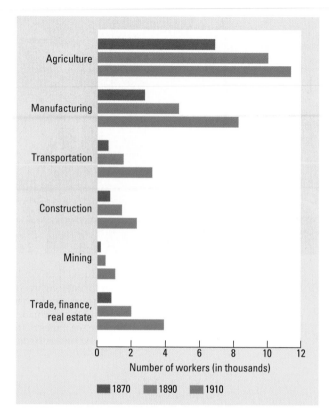

FIGURE 17.3 Industrial Distribution of the Work Force, 1870, 1890, 1910 The number of workers in every industry grew significantly after the Civil War. Though agriculture continued to employ more workers than any other industry, other industries were growing more rapidly than agriculture.

usually small and unproductive—were abandoned when their owners chose to take a job in a factory town or to move west.

The expanding economy, however, needed more workers than the nation itself could supply. As a result, the years from the Civil War to World War I (1865–1914) witnessed the largest influx of immigrants in American history: more than 26 million people, equivalent to three-quarters of the nation's entire population in 1865. By 1910, immigrants and their children made up more than 35 percent of the total population.

speed-up An effort to make employees produce more goods in the same time or for the same pay.

Child labor was widespread through much of the United States, including not just factories but also agriculture and mining. This photograph from the late 1860s is one of the few from that time period to show factory workers. These are probably all the workers in the factory behind them. The youngest seem to be about eight or ten, and at least ten of the thirty-seven people in the picture appear to be children. Note, too, the two men standing to the right side of the picture. The one in the suit is probably the owner of the factory, and the man next to him is likely the foreman. *William B. Becker Collection/American Museum of Photography.*

Large-scale immigration contributed many adult males to the work force—especially in mining, manufacturing, and transportation. But the expanding economy also pulled women and children into the industrial work force. They had often contributed to the work on family farms or business, but now increasing numbers became industrial wage earners. By 1880, a million children (under the age of 16) worked for wages, the largest number in agriculture. Others worked as newsboys, bootblacks, or domestic servants. Many children were employed in the textile industry, especially in the South. Mostly girls, they worked 70-hour weeks and earned 10 to 20 cents a day. Children worked in tobacco and cotton fields in the South, operated sewing machines in New York, and sorted vegetables in Delaware canneries. Other children worked at home, alongside their parents who brought home **piecework.** Most working children turned over all their wages to their parents.

Most of the women who found employment outside the home were unmarried. Data before 1890 are unreliable. In 1890, however, 40 percent of all single women worked for wages, along with 30 percent of widowed or divorced women. Among married women, only 5 percent did so. Black women were employed at much higher rates in all categories. Like child workers, most single young women who lived at home often turned over part or all of their wages to their parents.

A report of the Illinois Bureau of Labor Statistics for 1884 explained that some children and women worked for wages because of the "meager earnings of many [male] heads of families." A study in 1875 showed that the average male factory worker in Lawrence, Massachusetts, earned $500 per year. The study also showed that the average family in Lawrence required a minimum annual income of $600 to provide sufficient food, clothing, and shelter. In such circumstances, a family could not make ends meet without two or more incomes.

As more and more women entered the wage-earning work force, some occupations came to be filled mainly by women. By 1900, females—adults and children—made up more than 70 percent of the workers in clothing factories, knitting mills, and other

---

piecework   Work for which the pay is based on the number of items turned out, rather than by the hour.

textile operations. Women also dominated certain types of office work, accounting for more than 70 percent of the nation's secretaries and typists and 80 percent of telephone operators. However, as women moved into office work, displacing men, wage levels fell, along with the likelihood of promotion from clerical worker to managerial status. For women, office work usually paid less than factory work but was considered safer and of higher status. Women and children workers almost always earned less than their male counterparts. In most industries, work was separated by age and gender, and adult males usually held the jobs requiring the most skill and commanding the best pay. Even when men and women did the same work, they rarely received the same pay (see Fig. 17.4). This wage differential was often explained by the argument that a man had to support a family, whereas a woman worked to supplement the income of her husband or father.

Not all women earned money through working for wages. Some women were self-employed, for example, in making and selling women's hats or dresses. In factory towns or working-class neighborhoods of the cities, some married women rented a room to a boarder or charged to do other people's laundry or sewing. In rural areas, many married women kept chickens and sold eggs to supplement their family's income.

Despite rags-to-riches success stories, extreme mobility was highly unusual. Nearly all successful business leaders, in fact, came from middle-class or upper-class families. Few workers moved more than a step or so up the economic scale. An unskilled laborer might become a semiskilled worker, or a skilled worker might become a foreman, but few wage earners moved into the middle class. If they did, it was usually as the owner of a small and often struggling business.

Craft Unionism—and Its Limits

Just as the entrepreneurs of the late nineteenth century faced choices between competition and cooperation, so too did their employees. Like Frank Roney, some workers reacted to the far-reaching changes in the nature of work by joining with other workers in efforts to maintain or regain control over their working conditions.

Skilled workers remained indispensable in many fields. In construction, only an experienced carpenter could build stairs or hang doors properly. In publishing, only a skilled typesetter could quickly transform handwritten copy into lines of lead type. Only a skilled iron molder could set up the molds and know exactly when and how to pour the molten iron into them. Such workers took pride in the quality of their work and knew that their skill was crucial to their employer's success. One union leader was referring to such workers when he said, "The manager's brains are under the workman's cap."

Skilled workers formed the first unions, called **craft unions** or **trade unions** because membership was limited to skilled workers in a particular craft or trade. Before the Civil War, workers in most American cities created local trade unions in an attempt to regulate the quality of work, wages, hours, and working conditions within their craft. Local unions eventually formed national trade organizations—twenty-six of them by 1873, thirty-nine by 1880. They sometimes called themselves brotherhoods—for example, the United Brotherhood of Carpenters and Joiners, formed in 1881—and they drew on their craft traditions to forge bonds of unity.

The skills that defined craft unions' membership also provided the basis for their success. Skills that sometimes took years to develop made craft workers valuable to their employers and extremely difficult to replace. Such unions often limited their membership

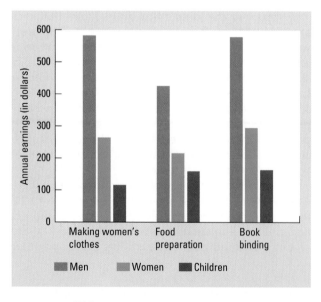

FIGURE 17.4 **Average Annual Earnings for Men, Women, and Children, in Selected Industries, 1890**

craft union, trade union Labor union that organizes skilled workers engaged in a specific craft or trade.

Local trade unions usually ordered elaborate banners, such as this one, which hung in their union hall during their meetings and which they carried in parades or displayed at funerals of members. Such organizations sometimes styled themselves brotherhoods, symbolizing not only the solidarity of the organization but also its masculine nature. © *Bettmann/Corbis.*

bargaining power. Without such skills, they could be replaced easily if they chose to strike. The most effective unions, therefore, were groups of skilled workers—sometimes called the "aristocracy of labor."

Shortly after the Civil War, in 1866, craft unionists representing a variety of local and national organizations joined with reformers to create the **National Labor Union** (NLU), headed by William Sylvis of the Iron Molders until his death in 1869. The NLU also included representatives of women's organizations and, after vigorous debate, decided to encourage the organization of black workers. The most important of the NLU objectives was to establish eight hours as the proper length for a day's work. In 1870 the NLU divided itself into a labor organization and a political party, the National Labor Reform Party, which Roney joined so hopefully when he was working in Omaha. In 1872 the political party nominated candidates for president and vice president, but the campaign was so unsuccessful and divisive that neither the NLU nor the party met again.

Politics: Parties, Spoils, Scandals, and Stalemate

■ What was the significance of political parties in the late nineteenth century?

■ Compare the presidencies of Grant and Hayes. Which was the more successful?

At a time when the nation's economy was changing at a breakneck pace, politics seemed to change very little. Political parties dominated nearly every aspect of the political process from the 1830s until the early 1900s, more so than before or since. During those years, Americans expected that politics meant party politics and that all meaningful political choices came through the structure of parties. Men were expected to hold intense party loyalties—allegiances so strong they were even seen as part of a man's gender role. (All states barred women from voting, as did nearly all the territories.) An understanding of politics, therefore, must begin with an analysis of political parties—what they were, what they did, what they stood for, and what choices they offered to voters.

not just to workers with particular skills but to white males with those skills. If most craft workers within a city belonged to the local union, a strike could badly disrupt or shut down the affected businesses. The strike, therefore, was a powerful weapon in the efforts of skilled workers to define working conditions.

A strike most often succeeded in times of prosperity, when the employer wanted to continue operating and was best able financially to make concessions to workers. When the economy experienced a serious downturn and employers sharply reduced work hours or laid off workers, craft unions usually disintegrated because they could not use the strike effectively. Only after the 1880s did local and national unions develop strategies that permitted them to survive depressions.

The craft union tradition served some skilled workers well but was of little help to most manufacturing workers. Unskilled or semiskilled workers—the majority of employees in many emerging industries—lacked the skills that gave the craft unions their

National Labor Union Federation of trade unions and reform societies organized at Baltimore in 1866; it lasted only six years but helped push through a law limiting government employees to an eight-hour workday.

A NICE FAMILY PARTY.

This cartoon, published in 1878, depicts government patronage as "cake" and all party leaders as greedily clamoring for a piece, despite President Hayes's efforts to maintain peace in his party. Such frantic scrambles eventually brought reform and, in 1882, a new system for appointing people to governmental positions based on their qualifications (see page 556). *Library of Congress.*

Parties, Conventions, and Patronage

The two major parties—Democrats and Republicans—had similar organizations and purposes. Both nominated candidates, tried to elect them to office, and attempted to write and enact their objectives into law.

After the 1830s, nominations for political offices came from **party conventions.** The process of selecting convention delegates began when neighborhood voters gathered in party **caucuses** to choose one or more delegates to represent them at local conventions. Conventions took place at county, state, and national levels and at the level of congressional districts and various state districts. At most conventions, the delegates listened to speech after speech glorifying their party and denouncing the opposition. They nominated candidates for elective offices or chose delegates to another convention further up the federal ladder. And they adopted a **platform,** a written explanation of their positions on important issues and their promises for policy change. Party leaders worked to create compromises that satisfied major groups within their party, and such deal-making sometimes occurred in informal settings—hotel rooms thick with cigar smoke and cluttered with whiskey bottles. Such behind-the-scenes bargaining reinforced the notion of political parties as all-male bastions into which no self-respecting women would venture.

After choosing their candidates, the parties conducted their campaigns. Party organizers tried to identify all their supporters and worked to get them to vote on election day. Such party organizing was sometimes done in places such as saloons, where males congregated and women were barred. Nominees campaigned as party candidates, and campaigns were almost entirely focused on party identity. Nearly every newspaper identified itself with a political party. A party expected to subsidize sympathetic newspapers and, in return, expected both wholehearted support for its candidates and officeholders and slashing criticism of the other party. During the month or so before an election, local party organizations tried to whip up enthusiasm among the party's supporters and to attract new or undecided voters through parades by marching clubs, free barbecues with speeches for dessert, and rallies capped by oratory that lasted for hours.

On election day, each party tried to mobilize all its supporters and make certain that they voted. This form of political campaigning produced very high

> **party convention**   Party meeting to nominate candidates for elective offices and to adopt a political platform.
>
> **caucus**   A gathering of people with a common political interest—for example, to choose delegates to a party convention or to seek consensus on party positions on issues.
>
> **platform**   A formal statement of the principles, policies, and promises on which a political party bases its appeal to voters.

levels of voter participation. In 1876 more than 80 percent of the eligible voters cast their ballots. Turnout sometimes rose even higher, although exact percentages were affected by poor record keeping or fraud. At the polling places, party workers distributed lists, or "tickets," of their party's candidates, which voters then used as ballots. Voting was not secret until the 1890s. Before then, everyone could see which party's ballot a voter deposited in the ballot box (see illustrations of voting on pages 474 and 560). Such a system obviously discouraged voters from crossing party lines.

Once the votes were counted, the winners turned to appointing people to government jobs. In the nineteenth century, government positions not filled by elections were staffed through the **patronage system**—that is, newly elected presidents or governors or mayors appointed their loyal supporters to government jobs, widely considered an appropriate reward for hard work during a campaign. Everyone also understood that those appointed to such jobs were expected to return part of their salaries to the party. The use of patronage for party purposes was often called the spoils system, after a statement by Senator William Marcy in 1831: "To the victor belong the spoils." Its defenders were labeled **spoilsmen.**

Party loyalists inevitably outnumbered the available patronage jobs, so competition for appointments was always fierce. When James A. Garfield became president in 1881, he was so overwhelmed with demands for jobs that he exclaimed in disgust, "My God! What is there in this place that a man should ever want to get into it?" The government jobs most in demand included those involving purchasing or government contracts. Purchasing and contracts became another form of spoils, awarded to entrepreneurs who supported the party. This system invited corruption, and the invitation was all too often accepted. One Post Office Department official, for example, pressured **postmasters** across the country to buy clocks from one of his political associates. Business owners hoping to receive government contracts sometimes paid bribes to the officials who made the decisions. Opportunities were limited only by the imagination of the spoilsmen.

Some critics found a more fundamental defect in the system, beyond its capacity for corruption. By concentrating so much on patronage, politics ignored principles and issues and revolved instead around greed for government employment. The spoils system had many defenders, however. One party loyalist explained, "You can't keep an organization together without patronage. Men ain't in politics for nothin'.

They want to get somethin' out of it." This spoilsman was describing the reality that all local party activists faced: given the enormous numbers of party workers needed to identify supporters and mobilize voters, politics required some sort of reward system.

Republicans and Democrats

Beneath the hoopla, fireworks, and interminable speeches, important differences characterized the two major parties. Some of those differences appeared in the ways the parties described themselves in their platforms, newspapers, speeches, and other campaign appeals.

During the years after the Civil War, Republicans asserted a virtual monopoly on patriotism by pointing to their defense of the Union during the war and claiming that Democrats—especially southern Democrats—had proven themselves disloyal during the conflict. Trumpeting this accusation was often called "waving the bloody shirt," after an instance when a Republican displayed the bloodstained shirt of a northerner (and Republican) beaten by southern white supremacists (who were Democrats). "Every man that shot a Union soldier," Robert Ingersoll, a Republican orator, proclaimed, "was a Democrat." Republicans exploited the Civil War legacy in other ways too. Republicans in Congress voted to provide generous federal pensions to disabled Union army veterans and to the widows and orphans of those who died. Republican Party leaders carefully cultivated the **Grand Army of the Republic** (GAR), the organization of Union veterans, attending their meetings and urging them to "vote as you shot." Republican presidential candidates were almost all Union veterans, as were many state and local officials throughout the North.

Prosperity was another persistent Republican campaign theme. Republicans pointed to the economic growth of the postwar era and insisted that it stemmed largely from their wise policies, especially the protective tariff. Many Republicans also claimed to be the

---

patronage system   System of appointment to government jobs that lets the winner in an election distribute nearly all appointive government jobs to loyal party members; also called the spoils system.

spoilsmen   Derogatory term for defenders of the patronage or spoils system.

postmaster   An official appointed to oversee the operations of a post office.

Grand Army of the Republic   Organization of Union army veterans.

Thomas Nast, the most influential cartoonist of the 1870s, and the most talented cartoonist of his age, began the practice of using an elephant to symbolize the Republicans and a donkey for the Democrats. At the time, however, Republicans often preferred an eagle, and Democrats usually chose a rooster. *Library of Congress.*

party of decency and morality. Senator George Hoar of Massachusetts once boasted that all upright and virtuous citizens "commonly, and as a rule, by the natural law of their being, find their place in the Republican party." Republican campaigners delighted in portraying as typical Democrats "the old slave-owner and slave-driver, the saloon-keeper, the ballot-box-stuffer, the Kuklux [Klan], the criminal class of the great cities, the men who cannot read or write."

Where Republicans defined themselves in terms of what their party did and who they were, Democrats typically focused on what they opposed. Most leading Democrats stood firm against "governmental interference" in the economy, especially the protective tariff and land grants, equating government activism with privileges for a favored few. The protective tariff, they charged, protected manufacturers from international competition at the expense of consumers who paid higher prices. The public domain, they argued, should provide farms for citizens, not subsidies for corporations. All in all, Democrats favored a strictly limited role for the government in the economy, a position much closer to laissez faire than that of the Republicans.

Just as the Democrats opposed governmental interference in the economy, so too did they oppose governmental interference in social relations and behavior. In the North, especially in Irish and German communities, they condemned **prohibition** (efforts to ban the sale of alcoholic beverages), which they called a violation of personal liberty. In the South, Democrats rejected federal enforcement of equal rights for African Americans, which they denounced as a violation of states' rights. There, Democrats called for white supremacy.

Most voters developed strong loyalties to one party or the other, often on the basis of **ethnicity**, race, or religion. Nearly all Catholics and many Irish, German, and other immigrants supported the Democrats. Poor voters in the cities usually supported the local party organization, whether Democratic or Republican— but far more were Democrats. Most southern whites

prohibition   A legal ban on the manufacture, sale, and use of alcoholic beverages.

ethnicity   Having to do with common racial, cultural, religious, or linguistic characteristics; an ethnic group is one that has some shared racial, religious, linguistic, cultural, or national heritage.

supported the Democrats as the party of white supremacy. The Democrats' opposition to the protective tariff attracted a few businessmen and professionals who favored more competition. The Democrats, all in all, comprised a very diverse coalition, one that held together primarily because its various components could unite to oppose government action on social or economic matters.

Outside the South, most **old-stock** Protestants voted Republican, as did most Scandinavian and British immigrants. Nearly all African Americans supported the Republicans as the party of emancipation, as did most veterans of the abolition movement. So many Union veterans supported the Republicans that someone suggested the initials *GAR* stood for "generally all Republicans." Republicans always did well among the voters of New England, Pennsylvania, and much of the Midwest. In California and New Mexico Territory, many Mexican Americans voted Republican. For the most part, the Republicans developed the more coherent political organization, united around a set of policies that involved action by the federal government to encourage economic growth and to protect blacks' rights. As one leading Republican put it, "The Republican party does things, the Democratic party criticizes." Neither party, however, advocated government action to regulate, restrict, or tax the newly developing industrial corporations.

During the Civil War and early years of Reconstruction, the dominant Republicans changed the very nature of the federal government. They significantly revised the nature of citizenship, relations between the federal government and the states, and the role of the federal government in the economy. Most of the economic policies established in the 1860s persisted with little change for more than a generation. The protective tariff and the use of the public domain to encourage rapid economic development both involved governmental action to stimulate economic development. Thus federal economic policy during these years should not be described as pure laissez faire, even though there was little regulation, restriction, or taxation of economic activity.

Grant's Troubled Presidency: Spoils and Scandals

Ulysses S. Grant's success as a general failed to prepare him for the presidency. During his two terms in office (elected in 1868, reelected in 1872), he rarely challenged congressional dominance of domestic policymaking. He often appointed friends or acquaintances to posts for which they possessed no particular qualifications. He proved unable to form a competent cabinet and faced constant turnover among his executive advisers. Many of his appointees seemed to view their positions as little more than the spoils of party victory, and Grant proved too willing to believe his appointees' denials of wrongdoing. He did choose a highly capable secretary of state, Hamilton Fish, and he eventually found in Benjamin Bristow a secretary of the Treasury who vigorously combated corruption.

Congress supplied its full share of scandal. Visiting Washington in 1869, young Henry Adams (great-grandson of the second president and grandson of the sixth) was surprised to hear a member of the cabinet bellow, "You can't use tact with a Congressman! A Congressman is a hog! You must take a stick and hit him on the snout!" Too many members of Congress behaved in a way that confirmed such a cynical view. In 1868, before Grant became president, several prominent congressional leaders had become stockholders in the **Crédit Mobilier,** a construction company created by the chief shareholders in the Union Pacific Railroad. The Union Pacific officers awarded to Crédit Mobilier a generous contract to build the railroad. Thus the company's chief shareholders paid themselves handsomely for constructing their own railroad. To protect this arrangement from congressional scrutiny, the company sold shares at cut-rate prices to key members of Congress. Purchasers included some leading Republicans. Revelation of these arrangements in 1872 and 1873 scandalized the nation. No sooner did that furor pass than Congress voted itself a 50 percent pay raise and made the increase two years retroactive. Only after widespread public protest did Congress repeal its "salary grab."

Public disgrace was not limited to the federal government or to Republicans. In New York City, the so-called **Tweed Ring,** accused of using bribery, **kickbacks,** and padded accounts to steal money from

---

old-stock   People whose ancestors have lived in the United States for several generations.

Crédit Mobilier   Company created to build the Union Pacific Railroad; in a scandalous deal uncovered in 1872–1873, it sold shares cheaply to congressmen who approved federal subsidies for railroad construction.

Tweed Ring   Name applied to the political organization of William Marcy Tweed.

kickback   An illegal payment by a contractor to the official who awarded the contract.

New York City, supplied a seemingly endless string of scandals involving city and state officials. At the center was **William Marcy Tweed,** whose name became synonymous with urban political corruption. Tweed entered New York City politics in the 1850s and became head of the Tammany Hall organization in 1863. By 1868, this organization dominated the local Democratic Party and controlled much of city and state government. Labeled "Boss Tweed" by his opponents, he and his associates built public support by spending tax funds on charities, and they gave to the poor from their own pockets—pockets often lined with public funds or bribes. Under Tweed's direction, city government launched major construction projects: public buildings, improvements in streets, parks, sewers, and docks. Much of the construction was riddled with corruption. Between 1868 and 1871, the Tweed **Ring** may have plundered $200 million from the city, mostly by giving bloated construction contracts to businesses that returned a kickback to the ring. In 1871 evidence of corruption led to Tweed's indictment and ultimately his conviction and imprisonment.

Though Grant won reelection without difficulty in 1872 (see pages 479–480), the midterm elections of 1874 were a different story. The congressional scandals alienated some voters. Moreover, the depression that began in 1873 gave Democrats in urban industrial areas a barbed response when Republicans claimed to be the party of prosperity. And throughout the South, political terrorism suppressed the Republican vote. All these factors combined to give Democrats widespread gains in the House of Representatives. Republicans previously had 194 seats to 92 for the Democrats, but now the Democrats held 169 seats to the Republicans' 109. For the next twenty years, from 1874 until 1894, Democrats generally commanded a majority in the House of Representatives. Even though Republicans usually won the presidency, Democratic control of the House made it difficult or impossible for the Republicans to push through major legislation. The scandals, depression, and political terrorism in the South had cost the Republicans control of Congress.

More scandals were to come. In 1875 Treasury Secretary Bristow took the lead in fighting widespread corruption in the collection of whiskey taxes. A **Whiskey Ring** of federal officials and distillers, centered in St. Louis, had conspired to evade payment of taxes. The 230 men indicted included several of Grant's appointees and even his private secretary. The next year, William Belknap, Grant's secretary of war, resigned shortly before he was impeached for accepting bribes.

President Rutherford B. Hayes and the Politics of Stalemate

Rutherford B. Hayes became president after the closely contested election of 1876 led to the Compromise of 1877 (see page 481). His personal integrity and principled stand on issues helped to restore the reputation of the Republican Party after the humiliations of the Grant administration, but any hope he had for significant change ran up against the Democratic majority in the House of Representatives and significant opposition within his own party. His harshest Republican critic was Roscoe Conkling, a flamboyant senator from New York and the boss of that state's large and hungry Republican organization. He became especially hostile after Hayes refused to install Conkling supporters in key federal patronage positions.

Hayes promised to serve only one term and probably could not have secured a second nomination had he sought one. His handling of patronage annoyed many Republicans, and he estranged reformers by not seeking a full-scale revision of the spoils system. When the White House stopped serving alcohol, Hayes's opponents blamed his wife, Lucy Webb Hayes, the first college-educated First Lady and a committed reformer, and dubbed her "Lemonade Lucy." By mid-1880, Hayes seemed to welcome the end of his presidency.

Challenges to Politics as Usual: Grangers, Greenbackers, and Silverites

Though political change seemed to move at a glacial pace, especially after 1874, at some times and in some places, groups emerged to challenge mainstream politics and to seek new policies and new ways of making political decisions. Given the large proportion of

> **William Marcy Tweed**   New York City political boss who used the Tammany organization to control city and state government from the 1860s until his downfall in 1871.
>
> **ring**   In this context, ring means a group of people who act together to exercise control over something.
>
> **Whiskey Ring**   Distillers and revenue officials in St. Louis who were revealed in 1875 to have defrauded the government of millions of dollars in whiskey taxes, with the cooperation of federal officials.

This poster appeared in 1869, two years after the founding of the Grange. It depicts the farmer as a member of the producing class, laboring in the soil to produce value. It shows a military officer, railroad magnate, physician, politician, lawyer, merchant, and preacher as living off the farmer's labor. *Library of Congress.*

the work force that was still engaged in agriculture, it should not be surprising that farmers were prominent in several influential movements.

After the Civil War, farmers joined organizations that they hoped would provide relief from the scourges of falling prices and high railroad freight rates. Oliver H. Kelley formed the first in 1867. Kelley called it the Patrons of Husbandry and wrote for it a secret ritual modeled on that of the Masons. Usually known as the **Grange,** the new organization extended full participation to women as well as men. Kelley hoped that the Grange would provide a social outlet for farm families and educate them in new methods of agriculture. Far exceeding his expectations, it soon led to political action.

The Grange grew rapidly, especially in the Midwest and the central South. In the 1870s, it became a leading proponent for cooperative buying and selling. Many local Grange organizations set up cooperative stores, and some even tried to sell their crops cooperatively. In a **cooperative** store (or consumers' cooperative), members agree to shop there and then divide any profits among themselves. In a producers' cooperative, farmers sought to hold their crops back from market and to negotiate over prices rather than

> **Grange** Organization of farmers that combined social activities with education about new methods of farming and cooperative economic efforts; formally called the Patrons of Husbandry.
>
> **cooperative** A business enterprise in which workers and consumers share in ownership and take part in management.

The Grange tries to awaken the public to the approaching locomotive (a symbol of monopoly power) that is bringing consolidation (mergers), extortion (high prices), bribery, and other evils. *Culver Pictures.*

simply to accept a buyer's offer. Two state Granges began manufacturing farm machinery, and Grangers laid ambitious plans for cooperative factories producing everything from wagons to sewing machines. Some Grangers formed mutual insurance companies, and a few experimented with cooperative banks.

The Grange defined itself as nonpartisan. However, as Grange membership rapidly climbed in the 1870s, its midwestern and western members began to move toward political action. New political parties emerged in eleven states. Usually called "Granger Parties," their central demand was state legislation to prohibit railroad rate discrimination. Other groups, especially merchants, also sought such laws, but the role of the Grangers was so prominent that the resulting state laws, most of them dating to 1872–1874, were usually called **Granger laws.** When the constitutionality of such regulation was challenged, the Supreme Court ruled, in *Munn v. Illinois* (1877), that businesses with "a public interest," including warehouses and railroads, "must submit to be controlled by the public for the common good."

The Grange reached its zenith in the mid-1870s. Hastily organized cooperatives soon began to suffer

financial problems that were compounded by the national depression, and the collapse of cooperatives often pulled down Grange organizations. Political activity brought some successes but also generated bitter disputes within the Granges. The organization lost many members, and after the late 1870s, the surviving Granges tended to avoid both cooperatives and politics.

With the decline of the Grange, some farmers looked to **monetary policy** for relief. After the Civil War, most prices fell (a situation called **deflation**) because of increased production, more efficient techniques in agriculture and manufacturing, and the failure of the money supply to grow as rapidly as the economy. Deflation has always injured debtors because it means that the money used to pay off a loan has greater purchasing power (and so is harder to come by) than the money of the original loan. The Greenback Party argued that printing more **greenbacks,** the paper money issued during the Civil War, would stabilize prices, and they found a receptive audience among farmers who were in debt. Greenbackers were arguing for the quantity theory of money. According to this view, if the currency (money in circulation, whether of paper or precious metal) grew more rapidly than the economy, the result was inflation (rising prices), but if the currency failed to grow as rapidly as the economy, the outcome was deflation (falling prices). Greenbackers hoped to control the monetary supply in such a way as to stabilize prices.

In the congressional elections of 1878, the Greenback Party received nearly a million votes and elected fourteen congressmen. In the 1880 presidential election, the Greenback Party not only endorsed inflation

---

Granger laws   State laws establishing standard freight and passenger rates on railroads, passed in several states in the 1870s in response to lobbying by the Grange and other groups, including merchants.

monetary policy   Now, the regulation of the money supply and interest rates by the Federal Reserve. In the late nineteenth century, federal monetary policy was largely limited to defining the medium of the currency (gold, silver, or paper) and the relations between the types of currency.

deflation   Falling prices, a situation in which the purchasing power of the dollar increases; the opposite of deflation is inflation, when prices go up and the purchasing power of the dollar declines.

greenbacks   Paper money, not backed by gold, that the federal government issued during the Civil War.

but also tried to attract urban workers by supporting the eight-hour workday, legislation to protect workers, and the abolition of child labor. They also called for regulation of transportation and communication, a **graduated income tax** (on the grounds that it was the fairest form of taxation), and woman suffrage. For president, they nominated James B. Weaver of Iowa, a Greenback congressman and former Union army general. Weaver got only 3.3 percent of the vote. In 1884, with a similar platform and the erratic Benjamin Butler as their presidential nominee, the Greenbackers fared even worse.

A similar monetary analysis motivated those who wanted the government to resume issuing silver dollars. Until 1873, federal law specified that federal mints would accept gold and silver and make them into coins as the easiest way to get money into circulation. Throughout the mid-nineteenth century, however, owners of silver made more money by selling it commercially than by taking it to the mints. Thus no silver dollars existed for many years. In 1873 Congress dropped the silver dollar from the list of approved coins, following the lead of Britain and Germany, which had specified that only gold was to serve as money. Some Americans believed that adhering to this **gold standard** was essential if American businesses were to compete effectively in international markets for capital and for the sale of goods. Soon after 1873, however, silver discoveries in the West drove down the commercial price of silver. Arguments for the coining of all available silver into dollars quickly found support not just among farmers but also among silver mining interests. Members of this farming-mining coalition were soon called "Silverites." In 1878, over Hayes's veto, Congress passed the **Bland-Allison Act** authorizing a limited amount of silver dollars, but the move failed to counteract deflation, and neither side was satisfied. Silverites condemned the action as too feeble, and gold supporters denounced it for diluting the gold standard.

The Great Railway Strike of 1877 and the Federal Response

During Hayes's first year in the presidency, the nation witnessed for the first time the implications of widespread labor strife. In response to the depression that began in 1873, railroad companies reduced operating costs by repeatedly cutting wages. Railroad workers' pay fell by more than a third from 1873 to 1877. Union leaders talked of organizing a strike but failed to bring one off.

Without union leadership, railway workers took matters into their own hands when companies announced additional pay cuts. On July 16, 1877, a group of firemen and brakemen on the Baltimore & Ohio Railroad stopped work in Maryland. The next day, nearby in West Virginia, a group of railway workers refused to work until the company restored their wages. Some members of the local community supported the strikers. The governor of West Virginia sent in the state **militia,** but the strikers prevented the trains from running. The governor then requested federal troops, and Hayes sent them.

Federal troops restored service on the Baltimore & Ohio, but the strike spread to other lines. Strikers shut down trains in Pittsburgh. When the local militia refused to act against the strikers, the governor of Pennsylvania sent militia units from Philadelphia. The troops killed twenty-six people. Strikers and their sympathizers then attacked the militia, forced the troops to retreat, and burned and looted railroad property throughout Pittsburgh.

Strikes erupted across Pennsylvania and New York and throughout the Midwest. Everywhere, the strikers drew support from their local communities. In various places, coal miners, factory workers, owners of small businesses, farmers, black workers, and women demonstrated their solidarity with the workers. In St. Louis, local unions declared a **general strike** to secure the eight-hour workday and to end child labor. State militia, federal troops, and local police eventually broke up the strikes, but not before hundreds had lost their lives. By the strikes' end, railroad companies had suffered property damage worth $10 million, half of the losses in Pittsburgh.

---

graduated income tax   Percentage tax that is levied on income and varies with income, so that individuals with the lowest income pay taxes at the lowest rates.

gold standard   A monetary system based on gold; under such a system, legal contracts typically called for the payment of all debts in gold, and paper money could be redeemed in gold at a bank.

Bland-Allison Act   Law passed by Congress in 1878 providing for federal purchase of limited amounts of silver to be coined into silver dollars.

militia   A military force consisting of civilians who agree to be mobilized into service in times of emergency; organized by state governments during the nineteenth century but now superseded by the National Guard.

general strike   A strike by members of all unions in a particular region.

This engraving depicts striking railroad workers in Martinsburg, West Virginia, as they stopped a freight train on July 17, 1877, in the opening days of the Great Railway Strike of that year. Engravings such as this, showing strikers to be heavily armed, may or may not have been accurate depictions of events. But the photography of that day could rarely capture live action, and the technology of the day could not reproduce photographs in newspapers, so the public's understanding of events such as the 1877 strike were formed through artists' depictions. *Library of Congress.*

The **Great Railway Strike of 1877** revealed widespread dislike for the new railroad companies and significant community support for striking workers. However, the strike alarmed many other Americans. Some considered the use of troops only a temporary expedient and, like Hayes, hoped for "education of the strikers," "judicious control of the capitalists," and some way to "remove the distress which afflicts laborers." Others saw in the strike a forecast of future labor unrest, and they called for better means to enforce law and order.

The United States and the World, 1865–1880

■ How did American policymakers define the role of the United States in North America during the period 1865 to 1880?

■ How did they define the role of the United States in other parts of the world?

During much of the nineteenth century, the U.S. role in world affairs was slight, and most Americans expected that their nation would avoid foreign conflicts, in keeping with the advice of George Washington to "steer clear of permanent alliances with any portion of the foreign world." In fact, Americans had few worries about being pulled into European wars, for Europe remained relatively peaceful. The insulation imposed by the Atlantic and Pacific reinforced Americans' feeling of security, and the powerful British navy provided a protective umbrella for American commercial shipping. Thus world events posed few threats to American interests. During the years 1865–1880, American involvement in world affairs began to expand, but gradually and uncertainly. However, the effect of America's economic transformation on its foreign relations, as on its domestic politics, was slow in appearing.

Alaska, Canada, and the *Alabama* Claims

In 1866 the Russian minister to the United States hinted to Secretary of State **William H. Seward** that Tsar Alexander II might dispose of Russian holdings in North America if the price were right. Seward, one of the most capable secretaries of state in the nine-

Great Railway Strike of 1877 Largely spontaneous strikes by railroad workers, triggered by wage cuts.

William H. Seward U.S. secretary of state under Lincoln and Johnson, a former abolitionist who had expansionist views and arranged the purchase of Alaska from Russia.

teenth century, had often voiced his belief in America's destiny to expand across the North American continent. He made an offer, and in 1867 the two diplomats agreed on slightly over $7 million—less than 2 cents per acre. The deal was done, and the land that was to become the state of Alaska was in U.S. hands.

The Alaska treaty differed from earlier agreements acquiring territory in one significant way. Previous treaties had specified that the inhabitants of the territories (except Indians) would immediately become American citizens and that the territories themselves would eventually become states. The Alaska treaty extended citizenship but carried no promise of eventual statehood. It therefore moved a half-step away from earlier patterns of territorial expansion and foreshadowed later patterns of colonial acquisition.

Some journalists derided the new purchase as a frozen, worthless wasteland and branded the bargain "Seward's Folly." The Senate, however, greeted the windfall with considerable enthusiasm. Charles Sumner, chairman of the **Senate Foreign Relations Committee,** looked on the purchase of Alaska as the first step toward the ultimate acquisition of Canada. Many others shared his hope.

Canada was on Sumner's mind as he considered claims against Great Britain arising out of the Civil War. Several Confederate warships, notably the *Alabama* and *Florida,* had badly disrupted northern shipping. British shipyards had built those ships for the Confederacy. British ports had also offered repairs and supplies to Confederate ships. The United States claimed that Britain had violated its neutrality by allowing these activities, but Britain refused to accept responsibility for the damage done by the Confederate cruisers. In 1869, however, as relations between Britain and Russia grew tense, the British began to fret that American shipyards might provide similar services for the Russians. Sumner argued that the damages caused by the Confederate navy included not just direct claims for shipping losses but many indirect claims as well, amounting, he insisted, to the entire cost of the last two years of the war. The total, by Sumner's calculations, was more than $2 billion—so much, he suggested, that Britain could best meet its obligation by ceding all its North American possessions, including Canada, to the United States.

Grant's secretary of state, Hamilton Fish, found Sumner's claims unrealistic and convinced Grant not to support them. Instead, in the Treaty of Washington (1871), the two countries agreed to **arbitration.** The 1872 arbitration decision held Britain responsible for the direct claims and set $15.5 million as damages to be paid to the United States.

The United States and Latin America

After the Civil War, American diplomats turned their attention to Latin America, partly because European powers were starting to exert influence in that direction and partly because some Americans wanted the United States to take a more prominent role in the region. In 1823 President James Monroe had announced that North and South America were not areas for colonial expansion by European powers, that the United States would consider any attempt by a European power to colonize in the Western Hemisphere a threat to the United States, and that the United States would not interfere with existing colonies nor become involved in European power politics. Though later a linchpin of American policy, the **Monroe Doctrine** was rarely mentioned by presidents over the next two-thirds of the nineteenth century.

In 1861, as the United States lurched into civil war, France, Spain, and Britain sent a joint force to Mexico to collect debts that Mexico could not pay. Spain and Britain soon withdrew, but French troops remained, occupying key areas despite resistance led by **Benito Juarez,** president of Mexico. Some of Juarez's political opponents cooperated with the French emperor, Napoleon III, to name Archduke **Maximilian** of Austria as emperor of Mexico. Maximilian, an idealistic young man, apparently believed that the Mexican people genuinely wanted him as their leader, and he hoped to serve them well. He antagonized some of his conservative supporters with talk of reform but failed to win other support. Resistance became war, and Maximilian held power only because the French army kept his enemies at bay.

Senate Foreign Relations Committee One of the standing (permanent) committees of the Senate; it deals with foreign affairs, and its chairman often wields considerable influence over foreign policy.

arbitration Process by which parties to a dispute submit their case to the judgment of an impartial person or group (the arbiter) and agree to abide by the arbiter's decision.

Monroe Doctrine Announcement by President James Monroe in 1823 that the Western Hemisphere was off-limits for future European colonial expansion.

Benito Juarez Elected president of Mexico who led resistance to the French occupation of his country in 1864–1867; the first Mexican president of Indian ancestry.

Maximilian Austrian archduke appointed by France to be emperor of Mexico in 1864; later executed by Mexican republicans.

As these events were unfolding, the United States was involved in its own civil war. The Union recognized Juarez as president of Mexico but could do little else. When the Civil War ended, Secretary of State Seward demanded that Napoleon III withdraw his troops. At the time, the United States possessed the most experienced, and perhaps the largest, army in the world. Seward underscored his demand when fifty thousand battle-hardened troops moved to the Mexican border. Thus confronted, Napoleon III agreed to withdraw. The last French soldiers sailed home in early 1867, but Maximilian unwisely remained behind, where he was defeated in battle by Juarez and then executed. Though Seward did not cite the Monroe Doctrine at any point, the withdrawal of the French troops in the face of substantial American military force renewed respect in Europe for the role of the United States in Latin America.

Some Americans had long regarded the Caribbean and Central America as potential areas for expansion. One vision was a canal through Central America to shorten the coast-to-coast shipping route around South America. In addition, after the Civil War, both the Caribbean and the Pacific attracted attention as regions where the navy might need bases. In 1867, seeking suitable sites, Secretary of State Seward negotiated treaties to buy part of the **Danish West Indies** and to secure a base site in **Santo Domingo,** but both efforts failed to win congressional approval.

In 1870, with Grant in the White House, Hamilton Fish became secretary of state. Rather than pursuing annexation of territory, Secretary of State Fish sought expansion of trade with Latin America. When the dictator of Santo Domingo offered either to annex his entire country to the United States or to lease a major bay for a naval base, Fish objected. Nonetheless, urged on by Americans eager to invest in the area, Grant asked the Senate to ratify a treaty of annexation. Approval required support of two-thirds of the Senate. With Sumner leading the opposition, the treaty failed by a vote of 28 to 28. Grant nevertheless proclaimed an extension, or **corollary,** of the Monroe Doctrine, specifying that no territory in the Western Hemisphere could ever be transferred to a European power.

Eastern Asia and the Pacific

Americans had long taken a strong commercial interest in eastern Asia. The China trade dated to 1784, and goods from Asia and the Pacific accounted for about 8 percent of all U.S. imports after the Civil War. Exports to that area were disappointing, however, less than 2 percent of the total, and some Americans dreamed of profits from selling to China's hundreds of millions of potential consumers. American missionaries began to preach in China in 1830. Although they counted few converts, their lectures back in the United States stimulated public interest in the Asian nation.

In 1839–1842, the British navy had humiliated Chinese forces in a naval war. The Chinese government had long placed severe restrictions on foreign trade. The war began over Chinese efforts to prevent British merchants from importing and selling **opium** in China, but the British defined the issue as the right to engage in trade without restraints. In defeat, China granted trading privileges to Britain and subsequently to other nations that wished to sell goods there. The first treaty between China and the United States, in 1844, included a provision granting **most-favored-nation status** to the United States. Japan and Korea had also refused to engage in trade, their way of deflecting Western influences and avoiding European power rivalries. In 1854 an American naval force convinced the Japanese government to open its ports to foreign trade. A similar navy action opened Korea in 1882.

Growing trade prospects between eastern Asia and the United States fueled American interest in the Pacific. Whether in sailing ships or steamships, the American merchant marine needed ports in the Pacific for supplies and repairs. Interest focused especially on Hawai`i. Hawai`i had attracted Christian missionaries from New England as early as 1819, shortly after King Kamehameha the Great united the islands into one nation. The **missionaries** were first concerned with preaching the Gospel and convincing the unabashed Hawaiians to wear clothes,

Danish West Indies Island group in the Caribbean, including St. Croix and St. Thomas, which the United States finally purchased from Denmark in 1917; now known as the U.S. Virgin Islands.

Santo Domingo Nation in the Caribbean that shares the island of Hispaniola with Haiti; it became independent from Spain in 1865; now known as the Dominican Republic.

corollary A proposition that follows logically and naturally from an already proven point.

opium An addictive drug made from poppies.

most-favored-nation status In a treaty between nation A and nation B, the provision that commercial privileges extended by A to other nations automatically become available to B.

King David Kalakaua of Hawai`i loved to pose in full military uniform, but he was, in fact, a weak monarch who yielded a good deal of power to the non-Hawaiians who dominated the islands' economy. *Bishop Museum.*

but later some missionaries and their descendants came to exercise great influence over several Hawaiian monarchs.

The islands' location near the center of the Pacific made them an ideal place to stockpile supplies of fresh food and water for ships crossing the Pacific and for whaling vessels. After 1848, ships traveling from New York around South America to San Francisco also routinely stopped in Hawai`i for supplies. As early as 1842, President John Tyler stated that the United States would not allow the islands to pass under the control of another power, but Britain and France continued to take a keen interest in them.

David Kalakaua became king of Hawai`i in 1874. During his reign, relations with the United States became much closer. Kalakaua was the first reigning monarch ever to visit the United States, in 1874, and in 1875 he approved a treaty of reciprocity that gave Hawaiian sugar duty-free access to the United States. The outcome was a rapid expansion of the Hawaiian sugar industry as the sons and daughters of New England missionaries joined representatives of American sugar refiners in developing huge sugar plantations. Soon Hawaiian sugar spawned a vertically integrated industry that included American-owned sugar plantations, ships to carry raw sugar to the mainland, and sugar refineries in California—and the economies of the two nations became closely linked.

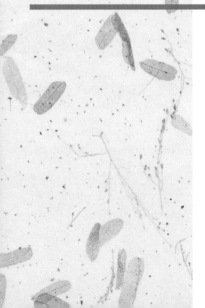

Individual Voices

Examining a Primary Source

Andrew Carnegie Explains the Gospel of Wealth

Unlike the typical industrial magnate, Andrew Carnegie wrote extensively about his ideas on a wide range of topics, including competition and wealth. Carnegie's views, from the vantage point of the boardroom, contrast sharply with those of Frank Roney down on the shop floor, as quoted from his autobiography in the Individual Choices feature at the beginning of this chapter. This selection, from an article written by Carnegie that he entitled "Wealth," appeared in *The North American Review* in June 1889.

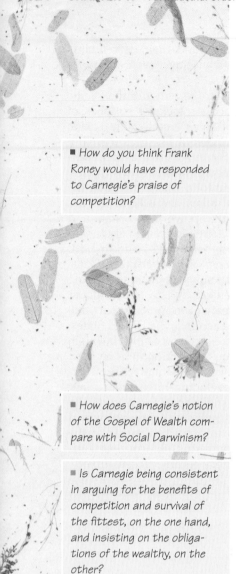

■ How do you think Frank Roney would have responded to Carnegie's praise of competition?

■ How does Carnegie's notion of the Gospel of Wealth compare with Social Darwinism?

■ Is Carnegie being consistent in arguing for the benefits of competition and survival of the fittest, on the one hand, and insisting on the obligations of the wealthy, on the other?

The price which society pays for the law of competition, like the price it pays for cheap comforts and luxuries, is also great; but the advantages of this law are also greater still, for it is to this law that we owe our wonderful material development, which brings improved conditions in its train. . . . It is here; we cannot evade it; no substitutes for it have been found; and while the law may be sometimes hard for the individual, it is best for the race, because it insures the survival of the fittest in every department. We accept and welcome, therefore, as conditions to which we must accommodate ourselves, great inequality of environment, the concentration of business, industrial and commercial, in the hands of a few, and the law of competition between these, as being not only beneficial, but essential for the future progress of the race. . . . ■

This, then, is held to be the duty of the man of Wealth: First, to set an example of modest unostentatious living, shunning display or extravagance; to provide moderately for the legitimate wants of those dependent upon him; and after doing so to consider all surplus revenues which come to him simply as trust funds, which he is called upon to administer, and strictly bound as a matter of duty to administer in the manner which, in his judgment, is best calculated to produce the most beneficial results for the community. . . . The best means of benefiting the community is to place within its reach the ladders upon which the aspiring can rise—parks, and means of recreation, by which men are helped in body and mind; works of art, certain to give pleasure and improve the public taste, and public institutions of various kinds, which will improve the general condition of the people. . . . Thus is the problem of the Rich and Poor to be solved. . . . Individualism will continue, but the millionaire will be but a trustee for the poor; intrusted for a season with a great part of the increased wealth of the community, but administering it for the community far better than it could or would have done for itself. . . . ■

The man who dies leaving behind him millions of available wealth, which was his to administer during life, will pass away "unwept, unhonored, and unsung," no matter to what uses he leaves the dross which he cannot take with him. Of such as these the public verdict will then be: "The man who dies thus rich dies disgraced." . . . Such, in my opinion, is the true Gospel concerning Wealth, obedience to which is destined some day to solve the problem of the Rich and the Poor, and to bring "Peace on earth, among men of Good-Will." ■

Summary

After 1865, large-scale manufacturing developed quite quickly in the United States, built on a foundation of abundant natural resources, a pool of skilled workers, expanding harvests, and favorable government policies. The outcome was the transformation of the U.S. economy.

Entrepreneurs improved and extended railway lines, creating a national transportation network. Manufacturers and merchants now began to think in terms of a national market for raw materials and fin-

ished goods. Railroads were the first businesses to grapple with the many problems related to size, and they made choices that other businesses imitated. Steel was the crucial building material for much of industrial America, and Andrew Carnegie revolutionized the steel industry. He became one of the best known of many entrepreneurs who developed manufacturing operations of unprecedented size and complexity. Social Darwinists acclaimed unrestricted competition for producing progress and survival of the fittest. Others criticized the negative aspects of the era's economy. At the time and later, some condemned the great entrepreneurs as robber barons, but more complex treatments by historians place such figures within the cultural context of their own time.

Industrial workers had little control over the pace or hours of their work and often faced unpleasant or dangerous working conditions. Even so, workers in both the United States and other parts of the world chose to migrate to expanding industrial centers from rural areas. The new work force included not only adult males but also women and children. Some workers formed labor organizations to seek higher wages, shorter hours, and better conditions. Trade unions, based on craft skills, were the earliest and most successful of such organizations.

Americans in the late nineteenth century expected political parties to dominate politics. All elected public officials were nominated by party conventions and elected through the efforts of party campaigners. Most civil service employees were appointed in return for party loyalty. Republicans used government to promote rapid economic development, but Democrats argued that government works best when it governs least. Most voters divided between the major parties largely along the lines of region, ethnicity, and race. The presidency of Ulysses S. Grant was plagued by scandals. President Rutherford B. Hayes restored Republican integrity but faced stormy conflict between Republican factions. Grangers, Greenbackers, and Silverites all challenged the major parties, appealing most to debt-ridden farmers. The Great Railway Strike of 1877 was the first indication of what widespread industrial strife could do to the nation's new transportation network based on railroads, and public officials resorted to federal troops to suppress the strike.

From 1865 to 1889, few Americans expected their nation to take a major part in world affairs, at least outside North America. The United States did acquire Alaska and convince the French to withdraw from Mexico, and some Americans hoped that Canada might become U.S. territory. At the same time, the United States took actions to encourage trade with the nations of eastern Asia, and the kingdom of Hawai`i became closely integrated with the American economy.

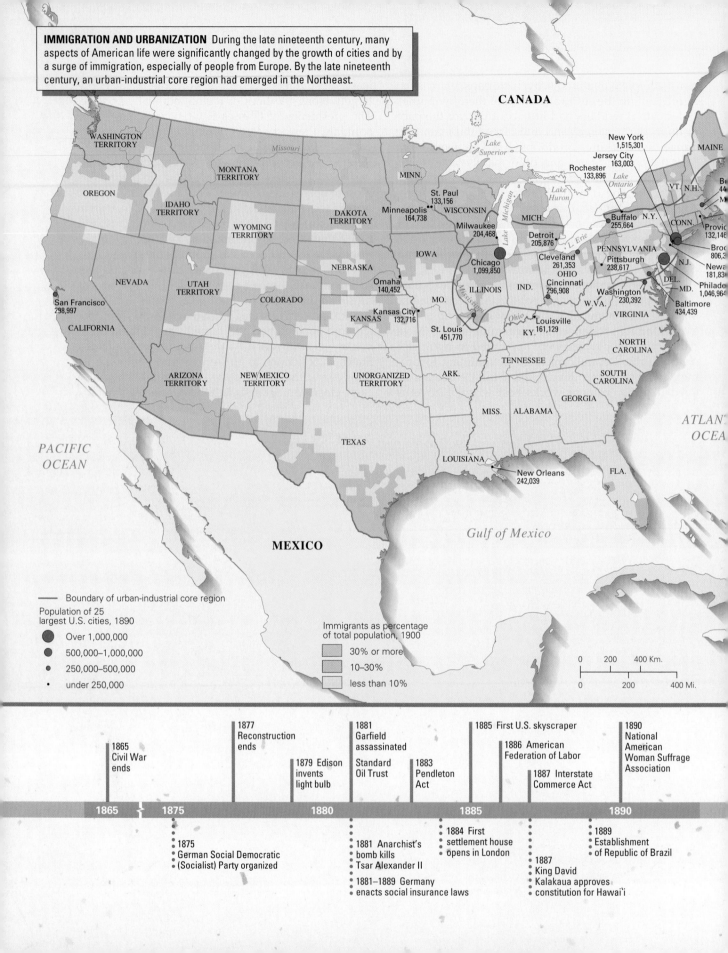

IMMIGRATION AND URBANIZATION During the late nineteenth century, many aspects of American life were significantly changed by the growth of cities and by a surge of immigration, especially of people from Europe. By the late nineteenth century, an urban-industrial core region had emerged in the Northeast.

CANADA

WASHINGTON TERRITORY

Missouri

MONTANA TERRITORY

MINN.

Lake Superior

New York 1,515,301
Jersey City 163,003
Rochester 133,896
Lake Ontario

MAINE

VT. N.H.

Be 44

OREGON

IDAHO TERRITORY

WYOMING TERRITORY

DAKOTA TERRITORY

St. Paul 133,156
Minneapolis 164,738
WISCONSIN
Milwaukee 204,468

Lake Michigan

MICH.

Lake Huron

Buffalo 255,664 N.Y.

CONN.

M

Provid 132,148

Detroit 205,876

L. Erie

PENNSYLVANIA
Pittsburgh 238,617

Bro 806,3

NEVADA

UTAH TERRITORY

NEBRASKA

IOWA

Chicago 1,099,850
ILLINOIS

IND.

Cleveland 261,353
OHIO
Cincinnati 296,908

N.J.

Newa 181,83

DEL.

Washington 230,392

Philade 1,046,96

CALIFORNIA

San Francisco 298,997

COLORADO

Omaha 140,452

MO.

KANSAS
Kansas City 132,716

Mississippi

St. Louis 451,770

Ohio

KY.

Louisville 161,129

MD.

Baltimore 434,439

W.VA.

VIRGINIA

ARIZONA TERRITORY

NEW MEXICO TERRITORY

UNORGANIZED TERRITORY

ARK.

TENNESSEE

NORTH CAROLINA

SOUTH CAROLINA

ATLANT OCEA

MISS. ALABAMA

GEORGIA

PACIFIC OCEAN

TEXAS

LOUISIANA
New Orleans 242,039

FLA.

MEXICO

Gulf of Mexico

— Boundary of urban-industrial core region

Population of 25 largest U.S. cities, 1890

⬤ Over 1,000,000
● 500,000–1,000,000
• 250,000–500,000
· under 250,000

Immigrants as percentage of total population, 1900

30% or more
10–30%
less than 10%

0   200   400 Km.
0   200   400 Mi.

1865 Civil War ends

1877 Reconstruction ends

1879 Edison invents light bulb

1881 Garfield assassinated

Standard Oil Trust

1883 Pendleton Act

1885 First U.S. skyscraper

1886 American Federation of Labor

1887 Interstate Commerce Act

1890 National American Woman Suffrage Association

1865   1875   1880   1885   1890

1875 German Social Democratic (Socialist) Party organized

1881 Anarchist's bomb kills Tsar Alexander II

1881–1889 Germany enacts social insurance laws

1884 First settlement house opens in London

1887 King David Kalakaua approves constitution for Hawai'i

1889 Establishment of Republic of Brazil

Becoming an Urban Industrial Society, 1880–1890

18

Immigration and Urbanization

The map on the facing page presents information about three central elements for this chapter: urbanization, immigration, and the emergence of an industrial core region. How do these three elements overlap? Compare these patterns with the patterns of manufacturing shown in the chapter-opening map for Chapter 17, with the agricultural expansion shown in Map 17.1, and with the expansion of railroads shown in Map 17.2.

527

Individual Choices

NIKOLA TESLA

Nikola Tesla was in his late 30s when he posed for this picture around 1895. He chose to show himself quietly sitting and reading in front of an enormous oscillating generator that he had designed. *Granger Collection.*

Nikola Tesla

Born in 1856, in a remote part of the Austro-Hungarian Empire, Nikola Tesla had become fascinated by electricity as a child. His parents were Serbian, and his father was an Orthodox priest who wanted Nikola to follow suit. Only with the greatest difficulty did Nikola persuade his father to permit him to study engineering. As a student, he had a crucial insight into the central problem with the electrical motors of his day, and he spent the next several years working through the solution.

At the age of 24 the answer came to him, and Tesla began to design a new kind of electric motor, powered not by direct current (DC), as was the case with electrical motors up to that time, but by alternating current (AC). Though Tesla had begun to achieve success as an engineer in Europe, he realized that he needed to collaborate with Thomas Edison if he were ever to develop the AC electric motor. Edison was by then famous in much of the world as the "wizard" who had invented the phonograph and the electric light. Tesla arrived in the United States in 1884 and was hired at Edison's research laboratory.

Tesla soon discovered that he and Edison were not very much alike. Tesla had graduated from one of the major engineering schools in Europe, become fluent in several languages, and lived in Prague, Budapest, and Paris. Edison was largely self-taught in science and engineering and often uninformed about other things, except the need for his work to be both practical and profitable. Further, Edison had based his inventions on DC and had no interest in Tesla's AC electric motor. Tesla later described his inefficient methods: "If he had a needle to find in a haystack," Tesla said about Edison, he would work "with the feverish diligence of a bee . . . to examine straw after straw." Tesla insisted that "just a little theory and calculation would have saved him 90 per cent of the labor." He could admire Edison's "instinct" and "practical American sense" but felt that Edison failed to appreciate Tesla's ability to conceptualize and solve complex engineering problems through reason rather than trial and error.

Disillusioned with his experience with Edison, Tesla set out on his own. He found support to build his AC electric motors, and in 1887 secured seven patents on his AC motors and generators—the first of Tesla's many patents and some of the most valuable patents in American history. Soon after, he struck up a working relationship with George Westinghouse, who had invented an effective brake for railroad cars and recognized the enormous importance of electricity for the future. Using AC solved many problems, not least the transmission of electrical power over long distances. Using Tesla's patents, Westinghouse's company soon challenged Edison's General Electric for dominance in the field of electricity. Ultimately AC won out over Edison's choice, DC. Today, throughout the world, the large majority of electrical devices operate on AC.

Tesla addressed other problems. Once he showed the possibility of transmitting electrical power over long distances, he set out to harness natural power sources,

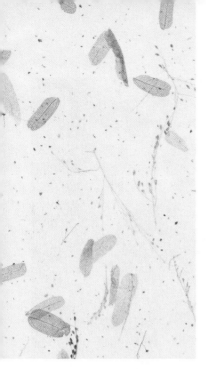

beginning with Niagara Falls. He sought forms of electrical lighting that did not waste energy on heat and developed some of the first neon and fluorescent lights. He was a pioneer in x-ray photography. He also received the first patents on devices to generate what we now know as radio waves. In 1898, he demonstrated his ability to transmit instructions, without wires, to a 4-foot-long boat that he had fitted up with an electric motor and electric lights. He could direct the boat to travel around a large tank, and he could transmit to the boat answers to questions—asked the cube root of 64, he flashed the boat's lights four times. Tesla's boat not only demonstrated the effectiveness of electrical transmission without wires (radio) but was also the first successful remotely controlled robot.

Tesla never developed Edison's ability to work cooperatively with investment bankers, and he never profited from his many patents as he might have done. Though he wanted to make money, he had other goals too—the substitution of machine power for human power, thus freeing people to be more creative, and the substitution of natural power sources for fossil fuels. He died nearly penniless in 1943, but some have traced President Ronald Reagan's Strategic Defense Initiative—nicknamed "Star Wars"—to one of Tesla's last efforts to design an electrical beam that could stop incoming warplanes.

INTRODUCTION

Nikola Tesla came to the United States during a time period that historians usually call the Gilded Age, after *The Gilded Age: A Tale of Today,* a novel by Samuel L. Clemens and Charles Dudley Warner, published in 1873. In the novel—the first for either writer—Clemens and Warner satirized the business and politics of their day. (Clemens went on to fame, under the pen name Mark Twain, as author of *Huckleberry Finn* and other classics.) Applying the term "the Gilded Age" to the years from the late 1860s through the 1890s suggests both the gleam of a **gilded** surface and the cheap nature of the base metal underneath. Among the aspects of late-nineteenth-century life that might justify the label "gilded" were the dramatic expansion of the economy, the spectacular accomplishments of new technologies, the extravagant wealth and great power of the new industrial entrepreneurs, and the rapid economic development of the West. The grim realities of life for most industrial workers and the plight of racial and ethnic minorities lay just below that thin golden surface.

This chapter, centered on the 1880s, examines the new patterns of life in American urban and industrial society that developed after Reconstruction. Most of the changes were related to the great transforming experiences of the late nineteenth century—industrialization, urbanization, massive immigration from Europe, and the development of the West. Technology, when joined to industry, regularly produced new marvels, many

of which soon became available to consumers. Cities expanded so rapidly that municipal governments sometimes proved unable to meet all the demands placed on them. Women entered into the public sphere on a scale not previously seen. The expansion of the educational system presented many Americans with new opportunities. In the South, where industrialization and urbanization lagged, some tried to develop a more diverse economy. The expanding industrial economy and mushrooming cities attracted migrants from throughout Europe who came to America hoping to acquire free land or earn high wages.

Expansion of the Industrial Economy

■ How did the industrial economy change from the 1870s to the 1880s?

■ How and why did companies expand their operations and control within an industry?

■ In what ways was the economy of the South distinctive?

The patterns of industry that emerged after the Civil War, especially railroad construction and expansion of the steel industry, continued to drive the economy

> **gild** To cover a cheaper metal with a very thin layer of gold.

in the 1880s, but important new developments emerged as well. John D. Rockefeller took the lead in bringing vertical and horizontal integration to the production of kerosene and other petroleum products. Innovative technologies and the integrated railway network began to affect other parts of the economy, changing the ways that Americans shopped for goods from clothing to food to home lighting products.

Standard Oil: Model for Monopoly

Just as Carnegie provided a model for other steel companies and for heavy industry in general, **John D. Rockefeller** revolutionized the petroleum industry and provided a model for other consumer-goods industries. Rockefeller was born in upper New York State in 1839 and educated in Cleveland, Ohio. After working as a bookkeeper and clerk, he became a partner in a grain and livestock business in 1859 and earned large profits during the Civil War. At that time, Cleveland was the center for refining oil from northwestern Pennsylvania, then the nation's main source for crude oil. (The first oil well in the nation was drilled in 1859 near Titusville, Pennsylvania.) The major product of oil refining was kerosene, which transformed home lighting as kerosene lamps replaced candles and oil lamps. Rockefeller, in 1863, invested his hefty wartime profits in a **refinery.** After the war, he bought control of more refineries and incorporated them as Standard Oil in 1870.

The refining business was relatively easy to enter and highly competitive. Aggressive competition became a distinctive Standard Oil characteristic. Recognizing that technology could bring a competitive advantage, Rockefeller recruited experts to make Standard the most efficient refiner. He secured reduced rates or rebates from railroads by offering a heavy volume of traffic on a predictable basis. He usually sought to persuade his competitors to join the **cartel** he was creating. If they refused, he often tried to drive them out of business.

By 1881, following a strategy of **horizontal integration,** Rockefeller and his associates controlled some forty oil refineries, accounting for about 90 percent of the nation's refining capacity. In the 1880s, Standard also moved toward vertical integration by gaining control of oil fields, building transportation facilities (including pipelines and oceangoing tanker ships), and creating retail marketing operations (see Fig. 18.1). By the early 1890s, Standard Oil had achieved almost complete vertical and horizontal in-

John D. Rockefeller posed for this portrait in 1884, when he was 47 years old and one of the most powerful industrialists in the nation. *Rockefeller Archive Center.*

tegration of the American petroleum industry—a virtual **monopoly** over an entire industry.

John D. Rockefeller American industrialist who amassed great wealth through the Standard Oil Company and donated much of his fortune to promote learning and research.

refinery An industrial plant that transforms raw materials into finished products; a petroleum refinery processes crude oil to produce a variety of products for use by consumers.

cartel A group of separate companies within an industry that cooperate to control the production, pricing, and marketing of goods within that industry; another name for a pool.

horizontal integration Merging one or more companies doing the same or similar activities as a way of limiting competition or enhancing stability and planning.

monopoly Exclusive control by an individual or company of the production or sale of a product.

Chronology

Urban Industrial America

1862	Land-Grant College Act
1865	Civil War ends 248,120 immigrants enter United States
1868	First medical school for women
1869	National Woman Suffrage Association and American Woman Suffrage Association formed Wyoming Territory adopts woman suffrage
1870	Utah Territory adopts woman suffrage Standard Oil incorporated 25 cities have populations exceeding 50,000
1871	Great Chicago Fire
1873	Samuel L. Clemens and Charles Dudley Warner name the Gilded Age
1874	Women's Christian Temperance Union founded
1875	Andrew Carnegie opens nation's largest steel plant
1876	Telephone invented
1877	Reconstruction ends
1879	Light bulb invented
1880	James A. Garfield elected president
1880s	Railroad expansion and consolidation
1881	Garfield assassinated Chester A. Arthur becomes president Standard Oil Trust organized 669,431 immigrants enter United States United Brotherhood of Carpenters and Joiners organized
1882–1885	Recession
1883	Pendleton Act
1884	Grover Cleveland elected president
1885	William LeBaron Jenney designs first U.S. skyscraper
1886	Last major railroad converts to standard gauge First Sears, Roebuck and Co. catalog *Wabash Railway v. Illinois* Knights of Labor reaches peak membership Haymarket Square bombing American Federation of Labor founded
1887	American Sugar Refining Company formed American Protective Association founded Interstate Commerce Act Congress disfranchises women in Utah Territory Tesla patents his AC electrical motors and generators
1888	First electric streetcar system Benjamin Harrison elected president
1888–1892	Australian ballot adopted
1889	North Dakota, South Dakota, Montana, and Washington become states
1890	58 cities have populations exceeding 50,000 Louis Sullivan designs Wainwright Building Idaho becomes a state Wyoming becomes a state, the first with woman suffrage National American Woman Suffrage Association formed
1893	Colorado voters (all male) adopt woman suffrage

Between 1879 and 1881, Rockefeller also centralized decision making among all his companies by creating the Standard Oil Trust. The **trust** was a new organizational form designed to get around state laws that prohibited one company from owning stock in another. To create the Standard Oil Trust, Rockefeller and others who held shares in the individual companies exchanged their stock for trust certificates issued by Standard Oil. Standard Oil thus controlled

trust A legal arrangement in which an individual (the trustor) gives control of property to a person or institution (the trustee); in the late nineteenth century, a legal device to get around state laws prohibiting a company chartered in one state from operating in another state, and often synonymous in common use with *monopoly*; first used by John D. Rockefeller to consolidate Standard Oil.

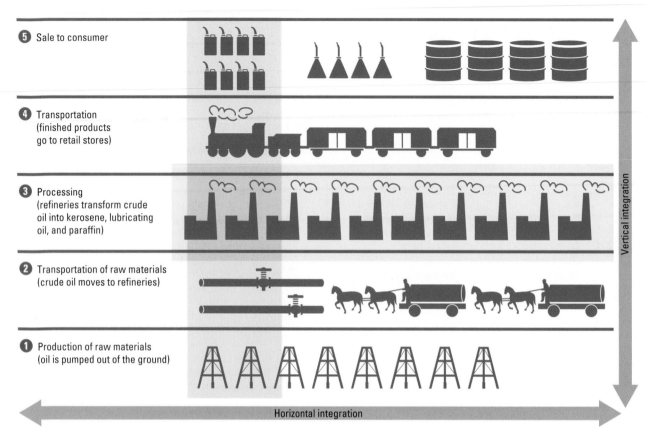

① Production of raw materials
(oil is pumped out of the ground)

② Transportation of raw materials
(crude oil moves to refineries)

③ Processing
(refineries transform crude
oil into kerosene, lubricating
oil, and paraffin)

④ Transportation
(finished products
go to retail stores)

⑤ Sale to consumer

Vertical integration

Horizontal integration

● Steps in petroleum production/distribution

FIGURE 18.1 Vertical and Horizontal Integration of the Petroleum Industry This
diagram represents the petroleum industry before Standard Oil achieved its dominance.
The symbols represent different specialized companies, each engaged in a different step
in the production of kerosene. Rockefeller entered the industry by investing in a refinery,
and first expanded *horizontally* by absorbing several other refineries (indicated by the
blue band). His Standard Oil Company then practiced *vertical integration* (indicated by
the green band) by acquiring oil leases, oil wells, pipelines, advantageous contracts with
railroads, and eventually even retail stores. For a time, Standard Oil controlled nearly 90
percent of the industry.

all the individual companies, though technically it did
not own them. Eventually, new laws in New Jersey
made it legal for corporations chartered in New Jersey to own stock in other companies. So Rockefeller
set up Standard Oil of New Jersey as a **holding company** for all the companies in the trust.

Once Rockefeller achieved his near-monopoly, Standard Oil consolidated its operations by closing many
of its older refineries and building larger plants that
incorporated the newest technology. These and other
innovations reduced the cost of producing petroleum
products by more than two-thirds, leading to a decline
by more than half in the price paid by consumers of

fuel and home lighting products. Standard also took
a leading role in the world market, producing nearly
all American petroleum products sold in Asia, Africa,
and Latin America during the 1880s.

Rockefeller retired from active participation in
business in the mid-1890s. Standard's petroleum monopoly was short-lived, however, because of the dis-

holding company A company that exists to own other
companies, usually through holding a controlling
interest in their stocks.

covery of new rich oil fields in Texas and elsewhere at the turn of the century. New companies emerged to tap those fields and quickly followed their own paths to vertical integration. Nonetheless, the "Rockefeller interests" (companies dominated by Rockefeller or his managers) steadily gained in power. They included the National City Bank of New York (an investment bank second only to the House of Morgan), railroads, mining, real estate, steel plants, steamship lines, and other industries.

Thomas Edison and the Power of Innovation

By the late nineteenth century, most American entrepreneurs had joined Rockefeller and Carnegie in viewing technology as a key competitive device. Railroads wanted more powerful locomotives, roomier freight cars, and stronger rails so they could carry more freight at a lower cost. Steel companies demanded larger and more efficient furnaces to make more steel more cheaply. Ordinary citizens as well as famous entrepreneurs seemed infatuated with technology. One invention followed another: an ice-making machine in 1865, the vacuum cleaner in 1869, the telephone in 1876, the phonograph in 1878, the electric light bulb in 1879, an electric welding machine in 1886, and the first American-made gasoline-engine automobile in 1895, to name only a few. By 1900, many Americans had come to expect a steady flow of ever-more-astounding creations, especially those that could be purchased by the middle and upper classes.

Many new inventions relied on electricity, and in the field of electricity one person stood out: **Thomas A. Edison.** Born in 1847, he became a telegraph operator as a teenager. He began to experiment with electrical devices and in 1869 secured the first of his thousand-plus **patents.** In 1876 Edison set up the first modern research laboratory, where he and his staff could work. He opened a new facility in 1887 that quickly became the world leader in research and development, especially for electricity. Edison promised "a minor invention every ten days and a big thing every six months," and he backed up his words with results. Sometimes building on the work of others, Edison's laboratories invented or significantly improved electrical lighting, electrical motors, the storage battery, the electric locomotive, the phonograph, the mimeograph, and many other products. Such research and development by Edison's laboratories and by others soon translated into production and sales. Nationwide, sales of electrical equipment were insignificant in 1870 but reached

This photograph from 1893 shows Thomas A. Edison in his laboratory, the world's leading research facility when it opened in 1876. By creating research teams, the Edison laboratories could pursue several projects at once. They developed a dazzling stream of new products, most based on electrical power. *Library of Congress.*

nearly $2 million ten years later and nearly $22 million in 1890.

The sale of new electrical devices depended on the availability of electricity. Generating and distribution systems had to be constructed, and wires for carrying electrical current had to be installed along city streets and in homes. The pace of this work picked up appreciably after Nikola Tesla demonstrated the superiority of alternating current to direct current for transmitting power over long distances. Early developers of electrical devices and electrical distribution systems realized quickly that they needed major financial assistance, and investment bankers came to

Thomas A. Edison American inventor, especially of electrical devices, among them the microphone (1877), the phonograph (1878), and the light bulb (1879).

patent A government grant that gives the creator of an invention the sole right to produce, use, or sell that invention for a set period of time.

play an important role in public utilities industries. General Electric, for example, developed out of Edison's company through a series of **mergers** arranged by the New York banking firm of J. P. Morgan.

Selling to the Nation

The expansion of manufacturing in the 1880s produced an acceleration of earlier trends toward a larger array of new and affordable consumer goods of many kinds, from household utensils to ready-made clothing and processed foodstuffs. Large, vertically integrated manufacturers of consumer products often produced items that differed little from one another and that cost virtually the same to produce. Often, such companies came to compete not on the basis of price but instead by using advertising to create different images for their products.

Much of the advertising in the mid-nineteenth century was for **patent medicines** and books. By the late nineteenth century, however, large-scale advertising also promoted packaged foods, clothing, soap, and petroleum products. Advertisements in newspapers and magazines became larger and more complex. In some cases—notably for cigarettes—advertising actually created demand and greatly expanded the market for the product. After the federal Patent Office registered the first **trademark** in 1870, companies rushed to develop brands and logos that they hoped would distinguish their products from nearly identical rivals.

Accompanying advertising came new ways of selling goods to customers. Before this time, most people expected to purchase whatever they needed directly from artisans who made goods on order (shoes, clothes, furniture), or from door-to-door peddlers (pots and pans), or in small specialty stores (hardware, dry goods) or general stores. In urban areas during the Gilded Age, the first American **department stores** appeared and flourished, offering a wide range of choices in ready-made products—ready-made clothing in fashionable styles, household furnishings, shoes, and much more. Department stores' products, unlike the wares in most previous retail outlets, not only had clearly marked prices but also could be returned or exchanged if the customer was dissatisfied. In the vanguard were R. H. Macy's in New York City, Wanamaker's in Philadelphia, Jordan Marsh in Boston, and Marshall Field in Chicago. Such stores relied heavily on newspaper advertising to attract large numbers of customers, especially women, from throughout the city and its suburbs. Although they targeted middle- and upper-class women, the stores especially appealed to young, single women who worked for wages, and

Mail-order companies led by Montgomery Ward and Sears, Roebuck and Co., both based in Chicago, issued advertising catalogs that brought the most remote farm family into contact with the latest fashions and the most recent developments in equipment. The cover for this 1899 catalog depicts a giant cornucopia, the traditional symbol of abundance, filled with consumer goods. *Granger Collection.*

had an eye for the fashions that were now within their financial reach.

merger   The joining together of two or more organizations.

patent medicine   A medical preparation that is advertised by brand name and available without a physician's prescription.

trademark   A name or symbol that identifies a product and is officially registered and legally restricted for use by the owner or manufacturer.

department store   Type of retail establishment that developed in cities in the late nineteenth century and featured a wide variety of merchandise organized in separate departments.

The variety presented by department stores paled, however, when compared with the vast array of goods available through the new mail-order catalogs. Led by Montgomery Ward (which issued its first catalog in 1872) and Sears, Roebuck and Co. (whose first catalogs appeared in the late 1880s)—both based in Chicago—mail-order houses aimed at rural America. They offered a wider range of choices than most rural-dwellers had ever before seen—everything from handkerchiefs to harnesses.

Department stores and mail-order houses became feasible because manufacturers had begun to produce many types of consumer goods in huge volumes. Mail-order houses also depended on railroads and the U.S. mail to deliver their catalogs and products across great distances, and department stores relied on railroads to bring consumer goods from distant factories. Together, advertising, mail-order catalogs (in rural areas), and the new department stores for consumer goods (in urban areas) began to change not only Americans' buying habits but also their thinking about what they expected to buy ready-made.

Railroads, Investment Bankers, and "Morganization"

Railroads expanded significantly in the 1880s, laying over 75,000 miles of new track, but some lines earned little profit. Some ran through sparsely populated areas of the West. Others spread into areas already saturated by rail service. In the 1880s, however, a few ambitious, talented, and occasionally unscrupulous railway executives maneuvered to produce great regional railway systems. The Santa Fe and the Southern Pacific, for example, came to dominate the Southwest, and the Great Northern and the Northern Pacific held sway in the Northwest. The Pennsylvania and the New York Central controlled much of the shipping in the Northeast. By consolidating many of the lines within a region, railway executives tried to create more efficient systems with less duplication, fewer price wars, and more dependable profits.

To raise the enormous amounts of capital necessary for construction and consolidation, railroad executives turned increasingly to **investment banks.** By the late 1880s, **John Pierpont Morgan** had emerged as the nation's leading investment banker. Born in Connecticut in 1837, he was the son of a successful merchant who turned to banking (and helped fund Andrew Carnegie's first big steel plant). After schooling in Switzerland and Germany, young Morgan began working in his father's bank in London. In 1857 he

J. P. Morgan Sr. was at the pinnacle of his power when this photograph was taken around 1900. In this photograph, as in others taken at that time, Morgan seems to exude both power and anger. The sense of anger may, in fact, reflect his anxiety over having his picture taken. Morgan was very sensitive about his appearance, especially his nose. He suffered from *acne rosacea*, which made his nose large and misshapen. He was so offended by one photograph, by the famous photographer Edward Steichen, that he tore it up when he first saw it. *New York Historical Society.*

moved to New York, where his father had arranged a banking position for him.

Morgan's background and his growing stature in banking gave him access to capital within the United States and abroad, in London and Paris. His investors

---

investment bank   An institution that acts as an agent for corporations issuing stocks and bonds.

John Pierpont Morgan   The most prominent and powerful American investment banker in the late nineteenth century.

wanted to put their money where it would be safe and would give them a reliable **return.** Morgan therefore tried to stabilize the railroad business, especially the cutthroat rate competition that often resulted when several companies served one market. Railroad companies that turned to Morgan for help in raising capital found strings attached to funding. Morgan regularly insisted that beneficiaries reorganize to simplify corporate structures and to combine small lines into larger, centrally controlled systems. He often demanded a seat on the board of directors as well, to guard against risky decisions in the future. Some began to refer to this process as "Morganization," and "Morganized" lines soon included some of the largest in the country. A few other investment bankers followed similar patterns.

Economic Concentration in Consumer-Goods Industries

Carnegie, Rockefeller, Edison, Morgan, and a few others helped to redefine the expectations of American entrepreneurs and provided models for their activities. In a number of industries, massive, complex companies—vertically integrated, sometimes horizontally integrated, often employing extensive advertising—appeared relatively suddenly in the 1880s. At first they were concentrated in consumer-goods industries.

The American Sugar Refining Company, created in 1887, imitated Rockefeller's organization to control three-quarters of the nation's sugar-refining capacity by the early 1890s. In the 1880s, James B. Duke used efficient machinery, extensive advertising, and vertical integration to become the largest manufacturer of cigarettes. In 1890 he merged with his four largest competitors to create the American Tobacco Company, which dominated the cigarette industry. Gustavus Swift in the early 1880s began to ship fresh meat from his slaughterhouse in Chicago to markets in the East, using his own refrigerated railcars. He eventually added refrigerated storage plants in each city, along with a sales and delivery staff. Other meatpacking companies followed Swift's lead. By 1890, half a dozen firms, all vertically integrated, dominated meatpacking. Such a market, in which a small number of firms dominate an industry, is called an **oligopoly.** Oligopolies were (and are) more typical than monopolies.

Some of the new manufacturing companies did not sell stock or use investment bankers to raise capital. Standard Oil, like Carnegie Steel, never "went public"—that is, Rockefeller chose not to sell stock on a stock exchange to raise capital. Instead, he expanded either through mergers or by making purchases capitalized by the profits of the business itself. Rockefeller, like Carnegie, concentrated ownership and control in his own hands. So did many others among the new manufacturing companies. As late as 1896, for example, the New York Stock Exchange sold stock in only twenty manufacturing concerns.

Gradually, however, with the passing of the first generation of industrial empire builders, ownership grew apart from management. Many new business executives were professional managers. Ownership rested with hundreds or thousands of stockholders, all of whom wanted a reliable return on their investment, even though the vast majority remained uninvolved with business operations. The huge size of the new companies also meant that most managers rarely saw or talked with most of their employees. Careful **cost analysis,** the desire for efficiency, and the need to pay shareholders regular **dividends** led many companies to treat most of their employees as expenses to be increased or cut as necessary, with little regard to the effect on individuals.

Laying an Economic Base for a New South

The term **New South** usually refers to efforts by some southerners to modernize their region during the years after Reconstruction. Some advocates of the New South promoted a more diverse economic base, with more manufacturing and less reliance on a few staple agricultural crops, as a way to strengthen the

---

return The yield on money that has been invested in an enterprise or product.

oligopoly A market or industry dominated by a few firms (from Greek words meaning "few sellers"); compare *monopoly* (from Greek words meaning "one seller").

cost analysis Study of the cost of producing manufactured goods in order to find ways to cut expenses.

dividend A share of a company's profits received by a stockholder; companies customarily announce dividends every quarter (three months).

New South Late-nineteenth-century term used by some southerners to promote the idea that the South should become industrialized, have a more diverse agriculture, and be thoroughly integrated into the economy of the nation.

Much of the new southern textile industry was based on child labor. These children were photographed by Lewis Hines in 1908. *National Archives/ Lewis Hines.*

southern economy and integrate it more thoroughly into the national economy.

Foremost among proponents of the New South was **Henry Grady,** who built the *Atlanta Constitution* into a powerful regional newspaper in the 1880s. Like Chicago, Atlanta grew as a railroad center. Though destroyed by Sherman's troops in 1864, Atlanta developed quickly once the war was over. It became the capital of Georgia in 1877. Thanks in part to Grady's skillful journalism, Atlanta's population boomed in the 1880s by 75 percent, and the city emerged as a symbol of the New South—a center for transportation, industry, and finance.

The importance of railroads in spurring Atlanta's growth was no coincidence. After the Civil War, inadequate transportation, especially railroads, posed a critical limit on the South's economic growth. During the 1880s, however, southern railroads more than doubled their miles of track. In the 1890s, J. P. Morgan led in reorganizing southern railroads into three large systems, dominated by the Southern Railway. With the emergence of better rail transportation, some entrepreneurs began to consider introducing new industries.

Some southerners had long advocated that their cotton be manufactured into cloth in the South. Early efforts to establish textile manufacturing in the region had been stymied by the economic chaos of the Civil War and its aftermath. The southern cotton textile industry finally boomed, however, during the 1880s and 1890s as the number of textile mills increased from 161 in 1880 to 400 in 1900. The new mills had more modern equipment and were larger and more productive than the mills of New England. Southern textile mills also had cheaper labor costs, partly because they relied extensively on child labor. An official of the American Cotton Manufacturers' Association estimated that 70 percent of southern cotton-mill workers were younger than 21, and another observer calculated that 75 percent of the cotton spinners in North Carolina were under the age of 14. Similar patterns characterized the emergence of cigarette manufacturing as a new southern industry. In the end, though, these enterprises did little to transform the regional economy. Most of the new companies paid low wages, and some located in the South specifically to take advantage of its cheap, unskilled, nonunion labor.

Other southerners tried to diversify the region's agriculture and to reduce its dependence on cotton and tobacco. Such efforts, however, ran up against the cotton textile and cigarette industries, both of which built factories in the South to be near their raw

Henry Grady Prominent Atlanta newspaper publisher and leading proponent of the concept of a New South.

materials. Thus southern agriculture changed little: owners and sharecroppers farmed small plots, obligated by their rental contracts or crop liens to raise cotton or tobacco. In some parts of the South, farmers became even more dependent on cotton than they had been before the Civil War. Parts of Georgia, for example, produced almost 200 percent more cotton in 1880 than in 1860.

Fencing laws brought some long-term improvement to southern livestock raising. States adopted such laws to keep farmers from allowing their cattle and hogs to run free in unfenced wooded areas. Fencing permitted more prosperous farmers to introduce new breeds, control breeding, and thereby improve the stock. But the law placed at a disadvantage many small-scale farmers who now had to fence their grazing areas but could not afford to buy the new breeds.

Despite repeated backing for the idea of a New South by some southern leaders, and despite growth of some new industries in the South, the late nineteenth century was also the time when the myth of the **Old South** and the so-called **Lost Cause** pervaded nearly every aspect of southern life. Popular fiction and song, in both the North and the South, romanticized the pre–Civil War Old South as a place of gentility and gallantry, where "kindly" plantation owners cared for "loyal" slaves. The Lost Cause myth portrayed the Confederacy as a heroic, even noble, effort to retain the life and values of the Old South. Leading southerners—especially Democratic Party leaders—promoted the nostalgic notion of the Lost Cause, and many white southerners embraced it as justification for the dislocation and suffering that so many of them had experienced during and after the Civil War. Hundreds of statues of Confederate soldiers appeared on courthouse lawns, and gala commemorative events and organizations reflected devotion to the myth among many white southerners.

Organized Labor in the 1880s

■ How did the Knights of Labor differ from craft unions in membership and objectives?

■ Which type of labor organization was more successful? Why?

The expansion of railroads and manufacturing and the growth of cities led to dramatic increases in the number of wage-earning workers. The Great Railway Strike of 1877 (see page 519) had suggested that working people could unite across lines of occupation, race, and gender, but no organization drew on that potential until the early 1880s, when the Knights of Labor

emerged as an alternative to craft unions. Though the Knights scored some organizing successes, they failed to sustain their organization against a challenge from craft unions.

The Knights of Labor

The **Knights of Labor** grew out of an organization of Philadelphia garment workers that dated to 1869. Abandoning their craft union origins, they proclaimed that labor was "the only creator of values or capital," and they opened their ranks to all whom they defined as part of "the producing class"—those who, by their labor, created value. Anyone joining the Knights was required to have worked for wages at some time, but the organization specifically excluded only professional gamblers, stockbrokers, lawyers, bankers, and liquor dealers.

The Knights accepted African Americans as members, and some sixty thousand joined by 1886. In many cases, local organizations of black workers seem to have organized themselves and joined the Knights rather than waiting to be approached by an organizer. Nearly all African Americans were enrolled in separate all-black local organizations, though some integrated local assemblies did exist. After one organizer formed a local organization of women in 1881, the Knights officially opened their ranks to women and enrolled about fifty thousand by 1886. Some women and African Americans held leadership positions at local and regional levels, and the Knights briefly appointed a woman as a national organizer. Through their activities, the Knights provided both women and African Americans with experience in labor organizing.

Terence V. Powderly, a machinist, directed the Knights from 1879 to 1893. Under his leadership, they focused on organization, education, and cooperation as their chief objectives. Powderly generally opposed strikes. A lost strike, he argued, often destroyed the local organization and thereby delayed the more important tasks of education and cooperation. The Knights

---

Old South Term used in both the South and the North for the antebellum (pre–Civil War) South, suggesting that it was a place of gentility and gallantry.

Lost Cause Term applied to the Confederate struggle in the Civil War, depicting it as a noble but doomed effort to preserve a way of life.

Knights of Labor Organization founded in 1869; membership, open to all workers, peaked in 1886; members favored a cooperative alternative to capitalism.

Terence V. Powderly Leader of the Knights of Labor.

This cartoon shows Terence Powderly, in the center, advocating the position of the Knights of Labor on arbitration. The Knights urged that labor and management (identified here as "capital") should settle their differences this way, rather than by striking. Note how the cartoonist has depicted labor and management as of equal size, and given both of them a large weapon; management's club is labeled "monopoly" and labor's hammer is called "strikes." In fact, labor and management were rarely equally matched when it came to labor disputes in the late nineteenth century. *From* Puck, *April 7, 1886.*

favored political action to accomplish a range of labor reforms, including health and safety laws for workers, the eight-hour workday, prohibition of child labor, equal pay for equal work regardless of gender, and the graduated income tax. They also endorsed government ownership of the telephone, telegraph, and railroad systems. In 1878, 1880, and 1882, Powderly won election as mayor of Scranton, Pennsylvania, as the candidate of a labor party. Other local labor parties sometimes appeared in other cities where the Knights were strong.

The Knights' endorsement of cooperation was related to the argument that only labor produces value. A major objective of the Knights was "to secure to the workers the full enjoyment of the wealth they create." Toward that end, they committed themselves in their first national meeting in 1878 to introduce a system of producers' and consumers' cooperatives, which they hoped would "supersede the wage-system." They established some 135 cooperatives by the mid-1880s, but few lasted very long. Like the Grangers' cooperatives in the 1870s (see page 517), some of the Knights' cooperatives folded because of lack of capital, some because of opposition from rival businesses, and some because of poor organization.

Despite the lackluster record of their cooperatives, the Knights of Labor quickly grew to be the largest labor organization in the country, expanding from 9,000 members in 1879 to a high point of 703,000 in 1886. This meteoric growth suggested that many working people were seeking ways to respond to the emerging corporate behemoths or to regain some control over their own working lives. Although the Knights opposed striking, much of the increase in membership in the mid-1880s came because local Knights organizers played major roles in helping to win strikes against prominent railroads in 1884 and 1885. Although many members seem to have joined in order to unite against their employers, the national leadership played down such conflicts in the interests of long-term economic and political change.

1886: Turning Point for Labor?

The railway strike of 1877 and the rise of the Knights of Labor seemed to signal a growing sense of common purpose among many working people. After 1886, however, labor organizations often found themselves on the defensive and were divided between those trying to adjust to the new realities of industrial capitalism and those seeking to change it.

On May 1, 1886, some eighty thousand Chicagoans marched through the streets in support of an eight-hour workday, a cause that united a wide variety of unions and radical groups. Three days later, Chicago police killed several strikers at the McCormick Harvester Works. Hoping to build on the May Day unity, a group of **anarchists** called a protest meeting for the next day at Haymarket Square. When police tried to break up the rally, someone tossed a bomb at the officers. The police then opened fire on the crowd, and some protesters fired back. Eight policemen died, along with an unknown number of demonstrators, and a hundred people suffered injuries.

The Haymarket bombing sparked public anxiety and antiunion feelings. Employers who had opposed unions before tried to discredit them now by playing on fears of terrorism. Some people who had supported what they saw as legitimate union goals now shrank back in horror. In Chicago, amid widespread furor over the violence, eight leading anarchists stood trial for inciting the bombing and, on flimsy evidence, were convicted. Four were hanged, one committed suicide, and three remained in jail until a sympathetic governor, John Peter Altgeld, released them in 1893.

Uniting the Craft Unions: The American Federation of Labor

Two weeks after the Haymarket bombing, trade union leaders met in Philadelphia to discuss the inroads that the Knights of Labor were making among their members. They proposed an agreement between the trade unions and the Knights: trade unions would recruit skilled workers, and the Knights would limit themselves to unskilled workers. When the Knights refused, the trade unions organized the **American Federation of Labor** (AFL) to coordinate their struggles with the Knights for the loyalty of skilled workers. Membership in the AFL was limited to national trade unions. The combined membership of the thirteen founding unions amounted only to 140,000.

Samuel Gompers became the AFL's first president. Born in London in 1850 to Dutch Jewish parents, he learned the cigarmaker's trade before coming to the United States in 1863. He joined the Cigarmakers' Union in 1864 and became its president in 1877. Except for one year, Gompers continued as president of the AFL from 1886 until his death in 1924. A socialist in his youth, Gompers became more conservative as AFL president, opposing labor involvement with radicalism or politics. Instead, he and other AFL leaders came to favor what Gompers called "pure and simple" unionism: higher wages, shorter hours, and improved working conditions for their own members. Most AFL unions did not challenge capitalism, but they did use strikes to achieve their goals and sometimes engaged in long and bitter struggles with employers.

After the 1880s, the AFL suffered little competition from the Knights of Labor. The decline of the Knights came swiftly: 703,000 members in 1886; 260,000 in 1888; 100,000 in 1890. The failure of several strikes involving the Knights in the late 1880s cost them many supporters. Some who abandoned the Knights were probably disappointed when a "cooperative commonwealth" was not quickly achieved. Some units of the Knights were organized much like trade unions, and these groups preferred the very practical AFL, rather than the more visionary Powderly. The most prominent was the United Mine Workers of America, which switched from the Knights to the AFL in 1890 but retained some central principles of the Knights, including commitments to include both whites and African Americans and to reach all workers, rather than only the most skilled.

---

anarchist   A person who believes that all forms of government are oppressive and should be abolished.

American Federation of Labor   National organization of trade unions founded in 1886; it used strikes and boycotts to improve the lot of craft workers.

Samuel Gompers   First president of the American Federation of Labor; he sought to divorce labor organizing from politics and stressed practical demands involving wages and hours.

New Americans from Europe

■ What expectations did immigrants have upon coming to the United States?

■ How did their expectations regarding assimilation compare with those of old-stock Americans?

Many of the members and leaders of both the Knights of Labor and the AFL craft unions were immigrants from Europe, reflecting the international flavor of the American work force in the Gilded Age. The United States had attracted large numbers of immigrants throughout its history, but it had never experienced a flood of immigrants like the one between the Civil War and World War I. Nearly all these immigrants came from Europe, and many settled in cities.

A Flood of Immigrants

The numbers of immigrants varied from year to year—higher in prosperous years, lower in depression years—but the trend was constantly upward. Nearly a quarter of a million arrived in 1865, two-thirds of a million in 1881, and a million in 1905. In the 1870s and 1880s, most immigrants came from Great Britain, Ireland, **Scandinavia,** Germany, and Canada, but during the 1890s and after, increasing numbers began to arrive from southern and eastern Europe. Fig. 18.2 shows the place of birth of the foreign-born population for the census years from 1870 through 1920. Note especially how the foreign-born population became increasingly diverse after the 1890s.

Immigrants left their former homes for a variety of reasons, but most came to the United States because it was known everywhere as the "land of opportunity." They came, as one bluntly said, for "jobs" and, as another declared, "for money." Some were also attracted by the reputation of the United States for toleration of religious difference and commitment to democracy. In fact, the reasons for immigrating to America varied from person to person, country to country, and year to year.

In Ireland, for example, a fourfold population increase between 1750 and 1850 combined with changes in agriculture to push people off the land. Repeated failure of potato crops after 1845 produced widespread famine and starvation, greatly increasing migration for several years. Irish immigrants, many desperately poor, arrived in greatest numbers before the Civil War, but Irish immigration continued at high levels until the 1890s. They settled at first in the cities of the Northeast, composing a quarter of the population in New York City and Boston as early as 1860.

Railroad companies, seeking to sell their land grants, advertised in Europe for immigrants to buy farmland in the West. This poster, issued by the Burlington and Missouri Railroad, probably in the 1880s, is in Czech, but the same poster was also issued in German and Swedish. The poster's sequence of drawings shows a six-year transition from bare prairie to prosperous farm. Such advertising helped to attract many European immigrants to the north-central states (see the map at the beginning of the chapter). *Nebraska State Historical Society.*

Scandinavia The region of northern Europe consisting of Norway, Sweden, Denmark, and Iceland.

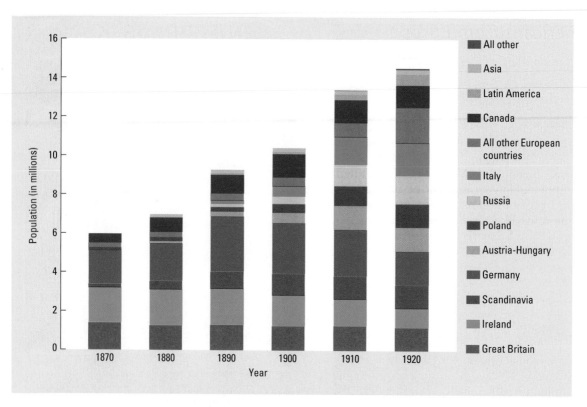

FIGURE 18.2 Foreign-Born Population of the United States, 1870–1920   This graph shows the largest foreign-born groups living in the United States at the time of the census every ten years. Note that the total number of foreign-born increased dramatically during these fifty years, and also that the foreign-born were increasingly diverse by country of origin. *Source:* U.S. Department of Commerce, Bureau of the Census, *Historical Statistics of the United States, Colonial Times to 1970,* Bicentennial edition, 2 vols. (Washington: Government Printing Office, 1975), 1: 116–117.

The chapter-opening map reveals concentrations of immigrants in the urban-industrial core region, or **manufacturing belt,** especially in urban areas, but distinctive immigrant communities were not limited to cities. Many of the immigrants who came in the 1870s and 1880s found that good farmland could still be acquired relatively easily in the north-central states, for there farmland was relatively cheap, or even free under the Homestead Act. Scandinavians, Dutch, Swiss, Czechs, and Germans were most likely to be farmers, but many other groups also formed rural farming settlements. One woman recalled that in rural Nebraska in the 1880s, her family could attend Sunday church services in Norwegian, Danish, Swedish, French, Czech, or German, as well as English.

Thus patterns of immigrant settlement reflect the expectations immigrants had about America, as well as the opportunities they found when they arrived.

After 1890, farmland was more difficult to obtain. The 1890s also marked a shift in the sources of immigration, with proportionately more coming from southern and eastern Europe and arriving with little or no capital. Newcomers after 1890 were more likely to find work in the rapidly expanding industrial sectors of the economy in mining, transportation, and manufacturing. Of course, individual variations on these patterns were many. Some immigrants coming after 1890 intended to become farmers and succeeded. Many

> **manufacturing belt**   A region that includes most of the nation's factories; in the late nineteenth century, the U.S. manufacturing belt also included most of the nation's large cities and railroad lines and much of its mining.

This sketch, from *Frank Leslie's Illustrated Newspaper* for July 2, 1887, shows immigrants from Europe passing the Statue of Liberty as they arrive in New York Harbor. In July 1887, the Statue of Liberty had been in place for less than a year. The newspaper provided the following caption: "Welcome to the land of freedom . . . Scene on the steerage deck." The steerage deck was the part of the ship where those who bought the cheapest ticket (and traveled in steerage) were permitted out on deck for fresh air and sunshine. Note how sympathetically the artist has depicted the immigrants, and the hopefulness that the artist has drawn onto their faces as they see this new symbol of freedom. *Library of Congress.*

who came before 1890 became industrial workers or took other urban jobs.

Hyphenated America

In the nineteenth century, most old-stock Americans assumed that immigrants should quickly learn English, become citizens, and restructure their lives and values to resemble those of longtime residents. Most immigrants, however, resisted rapid **assimilation.** For the majority, assimilation took place over a lifetime or even over generations. Most retained elements of their own cultures even as they embraced a new life in America. Their sense of identity drew on two elements—where they had come from and where they lived now—and they often came to think of themselves as hyphenated Americans: German-Americans, Irish-Americans, Norwegian-Americans.

On arriving in America, with its strange language and unfamiliar customs, many immigrants reacted by seeking others who shared their cultural values, practiced their religion, and, especially, spoke their language. Ethnic communities emerged throughout regions with large numbers of immigrants. These communities played a significant role in newcomers' transition from the old country to America. They gave immigrants a chance to learn about their new home with the assistance of those who had come before. At the same time, newcomers could, without apology or embarrassment, retain cultural values and behaviors from their homelands.

Hyphenated America developed a unique blend of ethnic institutions, often unlike anything in the old

> **assimilation** A process by which a minority or immigrant group is absorbed into another group or groups; among immigrants, the process of adopting some of the behaviors and values of the society in which they found themselves.

country but also unlike the institutions of old-stock America. Fraternal lodges based on ethnicity sprang up and provided not only social ties but sometimes also financial benefits in case of illness or death. Singing societies devoted to the music of the old country flourished. Foreign-language newspapers were vital in developing a sense of identity that connected the old country to the new, for they provided news from the old country as well as from other similar communities in the United States.

For members of nearly every **ethnic group,** religious institutions provided the most important building blocks of ethnic group identity. In most of Europe, a state church was officially sanctioned to perform certain functions. Membership in a religious body was voluntary in America, but religious ties often became stronger here, partly because religious organizations provided an important link among people with a similar language and cultural values. Protestant immigrant groups created new church organizations based on both theology and language. Catholic parishes in immigrant neighborhoods often took on the ethnic characteristics of the community. Their services were conducted in the native language, and special observances were transplanted from the old country. Jewish congregations, too, often differed according to the ethnic background of their members.

Nativism

Many Americans (including some only a generation removed from immigrant forebears themselves) expected immigrants to lay aside their previous identities, embrace the behavior and beliefs of old-stock Americans, and blend neatly into old-stock American culture. This view of immigrants eventually came to be identified with the image of the **melting pot** after the appearance of a play by that name in 1908. But the melting-pot metaphor rarely described the reality of immigrants' lives. Most immigrants changed in some ways, but most did so slowly, over lifetimes, gradually adopting new patterns of thinking and behavior or modifying previous beliefs and practices.

Few old-stock Americans appreciated or even understood the long-term nature of immigrants' adjustments to their new home. Instead of seeing the ways immigrants changed, many old-stock Americans saw only immigrants' efforts to retain their own culture. They fretted over the multiplication of newspapers published in German and Italian, feared to go into communities where they rarely heard an English sentence, and shuddered at the sprouting of Catholic schools. Such fears and misgivings fostered the growth

of **nativism:** the view that old-stock values and social patterns were preferable to those of immigrants. Nativists argued that only their values and institutions were genuinely American, and they feared that immigrants posed a threat to those traditions.

American nativism was often linked to anti-Catholicism. Irish and German immigrant groups, and later Italian and Polish groups, included large numbers of Catholics, and many old-stock Americans came to identify the Catholic Church as an immigrant church. The **American Protective Association,** founded in 1887, noisily proclaimed itself the voice of anti-Catholicism. Its members pledged not to hire Catholics, not to vote for them, and not to strike with them.

Jews, too, faced religious antagonism. In the 1870s, increasing numbers of organizations and businesses began to discriminate against Jews. Some employers refused to hire Jews. After 1900, such discrimination intensified. Many social organizations barred Jews from membership, and **restrictive covenants** kept them from buying homes in certain neighborhoods.

The New Urban America

- What were the key factors in the transformation of American cities in the late nineteenth century?
- What were some of the results of that transformation?

By 1890, immigrants made up more than 40 percent of the population of New York, San Francisco, and Chicago, and more than a third of the population in several other major cities. But immigrants were not the only people who thronged to the cities. Others came from rural areas and small towns. Thus Americans in the 1880s witnessed a burgeoning of their cities as Chicago doubled in size to take second rank, behind New York. In just ten years, Brooklyn grew by

---

ethnic group A group that shares a racial, religious, linguistic, cultural, or national heritage.

melting pot A concept that American society is a place where immigrants set aside their distinctive cultural identities and are absorbed into a homogeneous culture.

nativism The view that old-stock values and social patterns were preferable to those of immigrants.

American Protective Association An anti-Catholic organization founded in Iowa in 1887 and active during the next decade.

restrictive covenant Provision in a property title designed to restrict subsequent sale or use of the property, often specifying sale only to a white Christian.

more than 40 percent, St. Louis by nearly 30 percent, and San Francisco by almost as much. Cities not only added more people but also expanded upward and outward and became more complex, both socially and economically.

Surging Urban Growth

What Americans saw in their cities often fascinated them. Cities boasted the technological innovations that many equated with progress. But the lure of the city stemmed from far more than telephones, street-cars, and technological gadgetry. Samuel Lane Loomis in 1887 listed the many choices to be found in cities: "The churches and the schools, the theatres and con-certs, the lectures, fairs, exhibitions, and galleries . . . and the mighty streams of human beings that forever flow up and down the thoroughfares."

Not every urban vista was so appealing. Some vis-itors were shocked and repulsed by the poverty, crime, and filth that cluttered the urban landscape. Guil-lermo Prieto, visiting San Francisco in 1877, was struck by the contrast of luxurious wealth and des-perate poverty: "Behind the palaces run filthy alleys, or rather nasty dungheaps without sidewalks or illu-mination, whose loiterers smell of the gallows."

Filled with glamour and destitution, cities grew rapidly. Cities with more than 50,000 people were growing almost twice as fast as rural areas (see Fig. 18.3). The nation had twenty-five cities that large in 1870, with a total population of 5 million. By 1890, fifty-eight cities had reached that size and held nearly 12 million people. Most of these cities were in the Northeast and near the Great Lakes. This growth came largely through migration from rural areas in the United States and Europe. The mechanization of Amer-ican agriculture meant that farming required fewer workers. Rural birth rates remained high, however, and rural death rates were lower than death rates in the cities. America's farmlands contributed signifi-cantly to the growth of the cities, but many other new urban residents came from outside the United States, especially from Europe.

Jacob Riis, a Danish immigrant, provided this striking description of Manhattan in 1890:

A map of the city, colored to designate nationalities, would show more stripes than on the skin of a zebra, and more colors than any rainbow. The city on such a map would fall into two great halves, green for the Irish prevailing in the West Side tenement districts, and blue for the Germans on the East Side. But in-termingled with these ground colors would be an odd

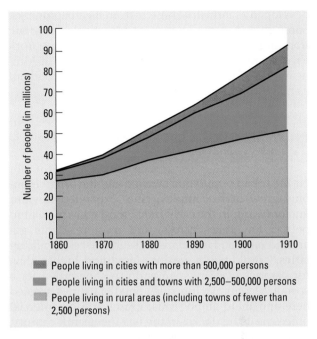

FIGURE 18.3 Urban and Rural Population of the United States, 1860–1910   Although much of the population increase between 1860 and 1910 came in urban areas, the number of people living in rural areas increased as well. Notice, too, that the largest increase was in towns and cities that had between 2,500 and 500,000 people. *Source:* U.S. Bureau of the Census, Department of Commerce, *Historical Statistics of the United States,* 2 vols. (Washington, D.C.: U.S. Government Printing Office, 1975), Series A-58, A-59, A-69, A-119.

variety of tints that would give the whole the appear-ance of an extraordinary crazy quilt.

Riis then pieced in some smaller parts of the ethnic patchwork by describing neighborhoods of Italians, African Americans, Jews, Chinese, Czechs, Arabs, Finns, Greeks, and Swiss.

The growth of manufacturing went hand in hand with urban expansion. By the late nineteenth century, the nation had developed a manufacturing belt. This region, which included nearly all the largest cities as well as the bulk of the nation's manufacturing and fi-nance, may be thought of as constituting the nation's urban-industrial "core" (see the chapter-opening map). Some of the cities in this region—Boston, New York, Baltimore, Buffalo, and St. Louis, for example—had long been among the busiest ports in the nation. Now manufacturing also flourished there and came to be nearly as important as trade. In other cases, cities developed as industrial centers from their beginnings. Some cities became known for a particular product: iron and steel in Pittsburgh, clothing in New York City, meatpacking in Chicago, flour milling in Minneapolis. A few cities, especially New York, stood out as major centers for finance.

New Cities of Skyscrapers and Streetcars

As the urban population swelled and the urban economy grew more complex, cities expanded upward and outward. In the early 1800s, most cities measured only a few miles across, and most residents got around on foot. Historians call such places **"walking cities."** Buildings were low (anything higher than four stories was unusual) and rarely designed for a specific economic function. Small factories existed here and there among warehouses and commercial offices near the docks. In the late nineteenth century, new technologies for construction and transportation transformed the cities.

Until the 1880s, construction techniques restricted building height because the lower walls carried the structure's full weight. The higher a building, the thicker its lower walls had to be. William LeBaron Jenney usually receives credit for designing the first skyscraper—ten stories high, erected in Chicago in 1885. Chicago architects also took the lead in designing other tall buildings. They could do so because of new construction technologies that allowed a steel frame to carry the weight of the walls. Another crucial technological advance was the elevator, a necessity for multistory buildings. Economical and efficient, skyscrapers created unique city skylines.

Among the Chicago architects who developed high-rise structures, **Louis Sullivan** stands out. He recognized the skyscraper as the architectural form of the future and introduced a new way of thinking about height. In the Wainwright Building (St. Louis, 1890), Sullivan emphasized height, creating what he called a "proud and soaring thing." He also tried to design exteriors that reflected the interior functions, in keeping to his rule that "form follows function." Frank Lloyd Wright, perhaps the greatest American architect of the twentieth century, applauded the Wainwright Building as signifying the birth of "the 'skyscraper' as a new thing under the sun."

Just as steel-frame buildings allowed cities to grow upward, so new forms of transportation permitted cities to expand outward. In the 1850s, horses pulled the first streetcars over iron rails laid in city streets.

Louis Sullivan designed the Wainwright Building (1890) with the intention of creating a new way of thinking about height and about the relationship between form and function. The building was widely acclaimed and often imitated. *Missouri Historical Society/Emil Boehl.*

Some cities also had **elevated rail lines** powered by steam locomotives, but the smoke and soot from the coal they burned made them unpopular in urban areas. By the 1870s and 1880s, some cities boasted streetcar lines powered by underground moving cables. Electricity, however, revolutionized urban transit. Frank Sprague, a protégé of Thomas Edison, designed a streetcar driven by an electric motor that drew its power from an overhead wire. Sprague's

walking city Term that urban historians use to describe cities before changes in urban transportation permitted cities to expand beyond the distance that a person could easily cover on foot.

Louis Sullivan American architect of the late nineteenth century whose designs reflected his theory that the outward form of a building should express its function.

elevated rail line A train that runs on a steel framework above a street, leaving the roadway free for other traffic.

This photograph shows snarled downtown traffic in Philadelphia in the 1890s. Note the mix of freight wagons (lower left), an electric streetcar (center right), a private carriage (center left), other vehicles, and pedestrians. *National Archives.*

system was first installed in Richmond, Virginia, in 1888. Electric streetcars replaced nearly all horse cars and cable cars within a dozen years. In the early 1900s, some large cities, choked with traffic, began to move their electrical streetcars above or below street level, thereby creating elevated trains and subways. Thus elaborate networks of rails came to crisscross most large cities, connecting suburban neighborhoods to central business districts. Middle-class women wearing white gloves and stylish hats rode on streetcars to well-stocked downtown department stores. Skilled workers took other streetcar lines to and from their jobs. Other lines carried the typists, bookkeepers, and corporate executives who filled the banks and offices in the city's center.

New construction technologies also launched bridges spanning rivers and bays that had once limited urban growth. When the Brooklyn Bridge was completed in 1883, it was hailed as a new wonder of the world. Other great bridges soon followed.

As bridges and streetcar lines pushed outward from the city's center, the old walking city expanded by annexing suburban areas. In 1860 Chicago had occupied 17 square miles; only thirty years later, it took in 178 square miles. During the same years, Boston grew from 5 square miles to 39, and St. Louis from 14 square miles to 61.

As streetcars expanded the city beyond distances that residents could cover on foot, suburban railroad lines began to bring more distant villages within commuting distance of urban centers. Wealthier urban residents who could afford the passenger fare now left the city at the end of the workday. As early as 1873, nearly a hundred suburban communities sent between five and six thousand commuters into Chicago each day, and by 1890 seventy thousand suburbanites were pouring in daily. At about the same time, commuter lines brought more than a hundred thousand workers daily into New York City just from its northern suburbs.

Building an Urban Infrastructure

Caught up in headlong growth, cities developed with only minimal planning. Local governments did little to regulate expansion or create building standards in the public interest, leaving to individual landowners, developers, and builders most decisions about land use and construction practices. Everywhere, builders and owners hoped to achieve a high return on their investment by producing the most square footage for the least cost. Such profit calculations rarely left room for such amenities as varied designs or open space. Most of the great urban parks that exist today, including Central Park in New York City, Prospect Park in Brooklyn, and Golden Gate Park in San Francisco, were established on the outskirts of their cities, before the surrounding areas were developed.

Given the rapid and largely unplanned nature of most urban growth, city governments usually found it difficult to meet all the demands for expanded municipal utilities and services—fire and police protection, schools, sewage disposal, street maintenance, water supply.

The quality and quantity of the water supply varied greatly from city to city. Some cities spent enormous sums to transport water over long distances, but water quality remained a problem in most locales. As city officials began to understand that germs caused diseases, cities introduced filtration and **chlorination** of their water. Even so, by the early twentieth century, only 6 percent of urban residents received filtered water.

City residents also faced major obstacles in disposing of sewage, cleaning streets (especially given the ever-present horse), and removing garbage. Even when cities built sewer lines, they usually dumped the untreated sewage into some nearby body of water. The disgusted mayor of Cleveland in 1881 called the Cuyahoga River "an open sewer through the center of the city," but similar situations existed in most large cities.

Few city streets were paved, and most became mud holes in the rain, threw up clouds of dust in dry weather, and froze into deep ruts in the winter. Chicago in 1890 included 2,048 miles of streets, but only 629 miles were paved, typically with wooden

blocks—and Chicago was not unusual. Only in the late nineteenth century did cities begin using asphalt paving. Sometimes it was easier to pave streets than to maintain them: after clearing garbage from a street in the 1890s, one Chicagoan discovered pavement buried under 18 inches of trash.

City utilities and services, including gas, public transit, sometimes water, and later electricity and telephone service, were typically provided by private companies operating under **franchises** from the city. Entrepreneurs eagerly competed for such franchises, sometimes bribing city officials to secure them. As a result, new residential areas sometimes had gas lines before sewers, and streetcars before paved streets.

Everywhere, urban growth seemed at first to outstrip the abilities of city officials and residents to provide for its consequences. Nonetheless most city utilities and services improved significantly between 1870 and 1900. New York City created the first uniformed police force in 1845, and other cities followed. By 1871, all major cities had switched from volunteer fire companies to paid professional firefighters, but the **Great Chicago Fire** of 1871 dramatically demonstrated that even the new system was inadequate. The fire devastated 3 square miles, including much of the downtown, killed more than 250 people, and left 18,000 homeless. Such disasters spurred efforts to improve fire protection. Pressured by citizens and fire insurance companies, many city officials worked to train and equip firefighters and to regulate construction so that buildings were more fire-resistant. By 1900, most American cities had impressive firefighting forces, especially compared with those in other parts of the world. Chicago had more firefighters and fire engines than London, a city three times its size.

The New Urban Geography

The new technologies that transformed the urban **infrastructure** interacted with the growth of manu-

---

chlorination The treatment of water with the chemical chlorine to kill germs.

franchise Government authorization allowing a company to provide a public service in a certain area.

Great Chicago Fire A fire that destroyed much of Chicago in 1871 and spurred national efforts to improve fire protection.

infrastructure Basic facilities that a society needs to function, such as transportation systems, water and power lines, and public institutions such as schools, post offices, and prisons.

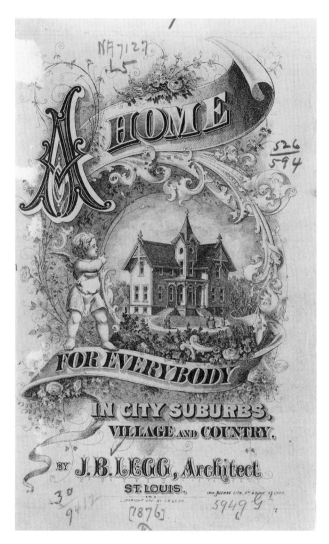

This cover for a book of architectural designs published in 1876 points to some of the appeal of the suburbs: a new, large, stylish house with a spacious, well-tended lawn and trees. Suburbs had an appeal that was both romantic (note Cupid holding the frame of the picture of the house) and countrylike. Furthermore, as this book cover proclaims, "everybody" could have a single-family home in the suburbs. *Library of Congress.*

facturing, commerce, and finance to change the geography of American cities. Within the largest cities, areas become increasingly specialized by economic function.

Early manufacturing in port cities was often scattered among warehouses near the waterfront. Clothing factories sometimes began in buildings formerly used by sail makers or as warehouses. Other manufacturing firms required specially designed facilities.

Iron and steel making, meatpacking, shipbuilding, and oil refining had to be established on the outskirts of a city. There, open land was plentiful and relatively cheap, freight transportation was convenient, and the city center suffered less from the noise, smoke, and odor of heavy industry.

Many manufacturing workers could not afford to ride the new streetcars, so they often had no choice but to live within walking distance of their work. Construction of industrial plants outside cities, therefore, usually meant working-class residential neighborhoods nearby. Some companies established planned communities: a manufacturing plant surrounded by residences, stores, and even parks and schools. Such company towns were sometimes well intended, but few earned good reputations among their residents. Workers whose employer was also their landlord and storekeeper usually resented the ever-present authority of the company—and the lack of alternatives to the rents and prices it charged.

At the same time that heavy manufacturing moved to the outskirts of the cities, areas in the city centers tended to become more specialized. By 1900 or so, the center of a large city usually had developed distinct districts. A district of light manufacturing might include clothing factories and printing plants. Next to or overlapping light manufacturing was often a wholesale trade district with warehouses and offices of **wholesalers.**

Retail shopping districts, anchored by the new department stores, emerged in a central location, where streetcar and railroad lines could bring middle-class and upper-class shoppers from the new suburbs. In the largest cities, banks, insurance companies, and headquarters of large corporations clustered to form a financial district. A hotel and entertainment district often lay close to the financial and retail blocks. These areas together made up a **central business district.**

Just as specialized downtown areas emerged according to economic function, so too did residential areas develop according to economic status. New suburbs ranged outward from the city center in order of wealth. Those who could afford to travel the farthest could also afford the most expensive homes.

wholesaler   Person engaged in the sale of goods in large quantities, usually for resale by a retailer.
retail   Related to the sale of goods directly to consumers.
central business district   The part of a city that includes most of its commercial, financial, and manufacturing establishments.

Those too poor to ride the new transportation lines lived in densely populated and deteriorating neighborhoods in the center of the city or clustered around industrial plants. Much of the burgeoning urban middle class lived between the two extremes, far enough from the central business district that many residents rode streetcars downtown to work or shop, but outside the least desirable ring of densely populated, deteriorating neighborhoods.

New Patterns of Urban Life

■ How did the middle class adjust to the changing demands and opportunities of the era?

■ What important new social patterns emerged in urban areas in the late nineteenth century?

The decades following the Civil War brought far-reaching social changes to nearly all parts of the nation. The burgeoning cities presented new vistas of opportunity for some, especially the middle class. In the new urban environments, some women questioned traditionally defined gender roles, as did gays and lesbians.

The New Middle Class

The Gilded Age brought significant changes to the lives of many middle-class Americans, especially urban-dwellers. The development of giant corporations and central business districts was accompanied by the appearance of an army of accountants, lawyers, secretaries, insurance agents, and middle-level managers, who staffed corporate headquarters and professional offices. The new department stores succeeded by appealing to the growing urban middle class. Streetcar lines allowed members of the middle class to live beyond walking distance of their work. Thus industrialization and urban expansion produced not only large neighborhoods of the industrial working class and enclaves of the very wealthy but also an expansion of distinctively middle-class neighborhoods and suburbs.

Single-family houses set amid wide and carefully tended lawns were common in many new middle-class neighborhoods, or **suburbs,** in the late nineteenth century. Such developments accelerated the tendency of American urban and suburban areas to sprawl for miles and to have population densities much lower than those of expanding European cities of the same time. Acquiring land had long been a cornerstone of the American dream. In the late nineteenth century, the single-family house became the realization of that dream for many middle-class families. Many members of the middle class found it especially attractive to acquire that house in a suburb, outside the city but connected to it by streetcar tracks or a commuter rail line. Moving to a middle-class suburb allowed them to avoid the congestion of the slums, the violence of labor conflicts, and the higher property taxes that funded city governments.

In the new middle-class suburbs and urban neighborhoods, households followed social patterns somewhat different from those of working-class or farm families. Middle-class families often employed a domestic servant to assist with household chores, and many middle-class women participated in social organizations outside the home. Middle-class parents rarely expected their children to contribute to the family's finances, and they usually insisted on their being educated at least through high school.

Middle-class families provided the major market for an expansion of daily newspapers, which began to include sections designed to appeal to women—household hints, fashion advice, and news of women's organizations—along with sports sections aimed largely at men and comics for the children. Joseph Pulitzer's *New York World* pioneered such innovations, and others soon emulated them. Urban middle-class households were also likely to subscribe to family magazines such as the *Ladies' Home Journal* and the *Saturday Evening Post,* which included household advice, fiction, and news. Much of the advertising (see page 534) in such publications was aimed at the middle class, fostering the emergence of a so-called **consumer culture** among middle-class women, who became responsible for nearly all their family's shopping. Such publications, through both their articles and their advertising, also helped to extend middle-class patterns to readers across the country.

Ferment in Education

Middle-class parents' concern for their children's education combined with other factors to produce impor-

suburb   A residential area lying outside the central city; many of the residents of suburbs work and shop in the central city even though they live outside it.

consumer culture   A consumer is an individual who buys products for personal use; a consumer culture emphasizes the values and attitudes that derive from the participants' roles as consumers.

tant changes in American education, from **kindergarten** through university. The number of kindergartens—first created outside the public schools to provide childcare for working mothers—grew from 200 in 1880 to 3,000 in 1900. Kindergartens also began to be included in the public school system in some cities, beginning with St. Louis in 1873. Between 1870 and 1900, most northern and western states and territories established school attendance laws, requiring children between certain ages (usually 8 to 14) to attend school for a minimum number of weeks each year, typically twelve to sixteen. In the 1880s, New York City schools began to provide textbooks rather than requiring students to buy their own, and the practice expanded slowly. By 1898, ten states required school districts to provide textbooks to students without charge.

The largest increase in school attendance was at the secondary level. There were fewer than 800 high schools in the entire nation in 1878, but 5,500 by 1898. The proportion of high school graduates in the population tripled in the late nineteenth century. By 1890, high schools offered grades 9 through 12 everywhere but in the South. The high school curriculum also changed significantly, adding courses in the sciences, civics, business, home economics, and skills needed by industry, such as drafting, woodworking, and the mechanical trades. From 1870 onward, women outnumbered men among high school graduates. The growth of high schools, however, was largely an urban phenomenon. In rural areas, few students continued beyond the eighth grade.

College enrollments also grew, with the largest gains in the new state universities created under the Land-Grant College Act of 1862. Even so, college students came disproportionately from middle-class and upper-class families and rarely from farms. The college curriculum changed greatly, from a set of classical courses required of all students (mostly Latin, Greek, mathematics, rhetoric, and religion) to a system in which students focused on a major subject and chose courses from a list of electives. The Land-Grant College Act required its universities to provide instruction in engineering and agriculture. Other new college subjects included economics, political science, modern languages, and laboratory sciences. Many universities also began to offer courses in business administration and teaching. In 1870 the curricula in most colleges still resembled those of a century before. By 1900, curricula looked more like those of today.

Despite the growing female majority through the high school level, far fewer women than men marched in college graduation processions. Only one college

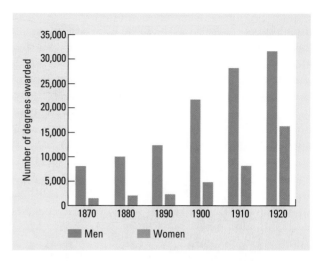

FIGURE 18.4 Number of First Degrees Awarded by Colleges and Universities, 1870–1920 This figure shows the change in the number of people receiving B.A., B.S., or other first college degrees, at ten-year intervals from 1870 to 1920. Notice that after 1890, the number of women increased more rapidly than the number of men. *Source:* U.S. Department of Commerce, Bureau of the Census, *Historical Statistics of the United States, Colonial Times to 1970,* Bicentennial edition, 2 vols. (Washington: Government Printing Office, 1975), 1: 385–386.

graduate in seven was a woman in 1870, and this ratio improved to only one in four by 1900 (see Fig. 18.4). In 1879 fewer than half of the nation's colleges admitted women, although most public universities did so. Twenty years later, four-fifths of all colleges, universities, and professional schools enrolled women.

Regardless of such impressive gains for coeducation, some colleges remained all-male enclaves, especially prestigious private institutions such as Harvard, Princeton, and Yale. Colleges exclusively for women began to appear after the Civil War, partly because so many colleges still refused to admit women and partly in keeping with the notion that men and women should occupy "separate spheres." The first, founded in 1861, was **Vassar College,** whose faculty of eight

---

kindergarten German for "children's garden"; a preschool program developed in the late nineteenth century initially as childcare for working mothers; based on programs first developed in Germany.

Vassar College The first collegiate institution for women, founded in Poughkeepsie, New York, in 1861.

FIGURE 18.13 The quilt pattern is called Drunkard's Path. The Drunkard's Path pattern became popular in the late 19th century, and some historians have connected its popularity at that time to the work of the Women's Christian Temperance Union (WCTU) in drawing attention to the evils of alcohol. Local chapters of the WCTU sometimes worked together (in a quilting party) to make a quilt, which they then sold as a fundraiser or used as a public banner for the temperance cause. This quilt was probably made in the 1890s in Maine, but has no known connection with the WCTU. *Picture Research Consultants & Archives.*

men and twenty-two women included Maria Mitchell, a leading astronomer and the first female member of the American Academy of Arts and Sciences.

Redefining Gender Roles

Greater educational opportunities for women marked only one part of a major reconstruction of gender roles. Throughout the nineteenth century, most Americans defined women's roles in domestic terms, as wife and mother and guardian of the family, responsible for its moral, spiritual, and physical well-being. This emphasis on **domesticity** also permitted women to take important roles in the church and the school. Business and politics, however, with their sometimes lax moral standards, were thought to pose a risk of cor-

ruption that might endanger women's roles as their families' spiritual guardians. Domesticity, some argued, required women to occupy a so-called **separate sphere,** immune from such dangers. The Illinois Supreme

> **domesticity** The notion common throughout much of the nineteenth century that women's activities were ideally rooted in domestic labor and the nurture of children.
>
> **separate sphere** The notion that men and women should engage in different activities: women were to focus on the family, church, and school, whereas men were to support the family financially and take part in politics, activities considered too competitive and corrupt for women.

Court even ruled, in 1870, that "God designed the sexes to occupy different spheres of action." Widely touted from the pulpits and in the journals of the day, the concepts of domesticity and separate spheres applied mostly to white middle-class and upper-class women in towns and cities. However, farm women and working-class women (including most women of color) witnessed too much of the world to fit easily into the patterns of dainty innocence prescribed by advocates of separate spheres.

Domesticity and, especially, separate spheres came under increasing fire in the late nineteenth century. One challenge came through education, especially at colleges. As more and more women finished college, some entered the professions. An early breakthrough came in medicine. In 1849 Elizabeth Blackwell became the first woman to complete medical school, and she helped to open a medical school for women in 1868. By the 1880s, some twenty-five hundred women held medical degrees. By the end of the century, about 3 percent of all physicians were women, proportionately more than during most of the twentieth century. After 1900, however, medical schools imposed enrollment practices that sharply reduced the number of female medical students and hence physicians. Access to the legal profession proved even more difficult. Arabella Mansfield was the first woman to be admitted to the bar, in 1869, but the entire nation counted only sixty practicing women attorneys ten years later. Most law schools refused to admit women until the 1890s. Other professions also yielded very slowly to women seeking admission.

Professional careers attracted a few women, but many middle-class and upper-class women in towns and cities became involved in other women's activities. Women's clubs became popular among middle- and upper-class women in the late nineteenth century, claiming 100,000 members nationwide by the 1890s. Ida Wells, a crusader for black civil rights who, after marrying, was known as Ida Wells-Barnett, actively promoted the development of black women's clubs. Such clubs often began within the separate women's sphere as forums in which to discuss literature or art, but they sometimes led women out of their insulation and into reform activities. (Of course, women had publicly participated in reform before, especially in the movement to abolish slavery.)

The **Women's Christian Temperance Union** (WCTU) was organized in 1874 by women who regarded alcohol as the chief reason for men's neglect and abuse of their families. WCTU members committed themselves to total abstinence from all alcohol and sought to protect the home and family by converting others

It Matters

The WCTU and Woman Suffrage Outside the United States

Drawing on the proselytizing traditions of Protestantism, the Women's Christian Temperance Union sent "round-the-world missionaries" to carry the message of prohibition and women's political rights to Hawai`i (then an independent kingdom), New Zealand, Australia, China, Japan, India, South Africa, and elsewhere. Their efforts had their greatest immediate success when local recruits secured the adoption of woman suffrage in New Zealand in 1893, in the Colony of South Australia in 1895, in Western Australia in 1899, and in the newly established Commonwealth of Australia in 1901. New Zealand and Australia were the first two nations to extend the suffrage to women. WCTU missionaries also made their presence felt in other parts of the world, helping to lay a basis for a women's movement in such places as Japan and India.

to abstinence and the legal prohibition of alcohol. The organization typically operated through such old-stock Protestant churches as the Methodists, Presbyterians, Congregationalists, and Baptists. From 1879 until her death in 1898, Frances Willard was the driving force in the organization. Her personal motto was "Do everything," and she was untiring in her work for the cause of temperance. By the early 1890s, the WCTU claimed 150,000 members, making it the largest women's organization in the nation. Yet for Willard the organization remained very much within the traditional women's arena of family and home. She once offered a simple statement of purpose for the WCTU: "to make the whole world homelike."

Women's church organizations, clubs, and reform societies all provided experience in working together toward a common cause and sometimes in seeking

Women's Christian Temperance Union Women's organization founded in 1874 that opposed alcoholic beverages and supported reforms such as woman suffrage.

changes in public policy. Through them, women developed networks of working relationships and cultivated leadership skills. These experiences and contacts contributed to the growing effectiveness of women's efforts to establish their right to vote (see pages 560–561). In 1882 the WCTU endorsed woman suffrage, the first support for that cause from a major women's organization other than those formed specifically to advocate woman suffrage.

Just as women's gender roles were undergoing reconstruction in the late nineteenth century, so too were those of men. In the early nineteenth century, manliness was defined largely in terms of "character," which included courage, honor, independence, duty, and loyalty (including loyalty to a political party), along with providing a good home for a family. With the growth of the urban industrial society, fewer men were self-employed (and thus no longer "independent"), and fewer men had the opportunity to demonstrate courage or boldness. The rise of big-city political organizations dominated by saloonkeepers and working-class immigrants caused some middle- and upper-class males to question older notions of party loyalty.

In response, some middle-class men seem to have turned to organizations and activities that emphasized male bonding or masculinity. Fraternal organizations modeled on the Masons multiplied in the late nineteenth century, usually providing both a ritualistic retreat to a preindustrial era and meager insurance benefits for widows and orphans. Professional athletics, including baseball and boxing, began to attract large numbers of middle- and upper-class male spectators. The Young Men's Christian Association (YMCA) spread rapidly in American cities after the Civil War, emphasizing Christian values, physical fitness, and service. Wilderness camping and hunting—necessities for many Americans in earlier times—became a middle-class and upper-class male sport, a demonstration of masculinity. Theodore Roosevelt delighted in hunting big game, claiming that it promoted the manly virtues of "nerve control" and "cool-headedness." He specified that such "bodily vigor" was necessary for "vigor of the soul."

Emergence of a Gay and Lesbian Subculture

Urbanization and economic change contributed to the social redefinition of gender roles for middle-class women and men, but a quite different redefinition oc-

curred at the same time, as burgeoning cities provided a setting for the development of gay and lesbian subcultures.

Homosexual behavior was illegal in all states and territories throughout the nineteenth and early twentieth centuries. At the same time, however, men and women engaged in a wide variety of socially acceptable same-sex relationships. The concept of separate spheres and the tendency for most schools and workplaces to be segregated by sex meant that many men and women spent much of their time with others of their own sex. Many occupations involved working closely with a partner, sometimes over long periods of time. Such partners—both male or both female—could speak of each other with deep affection without violating prevailing social norms. Same-sex relationships may not have involved physical contact, although kisses and hugs—and sleeping in the same bed—were common expressions of affection among young women. Participants in such same-sex relationships did not consider themselves to be committing what the laws called "an unnatural act," and most of them married partners of the opposite sex.

Same-sex relationships that involved genital contact, however, violated both the law and the expectations of society. In rural communities, where most people knew one another, people physically attracted to those of their own sex seem to have suppressed such tendencies or to have exercised them discreetly. The record of convictions for **sodomy** indicates, however, that some failed to conceal their activities. A few men and somewhat more women changed their dress and behavior, passed for a member of the other sex, and married someone of their own sex.

In the late nineteenth century, in parts of the United States and Europe, burgeoning cities permitted an anonymity not possible in rural societies. Homosexuals and lesbians gravitated toward the largest cities and began to create distinctive **subcultures.** By the 1890s, one researcher reported that "perverts of both sexes maintained a sort of social set-up in New

sodomy Varieties of sexual intercourse prohibited by law in the nineteenth century, typically including intercourse between two males.

subculture A group whose members differ from the dominant culture on the basis of some values or interests but who share most values and interests with the dominant culture.

York City, had their places of meeting, and [the] advantage of police protection." Reports of regular homosexual meeting places—clubs, restaurants, steam baths, parks, streets—also issued from Boston, Chicago, New Orleans, St. Louis, and San Francisco. Although most participants in these subcultures were secretive, some flaunted their sexuality. In a few places, "drag balls" featured cross-dressing, especially by men.

In the 1880s, physicians began to study members of these emerging subcultures and created medical names for them, including "homosexual," "lesbian," "invert," and "pervert." Earlier, law and religion had defined particular actions as illegal or immoral. The new, clinical definitions emphasized not the actions but instead the persons taking the actions. Some theorists in the 1880s and 1890s proposed that such behavior resulted from a mental disease, but others concluded that homosexuals and lesbians were born so.

New medical and legal definitions of homosexuality were accompanied by a similar delineation of heterosexuality. As medical and legal definitions shifted from actions to persons, the nature of same-sex relationships also changed. Once-acceptable behavior, including expressions of affection between heterosexuals of the same sex, became less common as individuals tried to avoid any suggestion that they were anything but heterosexual.

The Politics of Stalemate

■ Compare the presidencies of Garfield, Arthur, and Cleveland. Which do you consider more successful? Why?

■ What were some of the goals of the different reform groups, such as the Grangers and Greenbackers (discussed in Chapter 17), civil service reformers, prohibitionists, and supporters of woman suffrage? Why were some reformers able to accomplish more than others?

During the 1880s, as the nation's economy and social patterns changed with astonishing speed, American politics ironically seemed to be stalled at dead center. From the end of the Civil War to the mid-1870s, much of American politics had revolved around issues arising out of the war. By the late 1870s, other issues emerged as crucial, notably the economy and political corruption. After the mid-1870s, however, voters divided almost evenly between the two major political parties, beginning a long political **stalemate** during which neither party enacted significant new policies.

The Presidencies of Garfield and Arthur

As Rutherford B. Hayes neared the end of his term as president—a term made difficult by his conflicts with Roscoe Conkling and the railway strike of 1877 (see pages 516–520)—Republican leaders looked for a presidential candidate who could lead them to victory in 1880. James G. Blaine of Maine, a spellbinding orator who attracted loyal supporters and bitter enemies, sought the party's nomination. Conkling and his followers, calling themselves **Stalwarts**, tried to nominate former president Grant instead. Few major differences of policy separated Conkling from Blaine. Conkling showed more commitment to the spoils system and the defense of southern black voters, and Blaine took more interest in the protective tariff and economic policies, encouraging industrialization and western economic development. Conkling, however, dismissed Blaine and his supporters as **Half-Breeds**—not real Republicans.

After a frustrating convention deadlock, the Republicans compromised by nominating James A. Garfield, a congressman from Ohio. Born in a log cabin, Garfield had grown up in poverty. A minister, college president, and lawyer before the Civil War, he became the Union's youngest major general. For vice president, the delegates tried to placate the Stalwarts and secure New York's electoral votes by nominating Conkling's chief lieutenant, Chester A. Arthur.

The Democrats nominated Winfield Scott Hancock, a former Civil War general with little political experience. Both candidates worked at avoiding matters of substance during the campaign. Garfield won the popular vote by only half a percentage point. He won the electoral vote convincingly, however, even though he failed to carry a single southern state. Republicans, it appeared, could win the White House without the southern black vote.

Garfield brought to the presidency a solid understanding of Congress and a careful and studious

> **stalemate** A deadlock; in chess, a situation in which neither player can move.
>
> **Stalwarts** Faction of the Republican Party led by Roscoe Conkling of New York; Stalwarts claimed to be the genuine Republicans.
>
> **Half-Breeds** Insulting name that Roscoe Conkling gave to his opponents (especially James Blaine) within the Republican Party to suggest that they were not fully committed to Republican ideals.

approach to issues. Hoping to work cooperatively with both Stalwarts and Blaine supporters, he appointed Blaine as secretary of state, the most prestigious cabinet position. Discord soon threatened when Conkling demanded the right to name his supporters to key federal positions. In response, Garfield showed himself to be shrewder politically than any president since Lincoln. When Conkling acknowledged defeat by resigning from the Senate, Garfield scored a victory for a stronger presidency.

On July 2, 1881, four months after taking the oath of office, Garfield was shot while walking through a Washington railroad station. His assassin, Charles Guiteau, a mentally unstable religious fanatic, called himself "a Stalwart of the Stalwarts" and claimed he had acted to save the Republican Party. Two months later, Garfield died of the wound.

Chester A. Arthur became president. Long a close ally of Conkling, Arthur was probably best known as a capable administrator and a dapper dresser. However, as one of his former associates said, he soon showed that "He isn't 'Chet' Arthur any more; he's the President." In 1882 doctors diagnosed the president as suffering from Bright's disease, a kidney condition that produced fatigue, depression, and eventually death. Arthur kept the news secret from all but his family and closest friends. Overcoming both political liabilities and his own physical limitations, Arthur proved a competent president.

Reforming the Spoils System

The Republicans had slim majorities in Congress after the 1880 election, but the Democrats recovered control over the House of Representatives in 1882. Acting quickly, before the newly elected Democrats took their seats, the Republicans enacted the first major tariff revision in eight years and the **Pendleton Act,** reforming the civil service. Both measures had support from a few Democrats.

Named for its sponsor, Senator George Pendleton (an Ohio Democrat), the Pendleton Act had far-reaching consequences, for it brought into being a merit system for filling federal positions to replace the long-criticized spoils system. The new law designated certain federal positions, initially about 15 percent of the total, as "classified." **Classified civil service** positions were to be filled only through competitive examinations.

The law also authorized the president to add positions to the classified list. When an office was first classified, the patronage appointee then holding it was protected from removal for political reasons.

Presidents could therefore use the law to entrench their own appointees. When those appointees retired, however, their replacements came through the merit system. Thus the law used patronage in the short run to bring the long-term demise of the patronage system. Within twenty years, the law applied to 44 percent of federal employees. Most state and local governments eventually adopted merit systems as well. Arthur's approval of the measure marked his final break with the Stalwarts.

The most persistent critics of the spoils systems— and those who most loudly claimed credit for the Pendleton Act—were a group known as **Mugwumps** to their contemporaries. Centered in Boston and New York, most of these reformers were Republicans of high social status. They traced many of the defects of politics to the spoils system, and they argued that eliminating patronage would drive out the machines and opportunists. Only then, they insisted, could corruption be eliminated and political decency restored. Instead of basing appointments on political loyalty, the Mugwumps advocated a merit system based on a job seeker's ability to pass a comprehensive examination. Educated, dedicated civil servants, they believed, would stand above party politics and provide capable and honest administration.

Cleveland and the Democrats

In the end, Arthur proved more capable than anyone might have predicted. Given his failing health, he exerted little effort to win his party's nomination in 1884. Blaine—charming and quick-witted—secured the Republican nomination. The Democrats nominated Grover Cleveland, who as governor of New York had earned a reputation for integrity and political courage, particularly by attacking **Tammany Hall,**

> **Pendleton Act** Law passed by Congress in 1883 that created the Civil Service Commission and instituted the merit system for federal hiring and jobs.
>
> **classified civil service** Federal jobs filled through the merit system instead of by patronage.
>
> **Mugwumps** Reformers, mostly Republicans, who opposed political corruption and campaigned for reform, especially reform of the civil service, in the 1880s and 1890s, sometimes crossing party boundaries to achieve their goals.
>
> **Tammany Hall** A New York City political organization that dominated city and sometimes state politics by dominating the Democratic Party in New York City.

the dominant Democratic Party organization in New York City. Many Irish voters, who made up a large component in Tammany, retaliated by supporting Blaine even though they were staunch Democrats.

The 1884 campaign quickly turned nasty. Many Mugwumps disliked Blaine and revealed an old letter of his urging a cover-up of allegations that he had profited from prorailroad legislation. When the Mugwumps broke with their party, they drew the contempt of most party politicians. Blaine called them "conceited, foolish . . . pretentious but not powerful." Other party politicians questioned the Mugwumps' manhood, reflecting the extent to which being a loyal party member was closely tied to the male gender role in the minds of many.

Blaine supporters gleefully trumpeted that Cleveland had avoided military service during the Civil War and had fathered a child outside marriage. Democrats chanted, "Blaine, Blaine, James G. Blaine! The continental liar from the state of Maine." Republicans shouted back, "Ma! Ma! Where's my pa?"

The election hinged on New York State, where Blaine expected to cut deeply into the usually Democratic Irish vote. A few days before the election, however, Blaine heard a preacher in New York City call the Democrats the party of "rum, Romanism [Catholicism], and rebellion." Blaine ignored this insult to his Irish Catholic supporters until newspapers blasted it the next day. By then the damage was done. Cleveland won New York by a tiny margin, and New York's electoral votes gave him the presidency.

Cleveland enjoyed support from many who opposed the spoils system, already being whittled away by the Pendleton Act. Though Cleveland did not dismantle the patronage system, he did insist on demonstrated ability in those he appointed to office. He was also deeply committed to minimal government and cutting federal spending. Between 1885 and 1889, Cleveland vetoed 414 bills—most of them granting pensions to individual Union veterans—twice as many vetoes as all previous presidents combined. Cleveland provided little leadership regarding legislation but did approve several important measures produced by the Democratic House and Republican Senate, including the Dawes Severalty Act (see page 589) and the Interstate Commerce Act.

The Interstate Commerce Act grew out of political pressure from farmers and small businesses. In the early 1870s, several midwestern states passed laws regulating railroad freight rates (usually called Granger laws; see page 518). Though the Supreme Court, in *Munn v. Illinois*, had agreed that businesses with "a public interest" were subject to regulation, later in *Wabash Railway v. Illinois* (1886), the court significantly limited states' power to regulate railroad rates involving interstate commerce.

In response to the *Wabash* decision and continuing protests over railroad rate discrimination, Congress passed the Interstate Commerce Act in 1887. The new law created the **Interstate Commerce Commission** (ICC), the first federal regulatory commission. The law also prohibited pools, rebates, and differential rates for short and long hauls, and it required that rates be "reasonable and just." The ICC had little real power, however, until the Hepburn Act strengthened it in 1906.

Cleveland considered the nation's greatest problem to be the federal budget surplus. After the Civil War, the tariff usually generated more income than the country needed to pay federal expenses (see Fig.18.5). Throughout the 1880s, the annual surplus often exceeded $100 million. Worried that the surplus encouraged wasteful spending, Cleveland demanded in 1887 that Congress cut tariff rates. He hoped not only to reduce federal income but also, by reducing prices on raw materials, to encourage companies to compete with recently developed monopolies.

Cleveland's action provoked a serious division within his own party. So long as Democrats did not have responsibility for the tariff, they could criticize Republican policies without restraint. Urged to take positive action by their own party chief, however, they failed. Cleveland exerted little leadership, leaving the initiative to congressional leaders. The Democratic majority in the House of Representatives created a bill with little resemblance to Cleveland's proposal but with ample benefits for the South, and the Republican majority in the Senate responded with amendments targeting southern economic interests. In the end, Congress adjourned without voting on the bill, and Cleveland's call for tariff reform came to nothing.

In the 1888 presidential election, the Democrats renominated Cleveland, but he backed off from the tariff issue and did little campaigning. The Republicans nominated Benjamin Harrison, senator from Indiana and a former Civil War general. Known as thoughtful and cautious, Harrison also impressed many as cool and distant. The Republicans launched a vigorous campaign focused on the virtues of the

Interstate Commerce Commission The first federal regulatory commission, created in 1887 to regulate railroads.

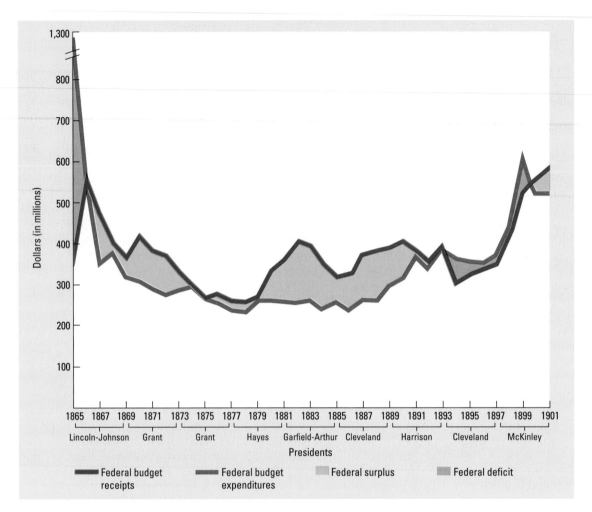

FIGURE 18.5 Federal Receipts and Expenditures, 1865–1901 The surplus usually shrank during economic downturns (the mid-1870s and mid-1890s) and grew in more prosperous periods (1880s). During the Harrison administration, however, the surplus virtually disappeared although the economy remained generally prosperous, reflecting efforts to reduce income and increase expenditures. *Source:* U.S. Department of Commerce, Bureau of the Census, *Historical Statistics of the United States, Colonial Times to 1970*, Bicentennial edition, 2 vols. (Washington, D.C.: U.S. Government Printing Office, 1975), 1: 1104.

protective tariff. They raised unprecedented amounts of campaign money by systematically approaching business leaders on the tariff issue, and they issued more campaign materials than ever before. Harrison received fewer popular votes than Cleveland (47.9 percent to Cleveland's 48.7 percent), but he won in the Electoral College. As important for the Republicans as their narrow presidential victory, however, were the majorities they secured in both the House and [[X-REF]] the Senate. (For the Fifty-first Congress, see page 605.)

The Mixed Blessings of Urban Machine Politics

In most cities, politics meant something very different from what it meant in the corridors and salons of Washington. Throughout the late nineteenth century, big-city politicians built loyal followings in poor neighborhoods by addressing the residents' needs directly and personally. In return, they wanted political loyalty from the poor. Such urban political organiza-

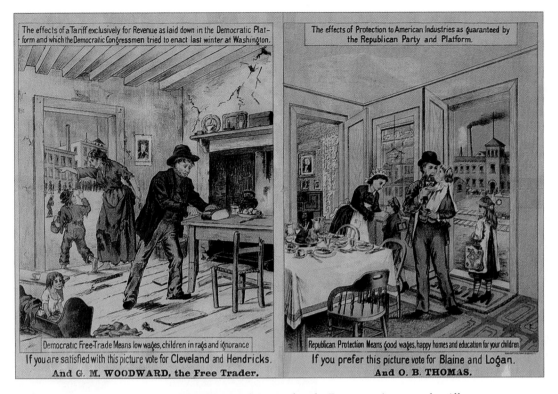

The effects of a Tariff exclusively for Revenue as laid down in the Democratic Platform and which the Democratic Congressmen tried to enact last winter at Washington.

The effects of Protection to American Industries as guaranteed by the Republican Party and Platform.

Democratic Free-Trade Means low wages, children in rags and ignorance

If you are satisfied with this picture vote for **Cleveland and Hendricks.** And G. M. WOODWARD, the Free Trader.

Republican Protection Means good wages, happy homes and education for your children

If you prefer this picture vote for **Blaine and Logan.** And O. B. THOMAS.

Republicans circulated this cartoon in 1884, claiming that the Democrats' proposed tariff reform would threaten wage levels and endanger little children, but Republicans' commitment to the protective tariff would protect wage levels and make families more secure. *Museum of American Political Life. Photograph by Steve Laschever.*

tions flourished during the years 1880–1910, and some survived long after that.

In 1905 a newspaper reporter published a series of conversations with a longtime participant in New York City politics, George W. Plunkitt. Plunkitt's observations provide insights into the nature of urban politics and its relation to urban poverty. Born in a poor Irish neighborhood of New York City, Plunkitt left school at the age of 11. He entered politics, eventually becoming a district leader of Tammany Hall, which dominated the city's Democratic Party. Between 1868 and 1904, he also served in a number of elected positions in state and city government. Plunkitt described to the reporter his formula for keeping the loyalty of the voters in his neighborhood.

> *Go right down among the poor families and help them in the different ways they need help. . . . It's philanthropy, but it's politics, too—mighty good politics. . . . The poor are the most grateful people in the world, and, let me tell you, they have more friends in their* neighborhoods *than the rich have in theirs. If there's a family in my district in want I know it before the charitable societies, and me and my men are first on the ground. . . . The consequence is that the poor look up to George W. Plunkitt as a father, come to him in trouble—and don't forget him on election day.*

Plunkitt typified many big-city politicians across the country. Because neighborhood saloons sometimes served as social gathering places for working-class men, would-be politicians frequented saloons—in fact, they sometimes owned them—and tried to build a personal rapport with the voters at the bar. They responded to the needs of the urban poor by providing a bucket of coal on a cold day, or a basket of food at Thanksgiving, or a job in some city department. In return, they expected the people they assisted to follow their lead in politics. Political organizations based among working-class and poor voters, usually led by men of poor immigrant parentage, emerged in nearly all large cities and experienced varying degrees of political success. Where they amassed great power, their rivals denounced the leader as a boss and the organization as a machine.

In every city, opponents of the machine charged corruption. Most bosses were cautious, but some accumulated sizable fortunes—sometimes through gifts or retainers from companies seeking franchises or city contracts (their critics called these bribes), sometimes through advance knowledge of city planning. Richard Croker, the boss of Tammany in the 1890s, accumulated an immense personal fortune, but he always insisted that he had never taken a dishonest dollar.

Above all, the bosses centralized political decision making. A machine politician in Boston, for example, insisted, "There's got to be in every ward somebody that any bloke can come to—no matter what he's done—to get help." If a pushcart vender needed a permit to sell tinware, or a railroad president needed permission to build a bridge, or a saloonkeeper wanted to stay open on Sunday in violation of the law, the machine could help them all—if they showed the proper gratitude in return. Always, the machine cultivated its base of support among poor and working-class voters.

Challenging the Male Bastion: Woman Suffrage

In the masculine political world of the Gilded Age, men expected one another to display strong loyalty to a political party, but they considered women—who could not vote—to stand outside the party system. The concepts of domesticity and separate spheres dictated that women avoid politics, especially party politics. In fact, some women did involve themselves in political struggles by taking part in reform efforts, even though they could not cast a ballot on election day, and a few even sought to take part in party activities. In the late nineteenth century, some women also pushed for full political participation through the right to vote.

The struggle for woman suffrage was of long standing. In 1848 Elizabeth Cady Stanton and four other women organized the world's first Women's Rights Convention, held at Seneca Falls, New York. The participants drafted a Declaration of Principles that announced, in part, "It is the duty of the women of this country to secure to themselves their sacred right to the elective franchise." Stanton became the most prominent leader in the struggle for women's rights, especially voting rights, from 1848 until her death in 1902. After 1851, Susan B. Anthony became her constant partner in these efforts. They achieved

This sketch of women voting in Cheyenne, Wyoming Territory, appeared in 1888. In 1869, Wyoming became the first state or territory to extend suffrage to women. This drawing appeared shortly before Wyoming requested statehood, a request made controversial by the issue of woman suffrage. *Library of Congress.*

some success in convincing lawmakers to modify laws that discriminated against women but failed to change laws that limited voting to men. During the nineteenth century, however, women increasingly participated in public affairs: movements to abolish slavery, mobilize support for the Union, improve educational opportunities, end child labor, and more.

In 1866 Stanton and Anthony unsuccessfully opposed inclusion of the word *male* in the Fourteenth Amendment (see page 471). In 1869 they formed the **National Woman Suffrage Association** (NWSA), its

National Woman Suffrage Association Women's suffrage organization formed in 1869 and led by Elizabeth Cady Stanton and Susan B. Anthony; it accepted only women as members and worked for related issues such as unionizing female workers.

membership open only to women. The NWSA sought an amendment to the federal Constitution as the only sure route to woman suffrage. It built alliances with other reform and radical organizations and worked to improve women's status. For example, members pressed for easier divorce laws and birth control (which Stanton called "self-sovereignty") and promoted women's trade unions. By contrast, the **American Woman Suffrage Association** (AWSA), organized by Lucy Stone and other suffrage advocates, also in 1869, concentrated strictly on winning the right to vote and avoided other issues. For twenty years, these two organizations led the suffrage cause, disagreeing not on the goal but on the way to achieve it. They merged in 1890, under Stanton's leadership, to become the National American Woman Suffrage Association. Until the early twentieth century, however, their support came largely from middle-class women—and men—who were largely of old-stock American Protestant descent.

The first victories for suffrage came in the West. In 1869, in Wyoming Territory, the territorial legislature extended the **franchise** to women. At the time, Wyoming was home to about seven thousand men but only two thousand women. Wyoming women had forged a well-organized suffrage movement, and they had persuaded some male legislators to support their cause. At the same time, other legislators may have hoped that woman suffrage would attract more women to Wyoming. Thus women in Wyoming Territory could—and did—vote, serve on juries, and hold elective office. In 1889, when Wyoming asked for statehood, some congressmen balked at admitting a state with woman suffrage. Wyoming legislators, however, bluntly stated, "We will remain out of the Union a hundred years rather than come in without the women." Finally Congress voted to approve Wyoming statehood—with woman suffrage—in 1890.

Utah Territory adopted woman suffrage in 1870. Mormon men formed the majority of Utah's voters, and Mormon women far outnumbered the relatively few non-Mormon women. By enfranchising women, Mormons strengthened their voting majority and may have hoped, at the same time, to silence the critics who claimed that **polygamy** degraded women. However, in an act aimed primarily at the Mormons, Congress outlawed polygamy in 1887 and simultaneously disfranchised the women in Utah. Not until Utah became a state, in 1896, did its women regain the vote. In 1893, Colorado voters (all male) approved woman suffrage, making Colorado the first state to adopt woman suffrage through a popular vote. In addition to a well-organized campaign by Colorado women,

their cause was assisted by support from the new Populist Party (see page 607). In Idaho, where both Mormon and Populist influences were strong, male voters approved woman suffrage in 1896.

In addition, several states began to extend limited voting rights to women, especially on matters outside party politics, such as school board elections and school bond issues. These concessions perhaps reflected the widespread assumption that women's gender roles included child rearing. By 1890, women could vote in school elections in nineteen states and on bond and tax issues in three.

Structural Change and Policy Change

The Grangers, Greenbackers (see pages 516–519), local labor parties with ties to the Knights of Labor, the WCTU, Mugwumps, and advocates of woman suffrage all challenged basic features of the party-bound political system of the Gilded Age. They and other groups sought political changes that the major parties ignored: abolition of the spoils system, woman suffrage, prohibition, the secret ballot, regulation of business, an end to child labor, changes in monetary policy, and more.

Most of these groups called themselves reformers, meaning that they wanted to change the form of politics. Most reforms fall into one of two categories—structural change and policy change. Structural change, or structural reform, modifies the *structure* of political decision making. Structural issues include the way in which public officials are chosen—for example, the convention system for making nominations, voting, and the appointment of government employees. Those seeking to eliminate the spoils system and substitute the merit system, therefore, addressed one element in the structure of politics. Woman suffrage was also a structural change.

American Woman Suffrage Association   Boston-based women's suffrage organization formed in 1869 and led by Lucy Stone, Julia Ward Howe, and others; it welcomed men and worked solely to win the vote for women.

franchise   As used here, the right to vote; another word for suffrage.

polygamy   The practice of a man having more than one wife; Mormons referred to this practice as plural marriage.

Policy issues, in contrast, have to do with the way that governmental power is used to accomplish particular objectives. The debate over federal economic policy in the Gilded Age provides an array of contrasting positions. Many Democrats favored a policy of laissez faire, believing that federal interference in the economy created a privileged class. Most Republicans favored a policy of distribution, meaning that they wanted to distribute benefits (land, tariff protection) to companies and individuals to encourage economic growth. Grangers favored regulation: they wanted the government to enforce basic rules governing economic activity—in this case, by prohibiting pools and rebates and setting maximum rates. Greenbackers wanted to use monetary policy to benefit debtors—or, as they would have put it, to replace a monetary policy that benefited lenders.

Groups seeking change may find they have little in common, or they may overlook differences to cooperate with other groups. Frances Willard of the WCTU, for example, embraced a wide range of reforms. One key distinction between the National Woman Suffrage Association and the American Woman Suffrage Association was that the NWSA often welcomed political alliances with groups such as the Greenbackers, who supported suffrage for all citizens in 1880. The AWSA, fearing that such alliances would lose more support for suffrage than they gained, chose a narrow focus on the suffrage issue.

Some groups combined structural and policy proposals. The tiny Prohibition Party, for example, wanted government to eliminate alcohol, but the Prohibitionists also favored woman suffrage because they assumed that most women voters would oppose alcohol. In this instance, they promoted a structural reform, woman suffrage, not just for its own sake but also to accomplish a policy reform, prohibition of alcohol. Advocates of woman suffrage also argued that enfranchising women would lead to a new approach to politics and to new policies.

One important structural change received widespread support from many political groups, and many states adopted it soon after its first appearance. The **Australian ballot**—printed and distributed by the government, not by political parties, listing all candidates of all parties, and marked in a private voting booth—was adopted by the first states in the late 1880s. The idea spread rapidly and was in use in most states by 1892. This reform carried important implications for political parties. No longer did voters find it difficult to cross party lines and vote a split ticket. No longer could party activists see which party's ballot a voter dropped into the ballot box. The switch to the Australian ballot

and the Pendleton Act marked the first significant efforts to limit parties' power and influence.

The United States and the World, 1880–1889

■ What reasons may there be for the lack of attention to foreign relations during this time period?

Presidents Garfield, Arthur, and Cleveland spent little time on foreign relations and paid little attention to the army and navy. After the end of most conflicts with American Indians in the late 1870s and early 1880s, the army was limited to a few garrisons, most of them near Indian reservations. The navy's wooden sailing vessels deteriorated to the point that some people ridiculed them as fit only for firewood. When a coal barge accidentally ran down a navy ship, one congressman joked that the worn-out navy was too slow even to get out of the way!

Whether from embarrassment or insight, Congress, in 1882, authorized construction of two steam-powered cruisers—the first new ships since the Civil War—and four more ships in 1883. Still, Secretary of the Navy William C. Whitney announced in 1885 that "we have nothing which deserves to be called a navy." Whitney persuaded Congress to fund several more cruisers and the first two modern battleships. Though Congress approved these ships, most federal decision makers still understood the role of the navy as limited to protecting American coasts.

Diplomacy was similarly routine. The most active American secretary of state also served the shortest term. James G. Blaine, Garfield's secretary of state, promoted closer relations with Latin America partly to encourage more trade among the nations of the Western Hemisphere—including more opportunities for the sale of products from the United States. He believed, too, that the United States should take a more active role among Latin American nations in resolving problems that might lead to war or European intervention. But when Garfield died, Arthur replaced Blaine at State, and Blaine's ambitious plans for hemispheric cooperation were scrapped.

policy A course of action adopted by a government, usually one that is pursued over a period of time and may involve several different laws and agencies.

Australian ballot A ballot printed by the government, rather then by political parties, and marked privately; so called because it originated there.

Hawai`i continued to attract the attention of some American entrepreneurs and policymakers. Despite the economic ties between Hawai`i and the United States that had developed through the sugar trade and other connections, relations between King David Kalakaua and the *haole* business and planter community of Hawai`i were never comfortable. Kalakaua wanted to preserve political power for **indigenous** Hawaiians, but haoles charged that he was ignoring the needs of business and the sugar plantations and that he protected corrupt officials.

In 1887 the news broke that Kalakaua himself had profited from bribery related to licenses for selling opium. Leaders of the haole community quickly forced a constitution on Kalakaua, reducing him to little more than a figurehead. Haoles soon dominated much of the government. That same year, Kalakaua approved the extension of the reciprocity treaty of 1875, with an additional provision giving the U.S. Navy exclusive rights to use Pearl Harbor. (The secretary of the navy admitted at the time, though, that he had no ships to send there.) Among some members of the royal family, resentment festered over the new constitution, the Pearl Harbor provision, and especially the extent of haole control, resentments that boiled over after Kalakaua's death in 1891.

Samoa, in the South Pacific, likewise attracted attention from the United States, and also from Britain and Germany. When German activity suggested an attempt at annexation, President Cleveland vowed to maintain Samoan independence. All three nations dispatched warships to the vicinity in 1889, and conflict seemed likely until a typhoon scattered the ships. A conference in Berlin then produced a treaty that provided for Samoan independence under the protection of the three Western nations.

---

haole   Hawaiian word for persons not of native Hawaiian ancestry, especially whites.
indigenous   Original to an area.
Samoa   A group of volcanic and mountainous islands in the South Pacific.

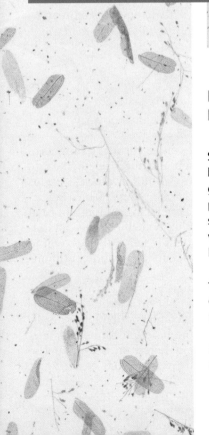

Individual Voices

Examining a Primary Source

Nikola Tesla Explores the Problems of Energy Resources and World Peace

Some of the leading figures of the Gilded Age seem to have been motivated largely by material concerns—how to organize an industry so as to produce more goods, at greater efficiency, and with greater profits. During that time, Nikola Tesla also applied the principles of physics to solving engineering problems so as to contribute to such goals. Tesla, however, also looked beyond the immediate circumstances in which he found himself and reflected on larger issues, some of which remain with humankind more than a century later.

In 1897, Tesla delivered an address entitled "On Electricity" at the launching of the great electrical generator he designed for Niagara Falls, which harnessed the energy of falling water without building a dam. His address was printed in the *Electrical Review*, January 27, 1897.

The development and wealth of a city, the success of a nation, the progress of the whole human race, is regulated by the power available. Think of the victorious

■ At that time, coal was the fossil fuel most widely used to drive most engines, including electrical generators. How does Tesla raise the issue of the exhaustion of supplies of fossil fuel? What do you think he proposed as the solution to the exhaustion of fossil fuels?

■ Compare Tesla's concerns here with the behavior of the United States in world affairs during the 1880s; after you complete Chapter 20, reconsider this issue.

■ How might Tesla's own experiences as an immigrant from Europe have affected his understanding of world affairs?

march of the British, the like of which history has never recorded. . . . They owe the conquest of the world to—coal. For with coal they produce their iron; coal furnishes them light and heat; coal drives the wheels of their immense manufacturing establishments, and coal propels their conquering fleets. But the stores are being more and more exhausted . . . , and the demand is continuously increasing. . . . We have to evolve means for obtaining energy from stores which are forever inexhaustible, to perfect methods which do not imply consumption and waste of any material whatever. . . . ■

Tesla was also concerned, throughout his life, with the human behavior that he considered the most serious impediment to the future progress of humankind. He addressed this issue in an article entitled "The Problem of Increasing Human Energy," published in *The Century Illustrated Monthly Magazine,* in June 1900.

There can be no doubt that, of all the frictional resistances, the one that most retards human movement is ignorance. . . . But however ignorance may have retarded the onward movement of man in times past, it is certain that, nowadays, negative forces have become of greater importance. Among these there is one of far greater moment than any other. It is called organized warfare. . . . It has been argued that the perfection of guns of great destructive power will stop warfare. So I myself thought for a long time, but now I believe this to be a profound mistake. . . . I think that every new arm that is invented, every new departure that is made in this direction, merely invites new talent and skill, engages new effort, offers new incentive, and so only gives a fresh impetus to further development. . . . ■

Again, it is contended by some that the advent of the flying-machine must bring on universal peace. This, too, I believe to be an entirely erroneous view. The flying-machine is certainly coming, and very soon, but the conditions will remain the same as before. In fact, I see no reason why a ruling power, like Great Britain, might not govern the air as well as the sea. . . . But, for all that, men will fight on merrily. ■

Summary

In the Gilded Age, as industrialization transformed the economy, urbanization and immigration challenged many established social patterns. John D. Rockefeller was one of the best known of many entrepreneurs who created manufacturing operations of unprecedented size and complexity, producing oligopoly and vertical integration in many industries. Technology and advertising emerged as important competitive devices. Investment bankers, notably J. P. Morgan, led in combining separate rail companies into larger and more profitable systems. Some southerners proclaimed the creation of a New South and promoted industrialization and a more diversified agricultural base. The outcome was mixed—the South did acquire

significant industry, but the region's poverty was little reduced.

Espousing cooperatives and reform, the Knights of Labor chose to open their membership to the unskilled, to African Americans, and to women—groups usually not admitted to craft unions. The Knights died out after 1890. The American Federation of Labor was formed by craft unions, and its leaders rejected radicalism and sought instead to work within capitalism to improve wages, hours, and conditions for its members.

Many Europeans immigrated to the United States because of economic and political conditions in their homelands and their expectations of better opportunities in America. Immigrants often formed distinct communities, frequently centered on a church. The flood of immigrants, particularly from eastern and southern Europe, spawned nativist reactions among some old-stock Americans.

As rural Americans and European immigrants sought better lives in the cities, urban America changed dramatically. New technologies in construction, transportation, and communication produced a new urban geography with separate retail, wholesale, finance, and manufacturing areas and residential neighborhoods defined by economic status.

Urban growth brought a new urban middle class. Education underwent far-reaching changes, from kindergartens through universities. Socially defined gender roles began to change as some women chose professional careers and took active roles in reform. Some men responded by redefining masculinity through organizations and athletics. Urbanization offered new choices to gay men and lesbians by making possible the development of distinctive urban subcultures. In response, medical specialists tried to define homosexuality and lesbianism.

The closely balanced strengths of the two parties contributed to a long-term political stalemate. Presidents James A. Garfield and Chester A. Arthur faced stormy conflict between factions in their own Republican Party. Mugwumps argued for the merit system in the civil service, accomplished through the Pendleton Act of 1883. As president, Grover Cleveland approved the Interstate Commerce Act. The growth of cities encouraged a particular variety of party organization, based on poor neighborhoods, where politicians traded favors for political support. By the late nineteenth century, a well-organized woman suffrage movement had emerged. A wide range of reform groups sought both structural changes and policy changes. Presidents during the 1880s largely neglected foreign relations because the period was one of stability in world affairs, and presidents saw little reason for the United States to become involved in foreign situations.

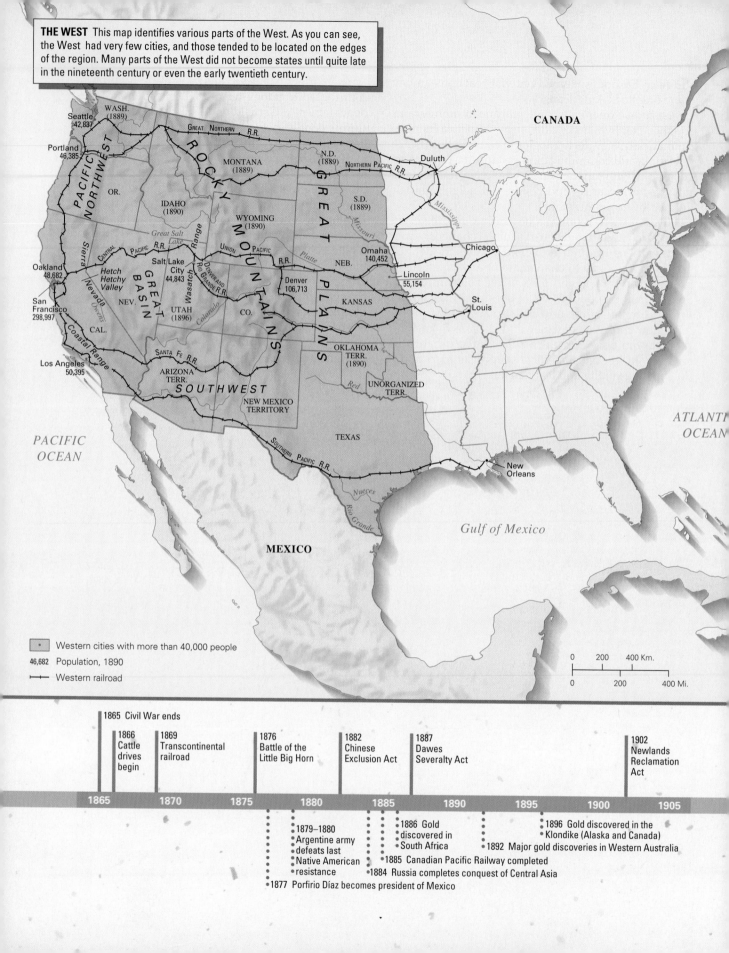

THE WEST This map identifies various parts of the West. As you can see, the West had very few cities, and those tended to be located on the edges of the region. Many parts of the West did not become states until quite late in the nineteenth century or even the early twentieth century.

CANADA

Seattle 42,837
WASH. (1889)

Portland 46,385

PACIFIC NORTHWEST

OR.

ROCKY MOUNTAINS

GREAT NORTHERN R.R.

MONTANA (1889)

N.D. (1889)

Duluth

Northern Pacific R.R.

IDAHO (1890)

WYOMING (1890)

S.D. (1889)

Great Salt Lake

Sierra Nevada

Central Pacific R.R.

Union Pacific R.R.

Salt Lake City 44,843

Hetch Hetchy Valley

GREAT BASIN

Rio Grande R.R.

Denver 106,713

Platte

NEB.

Omaha 140,452

Chicago

Oakland 48,682

Wasatch Range

UTAH (1896)

Denver & Rio Grande R.R.

Colorado

CO.

KANSAS

Lincoln 55,154

St. Louis

San Francisco 298,997

NEV.

Owens

CAL.

Coastal Range

Santa Fe R.R.

ARIZONA TERR.

Red

OKLAHOMA TERR. (1890)

UNORGANIZED TERR.

Los Angeles 50,395

SOUTHWEST

NEW MEXICO TERRITORY

TEXAS

PACIFIC OCEAN

Southern Pacific R.R.

New Orleans

ATLANTIC OCEAN

Nueces

Rio Grande

MEXICO

Gulf of Mexico

Mississippi

Missouri

• Western cities with more than 40,000 people

46,682 Population, 1890

━┿━ Western railroad

0   200   400 Km.

0   200   400 Mi.

1865 Civil War ends

1866 Cattle drives begin

1869 Transcontinental railroad

1876 Battle of the Little Big Horn

1882 Chinese Exclusion Act

1887 Dawes Severalty Act

1902 Newlands Reclamation Act

| 1865 | 1870 | 1875 | 1880 | 1885 | 1890 | 1895 | 1900 | 1905 |

1879–1880 Argentine army defeats last Native American resistance

1886 Gold discovered in South Africa

1896 Gold discovered in the Klondike (Alaska and Canada)

1892 Major gold discoveries in Western Australia

1885 Canadian Pacific Railway completed

1884 Russia completes conquest of Central Asia

1877 Porfirio Díaz becomes president of Mexico

Conflict and Change in the West, 1865–1902

The West

The map on the facing page includes all western cities with more than 40,000 people in 1890. What does the map tell you about the location of the western cities?

Individual Choices

The man known in legal history as Yick Wo apparently did not leave behind a photograph. This photograph shows an unnamed Chinese immigrant who worked as a laundryman in San Francisco at about the same time that Yick Wo was challenging the discriminatory city ordinance. Many Chinese laundries picked up and delivered laundry, and that is what this man is doing. Originally, laundrymen carried laundry in two large baskets, balanced on a pole over their shoulders, but a city ordinance in 1870 barred such poles from the public sidewalks. *Gabriel Moulin Studio, San Francisco, California.*

Yick Wo

The man known in history as Yick Wo was born in China and came to California in 1861. As a Chinese immigrant, he was not eligible to become a naturalized American citizen, because the law at that time limited naturalization to whites. A few years later, during Reconstruction, the law was changed to extend the opportunity for naturalization to persons of African descent—but not to persons born in Asia. Thus Yick remained a subject of the emperor of China. Soon after arriving in California, he engaged in the laundry business in San Francisco, under the name of Yick Wo, and he remained in that business, in the same building, for the next twenty-two years.

Running a small neighborhood laundry was not an unusual pursuit for a Chinese immigrant in San Francisco. Chinese were segregated both residentially and by occupation, and laundry work was a field dominated by them. Small laundries, usually run by Chinese immigrants, were scattered all across the city, in middle-class and upper-class neighborhoods. Historians know little about Yick—there is even disagreement over his actual name. Some claim it was Lee Yick and others that it was Yick Kwon Chang, but all agree that it was not Yick Wo. Regardless, the odds are that he lived alone in his laundry, perhaps with an employee. Few Chinese women came to the United States, partly because American customs officials discouraged Chinese women from entering the country. If Yick had a family, it was probably in China; if so, he likely sent them regular letters as well as money.

In 1885, Yick came up against a new San Francisco city ordinance that applied to laundries. Until then, he had always taken care to comply with laws regulating laundries. He had a license dated March 3, 1884, that specified his laundry had been inspected by city officials who had "found all proper arrangements for carrying on the business" and certified that it posed no fire danger. He also had had a certificate from the city health officer testifying that the laundry had been inspected and posed no risk to "the sanitary condition of the neighborhood."

However, when Yick applied to the San Francisco Board of Supervisors on June 1, 1885, for approval to continue his laundry business, he was refused. A city ordinance approved in 1880 required the Board of Supervisors to approve licenses for any laundries that operated in wooden buildings, on the grounds that laundries in wooden buildings posed a fire danger to their neighborhood. There were, at the time, about 320 laundries in the city, and 310 were in wooden buildings. About two-thirds of all the city's laundries were operated by Chinese immigrants. Given the new city ordinance, which purported to protect the city against the danger of fire, licenses were issued to all but one of the applicants who were not Chinese, but no licenses were issued to any Chinese laundry operators. When Yick and other Chinese laundry operators continued to operate, they were fined. When they did not pay their fines, they were jailed.

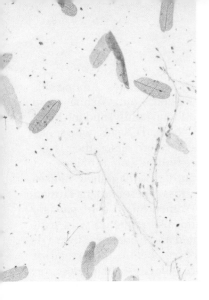

Yick and others challenged this discrimination. For their lawyer, they hired M. Hall McAllister, prominent in society and a leader of the bar, who had also defended some of the most powerful corporate tycoons in the West. Yick became the lead plaintiff in challenging the ordinance; his name was listed in all the legal documents as Yick Wo. McAllister filed for a **writ of habeas corpus** against Sheriff Peter Hopkins, but the California Supreme Court denied the request, so McAllister appealed to the U.S. Supreme Court.

In 1886, the United States Supreme Court reached its decision. Relying on the Fourteenth Amendment to the Constitution, the Court pronounced the behavior of the San Francisco Board of Supervisors to be unconstitutional because it discriminated on the basis of race, and ordered Yick to be freed. *Yick Wo v. Hopkins* stands as a major civil rights case (see Individual Voices, page 595), because the man known in history as Yick Wo was willing to challenge discrimination.

INTRODUCTION

In the same year as the *Yick Wo* decision, the army was eliminating the last major armed Indian resistance in the West, that of Geronimo and his followers. Eastern cities were burgeoning with immigrants from Europe, and Andrew Carnegie and John D. Rockefeller were building industrial empires. Western entrepreneurs were building their own empires. Americans have shown a long-lasting interest in the West of the late nineteenth century. Popular fiction and drama have glorified the West as a land where rugged individualism held sway and pioneers overcame great odds. The reality of western life was more complex.

For years before the Civil War, the issue of slavery had blocked efforts to develop the West. The secession of the southern states permitted the Republicans who took over the federal government in 1861 to open the West to economic development and white settlement, through measures such as the Pacific Railroad Act and the Homestead Act, both passed in 1862.

As Americans faced west, their prior experience suggested the steady westward extension of family farms. American farmers had taken more than a half-century to fill the area between the Appalachian Mountains and the Mississippi River. Some thought it would take as long to extend cultivation to the Rocky Mountains. In 1827 a cabinet officer had predicted that the nation would take five hundred years to fill up the West. However, travelers to the West had described it as an area of vast deserts, forbidding mountains, and well-armed, mounted Indian warriors, suggesting that parts of the West might never be developed like the eastern half of the nation.

In most of the West, rainfall was markedly less than in the eastern United States, where sufficient water was simply taken for granted. In the West, the scarcity of water presented new questions. What sort of development was appropriate in a region with little rain? How could water be harnessed to support development? Who would control the water, and who would benefit from it?

Similarly, the ethnic and racial composition of the West differed significantly from patterns in the East and South. At the end of the Civil War, the northeastern and north-central United States was almost entirely of European descent. The South was a biracial society—white and black. Some American Indians lived east of the Mississippi, but larger numbers had been pushed westward and were sharing parts of the West with tribal groups who claimed it as their ancestral homeland. The Southwest was home to significant numbers of people who spoke Spanish, who were often of mixed white and Native American ancestry, and whose families had lived in the region for generations. Santa Fe, New Mexico, for example, had been founded by Spanish conquistadores before 1610, and the first Spanish settlements in California dated to 1769. By the time of the Civil War, the Pacific Coast had attracted immigrants from Asia, especially China, who had crossed the Pacific going east in hopes of finding their fortune in America, much as European

writ of habeas corpus In law, the writ of habeas corpus is a court document challenging the legality of an incarceration.

immigrants crossed the Atlantic going west. In the late nineteenth century, these concentrations of ethnic groups marked the West as a distinctive place.

As individual Americans began to shape the development of the West—from seeking free land under the Homestead Act to speculating in mining stock to adjusting to an unfamiliar environment—federal officials had to decide what to do about the American Indians who occupied much of the region. Given the realities of the West, development there proved sometimes to be quite different from previous experience. The result was the transformation of the American West.

War for the West

▪ What did federal policymakers after the Civil War hope to accomplish regarding American Indians? How did western Indians respond?

▪ How can you explain the decisions of both federal policymakers and western Native Americans?

When Congress decided to use the public domain—western land—to encourage economic development, most white Americans considered the West to be largely vacant. In fact, American Indians lived throughout most of the West, and their understanding of their relationship to the land differed greatly from that of most white Americans. Certainly the most tragic outcome of the development of the West was the upheaval in the lives of the American Indians who lived there.

The Plains Indians

By the end of the Civil War, as many white Americans began to move west, the acquisition of horses and guns had already transformed the lives of western Native Americans. The transformation was most dramatic among the tribes living on or near the **Great Plains**—the vast, relatively flat, and treeless region that stretches from north to south across the center of the nation and that was the rangeland of huge herds of buffalo. The introduction of the horse to the Great Plains took place slowly, trickling northward from Spanish settlements in what is now New Mexico and eventually reaching the upper plains in the mid-eighteenth century. By that time, French and English traders working northeast of the plains had begun to provide guns to the Indians in return for furs. Together, horses and guns transformed the culture of some Plains tribes.

The Native Americans of the plains included both farmers and nomadic hunters. The farmers lived most of the year in large permanent villages. Among this group were the Arikaras, Pawnees, and Wichitas (who spoke languages of the Caddoan family) and the Mandans, Hidatsas, Omahas, Otos, and Osages (who spoke Siouan languages). On the northern plains, their large, dome-shaped houses were typically made of logs and covered with dirt. In southern areas, their houses were often covered with grass. These Indians farmed the fertile river valleys. Women raised corn, squash, pumpkins, and beans and also gathered wild fruit and vegetables. Men hunted and fished near their villages and cultivated tobacco. Before the arrival of horses, twice a year entire villages went, on foot, on extended hunting trips for buffalo—once in the early summer after their crops were planted, then again in the fall after the harvest. One favorite method of killing buffalo was to stampede an entire herd off a high cliff, causing large numbers to be killed or seriously injured. During these hunts, the people lived in **tipis,** cone-shaped tents of buffalo hide that were easy to move. Acquisition of horses changed the culture of these Indians only slightly.

The horse utterly revolutionized the lives of other Plains Indians. Because a hunter on horseback could kill twice as many buffalo as one on foot, the horse substantially increased the number of people the plains could support. The horse also increased mobility, permitting a band to follow the buffalo as they moved across the grasslands. The buffalo provided most essentials: food (meat), clothing and shelter (made from hides), implements (made from bones and horns), and even fuel for fires (dried dung). Some groups abandoned farming and became nomadic, living in tipis year-round and following the buffalo herds. The **Cheyennes,** for example, made this transition within a single generation after 1770. By the early nineteenth century, the **horse culture** existed throughout the Great Plains. The largest groups practicing this

---

Great Plains High grassland of western North America, stretching from roughly the 98th meridian to the Rocky Mountains; it is generally level, treeless, and fairly dry.

tipi Conical tent made from buffalo hide and used as a portable dwelling by Indians on the Great Plains.

Cheyenne Indian people who became nomadic buffalo hunters after migrating to the Great Plains in the eighteenth century.

horse culture The nomadic way of life of those American Indians, mostly on the Great Plains, for whom the horse brought significant changes in their ability to hunt, travel, and make war.

Chronology

Transforming the West

1700s	Horse culture spreads throughout Great Plains
1847	First Mormon settlements near Great Salt Lake
1848	Treaty of Guadalupe Hidalgo California gold rush begins
1862	Homestead Act Pacific Railroad Act
1865	Civil War ends
1866–1880	Cattle drives north from Texas
1867–1868	Treaties establish major western reservations
1868–1869	Army's winter campaign against southern Plains Indians
1869	First transcontinental railroad completed
Early 1870s	Cattle raising begins on northern plains
1870s	Destruction of buffalo herds Silver-mining boom in Nevada
1870s–1880s	Extension of farming to Great Plains
1871–1885	Anti-Chinese riots across West
1874	American Indian resistance ends on southern plains Patent issued for barbed wire Women's Christian Temperance Union founded
1876	Spring and summer campaign on northern plains Indian victory in Battle of Little Big Horn
1877	Reconstruction ends Army subdues last major Indian resistance on northern plains Surrender and death of Crazy Horse Chief Joseph and the Nez Perce flee Workingmen's Party of California attacks Chinese
1881	Surrender of Sitting Bull
1882	Chinese Exclusion Act
1883	Northern Pacific Railroad completed to Portland
1884	Federal court prohibits hydraulic mining
1885	First U.S. skyscraper
1886	Surrender of Geronimo *Yick Wo v. Hopkins*
1886–1887	Severe winter damages northern cattle business
1887	Dawes Severalty Act
Late 1880s	Reduced rainfall forces many homesteaders off western farms
1890	Sitting Bull killed Conflict at Wounded Knee Creek
1892	Sierra Club formed
1893	Great Northern Railway completed Frederick Jackson Turner presents his frontier thesis
1902	Reclamation Act

lifestyle included—from north to south—the Blackfeet, Crows, **Lakotas,** Cheyennes, Arapahos, Kiowas, and Comanches.

The Lakotas, largest of all the groups, were the westernmost members of a large group of Native American peoples often called Sioux; the eastern Sioux were called Dakotas or Nakotas. They did not call themselves *Sioux*—that name was applied to them by the French as a short version of an insulting name they were called by a neighboring, and enemy, tribe.

Their name for themselves can be translated as *allies,* reflecting their organization as a **confederacy.** All the Lakotas shared a common language. Membership in

> **Lakota** A confederation of Siouan Indian peoples who lived on the northern Great Plains.
>
> **confederacy** An organization of separate groups who have allied for mutual support or joint action.

John Mix Stanley painted this buffalo hunt in 1845, dramatically illustrating how the horse increased the ability of Native American hunters to kill buffalo. Before the horse, a hunter could not safely have gone into the midst of a stampeding herd to drive a lance into a buffalo's heart. *Smithsonian American Art Museum, Washington, D.C.; Art Resource, N.Y.*

the Lakota confederacy was not limited to those speaking a particular language, however, as the northern Cheyennes were generally considered members of the Lakota confederacy by the mid-nineteenth century.

Whether nomadic buffalo hunters or **sedentary** farming people, Indians living on the Great Plains and in other areas of North America understood the land differently from white settlers. From the time of the first European migrants to America, most white Americans had considered land to be a commodity to be bought and sold, owned and improved by individuals. According to Native American tradition, however, land was to be used but not individually owned. Horses, weapons, tipis, and clothing were all individually owned, but not land. Though they did not practice individual ownership of land, tribes did claim specific territories.

Before the arrival of horses, young men derived status from raiding a neighboring tribe to seize agricultural produce, capture a member of that tribe as a slave, or seek revenge for a raid. With the development of the horse culture, wealth was measured in horses. Now raids were staged primarily to steal horses, to retaliate, or both. A young man acquired status through demonstrations of daring and bravery in raids. Signs of success were the number of horses captured, the number of opponents defeated in battle, and success in returning home uninjured. An individual won special glory by **counting coup**—that

is, by touching an enemy, either with one's hand or with a stick.

Historians and anthropologists once thought that conflict between and among Plains tribes was largely related to stealing horses and seeking honor by counting coup. More recently, scholars have pointed to serious contests for territory—for example, the wars between Lakotas and Crows in the 1850s, when **Sitting Bull** first emerged as a leader. Conflicts over territory often developed as tribes were pushed to the west by other, more eastern tribes, who were also being pushed west by expanding European settlements along the Atlantic Coast. The Lakotas and Cheyennes, for example, once lived just east of the northern plains but were pushed onto the plains as the tribes to their east came west under pressure.

Among most of the Plains Indians, acquisition of goods was not a pressing goal. A person achieved

---

sedentary Living year-round in fixed villages and engaging in farming; as opposed to nomadic, or moving from camp to camp throughout the year.

counting coup Among Plains Indians, to win glory in battle by touching an enemy; *coup* is French for "blow," and the term comes from the French fur traders who were the first Europeans to describe the practice.

Sitting Bull Lakota war leader and holy man.

high social standing not by accumulating possessions but by sharing. Francis La Flesche, son of an Omaha leader, learned from his father that "the persecution of the poor, the sneer at their poverty is a wrong for which no punishment is too severe." His mother reinforced the lesson: "When you see a boy barefooted and lame, take off your moccasins and give them to him. When you see a boy hungry, bring him to your home and give him food."

The Plains Wars

In 1851 Congress approved a new policy intended to provide each tribe with a definite territory "of limited extent and well-defined boundaries," within which the tribe was to live. The government was to supply whatever needs the tribes could not meet themselves from the lands they were assigned. Federal officials first planned large reservations taking up much of the Great Plains. At a great conference held at Fort Laramie in 1868, they signed treaties that guaranteed extensive territory to the northern Plains tribes.

Before the 1851 policy, federal policymakers had considered the region west of Arkansas, Missouri, Iowa, and Minnesota and east of the Rocky Mountains to be a permanent Indian country. But farmers bound for Oregon and gold seekers on their way to California soon carved trails across the central plains, and some people began promoting a railroad to connect the Pacific Coast to the East. The policy initiated in 1851 was designed in part to open the central plains as a route to the Pacific.

Far more easterners thronged westward than federal officials had anticipated, and conflicts sometimes erupted along the trails. Then thousands of prospectors poured into Colorado after discovery of gold there in 1858. Withdrawal of many federal troops with the outbreak of the Civil War in 1861 may have encouraged some Plains Indians to believe they could expel the invaders. A series of Cheyenne and Lakota raids in 1864 brought demands for reprisals. Late in November, at Sand Creek in Colorado, a territorial militia unit massacred a band of Cheyennes who had not been involved in the raids. Soon after, the discovery of gold in Montana prompted construction of forts to protect a road, the **Bozeman Trail,** through Lakota territory. Cheyennes and Lakotas, led by **Red Cloud,** mounted a sustained war against the road.

In April 1868, many members of the northern Plains tribes met at Fort Laramie and agreed to a Great Sioux Reservation. They believed that they retained "unceded lands" for hunting in the Powder River country—present-day northeastern Wyoming

and southeastern Montana. In return, the army abandoned its posts along the Bozeman Trail, a victory for the Lakotas and Cheyennes.

The creation of the new reservation was part of a larger plan. With the end of the Civil War in 1865, railroad construction crews prepared to build westward (see pages 498, 581). Federal policymakers tried to head off hostilities by carving out a few great western reservations. One was to be for northern Plains tribes, north of the new state of Nebraska. Another was to be for southern Plains tribes, south of Kansas. A third was to be for the tribes of the mountains and the Southwest, in the Southwest. The remainder of the West was to be opened for development—railroad building, mining, and farming. Native Americans on the reservations were to receive food and shelter, and agents were to teach them how to farm and raise cattle.

The Fort Laramie Treaty of 1868 was one of several negotiated in 1867 and 1868 in fulfillment of the new policy. In 1867 a conference at Medicine Lodge Creek produced treaties by which the major southern Plains tribes accepted reservations in what is now western Oklahoma (see Map 19.1). In May 1868 the Crows agreed to a reservation in Montana. In June 1868 the Navajos accepted a large reservation in the Southwest. Given the highly fluid structure of authority among the Plains Indians, however, those who signed the treaties did not necessarily obligate those who did not.

As some federal officials were negotiating these treaties, other federal officials were permitting and even encouraging white buffalo hunters to kill the buffalo—for sport, for meat, for hides. Slaughter of the buffalo accelerated when **tanneries** in the East began to buy buffalo hides. In the mid-1870s more than 10 million buffalo were killed and stripped of their hides, which sold for a dollar or more. The southern herd was wiped out by 1878, the northern herd by 1883. Only two thousand survived, the remnant of a species whose numbers once seemed as vast as the stars. Given the importance of the buffalo in the lives of the Plains Indians, their way of life was doomed once the slaughter began.

Some members of the southern Plains tribes refused to accept the terms of the Medicine Lodge

---

Bozeman Trail   Trail that ran from Fort Laramie, Wyoming, to the gold fields of Montana.

Red Cloud   Lakota chief who led a successful fight to prevent the army from keeping forts along the Bozeman Trail.

tannery   An establishment where animal skins and hides are made into leather.

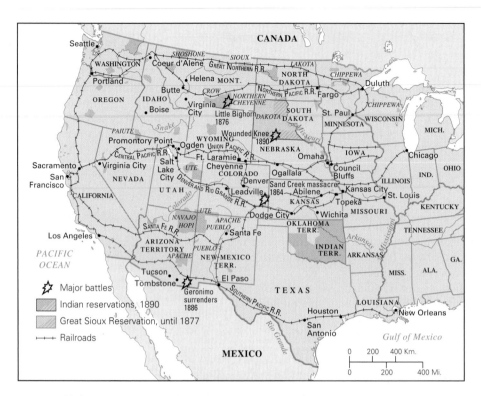

MAP 19.1 Indian Reservations This map indicates the location of most western Indian reservations in 1890, as well as the Great Sioux Reservation before it was broken up and severely reduced in size. Note how the development of a few large reservations on the northern plains and others on the southern plains opened the central plains for railroad construction and agricultural development.

Creek treaties and continued to live in their traditional territory. Resisting efforts to move them onto the reservations, they occasionally attacked stagecoach stations, ranches, travelers, and military units. General William Tecumseh Sherman, the Civil War general and now head of the army, planned military strategy on the plains. After a group of southern Cheyennes inflicted heavy losses on an army unit, Sherman decreed that all Native Americans not on reservations "are hostile and will remain so till killed off."

Sherman's response was the usual reaction of a conventional military force to guerrilla warfare: concentrate the friendly population in defined areas (in this case, reservations) and then open fire on anyone outside those areas. In the winter of 1868–1869, the army launched a southern plains campaign under the command of General Philip Sheridan, another Union army veteran, who directed his men to "destroy their villages and ponies, to kill and hang all warriors, and

bring back all women and children." The brutality that ensued convinced most southern Plains tribes to abandon further resistance.

In the early 1870s, however, sizable buffalo herds still roamed west and south of Indian Territory, in the Red River region of Texas. Though this was nonreservation land, the Medicine Lodge Creek treaties permitted Indians to hunt there. When white buffalo hunters began encroaching on the area in 1874, young men from the Kiowa, Comanche, and southern Cheyenne tribes attacked them. Sheridan responded with another **war of attrition,** destroying tipis, food,

> **war of attrition**   A form of warfare based on deprivation of food, shelter, and other necessities; if successful, it drives opponents to surrender out of hunger or exposure.

and animals. When winter came, the cold and hungry Indians surrendered to avoid starvation. Tribal war leaders were imprisoned in Florida, far from their families. Buffalo hunters then quickly exterminated the remaining buffalo on the southern plains.

Hunting grounds outside reservations were also a cause of conflict on the northern plains. Many Lakotas and some northern Cheyennes, led by **Crazy Horse** and Sitting Bull, lived on unceded hunting lands in the Powder River region. Complicating matters further, gold was discovered in the Black Hills, in the heart of the Great Sioux Reservation, in 1874, touching off an invasion of Indian land by miners. As the Northern Pacific Railroad prepared to lay track in southern Montana, federal authorities determined to force all Lakota and Cheyenne people onto the reservation, triggering a conflict sometimes called the **Great Sioux War.**

Military operations in the Powder River region began in the spring of 1876. Sheridan ordered troops to enter the area from three directions and converge on the Lakotas and Cheyennes. The offensive went dreadfully wrong when Lieutenant Colonel George A. Custer, without waiting for the other units, sent his Seventh Cavalry against a major village that his scouts had located. The encampment, on the **Little Big Horn River,** proved to be one of the largest ever on the northern plains. Custer unwisely divided his force, and more than two hundred men, including Custer, met their deaths.

That winter, U.S. soldiers unleashed another campaign of attrition on the northern plains. Troops defeated some Indian bands. Hunger and cold drove others to surrender. Crazy Horse and his band held out until spring and surrendered only when told that they could live in the Powder River region. A few months later, Crazy Horse was killed when he resisted being put into an army jail. Sitting Bull and his band escaped to Canada and remained there until 1881, when he finally surrendered. The government cut up the Great Sioux Reservation into several smaller units and took away the Powder River region, including the Black Hills (which the Lakotas considered sacred), and other lands.

The Last Indian Wars

After the Great Sioux War, no Native American group could muster the capacity for sustained resistance. Small groups occasionally left their reservations but were promptly tracked down by troops. In 1877 the Nez Perce, led by **Chief Joseph,** attempted to flee to Canada when the army tried to force them to leave their reservation in western Idaho. Between July and early October, they evaded the army as they traveled east and north through Montana. More than two hundred died along the way. Joseph surrendered on the specific condition that the Nez Perce be permitted to return to their previous home. His surrender speech is often quoted to illustrate the hopelessness of further resistance:

> *Our chiefs are killed. . . . The old men are dead. . . . It is cold and we have no blankets. The little children are freezing to death. . . . My heart is sick and sad. From where the sun now stands, I will fight no more forever!*

Federal officials sent the Nez Perce not back to Idaho but to Indian Territory, where, in an unfamiliar climate, many soon died of disease.

The last sizable group to refuse to live on a reservation was Geronimo's band of Chiricahua Apaches, who long managed to elude the army in the mountains of the Southwest. They finally gave up in 1886, and the men were sent to prison in Florida.

The last major confrontation between the army and Native Americans came in 1890, in South Dakota. Some Lakotas had taken up a new religion, the **Ghost Dance,** which promised to return the land to the Indians, restore the buffalo, and sweep away the whites. Fearing an uprising as the Ghost Dance gained popularity, federal authorities ordered the Lakotas to stop

Crazy Horse Lakota leader who resisted white encroachment in the Black Hills and fought at the Little Big Horn River in 1876; he was killed by U.S. soldiers in 1877.

Great Sioux War War between the tribes that took part in the Battle of Little Big Horn and the U.S. Army; it ended in 1881 with the surrender of Sitting Bull.

Little Big Horn River River in Montana where in 1876 Lieutenant Colonel George Custer attacked a large Indian encampment; Custer and most of his force died in the battle.

Chief Joseph Nez Perce chief who led his people in an attempt to escape to Canada in 1877; after a grueling journey they were forced to surrender and were exiled to Indian Territory.

Ghost Dance Indian religion centered on a ritual dance; it held out the promise of an Indian messiah who would banish the whites, bring back the buffalo, and restore the land to the Indians.

This painting by Yellow Nose, a Ute, was done in 1891. It depicts the Ghost Dance, a religion that promised to restore the buffalo and banish the whites. The dancers' shirts were thought to make them immune to harm. The cult began in Nevada in the 1880s and gained support throughout the West until the Wounded Knee massacre. *Smithsonian Institution.*

the ritual. Concerned that Sitting Bull might encourage defiance, federal authorities ordered his arrest; he was killed in the ensuing scuffle. A small band of Lakotas, led by Big Foot, fled but was surrounded by the Seventh Cavalry near **Wounded Knee Creek.** When one Lakota refused to surrender his gun, both Indians and soldiers fired their weapons. The soldiers, with their vastly greater firepower, quickly prevailed. As many as 250 Native Americans died, as did 25 soldiers.

The events at Wounded Knee marked the symbolic end of armed conflict on the Great Plains. In fact, the end of the horse culture was written long before. Once the federal government began to encourage rapid economic development in the West, displacement of the Indians was probably inevitable. From the beginning, the Indians faced overwhelming odds—they had a superior knowledge of the terrain, superior horsemanship and mobility, and great courage, but the U.S. Army had superior numbers and superior technology. The army was also often able to find allies among Native American groups who were traditional enemies of the defiant tribes. The desperate nature of Indian resistance suggests that they clearly understood that they were facing the loss not only of their hunting grounds but also of their culture and even their lives.

Transforming the West: Mormons, Cowboys, and Sodbusters

■ What did Mormons, cattle raisers, and farmers seek to accomplish in the West? How did they adapt their efforts to the western environment?

■ What were the motivations of these three groups in seeking to develop the West?

Long before the last battles between the army and the Indians, the economic development of the West was well under way. Quite different groups sought to transform the West and make it suit their needs—among them, Mormons, cattle ranchers, and farmers.

Zion in the Great Basin

By the end of the Civil War, development of the Great Basin region (between the Rocky Mountains and the Sierra Nevada) was well advanced owing to efforts by **Mormons.** Controversial because of their religious beliefs, which included **polygamy,** Mormons had been hounded out of one eastern state after another. In 1847 they finally settled near the Great Salt Lake, then part of northern Mexico. Led by Brigham Young, they planned to build a great Mormon state, which they called Deseret, in a region so remote that no one would interfere with them. The Treaty of Guadalupe Hidalgo (1848), which ended the Mexican War, incorporated the region into the United States. Congress created Utah Territory in 1850, with boundaries much smaller than those Young had envisioned for Deseret.

Nevertheless, in the remoteness of the Great Basin—isolated by mountains and deserts from the rest of the nation—the Mormons created their Zion, organizing themselves into a *theocracy* (a society governed by church officials). Church authority extended to politics, as a church-sponsored political party dominated elections for local and territorial officials.

Wounded Knee Creek Site of a conflict in 1890 between a band of Lakotas and U.S. troops, sometimes characterized as a massacre because the Lakotas were so outnumbered and overpowered; the last major encounter between Indians and the army.

Mormons Members of the Church of Jesus Christ of Latter-day Saints, founded in New York in 1830.

polygamy The practice of having more than one wife at a time; Mormons referred to this as "plural marriage."

Meager rainfall and poor soil made farming difficult. Young decreed communal ownership of both land and streams. Ignoring eastern laws that put limits on the amount of water that property owners could remove from streams running through their land, Young devised a system for creating farms and irrigation projects based on diverting water for irrigation. The communal ownership of land ended after 1869, when the Homestead Act of 1862 was extended to the territory, but Young's new system for water diversion remained.

With development firmly controlled by the church, the settlement thrived. By 1865, more than twenty thousand people lived in Utah Territory. The church established a consumers' cooperative known as Zion's Cooperative Mercantile Institute, or ZCMI. In addition to selling a variety of goods, ZCMI manufactured some products, including sugar made from sugar beets. Such cooperative enterprises mirrored practices within the 20 to 40 percent of families who practiced polygamy. Church officials urged some of the women in such households to take up home industries (such as silk production) or outside professional employment (such as teaching).

Mormons eventually came under strong federal pressure to renounce polygamy. Proposals for Utah statehood were repeatedly blocked because of that issue. Though Republican leaders branded polygamy as sinful, many politicians were also concerned about the political power of the Mormon Church. In 1890, to clear the way for statehood, church leaders dissolved their political party, encouraged Mormons to divide themselves among the national political parties, and disavowed polygamy. Utah became a state in 1896.

Cattle Kingdom on the Plains

As the Mormons were building their centralized and cooperative society in the Great Basin, a more individualistic enterprise was emerging on the Great Plains. There, cattle came to dominate the economy.

The expanding cities of the eastern United States were hungry for beef. At the same time, cattle were wandering the ranges of south Texas. Cattle had first been brought into south Texas—then part of New Spain (Mexico)—in the eighteenth century. The environment encouraged the herds to multiply, and Mexican ranchers developed an **open-range** system. The cattle grazed on unfenced plains, and *vaqueros* (cowboys) herded the half-wild longhorns from horseback. Many practices that developed in south Texas were subsequently transferred to the range-cattle industry, including **roundups** and **branding.**

At some time in the 1870s, these cowboys put on good clothes and sat for a photographer's portrait before a painted background. They probably worked together and were friends. Most cowboys were young African Americans, Mexican Americans, or poor southern whites. *Collection of William Gladstone.*

Between 1836, when Texas separated from Mexico, and the Civil War, few changes occurred in south Texas. Texans occasionally drove cattle to distant markets, but cattle drives ended during the Civil War. At the end of the war, 5 million cattle ranged across Texas. And in the slaughterhouses of Chicago, cattle brought ten times or more than their price in Texas.

To get cattle from south Texas to markets in the Midwest, Texans herded cattle north from Texas through Indian Territory (now Oklahoma) to the railroads being built westward (see Map 19.2). Half a

open range   Unfenced grazing lands on which cattle ran freely and cattle ownership was established through branding.

roundup   A spring event in which cowboys gathered together the cattle herds, branded newborn calves, and castrated most of the new young males.

branding   Burning a distinctive mark into an animal's hide using a hot iron as a way to establish ownership.

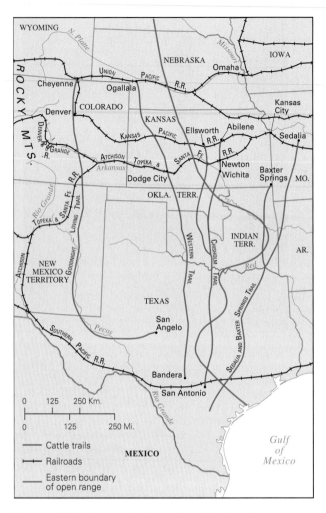

MAP 19.2 Western Cattle Trails and Railroads, 1865–1890   The demand for beef in northeastern cities encouraged Texans to drive cattle north to the railroads, which carried the cattle to eastern slaughterhouses. As railroad construction moved west, cattle trails did, too, creating a series of "cattle towns" where the trails met the tracks.

dime novels discovered and embroidered the exploits of town marshals like **James B. "Wild Bill" Hickok** and **Wyatt Earp,** giving them national reputations—deserved or not—as "town-tamers" of heroic dimensions. In fact, the most important changes in any cattle town came when middle-class residents—especially women—organized churches and schools, and determined to create law-abiding communities like those from which they had come.

Although most Texas cattle were eventually loaded on eastbound trains, some continued north to northern ranges where cattlemen had virtually free access to vast lands still in the public domain. One result of these "long drives" was the extension of open-range cattle raising from Texas into the northern Great Plains. By the early 1870s, the profits in cattle raising on the northern plains attracted attention in the East. From the East, England, and elsewhere swarmed investors eager to make a fortune. Some brought in new breeds of cattle, which they bred with Texas longhorns, producing hardy range cattle that yielded more meat.

By the early 1880s so many cattle ranches were operating that beef prices began to fall. Then, in the severe winter of 1886–1887, uncounted thousands of cattle froze or starved to death on the northern plains. Many investors went bankrupt. Cattle raising lost some of its romantic aura and afterward became more of a business than an adventure. Surviving ranchers fenced their ranges and made certain that they could feed their herds during the winter.

Another important change, both on the northern plains and in the Southwest, was the rise of sheep raising. By 1900, Montana had more sheep than any other state, and the western states accounted for more than half of the sheep raised in the nation.

As the cattle industry grew, the cowboy became a popular **icon.** Fiction after the 1870s, and motion pictures later, created the cowboy image: a brave, white,

dozen cowboys, a cook, and a foreman (the trail boss) could drive one or two thousand cattle. Not all the animals survived the drive, but enough did to yield a good profit. Between 1866 and 1880, some 4 million cattle plodded north from Texas.

As railroad construction crews pushed westward, cattle towns sprung up—notably Abilene and Dodge City, Kansas. In cattle towns, the trail boss sold his herd and paid off his cowboys, most of whom quickly headed for the cattle town's saloons, brothels, and gambling houses. Eastern journalists and writers of

dime novel   A cheaply produced novel of the mid-to-late nineteenth century, often featuring the dramatized exploits of western gunfighters.

James B. "Wild Bill" Hickok   Western gambler and gunfighter who for a time was the town marshal (law enforcement officer) in Abilene, Kansas.

Wyatt Earp   American frontier marshal and gunfighter involved in 1881 in a controversial shootout at the O.K. Corral in Tombstone, Arizona, in which several men were killed.

icon   A symbol, usually one with virtues considered worthy of copying.

Omer M. Kem (standing, slicing ripe watermelon) posed for the photographer with his children and his aged father outside his sod house in Custer County, Nebraska, in 1886. Such houses were made of sod cut into blocks and laid like bricks to make walls. Four years later, Kem was elected to the U.S. House of Representatives as a Populist, representing the grievances of western farmers (see p. 607). The photographer, Solomon Butcher, compiled a valuable collection of pictures illustrating the nature of life on what one historian termed "the sod-house frontier." *Nebraska State Historical Society.*

clean-cut hero who spent his time outwitting rustlers and rescuing fair-haired white women from snarling villains. In fact, most real cowboys were young and unschooled; many were African Americans or of Mexican descent, and others were former Confederate soldiers. On a cattle drive, they worked long hours (up to twenty a day), faced serious danger if a herd stampeded, slept on the ground, and ate biscuits and beans. They earned about a dollar a day and spent much of their working time in the saddle with no human companionship. Some joined the Knights of Labor.

Plowing the Plains

Removal of the Native Americans and buffalo from most of the Great Plains facilitated railroad construction and expansion of the cattle industry. When farmers entered this region, however, they encountered an environment significantly different from that to the east. Nevertheless, many first tried eastern farming methods. Some adapted successfully, but others failed and left.

After the Civil War, the land most easily available for new farms stretched from what is now the northern boundary of North Dakota and Minnesota southward through the current state of Oklahoma. Mapmakers in the early nineteenth century had labeled this region the Great American Desert. It was not a desert, however, and some parts of it were very fertile. But west of the line of **aridity**—roughly the 98th or 100th **meridian** (see Map 19.3)—sparse rainfall limited farming. Farmers who followed traditional farming practices risked not only failing but also damaging an unexpectedly fragile **ecosystem.**

When the vast region was opened for development by the Kansas-Nebraska Act (1854), the first settlers stuck to eastern areas, where the terrain and climate were similar to those they knew. After the Civil War, farmers pressed steadily westward, spurred by the offer of free land under the Homestead Act or lured by railroad advertising that promised fertile and productive land at little cost.

Those who came to farm were as diverse as the nation itself. Thousands of African Americans left the South, seeking farms of their own. Immigrants from Europe—especially Scandinavia, Germany, **Bohemia,** and Russia—also flooded in. Most homesteaders,

aridity   Dryness; lack of enough rainfall to support trees or woody plants.

meridian   Any of the imaginary lines representing degrees of longitude that pass through the North and South Poles and encircle the Earth.

ecosystem   A community of animals, plants, and bacteria, considered together with the environment in which they live.

Bohemia   A region of central Europe now part of the Czech Republic.

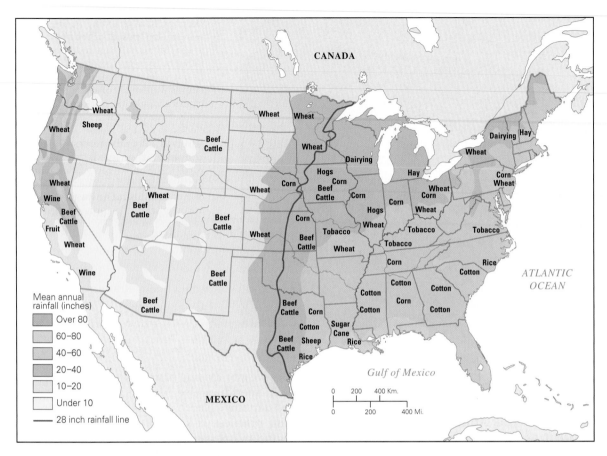

MAP 19.3 Rainfall and Agriculture, ca. 1890 The agricultural produce of any given area depended on the type of soil, the terrain, and the rainfall. Most of the western half of the nation received relatively little rainfall compared with the eastern half, and crops such as corn and cotton could not be raised in the West without irrigation. The line of aridity, beyond which many crops required irrigation, lies between twenty-eight inches and twenty inches of rain annually.

however, moved from areas a short distance to the east, where farmland had become too expensive for them to buy.

Single women could and did claim 160 acres of their own land. Sometimes the wife of a male homesteader did the same, claiming 160 acres in her own name next to the claim of her husband. By one estimate, one-third of all homestead claims in Dakota Territory were held by women in 1886. The prohibitive cost of farmland made such efforts almost impossible to the east. Some single women seem to have seen homesteading as a speculative venture, intending to sell the land and use the money for such purposes as starting a business, paying college tuition, or creating a nest egg for marriage.

The Homestead Act, together with cheap railroad land, brought many people west, but the Homestead Act had clear limits. The 160 acres that it provided were sufficient for a farm only east of the line of aridity. West of that line, it was often possible to raise wheat, but most of the land required irrigation for other crops or was suitable only for cattle raising, which required much more than 160 acres.

Federal officials were sometimes lax in enforcing the Homestead Act's requirements. Some cattle ranchers manipulated the law by having their cowboys file claims and then transfer the land to the rancher after they received title to it. Or ranchers claimed the land along both sides of streams, knowing that surrounding land was worthless without access to water, and thus they could control the whole watershed without establishing ownership.

Those who complied with the requirement to build a house and farm the land often faced an unfamiliar environment. The plains were virtually barren of trees. The new plains settlers, therefore, scavenged for substitutes for the construction material and fuel that eastern pioneers obtained without cost from the trees on their land.

Initially, many families carved homes out of the land itself. Some tunneled into the side of a low hill to make a cavelike dugout. Others cut the tough prairie **sod** into blocks from which they fashioned a small house. Many combined dugout and sod construction. "Soddies" became common throughout the plains but seldom made satisfactory dwellings. Years later, women told their grandchildren of their horror when snakes dropped from the ceiling or slithered out of walls. For fuel to use in cooking or heating, women burned dried cow dung or sunflower stalks. Sod houses were usually so dark that many household tasks were done outside whenever the weather permitted.

Plains families looked to technology to meet many of their needs. Barbed wire, first patented in 1874, provided a cheap and easy alternative to wooden fences. The barbs effectively kept ranchers' cattle off farmland. Ranchers eventually used it, too, to keep their herds from straying. Much of the plains had abundant groundwater, but the **water table** was deeper than in the East. Windmills pumped water from great depths. Because the sod was so tough, special plows were developed to make the first cut through it. These plows were so expensive that most farmers hired a specialist (a "sodbuster") to break their sod.

The most serious problem for pioneers on the Great Plains was a much-reduced level of rainfall compared with eastern farming areas. During the late 1870s and into the 1880s, when the central plains were farmed for the first time, the area received unusually heavy rainfall. Then, in the late 1880s, rainfall fell below normal, and crop failures drove many homesteaders off the plains. By one estimate, half of the population of western Kansas left between 1888 and 1892. Only after farmers learned better techniques of dry farming, secured improved strains of wheat (some brought by **Russian-German** immigrants), and began to practice irrigation did agriculture become viable. Even so, farming practices in some western areas failed to protect soil that had formerly been covered by natural vegetation. This exposed soil became subject to severe wind erosion in years of low rainfall.

Transforming the West: Railroads, Mining, Agribusiness, Logging, and Finance

■ What difficulties confronted western entrepreneurs engaged in mining, agriculture, or logging? What steps did those entrepreneurs take to develop their industries?

■ How did economic development in the West during the late nineteenth century compare with that taking place in the eastern United States at the same time?

At the end of the Civil War, most of the West was sparsely populated. (Many parts of it remain so at the beginning of the twenty-first century.) From 1865 onward, the West of the lone cowboy and solitary prospector was also a region in which most people lived in cities. In a region of great distances, few people, and widely scattered population centers, railroads were a necessity for economic development. Given the scarcity of water in much of the West, by 1900 many westerners had concluded that an adequate supply of water was as important for economic development as was their network of steel rails.

Western Railroads

In the eastern United States, railroad construction usually meant connecting already established population centers. Eastern railroads moved through areas with developed economies, connected major cities, and hauled freight to and from the many towns along their lines. At the end of the Civil War, this situation existed almost nowhere in the West.

Most western railroads were built first to connect the Pacific Coast to the eastern half of the country. Only slowly did they begin to find business along their routes. Railroad promoters understood that building a transcontinental line was very expensive

sod A piece of earth on which grass is growing; if grass has grown there a long time, the grass roots, dead grass from previous growing seasons, and the growing grass will be dense, tough, and fibrous, and the soil hard-packed.

water table The level at which the ground is completely saturated with water.

Russian-German Refers to people of German ancestry living in Russia; most had come to Russia in the eighteenth century at the invitation of the government to develop agricultural areas.

When the Central Pacific and Union Pacific companies raced to build their part of the tracks of the first transcontinental railroad, Chinese laborers were responsible for some of the most dangerous construction on the Central Pacific route through the Sierra Nevada. This photograph was taken, apparently by a photographer for the Union Pacific, when the two lines joined near Promontory Summit, in Utah Territory. *Denver Public Library, Western History Division.*

and that such a railway was unlikely at first to carry enough freight to justify the cost of construction. Thus they turned to the federal government for assistance with costs. The Pacific Railroad Act of 1862 provided loans and also 10 square miles (later increased to 20) of the public domain for every mile of track laid. Federal lawmakers promoted railroad construction to tie California and Nevada, with their rich deposits of gold and silver, to the Union and to stimulate the rapid economic development of other parts of the West.

Two companies received federal support for the first transcontinental railroad: the Union Pacific, which began laying tracks westward from Omaha, Nebraska, and the Central Pacific, which began building eastward from Sacramento, California. Construction began slowly, partly because crucial supplies—rails and locomotives—had to be brought to each starting point from the eastern United States, either by ship around South America to California or by riverboat to Omaha. Both lines experienced labor shortages. The Union Pacific solved its labor shortages only after the end of the Civil War, when former soldiers and construction workers flooded west. Many were Irish immigrants. The Central Pacific filled its rail gangs earlier by recruiting Chinese immigrants. By 1868, Central Pacific construction crews totaled six thousand workers, Union Pacific crews five thousand.

The Central Pacific laid only 18 miles of track during 1863, and the Union Pacific laid no track at all until mid-1864. The sheer cliffs and rocky ravines of the Sierra Nevada slowed construction of the Central Pacific. Chinese laborers sometimes dangled from ropes to create a roadbed by chiseling away the solid rock face of a mountain. Because the companies earned their federal subsidies by laying track, construction became a race in which each company tried to build faster than the other. In 1869, with the Sierra far behind, the Central Pacific boasted of laying 10 miles of track in a single day. The tracks of the two companies finally met at Promontory Summit, north of Salt Lake City (see Map 17.2, page 500), on May 10, 1869. Other lines followed during the next twenty years, bringing most of the West into the national market system.

Westerners greeted the arrival of a railroad in their communities with joyful celebrations, but some soon wondered if they had traded isolation for dependence on a greedy monopoly. The Southern Pacific, successor to the Central Pacific, became known as the "Octopus" because of its efforts to establish a monopoly over transportation throughout California. It had a reputation for charging the most that a customer could afford. James J. Hill of the Great Northern, by contrast, was called the "Empire Builder," for his efforts to build up the economy and prosperity of the region alongside his rails, which ran west from Minneapolis to Puget Sound. Whether "Octopus" or "Empire Builder," railroads provided the crucial transportation network for the economic development of the West. In their wake, western mining, agriculture, and lumbering all expanded rapidly.

Western Mining

During the forty years following the California gold rush (which began in 1848), prospectors discovered gold or silver throughout much of the mountainous West (see the chapter-opening map for Chapter 17). Any such discovery brought fortune seekers surging to the area, and boomtowns sprang up almost overnight. Stores that sold miners' supplies quickly appeared, along with boarding houses, saloons, gambling halls, and brothels. Once the valuable ore gave out, towns were sometimes abandoned. Discoveries of precious metals and valuable minerals in the mountainous regions of the West inevitably prompted the construction of rail lines to the sites of discovery, and the rail lines in turn permitted rapid exploitation of the mineral resources by bringing in supplies and heavy equipment. Many of the first miners found gold by **placer mining.** The only equipment they needed was a pan, and even a frying pan would do. Miners "panning" for gold simply washed gravel that they hoped contained gold. Any gold sank to the bottom of the pan as the lighter gravel was washed away by the water.

After the early gold seekers had taken the most easily accessible ore, elaborate mining equipment became necessary. Gold-mining companies in California developed hydraulic systems that used great amounts of water under high pressure to demolish entire mountainsides. One **hydraulic** mining operation used sixteen giant water cannon to bombard hillsides with 40 million gallons of water a day—about the same amount of water used daily by the people of Baltimore. Hydraulic mining wreaked havoc downstream, filling rivers with sediment and causing serious flooding. It ended only when a federal court ruled in 1884 that the technique inevitably damaged the property of others and had to stop.

In most parts of the West, the exhaustion of surface deposits led to construction of underground shafts and tunnels. In Butte, Montana, for example, a gold discovery in 1864 led to discoveries of copper, silver, and zinc in what has been called the richest hill on earth. Mine shafts there reached depths of a mile and required 3,000 miles of underground rail lines.

Such operations required elaborate machinery to move men and equipment thousands of feet into the earth and to keep the tunnels cool, dry, and safe. By the mid-1870s, some Nevada silver mines boasted the most advanced mining equipment in the world. There, temperatures soared to 120 degrees in shafts more than 2,200 feet deep. Mighty air pumps circulated air from the surface to the depths, and ice was used to reduce temperatures. Massive water pumps

It Matters

Western Environmental Pollution

The mining operations of the late nineteenth and early twentieth centuries left behind large amounts of debris, much of which was later found to be toxic, including significant levels of mercury (used to separate gold and silver from ore), arsenic, and lead. Some of this toxic material was found in the tailings—the material left over after the precious metals had been removed. Other toxic material was found in riverbeds and along rivers, where it had washed from the mining operations.

Several of these former mining areas are now federal **Superfund** sites, for cleanup of toxic materials. One such is the Carson River Mercury Site in Nevada, in the region of the most lucrative silver mines. Other Superfund sites for the cleanup of toxic mining debris are to be found throughout the West.

There is a major irony in this: the federal government underwrote the construction of railroads that made possible the development of western mining, and the federal government has taken final responsibility for cleaning up the toxic remnants of western mining. And yet it is in these same regions that political leaders today declaim vociferously about "getting the federal government off our backs."

kept the shafts dry. Powerful drills speeded the removal of ore, and enormous ore-crushing machines operated day and night on the surface.

placer mining   A form of gold mining that uses water to separate gold from gravel deposits; because gold is heavier, it settles to the bottom of a container filled with water when the container is agitated.

hydraulic   Having to do with water moved in pipes; hydraulic mining uses water under great pressure to wash away soil from underlying mineral deposits.

Superfund   Most common name for the federal Comprehensive Environmental Response, Compensation, and Liability Act (CERCLA) of 1980. The law requires polluters to clean up environmental contamination or reimburse the federal government for doing so. "Superfund" refers to the trust fund used to pay for cleanup.

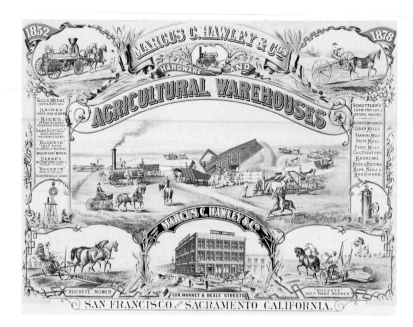

Mechanization greatly increased the amount of land that an individual could farm. This 1878 lithograph depicts a California crew setting a world's record for the amount of wheat harvested in a single day. *Department of Special Collections, F. Hal Higgins Library of Agricultural Technology, University of California, Davis.*

The mining industry changed rapidly. Solitary prospectors panning for gold in mountain streams gave way to gigantic companies whose operations were financed by banks in San Francisco and eastern cities. Mining companies became vertically integrated, operating mines, ore-crushing mills, railroads, and companies that supplied fuel and water for mining. Western miners organized too, forming strong unions. Beginning in Butte and spreading throughout the major mining regions of the West, miners' unions secured wages five to ten times higher than what miners in Britain or Germany earned.

The Birth of Western Agribusiness

Throughout the Northeast, the family farm was the typical agricultural unit. In the South after the Civil War, family-operated farms, whether run by owners or by sharecroppers, also became typical. Very large farming operations in the East and South tended to be exceptions. In California and other parts of the West, agriculture sometimes developed on a different scale, involving huge areas, the intensive use of heavy equipment, and wage labor. Today agriculture on such a large scale is known as **agribusiness.**

Wheat was the first major crop for which farming could be entirely mechanized. By 1880, in the Red River Valley of what is now North Dakota and in the San Joaquin Valley in central California, wheat farms were as large as 100 square miles. Such farming businesses required major capital investments in land, equipment, and livestock. One Dakota farm required 150 workers during spring planting and 250 or more at harvest time. By the late 1880s, some California wheat growers were using huge steam-powered tractors and **combines.**

Most of the great Dakota wheat farms had been broken into smaller units by the 1890s, but in some parts of California agriculture flourished on a scale unknown in most parts of the country. One California cattle-raising company, Miller and Lux, held more than a million acres, scattered throughout three states. Though California wheat raising declined in significance by 1900, large-scale agriculture employing many seasonal laborers became established for several other crops.

Growers of fruits and similar crops tended to operate small farms, but they still required a large work force at harvest time to pick the crops quickly so that they could be shipped to distant markets while still

agribusiness A large-scale farming operation typically involving considerable land holdings, hired labor, and extensive use of machinery; may also involve processing and distribution as well as growing.

combine A large harvesting machine that both cuts and threshes grain.

San Francisco rapidly emerged as the metropolis of the western United States. This 1905 photograph shows a San Francisco policeman talking to a young girl at one of the city's busiest intersections. Note the cable car on the right. *San Francisco Maritime National Historic Park, Muhrman Collection A22.16.824N.*

fresh. Fruit raising spread rapidly as California growers took advantage of refrigerated railroad cars and ships. By 1892, fresh fruit from California was for sale in London.

At first, growers relied on Chinese immigrants for such seasonal labor needs. After the Exclusion Act of 1882 (discussed later in this chapter), the number of Chinese fell, and growers turned to other groups—Japanese, **Sikhs** from India, and eventually Mexicans.

Logging in the Pacific Northwest

The coastal areas of the Pacific Northwest (see chapter-opening map and Map 19.3) are very different from other parts of the West. There, heavy winter rains and cool, damp, summer fogs nurture thick stands of evergreens, especially tall Douglas firs and coastal redwoods.

The growth of California cities and towns required lumber, and it came first from the coastal redwoods of central and northern California. When the most accessible stands of timber had been cut, attention shifted north to Oregon and Washington. Seattle developed as a lumber town from the late 1850s onward, as companies in San Francisco helped to finance an industry geared to providing lumber for California cities. By the late nineteenth century, some companies had become vertically integrated, owning **lumber mills** along the northwest coast, a fleet of schooners that hauled rough lumber down the coast to California, and lumberyards in the San Francisco Bay area.

In 1883, the Northern Pacific Railroad reached Portland, Oregon, and was extended to the Puget Sound area a few years later. The Great Northern completed its line to Seattle in 1893 (see Map 19.1). Both railroads promoted the development of the lumber industry by offering cheap rates to ship logs. Lumber production in Oregon and Washington boomed, leaving behind treeless hillsides subject to severe erosion during heavy winter rains. Westerners committed to rapid economic development seldom thought about ecological damage, for the long-term cost of such practices was not immediately apparent.

Western Metropolis: San Francisco

Lumber companies, the Miller and Lux cattle company, major mining companies, and the Southern Pacific Railroad all located their headquarters in San Francisco. Between the end of the Civil War and 1900, that city emerged as the **metropolis** of the West and was long unchallenged as the commercial, financial, and manufacturing center for much of the region west of the Rockies.

Sikh Follower of sikhism, a monotheistic religion founded in India in the 16th century.

lumber mill A factory or place where logs are sawed into rough boards.

metropolis An urban center, especially one that is dominant within a region.

From 1864 to 1875, the Bank of California, led by William Ralston, played a key role in the development in the West. Like many western entrepreneurs, Ralston saw himself as a visionary leader bringing civilization into the wilderness, and he expected to profit from his efforts. He once argued that "what is for the good of the masses will in the end be of equal benefit to the bankers." Seeking to build a diversified California economy, Ralston channeled profits from Nevada's silver mines into railroad and steamboat lines and factories that turned out furniture, sugar, woolen goods, and more. Other entrepreneurs pursued similar endeavors. By the 1880s, San Francisco was home to foundries that produced locomotives, technologically advanced mining equipment, agricultural implements for large-scale farming, and ships.

James Bryce, an English visitor, wrote in the 1880s that "California, more than any other part of the Union, is a country by itself, and San Francisco a capital." The city, he explained, "dwarfs" other western cities and is "more powerful over them than is any Eastern city over its neighbourhood." This power of San Francisco over much of the West came partly because it had headquarters of many leading western corporations and partly because it was the western center for finance capitalism—the Pacific Coast counterpart of Wall Street. By 1900, a few other western cities—Denver, Salt Lake City, Seattle, Portland, and especially Los Angeles—were challenging the economic dominance of San Francisco.

Water Wars

From the first efforts at western economic development, water was a central concern. Prospectors in the California gold rush needed water to separate worthless gravel from gold. On the Great Plains, a cattle rancher claimed grazing land by controlling a stream. Throughout much of the West, water was scarce, and competition for water sometimes produced conflict—usually in the form of courtroom battles.

Lack of water potentially posed stringent limits on western urban growth. Beginning in 1901, San Francisco sought federal permission to put a dam across the Hetch Hetchy Valley, on federal land adjacent to Yosemite National Park in the Sierra Nevada, in order to create a reservoir. Opposition came from the **Sierra Club,** formed in 1892 and dedicated to preserving Sierra Nevada wilderness. Congress finally approved the project in 1913, and the enormous construction project took another twenty-one years to complete. Los Angeles resolved its water problems in a similar way, by diverting the water of the Owens River to its use—even though Owens Valley residents tried to dynamite the **aqueduct** in resistance.

Throughout much of the West, irrigation was vital to the success of farming. As early as 1899, irrigated land in the eleven westernmost states produced $84 million in crops. Although individual entrepreneurs and companies undertook significant irrigation projects, the magnitude of the task led many westerners to look for federal assistance, just as they had sought federal assistance for railroad development. "When Uncle Sam puts his hand to a task, we know it will be done," wrote one irrigation proponent. "When he waves his hand toward the desert and says, 'Let there be water!' we know that the stream will obey his commands."

The National Irrigation Association, created in 1899, organized lobbying efforts, and Francis Newlands, a member of Congress from Nevada, introduced legislation. The **Reclamation Act** of 1902 promised federal construction of irrigation facilities. The Reclamation Service, established by the law, eventually became a major power in the West as it sought to move the region's water to areas where it could be used for irrigation. Reclamation projects sometimes drew criticism, however, for disproportionately benefiting large landowners.

Ethnicity and Race in the West

■ Compare the experiences of American Indians, Mexican Americans, and Chinese Americans between the end of the Civil War (1865) and about 1900.

In its ethnic and racial composition, the West has always differed significantly from the rest of the nation. In 1900 the western half of the United States included more than 80 percent of all Native Americans, Chinese Americans or Japanese Americans, and Mexican Americans. The northeastern quarter of the nation remained predominantly white until World War I, and the South was largely a biracial society of whites and African Americans. The West has long had greater ethnic diversity. (These patterns can be seen in Fig. 19.1.)

> **Sierra Club** Environmental organization formed in 1892; now dedicated to preserving and expanding parks, wildlife, and wilderness areas.
>
> **aqueduct** A pipe or channel designed to transport water from a remote source, usually by gravity.
>
> **Reclamation Act** Law passed by Congress in 1902 that provided funding for irrigation of western lands and created the Reclamation Service to oversee the process.

Immigrants to the Golden Mountain

Between 1854 and 1882, some 300,000 Chinese immigrants entered the United States. Most came from southern China, which in the 1840s and 1850s suffered from political instability, economic distress, and even **famine.** The fortune seekers who poured in from around the world as part of the California gold rush included significant numbers of Chinese. Among the early Chinese immigrants, California became known as "Land of the Golden Mountain."

Though many Chinese worked in mining, they also formed a major part of construction labor in the West, especially for railroad building. Chinese immigrants worked as agricultural laborers and farmers, too, especially in California, throughout the late nineteenth century. Some of them made important contributions to crop development, especially fruit growing.

In San Francisco and elsewhere in the West, they established **Chinatowns**—relatively autonomous and largely self-contained Chinese communities. In San Francisco's Chinatown, immigrants formed kinship organizations and district associations (whose members had come from the same part of China) to assist and protect each other. A confederation of such associations, the Chinese Consolidated Benevolent Association (often called the "Six Companies"), eventually dominated the social and economic life of Chinese communities in much of the West. Such communities were largely male, partly because immigration officials permitted only a few Chinese women to enter the country, apparently to prevent an American-born generation. As was true in many largely male communities, gambling and prostitution flourished, giving Chinatowns reputations as centers for vice.

Almost from the beginning, Chinese immigrants encountered discrimination and violence. In 1854 the California Supreme Court prohibited Chinese (along with Native Americans and African Americans) from testifying in court against a white person. A state tax on foreign-born miners posed a significant burden on Chinese (and also Latino) gold seekers. During the 1870s, many white workers blamed the Chinese for driving wages down and unemployment up. In fact, different economic factors depressed wage levels and brought unemployment, but white workers seeking a

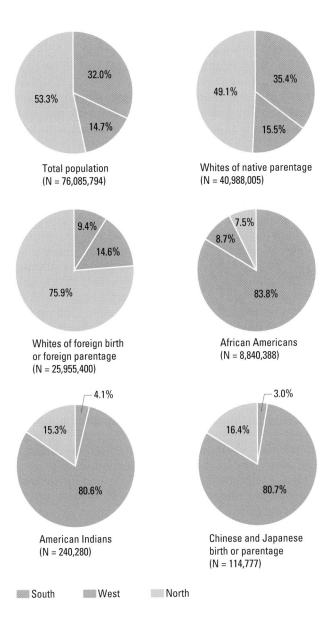

FIGURE 19.1 Regional Distribution of Population, by Race, 1900 These pie charts indicate the distinctiveness of the West with respect to race and ethnicity. Note that the West held about 15 percent of the nation's total population and about the same proportion of the nation's white population (including whites who were foreign-born or of foreign parentage) but included more than four-fifths of American Indians and those of Chinese and Japanese birth or parentage. *Source:* Data from *Twelfth Census of the United States: 1900* (Washington, D.C., 1901), Population Reports, vol. 1, p. 483, Table 9.

Total population
(N = 76,085,794)

Whites of native parentage
(N = 40,988,005)

Whites of foreign birth or foreign parentage
(N = 25,955,400)

African Americans
(N = 8,840,388)

American Indians
(N = 240,280)

Chinese and Japanese birth or parentage
(N = 114,777)

■ South ■ West ■ North

famine   A serious and widespread shortage of food.
Chinatown   A section of a city inhabited chiefly by people of Chinese birth or ancestry.

This public letter writer in San Francisco represents an institution that Chinese immigrants brought with them to America. By the 1880s, the Chinatowns of large western cities had become places of refuge that provided immigrants with some degree of safety from anti-Chinese agitation. *California Historical Society, San Francisco, E. N. Sewell FN-01003.*

scapegoat instigated anti-Chinese riots in Los Angeles in 1871 and in San Francisco in 1877. In 1885 anti-Chinese riots swept through much of the West. A mob of white miners burned the Chinatown in Rock Springs, Wyoming, and killed twenty-eight Chinese, mostly mine workers. This anti-Chinese violence prompted many Chinese to retreat to the largest Chinatowns, especially the one in San Francisco.

In these riots, the message was usually the same: "The Chinese Must Go." This slogan surfaced in San Francisco in 1877 as part of the appeal of the Workingmen's Party of California, a political organization that blamed unemployment and low wages on the Chinese and on the capitalists who hired them. In 1882 Congress responded to repeated pressures from unions, especially Pacific Coast unions, by passing the **Chinese Exclusion Act,** prohibiting entry to all Chinese people except teachers, students, merchants, tourists, and officials. The law also specified that Asian immigrants were not eligible to become naturalized citizens.

In some parts of the West, the Chinese were subjected to segregation similar to that imposed on blacks in the South, including residential and occupational segregation rooted in local custom rather than law. In 1871 the San Francisco school board barred Chinese students from that city's public schools. The ban lasted until 1885, when the parents of **Mamie Tape** convinced the courts to order the city to provide education for their daughter. The city then opened a segregated Chinese school. Segregated schools for Chinese American children were also set up in a few other places, but most school segregation began to break down in the 1910s and 1920s.

Among Chinese immigrants, merchants often took the lead in establishing a strong economic base. Organizations based on kinship, region, or occupation were sometimes successful in fighting anti-Chinese legislation. When San Francisco passed a city law restricting Chinese laundry owners, they brought a court challenge. In the case of *Yick Wo v. Hopkins* (1886), the U.S. Supreme Court for the first time declared a licensing law unconstitutional because local authorities had used it to discriminate on the basis of race.

When other immigrants began to arrive from Asia, they too concentrated in the West. Significant numbers of Japanese immigrants started coming to the United States after 1890. From 1891 through 1907, nearly 150,000 arrived, most through the Pacific Coast port cities. Whites in the West, especially organized labor, viewed Japanese immigrants in much the same way as they had earlier immigrants from China—with hostility and scorn. Pushed by western labor organizations, President Theodore Roosevelt in 1907 negotiated an agreement with Japan to halt immigration of Japanese laborers.

Forced Assimilation

As the headlines about the Great Sioux War, the Nez Perce, and Geronimo faded from the nation's newspapers, many Americans began to describe American Indians as a "vanishing race." But Indian people did not vanish. With the end of armed conflict, the relation between Native Americans and the rest of the nation entered a new phase, one appropriate to consider in the context of racial relations.

Chinese Exclusion Act   Law passed by Congress in 1882 that prohibited Chinese laborers from entering the United States; it was extended periodically until World War II.

Mamie Tape   Chinese girl in San Francisco whose parents sued the city in 1885 to end the exclusion of Chinese students from the public schools.

By the 1870s, federal policymakers were developing plans to **assimilate** Native Americans into white society. After 1871, federal policy shifted from treating Indian tribes as sovereign dependent nations, with whom federal officials negotiated treaties, to viewing them as wards of the federal government. Leading scholars, notably Lewis Henry Morgan of the Smithsonian Institution, viewed culture as an evolutionary process. Rather than seeing each culture as unique, they analyzed groups as being at one of three stages of development: savagery (hunters and gatherers), barbarism (those who practiced agriculture and made pottery), and civilization (those with a written language). All peoples, they thought, were evolving toward "higher" cultural types. Most white Americans probably agreed that western Europeans and their descendants throughout the world had reached the highest level of development. Not until the early years of the twentieth century did this perspective come under challenge, notably from Franz Boas, who held that every culture develops and should be understood on its own, rather than as part of an evolutionary chain.

Public support for a change in federal policy grew in response to speaking tours by American Indians and white reformers and to the publication of several exposés, notably Helen Hunt Jackson's *A Century of Dishonor* (1881) and *Ramona* (a novel, 1884). Soon federal policymakers accepted reformers' arguments for speeding up the evolutionary process for Native Americans. Apparently no reformers or federal policymakers understood that American Indians had complex cultures that were very different from—but not inferior to—the culture of Americans of European descent.

Education was an important element in the reformers' plans for "civilizing" the Indians. Federal officials worked with churches and philanthropic organizations to establish schools distant from the reservations, and many Native American children were sent to these institutions to live and study. The teachers' goal was to educate their students to become part of white society, and to that end they forbade the Indian students from speaking their languages, practicing their religions, or otherwise following their own cultural patterns. Other educational programs aimed to train adult Indian men to be farmers or mechanics. Federal officials also tried to prohibit some religious observances and traditional practices on reservations.

The **Dawes Severalty Act** (1887) was another important tool in the "civilizing" effort. Its objective was to make the Indians into self-sufficient, property-conscious, profit-oriented, individual farmers—model citizens of nineteenth-century white America. The law created a governmental policy of severalty—that is, individual ownership of land by Native Americans. Reservations were to be divided into individual family farms of 160 acres. Once each family received its allotment, surplus reservation land was to be sold by the government and the proceeds used for Indian education projects. This policy therefore found enthusiastic support among reformers urging rapid assimilation and among westerners who coveted Indian lands.

Individual landownership, however, was at odds with traditional Native American views that land was for the use of all and that sharing was a major obligation. Some Indian leaders urged Congress to defeat the Dawes Act. D. W. Bushyhead, leader of the Cherokee Nation, joined with delegates from the Cherokee, Creek, and Choctaw Nations in a petition to Congress. "Our people have not asked for or authorized this," they stressed, and they explained, "Our own laws regulate a system of land tenure suited to our condition."

Despite such protests, Congress approved the Dawes Act. The result bore out the warning of Senator Henry Teller of Colorado, who called it "a bill to despoil the Indians of their land." Once allotments to Indian families were made, about 70 percent of the land area of the reservations remained, and much of it was sold outright. In the end, the Dawes Act did not end the reservation system, nor did it reduce the Indians' dependence on the federal government. It did separate the Indians from a good deal of their land.

Native Americans responded to their situation in various ways. Some tried to cooperate with the assimilation programs. Susan La Flesche, for example, daughter of an Omaha leader, graduated from medical college in 1889 at the head of her class. But she disappointed her teachers, who wanted her to abandon Indian culture completely, when she set up her medical practice near the Omaha Reservation, treated both white and Omaha patients, took part in tribal affairs, and managed her land allotment and those of other family members. Dr. La Flesche also participated in the local white community through the

---

assimilate To absorb immigrants or members of a culturally distinct group into the prevailing culture.

Dawes Severalty Act Law passed by Congress in 1887 intended to break up Indian reservations to create individual farms (holding land in severalty) rather than maintaining common ownership of the land; surplus lands were to be sold and the proceeds used to fund Indian education.

Luther Standing Bear was called Ota K'te when he was born in 1868, the son of a chief who fought against Custer at the Battle of the Little Big Horn. He attended the Carlisle Indian School in Pennsylvania, toured with a Wild West Show, became an actor, and belonged to the Actors' Guild (a union). He was also a hereditary chief of the Oglala Lakota. In the 1920s, he began to write about his own experiences and the experiences of his people, seeking to improve their lives and to change federal policies. This photo was probably taken in Hollywood in the 1920s, showing him wearing a traditional Lakota headdress. *Nebraska State Historical Society.*

Susan La Flesche was the first Indian woman to graduate from medical college. Her sister, Susette, was a prominent crusader for Indian rights, and her brother, Francis, was a leading ethnologist. Well educated, they chose to live in and mediate between two societies—the Omaha and the whites. Dr. La Flesche, who became Susan La Flesche Picotte after her marriage in 1894, was also a leader in the local Presbyterian church and temperance movement. *Denver Public Library, Western History Division.*

temperance movement and sometimes by preaching in the local Presbyterian church.

Dr. La Flesche seems to have moved easily between two cultures. Some Native Americans preferred the old ways, hiding their children to keep them out of school and secretly practicing traditional religious ceremonies. Although Native American peoples' cultural patterns changed, it was not always in the way that federal officials anticipated. In Oklahoma, where many groups with different traditional cultures lived in close proximity, people began to borrow cultural practices from other groups. In some places, Indians became an important element in the wage-earning work force near their reservations, sometimes against the wishes of reservation officials. In the late nineteenth century, the **peyote cult,** based on the hallu-

cinogenic properties of the peyote cactus, emerged as an alternative religion. It evolved into the Native American Church, combining elements of traditional Indian culture, Christianity, and peyote use.

Mexican Americans in the Southwest

The United States annexed Texas in 1845 and soon after acquired vast territories from Mexico at the end of the Mexican War. Living in those territories were large numbers of people who spoke Spanish, many of

---

peyote cult   A religion that included ceremonial use of the hallucinogenic peyote cactus, native to Mexico and the Southwest.

In the late nineteenth and early twentieth centuries, Mexican Americans became a major part of the work force for constructing and maintaining railroads in the Southwest. This crew of Mexican American linemen was working in south Texas when this photograph was taken in 1910. They may have been employed by a railroad to put up and maintain its communication lines or by a telegraph or telephone company. *Texas State Library and Archives Commission.*

them **mestizos**—people of mixed Spanish and Native American ancestry. The treaties by which the United States acquired those territories specified that Mexican citizens living there automatically became American citizens.

Throughout the Southwest during the late nineteenth century, many Mexican Americans lost their land as the region attracted English-speaking whites (often called **Anglos** by those whose first language was Spanish). The Treaty of Guadalupe Hidalgo, which ended the war with Mexico, guaranteed Mexican Americans' landholdings, but the vagueness of Spanish and Mexican land grants encouraged legal challenges. Sometimes Mexican Americans were cheated out of their land through fraud.

In California, some **Californios**—Spanish-speaking people living in California—had welcomed the break

with Mexico. However, the California gold rush attracted fortune seekers from around the world, including Mexico and other parts of Latin America. Most came from the eastern United States and Europe. In northern California, a hundred thousand gold seekers inundated the few thousand Mexican Americans. Latinos (people from Latin America) who came to California as gold seekers were often driven from the mines by racist harassment and a tax on foreign miners. In southern California, however, there were fewer Anglos until late in the nineteenth century. There, Californios won election to local and state office, notably Romualdo Pacheco, who served as state treasurer and lieutenant governor and who succeeded to the governorship in 1875.

By the 1870s, many of the **pueblos** (towns created under Mexican or Spanish governments) had become **barrios**—some rural, some in inner cities—centered on a Catholic church. In some ways, the barrios resembled the neighborhoods of European immigrants in the eastern United States at the same time. Both had mutual benefit societies, political associations, and newspapers published in the language of the community, and the cornerstone of both was often a church. There was an important difference, however. Neighborhoods of European immigrants consisted of people who had come to a new land where they anticipated making some changes in their own lives in order to adjust. The residents of the barrios, in contrast, lived in regions that had been home to Mexicans for generations but now found themselves surrounded by English-speaking Americans who hired them for cheap wages, sometimes sneered at their culture, and pressured them to assimilate.

In Texas, as in California, some of the **Tejanos** (Spanish-speaking people born in Texas) had welcomed the break with Mexico. For example, Lorenzo de Zavala served briefly as the first vice president of the Texas Republic. Like the Californios, some

mestizo A person of mixed Spanish and Indian ancestry.

Anglo A term applied in the Southwest to English-speaking whites.

Californios Spanish-speaking people living in California at the time California was acquired by the United States.

pueblo Town created under Mexican or Spanish rules.

barrio A Spanish-speaking community, often a part of a larger city.

Tejanos Spanish-speaking people living in Texas at the time it was acquired by the United States.

This photograph, taken in San Antonio, Texas, shows Mexican American women preparing tortillas. The woman on the right is grinding corn using a *metate* (an Aztec word that designates the large, three-legged stone base) and *mano* (a Spanish word that designates the small stone held in her hand), a method of preparing cornmeal used by the indigenous peoples of Mexico and the Southwest for thousands of years. *William B. Becker Collection/American Museum of Photography.*

Tejanos lost their lands through fraud or coercion. By 1900, much of the land in south Texas had passed out of the hands of Tejano families—sometimes legally, sometimes fraudulently—but the new Anglo ranch owners usually maintained the social patterns characteristic of Tejano ranchers.

A large section of Texas—between the Nueces River and Rio Grande and west to El Paso—remained culturally Mexican, home to Tejanos and to two-thirds of all Mexican immigrants who came to the United States before 1900. In the 1890s, one journalist described the area as "an overlapping of Mexico into the United States." During the 1860s and 1870s, conflict sometimes broke out as Mexican Americans challenged the political and economic power of Anglo newcomers. In social relations and in politics, all but a few wealthy Tejanos came to be subordinate to the Anglos, who dominated the regional economy and the professions.

In New Mexico Territory, **Hispanos** (Spanish-speaking New Mexicans) were clearly the majority of the population and the voters throughout the nineteenth century. They consistently composed a majority in the territorial legislature and were frequently elected as territorial delegates to Congress (the only position elected by voters in the entire territory). Republicans usually prevailed in territorial politics, their party led by wealthy Hispanos and Anglos who began to arrive in significant numbers after the entrance of the first railroad in 1879. Although Hispanos were the majority and could dominate elections, many who had small landholdings lost their land in ways similar to patterns in California and Texas—except that some who enriched themselves in New Mexico were wealthy Hispanos.

In the 1880s, a secretive organization emerged dedicated to protecting the property—and lives—of

Hispanos Spanish-speaking New Mexicans.

poor Mexican Americans. Calling themselves *las Gorras Blancas* (the White Caps), they used violence at times to protect Mexican Americans' property or to fight the railroads. In 1889 three hundred Gorras Blancas destroyed extensive property belonging to the Santa Fe Railroad. Other Gorras Blancas aligned themselves with the Knights of Labor or tried to use electoral politics to accomplish their goals.

From 1856 to 1910, throughout the Southwest, the Latino population grew more slowly than the Anglo population. After 1910, however, that situation reversed itself as political and social upheavals in Mexico prompted massive migration to the United States. Probably a million people—equivalent to one-tenth of the entire population of Mexico in 1910—arrived over the next twenty years. More than half stayed in Texas, but significant numbers settled in southern California and throughout other parts of the Southwest. Inevitably, this new stream of immigrants changed some of the patterns of ethnic relations that had characterized the region since the mid-nineteenth century.

The West in American Thought

- How have historians' views of the West changed?
- How does the myth of the West compare with its reality?

The West has long fascinated Americans, and the "winning of the West" has become a national myth—one that has sometimes obscured or distorted the actual facts. Many Americans have thought of the West in terms of a frontier, an imaginary line marking the westward advance of mining, cattle raising, farming, commerce, and associated social patterns. According to this way of thinking, east of the frontier lay established society, and beyond it lay the wild, untamed West. Often this view was closely related to evolutionary notions of civilization like those put forth by Lewis Henry Morgan. For those who thought about the West in this way, the frontier represented the dividing point between barbarism and civilization.

The West as Utopia and Myth

During the nineteenth and much of the twentieth centuries, the West seemed a potential **utopia** to some who thought of the frontier as dividing emptiness from civilization. Generations of Americans dreamed of a better life on "new land" in the West, though relatively few ever ventured forth. In the popular mind of the late nineteenth century, the West was vacant, waiting to be filled and formed. Out there, it seemed,

nothing was predetermined. A person could make a fresh start. People who dreamed of creating communities based on new social values often looked to the West.

The West appealed as well to Americans who sought to improve their social and economic standing. The presence of free or cheap land, the ability to start over, the idea of creating a place of one's own, all were part of the West's attraction. Of course, not all who tried to fulfill their dreams succeeded, but enough did to justify the image of the West as a land of promise.

The West achieved mythical status in popular novels, movies, and later television. Stories about the "winning of the West" usually begin with the grandeur of wide grassy plains, towering craggy mountains, and vast silent deserts. In most versions, the western Indians face a tragic destiny. They often appear as a proud, noble people whose tragic but unavoidable demise clears the way for the transformation of the vacated land by bold men and women of European descent. The starring roles in this drama are played by miners, ranchers, cowboys, farmers, and railroad builders who struggle to overcome both natural and human obstacles. These pioneers personify rugged individualism—the virtues of self-reliance and independence—as they triumph through hard work and personal integrity. Many of the human obstacles are villainous characters: brutal gunmen, greedy speculators, vicious cattle rustlers, unscrupulous moneylenders, selfish railroad barons. Some are only doubters, too timid or too skeptical of the promise of the West to risk all in the struggle to succeed.

The novelist **Willa Cather** presents a sophisticated—and woman-centered—version of many of these elements. In *O Pioneers!* (1913), the major character is Alexandra Bergson, daughter of Swedish immigrant homesteaders on the Great Plains. When her father dies, Alexandra struggles with the land, the climate, and the skepticism of her brothers to create a lush and productive farm. Cather's *My Ántonia* (1918) presents Ántonia Shimerda, daughter of Czech immigrants, who survives run-ins with a land speculator, grain buyer, and moneylender, only to become pregnant outside marriage by a railroad conductor. Dishonored, Ántonia regains the respect of the community

utopia An ideally perfect place.
Willa Cather Early-twentieth-century writer, many of whose novels chronicle the lives of immigrants and others on the American frontier.

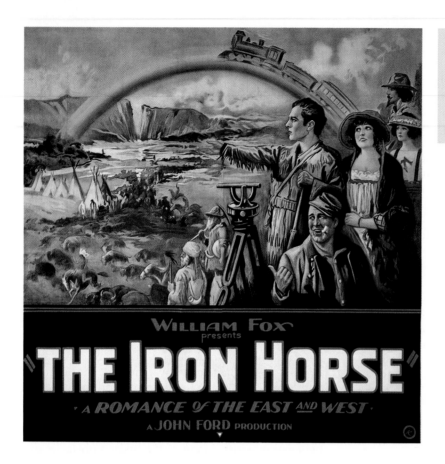

WILLIAM FOX
presents
"THE IRON HORSE"
· A ROMANCE OF THE EAST AND WEST ·
A JOHN FORD PRODUCTION

Popular fiction and Hollywood movies have contributed much to the creation of the "winning of the West" myth, which depicted much of the West as empty wilderness waiting for the transforming hand of bold white settlers. This myth either ignored or minimized previous inhabitants of the West. *Collection of Hershenson-Allen Archives.*

through her hard work. She builds a thriving farm, marries, raises a large family, and becomes "a rich mine of life, like the founders of early races." *My Ántonia* explicitly presents another aspect of the myth. Jim Burden, the narrator of the story, grows up on the frontier with Ántonia but becomes a prosperous New York lawyer whose own marriage is childless. Ántonia, symbolizing western fecundity, is thus contrasted with eastern sterility.

The Frontier and the West

Starting in the 1870s, accounts of the winning of the West suggested to many Americans the existence of an America more attractive than the steel mills and urban slums of their own day, a place where people were more virtuous than the barons of industry and corrupt city politicians, where individual success was possible without labor strife or racial and ethnic discord. The myth has evolved and exerts a hold on Americans' imagination even today. From at least the 1920s onward, the cowboy has been the most promi-

nent embodiment of the myth. The mythical cowboy is a brave and resourceful loner, riding across the West and dispelling trouble from his path and from the lives of others. He rarely does the actual work of a cowboy.

Like all myths, the myth of the winning of the West contains elements of truth but ignores others. The myth usually treats Indians as victims of progress. It rarely considers their fate after they meet defeat at the hands of the cavalry. Instead, they obligingly disappear. The myth rarely tempers its celebration of rugged individualism by acknowledging the fundamental role of government at every stage in the transformation of the West: dispossessing the Indians, subsidizing railroads, dispensing the public domain to promote economic development, and rerouting rivers to bring their precious water to both farmland and cities. The myth often overlooks the role of ethnic and racial minorities—from African American and Mexican cowboys to Chinese railroad construction crews—and it especially overlooks the extent to which these people were exploited as sources of cheap labor.

Women typically appear only in the role of helpless victim or noble helpmate. Finally, the myth generally ignores the extent to which the economic development of the West replicated economic conditions in the East, including monopolistic, vertically integrated corporations and labor unions. If such influences appear in the myth, they are usually as obstacles that the hardy pioneers overcame.

In 1893 **Frederick Jackson Turner,** a young historian, presented an influential essay called "The Significance of the Frontier in American History." In it, he challenged the prevailing idea that answers to questions about the nature of American institutions and values were to be found by studying the European societies to which white Americans traced their ancestry. Turner focused instead on the frontier as a uniquely defining factor. Turner argued that "American social development has been continually beginning over again on the frontier" and that these experiences constituted "the forces dominating American character." The western frontier, he claimed, was the region of maximum opportunity and widest equality, where individualism and democracy most flourished.

Turner's view of the West and the importance of the frontier dominated the thinking of historians for many years. Today, however, historians focus on many elements missing from Turner's analysis: the importance of cultural conflicts among different groups of people; the experiences of American Indians (the original inhabitants of the West), and of the Spanish-speaking mestizo peoples of the Southwest, and of Asian Americans; gender issues and the experiences of women; the natural environment and ecological issues, especially those involving water; the growth and development of western cities; and the ways in which the western economy resembles and differs from the economy of the East. If western individualism and mobility have been formative to the American experience, as Turner suggested, so too have been these other elements in the history of the West.

Frederick Jackson Turner American historian who argued that the frontier and cheap, abundant land were dominant factors in creating American democracy and shaping national character.

Individual Voices

Examining a Primary Source

Decision of the U.S. Supreme Court in *Yick Wo v. Hopkins*

The decision of the United States Supreme Court in the case of *Yick Wo v. Hopkins* (1886) is important in a number of ways. Following are excerpts from the decision, which was delivered by Justice Stanley Matthews.

The rights of the petitioners, as affected by the proceedings of which they complain, are not less, because they are aliens and subjects of the Emperor of China. The Fourteenth Amendment to the Constitution is not confined to the protection of citizens. It says: "Nor shall any State deprive any person of life, liberty, or property without due process of law; nor deny to any person within its jurisdiction the equal protection of the laws." These provisions are universal in their application, to all persons within the territorial jurisdiction, without regard to any differences

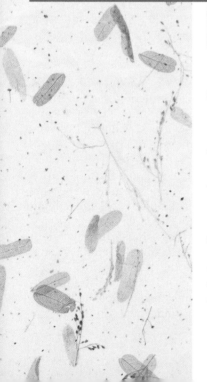

■ Here the Supreme Court rules that the Fourteenth Amendment applies to persons who are not citizens. What are the implications of this decision?

■ Here the Court is making a statement about the San Francisco Board of Supervisors' arbitrary power to grant or withhold laundry licenses. What are the implications of this statement?

■ This is the first time that the Court considered that the application of a law, separate from the law itself, might be unconstitutional. Does this represent a significant extension of the meaning of the Fourteenth Amendment?

■ Why is the Yick Wo decision so important in the history of civil rights in the United States?

of race, of color, or of nationality; and the equal protection of the laws is a pledge of the protection of equal laws. The questions we have to consider and decide in these cases, therefore, are to be treated as involving the rights of every citizen of the United States equally with those of the strangers and aliens who now invoke the jurisdiction of the court. ■

When we consider the nature and the theory of our institutions of government, the principles upon which they are supposed to rest, and review the history of their development, we are constrained to conclude that they do not mean to leave room for the play and action of purely personal and arbitrary power. . . . But the fundamental rights to life, liberty, and the pursuit of happiness, considered as individual possessions, are secured by . . . constitutional law . . . For, the very idea that one man may be compelled to hold his life, or the means of living, or any material right essential to the enjoyment of life, at the mere will of another, seems to be intolerable in any country where freedom prevails, as being the essence of slavery itself. ■ . . .

Though the law itself be fair on its face and impartial in appearance, yet, if it is applied and administered by public authority with an evil eye and an unequal hand, so as practically to make unjust and illegal discriminations between persons in similar circumstances, material to their rights, the denial of equal justice is still within the prohibition of the Constitution. ■ . . .

While this consent of the supervisors is withheld from [the petitioners] and from two hundred others who have also petitioned, all of whom happen to be Chinese subjects, eighty others, not Chinese subjects, are permitted to carry on the same business under similar conditions. The fact of this discrimination is admitted. No reason for it is shown, and the conclusion cannot be resisted, that no reason for it exists except hostility to the race and nationality to which the petitioners belong, and which in the eye of the law is not justified. The discrimination is, therefore, illegal, and the public administration which enforces it is a denial of the equal protection of the laws and a violation of the Fourteenth Amendment of the Constitution. ■

The imprisonment of the petitioners is, therefore, illegal, and they must be discharged.

Summary

The West underwent tremendous change during the thirty or forty years following the Civil War. Federal policymakers hoped for the rapid development of the region, and they often used the public domain to accomplish that purpose. Native Americans, especially those of the Great Plains, were initially seen as obstacles to development, but most were defeated by the army and relegated to reservations.

Patterns of development varied in different parts of the West. In the Great Basin, Mormons created a theocracy, organized cooperatives, and employed irrigation. A cattle kingdom emerged on the western

Great Plains, as railroad construction made it possible to carry cattle east for slaughter and processing. As farming moved west, lack of water led to new crops and improved farming methods.

Throughout the West, railroad construction overcame the vast distances, making possible most forms of economic development. As western mining became highly mechanized, control shifted to large mining companies able to secure the necessary capital. In California especially, landowners transformed western agriculture into a large-scale commercial undertaking. The coniferous forests of the Pacific Northwest attracted lumbering companies. By the 1870s, San Francisco had become the center of much of the western economy. Water posed a significant constraint on economic development in many parts of the West, prompting efforts to reroute natural water sources.

The western population included immigrants from Asia, American Indians, and Latino peoples in substantial numbers, but each group had significantly different expectations and experiences. White westerners chose to use politics and, sometimes, violence to exclude and segregate Asian immigrants. Federal policy toward American Indians proceeded from the expectation that they could and should be rapidly assimilated and must shed their separate cultural identities, but such policies largely failed. Latinos—descendants of those living in the Southwest before it became part of the United States and those who came later from Mexico or elsewhere in Latin America—often found their lives and culture under challenge.

Americans have viewed the West both as a utopia and as the source of a national myth. But those views frequently romanticize or overlook important realities in the nature of western development and in the people who accomplished it.

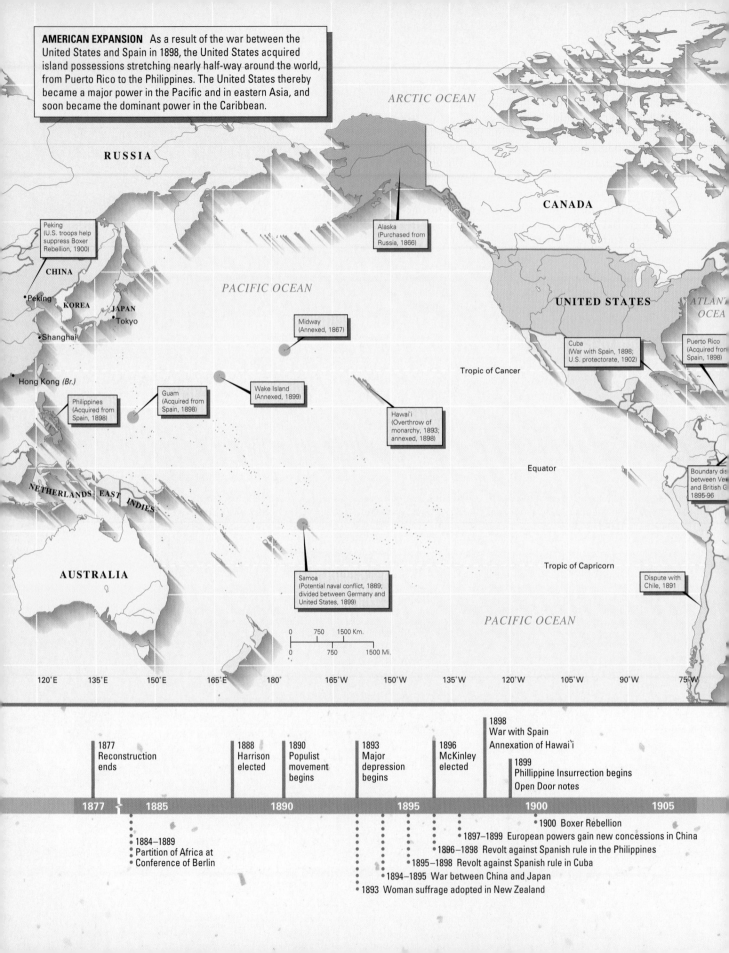

AMERICAN EXPANSION As a result of the war between the United States and Spain in 1898, the United States acquired island possessions stretching nearly half-way around the world, from Puerto Rico to the Philippines. The United States thereby became a major power in the Pacific and in eastern Asia, and soon became the dominant power in the Caribbean.

ARCTIC OCEAN

RUSSIA

CANADA

Alaska
(Purchased from
Russia, 1866)

Peking
(U.S. troops help
suppress Boxer
Rebellion, 1900)

CHINA

Peking

KOREA

JAPAN

Tokyo

Shanghai

PACIFIC OCEAN

UNITED STATES

*ATLANT
OCEA*

Midway
(Annexed, 1867)

Cuba
(War with Spain, 1898;
U.S. protectorate, 1902)

Puerto Rico
(Acquired from
Spain, 1898)

Tropic of Cancer

Hong Kong *(Br.)*

Guam
(Acquired from
Spain, 1898)

Wake Island
(Annexed, 1899)

Hawai`i
(Overthrow of
monarchy, 1893;
annexed, 1898)

Philippines
(Acquired from
Spain, 1898)

Equator

Boundary dis
between Ver
and British G
1895-96

NETHERLANDS EAST INDIES

Tropic of Capricorn

Dispute with
Chile, 1891

AUSTRALIA

Samoa
(Potential naval conflict, 1889;
divided between Germany and
United States, 1899)

PACIFIC OCEAN

| 0 | 750 | 1500 Km. |
| 0 | 750 | 1500 Mi. |

120°E 135°E 150°E 165°E 180° 165°W 150°W 135°W 120°W 105°W 90°W 75°W

1877
Reconstruction
ends

1888
Harrison
elected

1890
Populist
movement
begins

1893
Major
depression
begins

1896
McKinley
elected

1898
War with Spain
Annexation of Hawai`i

1899
Phillipine Insurrection begins
Open Door notes

1877   **1885**   **1890**   **1895**   **1900**   **1905**

1884–1889
Partition of Africa at
Conference of Berlin

1900 Boxer Rebellion

1897–1899 European powers gain new concessions in China

1896–1898 Revolt against Spanish rule in the Philippines

1895–1898 Revolt against Spanish rule in Cuba

1894–1895 War between China and Japan

1893 Woman suffrage adopted in New Zealand

Economic Crash and Political Upheaval, 1890–1900

20

American Expansion
How do the new acquisitions of the United States in the Pacific and in the Caribbean fit with the naval strategies outlined in this chapter by Alfred Thayer Mahan?

Individual Choices

ANNIE LE PORTE DIGGS

There are surprisingly few photographs of Annie Le Porte Diggs, given the prominent role that she played in Kansas politics in the 1890s. This one was probably taken in the mid-1890s. *Kansas State Historical Society.*

Annie Le Porte Diggs

In 1890 Annie Le Porte Diggs took a long step into party politics, though she may not have realized it at the time. Early that year, she was writing a weekly column for her local newspaper, the *Lawrence* [Kansas] *Journal.* Her column presented news from the Women's Christian Temperance Union (WCTU; see page 553), a cause she had supported for several years. In mid-February, however, she told her editor that she wanted to change her column and devote it instead to the activities of the Farmers' Alliance, a new organization. Fueled by abysmally low prices for corn and fanned by farmers' outrage at the refusal of Republican and Democratic politicians to address the problems of farmers, the Alliance was spreading like wildfire across Kansas and other Great Plains states.

Annie L. Diggs was no stranger to controversy. Born in Ontario, Canada, in 1853, daughter of a French-Canadian father and a New Jersey–born mother, she came to Kansas at the age of 19, married, had three children, and became active in the Unitarian Church and the temperance movement (including the WCTU and the Prohibition Party). Her church and temperance work led her into journalism. Soon after taking up the cause of the Farmers' Alliance, she became associate editor of the Kansas Alliance's state newspaper, the *Topeka Farmers Advocate,* and from there she moved into politics when the Farmers' Alliance sponsored the creation of the People's, or Populist, Party.

In her editorials for the *Advocate,* she ably promoted the ideals of the Populists, seeking to improve the situation of farmers and workers through state and federal legislation. Her editorials also staunchly supported woman suffrage and prohibition, and condemned capital punishment. She soon became a leading Populist campaign orator as well—one of her speeches in 1890 ran from 4:00 P.M. until sundown, perhaps three hours. Though she weighed only a bit over 90 pounds and, as one of her admirers said, "stood shoulder high to only the shortest men," she became a powerful figure in Kansas politics.

She attended all party gatherings and gained a reputation as a mediator, able to smooth over the various petty disputes that arose among the men who made up the vast majority of convention delegates. As one observer explained, "Thus she built up a hold on the Populists that was never broken, nor was her sincerity in the cause of the underdog ever questioned."

Diggs was a strong proponent of the tactic of *fusion* in Kansas—that is, a coalition between the Populists and Democrats (who ran a dismal third in state elections after the appearance of the Populists). She supported cooperation between the two parties in Kansas, gave strong support to the campaign of William Jennings Bryan (who won both the Democratic and Populist nominations for president in 1896), and emerged as the moving force in both the Democratic and Populist Parties of Kansas in the late 1890s. Along the way, she found time to serve as president of the Kansas Women's Free Silver League in 1896 and of the

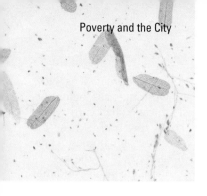

Kansas Equal Suffrage Association in 1899. In 1898 the Populist governor of Kansas (whom she had helped to elect) appointed her state librarian, the first woman to hold that position. In 1900 the *Kansas City Journal* said of her, "She has more political sagacity than the whole bunch of past party leaders put together. . . . In their day they tried to run things by dictating to the masses what they should do. She leads by first finding out what the common people of her party want and then going to the front to help them get it."

INTRODUCTION

In July 1892, a new political party, the People's Party, met in Omaha to choose its candidates for president and vice president. Born in protest against the economic and political events of the previous quarter-century, the new party—soon called the Populists—drafted a platform that boldly called for governmental action to aid the victims of industrialization. Most Americans, however, were unwilling to create a vastly more powerful federal government. Although most voters rejected the Populists' remedies, few doubted that industrialization, urbanization, immigration, and the development of the West had profoundly transformed the nation's social and economic life.

During the early 1890s, a number of other developments also affected the course of American politics. Urban poverty captured public attention, as did efforts to mitigate its worst features through settlement houses. Southern states approved new laws that disfranchised black voters and legitimized and extended racial segregation. Nativism took on political dimensions with efforts to limit immigration from Europe. A major contraction shook the economy, producing serious unemployment and deprivation. Eventually the Populists merged with the Democrats in support of the presidential candidacy of William Jennings Bryan in 1896. In 1896, however, voters chose William McKinley, the Republican candidate for president, thereby endorsing a more conservative approach to federal economic policy. The long-term outcome was a decisive shift in American politics.

During the 1890s, too, the United States emerged as a major world power, with a strong, modern navy. In war with Spain in 1898, the nation gained a colonial empire that stretched nearly halfway around the world, from Puerto Rico in the Caribbean to the Philippine Islands off the coast of eastern Asia. This, too, marked a major transformation of American politics, as henceforth foreign relations became an increasingly important part of the responsibility of federal policymakers.

Poverty and the City

■ What groups and movements arose to address urban poverty by the 1890s?

■ What do their different approaches tell you about each group?

The dramatic growth of cities in the 1870s and 1880s was accompanied by an equally dramatic growth of urban poverty. The slums of New York City had worried thoughtful Americans since before the Civil War, but the huge influx of people to the cities after the war multiplied the misery. By the 1890s, journalists and reformers began to focus on urban poverty, and new ways of addressing it captured national attention.

"How the Other Half Lives"

In 1890 Jacob Riis shocked many Americans with the revelations in *How the Other Half Lives*. In a city of a million and a half inhabitants, Riis claimed, half a million (136,000 families) had begged for food at some time over the preceding eight years. Of these, more than half were unemployed, but only 6 percent were physically unable to work. Most of Riis's book described the appalling conditions of **tenements**—home, he claimed, to three-quarters of the city's population.

Strictly speaking, a tenement is an apartment house occupied by three or more families, but the term came to imply overcrowded and badly maintained housing that was hazardous to the health and safety of its residents. Riis described the typical, cramped New York tenement of his day as

> *a brick building from four to six stories high on the street, frequently with a store on the first floor. . . . Four families occupy each floor, and a set of rooms consists of one or two dark closets, used as bedrooms, with a living room twelve feet by ten. The staircase is*

tenement   A multifamily apartment building, often unsafe, unsanitary, and overcrowded.

This photograph was either taken by Jacob Riis or taken at his direction, in the early 1890s. It shows an interior court on the Lower East Side of New York City, open to the sky above. As the photograph suggests, such busy places were often the playground for the children of the poor residents. On the far right is a water pump, perhaps the source of water for the residents of the building. Though the photographs in Riis's books were once attributed to him, it is now clear that most were taken by other people. Adding such powerful visual images to Riis's books—something made possible because of new printing technologies—greatly increased their effectiveness in mobilizing reform. *Museum of the City of New York.*

too often a dark well in the center of the house . . . no direct through ventilation is possible.

Such buildings, Riis insisted, "are the hotbeds of the epidemics that carry death to rich and poor alike; the nurseries of pauperism and crime that fill our jails and police courts. . . . Above all, they touch the family life with deadly moral contagion." He especially deplored the harmful influence of poverty and miserable housing conditions on children and families.

Crowded conditions in working-class sections of large cities developed in part because so many of the poor needed to live within walking distance of their work and of multiple sources of employment for various family members. By dividing buildings into small rental units, landlords packed in more tenants and collected more rent. To pay the rent, many tenants took in lodgers. Such practices produced shockingly high population densities in lower-income urban neighborhoods.

No other city was as densely populated as New York, but nearly all urban, working-class neighborhoods were crowded. Most Chicago stockyard workers, for example, lived in small row houses near the slaughterhouses. Many owned their own homes. A survey in 1911 revealed that three-quarters of the houses were subdivided into two or more living units, and that a small shanty often sat in the backyard. Half of all the living units had four rooms, a few had five, and none had more. More than half of all families took in lodgers, and lodgers who worked different shifts at the stockyards sometimes took turns sleeping in the same bed.

Few agreed on the causes of urban poverty, even fewer on its cure. Riis divided the blame, in New York City, among greedy landlords, corrupt officials, and the poor themselves. Henry George, a San Franciscan, in *Progress and Poverty,* pointed to the increase in the value of real estate due to urbanization and industrialization, which made it difficult or impossible for many to afford a home of their own. The Charity Organization Society (COS), by contrast, argued for individual responsibility. With chapters in a hundred cities by 1895, the COS claimed that, in most cases, individual character defects produced poverty and that assistance for such people only rewarded immorality or laziness. Public or private help should be given only after careful investigation, the COS insisted, and should be temporary, only until the person secured work. Moreover, COS officials expected the recipients of aid to be moral, thrifty, and hardworking.

Challenging Urban Poverty: The Settlement Houses

By the early 1890s, in several cities, young college-educated men and women began to confront poverty differently from the Charity Organization Societies. These humanitarians tried to provide a range of assistance for the poor to deal with the problems they faced in housing, nutrition, and sanitation. The **settlement house** idea originated in England in 1884, at Toynbee Hall, a house in London's slums where idealistic university graduates lived among the poor and tried to help them. The concept spread to New York in 1886 with the opening of a settlement house staffed by young male college graduates. In 1889 several women who had graduated from Smith College (a

settlement house Community center operated by resident social reformers in a slum area to help poor people in their own neighborhoods.

Chronology

The United States in the 1890s

1886	First U.S. settlement house opens
1887	American Protective Association founded Florida segregates railroads
1888	Benjamin Harrison elected president
late 1880s	Farmers' Alliances spread
1888–1892	Australian ballot adopted in most states
1889	North Dakota, South Dakota, Montana, and Washington become states Hull House opens Treaty of Berlin divides Samoa between Germany and the United States
1889–1891	Fifty-first Congress: McKinley Tariff, Sherman Anti-Trust Act, Sherman Silver Purchase Act, significant increase in naval appropriation; federal elections bill defeated
1890	Jacob Riis's *How the Other Half Lives* Alfred Thayer Mahan's *Influence of Sea Power upon History, 1660–1783* Second Mississippi Plan National American Woman Suffrage Association formed Idaho becomes a state Wyoming becomes a state, the first with woman suffrage Populist movement begins Wounded Knee
1891	Lili`uokalani becomes Hawaiian queen President Benjamin Harrison threatens war with Chile
1892	Homestead strike Cleveland elected president again
1893	Colorado men vote to adopt woman suffrage Sherman Silver Purchase Act repealed Queen Lili`uokalani overthrown

1893–1897	Depression
1894	Coxey's Army Pullman strike
1895	Booker T. Washington delivers Atlanta Compromise J. P. Morgan stabilizes gold reserve
1895–1896	Venezuelan boundary crisis
1896	Utah becomes a state, adopts woman suffrage Reconcentration policy in Cuba William Jennings Bryan's "Cross of Gold" speech William McKinley elected president Idaho adopts woman suffrage South Carolina adopts white primary *Plessy v. Ferguson*
1897	Dingley Tariff
1898	De Lôme letter published in the *New York Journal* U.S. warship *Maine* explodes War with Spain United States annexes Hawai`i by joint resolution Treaty of Paris signed
1899	Senate debates imperialism Treaty of Paris ratified Treaty of Berlin divides Samoa Open Door notes
1899–1902	Philippine insurrection suppressed
1900	Gold Standard Act Foraker Act McKinley reelected Boxer Rebellion
1901	United States Steel organized
1902	Insular cases Civil government in the Philippines Cuba becomes a protectorate

women's college) opened another settlement house in New York.

Also in 1889, two women opened **Hull House,** the first settlement house in Chicago. For many Americans,

---

Hull House   Settlement house founded by Jane Addams and Ellen Gates Starr in 1889 in Chicago.

This photo shows children from the Hull House kindergarten, probably from the 1890s. Kindergartens were first set up in Germany in the 1830s as a way to encourage learning through activities. In most American cities, settlement houses or other charitable organizations initially created kindergartens to provide daycare for children in poor and working-class neighborhoods. *The University of Illinois at Chicago, University Library, Jane Addams Memorial Collection, JAMC negative 109.*

its cofounder Jane Addams became synonymous with the settlement house movement. Born in 1860 in a small town in Illinois, the youngest daughter of a bank president, Addams attended college, then traveled in Europe. There she and Ellen Gates Starr, a friend from college, visited Toynbee Hall and learned about its approach to helping the urban poor. Inspired by that example, the two set up Hull House in a working-class, immigrant neighborhood in Chicago. Addams lived at Hull House for the rest of her life, attracting a circle of impressive associates and making Hull House the best-known example of settlement work. Hull House offered a variety of services to the families of its neighborhood: a nursery, a kindergarten (childcare for preschool children), classes in child rearing, a playground, and a gymnasium. Addams, Starr, and other Hull House activists also challenged the power of city bosses and lobbied state legislators, seeking cleaner streets, the abolition of child labor, health and safety regulations for factories, compulsory school attendance, and more. Their efforts brought national recognition.

Other settlement house workers across the country provided similar assistance to poor urban families: cooking and sewing classes, public baths, childcare facilities, instruction in English, and housing for unmarried working women. Some settlement houses were church sponsored, and others were secular. Nearly all tried to minimize class conflict because they agreed with Addams that "the dependence of classes on each other is reciprocal." Some historians have suggested that settlement house workers tried to bridge the gap between urban economic classes by imparting middle-class values to the poor and by persuading the wealthy to help mitigate poverty. Such a view suggests that their efforts reflected urban middle-class anxieties over growing extremes of wealth and poverty. Other historians have added that some settlement house workers drew on the bonds of gender solidarity to appeal to upper- and middle-class women for funds to assist working-class and poor women and children. Historians agree that, like Addams, many settlement house workers became forces for urban reform, promoting better education, improved public health and sanitation, and honest government.

Settlement houses spread rapidly, with some four hundred operating by 1910. By then, three-quarters of settlement house workers were women, and settlement houses became the first institutions created and staffed primarily by college-educated women. They led to a new profession—social work. When universities began to offer study in social work (first at Columbia, in 1902), women tended to dominate that field too. Women college graduates thus created a new and uniquely urban profession at a time when many other careers remained closed to them.

Church-affiliated settlement houses often reflected the influence of the **Social Gospel,** a movement popularized by urban Protestant ministers who were concerned about the social and economic problems of the cities. One of the best known, Washington Gladden, of Columbus, Ohio, called for "Applied Christianity," by which he meant the application to business of Christ's injunctions to love one another and to treat others as you would have them treat you. A similar strain of social activism appeared among some Catholics, especially those inspired by Pope Leo XIII's 1891 *Rerum Novarum* ("Of New Things"), a **papal encyclical** urging greater attention by the church to the problems of the industrial working class.

Political Upheaval, 1890–1892

■ What groups and which issues led to the formation of the Populist Party?

■ What accounts for the failure of the Republicans in the elections of 1890 and 1892?

Though urban poverty claimed the attention of many city-dwellers, it had little bearing on national politics. Benjamin Harrison had led the Republican Party to victory in the 1888 elections. When the new Congress convened late in 1889, the Republicans quickly set about writing their campaign promises into law. A torrent of new legislation began to pour out of Washington. Simultaneously, new elements in politics were developing. Nativism took political forms through the American Protective Association and efforts to restrict immigration. And in 1890–1891 the People's Party, or Populists, emerged, offering a radical political alternative.

Harrison and the Fifty-first Congress

With Harrison in the White House and Republican majorities in both houses of Congress, the Republicans set out to do a lot and to do it quickly. When the fifty-first session of Congress opened late in 1889, Harrison worked more closely with congressional leaders of his own party than any other president in recent memory. Democrats in the House of Representatives tried to delay progress on the administration's agenda, but Speaker Thomas B. Reed—an enormous man renowned for his wit—announced new rules designed to speed up House business.

The Republicans' first major task was tariff revision—to cut the troublesome federal surplus (see pages 557–558) without reducing protection. Led by representative William McKinley of Ohio, the **House Ways and Means Committee** drafted a tariff bill that moved some items to the free list (notably sugar, a major source of tariff revenue) but raised tariff rates on other items, sometimes so high as to be prohibitive. The House passed the **McKinley Tariff** in May 1890 and sent it on to the Senate.

In July the House also approved a federal elections bill, intended to protect the voting rights of African Americans in the South. Its Democratic opponents called it the "force bill," to emphasize its potential for federal intervention in southern affairs. Proposed by Representative Henry Cabot Lodge of Massachusetts, the bill would have permitted federal supervision over congressional elections to prevent disfranchisement, fraud, or violence. The measure passed the House and went to the Senate, where approval by the Republican majority seemed likely.

The Senate, meanwhile, was laboring over two measures named for Senator John Sherman of Ohio: the **Sherman Anti-Trust Act** and the **Sherman Silver Purchase Act.** The Silver Purchase Act somewhat increased the amount of silver being coined into dollars but stopped short of approving the coinage of all available silver (see page 519). The Anti-Trust Act, the

---

Social Gospel   A reform movement of the late nineteenth century led by Protestant clergy who drew attention to urban problems and advocated social justice for the poor.

papal encyclical   A letter from the pope to all Roman Catholic bishops, intended to guide them in the relations with the churches under their jurisdiction.

House Ways and Means Committee   One of the most significant standing committees (permanently organized committees) of the House of Representatives, responsible for initiating all taxation measures.

McKinley Tariff   Tariff passed by Congress in 1890 that sought not only to protect established industries but by prohibitory duties to stimulate the creation of new industries.

Sherman Anti-Trust Act   Law passed by Congress in 1890 authorizing the federal government to prosecute any "combination" "in restraint of trade"; because of adverse court rulings, at first it was ineffective as a weapon against monopolies.

Sherman Silver Purchase Act   Law passed by Congress in 1890 requiring the federal government to increase its purchases of silver to be coined into silver dollars.

work of several Republican senators close to Harrison, was approved with only a single dissenting vote. Created in response to growing public concern about the new trusts and monopolies, the law declared that "every contract, combination in the form of trust or otherwise, or conspiracy, in restraint of trade or commerce among the several states, or with foreign nations, is hereby declared to be illegal." Republicans thereby tried to be responsive to concerns about monopoly power, and the United States became the first industrial nation to attempt to prevent monopolies. In fact, however, the law proved difficult to interpret or enforce, and it had little effect on companies for more than ten years.

The tariff and elections bills still awaited Senate approval. Harrison wanted them passed as a party package, but some Senate Republicans feared that a Democratic **filibuster** against the elections bill would prevent passage of both measures. Finally a compromise emerged—if Republicans would table the elections bill, the Democrats would not delay the tariff bill. Despite strong protests from a few New England Republicans, their party sacrificed African Americans' voting rights to gain the revised tariff. (Some seventy more years passed before Congress finally acted to protect black voting rights in the South.) Harrison signed the McKinley Tariff on October 1, 1890, and the revised tariff soon produced the intended result: it reduced the surplus by cutting tariff income.

The McKinley Tariff and Sherman Anti-Trust Act were only the tip of the iceberg. In ten months the Republicans had passed what one Democrat called "a raging sea of ravenous legislation." Among the record number of new laws were a major increase in pension eligibility for disabled Union army veterans and their dependents, admission to statehood of Idaho and Wyoming, creation of territorial government in Oklahoma, and appropriations that laid the basis for a modern navy. Republicans hoped they had finally broken the political logjam that had clogged the capitol since 1875. However, as Congress labored in Washington, new and sometimes disturbing currents began to roil state and local politics.

The Politics of Nativism

During the 1890s, nativism (see page 544) became both more visible and more political. The American Protective Association (APA), the self-proclaimed voice of anti-Catholicism (see page 544), intensified its crusade against Catholics. A half-million strong by 1894, APA members sometimes fomented mob violence against Catholics. More often they tried to dominate the Republican Party, and they succeeded in several areas, especially in the Midwest, before they died out by the late 1890s.

In some parts of the Midwest in the early 1890s, nativists (not necessarily the APA) pushed through laws requiring schools to be taught only in English, a slap at German immigrants. The growth of prohibition sentiment was accompanied by unflattering nativist stereotypes of Irish saloonkeepers and German beer-brewers.

During the 1890s, a diverse political coalition emerged aimed at reducing immigration. Labor organizations began to look at immigration as a potential threat to jobs and wage levels. (Anti-Chinese grumblings among Pacific Coast unions had contributed to passage of the Chinese Exclusion Act in 1882; see page 588). At the same time, a few employers began to connect immigrants with unions and radicalism and to charge that unions represented foreign, un-American influences. Foreign-born radicals and especially anarchists were a special target, as newspapers claimed that "there is no such thing as an American anarchist." In 1901 Leon Czolgosz, an American-born anarchist with a foreign-sounding name, assassinated President William McKinley, and Congress promptly passed a bill barring anarchists from immigrating to the United States.

During the 1890s, the sources of European immigration began to shift from northwestern Europe to southern and eastern Europe, bringing larger numbers of Italians, Poles and other Slavs, and eastern European Jews (see Figure 18.2, page 542). This also furthered nativism. Anti-Catholicism and anti-Semitism combined with cruel stereotypes of those from southern and eastern Europe to create a sense that these **"new immigrants"** were less desirable than **"old immigrants"** from northwestern Europe.

The arrival of significant numbers of "new immigrants" after 1890 coincided with a wave of sentiment that glorified Anglo-Saxons (ancestors of the English)

> **filibuster** A long speech by a bill's opponents to delay legislative action; usually applies to extended speeches in the U.S. Senate, which has no time limit on speeches and where a minority may therefore try to "talk a bill to death" by holding up all other business.
>
> **"new immigrants"** Newcomers from southern and eastern Europe who began to arrive in the United States in significant numbers during the 1890s and after.
>
> **"old immigrants"** Newcomers from northern and western Europe who made up much of the immigration to the United States before the 1890s.

and accomplishments by the English and English Americans. Relying on Social Darwinism (see page 506) and its argument for survival of the fittest, proponents of Anglo-Saxonism were alarmed by statistics that showed old-stock Americans having fewer children than did immigrants. Some voiced fears of "race suicide" in which Anglo-Saxons allowed themselves to be bred out of existence. With such anxieties feeding their prejudices, some nativists became blatant racists.

By the 1890s, these economic, political, religious, and racist strains converged in demands that the federal government restrict immigration from Europe. Given stereotypes that immigrants were ignorant, advocates of restriction argued that immigrants should pass a literacy test before being admitted to the United States. In 1891 Henry Cabot Lodge (who had worked so hard to protect black voting rights) pushed the literacy test in Congress. The depression that began in 1893 apparently convinced the American Federation of Labor to endorse such a literacy test to reduce immigration. Many business leaders, however, opposed restrictions on immigration for fear that limits would cut into their supply of labor. Congress passed literacy bills in 1897 and 1913, but both met presidential vetoes. In 1917 President Woodrow Wilson vetoed another effort, but Congress overrode his veto and enacted the measure into law. When it failed to reduce the numbers coming from Europe, more sweeping restrictions came in the 1920s.

The Origins of the People's Party

As some southern politicians loudly promoted white supremacy and some midwestern politicians flirted with nativism, a quite different political movement was developing in response to the economic problems of southern and western farmers. In 1890 this movement sponsored the first **Populist** parties at a state level.

Populism grew out of the economic problems of farmers. During the 1870s and 1880s, farmers had become more and more dependent on the national railroad network, on national markets for grain and cotton, and on sources of credit in distant cities. At the same time, some of them felt increasingly apprehensive about the great concentrations of economic power that seemed to be dominating their lives. (For earlier farmers' organizations, see pages 516–519.)

Perhaps most troubling were the prices that farmers received for their crops. Crop prices fell steadily after the Civil War as production of wheat, corn, and cotton grew much faster than the population (see Fig-

ure 17.1 and page 495). Some farmers, however, denied that prices were falling solely because of overproduction, pointing to the hungry and ragged residents in the slums. Farmers also condemned the monopolistic practices of the **commodity markets** in Chicago and New York that determined crop prices. Farmers knew that the bushel of corn that they sold for 10 or 20 cents in October brought three or four times that amount in New York in December. When they brought their crops to market, however, they had to accept the price that was offered because they needed cash to pay their debts and because most of them had no way to store their crops for later sale at a higher price.

Farmers had accomplished much of the post–Civil War agricultural expansion on borrowed money, and falling prices magnified their indebtedness. For example, suppose a farmer borrowed $1,000 for five years in 1881. With corn selling at 63 cents per bushel, the $1,000 would have been equivalent to 1,587 bushels of corn. In 1886, when the loan came due, corn sold for 36 cents per bushel, requiring 2,777 bushels to repay the $1,000. Because prices for crops sank lower and lower, farmers raised more and more just to pay their mortgages and buy necessities. Given the relation between supply and demand, the more they raised, the lower prices fell. One historian compared the farmers' plight to the character in *Alice in Wonderland* who had to run faster and faster just to stay in the same place.

The railroads also angered many farmers. The railroads, farmers insisted, were greedy monopolies that charged as much as possible to deliver supplies to rural America and carry their crops to market. It sometimes cost four times as much to ship freight in the West as to ship the same amount over the same distance in the East. Farmers also protested the railroads' involvement in politics, claiming that they dominated state nominating conventions and state legislatures and distributed free passes to politicians in return for favorable treatment. One North Carolina farm editor in 1888 bemoaned the railroads' power in his state: "Do they not own the newspapers? Are not

Populists   Members of the People's Party, who held their first presidential nominating convention in 1892 and called for federal action to reduce the power of big business and to assist farmers and workers.

commodity market   Financial market in which brokers buy and sell agricultural products in large quantities, thus determining the prices paid to farmers for their harvests.

all the politicians their dependents? Has not every Judge in the State a free pass in his pocket?"

Crop prices, debt, and railroad practices were only some of the farmers' complaints. They protested, too, that local bankers charged 8, 9, or 10 percent interest—or even more—in western and southern states, compared with 6 percent or less in the Northeast. They argued that federal monetary policies contributed to falling prices and thereby compounded their debts. Farmers complained that the giant corporations that made farm equipment and fertilizer overcharged them. Even local merchants drew farmers' reproach for exorbitant markups. In the South, all these problems combined with sharecropping and crop liens (see page 467).

The Grange, the Greenback Party, and the silver movement in the late 1870s had expressed farmers' grievances, but those movements faded during the relatively prosperous 1880s. By 1890, however, falling crop prices and widespread indebtedness brought renewed concern among farmers and farm organizations. The Republicans' Silver Purchase Act of 1890 tried to calm this rising concern by increasing the amount of silver to be coined. As had been the case with the Bland-Allison Act (see page 519) before it, however, both silverites and advocates of the gold standard found the law unsatisfactory.

The People's Party

The Grange had demonstrated the possibility for united action, but its decline left an organizational vacuum among farmers, and the Greenback Party failed to fill it. In the 1880s, however, three new organizations emerged, all called **Farmers' Alliances.** One was centered in the north-central states. Another, the Southern Alliance, began in Texas in the late 1870s and spread eastward across the South, absorbing similar local groups along its way. Because the Southern Alliance limited its membership to white farmers, a third group, the Colored Farmers' Alliance, recruited southern black farmers. Like the Grange and Knights of Labor (see pages 517 and 539), the Alliances defined themselves as organizations of the "producing classes" and looked to cooperatives as a partial solution to their problems. Alliance stores were most common. The Texas Alliance also experimented with cooperative cotton selling, and some midwestern local Alliances built cooperative **grain elevators.**

Local Alliance meetings featured social and educational activities. By the late 1880s, a host of weekly newspapers across the South and West presented Alliance views. One Kansas woman described the out-

A PARTY OF PATCHES.
Grand Balloon Ascension—Cincinnati, May 20th, 1891.

When the Populists launched their new party, one cartoonist depicted them as a hot-air balloon of political malcontents. This cartoon may have inspired Frank Baum, author of *The Wizard of Oz,* whose wizard arrived in Oz in a hot-air balloon launched from Omaha, the site of the Populists' 1892 nominating convention. *Library of Congress.*

come: "People commenced to think who had never thought before, and people talked who had seldom spoken. . . . Thoughts and theories sprouted like weeds after a May shower."

The Alliances defined themselves as nonpartisan and expected their members to work for Alliance aims within the major parties. This was especially important in the South, where any white person who challenged the Democratic Party risked being condemned as a traitor to both race and region. Many midwestern Alliance leaders, however, came out of

Farmers' Alliances   Organizations of farm families in the 1880s and 1890s, similar to the Grange.

grain elevator   A storehouse for grain located near railroad tracks; such structures were equipped with mechanical lifting devices (elevators) that permitted the grain to be loaded into railcars.

the Granger Party tradition, and some had been Greenbackers. Others had aligned themselves with the Knights of Labor and took pride in its role in fostering local labor parties. Not until the winter of 1889–1890, however, did widespread support materialize for independent political action in the Midwest. By then, corn prices had fallen so low that some farmers found it cheaper to burn their corn than to sell it and buy fuel.

Through the hot summer of 1890, as the Fifty-first Congress argued over the McKinley Tariff and the Lodge federal elections bill, members of the Farmers' Alliance in Kansas, Nebraska, the Dakotas, Minnesota, and surrounding states formed new political parties to contest state and local elections. One leader explained that the political battle they waged was "between the insatiable greed of organized wealth and the rights of the great plain people."

Women took a prominent part in Populist campaigning, especially in Kansas and Nebraska. Mary Elizabeth Lease of Kansas was among the most effective. She acquired lasting fame when newspapers quoted her as urging farmers to "raise less corn and more hell!" Annie Diggs attracted less attention than Lease at first, but proved the more significant power within Kansas populism.

Soon dubbed the People's Party, or Populists, the new party emphasized three elements in their campaigns: **antimonopolism**, government action on behalf of farmers and workers, and increased popular control of government. Their antimonopolism drew on their own unhappy experiences with railroads, grain buyers, and manufacturing companies, but it also derived from a long American tradition of opposition to concentrated economic power. Populists quoted Thomas Jefferson on the need for equal rights for all, and they compared themselves to Andrew Jackson in his fight against the Bank of the United States.

"We believe the time has come," the Populists proclaimed in their 1892 platform, "when the railroad companies will either own the people or the people must own the railroads." The Populists' solution to the dangers of monopoly was government action on behalf of farmers and workers, including federal ownership of the railroads and the telegraph and telephone systems, and government alternatives to private banks. Some Populists also endorsed a proposal of the Southern Alliance called the Sub-Treasury Plan, under which crops stored in government warehouses might be **collateral** for low-interest loans to farmers. Populists also demanded currency inflation (through greenbacks, silver, or both) and a graduated income tax. Through such measures, they hoped, in the words of their 1892

platform, that "oppression, injustice, and poverty shall eventually cease in the land." They had some following within what remained of the Knights of Labor, and they hoped to gain broad support among other urban and industrial workers by calling for the eight-hour workday and for restrictions on companies' use of private armies in labor disputes.

Finally, the People's Party favored a series of structural changes to make government more responsive to the people, including expansion of the merit system for government employees, election of U.S. senators by the voters instead of by state legislatures, a one-term limit for the president, the secret ballot, and the **initiative** and **referendum.** Many of them also favored woman suffrage. In the South, the Populists not only opposed disfranchisement of black voters but also posed a serious challenge to the prevailing patterns of politics by seeking to forge a political alliance of the disadvantaged of both races.

Thus the Populists wanted to use government to control, even to own, the corporate behemoths that had evolved in their lifetimes. But they deeply distrusted the old parties and wanted to increase the influence of the individual voter in political decision making.

The Elections of 1890 and 1892

The issues in the 1890 elections for members of the House of Representatives and for state and local offices varied by region. In the West, the Populists stood at the center of the campaign, lambasting both major parties for ignoring the needs of the people. In the South, Democrats held up Lodge's "force bill" as a warning of the potential dangers if Southern whites should bolt the party of white supremacy. There, members of the Southern Alliance worked within the Democratic Party to secure candidates committed to the farmers' cause. In the Northeast, Democrats

---

antimonopolism   Opposition to great concentrations of economic power such as trusts and giant corporations, as well as to actual monopolies.

collateral   Property pledged as security for a loan, that is, something owned by the borrower that can be taken by the lender if the borrower fails to repay the loan.

initiative   Procedure allowing voters to petition to have a law placed on the ballot for consideration by the general electorate.

referendum   Procedure whereby a bill or constitutional amendment is submitted to the voters for their approval after having been passed by a legislative body.

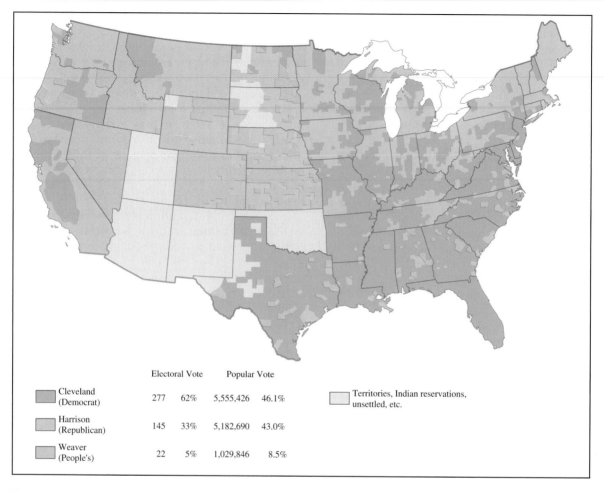

	Electoral Vote		Popular Vote	
Cleveland (Democrat)	277	62%	5,555,426	46.1%
Harrison (Republican)	145	33%	5,182,690	43.0%
Weaver (People's)	22	5%	1,029,846	8.5%

Territories, Indian reservations, unsettled, etc.

MAP 20.1 Popular Vote for Weaver, 1892   The Populist Party's presidential candidate, James B. Weaver, made a strong showing in 1892. This map indicates that his support was concentrated regionally in the West and South but that he had relatively little support in the northeastern states.

attacked the McKinley Tariff for producing higher prices for consumers. In the Rocky Mountain region, nearly all candidates pledged their support for unlimited silver coinage. In parts of the Midwest, Democrats scourged Republicans for supporting prohibition and school laws unpopular with German Americans.

The new Populist Party scored several victories, marking it as the most successful new party since the appearance of the Republicans in the 1850s. Kansas Republican senator John J. Ingalls had dismissed Populists as "a sort of turnip crusade," but Populists silenced Ingalls by winning enough seats in the Kansas legislature to elect a Populist to replace him in the

Senate. Elsewhere Populists elected state legislators, members of Congress, and one other U.S. senator. All across the South, where Alliance members had remained within the Democratic Party, the Alliance claimed that successful candidates owed their victories to Alliance voters.

Everywhere Republicans suffered defeat, losing to Populists in the West and to Democrats in the Midwest and Northeast. In the House of Representatives, the Republicans went from 166 seats in 1889 to only 88 in 1891. Many Republican candidates for state and local offices also lost. Republican disappointment in the results of the 1890 elections bred dissension within the party, and President Harrison could not maintain party unity.

For the 1892 presidential election, the Republicans renominated Harrison despite a lack of enthusiasm among many party leaders. The Democrats again chose Grover Cleveland as their candidate. Farmers' Alliance activists from the South joined western Populists to form a national People's Party and to nominate James Weaver, who had run for president as a Greenbacker twelve years earlier. Democrats and Populists scored the most impressive victories. Cleveland won with 46.1 percent of the popular vote, becoming the only president in American history to win two nonconsecutive terms. Harrison got 43 percent, and Weaver captured 8.5 percent. The Democrats kept control of the House of Representatives and won a majority in the Senate. Populists displayed particular strength in the West and South (see Map 20.1). The Democrats now found themselves where the Republicans had stood four years before: in control of the presidency and Congress and poised to translate their promises into law.

Economic Collapse and Restructuring

■ What were the short-term and long-term effects of the depression that began in 1893?

■ What conclusions might union leaders have drawn from Homestead and Pullman?

After the Democrats swept to power in the 1892 elections, they suddenly faced the collapse of the national economy. Labor organizations suffered major defeats in 1892 and 1894, putting unions on the defensive thereafter. As the nation began to recover from the depression, anxious entrepreneurs launched a merger movement intended to bolster economic stability that also brought much greater economic concentration.

Economic Collapse and Depression

Ten days before Cleveland took office, the Reading Railroad declared bankruptcy. A **financial panic** quickly set in. One business journal reported in August that "never before has there been such a sudden and striking cessation of industrial activity." Everywhere, industrial plants shut down in large numbers. More than fifteen thousand businesses failed in 1893, more proportionately than in any year since the depression of the 1870s.

At the time, no one really understood why the economy collapsed so suddenly and completely. In retrospect, the downturn seems to have resulted from both immediate events and underlying weaknesses. The collapse of a major English bank led some British investors to call back investments in the United States. This event in Britain meant that some gold was flowing out of the United States because British investors called back their U.S. investments, and this outflow of gold combined with the reduction in federal revenues caused by the McKinley Tariff to produce a sharp decline in federal **gold reserves.** This reduction in federal gold reserves, in turn, combined with the bankruptcies of a few large companies to trigger a stock market crash in May–June of 1893.

Beyond these immediate events, the most important underlying weaknesses included the slowing of agricultural expansion and railroad construction. Railroad building drove the industrial economy in the 1880s, but railroad construction first slowed and then fell by half between 1893 and 1895. The decline in railroad construction initiated a domino effect, toppling industries that supplied the railroads, especially steel. Production of steel rails fell by more than a third, and thirty-two steel companies closed their doors. (Figure 17.2, page 497, shows the drop in manufacturing in the mid-1890s.) In addition, some railway companies found they lacked sufficient traffic to pay their fixed costs, and several large lines declared bankruptcy, among them the Erie, Northern Pacific, Santa Fe, and Union Pacific. By 1894, almost one-fifth of the nation's railroad mileage had fallen into bankruptcy. Banks with investments in railroads and steel companies collapsed along with their client firms. Nearly five hundred banks failed in 1893 alone, and more than five hundred more closed by the end of 1897, equivalent to one bank out of every ten.

No agency kept careful national records on unemployment, but a third or more of the workers in manufacturing may have been out of work. During the winter of 1893–1894, Chicago counted one hundred thousand unemployed—roughly two workers out of five. Many who kept their jobs received smaller paychecks, as employers cut wages and hours. In 1892 the average nonfarm wage earner received $482 per year. By 1894, this sum had shrunk to $420. ($1 in 1893 is equivalent to nearly $20 today.)

financial panic   Widespread anxiety about financial and commercial matters; in a panic, investors often sell large amounts of stock to cut their own losses, which drives prices much lower.

gold reserves   The stockpile of gold with which the federal government backed up the currency.

In 1894, Jacob Coxey, an Ohio Populist, led his "petition in boots" on a march from Ohio to Washington, D.C., demanding that Congress provide public-works jobs to the unemployed. This rare photograph shows two of the banners that Coxey's Army carried on their march. The one in the foreground says, "Death to interest on Bonds," probably a reference to the interest that the nation was paying on the national debt. The larger one in the background seems to read, in part, "Work for Americans / More Money / Less Misery / Good Roads," a reference to Coxey's plan to end depression by putting unemployed Americans to work building public works and paying them with greenbacks. *William B. Becker Collection/American Museum of Photography.*

The depression produced widespread suffering. Many who lost their jobs had little to fall back on except charity. Newspapers told of people who chose suicide when faced with the dire options of starving to death or stealing food. Susan Orcutt, a Kansas farm wife nearly nine months pregnant, saw the worst of both farm poverty and depression unemployment:

> *I take my Pen In hand to let you know that we are Starving to death It is Pretty hard to do without any thing to Eat hear in this God for saken country we would have had Plenty to Eat if the hail hadent cut our rye down and ruined our corn and Potatoes . . . My Husband went a way to find work and came home last night and told me that we would have to Starve he has bin in ten countys and did not Get no work*

Like Orcutt's husband, many men and some women left home desperate to find work, hoping to send money to their families as soon as they could. Some walked the roads, and others hopped on freight trains, riding in **boxcars.**

A dramatic demonstration against unemployment began in January 1894, when Jacob S. Coxey, an Ohio Populist, proposed that the government hire the unemployed to build or repair roads and other public works and to pay them with greenbacks, thereby inflating the currency. He called on the unemployed to join him in a march on Washington to push this program. The response electrified the nation—all across the country, men and women tried to join the march. In the West, given the vast distances, some groups hijacked trains (fifty in all) and headed east, pulling boxcars loaded with unemployed men. (None of the pirated trains traveled far before authorities stopped them and arrested the leaders.) Several thousand people took part in **Coxey's Army** in some way, but most never reached Washington or reached it too late.

boxcar An enclosed railroad car with sliding side doors, used to transport freight.

Coxey's Army Unemployed workers led by Jacob S. Coxey, who marched on Washington to demand relief measures from Congress following the depression of 1893.

This drawing depicts troops firing on striking railway workers in Chicago, on July 7, 1894. The Pullman strike began with the employees of the Pullman factory near Chicago, but affected railway traffic from New York to California. Because of Chicago's position as the center of so much of the nation's railway traffic, and because of the strength of the unions in that area, the Chicago area was the flashpoint for much of the conflict of that strike. The intervention of federal troops, along with the use of thousands of U.S. marshals and the Illinois National Guard, effectively broke the strike. *Granger Collection.*

When Coxey and several hundred followers arrived in Washington, police arrested Coxey and others for trespassing and dispersed the rest. Never before had so many voices urged federal officials to create jobs for the unemployed, nor had so many protesters ever marched on Washington.

Labor on the Defensive: Homestead and Pullman

In the 1890s, workers often found that even the largest unions could not withstand the power of the new industrial companies. A major demonstration of this power came in 1892 in Homestead, Pennsylvania, at the giant Carnegie Steel plant that was managed by Henry Clay Frick, Carnegie's partner. The plant was a stronghold of the Amalgamated Association of Iron, Steel, and Tin Workers, the largest American Federation of Labor (AFL) union, which had a contract with Carnegie Steel. When Frick proposed major cuts in wages, the union balked. Frick then locked out the union members and prepared to bring in replacements.

Frick hired as guards three hundred agents of the Pinkerton National Detective Agency. They came by riverboat, but ten thousand strikers and community supporters resisted when the private army tried to land. Shots rang out. In the ensuing gun battle, seven Pinkertons and nine strikers were killed, and sixty

people were injured. The Pinkertons surrendered, leaving the strikers in control. Soon after, however, the governor of Pennsylvania sent in the state militia to patrol the city and incidentally to protect the strikebreakers. The Amalgamated Association never recovered. This crushing defeat suggested that no union could stand up to America's industrial giants, especially when those companies could call on the government for assistance.

A similar fate befell the most ambitious organizing drive of the 1890s. In 1893, under the leadership of **Eugene V. Debs,** railway workers launched the American Railway Union (ARU). Born in Indiana in 1855, Debs had served as an officer of the locomotive firemen's union. Railway workers had organized separate unions for engineers, firemen, switchmen, and conductors, but Debs hoped to bring all railway workers together into one union. Instead of using skill as the qualification for membership, he proposed employment anywhere in the railway industry as the basis for membership, thereby creating an **industrial union.**

Eugene V. Debs American Railway Union leader who was jailed for his role in the Pullman strike; he later became a leading socialist and ran for president.

industrial union Union that organizes all workers in an industry, whether skilled or unskilled, and regardless of occupation.

Success came quickly. Within a year, the ARU claimed 150,000 members and became the largest single union in the nation.

The twenty-four railway companies whose lines entered Chicago had formed the General Managers Association (GMA) as a way of addressing their common problems. Alarmed at the rise of the ARU, they found an opportunity to challenge the new union in 1894. Striking workers at the Pullman Palace Car Company (a manufacturer of luxury railway cars) asked the ARU to boycott **Pullman cars**—to disconnect them from trains and proceed without them. When the ARU agreed, it found itself on a collision course with the GMA. The managers threatened to fire any worker who observed the boycott, but their real purpose, as expressed by the GMA chairman, was to eliminate the ARU and "to wipe him [Debs] out."

Within a short time, all 150,000 ARU members were on strike in support of members who were fired for boycotting Pullman cars. Rail traffic in and out of Chicago came to a halt, affecting railways from the Pacific Coast to New York State. The companies, however, found an ally in U.S. Attorney General Richard Olney, a former railroad lawyer. Olney obtained an **injunction** against the strikers on two grounds: that the strike prevented delivery of the mail and that it violated the recently approved Sherman Anti-Trust Act. Olney convinced President Cleveland to use thousands of **U.S. marshals** and federal troops to protect trains operated by strikebreakers. In response, mobs lashed out at railroad property, especially in Chicago, burning trains and buildings. ARU leaders condemned the violence, but a dozen people died before the strike finally ended. Union leaders, including Debs, were jailed, and the ARU was destroyed.

The depression that began in 1893 further weakened the unions. In 1894 Gompers acknowledged that nearly all AFL affiliates "had their resources greatly diminished and their efforts largely crippled" through lost strikes and unemployment. Nevertheless, the AFL hung on. By 1897, the organization claimed fifty-eight national unions with a combined membership of nearly 270,000.

The "Merger Movement"

As the economy revived in the late 1890s, Americans witnessed an astonishing number of mergers in manufacturing and mining—a "merger movement" that lasted from 1898 until 1902. The high point came in 1899, with 1,208 mergers involving $2.3 billion in capital. The merger movement resulted partly from economic weaknesses revealed by the depression, es-

pecially among railroad companies. The threat of vicious competition among reviving manufacturing companies prompted reorganization there too.

The most prominent of the new corporations was United States Steel. As the economy edged out of the depression, J. P. Morgan began combining separate steel-related companies to create a vertically integrated operation (see pages 505, 532). Andrew Carnegie had never carried vertical integration to the point of manufacturing final steel products such as wire, barrels, or tubes. By vertically integrating to include that last step, Morgan threatened to close off a significant part of Carnegie's market. Faced with the formidable prospect of having to build his own manufacturing plants for finished products, Carnegie sold all his holdings to Morgan for $480 million. In 1901 Morgan combined Carnegie's company with his own to create United States Steel, the first corporation capitalized at over a billion dollars (see Figure 20.1).

As had been true with railroad reorganization in the 1880s, investment bankers usually sought two objectives in reorganizing an industry: first, to make the industry stable so that investments would yield predictable dividends, and second, to make the industry efficient and productive so that dividends would be high. Toward that end, investment bankers not only drove the mergers but also placed their representatives on the boards of directors of the newly created companies, to guarantee that those two objectives were top priority. By 1912, the three leading New York banking firms together occupied 341 directorships in 112 major companies. Investment bankers argued that benefits from their activities extended far beyond the dividends that shareholders received. One of Morgan's associates claimed in 1901 that as a result of mergers and restructuring, "production would become more regular, labor would be more steadily employed at better wages, and panics caused by over-production would become a thing of the past."

In fact, the new industrial combinations failed to produce long-term economic stability. The economy continued to alternate between expansion and contraction. After the severe depression of 1893–1897, for example, a period of general expansion was interrupted by downturns in 1903, 1907–1908, 1910–1911,

---

Pullman car A luxury railroad passenger car.

injunction A court order requiring an individual or a group to do something or to refrain from doing something.

U.S. marshal A federal law-enforcement official.

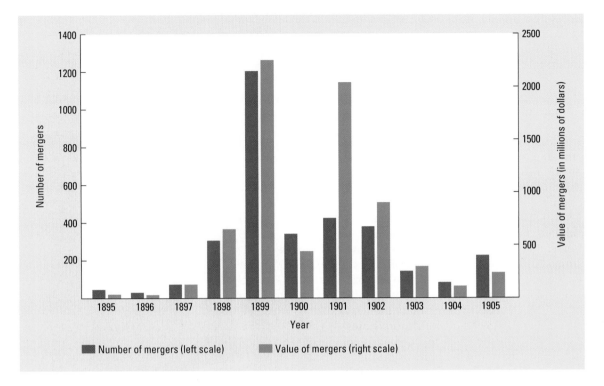

FIGURE 20.1 Recorded Mergers in Mining and Manufacturing, 1895–1905 The last few years of the 1890s and early 1900s witnessed the "merger movement," a restructuring of significant parts of corporate America. Note how the creation of United States Steel, the first "billion-dollar corporation," affects the bar for value for 1901.

and 1913–1914. Morgan's hopes for stability through centralized control failed to be realized, but his activities and those of his contemporaries created many of the characteristics of modern business. Many industries were oligopolistic, dominated by a few vertically integrated companies, and the stock market had moved beyond the sale of railroad securities to play an important role in raising capital for industry.

Political Realignment

- What main issues divided the candidates in the 1896 presidential election?

- What were the short-term and long-term results of the election?

During the 1890s, the nation underwent a series of political changes that, taken together, resulted in a significantly different political system. One set of changes took place in the South, where Mississippi Democrats led the way to disfranchisement and segregation of southern African Americans. Nationally,

Cleveland and the Democrats failed to stabilize the collapsing economy. Their failure opened the door to Republican victories in 1894. When the Democrats in 1896 adopted some of the Populists' issues and nominated a candidate sympathetic to many Populist goals, the People's Party threw in its lot with the Democrats, but the rebounding Republicans scored a major victory that year.

The Second Mississippi Plan and the Atlanta Compromise

In the 1890s, politics in the South underwent a major shift, toward writing white supremacy into law. Although Reconstruction came to an end in 1877 (see page 479), the Civil Rights Act of 1875, at least in theory, protected African Americans against discrimination in public places (see page 475). Some state laws required racial separation—for example, many states prohibited racial intermarriage. State or local law, or sometimes local practice, had produced racially separate school systems, cemeteries, hospitals, churches, and other voluntary organizations. Segregation existed throughout the South, frequently driven by local custom and the ever-present threat of violence against any African American who dared to challenge it. Restrictions on black political participation were also extralegal, enforced through coercion or intimidation.

Then, in the **Civil Rights cases** of 1883, the U.S. Supreme Court ruled the Civil Rights Act of 1875 unconstitutional. The Court said that the "equal protection" clause of the Fourteenth Amendment applied only to states and not to individuals and companies. Thus state governments were obligated to treat all citizens as equal before the law, but private businesses need not offer equal access to their facilities. Now southern lawmakers slowly began to require businesses to practice segregation. In 1887 the Florida legislature ordered separate accommodations on railroad trains. Mississippi passed a similar law the next year, as did Louisiana in 1890, and four more states followed in 1891. Law and social custom began to specify greater racial separation in other ways too.

Mississippi whites took a more brazen step in 1890, holding a state constitutional convention to eliminate African Americans' participation in politics. The new provisions did not mention the word *race*. Instead, they imposed a **poll tax,** a literacy test, and assorted other requirements for voting. Everyone understood, though, that these measures were designed to disfranchise black voters. Men who failed the literacy test could vote if they could understand a section of the state constitution or law when a local (white) official read it to them. The typical result was that the only illiterates who could vote were white. Most of the South watched this so-called Second Mississippi Plan unfold with great interest (see page 480 for the first Mississippi Plan). No other state moved immediately to imitate Mississippi, but the defeat of the Lodge bill in 1890 seemed to indicate that the federal government would not intervene to protect black rights.

In 1895 a black educator signaled his apparent willingness to accept disfranchisement and segregation for the moment. Born into slavery in 1856, **Booker T. Washington** had worked as a janitor while studying at Hampton Normal and Agricultural Institute in Virginia, a school that combined preparation for elementary school teaching with vocational education in agriculture and industrial work. Washington soon returned to Hampton as a teacher. In 1881 the Alabama legislature authorized a black **normal school** at Tuskegee. Washington became its principal,

This portrait of Booker T. Washington was taken in 1903. By the time of the photograph, he had already reached national fame as the leading black advocate for accommodation. *Library of Congress.*

Civil Rights cases A series of cases that came before the Supreme Court in 1883, in which the Court ruled that private companies could legally discriminate against individuals based on race.

poll tax An annual tax imposed on each citizen; used in some southern states as a way to disfranchise black voters, as the only penalty for not paying the tax was the loss of the right to vote.

Booker T. Washington Former slave who became an educator and founded Tuskegee Institute, a leading black educational institution; he urged southern African Americans to accept disfranchisement and segregation for the time being.

normal school A two-year school for preparing teachers for grades 1–8. The term is a direct translation from the French *école normale*, in which *école* means school and *normale* refers to norms or standards. Thus, an *école normale* was where future French teachers learned the standard curriculum that they were to teach to their students.

and he made Tuskegee Normal and Industrial Institute into a leading black educational institution.

In 1895 Atlanta played host to the Cotton States and International Exposition. The exposition directors invited Washington to speak at the opening ceremonies, hoping he could reach out to the anticipated crowd of southern whites, southern blacks, and northern whites. Washington did not disappoint the directors. In his speech, he seemed to accept an inferior status for blacks, at least for the present: "No race can prosper till it learns that there is as much dignity in tilling a field as in writing a poem. It is at the bottom of life we must begin, and not at the top." He also seemed to condone segregation: "In all things that are purely social, we can be as separate as the fingers, yet one as the hand in all things essential to mutual progress. The wisest among my race understand that the agitation of questions of social equality is the extremest folly." Furthermore, he implied that equal rights had to be earned: "It is important and right that all privileges of the law be ours, but it is vastly more important that we be prepared for the exercise of these privileges."

The speech—dubbed the **Atlanta Compromise**—won great acclaim for Washington. Southern whites were pleased to hear a black educator urge his race to accept segregation and disfranchisement. Northern whites too were receptive to the notion that the South would work out its thorny race relations by itself. Until his death in 1915, Washington was the most prominent black leader in the nation, at least among white Americans.

Among African Americans, Washington's message found a mixed reception. Some accepted his approach as the best that might be secured. Others criticized him for sacrificing black rights. Henry M. Turner, a bishop of the African Methodist Episcopal church in Atlanta, declared that Washington "will have to live a long time to undo the harm he has done our race." Privately, however, Washington never accepted disfranchisement and segregation as permanent fixtures in southern life.

Even as African Americans debated Washington's Atlanta speech, southern lawmakers were redefining the legal status of African Americans. The rise of southern Populism, with its support for a black and white political coalition of the poor, alarmed some southern conservatives. State after state followed the lead of Mississippi and disfranchised black voters. Louisiana, in 1898, added the infamous **grandfather clause,** which specified that men prevented from voting by the various new stipulations would be permitted to vote if their fathers or grandfathers had been eligible to vote in 1867 (before the Fourteenth Amendment extended the suffrage to African Americans). The rule reinstated poor or illiterate whites into the electorate but kept blacks out. Specific methods varied, but each southern state set up barriers to voting and then carved holes through which only whites could pass. Several southern states added an additional barrier in the form of the white primary, which specified that political parties had the right to limit participation in the process by which they chose their candidates. Southern Democrats, who had long proclaimed themselves to be the "white man's party" or the party of white supremacy, quickly restricted their primaries and conventions to whites only. South Carolina took this step first, in 1896, and other states soon followed. Even as southern states were removing African Americans from their political systems, some southern politicians sought to deflect the remaining attraction of populism by arguing for the unity of all white voters in support of white supremacy.

Southern lawmakers also began to extend segregation by law. They were given a major assist by the decision of the U.S. Supreme Court in ***Plessy v. Ferguson*** (1896), a case that involved a Louisiana law requiring segregated railroad cars. When the Court ruled that "separate but equal" facilities did not violate the equal protection clause of the Fourteenth Amendment, southern legislators soon applied that reasoning to other areas of life, eventually requiring segregation of everything from prisons to telephone booths—and especially such public places as parks and restaurants.

Violence directed against blacks accompanied the new laws, providing an unmistakable lesson in the

---

Atlanta Compromise Name applied to Booker T. Washington's 1895 speech in which he urged African Americans to temporarily accept segregation and disfranchisement and to work for economic advancement as a way to recover their civil rights.

grandfather clause Provision in Louisiana law that permitted a person to vote if his father or grandfather had been entitled to vote in 1867; designed to permit white men to vote who might otherwise be disfranchised by laws targeting blacks. Often applied to any law that permits some people to evade current legal provisions based on past practice.

Plessy v. Ferguson Supreme Court decision in 1896 that upheld a Louisiana law requiring the segregation of railroad facilities on the grounds that "separate but equal" facilities were constitutional under the Fourteenth Amendment.

The Defeat of the Lodge Bill

The failure of the Fifty-first Congress to approve the Lodge bill marked a retreat from federal enforcement of voting rights for seventy-five years. After the end of Reconstruction, some Republicans, especially those from New England, had continued to agitate for federal enforcement of voting rights but could do nothing about it given the Democrats' control of the House of Representatives. After the defeat of the Lodge bill in a Republican Congress, Republicans made no further effort to raise the issue.

In the absence of federal enforcement of voting rights, southern states systematically deprived African Americans of the voting rights supposedly guaranteed by the Fourteenth and Fifteenth Amendments to the Constitution, as well as legally requiring the segregation of nearly every aspect of southern life. Many African Americans and a few white allies continued to challenge this situation, but their efforts did not succeed until after World War II. Serious federal enforcement of voting rights came only with the Voting Rights Act of 1965, a measure that included a number of features similar to the Lodge bill. The 1965 act has since been amended, interpreted by the courts, and periodically extended, most recently in 1982, when it was extended for a term of twenty-five years.

consequences of resistance. From 1885 to 1900, when the South was redefining relations between the races, the region witnessed more than twenty-five hundred deaths by lynching—about one every two days. The victims were almost all African Americans, and the largest numbers were in the states with the most black residents. Once the new order was in place, lynching deaths declined slightly.

The Failure of the Divided Democrats

While the South was eliminating African Americans from state and local politics, very different political changes were under way elsewhere. When Congress met in 1893, the majority Democrats faced several controversial issues, especially silver coinage and the tariff. The depression and unemployment also demanded attention. President Cleveland, holding staunchly to his party's traditional commitment to minimal government and laissez faire, opposed any federal assistance to those in need. And, in the midst of the nation's financial crisis, Cleveland suffered a personal crisis. Doctors detected cancer in his mouth. Fearing that news of his condition might lead to further financial panic, the president kept his surgery and recuperation secret.

Many business leaders argued that the Sherman Silver Purchase Act (1890; see page 605) had caused the gold drain that set off the depression, but many western and southern Democrats supported it as better than no silver coinage at all. Convinced that silver coinage had contributed to the economic collapse, Cleveland asked Congress to repeal the Sherman Silver Purchase Act. In the House of Representatives, most Republicans voted for repeal, but more than a third of the Democrats voted against it. In the Senate, Republicans supported Cleveland by 2 to 1, but Democrats divided almost evenly. Cleveland won but divided his own party, pitting the Northeast against the West and much of the South.

The Democrats still faced the major challenge of the tariff. After their outspoken condemnation of the McKinley Tariff and commitment to cut tariff rates, they now had to demonstrate that they kept their word. The tariff bill produced by the House reduced duties, tried to balance sectional interests, and created an income tax to replace lost federal revenue. In the Senate, however, some Democrats tagged on so many amendments and compromises that Cleveland characterized the result as "party dishonor." He refused to sign it, and it became law without his signature in 1894. (The Supreme Court soon declared the income tax unconstitutional.)

Voters recorded their disgust with the disorganized Democrats in the 1894 elections. Democrats lost everywhere but in the Deep South, giving up 113 seats in the House of Representatives. Populists made few gains and suffered losses in some of their previous strongholds. Republicans scored their biggest gain in Congress ever, adding 117 House seats. Not surprisingly, Republicans looked forward eagerly to the approaching 1896 presidential election.

Repeal of the Sherman Act failed to stop the flow of gold from the Treasury, as investors responded to economic uncertainties by converting their securities to gold. The gold reserve fell dangerously low in 1895,

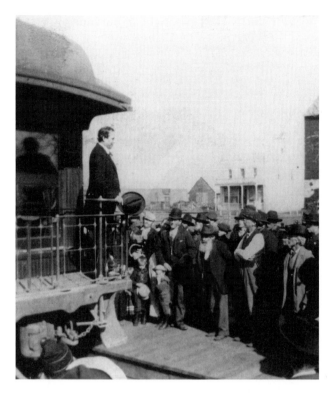 

In 1896, William Jennings Bryan (left), candidate for the Democratic, Populist, and Silver Republican Parties, traveled some eighteen thousand miles in three months, speaking to about 5 million people. William McKinley (right), the Republican, stayed home in Canton, Ohio, greeting thousands of well-wishers. *Bryan: Nebraska State Historical Society; McKinley: Ohio Historical Society.*

causing some to fear that the government might be unable to meet its obligations. In desperation, Cleveland turned to J. P. Morgan for assistance in floating a bond issue to restore the gold reserve. Cleveland now came under renewed criticism, both for the price paid to Morgan and for going to Morgan—symbol of Wall Street and the trusts—in the first place.

The 1896 Election: Bryan Versus McKinley, Silver Versus Protection

Republicans confidently anticipated victory in the presidential election of 1896. They nominated William McKinley, a Union veteran who had risen to the rank of major. McKinley had served fourteen years in Congress (where he had specialized in the tariff) and two terms as governor of Ohio. Known as a calm and competent leader, McKinley billed himself as the "Ad-

vance Agent of Prosperity." The Republican platform supported the gold standard and opposed silver, but McKinley preferred to focus on the tariff. When the convention voted against silver, several western Republicans walked out of the convention and out of the party.

When the Democratic convention met, silverites held the majority but were split among several candidates. Then the platform committee chose **William Jennings Bryan** of Nebraska to speak in a convention debate on silver. Blessed with a commanding voice, Bryan had won election to the House of Representatives in 1890 and 1892 and gained national attention

William Jennings Bryan Nebraska congressman who advocated free coinage of silver, opposed imperialism, and ran for president unsuccessfully three times on the Democratic ticket.

Political buttons with pins attached to the back were patented shortly before the 1896 presidential campaign, and they were in great abundance that year. The Bryan-Sewall button pictured shows a clock at 16 minutes to 1:00, a reference to the Democratic Party's commitment to increase the coinage of silver dollars, with a ratio of 16:1 between the weight of silver in a silver dollar to the weight of gold in a gold dollar. The McKinley campaign made a strenuous effort to reach all organized groups that might support their candidate and to appeal to their group's interest. This button celebrates support for McKinley by a wheelmen's club—that is, an organization of bicyclists, and the background of the button depicts a bicycle wheel. *Collection of Janice L. and David J. Frent.*

for his eloquent defense of silver. His speech was masterful. Defining the issue as a conflict between "the producing masses" and "the idle holders of idle capital," he argued that the first priority of federal policy should be "to make the masses prosperous," rather than to benefit the rich in the hope that "their prosperity will leak through on those below." His closing rang defiant: "We will answer their demand for a gold standard by saying to them: You shall not press down upon the brow of labor this crown of thorns. You shall not crucify mankind upon a cross of gold." The speech provoked an enthusiastic half-hour demonstration in support of silver—and Bryan. Only 36 years old, Bryan soon won the presidential nomination.

The Populists and the defecting western Republicans, who were quickly dubbed Silver Republicans, held nominating conventions next, amid frustration that the Democrats had stolen their thunder. Bryan favored silver, the income tax, and a broad range of reforms that Populists also favored, and he had worked closely with Populists. Populists felt compelled to give him their nomination too, and Silver Republicans did the same. Subsequently, a group of Cleveland supporters nominated a Gold Democratic candidate.

Bryan and McKinley fought all-out campaigns but used sharply contrasting tactics. Bryan, vigorous and young, knew that his speaking voice was his greatest campaign tool. He took his case directly to the voters in four grueling train journeys through twenty-six states and more than 250 cities. Speaking to perhaps 5 million people in all, he stressed over and over that the most important issue was silver and that other reforms would follow once it was settled. Large crowds of excited and enthusiastic supporters greeted him nearly everywhere.

McKinley stayed at home in Canton, Ohio, and campaigned from his front porch. The Republicans not only flooded the country with speakers, pamphlets, and campaign paraphernalia but also chartered trains and brought thousands of supporters to hear McKinley speak from his front porch. Many business leaders feared that Bryan and silver coinage would bring complete financial collapse, and they opposed Bryan's other proposals, such as the income tax and lower tariff rates. McKinley's campaign manager, Marcus Hanna, played on such fears to secure a campaign fund more than double the size of any previous effort, and many times what the Democrats were able to raise.

McKinley won by the largest margin of victory since 1872. As Map 20.2 shows, Bryan carried the South and nearly the entire West. McKinley's victory came in the urban, industrial Northeast (compare Map 20.2 with the Chapter 18 opening map on page 526). Of the twenty largest cities in the nation, only New Orleans went for Bryan. The crucial battleground was the Midwest, where McKinley carried not only the urban industrial regions but also many farming areas.

Bryan's defeat spelled the end of the Populist Party. Some Populists moved into Bryan's Democratic Party, but a few tried to hold together the tattered remnants of Populism. Others joined the Socialist Party, some returned to the Republican Party, and a few simply ignored politics. The issues they had raised—control of huge corporations, the extension of democratic processes, a fair monetary system—lived on, to be addressed by others. Their influence remained especially prominent in Bryan's wing of the Democratic Party.

After 1896: The New Republican Majority

The presidential election of 1896 focused on economic issues, sharpened by the depression. Bryan's

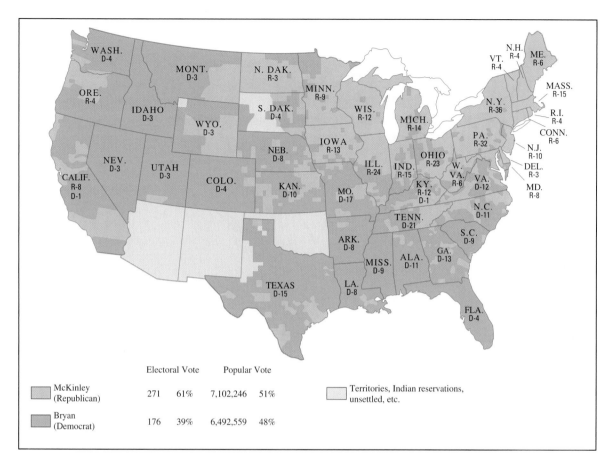

MAP 20.2 **Election of 1896**   Bryan could not win with just the votes of the South and West, for they had few electoral votes. Even if he had won all the West, South, and border states, he still would have needed one or more northeastern states. McKinley won in the urban, industrial core region and the more prosperous farming areas of the Midwest.

silver crusade appealed most to debt-ridden farmers, western miners, and traditional Democrats in the South and big cities. McKinley forged a broader appeal by emphasizing the gold standard and protective tariff as keys to economic recovery. For many urban residents— workers and the middle class alike—silver seemed to promise only higher prices, but the protective tariff meant manufacturing jobs. McKinley also won, in part, by restraining his party's nativist tendencies and denouncing the anti-Catholic American Protective Association, thereby gaining support among immigrants who approved of his stand on gold and the tariff.

McKinley's victory ushered in a generation of Republican dominance of national politics. The depression and the political campaigns of the 1890s caused some voters to reevaluate their partisan commitments

and to change parties. Republicans had majorities in the House of Representatives for twenty-eight of the thirty-six years after 1894, and in the Senate for thirty of those thirty-six years. Republicans also won seven of the nine presidential elections between 1896 and 1932. Similar patterns of Republican dominance appeared in state and local government, especially in the manufacturing belt.

The events of the 1890s brought about drastic changes in the Democratic Party. As Bryan led the Democrats over much of the next sixteen years, he and his allies moved the party away from its commitment to minimal government and laissez faire. While retaining Democrats' traditional distrust of monopoly and opposition to government favoritism toward business, Bryan and other new Democratic leaders agreed with the Populists that the solution to the

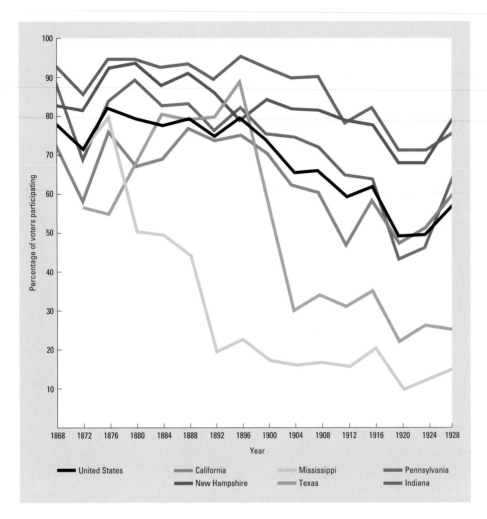

FIGURE 20.2 Voter Participation in Presidential Elections, 1868–1928, for the United States and for Selected States Note on the graph both the general pattern of declining participation and also the variation among states. For Mississippi and Texas, note the sharp decline that accompanied the disfranchisement of black voters. For California, note the short-term dip in 1912, the first year that women voted in that state. *Source:* U.S. Department of Commerce, Bureau of the Census, *Historical Statistics of the United States, Colonial Times to 1970,* Bicentennial edition, 2 vols. (Washington: Government Printing Office, 1975), 2:1071–72.

problems of economic concentration lay in a more active government that could limit monopoly power. "A private monopoly," Bryan never tired of repeating, "is indefensible and intolerable." Some traditional Democratic commitments persisted, however. The party clung to its version of states' rights, which permitted southern Democrats to perpetuate white-supremacist regimes. And most northern Democrats continued to oppose nativism and such moral reforms as prohibition.

McKinley provided strong executive leadership and worked closely with leaders of his party in Congress to develop and implement new policies. In 1897 a revised protective tariff, known as the Dingley Tariff for Nelson Dingley, the chair of the House Ways and Means Committee, fulfilled that Republican campaign promise, driving tariff rates sharply higher and reducing the list of imports that could enter the nation without charge. The surplus disappeared as an issue partly because of large naval expenditures. In

1900 the **Gold Standard Act** wrote that Republican pledge into law.

Although the majority of American voters now considered themselves Republicans, many of them held their new party commitments less intensely than before. For most voters before 1890, ethnicity and party went hand in hand. Now voters sometimes felt pulled toward one party by their economic situation and toward the other party by their ethnicity. Such voters sometimes supported Republicans for some offices and Democrats for others, choices now much easier because of the Australian ballot (see Chapter 18).

Sometimes voters resolved their conflicts by not voting. As more and more government positions became subject to the merit system, fewer and fewer party workers could be rewarded with jobs, so there were no legions of volunteers laboring to get people to the polls on election day. For these reasons and others, voter participation began to decline, dropping from 79 percent in 1896 to 65 percent in 1908, to 59 percent in 1912. Figure 20.2 shows this decline for the United States as a whole and for selected states. Part of this decline was caused by the disfranchisement of African Americans in the South (note Mississippi and Texas) and, during the early twentieth century, the disfranchisement of some northern voters through a variety of new voting rules. Some part of the falling turnout rate, however, reflected eligible voters who neglected to vote.

The political role of newspapers also changed. In the 1890s, technological advances in paper manufacturing and printing, together with increasing numbers of literate adults, brought the emergence of mass circulation newspapers. Enterprising publishers, notably William Randolph Hearst and Joseph Pulitzer, transformed large urban newspapers, competing for readership through eye-catching headlines and sensational stories. As they focused on increasing their circulation and advertising, they also played down their ties to political parties. Some journalists began to develop the idea of providing balanced coverage of both parties.

American politics in 1888 looked much like American politics in 1876 or even 1844. But in the 1890s, American politics changed. In the early 1900s, the continued decline of political parties and partisan loyalties among voters combined with the emergence of organized interest groups to create even more change, producing the major structural features of American politics in the twentieth century.

Stepping into World Affairs: Harrison and Cleveland

■ How and why did some Americans' attitudes about the U.S. role in world affairs begin to change between 1889 and 1897?

■ What were the policy implications of these changes?

During the 1890s, America's involvement in world affairs changed in important ways. One element revolved around a new role for the U.S. Navy and the commissioning of modern ships able to carry it out. Another related to the emergence and acceptance of new concepts of America's global status and foreign policy.

Building a Navy

Alfred Thayer Mahan played a key role in the development of a modern navy. President of the Naval War College, Captain Mahan exerted a powerful influence. In lectures to navy officers, in his book *The Influence of Sea Power upon History* (1890), and in articles in popular magazines and journals, Mahan argued that sea power had been the determining factor in the great European power struggles since the mid-seventeenth century. He also explored the significance of geography, population, and government as they related to establishing sea power, and he drew implications for his own day. He urged support for a strong merchant marine and advocated a large, modern navy centered on huge, powerful battleships capable of carrying American power to distant seas. He also stressed the need to extend American power beyond the national boundaries, to establish and control a canal through Central America, command the Caribbean, dominate strategic locations in the Pacific, and create naval bases at key points.

In 1889, with Harrison in the White House and Republican majorities in both houses of Congress, Secretary of the Navy Benjamin F. Tracy urged Congress to modernize the navy and to expand it significantly: eighteen more battleships (up from two), nearly fifty

Gold Standard Act Law passed by Congress in 1900 that made gold the monetary standard for all currency issued.

Alfred Thayer Mahan Naval officer and specialist on naval history who stressed the importance of sea power in international politics and diplomacy.

As late as 1880, the U.S. Navy specified that ship captains should use steam power only when "absolutely necessary" and should otherwise rely on sail. All this changed when Congress authorized the construction of several modern, steel, steam-powered ships, capable of carrying war to distant parts of the globe. This engraving shows the launching of the battleship *Maine* at the New York Navy Yard on November 12, 1889. The *Maine* was the nation's first modern battleship and the prototype for those that followed. *United States Naval Institute.*

more cruisers, and more smaller vessels. Tracy's ambitious proposal might have eliminated the federal budget surplus all by itself! Congress did not give him all that he asked for but did vote to create a modern navy centered on battleships. When construction was under way on three modern battleships, Tracy happily announced that "we shall rule [the sea] as certainly as the sun doth rise!"

A New American Mission?

Mahan's strategic arguments and Tracy's battleship launchings came as some Americans began, in Mahan's phrase, to "look outward." Appeals for change came from many sources: Protestant ministers, scholars, business figures, historians, politicians. Together they redefined the way American policymakers viewed the role of the nation in world affairs. Josiah Strong, for example, offered the perspective of a Protestant minister and missionary. His book *Our Country* (1885) argued that expansion of American Protestant ideals to the world constituted a Christian duty and was practically inevitable. "The world is to be Christianized

and civilized," he predicted, adding that "commerce follows the missionary."

Lewis Henry Morgan's book *Ancient Society* (1877) influenced not only federal Indian policy but also thinking about other parts of the world. Theodore Roosevelt, writing two years before he became president, implicitly accepted Morgan's analysis when he argued that conflict was inevitable when "civilized" and "barbarian" peoples came into contact because barbarians were inherently warlike. In such a situation, Roosevelt argued, expansion by "a great civilized power" not only extended peace but also meant "a victory for law, order, and righteousness."

Social Darwinism (see page 506) and the notion of "progress" merged with a belief in the superiority of the Anglo-Saxons—the people of England and their descendants. In the 1880s, popular books claimed that Anglo-Saxons had demonstrated a unique capacity for civilization and had a duty to enlighten and uplift other peoples. Albert Beveridge, a Republican senator from Indiana, blended some of these ideas with American nationalism when he proclaimed, "[God] has made us the master organizers of the world to establish system where chaos reigns." Rudyard Kipling, an English poet, expressed this feeling in 1899 when he urged the United States to "take up the white man's burden," a phrase that came to describe a self-imposed obligation to go into distant lands, bring the supposed blessings of Anglo-Saxon civilization to their peoples, Christianize them, and sell them Western products.

Today historians understand Anglo-Saxonism and the "white man's burden" as deeply tinged with racism. Such views assumed that some people, by virtue of race, possessed a superior capability for self-government and cultural accomplishment. This thinking elevated only one cultural pattern as "civilization," dismissing all others as inferior and ignoring their cultural accomplishments.

Revolution in Hawai`i

Belief in the "white man's burden," together with new understandings of the strategic significance of the Pacific, focused the attention of many Americans on Hawai`i when a revolution broke out there early in 1893. The most immediate causes of the revolution stemmed from changes in American tariff rates on sugar. In 1890, when the McKinley Tariff put sugar on the free list, all imported sugar entered the United States without paying a tariff. Previously only Hawaiian sugar had entered duty-free. Now it faced stiff competition in the American market, notably from Cuban sugar. The McKinley Tariff had also provided that sugar grown within the United States was to receive a subsidy of 2 cents per pound. Facing economic disaster, many Hawaiian planters began to talk of annexation to the United States.

In 1891 King Kalakaua died and was succeeded by his sister, **Lili`uokalani,** who hoped to restore Hawai`i to the indigenous Hawaiians and to return political power to the monarchy. Some haole entrepreneurs feared that they might lose both their political clout and their economic holdings. On January 17, 1893, a group of plotters proclaimed a republic and announced that they would seek annexation by the United States. John L. Stevens, the U.S. minister to Hawai`i, ordered the landing of 150 U.S. Marines. Lili`uokalani surrendered, as she put it, "to the superior force of the United States." Stevens immediately recognized the new republic, declared it a **protectorate** of the United States, and raised the American flag.

The Harrison administration **repudiated** Stevens's overzealous deeds but opened negotiations with representatives of the new republic. The Senate received a treaty of annexation shortly before Cleveland be-

Queen Lili`uokalani came to the Hawaiian throne in 1891 and hoped to regain royal power that had been lost by her predecessor, King Kalakaua. Instead, in 1893, haole planters and businessmen overthrew the monarchy, aided by 150 U.S. Marines ordered ashore by the American minister to Hawai`i. *The Lili`uokalani Trust.*

came president. Cleveland was willing to consider annexing Hawai`i if the Hawaiian people requested it, but he withdrew the annexation treaty to study it further. When he learned that the revolution could not have succeeded without the intervention of the marines, he asked the new officials to restore the queen. They refused, and Hawai`i continued as an independent republic, dominated by its haole business and planter community.

**Lili`uokalani**   Last reigning queen of Hawai`i, whose desire to restore land to the Hawaiian people and perpetuate the monarchy prompted haole planters to remove her from power in 1893.

protectorate   A country partially controlled by a stronger power and dependent on that power for protection from foreign threats.

repudiate   To reject as invalid or unauthorized.

Crises in Latin America

Although Harrison and Cleveland acted at cross-purposes regarding Hawai`i, they moved in similar directions with regard to Latin America. Both presidents extended American involvement, and both threatened the use of force.

A rebellion in Chile in 1891 ended with victory for the rebels. Because the American minister to Chile seemed to side against the rebels, anti-American feelings ran high. In October 1891, in Valparaiso, a mob set upon several American sailors on shore leave and beat them, injuring several and killing two. The Chilean government gave no sign of apologizing, so Harrison threatened "such action as may be necessary." Using language that Americans considered insulting, the Chilean government insinuated that Harrison was wrong. When Harrison responded with plans for a naval war and threats to cut off diplomatic relations, Chile gave in, apologized, and promised to pay damages and to meet other terms.

In 1895 and 1896, Cleveland also took the nation to the edge of war. At issue was a long-standing boundary dispute between Venezuela and British Guiana. Venezuela proposed arbitration, which Cleveland also favored, but Britain refused. Discovery of gold in the contested region intensified claims by both sides. In July 1895, Secretary of State Richard Olney demanded that Britain submit the issue to arbitration. Citing the Monroe Doctrine, he bombastically declared the United States to be preeminent throughout the Western Hemisphere. The British still refused. Cleveland then asked Congress for authority to determine the boundary and enforce it. Thus Britain faced the possibility of conflict with the United States—and at a time when it was increasingly concerned about the rising power of Germany and was facing war in South Africa against the Boer republics. Britain agreed to arbitration.

In both instances, American presidents behaved more forcefully than had any of their predecessors for twenty years. Both times, the American response surprised the other nation. Harrison's action toward Chile was a heavy-handed assertion of American power unlikely to encourage closer relations with Latin America. Cleveland's major objective was to serve notice to European imperial powers that the Western Hemisphere was off-limits in the ongoing scramble for colonies.

Cleveland faced a very different situation in Cuba. Cuba and Puerto Rico were all that remained of the once-mighty Spanish Empire in the Americas, and Cuba had rebelled against Spain repeatedly. In the early 1890s, when the McKinley Tariff permitted Cuban sugar to enter the United States without charge, the Cuban sugar industry boomed. By 1894, the United States was receiving nearly 90 percent of Cuba's exports, primarily sugar. That year, however, a new tariff law restored a high duty on Cuban sugar, removed the tariff on Hawaiian sugar, and caused a depression in Cuba. Fueled by economic distress, a new insurrection erupted against Spanish rule, and the advocates of *Cuba libre* ("a free Cuba") received support from sympathizers in the United States. In 1896, in response to the **insurgents' guerrilla warfare,** the Spanish commander, General Valeriano Weyler, established a **reconcentration** policy. The civilian population was ordered into fortified towns or camps. Everyone who remained outside these fortified areas was assumed to be an insurgent, subject to military action. Disease and starvation soon swept through the camps, killing many Cubans.

American newspapers—especially **Joseph Pulitzer's** *New York World* and **William Randolph Hearst's** *New York Journal*—vied in portraying Spanish atrocities. Papers sent their best reporters to Cuba and exaggerated the reports, a practice called **yellow journalism.** Sickened from the steady diet of such sensational stories, many Americans began clamoring for action to rescue the Cubans.

Cleveland reacted cautiously, intent on avoiding American involvement. He proclaimed American neutrality and warned Americans not to support the insurrection. When members of Congress pushed Cleveland to seek Cuban independence, he only urged

---

insurgents Rebels or revolutionaries.

guerrilla warfare An irregular form of war carried on by small bodies of men acting independently.

reconcentration Spanish policy in Cuba in 1896 that ordered the civilian population into fortified camps so as to isolate and annihilate the Cuban revolutionaries who remained outside the camps.

Joseph Pulitzer Hungarian-born newspaper publisher whose *New York World* printed sensational stories about Cuba that helped precipitate the Spanish-American War.

William Randolph Hearst Publisher and rival to Pulitzer whose newspaper, the *New York Journal,* sensationalized and distorted stories and actively promoted the war with Spain.

yellow journalism The use of sensational exposés, embellished reporting, and attention-grabbing headlines to sell newspapers.

On February 15, 1898, an explosion destroyed the American battleship *Maine* (see p. 624 for the launching of the *Maine*) as it lay at anchor in the harbor at Havana, Cuba. Some 260 Americans lost their lives. Many Americans blamed the Spanish government of Cuba, although there was no evidence to suggest who was responsible. *Library of Congress.*

Spain to grant some concessions to the insurgents. Cleveland doubted that the insurgents were capable of self-rule. Just as he had earlier opposed annexation of Samoa and Hawai`i, so now Cleveland resisted the notion of intervening in Cuba. He feared that such a move might lead to annexation regardless of the will of the Cuban people. Even so, by the time he left the presidency in early 1897, he had begun to warn Spain of possible American intervention.

Striding Boldly in World Affairs: McKinley, War, and Imperialism

■ What events led the United States into war with Spain?

■ What was the result of the war? Should Americans have been surprised about the outcome?

■ What new attitudes about America's role in world affairs appeared in the debate over the acquisition of new possessions?

In 1898 the United States went to war with Spain over Cuba. Far from combat, John Hay, the American ambassador to Great Britain, celebrated the conflict as "a splendid little war," and the description stuck. Some who promoted American intervention on behalf of the suffering Cubans envisioned a quick war to establish a Cuban republic. Others saw war with Spain as an opportunity to seize territory and acquire a colonial empire for the United States.

McKinley and War

William McKinley became president amid increasing demands for action regarding Cuba. He moved cautiously, however, gradually stepping up diplomatic efforts to resolve the crisis. Late that year Spain responded by softening the reconcentration policy and offering the Cubans limited self-government but not independence. In February 1898, however, two events scuttled progress toward a negotiated solution.

First, Cuban insurgents stole a letter written by **Enrique Dupuy de Lôme,** the Spanish minister to the United States, and released it to the *New York Journal.* In it, de Lôme criticized President McKinley as "weak and a bidder for the admiration of the crowd." The letter also implied that the Spanish government's commitment to reform in Cuba was not serious. Although de Lôme immediately resigned, the letter aroused intense anti-Spanish feeling among many Americans.

A few days later, on February 15, an explosion ripped open the American warship *Maine,* which

Enrique Dupuy de Lôme   Spanish minister to the United States whose private letter criticizing President McKinley was stolen and printed in the *New York Journal,* increasing anti-Spanish sentiment.

U.S.S. *Maine*   American warship that exploded in Havana Harbor in 1898, inspiring the motto "Remember the *Maine!*" which spurred the Spanish-American War.

was anchored in Havana Harbor, and it sank, killing more than 260 Americans. The yellow press accused Spain of sabotage but could produce no evidence. An official inquiry blamed a submarine mine but could not determine whose it may have been. (Years later, an investigation indicated that the blast was probably of internal origin, resulting from a fire.) Regardless of how the explosion occurred, those advocating intervention now had a rallying cry: "Remember the *Maine!*"

McKinley extended his demands: an immediate end to the fighting, an end to reconcentration, measures to relieve the suffering, and **mediation** by McKinley himself. He also specified that one possible outcome of mediation might be Cuban independence. In reply, the Spanish government promised reforms, agreed to end reconcentration, and consented to cease fighting if the insurgents asked for an **armistice.** Spain was silent, though, on mediation by McKinley and independence for Cuba.

On April 11, McKinley sent a message to Congress stating that "the war in Cuba must stop" and asking for authority to act. Congress answered on April 19 with four resolutions: (1) declaring that Cuba was and should be independent, (2) demanding that Spain withdraw "at once," (3) authorizing the president to use force to accomplish Spanish withdrawal, and (4) disavowing any intention to annex the island. The first three resolutions amounted to a declaration of war. The fourth is usually called the **Teller Amendment** for its sponsor, Senator Henry M. Teller, a Silver Republican from Colorado. In response, Spain declared war.

Most Americans wholeheartedly approved what they understood to be a war undertaken to bring independence and aid to the long-suffering Cubans. Some, however, distrusted the McKinley administration, fearing that a humanitarian war might become a struggle for the conquest of Cuba. In Congress, Democrats, Silver Republicans, and Populists sought recognition of the insurgents as the legitimate government of Cuba, but Republican congressional leaders squelched their efforts. The Teller Amendment also reflected a concern that the McKinley administration might try to make Cuba an American possession rather than granting it independence.

The "Splendid Little War"

Since 1895, Americans' attention had been riveted on Cuba. Thus many were surprised that the first engagement in the war occurred in the **Philippine Islands**— nearly halfway around the world from Cuba. A Spanish colony for three hundred years, the Philippines had rebelled repeatedly, most recently in 1896.

Some Americans understood the islands' strategic location with regard to eastern Asia—including Assistant Secretary of the Navy **Theodore Roosevelt.** In February 1898, six weeks before McKinley's war message to Congress, Roosevelt cabled George Dewey, the American naval commander in the Pacific, to crush the Spanish fleet at Manila Bay if war broke out.

At sunrise on Sunday, May 1, Dewey's squadron of four cruisers and three smaller vessels steamed into the harbor and quickly destroyed or captured ten Spanish cruisers and gunboats. The Spanish lost 381 men, and the Americans lost one, a victim of heat prostration. Dewey instantly became a national hero. A few weeks later, on June 21, an American cruiser secured the surrender of Spanish forces on the island of Guam, which is located in the Pacific roughly three-quarters of the way from Hawai`i to the Philippines (see the chapter-opening map on page 598).

Dewey's victory at Manila focused public attention on the Pacific and, for some, immediately raised the prospect of a permanent American presence there. This possibility, in turn, revived interest in the Hawaiian Islands—now seen as a crucial base halfway to the Philippines. The McKinley administration had negotiated a treaty of annexation with the Hawaiian government in 1897, shortly after Cleveland left the White House, but anti-imperialist sentiment in the Senate made approval unlikely. Now, with Dewey's victory and the prospect of an American base in the Philippines, McKinley revived the joint-resolution precedent by which Texas had been annexed in 1844. Only a majority vote in both houses of Congress was required to adopt a joint resolution, rather than the two-thirds vote of the Senate needed to approve a

mediation An attempt to bring about the peaceful settlement of a dispute through the intervention of a neutral party.

armistice An agreement to halt fighting, at least temporarily.

Teller Amendment Resolution approved by the U.S. Senate in 1898, by which the United States promised not to annex Cuba; introduced by Senator Henry Teller of Colorado.

Philippine Islands A group of islands in the Pacific Ocean southeast of China that came under U.S. control in 1898 after the Spanish-American War; they became an independent nation after World War II.

Theodore Roosevelt American politician and writer who advocated war against Spain in 1898; elected as McKinley's vice president in 1900, he became president in 1901 upon McKinley's assassination.

Theodore Roosevelt's Rough Riders, on foot because there was not room aboard ship for their horses, are shown in the background of this artist's depiction of the battle for Kettle Hill, a part of the larger battle for San Juan Hill, overlooking the city of Santiago, Cuba. The artist has put into the foreground members of the Ninth and Tenth Cavalry, both African American units, that also played a key role in that engagement, but one often overlooked because of the attention usually given Roosevelt and the Rough Riders. *Chicago Historical Society.*

treaty. Annexation of Hawai`i was accomplished on July 7.

Dewey's victory demonstrated that the American navy was clearly superior to Spain's. In contrast, the Spanish army in Cuba outnumbered the entire American army by more than five to one. The Spanish troops also had years of experience fighting in Cuba. When war was declared, McKinley called for volunteers, and nearly a million men responded—five times as many as the army could enlist. The army now needed many weeks to train and supply the new recruits.

Sent to training camps in the South, the new soldiers found chaos and confusion. Food, uniforms, and equipment arrived at one location while the men for whom they were intended stood hungry and idle at another. Uniforms were often of heavy wool, totally unsuited for the climate and season. Disease raged through some camps, killing many men. Others died from tainted food, called "embalmed beef" by the troops. Some African American soldiers refused to comply with racial segregation, and many white southerners objected to the presence in their communities of so many uniformed and armed black men. Congress declared war in late April, but not until June did the first troop transports head for Cuba.

When they finally arrived in Cuba, American forces tried to capture the port city of Santiago, where the Spanish fleet had taken refuge. Inexperienced, poorly equipped, and unfamiliar with the terrain, the Americans landed some distance from Santiago and then assaulted the fortified hills surrounding the city. Theodore Roosevelt had resigned as assistant secretary of the navy to organize a cavalry unit known as the **Rough Riders.** At Kettle Hill, he led a successful charge of Rough Riders and regular army units, including parts of the Ninth and Tenth Cavalry, made up of African Americans. All but Roosevelt were on foot because their horses had not yet arrived. Driving the Spanish from the crest of Kettle Hill cleared a serious impediment to the assault on nearby, and strategically more important, San Juan Heights and San Juan Hill. Roosevelt and his men were less prominent in that attack, but journalists loved Roosevelt—and newspapers all over the country declared Roosevelt the hero of the Battle of San Juan Hill.

Americans suffered heavy casualties during the first few days of the attack on Santiago. Nearly 10 percent of the troops were killed or wounded. Worsening the situation, the surgeon in charge of medical facilities refused assistance from Red Cross nurses

Rough Riders The First Volunteer Cavalry, a brigade recruited for action in the Spanish-American War by Theodore Roosevelt, who served first as the brigade's lieutenant colonel, then its colonel.

because he thought field hospitals were not appropriate places for women. He was later overruled. Red Cross nurses also helped care for injured Cuban insurgents and civilians.

Once American troops secured control of the high ground around Santiago harbor, the Spanish fleet (four cruisers and two destroyers) tried to escape. A larger American fleet under Admiral William Sampson and Commodore Winfield Schley met them and duplicated Dewey's rout at Manila—every Spanish ship was sunk or run aground. The Spanish suffered 323 deaths, the Americans one.

Their fleet destroyed, surrounded by American troops, the Spanish in Santiago finally surrendered on July 17. A week later American forces occupied Puerto Rico. Spanish land forces in the Philippines surrendered when the first American troops arrived in mid-August. The "splendid little war" lasted only sixteen weeks. More than 306,000 men served in the American forces. Only 385 of them died in battle, but more than 5,000 died of disease and other causes.

The Treaty of Paris

On August 12, the United States and Spain agreed to stop fighting and to hold a peace conference in Paris. The major question for the conference centered on the Philippines. Finley Peter Dunne, a popular humorist, parodied the national debate on the Philippines in a discussion between his fictional characters, Mr. Dooley (a Chicago saloonkeeper) and a customer named Hennessy. Hennessy insists that McKinley should take the islands. Dooley retorts that "it's not more than two months since you learned whether they were islands or canned goods," then confesses his own indecision: "I can't annex them because I don't know where they are. I can't let go of them because someone else will take them if I do. . . . It would break my heart to think of giving people I've never seen or heard tell of back to other people I don't know. . . . I don't know what to do about the Philippines. And I'm all alone in the world. Everybody else has made up his mind."

McKinley voiced as many doubts as Mr. Dooley. At first, he seemed to favor only a naval base, leaving Spain in control elsewhere. However, Spanish authority collapsed throughout the islands by mid-August as Filipino insurgents took charge. Britain, Japan, and Germany watched carefully, and one or another of them seemed likely to step in if the United States withdrew. By then, McKinley and his advisers had apparently decided that defending a naval base on Manila Bay would require control of the entire island group. No one seems to have seriously considered the Filipinos' desire for independence.

McKinley was well aware of the political and strategic importance of the Philippines for eastern Asia. He invoked other reasons, however, when he explained his decision to a group of visiting Methodists. He repeatedly prayed for guidance on the Philippine question, he told them. Late one night, he said, it came to him that "there was nothing left for us to do but to take them all, and to educate the Filipinos, and uplift and civilize and Christianize them and by God's grace do the very best we could by them." In fact, most Filipinos had been Catholics for centuries, but no one ever expressed more clearly the concept of the "white man's burden."

Spain resisted giving up the Philippines, but McKinley remained adamant. The Treaty of Paris, signed in December 1898, required Spain to surrender all claim to Cuba, cede Puerto Rico and Guam to the United States, and sell the Philippines for $20 million. For the first time in American history, a treaty acquiring new territory failed to confer U.S. citizenship on the residents. Nor did the treaty mention future statehood. Thus these acquisitions represented a new kind of expansion—America had become a colonial power.

The terms of the **Treaty of Paris** dismayed Democrats, Populists, and some conservative Republicans. They immediately sparked a public debate over acquisition of the Philippines in particular and **imperialism** in general. An anti-imperialist movement quickly formed, with William Jennings Bryan, Grover Cleveland, Andrew Carnegie, Mark Twain, and Jane Addams among its outspoken proponents. The treaty provisions, they argued, denied self-government for the newly acquired territories. For the United States to hold colonies, they claimed, threatened the very concept of democracy. "The Declaration of Independence," warned Carnegie, "will make every Filipino a thoroughly dissatisfied subject." Others worried over the perversion of American values. "God Almighty help the party that seeks to give civilization and Christianity hypodermically with 13-inch guns," prayed Senator

> **Treaty of Paris** Treaty ending the Spanish-American War, under which Spain granted independence to Cuba, ceded Puerto Rico and Guam to the United States, and sold the Philippines to the United States for $20 million.
>
> **imperialism** The practice by which a nation acquires and holds colonies and other possessions, denies them self-government, and usually exploits them economically.

William Morris of Illinois. Some anti-imperialists argued from a racist perspective that Filipinos were incapable of taking part in a Western-style democracy and that the United States would be corrupted by ruling people unable to govern themselves. Union leaders, fearing Filipino migration to the United States, repeated arguments once used to secure Chinese exclusion.

Those who defended acquisition of the Philippines echoed McKinley's lofty pronouncements about America's duty along with more mundane claims about economic benefits. Albert Beveridge, senator from Indiana after 1899, presented the commercial benefits: "We are raising more than we can consume, making more than we can use. Therefore we must find new markets for our produce." Such "new markets" were not limited to the Philippines or other new possessions. A strong naval and military presence in the Philippines would make the United States a leading power in eastern Asia. American business might therefore anticipate support for their continued access to markets in China.

William Jennings Bryan, the Democratic presidential candidate in 1896, urged senators to approve the treaty. That way, he reasoned, the United States alone could determine the future of the Philippines. Once the treaty was approved, he argued, the United States should immediately grant them independence. By a narrow margin, the Senate approved the treaty on February 6, 1899. Soon after, senators rejected a proposal for Philippine independence.

Republic or Empire: The Election of 1900

Bryan hoped to make independence for the Philippines the central issue in the 1900 presidential election. He easily won the Democratic nomination for a second time, and the Democrats' platform condemned the McKinley administration for its "imperialism." Bryan found, however, that many conservative anti-imperialists would not support his candidacy because he still insisted on silver coinage and attacked big business.

The Republicans renominated McKinley. For vice president, they chose Theodore Roosevelt, "hero of San Juan Hill." The McKinley reelection campaign seemed unstoppable. Republican campaigners pointed proudly to a short and highly successful war, legislation on the tariff and gold standard, and the return of prosperity. Bryan repeatedly attacked imperialism. McKinley and Roosevelt never used the term at all and instead took pride in expansion. Republican campaigners questioned the patriotism of anyone who proposed to pull down the flag where it had once been raised. McKinley easily won a second term with 51.7 percent of the vote, carrying not only the states that had given him his victory in 1896 but also many of the western states where Populism had flourished.

Organizing an Insular Empire

The Teller Amendment specified that the United States would not annex Cuba, but the McKinley administration refused to recognize the insurgents as a legitimate government. Instead, the U.S. Army took control. Among other tasks, the army undertook sanitation projects intended to reduce disease, especially yellow fever. After two years of army rule, the McKinley administration permitted Cuban voters to hold a constitutional convention.

The convention met in 1900 and drafted a constitution modeled on that of the United States. Nowhere did it define relations between Cuba and the United States. In response, the McKinley administration drafted, and Congress adopted, terms for Cuba to adopt before the army would withdraw. Called the **Platt Amendment** for Senate Orville Platt, who introduced the conditions as an amendment to an army appropriations bill, the terms specified that (1) Cuba was not to make any agreement with a foreign power that impaired the island's independence, (2) the United States could intervene in Cuba to preserve Cuban independence and maintain law and order, and (3) Cuba was to lease facilities to the United States for naval bases and coaling stations. Cubans reluctantly agreed, changed their constitution, and signed a treaty with the United States stating the Platt conditions. In 1902 Cuba thereby became a protectorate of the United States.

The Teller Amendment did not apply to Puerto Rico. There, the army provided a military government until 1900, when Congress approved the **Foraker Act.** That act made Puerto Ricans citizens of Puerto Rico but not citizens of the United States. Under its provisions Puerto Rican voters were to elect a legislature, but

---

Platt Amendment   An amendment to the Army Appropriations Act of 1901, sponsored by Senator Orville Platt, which set terms for the withdrawal of the U.S. Army from Cuba.

Foraker Act   Law passed by Congress in 1900 that established civilian government in Puerto Rico; it provided for an elected legislature and a governor appointed by the U.S. president.

The Spanish banished Emilio Aguinaldo from the Philippines because of his efforts to end Spanish rule. American naval officials returned him to the islands. There he helped to establish an independent Filipino government and later led armed resistance to American authority until he was captured in 1901. This photograph was taken in 1900, at the height of what American officials termed the "Philippine insurrection" and what many Filipinos considered a war for independence. *Brown Brothers.*

final authority was to rest with a governor and council appointed by the president of the United States. In 1901, in the **Insular cases,** the U.S. Supreme Court confirmed the colonial status of Puerto Rico and, by implication, the other new possessions. The Court ruled that they were not equivalent to earlier territorial acquisitions and that their people did not possess the constitutional rights of citizens.

Establishment of a civil government in the Philippines took longer. Between Dewey's victory and the arrival of the first American soldiers three months later, a Philippine independence movement led by **Emilio Aguinaldo** established a provisional government and took control everywhere but Manila. (Manila

remained in Spanish hands until American troops arrived.) Aguinaldo and his government wanted independence. When the United States determined to keep the islands, the Filipinos resisted.

Quelling what American authorities called the "Philippine insurrection" required three years (1899–1902), took the lives of 4,200 American soldiers (more losses than in the Spanish-American War) and perhaps 700,000 or more Filipinos (most through disease and other noncombat causes), and cost $400 million (twenty times the price of the islands). When some Filipinos resorted to guerrilla warfare, U.S. troops adopted the same practices that Spain had used in Cuba. Both sides committed atrocities, and anti-imperialists pointed to brutish behavior by American troops as proof that a colonial policy was corrupting American values. American troops captured Aguinaldo in 1901, but resistance continued into mid-1902.

With defeat of Aguinaldo, Congress set up a government for the Philippines similar to that of Puerto Rico. Filipinos became citizens of the Philippine Islands, but not of the United States. The president of the United States appointed the governor. Filipino voters elected one house in the two-house legislature, and the governor appointed the other. Both the governor and the U.S. Congress could veto laws passed by the legislature. **William Howard Taft,** governor of the islands from 1901 to 1904, tried to build local support for American control, secured limited land reforms, and started to build public schools, hospitals, and sanitary facilities. However, when the first Philippine legislature met, in 1907, more than half of its members favored independence.

The Open Door and the Boxer Rebellion in China

Late in 1899, Britain, Germany, and the United States signed the Treaty of Berlin, which divided Samoa between Germany and the United States. The new Pa-

---

Insular cases Cases concerning Puerto Rico, in which the U.S. Supreme Court ruled in 1901 that people in new island territories did not automatically receive the constitutional rights of U.S. citizens.

Emilio Aguinaldo Leader of unsuccessful struggles for Philippine independence, first against Spain and then against the United States.

William Howard Taft Governor of the Philippines from 1901 to 1904; he was elected president of the United States in 1908 and became chief justice of the Supreme Court in 1921.

cific acquisitions of the United States—Hawai`i, the Philippines, Guam, and Samoa—were all endowed with excellent harbors and suitable sites for naval bases. Combined with the modernized navy, these acquisitions greatly strengthened American ability to protect access to commercial markets in eastern Asia and to assert American power in the region. The United States now began to seek full participation in the East Asian **balance of power.**

Weakened by war with Japan in 1894–1895, the Chinese government could not resist European nations' demands for territory. By 1899, Britain, Germany, Russia, and France had all carved out **spheres of influence**—areas where they claimed special rights, usually a monopoly over trade. In keeping with the treaty of 1844, the United States claimed no such privileges in China and argued instead for the "Open Door"—a policy whereby citizens of all nations would have equal status in seeking trade. American diplomats, however, began to fear the breakup of China into separate European colonies and the subsequent exclusion of American commerce.

In 1899 Secretary of State John Hay circulated a letter to Germany, Russia, Britain, France, Italy, and Japan, asking them to preserve some semblance of Chinese sovereignty within their spheres of influence and urging them not to discriminate against citizens of other nations who were engaged in commerce within their spheres. Hay wanted both to prevent the dismemberment of China and to maintain commercial access for American entrepreneurs throughout China. Some replies proved less than fully supportive, but Hay announced in a second letter that all had agreed to his so-called Open Door principles. Hay's letters have usually been called the **Open Door notes.**

The next year, in 1900, a Chinese secret society tried to expel all foreigners from China. Because the rebels used a clenched fist as their symbol, westerners called them Boxers. The Boxers laid siege to the section of Beijing, the Chinese capital, that housed foreign **legations.** Hay feared that the major powers might use the rebellion as a pretext to take control and divide China permanently. To block such a move, the United States took full part in an international military expedition to rescue the besieged foreign diplomats and to crush the **Boxer Rebellion.**

Although China did not lose territory, the intervening nations required it to pay an **indemnity.** After compensating U.S. citizens for their losses, the United States government returned the remainder of its indemnity to China. To show its appreciation, the Chinese government used the money to send Chinese students to study in the United States.

A FAIR FIELD AND NO FAVOR!
UNCLE SAM: "I'M OUT FOR COMMERCE, NOT CONQUEST!"

In this 1899 cartoon celebrating the Open Door policy, Uncle Sam insists that the nations of Europe must compete fairly for China's commerce and must not seize Chinese territory. In the background, John Bull (Britain) lifts his hat in approval. *Library of Congress.*

balance of power   In international politics, the notion that nations may restrict one another's actions because of the relative equality of their naval or military forces, either individually or through alliance systems.

sphere of influence   A territorial area where a foreign nation exerts significant authority.

Open Door notes   An exchange of diplomatic letters in 1899–1900 by which Secretary of State John Hay announced American support for Chinese autonomy and opposed efforts by other powers to carve China into exclusive spheres of influence.

legation   Diplomatic officials representing their nation to another nation, and their offices and residences.

Boxer Rebellion   Uprising in China in 1900 directed against foreign powers who were attempting to dominate China; it was suppressed by an international army that included American participation.

indemnity   Payment for damage, loss, or injury.

Individual Voices

Examining a Primary Source

Annie Diggs Sympathizes with Filipinos Seeking Independence

Annie L. Diggs, a leading Populist, wrote this poem in 1899. By then, the United States was using its army to suppress Aguinaldo's government in the Philippines, and the expression "little brown brother" was in widespread use to designate the people of the Philippines.

Little Brown Brother

Little Brown Brothers across the sea
Running your race for liberty,
Here's to you,
We've been there ourselves.

Odd little Brown Men,
like "jack-rabbits" you run. ■
Bang the Krag-Jorgensen*;
"Pick 'em off, it's great fun!"
Halt!
"Jack-rabbits" are they? . . .
Well, even sparrows fall not unheeded.

Halt! Who goes there?
Not jack-rabbits, not rebels, but Men.
Fighting for life, liberty, homes.
Homes? Bamboo huts.
Well, homes are homes, brown stone or bamboo. . . .

A Brown Man lies dead 'neath his own island sky;
A Brown Wife utters a strange wild cry,
The billowy deep brings the piteous sound
Hearts are the same God's sweet world round. ■

O little Brown Child whose father lies low,
Just when will your love and your loyalty flow . . .
To the Flag and the Nation that made you an orphan?

Little Brown Brothers across the blue sea,
Are your bare, brown feet all bleeding and torn?
So were ours.
Valley Forge! Brandywine!
Where's Lafayette? . . . ■

*A type of rifle issued to U.S. forces in the Philippines.

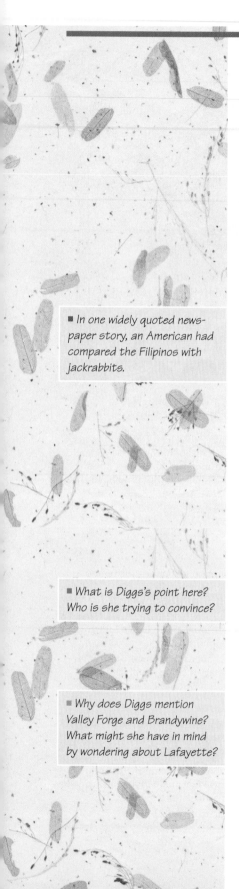

■ In one widely quoted newspaper story, an American had compared the Filipinos with jackrabbits.

■ What is Diggs's point here? Who is she trying to convince?

■ Why does Diggs mention Valley Forge and Brandywine? What might she have in mind by wondering about Lafayette?

■ In the Bible, Cain killed his brother Abel. What "mark of Cain" does Diggs refer to here?

■ What is Diggs's view on imperialism? What does she wish for the people of the Philippines?

God made of one blood all nations on earth,
Brothers all,
Lord God of Nations, spare us Cain's mark. ■

Little Brown Brothers across the blue sea,
Battling so bravely for liberty,
Here's to you.
We've been there ourselves—and won. ■

Summary

The 1890s saw important and long-lasting changes in American politics. In 1889–1890, Republicans wrote most of their campaign promises into law, breaking the political logjam of the preceding fourteen years. Nativism began to take political form in the 1890s, in the short-lived American Protective Association and the more successful immigration restriction movement. A political upheaval began when western and southern farmers joined the Farmers' Alliances and then launched a new political party, the Populist Party. In 1892 voters rejected the Republicans in many areas, choosing either the new Populist Party or the Democrats.

The nation entered a major depression in 1893. Organized labor suffered defeat in two dramatic encounters, one at the Homestead steel plant in 1892 and the other over the Pullman car boycott in 1894. At the end of the 1890s, entrepreneurs and investment bankers launched a merger movement that lasted until 1902, producing, among other massive new companies, United States Steel.

President Grover Cleveland proved unable to meet the political challenges of the depression, and his party, the Democrats, lost badly in the 1894 congressional elections. Southern Democrats began to write white supremacy into law by disfranchising black voters and requiring segregation of the races. In 1896 the Democrats chose as their presidential candidate William Jennings Bryan, a critic of Cleveland and supporter of silver coinage. The Republicans nominated William McKinley, who favored the protective tariff. McKinley won, beginning a period of Republican dominance in national politics that lasted until 1930. Under Bryan's long-term leadership, the Democratic Party discarded its commitment to minimal government and instead adopted a willingness to use government against monopolies and other powerful economic interests.

During the 1890s, the United States took on a new role in foreign affairs. During the administration of Benjamin Harrison, Congress approved creation of a modern navy. Although a revolution presented the United States with an opportunity to annex Hawai`i, President Cleveland rejected that course. However, Cleveland threatened war with Great Britain over a disputed boundary between Venezuela and British Guiana, and Britain backed down.

A revolution in Cuba led the United States into a one-sided war with Spain in 1898. The immediate result was acquisition of an American colonial empire that included the Philippines, Guam, and Puerto Rico. Congress annexed Hawai`i in the midst of the war, and the United States acquired part of Samoa by treaty in 1899. Filipinos resisted American authority, leading to a three-year war that cost more lives than the Spanish-American War. With the Philippines and an improved navy, the United States took on a new prominence in eastern Asia, especially in China, where U.S. diplomatic and commercial interests promoted the Open Door and where American troops took part in suppressing the Boxer Rebellion.

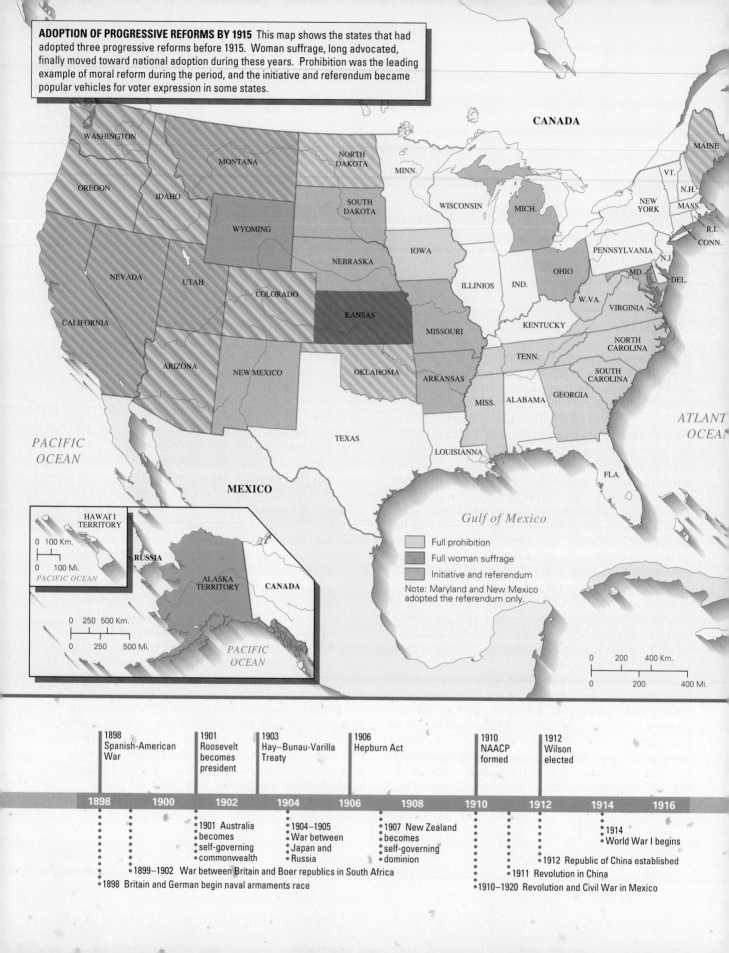

ADOPTION OF PROGRESSIVE REFORMS BY 1915 This map shows the states that had adopted three progressive reforms before 1915. Woman suffrage, long advocated, finally moved toward national adoption during these years. Prohibition was the leading example of moral reform during the period, and the initiative and referendum became popular vehicles for voter expression in some states.

CANADA

WASHINGTON

MONTANA

NORTH DAKOTA

MINN.

OREGON

IDAHO

SOUTH DAKOTA

WISCONSIN

MICH.

MAINE

VT.

N.H.

NEW YORK

MASS.

WYOMING

IOWA

R.I.

CONN.

NEVADA

UTAH

NEBRASKA

PENNSYLVANIA

N.J.

MD.

COLORADO

ILLINIOS

IND.

OHIO

DEL.

CALIFORNIA

KANSAS

MISSOURI

W.VA.

VIRGINIA

KENTUCKY

NORTH CAROLINA

ARIZONA

NEW MEXICO

OKLAHOMA

ARKANSAS

TENN.

SOUTH CAROLINA

MISS.

ALABAMA

GEORGIA

ATLANTIC OCEAN

PACIFIC OCEAN

TEXAS

LOUISIANNA

FLA.

MEXICO

Gulf of Mexico

HAWAI'I TERRITORY

0   100 Km.

0   100 Mi.

PACIFIC OCEAN

RUSSIA

ALASKA TERRITORY

CANADA

0   250   500 Km.

0   250   500 Mi.

PACIFIC OCEAN

Full prohibition

Full woman suffrage

Initiative and referendum

Note: Maryland and New Mexico adopted the referendum only.

0   200   400 Km.

0   200   400 Mi.

1898 Spanish-American War

1901 Roosevelt becomes president

1903 Hay–Bunau-Varilla Treaty

1906 Hepburn Act

1910 NAACP formed

1912 Wilson elected

| 1898 | 1900 | 1902 | 1904 | 1906 | 1908 | 1910 | 1912 | 1914 | 1916 |

1901 Australia becomes self-governing commonwealth

1904–1905 War between Japan and Russia

1907 New Zealand becomes self-governing dominion

1914 World War I begins

1899–1902 War between Britain and Boer republics in South Africa

1912 Republic of China established

1911 Revolution in China

1898 Britain and German begin naval armaments race

1910–1920 Revolution and Civil War in Mexico

The Progressive Era, 1900–1917

Adoption of Progressive Reforms by 1915
What regional patterns of progressive reform appear on the map on the facing page? Though woman suffrage and prohibition were often closely associated in the public mind at the time, they are not always closely associated on the map. What might explain the differences?

Individual Choices

THEODORE ROOSEVELT

President Theodore Roosevelt's distinctive face attracted photographers and cartoonists, and he was often shown with a big grin. He loved fun, and a friend of his once observed that "You must always remember that the President is about six." *Brown Brothers.*

Theodore Roosevelt

On September 7, 1901, President William McKinley was shaking the hands of well-wishers at an exposition in Buffalo, New York. Suddenly Leon Czolgosz, an American-born anarchist, opened fire with a small handgun. McKinley died a week later, and Theodore Roosevelt became president.

Roosevelt was only 42 years old, the youngest person ever to assume the presidency. He was unusual in other ways, too. His refined manners pointed to his distinguished family background, just as his thick spectacles hinted at his intellectual accomplishments. At a time when most presidents had been "practical men," Roosevelt had written more than a dozen books on history, natural history, and his own experiences as a rancher and hunter. Professors used his *Naval War of 1812* (1882) as a college textbook. His *Winning of the West* (4 vols., 1889–1896) won wide acclaim. Though he wrote a book, on average, every two years, he also made a career in Republican politics and captured the popular imagination as the "Hero of San Juan Hill" (see page 629).

Less than a year after assuming the presidency, Roosevelt faced a potential crisis, and he dealt with it in a way that set him apart from his predecessors. In June 1902, anthracite coal miners went on strike in Pennsylvania, seeking higher wages, an eight-hour workday, and union recognition. Mine owners refused to negotiate or even to meet with representatives of the United Mine Workers.

The railroads of the coal-mining region owned the mines, and the president of the Reading Railroad, George F. Baer, spoke for the mining companies. When urged to negotiate with the union, Baer replied,

> The rights and interests of the laboring men will be protected and cared for—not by the labor agitators, but by the Christian men to whom God in his infinite wisdom has given control of the property interests of this country.

Baer's claim to God-given control failed to impress the miners, much of the public, or Roosevelt.

As cold weather approached and coal prices edged upward, public concern grew because many people heated their homes with coal. Roosevelt knew that nothing in the Constitution or federal law required him to take action, but he did so nonetheless. In early October, Roosevelt called both sides to Washington, where he urged them to submit their differences to arbitration by a board that he would appoint. The owners haughtily refused and instead insisted that the army be used against the miners—the way that Cleveland had broken the Pullman strike ten years before, and that Hayes had put down the railroad strike of 1877. Roosevelt, now angry, blasted them as "insolent" and so "obstinate" as to be both "utterly silly" and "well-nigh criminal."

Roosevelt, instead of pitting troops against the strikers, began to consider using the army to dispossess the mine owners and reopen the mines. Roosevelt sent his secretary of war, Elihu Root, to talk with J. P. Morgan, the prominent investment

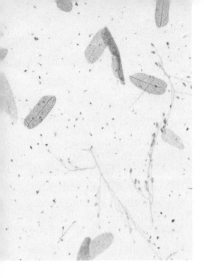

banker (see pages 535–536), who held a significant stake in the railroad companies. After talking with Root, Morgan convinced the companies to accept Roosevelt's offer of arbitration. The arbitration board granted the miners higher wages and a nine-hour workday but denied their other objectives. The companies were permitted to raise their prices to cover their additional costs.

No previous president had ever intervened in a strike by treating a union as equal to the owners, let alone threatening to use the army on the side of labor. By taking bold action and asserting the power of the presidency, Roosevelt acted as what he called "the steward of the people," mediating a conflict between organized interest groups in an effort to advance the public interest. In this and other ways, Roosevelt significantly changed both the office of the presidency and the authority of the federal government.

INTRODUCTION

Roosevelt became president at a time that historians call the Progressive Era—a time when "reform was in the air," as one small-town journalist later recalled. In 1912 Walter Weyl, a former settlement house worker, described American politics this way:

We are in a period of clamor, of bewilderment, of an almost tremulous unrest. We are hastily revising all our social conceptions. We are hastily testing all our political ideals.

Weyl's characterization, overstated as it was, reflected the widespread popular expectation for change. Reform was "in the air" almost everywhere, and many individuals and groups joined the crusade, often with quite different expectations. The variety of competing organizations seeking to reform politics could—and did—produce nearly as much clamor and bewilderment as Weyl described.

At the dawn of the new century, few Americans could have anticipated the extent of change that lay just ahead. Most probably expected a continuation of nineteenth-century political patterns, in which parties dominated politics, and the federal government did little in the economy other than to stimulate development through the tariff and land policies. At the same time, many Americans believed that something should be done to curb the power of the new industrial corporations and resolve the problems of the cities. Some Americans also came to identify traditional political practices as an impediment to reform.

Progressivism took shape through many decisions by voters and political leaders. A basic question loomed behind many of those decisions: Should government play a larger role in the lives of Americans?

This question lay behind debates over regulation of railroads in 1906 and regulation of banking in 1913, as well as behind proposals to prohibit alcoholic beverages and to limit working hours of women factory workers. Time after time, Americans chose a greater role for government. Often the consensus favoring government intervention was so broad that the only debate was over the form of intervention. As Americans gave government more power, they also tried to make it more responsive to ordinary citizens. They put limits on political parties and introduced ways for people to participate more directly in politics. Although progressives imposed new regulations on some businesses, traditional values of private property and individualism proved hardy. The political changes of the Progressive Era, following on the heels of the political realignment of the 1890s, fundamentally altered American politics and government in the twentieth century. The Progressive Era gave birth to many aspects of modern American politics.

Organizing for Change

■ What important changes transformed American politics in the early twentieth century?

■ What did women and African Americans seek to accomplish by creating new organizations devoted to political change?

During the early twentieth century, politics dramatically expanded to embrace wide-ranging concerns raised by a complex assortment of groups and individuals. In the swirl of proponents and proposals, politics more than ever before came to reflect the interaction of organized interest groups.

The Changing Face of Politics

As the United States entered the twentieth century, the lives of many Americans changed in important ways. The railroad, telegraph, and telephone had transformed concepts of time and space and fostered formation of new organizations. Executives of the new industrial corporations now thought in terms of regional or national markets. Union members allied with others of their trade in distant cities. Farmers in Kansas and Montana studied grain prices in Chicago and Liverpool. Physicians organized to establish nationwide standards for medical schools.

Manufacturers, farmers, merchants, carpenters, teachers, lawyers, physicians, and many others established or reorganized national associations to advance their economic or professional interests. Sometimes that meant seeking governmental assistance. As early as the 1870s, for example, associations of merchants, farmers, and oil producers had pushed for laws to regulate railroad freight rates (see page 518).

Other forms of associative activity also developed. Some graduates emerged from the recently transformed universities (see page 551) with the conviction that their knowledge and skills could improve society, and they formed professional associations to advance those objectives. Long-established church organizations sometimes fostered the emergence of new associations devoted to moral reform, especially prohibition. Some people formed groups with humanitarian goals such as ending child labor. Members of ethnic and racial groups set up societies to further their groups' interests. Reformers organized to limit the power of corporations or to defeat party bosses. Overlapping with many of these new associations were the organizational activities of women, including middle-class women, new college graduates, and factory and clerical workers.

Sooner or later, many of the new associations sought changes in laws to help them reach their objectives. Increasing numbers of citizens related to politics through such organized **interest groups,** even as the traditional political parties found they could no longer count on the voter loyalty typical of the Gilded Age (see Chapter 18).

Many of these new groups optimistically believed that responsible citizens, acting together, assisted by technical know-how, and sometimes drawing on the power of government, could achieve social progress—improvement of the human situation. As early as the 1890s, some had begun to call themselves "progressive citizens." By 1910, many were simply calling themselves "progressives."

Historians use the term *progressivism* to signify three related developments during the early twentieth century: (1) the emergence of new concepts of the purposes and functions of government, (2) changes in government policies and institutions, and (3) the political agitation that produced those changes. A progressive, then, was a person involved in one or more of these activities. The many individuals and groups promoting their own visions of change made progressivism a complex phenomenon. There was no single progressive movement. To be sure, an organized **Progressive Party** emerged in 1912 and sputtered for a brief time after, but it failed to capture the allegiance of all those who called themselves progressives. Although there was no typical progressive, many aspects of progressivism reflected concerns of the urban middle class, especially urban middle-class women.

Progressivism appeared at every level of government—local, state, and federal. And progressives promoted a wide range of new government activities: regulation of business, moral revival, consumer protection, conservation of natural resources, educational improvement, tax reform, and more. Through all these avenues, they brought government more directly into the economy and more directly into the lives of most Americans.

Women and Reform

Organizations formed by or dominated by women burst onto politics during the **Progressive Era.** By 1900 or so, a new ideal for women had emerged from women's colleges and clubs and from discussions on national lecture circuits and in the press. The New Woman stood for self-determination rather than unthinking acceptance of roles prescribed by the concepts of domesticity and separate spheres. By 1910, this attitude, sometimes called **feminism,** was accelerating the transition from the nineteenth-century

interest group   A coalition of people identified with a particular cause, such as an industry or occupational group, a social group, or a policy objective.

Progressive Party   Political party formed in 1912 with Theodore Roosevelt as its candidate for president; it fell apart when Roosevelt returned to the Republicans in 1916.

Progressive Era   Period of reform in the late nineteenth and early twentieth centuries.

feminism   The conviction that women are and should be the social, political, and economic equals of men.

Chronology

The Progressive Era

1885	Mark Twain's *The Adventures of Huckleberry Finn*
1889	Hazen Pingree elected mayor of Detroit
1890	National American Woman Suffrage Association formed
1893	Stephen Crane's *Maggie: A Girl of the Streets* World's Columbian Exposition, Chicago
1895	Anti-Saloon League formed *United States v. E. C. Knight*
1898	South Dakota adopts initiative and referendum War with Spain
1899	Permanent Court of Arbitration (the Hague Court) created Scott Joplin's "Maple Leaf Rag"
1900	First city commission, in Galveston, Texas Robert M. La Follette elected governor of Wisconsin President William McKinley reelected
1900–1901	Hay-Pauncefote Treaties signed by the United States and Britain
1901	Socialist Party of America formed McKinley assassinated; Theodore Roosevelt becomes president Formation of U.S. Steel by J. P. Morgan Frank Norris's *The Octopus*
1902	Muckraking journalism begins Oregon adopts initiative and referendum Antitrust action against Northern Securities Company Roosevelt intervenes in coal strike Reclamation Act Cuba becomes protectorate
1903	Women's Trade Union League formed W. E. B. Du Bois's *Souls of Black Folk* First World Series Panama becomes a protectorate Hay–Bunau-Varilla Treaty; construction begins on Panama Canal Elkins Act
1904	Roosevelt Corollary Lincoln Steffens's *The Shame of the Cities* Roosevelt elected president

1905	Niagara Movement formed Industrial Workers of the World organized Roosevelt mediates Russo-Japanese War Dominican Republic becomes third U.S. protectorate
1906	Upton Sinclair's *The Jungle* Hepburn Act Meat Inspection Act Pure Food and Drug Act
1907	Financial panic
1908	*Muller v. Oregon* Race riot in Springfield, Illinois First city manager government, in Staunton, Virginia William Howard Taft elected president
1909	Payne-Aldrich Tariff
1910	State of Washington approves woman suffrage National Association for the Advancement of Colored People formed Revolt against Cannonism Mann Act Taft fires Pinchot Hiram W. Johnson elected governor of California Mass woman suffrage movement
1911	Fire at Triangle Shirtwaist factory
1912	Progressive ("Bull Moose") Party formed Wilson elected president Nicaragua becomes a protectorate
1913	Sixteenth Amendment (federal income tax) ratified Seventeenth Amendment (direct election of U.S. senators) ratified Underwood Tariff Federal Reserve Act Armory Show
1914	Clayton Antitrust Act Federal Trade Commission Act Panama Canal completed
1915	National Birth Control League formed
1916	Louis Brandeis appointed to the Supreme Court Jeannette Rankin of Montana becomes first woman elected to U.S. House of Representatives Wilson reelected
1917	United States enters World War I

THE AWAKENING

This cartoon, entitled "The Awakening," shows a western woman, draped in a golden robe, bringing the torch of woman suffrage from the western states that had adopted suffrage to enlighten the darkness of the eastern states that had not done so. In the dark eastern states, women eagerly reach toward the light from the West. Yellow had become closely associated with the suffrage movement, and western suffrage advocates often depicted suffrage as a woman in a golden robe. *Library of Congress.*

movement for suffrage to the twentieth-century struggle for equality and individualism.

Women's increasing control over one aspect of their lives is evident in the birth rate, which fell steadily throughout the nineteenth and early twentieth centuries as couples (or, perhaps, women alone) chose to have fewer children. Abortion was illegal, and state and federal laws banned the distribution of information about contraception. As a result, women or couples seeking to prevent conception often had little reliable guidance. In 1915 a group of women formed the National Birth Control League to seek the repeal of laws that barred contraceptive information. In 1916 **Margaret Sanger,** a nurse practicing among the poor in New York City, attracted wide attention when she went to jail for informing women about birth control.

Other women also formed organizations to advance specific causes. Some, like the settlement houses, were oriented to service. The National Consumers' League (founded in 1890) and the Women's Trade Union

League (1903) tried to improve the lives of working women. Such efforts received a tragic boost in 1911 when fire roared through the Triangle Shirtwaist Company's clothing factory in New York City, killing 146 workers—nearly all young women—who were trapped in a building with no outside fire escapes and locked exit doors. The public outcry produced a state investigation and, in 1914, a new state factory safety law.

Some states passed laws specifically to protect working women. In *Muller v. Oregon* (1908), the Supreme

Margaret Sanger Birth-control advocate who believed so strongly that information about birth control was essential to help women escape poverty that she disobeyed laws against its dissemination.

Muller v. Oregon Supreme Court case in 1908, upholding an Oregon law that limited the hours of employment for women.

Viewing the unfortunates at the Morgue

When a fire swept through the Triangle Shirtwaist factory in New York City, on March 25, 1911, the workers, mostly young women, were unable to escape because of inadequate fire protection and inspection. Many believed that the fire escape doors had been purposefully locked to prevent workers from stealing. One hundred forty-six people died. This recently discovered lantern slide shows some of the victims. The "magic lantern," which showed slides such as this one, was a predecessor of the slide projector. *ILGWU Archives, Labor-Management Documentation Center, Cornell University.*

Court approved the constitutionality of one such law, limiting women's hours of work. Louis Brandeis, a lawyer working with the Consumers' League, defended the law on the grounds that women needed special protection because of their social roles as mothers. Such arguments ran contrary to the New Woman's rejection of separate spheres and ultimately raised questions for women's drive for equality. At the time, however, the decision was widely hailed as a vital and necessary protection for women wage earners. By 1917, laws in thirty-nine states restricted women's working hours.

Though prominent in reform politics, most women could neither vote nor hold office. Support for suffrage grew, however, as more women recognized the need for political action to bring social change. By 1896, four western states had extended the vote to women (see page 561). No other state did so until 1910, when Washington approved female suffrage. Seven more western states followed over the next five years. In 1916 **Jeannette Rankin** of Montana—born on a ranch, educated as a social worker, experienced as a suffrage campaigner—became the first woman elected to the U.S. House of Representatives. Suffrage scored few victories outside the West, however.

Convinced that only a federal constitutional amendment would gain the vote for all women, the **National American Woman Suffrage Association** (NAWSA), led by Carrie Chapman Catt and Anna Howard Shaw, developed a national organization geared to lobbying in Washington, D.C. Alice Paul advocated public demonstrations and civil disobedience, tactics she learned from suffragists in England, where she had been a settlement house worker from 1907 to 1910. In 1913 Paul and her followers formed the Congressional Union to pursue militant strategies. Some white suffragists tried to build an interracial movement for suffrage—NAWSA, for example, condemned lynching in 1917—but most feared that attention to other issues would weaken their position.

Although its leaders were predominantly white and middle class, the cause of woman suffrage ignited a mass movement during the 1910s, mobilizing women of all ages and socioeconomic classes. Opponents of woman suffrage argued that voting would bring women into the male sphere, expose them to corrupting influences, and render them unsuitable as guardians of the moral order. Some suffrage advocates now turned that argument on its head, claiming that women would make politics more moral and family oriented. Others, especially feminists, argued that women should vote because they deserved full equality with men.

Jeannette Rankin   Montana reformer who in 1916 became the first woman elected to Congress; she worked to pass the woman suffrage amendment and to protect women in the workplace.

National American Woman Suffrage Association   Organization formed in 1890 that united the two major women's suffrage groups of that time.

Moral Reform

Causes other than suffrage also stirred women to action. Moral reformers focused especially on banning alcohol, which they labeled Demon Rum. The temperance movement dated to at least the 1820s, but most early temperance advocates merely tried to persuade individuals to give up strong drink. By the late nineteenth century, however, they looked to government to prohibit the production, sale, or consumption of alcoholic beverages. Many saw prohibition as a progressive reform and expected government to safeguard what they saw as the public interest. Few reforms could claim as many women activists as prohibition.

The drive against alcohol developed a broad base during the Progressive Era. Some old-stock Protestant churches—notably the Methodists—termed alcohol one of the most significant obstacles to a better society. Most adherents of the Social Gospel (see page 605) viewed prohibition as urgently needed to save the victims of industrialization and urbanization. Others, appealing to concepts of domesticity, emphasized protecting the family and home from the destructive influence of alcohol on husbands and fathers. Scientists related alcohol to disease and publicized the **narcotic** and **depressive** qualities of the drug. Sociologists demonstrated links between liquor and prostitution, sexually transmitted diseases, poverty, crime, and broken families. Other evidence pointed to alcohol as contributing to industrial accidents, absenteeism, and inefficiency on the job.

Earlier prohibitionists had organized into the Prohibition Party and the Women's Christian Temperance Union (see page 553). By the late 1890s, however, the **Anti-Saloon League** became the model for successful interest-group politics. Proudly describing itself as "the Church in action against the saloon," the Anti-Saloon League usually operated through mainstream old-stock Protestant churches. The League focused its antagonism on the saloon, attacking it as the least defensible element in the liquor industry. Reformers viewed saloons as corrupting not only individuals—men who neglected their families—but politics as well. Saloons, where political cronies struck deals and mingled with voters, had long been identified with big-city political machines.

The League endorsed only politicians who opposed Demon Rum, regardless of their party or their stands on other issues. As the prohibition cause demonstrated its growing political clout, more politicians lined up against the saloon. At the same time, the League promoted statewide referendums to ban alcohol. Between 1900 and 1917, voters adopted prohibition in nearly half of the states, including nearly all of the West and the South. Elsewhere, many towns and rural areas voted themselves "dry" under **local option laws.**

Opposition to prohibition came especially from immigrants—and their American-born descendants—from Ireland, Germany, and southern and eastern Europe. These groups did not regard the use of alcohol as inherently sinful. For them, beer or wine was an accepted part of social life, and they resisted prohibition as an effort by some to impose their moral views on others. Companies that produced alcohol, especially beer-brewers, also organized to fight the prohibitionists and subsidized some associations, especially the German-American Alliance, to build a political coalition against the "dry" crusade. "Personal liberty" became the slogan for these "wets."

The drive against alcohol, ultimately successful at the national level, was not the only target for moral reformers. Reformers—many of them women—tried to eliminate prostitution through state and federal legislation. Beginning in Iowa in 1909, states passed "red-light abatement" laws designed to close brothels. In 1910 Congress passed the **Mann Act,** making it illegal to take a woman across a state line for "immoral purposes." Other moral reform efforts—to ban gambling or make divorces more difficult, for example—also represented attempts to use government power to regulate individual behavior.

Racial Issues

During the Progressive Era, racial issues were generally less prominent than other reform causes. Only a few white progressives actively opposed disfranchise-

---

narcotic A drug that reduces pain and induces sleep or stupor.

depressive Tending to lower a person's spirits and to lessen activity.

Anti-Saloon League Political interest group advocating prohibition, founded in 1895; it organized through churches.

local option law A state law that permitted the residents of a town or city to decide, by an election, whether to ban liquor sales in their community.

Mann Act Law passed by Congress in 1910, designed to suppress prostitution; it made transporting a woman across state lines for immoral purposes illegal.

An unknown photographer captured this lynching on film and preserved its brutality and depravity. Although there are many photographic records of lynch mobs, local authorities nearly always claimed that they were unable to determine the identity of those responsible for the murder. *Index Stock Photography.*

ment and segregation in the South. Indeed, southern white progressives often took the lead in enacting discriminatory laws. Journalist Ray Stannard Baker was one of the few white progressives to examine the situation of African Americans. In his book *Following the Color Line* (1908), Baker asked, "Does democracy really include Negroes as well as white men?" For most white Americans, the answer appeared to be no.

Lynchings and violence continued as facts of life for African Americans. Between 1900 and World War I, lynchings claimed more than eleven hundred victims, most in the South but many in the Midwest. During the same years, race riots wracked several cities. In 1906 Atlanta erupted into a riot as whites randomly attacked African Americans, killing four,

injuring many more, and vandalizing property. In 1908, in Springfield, Illinois (where Abraham Lincoln had made his home), a mob of whites lynched two black men, injured others, and destroyed black-owned businesses. In North and South alike, little effort was spent to prosecute the mob leaders.

During the Progressive Era, some African Americans challenged the accommodationist leadership of Booker T. Washington. **W. E. B. Du Bois,** the first African American to receive a Ph.D. degree from Harvard, wrote some of the first scholarly studies of African Americans. He emphasized the contributions of black men and women, disproved racial stereotypes, and urged African Americans to take pride in their accomplishments. A professor at Atlanta University after 1897, Du Bois used his book *Souls of Black Folk* (1903) to criticize Washington and to exhort African Americans to struggle for their rights "unceasingly." "The hands of none of us are clean," he argued, speaking to both whites and blacks, "if we bend not our energies to a righting of these great wrongs."

African American leaders organized in support of black rights. In 1905 Du Bois and others met in Canada, near Niagara Falls, and drafted demands for racial equality—including civil rights and equality in job opportunities and education—and an end to segregation. The Springfield riot so shocked some white progressives that they called a biracial conference to seek ways to improve race relations. In 1910 delegates formed the **National Association for the Advancement of Colored People** (NAACP), which later provided important leadership in the fight for black equality. Du Bois served as the NAACP's director of publicity and research.

The struggle against lynching occupied a central place in the life's work of **Ida B. Wells.** Born in Mississippi in 1862, Wells attended a school set up by the

W. E. B. Du Bois African American intellectual and civil rights leader, author of important works on black history and sociology, who helped to form and lead the NAACP.

National Association for the Advancement of Colored People Racially integrated civil rights organization founded in New York City in 1910; it continues to work to end discrimination in the United States.

Ida B. Wells African American reformer and journalist who crusaded against lynching and advocated racial justice and woman suffrage; upon marrying in 1895, she became Ida Wells-Barnett.

A brilliant young intellectual, W. E. B. Du Bois had to choose between leading the life of a quiet college professor or challenging Booker T. Washington's claim to speak on behalf of African Americans. *Schomburg Center for Research in Black Culture; New York Public Library; Astor, Lenox and Tilden Foundations.*

Freedmen's Bureau and worked as a rural teacher from 1884 to 1891. Then, in Memphis, Tennessee, she began to write for the black newspaper *Free Speech* and attacked lynching, arguing that several local victims had been targeted as a way of eliminating successful black businessmen. When a mob destroyed the newspaper office, she moved north. During the 1890s and early 1900s, Wells crusaded against lynching, speaking throughout the North and in England and writing *Southern Horrors* (1892) and *A Red Record* (1895). Her speeches and articles relentlessly challenged southern whites' justifications for lynching. Eventually she persuaded some white northerners to recognize and condemn the horror of lynching. She married in 1895, taking the name Ida Wells-Barnett, and lived in Chicago during the Progressive Era. There she promoted the development of black women's clubs and a black settlement house. Initially a supporter of the NAACP, she came to regard it as too cautious.

Challenging Capitalism: Socialists and Wobblies

Many progressive organizations reflected middle- and upper-class concerns, such as businesslike government, prohibition, and greater reliance on experts. Not so the **Socialist Party of America** (SPA), formed in 1901. Proclaiming themselves the political arm of workers and farmers, the Socialists argued that industrial capitalism had produced "an economic slavery which renders intellectual and political tyranny inevitable." They rejected most progressive proposals as inadequate to resolve the nation's problems and called instead for a cooperative commonwealth in which workers would control the means of production. Most looked to the political process and the ballot box as the means to accomplish this transformation.

The Socialists' best-known national leader was Eugene V. Debs, leader of the Pullman strike (see pages 613–614) and virtually the only person able to unite the many socialist factions, ranging from theoretical **Marxists** completely opposed to capitalism to Christian Socialists, who drew their inspiration from religion rather than from Marx. Strong among immigrants, some of whom had become socialists in their native lands, the SPA also attracted small numbers of trade unionists, municipal reformers, and intellectuals, including W. E. B. Du Bois, Margaret Sanger, and Upton Sinclair (see below). The party also had pockets of support among farmers, especially in Oklahoma and Kansas, where they attracted some former Populists.

In 1905 a group of unionists and radicals organized the Industrial Workers of the World (IWW, or "Wobblies"). IWW organizers boldly proclaimed, "We have been naught, we shall be all," as they set out to organize the most exploited unskilled and semiskilled workers. They aimed their message at **sweatshop** workers in eastern cities, **migrant** farm workers who harvested western crops, southern sharecroppers, women workers, African Americans, and the "new

---

Socialist Party of America Political party formed in 1901 and committed to socialism—that is, government ownership of most industries.

Marxist A believer in the ideas of Karl Marx and Friedrich Engels, who opposed private ownership of property and looked to a future in which workers would control the economy.

sweatshop A shop or factory in which employees work long hours at low wages under poor conditions.

migrant Traveling from one area to another.

THE I.W.W. is COMING!

JOIN THE ONE BIG UNION

This design appeared originally on a "stickerette," a small poster (2" X 3") with glue on the back. When the glue was moistened, the poster could be stuck on a fence post or inside a boxcar (where migratory workers often traveled). Wobblies sometimes called the stickerettes "silent agitators." *Courtesy of Labor Archives and Research Center, San Francisco State University.*

immigrants" from southern and eastern Europe. Such workers were usually ignored by the American Federation of Labor, which instead emphasized skilled workers, most of them white males. The Wobblies' objective was simple: when the majority of workers across the country had joined the IWW, they would call a general strike, labor would refuse to work, and capitalism would collapse.

The IWW did organize a few dramatic strikes and demonstrations and scored a handful of significant victories. Most AFL union leaders would have nothing to do with such radicals, however. The IWW often met brutal suppression by local authorities and made few lasting gains for its members.

The SPA counted considerably more victories than the Wobblies. Hundreds of cities and towns—ranging from Reading, Pennsylvania, to Milwaukee, Wisconsin, to Berkeley, California—elected Socialist mayors or council members. Socialists won election to state legislatures in several states. Districts in New York City and Milwaukee sent Socialists to the U.S. House of Representatives. Most Americans, however, had no interest in eliminating private property. Most progressive reformers looked askance at the Socialists

and sometimes tried to undercut their appeal with reforms that addressed some of their concerns but stopped short of challenging capitalism.

The Reform of Politics, the Politics of Reform

■ What did the muckrakers and new professional groups contribute to reform?

■ What were the characteristics of the reforms of city and state government?

■ How did the rise of interest groups reflect new patterns of politics and government?

Progressivism emerged at all levels of government as cities elected reform-minded mayors and states swore in progressive governors. Some reformers hoped only to make government more honest and efficient. Others wanted to change the basic structure and function of government, to make it more responsive to the needs of an urban industrial society. In their quest for change, reformers sometimes found themselves in conflict with the entrenched leaders of political parties and sought to limit the power of those parties.

Exposing Corruption: The Muckrakers

Journalists played an important role in preparing the ground for reform. By the early 1900s, magazine publishers discovered that their sales boomed when they presented dramatic exposés of scandal—political corruption, corporate wrongdoing, and other scandalous offenses. Those who practiced this provocative journalism acquired the name **muckrakers** in 1906 when President Theodore Roosevelt compared them to "the Man with the Muck-rake," a character in John Bunyan's classic allegory *Pilgrim's Progress.* Roosevelt intended the comparison as a rebuke, but journalists accepted the label with pride.

McClure's Magazine led the surge in muckraking journalism, especially after October 1902, when the

muckrakers Progressive Era journalists who wrote articles exposing corruption in city government, business, and industry. In John Bunyan's *Pilgrim's Progress,* "the Man with the Muck-rake" is so preoccupied with raking through the filth at his feet that he didn't notice he was being offered a celestial crown in exchange for his rake.

A NAUSEATING JOB, BUT IT MUST BE DONE
(President Roosevelt takes hold of the investigating muck-rake himself in the packing-house scandal.)

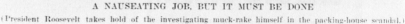

Upton Sinclair's novel *The Jungle* (1906) prompted President Theodore Roosevelt to order an investigation of Sinclair's allegations about unsanitary practices in the meatpacking industry. Roosevelt then used the results of that investigation to pressure Congress into approving new federal legislation to inspect meatpacking, including a stamp such as the one shown here for condemned meat. *Stamp: Chicago Historical Society; Cartoon: Utica Saturday Globe.*

magazine began a series by **Lincoln Steffens** on corruption in city governments. *McClure's* January 1903 issue featured Steffens's installment on Minneapolis, the first article in a series by **Ida Tarbell** on Standard Oil's sordid past, and a piece by Ray Stannard Baker revealing corruption and violence in labor unions. Sales of *McClure's* boomed, and other journals—including *Collier's* and *Cosmopolitan*—copied its style, publishing accounts of the defects of patent medicines, fraud in the insurance industry, the horrors of child labor, and more.

Muckraking soon extended from periodicals to books. Many muckraking books were simply reports on social problems. Both Steffens and Tarbell collected their articles and published them in book form (*The Shame of the Cities*, 1904; *The History of the Standard Oil Company*, 1904). The most famous muckraking book, however, was a novel: *The Jungle*, by **Upton Sinclair** (1906). In following the experiences of fictional immigrant laborers in Chicago, Sinclair exposed with disgusting accuracy the serious failings of the meat-

packing industry. He described in chilling detail the afflictions of packing-house workers—severed fingers, tuberculosis, blood poisoning. The nation was shocked to read of men who "fell into the vats" and "would be overlooked for days, till all but the bones of them had gone out to the world as Durham's Pure Leaf Lard!" Sinclair, a Socialist, hoped readers would recognize that the offenses he portrayed were the results of industrial capitalism.

Lincoln Steffens   Muckraking journalist and managing editor of *McClure's Magazine*, best known for investigating political corruption in city governments.

Ida Tarbell   Progressive Era journalist whose exposé revealed the ruthlessness of the Standard Oil Company.

Upton Sinclair   Socialist writer and reformer whose novel *The Jungle* exposed unsanitary conditions in the meatpacking industry and advocated socialism.

The Jungle horrified many Americans, and President Roosevelt appointed a commission to investigate its allegations. The report confirmed Sinclair's charges. Pressured by Roosevelt and the public, Congress passed the **Pure Food and Drug Act,** which banned impure and mislabeled food and drugs, and the **Meat Inspection Act,** which required federal inspection of meatpacking—a move the industry itself welcomed to reassure nauseated consumers. Sinclair, however, was disappointed because his revelations produced only regulation rather than converting readers to socialism. "I aimed at the public's heart," Sinclair later complained, "and by accident I hit it in the stomach."

Reforming City Government

In the early twentieth century, muckrakers, especially Lincoln Steffens, helped to focus public concern on city government. By the time of Steffens's first article (1902), advocates of **municipal reform** had already won office and brought changes to some cities, and municipal reformers soon appeared in many other cities.

Municipal reformers urged honest and efficient government, and many—perhaps most—also argued that corruption and inefficiency were inevitable without major changes in the structure of city government. **City councils** usually consisted of members elected from **wards** corresponding roughly to neighborhoods. Most voters lived in middle-class and working-class wards, which therefore dominated most city councils. Reformers, however, condemned the ward system as producing city council members unable to see beyond the needs of their own narrow neighborhoods. Reformers pointed to support for political bosses and machines in poor immigrant neighborhoods and concluded that the ward leaders' devotion to voter needs kept the machine in power despite its corruption. They argued that citywide elections, in which all city voters chose from one list of candidates, would produce city council members who could better address the problems of the city as a whole—men with citywide business interests, for example—and that citywide elections would undercut the influence of ward bosses and machines.

James Phelan of San Francisco provides an example of an early structural reformer. Son of a pioneer banker, he was equally at home in the worlds of politics, business, and the arts. Phelan attacked corruption in city government and won election as mayor in 1896. He then spearheaded the adoption of a new charter that strengthened the office of mayor and required citywide election of supervisors (equivalent to city council members).

Some municipal reformers proposed more fundamental changes in the structure of city government, notably the **commission system** and the **city manager plan.** Both reflect prominent traits of progressivism: a distrust of political parties and a desire for expertise and efficiency. The commission system first developed in Galveston, Texas, after a devastating hurricane and tidal wave in 1900. The governor appointed five businessmen to run the city, and they garnered widespread publicity for their efficiency and effectiveness. Within two years, some two hundred communities had adopted a commission system. Typically all the city's voters elected the commissioners, and each commissioner then managed a specific city function. The city manager plan—an application of the administrative structure of the corporation to city government—had similar objectives. It featured a professional city manager (similar to a corporate executive) who was appointed by an elected city council (similar to a corporate board of directors) to handle most municipal administration. Staunton, Virginia, tried such a system in 1908 but attracted little attention. In 1913 a serious flood prompted the citizens of Dayton, Ohio, to adopt a city manager plan, and other cities then followed.

Most municipal reformers hoped to bring about honest, efficient, and effective city administration by changing the structure of city government. A few re-

Pure Food and Drug Act   Law passed by Congress in 1906 forbidding the sale of impure and improperly labeled food and drugs.

Meat Inspection Act   Law passed by Congress in 1906 requiring federal inspection of meatpacking.

municipal reform   Political activity intended to bring about changes in the structure or function of city government.

city council   A body of representatives elected to govern a city.

ward   A division of a city or town, especially an electoral district, for administrative or representative purposes.

commission system   System of city government in which all executive and legislative power is vested in a small elective board, each member of which supervises some aspect of city government.

city manager plan   System of city government in which a small council, chosen on a nonpartisan ballot, hires a city manager who exercises broad executive authority.

The new profession of public health emerged in the early 20th century, in response to new knowledge about the transmission of disease and to conditions, especially in the cities, that encouraged the spread of disease. These men are rat catchers, working under the supervision of the public health professional on the left. Rats spread several diseases, especially the bubonic plague, which threatened San Francisco in 1907–1908 and New Orleans in 1914–1916. *Department of Health and Human Services/TimeLife Pictures/Getty Images*

formers went further to advocate social reforms. Hazen Pingree, a successful and socially prominent businessman, attracted national attention as mayor of Detroit. Elected in 1889 as an advocate of honest, efficient government, he soon began to criticize the city's gas, electric, and streetcar companies for overcharging customers and providing poor service. The depression of 1893 led him to address the needs of the unemployed with work projects and community vegetable gardens. A prosperous manufacturer, Samuel "Golden Rule" Jones, won election as mayor of Toledo, Ohio, in 1897. He boasted of running his factory in accordance with the Golden Rule—"Do unto others as you would have them do unto you"—and he brought the same standard to city government. Under his leadership, Toledo acquired free concerts, free public baths, kindergartens (childcare centers for working mothers), and the eight-hour workday for city employees. In addition, Phelan, Pingree, Jones, and a few others advocated city ownership of utilities—the gas, water, electricity, and streetcar systems.

The Progressive Era also saw early efforts at city planning. Throughout most of the nineteenth century, urban growth had been largely unplanned, driven primarily by the market economy. In the early twentieth century, city officials began to designate separate zones for residential, commercial, and industrial use (first in Los Angeles, in 1904–1908) and to plan more efficient transportation systems. A small number of cities tried to improve substandard housing. By 1910, a few cities had created city planning commissions, charged with planning on a continuing basis. The emergence of **city planning** represents an important transition in thinking about government and the economy, for it emphasized expertise and presumed greater government control over use of private property.

---

city planning The policy of planning urban development by regulating land use.

Saving the Future

The emergence of several new professions—especially public health, mental health, and social work—led to additional efforts to use government, especially local government, to solve some of the fundamental problems of an urban industrial society. Their objective was to use scientific and social scientific knowledge to control social forces and thereby to shape the future.

The public schools attracted a number of reformers. As university programs began graduating teachers and school administrators, these new professionals began to seek greater control over education, especially in the cities. Stressing the challenges of educating multiethnic urban students—many of whom did not speak English—and preparing them for life in a complex and technological society, professional educators pushed for greater centralization and professionalization in school administration. They particularly wanted to reduce the role of local, usually elected, **school boards** and to replace elected school superintendents with appointed professionals. Professional educators also began to rely on the recently developed intelligence tests as a way of identifying children unable to perform at average levels and to isolate them in special classes.

Advances in medical knowledge, together with efforts by the American Medical Association to raise the standards of medical colleges and to restrict access to the profession, improved the professional status of physicians. Professionals also worked to transform hospitals from charities that provided minimal care for the poor into centers for dispensing the most up-to-date treatment. New knowledge about disease and health, often developed in research universities, together with the facilities of modern hospitals, presented an opportunity to reduce disease on a significant scale. Physicians helped initiate public health programs to wipe out **hookworm** in the South, **tuberculosis** in the slums, and sexually transmitted diseases. Public health emerged as a new medical field, combining the knowledge of the medical doctor with the insight of the social scientist and the skills of the corporate manager.

Other emerging professional fields with important implications for public policy included mental health and social work. Mental health professionals—psychiatrists and psychologists—tried to transform **insane asylums** (places to confine the mentally ill) into places where patients could be treated and perhaps cured. Social workers often found themselves allied with public health and mental health professionals in their efforts to extend government control over urban health and safety codes.

Reforming State Government

As reformers launched changes in many cities and as new professionals considered ways to improve society, **Robert M. La Follette** pushed Wisconsin to the forefront of reform. A Republican, he entered politics soon after graduating from the University of Wisconsin. He served three terms in Congress in the 1880s but found his political career blocked when he accused the leader of the state Republican organization of unethical behavior. He finally won election as governor in 1900 and by then was convinced of the need for reform.

Conservative legislators, many of them Republicans like La Follette, defeated his proposals to regulate railroad rates and replace nominating conventions with the **direct primary** (in which the voters affiliated with a party choose that party's candidates through an election). La Follette threw himself into an energetic campaign to elect reformers to the state legislature. He earned the nickname "Fighting Bob" as he traveled the state and propounded his views wherever a crowd gathered. Most of his candidates won, and La Follette built a strong following among Wisconsin's farmers and urban wage earners, who returned him to the governor's mansion in 1902 and 1904.

La Follette secured legislation designed to limit both corporations and political parties. Acclaimed as

school board A board of policymakers who oversee the public schools of a local political unit.

hookworm A parasite, formerly common in the South, that causes loss of strength.

tuberculosis An infectious disease that attacks the lungs, causing coughing, fever, and weight loss; spread by unsanitary conditions and practices, such as spitting in public, it was common and often fatal in the nineteenth and early twentieth centuries and is reappearing today.

insane asylum In the nineteenth and early twentieth centuries, an institution for the incarceration of people with mental disorders.

Robert M. La Follette Governor of Wisconsin who instituted reforms such as direct primaries, tax reform, and anticorruption measures in Wisconsin.

direct primary An election in which voters who identify with a specific party choose that party's candidates to run later in the general election against the candidates of other parties.

Robert La Follette enjoyed taking his campaigns to the voters. He is shown here in 1900, campaigning for election as governor of Wisconsin. When he went to the voters, he saw his speechmaking as a process of education, and he often spent an hour or more explaining the intricacies of policy issues. *Library of Congress.*

a "laboratory of democracy," Wisconsin adopted the direct primary, set up a commission to regulate railroad rates, increased taxes on railroads and other corporations, enacted a merit system for state employees, and restricted lobbyists. In many of his efforts, La Follette drew on the expertise of faculty members at the University of Wisconsin. These reforms, along with reliance on experts, came to be called the **Wisconsin Idea.** La Follette won election to the U.S. Senate in 1905 and did his best to import the Wisconsin Idea to Capitol Hill until his death in 1925.

La Follette's success prompted imitation elsewhere. In 1901 Iowans elected Albert B. Cummins governor, and Cummins launched a campaign against railroad corporations that paralleled La Follette's. He too went on to the Senate. Reformers won office in other states as well, but only a few matched La Follette's legislative and political success.

Progressivism came to California relatively late. California reformers accused the Southern Pacific Railroad of running a powerful political machine that controlled the state by dominating the Republican Party. In 1906 and 1907 a highly publicized investigation revealed widespread bribery in San Francisco government. The ensuing trials made famous one of the prosecutors, **Hiram W. Johnson.** Reform-minded Republicans, organized as the Lincoln-Roosevelt Republican League, persuaded Johnson to run for governor in 1910. He conducted a vigorous campaign and won.

Once in power, California progressives produced a volume of reform that rivaled that of Wisconsin. Stubborn and principled, Johnson proved to be an uncompromising foe of corporate influence in politics. As governor, he pushed for regulation of railroads and public utilities, restrictions on political parties, protection for labor, and conservation. Progressives in the legislature sometimes went beyond Johnson's proposals, notably by sending a state constitutional amendment on woman suffrage to the voters, who approved the measure. Johnson showed more sympathy for labor than did most progressive reformers. He appointed union leaders to state positions and supported several measures to benefit working people, including an eight-hour workday law for women, **workers' compensation,** and restrictions on child labor. California progressives in both parties vied with each other, however, in the vehemence of their attacks on Asian immigrants and Asian Americans. In 1913 the progressive Republi-

Wisconsin Idea The program of reform sponsored by La Follette in Wisconsin, designed to decrease political corruption, foster direct democracy, regulate corporations, and increase expertise in governmental decision making.

Hiram W. Johnson Governor of California who promoted a broad range of reforms, including regulation of railroads and measures to benefit labor.

workers' compensation Payments that employers are required by law to award to workers injured on the job.

cans pushed through a law that prohibited Asian immigrants from owning land in California.

Like La Follette, Johnson moved on to national politics. In 1912 he was the vice-presidential candidate of the new Progressive Party. Reelected governor in 1914, he won election to the U.S. Senate in 1916 and served there until his death in 1945.

The Decline of Parties and the Rise of Interest Groups

Like California, many other states moved to restrict political parties. City and state reformers charged that bosses and machines manipulated nominating conventions, managed public officials, and controlled law enforcement. They claimed that bosses, in return for payoffs, used their influence on behalf of powerful interests. Articles by muckrakers and a few highly publicized bribery trials convinced many voters that the reformers were correct. The mighty party organizations that had dominated politics during the nineteenth century now came under attack along a broad front.

Progressives nearly everywhere proposed measures to enhance the power of individual voters and to reduce the power of party organizations. State after state adopted the direct primary, and many reformers sought to use the merit system to reduce the number of state positions filled through patronage. In many states, judgeships, school board seats, and educational offices were made nonpartisan.

A number of cities and states also adopted the initiative and referendum (see chapter-opening map). The initiative permitted voters to adopt a new law directly: if enough voters signed a petition, the proposed law would be voted on at the next election; if approved by the voters, it became law. The referendum permitted voters, through a petition, to have the final word on a law adopted by the legislature. Adopted first in South Dakota in 1898, the initiative and referendum gained national attention after Oregon voters adopted them in 1902. Oregon reformers led by William U'Ren, a former Populist turned progressive Republican, employed the initiative to create new laws. The Oregon reformers received so much attention that the initiative and referendum were sometimes called the **Oregon System.** Some states also adopted the **recall,** a procedure that permits voters through petitions to initiate a special election to remove an elected official from office. The direct primary, initiative and referendum, and recall are known collectively as **direct democracy** because they remove

intermediate steps between the voter and final political decisions.

One outcome of the switch to direct primaries and decline of party organizations was a new approach to campaigning for office. Candidates now appealed directly to voters rather than to party leaders and convention delegates. Individual candidates built up personal organizations (separate from party organizations) to win nomination and election. Formerly, the party leaders who managed nominating conventions had often insisted on informal **term limits,** but now voters sometimes returned the same individuals to office again and again. As campaigns focused more on individual candidates and less on parties, advertising supplanted the armies of party retainers who had mobilized voters in the nineteenth century (see page 512). At the same time, new voter registration laws and procedures disqualified some voters, especially transient workers. Voter turnout fell (see Figure 20.2, page 622). Ironically, the emergence of new channels for political participation created the illusion of a vast outpouring of public involvement in politics—but proportionally fewer voters actually cast ballots.

New avenues of political participation opened not only through direct democracy but also through organized interest groups. Such groups were often attracted to politics as the most direct way to advance their specialized concerns. Occasionally, groups cooperated when their political objectives coincided, as when merchants and farmers both favored regulation of railroad rates. Other times, they found themselves in conflict, perhaps over tariff policy. The many groups that advocated change sometimes fought among themselves over which reform goals were most important and how best to achieve them. More and more groups took up the tactics of the Anti-Saloon League—they ignored parties, pressured individual candidates to accept their group's position, and urged their members to vote only for candidates who did so. In 1904,

---

Oregon System   Name given to the initiative and referendum, first used widely in state politics in Oregon after 1902.

recall   Provision that permits voters, through the petition process, to hold a special election to remove an elected official from office.

direct democracy   Provisions that permit voters to make political decisions directly, including the direct primary, initiative, referendum, and recall.

term limit   A limit on the number of times one person can be elected to the same political office.

for example, the National Association of Manufacturers (NAM) targeted and defeated two key prolabor members of Congress, one in the House and one in the Senate. The American Federation of Labor (AFL) responded in 1906 with a similar strategy and managed to elect six union members to the House of Representatives.

Organized interest groups often focused their attention on the legislative process. When Congress was in session, they retained the services of full-time representatives, or **lobbyists,** in Washington. Lobbyists urged members of Congress to support their group's position on pending legislation, reminded senators and representatives of their group's electoral clout, and arranged campaign backing for those who supported their cause. Eventually many legislators became dependent on lobbyists for information about their **constituents** and sometimes relied on lobbyists to help draft legislation and raise campaign funds. Similar patterns developed in state legislatures.

Thus, as political parties receded from the dominant position they once occupied, organized interest groups moved in. Pushed one way by the AFL and the other by the NAM, under opposing pressure from the Anti-Saloon League and liquor interests, some elected officials came to see themselves less as loyal members of a political party and more as mediators among competing interest groups.

Roosevelt, Taft, and Republican Progressivism

▪ What did Theodore Roosevelt mean by a "Square Deal"? How do his accomplishments exemplify this description? Do any of his actions not fit this model?

▪ How did the role of the federal government in the economy and the power of the presidency change as a consequence of Theodore Roosevelt's activities in office?

When Theodore Roosevelt became president upon the death of William McKinley, his buoyant optimism and boundless energy fascinated Americans—one visitor reported that the most exciting things he saw in the United States were "Niagara Falls and the President . . . both great wonders of nature!" "TR" quickly became recognizable everywhere, as cartoonists delighted in sketching his bristling mustache, pince-nez glasses, and toothy grin.

Roosevelt later wrote, "I cannot say that I entered the Presidency with any deliberately planned and far-reaching scheme of social betterment." Nonetheless, Americans soon saw Roosevelt as the embodiment of progressivism. In seven years, he changed the nation's domestic policies more than any president since Lincoln—and made himself a legend.

Roosevelt: Asserting the Power of the Presidency

Roosevelt was unlike most politicians of his day. He had inherited wealth, and he had added to it from the many books he had written. He saw politics as a duty he owed the nation rather than as an opportunity for personal advancement, and he defined his political views in terms of character, morality, hard work, and patriotism. Uncertain whether to call himself a "radical conservative" or a "conservative radical," he considered politics a tool for forging an ethical and socially stable society. Confident in his own personal principles, Roosevelt did not hesitate to wield to the fullest the powers of the presidency. He also used the office as what he called a "bully pulpit," to bring attention to his concerns.

In his first message to Congress, in December 1901, Roosevelt sounded a theme that he repeated throughout his political career: the growth of powerful corporations was "natural," but some of them exhibited "grave evils" that the law needed to penalize. As Roosevelt later explained, "When I became President, the question as to the method by which the United States Government was to control the corporations was not yet important. The absolutely vital question was whether the Government had power to control them at all." He set out to establish that power.

The chief obstacle to regulating the new corporations was the Supreme Court decision in *United States v. E. C. Knight* (1895), preventing the Sherman Anti-Trust Act from being used against manufacturing monopolies. Roosevelt looked for an opportunity to challenge the *Knight* decision. Some of the nation's most prominent business leaders—J. P. Morgan, the Rockefeller interests, and railroad magnates James J. Hill and Edward H. Harriman—had joined forces to create the Northern Securities Company, which combined several railroad lines to create a railroad monopoly in the Northwest. The *Knight* case had involved

---

lobbyist   A person who tries to influence the opinions of legislators or other public officials for or against a specific cause.

constituents   Voters in the home district of a member of a legislature.

manufacturing; the Northern Securities Company, on the other hand, provided interstate transportation. If any industry could satisfy the Supreme Court that it fit the language of the Constitution authorizing Congress to regulate interstate commerce, Roosevelt believed, the railroads could.

In February 1902, Roosevelt advised Attorney General Philander C. Knox to seek dissolution of the Northern Securities Company for violating the Sherman Act. Wall Street leaders condemned Roosevelt's action, but most Americans responded positively. For the first time, the federal government was challenging a powerful corporation. In 1904 the Supreme Court agreed that the Sherman Act could be applied to the Northern Securities Company and ordered it dissolved.

Bolstered by this confirmation of federal power, Roosevelt launched additional antitrust suits and gloried in his reputation as a trustbuster. In all, he initiated more than forty antitrust actions, though not all were successful. He used **trustbusting** selectively, however. Large corporations, he thought, were natural, inevitable, and potentially beneficial. He thought regulation was preferable to breaking them up. Companies that met Roosevelt's standards of character and public service—and that acknowledged the power of the presidency—had no reason to fear antitrust action. Such nods to presidential power sometimes meant informal understandings between Roosevelt and corporate heads. In 1907, for example, in the midst of a financial panic, officials of United States Steel Corporation secured Roosevelt's consent before taking over the Tennessee Coal and Iron Company, arguing that the takeover would stabilize the industry.

Roosevelt's willingness to take bold action was not limited to trustbusting. In time of crisis, he felt, the president should "do whatever the needs of the people demand, unless the Constitution or the laws explicitly forbid him to do it." A year after he took office, he asserted new presidential powers to deal with a strike by coal miners (see Individual Choices, page 638). His bold action produced what he liked to call a **Square Deal,** fair treatment for all parties.

The Square Deal in Action: Creating Federal Economic Regulation

Roosevelt's trustbusting and handling of the coal strike brought him great popularity across the country. In 1903 Congress approved several measures he requested or endorsed: the Expedition Act, to speed up prosecution of antitrust suits; creation of a cabinet-level Department of Commerce and Labor, including a Bureau of Corporations to investigate corporate activities; and the **Elkins Act,** which amended the Interstate Commerce Act by setting penalties for railroads that paid rebates.

When Roosevelt sought election in 1904, he won by one of the largest margins up to that time, securing more than 56 percent of the popular vote. Conservatives had temporarily taken control of the Democratic Party and hoped to attract enough support from conservative voters to defeat Roosevelt. But Alton B. Parker, their drab nominee, made one of the Democrats' worst showings ever. Elected in his own right, with a powerful demonstration of public approval, Roosevelt set out to secure meaningful regulation of the railroads, largest of the nation's big businesses.

Roosevelt and reformers in Congress wanted to regulate railroad rates—the prices they charged for hauling freight and carrying passengers. In Roosevelt's year-end message to Congress in 1905, he asked for legislation to regulate railroad rates, open the financial records of railroads to government inspection, and increase federal authority in strikes involving interstate commerce. At the same time, the attorney general filed suits against some of the nation's largest corporations. Muckrakers (some of them friends of Roosevelt) also fired off scathing exposés of railroads and attacks on Senate conservatives.

Although Roosevelt compromised with conservative Republicans on some issues, he got most of what he wanted. On June 29, 1906, Congress passed the **Hepburn Act,** allowing the Interstate Commerce Commission (ICC) to establish maximum railroad rates and extending ICC authority to other forms of transportation. The act also limited railroads' ability to issue free passes, a practice reformers had long considered bribery. The next day, on June 30, Congress

trustbusting Use of antitrust laws to prosecute and dissolve big businesses ("trusts").

Square Deal Theodore Roosevelt's term for his efforts to deal fairly with all.

Elkins Act Law passed by Congress in 1903 that supplemented the Interstate Commerce Act of 1887 by penalizing railroads that paid rebates.

Hepburn Act Law passed by Congress in 1906 that authorized the Interstate Commerce Commission to set maximum railroad rates and to regulate other forms of transportation.

Gifford Pinchot, the first American to be trained in the new profession of forestry, believed in the careful management of natural resources, including the preservation of some wilderness areas and the carefully planned use of other natural resources. As head of the Forestry Service under Theodore Roosevelt, Pinchot influenced Roosevelt's conservation and preservation policies. *Library of Congress.*

approved the Pure Food and Drug Act and the Meat Inspection Act, as the aftermath to Sinclair's stomach-turning revelations. Congress also passed legislation defining employers' liability for workers injured on the job in the District of Columbia and on interstate railroads.

Regulating Natural Resources

An outspoken proponent of strenuous outdoor activities, Roosevelt took great pride in establishing five national parks and more than fifty wildlife preserves, to save what he called "beautiful and wonderful wild creatures whose existence was threatened by greed and wantonness." Preservationists, such as John Muir of the Sierra Club, applauded these actions and urged that wilderness areas be kept forever safe from developers. Setting aside parks and wildlife refuges, however, was only one element in Roosevelt's conservation agenda.

Roosevelt and **Gifford Pinchot,** the president's chief adviser on natural resources, believed conservation required not only preservation of wild and beautiful lands but also carefully planned use of resources. Trained in scientific forestry in Europe, Pinchot com-

bined scientific and technical expertise with a managerial outlook. He and Roosevelt withdrew large tracts of federal timber and grazing land from public sale or use. By establishing close federal management of these lands, they hoped to provide for the needs of the present and still leave resources for the future. While president, Roosevelt removed nearly 230 million acres from public sale, more than quadrupling the land under federal protection.

Roosevelt strongly supported the Reclamation Act of 1902 (see page 586). The act set aside proceeds from the sale of federal land in sixteen western states to finance irrigation projects, and it established a commitment later expanded many times: the federal government now undertook the construction of western dams, canals, and other facilities that made agriculture possible in areas of scant rainfall. Thus water, perhaps the single most important resource in the arid West, came to be managed. Far from preserv-

Gifford Pinchot Head of the Forestry Service from 1898 to 1910; he promoted conservation and urged careful planning in the use of natural resources.

This postcard depicts President Theodore Roosevelt, in command of the Republican Party, persuading his friend William Howard Taft to run for president in 1908. Taft was not eager for that office, but Roosevelt convinced him to seek it. With Roosevelt's strong support, Taft was elected, but he proved a disappointment to Roosevelt. *Collection of Janice L. and David J. Frent.*

ing the western landscape, federal water projects profoundly transformed it, vividly illustrating the vast difference between the preservation of wilderness that Muir advocated and the careful management of resources that Pinchot sought.

Taft's Troubles

Soon after Roosevelt won the election of 1904, he announced that he would not seek reelection in 1908. By 1908, he may have regretted this statement, but he kept his word. He remained immensely popular, however, and virtually named his successor. Republicans nominated William Howard Taft. A graduate of Yale and former federal judge, Taft had served as governor of the Philippines before joining Roosevelt's cabinet as secretary of war in 1904.

William Jennings Bryan, leader of the progressive wing of the Democratic Party, won his party's nomination for the third time. Roosevelt's popularity and his strong endorsement of Taft overcame a lackluster Republican campaign. Taft won just under 52 percent of the vote, and Republicans kept control of the Senate and the House. After turning the presidency over to Taft, Roosevelt set off to hunt big game in Africa.

Roosevelt had been Taft's mentor in politics, but Taft was far more restrained than his predecessor. Unlike Roosevelt, Taft hated campaigning and disliked

conflict. His legalistic approach often appeared timid when compared with Roosevelt's boldness. But Taft worked to demonstrate his support for Roosevelt's Square Deal. His attorney general initiated some ninety antitrust suits in four years, twice as many as during Roosevelt's seven years. And Taft approved legislation to strengthen regulatory agencies, as in 1910 when Congress extended the power of the Interstate Commerce Commission to cover most communication companies.

During the Taft administration, progressives amended the Constitution twice. Reformers had long considered an income tax to be the fairest means of raising federal revenues. With support from Taft, enough states ratified the **Sixteenth Amendment** (permitting a federal income tax) for it to take effect in 1913. By contrast, Taft took no position on the **Seventeenth Amendment,** proposed in 1912 and ratified

Sixteenth Amendment Constitutional amendment ratified in 1913 that gives the federal government the authority to establish an income tax.

Seventeenth Amendment Constitutional amendment ratified in 1913 that requires the election of U.S. senators directly by the voters of each state, rather than by state legislatures.

shortly after he left office in 1913. It changed the method of electing U.S. senators from election by state legislatures to election by voters, another long-time goal of reformers, who claimed that corporate influence and even outright bribery had swayed state legislatures and shaped the Senate.

Roosevelt had handed Taft a Republican Party divided by battles over the Hepburn Act and similar issues. Divisions between conservatives and progressives grew, and Taft increasingly sided with the conservatives. In 1909, he called on Congress to reform the tariff. Though the resulting **Payne-Aldrich Tariff** retained high rates on most imports, Taft signed the bill. When Republican progressives protested, Taft became defensive, alienating them further by calling it "the best bill that the Republican party ever passed."

The battle within the Republican Party intensified when Republican progressives attacked the high-handed exercise of power by Joseph Cannon, Speaker of the House of Representatives since 1902. Notorious for his profanity and poker playing, Cannon used the Speaker's power to support conservatives and stifle progressives. Taft first favored progressives' efforts to replace Cannon. He backed off, however, and he made his peace with Cannon, offending Republican progressives. In 1910 Nebraska representative George W. Norris led Republican progressives in a "revolt against Cannonism" that gained the support of the Democrats and permanently reduced the power of the Speaker.

A dispute over conservation further damaged Republican unity. Taft had kept Gifford Pinchot as head of the Forest Service. Pinchot soon charged that Taft's secretary of the interior, Richard A. Ballinger, had weakened the conservation program and favored corporate interests by opening reserved lands. Taft concluded, however, that Ballinger was reversing improper actions by Roosevelt's administration. Pinchot persisted, publicly airing charges against Ballinger. Taft now considered Pinchot "a radical and a crank" and fired him. An investigation by Congress cleared Ballinger, but the affair further estranged Taft from congressional progressives and undermined his generally strong record on conservation. By 1912, when Taft faced reelection, the Republican Party was in serious disarray, and he faced opposition from most progressive Republicans.

"Carry a Big Stick": Roosevelt, Taft, and World Affairs

■ What were Theodore Roosevelt's objectives for the United States in world affairs? What did he do to realize those objectives?

■ How did Roosevelt reshape America's foreign policy?

Theodore Roosevelt not only remolded the presidency and established new federal powers over the economy, he also significantly expanded America's role abroad. Few presidents have had so great an influence. He once expressed his fondness for what he referred to as a West African proverb: "Speak softly and carry a big stick; you will go far." As president, however, Roosevelt seldom spoke softly. Everything he did, it seemed, he did strenuously. Well read in history and current events, Roosevelt entered the presidency with definite ideas on the place of the United States in world affairs. As he advised Congress in 1902, "The increasing interdependence and complexity of international political and economic relations render it incumbent on all civilized and orderly powers to insist on the proper policing of the world." The United States, Roosevelt made clear, stood ready to do its share of "proper policing."

Taking Panama

While McKinley was still president, American diplomats began efforts to create a canal through Central America. Many people had long shared the dream of such a passage between the Atlantic and Pacific Oceans. A French company began construction in the late 1870s (building on the success of the Suez Canal), but abandoned the project when the task proved too great.

During the Spanish-American War, the battleship *Oregon* took well over two months to steam from the West Coast around South America to join the rest of the fleet off Cuba. A canal would have permitted the *Oregon* to reach Cuba in three weeks or less. McKinley pronounced an American-controlled canal "indispensable." In the Clayton-Bulwer Treaty of 1850,

Payne-Aldrich Tariff Tariff passed by Congress in 1909; the original bill was an attempt to reduce tariffs, but the final version retained high tariffs on most imports.

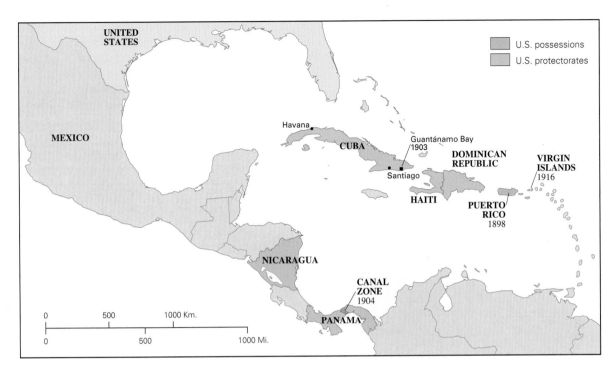

MAP 21.1 The United States and the Caribbean, 1898–1917   Between 1898 and 1917, the United States expanded into the Caribbean by acquiring possessions and establishing protectorates. As a result, the United States was the dominant power in the region throughout this time period.

however, Britain and the United States had agreed that neither would exercise exclusive control over a canal. Between 1900 and 1901, Secretary of State John Hay negotiated new agreements with Britain, the **Hay-Pauncefote Treaties,** which yielded the canal project to the United States alone.

Experts identified two possible locations for a canal, Nicaragua and Panama (then part of Colombia). The Panama route was shorter, and the French company had completed some of the work. **Philippe Bunau-Varilla**—formerly the chief project engineer for the French effort, now a major stockholder and indefatigable lobbyist—did his utmost to sell the French company's interests to the United States. Building through Panama, however, meant overcoming formidable mountains and fever-ridden swamps. Previous studies had preferred Nicaragua. Its geography posed fewer natural obstacles, and much of the route lay through Lake Nicaragua.

In 1902, shortly before Congress was to vote on the two routes, a volcano erupted in the Caribbean. Bunau-Varilla quickly distributed to all senators a Nicaraguan postage stamp showing a smoldering volcano loom-

ing over a lake. Bunau-Varilla's lobbying—and his stamps—reinforced efforts by prominent Republican senators. The Senate approved the route through the Colombian state of Panama.

Negotiations with Colombia bogged down over treaty language that limited Colombia's sovereignty. When American representatives applied pressure, the Colombian government offered to accept limitations on its sovereignty in return for more money. Outraged, Roosevelt called the offer "pure bandit morality." Bunau-Varilla and his associates then encouraged and financed a revolution in Panama. Roosevelt ordered

Hay-Pauncefote Treaties   Two separate treaties (1900 and 1901) signed by the United States and Britain that gave the United States the exclusive right to build, control, and fortify a canal through Central America.

Philippe Bunau-Varilla   Chief engineer of the French company that attempted to build a canal through the Panamanian isthmus, chief planner of the Panamanian revolt against Colombia, and later minister to the United States from the new Republic of Panama.

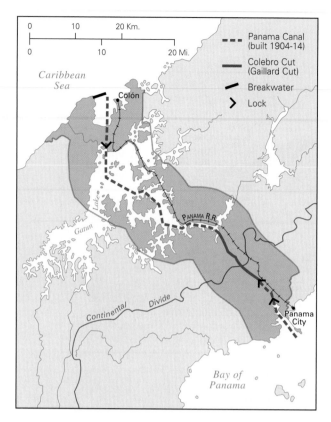

MAP 21.2 The Panama Canal The Panama Canal could take advantage of some natural waterways. The most difficult part of the construction, however, was devising some way to move ships over the mountains near the Pacific end of the canal (*lower right*). This problem was solved by a combination of cutting a route through the mountains and constructing massive locks to raise and lower ships over differences in elevation.

company and began construction. Roosevelt considered the canal his crowning deed in foreign affairs. "When nobody else could or would exercise efficient authority, I exercised it," he wrote in his *Autobiography* (1913). He always denied that he had any part in instigating the revolution, but he once bluntly claimed, "I took the canal zone."

Construction proved difficult. Just over 40 miles long, the canal took ten years to build and cost nearly $400 million. Completed in 1914, just as World War I began, it was considered one of the world's great engineering feats (see Map 21.2).

Making the Caribbean an American Lake

Well before the canal was finished, American policymakers considered how to protect it. Roosevelt determined to establish American dominance in the Caribbean and Central America, where the many harbors might permit a foreign power to prepare for a strike against the canal or even the Gulf Coast of the United States. Acquisition of Puerto Rico, protectorates over Cuba and Panama, and naval facilities in all three locations as well as on the Gulf Coast made the United States a powerful presence.

The Caribbean and the area around it contained twelve independent nations. Britain, France, Denmark, and the Netherlands held nearly all the smaller islands, and Britain had a coastal colony (British Honduras, now Belize). Several Caribbean nations had borrowed large amounts of money from European bankers, raising the prospect of intervention to secure loan payments. In 1902, for example, Britain and Germany declared a blockade of Venezuela over debts owed their citizens. In 1904 several European nations hinted that they might intervene in the Dominican Republic. Roosevelt waved his "big stick" and presented to Congress what became known as the **Roosevelt Corollary** to the Monroe Doctrine. He warned European nations against any intervention in the

U.S. warships to the area to prevent Colombian troops from crushing the uprising. The revolution quickly succeeded. Panama declared its independence on November 3, 1903, and the United States immediately extended diplomatic recognition. Bunau-Varilla became Panama's minister to the United States and promptly signed a treaty that gave the United States much the same arrangement earlier rejected by Colombia.

The **Hay–Bunau-Varilla Treaty** (1903) granted the United States perpetual control over the Canal Zone, a strip of Panamanian territory 10 miles wide, for a price of $10 million and annual rent of $250,000; it also made Panama the second American protectorate (Cuba was the first—see page 631; see also Map 21.1). The United States purchased the assets of the French

Hay–Bunau-Varilla Treaty 1903 treaty with Panama that granted the United States sovereignty over the Canal Zone in return for a $10 million payment plus an annual rent.

Roosevelt Corollary Extension of the Monroe Doctrine announced by Theodore Roosevelt in 1904, in which he proclaimed the right of the United States to police the Caribbean areas.

Theodore Roosevelt, in his 1904 Corollary to the Monroe Doctrine, asserted that the United States was dominant in the Caribbean. Here a cartoonist capitalized on Roosevelt's boyish nature, depicting the Caribbean as Roosevelt's pond. *Culver Pictures, Inc.*

Western Hemisphere, even if provoked by loan default or other action. If intervention by what he termed "some civilized nation" became necessary in the Caribbean or Central America in order to correct "chronic wrongdoing," Roosevelt insisted that the United States would handle it, acting as "an international police power."

Roosevelt acted forcefully to establish his new policy. In 1905 the Dominican Republic agreed to permit the United States to collect customs (the major source of governmental revenue) and supervise government expenditures, including debt repayment. Thus the island nation became the third U.S. protectorate. The Senate initially rejected this arrangement but approved an amended version in 1907. In the meantime, Roosevelt ordered the U.S. Navy to collect Dominican customs, claiming that he could do so under his presidential powers.

Roosevelt's successors, William Howard Taft and Woodrow Wilson, continued and expanded American domination in the Caribbean region. The Taft administration encouraged Americans to invest there. Taft hoped that diplomacy could open doors for American investments and that American investments would both block investment by other nations and stabilize and develop the Caribbean economies. Taft supported such **"dollar diplomacy"** throughout the region, especially in Nicaragua.

In 1912 Taft sent U.S. Marines to Nicaragua to suppress a rebellion against President Adolfo Díaz. They remained after the turmoil settled, ostensibly to guard the American legation but actually to prop up the Días government—making Nicaragua the fourth U.S. protectorate. A treaty was drafted giving the United States responsibility for collecting customs, but the Senate rejected it. At that point, the State Department, several American banks, and Nicaragua set up a **customs receivership** through the banks.

---

dollar diplomacy   Name applied by critics to the Taft administration's policy of supporting U.S. investments abroad.

customs receivership   An agreement whereby one nation takes over the collection of customs (taxes on imported goods) of another nation and exercises some control over that nation's expenditures of customs receipts, thus limiting the autonomy of the nation in receivership.

Japanese troops in Manchuria during the Russo-Japanese War of 1904–1905, in which Japanese military and naval forces scored major victories over the Russians. Theodore Roosevelt mediated the war, for which he received the Nobel Peace Prize in 1906. *Library of Congress.*

Roosevelt and Eastern Asia

In eastern Asia, Roosevelt built on the Open Door notes and American participation in the international force that suppressed the Boxer Rebellion. He was both concerned and optimistic about the rise of Japan as a major industrial and imperial power. Aware of Alfred Thayer Mahan's warnings of the potential danger that Japan posed to the United States in the Pacific, Roosevelt was also hopeful. He admired Japanese accomplishments and anticipated that Japan might exercise the same sort of international police power in its vicinity that the United States claimed under the Roosevelt Corollary.

In 1904 Russia and Japan went to war over **Manchuria,** part of northeastern China. Russia had pressured China to grant so many concessions in Manchuria that it seemed to be turning into a Russian colony. Russia seemed also to have designs on Korea, a nominally independent kingdom. Japan saw Russian expansion as a threat to its own interests and responded with force. The Japanese scored smashing

naval and military victories over the Russians but had too few resources to sustain a long-term war.

Roosevelt concluded that American interests were best served by reducing Russian influence in the region so as to maintain a balance of power. Such a balance, he thought, would also be most likely to preserve nominal Chinese sovereignty in Manchuria. Early in the war, he indicated some support for Japan, and as its resources ran low, Japan asked Roosevelt to act as mediator. The president agreed, concerned by then that Japanese victories might be as dangerous as Russian expansion. The peace conference took place in Portsmouth, New Hampshire. The **Treaty of Portsmouth** (1905) recognized Japan's dominance in Korea and gave Japan the southern half of Sakhalin Island and Russian concessions in southern Manchuria. Russia kept its railroad in northern Manchuria. China remained responsible for civil authority in Manchuria. For his mediation, Roosevelt received the 1906 Nobel Peace Prize.

That same year, Roosevelt mediated another dispute. The San Francisco school board ordered students of Japanese parentage to attend the city's segregated Chinese school. The Japanese government protested what it considered an insult, and some Japanese newspapers even hinted at war. Roosevelt brought the school officials to Washington and convinced them to withdraw the order. He promised in return to try to curtail Japanese immigration. He soon negotiated a so-called **gentlemen's agreement,** by which Japan agreed informally to limit the departure of laborers to the United States. In 1908 the American and Japanese governments further agreed to respect each other's territorial possessions (the Philippines and Hawai`i for the United States; Korea, Formosa, and southern Manchuria for Japan) and to honor as well "the independence and integrity of China" and the Open Door.

The Taft administration extended dollar diplomacy to China. Proponents sought Chinese permission for American citizens not only to trade with China but also to invest there, especially in railroad construc-

Manchuria   A region of northeastern China.

Treaty of Portsmouth   Treaty in 1905, ending the Russo-Japanese War; negotiated at a conference in Portsmouth, New Hampshire, through Theodore Roosevelt's mediation.

gentlemen's agreement   An agreement rather than a formal treaty; in this case, Japan agreed in 1907 to limit Japanese emigration to the United States.

"The Nations Pride"

This picture was issued as a penny postcard, expressing the nation's pride in the "Great White Fleet." The Post Office Department gave its approval to penny postcards in 1902, and the period between 1905 and 1915 is sometimes considered the "golden age" for penny postcards in the United States. The one-penny price for postage made them highly affordable, and the wide variety of subjects available made them collectable. *Collection of Picture Research Consultants and Archives.*

tion. Taft hoped that such investments could head off further Japanese expansion. The effort received Chinese government sanction, but little ever came of it.

The United States and the World, 1901–1913

Before the 1890s, the United States had few clear or consistent foreign-policy commitments or objectives. By 1905, its commitments were obvious to all. The Philippines, Guam, Hawai`i, Puerto Rico, eastern Samoa, and the Canal Zone were highly visible evidence that a new concept of America's role in world affairs had been born.

Central to that concept was a large, modern navy, without which every other commitment was merely a moral pronouncement. Roosevelt was so proud of the navy that in 1907 he dispatched sixteen battleships—painted white to signal their peaceful intent—on an around-the-world tour. He claimed that his primary purpose in sending the Great White Fleet "was to impress the American people." But Roosevelt was clearly interested in impressing other nations, especially Japan, and in demonstrating that the Ameri-

can navy was fully capable of moving quickly to distant parts of the globe.

Another aspect of America's new role in the world revolved around American control of the Panama Canal. The need to protect the canal led the United States to dominate the Caribbean and Central America to prevent any other major power from threatening the canal.

The new American role also focused on the Pacific. As Mahan and other naval strategists pointed out, just as the Atlantic Ocean had been the theater of conflict among European nations in the eighteenth century, so the Pacific Ocean was likely to be the theater of twentieth-century conflict. Thus considerations of commercial enterprise, such as the China trade, coincided with naval strategy and led the United States to acquire possessions at key locations in the Pacific and off eastern Asia (the Philippines).

American policymakers' new vision of the world seemed to divide nations into broad categories. In one class were the "civilized" nations. In the other were those nations that Theodore Roosevelt described, at various times, as "barbarous," "impotent," or simply unable to meet their obligations. When dealing with "civilized" countries—the European powers,

Political buttons continued to be ubiquitous in 1912. Roosevelt and his running mate, Hiram Johnson, the governor of California, are pictured with the Bull Moose that came to symbolize the Progressive Party after Roosevelt exclaimed that he felt as fit as a bull moose. Taft, the Republican candidate, and Wilson, the Democrat, are depicted with more traditional symbols of patriotism and party. *Collection of Janice L. and David J. Frent.*

Japan, the large, stable nations of Latin America, Canada, Australia, New Zealand—American diplomats focused on finding ways to realize mutual objectives, especially arbitration of disputes. In eastern Asia, McKinley, Roosevelt, and Taft looked to a balance of power among the contending "civilized" powers as most likely to realize the American objective of maintaining the "open door" in China.

The conviction that arbitration was the appropriate means to settle disputes among "civilized" countries was widespread. An international conference in 1899 created a Permanent Court of Arbitration in the Netherlands. Housed in a "peace palace" built through a donation from Andrew Carnegie, the **Hague Court** provided neutral arbitrators for international disputes. Both Roosevelt and Taft tried to negotiate arbitration treaties with major powers, but the Senate refused to ratify them for fear that arbitration might diminish the Senate's role in approving agreements with other countries.

The United States and Britain repeatedly used arbitration to settle their disputes. Throughout the late nineteenth and early twentieth centuries, American relations with Great Britain improved steadily, mostly as a result of British initiatives. As Germany expanded its army and navy, implicitly challenging Britain, British policymakers sought to improve relations with the United States, the only nation besides Britain with a navy comparable to Germany's. During the war with Spain, Britain alone among the major European powers sided with the United States and encouraged its acquisition of the Philippines. By signing the Hay-Pauncefote Treaties and reducing its naval forces in the Caribbean, Britain delivered a clear signal—it not only accepted American dominance there but now depended on the United States to protect its holdings in the region.

Wilson and Democratic Progressivism

■ What choices confronted American voters in the presidential election of 1912? What were the short-term and long-term outcomes of the election?

■ How did Wilson's views on reform evolve from the 1912 election through 1916?

■ How did the Wilson administration change the role of the federal government in the economy?

The presidential election of 1912 marks a moment when Americans actively and seriously debated their future. All three nominees were well educated and highly literate. Roosevelt and Wilson had written respected books on American history and politics. They approached politics with a sense of destiny and purpose, and they talked frankly to the American people about their ideas for the future.

Hague Court Body of delegates from about fifty member nations, created in the Netherlands in 1899 for the purpose of peacefully resolving international conflicts; also known as the Permanent Court of Arbitration.

Debating the Future: The Election of 1912

As Taft watched the Republican Party unravel, Theodore Roosevelt was traveling abroad, first hunting in Africa and then hobnobbing with European leaders. When he returned in 1910, he undertook a speaking tour and, without criticizing Taft, proposed a broad program of reform he labeled the **New Nationalism.** Roosevelt did not openly question Taft's reelection, but other Republican progressives began to do so. In the 1910 congressional elections, Republicans fared badly, plagued by divisions within their party and an economic downturn. For the first time since 1892, Democrats won a majority in the House of Representatives. Democrats, including Woodrow Wilson in New Jersey, also won a number of governorships.

By early 1911, many Republican progressives were looking to Robert La Follette to wrest the Republican nomination from Taft. Though Roosevelt found La Follette too radical and irresponsible, the former president had lost confidence in Taft. He began to criticize Taft for failing to maintain Republican unity and for his conservation and antitrust policies. Finally, in February 1912, Roosevelt announced he would oppose Taft for the Republican presidential nomination.

Thirteen states had established direct primaries to select delegates to the national nominating convention. There Roosevelt won 278 delegates to 48 for Taft and 36 for La Follette. Elsewhere, however, Taft had all the advantages of an incumbent president in control of the party machinery. At the Republican nominating convention, many states sent rival delegations, one pledged to Taft and one to Roosevelt. Taft's supporters controlled the **credentials committee** and gave most contested seats to Taft delegates. Roosevelt's supporters stormed out, complaining that Taft was stealing the nomination. The remaining delegates nominated Taft on the first ballot. Roosevelt refused to accept defeat. "We stand at Armageddon," he thundered, invoking the biblical prophecy of a final battle between good and evil. "And," he continued, "we battle for the Lord." His supporters quickly formed the Progressive Party, nicknamed the **Bull Moose Party** after Roosevelt's boast that he was "as fit as a bull moose." The delegates sang "Onward, Christian Soldiers" and issued a platform based on the New Nationalism, including tariff reduction, regulation of corporations, a minimum wage, an end to child labor, woman suffrage, and the initiative, referendum, and recall. Women were prominent at the Progressive convention and helped draft the platform—especially the sections dealing with labor. Settlement house pioneer Jane Addams addressed the convention to second the nomination of Roosevelt.

Democrats were overjoyed, certain that the Republican split gave them their best chance at the presidency in twenty years. The nomination was hotly contested, and the convention took forty-six ballots to nominate Woodrow Wilson, the governor of New Jersey. Their platform attacked monopolies, favored limits on campaign contributions by corporations, and called for major tariff reductions. Wilson labeled his program the **New Freedom.** Much of the campaign focused on Roosevelt and Wilson, ignoring Taft. Roosevelt continued to maintain that the behavior of corporations was the problem, not their size. After Wilson's nomination, he met with **Louis Brandeis,** a Boston attorney and leading critic of corporate consolidation. Brandeis convinced Wilson to center his campaign on the issue of big business and to offer a solution significantly different from the regulation promised by Roosevelt. Wilson depicted monopoly itself as the problem, not the misbehavior of individual corporations. Breaking up monopolies and restoring competition, he argued, would benefit consumers because competition would yield better products and lower prices. He also pointed to what he considered the most serious flaw in Roosevelt's proposals for regulation: as long as monopolies faced regulation, they would seek to control the regulator—the federal government. Only antitrust actions, Wilson argued, could protect democracy from this threat.

Though Roosevelt and Wilson presented quite different proposals for dealing with big business and

---

New Nationalism Program of labor and social reform that Theodore Roosevelt advocated before and during his unsuccessful bid to regain the presidency in 1912.

credentials committee Party convention committee that settles disputes arising when rival delegations from the same state demand to be seated.

Bull Moose Party Popular name given to the Progressive Party in 1912.

New Freedom Program of reforms that Woodrow Wilson advocated during his 1912 presidential campaign, including reducing tariffs and prosecuting trusts.

Louis Brandeis Lawyer and reformer who opposed monopolies and defended individual rights; in 1916 he became the first Jewish justice on the Supreme Court.

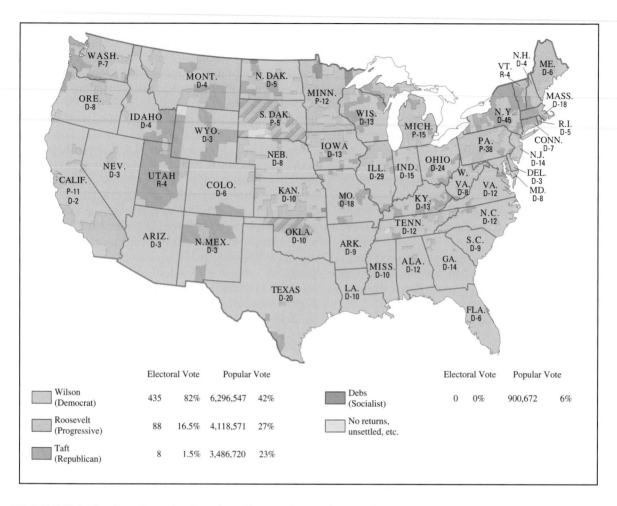

		Electoral Vote	Popular Vote				Electoral Vote	Popular Vote
	Wilson (Democrat)	435	82%	6,296,547	42%	Debs (Socialist)	0	0%	900,672	6%
	Roosevelt (Progressive)	88	16.5%	4,118,571	27%	No returns, unsettled, etc.			
	Taft (Republican)	8	1.5%	3,486,720	23%				

MAP 21.3 Election of 1912, by Counties   The presidential election of 1912 was complicated by the campaign of former president Theodore Roosevelt running as a Progressive. Roosevelt's campaign split the usual Republican vote without taking away much of the usual Democratic vote. Woodrow Wilson, the Democratic candidate, carried many parts of the West and Northeast that Democratic candidates rarely won.

attacked each other's right to claim the title "progressive," they agreed that Taft was not a progressive at all. Taft could claim a stronger record as a trustbuster than Roosevelt but was clearly the most conservative of the candidates. Eugene V. Debs, the Socialist candidate, rejected both regulation and antitrust actions and argued instead for government ownership of monopolies.

The real contest was between Roosevelt and Wilson. In the end, Wilson received most of the usual Democratic vote and won with 42 percent of the total. Democrats also won sizable majorities in both houses of Congress. Roosevelt and Taft split the traditional Republican vote, 27 percent for Roosevelt and 23 per-

cent for Taft. Debs, with only 6 percent, placed first in a few counties and city precincts (see Map 21.3).

Wilson and Reform, 1913–1914

Born in Virginia in 1856, Woodrow Wilson grew up in the South during the Civil War and Reconstruction. His father, a Presbyterian minister, impressed on him lessons in morality and responsibility that remained with him his entire life. Wilson earned a Ph.D. degree from Johns Hopkins University, and his first book, *Congressional Government,* analyzed federal lawmaking. A professor at Princeton University after 1890, he became president of Princeton in 1902 and intro-

derwood Act also implemented the income tax recently authorized by the Sixteenth Amendment.

The next matter facing Wilson and the Democrats was reform of banking. The national banking system dated to 1863, and periodic economic problems—most recently, a panic in 1907—had confirmed the system's major shortcomings: it had no real center to provide direction and no way to adjust the **money supply** to meet the needs of the economy. In 1913 a congressional investigation also revealed the concentration of a great power in the hands of the few investment bankers. Conservatives, led by Carter Glass of Virginia, joined with bankers in proposing a more centralized system with minimal federal regulation. Progressive Democrats, especially William Jennings Bryan (now Wilson's secretary of state) and Louis Brandeis, favored strong federal control.

The debate ended in compromise. In December 1913, Wilson approved the **Federal Reserve Act,** establishing twelve regional Federal Reserve Banks. These banks were "bankers' banks," institutions where commercial banks kept their reserves. All national banks were required to belong to the Federal Reserve System, and state banks were invited to join. The participating banks owned all the stock in their regional Federal Reserve Bank and named two-thirds of its board of directors; the president named the other third. The regional banks were to be regulated and supervised by the Federal Reserve Board, a new federal agency with members chosen by the president.

In 1914 Congress passed the **Clayton Antitrust Act,** which prohibited specified business practices, including **interlocking directorates** among large companies that could be proven to inhibit competition. It

It Matters

The Federal Reserve Act

The Federal Reserve Act stands as the most important domestic act of the Wilson administration, for it still provides the basic framework for the nation's banking and monetary system. Though the original act of 1913 has been amended many times, the Federal Reserve System remains an independent entity within the federal government, having both public purposes and private aspects.

Today, one central responsibility of the Federal Reserve is to carry out the nation's monetary policy, including regulating the money supply and interest rates to accomplish the congressionally determined goals of maximum employment, stable prices, and moderate long-term interest rates. The Federal Reserve also supervises and regulates banks and financial institutions to ensure their safety and soundness.

duced educational reforms that brought him wide attention.

In 1910 New Jersey Democrats needed a respectable candidate for governor. Party leaders picked Wilson because of his reputation as a conservative and a good public speaker. He won the election but shocked his party's conservative leaders by suddenly embracing reform. As governor, he led the legislature to adopt several progressive measures, including a direct primary and regulation of railroads and public utilities. His record won support from many Democratic progressives when he sought the 1912 presidential nomination.

Wilson firmly believed in party government and an active role for the president in policymaking. He set out to work closely with Democrats in Congress and succeeded to such an extent that, like Roosevelt, he changed the nature of the presidency itself. Confident in his oratorical skills, he became the first president since John Adams to address Congress in person.

Wilson first tackled tariff reform, arguing that high tariff rates fueled the creation of monopolies by reducing competition. Despite an outcry from manufacturers, Congress passed the **Underwood Tariff** in October 1913, establishing the most significant reductions since the Civil War. To offset federal revenue losses, the Un-

Underwood Act Law passed by Congress in 1913 that substantially reduced tariffs and made up for the lost revenue by providing for a graduated income tax.

money supply The amount of money in the economy, such as cash and the contents of checking accounts.

Federal Reserve Act Law passed by Congress in 1913 establishing twelve regional Federal Reserve Banks to hold the cash reserves of commercial banks and a Federal Reserve Board to regulate aspects of banking.

Clayton Antitrust Act Law passed by Congress in 1914 banning monopolistic business practices such as price fixing and interlocking directorates; it also exempted farmers' organizations and unions from prosecution under antitrust laws.

interlocking directorates Situation in which the same individuals sit on the boards of directors of various companies in one industry.

also exempted farmers' organizations and unions from antitrust prosecution under the Sherman Act. The antitrust sections in the final version of the Clayton Act, however, did little to break up big corporations. Instead of breaking up big business, Wilson now moved closer to Roosevelt's position favoring regulation. Wilson also supported passage of the **Federal Trade Commission Act** (1914), a regulatory measure intended to prevent unfair methods of competition.

Another Round of Reform and the Election of 1916

Progressives generally applauded the Wilson administration for tariff reform, the Federal Reserve System, and the Clayton Act. But many progressives criticized his appointees to the Federal Trade Commission and the Federal Reserve Board for their sympathies with business and banking. Congress fulfilled a Democratic campaign promise by creating a separate cabinet-level Department of Labor. As secretary of labor Wilson appointed William Wilson (not a relative), a union member and labor advocate. President Wilson did little more, however, to appeal to social reformers. He considered federal action to outlaw child labor to be unconstitutional, and he questioned the need to amend the Constitution for woman suffrage.

During his first year in office, Wilson drew sharp criticism from some northern social reformers when his appointees initiated racial segregation in several federal agencies. A southerner by birth and heritage, Wilson undoubtedly believed in segregation even though he resisted the most extreme racists in his party. At a cabinet meeting shortly after Wilson took office, the postmaster general (a southerner) proposed racial segregation of all federal employees. No cabinet member objected, and several federal agencies began to segregate African Americans. Wilson was surprised at the swell of protest, not just from African Americans but also from some white progressives in the North and Midwest. He never designated a change in policy, but the process of segregating federal facilities slowed significantly.

In 1912 Wilson had received less than half of the popular vote and had won the White House only because the Republicans split. As the 1916 election approached, he joined Democratic progressives in Congress—and social reformers outside Congress—in pushing measures intended to secure his claim as the true voice of progressivism and to capture the loyalty of all progressive voters.

In January 1916, Wilson nominated Louis Brandeis for the Supreme Court. Brandeis's reputation as a staunch progressive and critic of business aroused intense opposition from conservatives. He was the first Jewish nominee to the Court, and some dissent to his confirmation carried anti-Semitic overtones. The Senate vote on the nomination was close, but Brandeis was confirmed in June 1916 with support from a few progressive Republicans. Wilson followed up that victory with support for several reform measures—credit facilities for farmers, workers' compensation for federal employees, and the elimination of child labor. Under threat of a national railroad strike, Congress passed and Wilson signed the Adamson Act, securing an eight-hour workday for railroad employees.

The presidential election of 1916 was conducted against the background of the war that had been raging in Europe since 1914 (see Chapter 22). Wilson's shift toward social reform helped solidify his standing among progressives. His support for organized labor earned him strong backing among unionists, and labor's votes probably ensured his victory in a few states, especially California. In states where women could vote, many of them seem to have preferred Wilson, probably because he backed issues of interest to women, such as outlawing child labor and keeping the nation out of war. By 1916, Theodore Roosevelt had returned to the Republican Party, bringing many of his followers with him but losing some to Wilson, especially in the West. In a very close election, Wilson won with 49 percent of the popular vote to 46 percent for Charles Evans Hughes, a progressive Republican.

New Patterns in Cultural Expression

▪ How would you compare the influence of developments in the United States with the influence of developments in Europe with regard to cultural expression in the late nineteenth century?

▪ How did social and technological changes contribute to new patterns in mass entertainment?

Federal Trade Commission Act Law passed by Congress in 1914 that outlawed unfair methods of competition in interstate commerce and created a commission appointed by the president to investigate illegal business practices.

Mary Cassatt created this pastel portrait of a mother and child in 1897. Cassatt was one of the few Americans and few women, and the only American woman, to have a major role in the emergence of French Impressionism; some of her paintings were included in the Armory Show of 1913. Unlike other leading impressionists, her work often focused on women and children. Cassatt was also an important source of advice for a few American women whose wealth permitted them to collect important Impressionist paintings. She lived in France from the 1870s until the end of her life. © *Reunion des Musees Nationaux/Art Resource, NY.*

The changes sweeping American society also affected cultural expression. Shortly after 1900, the director of the nation's most prominent art museum, the Metropolitan Museum of New York, observed "a state of unrest" in art, literature, music, painting, and sculpture. "And," he added, "I dislike unrest." Unrest meant change, and Americans at that time witnessed dramatic changes in art, literature, and music—many of them directly influenced by the new urban industrial society, and some of them reflecting the concerns of the Progressive Era.

Realism, Impressionism, and Ragtime

At the turn of the century, American novelists increasingly turned to a realistic—and sometimes critical—portrayal of life, rejecting the romanticism characteristic of the earlier period. The towering figure of the era remained **Mark Twain** (pen name of Samuel L. Clemens), whose novel *The Adventures of Huckleberry Finn* (1885) may be read at many levels, ranging from a nostalgic account of boyhood adventures to profound social satire. In this masterpiece, Twain reproduced the everyday speech of unschooled whites and blacks, poked fun at social pretensions, scorned the Old South myth, and challenged prevailing, racially biased attitudes toward African Americans. Twain continued to be an important social commentator until his death in 1910. The novels of William Dean Howells and Henry James, by contrast, presented restrained, realistic portrayals of upper-class men and women, and Kate Chopin sounded feminist themes in *The Awakening* (1899), dealing with repression of a woman's desires. Stephen Crane, Theodore Dreiser, and Frank Norris showed the influence of Émile Zola, a prominent French novelist, as they sharpened the critical edge of fiction. Crane's *Maggie: A Girl of the Streets* (1893) depicted how urban squalor could turn a young woman to prostitution. Norris's *The Octopus* (1901) portrayed the abusive power that a railroad could wield over people.

As American literature moved toward realism and social criticism during these years, many American painters were also experimenting with new modes of expression. A notable exception was Thomas Eakins, a realist and probably the most accomplished painter working in the United States during much of the Gilded Age. Although he received limited recognition at the time, he is now considered a leading American painter. By 1900, many American painters had abandoned realism in response to French **impressionism,** which emphasized less an exact reproduction of the world and more the artist's impression of it. Mary

Mark Twain   Pen name of Samuel Clemens, prominent American author of the late nineteenth century; Twain wrote *The Adventures of Huckleberry Finn* and many other American literary classics.

impressionism   A style of painting that developed in France in the 1870s and emphasized the artist's impression of a subject.

Professional baseball developed a strong popular appeal in the years after the Civil War, as most major cities acquired one or more teams. Thomas Eakins, who depicted these ballplayers at work in 1875, was the most impressive realist painter in the country at the time. *"Baseball Players Practicing" by Thomas Eakins, 1875. Museum of Art, Rhode Island School of Design, Jesse Metcalf and Walter H. Kimball Funds. Photograph by Cathy Carver.*

Cassatt was the only American—and one of only two women—to rank among the leaders of impressionism, but she lived and painted mostly in France. Among prominent impressionists working in the United States was Childe Hassam, who often depicted urban scenes. Attention to the city was also characteristic of work by Robert Henri, John Sloan, and others. Labeled the **Ash Can School** because of their preoccupation with everyday urban life and people, they produced the artistic counterpart to critical realism in literature.

In 1913 the most widely publicized art exhibit of the era permitted Americans to view works by some of the most innovative European painters of the day. Known as the Armory Show, for its opening in New York's National Guard Armory (it was later displayed in Chicago and Boston), the exhibit presented works by Pablo Picasso, Henri Matisse, Marcel Duchamp, Wassily Kandinsky, and others. Sophisticated critics and popular newspapers alike dismissed them as either insane or anarchists. One reviewer scornfully suggested that Duchamp's cubist painting *Nude De-*

scending a Staircase be retitled "explosion in a shingle factory." The abstract, modernist style, however, soon became firmly established.

As with painting, many aspects of American music derived from European models. John Philip Sousa, who produced well over a hundred works between the 1870s and his death in 1932, was the most popular American composer of the day, best known for his stirring patriotic marches. Perhaps more significant in the long run was the African American composer Scott Joplin. Born in Texas, Joplin had formal instruction in the piano and then traveled through African American communities from New Orleans to Chicago. En route, he encountered **ragtime** music and soon began to write his own. In 1899 he published "Maple Leaf Rag" and quickly soared to fame as the leading ragtime composer in the country. Though condemned by some at the time as vulgar, ragtime contributed significantly to the later development of jazz.

Mass Entertainment in the Early Twentieth Century

By 1900, changes in transportation (the railroads) and communication (telegraph and telephone) combined with increased leisure time among the middle class and some skilled workers to foster new forms of entertainment. Traveling dramatic and musical troupes had long entertained some Americans, but now booking agencies could schedule such groups into nearly every corner of the country. Traveling actors, singers, and other performers offered everything from Shakespeare to **slapstick,** from opera to **melodrama.**

Booking agencies developed a star system: each traveling company had one or two popular performers who attracted the audience and helped to make up for the inadequacies of the other players. Other

Ash Can School   New York artists of varying styles who shared a focus on urban life.

ragtime   Style of popular music characterized by a syncopated rhythm and a regularly accented beat; considered the immediate precursor of jazz.

slapstick   A rowdy form of comedy marked by crude practical jokes and physical humor, such as falls.

melodrama   A sensational or romantic stage play with exaggerated conflicts and stereotyped characters.

traveling spectacles also took advantage of improved transportation and communication to establish regular circuits, including circuses and Wild West shows. One of the most popular traveling shows was the **Chautauqua,** a blend of inspirational oratory, educational lectures, and entertainment. The programs, often a week or two in length, attracted hundreds, even thousands, of people from the surrounding countryside.

During the late nineteenth century, a quite different form of mass entertainment appeared—professional baseball. Teams traveled by train from city to city, and urban rivalries built loyalty among fans. In 1876 team owners (often drawn initially from the ranks of players) formed the National League, as a way to monopolize the industry by excluding rival clubs from their territories and controlling the movement of players from team to team. Because African Americans were barred from the National League, separate black clubs and Negro leagues emerged. In the 1880s and 1890s, the National League warded off challenges from rival leagues and defeated a players' union. Not until 1901 did another league—the American League—successfully organize. In 1903 the two leagues merged into a new, stronger cartel and staged the first World Series—in which the Boston Red Sox beat the Pittsburgh Pirates. As other professional spectator sports developed, they often imitated the organization, labor relations, and racial discrimination first established in baseball.

Celebrating the New Age

In 1893, when the World's Columbian Exposition opened in Chicago, Hamlin Garland, a writer living there, wrote to his parents in South Dakota, "Sell the cook stove if necessary and come. . . . You must see this fair." Between 1876 and 1915, Americans repeatedly held great expositions, beginning with one in Philadelphia in 1876 that commemorated the centennial of independence and concluding with one in San Francisco in 1915 that celebrated the opening of the Panama Canal. Others took place in Atlanta, Buffalo, Omaha, Portland (Oregon), San Diego, and St. Louis. The most impressive and influential was the Columbian Exposition in Chicago, marking the four-hundredth anniversary of Columbus's voyage to the New World.

These expositions typically featured vast exhibition halls where companies demonstrated their latest technological marvels, artists displayed their creations, and farmers presented their most impressive

produce. In other halls, states and foreign nations showcased their accomplishments. The exhibits nearly always expressed the conviction that technology and industry would inevitably improve the lives of all. After 1898, most also included demeaning exhibits of "savage" or "barbarian" people from the nation's new overseas possessions.

Behind the gleaming machines in the imitation marble palaces, however, lurked troubling questions that never appeared in the exhibits glorifying "Progress." What should be the working conditions of those whose labor created such technological marvels? Were democratic institutions compatible with the concentration of power and control in industry and finance or with the acquisition of colonies?

Progressivism in Perspective

■ Was progressivism successful? How do you define success?

■ How did progressivism affect modern American politics?

The Progressive Era began with efforts at municipal reform in the 1890s and sputtered to a close during World War I. Some politicians who called themselves progressives remained in prominent positions afterward, and progressive concepts of efficiency and expertise continued to guide government decision making. But the war, which the United States entered in 1917, diverted public attention from reform, and by the end of the war political concerns had changed. By the mid-1920s, many of the major leaders of progressivism had passed from the political stage.

The changes of the Progressive Era transformed American politics and government. Before the Hepburn Act and the Federal Reserve Act, the federal government's role in the economy consisted largely of distributing land grants and setting protective tariffs. After the Progressive Era, the federal government became a significant and permanent player in the economy, regulating a wide range of economic activity and enforcing laws to protect consumers and some workers. The income tax quickly became the

Chautauqua A traveling show offering educational, religious, and recreational activities, part of a nationwide movement of adult education that began in the town of Chautauqua, New York.

At the center of the Columbian Exposition of 1893 was a great water-filled basin, with an elaborate sculpture representing Columbus at one end and this dramatic, 65-foot-tall depiction of the republic at the opposite end. The sculptor, Daniel Chester French, represented the American republic with one hand on a pole with a liberty cap at its end and with the other hand holding a globe surmounted by an American eagle. Though this view shows the entire statue as golden, in fact the head and arms were an ivory color and the rest of the statue was gilded. The statue may still be seen in Chicago's Jackson Park. *Chicago Historical Society.*

most significant source of federal funds, without which it is impossible to imagine the many activities that the federal government has assumed since then—from vast military expenditures to social welfare to support for the arts. Since the 1930s, the income tax has also been a potential instrument of social policy, by which the federal government can redistribute income.

During the Progressive Era, political parties declined in significance, and political campaigns were increasingly focused on personality and driven by advertising. These patterns accelerated in the second half of the twentieth century under the influence of television and public opinion polling. Organized pressure groups have proliferated and become ever more important. Women's participation in politics has continued to increase, especially in the last third of the twentieth century.

The assertion of presidential authority by Roosevelt and Wilson reappeared in the presidency of Franklin D. Roosevelt (1933–1945). The two Roosevelts and Wilson transformed Americans' expectations regarding the office of the presidency itself. Throughout the nineteenth century, Congress had dominated the making of domestic policy. During the twentieth century, Americans came to expect domestic policy to flow from forceful executive leadership in the White House.

Finley Peter Dunne, the leading political humorist of the Progressive Era, voiced a cynical view of reform when he observed that "a man that would expect to train lobsters to fly in a year is called a lunatic; but a man that thinks men can be turned into angels by an election is called a reformer." However, Dunne also realized that change is an integral part of American politics. He compared reform to housecleaning, and he quoted this conversation between a woman who ran a boarding house and one of her lodgers:

> *"I don't know what to do," says she. "I'm worn out, and it seems impossible to keep this house clean. What is the trouble with it?"*
>
> *"Madam," says my friend Gallagher, . . . "the trouble with this house is that it is occupied entirely by human beings. If it was a vacant house, it could easily be kept clean."*

Thus, Dunne concluded about progressive reform, "The noise you hear is not the first gun of a revolution. It's only the people of the United States beating a carpet."

Individual Voices

Examining a Primary Source

Theodore Roosevelt Asserts Presidential Powers

Theodore Roosevelt was one of the nation's most informed presidents. He read widely, especially in history and natural history, and he wrote extensively on those topics. Among his interests was the nature of executive power—a few years before he became president, he wrote a biography of Oliver Cromwell, who led the Puritan army that overthrew the British monarchy and who governed England in the mid-1600s. In Roosevelt's *Autobiography* (1913), he discussed some of his ideas about the nature of the presidency.

> *The most important factor in getting the right spirit in my Administration, next to the insistence upon courage, honesty, and a genuine democracy of desire to serve the plain people, was my insistence upon the theory that the executive power was limited only by specific restrictions and prohibitions appearing in the Constitution or imposed by the Congress under its Constitutional powers. . . . I declined to adopt the view that what was imperatively necessary for the Nation could not be done by the President unless he could find some specific authorization to do it. . . . I did and caused to be done many things not previously done by the President and the heads of the departments.* ■ *I did not usurp power, but I did greatly broaden the use of executive power. . . . I did not care a rap for the mere form and show of power; I cared immensely for the use that could be made of the substance. . . .*
>
> *There have long been two schools of political thought . . . The course I followed, of regarding the executive as subject only to the people, and, under the Constitution, bound to serve the people affirmatively in cases where the Constitu-*

■ Which of Roosevelt's actions were "things not previously done by a President"?

- What do you know about the presidencies of Jackson, Lincoln, and Buchanan that would support Roosevelt's views?

- Can you find examples of such behavior in U.S. foreign affairs? in domestic policy? Can you find contrary examples? How successful was Roosevelt in meeting his own standard?

- What dangers might result from Roosevelt's views of sweeping presidential powers?

tion does not explicitly forbid him to render the service, was substantially the course followed by both Andrew Jackson and Abraham Lincoln. Other honorable and well-meaning Presidents, such as James Buchanan, took the opposite and, as it seems to me, narrowly legal view that the President is the servant of Congress rather than of the people, and can do nothing, no matter how necessary it be to act, unless the Constitution explicitly commands the action. ■ Most able lawyers who are past middle age take this view. . . .

In foreign affairs the principle from which we never deviated was to have the Nation behave toward other nations precisely as a strong, honorable, and upright man behaves in dealing with his fellow-men. . . . ■

In internal affairs I cannot say that I entered the Presidency with any deliberately planned and far-reaching scheme of social betterment. I had, however, certain strong convictions . . . I was bent upon making the Government the most efficient possible instrument in helping the people of the United States to better themselves in every way, politically, socially, and industrially. I believed with all my heart in real and thoroughgoing democracy, and I wished to make this democracy industrial as well as political. . . . I believed that the Constitution should be treated as the greatest document ever devised by the wit of man to aid a people in exercising every power for its own betterment, and not as a straitjacket cunningly fashioned to strangle growth. . . . ■

Summary

Progressivism, a phenomenon of the late nineteenth and early twentieth centuries, refers to new concepts of government, to changes in government based on those concepts, and to the political process by which change occurred. Those years marked a time of political transformation, brought about by many groups and individuals who approached politics with often contradictory objectives. Organized interest groups became an important part of this process. Women broke through long-standing constraints to take a more prominent role in politics. The Anti-Saloon League was the most successful of several organizations that appealed to government to enforce morality. Some African Americans fought segregation and disfranchisement, notably W. E. B. Du Bois and the NAACP. Socialists and the Industrial Workers of the World saw capitalism as the source of many problems, but few Americans embraced their radical solutions.

Political reform took place at every level, from cities to states to the federal government. Muckraking journalists exposed wrongdoing and suffering. Municipal reformers introduced modern methods of city government in a quest for efficiency and effectiveness. Some tried to use government to remedy social problems by employing the expertise of new professions such as public health and social work. Reformers attacked the power of party bosses and machines by reducing the role of political parties.

At the federal level, Theodore Roosevelt set the pace for progressive reform. Relishing his reputation as a trustbuster, he challenged judicial constraints on federal authority over big business and promoted other forms of economic regulation, thereby increasing government's role in the economy. He also regulated the use of natural resources. His successor, William Howard Taft, failed to maintain Republican Party unity and eventually sided with conservatives against progressives.

Roosevelt played an important role in defining America's status as a world power, as he secured rights to build a U.S.-controlled canal through Panama and established Panama as an American protectorate. The Roosevelt Corollary declared that the United States was the dominant power in the Caribbean and Central America. In eastern Asia, Roosevelt tried to bolster the Open Door policy by maintaining a balance of power. Roosevelt and others sought arbitration treaties with leading nations but failed because of Senate opposition. Faced with the rise of German military and naval power, Great Britain improved relations with the United States.

In 1912 Roosevelt led a new political party, the Progressives, making that year's presidential election a three-way contest. Roosevelt called for regulation of big business, but Wilson, the Democrat, favored breaking up monopolies through antitrust action. Wilson won the election but soon preferred regulation over antitrust actions. He helped to create the Federal Reserve System to regulate banking nationwide. As the 1916 election approached, Wilson also pushed for social reforms in an effort to unify all progressives behind his leadership.

The new urban, industrial, multiethnic society contributed to critical realism in literature, new patterns in painting, and ragtime music, although many creative artists continued to look to Europe for inspiration. Urbanization and changes in transportation and communication also fostered the emergence of a mass entertainment industry.

Progressive reforms made a profound impression on later American politics. In many ways, progressivism marked the origin of modern American politics.

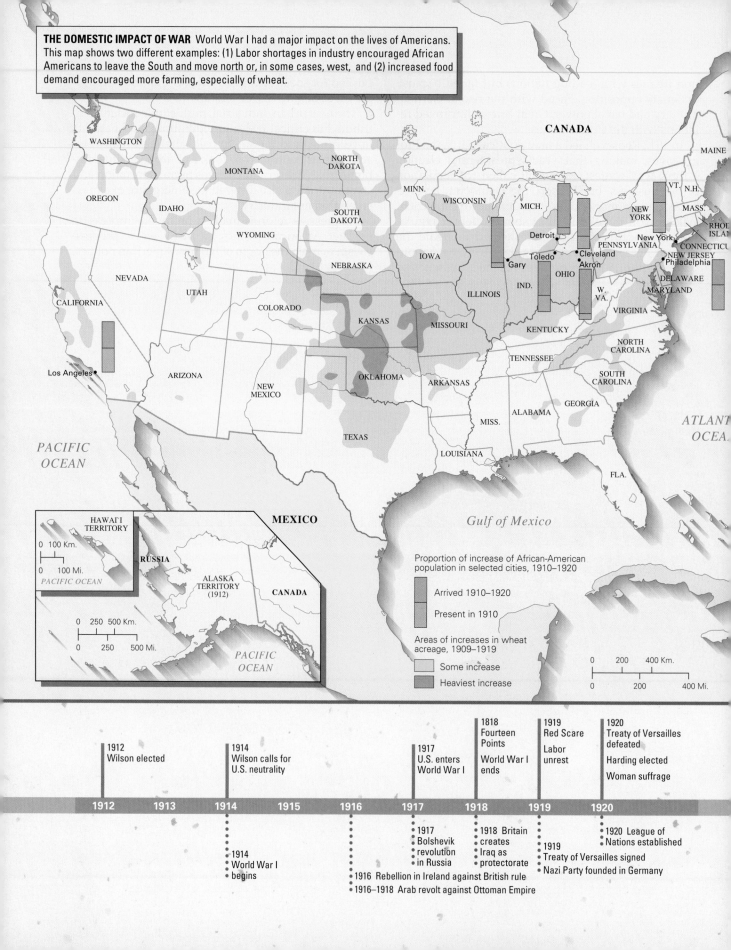

THE DOMESTIC IMPACT OF WAR World War I had a major impact on the lives of Americans. This map shows two different examples: (1) Labor shortages in industry encouraged African Americans to leave the South and move north or, in some cases, west, and (2) increased food demand encouraged more farming, especially of wheat.

CANADA

WASHINGTON

OREGON

IDAHO

MONTANA

NORTH DAKOTA

SOUTH DAKOTA

WYOMING

NEVADA

UTAH

COLORADO

NEBRASKA

IOWA

MINN.

WISCONSIN

MICH.

Detroit

Gary

Toledo

Cleveland

Akron

OHIO

IND.

ILLINOIS

MISSOURI

KANSAS

MAINE

VT. N.H.

MASS.

NEW YORK

New York

PENNSYLVANIA

Philadelphia

RHODE ISLAND

CONNECTICUT

NEW JERSEY

DELAWARE

MARYLAND

W. VA.

VIRGINIA

KENTUCKY

CALIFORNIA

ARIZONA

NEW MEXICO

Los Angeles

OKLAHOMA

ARKANSAS

TEXAS

TENNESSEE

NORTH CAROLINA

SOUTH CAROLINA

GEORGIA

ALABAMA

MISS.

LOUISIANA

FLA.

PACIFIC OCEAN

ATLANTIC OCEAN

Gulf of Mexico

HAWAI'I TERRITORY

0 100 Km.

0 100 Mi.

PACIFIC OCEAN

MEXICO

RUSSIA

ALASKA TERRITORY (1912)

CANADA

PACIFIC OCEAN

0 250 500 Km.

0 250 500 Mi.

Proportion of increase of African-American population in selected cities, 1910–1920

Arrived 1910–1920

Present in 1910

Areas of increases in wheat acreage, 1909–1919

Some increase

Heaviest increase

0 200 400 Km.

0 200 400 Mi.

1912
Wilson elected

1914
Wilson calls for U.S. neutrality

1917
U.S. enters World War I

1818
Fourteen Points

World War I ends

1919
Red Scare

Labor unrest

1920
Treaty of Versailles defeated

Harding elected

Woman suffrage

| 1912 | 1913 | 1914 | 1915 | 1916 | 1917 | 1918 | 1919 | 1920 |

1914
World War I begins

1917
Bolshevik revolution in Russia

1918 Britain creates Iraq as protectorate

1919
Treaty of Versailles signed

Nazi Party founded in Germany

1920 League of Nations established

1916 Rebellion in Ireland against British rule

1916–1918 Arab revolt against Ottoman Empire

The United States in a World at War, 1913–1920

The Domestic Impact of War

The map on the facing page shows two very different and
unrelated changes that came during World War I (WWI). Why
did the cities of the Midwest receive so many African American migrants from the South during WWI? Why was there
such a major expansion in wheat growing?

Individual Choices

ALVIN YORK

Alvin York, a devout Christian, had to choose between his moral compunctions about killing and his sense of obligation to his country. This photograph was taken in 1919, the year York was promoted to sergeant and received the Congressional Medal of Honor, as well as similar awards from many of the Allies for his exploits in battle. *Brown Brothers.*

Alvin York

On June 28, 1914, a Serbian terrorist killed Archduke Franz Ferdinand, heir to the throne of Austria-Hungary, and his wife, Sophie. The royal couple was visiting Sarajevo, in Bosnia-Herzegovina, which the Austrians had recently annexed against the wishes of the neighboring kingdom of Serbia. In response to the assassinations, Austria first consulted with its ally Germany and then made stringent demands on Serbia. Serbia sought help from Russia, which was allied with France. Tense diplomats invoked elaborate, interlocking alliances. Huge armies began to move. By August 4, most of Europe was at war.

Despite efforts to remain neutral, the United States entered the war in April 1917. Shortly after, Congress specified that all men ages 21 to 30 (later extended to 18 to 45) were subject to military service. Nearly 3 million men were drafted into service, including Alvin York.

Born in the Cumberland Mountains of Tennessee in 1887, York was raised in a backwoods community where people expected to secure some of the food on their tables through skill with their hunting rifles. He grew up with guns, remembering that his father "threatened to muss me up right smart if I failed to bring a squirrel down with the first shot or hit a [wild] turkey in the body instead of [shooting] its head off." From his youth, red-haired Alvin York was highly proficient with both rifle and pistol.

As a young man, York was known for his drinking, carousing, and recklessness. He put all that behind him when he became a **born-again Christian** in 1915 and joined a small **fundamentalist** church. He took his new faith seriously, and his commitment posed difficult choices for him when the war came:

> I loved and trusted old Uncle Sam and I have always believed he did the right thing. But I was worried clean through. I didn't want to go and kill. I believed in my Bible. And it distinctly said "thou shalt not kill." And yet old Uncle Sam wanted me. And he said he wanted me most awful bad. And I jest didn't know what to do. I worried and worried. I couldn't think of anything else. My thoughts just wouldn't stay a hitched.

York sought exemption from the draft as a conscientious objector but was refused.

Called to active duty, he made "good friends" with his new rifle and excelled at target practice. Still deeply troubled about the morality of war, he shared his concern with his battalion commander, Major Edward Buxton, who spent long hours discussing the Bible with York and trying to convince him that a good Christian might morally choose to go to war. Buxton recognized York's sincerity, however, and offered him the choice of noncombatant duty if he decided he could not kill on the battlefield. After struggling with his religious beliefs, York finally decided not only that he could fight in good conscience but that he was doing the Lord's work in helping to bring peace.

York's unit arrived on the front lines in France in June 1918 and took part in several major battles. On October 8, York—now a corporal—was part of a sixteen-man unit sent to take out some enemy machine guns in the Argonne Forest. They captured a small group of Germans, but a sudden burst of machine-gun fire killed or wounded nine of the Americans, including the sergeant, putting York in command. Leaving the surviving Americans to guard the prisoners, York coolly practiced his mountaineer sharpshooting, killing fourteen or so Germans as they trained machine-gun fire in his direction and tried to determine his position. When six Germans charged him with fixed bayonets, he dropped them all with his pistol. He then captured the German lieutenant in command and had him call on his men to surrender. York shot those who resisted. Prisoners in tow, York and other members of his unit then moved from position to position, using the German lieutenant to order each to surrender. Credited with killing twenty-five enemy soldiers and silencing thirty-five machine guns, York and the six other Americans marched 132 prisoners back to their astonished commanding officer.

The next day, York returned to the area searching for survivors. There he knelt and prayed for the souls of the dead, including those he had killed.

For his bravery and cool competence under fire, York received the Congressional Medal of Honor, the Croix de Guerre (France's highest decoration), and similar awards from other nations. Still, the blessings of his contemporaries were not enough to settle his conscience. Toward the end of his life, confined to bed, Alvin York pressed his son, a minister, for assurance that God would approve his deeds in the Argonne Forest.

INTRODUCTION

Before the events of August 1914, many Americans—including Theodore Roosevelt—had concluded that war had become unthinkable among what Roosevelt called the world's "civilized" nations. As president, Roosevelt had argued that the best way to preserve peace was by developing naval and military strength. Given the widely held expectation that war had become virtually obsolete, many Americans were shocked, saddened, and repelled in August 1914 when the leading "civilized" nations of the world—all of which had been busily accumulating arsenals—lurched into war.

When the nations of Europe went to war, the United States was no minor player on the international scene. Between 1898 and 1908, America acquired the Philippines and the Panama Canal, came to dominate the Caribbean and Central America, and actively participated in the balance of power in eastern Asia. The three presidents of the Progressive Era—Roosevelt, William Howard Taft, and Woodrow Wilson—agreed wholeheartedly that the United States should exercise a major role in world affairs.

Inherited Commitments and New Directions

■ Before the outbreak of war in Europe, how did Wilson conceive of America's role in dealing with other nations?

■ In what new directions did Wilson steer U.S. foreign policy before the coming of war in Europe?

When Woodrow Wilson entered the White House in 1913, he expected to spend most of his time dealing with domestic issues. Though well read on international affairs, he had neither significant international experience nor carefully considered foreign policies. For secretary of state he chose William Jennings Bryan,

born-again Christian   One whose life has been so changed by faith that he or she feels as if life has begun anew.

fundamentalism   A Christian religious movement that emphasizes the literal truth of the Bible and opposes those who seek to reconcile the Bible with scientific knowledge.

who also had devoted most of his political career to domestic matters and had little experience that qualified him as the nation's foreign-policy chief. Both Wilson and Bryan were devout Presbyterians, sharing a confidence that God had a plan for humankind. Both hoped—idealistically and perhaps naively—that they might make the United States a model among nations for the peaceful settlement of international disputes. Initially, Wilson fixed his attention on the three world regions of greatest American involvement: Latin America, the Pacific, and eastern Asia. There, he tried to balance the anti-imperialist principles of his Democratic Party against the expansionist practices of his Republican predecessors. He marked out some new directions, but in the end he extended many previous commitments.

Anti-Imperialism, Intervention, and Arbitration

Wilson's party had opposed many of the foreign policies of McKinley, Roosevelt, and Taft, especially imperialism. Secretary of State Bryan was a leading anti-imperialist who had criticized Roosevelt's "Big Stick" in foreign affairs. "The man who speaks softly does not need a big stick," Bryan said, adding, "If he yields to temptation and equips himself with one, the tone of his voice is very likely to change." Wilson shared Taft's support for American commercial expansion, but he faulted dollar diplomacy (see page 661) for using the State Department to advance the interests of particular companies.

During the Wilson administration, the Democrats' long-standing commitment to anti-imperialism produced two measures. In 1916 Congress established a bill of rights for residents of the Philippine Islands and promised them independence, though without specifying a date. The next year, Congress made Puerto Rico an American territory and extended American citizenship to its residents. Thus the Democrats wrote into law a limited version of the anti-imperialism they had proclaimed for some twenty years.

Democrats had criticized Roosevelt's actions in the Caribbean, but Wilson eventually intervened more in Central America and the Caribbean than did any other administration. In Nicaragua, Taft had used marines to prop up the rule of President Adolfo Días. Wilson now sought more authority for the United States within that country. Senate Democrats rejected his efforts, reminding him of their party's opposition to further protectorates. Even so, the **Bryan-Chamorro Treaty** of 1914 gave the United States significant concessions, including the right to build a canal through Nicaragua.

In Haiti, which owed a staggering debt to foreign bankers, the dictatorial president ordered many of his opponents put to death in 1915. When a mob tore him apart, Wilson sent in American marines. A treaty followed, making Haiti a protectorate in which American forces controlled most aspects of government until 1933. Wilson sent marines into the Dominican Republic in 1916, and U.S. naval officers exercised control there until 1924. In 1917, too, the United States bought the Virgin Islands from Denmark for $25 million.

Although Wilson made few changes in previous policies regarding the Caribbean, he enthusiastically encouraged Bryan to promote arbitration of international disputes. Roosevelt's and Taft's secretaries of state had sought arbitration treaties, but their efforts had foundered on the Senate's refusal to yield any of its role in foreign relations. Learning from those failures, Bryan drafted a model arbitration treaty and obtained approval of it from the Senate Foreign Relations Committee. The State Department then distributed the proposal—called "President Wilson's Peace Proposal"—to the forty nations that maintained diplomatic relations with the United States. Negotiations produced twenty-two ratified treaties, all of which featured a cooling-off period for disputes, typically a year, during which the nations agreed not to go to war and instead to seek arbitration. The treaties marked the beginning of a process by which Wilson sought to redefine international relations, substituting rational negotiations for raw power.

Wilson and the Mexican Revolution

In Mexico, Wilson attempted to influence internal politics but eventually found himself on the verge of war. **Porfirio Díaz** had ruled Mexico for a third of a century, supported by the great landholders, the

---

Bryan-Chamorro Treaty   Treaty in 1914 in which Nicaragua received $3 million in return for granting the United States exclusive rights to a canal route and a naval base.

Porfirio Díaz   Mexican soldier and politician who became president after a coup in 1876 and ruled Mexico until 1911.

Chronology

The United States and World Affairs, 1913–1920

1912	Woodrow Wilson elected president
1913	Victoriano Huerta takes power in Mexico Wilson denies U.S. recognition to Huerta Secretary of State Bryan proposes cooling-off treaties
1914	U.S. Navy occupies Veracruz War breaks out in Europe United States declares neutrality Stalemate on the western front Bryan-Chamorro Treaty
1915	German U-boat sinks the *Lusitania* United States occupies Haiti
1915–1920	Great Migration
1916	U.S. troops pursue Pancho Villa into Mexico National Defense Act *Sussex* pledge Sykes-Picot Agreement United States occupies Dominican Republic Wilson reelected
1917	Wilson calls for "peace without victory" American troops leave Mexico United States acquires Virgin Islands from Denmark Germany resumes submarine warfare Overthrow of tsar of Russia United States declares war on Germany Committee on Public Information War Industries Board Selective Service Act Espionage Act Race riot in East St. Louis Government crackdown on IWW Bolsheviks seize power in Russia

	Russia withdraws from the war Bolsheviks publish secret treaties Railroads placed under federal control
1917–1918	Union membership rises sharply
1918	Wilson presents Fourteen Points to Congress Lynchings increase Germans launch major offensive National War Labor Board Sedition Act U.S. troops in northern Russia and Siberia Successful Allied counteroffensive Republican majorities in Congress Armistice in Europe
1918–1919	Worldwide influenza epidemic
1918-1920	Civil war in Russia Rampant U.S. inflation
1919	Treaty of Versailles, including Covenant of the League of Nations Prohibition approved General strike in Seattle Urban race riots Wilson suffers stroke Boston police strike Senate defeats Versailles treaty
1919–1920	Steel strike Red Scare Palmer raids
1920	Senate defeats Versailles treaty again Nineteenth Amendment (woman suffrage) approved Warren G. Harding elected president

church, and the military. During his rule, and with his encouragement, many American companies invested in the Mexican economy. By the early twentieth century, however, discontent was brewing among peasants, workers, and intellectuals. Rebellion broke out, and mobs took to the streets demanding that Díaz resign. He did so in 1911. Francisco Madero, a leading advocate of reform, assumed the presidency to great acclaim but proved incapable of uniting the country. Discontent rolled across Mexico as peasant armies called for *tierra y libertad* ("land and liberty") and attacked the mansions of great landowners. Conservatives feared Madero as a reformer, but radicals dismissed him as too timid. Conservative forces launched an uprising in Mexico City in February 1913, working with the commander of the army,

Francisco "Pancho" Villa, shown here with his troops in 1914, raised an army in northern Mexico and helped to overthrow the dictatorial regimes of Porfirio Díaz and Victoriano Huerta. He also rebelled against the administration of Venustiano Carranza, whose reforms Villa found to be too moderate, and tried to incite a war between the United States and Mexico as a way to overthrow Carranza. *Brown Brothers.*

that he was withholding recognition because Huerta's regime did not rest on the consent of the governed.

Wilson's addition of a moral dimension to diplomatic recognition constituted something new in American foreign policy. Previous American presidents had automatically extended diplomatic recognition to governments in power. Labeled "missionary diplomacy," Wilson's approach implied that the United States would discriminate between pure and impure governments. Telling one visitor, "I am going to teach the South American republics to elect good men," Wilson engaged in what he called "watchful waiting," seeking an opportunity to act against Huerta. In the meantime, anti-Huerta forces led by **Venustiano Carranza** began to make significant gains.

In April 1914, Wilson found an excuse to intervene when Mexican officials in Tampico arrested a few American sailors who had come ashore. The city's army commander immediately released them and apologized. Wilson, however, used the incident to justify ordering the U.S. Navy to occupy **Veracruz** (see Map 22.1). As the leading Mexican port, Veracruz was the major source of the Huerta government's revenue (from customs) and the landing point for most government military supplies. The occupation cut these off. It also cost more than a hundred Mexican lives and turned many Mexicans against Wilson for violating their national sovereignty over a petty dispute. Facing Carranza's armies and without munitions and customs revenues, Huerta fled the country in mid-July. Wilson withdrew the last American forces from Veracruz in November.

Carranza succeeded Huerta as president, and Wilson officially recognized his government. Carranza faced armed opposition, however, from **Francisco "Pancho" Villa** in northern Mexico and Emiliano Za-

General **Victoriano Huerta.** Huerta took control of the government and had Madero executed.

Most European governments extended diplomatic recognition to Huerta because his government clearly held power in Mexico City. Taft—about to hand over the presidency—left that matter to his successor, so Wilson faced that decision soon after his inauguration. American companies with investments in Mexico, especially mining and oil, urged recognition because they considered Huerta likely to protect their holdings. Wilson, however, considered Huerta a murderer and privately vowed "not to recognize a government of butchers." In public, Wilson announced

Victoriano Huerta   Mexican general who overthrew President Francisco Madero in 1913 and established a military dictatorship until forced to resign in 1914.

Venustiano Carranza   Mexican revolutionary leader who helped to lead armed opposition to Victoriano Huerta and who succeeded to the presidency in 1914; his government was overthrown in 1920.

Veracruz   Major port city, located in east-central Mexico on the Gulf of Mexico; in 1914, Wilson ordered the U.S. Navy to occupy the port.

Francisco "Pancho" Villa   Mexican bandit and revolutionary who led a raid into New Mexico in 1916, which prompted the U.S. government to send troops into Mexico in unsuccessful pursuit.

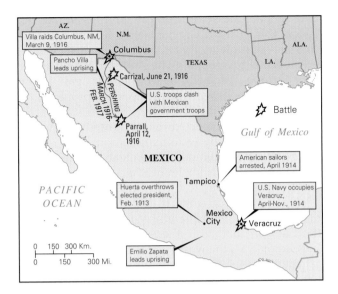

MAP 22.1 The United States and the Mexican Revolution
This map identifies the key locations for understanding relations between the United States and Mexico during 1913–1917.

pata in the south. When Villa suffered serious setbacks, he apparently decided to try to defeat Carranza by inciting a war with the United States. Villa's men murdered several Americans in Mexico and then, in March 1916, raided across the border and killed several Americans in Columbus, New Mexico. After securing reluctant approval from Carranza, Wilson sent an expedition of nearly seven thousand men, commanded by General John Pershing, into Mexico to punish Villa. Villa deftly evaded the American troops, but drew them ever deeper into Mexico.

Alarmed, Carranza protested the size of the American expedition and the distance it had penetrated into Mexico. When a clash between Mexican government forces and American soldiers produced deaths on both sides, Carranza asked Wilson to withdraw the American troops. Wilson refused. Villa then doubled behind the American army and raided into Texas, killing more Americans. Wilson sent more men into Mexico, though Carranza insisted that all American forces be withdrawn. Wilson still refused. Only in early 1917, when Wilson began to anticipate that America might soon be at war with Germany, did he order the troops to pull back, leaving behind a deep reservoir of Mexican resentment and suspicion toward the United States.

The United States in a World at War, 1914–1917

■ Why did Wilson proclaim American neutrality? What were the attitudes of Americans toward this objective?

■ What forces outside the United States made neutrality difficult? What forces within the United States were pushing for the nation to enter the war?

■ How did Wilson justify going to war?

At first, Americans paid only passing attention to the assassinations at Sarajevo. The nations of Europe, however, began methodically—sometimes regretfully, sometimes enthusiastically—to activate their intricate alliance networks. When Europe plunged into war, Wilson and all Americans faced difficult choices.

The Great War in Europe

Throughout much of the nineteenth and early twentieth centuries, most European governments had encouraged their citizens to identify strongly with their nation, thereby cultivating the intense patriotism known as **nationalism.** Within the ethnically diverse empires of Austria-Hungary, Russia, and Turkey, a different sort of nationalism fueled hopes for independence based on language and culture. Ethnic antagonisms and aspirations were especially powerful in the **Balkan Peninsula,** where the Ottoman (Turkish) Empire had lost territory as several groups had established their independence. Some of the new Balkan states, however, were weak, attracting the attention of the neighboring Austrian and Russian empires. As Austria-Hungary sought to annex new territories, Russia claimed the role of protector of other **Slavic** peoples.

nationalism   Intense patriotism, or a movement that favors a separate nation for an ethnic group that is part of a multiethnic state.

Balkan Peninsula   Region of southeastern Europe; once ruled by the Ottoman Empire, it included a number of relatively new and sometimes unstable states in the early twentieth century.

Slavic   Relating to the Slavs, a linguistic group that includes the Poles, Czechs, Slovaks, Slovenes, Serbs, Croats, Bosnians, and Bulgarians of Central Europe, as well as Russians, Ukrainians, Belarusians, and other groups in eastern Europe.

During the same years, competition for world markets and territory spawned an unprecedented arms buildup. After the 1870s, Germany had the most powerful army in Europe and, in 1898, launched a naval construction program designed to make its navy as powerful as Britain's. By 1900, most European powers had a thoroughly professional corps of military and naval officers and had instituted **universal military service.** Technological advances produced powerful weapons, including the machine gun, and designers quickly adapted automobiles and airplanes for combat.

The major powers of Europe had avoided armed conflict with one another since 1871, when Germany had humiliated France in the brief Franco-Prussian War, but they continued to prepare for war by lining up allies. Eventually European diplomats constructed two major alliance systems: the **Triple Entente** (Britain, France, and Russia; Britain was also allied with Japan) and the **Triple Alliance** (Germany, Austria-Hungary, and Italy).

Thus the events at Sarajevo occurred in the midst of an arms race between rival alliances. The assassinations themselves grew out of a territorial conflict between Austria-Hungary and Serbia. Austria-Hungary, whose empire included several restive Slavic groups, feared that Serbia might mold a strong Slavic state on its south. Russia, alarmed over Austrian expansion in the Balkans, presented itself as the protector of Serbia. Called the "powder keg of Europe," the Balkans lived up to their explosive nickname in 1914.

Austria first assured itself of Germany's backing, then declared war on Serbia. In turn, Russia confirmed France's support, then **mobilized** its army in support of Serbia. Germany declared war on Russia on August 1 and on France soon after. German strategists planned to bypass French defenses along their border by advancing through neutral Belgium (see Map 22.2). When the Belgian government refused permission to cross its territory, Germany invaded Belgium. Britain entered the conflict in defense of Belgium. By August 4, much of Europe was at war. Eventually Germany and Austria-Hungary combined with Bulgaria and the Ottoman Empire to form the **Central Powers.** Italy abandoned its Triple Alliance partners and joined Britain, France, Russia, Romania, and Japan as the Allies.

At first, Secretary of State Bryan took a hopeful view of events in Europe. "It may be," he suggested, "that the world needed one more awful object lesson to prove conclusively the fallacy of the doctrine that preparedness for war can give assurance for peace." Sir Edward Grey, Britain's foreign minister, was less optimistic. At twilight on August 3, 1914, he mourned to a friend, "The lamps are going out all over Europe. We shall not see them lit again in our lifetime." Grey proved a more accurate prophet than Bryan.

The Germans expected to roll through Belgium, a small and militarily weak nation, and land a quick knockout blow to France. The Belgians, however, resisted long enough for French and British troops to move into positions to block the Germans. The opposing armies soon settled into lines across 475 miles of Belgian and French countryside, extending from the English Channel to the Alps (see Map 22.2). By the end of 1914, the **western front** consisted of elaborate networks of trenches separated from the enemy's entrenchments by a desolate **no man's land** filled with coils of barbed wire, where any movement brought a burst of machine-gun fire. As the war progressed, terrible new weapons—poison gas, aerial bombings, tanks—took thousands of lives but failed to break the deadlock.

American Neutrality

Wilson's initial reaction to the European conflagration revealed his own deep religious beliefs—he wrote privately of his confidence that "Providence

---

universal military service   A governmental policy specifying that all adult males (or, rarely, all adults) are required to serve in the military for some period of time.

Triple Entente   Informal alliance that linked France, Great Britain, and Russia in the years before World War I.

Triple Alliance   Alliance that linked Germany, Italy, and Austria-Hungary in the years before World War I.

mobilize   To make ready for combat or other forms of action.

Central Powers   In World War I, the coalition of Germany, Austria-Hungary, Bulgaria, and the Ottoman Empire.

western front   The western line of battle between the Allies and Germany in World War I, located in French and Belgian territory; the **eastern front** was the line of battle between the Central Powers and Russia.

no man's land   The field of battle between the lines of two opposing, entrenched armies.

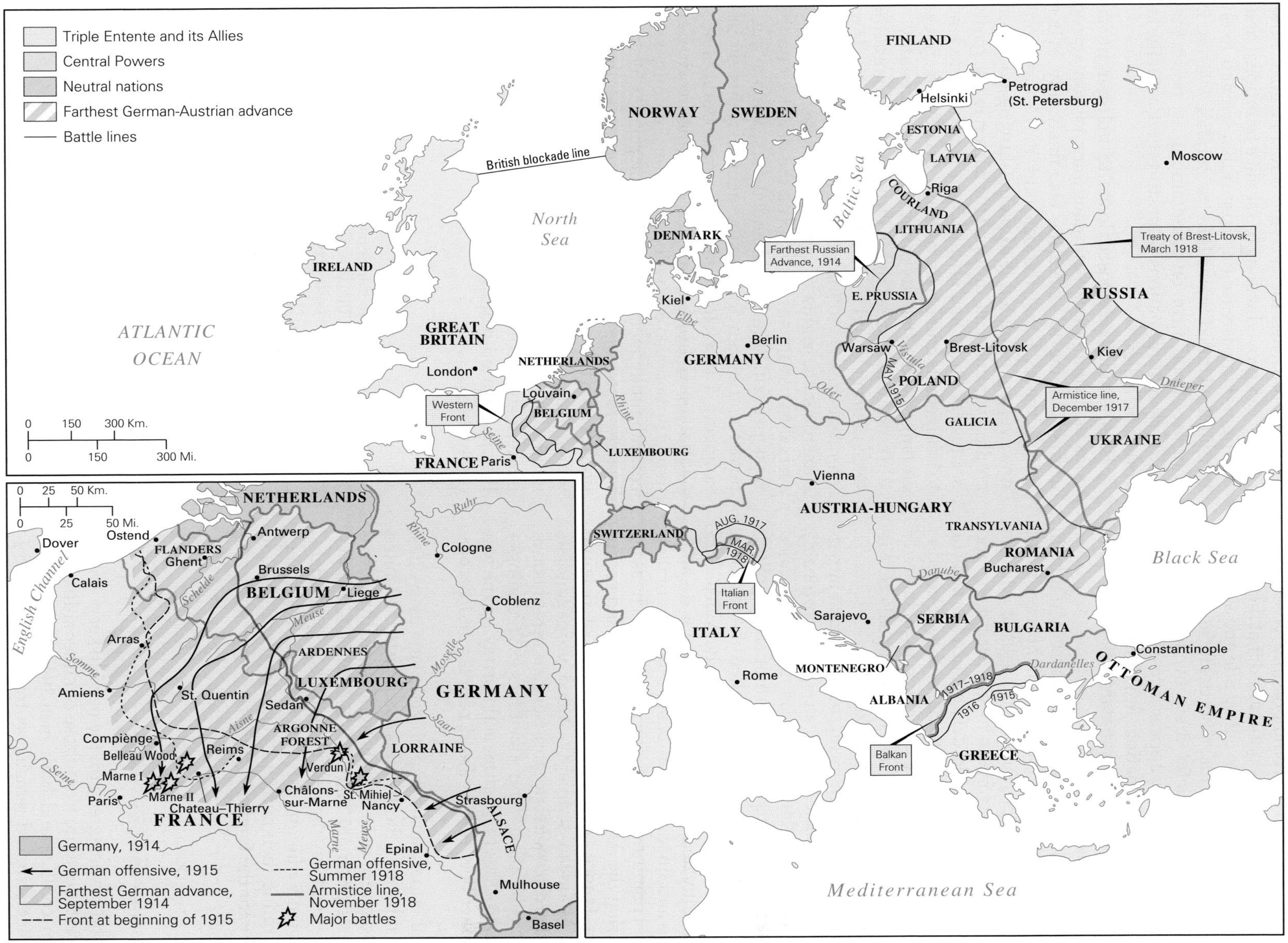
Triple Entente and its Allies
Central Powers
Neutral nations
Farthest German-Austrian advance
Battle lines
0 150 300 Km.
0 150 300 Mi.
ATLANTIC OCEAN
North Sea
Baltic Sea
Black Sea
Mediterranean Sea
British blockade line
IRELAND
GREAT BRITAIN
London
NORWAY
SWEDEN
FINLAND
Helsinki
Petrograd (St. Petersburg)
Moscow
ESTONIA
LATVIA
Riga
COURLAND
LITHUANIA
DENMARK
Kiel
Elbe
Farthest Russian Advance, 1914
E. PRUSSIA
Treaty of Brest-Litovsk, March 1918
RUSSIA
Berlin
GERMANY
Warsaw
Vistula
MAY 1915
POLAND
Brest-Litovsk
Kiev
Dnieper
Armistice line, December 1917
GALICIA
UKRAINE
Oder
NETHERLANDS
Louvain
BELGIUM
LUXEMBOURG
Rhine
Western Front
Seine
FRANCE
Paris
Vienna
AUSTRIA-HUNGARY
TRANSYLVANIA
ROMANIA
Bucharest
Danube
SWITZERLAND
AUG. 1917
MAR. 1918
Italian Front
Sarajevo
SERBIA
BULGARIA
Constantinople
Dardanelles
OTTOMAN EMPIRE
ITALY
Rome
MONTENEGRO
ALBANIA
1917–1918
1916
1915
GREECE
Balkan Front
0 25 50 Km.
0 25 50 Mi.
Dover
English Channel
Calais
Ostend
FLANDERS
Ghent
Antwerp
NETHERLANDS
Brussels
BELGIUM
Liege
Scheldt
Meuse
Ruhr
Rhine
Cologne
Coblenz
Arras
Somme
Amiens
St. Quentin
ARDENNES
LUXEMBOURG
Moselle
GERMANY
Sedan
Aisne
ARGONNE FOREST
Saar
LORRAINE
Compiègne
Belleau Wood
Reims
Verdun
Marne I
Marne II
Paris
Seine
Chateau–Thierry
FRANCE
Châlons-sur-Marne
St. Mihiel
Nancy
Strasbourg
ALSACE
Marne
Epinal
Mulhouse
Basel
Germany, 1914
German offensive, 1915
Farthest German advance, September 1914
Front at beginning of 1915
German offensive, Summer 1918
Armistice line, November 1918
Major battles

MAP 22.2 The War in Europe, 1914–1918 This map identifies the members of the two great military coalitions, the Central Powers and the Allies, and charts the progress of the war. Notice how much territory Russia lost by the Treaty of Brest-Litovsk as compared with the armistice line (the line between the two armies when Russia sought peace).

has deeper plans than we could possibly have laid for ourselves." On August 4, he announced that the United States was not committed to either side and was to be accorded all **neutral** rights. The death of his wife, Ellen, on August 6, briefly drew the grief-stricken Wilson away from public appearances. Later, on August 19, he spoke to the nation, urging Americans to be "neutral in fact as well as in name . . . impartial in thought as well as in action."

Wilson hoped not only that America would remain outside the conflict but also that he might serve as the peacemaker. Such hopes proved unrealistic. Most of the warring nations wanted to gain territory, and only a decisive victory could deliver such a prize. The longer they fought, the more territory they coveted to satisfy their losses. So long as they saw a chance of winning, they had no interest in the appeals of Wilson or other would-be peacemakers.

Wilson's hope that Americans could remain impartial was also unrealistic. American socialists probably came the closest to impartiality as they condemned all the warring nations for seeking imperial spoils at the expense of the workers who filled the trenches. Most Americans probably sided with the Allies. England had cultivated American friendship for decades, and trade and finance united many members of their business communities. Memories of French assistance during the American Revolution fueled enthusiasm for France. And the martyrdom of Belgium aroused American sympathy. Allied **propagandists** worked hard to generate anti-German sentiment in America, publicizing—and sometimes exaggerating— German atrocities in Belgium and portraying the war as a conflict between civilized peoples and barbarian **Huns.**

Not all Americans sympathized with the Allies. Nearly 8 million of the 97 million people in the United States had one or both parents from Germany or Austria. Not surprisingly, many of them disputed depictions of their cousins as bloodthirsty barbarians. Many of the 5 million Irish Americans disliked England for ruling their ancestral homeland and held no sympathy for the English.

Neutral Rights and German U-Boats

Wilson and Bryan agreed on the need to keep American interests separate from those of either side in the European conflict, and both men believed that the United States should remain neutral. They took dif-

ferent approaches for carrying out that goal, however. Bryan proved willing to sacrifice traditional neutral rights if insistence on those rights seemed likely to pull the United States into the conflict. Wilson, in contrast, stood firm on maintaining all traditional rights of neutral nations, a posture that actually favored the Allies.

Bryan initially opposed loans to **belligerent** nations as incompatible with neutrality. Wilson agreed at first, hoping to starve the war financially. When Wilson realized that the ban hurt the Allies more, however, he modified it to permit buying goods on credit. Eventually, he dropped the ban on loans, partly because neutrals had always been permitted to lend to belligerents and partly, perhaps, because the freeze endangered the stability of the American economy.

Traditional neutral rights included freedom of the seas: neutrals could trade with all belligerents. However, Wilson soon found himself in conflict with both sides over the rights of neutral ships, as both sides turned to naval warfare to break the deadlock on the western front. Britain commanded the seas at the war's outset and began to redefine neutral rights by announcing a blockade both of German ports and of neutral ports from which goods could reach Germany. Britain also expanded traditional definitions of **contraband** to include anything that might give indirect aid to its enemy—even cotton and food. In addition, Britain extended the right to "visit and search," which enabled belligerent nations to stop and search neutral ships for contraband. Insisting that large, modern ships could not be carefully searched at sea, Britain escorted neutral ships to port, thus imposing costly delays.

---

neutral   A neutral nation is one not aligned with either side in a war; traditionally, a neutral nation had the right to engage in certain types of trade with nations that were at war.

propagandist   A person who provides information in support of a cause, especially one-sided or exaggerated information.

Hun   Disparaging term used to describe Germans during World War I; the name came from a warlike tribe that invaded Europe in the fourth and fifth centuries.

belligerent   A nation formally at war.

contraband   Goods prohibited from being imported or exported; in time of war, contraband included materials of war.

Though New York newspapers carried warnings from the German embassy about the dangers of trans-Atlantic travel, the passengers who boarded the *Lusitania* on May 1, 1915, probably did not imagine themselves in serious danger from submarine attack. The ship was sunk on May 7. Of the 1,959 passengers and crewmembers, 1,198 died, including 128 Americans. *Warning: Cobb Heritage Centre, England. Photograph by Larry O. Nighswander/NGS; Sketch: Culver Pictures.*

Germany declared a blockade of the British Isles, to be enforced by its submarines, called **U-boats.** Because U-boats were relatively fragile, a lightly armed merchant ship might sink one that surfaced and ordered the merchant ship to stop in the traditional manner. Consequently, submarines struck from below the surface without issuing the warning called for by traditional rules of naval warfare. When Britain began disguising its ships by flying the flags of neutral countries, Germany specified that a neutral flag no longer guaranteed protection. Wilson had issued token protests over Britain's practices, but now he strongly denounced those of Germany. Because Germany's violations of neutrality produced loss of life, he considered them to be significantly different from Britain's, which caused only financial hardship.

On February 10, 1915, Wilson warned that the United States would hold Germany to "strict accountability" for its actions and would do everything necessary to "safeguard American lives and property and to secure to American citizens the full enjoyment of their acknowledged rights on the high seas." On May 7, 1915, a German U-boat torpedoed the British passenger ship **Lusitania.** More than a thousand people died, including 128 Americans. Americans reacted with shock and horror. When Bryan learned that the *Lusitania* carried rifle cartridges and other contraband, he urged restraint in protesting to Germany. Wilson, however, sent a message that stopped just short of demanding an end to submarine warfare against unarmed merchant ships. When the German response was noncommittal, Wilson composed an even stronger protest. Bryan feared it would lead to war, and he resigned as secretary of state rather than sign it.

Robert Lansing, Bryan's successor, strongly favored the Allies. Where Bryan had counseled restraint,

---

U-boat   A German submarine (in German, *Untersee-boot*).

Lusitania   British passenger liner torpedoed by a German submarine in 1915; more than one thousand drowned, including 128 Americans, creating a diplomatic crisis between the United States and Germany.

Lansing urged a show of strength. U-boat attacks continued, and Wilson sent more protests, but he knew that most Americans opposed going to war over that issue. The sinking of the unarmed French ship *Sussex* in March 1916, which injured several Americans, led Wilson to warn Germany that if unrestricted submarine warfare did not stop, "the United States can have no choice" but to sever diplomatic relations—usually the last step before declaring war. Germany responded with the *Sussex* **pledge,** promising that U-boats would no longer strike noncombatant vessels without warning, provided the United States convinced the Allies to obey "international law." Wilson accepted the pledge but did little to persuade the British to change their tactics.

The war strengthened America's economic ties to the Allies. Exports to Britain and France grew dramatically, from $756 million in 1914 to $2.7 billion in 1916. American companies exported $6 million worth of explosives in 1914 and $467 million in 1916. Even more significant was the transformation of the United States from a debtor to a **creditor nation.** By April 1917, American bankers had loaned more than $2 billion to the Allied governments. At the same time, the British blockade stifled Americans' trade with the Central Powers, which fell from around $170 million in 1914 to almost nothing two years later.

Convinced that the best way to keep the United States neutral was to end the war, Wilson sent his closest confidant, Edward M. House, to London and Berlin early in 1916. Wilson directed House to present proposals for peace, **disarmament,** and a league of nations to maintain peace in the future. House received no encouragement from either side and concluded that they were not interested in negotiations.

At the same time, increasing numbers of Americans began to demand "preparedness"—a military buildup. In the summer of 1916, Congress appropriated the largest naval expenditures in the country's peacetime history and approved the National Defense Act, which doubled the size of the army. Wilson accepted both measures.

The Election of 1916

By embracing preparedness, Wilson took control of an issue that otherwise might have helped the Republicans in the 1916 presidential campaign. The Democrats nominated Wilson for a second term, and they campaigned on their progressive domestic accomplishments and preparedness programs, frequently repeating the slogan "He kept us out of war."

Republicans nominated Charles Evans Hughes, a Supreme Court justice and former governor of New York with a reputation as a progressive. Hughes avoided taking a clear position on preparedness and neutrality, hoping for support both from German Americans upset with Wilson's harshness toward Germany and from those who wanted maximum assistance for the Allies. As a result, he failed to present a compelling alternative to Wilson. Hughes made other errors—in California, he slighted unions and Senator Hiram Johnson, both powerful forces, and Wilson narrowly carried California.

The contest was very close. Most voters identified themselves as Republicans, and Wilson needed support from at least some of them. First election reports— from eastern and midwestern states—gave Hughes such an edge that some Democrats conceded defeat. But Wilson won by uniting the always-Democratic South with the West, much of which was progressive. Wilson also received significant backing from unions, socialists, and women in states where women could vote. In the end, Wilson received 49.4 percent of the vote to 46.2 percent for Hughes.

The Decision for War

After the election, in January 1917, Wilson spoke to the Senate on the need to achieve and preserve peace. The galleries were packed as he eloquently called for a league of nations to keep peace in the future and to replace the old balance-of-power concept with "a community of power." He urged that the only lasting peace would be a "peace without victory" and a "peace among equals" in which neither side exacted gains from the other. He called for government by consent of the governed, freedom of the seas, and reductions in armaments. Wilson admitted privately that he had really aimed his speech toward "the people of the countries now at war," hoping to build public

---

Sussex **pledge** German promise in 1916 to stop sinking merchant ships without warning if the United States would compel the Allies to obey "international law."

creditor nation A nation whose citizens or government have loaned more money to the citizens or governments of other nations than the total amount that they have borrowed from the citizens or governments of other nations.

disarmament The reduction or dismantling of a nation's military forces or weaponry.

pressure on the governments to seek peace. He won praise from **left-wing** opposition parties in several countries, but the British, French, and German governments had no interest in "peace without victory."

In Germany, the initiative now passed to those who wanted to resume unrestricted submarine warfare. They expected that this would bring the United States into the war but gambled on being able to defeat the British and French before American troops could arrive in Europe. When Germany announced it was resuming unrestricted submarine warfare, Wilson broke off diplomatic relations. German U-boats began immediately to take a devastating toll on Atlantic shipping.

A few weeks later, on March 1, Wilson released a decoded message from the German foreign minister, **Arthur Zimmermann,** to the German minister in Mexico. Writing on January 16, Zimmermann proposed that if the United States went to war with Germany, Mexico should ally itself with Germany and attack the United States. Zimmermann went on to pledge that if Germany and Mexico won, Mexico would recover its "lost provinces" of Texas, Arizona, and New Mexico. Zimmermann also proposed that Mexico should encourage Japan to enter the war against the United States. The British had intercepted the message and, on February 24, gave it to American representatives. Zimmermann's suggestions outraged Americans, increasing public support for Wilson's proposal to arm American merchant ships for protection against the U-boats. A few senators, mostly progressives, blocked the measure, arguing that it was safer to bar merchant ships from the war zone. Wilson then acted on his own and authorized merchant ships to be armed.

Between February 3 and March 21, German U-boats sank six American ships. Wilson could now avoid war only by backing down from his previous insistence on "strict accountability." He did not retreat. On April 2, 1917, Wilson asked Congress to declare war on Germany. Wilson apparently thought that the nation was unlikely to go to war solely to protect American commerce with the Allies, and he himself probably felt the need to justify war in more noble terms. In fact, his major objective in going to war seems to have been to put the United States, and himself, in a position to demand the sort of peace he had outlined in January.

Thus, in asking for war, Wilson tried to unite Americans in a righteous, progressive crusade. He condemned German U-boat attacks as "warfare against mankind." "The world must be made safe for democracy," he proclaimed, and he promised that the United States would fight for self-government, "the rights and liberties of small nations," and a league of nations to "bring peace and safety to all nations and make the world itself at last free."

Not all members of Congress agreed that war was necessary, and not all were ready to join Wilson's crusade to transform the world. During the four days of debate that ensued, Senator George W. Norris, a progressive Republican from Nebraska, best voiced the arguments of the opposition. The nation, he claimed, was going to war "upon the command of gold" to "preserve the commercial right of American citizens to deliver munitions of war to belligerent nations." In the Senate, Norris, Robert La Follette, and four others voted no, but eighty-two senators voted for war. Jeannette Rankin of Montana, the first woman to serve in the House of Representatives, was among those who said no when the House voted 373 to 50 for war. In December, Congress also declared war against Austria-Hungary.

The Home Front

■ What steps did the federal government take to mobilize the economy and society in support of the war? How successful was the mobilization effort?

■ How did the war affect Americans, especially women, African Americans, and opponents of war?

Historians call World War I the first "total war" because it was the first war to demand mobilization of an entire society and economy. The war altered nearly every aspect of the economy as the progressive emphasis on expertise and efficiency produced unprecedented centralization of economic decision making. Mobilization extended beyond war production to the people themselves and especially to shaping their attitudes toward involvement in the war.

left-wing   Not conservative; usually implies socialist or otherwise radical leanings.

Arthur Zimmermann   German foreign minister who proposed in 1917 that if the United States declared war on Germany, Mexico should become a German ally and win back Texas, Arizona, and New Mexico and should try to persuade Japan to go to war with the United States.

Sow the seeds of Victory!
plant & raise your own vegetables

WRITE TO THE
NATIONAL
WAR GARDEN
COMMISSION ~
WASHINGTON, D.C.
for free books on
gardening, canning
& drying.

JAMES MONTGOMERY FLAGG

"Every Garden a Munition Plant"
Charles Lathrop Pack, President

In 1918, this poster by James Montgomery Flagg appealed to American women to contribute to victory by conserving food through raising and preserving food for their families. The woman is sowing seeds (in the way that grain was planted before the development of agricultural machinery for that task), garbed in a dress made from an American flag, and wearing a red Liberty cap, a symbol that originated in the French Revolution. *Ohio Historical Society.*

Mobilizing the Economy

The ability to wage war effectively depended on a fully engaged industrial economy. Thus warring nations sought to direct economic activities toward supplying their war machines. In the United States, shortages, railway transportation snarls, and delays in manufacturing led to increased federal direction over manufacturing, food and fuel production, and transportation. This was not unusual among the nations at war and in fact was probably less extreme than in other nations because the United States entered the

war later. Even so, the extent of direct federal control over so much of the economy has never been matched since World War I.

Though unprecedented, much of the government intervention was also voluntary. Business enlisted as a partner with government and supplied its cooperation and expertise. Some prominent entrepreneurs volunteered their full-time services for a dollar a year. Much of the wartime centralization of economic decision making came through new agencies composed of government officials, business leaders, and prominent citizens.

The **War Industries Board** (WIB) was established in 1917 to supervise production of war materials. At first, it had only limited success in increasing industrial productivity. Then, in early 1918, Wilson appointed Bernard Baruch, a Wall Street financier, to head the board. By pleading, bargaining, and sometimes threatening, Baruch usually managed to persuade companies to set and meet production quotas, allocate raw materials, develop new industries, and streamline their operations. Though Baruch once threatened steel company executives with a government takeover, he accomplished most goals without coercion. And industrial production increased by 20 percent.

Efforts to conserve fuel included the first use of **daylight saving time.** To improve rail transportation, the federal government consolidated the country's railroads in 1917 and ran them as a single system for the duration of the war. The government also took over the telegraph and telephone system and launched a huge shipbuilding program to expand the merchant marine.

The **National War Labor Board,** created in 1918, endorsed **collective bargaining** to resolve labor disputes and thereby facilitate production. The board also gave some support for an eight-hour workday in return for a no-strike pledge from unions. Many unions secured contracts with significant wage increases, and

War Industries Board Federal agency headed by Bernard Baruch that coordinated American production during World War I.

daylight saving time Setting of clocks ahead by one hour to provide more daylight at the end of the day during late spring, summer, and early fall.

National War Labor Board Federal agency created in 1918 to resolve wartime labor disputes.

collective bargaining Negotiation between the representatives of organized workers and their employer to determine wages, hours, and working conditions.

This poster encouraged Americans to buy Liberty Bonds (that is, loan money to the government) by emphasizing the image of the vicious and brutal Hun. This was part of a larger process of demonizing the people of the Central Powers that extended to condemning the music of Beethoven and the writings of Goethe. *Collection of Robert Cherny.*

Wheatless Wednesdays and to plant "war gardens" to raise vegetables. Farmers brought large areas under cultivation for the first time. (The chapter-opening map indicates the expansion of wheat growing.) Food shipments to the Allies tripled.

Some progressives urged that the Wilson administration pay for the war solely by taxing the wartime profits and earnings of corporations. That did not happen, but taxes—especially the relatively new income tax—did account for almost half of the $33 billion that the United States spent on the war between April 1917 and June 1920. The government borrowed the rest, most of it through **Liberty Loan** drives. Rallies, parades, and posters pushed all Americans to buy "Liberty Bonds." Groups such as the Red Cross and the YMCA urged people to donate time and energy in support of American soldiers.

Mobilizing Public Opinion

Not all Americans supported the war. Some German Americans were reluctant to see their sons sent to war against their cousins. Some Irish Americans took even less interest in saving Britain after the English brutally suppressed an attempt at Irish independence in 1916. When the Socialist Party determined to oppose the war, Socialist candidates greatly increased their share of the vote in several cities in 1917—to 22 percent in New York City and 34 percent in Chicago—suggesting that their antiwar stance attracted many voters.

To mobilize public opinion in support of the war, Wilson in 1917 created the Committee on Public Information, headed by George Creel. Once a muckraking journalist, Creel set out to sell the war to the American people. The **Creel Committee** eventually counted 150,000 lecturers, writers, artists, actors, and scholars championing the cause and whipping up hatred of the "Huns." Social clubs, movie theaters, and

union membership boomed from 2.7 million in 1916 to more than 4 million by 1919. Most union leaders fully supported the war. Samuel Gompers, president of the AFL, called it "the most wonderful crusade ever entered upon in the whole history of the world."

One crucial American contribution to the Allies was food, for the war had severely disrupted European agriculture. Wilson appointed **Herbert Hoover** as food administrator. A prominent mining engineer, Hoover had won wide praise for directing the relief program in Belgium. He now promoted conservation and increased production of food, urging families to conserve food through Meatless Mondays and

Herbert Hoover   U.S. food administrator during World War I, known for his proficient handling of relief efforts; he later served as secretary of commerce (1921–1928) and president (1929–1933).

Liberty Loan   One of four bond issues floated by the U.S. Treasury Department from 1917 to 1919 to help finance World War I.

Creel Committee   The U.S. Committee on Public Information (1917–1919), headed by journalist and editor George Creel; it used films, posters, pamphlets, and news releases to mobilize American public opinion in favor of World War I.

churches all joined what Creel called "the world's greatest adventure in advertising." "Four-Minute Men"—volunteers ready to make a four-minute patriotic speech anytime and anywhere a crowd gathered—made 755,190 speeches in 5,000 towns.

Wartime patriotism, fanned at times by the Creel Committee, sparked extreme measures against those considered "slackers" or pro-German. "Woe to the man or group of men that seeks to stand in our way," warned Wilson. "He who is not with us, absolutely and without reserve of any kind," echoed former president Theodore Roosevelt, "is against us, and should be treated as an alien enemy." Zealots everywhere took up the cry. "Americanization" drives promoted rapid assimilation among immigrants. Some states prohibited the use of foreign languages in public. Officials removed German books from libraries and sometimes publicly burned them. Some communities banned the music of Bach and Beethoven, and some dropped German classes from their schools. Even certain words became objectionable: sauerkraut, for example, became "liberty cabbage." Sometimes mobs hounded people with German names and occasionally attacked or even lynched people suspected of antiwar sentiments.

Civil Liberties in Time of War

German Americans suffered the most from the wartime hysteria, but pacifists, socialists, and other radicals also became targets for government repression and **vigilante** action. Congress passed the **Espionage Act** in 1917 and the **Sedition Act** in 1918, prohibiting interference with the draft and outlawing criticism of the government, the armed forces, or the war effort. Violators faced large fines and long prison terms. Officials arrested some fifteen hundred people for violating the Espionage and Sedition Acts, including Eugene V. Debs, leader of the Socialist Party. The Espionage Act permitted the postmaster general to decide what could pass through the nation's mails. By the war's end, the Post Office Department had denied mailing privileges to some four hundred periodicals, including, at least temporarily, the *New York Times* and other mainstream publications.

Dissenters found they could not rely on the courts for protection. When opponents of the war challenged the Espionage Act as unconstitutional, the Supreme Court ruled that freedom of speech was never absolute. Just as no one has the right to falsely shout "Fire!" in a theater and create panic, said Justice Oliver Wendell Holmes Jr., so in time of war

no one has a constitutional right to say anything that might endanger the security of the nation. The Court also upheld the Sedition Act in 1919, by a vote of 7 to 2.

Although the Industrial Workers of the World (IWW) made no public pronouncement against the war, most Wobblies probably opposed it. IWW members and leaders quickly came under relentless attack from employers, government officials, and patriotic vigilantes, most of whom had disliked the IWW before the war. In September 1917, Justice Department agents raided IWW offices nationwide and arrested the union's leaders, who were sentenced to jail terms of up to twenty-five years and to fines totaling millions of dollars. Deprived of most of its leaders and virtually bankrupted, the IWW never recovered.

A few Americans protested the abridgment of civil liberties. One group formed the Civil Liberties Bureau—forerunner of the American Civil Liberties Union, or ACLU—under the leadership of Roger Baldwin. Most Americans, however, did not object to the repression, and many who did kept silent.

Changes in the Workplace

Intense activism and remarkable productivity characterized American labor's wartime experience. Union membership almost doubled, and a significant number of women were among the surge of new cardholders. In addition, unions benefited from the encouragement that the National War Labor Board gave to collective bargaining between unions and companies as the most effective way to keep labor peace. The board also stepped in and helped to settle labor disputes. Never before had a federal agency interceded this way. Nevertheless, many workers felt that their purchasing power was not keeping pace with increases in prices.

---

vigilante   A person who takes law enforcement into his or her own hands, usually on the grounds that normal law enforcement has broken down.

Espionage Act   Law passed by Congress in 1917, mandating severe penalties for anyone found guilty of interfering with the draft or encouraging disloyalty to the United States.

Sedition Act   Law passed by Congress in 1918 to supplement the Espionage Act by extending the penalty to anyone deemed to have abused the government in writing.

Labor shortages attracted new people into the labor market and opened up some jobs to women and members of racial minorities. In May 1918, these women worked in the Union Pacific Railroad freight yard in Cheyenne, Wyoming. Most of them seem delighted to have their picture taken in their work clothes. *Wyoming State Archives.*

Demands for increased production at a time when millions of men were marching off to war opened opportunities for women in many fields. Employment of women in factory, office, and retail jobs had increased before the war, and the war accelerated those trends. At the war's end, many women's wartime jobs returned to male hands, but in office work and some retail positions women continued to predominate after the war.

Most women who worked outside the home were young and single. Some middle-class women who now entered the paid labor force gave up not only their homebound roles but also their parents' standards of morality and behavior. Some adopted instead the less restricted lifestyles that had long been experienced by many wage-earning, working-class women, taking control over their income and using it to establish autonomy from familial controls.

The Great Migration and White Reactions

The war had a great impact on African American communities. Until the war, about 90 percent of all African Americans lived in the South, 75 percent in rural areas. By 1920, perhaps as many as a half-million had moved north in what has been called the **Great Migration.** The largest increases in the African American population came in the industrial cities of the Midwest. Gary, Indiana, showed one of the greatest gains—1,284 percent between 1910 and 1920. Outside the Midwest, New York City, Philadelphia, and Los Angeles also attracted many blacks (see the chapter-opening map). Several factors combined to produce this migration, but the most important were the brutality of southern life and the economic opportunities in the cities of the North. "Every time a lynching takes place in a community down South," said T. Arnold Hill of Chicago's Urban League, "colored people will arrive in Chicago within two weeks." Southern agricultural hardships provided further incentive to leave. In 1915 and 1916, southern farmers alternately battled drought and severe rains and fought the **boll weevil.**

Perhaps the most significant factor in the Great Migration was American industry's desperate need for

Great Migration Movement of about a half-million black people from the rural South to the urban North during World War I.

boll weevil Small beetle that infests cotton plants and damages the cotton bolls, which contain the cotton fibers.

Labor shortages and high wages drew African Americans from the South to the North. This family, including members of three generations, posed for a photographer upon their arrival in Chicago from the South, as part of the Great Migration during World War I. *Schomburg Center for Research in Black Culture, New York Public Library.*

workers at the same time that European immigration declined sharply. The wartime labor needs of northern cities attracted hundreds of thousands of African Americans seeking better jobs and higher pay. In the North, one could earn almost as much in a day as in a week in the South—for example, industrial jobs often paid $3 a day, compared with 50 cents a day for picking cotton. The impact on some southern cities was striking. Jackson, Mississippi, for example, was estimated to have lost half of all working-class African Americans and between a quarter and a third of black business owners and professionals.

Severe wartime racial conflicts erupted in several cities at the northern end of the Great Migration trail. One of America's worst race riots swept through the industrial city of East St. Louis, Illinois, on July 2, 1917. Thousands of African American laborers, most from the South, had settled in the city during the previous two years. A least thirty-nine of them perished in the riot, and six thousand found themselves homeless. Incensed that such brutality could occur just weeks after the nation's moralistic entrance into the war, W. E. B. Du Bois charged, "No land that loves to lynch 'niggers' can lead the hosts of Almighty God," and the NAACP led a silent protest parade of ten thousand people through **Harlem.**

Americans "Over There"

■ What role did American ships and troops play in ending the war?

■ In what ways did Wilson try to keep America's participation in the war separate from that of the Allies? Why?

With the declaration of war, the United States needed to mobilize quickly for combat in a distant part of the world. The navy was already large and powerful after nearly three decades of shipbuilding, and preparedness measures in 1916 further strengthened it. The army, however, was tiny compared with the armies contesting in Europe. Millions of men and thousands of women had to be inducted, trained, and transported to Europe.

Harlem A section of New York City in the northern part of Manhattan; it became one of the largest black communities in the United States.

About 10,000 American Indians enlisted or were drafted into the army during World War I, including John Miller (*left*) and Charlie Wolf, members of the Omaha tribe. In some cases, the Indians who went to war first underwent tribal ceremonies, long unpracticed, for preparing warriors for battle, and thus may have contributed to the preservation of traditional customs. Indians' participation in the war led to increased demands for full citizenship and enfranchisement for all American Indians, a step that came in 1924. *Nebraska State Historical Society.*

the U.S. Army and National Guard stood at only 372,000 men. Many men volunteered but not enough. In May, therefore, Congress passed the **Selective Service Act,** requiring men ages 21 to 30 (later extended to 18 to 45) to register with local boards to determine who would be called to duty. Some, including members of Congress, objected that conscription (usually called "the draft") was undemocratic. The law exempted those who opposed war on religious grounds, but such **conscientious objectors** were sometimes badly treated.

Few people demonstrated against the draft, and most seemed to accept it as efficient and fair. Like Alvin York, 24 million men registered, and 2.8 million were drafted—about 72 percent of the entire army. By the end of the war, the combined army, navy, and Marine Corps counted 4.8 million members.

No women were drafted, but almost 13,000 joined the navy and marines, most serving in clerical capacities. For the first time, women held full naval and marine rank and status. The army, however, refused to enlist women, considering it a "most radical departure." Nearly 18,000 women served in the Army Corps of Nurses, but without army rank, pay, or benefits. At least 5,000 civilian women served in various capacities in France, sometimes near the front lines. The largest number served through the Red Cross, which helped to staff hospitals and rest facilities.

Nearly 400,000 African Americans served during World War I. Almost 200,000 served overseas, nearly 30,000 on the front lines. Emmett J. Scott, an African American and former secretary to Booker T. Washington, became special assistant to the secretary of war, responsible for the uniform application of the draft and the morale of African Americans. Nevertheless, black soldiers were often treated as second-class citizens. They served in segregated units in the army, were limited to food service in the navy, and were excluded altogether from the marines. More than 600 African Americans earned commissions as officers, but the army was reluctant to commission more. White officers commanded most black troops.

Mobilizing for Battle

Almost immediately the navy began to strike back at the German fleet. The American and British navies' convoy technique, in which several ships traveled together under the protection of destroyers, helped to cut shipping losses in half by late 1917. By spring 1918, U-boats ceased to pose a significant danger.

In April 1917, however, the combined strength of

Selective Service Act   Law passed by Congress in 1917 establishing compulsory military service for men ages 21 to 30.

conscientious objector   Person who refuses to bear arms or participate in military service because of religious beliefs or moral principles.

This is a stereoscope photograph. Such photographs were taken by a special camera with two lenses a short distance apart. When viewed through a stereoscope (a device found in most middle-class homes in the early twentieth century), the two photographs produced a three-dimensional image. The caption of this photo is "Our Answer to the Kaiser—3,000 of America's Millions Eager to Fight for Democracy." Such photographs were popular, both reflecting popular attitudes and helping to shape them. *Collection of George Kimball.*

"Over There"

By mid-1918, it seemed that Allied troops all along the western front had taken up a tune by the popular American composer George M. Cohan:

Over there, over there,
Send the word, send the word over there,
The Yanks are coming, the Yanks are coming,
And we won't come back 'til it's over over there.

A few Yanks—troops in the **American Expeditionary Force (AEF)**—arrived in France in June 1917, commanded by General John J. Pershing, recently returned from Mexico. Most American troops, however, were still to be inducted, supplied, trained, and transported across the Atlantic.

Throughout the war, Wilson held the United States apart from the Allies, referring to the United States as an Associated Power, rather than one of the Allies, and trying as much as possible to keep American troops separate. This distinction stemmed partly from his distrust of Allied war aims but more from

his wish to make the American contribution to victory as prominent as possible in order to maximize American influence in defining the peace.

As American troops began to trickle into France, the Central Powers seemed close to victory. French offensives in April 1917 had failed, and a British summer effort in Flanders produced enormous casualties but little gain. The Italians suffered a major defeat late in the year. A Russian drive in midsummer proved disastrous. Russia withdrew from the war late in 1917, and German commanders shifted troops moved from east to west (see Map 22.2). Hoping to win the war before many American troops could reinforce the Allies' battered lines, the Germans planned a massive offensive for spring 1918.

American Expeditionary Force   American army commanded by General John J. Pershing that served in Europe during World War I.

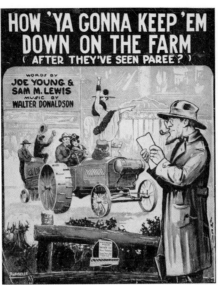

A black bandleader, James Reese Europe (*left*), went to France as a lieutenant, commanding a machine-gun company, and saw frontline action. When he and other black musicians were reassigned to present musical entertainment behind the lines, they were among the first to play jazz in France. Upon returning to the United States in 1919, he and his band recorded "How 'Ya Gonna Keep 'Em Down on the Farm After They've Seen Paree?" Many groups recorded the popular song, but black musicians may have given it a different emphasis: how can black soldiers be kept "down" after they experienced less oppressive racial patterns in France? *Left: Corbis/ Bettmann; right: The John Hay Library, Brown University. Photograph by Brooke Hammerle.*

The German thrust came in Picardy with sixty-four divisions smashing into the French and British lines and attempting to advance along the Marne River. AEF units were hurried to the front to block their advance. In mid-May, an AEF officer described trench life in a letter to his sister:

> We have to lay low all day to escape observation. . . .
> At nine p.m. we emerge and do various work all night: digging trenches, wiring, carrying ammunition, burying the dead. . . . It is scary . . . when the shelling begins, the rockets and flares all along the near horizon lighting up the weird scene, the Boche flashlights [German searchlights] simulating the aurora, the everlasting crack and roar of our own artillery . . . and the whine of the innumerable shells passing overhead, the sputtering of the machine guns, and in the midst of it all the persistent singing of a nightingale down in the ravine.

By late May, the Germans were within 50 miles of Paris. As French officials considered evacuating the capital, all available troops were rushed to the front. At Chateau-Thierry and at Belleau Wood, AEF units took 8,000 casualties during a month-long battle over a single square mile of wheat fields and woods. Of 310,000 AEF troops who fought in the Marne River region, 67,000 were killed or wounded.

The Allies launched a counteroffensive in July as American troops poured into France, topping the million mark. The American command insisted on having its own sector of the front, and in September, Pershing successfully launched a stunning one-day offensive against the St. Mihiel **salient** (see Map 22.2). AEF forces then joined a larger Allied offensive in the Meuse River–Argonne Forest region, the last major assault of the war and one of the fiercest battles in American military history. In the Argonne Forest on October 8, Alvin York became the most heroic American of the war, but his courage and coolness were not unique among the Americans who fought in the Meuse-Argonne campaign—Harry J. Adams, with only an empty pistol, captured 300 prisoners; Hercules Korgia, captured by the Germans, persuaded his captors to become his prisoners; and Samuel Woodfill single-handedly took out five machine guns. By October, German military leaders were urging their government to seek an armistice. Fighting ended at 11 A.M., November 11 (the eleventh hour of

salient A part of a battle line where the enemy has launched an offensive and pushed the line forward; a projection of the line.

the eleventh day of the eleventh month), 1918. By then, more than 2 million American soldiers were in France, giving the Allies an advantage of about 600,000 men.

By the time of the armistice, thirty-two nations had declared war on one or more of the Central Powers. Nearly 9 million men in uniform died: Germany lost 1.8 million, Russia 1.7 million, France 1.4 million, Austria-Hungary 1.2 million, the British Empire 908,400. France lost half its men between the ages of 20 and 32. More than 20 million combatants suffered wounds, producing many permanent disabilities. American losses were small in comparison—115,000 **casualties,** including 48,000 killed in action. Millions of people worldwide, including civilians, died from starvation and disease, especially during a global **influenza** epidemic in 1918 and 1919 that killed 500,000 Americans.

Some white Americans, including some military officers, worried that experiences in France might cause African American soldiers to resist segregation at home. Many black units were assigned to menial tasks behind the lines, although some saw action. In August 1918, AEF headquarters secretly requested that the French not prominently commend black units. The grateful French, however, awarded the **Croix de Guerre** to several all-black units that had distinguished themselves in combat and presented awards to individual soldiers for acts of bravery and heroism. When the Allies staged a grand victory parade down Paris's Champs Élysées, the British and French contingents included all races and ethnicities, but American commanders directed that no African American troops take part.

Wilson and the Peace Conference

▪ What were the American war objectives, and what factors influenced Wilson as he defined them?

▪ Do you think that Wilson was successful at the peace conference? On what basis?

▪ What caused the defeat of the treaty in the Senate? Who was responsible—Wilson, Lodge, or the irreconcilables?

When the war ended, Wilson hoped that the peace process would not sow the seeds of future wars. He hoped, too, to create an international organization to keep the peace. Most of the Allies, however, were more interested in grabbing territory and punishing Germany.

Bolshevism, the Secret Treaties, and the Fourteen Points

In March 1917, war-weary and hungry, Russians deposed their **tsar** and created a provisional government. In November, a group of radical socialists, the **Bolsheviks,** seized power. Soon renamed Communists, the Bolsheviks condemned capitalism and imperialism and sought to destroy them. **Vladimir Lenin,** the Bolshevik leader, immediately began separate peace negotiations with the Germans. The **Treaty of Brest-Litovsk,** in March 1918, was harsh and humiliating, requiring Russia to surrender vast territories—Finland, its Baltic provinces, parts of Poland and the Ukraine—in all, a third of its population, half of its industries, its most fertile agricultural land, and a quarter of its territory in Europe.

Condemning the war as nothing more than a scramble for imperial spoils, the Bolsheviks in December 1917 had published secret treaties by which the Allies agreed to strip colonies and territories from the Central Powers and divide those spoils among themselves. These exposés strengthened Wilson's intent to separate American war aims from those of the Allies and to impose his war objectives on the Allies.

On January 8, 1918, Wilson spoke to Congress. Elaborating on the war objectives he had presented earlier, he directly challenged the secret treaties and tried to seize the initiative in defining a basis for peace.

---

casualty   A member of the military lost through death, wounds, injury, sickness, or capture.

influenza   Contagious viral infection characterized by fever, chills, congestion, and muscular pain, nicknamed "the flu"; an unusually deadly strain, usually called "Spanish flu," swept across the world in 1918 and 1919.

Croix de Guerre   French military decoration for bravery in combat; in English, "the Cross of War."

tsar   The monarch of the Russian Empire; also spelled *czar.*

Bolsheviks   Radical socialists, later called Communists, who seized power in Russia in November 1917.

Vladimir Lenin   Leader of the Bolsheviks and of the Russian Revolution of 1917 and head of the Soviet Union until 1924.

Treaty of Brest-Litovsk   Humiliating treaty with Germany that Russia signed in March 1918 in order to withdraw from World War I; it required Russia to surrender vast territories along its western boundary with Germany.

He stressed that American goals derived from "the principle of justice to all peoples and nationalities, and their right to live on equal terms of liberty and safety with one another, whether they be strong or weak." Wilson presented fourteen objectives, soon called the **Fourteen Points.** Points one through five provided a general context for lasting peace: no secret treaties, freedom of the seas, reduction of barriers to trade, reduction of armaments, and adjustment of colonial claims based partly on the interests of colonial peoples. Point six dealt with Russia, calling for other nations to withdraw from Russian territory and to welcome Russia "into the society of free nations." Points seven through thirteen addressed particular situations: return of territories France had lost to Germany in 1871 and self-determination in Central Europe and the Middle East. The fourteenth point called for "a general association of nations" that could afford "mutual guarantees of political independence and territorial integrity to great and small states alike."

The Allies reluctantly accepted Wilson's Fourteen Points as a starting point for discussion but expressed little enthusiasm for them. The Germans were more interested. When they asked for an end to the fighting, they made clear that their request was based on the Fourteen Points.

The World in 1919

In December 1918, Wilson sailed for France—the first time that an American president in office had gone to Europe and the first time that a president had personally negotiated with other world leaders. Wilson brought along some two hundred experts on European history, culture, **ethnology,** and geography. In France, Italy, and Britain, huge welcoming crowds paid homage to the great "peacemaker from America."

Delegates to the peace conference assembled amid far-reaching change. The Austro-Hungarian Empire had crumbled, producing the new nations of Poland and Czechoslovakia and the republics of Austria and Hungary. The German monarch, Kaiser Wilhelm, had **abdicated,** and a republic was being formed. In January 1919, Berlin witnessed an unsuccessful communist uprising. Throughout the ruins of the Russian Empire, ethnic groups were proclaiming independent republics (most of which were eventually incorporated into the Soviet Union, often through intervention by the Bolsheviks' **Red Army**).

The Ottoman Empire was collapsing, too, as Arabs, with aid from Britain and France, had overthrown Turkish rule in many areas. Throughout Europe and the Middle East, national **self-determination** and gov-

ernment by the consent of the governed—part of Wilson's design for the postwar world—seemed to be lurching into reality. Nor were the British and French colonial empires immune, for both faced growing independence movements among their many possessions.

In Russia, civil war raged between the Bolsheviks and their opponents. When the Bolsheviks left the world war, the Allies pushed Wilson to join them in intervening in Russia, ostensibly to protect war supplies from falling into German hands. In mid-1918, Wilson had included American troops in Allied expeditions to northern Russia and eastern Siberia. In Siberia, his intent was primarily to head off a Japanese grab of territory. Lenin had initially accepted the intervention in northern Russia as necessary to block a German advance. However, the purpose of the Allied intervention soon changed, to support for the foes of the Bolsheviks. By late 1918, Wilson had begun to express concern over what he called "mass terrorism" directed by the Bolsheviks toward "peaceable Russian citizens." Before the last American troops were withdrawn—from northern Russia in May 1919 and from eastern Siberia in early 1920—they had engaged in conflict with units of the Red Army.

Wilson at Versailles

The peace conference opened on January 18, 1919, just outside Paris, at the glittering Palace of Versailles, once home to French kings. Representatives attended from all nations that had declared war against the Central Powers, but the major decisions were made by the Big Four: Wilson, David Lloyd George of Britain, Georges Clemenceau of France, and Vittorio Orlando of Italy. Germany was excluded. Terms of peace were

---

Fourteen Points   President Wilson's program for maintaining peace after World War I, which called for arms reduction, national self-determination, and a league of nations.

ethnology   The study of ethno-cultural groups.

abdicate   To relinquish a high office; usually said only of monarchs.

Red Army   The army created by the Bolsheviks to defend their communist government in their civil war and to reestablish control in parts of the Russian Empire that tried to create separate republics in 1917 and 1918; the Red Army was the army of the Soviet Union throughout its existence.

self-determination   The freedom of a given people to determine their own political status.

The victory of the Bolsheviks in Russia inspired radical revolutionaries elsewhere, including Germany and Hungary. Though Russia was not represented at the Versailles conference, the threat of Bolshevism was a major factor in some conference decisions. In this photo, Vladimir Lenin, the leader of the Bolsheviks, addresses a political rally in 1920. *Granger Collection.*

to be imposed, not negotiated. Russia, too, was absent, on the grounds that it had withdrawn from the war earlier and made a separate peace with Germany. Although Russia was barred from Versailles, the specter of anxiety about Bolshevism hung over the proceedings, affecting decisions about central and eastern Europe especially.

Wilson quickly learned that the European leaders were far more interested in pursuing their own national interests than in his Fourteen Points. Clemenceau, nicknamed "the Tiger," could recall Germany's humiliating defeat of France in 1871 and intended to disable Germany so thoroughly that it could never again threaten his nation. Lloyd George agreed in principle with many of Wilson's proposals but came to Paris with a **mandate** from British voters to exact heavy **reparations** from Germany. Orlando insisted on the territorial gains promised when Italy joined the Allies in 1915. Other war aims had been spelled out in the secret treaties, so various Allies were expecting to gain territory at the expense of Germany, Austria-Hungary, and the Ottoman Empire. In addition, the European Allies feared the spread of

Bolshevism and were intent on setting up buffers to keep it at bay.

Facing the insistent and acquisitive Allies, Wilson had no choice but to compromise. He did secure the creation of a **League of Nations.** Instead of "peace without victory," however, the **Treaty of Versailles** imposed harsh victors' terms, requiring Germany to accept the blame for starting the war, to pay repara-

mandate In politics, the understanding that a large electoral victory means that there is public support for the victorious party to carry out its program.

reparations Payments required as compensation for damage or injury.

League of Nations A world organization proposed by President Wilson and created by the Versailles peace conference; it worked to promote peace and international cooperation.

Treaty of Versailles Treaty signed in 1919 ending World War I; it imposed harsh terms on Germany, created several territorial mandates, and set up the League of Nations.

MAP 22.3 Postwar Boundary Changes in Central Europe and the Middle East This map shows the boundary changes in Europe and the Middle East that resulted from the defeat of the four large, multiethnic empires—Austria-Hungary, Germany, Russia, and the Ottoman Empire.

tions to the Allies (the exact amount to be determined later), and to surrender all its colonies along with Alsace-Lorraine (which Germany had taken from France in 1871), and other European territories (see Map 22.3.) The treaty also deprived Germany of its navy and merchant marine and limited its army to 100,000 men. German representatives signed on June 28, 1919.

Wilson reluctantly agreed to the massive reparations but insisted that colonies taken from Germany should not go to the Allies. Called **mandates,** they were to be administered by one of the Allies on behalf of the League of Nations. Mandates were intended to move toward self-government and independence. In nearly every case, however, the mandate went to the nation slated to receive the territory under the secret treaties. Wilson blocked Italy's most extreme territorial demands but gave in on others. The peace conference recognized the new nations of Central Europe, thereby creating a so-called quarantine zone between Russian Bolshevism and western Europe. But the treaty ignored other matters of self-determination. No one gave a hearing to people—from Ireland to Vietnam—seeking the right of self-determination in colonies held by one of the victorious Allies. Japan failed to secure a statement supporting racial equality.

In the end, Wilson compromised on nearly all of his Fourteen Points, but every compromise intensified his commitment to the League of Nations. The League, he hoped, would not only resolve future controversies without war but also solve problems created by the compromises. Even so, Wilson had to threaten a separate peace with Germany before the Allies agreed to incorporate the **League Covenant** into the treaty. Wilson was especially pleased with Article 10 of the League Covenant—he called it the League's "heart." It specified that League members agreed to protect one another's independence and territory against external attacks and to take joint economic and military action against aggressors.

The Senate and the Treaty

While Wilson was in Paris, opposition to his plans was percolating at home. The Senate, controlled by Republicans since the 1918 elections, had to approve any treaty. In response to concerns of some senators, Wilson added several provisions to the League Covenant.

Presented with the treaty, the Senate split into three groups. **Henry Cabot Lodge,** chairman of the Senate Foreign Relations Committee, led the largest faction, called reservationists after the *reservations*, or amend-

It Matters

Redrawing the Map of the Middle East

From the beginning of the war, in the Middle East, Britain had assisted Arabs to revolt against the Ottoman Empire, encouraging Arab wishes for self-determination. In 1916, in the secret Sykes-Picot Agreement, Britain and France divided much of the former Ottoman Empire between them, including areas that Britain had previously promised as part of an independent Arab state. At stake, both Britain and France knew, was oil in Iraq and along the Persian Gulf. In 1917, the British government made clear its support for "the establishment in Palestine of a national home for the Jewish people."

Britain and France were given League of Nations mandates in the Middle East. Britain received the mandate for Iraq, an entity that Britain had created by combining three former provinces of the Ottoman Empire; with the mandate came control of known oilfields. (Kuwait had become a British protectorate earlier, in 1914.) France, similarly, set up Syria and Lebanon as separate entities and received League mandates for them. Britain also received mandates for Palestine and Trans-Jordan (modern Jordan). The people of the newly created mandate of Iraq revolted against Britain in 1920 and achieved independence in 1932.

Thus many of the current nation-states and boundaries in the Middle East arose out of World War I and the mandate system created through the League of Nations.

mandate   Under the League of Nations, mandate referred to a territory that the League authorized a member nation to administer, with the understanding that the territory would move toward self-government.

League Covenant   The constitution of the League of Nations, which was incorporated in the 1919 Treaty of Versailles.

Henry Cabot Lodge   Prominent Republican senator from Massachusetts and chair of the Senate Foreign Relations Committee who led congressional opposition to Article 10 of the League of Nations.

ments, to the treaty that Lodge developed. Article 10 of the League Covenant especially bothered Lodge, for he feared it might be used to commit American troops to war without congressional approval. A small group, mostly Republicans, was called irreconcilables because they opposed any American involvement in European affairs. A third Senate group, nearly all Democrats, supported the president and his treaty.

Wilson decided to appeal directly to the American people. In September 1919, he undertook an arduous speaking tour—9,500 miles with speeches in twenty-nine cities. The effort proved too demanding for his fragile health, and he collapsed in Pueblo, Colorado. Soon after, he suffered a serious stroke.

Half-paralyzed and weak, Wilson could fulfill few of his duties. His wife, Edith Bolling Wilson, whom he had married in 1915, exercised what she later called a "stewardship," strictly limiting her ailing husband's contact with the outside world. Lodge now proposed that the Senate accept the treaty with fourteen reservations, his retort to the Fourteen Points. Some of his amendments were minor, but others would have permitted Congress to block action under Article 10. Wilson refused to compromise. On November 19, 1919, the Senate defeated the treaty with the Lodge reservations by votes of 39 to 55 and 41 to 50, with the irreconcilables joining the president's supporters in opposition. Then the Senate defeated the original version of the treaty by 38 to 53, with the irreconcilables joining the reservationists in voting no. The treaty with reservations came to a vote again in March 1920. By then, some treaty supporters had concluded that the League could never be approved without Lodge's reservations, so they joined the reservationists to produce a vote of 49 in favor to 35 opposed—still seven votes short of the two-thirds majority required for any treaty ratification. Enough Wilson loyalists—following their stubborn leader's order not to compromise—joined the irreconcilables to defeat the treaty once again. The United States did not join the League of Nations.

Legacies of the Great War

Roosevelt, Wilson, and most other prewar leaders had projected the progressive mood of optimism and confidence. Wilson invoked this tradition in claiming that the United States was going to war to make the world "safe for democracy." One of his supporters even described World War I as the "war to end war." Just as progressives defined their domestic policies in terms of progress, democracy, and social justice, so Wilson tried to invest his foreign policy with similarly enlightened values. In doing so, however, he fostered unrealistic expectations that world politics might be transformed overnight.

Many Americans became disillusioned by the contrast between Wilson's lofty idealism and the Allies' cynical opportunism at Versailles. The war to make the world "safe for democracy" turned out to be a chance for Italy to annex Austrian territory and for Japan to seize German concessions in China. In addition, the "war to end war" spun off several wars in its wake: Romania invaded Hungary in 1919, Poland invaded Russia in 1920, the Russian civil war continued until late 1920 with scattered resistance to the Bolsheviks afterward, and Greece and Turkey battled until 1923.

The peace conference left unresolved many problems. Wilson's promotion of self-government and self-determination encouraged aspirations for independence throughout the colonial empires retained by the Allies and among the new League mandates. Some of the new nations of Central Europe, supposedly based on ethnic self-determination, actually included different and sometimes antagonistic ethnic groups. Above all, the war and the treaty helped to produce economic and political instability in much of Europe, making it a breeding ground for totalitarian and nationalistic movements that eventually generated another world war.

America in the Aftermath of War, November 1918–November 1920

■ How did Americans react to the outcome of the war and the events of 1919? How did the war contribute to conflict within the nation in 1919?

■ How did the events of 1917–1920 affect the 1920 presidential election? What was unusual about that contest?

Almost as soon as French church bells pealed for the armistice, the United States began to demobilize. By November 1919, nearly 4 million men and women were out of uniform. Industrial demobilization occurred even more quickly, as officials canceled war contracts with no more than a month's notice. The year 1919 saw not only the return of American troops from Europe but also raging inflation that had begun in 1918, massive strikes, bloody race riots, widespread fear of radical **subversion**, violations of civil liberties,

subversion Efforts to undermine or overthrow an established government.

JOBS for FIGHTERS

U.S. Employment Service and Co-operating Agencies

BUREAU for RETURNING SOLDIERS and SAILORS -- WALK IN

HONORABLE DISCHARGE

WELCOME

Gordon Grant
Capt. USA

If You Need a Job
If You Need a Man

Inform the Official Central Agency

The Service is Free

The United States Employment Service

Bureau for Returning Soldiers and Sailors

United States Department of Labor—United States Employment Service   THOMSON-ELLIS CO., Baltimore, Md.

At the end of the war, the federal Employment Service tried to help returning soldiers and sailors to find jobs. Unemployment for 1918 and 1919 was less than 2 percent, but it rose above 5 percent in 1920 and to nearly 12 percent in 1921. *Picture Research Consultants & Archives.*

and at the same time, two new constitutional amendments that embodied important elements of progressivism—prohibition and woman suffrage.

"HCL" and Strikes

Inflation—described in newspapers as "HCL" for "High Cost of Living"—was the most pressing single problem Americans faced after the war. Between 1913

and 1919, prices almost doubled. Inflation contributed to labor unrest. The armistice ended unions' no-strike pledge, and organized labor made wage demands to match the soaring cost of living. In 1919, however, employers were ready for a fight.

Many companies wanted to return labor relations to prewar patterns. They blamed wage increases for inflation, and some linked unions to "dangerous foreign ideas" from Bolshevik Russia. In February 1919, Seattle's Central Labor Council called out all the city's unions in a five-day general strike to support striking shipyard workers. Seattle's mayor claimed the strike was a Bolshevik plot. Boston's police struck in September 1919 after the city's police commissioner fired nineteen policemen for joining an AFL union. The governor of Massachusetts, Calvin Coolidge, refused to negotiate and instead activated the national guard to maintain order and break the union. "There is no right to strike against the public safety by anybody, anywhere, anytime," he proclaimed. By mid-1919, many unionists concluded with dismay that conservative politicians had joined with business leaders in an effort to block further union organizing and to roll back the wartime gains.

The largest and most dramatic strike came against the United States Steel Corporation. Few steelworkers were represented by unions after the 1892 Homestead strike. Steel companies often hired recent immigrants, keeping the work force divided by language and culture. Most steelworkers put in twelve-hour workdays. Wages had not increased as fast as inflation—or as fast as company profits. In 1919 the AFL launched an ambitious unionization drive in the steel industry, and many steelworkers responded eagerly.

The men who ran the steel industry firmly refused to deal with the new organization. The workers went on strike in late September, demanding union recognition, collective bargaining, the eight-hour workday, and higher wages. United States Steel blamed the strike on radicals and effectively mobilized public opinion against the strikers. Company guards protected strikebreakers, and U.S. military forces moved into Gary, Indiana, to help round up what they called "the Red element." By January 1920, after eighteen workers had been killed and hundreds beaten, the strike was over and the unions were ousted.

Red Scare

The steel industry's charges of Bolshevism to discredit strikers came at a time when many government and corporate leaders vied in their depictions of the dangers of Bolshevism at home and abroad. And

On September 16, 1920, a bomb went off at the corner of Wall and Broad Streets in New York City—the symbolic center of American capitalism, opposite the headquarters of J. P. Morgan and the New York Stock Exchange. Thirty-three people died and some two hundred were injured. The bomb came as the Red Scare was subsiding. Like the bombs of 1919, the person responsible has never been positively identified. *Brown Brothers.*

a few anarchist bombers contributed their part in stirring up a widespread frenzy aimed at rooting out subversive radicals.

In late April 1919, thirty-four bombs addressed to prominent Americans—including J. P. Morgan, John D. Rockefeller, and Supreme Court justice Oliver Wendell Holmes—were discovered in various post offices after the explosion of two others addressed to a senator and to the mayor of Seattle. In June, bombs in several cities damaged buildings and killed two people. The explosions helped produce a panic over a supposed nationwide conspiracy to overthrow the government.

Attorney General A. Mitchell Palmer now organized an anti-Red campaign, hoping that success might enhance his chances for the 1920 presidential nomination. "Like a prairie fire," Palmer claimed, "the blaze of revolution was sweeping over every American institution." In August 1919, he appointed **J. Edgar Hoover,** a young lawyer, to head a new antiradical division in the Justice Department, the predecessor of the Federal Bureau of Investigation. In November, Palmer launched the first of what came to be called the **Palmer raids** to arrest suspected radicals. Authorities rounded up some five thousand people between

J. Edgar Hoover   Official appointed to head a new antiradical division in the Justice Department in 1919; he served as head of the FBI from its official founding in 1924 until his death in 1972.

Palmer raids   Government raids on individuals and organizations in 1919 and 1920 to search for political radicals and to deport foreign-born activists.

November 1919 and January 1920. Although officials found only a few firearms and no explosives, the raids led to the **deportation** of several hundred aliens who had some tie to a radical organization.

In May 1919, a group of veterans formed the American Legion, which not only lobbied on behalf of veterans but also condemned radicals and endorsed the deportations. Committing itself "to foster and perpetuate a one hundred percent Americanism," the Legion signed up a million members by the end of the year. Some of its branches gained a reputation for vigilante action against suspected radicals.

State legislatures joined in with their own antiradical measures, including **criminal syndicalism laws**—measures criminalizing the advocacy of Bolshevik or IWW ideologies. In January 1920, the assembly of the New York state legislature expelled five members elected as Socialists, solely because they were Socialists. However, after a wide range of respected public figures denounced the assembly action as undemocratic, public opinion regarding the **Red Scare** began to shift. With the approach of May 1, the major day of celebration for radicals, Palmer issued dramatic warnings for the public to be on guard against leftist activity, including a general strike and more bombings. When nothing happened, many concluded that the radical threat might have been overstated.

As the Red Scare sputtered to an end, in May 1920, police in Massachusetts arrested **Nicola Sacco and Bartolomeo Vanzetti,** both Italian-born anarchists, and charged them with robbery and murder. Despite inconclusive evidence and the accused men's protestations of innocence, a jury found them guilty, and they were sentenced to death. Many Americans argued that the two had been convicted because of their political beliefs and Italian origins. Further, many doubted that they had received a fair trial because of the nativism and antiradicalism that infected the judge and jury. Over loud protests at home and abroad and after long appeals, both men were executed in 1927. (Historians continue to debate the evidence in the case. Several have concluded that Sacco was probably guilty and Vanzetti innocent; others insist that both were innocent and that the state police concealed evidence.)

Race Riots and Lynchings

The racial tensions of the war years continued into the postwar period. Black soldiers encountered more acceptance and less discrimination in Europe than they had ever known at home. In May 1919, the NAACP journal *Crisis* expressed what the more militant returning soldiers felt:

We return. We return from fighting. We return fighting. Make way for Democracy! We saved it in France, and by the Great Jehovah, we will save it in the U.S.A., or know the reason why.

Some whites, North and South, greeted homecoming black troops with furious violence intended to restore prewar race relations. Southern mobs lynched ten returning black soldiers, some still in uniform. Rioters lynched more than seventy blacks in the first year after the war and burned eleven victims alive.

Rioting also struck outside the South. In July 1919, violence reached the nation's capital, where white mobs, many of them soldiers and sailors, attacked blacks throughout the city for three days, killing several. Unprotected, the city's African Americans organized their own defense, sometimes arming themselves. In Chicago in late July, war raged between white and black mobs for nearly two weeks, despite peacekeeping efforts by the militia. The rioting caused thirty-eight deaths (fifteen white, twenty-three black). More than a thousand families—nearly all black—were burned out of their homes. In Omaha in September, a mob tried to hang the mayor when he bravely stood between them and a black prisoner accused of rape. Police saved the mayor but not the prisoner.

By the end of 1919, race riots had flared in more than two dozen places. The year saw not only rampant lynchings but also the appearance of a new Ku Klux Klan (see page 730). Despite violence and coercion directed at African Americans, some things had changed. As W. E. B. Du Bois observed, black veterans "would never be the same again. You cannot ask them to go back to what they were before. They cannot, for they are not the same men."

---

deportation   Expulsion of an undesirable alien from a country.

criminal syndicalism laws   State laws that made membership in organizations that advocated communism or anarchism subject to criminal penalties.

Red Scare   Wave of anticommunism in the United States in 1919 and 1920.

Nicola Sacco and Bartolomeo Vanzetti   Italian anarchists convicted in 1921 of the murder of a Braintree, Massachusetts, factory paymaster and theft of a $16,000 payroll; in spite of public protests on their behalf, they were electrocuted in 1927.

Amending the Constitution: Prohibition and Woman Suffrage

In the midst of the turmoil at the end of the war, two of the great crusades of the Progressive Era finally realized their goals. Both had roots deep in the nineteenth century, and both had attracted numerous and diverse supporters during the Progressive Era. Prohibition was adopted as the Eighteenth Amendment to the Constitution, and woman suffrage as the Nineteenth Amendment. In some ways, these two measures marked the last gasp of the reforming zeal that had energized much of progressivism.

Spearheaded by the Anti-Saloon League (see page 644), prohibition advocates convinced Congress to pass a temporary prohibition measure in 1917, as a war measure to conserve grain. A more important victory for the "dry" forces came later that year, when Congress adopted and sent to the states the Eighteenth Amendment, prohibiting the manufacture, sale, or transportation of alcoholic beverages. Intense and single-minded lobbying by dry advocates persuaded three-fourths of the state legislatures to ratify the amendment in 1919, and it took effect in January 1920.

In June 1919, by a narrow margin, Congress proposed the Nineteenth Amendment, to enfranchise women over 21, and sent it to the states for ratification. After a grueling, state-by-state battle, ratification came in August 1920. Though many women by then already exercised the franchise, especially in western states, ratification meant that the electorate for the 1920 elections was significantly expanded.

The Election of 1920

Republicans confidently expected to regain the White House in 1920. The Democrats had lost their congressional majorities in the 1918 elections, and the postwar confusion and disillusionment often focused on Wilson. One reporter described the stricken president as the "sacrificial whipping boy for the present bitterness."

The reaction against Wilson almost guaranteed election for any competent Republican nominee. Several candidates attracted significant support, notably former army chief of staff General Leonard Wood, Illinois governor Frank Lowden, and California senator Hiram Johnson. However, no candidate could muster a majority of the convention delegates. Harry

Daugherty, campaign manager for Ohio senator Warren G. Harding, had foreseen such a deadlock months earlier and had predicted that it would be broken by a compromise candidate, chosen at about "eleven minutes after two o'clock on Friday morning," by about "fifteen or twenty men, bleary-eyed and perspiring profusely from the heat." And so it was. A small group of party leaders met late at night in a smoke-filled hotel room and picked Harding. Even some of his supporters were unenthusiastic—one called him "the best of the second-raters." For vice president, the Republicans nominated Calvin Coolidge, the Massachusetts governor who had broken the Boston police strike.

The Democrats also suffered severe divisions. After forty-four ballots, they chose James Cox, the governor of Ohio, as their presidential candidate. For vice president, they nominated Wilson's assistant secretary of the navy, Franklin D. Roosevelt, a remote cousin of Theodore Roosevelt.

Usually described as good-natured and likable—and sometimes as bumbling—Harding had published a small-town newspaper in Marion, Ohio, until his wife, Florence, and some of his friends pushed him into politics. He eventually won election to the Senate. Unhappy with his marriage, Harding apparently found contentment with a series of mistresses. The press knew of Harding's liaisons but never reported them.

An uproar arose, however, over a claim by an Ohio professor that Harding's ancestry included African Americans. The story spread rapidly, and a reporter soon asked Harding, "Do you have any Negro blood?" Harding replied mildly, "How do I know, Jim? One of my ancestors may have jumped the fence." The allegation, and Harding's response to it, apparently did not hurt his cause. Most of Harding's campaign reflected his promise to "return to normalcy," and the voters responded with enthusiasm to the notion of returning to "normal" after the stress of the war and the immediate postwar years.

Republicans won in a landslide. Harding took thirty-seven of the forty-eight states and 60 percent of the popular vote—the largest popular majority up to that time. Wilson had hoped the election might be a "solemn referendum" on the League of Nations, but it proved more a reaction to the war and its aftermath—a war launched with lofty ideals that turned sour at Versailles, the high cost of living, and the strikes and riots of 1919. Americans, it seemed, had tasted enough idealism and sacrifice for a while.

Individual Voices

Examining a Primary Source

Woodrow Wilson Proposes His Fourteen Points

President Woodrow Wilson spoke to a joint session of Congress on January 8, 1918, and presented his objectives for peace, including his Fourteen Points. This is a condensed version of that speech.

■ To what events does this passage refer? To whom is it directed?

. . . It will be our wish and purpose that the processes of peace, when they are begun, shall be absolutely open. . . . The day of conquest and aggrandizement is gone by; so is also the day of secret [treaties]. . . . ■

We entered this war because violations of right had occurred which touched us to the quick and made the life of our own people impossible unless they were corrected and the world secure once and for all against their recurrence. What we demand in this war, therefore, is nothing peculiar to ourselves. It is that the world be made fit and safe to live in; and particularly that it be made safe for every peace-loving nation which, like our own, wishes to live its own life, determine its own institutions, be assured of justice and fair dealing by the other peoples of the world as against force and selfish aggression. All the peoples of the world are in effect partners in this interest ■ . . . The program of the world's peace, therefore, is our program; and that program, the only possible program, as we see it, is this:

■ How do these statements compare with the outcome of the peace conference?

I. Open covenants of peace, openly arrived at, after which there shall be no private international understandings of any kind but diplomacy shall proceed always frankly and in the public view.

II. Absolute freedom of navigation upon the seas, outside territorial waters. . . .

III. The removal, so far as possible, of all economic barriers and the establishment of an equality of trade conditions among all the nations. . . .

IV. Adequate guarantees given and taken that national armaments will be reduced to the lowest point consistent with domestic safety.

■ What are the connections between Points I through V and the causes of the war in general, and the reasons for American's entrance into the war in particular?

V. A free, open-minded, and absolutely impartial adjustment of all colonial claims, based upon a strict observance of the principle that . . . the interests of the populations concerned must have equal weight with the equitable claims of the government whose title is to be determined. . . . ■

(Points VI–XIII laid out specific territorial restorations or adjustments.)

XIV. A general association of nations must be formed under specific covenants for the purpose of affording mutual guarantees of political independence and territorial integrity to great and small states alike. . . .

For such arrangements and covenants we are willing to fight and to continue to fight until they are achieved; but only because we wish the right to prevail and desire a just and stable peace such as can be secured only by removing the chief provocations to war. . . .

■ Was Wilson creating unrealistic expectations with statements such as these?

An evident principle runs through the whole program I have outlined. It is the principle of justice to all peoples and nationalities, and their right to live on equal terms of liberty and safety with one another, whether they be strong or weak. . . . ■

■ Compare Wilson's reasons, as stated here, for committing America to war with Alvin York's reasons, as he understood them, for his going to war.

The people of the United States could act upon no other principle. . . .

The moral climax of this the culminating and final war for human liberty has come. . . . ■

Summary

Woodrow Wilson took office expecting to focus on domestic policy, not affairs. He fulfilled some Democratic Party commitments to anti-imperialism but intervened extensively in the Caribbean. He also intervened in Mexico but failed to accomplish all of his objectives there.

When war broke out in Europe in 1914, Wilson declared the United States to be neutral, and most Americans agreed. German submarine warfare and British restrictions on commerce, however, threatened traditional definitions of neutrality. Wilson secured a German pledge to refrain from unrestricted submarine warfare. He was reelected in 1916 on the argument that "he kept us out of war." Shortly after he won reelection, however, the Germans violated their pledge, and in April 1917 Wilson asked for war against Germany.

The war changed nearly every aspect of the nation's economic and social life. To overcome inefficiency, the federal government developed a high degree of centralized economic planning. Fearing that opposition to the war might limit mobilization, the Wilson administration tried to mold public opinion and to restrict dissent. When the federal government backed collective bargaining, unions registered important gains. In response to labor shortages, more women and African Americans entered the industrial work force, and many African Americans moved to northern and Midwestern industrial cities.

Germany launched a major offensive in early 1918, expecting to achieve victory before American troops could make a difference. However, the AEF helped to break the German advance, and the Germans requested an armistice.

In his Fourteen Points, Wilson expressed his goals for peace. Facing opposition from the Allies, Wilson compromised at the Versailles peace conference but hoped that the League of Nations would be able to maintain the peace. Fearing the obligations that League membership might place on the United States, enough senators opposed the treaty to defeat it. Thus the United States did not become a member of the League.

In the United States, the end of the war brought disillusionment and a year of high prices, costly strikes, a Red Scare, and race riots and lynchings. In 1920 the nation returned to its Republican preference when it elected Warren G. Harding, a mediocre conservative, to the White House.

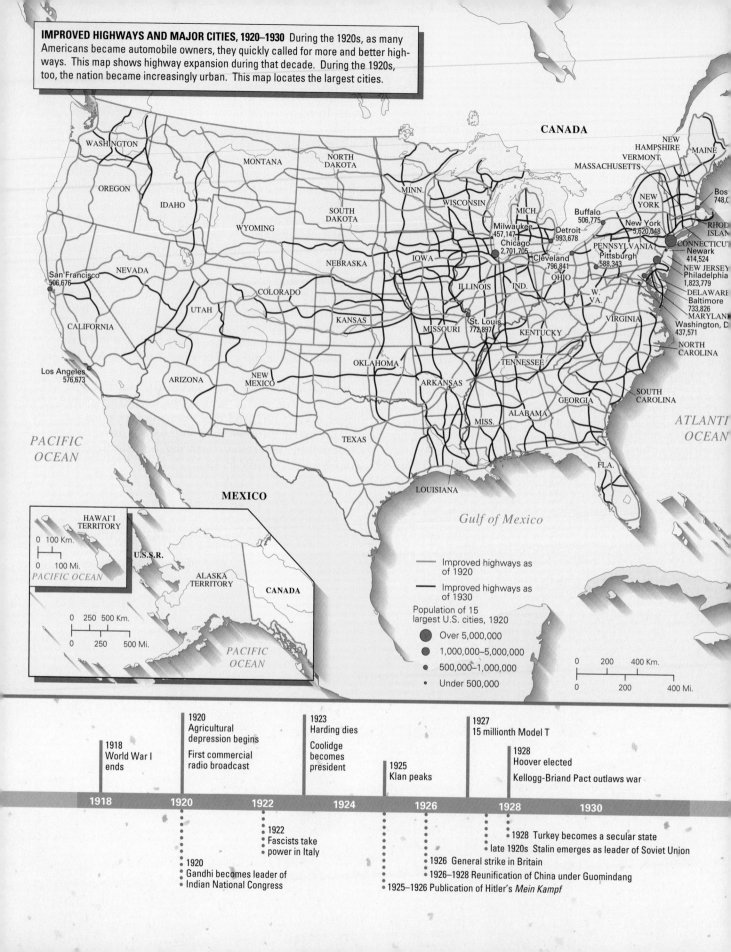

IMPROVED HIGHWAYS AND MAJOR CITIES, 1920–1930 During the 1920s, as many Americans became automobile owners, they quickly called for more and better highways. This map shows highway expansion during that decade. During the 1920s, too, the nation became increasingly urban. This map locates the largest cities.

CANADA

WASHINGTON
OREGON
IDAHO
MONTANA
NORTH DAKOTA
SOUTH DAKOTA
WYOMING
NEVADA
UTAH
COLORADO
NEBRASKA
KANSAS
CALIFORNIA
ARIZONA
NEW MEXICO
OKLAHOMA
TEXAS
MINN.
WISCONSIN
IOWA
MISSOURI
ARKANSAS
LOUISIANA
ILLINOIS
IND.
KENTUCKY
TENNESSEE
MISS.
ALABAMA
GEORGIA
MICH.
OHIO
W. VA.
VIRGINIA
NORTH CAROLINA
SOUTH CAROLINA
FLA.

NEW HAMPSHIRE
VERMONT
MAINE
MASSACHUSETTS
NEW YORK
RHODE ISLAND
CONNECTICUT
PENNSYLVANIA
NEW JERSEY
DELAWARE
MARYLAND

San Francisco 506,676
Los Angeles 576,673
Milwaukee 457,147
Chicago 2,701,705
Detroit 993,678
Cleveland 796,841
Buffalo 506,775
New York 5,620,048
Pittsburgh 588,343
St. Louis 772,897
Newark 414,524
Philadelphia 1,823,779
Baltimore 733,826
Washington, D 437,571
Bos 748,0

PACIFIC OCEAN

ATLANTIC OCEAN

MEXICO

Gulf of Mexico

Inset map:
HAWAI'I TERRITORY
0 100 Km.
0 100 Mi.
PACIFIC OCEAN

U.S.S.R.
ALASKA TERRITORY
CANADA
PACIFIC OCEAN
0 250 500 Km.
0 250 500 Mi.

Legend:
— Improved highways as of 1920
— Improved highways as of 1930

Population of 15 largest U.S. cities, 1920
● Over 5,000,000
● 1,000,000–5,000,000
● 500,000–1,000,000
• Under 500,000

0 200 400 Km.
0 200 400 Mi.

Timeline:

1918 World War I ends

1920 Agricultural depression begins
First commercial radio broadcast

1923 Harding dies
Coolidge becomes president

1925 Klan peaks

1927 15 millionth Model T

1928 Hoover elected
Kellogg-Briand Pact outlaws war

1918 1920 1922 1924 1926 1928 1930

1920 Gandhi becomes leader of Indian National Congress

1922 Fascists take power in Italy

1925–1926 Publication of Hitler's *Mein Kampf*

1926 General strike in Britain

1926–1928 Reunification of China under Guomindang

1928 Turkey becomes a secular state

late 1920s Stalin emerges as leader of Soviet Union

Prosperity Decade, 1920–1928

Improved Highways and Major Cities, 1920–1930
Compare the map on the facing page with Map 17.2 (p. 500), which shows railroads as of 1920. How would you compare the highway and railroad networks? Compare the map on the facing page with the map at the beginning of Chapter 18 (p. 526). What differences do you see in the locations of the nation's largest cities between 1890 and 1920?

Individual Choices

CLARA BOW

Clara Bow zoomed to stardom in Hollywood in the 1920s, and she came just as rapidly to symbolize a new and more open expression of sexuality and sensuality that Americans attributed to the movies and to popular magazines. This picture is undated, but seems to be from about 1925 or perhaps slightly later. © *Bettmann/Corbis.*

Clara Bow

At the age of 21, Clara Bow became the "It" Girl—star of the movie *It,* loosely based on Elinor Glyn's novel. "It" was sex appeal, or, in Glyn's words, "an inner magic, an animal magnetism." And Clara Bow, the "It" Girl, was the most popular movie star of the late 1920s.

Born in Brooklyn in 1905, Clara and her mother were frequently abandoned by her father. Clara's schizophrenic mother showed no affection for her daughter, and Clara grew up tough and streetwise, able to defend herself with her fists. Her mother engaged in prostitution; when she entertained a customer, she locked Clara in the cupboard for hours at a time. Clara left school at 13, without finishing the eighth grade, and began to work. At the age of 16, against her mother's orders, Clara entered a magazine contest for which the prize was a chance to appear in a film, and she won. Now Clara's mother threatened to kill her if she persisted in her goal of acting in movies. Her mother was confined to a mental institution in 1922 and died soon after. Left alone, Clara was raped by her father.

Movies allowed Bow to escape. By the time she was 17, she had a contract with a Hollywood studio, and she appeared in thirty-five movies before reaching the age of 21. Her first substantial role, in 1922, was as a tomboy, but by 1925 her studio labeled her "the hottest jazz baby in films." The *New York Times* agreed: "She radiates an elfin sensuousness." *It,* released in 1927, clinched her fame as the essential **flapper.** F. Scott Fitzgerald claimed that "Clara Bow is the quintessence of what the term 'flapper' signifies . . . pretty, impudent, superbly assured, as worldly-wise, briefly-clad and 'hard-berled' [tough] as possible." He added that thousands of young women were now "patterning themselves after her."

After *It,* Bow's films took on a formulaic quality derived from *It.* In each film, she set her sights on getting a handsome man, and she usually got what she wanted. On the screen, she was flirtatious and sensuous, conscious of her sexuality and willing to use it, and aggressive in accomplishing her goal. In the process, she usually revealed as much skin as the censors permitted. In her own life, she behaved in much the same way, attracting the most handsome men in Hollywood, making them her lovers, and discarding them for someone new. Perhaps reflecting on her parents' marriage, she told a reporter, "Marriage ain't woman's only job no more . . . I wouldn't give up *my* work for marriage."

Despite her huge popularity and her succession of famous lovers, Clara Bow remained deeply lonely. Her working-class behavior and speech and the gossip about her sex life made her a social outcast in Hollywood. When silent films gave way to the talkies, the looming overhead microphone became her enemy, reminding her of her childhood stutter and threatening her confidence in her performing ability. She made successful talking movies but never adjusted to the foreboding presence of the microphone. Several public scandals—an affair with a married man whose wife threatened a lawsuit, a dispute over a gambling debt, a court

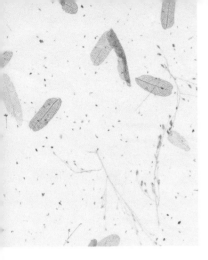

fight with her personal secretary—led to cancellation of her studio contract. At the age of 25, Clara Bow seemed a has-been.

She soon married Rex Bell, star of several low-cost western movies, and they moved to a remote ranch in Nevada. She made a comeback in 1933, starring in two films, both successful at the box office and with the critics. But Bow was done with Hollywood. She went into seclusion on the ranch. She and Bell had two children, but her mental well-being deteriorated, and she was diagnosed with schizophrenia and depression. She eventually returned to live in solitude in Los Angeles and died there, in 1965. In 1957, a poll of surviving silent-film directors, actors, and cameramen placed Clara Bow a close second to Greta Garbo as the greatest actress of the silent films.

INTRODUCTION

Called the "Jazz Age" and the "Roaring Twenties," the 1920s sometimes seem to be a swirl of conflicting images. Flappers—symbolized by Clara Bow—were flaunting new freedoms for women while prohibition marked an ambitious effort to preserve the values of nineteenth-century America. The booming stock market promised prosperity to all with money to invest even as thousands of farmers were abandoning the land because they could not survive financially. Business leaders celebrated the expansion of the economy while many wage earners in manufacturing endured the destruction of their unions and saw their legal protections evaporate. White-sheeted Klansmen marched as self-proclaimed defenders of Protestant American values and white supremacy, but African Americans' cultural expression in art, literature, and music was flowering.

Amid these seeming paradoxes, the economy roared along like a shiny new roadster, fueled by easy credit and consumer spending, virtually unregulated.

Prosperity Decade

- What was the basis for the economic expansion of the 1920s?
- What weaknesses existed within the economy?

By 1920, the industrialization of America was substantially achieved—the foundations of the corporate economy were in place, controlled by large industrial corporations, most of them run by professional managers. During the 1920s, the rise and growth of the automobile industry dramatized the new prominence of industries producing **consumer goods.** This significant change in direction carried implications for advertising, banking, and even the stock market.

The Economics of Prosperity

The end of the war in 1918 brought cancellation of orders for war supplies from ships to uniforms. At the same time, large numbers of recently discharged military and naval personnel swelled the ranks of job seekers. Such postwar conditions often bring on a recession or depression. At the end of World War I, however, no immediate economic collapse ensued. Given wartime shortages and overtime pay, many Americans had been earning more than they could spend. At the end of the war, their eagerness to spend helped to delay the postwar slump until 1920 and 1921. The **gross national product** (GNP) dropped by only 4.3 percent between 1919 and 1920, then fell by 8.6 percent between 1920 and 1921. During the war, unemployment affected only about 1 percent of the work force. The jobless rate increased to 5 percent in 1920 and 12 percent in 1921. Some employers also cut hours and wages. Figure 23.1 presents earnings for three groups of Americans and indicates the impact of recession in the early 1920s. However, reduced

flapper In the 1920s, a young woman with short hair and short skirts who flaunted her avant-garde dress and behavior.

consumer goods Products such as clothing, food, automobiles, and radios, intended for purchase and use by individuals or households, as opposed to products such as steel beams, locomotives, and electrical generators, intended for purchase and use by corporations.

gross national product The total market value of all goods and services that a nation produces during a specified period; now generally referred to as gross domestic product.

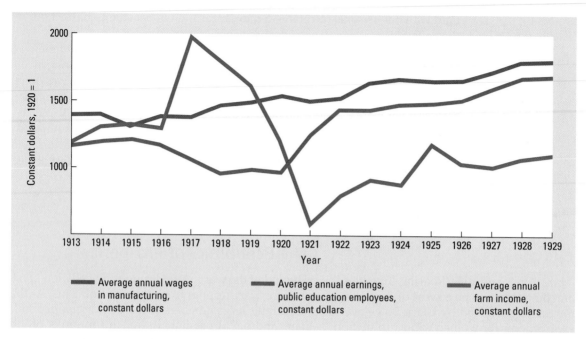

FIGURE 23.1 Patterns of Annual Income for Three Groups of Americans, 1913–1929 This graph depicts the patterns of annual income for three different groups of Americans. Income has been converted to constant dollars, meaning that the dollar amounts are adjusted for changes in the purchasing power of the dollar. In this case, 1920 is used as the base year for calculating the value of the dollar. Wages for manufacturing workers rose steadily during the war years, leveled during the recession of the early 1920s, then rose again. For public education employees—mostly teachers—real earnings fell dramatically with the inflation of the war years and the postwar recession, then rose to parallel those of manufacturing workers. Farmers, in 1913, had a boom in income during the war, but then saw their real earnings plunge at the end of the war with only a modest recovery after the recession of the early 1920s. *Source:* U.S. Department of Commerce, Bureau of Census, *Historical Statistics of the United States, Colonial Times to 1970,* Bicentennial Edition, 2 vols. (Washington: Government Printing Office, 1975), I:167, 170, 483.

earnings, unemployment, and declining demand halted the rampaging inflation of 1918 and 1919. In fact, consumer prices fell from 1920 to 1921, led by a 24 percent drop in the price of food.

The economy quickly rebounded. The gross national product increased by more than 15 percent between 1921 and 1922, a bigger jump than during the booming war years. Unemployment remained at 2–5 percent from 1923 through 1929, and prices for most manufactured goods remained relatively stable. Income for many increased. Thus many Americans seemed slightly better off by 1929 than in 1920: they earned more (at least in constant dollars) and paid somewhat less for necessities.

Targeting Consumers

By the 1920s, many business leaders understood that persuading Americans to consume an array of products was crucial to keeping the economy healthy. In 1921 General Foods Company invented Betty Crocker to give its baking products a womanly, domestic image. In 1924 General Mills first advertised Wheaties as the "Breakfast of Champions," thereby tying consumption of cold cereal to the popularity of sports. Americans responded by buying those products and others with similarly creative pitches. "We grew up founding our dreams on the infinite promises of American advertising," Zelda Sayre Fitzgerald later wrote.

The marketing of Listerine demonstrates a new dimension in advertising. Listerine had been devised as a general antiseptic, but in 1921 Gerard Lambert developed a more persuasive—and profitable—approach when he plucked the obscure term *halitosis* from a medical journal. Through aggressive advertising using the word, he fostered anxieties about the impact of bad breath on popularity and made millions by selling Listerine to combat the offensive condition. Until then, few Americans had been concerned about

Chronology

America in the 1920s

1908	Henry Ford introduces Model T General Motors formed
1914	Universal Negro Improvement Association founded War breaks out in Europe
1915	D. W. Griffith's *Birth of a Nation* Ku Klux Klan revives
1918	World War I ends
1920	Eighteenth Amendment (instituting Prohibition) takes effect Nineteenth Amendment (granting women the vote) takes effect Sinclair Lewis's *Main Street* Warren G. Harding elected president First commercial radio broadcasts
1920–1921	Nationwide recession
1921	Temporary immigration quotas Halitosis sells Listerine Farm Bloc formed
1921–1922	Washington Naval Conference
1922	Fordney-McCumber Tariff Nine-Power Pact Sinclair Lewis's *Babbitt* T. S. Eliot's *The Waste Land*
1923	Harding dies Calvin Coolidge becomes president Marcus Garvey convicted of mail fraud Jean Toomer's *Cane* American Indian Defense Association formed France occupies Ruhr Valley
1923–1927	Harding administration scandals revealed
1924	National Origins Act Coolidge elected First disposable handkerchiefs

	Wheaties marketed as "Breakfast of Champions" Crossword puzzle fad Full citizenship for American Indians Dawes Plan U.S. forces withdraw from Dominican Republic
1924–1929	Great Bull Market
1925	Scopes trial Bruce Barton's *The Man Nobody Knows* F. Scott Fitzgerald's *The Great Gatsby* Ku Klux Klan claims 5 million members Klan leader convicted of murder One automobile for every three residents in Los Angeles Chrysler Corporation formed
1926	Florida real-estate boom collapses Ernest Hemingway's *The Sun Also Rises* Gertrude Ederle swims English Channel United States intervenes in Nicaragua Railway Labor Act of 1926
1927	Clara Bow stars in *It* Coolidge vetoes McNary-Haugen bill Charles Lindbergh's transatlantic flight Duke Ellington conducts jazz at Cotton Club Peace of Titiapa Augusto Sandino begins guerrilla war in Nicaragua
1928	Coolidge vetoes McNary-Haugen bill again Ford introduces Model A Kellogg-Briand Pact Herbert Hoover elected
1929	Great Depression begins
1930	Rafael Trujillo seizes power in Dominican Republic
1931	Al Capone convicted and imprisoned
1933	Twenty-first Amendment repeals Prohibition
1934	U.S. forces withdraw from Haiti

freshening their breath. Afterward, other entrepreneurs also sought to sell products to meet needs that consumers had not identified before being alerted to them by advertising.

Changes in fashion also encouraged increased consumption. The chic new look of short hairstyles for women, for example, led to the development of hair salons and stimulated sales of the recently in-

She bags the *bouquets* but never a *Beau*

Many in Chicago society can remember when Mildred caught her second bouquet. The year was 1927. "Surely now, she will be the next to marry," they said, remembering the old adage. Everybody was marrying; war, romance and matrimony were in the air. It was almost a foregone conclusion that the groom would be one of the nice young men training at Fort Sheridan.

But somehow or other, none of them seemed interested in her after they really got to know her. The years rolled on . . . Mildred was still attractive, still catching bouquets. But there her luck ended. Matrimony seemed further off than ever. The truth was that Mildred repelled others without knowing why. And none of her friends had the courage to tell her.

You never have it? – *what colossal conceit!*

Surveys show that not one person in ten escapes halitosis (unpleasant breath). It may be absent one day and present the next. Its causes are many: excesses of eating or drinking, decaying teeth, pyorrhea, fermenting food particles in the mouth and slight infections of the gums, mouth, nose or throat, from which unpleasant odors arise.

Whatever the cause, halitosis is an unforgivable social fault. It is unforgivable because it is inexcusable. And it is inexcusable because it can be promptly overcome by the use of full strength Listerine, the safe antiseptic, as a mouth wash.

Being a germicide capable of killing 200,000,000 germs in 15 seconds, Listerine checks decay and infections which cause odors. Being also a powerful deodorant, it promptly gets rid of the odors themselves. The breath is left sweet and clean.

Rinse the mouth with Listerine before any business or social engagement. Keep a bottle handy in home and office. It puts you on the safe, polite and acceptable side. Lambert Pharmacal Co., St. Louis.

End halitosis with LISTERINE   THE SAFE ANTISEPTIC

Advertising promised that those who used Listerine to eliminate halitosis would gain friends and even romance. *Courtesy Warner-Lambert Company.*

vented **bobby pin.** Cigarette advertisers began to target women, as when the American Tobacco Company advised women to "Reach for a Lucky instead of a sweet" to attain a fashionably slim figure. Style and technology combined to create disposable products, thereby promoting regular, recurring consumer buying of throwaway items. Technological advances in the processing of wood cellulose fiber led in 1921 to the marketing of Kotex, the first manufactured disposable sanitary napkin, and in 1924 to the first disposable handkerchiefs, later known as Kleenex tissues.

Technological advances contributed in other ways to the growth of consumer-oriented manufacturing. In 1920 about one-third of all residences had electricity. By the end of the decade, electrical power had reached nearly all urban homes (but fewer than 10 percent of farm homes). As the number of residences with electricity increased, advertisers stressed the time and labor that housewives could save by using electric washing machines, irons, vacuum cleaners, and toasters. Between 1919 and 1929, consumer ex-

penditures for household appliances grew by more than 120 percent.

Increased consumption encouraged a change in people's spending habits. Before the war, most families saved their money until they could pay cash for what they needed, but in the 1920s many retailers urged buyers to "Buy now, pay later." And many consumers responded, taking home a new radio today and worrying about paying for it tomorrow. By the late 1920s, about 15 percent of all retail purchases were made through the installment plan, especially furniture, phonographs, washing machines, and refrigerators. Charge accounts in department stores also became popular, and **finance companies** (which made loans) grew rapidly.

The Automobile: Driving the Economy

The automobile epitomized the new consumer-oriented economy of the 1920s. Early automobiles were luxuries, but **Henry Ford** developed a mass-production system that drove down production costs.

Ford, a former mechanic, built his success on the **Model T,** introduced in 1908. A Model-T Ford was a dream come true for many middle-income Americans, and families came to love their ungraceful but reliable "Tin Lizzies" (so named because of their lightweight metal bodies). By 1927, Ford had produced more than 15 million of them, dominating the market by selling the largest possible number of cars at the lowest possible price. "Get the prices down to the buying power," Ford ordered. His dictatorial style of management combined with technological advances and high worker productivity to bring the price of a

bobby pin   Small metal hair clip with ends pressed tightly together, designed for holding short or "bobbed" hair in place.

finance company   Business that makes loans to clients based on some form of collateral, such as a new car, thus allowing a form of installment buying when sellers do not extend credit.

Henry Ford   Inventor and manufacturer who founded the Ford Motor Company in 1903 and pioneered mass production in the auto industry.

Model T   Lightweight automobile that Ford produced from 1908 to 1927 and sold at the lowest possible price on the theory that an affordable car would be more profitable than an expensive one.

"How did he ever get the money to buy a car"

Perhaps he *doesn't* make as much as you do—but he took advantage of this quick, easy, sure way to own an automobile

Ford Weekly Purchase Plan

Henry Ford constantly worked to reduce car prices on his cars. He also promoted installment buying, promising in this ad that "with even the most modest income, [every family] can now afford a car of their own." This ad also encouraged impulse buying: "You live but once and the years roll by quickly. Why wait for tomorrow for things that you rightfully should enjoy today?" Both installment buying and impulse buying, spurred by advertising, formed parts of the developing culture of consumerism. *Library of Congress.*

new Model T as low as $290 by 1927 (equivalent to about $2,900 today). Cheap to buy, the Model T sacrificed style and comfort for durability, ease of maintenance, and the ability to handle almost any road. It made Henry Ford into a folk hero—a wealthy one. By 1925, Ford Motor Company showed a *daily* profit of some $25,000.

Ford's company provides an example of efforts by American entrepreneurs to reduce labor costs by improving efficiency. In the process, however, work on Ford's assembly line became a thoroughly dehumanizing experience. Ford workers were prohibited from talking, sitting, smoking, singing, or even whistling while working. As one critic put it, workers were to "put nut 14 on bolt 132, repeating, repeating, repeating until their hands shook and their legs quivered."

Ford, however, paid his workers well, and they could increase their pay more by completing the company's Americanization classes. Ford workers earned enough, in fact, to afford their own Model T's. Ford's high wages pushed other automakers to increase pay for their workers as well, to keep their best workers from defecting to Ford. Auto workers thus came to

enjoy some of the consumer buying previously restricted to middle- and upper-income groups.

Not only streamlined production but also competition helped to keep auto prices low. Other automobile companies challenged Ford's predominance, notably General Motors (GM), founded by William Durant in 1908, and Chrysler Corporation, created by Walter Chrysler in 1925. GM and Chrysler adopted many of Ford's production techniques, but their cars also offered more comfort and style than the Model T. Ford only ended production of the Model T in 1927, when Chevrolet passed Ford in sales. The next year, Ford introduced the Model A, which incorporated some features touted by his competitors.

The automobile came to symbolize not only the ability of many Americans to acquire material goods but also technology, progress, and the freedom of the open road. The industry worked to promote this heady image. One car salesman remarked in 1926, "When I sold a car, I sold it with the honest conviction that I was doing the buyer a favor in helping him to take his place in a big forward movement." American consumers were receptive. By the late 1920s, about 80 percent of the world's registered vehicles were in the United States. By then, America's roadways sported nearly one automobile for every five people.

The automobile industry in the 1920s often led the way in devising new sales techniques. Installment buying became so widespread that by 1927 two-thirds of all American automobiles were sold on credit. GM led the way in introducing new models every year. This practice enticed owners to trade in their cars just to keep up with new fashions in design, color, and optional features. Dozens of small automakers closed when they could not compete with Chrysler, Ford, and GM—the Big Three. By 1929, the Big Three were making 83 percent of all cars manufactured in the country. The industry had become an oligopoly.

Changes in Banking and Business

Just as Henry Ford helped to bring automobiles within reach of most Americans, so did **A. P. Giannini**

> **A. P. Giannini**   Italian American who changed the banking industry by opening multiple branches and encouraging the use of banks for small accounts and personal loans.

The assembly line at Ford's main assembly plant in 1928. Model-A Fords are under production, as assembly-line workers quickly perform the same task on car after car, as the chassis moves past them at the rate of 6 feet per minute. Ford pioneered the assembly line as a way to reduce both cost and dependence on skilled workers. He paid the highest wages in Detroit but required complete obedience from his workers, even to the point of prohibiting whistling while at work. *From the Collections of Henry Ford Museum & Greenfield Village.*

revolutionize banking. The son of Italian immigrants, Giannini founded the Bank of Italy in 1904 as a bank for shopkeepers and workers in the Italian neighborhood of San Francisco. Until then, most banks had only one location, in the center of a city, and limited their services to businesses and substantial citizens with hefty accounts. Giannini not only based his bank on dealings with ordinary people but also opened branches throughout California, near people's homes and workplaces. Called the greatest innovator in twentieth-century American banking, Giannini broadened the base of banking by encouraging working people not only to open small checking and savings accounts but also to borrow for such investments as car purchases. In the process, his bank—later renamed the Bank of America—became the third largest in the nation by 1927.

Giannini's bank and Ford's auto factory survived as relics of family management in a new world of modern corporations with large bureaucracies. Ownership and control continued to grow apart, as salaried managers came to run most big businesses.

The number of corporations increased steadily throughout the 1920s, but a great corporate merger wave also accelerated as the 1920s progressed. These mergers continued earlier patterns toward greater economic concentration. By 1930, 5 percent of American corporations were receiving 85 percent of all net corporate income, up from 78 percent in 1921.

Leading entrepreneurs emerged as popular and respected public figures. Perhaps the ultimate glorification of the entrepreneur came in 1925, in a book entitled *The Man Nobody Knows*. The author, Bruce Barton (later founder of a leading advertising agency), suggested that Jesus Christ could best be understood as a business executive who "had picked up twelve men from the bottom ranks of business and forged them into an organization that conquered the world." Portraying Jesus' parables as "the most powerful advertisements of all time," Barton's book led the nonfiction bestseller lists for two years.

"Get Rich Quick"— Speculative Mania

More than ever before, the stock market captured people's imagination as the fast track to riches. Stock market speculation—buying a stock with the expectation of making money by selling it at a higher price—ran rampant. Articles in popular periodicals proclaimed that everyone could participate and get rich in no time, even with a small investment. By 1929, 4 million Americans owned stock, equivalent to about 10 percent of American households.

Just as Americans purchased cars and radios on the installment plan, some also bought stock on credit. It was possible to purchase stock listed at $100

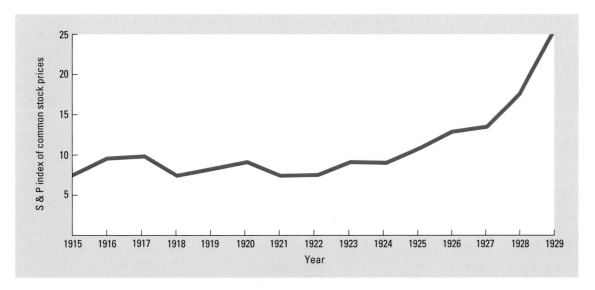

FIGURE 23.2 Stock Prices, 1915–1929 This graph shows the Standard and Poor index of common stock prices. This index is based on the years 1941–1942 as the base years (the index = 10 for those years). The figures for other years show stock prices in comparison to the base year. The Great Bull Market began in late 1924/early 1925 and roared upward until late 1929. *Source:* U.S. Department of Commerce, Bureau of Census, *Historical Statistics of the United States, Colonial Times to 1970,* Bicentennial Edition, 2 vols. (Washington: Government Printing Office, 1975), II:10–4.

a share with as little as $10 down and the other $90 "on margin"—that is, owed to the stockbroker. If the stock price advanced to $150, the investor could sell, pay off the broker, and gain a profit of $50 (500 percent!) on the $10 investment. Unfortunately, if the stock price fell to $50, the investor would still owe $90 to the broker. Actually, fewer than 1 percent of those who bought stocks did so on margin, and the size of the margin rarely exceeded 45 or 50 percent. A larger number of people borrowed money to buy stocks. Buying stocks with borrowed money, however, carried the same potential for disaster as buying on margin.

Driven partly by real economic growth and partly by speculation, stock prices rose higher and higher (see Figure 23.2). Standard and Poor's index of common stock prices tripled between 1920 and 1929. As long as the market stayed **bullish** and stock prices kept climbing, prosperity seemed endless.

The ease of borrowing funds and the ever-rising stock prices and corporate dividends of the 1920s encouraged the creation of holding companies—organizations designed not to sell actual goods or services but to keep dividends flowing to investors. Samuel Insull created a vast empire of electrical utilities companies. Much of his enterprise—and others like it—

consisted of holding companies, which existed solely to own the stock of another company, some of which existed primarily to own the stock of yet another company. The entire structure rested on the dividends that the underlying **operating companies** produced. Those dividends enabled the holding companies to pay dividends on their bonds. Any interruption in the flow of dividends from the operating companies was likely to bring the collapse of the entire pyramid, swallowing up the investments of speculators.

Although the stock market held the nation's attention as the most popular path to instant riches, other speculative opportunities abounded. One of the most prominent was a land boom in Florida. During the

bullish Optimistic or confident; when referring to the stock market, a bull market is when stock prices are going up, and a bear market is when stock prices come down.

operating company A company that exists to sell goods or services, as opposed to a holding company that exists to own other companies, including operating companies.

early 1920s, people poured into Florida, especially Miami, attracted by the climate, the beaches, and the ease of travel from the cities of the chilly Northeast. Speculators began to buy land—almost any land—amid predictions that its value would soar. Stories circulated of land whose value had increased 1,500 percent over ten years. Like stocks, land was bought with borrowed money, to be resold at a profit. Early in 1926, however, the population influx slowed, and the boom began to falter. It collapsed completely when a hurricane slammed into Miami in September 1926. By 1927, many Florida land speculators were facing bankruptcy.

Agriculture: Depression in the Midst of Prosperity

The prosperity never extended to agriculture, and farmers still made up nearly 30 percent of the work force in 1920. During the war, many farmers expanded their operations in response to government demands for more food, and exports of farm products nearly quadrupled. After the war, as European farmers resumed production, a glut of agricultural goods on world markets caused prices to fall. Exports of farm products dropped by half. Throughout the 1920s, American farmers consistently produced more than the domestic market could absorb, and this **overproduction** caused prices to fall.

The average farm's net income for the years 1917 to 1920 ranged between $1,196 and $1,395 (in current dollars) per year (see Figure 23.1, which is calculated in constant dollars rather than current dollars). Farm income fell to a dreadful $517 (see above) in 1921, then slowly began to rise but never reached the levels of 1917 to 1920 until World War II. Although farmers' net income, when adjusted for inflation, fell in the immediate postwar years and never recovered to prewar levels, their mortgage payments more than doubled over prewar levels, partly because of debts farmers had incurred to expand wartime production. Tax increases, purchases of tractors and trucks—now necessities on most farms—and the growing cost of fertilizer and other essential supplies bit further into farmers' meager earnings.

As the farm economy continued to hemorrhage, the average value of an acre of farmland, in constant dollars, fell by more than half between 1920 and 1928. The average farm was actually less valuable in 1928 than in 1912. Thousands of people left farming each year, and the proportion of farmers in the work force

fell from nearly 30 percent to less than 20 percent. The 1920s were not the prosperity decade for rural America.

The "Roaring Twenties"

■ What groups most challenged traditional social patterns during the 1920s? Why?

■ What role did technology play in social change during the 1920s?

"The world broke in two in 1922 or thereabouts," wrote novelist Willa Cather, and she indicated her distaste for much that came after. F. Scott Fitzgerald, another novelist, agreed with the date but embraced the change. He believed 1922 marked "the peak of the younger generation," who brought about an "age of miracles"—that, he admitted, became an "age of excess." For most Americans, evidence of sudden and dramatic social change was easy to see, from automobiles, radios, and movies to a new youth culture and an impressive cultural outpouring by African Americans in northern cities.

Putting a People on Wheels: The Automobile and American Life

The automobile profoundly changed American patterns of living. Highways significantly shortened the traveling time from rural areas to cities, reducing the isolation of farm life. One farm woman, when asked why her family had an automobile but no indoor plumbing, responded, "Why, you can't go to town in a bathtub." Trucks allowed farmers to take more products to market more quickly and conveniently than ever before. Tractors significantly expanded the amount of land that one family could cultivate. Because the spread of gasoline-powered farm vehicles reduced the need for human farm labor, they stimulated migration to urban areas.

If the automobile changed rural life, it made an even more profound impact on life in the cities. The 1920 census, for the first time, recorded more Americans living in urban areas (defined as places having

overproduction Production that exceeds consumer need or demand.

2,500 people or more) than in rural ones. As the automobile freed suburbanites from their dependence on commuter rail lines, new suburbs mushroomed and streetcars steadily declined. Most of the new suburban growth was in the form of single-family houses. From 1922 through 1928, construction began on an average of 883,000 new homes each year. New home construction rivaled the auto industry as a major driving force behind economic growth.

As early as 1913, the automobile demonstrated its ability to strangle urban traffic. One response was the development of traffic lights. Various versions were tried, but the four-directional, three-color traffic light first appeared in Detroit in 1920. Traffic lights spread rapidly to other large cities, but traffic congestion nonetheless worsened. By 1920, more than 250,000 cars entered Manhattan each day; by 1926, cars in the evening rush hour in Manhattan crawled along at less than 3 miles per hour—slower than a person could walk—and many commuters had returned to trains and subways.

Los Angeles: Automobile Metropolis

Most of Manhattan was not designed to handle automobile traffic, but the fastest-growing major city of the early twentieth century—Los Angeles—was. The population of Los Angeles increased tenfold between 1900 and 1920, then more than doubled by 1930, reaching 2.2 million. Expansion of citrus-fruit raising, major oil discoveries, and the development of the motion-picture industry laid an economic foundation for rapid population growth in southern California. Manufacturing also expanded—during the 1920s, the city moved from twenty-eighth to ninth place among American cities based on manufacturing.

Lack of sufficient water threatened to limit growth until city officials diverted the Owens River to Los Angeles through a 233-mile-long aqueduct, opened in 1913. Throughout the 1920s, southern California promoters attracted hundreds of thousands of people by presenting an image of perpetual summer, tall palm trees lining wide boulevards filled with automobiles, fountains gushing water into the sunshine, and broad sandy beaches.

The growth of Los Angeles came as the automobile industry was promoting the notion of a car for every family and real-estate developers were propounding

In the 1920s, civic leaders in Los Angeles cultivated an image of perpetual sunshine, warm weather the year-round, and abundant water. This photo from the late 1920s includes some of these and more—the personal automobile, and, in this case, a sporty touring car with its top down, and wide boulevards lined with palm trees and other semitropical vegetation to emphasize the warm climate. *Shades of L.A. Archives/Photo Collection/Los Angeles Public Library.*

the ideal of the single-family home. By 1930, about 94 percent of all residences in Los Angeles were single-family homes, an unprecedented level for a major city, and Los Angeles consequently had the lowest urban population density in the nation.

Life in Los Angeles came to be organized around the automobile in ways unknown in other major cities. The first modern supermarket, offering "one-stop shopping," appeared in Los Angeles, and the "Miracle Mile" along Wilshire Boulevard was the nation's first large shopping district designed for the automobile. Such innovations set the pace for new urban development everywhere. The *Los Angeles Times* put it this way in 1926: "Our forefathers in their immortal independence creed set forth 'the pursuit of happiness' as an inalienable right of mankind. And how can one pursue happiness by any swifter and surer means . . . than by the use of the automobile?" By then, Los Angeles had one automobile for every three residents, twice the national average.

Some movies provided more open expressions of sexuality and sensuality than had been available previously. Several of the biggest stars of the decade owed their fame to their sex appeal. Clara Bow, on the left, was the "It" girl, and "It" literally stood for sex appeal, though prevailing mores still prohibited using that term. Rudolph Valentino, on the right, was the leading male sex star of the 1920s. This poster advertises *The Sheik*, which appeared in 1921. The movie was so popular and influential that handsome young men came to be referred to for a time as sheiks. *Left: Collection of Hershenson-Allen Archives; right: Culver Pictures.*

A Homogenized Culture Searches for Heroes

As the automobile cut traveling time and more people moved to urban areas, restrictive immigration laws were closing the door to immigrants from abroad. These factors, together with the new technologies of radio and film, began to **homogenize** the culture—that is, to make it increasingly uniform by breaking down cultural differences based on region or ethnicity.

The first commercial radio station began broadcasting in 1920. Within six years, 681 were operating.

By 1930, 40 percent of all households had radios. By the mid-1920s, too, most towns of any size boasted at least one movie theater. Movie attendance increased rapidly, from a weekly average of 40 million people in 1922 to 80 million in 1929—the equivalent of two-thirds of the total population. As Americans all across the country tuned in to the same radio broadcast, and families in rural villages as well as urban neighborhoods laughed or wept at the same movie, radio and

homogenize To make something uniform throughout.

Charles Lindbergh chose photo settings in which he was alone with his plane, thereby emphasizing the individual nature of his flights. This photo was taken before his solo flight across the Atlantic. *Culver Pictures, Inc.*

film did their part to homogenize life in the United States.

Radio and film joined newspapers and magazines in creating and publicizing national trends and fashions as Americans pursued one fad after another. After the opening of the fabulous tomb of the Egyptian pharaoh Tutankhamen in 1922, Americans developed a passion for things Egyptian. In 1924, crossword puzzle books captured the attention of many Americans, and contract bridge, a card game, became the rage soon after, in 1926. Such fads created markets for new consumer goods, from Egyptian-style furniture to crossword dictionaries to folding card tables.

The media also helped to create national sports heroes. In the 1920s, spectator sports became an obsession. Baseball had long been the preeminent national sport, and radio now began to broadcast baseball games nationwide. Other sports vied with baseball for national favor and for fans' dollars. Most Americans were familiar with the exploits of Lou Gehrig and Babe Ruth on the baseball diamond, Jack Dempsey and Gene Tunney in boxing, and Bobby Jones, a golfer. Gertrude Ederle won national acclaim in 1926 when she became the first woman to swim the English

Channel and did so two hours faster than any previous man. Fame extended even to racehorses, notably Man o' War.

The rapid spread of movie theaters created a new category of fame—the movie star. Charlie Chaplin, Buster Keaton, Harold Lloyd, and others brought laughter to the screen. Tom Mix was the best known of those introducing the western as a rugged dramatic genre. Sex, too, sold movie tickets and made stars of Clara Bow, the "It" girl, and Theda Bara, the **vamp.** Rudolph Valentino soared to fame as a male sex symbol, with his most famous film, *The Sheik,* set in a fanciful Arabian desert.

The greatest popular hero of the 1920s, however, was neither an athlete nor an actor but a small-town airmail pilot named **Charles Lindbergh.** At the time, aviation was barely out of its infancy. The earliest regular airmail deliveries in the United States began in 1918, and night flying did not become routine until the mid-1920s. A few transatlantic flights had been logged by 1926, but the longest nonstop flight before 1927 was from San Diego to New York—2,500 miles.

Lindbergh, in 1927, decided to collect the prize of $25,000 offered by a New York hotel owner to the pilot of the first successful nonstop flight between New York and Paris—3,500 miles. His plane, *The Spirit of St. Louis,* was a stripped-down, one-engine craft. In a sleepless, 33½-hour flight, Lindbergh earned both the $25,000 and the adoration of crowds on both sides of the Atlantic. In an age devoted to materialism and dominated by a corporate mentality, Lindbergh's accomplishment suggested that old-fashioned individualism, courage, and self-reliance could still triumph over odds and adversity.

Alienated Intellectuals

Lindbergh flew to Paris and became a living legend. Other Americans, too, went to Paris and other European cities in the 1920s, but for different reasons. These **expatriates** left the United States to escape what they considered America's intellectual shallowness, dull materialism, and spreading uniformity. As

vamp A woman who uses her sexuality to entrap and exploit men.

Charles Lindbergh American aviator who made the first solo transatlantic flight in 1927 and became an international hero.

expatriate A person who takes up long-term residence in a foreign country.

In the 1920s, Ernest Hemingway lived the life of an expatriate, mostly in Paris but with excursions elsewhere in Europe. Here he is shown in Pamplona, Spain, in 1924, practicing to fight bulls. Hemingway is right of center, wearing white pants and a dark sweater. In his second novel, *The Sun Also Rises* (1926), a group of jaded, pleasure-seeking expatriates in Paris take a trip to Pamplona to run with the bulls and watch a bullfight. *Ernest Hemingway Collection/ John F. Kennedy Library.*

Malcolm Cowley put it in *Exile's Return* (1934), his memoir of his life in France, "by expatriating himself, by living in Paris, Capri or the South of France, the artist can break the puritan shackles, drink, live freely, and be wholly creative." He added that Paris in the 1920s "was a great machine for stimulating the nerves and sharpening the senses."

Though **Sinclair Lewis** and H. L. Mencken did not move to Paris, they were among the leading critics of middle-class materialism and uniformity. Lewis, in *Main Street* (1920), presented small-town, middle-class existence as not just boring but stifling. In *Babbitt* (1922), Lewis presented a suburban businessman (George F. Babbitt) as materialistic, narrow-minded, and complacent, speaking in clichés and buying every gadget on the market. H. L. Mencken, the influential editor of *The American Mercury*, relentlessly pilloried the "booboisie," jeered at all politicians (reformers and conservatives alike), and celebrated only those writers who shared his disdain for most of American life.

Other writers celebrated the seeking of pleasure and excitement. Edna St. Vincent Millay, a prominent poet, captured some of this spirit in 1920:

> *My candle burns at both ends;*
> *It will not last the night;*
> *But ah, my foes, and oh, my friends—*
> *It gives a lovely light!*

Where Millay celebrated social rebellion, F. Scott Fitzgerald, in *The Great Gatsby* (1925), revealed a grim side of the hedonism of the 1920s as he portrayed the pointless lives of wealthy pleasure seekers and their careless disregard for life and values. Ernest Hemingway, in *The Sun Also Rises* (1926), depicted disillusioned and frustrated expatriates. Other expatriates extended the theme of hopelessness. In *The Waste Land* (1922), T. S. Eliot, an American poet who had fled to England in 1915, presented the barrenness of modern life. Some writers even predicted the end of Western civilization.

Renaissance Among African Americans

For the most part, feelings of despair and disillusionment troubled white writers and intellectuals. Such sentiments were rarely apparent in the striking outpouring of literature, music, and art by African Americans in the 1920s.

Sinclair Lewis Novelist who satirized middle-class America in works such as *Babbitt* (1922) and became the first American to win the Nobel Prize for literature.

Many blacks moved to northern cities in the 1920s, continuing patterns begun earlier. Harlem emerged as the largest black neighborhood in New York City and quickly came to symbolize the new urban life of African Americans. The term **Harlem Renaissance,** or Negro Renaissance, refers to a literary and artistic movement in which black artists and writers insisted on the value of black culture and drew upon African and African American traditions in their writing, painting, and sculpture. Alain Locke, a leading black author, likened it to "a spiritual emancipation." Black actors, notably Paul Robeson, began to appear in serious theaters and earn acclaim for their abilities. Earlier black writers, especially Locke, James Weldon Johnson, and Claude McKay, encouraged and guided the novelists and poets of the Renaissance.

Among the movement's poets, Langston Hughes became the best known. His poetry rang with the voice of the people, for he sometimes used folk language to convey powerful images. Born in Joplin, Missouri, in 1902, Hughes began to write poetry in high school, briefly attended college, then worked and traveled in Africa and Europe. By 1925, he was a significant figure in the Harlem Renaissance, sometimes reading his poetry to the musical accompaniment of jazz. Some of his works present images from black history, such as "The Negro Speaks of Rivers" (1921), and others, such as "Song for a Dark Girl" (1927), vividly depict racism. Some of his poems look to the future with an expectation for change and for new choices, as in "I, Too" (1925):

> I, too, sing America.
> I am the darker brother.
> They send me
> To eat in the kitchen
> When company comes,
> But I laugh,
> And eat well,
> And grow strong.
> Tomorrow
> I'll sit at the table
> When company comes.
> Nobody'll dare
> Say to me,
> "Eat in the kitchen,"
> Then.
> Besides
> They'll see
> How beautiful I am
> And be ashamed.
> I, too, am America.

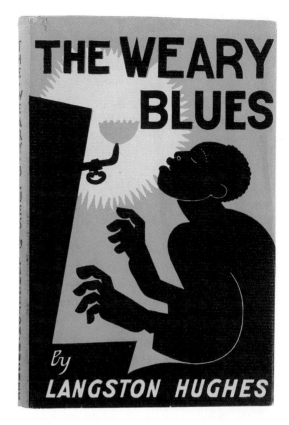

This is the original cover for *The Weary Blues,* the first book of poetry by Langston Hughes, published in 1926. Hughes later wrote that the book included some of the first blues that he had ever heard, dating to his childhood in Lawrence, Kansas. Both the reference to the blues in Hughes's poetry and the cover design for the book evoke the connection between music and poetry that was part of the Harlem Renaissance. *Picture Research Consultants & Archives.*

Other important writers included Zora Neale Hurston, who came from a poor southern family, won a scholarship to Barnard College, and began her long writing career with several short stories in the 1920s. Jean Toomer's novel *Cane* (1923), dealing with African Americans in rural Georgia and Washington, D.C., has been praised as "the most impressive product of the Negro Renaissance."

Harlem Renaissance   Literary and artistic movement in the 1920s, centered in Harlem, in which black writers and artists described and celebrated African American life.

This was the cover of a special issue of *Survey Graphic* in March 1925. A popular magazine of the period, *Survey Graphic* devoted the entire issue to Harlem and the emergence of a new consciousness among its African American residents. *Yale Collection of American Literature, Beinecke Rare Book Room and Manuscript Library, Yale University.*

Louis Armstrong, born in 1900, first began to play the trumpet in New Orleans but emerged as a leading innovator in jazz after 1924, when he joined Fletcher Henderson's orchestra in New York. Some of his recordings from the 1920s are among the most original and imaginative contributions to jazz. *Frank Driggs Collection.*

The 1920s have sometimes been called the Jazz Age. **Jazz** developed in the early twentieth century, drawing from several strains in African American music, particularly the blues and ragtime (see page 670). Created and nurtured by African American musicians in southern cities, especially New Orleans, jazz had been introduced to northern and white audiences by 1917. Jazz influenced leading white composers, notably George Gershwin, whose *Rhapsody in Blue* (1924) brought jazz into the symphony halls. Some attacked the new sound, claiming it encouraged people to abandon self-restraint, especially with regard to sex. But despite—or perhaps because of—such condemnation, the wail of the saxophone became as much a part of the 1920s as the roar of the roadster and the flicker of the movie projector.

The great black jazz musicians of the 1920s—Louis "Satchmo" Armstrong, Bessie Smith, Fletcher Henderson, Ferdinand "Jelly Roll" Morton, and others—

drew white audiences into black neighborhoods to hear them. Harlem came to be associated with exotic nightlife and glittering jazz clubs, with the Cotton Club the best known. There Edward "Duke" Ellington came in 1927 to lead the club band, and there he began to develop the works that made him one of the most respected American composers.

The fanfare of the Cotton Club was remote from the experience of most African Americans, but one Harlem black leader affected black people throughout the country and beyond. **Marcus Garvey,** born in

jazz Style of music developed in America in the early twentieth century, characterized by strong, flexible rhythms and improvisation on basic melodies.

Marcus Garvey Jamaican black nationalist active in America in the 1920s.

On the one hundred fiftieth anniversary of the Declaration of Independence, *Life* presented this cover parodying the famous painting *The Spirit of '76* by depicting "The Spirit of '26"—an uninhibited flapper with a jazz saxophonist and drummer, and banners with the snappy sayings of the day. The caption reads: "1776–1926: One Hundred and Forty-three Years of LIBERTY and Seven Years of PROHIBITION." *Private Collection.*

Jamaica, advocated a form of **black separatism.** His organization, the Universal Negro Improvement Association (UNIA), founded in 1914, stressed racial pride, the importance of Africa, and racial solidarity across national boundaries. Garvey supporters urged blacks from around the world to help Africans overthrow colonial rule and build a strong African state—which, they hoped, would become a powerful symbol of black accomplishment. Garvey established a steamship company, the Black Star Line, which he envisioned would carry African Americans to Africa, and he promoted other black enterprises. The UNIA message of racial pride and solidarity attracted wide support among African Americans, especially in the cities. However, black integrationist leaders, especially W. E. B. Du Bois of the NAACP, opposed Garvey's separatism and argued that the first task facing blacks

was integration and equality in the United States. Garvey and Du Bois each labeled the other a traitor to his race.

Federal officials eventually charged Garvey with irregularities in his fundraising, and he was convicted of mail fraud in 1923. He spent two years in jail and then was deported to his native Jamaica. Garvey continued to lead UNIA, but the organization lost members and influence.

"Flaming Youth"

Although African Americans created jazz, those who danced to it, in the popular imagination of the 1920s, were white—a male college student, clad in a stylish raccoon-skin coat with a hip flask of illegal liquor in his pocket, and his female counterpart, the uninhibited flapper with bobbed hair and a daringly short skirt. This stereotype of "flaming youth"—the title of a popular novel—reflected far-reaching changes among many white, college-age youths of middle- or upper-class background.

In the 1920s adolescence emerged as a separate subculture. The prosperity of the 1920s allowed many middle-class families to send their children to college. On the eve of World War I, just over 3 percent of the population ages 18 to 24 were enrolled in college. By 1930, that proportion had more than doubled, with larger increases among women, and women were receiving 40 percent of all bachelor's degrees. On campus, students reshaped colleges into youth centers, where football games and dances assumed as much significance as examinations and term papers.

For some young women—especially college students but also others from urban backgrounds—the changes of the 1920s seemed especially dramatic. Called "flappers" because of the flapping sound made by their fashionably unfastened galoshes, many young women scandalized their elders with skirts that stopped at the knee, stockings rolled below the knee, short hair often dyed black, and generous amounts of rouge and lipstick. Many observers assumed that this outrageous look reflected outrageous behavior and that young women were abandoning their parents' moral values. In fact, women's sexual activity outside marriage had begun to increase before

black separatism A strategy of creating separate black institutions, based on the assumption that African Americans can never achieve equality within white society.

the war, especially among working-class women and radicals. "Dating," too, owed its origins to prewar working-class young people. In the 1920s, these behaviors began to appear among college and high school students from middle-class families. About half of the women who came of age during the 1920s had intercourse before marriage, a marked increase from prewar patterns.

Such changes in behavior were often linked to the automobile. It brought greater freedom to young people, for behind the wheel they had no chaperone and could go where they wanted. Sometimes they went to a **speakeasy** (a place where illegal alcohol was sold). Before Prohibition, few women entered saloons, but Prohibition seemed to glamorize drinking. Men and women alike began to go to speakeasies, to drink and smoke together, and to dance to popular music derived from jazz. While some adults criticized the frivolities of the young, others emulated them, launching the first American youth culture. F. Scott Fitzgerald later called the years after 1922 "a children's party taken over by elders."

Traditional America Roars Back

■ Why and how did some Americans try to restore traditional social values during the 1920s?

■ What were some of the results of their efforts?

Americans embraced cars, electric appliances, movies, and radios, but many apparently felt threatened by the pace of change and the upheaval in social values that seemed centered in the cities. However, it is not accurate to see the 1920s as a time of cultural warfare between rural and urban values. In nearly every case, efforts to stop the tide of change were strong in cities as well as in rural areas, and many of those efforts dated to the prewar era. In the 1920s, several movements seeking to restore elements of an older America came to fruition at the same time as Fitzgerald's "age of excess."

Prohibition

The **Eighteenth Amendment** (Prohibition) took effect in January 1920, and it came to epitomize many of the cultural struggles of the 1920s to preserve white, old-stock, Protestant values. However, many Americans simply ignored the Eighteenth Amendment, and it grew less popular the longer it lasted. By 1926, a poll indicated that only 19 percent of Americans supported Prohibition, 50 percent wanted the amend-

ment modified, and 31 percent favored outright **repeal.** Prohibition, however, remained the law, if not the reality, from 1920 until 1933, when the Twenty-first Amendment finally did repeal it.

Prohibition did reduce drinking somewhat, and it apparently produced a decline in drunkenness and in the number of deaths from alcoholism. It was never well enforced anywhere, however, partly because of the immensity of the task and partly because Congress never provided enough money for more than token federal enforcement. In 1923 a federal agent visited major cities to see how long it took to find an illegal drink: it took only 35 seconds in New Orleans, 3 minutes in Detroit, and 3 minutes and 10 seconds in New York City.

Prohibition produced unintended consequences. Neighborhood saloons had often functioned as social centers for working-class and lower-middle-class men, but the new speakeasies were often more glamorous, attracting an upper- and middle-class clientele, women as well as men. **Bootlegging**—production and sale of illegal beverages—flourished. Some bootleggers brewed only small amounts of beer and sold it to their neighbors. In the cities, however, the thirst for alcohol provided criminals with a fresh and lucrative source of income, part of which they used to buy influence in city politics and protection from police.

In Chicago, the gang led by **Al Capone** counted nearly a thousand members and, in 1927, took in more than $100 million (equivalent to nearly a billion dollars today)—$60 million of it from bootlegged liquor. The scar-faced Capone systematically eliminated members of competing gangs through violence unprecedented in American cities. Gang warfare raged in Chicago throughout the 1920s, producing some five hundred slayings. In 1931 federal officials finally managed to convict Capone—of income-tax evasion—and send him to prison.

---

speakeasy   A place that illegally sells liquor and sometimes offers entertainment.

Eighteenth Amendment   Constitutional amendment, ratified in 1919, that forbade the manufacture, sale, or transportation of alcoholic beverages.

repeal   The act of making a law or regulation no longer valid and enforceable; repeal of a constitutional amendment requires a new amendment.

bootlegging   Illegal production, distribution, or sale of liquor.

Al Capone   Italian-born American gangster who ruthlessly ruled the Chicago underworld until he was imprisoned for tax evasion in 1931.

The blood-drenched mobs of Chicago had their counterparts elsewhere, as other gangsters—many of recent immigrant background, including Italians, Irish, Germans, and Jews—followed similar paths to wealth. Gangs also found riches in gambling, prostitution, and **racketeering.** Through racketeering they gained power in some labor unions. The gangs, killings, and corruption confirmed other Americans' long-standing distrust of cities and immigrants, and they clung to the vision of a dry America as the best hope for renewing traditional values.

Fundamentalism and the Crusade Against Evolution

Another effort to maintain traditional values came with the growth of fundamentalist Protestantism. Fundamentalism emerged from a conflict between Christian modernism and traditional beliefs. Modernists tried to reconcile their religious beliefs with modern science. Fundamentalists, however, rejected anything—including science—that they considered to be incompatible with a literal reading of the Scriptures. Every word of the Bible, they argued, is the revealed word of God. The fundamentalist movement grew throughout the first quarter of the twentieth century, led by figures such as Billy Sunday, a baseball player turned evangelist.

In the early 1920s, some fundamentalists focused on **evolution** as contrary to the Bible. Biologists cite the theory of evolution to explain how living things have developed over millions of years, but the Bible states that God created the world and all living things in six days. Fundamentalists saw in evolution not just a challenge to the Bible's account of creation but also a challenge to religion itself.

William Jennings Bryan, the former Democratic presidential candidate and secretary of state, fixed on the evolution controversy after 1920. Until his death, he provided fundamentalists with their greatest champion. His energy, eloquence, and enormous following—especially in the rural South—guaranteed that the issue received wide attention. "It is better," Bryan wrote, "to trust in the Rock of Ages than to know the age of rocks." Bryan played a central role in the most famous of the disputes over evolution—the Scopes trial.

In March 1925, the Tennessee legislature passed a law making it illegal for any public school teacher to teach evolution. When the American Civil Liberties Union (ACLU) offered to defend a teacher willing to challenge the law, John T. Scopes, a young biology teacher in Dayton, Tennessee, accepted. Bryan volunteered to assist the local prosecutors, who faced an ACLU defense team that included the famous attorney **Clarence Darrow.** Bryan claimed that the only issue was the right of the people to regulate public education as they saw fit, but Darrow insisted he was there to prevent "bigots and ignoramuses from controlling the education of the United States."

The court proceedings were carried nationwide, live, via radio. Toward the end of the trial, in a surprising move, Darrow called Bryan to the witness stand as an authority on the Bible. Under Darrow's withering questioning, Bryan revealed that he knew little about findings in archaeology, geology, and linguistics that cast doubt on Biblical accounts, and he also admitted, to the dismay of many fundamentalists, that he did not always interpret the words of the Bible literally. "Darrow never spared him," one reporter wrote, "It was masterful, but it was pitiful." Bryan died a few days later. Scopes was found guilty, but the Tennessee Supreme Court threw out his sentence on a technicality, preventing appeal.

Nativism and Immigration Restriction

Prohibition and laws against teaching evolution were efforts to use government to define individual behavior and beliefs. Laws designed to restrict immigration had a similar origin, resulting largely from nativist antagonism against immigrants, especially those from southern and eastern Europe (see page 542). After a hiatus in immigration during the war, 430,000 immigrants arrived in 1920 and 805,000 in 1921, more than half from southern and eastern Europe.

Efforts to cut off immigration were not new. However, the presence of so many German Americans during the war with Germany, the Red Scare and fear

racketeering   Commission of crimes such as extortion, loansharking, and bribery, sometimes behind the front of a seemingly legitimate business or union.

evolution   The central organizing theorem of the biological sciences, which holds that organisms change over generations, mainly as a result of natural selection; it includes the concept that humans evolved from nonhuman ancestors.

Clarence Darrow   A leading trial lawyer of the early twentieth century, who often defended those challenging the status quo.

Teaching Evolution in Public Schools

Following the Scopes trial, other state legislatures followed the lead of Tennessee and prohibited the teaching of evolution. Textbook publishers soft-pedaled or omitted treatment of evolution. Not until the 1950s, when the United States was in a technological competition with the Soviet Union and national science education standards were developed, did a thorough treatment of evolution return to most high school textbooks.

In 1968, the U.S. Supreme Court considered a case challenging an Arkansas law that prohibited the teaching of evolution. The court first found that the sole reason for the Arkansas law was that a particular religious group considered evolution to conflict with the Book of Genesis. The court therefore ruled that the law was intended to establish a particular religious view and consequently violated the First Amendment, which prohibits Congress from adopting any law which privileges one religious group, and the Fourteenth Amendment, which applies the prohibitions of the First Amendment to state governments.

Opponents of evolution then argued for the teaching of "creationism" as an alternative explanation to evolution. This the U.S. Supreme Court struck down in 1987, in a case involving a Louisiana law. In 1999, the Kansas state board of education voted to remove evolution from the state's biology curriculum. In elections the following year, however, most members of the board were not reelected, and evolution was returned to the Kansas state curriculum.

of foreign radicalism, and the continued influx of poor immigrants at a time of growing unemployment all combined in 1921 to win greater support for restriction. The result was an emergency act to limit immigration from any country to 3 percent of the number of people from that country living in the United States at the time of the 1910 census.

The act of 1921 slowed the arrival of immigrants, but advocates of restriction considered it temporary. In 1924 a permanent law, the **National Origins Act,** limited total immigration to 150,000 people each year.

Quotas for each country were to be based on 2 percent of the number of Americans whose ancestors came from that country, but the law completely excluded Asians. While statisticians worked at determining the ancestry of all Americans, quotas were based on the 1890 census (before the largest wave of immigrants from southern and eastern Europe). In attempting to freeze the ethnic composition of the nation, the law reflected the arguments of those nativists who contended that immigrants from southern and eastern Europe and Asia made less desirable citizens than people from northern and western Europe. The law did permit unrestricted immigration from Canada and Latin America.

Throughout the 1920s, nativism and discrimination flourished, sometimes taking violent forms. In West Frankfort, Illinois, for example, during three days in August 1920, rioting townspeople beat and stoned Italians, pulling them out of their homes and setting the houses on fire. Other times, discrimination took more subtle forms. **Restrictive covenants** attached to real-estate titles prohibited the future sale of the property to particular groups, typically African Americans and Jews. Exclusive eastern colleges placed quotas on the number of Jews admitted each year, and some companies refused to hire Jews. In 1920 Henry Ford, in a magazine for Ford dealers, accused Jewish bankers of controlling the American economy and then broadened his attack to suggest an international Jewish conspiracy to control virtually everything from baseball to bolshevism. After Aaron Sapiro, an attorney, sued Ford for defamation and challenged him to prove his claims, Ford retracted his charges and apologized in 1927.

The Ku Klux Klan

Nativism, anti-Catholicism, anti-Semitism, and fear of radicalism all contributed to the spectacular growth of the Ku Klux Klan in the early 1920s. The original Klan, created during Reconstruction to intimidate

National Origins Act   Law passed by Congress in 1924, establishing quotas for immigration to the United States; it limited immigration from southern and eastern Europe, permitted larger numbers of immigrants from northern and western Europe, and prohibited immigration from Asia.

restrictive covenant   Provision in a property title that prohibits the sale of property to specified groups of people, especially people of color and Jews.

This image is from a Ku Klux Klan pamphlet published in the mid-1920s, when the Klan claimed as many as 5 million members nationwide. The Klan portrayed itself as defending traditional, white, Protestant America against Jews, Catholics, and African Americans. *Private collection.*

ticipated actively in local politics. Its leaders sometimes exerted powerful political influence in communities and in state governments, notably in Texas, Oklahoma, Kansas, Oregon, and Indiana. In Oklahoma, the Klan led a successful impeachment campaign against a governor who tried to restrict its activities. In Oregon, the Klan claimed responsibility for a 1922 law aimed at eliminating Catholic schools. (The Supreme Court ruled the law unconstitutional.) Many local and state elections in 1924 divided along pro- and anti-Klan lines.

Although Klan members in 1923 hailed themselves as "the return of the Puritans in this corrupt, and jazz-mad age," extensive corruption underlay the Klan's self-righteous rhetoric. Some Klan leaders joined primarily for the profits, both legal (from recruiting) and illegal (mostly from political payoffs). Some shamelessly violated the morality they preached. In 1925, D. C. Stephenson, Grand Dragon of Indiana and one of the most prominent Klan leaders, was convicted of second-degree murder after the death of a woman who had accused him of raping her. When the governor refused to pardon him, Stephenson produced records proving the corruption of many Indiana officials, including the governor, a member of Congress, and the mayor of Indianapolis. Klan membership fell sharply amid factional disputes and further evidence of fraud and corruption.

Patterns of Ethnicity, Race, Class, and Gender

■ How did race relations during the 1920s show continuities with earlier patterns? What new elements appeared?

■ Is it appropriate to describe the 1920s as "the lean years" for working people?

■ How did gender roles and definitions change in the 1920s?

The "spiritual emancipation" that Alain Locke ascribed to the Harlem Renaissance, on the one hand, and the terror of Klan nightriders, on the other, represent the polar extremes of race relations in the 1920s. For most people of color, the realities of daily life fell somewhere in between. For working people, the 1920s represented what Irving Bernstein, a labor historian, has termed "the lean years," when gains from the Progressive Era and World War I were lost and unions remained largely on the defensive. For women, the 1920s opened with a political victory in the form of suffrage, but the unity mustered in support of that measure soon broke down.

former slaves, had long since died out, but D. W. Griffith's hugely popular film *The Birth of a Nation,* released in 1915, glorified the old Klan.

The new Klan portrayed itself as a patriotic order devoted to traditional American values, old-fashioned Protestant Christianity, and white supremacy. Attacking Catholics, Jews, immigrants, and blacks, along with bootleggers, corrupt politicians, and gamblers, the Klan fed on the insecurities of the day. Growth came slowly at first, to only five thousand members by 1920, but then a new recruiting scheme offered local organizers $4 out of every $10 initiation fee. This incentive combined with the postwar wave of nativism and antiradicalism to produce 5 million members nationwide by 1925.

The Klan was strong in the South, Midwest, West, and Southwest, and it mushroomed in towns and cities as well as in rural areas. The organization par-

African Americans intensified their efforts to put an end to lynching. This protest parade was held in Washington, D.C., in 1922. The NAACP's efforts to secure a federal antilynching law, however, were repeatedly defeated by southerners in Congress. © *Corbis/Bettmann.*

Ethnicity and Race: North, South, and West

Discrimination against Jews, violence against Italians, and the Klan's appeal to white Protestants all point to the continuing significance of ethnicity in American life during the 1920s. Throughout the decade, racial relations remained deeply troubled at best, violent at worst.

Although the Harlem Renaissance helped to produce greater appreciation for black music and other accomplishments, racial discrimination continued to confront most African Americans, no matter where they lived. A few gained better jobs by moving north, but many found work only in low-paying service occupations. In nearly every city, social pressures and restrictive covenants limited access to desirable housing. Those who did succeed sometimes found themselves the targets of racial hostility, like the black physician whose home was attacked by a white mob when he moved into a white Detroit neighborhood in 1925. A race riot devastated Tulsa, Oklahoma, in 1921, leaving nearly 40 confirmed dead (with blacks outnumbering whites by more than two to one), rumors

of hundreds more buried in mass graves, hundreds injured, and 1,400 black business and homes burned.

Throughout the 1920s, the NAACP tried to secure a federal antilynching law, but southern legislators defeated each attempt, arguing against any federal interference in the police power of the states. As part of its efforts to combat lynching, the NAACP tried to educate the public by publicizing crimes against blacks.

In the eastern United States, North and South, race relations usually meant black-white relations. In the West, race relations were always more complex, and became even more so in the years preceding and following World War I, when Filipinos began to arrive in Hawai`i and on the West Coast, most of them working in agriculture and aboard ships. In 1920 some eight thousand workers on Hawaiian sugar plantations, most of them Japanese and Filipino, went on strike for higher wages. After six months, however, most of the strikers gave up in defeat. Sikhs from India also entered the West Coast work force, mainly as agricultural laborers.

California had long led the way among western states in passing laws discriminating against Asian Americans. Westerners, especially Californians, had also compiled a lengthy record of violence aimed at Asians. By the 1920s, other western states had copied California laws forbidding Asian immigrants to own or lease land.

Some Asian immigrants and Asian Americans responded to discriminatory actions through court actions, but with little success. In the early 1920s, the U.S. Supreme Court affirmed that only white persons and persons of African descent could become naturalized citizens, denying citizenship to persons born in Japan or India. The U.S. Supreme Court also ruled that Mississippi could require a Chinese American schoolchild to attend the segregated school established for African Americans.

Beginnings of Change in Federal Indian Policy

Although Asian Americans made few gains in the 1920s, American Indians had more success, thanks in part to persistent and persuasive advocates. In the early 1920s, Interior Secretary Albert Fall tried to lease parts of reservations to white developers and to extinguish Pueblo Indians' title to lands along the Rio Grande. In the face of significant opposition, Fall's proposals were dropped or modified. The Pueblo land question led directly to the organization of the **American Indian Defense Association** (AIDA), created in 1923 by John Collier, an eastern social worker, to support the Pueblos.

Collier and AIDA soon emerged as leading voices calling for changes in federal Indian policy. They sought better health and educational services on the reservations, creation of tribal governments, tolerance of Indian religious ceremonies and other customs, and an end to land allotments—all in all, a major policy change, from assimilation to recognition of Indian cultures and values. The political pressure that the AIDA and similar groups applied, as well as political efforts by Indians themselves, secured several new laws favorable to Indians, including one in 1924 extending full citizenship to all Native Americans.

In 1926 Secretary of the Interior Hubert Work ordered a comprehensive study of Indian life. Completed in 1928, the report described widespread poverty and health problems among Indians, demonstrated the lack of adequate healthcare and education on the reservations, and condemned allotment as the single most important cause of Indian hardship. The efforts to support and extend Indian rights, especially the work of Collier, laid the basis for a significant shift in federal policy in the 1930s.

Mexican Americans

California and the Southwest, home to many Mexican and Mexican American families since the region was part of Mexico, attracted growing numbers of Mexican immigrants in the 1920s. Many Mexicans went north, most of them to Texas and California, to escape the revolution and civil war that devastated their nation from 1910 into the 1920s. Nearly 700,000 Mexicans legally fled to the United States between 1910 and 1930, and probably the same number came illegally.

The agricultural economies of the Southwest were also changing. In south Texas, some cattle ranches were converted to farms, especially for cotton but for fruit and vegetables too. By 1925, the Southwest was relying on irrigation to produce 40 percent of the nation's fruits and vegetables, crops that were highly labor-intensive. In the late 1920s, Mexicans made up 80 to 85 percent of farm laborers in that region. At the same time, the southwestern states also experienced large increases in their Anglo populations. These changes in population and economy reshaped relations between Anglos and Mexicans.

In south Texas, many Anglo newcomers looked on Mexicans as what one Anglo called a "partly colored race," and white newcomers tried to import elements of southern black-white relations, including disfranchisement and segregation. Disfranchisement was unsuccessful, but some schools and other social institutions were segregated despite Mexican opposition. Efforts organized through the League of United Latin American Citizens (LULAC) occasionally halted discrimination by businesses—but only occasionally.

In California, Mexican workers' efforts to organize and strike for better pay and working conditions often sparked violent opposition. Strikes in the early 1920s were broken quickly and brutally. Local authorities arrested and often beat strikers, and growers' private guards beat or kidnapped them. Leaders were likely to be deported. Nevertheless, Mexican labor had become vital to agriculture, and growers opposed any proposals to restrict immigration from Mexico. The landowners made certain that the revised immigration law of 1924 permitted unlimited immigration from the Western Hemisphere. In Lemon Grove, a

American Indian Defense Association Organization founded in 1923 to defend the rights of American Indians; it pushed for an end to land allotment and a return to tribal government.

This picture from 1924 shows Mexican farm workers, most of them women and children, pitting apricots in Los Angeles county. Immigration from Mexico increased significantly during the 1910s and 1920s, due to improvements in transportation within Mexico and to the social and economic dislocations produced by revolution and civil war in Mexico. By the 1920s, Mexicans made up much of the work force in California agriculture, and they often worked as family units, including women and children as well as adult males. *Seaver Center for Western History Research, Natural History Museum of Los Angeles County.*

small town near San Diego, in 1931, Mexican American parents mounted the first successful court challenge to school segregation.

Not all immigrants from Mexico stayed in the Southwest. As the doors to European immigration closed with the new immigration law, midwestern manufacturers began to recruit Mexican workers to work in steel mills, meatpacking plants, and auto factories. By 1930, significant numbers of Mexican Americans were to be found in such industrial cities as Chicago, Detroit, and Gary.

Labor on the Defensive

Difficulties in establishing unions among Mexican workers mirrored a larger failure of unions in the 1920s. When unions tried to recover lost purchasing power by striking in 1919 and 1920, nearly all failed. After 1921, employers took advantage of the conservative political climate to challenge Progressive Era legislation benefiting workers. The Supreme Court responded by limiting workers' rights, voiding laws that eliminated child labor, and striking down minimum wages for women and children.

Many companies undertook anti-union drives. Arguing that unions were not necessary and had become either corrupt or radical, some employers used the term **American Plan** to describe their refusal to

> **American Plan** Term that some employers in the 1920s used to describe their policy of refusing to negotiate with unions.

recognize unions as representing employees. At the same time, many companies began to provide workers with benefit programs such as insurance, retirement pensions, cafeterias, paid vacations, and stock purchase plans, an approach sometimes called **welfare capitalism.** Such innovations stemmed both from genuine concern about workers' well-being and from the expectation that such improvements would increase productivity and discourage unionization.

The 1920s marked the first period of prosperity since the 1830s when union membership declined, falling from 5 million in 1920 to 3.6 million in 1929, a 28 percent decline at a time when the total work force increased by 15 percent. Some unions lost members for reasons in addition to hostile government policies, the American Plan, and lost strikes. Prohibition devastated once-strong unions of brewery workers and bartenders. AFL leaders, holding fast to their concept of separate unions for each different skill group, made no serious effort to organize the great mass-production industries. Some unions suffered from internal battles—the International Ladies' Garment Workers' Union lost two-thirds of its members during power struggles between Socialists and Communists.

The Communists sought influence and power within other unions, but the membership of the **Communist Party** (CP) never approached the numbers claimed by the Socialist Party before World War I. In 1929 the CP counted only 9,300 members. Always closely tied to the leadership of the Soviet Union, the CP labored strenuously to organize workers throughout the 1920s, first by working within AFL unions and then by creating separate unions. CP operatives tried to organize the unskilled, people of color, women, and others outside AFL craft unions, but they had little success.

Changes in Women's Lives

The attention given to the flapper in accounts of the 1920s should not detract from important changes in women's gender roles during those years. Significant changes occurred in two arenas: family and politics.

Marriage among white middle-class women and men came increasingly to be valued as companionship between two partners. Although the ideal of marriage was often expressed in terms of man and woman taking equal responsibility for a relationship, the actual responsibility for the smooth functioning of the family typically fell on the woman. In addition, many women in the 1920s seem to have increased their control over decisions about childbearing.

Usually in American history, prosperity brings increases in the birth rate. In the 1920s, however, changing social values together with more options for birth control resulted in fewer births. Women who came of childbearing age in the 1910s and 1920s are distinctive in three ways, when compared with women of both earlier and later time periods: (1) they had fewer children on the average, (2) more of them had no children at all, and (3) far fewer had very large families (see Figure 23.3).

The declining birth rate in the 1920s reflected, in part, some degree of success for earlier efforts to secure wider availability of birth-control information and devices, for example, diaphragms. Margaret Sanger continued to carry the banner in the battle to extend birth-control information (see page 643), and she persuaded more doctors to join her efforts. As the birth-control movement gained the backing of male physicians, it became a more respectable, middle-class reform movement. By 1925, the American Medical Association, the New York Academy of Medicine, and the New York Obstetrical Society had all declared their support for birth control, and the Rockefeller Foundation began to fund medical research into contraception methods. Nevertheless, until 1936, federal law restricted public distribution of information about contraception. At the same time, during the 1920s, abortion continued to be an important way that some women terminated unwanted pregnancies. In Clara Bow's Hollywood, abortions were almost routine as a way for actresses both to meet their contractual obligations to perform in films and to avoid the public scandal that could end their careers.

Throughout the 1920s, working-class women still struggled to stretch their finances to cover their families' needs. As before, some women and children worked outside the home because the family needed additional income. The proportion of women working for wages remained quite stable during the 1920s, at about one in four. The proportion of married women working for wages increased, though, from 23 percent of the female labor force in 1920 to 29 percent in 1930.

---

welfare capitalism   Program adopted by some employers to provide to their employees benefits such as lunchrooms, paid vacations, bonuses, and profit-sharing plans.

"American Communist Party"   Party organized in 1919, devoted to destroying capitalism and private property and replacing them with a system of socialism.

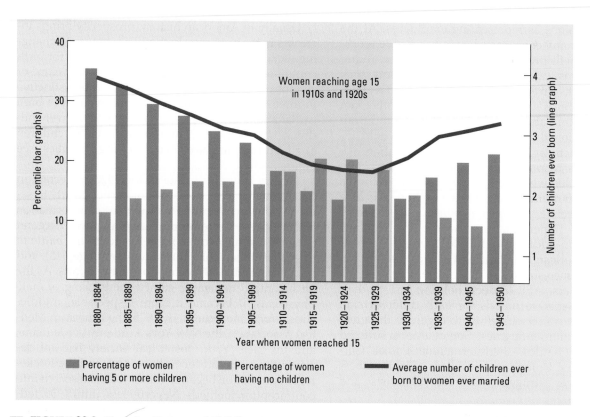

FIGURE 23.3 Changing Patterns of Childbearing Among Women This figure depicts three different choices regarding family size: (1) the number of children born to women ever married, (2) the percentage of women ever married having large families, and (3) the percentage of women ever married having no children at all. Childbearing ages are considered to be between 15 and 45. *Sources:* For women born in 1914 and before, Series B42–48, Percent Distribution of Ever-Married Women (Survivors of Birth Cohorts of 1835–39 to 1920–24) by Race and by Number of Children Ever Born, as Reported in Censuses of 1910, 1940, 1950, 1960, and 1970, U.S. Bureau of the Census, *Historical Statistics of the United States, Colonial Times to 1970,* Bicentennial Edition, 2 vols. (Washington, D.C.: U.S. Government Printing Office, 1975), I:53. For women born in 1916 and after, Table 270, Children Ever Born and Marital Status of Women by Age, Race, and Spanish Origin: 1980, U.S. Bureau of the Census, *1980 Census of Population: Detailed Population Characteristics: United States Summary* (Washington, D.C.: U.S. Government Printing Office, 1984), 1–103.

With the implementation of the **Nineteenth Amendment** (woman suffrage) in 1920, the unity of the suffrage movement disintegrated in disputes over the proper role for women voters. Both major political parties welcomed women as voters and modified the structure of their national committees to provide that each state be represented by both a national committeeman and a national committee-woman. Some suffrage activists joined the League of Women Voters, a nonpartisan group committed to social and political reform. The Congressional Union, led by Alice Paul (see page 643), had earlier converted itself into the National Woman's Party and, after 1923, focused its efforts largely on securing an **Equal Rights Amendment** to the Constitution. The

League of Women Voters disagreed, arguing that such an amendment would endanger laws that provided special rights and protections for women. In the end, woman suffrage seemed not to have dramatically changed either women or politics.

Nineteenth Amendment Constitutional amendment, ratified in 1919, that prohibited federal or state governments from restricting the right to vote on account of sex.

Equal Rights Amendment Proposed constitutional amendment, first advocated by the National Woman's Party in 1923, to give women in the United States equal rights under the law.

Development of Gay and Lesbian Subcultures

In the 1920s, gay and lesbian subcultures became more established and relatively open in some cities, including New York, Chicago, New Orleans, and Baltimore. *The Captive*, a play about lesbians, opened in New York in 1926, and some movies included unmistakable homosexual references. Novels with gay and lesbian characters circulated in the late 1920s and early 1930s. In Chicago, the Society for Human Rights was organized to advocate equal treatment. A relatively open gay and lesbian community emerged in Harlem, where some prominent figures of the Renaissance were gay or bisexual. In the early 1930s, the nation's largest gay event was the annual Hamilton Lodge drag ball in Harlem, which, at the height of its popularity, attracted as many as seven thousand revelers and spectators of all races.

At the same time, however, more and more psychiatrists and psychologists were labeling homosexuality a **perversion.** Shortly before World War I, as the work of **Sigmund Freud** became well known, the view that homosexuality was physiological in origin was replaced by a different explanation. Most psychiatrists and psychologists now labeled homosexuality a sexual disorder that required a cure, though no "cure" ever proved viable. Thus Freud's theories may have been a liberating influence with regard to heterosexual relations, but they proved harmful for same-sex relations.

The new medical definitions were slow to work their way into the larger society. The armed forces, for example, continued previous practices, making little effort to prevent homosexuals from enlisting and taking disciplinary action only against behavior that clearly violated the law.

The late 1920s and early 1930s brought increased suppression of gays and lesbians. New state laws gave police greater authority to prosecute open expressions of homosexuality. In 1927 New York City police raided *The Captive* and other plays with gay or lesbian themes, and the New York state legislature banned all such plays. In 1929 Adam Clayton Powell, a leading Harlem minister, launched a highly publicized campaign against gays. Motion-picture studios instituted a morality code that, among its wide-ranging provisions, prohibited any depiction of homosexuality. The end of Prohibition after 1933 brought increased regulation of businesses selling liquor, and local authorities used this regulatory power to close establishments that tolerated gay or lesbian customers.

Thus, by the 1930s, many gays and lesbians were becoming more secretive about their sexual identities.

The Politics of Prosperity

■ What was the basic attitude of the Harding and Coolidge administrations toward the economy? How does this mark a change from the administrations of Roosevelt and Wilson?

■ In what ways did the third-party candidacy of La Follette in 1924 resemble that of Roosevelt in 1912 and Weaver in 1892?

Sooner or later, nearly all the social and economic developments of the 1920s found their way into politics, from highway construction to prohibition, from immigration restriction to the teaching of evolution, from farm prices to lynching. After 1918, the Republicans returned to the majority role they had exercised from the mid-1890s to 1912, and they continued as the unquestioned majority party throughout the 1920s. Progressivism largely disappeared, although a few veterans of earlier struggles, led by Robert La Follette and George Norris, persisted in their efforts to limit corporate power. The Republican administrations of the 1920s shared a faith in the ability of business to establish prosperity and benefit the American people. Those in power considered government the partner of business, not its regulator.

Harding's Failed Presidency

Elected in 1920, Warren G. Harding looked presidential—handsome, gray-haired, dignified, warm, and outgoing—but had little intellectual depth. For some of his appointments, he chose the most respected leaders of his party, including Charles Evans Hughes for secretary of state, Andrew Mellon for secretary of the Treasury, and Herbert Hoover for secretary of commerce. Harding, however, was most at home playing poker with his friends, and he gave hundreds of government jobs to his cronies and political supporters. They turned his administration into one of the most corrupt in American history. As their misdeeds began to come to light, Harding put off taking action until

perversion Sexual practice considered abnormal or deviant.

Sigmund Freud Austrian who played a leading role in developing the field of psychoanalysis, known for his theory that the sex drive underlies much individual behavior.

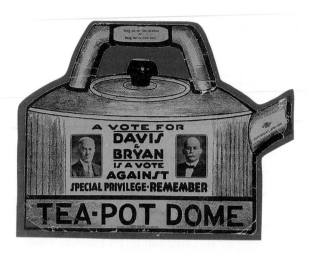

In 1924, the Democrats tried to capitalize on the Republicans' embarrassment over the Teapot Dome scandal. They received little response because the death of Harding brought Calvin Coolidge to the presidency, and Coolidge's personal honesty and morality were unquestioned. *Collection of David J. and Janice L. Frent.*

after a trip to Alaska. During his return, on August 2, 1923, he died when a blood vessel burst in his brain.

The full extent of the corruption became clear after Harding's death. Albert Fall, secretary of the interior, accepted huge bribes from oil companies for leases on federal oil reserves at Elk Hills, California, and Teapot Dome, Wyoming. Attorney General Harry Daugherty and others pocketed payoffs to approve the sale of government-held property for less than its value, and Daugherty may also have protected bootleggers. The head of the Veterans Bureau swindled the government out of more than $200 million. In all, three cabinet members resigned, four officials went to jail, and five men committed suicide. As if the financial dishonesty were not enough, in 1927 Nan Britton published a book claiming that she had been Harding's mistress, had borne his child, and had carried on trysts with him in the White House.

In the midst of these scandals, hard-pressed and debt-ridden farmers turned to the federal government for help. In 1921 farm organizations worked with a bipartisan group of senators and representatives to form a congressional **Farm Bloc,** which promoted legislation to assist farmers. The bloc enjoyed a substantial boost in the 1922 elections, when distraught farmers across the Midwest turned out conservatives and elected candidates who voiced sympathy for farmers' problems. Congress passed a few assistance

measures in the early 1920s, but none addressed the central problems of overproduction and low prices. By 1922, some farm organizations joined with unions, especially unions of railroad workers, to form the Conference for Progressive Political Action and agitate for a new Progressive Party.

The Three-Way Election of 1924

When Harding died, Vice President Calvin Coolidge became president. Fortunately for the Republican Party, the new president exemplified honesty, virtue, and sobriety. In 1924 Republicans quickly chose Coolidge as their candidate for president.

The Democratic convention, however, sank into a long and bitter deadlock. Since the Civil War, the party had divided between southerners (mostly Protestant and committed to white supremacy) and northerners (often city-dwellers and of recent immigrant descent, including many Catholics). In 1924 the Klan was approaching its peak membership and exercised significant influence among many Democratic delegates from the South and Midwest.

Northern Democrats tried to nominate **Al Smith** for president. Highly popular as governor of New York, Smith epitomized urban, immigrant America. Catholic and the son of immigrants, he was everything the Klan—and most of the southern convention delegates—hated. His chief opponent for the nomination, William G. McAdoo of California, boasted progressive credentials but had done legal work for an oil company executive tainted by the Elk Hills scandal. After nine hot days of stalemate and 103 ballots, the exhausted Democrats turned to a compromise candidate, John W. Davis. Davis had served in the Wilson administration and then became a leading corporate lawyer. All in all, the convention seemed to confirm the observation by the contemporary humorist Will Rogers: "I belong to no organized political party. I am a Democrat."

Americans committed to progressivism welcomed the independent candidacy of Senator Robert M. La

Farm Bloc   Bipartisan group of senators and representatives formed in 1921 to promote legislation to assist farmers.

Al Smith   New York governor who unsuccessfully sought the Democratic nomination for president in 1924 and was the unsuccessful Democratic candidate for president in 1928; his Catholicism and desire to repeal Prohibition were political liabilities.

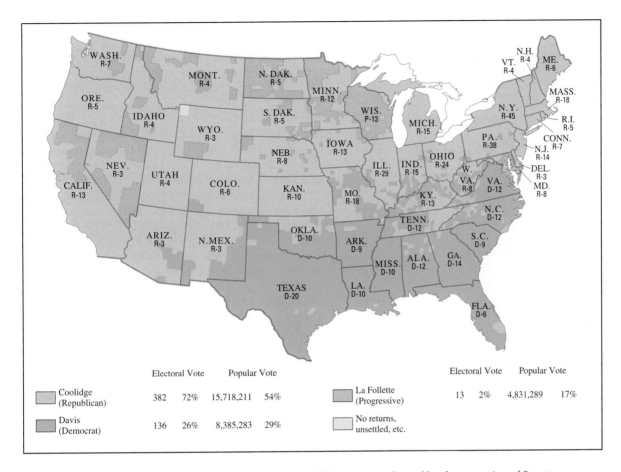

		Electoral Vote		Popular Vote	
☐	Coolidge (Republican)	382	72%	15,718,211	54%
☐	Davis (Democrat)	136	26%	8,385,283	29%

		Electoral Vote		Popular Vote	
☐	La Follette (Progressive)	13	2%	4,831,289	17%
☐	No returns, unsettled, etc.				

MAP 23.1 Election of 1924 The presidential election of 1924 was complicated by the campaign of Senator Robert La Follette of Wisconsin, who ran as a Progressive. As you can see, much of his support came from Republicans living in the north-central and northwestern regions where the agricultural economy was most hard-hit.

Follette as a Progressive. La Follette was nominated at a convention that expressed the concerns of farmers, unions, and an assortment of reformers dating back as far as the Populist Party of the 1890s. The La Follette Progressives attacked big business and promoted collective bargaining, reform of politics, public ownership of railroads and water power resources, and a public referendum on questions of war and peace. La Follette was the first presidential candidate to be endorsed by the American Federation of Labor, and the Socialist Party of America threw him its support as well.

Republican campaigners largely ignored Davis and focused on portraying La Follette as a dangerous radical. Coolidge claimed the key issue was "whether America will allow itself to be degraded into a communistic or socialistic state" or "remain American."

Coolidge won with nearly 16 million votes and 54 percent of the total, as voters seemed to champion the status quo. Davis held on to most traditional Democratic voters, especially in the South, receiving 8 million votes and 29 percent. La Follette carried only his home state of Wisconsin but garnered almost 5 million votes, 17 percent, and did well both in urban working-class neighborhoods and in parts of the rural Midwest and Northwest (see Map 23.1).

The Politics of Business

Committed to limited government and content to let problems work themselves out, Coolidge tried to reduce the significance of the presidency—and succeeded. Having once announced that "the business of America is business," he believed that the free market

This cartoon depicts Coolidge playing the praises of big business. Big business, dressed up like a flapper, responds by dancing the Charleston with wild abandon and singing a paraphrase of a popular song, "Yes Sir, He's My Baby." *Library of Congress.*

and free operation of business leadership would best sustain economic prosperity for all. As president, he set out to prevent government from interfering in the operation of business.

Firmly favoring an unfettered market economy, Coolidge had little sympathy for efforts to secure federal help for the faltering farm economy. Congress tried to address the related problems of low prices for farm products and persistent agricultural surpluses with the **McNary-Haugen bill,** which would have created federal price supports and authorized the government to buy farm surpluses and sell them abroad at prevailing world prices. The Farm Bloc finally pushed the bill through Congress in 1927, only to have Coolidge veto it. The same thing happened in 1928. By contrast, the **Railway Labor Act of 1926** drew on wartime experiences to establish collective bargaining for railroad employees. Passed by overwhelming margins in Congress, the new law met most of the railway unions' demands and effectively removed them from politics.

Andrew Mellon, an aluminum magnate and one of the wealthiest men in the nation, served as secretary of the Treasury throughout the Republican administrations of the 1920s. Acclaimed by Republicans and business leaders as the greatest secretary of the Treasury since Alexander Hamilton, Mellon argued that high taxes on the wealthy stifled the economy. He secured substantial tax breaks for the affluent, arguing that they would bring economic benefits to all as a result of the "productive investments" that the wealthy would make. Herbert Hoover, secretary of commerce during the Harding and Coolidge administrations, urged Coolidge to regulate the increasingly wild use of credit, which inflated stock values and produced rampant stock market speculation, but Coolidge refused.

Coolidge cut federal spending and staffed federal agencies with people who shared his distaste for too much government. Unlike Harding, Coolidge found honest and competent appointees. Like Harding, he named probusiness figures to regulatory commissions and put conservative, probusiness judges in the courts. The *Wall Street Journal* described the outcome: "Never before, here or anywhere else, has a government been so completely fused with business."

The 1928 Campaign and the Election of Hoover

In August 1927, President Coolidge, on vacation in South Dakota, told reporters, "I do not choose to run in 1928." Coolidge's announcement stunned the country and his party. Secretary of Commerce Herbert Hoover immediately declared his candidacy, and Republicans found him an ideal candidate, representing what most Americans believed was best about the United States: individual effort and honestly earned success.

McNary-Haugen bill   Farm relief bill that provided for government purchase of crop surpluses during years of large output; Coolidge vetoed it in 1927 and in 1928.

Railway Labor Act of 1926   Federal law that guaranteed collective bargaining for railroad employees, the first peacetime federal law to extend this guarantee to any group of workers.

Son of a Quaker blacksmith from Iowa, Hoover was orphaned at ten and raised by uncles. He grew up among thrifty farmers who believed that hard work was the only way to success. Graduating from Stanford University, he traveled the world as a mining engineer. By 1914 his fortune was more than $4 million. Having succeeded in business, Hoover turned to public service. When World War I broke out, he offered his organizational skills and energy to help provide relief to Belgium through the Committee for the Relief of Belgium. Hoover traveled across war-torn Europe seeking funds and supplies for Belgium. "This man is not to be stopped anywhere under any circumstance," the Germans noted on his passport. When the United States entered the war, President Wilson named Hoover to head the U.S. Food Administration (see page 691). By the end of the war, Hoover was an international hero. He served as secretary of commerce under Harding and Coolidge, and attracted wide support in the business community for his efforts to encourage economic growth through associationalism—voluntary cooperation among otherwise competing groups.

In launching his campaign before thousands of supporters gathered in the Stanford football stadium, Hoover sounded the theme of his candidacy: prosperity. "We in America today are nearer to the final triumph over poverty than ever before. . . . The poorhouse is vanishing among us," he boldly announced.

The Democrats nominated Al Smith, four-time governor of New York. Like Hoover, Smith was a self-made man. But unlike his opponent, who had gone to Stanford, Smith had received his education on the streets of the Lower East Side of New York City and as part of Tammany Hall, the Democratic machine that ran the city. As a reform-minded, progressive governor, Smith had streamlined state government, improved its efficiency, and supported legislation to set a minimum wage and maximum hours of work and to establish state ownership of hydroelectric plants.

In many places, Smith became the main issue in the campaign. Opponents attacked his Catholic religion, his big-city background, his opposition to Prohibition, his Tammany connections, and even his New York accent. Anti-Catholic sentiment burned hotly in many parts of the country, often fanned by the remnants of the Klan, whose fiery crosses marked the route of Smith's campaign train in some areas. Evangelist Billy Sunday called Smith supporters "damnable whiskey politicians, bootleggers, crooks, pimps and businessmen who deal with them." Thus, for many voters, the choice in 1928 seemed to be be-

tween a candidate who represented hard work and the pious values of small-town, old-stock, Protestant America and a candidate who represented Catholics, foreigners, machine politics, and the ugly problems of the cities.

Hoover won easily, with 58 percent of the popular vote. Prosperity and the nation's long-term Republican majority probably would have spelled victory for any competent Republican. Smith's religion and anti-Prohibition stance cost him support in the South, where Hoover carried some areas that had not voted Republican since the end of Reconstruction. Smith, however, helped Democrats make important gains in northern cities. In 1920 and 1924, the total vote in the twelve largest cities had been Republican by a large margin, but in 1928 Smith won a slim majority overall in those cities, partly by drawing to the polls Catholic women of immigrant descent who had not previously voted. As you can see in Figure 20.2 (page 622), voter participation spiked upward in 1928, temporarily interrupting a long-term downward trend.

The first president born west of the Mississippi River, Hoover came to the presidency with definite ideas about both domestic and foreign policy. More than Harding and Coolidge, he set out to be an active president at home and overseas. The role of government, he believed, was to promote cooperation without resorting to punitive measures like antitrust laws. He warned that once government, especially the federal government, stepped in to solve problems directly, the people gave up some of their freedom, and government became part of the problem. Hoover recognized that the federal government had a responsibility to help find solutions to social and economic problems, but the key word was *help:* Hoover looked to the government to help but not to solve problems by itself.

The Diplomacy of Prosperity

■ What is "independent internationalism"?

■ What role did the United States play in Latin America and Europe during the 1920s?

■ What were Hughes's goals for the Washington Naval Conference? How successful was he?

Two realities shaped American foreign policy in the 1920s: the rejection of Woodrow Wilson's internationalism following World War I and the continuing quest for economic expansion by American business. As president, Harding dismissed any American role in the League of Nations and refused to accept the

Treaty of Versailles (see page 702). Undamaged by the war, American firms outproduced and outtraded the rest of the world. U.S. trade amounted to 30 percent of the world's total, and American firms produced more than 70 percent of the world's oil and almost 50 percent of the world's coal and steel. American bankers loaned billions of dollars to other nations, expanding the global economy.

Because neither Harding nor Coolidge had any expertise or interest in foreign affairs, they left most foreign-policy decisions to their secretaries of state: Charles Evans Hughes and Frank Kellogg, respectively. Both were capable men interested in developing American business and influence abroad through "independent internationalism." Independent (or **unilateral**) internationalism had two central thrusts: avoidance of **multilateral** commitments—sometimes called **isolationism**—and expansion of economic opportunities overseas. The Commerce and State Departments promoted American business activities worldwide and encouraged private American investments in Japan and China. American officials also worked to make it possible for U.S. oil companies to drill in Iran, Iraq, the Persian Gulf region, and Saudi Arabia. Their efforts to expand Americans' economic position in Latin America and Europe were quite successful. As president, Hoover and his secretary of state, Henry L. Stimson, followed the approach that had characterized the earlier 1920s.

The United States and Latin America

When Harding took office in 1921, the United States had troops stationed in Panama, Haiti, the Dominican Republic, and Nicaragua (see Map 23.2). During the presidential campaign, Harding had criticized Wilson's "bayonet rule" in Haiti and the Dominican Republic and expressed his intention to end the occupation of those nations. To ensure continued American dominance in the Caribbean, however, U.S. officials wanted local governments that could keep order. Therefore, American administrators maintained some control over national finances and trained national guards as each nation's police force. American troops left the Dominican Republic in 1924, Nicaragua in 1932, and Haiti in 1934. In the Dominican Republic and in Haiti, however, the United States kept control of the customshouse—and tariff revenues—until the 1940s.

When American troops withdrew from the Do-minican Republic and Haiti, they left better roads, improved sanitation systems, governments favorable to the United States, and well-equipped national guards. But years of occupation had not advanced the educational systems, the national economies, or the standard of living for most residents. Nor did the United States do much to promote the cause of democracy, favoring stability over freedom even if it meant accepting dictators such as Rafael Trujillo, who seized power in the Dominican Republic in 1930 and ruled brutally until his death in 1961.

In Nicaragua, American forces left in 1925, only to be reintroduced in mid-1926 to protect the pro-American government when civil war broke out. Coolidge sent Henry L. Stimson to negotiate a peace agreement. The **Peace of Titiapa** (1927) ended most of the fighting, leaving only followers of **Augusto Sandino** continuing the war. Sandino, a nationalist who wanted to rid Nicaragua of American influence, rejected the Peace of Titiapa and continued guerrilla warfare.

When the United States withdrew from Nicaragua in 1933, it left an American-equipped and -trained national guard to maintain order. In 1934 the Nicaraguan president, Juan Bautista Sacasa, and **Anastasio Somoza,** his nephew and commander of the Guardia Nacional, arranged a peace conference with Sandino. Somoza, however, ordered Sandino and his aides seized and executed. Later Somoza turned against Sacasa and in 1936, using the U.S.-trained national guard as a political weapon, secured election as president. Somoza ruled either directly or

---

unilateral   An action taken by a country by itself, as opposed to actions taken jointly with other nations.

multilateral   Involving more than two nations.

isolationism   The notion that the United States should avoid political, diplomatic, and military entanglements with other nations.

Peace of Titiapa   Agreement negotiated by Henry L. Stimson in 1927 that sought to end factional fighting in Nicaragua.

Augusto Sandino   Nicaraguan guerrilla leader who resisted Nicaraguan and American troops in a rebellion from 1925 to 1933; he was murdered at the orders of Anastasio Somoza following a peace conference in 1934.

Anastasio Somoza   General who established a military dictatorship in Nicaragua in 1933, deposed his uncle to become president in 1934, and ruled the country for two decades, amassing a personal fortune and suppressing all opposition.

During the 1920s, American businesses greatly expanded their operations overseas. In Latin America, corporations such as United Fruit Company oversaw a wide range of enterprises, from running shipping lines to growing bananas. Here, recently picked bananas begin their journey from the field to American homes. *Benson Latin American Collection, University of Texas at Austin.*

through puppet presidents until his assassination in 1956. His family remained in power until 1979, when rebels calling themselves Sandinistas—after their hero Sandino—took power in Nicaragua.

Elsewhere in Latin America, the 1920s saw American interventions of another sort—not military, but commercial. Throughout Central America, American firms such as the United Fruit Company purchased thousands of acres of land for plantations on which to grow tropical fruit, especially bananas and coffee. In Venezuela and Colombia, American oil companies, with State Department help, negotiated profitable contracts for drilling rights, outmaneuvering European oil companies. U.S. investments in Latin America rose from nearly $2 billion in 1919 to over $3.5 billion in 1929.

Oil also played a key role in American relations with Mexico. Following the Mexican Revolution (see page 682), the Mexican constitution of 1917 limited foreign ownership, and Mexico moved to **nationalize** all of its subsurface resources, including oil. The United States, supported by American businessmen, strongly objected, especially to nationalization of oil. By 1925, American oilmen and some members of the Coolidge administration were calling for military action to protect American oil interests in northern Mexico from "bolshevism." Coolidge sent Dwight W. Morrow—a college friend—as ambassador to Mexico with instructions "to keep us out of war with Mex-

ico." Morrow understood Mexican nationalism and pride, knew some Spanish, and appreciated Mexico and its people. He cultivated a personal relationship with Mexican president Plutarco Calles, which reduced tensions and delayed Mexico's nationalization of oil properties until 1938.

In 1928, at a Pan-American Conference in Havana, American intervention in Latin America came under sharp challenge in a resolution introduced by the Argentine delegate. Secretary of State Hughes was prepared, and he handled the issue through a combination of accommodation and rebuttal. He supported some mild proposals but staunchly defended "taking action—I would call it interposition of a temporary character—for the purpose of protecting the lives and property of its nationals." And the anti-intervention resolution was voted down. Soon after, following the election of 1928, president-elect Hoover undertook a goodwill tour of eleven Latin American countries, seeking to build better relations.

America and the European Economy

While World War I was shattering much of Europe physically and economically, the American economy soared to unprecedented heights, and the United States became the world's leading creditor nation. After the war, Republican leaders joined with business figures to expand exports and restrict imports. In 1922 the **Fordney-McCumber Tariff** set the highest rates ever for most imported industrial goods. The tariff had the effect of not only limiting European imports but also making it difficult for Europeans to acquire the dollars needed to repay their war debts to the United States.

While Harding and Coolidge sought debt repayment, Secretary of State Hughes and Secretary of Commerce Hoover worked to expand American economic interests in Europe, especially Germany. They believed that if Germany recovered economically and paid its $33 billion war reparations, other European

---

nationalize   To convert an industry or enterprise from private to government ownership and control.

Fordney-McCumber Tariff   Tariff passed by Congress in 1922 to protect domestic production from foreign competitors; it raised tariff rates to record levels and provoked foreign tariff reprisals.

CANADA

UNITED STATES

ATLANTIC

OCEAN

Havana, Cuba
U.S. upholds right of intervention at
Pan American Conference, 1928

Cuba
Platt Amendment, 1902–1934
U.S. troops, 1906–1909, 1912, 1917–1922
U.S. companies invest in sugar

Haiti
U.S. troops, 1915–1934
U.S. financial supervision, 1916–1941

MEXICO

THE BAHAMAS
(BR.)

Gulf
of
Mexico

Dominican Republic
U.S. troops, 1916–1924
U.S. financial supervision, 1905–1941
Trujillo era, 1930–1961

Mexico
U.S. companies' investments, including railroads
and oil
Constitution of 1917 challenges U.S. interests
Nationalization of foreign oil companies, 1938

CUBA
JAMAICA
(BR.)
BRITISH HONDURAS
HONDURAS

DOMINICAN
REP.
HAITI

VIRGIN IS. (US,UK)
PUERTO
RICO (US)

Virgin Islands
U.S. possession since 1916

Guatemala
United Fruit Company, coffee
investments

GUATEMALA

Caribbean Sea

Puerto Rico
U.S. possession since 1898
Jones Act grants U.S. citizenship, 1917

El Salvador
U.S. companies invest in coffee

EL SALVADOR

NICARAGUA
COSTA
RICA

VENEZUELA

BRITISH GUIANA
DUTCH GUIANA
FRENCH GUIANA

Honduras
United Fruit Company investments

PANAMA

COLOMBIA

Nicaragua
U.S. financial supervision, 1911–1925
U.S. troops, 1912–1925, 1927–1933
War against Sandino, 1925–1933
Somoza era, 1936–1979

ECUADOR

U.S. companies
invest in oil

Panama
U.S. control of Canal Zone
since 1904

PERU

BRAZIL

PACIFIC

OCEAN

BOLIVIA

U.S. companies invest
in copper mining

CHILE

PARAGUAY

URUGUAY

ARGENTINA

0   500   1000 Km.

0   500   1000 Mi.

MAP 23.2 The United States and Latin America As this map indicates, during the 1920s, the United States continued to play an active role throughout Central America and the Caribbean and, to a lesser extent, in South America. In some cases, as in Nicaragua in the 1920s, this included military intervention. But during the 1920s and after, political and economic pressures largely replaced military force as the primary means for protecting U.S. interests.

nations would also recover and repay their debts. With government encouragement, over $4 billion in American investments flowed into Europe, doubling American investments there. General Motors purchased Opel, a German automobile firm. Ford built the largest automobile factory outside the United States, in England, and constructed a tractor factory in the Soviet Union.

Even with the infusion of American capital, Germany could not keep up its reparation payments, defaulting in 1923 to France and Belgium. France responded by sending troops to occupy Germany's **Ruhr Valley,** a key economic region, igniting an international crisis. Hughes sent Charles G. Dawes, a Chicago banker and prominent Republican, to resolve the situation. Under the **Dawes Plan,** American bankers loaned $2.5 billion to Germany for economic development, and the Germans promised to pay $2 billion in reparations to the European Allies, who, in turn, were to pay $2.5 billion in war debts to the United States. This circular flow of capital was the butt of jokes at the time, but the remedy worked fairly well until 1929, when the Depression ended nearly all loans and payments.

Encouraging International Cooperation

Although committed to independent internationalism, the Republican policymakers of the 1920s also understood that some international cooperation was necessary to achieve policy goals and solve international problems. On such issues, they were willing to cooperate with other nations and enter into international agreements, but only with the understanding that the United States was not entering any alliance or otherwise agreeing to commit resources or troops in defense of another nation.

Disarmament was such an issue. The destruction caused by World War I had spurred pacifism and calls for disarmament. Disarmament, advocates urged, was necessary—it would reduce the number of weapons and military spending, and might allow lower taxes. In the United States, support for arms cuts was widespread and vocal, as proponents pressed Harding to trim military budgets. In early 1921, Senator William E. Borah of Idaho suggested an international conference to reduce the size of the world's navies. Fearing that naval expenditures would prevent desirable tax cuts, Treasury Secretary Mellon and many members of Congress joined the disarmament chorus. In November 1921, Harding invited the major naval powers to Washington to discuss reducing "the crushing burdens of military and naval establishments."

There were other reasons for American interest in disarmament, notably concerns about Japan. Tied for first in naval strength, the United States and Britain had no desire to expand their navies. Japan, the third-place naval power, seemed inclined to continue its naval buildup. Americans worried about growing Japanese pressures on China that could endanger Chinese territory and the Open Door policy (see page 632). To block the Japanese, Harding and Hughes were willing to host international discussions aimed at limiting the size of navies and ensuring the status quo in China.

When the naval powers assembled for the **Washington Naval Conference,** Hughes shocked delegates with a radical proposal to scrap nearly 2 million tons of warships, primarily battleships. He also called for a ten-year ban on naval construction and for limits to the size of navies that would keep the Japanese navy well behind the British and American fleets. Hughes suggested a ratio of 5 to 5 to 3 for the United States, Britain, and Japan. Italy and France were allocated smaller ratios—1.7 each. Hughes's plan gained immediate support among the American public and most of the nations attending—but not Japan. The Japanese called it a national insult and demanded equality. Discussions dragged on for two months, but the Japanese finally agreed. U.S. intelligence had broken the Japanese diplomatic code, so Hughes knew that the Japanese delegates had orders to concede if he held firm.

By the end of the conference, in February 1922, the United States, Britain, Japan, France, and Italy agreed to build no more **capital ships** for ten years and to abide by the 5:5:3:1.7:1.7 ratio for future shipbuilding. A British observer commented that Hughes had sunk

---

Ruhr Valley   Region surrounding the Ruhr River in northwestern Germany, which contained many major industrial cities and valuable coal mines.

Dawes Plan   Arrangement for collecting World War I reparations from Germany; it scheduled annual payments and stabilized German currency.

Washington Naval Conference   International conference that in 1921–1922 produced a series of agreements to limit naval armaments and prevent conflict in the Far East and the Pacific.

capital ships   Generally, a navy's largest, most heavily armed ships; at the Washington Naval Conference, ships weighing over 10,000 tons and using guns with at least an 8-inch bore were classified as capital ships.

Secretary of State Frank Kellogg signs the Kellogg-Briand Pact on August 27, 1928. Fourteen other nations also signed renouncing war and agreeing to settle all of their future disputes peacefully, and other nations joined later. Within a few years, wars involved many of the signatories to this treaty to outlaw war. © *Bettmann/Corbis.*

more British ships in one speech "than all the admirals of the world have sunk in . . . centuries." In other treaties, the powers agreed to prohibit the use of poison gas and not to attack one another's Asian possessions. The **Nine-Power Pact** affirmed the sovereignty and territorial boundaries of China and guaranteed equal commercial access to China—the Open Door remained open.

Hughes considered the meetings successful, although critics complained that the agreements included no provisions for enforcement and no mention of smaller naval ships, including submarines. As it turned out, the Washington Naval Conference was the only successful disarmament conference of the 1920s. Other attempts to reduce naval and land forces had mixed outcomes. After a failure in 1927 to limit the number of smaller naval vessels, Britain, the United States, and Japan established a series of ratios at the 1930 London Conference similar to those of the Washington Naval Conference—but for cruisers and destroyers. Thereafter, competition reigned: by the mid-1930s, Japan's demands for naval equality ended British and American cooperation and spurred renewed naval construction by all three sea powers.

Many Americans and Europeans applauded the achievements of the Washington Naval Conference but wanted to go further, seeking a repudiation of war. In 1923 Senator Borah introduced a resolution in the Senate to outlaw war, and in 1924 La Follette campaigned for a national referendum as a requirement for declaring war. In 1927 the French foreign minister, Aristide Briand, suggested a pact formally outlawing war between the two nations, privately hoping that such an agreement would commit the United States to aid France, if attacked. Secretary of State Kellogg deflected the proposal by suggesting a multinational statement opposing war. Kellogg thereby removed any hint of an American commitment to any specific nation. On August 27, 1928, the United States and fourteen other nations, including Britain, France, Germany, Italy, and Japan, signed the Pact of Paris, or **Kellogg-Briand Pact.** By doing so, they renounced war "as an instrument of national policy" and agreed to settle disputes peacefully. Eventually sixty-four nations signed, but the pact included no enforcement provisions, and nearly every **signatory** reserved its right to defend itself and its possessions.

Thus, late in 1928, American independent interna-

Nine-Power Pact   Agreement signed in 1922 by Britain, France, Italy, Japan, the United States, China, the Netherlands, Portugal, and Belgium to recognize China and affirm the Open Door policy.

Kellogg-Briand Pact   Treaty signed in 1928 by fifteen nations, including Britain, France, Germany, the United States, and Japan, renouncing war as a means of solving international disputes.

signatory   One who has signed a treaty or other document.

tionalism seemed a success. Investments and loans by American businesses were fueling an expansive world economy and contributing to American prosperity. Avoiding entangling alliances, the United States had protected its Asian and Pacific interests against Japan, while protecting China and promoting disarmament and world peace. In Latin America, the United States had moderated its interventionist image by withdrawing American troops from the Caribbean, avoiding intervention in Mexico, and trying to broker a peace in Nicaragua. Foreign policies based on economic expansion and noncoercive diplomacy appeared to be establishing a promising era of cooperation and peace in world affairs.

Individual Voices

Examining a Primary Source

Middletown Parents Bemoan the Movies

Between 1923 and 1926, Robert S. Lynd and Helen Merrell Lynd conducted an elaborate study under the auspices of the Rockefeller Foundation. They moved to Muncie, Indiana, and interviewed scores of residents, asking them to talk about their lives and to compare their lives with life in the 1890s. They published the results as *Middletown: A Study in American Culture* (1929). According to the Lynds, Middletowners were especially anxious about the movies and sexuality.

■ How reliable do you think Middletowners' memories of the 1890s were likely to be? How would you test the validity of those memories?

The more sophisticated social life of today has brought with it another "problem" much discussed by Middletown parents, the apparently increasing relaxation of some of the traditional prohibitions upon the approaches of boys and girls to each other's persons. Here again new inventions of the last thirty-five years have played a part; in 1890 a "well-brought-up" boy and girl were commonly forbidden to sit together in the dark; but motion pictures and the automobile have lifted this taboo, and, once lifted, it is easy for the practice to become widely extended. . . . ■

[The following appeared in a footnote to the preceding paragraph:] *The impact of [magazines and movies] is apparent in the habits of such a girl as the following, a healthy seventeen-year-old high school girl, popular in school and the daughter of a high type of worker, who happened to be personally known to members of the research staff. She attends the movies twice a week (she had been home only one evening in the last seven) and reads regularly every week or month Snappy Stories, Short Stories, Cosmopolitan, True Story, Liberty, People's Popular Monthly, Woman's Weekly, Gentlewoman, and Collier's. She and her parents are at loggerheads most often, she says, about the way she dresses, and after that, about her use of the family Ford and about her boy and girl friends. Along with these evidences of divergence from the ways of her parents, she still maintains the family religious tradition, being an indefatigable church worker and Sunday School teacher.* ■

■ Is this evidence persuasive that magazines and movies have endangered family relationships? How would you compare this description to the behavior and attitudes of a 17-year-old today?

[At the movie theaters] Harold Lloyd comedies draw the largest crowds. . . . Next largest are the crowds which come to see the sensational society films. The kind of vicarious living brought to Middletown by these films may be inferred

■ *The Lynds seem to be infer-ring the content of the movies from the newspaper advertis-ing for them. How would you construct a research project to determine whether the movies were as titillating as their advertising suggested?*

■ *The Lynds infer changes in behavior from their interviews. What sources might you use to research whether there were actual changes in behav-ior among young people in the 1920s?*

from such titles as: "Alimony—brilliant men, beautiful jazz babies, champagne baths, midnight revels, petting parties in the purple dawn, all ending in one ter-rific smashing climax that makes you gasp." . . . It is the film with burning "heart interest," that packs Middletown's motion picture houses week after week. Young Middletown enters eagerly into the vivid experience of Flaming Youth: "neckers, petters, white kisses, red kisses, pleasure-mad daughters, sensation-craving moth-ers . . . the truth bold, naked, sensational" ■ *—so ran the press advertisement— under the spell of the powerful conditioning medium of pictures presented with music and all possible heightening of the emotional content, and the added factor of sharing this experience with a "date" in a darkened room. . . .*

Actual changes of habits resulting from the week-after-week witnessing of these films can only be inferred. . . . Some high school teachers are convinced that the movies are a powerful factor in bringing about the "early sophistication" of the young and the relaxing of social taboos. . . . The judge of the juvenile court lists the movies as one of the "big four" causes of juvenile delinquency, believing that the disregard of group mores by the young is definitely related to the wit-nessing week after week of fictitious behavior sequences that habitually link the taking of long chances and the happy ending. ■

Summary

The 1920s were a decade of prosperity. Unemploy-ment was low, productivity grew steadily, and many Americans fared well. Sophisticated advertising cam-paigns created bright expectations, and installment buying freed consumers from having to pay cash. Many consumers bought more and bought on credit— stimulating manufacturing and expanding personal debt. Expectations of continuing prosperity also en-couraged speculation. The stock market boomed, but agriculture did not share in this prosperity.

During the Roaring Twenties, Americans experi-enced significant social change. The automobile, radio, and movies, abetted by immigration restriction, pro-duced a more homogeneous culture. Many American intellectuals, however, rejected the consumer-oriented culture. During the 1920s, African Americans pro-duced an outpouring of significant art, literature, and music. Some young people rejected traditional con-straints, and one result was the emergence of a youth culture.

Not all Americans embraced change. Some tried instead to maintain or restore earlier cultural values. The outcomes were mixed. Prohibition was largely unsuccessful. Fundamentalism grew and prompted a campaign against the teaching of evolution. Nativism helped produce significant new restrictions on im-migration. The Ku Klux Klan, committed to nativism, traditional values, and white supremacy, experienced nationwide growth until 1925, but membership de-clined sharply thereafter.

Discrimination and occasional violence continued to affect the lives of people of color. Federal Indian policy had long stressed assimilation and allotment, but some groups successfully promoted different policies based on respect for Indian cultural values. Immigration from Mexico greatly increased the Latino population in California and the Southwest, and some Mexicans working in agriculture tried, in vain, to or-ganize unions. Nearly all unions faced strong opposi-tion from employers. Some older women's roles broke down as women gained the right to vote and exer-cised more control over the choice to have children.

An identifiable gay and lesbian subculture emerged, especially in cities.

The politics of the era were marked by greater conservatism than before World War I. Warren G. Harding was a poor judge of character, and some of his appointees accepted bribes and disgraced their chief. Harding and his successor, Calvin Coolidge, expected government to act as a partner with business, and their economic policies minimized regulation and encouraged speculation. With some exceptions, progressive reform disappeared from politics, and efforts to secure federal assistance for farmers fizzled. The federal government was strongly conservative, staunchly probusiness, and absolutely unwilling to intervene in the economy. Herbert Hoover defeated Al Smith in the 1928 presidential election, in which the values of an older rural America seemed to be pitted against those of the new, urban, immigrant society.

During the 1920s, the United States followed a policy of independent internationalism that stressed voluntary cooperation among nations, while at the same time enhancing opportunities for American business around the world. Relations with Latin America improved somewhat, and the Washington Naval Conference held out the hope for preventing a naval arms race.

THE GREAT DEPRESSION AND UNEMPLOYMENT As Herbert Hoover confronted Franklin D. Roosevelt and the Great Depression in the race for the presidency in 1932, the nation was experiencing historically high unemployment. This map shows the percentage of the work force unemployed by state, and how much unemployment jumped in some cities during a ten-month period.

CANADA

WASHINGTON
Seattle 23% / 9%

OREGON

MONTANA

IDAHO

NORTH DAKOTA

SOUTH DAKOTA

MINN. 21% / 9%
Minneapolis

WISCONSIN

MICH. 35% / 15%

MAINE 27%

VT.

N.H.

Buffalo 11%

NEW YORK 33%

MASS.

Boston 11%

RHODE ISLA

CONNECTI

NEW JERSEY

WYOMING

NEVADA

UTAH

COLORADO 19% / 9%
Denver

NEBRASKA

IOWA

Chicago 13%

ILLINOIS 25% / 10%

IND.

St. Louis

OHIO

Cleveland 31% / 15%

PENNSYLVANIA 12%
Pittsburgh

DELAWARE

MARYLAND

CALIFORNIA
Los Angeles 19% / 9%

ARIZONA

NEW MEXICO

KANSAS

MISSOURI

KENTUCKY

W. VA.

VIRGINIA

NORTH CAROLINA

OKLAHOMA

ARKANSAS

TENNESSEE 25%

SOUTH CAROLINA

TEXAS
Houston 23% / 8%

LOUISIANA
New Orleans 24% / 11%

MISS.

Birmingham 7%

ALABAMA

GEORGIA

FLA.

PACIFIC OCEAN

ATLANTIC OCEAN

MEXICO

Gulf of Mexico

HAWAI'I TERRITORY
0   100 Km.
0   100 Mi.
PACIFIC OCEAN

U.S.S.R.

ALASKA TERRITORY

CANADA

PACIFIC OCEAN

0   250   500 Km.
0   250   500 Mi.

State unemployment in 1930

- 25–30%
- 20–25%
- 15–20%
- Under 15%
- Percentage of population receiving more than 25% unemployment relief in 1934

Urban unemployment
January 1931 — 25%
April 1930 — 8%
— 20%
— 10%
— 0

0   200   400 Km.
0   200   400 Mi.

1928 Hoover elected
1929 Stock market crash
1932 Roosevelt elected
1933 First Hundred Days
1935 Second Hundred Days
1936 "Black Cabinet"
1937 Court-packing plan / Sit-down strikes
1938 Fair Labor Standards Act

1928 1929 1930 1931 1932 1933 1934 1935 1936 1937 1938

1931 Depression spreads to Europe

1934–1935 Mao Zedong leads "Long March"

1938 Mexico nationalizes oil industry

1930 Mahatma Gandhi's "Walk to the Sea"

1937 Sino-Japanese War begins

The Great Depression and the New Deal, 1929–1939

The Great Depression and Unemployment
It is correct to think of urban, industrial America being hit hard by the onslaught of the Great Depression, but how does the map on the facing page indicate that the loss of jobs was felt first in rural America?

Individual Choices

FRANCES PERKINS

Beginning in 1911, Frances Perkins sought to improve working conditions for the nation's men, women, and children. Perkins was the first woman cabinet member, and as secretary of labor, she tirelessly worked to create the Social Security system, establish a minimum wage for workers, and limit the number of hours people could be required to work. *New York Historical Society.*

Frances Perkins

On February 1, 1933, responding to a month-long flurry of rumors in the press and among "those in the know" that she was to be chosen secretary of labor, Frances Perkins wrote President-elect Franklin D. Roosevelt saying that she "honestly" hoped that the rumors were false. Informed of the letter and fearful that Perkins might reject a cabinet position, Mary Dewson, director of the Women's Division of the Democratic National Committee, visited Perkins. Dewson had recommended Perkins to Roosevelt for the labor post and went to convince her that as a high-ranking member of the administration she could make a difference in establishing a better life for the American worker. She reminded Perkins of the many years she had spent fighting to establish unemployment compensation and a minimum wage and to abolish child labor. "You want these things done," Dewson argued. "You have ideas. Nobody else will do it." She told Perkins, "You owe it to the women. Too many people count on what you do."

On February 22, Roosevelt asked Frances Perkins to be secretary of labor. A hesitant Perkins replied, only if she could push for the abolition of child labor, the establishment of unemployment insurance, old-age pensions, a minimum wage, and a limit on the maximum hours of work. Roosevelt agreed but told her that she would "have to invent the way to do these things" and that she should not "expect too much help from" him. She accepted the nomination. Confirmed by the Senate, Frances Perkins became "Madam Secretary," the first woman to serve in a president's cabinet.

She had arrived at the position through hard work and a commitment to improving workers' lives. The daughter of a conservative middle-class family, she had been introduced to her life's mission while taking an economics class at Mount Holyoke College in Massachusetts. She quickly immersed herself in the spirit of the Progressive Era, participating in the settlement house movement and investigating working conditions as part of the New York Factory Commission following the tragic fire at the Triangle Shirtwaist Company in 1911. Impressed by her work on the commission and with the Consumers' League, New York governor Al Smith appointed her to the state's Industrial Commission, which sought to improve the lives of workers. When Franklin D. Roosevelt replaced Smith as governor in 1929, he named her industrial commissioner, a state cabinet–level position—making her the first woman to hold such a position.

As secretary of labor, she threw herself into the first hundred days, seeking means to improve the life of the average American. She played key roles in supporting programs to provide jobs and relief, including the creation of the Civilian Conservation Corps and the Federal Emergency Relief Administration. She worked tirelessly for more public works and was instrumental in merging the Public Works Administration with the National Industrial Recovery Act. But these programs were temporary, and by 1934 she was forging an agenda to provide permanent benefits. As the chair of the newly created Committee on Economic Security, she

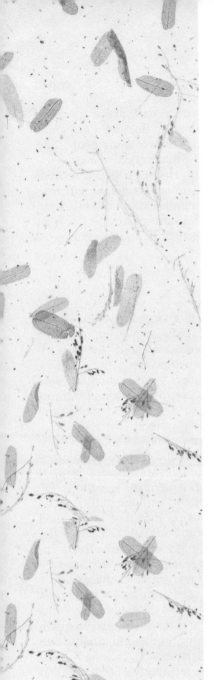

began to draft a social security bill that would provide workers with a retirement plan, increase unemployment compensation, and include support for children. An encouraging Roosevelt told her: "You care about this thing. You believe in it. Therefore I know you will put your back to it more than anyone else, and you'll drive it through."

The Social Security Act of 1935 was the outcome of many choices, most of which involved Perkins, **Harry Hopkins,** and Roosevelt. It was decided, for fiscal and political reasons, to have workers pay into the system as opposed to having the government pay for benefits out of taxes. Perkins had wanted to include medical coverage, but that option was excluded from the social security package, doused in large part by a hostile medical profession. To convince Congress to pass the bill, she made hundreds of public speeches and testified before countless congressional committees. With the bill's enactment on August 14, 1935, the relationship between the federal government and the people fundamentally and permanently changed.

Frances Perkins took pride in the passage of the Social Security Act, but she was overjoyed when the Fair Labor Standards Act became law in 1938. "A self-supporting and self-respecting democracy," she testified, "can plead no justification for the existence of child labor, no economic reason for chiseling workers' wages or stretching workers' hours." The bill was attacked as allowing too much government intrusion. Conservatives called it a form of socialism, while a few union leaders argued that collective bargaining—not the government—should gain wage and hour benefits for workers. Nevertheless, in the closing months of the New Deal, the bill became law on June 25, 1938. More than 12 million workers felt its effect. It immediately raised the pay of 300,000 people and shortened the workday for a million more. Equally important to Perkins, it barred industrial child labor under 16. Together, the Social Security Act and the Fair Labor Standards Act recast the economic and social values of the nation and established a new caretaker role for the government.

Frances Perkins continued to serve Roosevelt and his successor, Harry S. Truman, as an advocate of government support of workers and their families. Retiring in 1953, she wrote, lectured, and joined the faculty at Cornell University. She died in 1965, and her tombstone reflects the fateful choice she made in 1933:

FRANCES PERKINS WILSON
1880–1965
SECRETARY OF LABOR OF U.S.A.
1933–1945

INTRODUCTION

The Great Depression stretched across the thirties and affected all Americans, rich, poor, and in between. No segment of American society was untouched: lives were changed, traditions were challenged, and the function of the federal government was forever altered. When Herbert Clark Hoover became president, most Americans assumed that the United States would enjoy continued economic growth. Some even projected that domestic poverty would nearly disap-

pear. Those optimistic voices were wrong. Before the end of the 1930s, the American and world economy had collapsed and the Great Depression had begun.

Hoover faced the new challenges of the Depression with ideas he had expected would produce continued

Harry Hopkins   Close adviser to Roosevelt during his four administrations. He headed several New Deal agencies, including the Works Progress Administration.

growth. He found that they had little effect. He shifted policy but failed to change the course of the Depression. By 1932, the Depression had thwarted Hoover's hopes and ruined his political career as the American people chose a new path in the election of Franklin D. Roosevelt and a Democratic Congress.

Roosevelt, who would dominate American history for the next thirteen years, had few qualms about using the power of the government to combat the Depression and reform society. With a program called the "New Deal," the new administration unleashed a barrage of legislation along three paths: economic recovery, relief, and reform. By 1938, however, the New Deal was sputtering to an end. It had not rescued the economy, but it had totally transformed the role and function of government.

Against the backdrop of economic disaster, presidential actions, and partisan politics, Americans faced economic insecurity for the first time as the number of the unemployed and underemployed dramatically increased. Some feared that social values might be fundamentally changed, but their fears proved to be unfounded. The American people and society proved resilient; making do with less—getting by—many made new economic and social choices, and an increasing number looked for government intervention to ease their hardships and restore the economy. Most supported Roosevelt and the New Deal, although critics warned about the expanding power of government and its moving down the path toward socialism. By the end of the 1930s, most Americans had accepted a new activist role for government. Workers, farmers, women, and minorities had found new avenues of expression; and thousands of African Americans had joined the Democratic Party. Roosevelt and the New Deal had changed the definition of "liberalism" and had expanded the responsibilities and power of the federal government. Roosevelt would be both revered and reviled, but no one could deny his impact.

Campaigning for the presidency, Herbert Hoover had promised a "New Day" for America, but his sweeping victory was more a vote for the status quo. The United States had seen almost a decade of economic growth and rising standards of living, and people had voted for Hoover expecting that trend to continue under Republican leadership. Hoover believed it could be accomplished by promoting **associationalism**—that is, by encouraging voluntary cooperation among competing groups within American society. It was an approach soon tested by economic and social trauma.

The Great Crash and the Depression

Hoover assumed office as ever-rising stock prices, shiny new cars, and rapidly expanding suburbs seemed to verify his observation about "the final triumph over poverty." But behind the rush for radios, homes, and vacuum cleaners were economic weaknesses, overproduction, poor distribution of income, excessive credit buying, and weak and weakening sectors of the economy. Eight months later, on October 24, 1929, those hidden weaknesses became visible as the stock market crashed and the American economy stumbled and then fell. It was business as usual that Thursday morning as Americans went to work, most unconcerned about the rise and fall of stock prices on Wall Street. But on that day, later called Black Thursday, the bottom suddenly fell out of the stock market and nearly everyone's lives turned upside down. The value of stocks plummeted, and by noon the ticker tape that relayed stock prices across the nation was running nearly two and a half hours behind. Brokerage offices across the country were in a frenzy as brokers rushed to place sell orders. No place was untouched by the panic. In the mid-Atlantic, on board the passenger liner *Berengaria,* Helena Rubenstein watched stock prices fall and finally sold 50,000

Hoover and Economic Crisis

■ What were Americans' expectations when they elected Herbert Hoover president in 1928?

■ What was the impact of the stock market crash on the American economy, and what major economic weaknesses contributed to the crash and the Great Depression?

■ What choices did Hoover make in dealing with the problems created by the Depression, and why were Hoover's efforts to fight the Depression unsuccessful?

associationalism Hoover's belief that government could aid business organizations, farmers, professional groups, and others by coordinating their efforts to solve the nation's problems. The government would supply information and encourage discussions, but any solutions would originate from and be implemented by those groups involved. Any government role would be at the state and local levels.

Chronology

Depression and New Deal

1928	Herbert Hoover elected president
1929	Stock market crash
1929–1933	Depression deepens 9,000 U.S. banks fail 90,000 American businesses fail Unemployment rises from 9 to 25 percent
1930	Hawley-Smoot Tariff
1931	Mexican repatriation begins Scottsboro Nine convicted
1932	Glass-Steagall Act Federal Home Loan Bank Act Reconstruction Finance Corporation Emergency Relief Division of Reconstruction Finance Corporation created Milo Reno forms Farmers' Holiday Association Bonus Army marches to Washington Franklin D. Roosevelt elected president Erskine Caldwell's *Tobacco Road*
1933	Drought begins that turns Midwest into Dust Bowl Franklin D. Roosevelt inaugurated New Deal begins National Bank Holiday First fireside chat First Hundred Days (March 9–June 16) Civilian Conservation Corps created Agricultural Adjustment Administration created Tennessee Valley Authority created Home Owners' Loan Corporation (HOLC) created National Industrial Recovery Act passed (NRA and PWA) Twenty-first Amendment (repealing Prohibition) ratified Bank Act of 1933
1934	Huey Long's Share the Wealth plan Father Charles Coughlin forms National Union for

	Social Justice Indian Reorganization Act Securities and Exchange Commission (SEC) created American Liberty League established Dr. Francis Townsend's movement begins Federal Housing Administration
1935	Second Hundred Days Works Progress Administration created NRA ruled unconstitutional in Schechter case Rural Electrification Administration (REA) formed National Youth Administration created National Labor Relations Board created (Wagner Act) Social Security Act passed Long assassinated Committee of Industrial Organizations (CIO) established
1936	AAA ruled unconstitutional in Butler case Roosevelt reelected "Black Cabinet" organized Sit-down strikes begin
1937	Court-packing plan "Roosevelt's recession" U.S. unemployment climbs to 19 percent
1938	Works Progress Administration rolls double Fair Labor Standards Act AAA reestablished Republican victories in congressional elections Congress of Industrial Organizations formed
1939	Marian Anderson's concert at Lincoln Memorial John Steinbeck's *The Grapes of Wrath*
1940	Richard Wright's *Native Son*

shares of Westinghouse Company. She had lost more than a million dollars in a few hours.

The market rebounded, holding its own on Friday, but it slipped again on Monday. Then, on October 29—Black Tuesday—prices plunged and would continue to fall throughout the year. By mid-November, the *New York Times* industrials (selected industrial stocks chosen as indicators of trends in the economy) had declined from 469 to 221. Hundreds of brokers and speculators were ruined. Stories circulated of New York hotel clerks asking guests whether they wanted rooms for sleeping or jumping.

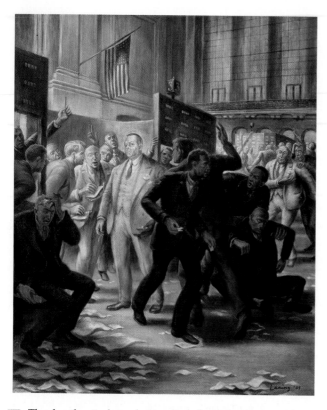

The day the stock market crashed, the entire nation suddenly became aware of Wall Street. The collapse of the stock market historically signals the beginning of the greatest depression in American history. Despite efforts of Hoover and Roosevelt, it was only the economic activity generated by World War II that revived the economy. *"Black Friday: Richard Whitney and the Stock Exchange," 1939 by Edward Laning. Collection of John P. Axelrod.*

The crash is a convenient starting point for the **Great Depression,** but it was not its cause. The Depression was a product of overproduction, poor distribution of income, too much credit buying, and uneven economic growth. The prosperity of the 1920s had in part rested on robust, expanding industries—chemical, automobile, and electronics, among others—that pushed the rest of the economy forward. But by 1927, even these industries were seeing a slowing of growth. Construction starts fell from 11 billion to 9 billion units between 1926 and 1929. Furniture companies, like many other producers of consumer merchandise, expecting an unlimited market, had by 1927 produced too many goods and by 1928 were reducing their labor forces to shave production costs. The impact of a slowing economy was even worse in less robust sectors of the economy. Throughout the 1920s, older industries such as railroads, textiles,

and iron and steel had barely made a profit, while agriculture and mining suffered steady losses. Workers in those jobs saw little increase in wages or standard of living. Agriculture was especially weak. The postwar economic expansion had totally bypassed agriculture, and farmers watched their incomes and property values slip to about half of their wartime highs. Compounding these problems, credit had virtually dried up in rural America because five thousand banks had closed between 1921 and 1928. By the end of 1928, thousands of people had left their farms, and agriculture was approaching an economic crisis.

Another weakness of the economy was a **maldistribution of wealth.** The nation had over 513 millionaires, but that concentration of wealth represented too much money in too few hands to maintain consumer spending. The **Brookings Institute** judged that an annual salary of $2,500 provided an American family a comfortable standard of living. It also found that 70 percent of American families earned less than that amount. When Hoover took office, most people were exhausting nearly all of their monthly income on food, housing, and a variety of consumer products and were supplementing their wages with credit buying. Increasingly, Americans were in debt. Americans had spent about $100 million in credit buying in 1919, but ten years later that amount had soared to over $7 billion. Still, few worried about debt as long as the economy seemed stable, unemployment remained low, and Americans had confidence in the economy. All that changed with the stock market crash.

When the market crashed, economic confidence was undermined, and the weaknesses of the economy were highlighted. Americans had viewed the

Great Depression   The years 1929 to 1941 when the economy of the United States suffered its greatest decline, millions of people were unemployed, and thousands of businesses went bankrupt; President Hoover used the term *depression* rather than the more traditional *panic* in hopes that it would reduce the public's fears.

maldistribution of wealth   Unequal distribution of wealth among population groups. In 1929, the richest fifth of the population controlled 52.3 percent of the nation's wealth, the middle fifth held only 14.4 percent, while the poorest fifth had access to only 5.4 percent.

Brookings Institute   A nonprofit, nonpartisan organization founded by Robert Brookings in 1916 that studies government, economic, and international issues.

TABLE 24.1 Unemployment Rates, 1929–1933 (percentage of each country's work force)

	1929	1930	1931	1932	1933
U.S.	3.2	8.7	15.9	23.6	24.9
Denmark	15.5	13.7	17.9	31.7	28.8
Germany	13.1	22.2	33.7	43.7	
Austria	12.3	15.0	20.3	26.1	29.0
Norway	15.4	16.6	22.2	30.8	33.4
Britain	10.4	16.1	21.3	22.1	19.9

soaring stock market as a symbol of the vigor of the economy and nation, but as the market continued to fall and the economy slumped, investors became wary. Corporations were more likely to cut production and lay off workers, who could ill afford any reduction in wages. Consumers were hesitant to spend their money. The Federal Reserve raised interest rates, and banks became less willing to lend money. As the economy spiraled downward in the months following the crash, the banking system appeared to be collapsing.

Many of the nation's banks were undercapitalized, had made too many loans and questionable investments, and were vulnerable to the slowing economy. Even before the stock market crash, "runs" on banks occurred as customers lined up at teller windows to empty their accounts. They intensified after the crash, and, unable to meet their obligations, more and more banks went into bankruptcy. The New York Bank of the United States had held over $280 million in savings accounts, but in December 1930 it closed its doors, and thousands of people lost all their money. The failure of the nation's banks forecast a serious economic crisis for the growing number of unemployed and jarred the well-being of many upper- and middle-class families, who suddenly found they had little or no savings—no buffer against hard times. Across the nation, Americans faced a deepening depression—the result of the stock market crash, too much credit, loss of economic confidence, and the existing weaknesses within the economy.

The declining American economy had an international dimension as well. During the last half of the 1920s, the European economy was recovering from

the devastation of the Great War, greatly aided by over $5.1 billion dollars borrowed from American sources. However, by the end of 1928, many American investors had reduced the amount of loans to Europe to half what they had been. The onset of the Depression in the United States made the contraction even worse. As the Depression spread, many nations took action to protect their industries from foreign goods by raising tariffs. Congress joined in when in 1930 it set the highest tariff rates in U.S. history with the Hawley-Smoot Tariff. Twenty-three foreign governments in turn raised their tariffs on American goods. While these actions may have protected domestic markets from foreign competition, it also undermined world trade. World trade was slowing to a crawl by 1931 as European banks and industries closed and unemployment exploded. In several countries, like Germany and Japan, new governments arose. Germany's newly installed chancellor, Adolf Hitler, initiated costly programs that pumped money into the economy, resulting in an impressive recovery within a few years.

Still, by 1933, the world and American economies were in shambles. American exports were at their lowest level since 1905, nearly ninety thousand businesses had failed, corporate profits were down 60 percent, and nine thousand banks closed, with depositors losing $2.5 billion. As the money supply shrank, dropping by a third between 1930 and 1933, the average expenditure for goods plummeted by 45 percent. Automobile purchases dropped by 75 percent. At the same time, unemployment rose from 3 percent in 1929 to 9 percent in 1930, to an unheard-of 25 percent by 1933 (see Table 24.1).

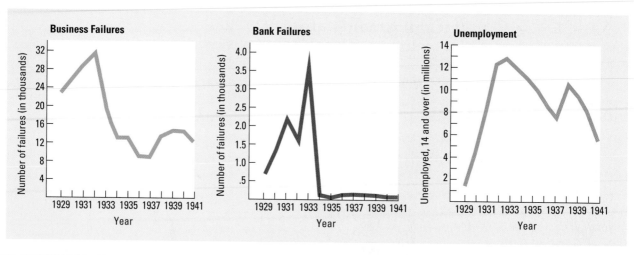

FIGURE 24.1 Charting the Economics of the Depression   Between 1929 and 1933, the number of people unemployed and of banks and businesses shutting down steadily increased. By 1933, over 9,000 banks had failed, unemployment had reached 24.9 percent, and over 90,000 firms had closed. As the New Deal began, not only did the statistics improve, but for most Americans a new sense of hope also emerged.

Hoover and the Depression

The most common and immediate response to the plunge in stock prices was voiced by Secretary of the Treasury Andrew Mellon, who stated that the economy remained strong and that the plunge of the market was temporary and would in fact strengthen the economy. Most experts believed the government should let the economy heal itself. Hoover disagreed and took an active role that reflected his belief in associationalism. He summoned the nation's economic leaders, asking them to help absorb the economic shock by reducing profits rather than the work force and wages. At the same time, he urged Congress, states, and cities to increase spending on **public works projects,** including buildings, highways, government facilities, and, in particular, the **Boulder Dam.** He called on local groups to raise money to help the unemployed as part of the President's Organization for Unemployment Relief program (POUR). The Agricultural Marketing Act (1929) attempted to solve farmers' problems with the creation of a Farm Board to help support agricultural prices. While initially there were some successes, they did not last long. As profits declined, businesses cut production and wages and laid off workers. At the same time, agricultural prices continued to collapse, and state, local, and private efforts to aid the growing number of unemployed were overwhelmed (see Figure 24.1).

With the country slipping further into the Depression, in 1931 Hoover took new steps. He asked Congress for banking reforms, financial support for home mortgages, the creation of the **Reconstruction Finance Corporation** (RFC), and higher taxes to pay for it all. Congress responded with the **Glass-Steagall Act** of 1932, which increased bank reserves to encourage lending, and the **Federal Home Loan Bank Act,** which allowed homeowners to remortgage their homes at

public works projects   Highways, dams, and other construction projects financed by public funds and carried out by the government.

Boulder Dam   Dam on the Colorado River between Nevada and Arizona, begun during Hoover's administration and completed in 1935.

Reconstruction Finance Corporation   Organization established at Hoover's request in 1932 to promote economic recovery; it provided emergency financing for banks, life insurance companies, railroads, and farm mortgage associations.

Glass-Steagall Act   Law passed by Congress in 1932 that expanded credit through the Federal Reserve System in order to counteract foreign withdrawals and domestic hoarding of money.

Federal Home Loan Bank Act   Law passed by Congress in 1932 that established twelve banks across the nation to supplement lending resources to institutions making home loans in an effort to reduce foreclosures and to stimulate the construction industry.

The Great Depression produced large-scale unemployment, reaching 25 percent in 1933; across the nation people scrambled to find other sources of revenue. In this picture a World War I vet sells apples on the street in Chicago. *Chicago Historical Society.*

Hoover accepted an Emergency Relief Division within the RFC. It was to provide $300 million in loans to states to pay for relief. Yet little money was used because the RFC loaned funds too cautiously, and few states wanted to borrow and put themselves deeper in debt. By the end of 1932, 90 percent of the relief fund was still intact. Whether for relief or recovery, the RFC did not make enough funds available to relieve the economic crisis.

The onslaught of the Depression had changed Hoover's and the nation's fortunes. Many Americans blamed the president and the Republicans for the worsening economy and a callousness toward the hardships faced by many Americans. In the traditionally conservative farm belt, militant farmers joined the **Farmers' Holiday Association,** led by **Milo Reno.** He accused the government of inaction and being in the "grip of Wall Street." Reno called on farmers to resist **foreclosures** and to destroy their crops. Farmers responded. On several occasions, they used numbers and threats of violence to force "penny auctions" that ensured that foreclosed farms were returned to their owners for a fraction of their value. In Ohio, Walter Crozier, backed by a crowd of angry neighbors, regained his farm for a high bid of $1.90. Farmers were not alone. Across the nation, strikes, protest rallies, "bread marches," and rent riots took place as citizens demanded more jobs, higher wages, and relief payments. In Detroit, three workers died when a workers' demonstration against Ford was attacked by police and security guards.

A larger expression of protest took place in Washington, D.C., as thousands of World War I veterans, the **Bonus Army,** converged to support the "bonus

lower rates and payments. But it was through the RFC that Hoover intended to fight the Depression by pumping money into the economy. Using federal funds, the RFC was to provide loans to banks, railroads, and large corporations to prevent their collapse and encourage expanded operations. Hoover and his advisers believed the money would "trickle down" to workers and the unemployed through higher wages and new jobs. Approved by Congress, within five months of operation, the RFC had loaned over $805 million, but little money seemed to be trickling down to workers. Liberal critics branded the program "welfare for the rich" and insisted Hoover do more for the poor and unemployed. Hoover opposed federal relief, the "dole," to the poor, believing that it was too expensive and eroded the work ethic. But with unemployment reaching nearly 25 percent and mounting pressure from Congress and the public,

Farmers' Holiday Association   Organization of farmers that called on members to take direct actions—such as destroying crops and resisting foreclosures—to protest the plight of agriculture and the lack of government support.

Milo Reno   Farm leader from Iowa who led the Farmers' Holiday Association and in 1932 called on farmers to strike, to "stay home, buy nothing, sell nothing"; he wanted government codes to control production but rejected President Roosevelt's farm program as a threat to independence and liberty; he died in 1936.

foreclosure   Confiscation of property by a bank when mortgage payments are delinquent.

Bonus Army   Unemployed World War I veterans who marched to Washington in 1932 to demand early payment of a promised bonus; Congress refused, and the army evicted protesters who remained.

The sign in front of the "Bonus Dugout" reads, "We have come to collect the gratitude that was promised us for participating in the World War." They received neither gratitude nor the bonus. Instead, Hoover commented: "Thank God we still have a government that knows how to deal with a mob." *Library of Congress.*

bill," which would provide them with an early payment of their $1,000 veteran's bonus, scheduled to be paid in 1945. The marchers set up their **Hooverville** across from Congress at Anacosta Flats and picketed Congress and the White House demanding passage of the bill. When the bill failed in mid-June, most of the Bonus Marchers left Washington, but nearly ten thousand stayed behind. To remove the protesters, Hoover turned to the army, led by Army Chief of Staff General Douglas MacArthur. Using sabers, rifles, tear gas, and fixed bayonets, the army drove the "squatters" from their encampment. In a one-sided fight, the soldiers forced the veterans and their families from the huts and tents while the smell of smoke and tear gas hung over the city. Over one hundred

veterans were injured, but rumors quickly swelled the number and added several fatalities, including the death of a baby who reportedly succumbed to tear gas. The rumors intensified the public's angry reaction. Upon hearing of the forced eviction of the marchers, the governor of New York, Franklin D. Roosevelt, crowed, "This will elect me."

> **Hooverville** Crudely built camp set up by the homeless on the fringes of a town or city during the Depression; the largest Hooverville was outside Oklahoma City and covered over 100 square miles.

The New Deal

■ How did the New Deal's "First Hundred Days" represent a change in the role of the federal government? In particular, what measures did it include, and how did they promote recovery?

■ What were the sources of opposition to Roosevelt's First Hundred Days, and how did the Second Hundred Days respond to those critics and differ from the first? Why did no Third Hundred Days follow Roosevelt's resounding victory in 1936?

■ How did the New Deal change the structure of government and Americans' expectations about the role of government?

Nearly any Democratic candidate could have defeated Hoover in 1932, but the Democrats had nominated an exceptional politician in Franklin D. Roosevelt. Born into wealth and privilege, he had attended Groton Academy and Harvard University, schools popular with America's aristocracy. Neither academically nor athletically gifted, Roosevelt was nonetheless popular and after graduation, with a recognizable name, entered New York politics. Tall, handsome, charming, glib, he quickly moved up the political ladder, being nominated for vice president in 1920. Even though he and James Cox were defeated, his future looked bright. Suddenly, in 1921, it appeared his political career was over when he was stricken with polio and paralyzed from the waist down. Greatly aided by his wife, Eleanor, he kept his political career alive and in 1928 ran for governor of New York. The current New York governor, Democrat Al Smith, lost his bid for the presidency that year, but Roosevelt won the governorship.

As governor of New York, Roosevelt was one of the few governors to mobilize his state's limited resources to help the unemployed and poor. While making little headway against the Depression, his efforts projected an image of a more caring and energetic leader than Hoover. His valiant struggle to overcome polio, combined with his actions as governor and cheery disposition, earned him a reputation as the champion of the "forgotten man" and made him appear the opposite of Hoover, who seemed to have little concern for the 11 million unemployed Americans.

When nominated for president in 1932, showing dynamic flair, Roosevelt broke with the tradition and flew to Chicago, site of the national convention. He emphasized two points in his acceptance speech: he was a man of action who promoted change, and his health was good and his paralysis in no way hindered his activity. He also established a theme for the coming campaign. Pointing to his tradition-breaking trip to the convention, Roosevelt emphatically announced that he and the Democratic Party had no

In the 1932 election, Roosevelt campaigned across the nation, always appearing confident and cheerful. Some said that his smile was the biggest political weapon he had—not only against Hoover but against the Depression. *FPG.*

fear of breaking "all foolish traditions." He closed by promising a "new deal for the American people." The media quickly picked up on the term, handing Roosevelt a memorable slogan for his campaign: the **New Deal.** Although the acceptance speech offered no concrete solutions to the problems facing the country, it stirred the desire for hope and instilled the belief that Roosevelt would move the nation along new paths.

> **New Deal**   Term applied to Roosevelt's policies to attack the problems of the Depression, which included relief for poor and unemployed, efforts to stimulate economic recovery, and social security; the term was coined by Roosevelt's adviser Raymond Moley.

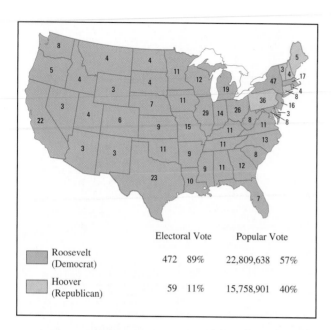

	Electoral Vote		Popular Vote	
Roosevelt (Democrat)	472	89%	22,809,638	57%
Hoover (Republican)	59	11%	15,758,901	40%

MAP 24.1 Election of 1932 In the election of 1932, Herbert Hoover faced not only Franklin D. Roosevelt but also the Great Depression. With many Americans blaming Hoover and the Republicans for the economic catastrophe and with Roosevelt promising a New Deal, the outcome was not close. Roosevelt won 42 of 48 states. While gaining no electoral votes, minor party candidates drew about 3 percent of the vote.

During the campaign, Roosevelt tried to avoid any commitments and policies that might offend voters or blocs within the Democratic Party. He supported direct federal relief while promising to balance the budget, but mostly he stressed hope and the prospect of change. Hoover, trying to overcome his opponent's popularity, emphasized their philosophical differences. He claimed that the campaign, "more than a contest between two men," was "a contest between two philosophies of government." The election was a huge success for the Democratic Party and Roosevelt. Across the nation, people voted for Democrats at every level, from local to national. Roosevelt won in a landslide, burying Hoover with 22.8 million votes, 57.4 percent of over 39.7 million votes cast. Hoover carried only six states—the rest belonged to Roosevelt (see Map 24.1).

Roosevelt Confronts the Depression

In the four months between the election and Inauguration Day, the people eagerly waited for the New Deal to start even as the economy worsened. To many, it appeared that Roosevelt and his advisers, labeled by the press as the **Brain Trust,** were developing a clear plan to restore prosperity. It was an illusion. There was no plan, and in fact the Brain Trust and Roosevelt's other advisers were frequently at odds about which path to follow. Some, like Rexford Tugwell and Raymond Moley, supported a collective approach, working with big businesses through increased regulation and joint economic planning. Others, like Harry Hopkins, Eleanor Roosevelt, and Felix Frankfurter, advocated social programs and a more competitive economic system. All agreed, however, that the worst path was doing nothing and that federal power must be used.

Riding a wave of popular support and great expectations, Roosevelt faced a unique political climate of almost total **bipartisanship.** The result was that within its first hundred days in office, the Roosevelt administration passed more legislation than any president before or since and forever changed the public's vision of the role of the federal government. Roosevelt took office on March 4, as the nation faced the possible collapse of its banking system. Nearly all the country's banks were closed, and the economy faced paralysis. The country waited anxiously to see how the new president would act. They were not disappointed. On Inauguration Day, Franklin D. Roosevelt spoke reassuring words to the American public and let the nation know that he was taking action. Millions listened to the radio as the president calmly stated that Americans had "nothing to fear but fear itself" and promised that the economy would revive. "We must act quickly," he added, announcing that he would ask Congress for sweeping powers to deal with the crisis. On March 6, Roosevelt declared a national **Bank Holiday** that closed all the country's banks. Three days later, as freshmen congressmen were still finding their seats, the president presented

Brain Trust Group of specialists in law, economics, and social welfare who, as advisers to President Roosevelt, helped develop the social and economic principles of the New Deal.

bipartisanship In American politics, it is when the two major parties agree on a set of issues and programs.

Bank Holiday Temporary shutdown of banks throughout the country by executive order of President Roosevelt in March 1933.

Congress with the **Emergency Banking Bill.** Without even seeing a written version of the bill, Democrats and Republicans gave Roosevelt what he wanted in less than four hours. It allowed the Federal Reserve and the Reconstruction Finance Corporation (which had outlasted Hoover) to support the nation's banks by providing funds and buying stocks of preferred banks. On Sunday evening, March 12, in the first of his **fireside chats,** the president said that the federal government was solving the banking crisis and banks would be safe again. He joked, "It is safer to keep your money in a reopened bank than under the mattress." Over 60 million Americans listened to the speech, and most believed in their leader. Confidence had been restored, and within a month nearly 75 percent of the nation's banks were operating again. In Atlanta on the day following the fireside chat, deposits outnumbered withdrawals by over 3 to 1. The New Deal had begun. Roosevelt signed fifteen major pieces of legislation over the next one hundred days. The legislation, he explained in another fireside chat, was moving along three paths: recovery, relief, and reform.

Seeking Recovery

Among the first bills Roosevelt offered Congress, on March 16, was the **Agricultural Adjustment Act.** Secretary of Agriculture Henry A. Wallace drafted a bill that used national planning and government payments to raise farm prices and provide a profit for agriculture. Passed by Congress on May 12, the act created the Agricultural Adjustment Administration (AAA), which encouraged farmers to reduce production by paying them *not* to plant. Focusing on wheat, cotton, field corn, rice, tobacco, hogs, and milk and milk products, a planning board set a domestic allotment and determined the amount to be removed from production. To pay for the program, a special tax on the industrial food processors was levied. Some critics argued that the AAA gave too much power to the government. Milo Reno, who still led the National Farmers' Association, rejected the AAA and called on farmers to strike. Others complained that the AAA did nothing to help small farmers, sharecroppers, and tenant farmers; they wanted the government to make the surplus food available for the needy.

Despite Reno's call for a strike, farmers and most of the nation put their trust in Roosevelt and the AAA. By 1935, it appeared that the program was working. Farm prices were climbing, and the purchasing power of farmers was increasing (see Figure 24.2).

Dorothea Lange became one of the most famous photographers of the Depression. Her photo of a mother and her children at a migrant camp in Nipomo, California, captured the human tragedy of the Depression. Seeking jobs and opportunities, over 350,000 people traveled to the state, most finding little relief. *Library of Congress.*

But there was a cost. Tenant farmers and sharecroppers usually received no share of the AAA payments paid to their landlords and found themselves evicted

Emergency Banking Bill   (Act) Law passed by Congress in 1933 that permitted sound banks in the Federal Reserve System to reopen and allowed the government to supply funds to support private banks.

fireside chats   Radio talks in which President Roosevelt promoted New Deal policies and reassured the nation; Roosevelt delivered twenty-eight fireside chats.

Agricultural Adjustment Act   Law passed by Congress in 1933 to reduce overproduction by paying farmers not to grow crops or raise livestock.

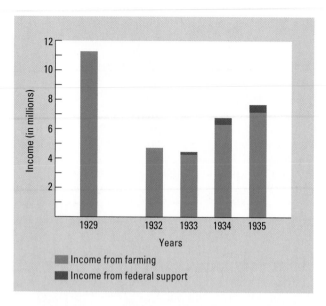

FIGURE 24.2 **Farm Income, 1929–1935** Prices for farm products fell rapidly as the Depression set in, but by 1933, with support from New Deal programs like the Agricultural Adjustment Act, some farm incomes were rising. Note, however, that some of the increase was a direct result of government payments. *Source:* U.S. Department of Commerce, *Historical Statistics of the United States, Colonial Times to 1970*, Bicentennial Edition, 2 vols. (Washington, D.C.: U.S. Government Printing Office, 1975), 1:483–484.

MAP 24.2 **The Dust Bowl** Throughout the 1930s, sun and wind eroded millions of acres of cropland, sending tons of topsoil into the air, generating tidal waves of dust—and the Dust Bowl. This map shows the regions most affected by the Dust Bowl and decreases in population, and Route 66, which many chose to travel, hoping that it would lead to a better life in California.

from their farms—a million by the end of 1935. In 1936, the whole plan to revitalize agriculture collapsed as the Supreme Court ruled the AAA unconstitutional in *Butler v. the United States.* In its 1936 decision the Court ruled that the federal government could not set production quotas and that the special tax on processing food was illegal. Quickly, the administration turned to other programs, including some existing ones such as the 1935 **Soil Conservation and Domestic Allocation Act** to reduce production. Nature also helped take land out of production as high winds swept across the drought-plagued Great Plains, creating what became known as the **Dust Bowl.** Dust storms sometimes stretched more than 200 miles across and over 7,000 feet high. In 1938 alone, over 850 million tons of topsoil were lost to wind erosion (see Map 24.2).

In 1938, as the Dust Bowl reached its worst point, Congress approved a second Agricultural Adjustment Act that reestablished the principle of federally set commodity quotas, acreage reduction, and **parity** payments. A year later, farm income had more than doubled since 1932, with the government providing over $4.5 billion in aid to farmers. Initially intended

as a short-term measure, federal support for farm prices lasted over fifty years and significantly changed the relationship between agricultural producers and the federal government.

Butler v. the United States Supreme Court decision (1936) declaring the Agricultural Adjustment Act invalid on the grounds that it unconstitutionally extended the powers of the federal government.

Soil Conservation and Domestic Allocation Act Legislation passed by Congress in 1935 that established an agency for the prevention of soil erosion by paying farmers to cut back on soil-depleting crops and to plant grasses and other crops that would help to hold the soil.

Dust Bowl Name given by a reporter in 1935 to the region devastated by drought and dust storms that began in 1932; the worst years (1936–1938) saw over sixty major storms per year, seventy-two in 1937.

parity A price paid to American farmers designed to give them the same income that they had between 1910 and 1914. The AAA provided parity prices on seven commodities: corn, cotton, wheat, rice, tobacco, hogs, and milk and milk products.

The National Recovery Administration was Roosevelt's main vehicle to restore industrial recovery during his First One Hundred Days. Headed by General Hugh Johnson, the NRA's goal was to mobilize management, workers, and consumers under the symbol of the Blue Eagle; establish national production codes; and get America moving again. *Collection of Janice L. and David J. Frent.*

The AAA addressed the problem of agriculture, and in May 1933, the Roosevelt administration offered Congress a program for dealing with the problem of industrial recovery. The **National Industrial Recovery Act** (NIRA) was approved in June, with Roosevelt calling it the "most important and far reaching legislation passed by the American Congress." The act created two agencies, the **National Recovery Administration** (NRA) for long-term economic revival and the **Public Works Administration** (PWA) for more immediate work relief. The goal of the National Recovery Administration, led by Gen-

eral Hugh "Ironpants" Johnson, was to stimulate the economy through national economic planning. "Industrial codes" were written that established prices, production levels, and wages for a variety of industries from steel to broomsticks. Business supported the NRA because it allowed **price fixing** that raised both prices and profits. Labor was attracted by prolabor codes—in Section 7a of the national codes—that gave workers the right to organize and bargain collectively, outlawed child labor, and established minimum wages and maximum hours of work. With the Blue Eagle as its symbol and "We Do Our Part" as its motto, the NRA **juggernaut** rolled forward.

Nearly overnight, the Blue Eagle appeared everywhere. By the beginning of 1935, over 700 industries and 2.5 million workers were covered by the NRA codes. But almost from the beginning, dissatisfaction brewed, and critics dubbed the NRA the "National Run Around." Workers complained that wages were too low, hours too long, and that employers resisted unionization. Consumers grumbled that prices rose without any noticeable growth in wages or jobs. Farmers griped that NRA-generated price increases ate up any AAA benefits they received. As production and profitability increased, businesses soon chafed under federal restrictions and regulations and questioned the government's right to impose such controls. Many opponents called the NRA unconstitutional, and on May 27, 1935, the Supreme Court

National Industrial Recovery Act Law passed by Congress in 1933 establishing the National Recovery Administration to supervise industry and the Public Works Administration to create jobs.

National Recovery Administration Agency created by the NIRA to draft national industrial codes and supervise their implementation.

Public Works Administration Headed by Harold Ickes, secretary of the interior, the Public Works Administration sought to increase employment and to stimulate economic recovery by putting people to work. It spent more than $4.25 million on 34,000 public works projects.

General Hugh Johnson Head of the National Recovery Administration; consumer and labor advocates accused him of being too favorable to business interests.

price fixing The artificial setting of commodity prices.

juggernaut An overwhelming, advancing force that crushes or seems to roll over everything in its path.

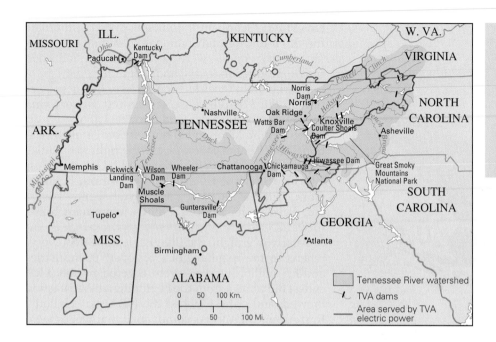

MAP 24.3 The Tennessee Valley Authority One of the most ambitious New Deal projects was developing the Tennessee Valley by improving waterways, building hydroelectric dams, and providing electricity to the area. This map shows the various components of the TVA and the region it changed.

agreed. In *Schechter Poultry Corporation v. the United States*, the Court held that the government could not set national codes or set wages and hours in local plants. Roosevelt was furious at the Court, saying it had a "horse and buggy" mentality.

Perhaps the most innovative and successful recovery program was the **Tennessee Valley Authority** (TVA). The goal was to showcase federally directed regional planning and development of a rural and impoverished 40,000-square-mile region. The most immediate benefit was new jobs, as flood controls were improved and dams repaired and built. But the TVA was much more. Hundreds of miles of river and lakes were made more navigable, soil erosion was reduced, and the TVA dams provided electricity through federally owned and operated hydroelectric systems (see Map 24.3). Critics opposed the government-owned agencies that operated factories and power companies, blasting the system as socialism. In the West, the federal government also reshaped water and electrical power usage, providing valuable water and electricity for the economic and demographic growth of the region. Boulder Dam served southern California, while the Central Valley Project in central California harnessed the Sacramento River and its tributaries. In Washington and Oregon, a series of dams and hydroelectric plants along the Columbia River, including the massive Grand Coulee Dam, provided the foundation for further growth.

Among the songs of the folk culture of the New Deal and the TVA was one, called "The Ballad of the T.V.A.," that spoke directly about the personal benefits gained from the Tennessee Valley Authority projects.

The Ballad of the T.V.A.
My name is William Edwards
I live down Cove Creek Way.
I'm working on the project
They call the T.V.A.

The government begun it
When I was a just a child;
But now they are in earnest
And the Tennessee's gone wild.

I meant to marry Sally
But work I could not find.
The T.V.A. was started
And surely eased my mind.

Schechter Poultry Corporation v. the United States Supreme Court decision (1935) declaring the NRA unconstitutional because it regulated companies not involved in interstate commerce.

Tennessee Valley Authority Independent public corporation created by Congress in 1933 and authorized to construct dams and power plants in the Tennessee River valley region.

I'm writing her a letter
These words I'll surely say,
"The government has surely saved us,
Just name our wedding day."

We'll build a little cabin
On Cove Creek near her home.
We'll settle down forever
And never care to roam.

The government employs us
Short hours and certain pay.
Things are up and comin'
God bless the T.V.A.

The TVA's electrification program provided a precedent, and in 1935, the Roosevelt administration committed itself to the electrification of rural America through the **Rural Electrification Administration** (REA). Utility companies had argued that rural America was too isolated and poor to make service profitable, and in the early 1930s only about 30 percent of farms had electricity. The REA bypassed opposition from private utility companies and state power commissions by aiding in the formation of rural and farmer electrical cooperatives. Twelve years later, electricity powered 45 percent of rural homes and farms. The electrification of rural America helped integrate those areas with the culture of modern urban America. Electricity improved education, health, and sanitation, and encouraged the diversification of agriculture and the introduction of new industries. It lessened the drudgery of farm life, giving families running water and access to a variety of electrical appliances. Within eight months, new electrical service customers bought about $180 in appliances—the first purchase usually was a washing machine.

Remembering the "Forgotten Man"

Recovery was only one thrust of Roosevelt's offensive against the Depression. He had campaigned on the slogan of helping the "forgotten man." In March 1933, unemployment was at a historic high—25 percent of the population, nearly 12 million people. In industrial states such as New York, Ohio, Pennsylvania, and Illinois, unemployment pushed toward 33 percent. Recognizing that state and private relief sources were unable to cope with people's needs, the administration accepted responsibility. During his First Hundred Days, Roosevelt proposed and Congress enacted four major relief programs. Though all

were temporary measures, they established a new role for the federal government. By the end of the decade, about 46 million people had received some form of relief support.

The first relief program enacted by Congress was the **Civilian Conservation Corps** (CCC), passed on March 31, 1933. It established over 2,650 army-style segregated camps to house and provide a healthy, moral environment for unemployed urban males ages 18 to 25. Within months it had enrolled over 300,000 men, paying them $30 a month, $25 of which had to be sent home. By 1941, enrollment was over 2 million men. The "Conservation Army" swept across the nation, building, developing, and improving national park facilities, constructing roads and firebreaks, erecting telephone poles, digging irrigation ditches, and planting trees. In the camps, 35,000 men were taught to read. But the CCC touched only a small percentage of those needing relief. To widen the range of assistance, the Roosevelt administration created the **Federal Emergency Relief Administration** (FERA), the Public Works Administration (PWA), and the short-lived Civil Works Administration.

The FERA provided states with money for their relief needs, even though some governors rejected the idea of relief and federal aid. But the FERA did more. In some cases it bypassed state and local governments and instituted federally administered programs. One such FERA program opened special centers to provide housing, meals, and medical care for many of the homeless roaming the nation. In the program's first year of operation, it cared for as many as 5 million people. Ed Paulson was one. Riding the rails, he and other hobos were pulled off a train in Omaha and forced into trucks by deputies. "You're not going to jail," they assured him. "You're going to

---

Rural Electrification Administration Government agency established in 1935 for the purpose of loaning money to rural cooperatives to produce and distribute electricity in isolated areas.

Civilian Conservation Corps Organization created by Congress in 1933 to hire young unemployed men for conservation work, such as planting trees, digging irrigation ditches, and maintaining national parks. The majority of those recruited were white, but African Americans, Latinos, and Native Americans also served in segregated camps, including more than 80,000 Native Americans who served on reservations.

Federal Emergency Relief Administration Agency created in May 1933 to provide direct grants to states and municipalities to spend on relief.

Here, Civilian Conservation Corps workers plant seedlings to reforest a section of forest destroyed by fire. Before its demise in 1942, the CCC enrolled over 2.75 million young men. In addition to its work in conservation, the CCC also taught around 35,000 men how to read and write. ©*Bettmann/Corbis.*

the Transient Camp." There, Paulson was deloused, given a bath, a bed, and "a spread with scrambled eggs, bacon, bread, coffee, and toast." "We ate a great meal," he recalled years later. "We thought we'd gone to heaven." In other programs, over half a million people attended literacy classes and 1 million received vaccinations and immunizations.

The Public Works Administration provided funds for a variety of projects that had social and community value. It paid 45 cents an hour for unskilled labor and $1.10 an hour for skilled workers, and sought, frequently unsuccessfully, equal pay regardless of race. Eventually the PWA provided over $4 billion to state and local governments for more than 34,000 projects, including sidewalks, roads, schools, and community buildings. PWA funds also constructed two aircraft carriers, the *Yorktown* and the *Enterprise.*

During the winter of 1933–1934, Roosevelt added another works program, the **Civil Works Administration** (CWA), directed by Harry Hopkins. The CWA ran its own programs and selected participants from the unemployed with only half coming from those on relief rolls. Some complained that people left lower-paying existing jobs for higher-paying CWA jobs. Before shutting down in February 1934, the CWA, Roosevelt's most controversial relief program, had employed over 4 million people, including paying the salaries of over fifty thousand teachers.

Not all relief programs were aimed at the homeless and poor. Two aided homeowners. The **Home Own-** ers' **Loan Corporation** (HOLC), established in May 1933, permitted homeowners to refinance their mortgages at lower interest rates through the federal government. Before it stopped making loans in 1936, the HOLC had refinanced 1 million homes, including 20 percent of all mortgaged urban homes. The National Housing Act, passed in June 1934, created the **Federal Housing Administration** (FHA), which still provides federally backed loans for home mortgages and repairs.

Interspersed among the recovery and relief programs were a number of reforms that sought to pre-

---

Civil Works Administration   Emergency unemployment relief program in 1933 and 1934; it hired 4 million jobless people for federal, state, and local work projects. Critics argued that it should not have bypassed state and local authorities and that in many cases it created useless jobs, like moving dirt from one place to another.

Home Owners' Loan Corporation   Government agency created in 1933 that refinanced home mortgage debts for nonfarm homeowners and allowed them to borrow money from the agency to pay property taxes and make repairs.

Federal Housing Administration   Agency created by the National Housing Act (1934) to insure loans made by banks and other institutions for new home construction, repairs, and improvements.

vent the recurrence of the events that had triggered the Depression and to place more constraints on the unfair practices of business. To correct problems within the banking and securities industries, the Bank Act of 1933 gave more power to the Federal Reserve System and created the **Federal Deposit Insurance Corporation** (FDIC). The act provided federal insurance for those who had deposited money in member banks. In less than six months, 97 percent of all commercial banks had joined the system. The **Securities and Exchange Commission** (SEC), created by the Securities Exchange Act of 1934, more closely regulated stock market activities.

Changing Focus

The New Deal started with almost total support in Congress and among the people. But as proposals flowed from the White House and the economy improved, opposition emerged. By mid-1933, most Republicans actively opposed relief programs, federal spending, and increased governmental controls over business. Conservatives fumed that Roosevelt threatened free enterprise, if not capitalism. The Hearst newspaper chain instructed its editors to tell the public that the New Deal was a "raw deal" and that Roosevelt planned to "Soak the Successful" and lead the nation down the path to socialism.

For the majority of the American people, however, Roosevelt and the New Deal still spelled hope and faith in the future. State and congressional elections held in 1934 showed Democrats gaining overwhelming victories. Supported by congressional Democrats and public opinion, Roosevelt continued to add to the New Deal and became less willing to cooperate with conservatives and business. The president was also aware that recovery was not progressing as rapidly as desired and that criticism was growing about the New Deal's failure to help the common man.

Three critics were especially popular: **Father Charles Coughlin,** Senator **Huey Long,** and **Dr. Francis Townsend.** At three o'clock every Sunday afternoon, Father Coughlin, a Roman Catholic priest, used the radio to preach to nearly 30 million Americans. The "radio priest" had strongly supported Roosevelt, but in mid-1934, he turned his influential voice against the New Deal and Roosevelt. His organization, the National Union for Social Justice, which he called the "people's lobby," advocated a guaranteed annual income, the redistribution of wealth, tougher antimonopoly laws, and the nationalization of banking. Within a year the organization claimed more than 5 million members. Senator Huey Long of

Louisiana suggested more radical programs to help the average American. His **"Share the Wealth"** plan included tempting provisions: every family would receive an annual check for $2,000, a home, a car, a radio, and a college education for each child. The system would be funded by taxing the rich, with incomes over $1 million to be taxed at 100 percent. Crying "Soak the Rich!" Share the Wealth societies mushroomed to over 4 million followers.

Coughlin's and Long's plans were broadly based, whereas Dr. Francis Townsend focused on the elderly. He advocated a federal old-age pension plan that would provide every American, age 60 and older, a monthly pension check for $200. To qualify, individuals could not work and had to spend the money within a month. A national sales tax of 2 percent on business transactions would finance the system. In support of Townsend's idea, thousands of clubs were created with an estimated membership of several million, including sixty members of Congress.

Roosevelt and his advisers were also aware of growing pressure from workers and unions for legislation that would support unionization and help industrial laborers. The national codes of the NRA had raised workers' expectations by promoting unions and

Federal Deposit Insurance Corporation Agency created by the Bank Act of 1933 to insure deposits up to a fixed sum in member banks of the Federal Reserve System and state banks that chose to participate.

Securities and Exchange Commission Agency created by the Securities Exchange Act of 1934 to license stock exchanges and supervise their activities, including the setting of margin rates.

Father Charles Coughlin Roman Catholic priest whose influential radio addresses in the 1930s at first emphasized social justice but eventually became anti-Semitic and profascist.

Huey Long Louisiana governor, then U.S. senator, who ran a powerful political machine and whose advocacy of redistribution of income was gaining him a national political following at the time of his assassination in 1935.

Dr. Francis Townsend California public health physician who proposed the Townsend Plan in 1933, under which every retired person over 60 would be paid a $200 monthly pension to be spent within the month.

Share the Wealth Movement that sprang up around the nation in the 1930s urging the redistribution of wealth through government taxes or programs; launched by Huey Long, its slogan was "Every man a king."

In 1934, Huey Long, a fiery politician from Louisiana, claimed that Roosevelt was not helping the common man enough. A dramatic and flamboyant speaker, Long proclaimed his support for the "little man" with the slogan "Every man a king" and the Share the Wealth program that would tax the rich and "spread the wealth among all our people." Before Long could become a real political threat to Roosevelt, he was assassinated in September 1935. *Corbis-Bettmann.*

Responding to these pressures, Roosevelt announced a change in priorities. He asked Congress to provide more **work relief,** to develop an old-age and unemployment insurance program, and to pass legislation regulating holding companies and utilities. A solidly Democratic and largely liberal Congress responded with a Second Hundred Days of legislation. In April 1935, Congress allocated nearly $5 billion for relief and created a new agency, the **Works Progress Administration** (WPA), led by Harry Hopkins. The WPA's goal was to put people to work, and it did. Between 1935 and 1938, the WPA employed over 2.1 million people a year. Most did manual labor, building roads, schools, and other public facilities. In its actions, the WPA established a maximum 140-hour work month and sought to pay wages higher than relief payments but lower than local wages. Wages for nonwhites and women were the exception—these generally exceeded the local rate. But the WPA went further than duplicating the PWA; it also created jobs for professionals, white-collar workers, writers, artists, actors and actresses, photographers, songwriters, and musicians. Historians conducted oral interviews, including those of ex-slaves, and wrote state and local histories and guidebooks. The WPA's Writers Project provided jobs for established and new novelists, including Saul Bellow and African American writer Richard Wright, author of *Native Son* (1940). Professional theater groups toured towns and cities, performing Shakespeare and other plays. By 1939 an estimated 30 million people had watched WPA productions.

"Art for the Millions" was a program designed to help artists and to elevate the public's awareness of art. It provided positive themes and images of Amer-

establishing higher wages. Workers had responded positively. Union membership doubled, with the fastest-growing unions in the mass-production industries, like Walter Reuther's **United Automobile Workers** (UAW), established in 1935. Also in 1935, leaders of the industrial unions formed the Committee of Industrial Organizations (CIO) within the AFL but left the AFL and formed their own independent labor organization in 1938, the **Congress of Industrial Organizations.** As workers became more dissatisfied with the application of NRA codes, a more militant and political worker emerged. Workers launched strikes, more than 1,800 in 1934, and union leaders increasingly asked their members to support, with votes and contributions, those politicians who were friends of labor and willing to promote workers' goals.

United Automobile Workers   Union of workers in the automobile industry; it used sit-down strikes in 1936 and 1937 to end work speed-ups and win recognition for the fledgling labor organization.

Congress of Industrial Organizations   Labor organization established in 1938 by a group of powerful unions that left the AFL to unionize workers by industry rather than by trade.

work relief   A system of governmental monetary support that provided work for the unemployed, who were usually paid a limited hourly or daily wage.

Works Progress Administration   Agency established in 1935 and headed by Harry Hopkins that hired the unemployed for construction, conservation, and arts programs.

The Works Progress Administration not only built roads and buildings but also provided employment for teachers, writers, and artists and supported the arts. *The Ivory Door* was a WPA production performed in Ohio in 1938. *Library of Congress.*

ican society, including over 2,500 murals—most adorning public buildings. Some objected to actors, artists, and writers receiving aid, arguing that their labor was not real work. But Hopkins bluntly responded, "Hell, they got to eat just like other people."

The WPA also made special efforts to help women, minorities, students, and young adults. Prodded by Eleanor Roosevelt, the WPA employed between 300,000 and 400,000 women a year. Although some were hired as teachers and nurses, the majority, especially in rural areas, worked on sewing and canning projects. Efforts to ensure African American employment met with success in the northeastern states but were less successful in the South. The **National Youth Administration** (NYA), created in 1935 and directed by Aubrey Williams, developed a successful program that provided aid for college and high school students and programs for young people not in school. **Mary McLeod Bethune,** an African American educator, directed the NYA's Division of Negro Affairs and through determination and constant, skillfully applied pressure obtained support for black schools and colleges and increased the number of African Americans enrolled in vocational and recreational programs.

The WPA reasserted Roosevelt's support for the common American, but it was the establishment of a federal old-age and survivor insurance program that set the tone of the Second Hundred Days and significantly modified the government's role in society. Frances Perkins (see Individual Choices, page 752–753) was a driving force behind the **Social Security Act** of 1935. Passed by Congress in August, the act's most controversial element was a pension plan for retirees 65 or older. The program would begin in 1937, and initial benefits would range from $10 to $85 per month, depending on how much the individual had paid in to the system.

Compared with Townsend's plan and many existing European systems, the U.S. Social Security system was limited and conservative. It required payments by workers, failed to cover domestic and agricultural laborers, and provided no health insurance. Nonetheless, it represented a major change in government's responsibility toward society.

Less controversial parts of the act provided federal aid to families with dependent children and the disabled, and helped fund state-run systems of unemployment compensation. Within two years, every state was part of the unemployment compensation

National Youth Administration   Program established by executive order in 1935 to provide employment for young people and to help needy high school and college students continue their educations.

Mary McLeod Bethune   African American educator who founded the Daytona Literary and Industrial School for Training Negro Girls in 1904 that became part of Bethune-Cookman College in 1923 and who, as director of the Division of Negro Affairs within the National Youth Administration, was a strong and vocal advocate for equality of opportunity for African Americans during the New Deal.

Social Security Act   Law passed by Congress in 1935 to create systems of unemployment, old-age, and disability insurance and to provide for child welfare.

It Matters

Social Security

Passage of the Social Security Act in 1935 established a new function for the federal government and is one of the most durable legacies of the New Deal. Since its initial payments in 1937, millions of Americans have benefited from its pension plan. In 2003, over 190 million people were covered by Social Security, and Social Security benefits amounted to over $746,750 million. As America's work force ages, many worry that by 2050 there will not be enough funds in the Social Security trust fund to cover all those eligible for Social Security benefits.

system, paying between $15 and $18 a week in unemployment compensation and supplying support to over 28 million people.

The Second Hundred Days also supported organized labor with the passage of the National Labor Relations Act (NLRA) in 1935, and quieted "Long's thunder" by raising taxes on corporations and the wealthy. Largely the work of Senator Robert Wagner, and called the **Wagner Act,** the National Labor Relations Act strengthened unions by putting the power of government behind workers' right to organize and to bargain with employers for wages and benefits. It created the National Labor Relations Board to ensure workers' rights—including their right to conduct elections to determine union representation—and to prevent unfair labor practices, such as firing or **blacklisting** workers for union activities. The act had its limitations. For example, it excluded many nonunionized workers as well as those in agriculture and service industries. Despite its limitations, the NLRA altered the relationships between business, labor, and the government and created a source of support for workers within the executive branch.

Waning of the New Deal

By the end of 1935, Roosevelt had effectively reasserted his leadership and popularity. The chances of a successful Republican or third-party challenge to the president were remote. In a less than enthusiastic convention, Republicans nominated **Alfred Landon**

of Kansas, the only Republican governor reelected in 1934. As governor, he had accepted and used most New Deal programs, but in keeping with party wishes he reluctantly attacked Roosevelt and the New Deal as destroying the values of America. As for Roosevelt's liberal critics, Huey Long was assassinated in 1935, and while Townsend and Coughlin continued to protest and formed a third party, the Union Party, they were no longer any threat to Roosevelt's reelection. Roosevelt followed a wise path, reminding voters of the New Deal's achievements and denouncing big business as greedy. It worked, and Roosevelt won in a landslide. Landon carried only two states, Maine and Vermont.

The Democratic victory demonstrated not only the personal appeal of Roosevelt but also the realignment of political forces accepting the concept of an activist New Deal that could provide social and economic gains. Roosevelt's second inaugural address, sometimes referred to as the "one-third speech," raised expectations of a Third Hundred Days. "I see millions of families trying to live on incomes so meager that the pall of family disaster hangs over them day by day," he announced. "I see one-third of a nation ill-housed, ill-clad, ill-nourished." The words seemed to promise new legislation aimed at helping the poor and the working class. But the Third Hundred Days failed to materialize.

Roosevelt did not have a good year in 1937, and the once-sprinting New Deal slowed to a crawl. Several factors contributed to the waning of public and political support for new programs. Roosevelt's mishandling of the Supreme Court and of the economy were two of the most important. Instead of promoting new social legislation, Roosevelt pitched his popularity against the Supreme Court—and lost. The president's anger at the High Court had been growing since the *Schechter* case, and as 1937 began, legal challenges to the Wagner Act and the Social Security Act were on the Court's docket. Roosevelt feared the

Wagner Act The National Labor Relations Act, a law passed by Congress in 1935 that defined unfair labor practices and protected unions against coercive measures such as blacklisting.

blacklisting Practice in which businesses share information to deny employment to workers known to belong to unions.

Alfred Landon Kansas governor who ran unsuccessfully for president on the Republican ticket in 1936.

Court was determined to undo the New Deal and sought to prevent it. Without consulting congressional leaders or close advisers, Roosevelt planned to enlarge the Court. His rationale was that the Court was overburdened and its elderly judges unable to meet the demands of the bench. He wanted the authority to add a new justice for every one over age 70 who had served more than ten years on the Court. Although changing the Court was a congressional power, many thought Roosevelt's "Court-packing plan" threatened the checks-and-balances system of government as established by the Constitution. The scheme was a major political miscalculation. Several Democrats, especially those in the South, saw an opportunity to safely break with the president and led opposition in the Senate. Roosevelt's effort was further weakened when the Court upheld a state's minimum wage law, the Wagner Act, and the Social Security system. After conservative justice Willis Van Devanter announced his retirement, Roosevelt dropped the issue and happily appointed Hugo Black, a southern New Dealer, to the Court. Justice Black was followed to the Court by eight other Roosevelt appointments.

Roosevelt now had a Court that accepted the philosophy of the New Deal, but he had lost valuable political control within his own party. Another setback that snagged the Roosevelt agenda was a recession, dubbed **Roosevelt's recession** by critics. Secretary of the Treasury Henry Morganthau pointed out that the economy was steady—industrial outputs had reached their 1929 levels, and unemployment had fallen to 14 percent—and he urged Roosevelt to reduce government spending. Hoping to move toward a more balanced budget, Roosevelt agreed and cut back programs. Relief programs were targeted, and nearly 1.5 million workers were released from the WPA. But the economy was not strong enough to cope with reduced government spending and thousands of people seeking jobs. Advocates thought that the private sector could absorb the released workers, but it could not and unemployment rapidly soared to 19 percent. The recovery collapsed, and in April 1938, Roosevelt restored spending. The WPA and other agencies subsequently rehired those released. But Roosevelt's sterling image of being able to manage recovery was tarnished. It was not just the Court-packing scheme and the recession that weakened the New Deal. People were also reacting to higher taxes, including payments into the Social Security system required by the Federal Insurance Contributions Act (FICA) of 1935, and labor strife. The public's mood had changed. The American

people, Hopkins observed, were now "bored with the poor, the unemployed, and the insecure."

Despite waning support for New Deal–style legislation, the administration managed to pass two more significant pieces of legislation (see Table 24.2). In 1938, a second Agricultural Adjustment Act that reestablished the principle of federally set quotas on specific commodities, acreage reduction, and parity payments was approved over conservative opposition. Frances Perkins considered passage of the **Fair Labor Standards Act** in 1938 as one of her major accomplishments. It addressed causes she had long championed, establishing a standard workweek (forty-four hours), setting a minimum wage (25 cents an hour), and outlawing child labor (under age 16). With its minimum-wage provision, the act was especially beneficial to unskilled, nonunion, and minority workers. It was also the last piece of New Deal legislation. In the November 1938 congressional elections, Roosevelt failed in his effort to get New Deal supporters elected and watched as Republicans increased in numbers and influence in Congress. The new Congress was more conservative and determined to derail any more of the president's "socialistic" ideas. Roosevelt recognized political reality and asked for no new domestic programs. The legislative New Deal was over, but the changes it generated would remain part of the American social, economic, and political culture. By 1939, the economy was recovering, reaching the point where it had been in 1929 and 1937, before the "Roosevelt recession." But unemployment and underemployment still persisted. Eight million were still unemployed, and there was no effort to provide more relief jobs or programs. Jobs and full "recovery" would have to wait until 1941, when the United States mobilized for a second world war. It would be spending connected with the war, and not the New Deal, that propelled the American economy out of the Depression and to new levels of prosperity.

Roosevelt's recession Economic downturn that occurred when Roosevelt, responding to improving economic figures, cut $4 billion from the federal budget, mostly by reducing relief spending.

Fair Labor Standards Act Law passed by Congress in 1938 that established a minimum wage and a maximum workweek and forbade labor by children under 16.

TABLE 24.2 Relief, Recovery, Reform, 1933–1938

Relief	Recovery	Reform
1933		
Civilian Conservation Corps (CCC)	Emergency Banking Relief Act	Beer and Wine Revenue Act (legalized the sale of beer and wine)
Federal Emergency Relief Act (FERA)	Tennessee Valley Authority Act (TVA)	Emergency Bank Act of 1933
Home Owners' Loan Corporation (HOLC)	Agricultural Adjustment Act (AAA)	
Public Works Administration (PWA)	National Recovery Administration (NRA)	Bank Act of 1933 (guaranteed deposits)
Civil Works Administration (CWA)		
1934		
National Housing Act	Gold Reserve Act (gold coins ceased to be legal tender)	Securities and Exchange Act Indian Reorganization Act
Federal Housing Administration (FHA)		Reciprocal Trade Agreements (encouraged bilateral treaties that lowered trade restrictions)
1935		
		National Labor Relations Act
Resettlement Administration (established model communities for those displaced by the Depression)		Rural Electrification Administration
National Youth Administration (NYA)		Social Security Act
Works Progress Administration (WPA)		Public Utility Holding Company Act (provided federal regulation of gas and electric holding companies)
Soil Conservation and Domestic Allocation Act		
1937		
Farm Security Administration (provided migrant camps for those displaced by the Depression)		National Housing Act (Wagner-Steagall Act) (established Housing Authority to provide funds to local agencies for low-income housing projects)
1938		
Second Agricultural Adjustment Act		Fair Labor Standards Act

When You
BUY an AUTOMOBILE
You GIVE
3 Months' Work
to Someone

Which
Allows
Him to
BUY
OTHER PRODUCTS

BUY A CAR NOW—HELP BRING BACK PROSPERITY

Recognizing the connection between sales and jobs, this ad asked readers to purchase an automobile and keep workers working so that they too could spend and stimulate the economy. Unfortunately, the number of people with enough money to spend was never enough to rekindle the economy and the Depression continued. *Private collection.*

Surviving the Depression

■ Amid the sweeping social changes taking place during the Depression, how did Americans manage to hold on to social and cultural values?

■ What opportunities opened for women and minorities— African Americans, Hispanics, Asians, and Native Americans— and what challenges faced these groups as an outcome of the Depression?

One reason the New Deal was able to establish new paths of government responsibility was that the Depression touched every segment of American life. Poverty and hardship were no longer reserved for those viewed as unworthy or relegated to remote ar-

eas and inner cities. Now poverty included blue- and white-collar workers, and even some of the once-rich. American industry, according to *Fortune,* suffered 46 percent unemployment, but in many areas it was much worse. In Gary, Indiana, nearly the entire working class was out of a job by 1932. Average annual income dropped 35 percent—from $2,300 to $1,500—by 1933. Although income rose after 1933, most Americans worried about their futures and economic insecurity. Would the next day bring a reduction in wages, the loss of a job, or the closing of a business? Some saw their businesses go bankrupt and found new careers. E. Y. Harburg lost his family's hardware store, borrowed $500 from a friend, and started writing songs—striking a common plea with "Brother, Can You Spare a Dime?" Others worked for less, lost and found other jobs, or, disheartened, accepted relief.

Coping with the Depression

To help those facing economic insecurity, magazines and newspapers provided useful hints and "Depression recipes" that stretched budgets and included information about nutrition. According to trained home economists, a careful shopper could feed a family of five on as little as $8 a week. This was comforting news for those with that much to spend, but for many families and for relief agencies $8 a week for food was beyond possibility. To feed his family of seven, Angelos Douvitos received work relief from Ann Arbor, Michigan, at 30 cents an hour and took home a mere $4.20 a week. New York City provided only $2.39 a week for each family. Things were bad, comedian Groucho Marx joked, when "pigeons started feeding people in Central Park."

Like New York, most towns and cities by 1933 had little ability to provide more than the smallest amount of relief and were unsuccessfully struggling to maintain basic city services. Experiencing a shrinking tax base, local, county, and state governments were forced to lay off teachers, policemen, and other workers. The city commissioner of Birmingham, Alabama, was typical when he said, "I am as much in favor of relief . . . as anyone, but I am unwilling to continue this relief at the expense of bankrupting . . . Birmingham." The New Deal provided relief for cities like Birmingham as programs such as the HOLC and the FHA saved homes, stimulated urban and suburban growth, and restored local tax bases. Federal relief agencies, especially the PWA and the WPA, not only provided civic improvements—constructing schools, post offices, and hospitals and repairing roads and bridges—but also through their jobs reduced local

Throughout the Depression, the most popular form of entertainment was the movies, providing escape from daily hardships into a prosperous world of fantasy. At 20 cents a ticket, movies attracted as many as 75 million people a week. In this photo, taken at a movie theater in San Diego, children display door prizes given during the matinee. *San Diego Historical Society, Photograph Collection.*

relief responsibilities. Chicago's Mayor Edward Kelly credited New Deal funds for saving Chicago. "Roosevelt is my religion," he announced during his campaign. In rural towns and city neighborhoods in the West, a variety of federal programs kept crumbling communities together. In North Dakota it was estimated that two-thirds of the people drew some form of federal relief. Use of the New Deal drastically altered the relationship between local and national government. Increasingly people saw the national government as having an obligation to support families and communities against economic adversity.

"Making Do"—Families and the Depression

With or without governmental aid, "Use it up, wear it out, make it do, or do without" became the motto of most American families. In many working-class and middle-class neighborhoods, "making do" meant that many homes sprouted signs announcing a variety of services—household beauty parlors, kitchen bakeries, rooms for boarders. A Milwaukee wife recalled, "I did baking at home to supplement our income. I got 9 cents for a loaf of bread and 25 cents for an apple cake. . . . I cleared about $65 a month." A

Singer sewing machine salesman commented that he was selling more and more machines to people who in the past would not have sewn. Feed sacks became a source of material. "I grew up in a small, exclusive suburb," recalled Florence Davis, who remembered her mother making a pretty new school dress out of one sack that had "a sky-blue background with gorgeous mallard ducks on it."

Still, even with "making do," many families—especially in the working class—failed, losing first jobs, then homes. Once evicted, fortunate families moved in with relatives. Don Blincoe remembered that during the Depression most households were like his, "where father, mother, children, aunts, uncles and grandma lived together." Approximately one-sixth of America's urban families "doubled up." Millions of others took to the road. Over 3 million, as in John Steinbeck's *Grapes of Wrath* (1939), loaded their meager possessions on their jalopies and traveled across the country looking for jobs. Many trekked toward California, whose population by the end of the decade had jumped by over a million. Others found their families and lives torn apart. Those called "hobos" rode the rails, hitching rides in boxcars, living in shantytowns—"Hoovervilles"—begging and scrounging for food and supplies along the road. Records show increased numbers of suicides, people admitted to state mental hospitals, and children placed in orphanages. Some worried about the psychological problems created as women and children replaced husbands and fathers as breadwinners. A social worker wrote: "I used to see men cry because they didn't have a job."

Despite the hardships and migrations, American society did not collapse, as some had predicted. The vast majority of Americans clung tightly to traditional social norms and even expanded family togetherness. Economic necessity kept families at home. They played board games and cards, read books and magazines, and tended vegetable and flower gardens. The game of *Monopoly* was introduced, allowing players to fantasize about becoming millionaires. Church attendance rose, and the number of divorces declined. Fewer people got married and the birth rate fell. But marriages were only delayed, and the lower birth rate resulted not so much from economic fears as from the increased availability of birth-control devices.

Movies and radio provided a break from the woes of the Depression. On a national average, 60 percent of the people saw a movie a week. Movies not only offered escape from the daily routine; some also reflected the social and political changes of the decade. The musical *Golddiggers of 1933* delighted audiences with its cheerful music, lavish sets, and attractive chorus line, but it also contained social commentary. As unemployed men march across the stage, a singer reminds viewers:

Remember my forgotten man,
You put a rifle in his hand,
You sent him far away,
You shouted, "Hip Hooray!"
But look at him today.

Gangster films remained popular but underwent a change as Roosevelt entered office. In the early thirties, the popular actors frequently played heroic but doomed gangsters, but by the mid-thirties many of those stars now played the brave government officials who brought villains to justice. James Cagney underwent such a character change in *G-Men*, abandoning his usual tough-guy mobster image to portray a dedicated FBI agent protecting average citizens. The plots of romantic comedies revolved around romances between people of opposite social and economic backgrounds, comparing the wisdom and honesty of the common American to the snobbish, selfish values of the upper class. Inevitably love and common sense prevailed.

Novels, however, were frequently more critical of American society, culture, and politics. Many authors stressed the immorality of capitalism and the inequities caused by racism and class differences. They focused on the plight of workers, minorities, and the poor and found heroes among those who refused to break under the strain of the Depression and society's inhumanity. Steinbeck's *The Grapes of Wrath* (1939), Erskine Caldwell's *Tobacco Road* (1932), and Richard Wright's *Native Son* (1940) featured "losers" but showed that their misery was not of their own making, but rather society's fault. In these and similar novels, writers assailed the rich and powerful and praised the humanitarian spirit and fair play of the poor.

The largest audience was reached by radio, which was heard in nearly 90 percent of American households. It provided another avenue of escape from the concerns of the Depression. Crooners like Rudy Vallee and Bing Crosby, afternoon soap operas, quiz shows, and "gloom chasers"—comedians such as the Marx Brothers and George Burns and Gracie Allen—filled the airways. Crime fighters like the Green Hornet, Dick Tracy, and the Lone Ranger and Tonto proved again and again that truth, justice, honor, and courage triumphed. Comic strip heroes Superman (1938) and Batman (1939) also protected downtrodden workers and minorities from harm and oppression. Radio was also a powerful means for both Franklin and Eleanor Roosevelt to reach huge audiences with their visions of government, the New Deal, and hopes for America.

Women and Minorities in the Depression

Depression and the New Deal provided mixed experiences for women and minorities. As unemployment rose, so too did pressures not to hire women or minorities. Emphasizing traditional roles in American society, public opinion polls consistently found that as unemployment rose, most people, including women, believed that men, not women, should have jobs. This was particularly true of married women, and in many cases companies chose not to hire married women, especially in professional and higher-paying jobs. The number of women in the professions declined from 14.2 to 12.3 percent during the Depression years. Teachers were particularly vulnerable. One survey found that of 1,500 school districts, 77 percent did not hire married women, and 63 percent had fired women when they married. By 1932, 2 million women were out of work, and an estimated 145,000 women were homeless, wandering across

Giving Her a Lift to Town · · · · · · · · —By Knott

President Franklin D. Roosevelt campaigned on helping the "forgotten man." As shown in this political cartoon, as First Lady, Eleanor Roosevelt did not forget women. She worked diligently to ensure that they benefited from the New Deal and had access to government and the Democratic Party. *Franklin D. Roosevelt Library.*

America. But employment patterns were uneven. Women in low-paying and low-status jobs were less likely to be laid off and more likely to find employment. In Detroit, automakers preferred to hire women at 4 cents an hour rather than pay a man 10 cents an hour. White women also took jobs away from minorities, especially in domestic service.

Few working women, however, found that bringing home the paycheck changed their status or role within the family. Husbands still maintained authority and dominance in the home, even if unemployed.

Rarely did husbands help with work around the house. One husband agreed to help with the laundry but refused to hang the wash outside for fear that neighbors might see him. At home women renewed and reaffirmed traditional roles: they sewed, baked bread, and canned fruits and vegetables. As wives and mothers, if not workers, women were praised as pillars of stability in a changing and perilous society. Reflecting on her own steadiness, one woman remembered, "I did what I had to do. I seemed to always find a way to make things work."

While the Depression's economic impact on women was mixed, it only intensified the economic and social difficulties for minorities. African Americans, Hispanics, and Asians faced increased racial hostility and demands that they give up their jobs to whites. In Tucson, Arizona, "Mexicans" were accused of "taking the bread out of our white children's mouths." Low-paying, frequently temporary jobs and high unemployment made life in the *colonias* deplorable, where, according to one observer, mothers and children went "up and down alleys, searching . . . for cast-off food." Throughout the Southwest, the United States Immigration Bureau worked with local authorities to facilitate repatriation of Mexican nationals to Mexico. To encourage their return to Mexico, many local and state agencies gave free transportation to the border for those willing to leave. In some cities, such as Los Angeles, as early as 1931, the Immigration Bureau conducted sweeps of Mexican American communities intended to scare Mexicans into leaving. Facing a lack of jobs and Anglo pressure, more than half a million Mexicans did leave the United States by 1937. Those who remained found fewer jobs and lower pay. On farms in California, the average yearly wage for Latinos was $289—about a third of what the government estimated it took to maintain a subsistence budget.

Officials made no effort to repatriate Asians living on the West Coast, but Asian immigrants and Asian Americans remained isolated, ignored in their ethnic enclaves, and received inadequate relief. In San Francisco, where nearly one-sixth of the Asian population picked up benefits, they received from 10 to 20 percent less than whites because relief agencies somehow concluded that Asians could subsist on a less

colonias   Village settlements of Mexicans and Mexican Americans, frequently constructed by or for migrant citrus workers in southern California.

expensive diet. Hoping to remove economic and social barriers, some sought to assimilate, becoming "200 percent Americans." The Japanese American Citizens League was organized in 1929 to overcome discrimination and oppose anti-Asian legislation, but by 1940 the group had made little headway.

Before 1929, African Americans working as sharecroppers, farm hands, and tenant farmers in the South already were experiencing depression conditions, earning only about $200 a year. Their lives worsened as farm prices continued to fall and as the number of evictions rose during the Depression. Many decided to leave and migrated to urban areas, seeking more economic security. Cities, however, provided few opportunities because whites were taking jobs previously held by African Americans, including low-paying and low-status domestic service jobs typically held by black women. In most cases, joblessness among African Americans in urban areas averaged 20 to 50 percent higher than for whites. Compounding the high unemployment, across the nation blacks faced increased racial hostility, violence, and intimidation. In 1931 the attention of the nation was drawn to Scottsboro, Alabama, where nine black men had been arrested and charged with raping two white prostitutes. Although no physical evidence linked the men to any crime, a jury of white males did not question the testimony of the women and quickly found the so-called **Scottsboro Nine** guilty. Eight were sentenced to death; the ninth, a minor, escaped the death penalty. Through appeals, intervention by the Supreme Court, retrials, parole, and escape, all those convicted were free by 1950.

A New Deal for Women and Minorities

Like the Depression, the New Deal impacted women and minorities in different ways, but generally it inspired a belief that the Roosevelt government cared and was trying to improve their lives. Eleanor Roosevelt was at the center of this image of compassion. She frequently acted as the social conscience of the administration and prodded her husband and other New Dealers not to forget women and minorities. "I'm the agitator," she said. "He's the politician." She crossed the country meeting and listening to people. She received thousands of letters that described people's hardships and asked for help. Although she was rarely able to provide any direct assistance, her replies emphasized hope and pointed to the changes being made by the New Deal.

Within the White House, she helped convene a special White House conference on the needs of women in 1933 and, with the help of Frances Perkins, Ellen Woodward, and other women in the administration, worked to ensure that women received more than just token consideration from New Deal agencies. Woodward, who served as assistant director of the FERA and the WPA, was especially successful in promoting women's programs, headed by women. With Eleanor Roosevelt as role model and advocate, the New Deal provided more opportunities for women in government and politics than at any other time in American history.

Yet the New Deal developed only a few programs for women and frequently paid women less than men for the same work. Women made up only 10 percent of the WPA's work force, and most of them were placed in programs that focused on traditional women's skills, such as sewing, which was the largest WPA program for women. In Texas, the state legislature mandated that women, especially minority women, were to be trained only in cooking, cleaning, and sewing. Passage of the Social Security Act and the Fair Labor Standards Act also ignored the needs of many women. Both acts excluded coverage of domestic workers and waitresses, professions largely composed of women.

For African Americans and Hispanics, the Roosevelts and the New Deal provided a large amount of hope and a lesser amount of change. More African Americans than ever before were appointed to government positions. Educator Mary Bethune headed the Division of Negro Affairs within the National Youth Administration and in 1936 organized African Americans in the administration into a **"Black Cabinet"** that met in her home and acted as a semiofficial advisory commission on racial relations. "We must think in terms of a 'whole' for the greatest service of our people," she said. Among the most pressing needs, the "Black Cabinet" concluded, was access to

Scottsboro Nine   Nine African Americans convicted of raping two white women in a freight train in Alabama in 1931; their case became famous as an example of racism in the legal system.

Black Cabinet   Semiofficial advisory committee on racial affairs organized by Mary McLeod Bethune in 1936 and made up of African American members of the Roosevelt administration.

In 1935 Mary McLeod Bethune (*front center*), became the first African American woman to hold a high-ranking government position, serving as the director of the Division of Negro Affairs in the National Youth Administration. Here, she is shown with the Council of Negro Women, which she helped organize in 1935 to focus on the problems faced by African Americans at the national level. *New York Public Library, Schomburg Center for Research in Black Culture.*

relief and jobs. The New Deal provided both, but never to the extent needed. Some New Deal administrators, notably Ickes and Hopkins, took steps to ensure that the PWA, WPA, and other New Deal agencies included minorities, especially African Americans. In northern cities, the WPA and the PWA nearly eliminated discrimination from their programs, but they had less success in other parts of the nation, where skilled African American workers were given menial minimum-wage jobs. Other agencies were less supportive. The Civilian Conservation Corps and the Tennessee Valley Authority practiced segregation and wage discrimination. Still, by 1938, nearly 30 percent of African Americans were receiving some federal relief, with the WPA alone supporting almost a million African American families. But even in the best of cases, it was not enough. In Cleveland, 40 percent of PWA jobs were reserved for African Americans, but there, as across the nation, black unemployment and poverty remained higher than for whites.

The Roosevelt administration also shrank from supporting civil rights legislation. When confronted by black leaders for his refusal to promote an anti-lynching law, Roosevelt explained, "If I come out for the anti-lynching bill now, they will block every bill I ask Congress to pass . . . I just can't take that risk." Again, acting as an advocate, Eleanor Roosevelt was willing to take more risks and visibly supported equality for minorities. In 1939, when the Daughters of the American Revolution refused to allow renowned black opera singer Marian Anderson to sing at their concert hall in Washington, the First Lady resigned her membership and helped arrange a public concert on the steps of the Lincoln Memorial. Anderson's performance before Lincoln's statue attracted more than 75,000 people.

Hispanics benefited from the New Deal in much the same way as African Americans—indirectly. In New Mexico and other western states, the Depression curtailed much of the migratory farm work for Mexican American workers, devastating local economies. New Deal agencies such as the CCC, PWA, and WPA provided welcome jobs and income. A worker in a CCC camp in northern New Mexico remembered, "I

In San Antonio, Texas, many Mexican Americans held jobs as pecan shellers and were among the worst paid in the nation—sometimes working a 54-hour week for only $3. *Benson Latin American Collection, University of Texas at Austin.*

had plenty to eat, . . . I had brand new clothes when I went to the CCC camps." Throughout the Southwest, federal relief agencies not only included Mexican Americans but also sometimes paid wages that exceeded what they received in the **private sector.** The WPA paid $8.54 a week for unskilled labor, whereas a comparable job in the private sector would have yielded an average of $6.02 or less. Discrimination, however, was still practiced, and enhanced by language differences.

New Deal legislation also helped union organizers trying to assist Hispanic workers throughout the West. San Antonio's Mexican American pecan shellers, mostly women, were among the lowest-paid workers in the country, earning less than 4 cents per pound of shelled pecans, which amounted to an annual wage of less than $180. In 1934, 1935, and again in 1938, CIO organizers, including local activist "Red" Emma Tenayuca, led the pecan shellers in strikes, finally gaining higher wages and union recognition in 1938. However, not every New Deal administrator or agency was committed to aiding minorities. In the fields of central California, local authorities supported growers; Mexican American unions had little success and received negligible support from the federal government. Nor did the New Deal lessen efforts to repatriate Mexicans to Mexico.

Despite its limitations, the New Deal provided hope and support for many women and minorities, who in turn praised Roosevelt. "The WPA came along, and Roosevelt came to be a god," said one African American. "You worked, you got a paycheck, and you had some dignity." Politically, such sentiments were more than praise because where they could vote, minorities voted for Roosevelt and the Democratic Party. Blacks bolted the Republican Party and enlisted in extraordinary numbers in the Democratic Party. In the 1936 presidential election, Roosevelt carried every black ward in Cleveland and, nationally, received nearly 90 percent of the black vote. By 1939, the Democratic Party again was emphasizing its working-class orientation, supplying a political vehicle for the aspirations of industrial workers, minorities, and farmers.

While most minorities benefited only indirectly from the New Deal, that was not the case for Native Americans. Native Americans had two strong supporters in Secretary of the Interior Ickes and Commissioner of Indian Affairs John Collier. Both opposed existing Indian policies that since 1887 had sought to destroy the reservation system and eradicate Indian cultures. At Collier's urging, Congress passed the **Indian Reorganization Act** in 1934. The act returned land and community control to tribal organizations. It provided Indian self-rule on the reservations and

private sector Businesses run by private citizens rather than by the government.
Indian Reorganization Act Law passed by Congress in 1934 that ended Indian allotment and returned surplus land to tribal ownership; it also sought to encourage tribal self-government and to improve economic conditions on reservations.

John Collier worked to ensure the passage of the Indian Reorganization Act. Designed to restore tribal sovereignty under federal authority, each tribe had to ratify the act to participate. Not all tribes did; seventy-seven rejected it, including the Navajos, the nation's largest tribe. This photo shows a group of Navajos meeting with Collier to discuss government-imposed limitations on the number of sheep each Navajo could own. *Wide World Photos.*

prevented individual ownership of tribal lands. To improve the squalid conditions found on most reservations and to provide jobs, Collier organized a CCC-type agency for Indians and ensured that other New Deal agencies played a part in improving Indian lands and providing jobs. He also promoted Native American culture. Working with tribal leaders, Collier took measures to protect, preserve, and encourage Indian customs, languages, religions, and folkways. Reservation school curricula incorporated Indian languages and customs, and Native Americans could once more openly and freely exercise their religions. While a positive effort, Collier's New Deal for Native Americans did little to improve the standard of living for most American Indians. Funds were too few, and the problems created by years of poverty and government neglect were too great. At best, Collier's programs slowed a long-standing economic decline and allowed Native Americans to regain some control over their cultures and societies.

Individual Voices

Examining a Primary Source

Frances Perkins Explains the Social Security Act

On September 2, 1935, Secretary of Labor Frances Perkins spoke over the radio to countless Americans to explain the importance of the recently passed Social Security Act. As the Social Security bill was being drafted and considered by Congress, it had come under attack from the right and the left. Conservatives argued that the bill imposed "big government" into an area best served by private and individual efforts. Liberals objected that it was not inclusive enough, leaving out large segments of the work force and providing no health benefits. Perkins's speech was for many Americans the first explanation they had heard of how the new act would change their lives. In this excerpt from her radio address, Madam Secretary Perkins underscores not only what the new law will accomplish for those participating in the program but also how the milestone legislation charts new territory for the federal government.

■What type of worker is most likely to receive an old-age pension? What type of worker would be less likely?

People who work for a living in the United States . . . can join with all other good citizens . . . in satisfaction that the Congress has passed the Social Security Act. . . . It provides for old-age pensions which mark great progress over the measures upon which we have hitherto depended in caring for those who have been unable to provide for the years when they no longer can work. It also provides security for dependent and crippled children, mothers, the indigent disabled and the blind.

■A Mississippi newspaper in 1935 argued that the Social Security plan was a bad one because it would provide a pension to African Americans, who would then live idly on their benefits "while cotton and corn crops are crying for workers." How do you think Perkins would have answered this charge?

Old-age benefits in the form of monthly payments are to be paid to individuals who have worked and contributed to the insurance fund in direct proportion to the total wages earned by such individuals in the course of their employment subsequent to 1936. The minimum monthly payment is to be $10, the maximum $85. These payments will begin in the year 1942 and will be to those who have worked and contributed. ■

Because of difficulty of administration not all employments are covered in this plan at this time . . . but it is sufficiently broad to cover all normally employed industrial workers. . . . It is a sound and reasonable plan. . . . It does not represent a complete solution to the problems of economic security, but it does represent a substantial, necessary beginning. ■

This is truly legislation in the interest of the national welfare . . . its enactment into law would not only carry us a long way toward the goal of economic security for the individual, but also a long way toward the promotion and stabilization of mass purchasing power without which the present economic system cannot endure. . . . ■

■The Roosevelt administration believed that the Social Security program was an important reform in preventing another depression. Why would they believe that?

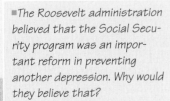

■*In what ways does Perkins's speech respond to the criticisms of conservatives? Of liberals?*

. . . The passage of this act . . . with so much intelligent public support is deeply significant of the progress which the American people have made in . . . using cooperation through government to overcome social hazards against which the individual alone is inadequate. ■

Summary

From 1929 to 1939, the Great Depression brought about significant changes in the nature of American life, altering expectations of government, society, and the economy. When Hoover assumed the presidency, most Americans believed that the economy and the quality of life would continue to improve. The Depression changed that. The flaws in the economy, largely hidden by the apparent prosperity of the 1920s, were suddenly exposed as the stock market crashed and legions of banks and businesses closed. Unemployment soared, and people lost their homes and their hope in the future.

More than previous presidents, Hoover expanded the role of the federal government to meet the economic and social crises. He initiated a series of measures, including the Reconstruction Finance Corporation, which tried to stimulate the economy. But Hoover's philosophy of limited government undermined the effort, and the economy continued to worsen. Losing faith in Hoover, most Americans put their faith instead in Roosevelt and his 1932 campaign promise of a New Deal. Roosevelt won easily and took office amid widespread expectations for a major shift in the role of government. The New Deal was launched, working to regenerate economic growth, aid millions of needy Americans, and institute reforms that further regulated the economy and ensured a more equitable society. The First Hundred Days witnessed a barrage of legislation, most dealing with the immediate problems of unemployment and economic collapse. The Agricultural Adjustment Administration (AAA) and the National Recovery Administration (NRA) were designed to restore the economy,

while a variety of relief programs such as the Civilian Conservation Corps (CCC) and the Public Works Administration (PWA) put people to work.

In 1935, assailed by both liberals and conservatives, Roosevelt responded with a second burst of legislation that focused more on social legislation and putting people to work than on programs for business-oriented recovery. The overwhelming Democratic victory in 1936 confirmed the popularity of Roosevelt and the changes brought by his New Deal, and raised expectations of further social and economic regulatory legislation. A Third Hundred Days, however, never materialized. The Court-packing scheme, an economic downturn, labor unrest, and growing conservatism generated more political opposition than New Deal forces could overcome. The outcome was that the New Deal wound down after 1937.

The Depression affected all Americans, as they had to adjust their values and lifestyles to meet the economic and psychological crisis. People worried about economic insecurity, but industrial workers and minorities were the most likely to face hard times and carried the extra burdens of discrimination and loss of status. Lives were disrupted, homes and businesses lost, but most people learned to cope with the Great Depression and hoped for better times.

Roosevelt and the New Deal provided new reasons for hope and made coping easier. Farmers, blue-collar workers, women, and minorities directly and indirectly benefited from the New Deal. The Home Owners' Loan Corporation (HOLC) and the Federal Housing Administration (FHA) saved thousands of homes; the Social Security Act provided some with retirement funds and established a national network of unemployment compensation; and the Fair Labor Standards Act guaranteed a minimum wage. But more than specific programs, the New Deal provided a sense of hope and a growing expectation about government's role in promoting the economy and providing for the welfare of those in need.

The New Deal never fully restored the economy, but it engineered a profound shift in the nature of government and in society's expectations about the federal government's role in people's lives. After the New Deal, neither the economy, nor society, nor government and politics would ever be the same.

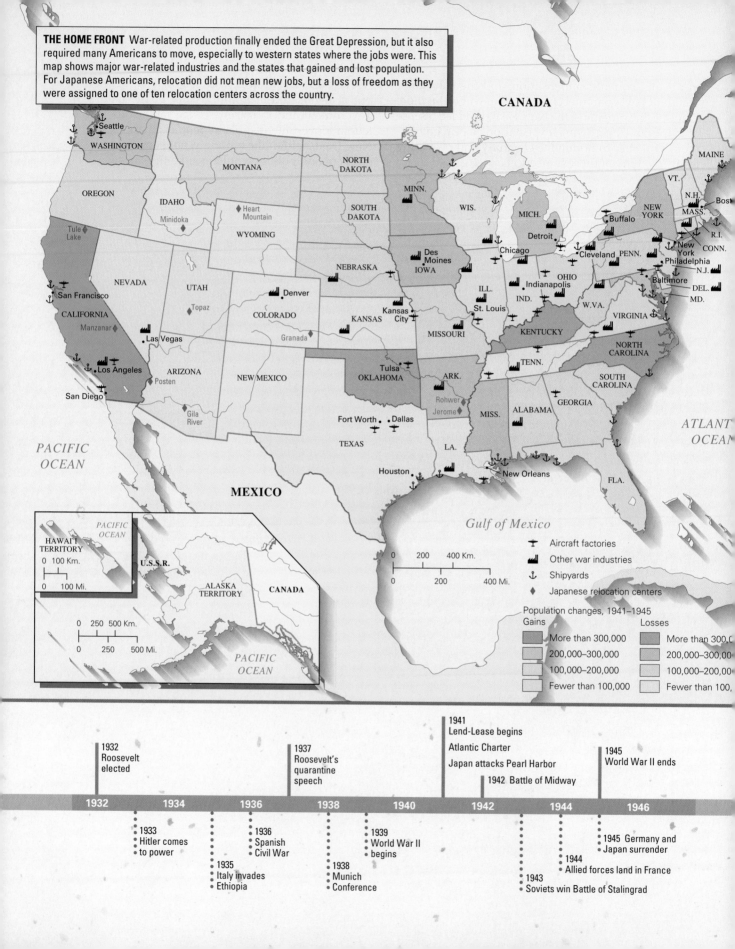

THE HOME FRONT War-related production finally ended the Great Depression, but it also required many Americans to move, especially to western states where the jobs were. This map shows major war-related industries and the states that gained and lost population. For Japanese Americans, relocation did not mean new jobs, but a loss of freedom as they were assigned to one of ten relocation centers across the country.

CANADA

WASHINGTON · Seattle

OREGON

MONTANA

IDAHO
Minidoka

Heart Mountain

WYOMING

NORTH DAKOTA

SOUTH DAKOTA

MINN.

WIS.

MICH.
· Buffalo
Detroit

MAINE

VT. N.H. Bos
NEW YORK MASS.
R.I.
New York CONN.
Philadelphia N.J.
Baltimore DEL.
MD.

Tule Lake

NEVADA

UTAH
Topaz

San Francisco

CALIFORNIA
Manzanar

· Las Vegas

Los Angeles

San Diego

ARIZONA
Posten

Gila River

COLORADO
· Denver

Granada

NEW MEXICO

NEBRASKA

Des Moines
IOWA

KANSAS

Kansas City

Chicago

ILL.

St. Louis

MISSOURI

Indianapolis
IND.

OHIO

KENTUCKY

TENN.

ARK.

Rohwer
Jerome

MISS.

ALABAMA

Tulsa
OKLAHOMA

Fort Worth · Dallas

TEXAS

LA.

Houston

New Orleans

W.VA.

VIRGINIA

NORTH CAROLINA

SOUTH CAROLINA

GEORGIA

PENN.
Cleveland

FLA.

PACIFIC OCEAN

MEXICO

ATLANT OCEAN

Gulf of Mexico

HAWAII TERRITORY

PACIFIC OCEAN

0 100 Km.
0 100 Mi.

U.S.S.R.

ALASKA TERRITORY

CANADA

PACIFIC OCEAN

0 250 500 Km.
0 250 500 Mi.

0 200 400 Km.
0 200 400 Mi.

Aircraft factories
Other war industries
Shipyards
Japanese relocation centers

Population changes, 1941–1945

Gains	Losses
More than 300,000	More than 300,0
200,000–300,000	200,000–300,00
100,000–200,000	100,000–200,00
Fewer than 100,000	Fewer than 100,

1932
Roosevelt elected

1937
Roosevelt's quarantine speech

1941
Lend-Lease begins
Atlantic Charter
Japan attacks Pearl Harbor
1942 Battle of Midway

1945
World War II ends

1932	1934	1936	1938	1940	1942	1944	1946

1933
Hitler comes to power

1936
Spanish Civil War

1939
World War II begins

1945 Germany and Japan surrender

1935
Italy invades Ethiopia

1938
Munich Conference

1944
Allied forces land in France

1943
Soviets win Battle of Stalingrad

America's Rise to World Leadership, 1929–1945

25

The Home Front

In 1941, the United States left the Depression behind and geared up to be the "arsenal of democracy." Examine the map on the facing page: What linkages do you see between population changes and the growth of the defense industry?

Individual Choices

SYBIL LEWIS

World War II caused a massive migration of African Americans to the West Coast, looking for jobs and a better life. Facing the possibility of a segregated life as a domestic worker, Sybil Lewis, like thousands of other black women, took the opportunity created by war. She found work in the defense industries of southern California, learning skills that before the war were denied to most, if not all, women. Echoing the views of Sybil Lewis, another African American stated, "Hitler was the one that got us out of the white folks' kitchen." For Sybil Lewis and others, the war provided an opportunity for a profound change in their lives—Sybil Lewis never returned to the kitchen. In this picture a pair of riveters work on a section of an airplane—both contributing to the war effort and changing American society. *Courtesy of the Boeing Company.*

Sybil Lewis

Sybil Lewis chose California. Out of 340,000 Americans who came to Los Angeles during the Second World War, she was among the over 140,000 African Americans. She, like others, had heard that California was a better place—a place with jobs for blacks and women, a place *without* segregation. Indeed, jobs were available, at first primarily for domestic workers, but by 1943 more and more wartime industries looked to African Americans to fill their labor shortages. Employers frequently preferred to hire black women for these industrial jobs instead of men. Reflecting the racism of the day, employers believed that hiring black men would threaten existing racial lines and set a worrisome precedent: African American men would no doubt seek similar employment once the war was finished. But women, everyone understood, clearly were only temporary hires and could be easily dismissed at war's end. The same was true of residential patterns. Although Los Angeles endorsed no legal segregation, African Americans found housing available only in a few areas of town and encountered white hostility if they sought to live outside those sections. Consequently, most blacks lived in the central part of Los Angeles, in areas like Watts and "Bronzeville." Bronzeville had been "Little Tokyo" before the war and had housed nearly 30,000 Japanese Americans. Following Japanese removal, Bronzeville became home to nearly 80,000 African Americans.

Sybil Lewis came from a small, segregated town in Oklahoma where she had worked as a maid, doing ironing and washing and earning $3.50 a week. Arriving in California, she saw both sides of Los Angeles. She noted that African Americans, especially women, were working in occupations unavailable to them in the South. She also observed white and "black people in the school system." It seemed a much more open society, where blacks had better opportunities and lives. But she also experienced prejudice and segregation, not only because she was black and a woman but because she was also an "Okie."

Vowing never to be a maid again, she searched the want ads for a job. Bending under federal pressure and the need for workers, Lockheed Aircraft was willing to hire and train minorities and women to work in their plant. Sybil Lewis applied, and after several attempts—"You had to be pretty persistent"—she was hired. Along with other women, she received a quick training program that taught her how to rivet. Riveting was a two-person operation. The riveter operated the rivet gun while another, the "bucker," used a heavy bar on the opposite side to expand and smooth the rivets as they came through. Sybil was selected to be a riveter and considered it a skilled position, unlike that of the bucker, which required more muscle than skill.

The new job not only provided Sybil a skill but placed her and others into a new environment that broke old patterns. She was paired with a white woman from Arkansas. Both had been raised in segregated societies and now found themselves working side by side as a team. It was a new experience. At first both were uncomfortable, but each learned to adapt. "I feel that the experience was meaningful to

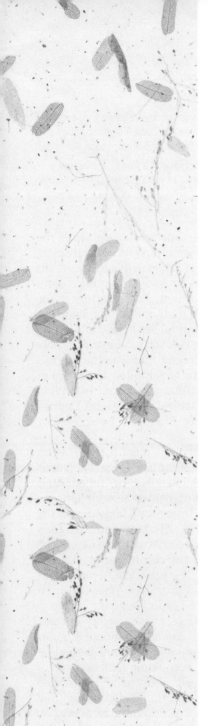

me and meaningful to her," Sybil wrote. "She learned that Negroes were people too, and I saw her as a person also, and we both gained from it." Another new experience was the pay, more money than she would ever have made in Oklahoma. She recalled, "When I got my first paycheck, I'd never seen that much money before." Overwhelmed to have made more than $350 in one month, she immediately treated herself to new clothes and shoes.

Sybil enjoyed working at Lockheed despite the occasional taunts, mostly from men, about her color and sex. Then, for no apparent reason, the foreman told her that she and her bucker were going to switch positions. "I wasn't failing as a riveter," she remembered. "In fact, the other girl learned to rivet from me." Although told that it was company policy to cross-train workers, she believed that "they gave me the job of bucker because I was black." Unwilling to accept what she considered a demotion, Sybil quit.

Next, Sybil Lewis became an arc welder in a shipyard. Arc welding was a higher skill and welders made more money ($1.20 an hour) than riveters. Again, she liked her job and her pay, but at the shipyards she encountered a form of discrimination that had been less obvious at Lockheed. Male welders made more money for doing the same job. While differential pay was a common practice, Sybil Lewis considered it unfair and asked why. "You'd ask about this," she said, "but they'd say . . . 'The men have to lift some heavy pieces of steel and you don't have to.'" She rejected that logic: "I had to help lift steel too." Not only was she getting less pay, she also noticed that she got less respect when she wore slacks. Confronting a male worker, she asked why. The response was, "You have a man's job and you're getting paid almost the same, so we don't have to give you a seat anymore, or show the common courtesies that men show women." That too, she thought, did not seem right. Less troublesome to Sybil Lewis was the knowledge that her position was temporary. "We were trained to do this kind of work because of the war. . . . We were all told that when the war was over we would not be needed anymore."

When Japan surrendered in August 1945, Sybil Lewis, like millions of other Americans, celebrated and cheered herself hoarse. When the cheering stopped, she planned her next move. "I realized that the good jobs, all of the advantages that had been offered because of the war . . . were over." She knew what she wanted to do, and with her savings to support her, she enrolled in college. Graduating, she found a position in the California civil service, where she worked until retirement. Looking back on her experiences, she stated, "The war changed my life, gave me an opportunity to leave my small town and discover there was another way of life. It . . . opened my eyes to opportunities I could take advantage of when the war was over." Sybil Lewis was not alone in having her life changed by the war. It had touched every American, altering their lives and society, but it also drastically changed the role of the United States in world affairs.

INTRODUCTION

The Great Depression was not only an American disaster—it impacted the entire world causing governments and the international system to collapse. Three nations especially seemed intent on changing the international system and almost eager to use military force to achieve their goals. Japan, seeking raw materials and markets, began the process of dismantling the peace when it annexed Manchuria in 1931. Adolf Hitler and the National Socialist (Nazi) Party assumed power in Germany, determined to make their country a major military power again. To the south in Italy, Benito Mussolini was using Italian nationalism to expand his imperial designs. When Hoover left office in 1933, the cheery optimism of a prosperous world at peace that had greeted him had vanished.

Between 1933 and 1939, Roosevelt wrestled with two problems: how to improve U.S. economic and political positions abroad while protecting economic and political interests at home. Although he wanted the country to take a more active role in world affairs, he understood the political realities: isolationist views among the public and in Congress were strong, and his first priority was American economic recovery. Focusing on the Depression, the president deferred to an isolationist Congress as world peace evaporated. The onslaught of the war in Europe in 1939 provided Roosevelt with new opportunities to chart a path toward international activism. Deciding that the United States must help Britain defeat Hitler, Roosevelt provided economic and military assistance to Britain. To check Japanese expansion, he used trade restrictions. Japan's attack on Pearl Harbor in December 1941 drew the United States into World War II.

The war managed to do what the New Deal had not—restore American prosperity. The full mobilization of the United States' resources resulted in full employment and unparalleled cooperation among business, labor, and government. As over 15 million Americans marched off to war, those at home, like Sybil Lewis, faced new challenges and opportunities. The result for women and minorities was mixed: they experienced greater opportunities, but they also were expected by most to relinquish their newfound status once the war ended.

In planning for a European and Pacific war, Roosevelt chose to allocate most of the nation's resources to defeat Hitler. Victory over Japan would have to wait. Allied with Britain and the Soviet Union, the United States began its efforts to liberate Europe by invading North Africa and Italy before invading France. In the Pacific, the victory at Midway gave the United States a naval and air advantage that allowed American forces to close the circle on Japan. By the end of May 1945, Hitler's Third Reich was in ruins, and American forces were on the verge of victory over Japan. Roosevelt had died. President Harry S. Truman, wanting to end the war as soon as possible and facing the prospect of huge casualties with an invasion of Japan, decided to use the atomic bomb. The destruction of Hiroshima and Nagasaki led to Japan's surrender. It also announced the beginning of a new age of atomic power, the United States' emergence as a superpower, and what many called "America's century."

The Road to War

■ How did Roosevelt's policies reflect those of Hoover, especially in Latin America? How was the Good Neighbor policy a change from previous American policies toward Latin America?

■ What obstacles did Roosevelt face in trying to implement a more interventionist foreign policy from 1933 to 1939?

■ Following the outbreak of World War II in 1939, how did Roosevelt reshape American neutrality?

When Herbert Hoover became president in 1929, the world appeared stable, peaceful, and increasingly prosperous. He saw no reason to change the policies of his predecessors. The United States would remain aloof from the political and diplomatic bickering of the world while expanding its trade and continuing to use economic and noncoercive policies to promote American interests. Supporting Hoover's international policies was a powerful economy that was the world's number one energy producer, supplied 46 percent of the world's industrial output, and led all nations in exports and foreign investments. The global Depression made a mockery of Hoover's foreign-policy expectations.

The initial response of the United States was reflected in the views of Senator George W. Norris (R.–Nebraska), who proclaimed that the United States should look out for its own interests and not to worry about Europe. Blaming Europe for a large part of the country's economic woes, Hoover and Congress adopted policies that sought to protect American business by raising tariffs and cutting back on foreign trade and investments. As president, Franklin D. Roosevelt did not blame Europe for America's troubles and initially appeared to implement a policy of working with Europe. He sent his secretary of state, Cordell Hull, to the 1933 London Economic Conference to help shore up international currencies and facilitate world trade. But even while Hull argued for increased trade, Roosevelt adopted a Hooverlike policy of economic nationalism. He announced that the United States would seek economic recovery "by means of a policy of **unilateralism.**" Without American cooperation, the conference collapsed, and the global economy worsened.

unilateralism A policy of acting alone, without consultation or agreement of others.

Chronology

A World at War

1929	Herbert Hoover becomes president
1931	Japan seizes Manchuria
1933	Franklin D. Roosevelt becomes president London Economic Conference Gerardo Machado resigns as president of Cuba United States recognizes Soviet Union Hitler and Nazi party take power in Germany
1934	Fulgencio Batista assumes power in Cuba
1935	First Neutrality Act Italy invades Ethiopia
1936	Germany reoccupies the Rhineland Italy annexes Ethiopia Spanish Civil War begins Second Neutrality Act
1937	Third Neutrality Act Roosevelt's quarantine speech Sino-Japanese War begins Japanese aircraft sink the U.S.S. *Panay*
1938	Germany annexes Austria and Sudetenland Munich Conference Pan-American Conference
1939	Germany invades Czechoslovakia German-Soviet Nonaggression Pact Germany invades Poland; Britain and France declare war on Germany; World War II begins Soviets invade Poland Neutrality Act of 1939
1939–1940	Russo-Finnish War
1940	Germany occupies most of Western Europe U.S. economic sanctions against Japan Burke-Wadsworth Act Destroyers-for-bases agreement Roosevelt reelected
1941	Lend-Lease Act Fair Employment Practices Commission created U.S. forces occupy Greenland and Iceland Germany invades Soviet Union Atlantic Charter U-boats attack U.S. warships Japan attacks Pearl Harbor United States enters World War II
1942	War Production Board created Manhattan Project begins Japanese conquer Philippines Japanese Americans interned Battles of Coral Sea and Midway Congress of Racial Equality founded U.S. troops invade North Africa
1943	U.S. forces capture Guadalcanal Soviets defeat Germans at Stalingrad Smith-Connally War Labor Disputes Act Detroit race riot U.S. and British forces invade Sicily and Italy; Italy surrenders Sept. 8 Tehran Conference
1944	Operation Overlord—June 6 invasion of Normandy Allies reach Rhine River G.I. Bill becomes law U.S. forces invade the Philippines Roosevelt reelected Soviet forces liberate Eastern Europe Battle of the Bulge
1945	Yalta Conference Roosevelt dies Harry S. Truman becomes president United Nations created Soviets capture Berlin Germany surrenders U.S. forces capture Iwo Jima and Okinawa Potsdam Conference United States drops atomic bombs on Hiroshima and Nagasaki Japan surrenders

Diplomacy in a Dangerous World

Roosevelt also followed Hoover's so-called **Good Neighbor policy** toward Latin America. Hoover stated that the United States would respect the interests of the nations of the hemisphere and affirmed that the Monroe Doctrine did not give the United States the right to intervene in regional affairs. On assuming office, Roosevelt's commitment to being a good neighbor and to noninterventionism was soon tested in Cuba and Mexico. Social and political unrest swept across Cuba in 1933, fed by opponents of Cuba's oppressive president, Gerardo "the Butcher" Machado. Seeking to stabilize Cuba and protect American interests, Roosevelt sent special envoy Sumner Welles to encourage Machado to resign. Bending under American pressure, Machado left office and was replaced by Ramón Grau San Martín. Welles considered the new Cuban leader too radical and wanted the United States to use military force to remove him. Roosevelt rejected armed intervention and instead continued political maneuvers. The United States' refusal to recognize the new government allowed Welles to argue that a more acceptable government was needed. Without too much effort, he convinced **Colonel Fulgencio Batista** to oust Grau and establish a new government. Batista's regime was immediately recognized by the United States and received a favorable trade agreement.

Mexico also tested Roosevelt's commitment to nonintervention in 1938 by nationalizing foreign-owned oil properties. American oil interests argued that Mexico had no right to seize their properties, demanded their return, and asked that Roosevelt intervene with military force if necessary. Roosevelt rejected the idea and instead accepted the principle of nationalization and sought a fair monetary settlement for the American companies. Not until 1941 did Mexico and the United States agree on the proper amount of compensation, but throughout, American relations with Mexico remained cordial. The Good Neighbor policy was also enhanced as the United States announced at the Pan-American Conference in 1938 that there were no acceptable reasons for armed intervention.

While Hoover and Roosevelt could point to successful and improved relations with Latin America, the same could not be said of policies toward Asia. In 1931, the long-standing American policy of supporting the unfettered trade and the sovereignty of China was tested by Japan. Rejecting most Western values and the ideal of free trade, many Japanese nationalists advocated a Japanese sphere of influence, or empire, and looked toward Manchuria. Situated north and west of Japanese-controlled Korea, Manchuria was rich in iron and coal, accounted for 95 percent of Japanese overseas investment, and also supplied large amounts of vital foodstuffs. In September 1931, the Japanese army stationed in Manchuria, the Guandong, seized control of the province.

World reaction was widespread condemnation, but little else. American humorist Will Rogers sarcastically wrote that world leaders would run out of stationery writing their protests before Japan would run out of soldiers. The League of Nations sheepishly called for peace. From Washington, Hoover's secretary of state Henry Stimson denounced the Japanese aggression and asked the Chinese and Japanese governments to halt the fighting. Following Japan's conquest of Manchuria, the United States invoked the **Stimson Doctrine.** Japan's success led to continued tensions with China and the idea of a **Greater East Asian Co-Prosperity Sphere** through which Japan would dominate most of Asia.

Roosevelt and Isolationism

In Europe, Germany and Italy also sought to alter the international status quo and expand their influence and power. Adolf Hitler had come to office in 1933, based on a promise to improve the economy and Germany's role in the world. Benito Mussolini, ruling Italy since 1921, argued that Italy needed to expand its influence abroad and to enlarge its interests in

---

Good Neighbor policy   An American policy toward Latin America that stressed economic ties and nonintervention; begun under Hoover but associated with Roosevelt.

Colonel Fulgencio Batista   Dictator who ruled Cuba from 1934 through 1958; his corrupt, authoritarian regime was overthrown by Fidel Castro's revolutionary movement.

Stimson Doctrine   Declaration by U.S. secretary of state Henry Stimson in 1932 that the United States would not recognize the Japanese-created state of Manchuko—a policy of nonrecognition—and that legally Manchuria was still Chinese territory.

Greater East Asian Co-Prosperity Sphere   Japan's plan to create and dominate an economic and defensive union in East Asia, using force if necessary. In defending the concept, the Japanese compared it to the United States' power in Latin America and advocated the idea of Asia for Asians.

"GERMANY SHALL NEVER BE ENCIRCLED."

Despite Hitler's assurances about the limited territorial goals of Nazi Germany, following the invasion of Poland, most people quickly realized that his true goal was world domination. *Frank & Marie-Therese Wood Print Collections, Alexandria, VA.*

tionists were in full cry. A Gallup poll revealed that 67 percent of Americans believed that the nation's intervention in World War I had been wrong, and a congressional investigation chaired by Senator Gerald P. Nye of North Dakota alleged that America's entry into the war had been the product of arms manufacturers, bankers, and war profiteers—"the merchants of death." Novelists such as Ernest Hemingway (*A Farewell to Arms*, 1929) and John Dos Passos (*Three Soldiers*, 1921) added to antiwar and isolationist sentiments with their powerful stories depicting the senseless horror of war.

Responding to increased tensions in Asia, Africa, and Europe, Congress in August 1935 passed the **Neutrality Act of 1935.** It prohibited the sale of arms and munitions to any nation at war, whether the aggressor or the victim. It also permitted the president to warn Americans traveling on ships of belligerent nations that they sailed at their own risk. If Roosevelt vetoed the legislation, announced Senator Key Pittman, he was "riding for a fall." Anxious to see the Second Hundred Days successfully through Congress, Roosevelt gave up his desire for **discriminatory neutrality** and accepted political reality. Isolationist senator Hiram Johnson of California declared the Neutrality Act would keep the United States "out of European controversies, European wars, and European difficulties."

Most Americans thought that the Neutrality Act came just in time. On October 3, 1935, Benito Mussolini's Italian troops invaded the African nation of Ethiopia. Roosevelt immediately announced American neutrality toward the Ethiopian conflict, denying the sale of war supplies to either side. Aware that Italy was buying increasing amounts of American nonwar goods, including coal and oil, Roosevelt asked Americans to apply a "moral **embargo**" on Italy. The request had no effect. American trade continued, as did Italian victories. On May 9, 1936, Italy formally annexed Ethiopia.

Africa. As the two dictators implemented policies to achieve their goals, American isolationists became more and more concerned that the United States might be drawn into another European conflict. Caught between Germany and Japan, the Soviet Union's Joseph Stalin sought to improve relations with the United States, western European states, and China. Roosevelt, seeking trade possibilities and hoping to stiffen Soviet resolve in the face of possible Japanese or German aggression, also sought improved relations. The result was minimal: American recognition of the Soviet Union in November 1933, but no expansion of U.S.-Soviet trade, nor any attempt to bridge the ideological gap and the decade of distrust that separated the two nations

Within the United States, Roosevelt's decision to establish relations with the Soviets prompted protests that he was abandoning isolationism. By 1934 isola-

Neutrality Act of 1935   Seeking to ensure that the events that pushed American into World War I would not be repeated, Congress forbade the sale and shipment of war goods to all nations at war and authorized the president to warn U.S. citizens against traveling on belligerents' vessels.

discriminatory neutrality   The ability to withhold aid and trade from one nation at war while providing it to another.

embargo   A ban on trade with a country or countries, usually ordered and enforced by a government.

As the Italian-Ethiopian war drew to a conclusion, international tensions were heightened when in March 1936, German troops violated the Treaty of Versailles by occupying the **Rhineland.** European stability was further weakened when in July civil war broke out in Spain. Roosevelt proclaimed that the re-militarization of the Rhineland was of no concern to the United States and then left on a planned fishing trip. Likewise, most Americans agreed when Roosevelt applied neutrality legislation to both sides of the Spanish Civil War. Taking no chances, Congress modified the neutrality legislation (the Second Neutrality Act) to require noninvolvement in civil wars and to forbid making loans to countries at war—whether victim or aggressor.

With the Italian conquest of Ethiopia, German re-militarization, and the war in Spain as background, both American political parties entered the 1936 elections as champions of neutrality. Roosevelt told an audience at Chautauqua, New York, that he hated war and that if it came to "the choice of profits over peace, the nation will answer—must answer—'We choose peace.'" The Republicans and their candidate, Alfred Landon, were equally adamant that they were the party best able to keep the nation out of war. Roosevelt easily defeated Landon and, with strong public support, approved the **Neutrality Act of 1937.** It required warring nations to pay cash for all "nonwar" goods and to carry them away on their own ships, and it barred Americans from sailing on belligerents' ships. Roosevelt would have liked a more flexible law, but because he was involved in his Supreme Court struggle (see pages 772–773), he signed the act. He did, however, appreciate a provision that allowed him to determine which nations were at war and which goods were nonwar goods.

Roosevelt used the provision in late July 1937, following a Japanese invasion of northern China. Ignoring reality and disregarding protests, he refused to recognize that China and Japan were fighting a war and allowed unrestricted American trade to continue with both nations. Hoping that isolationist views had softened, on October 5 Roosevelt suggested that the United States and other peace-loving nations should quarantine "bandit nations" that were contributing to "the epidemic of world lawlessness." The so-called quarantine speech was applauded in many foreign capitals, but not in Berlin, Rome, or Tokyo, and not at home. Within the United States, it only heightened cries for isolationism, while Japan continued gobbling up Chinese territory. On December 12, 1937, Japanese aircraft strafed, bombed, and sank the American gunboat *Panay*. Two Americans died, and

over thirty were wounded. Roosevelt was outraged and wanted to take some retaliatory action, but public opinion and Congress insisted otherwise. Within forty-eight hours of the *Panay* assault, isolationists in the House of Representatives pushed forward a previously proposed constitutional amendment drafted by Louis Ludlow of Indiana that would require a public referendum before Congress could declare war. Public opinion polls indicated that 70 percent of Americans supported the idea. Only after Roosevelt had expended a great deal of political effort did the House vote 209 to 188 to return the amendment to committee, effectively killing it. Understanding that he had no support for initiating any action against Japan, Roosevelt had no choice but to accept Japan's apology and payment of damages for the *Panay* attack.

World peace was crumbling fast as 1938 started. Fighting raged on in China and Spain with increased intensity. From Berlin, Hitler pronounced his intentions to unify all German-speaking lands and create a new German empire, or *Reich.* He first annexed Austria and then incorporated the Sudeten region of western Czechoslovakia into the German Reich (see Map 25.1). With a respectable military force and defense treaties with France and the Soviet Union, the Czechoslovakian government was prepared to resist. However, France, the Soviet Union, and Britain wanted no confrontation with Hitler. Choosing a policy of **appeasement,** in late September, Britain's prime minister, Neville Chamberlain, met with Hitler in Munich and accepted Germany's annexation of the Sudetenland. France concurred. Chamberlain returned to England smiling and promising that he had secured "peace for our time." Privately, Roosevelt was angry with the British and French, but publicly he congratulated them on defusing the crisis.

Within Germany, Hitler stepped up the persecution of the country's nearly half a million Jews. In

---

Rhineland   Region of western Germany along the Rhine River, which under the terms of the Versailles Treaty was to remain free of troops and military fortifications.

Neutrality Act of 1937   Law passed by Congress requiring warring nations to pay cash for "nonwar" goods and barring Americans from sailing on their ships; known as the Third Neutrality Act.

appeasement   A policy of granting concessions to potential enemies to maintain peace. Since the Munich agreement did not appease Hitler, it has become a policy that most nations avoid.

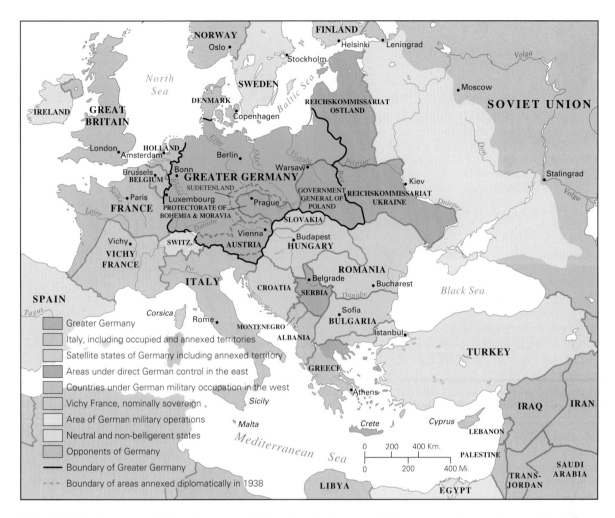

MAP 25.1 German and Italian Expansion, 1933–1942   By the end of 1942, the Axis nations of Italy and Germany, through conquest and annexation, had occupied nearly all of Europe. This map shows the political and military alignment of Europe as Germany and Italy reached the limit of their power.

1938 he launched government-sponsored violence against the German-Jewish population. Synagogues and Jewish businesses and homes were looted and destroyed. Detention centers—concentration camps—at Dachau and Buchenwald soon confined over 50,000 Jews. Thousands of German and Austrian Jews fled to other countries. Many applied to enter the United States, but most were turned away. American anti-Semitism was strong, and Congress rejected a bill designed to permit 20,000 Jews to come to the United States. The State Department, citing immigration requirements that no one be admitted to the country who would become "a public charge," routinely denied entry to German Jews whose property and as-

sets had been seized by the German government. Advocates of changing the immigration rules found Congress and the public uninterested. Opinion polls consistently indicated that large majorities objected to more Jewish immigration. One survey found that 85 percent of Protestants, 84 percent of Catholics, and even 25.8 percent of Jews in the United States opposed opening the door wider to more Jewish refugees. Roosevelt expressed concern but, like most politicians, did not translate that concern into any significant change in policy. In all, only about 60,000 Jewish refugees entered the United States between 1933 and 1938—many of them scientists, academics, and musicians.

In September 1939, Germany introduced the world to a new word and type of warfare, *blitzkrieg*—lightning war. Combining the use of tanks, aircraft, and infantry, German forces quickly overran first Poland, then most of Western Europe. This picture shows a German victory parade in Warsaw, Poland. *Hugo Jaeger/Timepix.*

Even so, Roosevelt was convinced that Hitler was a threat to humanity and sounded a dire warning to Americans in his 1939 State of the Union address. "Events abroad have made it increasingly clear to the American people that the dangers within are less to be feared than dangers without," he cautioned. "This generation will nobly save or meanly lose the last best hope of earth." He then asked Congress to increase military spending for the construction of aircraft and to repeal the arms embargo section of the 1937 Neutrality Act. Congress approved aircraft construction but rejected changing neutrality laws.

In quick succession, events seemed to verify Roosevelt's prediction of danger. Hitler ominously concluded a military alliance with Italy and a nonaggression pact with the Soviet Union. He seized what remained of Czechoslovakia and demanded that Poland turn over to Germany the Polish Corridor, which connected Poland to the Baltic Sea. Incensed by Warsaw's refusal and no longer worried about a Soviet attack, Hitler invaded Poland on September 1, 1939. Two days later, Britain and France declared war on Germany. Within a matter of days, German troops had overrun nearly all of Poland. On September 17, Soviet forces entered the eastern parts of Poland as they had secretly agreed to do in their **German-Soviet Nonaggression Pact.**

War and American Neutrality

As hostilities began in Europe, isolationism remained strong in the United States, with public opinion polls showing little desire to become involved. Just weeks before the invasion of Poland, in a poll taken by *Fortune* magazine, 54 percent of the respondents believed that no international question was important enough to involve the United States in a war. Sixty-six percent opposed the United States going to war to save France and Britain from defeat by an unnamed dictatorship. Roosevelt, however, was determined to do everything possible, short of war, to help those nations opposing Hitler.

After proclaiming neutrality, he called Congress into special session and asked that the cash-and-carry policy of the Neutrality Act of 1937 be modified to allow the sale of any goods, including arms, to any nation, provided the goods were paid for in cash and carried away in ships belonging to the purchasing country. A "peace bloc" argued that the request was a ruse to aid France and Britain and would certainly drag America into the war. Responding to the rapid collapse of Poland, Congress yielded to the president and passed the **Neutrality Act of 1939** in November. Any nation could now buy weapons from the United States. Roosevelt also worked with Latin American

---

German-Soviet Nonaggression Pact   Agreement in which Germany and the Soviet Union in 1939 pledged not to fight each other and secretly arranged to divide Poland after Germany conquered it.

Neutrality Act of 1939   Law passed by Congress repealing the arms embargo and authorizing cash-and-carry exports of arms and munitions even to belligerent nations.

Hitler ordered the German air force to attack British cities in an effort to break the will of the British people. London, like the British people, suffered tremendous damage but withstood the onslaught. By the end of 1942, the small British air force was winning the battle against Germany for the air space over Britain. *William Vandivert/Timepix.*

As Roosevelt shaped American neutrality, Hitler in April 1940 unleashed his forces on Denmark and Norway, which quickly fell under Nazi domination. On May 10 the German offensive against France began with an invasion of Belgium and the Netherlands (see Map 25.1). On May 26 Belgian forces surrendered, while French and British troops began their remarkable evacuation to England from the French port of Dunkirk. That 350,000 British and French forces avoided total defeat at Dunkirk was the only bright spot in an otherwise dismal showing by Britain and France. On June 10 Mussolini entered the war on Germany's side and invaded France from the southeast. Twelve days later, France surrendered.

Germany and Italy, called the **Axis powers,** controlled almost all of western and central Europe, leaving Britain to face the seemingly invincible German army and air force alone. England's new prime minister, **Winston Churchill,** pledged never to surrender until the Nazi scourge was destroyed. On August 8 the **Battle of Britain** began with the German air force bombing targets throughout England in preparation for an invasion of the island. Britain's Royal Air Force outfought the German *Luftwaffe* and denied them air superiority. Hitler eventually cancelled the invasion. To defend England and defeat Hitler, Churchill turned to Roosevelt for aid. His ultimate goal was to bring the United States into the war, but his first request was for war supplies. He needed forty or fifty destroyers and a huge number of aircraft. Roosevelt promised to help. He convinced Congress to increase the military budget, placed orders for the production of more than fifty thousand planes a year, and ordered National Guard units to active federal duty. In September he signed the **Burke-Wadsworth Act,** creating the first peacetime military draft in American history, and by executive order, he exchanged

neighbors to establish a 300-mile neutrality zone around the Western Hemisphere, excluding Canada and other British and French possessions. Within the zone, patrolled by the U.S. Navy, warships of the belligerent nations were forbidden.

Although neutral in appearance, both acts were designed to help France and England. While any nation could now theoretically buy weapons from the United States, German ships would be denied access to American ports by the British Royal Navy. The neutrality zone had to allow French and British warships to reach their Western Hemisphere possessions; therefore, it was only German warships that would be stopped by the navy. If the navy happened to sink any German submarines, Roosevelt joked to his cabinet, he would apologize like "the Japs do, 'So sorry. Never do it again.' Tomorrow we sink two."

Axis powers   Coalition of nations that opposed the Allies in World War II, first consisting of Germany and Italy and later joined by Japan.

Winston Churchill   Prime minister who led Britain through World War II; he was known for his eloquent speeches and his refusal to give in to the Nazi threat. He would be voted out of office in July 1945.

Battle of Britain   Series of battles between British and German planes fought over Britain from August to October 1940, during which English cities suffered heavy bombing.

Burke-Wadsworth Act   Law passed by Congress in 1940 creating the first peacetime draft in American history.

fifty old, mothballed destroyers for ninety-nine-year leases of British military bases in Newfoundland, the Caribbean, and British Guiana. By the end of the year, Congress had approved over $37 billion for military spending, more than the total cost of World War I.

As both parties prepared for the 1940 presidential election, opinion polls on American foreign policy showed public confusion. Ninety percent of those asked said they hoped the United States would stay out of the war, but 70 percent approved giving Britain the destroyers, and 60 percent wanted to support England, even if doing so led to war. Determined to prevent support for Britain from diminishing, Roosevelt chose to run for an unprecedented third term. Guided by their isolationist positions, Republicans, to the surprise of nearly everyone, bypassed leading Republicans such as Senators Robert Taft of Ohio and Arthur Vandenberg of Michigan and nominated as their candidate **Wendell Willkie,** an ex-Democrat from Indiana. Initially, Willkie accepted the bulk of the New Deal, supported aid to Britain and increased military spending, and focused on the issue of Roosevelt's third term. With Willkie trailing in the preference polls, Republican leaders convinced him to be more critical of the New Deal and to attack Roosevelt for pushing the nation toward war. Willkie's popularity surged upward. Roosevelt countered with a promise to American mothers: "Your boys are not going to be sent into any foreign wars." Hearing of the speech, Willkie remarked, "That is going to beat me." He was right. Roosevelt won easily, but his victory did not sweep other Democrats into office; Republicans gained seats in both the Senate and House of Representatives.

The Battle for the Atlantic

While Roosevelt relaxed during a postelection vacation in the Caribbean, he received an urgent message from Churchill. Britain was out of money to buy American goods, as required by the 1939 Neutrality Act. Churchill needed credit to pay for supplies. He also asked Roosevelt to allow American ships to carry goods to England and for American help to protect merchant ships from German submarines. Roosevelt agreed, but knowing that both requests would face tough congressional and public opposition, he turned to his powers of persuasion. In his December fireside chat, he told his audience that if England fell, Hitler would surely attack the United States next. He urged the people to make the nation the "arsenal of democracy" and to supply Britain with all the material help

it needed to defeat Hitler. He then presented Congress with a bill allowing the president to lend, lease, or in any way provide goods to any country considered vital to American security. The request drew the expected fire from isolationists. Senator Burton K. Wheeler called it a military Agricultural Adjustment Act that would "plow under every fourth American boy." Supporters countered with "Send guns, not sons." On March 11, 1941, the 60-year-old president breathed a sigh of relief when the **Lend-Lease Act** passed easily.

For a while it appeared that Lend-Lease might have come too late. German submarines were sinking so much cargo and so many irreplaceable ships that not even Britain's minimal needs were reaching its ports. In March 1941, Churchill warned Roosevelt that Germany's foes could not afford to lose the battle for the Atlantic. In response, Roosevelt sent part of the Pacific fleet to the Atlantic and extended the neutrality zone to include Greenland. By the summer of 1941, the United States Navy's patrols of the neutrality zone overlapped Hitler's Atlantic war zone. It was only a matter of time until American and German ships confronted each other.

Meanwhile, German forces plowed into Yugoslavia and Greece, heading toward the Mediterranean and North Africa. The nonaggression pact having served its role, Hitler planned to crush the Soviets with the largest military force ever assembled on a single front. On June 22, 1941, German forces, supported by allied Finnish, Hungarian, Italian, and Romanian armies, opened the eastern front. Claiming he would join even with the devil to defeat Hitler, Churchill made an ally of Stalin, while Roosevelt extended credits and lend-lease goods to the Soviet Union. Many worried that the Red Army would not last more than three months and that German troops would soon occupy Moscow. Yet despite initial crushing victories in which German soldiers surrounded Leningrad and advanced within miles of Moscow, by November it was becoming clear that the Soviets were not going to collapse.

Wendell Willkie Business executive and Republican presidential candidate who lost to Roosevelt in 1940; during the campaign, Roosevelt never publicly mentioned Willkie's name.

Lend-Lease Act Law passed by Congress in 1941 providing that any country whose security was vital to U.S. interests could receive arms and equipment by sale, transfer, or lease from the United States.

From the beginning of World War II, Roosevelt was determined to help defeat the forces of fascism. Meeting with Churchill, on board a cruiser off the coast of Newfoundland in August 1941, the two leaders signed the Atlantic Charter as a prelude to the United States waging war against Germany. *FDR Library.*

With the battle for the Atlantic reaching a turning point and Germany rolling through Russia, Roosevelt and Churchill met secretly off the coast of Newfoundland (the Argentia Conference, August 9–12, 1941). They discussed strategies, supplies, and future prospects. Churchill pleaded for an American declaration of war, but Roosevelt's main concern was more political than strategic. He urged Churchill to support the formation of a postwar world that subscribed to the goals of self-determination, freedom of trade and the seas, and the establishment of a "permanent system of general security" in the form of a new world organization. Roosevelt wanted the **Atlantic Charter** to highlight the distinctions between the open, multilateral world of the democracies and the closed, self-serving world of fascist expansion. Such a contrast, he believed, would help Americans support entry into the war. Churchill agreed to support the Atlantic Charter but reminded Roosevelt that Britain could not fully accept the goals of self-determination and free trade within its Commonwealth and the British Empire. Roosevelt, who saw the Atlantic Charter as a domestic tool and not as a blueprint for foreign policy, had no objection to the prime minister's exceptions. Returning to London, Churchill told his ministers that Roosevelt meant to "wage war, but not declare it, and that he would become more and more provocative . . . to force an incident . . . which would justify him in opening hostilities."

On September 4, 1941, an incident occurred that allowed the United States to step closer to officially ending its neutrality. In the North Atlantic, near Iceland, a German U-boat fired two torpedoes at the American destroyer *Greer*. Both missed, and the *Greer* counterattacked. Neither ship was damaged, but Roosevelt used the skirmish to get Congress to amend the neutrality laws to permit armed U.S. merchant ships to sail into combat zones. In October, following an attack on the U.S.S. *Kearney* and the sinking of the U.S.S. *Reuben James*, Congress rescinded all neutrality laws. As American ships were being attacked, the War Department sent its war plan, "the Victory Program," to the president. It concluded that the United States would have to fight a two-front war, one against Germany and another against Japan. It also stated that Hitler needed to be defeated before the Japanese, and that July 1943 was about the earliest date that American troops could be ready for any large-scale operation.

Pearl Harbor

Since 1937, Japanese troops had seized more and more of coastal China, while the United States did little but protest. By 1940, popular sentiment favored not only beefing up American defenses in the Pacific but also using economic pressure to slow Japanese aggression. In July 1940, Roosevelt began placing restrictions on Japanese-American trade, forbidding the sale and shipment of aviation fuel, steel, and scrap iron. Many Americans believed the action was too limited and pointed out that Japan was still allowed to buy millions of gallons of American oil, which it was using to "extinguish the lamps of China."

The situation in East Asia soon worsened. The **Vichy** French government, knuckling under to German and Japanese pressure, allowed Japanese troops

---

Atlantic Charter   Joint statement issued by Roosevelt and Churchill in 1941 to formulate American and British postwar aims of international economic and political cooperation.

Vichy   City in central France that was the capital of unoccupied France from 1940 to 1942; the Vichy government continued to govern French territories and was sympathetic to the fascists.

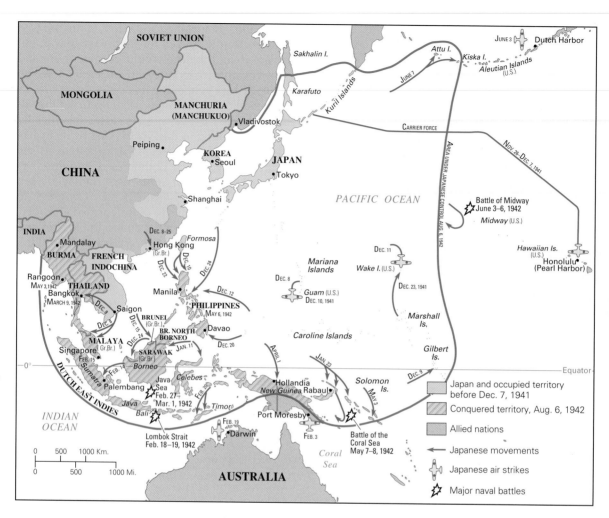

MAP 25.2 Japanese Advances, December 1941–1942 Beginning on December 7, 1941, Japanese forces began carving out a vast empire, the East Asian Co-Prosperity Sphere, by attacking American, British, Dutch, and Australian forces from Pearl Harbor to the Dutch East Indies. This map shows the course of Japanese expansion until the critical naval battles of the Coral Sea and Midway in the spring of 1942 that halted Japanese advances in the Pacific.

to enter French Indochina (see Map 25.2), and Japan signed a defense treaty with Germany and Italy. America promptly strengthened its forces in the Philippines, tightened trade restrictions on Japan, and sent long-range bombers to the Philippines to "set the paper cities of Japan on fire" as a deterrent. Within the Japanese government of Prime Minister Fumimaro Konoye, those fearful of confrontation with the United States sought to negotiate. The subsequent discussions between Hull and Admiral Kichisaburo Nomura, Japan's ambassador to the United States, were confused and nonproductive. The lack of progress in the negotiations convinced many in the Japanese government that war was un-

avoidable to break the "circle of force" that denied Japan its interests. High on the list of interests was Japanese control over Malaysia and the Dutch East Indies (Indonesia), sources of vital raw materials, including oil. Seizing those regions, they concluded, would probably involve fighting the United States.

For Minister of War Hideki Tojo, the choice had become simple: either submit to American demands, giving up the achievements of the past ten years and accepting a world order defined by the United States, or safeguard the nation's honor and achievements by initiating a war. In his mind, war could be averted only if the United States, which had frozen Japanese assets in July, agreed to suspend aid to China, cap its

Roosevelt called it "A Day of Infamy"—December 7, 1941, when Japanese planes attacked Pearl Harbor, Hawai`i, without warning and before a declaration of war. In this photo, the U.S.S. *West Virginia* sinks in flames, one of eight battleships sunk or badly damaged in the attack. *National Archives.*

military presence in the Pacific, and resume full trade with Japan. If these concessions did not occur, Tojo decided, Japan would begin military operations in the first week of December. Naval aircraft would strike the American fleet at Pearl Harbor, in Hawai`i, while the army would invade the Philippines, Malaya, Singapore, and the Dutch East Indies. Negotiations remained stalled until November 26, when Hull made it clear that the United States would make no concessions and insisted that Japan withdraw from China. The die was cast.

On November 26, Admiral Isoroku Yamamoto dispatched part of the Japanese fleet, including six aircraft carriers, toward Hawai`i. American observers, however, focused on the activity of a larger part of the Japanese fleet, which joined troop ships in sailing on December 5 toward the South China Sea and the Gulf of Siam. At 7:49 A.M. December 7 (Hawaiian time), before Japan's declaration of war had been received in Washington, Japanese planes struck the American fleet anchored at Pearl Harbor. By 8:12, seven battle-

ships of the American Pacific fleet lined up along Battleship Row were aflame, sinking, or badly damaged. Eleven other ships had been hit, nearly two hundred American aircraft had been destroyed, and twenty-five hundred Americans had lost their lives. Fortunately, U.S. aircraft carriers were not at Pearl Harbor, and Admiral Chuichi Nagumo decided to withdraw without launching further attacks that would have targeted the important support facilities—repair shops, dry docks, and oil storage tanks. These incurred only light damages.

The attack on Pearl Harbor, however, was only a small part of Japan's strategy. Elsewhere that day Japanese planes struck Singapore, Guam, the Philippines, and Hong Kong. Everywhere, British and American positions in the Pacific and East Asia were being overwhelmed. Roosevelt declared that the unprovoked, sneak attack on Pearl Harbor made December 7 "a day which will live in infamy" and asked Congress for a declaration of war against Japan. Only the vote of Representative Jeannette Rankin of Montana, a pacifist, kept the December 8 declaration of war from being unanimous. Three days later, Germany and Italy declared war on the United States. Americans were angry and full of fight. In England Churchill "slept the sleep of the saved and thankful." He knew that with the economic and human resources of the United States finally committed to war, the Axis would be "ground to powder."

America Responds to War

■ What actions did Roosevelt take to mobilize the nation for war? How did new wartime necessities affect the relationship between business and government?

■ What new social and economic choices did Americans confront as the nation became the "arsenal of democracy"? In particular, what doors opened and closed for women and minorities?

■ How were the military experiences of the Nisei, Mexican Americans, African Americans, and Indians different, and why?

The attack on Pearl Harbor unified the nation as no other event had done. Afterward, it was almost impossible to find an isolationist.

Thousands of young men rushed to enlist, especially into the navy and marines. On December 8, 1,200 applicants besieged the navy recruiting station in New York City, some having waited outside the doors all night. Eventually over 16.4 million Americans would serve in the armed forces during World War II.

The shock of Japan's attack on Pearl Harbor raised fears of further attacks, especially along the Pacific Coast. On the night of December 7 and throughout the next week, West Coast cities reported enemy planes overhead and practiced blackouts. Phantom Japanese planes were spotted above San Francisco and Los Angeles. In Seattle, crowds hurled rocks at an offending blue neon light that defied the blackout and then, venting both fear and rage, rioted across the city. The Rose Bowl game between Oregon State and Duke was moved from the bowl's home in Pasadena to Duke's stadium in Durham, North Carolina. Stores everywhere removed "made in Japan" goods from shelves. Alarm and anger were focused especially on Japanese Americans. Rumors circulated wildly that they intended to sabotage factories and military installations, paving the way for the invasion of the West Coast. Within a week, the FBI had arrested 2,541 citizens of Axis countries: 1,370 Japanese; 1,002 Germans; and 169 Italians.

Japanese American Internment

There were nearly 125,000 Japanese Americans in the country, about three-fourths of whom were *Nisei*— Japanese Americans who had been born in the United States. The remaining fourth were Japanese immigrants, or *Issei*—officially citizens of Japan, although nearly all had lived in the United States more than eighteen years. Almost immediately a belief emerged that they posed a threat. General John L. De Witt, commanding general of the Western Defense District, stated, "We must worry about the Japanese all the time . . . until he is wiped off the map." Echoing long-standing anti-Japanese sentiment, California moved to "protect" itself. Japanese Americans were fired from state jobs, and their law and medical licenses were revoked. Banks froze Japanese American assets, stores refused service, and loyal citizens vandalized Nisei and Issei homes and businesses The few voices that came forward to speak on behalf of Japanese Americans were shouted down by those demanding their removal from the West Coast. On February 19, 1942, Roosevelt signed **Executive Order #9066,** which allowed the military to remove anyone deemed a threat from official military areas. When the entire

Nisei   A person born in America of parents who emigrated from Japan.

Issei   A Japanese immigrant to the United States.

Executive Order #9066   Order of President Roosevelt in 1942 authorizing the removal of "enemy aliens" from military areas; it was used to isolate Japanese Americans in internment camps.

In February 1942, President Roosevelt signed an order sending all Japanese Americans living on the West Coast to internment camps. This photo, taken at a staging area for transportation to the internment camps, shows the quiet dignity of those waiting to be interned. *National Archives.*

look over all our possessions and offering such nominal amounts knowing we had no recourse but to accept." In the relocation it is estimated that Japanese American families lost from $810 million to $2 billion in property and goods.

Having disposed of a lifetime of possessions, Japanese Americans began the process of internment. Tags with numbers were issued to every family to tie to luggage and coats—no names, only numbers. "From then on," wrote one woman, "we were known as family #10710." In the camps, the Nisei and Issei were surrounded by barbed wire and watched over by guards. The internees were assigned to 20-by-25-foot apartments in long barracks of plywood covered with tarpaper, and each camp was expected to create a community complete with farms, shops, and small factories. Within a remarkably short period of time, they did. Making the desert bloom, by 1944 the internees at Manzanar, east of the Sierra in California's Owens Valley, were producing more than $2 million worth of agricultural products.

Some internees were able to leave the camps by working outside, supplying much-needed labor, especially farm work. By the fall of 1942, one-fifth of all males had left the camps to work. Others volunteered for military service. Japanese American units served in both the Pacific and European theaters, the most famous being the four-thousand-man 442nd Regimental Combat Team, which saw action in Italy, France, and Germany. The men of the 442nd would be among the most decorated in the army. Years later, in 2000, the federal government, citing racial bias during the war for the delay, awarded the Medal of Honor to twenty-one Asian Americans—most belonging to the 442nd Regiment. Included in the group was **Daniel Ken Inouye,** who was elected to the U.S. Senate from Hawai`i in 1960.

Aware of rabidly anti-Japanese public opinion, Roosevelt waited until after the off-year 1943 elections to allow internees who passed a loyalty review

West Coast was declared a military area, the eviction of the Japanese Americans from the region began. By the summer of 1942, over 110,000 Nisei and Issei had been transported to ten **internment camps** (see chapter-opening map). When tested in court, the executive order was upheld by the Supreme Court in *Korematsu v. the United States* (1944).

The orders to relocate allowed almost no time to prepare. Families could pack only a few personal possessions and had to store or sell the rest of their property, including homes and businesses. Finding storage facilities was nearly impossible, and most families had to liquidate their possessions at ridiculously low prices. "It is difficult to describe the feeling of despair and humiliation experienced," one man recalled, "as we watched the Caucasians coming to

internment camps   Camps to which more than 110,000 Japanese Americans living in the West were moved soon after the attack on Pearl Harbor; Japanese Americans in Hawai`i were not confined in internment camps.

Daniel Ken Inouye   A Japanese American from Hawai`i who served in the 422nd Regimental Combat Team and was badly wounded in Italy; he later became a U.S. senator from Hawai`i and received the Congressional Medal of Honor for his valor.

to go home. A year later, the camps were empty, each internee having been given train fare home and $25. Returning home, the Japanese Americans discovered that nearly everything was gone. Stored belongings had been stolen. Land, homes, and businesses had been confiscated by the government for unpaid taxes. Denied even an apology from the government, Japanese Americans nevertheless began to reestablish their homes and businesses. Decades later, in 1988, and after several lawsuits on behalf of victims, a semi-apologetic federal government paid $20,000 in compensation to each of the surviving sixty thousand internees.

Mobilizing the Nation for War

When President Roosevelt made his first fireside chat following Pearl Harbor, "Dr. New Deal" became "Dr. Win the War." He called on Americans to produce the goods necessary for victory—factories were to run twenty-four hours a day, seven days a week. Gone was every trace of the antibusiness attitude that had characterized much New Deal rhetoric, and in its place was the realization that only big business could produce the vast amount of armaments and supplies needed. Secretary of War Stimson noted: "You have to let business make money out of the process or business won't work." Overall, the United States paid over $240 billion in defense contracts, with 82 percent of them going to the nation's top one hundred corporations. At the same time more than half a million small businesses collapsed. Every part of the nation benefited from defense-based prosperity, but the South and the coastal West saw huge economic gains. The South experienced a remarkable 40 percent increase in its industrial capacity, and the West did even better.

The Depression and the New Deal had provided the West important resources such as electricity, experience in large-scale production projects, and a growing population. With the war, billions of dollars of government contracts flowed into the region. A corridor from San Diego to Los Angeles emerged as the country's "largest urban military-industrial complex." Wrote one observer, "It was [as] if someone had tilted the country: people, money, and soldiers all spilled west."

Among the contractors, few outdid Henry J. Kaiser, "Sir Launchalot." He took the expertise gained in building Boulder Dam and transformed the ship-building industry by constructing massive shipyards in California. By using **prefabricated** sections, he cut the time it took to build a merchant ship from about

The ability to wage war rests on a nation's resources, not only of men but of raw materials and production. In this political cartoon, the challenge is given, and over the next four years the United States easily produced more of the machines of war than either Germany or Japan. *Chicago Historical Society.*

three hundred days prior to the war to an average of eighty days in 1942. To supply his West Coast shipyards with steel, he utilized federal resources to build a new steel mill in Fontana, California. With men like Kaiser leading the way, by the end of 1942, one-third of all production was geared to the war, and the government had allocated millions of dollars to improve productivity by upgrading factories and generating new industries. When the war cut off some supplies of raw rubber, government and business cooperated to develop and produce synthetic rubber. By the end of the war, the United States had pumped more than $320 billion into the American economy, and the final

prefabricated   Manufactured in advance in standard sections that are easy to ship and assemble when and where needed.

production amounts exceeded almost everyone's expectations: U.S. manufacturers had built more than 300,000 aircraft; 88,140 tanks; and 86,000 warships. Neither Germany nor Japan could come close to matching the output of American products.

Aiding contractors in another way, the government also built towns to house workers. To provide living quarters for workers at Kaiser's three shipyards along the Columbia River, the government constructed Vanport City, Oregon. Construction began on September 14, 1942, and in ninety days "Vanport, . . . the war metropolis, appeared on the map." The *Portland Oregonian* called it "a triumph of American enterprise. Born of the national emergency, it will shelter 40,000 residents . . . becoming the most extensive mass housing experiment of all time." Vanport contained apartments and homes, schools, fire and police stations, a movie theater, a library, an infirmary, and icehouses. Couples lived in one-room apartments that were furnished with "a 'daveno' (also used as a bed), two . . . chairs and a dining table." Kitchens had a sink, an electric hot plate, small oven, and an icebox. Seven years old while living in Vanport, Earl Washington recalled: "If you had a wagon . . . people would ask you to go and get ice for them, you know, because everybody had iceboxes. So you could make a lot of money as a kid in Vanport. . . . You didn't get rich but if you went and got somebody a twenty-five pound block of ice they gave you a quarter. A quarter would go a long way in those days." Completed by August 12, 1943, Vanport was a robust "24-hour city," with a population of 40,000, including nearly 15,000 African Americans. Vanport barely survived the war: when the shipyards closed, most people moved away, and in 1948 a major flood destroyed what was left of the city.

Millions of dollars were also spent on research and development (R&D) to create and improve a variety of goods from weapons to medicines. In "science cities" constructed by the government across the country, researchers and technicians of the **Manhattan Project** harnessed atomic energy and built an atomic bomb. Hundreds of colleges and universities and private laboratories, such as Bell Labs, received research and development grants that created new technologies or enhanced the operation of a variety of products. Improved radar and sonar allowed American forces to detect and destroy enemy planes and ships. New medical techniques and new, more effective medicines, including penicillin, saved millions of lives. Potent pesticides fought insects that carried typhus, malaria, and other diseases at home and overseas. In Vanport, after residents complained of fleas, bed bugs, mice, and cockroaches, an experimental fumigation process that used a pint of DDT spray per apartment "yielded excellent results" with no further complaints. Some even boasted that insecticides such as DDT would be the "biggest contribution of military medicine to the civilian population" following the war.

As the economy retooled to provide the machines of war, Roosevelt acted to provide government direction and planning. His first steps were to establish an array of governmental agencies and boards to regulate prices and production. The size of the federal bureaucracy grew 400 percent. The War Production Board (WPB) and the War Labor Board (WLB), both created in January 1942, sought to coordinate and plan production, establish the allotment of materials, and ensure harmonious labor relations. An Office of Price Administration (OPA), established in 1941, sought to limit inflation and equalize consumption by setting prices and issuing ration books with coupons needed to buy a wide range of commodities, such as shoes, coffee, meat, and sugar. When the agencies failed to resolve problems and create a smoothly working economy, Roosevelt and Congress expanded the agencies' scope and created new ones. Seeking to improve coordination, in 1942 and 1943 Roosevelt added two new umbrella agencies, the Office of Economic Stabilization (OES) and the **Office of War Mobilization.** To direct both agencies, he appointed former Supreme Court justice **James F. Byrnes.** Armed with extensive powers and the president's trust, Byrnes, nicknamed the "Assistant President," controlled a far-flung economic empire of policies and programs that touched every American and produced the machinery to win wars. "If you want something done, go see Jimmie Byrnes" became the watchword. By the fall of 1943, production was

Manhattan Project   A secret scientific research effort begun in 1942 to develop an atomic bomb; much of the research was done in a secret community of scientists and workers near Oak Ridge, Tennessee, and Los Alamos, New Mexico.

Office of War Mobilization   Umbrella agency created in 1943 to coordinate the production, procurement, and distribution of civilian and military supplies.

James F. Byrnes   Supreme Court justice who left the Court to direct the nation's economy and war production; known as the "Assistant President," he directed the Office of Economic Stabilization and the Office of War Mobilization and later became secretary of state under President Truman.

booming, jobs were plentiful, wages and family incomes were rising, and inflation was under control. Even farmers were climbing out of debt as farm income had tripled since 1939.

The war provided full employment and new opportunities for both labor and its opponents. Unions, especially the CIO, grew rapidly during the war, and by 1945 union membership had reached a high of 15 million workers. Union leaders hoped the unions' voluntary agreements not to strike during wartime would persuade industry to agree to union recognition, collective bargaining, **closed shops,** and increased wages. Opponents argued that unions should be forbidden to strike or otherwise hinder war production and accept the open shop. In 1941, even before the United States entered the war, four thousand strikes had stopped work on defense production and had forced the government on one occasion—a strike at North American Aviation—to seize the plant and threaten the strikers with induction into the military if they did not return to work. Roosevelt hoped his war production agencies could find a middle ground between union advocates and opponents. In 1942 OPA, the WLB, and other agencies hammered out a compromise promoting union membership and accepting the closed shop and collective bargaining, but also expecting unions to control wages and oppose strikes. While most workers and employers accepted the guidelines, others did not, and strikes consistently plagued Roosevelt's administration. Every year nearly 3 million workers went on strike or conducted work slowdowns, but most lasted only a brief time and did not jeopardize production. Several strikes were more serious, generating the wrath of the president, Congress, and the public and prompting government intervention. The most serious confrontation occurred in 1943 when CIO president and head of the United Mine Workers John L. Lewis led a strike demanding higher wages and safer working conditions. An angry president threatened to take over the mines. Congress wanted Lewis jailed as a traitor and pushed through, over the president's veto, the **Smith-Connally War Labor Disputes Act.** It gave the president the power to seize and operate any strike-bound industries considered vital for war production. Eventually, the parties in the mine strike compromised, giving higher wages to the miners. By the end of the war, American workers had not only produced a massive amount of material but were receiving higher wages than ever before. Moreover, unions represented 35 percent of the labor force. Union leaders had gained unprecedented influence during the war and expected that it would continue

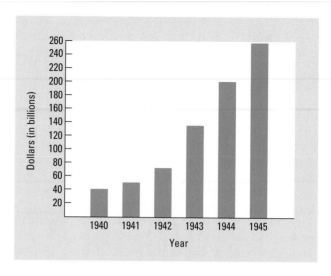

FIGURE 25.1 The National Debt, 1940–1945   As the United States fought to defeat the Axis nations, its national debt soared. Rather than further raise taxes, the government chose to borrow about 60 percent of the cost. By the end of the war the debt had reached near $260 billion.

into the postwar period. Unions, especially the CIO with its political action committee (PAC), intended to continue its key political role, especially within the Democratic Party.

Taxes were also up, reflecting Roosevelt's desire to fund the war through taxation. The 1942 and 1943 Revenue Acts increased the number of people paying taxes and raised rates. In 1939, 4 million Americans paid income taxes; by the end of the war, more than 40 million did so. Individuals making $500,000 or more a year paid 88 percent in taxes. Corporate taxes averaged 40 percent, with a 90 percent tax on excess profits.

These tax changes moderately altered the basic distribution of income by reducing the proportion held by the upper two-fifths of the population—but tax revenues paid for only about half of the cost of the war. The government borrowed the rest. The national debt jumped from $40 billion in 1940 to near $260 bil-

closed shop   A business or factory whose workers are required to be union members.
Smith-Connally War Labor Disputes Act   Law passed by Congress in 1943 authorizing the government to seize plants in which labor disputes threatened war production; it was later used to take over the coal mines.

lion by 1945 (see Figure 25.1). The most publicized borrowing effort encouraged the purchase of **war bonds.** Movie stars and other celebrities asked Americans to "do their part" and buy bonds, especially Series E bonds worth $25 and $50. The public responded by purchasing more than $40 billion in individual bonds, but the majority of bonds—$95 billion—were bought by corporations and financial institutions.

Wartime Politics

As Roosevelt mobilized the nation for war, Republicans and conservative Democrats moved to bury what was left of the New Deal. People secure in their jobs were no longer as concerned about social welfare programs. They griped about higher taxes, rents, and prices, the scarcity of some goods, and government inefficiency. Business-oriented publications like *Fortune* and the *Wall Street Journal* renewed their attacks on New Deal **statism,** especially social welfare programs. Congressional elections in November 1942 continued the trend started in 1937 and returned more Republicans to Congress. A more conservative Congress axed the Civilian Conservation Corps (CCC), the Works Progress Administration (WPA), and the National Youth Administration (NYA) and slashed the budgets of other government agencies.

Roosevelt, seeking an unprecedented fourth term in 1944, hoped to recapture some social activism and called for the passage of an economic bill of rights that included government support for higher-wage jobs, homes, and medical care, but his plea fell on deaf ears. Instead, Congress passed a smaller version that would reward veterans of the war. In June the **G.I. Bill** became law. It guaranteed a year's unemployment compensation for veterans while they looked for "good" jobs, provided economic support if they chose to go to school, and offered low-interest home loans.

Roosevelt brushed aside concerns about his age and health, but responding to conservatives in the party, he agreed to drop the too-liberal vice president, Henry Wallace, and replace him with a more conservative running mate. The choice was Senator **Harry S. Truman** from Missouri. Roosevelt campaigned on a strong wartime economy, his record of leadership, and by November 1944, a successful war effort.

Republicans nominated Governor Thomas Dewey of New York as their candidate, who attacked government inefficiency and waste and argued that his youth, 42, made him a better candidate than Roosevelt. A Republican-inspired "whispering campaign" hinted that at 62 Roosevelt was ill and close to death. Voters ignored the rumors and reelected Roosevelt, whose winning totals, although not as large as in 1940, were still greater than pollsters had predicted and proved that Roosevelt still generated widespread support.

A People at Work and War

America's entry into the war changed nearly everything about everyday life. Government agencies set prices and froze wages and rents. Cotton, silk, gasoline, and items made of metal, including hair clips and safety pins, became increasingly scarce. A rationing system was introduced, and by the end of 1942, most Americans had a ration book containing an array of different-colored coupons of various values that limited their purchases of such staples as meat, sugar, and gasoline. Explaining why most Americans received only 3 gallons of gasoline a week, Roosevelt explained that a bomber required nearly 1,100 gallons of fuel to bomb Naples, the equivalent of about 375 gasoline ration tickets. Also, the War Production Board changed fashion to conserve fabrics. In men's suits, lapels were narrowed, and vests and pant cuffs were eliminated. The amount of fabric in women's skirts was also reduced, and the two-piece bathing suit was introduced as "patriotic chic." Families collected scrap metal, paper, and rubber to be recycled for the war effort and grew **victory gardens** to support the war. When people complained about shortages and inconveniences, more would challenge, "Don't you know there's a war on?"

Even with rationing, most Americans were experiencing a higher-than-ever standard of living. Meat

war bonds   Bonds sold by the government to finance the war effort.

statism   The concept or practice of placing economic planning and policy under government control.

G.I. Bill   Law passed by Congress in 1944 to provide financial and educational benefits for American veterans after World War II; *G.I.* stands for "government issue."

Harry S. Truman   Democratic senator from Missouri whom Roosevelt selected in 1944 to be his running mate for vice president; in 1945, on Roosevelt's death, Truman became president.

victory garden   Small plot cultivated by a patriotic citizen during World War II to supply household food and allow farm production to be used for the war effort.

WE'RE SCRAPPERS TOO

Across the nation, Americans contributed to the war effort by cutting back on using rubber, tin cans, and hundreds of other products. And as illustrated in this poster, they also collected scrap materials that could be recycled into the machines of war. It was a way for even children to contribute to the war effort. *Chicago Historical Society.*

and 1945. Two hundred thousand people, many from the rural South, headed for Detroit, but more went west, where defense industries beckoned. Shipbuilding and the aircraft industry sparked boomtowns that could not keep pace with the growing need for local services and facilities. San Diego, California, once a small retirement community with a quiet naval base, mushroomed into a major military and defense industrial city almost overnight. Nearly 55,000 people flocked there each year of the war, with thousands living in small travel trailers leased by the federal government for $7 a month. Mobile, Alabama; Norfolk, Virginia; Seattle, Washington; Denver, Colorado—all experienced similar rapid growth (see chapter-opening map).

With the expanding populations, war industrial cities experienced massive problems providing homes, water, electricity, and sanitation. Crime flourished. Marriage, divorce, family violence, and juvenile delinquency rates soared. Twelve thousand sailors and soldiers looking for a good time gave Norfolk a reputation as a major sin city. Contributing to the social problems of the booming cities were those posed by many unsupervised teenage children. Juvenile crime increased dramatically during the war, much of it blamed on lockout and latchkey children whose working mothers left them alone during their job shifts. In Mobile, authorities speculated that two thousand children a day skipped school, some going to movies but most just hanging out looking for something to do.

Particularly worrisome to authorities were those nicknamed "V-girls." Victory girls were young teens, sometimes called "khaki-wacky teens," who hung around gathering spots like bus depots and drugstores to flirt with GIs and ask for dates. Wearing "sloppy-joe" sweaters, hair ribbons, bobby sox, and saddle shoes, their young faces thick with makeup and bright red lipstick, V-girls traded sex for movies, dances, and drinks. Seventeen-year-old Elvira Taylor of Norfolk took a different approach—she became an "Allotment Annie." She simply married the soldiers, preferably pilots, and collected their monthly **allotment checks.** Eventually, two American soldiers at an English pub showing off pictures of their wives discovered they had both married Elvira! It turned out she had wed six servicemen.

consumption increased to nearly 129 pounds a year, despite rationing that limited weekly consumption to 28 ounces. Consumer spending rose by 12 percent, and Americans were spending more than ever on entertainment, from books to movies to horse racing. Included in those discovering prosperity were women and minorities, who by 1943 were being hired because of severe labor shortages. Even the Nisei were allowed to leave their relocation camps when their labor was needed. To gain access to new jobs, 15 million Americans relocated between 1941

allotment checks Checks that a soldier's wife received from the government, amounting to a percentage of her husband's pay.

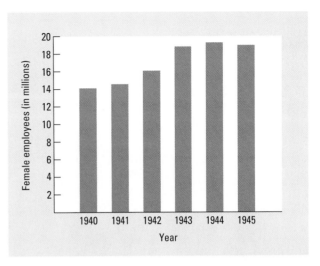

More than 350,000 women served in the military during the war, including Lt. Hazel Ying Lee, a Women's Airforce Service Pilot. WASPs flew "noncombat," ferrying planes and supplies across the United States and Canada. Already an experienced pilot in China, Lt. Lee is seated here in the cockpit of a trainer. Lt. Lee died in 1943, when her plane crashed. *Texas Woman's University.*

FIGURE 25.2 Women in the Work Force, 1940–1945   As men went to war, the nation turned increasingly to women to fill vital jobs. With government's encouragement, the number of women in the work force swelled from 14 million to nearly 20 million. With the war's end, however, many women left the workplace and returned to the home.

New Opportunities and Old Constraints

Mobilization forced the restructuring and redirecting of economic and human resources. Families had to adjust to new challenges. Minorities and women confronted new roles and accepted new responsibilities, both on the home front and in the military. Like men, many women were anxious to serve in the military. But the armed forces did not employ women except as nurses. To expand women's roles, Congresswoman Edith Norse Rogers prodded Congress and the Army, in March 1942, to create the Women's Auxiliary Army Corps (WAAC), which became the Women's Army Corps (WAC) a year later. The other services—with differing levels of enthusiasm—followed suit by creating the navy's Women Appointed for Volunteer Emergency Service (WAVES) and the marines' Women's Reserve. Relegated to noncombat roles, most women served as nurses and clerical workers, but there were notable exceptions. Women's Airforce Service Pilots (WASPS) tested planes, ferried planes across the United States and Canada, and trained male pilots. At the marine flight-training center at Cherry Point, North Carolina, all the flight instructors were women. By war's end,

over 350,000 women had donned uniforms, earned equal pay with men who held the same rank, and provided a new female image.

Women serving in the military were not the only break with tradition. With over 10 million men marching off to war, employers increasingly turned to women. Until 1943, employers did not actively recruit women, preferring to hire white males. But as the labor shortage deepened, they turned to women and minorities to work the assembly lines. The federal government applauded the move and conducted an emotional campaign, suggesting that women could shorten the war if they joined the work force. The image of Rosie the Riveter became the symbol of the patriotic woman doing her part. As more jobs opened, women did fill them—some because of patriotism, but most because they wanted both the job and the wages. Leaving home, Peggy Terry worked in a munitions plant and considered it "an absolute miracle. . . . We made the fabulous sum of $32 a week. . . . Before, we made nothing." Other women left menial jobs for better-paying positions with industries and the federal government. By 1944, 37 percent of all adult women were working, almost 19.4 million (see Figure 25.2). Of these, the majority (72.2 percent) were married, and over half were 35 or older. Despite

About 700,000 African Americans served in segregated units in all branches of the military, facing discrimination at all levels. Among those units were the four squadrons of the Tuskegee Airmen commanded by General Benjamin O. Davis. "We fought two wars" commented Airman Louis Parnell, "one with the enemy and the other back home." *National Archives.*

the number of women entering the work force, most stayed home. They supported the war effort in their homes and communities, providing volunteer efforts to organizations such as the Red Cross and Civil Defense.

Whether working or volunteering, however, women faced familiar constraints. Professional and supervisory positions were still dominated by men, and not all was rosy at work. Male workers resented and harassed women, who were generally paid lower wages than men, and constantly reminded their female coworkers that their jobs were temporary. Employers and most men expected that when the war was over, women would happily return to their traditional roles at home. Without adequate childcare and nursery facilities, worried about abandoning traditional family roles and their families, some women found it

difficult to balance family needs and work. Feeling regret or guilt, many gave up their jobs.

With the end of the war, the government reversed itself and pronounced that patriotism lay at home with the family. By the summer of 1945, many of the women who entered the work force during the war found themselves unemployed. Shipyards and the aircraft plants dismissed nearly three-fourths of their women employees. In Detroit, the automobile industry executed a similar cut in women workers, from 25 to 7.5 percent. Those who managed to remain at work were frequently transferred to less attractive, poorly paying jobs. Thus, for most women, the war experience was a mixed one of new choices cut short by changing circumstances.

Like the war experiences of women, those of minorities were mixed. New employment and social opportunities existed, but they were accompanied by racial and ethnic tensions and the knowledge that when the war ended, the opportunities were likely to vanish. Initially, the war provided few opportunities for African Americans. Shipyards and other defense contractors wanted white workers. North American Aviation Company spoke for the aircraft industry when, in early 1942, it announced that it would not hire blacks "regardless of their training."

The antiblack bias began to change by mid-1942 as businesses felt pressure from the worsening labor shortage, especially in the West, the growing unwillingness of African Americans to be denied the equality and rights due all Americans, and the efforts of the federal government. **A. Philip Randolph,** leader of the powerful Brotherhood of Sleeping Car Porters union, in early 1941 proposed that African Americans march en masse on Washington to demand equality in jobs and the armed forces. To avoid an embarrassing demonstration, Roosevelt issued Executive Order #8802 in June 1941, creating the **Fair Employment Practices Commission** (FEPC), and forbade racial job discrimination by the government and companies holding government contracts.

In California, these pressures dissolved the color line by the end of 1942. West Coast shipyards were

A. Philip Randolph African American labor leader who organized the 1941 march on Washington that pressured Roosevelt to issue an executive order banning racial discrimination in defense industries.

Fair Employment Practices Commission Commission established in 1941 to halt discrimination in war production and government.

the first to integrate. When Lockheed Aircraft broke the color barrier in August, even North American Aviation grudgingly complied. Word soon spread to the South that blacks could find work in California, and between the spring of 1942 and 1945, more than 340,000 African Americans moved to Los Angeles. Overall, nearly 400,000 African Americans abandoned the South for the West. Thousands of others went north to cities such as Chicago and Detroit.

The FEPC and increased access to jobs did not mean that segregation and discrimination ended. Black wages rose from an average of $457 to $1,976 a year but remained only about 65 percent of white wages. To continue their quest for equality, blacks advocated the "Double V" campaign: victory over racist Germany and victory over racism at home. Membership of the NAACP and Urban League increased as both turned to public opinion, the courts, and Congress to attack segregation, lynching, the poll tax, and discrimination. In 1942 the newly formed **Congress of Racial Equality** (CORE) adopted the sit-in tactic to attempt to integrate public facilities. Successes were minor, but still noteworthy. Led by black civil rights activist **James Farmer,** CORE integrated some public facilities in Chicago and Washington, although it failed in the South, where many CORE workers were badly beaten.

In many places across the nation, racial tensions increased as the population of African Americans grew. In Detroit, white workers went on strike when three black workers were promoted, harping, "We'd rather see Hitler and Hirohito win than work beside a nigger on the assembly line." A Justice Department examination reported, "White Detroit seems to be a particularly hospitable climate for native fascist-type movements." On a hot summer Sunday, June 20, 1943, the tensions in Detroit erupted into a major race riot. Before federal troops arrived on June 21 and restored order, twenty-five blacks and nine whites were dead.

The opportunities and difficulties of African Americans in uniform paralleled those of black civilians. Prior to 1940, blacks served at the lowest ranks and in the most menial jobs in a segregated army and navy. The Army Air Corps and the Marines Corps refused to accept blacks at all. Compounding the problem, most in the military openly agreed with Secretary of War Henry L. Stimson when he asserted, "Leadership is not embedded in the Negro race." The manpower needs of war changed the role of the black soldier, opening up new ranks and occupations. In April 1942, Secretary of the Navy James Forrestal permitted black **noncommissioned officers** in the U.S. Navy, although blacks would wait until 1944 before

being commissioned as officers. With only a small number of African American officers, in 1940 the army began to encourage the recruitment of black officers and promoted **Benjamin O. Davis Sr.** from colonel to brigadier general. By the beginning of 1942, the Army Air Corps had an all-black unit, the 99th Pursuit Squadron. Eventually six hundred African Americans were commissioned as pilots. The army also organized other African American units that fought in both the European and Pacific theaters of operations, such as the 371st Tank Battalion, which battled its way across France and into Germany and liberated the concentration camps of Dachau and Buchenwald.

Higher ranks and better jobs for a few still did not disguise that for most blacks, even officers, military life was often demeaning and brutal, and almost always segregated. In Indiana, more than a hundred black officers were arrested for trying to integrate an officers' club. Across the country, blacks objected to the Red Cross's practice of segregating its blood supply. In Salina, Kansas, German prisoners could eat at any local lunch counter and go to any movie theater, but their black guards could not. One dismayed soldier wrote, "The people of Salina would serve these enemy soldiers and turn away black American GIs. . . . If we were . . . in Germany, they would break our bones. As 'colored' men in Salina, they only break our hearts." In truth, many black soldiers had their bones broken, and their lives taken, on the home front. As in the civilian world, blacks in the military resisted discrimination and called on Roosevelt and the government for help. But their requests accomplished little.

Latinos, too, found new opportunities during the war while encountering continued segregation and hostility. Like other Americans, Latinos, almost invariably called "Mexicans" by their fellow soldiers, rushed to enlist as the war started. More than 300,000

Congress of Racial Equality   Civil rights organization founded in 1942 and committed to using nonviolent techniques, such as sit-ins, to end segregation.

James Farmer   Helped to organize the Congress of Racial Equality in 1942; led the organization from 1961 to 1966. In 1969 he became Assistant Secretary of Health, Education and Welfare.

noncommissioned officer   Enlisted member of the armed forces who has been promoted to a rank such as corporal or sergeant, conferring leadership over others.

Benjamin O. Davis, Sr.   Army officer who in 1940 became the first black general in the U.S. Army.

Secure communications on the battlefield are a necessity, and no communications were more secure than those provided by Navajo code talkers. Started in September 1942, members of the Navajo Code Talkers Program took part in every assault the U.S. Marines conducted in the Pacific from 1942 to 1945. The Japanese never were able to decode their telephone and radio transmissions on tactics and troop movements, and other vital battlefield information. *Colonel Charles H. Waterhouse/U.S. Marine Corps Art Collection.*

Latinos served—the highest percentage of any ethnic community—and seventeen won the nation's highest award for valor, the Medal of Honor. Although they faced some institutional and individual prejudices in the military, Latinos, unlike African Americans and most Nisei, served in integrated units and generally faced less discrimination in the military than in society.

For those remaining at home, more jobs were available, but still Latinos almost always worked as common laborers and agricultural workers. In the Southwest, it was not until 1943 that the FEPC attempted to open semiskilled and skilled positions to Mexican Americans. Jobs drew Mexican Americans to cities, creating a serious shortage of farm workers. After having deported Mexicans during the Depression repatriation program, the government had to ask Mexico to supply agricultural workers. Mexico agreed but insisted that the *braceros* (Spanish for "helping arms") receive fair wages and adequate housing, transportation, food, and medical care. In practice, whatever guarantees promised in *bracero* contracts mattered little. Most ranchers and farmers paid low wages and provided substandard facilities. The aver-

age Mexican American family earned about $800 a year, well below the government-established $1,130 annual minimum standard for a family of five.

Many young Mexican Americans, known as *pachucos,* expressed their rejection of Anglo culture and values by wearing **zoot suits**—long jackets with wide lapels and padded shoulders, worn over pleated trousers, pegged and cuffed at the ankle—topped off by a pancake hat and gold chains. In the summer of 1943, tensions between Anglos and Mexican Americans were running high in Los Angeles, which had a history of discrimination in housing, jobs, and education toward its large Mexican American population. Newspapers fanned racial tensions with articles highlighting a Mexican crime wave and depicting the "zooters" as dope addicts and draft dodgers. Anglo mobs, including several hundred servicemen, descended on East Los Angeles for three successive nights. They dragged zoot suiters out of movies, stores, even houses, beating them, and tearing apart their clothes. When the police acted, it was to arrest the victims—over six hundred Mexican American youths were taken into "preventive custody." The riot lasted a week. Afterward, the Los Angeles city council outlawed the wearing of zoot suits.

Like other disadvantaged groups, American Indians took advantage of new job opportunities and served gallantly during the war in the military. The availability of jobs and higher wages lured more than 40,000 American Indians away from their reservations, many of whom never returned following the war. In addition, over 25,000 Indians served in the military. Among the most famous were about four hundred Navajos who served as **code talkers** for the Marine Corps, using their native language as a secure means of communication. Although often called "chief," the American Indian, unlike other minorities, met little discrimination in the military. Whether in

---

braceros   Mexican nationals who worked on U.S. farms beginning in 1942 because of the labor shortage during World War II.

pachucos   A Spanish term originally meaning "bandits," it became associated with juvenile delinquents of Mexican American/Latino heritage.

zoot suit   A long jacket with wide lapels and padded shoulders, worn over pleated trousers, pegged and cuffed at the ankle.

code talkers   Navajos serving in the U.S. Marine Corps who communicated by radio in their native language, undecipherable by the enemy.

the armed forces or in the domestic work force, those who left the reservations saw their families' average incomes rise from $400 a year in 1941 to $1,200 in 1945, and many chose to assimilate into American culture, abandoning for good their old patterns of life.

Less visible in the military than women and minorities were homosexuals. Even though the military services had an official policy of not enlisting homosexuals, *Newsweek* complained that too many "inverts managed to slip through" an ineffective screening process that asked only if a person was a homosexual and looked for obvious effeminate behavior. In the military, many gays and lesbians discovered they could manage both military and personal needs, and that the military generally tolerated them—provided they were not caught in a sexual act. In a circular letter sent to military commanders, the surgeon general's office asked that homosexual relationships be overlooked as long as they did not disrupt the unit. During the war, gays' war records were much like those of other soldiers. "I was superpatriotic," said one gay combat veteran.

Waging World War

- What factors did Roosevelt consider in shaping America's strategy for global conflict?

- What stresses strained the Grand Alliance?

- Why did Truman and his advisers choose to use the atomic bomb?

The War Department's Victory Program, written prior to the Japanese attack on Pearl Harbor, argued that "the first major objective of the United States ought to be the complete military defeat of Germany." In the days that followed the attack, many Americans were convinced that defeating Japan should be the country's first priority. To Churchill's and Stalin's relief, Roosevelt remained committed to victory in Europe as the first priority. But the question remained, What was the best strategy to defeat Hitler? The Soviets fighting with 3.3 million Germans called for a northern European second front as soon as possible. Initially, American military planners supported such an operation in 1942, but the British vigorously opposed a cross-channel invasion. They considered it too risky and calculated that a year was not nearly enough time to assemble sufficient troops and supplies. Instead, the British promoted an Allied landing in western North Africa—Operation Torch. It would be an easier, safer venture that also would help the British army fighting in western Egypt. Be-

lieving the people needed a victory anywhere, Roosevelt ignored his chiefs of staff's opposition and approved the operation.

As planning began for the invasion of North Africa, the course of the war darkened for the Allies. German forces were advancing toward Egypt, while a renewed German offensive was penetrating deeper into the Soviet Union. In the Atlantic, German U-boats were sinking ships at an appalling rate. In April and May 1942, the majority of American forces in the Philippines surrendered, and elsewhere in the Pacific, Japanese successes continued. General Patrick Hurley admitted, "We were out-shipped, out-planed, out-manned, and out-gunned by the Japanese."

Halting the Japanese Advance

Despite the commitment to defeating Germany, the nation's first victory came in the Pacific on May 8, 1942, at the **Battle of the Coral Sea** (see Map 25.3). Having deciphered secret Japanese codes, American military planners were aware that Japan was preparing to invade Port Moresby, New Guinea. They sent the aircraft carriers *Lexington* and *Yorktown* to intercept the invasion fleet. The *Lexington* was sunk, but the Japanese invasion was halted. The success in the Coral Sea was soon duplicated in June at Midway. Again, reading top-secret Japanese messages, the United States learned of a Japanese thrust aimed at **Midway Island.**

The Battle of Midway, June 4–6, 1942, helped change the course of the war in the Pacific. The air-to-sea battle was several hours old when a flight of thirty-seven American dive-bombers attacked the Japanese carriers in the middle of rearming and refueling their planes. The result was cataclysmic. Their decks cluttered with planes, fuel, and bombs, the Japanese carriers suffered staggering casualties and damage. Three immediately sank, and a fourth sank later in the battle. Although the U.S.S. *Yorktown* was lost, the carriers and the air superiority of the Japanese had been destroyed. In the war of machines, the United States quickly replaced the *Yorktown* and by

Battle of the Coral Sea U.S. victory in the Pacific in May 1942; it prevented the Japanese from invading New Guinea and thus isolating Australia.

Midway Island Strategically located Pacific island that the Japanese navy tried to capture in June 1942; warned about Japanese plans by U.S. naval intelligence, American forces repulsed the attack and inflicted heavy losses on Japanese planes and carriers.

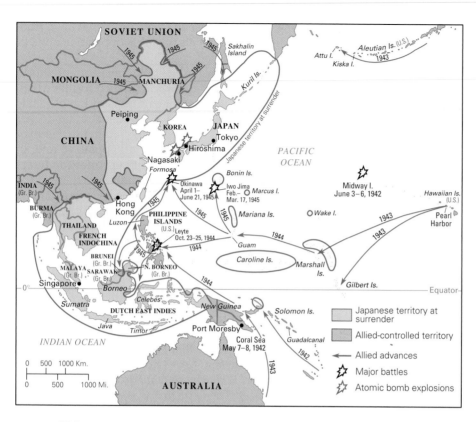

MAP 25.3 Closing the Circle on Japan, 1942–1945 Following the Battle of Midway, with the invasion of Guadalcanal (August 1942), American forces began the costly process of island-hopping. This map shows the paths of the American campaign in the Pacific, closing the circle on Japan. After the Soviet Union entered the war and Hiroshima and Nagasaki were destroyed by atomic bombs, Japan surrendered on August 14, 1945.

the end of the war had constructed fourteen additional large carriers—Japan was able to build only six.

With the victories at Coral Sea and Midway, the next step was to retake lost territory. **General Douglas MacArthur** and the army would take primary responsibility for an offensive beginning in New Guinea and advancing toward the Philippines from the south. The navy, under the direction of Admiral Chester Nimitz, would seize selected islands and atolls in the Solomon, Marshall, Gilbert, and Mariana island groups, approaching the Philippines from the east. Eventually, both forces would join for the final attack on Japan. On August 7, 1942, soldiers of the 1st Marine Division waded ashore on **Guadalcanal Island** in the Solomons (see Map 25.3). Japan, considering the invasion to be "the fork in the road that leads to victory for them or for us," furiously defended the island. Fierce fighting continued through November, but after heavy losses at sea and on land, Japan with-

drew its last troops from Guadalcanal in early February. In the horrendous face-to-face combat that characterized the war in the Pacific, both sides suffered significant losses, but Japanese casualties far outnumbered American. The tide had been turned against Japan.

General Douglas MacArthur Recalled to active duty in 1941, he was given command of American and Filipino troops in the Philippines; in 1942 he was appointed Supreme Commander of the Southwest Pacific Area; in 1945 he was appointed Supreme Commander for the Allied Powers (SCAP) and accepted Japan's formal surrender. As head of the Allied occupation he oversaw the rebuilding of Japan.

Guadalcanal Island Pacific island secured by U.S. troops in February 1943 in the first major U.S. offensive action in the Pacific.

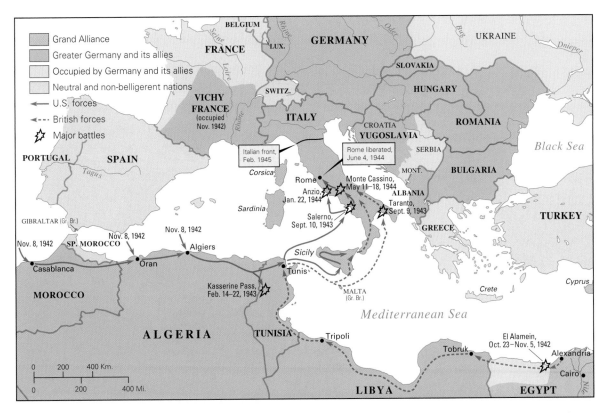

MAP 25.4 The North African and Italian Campaigns Having rejected a cross-channel attack on Hitler's "Atlantic Wall," British and American forces in 1942 and 1943 invaded North Africa and Italy, where victory seemed more assured. This map shows the British and American advances across North Africa and the invasions of Sicily and Italy. German forces fought stubbornly in Italy, slowing Allied advances up the peninsula. By February 1945, Allied forces were still advancing toward the Po Valley.

The Tide Turns in Europe

While American marines sweated in the jungles of Guadalcanal, British and American forces were closing in on German forces in North Africa (see Map 25.4). The British had halted the German advance at El Alamein on November 4, 1942, and had begun an offensive driving the Germans west toward Tunisia. On November 8, Operation Torch had successfully landed American troops in Morocco, who began to push eastward toward the British. Although temporarily halted by German forces at the Kasserine Pass in February 1943, by early May the Americans had linked up with the British, forcing the last German forces in North Africa to surrender on May 13, 1943.

German losses in North Africa were light compared with those in Russia, where Soviet and German forces were locked in a titanic struggle. Through the summer and fall of 1942, German armies advanced

steadily, but during the winter the Soviet army drove them from the Caucasus oil fields and trapped them at Stalingrad. On February 2, 1943, after a three-month Soviet counteroffensive in the dead of winter, 300,000 German soldiers surrendered, their 6th Army having lost more than 140,000 men. As German strength in Russia ebbed, Soviet strength grew. Although it was hard to predict in February, the tide of the war had turned in Europe. Soviet forces would continue to grind down the German army all the way to Berlin (see Map 25.5). But in February, Stalin knew only that the **Battle of Stalingrad** had cost the Russians dearly

Battle of Stalingrad   Battle for the Russian city that was besieged by the German army in 1942 and recaptured by Soviet troops in 1943; regarded by many as the key battle of the European war.

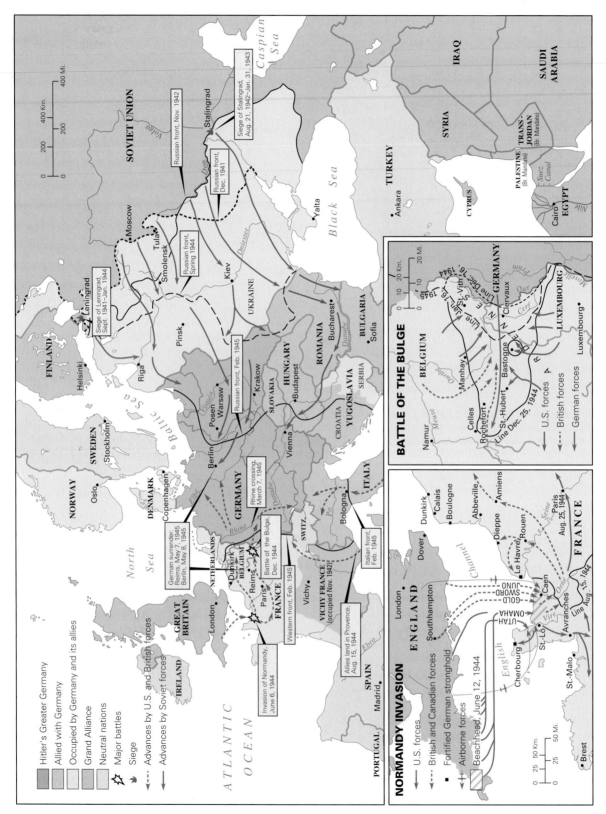

MAP 25.5   The Fall of the Third Reich   In 1943 and 1944, the war turned in favor of the Allies. On the eastern front, Soviet forces drove German forces back toward Germany. On June 6, 1944, D-Day, British, Canadian, and American forces landed on the coast of Normandy to begin the liberation of France. This map shows the course of the Allied armies as they fought their way toward Berlin. On May 7, 1945, Germany surrendered.

and that German strength was still formidable. He again demanded a second front in Western Europe. Again, he would be disappointed. Churchill meeting with Roosevelt at Casablanca (January 14–24, 1943) once more had overcome American desires for a cross-channel attack. Roosevelt agreed instead to invade Sicily and Italy, targets that Churchill called the "soft underbelly of the Axis." General Albert Wedemeyer expressed the U.S. military reaction to the Casablanca deal: "We lost our shirts . . . we came, we listened, and we were conquered."

The invasion of Sicily—Operation Husky—took place in early July 1943, and in a month the Allies controlled the island (see Map 25.4). In response, the Italians overthrew Mussolini and opened negotiations with Britain and the United States to change sides. Italy surrendered unconditionally on September 8, just hours before Allied troops landed at Salerno in Operation Avalanche. Immediately, German forces assumed the defense of Italy and halted the Allied advance just north of Salerno. Not until late May 1944 did Allied forces finally break through the German defenses in Italy. On June 4, U.S. forces under General Mark Clark entered Rome. Two days later, the world's attention turned toward Normandy along the west coast of France. The second front demanded by Stalin had, at long last, begun (see Map 25.5).

The leaders of the **Grand Alliance,** Roosevelt, Churchill, and Stalin, had affirmed their support for the cross-channel attack at the **Tehran Conference** (November 27–December 1, 1943). In the Iranian capital, Roosevelt and Churchill met with Stalin to discuss strategy and to consider the process of establishing a postwar settlement. Confident that he could handle that "old buzzard" Stalin, Roosevelt wanted to establish Soviet support for a new world organization and to obtain a Soviet commitment to declare war against Japan. Roosevelt left Tehran pleased. Stalin had agreed to support a world organization and to enter the Japanese war once the battle with Hitler was over. Militarily, the three had agreed on plans to coordinate a Soviet offensive with the Allied landings at Normandy.

The invasion of Normandy, France—**Operation Overlord**—was the grandest **amphibious** assault ever assembled: 6,483 ships, 1,500 tanks, and 200,000 men. Opposing the Allies were thousands of German troops behind the Atlantic Wall they had constructed along the coast to stop such an invasion. On D-Day, June 6, 1944, American forces landed on Utah and Omaha Beaches, while British and Canadian forces hit Sword, Gold, and Juno Beaches (see Map 25.5 inset). At the landing sites, German resistance varied:

the fiercest fighting was at Omaha Beach, where the American 1st Division suffered heavy casualties. One soldier from Arizona wrote:

> *Let the thunder roll,*
> *Smoke and flame, will show th' way.*
> *I am the Beach at Omaha.*
> *The gates of hell are open wide,*
> *For all who come to play.*
> *The stakes are high,*
> *The game is death,*
> *No winners here today.*

After a week of attacks and counterattacks, the five beaches finally were linked, and British and American forces coiled to break through the German positions blocking the roads to the rest of France. On July 25, American soldiers under General Omar Bradley pierced the stubbornly held German defensive lines at Saint-Lô. Paris was liberated on August 25, and on October 21, the German city of Aachen on the west side of the Rhine River fell to the Allies. From November 1944 to March 1945, American forces readied themselves to attack across the Rhine. While the British and Americans advanced across France, Allied bombers and fighter-bombers were doing what they had been doing since the spring of 1942: bombing German-held Europe night and day. They destroyed vital industries and transportation systems as well as German cities. In one of the worst raids, during the night of February 13–14, 1945, three flights of British and American bombers set Dresden aflame, creating a firestorm that killed more than 135,000 civilians. Nearly 600,000 German civilians would die in Allied air raids, with another 800,000 injured.

Grand Alliance   A term used to refer to those allied nations working to defeat Hitler; often used to refer to the Big Three: Britain, the United States, and the Soviet Union.

Tehran Conference   Meeting in Iran in 1943 at which Roosevelt, Churchill, and Stalin discussed the invasion of Western Europe and considered plans for a new international organization; Stalin also renewed his promise to enter the war against Japan.

Operation Overlord   The Allied invasion of Europe on June 6, 1944—D-Day—across the English Channel to Normandy; D-Day is short for "designated day."

amphibious   In historical context, a military operation that coordinates air, land, and sea military forces to land on a hostile shore.

Stresses in the Grand Alliance

As Allied forces struggled to move eastward toward the Rhine, the Soviets advanced rapidly westward, pushing the last German troops from Russia by the end of June 1944. Behind Germany's retreating eastern armies, the Soviets occupied parts of Poland, Romania, Bulgaria, Hungary, and Czechoslovakia. Following the Red Army were Soviet officials and Eastern European Communists who had lived in exile in the Soviet Union before and during the war. The Soviet goal was to establish new Eastern European governments that would be "friendly" to the Soviet Union. A Communist Lublin government (named after the town where the government was installed) was established in Poland, while in Romania and Bulgaria **"popular front"** governments, heavily influenced by local and returning Communist Party members, took command. Only Czechoslovakia and Hungary managed to establish non-Communist-dominated governments as the German occupation collapsed.

On February 4, 1945, the Big Three met at the Black Sea resort of **Yalta** amid growing Western apprehension about Soviet territorial and political goals in Eastern Europe. Confident that he could work with Stalin, Roosevelt wanted to ensure that the Soviet Union would enter the war against Japan and maintain its support for a new United Nations. He also wanted the Soviets to show some willingness to modify their controls over Eastern Europe. Stalin's goals were Western acceptance of a Soviet sphere of influence in Eastern Europe, the weakening of Germany, and the economic restoration of the Soviet Union. Central to Allied differences over Eastern Europe was the nature of the Polish government. The Soviet Union supported the Lublin government, whereas Roosevelt and Churchill supported a London-based government in exile. They considered the Lublin regime to be undemocratic and a puppet of the Soviet Union. Stalin labeled the London-based government hostile to the Soviet Union and demanded a friendly government in Poland. After considerable acidic haggling, the powers agreed on a compromise phrased in language that Admiral William Leahy, one of Roosevelt's primary advisers, ruefully noted was so vague that its meaning could be "stretched from Yalta to Washington" without breaking. Roosevelt reluctantly but realistically concluded that it was the best he could do for Poland at the moment. The Yalta Conference also left control over Eastern Europe firmly in Soviet hands.

Roosevelt was extremely tired and seriously ill with high blood pressure and a bad heart throughout

As Allied armies fought their way closer to Berlin, Roosevelt, Churchill, and Stalin met at the Black Sea resort of Yalta in February 1945 to discuss military strategy and postwar concerns. Among the most important issues were the Polish government, German reparations, and the formation of the United Nations. Two months later, Roosevelt died and Harry S. Truman assumed the presidency. *National Archives.*

the Yalta meetings. Nevertheless, he had negotiated well, achieving two of his major goals. He had maintained Soviet support in defeating Japan and promoting a new world organization. Although disappointed over the continued Soviet domination of Eastern Europe, Roosevelt realized that little could be done to prevent the Soviet Union from keeping what it already had, or could easily take. He hoped that his

popular front An organization or government composed of a wide spectrum of political groups; popular fronts were used by the Soviet Union in forming allegedly non-Communist governments in Eastern Europe.

Yalta Site in the Crimea of the last meeting, in 1945, between Roosevelt, Churchill, and Stalin; they discussed the final defeat of the Axis powers and the problems of postwar occupation.

good will would encourage Stalin to respond in kind, maintaining at least a semblance of representative government in Eastern Europe and continuing to cooperate with the United States.

Roosevelt understood that postwar stability and security were impossible without Soviet cooperation, and he was especially hopeful that the "spirit of Yalta" would contribute to the formation of an effective **United Nations** (UN). Roosevelt died shortly after his return from Yalta, thrusting Truman into the presidency. Truman brought a more assertive tone to American foreign policy but, like Roosevelt, was determined to see the creation of the world organization. Building on a series of high-level discussions in April 1945, a conference in San Francisco finished the task: the United Nations was born. The charter of the United Nations established an organization composed of six distinct bodies, the most important of which are the **General Assembly** and the **Security Council.** Composed of all member nations, the General Assembly was the weaker body, having the authority only to discuss issues but not to resolve them. More important was the smaller Security Council composed of eleven nations. Six were elected by the General Assembly, but the real power was held by five permanent members: the United States, the Soviet Union, the United Kingdom, China, and France. The Security Council established and implemented policies and could apply economic and military pressures against other nations. To protect their interests, each of the five permanent nations could veto Security Council decisions. The United Nations represented the concept of peace through world cooperation, but its structure clearly left the future of peace in the hands of the major powers.

Defeating Hitler

With his forces crumbling in the east, Hitler approved a last-ditch attempt to halt the Allied advance late in 1944. Taking advantage of bad weather that grounded Allied aircraft, on December 16 German forces launched an attack through the Ardennes Forest that drove a 50-mile "bulge" into the Allied lines in Belgium. If successful, the attack would have split American forces. It was a desperate gamble that failed. Although surprised by the attack, not all American forces were pushed aside. At Bastogne, a critical crossroads, Brigadier General A. C. McAuliffe, commander of the 101st Airborne Division, refused to retreat and when invited to surrender, simply told the Germans, "Nuts." After ten days, the weather improved, the German offensive slowed and halted,

and an American relief column reached Bastogne (see Map 25.5 inset). This last major Axis counteroffensive on the western front—known as the **Battle of the Bulge**—delayed **General Dwight D. Eisenhower's** eastward assault briefly, but by costing Germany valuable reserves and equipment, it hastened the end of the war. Also by the end of 1944, the war in Italy was about over as Allied forces pushed through the Po Valley.

On March 7, 1945, American forces crossed the Rhine at Remagen and began to battle their way into the heart of Germany. While American and British troops moved steadily eastward, Russian soldiers began the bloody, house-to-house conquest of Berlin. On April 25, American and Soviet infantrymen shook hands at the Elbe River 60 miles south of Berlin. Inside the city, unwilling to be captured, Hitler committed suicide on April 30 and had aides burn his body. On May 8, 1945, German officials surrendered. The war in Europe was over.

Although Roosevelt had worked since 1939 to ensure Hitler's defeat, he did not live to see it. On April 12, while relaxing and recovering from the strains of Yalta, he died of a massive cerebral hemorrhage at Warm Springs, Georgia. Nor did Roosevelt live to know the full horror of what came to be called the **Holocaust.** No atrocity of war could equal what advancing Allied armies found as they fought their way

---

United Nations International organization established in 1945 to maintain peace among nations and foster cooperation in human rights, education, health, welfare, and trade.

General Assembly Assembly of all members of the United Nations; it debates issues but neither creates nor executes policy.

Security Council The executive agency of the United Nations; it included five permanent members with veto power (China, France, the United Kingdom, the Soviet Union, and the United States) and ten members elected by the General Assembly for two-year terms.

Battle of the Bulge The last major Axis counteroffensive, in December 1944, against the Allied forces in Western Europe; German troops gained territory in Belgium but were eventually driven back.

Dwight David Eisenhower Supreme Commander of Allied forces in Europe during World War II, who planned D-Day invasion; later became president of the United States.

Holocaust Mass murder of European Jews and other groups systematically carried out by the Nazis during World War II.

Hitler ordered the "Final Solution"—the extermination of Europe's Jews—soon after the United States entered the war. In this picture, German troops arrest residents of the Warsaw ghetto for deportation to concentration camps. Few would survive the camps, where over 6 million Jews died. *YIVO Institute for Jewish Research.*

toward Berlin. In 1941 the Nazi political leadership had decided on what was called the **Final Solution** to rid German-occupied Europe of Jews. In concentration camps, Jews, along with homosexuals, gypsies, and the mentally ill, were brutalized, starved, worked as slave labor, and systematically exterminated. At Auschwitz, Nazis used gas chambers—disguised as showers—to execute 12,000 victims a day. American troops were among those to liberate the camps, inviting reporters and photographers to record the reality of the horror found there. Among the American units freeing Jewish survivors at Buchenwald and Dachau were the African American 761st Tank Battalion and the Japanese American 522nd Field Artillery Battalion. One survivor at first thought that the Japanese had won the war, until realizing they were Americans. "I had never seen black men or Japanese," another recalled. "They were riding in these tanks and jeeps; they were like angels who came down from heaven to save our lives." While thousands were saved, over 6 million Jews had been slaughtered in

the death camps, nearly two-thirds of prewar Europe's Jewish population.

Closing the Circle on Japan

Victory in Europe—**V-E Day**—touched off parades and rejoicing in the United States. But Japan still had to be defeated. Japan's defensive strategy was simple: force the United States to invade a seemingly endless number of Pacific islands before it could launch an invasion against Japan—with each speck of land costing the Americans dearly in lives and materials. The

---

Final Solution German plan to eliminate Jews through mass executions by isolating them in concentration camps; by the end of the war, the Nazis had killed 6 million Jews.

V-E Day May 8, 1945, the day marking the official end of the war in Europe, following the unconditional surrender of the German armies.

On November 21, 1943, marines stormed ashore on the atoll of Tarawa, soon to be called "Bloody Tarawa." The marines secured the island, but the cost was high. Of the 5,000 marines who fought in the battle, more than 1,000 were killed and another 2,000 wounded. Nearly all of the 5,000 Japanese defenders died, many in a final "death charge." *U.S. Marine Corps Museum.*

American military, however, realized that it had to seize only the most strategic of islands. With carriers providing mobile air superiority, the Americans could bypass and isolate others.

Throughout 1943, the army under General MacArthur advanced up the northern coast of New Guinea, while the navy and marines fought their way through the Solomon Islands. At the same time, far to the northeast, the U.S. Navy and the Marines Corps were establishing footholds in the Gilbert and Marshall Islands. Exemplifying the bitter fighting was "bloody Tarawa," where marines fought their way ashore on November 21, 1943. Overcoming 5,000 well-entrenched Japanese troops, nearly all of whom fought to the death, American marines suffered nearly 3,000 casualties. With the Gilbert and Marshall Islands neutralized, Admiral Nimitz approached Guam and Saipan in the Mariana Islands (see Map 25.3). In their effort to halt the American invasion of Saipan, the Japanese lost 243 planes and three more aircraft carriers. On Saipan itself, the Japanese defenders, including 22,000 Japanese civilians, ex-

pended all their ammunition and then committed suicide rather than surrender. Marines next seized the nearby islands of Tinian (August 1) and Guam (August 11). By July 1944, the southern and eastern approaches to the Philippines were in American hands, and MacArthur, who, ordered by President Roosevelt to evacuate the Philippines in March 1942, had vowed to return, was ready to fulfill his promise.

Airfields on Tinian, Saipan, and Guam provided for the systematic bombing of military and domestic targets. In February 1944, the War Department gave approval for American long-range bombers, the B-29s, to begin devastating raids against Japanese cities, with the intention of weakening the Japanese will to resist. Although the estimated number of Japanese civilians killed in the bombing by far exceeded the number of Japanese soldiers killed in combat, the bombing generated little Japanese citizen reduction in support for the war or the government. In October, American forces landed on Leyte in the center of the Philippine archipelago. Again, the Japanese navy acted to halt the invasion, and with the same results.

In the largest naval battle in history, the **Battle of Leyte Gulf** (October 23–25, 1944), American naval forces shattered what remained of Japanese air and sea power. On October 23, 1944, wading ashore with an escort of subordinates and at least one photographer, General MacArthur returned to the Philippines.

After the Battle of Leyte Gulf, the full brunt of the American Pacific offensive bore down on Iwo Jima and **Okinawa,** only 750 miles from Tokyo. To defend the islands, Japan resorted to a new tactic: the use of *kamikaze*—pilots who made suicide crashes on targets in explosive-laden airplanes. The American assault on Iwo Jima began on February 19 and became the worst experience faced by U.S. Marines in the war. Before the assault ended on March 17, virtually all of the 21,000 Japanese defenders had fought to the death, and American losses approached one-third of the landing force: 6,821 dead and 20,000 wounded.

On Okinawa, from April through June, the carnage was even worse. While American forces took heavy losses along Japanese defensive lines, nine hundred Japanese planes, including three hundred *kamikazes,* rained terror and destruction on the American fleet. Throughout May and June, the Japanese air onslaughts continued but became weaker each month as Japan ran out of planes and pilots. By the end of June, Okinawa was in American hands, but at a fearful price: 12,000 Americans, 110,000 Japanese soldiers, and 160,000 Okinawan and Japanese civilians dead.

Entering the Nuclear Age

Okinawa proved a painful warning for those planning the invasion of Japan. Fighting for their homeland, the Japanese could be expected to resist until death. American casualties would be extremely high, perhaps as many as a million. But by the summer of 1945, the United States had an alternative to invasion: a new and untried weapon—the atomic bomb. The A-bomb was the product of years of British-American research and development, the Manhattan Project. From the beginning of the conflict, science had played a vital role in the war effort by developing and improving the tools of combat. Among the outcomes were radar, sonar, flamethrowers, rockets, and a variety of other useful and frequently deadly products. But the most fearsome and secret of the projects was the drive started in 1941 to construct a nuclear weapon. Between then and 1945, the Manhattan Project scientists, led by physicists J. Robert Oppenheimer and Edward Teller, controlled a chain reaction involving

On August 6, 1945, the world entered the atomic age when the city of Hiroshima was destroyed by an atomic bomb. "We had seen the city when we went in," said the pilot of the *Enola Gay,* "and there was nothing to see when we came back." The city and most of its people had died. *National Archives.*

uranium and plutonium to create the atomic bomb. By the time Germany surrendered, the project had consumed more than $2 billion, but the bomb had been born. When it was tested at Alamogordo, New Mexico, on July 16, 1945, the results were spectacular. In the words of Brigadier General Leslie R. Groves, the U.S. Army engineer who headed the project: "The effect could well be called unprecedented, magnificent, beautiful, stupendous and terrifying. . . . The whole country was lighted by a searing light. . . . Thirty seconds after the explosion came . . . the air blast . . . followed almost immediately by the strong, sustained, awesome roar which warned of doomsday and made us feel that we puny things were blasphemous to dare tamper with the forces heretofore reserved to The

> **Battle of Leyte Gulf**   Naval battle in October 1944 in which American forces near the Philippines crushed Japanese air and sea power.
>
> **Okinawa**   Pacific island that U.S. troops captured in the spring of 1945 after a grueling battle in which over a quarter-million soldiers and civilians were killed.

TABLE 25.1   **Military War Dead**

Country	Dead
Soviet Union	13.5 million
China	7.4 million
Poland	6.0 million
Germany	4.6 million
Japan	1.2 million
Britain and Commonwealth	430,000
United States	220,000

Almighty." Word of the successful test was quickly relayed to Truman, who had assumed the presidency when Roosevelt died in April and who at the time was meeting with Churchill and Stalin at Potsdam, outside Berlin.

Truman had traveled to Potsdam with a new secretary of state, James F. Byrnes. Before leaving for Germany, they agreed not to tell Stalin any details about the atomic bomb (although both knew about a Soviet spy ring within the Manhattan Project) and to use the bomb as quickly as possible against Japan. Using the atomic bomb, Truman and Byrnes hoped, would serve two purposes. It would force Japan to surrender without an invasion, and it would impress the Soviets and, just maybe, make them more amenable to American views on the postwar world order.

Soon after his arrival for the Potsdam Conference (July 17–August 2), Truman met privately with Stalin and received the Soviet dictator's promise to enter the Japanese war in mid-August. Later, in a major understatement, Truman informed Stalin that the United States had a new and powerful weapon to use against Japan, never mentioning that it was an atomic bomb. Stalin appeared uninterested and told Truman to go ahead and use the weapon. Then, with Prime Minister Clement Attlee of Britain, Truman released the **Potsdam Declaration,** which called on Japan to surrender by August or face total destruction. The declaration reflected two developments—one Japan knew about, and the other it was soon to learn. Japanese officials had asked the "neutral" Soviets to try to persuade the Americans to consider negotiating a Japanese surrender. Stalin, Attlee, and Truman agreed instead to insist on unconditional surrender. In the

Potsdam Declaration, the Japanese could read the rejection of their overture, but they had no way of knowing that the utter destruction referred to in the declaration meant the A-bomb. On July 25, Truman ordered the use of the atomic bomb as soon after August 3 as possible, provided the Japanese did not surrender.

On the island of Tinian, B-29s were readied to carry the two available bombs to targets in Japan; a third was waiting to be assembled. A B-29 bomber named the *Enola Gay* dropped the first bomb over **Hiroshima** at 9:15 A.M. on August 6, 1945. Japan's eighth-largest city, Hiroshima had a population of over 250,000 and had not to that point suffered heavy bombing. In the atomic blast and fireball, almost 100,000 Japanese were killed or terribly maimed. Another 100,000 would eventually die from the effects of radiation. The United States announced that unless the Japanese surrendered immediately, they could "expect a rain of ruin from the air, the like of which has never been seen on this earth."

In Tokyo, peace advocates in the Japanese government again sought to use the Soviets as an intermediary. They wanted some guarantee that Emperor Hirohito would be allowed to remain as emperor and a symbol of Japan. The Soviet response was to declare war and advance into Japanese-held Manchuria on

Potsdam Declaration   The demand for Japan's unconditional surrender, made near the end of the Potsdam Conference.

Hiroshima   Japanese city that was the target, on August 6, 1945, of the first atomic bomb, called "Little Boy."

August 8, exactly three months after V-E Day. On August 9, as a high-level Japanese council considered surrender, a second atomic bomb destroyed **Nagasaki.** Nearly 60,000 people were killed. Although some within the Japanese army argued for continuing the fight, Emperor Hirohito, watching the Red Army slice through Japanese forces and afraid of losing more cities to atomic attacks, made the final decision. Japan must "bear the unbearable," he said, and surrender. On August 14, 1945, Japan officially surrendered, and the United States agreed to leave the position of emperor intact.

World War II was over, but much of the world now lay in ruins. Some 50 million people, military and civilian, had been killed (see Table 25.1). The United States was spared most of the destruction. It had suffered almost no civilian casualties, and its cities and industrial centers stood unharmed. In many ways, in fact, the war had been good to the United States. It had decisively ended the Depression, and although some economists predicted an immediate postwar recession, the overall economic picture was bright. Government regulation and planning for the economy that had their beginnings in the New Deal took root and flourished during the war. As the war ended, only a few wanted a return to the laissez-faire-style government that had characterized the 1920s. Big government was here to stay, and at the center of big government was a powerful presidency ready to direct and guide the nation.

> **Nagasaki** City in western Japan devastated on August 9, 1945, by the second atomic bomb, called "Fat Man."

Individual Voices

Examining a Primary Source

Rev. Clayton D. Russell Advocates Union Membership for Black Women

African American newspapers played key roles within black communities. Like other black newspapers, the *California Eagle* provided readers throughout the Los Angeles area with news about community social events and black athletes and sports teams, but it also informed its readers about issues relating to African Americans and sought to mobilize them for action. The publication championed a poll tax repeal, supported the Mexican Americans during the zoot suit riots, and, as in this document, urged African Americans to take full advantage of every opportunity to improve themselves that society offered. Reverend Russell's essay appeared in the *Eagle* on October 1, 1942.

Many of the women who are now going into industry have never worked before and if they did the majority . . . were engaged in that form of work which was open to them, namely, domestic work. They experienced a paternal relationship with employers. . . . In industry the boss will never be seen. . . . This is a new relationship and Negro women who face it, many of them will have difficulty.

I have no doubt as to the ability of Negro women to adjust to these new situations. Their whole history has been one of adjustment, but I raise these problems to show that the role of Negro women in this new field will not be an easy one and that there may be many who will fall by the wayside, both because of the new adjustments . . . and secondary because of racial discrimination that will be present in industry. ■

There will be many things of a racial nature that Negro women actually experienced [sic]. This will call for great broadness on the part of our women.

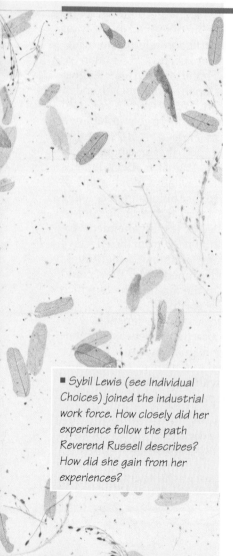

■ *Sybil Lewis (see Individual Choices) joined the industrial work force. How closely did her experience follow the path Reverend Russell describes? How did she gain from her experiences?*

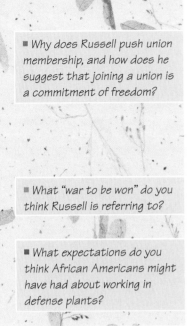

■ *Why does Russell push union membership, and how does he suggest that joining a union is a commitment of freedom?*

■ *What "war to be won" do you think Russell is referring to?*

■ *What expectations do you think African Americans might have had about working in defense plants?*

There is a way to beat racial discrimination. It cannot be broken down by individual effort. Racial discrimination can only be broken down by gradual every day organized action. In industry, the best weapon against racial discrimination, against all things undemocratic . . . is the trade union. Negro women must get into the new trade unions that will be formed of women workers. ■

Where the CIO is organized, Negro women must join, where the AFL is organized, Negro women must join. They must demand the right to join side by side with their white sister.

All over the country, CIO anti-discrimination committees have been active: white workers have left jobs because of discrimination against Negroes and have refused to return to work until these social injustices have been corrected.

. . . Today is the day of the industrial workers, the strength and the freedom of any people in America will depend on the amount of integration of that people in industry and the labor movement. Get into industry, there is a war to be won and much depends on you. ■ *. . . If you do not have a skill, you will be in an unskilled position or relegated to domestic work. But if you have a skilled position, you will be able to get a higher graded position. Now is the time to get the training and the training is free.* ■

Summary

As Herbert Hoover assumed office, he expected continued prosperity and peace. While he was able to further improve American relations with Latin America, he also sadly watched the global Depression destroy prosperity and peace. Both he and Franklin Roosevelt faced the collapse of the international system as Japan, Italy, and Germany sought to increase their territories, influence, and power. Japan seized Manchuria in 1931 and invaded China in 1937. Meanwhile Italy's Benito Mussolini conquered Ethiopia, and Adolph Hitler annexed Austria and sought to create a new German empire. In the lengthening shadow of world conflict, the majority of Americans maintained isolationism, and Congress passed neutrality laws designed to keep the nation from involvement in the faraway conflicts. Roosevelt wanted to take a more active role in world affairs but found himself hobbled by isolationist sentiment and by his own decision to fight the Depression at home first. Even as Germany invaded Poland in September 1939, the majority of Americans were still anxious to remain outside the conflict. Roosevelt, however, reshaped American neutrality to aid those nations fighting Germany, linking the United States' economic might first to England and then to the Soviet Union.

Roosevelt also increased economic and diplomatic pressures on Japan to halt its conquest of China and occupation of French Indochina. But the pressure only heightened the crisis, convincing many in the Japanese government that the best choice was to attack the United States before it grew in strength. Japan's attack on Pearl Harbor on December 7, 1941, brought a fully committed American public and government into World War II.

Mobilizing the nation for war ended the Depression and increased government intervention in the economy. Another outcome of the war was a range of new choices for women and minorities in the military and the workplace. Japanese Americans, however, suffered a loss of freedom and property as the government placed them in internment camps.

Fighting a two-front war, American planners gave first priority to defeating Hitler. The British and American offensive to recover Europe began in North Africa in 1942, expanded to Italy in 1943, and to France in 1944. By the beginning of 1945, Allied armies were threatening Nazi Germany from the west and the east, and on May 8, 1945, Germany surrendered. In the Pacific theater, the victory at Midway in mid-1942 checked Japan's offensive and allowed the use of aircraft carriers to begin tightening the noose around the enemy. To bring the war to a close without a U.S. invasion, Truman elected to use the atomic bomb. Following the destruction of Hiroshima and Nagasaki, Japan surrendered on August 14, 1945, ending the war and for many Americans ushering in the beginning of "America's century."

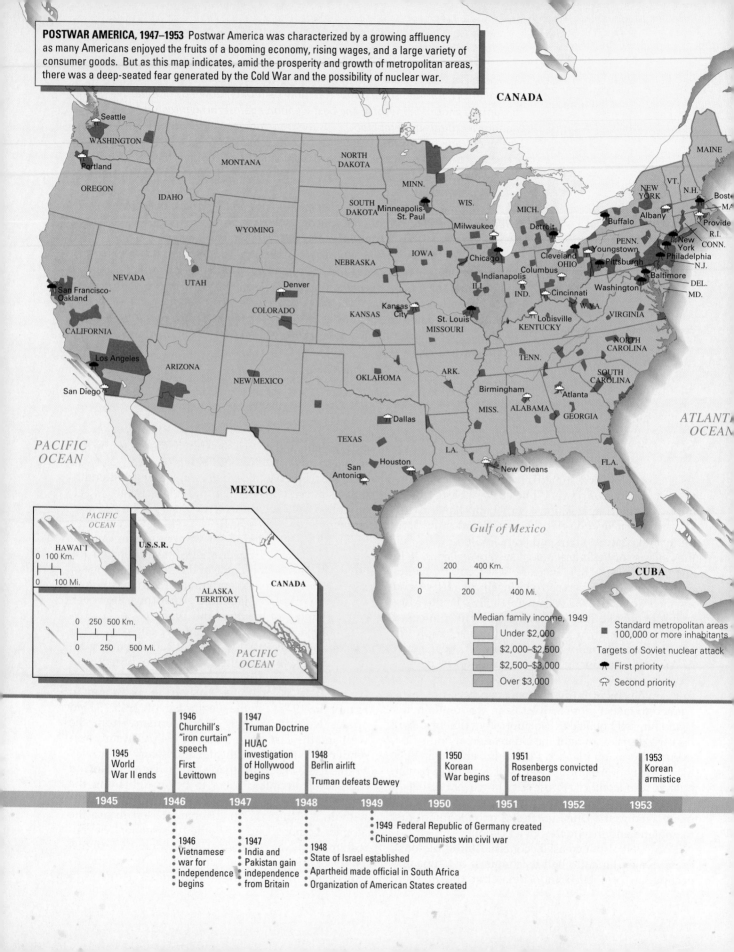

POSTWAR AMERICA, 1947–1953 Postwar America was characterized by a growing affluency as many Americans enjoyed the fruits of a booming economy, rising wages, and a large variety of consumer goods. But as this map indicates, amid the prosperity and growth of metropolitan areas, there was a deep-seated fear generated by the Cold War and the possibility of nuclear war.

CANADA

WASHINGTON
Seattle
Portland
OREGON
IDAHO
MONTANA
NORTH DAKOTA
SOUTH DAKOTA
MINN.
Minneapolis-St. Paul
WIS.
Milwaukee
MICH.
Detroit
NEW YORK
VT.
N.H.
MAINE
Buffalo
Albany
Bost
MA
Provide
R.I.
CONN.
NEVADA
UTAH
WYOMING
NEBRASKA
IOWA
Chicago
ILL.
Cleveland
OHIO
Columbus
Youngstown
Pittsburgh
PENN.
New York
Philadelphia
N.J.
San Francisco-Oakland
CALIFORNIA
Los Angeles
San Diego
Denver
COLORADO
KANSAS
Kansas City
MISSOURI
St. Louis
IND.
Indianapolis
Cincinnati
KENTUCKY
Louisville
W. VA.
Washington
DEL.
MD.
Baltimore
VIRGINIA
ARIZONA
NEW MEXICO
OKLAHOMA
ARK.
TENN.
NORTH CAROLINA
SOUTH CAROLINA
San Antonio
Houston
Dallas
TEXAS
LA.
New Orleans
MISS.
ALABAMA
Birmingham
GEORGIA
Atlanta
FLA.

PACIFIC OCEAN

MEXICO

Gulf of Mexico

ATLANT
OCEAN

CUBA

Inset:
PACIFIC OCEAN
HAWAI'I
0 100 Km.
0 100 Mi.
U.S.S.R.
ALASKA TERRITORY
CANADA
PACIFIC OCEAN
0 250 500 Km.
0 250 500 Mi.

0 200 400 Km.
0 200 400 Mi.

Median family income, 1949

	Under $2,000
	$2,000–$2,500
	$2,500–$3,000
	Over $3,000

Standard metropolitan areas 100,000 or more inhabitants

Targets of Soviet nuclear attack
🖤 First priority
☁ Second priority

Timeline:

1945 World War II ends

1946 Churchill's "iron curtain" speech
First Levittown

1946 Vietnamese war for independence begins

1947 Truman Doctrine
HUAC investigation of Hollywood begins

1947 India and Pakistan gain independence from Britain

1948 Berlin airlift
Truman defeats Dewey

1948 State of Israel established
Apartheid made official in South Africa
Organization of American States created

1949 Federal Republic of Germany created
Chinese Communists win civil war

1950 Korean War begins

1951 Rosenbergs convicted of treason

1953 Korean armistice

1945 1946 1947 1948 1949 1950 1951 1952 1953

Truman and Cold War America, 1945–1952

Postwar America, 1947–1953
Examine the map on the facing page. What relationship exists between expanding metropolitan areas and family wealth? What demographic and economic facts help explain why the South lagged in family income? How are income trends also reflecting of population changes, as indicated on the chapter-opening map for Chapter 25?

Individual Choices

GEORGE F. KENNAN

Following his graduation from Princeton University, George F. Kennan was trained by the State Department to be an expert on the Soviet Union. As such, he provided the Truman administration with evaluations of Soviet foreign policy that became the foundation of American foreign policy throughout the Cold War. He left the State Department in 1952 and became a respected historian, writer, and lecturer on foreign-policy issues. *National Portrait Gallery, Smithsonian Institution/Art Resource, NY.*

George Frost Kennan

It was a case, he concluded, "where nothing but the whole truth would do. They had asked for it. Now, by God, they would have it." Thus it was with a sense of urgency and expectation that George Frost Kennan, the American chargé d'affaires to the Soviet Union, sat down to write a reply to a request from the State Department. President Harry S. Truman and other high-level American policymakers were reexamining American policy toward the Soviet Union and wondering what factors determined Soviet foreign policy. They decided to ask their expert on Russia stationed in Moscow. Kennan's reply, called the "Long Telegram," written and dispatched to Washington on February 22, 1946, had a staggering impact among the inner circles of the Truman administration. The telegram contained a lucid, informative, and instructive evaluation of the motives behind Soviet policy and a positive suggestion about what course U.S. policy should take.

Kennan had entered the path that brought him to this critical juncture when, fresh from Princeton University, he joined the Foreign Service in 1926. He decided to become an expert on the Soviet Union and was sent to Riga, Latvia, to sharpen his Russian language skills and further his knowledge of Russia and the Soviet Union. His conversations with Russian exiles who had fled the Communist Revolution reinforced and sharpened his generally negative views about the Soviet Union and its leaders. When the United States established official relations with the Soviets in 1933, Kennan, who longed to be assigned to Moscow, was overjoyed to be part of the embassy's staff. Full of curiosity and enthusiasm, he was among the first contingent of Americans to arrive in Moscow. He would remain in the Soviet Union until 1937, when he returned to Washington. In those four years, he reached conclusions about the Soviet Union and its leaders that would shape his vision in the years to come and that were evident in his "Long Telegram." He rejected the view that revolutionary Communists would transform Russia. Communism, he wrote, "was not a turning point in history, but only another name, another milepost along the road of Russia's wasteful, painful" path toward an unknown future. Stalin and other leaders were copies of those who had ruled Russia for centuries—despotic, ruthless, and constantly beset by rivals who sought to topple them from power. Nor did Kennan hold out much optimism for positive Soviet-American relations, noting that their fundamental differences were too great.

Kennan returned to Moscow in 1944 at the request of William Averell Harriman, whom Roosevelt had appointed ambassador. Harriman wanted to draw on Kennan's expertise on the Soviet Union. Although Kennan appreciated the Soviets' key role in defeating Germany and understood the necessity of supplying the Union of Soviet Socialists Republics (USSR) with material aid, he disliked President Roosevelt's willingness to befriend and trust the Soviets. In memoranda and messages to Harriman and officials in the State Department, he repeated his fears of Soviet domination over Eastern and Central Europe and warned against a wrong-

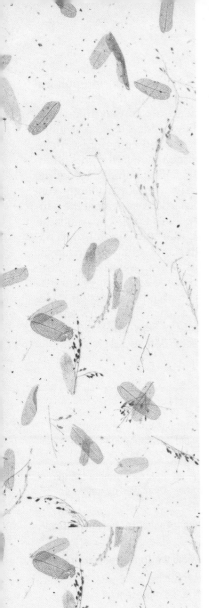

headed American policy. Moscow was determined "to have an extensive sphere of influence," he wrote, while the United States was "wandering about with our heads in the clouds of Wilsonian idealism." Although he liked Truman's view of the Soviets, which was harsher than Roosevelt's, Kennan was frustrated that his own opinions seemed to have little or no impact on policymakers. He considered resigning. Then came the request from Washington for his analysis of Soviet policy.

His eight-thousand-word telegraphed reply catapulted Kennan from a minor voice in American foreign policy to a major player. His lengthy analysis described Soviet policy as driven by traditional Russian goals and the need for Soviet leaders to maintain their control over the people and the state. He argued that there could be no permanent truce with the Soviets and that the United States should use its power to contain Russian expansionism. Secretary of State James Byrnes called the analysis "splendid." Secretary of the Navy James Forrestal made copies of the telegram and distributed it around Washington. For American policymakers, already angry with and suspicious of the Soviet Union, the report provided a clear, understandable, and logical explanation of Soviet behavior. The Soviets, not the United States, were responsible for the ominous hostility between the two nations, and the United States should take action to limit the growth of Soviet power and influence.

Kennan returned to the United States and was placed in charge of the Policy Planning Staff, whose task it was to formulate long-range policies, including the Marshall Plan. In July 1947, using the pen name "Mr. X," Kennan caught the attention of a wider national audience when he reformulated his views on the Soviet Union in an article, "The Sources of Soviet Conduct," published in the prestigious journal *Foreign Affairs*. Again he argued that the Soviets were expansionistic and that the United States needed to use "adroit and vigilant . . . counter-force" to contain Moscow's advances. He also speculated that American containment efforts, if applied correctly, would erode Soviet power.

Regarded by many as the "Father of Containment," Kennan left government service in 1953 to write, teach, and lecture. In 1975 he founded the Kennan Institute for Advanced Russian Studies in Washington, D.C. When the Soviet Union collapsed in 1991, many credited the policies advocated by George Kennan as the root cause, and he again enjoyed great popularity for his foreign-policy wisdom and insight.

INTRODUCTION

When World War II ended, Americans hoped for world peace and expected to experience the "American dream" of having a good job, owning a home, and enjoying the benefits of a consumer society. George Kennan's "Long Telegram" reflected one of the harsh realities of postwar America: there would not be world peace. Instead, the United States entered into a Cold War with the Soviet Union that would last nearly fifty years and affect every aspect of American life. The *Los Angeles Times* expressed the desire of most Americans: the United States would lead the postwar world because it had "no other direct interest" except a lasting and just peace. Seeking this lasting peace, Truman worked to forge an American vision of world affairs, but by the close of 1947, American and Soviet differences had ended their wartime cooperation and produced a bitter rivalry—the Cold War. Reflecting Kennan's recommendations, the United States began to implement a policy to contain

Soviet influence, first in Western Europe and then in Asia. The American isolationism that had existed after the First World War was now replaced by an expanded global role. When North Korea invaded South Korea, the Cold War suddenly became "hot" as Truman committed American troops to halt Communist aggression.

The Cold War not only changed American foreign policy, it also had an important impact on domestic life and politics, creating a second Red Scare and what some have called "an age of anxiety." Aided by a growing concern over communism abroad and at home, conservatives and others found it easier to reverse the economic and social strides made by minorities, women, and workers. Women, many argued, should give up their jobs and greater independence and return full-time to the roles of wife and mother. Postwar America, nearly everyone thought, would provide a prosperous economy with well-paying jobs, homes in newly constructed suburban communities, and stable families. These prospects, however, seemed out of reach to most African Americans and other minorities. They were expected to leave their wartime gains behind and return to their customary place at the foot of American society. Yet many remained optimistic about the future. The skills, experiences, and self-confidence gained by the war could not be taken away. The possibility loomed that President Truman's efforts to expand on the New Deal might bring increased opportunities for minorities, and, as evidence, by 1947 an African American athlete was playing professional baseball in what had been an all-white league.

For minorities and others, the key political question was whether Truman would indeed expand on the New Deal. Would he provide support for minorities, workers, and women in their quests for continued opportunity? Or would he buckle under conservative opposition that increasingly used the fears of the Cold War and New Deal socialism to press for fewer government controls and a retreat to traditional norms? Truman sought programs that expanded New Deal agencies and called for federal support for civil rights, education, and medical care. His plans proved too liberal for many, and Truman had to accept the "politics of the possible," an agenda that pleased neither ardent liberals nor staunch conservatives. It reflected what some called the "vital center" of American politics—an acceptance of, and even some expansion on, existing government activism, but little political or public support for any new programs.

The growing fear of communism also soon became a weapon to use against social, cultural, and political foes, who could be accused of being too liberal. Conservatives and businessmen asserted that unions had become too powerful—they needed to be restrained and purged of their socialist and communist members. Southern whites charged that civil rights advocates were tainted with socialistic values. Across the nation, change and diversity were increasingly suspect. Spearheading America's defense against the dangers of communism were the House Un-American Activities Committee (HUAC) and Republican senator Joseph McCarthy. Both claimed that American institutions were rife with disloyal Americans whose values threatened the existence and soul of the nation. By the end of the Truman administration, "McCarthyism" had exposed a fearful and dark side of American society and politics—an intolerance that limited civil liberties, dissent, and social change.

The Cold War Begins

- What were Americans' expectations for the postwar world and U.S.-Soviet relations? How did Soviet actions counter those expectations?

- What actions taken by the United States contributed to the Soviet Union's view that the United States was no longer an ally?

- How was the containment theory applied to Western Europe between 1947 and 1951?

- Outside Western Europe, how did the Truman administration promote and protect American interests?

- What changes in policy did NSC-68 represent?

Germany, Italy, and Japan had been defeated, and the world hoped that an enduring peace would follow. But could the cooperative relationship of the victorious Allies continue into the postwar era without a common enemy to unite them? Suspicion and distrust had already surfaced when Britain and the United States objected to the establishment of pro-Soviet governments in Eastern Europe. President Franklin D. Roosevelt believed he could work with the Soviets and had deemed their cooperation more important than the composition of Eastern European governments. But Roosevelt's death in April 1945 left Harry S. Truman the imposing tasks of finishing the war and creating the peace. Winning the war was mostly a matter of following existing policies and listening to the military planners, but establishing a new international system required new ideas and original policies. Unlike Roosevelt, Truman took a harsher position

Chronology

From World War to Cold War

1945   Yalta Conference
President Roosevelt dies
Harry S. Truman becomes president
Soviets capture Berlin
United Nations formed
Germany surrenders
Potsdam Conference
Japan surrenders

1946   Kennan's "Long Telegram"
Churchill's "iron curtain" speech
Iran crisis
Strikes by coal miners and railroad workers
Construction begins on first Levittown

1947   Truman Doctrine
Truman's Federal Employee Loyalty Program
National Security Act
Taft-Hartley Act
House Un-American Activities Committee begins
investigation of Hollywood
Jackie Robinson joins Brooklyn Dodgers
Marshall Plan announced
To Secure These Rights issued
Rio Pact organized

1948   Communist coup in Czechoslovakia
Western zones of Germany unified
State of Israel founded
Congress approves Marshall Plan

Shelly v. Kraemer
Berlin blockade begins
Truman defeats Dewey

1949   North Atlantic Treaty Organization created
Allied airlift causes Stalin to lift Berlin blockade
West Germany created
Soviet Union explodes atomic bomb
Communist forces win civil war in China
Alger Hiss convicted of perjury

1950   U.S. hydrogen bomb project announced
McCarthy's announcement of Communists in the
State Department
NSC–68
Korean War begins
Rosenbergs arrested for conspiracy to commit
espionage
Inchon landing
North Korean forces retreat from South Korea
UN forces cross into North Korea
China enters Korean War
McCarran Internal Security Act

1951   General MacArthur relieved of command
Korean War peace talks begin
Rosenbergs convicted of espionage
Dennis et al. v. the United States

1953   Korean War armistice signed

toward the Soviets and told a colleague, "The Soviet Union needs us more than we need them." Truman loved history and especially the notion that great individuals shaped it. Lazy men caused trouble, he wrote, and those who "worked hard had the job of rectifying their mistakes." A plaque on his desk proclaimed, "The buck stops here." Truman had read history; now he hoped to shape it.

Truman and the Soviets

Truman and other American leaders identified two overlapping paths to peace: international cooperation and **deterrence** based on military strength. They concluded that the United States must continue to field a strong military force with bases in Europe,

Asia, and the Middle East and maintain its atomic monopoly. But deterrence alone could not guarantee peace and a stable world. Policymakers needed to address the underlying causes of war. Drawing on lessons learned from World War II, especially the failed policies of appeasement and isolationism, American planners formulated a new international system. Aggressors would have to be halted, democratic governments supported, and a prosperous world economy created. These were the ideals of the Atlantic Charter,

deterrence   Measures that a state takes to discourage attacks by other states, often including a military buildup.

In July 1945, Truman met with Stalin and Churchill at Potsdam on the outskirts of Berlin. Meeting with Churchill and Stalin for the first time, Truman was surprised that the Soviet leader was shorter than he, and thought Churchill talked too much, giving him "a lot of hooey." Later, Truman wrote, "You never saw such pig-headed people as are the Russians." Here, Stalin and Truman (*left*) and advisers Byrnes and Molotov (*right*) pose for photographers. *Truman Library.*

and most Americans saw them as fundamental values on which to construct peace. To achieve these ends required that the United States assume a leadership role and work with individual nations or through regional organizations or the United Nations.

Not all nations accepted the American vision for peace and stability. The Soviets, given their different political and economic systems and historical experiences—two invasions from Western Europe in thirty years—had markedly different postwar objectives: they wanted to be treated as a major power, to have Germany reduced in power, and to see "friendly" governments in neighboring states, especially in Eastern Europe. While accepting the United Nations, the Soviets preferred to work bilaterally and to continue the relationship of the Big Three (Britain, the Soviet Union, and the United States) that was established during the war. The Soviets believed that the Truman administration was not as friendly as Roosevelt's and that the "spirit of Yalta" was decaying. Moscow also interpreted several American actions and policies as threatening and ideologically motivated. In September 1946, the Soviet ambassador in Washington, Nikolai Novikov, in a memorandum similar to Kennan's "Long Telegram," pictured the United States as globally aggressive, seeking to establish military bases around the world and keeping a monopoly over atomic technology. Novikov regarded the United States as using its economic power to further its capitalistic goals while forcing other countries to adopt

American interests, and he praised the Soviet Union for resisting the power and demands of the United States.

When Truman became president, he had little knowledge of diplomatic affairs or of Roosevelt's policies toward the Soviet Union. He turned to experienced advisers to learn the Soviet goals and how best to deal with them. Most of these advisers were critical of Soviet behavior and suspicious of aggressive and expansive Soviet aims. They noted that Moscow was ignoring the principles of the Atlantic Charter and following an "ominous course" in Eastern Europe that violated the Yalta agreements by creating undemocratic **puppet governments** and closing the region to free trade. By the end of 1945, Truman concluded that he was "tired of babying the Soviets," and expected them to accept American proposals more than halfway. Soviet attitudes appeared to be taking a more anti-Western stance as well. As 1946 began, Soviet officials and the press warned of "capitalist encirclement" and accused the United States of poisoning Soviet-American relations. Alarmed, the State Department asked its Russian expert, George Kennan, to evaluate Soviet policy.

---

puppet governments   Governments imposed, supported, and directed by an outside force, usually a foreign power.

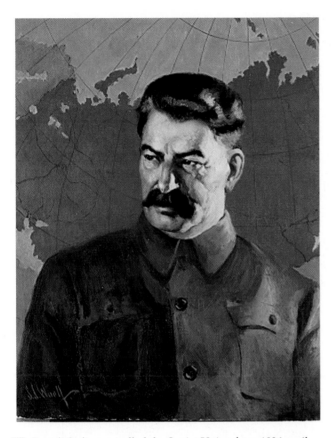

Joseph Stalin controlled the Soviet Union from 1926 until his death in 1953. During World War II, the popular image of the Soviet dictator was that of "Uncle Joe." By the time the Truman Doctrine was signed in March 1947, Stalin's image resembled Hitler's. At the Potsdam Conference in July 1945, Truman's first impression of Stalin was that he was "dishonest but smart as hell" and they could work together. One of Truman's closest advisers bluntly stated that Stalin was "a liar and a crook." *National Portrait Gallery, Smithsonian Institution, Gift of Muriel Woolf Hobson/ Art Resource, NY.*

Kennan responded with the "Long Telegram." He described Soviet totalitarianism as internally weak. Soviet leaders, he said, held communist ideology secondary to remaining in power, needing Western capitalism to serve as an enemy. But, he argued, Soviet leaders were not fanatics who wanted war and would retreat when met with opposition. He recommended a policy of **containment,** meeting head-on any attempted expansion of Soviet power. His report immediately drew high praise from Washington's official circles. Soon thereafter, Truman adopted a policy designed to "set will against will, force against force, idea against idea . . . until Soviet expansion is finally worn down."

Fear of Soviet expansion immediately became a bipartisan issue. Both Democrats and Republicans tried to educate the public about the Soviet threat—ending any possibility of a return to isolationism. One of the most dramatic warnings, however, came from Winston Churchill on March 5, 1946, at Westminster College in Fulton, Missouri. With President Truman sitting beside him, the former prime minister of Britain decried Soviet expansionism and stated that an **"iron curtain"** had fallen across Europe (see Map 26.1). Churchill called for a "fraternal association of the English-speaking peoples" to halt the Russians. Truman thought it was a wonderfully eloquent speech and would do "nothing but good." Churchill, *Time* magazine pronounced, had spoken with the voice of a "lion."

As Churchill spoke, it appeared that an "American lion" was needed in Iran. During World War II, the Big Three had stationed troops in Iran to ensure the safety of lend-lease materials going by that route to the Soviet Union. The troops were to be withdrawn by March 1946, but as that date neared, Soviet troops remained in northern Iran. Suddenly, on March 2, reports flashed from northern Iran that Soviet tanks were moving toward Tehran, the Iranian capital, as well as toward Iraq and Turkey. Some believed that war was imminent. Britain and the United States sent harshly worded telegrams to Moscow and petitioned the United Nations to consider an Iranian complaint against the Soviet Union. War did not break out, and Soviet forces soon evacuated Iran. The crisis was over, but it convinced many Americans that war with the Soviets was possible and that the United States had to assume a historically new leadership role in world affairs. *Woman's Home Companion* magazine reported that 3.5 million women believed war with the Soviets would occur within the next fifteen years. "Red Fascism" had replaced Nazi fascism, and for the sake of civilization there could be no more appeasement.

containment The U.S. policy of checking the expansion or influence of communist nations by making strategic alliances, aiding friendly nations, and supporting weaker states in areas of conflict. It often had three stages: political, economic, and military.

iron curtain Name given to the military, political, and ideological barrier established between the Soviet bloc and Western Europe after World War II.

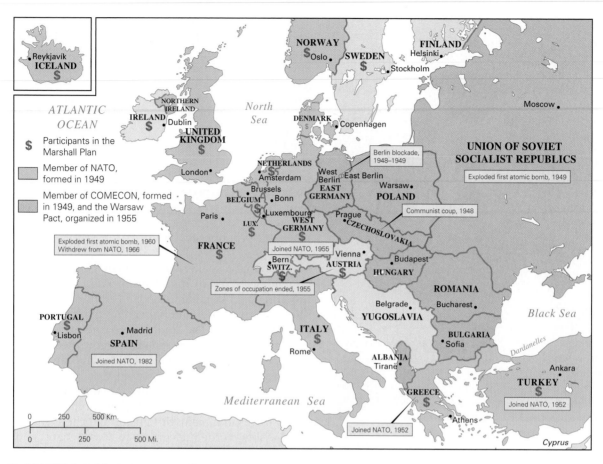

MAP 26.1 Cold War Europe Following World War II, Europe was divided by what Winston Churchill called the "iron curtain," which divided most of the continent politically, economically, and militarily into an eastern bloc (the Warsaw Pact) led by the Soviet Union and a western bloc (NATO) supported by the United States. This postwar division of Europe lasted until the collapse of the Soviet Union in the early 1990s.

The Division of Europe

As the crisis in Iran receded, events in Europe assumed priority. The deepening economic crisis across Europe appeared to favor leftist parties and their assertion that state controls and state planning led to quicker economic recovery. Politics had become economics, and the United States extended loans to nations on the basis of ideology. Western European nations received American loans, while those nations on the other side of the "iron curtain" were denied. The United States even used its influence to reduce United Nations–based aid to Eastern Europe. By the beginning of 1947, Greece and Turkey emerged as an international trouble spot. Turkey was being pressured by the neighboring Soviets to permit them some

control over the Dardanelles, the straits linking the Black Sea to the Mediterranean. In Greece, a civil war between Communist-backed rebels and the British-supported conservative government raged, and in February 1947, Britain informed Washington that it was no longer able to provide economic or military aid to the two eastern Mediterranean nations. Britain asked for the United States to assume its role in the region to prevent the expansion of communism. The Truman administration was eager to assume the responsibility of "world leadership with all of its burdens and all of its glory."

To convince Congress and gain public support for $400 million to support Greece and Turkey, Truman overstated the "crisis" and presented an image of the world under attack from the forces of evil. On

Appeasement

Prior to World War II, the Western democracies had appeased the dictators (Hitler, Mussolini, and Hirohito) in the hopes of avoiding war, but to no avail. By the end of the war, the policy of appeasement had lost its credibility. Americans no longer believed in isolationism and believed in the policy of nonappeasement. A new definition of national security was emerging that recognized the United States was no longer protected by two oceans and that an American global leadership was needed to maintain peace and Western values.

· ALL OUR COLOURS TO THE MAST ·

The goal of the Marshall Plan was to provide American economic support for the rebuilding of Europe's economy. By the time the plan ended, the United States had provided over $12.5 billion dollars to those European nations participating in the European Recovery Program. This poster demonstrated that with cooperation, Europe would soon be moving forward again. *Courtesy of the George C. Marshall Foundation.*

March 12, 1947, he set forth the **Truman Doctrine,** offering an ideological, black-and-white view of world politics, and blamed almost every threat to peace and stability on an unnamed but obvious villain: the Soviet Union. He said it was the duty of the United States "to support free people" who resisted subjugation "by armed minorities or by outside pressure." Congress accepted the president's request and provided aid for Greece and Turkey. Bolstered by American support, Turkey resisted Soviet pressure and retained control over the straits, and the Greek government was able to defeat the Communist rebels in 1949.

Although the Truman administration asked Congress only to support Greece and Turkey, officials admitted among themselves that the request was just the beginning. "It happens that we are having a little trouble with Greece and Turkey at the present time," stated a War Department official, "but they are just one of the keys on the keyboard of this world piano."

On June 5, 1947, in a commencement address at Harvard, Secretary of State George Marshall uncovered more of the keyboard. He offered Europe a program of economic aid, the **Marshall Plan,** to restore stability and prosperity. For the Truman administration, the difficult question was not whether to provide Western Europe with aid, but whether to include the Soviets and Eastern Europeans. To allow the Soviets and their satellites to participate seemed contrary to the intent of the Truman Doctrine. Would a Congress that had just spent $400 million to keep Greece and Turkey out of Soviet hands be willing to provide millions of American dollars to the Soviet Union? But

if the Soviets were excluded, the United States might seem to be encouraging the division of Europe, an image the State Department wanted to avoid. Chaired by Kennan, the State Department planning staff recommended that the United States take "a hell of a big gamble" and offer economic aid to all Europeans. Kennan was certain that the Soviets would reject the offer

Truman Doctrine   Anti-Communist foreign policy that Truman set forth in 1947; it called for military and economic aid to countries whose political stability was threatened by communism.

Marshall Plan   Program launched in 1948 to foster economic recovery in Western Europe in the postwar period through massive amounts of U.S. financial aid.

because it involved economic and political cooperation with capitalists. Thus, when Marshall spoke at Harvard, he invited all Europeans to work together and write a program "designed to place Europe on its feet economically."

The gamble worked. At a June 26, 1947, meeting in Paris of potential Marshall Plan participants, Soviet foreign minister Molotov rejected a British and French written proposal for an economically integrated Europe, joint economic planning, and a requirement to purchase mostly American goods. At first the Marshall Plan looked like a "tasty mushroom," commented one Soviet official, but on closer examination it turned out to be a "poisonous toadstool." Unwilling to participate in any form of economic integration, the Soviets and the Eastern Europeans left the conference. Over the next ten months the Soviet Union took steps to solidify their control over their satellite states. In July 1947, Moscow announced the Molotov Plan, which further incorporated Eastern European economies into the Soviet system. Throughout the region non-Communist elements were expelled from governments, an effort that culminated in February 1948 in a Soviet-engineered **coup** that toppled the Czechoslovakian government. "We are faced with exactly the same situation with which Britain and France were faced in 1938 and 1939 with Hitler," Truman announced. The Czech coup helped convince Congress to approve $12.5 billion in Marshall aid to Western Europe.

The "sovietization" of Eastern Europe prompted the United States, Britain, and France to economically and politically unify their German occupation zones. In March 1948, the United States announced that the western zones were eligible for Marshall Plan aid, would hold elections to select delegates to a constitutional convention, and would utilize a standard currency. The meaning of these actions seemed clear: a West German state was being formed. Faced with the prospect of a pro-Western, industrialized, and potentially remilitarized Germany, Stalin reacted. On June 24, the Russians blockaded all land traffic to and from Berlin, which had been divided into British-, French-, Soviet-, and U.S.-controlled zones after the war. With a population of more than 2 million, West Berlin lay isolated 120 miles inside the Soviet zone of Germany (see Map 26.2). The Soviet goal was to force the West either to abandon the creation of West Germany or to face the loss of Berlin. Americans viewed the blockade simply as further proof of Soviet hostility and were determined not to back down. Churchill affirmed the West's stand. We want peace, he stated, "but we should by now have learned that there is no

MAP 26.2 Cold War Germany This map shows how Germany and Berlin were divided into occupation zones. Meant as temporary divisions, they became permanent, transformed by the Cold War into East and West Germany. In 1948, with the Berlin airlift, and again in 1961, with the erection of the Berlin Wall, Berlin became the flash point of the Cold War. With the end of the Cold War, the division of Germany also ended. In 1989, the Berlin Wall was torn down, and in 1990 the two Germanies were reunified.

coup Sudden overthrow of a government by a group of people, usually with military support.

safety in yielding to dictators, whether Nazi or Communist." "We are very close to war," Truman wrote in his diary.

American strategists confronted the dilemma of how to stay in Berlin without starting a shooting war. Although some in the army recommended fighting their way across the Soviet zone to the city, Truman chose another option, one that would not violate Soviet-occupied territory or any international agreements. Marshaling a massive effort of men, provisions, and aircraft, British and Americans flew supply planes to three Berlin airports on an average of one flight every three minutes, month after month. To drive home to the Soviets the depth of American resolve, Truman ordered a wing of B-29 bombers, the "atomic bombers," to Britain. These planes carried no atomic weapons, but the general impression was that their presence lessened the likelihood of Soviet aggression.

The **Berlin airlift** was a victory for the United States in the Cold War. The increasing flow of airplanes and supplies into West Berlin's three airports testified not only to America's economic and military power but also to America's resolve to stand firm against the Soviets and protect Western Europe. In May 1949, Stalin, finding no gains from the blockade, without explanation ended it and allowed land traffic to cross the Soviet zone to Berlin. Berlin was saved, but the crisis bore other fruit too. It swept away most congressional opposition to the Marshall Plan and the creation of West Germany and silenced those who had protested a permanent American military commitment to Western Europe. In June 1949, Congress approved American entry into the **North Atlantic Treaty Organization** (NATO). Membership in the alliance ensured that American forces would remain in the newly created West Germany and that Western Europe would be eligible for additional American economic and military aid. The Mutual Defense Assistance Act passed in 1949 provided $1.5 billion in arms and equipment for NATO member nations. By 1952, 80 percent of American assistance to Europe was military aid.

A Global Presence

In order to facilitate fighting a global Cold War, Congress passed the National Security Act in 1947. It created the Air Force as a separate service and unified command of the military with a new cabinet position, the Department of Defense. To improve coordination between the State Department and the Department of Defense, the National Security Council was formed

When the Soviets blockaded the western zones of Berlin, in one of the first confrontations of the Cold War, the United States replied by staging one of the most successful logistical feats of the twentieth century, Operation Vittles, in which vital supplies were flown into the city. The airlift lasted 321 days, and American planes flew more than 272,000 missions and delivered 2.1 million tons of supplies. *Walter Sanders/Timpix.*

to provide policy recommendations to the president. The act also established the Central Intelligence Agency to collect and analyze foreign intelligence information and to carry out covert actions believed necessary for American national security. By mid-1948, covert operations were increasing in scope and

Berlin airlift Response to the Soviet blockade of West Berlin in 1948 involving tens of thousands of continuous flights by American and British planes to deliver supplies.

North Atlantic Treaty Organization Mutual defense alliance formed in 1949 among most of the nations of Western Europe and North America in an effort to contain communism.

number, including efforts to influence Italian elections (a success) and to topple the communist Albanian government (a failure).

While the Truman administration's primary foreign-policy concern was Europe, it could not ignore the rest of the world. As American policy crystallized, it became clear that the United States needed to promote economic and political stability around the world by removing barriers to the free movement of trade and people and by supporting governments that accepted Washington's goals.

In Latin America, the Truman administration rejected the requests of many Latin American nations for a Marshall Plan–style program and encouraged private firms to develop the region through business and trade. To ensure that the Western Hemisphere remained under the American eagle's wing, in 1947, the United States organized the **Rio Pact.** It established the concept of collective security for Latin America and created a regional organization—the **Organization of American States** (OAS)—to coordinate common defense, economic, and social concerns.

In the Middle East, fear of future oil shortages led the United States to promote the expansion of American petroleum interests. In Saudi Arabia, Kuwait, and Iran, the U.S. goal was to replace Britain as the major economic and political influence. At the same time, the United States became a powerful supporter of a new Jewish state. Truman's support for such a nation, to be created in **Palestine,** arose from several considerations—moral, political, and international. The area of Palestine had been administered by the British since the end of World War I and the fall of the Ottoman Empire (see page 700). Throughout the 1920s and 1930s, tensions and conflicts increased between the indigenous Arab population, the Palestinians, and an increasing number of Jews, largely immigrants from Europe. As World War II drew to a close, Britain faced growing pressure to create a new Jewish state in Palestine. Truman, for one, asked in August 1945 that at least 100,000 displaced European Jews be allowed to migrate to Palestine. Considering the Nazi terror against Jews, he believed that the Jews should have their own nation—a view strongly supported by a well-organized, pro-Jewish lobbying effort across the United States.

In May 1947, Britain turned the problem over to the United Nations, and the stage was set for the United Nations to divide the region into two nations: one Arab and one Jewish. When the United Nations voted to **partition** Palestine into Arab and Jewish states on May 14, 1948, Truman recognized the nation of Israel within fifteen minutes. War quickly broke out between Israel and the surrounding Arab nations—who refused to recognize the partition. Although outnumbered, the better-equipped Israeli army drove back the invading armies, and in January 1949 a cease-fire was arranged by UN mediator **Ralph Bunche.** When the fighting stopped, Israel had added 50 percent more territory to its emerging nation. More than 700,000 Arabs left Israeli-controlled territory during and after the war, many existing as refugees living in the Gaza Strip, Lebanon, Jordan, and Egypt. Bitter at the loss of what they regarded as their homeland, the majority of Palestinians were determined to destroy the Jewish state.

If Americans were pleased with events in Latin America and the Middle East, Asia provided several disappointments. Under American occupation, Japan's government had been reshaped into a democratic system and placed safely within the American orbit, but success in Japan was offset by diplomatic setbacks in China and Korea. During World War II, the **Nationalist Chinese government** of Jiang Jieshi (Chiang Kai-shek) and the Chinese Communists under

Rio Pact Considered the first Cold War alliance, it joined Latin American nations, Canada, and the United States in an agreement to prevent Communist inroads in Latin America and to improve political, social, and economic conditions among Latin American nations; it created the Organization of American States.

Organization of American States An international organization composed of most of the nations of the Americas, including the Caribbean, that deals with the mutual concerns of its members; Cuba is not currently a member.

Palestine Region on the Mediterranean that was a British mandate after World War I; the UN partitioned the area in 1948 to allow for a Jewish state (Israel) and a Palestinian state, which was never established.

partition To divide a country into separate, autonomous nations.

Ralph Bunche An African American scholar, teacher, and diplomat. Between 1948 and 1949, as a United Nations mediator he negotiated a settlement ending the Arab-Israeli War. In 1950, he received the Nobel Peace Prize for his efforts. He stated: "I have a bias against war, a bias for peace. . . . And I have a strong bias in favor of the United Nations." Until his death in 1971 he continued working for the United Nations.

Nationalist Chinese government The government of Jiang Jieshi, who fought the Communists for control of China in the 1940s; Jiang and his supporters were defeated and retreated to Taiwan in 1949, where they set up a separate government.

Mao Zedong (Mao Tse-tung) had collaborated to fight the Japanese. But when the war ended, old animosities quickly resurfaced, and the truce between the two forces collapsed. By February 1946, civil war had flared in China, and American supporters of Jiang were recommending that the United States increase its economic and military support for the Nationalist government. Especially vocal in promoting the cause of the Nationalists was the "China Lobby," led by *Time* and *Life* publisher Henry R. Luce and others who argued that Soviet power threatened China and the rest of Asia as much as it did Europe. Truman and Marshall (who was now secretary of state), aware of limited American resources, were of a different opinion. Though dreading Communist success in China, they questioned that the corrupt and inefficient Nationalist government under Jiang could ever effectively rule the vast country. While willing to continue some political, economic, and military support, neither wanted to commit American power to an Asian war. Providing more aid would be like "throwing money down a rat hole," Truman told his cabinet.

Faced with an efficient and popular opponent, unable to mobilize the Chinese people and resources, and denied additional American support, Jiang's forces steadily lost the civil war. In 1949 his army disintegrated, and the Nationalist government fled to the island of Taiwan. Conservative Democrats and Republicans labeled the rout of Jiang as a humiliating American defeat and complained that the Truman administration was too soft on communism. To quiet critics and to protect Jiang, Truman refused to recognize the People's Republic of China on the mainland and ordered the U.S. 7th Fleet to the waters near Taiwan.

Increasingly, Truman was feeling pressure to expand the containment policy to areas beyond Europe. The pressure intensified in late August 1949, when the Soviets detonated their own atomic bomb, shattering the American nuclear monopoly. Suddenly it seemed to many Americans that the United States was losing the Cold War. Calls came from inside and outside the administration for a more global and aggressive policy against communism. David Lilienthal, one of Truman's atomic advisers and head of the Atomic Energy Commission, in 1950 recommended building a **hydrogen bomb.** A joint Pentagon–State Department committee, headed by Paul Nitze, concluded that the Soviets were driven by "a new fanatic faith, antithetical to our own," whose objective was to dominate the world. The group speculated that the Soviets would be able to launch a nuclear attack on the United States as early as 1954. The committee's re-

port, NSC Memorandum #68, issued by the **National Security Council** (NSC), called for global containment and a massive buildup of American military force. In fact, NSC–68 called for an almost 400 percent increase in military spending for the next fiscal year, which would have raised military expenditures to nearly $50 billion. Truman studied the report but worried about the impact of such large-scale military production on the manufacture of domestic goods. A separate report concluded that the projected mobilization of industry for the Cold War would reduce automobile construction by nearly 60 percent and cut production of radios and television sets to zero. Truman eventually agreed to a "moderate" $12.3 billion military budget for 1950 that included building the hydrogen bomb. Proponents of NSC–68 won the final argument on June 25, 1950, when North Korean troops stormed across the 38th parallel.

The Korean War

■ As the North Koreans invaded South Korea, what choices did Truman face, and why did he decide to refer the issue to the United Nations?

■ What were Truman's and MacArthur's goals in Korea? What was the consequence of China's entry into the war?

When World War II ended, Soviet forces occupied Korea north of the **38th parallel** (see Map 26.3), and American forces remained south of it. The division of Korea was expected to be temporary, but like the division of Germany, it produced two nations. By mid-1946, an American-supported Republic of Korea (ROK), led by Syngman Rhee, existed in the south, with the Communist-backed Democratic People's Republic of Korea, headed by Kim Il Sung, in the north. Having established two Koreas, in 1949 the Soviet and American forces withdrew, leaving behind two hostile regimes. Both Koreas claimed to be Korea's rightful government and launched raids across

hydrogen bomb Nuclear weapon of much greater destructive power than the atomic bomb.
National Security Council Executive agency established in 1947 to coordinate the strategic policies and defense of the United States; it includes the president, vice president, and four cabinet members.
38th parallel Negotiated dividing line between North and South Korea; it was the focus of much of the fighting in the Korean War.

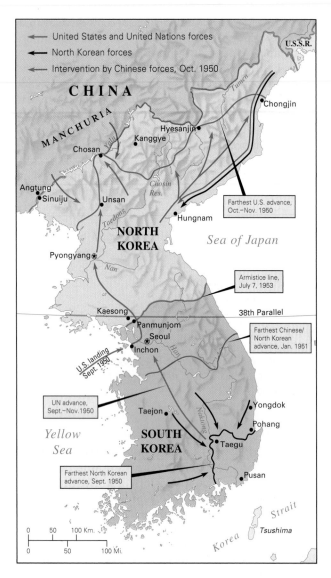

MAP 26.3 The Korean War, 1950–1953 Seeking to unify Korea, North Korean forces invaded South Korea in 1950. To protect South Korea, the United States and the United Nations intervened. After driving North Korean forces northward, Truman sought to unify Korea under South Korea. But as United Nations and South Korean forces pushed toward the Chinese border, Communist China intervened, forcing UN troops to retreat. This map shows the military thrusts and counterthrusts of the Korean War as it stalemated roughly along the 38th parallel.

the border. The raids accomplished little except to kill more than 100,000 Koreans and to expand each side's military capabilities.

Having received approval from the Soviets, on June 25, 1950, Kim Il Sung launched a full-scale inva-

sion of the south. Overwhelmed by superior forces, South Korean (ROK) forces rapidly retreated. Apprised of the invasion, Truman drew parallels to Manchuria and Ethiopia in the 1930s and quickly announced that Korea was vital to American interests and needed protection from Communist aggression. Fearful that a congressional declaration of war against North Korea might trigger a Chinese and Soviet response, Truman instead asked the UN Security Council to intervene. The Security Council complied and called for a cease-fire, asking member nations to provide assistance to South Korea.

Halting Communist Aggression

To blunt the Communist invasion, Truman ordered General Douglas MacArthur to ready American naval and air units for deployment south of the 38th parallel. Two days later (June 27), as North Koreans captured Seoul, the South Korean capital, the Security Council approved an international military force to defend South Korea—that is, to push the invaders back into North Korea and restore peace. General MacArthur was named commander of the United Nations forces. As a member of the UN Security Council, the Soviet Union could have blocked these actions with its veto, but at the time of the invasion the Russians were boycotting the council for its refusal to recognize the People's Republic of China. The Soviets returned to the Security Council in August 1950.

Although more than 70 percent of Americans polled supported Truman's decision to intervene in Korea, recruitment offices saw no rush to arms as they had in World War II. National guard and reserve forces had to be called to active duty to fill the ranks, and the draft was again used to ensure a monthly quota of 50,000 soldiers. General Lewis B. Hershey, head of the Selective Service, noted, "Everyone wants out; nobody wants in." On July 1, 1950, the first American soldiers, officially under United Nations control, arrived in Korea. Anxious not to provoke the Chinese and Russians with a formal declaration of war against North Korea, Truman never sought one. American troops served in Korea under United Nations resolutions and followed Truman's orders as commander in chief. For the record, the war was called the "Korean Conflict," a "police action" to defeat a "bandit raid." Few in Congress objected, and with little dissent the House and Senate approved large-scale expansions of the military and its budget.

The infusion of American troops did not halt the North Korean advance, and by the end of July, North Korean forces were occupying most of South Korea.

United Nations forces, including nearly 122,000 Americans and the whole South Korean army, held only the southeastern corner of the peninsula—the Pusan perimeter—and prepared for a last-ditch offensive. A bold maneuver on September 15 turned the tide. Seventy thousand American troops landed at Inchon, near Seoul, nearly 200 miles north of the Pusan defensive perimeter (see Map 26.3). MacArthur's brilliant tactical move surprised the enemy and not only threatened North Korean supply and communication lines but also potentially blocked the retreat of North Korean troops. Eleven days later, UN forces advancing north from Pusan joined forces driving east from Inchon. Their army collapsing, the North Koreans fled back across the 38th parallel. Seoul was liberated on September 27. The police action had achieved its purpose: the South Korean government was saved, and the 38th parallel was again a real border.

Seeking to Liberate North Korea

Now, however, restoring the conditions that had prevailed before the invasion was not enough. The South Korean leadership, MacArthur, Truman, and most Americans wanted to unify the peninsula under South Korean rule. Bending under American pressure, the United Nations approved the new goal on October 7, to "liberate" North Korea from Communist rule. MacArthur ordered UN and South Korean forces to cross the 38th parallel. With North Korean forces in disarray, in mid-October United Nations forces moved quickly northward toward the Korean-Chinese border at the Yalu River. The Chinese threatened intervention if the invaders approached the border, and some UN units had already encountered Chinese "volunteer" troops. Nevertheless, based on intelligence estimates, UN commander General MacArthur was supremely confident. If Chinese forces did cross the border, he explained to Truman, they would number less than 50,000 and easily could be defeated. Not entirely convinced, Truman ordered MacArthur to use only South Korean forces in approaching the Yalu River. The overconfident general, however, bridled at being restrained by his civilian commander, and on November 24, in violation of his orders, MacArthur moved American, British, and Korean forces to within a few miles of the Yalu. He also publicly promised to have victorious American soldiers home by Christmas. Two days later, nearly 300,000 Chinese soldiers entered the Korean Conflict.

With their bugles blowing, the Chinese attacked in waves, hurling grenades, taking massive casualties, and encircling and nearly trapping several American and South Korean units in the most brutal fighting of the war. MacArthur had assumed that vastly superior American air and fire power would stop any Chinese invaders. He had not foreseen the arrival of hundreds of thousands of Chinese soldiers, the bitter winter weather, or night battles that severely limited the role of American aircraft. Across northern North Korea, UN forces fell back in bitter combat. The U.S. 1st Marine Division, nearly surrounded at the Chosin Reservoir, battled its way to the port of Hungnam by leapfrogging units to clear the road in front of them. During the Communist offensive, American casualties exceeded 12,000, but the Chinese lost more than three times as many, lending grim proof to General O. P. "Slam" Smith's statement about the "retreat" from Chosin: "Gentlemen, we are not retreating. We are merely advancing in another direction."

Within three weeks, the North Koreans and Chinese had shoved the UN forces back to the 38th parallel. During the retreat, General MacArthur asked for permission to bomb bridges on the Yalu River and Chinese bases across the border. He also urged a naval blockade of China and the possible use of Nationalist Chinese forces against the mainland. Believing such escalation could trigger World War III, Truman allowed only the Korean half of the bridges to be targeted and flatly rejected MacArthur's other suggestions. In the face of the new military reality, Truman abandoned the goal of a unified pro-Western Korea and sought a negotiated settlement to end the conflict, even if it would leave two Koreas. The decision was not popular. Americans wanted victory. Encouraged by public opinion polls and vocal Republican critics of Truman, in March and April 1951, General MacArthur publicly took exception to the limitations his commander in chief had placed on him. He put it simply: there was "no substitute for victory." Already displeased by MacArthur's arrogance, Truman used the general's direct challenge to presidential power as grounds to relieve him of his command. General Matthew Ridgeway replaced the fired MacArthur.

The decision unleashed a storm of protest. Some called for Truman's impeachment and MacArthur's nomination for president. Congressional hearings to investigate the conduct of the war followed in June 1951, with MacArthur testifying that an expanded war could achieve victory. The administration responded by projecting nuclear world war alarmism and effectively made the case for a limited war and the need for civilian authority over the military. In the face-off between MacArthur and Truman there was no winner. Polls showed Truman's public approval rating continuing to fall, reaching a dismal 24 percent by

The Korean War was one of ebb and flow, advances and retreats—the movement of troops up and down the rugged Korean peninsula. The war also sped the integration of the American armed forces as African American troops served and fought alongside other Americans. *National Archives.*

late 1951. At the same time, MacArthur's hopes for a presidential candidacy collapsed because most Americans feared his aggressive policies might indeed result in World War III. By the beginning of 1952, frustrated by the war, the vast majority of Americans were simply tired of the "useless" conflict and wanted it to end.

The Korean front, meanwhile, stabilized along the 38th parallel. Four-power peace talks among the United States, South Korea, China, and North Korea began on July 10, 1951, amid sharp and ugly fighting. The negotiations did not go smoothly. For two years, the powers postured and argued about prisoners, cease-fire lines, and a multitude of lesser issues while soldiers fought and died over scraps of territory. UN casualties exceeded 125,000 during the two years of peace negotiations. When the Eisenhower administration finally concluded the cease-fire on July 26, 1953, the Korean Conflict had cost more than $20 billion and 33,000 American lives, but it had left South Korea intact.

The "hot war" in Korea had far-reaching military and diplomatic results for the United States. The expansion of military spending envisioned by NSC–68 had proceeded rapidly after the North Korean invasion. In Europe, Truman moved forward with plans to rearm West Germany and Italy and, in the name of anticommunism, improved relations with Spain's dictator, Francisco Franco. Throughout Asia and the Pa-

cific, a large American presence was made permanent. In 1951 the United States concluded a settlement with Japan that kept American forces in Japan and Okinawa. The Australian–New Zealand–United States (ANZUS) treaty of 1951 promised American military protection to Australia and New Zealand. At the same time, the United States was increasing its military aid and commitments to Nationalist China and French **Indochina.** The containment policy that George Kennan had envisioned to protect Western Europe had been expanded—formally and financially—to cover East Asia and the Pacific. Kennan objected to the growing number of commitments, but his arguments were more than offset by policymakers stressing the global struggle against the forces of communism. According to the philosophy of the day, a Communist victory anywhere threatened the national security of the United States.

Indochina   French colony in Southeast Asia, including present-day Vietnam, Laos, and Cambodia; it began fighting for its independence in the mid-twentieth century.

Postwar Politics

- In what ways did Truman attempt to maintain and expand the New Deal? How did the fear of communism strengthen conservative opposition to his programs?

- Why did Truman win the 1948 election?

When Roosevelt died, many wondered if Truman would continue the Roosevelt–New Deal approach to domestic policies. Would he work to protect the social and economic gains that labor, women, and minorities had earned during the Depression and World War II? Conservatives and some of Truman's friends predicted that the new president was "going to be quite a shock to those who followed Roosevelt—that the New Deal is as good as dead . . . and that the 'Roosevelt nonsense' was over." But Truman had no intention of extinguishing the New Deal.

Truman and Liberalism

In September 1945, Truman presented to Congress what one Republican critic called an effort to "out–New Deal the New Deal." Truman set forth an ambitious program designed to ease the transition to a peacetime economy and reenergize the New Deal. To prevent inflation and a recession, he wanted Congress to continue wartime economic agencies, such as the Office of Price Administration, that would help control wages and prices. To protect wartime gains by minorities, he asked that the Fair Employment Practices Commission be renewed. Furthering the New Deal, he recommended an expansion of Social Security coverage and benefits, an increase in the minimum wage, the development of additional housing programs, and a national health system to ensure medical care for all Americans.

Opposing Truman's proposals was a conservative coalition of southern Democrats and Republicans in Congress. Since 1937, they had successfully blocked extensions of the New Deal, and they were determined to continue their efforts to contain liberalism. They embarked on a campaign to persuade the American public of the dangers of socialism and communism and of the benefits of a return to business-directed free enterprise. The National Association of Manufacturers spent nearly $37 million on such propaganda in one year. "Public sentiment is everything," wrote an officer of Standard Oil. "He who molds public sentiment goes deeper than he who enacts statutes or pronounces decisions." A Truman official sadly agreed: "The consuming fear of communism fostered a widespread belief that change was subversive and that those who supported change were Communists or **fellow-travelers.**" Warning that Truman's "socialistic" program involved too much government, threatened private enterprise, and endangered existing class and social relations, Congress rejected or severely scaled back nearly all of his proposals. The Fair Employment Practices Commission faded away, allowing industries to return to prewar hiring practices that excluded minorities. Congress spurned any idea of a national health program and instead substituted a federal program to build hospitals. While Congress and Truman disagreed over the nation's domestic agenda, the country experienced economic and social dislocations caused by the conversion to a peacetime economy. Inflation quickly emerged as a principal issue, with prices rising 25 percent within 18 months after the defeat of Germany. At the same time, many workers watched their purchasing power fall—some by as much as 30 percent. The economic changes led to a wave of strikes, with nearly 4.5 million workers staging more than five thousand strikes. United Automobile Workers (UAW) strikers wanted a 30 percent increase in wages and a guarantee that car prices would not rise.

Unions like the UAW hoped their strikes would save wages and expand the power of the unions, but the opposite occurred. Congress and state and local governments responded to strikes and agitation with antilabor measures designed to weaken unions and end work stoppages. **Right-to-work laws** banned compulsory union membership and in some cases provided legal and police protection for workers crossing picket lines. In the spring of 1946, Truman joined the attack on strikes, squaring off against the coal miners' and railroad unions. In April 1946, he faced John L. Lewis and 400,000 striking United Mine Workers. Taking drastic action, the president seized the mines and ordered miners back to work. As miners returned to work, Truman wrote in his diary that Lewis had "folded" and was "as yellow as a dog pound pup." In reality, Truman pressured mine owners

fellow-traveler Individual who sympathizes with or supports the beliefs of the Communist Party without being a member.

right-to-work laws State laws that make it illegal for labor unions and employers to require that all workers are members of a union. Many state laws require that all employees must benefit from contract agreements made between the union and the employer, even if the employee is not a union member.

Workers march in New York City in support of unions and worldwide worker solidarity. As the war ended, business and government assumed a more hostile attitude toward organized labor—many claiming that unions were socialistic or communistic. The outcome of this attitude was laws, including the Taft-Hartley Act, that restricted union activities and contributed to a decline in union membership. *Corbis-Bettmann.*

to meet most of the union's demands. When locomotive engineers walked off the job in May, Truman asked Congress for power to draft the strikers. The railroad strike was settled before Congress responded, but momentum mounted in Congress to take legislative action to control strikes and disable unions.

Amid strikes, soaring inflation, divisions within Democratic ranks, and widespread dissatisfaction with Truman's leadership—"to err is Truman" was a common quip—Republicans asked the public, "Had enough?" Voters responded affirmatively, in 1946 filling both houses of the Eightieth Congress with more Republicans and anti–New Deal Democrats. Refusing to retreat, Truman opened 1947 by presenting Congress with a restatement of many of the programs he had offered in 1945. The political battle between the president and Congress fired up again. Congress rejected Truman's proposals, Truman vetoed 250 bills, and Congress overrode 12 of Truman's vetoes. Among the most critical vetoes cast by Truman and overridden by Congress was the **Taft-Hartley Act.** The Taft-Hartley Act, passed in June 1947, was a clear victory for management over labor. It banned the closed shop, prevented industry-wide collective bargaining, and legalized state-sponsored right-to-work laws that hindered union organizing. It also required that union officials sign **affidavits** that they were not Communists. Echoing Truman's actions in the coal strike, the law also empowered the president to use a court injunction to force striking workers back to

work for an eighty-day cooling-off period. Privately, Truman supported much of the bill and cast his veto knowing it would be overridden. He also knew his veto would help "hold labor support" for his 1948 run for the presidency.

Truman's veto of Taft-Hartley was an easy political decision. In contrast, the issue of civil rights was extremely complex and politically dangerous. Democrats were clearly divided on civil rights. Southern Democrats were opposed to any mention of civil rights, while African Americans and liberals, including Eleanor Roosevelt, demanded that Truman "speak" to the issue. Truman was cautious but supportive of civil rights and aware of Soviet criticism of American segregation. Confessing that he did not know how bad conditions were for African Americans and that "the top dog in a world . . . ought to clean his own house," Truman agreed in December 1946 to create a committee on civil rights to examine race relations in the country. The October 1947 report *To Secure These Rights* described the racial inequalities in American

Taft-Hartley Act Law passed by Congress in 1947 banning closed shops, permitting employers to sue unions for broken contracts, and requiring unions to observe a cooling-off period before striking.

affidavit A formal, written legal document made under oath; those signing the document state that the facts in the document are true.

society and called on the government to take steps to correct the imbalance. Among its recommendations were the establishment of a permanent commission on civil rights, the enactment of antilynching laws, and the abolition of the **poll tax.** The committee also called for integration of the U.S. armed forces and support for integrating housing programs and education. Truman asked Congress in February 1948 to act on the recommendations but provided no direction or legislation. Nor did the White House make any effort to fully integrate the armed forces until black labor leader A. Philip Randolph once again threatened a march on Washington (see page 810). Faced with the prospect of an embarrassing mass protest only months before the 1948 election, Truman issued an executive order instructing the military to integrate its forces. The navy and air force complied, but the army resisted until high casualties in the summer of 1950 in Korea forced the integration of black replacements into previously white combat units. Despite his caution, Truman had done more in the area of civil rights than any president since Lincoln, a record that ensured African American and liberal support for his 1948 bid to be elected president in his own right.

The 1948 Election

Republicans' hopes were high in 1948. They had done well in congressional elections in 1946 and 1947. To take on Truman they chose New York governor **Thomas E. Dewey.** In his loss to Roosevelt in 1944, Dewey had earned a respectable 46 percent of the popular vote, and Truman was not Roosevelt. The Democrats were also mired in bitter infighting over the direction of domestic policy. Many Democratic liberals and minorities were dissatisfied that Truman had not worked harder to sell his New Deal–type programs to the public and to push them through Congress. Truman was concerned that some liberals might switch their votes to Henry A. Wallace, the former vice president, who was running as a Progressive Party candidate. Southern Democrats, convinced that Truman was too liberal, opposed any efforts to support organized labor or civil rights. When a civil rights plank was inserted into the party's platform, many of them stalked out of the convention waving Confederate flags. Unwilling to support a Republican, they met in Birmingham and organized the States' Rights Democratic Party, better known as the **Dixiecrat Party,** nominating South Carolina governor J. Strom Thurmond for president.

With the Democratic Party so splintered and public opinion polls showing a large Republican lead,

Many considered Harry S. Truman's 1948 victory over Thomas E. Dewey a major political upset—nearly all of the major polls had named the Republican an easy winner. Here Truman holds up the *Chicago Tribune*'s incorrect headline announcing Dewey's triumph. *Corbis-Bettmann.*

Dewey, not known for his charm or speaking ability, conducted a low-key campaign almost devoid of debate on issues and contact with the public. In contrast, "Give 'Em Hell" Harry, running for his political life, crossed the nation by train, making hundreds of speeches that stressed the gains made under the progressive policies of the Democrats. He attacked the "do-nothing" Eightieth Congress and its business allies. He told one audience, "Wall Street expects its money to elect a Republican administration that will listen to the gluttons of privilege first and not to the

poll tax   A tax imposed by many states that required a fee to be paid as a prerequisite to voting; it was used to exclude the poor, especially minorities, from voting.

Thomas E. Dewey   New York governor who twice ran unsuccessfully for president as the Republican candidate, the second time against Truman in 1948.

Dixiecrat Party   Party organized in 1948 by southern delegates who refused to accept the civil rights plank of the Democratic platform; they nominated Strom Thurmond of South Carolina for president.

people at all." Touting the Berlin crisis, Truman also emphasized his expertise in foreign policy and his experience in standing up to Stalin.

Confounding the pollsters, Truman defeated Dewey. His margin of victory was the smallest since 1916—slightly over 2 million votes. Nevertheless, Truman's victory was a triumph for Roosevelt's New Deal coalition. Despite the Dixiecrat candidate, most southerners did not abandon the Democratic Party. Thurmond carried only four southern states; Wallace carried none (see Map 26.4). Democrats also won majorities in Congress, and Truman hoped that in 1949 he would succeed with his domestic program, which he called the **Fair Deal.**

In his inaugural address, Truman again held up the images of the New Deal. He asked for increases in Social Security, public housing, and the minimum wage, the repeal of the Taft-Hartley Act, and the creation of a national health program. He also gave civil rights and federal aid to education a place on the national agenda. Rewarding farmers for their role in his victory, Truman submitted the Brannan Plan, which included federal benefits for small farmers. Congress responded favorably to Truman's programs in areas already well established by the New Deal: a 65-cent minimum hourly wage, funds for low- and moderate-income housing, and increases in Social Security coverage and payments. Proposals going beyond the scope of the New Deal, however, encountered organized opposition from a coalition of southern Democrats and Republicans. They argued that too much government intrusion would move the country down a communistic path. Conservatives emphasized the "Communist" nature of a national health system and government intervention in education. Civil rights legislation was held captive by the southern wing of the Democratic Party, which considered it part of a Communist conspiracy to undermine American unity. Agribusiness leaders and conservatives attacked the Brannan Plan as socialistic and class oriented. The outbreak of the Korean War further strengthened opposition to Truman's liberal programs, limited available funds, and shifted the administration's priorities.

Cold War Politics

■ What fears and events heightened society's worries about internal subversion, and how did politicians respond to the public's concerns?

■ Why and how did Joseph McCarthy become so powerful by 1952?

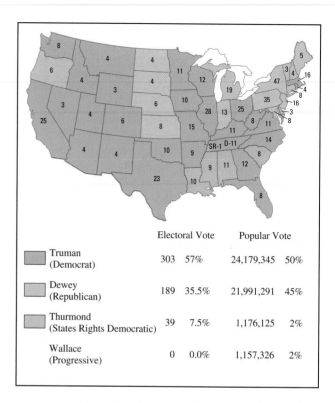

		Electoral Vote		Popular Vote	
Truman (Democrat)		303	57%	24,179,345	50%
Dewey (Republican)		189	35.5%	21,991,291	45%
Thurmond (States Rights Democratic)		39	7.5%	1,176,125	2%
Wallace (Progressive)		0	0.0%	1,157,326	2%

MAP 26.4 Election of 1948 In the 1948 presidential election, Harry S. Truman confounded the polls and analysts by upsetting his Republican opponent, Thomas Dewey, earning 50 percent of the popular vote and 57 percent of the electoral vote.

The development of the Cold War not only altered American foreign policy but also had significant political and social effects. As the Cold War began, fears arose that there were Communists and fellow-travelers throughout the government and society. Although the Soviets already had a well-developed system of **espionage** within U.S. government agencies, including the atomic bomb program, fears of Communist

Fair Deal President Truman said that "every segment of the population" deserved a "fair deal" from the government. He hoped the Democratic majority would provide an expansion of New Deal programs, including civil rights legislation, a fair employment practices act, a system for national health insurance, and appropriations for education.

espionage Usually an organized practice by governments to use spies to gain economic, military, and political information from enemies and rivals.

subversives quickly spread across the land. Linking communism and socialism to liberalism and calling for social change became widely used and effective weapons. Conservatives in Congress used them to resist Truman's efforts to expand the New Deal, while others used fears of socialism and communism to combat unionization and to maintain segregation. In 1946, tobacco giant R. J. Reynolds conducted a multi-million-dollar public ad campaign to defeat the CIO's "Operation Dixie" effort to organize southern workers. Unionization was characterized as a step toward socialism. In Pittsburgh, Pennsylvania, a local paper labeled those trying to integrate a public swimming pool "Commies." Across the country, neighborhoods and communities organized "watch groups," which screened books, movies, and public speakers and questioned teachers and public officials, seeking to ban or dismiss those considered suspect.

The Red Scare

Responding to increasing Republican accusations, including those of the **House Un-American Activities Committee** (HUAC), that his administration tolerated Communist subversion, Truman moved to beef up the existing loyalty program. Nine days after his Truman Doctrine speech (March 12, 1947), the president issued Executive Order #9835, establishing the Federal Employee Loyalty Program. The order stated that, after a hearing, a federal employee could be fired if "reasonable grounds" existed for believing he or she was disloyal in belief or action. Attorney General Tom Clark provided a lengthy list of subversive organizations, and government administrators screened their employees for membership. Soon supervisors and workers also began to accuse one another of "un-American" thoughts and activities. Between 1947 and 1951, the government discharged more than three thousand federal employees because of their supposed disloyalty. In almost every case, the accused had no right to confront the accusers or to refute the evidence. Few of those forced to leave government service were Communists. Fewer still were threats to American security.

Truman's loyalty program, despite all the discharges, intensified rather than calmed hysteria about an "enemy within." Federal Bureau of Investigation (FBI) director J. Edgar Hoover proclaimed that there was one American Communist for every 1,814 loyal citizens, while Attorney General Clark warned that Communists were everywhere, "in factories, offices, butcher shops, on street corners, in private businesses," carrying "the germs of death for society."

Grabbing headlines in 1947, the House Un-American Activities Committee (HUAC) targeted Hollywood. The committee's goals were to remove people with liberal, leftist viewpoints from the entertainment industry, and to ensure that the mass media promoted American capitalism and traditional American values. Just as World War II had required mobilization of the film industry, committee supporters reasoned, the Cold War necessitated that movies continue to promote the "right" images. With much fanfare, HUAC called Hollywood notables to testify about Communist influence in the industry. Many of those called used the opportunity to prove their patriotism and to denounce communism. Actor Ronald Reagan, president of the Screen Actors Guild, denounced Communist methods that "sucked" people into carrying out "red policy without knowing what they are doing" and testified that the Conference of Studio Unions was full of Reds.

Not all witnesses were cooperative. Some who were or had been members of the Communist Party, including the **"Hollywood Ten,"** took the Fifth Amendment and lashed out at the activities of the committee. Soon labeled "Fifth Amendment Communists," the ten were jailed for contempt of Congress and blacklisted by the industry. Eric Johnson, president of the Motion Picture Association, announced that no one would be hired who did not cooperate with the committee. He also stated that Hollywood would produce no more films like *The Grapes of Wrath*, featuring the hardships of poor Americans or "the seamy side of American life." Moviemakers soon issued a new code—*A Screen Guide for Americans*—that demanded, "Don't Smear the Free Enterprise System"; "Don't Deify the Common Man"; "Don't Show That Poverty Is a Virtue."

Just before the election of 1948, HUAC zeroed in on spies within the government, bringing forth a number of informants who had once been Soviet

---

House Un-American Activities Committee   Congressional committee, created in 1938, that investigated suspected Communists during the McCarthy era and that Richard Nixon used to advance his career.

Hollywood Ten   Ten screenwriters and producers who stated that the Fifth Amendment of the Constitution gave them the right to refuse to testify before the House Un-American Activies Committee in 1947. The House of Representatives disagreed and isssued citations for contempt. Found guilty in 1948, they served from 6 months to a year in prison.

Seeking to uncover those in the film industry who were subverting American values, in 1947 the House Un-American Activities Committee (HUAC) investigated Hollywood. While most in the industry agreed to testify and answer the committee's questions, ten did not and refused to testify, taking the Fifth Amendment. The Hollywood Ten were found guilty of contempt of Congress and sentenced to jail. In this picture a group Hollywood stars arrive in Washington to support the Hollywood Ten during the HUAC's hearings. This group included such stars as Humphrey Bogart, Lauren Bacall, Gene Kelly, Jane Wyatt, Sterling Hayden, and Danny Kay. ©*Bettmann/Corbis.*

agents and were now willing to name other Americans who allegedly had sold out the United States. The most sensational revelation came from one of the editors of *Time,* a repentant ex-Communist named Whittaker Chambers. Chambers accused **Alger Hiss,** a New Deal liberal and one-time State Department official who had been with Roosevelt at Yalta, of being a Communist. At first Hiss denied even knowing Chambers, but under interrogation by HUAC members, especially Congressman Richard M. Nixon of California, Hiss admitted an acquaintance with Chambers in the 1930s but denied he was or had been a Communist. When Hiss sued Chambers for libel, Chambers escalated the charges. He stated that Hiss had passed State Department secrets to him in the 1930s, and he produced rolls of microfilm that he said

Hiss had delivered to him. In a controversial and sensationalized trial, in 1949 Hiss was found guilty of **perjury** (the statute of limitations on espionage had expired) and was sentenced to five years in prison.

As the nation followed the Hiss case, news of the Communist victory in China and the Soviet explosion of an atomic bomb heightened American fears. Many people believed that such Communist successes could

Alger Hiss State Department official accused in 1948 of being a Communist spy; he was convicted of perjury and sent to prison.

perjury The deliberate giving of false testimony under oath.

have occurred only with help from American traitors. Congressman Harold Velde of Illinois proclaimed, "Our government from the White House down has been sympathetic toward the views of Communists and fellow-travelers, with the result that it has been infiltrated by a network of spies." Congress responded in 1950 by passing, over Truman's veto, the **McCarran Internal Security Act.** The law required all Communists to register with the attorney general and made it a crime to conspire to establish a totalitarian government in the United States. The following year the Supreme Court upheld the **Smith Act** (passed in June 1940) in *Dennis et al. v. the United States*, ruling that membership in the Communist Party was equivalent to conspiring to overthrow the American government and that no specific act of treason was necessary for conviction.

Congressman Velde's observation about spies seemed vindicated in February 1950, when English authorities arrested British scientist Klaus Fuchs for passing technical secrets to the Soviet Union. (A physicist, Fuchs had worked at Los Alamos, New Mexico, on the Manhattan Project.) Fuchs named an American accomplice, Harry Gold, who in turn named David Greenglass, an army sergeant at Los Alamos. Greenglass then claimed that his sister Ethel and her husband, Julius Rosenberg, were part of the Soviet atomic spy ring. In a controversial trial in 1951, the prosecution alleged that the information obtained and passed to the Soviets by **Ethel and Julius Rosenberg** was largely responsible for the successful Soviet atomic bomb. The Rosenbergs professed innocence but were convicted of espionage on the basis of Gold's and Greenglass's testimony. During the trial, J. Edgar Hoover asked that the death penalty not be considered for Ethel Rosenberg, but both she and her husband were executed in 1953. Soviet documents indicate that Julius Rosenberg was engaged in espionage but that Ethel was probably guilty only of being loyal to him.

Joseph McCarthy and the Politics of Loyalty

Feeding on the furor over the enemy within, Republican senator **Joseph McCarthy** of Wisconsin emerged at the forefront of the anti-Communist movement. He had entered the public arena as a candidate for Congress following World War II. Running for the Senate in 1946, he invented a glorious war record for himself that included the nickname "Tail-gunner Joe" and several wounds—he even walked with a fake limp—to

help himself win the election. Some regarded him as among the worst senators in Washington—available to lobbyists, totally lacking in moral principles, and absent most of the time. In February 1950, he was looking for an issue on which to peg his reelection bid. After conferring with friends, he settled on the internal Communist threat as an issue "with sex appeal."

The senator tried his gambit first in Wheeling, West Virginia. He announced to a Republican women's group that the United States was losing the Cold War because of traitors within the government. He claimed to know of 205 Communists working in the State Department. The senator next told a few curious reporters that in reality he had a list of "207 bad risks" in the State Department. McCarthy kept changing the number of people on his list but continued to hammer away at security risks, traitors who he could prove were employed by the State Department. He never produced his list of names for reporters.

McCarthy's charges were quickly examined by a Senate committee and shown to be at best inaccurate. When the chair of the committee, Democrat Millard Tydings of Maryland, pronounced McCarthy a hoax and a fraud, the Wisconsin senator countered by accusing Tydings of questionable loyalty. During Tydings's 1950 reelection campaign, McCarthy worked for his defeat, spreading false stories and pictures that supposedly showed connections to American Communists, including a faked photograph of the Democrat talking to Earl Browder, head of the American Communist Party. When Tydings lost by forty

McCarran Internal Security Act   Law passed by Congress in 1950 requiring Communists to register with the U.S. attorney general and making it a crime to conspire to establish a totalitarian government in the United States.

Smith Act   The Alien Registration Act, passed by Congress in 1940, which made it a crime to advocate or to belong to an organization that advocates the overthrow of the government by force or violence.

Ethel and Julius Rosenberg   Wife and husband who were arrested in 1950 and tried for conspiracy to commit espionage in 1951 after being accused of passing atomic bomb information to the Soviets; they were executed in 1953.

Joseph McCarthy   Republican senator from Wisconsin who in 1950 began a Communist witch-hunt that lasted until his censure by the Senate in 1954; *McCarthyism* is a term associated with attacks on liberals and others, often based on unsupported assertions and carried out without regard for basic liberties.

thousand votes, McCarthy's stature soared. Republicans and conservative Democrats rarely opposed him and frequently supported his wild allegations. The Senate's most powerful Republican, Robert Taft of Ohio, slapped McCarthy on the back saying, "Keep it up, Joe," and sent him the names of State Department officials who merited investigation. Taft encouraged him: "If one case doesn't work out, bring up another."

The outbreak of the Korean War and the reversals at the hands of the Chinese only increased the senator's popularity. Supported by Republican political gains in the 1950 elections, McCarthyism became a powerful political and social force. Politicians flocked to the anti-Communist bandwagon, making it ever more difficult for Truman to push his Fair Deal. Federal Trade Commissioner John Carson despaired that liberals "were on the run" and that reactionaries were "winning the fight."

By 1952, Truman's popularity was almost nonexistent: only 24 percent of those who were asked said they approved of his presidency. The Korean Conflict was stalemated, and Republicans were having a field day attacking "cowardly containment" and calling for victory in Korea. The Fair Deal was dead, and Truman had lost control over domestic policy. Compounding his problems, a probe of organized crime by a congressional committee chaired by Senator Estes Kefauver (D.–Tennessee) had found scandal, corruption, and links to the mob within the government. Presidential aide Harry Vaughan and other administration appointees were accused of accepting gifts and selling their influence.

When Truman lost the opening presidential primary in New Hampshire to Kefauver, he withdrew from the race, leaving the Democrats with no clear choice for a candidate. As in 1948, Republicans looked to the November election with great anticipation. At last, they were sure, voters would elect a Republican president—someone who, in Thomas Dewey's opinion, would "save the country from going to Hades in the handbasket of paternalism-socialism-dictatorship."

Homecoming and Social Adjustments

■ What social and economic expectations did most Americans have as the Second World War ended?

■ What was the nature of suburban America?

■ What adjustments did women and minorities have to make in postwar America?

Even before the war against Japan was over, Americans were returning home eager to resume normal lives. Organized "Bring Daddy Back" clubs flooded Washington with letters demanding a speedy return of husbands and fathers. With the defeat of Japan, soldiers in the Pacific sent letters and telegrams to their congressmen saying, "No boat; no vote." Twelve million men and women were still in uniform, and they wanted out. Despite protests from the military and the State Department, and against Truman's own better judgment, by November 1945, 1.25 million GIs were returning home each month. For Americans entering the postwar world, the homecoming was buoyed with expectations and fraught with anxieties. The United States had won the war and would oversee a peace, but would it last? The nation had experienced dramatic wartime economic growth and prosperity, but remembering the Depression, Americans wondered if the postwar economy would remain strong. Still, most were optimistic that any recession would be short-lived and they would be able to spend savings, find jobs, and enjoy the American dream. "Consumption is the frontier of the future," chirped one economic forecast.

Rising Expectations

Owning a home was for many the symbol of the American dream. Before 1945 the housing industry had focused on building custom homes or multifamily dwellings. But the postwar demand replaced custom homes with standardized ones. What people wanted were the charming "dream homes" in new planned communities that were advertised in popular magazines. To meet the demand, by mid-1946, William Levitt and other developers supplied mass-produced, prefabricated houses—the suburban **tract homes**. Using building techniques developed during the war, timber from his own forests, and nonunion workers, Levitt boasted that he could construct an affordable house on an existing concrete slab in sixteen minutes. Standardized, with few frills, the house was a two-story **Cape Cod** with four and a half rooms. Built on generous 60-by-100-foot lots, complete with

tract homes One of numerous houses of similar design built on small plots of land.

Cape Cod A style of two-story house that has a steep roof and a central chimney; it originated in colonial Massachusetts and became popular in suburbs after World War II.

As World War II ended, Americans flocked to the suburbs, creating a demand for new housing—a demand matched by developers of planned communities like Levittown, Pennsylvania. Developers kept the cost of the homes down using uniformity of style and of prefabricated materials. *Van Bucher/ Photo Researchers.*

a tree or two, Levitt homes cost slightly less than $8,000 and still provided Levitt with a $1,000 profit per house. The price was attractive, and hopeful buyers formed long lines as soon as the homes went on sale. The first Levittown sprang up in Hempstead, Long Island, and had more than seventeen thousand homes, seven village greens, fourteen playgrounds, and nine swimming pools. Hundreds of look-alike suburban neighborhoods were soon built across the nation, contributing to a growing migration from rural and urban America to the suburbs.

Nowhere were tract homes more prominent than in southern California. Fostered since the 1920s by the automobile, Los Angeles's development was different from urban development in eastern and midwestern cities. During and after the war, networks of roads extended out from southern California cities, which developed several "satellite" economic centers, pulling businesses, homes, and industries away from the central cities. Continuing the process, California governor Earl Warren in 1947 allocated nearly $300 million over a ten-year period to build 105 miles of freeways in southern California—most crisscrossing the Los Angeles area. Statewide gasoline taxes

and registration fees paid for the new roads. At the same time, in downtown Los Angeles and across the country, public transportation, especially streetcars and interurban rail systems, were vanishing and being replaced by bus lines that frequently provided only limited service to the poorer neighborhoods. The fate of downtown Los Angeles was not unique as it experienced a 50 percent loss in sales and revenues. Those still living and working in cities witnessed a parallel loss of jobs and wages.

Suburbs were not for everyone, and widespread discrimination kept some out by design. Whether it was the official policy of developers like Levitt, neighborhood covenants, or lack of home loans, almost every suburb in the nation was predominately white and Christian. Even though the Supreme Court ruled in *Shelly v. Kraemer* (1948) that restrictive housing

Shelly v. Kraemer Supreme Court ruling (1948) that barred lower courts from enforcing restrictive agreements that prevented minorities from living in certain neighborhoods; it had little impact on actual practices.

covenants written to exclude minorities could not be enforced by lower courts, the decision failed to have much impact. Neither did the Court's decision to prevent banks and the FHA from rejecting home loan applications from minorities trying to buy houses in typical white neighborhoods. Real-estate agents also continued to abide by the Realtors' Code of Ethics, which called it unethical to permit the "infiltration of inharmonious elements" into a neighborhood. Across the nation, fewer than 5 percent of suburban neighborhoods provided nonwhites access to the American dream house. In the San Francisco Bay Area, not even 1 percent of the more than 100,000 homes built between 1945 and 1950 were sold to nonwhites.

For many veterans a cozy home was only part of the postwar dream—so too was going to college. Armed with economic support through the G.I. Bill in September 1946, nearly 1 million veterans enrolled in college. New Jersey's Rutgers University saw its enrollment climb from 7,000 to 16,000. At Lehigh University in Pennsylvania, 940 veteran students outnumbered the 396 "civilians" and refused to don the traditional freshman beanie. Faculty and administrators soon discovered that veterans made exceptional students and rarely needed disciplinary action. Nonveteran students, however, complained that because of the veterans they had to work harder and "slave to keep up." Schools scrambled to respond to the influx of students, not only hiring more faculty and building more facilities but also providing special housing, daycare centers, and expanded health clinics for married students. By the time the G.I. Bill expired in 1952, over 2 million veterans, including 64,000 women, had earned their degrees under its umbrella.

Veterans expected jobs, too, and most figured that wartime workers, especially minorities and women, would relinquish their jobs and return to traditional roles. At first jobs seemed scarce. The cancellation of wartime contracts and the nationwide switch to domestic production resulted in 2.7 million workers being dismissed from their jobs within a month of Japan's surrender. Fortunately for veterans, the G.I. Bill provided unemployment compensation for a year until a job was found. And within a year, jobs were becoming more and more available. By 1947, 60 million people were working, 7 million more than at the peak of wartime production. But the work force had changed, with noticeably fewer women and minorities as industries and businesses resumed their prewar hiring habits.

From Industrial Worker to Homemaker

Across the nation in a variety of ways, women were told that they were no longer wanted in the workplace and that they would be most fulfilled by being wives and mothers again. A *Fortune* poll in the fall of 1945 revealed that 57 percent of women and 63 percent of men believed that married women should not work outside the home. Psychiatrists and marriage counselors argued that men wanted their wives to be feminine and submissive, not their fellow workers. Yet many women resisted these social pressures and rejected a return to the routine of housework. They wanted to keep their jobs. Despite their hopes, however, women experienced a rapid decline in employment, particularly in manufacturing. In the aircraft industry, women had made up 40 percent of the work force, but by 1948 they were only 12 percent, and most of those were now holding clerical positions. Women's wages declined too, from about $50 to $35 a week. Still, a significant majority of those women looking for work, 75 percent, found it, although in a more gender-segregated workplace than before the war. Rosie the Riveter had become Fran the File Clerk, and by 1950 the number of women working reached 29 million—a million less than at the wartime peak of women's employment.

At work or at home, Americans witnessed a renewed social emphasis on femininity, family, and a woman's proper role. Fashion designers, such as Christian Dior in his "New Look," lengthened skirts and accented waists and breasts to emphasize femininity. Marriage was more popular than ever: by 1950, two-thirds of the population were married and having children. Factors contributing to the rush to the altar were fears of "male scarcity" caused by war losses and a new attitude that viewed marriage as the ideal state for young people. Many women's magazines and marriage experts championed the idea that men should marry at around age 20 and women at age 18 or 19. With veterans returning home, with society celebrating family, and with prosperity increasing came the **"baby boom"** that would last for nearly twenty years. From a Depression level of under 19

---

baby boom   Sudden increase in the birth rate that occurred in the United States after World War II and lasted until roughly 1964.

"She's a gem—she used to work for Lockheed!"

Following World War II, a majority of women left the industrial work force and returned to the home and more "traditional" occupations. In this cartoon, a more affluent homemaker benefits from the wartime skills her new domestic servant acquired. Many women, like Sybil Lewis, were determined never to return to traditional roles. *Ellen Kaiper Collection, Oakland.*

births per 1,000 women per year, the birth rate rose to more than 25 births per 1,000 women by 1948 (see Figure 26.1).

Not all women accepted the role of contented, submissive wives and homemakers—the war experience had changed relationships. When one veteran informed his wife that she could no longer handle the finances because doing so was not "woman's work," she indignantly reminded him that she had successfully balanced the checkbook for four years and that his return had not made her suddenly stupid. Reflect-

ing such tensions and too many hasty wartime marriages, the divorce rate jumped dramatically. Twenty-five percent of all wartime marriages were ending in divorce in 1946, and by 1950 over a million GI marriages had dissolved. As the number of female heads of household rose, so also did the poverty and social stigma attached to single parenthood. Following her divorce, one suburban resident recalled that her neighbors "avoided" her and made remarks like "Why don't you get a job instead of taking tax monies?" She also noted that her children were singled out at school because they did not have a father at home.

Restrained Expectations

Like Sybil Lewis (see pages 788–789), nonwhites expected their wartime advances would dissipate as society forced them to return to prewar social and economic patterns. Most still lived in a distinctly segregated world. From housing to jobs, from healthcare to education, white society continued to deny nonwhites full participation in the American dream. Still, minorities looked eagerly toward the postwar period. Despite ongoing discrimination, they had achieved social and economic gains during the war, and despite immediate postwar adjustments, more progress seemed possible. In 1945, for example, Jackie Robinson broke the color barrier in professional baseball when team owner Branch Rickey signed him to play for the Brooklyn Dodgers' farm team, the Montreal Royals. Robinson joined the Dodgers in 1947 as the first African American player in the previously all-white major leagues and that season was voted the National League's Rookie of the Year.

Minorities also pursued activism to gain equality. Having fought for democracy overseas, Latino and African American veterans insisted that democracy be practiced at home. African American civil rights leader W. E. B. Du Bois echoed their feelings, stating that the real problems facing the United States came not from Stalin and Molotov, but from racists like Mississippi's Senator Theodore Bilbo and Congressman John Rankin. "Internal injustice done to one's brother," Du Bois warned, "is far more dangerous than the aggression of strangers from abroad." Confronting restrictions on the right to vote, some black veterans like Medgar Evers attempted to register to vote. Most failed, including Evers, who was barred from registering by armed whites, but some succeeded, especially in the Upper South and in urban areas. In several northern cities, while housing and race riots were one result of continuing black

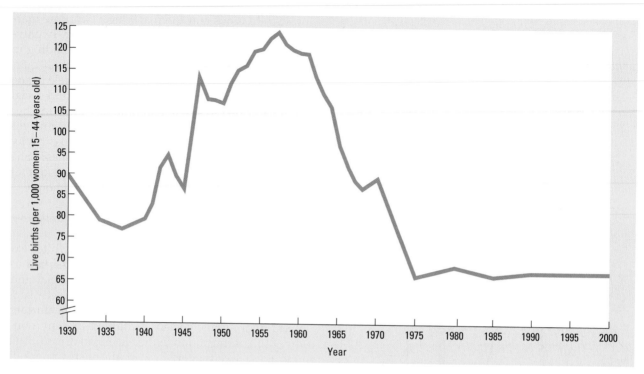

FIGURE 26.1 Birth Rate, 1930–2000 Between 1946 and 1964, rebounding from the low birth rate of the Depression, families chose to have more children. This increase is often called the "baby boom." In the 1960s, the birth rate slowed, and since the mid-1970s, it has remained fairly constant.

migration from the South, another was a growing political voice as African American neighborhoods elected black representatives such as Adam Clayton Powell Jr. to Congress.

While they cheered every at-bat and stolen base of Jackie Robinson, the reality for most African Americans was unchanged. They watched "fair employment" vanish as employers favored white males once the war was over. "Last hired, first fired" reflected job reality, especially in skilled and industrial jobs. In 1943 more than a million African Americans were employed in the aircraft industry. By 1950, the number had shrunk to 237,000. The decline was less marked in the automobile, rubber, and shipbuilding industries, but minority job levels dropped there too, as employers routinely chose to exclude nonwhites from many of the skilled and higher-paying positions.

Latinos, too, had limited expectations because of discrimination and limited job and educational opportunities. Anxious to gain the benefits of democracy, existing organizations such as the League of Latin American Citizens (LULAC) worked with new ones such as the **American GI Forum** to attack discrimination throughout the West and Southwest. The American GI Forum, organized in Texas in early 1948 by Mexican American veterans, worked to secure for Latino veterans the benefits provided by the G.I. Bill and to develop leadership within the Mexican American population. In California and Texas, LULAC and the American GI Forum successfully used federal courts to attack school systems that segregated Latino from white children. In *Mendez v. Westminster* (1946) and in *Delgado v. Bastrop School District* (1948), federal courts ruled that school systems could not educate Mexican Americans separately from Anglos.

American GI Forum Organization formed in Texas in 1948 by Mexican American veterans to overcome discrimination and provide support for veterans and all Hispanics; it led the court fight to end the segregation of Hispanic children in school systems in the West and Southwest.

Mendez v. Westminster and *Delgado v. Bastrop School District* Two federal court cases that overturned the establishment of separate schools for Mexican American children in California and Texas in 1946 and 1948, respectively.

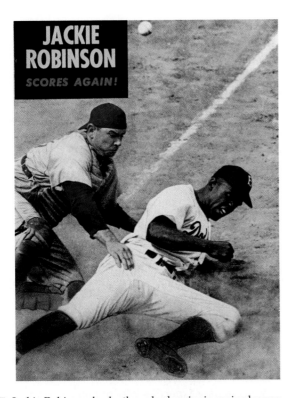

Jackie Robinson broke the color barrier in major-league baseball in 1947 when he joined the Brooklyn Dodgers. After serving as a lieutenant in the army during the war, Robinson, an All-American in football and baseball at UCLA, played with the Kansas City Monarchs of the Negro American Baseball League until he was signed by the Dodgers in 1945. Moved from the minors to the majors in 1947, he earned "Rookie of the Year" honors and later was inducted into the Baseball Hall of Fame. *Collection of Michael Barson/Past Perfect.*

Despite these rulings, throughout the Southwest and West, Latino students remained in predominantly "Mexican" schools and classrooms, perpetuating the lack of educational opportunities and contributing to high dropout rates.

For women and minorities, the immediate postwar period saw significant loss of income and status as society expected the "underclass" to return to its prewar existence. But the war had energized those left outside white suburbia and the nation's expanding affluence. Women, African Americans, Hispanics, and other minority groups had their own vision of the American dream, one that included not only growing prosperity but also a full and unfettered role in society and an unmuzzled voice in politics.

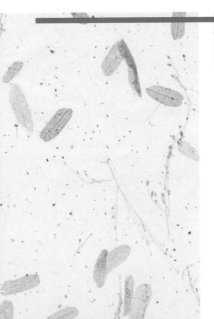

Individual Voices

Examining a Primary Source

George F. Kennan Analyzes the Soviets' Worldview

Kennan's "Long Telegram" is one of the most important documents in American foreign policy. It provided the Truman administration with an intellectual understanding of what drove the Soviet Union as the two superpowers inched toward a Cold War that would last nearly fifty years. Sent to the State Department on February 22, 1946, the document—excerpted here—was widely read within the administration and was instrumental in shaping U.S. policy toward the Soviet Union.

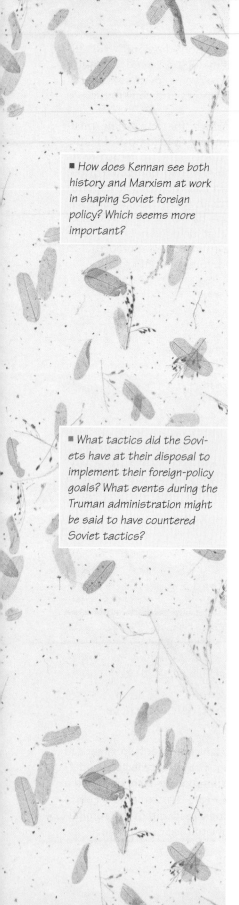

■ How does Kennan see both history and Marxism at work in shaping Soviet foreign policy? Which seems more important?

■ What tactics did the Soviets have at their disposal to implement their foreign-policy goals? What events during the Truman administration might be said to have countered Soviet tactics?

At the bottom of the Kremlin's neurotic view of world affairs is traditional and instinctive Russian sense of insecurity. . . . Russian rulers have invariably sensed that their rule was . . . fragile and . . . unable to stand comparison or contact with political systems of Western countries. For this reason they have always feared foreign penetrations, feared direct contact between Western world and their own.

. . . Marxist dogma . . . became the perfect vehicle for the sense of insecurity with which Bolsheviks, even more than previous Russian rulers, were afflicted. In this . . . they found justification for the dictatorship without which they did not know how to rule, for cruelties they did not dare to inflict, for sacrifices they felt bound to demand. . . . Today they cannot dispense with it [Marxism]. It is a fig leaf of their moral and intellectual respectability. Without it they would stand before history . . . as only the last of that long succession of cruel and wasteful Russian rulers. . . . ■

Soviet policy . . . is conducted on two planes: (1) official . . . and (2) subterranean. . . .

On official plane we must look for following:

(a) Internal policy devoted to increasing in every way strength and prestige of Soviet state. . . .

(b) Wherever it is considered timely and promising, efforts will be made to advance official limits of Soviet Power. . . .

(c) Russians will participate officially in international organizations where they see opportunity of extending Soviet power or of inhibiting or diluting power of others. . . .

Following May Be Said as to What We May Expect by Way of Implementation of Basic Soviet Policies on Unofficial, or Subterranean Plane . . .

(d) In foreign countries Communists will . . . work toward destruction of all forms of personal independence, economic, political, or moral. . . .

(e) Everything possible will be done to set major Western Powers against each other. . . .

(f) In general, all Soviet efforts on unofficial international plane will be negative and destructive, . . . designed to tear down sources of strength beyond reach of Soviet control. . . . ■

In summary, we have here a political force committed fanatically to the belief that with US there can be no permanent modus vivendi, that it is desirable and necessary that the internal harmony of our society be disrupted, our traditional way of life be destroyed, the international authority of our state be broken, if Soviet power is to be secure. . . .

Problem of how to cope with this force [is] undoubtedly greatest task our diplomacy has ever faced and probably greatest it will ever have to face. . . . I cannot attempt to suggest all answers here. But I would like to record my conviction that problem is within our power to solve—and that without recourse to any general military conflict. And in support of this conviction there are certain observations of a more encouraging nature I should like to make:

(1) Soviet power . . . is neither schematic nor adventuristic. It does not work by fixed plans. It does not take unnecessary risks. Impervious to logic of reason, and it is highly sensitive to logic of force. For this reason it can easily withdraw—and usually does when strong resistance is encountered. . . .

(2) Gauged against Western World . . . Soviets are still by far the weaker force. Thus their success will really depend on degree of cohesion, firmness and vigor which Western World can muster. . . .

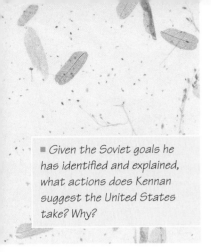

For those reasons I think we may approach calmly and with good heart problem of how to deal with Russia. As to how this approach should be made, I only wish to advance, by way of conclusion, following comments: . . .

(3) Much depends on health and vigor of our own society. World communism is like malignant parasite which feeds only on diseased tissue. . . .

(4) We must formulate and put forward for other nations a much more positive and constructive picture of world we would like to see than we have put forward in the past. . . . Many foreign peoples . . . are seeking guidance. . . . We should be better able than Russians to give them this. . . . And unless we do, the Russians certainly will. . . . ■

■ Given the Soviet goals he has identified and explained, what actions does Kennan suggest the United States take? Why?

Summary

People hoped that the end of World War II would usher in a period of international cooperation and peace. This expectation vanished as the world entered the Cold War, a period of armed and vigilant suspicion. To protect the country and the world from Soviet expansion, the United States asserted a primary economic, political, and military role around the globe. The Truman administration developed a containment policy that was first applied to Western Europe but eventually included Asia as well. By the end of Truman's presidency, the United States had begun to view its national security in global terms and vowed to use its resources to combat the spread of Communist power.

At home the Cold War had its impact as well, acting to curb the expansion of liberalism. Truman sought to expand on the New Deal but found success difficult. While existing New Deal programs such as Social Security, farm supports, and a minimum wage were extended, a conservative Congress blocked new programs, including national healthcare. Linking liberal ideas and programs with communism, moderates and conservatives alike promoted their own political, social, and economic interests. They often successfully attacked liberals, unions, and civil rights advocates as too radical and their proposals as smacking of communism. Ultraconservative groups such as the House Un-American Activities Committee and zealous individuals—especially Joseph McCarthy—led the way in promoting a Red Scare that not only attacked liberals in government but also deeply disturbed society.

Most Americans expected to enjoy the fruits of an expanding postwar economy that would bring increased prosperity and more consumer goods. For many the vision of the suburbs with its stable family structure and new-model car in every garage seemed obtainable and desirable. Women were encouraged to return to "domestic" life and raise a family. Postwar America saw a rise in marriages and births, the start of a baby boom. But alongside these trends were an increasing number of divorces and women dissatisfied with their traditional roles.

While jobs and homeownership multiplied for white males, and white families seemed poised to achieve the American dream, minorities seemed hemmed in, or nudged out, by discrimination that turned back many of the economic and social gains they had made during the war. Though ousted from the work force or into lesser jobs and still living in a socially segregated society, many minorities held their own more limited hopes for a future that would bring economic and educational improvement as well as full political and civil rights.

EISENHOWER'S AMERICA During the 1950s, Americans were on the move. White Americans were moving to the suburbs, especially in the South and West. Many African Americans were leaving the rural areas of the South; others were moving against long-existing patterns of segregation. This map shows the web of interstate highways as envisioned in the 1950s, the shifts of population from state to state, and the cities where the process of confronting legal segregation began.

CANADA

WASHINGTON 19%

MONTANA 14%

NORTH DAKOTA 2%

MINN. 14%

VT. 3%

MAINE 6%

OREGON 16%

IDAHO 13%

SOUTH DAKOTA 4%

WIS. 15%

MICH. 22%

N.H. 1

MASS

NEW YORK 13%

Wilkes-Barre /Hazleton, PA: 12% decrease in population, 1950–1960

WYOMING 13%

IOWA 5%

R.I.
CONN. 2

NEVADA 78%

UTAH 29%

NEBRASKA 6%

IND. 18%

OHIO 22%

PENNSYLVANIA 7%

N.J. 25%

Jersey City, N.J 6% decrease in population, 1950–1960

CALIFORNIA 48%

COLORADO 32%

ILL. 15%

W.VA. -7%

VIRGINIA 19%

Johnstown, PA 4% decrease in population, 1950–1960

KANSAS 14%

MISSOURI 9%

KENTUCKY 3%

DEL. 40%
MD. 32%

San Jose, CA: 121% increase in population, 1950–1960

ARIZONA 73%

NEW MEXICO 39%

OKLAHOMA 4%

ARK. 6%

TENN. 8%

NORTH CAROLINA 12%

Washington, D.C. -4

SOUTH CAROLINA 12%

ATLANT
OCEAN

PACIFIC OCEAN

TEXAS 24%

MISS. 1%

ALABAMA 6%

GEORGIA 14%

LA. 21%

Orlando, Florida: 125% increase in population, 1950–1960

Ft. Lauderdale /Hollywood, Florida: 298% increase in population, 1950–1960

FLA. 78%

Gulf of Mexico

HAWAI`I (1959) 26%

0   100 Km.

0   100 Mi.

PACIFIC OCEAN

U.S.S.R.

MEXICO

CUBA

ALASKA (1959) 75%

CANADA

0   250   500 Km.

0   250   500 Mi.

PACIFIC OCEAN

Interstate highway

Population changes, 1950–1960
Gains

Loss

Under 10%

Under 10%

10%–20%

20%–50%

Over 50%

0   200   400 Km.

0   200   400 Mi.

1950
Korean War begins

1952
Eisenhower elected

Hydrogen bomb tested

1953
Korean armistice

1954
Brown case

Army-McCarthy hearings

1955
Montgomery boycott

1957
Baby boom peaks

1950	1951	1952	1953	1954	1955	1956	1957	1958	1959	1960

1953
Stalin dies

1954
Battle of Dienbienphu

1956
Suez crisis

Soviets invade Hungary

1957
Common Market created

1959
Castro assumes power in Cuba

1960
OPEC created

Quest for Consensus, 1952–1960

27

Eishenhower's America
The 1950s saw population shifts and the rise of the Sunbelt. Examine the map on the facing page. What states experienced the largest gains, and what economic and social developments contributed to the population changes?

Individual Choices

RAY KROC

Having spent most of his life as a salesman, at 52 Ray Kroc chose to enter the restaurant business in 1955, purchasing the rights to franchise McDonald's name and system of fast-food production. Before he died in 1984, his small beginning had mushroomed into a multimillion-dollar enterprise and the "Golden Arches" had become a worldwide recognizable symbol of American culture. *Art Shay/Getty Images.*

Ray Kroc

It seemed astounding; a small drive-in restaurant located in southern California—the Mecca of drive-ins—was ordering two new milkshake-making machines. It already had eight, and Ray Kroc, who owned the marketing rights to the machine (Multimixer), wondered what the owners were doing to utilize so many machines. Traveling from Chicago to San Bernardino, California, to see for himself, he watched the small, eight-sided restaurant named McDonald's attract hundreds of customers. They flocked to windows to buy hamburgers, shakes, and fries, carrying them away in paper bags. What Kroc discovered was an assembly-line process of producing a very limited menu. He also saw opportunity, especially after interviewing the owners, Maurice (Mac) and Richard McDonald.

In 1940, the brothers operated a profitable, typical drive-in. It had eight sides, lots of glass, and employed twenty carhops who served food from a twenty-five-item menu. The restaurant made a good profit, but by 1948 sales were slipping as other drive-ins attracted their customers. To improve their profits, the McDonalds decided to cut costs and use the same assembly-line technique as Henry Ford. They fired all their carhops, opened take-out windows, and limited the menu. "If we gave people a choice . . . there would be chaos," explained Dick McDonald. The limited menu allowed for specialization: the French fry cook, the burger cook, the burger dresser, the shake maker, and the counterman—a total of twelve men (there were no women employed until 1968). The burgers were wrapped in paper, drinks were served in paper cups, and the order was put in paper bags (no need for dishes or a dishwasher). It was a revolutionary idea, and it worked. To expand their customer base, even at the expense of losing some teenagers, the brothers removed cigarette machines and jukeboxes, emphasized quick service, and kept clean premises—a place for the whole family. Later, in placing his franchises, Kroc focused on suburbs, looking for locations near schools and churches. "He saw the migration from downtown to the suburbs and the rise of the two-income families and how ideally those circumstances fit in with McDonald's," recounted Fred Turner, who became chairman of McDonald's.

Kroc was a salesman and had no experience in restaurants, but he decided to take a risk and convinced the McDonalds to give him the right to **franchise** the restaurant and open new ones in different places. Making enough money and satisfied with their business, the brothers had little desire to expand their system, but they were not opposed to letting Kroc do it. Kroc received the exclusive right to sell the McDonalds' idea and system, but there was a problem. The McDonalds demanded that he charge a low franchise fee and accept a service fee of less than

> **franchise**   Right granted by a company to an individual or group to sell the company's goods and services. The franchisee operates his or her own business and keeps most of the profits, although the franchiser receives part of the profit and may establish rules and guidelines for the running of the business.

2 percent of the profits of each restaurant, with one half of 1 percent paid to the brothers. It was not a formula for getting rich, but Kroc made his choice. "I went along with it because the Multimixer business was so bad, and I had to get into something that had a future."

Kroc's first franchise was his own, a McDonald's he opened in 1955 in Des Plaines, Illinois. Others followed, but profits lagged; selling franchises was not making a profit. Out of necessity, Kroc made another decision. In 1961, he paid the brothers $2,700,000 for the whole operation, including the name. In full control, Kroc applied a new approach to franchising. In most cases, the profit for the franchising company came from selling the franchise, with little interest in whether the franchise succeeded. However, because Kroc charged such a small franchising fee, he concluded that he needed to be most concerned about the success of the restaurants. Profits would come not from selling franchises but from profitable McDonald's restaurants.

To ensure quality and consistency, the McDonald's Corporation demanded the same look in buildings, the same menu, the same process of preparing and serving the food, and cleanliness. Cleanliness was critical to Kroc, who bragged of cleaning toilets in his restaurant. "If you have time to lean, you have time to clean." To improve profitability, McDonald's selected regional suppliers for all McDonald's, allowing for lower costs by buying in bulk. It was a formula for success, and within four years Kroc had 738 McDonald's franchised and open, and the demand for new franchises continued to grow—as did the menu. Over the years, new items were added to the basic menu—the first was the fish fillet in 1964—reflecting consumer desires and tastes.

As the number of McDonald's spread, its Golden Arches became an icon, representing not only America but hometown America. This view was clearly at the heart of a letter sent to McDonald's from a platoon fighting in Vietnam in the late 1960s. The letter stated: "We are the infantry. They call us grunts and we hump in the jungles and the rice paddies. . . . While thumbing through *Look* magazine we found a picture of a 'Big Mac'. . . . When we get back to the world . . . our first act [will be] going to McDonald's for a burger and a shake."

By the mid-seventies the war in Vietnam was over, but McDonald's had opened its 2,000th restaurant and had become one of the largest employers in the United States. By 2000, it was estimated that about 13 percent of the American work force was working for, or had worked for, McDonald's, and about 96 percent of the American population had eaten at a McDonald's. In 1971, McDonald's opened restaurants in Europe, Asia, and Australia. By 2004, there were 30,000 locations in 119 nations, from Paris to Moscow to Beijing. When asked in an interview why McDonald's was such a success, Kroc answered, "We take the hamburger business more seriously than anyone else."

INTRODUCTION

In the 1950s, the social landscape of America was changing, marked by roads, highways, and the automobile. It was characterized by the middle-class suburb, whose houses looked remarkably the same and whose conformity generated a needed sense of community and stability. Contributing to the security of conformity, Ray Kroc was shaping a new icon for America, the Golden Arches of McDonald's. Within a few years, those arches would become the second most recognizable symbol—second only to Coke—of an American way of life. Kroc recognized the shift to the suburbs and the desire for a more mobile America to have comfort points of stability. McDonald's would focus on suburban neighborhoods and the family. Value, quality, cleanliness, and a friendly environment attracted kids, parents, and grandparents. As Kroc explained, "family" is "where we get 90 percent of our business."

Indeed, much of the 1950s seemed to focus on nuclear families enjoying the fruits of democracy and capitalism. There was optimism that economic growth offered people like Kroc an opportunity to be a success or at least live free from economic want. Watching over and promoting the expanding economy was the Republican Party and President Dwight David Eisenhower. In 1952, Republicans claimed that they best represented American values and the new patriotism. A victory by Dwight David Eisenhower would end twenty years of Democratic control of the White House and reverse two "dangerous" trends: creeping socialism in the form of New Deal–style programs and appeasement of communism in the guise of containment. Eisenhower and a Republican Congress wanted to reduce government intervention in social and economic affairs, expand prosperity by supporting capitalism, conclude the war in Korea, and win victories in the Cold War. But most of all, Americans expected the government to foster and protect the values of America and allow them to live their lives to the fullest, in the strongest, most democratic, most prosperous nation in the world.

The United States of the 1950s was experiencing one of the longest periods of sustained economic growth in its history, one that in most people's opinion offered every citizen an opportunity to live free from the fear of economic want. This portrait of an affluent America meshed with the image of a gentle, quiet president who presided over a prosperous, stable nation.

Yet for Eisenhower and many other Americans, defining the **consensus** was not all that simple. Eisenhower himself was an example. Like the decade, President Eisenhower was more complex than commonly realized at the time. On the surface "Ike" seemed to live up to the popular joke: "What happens when you wind up an Eisenhower doll? Absolutely nothing!" But the real Eisenhower was an effective behind-the-scenes leader who recognized that a political and social consensus accepted the structure of government as shaped by the New Deal. Faced with this constraint on dismantling New Deal–style programs, he chose to modify some by cutting spending and to rein in government controls where possible. But he also increased Social Security benefits and the minimum wage, and initiated a massive highway-building project and federal aid to public education. Rather than roll back the principles of the New Deal, Eisen-

hower's inability to change served only to confirm and strengthen them.

In foreign policy, Eisenhower made similar choices. He decided to maintain the basic strategy of containment, placing new areas of the globe under an American nuclear umbrella. Desiring at the same time to balance the budget, he adopted the "New Look" in national security policy, stressing use of atomic weapons, the air force, alliances, and covert activities as foreign-policy tools. Thus, responding to political and international constraints established by the Great Depression, World War II, and the Truman years, Eisenhower shaped a modified—not a reinvented—foreign policy.

While Eisenhower sought to establish a political and international consensus, a large segment of the population thought that they lived in the best of times. Social and economic trends begun after the war continued. Unemployment was low, wages and spending were reaching new highs, and it seemed to many that all Americans, even those not living in the suburbs, had the chance to live prosperous, happy, stable, and fulfilling lives. The focus of that fulfilling life centered on the suburban nuclear family, Dad at work, Mom at home.

Yet that image of consensus was only partially valid. Many men and women were dissatisfied with their roles as husband and father, wife and mother. Dissatisfaction also struck many American youths, who rejected en masse the values of suburban culture, turning to the driving rhythms of rock 'n' roll and displaying antisocial behavior. At the same time, intellectual and cultural critics condemned the sameness and staleness of the suburban culture. The outcome was an American society fragmented by social realities that fed into, or starved, differing expectations.

Nor did prosperity touch all Americans. For minorities in 1950, the obstacles blocking their access to the American dream appeared insurmountable. Poverty, prejudice, and segregation remained the norm. Nevertheless, some groups nurtured expectations of change that would open new choices. By mid-decade, African Americans were tearing down barriers that excluded and isolated them. The outcome was a civil rights movement that attacked existing social and legal restrictions and forced government, political parties, and society to confront long-standing contradictions in the country's democratic image.

---

consensus Agreement of opinion.

Chronology

The Fifties

1948 Alfred Kinsey's *Sexual Behavior in the Human Male*

1950 Korean War begins
David Riesman's *The Lonely Crowd*

1951 J. D. Salinger's *The Catcher in the Rye*
Mattachine Society formed
Alan Freed's "Moondog's Rock 'n' Roll Party"

1952 Dwight David Eisenhower elected president
Eisenhower visits Korea
United States tests hydrogen bomb

1953 Korean armistice at Panmunjom
Mohammed Mossadegh overthrown in Iran
Joseph Stalin dies
Kinsey's *Sexual Behavior in the Human Female*
Termination policy for American Indians implemented
Earl Warren appointed chief justice of Supreme Court
Father Knows Best debuts on television
Playboy begins publication
Deptartment of Health, Education and Welfare created

1954 *Brown v. Board of Education*
St. Lawrence Seaway Act
Federal budget balanced
Army-McCarthy hearings
Jacobo Arbenz overthrown in Guatemala
Gamal Nasser assumes power in Egypt
Battle of Dienbienphu
Geneva Agreement (Vietnam)
SEATO founded

1955 Montgomery bus boycott
Salk vaccine approved for use
AFL-CIO merger

Warsaw Pact formed
Baghdad Pact formed
Geneva Summit
Eisenhower's Open Skies proposal
Montgomery, Alabama, bus boycott begins

1956 Federal Highway Act
Gayle et al. v. Browser
Southern Christian Leadership Conference formed
Eisenhower reelected
Suez crisis
Soviets invade Hungary
Allen Ginsberg's *Howl*
Grace Metalious's *Peyton Place*
Elvis Presley records "Heartbreak Hotel"

1957 Little Rock crisis
Civil Rights Act
Eisenhower Doctrine
United States joins Baghdad Pact
Soviets launch *Sputnik I*
Jack Kerouac's *On the Road*
Nevil Shute's *On the Beach*
Baby boom peaks at 4.3 million births

1958 Anti-U.S. demonstrations in Latin America
Berlin crisis
United States sends troops to Lebanon
National Defense Education Act
NASA established
Nuclear test moratorium

1959 Fidel Castro takes control in Cuba
CENTO formed
Alaska and Hawai`i become states
Nikita Khrushchev visits the United States
Cooper v. Aaron

1960 Soviets shoot down U-2 and capture pilot
Paris Summit

Politics of Consensus

■ What were the popular images of Eisenhower, and how did they compare with reality?

■ What were the goals of conservatives and Eisenhower as they sought to roll back the programs of the New Deal?

■ What programs were successful under Eisenhower's "Dynamic Conservatism"?

It was "time for a change," cried Republicans in 1952. Politically wounded by the lingering war in Korea and the soft-on-communism label, plus recent revelations of government corruption, the Democrats' twenty-year hold on the White House would finally be ended. Initially, the leading Republican candidate for the presidency was Senator Robert Taft, an ardent opponent of the New Deal and a prewar isolationist who remained suspicious of the new global role the nation was following. For those reasons, many moderate Republicans turned to General Dwight David Eisenhower. While politically inexperienced, "Ike" appeared to be the perfect candidate. He was well known, revered as a war hero, and carried the image of an honest man thrust into public service. Skillfully gaining the nomination at the Republican convention, Eisenhower chose Richard M. Nixon of California as his vice-presidential running mate. Nixon was young and had risen rapidly in the party because of his outspoken anticommunism and his aggressive role in the investigation of Alger Hiss. The Democrats nominated Adlai E. Stevenson, a liberal New Dealer and governor of Illinois.

Eisenhower Takes Command

The Republican campaign took two paths. One concentrated on the popular image of Eisenhower. Republicans introduced "spot commercials" on television and used them to stress Ike's honesty, integrity, and "American-ness." In public, Eisenhower crusaded for high standards and good government and posed as another George Washington. A war-weary nation applauded his promise to go to Korea "in the cause of peace." McCarthy, Nixon, and others who brutally attacked the Democrats' Cold War and New Deal records took the second campaign path. They blasted the Democrats as representing "plunder at home and blunder abroad." Proudly they boasted of "no Communists in the Republican Party." Nixon and others called the containment policy cowardly and promised to roll back communism. They also vowed to end the liberal spending of the Democrats and to dismantle the New Deal. Stevenson's effort to "talk sense" to the voters stood little chance.

The campaign's only tense moment came with an allegation that Nixon had accepted gifts from, and used a secret cash fund provided by, California business friends. To counter the accusations and to keep Eisenhower from dropping him from the ticket, Nixon explained his side of the story on television. In the "Checkers speech," a teary-eyed Nixon denied the fund existed and claimed that the only gift his family had ever received was a puppy, Checkers. His daughter loved the puppy, Nixon stated, and he would not make her give it back, no matter what it did to his career. It was an overly sentimental speech, but the public and Eisenhower rallied behind Nixon, and the Republicans easily won the election. Eisenhower buried Stevenson in popular (55 percent) and electoral (442 to 89) votes (see Map 27.1) and carried four

In this picture, the triumphant Republican nominees for the White House pose with smiles and wives—Pat Nixon and Mamie Eisenhower. Seen as a statesman and not a politician during the campaign, Eisenhower worked hard to ensure his nomination over Robert Taft, and then chose Richard Nixon to balance the ticket because he was a younger man, a westerner, and a conservative. *Corbis-Bettmann.*

traditionally Democratic southern states. Ike's broad political coattails also swept Republican majorities into Congress. Four years later, the 1956 presidential election was a repeat of 1952, with Eisenhower receiving 457 electoral votes and again swamping Stevenson, who carried only seven southern states. But in 1956, the Republican victory was Eisenhower's alone, as Democrats maintained the majorities in both houses of Congress they had won in the 1954 midterm races.

During both of his administrations, to the public Eisenhower was "Ike," a warm, friendly, slightly bumbling grandfather figure who projected middle-class values and habits. Critics complained that he seemed almost an absentee president, often leaving the government in the hands of Congress and his cabinet while he played golf or bridge. But to those who knew him and worked with him, he was far from bumbling or an absentee president. In military fashion, Eisenhower relied on his staff to provide a full discussion of any issue. We had a "good growl," he would say after especially heated cabinet talks, but he made the final decisions, and he expected them to be carried out.

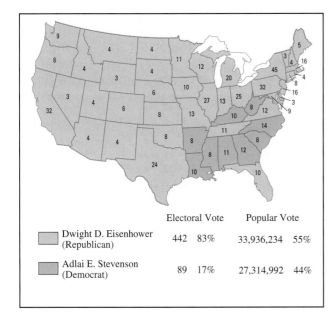

	Electoral Vote		Popular Vote	
Dwight D. Eisenhower (Republican)	442	83%	33,936,234	55%
Adlai E. Stevenson (Democrat)	89	17%	27,314,992	44%

MAP 27.1 Election of 1952 Dwight David Eisenhower and the Republicans swept into office in 1952. Leading the ticket, Eisenhower swamped his Democratic opponent, Adlai Stevenson, with 83 percent of the electoral vote and 55 percent of the popular vote. Republicans also won majorities in both houses of Congress. In the 1956 presidential election, Eisenhower beat Stevenson by even larger margins, but Democrats retained the majority status in Congress they had won in the 1954 midterm races.

Dynamic Conservatism

Eisenhower called himself a modern Republican and wanted to follow a "middle course" that was "conservative when it comes to money and liberal when it comes to human beings." He believed that government should be run efficiently, like a successful business, and he staffed the majority of his cabinet with businessmen, most of whom were millionaires. Among the president's key priorities was to reduce spending and the presence of the federal government. Federal controls over business and the economy would be limited and the authority of the states increased. Yet, like Truman, Eisenhower recognized the politics of the practical and understood that many New Deal agencies and functions could and should not be attacked. He meant to pick and choose his domestic battles, staying to the right but still in the "vital center."

Seeking to balance the budget, Eisenhower used a "meat ax" on Truman's projected budgets. He dismissed 200,000 workers from the government's pay-roll, cut domestic spending by 10 percent, and slashed the military budget. He succeeded in balancing the budget in 1954 and considered that and the balanced budget of 1960 among his greatest White House achievements.

Balancing the budget gave Eisenhower the means to reverse the "creeping socialism" of the New Deal and to return power and control to local and state governance. Among those areas he sought to remove from federal authority were energy, agriculture, the environment, and federal trusteeship for Indian reservations. Advocating private ownership and control, Congress approved—over Democratic opposition—private ownership of nuclear power plants and reduced federal controls. Congress also supported the return of much of the nation's offshore oil sources to state authority and opened federal lands to lumber and mining companies. Citing costs and expanding opportunities for Native Americans, Congress passed a resolution establishing a termination policy, which began to reduce federal economic support to tribes and the liquidation of selected reservations. Before the policy was reversed in the 1960s, sixty-one tribes were involved, with some losing valuable lands and resources. The Klamath tribe in Oregon sold much of their ponderosa pine lands to lumber companies. For many individuals in the affected tribes, the economic gains from such sales proved short-lived, and by the end of the decade conditions for Native Americans had worsened. By 1960 nearly half of all American Indians had abandoned their reservations.

Recognizing political reality, Eisenhower watched Congress increase agricultural subsidies, the minimum wage (to $1.00 an hour), and Social Security benefits. He told his brother that any political party that tried to "abolish Social Security and eliminate labor laws" would never be heard from again. The Democrats' return to power in Congress in 1954 also added to the president's willingness to accept and even expand such programs. He left the Tennessee Valley Authority intact and oversaw increased spending for urban housing and slum clearance and liberalized rules for Federal Housing Authority loans. Recognizing the government's role in public policy, in 1953 Eisenhower created the Department of Health, Education and Welfare—directed by Oveta Culp Hobby, who had commanded the Women's Army Corps during World War II. Still, Eisenhower's vision of the government's public policy role had limits. There were some things that were best left to the public, states, and communities—such as public health. In 1955, Jonas Salk developed a vaccine for polio, and many called for a nationwide federal program to inoculate

One of Eisenhower's goals was to reduce federal spending and controls. In line with this policy, he tried to turn Indian affairs over to the states and liquidate federal services and reservations. Between 1954 and 1960, sixty-one tribes were affected. This picture shows a 4-year-old Tuscarora boy protesting state and federal policies that attacked Indian rights. *Wide World.*

children from the disease, which in 1952 had infected 52,000 people, mostly children. Eisenhower, Secretary Hobby, and the American Medical Association, however, rejected such a program, calling it too socialistic and something that should be arranged by individuals, or state and local governments. Many state and local government did institute vaccination programs, and by the 1960s the number of polio cases had fallen to under a 1,000 a year.

Although he sought a balanced budget, Eisenhower also committed the nation to significant spending, usually explained as for economic and security needs. He signed into law the St. Lawrence Seaway Act (1954), which committed U.S. support for building an inland waterway to connect the Great Lakes with the Atlantic. He justified this act on the grounds that the seaway would benefit the nation by increasing trade.

He approved the **Federal Highway Act** (1956) to meet the needs of an automobile-driven nation and to provide the military with a usable nationwide transportation network. After the Soviet Union launched the space satellites *Sputnik I* (1957) and *Sputnik II* (1957), Eisenhower pointed to national security needs as grounds for increased federal spending on education.

The successful orbiting of the Soviet satellites— *Sputnik II* actually carried a dog into space—created a multilevel panic across the United States. Not only did the nation seem vulnerable to Soviet missiles, but also *Sputnik* seemed to underscore basic weaknesses in the American educational system. American schools, many critics argued, stressed "soft" subjects and social adjustment rather than "hard" subjects: science, languages, and mathematics. *Sputnik* spurred Eisenhower and Congress to pass the National Defense Education Act of 1958 to approve grants to schools developing strong programs in those areas. The act also provided $295 million in **National Defense Student Loans** for college students. Congress's creation in 1958 of the National Aeronautics and Space Administration (NASA) immediately made manned flight its major priority, unveiling Project Mercury with the goal of lifting an astronaut into space.

The Problem with McCarthy

While Eisenhower charted his "middle path," he also sought to diminish the influence of Joseph McCarthy, whom he personally disliked and whose activities, now that the election was over, he deplored. To weaken McCarthy's rhetoric, the administration increased loyalty requirements in 1953 and subsequently dismissed more than 2,000 federal employees—none of whom were proven to be Communists, but nearly all of whom were appointed during the Roosevelt

Federal Highway Act   Law passed by Congress in 1956, appropriating $32 billion for the construction of interstate highways.

Sputnik I   The first artificial satellite launched into space, it weighed 184 pounds; this feat by the Soviet Union in October 1957 marked the beginning of the space race. A month later, the larger *Sputnik II* was launched, weighing 1,120 pounds and carrying a dog named Laika.

National Defense Student Loans   Loans established by the U.S. government in 1958 to encourage the teaching and study of science and modern foreign languages.

At the heart of the Red Scare was Senator Joseph McCarthy. Using inquisition-style tactics to destroy opponents and bolster his own power, McCarthy had become one of the most powerful politicians in the nation by 1952. In his televised efforts to discredit the United States Army, McCarthy lost the public's approval, which hastened his censorship by Congress in 1954 and his ultimate fall from power. *Timepix.*

the 1954 **Army-McCarthy hearings** allowed more than 20 million viewers to see McCarthy's ruthless bullying firsthand. Public and congressional opposition to the senator rose, and when the army's lawyer, Joseph Welch, asked the brooding McCarthy, "Have you no sense of decency?" the nation burst into applause. Several months later, with Republicans evenly divided, the Senate voted 67 to 22 to censure McCarthy's "unbecoming conduct." Drinking heavily, shunned by his colleagues, and ignored by the media, McCarthy died in 1957. But for years McCarthyism, refined and tempered, remained a potent political weapon against liberal opponents.

Eisenhower and a Hostile World

■ What considerations contributed to the "New Look"?

■ What were the weaknesses of "massive retaliation," and how did Eisenhower address them?

■ What was the "Third World," and what problems did Third World nations pose for the Eisenhower administration?

■ What tactics did the Eisenhower administration pursue in the Middle East and Latin America to protect American interests?

During the 1952 campaign, part of Eisenhower's popularity reflected the widely held view that he and the Republicans would conduct a more forceful foreign policy. Truman's containment was denounced, and Republican spokesmen promised the rollback of communism and the liberation of peoples under Communist control. In a very popular move, Eisenhower promised—if elected—to go to Korea "in the cause of peace." He went—for three days. Many expected him to find a means to win the conflict, but after visiting the front lines, he was convinced that a negotiated peace was the only solution. The problem was how to persuade the North Koreans and Chinese that such a settlement would be in their best interests. Eisenhower came to the presidency well qualified to lead American foreign policy. His years in the military and as commander of NATO had made him not only an internationalist but also a realist, wary of too assertive and too simplistic solutions to international

and Truman years. With Ike taking action, he and most Republicans thought McCarthy would end his crusade against Communists. But the senator from Wisconsin enjoyed the spotlight and relished his power. He criticized the administration's foreign policy as too soft on communism and continued his search for subversives, especially in the State Department. When, in 1954, McCarthy claimed favoritism toward known Communists in the army, anti-McCarthy forces in Congress, quietly supported by Eisenhower, established a committee to examine the senator's claims.

The American Broadcasting Company's telecast of

Army-McCarthy hearings   Congressional investigation of Senator Joseph McCarthy televised in 1954; the hearings revealed McCarthy's villainous nature and ended his popularity.

problems. Despite the campaign rhetoric of liberation and rollback, Eisenhower embraced the principle of containment and sought to modify it to match what he believed to be the nation's capabilities and needs. His new policy was called the **New Look.**

The New Look

The core of the New Look was technology and nuclear deterrence—an enhanced arsenal of nuclear weapons and delivery systems, and the threat of **massive retaliation** to protect American international interests. In explaining the shift to more atomic weapons, Vice President Nixon stated, "Rather than let the Communists nibble us to death all over the world in little wars, we will rely . . . on massive mobile retaliation." Secretary of Defense Charles E. Wilson, noting that the nuclear strategy was cheaper than conventional forces, quipped that the policy ensured "more bang for the buck." Demonstrating the country's nuclear might, the United States exploded its first hydrogen bomb in November 1952 (the Soviets tested theirs in August 1953), expanded its arsenal of strategic nuclear weapons to 6,000, and developed tactical nuclear weapons of a lower destructive power that could be used on the battlefield.

The New Look was sold to the public as more positive than Truman's defensive containment policy, but insiders recognized that it had several flaws. The central problem was where the United States should draw the massive-retaliation line: "What if the enemy calls our bluff? How do you convince the American people and the U.S. Congress to declare war?" asked one planner. The answer was to make the bluff so convincing that it would never be called. Potential aggressors had to be convinced that the United States would strike back, raining nuclear destruction not only on the attackers but also on the Soviets and Chinese, who obviously would be directing any aggression. This policy was called **brinkmanship,** because it required the administration to be willing to take the nation to the brink of war, trusting that the opposition would back down. Thus Secretary of State **John Foster Dulles** and Eisenhower indulged in dramatic speeches explaining that nuclear weapons were as usable as conventional ones. It was necessary "to remove the taboo" from using nuclear weapons, Dulles informed the press.

To prod the North Koreans and Chinese to sign a Korean truce agreement, Eisenhower used aggressive images of liberation and through public and private channels suggested that the United States might use atomic weapons. By July 1953, it seemed the strategy

had worked. A truce signed at Panmunjom ended the fighting and brought home almost all the troops, but it left Korea divided by a **demilitarized zone.** It seemed to many that the nuclear threat, "atomic diplomacy," had worked. In reality, Stalin's death in March 1953 and the resolution of central issues, including the disposition of North Korean prisoners of war, were the deciding factors. Even so, Americans praised Eisenhower's new approach.

To strengthen the rationale for "going nuclear" and make the possibility of World War III less frightening, the administration introduced efforts related to surviving a nuclear war. Public and private underground **fallout shelters**—well stocked with food, water, and medical supplies—could, it was claimed, provide safety against an attack. A 32-inch-thick slab of concrete, *U.S. News & World Report* related, could protect people from an atomic blast "as close as 1,000 feet away." Across the nation, civil defense drills were established for factories, offices, and businesses. "Duck-and-cover" drills were held in schools: when their teachers shouted, "Drop!" students immediately got into a kneeling or prone position and placed their hands behind their necks.

While educators and government agencies worked to convince people that they could survive a nuclear war, movies and novels showed the horror of nuclear death and destruction. Nevil Shute realistically portrayed the extinction of humankind in his novel *On*

New Look   National security policy under Eisenhower that called for a reduction in the size of the army, development of tactical nuclear weapons, and the buildup of strategic air power employing nuclear weapons.

massive retaliation   Term that Secretary of State John Foster Dulles used in a 1954 speech, implying that the United States was willing to use nuclear force in response to Communist aggression anywhere.

brinkmanship   Practice of seeking to win disputes in international politics by creating the impression of being willing to push a highly dangerous situation to the limit.

John Foster Dulles   Secretary of state under Eisenhower; he used the threat of nuclear war to deter Soviet aggression.

demilitarized zone   An area from which military forces, operations, and installations are prohibited.

fallout shelter   Underground shelter stocked with food and supplies that was intended to provide safety in case of atomic attack; *fallout* refers to the irradiated particles falling through the atmosphere after a nuclear attack.

As the Cold War intensified, as the Soviets became a nuclear power, and as the threat of nuclear war heightened, the government, to ease the fears of the public, stressed civil defense as a means of surviving a nuclear war. *Collection of Janice L. and David J. Frent.*

forces of regional allies, perhaps supported with American naval and air strength, would snuff them out.

Mindful of existing tensions in Asia, Eisenhower concluded **bilateral** defense pacts with South Korea (1953) and Taiwan (1955) and a **multilateral** agreement, the Southeast Asia Treaty Organization (SEATO, 1954), that linked the United States, Australia, Thailand, the Philippines, Pakistan, New Zealand, France, and Britain. In the Middle East, the United States officially joined Britain, Iran, Pakistan, Turkey, and Iraq in the **Baghdad Pact** in 1957, later called the Central Treaty Organization (CENTO) after Iraq withdrew in 1959. In Europe, the United States helped to rearm West Germany and welcomed it into NATO. The Soviet bloc responded to that last move with the formation of a military alliance between Eastern European nations and the Soviet Union, the Warsaw Pact, in 1955. In all, the Eisenhower administration signed forty-three pacts to help defend regions or individual countries from Communist aggression (see Map 27.2).

The Third World

Brinkmanship was also of little use in dealing with Soviet and Chinese efforts to enlist the support of emerging nations. When the United Nations was created at the end of WWII, 51 nations signed its charter. Most were located in Europe and the Western Hemisphere. Over the next ten years, 25 more nations entered, about a third of them having achieved independence from European nations through revolution and political and social protests. By 1960, 37 new nations existed in Africa, Asia, and the Middle East. For many of the newly emerging nations, independence did not bring peace, prosperity, or stability. Despite a unifying sense of nationalism, political, social, religious, and ethnic factors divided loyalties and frequently led to violence. Internal warfare raged in 28 countries

the Beach (1957). In *Them!* (1954) and dozens of other **B movies,** giant ants and other hideous creatures mutated by atomic fallout threatened the world.

Despite the massive-retaliation talk, Eisenhower recognized the limits of American power—areas under Communist control could not be liberated, and a thermonuclear war would yield no winners. Consequently, the administration sought ways to avoid a nuclear solution to international problems. Alliances and **covert operations** seemed logical alternatives. Alliances would identify areas protected by the American nuclear umbrella, and they would protect the United States from being drawn into limited "brushfire" wars. When small conflicts erupted, the ground

B movies   Poorer quality, more cheaply made films that were shown in addition to the main movies.

covert operation   A program or event carried out not openly but in secret.

bilateral   Involving two parties.

multilateral   Involving more than two parties.

Baghdad Pact   A regional defensive alliance signed between Turkey and Iraq in 1955; Great Britain, Pakistan, and Iran soon joined; the United States supported the pact but did not officially join until mid-1957.

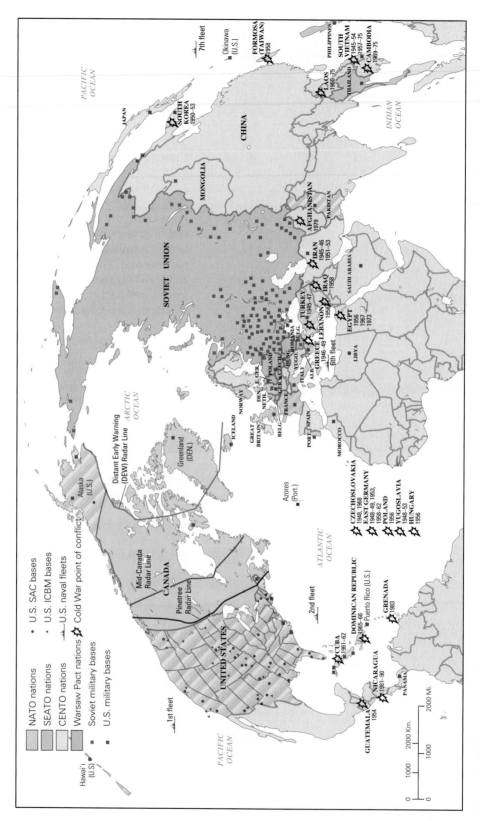

MAP 27.2 The Global Cold War During the Cold War, the United States and the Soviet Union faced each other as enemies. The United States attempted to construct a ring of containment around the Soviet Union and its allies, while the Soviets worked to expand their influence and power. This map shows the nature of this military confrontation—the bases, alliances, and flash points of the Cold War.

in 1958 alone. Efforts to achieve stability in these so-called **Third World** nations were often compounded by their economic dependency on industrial nations and the Cold War. Both the capitalistic West, led by the United States, and the Communist bloc, led by the Soviet Union, competed for the "hearts and minds" of the emerging nations. In many cases, although nonaligned, Third World nations—associating capitalism and the West with colonialism, racism, and economic exploitation—moved toward the left. For the Eisenhower administration this was a new problem. Commenting on nationalistic movements in Latin America, Secretary of State Dulles said: "In the old days we used to be able to let South America go through the wringer of bad times . . . but the trouble is, now, when you put it through the wringer, it comes out red." One solution to the problem was to use economic and military aid, political pressure, and the **Central Intelligence Agency** (CIA) to support those nationalist governments that were anti-Communist and provided stability, even if that stability was achieved through ruthless and undemocratic means. It seemed a never-ending and largely thankless task. "While we are busy rescuing Guatemala or assisting Korea and Indochina," Eisenhower observed, the Communists "make great inroads in Burma, Afghanistan, and Egypt." The growing use of the CIA resulted in the size of the agency expanding by 500 percent and a shifting of resources to covert activities. By 1957, nearly 80 percent of the agency's funds were funneled into covert activities. In its conduct of activities the CIA, headed by Allen Dulles, operated with almost no congressional oversight or restrictions.

Turmoil in the Middle East

In the Middle East, Arab nationalism, fired by anti-Israeli and anti-Western attitudes, posed a serious threat to American interests. Iran and Egypt offered the greatest challenges. In Iran, Prime Minister Mohammed Mossadegh had nationalized British-owned oil properties and seemed likely to sell oil to the Soviets. Eisenhower considered him to be "neurotic and periodically unstable" and, along with the British, favored forcing him from power. Eisenhower gave the CIA the green light to overthrow the Iranian leader and replace him with a pro-Western government. On August 18, 1953, a mass demonstration funded and orchestrated by the CIA toppled the Mossadegh government. Quickly, millions in American money flowed into Iran to support the new regime. A thankful Iranian government, headed by **Shah Mohammed Reza Pahlevi,** awarded the United States 40 percent of Iranian oil production.

Like Mohammed Mossadegh, Egyptian leader Gamal Abdel Nasser, who assumed power in 1954, also attempted to develop his nation's economic resources independent of European controls and influence. At first the United States supported Nasser, hoping to woo him with loans, cash, arms, and an offer to help build the High Aswan Dam on the Nile. Eventually Nasser rejected the American offers—in large part because Americans pushed for an Egyptian-Israeli peace and closer ties with Britain—and turned to the Soviets for support. Eisenhower concluded that he was an "evil influence" in the region and canceled the Aswan Dam project (July 1956). Days later, claiming the need to finance the dam, Nasser nationalized the Anglo-French-owned Suez Canal, through which the majority of European-bound oil passed. Some within the administration suggested that Nasser be assassinated, but Eisenhower rejected that option. Egypt had, he explained, no suitable replacement.

Israel, France, and Britain, however, responded with military action to regain control of the canal. On October 29, 1956, Israeli forces sliced through the Sinai Desert toward Egypt. Over the next week, French and British forces bombed Egyptian targets and seized the canal. Eisenhower was furious. He disliked Nasser but could not approve armed aggression. Joined by the Soviets, Eisenhower sponsored a UN General Assembly resolution (November 2, 1956) calling for an end to the fighting, the removal of foreign troops from Egyptian soil, and the assignment of a United Nations peacekeeping force there. Faced with worldwide opposition and intense pressure from the United States—including a threat to withhold oil shipments—France, Britain, and Israel withdrew their forces. Nasser regained control of the canal and, as Eisenhower had feared, emerged as the

---

Third World   Nations in the Third World claim to be independent and not part of either the Western capitalist or Communist blocs. This Cold War neutrality was tested by both sides in the Cold War, as each used a variety of means to include them in their camps.

Central Intelligence Agency   An agency created in 1947 to gather and evaluate of military, political, social, and economic information on foreign nations.

Shah Mohammed Reza Pahlevi   Iranian ruler who received the hereditary title *shah* from his father in 1941 and with CIA support helped to oust the militant nationalist Mohammed Mossadegh in 1953.

Implementing the Eisenhower Doctrine, American forces landed troops in Lebanon in July 1958. The intervention and withdrawal was without incident, but not before some soldiers enjoyed the warm waters of the Mediterranean. American forces in Beirut in 1983 were not so lucky. *Paul Schutzer/Timepix.*

Congress for permission to commit American forces, if requested, to resist "armed attack from any country controlled by internationalism" (by *internationalism* Eisenhower meant the forces of communism). Congress agreed in March 1957, establishing the so-called **Eisenhower Doctrine** and providing $200 million in military and economic aid to improve military defenses in the nations of the Middle East.

It did not take long for Eisenhower to use his powers. When an internal revolt threatened Jordan's King Hussein in 1957, the White House announced Jordan was "vital" to American interests, moved the U.S. 6th Fleet into the eastern Mediterranean, and supplied more than $10 million in aid. King Hussein put down the revolt, dismissed parliament and all political parties, and instituted authoritarian rule. In 1958, when Lebanon's Christian president Camile Chamoun ignored his country's constitution and ran for a second term, opposition leaders—including Muslim nationalistic, anti-West elements—rebelled. Chamoun requested American intervention, and Eisenhower committed nearly fifteen thousand troops to protect the pro-American government. The American forces left in three months—after Chamoun had stepped down and, with American approval, been replaced by General Fuad Chehab. Eisenhower had demonstrated his willingness to protect American interests but had done little to resolve the problems that plagued Lebanon and the rest of the Middle East.

A Protective Neighbor

During the 1952 presidential campaign, Eisenhower charged Truman with following a "Poor Neighbor policy" toward Latin America, allowing the development of economic problems and popular uprisings that had been "skillfully exploited by the Communists." He was most concerned about Guatemala, disapproving of the reformist president, Jacobo Arbenz, who had instituted agrarian reforms by nationalizing thousands of acres of land, much of it owned by the American-based United Fruit Company. These radical actions convinced the administration to use the CIA

uncontested leader of those opposing Western influence in Arab countries.

The decline of British and French power, Nasser's enhanced prestige, and the growth of Soviet influence in the Middle East forced the Eisenhower administration to affirm American interests in the region and to support a regional anti-Soviet alliance with the northern tier of Middle Eastern states: the Baghdad Pact/CENTO. Eisenhower also redoubled his effort to contain Nasser's **pan-Arab movement** and an expanding Soviet presence. To protect Arab friends from Communist-nationalist revolutions, Eisenhower asked

pan-Arab movement Attempts to politically unify the Arab nations of the Middle East; its followers advocated freedom from Western control and opposition to Israel.

Eisenhower Doctrine Policy formulated by Eisenhower of providing military and economic aid to Arab nations in the Middle East to help defeat Communist-nationalistic rebellions.

For nearly four decades, Fidel Castro has plagued American presidents and policymakers. Gaining power in a popular revolution against the dictator Batista in 1959, Castro quickly moved Cuba into the Soviet bloc. Eisenhower sought to use a CIA-trained army to overthrow Castro but left office before the plan could be executed. President John F. Kennedy implemented the plan, but it failed miserably. *Andrew St. George/Magnum Photo, Inc.*

had controlled Cuba through the 1940s and 1950s, was beset by a rebellion led by **Fidel Castro.**

The corrupt and dictatorial Batista had become an embarrassment to the United States, and many Americans believed that Castro could be a pro-American reformist leader. By 1959, rebel forces had control of the island, but by midyear many of Castro's economic and social reforms were endangering American investments and interests. American interests dominated Cuba's economy, controlling 40 percent of Cuba's sugar industry, 90 percent of Cuba's telephone and electric companies, 50 percent of its railroads, and 25 percent of its banking. In addition, 70 percent of Cuba's imports came from the United States. Concerned about Castro's political leanings, Washington tried to push Cuba in the right direction by applying economic pressure. In February 1960, Castro reacted to the American arm-twisting by signing an economic pact with the Soviet Union. Eisenhower seethed: Castro was a "madman . . . going wild and harming the whole American structure." In March, Eisenhower approved a CIA plan to prepare an attack against Castro. Actual implementation of the plot to overthrow the Cuban leader, however, was left to Eisenhower's successor.

The New Look in Asia

When Eisenhower took office, Asia was the focal point of Cold War tensions. Fighting continued in Korea, and in Indochina the Communist **Viet Minh,** directed by Ho Chi Minh, was fighting a "war of national liberation" against the French. Truman had supported France, and Eisenhower saw no reason to alter American policy. By 1954, the United States had dispatched more than three hundred advisers to Vietnam, was paying nearly 78 percent of the war's cost, and was watching the French military position worsen. A believer in the **domino theory,** Eisenhower warned that if Indochina fell to communism, the loss

to remove Arbenz. The CIA organized and supplied a rebel army in Honduras, led by Guatemalan Colonel Carlos Castillo Armas. Colonel Armas launched the effort to "liberate" Guatemala on June 18, 1954, and within two weeks a new, pro-American government was installed in Guatemala City. On July 8, 1954, a military **junta** named Colonel Armas president. Eisenhower had created a pro-American government in Guatemala but had failed to reduce the social and economic inequalities, blunt the cry for revolution, or foster good will toward the United States among Latin Americans. When Vice President Nixon toured Latin America in 1958, demonstrators in Lima, Peru, stoned his car, and an angry mob in Caracas, Venezuela, almost overturned it. Nixon called the demonstrators "Communist thugs." And while Nixon toured Latin America, Fulgencio Batista, who

junta   Group of military officers ruling a country after seizing power.

Fidel Castro   Cuban revolutionary leader who overthrew the corrupt regime of dictator Fulgencio Batista in 1959 and established a Communist state.

Viet Minh   Vietnamese army made up of Communist and other nationalist groups that fought from 1946 to 1954 for independence from French rule.

domino theory   The idea that if one nation came under Communist control, then neighboring nations would also fall to the Communists.

"of Burma, of Thailand, of the [Malay] Peninsula, and Indonesia" would certainly follow, endangering Australia and New Zealand.

In Vietnam, Viet Minh forces led by General Vo Nguyen Giap encircled the French fortress at Dienbienphu and launched murderous attacks on the beleaguered garrison. Asserting, "My God, we must not lose Asia," Eisenhower transferred forty bombers and detailed two hundred air force mechanics to bolster the French in Vietnam. The French—and some members of the Eisenhower administration—wanted a more direct American role, but Eisenhower believed that "no military victory is possible in that kind of theater" and rejected such options. After a fifty-five-day siege, Dienbienphu fell on May 7, 1954, and Eisenhower was left no option but to try to salvage a partial victory at an international conference in Geneva.

But the West could piece together no victory at Geneva either. The **Geneva Agreement** "temporarily" partitioned Vietnam along the 17th parallel and created the neutral states of Cambodia and Laos. Within two years, the two Vietnams were to hold elections to unify the nation, and neither was to enter into military alliances or allow foreign bases on its territory. American strategists called the settlement a "disaster"—half of Vietnam was lost to communism. Showing its displeasure, the United States refused to sign the agreement. Eisenhower rushed advisers and aid to South Vietnam's new prime minister, Ngo Dinh Diem. With American blessings, Diem ignored the Geneva-mandated unification elections, quashed his political opposition, and in October 1955 staged a **plebiscite** that created the Republic of Vietnam and elected him president.

The Soviets and Cold War Politics

Eisenhower believed, like Truman, that one method to halt the spread of communism was through deterrence. Within the context of the New Look and the prospect of nuclear war, the Eisenhower administration worked to develop a three-way system to attack the Soviet Union and China. Efforts were intensified to develop an intercontinental and intermediate-range ballistic missile system that could be fired from land bases and from submarines. At the same time, the nation's bomber fleet was improved, introducing the jet-powered B-47. While the New Look stressed nuclear force as a means of deterrence, Eisenhower realized that improving American-Soviet relations was

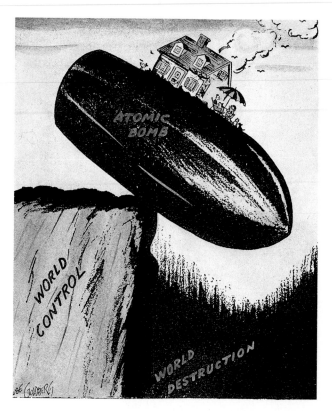

In this cartoon, an American suburban family sits contentedly next to their cozy home with little concern about the delicate Cold War balance between peace and destruction. By 1953, both the United States and the Soviet Union had tested hydrogen bombs and seemed willing to use the A-bomb to protect national interests. *Granger Collection.*

important. It would reduce the expanding and expensive arms race and limit points of conflict throughout the world. Both Eisenhower and Secretary of State Dulles, however, questioned the Soviets' commitment to peace and their willingness to keep agreements, and both knew that adversaries in the U.S. military and Congress and among the American public would condemn any softening of U.S. policy toward the Soviets. Still, growing Soviet nuclear capabilities and the death of Stalin in 1953 provided the need and the opportunity to reduce tensions.

> **Geneva Agreement**   Truce signed at Geneva in 1954 by French and Viet Minh representatives, dividing Vietnam along the 17th parallel into the Communist North and the anti-Communist South.
>
> **plebiscite**   Special election that allows people to either approve or reject a particular proposal.

Freedom Has a New Sound!

ALL OVER AMERICA these days the blast of supersonic flight is shattering the old familiar sounds of city and countryside.
At U.S. Air Force bases strategically located near key cities our Airmen maintain their *round the clock* vigil, ready to take off on a moment's notice in jet aircraft like Convair's F-102A all-weather interceptor. Every flight has only one purpose —your personal protection! The next time jets thunder overhead, remember that the pilots who fly them are not willful disturbers of your peace; they are patriotic young Americans affirming *your New Sound of Freedom!*

PUBLISHED FOR BETTER UNDERSTANDING OF THE MISSION OF THE U.S.A.F. AIR DEFENSE COMMAND

CONVAIR

Promoting its new fighter, the F-102 Delta Dagger, Convair provided this image of the American way of life being protected by its newest jet. Rather than being annoyed by the sonic booms produced by the fighter, Convair asked Americans to hear the noise as "the New Sound of Freedom." *Gaslight Advertising Archives.*

Soon after Stalin's death, the new Soviet leader, Georgy Malenkov, called for "peaceful coexistence." Dulles dismissed the suggestion, but Eisenhower, with an eye on world opinion, called on the Soviets to demonstrate openly a change of policy and their willingness to cooperate with the West. Malenkov complied. He agreed to consider some form of on-site inspection to verify any approved arms reductions. Eisenhower responded by asking the Soviets in December 1953 to join him in the **Atoms for Peace plan** and to work toward universal disarmament.

Both countries by then were testing hydrogen **thermonuclear** bombs hundreds of times more powerful than atomic bombs. And world concern was growing, not only about the threat of nuclear war but about the dangers of radiation from the testing. Throughout 1954, worldwide pressure grew for a summit meeting to deal with the "balance of terror." In 1955 Eisenhower agreed to a summit meeting in Geneva with the new Soviet leadership team of Nikolai Bulganin and **Nikita Khrushchev**, who had replaced Malenkov. Eisenhower expected no resolution of the two major issues—disarmament and Berlin—and instead saw the meeting as good public relations. He intended to make a bold disarmament initiative—the Open Skies proposal—that would certainly earn broad international support. In a dramatic presentation, highlighted by a sudden thunderstorm that momentarily blacked out the conference room, Eisenhower asked the Soviets to share information about military installations and to permit aerial reconnaissance to verify the information while work began on general disarmament. Bulganin voiced official interest, but Khrushchev, speaking privately, called the proposal a "very transparent espionage device."

Eisenhower recognized that Khrushchev represented the real power in the Soviet Union and that his disapproval meant rejection of the proposal. Thus the Geneva Summit went as expected: the Americans and Soviets agreed to disagree. Nevertheless, Eisenhower was pleased. The Open Skies proposal was popular, and the meeting had generated a "spirit of Geneva" that reduced East-West tensions without appeasing the Communist foe. Besides, he knew that the United States would soon have in service a new high-altitude jet plane, the U-2, which it was thought could safely fly above Soviet anti-aircraft missiles while taking close-up photographs of Soviet territory. This was Cold War gamesmanship at its best.

The spirit of Geneva vanished when Soviet forces invaded Hungary in November 1956 to quell an anti-Soviet revolt. Many Americans favored supporting the Hungarian freedom fighters, but facing the Suez crisis and seeing no way to send aid to the Hungarians without risking all-out war, the administration could only watch as the Soviets crushed the revolt.

Atoms for Peace plan   Eisenhower's proposal to the United Nations in 1953 that the United States and other nations cooperate to develop peaceful uses of atomic energy.

thermonuclear   Relating to the fusion of atomic nuclei at high temperatures, or to weapons based on fusion, such as the hydrogen bomb (as distinct from weapons based on fission).

Nikita Khrushchev   Soviet leader who denounced Stalin in 1956 and improved the Soviet Union's image abroad; he was deposed in 1964 after six years as premier for his failure to improve the country's economy.

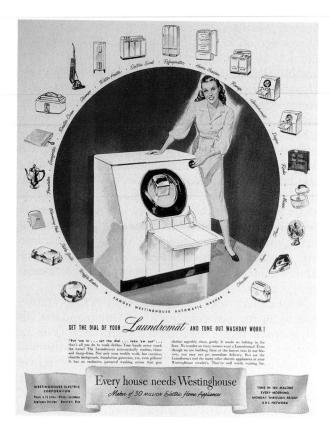

SET THE DIAL OF YOUR *Laundromat* AND TUNE OUT WASHDAY WORK!

Every house needs Westinghouse
Maker of 30 million Electric Home Appliances

In September 1959, Vice President Nixon in the "kitchen debates" argued with Soviet premier Nikita Khrushchev about the types of appliances the average working family in America had in their kitchens. This advertisement showing the range of consumer products made by Westinghouse clearly supports Nixon's claim that American families were affluent enough to furnish their homes with a wide range of products. *Picture Research Consultants & Archives.*

After the Hungary crisis, Soviet-American relations cooled and rivalry intensified. Seeking to gain an advantage while gathering worldwide public support, Eisenhower and Khrushchev jousted with each other over nuclear testing and disarmament. First one, and then the other, with little belief in success, offered to end nuclear testing and eliminate nuclear weapons if certain provisions were met. In the spring of 1958, both sides temporarily ended nuclear testing, but when discussion on how to implement and verify a test-ban treaty failed, the race resumed.

The simmering issue of Berlin was also aggravating tensions. In November 1958, the Soviets reported that they would soon sign a treaty with East Germany terminating the West's right to occupy West Berlin and unifying the city under East German control. For Eisenhower, this was unthinkable. Supported by the British and French, he declared that Western Allies would remain in West Berlin, and American and NATO forces made plans for the defense of the city. Faced with unflinching Western determination, Khrushchev noted a permanent delay in the treaty and suggested that he and Eisenhower exchange visits and hold a summit meeting. During Khrushchev's twelve-day tour of the United States in September 1959, the Soviet leader and Eisenhower announced that they would attend a summit in Paris in May and that Eisenhower would later visit the Soviet Union. There was even consideration of opening air travel to and from the Soviet Union and the United States by Pan American Airlines and Aeroflot.

Khrushchev did tour the United States, but as the summit began on May 1, 1960, the Soviets shot down an American U-2 spy plane over the Soviet Union and captured its pilot, Major Francis Gary Powers. At first, the United States feebly denied the purpose of the flight, saying the U-2 was a weather plane that had strayed from its Turkish flight plan. Khrushchev then showed pictures of the plane's wreckage and presented Major Powers, clearly proving the American spy mission. In Paris, Eisenhower took full responsibility but refused to apologize for such flights, which he contended were necessary to prevent a "nuclear Pearl Harbor." Khrushchev withdrew from the summit, and Eisenhower canceled his trip to the Soviet Union. The Cold War thaw was over.

Eisenhower returned home a hero, having stood up to the Soviets. But public support was temporary. The loss of the U-2, Soviet advances in missile technology and nuclear weaponry, and a Communist Cuba only 90 miles from Florida provided the Democrats with strong reasons to claim that the Republicans and Eisenhower had been deficient in meeting Soviet threats. In 1960, turning the Republicans' tactics of 1952 against them, Democrats cheerfully accused their opponents of endangering the United States by being too soft on communism.

The Best of Times

■ What factors contributed to prosperity in the 1950s, and what was new about the "new economics"?

■ Why did Americans embrace suburban culture? What stresses were at work beneath the placid surface of suburbia?

■ Who were some of the critics of suburban culture, and what were their complaints? Why were rock 'n' roll and rebellious teens seen as threats to social norms?

According to the middle-class magazine *Reader's Digest*, in 1954 the average American male stood 5 feet 9 inches tall and weighed 158 pounds. He liked brunettes, baseball, bowling, and steak and French fries. In seeking a wife, he could not decide if brains or beauty was more important, but he definitely wanted a wife who could run a home efficiently. The average female was 5 feet 4 inches tall and weighed 132 pounds. She preferred marriage to career, but she wanted to remove the word *obey* from her marriage vows. Both were enjoying life to the fullest, according to the *Digest*, and buying more of just about everything. The economy appeared to be bursting at the seams, providing jobs, good wages, a multitude of products, and profits.

The Web of Prosperity

The nation's "easy street" was a product of trends and developments that followed World War II. At the center of the activity was big government, big business, cheap energy, and an expanding population. World War II and the Cold War had created military-industrial-governmental linkages that primed the economy through government spending, what some have labeled "military **Keynesianism.**" National security needs by 1955 accounted for half of the U.S. budget, equaling about 17 percent of the gross national product, and exceeded more than the total net incomes of all American corporations. The connection between government and business went beyond spending, however. Government officials and corporate managers moved back and forth in a vast network of jobs and directorships. Few saw any real conflict of interest. Frequently, people from the businesses to be regulated also staffed cabinet positions and regulatory agencies. Secretary of Defense Wilson, who had been the president of General Motors, voiced the common view: "What was good for our country was good for General Motors and vice versa." It was an era of "new economics," in which, according to a 1952 ad in the *New York Times*, industry's "efforts are not in the selfish interest" but "for the good of many . . . the American way."

Direct military spending was only one aspect of government involvement in the economy. Federal research and development (R&D) funds flowed into colleges and industries. The rapidly expanding electronics industry drew 70 percent of its research funds from the government, producing not only new scientific and military technology but marketable consumer goods like the transistor radio and computers. Plastics invaded the home, providing everything from toys to flooring. Stressing style, color, and washability, vinyl floors and Formica countertops became standard features of new kitchens. In 1953 *McCall's* magazine published an entire issue on the wonders of plastic throughout the home. Monsanto, one of the nation's largest plastics producers, constructed and furnished a "home of the future" featuring nearly everything made of plastic in "Tomorrowland," one section of a new theme park named Disneyland. Technological advances also increased profits and productivity. Profits doubled between 1948 and 1958, with 574 of the largest corporations making nearly 53 percent of all business income. Many small companies, however, could not afford to keep up with technology and **automation.** During the 1950s, more than four thousand mergers took place as large corporations swallowed up less-well-off competitors. By 1960, only 5 percent of American corporations were generating 90 percent of corporate income. Meanwhile, the number of American multinational corporations increased as American firms constructed plants overseas, closer to growing markets, raw materials, and cheaper labor.

Expanding prosperity and productivity and the growth of the service sector characterized the work force. While salaries for industrial workers increased steadily, from about $55 a week in 1950 to nearly $80 in 1960, their numbers declined. More and more jobs were created in the public and service sectors, and by 1956 white-collar workers outnumbered blue-collar workers for the first time. Unions responded to these changes and to the accusations made in the late 1940s of being too communistic by altering their goals. Wishing to avoid strikes and confrontation, they focused on negotiating better pensions, cost-of-living raises, and paid vacations for their members while giving up efforts to gain some control over the workplace and production. Despite favorable contracts, however, union membership as a percentage of the work force fell from about 35.5 percent in 1950 to about 31 percent by 1960. Although the AFL and the CIO

Keynesianism Refers to economic theories of Lord John Maynard Keynes, who in the 1920s and 1930s argued for government intervention in the economy; he believed that government expansion and contraction of the money supply and regulation of interest rates could stimulate economic growth during periods of recession and inflation.

automation A process or system designed so that equipment functions automatically; one outcome of automation is the replacement of workers with machines.

merged in 1955, they made little effort to organize agricultural workers, the growing number of white-collar workers, or people working in the **Sunbelt.**

Suburban and Family Culture

Across the Sunbelt and in the Pacific Northwest, defense contracts played a key role in the booming economy. Rather than business being concentrated in a center city, towns, suburbs, and industrial parks were linked by an ever-growing system of roads and highways. The economy thrived in these hubs of businesses, shopping and entertainment, homes, administrative centers, and industry. In northern California, Stanford University, specialized firms, and federal grants combined to open new industrial areas—which became Silicon Valley—that focused on developing technology, especially electronics. By 1960 electronics was the fifth-largest industry in the United States.

In the metropolitan areas and across the country, people continued the postwar desire to live in the suburbs, and by 1960 more than 214 million single-family homes had been built. By the 1950s, Levitt's original Cape Cod–style home had given way to the **"ranch" or California-style home.** Levitt's new ranch-style developments also helped reshape home life by including a television in each "living" room and by relocating the kitchen to a central place in the house. Other developers followed his example. A California builder advertised his Lakewood as the "perfect place to raise children." Communities like Lakewood represented a fresh start, a commitment to community and the American dream. "We were thrilled to death," recalled one newly arrived suburbanite. "Everyone else was moving in at the same time. . . . It was a whole new adventure for us. Everyone was arriving with a sense of forward momentum. Everyone was taking courage from the sight of another orange moving van pulling in next door, a family just like us, unloading pole lamps and cribs and Formica dining tables like our own, reflections of ourselves multiplying around us. . . ." When, in 1960, Lakewood opened its first major shopping center, complete with an upscale department store, it was a community event with the high school band and cheerleaders highlighting the opening ceremony.

At the center of this view of America rested an expanding consumer economy; the modern ranch home; the nuclear, homeowning family; and the church. Religion, with an emphasis on family life, enjoyed new popularity. Church attendance rose to 59.5 percent in 1953, a historic high. Religious leaders were rated as the most important members of society, especially those who used television to reach huge audiences. Such preachers stressed positive, religious, and patriotic themes. In 1954 the **Reverend Norman Vincent Peale** was named one of the nation's ten most successful salesmen. In keeping with the spirit of the times, Congress added "under God" to the Pledge of Allegiance in 1954 and "In God We Trust" to the American currency in 1955.

Increasingly, television invaded American society and redefined America in its suburban, middle-class image. Although television was developed in the 1930s, it was not until World War II ended that televisions became available to the consumer, and at first they were very expensive. As demand and production increased, prices fell, and more and more people regarded "the box" as a necessity. In 1950 only about 9 percent of homes had a television, but at the end of the decade the percentage had risen to nearly 90 percent, and most people watched for five hours a day. As Levitt had understood, television would be at the heart of the home, in the living room, and would shape American society.

Every evening, families by the millions watched domestic situation comedies ("sitcoms") in which the home was invariably the center of togetherness. As defined in 1954 by *McCall's* magazine, "togetherness" reflected the popular vision of family life in the suburbs. There, husband and wife shared responsibilities from housekeeping and shopping to decision making and fulfilling the needs and desires of their children. In popular television shows like *Father Knows Best* (1953), *Leave It to Beaver* (1957), and *The Donna Reed Show* (1958), the ideal middle-class TV families were white and had hardworking, earnest fathers and attractive, savvy mothers who shared household chores. Their children, usually numbering between two and four, did well in school, were not overly concerned about the future, and provided the usually humorous dilemmas that Mom's common sense and sensitivity

---

Sunbelt   A region stretching from Florida in a westward arc across the South and Southwest.

ranch or California-style home   A single-story rectangular or L-shaped house with a low-pitched roof, simple floor plan, and an attached garage.

Norman Vincent Peale   Minister who told his congregations that positive thinking could help them overcome all their troubles in life; his book *The Power of Positive Thinking* was an immediate bestseller.

The 1950s witnessed the beginning of the "freeway," super, divided, limited-access highways. As part of the state and interstate highway systems, the superhighway reshaped American travel as well as residential and business locations. Southern California led the nation in construction, and by 1960 Los Angeles had over 250 miles of freeway. Here the Santa Monica Freeway cuts across the landscape. *California Department of Transportation.*

untangled. During the day, **soap operas,** most also set in middle-class settings, revolved around personal problems that eventually were worked out in a manner that affirmed family values.

Families were seen as the strength of the nation, and the number of American families was growing. As the divorce rate slowed, the numbers of marriages and births climbed, and the baby boom continued, peaking at 4.3 million births in 1957. Popular images of the family focused on the wife managing the house and raising the children, while the husband worked in an office and directed weekend events. "There was this pressure to be the perfect housekeeper. I mean, now I had this home I *had* to be Donna Reed," remembered one Levittown resident. For guidance on how to raise

babies and children, millions of Americans turned to Dr. Benjamin Spock's popular book *Baby and Child Care* (1946). A mother's love and positive parental guidance were keys to healthy and well-adjusted children. Strict rules and corporal punishment were to be avoided. And to ensure proper gender identity, boys should participate in sports and outdoor activities, whereas girls should concentrate on their appearance and domestic skills. Toy guns and doctor bags were for boys; dolls, tea sets, and nurse kits were for girls. Conforming—being part of the group—was as important for parents as for children. Those unwilling to fulfill those roles, especially women, were suspected of being homosexual, neurotic, emotionally immature, too involved in a career, or simply irresponsible.

Consumerism

Another dimension of suburbia was consumerism. Radio and television bombarded their audiences with images not only of the average American but of the products those Americans used. Commercials provided the average television watcher with over five hours a week of ads that enticed viewers to indulge themselves, enjoy life, and own more.

And Americans were in a buying mood, especially the suburbanite. New goods were a sign of progress and a matter of status. Moving into a new housing development involved buying more than a new house: often it required the purchase of a variety of household furnishings and appliances and, of course, a new car. One resident noted, "Our old car just didn't cut it . . . a car was a real status symbol and who didn't want to impress the neighbors?" Those producing the goods responded by emphasizing style and "the latest model." The automobile industry was especially effective in upgrading and changing the styles of their cars. Market research showed that it was mostly the middle and upper classes that bought new cars and encouraged the automobile makers to close the gap between luxury and nonluxury cars. Cadillac introduced fins in 1948, and by the mid-1950s nearly every car had fins and dealer showrooms were waging a fin-war.

The automobile industry also benefited from and contributed to the development of both roads and

soap opera A daytime serial drama so nicknamed because it was sponsored by cleaning products, aimed at its housewife audience.

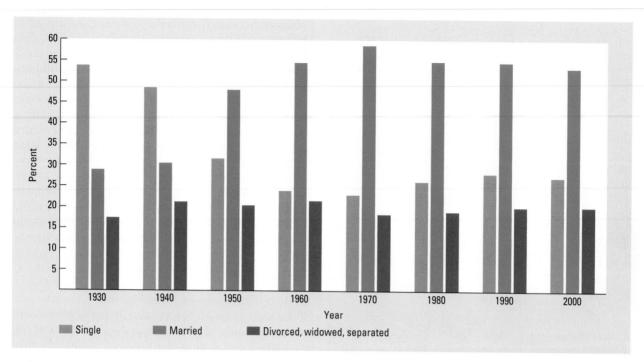

FIGURE 27.1 Marital Status of Women in the Work Force, 1930–2000   This figure shows the percentage of women in the work force from the Great Depression through 2000. While the number of women who fall into the category of divorced, widowed, and separated remained fairly constant, there was a significant shift in the number of single and married women in the work force, with the number of single women declining as the number of married women increased. *Source:* U.S. Department of Commerce, *Historical Statistics of the United States, Colonial Times to 1970*, Vol. I (Washington, D.C.: U.S. Government Printing Office, 1970), pp. 20–21, 131–132; and U.S. Department of Commerce, *Statistics of the United States, 1993* (Washington, D.C.: U.S. Government Printing Office, 1993), pp. 74, 399; U.S. Department of Commerce, *Statistical Abstract of the United States: 2003* (Washington, D.C.: U.S. Government Printing Office, 2003), pp. 390–391.

suburbs. By 1960, 75 percent of all Americans had at least one car, increasing the pressure on all levels of government to build new roads and highways. Eisenhower's greatest spending program, the Federal Highway Act of 1956, allocated over $32 billion to begin a federal interstate highway system. New industries arose to service the needs of the automobile-driving family—motels, amusement parks, drive-in theaters, and fast-food restaurants. Walt Disney opened Disneyland in 1955, in a televised extravaganza, with the intention of providing family entertainment in a sparkling, clean-cut setting that reflected the spirit of America. In a similar vein, McDonald's changed the nation's eating habits while providing "Mom a Night Off," in a clean and wholesome environment without cigarette machines, jukeboxes, and beer.

To sell cars and hamburgers and other products, advertisers continued to use images of youth, glamour, sex appeal, and sophistication. In the forefront of the advertising onslaught was the tobacco industry, persuading people that smoking cigarettes was a styl-ish way to relax from the rigors of work and family. When medical reports surfaced about health risks connected to smoking, the tobacco giants intensified their advertising and stressed that new, longer, filtered cigarettes were milder and posed no health hazard. Cigarette advertising increased 400 percent between 1945 and 1960, whereas advertising in general increased "only" a little more than 250 percent.

Helping to pay for cars, televisions, washing machines, toys, and "Mom's night out" were increasing wages and credit. Why pay cash when consumer credit was available? The Diner's Club credit card made its debut in 1950 and was soon followed by American Express and a host of other plastic cards. Credit purchases leaped from $8.4 billion in 1946 to more than $44 billion in 1958.

Another View of Suburbia

Unlike the wives shown on television, more and more married women were working outside the home even though they had young children (see Figure 27.1). Some desired careers, but the majority worked to safeguard their family's existing **standard of living.** The percentage of middle-class women who worked for wages rose from 7 percent in 1950 to 25 percent in 1960. Most held part-time jobs or sales-clerk and clerical positions that paid low wages and provided few benefits. Women represented 46 percent of the banking work force—filling most secretary, teller, and receptionist slots—but held only 15 percent of upper-level positions.

Togetherness and suburban expectations did not make all homemakers happy. A study found that of eighteen household chores, men were willing to do three—lock up at night, do yard work, and make repairs. Other surveys discovered that more than one-fifth of suburban wives were unhappy with their marriages and lives. Many women complained of the drudgery and boredom of housework and the lack of understanding and affection from their husbands. Women were also more sexually active than generally thought, shattering the image of loyal wife and pure mother. Research on women's sexuality conducted by **Alfred Kinsey** and described in his book *Sexual Behavior in the Human Female* (1953) indicated that a majority of American women had had sexual intercourse before marriage, and 25 percent were having affairs while married.

Reflecting the shadier side of middle-class life in fiction, the best-selling novel *Peyton Place* (1956), by Grace Metalious, set America buzzing over the licentious escapades of the residents of a quiet town in New England. Hollywood kept pace with stars like Marilyn Monroe. Starting in 1952, the "blonde bombshell" was repeatedly cast in slightly dumb but very sexy roles in which older, more worldly men usually romanced her.

Rejecting Consensus

Americans seemed to consider sex symbols in the movies and men's magazines as a minor threat to the image of family, community, and nation. Homosexuality, however, was another matter. Many people believed it damaged the moral and social fabric of society. Kinsey's 1948 study of male sexuality shocked readers by claiming that nearly 8 percent of the population lived a gay lifestyle and that homosexuality existed throughout American society. An increasingly open gay subculture that centered around gay bars in every major city seemed to support his findings.

In a postwar society that emphasized the traditional family and feared internal subversion, homo-

sexuals represented a double menace. A Senate investigating committee concluded that because of sexual perversions and lack of moral fiber, one homosexual could "pollute a Government office." Responding to such views, the Eisenhower administration barred homosexuals from most government jobs. Taking their cue from the federal government, state and local authorities intensified their efforts to control homosexuals and, if possible, purge them from society. **Vice squads** made frequent raids on gay and lesbian bars, and newspapers often listed the names, addresses, and employers of those arrested. In response to the virulent attacks, many took extra efforts to hide their homosexuality, but some organized to confront the offensive. In Los Angeles, Henry Hay formed the Mattachine Society in 1951 to fight for homosexual rights, and in San Francisco in 1955 Del Martin and Phyllis Lyon organized a similar organization for lesbians, the Daughters of Bilitis.

Also viewed as extreme were the **Beats,** or "beatniks," a group of often-controversial artists, poets, and writers. Allen Ginsberg in his poem *Howl* (1956) and Jack Kerouac in his novel *On the Road* (1957) denounced American materialism and sexual repression and glorified a freer, natural life. In an interview in the New York alternative newsweekly *The Village Voice,* Ginsberg praised the few "hipsters" who were battling "an America gone mad with materialism, a police-state America, a sexless and soulless America."

A minority, especially among young college students, found the beatnik critique of "square America" meaningful. Most, however, had few qualms about rejecting the Beats' message and lifestyles. In an article in *Life* magazine in 1959, journalist Paul O'Neil described beatniks as smelly, dirty people in beards and sandals, who were "sick little bums" and "hostile little

standard of living   Level of material comfort as measured by the goods, services, and luxuries currently available.

Alfred Kinsey   Biologist whose studies of human sexuality attracted great attention in the 1940s and 1950s, especially for his conclusions on infidelity and homosexuality.

vice squad   Police unit charged with the enforcement of laws dealing with vice—that is, immoral practices such as gambling and prostitution.

Beats   Group of American writers, poets, and artists in the 1950s, including Jack Kerouac and Allen Ginsberg, who rejected traditional middle-class values and championed nonconformity and sexual experimentation.

females." FBI director J. Edgar Hoover thought otherwise and told the Republican presidential convention in 1960 that beatniks were a major threat to the nation.

Most Americans could justify the suppression of beatniks and homosexuals because they appeared to mock traditional values of family and community. Other critics of American society, however, were more difficult to dismiss. Several respected writers and intellectuals claimed that the suburban and consumer culture was destructive—stifling diversity and individuality in favor of conformity. Mass-produced homes, meals, toys, fashions, and the other trappings of suburban life, they said, created a gray sameness about Americans. Sociologist David Riesman argued in *The Lonely Crowd* (1950) that postwar Americans, unlike earlier generations, were "outer-directed"— less sure of their values and morals and overly concerned about fitting into a group. Peer pressure, he suggested, had replaced individual thinking, and he urged readers to reassert their own identities. Serious literature also highlighted a sense of alienation from the conformist society. Much of Sylvia Plath's poetry and her novel *The Bell Jar* (1963) reflect those forces, especially as they affected women torn between the demands of society and the quest for individual freedom. Similar themes were central to many contemporary novels, including J. D. Salinger's *The Catcher in the Rye* (1951), whose hero, Holden Caulfield, concludes that the major features of American life are all phony.

The Trouble with Kids

While a small percentage of the nation's youth adopted the views of the Beats or turned their backs on middle-class values and consumerism, many parents and adults were concerned about teenagers, their behavior, and juvenile delinquency. Juvenile crime and gangs were not new topics, but for the first time many people worried that these problems were taking hold outside of the city and the urban poor and minorities. To the suburban middle-class parent, the violent crime associated with inner-city gangs was not the concern; instead, it was the behavior of their own teens as they seemed to flaunt traditional values and behavior. At the center of the problem, many believed, was a developing youth culture characterized by the car, **rock 'n' roll,** and disrespect for adults. One study of middle-class delinquency concluded that the automobile not only allowed teens to escape adult controls but also provided "a private lounge for drinking and for petting or sex episodes." Critics also

In 1954, Elvis Presley's first record was released, and within a year a new rock 'n' roll star had burst onto the music scene. Elvis's style blended rhythm and blues, country, and gospel into a unique sound that, along with his body language, created an American icon. *Michael Barson Collection/Past Perfect.*

blamed misbehavior on rock 'n' roll, comic books, television, and lack of proper family upbringing. In the film *Rebel Without a Cause* (1955), which featured soon-to-be teen idol James Dean, the rebellious characters came from atypical suburban homes where gender roles were reversed. Audiences saw a dominating mother and a father who cooked and assumed many traditional housewifely duties. To the adult audience, the message was clear: an "improper" family environment bred juvenile delinquents.

> **rock 'n' roll**   Style of music that developed out of rhythm and blues in the 1950s, with a fast beat and lyrics appealing to teenagers.

The problem with kids also seemed wedded to rock 'n' roll. Cleveland disc jockey Alan Freed coined the term in 1951. He had noticed that white teens were buying rhythm and blues (R&B) records popular among African Americans, but he also knew that few white households would listen to a radio program playing "black music." Freed decided to play the least sexually suggestive of the R&B records and call the music rock 'n' roll. His radio program, "Moondog's Rock 'n' Roll Party," was a smash hit. Quickly the barriers between "black music" and "white music" began to blur as white singers copied and modified R&B songs to produce **cover records.**

Cover artists like Pat Boone and Georgia Gibbs sold millions of records that avoided suggestive lyrics and were heard on hundreds of radio stations that had refused to play the original versions created by black artists. By mid-decade, African American artists like Chuck Berry, Little Richard, and Ray Charles were successfully "crossing over" and being heard on "white" radio stations. At the same time, white artists, including the 1950s' most dynamic star, **Elvis Presley,** were making their own contributions. Beginning with "Heartbreak Hotel" in 1956, Presley recorded fourteen **gold records** within two years. In concerts, he drove his audiences into frenzies with sexually suggestive movements that earned him the nickname "Elvis the Pelvis."

Some sociologists argued that because of its roots in lower-class society, especially among African Americans, rock 'n' roll glamorized behavior that led to crime and delinquency. Blaming rock 'n' roll for a decline in morals, if not civilization, a Catholic Youth Center newspaper asked readers to "smash" rock 'n' roll records because they promoted "a pagan concept of life." But such opponents were waging a losing battle. Rock 'n' roll continued to surge in popularity, and by the end of the decade Dick Clark's *American Bandstand,* a weekly television show featuring teens dancing to rock 'n' roll, was one of the nation's most watched and most accepted programs.

The average American depicted by *Reader's Digest* was a white, middle-class suburbanite. This portrait excluded a huge part of the population, especially minorities and the poor. Although the percentage of those living below the poverty line—set during the 1950s at around $3,000 a year—was declining, it was still over 22 percent and included large percentages of the elderly, minorities, and women heads of households. Even with Social Security payments, as 1959 ended nearly 31 percent of those over 65 lived below the poverty line, with 8 million receiving less than $1,000 a year. Women heads of households constituted about 23 percent of those making less than $3,000 annually. Throughout rural America, especially among small farmers and farm workers, poverty was common, with most earning $1,000 below the national average of about $3,500. In rural Mississippi, the annual per capita income was less than $900.

Poverty also increased in major cities as minorities continued to migrate seeking jobs and a less segregated society. Blacks continued their exodus from the rural South, and by 1960 half of African Americans lived in urban areas. Latinos also flocked to urban areas; only 20 percent of all Latinos did not live in cities by the end of the 1950s. New York's Puerto Rican community, for example, increased more than 1,000 percent. In some cities, including Atlanta and Washington, D.C., minorities became the majority, but they rarely exercised any political power proportionate to their numbers. No matter what the city, minority job seekers still found few openings and little economic opportunity, and it was common for nonwhite unemployment in cities to reach 40 percent.

At the same time, cities were less able or willing to provide services. Cities lost tax revenues and deteriorated at an accelerating rate as white middle- and working-class families moved into the suburbs and were followed by shopping centers and businesses. When funds were available for urban renewal and development, many city governments, like Miami

Outside Suburbia

▪ What groups existed outside of the popular image of the nation?

▪ How did African Americans attack de jure segregation in American society during the 1950s?

▪ What role did the federal government play in promoting civil rights?

cover record A new version of a song already recorded by an original artist.

Elvis Presley Immensely popular rock 'n' roll musician from a poor white family in Mississippi; many of his songs and concert performances were considered sexually suggestive.

gold record Status that is awarded when 500,000 records have been sold.

and Los Angeles, used those funds to relocate and isolate minorities in specific neighborhoods away from developing entertainment, administrative, and shopping areas and upscale apartments. Cities also chose to build wider roads connecting the city to the suburbs rather than invest in mass transit within the city. In South and East Central Los Angeles, freeway interchanges gobbled up 10 percent of the housing space and divided neighborhoods and families. For nearly all minorities, discrimination and **de facto** segregation put upward mobility and escaping poverty even further out of reach.

Integrating Schools

For many African Americans, poverty was just one facet of life. They also faced a legally sanctioned segregated society. Legal, or **de jure,** segregation existed not only in the South but also in the District of Columbia and several western and midwestern states. Changes had occurred, but most African Americans regarded them as minor victories, indicating no real shift in white America's racial views. By 1952 the NAACP had won cases permitting African American law and graduate students to attend white colleges and universities, even though the separate-but-equal ruling established in 1896 by the Supreme Court in *Plessy v. Ferguson* (see page 617) remained intact.

A step toward more significant change came in 1954 when the Supreme Court considered the case of *Brown v. Board of Education, Topeka, Kansas.* The *Brown* case had started four years earlier, when Oliver Brown sued to allow his daughter to attend a nearby white school. The Kansas courts had rejected his suit, pointing out that the availability of a school for African Americans fulfilled the Supreme Court's separate-but-equal ruling. The NAACP appealed. In addressing the Supreme Court, NAACP lawyer **Thurgood Marshall** argued that the concept of "separate but equal" was inherently self-contradictory. He used statistics to show that black schools were separate and *un*equal in financial resources, quality and number of teachers, and physical and educational resources. He also read into the record a psychological study indicating that black children educated in a segregated environment suffered from low self-esteem. Marshall stressed that segregated educational facilities, even if physically similar, could never yield equal results.

In 1952 a divided Court was unable to make a decision, but two years later the Court heard the case again. Now sitting as chief justice was **Earl Warren,**

As Elizabeth Eckford approached Little Rock's Central High School, the crowd began to hurl curses, yelling "Lynch her! Lynch her!" and a National Guardsman blocked her entrance into the school with his rifle. Terrified, she retreated down the street away from the threatening mob. Weeks later, with army troops protecting her, Elizabeth Eckford finally attended—and integrated— Central High School. *Francis Miller, LIFE Magazine ©Time Warner Inc.*

---

de facto   Existing in practice, though not officially established by law.

de jure   According to, or brought about by, law, such as "Jim Crow" laws that separated the races throughout the South until passage of the 1964 Civil Rights Act.

Brown v. Board of Education   Case in 1954 in which the Supreme Court ruled that separate educational facilities for different races were inherently unequal.

Thurgood Marshall   Civil rights lawyer who argued thirty-two cases before the Supreme Court and won twenty-nine; he became the first African American justice of the Supreme Court in 1967.

Earl Warren   Chief justice of the Supreme Court from 1953 to 1969, under whom the Court issued decisions protecting civil rights, the rights of criminals, and First Amendment rights.

the Republican former governor of California who had been appointed to the Court by Eisenhower in 1953. To the dismay of many who had considered Warren a legal conservative, the chief justice moved the Court away from its longtime preoccupation with economic and regulatory issues and down new judicial paths. Rejecting social and political consensus, the activism of the Supreme Court promoted new visions of society as it deliberated racial issues and individual rights. Reflecting the opinion of a unanimous Court, the *Brown* decision stated that "separate educational facilities are inherently unequal." In 1955, in addressing how to implement *Brown*, the Court gave primary responsibility to local school boards. Not expecting integration overnight, the Court ordered school districts to proceed with "all deliberate speed." The justices instructed lower federal courts to monitor progress according to this vague guideline.

Reactions to the case were predictable. African Americans and liberals hailed the decision and hoped that segregated schools would soon be an institution of the past. Southern whites vowed to resist integration by all possible means. Virginia passed a law closing any integrated school. Southern congressional representatives issued the **Southern Manifesto,** in which they proudly pledged to oppose the *Brown* ruling. Eisenhower, who believed the Court had erred, refused to support the decision publicly.

While both political parties carefully danced around school integration and other civil rights issues, school districts in Little Rock, Arkansas, moved forward with "all deliberate speed." Central High School was scheduled to integrate in 1957. Opposing integration were the parents of the school's students and Governor Orval Faubus, who ordered National Guard troops to surround the school and prevent desegregation. When Elizabeth Eckford, one of the nine integrating students, walked toward Central High, National Guardsmen blocked her path as a hostile mob roared, "Lynch her! Lynch her!" Spat on by the jeering crowd, she retreated to her bus stop. Central High remained segregated.

For three weeks the National Guard prevented the black students from enrolling. Then on September 20 a federal judge ordered the integration of Central High School. Faubus complied and withdrew the National Guard. But the crisis was not over. Segregationists remained determined to block integration and were waiting for the black students on Monday, September 23, 1957. When they discovered that the nine had slipped into the school unnoticed, the mob rushed the police lines and battered the school doors

open. Inside the school, Melba Patella Beaus thought, "We were trapped. I'm going to die here, in school." Hurriedly, the students were loaded into cars and warned to duck their heads. School officials ordered the drivers to "start driving, do not stop. . . . If you hit somebody, you keep rolling, 'cause [if you stop] the kids are dead."

Integration had lasted almost three hours and was followed by rioting throughout the city, forcing the mayor to ask for federal troops to restore order. Faced with insurrection, Eisenhower, on September 24, nationalized the Arkansas National Guard and dispatched a thousand troops of the 101st Airborne Division to Little Rock. Speaking to the nation, the president emphasized that he had sent the federal troops not to integrate the schools but to uphold the law and to restore order. The distinction was lost on most white southerners, who fumed as soldiers protected the nine black students for the rest of the school year.

In the school year that followed (1957–1958), the city closed its high schools rather than integrate them. To prevent such actions, the Supreme Court ruled in *Cooper v. Aaron* (1959) that an African American's right to attend school could not "be nullified openly and directly by state legislators or state executive officials nor nullified indirectly by them by evasive schemes for segregation." Little Rock's high schools reopened, and integration slowly spread to the lower grades. But in Little Rock, as in other communities, many white families fled the integrated public schools and enrolled their children in private schools that were beyond the reach of the federal courts. With no endorsement from the White House and entrenched southern opposition, "all deliberate speed" amounted to a snail's pace. By 1965, less than 2 percent of all southern schools were integrated.

Southern Manifesto   Statement issued by one hundred southern congressmen in 1954 after the *Brown v. Board of Education* decision, pledging to oppose desegregation.

Cooper v. Aaron   Supreme Court decision (1959) that barred state authorities from interfering with desegregation either directly or through strategies of evasion.

It Matters

The *Brown* Decision

The *Brown v. Board of Education* decision by the Supreme Court remains a milestone in American history. It helped to propel a mass movement seeking racial equality. It raised expectations, but it also fell short of those expectations. It forced desegregation, but it did not provide effective integration or equality. Fifty years later, only a few Americans have experienced a racially and culturally inclusive education. Despite the shortcomings of the decision, however, few can disagree with its stated goal: "It is doubtful that any child may reasonably be expected to succeed in life if he is denied the opportunity of an education. Such an opportunity . . . is a right which must be made available to all in equal terms."

The Montgomery Bus Boycott

1955 was not only the year the Supreme Court issued its second *Brown* decision, it was a year that focused the nation's attention on southern opposition to racial equality. The first incident took place when Emmett Till, a teenager from Chicago visiting relatives in Mississippi, was brutally tortured and murdered for speaking to a white girl without her permission. In the trial that followed, the two confessed murderers were acquitted. It was not an unexpected verdict in Mississippi, but it and the brutality of the murder shocked much of the nation.

In Montgomery, Alabama, African Americans were aware of the Till murder but were determined to confront another form of white social control: segregation on the city bus line. The confrontation began almost imperceptibly on December 1, 1955, when **Rosa Parks** refused to give up her seat on the bus so that a white man could sit. At 42, Mrs. Parks, a high school graduate who earned $23 a week as a seamstress, had not boarded the bus with the intention of disobeying the law, although she strongly opposed it. But that afternoon, her fatigue and humiliation were suddenly too much. She refused to move and was arrested.

Hearing of her arrest, local African American leaders Jo Ann Robinson and Edward Nixon felt they had found the right person committed enough to contest segregation. African American community leaders called for a boycott of the buses to begin on the day of Mrs. Parks's court appearance. Accordingly, they submitted a list of proposals to city and bus officials calling for courteous drivers, the hiring of black drivers, and a more equitable system of bus seating.

On December 5, 1955, the night before the boycott was to begin, nearly four thousand people filled and surrounded Holt Street Baptist Church to hear **Martin Luther King Jr.,** the newly selected leader of the boycott movement—now called the Montgomery Improvement Association. The 26-year-old King firmly believed that the church had a social justice mission and that violence and hatred, even when considered justified, brought only ruin. In shaping that evening's speech, he wrestled with the problem of how to balance disobedience with peace, confrontation with civility, and rebellion with tradition—and won. His words electrified the crowd: "We are here this evening to say to those who have mistreated us so long that we are tired of being segregated and humiliated, tired of being kicked about by the brutal feet of oppression." King asked the crowd to boycott the buses, urging his listeners to protest "courageously, and yet with dignity and Christian love," and when confronted with violence, to "bless them that curse you."

On December 6, Rosa Parks was tried, found guilty, and fined $10, plus $4 for court costs. She appealed, and the boycott, 90 percent effective, stretched into days, weeks, and finally months. Police issued basketfuls of traffic tickets to drivers taking part in the car pools that provided transportation for the boycotters. Insurance companies canceled their automobile coverage, and acid was poured on their cars. On January 30, 1956, a stick of dynamite was thrown onto King's front porch, destroying it and almost injuring King's wife and a friend. King nevertheless remained calm, reminding supporters to avoid violence and persevere. Finally, as the boycott approached its

Rosa Parks Black seamstress who refused to give up her seat to a white man on a bus in Montgomery, Alabama, in 1955, triggering a bus boycott that stirred the civil rights movement.

Martin Luther King Jr. Ordained Baptist minister, brilliant orator, and civil rights leader committed to nonviolence; he led many of the important protests of the 1950s and 1960s.

On December 1, 1955, Rosa Parks made a fateful choice—she refused to give up her seat to a white man on a Montgomery, Alabama, bus. She was arrested and fined $14 as a result of her decision. Her act of defiance ignited a grassroots effort by African Americans to eliminate discrimination, and with it Martin Luther King Jr. emerged as a national leader for civil rights. These pictures show the Montgomery Police Department's mug shots of Rosa Parks and Martin Luther King Jr., following their arrests. "I had no idea history was being made," Parks stated later. "I was just tired of giving in." *AP/Montgomery County (Alabama Sheriff's Office)/ Wide World.*

first anniversary, the Supreme Court ruled in *Gayle et al. v. Browser* (1956) that the city's and bus company's policy of segregation was unconstitutional. "Praise the Lord. God has spoken from Washington, D.C.," cried one boycotter.

The Montgomery bus boycott shattered the traditional white view that African Americans accepted segregation, and it marked the beginning of a pattern of nonviolent resistance. King himself was determined to build on the energy generated by the boycott to fight segregation throughout American society. In 1956 he and other black leaders formed a new civil rights organization, the **Southern Christian Leadership Conference** (SCLC), and across the South thousands of African Americans were ready and eager to take to the streets and to use the federal courts to achieve equality.

Ike and Civil Rights

As the Montgomery boycott steamrolled into the headlines month after month, from the White House came either silence or carefully selected platitudes. When asked, Eisenhower gave elusive replies: "I believe we should not stagnate. . . . I plead for understanding, for really sympathetic consideration of a problem. . . . I am for moderation, but I am for progress; that is exactly what I am for in this thing." Personally,

> **Southern Christian Leadership Conference** Group formed by Martin Luther King Jr. and others after the Montgomery bus boycott; it became the backbone of the civil rights movement in the 1950s and 1960s.

Eisenhower believed that government, especially the executive branch, had little role in integration. Max Rabb, the president's adviser on minority affairs, thought the "Negroes were being too aggressive." On a political level, cabinet members and Eisenhower were disappointed in the low number of blacks who had voted Republican in 1952 and 1956.

But not all within the administration were so unsympathetic toward civil rights. Attorney General Herbert Brownell drafted the first civil rights legislation since Reconstruction. The **Civil Rights Act of 1957** passed Congress after a year of political maneuvering, having gained the support of Democratic majority leader Lyndon B. Johnson of Texas. A moderate law, it provided for the formation of a Commission on Civil Rights and opened the possibility of using federal lawsuits to ensure voter rights. The SCLC had hoped to enroll 3 million new black voters in the South but fell far short of the goal, enrolling only 160,000 between 1958 and 1960. Ella Baker, who headed the underfunded and understaffed effort, faced effective opposition from southern whites and local and state officials. In 1960 Congress passed a voting rights act that offered little help. To remove the barriers to black voting, the act mandated the use of the cumbersome and expensive judiciary system—again placing the burden of forcing change on African Americans. Critics acknowledged that Eisenhower had sent troops to Little Rock and signed two civil rights acts, but they argued that the president had provided little political or moral leadership. If the nation was to commit itself to civil rights, such leadership was imperative.

The activism of the civil rights movement and the Warren Court was at odds with the popular image of the 1950s, a picture of consensual solutions, political inaction, and Eisenhower's blandness. By the end of the decade an increasing number of people were calling for more activism and decisive direction from the White House. As the 1960 presidential election neared, Democrats and other critics of the Eisenhower years called for a new, involved government that would protect American interests abroad and solve social problems at home.

Civil Rights Act of 1957   Created the U.S. Commission on Civil Rights and the Civil Rights Division of the Department of Justice; the Commission on Civil Rights primarily investigated restrictions on voting.

Individual Voices

Examining a Primary Source

Ray Kroc Explains the McDonald's Approach to Business

Around the world few symbols are better known than the Golden Arches of McDonald's. Since its humble origins in San Bernardino, California, more than 12,000 restaurants now exist in the United States and 7,000 in foreign nations. Unlike the original (see below), today's McDonald's menus provide a wide variety of choices, from Big Macs to salads to vegetarian burgers in India and Shogun Burgers in Japan.

In 1977, as McDonald's spread across the nation, Ray Kroc wrote his autobiography, *Grinding It Out*. It not only explained his personal long climb to prominence but provided insight into the many innovations that have shaped the fast-food industry and changed America's and the world's eating habits. The following excerpts demonstrate not only some of the techniques McDonald's used but provide a glimpse of Kroc's enthusiasm for his product.

■ *Compare this original McDonald's menu to a menu at today's McDonald's. What do the differences suggest about McDonald's and American eating habits?*

McDonald's Menu ■

1956

Hamburgers	15 cents
Cheeseburgers	19 cents
Malt Shakes	20 cents
French Fries	10 cents
Orange	10 cents
Root Beer	10 cents
Coke	10 cents
Milk	10 cents
Coffee	10 cents

It requires a certain kind of mind to see beauty in a hamburger bun. Yet, is it any more unusual to find grace in the texture and softly curved silhouette of a bun than [in] . . . a favorite fishing fly? Or the arrangement of textures and colors of a butterfly wing? Not if you are a McDonald's man. Not if you view the bun as an essential material in the art of serving a great many meals fast. Then this plump, yeasty mass becomes an object worthy of somber study. . . .

We set the standards of quality and recommended methods for packaging. . . . Our stores are selling only nine items, and they were buying only thirty-five or forty items with which to make the nine. So although a McDonald's restaurant's purchasing power was not greater in total than that of any other restaurant in a given area, it was concentrated. A McDonald's bought more buns, more catsup, more mustard, and so forth, and this gave it a terrific position in the marketplace for those items. We enhanced that position by figuring out ways a supplier could lower his costs, which meant . . . that he could afford to sell to a McDonald's for

- In what ways is McDonald's seeking to lower their costs and make their product more competitive?

- How does Ray Kroc's statement on American capitalism reflect the hopes and values of the 1950s in America?

- Ray Kroc said that a major reason McDonald's was successful what that they took "the hamburger business more seriously than anyone else." How does this excerpt support that point of view?

less. Bulk packaging was one way; another was making it possible for him to deliver more items per stop. . . . ■

. . . [A] McDonald's hamburger patty is a piece of meat with character. The first thing that distinguishes it from the patties that many other places pass off as hamburgers is that it is all beef. There are no hearts or other alien goodies ground into our patties. The fat content . . . is a prescribed nineteen percent. . . . We decided that our patties would be ten to a pound. . . . There was also a science in stacking patties. If you made the stack too high, the ones at the bottom would be misshapen and dried out. So we arrived at the optimum stack, and that determined the height of our meat suppliers' packages. The purpose of all these refinements . . . was to make our griddle man's job easier to do quickly and well. . . .

Since a McDonald's restaurant is a prime example of American small business in action, the husband-wife team is basic to us. Typically, the husband will look after operations and maintenance while his wife keeps the books and handles personnel. . . . ■

My way of fighting the competition is the positive approach. Stress your own strengths, emphasize quality, service, cleanliness and value, and the competition will wear itself out trying to keep up. ■

Ray Kroc, *Grinding It Out: The Making of McDonald's* (Chicago, Henry Regnery, 1977), pp. 92–97, 107.

Summary

"Had enough?" Republicans asked voters in 1952, offering the choice of a new vision of domestic and foreign policy. Americans answered by electing Eisenhower. Though promising change, Eisenhower in practice chose foreign and domestic policies that continued the basic patterns established by Roosevelt and Truman. Republican beliefs, pervasive anticommunism, and budget concerns allowed reductions in some domestic programs, but public acceptance of existing federal responsibilities prevented any large-scale dismantling of the New Deal. The New Look relied on new tactics, but Cold War foreign policies did not change significantly. Using alliances, military force, nuclear deterrence, and covert activities, Eisenhower continued containment and expanded American influence in southern Asia and the Middle East. Meanwhile, relations with the Soviet Union deteriorated with the launching of *Sputnik,* another Berlin crisis, Castro's victory in Cuba, and the U-2 incident. By the end of the decade, many questioned the effectiveness of the administration, especially the president, to lead in the fight against communism and solve what seemed to be a growing number of social and political problems at home.

Reflecting the image of Ike in the White House, the 1950s spawned comforting, if not entirely accurate, images of America centered on affluent suburbs and a growing consumer culture. To be sure, many white working-class and middle-class Americans fulfilled their expectations by moving to the suburbs and living the American dream. Suburbs continued to expand, and a society shaped by cars, expanded purchasing power, and middle-class values seemed to be what America "was about." Critics of this benign vision stated that such a consensual society bred a social grayness and stifled individualism. They argued that rather than trying to conform to society, individuals should work to change society. Yet life in suburbia did not necessarily fit either the popular or the critics' image. Many men, women, and children behaved contrary to the supposed norms of family and suburban culture. Teens and young adults, especially, turned to forms of expression that seemed to reject established norms and values.

Outside the suburbs another America existed, where economic realities, social prejudices, and old-fashioned politics blocked equality and upward mobility. Although declining, poverty still persisted, especially in rural America and among minorities living in urban areas. While poverty remained largely ignored, it became increasingly difficult to ignore the actions taken by African Americans to overturn decades of segregation. By the end of the decade, civil rights had emerged as an issue that neither political party nor white, suburban America could avoid.

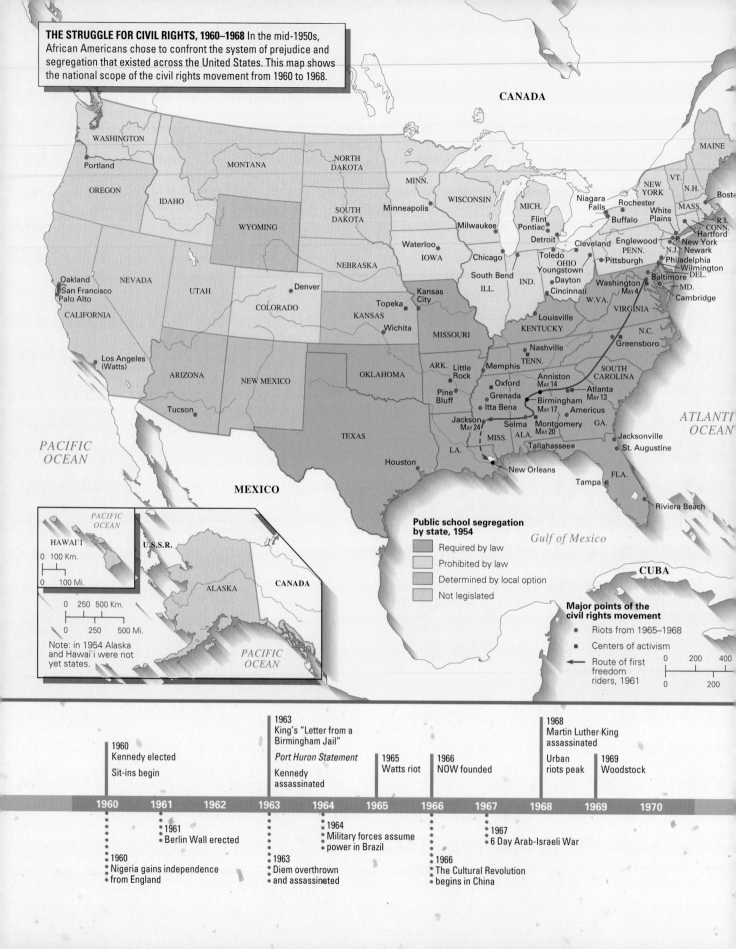

THE STRUGGLE FOR CIVIL RIGHTS, 1960–1968 In the mid-1950s, African Americans chose to confront the system of prejudice and segregation that existed across the United States. This map shows the national scope of the civil rights movement from 1960 to 1968.

CANADA

WASHINGTON
Portland
OREGON
IDAHO
MONTANA
NORTH DAKOTA
SOUTH DAKOTA
WYOMING
NEBRASKA
MINN.
Minneapolis
WISCONSIN
MICH.
Flint
Pontiac
Milwaukee
Waterloo
IOWA
Detroit
Chicago
Cleveland
South Bend
ILL.
IND.
OHIO
Youngstown
Toledo
Dayton
Cincinnati
NIAGARA Falls
NEW YORK
Rochester
Buffalo
White Plains
VT.
N.H.
MAINE
Bost
MASS.
R.I.
CONN.
Hartford
New York
Newark
Englewood
N.J.
PENN.
Pittsburgh
Philadelphia
Wilmington
DEL.
Baltimore
MD.
Cambridge
W.VA.
VIRGINIA
Washington
May 4

OAKLAND
San Francisco
Palo Alto
NEVADA
UTAH
CALIFORNIA
Denver
COLORADO
Topeka
KANSAS
Wichita
Kansas City
MISSOURI
KENTUCKY
Louisville
Nashville
TENN.
N.C.
Greensboro

Los Angeles (Watts)
ARIZONA
NEW MEXICO
OKLAHOMA
ARK.
Little Rock
Memphis
Oxford
Pine Bluff
Grenada
Itta Bena
Anniston
May 14
Birmingham
May 17
Americus
SOUTH CAROLINA
Atlanta
May 13
GA.
Tucson
Jackson
May 24
Selma
Montgomery
May 20
ALA.
MISS.
Tallahassee
Jacksonville
St. Augustine

TEXAS
LA.
Houston
New Orleans
Tampa
FLA.
Riviera Beach

PACIFIC OCEAN

MEXICO

ATLANTIC OCEAN

Gulf of Mexico

CUBA

Public school segregation by state, 1954
- Required by law
- Prohibited by law
- Determined by local option
- Not legislated

Major points of the civil rights movement
- • Riots from 1965–1968
- ■ Centers of activism
- ← Route of first freedom riders, 1961

PACIFIC OCEAN
HAWAI'I
0 100 Km.
0 100 Mi.

U.S.S.R.
ALASKA
CANADA
PACIFIC OCEAN

0 250 500 Km.
0 250 500 Mi.

Note: in 1954 Alaska and Hawai'i were not yet states.

0 200 400
0 200

Timeline

1960
Kennedy elected
Sit-ins begin

1963
King's "Letter from a Birmingham Jail"
Port Huron Statement
Kennedy assassinated

1965
Watts riot

1966
NOW founded

1968
Martin Luther King assassinated
Urban riots peak

1969
Woodstock

| 1960 | 1961 | 1962 | 1963 | 1964 | 1965 | 1966 | 1967 | 1968 | 1969 | 1970 |

1961
Berlin Wall erected

1964
Military forces assume power in Brazil

1967
6 Day Arab-Israeli War

1960
Nigeria gains independence from England

1963
Diem overthrown and assassinated

1966
The Cultural Revolution begins in China

Great Promises, Bitter Disappointments, 1960–1968

28

The Struggle for Civil Rights, 1960–1968
How does the map on the facing page indicate the national nature of discrimination and segregation? What can be determined about the "de facto" and "de jure" phases of the civil rights movement?

Individual Choices

Stokely Carmichael (Kwame Ture)

STOKELY CARMICHAEL

Stokely Carmichael was one of the most influential African American leaders of the 1960s and 1970s. Born in Trinidad in 1941, Carmichael attended Howard University, where he immersed himself in the civil rights movement. He participated in one of the first freedom rides and was arrested the first of thirty-five times for civil rights activism. He graduated with a degree in philosophy in 1964 and two years later became nationally recognized as an advocate of "Black Power." Black Power was, he told a London newspaper, "the coming together of black people to fight for their liberation by any means necessary." *Marc Vignes/Timepix.*

It was an idea whose time had come. That was the decision of Stokely Carmichael and other leaders of the Student Nonviolent Coordinating Committee (SNCC) in the summer of 1966. Participating in the James Meredith "March Against Fear" on June 16, Carmichael was arrested by Greenwood, Mississippi, police following a rally—it was his twenty-seventh arrest. Later that day, following his release, he spoke to a crowd of about three thousand assembled marchers and local blacks. In a fiery speech, he called to the crowd to move away from the passive disobedience associated with Dr. Martin Luther King Jr.'s "Freedom Now" crusade and adopt a more militant and separatist vision of "Black Power." "The only way we gonna stop them white men from whuppin' us is to take over," he roared to the crowd. "We been saying freedom for six years—and we ain't got nothin'. What we gonna start saying now is 'Black Power.'" The crowd roared back, "Black Power!" Carmichael's call did more than energize a crowd of demonstrators. It also defiantly challenged the leadership and tactics of King and the Southern Christian Leadership Council. The nation suddenly was aware of another dimension of the civil rights movement. A white civil rights marcher listening to the thundering demand for Black Power reflected, "[S]uddenly I was a 'honky'" rather than a comrade.

The idea of Black Power had been building in Carmichael since his arrival in the United States at age 11. Born in Trinidad, where blacks held positions of power, he discovered the reverse was true in America when he moved to Harlem in 1952. Graduating from high school in 1960, he was motivated by the sit-in students to join the Congress of Racial Equality on picket lines. As a freshman at Howard University, he joined one of the first "freedom rides," and in Mississippi he was arrested—the first of thirty-five times. Graduating from Howard in 1964, he helped organize SNCC and launch a voter registration drive in Lowndes County, Alabama.

Lowndes was a rural, impoverished county dominated by the Klan and white supremacy. The white minority—fewer than 1,000 of the total 13,000—owned 90 percent of the land. Over 12,000 African Americans lived in Lowndes, and in January of 1965, none were registered to vote. SNCC decided to organize a voters' movement there, and Carmichael arrived to implement the effort, which included founding a new black political party and power base. The goal was "to register as many Blacks as we could . . . and take over the county." The effort moved at a crawl until passage of the 1965 Voting Rights Act and the arrival of federal registrars to oversee the end of the literacy test. Blacks surged forward to register and despite increased jailings and beatings—and one murder—formed a political organization in March 1966, the Lowndes County Freedom Organization. The goal of the new party and its symbol reflected Carmichael's growing sense of black power. The goal was to gain power; the symbol was the black panther, selected because, according to one organizer, it was "a vicious animal, who if he was attacked, would not back up. It said we would fight back if we had to." Soon afterward, in a contested election, SNCC members elected Carmichael as their chairman.

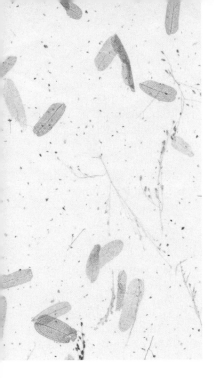

Under Carmichael's direction, SNCC reshaped itself along new, more militant, Black Nationalist, Black Power lines. The organization purged itself of white membership, abandoned nonviolence, promoted Black Nationalism, and clarified the term *Black Power*. While Carmichael had first used the term in Mississippi, he recognized it had a more significant impact in northern urban areas where Black Nationalism and militancy had exploded in the mid-1960s. A spokesman for Black Power and Black Nationalism, Carmichael directed SNCC for a year, leaving it in 1968. He became the honorary prime minister of the Black Panther Party and traveled overseas, speaking out against social, political, and economic repression and American imperialism and denouncing the Vietnam War. Under FBI surveillance and feeling harassed by efforts to neutralize the movement, Carmichael left the United States in 1969 and moved to Guinea, West Africa. He became deeply involved in African politics, helping to establish the All-African People's Revolutionary Party, an international organization dedicated to Pan-Africanism and the worldwide plight of Africans. In 1978 he changed his name to Kwame Ture in honor of two African leaders and supporters of Pan-Africanism, Ghana's Kwame Nkrumah and Guinea's Sékou Turé. Carmichael died of cancer in Guinea in November 1998.

INTRODUCTION

The 1960s stand out as a unique decade in American history, evoking visions of change; of protest marches, demonstrations, and governmental intervention; of New Frontiers and Great Societies. It seemed to Stokely Carmichael and thousands of others that the sixties provided an opportunity to generate change through individual, group, and governmental activism. The election of President John F. Kennedy in 1960 symbolized a new level of youth and vigor in government that raised expectations and created the "politics of hope." Kennedy represented a more interventionist government in both foreign and domestic affairs. Perhaps the activism found in the streets would be joined by that of government—and real change would occur.

Indeed, President Kennedy called for a New Frontier that promised a better society for all Americans and, especially among the poor and minorities, raised expectations that his administration would stimulate the economy, reduce poverty and discrimination, and improve education. But Kennedy faced political opposition from conservatives in Congress who objected to an expansion of liberal programs and who obstructed civil rights legislation. The economy grew, but faced with Republican and southern Democratic

opposition, Kennedy's legislative record generally expanded on existing programs. Policies that charted new paths such as civil rights, healthcare, and aid to education were delayed or abandoned. Still, among many, especially minorities and women, there remained a heightened level of activism and expectations.

Finding fewer political obstacles in foreign policy, Kennedy preferred being a foreign-policy president than a domestic-policy one. He promised to overcome the "missile gap" and regain ground lost to communism. He chose "flexible response" over massive retaliation to confront the global Communist threat. As part of the Cold War, he placed new emphasis on the developing regions of the world, especially Latin America and South Vietnam. To fund new foreign aid and military spending, Kennedy loosened constraints on the military budget, entering into both an arms race and a space race with the Soviets. Yet despite his administration's self-confidence and bold efforts, the outcome was not a safer and less divided world. The erection of the Berlin Wall, the Cuban missile crisis, and events in Vietnam heightened Cold War tensions while stretching American commitments.

Lyndon Johnson inherited two broad issues from Kennedy: completion of the New Frontier and continuation of the struggle against communism, especially in Vietnam. He attacked the domestic agenda immediately while postponing foreign-policy decisions. He called on Congress to pass the civil rights bill and to fund a broad antipoverty campaign. In the months before and after the 1964 presidential election, Johnson presented the nation with his proposals for a Great Society. In an onslaught of legislation, he waged war on poverty and discrimination, developed federal welfare programs, increased federal support for education, and created a national system of healthcare for the aged and poor. But 1965 was the high tide for Johnson and the politics of hope. Unfulfilled expectations, an expanding war in Vietnam, and controversial social and political issues drained away faith in the politics of hope and the effectiveness of the Great Society.

A wave of angry voices—including Stokely Carmichael's—began to challenge the assumptions of the Democratic social and political agenda. Black Power leaders chose confrontation over compromise. Urban riots and violence drove wedges between African American leaders and some white supporters. The emergence of a youth-centered counterculture that rejected traditional social and moral values and stressed personal freedoms also worked to fragment American society. The result was a decade that began with great optimism but ended with diminished expectations.

The Politics of Action

■ What images did John F. Kennedy and his advisers project, and how did those images contribute to the flavor of the 1960s?

■ What were the domestic goals of the Kennedy administration? How successful was the president on the home front, and why?

■ What form of African American activism pushed the civil rights movement forward, and how did Kennedy respond to those efforts?

Republicans had every reason to worry as the 1960 presidential campaign neared. The last years of the 1950s had not been kind to the Republican Party. Domestically, neither the president nor Republicans nor Congress appeared able to deal with the problems of the country—civil rights agitation, a slowing economy, and a soaring national debt that had reached $488 billion. The United States also saw few Cold War victories as the Soviets downed an American spy plane over the Soviet Union, launched *Sputnik* into

space, and supported Castro in Cuba. Democratic gains in the congressional elections of 1958 signaled that the Democrats were again the majority, if not the dominant, party. Vice President Richard Nixon calculated that for a Republican presidential victory, the "candidate would have to get practically all Republican votes, more than half of the independents—and, in addition the votes of five to six million Democrats."

The 1960 Campaign

On the Democratic side stood John Fitzgerald Kennedy, a youthful, vigorous senator from Massachusetts. A Harvard graduate, Kennedy came from a wealthy Catholic family. Some worried about his young age (43) and lack of experience. Others worried about his religion—no Catholic had ever been elected president. To offset these possible liabilities, Kennedy astutely added the politically savvy Senate majority leader Lyndon Johnson of Texas to the ticket, called for a new generation of leadership, and suggested that those who were making religion an issue were bigots. Drawing on the legacy of Franklin Roosevelt, he challenged the nation to enter a **New Frontier** to improve the overall quality of life of all Americans, and to reenergize American foreign policy to stand fast against the Communist threat. He offered action, and empowerment to the government, people, and institutions.

Facing Kennedy was Eisenhower's vice president, Richard M. Nixon. Trying to distance himself from the image of Eisenhower's elderly leadership, Nixon promised a forceful, energetic presidency and emphasized his executive experience and history of anticommunism. He, too, vowed to improve the quality of life, to support civil rights, and to defeat international communism. Several political commentators called the candidates "two peas in a pod" and speculated that the election would probably hinge on appearances more than on issues.

Trailing in the opinion polls and hoping to give his campaign a boost, Nixon agreed to televised debates with Kennedy. He was proud of his debating skills and thought he could adapt them successfully to radio and television. Kennedy seized the opportunity,

New Frontier Program for social and educational reform put forward by President John F. Kennedy; though charismatically presented, it was largely resisted by Congress.

Chronology

New Frontiers

1960	Sit-ins begin
	SNCC formed
	Students for a Democratic Society formed
	Boynton v. Virginia
	John F. Kennedy elected president
1961	Peace Corps formed
	Alliance for Progress
	Yuri Gagarin orbits the Earth
	Bay of Pigs invasion
	Freedom rides begin
	Vienna summit
	Berlin Wall erected
1962	Michael Harrington's *The Other America*
	SDS's *Port Huron Statement*
	James Meredith enrolls at the University of Mississippi
	Cuban missile crisis
	Rachel Carson's *Silent Spring*
1963	Report on the status of women
	Betty Friedan's *The Feminine Mystique*
	Equal Pay Act
	Martin Luther King's "Letter from a Birmingham Jail"
	Limited Test Ban Treaty
	March on Washington
	16,000 advisers in Vietnam
	Diem assassinated

	Kennedy assassinated; Lyndon Baines Johnson becomes president
1964	War on Poverty begins
	Freedom Summer in Mississippi
	Civil Rights Act
	Office of Economic Opportunity created
	Johnson elected president
1965	Malcolm X assassinated
	Selma freedom march
	Elementary and Secondary Education Act
	Medicaid and Medicare
	Voting Rights Act
	Watts riot
	Immigration Act
1966	Black Panther Party formed
	National Organization for Women founded
	Stokely Carmichael announces Black Power
	Model Cities Act
1967	Urban riots in over 75 cities
1968	Kerner Commission Report
	Martin Luther King Jr. assassinated
1969	Woodstock
	Stonewall Riot
	Neil Armstrong lands on moon

recognizing that the candidate who appeared most calm and knowledgeable—more "presidential"— would "win" each debate. Before the camera's eye, in the war of images, Kennedy appeared fresh and confident, while Nixon, having been ill, appeared tired and haggard. The contrasts were critical. Unable to see Nixon, the radio audience believed he won the debates, but to the 70 million television viewers, the winner was the self-assured and sweat-free Kennedy.

The televised debates helped Kennedy, but victory depended on his ability to hold the Democratic coalition together, maintaining southern Democratic support while wooing African American and liberal voters. The Texan Johnson used his political clout to keep the South largely loyal while Kennedy blasted the lack of Republican leadership on civil rights. Martin Luther King Jr. had been arrested for civil rights activities in Atlanta, and in a grand gesture, Kennedy telephoned Coretta Scott King to express his concern about her husband's jailing. Kennedy's brother Robert used his influence to get King freed, convincing even the staunchest Protestant black ministers, including Martin Luther King Sr., to overlook Kennedy's religion and endorse him. Every vote was critical. When the ballots were counted, Kennedy had scored the slimmest of victories (see Map 28.1). Nixon carried more states, 25 to 21, but Kennedy had a narrow margin over Nixon in popular votes and won the electoral count, 303 to 219. (Independent southern candidate Harry Byrd earned 15 electoral votes.)

The 1960 presidential race was at the time the closest in recent history, with many people believing that the outcome hinged on the public's perception of the candidates during their nationally televised debates. The majority of viewers believed that Kennedy won the debates and looked more in control and presidential than Nixon. Kennedy won the election by fewer than 119,000 popular votes. *Left: Corbis-Bettmann; right: © Bettmann/Corbis.*

The New Frontier

The weather in Washington was frigid when Kennedy gave his inaugural address, but his speech fired the imagination of the nation. Speaking in idealistic terms, avoiding any mention of specific programs, he pledged to march against "the common enemies of man: tyranny, poverty, disease, and war itself." He invited all Americans to participate, exhorting them to "ask not what your country can do for you; ask what you can do for your country." In this speech and throughout the campaign, Kennedy had tapped into a growing sense that activism and change were to be embraced and not avoided. This optimistic view was a product of the country's growing affluence and a youthful confidence that science and technology could solve whatever ills faced society. "Science and technology are making the problems of today ir-

relevant. . . . The basic miracle of modern technology . . . is a magic wand that gives us what we desire," stated Adlai Stevenson. Kennedy believed that most national problems were "technical" and "administrative" and would be solved by experts. In keeping with his view, he selected for his cabinet and advisers those with "know-how," people who were willing to take action to get the nation moving again. Kennedy chose Rhodes scholars, successful businessmen, and Harvard professors. Harvard supplied economist John Kenneth Galbraith (a personal adviser) and Dean Rusk (secretary of state). The successful Ford Motor Company president Robert McNamara was tapped for secretary of defense. In a controversial move, Kennedy named his younger brother Robert as attorney general. Many hailed Kennedy's choices as representing "the best and the brightest." But not everyone thought so. Referring to the lack of political

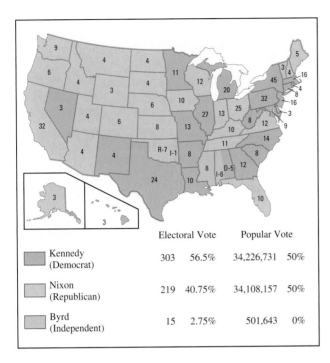

	Electoral Vote		Popular Vote	
Kennedy (Democrat)	303	56.5%	34,226,731	50%
Nixon (Republican)	219	40.75%	34,108,157	50%
Byrd (Independent)	15	2.75%	501,643	0%

MAP 28.1 Election of 1960 Although Richard Nixon won in more states than John F. Kennedy, in the closest presidential election in the twentieth century, Kennedy defeated his Republican opponent by a slim 84 electoral votes and fewer than 119,000 popular votes.

background among appointees, Speaker of the House Sam Rayburn, a Democrat, remarked that he would "feel a whole lot better . . . if just one of them had run for sheriff once."

Kennedy and his staff wanted to be activists leading the nation along new paths, but they also realized that it would be difficult to convince Congress to accept new programs that went beyond the familiar boundaries of the New Deal and the vital center. Consequently, Kennedy decided to focus on legislation within the "vital center"—neither overly liberal nor overly conservative—that would improve the economy and the services provided under existing New Deal–style programs. Like Truman, he asked Congress for a wide range of domestic programs, but he received only a modest Eisenhower-like result. By 1963, Congress had approved small increases in Social Security coverage and benefits and in the minimum wage (to $1.25 an hour), an extension of unemployment insurance, and a housing and **urban renewal** bill. Attempts to introduce national health coverage, federal aid to education, and civil rights remained bottled up in Congress.

Kennedy had better luck in spurring economic recovery. He turned to the "**new economics**" advocated by Walter Heller, his chairman of the Council of Economic Advisers. Heller recommended a more aggressive use of **fiscal** and monetary policies as well as tax cuts to stimulate the economy. In 1962, Kennedy managed to push through Congress a reduction in business taxes but failed the following year to gain congressional approval of broad cuts in the income tax. The biggest contribution to the expanding economy, however, was military and Cold War–related spending. In the face of a seemingly more aggressive Soviet Union, Congress raised the defense budget by almost 20 percent ($6 billion), funded an expensive space program, and provided millions of dollars for research and development (R&D). By 1965, government-sponsored R&D for a wide variety of potential defense-related products amounted to one-sixth of the federal budget. These developments brought a boom in the economy, which expanded by 13 percent.

Although Eisenhower had created the National Aeronautics and Space Administration (NASA), it appeared that the Soviets were still leading the space race. In 1961, the Soviet cosmonaut Yuri Gagarin orbited the Earth, while the United States' Mercury project only managed to lift its astronauts into space for fifteen minutes. Kennedy was determined not to lose the space race and called upon Congress to fund a program for a manned space flight to the moon and back. In his message to Congress, he emphasized that success in the program, Project Apollo, would have a positive effect on the peoples of the Third World. In 1969, after spending nearly $33 billion, Neil Armstrong won the race and became the first human to step on the surface of the moon.

Kennedy and Civil Rights

Promotion of a robust economy and flights to the moon were only part of the image of the New Frontier. There was a confidence that improving society

urban renewal Effort to revitalize run-down areas of cities by providing federal funding for the construction of apartment houses, office buildings, and public facilities.
new economics Planning and shaping the national economy through the use of tax policies and federal spending as recommended by Keynesian economics.
fiscal policy The use of government spending to stimulate or slow down the economy.

was possible through a combination of individual, group, and governmental action. As Kennedy took office, nowhere were these ideas more applauded than within the civil rights movement.

Although their hopes had been raised by Kennedy's promises of executive action, most African Americans knew that progress depended on their own actions, that the movement must be generated at the grassroots level and could not wait for or depend on government. Even as Kennedy campaigned, a new wave of black activism swept across the South in the form of sit-ins. The **sit-ins** began when four black freshmen at North Carolina Agricultural and Technical College in Greensboro, North Carolina, decided to integrate the public lunch counter at the local F. W. Woolworth store. On February 1, 1960, they entered the store, sat down at the counter, and ordered a meal. A black waitress told them she could not serve them, but still they sat and waited for service until the store closed. They were not served, but no one tried to remove or arrest them. The next day twenty Black A&T students sat at the lunch counter demanding service. The movement quickly spread to more than 140 cities, including some outside the South, in Nevada, Illinois, and Ohio. In some cities, including Greensboro, integration was achieved with a minimum of resistance. But elsewhere, particularly in the Deep South, whites resisted violently in order to protect segregation. Thousands of participants in sit-ins were beaten, blasted with high-pressure fire hoses, and jailed. Most of those taking part were young and initially unorganized, but as the movement grew, organized civil rights groups moved to incorporate the new tactic and its practitioners. In April 1960, SCLC official Ella Baker helped form the **Student Nonviolent Coordinating Committee** (SNCC, pronounced "snick"), a new civil rights organization built around the sit-in movement. Although its statement of purpose emphasized **nonviolence,** SNCC members were more militant than other civil rights activists. As one stated, "We do not intend to wait placidly for those rights which are already legally and morally ours." SNCC workers quickly spread across the South, emphasizing action.

The new administration was not rushing to action nor rushing to ask Congress for civil rights legislation. With southern Democrats entrenched in Congress, Kennedy saw little reason to "raise hell" and waste legislative efforts on civil rights. Instead, he relied on limited executive action. He appointed more African Americans to federal positions than any previous president, including over forty to major posts, and named NAACP lawyer **Thurgood Marshall** to the U.S. circuit court, although Congress delayed

When Kennedy took office, the sit-in movement was spreading across the South as students from colleges and universities sought to integrate places of public accommodation. In this picture, whites harass students from Tougaloo College as they "sit-in" at a Woolworth lunch counter in Jackson, Mississippi. *State Historical Society of Wisconsin.*

Marshall's appointment for over a year. But Kennedy also took until November 1962 to fulfill a campaign pledge to lift his pen to ban segregation in federal housing.

Seeking to stimulate executive action, James Farmer of the Congress of Racial Equality (CORE) (see page 811) announced a series of "**freedom rides**" to force

sit-in   The act of occupying the seats or an area of a segregated establishment to protest racial discrimination; CORE had used the tactic in the 1940s to integrate public facilities.

Student Nonviolent Coordinating Committee   Organization formed in 1960 to give young blacks a greater voice in the civil rights movement; it initiated black voter registration drives, sit-ins, and freedom rides.

nonviolence   The rejection of violence in favor of peaceful tactics as a means of achieving political objectives.

Thurgood Marshall   African American lawyer who argued the *Brown* case before the Supreme Court; appointed to the federal court system by President Kennedy, he became the first African American Supreme Court justice.

freedom rides   An effort by civil rights protesters who, by riding buses throughout the South in 1961, sought to achieve the integration of bus terminals.

integration in southern bus lines and bus stations. In December 1960, the Supreme Court had ruled in *Boynton v. Virginia* that all interstate buses, trains, and terminals were to be desegregated, and Farmer intended to make that decision a reality. The buses of riders left Washington, D.C., in May 1961, headed toward Alabama and Mississippi. Trouble was anticipated, and in Anniston, Alabama, angry whites attacked the buses, setting them on fire and severely beating several freedom riders. The savagery continued in Birmingham, Alabama, where one freedom rider needed fifty-three stitches to close his head wound. As expected, the violence forced a response by the administration. Having failed to stop the ride for a "cooling-off" period, U.S. Attorney General Robert Kennedy negotiated state and local protection for the riders through Alabama and placed federal agents on the buses. It did little good. When the buses arrived in Montgomery, Alabama, the police and National Guard escorts vanished, and a large mob attacked the riders again. Furious, the attorney general deputized local federal officials as marshals and ordered them to escort the freedom riders to the state line, where Mississippi forces would take over. Battered and bloodied, the riders continued to the state capital, Jackson. There they were peacefully arrested for violating Mississippi's recently passed **public order laws.** The jails quickly filled as more freedom riders arrived and were arrested—328 by the end of the summer. The freedom rides ended in September 1961 when the administration declared that the Interstate Commerce Commission would uphold the Supreme Court decision prohibiting segregation. Faced with direct federal involvement, most state and local authorities desegregated bus and train terminals.

Robert Kennedy hoped to use that direct involvement to support the integration of the University of Mississippi by **James Meredith** in September 1962. The attorney general sent a hundred federal marshals to guard Meredith, but the tactic did not work. Thousands of white students and nonstudents attacked Meredith and the marshals. Two people were killed, and 166 marshals were wounded before five thousand army troops arrived and restored order. Protected by federal forces, Meredith finished the year. In May 1963, the University of Mississippi had its first African American graduate.

As Meredith prepared to graduate, Martin Luther King Jr. organized a series of protest marches to overturn segregation in Birmingham. King expected a violent white reaction, which would force federal intervention and raise national awareness and support. On Good Friday, 1963, King led the first march. He

Anniston, Alabama, was the end of the line for this bus of freedom riders. As riders got off the bus, they were pelted by stones and savagely beaten by a white mob. The bus was fire-bombed and its tires slashed. A second bus continued on to Montgomery. *Corbis-Bettmann.*

was quickly arrested and, from his cell, wrote a nineteen-page "letter" defending his confrontational tactics, aimed at those who denounced his activism in favor of patience. The "Letter from a Birmingham Jail" called for immediate and continuous peaceful civil disobedience. Freedom was "never given voluntarily by the oppressor," King asserted, but "must be demanded by the oppressed." Smuggled out of jail and read aloud in churches and printed in newspapers across the nation, the letter rallied support for King's efforts. In Birmingham the marches continued, and on May 3 young and old alike filled the city's streets. Sheriff "Bull" Connor's police attacked the marchers with nightsticks, attack dogs, and high-pressure fire hoses. Television caught it all, including the arrest of more than thirteen hundred battered and bruised children. Connor's brutality not only horrified much of the American public but also caused

public order laws   Laws passed by many southern communities to discourage civil rights protests; the laws allowed the police to arrest anyone suspected of intending to disrupt public order.

James Meredith   Black student admitted to the University of Mississippi under federal court order in 1962; in spite of rioting by racist mobs, he finished the year and graduated in 1963.

On August 28, 1963, one-quarter of a million people gathered in Washington, D.C., to support racial equality. Martin Luther King Jr. electrified the crowd by saying, "I have a dream that my four little children will one day live . . . where they will not be judged by the color of their skin but by the content of their character." *Francis Miller, LIFE Magazine ©Time Warner Inc.*

many Birmingham blacks to reject the tactic of nonviolence. The following day, many African Americans fought the police with stones and clubs. Fearing more violence, King and Birmingham's business element met on May 10, and white business owners agreed to hire black salespeople. Neither the agreement nor King's pleading, however, halted the violence, and two days later President Kennedy ordered three thousand troops to Birmingham to maintain order and to uphold the integration agreement. "The sound of the explosion in Birmingham," King observed, "reached all the way to Washington."

Indeed, Birmingham encouraged Kennedy to fulfill his campaign promise to make civil rights a priority. In June 1963, he announced that America could not be truly free "until all its citizens were free" and sent Congress civil rights legislation that would mandate integration in public places. To pressure Congress to act on the bill, King and other civil rights leaders organized a **March on Washington.** During the August 28 march, King gave an address that electrified the throng. He promised to continue the struggle until justice flowed "like a mighty stream," and he warned about a "whirlwind of revolt" if black rights were denied. "I have a dream," he offered, "that even Mississippi could become an oasis of freedom and justice" and that "all of God's children, black men and white men, Jews and Gentiles, Protestants and Catholics, will be able to join hands and sing . . . 'Free

at last! Free at last! Thank God almighty, we are free at last!'" It was a stirring speech, but it did not move Congress to act. The civil rights bill stalled in committee, while in the South whites vowed to maintain segregation, and racial violence continued. In Birmingham, within weeks of King's "I Have a Dream" speech, a church bombing killed four young black girls attending Sunday school.

Flexible Response

▪ How did the Cold War shape Kennedy's foreign policy?

▪ What challenges did the Third World and developing nations provide Kennedy?

▪ What actions did Kennedy take in Latin America and Vietnam to promote American interests?

From day one, President Kennedy favored foreign over domestic policy. In his inaugural address, he dropped most of the material on domestic policy and concentrated on foreign policy, generating the power-

March on Washington Meeting of a quarter of a million civil rights supporters in Washington in 1963, at which Martin Luther King Jr. delivered his "I Have a Dream" speech.

It Matters

Letter from Jail

In 1963, Martin Luther King Jr. wrote and smuggled out of a Birmingham jail a lengthy letter calling for support for the ongoing civil rights struggle. His letter provides a lasting statement about oppression and freedom that places the African American struggle in the context of America's history and provides an enduring guide for other groups and peoples. "Oppressed people cannot remain oppressed forever," King wrote. "The yearning for freedom eventually manifests itself, and that is what has happened to the American Negro . . . and with his black brothers of Africa and his brown and yellow brothers of Asia, South America and the Caribbean."

ful lines: "We shall pay any price, bear any burden, meet any hardship, support any friend, oppose any foe to assure the survival and success of liberty." Advised by his close circle of "action intellectuals," Kennedy was anxious to meet whatever challenges the United States faced, from the arms race to the space race, to winning the allegiance of Third World countries.

To back up his foreign policies, Kennedy instituted a new defense strategy called **flexible response** and significantly expanded military spending to pay for it. Flexible response involved continuing support for NATO and other multilateral alliances, plus further development of nuclear capabilities and intercontinental **ballistic missiles** (ICBMs). Another aspect of flexible response centered on conventional, nonnuclear warfare. With increased budgets, each branch of the service sought new weapons and equipment and developed new strategies for deploying them. Of special urgency was how to win the Cold War in the world's developing and Third World nations. In that volatile arena of political instability, economic inequalities, and social conflicts, the opportunity was ripe for the West and the Communist bloc to expand their influence. It was a struggle that Kennedy meant to win. To strengthen pro-Western governments with advisers and to combat revolutionaries, special counterinsurgency forces, such as the Green Berets, were developed. The military commitment, though, was second to wider economic strategies that provided direct government aid and private investment to "friendly" nations. This effort also included the personal involvement of American volunteers participating in the **Peace Corps.** Beginning in March 1961, more than ten thousand idealistic young Americans enrolled for two years to help win the "hearts and minds" of what Kennedy called "the rising peoples" around the world, staffing schools, constructing homes, building roads, and making other improvements.

Confronting Castro and the Soviets

Kennedy saw Latin America as an important part of the Cold War struggle for influence in developing nations. Castro's success in Cuba reinforced the idea that Latin America and the Caribbean were important battlegrounds in the struggle against communism. Seeking a new approach to Latin America, in 1961 Kennedy introduced the **Alliance for Progress,** a foreign-aid package promising more than $20 billion to show that "liberty and progress walk hand in hand." In return, Latin American governments were to introduce land and tax reforms and commit themselves to improving education and their people's standard of living. Overall, it was a plan that, Kennedy noted, could "successfully counter the Communists in the Americas." Results fell short of expectations. The United States granted far less aid than proposed, and Latin American governments implemented few reforms and frequently squandered the aid. Throughout the 1960s in Latin America, the gap between rich and poor widened, and the number of military dictatorships increased.

flexible response   Kennedy's strategy of considering a variety of military and nonmilitary options when facing foreign-policy decisions.

ballistic missiles   Missiles without fins or wings whose path cannot be changed once launched; their range can be from a few miles to intercontinental. In 2003 an estimated 35 nations had ballistic missiles.

Peace Corps   Program established by President Kennedy in 1961 to send young American volunteers to other nations as educators, health workers, and technicians.

Alliance for Progress   Program proposed by Kennedy in 1961 through which the United States provided aid for social and economic programs in Latin American countries; Congress trimmed appropriations following Kennedy's death.

Soviet leader Nikita Khrushchev met with John Kennedy at the Vienna Summit in June 1961. After their first meetings, Kennedy, who had been warned that Khrushchev's style ranged from "cherubic to choleric," was convinced that the Soviet leader had bested him, and that he had appeared to be a man "with no guts." Following the Vienna Summit, Kennedy was determined to be tougher with the Soviets. "If Khrushchev wants to rub my nose in the dirt, it's all over," Kennedy stated after their meeting. *Wide World Photos.*

The Alliance for Progress, however, would not deal with the problem of Castro. Determined to remove the Cuban dictator, Kennedy decided to implement the Eisenhower administration's covert plan to topple the Cuban leader (see page 873). In March 1960, the Central Intelligence Agency began training Cuban exiles and mercenaries for an invasion of Cuba, which included a scheme to assassinate Castro.

The invasion of Cuba began on April 17, 1961. More than fourteen hundred Cuban exiles landed at the Bahía de Cochinos, the **Bay of Pigs.** The strike was a failure, and within three days Castro's forces had captured or killed most of the invaders. Kennedy took responsibility for the fiasco but indicated no regrets for his aggressive policy and the violation of Cuban territory, vowing to continue the "relentless struggle" against Castro and communism. Responding to Kennedy's orders to disrupt Cuba, **Operation Mongoose** was devised. It and other operations sponsored CIA-backed raids that destroyed roads, bridges, factories, and crops, and about thirty attempts to assassinate Castro.

After the Bay of Pigs disaster, in early June 1961, Kennedy met with Soviet leader Nikita Khrushchev in Vienna. Both men were eager to show their toughness. Kennedy stressed American determination to protect its interests and fulfill its international commitments. The issue of Berlin was especially worrisome because Khrushchev was threatening to sign a peace treaty with East Germany that would give it full control of all four zones of the city.

Returning home, Kennedy asked for massive increases in military spending, tripled the draft, and called fifty-one thousand reservists to active duty. Back in Moscow, Khrushchev renewed atmospheric nuclear weapons testing and reaffirmed his commitment to East Germany and his determination to oust the Allies from Berlin. Kennedy responded by beginning American nuclear testing and voicing his strong support for West Berlin. Some within the administration advocated the use of force if the East Germans or the Soviets interfered with West Berlin. With both sides posturing, many feared armed confrontation over Berlin.

In August 1961, the tension finally broke. The Soviets and East Germans suddenly erected a wall between East and West Berlin to choke off the flow of

Bay of Pigs Site of a 1961 invasion of Cuba by Cuban exiles and mercenaries sponsored by the CIA; the invasion was crushed within three days and embarrassed the United States.

Operation Mongoose Mission authorized by President Kennedy in November 1961, and funded with a $50 million budget, to create conditions for the overthrow of Castro.

refugees fleeing East Germany and Eastern Europe. Although the Berlin Wall challenged Western ideals of freedom, it did not directly threaten the West's presence in West Berlin.

Far more serious than the Berlin crisis was the possibility of nuclear confrontation over Cuba in October 1962. On October 14, an American U-2 spy plane flying over the island discovered that medium-range nuclear missile sites were being built there. Launched from Cuba, such missiles would drastically reduce the time for mobilizing a U.S. counterattack on the Soviet Union. Kennedy promptly decided on a showdown with the Soviets and mustered a small crisis staff.

Negotiations were out of the question until the missiles were removed or destroyed. The military offered a series of recommendations ranging from a military invasion to a "surgical" air strike to destroy the missiles. All proposals were rejected as too dangerous, possibly inviting a Soviet attack on West Berlin or on American nuclear missile sites in Turkey. President Kennedy, supported by his brother, the attorney general, decided to impose a naval blockade around Cuba until Khrushchev met the U.S. demand to remove the missiles. On Monday, October 22, Kennedy went on television and radio to inform the public of the missile sightings and his decision to quarantine Cuba. As 180 American warships got into position to stop Soviet ships carrying supplies for the missiles, army units converged on Florida. The **Strategic Air Command** (SAC) kept a fleet of nuclear-armed B-52s in the air at all times. On Wednesday, October 24, confrontation and perhaps war seemed imminent as two Soviet freighters and a Russian submarine approached the quarantine line. Robert Kennedy recalled, "We were on the edge of a precipice with no way off." Voices around the world echoed his anxiety.

The Soviet vessels, however, stopped short of the blockade. Khrushchev had decided not to test Kennedy's will. After a series of diplomatic maneuvers, the two sides reached an agreement based on an October 26 message from Khrushchev: if the United States agreed not to invade Cuba, the Soviets would remove their missiles. Khrushchev sent another letter the following day that called for the United States to remove existing American missiles in Turkey. Kennedy chose to ignore the second message, and the Soviets agreed to remove their missiles without the United States publicly linking the agreement to withdrawing missiles in Turkey. Privately, the Soviets told Washington that they expected the United States to uphold its agreement to remove American missiles in Turkey. The world breathed a collective sigh of relief.

Kennedy basked in what many viewed as a victory, but he recognized how near the world had come to nuclear war and concluded that it was time to improve Soviet-American relations. A "hot line" telephone link was established between Moscow and Washington to allow direct talks in case of another East-West crisis.

In a major foreign-policy speech in June 1963, Kennedy suggested an end to the Cold War and offered that the United States, as a first step toward improving relations, would halt its nuclear testing. By July, American-Soviet negotiations had produced the **Limited Test Ban Treaty,** which forbade those who signed to conduct nuclear tests in the atmosphere, in space, and under the seas. Underground testing, with its verification problems, was still allowed. By October 1963, one hundred nations had signed the treaty, although the two newest atomic powers, France and China, refused to participate and continued to test in the atmosphere.

Vietnam

South Vietnam represented one of the most challenging issues Kennedy faced. Like Eisenhower, Kennedy saw it as a place where the United States' flexible response could stem communism and develop a stable, democratic nation. But by 1961, President **Ngo Dinh Diem** was losing control of his nation. South Vietnamese Communist rebels, the **Viet Cong,** controlled a large portion of the countryside, having battled Diem's troops, the Army of the Republic of Vietnam (ARVN), to a standstill. Military advisers argued that

---

Strategic Air Command U.S. military unit formed in March 1946 to conduct long-range bombing operations anywhere in the world; its first strategic plan, completed in 1949, projected nuclear attacks on seventy Soviet cities. The Strategic Air Command was abolished in 1992 as part of the reorganization of the Department of Defense. The much smaller interservice U.S. Strategic Command (StratCom) now coordinates nuclear plans for both the army and the navy.

Limited Test Ban Treaty Treaty signed by the United States, the USSR, and nearly one hundred other nations in 1963; it banned nuclear weapons tests in the atmosphere, in outer space, and underwater.

Ngo Dinh Diem President of South Vietnam (1954–1963) who jailed and tortured opponents of his rule; he was assassinated in a coup in 1963.

Viet Cong Vietnamese Communist rebels in South Vietnam.

the use of American troops was necessary to turn the tide. Kennedy was more cautious. "The troops will march in, the bands will play," he said privately, "the crowds will cheer; and in four days everyone will have forgotten. Then we will be told we have to send in more troops. It's like taking a drink. The effect wears off and you have to take another." The South Vietnamese forces would have to continue to do the fighting, but the president agreed to send more "advisers." By November 1963, the United States had sent $185 million in military aid and had committed sixteen thousand advisers to Vietnam—compared with only a few hundred in 1961.

The Viet Cong was only part of the problem. Diem's administration was unpopular, out of touch with the people, and unwilling to heed Washington's pleas for political and social reforms. Some were even concerned that Diem might seek an accord with North Vietnam, and by autumn of 1963, Diem and his inner circle seemed more a liability than an asset. American officials in Saigon secretly informed several Vietnamese generals that Washington would support a change of government. The army acted on November 1, killing Diem and installing a new military government. The change of government, however, brought neither political stability nor improvement in the ARVN's capacity to fight the Viet Cong.

Death in Dallas

With his civil rights and tax-cut legislation in limbo in Congress, a growing military commitment shackling the country to Vietnam, and the economy languishing, Kennedy in late 1963 watched his popularity rating drop below 60 percent. He decided to visit Texas in November to try to heal divisions within the Texas Democratic Party. He was assassinated there on November 22, 1963. The police quickly captured the reputed assassin, Lee Harvey Oswald. The next day a local nightclub owner and gambler, Jack Ruby, shot Oswald to death in the basement of the police station.

Many wondered whether Kennedy's assassination was the work of Oswald alone or part of a larger conspiracy. To dispel rumors, the government hastily formed a commission headed reluctantly by Chief Justice Earl Warren to investigate the assassination and determine if others were involved. The commission hurriedly examined most, but not all, of the available evidence and announced that Oswald was a psychologically disturbed individual who had acted alone. No other gunmen were involved, nor was there any conspiracy. While many Americans accepted the conclusions of the Warren Commission,

others continued to find errors in the report and to suggest additional theories about the assassination.

Kennedy's assassination traumatized the nation. Many people canonized the fallen president as a brilliant, innovative chief executive who combined vitality, youth, and good looks with forceful leadership and good judgment. Lyndon B. Johnson, sworn in as president as he flew back to Washington on the plane carrying Kennedy's body, did not appear to be cut from the same cloth. Kennedy had attended the best eastern schools, enjoyed the cultural and social life associated with wealth, and liked to surround himself with intellectuals. Johnson, a product of public schools and a state teachers college, distrusted intellectuals. Raised in the hill country of Texas, his passion was politics. By 1960, his congressional experiences were unrivaled: he had served from 1937 to 1948 in the House of Representatives and from 1949 to 1961 in the Senate, where he had become Senate majority leader. Johnson knew how to wield political power and get things done in Washington.

Defining a New Presidency

■ How did Johnson's programs build on those started by Kennedy?

■ In what ways did the legislation associated with Johnson's Great Society differ from New Deal programs?

■ How did Johnson's War on Poverty and Great Society further the civil rights movement?

As president, Johnson made those around him aware that he was a liberal. He described himself as a New Dealer and told one adviser that Kennedy was "a little too conservative to suit my taste." Johnson wanted to build a better society, "where progress is the servant of the neediest." Recognizing the political opening generated by the assassination, Johnson immediately committed himself to Kennedy's agenda, and in January 1964 he expanded on it by announcing an "unconditional war on poverty."

Old and New Agendas

Throughout 1964, Johnson transformed Kennedy's quest for action into his own quest for social reform. Wielding the political skill for which he was renowned, he moved Kennedy's tax cut and civil rights bill out of committee and toward passage. The Keynesian tax cut (the Tax Reduction Act), designed to generate more economic growth, became law in February. The civil rights bill moved more slowly, especially in the Senate,

In implementing his Great Society, Johnson sought to reduce poverty and provide more opportunities for those at the bottom of the economic ladder. In 1965, Johnson signed the Appalachian Regional Development Act designed to provide economic development to a region that contained more than 17 million people, many living well below the poverty level. Seen here, President and Mrs. Johnson visit a family of ten that made only $400 a year. © *Bettmann/Corbis.*

where it faced a stubborn southern filibuster. Johnson traded political favors for Republican backing to silence the fifty-seven-day filibuster, and the **Civil Rights Act of 1964** became law on July 2. The act made it illegal to discriminate for reasons of race, religion, or gender in places and businesses that served the public. Putting force behind the law, Congress established a federal Fair Employment Practices Committee (FEPC) and empowered the executive branch to withhold federal funds from institutions that violated its provisions.

By August 1964, the War on Poverty had begun, aimed at benefiting the 20 percent of the population who were classified as poor. In 1962, social critic Michael Harrington had alerted the public to widespread poverty in America with his book *The Other America,* which indicated that 35 million people lived in poverty. His findings were confirmed by a government study that defined the poverty line at $3,130 for an urban household of four and at $1,925 for a rural family; the study also found that almost 40 percent of the poor (15.6 million) were under the age of 18.

The **War on Poverty** was to be fought on two fronts: expanding economic opportunities and improving the

Civil Rights Act of 1964   Law that barred segregation in public facilities and forbade employers to discriminate on the basis of race, religion, sex, or national origin.

War on Poverty   Lyndon Johnson's program to help Americans escape poverty through education, job training, and community development.

social environment. In March, after having selected **Sargent Shriver** to direct the offensive, the administration introduced to Congress the economic opportunity bill. Passed in August, the Economic Opportunity Act established a variety of programs to be coordinated by an Office of Economic Opportunity. The cornerstones of the effort were education and job training. Improved "training and . . . job opportunities," Johnson stated, would "help more Americans, especially young Americans, to escape from squalor and misery." Johnson was, according to Vice President Hubert Humphrey, "a nut on education . . . he just believed in it, just like some people believe in miracle cures." Under Shriver's direction, the Job Corps, Head Start, and the Work Incentive Program provided new educational and economic opportunities for the disadvantaged. Job Corps branches enrolled unemployed teens and young adults (16 to 21) lacking skills, while Head Start reached out to pre-kindergarten children to provide disadvantaged preschoolers an opportunity to gain important thinking and social skills. Another program called Volunteers in Service to America (VISTA), modeled after the Peace Corps, sent service-minded Americans to help improve life in regions of poverty. Among the most unique and ambitious programs was the Community Action Program (CAP). It allowed disadvantaged community organizations to target local needs by allowing direct access to federal funds. The program was never as effective as projected because of poor local leadership and opposition from state and local governments that wanted to control the funds. CAP did, however, generate local activism and agencies, including legal aid and community health clinics.

To assure his election in November, Johnson figured he needed passage of Kennedy's tax cuts, the civil rights bill, and his War on Poverty. By August Congress had approved all three, and public opinion polls showed significant support for the president in all parts of the nation, except the South. They also indicated that he would win easily against any Republican opponent. Conservative Republicans made his election even more likely by nominating U.S. senator **Barry Goldwater.** To some it appeared that conservatives were more interested in promoting their ideology than in winning the White House, and one prominent Democrat noted that the Republicans were "going on a Kamikaze mission."

Plainspoken and direct, Goldwater had voted against the 1964 Civil Rights Act and was an outspoken opponent of "Big Government" and New Deal–style programs. On the world stage, the Ari-

zona Republican promised a more intense anti-Communist crusade and appeared willing not only to commit American troops in Vietnam but also to use nuclear weapons against Communist nations, including Cuba and North Vietnam. The Democrats presented Goldwater as a dangerous radical. Meanwhile, Johnson promoted his Great Society and promised that "American boys" would not "do the fighting for Asian boys." Johnson won easily in a lopsided election.

Implementing the Great Society

Not only did Goldwater lose, but so too did many Republicans—moderates and conservatives—as more than forty new Democrats entered Congress. Armed with a seeming mandate for action and reform, Johnson pushed forward legislation to enact his **Great Society.** He told aides that they must hurry before the natural opposition of politics returned. Between 1964 and 1968, more than sixty Great Society programs were put in place (see Table 28.1). Most sought to provide better economic and social opportunities by removing barriers thrown up by health, education, region, and race.

One of Johnson's Great Society goals was to further equality for African Americans. Within months of his election, he signed an executive order that, like the old Fair Employment Practices Commission, required government contractors to practice nondiscrimination in hiring and on the job. He also appointed the first African American to the cabinet, Secretary of Housing and Urban Development Robert Weaver; the first African American woman to the federal courts, Judge Constance Baker Motley; and the first African American to the Supreme Court, Justice Thurgood Marshall.

Sargent Shriver Married into the Kennedy family, he held many positions during the Kennedy-Johnson years; served as Director of the Peace Corps, 1961–1966; Director of Office of Economic Opportunity, 1964–1968; and ambassador to France, 1968–1970. In 1972 the was nominated by the Democratic Party to be vice president.

Barry Goldwater Conservative Republican senator from Arizona who ran unsuccessfully for president in 1964.

Great Society Social program that Johnson announced in 1964; it included the War on Poverty, protection of civil rights, and funding for education.

TABLE 28.1 War on Poverty and Great Society Programs, 1964–1966

1964	1965	1966
Tax Reduction Act	Elementary and Secondary Education Act	Demonstration Cities and Metropolitan Development Act
Civil Rights Act	Voting Rights Act	Motor Vehicle Safety Act
Economic Opportunity Act	Medical Care Act (Medicare and Medicaid)	Truth in Packaging Act
Equal Employment Opportunity Commission	Head Start (Office of Economic Opportunity)	Model Cities Act
Twenty-fourth Amendment	Upward Bound (Office of Economic Opportunity)	Clean Water Restoration Act
Job Corps (Office of Economic Opportunity)	Water Quality Act and Air Quality Act	Department of Transportation
Legal services for the poor	Department of Housing and Urban Development	
VISTA	National Endowment for the Arts and Humanities	
Wilderness Act	Immigration and Nationality Act	

Blacks applauded the president's actions but vowed to continue their activism, realizing that passage of a civil rights act did not end discrimination or poverty and were all too aware that large pockets of active opposition to civil rights remained—especially in Alabama and Mississippi. To keep up the pressure, Martin Luther King Jr. explained, African Americans would peacefully press for change and would be physically attacked, and Americans, "in the name of decency," would demand federal intervention and "remedial legislation."

A major goal was to expand black voting in the South. For nearly one hundred years, most southern whites had viewed voting as an activity for whites only and, through the poll tax and their control of the ballot, had maintained their political power and a segregated society. The ratification of the Twenty-fourth Amendment (banning the poll tax) in January 1964 was a major step toward dismantling that system, and by mid-1964 plans were under way for black voters to gain access to the ballot. One effort was led by Bob Moses of SNCC, who organized a **Freedom Summer** in Mississippi. Whites and blacks opened "Freedom Schools" to teach literacy and black history, stress black pride and achievements, and help residents register to vote. In Mississippi, as in several other southern states, a voter literacy test required that all questions be answered to the satisfaction of a white registrar. Thus a question calling for "a reasonable interpretation" of an obscure section of the state constitution could be used to block blacks from registering.

Freedom Summer Effort by civil rights groups in Mississippi to register black voters and cultivate black pride during the summer of 1964.

President Johnson's Great Society greatly expanded the role of society in the lives of Americans through passage of civil rights, welfare, and education legislation. In this picture, President Johnson signs legislation establishing Medicare. His wife, Lady Bird, and Vice President Hubert Humphrey watch in the background. *Lyndon B. Johnson Presidential Library.*

In the face of white hostility, voter registration was dangerous work. "You talk about fear," an organizer told recruits. "It's like the heat down there, it's continually oppressive. You think they're rational. But, you know, you suddenly realize, they want to kill you." Indeed, from June through August of 1964, Mississippi was rocked by more than thirty-five shooting incidents, and thirty buildings, many of them churches, were bombed. Hundreds were beaten and arrested, and three Freedom Summer workers were murdered. But the crusade drew national support and registered nearly sixty thousand new African American voters.

Keeping up the pressure, King announced that a voter registration drive was to take place in Selma, Alabama, where only 2.1 percent of eligible black voters were registered. As expected, the police, led by Sheriff Jim Clark, who wore mirrored sunglasses and a helmet and carried a swagger stick, confronted protesters, arresting nearly 2,000. King then called for a **freedom march** from Selma to Montgomery. On March 7, 1965, as scores of reporters watched, hun-

dreds of freedom marchers faced fifty Alabama state troopers and Clark's mounted forces at Pettus Bridge. After ordering the marchers to halt and firing tear gas, Clark's men, brandishing clubs and whips, chased them down. Television coverage of the assault stirred nationwide condemnation of Clark's tactics and support for King and the marchers. When Alabama's staunch segregationist governor George Wallace told President Johnson that he could not provide protection for the marchers, Johnson ordered the National Guard, two army battalions, and 250 federal marshals to escort the protesters. The march resumed on March 21 with about 3,200 marchers. When it arrived in Montgomery on March 27, more than 25,000 had joined.

> **freedom march** Civil rights march from Selma to Montgomery, Alabama, in March 1965; the violent treatment of protesters by local authorities helped galvanize national opinion against segregationists.

The summer of 1964 was called "Freedom Summer," as hundreds of civil rights volunteers—many of them college students—converged on Alabama and Mississippi to conduct voter registration drives, often facing violent opposition. Many were beaten, some were jailed, and some lost their lives, but as Anne Moody wrote in her autobiography, *Coming of Age in Mississippi*, "threats did not stop them." *Art and Artifacts Division, Schomburg Center for Research in Black Culture, the New York Public Library, Astor, Lenox, and Tilden Foundations.*

Johnson used the violence in Selma to pressure Congress to pass the **Voting Rights Act,** which he signed into law in August 1965. It banned a variety of methods that states had been using to deny blacks the right to vote, including Mississippi's literacy test, and had immediate effect. Across the South, the percentage of African Americans registered to vote rose an average of 30 percent between 1965 and 1968 (see Map 28.2). In Mississippi, it went from 7 to 59 percent, and in Selma, more than 60 percent of qualified African Americans voted in 1968, stopping Sheriff Clark's bid for reelection.

But civil rights legislation was only one of many facets of the Great Society. The Appalachian Regional Development Act (1965), the Public Works and Development Act (1965), and the Model Cities Act (1966) focused on developing economic growth in cities and long-depressed regional areas. An Omnibus Housing Bill (1965) provided $8 billion for constructing low- and middle-income housing and supplementing low-income rent programs. In a related move, a cabinet-level Department of Housing and Urban Development was created in 1965. Mass-transit laws (1964 and 1966) provided needed funds for the nation's bus and rail systems, and consumer protection legislation established new and higher standards for product safety and truth in advertising. Immigration laws also underwent major modification. The Immigration and Nationality Act of 1965 dropped the racial and ethnic discrimination in immigration policies that had been in effect since the 1920s by setting a uniform yearly limit on immigration from any one nation.

Responding to his own concerns and to rising voices, Johnson also worked to have environmental law enacted. It was increasingly clear that many of the products developed during the war and commonly used by the 1950s, such as plastics, fertilizers, and pesticides, carried with them health problems. Efforts to protect the environment and America's wilderness had intensified since the Eisenhower administration's efforts to make it easier for business interests to have access to wilderness areas that contained raw materials, like oil, gas, and timber. In the mid-1950s, environmentalists effectively prevented two dams from being built in Dinosaur National Park. Kennedy supported bettering the environment and the idea of preserving more wilderness areas. In 1963, a Clear Air Act was passed, and under Johnson in 1964, the Wilderness Act designated 9 million acres of land that people could only visit. Not only were more and more Americans concerned about saving the wilderness, they were also becoming aware of chemical pollutants that threatened the environment and the health of the nation.

In 1962, biologist Rachel Carson's book *Silent Spring* alerted readers to the health dangers of the pesticide DDT and helped fuel a growing movement to protect the environment. While a Kennedy-appointed committee supported Carson's findings, it

Voting Rights Act   Law passed by Congress in 1965 that outlawed literacy and other voting tests and authorized federal supervision of elections in areas where black voting had been restricted.

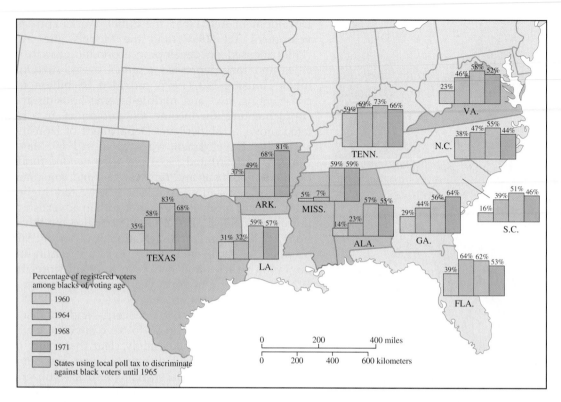

MAP 28.2 African Americans and the Southern Vote, 1960–1971 An important part of the civil rights movement was to reestablish the African American vote that had been stripped away in the South following Reconstruction. Between 1960 and 1971, with the outlawing of the poll tax and other voter restrictions, African American voter participation rose significantly across the South.

was not until 1972 that the federal government banned its use. Johnson also supported the growing movement to improve the environment, and wanted to impose national standards to prevent environmental pollution. His proposals met stiff opposition from industry and underwent modifications in Congress. Still, the Water Quality and Air Quality Acts signed by Johnson in October 1965 were a beginning. Over the next three years, he would guide through Congress acts that improved water quality, expanded wilderness areas, and removed billboards from federal highways.

At the top of Johnson's priorities, however, were health and education. Above all, he wanted those two "coonskins on the wall." The Elementary and Secondary Education Act (1965) was the first general educational funding act by the federal government. It granted more than a billion dollars to public and parochial schools for textbooks, library materials, and special education programs. Poor and rural school districts were supposed to receive the highest per-

centage of federal support. But, as with many Great Society programs, implementation fell short of intention, and much of the money went to affluent suburban school districts. Johnson's biggest "coonskin" was the Medical Care Act (1965), which established **Medicaid** and **Medicare** to help pay healthcare costs for the elderly and individuals on welfare. In 1966 Democrats were calling the Eighty-ninth Congress "the Congress of accomplished hopes." They were overly optimistic. Despite the flood of legislation,

Medicaid Program of health insurance for the poor established in 1965; it provides states with money to buy healthcare for people on welfare.

Medicare Program of health insurance for the elderly and disabled established in 1965; it provides government payment for healthcare supplied by private doctors and hospitals.

most of the Great Society's programs were under-funded and diminishing in popularity. Republicans and conservative Democrats had enough votes in Congress to effectively oppose further "welfare state" proposals. Supporting the opposition was the growing cost and dissatisfaction with the war in Vietnam, a backlash against urban riots and feminist militancy, and an expanding view that the federal government's efforts to wage war on poverty and build a "Great Society" were futile. Still, Johnson's programs had contributed to a near 10 percent decrease in the number of people living in poverty and a one-third drop in infant mortality. For African Americans there were also good statistics: unemployment dropped over four years to 42 percent while average family income rose 53 percent.

New Voices

▪ How do the urban riots and the emergence of the Black Power movement reflect a new agenda for the civil rights movement? In what ways were the voices of Black Power new?

▪ What limitations on equality did women face, and how did they organize to overcome those barriers? What was the critique of American values made by some women and homosexuals?

▪ What changes did the youth movement seek? How did the counterculture reject traditional social norms?

By the end of 1965, legislation had ended de jure segregation and voting restrictions. Equality, however, depended on more than laws. Neither the Civil Rights Act nor the Voting Rights Act guaranteed justice, removed oppressive poverty, provided jobs, or ensured a higher standard of living. De facto discrimination and prejudice remained, and African American frustrations—born of raised expectations—poverty, prejudice, and violence soon changed the nature of civil rights protest and ignited northern cities. During the 1960s, more than a million mostly poor and unskilled African Americans left the South each year. Most sought a better life in northern and western cities, but they mostly found soaring unemployment and cities unable or unwilling to provide adequate social services. Economics, not segregation, was the key issue: "I'd eat at your lunch counter—if only I had a job," spelled out the problem for many urban blacks. By the mid-1960s, the nation's cities were primed for racial trouble. Minor race riots occurred in Harlem and Rochester, New York, during the summer of 1964, but it was the Watts riot and the militant new voices that shook the nation.

Urban Riots and Black Power

In Los Angeles, African Americans earned more per capita and owned more homes than African Americans in any other American city. Within Los Angeles, most African Americans lived in a 50-square-mile area called **Watts.** To most outside observers, Watts did not look like a ghetto. It was a community of well-maintained single-family homes and duplexes. But looks were deceptive. With a population exceeding 250,000, Watts had a population density more than four times higher per block than the rest of the city. Schools were overcrowded, and male unemployment hovered at 34 percent. Patrolling Watts was the nearly all-white L.A. police force, which had a reputation for racism and brutality.

In this climate, on August 11, 1965, what began as a drunk driving arrest became a riot. Stores were looted and set on fire, cars were overturned and set ablaze, firefighters and police were attacked and unable to either put out the flames or restore order. Thirty-six hours passed until sixteen thousand poorly trained and equipped members of the California National Guard, along with police and sheriff's deputies, began to calm the storm. The costs of the Watts riot were high: 34 dead, including 28 African Americans, more than 900 injured, and $45 million in property destroyed.

The Watts riot also signaled a change in attitude among African Americans and shattered the complacency of many whites who thought civil rights was just a southern problem. In addition, the riot demonstrated a growing willingness of African Americans to reject nonviolence. The debate about goals and tactics intensified, with concrete goals gaining favor over "dreams" and force becoming the tool of choice. In 1964 Martin Luther King Jr. had received the Nobel Peace Prize, but in 1965, when he spoke to the people of Watts after the rioting, he discovered they had little use for his "dreams." He was shouted down and jeered. "Hell, we don't need no damn dreams," one skeptic remarked. "We want jobs."

Watts Predominantly black neighborhood of Los Angeles where a race riot in August 1965 did $45 million in damage and took the lives of twenty-eight blacks.

Dropping his "slave name," Malcolm Little took the name Malcolm X—the letter "X" representing the stolen identities of African slaves. A member of the Black Muslims, he became one of the most recognized and controversial African American nationalist leaders. He was assassinated in 1963 by members of the Nation of Islam after forming a rival organization. *John Launois/Black Star/Stockphoto.com.*

dependence from white allies and the violent rhetoric widened the gap between moderates and radicals.

The new voices also found advocates among the Nation of Islam, or **Black Muslims.** Founded by Elijah Muhammad in the 1930s, the movement attracted mostly young males and demanded adherence to a strict moral code that prohibited the use of drugs and alcohol. Black Muslims preached black superiority and separatism from an evil white world. By the early 1960s, there were nearly a hundred thousand Black Muslims, including **Malcolm X.**

A life of hard drugs, pimping, and burglary landed Malcolm Little in prison by the age of 20. Behind bars, his intellectual abilities blossomed. He devoured the prison library, took correspondence courses, and converted to the Nation of Islam—becoming Malcolm X. On his release in 1952 at age 27, he quickly became one of the Black Muslims' most powerful and respected leaders. A mesmerizing speaker, he rejected integration with a white society that, he said, emasculated blacks by denying them power and personal identity. "Our enemy is the white man!" he roared. But in 1964 he reevaluated his policy. Though still a Black Nationalist, he admitted that to achieve their goals Black Muslims needed to cooperate with other civil rights groups and with some whites. He broke with Elijah Muhammad, and the defection cost him his life. On February 21, 1965, three Black Muslims assassinated him in Harlem. After his death, Malcolm X's *Autobiography* (1965), chronicling his personal triumph over white oppression, became a revered guide for many blacks.

Carmichael and Malcolm X represented only two

Competing with King were new voices that called on blacks to seek power through solidarity, independence, and, if necessary, violence. They called for **Black Power.**

African Americans needed to use the same means as whites, argued one veteran of the battle to integrate Mississippi: "If he pose with a smile, meet him with a smile, and if he pose with a gun, meet him with a gun." Many in SNCC and CORE agreed and embraced Black Power. The new leader of SNCC was **Stokely Carmichael** (see Individual Choices, pages 894–895), who exalted Black Power: "I'm not going to beg the white man for anything I deserve," he announced in 1966. "I'm going to take it." SNCC and CORE quickly changed from biracial, nonviolent organizations to Black Power resistance movements that stressed Black Nationalism. The insistence on in-

Black Power   Movement begun in 1966 that rejected the nonviolent, coalition-building approach of traditional civil rights groups and advocated black control of black organizations; the self-determination approach was adopted by Latinos (Brown Power) and Native Americans (Red Power) as well.

Stokely Carmichael   Civil rights activist who led SNCC and popularized the term "Black Power" to describe the need for blacks to use militant tactics to force whites to accept political change.

Black Muslims   Popular name for the Nation of Islam, an African American religious group founded by Elijah Muhammad, which professed Islamic religious beliefs and emphasized black separatism.

Malcolm X   Black activist who advocated black separatism as a member of the Nation of Islam; in 1963 he converted to orthodox Islam and two years later was assassinated.

of the strident African American voices advocating direct—and, if necessary, violent—action. Adopting the name and symbol of the Mississippi Freedom Party, Huey P. Newton, Eldridge Cleaver, and Bobby Seale organized the **Black Panthers** in Oakland, California, in 1966. Although they pursued community action, such as developing school lunch programs, they were more noticeable for being well armed and willing to use their weapons. FBI director J. Edgar Hoover called them "the most dangerous . . . of all extremist groups."

The militant black nationalism and calls for self-defense by a new wave of black leaders appeared to fuel a growing number of race riots that shook more than three hundred cities between 1965 and 1968. The summer of 1967 marked the worst year, with more than seventy-five major riots. The deadliest occurred in Detroit. With its mayor strongly supporting civil rights and working closely with civil rights organizations, Detroit appeared to be a stable city. It had received more than $200 million in federal grants for urban renewal, job training, and schools. Yet, as in Watts, tensions simmered beneath the surface. Jobs were few, urban renewal projects and a new highway system were breaking apart black neighborhoods, and the police were widely seen as racist. When in July the police raided an after-hours bar, the black neighborhoods exploded. In the five days it took the army to quell the riot, thirty-four people died, seven thousand were arrested, and millions of dollars' worth of property was destroyed.

Responding to the riots in Detroit and elsewhere, Johnson created a special commission, chaired by Governor Otto Kerner of Illinois, to investigate their causes. The commission report, issued in March 1968, put the primary blame on the racist attitudes of white America. The study described two Americas, one white and one black, and concluded: "Pervasive discrimination and segregation in employment, education, and housing have resulted in the continuing exclusion of great numbers of Negroes from the benefits of economic progress."

Just a month later, a new wave of riots spread across the United States following the assassination of Martin Luther King Jr. by a white racist. King had worked hard to regain his leadership of the civil rights movement after the Watts riot and the emergence of Black Power. Shifting from legal rights to economic rights, he had become a champion of the black urban **underclass,** criticizing the capitalistic system that relegated millions of people to poverty. Still an advocate of nonviolence, King called for mass demonstrations to compel economic and social jus-

tice. He was in Memphis supporting striking black sanitation workers when, on April 4, 1968, he was killed by James Earl Ray. Spontaneously, African Americans took to the streets in 168 cities, including Washington, D.C.

Before long, the flames engulfing American cities and the fiery cries of "Burn, baby, burn!" and "Black Power!" sparked a white backlash. Many Americans, fearful of Black Power advocates and increasing urban violence, backed away from supporting civil rights. Republican politicians were especially vocal. California governor Ronald Reagan argued the "riff-raff" theory of urban problems: "mad dogs" and "lawbreakers" were the sole cause of the trouble. Most Americans applauded as the FBI and police cracked down on the radicals, especially the Black Panther Party, many of whose members were arrested or killed in battles with authorities. Others, including Cleaver and Carmichael, left for Africa.

From King to Carmichael, African Americans confronted the old order. But they were not alone. The 1960s found many other individuals and groups arguing and protesting for change. Young adults questioned social and cultural values and voiced demands for a more liberated society, one that placed few barriers on individual actions. Women in increasing numbers were seeking to alter the status quo and were rejecting the notion that they were fulfilled by running their homes and serving their families. For some, what began as an effort to gain equality resulted in a larger critique of traditional American views about sexuality and gender.

Rejecting the Feminine Mystique

The willingness of women to question their popular image was partially a response to the changing reality of society and the workplace. Since the 1950s, more women were entering the work force, graduating from college, getting divorces, and becoming heads of households. Households headed by single women

---

Black Panthers   Black revolutionary party founded in 1966 that endorsed violence as a means of social change; many of its leaders were killed in confrontations with police or imprisoned.

underclass   The lowest economic class; the term carries the implication that members of this class are so disadvantaged by poverty that they have little or no chance to escape it.

In 1972, Title IX of the Education Amendments of 1972 required gender equality in school and college sports, dramatically changing the nature of women's athletics by igniting a women's sports boom. In this 1967 picture, the first woman to attempt the running of the Boston Marathon—a previously all-male event—is attacked by a race official and prevented from finishing the race. Today, the Boston Marathon celebrates both men and women marathon runners. © Bettmann/Corbis.

were among the most impoverished group in America. Women complained that gender stereotyping denied them access to better-paying career jobs. The Kennedy administration's 1963 report of the Presidential Commission on the Status of Women confirmed in stark statistics that women constituted a social and economic underclass. They worked for less pay than white males (on average 40 percent less), were more likely to be fired or laid off, and rarely reached top career positions. It was not solely in the workplace that women faced discrimination. Throughout the country, divorce, credit, and property laws generally favored men, and in several states women were not even allowed to serve on juries. The president's commission provided statistics, but it was **Betty Friedan's** 1963 bestseller *The Feminine Mystique* that many regard as the beginning of the women's movement. After reviewing the responsibilities of the housewife (making beds, grocery shopping, driving children everywhere, preparing meals and snacks, and pleasing her husband), Friedan asked: "Is this all?" She concluded it was not enough. Women needed to overcome the "feminine mystique" that promised them fulfillment in the domestic arts. She called on women to set their own goals and seek careers outside the home. Her book, combined with the presidential report, provided new perspectives to women and contributed to a renewed women's movement.

In 1963, Congress began to address women's issues when it passed the **Equal Pay Act.** Also engendering more activism was the passage of the 1964 Civil Rights Act with the inclusion of **Title VII.** The original version of the bill made no mention of discrimination on account of sex, but Representative

Martha Griffins (D-Michigan) joined with conservative Democrat Howard Smith of Virginia to add the word *sex* to the civil rights act. As finally approved, Title VII prohibited discrimination on the basis of race, religion, creed, national origin, or sex.

Many people hoped Title VII marked the beginning of a serious effort by government to provide gender equality. But when the Equal Employment Opportunity Commission, established in 1964 to support the law, and the Johnson administration showed little interest in dealing with gender discrimination, women formed organizations to promote their interests and to persuade the government to enforce Title VII. The most prominent women's organization to emerge was the **National Organization for Women (NOW)**, formed in 1966. With Betty Friedan as presi-

Betty Friedan Feminist who wrote *The Feminine Mystique* in 1963 and helped found the National Organization for Women in 1966.

Equal Pay Act Forbids employers engaged in commerce or in the production of goods for commerce to pay different wages for equal work based on sex. Some employers continued to pay lower wages to women arguing that the jobs were not exactly equal.

Title VII Provision of the Civil Rights Act of 1964 that guarantees women legal protection against discrimination.

National Organization for Women Women's rights organization founded in 1966 to fight discrimination against women; to improve educational, employment, and political opportunities for women; and to fight for equal pay for equal work.

dent, NOW launched an aggressive campaign to draw attention to sex discrimination and redress wrongs. It demanded an Equal Rights Amendment to the Constitution to ensure gender equality and pushed for easier access to birth-control devices and the right to have an abortion. NOW grew rapidly from about 300 in 1966 to 175,000 in 1968. But the women's movement was larger than NOW and represented a variety of voices.

Rejecting Gender Roles

By the end of the decade, some of those seeking change went beyond economics and politics in their critique of American society, taking aim at existing norms of sex and gender roles. Radical feminists, for example, called for a redefinition of sexuality and repudiated America's enchantment with family, marriage, and male-dominated society. "We identify the agents of our oppression as men, ... We are exploited as sex objects, breeders, domestic servants and cheap labor," declared the Redstocking Manifesto in 1969. The New York group that issued the manifesto was among the first to use **"consciousness-raising"** groups to educate women about the oppression they faced because of the sex-gender system. Rita Mae Brown went further, leaving the Redstockings in order to advocate lesbian rights. In 1973 she published her first, acclaimed novel, *Rubyfruit*, which presented lesbianism in a positive light and provided a literary basis for discussion of lesbian life and attitudes.

By the late 1960s, Rita Brown and radical feminists were not the only ones asking society to reconsider its traditional views toward sexuality and gender. Since the 1950s, organizations such as the Daughters of Bilitis and the Mattachine Society had worked quietly to promote new attitudes toward homosexuality and to overturn laws that punished homosexual activities. But most homosexuals remained "in the closet," fearful of reprisals by the "straight" community and its institutions. The Stonewall Riot in 1969, however, brought increased visibility and renewed activism to the homosexual community.

The police raid on the Stonewall Inn in New York City resulted in an unexpected riot as gay patrons fought the police and were joined by other members of the community. A Gay Manifesto called for gays and lesbians to raise their consciousness and rid their minds of "garbage" poured into them by old values. "Liberation . . . is defining for ourselves how and with whom we live. . . . We are only at the beginning."

It was a beginning, and success came slowly. Polls indicated that the majority of Americans still consid-ered homosexuality immoral and even a disease. But by the mid-1970s, those polls indicated a shift as a slight majority of Americans opposed job discrimination based on sexual orientation and seemed willing to show more tolerance of gay lifestyles. Responding to gay rights pressure in 1973, the American Psychiatric Association ended its classification of homosexuality as a mental disorder.

The Youth Movement

Within the civil rights, feminist, and gay rights movements, young college-age adults were among the loudest and most militant calling for change. Across the nation during the 1960s, the impact of an activist youth culture was instrumental in shaping the decade. The "youth culture" was a product of the baby boom as the leading edge of that generation went off to college. More than ever, Americans were pursuing post–high school education—and postponing full-time employment and marriage.

In 1965, more than 40 percent of the nation's high school graduates were attending college, a leap of 13 percent from 1955 and of nearly 30 percent since World War II. Graduate and professional schools were churning out record numbers of advanced degrees. Although the majority of young adults remained quite traditional, an expanding number chose alternative careers and values. Some joined the Peace Corps and VISTA; others led sit-ins, protested injustices, and joined organizations like SNCC and NOW. But all believed that the actions of one person or group could make a difference in transforming society and the world. As they enrolled in colleges in record numbers, some began to question the role of the university and the goals of education. Particularly at huge institutions like the University of California at Berkeley and Los Angeles and the University of Michigan, students complained that humanism and concern for individuals were missing from education. Education seemed sterile, an assembly line producing standardized products, not a crucible of ideas creating independent, thinking individuals. Paul Goodman, in *Growing Up Absurd* (1960), argued that schools destroyed natural creativity and replaced it with a highly structured system that stressed order, conformity, and pragmatism. Education was designed to

---

consciousness-raising   Achieving greater awareness of the nature of political or social issues through group interaction.

meet the needs of administrators and teachers, not students, he charged. Reflecting Goodman's view, many students demanded freedom of expression and a new, more flexible attitude from college administrators and faculty.

Campus activists denounced course requirements and restrictions on dress, behavior, and living arrangements. On some campuses they led protests and staged sit-ins in campus buildings, demanding changes and more student freedoms. By the end of the decade, many colleges and schools had relaxed or eliminated dress codes. Long hair was accepted for males, and casual clothes like faded blue jeans and shorts were common dress for both sexes on most college campuses. Colleges also lifted dorm curfews, visitation restrictions, and other residence rules. Some dorms became coed. Academic departments reduced the number of required courses. By the beginning of the 1970s, many colleges and even some high schools had introduced programs in nontraditional fields such as African American, Native American, and women's studies.

Setting their sights beyond the campus community, some student activists urged that the campus should be a haven for free thought and a marshaling ground for efforts to change society significantly. At the University of Michigan in 1960, Tom Hayden and Al Haber organized **Students for a Democratic Society** (SDS). SDS members insisted that Americans recognize that their affluent nation was also a land of poverty and want and that business and government chose to ignore social inequalities. In 1962 SDS issued its *Port Huron Statement*, which maintained, "The search for truly democratic alternatives to the present, and a commitment to social experimentation with them, is a worthy and fulfilling human enterprise, one which moves us and, we hope, others today." Hayden argued that the country should reallocate its resources according to social need and strive to build "an environment for people to live in with dignity and creativeness."

The youth movement's discontent with social and cultural norms also found expression in what was called the **counterculture.** Many young people spurned the traditional moral and social values of their parents and the 1950s. "Don't trust anyone over 30" was the motto of the young generation. Counterculture thinking grated at conformity and glorified freedom of the spirit and self-knowledge. A large number of teens and young adults began to accuse American society of being "plastic" in its materialism and blind to change, and they sought ways to express their dissatisfaction.

Music was one of the most prominent forms of defiance. Some musicians, like Bob Dylan and Joan Baez, challenged society with protest and antiwar songs rooted in folk music and aimed at specific problems. For the majority, however, rock 'n' roll, which took a variety of forms, remained dominant. Performers like the **Beatles,** an English group that exploded on the American music scene in 1964, were among the most popular, sharing the stage with other British imports such as the Rolling Stones and the Animals, whose behavior and songs depicted a life of pleasure and lack of social restraints. Other musicians, like the Grateful Dead and Jimi Hendrix, turned rock 'n' roll into a new form of music, psychedelic **acid rock,** which acclaimed an uninhibited drug culture.

The Counterculture

The message of much music of the 1960s was that drugs offered another way to be free of the older generation's values. For many coming of age in the 1960s, marijuana, or "pot," was the primary means to get "stoned" or "high." Marijuana advocates claimed that it was nonaddictive and that, unlike the nation's traditional drug—alcohol—it reduced aggression and heightened perception. Thus, they argued, marijuana reinforced the counterculture's ideals of peace, serenity, and self-awareness. A more dangerous and unpredictable drug also became popular with some members of the counterculture: LSD, lysergic acid diethylamide, or "acid," a hallucinogenic drug that alters perception. Harvard psychology professor

---

Students for a Democratic Society   Left-wing student organization founded in 1960 to criticize American materialism and work for social justice.

Port Huron Statement   A 1962 critique of the Cold War and American materialism and complacency by Students for a Democratic Society; it called for "participatory democracy" and for universities to be centers of free speech and activism.

counterculture   A subculture espousing values or lifestyles in opposition to those of the established culture; prominent in the 1960s as members adopted lifestyles that stressed communal living, drugs, Asian religions, and free sexual expression.

Beatles   English rock group that gained international fame in 1964 and disbanded in 1970; they were known for the intelligence of their lyrics and their sophisticated instrumentation.

acid rock   Rock music having a driving, repetitive beat and lyrics that suggest psychedelic drug experiences.

To many, the counterculture was defined by "hippie" communes, where groups of young people left conventional society to establish alternative lifestyles, often close to nature, like the setting shown. In this picture, members of a commune use a bus named "The Road Hog" to participate in a Fourth of July parade in New Mexico. *Lisa Law/The Image Works.*

Timothy Leary argued that by "tripping" on LSD people could "turn on, tune in, and drop out" of the rat race that was American society. Although most youths did not use drugs, drugs offered some within the counterculture and the nation a new experience that many believed was liberating. Drugs also proved to be destructive and deadly, contributing to the deaths of several counterculture figures, including musicians Jimi Hendrix, Jim Morrison, and Janis Joplin.

Another realm of traditional American values the counterculture overturned was sex. Some young people appalled their parents and society by questioning, if not rejecting, the values that placed restrictions on sexual activities. Sex was a form of human expression, they argued, and if it felt good, why stifle it? New openness about sexuality and relaxation of the stigma on extramarital sex turned out to be significant legacies of the 1960s. But the philosophy of **free love** also had a negative side as increased sexual activity contributed to a rapid rise in cases of sexually transmitted diseases. The notion of free love also exposed women to increased sexual assault as some men assumed that all "liberated" women desired sexual relations.

Perhaps the most colorful and best-known advocates of the counterculture and its ideals were the **"hippies."** Seeking a life of peace, love, and self-awareness—governed by the law of "what feels good" instead of by the rules of traditional behavior—hippies tried to distance themselves from traditional society. They flocked in large numbers to northern California, congregating especially in the Haight-Ashbury neighborhood of San Francisco, where they frequently carried drug abuse and free love to excess. Elsewhere, some hippie groups abandoned the "old-fashioned" nuclear family and lived together as extended families on communes. Hippies expressed their nonconformity in their appearance, favoring long, unkempt hair and ratty blue jeans or long flowered dresses. Although the number of hippie dropouts was small, their style of dress and grooming greatly influenced young Americans.

The influence of the counterculture peaked, at least in one sense, in the summer of 1969, when an army of teens and young adults converged on **Woodstock,** New York, for the largest free rock concert in history. For three days, through summer rains and deepening mud, more than 400,000 came together in

Timothy Leary Harvard professor and counterculture figure who advocated the expansion of consciousness through the use of drugs such as LSD.

free love Popular belief among members of the counterculture in the 1960s that sexual activities should be unconstrained.

hippies Members of the counterculture in the 1960s who rejected the competitiveness and materialism of American society and searched for peace, love, and autonomy.

Woodstock Free rock concert in Woodstock, New York, in August 1969; it attracted 400,000 people and was remembered as the classic expression of the counterculture.

a temporary open-air community, where many of the most popular rock 'n' roll bands performed day and night. Touted as three days of peace and love, sex, drugs, and rock 'n' roll, Woodstock symbolized the power of counterculture values to promote cooperation and happiness.

The spirit of Woodstock was fleeting. For most people, at home and on campus, the communal ideal was impractical, if not unworkable. Nor did the vast majority of young people who took up some counterculture notions completely reject their parents' society. Most stayed in school and continued to participate in the society they were criticizing. To be sure, the counterculture had a lasting impact on American society—on dress, sexual attitudes, music, and even personal values—but it did not reshape America in its image.

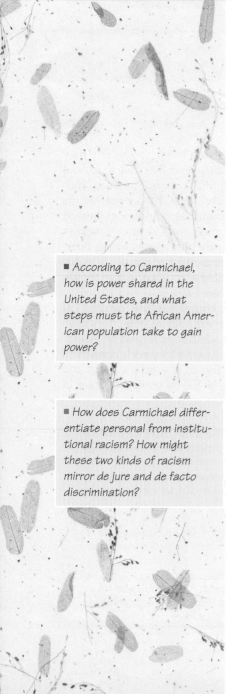

Individual Voices

Examining a Primary Source

Stokely Carmichael Justifies Black Power

The pivotal catch phrase that redefined race relations in the sixties burst onto the front pages on June 16, 1966, when Stokely Carmichael renewed the call for "Black Power." Black Power conjured up a variety of images, depending on who said it. To many whites the term seemed threatening; to many African Americans it signaled the need to understand the race issue in a different way and to consider new choices. In the speech excerpted below, entitled "Toward Black Liberation," Carmichael defines Black Power and distinguishes its goals from those of other civil rights organizations.

■ According to Carmichael, how is power shared in the United States, and what steps must the African American population take to gain power?

■ How does Carmichael differentiate personal from institutional racism? How might these two kinds of racism mirror de jure and de facto discrimination?

Negroes are defined by two forces, their blackness and their powerlessness. There have been traditionally two communities in America. The White community, which controlled and defined the forms that all institutions within the society would take, and the Negro community, which has been excluded from participation in the power decisions that shaped the society, and has traditionally been dependent upon, and subservient to the White community. ■

This has not been accidental. . . . This has not been on the level of individual acts of discrimination between individual whites against individual Negroes, but as total acts by the White Community against the Negro community. . . .

Let me give an example of the difference between individual racism and institutionalized racism, and the society's response to both. When . . . White terrorists bomb a Negro Church and kill five children, that is an act of individual racism, widely deplored by . . . society. But when in that same city . . . not five but 500 Negro babies die each year because of a lack of proper food, shelter, and medical facilities . . . that is a function of institutionalized racism. ■ *But the society either pretends it doesn't know of this situation, or is incapable of doing anything meaningful about it. And, the resistance to do anything meaningful . . . is . . . a product of . . . forces and special interests in the White community, and the groups that have . . . resources and power to change that situation benefit, politically and economically, from the existence of that ghetto. . . . The people of the Negro community do not control the resources of that community, its political decisions, its law enforcement, its housing standards, and even the physical ownership of the land, houses and stores lie outside that community. . . .*

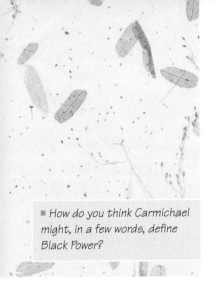

■ *How do you think Carmichael might, in a few words, define Black Power?*

In recent years the answer to these questions which has been given by the most articulate groups of Negroes and their white allies . . . has been in terms of something called "integration" . . . social justice will be accomplished by "integrating the Negro into the mainstream institutions of the society. . . ."

This concept . . . had to be based on the assumption that there was nothing of value in the Negro community and that little of value could be created among Negroes, so the thing to do was to siphon off the "acceptable" Negroes into the surrounding middle-class white communities. . . . It is true . . . SNCC . . . had a similar orientation. But while it is hardly a concern of a black sharecropper, dishwasher, or welfare recipient whether a certain fifteen-dollar-a-day motel offers accommodations to Negroes, the overt symbols of white superiority . . . had to be destroyed. Now, black people must look beyond these goals, to the issue of collective power. ■

Summary

Kennedy's election generated a renewed wave of activism and optimism. Many hoped that the nation's and the world's problems could be solved by combinations of individual, institutional, and governmental actions. It fueled the heart of the New Frontier, the War on Poverty, and the Great Society and raised the expectations of a nation. Heightened expectations were clearly visible among the African Americans who looked to Kennedy, and later to Johnson, for legislation to end segregation and discrimination. As Kennedy took office, African American leaders launched a series of sit-ins and freedom marches designed to keep the pressure on American society and the government. Kennedy's domestic options, however, were limited by a narrow Democratic margin in Congress, and a comprehensive civil rights bill was not introduced until mid-1963. It was quickly mired in congressional politics, as were several other pieces of Kennedy's domestic agenda, including aid to education and a tax cut. Like Eisenhower, Kennedy had to settle for modest legislative successes that merely expanded existing programs and **entitlements.**

Hampered by congressional opposition, Kennedy favored foreign policy. In implementing flexible response, Kennedy adopted a more comprehensive strategy to confront communism. Confrontations over Berlin and Cuba, an escalating arms and space race, and an expanded commitment to Vietnam were accepted as part of the United States' global role and passed intact to Johnson.

As president, Johnson expanded on the slain president's agenda, announcing a War on Poverty and the implementation of a Great Society. Between 1964 and 1966 Johnson pushed through Congress a series of acts that extended New Deal liberalism into new areas of public policy. The 1964 Civil Rights Act and the 1965 Voting Rights Act reshaped society and politics. Other Great Society legislation tackled poverty and discrimination, expanded educational opportunities, and created a national system of health insurance for the poor and elderly.

The decade's emphasis on activism, the New Frontier, and the Great Society encouraged more Americans to seek equality and raise new agendas. Within the African American movement, more emphasis was centered on economic and social issues. Some African American activists rejected assimilation and expressed more militant demands for basic institutional social and economic changes. Drawing from the civil rights movement, consciousness-raising efforts, and the inclusion of gender in the civil rights act, the decade also saw the reemergence of a women's movement. Many women also began to question the framework of gender roles in a male-dominated society as they sought economic, legal, and social equality. Within the civil rights and feminist movements, much of the activism came from young adults. The nation's youth, too, seemed unwilling to accept the traditional values of society and demanded change.

Some Americans, as the decade drew to a close, recoiled from the incessant demands for change. Disturbed by race riots and other attacks on the status quo, an increasing number of people were questioning government programs that appeared to favor the poor and minorities at the majority's expense. The result was that a decade that had begun with great promise produced, for many, disappointment and disillusionment.

entitlements Government programs and benefits provided to particular groups, such as the elderly, farmers, the disabled, and the poor.

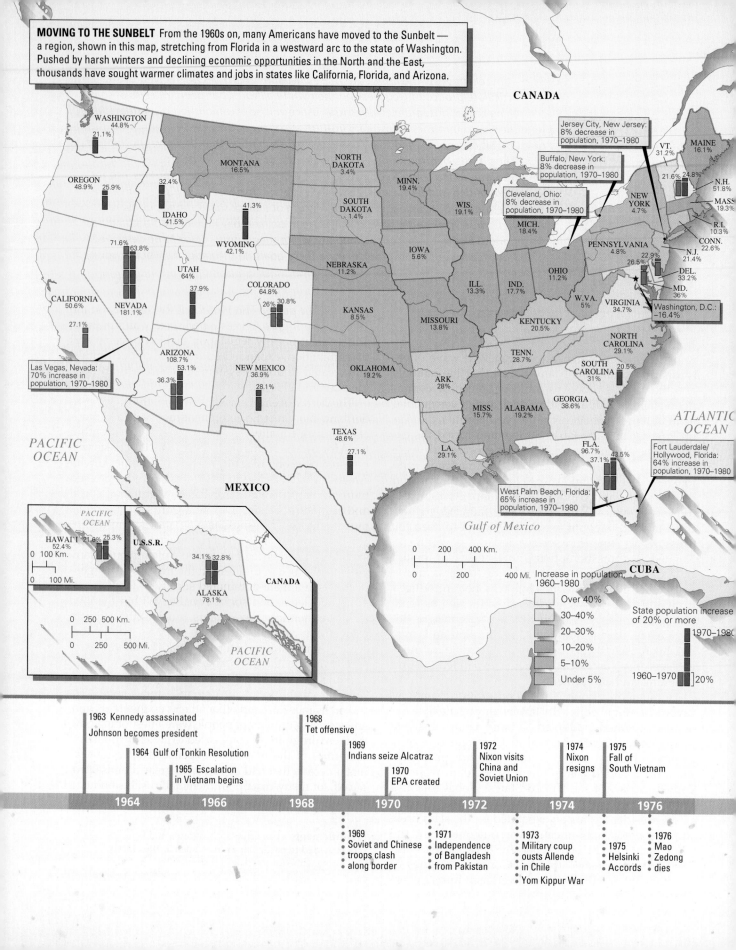

MOVING TO THE SUNBELT From the 1960s on, many Americans have moved to the Sunbelt — a region, shown in this map, stretching from Florida in a westward arc to the state of Washington. Pushed by harsh winters and declining economic opportunities in the North and the East, thousands have sought warmer climates and jobs in states like California, Florida, and Arizona.

CANADA

WASHINGTON 44.8%
21.1%

OREGON 48.9% 25.9%

IDAHO 41.5%
32.4%

MONTANA 16.5%

NORTH DAKOTA 3.4%

MINN. 19.4%

WIS. 19.1%

MICH. 18.4%

WYOMING 42.1%
41.3%

SOUTH DAKOTA 1.4%

IOWA 5.6%

NEBRASKA 11.2%

UTAH 64%
37.9%

CALIFORNIA 50.6%
71.6% 63.8%

NEVADA 181.1%
27.1%

COLORADO 64.8%
26% 30.8%

KANSAS 8.5%

ILL. 13.3%

IND. 17.7%

OHIO 11.2%

MISSOURI 13.8%

KENTUCKY 20.5%

W.VA. 5%

VIRGINIA 34.7%

PENNSYLVANIA 4.8%
22.9% 26.5%

NEW YORK 4.7%

N.J. 21.4%

DEL. 33.2%

MD. 36%

VT. 31.2%
21.6% 24.8%

MAINE 16.1%

N.H. 51.8%

MASS 19.3%

R.I. 10.3%

CONN. 22.6%

NORTH CAROLINA 29.1%
20.5%

SOUTH CAROLINA 31%

ARIZONA 108.7%
36.3% 53.1%

NEW MEXICO 36.9%
28.1%

OKLAHOMA 19.2%

ARK. 28%

TENN. 28.7%

GEORGIA 38.6%

MISS. 15.7%

ALABAMA 19.2%

TEXAS 48.6%
27.1%

LA. 29.1%

FLA. 96.7%
37.1% 43.5%

Jersey City, New Jersey: 8% decrease in population, 1970–1980

Buffalo, New York: 8% decrease in population, 1970–1980

Cleveland, Ohio: 8% decrease in population, 1970–1980

Washington, D.C.: –16.4%

Las Vegas, Nevada: 70% increase in population, 1970–1980

Fort Lauderdale/Hollywood, Florida: 64% increase in population, 1970–1980

West Palm Beach, Florida: 65% increase in population, 1970–1980

PACIFIC OCEAN

MEXICO

ATLANTIC OCEAN

Gulf of Mexico

CUBA

PACIFIC OCEAN
HAWAI'I 52.4%
21.6% 25.3%
0 100 Km.
0 100 Mi.

U.S.S.R.

34.1% 32.8%
ALASKA 78.1%
0 250 500 Km.
0 250 500 Mi.

CANADA

PACIFIC OCEAN

0 200 400 Km.
0 200 400 Mi.

Increase in population, 1960–1980
Over 40%
30–40%
20–30%
10–20%
5–10%
Under 5%

State population increase of 20% or more
1970–1980
1960–1970 20%

1963 Kennedy assassinated
Johnson becomes president

1964 Gulf of Tonkin Resolution

1965 Escalation in Vietnam begins

1968 Tet offensive

1969 Indians seize Alcatraz

1970 EPA created

1972 Nixon visits China and Soviet Union

1974 Nixon resigns

1975 Fall of South Vietnam

1964   1966   1968   1970   1972   1974   1976

1969 Soviet and Chinese troops clash along border

1971 Independence of Bangladesh from Pakistan

1973 Military coup ousts Allende in Chile
Yom Kippur War

1975 Helsinki Accords

1976 Mao Zedong dies

America Under Stress, 1967–1976

Moving to the Sunbelt
How does the map on the facing page reflect the economic
and demographic changes that began during the Second
World War? What were the political changes that the emergence of the Sunbelt created?

Individual Choices

CÉSAR CHÁVEZ

César Chávez organized the first successful farm workers' union in America in 1962, the National Farm Workers Association. Choosing to confront opponents by using the non-violent tactics of the civil rights movement, Chávez sought to give power and dignity to Mexican American workers. *Bob Fitch/Black Star.*

César Chávez

"*Viva la huelga!*" With these words, in September 1965, César Chávez began the strike (*huelga*) against the grape growers in California's Central Valley. Although a new organization, the National Farm Workers Association (NFWA) mobilized more than 2,700 workers and activists, carrying red banners bearing the black thunderbird, to picket vineyards and encourage other workers not to pick grapes. It was the beginning of a five-year effort to force California agribusiness to pay higher wages, provide better working conditions, and give workers some control over their employment.

Chávez knew what it meant to be a migrant worker, to be trapped at the bottom of the economic and social ladder—without choices. "The work is backbreaking, it is temporary, and it still leaves us almost at the bottom, standing ahead only of even more destitute farm workers in other states." The "whole fight if you're poor, and if you're a minority group," Chávez believed, "is economic power." But the strike was about more than wages—the average farm laborer in 1965 earned about $1,350 a year. It was *La Causa Para La Raza* (literally, "the cause for the race"). *La Causa,* initially associated with Chávez's effort to organize farm workers, soon became linked to the broader effort to promote Hispanic and Latino lives.

Chávez also knew what it meant to have little control over one's life. During the Depression he had watched his family evicted from their Arizona farm. His parents had moved to California and become migrant workers, never able to break the cycle of poverty. César Chávez dropped out of school after the eighth grade to work in the fields. Education, instead of being an escape route from poverty, was, Chávez recalled, a "nightmare." He had attended thirty-seven different schools, a succession of classes ruled over by Anglo teachers who had little concern about the unique problems of Spanish-speaking migrant children. "When we spoke Spanish," Chávez remembered, "the teacher swooped down on us. I remember the ruler whistling through the air as its edge came down sharply across my knuckles."

In 1962, after serving in the navy and working to mobilize poor Mexican American communities for the Community Service Organization, Chávez decided to form a farm workers' union. With no funds, while his wife, Helen, continued to work in the fields, he drove up and down the San Joaquin Valley in central California, talking to workers in the fields. He asked about their work conditions, aspirations, and thoughts about a union. When asked about strikes, he replied, "Not right away, but eventually." Within six months he had recruited three hundred members and formed the **National Farm Workers Association.** From the beginning the goal was to create a different type of union, one that spoke to the total needs of the Latino farm worker community. At their opening convention, the union agreed on a red background flag with black eagle on a white circle as a symbol for the union and *La Causa.*

Created in 1962 with no contracts or credibility with growers, the new union sought to supply other services to its growing membership. It provided a credit

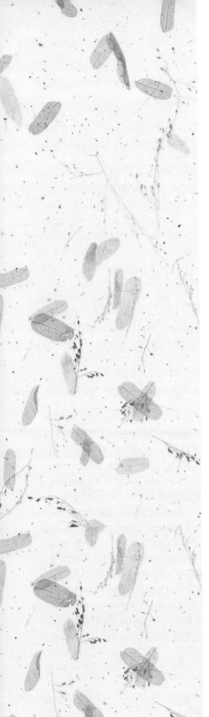

union, insurance, and a wide range of other services. "We help to get a guy a driver's license," stated Chávez, and "help . . . with such problems as translation from Spanish to English, securing welfare and other benefits." As membership increased and the growers ignored the demands for improved wages, and working conditions did not improve, pressure grew to strike. In 1965, a strike was called, and workers left the fields. Growers brought in other workers to harvest the grapes. Immediately the strike became bitter and violent. Workers and union leaders were jailed and attacked while on the picket lines. Recognizing their lack of power and visibility, Chávez decided to try and enlist a wider audience. "Alone," he explained, "the farm workers have no economic power, but with the help of the public they can develop the economic power to counter that of the growers."

To gain more power and support Chávez organized marches throughout the state, went on hunger strikes—one fast lasting nearly a month—and asked consumers to boycott nonunion-picked grapes. "Our best hope is the boycott," he said. Boycotting was something that anyone could do; it required no walking in marches or on picket lines, and it did not require giving money to the union. Chávez concluded that it was a "most effective weapon." Responding to the union's tactics, one growers' association announced: "We will not sell out the American consumer or our workers to Chávez."

The strike lasted five years, but Chávez's energy and persistence, along with marches and an effective boycott, finally produced results. Indeed, the boycott had been a powerful tool, and by 1970, when the strike ended, an estimated 12 percent of the public had refused to buy nonunion grapes, and many grape growers had gone out of business. In return for a union promise not to strike, growers agreed to higher wages, some health benefits, and improved conditions at work—including providing portable toilets and restricting the use of pesticides, including DDT. California and the Environmental Protection Agency began to restrict the use of DDT in agricultural products in 1970. However, a total ban on DDT was not implemented in California until 1973, with a total ban by the federal government coming in 1974.

The success of the grape strike soon faded as the United Farm Workers Union launched a strike against lettuce growers in 1979, fought a rival union (the Teamsters), experienced internal conflicts, and lost public support. Membership in the union dropped from 100,000 members to less than 20,000 by the end of the 1980s. But in 1996, the United Farm Workers finally won their seventeen-year lettuce strike, and under the leadership of Arturo Rodriquez, Chávez's son-in-law, saw their membership and influence begin to return.

César Chávez died in 1993, knowing that the struggle for economic, social, and political equality would not be easy or won overnight. "The work for social change and against social injustice," he said, "is never ended."

INTRODUCTION

The 1960s began with a wave of optimism and confidence in the ability of individuals and government to improve society and promote American interests abroad. For many, that optimism did not last throughout the decade. By 1968, American efforts to mold the

National Farm Workers Association   The initial name for the farm workers' union; from 1966 to 1972, as it grew, the union was named the United Farm Workers Organizing Committee; upon becoming part of the American Federation of Labor in 1972 the union altered its name to the United Farm Workers of America.

emerging nation of Vietnam, to reshape American society along more egalitarian lines, and to banish poverty seemed either a lost cause or a venture that was flawed from the beginning. The Supreme Court under Chief Justice Earl Warren had in a series of controversial decisions expanded the rights of individuals while limiting the power of the state. Its rulings protected those accused of crimes, separated church and state, and expanded the legal right of privacy. But by the end of the decade, the Court was undergoing change as new justices replaced those leaving the bench. Activists like César Chávez, however, continued to believe that group and individual efforts could persuade government and society to promote social and economic justice, improving not only the lives of minorities and the poor but the overall quality of American life.

Like African Americans, many Latinos and American Indians were encouraged by the 1960 election of John Kennedy, who promised increased government activism and social change. Also, like African Americans, Latinos and American Indians also recognized that continued grassroots organizing and the mobilization of public opinion were needed to prod governmental action. To varying degrees these groups were successful—gaining national visibility; forcing local, state, and federal governments to respond; and providing paths for further gains.

In 1963, President Kennedy's assassination brought Lyndon Baines Johnson to the White House. As described in Chapter 28, Johnson's political skills enabled him to go beyond the New Frontier to fight a war on poverty and to formulate his Great Society. Johnson was comfortable dealing with domestic affairs, but foreign affairs were a different matter. In that arena Johnson seemed content to continue Kennedy's policies as he understood them, especially in Vietnam, where he was determined that the United States would not be beaten by a "two-bit" nation like North Vietnam. Johnson agreed with his advisers that the commitment of American forces was the only effective solution to defeat the Communists.

Certain political circumstances initially made that commitment difficult. A sudden buildup could weaken support for Johnson's domestic program and might drive the Chinese and the Soviets to increase their support of North Vietnam. To Johnson, the best choice seemed a carefully controlled, gradual escalation of American forces that would convince the North Vietnamese that the cost of the war was too high. The administration expected that the North Vietnamese would then abandon their efforts to unify Vietnam

and that an American-supported South Vietnam would prevail.

The strategy failed miserably. North Vietnam chose to meet escalation with escalation until many Americans turned against both the war and Johnson. In 1968, watching opposition to the war mount, Johnson chose to break the momentum of escalation and started peace negotiations with North Vietnam. Unexpectedly, he also announced his withdrawal from the presidential campaign. The turbulent 1968 Democratic convention symbolized the outcome of Johnson's presidency—a divided nation and an end to liberal optimism.

Republicans rallied behind Richard Nixon, who, they said, would provide the leadership necessary to restore national unity and global prestige and reassert the traditions and values that had made the nation strong. Nixon's call for unity played on the uneasy expectations of a society that was fragmented by the Vietnam War, urban and campus unrest, and an array of groups clamoring for political, economic, and social changes.

Despite their unity rhetoric, Nixon and the Republicans inflamed social divisions to ensure their victories in 1968 and in 1972. They wanted to construct a solid political base around a Silent Majority—composed largely of middle-class white Americans living in suburbs, the South, and the West—who supported the war, opposed antiwar protesters and "hippies," and rejected justifications for urban riots and campus demonstrations. Promising a new, pragmatic conservatism that accepted legitimate government activism, Nixon's first administration achieved generally successful results. Nixon improved relations with the Soviet Union and the People's Republic of China and withdrew American forces from Vietnam. Domestically, his policy choices showed flexibility, expanding some Great Society programs and following Keynesian guidelines to confront inflation and a sluggish economy.

Nixon, despite his successes, was not satisfied. He wanted his political enemies ruined, and this desire contributed to the illegal activities surrounding the Watergate break-in at the offices of the Democratic Party National Committee. Watergate produced a bitter harvest: not only the unprecedented resignation of a president but a nationwide wave of disillusionment with politics and government.

Vice President Gerald Ford assumed the presidency after Nixon's resignation in 1974. The first unelected president, he faced a floundering economy and a cynical public disgusted with politics. Regarded

Chronology

From Camelot to Watergate

1960	Kennedy elected president
1962	César Chávez forms National Farm Workers Association *Baker v. Carr* *Engel v. Vitale*
1963	*Abington v. Schempp* *Gideon v. Wainright* *Jacobvellis v. Ohio* La Raza Unida formed in Texas John F. Kennedy assassinated Lyndon B. Johnson becomes president
1964	*Griswold v. Connecticut* *Escobedo v. Illinois* Civil Rights Act Gulf of Tonkin Resolution Johnson elected president
1965	U.S. air strikes against North Vietnam begin American combat troops arrive in South Vietnam Anti-Vietnam "teach-ins" begin Dominican Republic intervention National Farm Workers Association begins strike Voting Rights Act
1966	*Miranda v. Arizona*
1967	Antiwar march on Washington
1968	Tet offensive My Lai massacre Johnson withdraws from presidential race Peace talks begin in Paris Robert Kennedy assassinated Mexican American student walkouts American Indian Movement founded Anti-Vietnam march on Washington Richard Nixon elected president
1969	Secret bombing of Cambodia Warren Burger appointed chief justice of Supreme Court Nixon Doctrine First American troop withdrawals from Vietnam *Alexander v. Holmes* American Indians occupy Alcatraz
1970	U.S. troops invade Cambodia Kent State and Jackson State killings First Earth Day observed Harry Blackmun appointed to Supreme Court Environmental Protection Agency created Clean Air and Water Quality Improvement Act
1971	Nixon enacts price and wage controls *New York Times* publishes Pentagon Papers *Swann v. Charlotte-Mecklenburg* William Rehnquist and Lewis Powell appointed to Supreme Court Twenty-sixth Amendment ratified
1972	Nixon visits China and Soviet Union Bombing of North Vietnam resumes Watergate break-in Nixon reelected SALT I treaty
1973	Vietnam peace settlement "Second Battle of Wounded Knee" Watergate hearings Salvador Allende overthrown in Chile War Powers Act Vice President Spiro Agnew resigns and Nixon appoints Representative Gerald R. Ford as vice president Arab oil boycott
1974	Nixon resigns Gerald Ford becomes president Brezhnev-Ford Summit at Vladivostok
1975	South Vietnam government falls to North Vietnamese Helsinki Summit

by many, even fellow Republicans, as an interim president, Ford gained few domestic or foreign-policy victories. Nevertheless, after a sharp challenge from within his own party, he won the Republican Party nomination at their 1976 presidential convention.

Liberal Forces at Work

■ In what ways did the Supreme Court work to expand and protect rights of individuals during the 1960s? How did its decisions restrict the actions of local and state governments?

■ What problems did Hispanics and American Indians face in American society, and how did they organize to bring about change?

■ How did the federal government respond to the needs of Hispanics and American Indians?

The 1960s provided many groups in American society with hope that they, together with the federal government, might successfully challenge inequities and expand their rights in American society. The civil rights movement demonstrated how grassroots activism could gain support from the federal government, especially from the Supreme Court and the executive branch, to achieve change.

The Warren Court

Until joined in the 1960s by the executive branch, the Supreme Court—the **Warren Court**—was at the forefront of liberalism, altering the obligations of the government and the rights of citizens. The Court's decisions in the 1950s redefined race relations and contributed a legal base to the 1964 Civil Rights Act. Also in the 1950s, the Court's *Yates v. the United States* (1957) ruling began a reversal of earlier decisions about the rights of those accused of crimes and started to require that states accept many of the protections accorded individuals under the Bill of Rights. For the next decade and a half, the Court expanded freedom of expression, separated church and state, redrew voting districts, and increased protection to those accused of violating the law.

In the *Yates* case, the Court released American Communist Party officials from prison who had advocated the overthrow of the American government but had not taken any actions to support their rhetoric: actions, not words, constituted a crime. Between 1961 and 1969, the Court issued over two hundred criminal justice decisions that, according to critics, hampered law enforcement. Among the most important were *Gideon v. Wainwright* (1963), *Escobedo v. Illinois* (1964), and *Miranda v. Arizona* (1966). In those rulings the Court declared that all defendants have a right to an attorney, even if the state must provide one, and that those arrested must be informed of their right to remain silent and to have an attorney present during questioning (the *Miranda* warning).

The Warren Court's actions involving church and state also angered many. In *Engel v. Vitale* (1962) and *Abington v. Schempp* (1963), the Court applied the First Amendment—separation of church and state—to state and local actions that allowed prayer and the reading of the Bible in public schools. Both decisions produced outcries of protest across the nation and from Democrats and Republicans in Congress. Governor George Wallace of Alabama stated, "We find the court ruling against God." Congress introduced over 150 resolutions demanding that reading the Bible and praying aloud be permitted in schools. Still, the Court's decisions remained the law, and communities and classrooms complied.

Critics also complained that the Court's actions not only undermined the tradition of religion but, perhaps worse, condoned and promoted immorality. The Court's weakening of "community standards" in favor of broader ones regarding "obscene" and sexually explicit materials in *Jacobvellis v. Ohio* (1963) was compounded in the 1964 *Griswold v. Connecticut* decision. In the latter case, the Court attacked the state's responsibility to establish moral standards by overturning Connecticut's laws that forbade the sale of contraceptives, arguing that individuals have a right to privacy that the state cannot abridge.

The Court's rejection of statewide gerrymandering, or redrawing voting districts so as to favor one party, was less controversial but equally lasting in importance. It was the 1962 *Baker v. Carr* ruling that established the goal of making congressional districts "as nearly as practicable" equal in population—"one person, one vote." Two years later in *Reynolds v. Sims* the Court applied the same rule to state election districts. Still, by 1966, the Court's judicial activism had earned growing opposition. One poll found that 52 percent of the public considered the Court was doing a poor job. But for minorities and women and other

> **Warren Court** Term applied to the Supreme Court under Chief Justice Earl Warren; during this period the Court was especially active in expanding individual rights, often at the expense of state and local governments.

TABLE 29.1 Whites, African Americans, and Latinos, 1992

	Whites	African Americans	Latinos
Average income	$30,513	$18,676	$22,330
Female-headed households	11.4%	47.8%	19.1%
High school education	80.5%	66.7%	51.3%
College	22.5%	11.5%	9.7%
Unemployment	6.9%	12.4%	10.0%
Below poverty line	12.1%	31.9%	28.1%

Source: Congressional Quarterly Researcher, October 30, 1992, p. 936.

groups outside the economic, social, and political mainstream, the Court remained a valuable ally.

The Emergence of *La Causa*

The roots of *La Causa*, as the farm workers' movement came to be called, preceded the 1960s. In the 1920s and 1930s, Latino activists had attempted to organize Mexican American workers in the fields and factories. With varying degrees of success, organizations such as the League of Latin American Citizens and the American GI Forum turned to the government and the court system to gain political, economic, and social legitimacy. Still, Hispanics and Latinos remained a largely ignored minority mired near society's lowest levels of income and education (see Table 29.1). Kennedy's candidacy, however, brought hope. Kennedy had initiated the "Viva Kennedy" movement to mobilize the Hispanic, especially the Mexican American, vote. This resulted in new organizations, like the Political Association of Spanish-Speaking Organizations (PASO), that worked to increase Hispanic political representation and recognition of Hispanic issues.

Initially expectant, Hispanic leaders soon were disappointed. The Kennedy administration named few Hispanics to government positions and seemed little interested in listening to their voices or promoting their civil rights. Johnson was seen as more of an "amigo." He quickly gained praise for appointing several prominent Mexican Americans to the administration and for guaranteeing that programs established under the War on Poverty and the Great Society reached into Hispanic communities. The praise be-

came muted by 1966, however, as many Mexican Americans believed they were still being ignored, particularly in the West and Southwest. There, federal agencies appeared to defer to local and state governments that frequently opposed increased Mexican American political power and activism. Despite being the largest minority in the western states (see Map 29.1), they were still, according to one Mexican American leader, the "invisible minority."

Encouraged by Kennedy and Johnson, but unwilling to wait for Anglo politics or the federal government, many Mexican Americans turned to more direct action. For many the beginning of the "revolution" came in 1963 when the Mexican American majority in Crystal City, Texas, toppled the established Anglo political machine and elected an all–Mexican American slate to the city council. Despite claims that they were Communists who wanted to create a "little Cuba" in South Texas, Crystal City was the product of a growing grassroots militancy among Mexican Americans, especially among young adults, who called themselves **Chicanos.** They stressed pride in their heritage and Latino culture and called for resistance to the dictates of Anglo society.

Chicano A variation of mexicano, a man or boy of Mexican decent. The feminine form in Chicana. Many Mexican Americans used the term during the late 1960s to signify their ethinic idenity; the name was associated with the promotion of Mexican American heritage and rights.

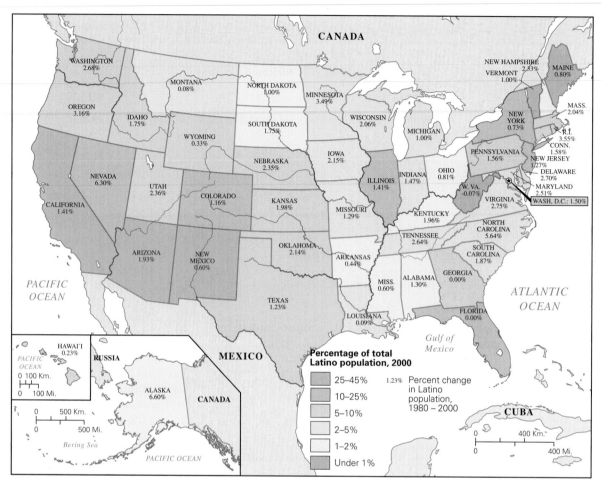

MAP 29.1 Changing Latino Population Growing rapidly, the Latino population became the largest minority population in the United States by 2000, reaching 12.5 percent of the total population.

By the mid-1960s, many Latinos were becoming more visible. In the urban Northeast, the Puerto Rican population had increased to about a million. At the same time, however, especially in New York City, economic opportunities declined as manufacturing jobs, especially in the garment industry, relocated. The Puerto Rican Forum attempted to coordinate federal grants and to find jobs, while the more militant Young Lords organized younger Puerto Ricans in Chicago and New York with an emphasis on their island culture and Hispanic heritage.

In the West, similar actions were taking place. In Colorado, Rodolfo "Corky" Gonzales formed the Crusade for Justice in 1965 to work for social justice for Mexican Americans, to integrate Colorado's schools, and to foster pride in the Mexican heritage. In New

Mexico, Reies Lopez Tijerina demanded that Mexican Americans be allowed to enjoy the rights, including land grants, promised under the Treaty of Guadalupe Hidalgo (which had ended the Mexican War in 1848) and to that end formed the Alianza Federal de Mercedes (the Federal Alliance of Land Grants). The nationalistic Brown Berets, formed in Los Angeles in 1967, expressed a militant view that rejected assimilation into the Anglo world: "We're not in the melting pot. . . . Chicanos don't melt."

For most Mexican Americans, however, it was education, jobs, and wages—not assimilation or land grievances—that were key issues. They argued that discrimination and segregation still barred their children from a decent education; school districts needed to provide better educational opportunities for His-

For most Mexican American farm laborers, working in the fields was a family affair. Children as well as adults played a necessary economic role, traveling along with their families from location to location as the need for farm labor dictated. In this picture, children work in the onion fields of California. *Walter P. Reuther Library/Wayne State University.*

panics and to offer programs that would meet special needs of Hispanic students, including bilingual education. Raul Ruiz mobilized Mexican American students in Los Angeles in 1967: "If you are a student you should be angry! You should demand! You should protest! You should organize for a better education! This is your right!" He called for students to walk out of class if schools did not meet their demands. "Walkouts" spread in California and Texas.

In November 1968, Mexican American students walked out of the high school in the small South Texas school district of Edcouch-Elsa. The activists demanded dignity, respect, and an end to "blatant discrimination," including corporal punishment— paddling—for speaking Spanish outside Spanish class. The school board blamed "outside agitators" and suspended more than 150 students. But as in

other school districts, the protests brought results. The Edcouch-Elsa school district implemented Mexican American studies and bilingual programs, hired more Mexican American teachers and counselors, and created programs to meet the peculiar needs of migrant farm worker children, who moved from one school to another during picking season. In 1968, as Title VII of the Elementary and Secondary Education Act, bilingual education in public schools was approved. It required and provided funds for schools to meet the "special educational needs" of students with limited English-speaking ability. The act, which expired in 2002, aided education not only for those speaking Spanish but also for those speaking other languages—minorities for whom the dominant language spoken in the home was not English.

Cries for dignity, better working conditions, and a living wage were also heard in the fields, where many of the poorest Mexican Americans worked as laborers. Trapped at the bottom of the occupational ladder, not covered by Social Security or minimum wage and labor laws, unskilled and uneducated farm laborers—nearly one-third of all Mexican Americans— toiled long hours for little wages under often deplorable conditions. Drawing from a traditional base of farm worker organizations, especially in Texas and California, in 1962 **César Chávez** created the National Farm Workers Association (NFWA) in the fields of central California. Chávez's union gained national recognition three years later when he called a strike against the grape growers. The union demanded a wage of $1.40 an hour and asked the public to buy only union-picked grapes. After five years, the strike and the nationwide boycott forced most of the major growers to accept unionization and to improve wages and working conditions. Chávez emerged as a national figure promoting *La Causa*, not only for farm workers but for all Latinos and other exploited minorities. Eventually, California and other states passed legislation to recognize farm workers' unions and to improve the wages and conditions of work for field workers, but agricultural workers, especially migrants, remain among the lowest-paid workers in the nation.

César Chávez   Labor organizer who in 1962 founded the National Farm Workers Association; Chávez believed in nonviolence and used marches, boycotts, and fasts to bring moral and economic pressure to bear on growers.

American Indian Activism

American Indians, responding to poverty, federal and state termination policies, and efforts by state government to seize land for development, also organized and asserted their rights with new vigor in the 1960s. In 1961, reservation and nonreservation Indians, including those not officially recognized as tribes, held a national convention in Chicago to discuss problems and consider plans of action (see Map 29.2). They agreed on a "Declaration of Indian Purpose" that called for a reversal of termination policies and better education, economic, and health opportunities. "What we ask of America is not charity, not paternalism . . . we ask only that . . . our situation be recognized and be made a basis . . . of action." Presidents Kennedy and Johnson recognized the plight of the American Indian and took steps to ensure that they benefited from New Frontier and Great Society programs. Johnson, in 1968, declared that Native Americans should have the same "standard of living" as the rest of the nation and signed the Indian Civil Rights Act. It officially ended the termination program and gave more power to tribal organizations (see p. 865).

Kennedy's and Johnson's support for an increased standard of living and tribal and individual rights was a good beginning, but many activists wanted to redress old wrongs. The National Indian Youth Council, founded shortly after the Chicago conference, called for "Red Power"—that is, for Indians to use all means possible to resist further loss of their lands, rights, and traditions. They began "fish-ins" in 1964 when the Washington state government, in violation of treaty rights, barred Indians from fishing in certain areas. Protests, arrests, and violence continued until 1975, when the state complied with a federal court decision (*United States v. Washington*) upholding treaty rights. Indian leaders also demanded the protection and restoration of their water and timber rights and ancient burial grounds. Museums were asked to return for proper burial the remains and grave goods of Indians on display. But for most, the crucial issue was self-determination, which would allow Indians control over their lands and over federal programs that served the reservations.

In 1969 a group of San Francisco Indian activists, led by **Russell Means,** gained national attention by seizing **Alcatraz Island** and holding it until 1971, when, without bloodshed, federal authorities regained control. Two years later, in a more violent confrontation, **American Indian Movement** (AIM) leaders Means and Dennis Banks led an armed occupation of

In 1973, over two hundred Sioux organized by the American Indian Movement (AIM) took over Wounded Knee, South Dakota, the site of the 1890 massacre, holding out for seventy-one days against state and federal authorities. The confrontation ended after two protesters were killed and the government agreed to examine the treaty rights of the Oglala Sioux. In this picture, AIM leader Russell Means receives a blessing and symbolic red paint during the siege. *Dirck Halstead, TIME Magazine,* © *Time Warner.*

Russell Means Indian activist who helped organize the seizures of Alcatraz in 1969 and Wounded Knee in 1973.

Alcatraz Island Rocky island, formerly a federal prison, in San Francisco Bay that was occupied in 1969 by Native American activists who demanded that it be made available to them as a cultural center.

American Indian Movement Militant Indian movement founded in 1968 that was willing to use confrontation to obtain social justice and Indian treaty rights; organized the seizure of Wounded Knee.

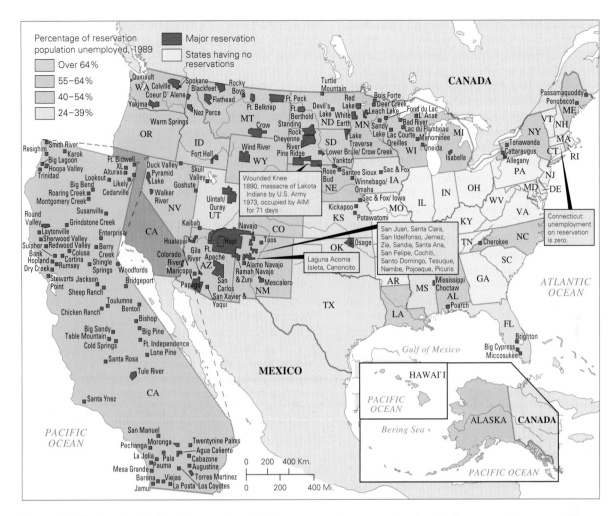

MAP 29.2 American Indian Reservations   In the seventeenth century, American Indians roamed over an estimated 1.9 billion acres, but by 1990 that area had shrunk to about 46 million acres spread across the United States. This area constitutes the federal reservation system. Composing about 1 percent of the population, American Indians are among the most impoverished people in society, facing a life expectancy of about twenty fewer years than the average non-Indian American. This map shows the location of most of the federal Indian reservations and highlights the high unemployment found on nearly every reservation. (*Note:* California is enlarged to show the many small reservations located there.)

Wounded Knee, South Dakota, the site of the 1890 massacre of the Lakotas by the army (see page 576). AIM controlled the town for seventy-one days before surrendering to federal authorities. Two Indians were killed, and over 230 activists arrested, in the "Second Battle of Wounded Knee."

While President Nixon opposed AIM's actions at Wounded Knee, he agreed with many of the activists

that more needed to be done to improve tribal and individual lives. He doubled funding for the Bureau of Indian Affairs and sought to promote tribal economies. He condemned the termination program and supported acts that returned 40 million acres of Alaskan land to Eskimos and other native peoples. He also supported the restoration of the Menominees as a tribe after it had been terminated in 1953. In 1974 Congress passed the **Indian Self-Determination and Education Assistance Act,** which gave tribes control and operation of many federal programs on their reservations

As federal courts asserted Indian treaty rights in the 1970s, an increasing number of tribes found new economic resources in commercial and industrial ventures operated on reservations. Among the most lucrative and controversial were casinos, which started to open in the 1990s. The profits from such enterprises greatly improved the conditions of life of those involved. As Native Americans enter the twenty-first century, they remain among the nation's most impoverished and poorly educated minority, but there are reasons for optimism. Disease and mortality rates are declining, and Indian populations are increasing. Tribal and pan-Indian movements have sparked cultural pride and awareness; Indian languages are being revived and taught to the younger generations. "We're a giant that's been asleep because we've been fed through our veins by the federal government," stated a Navajo leader. "But now that's ending, and we're waking up and flexing muscles we never knew we had. And no one knows what we're capable of."

Johnson and the War

■ How did foreign-policy decisions made by Kennedy influence Johnson's decisions regarding Latin America and Southeast Asia? In what ways were Johnson's policies different from Kennedy's?

■ What considerations led Johnson to escalate America's role in Vietnam in 1965? How did the North Vietnamese respond to the escalation?

Suddenly thrust into the presidency by Kennedy's assassination, Lyndon Johnson moved quickly to breathe life into Kennedy's domestic programs and to launch the more extensive Great Society. He was comfortable dealing with domestic issues and politics. In foreign policy, however, Johnson relied more heavily on his advisers—the "wise men," as he called them. Johnson was determined not to deviate significantly from past policies or allow further erosion of American power. Two regions of special concern were Latin America and Vietnam, where, like his predecessors, Johnson was determined to prevent further Communist inroads.

In the Western Hemisphere, Castro and his determination to export revolution remained the biggest issue. Johnson agreed to continue Kennedy's economic boycott of Cuba and the CIA's efforts to desta-

bilize the Castro regime. Concerned about instability in Latin America and the growth of communism, Johnson refocused Kennedy's Alliance for Progress. Stability became more important than reform. Assistant Secretary of State Thomas Mann told Latin American leaders that political, social, and economic reforms were no longer a central requirement for American aid and support. This new perspective, labeled the **Mann Doctrine,** resulted in increased amounts of American military equipment and advisers in Latin America to aid various regimes to suppress those disruptive elements they labeled "Communist." The new policy led to direct military intervention in the Dominican Republic in 1965. There, supporters of deposed, democratically elected president Juan Bosch rebelled against a repressive, pro-American regime. Johnson and his advisers decided that the pro-Bosch coalition was dominated by Communists, asserted the right to protect the Dominican people from an "international conspiracy," and sent in twenty-two thousand American troops. They restored order; monitored elections that put a pro-American president, Joaquin Balaguer, in power; and left the island in mid-1966. Johnson claimed to have saved the Dominicans from communism, but many Latin Americans saw the American intervention only as an example of Yankee arrogance and the intrusive uses of its power.

Americanization of the Vietnam War

Kennedy had left Johnson a crisis in Vietnam. The South Vietnamese government remained unstable and its army ineffective, and the Viet Cong, supported by men and supplies from North Vietnam, were winning the conflict. Without a larger and more direct American involvement, Johnson's advisers saw little hope for improvement. Johnson felt trapped: "I

Indian Self-Determination and Education Assistance Act   Law passed by Congress in 1974 giving Indian tribes control over federal programs carried out on their reservations and increasing their authority in reservation schools.

Mann Doctrine   U.S. policy outlined by Thomas Mann during the Johnson administration that called for stability in Latin America rather than economic and political reform.

Unlike previous wars, Vietnam was a war without fixed frontlines. In this picture, marines work their way through the jungle south of the demilitarized zone (DMZ) trying to cut off North Vietnamese supplies and reinforcements moving into South Vietnam. *Larry Burrows/Timepix.*

don't think it is worth fighting for," he told an adviser, "and I don't think we can get out." "I am not going to be the president who saw Southeast Asia go the way China went," he asserted. But in 1964 he was focused on domestic issues and the upcoming election. Increasing the American role in Vietnam would come only after more strategic planning, increased covert raids against North Vietnam, and a public awareness campaign to generate support for a larger American role there. Aware of the need for more direct American involvement, the White House awaited an event that would allow asking Congress for permission to use whatever force would be necessary to defend South Vietnam.

The chance came in August 1964 off the coast of North Vietnam. Following a covert attack on its territory, North Vietnamese torpedo boats skirmished with the American destroyer *Maddox* in the Gulf of Tonkin on August 2 (see Map 29.3). On August 4, experiencing rough seas and poor visibility, radar operators on the *Maddox* and another destroyer, the *C. Turner Joy*, concluded that the patrol boats were making another attack. Confusion followed. Both ships fired wildly at targets shown only on radar screens. Johnson immediately ordered retaliatory air strikes on North Vietnam and prepared a resolution for Congress. Although within hours he learned that the second incident probably had not occurred, Johnson told the public and Congress that Communist attacks against "peaceful villages" in South Vietnam had been "joined by open aggression on the high seas against the United States of America." On August 7, Congress approved the **Gulf of Tonkin Resolution,** allowing the United States "to take all necessary measures to repel" attacks against American forces in Vietnam and "to prevent further aggression." It was, in Johnson's terms, "like Grandma's nightgown, it covered everything." Public opinion polls showed strong support for the president, and only two senators opposed the resolution: Wayne Morse of Oregon and Ernest Gruening of Alaska.

The resolution gave Johnson freedom to take whatever measures he wanted in Vietnam, but he remained unsure about what course of action to take and when. His advisers recommended committing American combat troops and bombing North Vietnam. To do nothing, Secretary of Defense Robert McNamara warned, was the "worst course of action" and would "lead only to a disastrous defeat." Johnson agreed and decided to limit the American commitment to air attacks on targets in North Vietnam. A Viet Cong attack on the American base at Pleiku on February 7, 1965, that killed eight Americans provided a hoped-for provocation for unleashing the air assault.

Operation Rolling Thunder began on March 2. On March 8, the 3rd Marine Division arrived to take up positions around the American base at Da Nang. By July, American planes were flying more than nine hundred missions a week, and a hundred thousand American ground forces had reached Vietnam. Near their bases, American infantry and armored units patrolled aggressively, searching out the enemy. Johnson's strategy soon showed its flaws. As the United

Gulf of Tonkin Resolution   Decree passed by Congress in 1964 authorizing the president to take any measures necessary to repel attacks against U.S. forces in Vietnam.

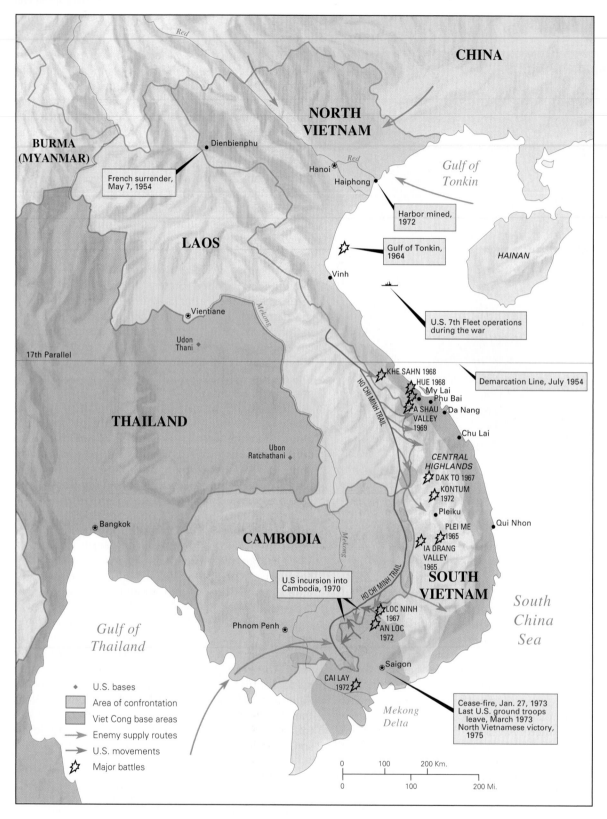

MAP 29.3 The Vietnam War, 1954–1975 Following the French defeat at Dienbienphu in 1954, the United States became increasingly committed to defending South Vietnam. This map shows some of the major battle sites of the Vietnam War from 1954 to the fall of Saigon and the defeat of the South Vietnamese government in 1975.

States escalated the war, so too did the enemy, which committed units of the North Vietnamese army (NVA) to the fighting in South Vietnam. The U.S. commanding general in Vietnam, **William Westmoreland,** and others insisted that victory required taking the offensive, which necessitated even more American soldiers. Reluctantly, Johnson gave the green light. Vietnam had become an American war.

Westmoreland's plan was to use overwhelming numbers and firepower to destroy the enemy. The first major American offensive was a large-scale sweep of the Ia Drang Valley in November 1965. Ten miles from the Cambodian border, the Ia Drang Valley contained no villages and was a longtime sanctuary for Communist forces. The goal was to airlift in units of the air cavalry and search out and destroy the enemy.

The initial landing went without incident, but soon the Americans came under fierce attack from North Vietnamese troops. One soldier recalled that his "assault line [that] had started out erect went down to . . . a low crawl." The battle raged for three days with air and artillery supporting the outnumbered Americans. "There was very vicious fighting," North Vietnamese commander Nguyen Huu noted. The "soldiers fought valiantly. They had no choice, you were dead if not." Both sides claimed victory and drew different lessons from the engagement. Examining the losses, 305 Americans versus 3,561 Vietnamese, American officials embraced the strategy of search and destroy—the enemy would be ground down. *Time* magazine named Westmoreland "Man of the Year" for 1965. Hanoi concluded that its "peasant army" had withstood America's best firepower and had fought U.S. troops to a draw. The North Vietnamese were confident: the costs would be great, but they would wear down the Americans. Both sides, believing victory was possible, committed more troops and prepared for a lengthy war.

Thus the war spiraled upward in 1966 and 1967. The United States and the North Vietnamese committed more troops, while American aircraft rained more bombs on North Vietnam and supply routes, especially the **Ho Chi Minh Trail** (see Map 29.3). The strategic bombing of North Vietnam produced great results—on paper. Nearly every target in North Vietnam had been demolished by 1968, but the North Vietnamese continued the struggle. China and the Soviet Union increased their support, while much of North Vietnamese industrial production was moved underground. It seemed that the more the United States bombed, the more North Vietnamese determination continued to increase. By mid-1966, it appeared to

some in Washington that the war had reached a stalemate, with neither side able to win nor willing to lose. Some speculated that any victory would be a matter of will, and feared that growing opposition to the war in the United States might be a deciding factor.

The Antiwar Movement

Throughout 1964, support at home for an American role in Vietnam was widespread. Most Americans accepted the domino theory and predictions that horrible reprisals against non-Communists would follow a Communist victory. The escalation of the war in 1965 saw a largely college-based opposition to the war arise—with Students for a Democratic Society (SDS) the prime instigators. The University of Michigan held the first Vietnam "teach-in" to mobilize opposition to American policy on March 24, 1965. In April, SDS organized a protest march of nearly twenty thousand past the White House, and by October its membership had increased 400 percent. But by mid-1966, SDS was losing its leadership of the movement and was only one of many groups and individuals demonstrating against the expanding war.

Those opposing the war fell into two major types who rarely agreed on anything other than that the war should be ended. Pacifists and radical liberals on the political left opposed the war for moral and ideological reasons. Others, as the American military commitment grew and the military draft claimed more young men, opposed the war for more pragmatic reasons: the draft, the loss of lives and money, and the inability of the United States either to defeat the enemy or to create a stable, democratic South Vietnam. A University of Michigan student complained that if he were drafted and spent two years in the army, he would lose more than $16,000 in income. "I know I sound selfish," he explained, "but . . . I paid $10,000 to get this education."

Yet college students and graduates were not the most likely to be drafted or go to Vietnam. Far more often, minorities and the poor served in Vietnam, especially in combat roles. African Americans constituted about 12 percent of the population but in Vietnam sometimes made up to 50 percent of frontline

William Westmoreland   Commander of all American troops in Vietnam from 1964 to 1968.

Ho Chi Minh Trail   Main infiltration route for North Vietnamese soldiers and supplies into South Vietnam; it ran through Laos and Cambodia.

THE AMERICANS ARE COMING

T. UNGERER

As the American involvement in Vietnam increased, so too did the opposition to the war. Some protesters argued that the Viet Cong were fighting for national independence, like the American revolutionaries. Here, a Vietnamese Paul Revere raises the alarm that the enemy is coming. *Library of Congress.*

units and accounted for about 25 percent of combat deaths. Stokely Carmichael and SNCC had supported SDS actions against the war as early as 1965, but it was Martin Luther King Jr.'s denouncement of the war in 1967 that made international headlines and shook the administration. King called the war immoral and preached that "the Great Society has been shot down on the battlefields of Vietnam." He stated that it was wrong to send young blacks to defend democracy in Vietnam when they were denied it in Georgia.

Johnson labeled King a "crackpot," but he knew he had to win the struggle at home to successfully win the war in Vietnam. Watching the antiwar movement grow and public opinion polls register increasing dis-

approval of the war effort, the administration responded with **COINTELPRO** and **Operation Chaos** actions, in which federal agents infiltrated, spied on, and tried to discredit antiwar groups. FBI reports showing antiwar groups in league with Communists were leaked to the press and counterdemonstrations planned. Nevertheless, opposition to the war swelled. A "Stop-the-Draft Week" in October 1967 prompted more than 10,000 demonstrators to block the entrance of an induction center in Oakland, California, while over 200,000 people staged a massive protest march in Washington against "Lyndon's War."

The administration itself was torn by increasing disagreement about the course of the war. Hawks supported General Westmoreland's assertions that the war was being won, that by 1968 half of the enemy's forces were no longer capable of combat, and that more troops were needed to complete the job. Yet by late 1967 some of Johnson's wise men were taking a different view. In November, Secretary of War Robert McNamara recommended a sharp reduction in the war effort, including a permanent end to the bombing of North Vietnam. Johnson rejected his position, and McNamara left the administration. Still, Johnson decided to consider a "withdrawal strategy" that would reduce American support while the South Vietnamese assumed a larger role. But first it was necessary to commit more troops, intensify the bombing, and put more pressure on the South Vietnamese to make domestic reforms. "The clock is ticking," he said.

Tet and the 1968 Presidential Campaign

- What were the political, social, and military outcomes of the Tet offensive?
- What key issues shaped the 1968 campaign? What strategy did Richard Nixon use to win?

COINTELPRO Acronym (COunterINTELligence PROgram) for an FBI program begun in 1956 and continued until 1971 that sought to expose, disrupt, and discredit groups considered to be radical political organizations; it targeted various antiwar groups during the Vietnam War.

Operation Chaos CIA operation within the country from 1965 to 1973 that collected information on and disrupted anti–Vietnam War elements; although it is illegal for the CIA to operate within the United States, it collected files on over 7,000 Americans.

Johnson was correct: the clock was ticking—not only for the United States but also for North Vietnam. As Westmoreland reported success, North Vietnamese leaders were planning an immense campaign to capture South Vietnamese cities during **Tet,** the Vietnamese lunar New Year holiday, a maneuver that would catch American intelligence agencies totally off-guard.

The Tet Offensive

In January 1968, the Viet Cong struck forty-one cities throughout South Vietnam, including the capital, Saigon. In some of the bloodiest fighting of the war, American and South Vietnamese forces recaptured the lost cities and villages. It took twenty-four days to oust the Viet Cong from the old imperial city of Hue, leaving the city in ruins and costing more than 10,000 civilian, 5,000 Communist, 384 South Vietnamese, and 216 American lives.

The Tet offensive was a military defeat for North Vietnam and the Viet Cong. It provoked no popular uprising against the South Vietnamese government, the Communists held no cities or provincial capitals, and they suffered staggering losses. More than 40,000 Viet Cong were killed. Tet was, nevertheless, a "victory" for the North Vietnamese, for it seriously weakened American support for the war. Amid official pronouncements of "victory just around the corner," Tet destroyed the Johnson administration's credibility and inflamed a growing antiwar movement. The highly respected CBS news anchor Walter Cronkite had supported the war, but Tet changed his mind. He announced on the air that there would be no victory in Vietnam and that the United States should make peace. "If I have lost Walter Cronkite, then it's over. I have lost Mr. Average Citizen," Johnson lamented.

By March 1968, Johnson and most of his "wise men" had also concluded that the war was not going to be won. The new secretary of defense, Clark Clifford, admitted that four years of "enormous casualties" and "massive destruction from our bombing" had not weakened "the will of the enemy." The emerging strategy was to place more responsibility on South Vietnam, send fewer troops than Westmoreland had asked for, and seek a diplomatic end to the war.

Changing of the Guard

Two months after Tet came the first presidential primary in New Hampshire. There, Minnesota senator **Eugene McCarthy** was campaigning primarily on the antiwar issue. At the heart of his New Hampshire effort were hundreds of student volunteers who, deciding to "go clean for Gene," cut their long hair and shaved their counterculture beards. They knocked on doors and distributed bales of flyers and pamphlets touting their candidate and condemning the war. Johnson had not entered the New Hampshire primary, but as McCarthy's antiwar candidacy strengthened, Johnson's political advisers organized a **write-in campaign** for the president. Johnson won, but by only 6 percent of the votes cast. Political commentators promptly called McCarthy the real winner. New York senator **Robert Kennedy's** announcement of his candidacy and his surging popularity in the public opinion polls added to the pressure on Johnson. Quietly, Johnson decided to not run for the presidency.

On March 31, 1968, a haggard-looking president delivered a major televised speech announcing changes in his Vietnam policy. The United States was going to seek a political settlement through negotiations in Paris with the Viet Cong and North Vietnamese. The escalation of the ground war was over, and the South Vietnamese would take a larger role in the war. The bombing of northern North Vietnam was going to end, and a complete halt of the air war would follow the start of negotiations. At the end of his speech, Johnson calmly made this announcement: "I shall not seek, and I will not accept, the nomination of my party for another term as president." Listeners were shocked. Lyndon B. Johnson had thrown in the towel. Although he later claimed that his fear of having a heart attack while in office was the primary reason for his decision not to run, nearly everyone agreed that the Vietnam War had ended Johnson's political career and undermined his Great Society.

Tet The lunar New Year celebrated as a huge holiday in Vietnam; the Viet Cong–North Vietnamese attack on South Vietnamese cities during Tet in January 1968 was a military defeat for North Vietnam, but it seriously undermined U.S. support for the war.

Eugene McCarthy Senator who opposed the Vietnam War and made an unsuccessful bid for the 1968 Democratic nomination for president.

write-in campaign An attempt to elect a candidate in which voters are urged to write the name of an unregistered candidate directly on the ballot.

Robert Kennedy Attorney general during the presidency of his brother John F. Kennedy; elected to the Senate in 1964, his campaign for the presidency was gathering momentum when he was assassinated in 1968.

The Election of 1968

There were now three Democratic candidates. McCarthy campaigned against the war and the "imperial presidency." Kennedy opposed the war, but not executive and federal power, and he called on the government to better meet the needs of the poor and minorities. Vice President Hubert H. Humphrey, running in the shadow of Johnson, stood behind the president's foreign and domestic programs.

By June, Kennedy was winning the primary race, drawing heavily from minorities and urban Democratic voters. In the critical California primary, Kennedy gained a narrow victory over McCarthy, 46 to 41 percent, but the victory was all too short. As the winner left his campaign headquarters, he was shot by Sirhan Sirhan, a Jordanian immigrant. Kennedy died the next day. His death stunned the nation and ensured Humphrey's nomination. McCarthy continued his campaign but did not generate much support among party regulars. By the time of the national convention in Chicago in August, Humphrey had enough pledged votes to guarantee his nomination. Nevertheless, the convention was dramatic. Inside and outside the convention center, antiwar and anti-establishment groups demonstrated for McCarthy, peace in Vietnam, and social justice. Radical factions within the Students for a Democratic Society promised physical confrontation and threatened to contaminate the water supply with drugs. Chicago mayor Richard Daley, determined to maintain order, called in twelve thousand police. By August 24, the second day of the convention, clashes between the police and protesters started and grew more belligerent every day. Protesters threw eggs, bottles, rocks, and balloons filled with water, ink, and urine at the police, who responded with tear gas and nightsticks. On August 28, the police responded with force, indiscriminately attacking protesters and bystanders alike as television cameras recorded the scene. The violence in Chicago's streets overshadowed Humphrey's nomination and acceptance speech—and much of his campaign.

Many Americans were disgusted by the chaos in Chicago and saw it as typical of the general disruption that was plaguing the nation. The politics of hope that had begun the 1960s was losing its appeal by 1968. From both the political left and right came criticisms of the social policies of the Great Society and the foreign policies that mired the nation in the war in Vietnam.

Representing growing dissatisfaction with liberal social policies within Democratic ranks, Governor **George Wallace** of Alabama left the Democratic Party

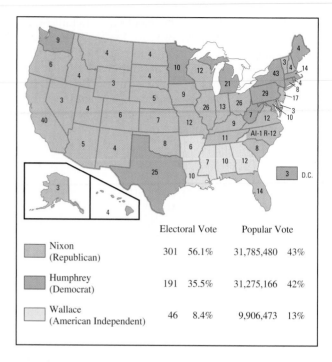

	Electoral Vote		Popular Vote	
Nixon (Republican)	301	56.1%	31,785,480	43%
Humphrey (Democrat)	191	35.5%	31,275,166	42%
Wallace (American Independent)	46	8.4%	9,906,473	13%

MAP 29.4 Election of 1968 In winning the 1968 election against Hubert Humphrey, Richard Nixon received fewer popular votes than he did in 1960, when he won more than 34 million votes. But in the all-important electoral vote, Nixon easily defeated his Democratic rival. As they did in the 1960 election, some southerners opted for a third choice, unwilling to vote for a Republican or a liberal Democrat. The third choice was George Wallace.

and ran for president as the American Independent Party's candidate. He aimed his campaign at southern whites, blue-collar workers, and low-income white Americans, all of whom deplored the "loss" of traditional American values and society. On the campaign trail, Wallace called for victory in Vietnam and took special glee in attacking the counterculture and the "rich-kid" war protesters who avoided serving in Vietnam while the sons of working-class Americans died there. He also opposed federal civil rights and welfare legislation. Two months before the election, Wallace commanded 21 percent of the vote, according to national opinion polls. "On November 5," he

George Wallace Conservative Alabama governor who opposed desegregation in the 1960s and ran unsuccessfully for the presidency in 1968 and 1972.

Violence erupted during the 1968 Democratic National Convention in Chicago. Using nightsticks, police attacked antiwar and anti-establishment protesters in Grant Park, near the convention hotel. The violent confrontations in Chicago did little to quell similar protests, unify the Democratic Party, or help Hubert Humphrey's chances for election. *Jeffrey Blankfort/Jeroboam.*

confidently predicted, "they're going to find out there are a lot of rednecks in this country."

Richard Nixon was the Republican candidate, having easily won his party's nomination at an orderly convention. He also intended to tap the general dissatisfaction, but without the antagonism of the Wallace campaign. He and **Spiro Agnew,** his vice-presidential running mate, focused the Republican campaign on the need for effective international leadership and law and order at home, while denouncing pot, pornography, protesters, and permissiveness. Nixon announced that he would "end the war and win the peace in Vietnam" but refused to comment further. Nixon won with a comfortable margin in the Electoral College although he received only 43 percent of the popular vote (see Map 29.4). Conservatives were pleased. Together, Nixon and Wallace attracted almost 56 percent of the popular vote, which conservatives interpreted as wide public support for an end to liberal social programs and a return to traditional values.

Nixon Confronts the World

■ How did Richard Nixon plan to achieve an "honorable" peace in Vietnam?

■ How did Nixon's Cold War policies differ from those favored by earlier administrations?

As 1969 started, Nixon declared himself a happy man. He had achieved the dream that had been denied him in 1960. As president, he was determined to be the center of decision making, using a few close and loyal advisers to make policy. For domestic affairs, he relied on John Mitchell, his choice for attorney general, and longtime associates H. R. "Bob" Haldeman and

Spiro Agnew Vice president under Richard Nixon; he resigned in 1973 amid charges of illegal financial dealings during his governorship of Maryland.

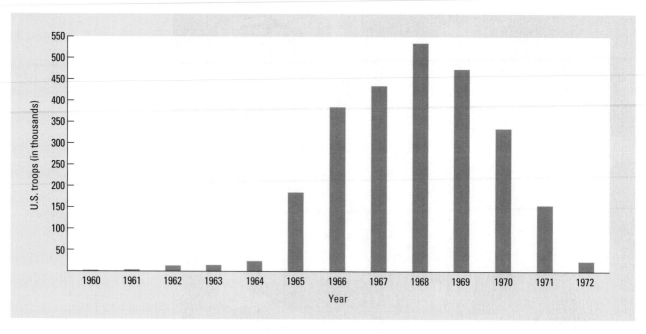

FIGURE 29.1 Troop Levels by Year For America, the Vietnam War went through two major phases: Americanization from 1960 to 1968 and Vietnamization from 1969 to 1972.

John Ehrlichman. In foreign affairs, he tapped Harvard professor **Henry Kissinger,** as his national security adviser, and later made him secretary of state.

Repeating his campaign pledges, President Nixon promised to work for national unity and to promote minority rights. But he also wanted to consolidate a new conservative majority that linked long-term Republicans with those recently dissatisfied with protests, the Great Society, and the "liberal" attacks on traditional American society. While he presented himself as a pragmatic politician who could balance liberal and conservative views, his close circle of advisers knew that Nixon had little desire to incorporate liberal views with his own. Instead, he would court what he called the **"Silent Majority."**

Vietnamization

Nixon took office and faced not only a Democratic Congress but the looming specter of Vietnam. Vietnam influenced nearly all other issues—the budget, public and congressional opinion, foreign policy, and domestic stability—and Nixon needed a solution before he could move ahead on other fronts. No one in the administration questioned whether American

troops would be withdrawn, but there was considerable debate over the exit speed and how to ensure that the government of Nguyen Van Thieu remained intact. There was also the issue of international credibility. If the United States just left Vietnam, Nixon believed, it would harm American relations with its friends. "A nation cannot remain great, if it betrays its allies and lets down its friends."

The product was **Vietnamization.** As American troops left, better-trained, better-led, and better-

Henry Kissinger German-born American diplomat who was President Nixon's national security adviser and secretary of state; he helped negotiate the cease-fire in Vietnam.

Silent Majority Name given to the majority of Americans who supported the government and did not protest or riot; a typical member of the Silent Majority was believed to be white, middle class, average in income and education, and moderately conservative in values and attitudes.

Vietnamization U.S. policy of scaling back American involvement in Vietnam and helping Vietnamese forces fight their own war.

Together, Richard Nixon and Secretary of State Henry Kissinger (shown here) sought to refocus American foreign policy by ending the war in Vietnam and improving relations with the Soviet Union and the People's Republic of China. *Camera Press/Retna, Ltd.*

equipped South Vietnamese units would resume the bulk of the fighting (see Figure 29.1). In direct support of the South Vietnamese, the United States would provide increased air support, including if necessary the resumption of bombing North Vietnam. Changing the "color of bodies" and bringing American soldiers home, Nixon believed, would rebuild public support and diminish the crowds of protesters. Expanding the theme of limiting American involvement, in July Nixon developed the **Nixon Doctrine:** countries warding off communism would have to shoulder most of the military burden, with the United States providing political and economic support and limited naval and air support.

Nixon publicly announced Vietnamization in the spring of 1969, telling the public that 25,000 American soldiers were coming home. At the same time, he convinced some in the media to alter their coverage of the war. ABC's news director instructed his staff to downplay the fighting and emphasize "themes and stories under the general heading: We are on our way out of Vietnam." By the end of the year, American forces in

Vietnam had declined by over 110,000, and public opinion polls indicated support for Nixon's policy.

The other dimensions of Nixon's Vietnam policy, however, were unknown to either the public or the press. Quietly, Kissinger and Nixon began work to improve relations with the Soviets and Chinese and to encourage them to reduce their support for North Vietnam. More significantly, the United States expanded its air war in two directions: targeting enemy bases inside Cambodia and Laos and resuming the bombardment of North Vietnam. The secret attacks on Communist sanctuaries inside Cambodia (Operation Menu) began in March 1969, with air force records being falsified to aid in official denials of stories about any such strikes. The intense air assault

---

Nixon Doctrine   Nixon's policy of requiring countries threatened by communism to shoulder most of the military burden, with the United States offering mainly political and economic support.

On May 4, 1970, Ohio National Guard troops opened fire on a crowd of Kent State students protesting the American incursion into Cambodia, killing four of them. Here, a student screams in horror as she hovers over the body of one of the dead students. In outrage, campuses throughout the nation closed and students flocked to Washington to protest the war. *John Filo.*

As Nixon assumed office, antiwar protests heated up as protests occurred around the nation, culminated by the March on Washington in 1969. In 1970 news about the invasion also refueled antiwar protests across the United States, especially on college campuses. Demonstrations at Kent State University in Ohio and at Jackson State University in Mississippi resulted in the deaths of six protesters. An angry Senate repealed the Gulf of Tonkin Resolution, which had provided the legislative foundation for the war, and forbade the further use of American troops in Laos or Cambodia.

Also adding to a broad opposition to the continued American role in Vietnam were reports of American atrocities around the village of **My Lai** and the release of the **Pentagon Papers.** In 1968, American units, including a platoon commanded by Lieutenant William Calley, had killed over 500 hundred men, women, and children in and around the village of My Lai. The death toll would have been greater if army helicopter pilot Hugh Thompson and his crew had not rescued eleven civilians about to be killed by American soldiers. "It had to happen then, Thompson said, "'cause they were fixin' to die." Later, an official evaluation stated that some units and officers were "eager participants in the body-count game." The massacre, stories about drug use, **fragging,** and seemingly mindless slaughter strengthened the belief that the war was unraveling the morality of American soldiers. As Thompson explained, "This is not what the American soldier does." The moral fiber of American leadership also was questioned with the unauthorized publishing of secret documents (the

was part of a "madman strategy" that Nixon designed to convince the North Vietnamese to negotiate. Nixon said he wanted Hanoi "to believe that I've reached the point where I might do anything to stop the war." "We'll just slip the word," Nixon told his advisers, "that 'for God's sake, you know Nixon. . . . We can't restrain him when he's angry—and he has his hand on the nuclear button.'"

The strategy did not work. The North Vietnamese appeared unconcerned about Nixon's "madness," the increased bombing, or decreasing support from China and the Soviet Union. They believed that victory was only a matter of patiently waiting until America was fed up with the war. Consequently, **peace talks** between Kissinger and the North Vietnamese in Paris produced only bitter feelings. Despite such setbacks, Nixon continued his strategy, and in 1970 ordered American troops to cross the border into Cambodia and destroy Communist bases and supply areas. Nearly eighty thousand American and South Vietnamese troops entered Cambodia and demolished enemy bases and large amounts of supplies. The mission, however, failed to halt the flow of supplies or weaken North Vietnam's resolve.

peace talks   Began in 1968 under the Johnson administration and continued by Nixon's; they produced little agreement until 1972 when Kissinger and North Vietnamese foreign minister Le Doc Tho began to work out a final accord that was signed in 1973.

My Lai   Site of a massacre of South Vietnamese villagers by U.S. infantrymen in 1968. Of those brought to trial for the murders, only Lieutenant William Calley was found guilty of murder. Originally sentenced to life in prison, he was paroled in 1974.

Pentagon Papers   Classified government documents on policy decisions leaked to the press by Daniel Ellsberg and printed by the *New York Times* in 1971. Efforts to block the papers' publication was rejected by a Supreme Court ruling.

fragging   An effort to kill fellow soldiers, frequently officers, by using a grenade. It may have accounted for over a thousand American deaths in Vietnam.

As North Vietnamese forces entered Saigon in April 1975, the last American evacuees left by helicopter. Here, they scramble to the roof of the Pittman apartments in Saigon; others left from the roof of the American embassy. Henry Kissinger asked the nation "to put Vietnam behind us." ©*Bettmann/Corbis.*

Pentagon Papers) that indicated that American administrations from Truman to Nixon had not told the truth about Vietnam to the American people.

Despite public opinion polls indicating that two-thirds of the American people wanted to get out of Vietnam, Nixon's determination to maintain his policies never wavered. His resolve, however, was matched by North Vietnam. With peace discussions in Paris stalemated, the North Vietnamese in March 1972 launched its "Easter Offensive." Pushing aside Army of South Vietnam (ARVN) troops, Communist forces advanced toward Saigon. A livid Nixon ordered massive bombing raids against North Vietnam and Communist forces in South Vietnam. By mid-June 1972, American air power had stalled the offensive and enabled ARVN forces to regroup and drive back the North Vietnamese. With their cities under almost continuous air attacks, the North Vietnamese became more flexible in negotiations. By October, with both sides offering some concessions, a peace settlement was ready. "Peace is at hand," Kissinger announced—just in time for the 1972 presidential election.

South Vietnamese president Nguyen Van Thieu, however, rejected the plan. Reluctantly, Nixon supported Thieu and ordered the Christmas bombing of Hanoi and North Vietnam. One goal was to put additional pressure on Hanoi. Another was to convince

Thieu that the United States would use its air power to protect South Vietnam. After eleven days the bombing stopped, and Washington advised Thieu that if he did not accept the next peace settlement, the United States would leave him to fend for himself. On January 27, 1973, Thieu accepted a peace settlement that did not differ significantly from the one offered in October. Nixon and Kissinger proclaimed peace with honor, and Kissinger shared the 1973 Nobel Peace Prize with his North Vietnamese counterpart.

The peace settlement imposed a cease-fire; required the removal of the twenty-four thousand remaining American troops, but not North Vietnamese troops; and promised the return of American prisoners of war. The peace terms permitted the United States to complete its military and political withdrawal, but the pact did little to ensure the continued existence of Thieu's government or South Vietnam. The cease-fire, everyone expected, would be temporary. When Haldeman asked Kissinger how long the South Vietnamese government could last, Kissinger answered bluntly, "If they're lucky, they can hold out for a year and a half."

As expected, the cease-fire soon collapsed. North Vietnam continued to funnel men and supplies to the south, but substantial American air and naval support for South Vietnam never arrived. Neither Congress nor the public was eager to help Thieu's government.

TABLE 29 . 2   The Vietnam Generation, 1964–1975

	Men	Women
Total in military service	8,700,000	250,000
Served in Vietnam	2,700,000	6,431
Killed in Vietnam	300,635*	
Wounded	46,000	9
Missing in action	2,330	—
Draft resisters (estimate)	570,000	—
Accused	210,000	—
Convicted	8,750	—

*Combined men and women

Source: Department of Defense and Veterans Administration.

Instead, Congress cut aid to South Vietnam and in November 1973 passed the **War Powers Act.** The law requires the president to inform Congress within forty-eight hours of the deployment of troops overseas and to withdraw those troops within sixty days if Congress fails to authorize the action. In March 1975, North Vietnam began its final campaign to unify the country. A month later, North Vietnamese troops entered Saigon as a few remaining Americans and some South Vietnamese were evacuated by helicopter—some dramatically from the roof of the American embassy. The Vietnam War ended as it had started, with Vietnamese fighting Vietnamese (see Table 29.2).

Modifying the Cold War

Ending the Vietnam War was a political and diplomatic necessity for Nixon and was part of his plan to reshape the Cold War. In his first inaugural address, Nixon urged that an "era of confrontation" give way to an "era of negotiation." To this end, he pursued **détente,** a policy that reduced tensions with the two Communist superpowers. China, with which the United States had had virtually no diplomatic contact since the end of the Chinese civil war in 1949, was the key to the Nixon-Kissinger strategy. The Soviets and Chinese had engaged in several bloody clashes along their border, and the Chinese feared a broader border war. Wanting American technology and believing

that better relations with the United States would help deter Soviet aggression, the Chinese were ready to open diplomatic discussions with Nixon.

Nixon believed that American friendship with the Chinese would encourage the Soviets to improve their relations with the United States, leading to détente, and opening a great potential market for American producers. Sending a signal to China, Nixon lowered restrictions on trade, and in April 1971 the Chinese responded by inviting an American Ping-Pong team to tour China. A few months later, Kissinger secretly flew to Beijing to meet with Premier Zhou Enlai. The result would, as Kissinger phrased it, "send a shock wave around the world": Nixon was going to China. In February 1972, Nixon arrived in Beijing and met with Communist Party chairman Mao Zedong and Zhou. Suddenly the "Red Chinese" were no longer the enemy but "hard-working, intelligent . . . and practical" people. The Cold War was thawing a little in the East.

War Powers Act   Law passed by Congress in 1973 to prevent the president from involving the United States in war without authorization by Congress.

détente   Relaxing of tensions between the superpowers in the early 1970s, which led to increased diplomatic, commercial, and cultural contact.

In efforts to redirect the Cold War, Nixon became the first president to visit China, meeting with Mao Zedong and Zhou Enlai in 1972. With regard to Chinese-Soviet relations, Nixon confided to Zhou that if Moscow marched either east or west, he was ready to "turn like a cobra on the Russians." Nixon's visit to China began the process of normalizing relations with the People's Republic of China that was finalized under Carter. *John Dominis, LIFE Magazine ©Time Warner, Inc.*

However, in some areas, America's traditional Cold War stance was unwavering. In Latin America, Nixon followed closely in Johnson's footsteps, working to isolate Cuba and to prevent any additional Communist-style leaders from gaining power. Borrowing from Eisenhower's foreign policy, he used covert operations to disrupt the democratically elected socialist-Marxist government of **Salvador Allende** in Chile. For three years the CIA squeezed the Chilean economy "until it screamed," producing food riots, numerous strikes, and massive inflation. Finally, in September 1973, Chilean armed forces bombed and stormed the presidential palace, killing Allende. Kissinger denied any direct American role in the coup and quickly recognized the repressive military government of General Augusto Pinochet, who promptly reinstated a free-market economy.

Nixon and the Presidency

■ How did Nixon's choices in dealing with welfare reform, the economy, and the environment reflect traditional Republican policies?

■ What led to Nixon's success in the 1972 election?

■ How did Nixon expect to create a new conservative base for the Republican Party, and what actions did he take to accomplish that goal?

■ What actions led to the Watergate investigation and Nixon's resignation?

■ What success did Gerald Ford have in continuing the policies of the Nixon administration?

In his foreign policy, Nixon followed new paths in dealing with the Chinese and Soviets that did not reflect traditional Republican policies. This was also true in domestic affairs. Nixon had complex views of a new Republican domestic agenda that needed to be

Nixon's China policy, as hoped, contributed to détente with the Soviet Union. Kissinger followed his secret visit to China with one to Moscow, where he discussed improving relations with President **Leonid Brezhnev.** Nixon flew to Moscow in May 1972 and told Brezhnev that he believed that the two nations should "live together and work together." Needing to reduce military spending, develop the Soviet domestic economy, and increase American trade, Brezhnev agreed. The meeting was a success. Brezhnev obtained increased trade with the West, including shipments of American grain, and the superpowers announced the **Strategic Arms Limitation agreement** (SALT I), which restricted antimissile sites and established a maximum number of intercontinental ballistic missiles (ICBMs) and submarine-launched ballistic missiles (SLBMs) for each side. It seemed as if Nixon was reshaping world affairs.

Leonid Brezhnev Leader of the Soviet Union (first as Communist Party secretary, and then also as president) from 1964 to his death in 1982; he worked to foster détente with the United States during the Nixon era.

Strategic Arms Limitation agreement Treaty between the United States and the Soviet Union in 1972 to limit offensive nuclear weapons and defensive antiballistic missile systems; known as SALT I.

Salvador Allende Chilean president who was considered the first democratically elected Marxist to head a government; he was killed in a coup in 1973.

more receptive to social responsibility and executive activism. Domestic adviser Daniel Patrick Moynihan pointed out that with the Democrats controlling Congress, it was "time to consolidate, not innovate." Nonetheless, Nixon told his advisers to plan new initiatives; he wanted "game plans" and not reactions.

Nixon as Pragmatist

For most of his first term, Nixon played **pragmatic** politics. Without fanfare, his administration increased welfare support and approved legislation that enhanced the regulatory powers of the federal government. Food stamps became more accessible, and Social Security, Medicare, and Medicaid payments were increased. In October 1969, Nixon established a new approach to affirmative action with the "Philadelphia Plan," which required construction unions in that city working under government contracts to hire black apprentices. The following year, the plan became national in scope, involving all government hiring and contracting and setting aside jobs for minorities. Nixon also supported subsidized housing for low- and middle-income families, expanded the Job Corps, and oversaw the formation of the Occupational Safety and Health Administration (OSHA).

At the same time, he abolished Johnson's Office of Economic Opportunity and sought a way to eliminate the welfare bureaucracy. He believed the welfare system robbed people of their self-esteem, contributed to the breakup of nuclear families, and punished people for working. The Family Assistance Plan introduced in 1969 sought to replace existing programs and agencies with a direct payment, provided the recipient accepted work or job training. It was an innovative plan, but neither conservatives nor liberals adopted the idea, and it was defeated in the Senate in 1969 and 1971. Despite that defeat, Nixon believed that the Republican Party could not afford to ignore social needs and public concerns.

The environmental issue was a case in point. When Nixon took office in 1969, the condition of the environment was an increasingly serious public issue. Urban air pollution, an oil slick off Santa Barbara, California, the declaration that Lake Erie was ecologically dead, and growing mountains of garbage everywhere provided graphic reminders of the ecological dangers facing the nation. Though constituting less than 6 percent of the world's population, environmentalists complained, Americans consumed 40 percent of the globe's resources and created 50 percent of the world's trash. During the first celebra-

On April 22, 1970, the nation celebrated the first national Earth Day. Part of the environmental movement, Earth Day emphasized the things that ordinary people could do to improve the environment. A few days later, President Nixon created the Environmental Protection Agency. *Ken Regan/Camera 5.*

tion of Earth Day, in April 1970, nearly every community in the nation and more than ten thousand schools and two thousand colleges hosted some type of Earth Day activities, emphasizing a national call for government action to improve environmental quality.

Nixon was not an environmentalist, but he recog-

pragmatic Concerned with facts and actual events; in this case, refers to a willingness to adopt policies that could be either liberal or conservative, depending on the need.

nized a new national agenda topic. Seizing the opportunity, two days after Earth Day 1970, he proposed the creation of the **Environmental Protection Agency** (EPA). Congress joined in, approving five major environmental acts before the year was finished, including the Clean Air Act and the Water Quality Improvement Act. Both acts directed the EPA, which was rapidly growing into the third-largest government agency, to establish standards on the amount of pollutants that business and industry could discharge. Conservatives grumbled that the standards placed too great a burden on business, and liberals objected that the guidelines did not go far enough to protect the environment.

Nixon also proved flexible in economic matters. When he took office, he faced a budget deficit of nearly $25 billion and a climbing rate of inflation. Nixon cut spending, increased interest rates, and balanced the budget in 1969. But economic recovery failed to follow, and inflation rose as economic growth slowed—giving rise to a new phenomenon, **stagflation.** By 1971, the economy was in its first recession since 1958. Unemployment and bankruptcies increased, but inflation still climbed, approaching 5.3 percent. Fearing that economic woes would erode his support, Nixon radically shifted his approach. In April 1971, he asked for increased federal spending to boost recovery and for wage and price controls to stall advancing inflation. Conservatives were shocked and complained bitterly at the betrayal of their values. The public and the economy responded positively, however, as inflation and unemployment declined. At the end of ninety days, Nixon replaced the wage and price freeze with recommended guidelines. Freed from federal restrictions, wages and prices began to climb again.

Nixon's battle with inflation was a losing one, in part because of events over which he had no control. A global drought pushed up farm prices, while Arab nations raised oil prices and limited oil sales in response to the devaluation of the American dollar and continued U.S. support for Israel. After the October 1973 Arab-Israeli **Yom Kippur War,** Arab nations instituted an oil embargo on the United States that, before it was over in 1974, nearly doubled gasoline prices and forced many Americans to wait in long lines to gas up their cars. Increases in food and oil prices pushed the 1974 inflation rate over 10 percent. That same year, 85 percent of those asked said not only that the economy was the nation's most pressing problem but also that they expected the situation to get worse.

It Matters

Improving the Environment

The formation of the Environmental Protection Agency affirmed the importance of improving the public's health and protecting the environment by the federal government. Among its most prominent goals are clean air and water, safe food, and reducing global environmental risks. A central part of the EPA's actions have been to enforce regulations, such as the clean-air acts, that seek to reduce the emission of carbon dioxide and other carbon-based emissions. Between 1970 and 2002, EPA efforts have overseen a 48 percent reduction in carbon dioxide levels in the United States. Environmentalists call for more to be done to reduce the emission of pollutants. But critics argue that the existing environmental regulations are too stringent and hamper economic growth, energy production, and product innovation. While most administrations have favored some toughening of air- and water-quality standards, in 2002 that trend began to be reversed as the George W. Bush administration decided to weaken existing regulations for air pollutants. While administrations promote different priorities and policies, contracting or expanding the agenda, no administration can ignore the issue—environmentalism has become a recognized movement and part of American life.

Environmental Protection Agency Agency created in 1970 to consolidate all major governmental programs controlling pollution and other programs to protect the environment.

stagflation Persistent inflation combined with stagnant consumer demand and relatively high unemployment.

Yom Kippur War On October 6, 1973, Egypt and Syria suddenly invaded Israel; after initial losses, the Israeli military defeated the Arab armies; with U.S. support, negotiations finally led to a cease-fire on October 22.

Building the Silent Majority

During the 1968 campaign, Nixon had presented himself as the law-and-order candidate who would use the resources and power of government to combat crime and restore social stability. Nixon also hoped to use this issue to build a new, broader conservative base for the Republican Party. An aide to Attorney General **John Mitchell,** Kevin Phillips, argued in *The Emerging Republican Majority* (1969) that the future of the Republican Party rested on the support of people living in suburbs, working-class neighborhoods, the South, and the Sunbelt. In those areas, Phillips asserted, there was little sympathy for student activists, antiwar protesters, welfare recipients, or civil rights advocates. The parts of the new coalition of southern and other disaffected Democrats and Republicans could, in Nixon's terms, gain control of Congress by realignment rather than by election.

Zealously, Vice President Spiro Agnew denounced antiwar protesters for aiding the enemy and undermining the nation's social and patriotic values, and he challenged the Silent Majority to reassert traditional values and restore stability to America. In many areas, blue-collar and middle-class America responded to Agnew's plea. Fearing integration and experiencing a slowing of economic gains, more and more of suburban America voted Republican. In southern California, residents of Lakewood (see Chapter 30) felt threatened by a seeming "invasion" of blacks and Latinos, who used "their" parks and swimming pools, encroaching on what had once been a model, modern, and upwardly mobile suburb.

As part of an ongoing **"southern strategy"**—an attempt to lock up the once solidly Democratic South for Republicans—the Nixon administration opposed busing to achieve school integration. In response to a 1969 request from Mississippi to postpone court-ordered integration of several school systems, Attorney General John Mitchell petitioned the Supreme Court for a delay. At the same time, the administration lobbied Congress for a revision of the 1965 Voting Rights Act that would have weakened southern compliance. Neither effort was successful. In October 1969, the Supreme Court unanimously decreed in *Alexander v. Holmes* that it was "the obligation of every school district to terminate dual school systems at once." The White House suffered another loss in 1971 when the Burger Court reaffirmed the use of busing to achieve integration in a North Carolina case, *Swann v. Charlotte-Mecklenburg.* The Nixon administration criticized the decisions but agreed to "carry

out the law." By 1973, most African American children in the South were attending integrated public schools. Even though Nixon was unable to slow the process of integration, he won increasing political support among white southerners.

A second part of Nixon's southern strategy was to alter the composition of the Supreme Court. He wanted a more conservative Court that would more narrowly interpret the Constitution and move away from the social interventionism of the Warren Court. His first opportunity came in 1969 when Chief Justice Earl Warren retired. To take Warren's place, Nixon nominated Warren Burger, a respected, conservative federal judge, who was easily confirmed by the Senate. The resignation of liberal justice Abe Fortas soon after gave Nixon a second chance to alter the Court.

For political reasons, Nixon nominated Clement Haynesworth of South Carolina. Haynesworth's history of antilabor and anti–civil rights statements and decisions raised predictable trouble in the Senate. Democrats and several Republicans joined forces to deny his confirmation. The rejection incensed Nixon, who was determined to force a southerner down the Senate's throat. His second choice was worse than the first. Not only was G. Harrold Carswell of Florida opposed to civil rights and labor, but his ratings as a lawyer and judge were below average. Carswell, too, failed confirmation. On his third try, Nixon stopped looking for a southerner and selected Harry Blackmun, a conservative from Minnesota. Blackmun was confirmed easily. In 1971 Nixon appointed two more justices, Lewis Powell of Virginia and William Rehnquist of Arizona, creating a more conservative Supreme Court.

An Embattled President

By the end of Nixon's first term, Republicans had every reason to gloat. Nearly 60 percent of respondents in national opinion polls said they approved of Nixon's record. The efforts on behalf of southern

---

John Mitchell Nixon's attorney general, who eventually served four years in prison for his part in the Watergate scandal.

southern strategy A plan to entice southerners into the Republican Party by appointing white southerners to the Supreme Court and resisting the policy of busing to achieve integration.

FIFTY CENTS   APRIL 30, 1973

WATERGATE
BREAKS WIDE OPEN

TIME

ISRAEL AT 25

As the Watergate investigation uncovered a host of "dirty tricks" and other unethical and illegal activities by the Nixon administration, it seemed that passing the blame became an administration pastime. *TimeLife Pictures/Getty Images.*

The 1972 campaign was marked by a confident Republican Party and the continued disarray of the Democratic Party. Most of the enthusiastic Democrats had migrated to the two wings of the party, led by the liberal **George McGovern** and the conservative George Wallace. Moderate Democrats seemed unable to energize the voters, especially the new group of first-time voters—those between 18 and 21. The newest category of voter was a result of the Twenty-sixth Amendment, ratified in 1971, which had lowered the voting age to 18.

Senator McGovern of South Dakota gained the presidential nomination after several bruising primaries and a divided nominating convention. Many Democrats believed he was too liberal and refused to support him. George Wallace—confined to a wheelchair following an assassination attempt that left him paralyzed—again bolted the party to run as a third-party candidate on the American Independent ticket.

Despite almost certain victory, as he had been since taking office, Nixon was convinced that enemies surrounded him: bureaucrats, Democrats, social activists, liberals, most of the press, and even some members of his own staff and party. Repeatedly, he spoke about "screwing" his domestic enemies before they got him. He kept an "enemies list," used illegal wiretaps and infiltration to spy on suspect organizations and people, and instructed the FBI, the Internal Revenue Service, and other governmental organizations to intimidate and punish his opponents.

Nixon and his campaign coordinators longed to humiliate the Democrats. To achieve this, Nixon's staff and the **Committee to Re-elect the President** (CREEP), directed by John Mitchell, stepped outside the normal bounds of election behavior. They turned to a Special Investigations Unit, known informally as the "Plumbers," who conducted "dirty tricks" to disrupt the Democrats. They sponsored hecklers to attack Democratic candidates who supported McGovern. Seeking inside information on the opposition, CREEP approved a burglary of the Democratic

whites had ensured growing support in what had once been the "solid Democratic South." The law-and-order campaign appealed to so-called Middle America, and protesters and activists were losing strength. The economy, though still a worry, seemed under control: unemployment was dropping, and inflation was being held in check. Diplomatically, Nixon had scored major successes: the opening of relations with China, détente with the Soviets, the reduction of American forces in Vietnam, and the possibility of a peace agreement in Paris. Nixon projected that his second term would hold few obstacles, especially since he did not have to run for office again.

George McGovern   South Dakota senator who opposed the Vietnam War and was the unsuccessful Democratic candidate for president in 1972.

Committee to Re-elect the President   Nixon's campaign committee in 1972, which enlisted G. Gordon Liddy and others to spy on the Democrats and break into the offices of the Democratic National Committee.

National Committee headquarters in the **Watergate** building in Washington, D.C., to copy documents and tap phones.

On June 17, 1972, a Watergate security guard detected the burglars and notified the police, who arrested five men carrying "bugging" equipment. Soon the burglars were linked to the Plumbers and then to CREEP. CREEP and the White House denied any connection to the burglars, while Mitchell and White House staffers destroyed documents indicating the opposite and encouraged the FBI to limit its investigation. "I want you all to stonewall it," Nixon told John Mitchell. "Cover it up." The furor passed, and in November, Nixon buried McGovern in an avalanche of electoral votes, winning every state except Massachusetts. It was a personal victory, however, as Democrats still held majorities in Congress.

Nixon was overjoyed with the results. He had demolished his enemies and claimed a public mandate for his policies. Within the White House, however, the cheers were tempered with concerns about the trial of the Watergate burglars. The cover-up was unraveling. Key Republicans were being implicated in the planning of the operation and in paying "hush money" to the burglars. *Washington Post* reporters Bob Woodward and Carl Bernstein investigated the suspicious payments and found a path leading to John Mitchell, CREEP, and the White House. To investigate allegations of White House involvement, the Senate convened a special committee to investigate the break-in, chaired by a Democrat, Senator Sam Ervin Jr. of North Carolina. Among those testifying was White House staffer John Dean, who implicated top White House officials, including Nixon, in the cover-up.

Adding to Nixon's troubles were accusations he had improperly taken tax deductions and that Vice President Agnew was guilty of income-tax evasion and influence peddling. "I am not a crook," Nixon announced, as both denied any wrongdoing. Nevertheless, Nixon agreed that he had made errors in his income-tax deductions and that he owed the government an additional half-million dollars. Agnew, certain to be convicted, pleaded no contest to the charges against him and resigned. In October 1973, Nixon named Representative Gerald R. Ford of Michigan to be vice president.

As Ford assumed office, the cover-up rapidly disintegrated. The revelation that Nixon had secretly recorded meetings in the Oval Office, including those with John Dean, raised demands for the release of the tapes. Responding to public pressure, Nixon appointed Archibald Cox, a Harvard law professor, as

special Justice Department prosecutor to investigate Watergate, promising full cooperation. But when Cox demanded the Oval Office tapes, Nixon ordered him fired. Following the October 20, 1973, **"Saturday Night Massacre,"** Nixon's popularity shrank to 30 percent, and calls for his resignation or impeachment intensified.

In March 1974, the grand jury investigating the Watergate break-in **indicted** Mitchell, Haldeman, and Ehrlichman and named Nixon as an "unindicted co-conspirator." Nixon, under tremendous pressure, released transcripts of selected tapes. The outcome was devastating. The transcripts contradicted some official testimony, and Nixon's apparent callousness, lack of decency, and profane language shocked the nation. By the end of July, the House Judiciary Committee had charged Nixon with three impeachable crimes: obstructing justice, abuse of power, and defying subpoenas. Nixon's remaining support evaporated, and once-loyal Republicans told him that he could either resign or face impeachment. Nixon resigned on August 9, 1974, making Nixon's vice-presidential appointee, Gerald Ford, an unelected president. Eventually, twenty-nine people connected to the White House were convicted of crimes related to Watergate and the 1972 campaign. Ex-president Nixon was spared from any further legal actions by a presidential pardon granted by Ford upon assuming office.

An Interim President

Most saw Gerald Ford as an honest man, a good administrator, a compassionate person to heal a nation, but as only an interim president. Ford's most immediate issue was the sluggish economy, and his approach was the traditional Republican one: cutting

Watergate   Apartment and office complex in Washington, D.C., that housed the headquarters of the Democratic National Committee; its name became synonymous with the scandal over the Nixon administration's involvement in a break-in there and the president's part in the cover-up that followed.

Saturday Night Massacre   Events on October 20, 1973, when Nixon ordered the firing of Watergate special prosecutor Archibald Cox; rather than carry out Nixon's order, both the U.S. attorney general and deputy attorney general resigned.

indict   To make a formal charge of wrongdoing against a person or party.

business taxes and federal spending while raising interest rates. Democrats rejected the formula and instead introduced legislation to create jobs and to increase spending for social and educational programs. Ford vetoed the bills and conducted a public opinion campaign to mobilize support for his program. The result was a political stalemate. In two years, Ford successfully blocked thirty-seven bills but never generated enough public support to advance his own programs. At the same time, the economy continued to worsen. Oil prices rose 350 percent after the **Organization of Petroleum Exporting Countries** (OPEC) placed an embargo on the sale of oil to the United States in order to modify American support to Israel during the Yom Kippur War.

In his foreign policy, Ford relied heavily on Henry Kissinger, who was now national security adviser and secretary of state. Kissinger played a key role in negotiating a cease-fire to the Yom Kippur War and continued to work for a reduction of tensions in the Middle East. Shuttling between Israel and Egypt and Israel and Syria, Kissinger brokered a peace agreement that removed Israeli forces from Egyptian territory (January 1974) and Syria (May, 1974). His efforts paid off in September 1975, when Israel and Egypt signed a pact whereby Israeli troops withdrew from some occupied areas and Egypt resigned from the anti–Israeli-Arab coalition. An added benefit of the agreement was that it convinced OPEC to increase oil production and lower prices. Other foreign-policy efforts, however, produced few positive results, in part due to opposition from the right and the left in Congress.

Ford's efforts to maintain economic and military support for South Vietnam also met with congressional opposition and delays, and when Saigon fell to Communist forces in April 1975, Ford blamed Congress for the defeat. On the Russian front, trying to maintain the Nixon-Kissinger effort to arrive at détente with Moscow, he met with Soviet premier Brezhnev at Vladivostok in Siberia, and in Helsinki, Finland. At the summits he made progress toward strategic arms limitation and improved East-West relations but received little credit at home. In Congress and within his own party, Ford's actions drew fire from those who wanted a tougher, more traditional Cold War policy toward the Soviet Union.

Among the most forceful Republican critics was presidential hopeful Ronald Reagan. Embarrassing a sitting president, Reagan sought the Republican nomination in 1976 and won several primaries in the West and South. The ex-governor of California represented the conservative wing of the party and attacked the Ford-Kissinger policy of détente as well as Ford's political ineffectiveness. Ford managed to eke out a victory at the convention, embracing a conservative agenda that called for smaller government and tougher policies toward communism, but few expected the interim president to win the election.

Organization of Petroleum Exporting Countries
Economic alliance of oil-producing countries, mostly Arab, formed in 1960, powerful enough to influence the world price of oil by controlling oil supplies; in 1973 its members placed an embargo on the sale of oil to countries allied with Israel.

Individual Voices

Examining a Primary Source

Striking Grape Workers Proclaim Their Goals

In 1965 César Chávez called a strike of the National Farm Workers Association against the grape growers in Delano, California. When traditional labor protests such as picket lines failed to work, he moved to mobilize public opinion. He fasted, held parades and rallies, and called on consumers to buy only union-picked grapes. This document, which appeared in the NFWA newspaper, *El Malcriado* ("The Unruly One") in May 1969, was printed in Spanish and English to rally those supporting *la huelga,* the strike, and to explain in revolutionary terms the efforts of the strikers. The strike was settled in 1970.

■ What do the writers of the proclamation mean when they call themselves "pilgrims"?

■ What changes in society are the strikers seeking?

■ According to the document, why did the traditional tool of labor, the strike, fail, and why did the strikers turn to using a boycott?

■ How do the sentiments in this document compare with César Chávez's goals for La Causa?

We the striking grape workers of California join . . . with consumers across the continent in planning the steps that lie ahead on the road to our liberation. . . .

We have been farm workers for hundreds of years and pioneers for seven. Mexicans, Filipinos, Africans, and others, our ancestors were among those who founded this land and tamed its wilderness. But we are still pilgrims on this land, and we are pioneers who blaze a trail out of the wilderness of hunger and deprivation. . . . ■ *If this road we chart leads to the rights and reforms we demand, if it leads to just wages, humane working conditions, protection from the misuse of pesticides, and to the fundamental right of collective bargaining, if it changes the social order that relegates us to the bottom reaches of society, then in our wake will follow thousands of American farm workers.* ■ *Our example will make them free. But if our road does not bring us victory and social change, it will not be because . . . our resolve is too weak, but only because our bodies are mortal and our journey hard. For we are in the midst of a great social movement, and we will not stop struggling 'til we die, or win!*

We have been farm workers for hundreds of years and strikers for four. It was four years ago that we threw down our plowshares and pruning hooks. These Biblical symbols of peace and tranquility to us represent too many lifetimes of unprotesting submission to a degrading social system that allows us no dignity, no comfort, no peace. . . . So we went and stood tall outside the vineyards where we had stooped for years. But the tailors of national labor legislation left us naked . . . our picket lines crippled by injunctions and harassed by growers; our strike was broken by imported scabs; our overtures to our employers were ignored. Yet we knew the day must come when they would talk to us as equals.

We have been farm workers for hundreds of years and boycotters for two. We did not choose the grape boycott, but we had chosen to leave our peonage, poverty, and despair behind. Though our first bid for freedom, the strike, was weakened, we would not turn back. The boycott was the only way forward the growers left to us. ■ *We called upon our fellow men and were answered by consumers who said—as all men of conscience must—that they would no longer allow their tables to be subsidized by our sweat and our sorrow. They shunned the grapes, fruit of our affliction.*

. . . The grapes grow sweet and heavy on the vines, but they will have to wait while we reach out first for our freedom. The time is ripe for our liberation. ■

Summary

When President Johnson assumed the presidency in 1963, the forces of liberalism that had given substance to the Kennedy administration continued their efforts to reform society. Encouraged by Johnson's Great Society and War on Poverty, Hispanics and American Indians organized, demonstrated, and turned to the government—especially the federal courts—to further their causes. The activism associated with the Warren Court intensified as the Court continued to issue controversial decisions that expanded individual rights and protections. By the mid-1960s, however, liberals increasingly were divided and critical of the Johnson administration. At the heart of a growing disillusionment was the war in Vietnam.

Johnson continued Kennedy's foreign policies, expanding commitments to oppose communism around the world. Unable to find options that would save South Vietnam and reduce the American role, Johnson eventually implemented a series of planned escalations that Americanized the war. The expectation that American military superiority would defeat Ho Chi Minh's Communists proved disastrous. As the United States escalated its efforts, North Vietnam forces kept pace and showed no slackening of resolve or resources. Within the United States, however, as the American commitment grew, a significant antiwar movement developed. The combination of the Tet offensive and presidential politics cost Johnson his presidency, divided the Democratic Party, and compounded the divisions in American society.

But more than the debate over the war divided the nation. By 1968, the country was aflame with riots in urban centers, and an increasing number of groups were seeking better social, economic, and political choices. Those advocating social reforms, however, faced a resurgence of conservatism that helped elect Nixon. Hoping to find a strategy for withdrawing from Vietnam, Nixon implemented a policy of Vietnamization. He also wanted to restructure international relations by working to improve relations with the Soviet Union and China.

At home, Nixon charted an uneven course, switching between maintaining government activism and reducing the power of government. Though opposed to government intervention, he created the Environmental Protection Agency. Politically, he sought a broader base for the Republican Party by pursuing a southern strategy that curtailed federal support for civil rights.

Despite Nixon's domestic and foreign-policy successes, however, his desire to crush his enemies led to the Watergate scandal and his downfall. Facing impeachment, the president resigned. President Ford tried to restore confidence in government but faced too many obstacles to be successful. As the nation approached the 1976 bicentennial election, many wondered if the optimism that began the 1960s would ever return. The nation seemed mired in a slowing economy and a public cynicism toward government and politics generated by Vietnam and Watergate.

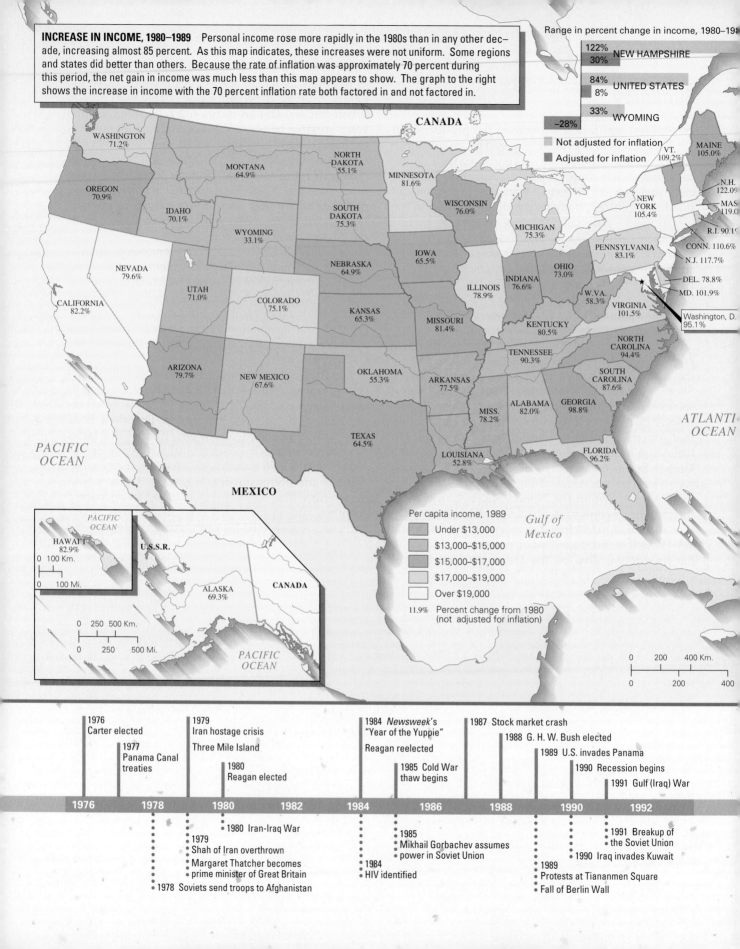

INCREASE IN INCOME, 1980–1989   Personal income rose more rapidly in the 1980s than in any other dec-ade, increasing almost 85 percent. As this map indicates, these increases were not uniform. Some regions and states did better than others. Because the rate of inflation was approximately 70 percent during this period, the net gain in income was much less than this map appears to show. The graph to the right shows the increase in income with the 70 percent inflation rate both factored in and not factored in.

Range in percent change in income, 1980–198

122% / 30%	NEW HAMPSHIRE
84% / 8%	UNITED STATES
33% / −28%	WYOMING

Not adjusted for inflation
Adjusted for inflation

CANADA

WASHINGTON 71.2%
MONTANA 64.9%
NORTH DAKOTA 55.1%
MINNESOTA 81.6%
OREGON 70.9%
IDAHO 70.1%
SOUTH DAKOTA 75.3%
WISCONSIN 76.0%
WYOMING 33.1%
MICHIGAN 75.3%
MAINE 105.0%
VT. 109.2%
N.H. 122.0%
MASS. 119.0
NEW YORK 105.4%
NEVADA 79.6%
IOWA 65.5%
NEBRASKA 64.9%
PENNSYLVANIA 83.1%
R.I. 90.1%
CONN. 110.6%
CALIFORNIA 82.2%
UTAH 71.0%
COLORADO 75.1%
ILLINOIS 78.9%
INDIANA 76.6%
OHIO 73.0%
N.J. 117.7%
DEL. 78.8%
MD. 101.9%
KANSAS 65.3%
MISSOURI 81.4%
KENTUCKY 80.5%
W.VA. 58.3%
VIRGINIA 101.5%
Washington, D. 95.1%
ARIZONA 79.7%
NEW MEXICO 67.6%
OKLAHOMA 55.3%
ARKANSAS 77.5%
TENNESSEE 90.3%
NORTH CAROLINA 94.4%
SOUTH CAROLINA 87.6%
MISS. 78.2%
ALABAMA 82.0%
GEORGIA 98.8%
ATLANTIC OCEAN
TEXAS 64.5%
LOUISIANA 52.8%
FLORIDA 96.2%

PACIFIC OCEAN

MEXICO

Gulf of Mexico

Per capita income, 1989
Under $13,000
$13,000–$15,000
$15,000–$17,000
$17,000–$19,000
Over $19,000

11.9% Percent change from 1980 (not adjusted for inflation)

PACIFIC OCEAN
HAWAI'I 82.9%
0 100 Km.
0 100 Mi.

U.S.S.R.
CANADA
ALASKA 69.3%
PACIFIC OCEAN

0 250 500 Km.
0 250 500 Mi.

0 200 400 Km.
0 200 400

Facing Limits, 1976–1992

Increase in Income, 1980–1989

As indicated in this map on the facing page, every state in the country saw significant income growth between 1980 and 1989. But because of inflation, not every state experienced an increase in real wages. Factoring in inflation, what states still experienced growth in income?

Individual Choices

FRANKLIN CHANG-DÌAZ

Born in Costa Rica, Franklin Chang-Dìaz grew up wanting to travel into space. To fulfill his dream, he immigrated to the United States after finishing high school to continue his education. Eventually he received a Ph.D. degree from the Massachusetts Institute of Technology and became a scientist-astronaut. *NASA.*

Franklin Chang-Dìaz

Twenty-one years separated the young child looking into space from a mango tree in Venezuela and the young man who looked down toward Latin America from space. Franklin Chang-Dìaz's wish had come true—he was an astronaut. It was January 1986 and he was on board the space shuttle *Columbia*, chasing Halley's comet.

Born in Costa Rica in 1950, Franklin Chang-Dìaz was living in Venezuela with his parents when the Soviets launched *Sputnik* in 1957. His mother told him that man had placed a new star in the heavens and that someday man would explore the stars. Like other children around the world, Franklin dreamed of exploring space.

His family returned to Costa Rica, where his Chinese grandfather had settled, seeking a better life in the late nineteenth century. Growing up in Costa Rica, "I was a normal boy, living a normal life," he later recounted. In school, he was successful at both athletics and academics. He especially liked doing science experiments, and at home, he experimented with model rockets, using gunpowder as fuel. His fascination with space continued as he watched the Soviets and the Americans send astronauts into space. He too wanted to go into space, but that was impossible in Costa Rica. When he told his friends he planned to go to the United States, they said he was crazy. Pursuing his goal, he worked in a bank after high school each day to save money for his journey to America.

In nine months, he had saved $50.00 and had convinced his parents to buy him an airline ticket to the United States. He arrived in Hartford in 1968 and moved in with relatives, but he faced a major hurdle in trying to enter the local high school. Finally, he convinced school officials to place him in the senior class as a regular student. He initially failed his classes, but soon his English and his grades improved significantly. The second hurdle was to get into college. He knew it would be impossible to become an astronaut with just a high school diploma.

With superior grades and support from his teachers, Franklin Chang-Dìaz received a scholarship to attend the University of Connecticut. Disappointment soon followed, however, for the scholarship was for citizens of the United States. His application had been read incorrectly; the scholarship board thought he was Puerto Rican. The scholarship was then withdrawn. But university officials and other supporters petitioned the Connecticut legislature to grant him a waiver of citizenship. In the fall of 1969, he entered the university intending to major in science, engineering, or mathematics. He chose mechanical engineering and graduated in 1973.

The next step was to attend graduate school. Chang-Dìaz determined that if he were a scientist, he would have a better chance of joining the National Aeronautics and Space Administration (NASA). Receiving a scholarship from the Massachusetts Institute of Technology, he entered the doctoral program. His area of interest and research was applied plasma physics and fusion technology. Watching space probes being sent to Mars and deeper into space, he concluded that nuclear

power would be needed for long-range voyages and that "plasma physics would play a key role." After receiving his Ph.D. degree in 1977, an optimistic Dr. Franklin Chang-Dìaz applied to the astronaut program. "All of a sudden the space program was so close, I felt I could touch it."

The space program was in a period of limited funding and support and accepted only a handful of candidates into the program. Franklin Chang-Dìaz was rejected; again, not being an American citizen had worked against him. He continued his scientific research, contributing to the concepts of how to make a fusion reactor. Two years later, now a naturalized U.S. citizen, he applied again to the NASA program, one of four thousand applicants for nineteen open slots. This time, he made the program and in 1981 earned his astronaut status. Still, however, there was disappointment. Chang-Dìaz wanted to participate in space flights, but NASA kept finding other duties for him. He served as part of the support team for other missions, and he continued to conduct research on nuclear propulsion, developing a new technology for manned missions to Mars. Finally, in January 1986, his dream came true. The space shuttle *Columbia* lifted off from the Kennedy Space Center in Florida with Dr. Franklin Chang-Dìaz on board for a six-day flight.

Since his first flight in 1986, Chang-Dìaz has made six additional flights, logging more than 1,601 hours in space, including 19 hours and 31 minutes in three spacewalks. He currently serves as the director of the Advanced Space Propulsion Laboratory at the Johnson Space Center in Houston, Texas. Once asked about his journey from Costa Rica to Houston, he replied: "I cannot think of a better job. . . . I'm just having the time of my life. This is what I planned for all my life and I'm really enjoying it, and to me, I guess I feel I have the best of both worlds because I also continue my research, and so I am able to be a scientist at the same time that I am also an astronaut, and that is to me the perfect combination."

INTRODUCTION

As the nation celebrated its two-hundredth birthday in 1976, television networks showed 30-second clips of proud moments in American history. Watching those clips, Franklin Chang-Dìaz was full of optimism about his future in America. In a year, he would have his doctorate and apply to be an astronaut. His optimism, and the dreams of many Americans and immigrants, seemed overblown, though, as limits seemed to loom everywhere. A sluggish economy, increasing intolerance, and rising unemployment appeared to make achieving—or even maintaining—the American dream more difficult. Support for the liberalism that had attacked racism and poverty was waning, challenged by the belief that an activist government was part of the nation's problems. Even James Earl Carter, the Democratic candidate for the presidency in 1976, argued that government could not solve every problem. He urged Americans to make sacrifices to overcome problems at home and abroad.

Arriving in Washington as a political outsider in 1977, President Carter failed to lead the Democratic Congress and proved ineffective in reversing the slowing economy. His administration also failed to match the expectations of those seeking an activist government to support their goals. Carter's efforts to refocus American foreign policy fared only slightly better, and to many Americans Carter's foreign policy resulted in a near-eclipse of American prestige abroad.

A resurgent conservatism led by the New Right and Ronald Reagan defeated Carter in the 1980 presidential contest. Reagan had gained high public approval ratings by promising a renewed America, powerful and prosperous. He attacked liberal economic and social policies and reemphasized a Cold War–style foreign policy that would "stand tall" against the Soviet "evil empire." During Reagan's administration, the economy was revitalized, and government spending was directed away from social programs toward military spending. Many Americans believed that his conservative values had freed businesses of many needless government controls and reasserted traditional social and family values. Reagan's foreign policy, supporters argued, promoted American interests in Central America and weakened the Soviet Union, which was ending the Cold War with an American victory.

Not everyone agreed that Reagan's choices produced favorable results. Critics argued that he placed too much emphasis on satisfying the wealthy and too little on the needs of minority groups, the less well off, and the poor. Others pointed to a massive national debt and the growing trade deficit as serious economic problems. Despite Reagan's personal popularity, as his administration ended, more and more Americans were uncertain about the ultimate outcome of Reagan's economic and social policies.

Running in the shadow of Reagan in 1988, Vice President George Bush gained the Republican presidential nomination in a nation that seemed dissatisfied but unable to pinpoint what was wrong or how to fix it. He offered the nation experienced leadership and promised to maintain American strength abroad. At home he would institute a "kinder, gentler nation" that would show more concern for minorities, the poor, education, and the environment. He easily defeated Democratic candidate Michael Dukakis, but as president he showed little desire to implement domestic policy changes. Instead, he chose to focus on foreign policy. Taking office as the Soviet Union collapsed, he charted a foreign policy in a new international setting with the United States as the only superpower. Bush cautiously supported democratic change in Eastern Europe and Central America. To promote American interests he committed American military forces in Panama and Kuwait. As Bush prepared for his reelection, he was confident that his foreign-policy success, including the invasion of Iraq, would carry him to victory.

The Carter Presidency

■ What new directions in foreign policy did Carter take, and how did his policies toward Central America reflect that direction?

■ What successes and failures did Carter experience in dealing with the Middle East?

■ What domestic problems did Carter face on assuming the presidency? How did Carter's status as an "outsider" shape his goals and leadership?

The United States celebrated the two-hundredth anniversary of its independence in 1976. Amid the fes-

tivities and praise for its institutions and accomplishments, however, lurked a deepening sense of cynicism, uneasiness, and uncertainty. The social activism and turmoil of the 1960s, Vietnam, and Watergate had shaken the nation's belief in government's ability to solve problems. President Ford's efforts to restore faith in government had not succeeded, as indicated by responses to a 1975 survey: most people said they believed that politicians consistently lied to them. Other surveys found that the same lack of faith had spread to other institutions. Americans were now questioning the motives and credibility of the medical and legal professions, business leaders, and even educators. The public's lack of trust and confidence was heightened by a slowing economy that raised concerns about the future. For the first time since the Depression, many parents worried that their children would not enjoy a higher standard of living. The optimism that had characterized the 1960s had faded into frustration and apathy, and a sense that the nation no longer shaped events but reacted to them.

To many Americans the political forecast did not look especially promising as the two presidential contenders began their race for the White House. Gerald Ford had his party's nomination for the presidency, after overcoming a stiff challenge from the more conservative Ronald Reagan. Polls showed that people liked Ford but considered him an ineffective president. His Democratic opponent, James Earl Carter, boasted about his lack of political experience, aside from being a one-time governor of Georgia. People seemed to like Carter's nonpolitical, folksy background but wondered if he had the political strength to lead Congress and the nation. Both men seemed full of good intentions, but neither appeared up to the task of implementing them.

The presidential contest between Ford and Carter lacked drama. In the debates and throughout the campaign, the candidates were vague on issues but expansive on smiles and photo sessions. The result was a very close election. Ford won more states than Carter but lost the electoral count by 56 votes. Reflecting the political apathy of the nation, only 54.4 percent of eligible voters cast their ballots. One Californian explained that he had not voted because he did not want "to force a second-class decision on my neighbors."

Jimmy Carter arrived in the nation's capital in January 1977 brimming with enthusiasm and stressing that he was free of Washington politics and the lures of special interests. On Inauguration Day he led the people from Capitol Hill to the White House by walking rather than riding in a limousine. As president, he

Chronology

New Directions, New Limits

1976	Jimmy Carter elected president
1977	Department of Energy created
	Panama Canal treaties
	SALT I treaty expires
1978	Camp David Accords
1979	Revolution in Iran topples shah
	Ayatollah Khomeini assumes power in Iran
	United States recognizes People's Republic of China
	Nuclear accident at Three Mile Island, Pennsylvania
	Egyptian-Israeli peace treaty signed in Washington, D.C.
	SALT II treaty signed in Vienna
	Hostages seized in Iran
	Soviet Union invades Afghanistan
1980	Carter applies sanctions against Soviet Union
	SALT II treaty withdrawn from Senate
	Carter Doctrine
	Iran-Iraq War begins
	Ronald Reagan elected president
1981	Iran releases American hostages
	Economic Recovery Tax Act
1982	United States sends marines to Beirut
1983	Congress funds Strategic Defense Initiative
	Marine barracks in Beirut destroyed
	United States invades Grenada

1984	Withdrawal of U.S. forces from Lebanon
	Boland Amendment
	Reagan reelected
	Newsweek's "Year of the Yuppie"
	Mikhail Gorbachev assumes power in Soviet Union
	Secret arms sales to Iran in exchange for U.S. hostages
	Gorbachev-Reagan summit in Geneva
1986	U.S. bombing raid on Libya
	Gorbachev-Reagan summit in Reykjavik, Iceland
1987	Iran-Contra hearings
	Stock market crash
	Intermediate Nuclear Force Treaty
1988	George Bush elected president
1989	Chinese government represses democracy movement in Tiananmen Square
	Berlin Wall pulled down
	Gorbachev-Bush summit on Malta
	United States invades Panama
1990	Recession begins
	Free elections in Nicaragua
	Clean Air Act
	Iraq invades Kuwait
	Americans with Disabilities Act
1991	Breakup of the Soviet Union
	Gorbachev resigns
	First Iraqi War

pledged honesty and hard work. Anxious to get started, he wrote in his diary: "It's almost impossible for me to delay something that I see needs to be done."

New Directions in Foreign Policy

In international relations, Carter saw a lot that needed to be done. First and foremost, American foreign policy needed to be redirected. It was too European and Cold War–oriented, shaped too much by an "inordi-

nate fear of communism." He sought a more open and moral diplomacy that would pay greater attention to the economic and social problems of the non-European world, including abuses of **human rights.**

> **human rights** Basic rights and freedoms to which all human beings are entitled, such as the right to life and liberty, to freedom of thought and expression, and to equality before the law.

Latin America seemed a good place to set the new tone. The United States would work harder to consider the interests of Latin Americans. Carter believed that the Panama Canal presented an excellent opportunity to chart a fresh Latin American policy. The Panama Canal Zone lay like an affluent, foreign-occupied island within Panama. To Panamanians it was a reminder of the inequalities between themselves and the United States. Panama wanted control over the canal, and for years negotiations on the issue had stalled because of American opposition. An agreement with Panama was one of Carter's highest priorities, and within a year two treaties were complete. Carter was pleased, although almost 80 percent of the American public was not and opposed giving up the canal. Most thought that the canal was American-built and American-run and should remain that way. Under the terms of the new treaties, the Panamanians gained control of the canal in 1999.

Carter's emphasis on moral governments and human rights also drew widespread opposition. Critics warned that letting human rights drive American policy might undermine pro-American but abusive governments, especially in developing countries. Some liberals and moderates also expressed concern that the human rights issue might harm improving relations with the Soviets and Chinese. Both were correct. In Nicaragua, Carter's emphasis on human rights contributed to the United States' halting military and economic aid, which in turn was a factor in the ouster of Anastasio Somoza, who had ruled the nation with an iron hand for years. Fulfilling some Americans' worst fears, replacing Somoza in power was the largely Marxist **Sandinista Liberation Front,** led by Daniel Ortega.

Carter's criticism of Soviet and Eastern European violations of human rights led to an almost immediate cooling of relations with the Soviets that threatened the continuation of détente and efforts at arms limitations. Yet the talks continued, and despite chilly relations and difficult discussions, the two superpowers agreed to place some limits on long-range missiles, bombers, and nuclear warheads. Carter and Leonid Brezhnev signed the second **Strategic Arms Limitation Treaty** (SALT II) during their Vienna summit in June 1979. The agreement encountered stubborn and bipartisan congressional opposition. Conservatives concluded it gave too many advantages to the Soviets, while liberals argued that it was not encompassing enough. Hopes that the Senate would approve the treaty faded quickly when the Soviets invaded Afghanistan in December 1979. Calling the Soviet incursion the "gravest threat to peace since 1945," Carter

withdrew the treaty from consideration, imposed **economic sanctions** on the Soviet Union, and boycotted the 1980 Olympic Games held in Moscow. He also provided aid to the **mujahedeen,** who were fighting the Soviets, and announced the "**Carter Doctrine.**" Any nation that attempted to take control of the **Persian Gulf,** Carter stated, would "be repelled by any means necessary, including the use of force." Relations with the other Communist superpower, however, got progressively better as Carter worked with China's new leader, Deng Xiaoping, and restored full diplomatic relations with the People's Republic of China in January 1979.

Middle Eastern Crises

Carter credited the Panama Canal treaty to his ability to take a new approach to an old issue. He believed that such a tactic would also move Israel and its Arab neighbors toward a peace settlement (see Map 30.1). To this end, Carter invited Egyptian president Anwar Sadat and Israeli prime minister Menachem Begin for talks at the presidential retreat at Camp David in Maryland. Surprisingly both accepted.

Meeting in September 1978, Sadat and Begin did not get along well. Carter shuttled between the two

Sandinista Liberation Front Leftist guerrilla movement that overthrew Anastasio Somoza in Nicaragua in 1979 and established a revolutionary government under Daniel Ortega.

Strategic Arms Limitation Treaty Agreement, known as SALT II, between the United States and the Soviet Union in 1979 to limit the number of strategic nuclear missiles in each country; these strategic missiles contained warheads that had large-scale destructive capability and the probability of changing the course of a war; during the Cold War these weapons carried nuclear warheads and were considered weapons of mass destruction; Congress never approved the treaty.

economic sanctions Trade restrictions imposed on a country that has violated international law.

mujahedeen Afghan resistance group supplied with arms by the United States to assist in its fight against the Soviets following their 1979 invasion of Afghanistan.

Carter Doctrine Carter's announced policy that the United States would use force to repel any nation that attempted to take control of the Persian Gulf.

Persian Gulf Arm of the Arabian Sea and location of the ports of several major oil-producing Arab countries; its security is crucial to the flow of oil from the Middle East to the rest of the world.

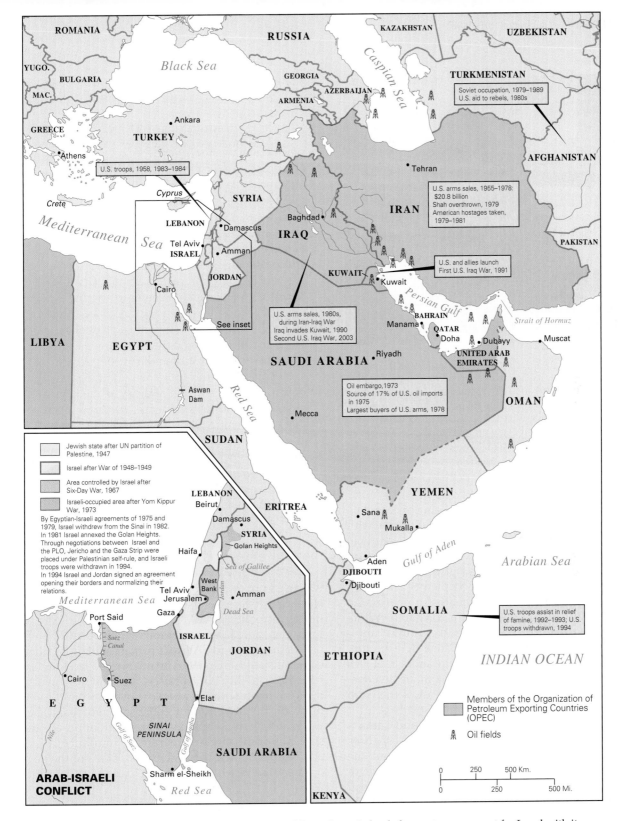

MAP 30.1 The Middle East Since 1946, the United States has tried to balance strong support for Israel with its need for oil from the Arab states. To support U.S. interests in this volatile region, the United States has funneled in large amounts of financial and military aid and used overt and covert force to shape regional governments. Agreements signed in Washington in 1993 and 1994 between Israel and the Palestine Liberation Organization and between Israel and the Kingdom of Jordan reduced tensions in the region.

One of President Carter's greatest triumphs was the signing of the 1978 peace accords between President Anwar Sadat of Egypt (*left*) and Prime Minister Menachem Begin of Israel (*right*). The agreement followed days of personal diplomacy by Carter at the Camp David presidential retreat. Both Sadat and Begin received the Nobel Peace Prize for their efforts. *Jimmy Carter Presidential Library.*

It Matters

Islamic Fundamentalism

When the shah of Iran was overthrown, most Americans were first introduced to a "new" world movement, Islamic fundamentalism. With the seizure of American hostages in Iran and proclamations that the United States represented the "Great Satan," it appeared to many in the United States that Islamic fundamentalism was anti-American, antidemocratic, and militant, advocating violence, even the use of terrorism, to accomplish its goals. Since 1979, that belief has been hardened by a series of terrorist attacks against the United States, including those against American embassies in Africa and the attacks on the World Trade Center and Pentagon. Emphasizing the use of terrorism, some argue that "their objective is nothing less than the total destruction of the West" and there can be "no peaceful coexistence." Others respond that the extremists within the Islamic fundamentalist movement are a small minority and that the movement is neither antidemocratic nor anti-Western. Whether benign or hostile to American interests in the Islamic world, Islamic fundamentalism had become a powerful force.

leaders, smoothing relations and stressing his personal commitment to both nations. Personally friendly with Sadat, he frequently exchanged harsh words with Begin. But he carefully negotiated agreements by which Egypt would recognize Israel's right to exist and Israel would return the Israeli-occupied Sinai Peninsula to Egypt. It took several months to finalize the **Camp David Accords,** but in a ceremony at the White House on March 26, 1979, acting like a proud midwife, Carter watched Begin and Sadat sign the first peace treaty between an Arab state and Israel. Although the treaty was a major diplomatic achievement for Carter, Arab leaders and most of the Arab world condemned it.

The Soviet intervention in Afghanistan and Carter's announcement of the Carter Doctrine were responses to more than just events in Afghanistan. Both the Americans and the Soviets were reacting to the revolution in Iran, which had toppled the pro-American ruler, Mohammad Reza Shah Pahlavi, in early 1979. The shah had been restored to power by the United States in 1953 and had become America's staunchest ally in the Persian Gulf region. Buying arms from the United States, the shah created the largest military force in the region. On several occasions, the military

was used not to protect Iran from invasion but to increase the government's control over its people. Using his secret police, SAVAK, the shah became increasingly despotic. Despite obvious widespread opposition to the shah and SAVAK's brutal reputation, when Carter visited Iran in 1977, he not only called Iran "an island of stability" but praised the "love" shown to the shah by the Iranian people. Love for, and the stability of, the government collapsed two years later when Iran's religious leaders, who opposed the shah's efforts to modernize Iran and introduce "Western" values, joined with other opponents of the government and drove the shah into exile.

Camp David Accords   Treaty, signed at Camp David in 1978, under which Israel returned territory captured from Egypt and Egypt recognized Israel as a nation.

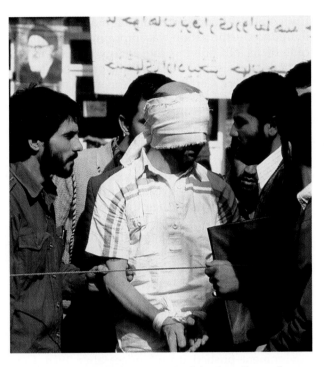

In November 1979, Iranians seized the American embassy in Tehran and took sixty-six hostages. Thirteen were soon released through the effort of Yasir Arafat, but negotiations to release more failed. Held more than a year, the hostages were released as Ronald Reagan was being sworn in as president. When one hostage was asked if he would ever return to Iran, he said yes, but only in an American bomber. *Alain Mingam/Gamma Liaison.*

The revolution was led by **Ayatollah Ruhollah Khomeini,** who assumed power and began to establish an Islamic fundamentalist state that was diametrically opposed to Western ideas and values.

Tensions between Iran and the United States increased as the revolutionary government called the United States the main source of evil in the world. Carter cut off economic and military aid to Iran, ordered Americans home, and reduced the embassy staff in Tehran. On October 22, the exiled shah, who was dying, entered a New York hospital to receive cancer treatments, amid warnings of Iranian reprisals. On November 4 an angry mob stormed the American embassy in Tehran and abducted the remaining staff. The sixty-six American hostages were paraded through the streets and subjected to numerous abuses as the Iranians demanded the return of the shah for trial. The press quickly dubbed the crisis "America Held Hostage," and television accounts flooded American homes.

Carter's foreign-policy advisers, Secretary of State **Cyrus Vance** and National Security Adviser **Zbigniew Brzezinski,** offered conflicting options. Brzezinski wanted to use military force to free the hostages. Vance argued for negotiation, hoping that Iranian moderates would find a way to release the captives. Carter sided with Vance and was able to negotiate freedom for thirteen hostages, mostly women and African Americans. As further discussions failed, American frustration and anger grew, and Carter's popularity ratings fell to near 30 percent. It was time to "lance the boil," concluded Brzezinski. Carter ordered a military rescue mission. It was a disaster. After losing three helicopters in a violent dust storm in Iran, Carter scrapped the mission.

Diplomatic efforts through the Canadians and the Algerians eventually resulted in an agreement in late 1980 to release the hostages. By that time the shah had died of cancer, and Iran was at war against Iraq and needed the assets that Carter had frozen. Seen by many as a personal insult to Carter, Iran released the hostages on January 20, 1981, the day he left the presidency, ending 444 days of captivity.

Domestic Priorities

Domestically, Carter immediately faced two significant problems: a resurgent Congress anxious to exert leadership, and the declining economy. Compounding the problems, Carter and his staff frequently ignored Congress and its leaders. Relations with the Democratic Congress quickly deteriorated. "I don't see this Congress rolling over and playing dead," announced one Democratic leader. "Carter is going to set up his priorities and we are going to set up ours. We'll see where we go from there." Dealing with the economy was one issue in dispute. In the third year of what some have called the "Great Stagflation," Carter adopted several approaches that some called more Republican

Ayatollah Ruhollah Khomeini Religious leader of Iran's Shiite Muslims; the Shiites toppled the shah in 1979, and the ayatollah (a title of respect given to a high-ranking Shiite religious authority and leader) established a new constitution that gave him supreme powers.

Cyrus Vance Carter's secretary of state, who wanted the United States to defend human rights and promote economic development of lesser-developed nations.

Zbigniew Brzezinski Carter's national security adviser, who favored confronting the Soviet Union with firmness.

When OPEC reduced production in 1973 and drove up gas prices by 350 percent, the impact on the American economy and motorists was staggering, as a gas and oil shortage swept across the nation. Lucky were those who drove fuel-efficient cars. © *Owen Franklin/Corbis.*

than Democratic. He raised interest rates, cut taxes, and trimmed federal spending, especially for social programs. When he proposed only a twenty-cent raise in the minimum wage, Democrats in Congress rebelled and pushed through a ninety-five-cent increase.

Another issue separating Carter from many Democrats concerned governmental regulation of industry. There was a growing view that one way to stimulate the economy was to reduce or remove federal regulations over many industries. Many Democrats opposed trimming New Deal and Great Society programs, but supporters argued that regulations kept prices high and removed incentives for growth and innovation. Carter agreed and began a process of removing regulations from several sectors of the economy. He deregulated the transportation industry: railroads, trucking, and airlines. The result appeared positive as airfares dropped almost immediately and a new level of competition swept across the airline industry. There was also a similar benefit from Carter's deregulation of the natural-gas industry. Consumer prices fell, and energy companies widened their search for new sources of gas. Another longer-range result of deregulation, however, was consolidations within the industries as stronger companies bought weaker ones and reduced competition.

A more important part of Carter's economic plan was to reduce the nation's dependency on foreign sources of oil. He concluded that the economy could not improve and unemployment be reduced until the

United States stopped consuming more energy than it produced—the nation was importing about 60 percent of its oil. Solving the **energy crisis** was the "moral equivalent of war" and the only road to economic recovery, Carter told the American people. He offered Congress 113 energy proposals, including the creation of a cabinet-level Department of Energy, support for research and development of fuels other than oil, and special regulations and taxes to prevent the energy industry from reaping excess profits. He also asked individuals to reduce their energy consumption by wearing sweaters, using public transportation, and lowering their thermostats in winter.

Few liked Carter's solutions. Almost everyone, including industry and Congress, favored increasing the production of domestic gas and oil. Buoyed by the potential of new oil fields in Alaska, Congress found it easy to dismiss most of Carter's recommendations. Only fragments of his plan were passed in 1977, including the formation of the Department of Energy, a few incentives for conservation, and deregulation of the natural-gas industry. When the Iranian government pushed up oil prices after 1978, Congress agreed to approve funds for **alternative fuels** (including nuclear energy) and an excess-profits tax on the oil and gas industry.

Nuclear power was an alternative source that many argued would be the most successful in reducing dependency on gas and oil. Advocates argued that it was cheap and environmentally safe and called for funds to build new and larger facilities. Opponents replied that nuclear energy was expensive and potentially dangerous. On March 28, 1979, the critics' case was clinched when a serious accident at a nuclear power plant at **Three Mile Island** in central Pennsylvania released a cloud of radioactive gas and nearly caused a **meltdown.** Fortunately, no one was injured in the accident, but it took two weeks to shut

energy crisis Vulnerability to dwindling oil supplies, wasteful energy consumption, and potential embargoes by oil-producing countries.

alternative fuels Sources of energy other than coal, oil, and natural gas, such as solar, geothermal, hydroelectric, and nuclear energy.

Three Mile Island Site of a nuclear power plant near Harrisburg, Pennsylvania; an accident at the plant in 1979 led to a release of radioactive gases and almost caused a meltdown.

meltdown Severe overheating of a nuclear reactor core, resulting in the melting of the core and the escape of life-threatening radiation.

down the reactor, and more than a hundred thousand people were evacuated from the surrounding area. Suddenly, nuclear power became a less attractive energy source, as more than thirty energy companies canceled their nuclear energy projects. The nation remained dependent on natural gas, oil, and coal for most of its energy.

Despite taking new approaches to improve the economy, most of Carter's efforts failed. Stagflation continued, and by 1980 inflation stood at 14 percent—the highest rate since 1947—while unemployment rose to nearly 7.6 percent. Many Democrats, especially liberals, denounced his lack of leadership. Carter admitted he had not provided enough leadership, but he also blamed the public's unwillingness to sacrifice for much of the nation's woes. The public, in turn, gave Carter only a 19 percent approval rating. Republicans were hopeful that Carter's low popularity would translate into a Republican victory.

A Society in Transition

■ What changes were taking place in the American economy during the 1970s, and what was their impact on American families and communities?

■ Why did women, minorities, and liberals criticize Carter's social policies?

■ Who were the "new immigrants," and what problems did they face?

More than a leadership deficit, however, caused Carter's political problems. He and the American people were caught in a changing economy and society. The period from the end of World War II to the 1970s had been the longest era of consistent economic growth in the history of the United States. Despite occasional recessions and setbacks, the gross national product and productivity rose at a rate slightly higher than 2.5 percent. In personal terms, it meant that wages increased, as did the American standard of living and homeownership. A college education for their children seemed possible for nearly all Americans who held a steady job. But during the 1970s, the economy grew at a slower rate, dipping to slightly over 1 percent, while the cost of living increased over 200 percent. In personal terms, this meant higher prices, fewer jobs, and less optimism.

Economic Slowdown

The problems with the economy varied, but many were the product of a shift in the economic base from manufacturing to service industries and what was being called **globalization,** a changing world and American economy over which there seemed little control. Economically, the changes had started in the late 1960s with the expanding economies of West Germany, Japan, Korea, and Taiwan cutting into American domestic and foreign markets—reducing American profits and prosperity. In the new global economy, many American industries were unable to match the production costs, retail prices, or quality of goods produced overseas. The United States produced nearly two-thirds of the world's steel in 1946, but as Carter took office it made only 15 percent. Aggravating the situation were the high oil prices set by the Organization of Petroleum Exporting Countries (OPEC), which added to inflation and unemployment and threatened the nation's industrial base, which depended on inexpensive fuels. As a result of these pressures, many of the nation's primary industries (iron and steel, rubber, automobiles and their parts, clothing, coal), especially those located in the Great Lakes region, cut back production, laid off workers, and closed plants. Corporate profits fell from highs of 10 percent in the mid-1960s to under 5 percent by the end of the 1970s.

Adjusting to globalization and what some called the **postindustrial economy,** corporations devised new strategies for survival and profitability. One tactic was to refocus resources. Many corporations rid themselves of less profitable manufacturing operations and invested more heavily in service industries. Implementing these strategies, during the 1970s and 1980s General Electric, one of the largest American manufacturing firms, sold off most of its manufacturing divisions and moved its resources into the service sector by buying the entertainment giant RCA as well as a number of investment and insurance firms.

At the same time, many companies shifted their production sites to locales where operating costs were lower and closed less-productive plants. Some companies kept their plants in the United States, moving their factories to southern and western states, but an increasing number moved their operations overseas, where expenses were even lower than in

globalization The process of opening national borders to the free flow of trade, capital, ideas and information, and people.

postindustrial economy An economy whose base is no longer driven by manufacturing but by service and information industries.

the Sunbelt. A so-called **Rust Belt** formed in the Northeast out of what had been the vibrant industrial center of the United States. Philadelphia from 1969 to 1981, for example, lost 42 percent of its factory jobs and 14 percent of its population, and its crime rate jumped by nearly 200 percent. Japanese goods, once the joke of international commerce, were gobbling up the electronics industry and cutting deeply into the American automobile market as Americans decided to purchase more-gas-efficient Japanese automobiles. Many of those facilities that did not close or move overseas cut production costs by becoming more automated.

As the higher-paying manufacturing jobs declined, the number of service jobs—which paid about one-third less and used more part-time help—increased. McDonald's became one of the largest employers in the nation. The changes were felt everywhere. Lakewood, California, which had seen great economic success in the three decades after World War II, underwent significant economic and social changes (see Chapter 27). By the 1980s, wages were falling as jobs in defense-related and other nearby industries disappeared. Individuals who landed service-related jobs found that they were paid less and provided few benefits. As the economic vitality of the community declined, the largest department store in Lakewood's central mall closed, and discount stores like Kmart and Wal-Mart took its place. It seemed to many of Lakewood's residents that their town had been transformed almost overnight from an optimistic middle-class community into a depressed lower-class one. Fear and anger replaced hope. A local minister observed that the combination of economic decline, growth in minority residents, and the expanding permissiveness of society had generated a "feeling of being encroached upon . . . overwhelmed." Politically, Lakewood shifted from moderate and generally Democratic to more conservative and mostly Republican.

Social Divisions

The problems of the changing economic structure were matched by the social and political problems of a disillusioned and diverse society. The late 1960s and 1970s saw a blunting of New Deal–Great Society liberalism. Nixon's election, in part, was a political reaction to the activism, protests, and policies of the Kennedy and Johnson administrations. Nixon had left the political scene, but the political successes of Reagan, Wallace, and other conservative politicians demonstrated that many Americans, especially working- and middle-class whites, thought that too

In 1974, Bill Gates decided to drop out of Harvard and with high school friend Paul Allen wrote operating software for the newly emerging personal computers. They formed Microsoft and created MSDOS. Twelve years later, Microsoft dominated the personal computer market and Gates became the nation's richest billionaire. © *Bettmann/Corbis.*

many governmental programs favored minorities over the majority.

Domestically, Carter's problem arose from the interaction of the changing economy, calls for more governmental social intervention, and the limits, especially financial, he saw on the ability of government to correct social problems. "Government cannot eliminate poverty or provide a bountiful economy," he stated, "or save our cities or cure literacy." Liberalism, he argued, had its limits. Liberal Democratic critics disagreed. Senator Edward Kennedy and others thought

Rust Belt Industrialized Middle Atlantic and Great Lakes region whose old factories are barely profitable or have closed.

that Carter had unwisely put the brakes on needed social programs. Carter's supporters pointed out that he had appointed more minorities and women to government and judicial positions than previous presidents, and instead of new or expanded programs, the president improved minority and other social conditions by improving regulatory agencies and better enforcement of existing regulations and laws.

Despite Carter's appointees and improved enforcement efforts, Latinos and African American leaders considered his efforts too weak and continued to lament his lack of legislation and his cuts in funding for social programs. Economically, they pointed out, minorities were experiencing the negative effects of the changing economy, higher unemployment, declining wages, and general lack of jobs. As one African American spokesman put it, "It's not whether there is equal opportunity to get a job, but whether there's a job to be got." It seemed that minority social needs were being sacrificed for the cause of **fiscal stringency.**

Another concern worrying liberals and minorities was the growing campaign against **affirmative action,** and the anti-affirmative-action *Bakke* case, which had made its way to the Supreme Court. **Alan Bakke** was suing the University of California at Davis Medical School for reverse discrimination. Since the mid-1960s, in an effort to provide more opportunities, many businesses and colleges had established affirmative action slots for minorities. But as the economy slowed, a growing number of middle-class and blue-collar whites believed that these programs limited their own job and educational opportunities and constituted preferential treatment for minorities. Bakke claimed that he had been denied admission because he was white, and that in his place the medical school had accepted less-qualified black students. Supporters of affirmative action pleaded with Carter to back the university. The **Justice Department** eventually petitioned the Court to uphold affirmative action, but not until after Carter had publicly stated, "I hate to endorse the proposition of quotas." In 1978, despite the Justice Department's **brief,** the Supreme Court, in a 5-to-4 decision, found in Bakke's favor and ruled that the university should admit him to the medical school.

Carter's lack of zeal in promoting minority needs, many feminists argued, was equally true when it came to the abortion issue. They applauded the president's support for extending the time needed to ratify the **Equal Rights Amendment** (ERA) but thought he should be more supportive on the abortion issue. The ERA was needed, advocates argued, to overcome state and local practices that blocked equality for women. Congress in 1972 drafted a proposed amendment and sent it to the states for ratification. Thirty-eight states needed to approve the amendment to make it law, and at first, ratification appeared almost certain. Thirty-three states had approved it by 1974. But opposition stiffened under the leadership of conservative **Phyllis Schlafly,** and when the deadline for ratification expired in 1979, the amendment had only thirty-five states in its corner. Carter joined with Congress to extend the ratification deadline to 1982, but it did no good. In 1982 the amendment remained three states short of the thirty-eight required for ratification.

Part of the "Stop-ERA" movement's success was a growing conservative reaction to a variety of social issues that appeared, in Schlafly's words, to diminish the rights and status of women and to alter the "role of the American woman as wife and mother." Foremost among these issues was the acrid debate over abortion. In 1973, in a 5-to-2 decision, the Supreme Court in *Roe v. Wade* invalidated a Texas law that prevented abortion. Justice Harry Blackmun, writing

---

fiscal stringency   The need because of real or perceived economic conditions to restrict, cut, or eliminate funding for programs.

affirmative action   Policy that seeks to redress past discrimination through active measures to ensure equal opportunity, especially in education and employment.

Alan Bakke   Rejected white medical school applicant who filed a lawsuit against the University of California at Davis for reverse discrimination; he claimed that he was denied admittance to medical school because of school policy that set aside admission slots for less-qualified minorities; the Supreme Court agreed in 1978.

Justice Department   Part of the executive branch that has responsibility to enforce the law, defend the interests of the United States according to the law, and to ensure fair and impartial administration of justice for all Americans. It is administered by the attorney general who was one of the original members of the cabinet.

brief   A summary or statement of a legal position or argument.

Equal Rights Amendment   Proposed constitutional amendment giving women equal rights under the law; Congress approved it in 1972, but it failed to achieve ratification by the required thirty-eight states.

Phyllis Schlafly   Leader of the movement to defeat the Equal Rights Amendment; she believed that the amendment threatened the domestic role of women.

Roe v. Wade   Supreme Court ruling (1973) that women have an unrestricted right to choose an abortion during the first three months of pregnancy.

for the majority, held that "the right to privacy" gave women the freedom to choose to have an abortion during the first three months of pregnancy. The controversial ruling struck down laws in forty-six states that had made abortions nearly impossible to obtain except in cases of rape or to save the life of the mother. As the number of legal abortions rose from about 750,000 in 1973 to nearly a million and a half by 1980, so too did opposition.

Although most public opinion polls indicated that a majority of Americans favored giving women the right to choose an abortion, at least under some circumstances, Catholics, Mormons, some Orthodox Jews, and many Protestant churches worked with conservative groups to organize a "Right to Life" campaign to oppose abortion rights on moral and legal grounds. The **Right to Life movement** easily merged with the conservative critique of American society and liberalism. Responding to conservative and anti-abortion pressure, Congress in 1976 passed the Hyde Amendment, which prohibited the use of federal Medicaid funds to pay for abortions. In 1980 the Supreme Court upheld Hyde in *Harris v. McRae*. Feminists had lobbied Carter to oppose the Hyde Amendment, and when he refused, some within the NOW camp argued that their organization should support anyone but Carter in the forthcoming 1980 election.

Latinos, Asians, and people from the Caribbean make up the majority of immigrants arriving in the United States today. Critics of immigration worry that these groups will not assimilate easily and want to limit further immigration. Supporters argue that assimilation is taking place and point to increased rates of nationalization and citizenship. Here, a Vietnamese family participates in the all-American sport of baseball (T-Ball). *Bob Daemmrich.*

New Immigrants

As American society became less tolerant and government less supportive of social programs, a new wave of immigrants started to arrive in the United States. The 1965 Immigration Act ended the national quota system for immigration and opened access to the United States from areas other than Europe. In 1960, three of every four immigrants had come from Europe, but that quickly changed as increasing numbers arrived from Mexico, Latin America, the Caribbean, and Asia. Within two decades, more than half of all immigrants arrived from Mexico, the Caribbean, and Central and South America. In the border city of Laredo, Texas, the Latino population exceeded 95 percent, compared with 63 percent in Miami, Florida, and 40 percent in Los Angeles.

They came to the United States mostly for the traditional reasons: jobs and security. As one immigrant stated simply: "It was better in America." Many immigrants were uneducated and unskilled, especially those who were refugees or from Latin America. But because immigration law favored professionals, many others were highly educated and skilled. Whether skilled or not, new immigrants fit nicely into the structure of the postindustrial economy. Those with few skills found jobs in the service and agriculture sectors, whereas the skilled newcomers filled the ranks of professionals and technicians.

Changes in immigration laws also allowed the Asian population to grow rapidly. In 1960, half a million Asians came to the United States, twenty years later the number had risen to more than 2.5 million, and by 2000, Asian immigrants became the second-largest immigration group—5 million—surpassing those arriving from Europe. Most came as families and clustered in ethnic communities in major urban areas, especially along the Pacific Coast. Those who were well educated and had marketable skills found economic

> **Right to Life movement** Anti-abortion movement that favors a constitutional amendment to prohibit abortion; some adherents grew increasingly militant during the 1980s and 1990s; also called the pro-life movement.

success as medical professionals, engineers, and owners of small businesses. This was especially true of those from Japan, China, Korea, and India. Many considered these populations the "model minority."

This view ignored the very different experiences of many other Asians, particularly those from Vietnam, Laos, and Cambodia. Coming as refugees, they arrived with few possessions, little education, and few skills. Mired in poverty and having difficulty assimilating into American society, they faced growing intolerance and hostility. The slowing economy contributed to the problem along the Gulf Coast, where whites, objecting to the employment competition, attacked Vietnamese fishermen.

Tensions also rose in inner cities between Asians and other minorities when they competed for jobs, housing, public resources, and political influence. This was the case in South Central Los Angeles as it became a multiracial area with significant African American, Hispanic, and Asian populations. When a riot swept through the community in 1992, many of the rioters targeted Asians, especially Koreans. Latino and African American rioters justified their attacks by claiming Asian landlords and shop owners discriminated against and exploited them. "We hate [the Koreans]," one rioter explained. "Everyone does."

If some Asians were regarded as model immigrants, the opposite was true concerning most immigrants from Mexico, Latin America, and the Caribbean. Coming as both legal and illegal immigrants, Hispanics represented the largest number of the new immigrants. Like Franklin Chang-Dìaz, most came for new and better opportunities while speaking little or no English. Franklin Chang-Dìaz fulfilled his dream of becoming an astronaut, but for most Hispanic immigrants the outcome was vastly different. Arriving with few skills and little education, most immigrants from the Caribbean, Mexico, and Latin America found themselves taking one or more low-paying jobs just to survive. Even with two jobs, stated one Mexican American activist, the social and economic "ladder isn't there" for most Latino immigrants.

Illegal immigration, primarily from Mexico, added to the growing hostility toward Hispanics and calls for immigration limits. Attempting to stem the flood of "illegals" into the United States, Congress passed the **Immigration Reform and Control Act** in 1986. It provided amnesty to illegal aliens who had been in the United States before 1982 and made them eligible for citizenship. It also provided criminal punishment for those who hired illegal aliens and strengthened controls to prevent illegal entry into the United States. The crackdown did not work: the flow of immigrants

entering the country illegally was unaffected. As the 1980s ended, demands for immigration restrictions increased—in a 1991 poll, 69 percent of those asked believed there were too many Latinos in the country.

Resurgent Conservatism

■ What issues and forces contributed to the emergence of the New Right? How did the New Right shape American politics?

■ How did the candidacy and goals of Ronald Reagan match those of the New Right?

■ What is "Reaganomics," and what were the consequences of Reagan's economic policies?

Traditional liberals criticized Carter for his lack of zeal and continued to espouse government activism as a means to promote social equality and **cultural pluralism.** But their voices found little support as growing numbers of people began to argue that government activism was not the solution. "Liberalism is no longer the answer—it is the problem," insisted Ronald Reagan. Conservatives like Reagan argued that government was inefficient and that liberal programs made victims of middle-class Americans who worked hard, saved their money, and believed in strong, traditional family values. The activism of the 1960s, they believed, had made the nation a collection of interest groups clamoring for rights and power and had produced a loss of national identity and a moral breakdown. Conservatives argued that liberal views threatened "to destroy everything that is good and moral here in America."

Conservatives had no trouble pinpointing the problems: a hedonistic society, the decline of marriage and the breakdown of the traditional family, the rise in abortions and divorces. To support their concerns, they pointed to a 1973 public television (PBS) program that followed the disintegration of the Loud family. In a series of installments, a twenty-year marriage broke apart because of incompatibility, a son announced his

Immigration Reform and Control Act   Law passed by Congress in 1986 that prohibits the hiring of illegal aliens; it offered amnesty and legal residence to any who could prove that they had entered the country before January 1, 1982.

cultural pluralism   The coexistence of many cultures in a locality, without any one culture dominating the region; it seeks to reduce racism, sexism, and other forms of discrimination.

homosexuality, and teenage children went their own aimless ways. By the mid-1970s, many conservatives had grouped around the **New Right.**

The New Right

The New Right emerged as a highly centralized alliance of political and social conservatives. Economically and politically, it embraced a retreat from government activism and a reduction of taxes. By 1979, lowering taxes had become a hot national issue. Throughout the 1970s, Americans were aware that they were paying more taxes than ever. Social Security taxes to pay for entitlements, now including Medicare, grew by 30 percent. At the same time, because of inflation and "**bracket creep,**" income taxes rose by about 20 percent. In addition, state and local taxes kept going up. Responding to the tax avalanche, Californians led a tax revolt in 1978. Using a referendum to bypass the legislature, California voters passed **Proposition 13,** which placed limits on property taxes and state spending. Recognizing the importance of the movement, a Carter aide confided: It "isn't just a tax revolt, it is a revolution against government."

Reducing taxes was a broad-based issue, but the New Right's passion came from rejecting "liberal" moral and social values that, among other things, advocated abortion and condoned homosexuality. The nation's schools, it charged, had retreated from teaching a positive work ethic and moral habits and needed to return to the basics: reading, writing, arithmetic, and traditional values. To mobilize support, the New Right pioneered the effective political use of **direct mail** aimed at specific segments of the population.

Highly visible among New Right groups were evangelical Christian sects, many of whose ministers were **televangelists**—preachers who used radio and television to spread the gospel. Receiving donations that exceeded a billion dollars a year, they did not hesitate to mix religion and politics. Jerry Falwell's **Moral Majority** promoted New Right views on more than five hundred television and radio stations. Reaching millions of Americans, Falwell called on his listeners to wage political war against government officials whose views on the Bible, homosexuality, prayer in school, abortion, and communism were too liberal. Falwell told his religious colleagues to get people "saved, baptized, and registered."

The conservative resurgence aided Ronald Reagan more than any other Republican candidate. He promised to restore America by reducing government involvement and freeing American ingenuity and

In the 1970s and into the 1990s, the "electronic church" developed an audience of over 100 million viewers. With fancy, high-tech showmanship, televangelists like Jerry Falwell, pictured here, damned liberalism, feminism, sex education, homosexuality, and the teaching of evolution while demanding a return to traditional Christian values and prayer in school. Praising the power of the modern media pulpit, Falwell stated, "You can explain the issues. . . . And you can endorse candidates, right there in church on Sunday morning." *Steve McCurry/ Magnum Photos.*

New Right   Conservative movement opposing the political and social reforms that developed in the late 1960s and demanding less government intervention in the economy and a return to traditional values; it was a major political force by the 1980s.

bracket creep   Inflation of salaries pushing individuals into higher tax brackets.

Proposition 13   Measure adopted by referendum in California in 1978 cutting local property taxes by more than 50 percent.

direct mail   Advertising or promotional matter mailed directly to potential customers or audiences chosen because they are likely to respond favorably.

televangelist   Protestant evangelist minister who conducts televised worship services; many such ministers used their broadcasts as a forum for promoting conservative values.

Moral Majority   Conservative religious organization led by televangelist Jerry Falwell; it had an active political lobby in the 1980s promoting such issues as opposition to abortion and to the Equal Rights Amendment.

competitiveness, and he embraced the social positions of the New Right. Carter, according to Republicans, was a failure. He had failed to free the hostages, and he had failed to restore the nation's economy. Reagan, on the other hand, smacked of success: he was an effective campaigner who communicated confidence and a sense of humor. "A recession," he quipped, "is when your neighbor loses his job. A depression is when you lose yours. A recovery is when Jimmy Carter loses his." Reagan presented himself as the "citizen politician, speaking out for the ideas, values, and common sense of everyday Americans." A vote for Reagan, his supporters claimed, would restore American pride, power, and traditions.

Reagan's message was welcome news not only to those who routinely voted Republican but also to many living in the Sunbelt and to Democrats seeking a new approach to solving the economic problem. By 1980, the Sunbelt's population exceeded that of the industrial North and East. Politically, the region was more conservative and opposed the intrusive power of the federal government. White southerners equated "liberal" government with altering traditional racial norms, and a "**sagebrush rebellion**" in the western Sunbelt contested federal control and regulation of land and natural resources. Many westerners argued that federal environmental and land-use regulations blocked growth and economic development in the West. Further contributing to Republican totals were younger voters attracted by the economic goals and social stability Republicans represented. Except for the size of Reagan's majority and how many Republicans his **political coattails** would carry into office, the outcome of the election of 1980 was never in doubt.

When the voting ended, Reagan had 51 percent of the popular vote and an impressive 91 percent of the electoral count. Republicans held their majority in the Senate and substantially narrowed the Democratic majority in the House of Representatives. Many political observers believed the election of 1980 was the beginning of a new conservative era.

Reaganism

Reagan brought to the White House two distinct advantages lacked by Nixon, Ford, and Carter: he had a clear and simple vision of the type of America he wanted and an unusual ability to convey that image to the American public. Called the "Great Communicator" by the press, Reagan expertly presented images and visions, setting the grand agenda, but left to his cabinet and executive staff the fine-tuning and implementation of programs and legislation. Reagan

A former movie star and host of television shows, Ronald Reagan used television and radio very effectively to outline his visions of American domestic and foreign policies. Because of his communication style, he was called "the Great Communicator." *Corbis-Bettmann.*

rode to the presidency on a wide domestic platform promising not just prosperity and less government but also morality, tapping the New Right's political strength on issues of family and gender. In office, however, he virtually ignored the New Right's social agenda and concentrated on the economy and foreign policy. The administration's plan to improve the

sagebrush rebellion A 1980s political movement in western states opposing federal regulations governing land use and natural resources, seeking state jurisdiction instead.

political coattails Term referring to the ability of a presidential candidate to attract voters to other office seekers from the same political party.

economy was simple: cut the number and cost of social programs, increase military spending, and reduce taxes and government restrictions. "If we can do that, the rest will take care of itself," Reagan's chief of staff, James A. Baker III, argued.

Much of the administration's formula for restoring economic vitality rested on improving productivity and reducing inflation. To combat inflation, the Federal Reserve ("the Fed") kept interest rates high—spiking at 18 percent, the highest in the twentieth century. While the Fed squeezed inflation, Reagan introduced **supply-side economics,** intending to reduce federal regulations, taxes, and social programs. The 1981 **Economic Recovery Tax Act** lowered income taxes and most business taxes by an average of 25 percent. Supported by conservative Democrats in the House, Reagan raised military spending and slashed $25 billion from federal spending on social programs. Among the programs affected were food stamps, **Aid to Families with Dependent Children,** jobs, and housing. Yet despite these efforts, the cost of social programs continued to rise, largely because of increases in entitlement programs like Social Security and Medicare, which were politically untouchable.

Another aim of **Reaganomics** was deregulation—freeing businesses and corporations from restrictive federal regulations. Appointees to regulatory agencies were selected because of their support for deregulation and for business. Among the areas affected by deregulation were banking, communications, and oil. But its impact was most visible in the area of environmental regulation. Secretary of the Interior James Watt sought to open federally controlled land, coastal waters, and wetlands to mining, lumber, oil, and gas companies—a policy strongly advocated by many in the West. The Environmental Protection Agency relaxed enforcement of federal guidelines for reducing air and water pollution and cleaning up toxic-waste sites.

Reagan's economic policies were not immediately effective. Indeed, it appeared that the economy had gotten worse, as unemployment climbed to over 12 percent, the **trade deficit** soared, and bankruptcies for small businesses and farmers increased. Also, growing at an alarming rate was the **federal deficit,** pushed by declining tax revenues and increases in military spending. Reagan called for patience, assuring the public that his economic programs eventually would work.

As Reagan predicted in 1983, the recession ended and the economy recovered. Contributing to the resurgence were lower interest rates and oil prices. Inflation dropped to 4 percent, and unemployment fell to 7.5 percent. Reagan's economic policies and his support of a positive business culture now received widespread praise. Corporate leaders especially cheered, applauding fewer government controls, changes in antimonopoly policy, and increases in defense spending—most of which went to firms located in the Sunbelt. The deregulating of financial institutions was seen as especially positive because it spurred investment and speculation, which drove the stock market upward—the Great Bull Market. "I think we hit the jackpot," Reagan announced when he signed the Garn–St. Germain Act in 1982, which deregulated the **savings and loan industry.** Deregulation allowed savings and loan institutions (S&Ls) to make loans for all types of investment rather than just single-family homes, providing a new source of capital for the construction of office buildings, shopping malls, and industrial parks.

Another boon for big business was a change in antimonopoly implementation. Since the New Deal, justice departments and courts had generally hampered mergers of companies in the same or related fields. But in the 1980s a new approach became prominent that allowed such mergers, provided they did not obstruct eventual competition. Within three years of the Reagan administration's adopting the new approach,

supply-side economics Theory that reducing taxes on the wealthy and increasing the money available for investment will stimulate the economy and eventually benefit everyone.

Economic Recovery Tax Act Law passed by Congress in 1981 that cut income taxes over three years by 25 percent across the board and lowered the rate for the highest bracket from 78 percent to 28 percent.

Aid to Families with Dependent Children A program created by the Social Security Act of 1935; it provided states with matching federal funds and became one of the states' main welfare programs.

Reaganomics Economic beliefs and policies of the Reagan administration, including the belief that tax cuts for the wealthy and deregulation of industry benefit the economy.

trade deficit Amount by which the value of a nation's imports exceeds the value of its exports.

federal deficit The total amount of debt owed by the national government.

savings and loan industry Network of financial institutions, known as S&Ls, originally founded to provide home mortgage loans; deregulation during the Reagan era allowed them to speculate in risky ventures and led to many S&L failures.

twenty-one mergers had been completed, each worth over $1 billion. Business opportunities also multiplied as technological developments opened new fields, especially in communications and electronics. In those two areas, advances in miniaturization, satellite transmissions, videocassette recorders (VCRs), and computers touched almost every American—and provided new avenues of wealth. With Apple and IBM leading the way, office and personal computers restructured the process of handling information and communications, spawning a new wave of "tech" companies and a new crop of millionaires such as Bill Gates. Gates dropped out of Harvard to develop software for IBM's entry into the new field of personal computers and became America's youngest billionaire and founder of Microsoft.

Gates was not alone. It seemed that thousands of people were riding the expanding economy to wealth and power, from inventors to financial "wizards" who brokered mergers. Stories of economic success filled newspapers, magazines, television, and movies, creating a money culture. "Buy high, sell higher," *Fortune* magazine proclaimed. The pursuit of wealth and the goods that it could buy became a lifestyle sought after by many young Americans, particularly the baby boomers, who were reaching peak earning and spending levels. *Money* magazine saw its circulation jump from 800,000 in 1980 to 1.85 million in 1987.

Some called the 1980s the "Me Decade," in which acquiring money and state-of-the-art high-tech gadgetry mattered very much and led to self-satisfaction. In 1974 only 46 percent of college freshmen and high school seniors listed being "financially successful" as the first priority in their lives. Twelve years later, in 1986, 73 percent of college freshmen considered being "very well off financially" as their number one priority. Income-conscious college graduates hoping to become highly paid, aggressive professionals eagerly applied to law, business, and other postgraduate schools. The number of doctors and lawyers swelled, executive salaries quickly broke $40 million, and everyone needed to have cell phones, Walkmans, videos, computers, and fax machines. Some lamented the loss of the activism of the 1960s, but many agreed with *Newsweek* when it declared 1984 the "Year of the **Yuppie**"—the young, upwardly mobile urban professional who was on the leading edge of the new economic vitality.

Not everyone applauded the new economy. Some warned of serious weaknesses—revenues had shrunk while spending continued to expand, creating an alarming federal deficit. Critics also pointed out that the economic boom was selective. Regionally, the

West Coast and Sunbelt did well, but the Northeast—the Rust Belt—still rusted, and the farm belt experienced farm foreclosures at levels near that of the Great Depression. Socially, the gap between rich and poor was widening as the percentage of the nation's wealth held by the top 10 percent of American families climbed from 67 to 73 percent between 1980 and 1988. At the same time, many American workers found their wages and employment opportunities declining; thus the number of people living below the poverty line of $9,885 increased. Across the country, the number of homeless increased, placing more pressure on social programs that found their budgets being reduced. With 15 percent blue-collar unemployment in Los Angeles, Juan Sanchez was happy to have a good job at a furniture factory, although he and his wife and three children were unable to afford a home and had to live in his brother-in-law's garage.

By the end of Reagan's second term, the economy began to slow and expose important weaknesses. The federal deficit reached $1,065 billion a year, adding to a national debt that stood at nearly $3 trillion, requiring an annual interest payment of $200 million. The savings and loan industry was tottering on the verge of collapse resulting from aggressive investment and loan policies encouraged by deregulation. In 1988, the Lincoln Savings and Loan in California disclosed that it had lost more than $2.6 billion of depositors' money. Although the federal government provided more than $500 billion to cover the S&L losses, many now questioned the reality of Reaganomics, the administration's concern for the less privileged, and the ethics of many within the administration—over a hundred members of the administration were found guilty of unethical or illegal behavior. Throughout it all, Reagan remained untouched and popular with the public, causing some to refer to him as the "Teflon president."

A Second Term

The recession ended just in time for Reagan's second quest for the presidency. Republicans faced the 1984 election with great anticipation. Reagan was personally popular with the people, reflecting what some called "Main Street America." Using the theme "Morning in America," his reelection campaign projected

---

yuppie Young urban professional with a high-paying job and a materialistic lifestyle.

continued economic growth and affirmed his commitment to a strong America abroad. Democrats nominated a traditional liberal, Walter Mondale, who selected Representative Geraldine Ferraro of New York as his vice-presidential candidate. Immediately, Republicans defined liberalism, and Mondale, as "tax and spend." When Mondale did call for expanded social programs and higher taxes, Republican saw a potential political landslide. They were correct. President Reagan won an overwhelming victory, taking 59 percent of the popular vote and carrying every state except Mondale's Minnesota.

Asserting World Power

■ What did the Reagan administration view as the main source of trouble in world affairs?

■ In what ways did the Reagan administration attempt to implement a more assertive foreign policy?

■ How did Reagan shift U.S.-Soviet policy during his second term? What role did Gorbachev play in promoting change in the Soviet Union?

Reagan's victories in 1980 and 1984 resulted not only from the popularity of his domestic agenda but also from public support for his views on the role of the United States in world affairs. Throughout the 1980 presidential campaign, the Republicans had hammered at Carter's ineffective foreign policy and at slipping American prestige in the world. As president, Reagan promised to restore American power and influence. With little expertise in foreign policy, Reagan set the broad patterns of American policy but left the specifics to his foreign-policy staff, especially CIA director William Casey and Secretary of State George Shultz.

Cold War Renewed

At the center of Reagan's view of the world were two threats, the Soviet Union and nuclear war. The Soviet Union, he stated, constituted an "evil empire" and was the "focus of evil in the modern world." He believed that America's grand role was to defend the world from the Soviets and communism. Large increases in the military budget were necessary to back up the nation's diplomacy and to close the "window of vulnerability" that Carter had opened by allowing the Soviets to pull ahead in the arms race.

Congress quickly funded Reagan's military budget, which added more than $100 billion a year in appropriations, going from $164 billion in 1980 to $228 billion by 1985. By 1985, a million dollars was being spent on weapons every minute, and much of that money was flowing into the Sunbelt. Seeking a method to move from "assured destruction to one of assured survival," Reagan had asked Congress in 1983 to fund a controversial system of defense against Soviet missiles: the **Strategic Defense Initiative** (SDI). Between 1983 and 1989, Congress provided more than $17 billion for SDI research amid complaints that the concept was conceptually and technologically flawed. Critics pointed out that even if the system could work and was 95 percent effective, the 5 percent of Soviet warheads that would hit the United States would still destroy the nation, if not civilization.

With a stronger military and Cold War commitment, Reagan was determined to confront the Soviet menace and to roll back communism, especially in the Third World. The Reagan Doctrine promised economic and military aid, including covert operations funded by the CIA, to those fighting Communist tyranny. Quickly, the United States initiated or increased support and funding for "freedom fighters" opposing communism in Afghanistan, Angola, Ethiopia, and several Central American countries. In the Caribbean, Reagan approved a military strike against the island nation of **Grenada**. Grenada's Marxist government posed a direct threat to nearly five hundred American students attending medical school on the island and also a potential threat to American interests because it was accepting Cuban help in building an extended airport runway, one that Reagan feared might also serve as a staging area for enemy aircraft. On October 25, 1983, more than two thousand American soldiers quickly overcame minimal opposition, brought home the American students, and installed a pro-American government on the island. The administration basked in the light of public approval.

The nation applauded the administration for its action in Grenada, but some were concerned about American policies in Central America (see Map 30.2). They worried about the disturbing reports of human rights violations by "death squads" linked to the Salvadoran military and feared that Central America

---

Strategic Defense Initiative   Research program to create an effective laser-based defense against nuclear missile attack.

Grenada   Country in the West Indies that achieved independence from Britain in 1974 and was invaded briefly by U.S. forces in 1983.

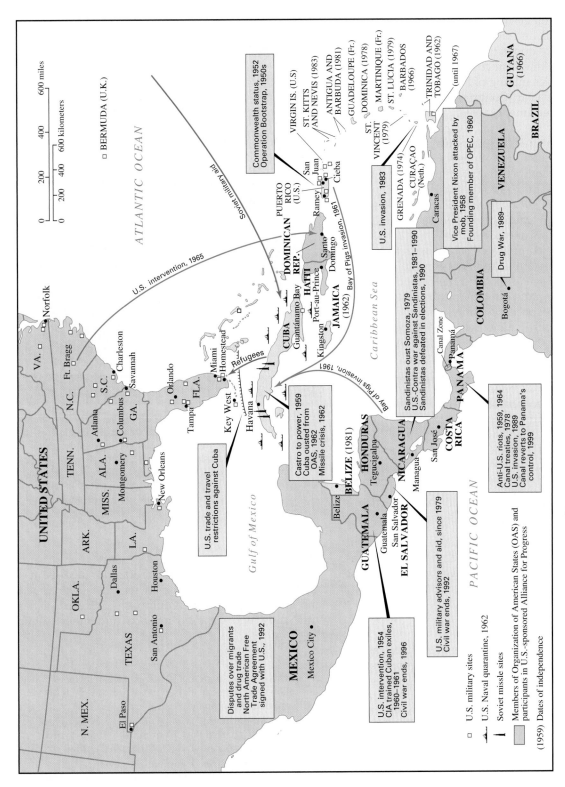

MAP 30.2 The United States and Central America and the Caribbean Geographical nearness, important economic ties, security needs, and the drug trade continue to make Central America and the Caribbean a critical region for American interests. This map shows some of the American economic, military, and political actions taken in the region since the end of World War II.

Map labels:

ATLANTIC OCEAN

600 miles
600 kilometers

BERMUDA (U.K.)

Commonwealth status, 1952
Operation Bootstrap, 1950s

VIRGIN IS. (U.S)
ST. KITTS
AND NEVIS (1983)
ANTIGUA AND
BARBUDA (1981)
GUADELOUPE (Fr.)
DOMINICA (1978)
MARTINIQUE (Fr.)
ST. LUCIA (1979)
ST. VINCENT (1979)
BARBADOS (1966)
TRINIDAD AND
TOBAGO (1962)
(until 1967)

GUYANA (1966)
BRAZIL
VENEZUELA

San Juan
Ramey   Cieba
PUERTO RICO (U.S.)

U.S. invasion, 1983

GRENADA (1974)
CURAÇAO (Neth.)
Caracas

Vice President Nixon attacked by
mob, 1958
Founding member of OPEC, 1960

Drug War, 1989–

COLOMBIA
Bogotá

DOMINICAN REP.
HAITI
Port-au-Prince
Santo Domingo
JAMAICA
Kingston
Bay of Pigs invasion, 1961

Caribbean Sea

U.S. intervention, 1965

Soviet military aid

CUBA
Guantánamo Bay

Sandinistas oust Somoza, 1979
U.S.-Contra war against Sandinistas, 1981–1990
Sandinistas defeated in elections, 1990

Canal Zone
Panamá
PANAMA

UNITED STATES
Norfolk
VA.
Ft. Bragg
N.C.
Charleston
S.C.
Savannah
Atlanta
GA.
Columbus
Orlando
FLA.
Tampa
Miami
Homestead
Key West
Refugees
Havana
Gulf of Mexico

TENN.
ALA.
Montgomery
MISS.
New Orleans
ARK.
LA.

Castro to power, 1959
Cuba ousted from
OAS, 1962
Missile crisis, 1962

U.S. trade and travel
restrictions against Cuba

Bay of Pigs invasion, 1961

BELIZE (1981)
Belize
HONDURAS
Tegucigalpa
NICARAGUA
Managua
COSTA RICA
San José

Anti-U.S. riots, 1959, 1964
Canal treaties, 1978
U.S. invasion, 1989
Canal reverts to Panama's
control, 1999

GUATEMALA
Guatemala
San Salvador
EL SALVADOR

U.S. military advisors and aid, since 1979
Civil war ends, 1992

PACIFIC OCEAN

OKLA.
Dallas
Houston
TEXAS
San Antonio
N. MEX.
El Paso

Disputes over migrants
and drug trade
North American Free
Trade Agreement
signed with U.S., 1992

MEXICO
Mexico City

U.S. intervention, 1954
CIA trained Cuban exiles,
1960–1961
Civil war ends, 1996

Legend:
□ U.S. military sites
⚓ U.S. Naval quarantine, 1962
| Soviet missile sites
▨ Members of Organization of American States (OAS) and participants in U.S.-sponsored Alliance for Progress
(1959) Dates of independence

0   200   400   600 miles
0   200   400   600 kilometers

might become another Vietnam, with American troops following the aid and advisers already being sent. Concern turned to opposition when the press uncovered large-scale American covert aid to the **Contras,** including the CIA's mining of Nicaraguan harbors in 1984. That same year, Congress passed legislation, the **Boland Amendment,** which allowed only humanitarian aid to the Contras. Reagan and CIA director William Casey quickly sought ways to continue to arm the Contras without Congress's knowledge. One plan involved a complicated system of secretly selling arms to the Iranians and then using the money to fund the Contras. The operation also involved securing Iran's help in gaining the release of American hostages held in Lebanon.

As news of the complicated sale of arms to Iran increased (the Iran-Contra Affair), it became clear that the administration had violated the Boland Amendment. Responding to a growing public concern, Reagan appointed a special commission and Congress began its own investigation. By mid-1987, both investigations agreed that members of the CIA and the National Security Council (NSC) had acted independently, without the knowledge or approval of Congress, and had lied to Congress to hide their operation. Eventually, fourteen people were charged with committing crimes, and eleven—including several top-level advisers to Reagan—were convicted of violating a variety of federal laws and were sentenced to prison terms. Investigators found no direct proof of Reagan's involvement in the undercover arrangement but concluded that he had set the stage for others' illegal activities by encouraging and, in general terms, ordering support for the Contras. Reagan protested, "I just didn't know." The Iran-Contra investigations showed a president out of touch with what was happening, and for once the image of Reagan was tarnished.

Terrorism

The hope of using Iran to help obtain the release of Americans held hostage by terrorists reflected one of the most difficult problems complicating American policy—how to deal with terrorism directed against the United States. In 1985, over 800 terrorist attacks around the world killed over 900 people, including 23 Americans. The rise in terrorism was largely a product of the struggle between Israel and the **Palestine Liberation Organization** (PLO) and its Arab supporters. By the late 1970s, shadowy militant Islamic groups that had previously confined their assaults to Israel were launching campaigns of terrorism against

Like Eisenhower twenty years before, President Reagan in 1983 committed American troops to Beirut, Lebanon, as part of a peacekeeping operation. This intervention, however, was not successful. In October, terrorists blew up the marine barracks, killing 241 soldiers. "Too few to fight and too many to die," said one congressional critic, as four months later Reagan withdrew the remaining American forces from the war-torn nation. *Corbis-Bettmann.*

Israel's Western supporters. Throughout the Mediterranean region, pro-Palestinian terrorists kidnapped and killed Americans and Europeans, hijacked planes and ships, and attacked airports and other public

Contras Nicaraguan rebels, many of them former followers of Somoza, fighting to overthrow the leftist Sandinista government.

Boland Amendment Motion, approved by Congress in 1984, that barred the CIA from using funds to give direct or indirect aid to the Nicaraguan Contras.

Palestine Liberation Organization Political and military organization of Palestinians, originally dedicated to opposing the state of Israel through terrorism and other means.

places. American troops became a direct target when in 1982 they arrived as part of a United Nations peacekeeping force in Lebanon. The first attack came in April 1983 when Muslim terrorists attacked the American embassy in Beirut, killing 63 people. Six months later, in October, a suicide driver rammed a truck filled with explosives into the marine barracks at the Beirut airport, killing 241 marines. Two miles away another suicide attack killed 50 French troops, who like the Americans were part of a peacekeeping effort. Reagan vehemently denounced the terrorist attacks but found no solution to the problem except to remove American troops in January 1984.

The Reagan administration came up with a more satisfying response two years later when it bombed targets in Libya. The attack was in retribution for a terrorist bombing of a disco in West Berlin that killed an American soldier. Intelligence sources linked the terrorists to the anti-American ruler of Libya, **Muammar Qaddafi.** Reagan condemned Qaddafi as the "mad dog of the Middle East" and, calling Libya a "rogue nation," ordered a reprisal raid. American navy and air force planes hit several targets in Libya, including Qaddafi's quarters, killing his daughter. Qaddafi remained anti-American and continued to support the PLO and terrorist groups, but one American official bragged that they had shown Qaddafi "that we could get people close to him." To terrorists Reagan declared, "You can run but you can't hide." Neither the declaration of the president nor the attack on Libya deterred the terrorists, who continued their activities.

Reagan and Gorbachev

Until 1985, Reagan's foreign policy had focused on combating the power of the Soviet Union around the globe. Then, unexpectedly, the president executed a reversal of policy toward the Soviet Union. He called for the resumption of arms limitation talks and invited the Soviet leader, **Mikhail Gorbachev,** to the United States. Gorbachev was different from previous Soviet leaders. He was younger and committed to changing the Soviet Union. With his policy of *perestroika* ("restructuring"), he wanted to breathe new life into an economy that was stagnating under the weight of military spending and state planning. And under his new policy of *glasnost* ("openness"), he instituted reforms that provided more political and civil rights to the Soviet people. To demonstrate to the West that he was a new type of Soviet leader, Gorbachev unilaterally stopped nuclear testing and deployment of missiles from Eastern Europe and embarked on

After declaring the Soviet Union an "evil empire" responsible for nearly all the world's problems, President Reagan reversed course in 1988 and opened productive discussions with Soviet reformer Mikhail Gorbachev. The outcome was an intermediate-range nuclear force treaty that helped to end the Cold War as well as to reduce the overall number of nuclear missiles. Here, the two superpower leaders pose in front of St. Basil's Cathedral in Moscow. *Bettmann/Corbis.*

goodwill trips to Europe and the Americas. By the time he was forced from office in 1991, Gorbachev had been awarded the Nobel Peace Prize for his role in ending the Cold War, and the first McDonald's had opened in Moscow.

Muammar Qaddafi   Political leader who seized power in a 1969 military coup and imposed a socialist regime and Islamic orthodoxy on Libya.

Mikhail Gorbachev   As Soviet General Secretary of the Communist Party assumed power in 1985, he introduced political and economic reforms and then found himself presiding over the breakup of the Soviet Union.

In 1985, Gorbachev declined Reagan's invitation to visit the United States but agreed to a summit meeting in Geneva. The two leaders at first jousted with each other. Reagan condemned the Soviets for human rights abuses, their involvement in Afghanistan, and their aid to Communist factions fighting in Angola and Ethiopia. Gorbachev attacked the proposed development of SDI. But both were concerned over the possibility of nuclear war, and slowly they gained a respect and fondness for each other. Soviet-American negotiations on arms limitations continued with new optimism. A year later, in October 1986, the two leaders met again in Reykjavik, Iceland, to discuss reductions of strategic weapons. They reached no accord but agreed to keep working on arms limitations. Both leaders left the meeting more trusting of the other and increasingly determined to reduce the possibility of nuclear war. In December 1987, a breakthrough occurred. During a Washington summit, Reagan and Gorbachev signed the **Intermediate Nuclear Force Treaty,** which removed their intermediate-range missiles from Europe.

Throughout 1988, Soviet-American relations continued to improve. Gorbachev withdrew Soviet forces from Afghanistan, the Senate approved the Intermediate Nuclear Force Treaty, and Reagan visited Moscow. Assessing the changes in Russia and Soviet policy, Secretary Shultz noted that the Cold War "was all over but the shouting."

In Reagan's Shadow

■ What new foreign-policy choices did the United States face as a result of the collapse of the Soviet Union?

■ How did Reagan's domestic policies affect expectations and outcomes for the Bush administration?

"Was it all over but the shouting?" could have been a question that many Republicans were asking by 1988. The Reagan presidency was coming to an end, and as Nancy Reagan said of 1987, "It's not been a great year." Despite the apparent thaw in the Cold War, for the first time in the Reagan administration a combination of events had dented the image of Reagan and Republican leadership. The stock market collapse in October 1987 and the Iran-Contra revelations created the impression that the administration was not in control of events or of itself and that the president had little grasp of what was happening. Still, most Republicans believed that their conservative revolution was still strong, that they would defeat the Democrats and continue to strengthen the nation.

Bush Assumes Office

Republicans passed the torch to Vice President George Bush, although some worried that he was not conservative enough to push the New Right's social agenda. Nonetheless, Bush had been the loyal vice president and had served the party faithfully, holding important posts under Presidents Nixon and Ford: ambassador to the United Nations, chairman of the Republican National Committee, ambassador to China, and director of the Central Intelligence Agency. Several Democrats eagerly contended to confront Bush, whose popularity seemed a faint shadow of Reagan's. Eventually, Governor Michael Dukakis of Massachusetts gained the Democratic nomination.

The 1988 campaign was dull. Both candidates lacked flair, and neither was unable to energize the voters. Both candidates avoided most social and international issues, while claiming that they were the best suited to fight crime and drugs. While both vowed not to raise taxes, Bush's promise "Read my lips . . . no new taxes" was best received. To motivate voters, the candidates relied on television and negative campaigning, which aimed at discrediting the opponent rather than addressing issues and policies. Republican ads were more effective and, combined with falling unemployment and inflation rates, contributed to Bush's easy victory. With 79.2 percent of the electoral vote and 54 percent of the popular vote, he became the first sitting vice president to be elected president since Martin Van Buren in 1836. Although Bush trounced Dukakis, the victory was not as sweet as Bush had hoped. Democrats controlled the House and the Senate.

Bush and a New International Order

Bush's own preferences and international events dictated that foreign affairs would consume most of his attention. The world was changing rapidly, and Bush considered the management of international relations to be one of his strengths. Unlike Reagan, he focused on specific policies. The immediate problems were

Intermediate Nuclear Force Treaty   Treaty (1987) that provided for the destruction of all U.S. and Soviet medium-range nuclear missiles and for verification with on-site inspections.

With the collapse of the Soviet Union and communism across Eastern Europe, the symbol of the iron curtain and the Cold War came tumbling down in Berlin. Jubilant Berliners sit atop the Berlin Wall, which had divided the city from 1962 to November 1989. *AP/Wide World.*

those resulting from Gorbachev's reforms, which had produced significant political and economic changes through the Communist world. His withdrawal of Soviet forces from Afghanistan and Eastern Europe, combined with his announcement that the Soviets would not intervene to prevent political change in Eastern Europe, unleashed a series of events that undermined Communist systems in operation since the end of World War II.

Communism was in retreat throughout Eastern Europe by 1989. Poland had a new constitution, a free-market economy, and a non-Communist government. In Berlin the symbol of the Cold War, the **Berlin Wall,** was torn down on November 9, 1989, by jubilant Germans. As the wall crumbled, so too did the Communist governments of East Germany, Hungary, Bulgaria, Czechoslovakia, and Romania (see Map 30.3). On December 2–3, 1989, Gorbachev met with Bush on the island of Malta in the Mediterranean Sea and declared that the Cold War was over. A year later, Germany had been unified and the Baltic states—Latvia, Estonia, and Lithuania—had declared their independence from the Soviet Union.

Throughout most of the Eastern bloc the change in governments was accompanied with little violence or territorial adjustments, but not in the case of Yugoslavia and the Soviet Union. When Yugoslavia's Communist regime collapsed in 1991, ethnic separatist movements demanded independence for the regions of Slovenia, Croatia, Bosnia-Herzegovina, and Macedonia. Serbian leader Slobodan Milosevic attempted to use the army to maintain unity under Serbian **hegemony.** Warfare ignited and quickly spread across the region. Slovenia, Croatia, and Macedonia gained independence by 1992. But in Bosnia-Herzegovina the fighting continued to rage as Serb forces instituted a policy of "ethnic cleansing" to remove the Muslim Bosnians from the country. By 1995 more than 200,00 people were dead and nearly 2 million left homeless.

The demise of the Soviet Union was almost as dramatic but less violent. Gorbachev's policies that permitted Eastern Europe to break free also caused the republics of the Soviet Union to demand greater autonomy and even independence. In August 1991, Communist hard-liners attempted a coup to topple Gorbachev. It failed, in large part because of the actions of **Boris Yeltsin,** who declared the coup illegal and called on the Russian people to resist. Faced with popular opposition in Moscow and other cities, the coup collapsed within seventy-two hours. The aborted coup accelerated the Soviet republics' movement toward independence. Pleas by Gorbachev to maintain Soviet unity were rejected, and by the end of 1991, Gorbachev had resigned and the Soviet Union had ceased to exist. In its place was the **Commonwealth of Independent States** (CIS), a weak federation led by Yeltsin, the president of the Russian Republic.

The forces that promoted change in the Soviet bloc were alive throughout the globe. University students

Berlin Wall   Barrier that the Communist East German government built in 1961 to divide East and West Berlin; it was torn down in November 1989 as the Cold War was ending.

hegemony   The dominance of one group over other groups.

Boris Yeltsin   Russian parliamentary leader who was elected president of the new Russian Republic in 1991 and provided increased democratic and economic reforms.

Commonwealth of Independent States   Weak federation of the former Soviet republics; it replaced the Soviet Union in 1992 and soon gave way to total independence of the member countries.

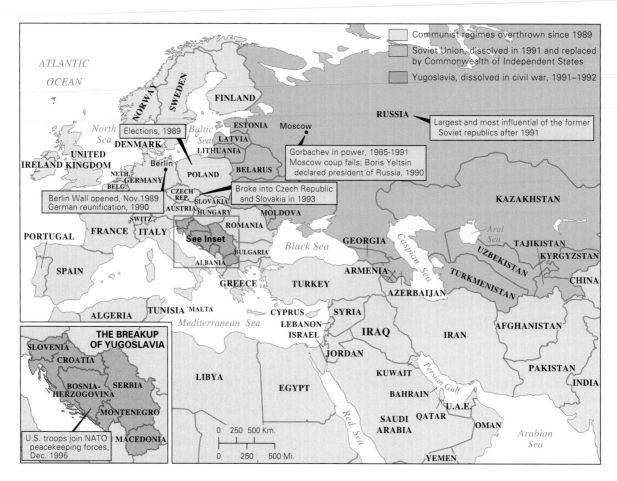

MAP 30.3 The Fall of Communism   As the Soviet Union collapsed and lost its control over the countries of Eastern Europe, the map of Eastern Europe and Central Asia changed. The Soviet Union disappeared into history, replaced by fifteen new national units. In Eastern Europe, West and East Germany merged, Czechoslovakia divided into two nations, and Yugoslavia broke into five feuding states.

in China led a series of demonstrations in 1989 demanding democracy and economic and governmental reform. In Beijing that June, thousands of student protesters filled the massive expanse of Tiananmen Square. China's leaders chose to restore order by using force, killing hundreds as the world watched on television. Under political and public pressure to impose sanctions against China for the massacre, President Bush merely condemned Beijing. He argued that harsh action toward China would further isolate its leadership and make it even more brutal.

Criticized by some for his lenient China policy, Bush's policies in Central America gained widespread support. There he reduced American military assistance, pushed for political negotiations, and backed the **Contadora Plan,** a formula for peace in Nicaragua

negotiated by a coalition of Central American nations. These actions contributed to the Contras' halting military operations and the Marxist Ortega government's accepting free elections. Those elections, in February 1990, saw opposition candidate Violeta de Chamorro defeat Daniel Ortega. In neighboring El Salvador, American-supported peace negotiations also ended the civil war.

Contadora Plan   Pact signed by the presidents of five Central American nations in 1987 calling for a cease-fire in conflicts in the region and for democratic reforms.

Protecting American Interests Abroad

Promoting democracy and free trade were still clearly in the interests of the United States, but with the collapse of the Soviet Union, many wondered what goals and interests would now shape American foreign and military policies. Some called for a "peace dividend," asking that the United States reduce its global role and the military's budget. Bush resisted these suggestions and warned that the world was still a dangerous place. The bloody conflict in the Balkans, continued tensions in the Middle East, and the ever-present threat of nuclear weapons each demanded a strong, activist U.S. foreign policy. Less traditional foreign-policy concerns included the drug trade, terrorism, and a variety of issues related to the global economy.

President Bush had made drugs a key issue during his campaign and had promised to crack down on the flow of cocaine into the United States. In December 1989, he ordered American troops into Panama, in Operation Just Cause, to arrest Panamanian dictator Manuel Noriega on drug-related charges. Once praised by Reagan and Bush, Noriega had been implicated in the torture and murder of his political enemies and the shipment of drugs from Colombia through Panama to the United States. Within seventy-two hours, American forces had accomplished their mission and had Noriega in custody. American casualties were light (only twenty-three lost their lives), but more than three thousand Panamanians, almost all civilians, died. A Miami court later found Noriega guilty of drug-related offenses and sentenced him to prison in 1992. Panama, however, remained a major route in the smuggling of drugs into the United States.

In the fall of 1990, President Bush faced a more traditional and serious threat. Iraq's Saddam Hussein invaded the oil-rich sheikdom of Kuwait and overran the country. Many worried that Hussein intended to dominate the Persian Gulf and thus gain control over the flow of more than 40 percent of the world's oil supply. Within hours of the invasion, Bush warned, "This will not stand," and he organized a United Nations response. A multinational force of more than 700,000, including 500,000 Americans, went to Saudi Arabia in Operation Desert Shield to protect Saudi borders and oil sources and to pressure Iraq to withdraw from Kuwait. Nearly 80 percent of the American public supported protecting Saudi Arabia, but most wanted to avoid war by using economic and diplomatic sanctions to force Iraq to leave Kuwait. Bush thought otherwise. He worked with other coalition nations to set a deadline for Iraqi withdrawal. If by January 15, 1991, Iraq still occupied Kuwait, the allies would use force.

Eighteen hours after the deadline expired, with Iraq making no move to pull out, aircraft of the UN coalition began devastating attacks on Iraqi positions in Kuwait and on Iraq itself. American public support immediately rallied behind the **Persian Gulf War.** After nearly forty days of air attacks, United Nations ground forces prepared to push Saddam Hussein's forces out of Kuwait (see Map 30.4). Saddam had promised that the ground war would be the "mother of all battles," but General Norman Schwarzkopf, coalition force commander, was confident of victory. He ridiculed the Iraqi leader's military ability: Hussein is "neither a strategist, nor is he schooled in the operational arts, nor is he a tactician, nor is he a general, nor is he a soldier. Other than that, he is a great military man."

The ground offensive of the war against Iraq, called by U.S. forces Operation Desert Storm, started the night of February 23. Within a hundred hours, coalition forces liberated Kuwait, where thousands of demoralized Iraqi soldiers, many of whom had gone without food and water for days, surrendered to advancing coalition forces. Estimates of Iraqi losses ranged from 70,000 to 115,000 killed. The United States lost fewer than 150. It was the "mother of all victories," quipped many Americans as President Bush's popularity momentarily soared above 90 percent. Some, less euphoric, speculated that the offensive had ended too soon and should have continued until all, or nearly all, of the Iraqi army had been destroyed and Hussein ousted from power.

By the summer of 1991, the United States could claim victory in two wars, the one against Iraq and the Cold War, and was clearly the diplomatic and military leader of the world. Riding a wave of popularity and foreign-policy successes, the White House looked hopefully toward the forthcoming presidential campaign.

Persian Gulf War   War in the Persian Gulf region in 1991, triggered by Iraq's invasion of Kuwait; a U.S.-led coalition defeated Iraqi forces and freed Kuwait.

In Operation Desert Shield, regarded by many as Bush's most successful action as president, United Nations forces led by the United States successfully pushed back the Iraqi army and liberated Kuwait. In this picture, U.S. Marines and their "humvees" prepare for action in Saudi Arabia, along the Kuwait border. *Bill Gentile/Spia Press.*

A Kinder, Gentler Nation

Bush had entered the White House in 1989 promising a "kinder, gentler nation," an administration concerned about the nation's social problems. But the Bush administration made no move to improve America's society or economy. The goal was not "to remake society" but to manage the presidency, avoid "stupid mistakes," and "see that government doesn't get in the way." More government and more money were not always the best solutions to the country's ills, Bush frequently reminded his listeners. The message echoed Reagan's, but Bush was not as effective a communicator—he liked talking to people over the phone rather than face-to-face. Without Reagan's stage presence, Bush seemed to lack vision.

By the end of his first year in office, Bush and his advisers were confident they were managing well. They pointed to successful legislation that protected disabled Americans against discrimination (the Americans with Disabilities Act of 1990) and reduced smokestack and auto emissions and acid rain (the Clean Air Act of 1990). Bush also noted that under his administration, the minimum wage had risen from $3.35 to $4.25 an hour, and more funding had been provided for the Head Start program. Only two problem areas seemed to exist: the sluggish economy and his broken pledge on taxes.

In mid-1990, in part because of oil price increases caused by Iraq's invasion of Kuwait, the nation entered into a recession. The recession, plus the growing federal deficit, had convinced Bush to work with Congress to raise taxes, despite his "no new taxes" pledge. Bush believed that by 1992 the recession would be over, the national debt would be reduced, and forgiving or forgetful voters would happily reelect him. The recession, however, continued into 1992.

The recession lasted longer than Bush had expected for several reasons. The world economy was slowing, and one result was that fewer American goods were being sold overseas. A restructuring of the American economy forced many businesses to declare bankruptcy or downsize, releasing both blue-collar and white-collar workers. Between July 1990 and July 1993, more than 1.9 million people lost their jobs, and 63 percent of American corporations cut their staffs. IBM and General Motors were among those that faced huge losses and dismissed thousands of workers. "I don't see the United States regaining a substantial percentage of the jobs lost for five to ten years," said one chief executive.

Sharply rising federal spending and the ever-swelling deficit helped to lengthen and deepen the recession. Despite Bush's pledges to hold down federal spending and reduce the deficit, the budget skyrocketed during his term, reaching $1.5 trillion in 1992. At the same time, family income dropped below 1980 levels, to $37,300 from a 1980 high of $38,900. Consumers—caught between rising unemployment, falling wages, and nagging inflation—saw their savings shrink, and their confidence in the economy followed suit.

Bush did little to respond to the economic slide. Apart from saying that the American economy would

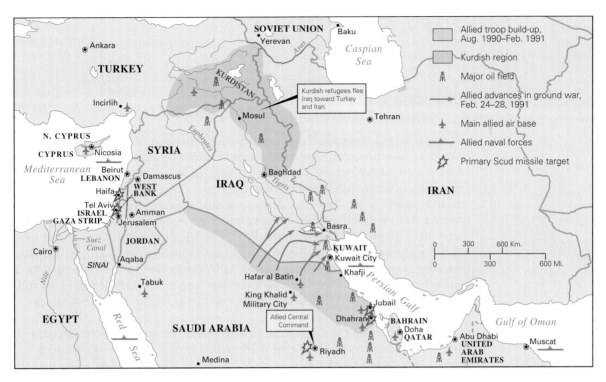

MAP 30.4 The Gulf War   On August 2, 1990, Iraq invaded Kuwait, threatening Saudi Arabia and the Persian Gulf region. In response, the United States and other nations formed an international coalition to restore Kuwait's independence. In January 1991, the coalition forces of Operation Desert Storm began to attack the forces of Saddam Hussein. The outcome was the destruction of most of the Iraqi army and Kuwait's liberation, but Saddam Hussein maintained control of Iraq.

rebound, Bush relied on raising interest rates and promoted globalization by reducing tariff barriers to allow foreign trade to expand. Negotiations went forward to establish a North American free trading zone with Mexico and Canada and to eliminate Japanese barriers to American trade, but these negotiations had little impact on the economy. As the recession wore on, Democrats called for tax cuts on the middle class, increased and extended unemployment benefits, and other social programs. Bush responded with the veto. When House majority leader Richard Gephardt was asked to define Bush's domestic program, the Democrat icily commented that it was "the veto pen." Congressional Democrats replied by blocking Bush's attempts to reduce **capital gains taxes.** The result was political gridlock. As 1992 began, Bush faced his lowest approval rating ever in public opinion polls—around 40 percent. Political observers noted, and Republicans lamented, that Bush, unlike Reagan,

seemed unable to project the image of an effective leader who had a vision of where the nation or the world should be going. Still, as a sitting president with important foreign-policy successes, most observers believed he would have little problem winning the next presidential election.

capital gains tax   Tax on profits resulting from the sale of assets such as securities and real estate.

Individual Voices

Examining a Primary Source

Diameng Pa Tells His Story

The patterns of immigration that began with the passage of the 1965 Immigration Act continued throughout the 1990s, with increasing numbers of Asians and Latin Americans migrating to the United States. Amid growing calls for limitations on immigration, a Senate subcommittee heard testimony on Ellis Island, New York, from those supporting the idea that America should remain a nation of immigrants. Among those presenting their views before the Senate Judicial Committee's Subcommittee on Immigration were New York City mayor Rudolph Giuliani and New York State governor George Pataki, both of whom pointed out that their families too were once immigrants. On August 11, 1997, Cambodian refugee Diameng Pa, a senior from Wakefield High School in Arlington, Virginia, described before the subcommittee the hope and opportunity afforded him as an immigrant in America.

I would like to thank the Committee on Immigration for giving me this opportunity to tell . . . my strong belief that America should continue to be a nation of immigrants. This institution is hope for those still seeking a new beginning similar to the one I received.

I was born in Batdambang, Cambodia, on November 23, 1978 . . . a rural village . . . several miles from the Thai border. . . . This period produced a Cambodian Communist faction known as the Khmer Rouge, who killed more than 400,000 Cambodians and forced many more to flee to refugee camps in Thailand, including my family.

To acquire a better life for their family, my parents fled to a refugee camp in Thailand, fortunately able to escape from the constant threat of guerrilla attacks by the Khmer Rouge . . . and then to escape to the United States. . . . By coming to the United States of America, we were traveling to a land that was foreign to us and whose language we did not speak. However, it would be a place that we would receive new identities and a new chance of a better life. It is a land that would take time to adapt to, however, it is a land of opportunity. ▪

My family initially settled in a minority neighborhood of South Arlington, Virginia, not far from Strayer College where my father, Mong Pa, pursued a degree in business administration. However, unfortunately, he abandoned his goals to support the family. My father would also mention the importance of education and its correlation with success. Though quite young, I realized that my father sacrificed his opportunity to pursue his business degree so that the family was financially stable. He encouraged me to reach out and to appreciate one of the many precious gifts that America offered—formal education.

Two years after I started school, I settled into the language thanks to my teachers and the miracle of TV. I remember adopting a few phrases here and there and soon enough I became accustomed to the English language and American culture. Bugs Bunny's "What's up, Doc" was my most favorite phrase during that time.

. . . [W]hile attending Thomas Jefferson Middle School . . . I accelerated in my studies and took the most demanding courses possible . . . I developed an interest in science activities. ▪

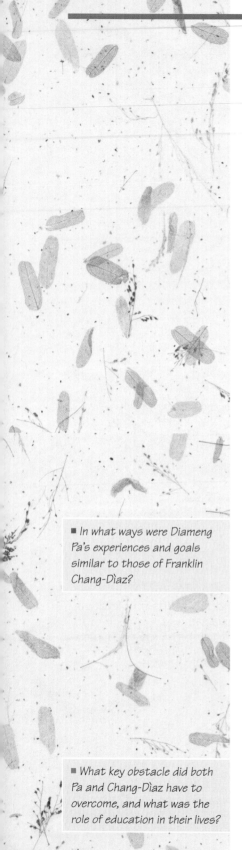

■ In what ways were Diameng Pa's experiences and goals similar to those of Franklin Chang-Díaz?

■ What key obstacle did both Pa and Chang-Díaz have to overcome, and what was the role of education in their lives?

■ *Do you agree with the statement that immigrants are underdogs and have a special drive for success? In your opinion, are the success stories of Pa and Chang-Dìaz proof that America is a land of opportunity, or are these two immigrants exceptions to the rule?*

As a sophomore at Wakefield High School I was privileged to be the first student in Wakefield history to attend the international Science and Engineer Fair in . . . Canada and to win second place in the category of environmental science.

As an immigrant, valedictorian of my senior class and now a proud American citizen, I realize that becoming an American took time. I feel that pursuing a dream takes dedication and will to strive and succeed. Only in America are you given this generous privilege. A world-renowned . . . researcher by the name of David Da-i Ho states, "Success is a result of immigrant drive. People get in this new world, they want to carve out their place in it. . . . You always retain a bit of underdog mentality. And if they work assiduously and lie low long enough, even underdogs will have their day." ■

Summary

The years between Carter's inauguration and Bush's farewell were ones of changing expectations based in part on the health of the American economy. The economic growth that had characterized the postwar period was slowing, making the American dream harder and harder to attain. During Carter's presidency the nation seemed beset by blows to its domestic prosperity and international status. Carter seemed unable to lead Congress and unsure of the government's ability to solve the country's social and economic problems. In his foreign policy, Carter de-emphasized Cold War relationships and gave more attention to human rights and Third World problems. Many believed the result was a weakening of America's international status, exemplified by the hostage crisis in Iran.

Reagan rejected Carter's notion that the nation was being held in check by some ill-defined limits. Instead, he argued that the only constraint on American greatness was government's excessive regulation and interference in society. He promised to reassert American power and renew the offensive in the Cold War. It was a popular message and contributed to a conservative resurgence that elevated Reagan to the presidency. As president, Reagan fulfilled many conservative expectations by reducing support for some social programs, easing and eliminating some government regulations, and exerting American power around the world—altering the structure of Soviet-American relations. Supporters claimed that the outcome of Reagan's choices was a prosperous nation that faced few constraints. They applauded Reagan's assessment that his administration had chosen to "change a nation, and instead . . . changed a world."

Bush inherited the expectations that the Reagan administration had generated. But, unlike Reagan, he could not project an image of strong and visionary leadership. Finding fewer constraints in conducting foreign policy, Bush directed most of his attention to world affairs. As the Soviet Union and communism in Eastern Europe collapsed, Bush gained public approval for his foreign policies, also demonstrating American strength and resolve in Panama and the Persian Gulf. His foreign-policy successes, however, only highlighted his weakness in domestic economic policy as the nation found itself mired in a nagging recession that sapped the public's confidence in Republican leadership and the economy.

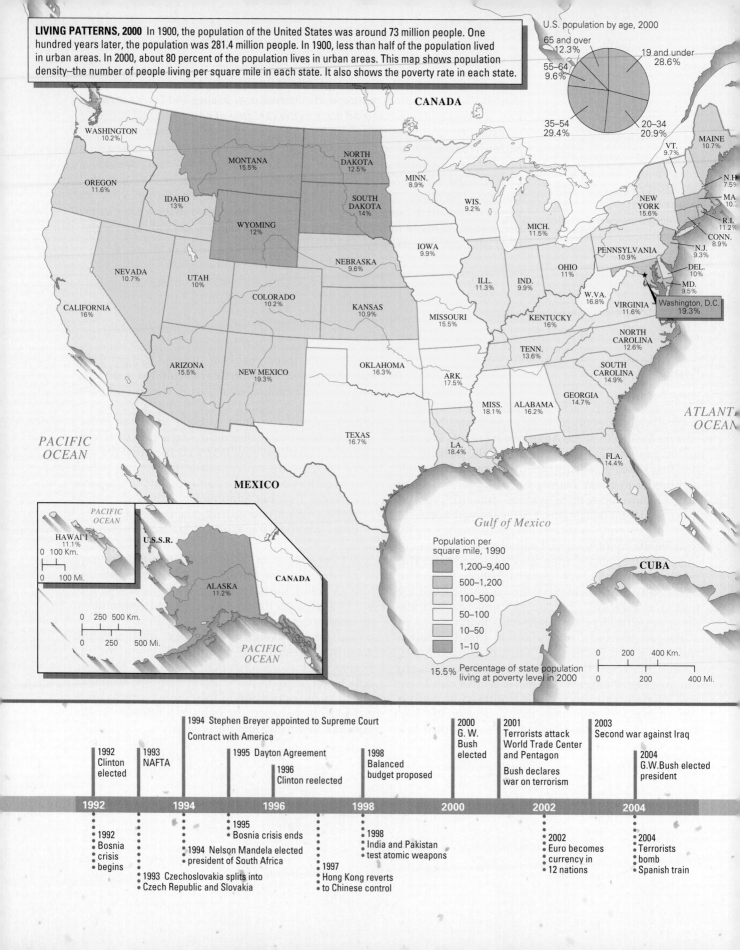

LIVING PATTERNS, 2000 In 1900, the population of the United States was around 73 million people. One hundred years later, the population was 281.4 million people. In 1900, less than half of the population lived in urban areas. In 2000, about 80 percent of the population lives in urban areas. This map shows population density—the number of people living per square mile in each state. It also shows the poverty rate in each state.

U.S. population by age, 2000

- 65 and over 12.3%
- 55–64 9.6%
- 35–54 29.4%
- 19 and under 28.6%
- 20–34 20.9%

CANADA

WASHINGTON 10.2%
OREGON 11.6%
IDAHO 13%
MONTANA 15.5%
NORTH DAKOTA 12.5%
SOUTH DAKOTA 14%
WYOMING 12%
NEVADA 10.7%
UTAH 10%
CALIFORNIA 16%
COLORADO 10.2%
NEBRASKA 9.6%
KANSAS 10.9%
ARIZONA 15.5%
NEW MEXICO 19.3%
OKLAHOMA 16.3%
TEXAS 16.7%
MINN. 8.9%
WIS. 9.2%
IOWA 9.9%
MISSOURI 15.5%
ARK. 17.5%
LA. 18.4%
MISS. 18.1%
ALABAMA 16.2%
MICH. 11.5%
ILL. 11.3%
IND. 9.9%
OHIO 11%
KENTUCKY 16%
TENN. 13.6%
GEORGIA 14.7%
W.VA. 16.8%
VIRGINIA 11.6%
NORTH CAROLINA 12.6%
SOUTH CAROLINA 14.9%
FLA. 14.4%
PENNSYLVANIA 10.9%
NEW YORK 15.6%
MAINE 10.7%
VT. 9.7%
N.H 7.5%
MA 10.?
R.I. 11.2%
CONN. 8.9%
N.J. 9.3%
DEL. 10%
MD. 9.5%
Washington, D.C. 19.3%

PACIFIC OCEAN

MEXICO

ATLANTIC OCEAN

PACIFIC OCEAN
HAWAI'I 11.1%
0 100 Km.
0 100 Mi.

U.S.S.R.
CANADA
ALASKA 11.2%
0 250 500 Km.
0 250 500 Mi.
PACIFIC OCEAN

Gulf of Mexico

CUBA

Population per square mile, 1990

- 1,200–9,400
- 500–1,200
- 100–500
- 50–100
- 10–50
- 1–10

15.5% Percentage of state population living at poverty level in 2000

0 200 400 Km.
0 200 400 Mi.

1992 Clinton elected

1993 NAFTA

1994 Stephen Breyer appointed to Supreme Court
Contract with America

1995 Dayton Agreement

1996 Clinton reelected

1998 Balanced budget proposed

2000 G. W. Bush elected

2001 Terrorists attack World Trade Center and Pentagon
Bush declares war on terrorism

2003 Second war against Iraq

2004 G.W.Bush elected president

1992	1994	1996	1998	2000	2002	2004

1992 Bosnia crisis begins

1993 Czechoslovakia splits into Czech Republic and Slovakia

1994 Nelson Mandela elected president of South Africa

1995 Bosnia crisis ends

1997 Hong Kong reverts to Chinese control

1998 India and Pakistan test atomic weapons

2002 Euro becomes currency in 12 nations

2004 Terrorists bomb Spanish train

Entering a New Century, 1992–2004

31

Living Patterns, 2000
Since the end of World War II, Americans have been moving into the Sunbelt. To better understand these changes, compare the chapter-opening map for Chapter 25, which shows population changes, with the map on the facing page, which shows the population density of each state.

Individual Choices

FATHER MYCHAL JUDGE

In 1996 Father Mychal Judge became a symbol for those seeking solace and reconciliation after a great tragedy—the crash of TWA flight #800 into Long Island Sound that killed all passengers on board. He told relatives of those lost: "Open your hearts, and let their spirit and life keep you going." Little did he know at the time that on September 11, 2001, his actions and words would provide meaning to a whole nation. Father Mychal Judge, who had grown up on the streets of New York, became the first "official" casualty of the terrorist attack that destroyed the World Trade Center. *Ed Betz/Wide World.*

Father Mychal Judge

In 1868 Horatio Alger wrote the first of his many works about young men with few prospects finding the road to success and respectability. In that novel, *Ragged Dick,* a vagabond shoeshine boy on the streets of New York, eventually found a sponsor, gained an education, and got a responsible job—fame and fortune were within reach. Mychal Judge followed a similar path but discovered a very different fame and fortune. Born of Irish immigrant parents in 1933, he grew up in Brooklyn during the Great Depression, and money was scarce. Things got worse when in 1936 his father became gravely ill and was unable to work. When his father died three years later, Judge's childhood ended. "I never had a father growing up, someone I would play catch with or go for a walk with," he remembered. Instead of playing, he went to work as a shoeshine boy, earning money for his mother and family. He considered being a fireman when he grew up. Working the streets of Brooklyn and Manhattan, he would sometimes duck into neighboring Catholic churches to rest and find solace. He later recalled that he liked going to church—"I just felt good there." Despite his mother's favorite saying, "Too much religion is no good for anybody," he found himself drawn to a religious life. At one of the churches he used to visit, St. Francis of Assisi in Lower Manhattan, he met Father Teddy, who took him under his wing and became his mentor. "Watching him," Judge remembered, "I realized that I didn't care for material things all that much."

For a poor Irish boy, the church provided a path to a different world, and in 1948, at the age of 15, Mychal Judge took it. He joined the Franciscan friars and eleven years later became Friar Judge, officially entering the order. In 1961 he was ordained as a priest and assigned to a parish in East Rutherford, New Jersey. It was a learning experience. "In seminary, you can get all the theology and Scripture in the world, and you land in your first parish," he recalled, "and you find out it's you—the personality and the gifts that God gave you."

Almost immediately the new priest became known for his "snappy laugh," charismatic personality, and "hands-on" concern for people. He would put his big Irish hand on you and give you a blessing, even if you didn't ask for one, recalled a friend. In 1974 he received national attention for helping talk a man into surrendering who was holding his wife and children at gunpoint. He also displayed a unique talent for being a peacemaker and helping people cope with grief. Recalled a colleague, "Mychal was really intuitive by diagnosing people's pain, their confusion, and guiding them to inner peace and inner strength. . . ."

In 1986 "Father Mike" returned to his roots—St. Francis of Assisi Church in Manhattan—and immersed himself in a wide variety of ministries, including working in local hospitals and among the poor, and running an AIDS ministry when many in society condemned and avoided people with AIDS. As an advocate of gay rights, he worked with gay organizations in New York, even marching in a gay St. Patrick's Day Parade.

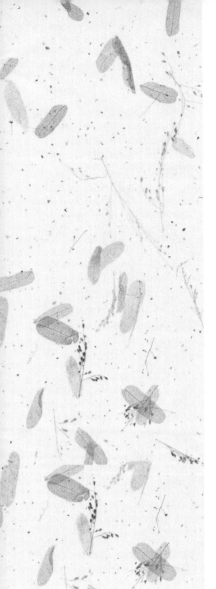

Father Mike gained recognition for his ability to build bridges between opposing parties and to bring comfort to the bereaved. In New York he became a close friend and confessor to Steven McDonald, a New York police detective who was shot and paralyzed in 1986, helping him to accept his condition and forgive his assailant. Later the two became involved in peace missions to Northern Ireland, trying to reconcile Protestants and Catholics and meeting with leaders on both sides, including the prime minister of Ireland. In 1996 Father Mike received national attention for working with the relatives and friends of the victims of TWA flight 800, which had crashed into Long Island Sound. "What a beacon of light," recalled Senator Hillary Clinton, remembering a time when Mychal Judge and other clergy were invited to Washington. "He lit up the White House."

In 1992 Father Mike chose to become a chaplain to the New York Fire Department. According to one fireman, "He was a real fire buff. . . . He just loved firemen and their jobs." He became part of the firefighters' families, marrying (by one account, 2,500 weddings), burying, and baptizing them. He lived in the Franciscan friary, sleeping on an old couch in a sparsely furnished room with a fire/police scanner. Across the street was his firehouse, Engine Company 1 and Ladder Company 24.

On September 11, 2001, he was with his squad as they responded to news that an airplane had just crashed into the World Trade Center's North Tower. There was orderly panic as people fled the towers and as firemen and police rushed inside to facilitate the evacuation and help the injured. As Father Mike headed to the North Tower, he passed Rudolph Giuliani, mayor of New York, who shouted, "Pray for us, Mychal." "I always do," he yelled back. Although there is no conclusive eyewitness account of how Father Mike died, a popular account states that a few minutes after passing Mayor Giuliani, he knelt and removed his helmet to administer last rites to a fallen firefighter, and he was struck in the head by a falling piece of debris. He died instantly, "doing," Senator Clinton said later, "what he was called to do." While the above story of Father Mike's death may not be true and questions remain about exactly how he died, there is little question that in the immediate aftermath of the collapse of the Twin Towers, the "story of Father Mike's death provided a symbol of the self-sacrificing policemen and firemen who did their duty "as usual" as the nation responded to a new threat.

INTRODUCTION

When the 1990s began, it appeared in many ways that the country was divided and unsure of the future—the American vision needed to be rediscovered or redefined. Trends that had started two decades earlier were continuing to change the society, politics, and economy of the nation. The industrial economy that had characterized the United States for most of the twentieth century was shifting toward postindustrialism, in which service jobs and information-based technology—not manufacturing—shaped the economy. Globalization, too, provided new realities for society and the economy as nations loosened their restrictions on the flow of goods, services, capital, ideas, and people.

These changes, as they had for the previous two decades, provided new opportunities for some but also added to the growing disparities in income. The number of people living near or at the poverty level increased, while the middle class shrank slightly. Geographically, the Sunbelt, the suburbs, and the new "boomburbs" continued to accumulate population, political power, and wealth, while many cities, especially those in the industrial states, continued to decline and sought to redefine their images and economies.

Throughout the 1990s, American population growth accelerated as many Asian and Latino immigrants continued to arrive. Newcomers with technical and professional skills often moved into the suburbs. Most, however, settled in the cities, frequently joining the ranks of the underclass, finding few full-time, well-paying jobs and often making do with public assistance and part-time employment. Whether in suburbs or cities, many new immigrants experienced growing intolerance and sometimes ethnic and racial violence.

Across the nation, discussions about the economy, poverty, and society frequently revolved around redefining the nation's social and political vision. A resurgent conservatism challenged New Deal and Great Society visions of social policy. Conservatives maintained that liberal policies were too expensive and were destroying the nation's basic value system. The product of liberal activism, they charged, was a breakdown of values, which resulted in increasing rates of divorce, abortion, crime, drug abuse, and violence. Increasingly beleaguered liberals argued that government activism remained the prime force for improving American society and that social programs needed to be expanded and effectively funded.

Conservatives predicted that the 1992 presidential election would be a clash between liberal and conservative values, a cultural and social war for the soul of the nation. Running for reelection, President George Bush counted on the strong support of conservatives and expected that his foreign-policy achievements would attract more than enough moderates to ensure his success. However, that expectation faded quickly when it became obvious that the public was most interested in economic issues. Whereas Bush offered few answers to troubling economic issues, his main opponent—the Democratic governor of Arkansas, William Jefferson (Bill) Clinton—focused on the economy and promised to support social needs, to control the federal budget, and to reduce the national debt. Clinton pulled ahead of Bush in public opinion polls and won the election.

Once in office, the new president made implementation of a national health system and reduction of the federal deficit his primary goals. However, his efforts met with opposition from both Republicans and Democrats. In 1994 Republicans gained control of both houses of Congress and announced a "Contract with America" to capture the legislative initiative. Clinton, however, proved politically adept, shedding liberal trappings and establishing himself as a centrist. He adopted the issue of welfare reform, oversaw an improvement of the economy, and proved successful in foreign policy. As Americans headed back into the polls for the presidential election of 1996, the United States was at peace, and the economy was prospering. It was an unbeatable combination, and Clinton easily defeated Robert Dole.

Clinton's second term polarized America politically and nearly saw the removal of a president through the process of **impeachment.**

The events leading to the impeachment revolved around the investigation of a sexual affair between Clinton and a White House intern, Monica Lewinsky. Charging the president with perjury, obstruction of justice, and witness tampering, the Republican-controlled House in December 1998 voted to impeach Clinton and recommended to the Senate that he be removed from office. The Senate thereupon began an impeachment trial against Clinton and in February 1999 acquitted him of all charges. Basking in an expanding economy, Clinton left office with high approval ratings and credit for balancing the budget.

Following Clinton's example, the 2000 presidential candidates—the Republican governor of Texas, George W. Bush, and the Democratic vice president, Albert Gore—worked to occupy the center of the political spectrum, producing a close campaign and an even closer vote. Gore won the popular vote, but Bush, in a decision facilitated by the U.S. Supreme Court, won the Electoral College count. With Republican and a few Democratic votes, Bush pushed through a broad tax cut and an education reform act, but most of the rest of his agenda fell victim to Democratic roadblocks. However, partisan debate on Bush's domestic agenda was eclipsed on September 11, 2001, when nineteen terrorists hijacked domestic airliners and used them to attack the World Trade Center in New York City and the Pentagon in Washington, D.C.

The attacks killed over three thousand people and were quickly linked to **Al Qaeda,** a terrorist organization led by Osama bin Laden, who directed operations from Afghanistan. The war against terrorism

impeachment A Congressional power to remove the president, vice president, and civil officers of the United States. If the House of Representatives determines that a federal official has committed "high crimes and misdemeanors," it can vote for Articles of Impeachment. If a majority agree, the House recommends to the Senate that the official be removed from office. If two-thirds of the Senate agree the official may be removed from office. From 1789 to 2004, the House has voted only 18 impeachments and only seven officials have been removed from office by the Senate.

Al Qaeda Established by Saudi Osama bin Laden in 1989 as a terrorist network that organizes the activities of militant Islamic groups which seek to establish a global fundamentalist Islamic order.

Chronology

A New Century with New Challanges

1992	U.S. troops sent to Somalia
	Bill Clinton elected president
	Planned Parenthood of Southeastern Pennsylvania v. Casey
1993	Congress ratifies North American Free Trade Agreement
	Clinton introduces national healthcare package
	Harris v. Forklift Systems
1994	Withdrawal of U.S. troops from Somalia
	U.S. troops sent to Haiti
	Violence Against Women Act
	"Contract with America"
1995	Bombing of Oklahoma City federal building
	Dayton Agreement
1996	Welfare reform passed
	Clinton reelected
	Reno v. ACLU
	Clinton proposes balanced budget
1998	House of Representatives votes to impeach Clinton
	Terrorists attack U.S. embassies in Kenya and Tanzania
1999	NATO bombs Serbia over Kosovo crisis
	Senate votes not to remove Clinton from office
	Columbine High School shooting

2000	Terrorists attack U.S.S. *Cole*
	George W. Bush elected president
	Nation experiences longest economic expansion in its history
2001	Bush's tax cut bill passed
	Terrorists associated with Al Qaeda attack World Trade towers and Pentagon
	Office of Homeland Security established
	U.S. launches operation against Al Qaeda and the Taliban government of Afghanistan
	Economy in a recession
	USA Patriot Act
2002	Taliban regime collapses and is replaced by interim government
2003	U.S. invades Iraq, removes Saddam Hussein regime
2004	Massachusetts Supreme Court permits same-sex marriage
	U.S. turns over authority to interim Iraqi government
	George W. Bush elected president

provided the president with a new agenda that solidified public and political support. To provide increased security within the United States, Bush established by executive order an Office of Homeland Security, and Congress approved the Patriot Act. Internationally, the administration worked to create a global war against terrorism and demanded that the Taliban government of Afghanistan surrender bin Laden and other Al Qaeda leaders. When the Taliban refused to do so, in October 2001 the United States and its allies invaded Afghanistan, with the purpose of destroying Al Qaeda and overthrowing the Taliban. By mid-November the Taliban government had collapsed, and the United States began the process of building a democratic Afghanistan. Osama bin Laden, however, eluded capture and vanished from sight.

Bush announced that in fighting the war against terrorism, the United States would have to change its method of responding to threats. In some cases, the nation could not wait until it was attacked but must strike first, taking preemptive action. He also declared that three nations—Iran, North Korea, and Iraq—constituted an "axis of evil" that posed a serious threat to the United States and to world stability. Behind the scenes, members of the administration were planning an attack to remove Iraq's brutal dictator, Saddam Hussein. In March 2003, claiming that Saddam Hussein possessed weapons of mass destruction that threatened regional and world security, the United States and its allies began military action in Iraq to oust Saddam and establish a democratic and prosperous Iraq.

Three weeks into the invasion, U.S. forces entered the capital city of Baghdad with little resistance; the Iraqi government disintegrated, with the dictator and his advisers going into hiding. Saddam and most of his advisers were captured or killed, but the quest to remake Iraq proved difficult. While nearly all Iraqis were pleased that Saddam was removed from power, a significant and growing number of Iraqis resented American occupation. Within weeks of President Bush's announcing the end of major combat operations, a civil and guerrilla war broke out, targeting American and other occupational forces, as well as those Iraqis who supported the occupation. By the summer of 2004, more Americans had been killed during the occupation than during the war.

The terrorist attacks and the following war on terrorism had economic and political consequences as well. As Bush took office, the economy that had boomed for Clinton began to slow, and the nation entered a recession. The attacks of 9/11, combined with corporate scandals, a growing federal deficit, and rising unemployment, strengthened the recession and ignited partisan politics. Democrats believed the weak economy would provide a platform for defeating Bush in 2004. Not only did Democrats intend to focus on the economy, but by the beginning of 2004 they thought they could use a growing public concern about Bush's conduct of the war against terrorism and the war in Iraq to gain support. By April, Senator John Kerry had emerged as the Democratic candidate and began attacking the administration on its economic and foreign policy. Republicans responded that Kerry was inconsistent on issues, a flip-flopper, and a "tax-and-spend" Democrat. They also stressed that Bush was far better suited to fight the war on terrorism. As the election neared, the candidates appeared evenly matched in public opinion polls, and the two parties focused on seventeen battleground states, hoping to energize their own party members and attract independents.

The 2004 election saw more Americans vote than ever before; and when the ballots were tallied, George W. Bush was re-elected president with 51 percent of the vote. With larger Republican majorities in Congress, Bush announced that the nation was "entering a season of hope" and the people had given him a mandate to finish the job in Iraq and to reform the tax codes and the social security system. Many conservative Republicans hoped that the president's program would go further and implement a social agenda and replace retiring Supreme Court Justices with those who would restore moral and family values.

Old Visions and New Realities

■ What changes took place in the American economy during the 1990s? How did the slowing economy affect people's lives and expectations?

■ What debates surrounded issues faced by women and minorities, and what were the political implications?

As the two major political parties readied themselves for the 1992 presidential election, they presented two distinct visions of the critical issues and the condition of American society. Republicans hoped the alignment of voters that had elected Reagan and Bush would continue to reject liberal activism and big government in favor of conservative social values. The party platform forcefully attacked permissiveness in American society, opposed abortion and alternative lifestyles, advocated less government, and stressed the "traditional American values" that emphasized family and religion. Conservative journalist and political commentator Pat Buchanan roused the convention by calling for a "**cultural war** . . . for the soul of the nation." Confident in their agenda, conservatives rallied around President George Bush. Bush accepted the social agenda but preferred to emphasize his experience and to bask in the afterglow of Operation Desert Storm and the fall of communism. Looking forward, he called for tax cuts and reduced government spending to stimulate the economy. Republicans expected Bush to win easily.

Many prominent Democrats agreed with the Republican assessment, leaving the door open for Governor William (Bill) Clinton of Arkansas, a 46-year-old baby boomer who easily won the nomination. In his campaign, Clinton and his young team of political advisers focused on a different vision of American society and its needs. Unlike Republicans, they saw a vital need for an activist government to deal with social problems. They avoided "cultural war" slogans, targeting instead the slowing economy's impact on society. James Carvell, Clinton's chief political adviser, tacked reminders over his own desk reading, "It's the Economy, Stupid," "Change vs. More of the Same," and "Don't Forget Healthcare."

The Shifting Economy

While Republicans and Democrats honed their political messages about who could best solve America's

---

cultural war A belief that the nation is divided over liberal and conservative values that stress moral issues as an important part of the political debate.

Opponents of globalization argue that the primary benefactors of the new economy are the industrialized nations and big business and that among the victims are the environment and the poor. Many antiglobalization protestors took to the streets in Seattle, Washington, in November 1999, protesting the meeting of the World Trade Organization. *Karie Hamilton/ CorbisSygma.*

problems, many people grew ever more concerned over their economic future. The conventional vision of an American economy resting on industrial growth and robust sales of U.S. goods in foreign markets was giving way to a new reality. The postindustrial economy was replacing the nation's manufacturing firms with service and technology companies as the driving economic force. Compounding the shift to a new economy was the impact of globalization. As the economy changed, so too did many of the nation's social, cultural, and economic underpinnings.

To many, the globalization of trade, information, services, and people provided a variety of benefits to the United States and the world. Advocates believed it reduced world poverty, promoted the spread of knowledge, improved international understanding, and provided solutions for global problems such as world hunger, human rights, and environmental threats. An expanding Internet used by over 250 million people around the world to communicate with a simple "point and click," supporters argued, was just one example of the benefits of new technology sup-

porting globalization and the lowering of barriers between nations. Another aspect of globalization was the reduction of trade barriers and the establishment of regional free-trade areas. Such areas in North America began under President Reagan, who in 1988 signed a free-trade agreement with Canada, and were continued by President Bush, who sought to include Mexico in an expanded free-trade community. His efforts generated strong opposition from labor unions, environmentalists, and various American businesses that feared Mexico's participation. By the end of Bush's administration, the **North American Free Trade Agreement** (NAFTA) existed, although opposition in Congress prevented the United States from ratifying the treaty until November 1993.

> **North American Free Trade Agreement**   Agreement approved by the Senate in 1993 that eliminated most tariffs and other trade barriers between the United States, Mexico, and Canada.

The globalization of technology and trade are central parts of the new world economy. Few developments better reflect the globalization of communications and technology than the spread of the Internet. In Ho Chi Minh City, Internet access is available in public offices, while the Vietnamese government has a five-year plan to develop high-tech industrial parts to attract software industries. *Hoang Dinh Man-AFP.*

Opponents of globalization, while accepting that some of its ideals were positive, argued that in practice its consequences were negative. Some were convinced that it primarily benefited rich multinational corporations that relocated their factories to less developed nations where wages were low and laws to protect the environment and workers' rights were absent. Emphasizing the threats to human rights, exploitation of workers, loss of jobs, and harm to the environment, in the 1990s antiglobalization organizations targeted the symbols of globalization—meetings of the leaders of the industrial nations, the **G-8 na-**

tions and the **World Trade Organization** (WTO); in November 1999, fifty thousand protesters carried out a massive demonstration against the WTO and globalization at a conference in Seattle, Washington. Less concerned with global issues, others feared that open borders invited more narcotics, diseases, terrorism, and immigrants, thus weakening the United States' ability to protect its economy, interests, and culture.

Yet others, especially foreign critics, saw globalization as an extension of American **cultural imperialism,** with its emphasis on materialism, individualism, and other social and cultural values. The Internet, they pointed out, not only facilitated communication and trade but also further solidified English as the world's dominant language, especially for communications and commerce. They saw the spread of American products and businesses as contributing to a cultural conformity that displaced traditional foods and cultures, local production, independent thinking, and alternative political ideologies. Between 1995 and 2000, for example, McDonald's restaurants around the world were the targets of violent protests in over fifty nations, from France to Brazil to Indonesia.

Within the United States, the shift from an industrial base to a more global postindustrial economy had a significant impact on where people worked and lived. As the economy became increasingly based on service and **information technology** (IT) industries, blue-collar manufacturing jobs declined, while jobs in the service sector rose. In 1960, factories ac-

G-8 nations   Term given to the leading industrial nations (Canada, China, France, Germany, Italy, Japan, the United Kingdom, and the United States), which meet periodically to deal with major economic and political problems facing their countries and the international community; the first summit, in 1975, included only six nations (the G-6), since Canada and China were not yet part of the group.

World Trade Organization   Geneva-based organization that oversees world trading systems; founded in 1995 by 135 countries to replace the 1948 General Agreement on Tariffs and Trades (GATT).

cultural imperialism   The idea that around the world there is expanding acceptance, adoption, and usage of American ideals, products, values, and culture; many point to the growing use of the Internet and the continued popularity of American food, movies, and music as a major cause of its spread.

information technology   A broad range of businesses concerned with managing and processing information, especially with the use of computers and other forms of telecommunications.

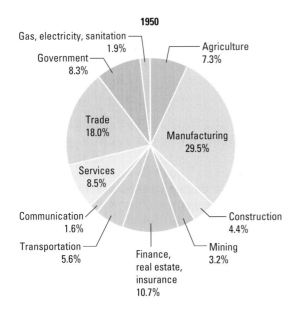

1950

Gas, electricity, sanitation
1.9%

Government
8.3%

Agriculture
7.3%

Trade
18.0%

Manufacturing
29.5%

Services
8.5%

Communication
1.6%

Transportation
5.6%

Finance,
real estate,
insurance
10.7%

Mining
3.2%

Construction
4.4%

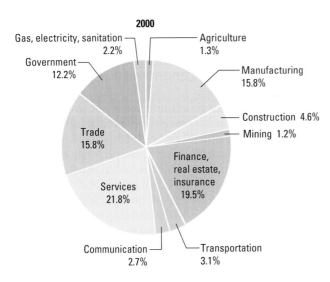

2000

Gas, electricity, sanitation
2.2%

Government
12.2%

Agriculture
1.3%

Manufacturing
15.8%

Construction 4.6%

Mining 1.2%

Trade
15.8%

Finance,
real estate,
insurance
19.5%

Services
21.8%

Communication
2.7%

Transportation
3.1%

FIGURE 31.1 Main Sectors of U.S. Economy   A comparison of the 1950 and 2000 graphs shows that many of the economic sectors that deal with the production and marketing of goods—such as manufacturing, agriculture, transportation, and trade—have declined, while those sectors that mainly provide services have increased, especially government, services, and finance.

numbers were similar for the larger service industry, which employed only about 15 percent of the work force in the early 1960s, but about 25 percent by 1997.

Many of those classified as technical and professional workers were part of the fastest-growing segment of the economy, the information-based industries associated with computers and global networking. Almost overnight, companies associated with computer technology, software, and the Internet proliferated and saw the value of their stocks skyrocket—pushing the stock market and the **Nasdaq** index, which tracks the stock of many of the new high-tech companies, to record highs. Suddenly, the ranks of the rich included large numbers of new millionaires—"dot-com millionaires"—men and women who owned businesses focused on the exchange of services, information, and goods over the Internet or who invested in those businesses. Northern California's Silicon Valley, a center for the microprocessing industry, boasted the greatest concentration of new wealth in the nation.

The growth of Silicon Valley was duplicated throughout the Sunbelt as the new economy pushed wealth and population upward. Phoenix became the nation's sixth-largest city, acquiring professional football and baseball teams. But surrounding Phoenix and many other western cities, the suburbs grew even faster. By the end of the 1990s, many suburbs had populations larger than traditional cities, becoming "**boomburbs**." In 2000 there were fifty-three boomburbs, each with populations larger than 100,000, and four larger than 300,000, including Mesa, Arizona, and Arlington, Texas. No longer bedroom communities, these boomburbs have the same functions and offer the same facilities as traditional cities while matching the needs of a drive-through society.

In boomburbs like Mesa and throughout the rest of the country, diversity was more apparent than ever. More minorities were joining the middle class—graduating from colleges; enrolling in medical, law, and graduate programs; and entering the professions.

Nasdaq   A stock exchange, launched in 1971, that focuses on companies in technological fields; *Nasdaq* stands for National Association of Securities Dealers Automated Quotation.

boomburbs   Term used to describe suburban cities with populations of over 100,000 and double-digit growth every decade since they first exceeded a population of 2,500; other terms for this new classification of city are "fringe cities" and "technoburbs."

counted for about 19 percent of the work force, whereas only about 11 percent was defined as technical or professional workers. By mid-1990, those numbers had been reversed: 18 percent of the work force was classified as technical or professional, and only 10 percent still labored in factories (see Figure 31.1). The

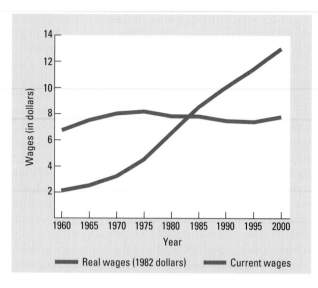

FIGURE 31.2 Real Versus Current Wages Reflecting the growing economic uneasiness that many Americans began to feel in the mid-1980s, purchasing power generated by wages began to decline, even though wages themselves continued to climb. In 1999 the average wage of about $13.00 an hour was worth only about $7.80, based on the amounts of goods that a dollar in 1982 could buy. Adjusted for inflation, the increase in wages from 1960 to the present has remained fairly constant. Real wages grew about .7% as the nation recovered from recession, 2002–2003, but fell about .7% by September 2004.

By the end of the 1990s, 40 percent of African Americans considered themselves middle or upper class. The nation's diversity and the purchasing power of minorities found expression in advertising campaigns and the spread of ethnic culture as Americans enjoyed Mexican, Asian, and Indian foods and listened to rap and salsa music. Responding to the growing diversity of the American population, in 2000 the census included the category "multiracial." The new category seemed tailor-made for champion golfer Tiger Woods, a southern Californian who describes himself as "Cablinasian"—Caucasian, black, Indian, and Asian.

Rich and Poor

The ongoing changes in the economy produced a three-level economy and society. At the top were highly trained professionals, while poorly paid service and assembly plant workers peopled the bottom tier. The rich were getting richer while the poor be-

came poorer. Between 1979 and 1995, the wealthiest 20 percent of the population increased their wealth by 26 percent, while the poorest 20 percent became 9 percent poorer. Put in more dramatic terms, by 1996 many company executives received 209 times more income than a factory worker. Between the two tiers was a changing and increasing fearful middle class whose incomes were barely holding steady (see Figure 31.2). Not only did middle- and working-class families see their economic status jeopardized, many also doubted that the Social Security system would be able to provide them an adequate retirement. As baby boomers were getting older and approaching retirement age, fewer and fewer younger workers were paying into the Social Security system. Many worried that without a major overhaul, both Social Security and Medicare would go broke before the boomer generation could benefit from them. In the 1980s, a 25 percent increase in Social Security taxes helped make the system more solvent, but the tax increase also had drawn down take-home wages. Even more worrisome, medical costs were among the fastest rising in the country. In 1990, federal healthcare costs amounted to about 2.8 percent of the **gross domestic product** (GDP); in 1998 the percentage had soared to 40 percent.

Concerns about retirement were not in the minds of the more than 15 percent of the population who lived below the official poverty line of $14,335 (for a family of four) in 1995. Among the poorest were those living in the inner city. They included minorities, immigrants, those with little education and few skills, and single female heads of households. As in the 1980s, throughout the 1990s and into the new millennium the number of legal immigrants continued to rise (see Figure 31.3). One of the chief causes was the **Immigration Act of 1990,** which increased the number of immigrants who could come to the United States each year to nearly 700,000.

gross domestic product The total value of goods and services produced in one year within a nation's borders. In 1999, the GDP of the United States was slightly more than $9.2 trillion.

Immigration Act of 1990 Law reforming the Immigration Act of 1965; it increased the number of immigrants allowed annually into the United States to around 700,000 from the 290,000 level established in 1968 and gave preference to skilled workers and those with families already living in the country.

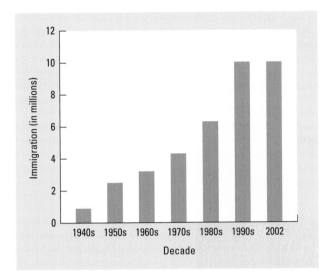

FIGURE 31.3 Immigration to the United States Since 1940   Since the 1940s, the number of immigrants coming to the United States has grown steadily. Changes in immigration laws in 1965 and 1990 not only allowed more immigrants to enter the country but also changed the point of departure for most of those immigrants from Europe to Latin America and Asia.

Most settled in the boomburbs and in cities like Los Angeles, where the largest immigrant groups were Mexicans, Iranians, Salvadorans, Japanese, Chinese, and Filipinos. One writer commented that Los Angeles was an ethnic and cultural borderland "on a frontier between Europe and Asia and between Anglo and Hispanic." In places like Los Angeles, immigrants encountered unemployment, crime, and dropout rates that surpassed the national level—and wages, educational achievement, and opportunity that lagged behind the national average. Because of the lack of jobs and job training, 6 percent of immigrants ended up on the welfare rolls—double the percentage of those born in the United States.

For some African American males, one inner-city response was rap music. Rap, with its vivid and angry vocals that attacked racism, the police, and society, originated in the South Bronx in the 1970s. By the mid-1990s, while it still carried its harsh edge, rap had become popular with white audiences as well as black and Latino ones. It even was heard on *Sesame Street* and generated its own style of clothes.

The increasing numbers of women heads of households among the poor, a "feminization of poverty," was of particular concern. Nationally, over 30 percent of single women were living in poverty, contributing to an alarming increase in the percentage of children living in poverty—26.3 percent by 1993. The causes were varied. Lack of skills was a general cause for the poverty, forcing people into service industry jobs in which wages were low and benefits scarce. But, especially for women, there were other reasons: more children were being born to unwed mothers, more marriages were ending in divorce, and less money was being paid in alimony and child support. Changes in divorce laws eliminated or reduced alimony, and child support payments were often not paid. In 1990, for example, more than a fourth of spouses who owed child support, mostly men, paid nothing. Another problem, faced not just by those living in poverty, was that women still encountered position and pay inequality. In many companies, women were not promoted to management positions or paid the same for comparable jobs. In California, a woman manager discovered that she made less than half the salary of one of the male assistant managers. When she confronted the company, a spokesman stated that the assistant manager had a wife and two children. She responded that she was a single mother with one child to support. Failing to resolve such inequalities, women brought class-action lawsuits against a variety of companies for sex discrimination, including the Publix chain of supermarkets and Wal-Mart.

Women and Family Values

Throughout American history, people and politicians have expressed concern about the poor and about social change. The liberal activism of the 1960s provided one vantage point, and the conservative reaction on the New Right provided another. For the past two decades, conflict between the two views has raged around issues of economic and social opportunity, welfare, sexuality, and family values. Connecting several of the issues, Kate O'Beirne of the conservative Heritage Foundation stressed the importance of the traditional American family. "Why experiment with new antipoverty programs," she asked, "when the most important indicator of poverty is whether there are two parents at home?" She and others firmly advocated what they labeled strong family values and blamed feminism for many of society's problems.

O'Beirne's antifeminist attitude seemed by the 1990s to be gaining acceptance as a backlash against feminism gained momentum. By 1995, only 20 percent of women college freshmen accepted the label

Ever since the controversial *Roe v. Wade* decision in 1973, opponents of abortion have petitioned the Supreme Court, lobbied Congress, and demonstrated to ban abortions. Some radical pro-life supporters have even advocated violence against and murder of those performing abortions as a moral choice in the "war" against abortion. *Evan Richman/The Boston Globe. Published with permission of the Globe Newspaper Company, Inc.*

"feminist," and in an article titled "What Happened to the Women's Movement?" *Newsweek* suggested the death of feminism. Central to the conservative attack on feminism was that it presented women as victims of a heterosexual, male-dominated culture. Unwilling to make a distinction between the radical "**gender feminists**" and the feminist movement, conservative groups like Concerned Women of America in large part blamed the women's movement for the decline in moral values and "traditional" families. As one antifeminist explained: "It all comes down to values. Traditional values work because they are the guidelines most consistent with human nature."

Abortion remained one of the most divisive issues. Since *Roe v. Wade* (1972), pro-choice supporters had worried that the growing power of the New Right and an increasingly conservative Supreme Court might restrict access to abortions (see Chapter 30). In 1992, the Supreme Court's decision in *Planned Parenthood of Southeastern Pennsylvania v. Casey* confirmed a woman's right to have an abortion. But it offset that affirmation with the condition that, in some cases, the state could modify that right. Advocates of a "woman's right to choose" also worried about the violent tactics that some opponents were adopting.

Opponents of abortion, on the other hand, were more and more frustrated and angered by the inability of the Court and Congress to ban, or at least limit, abortions. Acting on their anger, a minority within the Right to Life movement decided to take more direct and forceful tactics. Abortion clinic doctors, staff, and patients became targets. By 1994, more than half of all abortion clinics reported varied cases of intimidation and violence, and a hundred clinics had been targets of arson or bombings. In an effort to prevent these occurrences, in 1994 the federal government passed the Freedom of Access to Clinic Entrances Act. It restricted the tactics of intimidation that pro-life supporters such as **Operation Rescue** could use. None-

gender feminists Term applied to those within the feminist movement who focus on the subordination of women and on the need for radical changes in gender-related roles and traditions.

Operation Rescue A militant anti-abortion group that advocates intimidation and physical confrontation as a means to stop abortion.

theless, opponents vowed to maintain the struggle against abortion and feminism.

Many feminist leaders, however, asserted that the women's movement was alive and well, despite internal tensions. They pointed out that most within the women's movement disagreed with the views held by gender feminists, and that a "new wave" of more inclusive and less ideological feminism was emerging. Most women, they said, including the vast majority who worked, wanted to "fit their new gains at work and in the public world into . . . the story of marriage and family that they . . . inherited from their mothers." They wanted to keep the gains women had made, while at the same time strengthening marriage and family, reducing sexual permissiveness, and softening the impact on young children whose mothers worked. As signs of the movement's continuing achievements, new-wave feminists pointed to efforts to combat **sexual harassment,** changes in the workplace, women's breaking through the "**glass ceiling,**" and the growing number of women in the professions.

A poll conducted in 1991 revealed that 42 percent of women had been sexually harassed, and the National Organization for Women claimed that physical abuse of women was a cultural norm. Responding to sexual harassment lawsuits, courts began to define its legal dimensions. In 1993 the Supreme Court decided in *Harris v. Forklift Systems* that sexual harassment involved not only "verbal and physical conduct" but also the creation of a "hostile environment." The following year, Congress passed the **Violence Against Women Act.** Part of a larger anticrime bill, the act provided funds and federal support for efforts to more harshly punish sexual violence and other attacks on women and to provide resources to aid victims and prevent future attacks.

Supporters of the women's movement also stated that their efforts to fight harassment were only one part of a continuing effort to improve the workplace for women. The gap between salaries for men and women was narrowing, and greater numbers of women were entering the professions, but more needed to be done to adjust the workplace to fit the needs of women with families. Programs such as **flextime** and **flexplace,** job sharing, and family leave needed to be more widely adopted and more accessible daycare provided. The editor of *Ms.* magazine noted that the central issues for working women were recognizing choices and their consequences and promoting a "woman-friendly family and a family-friendly workplace."

While feminists listed their accomplishments on behalf of women, their critics remained focused on the "threats" to the family and the need for a moral society. They argued that even "mommy-friendly" workplaces were not a replacement for full-time mothers and an environment that respected moral values. Echoing the concerns of many in the public, they pressed for more controls to ban pornography and to limit the amount of sex and violence in the media. During the 1980s, sexual content had become standard fare in books, magazines, music, movies, and television. In 1987 it was estimated that more than sixty-five thousand sexual references were broadcast each year on prime-time television programs. During the day, sex and sex-related issues became more daring and numerous on the soaps, and talk-show hosts probed guests for intimate details about their sex lives. Violence, too, seemed everywhere, including on video games. A 1997 study indicated that 44 percent of all network programming had violent content, 73 percent of which went unpunished in the story line. On cable and satellite television, another study concluded, it was worse, with 85 percent of the programming having violent content. As usage of the Internet expanded, many argued that legislation was needed to keep some types of sexual content from being easily accessed.

The impact of a climate of sex and violence, some believed, was especially detrimental to children and

---

sexual harassment Unwanted sexual advances, sexually derogatory remarks, gender-related discrimination, or the existence of a sexually hostile work environment.

glass ceiling Term used to express an intangible barrier within the hierarchy of a company that prevents women or minorities from rising to upper-level positions.

Violence Against Women Act Law passed by Congress in 1994 that provided federal funds and support to judicial and law-enforcement agencies to prevent violence against women, to aid victims, and to punish those convicted of sexual violence and attacks on women.

flextime Allows an employee to select the hours of work. There are usually specified limits set by the employer. Employees on a flexible schedule may work a condensed workweek or may work a regular workweek. In 2001 approximately 30 percent of the national work force was using some type of flextime.

flexplace Allows employees to work at the office or from an alternate work site during part of their scheduled hours. Working at home is the most common alternative site, and in 2001 about 15 percent of the work force was paid to work at home.

contributed to increasingly violent incidents involving children, such as the April 1999 shooting at **Columbine High School** in Colorado. Although admitting that these problems existed, the nation, as expected, responded in varying ways. Many conservatives wanted tougher laws and more stringent enforcement. Some proposed that juveniles who committed violent crimes be tried as adults. Others believed that more gun-control measures were the best means to reduce crime and violence. To some, the best way to combat the amount of sex and violence in society was to curb the amount of sex and violence in the media. But efforts to impose censorship usually were rejected by the courts, as in 1997 when the Supreme Court declared unconstitutional an effort to censor the Internet in *Reno v. ACLU*. Rather than governmental censorship, others supported technology that would allow individual or parental control within the home, and rating systems that indicated the level of sex and violence in songs, music videos, movies, and television shows.

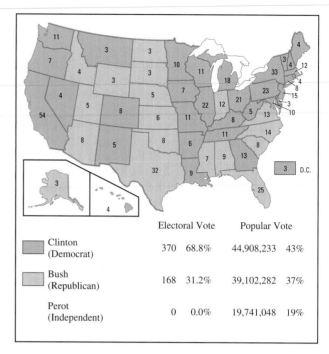

		Electoral Vote		Popular Vote	
Clinton (Democrat)		370	68.8%	44,908,233	43%
Bush (Republican)		168	31.2%	39,102,282	37%
Perot (Independent)		0	0.0%	19,741,048	19%

MAP 31.1 Election of 1992   Bill Clinton received almost 69 percent of the Electoral College votes—almost double the electoral votes received by George Bush. Nevertheless, Clinton received only 43 percent of the popular vote—the lowest popular vote percentage since Wilson's victory in 1912 over Theodore Roosevelt and William Taft. Third-party candidate H. Ross Perot drew votes from both Democrats and Republicans in equal numbers and had no impact on the electoral vote.

The Clinton Years

■ How did Clinton redefine himself politically during his two terms? What was the effect on his administration of an improving economy? What was the impact of his personal life on his presidency?

■ What did the "Contract with America" represent, and in what ways did the decisions of the Rehnquist Court support its agenda?

■ What policies did Clinton promote to expand democracy and the globalization of trade?

As the 1992 presidential campaign began, it appeared that the two candidates epitomized the visions of the country projected by their political parties. Republicans were fond of saying that Clinton had opposed the war in Vietnam, had avoided military service, had used drugs, and was a womanizer. He represented the moral weakness that infected America. George Bush had served gallantly in World War II, had the needed experience and maturity to be president, and was a family man. Clinton ignored most of the attacks on his character and focused on the economy and the need to revitalize the nation. In typical Democratic fashion, he promised welfare reform, support of minority goals, a national healthcare system, and a smaller federal deficit. In February, a new contender entered the battle when **H. Ross Perot** launched his campaign as a third-party candidate. Perot's message was simple: politicians had messed

up the nation, and control had to be returned to the people.

The campaign culminated in three televised debates between the candidates. An estimated 88 million people watched the third debate. Both Bush and

Columbine High School   Located in Littleton, Colorado, this was the sight of one of the most violent school shootings, when two students entered the lunchroom with a variety of weapons and homemade bombs. They killed 1 teacher and 12 students, and injured 12 others before they committed suicide. 34 students escaped.

H. Ross Perot   Texas billionaire who used large amounts of his own money to run as an Independent candidate for president in 1992 and who created the Reform Party for his 1996 bid for the presidency.

Even though Bush, Clinton, and Perot dressed alike in the 1992 presidential debates, many observers believed Clinton emerged the strongest. Although a candidate for the presidency again in 1996, Perot was not invited to participate in the presidential debates between Clinton and Dole—a decision upheld by a federal court that concluded he did not have enough support to be a credible candidate. *Wide World Photos.*

Perot gained in the public opinion polls following the head-to-head encounters, but they could not overtake the front-running Clinton. In a three-way race, Clinton earned 43 percent of the popular vote, compared with Bush's 37 percent and Perot's 19 percent (see Map 31.1). Clinton swept to victory with 370 votes in the Electoral College, 100 more than he needed to win. While Democrats still held the majority in Congress, Clinton's victory provided no real Democratic coattails as Republicans gained nine seats in the House of Representatives. In both parties, a record number of women and minorities were elected to Congress.

Clinton and Congress

From the start it was clear that Clinton relished being president and was eager to begin. "I want to get something done," he told a press conference. Setting

an ambitious agenda, he dove into producing an economic recovery plan, welfare reform, and a national healthcare system. Setting a liberal tone to his administration, in February 1993 he signed into law the Family and Medical Leave Act, which had previously been vetoed by Bush, and asked Congress to lift the ban against homosexuals in the military. Although public opinion polls showed that many Americans tolerated homosexuality as a lifestyle, there seemed much less support for broad antidiscriminatory laws that favored gay rights. The proposal met immediate and irresistible opposition from both political parties, the military, and the public. Faced with such opposition, Clinton retreated and accepted a compromise. The armed forces were not to ask recruits about sexual preferences, and gays and lesbians in the service were expected to refrain from homosexual activities. It was a system that did not work and failed to please either side of the debate.

Outside of the military, gay-rights activists continued their efforts to gain antidiscriminatory laws that would protect jobs, provide work-related benefits for partners, and allow same-sex marriages. By the end of 2003, they could count some major victories as 14 states and the District of Columbia and over 140 cities and counties had passed legislation banning employment discrimination based on sexual orientation, and the Supreme Court in *Lawrence v. Texas* (2003) declared sodomy laws unconstitutional.

On a related issue, Clinton and Congress supported more funds to fight the AIDS epidemic. AIDS, or **acquired immune deficiency syndrome,** began to be noticed in American cities in the early 1980s. Because the disease infected mostly gays and drug users and seemed confined to the inner cities, official and public response was at first largely apathetic. Linking AIDS to the "morality battle," some, like Pat Buchanan and Senator Jesse Helms (R.–North Carolina), even suggested that those with the disease were being punished for their unnatural perversions. Responding to conservative pressure, the Reagan administration did little to fight AIDS. However, as the number of victims climbed and the disease spread to the heterosexual population, the public's fear of AIDS

acquired immune deficiency syndrome (AIDS)
Gradual and eventually fatal breakdown of the immune system caused by the human immunodeficiency virus (HIV); HIV/AIDS is transmitted by the exchange of body fluids through such means as sexual intercourse or needle sharing.

grew rapidly, and in the 1990s federal support became available for education and prevention programs and research. By the mid-1990s, AIDS had claimed more than 280,000 American lives and had infected 20 million people worldwide, especially in Africa. At the same time, significant advances were being made in research toward controlling AIDS. Combinations of drugs seemed to have a positive effect in slowing the advance and death rate of the disease, but their experimental nature and high costs severely limited their availability.

The AIDS crisis dramatized Americans' uneven access to healthcare. Studies showed that large segments of the population, especially among the working poor who did not qualify for Medicaid, were virtually unprotected should disease or serious injury occur. During the campaign, Clinton had made a national healthcare system a priority of his administration. Soon after assuming office, he announced a task force, chaired by First Lady Hillary Clinton, to draft legislation. In September 1993, President Clinton asked Congress to write a "new chapter in the American story" and "guarantee every American comprehensive health benefits that can never be taken away." The plan was complicated, with one Democratic congressional leader dubbing it "Godzilla." Republicans attacked the bill with gusto, saying that it affirmed that Clinton was an advocate of big government and big spending, and announced that healthcare was too important an issue to leave to the federal government. After a year of public and congressional hearings and debate, President Clinton admitted defeat and abandoned the effort.

Clinton also struggled with Congress over his economic programs. Having made the economy the focal point of his campaign, he considered balancing the budget and reducing the deficit a primary priority. One step was to increase international trade by selectively lowering trade barriers. Continuing initiatives started by Bush, Clinton pushed for congressional approval of the North American Free Trade Agreement (NAFTA) and the **General Agreement on Tariffs and Trade** (GATT). Both were part of the trend toward globalization and were designed to reduce or eliminate trade barriers and increase international trade—NAFTA for the United States, Mexico, and Canada; GATT for most of the world, including the members of NAFTA. Opponents claimed that both would harm the American economy by encouraging U.S. companies to relocate their factories to nations with lower environmental, worker, and product standards. Organized labor was especially vocal about the potential loss of jobs. Unable to convince many

Democrats to support the bills, Clinton was forced to rely on Republican votes for their passage.

While Republicans supported NAFTA, they staunchly opposed most of Clinton's budget and economic recovery plan. Based on his conviction that reducing the deficit was necessary to end the recession and promote future growth, Clinton raised taxes on the wealthiest Americans—those making over $180,000 a year—and expanded tax credits for low-income families. He also made major spending cuts throughout the budget, especially in defense spending. Republicans denounced the budget as a typical liberal Democratic "tax and spend" measure that would create a "job-killing recession" and put the nation's economy in the "gutter." Six months later, with Vice President Albert Gore casting the tie-breaking vote in the Senate, the Clinton budget passed without the votes of any Republican senators.

The fights over the budget, healthcare, and gays in the military—combined with allegations of wrongdoing by the Clintons in a land-investment scheme (**Whitewater**) and Clinton's womanizing—had by the end of 1993 eroded the president's popularity. Republicans led by Newt Gingrich, a conservative representative from Georgia, seized the opportunity to regain the political initiative and drafted a political agenda called the "**Contract with America.**" It called for reduced federal spending (especially for welfare), a balanced budget by 2002, and support for family values. The public responded by electing nine new Republican senators and fifty-two new Republican representatives in 1994. Republicans had a majority in both houses of Congress for the first time in forty years. Gingrich, the new Republican Speaker of the House, predicted that the conservative majority was "going to change the world."

General Agreement on Tariffs and Trade First signed in 1947, the agreement sought to provide an international forum to encourage free trade between member states by regulating and reducing tariffs on traded goods and by providing a common mechanism for resolving trade disputes. GATT membership now includes more than 110 countries.

Whitewater A scandal involving a failed real-estate development in Arkansas in which the Clintons had invested.

Contract with America Pledge taken in 1994 by some three hundred Republican candidates for the House, who promised to reduce the size and scope of the federal government and to balance the federal budget by 2002.

The North American Free Trade Agreement eliminated many trade barriers between the United States, Canada, and Mexico. Here, a Mexican worker sews garments to be shipped and sold north of the border. American supporters of the agreement argue that it has led to an overall increase in trade, while critics argue that it cost American jobs as American companies used Mexican plants and workers to produce what was once made in the United States. *Keith Dannemiller/Corbis/SABA.*

Judicial Restraint and the Rehnquist Court

Part of the Republican hopes for reconstructing government rested with the Supreme Court under Chief Justice William Rehnquist. Since the Nixon administration, Republican presidents had made an effort, not always successful, to appoint Supreme Court justices who rejected the social and political activism of the Warren Court. They believed that since the New Deal, the Court had worked to strengthen the power of the federal government over areas that had traditionally been reserved for state and local controls. It was a trend that conservatives and most Republicans believed needed to be reversed. What was needed was a Court that practiced **judicial restraint,** restricting federal authority and returning executive power to individuals and state and local governments. Using those criteria, Presidents Reagan and Bush had appointed six justices to the Court, consti-

tuting a narrow, but not always stable, conservative majority.

By 1992, the Rehnquist Court had modified many of the principles behind the Warren Court's decisions that had promoted forced desegregation and affirmative action. During the 1980s, the Reagan and Bush administrations had backed away from supporting court-ordered busing to integrate schools. "We aren't going to compel children who don't want to have an integrated education to have one," said a Reagan Justice Department official. In 1992 the Court agreed in the *DeKalb County, Georgia,* case, stating that busing should not be used to integrate schools segregated by de facto housing patterns.

judicial restraint   Refraining from using the courts as a forum for implementing social change but instead deferring to Congress, the president, and the consensus of the people.

Those supporting affirmative action were overwhelmed by California voters in 1997, who voted to eliminate consideration of race or gender in state hiring and contracting, and in admission to the state's colleges and universities. *Lou Dematteis/The Image Works.*

Similarly, the Reagan and Bush administrations had echoed increasingly popular opposition to **affirmative action,** saying that it undermined freedom of action and merit-based achievement. Reflecting that view, in 1989, in the *Croson* decision, the Supreme Court ruled that state and local government affirmative action guidelines that set aside jobs and contracts for minorities were unconstitutional. Six years later, in the *Adarand* decision, the Court reaffirmed its decision and further limited the criteria for providing "set-asides" for minorities. The Court's 1995 decision matched public opinion poll results: 77 percent of those surveyed, including 66 percent of African Americans, believed that affirmative action discriminated against whites. Following California's lead (Proposition 209 in 1996), Washington (1998) and Florida (1999)

passed legislation forbidding special consideration for race and/or gender in state hiring and admissions to state colleges and universities.

The Rehnquist Court also chipped away at the federal government's power to make state and local governments comply with its directives. In several cases throughout the 1990s, the Court upheld state sovereignty by deciding that states and municipalities could resist implementing executive and congressional directives. In *Printz v. the United States* (1997), the Court declared unconstitutional certain provisions in the so-called Brady Bill that required state police to do a background search of anyone wanting to buy a handgun. Continuing the pattern, in 2000 a divided Court invalidated provisions in the Violence Against Women Act that permitted suits in federal courts by victims of gender-motivated crimes. In writing for the majority, Chief Justice Rehnquist announced that distinctions must be made between "what is truly national and what is truly local."

Clinton's Comeback

The 1994 election results were a blow to Democrats and to Clinton. Assured of their mandate, Republicans assumed the political offensive, seeing no need to compromise with the White House. Wanting to roll back social programs, Republicans focused on balancing the budget. "You cannot sustain the old welfare state" with a balanced budget, Gingrich proclaimed. Immediately, Republicans began work on an economic plan that would slash government spending on education, welfare, Medicare, Medicaid, and the environment while reducing taxes—especially for the more affluent.

Clinton responded by emphasizing his fiscally conservative centrist position, calling it the "dynamic center." In the "battle of the budget," Clinton agreed that balancing the budget was the first priority and made additional spending cuts. But he also sought to draw a distinction between himself and Republicans, saying that Gingrich Republicans were too extreme in their cuts. As president, Clinton vowed it was necessary to protect spending for education, Medicare, Social Security, and the environment.

affirmative action   Policy that seeks to redress past discrimination through active measures to ensure equal opportunity, especially in education and employment.

On April 19, 1995, a terrorist truck bomb exploded in front of the Murrah Federal Building in Oklahoma City, killing 168 people. Here, a fireman carries the lifeless body of one of the 19 children who lost their lives in a daycare center housed in the building. *Charles H. Porter IV/Sygma.*

As Clinton reaffirmed his centrist position, an act of domestic terrorism offered an opportunity for him to reassert his presidential leadership. On April 19, 1995, Americans were stunned when an explosion destroyed the Murrah Federal Building in Oklahoma City, killing 168 people, 19 of them children. Many initially concluded that the powerful bomb was the work of Islamic terrorists, but it soon became clear that it was the work of Timothy McVeigh, an American extremist who believed that the federal government was a threat to the freedom of the American people. His heinous crime seemed to symbolize the depth of division and the dangers of extremism in the nation. Clinton asked that people reject extremism and stressed national unity. Public opinion polls again gave the president positive numbers.

Continuing his emphasis on a centrist position, Clinton, in a series of "common ground" speeches, supported what many saw as generally Republican goals. He committed himself to passing anticrime legislation, finding methods to limit sex and violence on television, reforming welfare, and fixing affirmative action. The battle over welfare reform was one example of Clinton's successful strategy. Critics of the Republican plan questioned whether the private sector would be able to hire all those shaved from the welfare rolls. Conservatives argued that welfare programs created a class of welfare-dependent people, "welfare mothers" with little integrity and no work ethic who represented "spiritual and moral poverty." Clinton and other Democrats denounced such statements as mean-spirited and blind to the reality of those on welfare—especially regarding the number of children on welfare. They argued that to replace relief with jobs, it was vital to increase funds for job training, educational programs, and daycare. Clinton's efforts brought success. By the fall of 1995, when the battle over the 1995–1996 budget began in earnest, Clinton successfully had portrayed many aspects of the Republican's program as too extreme.

For their part, as promised, Republicans slashed spending for many social programs. Clinton refused the congressional budget and sent it back to Congress. Overconfident, Republicans in turn refused to pass a temporary measure to keep the government operating unless the president accepted their budget. Unmoved, and with no operating funds, Clinton shut down all nonessential functions of the government— first, for six days in November, then for a twenty-one-day standoff lasting from December 16 to January 6, 1996, after which Congress and the president compromised. Clinton accepted some Republican cuts, including those on housing and the arts, while Congressional Republicans accepted most of the president's requests, including those for education, Medicare, and Medicade. Most of the nation blamed Gingrich and his followers for the budget impasse and the government shutdown.

Having won the battle of the budget, Clinton solidified his position in the center. He publicly stated that the "era of big government was over" and committed himself to balancing the budget by 2002. As the 1996 presidential election approached, disgruntled Republicans claimed that Clinton had stolen much of their agenda. However, they still argued that Clinton's cuts were not enough and that his big spending had "sucked the life out of the economy, eaten up the American workers' pay, and given money to the government instead." The problem with that approach was that the economy was beginning to boom, and Clinton was boasting that his administration had created 10 million new jobs and had reduced poverty.

A Revitalized Economy

The economy had started to climb out of the recession (see Figure 31.4) as Clinton took office. It would continue to improve for almost a decade before slowing again in 2001, one of the longest periods of sustained economic growth in the nation's history. The revitalized economy was in large part the product of the transition to an information and service economy and the result of technological innovations, especially in communications, biology, and medicine. American leadership in the computer software, microprocessing, and telecommunications industries, plus growth in the retail markets at home and overseas, sparked the economy boom. Beginning in 1992, the economy grew at about 3 percent per year, the strongest showing since World War II. The rapid growth of technology stocks spurred the stock market to reach new heights. **Standard and Poor's 500** (the S&P 500) averaged unprecedented increases of 33 percent per year between 1994 and 1998. Stories about individual investors becoming overnight millionaires by investing in Internet-connected stocks, the "dot-coms," convinced many to invest. In 1999 the number of Americans participating in the stock market reached 43 percent, whereas in 1965 only about 10 percent of the public owned stock.

The surging stock market seemed matched by increasing prosperity and wages, and by falling unemployment and inflation rates. In 1996, national prosperity matched that of the peak year of 1989 and continued upward as take-home pay mushroomed. Average wages for men grew at about 4 percent beginning in 1997, with low-income workers' incomes growing by 6 percent between 1993 and 1998. The median household income in 2000 was $42,151, with Hispanic and black incomes reaching new highs ($33,455 and $30,436, respectively). Unemployment shrank throughout the 1990s, declining to only 4.1 percent in 1999, the lowest figure since 1968. Minority unemployment rates also recorded new lows, 7.2 percent for Hispanics and 8.9 percent for African Americans. With more jobs and higher wages, the number of Americans living in poverty (incomes below $17,029 for a family of four) fell to 11.8 percent, the lowest rate since 1979. Hidden within the statistics were grim realities: African American and Hispanic poverty rates still averaged above 20 percent, the income gap between the poor and the upper class continued to widen, and middle-class incomes, when adjusted for inflation, stayed the same or declined slightly.

Clinton's Second Term

Despite the improving economy and Clinton's shrewd shift to the center, Republicans were confident that they could regain the presidency in the 1996 election. Conservative Republicans dominated the convention, once again declaring a "cultural war" and focusing on Clinton's moral shortcomings. Robert Dole, a strict conservative who had resigned his Senate seat and his position as Senate majority leader to become the Republican candidate, generally avoided the cultural-war issues and stressed the economy and ethics. The moral issues—accusations of sexual harassment by Clinton when he was governor of Arkansas, and Whitewater—drew headlines but had little impact on the election. Public opinion polls found that over 60 percent of those questioned approved Clinton's running of the nation, even though 54 percent thought Clinton was not "honest" or "trustworthy." As in 1992, it was the economy, not moral issues, that shaped the election. Facing Clinton's popularity and economic prosperity, Dole would have to run an amazingly effective campaign to win. It did not happen. His campaign lacked energy from the start, as did Perot's second run for office. In an election marked by low voter turnout, Clinton became the first Democratic president to be reelected since Franklin D. Roosevelt. He captured 379 electoral votes and 49 percent of the popular vote.

As Clinton started his second term, he recognized that his support rested on his centrist position and the expanding growth of the economy. In his 1997 State of the Union address, he focused on the economic strength of the nation and projected the first balanced budget in thirty years. The balanced budget, he stated, marked "an end to decades of deficits that have shackled our economy, paralyzed our policies, and held our people back." To undermine Republican calls for tax cuts, Clinton stressed that any surplus should be set aside to ensure the viability of Social Security. "Let's save Social Security first," he told Congress. Calling for an end to "bickering and extreme partisanship," he asked Congress to approve programs to improve education, daycare, Medicare, and Medicaid. Finding some common ground, Republicans and Democrats managed to approve the budget, pass the Balanced Budget Act of 1997, provide a small

Standard and Poor's 500 An index of five hundred widely held stocks.

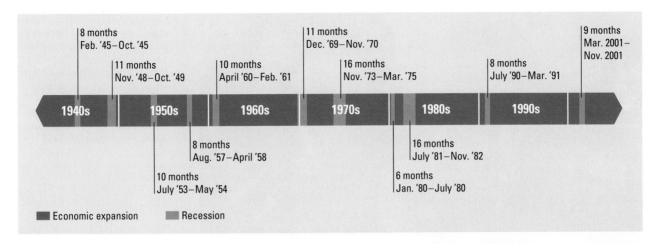

FIGURE 31.4 Expansion and Recession, 1940–2001 Economists define a recession as a contraction in the economy that is characterized by rising unemployment and decreasing production. Since the end of World War II, the average recession has lasted about 10 months. As this figure shows, the period of economic expansion that ended in March 2001 was the longest period of growth since the end of World War II. Source: *New York Times*, November 27, 2001, C-18.

cut in taxes (the Taxpayer Relief Act of 1997), and make minor reforms to the healthcare system that helped to limit growing costs. Beyond those agreements, however, Republicans and Democrats marched to different agendas and expressed bitter partisanship.

In January 1998, many Republicans seized on an opportunity not only to discredit and weaken Clinton politically but also to remove him from office. The issue was sexual misconduct involving the president and a White House intern, **Monica Lewinsky.** Their affair, including meetings in the Oval Office, had occurred between 1995 and 1997. When the allegations first arose, Clinton denied them as ugly rumors, telling the nation that he had not had "sexual relations with that woman, Miss Lewinsky." His denial drew heavy doses of public and Republican skepticism. An investigation headed by Independent Counsel Kenneth Starr, who in 1994 had examined the Whitewater matter, clearly proved the case, and in August, Clinton finally admitted that he had had "inappropriate relations" with Lewinsky and that he had "misled" the public.

Starr's 445-page report identified eleven possible grounds for impeaching the president. As the political momentum for impeachment grew, many of Clinton's supporters argued that the Lewinsky affair was a private matter that in no way obstructed his running of the government. Public opinion polls confirmed that a majority of Americans agreed and continued to

give Clinton high marks as president, even as they gave him low marks for integrity. The November 1998 congressional elections also indicated that most Americans did not see politics as revolving solely around Clinton. Republicans had projected large gains in Congress because of Clinton's behavior but were disappointed, although Republicans still held majorities in both houses of Congress. Undeterred by the polls and election results, and anxious to continue the attack on Clinton, Republicans in the House of Representatives—in a purely partisan vote—agreed in December to ask for impeachment. Believing that while the sexual indiscretions were minor, the lies were major, they cited two offenses, perjury and obstruction of justice. Clinton was the second president to face trial in the Senate (the first was Andrew Johnson, in 1868), which with a two-thirds vote could remove him from office.

The Republicans had a 55-to-45 majority in the Senate, but it was not enough to ensure Clinton's removal from office. The trial consumed five weeks,

Monica Lewinsky White House intern who had a two-year sexual affair with President Clinton; Clinton's misleading testimony about the affair contributed to his impeachment.

A Balanced Budget
That Protects Our Families, Invests in Our People
and Cuts Taxes for Middle Class Families

On August 5, 1997, Bill Clinton signed the Balanced Budget Act. Applauding the president are Vice President Albert Gore (*left*) and House Speaker Newt Gingrich (*right*). In the fall of 1998, Clinton announced a federal budget surplus of $70 billion, the first surplus since 1969. *Ron Edmonds/World Wide.*

and to many it seemed to confirm the view that Republicans were more interested in destroying Clinton politically than in governing. On February 19, 1998, the Senate voted against removing Clinton from office. On the issue of perjury, 10 Republicans voted with the Democrats to defeat the charge, 55 to 44. The vote on obstruction of justice was closer, 50 to 50, but nowhere near a two-thirds majority. Following the Senate's decision, Clinton expressed his sorrow for the burden he had placed on the nation.

With the high drama and low tragedy of impeachment over, politics returned to the issues of government spending and tax cuts, how best to "save" Social Security and improve education and the environment, the role of the military in foreign affairs, and jockeying for position in the upcoming 2000 election.

Clinton's Foreign Policy

When Clinton assumed control of America's foreign policy, it still was not clear what general policy would replace that of the Cold War. Americans wanted to maintain status and influence as a superpower but were divided over what situations warranted Ameri-

can attention or intervention. Inexperienced in foreign affairs, Clinton proceeded cautiously and followed the general outline set by President Bush.

Seeking to expand the American economy, Clinton worked to reduce trade barriers and to enhance global economic stability. Congress passed the NAFTA and GATT agreements, while Clinton worked to improve trade with China and to encourage Japan to buy more American goods. To promote global economic stability, the Clinton administration provided loans and supported the **International Monetary Fund** to support the economies of several countries, including Mexico, Russia, and Indonesia by providing loans.

Clinton also continued efforts to ease tensions in the Middle East and to resolve disputes between Is-

International Monetary Fund An agency of the United Nations established in 1945 to help promote the health of the world economy; it seeks to expand international trade by stabilizing exchange rates between international currencies; it also provides temporary loans for nations unable to maintain their balance of trade. Currently, 184 countries are members of the IMF.

American forces played a key role in the United Nations and NATO peacekeeping effort in Bosnia and Kosovo. In this picture, an American patrol greets Albanian children from a Kosovo village. *Alexander Zemlianichenko/Wide World.*

rael and the Palestinians. The Clinton State Department played a role in reaching an accord that established Palestinian self-rule in some Israeli-occupied areas and in a treaty in which Jordan and Israel pledged cooperation. Despite the administration's efforts, however, solutions to differences between the Palestine Liberation Organization and Israel deteriorated as hard-liners on each side opposed peace initiatives and violence escalated.

Clinton's efforts to promote democracy in Haiti proved more successful. A 1991 military coup had ousted the democratically elected government headed by President Jean Bertrand Aristide. When isolation and economic pressure failed to convince the ruling junta, which was brutally repressing its opponents, to restore democracy, Clinton obtained UN support for an invasion. Under this threat, the junta opened discussions in October 1994 with a delegation led by former president Jimmy Carter. The resulting agreement allowed the junta members to leave the country and Aristide to return. Elections followed, and U.S. troops withdrew after helping Haiti make the transition back to democracy.

Clinton also inherited two additional, and highly controversial, foreign-policy commitments from Bush. One was in the East African nation of Somalia; the other dealt with Bosnia, once part of Yugoslavia. U.S. troops had intervened in Somalia in 1992 as part of a United Nations undertaking to provide humanitar-ian aid and to keep the peace between factions in a civil war. In October 1993, eighteen American soldiers were ambushed and killed. Seeing little direct American interest in Somalia and responding to public outrage and congressional pressure, Clinton withdrew American forces in April 1994.

In the Balkan nation of Bosnia, Clinton faced a similar problem: how to justify and use American forces in a region where few Americans believed the United States had a direct interest. During the 1992 campaign, Clinton had chided Bush for not promoting peace in Bosnia more assertively. Once in office, however, he too became cautious and moved slowly in supporting UN peacekeeping and relief efforts there. As the carnage increased, however, the Clinton administration agreed to allow American forces to participate in a UN campaign to establish and protect "safe areas" for refugees displaced by the fighting. In the fall of 1995, the United States sponsored talks between the warring elements—the Serbs, the Muslim Bosnians, and the Croats. The resulting **Dayton Agreement** partitioned the country into a Bosnian-Croat federation

Dayton Agreement Agreement signed in Dayton, Ohio, in November 1995 by the three rival ethnic groups in Bosnia that pledged to end the four-year-old civil war there.

I t   M a t t e r s

The Impeachment Process

The Senate's decision not to remove Clinton from office reaffirmed the principle that the process of impeachment and removal of a president, or any government official, should not rest on political passions. In writing the Constitution, the drafters in Article II, Section 4, stated: "The President . . . and all civil Officials of the United States, shall be removed from Office on Impeachment for, and Conviction of, Treason, Bribery, or other high Crimes and Misdemeanors." While the Constitution does not provide a definition of "high Crimes and Misdemeanors," Congress historically has required a high standard of guilt, preventing the process from being used as a political weapon by a Congressional majority.

and a Serb republic, and called for UN forces, including twenty thousand Americans, to police the peace. By the summer of 1996, when most American forces were withdrawn, much had been accomplished to rebuild the shattered region. Although Clinton assured Americans that efforts in Bosnia had been successful, in December 1997 he announced that a continued American presence in that nation was necessary to continue with the task of nation building.

Clinton's commitment to peace in the Balkans was soon tested again. President Slobodan Milosevic of Serbia was intent on crushing dissent and insurgent forces in the Serbian province of Kosovo. The conflict that erupted in 1998 involved ancient hostilities between Serbian Orthodox Christians and Muslim ethnic Albanians, who made up 90 percent of Kosovo's population. When the Kosovo Liberation Army (KLA) began to fight for independence in 1998, Milosevic responded with force—targeting both members of the KLA and the Muslim population. As the bloodshed increased, NATO leaders sought a diplomatic solution before events ignited another war in the Balkans. When negotiations with Milosevic proved unsuccessful, Secretary of State Madeleine Albright called for "humanitarian intervention" and the establishment of autonomy for Kosovo within Serbia. Unwilling to use ground forces, NATO began a bombing campaign in March 1999, with American air power

providing the bulk of planes and bombs. The goal, the president announced, was to halt Serbian aggression.

Milosevic responded by sending more troops into Kosovo and stepping up his program of "**ethnic cleansing**."

The NATO bombing intensified and expanded to include the Serbian capital of Belgrade, and in June 1999, Milosevic agreed to withdraw his troops, recognize Kosovo's autonomy, and allow United Nations peacekeeping forces into the area to ensure the peace. Clinton called it "a victory for a safer world, for our democratic values, and a stronger America." Later investigations estimated that more than ten thousand ethnic Albanian civilians had been killed in ethnic cleansing between January 1998 and 2000. And in May 1999 the International War Crimes Tribunal at The Hague charged Milosevic with crimes against humanity. In October 2000 a popular uprising overthrew Milosevic in a bloodless coup, and in April 2001 he was arrested and later extradited to stand trial at The Hague. As the trial started, Milosevic pleaded not guilty to all charges. (The trial continues.)

Also contributing to a safer world were American efforts to maintain economic sanctions against Iraq. In January 1998, Saddam Hussein refused to allow United Nations inspection teams access to several sites where, some suspected, he was manufacturing or stockpiling biological and chemical weapons. Clinton stated that the United States was willing to attack Iraq to force compliance with a United Nations mandate requiring Iraq to eliminate all such weapons. As the United States moved military units into the Persian Gulf region, one navy pilot was heard to say: "I don't think you can find a more powerful tool to make a statement than to park an airplane twenty miles off a guy's beach." No direct attack took place, but the Clinton administration worked with Britain and other allies to contain Hussein by maintaining UN-sanctioned economic boycotts and patrolling the skies over Iraq.

By 1999, Clinton believed he had moved well along the path of fulfilling his broad foreign-policy goals of promoting peace, democracy, and economic globalization. In the effort to make the world safer, he had continued previous administration support for international efforts to control and eliminate biological and chemical weapons. And in 1997 with the help

ethnic cleansing   An effort to eradicate an ethnic or religious group from a country or region, often through mass killings.

of key Republican leaders, Clinton pushed through the Senate a Chemical Weapons Convention treaty that provided stronger sanctions against countries continuing to maintain and develop chemical weapons. The following year, however, Clinton, despite failing to obtain Senate approval, committed the United States to the **Kyoto Protocol** to reduce global air pollution.

As Clinton left office in 2000, he pointed to several important legacies that made the world safer and more democratic. In Haiti, Bosnia, and Kosovo, American actions had helped establish democracy and restore stability. In the economic arena, Clinton pointed to NAFTA, improved trade with China and Japan, and the more than 270 trade agreements he had signed lowering trade barriers around the globe. Still, as the political campaign for 2000 began, Republicans and some Democrats voiced criticism of his foreign policies, arguing that they harmed the economy, weakened American freedom of action around the globe, and dangerously extended the responsibilities of the military to include nation building.

The Testing of President Bush

- To what degree did Bush and Gore represent the political centers of their respective parties? How did their solutions to America's problems differ?

- What were Democratic criticisms of President Bush's domestic and foreign policies?

- How did the events of September 11, 2001, affect politics, the public, and foreign policy?

Americans welcomed the twenty-first century with celebrations and optimism. With the economy growing and providing more jobs and prosperity, President Clinton was more popular than ever, with a 63 percent approval rating in the polls. Thus it was an upbeat president who, on January 27, 2000, presented his State of the Union address: "We have restored the vital center, replacing outdated ideologies with a new vision anchored in basic enduring values: opportunity for all, responsibility from all, and a community for all Americans. . . . We begin the new century with over 20 million new jobs. The fastest economic growth in more than 30 years; the lowest unemployment rates in 30 years; the lowest poverty rates in 20 years; the lowest African American and Hispanic unemployment rates on record. . . ." He called for improving Social Security, healthcare, and the quality of education. It seemed an agenda that Vice President Al Gore could expand on in his campaign for the

presidency. Gore occupied the Democratic center, seeing a major role for government in solving national problems and advocating selected tax cuts.

The 2000 Election

Normally, under such circumstances, Republicans would not have had great expectations of successfully challenging the vice president. But 2000 was hardly an ordinary year, and many Republicans believed that Gore was vulnerable exactly *because* he was the vice president. They focused their campaign not only on cutting taxes and the dangers of big-government and "tax-and-spend" Democrats but also on the Clinton-Gore connection and the need to restore integrity to the White House.

Leading the Republican hopefuls was George W. Bush, governor of Texas and son of the former president. Others challenged Bush, most importantly Senator John McCain from Arizona, but support from party regulars and money from a massive campaign fund allowed Bush to outdistance his rivals and win the nomination. To quiet those who thought he lacked enough national experience, especially in foreign policy, he selected a veteran Republican statesman, Dick Cheney, as his vice president.

Running for the presidency, Bush announced a policy of "compassionate conservatism" that avoided the militancy of the cultural war and moved away from opposing most government programs. He stressed the use of private initiatives to improve education, Social Security, and healthcare. At the heart of this campaign was a promise to reduce taxes and restore dignity to the White House.

The campaign generated a lot of spending and almost no heated rhetoric or sharp debates between the two contenders. Even the three televised debates failed to generate much excitement or change people's minds. On the issues, their differences were largely matters of "how to," reflecting party ideologies. To improve education, Bush supported state initiatives and more stringent testing, whereas Gore wanted federal funds to hire more teachers and repair school facilities. On how to spend the budget surplus, Bush

Koyto Protocol   Drafted by the United Nations in 1997 were a set of international agreements in which participating nations agreed to reduce their emissions rates of carbon dioxide and other industrial-produced gases that are linked to global climate change; the United States was to reduce its emissions 7 percent by 2012.

The winner of the 2000 presidential election was determined by a disputed vote count in Florida that was later upheld by the U.S. Supreme Court. As the justices considered their decision, supporters of Gore and Bush confronted one another outside the Supreme Court building. *Michael DiBari Jr./AP/Wide World.*

advocated a tax cut to give money back to the people. Gore called the tax cut dangerous and unfair—it favored the rich, he insisted—and said he would use the surplus to reduce the national debt and fund government programs.

Nationally, the two candidates ran a dead heat, but the geography of support told a different story—of a confrontation between two Americas. Bush ran strong in the less populated states. Gore's strength was in urban areas (he received over 70 percent of the vote in large metropolitan areas) and in the Northeast and Pacific Coast. Bush was particularly popular with white males, who voted for him 5 to 3. Gore, as expected, did exceedingly well among minorities, with Bush receiving fewer African American votes than any Republican candidate since 1960. On election day Gore received a minuscule majority of votes—half a million more out of the 10.5 million votes cast—but Bush won the Electoral College vote with 271 votes to 267, one vote more than necessary to win (see Map 31.2).

Before the final votes were in, the nation's attention was centered on the results in Florida, whose 25 electoral votes gave Bush the victory. Because of Bush's narrow margin of less than 1,000 popular votes in the state, Florida law required a recount. As the recount proceeded, Gore supporters claimed that voting irregularities had occurred and asked the Florida Supreme Court to set aside certification of the vote until hand counts were completed in several largely Democratic counties. When the court agreed, Bush supporters protested that Gore was trying to "steal" the election by including in the count votes that had not been clearly marked or punched through the ballot. To halt the hand recount and certify existing totals that made Bush the victor, Bush supporters filed suit in federal court. On December 4, a month after the election, the federal district court set aside the Florida Supreme Court's decision. The existing count would be certified. But the legal struggle was not finished, and there was the issue of which court—the federal district court or the Florida Supreme Court—should decide the outcome. The question of jurisdiction was heard by a special session of the U.S. Supreme Court. On December 4, the justices decided, 5 to 4, in favor of accepting the existing count and allowing Florida officials to certify that Bush had won Florida's electoral votes and the presidential election. Gore conceded, and an hour later President-elect Bush stated, "Whether you voted for me or not, I will do my best to serve your interest, and I will work to earn your respect."

Establishing the Bush Agenda

George Walker Bush entered the presidency with the flimsiest national support, but as determined to implement his campaign promises as if he had received a clear mandate from the voters. In establishing his program, Bush expected to be able to work with a Republican majority in the House of Representatives and a 50-50 tie in the Senate (which, if necessary, could be broken by the vote of the vice president). Observing that Bush's administration was "more Reaganite than the Reagan administration," conser-

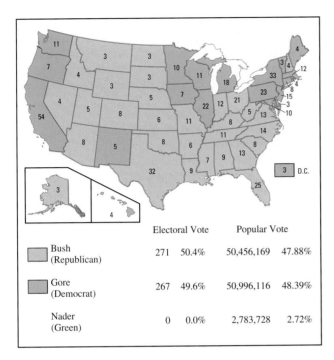

Electoral Vote | Popular Vote

	Electoral Vote		Popular Vote	
Bush (Republican)	271	50.4%	50,456,169	47.88%
Gore (Democrat)	267	49.6%	50,996,116	48.39%
Nader (Green)	0	0.0%	2,783,728	2.72%

MAP 31.2 Election of 2000 Democratic candidate Al Gore won the popular vote, but George W. Bush succeeded in gaining victory in the Electoral College by four votes. Among white males, Bush ran extremely well, while Gore won a majority of minority and women voters. Ralph Nader's Green Party won less than 3 percent of the popular vote, but his votes in Florida may have detracted from the Gore tally, helping Bush win the critical electoral votes.

vatives were anxious to shape the nation's new path. Among the highest priorities were tax cuts and education reform, two issues that had some degree of bipartisan support. Bush's tax cut called for reducing the federal government's revenue by $1.6 trillion over a six-year period. Such a reduction, most Republicans cheerfully reasoned, would limit government spending and stimulate the economy, which was slipping into a recession.

Democrats rejected the projected tax cut, arguing that it was too large and favored the rich. But, finding it difficult to oppose a tax cut in a period of government surplus, several Democrats voted with the Republicans to approve a slightly smaller $1.35 trillion tax cut in June. Bush had succeeded in making good on one of his key campaign promises. Next, Bush pushed forward on his education bill. Many Republicans sought a major shakeup in the structure of education, supporting a voucher system that provided a means for people to take their children out of "failing" public schools and enroll them in private and al-

ternative schools, with some form of financial support from local, state, or federal education funds. Democrats wanted more federal spending for additional teachers and improved schools. As the debate on education intensified, in June, Vermont senator James Jeffords shocked and angered his party by leaving the Republican fold and becoming an Independent. His switch gave the Democrats a one-vote majority in the Senate and, equally important, leadership in the Senate and all its committees. Congressional gridlock followed. Caught in the gridlock were proposals for education, campaign financing reform, energy, and healthcare.

Adding to the bipartisanship was the declining economy. Led by heavy losses in high-tech stocks on the Nasdaq—highlighted by the rapid devaluation of dot-com stocks—the stock market plummeted in March 2001. An abrupt slowdown in sales in the service and technological sectors of the economy, combined with higher oil prices, produced widespread layoffs, climbing unemployment, and a loss of investor and consumer confidence. Democrats quickly blamed Bush's handling of the economy and his tax cut for the recession. Republicans responded that further tax cuts were needed to help restore the economy and that the Bush administration was more fiscally responsible than the tax-and-spend Democrats. Speaking to a crowd in California, President Bush sounded like his father in promising no new taxes: "Not over my dead body will they raise your taxes." Some chuckled about the president's verbal misstatement, but no one misunderstood what he meant.

Charting New Foreign Policies

As with domestic policy, the Bush administration had fundamental differences with Clinton's foreign policy. The Republicans believed that Clinton had been too cautious and too interested in international cooperation, which had weakened the nation's power and failed to promote national interests. Bush meant to reverse the direction. Upon taking office, he assumed a cooler attitude toward Russia and rejected Clinton's policies on **global warming** and international controls on biological and chemical weapons. In rejecting

global warming The gradual warming to the surface of the Earth; most scientists argue that over the past 20 years the Earth's temperature has risen at a more rapid rate because of industrial emission of gases that trap heat; the consequence of continued emissions, they argue, could be major ecological changes.

provisions of the Kyoto Protocol that called for a reduction in carbon dioxide emissions, Bush stated, "We will not do anything that harms our economy."

Because the world was too dangerous to rely on others to protect the United States and its interests, the Bush administration believed that multilateralism, past agreements, and treaty obligations were less important than a strong and determined America promoting its own interests. Following such logic, Bush decided to reenergize Reagan's goal of implementing an antiballistic missile defense system. Many, including the Russians, believed that Bush's decision violated a 1972 antiballistic missile pact with the Soviet Union (SALT I), thereby destabilizing the international system of arms reduction and control and possibly starting a new arms race with Russia and China.

Democratic leader Richard Gephardt warned that Bush's "go-it-alone policy" undermined national security. Administration officials denied the charges and said that the administration was practicing "**à la carte** multilateralism" sensitive to American interests. At the same time, some insiders spoke about divisions within the administration between such individuals as Secretary of State **Colin Powell,** who favored a more international role for the United States, and National Security Adviser Condoleezza Rice and Secretary of Defense Donald Rumsfeld, who preferred a more unilateral approach and wanted to reduce the United States' commitment to multilateralism. With Vice President Cheney's views nearer to those of Rice and Rumsfeld, many thought that Powell would lose the struggle.

An Assault Against a Nation

It was an event that no one thought possible. On the morning of September 11, 2001, the world changed for the United States as four hijacked airplanes became flying bombs aimed at symbols of American financial and military power. At 8:48 A.M., a group of five terrorists led by Mohammed Atta crashed American Airlines Flight 11 into the North Tower of the World Trade Center. As New York fire and police departments responded to the disaster, a second airliner struck the South Tower of the World Trade Center at 9:06 A.M. The second crash confirmed that the first had not been an accident and that the United States was being attacked by terrorists. The extent of the planned attack was further dramatized thirty-nine minutes later when a third hijacked plane slammed into the Pentagon, just outside Washington, D.C., at 9:45 A.M. A fourth plane, United Airlines Flight 93,

was seized by four hijackers, altered course toward the nation's capital, and crashed into a field southeast of Pittsburgh, Pennsylvania. On that flight, passengers, having learned about the three other hijackings by cell phone, attempted to regain control of the aircraft—a struggle ending in the crash of the plane short of its targeted destination.

In New York City the tragedy was soon magnified when the twin towers of the World Trade Center, the tallest structures in the city, collapsed, engulfing and killing thousands, including many of the firefighters and policemen who had rushed to the scene and had entered the towers to provide help (see Individual Choices, pages 990–991). Over three thousand people died that morning, and Americans began to realize that the United States had entered a new kind of war.

President Bush, speaking to a stunned and concerned nation, declared that Americans had witnessed "evil, the very worst of human nature" and vowed to track down those responsible and bring them to justice. Patriotism and support for the president swept across the country, American flags flew from homes and car antennas, and President Bush's approval rating soared to over 86 percent.

Among Democrats and Republicans, the battles over education, Social Security, missile defense, and the budget were set aside. "The political war will cease," said Democrat John Breaux of Louisiana. "The war we have now is against terrorism." Congress quickly appropriated $40 billion for disaster relief and support for the effort to fight terrorism. Within days, the horrifying events were linked to Al Qaeda, a worldwide Islamic militant organization led by **Osama bin Laden.** The son of a wealthy Saudi Arabian family, bin Laden fought against Soviet forces in

---

à la carte Term used to explain selecting items one at a time instead of as a group or set; as used here, meaning that Bush selected allies as he needed them and ignored including existing combinations and organizations.

Colin Powell First African American to hold the position of secretary of state; a career army officer, Powell served as national security adviser to President Reagan and as chairman of the Joint Chiefs of Staff under the first President Bush.

Osama bin Laden Muslim fundamentalist whose Islamic militant organization, Al Qaeda, has organized terrorist attacks on Americans at home and abroad, including those against the American embassies in Kenya and Tanzania in 1998.

The September 11, 2001, attack on the World Trade Center by terrorists who hijacked two civilian airliners and used them as missiles against the twin towers left the nation stunned, angry, and determined to bring those who had orchestrated the attack to justice. *Robert Clark/Aurora.*

Afghanistan, but after the Gulf War, angered by American forces remaining in his homeland, he dedicated himself to conducting a war of terror against the United States. At the root of his decision was his conversion to Muslim fundamentalism and his belief that U.S. forces in Saudi Arabia defiled the holy ground of Islam. By the early 1990s, he and Al Qaeda were linked to several terrorist attacks on the United States, including the 1993 attempt to car-bomb the World Trade Center. In this attempt, the terrorists were caught and eventually sentenced (October 2001) to life in prison.

Three years later, in 1996, bin Laden's organization was involved in the truck bombing of an apartment complex in Saudi Arabia that housed American servicemen and their families. Nineteen Americans died in the explosion, a grievous loss, but even worse casualties were suffered when Al Qaeda terrorists attacked the American embassies in Kenya and Tanzania in August 1998, killing 224 and wounding over 5,000.

Following that attack, President Clinton ordered missile strikes against bin Laden and his training camps in Afghanistan. The attacks destroyed the camps but did not deter bin Laden or terrorism. Threats and rumors of schemes to attack American targets continued, and in October 2000 those associated with bin Laden damaged the American destroyer U.S.S. *Cole* while it was at anchor in a Yemen port. Seventeen sailors died, and over thirty were injured.

Unknown to American intelligence, in 1999 a group of terrorists in Germany led by Mohammed Atta were already formulating their plan to attack the United States. For more than a year, the nineteen known terrorists who hijacked the planes on September 11, 2001, lived openly in the United States, several of them taking lessons at U.S. flight schools to become airline pilots. In 2004, a congressional investigation concluded that the 9/11 attacks might have been prevented if intelligence and law enforcements had exchanged information and given the possibility of a terrorist attack on the United States a higher priority.

As the magnitude of the September 11 disasters unfolded, another kind of deadly attack took place, this time focusing American fears on bioterrorism. Letters tainted with deadly **anthrax** spores were being sent through the mail. The first case of anthrax infection, and death, occurred in Florida in September 2001, when a letter containing anthrax was sent to a media company. Other cases appeared in October, including an exposure at the NBC Nightly News headquarters in New York and one in Senator Tom Daschle's office in Washington, D.C. By the end of October, three people had died of anthrax, thirteen others had been infected, and twenty-eight had tested positive for exposure. Many people assumed that bin Laden was behind the anthrax letters, and fears and rumors of more terrorist attacks spread across the country. Later, investigators concluded that the anthrax letters were most likely the work of an unknown domestic terrorist. In the wake of the 9/11 attacks and the repeated anthrax alerts, it seemed that America's sense of safety had been lost and was being replaced with feelings of vulnerability and fear. Sales of guns, gas masks, and biological warfare detection kits increased. Assaults and threats against Arab Americans and

anthrax An infectious disease caused by spore-forming bacteria. Usually associated with livestock, anthrax can be contracted through touching or breathing anthrax spores and can be deadly to humans.

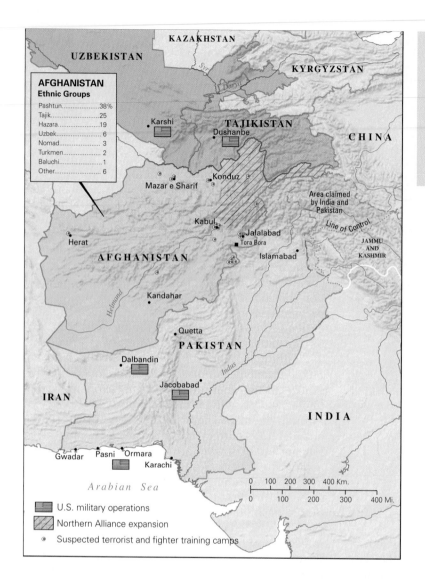

MAP 31.3 Afghanistan Not long after 9/11, the Bush administration was able to link the attacks on the Pentagon and World Trade Center to the terrorist organization Al Qaeda. When Taliban leaders refused to turn over bin Laden and other Al Qaeda leaders, the United States and its allies joined with anti-Taliban forces in a military action in Afghanistan. By the end of December 2001, the Taliban government and Al Qaeda forces had collapsed, although leaders of both organizations eluded capture.

those who looked Middle Eastern occurred. The Justice Department, in the eleven months following 9/11, arrested over 1,200 immigrants, mostly from Arab nations. Defending the action, Attorney General Ashcroft stated: "Taking suspected terrorists in violation of the law off the streets and keeping them locked up is our clear strategy to prevent terrorism within our borders."

Inside the White House, planning had started on how best to fight global terrorism. Some in the administration called for an immediate military response against bin Laden and other supporters of terrorism throughout the Middle East, especially Iraq. Secretary of State Powell led another faction, urging the president to move more slowly and build an international coalition based on evidence of bin Laden's role in the September 11 attacks. "We can't

solve everything with one blow," stated a White House supporter of Powell's position.

President Bush took both paths. He began planning for a major strike to remove the **Taliban** government in Afghanistan, which was protecting Osama bin Laden, and to capture the terrorist leader. At the same time, he worked to form a global coalition that would take action against terrorists in their own countries and would accept, if not support, an American military retaliation. The effort to build a global

Taliban An organization of Muslim fundamentalists that gained control over Afghanistan in 1996 after the Soviets withdrew and which established a strict Islamic government.

In the war on terrorism, American forces joined with anti-Taliban forces in Afghanistan in attacking government and Al Qaeda forces. In this picture, American Special Forces personnel work with members of the Northern Alliance in directing operations north of the capital city of Kabul. © *Sigma/Corbis.*

coalition against terrorism was extremely successful, with nearly every nation agreeing to cooperate in rooting out terrorism at home. As expected, however, fewer nations agreed to participate in the military dimension of a war on terrorism. Without hesitation, British prime minister Tony Blair offered direct military support to attack terrorist targets, noting that more than two hundred British citizens had been killed in the attack on the World Trade Center. France, Germany, Australia, and Canada also agreed to supply some type of military support.

On October 7, 2001, the United States and Britain launched bombing and missile attacks on selected targets in Afghanistan. On the ground, American military and Special Forces units provided support to anti-Taliban groups, especially the Northern Alliance, which held a section of northeast Afghanistan. By mid-November the major cities of Mazar-i-Sharif and Kabul were under Northern Alliance control, and the Taliban government had collapsed. By January 2002 a new interim government for Afghanistan had been established, hundreds of Taliban and Al Qaeda fighters had been captured, and Al Qaeda positions in the Tora Bora Mountains were under relentless attack. However, the whereabouts of Osama bin Laden remained unknown, and some speculated that he had successfully fled Afghanistan (see Map 31.3). Despite U.S. success in Afghanistan, President Bush reminded Americans that the war against terrorism had just begun and that the search for Osama bin Laden, Al Qaeda, and other terrorist organizations would continue around the globe.

As the assault on the Taliban commenced, Bush reassured the world that this was not an attack on Islam but an attack on terrorists and those who harbored them. He told the American people that the war against terrorism would be lengthy, multifaceted, and not limited to actions in Afghanistan. He also warned there could be more acts of terrorism against the United States and appointed Tom Ridge, the governor of Pennsylvania, to assume the new post of director of homeland security. Ridge's job was to coordinate and direct various governmental agencies in efforts to prevent further acts of terrorism against the United States. The administration's efforts to deter and apprehend terrorists were improved on October 26, 2001, when Congress passed the **USA Patriot Act.** The Patriot Act provided law-enforcement agencies wider discretion in dealing with those suspected of terrorism; loosened restrictions on wiretaps, monitoring the Internet, and searches; and allowed the Attorney General's Office to detain and deport noncitizens thought to be a security risk. The passage of the act and the decision to try noncitizens accused of terrorism in military courts caused some to protest

USA Patriot Act (Uniting and Strengthening America by Providing Appropriate Tools Required to Intercept and Obstruct Terrorism) Legislation passed by Congress in 2001 that reduced constraints on the Justice Department and other law-enforcement agencies in dealing with individuals who had suspected links to terrorism.

that the new rules were a threat to civil liberties and unconstitutional. Those against the act pointed to cases of Arab Americans being targeted because of public anxiety and not solid evidence. In Houston, for example, two Palestinian Americans were detained for two months because their passports looked suspicious—they were released after tests showed that their passports were valid. Most Americans, however, agreed with the government and supported the new, tougher antiterrorism measures.

Bush vowed that the United States would continue the war on terrorism, saying that the world was still full of "dangerous killers . . . set to go off without warning." Focusing on what he termed an "axis of evil," he referred to Iraq, Iran, and North Korea as nations that represented threats to world peace. To protect the nation, he asked for large increases in security spending for the military and for homeland defense. He admitted that such spending would result in a deficit but maintained that the price of freedom was "never too high." "We have clear priorities," he told Americans in his State of the Union address in January 2002. "History has called America . . . to action, and it is both our responsibility and our privilege to fight freedom's fight."

To those most involved in shaping "freedom's fight," it was clear that the United States needed to implement a new aspect of national security policy—the **preemptive strike.** In the war on terrorism, the nation could not wait until an attack came; it must take positive steps to halt such attacks before they occurred. Clinton's policy had been "reflexive pullback," said Secretary of Defense Donald Rumsfeld, but the Bush policy would be "forward-leaning." The reasons for the focus on Iraq and Saddam Hussein were varied. Saddam was unfinished business, left over from the war to liberate Kuwait. He was a vile dictator who had used chemical and biological weapons against his enemies, including citizens of his own country, and it was thought that he still possessed **weapons of mass destruction** and was also trying to obtain nuclear weapons. By March 2002, a consensus was developing within the administration that Saddam did have weapons of mass destruction, that he represented a direct threat to American interests in the Middle East, and that he had links to Al Qaeda. Many within the administration also believed that the United States should use force, if necessary, to remove Saddam from power, and steps were being implemented to build up American military capabilities in the Persian Gulf region. Those advocating the use of force, however, were faced with opposition from Secretary of State Powell and most of the inter-

national community, who favored diplomacy, the tightening of United Nations economic sanctions, and the reestablishment of United Nations weapons inspectors in Iraq to determine if Saddam did indeed have weapons of mass destruction.

Pressured by the United Nations and Bush's threat to use force, Saddam promised cooperation and agreed to allow the weapons inspectors back into Iraq. There was little cooperation forthcoming, and the weapons inspectors found nothing, but they could not rule out that Iraq did not have such weapons. Claiming that American and British intelligence sources proved the weapons did exist, the Bush administration argued that it was fruitless to continue diplomacy and that the United Nations must demand that Iraq comply immediately and allow full access to arms inspection teams and reveal the existence of any weapons of mass destruction. Speaking just before the first anniversary of 9/11, Vice President Cheney warned that "time is not on our side." He stated that Iraq was reviving its "nuclear weapons program" and that it "directly threatened the United States." Condoleezza Rice said that although the status of Saddam Hussein's nuclear weapons project was not known, "We don't want the smoking gun to be a mushroom cloud." In October 2002, stressing the threat of weapons of mass destruction, Bush obtained a congressional resolution permitting the use of force against Iraq. A majority of the public agreed that Iraq was a real threat and part of the terrorist war against the United States. With American troop strength in the Persian Gulf reaching about 250,000 in March 2003, the Bush administration, tired of playing "pattycake" with the United Nations and Iraq, gave Saddam Hussein notice to leave the country within forty-eight hours. If he did not, he would face a military onslaught that would "shock and awe" those who witnessed it.

Hoping to shorten the war by removing Saddam and his henchmen, on March 20, 2003, Bush launched an attack on Baghdad buildings believed to be housing Saddam and many members of his government. The raid failed to kill Saddam but served as the be-

---

preemptive strike Policy adopted by the Bush administration allowing the United States to use force against suspected threats before the threats occurred.

weapons of mass destruction Nuclear, chemical, and biological weapons that have the potential to injure or kill large numbers of people—civilians as well as military personnel.

On March 20, 2003, U.S. and British forces crossed from Kuwait into Iraq in the second Iraq war. (*Left*) By May 1, on board the U.S.S. *Abraham Lincoln,* President Bush declared the war in Iraq over. But for thousands of American soldiers in Iraq, the conflict continued as insurgents continued the struggle. (*Right*) An Iraqi armed with a rocket-propelled grenade (RPG) stands by a burning vehicle in Basra. Between May 2003 and October 2004, more Americans have been killed in Iraq than during the "official" war. *Left: © Joseph Sohm; Visions of America/CORBIS. Right: © ATEF HASSAN/Reuters/Corbis.*

ginning of an aerial and land campaign to free Iraq of Saddam Hussein and establish a new and democratic Iraqi nation. Advancing up the Tigris and Euphrates Rivers toward Baghdad, U.S. army and marine troops met moderate resistance from regular and irregular Iraqi units. However, there was never any doubt of the outcome. The Iraqis were outmatched in every category, and on April 9, Baghdad was in American hands. Saddam and his government fled into hiding. The official war ended, and the task of building a stable and democratic Iraq began. A public opinion poll found that an overwhelming number of Americans considered the war a success and approved of Bush as president. Unfortunately, the war was not over, and the battle to remake Iraq was much more difficult than toppling Saddam Hussein.

It quickly became apparent that American planners and forces were not well prepared for the duties of occupation. There were not enough soldiers and not enough planning. Damage to the Iraqi infrastructure caused by the war, **saboteurs,** and looters was extensive and not easily or quickly fixed. Although most Iraqis thanked the United States for Saddam's removal—he was found hiding in a small "spider hole" in the ground on December 14, 2003, and taken into custody—they quickly grew impatient with the occupation. They criticized the slowness in restoring electricity, water, and other necessities and, importantly, the lack of security. Many disagreed with the U.S.-selected interim government and called for the formation of an Islamic-based government and state.

Occupation costs swelled to almost $4 billion a month, and it became necessary to extend the tour of duty for many American troops to provide security and fight guerrilla insurgents, some of whom entered Iraq just to fight Americans. The goal of the insurgents was to attack American and allied forces, forcing them to withdraw from Iraq. Initially, much of the resistance came from pro-Hussein elements centered in the Sunni Triangle north and east of Baghdad, but it soon spread to most of the country (see Map 31.4). Using car bombs and hit-and-run tactics, the insurgents ambushed American troops and attacked Iraqi civilians and security forces. The number of dead and wounded increased daily, and by June more Americans had been killed during the occupation than during the official fighting. American losses, however,

saboteurs Individuals who damage property or interfere with procedures to obstruct productivity and normal functions.

paled in comparison to Iraqis, who had lost over 10,000 people since the end of the official hositilities.

Making the situation more complicated, in April 2004 anti-American radical Shiite religious leader Moktada al-Sadr called for his followers to "terrorize your enemies," with the goal of ending the occupation and creating an Islamic republic. Al-Sadr's private militia launched attacks on occupation forces in several cities near and south of Baghdad. "The occupation is over," yelled supporters on the streets, "Americans should stay out." In mid-June, the United States turned over political control of Iraq to a civilian interim government, promising to support the Iraqis as they regained control of their nation and to continue to provide necessary peacekeeping forces. The turnover of authority did little to halt the violence. Throughout August and September, American forces continued to confront insurgents across the country and take casualities, causing some analysts to argue that the number of insurgents had doubled or tripled since April. Many Americans now doubted that the war for Iraq would be easily won and feared that it would be years before American troops could come home.

With slightly more than two months to go before the scheduled January 30, 2005, Iraqi national elections, American and Iraqi forces attacked major insurgent centers in the town of Falluja. Some saw the battle as a microcosm for the problems the United States faced in Iraq. American forces in bitter, street-to-street fighting took control of the city, but many feared there would be no reduction of the insurgency, and unless the city was made safe and its economy rebuilt, many of its near 300,000 population would continue to oppose the American occupation, boycott the elections, and resist the national government. Even if the struggle for Falluja was successful, no one thought the American presence in Iraq or the war on terrorism would end soon—both would remain long-term commitments of American foreign policy.

A Political Race

Like his father, George W. Bush enjoyed a high public approval rate for his actions in fighting terrorism and as the official war in Iraq ended in mid-April 2003. And like his father, the president also faced a worsening economic condition as employment continued to fall, almost as fast as the deficit grew. The parallel encouraged several Democrats to run for the presidency. Howard Dean, former governor of Vermont, began the assault on the Bush-Cheney ticket, focusing not only on the economy but also on Bush's Iraqi policy. Dean found growing public support for the view that Bush

had rushed to war and had dramatically oversold the danger that Saddam Hussein and his alleged weapons of mass destruction posed to the United States. Dean energized many Democrats, but it was the campaign of the more politically experienced and better-funded Senator John Kerry of Massachusetts that swept through the primaries. By April 2004, Kerry's two primary rivals, Howard Dean and North Carolina senator John Edwards, had ended their campaigns and thrown their support to Kerry. In July, Kerry chose Edwards to be his vice-presidential candidate.

The health of the economy was a critical issue. The recession that started in March 2001 had been declared officially over in November 2001, but to many Americans it seemed as if the economic news was worsening. "We've declared victory over the recession," said a Democratic representative, but "we're still laying off a couple of hundred thousand workers a month." It was a jobless recovery, compounded by a growing number of American businesses outsourcing their products to foreign workers. Overall, in 2002, the poverty rate increased to 12.1 percent from a low of 11.3 percent in 2000 while household incomes fell by 3.4 percent. By the summer of 2004, however, the economy was improving, spurred forward by low interest rates, the president's tax cuts, and military spending, which had pushed up overall federal spending by 25 percent. Still, many argued that it was a selective recovery and that the number of new jobs being created lagged behind demand and that real wages continued to decline. In June 2004, a majority of those polled believed that Kerry and the Democrats could deal with the economic problems better than the Bush administration.

Also by the summer of 2004, politicians and the public were both questioning the president's Iraqi policies, especially his rationale for going to war. No weapons of mass destruction had been found in Iraq, and various sources agreed that the intelligence committee had overestimated Iraq's capabilities, giving the White House incorrect information on Iraq's weapons of mass destruction. Several Republican and Democratic congressmen said they would not have voted for war and would have supported further United Nations efforts if they had known the truth about Saddam Hussein's weapons program. Bush responded to the growing criticism of his decision to go to war by stating that weapons of mass destruction would be found and by emphasizing that Iraq had the potential to develop such weapons and had connections with Al Qaeda. Most important, the administration argued that regime change, the removal of the dictator Saddam Hussein, was worth

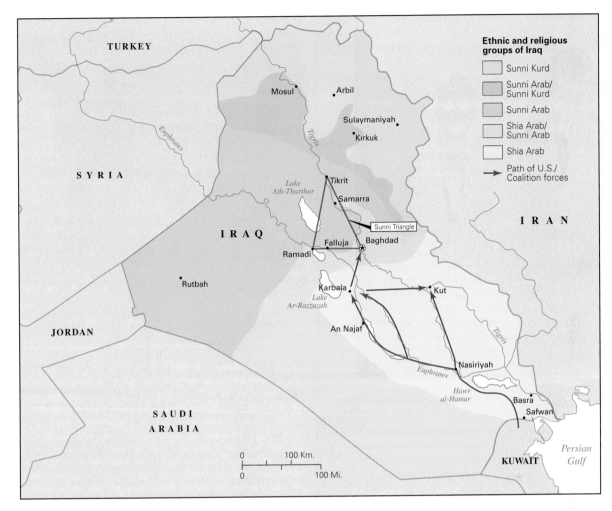

MAP 31.4 Second Iraq War Saddam Hussein's regime collapsed within weeks of the beginning of the invasion north along the Tigris and Euphrates Rivers. Although the official hostilities ended, insurgents continued to resist the American occupation and the control of the interim Iraqi government, especially in the Sunni Triangle.

the war. However, even as the administration tried to focus attention on the importance of regime change and building a democratic Iraq, public opinion became more and more critical of the president's handling of the war, and costs of the U.S. military occupation.

As the political campaigns heated up during the summer of 2004, Kerry argued that he would have the best policies to fix the economy, improve society, and restore international support for American foreign policy. Bush and his supporters emphasized the rebounding economy, arguing that the president's tax cuts were responsible. On Iraq, Bush stated, "We acted. We led," and accused Kerry of having no real foreign-policy experience or policies. Republicans also attempted to energize the cultural war of previous campaigns, using the issue of gay marriage.

In November 2003, the Massachusetts Supreme Court ruled that banning same-sex marriage violated the state's constitution and stated that the state legislature had 180 days to act on the Court's decision. In April the Massachusetts legislature approved a constitutional amendment that would permit same-sex civil unions but defined marriage as a union only between a man and a woman. Because the amendment could not be ratified until 2006, Massachusetts became the first state to issue marriage licenses to same-sex couples. Gay and lesbian couples rushed to get married. The response across the nation was generally negative, with thirty-five states hurrying to strengthen legislation or to pass amendments to their constitutions that would prevent same-sex marriage. In most states, laws against same-sex marriage already

Having received Kerry's call conceding the election, President Bush and Vice President Cheney address the crowd at a victory celebration.

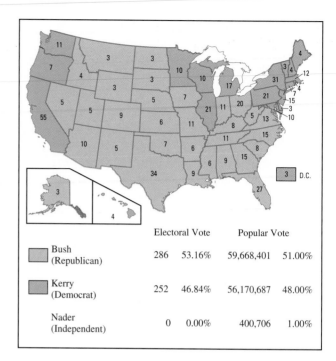

	Electoral Vote		Popular Vote	
Bush (Republican)	286	53.16%	59,668,401	51.00%
Kerry (Democrat)	252	46.84%	56,170,687	48.00%
Nader (Independent)	0	0.00%	400,706	1.00%

MAP 31.5 Election of 2004 With more people voting than in any previous election, George W. Bush stated "results really do matter" and argued that his 51 percent of the popular vote represented a mandate from the people for the vision of America which he presented during the hard fought presidential campaign. Unlike the results of the 2000 election, President Bush defeated John Kerry in both the popular and electoral vote with the third party candidacy of Ralph Nader having virtually no impact on the election results. While many thought that the economy and the war in Iraq would play key roles in deciding the vote, many post-election polls indicated that the primary factors for many voters were moral and family issues.

existed, based on the 1996 federal **Defense of Marriage Act,** which bans federal recognition of same-sex marriages and allows states to ignore such marriages performed in other states. In addition, many opponents of same-sex marriage believed that **civil unions,** allowing legal, medical, and financial benefits to same-sex partners, should also be banned. In February 2004, President Bush endorsed the idea of a constitutional amendment that would restrict marriage to two people of the opposite sex. John Kerry, a Roman Catholic, took the position that it should be left to the states to legislate on the issue and said that he personally opposed same-sex marriage but supported the right for a civil union. In July, the Senate failed to approve a House bill creating a constitutional amendment banning gay marriage while public opinion polls indicated that among most Americans the gay and lesbian marriage issue held little priority. Nonetheless, many Republicans continued claims that Kerry's nonsupport for the constitutional ban proved he was too liberal and his values did not reflect those of the majority of the nation.

Targeting their efforts at battleground, swing states, both parties poured vast amounts of time and campaign money into a few states. With increasingly venomous campaign ads, the candidates and their representatives paid repeated visits to states like Pennsylvania, Ohio, Florida, and Wisconsin, trying

Defense of Marriage Act Passed in 1996, the law defines marriage as between a man and a woman for the purpose of federal law, and prevents other jurisdictions (states, counties, cities) from being forced to accept any other definition of marriage.

civil unions Term for a civil status similar to marriage and provides homosexual couples access to the benefits enjoyed by married heterosexuals.

to lure a few more votes into their column. Days before the election, most polls showed the candidates tied in popular support. Voters who placed an emphasis on fighting terrorism and the war in Iraq slightly favored President Bush, while those focusing on domestic issues gave Kerry a small lead. Some Democrats, however, found hope, if not an omen, in the Boston Red Sox winning their first world series since 1918. Adding to the election drama were significantly large numbers of people registering to vote for the first time and pre-election allegations of voter fraud. Some worried that as in the 2000 election, the winner might not be known until days after the election.

On November 2, 2004, more Americans voted than ever before and re-elected George W. Bush with 51 percent of the vote (see Map 31.5). Bush had effectively mobilized his party's loyalists and won most of the battleground states, but to the surprise of most observers, a majority of those supporting Bush stated that moral issues and family values were critical reasons for voting. Supporting this observation, in Ohio—

which was critical to the president's reelection—and ten other states, voters affirmed their support for constitutional amendments to state constitutions prohibiting same-sex marriages and unions. "Make no mistake—conservative Christians and 'value voters' won this election," stated Richard Viguerie, who had pioneered the direct-mail strategy that contributed to the emergence of the New Right.

With larger Republican majorities in the House of Representatives and the Senate, President Bush said he was eager to use his "political capital" to implement policies which promoted an "ownership society" that placed more control in the hands of individuals regarding health care, social security retirement funds, and education. "Now comes the revolution," voiced some conservatives when the president announced that strengthening family values and reforming social security, tax codes, and education were agenda priorities. Others argued that with the on-going war against terrorism, the conflict in Iraq, and a soaring deficit, he should reach out to Democrats and moderates fostering bipartisanship.

Individual Voices

Examining a Primary Source

President George W. Bush Consoles a Nation

History is full of dates, but only a few have special meaning to a whole society. Such days usually are connected with a great tragedy or a thrilling triumph. September 11, 2001, will probably be one of those dates in American history—one that people will remember without the prompting of a history book. To commemorate that tragic day, on September 14, 2001, President George W. Bush spoke at the National Cathedral in Washington, D.C., joining millions of others who were observing a National Day of Prayer and Remembrance in churches, synagogues, mosques, and other places of worship all across the United States. In his remarks, he not only lamented a nation's sorrow but stated a nation's determination to exact justice on those who had attacked the soul of America.

On Tuesday, our country was attacked with deliberate and massive cruelty. We have seen the images of fire and ashes, and bent steel.

Now come the names, the list of casualties we are only beginning to read. They are the names of men and women who began their day at a desk or in an airport, busy with life. They are the names of people who faced death, and in their last moments called home to say, be brave, and I love you. . . .

■ *How does President Bush characterize the perpetrators of the September 11 attacks?*

Just three days removed from these events, Americans do not yet have the distance of history. But our responsibility to history is already clear: to answer these attacks and rid the world of evil.

War has been waged against us by stealth and deceit and murder. This nation is peaceful, but fierce when stirred to anger. This conflict was begun on the timing and terms of others. It will end in a way, and at an hour, of our choosing. . . . ■

It is said that adversity introduces us to ourselves. This is true of a nation as well. In this trial, we have been reminded, and the world has seen, that our fellow Americans are generous and kind, resourceful and brave. We see our national character in rescuers working past exhaustion; in long lines of blood donors; in thousands of citizens who have asked to work and serve in any way possible.

■ *If Father Mychal Judge had been able to address the crowd gathered in the cathedral, how might his speech have differed from the president's?*

And we have seen our national character in eloquent acts of sacrifice. Inside the World Trade Center, one man who could have saved himself stayed until the end at the side of his quadriplegic friend. A beloved priest died giving the last rites to a firefighter. Two office workers, finding a disabled stranger, carried her down sixty-eight floors to safety. . . . ■

In these acts, and in many others, Americans showed a deep commitment to one another, and an abiding love for our country. Today, we feel what Franklin Roosevelt called the warm courage of national unity. . . .

It has joined together political parties in both houses of Congress. It is evident in services of prayer and candlelight vigils, and American flags, which are displayed in pride, and wave in defiance. ■

■ *How does President Bush want the American people to respond to the attacks?*

Our unity is a kinship of grief, and a steadfast resolve to prevail against our enemies. . . .

America is a nation full of good fortune, with so much to be grateful for. But we are not spared from suffering. In every generation, the world has produced enemies of human freedom. They have attacked America, because we are freedom's home and defender. And the commitment of our fathers is now the calling of our time. . . . ■

■ *Who, according to President Bush, are the victims of the terrorist attacks?*

Summary

Clinton's chief political adviser, James Carvell, said during the 1992 election that the central issue was the economy, and he was right. Throughout the 1990s, it was the economy that shaped political and social issues. At the beginning of the decade, a shifting and slowing economy provided new opportunities and old challenges; it underlined divisions within the nation, contributing to what some called an hourglass-shaped society. Those at the top of society continued to prosper, while others, including the middle class, worried about their and their children's future. In urban areas, changes in the economy, continuing poverty, and reduced social services created a volatile and dangerous environment. The debate over the causes and cures of social problems continued to divide liberals and conservatives, and provided the framework for political debate.

The 1992 presidential election, however, was more about economics than social values as people voted their pocketbooks. It was the economy that helped to elect Clinton, and it was the economy that helped to reelect him and that saved him from being removed from office following his impeachment.

Clinton's first administration provided images of indecisiveness and ineffective leadership as efforts to expand the welfare state by implementing a national healthcare system failed. Clinton's political problems worsened in 1994 when Republicans gained control of Congress and announced their "Contract with America" legislative agenda. Clinton, however, proved politically adept in moving toward the political center and painting Republicans as extremists. After facing down Republicans over the budget, Clinton shifted again and adopted aspects of the Republican Party's plans for the budget and welfare reform. His political shifts, a resurgent economy, and a successful foreign policy made his reelection over Bob Dole almost a sure thing.

The political momentum Clinton gained in the 1996 election was soon lost, however, when he became entangled in the Monica Lewinsky scandal. In a partisan debate, the House of Representatives voted to impeach the president, but he survived the Senate trial, remaining in office; throughout it all, to the amazement of many, he stayed popular with the public. Contributing to Clinton's popularity and high approval ratings was a booming economy that restored prosperity, reduced poverty, and resulted in a balanced budget and a smaller national debt.

Seeing the benefits Clinton had gained, during the 2000 presidential election both Gore and Bush moved to occupy the political center of their parties. The closeness of the election only seemed to strengthen the view of some political observers that while the "age of the New Deal" was over, there was little support for eliminating or reducing government programs. As President Bush implemented a tax cut and sought legislation on education and other agenda items, the nation was overwhelmed by the events of 9/11.

On September 11, 2001, terrorists affiliated with Osama bin Laden attacked the World Trade Center and the Pentagon, killing over three thousand people. Soon after that shock, anthrax-laced letters put the postal system and the country at large on high alert. The nation was under siege, and the Bush administration responded by establishing an Office of Homeland Security to secure Americans from further terrorist attacks at home, and a global coalition to fight terrorist organizations abroad. In October 2001 the United States joined forces with others, including anti-Taliban elements in Afghanistan, to conduct a successful war that brought down the Taliban government and much of the Al Qaeda organization—although Osama bin Laden himself remained at large.

As the war in Afghanistan ended, the Bush administration focused its concern on Saddam Hussein and Iraq. Claiming that the dictator possessed weapons of mass destruction and was linked to Al Qaeda, the United States set plans in motion to remove Saddam from power. In March 2003, having moved a quarter of a million American troops to the Persian Gulf region, President Bush gave the order to invade Iraq. The second Iraq war lasted less than three weeks. Saddam Hussein's government was toppled. It was a job well done, Bush told military personnel and the public. However, the effort to transform Iraq into a stable, Western-style democracy and society met with growing opposition from Saddam supporters and a variety of anti-American elements, several important Islamic religious leaders, and the Iraqi public. American soldiers and Iraqis came under attack from insurgents, and as the violence continued and American casualties increased, more and more Americans began to question the American role in Iraq and the justifications for the war.

Growing dissatisfaction with Bush's Iraqi policy paralleled an increasing frustration with the president's handling of the economy. Although the recession had ended, there was little real economic growth, and many Americans watched as their jobs were shipped to foreign countries. Both of these developments caused John Kerry and Democrats to hope that history would repeat itself and that George Walker Bush would follow in the one-term footsteps of his father. In November, Democrats not only lost their wish as Bush received 51 percent of the vote but watched as Republicans gained seats in the House and Senate. Speaking of a political mandate, many Republicans hoped that George W. Bush's second term would not only continue its effective foreign policy and war on terrorism, but emphasize a more conservative approach to domestic issues, placing more control in the hands of individuals and state and local governments while limiting the responsibilities of the federal government. Whatever course President Bush took, all agreed, he would continue to make America.

CHAPTER 1 Making a "New" World, to 1588

Marvin B. Becker. *Civility and Society in Western Europe, 1300–1600* (1988).
A brief but comprehensive look at social conditions in Europe during the period leading up to and out of the exploration of the New World.

Alfred W. Crosby. *The Columbian Exchange: Biological and Cultural Consequences of 1492* (1972).
The landmark book that brought the Columbian impact into focus for the first time. Parts of the book are technical, but the explanations are clear and exciting.

Alvin M. Josephy. *America in 1492: The World of the Indian Peoples before the Arrival of Columbus* (1992).
An overview of American civilizations prior to Columbus's and subsequent European intrusions. Nicely written, comprehensive, and engaging.

Kupperman, Karen Ordahl, ed. *America in European Consciousness, 1493–1750* (1995).
A collection of essays by leading scholars tracing the impact of America on the European intellectual world from the time of discovery through the colonization period.

William H. McNeill. *Plagues and Peoples* (1976).
A fascinating history of disease and its impact on people throughout the period of European expansion and New World colonization.

Roland Oliver and J. D. Fage. *A Short History of Africa* (1988).
The most concise and understandably written comprehensive history of Africa available.

CHAPTER 2 A Continent on the Move, 1400–1725

Peter N. Moogk. *La Nouvelle France: The Making of French Canada—A Cultural History* (2000).
An excellent overview of French activities in Canada during the colonial era.

Oliver A. Rink. *Holland on the Hudson: An Economic and Social History of Dutch New York* (1986).
A comprehensive overview of Dutch colonial activities in New Netherland with an emphasis on both the activities of the Dutch West India Company and private traders in creating the culture of Dutch New York.

Daniel H. Usner, Jr. *Indians, Settlers, and Slaves in a Frontier Exchange Economy: The Lower Mississippi Valley before 1783* (1992).
A highly acclaimed study of the complex world of colonial Louisiana.

David Weber. *The Spanish Frontier in North America* (1992).
A broad synthesis of the history of New Spain by the foremost scholar in the field.

Richard White. *The Middle Ground: Indians, Empires, and Republics in the Great Lakes Region, 1650–1815* (1991).
Although it covers material far beyond the chronological scope of this chapter, students interested in the relations between Indians and Europeans in the colonial era will find this book extraordinarily rich.

CHAPTER 3 Founding the English Colonies in the Eighteenth Century, 1585–1732

Philip Barbour. *Pocahontas and Her World* (1970).
A factual account of the life of an American Indian princess celebrated in folklore.

Elaine G. Breslaw. *Tituba, Reluctant Witch of Salem: Devilish Indians and Puritan Fantasies* (1996).
The author reconstructs the life of the Caribbean-born Indian slave who was a central figure in the Salem witch trials.

John Demos. *A Little Commonwealth: Family Life in Plymouth Colony* (1970).
A beautifully written and very engaging portrait of family and community life in Plymouth Plantations.

Kai T. Erikson. *Wayward Puritans: A Study in the Sociology of Deviance* (1966).
The author discovers the values and ideals of Massachusetts Puritan society by examining the behavior and ideas these Puritans condemned, including witchcraft and Quakerism.

Mary Beth Norton. *In the Devil's Snare* (2003).
Unlike earlier scholars of the Salem witch trials, Norton places the events of 1692 in the context of European imperial rivalries, especially the intense struggles between England and France for control of North America.

CHAPTER 4 The English Colonies in the Eighteenth Century, 1689–1763

Bernard Bailyn. *Voyagers to the West: A Passage in the Peopling of America on the Eve of the Revolution* (1986).
Bailyn won a Pulitzer Prize for this survey of the character of, and motives for, emigration from the British Isles to America during the eighteenth century.

Patricia Bonomi. *Under the Cope of Heaven: Religion, Society, and Politics in Colonial America* (1986).
Bonomi provides an overview of the role of religion in colonial society and a close look at the leaders of the Great Awakening and the impact of that religious revival movement on pre-Revolutionary politics in the 1760s and 1770s.

Richard Hofstadter. *America at 1750: A Social Portrait* (1971).
This highly accessible work includes chapters on indentured servitude, the slave trade, the middle-class world of the colonies, the Great Awakening, and population growth and immigration patterns.

Thomas A. Lewis. *For King and Country: The Maturing of George Washington, 1748–1760* (1993).
This look at the early career of George Washington follows him as a colonial soldier of the Crown, a Virginia planter, and a young man of ambition.

Jane T. Merritt. *At the Crossroads: Indians and Empires on a Mid-Atlantic Frontier, 1700–1763* (2003).
Merritt takes a close look at the interaction between Indians and colonists in the backcountry of Pennsylvania and narrates the growing tensions between settlers and Native Americans.

Betty Wood. *The Origins of American Slavery* (1998).
This is a brief but excellent look at the use of enslaved labor in the West Indies and in the English mainland colonies and at the laws that arose to institutionalize slavery.

CHAPTER 5 Deciding Where Loyalties Lie, 1763–1776

Carol Berkin. *Revolutionary Mothers: Women in the Struggle for America's Independence* (2005).

This book recounts the role of colonial women in the boycotts of the 1760s and 1770s. In separate chapters it tells the story of Indian, African American, and Loyalist women as well as the stories of camp followers, generals' wives, spies, and female soldiers during the Revolution.

Colin G. Calloway. *The American Revolution in Indian Country: Crisis and Diversity in Native American Communities* (1995).
A well-written account of the variety of Indian experiences during the American revolutionary era.

Edward Countryman. *The American Revolution* (1985).
An excellent narrative of the causes and consequences of the Revolutionary War.

David Hackett Fischer. *Paul Revere's Ride* (1994).
This lively account details the circumstances and background of the efforts to rouse the countryside in response to the march of British troops toward Lexington.

Woody Holton. *Forced Founders: Indians, Debtors, Slaves and the Making of the American Revolution in Virginia* (1999).
Holton provides a new interpretation of the factors that went into transforming wealthy planters into revolutionaries. He examines the importance of mounting debts, fear of slave revolts and Indian attacks, and pressures from small farmers in radicalizing the men we often think of as leading "founding fathers."

"Liberty!" PBS series on the American Revolution.
Using the actual words of revolutionaries, loyalists, and British political leaders, this six-hour series follows events from the Stamp Act to the Constitution.

Pauline Maier. *American Scripture: Making the Declaration of Independence* (1998).
This path-breaking book points out that the ideas expressed in the Declaration of Independence were widely accepted by Americans, and proclaimed in state declarations of independence before Jefferson set them down in July 1776. Maier also traces the history of the Declaration in the decades following the revolution.

Edmund Morgan. *Benjamin Franklin* (2002).
A distinguished historian of colonial America draws a compelling portrait of Benjamin Franklin, following the printer-writer-scientist-diplomat through major crises and turning points in his life and the life of his country.

CHAPTER 6 Recreating America: Independence and a New Nation, 1775–1783

Sylvia Frey. *Water From a Rock: Black Resistance in a Revolutionary Age* (1991).
This scholar of African American religion and culture examines the experiences of African Americans during the Revolution and the repression that followed in the Southern states that continued to rely on slave labor.

Joseph Plumb Martin. *Ordinary Courage: The Revolutionary War Adventures of Joseph Plumb Martin,* ed. James Kirby Martin (1993).
The military experiences of a Massachusetts soldier who served with the Continental Army during the American Revolution.

William Nelson. *The American Tory* (1961).
An account of those who chose to align themselves with the British during the war.

Charles Royster. *A Revolutionary People at War: The Continental Army and American Character, 1775–1783* (1996).
Royster's in-depth account of military life during the Revolution provides insights into both the American character and the changing understanding of the political ideals of the war among the common soldiers.

Alfred Young. *The Shoemaker and the Tea Party: Memory and the American Revolution* (2000).

Young looks at the memories of an aging shoemaker who witnessed the Boston Tea Party. These memories reveal the meaning of the Revolution to ordinary Americans.

CHAPTER 7 Competing Visions of the Virtuous Republic, 1770–1796

Carol Berkin. *A Brilliant Solution: Inventing the American Constitution* (2002).
A highly readable account of the crises that led to the constitutional convention and the men who created a new national government.

Lyman Butterfield, et al., eds. *The Book of Abigail and John: Selected Letters of the Adams Family, 1762–1784* (1975).
The editors of the Adams Papers have collected part of the extensive correspondence between John and Abigail Adams during the critical decades of the independence movement.

Joseph Ellis. *Founding Brothers: The Revolutionary Generation* (2002).
An award-winning study of the most notable leaders of the American Revolution, and an examination of their political ideas and actions.

Richard B. Morris. *Witness at the Creation* (1985).
A distinguished scholar re-creates the drama of the Constitutional Convention by focusing on the personalities and motives of the framers.

Thomas P. Slaughter. *The Whiskey Rebellion* (1986).
A vivid account of the major challenge to the Washington government.

Gary Wills. *Cincinnatus: George Washington and the Enlightenment* (1984).
A beautifully written intellectual biography of America's first president and his times.

CHAPTER 8 The Early Republic, 1796–1804

Stephen E. Ambrose. *Undaunted Courage: Meriwether Lewis, Thomas Jefferson, and the Opening of the American West* (1996).
A critically acclaimed and highly readable narrative exploring the relationship between Jefferson and Lewis and their efforts to acquire and explore Louisiana.

Alexander DeConde. *This Affair of Louisiana* (1976).
Dated, but still the best overview of the diplomacy surrounding the Louisiana Purchase.

Joseph J. Ellis. *American Sphinx: The Character of Thomas Jefferson* (1996).
Winner of the National Book Award, this biography focuses on Jefferson's personality seeking to expose his inner character; highly readable.

Joanne B. Freeman. *Affairs of Honor: National Politics in the New Republic* (2001).

Jeffrey L. Pasley. *"The Tyranny of Printers": Newspaper Politics in the Early American Republic* (2001).
Taken together, these two groundbreaking studies of political culture in the Early Republic bring a whole set of new perspectives to the topic. Freeman concentrates on honor as a political force, while Pasley illustrates the power of an increasingly self-conscious press in shaping the political landscape.

Richard Hofstadter. *The Idea of a Party System* (1969).
The classic account of the rise of legitimate opposition in the American party system.

David McCullough. *John Adams* (2001).
A highly acclaimed and extremely readable biography of one of America's true founding fathers.

Gary B. Nash. *Forging Freedom: The Formation of Philadelphia's Black Community, 1720–1840* (1990).

A brilliant and exciting exploration of how African Americans in early Philadelphia created their own urban community.

James Ronda. *Lewis and Clark Among the Indians* (1984).
   A bold retelling of the expedition's story, showcasing the Indian role in both Lewis and Clark's and the nation's successful expansion into the Louisiana Territory and beyond.

CHAPTER 9   Increasing Conflict and War, 1805–1815

Gregory E. Dowd. *A Spirited Resistance: The North American Indian Struggle for Unity, 1745–1815* (1992).
   Hailed by many as one of the best works on Native American history, this well-written study covers the efforts by Indians to unite in defense of their lands and heritages, culminating in the struggles during the War of 1812.

R. David Edmunds. *The Shawnee Prophet* (1983); *Tecumseh and the Quest for Indian Leadership* (1984).
   Each of these biographies is a masterpiece, but taken together, they present the most complete recounting of the lives and accomplishments of these two fascinating Shawnee brothers and their historical world.

John Denis Haeger. *John Jacob Astor; Business and Finance in the Early Republic* (1991).

William E. Foley and C. David Rice. *The First Chouteaus: River Barons of Early St. Louis* (1983).
   Taken together, these two books provide a comprehensive overview of the fur trade during its early years, showcasing the importance of business tycoons like Astor and the Chouteaus and demystifying this huge business enterprise.

Donald Hickey. *The War of 1812: A Forgotten Conflict* (1989).
   Arguably the best single-volume history of the war, encyclopedic in content, but so colorfully written that it will hold anyone's attention.

Robert A. Rutland. *Madison's Alternatives: The Jeffersonian Republicans and the Coming of War, 1805–1812* (1975).
   An interesting review of the events leading up to the outbreak of war in 1812 and the various alternatives Jefferson and Madison had to choose from in facing the evolving diplomatic and political crises.

CHAPTER 10   The Rise of a New Nation, 1815–1836

George Dangerfield. *The Era of Good Feelings* (1952).
   An older book, but so well written and informative that it deserves its status as a classic. All students will enjoy this grand overview.

Angie Debo. *And Still the Waters Run: The Betrayal of the Five Civilized Tribes* (1940; reprint, 1972).
   A classic work by one of America's most talented and sensitive historical writers, a truly engaging history of this tragic sequence of events.

Richard E. Ellis. *The Union at Risk: Jacksonian Democracy, States' Rights, and the Nullification Crisis* (1987).
   An invigorating reconsideration of the Nullification Crisis set in context with the other problems that beset the Jackson administration, suggesting how close the nation came to civil war in the 1830s.

Theda Perdue and Michael D. Green. *The Cherokee Removal* (2005).
   Designed for classroom use, this brief history with selected documents is an excellent and interesting resource for students who wish to know more about this tragedy in American history. The new Second Edition has expanded coverage and additional documents.

Charles G. Sellers. *The Market Revolution: Jacksonian America, 1815–1846* (1991).

A far-reaching reassessment of economics and politics during this period focusing on the rise of the market economy and the responses, both positive and negative, that led to the rise of Jacksonian democracy.

John William Ward. *Andrew Jackson: Symbol for an Age* (1955).
   More a study of American culture during the age of Jackson than a biography of the man himself, Ward seeks to explain Old Hickory's status as a living myth during his own time and as a continuing monument in American history.

CHAPTER 11   The Great Transformation, 1828–1840

Ira Berlin. *Slaves Without Masters* (1975).
   A masterful study of a forgotten population: free African Americans in the Old South. Lively and informative.

Stuart M. Blumin. *The Emergence of the Middle Class: Social Experience in the American City, 1760–1900* (1989).
   Considered by many to be the most comprehensive overview of the emergence of the middle class in America during the nineteenth century.

Bill Cecil-Fronsman. *Common Whites: Class and Culture in Antebellum North Carolina* (1992).
   A pioneering effort to describe the culture, lifestyle, and political economy shared by the antebellum South's majority population: nonslaveholding whites. Though confined in geographical scope, the study is suggestive of conditions that may have prevailed throughout the region.

Nancy M Cott. *The Bonds of Womanhood: "Woman's Sphere" in New England, 1780–1835* (1977).
   A classic work on the ties that held the woman's world together, but collectively bound them into a secondary position in American life.

Thomas Dublin. *Women at Work: The Transformation of Work and Community in Lowell, Massachusetts, 1826–1860* (1979).
   An interesting look at the way in which the nature of work changed and the sorts of changes that were brought to one manufacturing community.

Elizabeth Fox-Genovese. *Within the Plantation Household* (1988).
   A look at the lives of black and white women in the antebellum South. This study is quite long, but is well written and very informative.

Isabel Lehuu. *Carnival on the Page: Popular Print Media in Antebellum America* (2000).
   An overview of the explosion in print media during the early nineteenth century and its role in shaping national culture.

Margaret Mitchell. *Gone With the Wind* (1936).
   Arguably the most influential book in conveying a stereotyped vision of antebellum southern life. The film version, directed by Victor Fleming in 1939, was even more influential.

Mary P. Ryan. *Cradle of the Middle Class: The Family in Oneida County, New York, 1790–1865* (1981).
   A marvelous synthesis of materials focusing on the emergence of a new social and economic class in the midst of change from a traditional to a modern society.

George Rogers Taylor. *The Transportation Revolution, 1815–1860* (1951).
   The only comprehensive treatment of changes in transportation during the antebellum period and their economic impact. Nicely written.

CHAPTER 12   Responses to the Great Transformation, 1828–1840

Eugene D. Genovese. *From Rebellion to Revolution: Afro-American Slave Revolts in the Making of the Modern World* (1979).

Although it focuses somewhat narrowly on confrontation, as opposed to more subtle forms of resistance, this study traces the emergence of African American political organization from its roots in antebellum slave revolts.

Karen Haltunen. *Confidence Men and Painted Women: A Study of Middle-Class Culture in America, 1830–1870* (1982).
A wonderfully well-researched study of an emerging class defining and shaping itself in the evolving world of early nineteenth-century urban space.

Edward Pessen. *Most Uncommon Jacksonians: The Radical Leaders of the Early Labor Movement* (1967).
A look at early labor movements and reform by one of America's leading radical scholars.

Anthony F. C. Wallace. *Rockdale: The Growth of an American Village in the Early Industrial Revolution* (1978).
A noted anthropologist's reconstruction of a mill town and the various class, occupational, and gender cultures that developed there during its transition from a traditional village to a mill town.

Ronald G. Walters. *American Reformers, 1815–1860* (1978).
The best overview of the reform movements and key personalities who guided them during this difficult period in American history.

Sean Wilentz. *Chants Democratic: New York City and the Rise of the American Working Class, 1788–1850* (1984).
An insightful view of working-class culture and politics in the dynamic setting of Erie Canal–era New York City.

Susan Zaeske. *Signatures of Citizenship: Petitioning, Antislavery, and Women's Political Identity* (2003).
A fascinating study of how participation in reform campaigns helped lead early nineteenth-century women into a new sense of political identity.

CHAPTER 13 Westward Expansion and Manifest Destiny, 1841–1848

Ray Allen Billington. *America's Frontier Heritage* (1966).
A broad overview of America's Western experience from a Turnerian point of view.

Thomas R. Hietala. *Manifest Design* (1985).
An interesting and well-written interpretation of the Mexican War and the events leading up to it.

Patricia Nelson Limerick. *The Legacy of Conquest* (1988).
Considered by many to be the Bible of the New Western History, this wonderfully written interpretation of events in the West challenges many assumptions and stereotypes.

Donald W. Meinig. *Imperial Texas* (1969).
A fascinating look at Texas history by a leading historical geographer.

Christopher L. Miller. *Prophetic Worlds* (2003).
This new edition includes commentary that helps to define the debates that this book has sparked about the history of the Pacific Northwest during the pioneer era.

Kenneth N. Owens, ed. *Riches for All: The California Gold Rush and the World* (2002).
A collection of essays by leading scholars about the California Gold Rush and its impact on both national and international life.

Wallace E. Stegner. *The Gathering of Zion* (1964).
A masterfully written history of the Mormon Trail by one of the West's leading literary figures.

John David Unruh. *The Plains Across* (1979).
Arguably the best one-volume account of the overland passage to Oregon. The many pages melt as the author captures the reader in the adventure of the Oregon Trail.

CHAPTER 14 Sectional Conflict and Shattered Union, 1848–1860

Don E. Fehrenbacher. *Prelude to Greatness* (1962).
A well-written and interesting account of Lincoln's early career.

Don E. Fehrenbacher. *Slavery, Law, and Politics: The Dred Scott Case in Historical Perspective* (1981).
An excellent interpretive account of this landmark antebellum legal decision, placing it firmly into historical context.

William E. Gienapp, et al. *Essays in American Antebellum Politics, 1840–1860* (1982).
A collection of essays by the rising generation of new political scholars. Exciting and challenging reading.

Michael F. Holt. *The Political Crisis of the 1850s* (1978).
Arguably the best single-volume discussion of the political problems besetting the nation during this critical decade.

Stephen B. Oates. *To Purge This Land with Blood* (1984).
The best biography to date on John Brown, focusing on his role in the emerging sectional crisis during the 1850s.

David Potter. *The Impending Crisis, 1848–1861* (1976).
An extremely long and detailed work but beautifully written and informative.

James Rawley. *Race and Politics: "Bleeding Kansas" and the Coming of the Civil War* (1969).
An interesting look at the conflicts in Kansas, centering upon racial attitudes in the West. Insightful and captivating reading.

Harriet Beecher Stowe. *Uncle Tom's Cabin* (1852; reprint, 1982).
This edition includes notes and chronology by noted social historian Kathryn Kish Sklar, making it especially informative. See also the one-hour film version produced by the Program for Culture at Play, available from Films for the Humanities and Sciences.

CHAPTER 15 A Violent Choice: Civil War, 1861–1865

Annie Heloise Abel. *The Slaveholding Indians*, 3 vols. (1919–1925; reprint, 1992–1993).
This long-ignored classic work focuses on Indians as slaveholders, participants in the Civil War, and subjects of Reconstruction. Its three volumes have recently been updated by historians Theda Purdue and Michael Green. Each volume can stand on its own and will reward the patient reader.

Bruce Catton. *This Hallowed Ground: The Story of the Union Side of the Civil War* (1956).
Catton is probably the best in the huge company of popular writers on the Civil War. This is his most comprehensive single-volume work. More detailed but still very interesting titles by Catton include *Glory Road: The Bloody Route from Fredericksburg to Gettysburg* (1952), *Mr. Lincoln's Army* (1962), *A Stillness at Appomattox* (1953), and *Grant Moves South* (1960).

Paul D. Escott. *After Secession: Jefferson Davis and the Failure of Confederate Nationalism* (1978).
An excellent overview of internal political problems in the Confederacy by a leading Civil War historian.

Ann Giesberg. *Civil War Sisterhood: The U.S. Sanitary Commission and Women's Politics in Transition* (2000).
A study of how women's activism in forming the sanitary movement during the Civil War recast their view of themselves as political figures and helped shape an emerging women's movement.

Alvin M. Josephy. *The Civil War in the American West* (1991).
A former editor for *American Heritage*, Josephy writes an interesting and readable story about this little-known chapter in Civil War history.

William Marvel. *The* Alabama *& the* Kearsarge: *The Sailor's Civil War* (1996).

Military and social historians have compared this new study favorably with *The Life of Billy Yank* (1952) and *The Life of Johnny Reb* (1943), Bell Irvin Willey's classic studies of life for the common soldier, calling it an insightful narrative of the Civil War experience for the common sailor.

James McPherson. *Battle Cry of Freedom: The Civil War Era* (1988).

Hailed by many as the best single-volume history of the Civil War era; comprehensive and very well written.

Emory M. Thomas. *The Confederate Nation* (1979).

A classic history of the Confederacy by an excellent southern historian.

Garry Wills. *Lincoln at Gettysburg: The Words That Remade America* (1992).

A prize-winning look at Lincoln's rhetoric and the ways in which his speeches, especially his Gettysburg Address, recast American ideas about equality, freedom, and democracy. Exquisitely written by a master biographer.

Gettysburg (the movie)

Ronald Maxwell directed this four-hour epic detailing one of the Civil War's most famous battles. Based on Michael Shaara's Pulitzer Prize–winning novel *The Killer Angels*, this ambitious film seeks to capture not only the historical events but also the atmosphere and personalities of the era.

CHAPTER 16 Reconstruction: High Hopes and Shattered Dreams, 1865–1877

David Donald. *Charles Sumner and the Rights of Man* (1970).

Deals both with this important Radical leader and with Reconstruction issues.

W. E. B. Du Bois. *Black Reconstruction in America: An Essay Toward a History of the Part Which Black Folk Played in the Attempt to Reconstruct Democracy in America, 1860–1880* (1935; reprint, 1999).

Written more than a half-century ago, Du Bois's book is a classic and still useful for both information and insights.

Carol Faulkner. *Women's Radical Reconstruction: The Freedmen's Aid Movement* (2004).

A new study of the role of women in the Freedmen's Bureau and in federal Reconstruction policy more generally.

Eric Foner. *Reconstruction: America's Unfinished Revolution, 1863–1877* (1988; reprint, 2002).

The most thorough of recent treatments, incorporating insights from many historians who have written on the subject during the past fifty years.

Leon F. Litwack. *Been in the Storm So Long: The Aftermath of Slavery* (1979).

An account that focuses especially on the experience of the freed people.

William S. McFeely. *Frederick Douglass* (1991).

A highly readable biography of the most prominent black political leader of the nineteenth century.

Michael Perman. *Emancipation and Reconstruction*, 2nd ed. (2003).

Short, readable, and recently revised.

C. Vann Woodward. *Reunion and Reaction: The Compromise of 1877 and the End of Reconstruction*, rev. ed. (1956; reprint, 1991).

The classic account of the Compromise of 1877.

CHAPTER 17 An Industrial Order Emerges, 1865–1880

Edward L. Ayers. *The Promise of the New South: Life After Reconstruction* (1992).

A comprehensive survey of developments in the South.

Robert V. Bruce. *1877: Year of Violence* (1959, 1989).

The classic account of the 1877 railroad strike.

Alfred D. Chandler, Jr., with Takashi Hikino. *Scale and Scope: The Dynamics of Industrial Capitalism* (1990).

Alfred Chandler's writings changed historians' thinking about the emergence of industrial capitalism in the United States; this is one of his key works.

Melvyn Dubofsky. *Industrialism and the American Worker, 1865–1920*, 3rd ed. (1996).

A brief introduction to the topic, organized chronologically.

Ari Hoogenboom. *Rutherford B. Hayes: Warrior and President* (1995).

An excellent biography that also includes a good deal of important information on the politics of the era.

Harold C. Livesay. *Andrew Carnegie and the Rise of Big Business*, 2nd ed. (2000).

A brief biography of a key figure in the transformation of the American economy.

William S. McFeely. *Grant: A Biography* (1981, 2002).

The standard biography of Grant, including his troubled presidency.

David Montgomery. *Workers' Control in America: Studies in the History of Work, Technology, and Labor Struggles* (1979).

An important book for understanding craft unions and labor more generally.

Glenn Porter. *The Rise of Big Business, 1860–1910*, 2nd ed. (1992).

A brief introduction, surveying the role of the railroads, vertical and horizontal integration, and the merger movement.

Frank Roney. *Frank Roney: Irish Rebel and California Labor Leader, an Autobiography*, edited by Ira B. Cross (1931).

Roney's life as an iron molder and labor leader, in his own words.

CHAPTER 18 Becoming an Urban Industrial Society, 1880–1890

Ron Chernow. *The House of Morgan: An American Banking Dynasty and the Rise of Modern Finance* (1990).

An award-winning account of Morgan's bank and Morgan's role in the emergence of finance capitalism.

_____. *Titan: The Life of John D. Rockefeller, Sr.* (1998).

Well written and engaging, based on extensive research in Rockefeller family papers.

Robert W. Cherny. *American Politics in the Gilded Age, 1868–1900* (1997).

A recent, brief survey of the politics of this period.

Ellen Carol DuBois. *Woman Suffrage and Women's Rights* (1998).

Wide-ranging essays on women and politics in the late 19th and early 20th centuries.

Leon Fink. *Workingmen's Democracy: The Knights of Labor and American Politics* (1983).

The best overall treatment of the Knights of Labor.

John Higham. *Strangers in the Land: Patterns of American Nativism, 1860–1925* (1965).

This classic book first defined the contours of American nativism and still provides an excellent introduction to the subject.

Jill Jonnes. *Empires of Light: Edison, Tesla, Westinghouse, and the Race to Electrify the World* (2003).

A recent and popular account of the battles over DC and AC current, and of the larger corporate and financial economy within which the key figures worked.

Alan M. Kraut. *The Huddled Masses: The Immigrant in American Society, 1880–1921* (1982).

A helpful introduction to immigration, especially the so-called new immigration.

Raymond A. Mohl. *The New City: Urban America in the Industrial Age, 1860–1920* (1985).

An excellent introduction to nearly all aspects of the growth of the cities.

Mark Wahlgren Summers. *Party Games: Getting, Keeping, and Using Power in Gilded Age Politics* (2004).

A fascinating account of political parties during the late 19th century.

CHAPTER 19   Conflict and Change in the West, 1865–1902

Dee Brown. *Bury My Heart at Wounded Knee: An Indian History of the American West* (1971).

One of the first efforts to write western history from the Indians' perspective, drawing on oral histories.

Charles J. McClain. *In Search of Equality: The Chinese Struggle Against Discrimination in Nineteenth-Century America* (1994).

Focuses on Chinese immigrants' use of the legal system to combat discrimination.

Juan Gómez-Quiñones. *Roots of Chicano Politics, 1600–1940* (1994).

The political history of Mexican Americans from the first Spanish settlements in the Southwest up to the eve of World War II.

Norris Hundley, Jr. *The Great Thirst: Californians and Water, 1770s–1990s* (1992).

Among the best of recent studies surveying the role of water in the West.

Patricia Nelson Limerick. *The Legacy of Conquest: The Unbroken Past of the American West* (1987).

A major recent criticism of the Turner thesis, posing an alternative framework for viewing western history.

Glenda Riley. *The Female Frontier* (1988).

A survey of women's experiences on the western frontier.

Robert M. Utley. *The Lance and the Shield: The Life and Times of Sitting Bull* (1993).

An exhaustively researched biography of the Lakota leader that incorporates much of the history of the northern plains from the early nineteenth century to the end of the Indian wars.

Richard White. *"It's Your Misfortune and None of My Own": A History of the American West* (1991).

Like Limerick, White seeks to reconsider the history of the West, from the first European contact to the late 1980s.

CHAPTER 20   Economic Crash and Political Upheaval, 1890–1900

Jane Addams. *Twenty Years at Hull House* (1910, reprint, 1960).

Nothing conveys the complex world of Hull House and the striking personality of Jane Addams as well as her own account. It is available online.

Robert L. Beisner. *From the Old Diplomacy to the New, 1865–1900*, 2nd ed. (1986).

A concise introduction to American foreign relations in this period, challenging some of LaFeber's conclusions.

Robert W. Cherny. *A Righteous Cause: The Life of William Jennings Bryan* (1985, 1994).

Includes a survey of the politics of the 1890s, especially the election of 1896.

Lewis Gould. *The Presidency of William McKinley* (1980).

A major contribution to historians' understanding of McKinley's presidency.

Louis R. Harlan. *Booker T. Washington: The Making of a Black Leader, 1856–1901* (1975).

The standard biography of Washington, which includes a good account of the racial situation in the South in the 1890s.

Walter LaFeber. *The New Empire: An Interpretation of American Expansion, 1860–1898* (1963).

A classic account, the first to emphasize the notion of a commercial empire.

Naomi Lamoreaux. *The Great Merger Movement in American Business, 1895–1904* (1985).

An impressive study of the merger movement using detailed case histories of particular industries.

Robert C. McMath, Jr. *American Populism: A Social History, 1877–1898* (1993).

A good, recent introduction to Populism.

Stuart Creighton Miller. *"Benevolent Assimilation": The American Conquest of the Philippines, 1899–1903* (1982).

A thorough account.

CHAPTER 21   The Progressive Era, 1900–1917

John Whiteclay Chambers, II. *The Tyranny of Change: Americans in the Progressive Era, 1890–1920*, 2nd ed. (2000).

A concise overview of American life during the Progressive Era.

K. Austin Kerr. *Organized for Prohibition: A New History of the Anti-Saloon League* (1985).

A recent treatment of the organization that formed the prototype for many organized interest groups.

Lester D. Langley. *The Banana Wars: United States' Intervention in the Caribbean, 1898–1934*, 2nd ed. (2001).

A sprightly and succinct account of the role of the United States in the Caribbean and Central America.

David Levering Lewis. *W. E. B. Du Bois: Biography of a Race, 1868–1919* (1993).

A powerful biography of Du Bois that delivers on its promise to present the "biography of a race" during the Progressive Era.

Arthur S. Link and Richard L. McCormick. *Progressivism* (1983).

A thorough survey of progressivism, including the views of historians.

David G. McCullough. *The Path between the Seas: The Creation of the Panama Canal, 1870–1914* (1977).

Perhaps the most lively and engrossing coverage of this subject.

Theodore Roosevelt. *An Autobiography* (1913; abridged ed. reprint, 1958).

Roosevelt's account of his actions sometimes needs to be taken with a grain of salt but nevertheless provides insight into Roosevelt the person. Available online.

Upton Sinclair. *The Jungle: The Uncensored Original Edition*, ed. by Kathleen De Grave and Earl Lee (1905, 2003).

This socialist novel about workers in Chicago's packinghouses is a classic example of muckraking; this edition includes the full, unexpurgated version that was originally published in serial form in a muckraking journal. The shorter version is available online in several places.

CHAPTER 22   The United States in a World at War, 1913–1920

Kendrick A. Clements. *The Presidency of Woodrow Wilson* (1992).

More than half of this recent account of Wilson's presidency is devoted to foreign-policy matters and the war.

Frank Freidel. *Over There: The Story of America's First Great Overseas Crusade*, rev. ed. (1990).

A vivid survey of American participation in the fighting in Europe, with many firsthand accounts.

David D. Lee. *Sergeant York: An American Hero* (1985).
  The best and most carefully researched biography of York.
Sinclair Lewis. *Main Street* (1920; reprint, 1961).
  An absorbing novel about a woman's dissatisfaction with her life and her decision to work in Washington during the war.
Arthur S. Link. *Woodrow Wilson: Revolution, War, and Peace* (1979).
  A concise introduction to Wilson's role in and thinking about foreign affairs.
Erich Maria Remarque. *All Quiet on the Western Front*, trans. A. W. Wheen (1930; reprint, 1982).
  The classic and moving novel about World War I, seen through German eyes.
Barbara W. Tuchman. *The Guns of August* (1962; reprint, 1976).
  A popular and engaging account of the outbreak of the war, focusing on events in Europe.
_____. *The Zimmermann Telegram* (1958, 1985).
  Highly readable and carefully researched.

CHAPTER 23 Prosperity Decade, 1920–1928

Frederick Lewis Allen. *Only Yesterday: An Informal History of the 1920s* (1931, 2000).
  An anecdote-filled account that brings the decade to life.
Robert H. Ferrell. *The Presidency of Calvin Coolidge* (1998).
  A good treatment of national politics during the 1920s.
F. Scott Fitzgerald. *The Great Gatsby* (1925).
  A fictional portrayal of high living and pleasure seeking among the wealthy of New York.
Nathan Irvin Huggins. *Harlem Renaissance* (1971).
  A thorough and thoughtful work that places the Harlem Renaissance into the larger context of race relations in the 1920s.
William E. Leuchtenburg. *The Perils of Prosperity, 1914–1932*, 2nd ed. (1993).
  A comprehensive and lively account by a leading historian.
The Smithsonian Collection of Classic Jazz. Five compact disks (1987).
  An outstanding collection that reflects the development of American jazz, with annotations and biographies of performers.
David Stenn. *Clara Bow: Runnin' Wild* (1990).
  The best and most carefully researched of the biographies of Bow.
Jules Tygiel. *The Great Los Angeles Swindle: Oil, Stocks, and Scandal During the Roaring Twenties* (1996).
  A recent, engagingly written account of Los Angeles in the 1920s.

CHAPTER 24 The Great Depression and the New Deal, 1929–1939

Michael A. Bernstein. *The Great Depression* (1987).
  A detailed economic examination of the causes and effects of the Depression, with American manufacturing as a primary focus.
Caroline Bird. *The Invisible Scar* (1966).
  An excellent study of how people responded to the impact of the Depression.
Julia Kirk Blackwelder. *Women of the Depression: Caste and Culture in San Antonio, 1929–1939* (1984).
  A tightly focused study on Mexican American, African American, and Anglo women in the world of San Antonio during the Depression.
Lizabeth Cohen. *Making a New Deal: Industrial Workers in Chicago, 1919–1939* (1990).
  A detailed examination of the inclusion of African American and immigrant workers in the CIO and in New Deal politics.
David Kennedy. *Freedom from Fear: The American People in Depression and War, 1929–1945* (1999).
  A well-written and researched comprehensive examination of a period that shaped recent American history.
Maury Klein. *Rainbow's End: The Crash of 1929* (2001).
  A compelling account of the stock market crash set within the framework of the many social, political, cultural, and economic events that surrounded it.
Robert McElvaine. *The Great Depression: America, 1929–1941* (1984).
  An excellent overview of the origins of and responses to the Depression.
George McJimsey. *The Presidency of Franklin Delano Roosevelt* (2000).
  A brief and positive account of Roosevelt's struggles to combat the Depression and the Second World War, contains a well-presented annotated bibliography.
Studs Terkel. *Hard Times: An Oral History of the Great Depression* (1970).
  A classic example of how oral histories can provide the human dimension to history.
Harvard Sitkoff. *A New Deal for Blacks* (1978).
  A review of how African Americans benefited from and were otherwise affected by the New Deal and the Roosevelts.
Susan Ware. *Holding Their Own: American Women in the 1930s* (1982).
  An examination of the impact of the Depression on the lives and lifestyles of women.
Joan Hoff Wilson. *Herbert Hoover: Forgotten Progressive* (1970).
  A positive evaluation of the life of Herbert Hoover that stresses his accomplishments as well as his limitations.

CHAPTER 25 America's Rise to World Leadership, 1929–1945

Robert Dallek. *Franklin D. Roosevelt and American Foreign Policy, 1932–1945* (1979).
  An excellent, balanced study of Franklin Roosevelt's foreign policy.
Justus D. Doenecke. *Storm on the Horizon: The Challenge to American Intervention, 1939–1941* (2001).
  Well-documented and -written examination of American isolationists prior to Pearl Harbor that shows the complexity of the movement and the issues.
Sherna B. Gluck. *Rosie the Riveter Revisited: Women, the War, and Social Change* (1987).
  An important work examining the changes that took place among women in society during the war.
John Keegan. *The Second World War* (1990).
  An excellent one-volume work that summarizes the military and diplomatic aspects of World War II.
William O'Neill. *A Democracy at War: America's Fight at Home and Abroad in World War II* (1993).
  A good introduction to American society and politics during the war as well as an excellent view of the military campaigns against the Axis powers.
Ronald Spector. *Eagle Against the Sun* (1988).
  One of the best-written general accounts of the war in the Pacific.
Ronald Takiaki. *Double Victory* (2002).
  A wide-ranging look at American minorities' contribution to the war effort at home and abroad. Clearly demonstrates how these efforts set the foundation for the civil rights movements that followed.

David Wyman. *The Abandonment of the Jews* (1985).
   A balanced account of the Holocaust.

CHAPTER 26   Truman and Cold War America, 1945–1952

Paul Boyer. *By the Bomb's Early Light: American Thought and Culture at the Dawn of the Atomic Age* (1985).
   A useful analysis of the impact of atomic energy and the atomic bomb on American society, from advertising to mock "atomic air bomb drills."

Fraser Harbutt. *The Cold War Era* (2002).
   An informative comprehensive view of the Cold War that provides not only a balanced view, but provides examples of other viewpoints on several important issues.

Max Hastings. *The Korean War* (1987).
   A short, well-written study of the military dimension of the Korean War.

Marc Trachtenberg. *A Constructed Peace: The Making of the European Settlements, 1945–1963* (1999).
   A well-researched study of the politics and issues that surrounded the origins of the Cold War from a multinational perspective.

David McCullough. *Truman* (1992).
   A highly acclaimed biography of Truman.

James Patterson. *Grand Expectations: The United States, 1945–1974* (1996).
   A general, readable view of American society and politics in the postwar period.

Ellen W. Schrecker. *Many Are the Crimes: McCarthyism in America* (1998).
   A complex study of the relationship between American communism and anticommunism and the consequence of both on American society and politics.

Jules Tygiel. *Baseball's Great Experiment: Jackie Robinson and His Legacy* (1983).
   Reflections on the life experiences and decisions that brought Jackie Robinson to break the color barrier in professional baseball.

Stephen J. Whitfield. *The Culture of the Cold War* (1991).
   A critical account of the impact of the Cold War on the United States that argues that a cultural, social, and political consensus that equated "Americanism" with militant anticommunism dominated American life. Especially useful is the examination of the effect of the Cold War on American social values and popular culture.

CHAPTER 27   Quest for Consensus, 1952–1960

Stephen E. Ambrose. *Eisenhower: The President* (1984).
   A generally positive and well-balanced biography of Eisenhower as president by one of the most respected historians of the Eisenhower period.

Michael Bertrand. *Race, Rock, and Elvis* (2000).
   Provides a view of how Elvis and his music not only shaped American music but altered views about class, race, and gender.

Taylor Branch. *Parting the Waters: America in the King Years, 1954–1963* (1988).
   An interesting and useful description of the development of the civil rights movement that focuses on the role of Martin Luther King Jr.

Robert F. Burk. *The Eisenhower Administration and Black Civil Rights* (1984).
   An insightful examination of federal policy and the civil rights movement.

Lizabeth Cohen. *A Consumer's Republic: The Politics of Mass Consumption in Postwar America* (2003).
   An important study of the connections between business, politics, and culture that have shaped American society following World War II to the mid-1960s.

Robert A. Devine. *Eisenhower and the Cold War* (1981).
   A solid and brief account of Eisenhower's foreign policy, especially toward the Soviet Union.

David Halberstam. *The Fifties* (1993).
   A positive interpretive view of the 1950s by a well-known journalist and author, especially recommended for its description of famous and not-so-famous people.

Eugenia Kaledin. *Mothers and More: American Women in the 1950s* (1984).
   A thoughtful look at the role of American women in society during the 1950s.

Joanne J. Meyerowitz, ed. *Not June Cleaver: Women and Gender in Postwar America, 1945–1960* (1994).
   An excellent collection of essays that explore the variety of views on women's roles in American culture, society, and politics.

James Patterson. Brown v. Board of Education: *A Civil Rights Milestone and Its Troubled Legacy* (2001).
   A timely study of the events and decisions that led to the *Brown* case as well as an examination of the role the *Brown* decision has had on American politics, society, and race relations.

CHAPTER 28   Great Promises, Bitter Disappointments, 1960–1968

Peter Braunstein and Michael Doyle, eds. *Imagine Nation: The American Counterculture of the 1960s and 1970s* (2001).
   A wide range of essays that provide useful evaluations on the many aspects of the counterculture.

Irving Bernstein. *Promises Kept: John F. Kennedy's New Frontier* (1991).
   A brief and balanced account of Kennedy's presidency that presents a favorable report of the accomplishments and legacy of the New Frontier.

Michael Beschloss. *The Crisis Years: Kennedy and Khrushchev, 1960–1963* (1991).
   A strong narrative account of the Cold War during the Kennedy administration and the personal duel between the leaders of the two superpowers.

Clayborne Carson. *In Struggle: SNCC and the Black Awakening of the 1960s* (1981).
   A useful study that uses the development of SNCC to examine the changing patterns of the civil rights movement and the emergence of black nationalism.

Margaret Cruikshank. *The Gay and Lesbian Liberation Movement* (1992).
   Provides a good introduction and insight into the gay and lesbian movement.

Robert Dallek. *Flawed Giant: Lyndon B. Johnson, 1960–1973* (1998).
   An important biography that focuses on politics and foreign policy.

Alice Echols. *Daring to Be Bad* (1989).
   An insightful and interesting account of the radical dimension of the women's movement.

David Horowitz. *Betty Friedan and the Making of the Feminist Movement* (1998).
   Uses the central figure of the women's movement to examine the beginnings and development of the movement.

Michael Kazin and Maurice Isserman. *America Divided: The Civil War of the 1960s* (2000).
   The social and cultural currents of the 1960s are skillfully woven into an overall picture of American society.

William L. Van Deburg. *New Day in Babylon: The Black Power Movement and American Culture, 1965–1975* (1992).

A well-written study of the varieties of the Black Power movement and the development of an American consciousness.

CHAPTER 29   America Under Stress, 1967–1976

Stephen Ambrose. *Nixon: The Triumph of a Politician, 1962–1972* (1989).

An excellent examination of Nixon and his politics—the second volume of Ambrose's three-volume biography.

Larry Berman. *No Peace, No Honor: Nixon, Kissinger, and Betrayal in Vietnam* (2001).

A critical view of Vietnamization and the politics of ending the American presence in Vietnam.

Philip Caputo. *Rumor of War* (1986).

The author's account of his own changing perspectives on the war in Vietnam. Caputo served as a young marine officer in Vietnam and later covered the final days in Saigon as a journalist. His views frequently reflected those of the American public.

Ian F. Haney Lopez. *Racism on Trial: The Chicano Fight for Justice* (2003).

An interesting use of two trials to examine the development of Chicano identity and the idea of race and violence.

Burton Kaufman. *The Presidency of James Earl Carter, Jr.* (1993).

A well-balanced account and analysis of Carter's presidency and the changing political values of the 1970s.

Stanley Kutler. *The Wars of Watergate* (1990) and *Abuse of Power: The New Nixon Tapes* (1997).

The former work details the events surrounding the Watergate break-in and the hearings that led to Nixon's resignation. The latter provides transcripts of selected Nixon tapes.

Joanne Nagel. *American Indian Ethnic Revival: Red Power and the Resurgence of Identity and Culture* (1996).

A thorough analysis of the Red Power movement and how it helped to shape cultural and political change.

Marylin Young. *The Vietnam Wars, 1945–1990* (1991).

A brief, well-written and a carefully documented history of Vietnam's struggle for nationhood with a focus on American policy toward Vietnam since near the end of WWII.

CHAPTER 30   Facing Limits, 1976–1992

A. J. Bacevich, et al. *The Gulf Conflict of 1991 Reconsidered* (2003).

A collection of essays that provide both insight and an excellent overview of the Gulf War.

Lou Cannon. *President Reagan: The Role of a Lifetime* (1992).

The most complete and detailed account of the Reagan presidency from a generally positive perspective.

Roger Daniels. *Coming to America* (1990).

A solid analysis of the new immigrants seeking a place in American society; especially effective on Asian immigration.

Michael Duffy and Don Goodgame. *Marching in Place: The Status Quo Presidency of George Bush* (1992).

An insightful but critical analysis of the Bush presidency.

John L. Gaddis. *The United States and the End of the Cold War* (1992).

An excellent narrative of events in the Soviet Union and the United States that led to the end of the Cold War, as well as a useful analysis of the problems facing the United States in the post–Cold War world.

David J. Garrow. *Liberty and Sexuality: The Right to Privacy and the Making of* Roe v. Wade (1994).

An in-depth and scholarly account of the origins and impact of *Roe v. Wade* and the legal and political issues dealing with privacy, gender, and abortion.

Lisa McGirr. *Suburban Warriors: The Origins of the New American Right* (2001).

A study of how the ideology and issues of the New Right found fertile soil within the American middle suburban class.

Michael Schaller. *Reckoning with Reagan* (1992).

A brief but scholarly analysis of the Reagan administration and the society and values that supported the Reagan revolution.

Bruce Schulman. *The Seventies: The Great Shift in American Culture, Society, and Politics* (2001).

A readable and comprehensive overview of the central issues that defined the decade.

Studs Terkel. *The Great Divide* (1988).

An interesting and informative collection of oral interviews that provide a personal glimpse of changes recently taking place in American society.

CHAPTER 31   Entering a New Century, 1992–2004

Michael Bernstein and David A. Adler, eds. *Understanding American Economic Decline* (1994).

A collection of essays by economists and knowledgeable observers who analyze the slowing down of the American economy and its impact.

Colin Campbell and Bert A. Rockman, eds. *The Clinton Presidency: First Appraisals* (1995).

An informative and speculative group of wide-ranging essays that explore many aspects of Clinton's first years in office and examine broader political issues.

Congressional Quarterly's Research Reports.

A valuable monthly resource for information and views on issues facing the United States and the world.

Anthony Gidden. *Runaway World: How Globalization is Reshaping Our World* (2002).

A readable and positive appraisal of globalization and its effects on a world society and its people.

David Halberstam. *War in Time of Peace: Bush, Clinton, and the Generals* (2001).

An understandable account of American foreign policy and policymakers coming to dealing with a post–Cold War world where the major issues are terrorism, genocide, and nation-building.

Randy Shilts. *And the Band Played On: Politics, People and the AIDS Epidemic* (1987).

A compelling book on the AIDS epidemic and the early lack of action by society; written by a victim of AIDS.

Strobe Talbott and Nayan Chanda, eds. *The Age of Terror: America and the World After September 11* (2001).

An informative collection of essays that place the attacks of September 11 in historical and political context.

Bob Woodward. *Plan of Attack* (2004).

Based on interviews, an account of the internal decisions the Bush administration made that led to the decision to go to war with Iraq.

Declaration of Independence in Congress, July 4, 1776

When, in the course of human events, it becomes necessary for one people to dissolve the political bonds which have connected them with another, and to assume, among the powers of the earth, the separate and equal station to which the laws of nature and of nature's God entitle them, a decent respect to the opinions of mankind requires that they should declare the causes which impel them to the separation.

We hold these truths to be self-evident: That all men are created equal; that they are endowed by their Creator with certain unalienable rights; that among these are life, liberty, and the pursuit of happiness; that, to secure these rights, governments are instituted among men, deriving their just powers from the consent of the governed; that whenever any form of government becomes destructive of these ends, it is the right of the people to alter or to abolish it, and to institute new government, laying its foundation on such principles, and organizing its powers in such form, as to them shall seem most likely to effect their safety and happiness. Prudence, indeed, will dictate that governments long established should not be changed for light and transient causes; and accordingly all experience hath shown that mankind are more disposed to suffer, while evils are sufferable, than to right themselves by abolishing the forms to which they are accustomed. But when a long train of abuses and usurpations, pursuing invariably the same object, evinces a design to reduce them under absolute despotism, it is their right, it is their duty, to throw off such government, and to provide new guards for their future security. Such has been the patient sufferance of these colonies; and such is now the necessity which constrains them to alter their former systems of government. The history of the present King of Great Britain is a history of repeated injuries and usurpations, all having in direct object the establishment of an absolute tyranny over these states. To prove this, let facts be submitted to a candid world.

He has refused his assent to laws, the most wholesome and necessary for the public good.

He has forbidden his governors to pass laws of immediate and pressing importance, unless suspended in their operation till his assent should be obtained; and, when so suspended, he has utterly neglected to attend to them.

He has refused to pass other laws for the accommodation of large districts of people, unless those people would relinquish the right of representation in the legislature, a right inestimable to them, and formidable to tyrants only.

He has called together legislative bodies at places unusual, uncomfortable, and distant from the depository of their public records, for the sole purpose of fatiguing them into compliance with his measures.

He has dissolved representative houses repeatedly, for opposing, with manly firmness, his invasions on the rights of the people.

He has refused for a long time, after such dissolutions, to cause others to be elected; whereby the legislative powers, incapable of annihilation, have returned to the people at large for their exercise; the state remaining, in the mean time, exposed to all the dangers of invasions from without and convulsions within.

He has endeavored to prevent the population of these states; for that purpose obstructing the laws for naturalization of foreigners; refusing to pass others to encourage their migration hither, and raising the conditions of new appropriations of lands.

He has obstructed the administration of justice, by refusing his assent to laws for establishing judiciary powers.

He has made judges dependent on his will alone, for the tenure of their offices, and the amount and payment of their salaries.

He has erected a multitude of new offices, and sent hither swarms of officers to harass our people and eat out their substance.

He has kept among us, in times of peace, standing armies, without the consent of our legislatures.

He has affected to render the military independent of, and superior to, the civil power.

He has combined with others to subject us to a jurisdiction foreign to our constitution, and unacknowledged by our laws, giving his assent to their acts of pretended legislation:

For quartering large bodies of armed troops among us;

For protecting them, by a mock trial, from punishment for any murders which they should commit on the inhabitants of these states;

For cutting off our trade with all parts of the world;

For imposing taxes on us without our consent;

For depriving us, in many cases, of the benefits of trial by jury;

For transporting us beyond seas, to be tried for pretended offenses;

For abolishing the free system of English laws in a neighboring province, establishing therein an arbitrary government, and enlarging its boundaries, so as to render it at once an example and fit instrument for introducing the same absolute rule into these colonies;

For taking away our charters, abolishing our most valuable laws, and altering fundamentally the forms of our governments;

For suspending our own legislatures, and declaring themselves invested with power to legislate for us in all cases whatsoever.

He has abdicated government here, by declaring us out of his protection and waging war against us.

He has plundered our seas, ravaged our coasts, burned our towns, and destroyed the lives of our people.

He is at this time transporting large armies of foreign mercenaries to complete the works of death, desolation, and tyranny already begun with circumstances of cruelty and perfidy scarcely paralleled in the most barbarous ages, and totally unworthy the head of a civilized nation.

He has constrained our fellow-citizens, taken captive on the high seas, to bear arms against their country, to become the executioners of their friends and brethren, or to fall themselves by their hands.

He has excited domestic insurrection among us, and has endeavored to bring on the inhabitants of our frontiers the merciless Indian savages, whose known rule of warfare is an undistinguished destruction of all ages, sexes, and conditions.

In every stage of these oppressions we have petitioned for redress in the most humble terms; our repeated petitions have been answered only by repeated injury. A prince, whose character is thus marked by every act which may define a tyrant, is unfit to be the ruler of a free people.

Nor have we been wanting in our attentions to our British brethren. We have warned them, from time to time, of attempts by their legislature to extend an unwarrantable jurisdiction over us. We have reminded them of the circumstances of our emigration and settlement here. We have appealed to their native justice and magnanimity; and we have conjured them, by the ties of our common kindred, to disavow these usurpations, which would inevitably interrupt our connections and correspondence. They, too, have been deaf to the voice of justice and of consanguinity. We must, therefore, acquiesce in the necessity which denounces our separation, and hold them, as we hold the rest of mankind, enemies in war, in peace friends.

We, therefore, the representatives of the United States of America, in General Congress assembled, appealing to the Supreme Judge of the world for the rectitude of our intentions, do, in the name and by the authority of the good people of these colonies, solemnly publish and declare, that these United Colonies are, and of right ought to be, FREE AND INDEPENDENT STATES; that they are absolved from all allegiance to the British crown, and that all political connection between them and the state of Great Britain is, and ought to be, totally dissolved; and that, as free and independent states, they have full power to levy war, conclude peace, contract alliances, establish commerce, and do all other acts and things which independent states may of right do. And for the support of this declaration, with a firm reliance on the protection of Divine Providence, we mutually pledge to each other our lives, our fortunes, and our sacred honor.

JOHN HANCOCK
and fifty-five others

Articles of Confederation

Whereas the Delegates of the United States of America in Congress assembled did on the fifteenth day of November in the Year of our Lord One Thousand Seven Hundred and Seventy seven, and in the Second Year of the Independence of America agree to certain articles of Confederation and perpetual Union between the States of Newhampshire, Massachusetts-bay, Rhode-island and Providence Plantations, Connecticut, New-York, New-Jersey, Pennsylvania, Delaware, Maryland, Virginia, North-Carolina, South-Carolina and Georgia in the Words following, viz. "Articles of Confederation and perpetual Union between the states of Newhampshire, Massachusetts-bay, Rhodeisland and Providence Plantations, Connecticut, New-York, New-Jersey, Pennsylvania, Delaware, Maryland, Virginia, North-Carolina, South-Carolina and Georgia.

Article I   The Stile of this confederacy shall be "The United States of America."

Article II   Each state retains its sovereignty, freedom and independence, and every Power, Jurisdiction and right, which is not by this confederation expressly delegated to the United States, in Congress assembled.

Article III The said states hereby severally enter into a firm league of friendship with each other, for their common defence, the security of their Liberties, and their mutual and general welfare, binding themselves to assist each other, against all force offered to, or attacks made upon them, or any of them, on account of religion, sovereignty, trade, or any other pretence whatever.

Article IV The better to secure and perpetuate mutual friendship and intercourse among the people of the different states in this union, the free inhabitants of each of these states, paupers, vagabonds and fugitives from Justice excepted, shall be entitled to all privileges and immunities of free citizens in the several states; and the people of each state shall have free ingress and regress to and from any other state, and shall enjoy therein all the privileges of trade and commerce, subject to the same duties, impositions and restrictions as the inhabitants thereof respectively, provided that such restriction shall not extend so far as to prevent the removal of property imported into any state, to any other state of which the Owner is an inhabitant; provided also that no imposition, duties or restriction shall be laid by any state, on the property of the united states, or either of them.

If any Person guilty of, or charged with treason, felony, or other high misdemeanor in any state, shall flee from Justice, and be found in any of the united states, he shall upon demand of the Governor or executive power, of the state from which he fled, be delivered up and removed to the state having jurisdiction of his offence.

Full faith and credit shall be given in each of these states to the records, acts and judicial proceedings of the courts and magistrates of every other state.

Article V For the more convenient management of the general interests of the united states, delegates shall be annually appointed in such manner as the legislature of each state shall direct, to meet in Congress on the first Monday in November, in every year, with a power reserved to each state, to recall its delegates, or any of them, at any time within the year, and to send others in their stead, for the remainder of the Year.

No state shall be represented in Congress by less than two, nor by more than seven Members; and no person shall be capable of being a delegate for more than three years in any term of six years; nor shall any person, being a delegate, be capable of holding any office under the united states, for which he, or another for his benefit receives any salary, fees or emolument of any kind.

Each state shall maintain its own delegates in a meeting of the states, and while they act as members of the committee of the states.

In determining questions in the united states, in Congress assembled, each state shall have one vote.

Freedom of speech and debate in Congress shall not be impeached or questioned in any Court, or place out of Congress, and the members of congress shall be protected in their persons from arrests and imprisonments, during the time of their going to and from, and attendance on congress, except for treason, felony, or breach of the peace.

Article VI No state without the Consent of the united states in congress assembled, shall send any embassy to, or receive any embassy from, or enter into any conference, agreement, or alliance or treaty with any King, prince or state; nor shall any person holding any office of profit or trust under the united states, or any of them, accept of any present, emolument, office or title of any kind whatever from any king, prince or foreign state; nor shall the united states in congress assembled, or any of them, grant any title of nobility.

No two or more states shall enter into any treaty, confederation or alliance whatever between them, without the consent of the united states in congress assembled, specifying accurately the purposes for which the same is to be entered into, and how long it shall continue.

No state shall lay any imposts or duties, which may interfere with any stipulations in treaties, entered into by the united states in congress assembled, with any king, prince or state, in pursuance of any treaties already proposed by congress, to the courts of France and Spain.

No vessels of war shall be kept up in time of peace by any state, except such number only, as shall be deemed necessary by the united states in congress assembled, for the defence of such state, or its trade; nor shall any body of forces be kept up by any state, in time of peace, except such number only, as in the judgment of the united states, in congress assembled, shall be deemed requisite to garrison the forts necessary for the defence of such state; but every state shall always keep up a well regulated and disciplined militia, sufficiently armed and accoutred, and shall provide and constantly have ready for use, in public stores, a due number of field pieces and tents, and a proper quantity of arms, ammunition and camp equipage.

No state shall engage in any war without the consent of the united states in congress assembled, unless such state be actually invaded by enemies, or shall have received certain advice of a resolution being formed by some nation of Indians to invade such state, and the danger is so imminent as not to admit of a delay, till the united states in congress assembled can be consulted: nor shall any state grant commissions to any ships or vessels of war, nor letters of marque or reprisal, except it be after a declaration of war by the united states in congress assembled, and then only against the kingdom or state and the subjects thereof, against which war has been so declared, and under such regulations as shall be established by the united states in congress assembled, unless such state be infested by pirates, in which case vessels of war may be fitted out for that occasion, and kept so long as the danger shall continue, or until the united states in congress assembled shall determine otherwise.

Article VII   When land-forces are raised by any state for the common defence, all officers of or under the rank of colonel, shall be appointed by the legislature of each state respectively by whom such forces shall be raised, or in such manner as such state shall direct, and all vacancies shall be filled up by the state which first made the appointment.

Article VIII   All charges of war, and all other expences that shall be incurred for the common defence or general welfare, and allowed by the united states in congress assembled, shall be defrayed out of a common treasury, which shall be supplied by the several states, in proportion to the value of all land within each state, granted to or surveyed for any Person, as such land and the buildings and improvements thereon shall be estimated according to such mode as the united states in congress assembled, shall from time to time direct and appoint. The taxes for paying that proportion shall be laid and levied by the authority and direction of the legislatures of the several states within the time agreed upon by the united states in congress assembled.

Article IX   The united states in congress assembled, shall have the sole and exclusive right and power of determining on peace and war, except in the cases mentioned in the sixth article—of sending and receiving ambassadors—entering into treaties and alliances, provided that no treaty of commerce shall be made whereby the legislative power of the respective states shall be restrained from imposing such imposts and duties on foreigners, as their own people are subjected to, or from prohibiting the exportation or importation of any species of goods or commodities whatsoever—of establishing rules for deciding in all cases, what captures on land or water shall be legal, and in what manner prizes taken by land or naval forces in the service of the united states shall be divided or appropriated.—of granting letters of marque and reprisal in times of peace—appointing courts for the trial of piracies and felonies committed on the high seas

and establishing courts for receiving and determining finally appeals in all cases of captures, provided that no member of congress shall be appointed a judge of any of the said courts.

The united states in congress assembled shall also be the last resort on appeal in all disputes and differences now subsisting or that hereafter may arise between two or more states concerning boundary, jurisdiction or any other cause whatever; which authority shall always be exercised in the manner following. Whenever the legislative or executive authority or lawful agent of any state in controversy with another shall present a petition to congress, stating the matter in question and praying for a hearing, notice thereof shall be given by order of congress to the legislative or executive authority of the other state in controversy, and a day assigned for the appearance of the parties by their lawful agents, who shall then be directed to appoint by joint consent, commissioners or judges to constitute a court for hearing and determining the matter in question: but if they cannot agree, congress shall name three persons out of each of the united states, and from the list of such persons each party shall alternately strike out one, the petitioners beginning, until the number shall be reduced to thirteen; and from that number not less than seven, nor more than nine names as congress shall direct, shall in the presence of congress be drawn out by lot, and the persons whose names shall be so drawn or any five of them, shall be commissioners or judges, to hear and finally determine the controversy, so always as a major part of the judges who shall hear the cause shall agree in the determination: and if either party shall neglect to attend at the day appointed, without shewing reasons, which congress shall judge sufficient, or being present shall refuse to strike, the congress shall proceed to nominate three persons out of each state, and the secretary of congress shall strike in behalf of such party absent or refusing; and the judgment and sentence of the court to be appointed, in the manner before prescribed, shall be final and conclusive; and if any of the parties shall refuse to submit to the authority of such court, or to appear to defend their claim or cause, the court shall nevertheless proceed to pronounce sentence, or judgment, which shall in like manner be final and decisive, the judgment or sentence and other proceedings being in either case transmitted to congress, and lodged among the acts of congress for the security of the parties concerned: provided that every commissioner, before he sits in judgment, shall take an oath to be administered by one of the judges of the supreme or superior court of the state, where the cause shall be tried, "well and truly to hear and determine the matter in question, according to the best of his judgment, without favour, affection or hope of reward:" provided also that no state shall be deprived of territory for the benefit of the united states.

All controversies concerning the private right of soil claimed under different grants of two or more states, whose jurisdictions as they may respect such lands, and the states which passed such grants are adjusted, the said grants or either of them being at the same time claimed to have originated antecedent to such settlement of jurisdiction, shall on the petition of either party to the congress of the united states, be finally determined as near as may be in the same manner as is before prescribed for deciding disputes respecting territorial jurisdiction between different states.

The united states in congress assembled shall also have the sole and exclusive right and power of regulating the alloy and value of coin struck by their own authority, or by that of the respective states—fixing the standard of weights and measures throughout the united states.—regulating the trade and managing all affairs with the Indians, not members of any of the states, provided that the legislative right of any state within its own limits be not infringed or violated—establishing and regulating post-offices from one state to another, throughout all the united states, and exacting such postage on the papers passing thro' the same as may be requisite to defray the expences of the said office—appointing all officers of the land forces, in the service of the united states, excepting regimental officers.—appointing all the officers of the naval forces, and commissioning all officers whatever in the service of the united states—making rules for the government and regulation of the said land and naval forces, and directing their operations.

The united states in congress assembled shall have authority to appoint a committee, to sit in the recess of congress, to be denominated "A Committee of the States," and to consist of one delegate from each state; and to appoint such other committees and civil officers as may be necessary for managing the general affairs of the united states under their direction—to appoint one of their number to preside, provided that no person be allowed to serve in the office of president more than one year in any term of three years; to ascertain the necessary sums of Money to be raised for the service of the united states, and to appropriate and apply the same for defraying the public expences—to borrow money, or emit bills on the credit of the united states, transmitting every half year to the respective states an account of the sums of money so borrowed or emitted,—to build and equip a navy—to agree upon the number of land forces, and to make requisitions from each state for its quota, in proportion to the number of white inhabitants in such state; which requisition shall be binding, and thereupon the legislature of each state shall appoint the regimental officers, raise the men and cloath, arm and equip them in a soldier like manner, at the expence of the united states, and the officers and men so cloathed, armed and equipped shall march to the place appointed, and within the time agreed on by the united states in congress assembled: But if the united states in congress assembled shall, on consideration of circumstances judge proper that any state should not raise men, or should raise a smaller number than its quota, and that any other state should raise a greater number of men than the quota thereof, such extra number shall be raised, officered, cloathed, armed and equipped in the same manner as the quota of such state, unless the legislature of such state shall judge that such extra number cannot be safely spared out of the same, in which case they shall raise, officer, cloath, arm and equip as many of such extra number as they judge can be safely spared. And the officers and men so cloathed, armed and equipped, shall march to the place appointed, and within the time agreed on by the united states in congress assembled.

The united states in congress assembled shall never engage in a war, nor grant letters of marque and reprisal in time of peace, nor enter into any treaties or alliances, nor coin money, nor regulate the value thereof, nor ascertain the sums and expences necessary for the defence and welfare of the united states, or any of them, nor emit bills, nor borrow money on the credit of the united states, nor appropriate money, nor agree upon the number of vessels of war, to be built or purchased, or the number of land or sea forces to be raised, nor appoint a commander in chief of the army or navy, unless nine states assent to the same: nor shall a question on any other point, except for adjourning from day to day be determined, unless by the votes of a majority of the united states in congress assembled.

The congress of the united states shall have power to adjourn to any time within the year, and to any place within the united states, so that no period of adjournment be for a longer duration than the space of six Months, and shall publish the Journal of their proceedings monthly, except such parts thereof relating to treaties, alliances or military operations as in their judgment require secresy; and the yeas and nays of the delegates of each state on any question shall be entered on the Journal, when it is desired by any delegate; and the delegates of a state, or any of them, at his or their request shall be furnished with a transcript of the said Journal, except such parts as are above excepted, to lay before the legislatures of the several states.

Article X The committee of the states, or any nine of them, shall be authorised to execute, in the recess of congress, such of the powers of congress as the united states in congress assembled, by the consent of nine states, shall from time to time think expedient to vest them with; provided that no power be delegated to the said committee, for the exercise of which, by the articles of confederation, the voice of nine states in the congress of the united states assembled is requisite.

Article XI Canada acceding to this confederation, and joining in the measures of the united states, shall be admitted into, and entitled to all the advantages of this union: but no other colony shall be admitted into the same, unless such admission be agreed to by nine states.

Article XII All bills of credit emitted, monies borrowed and debts contracted by, or under the authority of congress, before the assembling of the united states, in pursuance of the present confederation, shall be deemed and considered as a charge against the united states, for payment and satisfaction whereof the said united states, and the public faith are hereby solemnly pledged.

Article XIII Every state shall abide by the determinations of the united states in congress assembled, on all questions which by this confederation are submitted to them. And the Articles of this confederation shall be inviolably observed by every state, and the union shall be perpetual; nor shall any alteration at any time hereafter be made in any of them; unless such alteration be agreed to in a congress of the united states, and be afterwards confirmed by the legislatures of every state.

AND WHEREAS it hath pleased the Great Governor of the World to incline the hearts of the legislatures we respectively represent in congress, to approve of, and to authorize us to ratify the said articles of confederation and perpetual union. Know Ye that we the under-signed delegates, by virtue of the power and authority to us given for that purpose, do by these presents, in the name and in behalf of our respective constituents, fully and entirely ratify and confirm each and every of the said articles of confederation and perpetual union, and all and singular the matters and things therein contained: And we do further solemnly plight and engage the faith of our respective constitutents, that they shall abide by the determinations of the united states in congress assembled, on all questions, which by the said confederation are submitted to them. And that the articles thereof shall be inviolably observed by the states we respectively represent, and that the union shall be perpetual. In Witness whereof we have hereunto set our hands in Congress. Done at Philadelphia in the state of Pennsylvania the ninth Day of July in the Year of our Lord one Thousand seven Hundred and Seventy-eight, and in the third year of the independence of America.

Constitution of the United States of America and Amendments[*]

Preamble

We the people of the United States, in order to form a more perfect union, establish justice, insure domestic tranquillity, provide for the common defense, promote the general welfare, and secure the blessings of liberty to ourselves and our posterity, do ordain and establish this Constitution for the United States of America.

Article I

Section 1 All legislative powers herein granted shall be vested in a Congress of the United States, which shall consist of a Senate and a House of Representatives.

Section 2 The House of Representatives shall be composed of members chosen every second year by the people of the several States, and the electors in each State shall have the qualifications requisite for electors of the most numerous branch of the State Legislature.

No person shall be a Representative who shall not have attained to the age of twenty-five years, and been seven years a citizen of the United States, and who shall not, when elected, be an inhabitant of that State in which he shall be chosen.

Representatives and direct taxes shall be apportioned among the several States which may be included within this Union, according to their respective numbers, *which shall be determined by adding to the whole number of free persons, including those bound to service for a term of years and excluding Indians not taxed, three-fifths of all other persons.* The actual enumeration shall be made within three years after the first meeting of the Congress of the United States, and within every subsequent term of ten years, in such manner as they shall by law direct. The number of Representatives shall not exceed one for every thirty thousand, but each State shall have at least one Representative; *and until such enumeration shall be made, the State of New Hampshire shall be entitled to choose three, Massachusetts eight, Rhode Island and Providence Plantations one, Connecticut five, New York six, New Jersey four, Pennsylvania eight, Delaware one, Maryland six, Virginia ten, North Carolina five, South Carolina five, and Georgia three.*

When vacancies happen in the representation from

---

[*] Passages no longer in effect are printed in italic type.

any State, the Executive authority thereof shall issue writs of election to fill such vacancies.

The House of Representatives shall choose their Speaker and other officers; and shall have the sole power of impeachment.

Section 3 The Senate of the United States shall be composed of two Senators from each State, *chosen by the legislature thereof,* for six years; and each Senator shall have one vote.

Immediately after they shall be assembled in consequence of the first election, they shall be divided as equally as may be into three classes. The seats of the Senators of the first class shall be vacated at the expiration of the second year, of the second class at the expiration of the fourth year, and of the third class at the expiration of the sixth year, so that one-third may be chosen every second year; *and if vacancies happen by resignation or otherwise, during the recess of the legislature of any State, the Executive thereof may make temporary appointments until the next meeting of the legislature, which shall then fill such vacancies.*

No person shall be a Senator who shall not have attained to the age of thirty years, and been nine years a citizen of the United States, and who shall not, when elected, be an inhabitant of that State for which he shall be chosen.

The Vice-President of the United States shall be President of the Senate, but shall have no vote, unless they be equally divided.

The Senate shall choose their other officers, and also a President *pro tempore,* in the absence of the Vice-President, or when he shall exercise the office of President of the United States.

The Senate shall have the sole power to try all impeachments. When sitting for that purpose, they shall be on oath or affirmation. When the President of the United States is tried, the Chief Justice shall preside: and no person shall be convicted with-out the concurrence of two-thirds of the members present.

Judgment in cases of impeachment shall not extend further than to removal from the office, and disqualification to hold and enjoy any office of honor, trust or profit under the United States: but the party convicted shall nevertheless be liable and subject to indictment, trial, judgment and punishment, according to law.

Section 4 The times, places and manner of holding elections for Senators and Representatives shall be prescribed in each State by the legislature thereof; but the Congress may at any time by law make or alter such regulations, except as to the places of choosing Senators.

The Congress shall assemble at least once in every year, and such meeting *shall be on the first Monday in December, unless they shall by law appoint a different day.*

Section 5 Each house shall be the judge of the elections, returns and qualifications of its own members, and a majority of each shall constitute a quorum to do business; but a smaller number may adjourn from day to day, and may be authorized to compel the attendance of absent members, in such manner, and under such penalties, as each house may provide.

Each house may determine the rules of its proceedings, punish its members for disorderly behavior, and with the concurrence of two-thirds, expel a member.

Each house shall keep a journal of its proceedings, and from time to time publish the same, excepting such parts as may in their judgment require secrecy; and the yeas and nays of the members of either house on any question shall, at the desire of one-fifth of those present, be entered on the journal.

Neither house, during the session of Congress, shall, without the consent of the other, adjourn for more than three days, nor to any other place than that in which the two houses shall be sitting.

Section 6 The Senators and Representatives shall receive a compensation for their services, to be ascertained by law and paid out of the treasury of the United States. They shall in all cases except treason, felony and breach of the peace, be privileged from arrest during their attendance at the session of their respective houses, and in going to and returning from the same; and for any speech or debate in either house, they shall not be questioned in any other place.

No Senator or Representative shall, during the time for which he was elected, be appointed to any civil office under the authority of the United States, which shall have been created, or the emoluments whereof shall have been increased, during such time; and no person holding any office under the United States shall be a member of either house during his continuance in office.

Section 7 All bills for raising revenue shall originate in the House of Representatives; but the Senate may propose or concur with amendments as on other bills.

Every bill which shall have passed the House of Representatives and the Senate, shall, before it become a law, be presented to the President of the United States; if he approve he shall sign it, but if not he shall return it with objections to that house in which it originated, who shall enter the objections at large on their journal, and proceed to reconsider it. If after such reconsideration two-thirds of that house shall agree to pass the bill, it shall be sent, together with the objections, to the other house, by which it shall likewise be reconsidered, and, if approved by two-thirds of that house, it shall become a law. But in all such cases the votes of both houses shall be determined by yeas and nays, and the names of the persons voting for and against the bill shall be entered on the journal of each house respectively. If any bill shall not be returned by the President within ten days (Sundays excepted) after it shall have been presented to him, the same shall be a law, in like manner as if he had signed it, unless the Congress by their adjournment prevent its return, in which case it shall not be a law.

Every order, resolution, or vote to which the concurrence of the Senate and House of Representatives may be necessary (except on a question of adjournment) shall be presented to the President of the United States; and before the same shall take effect, shall be approved by him, or being disapproved by him, shall be repassed by two-thirds of the Senate and House of Representatives, according to the rules and limitations prescribed in the case of a bill.

Section 8 The Congress shall have power

To lay and collect taxes, duties, imposts, and excises, to pay the debts and provide for the common defense and general welfare of the United States; but all duties, imposts and excises shall be uniform throughout the United States;

To borrow money on the credit of the United States;

To regulate commerce with foreign nations, and among the several States, and with the Indian tribes;

To establish an uniform rule of naturalization, and uniform laws on the subject of bankruptcies throughout the United States;

To coin money, regulate the value thereof, and of foreign coin, and fix the standard of weights and measures;

To provide for the punishment of counterfeiting the securities and current coin of the United States;

To establish post offices and post roads;

To promote the progress of science and useful arts by securing for limited times to authors and inventors the exclusive right to their respective writings and discoveries;

To constitute tribunals inferior to the Supreme Court;

To define and punish piracies and felonies committed on the high seas and offenses against the law of nations;

To declare war, grant letters of marque and reprisal, and make rules concerning captures on land and water;

To raise and support armies, but no appropriation of money to that use shall be for a longer term than two years;

To provide and maintain a navy;

To make rules for the government and regulation of the land and naval forces;

To provide for calling forth the militia to execute the laws of the Union, suppress insurrections, and repel invasions;

To provide for organizing, arming, and disciplining the militia, and for governing such part of them as may be employed in the service of the United States, reserving to the States respectively the appointment of the officers, and the authority of training the militia according to the discipline prescribed by Congress;

To exercise exclusive legislation in all cases whatsoever, over such district (not exceeding ten miles square) as may, by cession of particular States, and the acceptance of Congress, become the seat of government of the United States, and to exercise like authority over all places purchased by the consent of the legislature of the State, in which the same shall be, for erection of forts, magazines, arsenals, dockyards, and other needful buildings; — and

To make all laws which shall be necessary and proper for carrying into execution the foregoing powers, and all other powers vested by this Constitution in the government of the United States, or in any department or officer thereof.

Section 9 *The migration or importation of such persons as any of the States now existing shall think proper to admit shall not be prohibited by the Congress prior to the year 1808; but a tax or duty may be imposed on such importation, not exceeding $10 for each person.*

The privilege of the writ of habeas corpus shall not be suspended, unless when in cases of rebellion or invasion the public safety may require it.

No bill of attainder or ex post facto law shall be passed.

No capitation, or other direct, tax shall be laid, unless in proportion to the census or enumeration herein before directed to be taken.

No tax or duty shall be laid on articles exported from any State.

No preference shall be given by any regulation of commerce or revenue to the ports of one State over those of another; nor shall vessels bound to, or from, one State, be obliged to enter, clear, or pay duties in another.

No money shall be drawn from the treasury, but in consequence of appropriations made by law; and a regular statement and account of the receipts and expenditures of all public money shall be published from time to time.

No title of nobility shall be granted by the United States: and no person holding any office of profit or trust under them, shall, without the consent of the Congress, accept of any present, emolument, office, or title, of any kind whatever, from any king, prince, or foreign state.

Section 10 No State shall enter into any treaty, alliance, or confederation; grant letters of marque and reprisal; coin money; emit bills of credit; make anything but gold and silver coin a tender in payment of debts; pass any bill of attainder, ex post facto law, or law impairing the obligation of contracts, or grant any title of nobility.

No State shall, without the consent of Congress, lay any imposts or duties on imports or exports, except what may be absolutely necessary for executing its inspection laws: and the net produce of all duties and imposts, laid by any State on imports or exports, shall be for the use of the treasury of the United States; and all such laws shall be subject to the revision and control of the Congress.

No State shall, without the consent of Congress, lay any duty of tonnage, keep troops or ships of war in time of peace, enter into any agreement or compact with another State, or with a foreign power, or engage in war, unless actually invaded, or in such imminent danger as will not admit of delay.

Article II

Section 1 The executive power shall be vested in a President of the United States of America. He shall hold his office during the term of four years, and, together with the Vice-President, chosen for the same term, be elected as follows:

Each State shall appoint, in such manner as the legislature thereof may direct, a number of electors, equal to the whole number of Senators and Representatives to which the State may be entitled in the Congress; but no Senator or Representative, or person holding an office of trust or profit under the United States, shall be appointed an elector.

The electors shall meet in their respective States, and vote by ballot for two persons, of whom one at least shall not be an inhabitant of the same State with themselves. And they shall make a list of all the persons voted for, and of the number of votes for each; which list they shall sign and certify, and transmit sealed to the seat of government of the United States, directed to the President of the Senate. The President of the Senate shall, in the presence of the Senate and House of Representatives, open all the certificates, and the votes shall then be counted. The person having the greatest number of votes shall be the President, if such number be a majority of the whole number of electors appointed; and if there be more than one who have such majority, and have an equal number of votes, then the House of Representatives shall immediately choose by ballot one of them for President; and if no person have a majority, then from the five highest on the list said house shall in like manner choose the President. But in choosing the President the votes shall be taken by States, the representation from each State having one vote; a quorum for this purpose shall consist of a member or members from two-thirds of the States, and a majority of all the States shall be necessary to a choice. In every case, after the choice of the President, the person having the greatest number of votes of the electors shall be the Vice-President. But if there should remain two or more who have equal votes, the Senate shall choose from them by ballot the Vice-President.

The Congress may determine the time of choosing the electors and the day on which they shall give their votes; which day shall be the same throughout the United States.

No person except a natural-born citizen, *or a citizen of the United States at the time of the adoption of this Constitution,* shall be eligible to the office of President; neither shall any person be eligible to that office who shall not have attained to the age of thirty-five years, and been fourteen years a resident within the United States.

In cases of the removal of the President from office or of his death, resignation, or inability to discharge the powers and duties of the said office, the same shall devolve on the Vice-President, and the Congress may by law provide for the case of removal, death, resignation, or inability, both of the President and Vice-President, declaring what officer shall then act as President, and such officer shall act accordingly, until the disability be removed, or a President shall be elected.

The President shall, at stated times, receive for his services a compensation, which shall neither be increased nor diminished during the period for which he shall have been elected, and he shall not receive within that period any other emolument from the United States, or any of them.

Before he enter on the execution of his office, he shall take the following oath or affirmation:—"I do solemnly swear (or affirm) that I will faithfully execute the office of the President of the United States, and will to the best of my ability preserve, protect and defend the Constitution of the United States."

Section 2 The President shall be commander in chief of the army and navy of the United States, and of the militia of the several States, when called into the actual service of the United States; he may require the opinion, in writing, of the principal officer in each of the executive departments, upon any subject relating to the duties of their respective offices, and he shall have power to grant reprieves and pardons for offenses against the United States, except in cases of impeachment.

He shall have power, by and with the advice and consent of the Senate, to make treaties, provided two-thirds of the Senators present concur; and he shall nominate, and by and with the advice and consent of the Senate, shall appoint ambassadors, other public ministers and consuls, judges of the Supreme Court, and all other officers of the United States, whose appointments are not herein otherwise provided for, and which shall be established by law: but Congress may by law vest the appointment of such inferior officers, as they think proper, in the President alone, in the courts of law, or in the heads of departments.

The President shall have power to fill up all vacancies that may happen during the recess of the Senate, by granting commissions which shall expire at the end of their next session.

Section 3   He shall from time to time give to the Congress information of the state of the Union, and recommend to their consideration such measures as he shall judge necessary and expedient; he may, on extraordinary occasions, convene both houses, or either of them, and in case of disagreement between them, with respect to the time of adjournment, he may adjourn them to such time as he shall think proper; he shall receive ambassadors and other public ministers; he shall take care that the laws be faithfully executed, and shall commission all the officers of the United States.

Section 4   The President, Vice-President and all civil officers of the United States shall be removed from office on impeachment for, and on conviction of, treason, bribery, or other high crimes and misdemeanors.

Article III

Section 1   The judicial power of the United States shall be vested in one Supreme Court, and in such inferior courts as the Congress may from time to time ordain and establish. The judges, both of the Supreme and inferior courts, shall hold their offices during good behavior, and shall, at stated times, receive for their services a compensation which shall not be diminished during their continuance in office.

Section 2   The judicial power shall extend to all cases, in law and equity, arising under this Constitution, the laws of the United States, and treaties made, or which shall be made, under their authority;—to all cases affecting ambassadors, other public ministers and consuls;—to all cases of admiralty and maritime jurisdiction;—to controversies to which the United States shall be a party;—to controversies between two or more States;—*between a State and citizens of another State*;—between citizens of different States;—between citizens of the same State claiming lands under grants of different States, and between a State, or the citizens thereof, and foreign states, citizens or subjects.

In all cases affecting ambassadors, other public ministers and consuls, and those in which a State shall be party, the Supreme Court shall have original jurisdiction. In all the other cases before mentioned, the Supreme Court shall have appellate jurisdiction, both as to law and fact, with such exceptions, and under such regulations, as the Congress shall make.

The trial of all crimes, except in cases of impeachment, shall be by jury; and such trial shall be held in the State where said crimes shall have been committed; but when not committed within any State, the trial shall be at such place or places as the Congress may by law have directed.

Section 3   Treason against the United States shall consist only in levying war against them, or in adhering to their enemies, giving them aid and comfort. No person shall be convicted of treason unless on the testimony of two witnesses to the same overt act, or on confession in open court.

The Congress shall have power to declare the punishment of treason, but no attainder of treason shall work corruption of blood, or forfeiture except during the life of the person attainted.

Article IV

Section 1   Full faith and credit shall be given in each State to the public acts, records, and judicial proceedings of every other State. And the Congress may by general laws prescribe the manner in which such acts, records, and proceedings shall be proved, and the effect thereof.

Section 2   The citizens of each State shall be entitled to all privileges and immunities of citizens in the several States.

A person charged in any State with treason, felony, or other crime, who shall flee from justice, and be found in another State, shall on demand of the executive authority of the State from which he fled, be delivered up, to be removed to the State having jurisdiction of the crime.

No person held to service or labor in one State, under the laws thereof, escaping into another, shall, in consequence of any law or regulation therein, be discharged from such service or labor, but shall be delivered up on claim of the party to whom such service or labor may be due.

Section 3   New States may be admitted by the Congress into this Union; but no new State shall be formed or erected within the jurisdiction of any other State; nor any State be formed by the junction of two or more States, or parts of States, without the consent of the legislatures of the States concerned as well as of the Congress.

The Congress shall have power to dispose of and make all needful rules and regulations respecting the territory or other property belonging to the United States; and nothing in this Constitution shall be so construed as to prejudice any claims of the United States, or of any particular State.

Section 4 The United States shall guarantee to every State in this Union a republican form of government, and shall protect each of them against invasion; and on application of the legislature, or of the executive (when the legislature cannot be convened), against domestic violence.

Article V

The Congress, whenever two-thirds of both houses shall deem it necessary, shall propose amendments to this Constitution, or, on the application of the legislatures of two-thirds of the several States, shall call a convention for proposing amendments, which, in either case, shall be valid to all intents and purposes, as part of this Constitution, when ratified by the legislatures of three-fourths of the several States, or by conventions in three-fourths thereof, as the one or the other mode of ratification may be proposed by the Congress; provided *that no amendments which may be made prior to the year one thousand eight hundred and eight shall in any manner affect the first and fourth clauses in the ninth section of the first article;* and that no State, without its consent, shall be deprived of its equal suffrage in the Senate.

Article VI

All debts contracted and engagements entered into, before the adoption of this Constitution, shall be as valid against the United States under this Constitution, as under the Confederation.

This Constitution, and the laws of the United States which shall be made in pursuance thereof; and all treaties made, or which shall be made, under the authority of the United States, shall be the supreme law of the land; and the judges in every State shall be bound thereby, anything in the Constitution or laws of any State to the contrary notwithstanding.

The Senators and Representatives before mentioned, and the members of the several State legislatures, and all executive and judicial officers, both of the United States and of the several States, shall be bound by oath or affirmation to support this Constitution; but no religious test shall ever be required as a qualification to any office or public trust under the United States.

Article VII

The ratification of the conventions of nine States shall be sufficient for the establishment of this Constitution between the States so ratifying the same.

Done in Convention by the unanimous consent of the States present, the seventeenth day of September in the year of our Lord one thousand seven hundred and eighty-seven and of the Independence of the United States of America the twelfth. In witness whereof we have hereunto subscribed our names.

GEORGE WASHINGTON
and thirty-seven others

Amendments to the Constitution[*]

Amendment I

Congress shall make no law respecting an establishment of religion, or prohibiting the free exercise thereof; or abridging the freedom of speech, or of the press; or the right of the people peaceably to assemble, and to petition the government for a redress of grievances.

Amendment II

A well-regulated militia being necessary to the security of a free State, the right of the people to keep and bear arms shall not be infringed.

Amendment III

No soldier shall, in time of peace, be quartered in any house without the consent of the owner, nor in time of war, but in a manner to be prescribed by law.

Amendment IV

The right of the people to be secure in their persons, houses, papers, and effects, against unreasonable searches and seizures, shall not be violated, and no warrants shall issue but upon probable cause, supported by oath or affirmation, and particularly describing the place to be searched, and the persons or things to be seized.

Amendment V

No person shall be held to answer for a capital, or otherwise infamous crime, unless on a presentment or indictment of a grand jury, except in cases arising in the land or naval forces, or in the militia, when in actual service in time of war or public danger; nor shall any person be subject for the same offense to be twice put in jeopardy of life or limb; nor shall be compelled in any criminal case to be a witness against himself, nor be deprived of life, liberty, or property, without due process of law; nor shall private property be taken for public use without just compensation.

Amendment VI

In all criminal prosecutions, the accused shall enjoy the right to a speedy and public trial, by an impartial jury of

---

[*] The first ten Amendments (the Bill of Rights) were adopted in 1791.

the State and district wherein the crime shall have been committed, which district shall have been previously ascertained by law, and to be informed of the nature and cause of the accusation; to be confronted with the witnesses against him; to have compulsory process for obtaining witnesses in his favor, and to have the assistance of counsel for his defense.

Amendment VII

In suits at common law, where the value in controversy shall exceed twenty dollars, the right of trial by jury shall be preserved, and no fact tried by a jury shall be otherwise reexamined in any court of the United States, than according to the rules of the common law.

Amendment VIII

Excessive bail shall not be required, nor excessive fines imposed, nor cruel and unusual punishments inflicted.

Amendment IX

The enumeration in the Constitution, of certain rights, shall not be construed to deny or disparage others retained by the people.

Amendment X

The powers not delegated to the United States by the Constitution, nor prohibited by it to the States, are reserved to the States respectively, or to the people.

Amendment XI

[Adopted 1798]

The judicial power of the United States shall not be construed to extend to any suit in law or equity, commenced or prosecuted against one of the United States by citizens of another State, or by citizens or subjects of any foreign state.

Amendment XII

[Adopted 1804]

The electors shall meet in their respective States, and vote by ballot for President and Vice-President, one of whom, at least, shall not be an inhabitant of the same State with themselves; they shall name in their ballots the person voted for as President, and in distinct ballots the person voted for as Vice-President, and they shall make distinct lists of all persons voted for as President, and of all persons voted for as Vice-President, and of the number of votes for each, which lists they shall sign and certify, and transmit sealed to the seat of government of the United States, directed to the President of the Senate;—the President of the Senate shall, in the presence of the Senate and House of Representatives, open all the certificates and the votes shall then be counted;—the person having the great-

est number of votes for President shall be the President, if such number be a majority of the whole number of electors appointed; and if no person have such majority, then from the persons having the highest numbers not exceeding three on the list of those voted for as President, the House of Representatives shall choose immediately, by ballot, the President. But in choosing the President, the votes shall be taken by States, the representation from each State having one vote; a quorum for this purpose shall consist of a member or members from two-thirds of the States, and a majority of all the States shall be necessary to a choice. And if the House of Representatives shall not choose a President whenever the right of choice shall devolve upon them, before the fourth day of March next following, then the Vice-President shall act as President, as in the case of the death or other constitutional disability of the President.

The person having the greatest number of votes as Vice-President shall be the Vice-President, if such number be a majority of the whole number of electors appointed; and if no person have a majority, then from the two highest numbers on the list the Senate shall choose the Vice-President; a quorum for the purpose shall consist of two-thirds of the whole number of Senators, and a majority of the whole number shall be necessary to a choice. But no person constitutionally ineligible to the office of President shall be eligible to that of Vice-President of the United States.

Amendment XIII

[Adopted 1865]

Section 1   Neither slavery nor involuntary servitude, except as a punishment for crime whereof the party shall have been duly convicted, shall exist within the United States, or any place subject to their jurisdiction.

Section 2   Congress shall have power to enforce this article by appropriate legislation.

Amendment XIV

[Adopted 1868]

Section 1   All persons born or naturalized in the United States, and subject to the jurisdiction thereof, are citizens of the United States and of the State wherein they reside. No State shall make or enforce any law which shall abridge the privileges or immunities of citizens of the United States; nor shall any State deprive any person of life, liberty, or property, without due process of law; nor deny to any person within its jurisdiction the equal protection of the laws.

Section 2   Representatives shall be apportioned among the several States according to their respective numbers, counting the whole number of persons in each State, excluding Indians not taxed. But when the right to vote at any election for the choice of Electors for President and Vice-President of the United States, Representatives in Congress, the executive and judicial officers of a State, or the members of the legislature thereof, is denied to any of the male inhabitants of such State, being twenty-one years of age and citizens of the United States, or in any way abridged, except for participation in rebellion, or other crime, the basis of representation therein shall be reduced in the proportion which the number of such male citizens shall bear to the whole number of male citizens twenty-one years of age in such State.

Section 3   No person shall be a Senator or Representative in Congress, or Elector of President and Vice-President, or hold any office, civil or military, under the United States, or under any State, who, having previously taken an oath, as a member of Congress, or as an officer of the United States, or as a member of any State legislature, or as an executive or judicial officer of any State, to support the Constitution of the United States, shall have engaged in insurrection or rebellion against the same, or given aid or comfort to the enemies thereof. Congress may, by a vote of two-thirds of each house, remove such disability.

Section 4   The validity of the public debt of the United States, authorized by law, including debts incurred for payment of pensions and bounties for services in suppressing insurrection or rebellion, shall not be questioned. But neither the United States nor any State shall assume or pay any debt or obligation incurred in aid of insurrection or rebellion against the United States, or any claim for the loss or emancipation of any slave; but all such debts, obligations, and claims shall be held illegal and void.

Section 5   The Congress shall have power to enforce, by appropriate legislation, the provisions of this article.

Amendment XV

[Adopted 1870]

Section 1   The right of citizens of the United States to vote shall not be denied or abridged by the United States or by any State on account of race, color, or previous condition of servitude.

Section 2   The Congress shall have power to enforce this article by appropriate legislation.

Amendment XVI

[Adopted 1913]

The Congress shall have power to lay and collect taxes on incomes, from whatever source derived, without apportionment among the several States, and without regard to any census or enumeration.

Amendment XVII

[Adopted 1913]

Section 1   The Senate of the United States shall be composed of two Senators from each State, elected by the people thereof, for six years; and each Senator shall have one vote. The electors in each State shall have the qualifications requisite for electors of [voters for] the most numerous branch of the State legislatures.

Section 2   When vacancies happen in the representation of any State in the Senate, the executive authority of such State shall issue writs of election to fill such vacancies: Provided, that the Legislature of any State may empower the executive thereof to make temporary appointments until the people fill the vacancies by election as the Legislature may direct.

Section 3   This amendment shall not be so construed as to affect the election or term of any Senator chosen before it becomes valid as part of the Constitution.

Amendment XVIII

[Adopted 1919; Repealed 1933]

Section 1   After one year from the ratification of this article the manufacture, sale, or transportation of intoxicating liquors within, the importation thereof into, or the exportation thereof from the United States and all territory subject to the jurisdiction thereof, for beverage purposes, is hereby prohibited.

Section 2   The Congress and the several States shall have concurrent power to enforce this article by appropriate legislation.

Section 3   This article shall be inoperative unless it shall have been ratified as an amendment to the Constitution by the legislatures of the several States, as provided by the Constitution, within seven years from the date of the submission thereof to the States by the Congress.

Amendment XIX

[Adopted 1920]

Section 1   The right of citizens of the United States to vote shall not be denied or abridged by the United States or by any State on account of sex.

Section 2   The Congress shall have power to enforce this article by appropriate legislation.

Amendment XX

[Adopted 1933]

Section 1   The terms of the President and Vice-President shall end at noon on the 20th day of January, and the terms of Senators and Representatives at noon on the 3rd day of January, of the years in which such terms would have ended if this article had not been ratified; and the terms of their successors shall then begin.

Section 2   The Congress shall assemble at least once in every year, and such meeting shall begin at noon on the 3d day of January, unless they shall by law appoint a different day.

Section 3   If, at the time fixed for the beginning of the term of the President, the President-elect shall have died, the Vice-President-elect shall become President. If a President shall not have been chosen before the time fixed for the beginning of his term, or if the President-elect shall have failed to qualify, then the Vice-President-elect shall act as President until a President shall have qualified; and the Congress may by law provide for the case wherein neither a President-elect nor a Vice-President-elect shall have qualified, declaring who shall then act as President, or the manner in which one who is to act shall be selected, and such persons shall act accordingly until a President or Vice-President shall have qualified.

Section 4   The Congress may by law provide for the case of the death of any of the persons from whom the House of Representatives may choose a President whenever the right of choice shall have devolved upon them, and for the case of the death of any of the persons from whom the Senate may choose a Vice-President whenever the right of choice shall have devolved upon them.

Section 5   Sections 1 and 2 shall take effect on the 15th day of October following the ratification of this article.

Section 6   This article shall be inoperative unless it shall have been ratified as an amendment to the Constitution by the Legislatures of three-fourths of the several States within seven years from the date of its submission.

Amendment XXI

[Adopted 1933]

Section 1   The eighteenth article of amendment to the Constitution of the United States is hereby repealed.

Section 2   The transportation or importation into any State, Territory, or Possession of the United States for delivery or use therein of intoxicating liquors, in violation of the laws thereof, is hereby prohibited.

Section 3   This article shall be inoperative unless it shall have been ratified as an amendment to the Constitution by conventions in the several States, as provided in the Constitution, within seven years from the date of submission thereof to the States by the Congress.

Amendment XXII

[Adopted 1951]

Section 1   No person shall be elected to the office of President more than twice, and no person who has held the office of President, or acted as President, for more than two years of a term to which some other person was elected President shall be elected to the office of President more than once. But this article shall not apply to any person holding the office of President when this article was proposed by the Congress, and shall not prevent any person who may be holding the office of President, or acting as President, during the term within which this article becomes operative from holding the office of President or acting as President during the remainder of such term.

Section 2   This article shall be inoperative unless it shall have been ratified as an amendment to the Constitution by the legislatures of three-fourths of the several States within seven years from the date of its submission to the States by the Congress.

Amendment XXIII

[Adopted 1961]

Section 1   The District constituting the seat of Government of the United States shall appoint in such manner as the Congress may direct:

A number of electors of President and Vice-President equal to the whole number of Senators and Representatives in Congress to which the District would be entitled if it were a State, but in no event more than the least populous State; they shall be in addition to those appointed by the States, but they shall be considered for the purposes of the election of President and Vice-President, to be electors appointed by a State; and they shall meet in the District and perform such duties as provided by the twelfth article of amendment.

Section 2   The Congress shall have the power to enforce this article by appropriate legislation.

Amendment XXIV

[Adopted 1964]

Section 1   The right of citizens of the United States to vote in any primary or other election for President or Vice-President, for electors for President or Vice-President, or for Senator or Representative in Congress, shall not be denied or abridged by the United States or any State by reason of failure to pay any poll tax or other tax.

Section 2   The Congress shall have the power to enforce this article by appropriate legislation.

Amendment XXV

[Adopted 1967]

Section 1   In case of the removal of the President from office or of his death or resignation, the Vice-President shall become President.

Section 2   Whenever there is a vacancy in the office of the Vice-President, the President shall nominate a Vice-President who shall take office upon confirmation by a majority vote of both Houses of Congress.

Section 3   Whenever the President transmits to the President pro tempore of the Senate and the Speaker of the House of Representatives his written declaration that he is unable to discharge the powers and duties of his office, and until he transmits to them a written declaration to the contrary, such powers and duties shall be discharged by the Vice-President as Acting President.

Section 4   Whenever the Vice-President and a majority of either the principal officers of the executive departments or of such other body as Congress may by law provide, transmit to the President pro tempore of the Senate and the Speaker of the House of Representatives their written declaration that the President is unable to discharge the powers and duties of his office, the Vice-President shall immediately assume the powers and duties of the office as Acting President.

Thereafter, when the President transmits to the President pro tempore of the Senate and the Speaker of the House of Representatives his written declaration that no inability exists, he shall resume the powers and duties of his office unless the Vice-President and a majority of either the principal officers of the executive department[s] transmit within four days to the President pro tempore of the Senate and the Speaker of the House of Representatives their written declaration that the President is unable to discharge the powers and duties of his office. Thereupon Congress shall decide the issue, assembling within forty-eight hours for that purpose if not in session. If the Congress, within twenty-one days after receipt of the latter written declaration, or, if Congress is not in session, within twenty-one days after Congress is required to assemble, determines by two-thirds vote of both Houses that the President is unable to discharge the powers and duties of his office, the Vice-President shall continue to discharge the same as Acting President; otherwise, the President shall resume the powers and duties of his office.

Amendment XXVI

[Adopted 1971]

Section 1   The right of citizens of the United States, who are eighteen years of age or older, to vote shall not be denied or abridged by the United States or by any State on account of age.

Section 2   The Congress shall have power to enforce this article by appropriate legislation.

Amendment XXVII

[Adopted 1992]

No law, varying the compensation for the services of the Senators and Representatives, shall take effect, until an election of Representatives shall have intervened.

Territorial Expansion of the United States

Territory	Date Acquired	Square Miles	How Acquired
Original states and territories	1783	888,685	Treaty with Great Britain
Louisiana Purchase	1803	827,192	Purchase from France
Florida	1819	72,003	Treaty with Spain
Texas	1845	390,143	Annexation of independent nation
Oregon	1846	285,580	Treaty with Great Britain
Mexican Cession	1848	529,017	Conquest from Mexico
Gadsden Purchase	1853	29,640	Purchase from Mexico
Alaska	1867	589,757	Purchase from Russia
Hawai`i	1898	6,450	Annexation of independent nation
The Philippines	1899	115,600	Conquest from Spain (granted independence in 1946)
Puerto Rico	1899	3,435	Conquest from Spain
Guam	1899	212	Conquest from Spain
American Samoa	1900	76	Treaty with Germany and Great Britain
Panama Canal Zone	1904	553	Treaty with Panama (returned to Panama by treaty in 1978)
Corn Islands	1914	4	Treaty with Nicaragua (returned to Nicaragua by treaty in 1971)
Virgin Islands	1917	133	Purchase from Denmark
Pacific Islands Trust (Micronesia)	1947	8,489	Trusteeship under United Nations (some granted independence)
All others (Midway, Wake, and other islands)		42	

Admission of States into the Union

State	Date of Admission	State	Date of Admission
1. Delaware	December 7, 1787	26. Michigan	January 26, 1837
2. Pennsylvania	December 12, 1787	27. Florida	March 3, 1845
3. New Jersey	December 18, 1787	28. Texas	December 29, 1845
4. Georgia	January 2, 1788	29. Iowa	December 28, 1846
5. Connecticut	January 9, 1788	30. Wisconsin	May 29, 1848
6. Massachusetts	February 6, 1788	31. California	September 9, 1850
7. Maryland	April 28, 1788	32. Minnesota	May 11, 1858
8. South Carolina	May 23, 1788	33. Oregon	February 14, 1859
9. New Hampshire	June 21, 1788	34. Kansas	January 29, 1861
10. Virginia	June 25, 1788	35. West Virginia	June 20, 1863
11. New York	July 26, 1788	36. Nevada	October 31, 1864
12. North Carolina	November 21, 1789	37. Nebraska	March 1, 1867
13. Rhode Island	May 29, 1790	38. Colorado	August 1, 1876
14. Vermont	March 4, 1791	39. North Dakota	November 2, 1889
15. Kentucky	June 1, 1792	40. South Dakota	November 2, 1889
16. Tennessee	June 1, 1796	41. Montana	November 8, 1889
17. Ohio	March 1, 1803	42. Washington	November 11, 1889
18. Louisiana	April 30, 1812	43. Idaho	July 3, 1890
19. Indiana	December 11, 1816	44. Wyoming	July 10, 1890
20. Mississippi	December 10, 1817	45. Utah	January 4, 1896
21. Illinois	December 3, 1818	46. Oklahoma	November 16, 1907
22. Alabama	December 14, 1819	47. New Mexico	January 6, 1912
23. Maine	March 15, 1820	48. Arizona	February 14, 1912
24. Missouri	August 10, 1821	49. Alaska	January 3, 1959
25. Arkansas	June 15, 1836	50. Hawai`i	August 21, 1959

Presidential Elections

Year	Number of States	Candidates	Parties	Popular Vote	% of Popular Vote	Electoral Vote	% Voter Participation[a]
1789	11	**George Washington**	No party			69	
		John Adams	designations			34	
		Other candidates				35	
1792	15	**George Washington**	No party			132	
		John Adams	designations			77	
		George Clinton				50	
		Other candidates				5	
1796	16	**John Adams**	Federalist			71	
		Thomas Jefferson	Democratic-Republican			68	
		Thomas Pinckney	Federalist			59	
		Aaron Burr	Democratic-Republican			30	
		Other candidates				48	
1800	16	**Thomas Jefferson**	Democratic-Republican			73	
		Aaron Burr	Democratic-Republican			73	
		John Adams	Federalist			65	
		Charles C. Pinckney	Federalist			64	
		John Jay	Federalist			1	
1804	17	**Thomas Jefferson**	Democratic-Republican			162	
		Charles C. Pinckney	Federalist			14	
1808	17	**James Madison**	Democratic-Republican			122	
		Charles C. Pinckney	Federalist			47	
		George Clinton	Democratic-Republican			6	
1812	18	**James Madison**	Democratic-Republican			128	
		DeWitt Clinton	Federalist			89	
1816	19	**James Monroe**	Democratic-Republican			183	
		Rufus King	Federalist			34	
1820	24	**James Monroe**	Democratic-Republican			231	
		John Quincy Adams	Independent-Republican			1	
1824	24	**John Quincy Adams**	Democratic-Republican	108,740	30.5	84	26.9
		Andrew Jackson	Democratic-Republican	153,544	43.1	99	

Presidential Elections *(continued)*

Year	Number of States	Candidates	Parties	Popular Vote	% of Popular Vote	Electoral Vote	% Voter Participation[a]
		Henry Clay	Democratic-Republican	47,136	13.2	37	
		William H. Crawford	Democratic-Republican	46,618	13.1	41	
1828	24	**Andrew Jackson**	Democratic	647,286	56.0	178	57.6
		John Quincy Adams	National Republican	508,064	44.0	83	
1832	24	**Andrew Jackson**	Democratic	688,242	54.5	219	55.4
		Henry Clay	National Republican	473,462	37.5	49	
		William Wirt	Anti-Masonic	101,051	8.0	7	
		John Floyd	Democratic			11	
1836	26	**Martin Van Buren**	Democratic	765,483	50.9	170	57.8
		William H. Harrison	Whig			73	
		Hugh L. White	Whig			26	
		Daniel Webster	Whig	739,795	49.1	14	
		W. P. Mangum	Whig			11	
1840	26	**William H. Harrison**	Whig	1,274,624	53.1	234	80.2
		Martin Van Buren	Democratic	1,127,781	46.9	60	
1844	26	**James K. Polk**	Democratic	1,338,464	49.6	170	78.9
		Henry Clay	Whig	1,300,097	48.1	105	
		James G. Birney	Liberty	62,300	2.3		
1848	30	**Zachary Taylor**	Whig	1,360,967	47.4	163	72.7
		Lewis Cass	Democratic	1,222,342	42.5	127	
		Martin Van Buren	Free-Soil	291,263	10.1		
1852	31	**Franklin Pierce**	Democratic	1,601,117	50.9	254	69.6
		Winfield Scott	Whig	1,385,453	44.1	42	
		John P. Hale	Free-Soil	155,825	5.0		
1856	31	**James Buchanan**	Democratic	1,832,955	45.3	174	78.9
		John C. Frémont	Republican	1,339,932	33.1	114	
		Millard Fillmore	American	871,731	21.6	8	
1860	33	**Abraham Lincoln**	Republican	1,865,593	39.8	180	81.2
		Stephen A. Douglas	Democratic	1,382,713	29.5	12	
		John C. Breckinridge	Democratic	848,356	18.1	72	
		John Bell	Constitutional Union	592,906	12.6	39	
1864	36	**Abraham Lincoln**	Republican	2,206,938	55.0	212	73.8
		George B. McClellan	Democratic	1,803,787	45.0	21	
1868	37	**Ulysses S. Grant**	Republican	3,013,421	52.7	214	78.1
		Horatio Seymour	Democratic	2,706,829	47.3	80	
1872	37	**Ulysses S. Grant**	Republican	3,596,745	55.6	286	71.3
		Horace Greeley	Democratic	2,843,446	43.9	[b]	
1876	38	**Rutherford B. Hayes**	Republican	4,036,572	48.0	185	81.8

Presidential Elections (continued)

Year	Number of States	Candidates	Parties	Popular Vote	% of Popular Vote	Elec-toral Vote	% Voter Partici-pation[a]
		Samuel J. Tilden	Democratic	4,284,020	51.0	184	
1880	38	**James A. Garfield**	Republican	4,453,295	48.5	214	79.4
		Winfield S. Hancock	Democratic	4,414,082	48.1	155	
		James B. Weaver	Greenback-Labor	308,578	3.4		
1884	38	**Grover Cleveland**	Democratic	4,879,507	48.5	219	77.5
		James G. Blaine	Republican	4,850,293	48.2	182	
		Benjamin F. Butler	Greenback-Labor	175,370	1.8		
		John P. St. John	Prohibition	150,369	1.5		
1888	38	**Benjamin Harrison**	Republican	5,477,129	47.9	233	79.3
		Grover Cleveland	Democratic	5,537,857	48.6	168	
		Clinton B. Fisk	Prohibition	249,506	2.2		
		Anson J. Streeter	Union Labor	146,935	1.3		
1892	44	**Grover Cleveland**	Democratic	5,555,426	46.1	277	74.7
		Benjamin Harrison	Republican	5,182,690	43.0	145	
		James B. Weaver	People's	1,029,846	8.5	22	
		John Bidwell	Prohibition	264,133	2.2		
1896	45	**William McKinley**	Republican	7,102,246	51.1	271	79.3
		William J. Bryan	Democratic	6,492,559	47.7	176	
1900	45	**William McKinley**	Republican	7,218,491	51.7	292	73.2
		William J. Bryan	Democratic; Populist	6,356,734	45.5	155	
		John C. Wooley	Prohibition	208,914	1.5		
1904	45	**Theodore Roosevelt**	Republican	7,628,461	57.4	336	65.2
		Alton B. Parker	Democratic	5,084,223	37.6	140	
		Eugene V. Debs	Socialist	402,283	3.0		
		Silas C. Swallow	Prohibition	258,536	1.9		
1908	46	**William H. Taft**	Republican	7,675,320	51.6	321	65.4
		William J. Bryan	Democratic	6,412,294	43.1	162	
		Eugene V. Debs	Socialist	420,793	2.8		
		Eugene W. Chafin	Prohibition	253,840	1.7		
1912	48	**Woodrow Wilson**	Democratic	6,296,547	41.9	435	58.8
		Theodore Roosevelt	Progressive	4,118,571	27.4	88	
		William H. Taft	Republican	3,486,720	23.2	8	
		Eugene V. Debs	Socialist	900,672	6.0		
		Eugene W. Chafin	Prohibition	206,275	1.4		
1916	48	**Woodrow Wilson**	Democratic	9,127,695	49.4	277	61.6
		Charles E. Hughes	Republican	8,533,507	46.2	254	
		A. L. Benson	Socialist	585,113	3.2		
		J. Frank Hanly	Prohibition	220,506	1.2		
1920	48	**Warren G. Harding**	Republican	16,143,407	60.4	404	49.2
		James M. Cox	Democratic	9,130,328	34.2	127	

Presidential Elections (continued)

Year	Number of States	Candidates	Parties	Popular Vote	% of Popular Vote	Electoral Vote	% Voter Participation[a]
		Eugene V. Debs	Socialist	919,799	3.4		
		P. P. Christensen	Farmer-Labor	265,411	1.0		
1924	48	**Calvin Coolidge**	Republican	15,718,211	54.0	382	48.9
		John W. Davis	Democratic	8,385,283	28.8	136	
		Robert M. La Follette	Progressive	4,831,289	16.6	13	
1928	48	**Herbert C. Hoover**	Republican	21,391,993	58.2	444	56.9
		Alfred E. Smith	Democratic	15,016,169	40.9	87	
1932	48	**Franklin D. Roosevelt**	Democratic	22,809,638	57.4	472	56.9
		Herbert C. Hoover	Republican	15,758,901	39.7	59	
		Norman Thomas	Socialist	881,951	2.2		
1936	48	**Franklin D. Roosevelt**	Democratic	27,752,869	60.8	523	61.0
		Alfred M. Landon	Republican	16,674,665	36.5	8	
		William Lemke	Union	882,479	1.9		
1940	48	**Franklin D. Roosevelt**	Democratic	27,307,819	54.8	449	62.5
		Wendell L. Wilkie	Republican	22,321,018	44.8	82	
1944	48	**Franklin D. Roosevelt**	Democratic	25,606,585	53.5	432	55.9
		Thomas E. Dewey	Republican	22,014,745	46.0	99	
1948	48	**Harry S Truman**	Democratic	24,179,345	49.6	303	53.0
		Thomas E. Dewey	Republican	21,991,291	45.1	189	
		J. Strom Thurmond	States' Rights	1,176,125	2.4	39	
		Henry A. Wallace	Progressive	1,157,326	2.4		
1952	48	**Dwight D. Eisenhower**	Republican	33,936,234	55.1	442	63.3
		Adlai E. Stevenson	Democratic	27,314,992	44.4	89	
1956	48	**Dwight D. Eisenhower**	Republican	35,590,472	57.6	457	60.6
		Adlai E. Stevenson	Democratic	26,022,752	42.1	73	
1960	50	**John F. Kennedy**	Democratic	34,226,731	49.7	303	62.8
		Richard M. Nixon	Republican	34,108,157	49.5	219	
1964	50	**Lyndon B. Johnson**	Democratic	43,129,566	61.1	486	61.7
		Barry M. Goldwater	Republican	27,178,188	38.5	52	
1968	50	**Richard M. Nixon**	Republican	31,785,480	43.4	301	60.6
		Hubert H. Humphrey	Democratic	31,275,166	42.7	191	
		George C. Wallace	American Independent	9,906,473	13.5	46	
1972	50	**Richard M. Nixon**	Republican	47,169,911	60.7	520	55.2
		George S. McGovern	Democratic	29,170,383	37.5	17	
		John G. Schmitz	American	1,099,482	1.4		
1976	50	**Jimmy Carter**	Democratic	40,830,763	50.1	297	53.5
		Gerald R. Ford	Republican	39,147,793	48.0	240	
1980	50	**Ronald Reagan**	Republican	43,899,248	50.8	489	52.6
		Jimmy Carter	Democratic	35,481,432	41.0	49	
		John B. Anderson	Independent	5,719,437	6.6	0	
		Ed Clark	Libertarian	920,859	1.1	0	

Presidential Elections *(continued)*

Year	Number of States	Candidates	Parties	Popular Vote	% of Popular Vote	Electoral Vote	% Voter Participation[a]
1984	50	**Ronald Reagan**	Republican	54,455,075	58.8	525	53.1
		Walter Mondale	Democratic	37,577,185	40.6	13	
1988	50	**George Bush**	Republican	48,901,046	53.4	426	50.2
		Michael Dukakis	Democratic	41,809,030	45.6	111[c]	
1992	50	**Bill Clinton**	Democratic	44,908,233	43.0	370	55.0
		George Bush	Republican	39,102,282	37.4	168	
		Ross Perot	Independent	19,741,048	18.9	0	
1996	50	**Bill Clinton**	Democratic	47,401,054	49.2	379	49.0
		Robert Dole	Republican	39,197,350	40.7	159	
		Ross Perot	Independent	8,085,285	8.4	0	
		Ralph Nader	Green	684,871	0.7	0	
2000	50	**George W. Bush**	Republican	50,456,169	47.88	271	50.7
		Albert Gore, Jr.	Democratic	50,996,116	48.39	267	
		Ralph Nader	Green	2,783,728	2.72	0	
2004	50	George W. Bush	Republican	59,668,401[d]	51	286	58[e]
		John F. Kerry	Democratic	56,170,687[d]	48	252	
		Ralph Nader	Independent	400,706[d]	1	0	

Candidates receiving less than 1 percent of the popular vote have been omitted. Thus the percentage of popular vote given for any election year may not total 100 percent.

Before the passage of the Twelfth Amendment in 1804, the Electoral College voted for two presidential candidates; the runner-up became vice president.

Before 1824, most presidential electors were chosen by state legislatures, not by popular vote.

[a]Percent of voting-age population casting ballots (eligible voters).

[b]Greeley died shortly after the election; the electors supporting him then divided their votes among minor candidates.

[c]One elector from West Virginia cast her Electoral College presidential ballot for Lloyd Bentsen, the Democratic Party's vice-presidential candidate.

[d]At press time.

[e]Estimate at press time.

Presidents, Vice Presidents, and Cabinet Members

The Washington Administration

President	George Washington	1789–1797
Vice President	John Adams	1789–1797
Secretary of State	Thomas Jefferson	1789–1793
	Edmund Randolph	1794–1795
	Timothy Pickering	1795–1797
Secretary of Treasury	Alexander Hamilton	1789–1795
	Oliver Wolcott	1795–1797
Secretary of War	Henry Knox	1789–1794
	Timothy Pickering	1795–1796
	James McHenry	1796–1797
Attorney General	Edmund Randolph	1789–1793
	William Bradford	1794–1795
	Charles Lee	1795–1797
Postmaster General	Samuel Osgood	1789–1791
	Timothy Pickering	1791–1794
	Joseph Habersham	1795–1797

The John Adams Administration

President	John Adams	1797–1801
Vice President	Thomas Jefferson	1797–1801
Secretary of State	Timothy Pickering	1797–1800
	John Marshall	1800–1801
Secretary of Treasury	Oliver Wolcott	1797–1800
	Samuel Dexter	1800–1801
Secretary of War	James McHenry	1797–1800
	Samuel Dexter	1800–1801
Attorney General	Charles Lee	1797–1801
Postmaster General	Joseph Habersham	1797–1801
Secretary of Navy	Benjamin Stoddert	1798–1801

The Jefferson Administration

President	Thomas Jefferson	1801–1809
Vice President	Aaron Burr	1801–1805
	George Clinton	1805–1809
Secretary of State	James Madison	1801–1809
Secretary of Treasury	Samuel Dexter	1801
	Albert Gallatin	1801–1809
Secretary of War	Henry Dearborn	1801–1809
Attorney General	Levi Lincoln	1801–1805
	Robert Smith	1805
	John Breckinridge	1805–1806
	Caesar Rodney	1807–1809
Postmaster General	Joseph Habersham	1801
	Gideon Granger	1801–1809
Secretary of Navy	Robert Smith	1801–1809

The Madison Administration

President	James Madison	1809–1817
Vice President	George Clinton	1809–1813
	Elbridge Gerry	1813–1817
Secretary of State	Robert Smith	1809–1811
	James Monroe	1811–1817
Secretary of Treasury	Albert Gallatin	1809–1813
	George Campbell	1814
	Alexander Dallas	1814–1816
	William Crawford	1816–1817
Secretary of War	William Eustis	1809–1812
	John Armstrong	1813–1814
	James Monroe	1814–1815
	William Crawford	1815–1817
Attorney General	Caesar Rodney	1809–1811
	William Pinkney	1811–1814
	Richard Rush	1814–1817
Postmaster General	Gideon Granger	1809–1814
	Return Meigs	1814–1817
Secretary of Navy	Paul Hamilton	1809–1813
	William Jones	1813–1814
	Benjamin Crowninshield	1814–1817

The Monroe Administration

President	James Monroe	1817–1825
Vice President	Daniel Tompkins	1817–1825
Secretary of State	John Quincy Adams	1817–1825
Secretary of Treasury	William Crawford	1817–1825
Secretary of War	George Graham	1817
	John C. Calhoun	1817–1825
Attorney General	Richard Rush	1817
	William Wirt	1817–1825
Postmaster General	Return Meigs	1817–1823
	John McLean	1823–1825
Secretary of Navy	Benjamin Crowninshield	1817–1818
	Smith Thompson	1818–1823
	Samuel Southard	1823–1825

The John Quincy Adams Administration

President	John Quincy Adams	1825–1829
Vice President	John C. Calhoun	1825–1829

Presidents, Vice Presidents, and Cabinet Members *(continued)*

Secretary of State	Henry Clay	1825–1829
Secretary of Treasury	Richard Rush	1825–1829
Secretary of War	James Barbour	1825–1828
	Peter Porter	1828–1829
Attorney General	William Wirt	1825–1829
Postmaster General	John McLean	1825–1829
Secretary of Navy	Samuel Southard	1825–1829

The Jackson Administration

President	Andrew Jackson	1829–1837
Vice President	John C. Calhoun	1829–1833
	Martin Van Buren	1833–1837
Secretary of State	Martin Van Buren	1829–1831
	Edward Livingston	1831–1833
	Louis McLane	1833–1834
	John Forsyth	1834–1837
Secretary of Treasury	Samuel Ingham	1829–1831
	Louis McLane	1831–1833
	William Duane	1833
	Roger B. Taney	1833–1834
	Levi Woodbury	1834–1837
Secretary of War	John H. Eaton	1829–1831
	Lewis Cass	1831–1837
	Benjamin Butler	1837
Attorney General	John M. Berrien	1829–1831
	Roger B. Taney	1831–1833
	Benjamin Butler	1833–1837
Postmaster General	William Barry	1829–1835
	Amos Kendall	1835–1837
Secretary of Navy	John Branch	1829–1831
	Levi Woodbury	1831–1834
	Mahlon Dickerson	1834–1837

The Van Buren Administration

President	Martin Van Buren	1837–1841
Vice President	Richard M. Johnson	1837–1841
Secretary of State	John Forsyth	1837–1841
Secretary of Treasury	Levi Woodbury	1837–1841
Secretary of War	Joel Poinsett	1837–1841
Attorney General	Benjamin Butler	1837–1838
	Felix Grundy	1838–1840
	Henry D. Gilpin	1840–1841
Postmaster General	Amos Kendall	1837–1840
	John M. Niles	1840–1841
Secretary of Navy	Mahlon Dickerson	1837–1838
	James Paulding	1838–1841

The William Harrison Administration

President	William H. Harrison	1841
Vice President	John Tyler	1841
Secretary of State	Daniel Webster	1841
Secretary of Treasury	Thomas Ewing	1841
Secretary of War	John Bell	1841
Attorney General	John J. Crittenden	1841
Postmaster General	Francis Granger	1841
Secretary of Navy	George Badger	1841

The Tyler Administration

President	John Tyler	1841–1845
Vice President	None	
Secretary of State	Daniel Webster	1841–1843
	Hugh S. Legaré	1843
	Abel P. Upshur	1843–1844
	John C. Calhoun	1844–1845
Secretary of Treasury	Thomas Ewing	1841
	Walter Forward	1841–1843
	John C. Spencer	1843–1844
	George Bibb	1844–1845
Secretary of War	John Bell	1841
	John C. Spencer	1841–1843
	James M. Porter	1843–1844
	William Wilkins	1844–1845
Attorney General	John J. Crittenden	1841
	Hugh S. Legaré	1841–1843
	John Nelson	1843–1845
Postmaster General	Francis Granger	1841
	Charles Wickliffe	1841
Secretary of Navy	George Badger	1841
	Abel P. Upshur	1841
	David Henshaw	1843–1844
	Thomas Gilmer	1844
	John Y. Mason	1844–1845

The Polk Administration

President	James K. Polk	1845–1849
Vice President	George M. Dallas	1845–1849
Secretary of State	James Buchanan	1845–1849
Secretary of Treasury	Robert J. Walker	1845–1849
Secretary of War	William L. Marcy	1845–1849
Attorney General	John Y. Mason	1845–1846
	Nathan Clifford	1846–1848
	Isaac Toucey	1848–1849

Presidents, Vice Presidents, and Cabinet Members *(continued)*

Postmaster General	Cave Johnson	1845–1849
Secretary of Navy	George Bancroft	1845–1846
	John Y. Mason	1846–1849

The Taylor Administration

President	Zachary Taylor	1849–1850
Vice President	Millard Fillmore	1849–1850
Secretary of State	John M. Clayton	1849–1850
Secretary of Treasury	William Meredith	1849–1850
Secretary of War	George Crawford	1849–1850
Attorney General	Reverdy Johnson	1849–1850
Postmaster General	Jacob Collamer	1849–1850
Secretary of Navy	William Preston	1849–1850
Secretary of Interior	Thomas Ewing	1849–1850

The Fillmore Administration

President	Millard Fillmore	1850–1853
Vice President	None	
Secretary of State	Daniel Webster	1850–1852
	Edward Everett	1852–1853
Secretary of Treasury	Thomas Corwin	1850–1853
Secretary of War	Charles Conrad	1850–1853
Attorney General	John J. Crittenden	1850–1853
Postmaster General	Nathan Hall	1850–1852
	Sam D. Hubbard	1852–1853
Secretary of Navy	William A. Graham	1850–1852
	John P. Kennedy	1852–1853
Secretary of Interior	Thomas McKennan	1850
	Alexander Stuart	1850–1853

The Pierce Administration

President	Franklin Pierce	1853–1857
Vice President	William R. King	1853–1857
Secretary of State	William L. Marcy	1853–1857
Secretary of Treasury	James Guthrie	1853–1857
Secretary of War	Jefferson Davis	1853–1857
Attorney General	Caleb Cushing	1853–1857
Postmaster General	James Campbell	1853–1857
Secretary of Navy	James C. Dobbin	1853–1857
Secretary of Interior	Robert McClelland	1853–1857

The Buchanan Administration

President	James Buchanan	1857–1861
Vice President	John C. Breckinridge	1857–1861
Secretary of State	Lewis Cass	1857–1860
	Jeremiah S. Black	1860–1861
Secretary of Treasury	Howell Cobb	1857–1860
	Philip Thomas	1860–1861
	John A. Dix	1861
Secretary of War	John B. Floyd	1857–1861
	Joseph Holt	1861
Attorney General	Jeremiah S. Black	1857–1860
	Edwin M. Stanton	1860–1861
Postmaster General	Aaron V. Brown	1857–1859
	Joseph Holt	1859–1861
	Horatio King	1861
Secretary of Navy	Isaac Toucey	1857–1861
Secretary of Interior	Jacob Thompson	1857–1861

The Lincoln Administration

President	Abraham Lincoln	1861–1865
Vice President	Hannibal Hamlin	1861–1865
	Andrew Johnson	1865
Secretary of State	William H. Seward	1861–1865
Secretary of Treasury	Salmon P. Chase	1861–1864
	William P. Fessenden	1864–1865
	Hugh McCulloch	1865
Secretary of War	Simon Cameron	1861–1862
	Edwin M. Stanton	1862–1865
Attorney General	Edward Bates	1861–1864
	James Speed	1864–1865
Postmaster General	Horatio King	1861
	Montgomery Blair	1861–1864
	William Dennison	1864–1865
Secretary of Navy	Gideon Welles	1861–1865
Secretary of Interior	Caleb B. Smith	1861–1863
	John P. Usher	1863–1865

The Andrew Johnson Administration

President	Andrew Johnson	1865–1869
Vice President	None	
Secretary of State	William H. Seward	1865–1869
Secretary of Treasury	Hugh McCulloch	1865–1869
Secretary of War	Edwin M. Stanton	1865–1867
	Ulysses S. Grant	1867–1868

Presidents, Vice Presidents, and Cabinet Members *(continued)*

	Lorenzo Thomas	1868
	John M. Schofield	1868–1869
Attorney General	James Speed	1865–1866
	Henry Stanbery	1866–1868
	William M. Evarts	1868–1869
Postmaster General	William Dennison	1865–1866
	Alexander Randall	1866–1869
Secretary of Navy	Gideon Welles	1865–1869
Secretary of Interior	John P. Usher	1865
	James Harlan	1865–1866
	Orville H. Browning	1866–1869

The Grant Administration

President	Ulysses S. Grant	1869–1877
Vice President	Schuyler Colfax	1869–1873
	Henry Wilson	1873–1877
Secretary of State	Elihu B. Washburne	1869
	Hamilton Fish	1869–1877
Secretary of Treasury	George S. Boutwell	1869–1873
	William Richardson	1873–1874
	Benjamin Bristow	1874–1876
	Lot M. Morrill	1876–1877
Secretary of War	John A. Rawlins	1869
	William T. Sherman	1869
	William W. Belknap	1869–1876
	Alphonso Taft	1876
	James D. Cameron	1876–1877
Attorney General	Ebenezer Hoar	1869–1870
	Amos T. Ackerman	1870–1871
	G. H. Williams	1871–1875
	Edwards Pierrepont	1875–1876
	Alphonso Taft	1876–1877
Postmaster General	John A. J. Creswell	1869–1874
	James W. Marshall	1874
	Marshall Jewell	1874–1876
	James N. Tyner	1876–1877
Secretary of Navy	Adolph E. Borie	1869
	George M. Robeson	1869–1877
Secretary of Interior	Jacob D. Cox	1869–1870
	Columbus Delano	1870–1875
	Zachariah Chandler	1875–1877

The Hayes Administration

President	Rutherford B. Hayes	1877–1881
Vice President	William A. Wheeler	1877–1881
Secretary of State	William B. Evarts	1877–1881

Secretary of Treasury	John Sherman	1877–1881
Secretary of War	George W. McCrary	1877–1879
	Alex Ramsey	1879–1881
Attorney General	Charles Devens	1877–1881
Postmaster General	David M. Key	1877–1880
	Horace Maynard	1880–1881
Secretary of Navy	Richard W. Thompson	1877–1880
	Nathan Goff, Jr.	1881
Secretary of Interior	Carl Schurz	1877–1881

The Garfield Administration

President	James A. Garfield	1881
Vice President	Chester A. Arthur	1881
Secretary of State	James G. Blaine	1881
Secretary of Treasury	William Windom	1881
Secretary of War	Robert T. Lincoln	1881
Attorney General	Wayne MacVeagh	1881
Postmaster General	Thomas L. James	1881
Secretary of Navy	William H. Hunt	1881
Secretary of Interior	Samuel J. Kirkwood	1881

The Arthur Administration

President	Chester A. Arthur	1881–1885
Vice President	None	
Secretary of State	F. T. Frelinghuysen	1881–1885
Secretary of Treasury	Charles J. Folger	1881–1884
	Walter Q. Gresham	1884
	Hugh McCulloch	1884–1885
Secretary of War	Robert T. Lincoln	1881–1885
Attorney General	Benjamin H. Brewster	1881–1885
Postmaster General	Timothy O. Howe	1881–1883
	Walter Q. Gresham	1883–1884
	Frank Hatton	1884–1885
Secretary of Navy	William H. Hunt	1881–1882
	William E. Chandler	1882–1885
Secretary of Interior	Samuel J. Kirkwood	1881–1882
	Henry M. Teller	1882–1885

The Cleveland Administration

President	Grover Cleveland	1885–1889
Vice President	Thomas A. Hendricks	1885–1889
Secretary of State	Thomas F. Bayard	1885–1889

Presidents, Vice Presidents, and Cabinet Members *(continued)*

Secretary of Treasury	Daniel Manning	1885–1887
	Charles S. Fairchild	1887–1889
Secretary of War	William C. Endicott	1885–1889
Attorney General	Augustus H. Garland	1885–1889
Postmaster General	William F. Vilas	1885–1888
	Don M. Dickinson	1888–1889
Secretary of Navy	William C. Whitney	1885–1889
Secretary of Interior	Lucius G. C. Lamar	1885–1888
	William F. Vilas	1888–1889
Secretary of Agriculture	Norman J. Colman	1889

The Benjamin Harrison Administration

President	Benjamin Harrison	1889–1893
Vice President	Levi P. Morton	1889–1893
Secretary of State	James G. Blaine	1889–1892
	John W. Foster	1892–1893
Secretary of Treasury	William Windom	1889–1891
	Charles Foster	1891–1893
Secretary of War	Redfield Proctor	1889–1891
	Stephen B. Elkins	1891–1893
Attorney General	William H. H. Miller	1889–1891
Postmaster General	John Wanamaker	1889–1893
Secretary of Navy	Benjamin F. Tracy	1889–1893
Secretary of Interior	John W. Noble	1889–1893
Secretary of Agriculture	Jeremiah M. Rusk	1889–1893

The Cleveland Administration

President	Grover Cleveland	1893–1897
Vice President	Adlai E. Stevenson	1893–1897
Secretary of State	Walter Q. Gresham	1893–1895
	Richard Olney	1895–1897
Secretary of Treasury	John G. Carlisle	1893–1897
Secretary of War	Daniel S. Lamont	1893–1897
Attorney General	Richard Olney	1893–1895
	James Harmon	1895–1897
Postmaster General	Wilson S. Bissell	1893–1895
	William L. Wilson	1895–1897
Secretary of Navy	Hilary A. Herbert	1893–1897
Secretary of Interior	Hoke Smith	1893–1896
	David R. Francis	1896–1897
Secretary of Agriculture	Julius S. Morton	1893–1897

The McKinley Administration

President	William McKinley	1897–1901
Vice President	Garret A. Hobart	1897–1901
	Theodore Roosevelt	1901
Secretary of State	John Sherman	1897–1898
	William R. Day	1898
	John Hay	1898–1901
Secretary of Treasury	Lyman J. Gage	1897–1901
Secretary of War	Russell A. Alger	1897–1899
	Elihu Root	1899–1901
Attorney General	Joseph McKenna	1897–1898
	John W. Griggs	1898–1901
	Philander C. Knox	1901
Postmaster General	James A. Gary	1897–1898
	Charles E. Smith	1898–1901
Secretary of Navy	John D. Long	1897–1901
Secretary of Interior	Cornelius N. Bliss	1897–1899
	Ethan A. Hitchcock	1899–1901
Secretary of Agriculture	James Wilson	1897–1901

The Theodore Roosevelt Administration

President	Theodore Roosevelt	1901–1909
Vice President	Charles Fairbanks	1905–1909
Secretary of State	John Hay	1901–1905
	Elihu Root	1905–1909
	Robert Bacon	1909
Secretary of Treasury	Lyman J. Gage	1901–1902
	Leslie M. Shaw	1902–1907
	George B. Cortelyou	1907–1909
Secretary of War	Elihu Root	1901–1904
	William H. Taft	1904–1908
	Luke E. Wright	1908–1909
Attorney General	Philander C. Knox	1901–1904
	William H. Moody	1904–1906
	Charles J. Bonaparte	1906–1909
Postmaster General	Charles E. Smith	1901–1902
	Henry C. Payne	1902–1904
	Robert J. Wynne	1904–1905
	George B. Cortelyou	1905–1907
	George von L. Meyer	1907–1909
Secretary of Navy	John D. Long	1901–1902
	William H. Moody	1902–1904
	Paul Morton	1904–1905
	Charles J. Bonaparte	1905–1906
	Victor H. Metcalf	1906–1908
	Truman H. Newberry	1908–1909

Presidents, Vice Presidents, and Cabinet Members *(continued)*

Secretary of Interior	Ethan A. Hitchcock	1901–1907
	James R. Garfield	1907–1909
Secretary of Agriculture	James Wilson	1901–1909
Secretary of Labor and Commerce	George B. Cortelyou	1903–1904
	Victor H. Metcalf	1904–1906
	Oscar S. Straus	1906–1909
	Charles Nagel	1909

The Taft Administration

President	William H. Taft	1909–1913
Vice President	James S. Sherman	1909–1913
Secretary of State	Philander C. Knox	1909–1913
Secretary of Treasury	Franklin MacVeagh	1909–1913
Secretary of War	Jacob M. Dickinson	1909–1911
	Henry L. Stimson	1911–1913
Attorney General	George W. Wickersham	1909–1913
Postmaster General	Frank H. Hitchcock	1909–1913
Secretary of Navy	George von L. Meyer	1909–1913
Secretary of Interior	Richard A. Ballinger	1909–1911
	Walter L. Fisher	1911–1913
Secretary of Agriculture	James Wilson	1909–1913
Secretary of Labor and Commerce	Charles Nagel	1909–1913

The Wilson Administration

President	Woodrow Wilson	1913–1921
Vice President	Thomas R. Marshall	1913–1921
Secretary of State	William J. Bryan	1913–1915
	Robert Lansing	1915–1920
	Bainbridge Colby	1920–1921
Secretary of Treasury	William G. McAdoo	1913–1918
	Carter Glass	1918–1920
	David F. Houston	1920–1921
Secretary of War	Lindley M. Garrison	1913–1916
	Newton D. Baker	1916–1921
Attorney General	James C. McReynolds	1913–1914
	Thomas W. Gregory	1914–1919
	A. Mitchell Palmer	1919–1921
Postmaster General	Albert S. Burleson	1913–1921
Secretary of Navy	Josephus Daniels	1913–1921
Secretary of Interior	Franklin K. Lane	1913–1920
	John B. Payne	1920–1921

Secretary of Agriculture	David F. Houston	1913–1920
	Edwin T. Meredith	1920–1921
Secretary of Commerce	William C. Redfield	1913–1919
	Joshua W. Alexander	1919–1921
Secretary of Labor	William B. Wilson	1913–1921

The Harding Administration

President	Warren G. Harding	1921–1923
Vice President	Calvin Coolidge	1921–1923
Secretary of State	Charles E. Hughes	1921–1923
Secretary of Treasury	Andrew Mellon	1921–1923
Secretary of War	John W. Weeks	1921–1923
Attorney General	Harry M. Daugherty	1921–1923
Postmaster General	Will H. Hays	1921–1922
	Hubert Work	1922–1923
	Harry S. New	1923
Secretary of Navy	Edwin Denby	1921–1923
Secretary of Interior	Albert B. Fall	1921–1923
	Hubert Work	1923
Secretary of Agriculture	Henry C. Wallace	1921–1923
Secretary of Commerce	Herbert C. Hoover	1921–1923
Secretary of Labor	James J. Davis	1921–1923

The Coolidge Administration

President	Calvin Coolidge	1923–1929
Vice President	Charles G. Dawes	1925–1929
Secretary of State	Charles E. Hughes	1923–1925
	Frank B. Kellogg	1925–1929
Secretary of Treasury	Andrew Mellon	1923–1929
Secretary of War	John W. Weeks	1923–1925
	Dwight F. Davis	1925–1929
Attorney General	Henry M. Daugherty	1923–1924
	Harlan F. Stone	1924–1925
	John G. Sargent	1925–1929
Postmaster General	Harry S. New	1923–1929
Secretary of Navy	Edwin Derby	1923–1924
	Curtis D. Wilbur	1924–1929
Secretary of Interior	Hubert Work	1923–1928
	Roy O. West	1928–1929
Secretary of Agriculture	Henry C. Wallace	1923–1924
	Howard M. Gore	1924–1925
	William M. Jardine	1925–1929

Presidents, Vice Presidents, and Cabinet Members *(continued)*

Secretary of Commerce	Herbert C. Hoover	1923–1928
	William F. Whiting	1928–1929
Secretary of Labor	James J. Davis	1923–1929

The Hoover Administration

President	Herbert C. Hoover	1929–1933
Vice President	Charles Curtis	1929–1933
Secretary of State	Henry L. Stimson	1929–1933
Secretary of Treasury	Andrew Mellon	1929–1932
	Ogden L. Mills	1932–1933
Secretary of War	James W. Good	1929
	Patrick J. Hurley	1929–1933
Attorney General	William D. Mitchell	1929–1933
Postmaster General	Walter F. Brown	1929–1933
Secretary of Navy	Charles F. Adams	1929–1933
Secretary of Interior	Ray L. Wilbur	1929–1933
Secretary of Agriculture	Arthur M. Hyde	1929–1933
Secretary of Commerce	Robert P. Lamont	1929–1932
	Roy D. Chapin	1932–1933
Secretary of Labor	James J. Davis	1929–1930
	William N. Doak	1930–1933

The Franklin D. Roosevelt Administration

President	Franklin D. Roosevelt	1933–1945
Vice President	John Nance Garner	1933–1941
	Henry A. Wallace	1941–1945
	Harry S Truman	1945
Secretary of State	Cordell Hull	1933–1944
	Edward R. Stettinius, Jr.	1944–1945
Secretary of Treasury	William H. Woodin	1933–1934
	Henry Morgenthau, Jr.	1934–1945
Secretary of War	George H. Dern	1933–1936
	Henry A. Woodring	1936–1940
	Henry L. Stimson	1940–1945
Attorney General	Homer S. Cummings	1933–1939
	Frank Murphy	1939–1940
	Robert H. Jackson	1940–1941
	Francis Biddle	1941–1945
Postmaster General	James A. Farley	1933–1940
	Frank C. Walker	1940–1945
Secretary of Navy	Claude A. Swanson	1933–1940
	Charles Edison	1940
	Frank Knox	1940–1944
	James V. Forrestal	1944–1945

Secretary of Interior	Harold L. Ickes	1933–1945
Secretary of Agriculture	Henry A. Wallace	1933–1940
	Claude R. Wickard	1940–1945
Secretary of Commerce	Daniel C. Roper	1933–1939
	Harry L. Hopkins	1939–1940
	Jesse Jones	1940–1945
	Henry A. Wallace	1945
Secretary of Labor	Frances Perkins	1933–1945

The Truman Administration

President	Harry S Truman	1945–1953
Vice President	Alben W. Barkley	1949–1953
Secretary of State	Edward R. Stettinius, Jr.	1945
	James F. Byrnes	1945–1947
	George C. Marshall	1947–1949
	Dean G. Acheson	1949–1953
Secretary of Treasury	Fred M. Vinson	1945–1946
	John W. Snyder	1946–1953
Secretary of War	Robert P. Patterson	1945–1947
	Kenneth C. Royall	1947
Attorney General	Tom C. Clark	1945–1949
	J. Howard McGrath	1949–1952
	James P. McGranery	1952–1953
Postmaster General	Frank C. Walker	1945
	Robert E. Hannegan	1945–1947
	Jesse M. Donaldson	1947–1953
Secretary of Navy	James V. Forrestal	1945–1947
Secretary of Interior	Harold L. Ickes	1945–1946
	Julius A. Krug	1946–1949
	Oscar L. Chapman	1949–1953
Secretary of Agriculture	Clinton P. Anderson	1945–1948
	Charles F. Brannan	1948–1953
Secretary of Commerce	Henry A. Wallace	1945–1946
	W. Averell Harriman	1946–1948
	Charles W. Sawyer	1948–1953
Secretary of Labor	Lewis B. Schwellenbach	1945–1948
	Maurice J. Tobin	1948–1953
Secretary of Defense	James V. Forrestal	1947–1949
	Louis A. Johnson	1949–1950
	George C. Marshall	1950–1951
	Robert A. Lovett	1951–1953

The Eisenhower Administration

President	Dwight D. Eisenhower	1953–1961
Vice President	Richard M. Nixon	1953–1961

Presidents, Vice Presidents, and Cabinet Members *(continued)*

Secretary of State	John Foster Dulles	1953–1959
	Christian A. Herter	1959–1961
Secretary of Treasury	George M. Humphrey	1953–1957
	Robert B. Anderson	1957–1961
Attorney General	Herbert Brownell, Jr.	1953–1958
	William P. Rogers	1958–1961
Postmaster General	Arthur E. Summerfield	1953–1961
Secretary of Interior	Douglas McKay	1953–1956
	Fred A. Seaton	1956–1961
Secretary of Agriculture	Ezra T. Benson	1953–1961
Secretary of Commerce	Sinclair Weeks	1953–1958
	Lewis L. Strauss	1958–1959
	Frederick H. Mueller	1959–1961
Secretary of Labor	Martin P. Durkin	1953
	James P. Mitchell	1953–1961
Secretary of Defense	Charles E. Wilson	1953–1957
	Neil H. McElroy	1957–1959
	Thomas S. Gates, Jr.	1959–1961
Secretary of Health, Education, and Welfare	Oveta Culp Hobby	1953–1955
	Marion B. Folsom	1955–1958
	Arthur S. Flemming	1958–1961

The Kennedy Administration

President	John F. Kennedy	1961–1963
Vice President	Lyndon B. Johnson	1961–1963
Secretary of State	Dean Rusk	1961–1963
Secretary of Treasury	C. Douglas Dillon	1961–1963
Attorney General	Robert F. Kennedy	1961–1963
Postmaster General	J. Edward Day	1961–1963
	John A. Gronouski	1963
Secretary of Interior	Stewart L. Udall	1961–1963
Secretary of Agriculture	Orville L. Freeman	1961–1963
Secretary of Commerce	Luther H. Hodges	1961–1963
Secretary of Labor	Arthur J. Goldberg	1961–1962
	W. Willard Wirtz	1962–1963
Secretary of Defense	Robert S. McNamara	1961–1963
Secretary of Health, Education, and Welfare	Abraham A. Ribicoff	1961–1962
	Anthony J. Celebrezze	1962–1963

The Lyndon Johnson Administration

President	Lyndon B. Johnson	1963–1969
Vice President	Hubert H. Humphrey	1965–1969

Secretary of State	Dean Rusk	1963–1969
Secretary of Treasury	C. Douglas Dillon	1963–1965
	Henry H. Fowler	1965–1969
Attorney General	Robert F. Kennedy	1963–1964
	Nicholas Katzenbach	1965–1966
	Ramsey Clark	1967–1969
Postmaster General	John A. Gronouski	1963–1965
	Lawrence F. O'Brien	1965–1968
	Marvin Watson	1968–1969
Secretary of Interior	Stewart L. Udall	1963–1969
Secretary of Agriculture	Orville L. Freeman	1963–1969
Secretary of Commerce	Luther H. Hodges	1963–1964
	John T. Connor	1964–1967
	Alexander B. Trowbridge	1967–1968
	Cyrus R. Smith	1968–1969
Secretary of Labor	W. Willard Wirtz	1963–1969
Secretary of Defense	Robert S. McNamara	1963–1968
	Clark Clifford	1968–1969
Secretary of Health, Education, and Welfare	Anthony J. Celebrezze	1963–1965
	John W. Gardner	1965–1968
	Wilbur J. Cohen	1968–1969
Secretary of Housing and Urban Development	Robert C. Weaver	1966–1969
	Robert C. Wood	1969
Secretary of Transportation	Alan S. Boyd	1967–1969

The Nixon Administration

President	Richard M. Nixon	1969–1974
Vice President	Spiro T. Agnew	1969–1973
	Gerald R. Ford	1973–1974
Secretary of State	William P. Rogers	1969–1973
	Henry A. Kissinger	1973–1974
Secretary of Treasury	David M. Kennedy	1969–1970
	John B. Connally	1971–1972
	George P. Shultz	1972–1974
	William E. Simon	1974
Attorney General	John N. Mitchell	1969–1972
	Richard G. Kleindienst	1972–1973
	Elliot L. Richardson	1973
	William B. Saxbe	1973–1974
Postmaster General	Winton M. Blount	1969–1971
Secretary of Interior	Walter J. Hickel	1969–1970
	Rogers Morton	1971–1974
Secretary of Agriculture	Clifford M. Hardin	1969–1971
	Earl L. Butz	1971–1974

Presidents, Vice Presidents, and Cabinet Members *(continued)*

Secretary of Commerce	Maurice H. Stans	1969–1972
	Peter G. Peterson	1972–1973
	Frederick B. Dent	1973–1974
Secretary of Labor	George P. Shultz	1969–1970
	James D. Hodgson	1970–1973
	Peter J. Brennan	1973–1974
Secretary of Defense	Melvin R. Laird	1969–1973
	Elliot L. Richardson	1973
	James R. Schlesinger	1973–1974
Secretary of Health, Education, and Welfare	Robert H. Finch	1969–1970
	Elliot L. Richardson	1970–1973
	Casper W. Weinberger	1973–1974
Secretary of Housing and Urban Development	George Romney	1969–1973
	James T. Lynn	1973–1974
Secretary of Transportation	John A. Volpe	1969–1973
	Claude S. Brinegar	1973–1974

The Ford Administration

President	Gerald R. Ford	1974–1977
Vice President	Nelson A. Rockefeller	1974–1977
Secretary of State	Henry A. Kissinger	1974–1977
Secretary of Treasury	William E. Simon	1974–1977
Attorney General	William Saxbe	1974–1975
	Edward Levi	1975–1977
Secretary of Interior	Rogers Morton	1974–1975
	Stanley K. Hathaway	1975
	Thomas Kleppe	1975–1977
Secretary of Agriculture	Earl L. Butz	1974–1976
	John A. Knebel	1976–1977
Secretary of Commerce	Frederick B. Dent	1974–1975
	Rogers Morton	1975–1976
	Elliot L. Richardson	1976–1977
Secretary of Labor	Peter J. Brennan	1974–1975
	John T. Dunlop	1975–1976
	W. J. Usery	1976–1977
Secretary of Defense	James R. Schlesinger	1974–1975
	Donald Rumsfeld	1975–1977
Secretary of Health, Education, and Welfare	Casper Weinberger	1974–1975
	Forrest D. Mathews	1975–1977
Secretary of Housing and Urban Development	James T. Lynn	1974–1975
	Carla A. Hills	1975–1977
Secretary of Transportation	Claude Brinegar	1974–1975
	William T. Coleman	1975–1977

The Carter Administration

President	Jimmy Carter	1977–1981
Vice President	Walter F. Mondale	1977–1981
Secretary of State	Cyrus R. Vance	1977–1980
	Edmund Muskie	1980–1981
Secretary of Treasury	W. Michael Blumenthal	1977–1979
	G. William Miller	1979–1981
Attorney General	Griffin Bell	1977–1979
	Benjamin R. Civiletti	1979–1981
Secretary of Interior	Cecil D. Andrus	1977–1981
Secretary of Agriculture	Robert Bergland	1977–1981
Secretary of Commerce	Juanita M. Kreps	1977–1979
	Philip M. Klutznick	1979–1981
Secretary of Labor	F. Ray Marshall	1977–1981
Secretary of Defense	Harold Brown	1977–1981
Secretary of Health, Education, and Welfare	Joseph A. Califano	1977–1979
	Patricia R. Harris	1979
Secretary of Health and Human Services	Patricia R. Harris	1979–1981
Secretary of Education	Shirley M. Hufstedler	1979–1981
Secretary of Housing and Urban Development	Patricia R. Harris	1977–1979
	Moon Landrieu	1979–1981
Secretary of Transportation	Brock Adams	1977–1979
	Neil E. Goldschmidt	1979–1981
Secretary of Energy	James R. Schlesinger	1977–1979
	Charles W. Duncan	1979–1981

The Reagan Administration

President	Ronald Reagan	1981–1989
Vice President	George Bush	1981–1989
Secretary of State	Alexander M. Haig	1981–1982
	George P. Shultz	1982–1989
Secretary of Treasury	Donald Regan	1981–1985
	James A. Baker III	1985–1988
	Nicholas F. Brady	1988–1989
Attorney General	William F. Smith	1981–1985
	Edwin A. Meese III	1985–1988
	Richard L. Thornburgh	1988–1989
Secretary of Interior	James G. Watt	1981–1983
	William P. Clark, Jr.	1983–1985
	Donald P. Hodel	1985–1989

Presidents, Vice Presidents, and Cabinet Members *(continued)*

Secretary of Agriculture	John Block	1981–1986
	Richard E. Lyng	1986–1989
Secretary of Commerce	Malcolm Baldrige	1981–1987
	C. William Verity, Jr.	1987–1989
Secretary of Labor	Raymond J. Donovan	1981–1985
	William E. Brock	1985–1987
	Ann Dore McLaughlin	1987–1989
Secretary of Defense	Casper Weinberger	1981–1987
	Frank C. Carlucci	1987–1989
Secretary of Health and Human Services	Richard S. Schweiker	1981–1983
	Margaret Heckler	1983–1985
	Otis R. Bowen	1985–1989
Secretary of Education	Terrel H. Bell	1981–1984
	William J. Bennett	1985–1988
	Lauro F. Cavazos	1988–1989
Secretary of Housing and Urban Development	Samuel R. Pierce, Jr.	1981–1989
Secretary of Transportation	Drew Lewis	1981–1982
	Elizabeth Hanford Dole	1983–1987
	James H. Burnley IV	1987–1989
Secretary of Energy	James B. Edwards	1981–1982
	Donald P. Hodel	1982–1985
	John S. Herrington	1985–1989

The George Bush Administration

President	George Bush	1989–1993
Vice President	Dan Quayle	1989–1993
Secretary of State	James A. Baker III	1989–1992
	Lawrence Eagleburger	1992–1993
Secretary of Treasury	Nicholas F. Brady	1989–1993
Attorney General	Richard L. Thornburgh	1989–1992
	William P. Barr	1992–1993
Secretary of Interior	Manuel Lujan, Jr.	1989–1993
Secretary of Agriculture	Clayton K. Yeutter	1989–1991
	Edward Madigan	1991–1993
Secretary of Commerce	Robert A. Mosbacher	1989–1992
	Barbara Hackman Franklin	1992–1993
Secretary of Labor	Elizabeth Hanford Dole	1989–1991
	Lynn Martin	1991–1993
Secretary of Defense	Richard B. Cheney	1989–1993
Secretary of Health and Human Services	Louis W. Sullivan	1989–1993

Secretary of Education	Lauro F. Cavazos	1989–1991
	Lamar Alexander	1991–1993
Secretary of Housing and Urban Development	Jack F. Kemp	1989–1993
Secretary of Transportation	Samuel K. Skinner	1989–1992
	Andrew H. Card	1992–1993
Secretary of Energy	James D. Watkins	1989–1993
Secretary of Veterans Affairs	Edward J. Derwinski	1989–1993

The Clinton Administration

President	Bill Clinton	1993–2000
Vice President	Albert Gore, Jr.	1993–2000
Secretary of State	Warren M. Christopher	1993–1997
	Madeleine K. Albright	1997–2000
Secretary of Treasury	Lloyd Bentsen	1993–1995
	Robert E. Rubin	1995–2000
Attorney General	Janet Reno	1993–2000
Secretary of the Interior	Bruce Babbitt	1993–2000
Secretary of Agriculture	Mike Espy	1993–1995
	Daniel R. Glickman	1995–2000
Secretary of Commerce	Ronald H. Brown	1993–1996
	Mickey Kantor	1996–1997
	William Daley	1997–2000
Secretary of Labor	Robert M. Reich	1993–1997
	Alexis M. Herman	1997–2000
Secretary of Defense	Les Aspin	1993–1994
	William J. Perry	1994–1997
	William S. Cohen	1997–2000
Secretary of Health and Human Services	Donna E. Shalala	1993–2000
Secretary of Education	Richard W. Riley	1993–2000
Secretary of Housing and Urban Development	Henry G. Cisneros	1993–1996
	Andrew Cuomo	1997–2000
Secretary of Transportation	Federico F. Peña	1993–1997
	Rodney E. Slater	1997–2000
Secretary of Energy	Hazel O'Leary	1993–1997
	Federico F. Peña	1997–1998
Secretary of Veterans Affairs	Jesse Brown	1993–2000

Presidents, Vice Presidents, and Cabinet Members *(continued)*

The George W. Bush Administration

President	George W. Bush	2001–
Vice President	Richard Cheney	2001–
Secretary of State	Colin Powell	2001–2005
Secretary of Treasury	Paul O'Neill	2001–2002
	John Snow	2003–
Attorney General	John Ashcroft	2001–2005
Secretary of Interior	Gale Norton	2001–
Secretary of Agriculture	Ann Veneman	2001–2005
Secretary of Commerce	Donald Evans	2001–2005
Secretary of Labor	Elaine Chao	2001–
Secretary of Defense	Donald Rumsfeld	2001–
Secretary of Health and Human Services	Tommy Thompson	2001–2005
Secretary of Education	Rodney Paige	2001–2005
Secretary of Housing and Urban Development	Melvin Martinez	2001–2003
	Alphonso Jackson	2003–
Secretary of Transportation	Norman Mineta	2001–
Secretary of Energy	Spencer Abraham	2001–2005
Secretary of Veterans Affairs	Anthony Principi	2001–2005
Secretary of Homeland Security	Tom Ridge	2001–2005

Party Strength in Congress, 1789–2004

Year	President and vice president	Party of president	Congress	House Majority party	House Minority party	Senate Majority party	Senate Minority party
1789–1797	George Washington John Adams	None	1st 2d 3d 4th	38 Admin 37 Fed 57 Dem-Rep 54 Fed	26 Opp 33 Dem-Rep 48 Fed 52 Dem-Rep	17 Admin 16 Fed 17 Fed 19 Fed	9 Opp 13 Dem-Rep 13 Dem-Rep 13 Dem-Rep
1797–1801	John Adams Thomas Jefferson	Federalist	5th 6th	58 Fed 64 Fed	48 Dem-Rep 42 Dem-Rep	20 Fed 19 Fed	12 Dem-Rep 13 Dem-Rep
1801–1809	Thomas Jefferson Aaron Burr (to 1805) George Clinton (to 1809)	Dem-Rep	7th 8th 9th 10th	69 Dem-Rep 102 Dem-Rep 116 Dem-Rep 118 Dem-Rep	36 Fed 39 Fed 25 Fed 24 Fed	18 Dem-Rep 25 Dem-Rep 27 Dem-Rep 28 Dem-Rep	13 Fed 9 Fed 7 Fed 6 Fed
1809–1817	James Madison George Clinton (to 1813) Elbridge Gerry (to 1817)	Dem-Rep	11th 12th 13th 14th	94 Dem-Rep 108 Dem-Rep 112 Dem-Rep 117 Dem-Rep	48 Fed 36 Fed 68 Fed 65 Fed	28 Dem-Rep 30 Dem-Rep 27 Dem-Rep 25 Dem-Rep	6 Fed 6 Fed 9 Fed 11 Fed
1817–1825	James Monroe Daniel D. Tompkins	Dem-Rep	15th 16th 17th 18th	141 Dem-Rep 156 Dem-Rep 158 Dem-Rep 187 Dem-Rep	42 Fed 27 Fed 25 Fed 26 Fed	34 Dem-Rep 35 Dem-Rep 44 Dem-Rep 44 Dem-Rep	10 Fed 7 Fed 4 Fed 4 Fed
1825–1829	John Quincy Adams John C. Calhoun	Nat-Rep	19th 20th	105 Admin 119 Jack	97 Jack 94 Admin	26 Admin 28 Jack	20 Jack 20 Admin
1829–1837	Andrew Jackson John C. Calhoun (to 1833) Martin Van Buren (to 1837)	Democratic	21st 22d 23d 24th	139 Dem 141 Dem 147 Dem 145 Dem	74 Nat Rep 58 Nat Rep 53 AntiMas 98 Whig	26 Dem 25 Dem 20 Dem 27 Dem	22 Nat Rep 21 Nat Rep 20 Nat Rep 25 Whig
1837–1841	Martin Van Buren Richard M. Johnson	Democratic	25th 26th	108 Dem 124 Dem	107 Whig 118 Whig	30 Dem 28 Dem	18 Whig 22 Whig
1841	William H. Harrison* John Tyler	Whig					
1841–1845	John Tyler (VP vacant)	Whig	27th 28th	133 Whig 142 Dem	102 Dem 79 Whig	28 Whig 28 Whig	22 Dem 25 Dem
1845–1849	James K. Polk George M. Dallas	Democratic	29th 30th	143 Dem 115 Whig	77 Whig 108 Dem	31 Dem 36 Dem	25 Whig 21 Whig

NOTES: Only members of two major parties in Congress are shown; omitted are independents, members of minor parties, and vacancies.

Party balance as of beginning of Congress.

Congresses in which one or both houses are controlled by party other than that of the president are shown in color.

During administration of George Washington and (in part) John Quincy Adams, Congress was not organized by formal parties; the split shown is between supporters and opponents of administration.

ABBREVIATIONS: **Admin** = Administration supporters; **AntiMas** = Anti-Masonic; **Dem** = Democratic; **Dem-Rep** = Democratic-Republican; **Fed** = Federalist; **Jack** = Jacksonian Democrats; **Nat-Rep** = National Republican; **Opp** = Opponents of administration; **Rep** = Republican; **Union** = Unionist; **Whig** = Whig.

*Died in office.

Party Strength in Congress, 1789–2004 *(continued)*

Year	President and vice president	Party of president	Congress	House Majority party	House Minority party	Senate Majority party	Senate Minority party
1849–1850	Zachary Taylor[*] Millard Fillmore	Whig	31st	112 Dem	109 Whig	35 Dem	25 Whig
1850–1853	Millard Fillmore (VP vacant)	Whig	32d	140 Dem	88 Whig	35 Dem	24 Whig
1853–1857	Franklin Pierce William R. King	Democratic	33d 34th	159 Dem 108 Rep	71 Whig 83 Dem	38 Dem 40 Dem	22 Whig 15 Rep
1857–1861	James Buchanan John C. Breckinridge	Democratic	35th 36th	118 Dem 114 Rep	92 Rep 92 Dem	36 Dem 36 Dem	20 Rep 26 Rep
1861–1865	Abraham Lincoln[*] Hannibal Hamlin (to 1865) Andrew Johnson (1865)	Republican	37th 38th	105 Rep 102 Rep	43 Dem 75 Dem	31 Rep 36 Rep	10 Dem 9 Dem
1865–1869	Andrew Johnson (VP vacant)	Republican	39th 40th	149 Union 143 Rep	42 Dem 49 Dem	42 Union 42 Rep	10 Dem 11 Dem
1869–1877	Ulysses S. Grant Schuyler Colfax (to 1873) Henry Wilson (to 1877)	Republican	41st 42d 43d 44th	149 Rep 134 Rep 194 Rep 169 Dem	63 Dem 104 Dem 92 Dem 109 Rep	56 Rep 52 Rep 49 Rep 45 Rep	11 Dem 17 Dem 19 Dem 29 Dem
1877–1881	Rutherford B. Hayes William A. Wheeler	Republican	45th 46th	153 Dem 149 Dem	140 Rep 130 Rep	39 Rep 42 Dem	36 Dem 33 Rep
1881	James A. Garfield[*] Chester A. Arthur	Republican	47th	147 Rep	135 Dem	37 Rep	37 Dem
1881–1885	Chester A. Arthur (VP vacant)	Republican	48th	197 Dem	118 Rep	38 Rep	36 Dem
1885–1889	Grover Cleveland Thomas A. Hendricks	Democratic	49th 50th	183 Dem 169 Dem	140 Rep 152 Rep	43 Rep 39 Rep	34 Dem 37 Dem
1889–1893	Benjamin Harrison Levi P. Morton	Republican	51st 52d	166 Rep 235 Dem	159 Dem 88 Rep	39 Rep 47 Rep	37 Dem 39 Dem
1893–1897	Grover Cleveland Adlai E. Stevenson	Democratic	53d 54th	218 Dem 244 Rep	127 Rep 105 Dem	44 Dem 43 Rep	38 Rep 39 Dem
1897–1901	William McKinley[*] Garret A. Hobart (to 1901) Theodore Roosevelt (1901)	Republican	55th 56th	204 Rep 185 Rep	113 Dem 163 Dem	47 Rep 53 Rep	34 Dem 26 Dem
1901–1909	Theodore Roosevelt (VP vacant, 1901–1905) Charles W. Fairbanks (1905–1909)	Republican	57th 58th 59th 60th	197 Rep 208 Rep 250 Rep 222 Rep	151 Dem 178 Dem 136 Dem 164 Dem	55 Rep 57 Rep 57 Rep 61 Rep	31 Dem 33 Dem 33 Dem 31 Dem

[*]Died in office.

Party Strength in Congress, 1789–2004 (continued)

Year	President and vice president	Party of president	Congress	House Majority party	House Minority party	Senate Majority party	Senate Minority party
1909–1913	**William Howard Taft** James S. Sherman	Republican	61st 62d	219 Rep 228 Dem	172 Dem 161 Rep	61 Rep 51 Rep	32 Dem 41 Dem
1913–1921	**Woodrow Wilson** Thomas R. Marshall	Democratic	63d 64th 65th 66th	291 Dem 230 Dem 216 Dem 240 Rep	127 Rep 196 Rep 210 Rep 190 Dem	51 Dem 56 Dem 53 Dem 49 Rep	44 Rep 40 Rep 42 Rep 47 Dem
1921–1923	**Warren G. Harding**[*] Calvin Coolidge	Republican	67th	301 Rep	131 Dem	59 Rep	37 Dem
1923–1929	**Calvin Coolidge** (VP vacant, 1923–1925) Charles G. Dawes (1925–1929)	Republican	68th 69th 70th	225 Rep 247 Rep 237 Rep	205 Dem 183 Dem 195 Dem	51 Rep 56 Rep 49 Rep	43 Dem 39 Dem 46 Dem
1929–1933	**Herbert Hoover** Charles Curtis	Republican	71st 72d	267 Rep 220 Dem	167 Dem 214 Rep	56 Rep 48 Rep	39 Dem 47 Dem
1933–1945	**Franklin D. Roosevelt**[*] John N. Garner (1933–1941) Henry A. Wallace (1941–1945) Harry S Truman (1945)	Democratic	73d 74th 75th 76th 77th 78th	310 Dem 319 Dem 331 Dem 261 Dem 268 Dem 218 Dem	117 Rep 103 Rep 89 Rep 164 Rep 162 Rep 208 Rep	60 Dem 69 Dem 76 Dem 69 Dem 66 Dem 58 Dem	35 Rep 25 Rep 16 Rep 23 Rep 28 Rep 37 Rep
1945–1953	**Harry S Truman** (VP vacant, 1945–1949) Alben W. Barkley (1949–1953)	Democratic	79th 80th 81st 82d	242 Dem 245 Rep 263 Dem 234 Dem	190 Rep 188 Dem 171 Rep 199 Rep	56 Dem 51 Rep 54 Dem 49 Dem	38 Rep 45 Dem 42 Rep 47 Rep
1953–1961	**Dwight D. Eisenhower** Richard M. Nixon	Republican	83d 84th 85th 86th	221 Rep 232 Dem 233 Dem 283 Dem	211 Dem 203 Rep 200 Rep 153 Rep	48 Rep 48 Dem 49 Dem 64 Dem	47 Dem 47 Rep 47 Rep 34 Rep
1961–1963	**John F. Kennedy**[*] Lyndon B. Johnson	Democratic	87th	263 Dem	174 Rep	65 Dem	35 Rep
1963–1969	**Lyndon B. Johnson** (VP vacant, 1963–1965) Hubert H. Humphrey (1965–1969)	Democratic	88th 89th 90th	258 Dem 295 Dem 247 Dem	177 Rep 140 Rep 187 Rep	67 Dem 68 Dem 64 Dem	33 Rep 32 Rep 36 Rep
1969–1974	**Richard M. Nixon**[†] Spiro T. Agnew[††] Gerald R. Ford[§]	Republican	91st 92d	243 Dem 254 Dem	192 Rep 180 Rep	57 Dem 54 Dem	43 Rep 44 Rep

[*]Died in office.　[†]Resigned from the presidency.　[††]Resigned from the vice presidency.　[§]Appointed vice president.

Party Strength in Congress, 1789–2004 *(continued)*

Year	President and vice president	Party of president	Congress	House Majority party	House Minority party	Senate Majority party	Senate Minority party
1974–1977	Gerald R. Ford Nelson A. Rockefeller§	Republican	93d 94th	239 Dem 291 Dem	192 Rep 144 Rep	56 Dem 60 Dem	42 Rep 37 Rep
1977–1981	Jimmy Carter Walter Mondale	Democratic	95th 96th	292 Dem 266 Dem	143 Rep 157 Rep	61 Dem 58 Dem	38 Rep 41 Rep
1981–1989	Ronald Reagan George Bush	Republican	97th 98th 99th 100th	243 Dem 269 Dem 253 Dem 257 Dem	192 Rep 165 Rep 182 Rep 178 Rep	53 Rep 54 Rep 53 Rep 54 Dem	46 Dem 46 Dem 47 Dem 46 Rep
1989–1993	George Bush Dan Quayle	Republican	101st 102d	262 Dem 267 Dem	173 Rep 167 Rep	55 Dem 56 Dem	45 Rep 44 Rep
1993–2000	Bill Clinton Albert Gore, Jr.	Democratic	103d 104th 105th 106th	258 Dem 230 Rep 228 Rep 223 Rep	176 Rep 204 Dem 206 Dem 211 Dem	57 Dem 53 Rep 55 Rep 54 Rep	43 Rep 47 Dem 45 Dem 46 Dem
2000–	George W. Bush Richard Cheney	Republican	107th 108th***	221 Rep 230 Rep	212 Dem 201 Dem	50 Rep* 55 Rep	50 Dem** 44 Dem

§Appointed vice president.

*On June 6, 2001, Republican John Jeffords become an Independent, reducing the Republican total in the Senate to 49. In the November 5, 2002, election, the Republicans gained a seat, bringing the final total of Republicans in this session again to 50.

**On October 25, 2002, Democrat Paul Wellstone died; an Independent was appointed as his replacement, reducing the Democrat total in the Senate to 49. In the November 5, 2002, election, the Democrats lost a seat, bringing the final total of Democrats in this session to 48.

***At press time, two seats in Louisiana had not yet been decided.

A

à la carte   Term used to explain selecting items one at a time instead of as a group or set; as used here, meaning that Bush selected allies as he needed them and ignored including existing combinations and organizations.

A. P. Giannini   Italian American who changed the banking industry by opening multiple branches and encouraging the use of banks for small accounts and personal loans.

A. Philip Randolph   African American labor leader who organized the 1941 march on Washington that pressured Roosevelt to issue an executive order banning racial discrimination in defense industries.

Aaron Burr   New York lawyer and vice-presidential candidate in 1796; he became Thomas Jefferson's vice president in 1801 after the House of Representatives broke a deadlock in the Electoral College.

abdicate   To relinquish a high office; usually said only of monarchs.

abolitionist   An individual who condemns slavery as morally wrong and seeks to abolish (eliminate) slavery; an individual who supported national legislation outlawing slavery, either gradually or immediately, with or without compensation to slave owners.

Abraham Lincoln   Illinois lawyer and politician who argued against popular sovereignty in debates with Stephen Douglas in 1858; he lost the senatorial election to Douglas but was elected president in 1860.

absentee planters   An estate owner who collects profits from farming or rent but does not live on the land or help cultivate it.

absolute monarch   The ruler of a kingdom in which every aspect of national life—including politics, religion, the economy, and social affairs—comes under royal authority.

acculturation   Changes in the culture of a group or an individual as a result of contact with a different culture.

acid rock   Rock music having a driving, repetitive beat and lyrics that suggest psychedelic drug experiences.

Ácoma pueblo   Pueblo Indian community that resisted Spanish authority in 1598 and was subdued by the Spanish.

acquired immune deficiency syndrome (AIDS)   Gradual and eventually fatal breakdown of the immune system caused by the human immunodeficiency virus (HIV); HIV/AIDS is transmitted by the exchange of body fluids through such means as sexual intercourse or needle sharing.

acquired immunity   Resistance or partial resistance to a disease; acquired immunity develops in a population over time as a result of exposure to harmful bacteria and viruses.

ad hoc   Created for, or concerned with, one specific purpose; Latin for "to this [end]."

Adams-Onís Treaty   Treaty between the United States and Spain in 1819 that ceded Florida to the United States, ended any Spanish claims in Oregon, and recognized Spanish rights in the American Southwest.

Adena culture   An early nonagricultural American Indian society centered in the Ohio River Valley and spreading as far as West Virginia; it is known for having built large trading centers, where artifacts from all over North America have been found.

affidavit   A formal, written legal document made under oath; those signing the document state that the facts in the document are true.

affirmative action   Policy that seeks to redress past discrimination through active measures to ensure equal opportunity, especially in education and employment.

African Methodist Episcopal Church   African American branch of Methodism established in Philadelphia in 1816 and in New York in 1821.

agrarian capitalism   A system of agriculture based on the efficient, specialized production of crops intended to generate profits rather than subsistence.

agribusiness   A large-scale farming operation typically involving considerable land holdings, hired labor, and extensive use of machinery; may also involve processing and distribution as well as growing.

Agricultural Adjustment Act   Law passed by Congress in 1933 to reduce overproduction by paying farmers not to grow crops or raise livestock.

Aid to Families with Dependent Children   A program created by the Social Security Act of 1935; it provided states with matching federal funds and became one of the states' main welfare programs.

Al Capone   Italian-born American gangster who ruthlessly ruled the Chicago underworld until he was imprisoned for tax evasion in 1931.

Al Qaeda   Established by Saudi Osama bin Laden in 1989 as a terrorist network that organizes the activities of militant Islamic groups which seek to establish a global fundamentalist Islamic order.

Al Smith   New York governor who unsuccessfully sought the Democratic nomination for president in 1924 and was the unsuccessful Democratic candidate for president in 1928; his Catholicism and desire to repeal Prohibition were political liabilities.

Alamo   A fortified Franciscan mission at San Antonio; rebellious Texas colonists were besieged and annihilated there by Santa Anna's forces in 1836.

Alan Bakke   Rejected white medical school applicant who filed a lawsuit against the University of California at Davis for reverse discrimination; he claimed that he was denied admittance to medical school because of school policy that set aside admission slots for less-qualified minorities; the Supreme Court agreed in 1978.

Albert Gallatin   Treasury secretary in Jefferson's administration; he favored limited government and reduced the federal debt by cutting spending.

Alcatraz Island   Rocky island, formerly a federal prison, in San Francisco Bay that was occupied in 1969 by Native American activists who demanded that it be made available to them as a cultural center.

Alexis de Tocqueville   French traveler and historian who toured the United States in 1831 and wrote *Democracy in America*, a classic study of American institutions and the American character.

Alfred Kinsey   Biologist whose studies of human sexuality attracted great attention in the 1940s and 1950s, especially for his conclusions on infidelity and homosexuality.

Alfred Landon   Kansas governor who ran unsuccessfully for president on the Republican ticket in 1936.

Alfred Thayer Mahan   Naval officer and specialist on naval history who stressed the importance of sea power in international politics and diplomacy.

Alger Hiss   State Department official accused in 1948 of being a Communist spy; he was convicted of perjury and sent to prison.

Alien and Sedition Acts   Collectively, the four acts—Alien Act, Alien Enemies Act, Naturalization Act, and Sedition Act—passed by Congress in 1798 designed to prevent immigrants from participating in politics and to silence the anti-Federalist press.

Allegheny Portage Railroad   A rail line that carried canal boats over the Allegheny Mountains as part of the Main Line Canal system.

allegory   A story in which characters and events stand for abstract ideas and suggest a deep, symbolic meaning.

Alliance for Progress   Program proposed by Kennedy in 1961 through which the United States provided aid for social and economic programs in Latin American countries; Congress trimmed appropriations following Kennedy's death.

allotment checks   Checks that a soldier's wife received from the government, amounting to a percentage of her husband's pay.

alma mater   The college or school from which a person graduates.

almshouse   A public shelter for the poor.

alternative fuels   Sources of energy other than coal, oil, and natural gas, such as solar, geothermal, hydroelectric, and nuclear energy.

amenities   Conveniences, comforts, and services.

American Colonization Society   Organization founded in 1817 to end slavery gradually by assisting individual slave owners to liberate their slaves and then transporting them to Africa.

American Communist Party   Party organized in 1919, devoted to destroying capitalism and private property and replacing them with a system of socialism.

American Expeditionary Force   American army commanded by General John J. Pershing that served in Europe during World War I.

American Federation of Labor   National organization of trade unions founded in 1886; it used strikes and boycotts to improve the lot of craft workers.

American GI Forum   Organization formed in Texas in 1948 by Mexican American veterans to overcome discrimination and provide support for veterans and all Hispanics; it led the court fight to end the segregation of Hispanic children in school systems in the West and Southwest.

American Indian Defense Association   Organization founded in 1923 to defend the rights of American Indians; it pushed for an end to land allotment and a return to tribal government.

American Indian Movement   Militant Indian movement founded in 1968 that was willing to use confrontation to obtain social justice and Indian treaty rights; organized the seizure of Wounded Knee.

American Plan   Term that some employers in the 1920s used to describe their policy of refusing to negotiate with unions.

American Prohibitory Act   British law of 1775 that authorized the royal navy to seize all American ships engaged in trade; it amounted to a declaration of war

American Protective Association   An anti-Catholic organization founded in Iowa in 1887 and active during the next decade.

American System   An economic plan sponsored by nationalists in Congress following the War of 1812; it was intended to capitalize on regional differences to spur U.S. economic growth and the domestic production of goods previously bought from foreign manufacturers.

American Woman Suffrage Association   Boston-based women's suffrage organization formed in 1869 and led by Lucy Stone, Julia Ward Howe, and others; it welcomed men and worked solely to win the vote for women.

Amerigo Vespucci   Italian explorer of the South American coast; Europeans named America after him.

amnesty   A general pardon granted by a government, especially for political offenses.

amphibious   In a historical context, a military operation that coordinates air, land, and sea military forces to land on a hostile shore.

anaconda plan   Winfield Scott's plan (named after a snake that smothers prey in its coils) to blockade southern ports and take control of the Mississippi River, thus splitting the Confederacy, cutting off southern trade, and causing an economic collapse.

anarchist   A person who believes that all forms of government are oppressive and should be abolished.

Andersonville   Confederate prisoner-of-war camp in northern Georgia where some fourteen thousand Union prisoners died of disease and malnutrition.

Andrew Carnegie   Scottish-born industrialist who made a fortune in steel and believed the rich had a duty to act for the public benefit.

Andrew Jackson   General who defeated the Creeks at Horseshoe Bend in 1814 and the British at New Orleans in 1815; he later became the seventh president of the United States.

Andrew Johnson   Tennessee senator who became Lincoln's running mate in 1864 and who succeeded to the presidency after Lincoln's assassination.

Anglo   A term applied in the Southwest to English-speaking whites.

Anne Hutchinson   A religious leader banished from Massachusetts in 1637 because of her criticism of the colonial government and what were judged to be heretical beliefs.

annexation   The incorporation of a territory into an existing political unit such as a neighboring country.

annuity   An allowance or income paid annually.

annul   To declare a law or contract invalid.

antebellum   The decades before the Civil War, the period from 1815 to 1860; Latin for "before the war."

anthrax   An infectious disease caused by spore-forming bacteria; usually associated with livestock, anthrax can be contracted through touching or breathing anthrax spores and can be deadly to humans.

anthropologist   A scholar who studies human behavior and culture in the past or the present.

Antietam Creek   Site of a battle that occurred in September 1862 when Lee's forces invaded Maryland; both sides suffered heavy losses, and Lee retreated into Virginia.

anti-expansionist   Opposed to the policy of expanding a country by acquiring new territory.

Antifederalists   Opponents of the ratification of the Constitution; they believed a strong central government was a threat to American liberties and rights.

Antimasonic Party   Political party formed in 1827 to capitalize on popular anxiety about the influence of the Masons; it opposed politics-as-usual without offering any particular substitute.

antimonopolism   Opposition to great concentrations of economic power such as trusts and giant corporations, as well as to actual monopolies.

Anti-Saloon League   Political interest group advocating prohibition, founded in 1895; it organized through churches.

Antonio López de Santa Anna   Mexican general who was president of Mexico when he led an attack on the Alamo in 1836; he again led Mexico during its war with the United States in 1846–1848.

appeasement   A policy of granting concessions to potential enemies to maintain peace. Since the Munich agreement did not appease Hitler, it has become a policy that most nations avoid.

apprentice   A person who is bonded to a craftsman, providing labor in exchange for learning the skills associated with the craft.

appropriation   Public funds authorized for a specific purpose.

aqueduct   A pipe or channel designed to transport water from a remote source, usually by gravity; an elevated structure raising a canal to bridge rivers, canyons, or other obstructions.

arbitration   Process by which parties to a dispute submit their case to the judgment of an impartial person or group (the arbiter) and agree to abide by the arbiter's decision.

aridity   Dryness; lack of enough rainfall to support trees or woody plants.

armada   A fleet of warships.

armistice   An agreement to halt fighting, at least temporarily.

Army of the Potomac   Army created to guard the U.S. capital after the Battle of Bull Run in 1861; it became the main Union army in the East.

Army-McCarthy hearings   Congressional investigation of Senator Joseph McCarthy televised in 1954; the hearings revealed McCarthy's villainous nature and ended his popularity.

Arthur Zimmermann   German foreign minister who proposed in 1917 that if the United States declared war on Germany, Mexico should become a German ally and win back Texas, Arizona, and New Mexico and should try to persuade Japan to go to war with the United States.

Articles of Confederation   The first constitution of the United States; it created a central government with limited powers, and it was replaced by the Constitution in 1788.

artisan   A skilled worker, whether self-employed or working for wages; a person whose primary employment is the specialized production of hand-manufactured items; a craftsperson.

ascetic   Practicing severe abstinence or self-denial, generally in pursuit of spiritual awareness.

Ash Can School   New York artists of varying styles who shared a focus on urban life.

assimilate   To absorb immigrants or members of a culturally distinct group into the prevailing culture.

assimilation   A process by which a minority or immigrant group is absorbed into another group or groups; among immigrants, the process of adopting some of the behaviors and values of the society in which they found themselves.

associationalism   Hoover's belief that government could aid business organizations, farmers, professional groups, and others by coordinating their efforts to solve the nation's problems. The government would supply information and encourage discussions, but any solutions would originate from and be implemented by those groups involved. Any government role would be at the state and local levels.

astrolabe   An instrument for measuring the position of the sun and stars; using these readings, navigators could calculate their latitude—their distance north or south of the equator.

Atlanta Compromise   Name applied to Booker T. Washington's 1895 speech in which he urged African Americans to temporarily accept segregation and disfranchisement and to work for economic advancement as a way to recover their civil rights.

Atlantic Charter   Joint statement issued by Roosevelt and Churchill in 1941 to formulate American and British postwar aims of international economic and political cooperation.

Atoms for Peace plan   Eisenhower's proposal to the United Nations in 1953 that the United States and other nations cooperate to develop peaceful uses of atomic energy.

Augusto Sandino   Nicaraguan guerrilla leader who resisted Nicaraguan and American troops in a rebellion from 1925 to 1933; he was murdered at the orders of Anastasio Somoza following a peace conference in 1934.

Australian ballot   A ballot printed by the government, rather than by political parties, and marked privately; so called because it originated there.

automation   A process or system designed so that equipment functions automatically; one outcome of automation is the replacement of workers with machines.

autonomy Control of one's own affairs.

Axis powers Coalition of nations that opposed the Allies in World War II, first consisting of Germany and Italy and later joined by Japan.

Ayatollah Ruhollah Khomeini Religious leader of Iran's Shiite Muslims; the Shiites toppled the shah in 1979, and the ayatollah (a title of respect given to a high-ranking Shiite religious authority and leader) established a new constitution that gave him supreme powers.

Aztecs An Indian group living in central Mexico; the Aztecs used military force to dominate nearby tribes; their civilization was at its peak at the time of the Spanish conquest.

B

B movies Poorer quality, more cheaply made films that were shown in addition to the main movies.

baby boom Sudden increase in the birth rate that occurred in the United States after World War II and lasted until roughly 1964.

Baghdad Pact A regional defensive alliance signed between Turkey and Iraq in 1955; Great Britain, Pakistan, and Iran soon joined; the United States supported the pact but did not officially join until mid-1957.

Bahamas A group of islands in the Atlantic Ocean east of Florida and Cuba.

balance of payments The difference between a nation's total payments to foreign countries and its total receipts from abroad.

balance of power In international politics, the notion that nations may restrict one another's actions because of the relative equality of their naval or military forces, either individually or through alliance systems.

Balkan Peninsula Region of southeastern Europe; once ruled by the Ottoman Empire, it included a number of relatively new and sometimes unstable states in the early twentieth century.

ballistic missiles Missiles without fins or wings whose path cannot be changed once launched; their range can be from a few miles to intercontinental. In 2003 an estimated 35 nations had ballistic missiles.

Baltimore and Ohio Railroad First steam railroad commissioned in the United States; it resorted to using horse-drawn cars after a stagecoach horse beat its pioneer locomotive in a race.

Bank Holiday Temporary shutdown of banks throughout the country by executive order of President Roosevelt in March 1933.

Bank War The political conflict that occurred when Andrew Jackson tried to destroy the Second Bank of the United States, which he thought represented special interests at the expense of the common man.

Barbary pirates Pirates along the Barbary Coast of North Africa who attacked European and American vessels engaged in Mediterranean trade.

Baron Friedrich von Steuben Prussian military officer who served as Washington's drillmaster at Valley Forge.

barrio A Spanish-speaking community, often a part of a larger city.

Barry Goldwater Conservative Republican senator from Arizona who ran unsuccessfully for president in 1964.

battery An army artillery unit, usually supplied with heavy guns.

Battle of Britain Series of battles between British and German planes fought over Britain from August to October 1940, during which English cities suffered heavy bombing.

Battle of Buena Vista Battle in February 1847 during which U.S. troops led by Zachary Taylor forced Santa Anna's forces to withdraw into the interior of Mexico.

Battle of Bunker Hill British assault on American troops on Breed's Hill near Boston in June 1775; the British won the battle but suffered heavy losses.

Battle of Fallen Timbers 1794 battle in which Kentucky riflemen defeated Indians of several tribes, helping to end Indian resistance in the Northwest.

Battle of Horseshoe Bend Battle in 1814 in which Tennessee militia massacred Creek Indians in Alabama, ending Red Stick resistance to white westward expansion.

Battle of King's Mountain Battle fought in October 1780 on the border between the Carolinas in which revolutionary troops defeated loyalists.

Battle of Leyte Gulf Naval battle in October 1944 in which American forces near the Philippines crushed Japanese air and sea power.

Battle of Monmouth New Jersey battle in June 1778 in which Charles Lee wasted a decisive American advantage.

Battle of New Orleans Battle in the War of 1812 in which American troops commanded by Andrew Jackson destroyed the British force attempting to seize New Orleans.

Battle of Shiloh Battle in Tennessee in April 1862 that ended with an unpursued Confederate withdrawal; both sides suffered heavy casualties for the first time, but neither side gained ground.

Battle of Stalingrad Battle for the Russian city that was besieged by the German army in 1942 and recaptured by Soviet troops in 1943; regarded by many as the key battle of the European war.

Battle of the Bulge The last major Axis counteroffensive, in December 1944, against the Allied forces in Western Europe; German troops gained territory in Belgium but were eventually driven back.

Battle of the Coral Sea U.S. victory in the Pacific in May 1942; it prevented the Japanese from invading New Guinea and thus isolating Australia.

Battle of Tippecanoe Battle near Prophetstown in 1811, where American forces led by William Henry Harrison defeated the followers of the Shawnee Prophet and destroyed the town.

Battle of Trenton Battle on December 26, 1776, when Washington led his troops by night across the Delaware River and captured a Hessian garrison wintering in New Jersey.

Battles of Lexington and Concord Two confrontations in April 1775 between British soldiers and patriot Minutemen; the first recognized battles of the Revolution.

Bay of Pigs Site of a 1961 invasion of Cuba by Cuban exiles and mercenaries sponsored by the CIA; the invasion was crushed within three days and embarrassed the United States.

Beatles   English rock group that gained international fame in 1964 and disbanded in 1970; they were known for the intelligence of their lyrics and their sophisticated instrumentation.

Beats   Group of American writers, poets, and artists in the 1950s, including Jack Kerouac and Allen Ginsberg, who rejected traditional middle-class values and championed nonconformity and sexual experimentation.

belligerent status   Recognition that a participant in a conflict is a nation engaged in warfare rather than a rebel against a legally constituted government; full diplomatic recognition is one possible outcome.

belligerent   A nation formally at war.

Benedict Arnold   Pharmacist-turned-military-leader whose bravery and daring made him an American hero and a favorite of George Washington until he committed treason in 1780.

benevolent society   An organization of people dedicated to some charitable purpose.

Benito Juarez   Elected president of Mexico who led resistance to the French occupation of his country in 1864–1867; the first Mexican president of Indian ancestry.

Benjamin Franklin   American writer, inventor, scientist, and diplomat instrumental in bringing about a French alliance with the United States in 1778 and who later helped negotiate the treaty ending the war.

Benjamin O. Davis Sr.   Army officer who in 1940 became the first black general in the U.S. Army.

Berlin airlift   Response to the Soviet blockade of West Berlin in 1948 involving tens of thousands of continuous flights by American and British planes to deliver supplies.

Berlin Decree   Napoleon's order declaring the British Isles under blockade and authorizing the confiscation of British goods from any ship found carrying them.

Berlin Wall   Barrier that the Communist East German government built in 1961 to divide East and West Berlin; it was torn down in November 1989 as the Cold War was ending.

Betty Friedan   Feminist who wrote *The Feminine Mystique* in 1963 and helped found the National Organization for Women in 1966.

bicameral   Having a legislature with two houses.

bilateral   Involving two parties.

bill of rights   A formal statement of essential rights and liberties under law.

Bill of Rights   The first ten amendments to the U.S. Constitution, added in 1791 to protect certain basic rights of American citizens.

bipartisanship   In American politics, it is when the two major parties agree on a set of issues and programs.

Black Cabinet   Semiofficial advisory committee on racial affairs organized by Mary McLeod Bethune in 1936 and made up of African American members of the Roosevelt administration.

black codes   Laws passed by the southern states after the Civil War to define the status of freed people as subordinate to whites.

Black Hawk   Sauk leader who brought his people back to their homeland in Illinois; he was captured in 1832 when U.S. troops massacred his followers.

black market   The illegal business of buying and selling goods that are banned or restricted.

Black Muslims   Popular name for the Nation of Islam, an African American religious group founded by Elijah Muhammad, which professed Islamic religious beliefs and emphasized black separatism.

Black Panthers   Black revolutionary party founded in 1966 that endorsed violence as a means of social change; many of its leaders were killed in confrontations with police or imprisoned.

Black Power   Movement begun in 1966 that rejected the nonviolent, coalition-building approach of traditional civil rights groups and advocated black control of black organizations; the self-determination approach was adopted by Latinos (Brown Power) and Native Americans (Red Power) as well.

Black Reconstruction   The period of Reconstruction when African Americans took an active role in state and local government.

black separatism   A strategy of creating separate black institutions, based on the assumption that African Americans can never achieve equality within white society.

blacklisting   Practice in which businesses share information to deny employment to workers known to belong to unions.

Bland-Allison Act   Law passed by Congress in 1878 providing for federal purchase of limited amounts of silver to be coined into silver dollars.

blandishments   The use of flattery or manipulation to convince others to support a particular project or point of view.

bloc   A group of people united for common action.

block voting   The practice by organized groups of people to coordinate their voting so that all members vote the same way, thereby enhancing the group's political influence.

blue laws   Local legislation designed to enforce Christian morality by forbidding certain activities, including traveling, on Sunday.

blue-collar workers   Workers who wear work clothes, such as coveralls and jeans, on the job; their work is likely to involve manual labor.

bobby pin   Small metal hair clip with ends pressed tightly together, designed for holding short or "bobbed" hair in place.

Bohemia   A region of central Europe now part of the Czech Republic.

Boland Amendment   Motion, approved by Congress in 1984, that barred the CIA from using funds to give direct or indirect aid to the Nicaraguan Contras.

boll weevil   Small beetle that infests cotton plants and damages the cotton bolls, which contain the cotton fibers.

Bolsheviks   Radical socialists, later called Communists, who seized power in Russia in November 1917.

bond   A certificate of debt issued by a government or corporation guaranteeing payment of the original investment plus interest at a specified future date.

Bonus Army   Unemployed World War I veterans who marched to Washington in 1932 to demand early payment of a promised bonus; Congress refused, and the army evicted protesters who remained.

Booker T. Washington   Former slave who became an educator and founded Tuskegee Institute, a leading black educational institution; he urged southern African Americans to accept disfranchisement and segregation for the time being.

boomburbs   Term used to describe suburban cities with populations of over 100,000 and double-digit growth every decade since they first exceeded a population of 2,500; other terms for this new classification of city are "fringe cities" and "technoburbs."

bootlegging   Illegal production, distribution, or sale of liquor.

border states   The slave states of Delaware, Maryland, Virginia, Kentucky, and Missouri, which shared a border with states in which slavery was illegal.

Boris Yeltsin   Russian parliamentary leader who was elected president of the new Russian Republic in 1991 and provided increased democratic and economic reforms.

born-again Christian   One whose life has been so changed by faith that he or she feels as if life has begun anew.

bosch loopers   Dutch term meaning "woods runners"; independent Dutch fur traders.

Boulder Dam   Dam on the Colorado River between Nevada and Arizona, begun during Hoover's administration and completed in 1935.

boxcar   An enclosed railroad car with sliding side doors, used to transport freight.

Boxer Rebellion   Uprising in China in 1900 directed against foreign powers who were attempting to dominate China; it was suppressed by an international army that included American participation.

boycott   An organized political protest in which people refuse to buy goods from a nation or group of people whose actions they opposed.

Bozeman Trail   Trail that ran from Fort Laramie, Wyoming, to the gold fields of Montana.

braceros   Mexican nationals who worked on U.S. farms beginning in 1942 because of the labor shortage during World War II.

bracket creep   Inflation of salaries pushing individuals into higher tax brackets.

Brain Trust   Group of specialists in law, economics, and social welfare who, as advisers to President Roosevelt, helped develop the social and economic principles of the New Deal.

branding   Burning a distinctive mark into an animal's hide using a hot iron as a way to establish ownership.

brief   A summary or statement of a legal position or argument.

Brigham Young   Mormon leader who took over in 1844 after Joseph Smith's death and guided the Mormons from Illinois to Utah, where they established a permanent home for the church.

brinkmanship   Practice of seeking to win disputes in international politics by creating the impression of being willing to push a highly dangerous situation to the limit.

broad constructionist   A person who believes the government can exercise any implied powers that are in keeping with the spirit of the Constitution.

broadside   An advertisement, public notice, or other publication printed on one side of a large sheet of paper. Also, the simultaneous discharge of all the guns on one side of a warship.

Brook Farm   An experimental farm based on cooperative living; established in 1841, it first attracted transcendentalists and then serious farmers before fire destroyed it in 1845.

Brookings Institute   A nonprofit, nonpartisan organization founded by Robert Brookings in 1916 that studies government, economic, and international issues.

Brown v. Board of Education   Case in 1954 in which the Supreme Court ruled that separate educational facilities for different races were inherently unequal.

Bryan-Chamorro Treaty   Treaty in 1914 in which Nicaragua received $3 million in return for granting the United States exclusive rights to a canal route and a naval base.

buffalo   The American bison, a large member of the ox family, native to North America and the staple of the Plains Indian economy between the fifteenth and mid-nineteenth centuries.

Bull Moose Party   Popular name given to the Progressive Party in 1912.

Bull Run   A creek in Virginia not far from Washington, D.C., where Confederate soldiers forced federal troops to retreat in the first major battle of the Civil War, fought in July 1861.

bullish   Optimistic or confident; when referring to the stock market, a bull market is when stock prices are going up, and a bear market is when stock prices come down.

bureaucrat   A government official, usually appointed, who is deeply devoted to the details of administrative procedures.

burghers   Town-dwellers who were free from feudal obligations and were responsible for civic government during the medieval period in Europe; in New Amsterdam these were men who were not Dutch West India Company officials, but who governed civic affairs through their political influence.

Burke-Wadsworth Act   Law passed by Congress in 1940 creating the first peacetime draft in American history.

Butler v. the United States   Supreme Court decision (1936) declaring the Agricultural Adjustment Act invalid on the grounds that it unconstitutionally extended the powers of the federal government.

C

cabildo secular   Secular municipal council that provided local government in Spain's New World empire.

cabinet   A body of officials appointed by the president to run the executive departments of the government and to act as the president's advisers.

Caddoan   A family of languages spoken by the Wichitas, Pawnees, Arikaras, and other Plains Indians.

Californios   Spanish-speaking people born in California before California was acquired by the United States; Spanish colonists in California in the eighteenth and nineteenth centuries.

Calvinists   Protestant followers of John Calvin, whose theology emphasizes the absolute power of God, human sinfulness, and people's inability to effect salvation.

Camp David Accords   Treaty, signed at Camp David in 1978, under which Israel returned territory captured from Egypt and Egypt recognized Israel as a nation.

canvass   A survey that is taken.

Cape Cod   A style of two-story house that has a steep roof and a central chimney; it originated in colonial Massachusetts and became popular in suburbs after World War II.

Cape of Good Hope A point of land projecting into the Atlantic Ocean at the southern tip of Africa; to trade with Asia, European mariners had to sail around the cape to pass from the South Atlantic into the Indian Ocean.

capital Money, especially the money invested in a commercial enterprise; money needed to start or sustain a commercial enterprise.

capital gains tax Tax on profits resulting from the sale of assets such as securities and real estate.

capital ships Generally, a navy's largest, most heavily armed ships; at the Washington Naval Conference, ships weighing over 10,000 tons and using guns with at least an 8-inch bore were classified as capital ships.

caricature An exaggerated image of a person, usually enhancing their most uncomplimentary features.

carpetbagger Derogatory term for the northerners who came to the South after the Civil War to take part in Reconstruction.

carrying trade The business of transporting goods across the Atlantic or to and from the Caribbean.

cartel A group of separate companies within an industry that cooperate to control the production, pricing, and marketing of goods within that industry; another name for a pool.

Carter Doctrine Carter's announced policy that the United States would use force to repel any nation that attempted to take control of the Persian Gulf.

cash crop A crop raised in large quantities for sale rather than for local or home consumption.

casualty A member of the military lost through death, wounds, injury, sickness, or capture.

caucus A gathering of people with a common political interest—for example, to choose delegates to a party convention or to seek consensus on party positions on issues.

censure To issue an official rebuke, as by a legislature to one of its members.

central business district The part of a city that includes most of its commercial, financial, and manufacturing establishments.

Central Intelligence Agency An agency created in 1947 to gather and evaluate of military, political, social, and economic information on foreign nations.

Central Powers In World War I, the coalition of Germany, Austria-Hungary, Bulgaria, and the Ottoman Empire.

Chancellorsville Site in Virginia where in May 1863 Confederate troops led by Lee defeated a much larger Union force.

charismatic Having a spiritual power or personal quality that stirs enthusiasm and devotion in large numbers of people.

Charles Cornwallis British general who was second in command to Henry Clinton; his surrender at Yorktown in 1781 brought the American Revolution to a close.

Charles Cotesworth Pinckney Federalist politician and brother of Thomas Pinckney; he was sent on a diplomatic mission to Paris in 1796 during a period of unfriendly relations between France and the United States.

Charles Lee Revolutionary general who tried to undermine Washington's authority on several occasions; he was eventually dismissed from the military.

Charles Lindbergh American aviator who made the first solo transatlantic flight in 1927 and became an international hero.

Charles Maurice de Talleyrand-Périgord French foreign minister appointed by the revolutionary government in 1797; he later aided Napoleon Bonaparte's overthrow of that government and served as his foreign minister.

Charles Sumner Massachusetts senator who was brutally beaten by a southern congressman in 1856 after delivering a speech attacking the South.

chattel slavery The bondage of people who are considered to be the movable personal property of their owners.

Chautauqua A traveling show offering educational, religious, and recreational activities, part of a nationwide movement of adult education that began in the town of Chautauqua, New York.

cheap money Paper money that is readily available but has declined in value.

Cherokee Nation v. Georgia Supreme Court case (1831) concerning Georgia's annulment of all Cherokee laws; the Supreme Court ruled that Indian tribes did not have the right to appeal to the federal court system.

Chesapeake The Chesapeake was the common term for the two colonies of Maryland and Virginia, both of which border on the Chesapeake Bay.

Cheyenne Indian people who became nomadic buffalo hunters after migrating to the Great Plains in the eighteenth century.

Chicano A variation of *mexicano,* a man or boy of Mexican descent. The feminine form is Chicana. Many Mexican Americans used the term during the late 1960s to signify their ethnic identity; it was associated with the promotion of Mexican American heritage and rights.

Chief Joseph Nez Perce chief who led his people in an attempt to escape to Canada in 1877; after a grueling journey they were forced to surrender and were exiled to Indian Territory.

Chinatown A section of a city inhabited chiefly by people of Chinese birth or ancestry.

Chinese Exclusion Act Law passed by Congress in 1882 that prohibited Chinese laborers from entering the United States; it was extended periodically until World War II.

chivalry The code of honor among medieval knights that was central to the romantic self-image among southern planters.

chlorination The treatment of water with the chemical chlorine to kill germs.

Choctaw Indians A mound-building people who became a society of hunters after 1400; they were steadfast allies of the French in wars against the Natchez and Chickasaws.

cholera Infectious and often fatal disease associated with poor sanitation.

Christian benevolence A tenet in some Christian theology teaching that the essence of God is self-sacrificing love and that the ultimate duty for Christians is to perform acts of kindness with no expectation of reward in return.

Christopher Columbus (Cristoforo Colombo) Italian explorer in the service of Spain who attempted to reach Asia by sailing west from Europe, thereby arriving in America in 1492.

Church of England The Protestant church established in the sixteenth century by King Henry VIII as England's official church; also known as the Anglican Church.

circuit court A court of appeals that has the power to review and either uphold or overturn decisions made by lower courts; in terms of authority, these stand between federal district courts and the Supreme Court.

circulation The number of copies of a publication sold or distributed.

city council A body of representatives elected to govern a city.

city manager plan System of city government in which a small council, chosen on a nonpartisan ballot, hires a city manager who exercises broad executive authority.

city planning The policy of planning urban development by regulating land use.

civil chiefs In many Native American societies, leadership was shared among different classes of chiefs, each of which was responsible for specific political tasks; civil chiefs generally were responsible for overseeing domestic affairs, while war chiefs were responsible for diplomacy.

civil court Any court that hears cases regarding the rights of private citizens.

civil liberties Fundamental individual rights such as freedom of speech and religion, protected by law against interference from the government.

civil rights The rights, privileges, and protections that are a part of citizenship.

Civil Rights Act of 1875 Law passed by Congress in 1875 prohibiting racial discrimination in selection of juries and in transportation and other businesses open to the general public.

Civil Rights Act of 1957 Created the U.S. Commission on Civil Rights and the Civil Rights Division of the Department of Justice; the Commission on Civil Rights primarily investigated restrictions on voting.

Civil Rights Act of 1964 Law that barred segregation in public facilities and forbade employers to discriminate on the basis of race, religion, sex, or national origin.

Civil Rights cases A series of cases that came before the Supreme Court in 1883, in which the Court ruled that private companies could legally discriminate against individuals based on race.

civil union Term for a civil status similar to *marriage* and provides *homosexual* couples access to the benefits enjoyed by married heterosexuals.

Civil Works Administration Emergency unemployment relief program in 1933 and 1934; it hired 4 million jobless people for federal, state, and local work projects. Critics argued that in many cases it created useless jobs, like moving dirt from one place to another.

Civilian Conservation Corps Organization created by Congress in 1933 to hire young unemployed men for conservation work, such as planting trees, digging irrigation ditches, and maintaining national parks. The majority of those recruited were white, but African Americans, Latinos, and Native Americans also served in segregated camps, including more than 80,000 Native Americans who served on reservations.

Clara Barton Organizer of a volunteer service to aid sick and wounded Civil War soldiers; she later founded the American branch of the Red Cross.

Clarence Darrow A leading trial lawyer of the early twentieth century, who often defended those challenging the status quo.

classified civil service Federal jobs filled through the merit system instead of by patronage.

Clayton Antitrust Act Law passed by Congress in 1914 banning monopolistic business practices such as price fixing and interlocking directorates; it also exempted farmers' organizations and unions from prosecution under antitrust laws.

closed shop A business or factory whose workers are required to be union members.

coalition An alliance, especially a temporary one of different people or groups.

code talkers Navajos serving in the U.S. Marine Corps who communicated by radio in their native language, undecipherable by the enemy.

coercion Use of threats or force to compel action.

COINTELPRO Acronym (COunterINTELligence PROgram) for an FBI program begun in 1956 and continued until 1971 that sought to expose, disrupt, and discredit groups considered to be radical political organizations; it targeted various antiwar groups during the Vietnam War.

Cold Harbor Area of Virginia, about 10 miles from Richmond, where Grant made an unsuccessful attempt to drive his forces through Lee's center.

Colin Powell First African American to hold the position of secretary of state; a career army officer, Powell served as national security adviser to President Reagan and as chairman of the Joint Chiefs of Staff under the first President Bush.

collateral Property pledged as security for a loan, that is, something owned by the borrower that can be taken by the lender if the borrower fails to repay the loan.

collective bargaining Negotiation between the representatives of organized workers and their employer to determine wages, hours, and working conditions.

Colonel Fulgencio Batista Dictator who ruled Cuba from 1934 through 1958; his corrupt, authoritarian regime was overthrown by Fidel Castro's revolutionary movement.

colonias Village settlements of Mexicans and Mexican Americans, frequently constructed by or for migrant citrus workers in southern California.

Columbian Exchange The exchange of people, plants, and animals between Europe, Africa, and North America that occurred after Columbus's arrival in the New World.

Columbine Columbine High School located in Littleton, Colorado, was the sight of one of the most violent school shootings, when two students entered the lunchroom with a variety of weapons and homemade bombs. They killed 1 teacher and 12 students, and injured 12 others before they committed suicide.

combine A large harvesting machine that both cuts and threshes grain.

commission system System of city government in which all executive and legislative power is vested in a small elective board, each member of which supervises some aspect of city government.

Committee to Re-elect the President Nixon's campaign committee in 1972, which enlisted G. Gordon Liddy and others to spy on the Democrats and break into the offices of the Democratic National Committee.

commodity market Financial market in which brokers buy and sell agricultural products in large quantities, thus determining the prices paid to farmers for their harvests.

Common Sense Revolutionary pamphlet written by Thomas Paine in 1776; it attacked George III, argued against monarchy, and advanced the patriot cause.

Commonwealth The republic established after the victory of Oliver Cromwell in the English civil war; the Commonwealth lasted from 1649 until the monarchy was restored in 1660.

Commonwealth of Independent States Weak federation of the former Soviet republics; it replaced the Soviet Union in 1992 and soon gave way to total independence of the member countries.

Community of Habitants of New France Company chartered by Anne of Austria to make operations in New France more efficient and profitable; it gave significant political power to local officials in Canada.

Company of New France Company established by Cardinal Richelieu to bring order to the running of France's North American enterprises.

Company of the West Company chartered by Colbert after New France became a royal colony; modeled on the Dutch West India Company, it was designed to maximize profits to the Crown.

company town A town built and owned by a single company; its residents depend on the company not only for jobs but for stores, schools, and housing.

Compromise of 1850 Plan intended to reconcile North and South on the issue of slavery; it recognized the principle of popular sovereignty and included a strong fugitive slave law.

Compromise of 1877 Name applied by historians to the resolution of the disputed presidential election of 1876; it gave the presidency to the Republicans and made concessions to southern Democrats.

concession In diplomacy, something given up during negotiations.

conciliatory Striving to overcome distrust or to regain good will.

confederacy An organization of separate groups who have allied for mutual support or joint action.

Confederate States of America Political entity formed by the seceding states of South Carolina, Georgia, Florida, Alabama, Mississippi, and Louisiana in February 1861; Texas, Virginia, Arkansas, Tennessee, and North Carolina joined later.

Congregationalism A form of Protestant church government in which the local congregation is independent and self-governing; in the colonies, the Puritans were Congregationalists.

Congress of Industrial Organizations Labor organization established in 1938 by a group of powerful unions that left the AFL to unionize workers by industry rather than by trade.

Congress of Racial Equality Civil rights organization founded in 1942 and committed to using nonviolent techniques, such as sit-ins, to end segregation.

Congress of Vienna Conference between ambassadors from the major powers in Europe to redraw the continent's political map after the defeat of Napoleon; it also sought to uproot revolutionary movements and restore traditional monarchies.

conquistadors Spanish soldiers who conquered Indian civilizations in the New World.

conscience Whigs Members of the Whig Party who supported moderate abolitionism, as opposed to cotton Whigs, members who opposed abolitionism.

conscientious objector Person who refuses to bear arms or participate in military service because of religious beliefs or moral principles.

consciousness-raising Achieving greater awareness of the nature of political or social issues through group interaction.

Conscription Act Law passed by Congress in 1863 that established a draft but allowed wealthy people to escape it by hiring a substitute or paying the government a $300 fee.

consensus Agreement of opinion.

constituents Voters in the home district of a member of a legislature.

Constitutional Union Party Political party that organized on the eve of the Civil War with no platform other than preservation of the Constitution, the Union, and the law.

constitutionality Accordance with the principles or provisions of the Constitution.

consumer culture A consumer is an individual who buys products for personal use; a consumer culture emphasizes the values and attitudes that derive from the participants' roles as consumers.

consumer goods Products such as clothing, food, automobiles, and radios, intended for purchase and use by individuals or households, as opposed to products such as steel beams, locomotives, and electrical generators, intended for purchase and use by corporations.

consumer revolution The rising market for manufactured goods, particularly luxury items, that occurred in the early eighteenth century in the colonies.

Contadora Plan Pact signed by the presidents of five Central American nations in 1987 calling for a cease-fire in conflicts in the region and for democratic reforms.

containment The U.S. policy of checking the expansion or influence of communist nations by making strategic alliances, aiding friendly nations, and supporting weaker states in areas of conflict. It often had three stages: political, economic, and military.

contraband Goods prohibited from being imported or exported; in time of war, contraband included materials of war.

Contract with America Pledge taken in 1994 by some three hundred Republican candidates for the House, who promised to reduce the size and scope of the federal government and to balance the federal budget by 2002.

contraction In the economic cycle, a time when the economy has ceased to grow, characterized by decreased production of goods and services and often by high rates of unemployment.

Contras Nicaraguan rebels, many of them former followers of Somoza, fighting to overthrow the leftist Sandinista government.

cooper A person who makes or repairs wooden barrels.

Cooper v. Aaron Supreme Court decision (1959) that barred state authorities from interfering with desegregation either directly or through strategies of evasion.

cooperative A business enterprise in which workers and consumers share in ownership and take part in management.

Copperheads Derogatory term (the name of a poisonous snake) applied to northerners who supported the South during the Civil War.

corollary A proposition that follows logically and naturally from an already proven point.

corporate colony A self-governing colony, not directly under the control of proprietors or the Crown.

cost analysis Study of the cost of producing manufactured goods in order to find ways to cut expenses.

Cotton Belt The region in the southeastern United States in which cotton is grown.

cotton boll The pod of the cotton plant; it contains the plant's seeds surrounded by the fluffy fiber that is spun into yarn.

counterculture A subculture espousing values or lifestyles in opposition to those of the established culture; prominent in the 1960s as members adopted lifestyles that stressed communal living, drugs, Asian religions, and free sexual expression.

counting coup Among Plains Indians, to win glory in battle by touching an enemy; *coup* is French for "blow," and the term comes from the French fur traders who were the first Europeans to describe the practice.

coup Sudden overthrow of a government by a group of people, usually with military support.

coureurs de bois Literally, "runners of the woods"; independent French fur traders who lived among the Indians and sold furs to the French.

courier A messenger carrying official information, sometimes secretly.

Covenant Chain An alliance of Indian tribes established to resist colonial settlement in the Ohio Valley and Great Lakes region and to oppose British trading policies.

cover record A new version of a song already recorded by an original artist.

covert operation A program or event carried out not openly but in secret.

Coxey's Army Unemployed workers led by Jacob S. Coxey, who marched on Washington to demand relief measures from Congress following the depression of 1893.

craft union, trade union Labor union that organizes skilled workers engaged in a specific craft or trade.

Crazy Horse Lakota leader who resisted white encroachment in the Black Hills and fought at the Little Big Horn River in 1876; he was killed by U.S. soldiers in 1877.

credentials committee Party convention committee that settles disputes arising when rival delegations from the same state demand to be seated.

Crédit Mobilier Company created to build the Union Pacific Railroad; in a scandalous deal uncovered in 1872–1873, it sold shares cheaply to congressmen who approved federal subsidies for railroad construction.

creditor nation A nation whose citizens or government have loaned more money to the citizens or governments of other nations than the total amount that they have borrowed from the citizens or governments of other nations.

Creek Confederacy Alliance of Indians living in the Southeast; formed after the lethal spread of European diseases to permit a cooperative economic and military system among survivors.

Creel Committee The U.S. Committee on Public Information (1917–1919), headed by journalist and editor George Creel; it used films, posters, pamphlets, and news releases to mobilize American public opinion in favor of World War I.

creole In colonial times, a term referring to anyone of European or African heritage who was born in the colonies; in Louisiana, refers to the ethnic group resulting from intermarriage by people of mixed languages, races, and cultures.

criminal syndicalism laws State laws that made membership in organizations that advocated communism or anarchism subject to criminal penalties.

Croix de Guerre French military decoration for bravery in combat; in English, "the Cross of War."

crop lien A legal claim to a farmer's crop, similar to a mortgage, based on the use of crops as collateral for extension of credit by a merchant.

Crusades Military expeditions undertaken by European Christians in the eleventh through the thirteenth centuries to recover the Holy Land from the Muslims.

cult of domesticity The belief that women's proper role lies in domestic pursuits.

cultural imperialism The idea that around the world there is expanding acceptance, adoption, and usage of American ideals, products, values, and culture; many point to the growing use of the Internet and the continued popularity of American food, movies, and music as a major cause of its spread.

cultural pluralism The coexistence of many cultures in a locality, without any one culture dominating the region; it seeks to reduce racism, sexism, and other forms of discrimination.

cultural war A belief that the nation is divided over liberal and conservative values that stress moral issues as an important part of the political debate.

Cumberland Road A national highway built with federal funds; it eventually stretched from Cumberland, Maryland, to Vandalia, Illinois, and beyond.

cupidity The extreme desire for wealth; greed.

Currency Act British law of 1764 banning the printing of paper money in the American colonies.

customs receivership An agreement whereby one nation takes over the collection of customs (taxes on imported goods) of another nation and exercises some control over that nation's expenditures of customs receipts, thus limiting the autonomy of the nation in receivership.

customs service A government agency authorized to collect taxes on foreign goods entering a country.

Cyrus McCormick Virginia inventor and manufacturer who developed and mass-produced the McCormick reaper, a machine that harvested grain.

Cyrus Vance Carter's secretary of state, who wanted the United States to defend human rights and promote economic development of lesser-developed nations.

D

dandyism Dressing and behaving in an overly ornate and flamboyant fashion.

Daniel Ken Inouye A Japanese American from Hawai`i who served in the 422nd Regimental Combat Team and was badly wounded in Italy; he later became a U.S. senator from Hawai`i and received the Congressional Medal of Honor for his valor.

Daniel Shays Revolutionary War veteran considered the leader of the farmers' uprising in western Massachusetts called Shays's Rebellion.

Daniel Webster Massachusetts senator and lawyer who was known for his forceful speeches and considered nullification a threat to the Union.

Danish West Indies Island group in the Caribbean, including St. Croix and St. Thomas, which the United States finally purchased from Denmark in 1917; now known as the U.S. Virgin Islands.

dark horse A political candidate who has little organized support and is not expected to win.

Dartmouth College v. Woodward Supreme Court case (1819) in which the majority ruled that private contracts are sacred and cannot be modified by state legislatures.

Dawes Plan Arrangement for collecting World War I reparations from Germany; it scheduled annual payments and stabilized German currency.

Dawes Severalty Act Law passed by Congress in 1887 intended to break up Indian reservations to create individual farms (holding land in severalty) rather than maintaining common ownership of the land; surplus lands were to be sold and the proceeds used to fund Indian education.

daylight-saving time Setting of clocks ahead by one hour to provide more daylight at the end of the day during late spring, summer, and early fall.

Dayton Agreement Agreement signed in Dayton, Ohio, in November 1995 by the three rival ethnic groups in Bosnia that pledged to end the four-year-old civil war there.

de facto Existing in practice, though not officially established by law.

de jure According to, or brought about by, law, such as "Jim Crow" laws that separated the races throughout the South until passage of the 1964 Civil Rights Act.

Declaration of Independence A formal statement, adopted by the Second Continental Congress in 1776, that listed justifications for rebellion and declared the American mainland colonies to be independent of Britain.

Deep South The region of the South farthest from the North, usually said to be the states of Alabama, Florida, Georgia, Louisiana, Mississippi, and South Carolina.

Defense of Marriage Act Passed in 1996, the law defines marriage as between a man and a woman for the purpose of federal law, and prevents other jurisdictions (states, counties, cities) from being forced to accept any other definition of marriage.

deference Yielding to the judgment or wishes of a social or intellectual superior.

deflation Falling prices, a situation in which the purchasing power of the dollar increases; the opposite of deflation is inflation, when prices go up and the purchasing power of the dollar declines.

deism The belief that God created the universe in such a way that it could operate without any further divine intervention.

delusion A false belief strongly held in spite of evidence to the contrary.

demilitarization The removal of military forces from a region and the restoration of civilian control.

demilitarized zone An area from which military forces, operations, and installations are prohibited.

Democratic-Republican societies Political organizations formed in 1793 and 1794 to demand greater responsiveness by the state and federal governments to the needs of the citizens.

Democrats Political party that brought Andrew Jackson into office; it recalled Jeffersonian principles of limited government and drew its support from farmers, craftsmen, and small businessmen.

demographic disaster The outcome of a high death rate and an unbalanced ratio of men to women in the seventeenth-century Chesapeake colonies.

demographic The statistical distribution of subpopulations (ethnic groups, for example) among the larger population of a community or nation.

denomination A group of religious congregations that accept the same doctrines and are united under a single name.

department store Type of retail establishment that developed in cities in the late nineteenth century and featured a wide variety of merchandise organized in separate departments.

deploy To position military resources (troops, artillery, equipment) in preparation for action.

deportation Expulsion of an undesirable alien from a country.

depression A period of economic contraction, characterized by decreasing business activity, falling prices, and high unemployment.

depressive Tending to lower a person's spirits and to lessen activity.

despotism Rule by a tyrant.

détente Relaxing of tensions between the superpowers in the early 1970s, which led to increased diplomatic, commercial, and cultural contact.

deterrence Measures that a state takes to discourage attacks by other states, often including a military buildup.

dime novel A cheaply produced novel of the mid-to-late nineteenth century, often featuring the dramatized exploits of western gunfighters.

direct democracy Provisions that permit voters to make political decisions directly, including the direct primary, initiative, referendum, and recall.

direct mail Advertising or promotional matter mailed directly to potential customers or audiences chosen because they are likely to respond favorably.

direct primary An election in which voters who identify with a specific party choose that party's candidates to run later in the general election against the candidates of other parties.

direct tax A tax imposed to raise revenue rather than to regulate trade.

disarmament The reduction or dismantling of a nation's military forces or weaponry.

discretion The power or right to act according to one's own judgment.

discretionary powers Powers to be used at one's own judgment; in government, powers given to an administrative official to be used without outside consultation or oversight.

discrimination Denial of equal treatment based on prejudice or bias; treatment based on class, gender, or racial category rather than on merit; prejudice.

discriminatory neutrality The ability to withhold aid and trade from one nation at war while providing it to another.

disfranchisement The taking away of an individual's or group's right to vote.

dissenter A person who does not accept the doctrines of an established or national church.

dividend A share of a company's profits received by a stockholder; companies customarily announce dividends every quarter (three months).

divine right The idea that monarchs derive their authority to rule directly from God and are accountable only to God.

Dixiecrat Party Party organized in 1948 by southern delegates who refused to accept the civil rights plank of the Democratic platform; they nominated Strom Thurmond of South Carolina for president.

dollar diplomacy Name applied by critics to the Taft administration's policy of supporting U.S. investments abroad.

domesticity The notion common throughout much of the nineteenth century that women's activities were ideally rooted in domestic labor and the nurture of children.

Dominion of New England A megacolony created in 1686 by James II that brought Massachusetts, Plymouth Plantations, Connecticut, Rhode Island, New Jersey, and New York under the control of one royal governor; William and Mary dissolved the Dominion when they came to the throne in 1689.

domino theory The idea that if one nation came under Communist control, then neighboring nations would also fall to the Communists.

Don Juan de Oñate Spaniard who conquered New Mexico and claimed it for Spain in the 1590s.

Dorothea Dix Philanthropist, reformer, and educator who was a pioneer in the movement for specialized treatment of the mentally ill.

Dr. Francis Townsend California public health physician who proposed the Townsend Plan in 1933, under which every retired person over 60 would be paid a $200 monthly pension to be spent within the month.

Dred Scott Slave who sued for his liberty in the Missouri courts, arguing that four years on free soil had made him free; the Supreme Court's 1857 ruling against him negated the Missouri Compromise.

Duke of Wellington The most respected military leader in Great Britain in the early nineteenth century, Wellington was responsible for the defeat of Napoleon.

Dust Bowl Name given by a reporter in 1935 to the region devastated by drought and dust storms that began in 1932; the worst years (1936–1938) saw over sixty major storms per year, seventy-two in 1937.

Dutch Reform Church Calvinistic Protestant denomination; the established church in the Dutch Republic and the official church in New Netherland.

Dutch West India Company Dutch investment company formed in 1621 to develop colonies for the Netherlands in North America.

Dwight David Eisenhower Supreme Commander of Allied forces in Europe during World War II, who planned D-Day invasion; later became president of the United States.

E

Earl Warren Chief justice of the Supreme Court from 1953 to 1969, under whom the Court issued decisions protecting civil rights, the rights of criminals, and First Amendment rights.

Ebenezer McIntosh Boston shoemaker whose working-man's organization, the South End "gang," became the core of the city's Sons of Liberty in 1765.

Ecology Relating to the interactive relationships between organisms (animals, plants, microorganisms, etc.) and the physical environment in which they are found.

Economic Recovery Tax Act Law passed by Congress in 1981 that cut income taxes over three years by 25 percent across the board and lowered the rate for the highest bracket from 78 percent to 28 percent.

economic sanctions Trade restrictions imposed on a country that has violated international law.

ecosystem A community of animals, plants, and bacteria, considered together with the environment in which they live.

Edmund Genêt Diplomat sent by the French government to bring the United States into France's war with Britain and Spain.

egalitarianism A belief in human equality.

Eighteenth Amendment Constitutional amendment, ratified in 1919, that forbade the manufacture, sale, or transportation of alcoholic beverages.

Eisenhower Doctrine Policy formulated by Eisenhower of providing military and economic aid to Arab nations in the Middle East to help defeat Communist-nationalistic rebellions.

Elect, the According to Calvinism, the people chosen by God for salvation.

Electoral College A body of electors chosen by the states to elect the president and vice president; each state may select a number of electors equal to the number of its senators and representatives in Congress.

electorate The portion of the population that possesses the right to vote.

electric telegraph Device invented by Samuel F. B. Morse in 1836 that transmits coded messages along a wire over long distances; the first electronic communications device.

elevated rail line   A train that runs on a steel framework above a street, leaving the roadway free for other traffic.

Eli Whitney   American inventor and manufacturer; his perfecting of the cotton gin revolutionized the cotton industry.

Elizabeth Cady Stanton   A founder and leader of the American woman suffrage movement from 1848, and the Seneca Falls Conference, until her death in 1902.

Elizabeth I   Queen of England (r. 1558–1603); she succeeded the Catholic Mary I and reestablished Protestantism in England; her reign was a time of domestic prosperity and cultural achievement.

Elkins Act   Law passed by Congress in 1903 that supplemented the Interstate Commerce Act of 1887 by penalizing railroads that paid rebates.

Elvis Presley   Immensely popular rock 'n' roll musician from a poor white family in Mississippi; many of his songs and concert performances were considered sexually suggestive.

emancipation   Release from slavery.

Emancipation Proclamation   Lincoln's order abolishing slavery as of January 1, 1863, in states "in rebellion" but not in border territories still loyal to the Union.

embargo   A ban on trade with a country or countries, usually ordered and enforced by a government.

Embargo Act   Embargo (a government-ordered trade ban) announced by Jefferson in 1807 in order to pressure Britain and France to accept neutral trading rights; it went into effect in 1808 and closed down all U.S. foreign trade.

Embargo of 1813   An absolute embargo on all American trade and British imports.

Emergency Banking Bill   Law passed by Congress in 1933 that permitted sound banks in the Federal Reserve System to reopen and allowed the government to supply funds to support private banks.

Emilio Aguinaldo   Leader of unsuccessful struggles for Philippine independence, first against Spain and then against the United States.

empower   To increase the power or authority of some person or group.

encomienda system   A system of bonded labor in which Indians were assigned to Spanish plantation and mine owners in exchange for a tax payment and an agreement to "civilize" and convert them to Catholicism.

endemic   Present among a particular group or groups of people or geographical area.

energy crisis   Vulnerability to dwindling oil supplies, wasteful energy consumption, and potential embargoes by oil-producing countries.

enfranchise   To grant the right to vote to an individual or group.

Enlightenment   An eighteenth-century intellectual movement that stressed the pursuit of knowledge through reason and challenged the value of religious belief, emotion, and tradition.

Enrique Dupuy de Lôme   Spanish minister to the United States whose private letter criticizing President McKinley was stolen and printed in the *New York Journal,* increasing anti-Spanish sentiment.

entail   A legal limitation that prevents property from being divided, sold, or given away.

entitlements   Government programs and benefits provided to particular groups, such as the elderly, farmers, the disabled, and the poor.

entrepreneur   A person who takes on the risks of creating, organizing, and managing a business enterprise; a person who organizes and manages a business enterprise that involves risk and requires initiative.

enumerate   To count.

Environmental Protection Agency   Agency created in 1970 to consolidate all major governmental programs controlling pollution and other programs to protect the environment.

envoy   A government representative charged with a special diplomatic mission.

equal access   The right of any person to use a public facility, such as streetcars, as freely as other people in the society.

Equal Pay Act   Forbids employers engaged in commerce or in the production of goods for commerce to pay different wages for equal work based on sex. Some employers continued to pay lower wages to women arguing that the jobs were not exactly equal.

Equal Rights Amendment   Proposed constitutional amendment, first advocated by the National Woman's Party in 1923, to give women in the United States equal rights under the law; Congress approved it in 1972, but it failed to achieve ratification by the required thirty-eight states.

Era of Good Feelings   The period from 1816 to 1823, when the decline of the Federalist Party and the end of the War of 1812 gave rise to a time of political cooperation.

Erie Canal   A 350-mile canal stretching from Buffalo to Albany; it revolutionized shipping in New York State.

espionage   Usually an organized practice by governments to use spies to gain economic, military, and political information from enemies and rivals.

Espionage Act   Law passed by Congress in 1917, mandating severe penalties for anyone found guilty of interfering with the draft or encouraging disloyalty to the United States.

Esquire   A term used to indicate that a man was a gentleman.

Essex Junto   Junto—A group of political conspirators who seek power outside of the regular political process—composed of radical Federalists in Essex County, Massachusetts, who at first advocated constitutional changes that would favor New England politically and later called for New England and New York to secede from the United States.

established church   The official church of a nation or colony, usually supported by taxes collected from all citizens, no matter what their religious affiliation.

Ethel and Julius Rosenberg   Wife and husband who in 1950 were arrested and tried for conspiracy to commit espionage in 1951 after being accused of passing atomic bomb information to the Soviets; they were executed in 1953.

ethnic cleansing   An effort to eradicate an ethnic or religious group from a country or region, often through mass killings.

ethnic group   A group that shares a racial, religious, linguistic, cultural, or national heritage.

ethnicity   Having to do with common racial, cultural, religious, or linguistic characteristics; an ethnic group is one that has some shared racial, religious, linguistic, cultural, or national heritage.

ethnology   The study of ethno-cultural groups.

Eugene McCarthy   Senator who opposed the Vietnam War and made an unsuccessful bid for the 1968 Democratic nomination for president.

Eugene V. Debs   American Railway Union leader who was jailed for his role in the Pullman strike; he later became a leading socialist and ran for president.

evangelical sects   Protestant groups that emphasized the sole authority of the Bible and the necessity of actively striving to convert others.

evangelicalism   A Protestant religious persuasion that emphasizes the literal truth of the Gospels and salvation through faith alone; in the early nineteenth century it became infused with increasing amounts of romantic emotionalism and an emphasis on converting others.

evolution   The central organizing theorem of the biological sciences, which holds that organisms change over generations, mainly as a result of natural selection; it includes the concept that humans evolved from nonhuman ancestors.

excise   A tax on the production, sale, or consumption of a commodity or on the use of a service within a country.

excise men   Men who collected taxes on an article of trade or sale.

Executive Order #9066   Order of President Roosevelt in 1942 authorizing the removal of "enemy aliens" from military areas; it was used to isolate Japanese Americans in internment camps.

executive powers   Powers given to the president by the Constitution.

expansion   In the economic cycle, a time when the economy is growing as indicated by increased production of goods and services and usually by low rates of unemployment.

expatriate   A person who takes up long-term residence in a foreign country.

extended family   A family group consisting of various close relatives as well as the parents and children.

external taxation   Revenue raised in the course of regulating trade with other nations.

extractive industry   An industry, such as fur trapping, logging, or mining, that removes natural resources from the environment.

F

faction   A political group with shared opinions or interests.

factionalism   In politics, the emergence of various self-interested parties (factions) that compete to impose their own views onto either a larger political party or the nation at large.

Fair Deal   President Truman said that "every segment of the population" deserved a "fair deal" from the government. He hoped the Democratic majority would provide an expansion of New Deal programs, including civil rights legislation, a fair employment practices act, a system for national health insurance, and appropriations for education.

Fair Employment Practices Commission   Commission estab-lished in 1941 to halt discrimination in war production and government.

Fair Labor Standards Act   Law passed by Congress in 1938 that established a minimum wage and a maximum workweek and forbade labor by children under 16.

fait accompli   An accomplished deed or fact that cannot be reversed or undone.

fallout shelter   Underground shelter stocked with food and supplies that was intended to provide safety in case of atomic attack; *fallout* refers to the irradiated particles falling through the atmosphere after a nuclear attack.

famine   A serious and widespread shortage of food.

Far West   In North America, the lands west of the Mississippi River.

Farm Bloc   Bipartisan group of senators and representatives formed in 1921 to promote legislation to assist farmers.

Farmers' Alliances   Organizations of farm families in the 1880s and 1890s, similar to the Grange.

Farmers' Holiday Association   Organization of farmers that called on members to take direct actions—such as destroying crops and resisting foreclosures—to protest the plight of agriculture and the lack of government support.

farthing   A British coin worth one-fourth of a penny and thus a term used to indicate something of very little value.

Father Charles Coughlin   Roman Catholic priest whose influential radio addresses in the 1930s at first emphasized social justice but eventually became anti-Semitic and profascist.

favorite son   A candidate nominated for office by delegates from his or her own region or state.

federal deficit   The total amount of debt owed by the national government.

Federal Deposit Insurance Corporation   Agency created by the Bank Act of 1933 to insure deposits up to a fixed sum in member banks of the Federal Reserve System and state banks that choose to participate.

Federal Emergency Relief Administration   Agency created in May 1933 to provide direct grants to states and municipalities to spend on relief.

Federal Highway Act   Law passed by Congress in 1956, appropriating $32 billion for the construction of interstate highways.

Federal Home Loan Bank Act   Law passed by Congress in 1932 that established twelve banks across the nation to supplement lending resources to institutions making home loans in an effort to reduce foreclosures and to stimulate the construction industry.

Federal Housing Administration   Agency created by the National Housing Act (1934) to insure loans made by banks and other institutions for new home construction, repairs, and improvements.

federal Indian agents   Government officials who were responsible for negotiating treaties with Native American groups; in the nineteenth century they were employed by the War Department.

Federal Reserve Act   Law passed by Congress in 1913 establishing twelve regional Federal Reserve Banks to hold the cash reserves of commercial banks and a Federal Reserve Board to regulate aspects of banking.

Federal Trade Commission Act   Law passed by Congress in 1914 that outlawed unfair methods of competition in interstate commerce and created a commission appointed by the president to investigate illegal business practices.

Federalist Papers   Essays written by Alexander Hamilton, John Jay, and James Madison in support of the Constitution.

Federalists   Supporters of the Constitution; they desired a strong central government.

fellow-traveler   Individual who sympathizes with or supports the beliefs of the Communist Party without being a member.

feminism   The conviction that women are and should be the social, political, and economic equals of men.

femme couverte   From the French for "covered woman"; a legal term for a married woman; this legal status limited women's rights, denying them the right to sue or be sued, own or sell property, or earn wages.

femme sole   From the French for "woman alone"; a legal term for an unmarried, widowed, or divorced woman with the legal right to own or sell property, sue or be sued, or earn wages.

Ferdinand and Isabella   Joint rulers of Spain (r. 1469–1504); their marriage in 1469 created a united Spain from the rival kingdoms of Aragon and Castile.

feudal   Relating to a system in which landowners held broad powers over peasants or tenant farmers, providing protection in exchange for loyalty and labor.

fictive ancestor   A mythical figure believed by a social group to be its founder and from whom all members are believed to be biologically descended.

Fidel Castro   Cuban revolutionary leader who overthrew the corrupt regime of dictator Fulgencio Batista in 1959 and established a Communist state.

field hands   People who do agricultural work such as planting, weeding, and harvesting.

Fifteenth Amendment   Constitutional amendment, ratified in 1870, that prohibited states from denying the right to vote because of a person's race or because a person had been a slave.

54th Massachusetts   Civil War regiment of African American troops from Massachusetts commanded by abolitionist Colonel Robert Gould Shaw; it led an assault on Fort Wagner at Charleston Harbor.

filibuster   A long speech by a bill's opponents to delay legislative action; usually applies to extended speeches in the U.S. Senate, which has no time limit on speeches and where a minority may therefore try to "talk a bill to death" by holding up all other business; to use obstructionist tactics, especially prolonged speechmaking, in order to delay legislative action.

Final Solution   German plan to eliminate Jews through mass executions by isolating them in concentration camps; by the end of the war, the Nazis had killed 6 million Jews.

finance company   Business that makes loans to clients based on some form of collateral, such as a new car, thus allowing a form of installment buying when sellers do not extend credit.

financial panic   Widespread anxiety about financial and commercial matters; in a panic, investors often sell large amounts of stock to cut their own losses, which drives prices much lower.

fireside chats   Radio talks in which President Roosevelt promoted New Deal policies and reassured the nation; Roosevelt delivered twenty-eight fireside chats.

First Organic Laws   A constitution adopted by American settlers in the Oregon Country on July 5, 1843, establishing a government independent from Great Britain and requesting annexation by the United States.

fiscal   Relating to finances.

fiscal policy   The use of government spending to stimulate or slow down the economy.

fiscal stringency   The need because of real or perceived economic conditions to restrict, cut, or eliminate funding for programs.

Five Civilized Tribes   Term used by whites to describe the Cherokee, Choctaw, Seminole, Creek, and Chickasaw Indians, many of whom were planters and merchants.

fixed costs   Costs that a company must pay even if it closes down all its operations—for example, interest on loans, dividends on bonds, and property taxes.

flagship   The ship that carries the fleet commander and bears the commander's flag.

Fletcher v. Peck   Supreme Court case (1810) growing out of the Yazoo affair in which the majority ruled that the original land sale contract rescinded by the Georgia legislature was binding, establishing the superiority of contracts over legislation.

flexible response   Kennedy's strategy of considering a variety of military and nonmilitary options when facing foreign-policy decisions.

flexplace   Allows employees to work at the office or from alternate work site during part of their scheduled hours. Working at home is the most common alternative site, and in 2001 about 15 percent of the work force was paid to work at home.

flextime   Allows an employee to select the hours of work. There are usually specified limits set by the employer. Employees on a flexible schedule may work a condensed workweek or may work a regular workweek. In 2001 approximately 30 percent of the national work force was using some type of flextime.

Foraker Act   Law passed by Congress in 1900 that established civilian government in Puerto Rico; it provided for an elected legislature and a governor appointed by the U.S. president.

Fordney-McCumber Tariff   Tariff passed by Congress in 1922 to protect domestic production from foreign competitors; it raised tariff rates to record levels and provoked foreign tariff reprisals.

foreclosure   Confiscation of property by a bank when mortgage payments are delinquent.

Fort Orange   Dutch trading post established near present-day Albany, New York, in 1614.

Fort Sumter   Fort at the mouth of the harbor of Charleston, South Carolina; it was the scene of the opening engagement of the Civil War in April 1861.

forty-niners   Prospectors who streamed into California in 1849, after the discovery of gold at New Helvetia in 1848.

Fourierism Social system advanced by Frenchman Charles Fourier, who argued that people were capable of living in perfect harmony under the right conditions, which included communal life and republican government.

Fourteen Points President Wilson's program for maintaining peace after World War I, which called for arms reduction, national self-determination, and a league of nations.

Fourteenth Amendment Constitutional amendment, ratified in 1868, defining American citizenship and placing restrictions on former Confederates.

fragging An effort to kill fellow soldiers, frequently officers, by using a grenade. It may have accounted for over a thousand American deaths in Vietnam.

Frances (Fanny) Wright Nineteenth-century reformer who advocated what at the time were considered radical causes, including racial equality, equality for women, birth control, and open sexuality.

franchise As used here, the right to vote; another word for suffrage. Also, government authorization allowing a company to provide a public service in a certain area. Right granted by a company to an individual to sell the company's goods and services. The franchisee operates his or her own business and keeps most of the profits, although the franchiser receives part of the profit and may establish rules and guidelines for the running of the business.

Francis Marion South Carolina leader of guerrilla forces during the Revolutionary War; known as the "Swamp Fox," he harassed British forces during the second southern campaign.

Francis Scott Key Author of "The Star-Spangled Banner," which chronicles the British bombardment of Fort McHenry in 1814; Key's poem, set to music, became the official U.S. national anthem in 1931.

Francisco "Pancho" Villa Mexican bandit and revolutionary who led a raid into New Mexico in 1916, which prompted the U.S. government to send troops into Mexico in unsuccessful pursuit.

François Dominique Toussaint L'Ouverture Black revolutionary who liberated the island of Santo Domingo in 1791, only to see it reinvaded by the French in 1802.

Franklin Pierce New Hampshire lawyer and Democratic politician nominated as a compromise candidate and elected president in 1852.

fraternal Describes a group of people with common purposes or interests.

fraternal order An organization of men, often with a ceremonial initiation, that typically provided rudimentary life insurance; many fraternal orders also had auxiliaries for the female relatives of members.

Frederick Douglass Abolitionist and journalist who escaped from slavery in 1838 and became an influential lecturer in the North and abroad.

Frederick Jackson Turner American historian who argued that the frontier and cheap, abundant land were dominant factors in creating American democracy and shaping national character.

Fredericksburg Site in Virginia of a Union defeat in December 1862, which demonstrated the incompetence of the new Union commander, Ambrose E. Burnside.

free love Popular belief among members of the counterculture in the 1960s that sexual activities should be unconstrained.

free trade Trade between nations without any protective tariffs.

freed people Former slaves; *freed people* is the term used by historians to refer to former slaves, whether male or female.

Freedmen's Bureau Agency established in 1865 to aid former slaves in their transition to freedom, especially by administering relief and sponsoring education.

freedom march Civil rights march from Selma to Montgomery, Alabama, in March 1965; the violent treatment of protesters by local authorities helped galvanize national opinion against segregationists.

freedom rides An effort by civil rights protesters who by riding buses throughout the South in 1961 sought to achieve the integration of bus terminals.

Freedom Summer Effort by civil rights groups in Mississippi to register black voters and cultivate black pride during the summer of 1964.

Freeport Doctrine Stephen Douglas's belief, stated at Freeport, Illinois, that a territory could exclude slavery by writing local laws or regulations that made slavery impossible to enforce.

Free-Soil Party A political party that opposed the extension of slavery into any of the territories newly acquired from Mexico.

French Revolution Political rebellion against the French monarchy and aristocratic privileges; it began in 1789 and ended in 1799.

Fries's Rebellion A tax revolt by Pennsylvania citizens in 1799 that was suppressed by federal forces; leader John Fries was condemned to death for treason but received a presidential pardon from John Adams.

frigate A very fast warship, rigged with square sails and carrying from thirty to fifty cannon on two gun decks.

frontier line The outer limit of agricultural settlement bordering on areas still under Indian control or unoccupied.

frugality An unwillingness to spend money for unnecessary things; by stereotype, New Englanders (Yankees) supposedly have an ingrained tendency to frugality.

fugitive slave law Law providing for the return of escaped slaves to their owners.

fundamentalism A Christian religious movement that emphasizes the literal truth of the Bible and opposes those who seek to reconcile the Bible with scientific knowledge.

G

G-8 nations Term given to the leading industrial nations (Canada, China, France, Germany, Italy, Japan, the United Kingdom, and the United States) that meet periodically to deal with major economic and political problems facing their countries and the international community; the first summit meeting, in 1975, had only six members, as Canada and China were not yet members.

G.I. Bill Law passed by Congress in 1944 to provide financial and educational benefits for American veterans after World War II; *G.I.* stands for "government issue."

Gadsden Purchase A strip of land in present-day Arizona and New Mexico that the United States bought from Mexico in 1853 to secure a southern route for a transcontinental railroad.

gag rule A rule that limits or prevents debate on an issue.

gauge In this usage, the distance between the two rails making up railroad tracks.

gender feminists Term applied to those within the feminist movement who focus on the subordination of women and on the need for radical changes in gender-related roles and traditions.

General Agreement on Tariffs and Trade (GATT) First signed in 1947, the agreement sought to provide an international forum to encourage free trade between member states by regulating and reducing tariffs on traded goods and by providing a common mechanism for resolving trade disputes. GATT membership now includes more than 110 countries.

General Assembly Assembly of all members of the United Nations; it debates issues but neither creates nor executes policy.

General Douglas MacArthur Recalled to active duty in 1941, he was given command of American and Filipino troops in the Philippines; in 1942 he was appointed Supreme Commander of the Southwest Pacific Area; in 1945 he was appointed Supreme Commander for the Allied Powers (SCAP) and accepted Japan's formal surrender. As head of the Allied occupation he oversaw the rebuilding of Japan. Commanded UN forces in Korea until a dispute over strategy led Truman to dismiss him.

General Hugh Johnson Head of the National Recovery Administration; consumer and labor advocates accused him of being too favorable to business interests.

general strike A strike by members of all unions in a particular region.

Geneva Agreement Truce signed at Geneva in 1954 by French and Viet Minh representatives, dividing Vietnam along the 17th parallel into the Communist North and the anti-Communist South.

genteel The manner and style associated with elite classes, usually characterized by elegance, grace, and politeness.

gentlemen's agreement An agreement rather than a formal treaty; in this case, Japan agreed in 1907 to limit Japanese emigration to the United States.

gentry The class of English landowners ranking just below the nobility.

George III King of England (r. 1760–1820); his government's policies produced colonial discontent that led to the American Revolution in 1776.

George B. McClellan U.S. general who replaced Winfield Scott as general in chief of Union forces; a skillful organizer, but slow and indecisive as a field commander.

George Grenville British prime minister who sought to tighten controls over the colonies and to impose taxes to raise revenues.

George Guess (Sequoyah) Cherokee silversmith and trader who created an alphabet that made it possible to transcribe the Cherokee language according to the sounds of its syllables.

George McGovern South Dakota senator who opposed the Vietnam War and was the unsuccessful Democratic candidate for president in 1972.

George Rogers Clark Virginian who led his troops to successes against the British and Indians in the Ohio Territory in 1778.

George Wallace Conservative Alabama governor who opposed desegregation in the 1960s and ran unsuccessfully for the presidency in 1968 and 1972.

George Washington Commander in chief of the Continental Army; he led Americans to victory in the Revolution and later became the first president of the United States.

George Whitefield English evangelical preacher of the Great Awakening whose charismatic style attracted huge crowds during his preaching tours of the colonies.

German-Soviet Nonaggression Pact Agreement in which Germany and the Soviet Union in 1939 pledged not to fight each other and secretly arranged to divide Poland after Germany conquered it.

Gettysburg Site in Pennsylvania where in July 1863 Union forces under General George Meade defeated Lee's Confederate forces, turning back Lee's invasion of the North.

Gettysburg Address A speech given by Abraham Lincoln on November 19, 1863, dedicating a national cemetery in Gettysburg, Pennsylvania; it enunciated Lincoln's maturing view of the war and its purpose.

Ghost Dance Indian religion centered on a ritual dance; it held out the promise of an Indian messiah who would banish the whites, bring back the buffalo, and restore the land to the Indians.

Gibbons v. Ogden Supreme Court case (1824) in which the majority ruled that the authority of Congress is absolute in matters of interstate commerce.

Gifford Pinchot Head of the Forestry Service from 1898 to 1910; he promoted conservation and urged careful planning in the use of natural resources.

gild To cover a cheaper metal with a very thin layer of gold.

glass ceiling Term used to express an intangible barrier within the hierarchy of a company that prevents women or minorities from rising to upper-level positions.

Glass-Steagall Act Law passed by Congress in 1932 that expanded credit through the Federal Reserve System in order to counteract foreign withdrawals and domestic hoarding of money.

global warming The gradual warming to the surface of the Earth; most scientists argue that over the past 20 years the Earth's temperature has risen at a more rapid rate because of industrial emission of gases that trap heat; the consequence of continued emissions, they argue, could be major ecological changes.

globalization The process of opening national borders to the free flow of trade, capital, ideas and information, and people.

Glorious Revolution A term used to describe the removal of James II from the English throne and the crowning of the Protestant monarchs, William and Mary.

gold record Status that is awarded when 500,000 records have been sold.

gold reserves The stockpile of gold with which the federal government backed up the currency.

gold standard A monetary system based on gold; under such a system, legal contracts typically called for the payment of all debts in gold, and paper money could be redeemed in gold at a bank.

Gold Standard Act Law passed by Congress in 1900 that made gold the monetary standard for all currency issued.

Good Neighbor policy An American policy toward Latin America that stressed economic ties and nonintervention; begun under Hoover but associated with Roosevelt.

Gospel of Wealth Andrew Carnegie's idea that all possessors of great wealth have an obligation to spend or otherwise disburse their money to help people help themselves.

gradualism The belief that slavery in the United States should be abolished gradually, by methods such as placing territorial limits on slavery or settling free blacks in Africa.

graduated income tax Percentage tax that is levied on income and varies with income, so that individuals with the lowest income pay taxes at the lowest rates.

graft Unscrupulous use of one's position for profit or advantage.

grain elevator A storehouse for grain located near railroad tracks; such structures were equipped with mechanical lifting devices (elevators) that permitted the grain to be loaded into railcars.

Grand Alliance A term used to refer to those allied nations working to defeat Hitler; often used to refer to the Big Three: Britain, the United States, and the Soviet Union.

Grand Army of the Republic Organization of Union army veterans.

grandfather clause Provision in Louisiana law that permitted a person to vote if his father or grandfather had been entitled to vote in 1867; designed to permit white men to vote who might otherwise be disfranchised by laws targeting blacks. Often applied to any law that permits some people to evade current legal provisions based on past practice.

Grange Organization of farmers that combined social activities with education about new methods of farming and cooperative economic efforts; formally called the Patrons of Husbandry.

Granger laws State laws establishing standard freight and passenger rates on railroads, passed in several states in the 1870s in response to lobbying by the Grange and other groups, including merchants.

Great Awakening A series of religious revivals based on fiery preaching and emotionalism that swept across the colonies during the second quarter of the eighteenth century.

Great Basin A desert region of the western United States including most of Nevada and parts of Utah, California, Idaho, Wyoming, and Oregon.

Great Chicago Fire A fire that destroyed much of Chicago in 1871 and spurred national efforts to improve fire protection.

Great Compromise A proposal calling for a bicameral legislature with equal representation for the states in one house and proportional representation in the other.

Great Migration The movement of Puritans from England to America in the 1630s, caused by political and religious unrest in England. Also, movement of about a half-million black people from the rural South to the urban North during World War I.

Great Plains High grassland of western North America, stretching from roughly the 98th meridian to the Rocky Mountains; it is generally level, treeless, and fairly dry.

Great Railway Strike of 1877 Largely spontaneous strikes by railroad workers, triggered by wage cuts.

Great Salt Lake A shallow, salty lake in the Great Basin near which the Mormons established a permanent settlement in 1847.

Great Sioux War War between the tribes that took part in the Battle of Little Big Horn and the U.S. Army; it ended in 1881 with the surrender of Sitting Bull.

Great Society Social program that Johnson announced in 1965; it included the War on Poverty, protection of civil rights, and funding for education.

Greater East Asian Co-Prosperity Sphere Japan's plan to create and dominate an economic and defensive union in East Asia, using force if necessary. In defending the concept, the Japanese compared it to the United States' power in Latin America and advocated the idea of Asia for Asians.

greenbacks Paper money, not backed by gold, that the federal government issued during the Civil War; paper money issued by the Union; it was not backed by gold.

Grenada Country in the West Indies that achieved independence from Britain in 1974 and was invaded briefly by U.S. forces in 1983.

gross domestic product (GDP) The total value of goods and services produced in one year within a nation's borders. In 2003, the GDP of the United States was slightly more than $10.9 trillion.

gross national product The total market value of all goods and services that a nation produces during a specified period; now generally referred to as gross domestic product.

Guadalcanal Island Pacific island secured by U.S. troops in February 1943 in the first major U.S. offensive action in the Pacific.

guerrilla tactics A method of warfare in which small bands of fighters in occupied territory harass and attack their enemies, often in surprise raids; the Indians used these tactics during King Philip's War.

guerrilla warfare An irregular form of war carried on by small bodies of men acting independently.

guild An association of craftspeople with the same skills who join together to protect their mutual interests.

Gulf of Tonkin Resolution Decree passed by Congress in 1964 authorizing the president to take any measures necessary to repel attacks against U.S. forces in Vietnam.

H

H. Ross Perot Texas billionaire who used large amounts of his own money to run as an Independent candidate for president in 1992 and who created the Reform Party for his 1996 bid for the presidency.

Hague Court Body of delegates from about fifty member nations, created in the Netherlands in 1899 for the purpose of peacefully resolving international conflicts; also known as the Permanent Court of Arbitration.

Half-Breeds Insulting name that Roscoe Conkling gave to his opponents (especially James Blaine) within the Republican Party to suggest that they were not fully committed to Republican ideals.

Half-Way Covenant An agreement (1662) that gave partial membership in Puritan churches to the children of church members even if they had not had a "saving faith" experience.

hang in effigy To hang, as if on a gallows, a crude likeness or dummy—an effigy—representing a hated person.

haole Hawaiian word for persons not of native Hawaiian ancestry, especially whites.

Harlem A section of New York City in the northern part of Manhattan; it became one of the largest black communities in the United States.

Harlem Renaissance Literary and artistic movement in the 1920s, centered in Harlem, in which black writers and artists described and celebrated African American life.

Harpers Ferry Town in present-day West Virginia and site of the U.S. arsenal that John Brown briefly seized in 1859.

Harriet Beecher Stowe American novelist and abolitionist whose novel *Uncle Tom's Cabin* fanned antislavery sentiment in the North.

Harriet Tubman One of the most famous and most effective of the many African American "conductors" on the Underground Railroad in the years before the Civil War; she is thought to have been personally responsible for leading at least three hundred slaves into freedom.

Harry S. Truman Democratic senator from Missouri whom Roosevelt selected in 1944 to be his running mate for vice president; in 1945, on Roosevelt's death, Truman became president.

Hay–Bunau-Varilla Treaty 1903 treaty with Panama that granted the United States sovereignty over the Canal Zone in return for a $10 million payment plus an annual rent.

Hay-Pauncefote Treaties Two separate treaties (1900 and 1901) signed by the United States and Britain that gave the United States the exclusive right to build, control, and fortify a canal through Central America.

head right system The grant of 50 acres of land for each settler brought over to Virginia by a colonist.

hegemony The dominance of one group over other groups.

Henry VIII King of England (r. 1509–1547); his desire to divorce his first wife led him to break with Catholicism and establish the Church of England.

Henry Cabot Lodge Prominent Republican senator from Massachusetts and chair of the Senate Foreign Relations Committee, who led congressional opposition to Article 10 of the League of Nations.

Henry David Thoreau Writer and naturalist and friend of Ralph Waldo Emerson; his best-known work is *Walden* (1854).

Henry Ford Inventor and manufacturer who founded the Ford Motor Company in 1903 and pioneered mass production in the auto industry.

Henry Grady Prominent Atlanta newspaper publisher and leading proponent of the concept of a New South.

Henry Hudson Dutch ship captain and explorer who sailed up the Hudson River in 1609, giving the Netherlands a claim to the area now occupied by New York.

Henry Kissinger German-born American diplomat who was President Nixon's national security adviser and secretary of state; he helped negotiate the cease-fire in Vietnam.

Henry the Navigator Prince who founded an observatory and school of navigation and directed voyages that helped build Portugal's colonial empire.

Henry Ware Liberal Congregationalist who was elected senior theologian at Harvard College in 1805, making Unitarianism the dominant religious view at the previously Calvinist stronghold.

Hepburn Act Law passed by Congress in 1906 that authorized the Interstate Commerce Commission to set maximum railroad rates and to regulate other forms of transportation.

Herbert Hoover U.S. food administrator during World War I, known for his proficient handling of relief efforts; he later served as secretary of commerce (1921–1928) and president (1929–1933).

heretic A person who does not behave in accordance with an established attitude, doctrine, or principle, usually in religious matters.

Hernando Cortés Spanish soldier and explorer who conquered the Aztecs and claimed Mexico for Spain.

Hessian troops German soldiers from the state of Hesse who were hired by Britain to fight in the American Revolution.

hierarchical A system in which people or things are ranked above one another.

hippies Members of the counterculture in the 1960s who rejected the competitiveness and materialism of American society and searched for peace, love, and autonomy.

Hiram W. Johnson Governor of California who promoted a broad range of reforms, including regulation of railroads and measures to benefit labor.

Hiroshima Japanese city that was the target, on August 6, 1945, of the first atomic bomb, called "Little Boy."

Hispanos Spanish-speaking New Mexicans.

Ho Chi Minh Trail Main infiltration route for North Vietnamese soldiers and supplies into South Vietnam; it ran through Laos and Cambodia.

holding company A company that exists to own other companies, usually through holding a controlling interest in their stocks.

Hollywood Ten Ten screenwriters and producers who stated that the Fifth Amendment of the Constitution gave them the right to refuse to testify before the House Un-American Activies Committee in 1947. The House of Representatives disagreed and isssued citations for contempt. Found guilty in 1948, they served from 6 months to a year in prison.

Holocaust Mass murder of European Jews and other groups systematically carried out by the Nazis during World War II.

Holy Land Palestine, which now is divided between Israel, Jordan, and Syria; called the Holy Land because it is the region in which the events described in the Old and New Testaments of the Bible took place; it is sacred to Christians, Jews, and Muslims.

Holy Roman Empire A political entity, authorized by the Catholic Church in 1356, unifying central Europe under an emperor elected by four princes and three Catholic archbishops.

Home Owners' Loan Corporation Government agency created in 1933 that refinanced home mortgage debts for non-farm homeowners and allowed them to borrow money from the agency to pay property taxes and make repairs.

Homestead Act Law passed by Congress in 1862 that offered ownership of 160 acres of designated public lands to any citizen who lived on and improved the land for five years.

homogenize To make something uniform throughout.

hookworm A parasite, formerly common in the South, that causes loss of strength.

Hooverville Crudely built camp set up by the homeless on the fringes of a town or city during the Depression; the largest Hooverville was outside Oklahoma City and covered over 100 square miles.

Hopewell culture A successor to the Adena culture also centered in the Ohio River Valley and spreading as far as New York; Hopewell Indians introduced maize agriculture in about 200 BCE and built larger and more elaborate mound cities in which large-scale trading activities continued.

Hopewell Treaties Treaties signed by 1785 in which the Choctaws, Chickasaws, and Cherokees granted American settlement rights in the Southwest.

Hopi Indians Indians who were related to the Comanches and Shoshones and took up residence among the Pueblo Indians as agricultural town-dwellers; their name means "peaceful ones."

Horace Greeley Journalist and politician who helped found the Republican Party; his newspaper, the *New York Tribune,* was known for its antislavery stance.

Horace Mann Educator who called for publicly funded education for all children and was head of the first public board of education in the United States.

Horatio "Granny" Gates Elderly Virginia general who led the American troops to victory in the Battle of Saratoga in 1777.

horizontal integration Merging one or more companies doing the same or similar activities as a way of limiting competition or enhancing stability and planning.

horse culture The nomadic way of life of those American Indians, mostly on the Great Plains, for whom the horse brought significant changes in their ability to hunt, travel, and make war.

House of Burgesses The elected lawmaking body of Virginia, established by the Virginia Company in 1618; the assembly first met in 1619.

House Un-American Activities Committee Congressional committee, created in 1938, that investigated suspected Communists during the McCarthy era and that Richard Nixon used to advance his career.

House Ways and Means Committee One of the most significant standing committees (permanently organized committees) of the House of Representatives, responsible for initiating all taxation measures.

house slaves People who did domestic work such as cleaning and cooking.

Hudson River school The first native school of landscape painting in the United States (1825–1875); it attracted artists rebelling against the neoclassical tradition.

Huey Long Louisiana governor, then U.S. senator, who ran a powerful political machine and whose advocacy of redistribution of income was gaining him a national political following at the time of his assassination in 1935.

Hull House Settlement house founded by Jane Addams and Ellen Gates Starr in 1889 in Chicago.

human rights Basic rights and freedoms to which all human beings are entitled, such as the right to life and liberty, to freedom of thought and expression, and to equality before the law.

Hun Disparaging term used to describe Germans during World War I; the name came from a warlike tribe that invaded Europe in the fourth and fifth centuries.

hydraulic Having to do with water moved in pipes; hydraulic mining uses water under great pressure to wash away soil from underlying mineral deposits.

hydrogen bomb Nuclear weapon of much greater destructive power than the atomic bomb.

I

icon A symbol, usually one with virtues considered worthy of copying.

Ida B. Wells African American reformer and journalist who crusaded against lynching and advocated racial justice and woman suffrage; upon marrying in 1895, she became Ida Wells-Barnett.

Ida Tarbell Progressive Era journalist whose exposé revealed the ruthlessness of the Standard Oil Company.

idolater A person who worships idols.

idolatry The worship of idols, a practice forbidden in the Judeo-Christian tradition.

Immigration Act of 1990 Law reforming the Immigration Act of 1965; it increased the number of immigrants allowed annually into the United States to around 700,000 and gave preference to skilled workers and those with families already living in the country.

Immigration Reform and Control Act Law passed by Congress in 1986 that prohibits the hiring of illegal aliens; it offered amnesty and legal residence to any who could prove that they had entered the country before January 1, 1982.

impeach To charge a public official with improper, usually criminal, conduct; to formally charge a public official with criminal conduct in office; once Congress has impeached a federal official, the official is then tried in the Senate on the stated charges.

impeachment A Congressional power to remove the president, vice president, and civil officers of the United States. If the House of Representatives determines that a federal official has committed "high crimes and misdemeanors," it can vote for Articles of Impeachment. If a majority agree, the House recommends to the Senate that the official be removed from office. If two-thirds of the Senate agree, the official may be removed from office. From 1789 to 2004, the House has voted only 18 impeachments and only 7 officials have been removed from office by the Senate.

imperialism The practice by which a nation acquires and holds colonies and other possessions, denies them self-government, and usually exploits them economically.

implied power Power that is not specifically granted to the government by the Constitution but can be viewed as necessary to carry out the governing duties listed in the Constitution.

import duties A tax on imported goods.

impressionism A style of painting that developed in France in the 1870s and emphasized the artist's impression of a subject.

impressment Procedure permitted under British maritime law that authorized commanders of warships to force English civilian sailors into military service.

indemnity Payment for damage, loss, or injury.

indentured servants Compulsory service for a fixed period of time, usually from four to seven years, most often agreed to in exchange for passage to the colonies; a labor contract called an indenture spelled out the terms of the agreement.

Indian Removal Act Law passed by Congress in 1830 providing for the removal of all Indian tribes east of the Mississippi and the purchase of western lands for their resettlement.

Indian Reorganization Act Law passed by Congress in 1934 that ended Indian allotment and returned surplus land to tribal ownership; it also sought to encourage tribal self-government and to improve economic conditions on reservations.

Indian Self-Determination and Education Assistance Act Law passed by Congress in 1974 giving Indian tribes control over federal programs carried out on their reservations and increasing their authority in reservation schools.

indigenous Original to an area.

indigo Shrublike plant with clusters of red or purple flowers, grown on plantations in the South; a primary source of blue dye.

Indochina French colony in Southeast Asia, including present-day Vietnam, Laos, and Cambodia; it began fighting for its independence in the mid-twentieth century.

industrial union Union that organizes all workers in an industry, whether skilled or unskilled, and regardless of occupation.

industry A basic unit of business activity in which the various participants do similar activities; for example, the railroad industry consists of railroad companies and the firms and factories that supply their equipment.

inequities Unfair circumstances or proceedings.

infant depravity The idea that children are naturally sinful because they share in the original sin of the human race but have not learned the discipline to control their evil instincts.

inflation Rising prices that occur when the supply of currency or credit grows faster than the available supply of goods and services.

influence peddling Using one's influence with people in authority to obtain favors or preferential treatment for someone else, usually in return for payment.

influenza Contagious viral infection characterized by fever, chills, congestion, and muscular pain, nicknamed "the flu"; an unusually deadly strain, usually called "Spanish flu," swept across the world in 1918 and 1919.

information technology A broad range of businesses concerned with managing and processing information, especially with the use of computers and other forms of telecommunications.

infrastructure Basic facilities that a society needs to function, such as transportation systems, water and power lines, and public institutions such as schools, post offices, and prisons.

initiative Procedure allowing voters to petition to have a law placed on the ballot for consideration by the general electorate.

injunction A court order requiring an individual or a group to do something or to refrain from doing something.

insane asylum In the nineteenth and early twentieth centuries, an institution for the incarceration of people with mental disorders.

installment Partial payments of a debt to be made at regular intervals until the entire debt is repaid.

insubordination Resistance to authority; disobedience.

Insular cases Cases concerning Puerto Rico, in which the U.S. Supreme Court ruled in 1901 that people in new island territories did not automatically receive the constitutional rights of U.S. citizens.

insurgents Rebels or revolutionaries.

insurrection An uprising against a legitimate authority or government.

interchangeable parts Mechanical parts that are identical and can be substituted for one another.

interest group A coalition of people identified with a particular cause, such as an industry or occupational group, a social group, or a policy objective.

interlocking directorates Situation in which the same individuals sit on the boards of directors of various companies in one industry.

Intermediate Nuclear Force Treaty Treaty (1987) that provided for the destruction of all U.S. and Soviet medium-range nuclear missiles and for verification with on-site inspections.

internal taxes Taxes collected directly from citizens, like Alexander Hamilton's various excise taxes, as opposed to tariffs or other taxes collected in connection with foreign trade.

International Monetary Fund An agency of the United Nations established in 1945 to help promote the health of the world economy; it seeks to expand international trade by stabilizing exchange rates between international currencies; it also provides temporary loans for nations unable to maintain their balance of trade. Currently, 184 countries are members of the IMF.

internment camps Camps to which more than 110,000 Japanese Americans living in the West were moved soon after the attack on Pearl Harbor; Japanese Americans in Hawai'i were not confined in internment camps.

interpose To place a barrier between two objects or forces; to

Jefferson, the principle of interposition meant that states had the right to use their sovereign power as a barrier between the federal government and the states' citizens when the natural rights of those citizens were at risk.

Interstate Commerce Commission The first federal regulatory commission, created in 1886 to regulate railroads.

investment bank An institution that acts as an agent for corporations issuing stocks and bonds.

iron curtain Name given to the military, political, and ideological barrier established between the Soviet bloc and Western Europe after World War II.

irreligious Hostile or indifferent to religion.

isolationism The notion that the United States should avoid political, diplomatic, and military entanglements with other nations.

Issei A Japanese immigrant to the United States.

itinerant Traveling from place to place.

J

J. Edgar Hoover Official appointed to head a new antiradical division in the Justice Department in 1919; he served as head of the FBI from its official founding in 1924 until his death in 1972.

Jacob Leisler German merchant who led a revolt in New York in 1689 against royal officials representing the Dominion of New England; he was executed as a traitor when he refused to surrender control of the colony to a governor appointed by William and Mary.

Jacques Cartier French explorer who, by navigating the St. Lawrence River in 1534, gave France its primary claim to territories in the New World.

James B. "Wild Bill" Hickok Western gambler and gunfighter who for a time was the town marshal (law enforcement officer) in Abilene, Kansas.

James Buchanan Pennsylvania senator who was elected president in 1856 after gaining the Democratic nomination as a compromise candidate.

James F. Byrnes Supreme Court justice who left the Supreme Court to direct the nation's economy and war production; known as the "Assistant President," he directed the Office of Economic Stabilization and the Office of War Mobilization and later became secretary of state under President Truman.

James Farmer Helped to organize the Congress of Racial Equality in 1942; led the organization from 1961 to 1966. In 1969 he became Assistant Secretary of Health, Education and Welfare.

James Forten African American entrepreneur with a successful sailmaking business in Philadelphia who provided leadership for black business enterprises and advocated both racial integration and equal rights during the Jeffersonian era.

James K. Polk Tennessee congressman who was a leader of the Democratic Party and the dark-horse winner of the presidential campaign in 1844.

James Madison Virginia planter and political theorist known as the "father of the Constitution"; he became the fourth president of the United States.

James Meredith Black student admitted to the University of Mississippi under federal court order in 1962; in spite of rioting by racist mobs, he finished the year and graduated in 1963.

James Monroe Republican politician from Virginia who served in diplomatic posts under George Washington, John Adams, and Thomas Jefferson; he later became the fifth president of the United States.

James Oglethorpe English philanthropist who established the colony of Georgia in 1732 as a refuge for debtors.

Jamestown First permanent English settlement in mainland America, established in 1607 by the Virginia Company and named in honor of King James I.

Jay's Treaty Controversial 1794 treaty negotiated between the United States and Great Britain by John Jay to ensure American neutrality in the French and English war.

Jean Laffite Leader of a band of pirates in southeast Louisiana; he offered to fight for the Americans at New Orleans in return for the pardon of his men.

Jeannette Rankin Montana reformer who in 1916 became the first woman elected to Congress; she worked to pass the woman suffrage amendment and to protect women in the workplace.

Jefferson Davis Secretary of war under Franklin Pierce; he later became president of the Confederacy.

John Brown Abolitionist who fought proslavery settlers in Kansas in 1855; he was hanged for treason after seizing the U.S. arsenal at Harpers Ferry in 1859 as part of an effort to liberate southern slaves.

John Burgoyne British general forced to surrender his entire army at Saratoga, New York, in October 1777.

John C. Calhoun Congressman from South Carolina who was a leader of the War Hawks and the author of the official declaration of war in 1812.

John C. Frémont Explorer, soldier, and politician who explored and mapped much of the American West and Northwest; he later ran unsuccessfully for president.

John Cabot (Giovanni Caboto) Italian explorer who led the English expedition that sailed along the North American mainland in 1497.

John Coode Leader of a rebel army, the Protestant Association, that won control of Maryland in 1691.

John D. Rockefeller American industrialist who amassed great wealth through the Standard Oil Company and donated much of his fortune to promote learning and research.

John Deere Nineteenth-century American industrialist who pioneered the manufacture of steel plows especially suited for working hard-packed prairie soil.

John Dickinson Philadelphia lawyer and revolutionary pamphleteer who drafted the Articles of Confederation.

John Foster Dulles Secretary of state under Eisenhower; he used the threat of nuclear war to deter Soviet aggression.

John J. Crittenden Kentucky senator who made an unsuccessful attempt to prevent the Civil War by proposing a series of constitutional amendments protecting slavery south of the Missouri Compromise line.

John Jay New York lawyer and diplomat who negotiated with Great Britain and Spain on behalf of the Confederation;

he later became the first chief justice of the Supreme Court and negotiated the Jay Treaty with England.

John Marshall   Virginia lawyer and politician whom President John Adams made chief justice of the Supreme Court; his legal decisions helped shape the role of the Supreme Court in American government.

John Mitchell   Nixon's attorney general, who eventually served four years in prison for his part in the Watergate scandal.

John Pierpont Morgan   The most prominent and powerful American investment banker in the late nineteenth century.

John Randolph   Virginia Republican politician who was a cousin of Thomas Jefferson; he believed in limited government and objected to several of Jefferson's policies.

John Ross   Cherokee leader who had reluctantly directed the forced removal of the Cherokees from Georgia to Oklahoma Territory in the 1830s; he signed an alliance between some groups in Indian Territory and the Confederacy.

John Sutter   Swiss immigrant who founded a colony in California; the discovery of gold on his property in Coloma Valley, northeast of New Helvetia (Sacramento), in 1848 attracted hordes of miners who seized his land, leaving him financially ruined.

John Tyler   Virginia senator who left the Democratic Party after conflicts with Andrew Jackson; he was elected vice president in 1840 and became president when William Henry Harrison died in office.

John Wilkes Booth   Actor and southern sympathizer who on April 14, 1865, five days after Lee's surrender, fatally shot President Lincoln at Ford's Theater in Washington.

John Winthrop   One of the founders of Massachusetts Bay Colony and the colony's first governor.

joint resolution   A formal statement adopted by both houses of Congress and subject to approval by the president; if approved, it has the force of law.

joint-stock company   A business financed through the sale of shares of stock to investors; the investors share in both the profits and losses from a risky venture.

Joseph McCarthy   Republican senator from Wisconsin who in 1950 began a Communist witch-hunt that lasted until his censure by the Senate in 1954; *McCarthyism* is a term associated with attacks on liberals and others often based on unsupported assertions and carried out without regard for basic liberties.

Joseph Pulitzer   Hungarian-born newspaper publisher whose *New York World* printed sensational stories about Cuba that helped precipitate the Spanish-American War.

Joseph Smith Jr.   Founder of the Church of Jesus Christ of Latter-day Saints, also known as the Mormon Church, who transcribed the Book of Mormon and led his congregation westward from New York to Illinois; he was later murdered by an anti-Mormon mob.

journeyman   A person who has finished an apprenticeship in a trade or craft and is a qualified worker in the employ of another.

judicial restraint   Refraining from using the courts as a forum for implementing social change but instead deferring to Congress, the president, and the consensus of the people.

judicial review   The power of the Supreme Court to review the constitutionality of laws passed by Congress and by the states.

Judiciary Act of 1789   Law establishing the Supreme Court and the lower federal courts; it gave the Supreme Court the right to review state laws and state court decisions to determine their constitutionality.

Judiciary Act of 1801   Law that the Federalist Congress passed to increase the number of federal courts and judicial positions; President John Adams rushed to fill these positions with Federalists before his term ended.

juggernaut   An overwhelming, advancing force that crushes or seems to roll over everything in its path.

Junípero Serra   Spanish missionary who went to California in 1769; he and his successors established near the California coast a chain of missions that depended on Indian labor.

junta   Group of military officers ruling a country after seizing power.

Justice Department   Part of the executive branch that has responsibility to enforce the law, defend the interests of the United States according to the law, and to ensure fair and impartial administration of justice for all Americans. It is administered by the attorney general who was one of the original members of the cabinet.

justice of the peace   The lowest level of judge in some state court systems, usually responsible for hearing small claims and minor criminal cases; because Washington, D.C., is a federal territory rather than a state, the justice of the peace for that district is a federal appointee.

K

Kansas-Nebraska Act   Law passed by Congress in 1854 that allowed residents of Kansas and Nebraska Territories to decide whether to allow slavery within their borders.

katsina dolls   Painted wooden models that represent important spirit beings in Pueblo beliefs, often used in ceremonies and possessing great cultural significance.

Kellogg-Briand Pact   Treaty signed in 1928 by fifteen nations, including Britain, France, Germany, the United States, and Japan, renouncing war as a means of solving international disputes.

Kenniwick Man   The name given to a human skeleton discovered next to the Columbia River near Kenniwick, Washington, in 1996. The skeleton is believed to be over 9,000 years old and appears to have facial features unlike those of other ancient Indian relics.

Keynesianism   Refers to economic theories of Lord John Maynard Keynes, who in the 1920s and 1930s argued for government intervention in the economy; he believed that government expansion and contraction of the money supply and regulation of interest rates could stimulate economic growth during periods of recession and inflation.

kickback   An illegal payment by a contractor to the official who awarded the contract.

kindergarten   German for "children's garden"; a preschool program developed in the late nineteenth century initially as childcare for working mothers; based on programs first developed in Germany.

Kitchen Cabinet President Jackson's informal advisers, who helped him shape both national and Democratic Party policy.

Knights of Labor Organization founded in 1869; membership, open to all workers, peaked in 1886; members favored a cooperative alternative to capitalism.

Know-Nothings Members of anti-Catholic, anti-immigrant organizations who eventually formed themselves into a national political party.

Koyto Protocol Drafted by the United Nations in 1997 were a set of international agreements in which participating nations agreed to reduce their emissions rates of carbon dioxide and other industrial-produced gases that are linked to global climate change; the United States was to reduce its emissions 7 percent by 2012.

Ku Klux Klan A secret society organized in the South after the Civil War to resurrect white supremacy by means of violence and intimidation.

L

labor glut Oversupply of labor in relation to the number of jobs available.

laissez faire The principle that the government should not interfere in the workings of the economy.

Lakota A confederation of Siouan Indian peoples who lived on the northern Great Plains.

Lakotas/Dakotas Subgroups of the Sioux Nation of Plains Indians; Lakotas make up the western branch, living mostly on the Great Plains; Dakotas, the eastern branch, live mostly in the prairie and lakes region of the Upper Midwest.

lame duck An officeholder who has failed to win, or is ineligible for, reelection but whose term in office has not yet ended.

land redistribution The division of land held by large landowners into smaller plots that are turned over to people without property.

Land-Grant College Act Law passed by Congress in 1862 that gave states land to use to raise money to establish public universities that were to offer courses in engineering and agriculture and to train military officers.

lay exhorter A church member who preaches but is not an ordained minister.

League Covenant The constitution of the League of Nations, which was incorporated in the 1919 Treaty of Versailles.

League of Nations A world organization proposed by President Wilson and created by the Versailles peace conference; it worked to promote peace and international cooperation.

Lecompton constitution State constitution written for Kansas in 1857 at a convention dominated by proslavery forces; it would have allowed slavery, but Kansas voters rejected it.

left-wing Not conservative; usually implies socialist or otherwise radical leanings.

legation Diplomatic officials representing their nation to another nation, and their offices and residences.

Lend-Lease Act Law passed by Congress in 1941 providing that any country whose security was vital to U.S. interests could receive arms and equipment by sale, transfer, or lease from the United States.

Leonid Brezhnev Leader of the Soviet Union (first as Communist Party secretary, and then also as president) from 1964 to his death in 1982; he worked to foster détente with the United States during the Nixon era.

Liberty Loan One of four bond issues floated by the U.S. Treasury Department from 1917 to 1919 to help finance World War I.

Liberty Party The first antislavery political party; it was formed in Albany, New York, in 1840.

**Lili`uokalani** Last reigning queen of Hawai`i, whose desire to restore land to the Hawaiian people and perpetuate the monarchy prompted *haole* planters to remove her from power in 1893.

Limited Test Ban Treaty Treaty signed by the United States, the USSR, and nearly one hundred other nations in 1963; it banned nuclear weapons tests in the atmosphere, in outer space, and underwater.

Lincoln Steffens Muckraking journalist and managing editor of *McClure's Magazine,* best known for investigating political corruption in city governments.

Little Big Horn River River in Montana where in 1876 Lieutenant Colonel George Custer attacked a large Indian encampment; Custer and most of his forces died in the battle.

lobby To try to influence the thinking of public officials for or against a specific cause.

lobbyist A person who tries to influence the opinions of legislators or other public officials for or against a specific cause.

local option law A state law that permitted the residents of a town or city to decide, by an election, whether to ban liquor sales in their community.

lock A section of canal with gates at each end, used to raise or lower boats from one level to another by admitting or releasing water; locks allow canals to compensate for changes in terrain.

lockjaw A popular name for tetanus, an often fatal disease resulting primarily from deep wounds.

longhouse A communal dwelling, usually built of poles and bark and having a central hallway with family apartments on either side.

long-staple cotton A variety of cotton with long and loosely packed pods of fiber that is easy to comb out and process.

Lost Cause Term applied to the Confederate struggle in the Civil War, depicting it as a noble but doomed effort to preserve a way of life.

Louis XVI The king of France (r. 1774–1792) when the French Revolution began; he and his wife, Marie Antoinette, were executed in 1793 by the revolutionary government.

Louis Brandeis Lawyer and reformer who opposed monopolies and defended individual rights; in 1916 he became the first Jewish justice on the Supreme Court.

Louis Sullivan American architect of the late nineteenth century whose designs reflected his theory that the outward form of a building should express its function.

Louisiana French colony south of New France; it included the entire area drained by the Mississippi River and all its tributary rivers.

Louisiana Purchase The U.S. purchase of Louisiana from France for $15 million in 1803; the Louisiana Territory extended from the Mississippi River to the Rocky Mountains.

loyalist An American colonist who remained loyal to the king during the Revolution.

Lucretia Mott Quaker minister who founded the Philadelphia Female Anti-Slavery Society (1833) and co-organized the Seneca Falls Women's Rights Convention in 1848.

lumber mill A factory or place where logs are sawed into rough boards.

Lusitania British passenger liner torpedoed by a German submarine in 1915; more than one thousand drowned, including 128 Americans, creating a diplomatic crisis between the United States and Germany.

Lydia Sigourney Nineteenth-century Romantic and sentimental author who was one of the first women in American history to make a living as a professional writer.

M

machine politics The aggressive use of influence, favors, and tradeoffs by a political organization, or "machine," to mobilize support among its followers.

Macon's Bill No. 2 Law passed by Congress in 1810 that offered exclusive trading rights to France or Britain, whichever recognized American neutral rights first.

magistrate A civil officer charged with administering the law.

mail-order sales The business of selling goods using the mails; mail-order houses send out catalogs, customers submit orders, and the products are delivered all by mail.

Main Line Canal Ambitious canal-building enterprise by the state of Pennsylvania to connect the Delaware River at Philadelphia with the Ohio River at Pittsburgh.

maize Corn; the word *maize* comes from an Indian word for this plant.

malarial Related to malaria, an infectious disease characterized by chills, fever, and sweating; malaria is often transmitted through mosquito bites.

Malcolm X Black activist who advocated black separatism as a member of the Nation of Islam; in 1963 he converted to orthodox Islam and two years later was assassinated.

maldistribution of wealth Unequal distribution of wealth among population groups. In 1929, the richest fifth of the population controlled 52.3 percent of the nation's wealth, the middle fifth held only 14.4 percent, while the poorest fifth had access to only 5.4 percent.

Mamie Tape Chinese girl in San Francisco whose parents sued the city in 1885 to end the exclusion of Chinese students from the public schools.

Manchuria A region of northeastern China.

Mandan Indians A Siouan-speaking Native American group that lived in permanent villages and practiced agriculture in the Red River Valley in present-day North Dakota; they hosted the Lewis and Clark expedition during the winter of 1804.

mandate In politics, the understanding that a large electoral victory means that there is public support for the victorious party to carry out its program. Under the League of Nations, *mandate* referred to a territory that the League authorized a member nation to administer, with the understanding that the territory would move toward self-government.

Manhattan Project A secret scientific research effort begun in 1941 to develop an atomic bomb; much of the research was done in a secret community of scientists and workers near Oak Ridge, Tennessee, and Los Alamos, New Mexico.

manifest destiny Term first used in the 1840s to describe the right and duty of the United States to expand westward.

manifesto A written statement publicly declaring the views of its author.

manioc Also called cassava, a root vegetable native to South America that became a staple food source throughout the tropical world after 1500.

Mann Act Law passed by Congress in 1910, designed to suppress prostitution; it made transporting a woman across state lines for immoral purposes illegal.

Mann Doctrine U.S. policy outlined by Thomas Mann during the Johnson administration that called for stability in Latin America rather than economic and political reform.

manufacturing belt A region that includes most of the nation's factories; in the late nineteenth century, the U.S. manufacturing belt also included most of the nation's large cities and railroad lines and much of its mining.

manumit To free from slavery or bondage; to emancipate.

Marbury v. Madison Supreme Court decision (1803) declaring part of the Judiciary Act of 1789 unconstitutional, thereby establishing an important precedent in favor of judicial review.

March on Washington Meeting of a quarter of a million civil rights supporters in Washington in 1963, at which Martin Luther King Jr. delivered his "I Have a Dream" speech.

March to the Sea Sherman's march through Georgia from Atlanta to Savannah from November 15 to December 21, 1864, during which Union soldiers carried out orders to destroy everything in their path.

Marcus Garvey Jamaican black nationalist active in America in the 1920s.

Margaret Sanger Birth-control advocate who believed so strongly that information about birth control was essential to help women escape poverty that she disobeyed laws against its dissemination.

Mark Twain Pen name of Samuel Clemens, prominent American author of the late nineteenth century; Twain wrote *The Adventures of Huckleberry Finn* and many other American literary classics.

market economy An economic system based on the buying and selling of goods and services, in which prices are determined by the forces of supply and demand.

Marshall Plan Program launched in 1948 to foster economic recovery in Western Europe in the postwar period through massive amounts of U.S. financial aid.

martial law Temporary rule by military authorities, imposed on a civilian population in time of war or when civil authority has broken down.

Martin Luther King Jr. Ordained Baptist minister, brilliant orator, and civil rights leader committed to nonviolence; he led many of the important protests of the 1950s and 1960s.

Martin Van Buren New York politician known for his skillful handling of party politics; he helped found the Democratic Party and later became the eighth president of the United States.

Marxist A believer in the ideas of Karl Marx and Friedrich Engels, who opposed private ownership of property and looked to a future in which workers would control the economy.

Mary Ludwig Howe Wife of a soldier at Fort Monmouth; one of many women known popularly as "Molly Pitchers" because they carried water to cool down the cannon their husbands fired in battle.

Mary McLeod Bethune African American educator who founded the Daytona Literary and Industrial School for Training Negro Girls in 1904 that became part of Bethune-Cookman College in 1923 and who, as director of the Division of Negro Affairs within the National Youth Administration, was a strong and vocal advocate for equality of opportunity for African Americans during the New Deal.

Mason-Dixon Line The boundary between Pennsylvania and Maryland; it marked the northern division between free and slave states before the Civil War.

Masons An international fraternal organization with many socially and politically prominent members, including a number of U.S. presidents.

massive retaliation Term that Secretary of State John Foster Dulles used in a 1954 speech, implying that the United States was willing to use nuclear force in response to Communist aggression anywhere.

materialism Excessive interest in worldly matters, especially in acquiring goods.

mawkish Mushy, exaggerated, and insincere sentimentality.

Maximilian Austrian archduke appointed by France to be emperor of Mexico in 1864; later executed by Mexican republicans.

Mayflower Compact An agreement drafted in 1620 when the Pilgrims reached America that granted political rights to all male colonists who would abide by the colony's laws.

McCarran Internal Security Act Law passed by Congress in 1950 requiring Communists to register with the U.S. attorney general and making it a crime to conspire to establish a totalitarian government in the United States.

McCulloch v. Maryland Supreme Court case (1819) in which the majority ruled that federal authority is superior to that of individual states and that states cannot control or tax federal operations within their borders.

McKinley Tariff Tariff passed by Congress in 1890 that sought not only to protect established industries but by prohibitory duties to stimulate the creation of new industries.

McNary-Haugen bill Farm relief bill that provided for government purchase of crop surpluses during years of large output; Coolidge vetoed it in 1927 and in 1928.

Meat Inspection Act Law passed by Congress in 1906 requiring federal inspection of meatpacking.

meatpacking The business of slaughtering animals and preparing their meat for sale as food.

mechanize To substitute machinery for human labor.

mediation An attempt to bring about the peaceful settlement of a dispute through the intervention of a neutral party.

Medicaid Program of health insurance for the poor established in 1965; it provides states with money to buy healthcare for people on welfare.

Medicare Program of health insurance for the elderly and disabled established in 1965; it provides government payment for healthcare supplied by private doctors and hospitals.

melodrama A sensational or romantic stage play with exaggerated conflicts and stereotyped characters.

meltdown Severe overheating of a nuclear reactor core, resulting in the melting of the core and the escape of life-threatening radiation.

melting pot A concept that American society is a place where immigrants set aside their distinctive cultural identities and are absorbed into a homogeneous culture.

Mendez v. Westminster **and** *Delgado v. Bastrop School District* Two federal court cases that overturned the establishment of separate schools for Mexican American children in California and Texas in 1946 and 1948.

mercantile theory The economic notion that a nation should amass wealth by exporting more than it imports; colonies are valuable in a mercantile system as a source of raw materials and as a market for manufactured goods.

merchant marine A nation's commercial ships.

Mercy Otis Warren Writer and historian known for her influential anti-British plays and essays during the prerevolutionary era; an active opponent of the Constitution.

merger The joining together of two or more organizations.

meridian Any of the imaginary lines representing degrees of longitude that pass through the North and South Poles and encircle the Earth.

Meriwether Lewis Jefferson aide who was sent to explore the Louisiana Territory in 1803; he later served as its governor.

mestizo A person of mixed Spanish and Indian ancestry.

Metacomet A Wampanoag chief, known to the English as King Philip, who led the Indian resistance to colonial expansion in New England in 1675.

metropolis An urban center, especially one that is dominant within a region.

middle passage The transatlantic voyage of indentured servants or African slaves to the Americas.

Midway Island Strategically located Pacific island that the Japanese navy tried to capture in June 1942; warned about Japanese plans by U.S. naval intelligence, American forces repulsed the attack and inflicted heavy losses on Japanese planes and carriers.

midwifery The practice of assisting women in childbirth.

migrant Traveling from one area to another.

Mikhail Gorbachev As Soviet General Secretary of the Communist Party assumed power in 1985, he introduced political and economic reforms and then found himself presiding over the breakup of the Soviet Union.

Milan Decree Napoleon's order authorizing the capture of any neutral vessels sailing from British ports or submitting to British searches.

militia A military force consisting of civilians who agree to be mobilized into service in times of emergency; organized by state governments during the nineteenth century but now superseded by the National Guard.

militiamen Soldiers who were not members of a regular army but ordinary citizens called out in case of an emergency.

millennia The plural of *millennium,* a period of one thousand years.

millet A large family of grain grasses that produce nutritious, carbohydrate-rich seeds used for both human and animal feed.

milliner A maker or designer of hats.

millrace The channel for the fast-moving stream of water that drives a mill wheel.

millwright A person who designs, builds, or repairs mills or mill machinery.

Milo Reno Farm leader from Iowa who led the Farmers' Holiday Association and in 1932 called on farmers to strike, to "stay home, buy nothing, sell nothing"; he wanted government codes to control production but rejected President Roosevelt's farm program as a threat to independence and liberty; he died in 1936.

minstrel show A variety show in which white actors made up as blacks presented jokes, songs, dances, and comic skits.

Minutemen Nickname first given to the Concord militia because of their speed in assembling and later applied generally to colonial militia during the Revolution.

Mississippi Plan Use of threats, violence, and lynching by Mississippi Democrats in 1875 to intimidate Republicans and bring the Democratic Party to power.

Mississippian tradition A culture shared by a number of American Indian societies centered in the southern Mississippi River Valley; influenced by Mexican culture, it is known for its pyramid building and urban centers.

Missouri Compromise Law proposed by Henry Clay in 1820 admitting Missouri to the Union as a slave state and Maine as a free state and banning slavery in the Louisiana Territory north of latitude 36°30′.

mobilize To make ready for combat or other forms of action.

Model T Lightweight automobile that Ford produced from 1908 to 1927 and sold at the lowest possible price on the theory that an affordable car would be more profitable than an expensive one.

moderates People whose views are midway between two more-extreme positions; in this case, Republicans who favored some reforms but not all the Radicals' proposals.

mogul An important or powerful person, especially the head of a major company.

Mohammed Born ca. 570 into an influential family in Mecca, on the Arabian Peninsula; around 610 Mohammed began having religious visions in which he was revealed as "the Messenger of God." The content of his various visions was recorded as the Qur'an, the sacred text that is the foundation for the Islamic religion.

Mohicans Algonquin-speaking Indians who lived along the Hudson River, were dispossessed in a war with the Iroquois confederacy, and eventually were all but exterminated.

monetary policy Now, the regulation of the money supply and interest rates by the Federal Reserve. In the late nineteenth century, federal monetary policy was largely limited to defining the medium of the currency (gold, silver, or paper) and the relations between the types of currency.

money supply The amount of money in the economy, such as cash and the contents of checking accounts.

Monica Lewinsky White House intern who had a two-year sexual affair with President Clinton; Clinton's misleading testimony about the affair contributed to his impeachment.

monopoly Exclusive control by an individual or company of the production or sale of a product.

Monroe Doctrine Announcement by President James Monroe in 1823 that the Western Hemisphere was off-limits for future European colonial expansion.

Moors Natives of northern Africa who converted to Islam in the eighth century, becoming the major carriers of the Islamic religion and culture both to southern Africa and to the Iberian Peninsula (Spain and Portugal), which they conquered and occupied from the eighth century until their ouster in the late fifteenth century.

Moral Majority Conservative religious organization led by televangelist Jerry Falwell; it had an active political lobby in the 1980s promoting such issues as opposition to abortion and to the Equal Rights Amendment.

Mormons Members of the Church of Jesus Christ of Latterday Saints, founded in New York in 1830.

mortar A portable, muzzle-loading cannon that fires large projectiles at high trajectories over a short range; traditionally used by mobile troops against fixed fortifications.

most-favored-nation status In a treaty between nation A and nation B, the provision that commercial privileges extended by A to other nations automatically become available to B.

mound builder Name applied to a number of Native American societies, including the Adena, Hopewell, and Mississippian cultures, that constructed massive earthen mounds as monuments and building foundations.

Muammar Qaddafi Political leader who seized power in a 1969 military coup and imposed a socialist regime and Islamic orthodoxy on Libya.

muckrakers Progressive Era journalists who wrote articles exposing corruption in city government, business, and industry. In John Bunyan's *Pilgrim's Progress,* "the Man with the Muck-rake" is so preoccupied with raking through the filth at his feet that he didn't notice he was being offered a celestial crown in exchange for his rake.

Mugwumps Reformers, mostly Republicans, who opposed political corruption and campaigned for reform, especially reform of the civil service, in the 1880s and 1890s, sometimes crossing party boundaries to achieve their goals.

mujahedeen Afghan resistance group supplied with arms by the United States to assist in its fight against the Soviets following their 1979 invasion of Afghanistan.

Muller v. Oregon Supreme Court case in 1908, upholding an Oregon law that limited the hours of employment for women.

multilateral Involving more than two nations.

municipal reform Political activity intended to bring about changes in the structure or function of city government.

Muslims People who practice the religion of Islam, a monotheistic faith that accepts Mohammed as the chief and last prophet of God.

My Lai Site of a massacre of South Vietnamese villagers by U.S. infantrymen in 1968. Of those brought to trial for the murders, only Lieutenant William Calley was found guilty of murder. Originally sentenced to life in prison, he was paroled in 1974.

N

Nagasaki   City in western Japan devastated on August 9, 1945, by the second atomic bomb, called "Fat Man."

Napoleon Bonaparte   General who took control of the French government in November 1799, at the end of France's revolutionary period; he eventually proclaimed himself emperor of France and conquered much of the continent of Europe.

Napoleonic wars   Wars in Europe waged by or against Napoleon Bonaparte between 1803 and 1815.

narcotic   A drug that reduces pain and induces sleep or stupor.

Nasdaq   A stock exchange, launched in 1971, that focuses on companies in technological fields; *Nasdaq* stands for National Association of Securities Dealers Automated Quotation.

Natchez Indians   An urban, mound-building Indian people who lived on the lower Mississippi River until they were destroyed in a war with the French in the 1720s; survivors joined the Creek Confederacy.

Natchez Trace   A road connecting Natchez, Mississippi, with Nashville, Tennessee; it was commercially and strategically important in the late eighteenth and early nineteenth centuries.

Nathanael Greene   American general who took command of the Carolinas campaign in 1780.

National American Woman Suffrage Association   Organization formed in 1890 that united the two major women's suffrage groups of that time.

National Association for the Advancement of Colored People   Racially integrated civil rights organization founded in New York City in 1910; it continues to work to end discrimination in the United States.

National Defense Student Loans   Loans established by the U.S. government in 1958 to encourage the teaching and study of science and modern foreign languages.

National Farm Workers Association   The initial name for the farm workers' union; from 1966 to 1972, as it grew, the union was named the United Farm Workers Organizing Committee; upon becoming part of the American Federation of Labor in 1972, the union altered its name to the United Farm Workers of America**.**

National Industrial Recovery Act   Law passed by Congress in 1933 establishing the National Recovery Administration to supervise industry and the Public Works Administration to create jobs.

National Labor Union   Federation of trade unions and reform societies organized at Baltimore in 1866; it lasted only six years but helped push through a law limiting government employees to an eight-hour workday.

National Organization for Women   Women's rights organization founded in 1966 to fight discrimination against women; to improve educational, employment, and political opportunities for women; and to fight for equal pay for equal work.

National Origins Act   Law passed by Congress in 1924, establishing quotas for immigration to the United States; it limited immigration from southern and eastern Europe, permitted larger numbers of immigrants from northern and western Europe, and prohibited immigration from Asia.

National Recovery Administration   Agency created by the NIRA to draft national industrial codes and supervise their implementation.

National Security Council   Executive agency established in 1947 to coordinate the strategic policies and defense of the United States; it includes the president, vice president, and four cabinet members.

National Trades' Union   The first national association of trade unions in the United States; it was formed in 1834.

National War Labor Board   Federal agency created in 1918 to resolve wartime labor disputes.

National Woman Suffrage Association   Women's suffrage organization formed in 1869 and led by Elizabeth Cady Stanton and Susan B. Anthony; it accepted only women as members and worked for related issues such as unionizing female workers.

National Youth Administration   Program established by executive order in 1935 to provide employment for young people and to help needy high school and college students continue their educations.

nationalism   Intense patriotism, or a movement that favors a separate nation for an ethnic group that is part of a multiethnic state.

Nationalist Chinese government   The government of Jiang Jieshi, who fought the Communists for control of China in the 1940s; Jiang and his supporters were defeated and retreated to Taiwan in 1949, where they set up a separate government.

nationalists   Americans who preferred a strong central government rather than the limited government prescribed in the Articles of Confederation.

nationalize   To convert an industry or enterprise from private to government ownership and control.

nativism   The view that old-stock values and social patterns were preferable to those of immigrants.

nativist   Favoring native-born inhabitants of a country over immigrants.

nativity   Place of birth.

naturalized   Granted full citizenship (after having been born in a foreign country).

neoclassicism   A revival in architecture and art in the eighteenth and nineteenth centuries inspired by Greek and Roman models and characterized by order, symmetry, and simplicity of style.

Netherlands, the/Holland/Dutch   Often used interchangeably, the first two terms refer to the low-lying area in western Europe north of France and Belgium and across the English Channel from Great Britain; the Dutch are the inhabitants of the Netherlands.

neutral   A neutral nation is one not aligned with either side in a war; traditionally, a neutral nation had the right to engage in certain types of trade with nations that were at war.

neutrality   The policy of treating both sides in a conflict the same way and thus favoring neither.

Neutrality Act of 1935   Seeking to ensure that the events that pushed America into World War I would not be repeated, Congress forbade the sale and shipment of war goods to all nations at war and authorized the president to warn U.S. citizens against traveling on belligerents' vessels.

Neutrality Act of 1937 Law passed by Congress requiring warring nations to pay cash for "nonwar" goods and barring Americans from sailing on their ships; known as the Third Neutrality Act.

Neutrality Act of 1939 Law passed by Congress repealing the arms embargo and authorizing cash-and-carry exports of arms and munitions even to belligerent nations.

New Deal Term applied to Roosevelt's policies to attack the problems of the Depression, which included relief for poor and unemployed, efforts to stimulate economic recovery, and social security; the term was coined by Roosevelt's adviser Raymond Moley.

New Departure Strategy of cooperation with some Reconstruction measures adopted by some leading southern Democrats in the hope of winning compromises favorable to their party.

new economics Planning and shaping the national economy through the use of tax policies and federal spending as recommended by Keynesian economics.

New France The colony established by France in what is now Canada and the Great Lakes region of the United States.

New Freedom Program of reforms that Woodrow Wilson advocated during his 1912 presidential campaign, including reducing tariffs and prosecuting trusts.

New Frontier Program for social and educational reform put forward by President John F. Kennedy; though charismatically presented, it was largely resisted by Congress.

New Harmony Utopian community that Robert Owen established in Indiana in 1825; economic problems and discord among members led to its failure two years later.

"new immigrants" Newcomers from southern and eastern Europe who began to arrive in the United States in significant numbers during the 1890s and after.

New Jersey Plan A proposal submitted by the New Jersey delegation at the Constitutional Convention for creating a government in which the states would have equal representation in a unicameral legislature.

New Look National security policy under Eisenhower that called for a reduction in the size of the army, development of tactical nuclear weapons, and the buildup of strategic air power employing nuclear weapons.

New Nationalism Program of labor and social reform that Theodore Roosevelt advocated before and during his unsuccessful bid to regain the presidency in 1912.

New Netherland The colony founded by the Dutch West India Company in present-day New York; its capital was New Amsterdam on Manhattan Island.

New Right Conservative movement opposing the political and social reforms that developed in the late 1960s and demanding less government intervention in the economy and a return to traditional values; it was a major political force by the 1980s.

New South Late-nineteenth-century term used by some southerners to promote the idea that the South should be-

come industrialized, have a more diverse agriculture, and be thoroughly integrated into the economy of the nation.

New World A term that Europeans used during the period of early contact and colonization to refer to the Americas, especially in the context of their discovery and colonization.

Ngo Dinh Diem President of South Vietnam (1954–1963) who jailed and tortured opponents of his rule; he was assassinated in a coup in 1963.

Nicholas Biddle President of the Second Bank of the United States; he struggled to keep the bank functioning when President Jackson tried to destroy it.

Nicola Sacco and Bartolomeo Vanzetti Italian anarchists convicted in 1921 of the murder of a Braintree, Massachusetts, factory paymaster and theft of a $16,000 payroll; in spite of public protests on their behalf, they were electrocuted in 1927.

Nikita Khrushchev Soviet leader who denounced Stalin in 1956 and improved the Soviet Union's image abroad; he was deposed in 1964 after six years as premier for his failure to improve the country's economy.

Nine-Power Pact Agreement signed in 1922 by Britain, France, Italy, Japan, the United States, China, the Netherlands, Portugal, and Belgium to recognize China and affirm the Open Door policy.

Nineteenth Amendment Constitutional amendment, ratified in 1919, that prohibited federal or state governments from restricting the right to vote on account of sex.

Ninety-five Theses A document prepared by Martin Luther in 1517 protesting certain Roman Catholic practices that he believed were contrary to the will of God as revealed in Scripture.

Nisei A person born in America of parents who emigrated from Japan.

Nixon Doctrine Nixon's policy of requiring countries threatened by communism to shoulder most of the military burden, with the United States offering mainly political and economic support.

noblesse oblige The belief that members of the elite are duty-bound to treat others charitably, especially those of lower status than themselves.

no man's land The field of battle between the lines of two opposing, entrenched armies.

noncommissioned officer Enlisted member of the armed forces who has been promoted to a rank such as corporal or sergeant, conferring leadership over others.

noncompliance Failure or refusal to obey a law or request.

nonconformity Refusal to accept or conform to the beliefs and practices of the majority.

Non-Intercourse Act Law passed by Congress in 1809 reopening trade with all nations except France and Britain and authorizing the president to reopen trade with them if they lifted restrictions on American shipping.

nonliterate Lacking a system of reading and writing, relying instead on storytelling and mnemonic (memory-assisting) devices such as pictures.

nonviolence The rejection of violence in favor of peaceful tactics as a means of achieving political objectives.

normal school A two-year school for preparing teachers for grades 1–8. The term is a direct translation from the French *école normale*, in which *école* means school and *normale* refers to norms or standards. Thus, an *école normale* was where future French teachers learned the standard curriculum that they were to teach to their students.

Norman Vincent Peale   Minister who told his congregations that positive thinking could help them overcome all their troubles in life; his book *The Power of Positive Thinking* was an immediate bestseller.

North American Free Trade Agreement   Agreement approved by the Senate in 1993 that eliminated most tariffs and other trade barriers between the United States, Mexico, and Canada.

North Atlantic Treaty Organization   Mutual defense alliance formed in 1949 among most of the nations of Western Europe and North America in an effort to contain communism.

Northwest Ordinances   Three laws (1784, 1785, 1787) that dealt with the sale of public lands in the Northwest Territory and established a plan for the admission of new states to the Union.

Northwest Passage   The rumored and much-hoped-for water route from Europe to Asia by way of North America sought by early explorers.

nullification   Refusal by a state to recognize or enforce a federal law within its boundaries.

O

Office of War Mobilization   Umbrella agency created in 1943 to coordinate the production, procurement, and distribution of civilian and military supplies.

Ohio Canal   A canal connecting Cleveland to Portsmouth, completing a network of waterways linking the Hudson River, the Great Lakes, and the Mississippi River system.

Okinawa   Pacific island that U.S. troops captured in the spring of 1945 after a grueling battle in which over a quarter-million soldiers and civilians were killed.

"old immigrants"   Newcomers from northern and western Europe who made up much of the immigration to the United States before the 1890s.

Old Ironsides   Nickname of the U.S.S. *Constitution, the forty-four-gun American frigate whose victory over the Guerrière bolstered sagging national morale during the War of 1812.*

Old Northwest   The area of the United States referred to at the time as the Northwest Territory, it would eventually be broken into the states of Indiana, Illinois, Michigan, and Wisconsin.

Old South   Term used in both the South and the North for the antebellum (pre–Civil War) South, suggesting that it was a place of gentility and gallantry.

old-stock   People whose ancestors have lived in the United States for several generations.

oligarchy   A small group of people or families who hold power.

oligopoly   A market or industry dominated by a few firms (from Greek words meaning "few sellers"); compare *monopoly* (from Greek words meaning "one seller").

Olive Branch Petition   Resolution, adopted by the Second Continental Congress in 1775 after the Battles of Lexington and Concord, that offered to end armed resistance if the king would withdraw his troops and repeal the Intolerable Acts.

Oliver Hazard Perry   American naval officer who led the fleet that defeated the British in the Battle of Put-in-Bay during the War of 1812.

omnibus   Including or covering many things; an omnibus bill is a piece of legislation with many parts.

Oneida Community   A religious community established in central New York in 1848; its members shared property, practiced group marriage, and reared children under communal care.

Open Door notes   An exchange of diplomatic letters in 1899–1900 by which Secretary of State John Hay announced American support for Chinese autonomy and opposed efforts by other powers to carve China into exclusive spheres of influence.

open range   Unfenced grazing lands on which cattle ran freely and cattle ownership was established through branding.

operating company   A company that exists to sell goods or services, as opposed to a holding company that exists to own other companies, including operating companies.

Operation Chaos   CIA operation within the country from 1965 to 1973 that collected information on and disrupted anti–Vietnam War elements; although it is illegal for the CIA to operate within the United States, it collected files on over 7,000 Americans.

Operation Mongoose   Mission authorized by President Kennedy in November 1961, and funded with a $50 million budget, to create conditions for the overthrow of Castro.

Operation Overlord   The Allied invasion of Europe on June 6, 1944—D-Day—across the English Channel to Normandy; D-Day is short for "designated day."

Operation Rescue   A militant anti-abortion group that advocates intimidation and physical confrontation as a means to stop abortion.

opium   An addictive drug made from poppies.

opposition party   A political party opposed to the party or government in power.

oratorical   Related to the art of persuasive and eloquent public speaking.

ordnance   Weapons, ammunition, and other military equipment.

Oregon Country   The region to the north of Spanish California extending from the crest of the Rocky Mountains to the Pacific Coast.

Oregon Question   The question of the national ownership of the Pacific Northwest; the United States and England renegotiated the boundary in 1846, establishing it at 49° north latitude.

Oregon System   Name given to the initiative and referendum, first used widely in state politics in Oregon after 1902.

Oregon Trail   The overland route from St. Louis to the Pacific Northwest followed by thousands of settlers in the 1840s.

Organization of American States   An international organization composed of most of the nations of the Americas, including the Caribbean, that deals with the mutual concerns of its members; Cuba is not currently a member.

Organization of Petroleum Exporting Countries Economic alliance of oil-producing countries, mostly Arab, formed in 1960, powerful enough to influence the world price of oil by controlling oil supplies; in 1973 its members placed an embargo on the sale of oil to countries allied with Israel.

original sin In Christian doctrine, the condition of sinfulness that all humans share because of Adam and Eve's disobedience to God in the Garden of Eden.

Osama bin Laden Muslim fundamentalist whose Islamic militant organization, Al Qaeda, has organized terrorist attacks on Americans, including those against the American embassies in Kenya and Tanzania in 1998.

Osceola Seminole leader in Florida who opposed removal of his people to the West and led resistance to U.S. troops; he was captured by treachery while bearing a flag of truce.

Ostend Manifesto Declaration by American foreign ministers in 1854 that if Spain refused to sell Cuba, the United States might be justified in taking it by force.

overproduction Production that exceeds consumer need or demand.

P

pachucos A Spanish term originally meaning "bandits," it became associated with juvenile delinquents of Mexican American/Latino heritage.

Pacific Railway Act Law passed by Congress in 1862 that gave loans and land to the Central Pacific and Union Pacific Railroad companies to subsidize construction of a rail line between Omaha and the Pacific Coast.

pacifism Opposition to war or violence of any kind.

Palestine Region on the Mediterranean that was a British mandate after World War I; the UN partitioned the area in 1948 to allow for a Jewish state (Israel) and a Palestinian state, which was never established.

Palestine Liberation Organization Political and military organization of Palestinians, originally dedicated to opposing the state of Israel through terrorism and other means.

Palmer raids Government raids on individuals and organizations in 1919 and 1920 to search for political radicals and to deport foreign-born activists.

pan-Arab movement Attempts to politically unify the Arab nations of the Middle East; its followers advocated freedom from Western control and opposition to Israel.

Panic of 1819 A financial panic that began when the Second Bank of the United States tightened credit and recalled government loans.

Panic of 1837 An economic collapse that came as the result of Andrew Jackson's fiscal policies and led to an extended national economic depression.

Papal encyclical A letter from the pope to all Roman Catholic bishops, intended to guide them in the relations with the churches under their jurisdiction.

pardon A governmental directive canceling punishment for a person or people who have committed a crime.

parity A price paid to American farmers designed to give them the same income that they had between 1910 and 1914. The AAA provided parity prices on seven commodities: corn, cotton, wheat, rice, tobacco, hogs, and milk and milk products.

Parliament The lawmaking branch of the English government, composed of the House of Lords, representing England's nobility, and the House of Commons, an elected body of untitled English citizens.

parochial school A school supported by a church parish; in the United States, the term usually refers to a Catholic school.

partisan Taking a strong position on an issue out of loyalty to a political group or leader.

partition To divide a country into separate, autonomous nations.

party caucus A meeting of members of a political party to decide on questions of policy or leadership or to register preferences for candidates running for office.

party convention Party meeting to nominate candidates for elective offices and to adopt a political platform.

party platform A formal statement of the principles, policies, and promises on which a political party bases its appeal to the public.

pass system Laws that forbade slaves from traveling without written authorization from their owners.

passive resistance Resistance by nonviolent methods.

patent A government grant that gives the creator of an invention the sole right to produce, use, or sell that invention for a set period of time.

patent medicine A medical preparation that is advertised by brand name and available without a physician's prescription.

paternalistic Treating social dependents as a father treats his children, providing for their needs but denying them rights or responsibilities.

Patrick Henry Member of the Virginia House of Burgesses and American revolutionary leader noted for his oratorical skills.

patrollers During the era of slavery, white guards who made the rounds of rural roads to make certain that slaves were not moving about the countryside without written permission from their masters.

patronage Jobs or favors distributed on a political basis, usually as rewards for loyalty or service.

patronage system System of appointment to government jobs that lets the winner in an election distribute nearly all appointive government jobs to loyal party members; also called the spoils system.

patroonship A huge grant of land given to any Dutch West India Company stockholder who, at his own expense, brought fifty colonists to New Netherland; the colonists became the tenants of the estate owner, or patroon.

paupers A term popular in the eighteenth and nineteenth centuries to describe poor people; cities like New York and Boston often registered paupers so as to provide local relief.

Paxton Boys Settlers in Paxton, Pennsylvania, who massacred Conestoga Indians in 1763 and then marched on Philadelphia to demand that the colonial government provide better defense against the Indians.

payload The part of a cargo that generates revenue, as opposed to the part needed to fire the boiler or supply the crew.

Payne-Aldrich Tariff Tariff passed by Congress in 1909; the original bill was an attempt to reduce tariffs, but the final version retained high tariffs on most imports.

Peace Corps Program established by President Kennedy in 1961 to send young American volunteers to other nations as educators, health workers, and technicians.

Peace of Titiapa Agreement negotiated by Henry L. Stimson in 1927 that sought to end factional fighting in Nicaragua.

Pendleton Act Law passed by Congress in 1883 that created the Civil Service Commission and instituted the merit system for federal hiring and jobs.

Peninsular Campaign McClellan's attempt in the spring and summer of 1862 to capture Richmond by advancing up the peninsula between the James and York Rivers; Confederate forces under Robert E. Lee drove his troops back.

Pentagon Papers Classified government documents on policy decisions leaked to the press by Daniel Ellsberg and printed by the *New York Times* in 1971. Efforts to block the papers' publication was rejected by a Supreme Court ruling.

Pequot War Conflict in 1636 between the Pequot Indians inhabiting eastern Connecticut and the colonists of Massachusetts Bay and Connecticut: the Indians were destroyed and driven from the area.

percussion cap A thin metal cap containing an explosive compound, needed to fire the guns used in the Civil War.

perjury The deliberate giving of false testimony under oath.

Persian Gulf Arm of the Arabian Sea and location of the ports of several major oil-producing Arab countries; its security is crucial to the flow of oil from the Middle East to the rest of the world.

Persian Gulf War War in the Persian Gulf region in 1991, triggered by Iraq's invasion of Kuwait; a U.S.-led coalition defeated Iraqi forces and freed Kuwait.

perversion Sexual practice considered abnormal or deviant.

pet banks State banks into which Andrew Jackson ordered federal deposits to be placed to help deplete the funds of the Second Bank of the United States.

peyote cult A religion that included ceremonial use of the hallucinogenic peyote cactus, native to Mexico and the Southwest.

Philippe Bunau-Varilla Chief engineer of the French company that attempted to build a canal through the Panamanian isthmus, chief planner of the Panamanian revolt against Colombia, and later minister to the United States from the new Republic of Panama.

Philippine Islands A group of islands in the Pacific Ocean southeast of China that came under U.S. control in 1898 after the Spanish-American War; they became an independent nation after World War II.

philosophe Any of the popular French intellectuals or social philosophers of the Enlightenment, such as Voltaire, Diderot, or Rousseau.

Phyllis Schlafly Leader of the movement to defeat the Equal Rights Amendment; she believed that the amendment threatened the domestic role of women.

piecework Work for which the pay is based on the number of items turned out, rather than by the hour.

piedmont Land lying at the foot of a mountain range.

Piegan Indians The branch of the Blackfoot Indians who resided in areas of what is now Montana during the late eighteenth and early nineteenth centuries.

pig iron Crude iron, direct from a blast furnace, that is cast into rectangular molds called pigs in preparation for conversion into steel, cast iron, or wrought iron.

Pilgrims A small group of separatists who left England in search of religious freedom and sailed to America on the *Mayflower* in 1620.

placer mining A form of gold mining that uses water to separate gold from gravel deposits; because gold is heavier, it settles to the bottom of a container filled with water when the container is agitated.

plank One of the articles of a political platform.

platform A formal statement of the principles, policies, and promises on which a political party bases its appeal to voters.

Platt Amendment An amendment to the Army Appropriations Act of 1901, sponsored by Senator Orville Platt, which set terms for the withdrawal of the U.S. Army from Cuba.

plebiscite Special election that allows people to either approve or reject a particular proposal.

Plessy v. Ferguson Supreme Court decision in 1896 that upheld a Louisiana law requiring the segregation of railroad facilities on the grounds that "separate but equal" facilities were constitutional under the Fourteenth Amendment.

plurality In an election with three or more candidates, the number of votes received by the winner when the winner receives less than half of the total number of votes cast.

policy A course of action adopted by a government, usually one that is pursued over a period of time and may involve several different laws and agencies; a course of action taken by a government or a ruler.

political coattails Term referring to the ability of a presidential candidate to attract voters to other office seekers from the same political party.

poll tax A tax imposed by many states that required a fee be paid as a prerequisite to voting and that was used to exclude the poor, especially minorities, from voting. Also, used in some southern states as a way to disfranchise black voters, as the only penalty for not paying the tax was the loss of the right to vote.

polygamy The practice of a man having more than one wife at a time; Mormons referred to this as "plural marriage."

Pontiac Ottawa chief who led the unsuccessful resistance against British policy in 1763.

pool An agreement among businesses in the same industry to divide up the market and charge equal prices instead of competing.

popular front An organization or government composed of a wide spectrum of political groups; popular fronts were used by the Soviet Union in forming allegedly non-Communist governments in Eastern Europe.

popular sovereignty The doctrine that the people of a territory had the right to determine whether slavery would exist within their territory.

Populists Members of the People's Party, who held their first presidential nominating convention in 1892 and called for federal action to reduce the power of big business and to assist farmers and workers.

Porfirio Díaz Mexican soldier and politician who became president after a coup in 1876 and ruled Mexico until 1911.

Port Hudson Confederate garrison in Louisiana that surrendered to Union forces in July 1863, thus giving the Union unrestricted control of the Mississippi River.

Port Huron Statement A 1962 critique of the Cold War and American materialism and complacency by Students for a Democratic Society; it called for "participatory democracy" and for universities to be centers of free speech and activism.

portage The carrying of boats or supplies overland between two waterways.

posse A group of people usually summoned by a sheriff to aid in law enforcement.

postindustrial economy An economy whose base is no longer driven by manufacturing but by service and information industries.

postmaster An official appointed to oversee the operations of a post office.

post-millennialism The tenet in some Christian theology teaching that Christ will return to Earth after religious activists have succeeded in converting all people to Christianity and following a thousand years under their godly rule.

Potsdam Declaration The demand for Japan's unconditional surrender, made near the end of the Potsdam Conference.

power of the purse The political power that is enjoyed by the branch of government that controls taxation and the use of tax monies.

pragmatic Concerned with facts and actual events; in this case, refers to a willingness to adopt policies that could be either liberal or conservative, depending on the need.

preamble An introductory paragraph in a formal document setting out its underlying justification and purpose.

precedent An event or decision that may be used as an example in similar cases later on.

pre-Columbian Existing in the Americas before the arrival of Columbus.

preemption bill A temporary law that gave squatters the right to buy land they had settled on before it was offered for sale at public auction.

prefabricated Manufactured in advance in standard sections that are easy to ship and assemble when and where needed.

Presbyterians Members of a Protestant sect that eventually became the established church of Scotland but which in the seventeenth century was sometimes persecuted by Scotland's rulers.

price fixing The artificial setting of commodity prices.

primogeniture The legal right of the eldest son to inherit the entire estate of his father.

private sector Businesses run by private citizens rather than by the government.

privateer A ship captain who owned his own boat, hired his own crew, and was authorized by his government to attack and capture enemy ships.

probate court A court that establishes the validity of wills and administers the estates of people who have died.

Proclamation Line of 1763 Temporary boundary that Britain established in the Appalachian Mountains, west of which white settlement was banned; it was intended to reduce conflict between Indians and colonists.

Progressive Era Period of reform in the late nineteenth and early twentieth centuries.

Progressive Party Political party formed in 1912 with Theodore Roosevelt as its candidate for president; it fell apart when Roosevelt returned to the Republicans in 1916.

prohibition A legal ban on the manufacture, sale, and use of alcoholic beverages.

propagandist A person who provides information in support of a cause, especially one-sided or exaggerated information.

property requirement The limitation of voting rights to citizens who own certain kinds or amounts of property.

Prophet, The Shawnee religious visionary who called for a return to Indian traditions and founded the community of Prophetstown on Tippecanoe Creek in Indiana.

proportional representation Representation in the legislature based on the population of each state.

Proposition 13 Measure adopted by referendum in California in 1978 cutting local property taxes by more than 50 percent.

proprietor A person who owns something.

protective tariff Tax on imported goods intended to make them more expensive than similar domestic goods, thus protecting the market for goods produced at home.

protectorate A country partially controlled by a stronger power and dependent on that power for protection from foreign threats.

protégé An individual whose welfare or career is promoted by an influential person.

Protestantism From the root word *protest*, the beliefs and practices of Christians who broke with the Roman Catholic Church; rejecting church authority, the doctrine of "good works," and the necessity of the priesthood, Protestants accepted the Bible as the only source of revelation, salvation as God's gift to the faithful, and a direct, personal relationship with God as available to every believer.

provincialism The limited and narrow perspective thought to be characteristic of people in rural areas.

provisional Temporary.

proviso A clause making a qualification, condition, or restriction in a document.

Prussia A northern European state that became the basis for the German Empire in the late nineteenth century.

public accommodations Hotels, bars and restaurants, theaters, and other places set up to do business with anyone who can pay the price of admission.

public domain Land owned by the federal government; land owned and controlled by the federal government.

public order laws Laws passed by many southern communities to discourage civil rights protests; the laws allowed the police to arrest anyone suspected of intending to disrupt public order.

public prosecutor A lawyer appointed by the government to prosecute criminal actions on behalf of the state.

Public Works Administration Headed by Harold Ickes, secretary of the interior, the Public Works Administration sought to increase employment and to stimulate economic recovery by putting people to work. It spent more than $4.25 million on 34,000 public works projects.

public works projects Highways, dams, and other construction projects financed by public funds and carried out by the government.

Pueblo Revolt Indian rebellion against Spanish authority in 1680 led by Popé; succeeded in driving the Spanish out of New Mexico for nearly a decade.

pueblo Town created under Mexican or Spanish rules.

Pullman car A luxury railroad passenger car.

puppet government A government imposed, supported, and directed by an outside force, usually a foreign power.

Pure Food and Drug Act Law passed by Congress in 1906 forbidding the sale of impure and improperly labeled food and drugs.

putting-out system Manufacturing system through which machine-made components were distributed to individual families who used them to craft finished goods.

Q

Quakers Members of the Society of Friends, a radical Protestant sect that believed in the equality of men and women, pacifism, and the presence of a divine "inner light" in every individual.

Quasi-War Diplomatic crisis triggered by the XYZ affair; fighting occurred between the United States and France between the early summer of 1798 and the official end of the conflict in September 1800, but neither side issued a formal declaration of war.

quill pen A pen made from the shaft of a feather; the end of the quill is sharpened with a knife and then dipped in ink.

R

racial integration Equal opportunities to participate in a society or organization by people of different racial groups; the absence of race-based barriers to full and equal participation.

racketeering Commission of crimes such as extortion, loan-sharking, and bribery, sometimes behind the front of a seemingly legitimate business or union.

Radical Republicans A group within the Republican Party during the Civil War and Reconstruction who advocated abolition of slavery, citizenship for the former slaves, and sweeping alteration of the South; Republican faction that tried to limit presidential power and enhance congressional authority during the Civil War; Radicals opposed moderation toward the South or any toleration of slavery.

ragtime Style of popular music characterized by a syncopated rhythm and a regularly accented beat; considered the immediate precursor of jazz.

rail gauge The distance between train tracks.

Railway Labor Act of 1926 Federal law that guaranteed collective bargaining for railroad employees, the first peacetime federal law to extend this guarantee to any group of workers.

Ralph Bunche An African American scholar, teacher, and diplomat. Between 1948 and 1949, as a United Nations mediator he negotiated a settlement ending the Arab-Israeli War. In 1950, he received the Nobel Peace Prize for his efforts. He stated: "I have a bias against war, a bias for peace. . . . And I have a strong bias in favor of the United Na-

tions." Until his death in 1971 he continued working for the United Nations.

Ralph Waldo Emerson Philosopher, writer, and poet whose essays and poems made him a central figure in the transcendentalist movement and an important figure in the development of literary expression in the United States.

ranch or California-style home A single-story rectangular or L-shaped house with a low-pitched roof, simple floor plan, and an attached garage.

ratification The act of approving or confirming a proposal.

ratifying conventions A meeting of delegates in each state to determine whether that state would ratify the Constitution.

rationalism The theory that the exercise of reason, rather than the acceptance of authority or spiritual revelation, is the only valid basis for belief and the best source of spiritual truth.

Reaganomics Economic beliefs and policies of the Reagan administration, including the belief that tax cuts for the wealthy and deregulation of industry benefit the economy.

rebate The refund of part of a payment.

rebellion Open, armed, and organized resistance to a legally constituted government.

recall Provision that permits voters, through the petition process, to hold a special election to remove an elected official from office.

recession/depression A recession is an economic contraction of relatively short duration; a depression is an economic contraction of longer duration.

reciprocal trade A system of trading in which the objective is equal exchange of commodities rather than profit.

Reclamation Act Law passed by Congress in 1902 that provided funding for irrigation of western lands and created the Reclamation Service to oversee the process.

reconcentration Spanish policy in Cuba in 1896 that ordered the civilian population into fortified camps so as to isolate and annihilate the Cuban revolutionaries who remained outside the camps.

Reconquista The campaign undertaken by European Christians to recapture the Iberian Peninsula from the Moors.

Reconstruction Term applied by historians to the years 1865–1877, when the Union was restored from the Civil War; important changes were made to the federal Constitution; and social, economic, and political relations between the races were transformed in the South.

Reconstruction Finance Corporation Organization established at Hoover's request in 1932 to promote economic recovery; it provided emergency financing for banks, life insurance companies, railroads, and farm mortgage associations.

Red Army The army created by the Bolsheviks to defend their Communist government in their civil war and to reestablish control in parts of the Russian Empire that tried to create separate republics in 1917 and 1918; the Red Army was the army of the Soviet Union throughout its existence.

Red Cloud Lakota chief who led a successful fight to prevent the army from keeping forts along the Bozeman Trail.

Red Scare Wave of anticommunism in the United States in 1919 and 1920.

redeem To pay a specified sum in return for something; in this case, to make good on paper money issued by the government by exchanging it for hard currency, silver or gold.

Redeemers Southern Democrats who hoped to bring the Democratic Party back into power and to suppress Black Reconstruction.

re-exports Products shipped from one nation to another by way of a third; during wartime, neutral nations can be used as third parties to carry goods to combatants.

referendum Procedure whereby a bill or constitutional amendment is submitted to the voters for their approval after having been passed by a legislative body.

refinery An industrial plant that transforms raw materials into finished products; a petroleum refinery processes crude oil to produce a variety of products for use by consumers.

Reformation The sixteenth-century rise of Protestantism, with the establishment of state-sponsored Protestant churches in England, the Netherlands, parts of Germany and Switzerland, and elsewhere.

regionalism Loyalty to the interests of a particular region of the country.

Regulators Frontier settlers in the Carolinas who protested the lack or abuse of government services in their area; the North Carolina Regulators were suppressed by government troops in 1771.

Reign of Terror The period from 1793 to 1794 in the French Revolution when thousands of people were executed as enemies of the state.

reparations Payments required as compensation for damage or injury.

repeal The act of making a law or regulation no longer valid and enforceable; repeal of a constitutional amendment requires a new amendment.

repossession The reclaiming of land or goods by the seller or lender after the purchaser fails to pay installments due.

republic A nation in which supreme power resides in the citizens, who elect representatives to govern them.

Republican Party Political party formed in 1854 that opposed the extension of slavery into the western territories.

"Republican womanhood" A role for mothers that became popularized following the Revolution; it stressed women's importance in instructing children in republican virtues such as patriotism and honor.

Republicans Political group formed during Washington's first administration; led by Thomas Jefferson and James Madison, they favored limited government involvement in encouraging manufacturing and the continued dominance of agriculture in the national economy.

repudiate To refuse to acknowledge or pay; also, to reject as invalid or unauthorized.

repudiation The act of rejecting the validity or the authority of something.

requisition To demand for military use.

Restoration The era following the return of monarchy to England, beginning in 1660 with King Charles II and ending in 1688 with the exile of King James II.

restrictive covenant Provision in a property title designed to restrict subsequent sale or use of the property, often specifying sale only to a white Christian.

retail Related to the sale of goods directly to consumers.

retaliatory tariff A tariff on imported goods imposed neither to raise revenue nor control commerce but to retaliate against tariffs charged by another nation.

retrenchment In government, the elimination of unnecessary jobs or functions for reform or cost-cutting purposes.

return The yield on money that has been invested in an enterprise or product.

return on capital The yield on money that has been invested in an enterprise or product.

revenue cutter A small, lightly armed boat used by government customs agents to apprehend merchant ships violating customs laws.

revenue stamps Stickers affixed to taxed items by government officials indicating that the tax has been paid.

revival meeting A meeting for the purpose of reawakening religious faith, often characterized by impassioned preaching and emotional public testimony by converted sinners.

Rhineland Region of western Germany along the Rhine River, which under the terms of the Versailles Treaty was to remain free of troops and military fortifications.

Richard Howe British admiral who commanded British naval forces in America; he was General William Howe's brother.

Richmond Port city on the James River in Virginia; already the state capital, it became the capital of the Confederacy.

rifled Having a series of spiral grooves inside the barrel of a gun that causes the bullet to spin, giving it greater range and accuracy.

Right to Life movement Anti-abortion movement that favors a constitutional amendment to prohibit abortion; some adherents grew increasingly militant during the 1980s and 1990s; also called the pro-life movement.

Right-to-work laws State laws that make it illegal for labor unions and employers to require that all workers are members of a union. Many state laws require that all employees must benefit from contract agreements made between the union and the employer, even if the employee is not a union member.

ring In this context, ring means a group of people who act together to exercise control over something.

Rio Bravo The Spanish and then Mexican name for the river that now forms the border between Texas and Mexico; the Rio Grande.

Rio Pact Considered the first Cold War alliance, it joined Latin American nations, Canada, and the United States in an agreement to prevent Communist inroads in Latin America and to improve political, social, and economic conditions among Latin American nations; it created the Organization of American States.

Roanoke Island Island off North Carolina that Raleigh sought to colonize beginning in 1585.

robber baron In medieval times, a feudal aristocrat who laid exorbitant charges on all who crossed his territory; in the late nineteenth century, an insulting term applied to powerful industrial and financial figures, especially those who disregarded the public interest in their haste to make profits.

Robert Cavelier, Sieur de La Salle French explorer who followed the Mississippi River from its origin in present-day Illinois to the Gulf of Mexico in 1683, giving France a claim to the entire river way and adjoining territory.

Robert E. Lee A Virginian with a distinguished career in the U.S. Army who resigned to assume command of the Confederate army in Virginia when the Civil War began.

Robert Kennedy Attorney general during the presidency of his brother John F. Kennedy; elected to the Senate in 1964, his campaign for the presidency was gathering momentum when he was assassinated in 1968.

Robert M. La Follette Governor of Wisconsin who instituted reforms such as direct primaries, tax reform, and anticorruption measures in Wisconsin.

Robert Morris Pennsylvania merchant and financial expert who advised the Continental Congress during the Revolution and served as a fundraiser for the Confederation government.

rock 'n' roll Style of music that developed out of rhythm and blues in the 1950s, with a fast beat and lyrics appealing to teenagers.

Roe v. Wade Supreme Court ruling (1973) that women have an unrestricted right to choose an abortion during the first three months of pregnancy.

Roger Williams Puritan minister banished from Massachusetts for criticizing its religious rules and government policies; in 1635, he founded Providence, a community based on religious freedom and the separation of church and state.

romanticism Artistic and intellectual movement characterized by interest in nature, emphasis on emotion and imagination over rationality, and rebellion against social conventions.

Roosevelt Corollary Extension of the Monroe Doctrine announced by Theodore Roosevelt in 1904, in which he proclaimed the right of the United States to police the Caribbean areas.

Roosevelt's recession Economic downturn that occurred when Roosevelt, responding to improving economic figures, cut $4 billion from the federal budget, mostly by reducing relief spending.

Rosa Parks Black seamstress who refused to give up her seat to a white man on a bus in Montgomery, Alabama, in 1955, triggering a bus boycott that stirred the civil rights movement.

Rough Riders The First Volunteer Cavalry, a brigade recruited for action in the Spanish-American War by Theodore Roosevelt, who served first as the brigade's lieutenant colonel, then its colonel.

roundup A spring event in which cowboys gathered together the cattle herds, branded newborn calves, and castrated most of the new young males.

Ruhr Valley Region surrounding the Ruhr River in northwestern Germany, which contained many major industrial cities and valuable coal mines.

runoff election A final election held to determine a winner after an earlier election has eliminated the weakest candidates.

Rural Electrification Administration Government agency established in 1935 for the purpose of loaning money to rural cooperatives to produce and distribute electricity in isolated areas.

Russell Means Indian activist who helped organize the seizures of Alcatraz in 1969 and Wounded Knee in 1973.

Russian-German Refers to people of German ancestry living in Russia; most had come to Russia in the eighteenth century at the invitation of the government to develop agricultural areas.

Rust Belt Industrialized Middle Atlantic and Great Lakes region whose old factories are barely profitable or have closed.

Rutherford B. Hayes Ohio governor and former Union general who won the Republican nomination in 1876 and became president of the United States in 1877.

S

S&P 500 An index of five hundred widely held stocks.

saboteurs Individuals who damage property or interfere with procedures to obstruct productivity and normal functions.

Sacajawea Shoshone woman who served as guide and interpreter on the Lewis and Clark expedition.

sagebrush rebellion A 1980s political movement in western states opposing federal regulations governing land use and natural resources, seeking state jurisdiction instead.

Saint Augustine First colonial city in the present-day United States; located in Florida and founded by Pedro Menéndez de Aviles for Spain in 1565.

sainthood Full membership in a Puritan church.

salient A part of a battle line where the enemy has launched an offensive and pushed the line forward; a projection of the line.

salutary neglect The British policy of relaxed enforcement of most colonial trade regulations as long as the mainland colonies remained loyal to the government and profitable within the British economy.

Salvador Allende Chilean president who was considered the first democratically elected Marxist to head a government; he was killed in a coup in 1973.

Sam Houston American general and politician who fought in the struggle for Texas's independence from Mexico and became president of the Republic of Texas.

Samoa A group of volcanic and mountainous islands in the South Pacific.

Samuel Adams Massachusetts revolutionary leader and propagandist who organized opposition to British policies after 1764.

Samuel de Champlain French explorer who traced the St. Lawrence River inland to the Great Lakes, founded the city of Quebec, and formed the French alliance with the Huron Indians.

Samuel Gompers First president of the American Federation of Labor; he sought to divorce labor organizing from politics and stressed practical demands involving wages and hours.

sanctity Saintliness or holiness; the quality of being sacred or beyond reproach.

Sandinista Liberation Front Leftist guerrilla movement that overthrew Anastasio Somoza in Nicaragua in 1979 and established a revolutionary government under Daniel Ortega.

Santa Fe Spanish colonial town established in 1609; eventually the capital of the province of New Mexico.

Santo Domingo Nation in the Caribbean that shares the island of Hispaniola with Haiti; it became independent from Spain in 1865; now known as the Dominican Republic.

Sargent Shriver Married into the Kennedy family, he held many positions during the Kennedy-Johnson years; served as Director of the Peace Corps, 1961–1966; Director of Office of Economic Opportunity, 1964–1968; and ambassador to France, 1968–1970. In 1972 the was nominated by the Democrats to be vice president.

Saturday Night Massacre Events on October 20, 1973, when Nixon ordered the firing of Watergate special prosecutor Archibald Cox; rather than carry out Nixon's order, both the U.S. attorney general and deputy attorney general resigned.

savings and loan industry Network of financial institutions, known as S&Ls, originally founded to provide home mortgage loans; deregulation during the Reagan era allowed them to speculate in risky ventures and led to many S&L failures.

scalawag Derogatory term for white southerners who aligned themselves with the Republican Party during Reconstruction.

Scandinavia The region of northern Europe consisting of Norway, Sweden, Denmark, and Iceland.

Schechter Poultry Corporation v. the United States Supreme Court decision (1935) declaring the NRA unconstitutional because it regulated companies not involved in interstate commerce.

school board A board of policymakers who oversee the public schools of a local political unit.

Scots-Irish Protestant Scottish settlers in British-occupied northern Ireland, many of whom migrated to the colonies in the eighteenth century.

Scottsboro Nine Nine African Americans convicted of raping two white women in a freight train in Alabama in 1931; their case became famous as an example of racism in the legal system.

seasoning A period during which slaves from Africa were held in the West Indies so they could adjust to the climate and disease environment of the American tropics.

secede To withdraw from membership in an organization; in this case, the attempted withdrawal of eleven southern states from the United States in 1860–1861, giving rise to the Civil War; to withdraw formally from membership in a political union; threats of secession were used frequently during the early nineteenth century to bring attention to political issues.

secession Withdrawal from the United States.

Second Battle of Bull Run Union defeat near Bull Run in August 1862; Union troops led by John Pope were outmaneuvered by Lee.

Second Great Awakening An upsurge in religious fervor that began around 1800 and was characterized by revival meetings.

sectionalism Excessive concern for local or regional interests.

Securities and Exchange Commission Agency created by the Securities Exchange Act of 1934 to license stock exchanges and supervise their activities, including the setting of margin rates.

Security Council The executive agency of the United Nations; it includes five permanent members with veto power (China, France, the United Kingdom, Russia [formerly the Soviet Union], and the United States) and ten members elected by the General Assembly for two-year terms.

sedentary Living year-round in fixed villages and engaging in farming; as opposed to nomadic, or moving from camp to camp throughout the year.

sedition Conduct or language inciting rebellion against the authority of a state.

Sedition Act Law passed by Congress in 1918 to supplement the Espionage Act by extending the penalty to anyone deemed to have abused the government in writing.

segregation Separation on account of race or class from the rest of society, such as the separation of blacks from whites in most southern school systems.

Selective Service Act Law passed by Congress in 1917 establishing compulsory military service for men ages 21 to 30.

self-determination The freedom of a given people to determine their own political status.

Senate Foreign Relations Committee One of the standing (permanent) committees of the Senate; it deals with foreign affairs, and its chairman often wields considerable influence over foreign policy.

separate sphere The notion that men and women should engage in different activities: women were to focus on the family, church, and school, whereas men were to support the family financially and take part in politics, activities considered too competitive and corrupt for women.

separatists English Protestants who chose to leave the Church of England because they believed it was corrupt.

serfs Peasants who were bound to a particular estate but, unlike slaves, were not the personal property of the estate owner and received traditional feudal protections.

settlement house Community center operated by resident social reformers in a slum area to help poor people in their own neighborhoods.

Seventeenth Amendment Constitutional amendment ratified in 1913 that requires the election of U.S. senators directly by the voters of each state, rather than by state legislatures.

sexual harassment Unwanted sexual advances, sexually derogatory remarks, gender-related discrimination, or the existence of a sexually hostile work environment.

Shah Mohammed Reza Pahlevi Iranian ruler who received the hereditary title *shah* from his father in 1941 and with CIA support helped to oust the militant nationalist Mohammed Mossadegh in 1953.

Shakers A mid-eighteenth-century offshoot of the Quakers, founded in England by Mother Ann Lee; Shakers engaged in spirited worship, including dancing and rhythmic shaking, hence their name, and practiced communal living and strict celibacy.

shaman A person who acts as a link between the visible material world and an invisible spirit world; a shaman's duties include healing, conducting religious ceremonies, and foretelling the future.

Share the Wealth Movement that sprang up around the

nation in the 1930s urging the redistribution of wealth through government taxes or programs; launched by Huey Long, its slogan was "Every man a king."

sharecropping A system for renting farmland in which tenant farmers give landlords a share of their crops, rather than cash, as rent.

Shelly v. Kraemer Supreme Court ruling (1948) that barred lower courts from enforcing restrictive agreements that prevented minorities from living in certain neighborhoods; it had little impact on actual practices.

Sherman Anti-Trust Act Law passed by Congress in 1890 authorizing the federal government to prosecute any "combination" "in restraint of trade"; because of adverse court rulings, at first it was ineffective as a weapon against monopolies.

Sherman Silver Purchase Act Law passed by Congress in 1890 requiring the federal government to increase its purchases of silver to be coined into silver dollars.

short-staple cotton A variety of cotton with short and tightly packed pods of fiber in which the plant's seeds are tangled.

Sierra Club Environmental organization formed in 1892; now dedicated to preserving and expanding parks, wildlife, and wilderness areas.

Sigmund Freud Austrian who played a leading role in developing the field of psychoanalysis, known for his theory that the sex drive underlies much individual behavior.

signatory One who has signed a treaty or other document.

Sikhs Follower of Sikhism, a monotheistic religion founded in India in the 16th century.

Silent Majority Name given to the majority of Americans who supported the government and did not protest or riot; a typical member of the Silent Majority was believed to be white, middle class, average in income and education, and moderately conservative in values and attitudes.

Sinclair Lewis Novelist who satirized middle-class America in works such as *Babbitt* (1922) and became the first American to win the Nobel Prize for literature.

Sir Henry Clinton General who replaced William Howe as commander of the British forces in America in 1778 after the British surrender at Saratoga.

Sir Walter Raleigh English courtier, soldier, and adventurer who attempted to establish the Virginia Colony.

sit-in The act of occupying the seats or an area of a segregated establishment to protest racial discrimination; CORE had used the tactic in the 1940s to integrate public facilities.

Sitting Bull Lakota war leader and holy man.

Sixteenth Amendment Constitutional amendment ratified in 1913 that gives the federal government the authority to establish an income tax.

slapstick A rowdy form of comedy marked by crude practical jokes and physical humor, such as falls.

Slave Coast A region of coastal West Africa adjacent to the Gold Coast; it was the principal source of the slaves taken out of West Africa from the sixteenth to the early nineteenth century.

slave codes Laws that established the status of slaves, denying them basic rights and classifying them as the property of slaveowners.

Slavic Relating to the Slavs, a linguistic group that includes the Poles, Czechs, Slovaks, Slovenes, Serbs, Croats, Bosnians, and Bulgarians of Central Europe, as well as Russians, Ukrainians, Belarusians, and other groups in eastern Europe.

Smith Act The Alien Registration Act, passed by Congress in 1940, which made it a crime to advocate or to belong to an organization that advocates the overthrow of the government by force or violence.

Smith-Connally War Labor Disputes Act Law passed by Congress in 1943 authorizing the government to seize plants in which labor disputes threatened war production; it was later used to take over the coal mines.

soap opera A daytime serial drama so nicknamed because it was sponsored by cleaning products, aimed at its housewife audience.

social contract A theoretical agreement between the governed and the government that defines and limits the rights and obligations of each.

Social Darwinism The philosophical argument, inspired by Charles Darwin's theory of evolution, that competition in human society produced "the survival of the fittest" and therefore benefited society as a whole; Social Darwinists opposed efforts to regulate competitive practices.

Social Gospel A reform movement of the late nineteenth century led by Protestant clergy who drew attention to urban problems and advocated social justice for the poor.

Social Security Act Law passed by Congress in 1935 to create systems of unemployment, old-age, and disability insurance and to provide for child welfare.

socialist Practicing socialism, the public ownership of manufacturing, farming, and other forms of production so that they benefit society rather than produce individual or corporate profits.

Socialist Party of America Political party formed in 1901 and committed to socialism—that is, government ownership of most industries.

sod A piece of earth on which grass is growing; if grass has grown there a long time, the grass roots, dead grass from previous growing seasons, and the growing grass will be dense, tough, and fibrous, and the soil hard-packed.

sodomy Varieties of sexual intercourse prohibited by law in the nineteenth century, typically including intercourse between two males.

Soil Conservation Act Legislation passed by Congress in 1935 that established an agency for the prevention of soil erosion by paying farmers to cut back on soil-depleting crops and to plant grasses and other crops that would help to hold the soil.

Sojourner Truth Abolitionist and feminist who was freed from slavery in 1827 and became a leading preacher against slavery and for the rights of women.

Songhai Empire A large empire in West Africa whose capital was Timbuktu; its rulers accepted Islam around the year 1000.

Sons of Liberty A secret organization first formed in Boston to oppose the Stamp Act.

Southern Christian Leadership Conference Group formed by Martin Luther King Jr. and others after the Montgomery bus boycott; it became the backbone of the civil rights movement in the 1950s and 1960s.

Southern Manifesto Statement issued by one hundred southern congressmen in 1954 after the *Brown v. Board of Education* decision, pledging to oppose desegregation.

southern strategy A plan to entice southerners into the Republican Party by appointing white southerners to the Supreme Court and resisting the policy of busing to achieve integration.

sovereignty The ultimate power in a nation or a state.

speakeasy A place that illegally sells liquor and sometimes offers entertainment.

special interest A person or organization that seeks to benefit by influencing legislators.

specie Coins minted from precious metals.

Specie Circular Order issued by President Jackson in 1836 stating that the federal government would accept only specie—gold and silver—as payment for public land; one of the causes of the Panic of 1837.

speculator A person who buys and sells land or some other commodity in the hope of making a profit.

speed-up An effort to make employees produce more goods in the same time or for the same pay.

spendthrift A person who spends money recklessly or wastefully.

sphere of influence A territorial area where a foreign nation exerts significant authority.

spiritual A religious folk song originated by African Americans, often expressing a longing for deliverance from the constraints and hardships of their lives.

Spiro Agnew Vice president under Richard Nixon; he resigned in 1973 amid charges of illegal financial dealings during his governorship of Maryland.

spoils Jobs and other rewards for political support.

spoilsmen Derogatory term for defenders of the patronage or spoils system.

Squanto A Patuxet Indian who taught the Pilgrims survival techniques in America and acted as translator for the colonists.

Sputnik I The first artificial satellite launched into space, it weighed 184 pounds; this feat by the Soviet Union in October 1957 marked the beginning of the space race. A month later, the larger *Sputnik II* was launched, weighing 1,120 pounds and carrying a dog named Laika.

Square Deal Theodore Roosevelt's term for his efforts to deal fairly with all.

squatter A person who settles on unoccupied land to which he or she has no legal claim.

stagflation Persistent inflation combined with stagnant consumer demand and relatively high unemployment.

stalemate A deadlock; in chess, a situation in which neither player can move.

Stalwarts Faction of the Republican Party led by Roscoe Conkling of New York; Stalwarts claimed to be the genuine Republicans.

Stamp Act British law of 1765 that directly taxed a variety of items, including newspapers, playing cards, and legal documents.

standard-bearer The recognized leader of a movement, organization, or political party.

standard of living Level of material comfort as measured by the goods, services, and luxuries currently available.

staple crop A basic or necessary agricultural item, produced for sale or export.

states' rights A political position favoring limitation of the federal government's power and the greatest possible self-government by the individual states.

statesman A political leader who acts out of concern for the public good and not out of self-interest.

statism The concept or practice of placing economic planning and policy under government control.

stay laws Laws suspending the right of creditors to foreclose on debtors; they were designed to protect indebted farmers from losing their land.

Stephen A. Douglas Illinois senator who tried to reconcile northern and southern differences over slavery through the Compromise of 1850 and the Kansas-Nebraska Act.

Stephen F. Austin American colonizer in Texas and leading voice in the Texas Revolution.

Stimson Doctrine Declaration by U.S. secretary of state Henry Stimson in 1932 that the United States would not recognize the Japanese-created state of Manchuko—a policy of nonrecognition—and that legally Manchuria was still Chinese territory.

stock exchange A place where people buy and sell stocks (shares in the ownership of companies); stockholders may participate in election of the company's directors and share in the company's profits.

Stokely Carmichael Civil rights activist who led SNCC and popularized the term "Black Power" to describe the need for blacks to use militant tactics to force whites to accept political change.

Stono Rebellion Slave revolt in South Carolina in 1739; it prompted the colony to pass harsher laws governing the movement of slaves and the capture of runaways.

Strategic Air Command U.S. military unit formed in March 1946 to conduct long-range bombing operations anywhere in the world; its first strategic plan, completed in 1949, projected nuclear attacks on seventy Soviet cities. The Strategic Air Command was abolished in 1992 as part of the reorganization of the Department of Defense. The much smaller interservice U.S. Strategic Command (StratCom) now coordinates nuclear plans for both the army and the navy.

Strategic Arms Limitation agreement Treaty between the United States and the Soviet Union in 1972 to limit offensive nuclear weapons and defensive antiballistic missile systems; known as SALT I.

Strategic Arms Limitation Treaty Agreement, known as SALT II, between the United States and the Soviet Union in 1979 to limit the number of strategic nuclear missiles in each country; these strategic missiles contained warheads that had large-scale destructive capability and the probability of changing the course of a war; during the Cold War these weapons carried nuclear warheads and were considered weapons of mass destruction; Congress never approved the treaty.

Strategic Defense Initiative Research program to create an effective laser-based defense against nuclear missile attack.

strict constructionist A person who believes the government has only the powers specifically named in the Constitution.

Stuart kings The dynasty of English kings who claimed the throne after the death of Elizabeth I, who left no heirs.

Students for a Democratic Society Left-wing student organization founded in 1960 to criticize American materialism and work for social justice.

subculture A group whose members differ from the dominant culture on the basis of some values or interests but who share most values and interests with the dominant culture.

subpoena A writ, or order, requiring an individual to appear in court to give testimony.

sub-Saharan Africa The region of Africa south of the Sahara Desert.

subsidy Financial assistance that a government grants to an enterprise considered to be in the public interest.

subsistence farming Farming that produces enough food for survival but no surplus that can be sold.

subsistence society A society that produces the food and supplies necessary for its survival but which does not produce a surplus that can be marketed.

suburb A residential area lying outside the central city; many of the residents of suburbs work and shop in the central city even though they live outside it.

subversion Efforts to undermine or overthrow an established government.

suffrage The right to vote.

Sugar Act British law of 1764 that taxed sugar and other colonial imports to pay for some of Britain's expenses in protecting the colonies.

Sunbelt A region stretching from Florida in a westward arc across the South and Southwest.

Superfund Most common name for the federal Comprehensive Environmental Response, Compensation, and Liability Act (CERCLA) of 1980. The law requires polluters to clean up environmental contamination or reimburse the federal government for doing so. "Superfund" refers to the trust fund used to pay for cleanup.

supply and demand The two factors that determine price in an economy based on private property: (1) how much of a commodity is available (supply) and (2) how many people want it (demand).

supply-side economics Theory that reducing taxes on the wealthy and increasing the money available for investment will stimulate the economy and eventually benefit everyone.

survey To determine the area and boundaries of land through measurement and mathematical calculation.

Susan B. Anthony Tireless campaigner for woman suffrage and close associate of Elizabeth Cady Stanton.

Sussex pledge German promise in 1916 to stop sinking merchant ships without warning if the United States would compel the Allies to obey "international law."

sweatshop A shop or factory in which employees work long hours at low wages under poor conditions.

syphilis An infectious disease usually transmitted through sexual contact; if untreated, it can lead to paralysis and death.

T

table Action taken by a legislative body (Congress, for example) to postpone debate on an issue until a positive vote to remove the topic from the table is taken.

Taft-Hartley Act Law passed by Congress in 1947 banning closed shops, permitting employers to sue unions for broken contracts, and requiring unions to observe a cooling-off period before striking.

Taliban An organization of Muslim fundamentalists that gained control over Afghanistan in 1996 after the Soviets withdrew and which established a strict Islamic government.

Tallmadge Amendment An amendment to a statehood bill for Missouri proposed by New York congressman James Tallmadge Jr. that would have banned slavery from the new state; it created a deadlock in Congress that necessitated the Missouri Compromise.

tallow Hard fat obtained from the bodies of cattle and other animals and used to make candles and soap.

tannery An establishment where animal skins and hides are made into leather.

tariff A tax on imported or exported goods.

Tariff of 1816 First protective tariff in U.S. history; its purpose was to protect America's fledgling textile industry.

Tariff of Abominations Tariff package designed to win support for anti-Adams forces in Congress; its passage in 1828 discredited Adams but set off sectional tension over tariff issues.

Tecumseh Shawnee leader and brother of The Prophet; he established an Indian confederacy along the frontier that he hoped would be a barrier to white expansion.

Tehran Conference Meeting in Iran in 1943 at which Roosevelt, Churchill, and Stalin discussed the invasion of Western Europe and considered plans for a new international organization; Stalin also renewed his promise to enter the war against Japan.

Tejanos Spanish-speaking people born in Texas before it was acquired by the United States; Mexican settlers in Texas in the nineteenth century.

televangelist Protestant evangelist minister who conducts televised worship services; many such ministers used their broadcasts as a forum for promoting conservative values.

Teller Amendment Resolution approved by the U.S. Senate in 1898, by which the United States promised not to annex Cuba; introduced by Senator Henry Teller of Colorado.

temperance Moderation or abstinence in the consumption of alcoholic drinks.

tenement A multifamily apartment building, often unsafe, unsanitary, and overcrowded; an urban apartment house, usually with minimal facilities for sanitation, safety, and comfort.

Tennessee Valley Authority Independent public corporation created by Congress in 1933 and authorized to construct dams and power plants in the Tennessee River valley region.

Terence V. Powderly Leader of the Knights of Labor.

term limit A limit on the number of times one person can be elected to the same political office.

terrorists Those who use threats and violence to achieve ideological or political goals.

Tertium Quid Republican faction formed by John Randolph in protest against Jefferson's plan for acquiring Florida from Spain; the name is Latin and means a "third thing," indicating Randolph's rejection of both the Federalist and Republican Parties.

Tet The lunar New Year celebrated as a huge holiday in Vietnam; the Viet Cong–North Vietnamese attack on South Vietnamese cities during Tet in January 1968 was a military defeat for North Vietnam, but it seriously undermined U.S. support for the war.

Texas Revolution A revolt by American colonists in Texas against Mexican rule; it began in 1835 and ended with the establishment of the Republic of Texas in 1836.

Texians Non-Hispanic settlers in Texas in the nineteenth century.

Thaddeus Stevens Pennsylvania congressman who was a leader of the Radical Republicans during the Civil War and Reconstruction.

Thayendanegea Mohawk chief known to the Americans as Joseph Brant; his combined forces of loyalists and Indians defeated John Sullivan's expedition to upstate New York in 1779.

Theodore Roosevelt American politician and writer who advocated war against Spain in 1898; elected as McKinley's vice president in 1900, he became president in 1901 upon McKinley's assassination.

thermonuclear Relating to the fusion of atomic nuclei at high temperatures, or to weapons based on fusion, such as the hydrogen bomb (as distinct from weapons based on fission).

Third World Nations in the Third World claim to be independent and not part of either the Western capitalist or Communist blocs. This Cold War neutrality was tested by both sides in the Cold War, as each used a variety of means to include them in their camps.

Thirteenth Amendment Constitutional amendment, ratified in 1865, that abolished slavery in the United States and its territories.

38th parallel Negotiated dividing line between North and South Korea; it was the focus of much of the fighting in the Korean War.

Thomas A. Edison American inventor, especially of electrical devices, among them the microphone (1877), the phonograph (1878), and the light bulb (1879).

Thomas E. Dewey New York governor who twice ran unsuccessfully for president as the Republican candidate, the second time against Truman in 1948.

Thomas Gage British general who was military governor of Massachusetts and commander of the army occupying Boston in 1775.

Thomas Hart Benton U.S. senator from Missouri and legislative leader of the Democrats; he was a champion of President Jackson and a supporter of westward expansion.

Thomas Hutchinson Boston merchant and judge who served as lieutenant governor and later governor of Massachusetts; Stamp Act protesters destroyed his home in 1765.

Thomas J. Jackson Confederate general nicknamed "Stonewall"; he commanded troops at both battles of Bull Run and was mortally wounded by his own soldiers at Chancellorsville in 1863.

Thomas Pinckney South Carolina politician and diplomat who was an unsuccessful Federalist candidate for president in 1796.

Three Mile Island Site of a nuclear power plant near Harrisburg, Pennsylvania; an accident at the plant in 1979 led to a release of radioactive gases and almost caused a meltdown.

Three-Fifths Compromise An agreement to count three-fifths of a state's slave population for purposes of determining a state's representation in the House of Representatives.

Thurgood Marshall African American civil rights lawyer who argued thirty-two cases before the Supreme Court and won twenty-nine; appointed to the federal court system by President Kennedy, he became the first African American justice of the Supreme Court in 1967.

tidewater Low coastal land drained by tidal streams in Maryland and Virginia.

Timothy Leary Harvard professor and counterculture figure who advocated the expansion of consciousness through the use of drugs such as LSD.

tipi Conical tent made from buffalo hide and used as a portable dwelling by Indians on the Great Plains.

Title VII Provision of the Civil Rights Act of 1964 that guarantees women legal protection against discrimination.

total war War waged with little regard for the welfare of troops on either side or for enemy civilians; the objective is to destroy both the human and the economic resources of the enemy.

tract homes One of numerous houses of similar design built on small plots of land.

trade deficit Amount by which the value of a nation's imports exceeds the value of its exports.

trade union A labor organization whose members work in a specific trade or craft.

trademark A name or symbol that identifies a product and is officially registered and legally restricted for use by the owner or manufacturer.

Trail of Tears Forced march of the Cherokee people from Georgia to Indian Territory in the winter of 1838, during which thousands of Cherokees died.

transcendent Lying beyond the normal range of experience.

transcendentalism A philosophical and literary movement asserting the existence of God within human beings and in nature and the belief that intuition is the highest source of knowledge.

transship The practice of shipping cargo to a secondary port and then transferring it to other ships for transport to a final destination; cargos from up the Mississippi River were shipped by barge to New Orleans and then loaded onto ocean-going vessels to be carried to American ports along the Atlantic Coast.

Treaty of Brest-Litovsk Humiliating treaty with Germany that Russia signed in March 1918 in order to withdraw from

World War I; it required Russia to surrender vast territories along its western boundary with Germany.

Treaty of Fort Stanwix Treaty signed in 1784 that opened all Iroquois lands to white settlement.

Treaty of Ghent Treaty ending the War of 1812, signed in Belgium in 1814; it restored peace but was silent on the issues over which the United States and Britain had gone to war.

Treaty of Greenville 1795 treaty in which the United States agreed to pay northwestern Indians about $10,000 for the land that later became the state of Ohio.

Treaty of Guadalupe Hidalgo Treaty (1848) in which Mexico gave up Texas above the Rio Grande and ceded New Mexico and California to the United States in return for $15 million.

Treaty of New Echota Treaty in 1835 by which a minority faction gave all Cherokee lands east of the Mississippi to the U.S. government in return for $5 million and land in Indian Territory.

Treaty of Paris Treaty ending the Spanish-American War, under which Spain granted independence to Cuba, ceded Puerto Rico and Guam to the United States, and sold the Philippines to the United States for $20 million.

Treaty of Paris of 1763 The treaty ending the French and Indian War in 1763; it gave all of French Canada and Spanish Florida to Britain.

Treaty of Paris of 1783 Treaty that ended the Revolutionary War in 1783 and secured American independence.

Treaty of Portsmouth Treaty in 1905, ending the Russo-Japanese War; negotiated at a conference in Portsmouth, New Hampshire, through Theodore Roosevelt's mediation.

Treaty of San Lorenzo Treaty between the United States and Spain, negotiated in 1795 by Thomas Pinckney; Spain granted the United States the right to navigate the Mississippi River and use the port of New Orleans as an outlet to the sea.

Treaty of Tordesillas The agreement, signed by Spain and Portugal in 1494, that moved the line separating Spanish and Portuguese claims to territory in the non-Christian world, giving Spain most of the Western Hemisphere.

Treaty of Velasco Treaty that Santa Anna signed in May 1836 after his capture at the San Jacinto River; it recognized the Republic of Texas but was later rejected by the Mexican congress.

Treaty of Versailles Treaty signed in 1919 ending World War I; it imposed harsh terms on Germany, created several territorial mandates, and set up the League of Nations.

tributary empire An empire in which subjects rule themselves but make payments, called tribute, to an imperial government in return for protection and services.

tribute A payment of money or other valuables that one group makes to another as the price of security.

trickster tales Stories that feature as a central character a clever figure who uses his wits and instincts to adapt to changing times; a survivor, the trickster is used by traditional societies, including African cultures, to teach important cultural lessons.

Trinity In Christian doctrine, the belief that God has three divine aspects—Father, Son, and Holy Spirit.

Triple Alliance Alliance that linked Germany, Italy, and Austria-Hungary in the years before World War I.

Triple Entente Informal alliance that linked France, Great Britain, and Russia in the years before World War I.

Truman Doctrine Anti-Communist foreign policy that Truman set forth in 1947; it called for military and economic aid to countries whose political stability was threatened by communism.

trust A legal arrangement in which an individual (the trustor) gives control of property to a person or institution (the trustee); in the late nineteenth century, a legal device to get around state laws prohibiting a company chartered in one state from operating in another state, and often synonymous in common use with *monopoly*; first used by John D. Rockefeller to consolidate Standard Oil.

trustbusting Use of antitrust laws to prosecute and dissolve big businesses ("trusts").

tsar The monarch of the Russian Empire; also spelled *czar*.

tuberculosis An infectious disease that attacks the lungs, causing coughing, fever, and weight loss; spread by unsanitary conditions and practices, such as spitting in public, it was common and often fatal in the nineteenth and early twentieth centuries and is reappearing today.

turnpike A road on which tolls are collected at gates set up along the way; private companies hoping to make a profit from the tolls built the first turnpikes.

Tweed Ring Name applied to the political organization of William Marcy Tweed, accused of using bribery, kickbacks, and padded accounts to steal money from New York City.

Twelfth Amendment Constitutional amendment, ratified in 1804, that provides for separate balloting in the Electoral College for president and vice president.

Twenty Negro Law Confederate law that exempted planters owning twenty or more slaves from the draft on the grounds that overseeing farm labor done by slaves was necessary to the war effort.

typhoid fever An infectious disease transmitted through contact with contaminated water, milk, or food; causes severe intestinal distress and high fever.

U

U-boat A German submarine (in German, *Unterseeboot*).

U.S. marshal A federal law-enforcement official.

U.S.S. *Maine* American warship that exploded in Havana Harbor in 1898, inspiring the motto "Remember the *Maine*!" which spurred the Spanish-American War.

Ulysses S. Grant U.S. general who became general in chief of the Union army in 1864 after the Vicksburg campaign; he later became president of the United States.

underclass The lowest economic class; the term carries the implication that members of this class are so disadvantaged by poverty that they have little or no chance to escape it.

Underground Railroad The secret network of northerners who helped fugitive slaves escape to Canada or to safe areas in free states.

Underwood Act Law passed by Congress in 1913 that substantially reduced tariffs and made up for the lost revenue by providing for a graduated income tax.

underwrite To assume financial responsibility for; in this case, to guarantee the purchase of bonds so that a project can go forward.

unicameral Having a single legislative house.

unilateral An action taken by a country by itself, as opposed to actions taken jointly with other nations.

unilateralism A policy of acting alone, without consultation or agreement of others.

Unionist Loyal to the United States of America.

Unitarianism A religion that denies the Trinity, teaching that God exists only in one person; it also stresses individual freedom of belief and the free use of reason in religion.

United Automobile Workers Union of workers in the automobile industry; it used sit-down strikes in 1936 and 1937 to end work speed-ups and win recognition for the fledgling labor organization.

United Nations International organization established in 1945 to maintain peace among nations and foster cooperation in human rights, education, health, welfare, and trade.

United States Sanitary Commission Government commission established by Abraham Lincoln to improve public health conditions in military camps and hospitals.

universal military service A governmental policy specifying that all adult males (or, rarely, all adults) are required to serve in the military for some period of time.

unprecedented Unheard of or novel.

Upton Sinclair Socialist writer and reformer whose novel *The Jungle* exposed unsanitary conditions in the meatpacking industry and advocated socialism.

urban renewal Effort to revitalize run-down areas of cities by providing federal funding for the construction of apartment houses, office buildings, and public facilities.

urbanization The growth of cities in a nation or region and the shifting of the population from rural to urban areas.

USA PATRIOT Act (Uniting and Strengthening America by Providing Appropriate Tools Required to Intercept and Obstruct Terrorism) Legislation passed by Congress in 2001 that reduced constraints on the Justice Department and other law-enforcement agencies dealing with individuals with suspected links to terrorism.

utopia An ideally perfect place.

utopian Idealistic reform sentiment based on the belief that a perfect society can be created on Earth and that a particular group or leader has the knowledge to actually create such a society.

V

V-E Day May 8, 1945, the day marking the official end of the war in Europe, following the unconditional surrender of the German armies.

vagrancy The legal condition of having no fixed place of residence or means of support.

Valley Forge Winter encampment of Washington's army in Pennsylvania in 1777–1778; because the soldiers suffered greatly from cold and hunger, the term *Valley Forge* has become synonymous with "dire conditions."

vamp A woman who uses her sexuality to entrap and exploit men.

vanguard The foremost position in any army advancing into battle.

Vassar College The first collegiate institution for women, founded in Poughkeepsie, New York, in 1861.

Venustiana Carranza Mexican revolutionary leader who helped to lead armed opposition to Victoriano Huerta and who succeeded to the presidency in 1914; his government was overthrown in 1920.

Veracruz Major port city, located in east-central Mexico on the Gulf of Mexico; in 1914, Wilson ordered the U.S. Navy to occupy the port.

vertical integration The process of bringing together into a single company several of the activities in the process of creating a manufactured product, such as the acquiring of raw materials, the manufacturing of products, and the marketing, selling, and distributing of finished goods.

veto The power or right of one branch of government to reject the decisions of another branch.

vice squad Police unit charged with the enforcement of laws dealing with vice—that is, immoral practices such as gambling and prostitution.

vice-admiralty court Nonjury British court in which a judge heard cases involving shipping.

Vichy City in central France that was the capital of unoccupied France from 1940 to 1942; the Vichy government continued to govern French territories and was sympathetic to the fascists.

vicissitudes Sudden or unexpected changes encountered during the course of life.

Vicksburg Confederate-held city on the Mississippi River that surrendered on July 4, 1863, after a lengthy siege by Grant's forces.

Victoriano Huerta Mexican general who overthrew President Francisco Madero in 1913 and established a military dictatorship until forced to resign in 1914.

victory garden Small plot cultivated by a patriotic citizen during World War II to supply household food and allow farm production to be used for the war effort.

Viet Cong Vietnamese Communist rebels in South Vietnam.

Viet Minh Vietnamese army made up of Communist and other nationalist groups that fought from 1946 to 1954 for independence from French rule.

Vietnamization U.S. policy of scaling back American involvement in Vietnam and helping Vietnamese forces fight their own war.

vigilance committees Groups of armed private citizens who use the threat of mob violence to enforce their own interpretation of the law.

vigilante A person who takes law enforcement into his or her own hands, usually on the grounds that normal law enforcement has broken down.

Vikings Late-medieval Danish, Swedish, and Norwegian groups who responded to land shortages and climatic conditions in Scandinavia by taking to the sea and establishing communities in various parts of western Europe, Iceland, Greenland, and North America.

Violence Against Women Act Law passed by Congress in

1994 that provided federal funds and support to judicial and law-enforcement agencies to prevent violence against women, to aid victims, and to punish those convicted of sexual violence and attacks on women.

Virginia and Kentucky Resolutions Statements that the Virginia and Kentucky legislatures issued in 1798 in response to the Alien and Sedition Acts; they asserted the right of states to overrule the federal government.

Virginia Dynasty Term applied to the U.S. presidents from Virginia in the period between 1801 and 1825: Jefferson, Madison, and Monroe.

Virginia Plan Fourteen proposals by the Virginia delegation to the Constitutional Convention for creating a more powerful central government and giving states proportional representation in a bicameral legislature.

Vladimir Lenin Leader of the Bolsheviks and of the Russian Revolution of 1917 and head of the Soviet Union until 1924.

voluntary association An organization or club through which individuals engage in voluntary service, usually associated with charity or reform.

voting fraud Altering election results by illegal measures to bring about the victory of a particular candidate.

Voting Rights Act Law passed by Congress in 1965 that outlawed literacy and other voting tests and authorized federal supervision of elections in areas where black voting had been restricted.

W

W. E. B. Du Bois African American intellectual and civil rights leader, author of important works on black history and sociology, who helped to form and lead the NAACP.

wage slavery The bondage of workers who, though legally free, are underpaid, trapped in debt, and living in extreme poverty.

Wagner Act The National Labor Relations Act, a law passed by Congress in 1935 that defined unfair labor practices and protected unions against coercive measures such as blacklisting.

walking city Term that urban historians use to describe cities before changes in urban transportation permitted cities to expand beyond the distance that a person could easily cover on foot.

war bond Bonds sold by the government to finance the war effort.

War Hawks Members of Congress elected in 1810 from the West and South who campaigned for war with Britain in the hopes of stimulating the economy and annexing new territory.

War Industries Board Federal agency headed by Bernard Baruch that coordinated American production during World War I.

war of attrition A form of warfare based on deprivation of food, shelter, and other necessities; if successful, it drives opponents to surrender out of hunger or exposure.

War on Poverty Lyndon Johnson's program to help Americans escape poverty through education, job training, and community development.

War Powers Act Law passed by Congress in 1973 to prevent the president from involving the United States in war without authorization by Congress.

ward A division of a city or town, especially an electoral district, for administrative or representative purposes; a child who is legally put into the care of someone other than a parent.

Warren Court Term applied to the Supreme Court under Chief Justice Earl Warren; during this period the Court was especially active in expanding individual rights, often at the expense of state and local governments.

Washington Naval Conference International conference that in 1921–1922 produced a series of agreements to limit naval armaments and prevent conflict in the Far East and the Pacific.

water table The level at which the ground is completely saturated with water.

Watergate Apartment and office complex in Washington, D.C., that housed the headquarters of the Democratic National Committee; its name became synonymous with the scandal over the Nixon administration's involvement in a break-in there and the president's part in the cover-up that followed.

Watts Predominantly black neighborhood of Los Angeles where a race riot in August 1965 did $45 million in damage and took the lives of twenty-eight blacks.

weapons of mass destruction Nuclear, chemical, and biological weapons that have the potential to injure or kill large numbers of people—civilians as well as military personnel.

Webster-Ashburton Treaty Treaty that in 1842 established the present border between Canada and northeastern Maine.

welfare capitalism Program adopted by some employers to provide to their employees benefits such as lunchrooms, paid vacations, bonuses, and profit-sharing plans.

Wendell Willkie Business executive and Republican presidential candidate who lost to Roosevelt in 1940; during the campaign, Roosevelt never publicly mentioned Willkie's name.

West Point Site of a fort overlooking the Hudson River, north of New York City.

western front The western line of battle between the Allies and Germany in World War I, located in French and Belgian territory; the **eastern front** was the line of battle between the Central Powers and Russia.

Western Hemisphere Geographers speak of the world as being divided into two halves (hemispheres). The Western Hemisphere includes North America, Mexico, Central America, and South America; the Eastern Hemisphere includes Europe, Asia, and Africa.

wheelwright A person who makes or repairs wheels for carts, wagons, or other vehicles.

Whig Party Political party that came into being in 1834 as an anti-Jackson coalition and that charged "King Andrew" with executive tyranny.

Whiskey Rebellion A protest by grain farmers against the

1794 federal tax on whiskey; militia forces led by President Washington put down this Pennsylvania uprising.

Whiskey Ring Distillers and revenue officials in St. Louis who were revealed in 1875 to have defrauded the government of millions of dollars in whiskey taxes, with the cooperation of federal officials.

white supremacy The racist belief that whites are inherently superior to all other races and are therefore entitled to rule over them.

white-collar workers Workers able to wear white shirts on the job because they do no grubby manual labor.

Whitewater A scandal involving a failed real-estate development in Arkansas in which President Clinton invested.

wholesaler Person engaged in the sale of goods in large quantities, usually for resale by a retailer.

Wilderness, The Densely wooded region of Virginia that was the site in May 1864 of a devastating but inconclusive battle between Union forces under Grant and Confederates under Lee.

Willa Cather Early-twentieth-century writer, many of whose novels chronicle the lives of immigrants and others on the American frontier.

William Bradford The separatist who led the Pilgrims to America; he became the first governor of Plymouth Plantations.

William Clark Soldier and explorer who joined Meriwether Lewis as coleader on the expedition to explore the Louisiana Territory; he was responsible for mapmaking.

William H. Seward U.S. secretary of state under Lincoln and Johnson, a former abolitionist who had expansionist views and arranged the purchase of Alaska from Russia.

William Howard Taft Governor of the Philippines from 1901 to 1904; he was elected president of the United States in 1908 and became chief justice of the Supreme Court in 1921.

William Howe British general in command at the Battle of Bunker Hill; three years later he became commander in chief of British forces in America.

William Jennings Bryan Nebraska congressman who advocated free coinage of silver, opposed imperialism, and ran for president unsuccessfully three times on the Democratic ticket.

William Lloyd Garrison Abolitionist leader who founded and published *The Liberator,* an antislavery newspaper.

William Marcy "Boss" Tweed New York City political boss who used the Tammany organization to control city and state government from the 1860s until his downfall in 1871.

William Penn English Quaker who founded the colony of Pennsylvania in 1681.

William Randolph Hearst Publisher and rival to Pulitzer whose newspaper, the *New York Journal,* sensationalized and distorted stories and actively promoted the war with Spain.

William Tecumseh Sherman U.S. general who captured Atlanta in 1864 and led a destructive march to the Atlantic Coast.

William Westmoreland Commander of all American troops in Vietnam from 1964 to 1968.

Wilmot Proviso Amendment to an appropriations bill in 1846 proposing that any territory acquired from Mexico be closed to slavery; it was defeated in the Senate.

Winfield Scott Virginia soldier and statesman who led troops in the War of 1812 and the War with Mexico; he was still serving as a general at the start of the Civil War.

Winston Churchill Prime minister who led Britain through World War II; he was known for his eloquent speeches and his refusal to give in to the Nazi threat. He would be voted out of office in July 1945.

Wisconsin Idea The program of reform sponsored by La Follette in Wisconsin, designed to decrease political corruption, foster direct democracy, regulate corporations, and increase expertise in governmental decision making.

Women's Christian Temperance Union Women's organization founded in 1874 that opposed alcoholic beverages and supported reforms such as woman suffrage.

Woodstock Free rock concert in Woodstock, New York, in August 1969; it attracted 400,000 people and was remembered as the classic expression of the counterculture.

Worcester v. Georgia Supreme Court case (1832) concerning the arrest of two missionaries to the Cherokees in Georgia; the Court found that Georgia had no right to rule in Cherokee territory.

work relief A system of governmental monetary support that provided work for the unemployed, who were usually paid a limited hourly or daily wage.

workers' compensation Payments that employers are required by law to award to workers injured on the job.

Works Progress Administration Agency established in 1935 and headed by Harry Hopkins that hired the unemployed for construction, conservation, and arts programs.

World Trade Organization Geneva-based organization that oversees world trading systems; founded in 1995 by 135 countries to replace the 1948 General Agreement on Tariffs and Trades (GATT).

Wounded Knee Creek Site of a conflict in 1890 between a band of Lakotas and U.S. troops, sometimes characterized as a massacre because the Lakotas were so outnumbered and overpowered; the last major encounter between Indians and the army.

writ of habeas corpus In law, the writ of habeas corpus is a court document challenging the legality of an incarceration.

write-in campaign An attempt to elect a candidate in which voters are urged to write the name of an unregistered candidate directly on the ballot.

Wyatt Earp American frontier marshal and gunfighter involved in 1881 in a controversial shootout at the O.K. Corral in Tombstone, Arizona, in which several men were killed.

X

xenophobic Fearful of or hateful toward foreigners or those seen as being different.

XYZ affair A diplomatic incident in which American envoys to France were told that the United States would have to loan France money and bribe government officials as a precondition for negotiation.

Y

Yalta   Site in the Crimea of the last meeting, in 1945, between Roosevelt, Churchill, and Stalin; they discussed the final defeat of the Axis powers and the problems of postwar occupation.

Yazoo affair   Corrupt deal in which the Georgia legislature sold a huge tract of public land to speculators for a low price but later overturned the sale; the basis for the Supreme Court case of *Fletcher v. Peck,* which in 1810 supported Jefferson's position favoring compensation and helped establish the sanctity of civil contracts over state legislation.

yellow journalism   The use of sensational exposés, embellished reporting, and attention-grabbing headlines to sell newspapers.

yeoman   Independent landowner entitled to suffrage.

Yom Kippur War   On October 6, 1973, Egypt and Syria suddenly invaded Israel; after initial losses, the Israeli military defeated the Arab armies; with U.S. support, negotiations finally led to a cease-fire on October 22.

Yorktown   Site of the last major battle of the Revolution; American and French troops trapped Cornwallis's army here, on a peninsula on the York River near the Chesapeake Bay, and forced him to surrender.

Young America movement   A political movement popular among young voters during the 1840s and early 1850s that advocated free-market capitalism, national expansionism, and American patriotism; a strong force within the Democratic Party, Young America leaders tried to avoid antislavery debates and other divisive controversies.

yuppie   Young urban professional with a high-paying job and a materialistic lifestyle.

Z

Zachary Taylor   American general whose defeat of Santa Anna at Buena Vista in 1847 made him a national hero and the Whig choice for president in 1848.

Zbigniew Brzezinski   Carter's national security adviser, who favored confronting the Soviet Union with firmness.

zoot suit   A long jacket with wide lapels and padded shoulders, worn over pleated trousers, pegged and cuffed at the ankle.

INDEX

Boldfaced terms indicate glossary terms that are defined on that page.